D0290964

LUTHERAN STUDY BIBLE

Presented to

Alec Towse

By

Date

LUTHERAN STUDY BIBLE

New Revised Standard Version

AUGSBURG FORTRESS
MINNEAPOLIS

LUTHERAN STUDY BIBLE
New Revised Standard Version

Copyright © 2009 Augsburg Fortress. All rights reserved. Except for brief quotations in critical articles or reviews, no part of this book may be reproduced in any manner without prior written permission from the publisher. Visit http://www.augsburgfortress.org/copyrights/contact.asp or write to Permissions, Augsburg Fortress, Box 1209, Minneapolis, MN 55440.

The NRSV is published by arrangement with HarperOne, an imprint of HarperCollins Publishers. All rights reserved. Unless otherwise noted, Scripture quotations are from the New Revised Standard Version Bible, copyright © 1989 by the Division of Christian Education of the National Council of the Churches of Christ in the United States of America and used by permission. All rights reserved.

Augsburg Fortress Publishing Team for Lutheran Study Bible: Scott Tunseth, Project Director; Laurie J. Hanson, Development Editor; Tim Larson, Project Manager; John W. Goodman, Designer; Madeleine Sasseville, Technical Illustrator; Here We Stand Edition cover designer: Joe Vaughan

Book opener illustrations: Julie Lonneman
Maps: Paul LoBue/Mapping Specialists
Cover design: Spunk Design Machine
Typesetting: CouGrrr Graphics, Thomas Ristow, Kathleen Ristow
Copyediting: Donn McLellan
Proofreading: Peachtree Editorial, Rebecca Lowe

ISBN 978-0-8066-9846-5 Here We Stand Edition
ISBN 978-0-8066-9742-0 Deluxe Edition
ISBN 978-0-8066-9743-7 Large Print Edition

Library of Congress Cataloging-in-Publication Data

Bible. English. New Revised Standard. 2009.
Lutheran study Bible : New Revised Standard Version.
p. cm.
ISBN 978-0-8066-8059-0 (hardcover : alk. paper) — ISBN 978-0-8066-8060-6 (softcover : alk. paper)
I. Title.

BS191.5.A12009 M56 2009b 2008053105

Printed in Canada.

13 12 11 10 1 2 3 4 5 6 7 8 9

CONTENTS

CONTRIBUTORS

Board of Consultants

James W. Aageson
Norma Cook Everist
Diane L. Jacobson
Rolf A. Jacobson
Mark Allan Powell
Barbara R. Rossing
Nelson T. Strobert
Jane E. Strohl
Timothy J. Wengert

Book Introductions and Study Notes

Terence E. Fretheim	Genesis
Esther M. Menn	Exodus
Rodney R. Hutton	Leviticus
Wilda C. Gafney	Numbers
Richard D. Nelson	Deuteronomy
Burton L. Everist	Joshua
James Limburg	Judges
Diane L. Jacobson	Ruth and Ecclesiastes
Jeanette Bialas Strandjord	1 and 2 Samuel
Ralph W. Klein	1 and 2 Kings
Mark A. Throntveit	1 and 2 Chronicles
Lamontte Luker	Ezra and Nehemiah
Elna K. Solvang	Esther
Kathryn Schifferdecker	Job
Rolf A. Jacobson	Psalms
John S. Kerr	Proverbs
Ann Fritschel	Song of Solomon
Frederick J. Gaiser	Isaiah
Foster R. McCurley	Jeremiah
Walter C. Bouzard	Lamentations
Samuel D. Giere	Ezekiel
Richard Nysse	Daniel
Marty E. Stevens	Hosea
Karl N. Jacobson	Joel and Obadiah
Peter T. Nash	Amos
Kristin Johnston Largen	Jonah
Fred Strickert	Micah
Gwen Sayler	Nahum and Habakkuk
Steed Vernyl Davidson	Zephaniah, Haggai, Zechariah, and Malachi
Duane A. Priebe	Matthew
Mark G. Vitalis Hoffman	Mark
Richard W. Swanson	Luke
Karoline M. Lewis	John
Theodore W. Schroeder	Acts
Walter F. Taylor, Jr.	Romans
David E. Fredrickson	1 and 2 Corinthians
David L. Tiede	Galatians
Eliseo Pérez Álvarez	Ephesians
Roy A. Harrisville III	Philippians
Richard Carlson	Colossians
Karl P. Donfried	1 and 2 Thessalonians
Christian Eberhart	1 and 2 Timothy
Dena L. Williams	Titus and Jude
David A. Brondos	Philemon
Erik M. Heen	Hebrews
James L. Boyce	James
Raymond L. Schultz	1 and 2 Peter
Wayne C. Kannaday	1, 2, and 3 John
Nathan Aaseng	Revelation

Additional Content

Walter C. Bouzard	Old Testament: Overview and Section Introductions
Hans Dahl	Article: Introduction to the Bible
Samuel D. Giere	Article: The Shape of the Sacred Bible
Mary Jane Haemig	Article: Martin Luther on the Bible
Arland J. Hultgren	New Testament: Overview and Section Introductions
Darrell Jodock	Article: What Should We Expect When We Read the Bible?
Beth Kreitzer	Additional content for Lutheran Perspectives notes
Winston D. Persaud	Article: The Bible and God's Mission
Mark Allan Powell	Article: Lutheran Insights that Open the Bible
Duane A. Priebe	Article: The Shape of the Sacred Bible
Doris Rikkers	Subject Guide
Martha E. Stortz	Additional content for Lutheran Perspectives notes
Jane E. Strohl	Additional content for Lutheran Perspectives notes
Walter Sundberg	Article: Martin Luther on the Bible
Timothy J. Wengert	Article: The Small Catechism: A Simple Guide for the Book of Faith
Hans Wiersma	Additional content for Lutheran Perspectives notes

ABBREVIATIONS

BC — *The Book of Concord: The Confessions of the Evangelical Lutheran Church.* Robert Kolb, Timothy J. Wengert, eds. (Fortress, 2000).

B.C.E. — Before the Common Era

C.E. — Common Era

ELCA — Evangelical Lutheran Church in America

ELW — *Evangelical Lutheran Worship*, pew edition (Augsburg Fortress, 2006).

LBW — *Lutheran Book of Worship*, pew edition (Augsburg Fortress, 1978).

LW — *Luther's Works.* 55 volumes. Helmut Lehmann and Jaroslav Pelikan, eds. (Fortress and Concordia, 1955-1986). (The abbreviation is followed by volume number, colon, and page number.)

NRSV — New Revised Standard Version (Division of Christian Education of the National Council of the Churches of Christ in the United States of America, 1989).

OBF — *Opening the Book of Faith: Lutheran Insights for Bible Study.* Diane L. Jacobson, Stanley N. Olson, and Mark Allan Powell. (Augsburg Fortress, 2008).

RSV — Revised Standard Version (Division of Christian Education of the National Council of the Churches of Christ in the United States of America, 1946, 1952, 1971).

SC — *Luther's Small Catechism with* Evangelical Lutheran Worship *texts.* Gift edition. Timothy J. Wengert, trans. (Augsburg Fortress, 2008).

v. — verse

vv. — verses

WLS — *What Luther Says: An Anthology.* Vol. III. Ewald M. Plass, comp. (Concordia, 1959).

Old Testament

Gen	Genesis
Exod	Exodus
Lev	Leviticus
Num	Numbers
Deut	Deuteronomy
Josh	Joshua
Judg	Judges
Ruth	Ruth
1 Sam	1 Samuel
2 Sam	2 Samuel
1 Kgs	1 Kings
2 Kgs	2 Kings
1 Chr	1 Chronicles
2 Chr	2 Chronicles
Ezra	Ezra
Neh	Nehemiah
Esth	Esther
Job	Job
Ps/Pss	Psalm/Psalms
Prov	Proverbs
Eccl	Ecclesiastes
Song	Song of Solomon
Isa	Isaiah
Jer	Jeremiah
Lam	Lamentations
Ezek	Ezekiel
Dan	Daniel
Hos	Hosea
Joel	Joel
Amos	Amos
Obad	Obadiah
Jonah	Jonah
Mic	Micah
Nah	Nahum
Hab	Habakkuk
Zeph	Zephaniah
Hag	Haggai
Zech	Zechariah
Mal	Malachi

New Testament

Matt	Matthew
Mark	Mark
Luke	Luke
John	John
Acts	Acts of the Apostles
Rom	Romans
1 Cor	1 Corinthians
2 Cor	2 Corinthians
Gal	Galatians
Eph	Ephesians
Phil	Philippians
Col	Colossians
1 Thess	1 Thessalonians
2 Thess	2 Thessalonians
1 Tim	1 Timothy
2 Tim	2 Timothy
Titus	Titus
Phlm	Philemon
Heb	Hebrews
Jas	James
1 Pet	1 Peter
2 Pet	2 Peter
1 John	1 John
2 John	2 John
3 John	3 John
Jude	Jude
Rev	Revelation

LUTHERAN STUDY BIBLE
An Introduction

Lutherans share with other Christians this foundational understanding: The Bible is the Word of God, and through it God's Spirit speaks to us to create and sustain Christian faith and fellowship for service in the world. The Bible shapes our lives individually and together as the church of Christ. The "Confession of Faith" in The Constitution of the Evangelical Lutheran Church in America states:

> This church accepts the canonical Scriptures of the Old and New Testaments as the inspired Word of God and the authoritative source and norm of its proclamation, faith, and life. (2.03)

With this clear view of the Scriptures comes the impetus to develop a new study Bible for use in the church. We are a gifted church with many talented and influential teaching theologians. This study Bible provides a means to display these gifts and insights for the sake of all who seek to study, read, and reflect on God's Word. Like other study Bibles, the notes utilize the best of modern biblical scholarship. To this are added Lutheran perspectives and articles that make Lutheran Study Bible truly unique. Drawing on the rich catechetical traditions of Martin Luther, this study Bible brings together Bible insights with theological reflection on foundational teachings important to Lutherans and relevant for all.

Book of Faith Connections

Development of this Bible was well underway when the ELCA decided to support a new initiative called Book of Faith in 2007. The emergence of this initiative lent further support to the need for this new study Bible. In fact, the guiding principles of the initiative have helped shape the ongoing development, design, and content of Lutheran Study Bible. The release of Lutheran Study Bible to coincide with the Book of Faith initiative is truly an opportune moment for the church. The initiative's vision is "that the whole church becomes more fluent in the first language of faith, the language of Scripture . . . ." What better way to support this vision than by reading and studying Scripture together under the guidance of some of our very best Bible teachers.

The Book of Faith initiative invites all to "Open Scripture. Join the Conversation." In the spirit of this invitation, Lutheran Study Bible also includes questions for individual reflection and group conversation. The Bible comes alive and God's Word does its work of renewing and changing lives, especially when we talk about it and share it with one another. In this way Lutheran Study Bible is also a study guide.

What to Look For

Lutheran Study Bible has several unique features that can be used to support individual study and reflection as well as group study ranging from confirmation to various adult learning settings. You will note the following features:

Introductions

Each major section and each book of the Bible will begin with a summary introduction. Here you will discover historical and contextual background, as well as insights into the key themes and messages. Use these introductions as helpful guides to approaching the sections or books of the Bible.

Study Notes

Each book of the Bible is accompanied by three types of study notes and by faith-reflection questions. These study notes and questions are designated by the following icons and provided in the margin near the corresponding Bible text.

World of the Bible notes explore people, places, events, and artifacts that are mentioned in the Bible. These may also describe how a particular book may have been written and what literary form it takes.

Bible Concepts notes focus on ideas and theological insights. Here you will find connections between how such concepts are expressed in different books and how Old Testament themes influence the New Testament.

Lutheran Perspectives notes are introduced by a key question that connects a Bible verse or passage with Lutheran theological perspectives, teachings, or practices.

Faith Reflection questions encourage individuals and groups to think about and discuss the meaning of some Bible texts or study notes.

Charts, Illustrations, Diagrams, and Maps

Found throughout the study Bible, these resources will provide helpful summaries and views to help you picture what is introduced in the Bible text.

A set of four-color maps and occasional spot maps are provided to help you follow the action.

Bible Reading Plan and Subject Guide

For those who wish to engage in a daily Bible reading plan, a detailed plan is provided for three different levels (see pp. 2081-2093).

The Subject Guide (pp. 2055-2078) provides a concordance-like listing of key Bible terms and cross-references.

Articles

Many helpful articles can be found in the first and second four-color sections of the Bible (pp. 15–32 and 1521–1553). The first section includes a detailed Introduction to the Bible, a chart describing the various canons of the Hebrew Scripture (Old Testament), and a helpful three-page Bible History Timeline. The second section highlights Martin Luther and the Bible, provides a helpful view of Luther's Small Catechism and the Bible, and offers several short articles that focus on how Lutherans and others may read, interpret, and study the Bible. Helpful hints for personal Bible reading and study can be found here as well. Be sure to spend some time reviewing this rich collection of articles and resources.

A Word about Dates

In Lutheran Study Bible, dates are designated by the initials B.C.E. (Before the Common Era) and C.E. (Common Era). These correspond to the traditional dating convention of B.C. and A.D. The abbreviation B.C. stands for "before Christ," while A.D. stands for the Latin phrase *anno domine* ("in the year of our Lord"). A monk named Dionysius Exiguus invented this dating system in Rome in 525, based on his work on calculating the date of Easter. While the system attempted to mark Jesus' birth as the transition point in history, it was later discovered that the calculation of Jesus' birth year was incorrect. It is now believed that Jesus was more likely born in about 4 B.C. (B.C.E.).

We recognize that some readers may prefer the traditional dating abbreviations, which call attention to the importance of Christ's incarnation and center human history around that event. We also recognize that we share history with people of many faiths, including Jewish brothers and sisters with whom we share sacred Scripture. Therefore, we have chosen to follow the lead of several other study Bibles and scholars today and use the B.C.E. and C.E. dating abbreviations.

A Word about the Translation

The New Revised Standard Version translation of the Bible (NRSV) was chosen because of its continued wide use in the church. Research revealed a strong preference for the use of this translation in a new Lutheran Study Bible. The NRSV is acclaimed for its accuracy, clarity, and inclusivity. It continues to be an important translation for use in various teaching settings.

Using this Bible

Lutheran Study Bible has been designed to support confirmation study and various adult learning settings. Here are some additional ways to use the resources:

- Consider using various articles as the basis for teaching activities.

- Make use of the helpful hints for individual study.

- Discuss the Faith Reflection questions with others.

- Adopt a personal reading plan. Use the study notes for guidance as you read. Consider writing your reflections and your questions in a journal.

- Read and think about the many Lutheran Perspectives notes. Use them to learn or review important Lutheran teachings and practices. Those who are new to the Lutheran faith may find these perspectives to be particularly helpful.

The Bible is an exciting but challenging book. It can be difficult to understand. We hope Lutheran Study Bible will be a valuable guide and companion to your reading and study of the Bible. We hope it does indeed help you become more fluent in Scripture, the first language of faith. As we become more fluent in God's life-giving, renewing Word, we are better equipped to live out our Christian faith for the sake of the world.

Acknowledgments

You will see the large number of contributors on pp. 10-11. We thank them for their work and for their willingness to participate in this major undertaking. We also thank the board of consultants for helping shape the design of the project and for reviewing selected material. Their insights and ongoing counsel were invaluable.

INTRODUCTION to the Bible

What Is the Bible?

The Bible is a book, or more accurately it is a collection of books. In fact, the word *Bible* comes from the Greek word *biblia* (BIB-lee-ah), which means "books." But reading the Bible isn't like reading a history book, a rulebook, or a self-help book of wise sayings. Why not? Because the Bible is also holy. It is the sacred Scripture for those who practice both the Jewish and Christian religions. What makes it holy or sacred? It is not holy because we say so; it is holy because God speaks through the Bible.

The Bible is also called the Word of God because it is God's Word for humankind, and through it God acts to change lives. Many Lutherans describe the Bible as follows:

> The canonical Scriptures of the Old and New Testaments are the written Word of God. Inspired by God's Spirit speaking through their authors, they record and announce God's revelation centering in Jesus Christ. Through them God's Spirit speaks to us to create and sustain Christian faith and fellowship for service in the world. (From "Confession of Faith," The Constitution of the Evangelical Lutheran Church in America, 2.02c).

This confession statement means several things. It means that the Bible is God's Word, but human beings were inspired by God's Spirit to write the words. The Spirit speaks through the words to create and sustain faith and to encourage people of faith to be active in serving in the world. Finally, Lutheran Christians see the Bible as centering on Jesus Christ and how he reveals God's Word for the world. In fact, the Bible itself speaks of the Word who became flesh and lived among us (John 1:1, 14).

Above all for Christians, the Bible communicates the grace of God in Jesus Christ. By speaking and hearing the words printed in the Bible, Christ is made alive for us. The church's confession also describes the Bible as "the authoritative source and norm of [the church's] proclamation, faith, and life" ("Confession of Faith," 2.03). That means the Bible guides our thinking about matters of faith and life. So Lutherans begin with what the Bible does. Trying to discover who wrote the Bible is important. Exploring the process of how the Bible came to be is useful. But even more important is the way it reveals God's power. Its message can change lives.

A book of faith

The Bible can also be described as a book of faith. That means three things. First, the Bible comes *from* faith. The Bible is a product of communities of faith who gathered the writings of authors inspired by God and regarded them as having authority as sacred Scriptures. Secondly, we are invited to read and study and listen to the Bible *in* faith. That means that we approach the Bible as a book of faith. Through it we are connected with all the people of faith—today and in the past. Finally, the Bible is written primarily *for* faith. The great story of God's love and the promises of new life found in the Bible are meant to be heard and shared. That means the Bible creates individuals and communities of faith for a purpose—so that the good news of God's love will be shared in both words and actions.

Handed down from generation to generation

The stories found in the books of the Bible were handed down from generation to generation, first by word of mouth. Eventually, after hundreds of years, the stories were written down into books and finally collected into a "canon" (a list of writings) that we now recognize as the Bible. These books were first written on scrolls made of dried animal skins or crude paper made of reeds. Portions of these books date as far back as the thirteenth century B.C.E. and as late as the second century C.E. The books of the Bible are varied in many ways. The diversity of the literature reflects the number of authors who contributed to the Bible and the wide range of times in which they wrote. Together the books of the Bible give witness to God and God's relationship to humanity. For more, see "What Is in the Bible?" (pp. 24–25).

The Bible is inspired

Although the Bible was written down by human hands, God inspired the writings of the Bible: "All scripture is inspired by God" (2 Tim 3:16). Christians may disagree on what this means, because the Bible does not explain how this inspiration occurred. Some believe the Bible's words were communicated directly by God to its authors, and the authors wrote them down as if listening to a recording. Others argue that the message of the Bible is what God inspired, but the actual words were the work of the authors. Still others believe the authors themselves were inspired by God, but not necessarily the words. As stated above, the church's confession of faith says it this way: "Inspired by God's Spirit speaking through their authors, they [the Scriptures] record and announce God's revelation centering in Jesus Christ."

During the sixteenth century, Martin Luther described the key center of the entire Scripture when he said of the Bible: "Here you will find the swaddling cloths and manger in which Christ lies, and to which the angel points the shepherds. Simple and lowly are these swaddling cloths, but dear is the treasure, Christ, who lies in them" (*LW* 35: 236). The point Luther was making is that the Bible is not to be worshiped in and of itself. Instead, he argued that the Bible is the place where Christ is revealed. So the Bible is both human and divine at the same time. As a human book, it was written in languages spoken by ordinary people who had different styles, passions, and experiences. In the Bible's stories, songs, prophecies, poems, and narratives we encounter the "dear treasure," the living Christ. We are introduced to Jesus, who came into the world to reveal God and to save humans from sin and death, and who now lives and reigns forever. The biblical authors wrote inspired stories of faith meant to create new realities in the lives of their readers through encounters with God. The Old Testament authors gave witness to this new reality in the stories of God's continual faithfulness to the people of Israel. For the New Testament authors, the life, death, and resurrection of Jesus Christ shaped this new reality.

Reading and interpreting the Bible

Because the Bible is authoritative for faith and daily life, the Bible requires careful reading and interpretation. It is an ancient book written by people who lived in a very different time and place. This makes reading the Bible today both challenging and exciting. Some portions of the Bible have a more literal meaning. That is, they are meant to be read and understood as the original readers would have understood them. Other portions contain images, metaphors, and stories that convey important truths, but they are to be understood not as literally happening. When "the trees of the forest sing for joy" (Ps 96:12), we know this didn't literally happen, but it is a metaphor used by the writer to express great joy.

The Bible was written long ago in a time and culture different from our own. So along with careful reading of the Bible's words, we also read with the historical and social setting of the Bible in mind. Like viewing a great painting, each time we come to the Bible we may see something we might not have noticed before. When we read and discuss it with others, we encounter it differently and add to our understanding of it. Ages ago the Holy Spirit inspired the authors of the Bible to paint the portrait of God and God's relationship to humanity that we find in the Bible. That same Holy Spirit continues to inspire us, here and now, as we read through the pages of this holy book and work at understanding the words in the context of our lives with other believers. For more on reading and understanding the Scriptures, see the articles on pages 1521–1553.

When we read the Bible, the Holy Spirit uses the writings of the biblical authors to awaken and strengthen faith in us and those around us. For some, reading the Bible results in a dramatic conversion experience. For most, though, faith is not realized so easily or quickly. Rather, when we read carefully the stories of faith found in the Bible over an extended period of time, they take root in our lives. We discover that faith comes to us in God's own time and as a gift from God alone. When we encounter these stories of faith, they are planted in our lives like seeds. Through the work of the Holy Spirit, the seeds of faith are nurtured over a lifetime of being challenged and renewed by God's Word.

How Did the Bible Come to Be?

The Bible as we know it today came to be during a long and complex process. The books that make up the Bible were written by many different authors over hundreds of years. And even after the manuscripts were written down, it took several hundred years before all the books that make up the Bible were put together in one complete volume. But that is getting ahead of the story.

Oral tradition

Long before a single word of the Bible was written down, people of faith told stories, created poems, and sang songs of faith. Generations passed on the stories of God and God's relationship with the people we now read about in the Bible. People passed along these stories, teachings, songs, poems, codes of law, and wisdom for living from one generation to the next by word of mouth. It is likely that some of the Old Testament stories were told for centuries before they were written down. Even the Gospels, which tell the story of Jesus' life and teachings, were written down a few decades after Jesus lived, died, and was raised from the dead.

Creating manuscripts

The very first manuscripts of books of the Bible have never been found. What is remarkable is that God's faithful people preserved the message of these books by making copies of those manuscripts. The first manuscripts were written on papyrus, a kind of paper made from reeds. Later, manuscripts were also written on vellum, made from dried animal skins. Because these manuscripts were created over a long period of time, some portions of the Old Testament date as far back as the thirteenth century B.C.E., while the last book of the Old Testament was penned during the second century B.C.E. The earliest New Testament writings came about two hundred years later. The letters of the apostle Paul are considered the earliest New Testament writings and can be dated from the early-to-late 50s C.E. The four Gospels were probably written sometime between 70 and 90 C.E., while the latest New Testament book may have been written sometime in the first half of the second century C.E.

Ancient Greek papyrus manuscript from the second or third century C.E. showing portions of chapters 11 and 12 of Paul's Letter to the Romans.

We tend to think of all the authors of the Bible as living in a similar time and place, experiencing culture and society in similar ways. But imagine someone writing a novel by candlelight in a small village in Italy more than one thousand years ago and a modern-day writer doing the same in an apartment in a modern European city. How would their experiences and view of the world differ?

The authors of the biblical writings also lived in vastly different times and places. They were influenced by their own cultures and times and personal circumstances. As a result, some early stories of the Bible tell of nomadic people being led by and following God from place to place. Other Old Testament writings reflect the view of temple officials writing at a time when the people were more settled and their life of faith centered in the temple in Jerusalem. Other authors wrote sad songs (laments) while they and the people were living in exile in Babylon or some other foreign land. Still others wrote down the laws and rules that were intended to set the people apart as God's holy people. The biblical writings reflect the events and the experiences that their authors encountered and tried to interpret.

A few lines (in Hebrew square writing) from an Isaiah scroll found in the cave of the scrolls of Qumran, northwest of the Dead Sea. Of the Herodian period, the piece is now housed at Israel Museum (IDAM), Jerusalem.

Creating a canon

Before the Bible became a single volume, its manuscripts (books) underwent a process called "canonization." The word *canon* (only one *n* in the middle) comes from a Greek word meaning "measure" or "standard." A canon is a list of writings considered to be the standard for a community, so they have special significance. Developing this standard list was a very slow process. Over a long period the people of Israel and the early church found themselves drawn to certain books that seemed to speak the Word of God most clearly and with greatest authority. Eventually these books became authoritative and ultimately considered canon.

The canon of the Hebrew Scriptures, or Old Testament, began with the adoption of the Torah, the first five books of our Bible today. It is believed by some people that it took at least five centuries for the rest of the books that make up the Hebrew Scriptures to be adopted as "canon," probably by the end of the first century C.E. There still remains some controversy about exactly when the canon of the Hebrew Scriptures was set. The Hebrew Scriptures closely correspond to the content of what Protestants usually define as the Old Testament. See the chart Different Canons of the Hebrew Bible (Old Testament), pp. 28–29.

The canon of the Christian New Testament gathers together writings centered in the ministry and meaning of Jesus. Though the last New Testament book was likely written early in the second century C.E. (see above), the process of creating a New Testament canon went on for many years. While some books were agreed on quite early as being authentic and authoritative, different parts of the church used different books. This process continued even into the time of the Reformation (see "The Shape of the Sacred Bible," pp. 26–27). In an Easter letter written in 367 C.E., Athanasius, the bishop of Alexandria, offered up a list of twenty-seven books that he believed should be authoritative for Christian faith and life. Even so, this list by no means settled the issue of which books should make up the Christian canon. That list does, however, correspond to the twenty-seven books included in the New Testament today.

It is important to remember that Jesus and his followers were Jewish, and the Hebrew Scriptures were their authoritative writings. However, early Christians were familiar with and used the Greek translation of the Hebrew Scriptures, called the Septuagint. This translation is quoted many times in the New Testament. The Christian church saw the important connection between the Hebrew Scriptures and the new authoritative books centering on the message of Jesus. So, eventually, these manuscripts were combined into one Bible.

For Martin Luther and other Protestant reformers in the sixteenth century, the biblical canon became especially important. These reformers emphasized biblical authority as primary, meaning church teachings, church councils, or the pronouncements of church leaders were to be shaped by the Bible. It is no secret that Luther was troubled by four books—Jude, James, Hebrews, and Revelation—so he wrestled with their inclusion in the canon. He did choose to include those books in his translation of the Bible. Luther also promoted the idea that the Bible contains a "canon within a canon." He recognized that within the biblical canon there are books, such as the letters of Paul and the Gospel of John, that hold greater authority than others because they convey more clearly who Christ is and what Christ came to do. For more on Luther's Bible, see the article "Martin Luther on the Bible," pp. 1521–1529.

The Bible lives on

By the late second century C.E., hand-written copies of the Bible were already translated into a variety of local languages. Today the Bible is found in more than one-third of the world's languages, and several new versions of the Bible have been created in the last fifty years. The work of translating the Bible continues. As the Word of God, the Bible continues to endure the test of time. Regardless of which version, edition, or translation of the Bible you read, the Holy Spirit continues to use these human words to reveal Christ and keep the story of God's people alive.

What Is in the Bible?

The contents of the Bible can be described in several ways—by its books, by the sections of books, and by the different kinds of literature, or writing, found in those books. Each section and each individual book is described in detail in this Bible, so this article will focus on the big picture. First, the Bible is divided into two major sections: the Old Testament and the New Testament. Each testament bears witness ("testifies") to God's relationship with the world and humankind. In the Old Testament, the focus is on the ancient people of Israel and the promises God made to their ancestors. The New Testament focuses on Jesus Christ, God's Son, and the meaning of his life, death, and resurrection.

The Old Testament

What Christians call the Old Testament is similar to but not identical to the books of the Jewish *Tanak* (ta-NAK). "Hebrew Bible" is another term that refers to the portions of the Jewish canon held in common with the Christian canon. The Tanak organizes this material into twenty-four books; the Old Testament refers to thirty-nine books. For some time, Old Testament writings were divided into the Law or Teachings (Torah), the Prophets (Nevi'im), and the Writings (Ketuvim). The name *Tanak* is formed from the initial Hebrew letters of these three traditional subdivisions. We find reference to these divisions in the New Testament (Luke 24:44). Today, Christians organize the books of the Old Testament into four groups: Pentateuch, Historical Books, Writings, and Prophets. Christians continue to have differences about which books are to be included in the Old Testament and how they will be named. It is a complex picture. See the chart on pp. 28–29.

How the books of the Old Testament are grouped

The thirty-nine books of the Old Testament were originally written in the Hebrew and Aramaic languages and composed over several centuries. These books and others were translated into Greek (the Septuagint). The first five books of the Old Testament are called the **Pentateuch** (Greek for "five books"), which includes the books of Genesis, Exodus, Leviticus, Numbers, and Deuteronomy. These five books made up the first official canon (set of authoritative writings) of the Jewish people, which they called the *Torah* ("law" or "instruction"). The Pentateuch leads us through the stories of creation, describes the adventures of the Israelite people in slavery in Egypt, and ends as they are led out of slavery to the promised land.

The next group of Old Testament books includes the twelve **Historical Books**. These books cover the history of the Israelite people from the time of Israel's emergence in the promised land (thirteenth century B.C.E.), down to the period when the Persians controlled Israel (late fifth century B.C.E.). Early portions of this material, Joshua–Kings, draw on the values of Deuteronomy to interpret history and ask, "Why did God allow us to be taken from our land into exile in a foreign land? Is God still with us? What is our future now?" Later portions of the Historical Books, Chronicles–Esther, are much more optimistic, and concerns move toward worship, the temple, faithfulness, and purity. The short books of Ruth and Esther are inserted within this grouping and tell the powerful stories of brave and bold women of faith.

The third group of Old Testament books is a collection of poetry known as the **Writings**. This diverse group of books includes many types of literature and a variety of historical perspectives. For example, Psalms is Israel's prayer book. It is filled with songs of praise, songs of sadness (lament), and much more (see the chart Types of Psalms, pp. 849–850). The Song of Solomon is affectionate love poetry. Job, Proverbs, and Ecclesiastes are often called wisdom literature and focus on experiences of daily life.

The Prophets are a collection of books that report the words of the LORD that came to the prophets of Israel and Judah from the eighth to the fifth centuries B.C.E. Prophets were not fortune-tellers, as some believe. Rather, prophets were those called by God to deliver God's message to God's people. The books of the Prophets include three Major Prophets ("major" referring to length, not importance)—Isaiah, Jeremiah, and Ezekiel—as well as Daniel, Lamentations, and a collection of twelve Minor Prophets. Though grouped with the prophetic books in the Christian Bible, the books of Daniel and Lamentations are actually found among the "Writings" in the Hebrew Bible. Daniel, likely written as late as the second century B.C.E., includes stories of faithful Daniel and his friends, but it also includes a form of writing that is similar to the New Testament book of Revelation. Known as "apocalyptic" literature, it uses symbols and images as a kind of code language for historic people and events. It also intends to provide hope for those who remain faithful in difficult times. The book of Lamentations is a collection of five poems that mourn the destruction of Jerusalem in 586 B.C.E.

The New Testament

The New Testament contains the stories of the life of Jesus Christ, the dominant figure of the Christian faith, and people's encounters with Jesus and his teachings. Following Christ's death and resurrection, oral stories were written down. These stories and many letters eventually became the twenty-seven books of the New Testament. The books of the New Testament can be grouped in different ways. Lutheran Study Bible uses three groups.

The first group of books is the Gospels and Acts. At the heart of the Bible are the first four books of the New Testament, called the Gospels. The word "gospel" means "good news." These books share stories of the good news of Jesus Christ's teaching and ministry, as well as his death and resurrection. The Gospel writers produced their books decades after Jesus' death and resurrection in about 30 C.E. Each of the Gospel writers paints a portrait of the life and ministry of Jesus that reflects a unique perspective. When these writings are viewed together, the Gospels give us a complete picture of Jesus' ministry that none of the individual books could provide by itself. The book of Acts is a companion or second volume to the Gospel of Luke. It is believed that the same person who wrote Luke is also responsible for this brief historical narrative of the early church (compare Luke 1:1-4 and Acts 1:1). Acts covers the story of the early church from about 30 to 60 C.E. The main concern of this book is the development of the early church and the outreach of the early Christians, especially Peter, Stephen, and Paul.

The second group is the Letters of Paul. These are actual letters written during the first century to Christian communities around the Mediterranean Sea. Paul is named as author of these letters, though some may have been written by his close followers. Paul is the most influential author of the New Testament and responsible for the earliest books of the New Testament.

The final group of New Testament books is the General Letters and Revelation. The General Letters are called "general" because they mention no specific audience. Revelation is sometimes called the "Apocalypse" (Greek for "revelation"). Apocalypses are marked by bizarre visions and code language for historic people, places, and events. It is easy to be confused by this type of literature when we read it today. The author of Revelation wrote to encourage late-first-century Christians who were threatened by government authorities because of their beliefs. Some were tortured, imprisoned, or killed. Apocalyptic literature is meant to provide hope for those who remain faithful during such difficult times. The word "revelation" means to unveil (or reveal). The book of Revelation seeks to unveil God's peace, justice, and renewal for creation and all people in the life, death, and resurrection of Jesus Christ.

The Shape of the Sacred Bible

The Bible is a collection of sacred writings that serves as the ultimate source and norm of Christian thought and life. Other major religious traditions also have "scriptures" with similar functions. The Jews have the TANAK, Hindus have the Vedas, and Islam has the Qur'an (Koran), to name a few. While each religion has other important writings, those called "scripture" are considered to be God's word in human language. Fundamental to scripture in all these traditions is that its meaning expands through interpretation. Scripture occupies a different place in Christianity than it does in these other traditions. Why? God's Word is a person, not a book. God's Word is God's Son, the second person of the Trinity. Jesus Christ is the incarnation of God's Word that is with God and is God, through whom all things were created. This Word became fully human without ceasing to be fully God (John 1:1-14). The Bible is God's word as the bearer of this Word. Jesus Christ and the Bible mutually interpret one another.

Many shapes and sizes

As mentioned above, Israel's Bible was the Scripture for Jesus, the disciples, and early Christians. Through Israel's Scriptures, Christians interpreted Jesus Christ as God's saving action, fulfilling God's ancient promises. The process by which books were written and came to be understood as Scripture was a centuries-long process. Books that formed the core of the Bible came to be understood as Scripture shortly after they were written. They carried inherent authority. In Israel's Scripture, these were the Pentateuch, prophets, Psalms, and some of the writings. For the early Christians, this included the books in the Jewish Bible, four Gospels, 13 letters of Paul, Acts, 1 Peter and 1 John. Other books were included by some and excluded by others, and have remained so. Throughout the centuries, Christians and Jews have maintained that the books included in Scripture were self-authenticating. This meant that their authority was inherent; it was not grounded in human choice. While this particular study Bible includes thirty-nine Old Testament books and twenty-seven New Testament books, this is not the size or shape of all Christian Bibles today. To understand why this is so, we need to go back in history once again.

The Old Testament

Most early Christians used a Greek translation of the Israel's Scriptures, called the Septuagint. This was translated by Greek-speaking Jews starting in the third century B.C.E., and it came to include some books that were not found in the Jewish Bible. Most of these additional books were written between the third century B.C.E. and the first century C.E.

For Christians the list of accepted Old Testament books remained fluid. Many of the lists had twenty-two books, one for each letter of the Hebrew alphabet. Josephus, a Jew writing in the late first century C.E., is the earliest example of this idea. He does not list the books but identifies them as the five books of Moses, thirteen prophetic books, and four poetic books. When the early Christian lists included twenty-two books, these were the same as the Jewish Bible. The number twenty-two was reached by counting Judges and Ruth, 1 and 2 Samuel, 1 and 2 Kings, Ezra and Nehemiah, and the twelve minor prophets each as one book.

The lists that included many of those books found in the Septuagint varied. The Roman Catholic, Greek, and Slavonic Bibles included different books (see the chart on pp. 28–29). When the Scriptures were translated into Latin by Jerome around the year 400 C.E., he included only the books found in the Jewish Bible in his Old Testament. The others he placed in a section called the Apocrypha, which means "hidden." Still today many Protestants include these books in a separate section of books.

The New Testament

The canon of the New Testament is far more uniform among Christians, but its development is no less complex. In the early centuries of the church, the lists of New Testament books were divided into books that were accepted, books that were disputed, and books that were rejected. Disputed books that came to be included in the New Testament were Hebrews, James, 2 Peter, 2 and 3 John, Jude, and Revelation. In isolated instances, the epistles called 1 and 2 Clement and Barnabas were also included. In some lists the Shepherd of Hermas and the Didache are listed as books that were not considered to be Scripture but could be read in worship. Still other writings were rejected by all except some smaller groups that may have regarded them as Scripture. Among others, these included gospels such as the Gospel of Thomas and the Gospel of the Egyptians.

By the fifth century C.E., the twenty-seven books in the New Testament, including the seven disputed books, became standard in the Greek and Latin tradition. However, the seven (mentioned above) continued to be remembered as disputed into the Reformation era. While the Greek and Latin traditions accepted the twenty-seven books, others did not. The Syriac New Testament, used widely in Asia, included only the twenty books that were not disputed. For a while they substituted a harmony of the four New Testament Gospels. This is known as Tatian's *Diatessaron*, which combined the four into a single Gospel. The Ethiopian Orthodox Church still today includes the largest number of books in its Bible. It has eighty-one in all, forty-five in the Old Testament and thirty-six in the New.

Criteria for "accepted" books

Many books were being written by Christians as they sought to understand and communicate the gospel of Jesus Christ. Although regarded as inspired, most of these books played no role in the formation of the New Testament. Criteria also played little role in the early formation of the New Testament. Use played the primary role. The twenty main books were, in effect, self-authenticating, in contrast to those everyone rejected. They quickly become central to the life and faith of the Christian community. Early in the fourth century C.E., Eusebius, considered the "father" of church history (who lived about 260–340 C.E.), identified criteria for deciding which books were to be regarded as Christian Scripture. He identified three primary criteria by asking three questions. First, was a particular book used as Scripture by all the churches? Second, did a book accurately communicate the gospel of Jesus Christ? Third, did the book have a clear connection back to early apostles of Jesus? Writing style and consistency of key themes and message were also considered important.

Luther's translation of the Bible

When Luther translated the Bible, he used these same criteria. With regard to the Old Testament, he included the apocryphal writings in a separate section, just as Jerome had done centuries earlier. According to Luther, they were good to read but did not have the same authority as the books included in the Jewish canon and accepted by all in the early church. He did the same in the New Testament for Hebrews, James, Jude, and Revelation. It is no secret that Luther was troubled by these four books, so he wrestled with their inclusion in the canon. While he first noted that they were not accepted by all, Luther then argued that each of the four contradicts the main books in their theology. He also added questions of style and denied that they could be apostolic. He placed these four books in the same category as he did the Old Testament Apocrypha. He saw no reason in the content of 2 Peter and 2 and 3 John for not treating them as apostolic. In response to the Protestant Reformation, at the Council of Trent (1546), the Roman Catholic Church for the first time formally defined its canon of Scripture (see the chart on pp. 28–29).

Different Canons of the Hebrew Bible (Old Testament)

Jewish Tanakh	Protestant Old Testament	Roman Catholic Old Testament	Greek Septuagint (LXX)
Torah (The Law)	**Pentateuch**	**Pentateuch**	**Pentateuch**
Genesis	Genesis	Genesis	Genesis
Exodus	Exodus	Exodus	Exodus
Leviticus	Leviticus	Leviticus	Leviticus
Numbers	Numbers	Numbers	Numbers
Deuteronomy	Deuteronomy	Deuteronomy	Deuteronomy
The Prophets	**Historical Books**	**Historical Books**	**Historical Books**
Joshua	Joshua	Joshua	Joshua
Judges	Judges	Judges	Judges
	Ruth	Ruth	Ruth
Samuel	1 & 2 Samuel	1 & 2 Samuel	1 & 2 Kingdoms
Kings	1 & 2 Kings	1 & 2 Kings	3 & 4 Kingdoms
	1 & 2 Chronicles	1 & 2 Chronicles	1 & 2 Paraliopmenom
Isaiah			1 Esdras
Jeremiah	Ezra	Ezra	2 Esdras (Ezra & Nehemiah)
Ezekiel	Nehemiah	Nehemiah	
	Esther	Esther and Additions	Esther and Additions
The Twelve		Tobit	Tobit
Hosea		Judith	Judith
Joel		1 & 2 Maccabees	1 & 2 Maccabees
Amos			3 Maccabees & 4 Macc.
Obadiah	**Poetry/Wisdom**	**Poetry/Wisdom**	**Poetry/Wisdom**
Jonah	Job	Job	Job
Micah Nahum Habukkuk	Psalms	Psalms	Psalms/Psalm 151 Odes, including the Prayer of Manasseh
Zephaniah	Proverbs	Proverbs	Proverbs
Haggai	Ecclesiastes	Ecclesiastes	Ecclesiastes
Zechariah	Song of Songs	Song of Songs	Song of Songs
Malachi		Wisdom of Solomon	Wisdom of Solomon
		Ecclesiasticus (Sirach)	Ecclesiasticus (Sirach)
			Psalms of Solomon
The Writings	**Prophets**	**Prophets**	**Prophets**
Psalms	Isaiah	Isaiah	Isaiah
Job	Jeremiah	Jeremiah	Jeremiah
Proverbs	Lamentations	Lamentations	Lamentations
Ruth Song of Songs		Baruch and the Letter of Jeremiah	Baruch and the Letter of Jeremiah
Ecclesiastes	Ezekiel	Ezekiel	Ezekiel

Lamentations	Daniel	Daniel with the Prayer of Azariah and the Song of the Three Young Men, Susanna, Bel and the Dragon	Daniel with the Prayer of Azariah and the Song of the Three Young Men, Susanna, Bel and the Dragon
Esther			
Daniel			
Ezra-Nehemiah			
Chronicles			
	Hosea	Hosea	Hosea
	Joel	Joel	Joel
	Amos	Amos	Amos
	Obadiah	Obadiah	Obadiah
	Jonah	Jonah	Jonah
	Micah	Micah	Micah
	Nahum	Nahum	Nahum
	Habakkuk	Habakkuk	Habakkuk
	Zephaniah	Zephaniah	Zephaniah
	Haggai	Haggai	Haggai
	Zechariah	Zechariah	Zechariah
	Malachi	Malachi	Malachi

KEY TO THE CHART AND NOTES

Black - Books common to the Jewish Tanakh and Christian Old Testaments.

Blue - Catholic deuterocanonical books; Protestant Apocrypha; common to other Christian Old Testaments.

Brown - Books in the Greek Septuagint, included in some Christian Old Testaments, but not in the Roman Catholic Old Testament.

Green - Books in the Greek Septuagint, but not in Christian Old Testaments.

Red - Books not in the Greek Septuagint, but included in some Christian Old Testaments (see below).

1. Notice that the Jewish Tanakh and the Protestant Old Testament include the same books, but in a different sequence.

2. The Septuagint (LXX), which included some variations, was the scripture of Greek-speaking Judaism and of the early Christians. The sequence here is adjusted slightly to match the Protestant and Catholic Bibles. In the LXX, Job follows the Song of Songs, and The Twelve Minor Prophets are before the Major Prophets.

3. The Christian Old Testament included the books of the Jewish Tanakh. Differences largely circled around which, if any, of the additional books in the LXX to include.

4. The names of the books associated with Ezra are very confusing. The names used in the NRSV are listed first.
   a. Latin Vulgate: Ezra = 1 Esdras; Nehemiah = 2 Esdras; 1 Esdras = 3 Esdras; 2 Esdras = 4 Esdras
   b. Greek Septuagint: Ezra + Nehemiah = 2 Esdras; 1 Esdras = 1 Esdras
   c. Slavonic/Russian Orthodox Bibles: Ezra + Nehemiah = 1 Esdras; 1 Esdras = 2 Esdras; 2 Esdras = 3 Esdras.

5. The Roman Catholic Old Testament includes the books in the Jewish Tanakh plus the deuterocanonical (written later) books listed in blue.

The Latin Vulgate Appendix includes: 1 Esdras (3 Esdras), 2 Esdras (4 Esdras), and The Prayer of Manasseh.

6. For Protestants, the Roman Catholic deuterocanonical books are the Apocrypha. They are useful to read, but not authoritative for doctrine.

This was true of Luther's Bible. Later Lutherans sometimes included The Prayer of Manasseh as an Appendix.

The Anglican Apocrypha also includes 1 Esdras (3 Esdras), 2 Esdras (4 Esdras), and The Prayer of Manasseh.

7. The Greek Orthodox Old Testament also includes: 1 Esdras, The Prayer of Manasseh, Psalm 151, and 3 Maccabees. In an Appendix: 4 Maccabees.

8. In addition, the Russian Orthodox/Slavonic Old Testament includes: 2 Esdras (3 Esdras).

9. Unique to the Syriac Peshitta: 2 Baruch and Psalms 152-155.

10. Unique to the Ethiopian Orthodox Old Testament (R.W. Cowley): Enoch, Jubilees, Ezra Apocalypse (2 Esdras 3-14), 1-2 Meqabyan (with 2 and 3 Meqabyan combined as 2 Meqabyan). Not included: 1-3 Maccabees.

BIBLE HISTORY TIMELINE

Key Bible events and people are listed along with the ruling powers and kingdoms influential in the world of the Bible. All dates are approximate.

2500 B.C.E. | 2000 B.C.E. | 1500 B.C.E. | 1250 B.C.E. | 1000 B.C.E.

KEY BIBLE EVENTS

PREHISTORY
- CREATION, FALL AND FLOOD
- TOWER OF BABEL

TIME OF PATRIARCHS AND MATRIARCHS
- God calls Abraham and Sarah (1850)
- Jacob's descendants settle in Egypt (1750)

EXODUS PERIOD
- Moses leads Exodus from Egypt (1290)
- Ten Commandments at Mount Sinai (1289)

PERIOD OF JUDGES
- Joshua invades Canaan (1250)
- Judges lead Israelite Tribes in Canaan (1200)

UNITED KINGDOM
- Saul first king of Israel (1020)
- David takes Jerusalem as capital (1000)

KEY BIBLE PEOPLE

Adam
Eve
Cain
Abel
Noah

Isaac
Rebekah
Jacob
Leah
Rachel
Joseph

Moses
Aaron
Miriam

Deborah
Gideon
Samson
Samuel

POWERS AND KINGDOMS

Ancient Egyptian Kingdoms
2500–1086 B.C.E.

- Pyramids built (2500)

Biblical Prophets
Key People
World Rulers

900 B.C.E. | 800 B.C.E. | 700 B.C.E. | 600 B.C.E. | 500 B.C.E. | 400 B.C.E.

Divided Kingdom

- Kingdom divides into Israel and Judah (922)
- Assyrians capture Samaria, ending the kingdom of Israel (721)
- Solomon rules Kingdom, builds Temple (961)

Exile and Post-Exilic Period

- Jerusalem surrenders to Babylonians (598/7) Exile begins
- Judah falls to Babylonians and temple is destroyed (587/6)
- Cyrus of Persia frees Jews to return to Judah (538)
- Israelites return to Judah (538–445)
- People of Judah rebuild Temple in Jerusalem (515)
- Ezra brings Torah to Jerusalem (458 or 398)
- Nehemiah becomes governor of Judah, rebuilds walls of Jerusalem (445)

Kings of Judah and Israel

(see chart, p. 545)

- Elijah
- Elisha
- Amos
- Hosea
- First Isaiah
- Micah
- Zephaniah
- Nahum
- Habakkuk
- Jeremiah
- Ezekiel
- Second Isaiah
- Haggai
- First Zechariah
- Third Isaiah?
- Obadiah
- Joel
- Malachi

Assyrian Empire
1000–612

- Tiglath-Pileser III (745-727)
- Shalmaneser V (727-722)
- Sargon II (721-705)
- Sennacherib (704-681)

Babylonian Empire
747–539

- Nebuchadnezzer II (605-562)

Persian Empire
559–331

- Cyrus (559-330)
- Darius I (522-486)
- Xerxes (485-65)
- Artaxerxes I (465-24)

BIBLE HISTORY TIMELINE

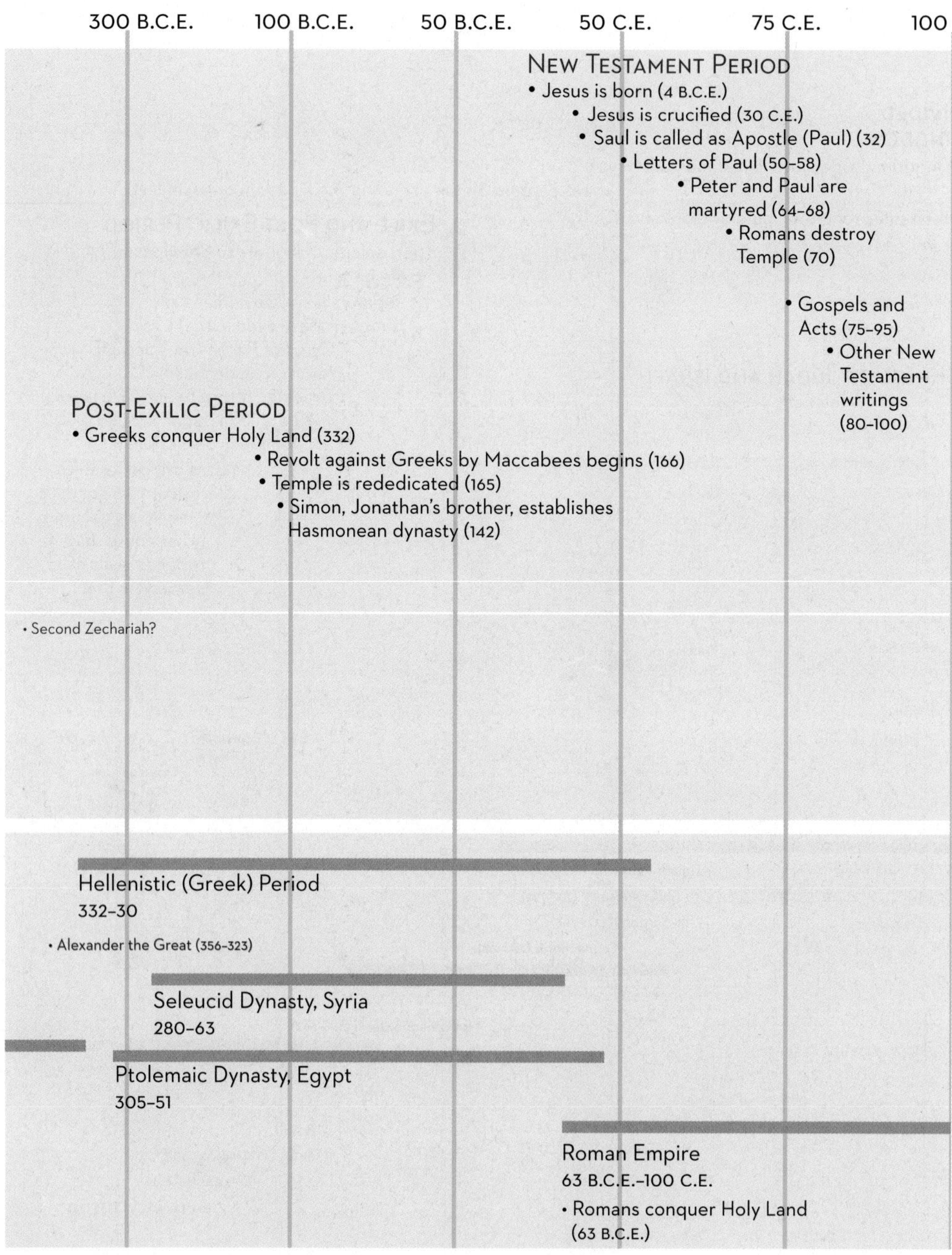

300 B.C.E.
100 B.C.E.
50 B.C.E.
50 C.E.
75 C.E.
100
NEW TESTAMENT PERIOD
• Jesus is born (4 B.C.E.)
• Jesus is crucified (30 C.E.)
• Saul is called as Apostle (Paul) (32)
• Letters of Paul (50–58)
• Peter and Paul are martyred (64–68)
• Romans destroy Temple (70)
• Gospels and Acts (75–95)
• Other New Testament writings (80–100)
POST-EXILIC PERIOD
• Greeks conquer Holy Land (332)
• Revolt against Greeks by Maccabees begins (166)
• Temple is rededicated (165)
• Simon, Jonathan's brother, establishes Hasmonean dynasty (142)
• Second Zechariah?
Hellenistic (Greek) Period
332–30
• Alexander the Great (356–323)
Seleucid Dynasty, Syria
280–63
Ptolemaic Dynasty, Egypt
305–51
Roman Empire
63 B.C.E.–100 C.E.
• Romans conquer Holy Land (63 B.C.E.)

PREFACE
to the
New Revised Standard Version

This preface is addressed to you by the Committee of translators, who wish to explain, as briefly as possible, the origin and character of our work. The publication of our revision is yet another step in the long, continual process of making the Bible available in the form of the English language that is most widely current in our day. To summarize in a single sentence: the New Revised Standard Version of the Bible is an authorized revision of the Revised Standard Version, published in 1952, which was a revision of the American Standard Version, published in 1901, which, in turn, embodied earlier revisions of the King James Version, published in 1611.

In the course of time, the King James Version came to be regarded as "the Authorized Version." With good reason it has been termed "the noblest monument of English prose," and it has entered, as no other book has, into the making of the personal character and the public institutions of the English-speaking peoples. We owe to it an incalculable debt.

Yet the King James Version has serious defects. By the middle of the nineteenth century, the development of biblical studies and the discovery of many biblical manuscripts more ancient than those on which the King James Version was based made it apparent that these defects were so many as to call for revision. The task was begun, by authority of the Church of England, in 1870. The (British) Revised Version of the Bible was published in 1881-1885; and the American Standard Version, its variant embodying the preferences of the American scholars associated with the work, was published, as was mentioned above, in 1901. In 1928 the copyright of the latter was acquired by the International Council of Religious Education and thus passed into the ownership of the Churches of the United States and Canada that were associated in this Council through their boards of education and publication.

The Council appointed a committee of scholars to have charge of the text of the American Standard Version and to undertake inquiry concerning the need for further revision. After studying the questions whether or not revision should be undertaken, and if so, what its nature and extent should be, in 1937 the Council authorized a revision. The scholars who served as members of the Committee worked in two sections, one dealing with the Old Testament and one with the New Testament. In 1946 the Revised Standard Version of the New Testament was published. The publication of the Revised Standard Version of the Bible, containing the Old and New Testaments, took place on September 30, 1952. A translation of the Apocryphal/Deuterocanonical Books of the Old Testament followed in 1957. In 1977 this collection was issued in an expanded edition, containing three additional texts received by Eastern Orthodox communions (3 and 4 Maccabees and Psalm 151). Thereafter the Revised Standard Version gained the distinction of being officially authorized for use by all major Christian churches: Protestant, Anglican, Roman Catholic, and Eastern Orthodox.

The Revised Standard Version Bible Committee is a continuing body, comprising about thirty members, both men and women. Ecumenical in representation, it includes scholars affiliated with various Protestant denominations, as well as several Roman Catholic members, an Eastern Orthodox member, and a Jewish member who serves in the Old Testament section. For a period of time, the Committee included several members from Canada and from England.

Because no translation of the Bible is perfect or is acceptable to all groups of readers, and because discoveries of older manuscripts and further investigation of linguistic features of the text continue to become available, renderings of the Bible have proliferated. During the years following the publication of the Revised Standard Version, twenty-six other English translations and revisions of the Bible were produced by committees and by individual scholars—not to mention twenty-five other translations and revisions of the New Testament alone. One of the latter was the second edition of the RSV New Testament, issued in 1971, twenty-five years after its initial publication.

Following the publication of the RSV Old Testament in 1952, significant advances were made in the discovery and interpretation of documents in Semitic languages related to Hebrew. In addition to the information that had become available in the late 1940s from the Dead Sea texts of Isaiah and Habakkuk, subsequent acquisitions from the same area brought to light many other early copies of all the books of the Hebrew Scriptures (except Esther), though most of these copies are fragmentary. During the same period early Greek manuscript copies of books of the New Testament also became available.

In order to take these discoveries into account, along with recent studies of documents in Semitic languages related to Hebrew, in 1974 the Policies Committee of the Revised Standard Version, which is a standing committee of the National Council of the Churches of Christ in the U.S.A., authorized the preparation of a revision of the entire RSV Bible.

For the Old Testament the Committee has made use of the Biblia Hebraica Stuttgartensia (1977; ed. sec. emendata, 1983). This is an edition of the Hebrew and Aramaic text as current early in the Christian era and fixed by Jewish scholars (the "Masoretes") of the sixth to the ninth centuries. The vowel signs, which were added by the Masoretes, are accepted in the main, but where a more probable and convincing reading can be obtained by assuming different vowels, this has been done. No notes are given in such cases, because the vowel points are less ancient and reliable than the consonants. When an alternative reading given by the Masoretes is translated in a footnote, this is identified by the words "Another reading is."

Departures from the consonantal text of the best manuscripts have been made only where it seems clear that errors in copying had been made before the text was standardized. Most of the corrections adopted are based on the ancient versions (translations into Greek, Aramaic, Syriac, and Latin), which were made prior to the time of the work of the Masoretes and which therefore may reflect earlier forms of the Hebrew text. In such instances a footnote specifies the version or versions from which the correction has been derived and also gives a translation of the Masoretic Text. Where it was deemed appropriate to do so, information is supplied in footnotes from subsidiary Jewish traditions concerning other textual readings (the Tiqqune Sopherim, "emendations of the scribes"). These are identified in the footnotes as "Ancient Heb tradition."

Occasionally it is evident that the text has suffered in transmission and that none of the versions provides a satisfactory restoration. Here we can only follow the best judgment of competent scholars as to the most probable reconstruction of the original text. Such reconstructions are indicated in footnotes by the abbreviation Cn ("Correction"), and a translation of the Masoretic Text is added.

For the Apocryphal/Deuterocanonical Books of the Old Testament, the Committee has made use of a number of texts. For most of these books, the basic Greek text from which the present translation was made is the edition of the Septuagint prepared by Alfred Rahlfs and published by the Württemberg Bible Society (Stuttgart, 1935). For several of the books, the more recently published individual volumes of the Göttingen Septuagint project were utilized. For the book of Tobit, it was decided to follow the form of the Greek text found in codex Sinaiticus (supported as it is by evidence from Qumran); where this text is defective, it was supplemented and corrected by other Greek manuscripts. For the three Additions to Daniel (namely, Susanna, the Prayer of Azariah and the Song of the Three Jews, and Bel and the Dragon) the Committee continued to use the Greek version attributed to Theodotion (the so-called "Theodotion-Daniel"). In translating Ecclesiasticus (Sirach), while constant reference was made to the Hebrew fragments of a large portion of this book (those discovered at Qumran and Masada as well as those recovered from the Cairo Geniza), the Committee generally followed the Greek text (including verse numbers) published by Joseph Ziegler in the Göttingen Septuagint (1965). But in many places the Committee has translated the Hebrew text when this provides a reading that is clearly superior to the Greek; the Syriac and Latin versions were also consulted throughout and occasionally adopted. The basic text adopted in rendering 2 Esdras is the Latin version given in Biblia Sacra, edited by Robert Weber (Stuttgart, 1971). This was supplemented by consulting the Latin text as edited by R. L. Bensly (1895) and by Bruno Violet (1910), as well as by taking into account the several Oriental versions of 2 Esdras, namely, the Syriac, Ethiopic, Arabic (two forms, referred to as Arabic 1 and Arabic 2), Armenian, and Georgian versions. Finally, since the Additions to the Book of Esther are disjointed and quite unintelligible as they stand in most editions of the Apocrypha, we have provided them with their original context by translating the whole of the Greek version of Esther from Robert Hanhart's Göttingen edition (1983).

For the New Testament the Committee has based its work on the most recent edition of The Greek New Testament, prepared by an interconfessional and international committee and published by the United Bible Societies (1966; 3rd ed. corrected, 1983; information concerning changes to be introduced into the critical apparatus of the forthcoming 4th edition was available to the Committee). As in that edition, double brackets are used to enclose a few passages that are generally regarded to be later additions to the text, but which we have retained because of their evident antiquity and their importance in the textual tradition. Only in very rare instances have we replaced the text or the punctuation of the Bible Societies' edition by an alternative that seemed to us to be superior. Here and there in the footnotes, the phrase "Other ancient authorities read," identifies alternative readings preserved by Greek manuscripts and early versions. In both Testaments alternative renderings of the text are indicated by the word "Or."

As for the style of English adopted for the present revision, among the mandates given to the Committee in 1980 by the Division of Education and Ministry of the National Council of Churches of Christ (which now holds the copyright of the RSV Bible) was the directive to continue in the tradition of the King James Bible, but to introduce such changes as are warranted on the basis of accuracy, clarity, euphony, and current English usage. Within the constraints set by the original texts and by the mandates of the Division, the Committee has followed the maxim, "As literal as possible, as free as necessary." As a consequence, the New Revised Standard Version (NRSV) remains essentially a literal translation. Paraphrastic renderings have been adopted only sparingly, and then chiefly to compensate for a deficiency in the English language—the lack of a common gender third person singular pronoun.

During the almost half a century since the publication of the RSV, many in the churches have become sensitive to the danger of linguistic sexism arising from the inherent bias of the English language towards the masculine gender, a bias that in the case of the Bible has often restricted or obscured the meaning of the original text. The mandates from the Division specified that, in references to men and women, masculine-oriented language should be eliminated as far as this can be done without altering passages that reflect the historical situation of ancient patriarchal culture. As can be appreciated, more than once the Committee found that the several mandates stood in tension and even in conflict. The various concerns had to be balanced case by case in order to provide a faithful and acceptable rendering without using contrived English. Only very occasionally has the pronoun "he" or "him" been retained in passages where the reference may have been to a woman as well as to a man; for example, in several legal texts in Leviticus and Deuteronomy. In such instances of formal, legal language, the options of either putting the passage in the plural or of introducing additional nouns to avoid masculine pronouns in English seemed to the Committee to obscure the historic structure and literary character of the original. In the vast majority of cases, however, inclusiveness has been attained by simple rephrasing or by introducing plural forms when this does not distort the meaning of the passage. Of course, in narrative and in parable no attempt was made to generalize the sex of individual persons.

Another aspect of style will be detected by readers who compare the more stately English rendering of the Old Testament with the less formal rendering adopted for the New Testament. For example, the traditional distinction between shall and will in English has been retained in the Old Testament as appropriate in rendering a document that embodies what may be termed the classic form of Hebrew, while in the New Testament the abandonment of such distinctions in the usage of the future tense in English reflects the more colloquial nature of the koine Greek used by most New Testament authors except when they are quoting the Old Testament.

Careful readers will notice that here and there in the Old Testament the word LORD (or in certain cases GOD) is printed in capital letters. This represents the traditional manner in English versions of rendering the Divine Name, the "Tetragrammaton" (see the notes on Exodus 3:14, 15), following the precedent of the ancient Greek and Latin translators and the long established practice in the reading of the Hebrew Scriptures in the synagogue. While it is almost if not quite certain that the Name was originally pronounced "Yahweh," this pronunciation was not indicated when the Masoretes added vowel sounds to the consonantal Hebrew text. To the four consonants YHWH of the Name, which had come to be regarded as too sacred to be pronounced, they attached vowel signs indicating that in its place should be read the Hebrew word Adonai meaning "Lord" (or Elohim meaning "God"). Ancient Greek translators employed the word Kyrios ("Lord") for the Name. The Vulgate likewise used the Latin word Dominus ("Lord"). The form "Jehovah" is of late medieval origin; it is a combination of the consonants of the Divine Name and the vowels attached to it by the Masoretes but belonging to an entirely different word. Although the American Standard Version (1901) had used "Jehovah" to render the Tetragrammaton (the sound of Y being represented by J and the sound of W by V, as in Latin), for two reasons the Committees that produced the RSV and the NRSV returned to the more familiar usage of the King James Version. (1) The word "Jehovah" does not accurately represent any form of the Name ever used in Hebrew. (2) The use of any proper name for the one and only God, as though there were other gods from whom the true God had to be distinguished, began to be discontinued in Judaism before the Christian era and is inappropriate for the universal faith of the Christian Church.

It will be seen that in the Psalms and in other prayers addressed to God, the archaic second person singular pronouns (thee, thou, thine) and verb forms (art, hast, hadst) are no longer used. Although some readers may regret this change, it should be pointed out that in the original languages neither the

Old Testament nor the New makes any linguistic distinction between addressing a human being and addressing the Deity. Furthermore, in the tradition of the King James Version one will not expect to find the use of capital letters for pronouns that refer to the Deity—such capitalization is an unnecessary innovation that has only recently been introduced into a few English translations of the Bible. Finally, we have left to the discretion of the licensed publishers such matters as section headings, cross-references, and clues to the pronunciation of proper names.

This new version seeks to preserve all that is best in the English Bible as it has been known and used through the years. It is intended for use in public reading and congregational worship, as well as in private study, instruction, and meditation. We have resisted the temptation to introduce terms and phrases that merely reflect current moods, and have tried to put the message of the Scriptures in simple, enduring words and expressions that are worthy to stand in the great tradition of the King James Bible and its predecessors.

In traditional Judaism and Christianity, the Bible has been more than a historical document to be preserved or a classic of literature to be cherished and admired; it is recognized as the unique record of God's dealings with people over the ages. The Old Testament sets forth the call of a special people to enter into covenant relation with the God of justice and steadfast love and to bring God's law to the nations. The New Testament records the life and work of Jesus Christ, the one in whom "the Word became flesh," as well as describes the rise and spread of the early Christian Church. The Bible carries its full message, not to those who regard it simply as a noble literary heritage of the past or who wish to use it to enhance political purposes and advance otherwise desirable goals, but to all persons and communities who read it so that they may discern and understand what God is saying to them. That message must not be disguised in phrases that are no longer clear, or hidden under words that have changed or lost their meaning; it must be presented in language that is direct and plain and meaningful to people today. It is the hope and prayer of the translators that this version of the Bible may continue to hold a large place in congregational life and to speak to all readers, young and old alike, helping them to understand and believe and respond to its message.

For the Committee,
BRUCE M. METZGER

THE OLD TESTAMENT

The Hebrew Scriptures Commonly Called the Old Testament

OLD TESTAMENT OVERVIEW

When the earliest Christians thought about the Scriptures, they did not consider the New Testament Gospels or the letters from Paul. They thought instead of "the law of Moses, the prophets, and the psalms" (Luke 24:44). In other words, they had in mind many of the books of what we now call the Old Testament. Even so, the earliest Christians would not have agreed on what books made up that collection, for it was not until about the close of the first century C.E. that communities of faith began to reach a consensus about what was and was not "Scripture."

What eventually came to be the Old Testament is made up of thirty-nine books that correspond to the Hebrew Bible. The Hebrew Bible, however, combines several books—1 and 2 Samuel, for example—so that the count of books in that collection is twenty-four. Moreover, the arrangement and order of the books differs between those two collections (see chart, pp. 14-15).

Roman Catholics and the Eastern Orthodox include more books in the Old Testament sections of their Bibles than do Protestants. Protestants have traditionally not considered those extra books to be authoritative for faith and life. Accordingly, if the disputed books are printed in a Protestant Bible at all, they are gathered into a section called the Apocrypha (or Deuterocanon). In this respect, the Protestant tradition has followed Martin Luther. Luther's 1534 edition of the complete Bible included these additional books in a section called the Apocrypha, printed between the Old and New Testaments. Luther believed these books should not be regarded as Scripture because they did not appear in the Jewish canon.

The Old Testament books were written in Hebrew, an ancient Semitic language. In addition, and for reasons that are not fully understood, a few scattered passages were written in Aramaic, a common language in the Middle East for much of the Old and New Testament periods (see NRSV footnotes to Jer 10:11; Dan 2:4b–7:28; Ezra 4:8–6:18).

The books of the Old Testament were composed by numerous authors between the tenth and second centuries B.C.E. In the third century B.C.E., the Hebrew Scriptures began to be translated into Greek, a language that became more common in the wake of the conquests of Alexander the Great (died 323 B.C.E.). The Greek translation of the Hebrew Bible is called the Septuagint. The Septuagint version was most familiar to New Testament writers who quoted this Greek version rather than the Hebrew original.

The Old Testament sections

Christians divide the Old Testament into four major sections. First is the Pentateuch, made up of Genesis through Deuteronomy. The narrative of these books begins "In the beginning" with creation and ends with the ancient Hebrews standing on the border of the Promised Land. Next come the Historical Books, Joshua through 2 Chronicles. These books report the history of Israel, told through the lens of faith in the LORD. The period covered by these books begins in the thirteenth century B.C.E. when the Israelites entered Canaan after their years of wandering in the wilderness following the exodus from Egypt. The history continues through several hundred years, to the destruction of Jerusalem, when many of the Jewish people were forced to leave their homeland and go into exile to Babylonia. This difficult time lasted from 587 to 539 B.C.E., when the people were allowed to return to Jerusalem and rebuild their temple and city walls. This rebuilding and the reorganization of the people around the law, reported in the books of Ezra and Nehemiah, took place over the next seventy-five years.

Various poetic books are collected in the section known as the Writings (Job to the Song of Solomon). This section includes Israel's prayer book, the Psalms. Finally comes the Prophets, a collection of books that report the word of the LORD to the prophets of Israel and Judah from the eighth to the second centuries B.C.E. Further details on these Christian divisions of the Old Testament are found in essays elsewhere in this study Bible.

Why is it called "Old"?

To call the Old Testament *Old* signals a Christian view of these writings. Jewish people, of course, do not call these books the Old Testament. Instead, Jewish people refer to these Scriptures as the *Tanak*. The consonants of that word form an acronym representing the Hebrew words for, respectively, the law, the prophets, and the writings. Knowing this and understanding that the Jewish *Tanak* locates some books in different sections of the collection has interpretive significance for Christians. The book of Daniel, for example, is counted among the prophetic works in the Christian Old Testament, while the Hebrew Bible lists Daniel in the Writings. Thus, Daniel is not really a prophetic work, and it is better understood as an apocalyptic work addressed to persecuted people.

The Old Testament was composed over centuries and penned by more authors than we know. The biblical writers do not always share a common understanding of the events in Israel's history. At times biblical writers questioned God's management of the world. On other occasions, the Bible records songs of praise and thanksgiving for God's deliverance. Sometimes the Old Testament records God's pronouncement of wrath and coming judgment on account of the sins of the people. Other times, the Bible records God's promise of salvation. But within the diversity of the Old Testament, there remains a conviction that God has decided to be intimately involved with the world and with God's people, Israel. God is determined to rescue and to return the whole creation and all of humanity to the wholeness that God intended all along. For Christians, the entire Old Testament—Pentateuch, Historical Books, Poetic Books, and the Prophets—remains the *Old* Testament, because it is only in view of the New Testament that we can see the breadth and depth of God's determination to have us as God's own.

How do Lutherans read the Old Testament (or "Hebrew Scripture")?

In his own introduction to the Old Testament, Luther suggested that readers not be put off by the "simplicity of language and stories" of the Old Testament, since they are "the swaddling cloths and the manger in which Christ lies.... Simple and lowly are these swaddling cloths, but dear is the treasure, Christ, who lies in them" (*LW* 35:236). Modern Lutherans may not be as daring as Luther was in looking for and finding Jesus Christ prefigured in each story of Genesis or predicted everywhere in the Psalms and Prophets. Nevertheless, Lutherans read the Old Testament in much the same way they read the New Testament: distinguishing Law and Gospel. That is, Lutherans read the Old Testament instructed and convicted by God's commandments, so that they might be pointed toward the promised Messiah, the one the Prophet Isaiah called "Wonderful Counselor, Mighty God, Everlasting Father, Prince of Peace" (9:6).

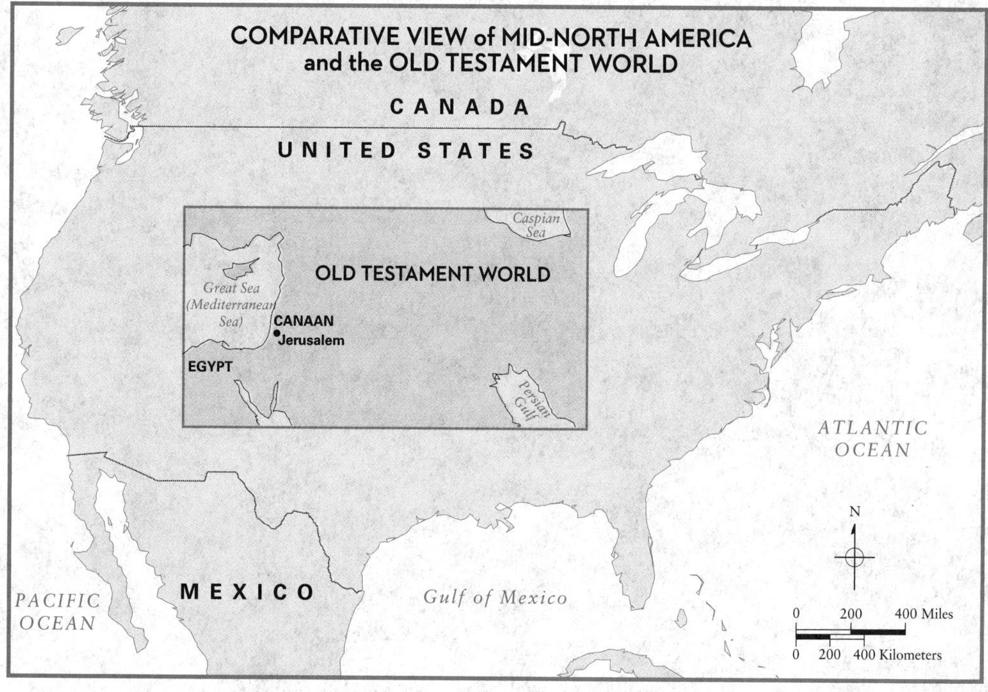

PENTATEUCH

Genesis to Deuteronomy

The first five books of the Old Testament are known by several names. Christians refer to them as the Pentateuch, a word derived from Greek that means a collection of five scrolls. Jews refer to these books as the *Torah*, a word that is too narrowly translated as "law," as in the "books of the law." That translation is unfortunate, because *torah* cannot be summed up in the single word *law*. *Torah* also includes ideas like direction, instruction, and teaching. Moreover, thinking of the content of the Pentateuch only as law is not helpful. It is true that many of the chapters in these books are filled with legal material, but they include much more than that. Between Genesis and Deuteronomy we find stories, poems, genealogies, folk tales, and other types of literature.

Nowhere in the Pentateuch is it claimed that Moses authored these books. Still, the Pentateuch has often been referred to as the "Books of Moses," a title that implies that Moses authored all five books. Indeed, the King James Version of the Bible (published in 1611) helped broadcast that idea when it added words suggesting Mosaic authorship to the original titles such as "The first book of Moses called Genesis." And there are a few late passages in the Bible that seem to claim Moses' authorship (Ezra 3:2; 6:18; Luke 24:44). These passages are better understood as declaring Moses' authority rather than his authorship.

As early as the medieval period (1200–1450 C.E.) scholars wondered whether Moses wrote these books after all. People noticed that Genesis 12:6, for example, refers to the Canaanites' occupation of the land "at that time" (of Abram). Moses could not have written that, because when Moses died the Canaanites had not yet been expelled. Genesis 36:31 implies that the author knew of Israelite kings, even though there were none until centuries after Moses lived. Deuteronomy 1:1 indicates that Moses spoke "beyond the Jordan." But since Moses died in Moab, east of the river Jordan (Deut 34:5), the author must have been west of the Jordan, where Moses never stepped foot.

All these details, coupled with differences in literary style, the various names used for God, and other evidence led scholars to suspect that the Pentateuch was not composed by Moses, but rather represents the writings of several writers (or schools of writers) whose work has been woven into a whole. The main strands were identified as follows: a Yahwistic author (J) writing in tenth century B.C.E. Judah; an Elohistic author (E), likely originating in Israel; a Priestly (P) composer, writing during the time of the Babylonian exile and after; and a fourth writer (D), primarily responsible for Deuteronomy, a book associated with the reforms of Josiah in the late seventh century B.C.E. (2 Kgs 22:8-20). So, the five books of the Pentateuch are a combination of these J, E, P, and D sources.

In recent decades, a few respected scholars have challenged aspects of the JEPD theory. Nevertheless, virtually all agree that the Pentateuch is made up of multiple literary strands. Thus, the Pentateuch is like a mosaic created of many colored stones or pieces of glass. The different sources combine, creating a wondrous picture of what God has done in the life of ancient Israel. The literary pieces provide us with a work that is greater than the sum of its individual parts.

Christians affirm that the creation of this literary mosaic was guided by the Holy Spirit. It is certainly true that the main lines of the Pentateuch's story form a consistent whole. Stories of primeval times (Gen 1–11) lead deliberately to accounts of Israel's ancestors (Gen 12–50). The Israelites' time as slaves in Egypt and their rescue by God is reported in Exodus 1–18. Exodus 19 to Numbers 10:10 describe events set around Mount Sinai, including the giving of the Ten Commandments and other laws. Finally, Numbers 10:11 through Deuteronomy record the Israelites' wilderness wandering from Sinai until the day they stood on the edge of the Promised Land. There Moses repeats and amplifies the *torah* in Deuteronomy (from the Greek, meaning "second law") in anticipation of the Israelites crossing to Canaan, the land God promised Abraham (Gen 12:1-3).

In sum, the pieces of the Pentateuch combine to tell a story about God's relationship with the world and with the Hebrew people. It is a story about a creation gone astray and about a series of promises God made about the creation (Gen 9:1-7) and to the ancient Hebrews (Gen 12:1-3; Exod 19–24) to set things right again. It is a story whose middle will not come until the New Testament and the presence of God in Christ. And it is a story that is yet to end. We watch and wait for the end that will be realized when God's kingdom comes in all its fullness.

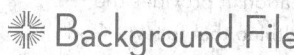

Genesis 1:3

GENESIS

Background File

Moses has traditionally been considered the author of Genesis, which is part of the Pentateuch, the first five books of the Bible. For about five hundred years, since the Reformation, the question of who wrote Genesis has been seen to be more complex. Genesis is now usually understood to have been written and compiled over the course of more than five centuries, being completed shortly after the Babylonian exile (587–538 B.C.E.), when many of the Jewish people returned to their homeland of Judah and rebuilt Jerusalem and the temple.

What's the Story?

The book of Genesis is divided into two primary sections: Genesis 1–11 portrays the beginnings of the world, including creation, the fall into sin, and the flood and its aftermath. Genesis 12–50 tells the story of Israel's ancestors and is especially concerned to speak of God's promises to this family. The book may be outlined as follows:

The Primeval Story (Gen 1:1—11:26). God, with the help of various agents, creates the world. Human sin intrudes on the creation, with social and cosmic effects. God promises a new world order.

The Story of Abraham and Sarah (Gen 11:27—25:18). God calls Abraham and makes promises to him and his descendants through both Hagar and Sarah, though it is only through his son Isaac that the covenant is established.

The Story of Jacob, Leah, and Rachel (Gen 25:19—36:43). God renews the promises to Jacob/Israel, whose twelve sons become the tribes of Israel.

The Story of Jacob's Sons, Especially Joseph (Gen 37:1—50:26). The development of Jacob's family is seen mainly through the prism of the story of Joseph.

The scholarly effort to reconstruct the history that lies behind the book of Genesis has had mixed results, because the materials have been edited over many centuries and because these chapters are more story than historical account. Especially regarding Genesis 1–11, we cannot determine its specific historical background with any confidence. As for Genesis 12–50, it is reasonable to claim that the stories carry authentic memories of Israel's ancient history prior to the Exodus from Egypt (about 2000–1500 B.C.E.). Yet, because these stories come from so long ago, it is difficult to verify the extent to which the stories of the women and men of Genesis reflect actual historical figures and events.

What's the Message?

Genesis is the first "chapter" of the Bible. Like the first chapter of any book, the placement of Genesis at the beginning is important for understanding both Genesis and the Bible as a whole.

The Bible begins, not with the chosen people (Israel), but with the entire creation. It provides the reader with a universal frame of reference. Through it we can interpret everything that follows. God's purposes—at work among the people of Israel and in Jesus Christ—have to do with all of God's good creation. "For God so loved the world..." (see John 3:16).

Genesis continues with a sad story that has tragic effects. God created a good world with no sin and evil. Human beings did not trust God, and this sin disrupted the life of God's good world. Relationships at every level fell apart: between human beings and God, among human beings, and between human beings and other creatures, including land and animals. Sin and evil are now powerful forces at work in the life of the world. Even so, God continues to shower blessings at every turn.

Genesis continues with a divine strategy to save a world broken by sin and evil. To this end, God chooses the family of Abraham and Sarah. Their task is stated clearly in Genesis 12:3: "in you all the families of the earth [listed in Gen 10] shall be blessed." God chooses one family as a means to save all families. Initially, God makes an exclusive move (choosing one family) to achieve an inclusive end: salvation of the entire creation, both human and nonhuman.

Genesis focuses on God's promises. After the flood God promises never to judge the world like this again. This promise is the foundation for God's later promises to the chosen family: blessing, descendants, a great name and nation, and a land to call their own. These promises, repeated throughout Genesis, begin to be fulfilled in this family's growth.

Genesis focuses on families. This interest in family life begins with Cain and Abel but centers on the families of Abraham and Sarah, Isaac and Rebekah, Jacob and Leah/Rachel, and their children. But these stories do not present families in ideal terms. The chosen family is dysfunctional! Yet God chooses to work in and through them, with all their flaws and weaknesses, on behalf of God's purposes for the world. Readers from every generation can recognize themselves in these families.

Genesis has an interest in the outsider, on families not chosen. Genesis often portrays the chosen family in relationships with outsiders (Egyptians, Canaanites, Philistines, Aramaeans), especially in view of its call to be a blessing to all families. Sometimes the chosen fulfill their responsibilities in exceptional ways; at other times they alienate the outsider and frustrate God's purposes. These stories help readers think carefully about how they are relating to the outsiders in our communities.

Six Days of Creation and the Sabbath

1 In the beginning when God created[a] the heavens and the earth, [2]the earth was a formless void and darkness covered the face of the deep, while a wind from God[b] swept over the face of the waters. [3]Then God said, "Let there be light"; and there was light. [4]And God saw that the light was good; and God separated the light from the darkness. [5]God called the light Day, and the darkness he called Night. And there was evening and there was morning, the first day.

6 And God said, "Let there be a dome in the midst of the waters, and let it separate the waters from the waters." [7]So God made the dome and separated the waters that were under the dome from the waters that were above the dome. And it was so. [8]God called the dome Sky. And there was evening and there was morning, the second day.

9 And God said, "Let the waters under the sky be gathered together into one place, and let the dry land appear." And it was so. [10]God called the dry land Earth, and the waters that were gathered together he called Seas. And God saw that it was good. [11]Then God said, "Let the earth put forth vegetation: plants yielding seed, and fruit trees of every kind on earth that bear fruit with the seed in it." And it was so. [12]The earth brought forth vegetation: plants yielding seed of every kind, and trees of every kind bearing fruit with the seed in it. And God saw that it was good. [13]And there was evening and there was morning, the third day.

14 And God said, "Let there be lights in the dome of the sky to separate the day from the night; and let them be for signs and for seasons and for days and years, [15]and let them be lights in the dome of the sky to give light upon the earth." And it was so. [16]God made the two great lights—the greater light to rule the day and the lesser light to rule the night—and the stars. [17]God set them in the dome of the sky to give light upon the earth, [18]to rule over the day and over the night, and to separate the light from the darkness. And God saw that it was good. [19]And there was evening and there was morning, the fourth day.

20 And God said, "Let the waters bring forth swarms of living creatures, and let birds fly above the earth across the dome of the sky." [21]So God created the great sea monsters and every living creature that moves, of every kind, with which the waters swarm, and every winged bird of every kind. And God saw that it was good. [22]God blessed them, saying, "Be fruitful and multiply and fill the waters in the seas, and let birds multiply on the earth." [23]And there was evening and there was morning, the fifth day.

24 And God said, "Let the earth bring forth living creatures of

---

[a] Or *when God began to create* or *In the beginning God created* [b] Or *while the spirit of God* or *while a mighty wind*

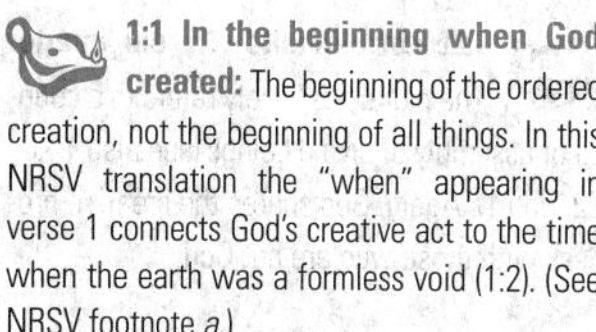

1:1 In the beginning when God created: The beginning of the ordered creation, not the beginning of all things. In this NRSV translation the "when" appearing in verse 1 connects God's creative act to the time when the earth was a formless void (1:2). (See NRSV footnote *a.*)

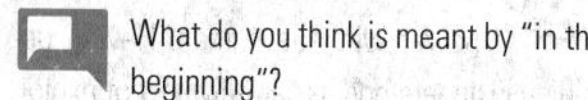

What do you think is meant by "in the beginning"?

1:2 a formless void: This phrase refers to the earth being desolate and unproductive. It doesn't mean that nothing existed (for earth, waters, and darkness exist). It simply describes the situation before God ordered the cosmos.

1:2 a wind from God: Better translated *spirit,* its link to God suggests purposeful, creative activity, preparing for the ordering to follow.

1:3 God said: God's speaking does not stand isolated from God's creating (see also 1:6-7). The word is not the only way of expressing God's creative modes. God often speaks with things and people *already* created (1:11, 20, 24, 26, 28), so the creature participates in the creative activity initiated by God.

1:4 God saw...was good: Notice how God evaluates the work of creating. This implies an ongoing process. The word *good* does not mean perfect (see "subdue" in 1:28); it carries the sense of purposefulness and beauty.

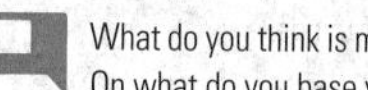

What do you think is meant by "day"? On what do you base your response?

1:7 the dome: A solid, curved sky, held up by pillars (Job 26:11) over a flat earth, providing space between waters above (the source of rain and snow) and the earth.

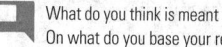

1:12 earth brought forth: God's creatures participate in creative activity.

1:14 lights: As "signs" they mark time. Some of ancient Israel's neighbors worshiped the sun, moon, and stars. For this reason, these may not have been mentioned specifically in Israel's account of creation.

1:22 God blessed: God gives power to creatures to reproduce themselves.

How have you experienced blessing in your own life?

1:26 Let us make…in our image: The plural "us" likely refers to a council or assembly of divine beings (see also 1 Kgs 22; Job 1). Again, God shares the creative process with those who are not God.

1:28 subdue…dominion: God shares power with the human. Having dominion is understood as care-giving, not exploitation. To subdue implies that God's creation was not perfect and continued to need work.

What do Lutherans believe about creation and evolution? Worldwide, there is diversity among Lutherans regarding the interpretation of the days of creation in Genesis 1. The Lutheran Confessions do not mandate the belief that God created the world in six twenty-four hour days. Many Lutherans understand that science helps us understand how God created the heavens and the earth. Whatever the case, all Lutherans are united on the confession that God created it all. *Genesis 1-2*

In your view, how does the story of creation in Genesis 1 and 2 fit with modern scientific evidence that attempts to describe how the world was created?

2:2 seventh day: God's resting, letting the creation be itself, concludes the creative process. Sabbath belongs to the created order of things.

2:4b-25 In the day the Lord God made: Originally a separate account, this chapter was composed by a different author from the one of the story in 1:1—2:4a. This has led to theories about the two accounts of creation coming from different traditions and being written at different times.

2:8 a garden in Eden: Eden, probably meaning "luxuriant," is of uncertain location (see 13:10).

2:9 tree of life: Mentioned again in 3:22-24, where eating its fruit grants immortality This tree shows that human beings were not created immortal but could continue to live by eating its fruit.

2:9 knowledge of good and evil: God has this "knowledge" (3:22), the serpent recognizes it (3:5), and humans gain it through eating, but they do not handle it well.

every kind: cattle and creeping things and wild animals of the earth of
every kind." And it was so. 25 God made the wild animals of the earth
of every kind, and the cattle of every kind, and everything that creeps
upon the ground of every kind. And God saw that it was good.

26 Then God said, "Let us make humankind[a] in our image, according to our likeness; and let them have dominion over the fish
of the sea, and over the birds of the air, and over the cattle, and over
all the wild animals of the earth,[b] and over every creeping thing that
creeps upon the earth."

27 So God created humankind[a] in his image,
in the image of God he created them;[c]
male and female he created them.

28 God blessed them, and God said to them, "Be fruitful and multiply,
and fill the earth and subdue it; and have dominion over the fish of
the sea and over the birds of the air and over every living thing that
moves upon the earth." 29 God said, "See, I have given you every plant
yielding seed that is upon the face of all the earth, and every tree with
seed in its fruit; you shall have them for food. 30 And to every beast of
the earth, and to every bird of the air, and to everything that creeps
on the earth, everything that has the breath of life, I have given every
green plant for food." And it was so. 31 God saw everything that he had
made, and indeed, it was very good. And there was evening and there
was morning, the sixth day.

2 Thus the heavens and the earth were finished, and all their multitude. 2 And on the seventh day God finished the work that he
had done, and he rested on the seventh day from all the work that he
had done. 3 So God blessed the seventh day and hallowed it, because
on it God rested from all the work that he had done in creation.

4 These are the generations of the heavens and the earth when
they were created.

Another Account of the Creation

In the day that the Lord[d] God made the earth and the heavens,
5 when no plant of the field was yet in the earth and no herb of the
field had yet sprung up—for the Lord God had not caused it to rain
upon the earth, and there was no one to till the ground; 6 but a stream
would rise from the earth, and water the whole face of the ground—
7 then the Lord God formed man from the dust of the ground,[e] and
breathed into his nostrils the breath of life; and the man became a living being. 8 And the Lord God planted a garden in Eden, in the east;
and there he put the man whom he had formed. 9 Out of the ground
the Lord God made to grow every tree that is pleasant to the sight

[a] Heb *adam* [b] Syr: Heb *and over all the earth* [c] Heb *him* [d] Heb *YHWH*, as in other places where "Lord" is spelled with capital letters (see also Ex 3.14–15 with notes). [e] Or *formed a man* (Heb *adam*) *of dust from the ground* (Heb *adamah*)

and good for food, the tree of life also in the midst of the garden, and
the tree of the knowledge of good and evil.

10 A river flows out of Eden to water the garden, and from there it
divides and becomes four branches. 11The name of the first is Pishon;
it is the one that flows around the whole land of Havilah, where there
is gold; 12and the gold of that land is good; bdellium and onyx stone
are there. 13The name of the second river is Gihon; it is the one that
flows around the whole land of Cush. 14The name of the third river
is Tigris, which flows east of Assyria. And the fourth river is the Euphrates.

15 The LORD God took the man and put him in the garden of
Eden to till it and keep it. 16And the LORD God commanded the man,
"You may freely eat of every tree of the garden; 17but of the tree of the
knowledge of good and evil you shall not eat, for in the day that you
eat of it you shall die."

18 Then the LORD God said, "It is not good that the man should
be alone; I will make him a helper as his partner." 19So out of the
ground the LORD God formed every animal of the field and every
bird of the air, and brought them to the man to see what he would call
them; and whatever the man called every living creature, that was its
name. 20The man gave names to all cattle, and to the birds of the air,
and to every animal of the field; but for the man[a] there was not found
a helper as his partner. 21So the LORD God caused a deep sleep to fall
upon the man, and he slept; then he took one of his ribs and closed up
its place with flesh. 22And the rib that the LORD God had taken from
the man he made into a woman and brought her to the man. 23Then
the man said,

"This at last is bone of my bones
and flesh of my flesh;
this one shall be called Woman,[b]
for out of Man[c] this one was taken."

24Therefore a man leaves his father and his mother and clings to his
wife, and they become one flesh. 25And the man and his wife were
both naked, and were not ashamed.

The First Sin and Its Punishment

3 Now the serpent was more crafty than any other wild animal
that the LORD God had made. He said to the woman, "Did God
say, 'You shall not eat from any tree in the garden'?" 2The woman said
to the serpent, "We may eat of the fruit of the trees in the garden; 3but
God said, 'You shall not eat of the fruit of the tree that is in the middle
of the garden, nor shall you touch it, or you shall die.'" 4But the serpent
said to the woman, "You will not die; 5for God knows that when you

[a] Or *for Adam* [b] Heb *ishshah* [c] Heb *ish*

2:10-11: A river…four branches: Rivers and places not known to us combine with the known (Assyria and the Tigris-Euphrates River valleys, which are in modern-day Iraq and beyond). Blessings flow out to the rest of the world from Eden. Human beings will not move from a world of blessing to one without blessing.

2:15 to till…keep: Human responsibility for the care of the earth is closely described (*till* could be translated "serve"); it is crucial for earth's future.

What do you think it means for human beings to "keep" the earth?

2:17 you shall die: Death here has to do with the all-encompassing breakdown in relationships (for example, between humans and God, other humans, animals, or the earth and shame within the self).

2:18 a helper: God is often called a helper (see, for example, Ps 121:1-2), so this word does not imply that the woman is an inferior assistant to the man. She is a partner and companion.

2:22 the rib: Perhaps to be translated "side." Again, this does not imply that the woman is subordinate to the man, any more than the man is subordinate to the ground from which he is made (2:7).

2:24 one flesh: A reference to sexual intimacy as part of a close relationship.

3:1 serpent: Though traditionally associated with the devil, the serpent is explicitly an animal God made (at 2:19). It is nowhere said to be evil. The serpent represents anything in God's good creation that could present tempting options to human beings, and it bears the consequences (3:14-15).

How would you describe temptation?

3:4 You will not die: A more likely translation is "You will not surely die" (NIV, RSV). So (in view of 3:22) the serpent never lies. He does not tell the full truth either (if he knew it), but neither does God. God's withholding knowledge from the humans ("for God knows") becomes the key point of temptation. Mistrust follows and is the first sin, and disobedience is a symptom of this sin.

3:6 husband, who was with her: The man was silently present during the entire conversation (the "you" is plural). He bears as much responsibility for what happens as the woman, who seduces no one.

The woman has often been blamed for introducing sin into the world. Do you think that blame is justified on the basis of this text? Why or why not?

3:14-19 The Lord God said: Following upon God's investigation (3:8-13), God announces, not *prescribes*, the consequences of sin, namely, disruptions in every relationship.

3:14-15 the serpent: The serpent (and its seed) becomes a symbol for the ongoing struggle with temptation. Sometimes this verse is linked to the victory of Christ over the devil, but no victory is in sight here. Crushing the head of the snake and a bite on the heel from a poisonous snake will have equally fatal effects.

3:16 he shall rule over you: The "rule" over the woman is a consequence of sin; it is not a prescription for their future relationship. Both man and woman will experience hardship in their primary roles in that culture (wife/mother; laborer). The pain in childbirth will "increase," implying that pain would have been experienced before sin.

How would you describe God's relationship to sinful human beings in 3:21?

eat of it your eyes will be opened, and you will be like God,[a] knowing
good and evil." 6So when the woman saw that the tree was good for
food, and that it was a delight to the eyes, and that the tree was to be
desired to make one wise, she took of its fruit and ate; and she also
gave some to her husband, who was with her, and he ate. 7Then the
eyes of both were opened, and they knew that they were naked; and
they sewed fig leaves together and made loincloths for themselves.

8 They heard the sound of the Lord God walking in the garden
at the time of the evening breeze, and the man and his wife hid themselves from the presence of the Lord God among the trees of the garden. 9But the Lord God called to the man, and said to him, "Where
are you?" 10He said, "I heard the sound of you in the garden, and I
was afraid, because I was naked; and I hid myself." 11He said, "Who
told you that you were naked? Have you eaten from the tree of which
I commanded you not to eat?" 12The man said, "The woman whom
you gave to be with me, she gave me fruit from the tree, and I ate."
13Then the Lord God said to the woman, "What is this that you have
done?" The woman said, "The serpent tricked me, and I ate." 14The
Lord God said to the serpent,

"Because you have done this,
cursed are you among all animals
and among all wild creatures;
upon your belly you shall go,
and dust you shall eat
all the days of your life.
15 I will put enmity between you and the woman,
and between your offspring and hers;
he will strike your head,
and you will strike his heel."

16To the woman he said,

"I will greatly increase your pangs in childbearing;
in pain you shall bring forth children,
yet your desire shall be for your husband,
and he shall rule over you."

17And to the man[b] he said,

"Because you have listened to the voice of your wife,
and have eaten of the tree
about which I commanded you,
'You shall not eat of it,'
cursed is the ground because of you;
in toil you shall eat of it all the days of your life;
18 thorns and thistles it shall bring forth for you;
and you shall eat the plants of the field.

---

[a] Or *gods* [b] Or *to Adam*

19 By the sweat of your face
you shall eat bread
until you return to the ground,
for out of it you were taken;
you are dust,
and to dust you shall return."

20 The man named his wife Eve,[a] because she was the mother of
all living. 21 And the LORD God made garments of skins for the man[b]
and for his wife, and clothed them.

22 Then the LORD God said, "See, the man has become like one
of us, knowing good and evil; and now, he might reach out his hand
and take also from the tree of life, and eat, and live forever"— 23 therefore the LORD God sent him forth from the garden of Eden, to till the
ground from which he was taken. 24 He drove out the man; and at the
east of the garden of Eden he placed the cherubim, and a sword flaming and turning to guard the way to the tree of life.

Cain Murders Abel

4 Now the man knew his wife Eve, and she conceived and bore
Cain, saying, "I have produced[c] a man with the help of the
LORD." 2 Next she bore his brother Abel. Now Abel was a keeper of
sheep, and Cain a tiller of the ground. 3 In the course of time Cain
brought to the LORD an offering of the fruit of the ground, 4 and Abel
for his part brought of the firstlings of his flock, their fat portions. And
the LORD had regard for Abel and his offering, 5 but for Cain and his
offering he had no regard. So Cain was very angry, and his countenance fell. 6 The LORD said to Cain, "Why are you angry, and why has
your countenance fallen? 7 If you do well, will you not be accepted?
And if you do not do well, sin is lurking at the door; its desire is for
you, but you must master it."

8 Cain said to his brother Abel, "Let us go out to the field."[d] And
when they were in the field, Cain rose up against his brother Abel,
and killed him. 9 Then the LORD said to Cain, "Where is your brother
Abel?" He said, "I do not know; am I my brother's keeper?" 10 And the
LORD said, "What have you done? Listen; your brother's blood is crying out to me from the ground! 11 And now you are cursed from the
ground, which has opened its mouth to receive your brother's blood
from your hand. 12 When you till the ground, it will no longer yield to
you its strength; you will be a fugitive and a wanderer on the earth."
13 Cain said to the LORD, "My punishment is greater than I can bear!
14 Today you have driven me away from the soil, and I shall be hidden from your face; I shall be a fugitive and a wanderer on the earth,

[a] In Heb *Eve* resembles the word for *living* [b] Or *for Adam* [c] The verb in Heb resembles the word for *Cain* [d] Sam Gk Syr Compare Vg: MT lacks *Let us go out to the field*

3:24 cherubim: They are a human/animal/bird composite, functioning as guardians of sanctuaries in Israel and its world. The close relationship the first humans enjoyed in the presence of God is no longer accessible. There can be no return to Eden.

What is the basic Lutheran understanding of sin? The Lutheran Confessions define sin as the inability to fear, love, and trust God. Human beings turn away from God and in on themselves, seeking their own will first and using the gifts of creation, including other people, to gratify their own desires. It is God's acting in Christ that brings us to repentance and gives us renewed vision of ourselves and our world. *Genesis 3*

How would you describe your relationship with God?

4:1 I have produced…the help of the LORD: This word from Eve implies divine-human cooperation in the fulfillment of 1:28.

4:5 had no regard: The reason for God's rejection of Cain's offering may be rooted in Cain's motivation, or it may simply be a random choice, such as God's choice of the second born elsewhere—Isaac in place of firstborn Ishmael (Gen 16:15; 21:10-13; 22:15-18) and Jacob over Esau (Gen 25:22-23).

4:9 brother's keeper: Only God "keeps" humans in the Old Testament (for example, see Ps 121:3-8). So Cain may be focusing on *God's* responsibility for (not) keeping Abel safe, and playing down his (Cain's) own responsibility.

What has been your understanding of "brother's keeper"? How would that be affected by this interpretation given here?

4:13 punishment…than I can bear: God's claim that Cain is "cursed" is not a description of punishment. Rather, it is an announcement of the consequence of Cain's action.

What difference does it make in your thinking about God if you use the language of consequence rather than punishment?

4:15 mark on Cain...land of Nod: The mark is an uncertain external sign designed by a gracious God to protect Cain from those who would take vengeance. Nod, a place of uncertain location, is a play on the Hebrew verb for "wander."

and anyone who meets me may kill me." 15 Then the LORD said to
him, "Not so![a] Whoever kills Cain will suffer a sevenfold vengeance."
And the LORD put a mark on Cain, so that no one who came upon
him would kill him. 16 Then Cain went away from the presence of the
LORD, and settled in the land of Nod,[b] east of Eden.

Beginnings of Civilization

4:17 Cain knew his wife: The questions about who could have endangered Cain, where he got his wife, and for whom he built his city are difficult. As with 2:24, these references may collapse the "then" of the story and the author's own time.

4:18-24 lyre...tools...killed a man: The cultural advancements described are positive developments in God's good creation. Alongside these is the negative development evident in Lamech's revengeful response.

17 Cain knew his wife, and she conceived and bore Enoch; and
he built a city, and named it Enoch after his son Enoch. 18 To Enoch
was born Irad; and Irad was the father of Mehujael, and Mehujael the
father of Methushael, and Methushael the father of Lamech. 19 Lamech took two wives; the name of the one was Adah, and the name
of the other Zillah. 20 Adah bore Jabal; he was the ancestor of those
who live in tents and have livestock. 21 His brother's name was Jubal;
he was the ancestor of all those who play the lyre and pipe. 22 Zillah
bore Tubal-cain, who made all kinds of bronze and iron tools. The
sister of Tubal-cain was Naamah.

23 Lamech said to his wives:
"Adah and Zillah, hear my voice;
    you wives of Lamech, listen to what I say:
I have killed a man for wounding me,
    a young man for striking me.
24 If Cain is avenged sevenfold,
    truly Lamech seventy-sevenfold."

4:26 Seth: Seth's importance is signaled by the reference to the worship of God under the name Yahweh (LORD), a testimony to a pre-Israel worship of Israel's God.

25 Adam knew his wife again, and she bore a son and named him
Seth, for she said, "God has appointed[c] for me another child instead
of Abel, because Cain killed him." 26 To Seth also a son was born, and
he named him Enosh. At that time people began to invoke the name
of the LORD.

Adam's Descendants to Noah and His Sons

5:1-32 descendants of Adam: Genealogies, or family trees, occur at important points in Genesis (for example, see 11:10-26; 46:8-27).

5 This is the list of the descendants of Adam. When God created
humankind,[d] he made them[e] in the likeness of God. 2 Male and
female he created them, and he blessed them and named them "Humankind"[d] when they were created.

3 When Adam had lived one hundred thirty years, he became the
father of a son in his likeness, according to his image, and named him
Seth. 4 The days of Adam after he became the father of Seth were eight
hundred years; and he had other sons and daughters. 5 Thus all the
days that Adam lived were nine hundred thirty years; and he died.

6 When Seth had lived one hundred five years, he became the
father of Enosh. 7 Seth lived after the birth of Enosh eight hundred

[a] Gk Syr Vg: Heb *Therefore* [b] That is *Wandering* [c] The verb in Heb resembles the word for *Seth*
[d] Heb *adam* [e] Heb *him*

seven years, and had other sons and daughters. [8]Thus all the days of Seth were nine hundred twelve years; and he died.

9 When Enosh had lived ninety years, he became the father of Kenan. [10]Enosh lived after the birth of Kenan eight hundred fifteen years, and had other sons and daughters. [11]Thus all the days of Enosh were nine hundred five years; and he died.

12 When Kenan had lived seventy years, he became the father of Mahalalel. [13]Kenan lived after the birth of Mahalalel eight hundred and forty years, and had other sons and daughters. [14]Thus all the days of Kenan were nine hundred and ten years; and he died.

15 When Mahalalel had lived sixty-five years, he became the father of Jared. [16]Mahalalel lived after the birth of Jared eight hundred thirty years, and had other sons and daughters. [17]Thus all the days of Mahalalel were eight hundred ninety-five years; and he died.

18 When Jared had lived one hundred sixty-two years he became the father of Enoch. [19]Jared lived after the birth of Enoch eight hundred years, and had other sons and daughters. [20]Thus all the days of Jared were nine hundred sixty-two years; and he died.

21 When Enoch had lived sixty-five years, he became the father of Methuselah. [22]Enoch walked with God after the birth of Methuselah three hundred years, and had other sons and daughters. [23]Thus all the days of Enoch were three hundred sixty-five years. [24]Enoch walked with God; then he was no more, because God took him.

25 When Methuselah had lived one hundred eighty-seven years, he became the father of Lamech. [26]Methuselah lived after the birth of Lamech seven hundred eighty-two years, and had other sons and daughters. [27]Thus all the days of Methuselah were nine hundred sixty-nine years; and he died.

28 When Lamech had lived one hundred eighty-two years, he became the father of a son; [29]he named him Noah, saying, "Out of the ground that the LORD has cursed this one shall bring us relief from our work and from the toil of our hands." [30]Lamech lived after the birth of Noah five hundred ninety-five years, and had other sons and daughters. [31]Thus all the days of Lamech were seven hundred seventy-seven years; and he died.

32 After Noah was five hundred years old, Noah became the father of Shem, Ham, and Japheth.

The Wickedness of Humankind

6 When people began to multiply on the face of the ground, and daughters were born to them, [2]the sons of God saw that they were fair; and they took wives for themselves of all that they chose. [3]Then the LORD said, "My spirit shall not abide[a] in mortals forever,

[a] Meaning of Heb uncertain

5:24 Enoch...God took him: The phrase is uncertain. He either died prematurely or disappeared unexpectedly. Some have compared his departure to the way God took the prophet Elijah away into heaven (2 Kgs 2:11-12).

5:27 Methuselah...nine hundred sixty-nine years: The long ages of the pre-flood patriarchs were probably understood literally (though similar descriptions can be found in ancient Babylonian literature). The decreasing life spans in this list (969–777 years, except Enoch) compared to those in 11:10-32 (six hundred to two hundred years) witnesses to the effects of sin over time.

6:2, 4 sons of God...Nephilim: The effects of sin become cosmic. This difficult text suggests that sin's devastating effects go beyond the human sphere. The "sons of God" may be divine beings who breach the earth-heaven boundary by taking human wives. Their offspring are "warriors of renown." The Nephilim, probably a race of giants, are compared to these sons of God.

for they are flesh; their days shall be one hundred twenty years." [4]The
Nephilim were on the earth in those days—and also afterward—when
the sons of God went in to the daughters of humans, who bore children
to them. These were the heroes that were of old, warriors of renown.
5 The LORD saw that the wickedness of humankind was great in
the earth, and that every inclination of the thoughts of their hearts
was only evil continually. [6]And the LORD was sorry that he had made
humankind on the earth, and it grieved him to his heart. [7]So the LORD
said, "I will blot out from the earth the human beings I have created—
people together with animals and creeping things and birds of the air,
for I am sorry that I have made them." [8]But Noah found favor in the
sight of the LORD.

Noah Pleases God

9 These are the descendants of Noah. Noah was a righteous man,
blameless in his generation; Noah walked with God. [10]And Noah had
three sons, Shem, Ham, and Japheth.
11 Now the earth was corrupt in God's sight, and the earth was
filled with violence. [12]And God saw that the earth was corrupt; for all
flesh had corrupted its ways upon the earth. [13]And God said to Noah,
"I have determined to make an end of all flesh, for the earth is filled
with violence because of them; now I am going to destroy them along
with the earth. [14]Make yourself an ark of cypress[a] wood; make rooms
in the ark, and cover it inside and out with pitch. [15]This is how you are
to make it: the length of the ark three hundred cubits, its width fifty
cubits, and its height thirty cubits. [16]Make a roof[b] for the ark, and
finish it to a cubit above; and put the door of the ark in its side; make
it with lower, second, and third decks. [17]For my part, I am going to
bring a flood of waters on the earth, to destroy from under heaven all
flesh in which is the breath of life; everything that is on the earth shall
die. [18]But I will establish my covenant with you; and you shall come
into the ark, you, your sons, your wife, and your sons' wives with you.
[19]And of every living thing, of all flesh, you shall bring two of every
kind into the ark, to keep them alive with you; they shall be male and
female. [20]Of the birds according to their kinds, and of the animals according to their kinds, of every creeping thing of the ground according to its kind, two of every kind shall come in to you, to keep them
alive. [21]Also take with you every kind of food that is eaten, and store
it up; and it shall serve as food for you and for them." [22]Noah did this;
he did all that God commanded him.

The Great Flood

7 Then the LORD said to Noah, "Go into the ark, you and all your
household, for I have seen that you alone are righteous before

---

[a] Meaning of Heb uncertain [b] Or *window*

6:5—8:22 the wickedness of humankind: The next chapters describe the flood that God sends on the earth in response to humankind's "wickedness" (6:5). This universal sinful condition of humans is repeated after the flood (8:21), so the flood did not rid the world of sin. The sinful human heart displays itself especially in violence (6:11-13), with consequences that affect the entire created order. Divine judgment takes the form of an environmental catastrophe, with possible parallels to other ancient stories. For example, the Babylonian Epic of Gilgamesh describes a great flood, though no geological evidence exists of a worldwide flood.

6:6 the LORD was sorry...and it grieved him to his heart: God's response to the sinful human situation and anticipated consequences portrays a God whose heart is deeply pained. This divine agony leads God to choose Noah and to save some.

How would you include sorrow and grief in your understanding of God?

6:15 cubits: Each is eighteen to twenty-one inches, or the lenth of an adult man's forearm from elbow to finger tip. The dimensions of the multi-decked ark would be approximately 450 x 75 x 45 feet.

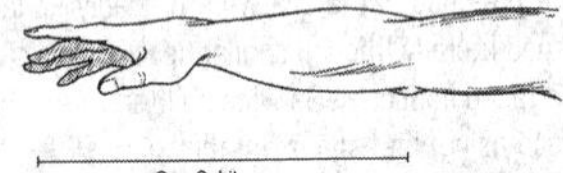

One Cubit

6:19 two of every kind: This number may refer to pairs generally, while the command in 7:2-3 to take seven pairs of clean animals (compare the need in 8:20) is a subset within that general instruction. God determines to save both humans and animals.

me in this generation. [2]Take with you seven pairs of all clean animals,
the male and its mate; and a pair of the animals that are not clean, the
male and its mate; [3]and seven pairs of the birds of the air also, male
and female, to keep their kind alive on the face of all the earth. [4]For in
seven days I will send rain on the earth for forty days and forty nights;
and every living thing that I have made I will blot out from the face of
the ground." [5]And Noah did all that the LORD had commanded him.

6 Noah was six hundred years old when the flood of waters came
on the earth. [7]And Noah with his sons and his wife and his sons' wives
went into the ark to escape the waters of the flood. [8]Of clean animals,
and of animals that are not clean, and of birds, and of everything that
creeps on the ground, [9]two and two, male and female, went into the
ark with Noah, as God had commanded Noah. [10]And after seven days
the waters of the flood came on the earth.

11 In the six hundredth year of Noah's life, in the second month,
on the seventeenth day of the month, on that day all the fountains
of the great deep burst forth, and the windows of the heavens were
opened. [12]The rain fell on the earth forty days and forty nights. [13]On
the very same day Noah with his sons, Shem and Ham and Japheth,
and Noah's wife and the three wives of his sons entered the ark, [14]they
and every wild animal of every kind, and all domestic animals of every
kind, and every creeping thing that creeps on the earth, and every bird
of every kind—every bird, every winged creature. [15]They went into
the ark with Noah, two and two of all flesh in which there was the
breath of life. [16]And those that entered, male and female of all flesh,
went in as God had commanded him; and the LORD shut him in.

17 The flood continued forty days on the earth; and the waters increased, and bore up the ark, and it rose high above the earth.
[18]The waters swelled and increased greatly on the earth; and the ark
floated on the face of the waters. [19]The waters swelled so mightily on
the earth that all the high mountains under the whole heaven were
covered; [20]the waters swelled above the mountains, covering them fifteen cubits deep. [21]And all flesh died that moved on the earth, birds,
domestic animals, wild animals, all swarming creatures that swarm on
the earth, and all human beings; [22]everything on dry land in whose
nostrils was the breath of life died. [23]He blotted out every living thing
that was on the face of the ground, human beings and animals and
creeping things and birds of the air; they were blotted out from the
earth. Only Noah was left, and those that were with him in the ark.
[24]And the waters swelled on the earth for one hundred fifty days.

7:17-24 flood continued forty days…one hundred fifty days: Some scholars have suggested that two versions of the story have been combined, as in the description of creation (Gen 1–2).

The Flood Subsides

8 But God remembered Noah and all the wild animals and all the
domestic animals that were with him in the ark. And God made
a wind blow over the earth, and the waters subsided; [2]the fountains

8:1 God remembered Noah and all…animals: This notice is the turning point in the story. The water begins to subside. God's remembrance includes animals, both wild and domestic, not just humans.

8:4 Ararat: Not one specific mountain but a range in northeastern Turkey.

of the deep and the windows of the heavens were closed, the rain
from the heavens was restrained, [3]and the waters gradually receded
from the earth. At the end of one hundred fifty days the waters had
abated; [4]and in the seventh month, on the seventeenth day of the
month, the ark came to rest on the mountains of Ararat. [5]The waters
continued to abate until the tenth month; in the tenth month, on the
first day of the month, the tops of the mountains appeared.

6 At the end of forty days Noah opened the window of the ark
that he had made [7]and sent out the raven; and it went to and fro until the waters were dried up from the earth. [8]Then he sent out the
dove from him, to see if the waters had subsided from the face of the
ground; [9]but the dove found no place to set its foot, and it returned
to him to the ark, for the waters were still on the face of the whole
earth. So he put out his hand and took it and brought it into the ark
with him. [10]He waited another seven days, and again he sent out the
dove from the ark; [11]and the dove came back to him in the evening,
and there in its beak was a freshly plucked olive leaf; so Noah knew
that the waters had subsided from the earth. [12]Then he waited another seven days, and sent out the dove; and it did not return to him
any more.

13 In the six hundred first year, in the first month, on the first day
of the month, the waters were dried up from the earth; and Noah removed the covering of the ark, and looked, and saw that the face of
the ground was drying. [14]In the second month, on the twenty-seventh
day of the month, the earth was dry. [15]Then God said to Noah, [16]"Go
out of the ark, you and your wife, and your sons and your sons' wives
with you. [17]Bring out with you every living thing that is with you of
all flesh—birds and animals and every creeping thing that creeps on
the earth—so that they may abound on the earth, and be fruitful and
multiply on the earth." [18]So Noah went out with his sons and his wife
and his sons' wives. [19]And every animal, every creeping thing, and
every bird, everything that moves on the earth, went out of the ark
by families.

God's Promise to Noah

20 Then Noah built an altar to the LORD, and took of every clean
animal and of every clean bird, and offered burnt offerings on the altar. [21]And when the LORD smelled the pleasing odor, the LORD said
in his heart, "I will never again curse the ground because of humankind, for the inclination of the human heart is evil from youth; nor
will I ever again destroy every living creature as I have done.

22 As long as the earth endures,
seedtime and harvest, cold and heat,
summer and winter, day and night,
shall not cease."

8:21-22 As long as the earth endures: God's faithfulness is shown in this eternal self-limiting promise to never again respond to human sin in flood-like ways. The promise focuses on environmental matters. Come what may, the cosmic order will remain steady and regular.

What do you think of this statement: The promise in 8:22 limits God's options regarding any future actions. Relate this to promises you have made.

The Covenant with Noah

9 God blessed Noah and his sons, and said to them, "Be fruitful and multiply, and fill the earth. [2]The fear and dread of you
shall rest on every animal of the earth, and on every bird of the air,
on everything that creeps on the ground, and on all the fish of the
sea; into your hand they are delivered. [3]Every moving thing that lives
shall be food for you; and just as I gave you the green plants, I give you
everything. [4]Only, you shall not eat flesh with its life, that is, its blood.
[5]For your own lifeblood I will surely require a reckoning: from every
animal I will require it and from human beings, each one for the blood
of another, I will require a reckoning for human life.

6 Whoever sheds the blood of a human,
by a human shall that person's blood be shed;
for in his own image
God made humankind.

[7]And you, be fruitful and multiply, abound on the earth and multiply
in it."

8 Then God said to Noah and to his sons with him, [9]"As for me,
I am establishing my covenant with you and your descendants after
you, [10]and with every living creature that is with you, the birds, the
domestic animals, and every animal of the earth with you, as many as
came out of the ark.[a] [11]I establish my covenant with you, that never
again shall all flesh be cut off by the waters of a flood, and never again
shall there be a flood to destroy the earth." [12]God said, "This is the
sign of the covenant that I make between me and you and every living creature that is with you, for all future generations: [13]I have set
my bow in the clouds, and it shall be a sign of the covenant between
me and the earth. [14]When I bring clouds over the earth and the bow
is seen in the clouds, [15]I will remember my covenant that is between
me and you and every living creature of all flesh; and the waters shall
never again become a flood to destroy all flesh. [16]When the bow is in
the clouds, I will see it and remember the everlasting covenant between God and every living creature of all flesh that is on the earth."
[17]God said to Noah, "This is the sign of the covenant that I have established between me and all flesh that is on the earth."

Noah and His Sons

18 The sons of Noah who went out of the ark were Shem, Ham,
and Japheth. Ham was the father of Canaan. [19]These three were the
sons of Noah; and from these the whole earth was peopled.

20 Noah, a man of the soil, was the first to plant a vineyard. [21]He
drank some of the wine and became drunk, and he lay uncovered in
his tent. [22]And Ham, the father of Canaan, saw the nakedness of his

---

[a] Gk: Heb adds *every animal of the earth*

9:1-5: Be fruitful...shall be food for you: Just as God had commanded the first humans (Gen 1:28), God calls Noah and his family to repopulate the earth. God extends the vegetarian diet of 1:29-30 to include meat (9:3), except for lifeblood. For ancient peoples, life was thought to reside in the blood. This is apparent in the restrictions on eating blood that are part of Israel's laws (see Lev 17:11). Could this have been a concession in a famine-ridden world? The restriction against eating blood is a reminder that killing animals is not taken lightly, for God is the source of their life. The animals fear human beings, and animal violence against humans also occurs.

9:8-17: my covenant with you: The promise of 8:21-22 is told to Noah and his family. This unconditional, eternal promise is made to humans and "every living creature" ("all flesh"). The rainbow is a sign of God's ongoing commitment to the preservation of creation.

What does God's commitment to all nonhuman creatures mean for our response to the environment?

father, and told his two brothers outside. 23 Then Shem and Japheth
took a garment, laid it on both their shoulders, and walked backward
and covered the nakedness of their father; their faces were turned
away, and they did not see their father's nakedness. 24 When Noah
awoke from his wine and knew what his youngest son had done to
him, 25 he said,

"Cursed be Canaan;
lowest of slaves shall he be to his brothers."

26 He also said,

"Blessed by the LORD my God be Shem;
and let Canaan be his slave.
27 May God make space for[a] Japheth,
and let him live in the tents of Shem;
and let Canaan be his slave."

28 After the flood Noah lived three hundred fifty years. 29 All the
days of Noah were nine hundred fifty years; and he died.

Nations Descended from Noah

10 These are the descendants of Noah's sons, Shem, Ham, and
Japheth; children were born to them after the flood.

2 The descendants of Japheth: Gomer, Magog, Madai, Javan, Tubal, Meshech, and Tiras. 3 The descendants of Gomer: Ashkenaz, Ri-
phath, and Togarmah. 4 The descendants of Javan: Elishah, Tarshish,
Kittim, and Rodanim.[b] 5 From these the coastland peoples spread.
These are the descendants of Japheth[c] in their lands, with their own
language, by their families, in their nations.

6 The descendants of Ham: Cush, Egypt, Put, and Canaan. 7 The
descendants of Cush: Seba, Havilah, Sabtah, Raamah, and Sabteca.
The descendants of Raamah: Sheba and Dedan. 8 Cush became the
father of Nimrod; he was the first on earth to become a mighty warrior. 9 He was a mighty hunter before the LORD; therefore it is said,
"Like Nimrod a mighty hunter before the LORD." 10 The beginning
of his kingdom was Babel, Erech, and Accad, all of them in the land
of Shinar. 11 From that land he went into Assyria, and built Nineveh,
Rehoboth-ir, Calah, and 12 Resen between Nineveh and Calah; that
is the great city. 13 Egypt became the father of Ludim, Anamim, Lehabim, Naphtuhim, 14 Pathrusim, Casluhim, and Caphtorim, from
which the Philistines come.[d]

15 Canaan became the father of Sidon his firstborn, and Heth,
16 and the Jebusites, the Amorites, the Girgashites, 17 the Hivites, the
Arkites, the Sinites, 18 the Arvadites, the Zemarites, and the Hamathites. Afterward the families of the Canaanites spread abroad. 19 And

[a] Heb *yapht,* a play on *Japheth* [b] Heb Mss Sam Gk See 1 Chr 1.7: MT *Dodanim* [c] Compare verses 20, 31. Heb lacks *These are the descendants of Japheth* [d] Cn: Heb *Casluhim, from which the Philistines come, and Caphtorim*

9:25-27 Canaan…slave: The issue in this story has to do with respect, not sexual activity. This affects both family and national life (Noah's sons are both individuals and nations). Canaan is the father of the peoples who are Semitic or Indo-European (10:15-19). Any attempts to justify the slavery of African peoples misuses this text. The enslavement of Canaan (9:26) probably anticipates the future when other peoples, including the Israelites who descended from Shem, would conquer and rule over the Canaanite people.

10:5, 20, 31-32 families…nations: This genealogy of Noah's sons gathers all peoples known at that time. The repeated word "families" links this text to the call of Abraham, through whom all the families of the earth will be blessed (12:3). The descendants of Japheth included peoples who lived to the north and west. This included the peoples of Greece and Asia Minor and the Philistines who lived along the Mediterranean Sea. Ham's descendants included peoples of Egypt and Mesopotamia. The legendary warrior Nimrod conquered the land of Shinar, which included Babylon and Assyria (10:9-11), both of which became enemies of Israel. Shem's descendants included the children of Eber (10:21), which may be related to the name for the wandering peoples known as the Hebrews (see also 11:10-32). See Map 1, p. 2098, for some of the locations mentioned.

the territory of the Canaanites extended from Sidon, in the direction
of Gerar, as far as Gaza, and in the direction of Sodom, Gomorrah,
Admah, and Zeboiim, as far as Lasha. [20]These are the descendants of
Ham, by their families, their languages, their lands, and their nations.
21 To Shem also, the father of all the children of Eber, the elder
brother of Japheth, children were born. [22]The descendants of Shem:
Elam, Asshur, Arpachshad, Lud, and Aram. [23]The descendants of
Aram: Uz, Hul, Gether, and Mash. [24]Arpachshad became the father
of Shelah; and Shelah became the father of Eber. [25]To Eber were born
two sons: the name of the one was Peleg,[a] for in his days the earth
was divided, and his brother's name was Joktan. [26]Joktan became the
father of Almodad, Sheleph, Hazarmaveth, Jerah, [27]Hadoram, Uzal,
Diklah, [28]Obal, Abimael, Sheba, [29]Ophir, Havilah, and Jobab; all these
were the descendants of Joktan. [30]The territory in which they lived
extended from Mesha in the direction of Sephar, the hill country of
the east. [31]These are the descendants of Shem, by their families, their
languages, their lands, and their nations.
32 These are the families of Noah's sons, according to their genealogies, in their nations; and from these the nations spread abroad on
the earth after the flood.

The Tower of Babel

11 Now the whole earth had one language and the same words.
[2]And as they migrated from the east,[b] they came upon a plain
in the land of Shinar and settled there. [3]And they said to one another,
"Come, let us make bricks, and burn them thoroughly." And they had
brick for stone, and bitumen for mortar. [4]Then they said, "Come, let
us build ourselves a city, and a tower with its top in the heavens, and let
us make a name for ourselves; otherwise we shall be scattered abroad
upon the face of the whole earth." [5]The LORD came down to see the
city and the tower, which mortals had built. [6]And the LORD said,
"Look, they are one people, and they have all one language; and this
is only the beginning of what they will do; nothing that they propose
to do will now be impossible for them. [7]Come, let us go down, and
confuse their language there, so that they will not understand one another's speech." [8]So the LORD scattered them abroad from there over
the face of all the earth, and they left off building the city. [9]Therefore
it was called Babel, because there the LORD confused[c] the language
of all the earth; and from there the LORD scattered them abroad over
the face of all the earth.

Descendants of Shem

10 These are the descendants of Shem. When Shem was one
hundred years old, he became the father of Arpachshad two years

[a] That is *Division* [b] Or *migrated eastward* [c] Heb *balal*, meaning *to confuse*

11:4-8 make a name ...scattered them abroad: Those who spoke one common language wanted to build to the heavens and make a name for themselves. God does not allow people to become one people with one language. Rather, the LORD scatters them all over the earth, and many languages result. The tower-builders of Babel were challenging God's command to fill the earth (1:28), which is necessary in order to be caretakers of the earth. God's action challenges an isolationist perspective and promotes diversity for the sake of the care of the earth and its creatures.

11:9 Babel: In the land of Shinar (10:10), Babel is a play on the word "confuse." This could also be a bit of sarcastic humor aimed at the later Babylonia.

11:10-26 descendants of Shem... Terah: This variation of the family tree in 10:21-31 is designed to lead to the family of Terah, the father of sons Abram (Abraham), Nahor, and Haran.

after the flood; 11 and Shem lived after the birth of Arpachshad five
hundred years, and had other sons and daughters.
12 When Arpachshad had lived thirty-five years, he became the
father of Shelah; 13 and Arpachshad lived after the birth of Shelah four
hundred three years, and had other sons and daughters.
14 When Shelah had lived thirty years, he became the father of
Eber; 15 and Shelah lived after the birth of Eber four hundred three
years, and had other sons and daughters.
16 When Eber had lived thirty-four years, he became the father
of Peleg; 17 and Eber lived after the birth of Peleg four hundred thirty
years, and had other sons and daughters.
18 When Peleg had lived thirty years, he became the father of
Reu; 19 and Peleg lived after the birth of Reu two hundred nine years,
and had other sons and daughters.
20 When Reu had lived thirty-two years, he became the father
of Serug; 21 and Reu lived after the birth of Serug two hundred seven
years, and had other sons and daughters.
22 When Serug had lived thirty years, he became the father of
Nahor; 23 and Serug lived after the birth of Nahor two hundred years,
and had other sons and daughters.
24 When Nahor had lived twenty-nine years, he became the father of Terah; 25 and Nahor lived after the birth of Terah one hundred
nineteen years, and had other sons and daughters.
26 When Terah had lived seventy years, he became the father of
Abram, Nahor, and Haran.

Descendants of Terah

27 Now these are the descendants of Terah. Terah was the father of Abram, Nahor, and Haran; and Haran was the father of Lot.
28 Haran died before his father Terah in the land of his birth, in Ur of
the Chaldeans. 29 Abram and Nahor took wives; the name of Abram's
wife was Sarai, and the name of Nahor's wife was Milcah. She was the
daughter of Haran the father of Milcah and Iscah. 30 Now Sarai was
barren; she had no child.
31 Terah took his son Abram and his grandson Lot son of Haran,
and his daughter-in-law Sarai, his son Abram's wife, and they went out
together from Ur of the Chaldeans to go into the land of Canaan; but
when they came to Haran, they settled there. 32 The days of Terah were
two hundred five years; and Terah died in Haran.

The Call of Abram

12 Now the LORD said to Abram, "Go from your country and
your kindred and your father's house to the land that I will
show you. 2 I will make of you a great nation, and I will bless you, and
make your name great, so that you will be a blessing. 3 I will bless those

11:30 barren: A theme in Genesis, describing Sarah, Rebekah, and Rachel. The word refers to childlessness, not necessarily infertility.

11:31—12:9 Ur...Haran...Negeb: Ur is likely a city south of Babylon. From there Terah and his family departed for Canaan, but stopped in Haran (southeastern Turkey). In response to God's call, Abram goes to Canaan (the destination in 11:31) and passes worshipfully through the entire land that God promised. Shechem, Bethel, Mamre, and Negeb are locations in Canaan. See Map 1, p. 2098.

12:1-3 I will bless you: God's promises, an interpretive key to Genesis, punctuate the texts that follow (see 28:13-14). God's choice of one individual for the sake of "all the families of the earth" looks back to previous chapters. The centrality of "blessing" in the promises links back to the blessing of 1:28. In and through this family, God's original intention in creation is to be brought forward in the lives of all.

who bless you, and the one who curses you I will curse; and in you all
the families of the earth shall be blessed."[a]
4 So Abram went, as the LORD had told him; and Lot went with
him. Abram was seventy-five years old when he departed from Haran. [5]Abram took his wife Sarai and his brother's son Lot, and all the
possessions that they had gathered, and the persons whom they had
acquired in Haran; and they set forth to go to the land of Canaan.
When they had come to the land of Canaan, [6]Abram passed through
the land to the place at Shechem, to the oak[b] of Moreh. At that time
the Canaanites were in the land. [7]Then the LORD appeared to Abram,
and said, "To your offspring[c] I will give this land." So he built there an
altar to the LORD, who had appeared to him. [8]From there he moved
on to the hill country on the east of Bethel, and pitched his tent, with
Bethel on the west and Ai on the east; and there he built an altar to the
LORD and invoked the name of the LORD. [9]And Abram journeyed on
by stages toward the Negeb.

Abram and Sarai in Egypt

10 Now there was a famine in the land. So Abram went down to
Egypt to reside there as an alien, for the famine was severe in the land.
[11]When he was about to enter Egypt, he said to his wife Sarai, "I know
well that you are a woman beautiful in appearance; [12]and when the
Egyptians see you, they will say, 'This is his wife'; then they will kill
me, but they will let you live. [13]Say you are my sister, so that it may
go well with me because of you, and that my life may be spared on
your account." [14]When Abram entered Egypt the Egyptians saw that
the woman was very beautiful. [15]When the officials of Pharaoh saw
her, they praised her to Pharaoh. And the woman was taken into Pharaoh's house. [16]And for her sake he dealt well with Abram; and he had
sheep, oxen, male donkeys, male and female slaves, female donkeys,
and camels.
17 But the LORD afflicted Pharaoh and his house with great
plagues because of Sarai, Abram's wife. [18]So Pharaoh called Abram,
and said, "What is this you have done to me? Why did you not tell me
that she was your wife? [19]Why did you say, 'She is my sister,' so that
I took her for my wife? Now then, here is your wife, take her, and be
gone." [20]And Pharaoh gave his men orders concerning him; and they
set him on the way, with his wife and all that he had.

Abram and Lot Separate

13 So Abram went up from Egypt, he and his wife, and all that
he had, and Lot with him, into the Negeb.
2 Now Abram was very rich in livestock, in silver, and in gold. [3]He

What does it mean to be "called" by God? How does your call compare with Abram's call in Genesis 12?

12:13 my sister: In this text Abram endangers the promise (compare with 20:1-18; 26:1-11). His presentation of Sarah assumes a situation where adultery is forbidden but a murder might be arranged. His life is preserved, and he becomes a wealthy man (12:16), but his deception costs Sarah her honor as she becomes Pharaoh's "wife" (12:19) and has no voice in the narrative. God's action (Pharaoh's house is afflicted with plagues) redeems the situation, and Pharaoh's gracious response serves God's purposes.

13:1-4 Egypt...Ai: Abram retraces his journey back to Canaan with Sarai and nephew Lot. See Map 1, p. 2098.

---

[a] Or *by you all the families of the earth shall bless themselves* [b] Or *terebinth* [c] Heb *seed*

journeyed on by stages from the Negeb as far as Bethel, to the place
where his tent had been at the beginning, between Bethel and Ai, 4to
the place where he had made an altar at the first; and there Abram
called on the name of the LORD. 5Now Lot, who went with Abram,
also had flocks and herds and tents, 6so that the land could not support both of them living together; for their possessions were so great
that they could not live together, 7and there was strife between the
herders of Abram's livestock and the herders of Lot's livestock. At that
time the Canaanites and the Perizzites lived in the land.

13:8 no strife: The strife between Abram and Lot leads to a decision regarding land that has wide-ranging effects. The blessings that God showers on people create problems as well as possibilities. Abraham and Lot have been blessed with many possessions, but that very blessing leads to strife and separation. A situation of material well-being raises its own set of problems, and special care is needed in working with others in a way that will bring blessing rather than curse.

How can blessings bring problems? How can problems lead to possibilities? How have you experienced one or both situations?

8 Then Abram said to Lot, "Let there be no strife between you
and me, and between your herders and my herders; for we are kindred. 9Is not the whole land before you? Separate yourself from me.
If you take the left hand, then I will go to the right; or if you take the
right hand, then I will go to the left." 10Lot looked about him, and
saw that the plain of the Jordan was well watered everywhere like the
garden of the LORD, like the land of Egypt, in the direction of Zoar;
this was before the LORD had destroyed Sodom and Gomorrah. 11So
Lot chose for himself all the plain of the Jordan, and Lot journeyed
eastward; thus they separated from each other. 12Abram settled in the
land of Canaan, while Lot settled among the cities of the Plain and
moved his tent as far as Sodom. 13Now the people of Sodom were
wicked, great sinners against the LORD.

13:10 Sodom and Gomorrah: These "wicked" cities probably lay southeast of the Dead Sea; the behaviors of their residents lead to environmental disaster for that region and for Lot's family (see Gen 18–19).

14 The LORD said to Abram, after Lot had separated from him,
"Raise your eyes now, and look from the place where you are, northward and southward and eastward and westward; 15for all the land
that you see I will give to you and to your offspring[a] forever. 16I will
make your offspring like the dust of the earth; so that if one can count
the dust of the earth, your offspring also can be counted. 17Rise up,
walk through the length and the breadth of the land, for I will give
it to you." 18So Abram moved his tent, and came and settled by the
oaks[b] of Mamre, which are at Hebron; and there he built an altar to
the LORD.

Lot's Captivity and Rescue

14:1-17 King Amraphel of Shinar…Damascus: Abraham is portrayed as a military leader on the world stage, engaged in an act of deliverance similar to later judges (see Gideon, for example, in Judg 6–8). Many of the persons and places are of uncertain reference. The setting is a war between four kings from the Mesopotamian region to the east (Shinar, which is Babylonia) and five kings from the Sodom area. During the battle Lot is captured. With the help of allies, Abram defeats the four kings, rescues Lot and the booty, and liberates the region around Sodom. He pushes the enemies far north past Damascus. The effect of Abram's action: he gains control over much of the promised land.

14 In the days of King Amraphel of Shinar, King Arioch of Ellasar, King Chedorlaomer of Elam, and King Tidal of Goiim,
2these kings made war with King Bera of Sodom, King Birsha of Gomorrah, King Shinab of Admah, King Shemeber of Zeboiim, and
the king of Bela (that is, Zoar). 3All these joined forces in the Valley of Siddim (that is, the Dead Sea).[c] 4Twelve years they had served
Chedorlaomer, but in the thirteenth year they rebelled. 5In the fourteenth year Chedorlaomer and the kings who were with him came
and subdued the Rephaim in Ashteroth-karnaim, the Zuzim in Ham,

[a] Heb *seed* [b] Or *terebinths* [c] Heb *Salt Sea*

the Emim in Shaveh-kiriathaim, 6 and the Horites in the hill country
of Seir as far as El-paran on the edge of the wilderness; 7 then they
turned back and came to En-mishpat (that is, Kadesh), and subdued
all the country of the Amalekites, and also the Amorites who lived
in Hazazon-tamar. 8 Then the king of Sodom, the king of Gomorrah,
the king of Admah, the king of Zeboiim, and the king of Bela (that is,
Zoar) went out, and they joined battle in the Valley of Siddim 9 with
King Chedorlaomer of Elam, King Tidal of Goiim, King Amraphel of
Shinar, and King Arioch of Ellasar, four kings against five. 10 Now the
Valley of Siddim was full of bitumen pits; and as the kings of Sodom
and Gomorrah fled, some fell into them, and the rest fled to the hill
country. 11 So the enemy took all the goods of Sodom and Gomorrah,
and all their provisions, and went their way; 12 they also took Lot, the
son of Abram's brother, who lived in Sodom, and his goods, and departed.

13 Then one who had escaped came and told Abram the Hebrew,
who was living by the oaks[a] of Mamre the Amorite, brother of Eshcol
and of Aner; these were allies of Abram. 14 When Abram heard that
his nephew had been taken captive, he led forth his trained men, born
in his house, three hundred eighteen of them, and went in pursuit as
far as Dan. 15 He divided his forces against them by night, he and his
servants, and routed them and pursued them to Hobah, north of Damascus. 16 Then he brought back all the goods, and also brought back
his nephew Lot with his goods, and the women and the people.

Abram Blessed by Melchizedek

17 After his return from the defeat of Chedorlaomer and the
kings who were with him, the king of Sodom went out to meet him at
the Valley of Shaveh (that is, the King's Valley). 18 And King Melchizedek of Salem brought out bread and wine; he was priest of God Most
High.[b] 19 He blessed him and said,

"Blessed be Abram by God Most High,[b]
maker of heaven and earth;
20 and blessed be God Most High,[b]
who has delivered your enemies into your hand!"

And Abram gave him one-tenth of everything. 21 Then the king of
Sodom said to Abram, "Give me the persons, but take the goods for
yourself." 22 But Abram said to the king of Sodom, "I have sworn to the
LORD, God Most High,[b] maker of heaven and earth, 23 that I would
not take a thread or a sandal-thong or anything that is yours, so that
you might not say, 'I have made Abram rich.' 24 I will take nothing but
what the young men have eaten, and the share of the men who went
with me—Aner, Eshcol, and Mamre. Let them take their share."

---

[a] Or *terebinths* [b] Heb *El Elyon*

14:18-20 Melchizedek: The king of Salem (another name for Jerusalem, Ps 76:2) serves as priest of God Most High, which in Hebrew is *El Elyon*, the name of a pre-Israelite god. Abram identifies El Elyon with his god Yahweh as the creator of the world (14:22). Melchizedek blesses Abram in the name of this God and blesses (praises) Abram's God for this deliverance. Abram responds with a tithe (one-tenth) of his goods. Melchizedek is a mysterious figure, but was probably considered a forerunner of the royal and priestly lines in the empire of Israel's later King David (see Ps 110:4). This is also why Jesus is compared with Melchizedek in Hebrews 5–7.

14:24 I will take nothing: Abram, with an issue of justice at stake, refuses to make himself rich by taking booty from a region belonging to Lot.

What might this story say to Christians about the positive impact that outsiders commonly have on their lives?

God's Covenant with Abram

15 After these things the word of the LORD came to Abram in
a vision, "Do not be afraid, Abram, I am your shield; your
reward shall be very great." 2 But Abram said, "O Lord GOD, what will
you give me, for I continue childless, and the heir of my house is Eliezer of Damascus?"[a] 3 And Abram said, "You have given me no offspring, and so a slave born in my house is to be my heir." 4 But the
word of the LORD came to him, "This man shall not be your heir;
no one but your very own issue shall be your heir." 5 He brought him
outside and said, "Look toward heaven and count the stars, if you are
able to count them." Then he said to him, "So shall your descendants
be." 6 And he believed the LORD; and the LORD[b] reckoned it to him as
righteousness.

7 Then he said to him, "I am the LORD who brought you from
Ur of the Chaldeans, to give you this land to possess." 8 But he said,
"O Lord GOD, how am I to know that I shall possess it?" 9 He said to
him, "Bring me a heifer three years old, a female goat three years old,
a ram three years old, a turtledove, and a young pigeon." 10 He brought
him all these and cut them in two, laying each half over against the
other; but he did not cut the birds in two. 11 And when birds of prey
came down on the carcasses, Abram drove them away.

12 As the sun was going down, a deep sleep fell upon Abram,
and a deep and terrifying darkness descended upon him. 13 Then the
LORD[b] said to Abram, "Know this for certain, that your offspring shall
be aliens in a land that is not theirs, and shall be slaves there, and they
shall be oppressed for four hundred years; 14 but I will bring judgment
on the nation that they serve, and afterward they shall come out with
great possessions. 15 As for yourself, you shall go to your ancestors in
peace; you shall be buried in a good old age. 16 And they shall come
back here in the fourth generation; for the iniquity of the Amorites is
not yet complete."

17 When the sun had gone down and it was dark, a smoking fire
pot and a flaming torch passed between these pieces. 18 On that day
the LORD made a covenant with Abram, saying, "To your descendants I give this land, from the river of Egypt to the great river, the
river Euphrates, 19 the land of the Kenites, the Kenizzites, the Kad-
monites, 20 the Hittites, the Perizzites, the Rephaim, 21 the Amorites,
the Canaanites, the Girgashites, and the Jebusites."

The Birth of Ishmael

16 Now Sarai, Abram's wife, bore him no children. She had an
Egyptian slave-girl whose name was Hagar, 2 and Sarai said to
Abram, "You see that the LORD has prevented me from bearing chil-

[a] Meaning of Heb uncertain [b] Heb *he*

15:2 I continue childless: Abraham responds to God's reassuring word by wondering what use it will be if he has no children. In response, God promises him offspring as numerous as the stars.

15:6 believed the LORD; and the LORD reckoned it...as righteousness: Abram trusts in the promise-giver. In response to Abram's faith, God formally declares that Abram is righteous, that is, in a right relationship with God (see Rom 4:3, 20-24; Gal 3:6; Jas 2:23).

What do you mean when you say that you "believe" in God?

How do Lutherans understand God's promise to Abraham? The key matter regarding God's assurances to Abraham is not the location of the promised land or the bloodline of the promised descendants. Instead, for Lutherans, the key matter is summed up in 15:6: "And he [Abraham] believed the LORD; and the LORD reckoned it to him as righteousness." Since this is the first instance in Scripture that faith is commended, according to Luther, "this is therefore one of the foremost passages in all of scripture" (*LW* 3:19). How does Abraham "obtain righteousness" here? "In this way," said Luther: "God speaks and Abraham believes what God is saying" (*LW* 3:21). See also Romans 4. *Genesis 15:6*

15:8 How am I to know?: Abraham asks God another question. God responds by asking Abram to perform a ritual. After Abram prepares the sacrifice, he falls asleep, but God proceeds to make the covenant.

15:13-16 Know this for certain: God reassures Abram by sketching the long journey of his offspring that would lie ahead before they settle in the land: being oppressed in Egypt for four hundred years, plagues, the exodus, and the return to Canaan in the fourth generation. The sin of the Amorites (Canaanites) will cause disastrous effects for them. The specifics of the disaster are not made clear here, just that there will be disastrous effects. You reap what you sow. Eventually we learn what those effects will be (Deut 9:4).

15:17 smoking firepot and a flaming torch: Symbols for the presence of God, who alone passes through the cut animals (see Jer 34:18-20). God makes the cov-

dren; go in to my slave-girl; it may be that I shall obtain children by
her." And Abram listened to the voice of Sarai. 3 So, after Abram had
lived ten years in the land of Canaan, Sarai, Abram's wife, took Hagar
the Egyptian, her slave-girl, and gave her to her husband Abram as a
wife. 4 He went in to Hagar, and she conceived; and when she saw that
she had conceived, she looked with contempt on her mistress. 5 Then
Sarai said to Abram, "May the wrong done to me be on you! I gave my
slave-girl to your embrace, and when she saw that she had conceived,
she looked on me with contempt. May the LORD judge between you
and me!" 6 But Abram said to Sarai, "Your slave-girl is in your power;
do to her as you please." Then Sarai dealt harshly with her, and she ran
away from her.

7 The angel of the LORD found her by a spring of water in the wilderness, the spring on the way to Shur. 8 And he said, "Hagar, slave-girl
of Sarai, where have you come from and where are you going?" She
said, "I am running away from my mistress Sarai." 9 The angel of the
LORD said to her, "Return to your mistress, and submit to her." 10 The
angel of the LORD also said to her, "I will so greatly multiply your offspring that they cannot be counted for multitude." 11 And the angel of
the LORD said to her,

"Now you have conceived and shall bear a son;
  you shall call him Ishmael,[a]
  for the LORD has given heed to your affliction.
12 He shall be a wild ass of a man,
with his hand against everyone,
  and everyone's hand against him;
and he shall live at odds with all his kin."

13 So she named the LORD who spoke to her, "You are El-roi";[b] for she
said, "Have I really seen God and remained alive after seeing him?"[c]
14 Therefore the well was called Beer-lahai-roi;[d] it lies between Kadesh
and Bered.

15 Hagar bore Abram a son; and Abram named his son, whom
Hagar bore, Ishmael. 16 Abram was eighty-six years old when Hagar
bore him[e] Ishmael.

The Sign of the Covenant

17 When Abram was ninety-nine years old, the LORD appeared
to Abram, and said to him, "I am God Almighty;[f] walk before
me, and be blameless. 2 And I will make my covenant between me and
you, and will make you exceedingly numerous." 3 Then Abram fell on
his face; and God said to him, 4 "As for me, this is my covenant with
you: You shall be the ancestor of a multitude of nations. 5 No longer

---

[a] That is *God hears* [b] Perhaps *God of seeing* or *God who sees* [c] Meaning of Heb uncertain [d] That is *the Well of the Living One who sees me* [e] Heb *Abram* [f] Traditional rendering of Heb *El Shaddai*

enant with Abram—an unconditional promise of land (detailed in 15:18-21, the broadest such list in the Bible). The ritual formalizes God's promises in an already existing relationship.

16:2 The LORD has prevented me: Sarai seeks to obtain an heir through her slave-girl, Hagar. This is a custom of the time (see 30:3-13), not a lack of faith. The promise to Abram did not specify the identity of the mother.

16:6 Sarai dealt harshly: Sarai's oppression of the Egyptian slave-girl Hagar is parallel to the Egyptians' oppression of Israel in Egypt (Exod 1:11).

16:7-9 The angel...Return to your mistress: God in human form (see 16:13) appears to an "outsider," makes promises, and commands that she return to Sarai. God makes promises to these "outsiders," showing that God is graciously at work outside the chosen community.

What might it mean that God makes promises to Hagar and Ishmael?

16:7 Shur: A wilderness between Canaan and Egypt. Hagar was going home.

16:13 named the LORD...El-roi: Hagar is the only human being to give God a name. Her naming is based on her reflection after remaining alive upon seeing God.

16:14 Beer-lahai-roi: See the NRSV footnote. This place is later associated with Isaac (24:62).

17:2-9 covenant: This *revision* of the covenant of Genesis 15, in view of a new situation, includes: a new name for God ("God Almighty"), new names for Sarah and Abraham, the naming of Sarah as the mother of the child of promise (17:15-16), the everlastingness of the covenant with Isaac (17:19), still more promises for Ishmael (17:20), and the institution of the rite of circumcision. Abraham was to keep the covenant by making sure males from his people are circumcised.

17:10 circumcision: Circumcision is to be a sign of Abraham's and his descendants' faithfulness to the covenant. Not circumcising would result in excommunication from the community (17:14). God's promise is unconditional, but people could remove themselves from the sphere of the promise by being unfaithful. Circumcision was common among Israel's neighbors.

What promises affect or shape your life?

17:15-21 Sarai your wife: For the first time in the story, Sarah is named by God to be the mother of Abraham's child. She receives a new name and promises of blessing (twice!), nations, and kings. For God to repeat these promises with respect to Sarah means that Sarah is important in her own right, not only because of her relationship to Abraham. Moreover, God speaks promises not only with respect to Isaac (17:19, 21), but also with respect to Ishmael (17:20; see also 16:10; 21:13, 18).

What does it mean for God to make promises to an outsider like Ishmael?

shall your name be Abram,[a] but your name shall be Abraham;[b] for I
have made you the ancestor of a multitude of nations. 6 I will make
you exceedingly fruitful; and I will make nations of you, and kings
shall come from you. 7 I will establish my covenant between me and
you, and your offspring after you throughout their generations, for
an everlasting covenant, to be God to you and to your offspring[c] after
you. 8 And I will give to you, and to your offspring after you, the land
where you are now an alien, all the land of Canaan, for a perpetual
holding; and I will be their God."

9 God said to Abraham, "As for you, you shall keep my covenant,
you and your offspring after you throughout their generations. 10 This
is my covenant, which you shall keep, between me and you and your
offspring after you: Every male among you shall be circumcised.
11 You shall circumcise the flesh of your foreskins, and it shall be a sign
of the covenant between me and you. 12 Throughout your generations
every male among you shall be circumcised when he is eight days old,
including the slave born in your house and the one bought with your
money from any foreigner who is not of your offspring. 13 Both the
slave born in your house and the one bought with your money must
be circumcised. So shall my covenant be in your flesh an everlasting
covenant. 14 Any uncircumcised male who is not circumcised in the
flesh of his foreskin shall be cut off from his people; he has broken
my covenant."

15 God said to Abraham, "As for Sarai your wife, you shall not call
her Sarai, but Sarah shall be her name. 16 I will bless her, and moreover
I will give you a son by her. I will bless her, and she shall give rise to
nations; kings of peoples shall come from her." 17 Then Abraham fell
on his face and laughed, and said to himself, "Can a child be born to a
man who is a hundred years old? Can Sarah, who is ninety years old,
bear a child?" 18 And Abraham said to God, "O that Ishmael might live
in your sight!" 19 God said, "No, but your wife Sarah shall bear you a
son, and you shall name him Isaac.[d] I will establish my covenant with
him as an everlasting covenant for his offspring after him. 20 As for Ishmael, I have heard you; I will bless him and make him fruitful and
exceedingly numerous; he shall be the father of twelve princes, and I
will make him a great nation. 21 But my covenant I will establish with
Isaac, whom Sarah shall bear to you at this season next year." 22 And
when he had finished talking with him, God went up from Abraham.

23 Then Abraham took his son Ishmael and all the slaves born in
his house or bought with his money, every male among the men of
Abraham's house, and he circumcised the flesh of their foreskins that
very day, as God had said to him. 24 Abraham was ninety-nine years
old when he was circumcised in the flesh of his foreskin. 25 And his

[a] That is *exalted ancestor* [b] Here taken to mean *ancestor of a multitude* [c] Heb *seed* [d] That is *he laughs*

son Ishmael was thirteen years old when he was circumcised in the
flesh of his foreskin. 26 That very day Abraham and his son Ishmael
were circumcised; 27 and all the men of his house, slaves born in the
house and those bought with money from a foreigner, were circumcised with him.

A Son Promised to Abraham and Sarah

18 The LORD appeared to Abraham[a] by the oaks[b] of Mamre, as
he sat at the entrance of his tent in the heat of the day. 2 He
looked up and saw three men standing near him. When he saw them,
he ran from the tent entrance to meet them, and bowed down to
the ground. 3 He said, "My lord, if I find favor with you, do not pass
by your servant. 4 Let a little water be brought, and wash your feet,
and rest yourselves under the tree. 5 Let me bring a little bread, that
you may refresh yourselves, and after that you may pass on—since
you have come to your servant." So they said, "Do as you have said."
6 And Abraham hastened into the tent to Sarah, and said, "Make ready
quickly three measures[c] of choice flour, knead it, and make cakes."
7 Abraham ran to the herd, and took a calf, tender and good, and gave
it to the servant, who hastened to prepare it. 8 Then he took curds and
milk and the calf that he had prepared, and set it before them; and he
stood by them under the tree while they ate.
9 They said to him, "Where is your wife Sarah?" And he said,
"There, in the tent." 10 Then one said, "I will surely return to you in due
season, and your wife Sarah shall have a son." And Sarah was listening at the tent entrance behind him. 11 Now Abraham and Sarah were
old, advanced in age; it had ceased to be with Sarah after the manner
of women. 12 So Sarah laughed to herself, saying, "After I have grown
old, and my husband is old, shall I have pleasure?" 13 The LORD said to
Abraham, "Why did Sarah laugh, and say, 'Shall I indeed bear a child,
now that I am old?' 14 Is anything too wonderful for the LORD? At the
set time I will return to you, in due season, and Sarah shall have a son."
15 But Sarah denied, saying, "I did not laugh"; for she was afraid. He
said, "Oh yes, you did laugh."

Judgment Pronounced on Sodom

16 Then the men set out from there, and they looked toward
Sodom; and Abraham went with them to set them on their way. 17 The
LORD said, "Shall I hide from Abraham what I am about to do, 18 seeing that Abraham shall become a great and mighty nation, and all the
nations of the earth shall be blessed in him?[d] 19 No, for I have chosen[e]
him, that he may charge his children and his household after him to

[a] Heb *him* [b] Or *terebinths* [c] Heb *seahs* [d] Or *and all the nations of the earth shall bless themselves by him* [e] Heb *known*

18:1-2 The LORD appeared...three men: Two points of view are presented regarding the three visitors—the narrator's (18:1) and Abraham's (18:2). God assumes human form and appears as one of the three; the other two are angels (see 19:1).

18:11 after the manner of women: Refers to menopause.

18:14 too wonderful: "Wonderful" can refer to competence, power, or awesomeness (Ps 118:23). The force of this verse: God's promises will not fail; God will always find a way into the future.

18:17 hide from Abraham: God consults with Abraham, because God does not want to keep him ignorant of God's ways. God has chosen him to have a role among the nations (12:3) and charged him to teach his children justice.

keep the way of the LORD by doing righteousness and justice; so that
the LORD may bring about for Abraham what he has promised him."
20 Then the LORD said, "How great is the outcry against Sodom and
Gomorrah and how very grave their sin! 21 I must go down and see
whether they have done altogether according to the outcry that has
come to me; and if not, I will know."

22 So the men turned from there, and went toward Sodom, while
Abraham remained standing before the LORD.[a] 23 Then Abraham
came near and said, "Will you indeed sweep away the righteous with
the wicked? 24 Suppose there are fifty righteous within the city; will
you then sweep away the place and not forgive it for the fifty righteous
who are in it? 25 Far be it from you to do such a thing, to slay the righteous with the wicked, so that the righteous fare as the wicked! Far
be that from you! Shall not the Judge of all the earth do what is just?"
26 And the LORD said, "If I find at Sodom fifty righteous in the city, I
will forgive the whole place for their sake." 27 Abraham answered, "Let
me take it upon myself to speak to the Lord, I who am but dust and
ashes. 28 Suppose five of the fifty righteous are lacking? Will you destroy the whole city for lack of five?" And he said, "I will not destroy
it if I find forty-five there." 29 Again he spoke to him, "Suppose forty
are found there." He answered, "For the sake of forty I will not do
it." 30 Then he said, "Oh do not let the Lord be angry if I speak. Suppose thirty are found there." He answered, "I will not do it, if I find
thirty there." 31 He said, "Let me take it upon myself to speak to the
Lord. Suppose twenty are found there." He answered, "For the sake of
twenty I will not destroy it." 32 Then he said, "Oh do not let the Lord
be angry if I speak just once more. Suppose ten are found there." He
answered, "For the sake of ten I will not destroy it." 33 And the LORD
went his way, when he had finished speaking to Abraham; and Abraham returned to his place.

The Depravity of Sodom

19 The two angels came to Sodom in the evening, and Lot was
sitting in the gateway of Sodom. When Lot saw them, he rose
to meet them, and bowed down with his face to the ground. 2 He said,
"Please, my lords, turn aside to your servant's house and spend the
night, and wash your feet; then you can rise early and go on your way."
They said, "No; we will spend the night in the square." 3 But he urged
them strongly; so they turned aside to him and entered his house;
and he made them a feast, and baked unleavened bread, and they ate.
4 But before they lay down, the men of the city, the men of Sodom,
both young and old, all the people to the last man, surrounded the
house; 5 and they called to Lot, "Where are the men who came to you

[a] Another ancient tradition reads *while the LORD remained standing before Abraham*

18:21 I must...see whether: God knows of injustice in Sodom but determines to consult with Abraham about it before making a final decision. God admits the possibility of an "if not," so the future of Sodom is at least somewhat open.

Concerning God's knowledge and understanding of future events, what may this "if" (18:21, 26) mean to you (see also 22:12)?

18:24-32 fifty righteous...ten: The issue is critical mass. Are there enough righteous people in the city to outweigh the effects of the wicked? In this case, as few as ten righteous persons are a sufficient number to turn the judgment situation around.

18:25 Judge of all the earth do what is just?: Abraham's question assumes that God must act in a just way regarding divinely established relationships. This especially includes recognizing the differences between the righteous and the wicked, and treating them according to their deeds.

How can we explain or deal with the fact that difficult and painful things happen to good people? Why doesn't God act to make sure everyone gets exactly what they deserve?

19:1-11 two angels...struck with blindness: This scene is an illustration of Sodom's wickedness. The verb *know* refers to sexual activity. With *every* man involved, the result would have been gang rape (19:4-5). Sexual abuse of strangers demonstrated who was in charge (as in prisons). The sins of Sodom are most explicit in Ezekiel 16:49: pride, gluttony, prosperous ease, and not aiding the poor and needy (compare with Matt 10:14-15). That Lot would substitute his *betrothed* (engaged) daughters is another sign of Sodom's immorality. In 19:30-38, Lot himself is sexually abused.

tonight? Bring them out to us, so that we may know them." [6]Lot went out of the door to the men, shut the door after him, [7]and said, "I beg you, my brothers, do not act so wickedly. [8]Look, I have two daughters who have not known a man; let me bring them out to you, and do to them as you please; only do nothing to these men, for they have come under the shelter of my roof." [9]But they replied, "Stand back!" And they said, "This fellow came here as an alien, and he would play the judge! Now we will deal worse with you than with them." Then they pressed hard against the man Lot, and came near the door to break it down. [10]But the men inside reached out their hands and brought Lot into the house with them, and shut the door. [11]And they struck with blindness the men who were at the door of the house, both small and great, so that they were unable to find the door.

Sodom and Gomorrah Destroyed

12 Then the men said to Lot, "Have you anyone else here? Sons-in-law, sons, daughters, or anyone you have in the city—bring them out of the place. [13]For we are about to destroy this place, because the outcry against its people has become great before the LORD, and the LORD has sent us to destroy it." [14]So Lot went out and said to his sons-in-law, who were to marry his daughters, "Up, get out of this place; for the LORD is about to destroy the city." But he seemed to his sons-in-law to be jesting.

15 When morning dawned, the angels urged Lot, saying, "Get up, take your wife and your two daughters who are here, or else you will be consumed in the punishment of the city." [16]But he lingered; so the men seized him and his wife and his two daughters by the hand, the LORD being merciful to him, and they brought him out and left him outside the city. [17]When they had brought them outside, they[a] said, "Flee for your life; do not look back or stop anywhere in the Plain; flee to the hills, or else you will be consumed." [18]And Lot said to them, "Oh, no, my lords; [19]your servant has found favor with you, and you have shown me great kindness in saving my life; but I cannot flee to the hills, for fear the disaster will overtake me and I die. [20]Look, that city is near enough to flee to, and it is a little one. Let me escape there—is it not a little one?—and my life will be saved!" [21]He said to him, "Very well, I grant you this favor too, and will not overthrow the city of which you have spoken. [22]Hurry, escape there, for I can do nothing until you arrive there." Therefore the city was called Zoar.[b] [23]The sun had risen on the earth when Lot came to Zoar.

24 Then the LORD rained on Sodom and Gomorrah sulfur and fire from the LORD out of heaven; [25]and he overthrew those cities, and all the Plain, and all the inhabitants of the cities, and what grew

[a] Gk Syr Vg: Heb *he* [b] That is *Little*

19:24-26 rained...sulfur and fire: The cities' devastation may have been caused by an earthquake with associated fires that ignited bitumen deposits (see 14:10). Lot's hesitant wife may have been engulfed in the explosion. The environmental disaster changed the area from garden (13:10) to wasteland is due to *human* wickedness.

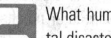

What human causes of environmental disaster today can you cite?

on the ground. [26]But Lot's wife, behind him, looked back, and she
became a pillar of salt.
27 Abraham went early in the morning to the place where he had
stood before the LORD; [28]and he looked down toward Sodom and
Gomorrah and toward all the land of the Plain and saw the smoke of
the land going up like the smoke of a furnace.
29 So it was that, when God destroyed the cities of the Plain, God
remembered Abraham, and sent Lot out of the midst of the overthrow, when he overthrew the cities in which Lot had settled.

The Shameful Origin of Moab and Ammon

30 Now Lot went up out of Zoar and settled in the hills with his
two daughters, for he was afraid to stay in Zoar; so he lived in a cave
with his two daughters. [31]And the firstborn said to the younger, "Our
father is old, and there is not a man on earth to come in to us after the
manner of all the world. [32]Come, let us make our father drink wine,
and we will lie with him, so that we may preserve offspring through
our father." [33]So they made their father drink wine that night; and the
firstborn went in, and lay with her father; he did not know when she
lay down or when she rose. [34]On the next day, the firstborn said to the
younger, "Look, I lay last night with my father; let us make him drink
wine tonight also; then you go in and lie with him, so that we may preserve offspring through our father." [35]So they made their father drink
wine that night also; and the younger rose, and lay with him; and he
did not know when she lay down or when she rose. [36]Thus both the
daughters of Lot became pregnant by their father. [37]The firstborn
bore a son, and named him Moab; he is the ancestor of the Moabites
to this day. [38]The younger also bore a son and named him Ben-ammi;
he is the ancestor of the Ammonites to this day.

Abraham and Sarah at Gerar

20 From there Abraham journeyed toward the region of the
Negeb, and settled between Kadesh and Shur. While residing in Gerar as an alien, [2]Abraham said of his wife Sarah, "She is my
sister." And King Abimelech of Gerar sent and took Sarah. [3]But God
came to Abimelech in a dream by night, and said to him, "You are
about to die because of the woman whom you have taken; for she is
a married woman." [4]Now Abimelech had not approached her; so he
said, "Lord, will you destroy an innocent people? [5]Did he not himself
say to me, 'She is my sister'? And she herself said, 'He is my brother.' I
did this in the integrity of my heart and the innocence of my hands."
[6]Then God said to him in the dream, "Yes, I know that you did this in
the integrity of your heart; furthermore it was I who kept you from
sinning against me. Therefore I did not let you touch her. [7]Now then,
return the man's wife; for he is a prophet, and he will pray for you and

19:37-38 Moabites...Ammonites: Transjordanian peoples. Ruth, whose descendants include David and Jesus, comes from the line of Moab (Ruth 4:18-22; Matt 1:5).

How can God bring blessing from even the worst of family situations?

20:1-2 King Abimelech...Gerar: Gerar was probably in south Canaan, where Isaac settled (26:6), in what later became Philistine territory. Abimelech, the king of Gerar, has several dealings with Abraham's family (21:22-34; 26:1-11).

20:3 God came...in a dream: Dreams could be a medium of divine revelation, meaning God uses dreams to reveal messages to people. Here, God communicated with Abimelech to protect Sarah. God acknowledges Ambimelech's innocence in this matter, but death will come if he does not restore Sarah (20:3, 7).

20:7 a prophet: Though Abraham is not actually a prophet he is described as one because he does what later prophets do—speak with God on behalf of others.

you shall live. But if you do not restore her, know that you shall surely die, you and all that are yours."

8 So Abimelech rose early in the morning, and called all his servants and told them all these things; and the men were very much afraid. [9]Then Abimelech called Abraham, and said to him, "What have you done to us? How have I sinned against you, that you have brought such great guilt on me and my kingdom? You have done things to me that ought not to be done." [10]And Abimelech said to Abraham, "What were you thinking of, that you did this thing?" [11]Abraham said, "I did it because I thought, There is no fear of God at all in this place, and they will kill me because of my wife. [12]Besides, she is indeed my sister, the daughter of my father but not the daughter of my mother; and she became my wife. [13]And when God caused me to wander from my father's house, I said to her, 'This is the kindness you must do me: at every place to which we come, say of me, He is my brother.' " [14]Then Abimelech took sheep and oxen, and male and female slaves, and gave them to Abraham, and restored his wife Sarah to him. [15]Abimelech said, "My land is before you; settle where it pleases you." [16]To Sarah he said, "Look, I have given your brother a thousand pieces of silver; it is your exoneration before all who are with you; you are completely vindicated." [17]Then Abraham prayed to God; and God healed Abimelech, and also healed his wife and female slaves so that they bore children. [18]For the LORD had closed fast all the wombs of the house of Abimelech because of Sarah, Abraham's wife.

20:9 What have you done? This outsider, Abimelech, calls Abraham, God's chosen one, to account for his behavior and its ill effects (see 20:17-18). Abraham's rationalizing response is self-serving and its information cannot be trusted.

In your experience, can a non-Christian have a strong or even stronger sense of justice than that of many Christians? Why or why not?

The Birth of Isaac

21 The LORD dealt with Sarah as he had said, and the LORD did for Sarah as he had promised. [2]Sarah conceived and bore Abraham a son in his old age, at the time of which God had spoken to him. [3]Abraham gave the name Isaac to his son whom Sarah bore him. [4]And Abraham circumcised his son Isaac when he was eight days old, as God had commanded him. [5]Abraham was a hundred years old when his son Isaac was born to him. [6]Now Sarah said, "God has brought laughter for me; everyone who hears will laugh with me." [7]And she said, "Who would ever have said to Abraham that Sarah would nurse children? Yet I have borne him a son in his old age."

21:3-6 circumcised his son Isaac...God has brought laughter: Isaac is born as God had promised (17:19; 18:14); Isaac's name is a play on the word *laughter*, in view of his parents' incredulous laughter at God's promise and joy at his birth (17:17; 18:12).

Hagar and Ishmael Sent Away

8 The child grew, and was weaned; and Abraham made a great feast on the day that Isaac was weaned. [9]But Sarah saw the son of Hagar the Egyptian, whom she had borne to Abraham, playing with her son Isaac.[a] [10]So she said to Abraham, "Cast out this slave woman with her son; for the son of this slave woman shall not inherit along with

21:10 Cast out: Isaac's birth raises a problem regarding Ishmael since both had received God's promises. Sarah, concerned about Isaac's inheritance, successfully urges that Ishmael be sent away, with God's support. Yet Ishmael is not forgotten, as God "was with the boy" (21:20) and repeats promises regarding his future (21:13, 18). Muslims understand themselves to be descendants of Ishmael.

[a] Gk Vg: Heb lacks *with her son Isaac*

Given that God keeps promises, what might this mean for our understanding of the growth of Islam?

my son Isaac." [11]The matter was very distressing to Abraham on account of his son. [12]But God said to Abraham, "Do not be distressed because of the boy and because of your slave woman; whatever Sarah says to you, do as she tells you, for it is through Isaac that offspring shall be named for you. [13]As for the son of the slave woman, I will make a nation of him also, because he is your offspring." [14]So Abraham rose early in the morning, and took bread and a skin of water, and gave it to Hagar, putting it on her shoulder, along with the child, and sent her away. And she departed, and wandered about in the wilderness of Beer-sheba.

15 When the water in the skin was gone, she cast the child under one of the bushes. [16]Then she went and sat down opposite him a good way off, about the distance of a bowshot; for she said, "Do not let me look on the death of the child." And as she sat opposite him, she lifted up her voice and wept. [17]And God heard the voice of the boy; and the angel of God called to Hagar from heaven, and said to her, "What troubles you, Hagar? Do not be afraid; for God has heard the voice of the boy where he is. [18]Come, lift up the boy and hold him fast with your hand, for I will make a great nation of him." [19]Then God opened her eyes and she saw a well of water. She went, and filled the skin with water, and gave the boy a drink.

20 God was with the boy, and he grew up; he lived in the wilderness, and became an expert with the bow. [21]He lived in the wilderness of Paran; and his mother got a wife for him from the land of Egypt.

Abraham and Abimelech Make a Covenant

22 At that time Abimelech, with Phicol the commander of his army, said to Abraham, "God is with you in all that you do; [23]now therefore swear to me here by God that you will not deal falsely with me or with my offspring or with my posterity, but as I have dealt loyally with you, you will deal with me and with the land where you have resided as an alien." [24]And Abraham said, "I swear it."

25 When Abraham complained to Abimelech about a well of water that Abimelech's servants had seized, [26]Abimelech said, "I do not know who has done this; you did not tell me, and I have not heard of it until today." [27]So Abraham took sheep and oxen and gave them to Abimelech, and the two men made a covenant. [28]Abraham set apart seven ewe lambs of the flock. [29]And Abimelech said to Abraham, "What is the meaning of these seven ewe lambs that you have set apart?" [30]He said, "These seven ewe lambs you shall accept from my hand, in order that you may be a witness for me that I dug this well." [31]Therefore that place was called Beer-sheba;[a] because there both of them swore an oath. [32]When they had made a covenant at

21:31-33 Beersheba: A well (later a city) in southern Judah commemorating the covenant between Abraham and Abimelech (see also 26:12-33).

21:32, 34 Philistines: A reference to sea people (see 26:1) who settled in Canaan about 1200 B.C.E. and were often in conflict with the Israelites. They were not yet in the land when Abraham was in this area.

[a] That is *Well of seven* or *Well of the oath*

Beer-sheba, Abimelech, with Phicol the commander of his army, left
and returned to the land of the Philistines. 33 Abraham[a] planted a tamarisk tree in Beer-sheba, and called there on the name of the LORD,
the Everlasting God.[b] 34 And Abraham resided as an alien many days
in the land of the Philistines.

The Command to Sacrifice Isaac

22 After these things God tested Abraham. He said to him,
"Abraham!" And he said, "Here I am." 2 He said, "Take your
son, your only son Isaac, whom you love, and go to the land of Moriah, and offer him there as a burnt offering on one of the mountains
that I shall show you." 3 So Abraham rose early in the morning, saddled his donkey, and took two of his young men with him, and his son
Isaac; he cut the wood for the burnt offering, and set out and went
to the place in the distance that God had shown him. 4 On the third
day Abraham looked up and saw the place far away. 5 Then Abraham
said to his young men, "Stay here with the donkey; the boy and I will
go over there; we will worship, and then we will come back to you."
6 Abraham took the wood of the burnt offering and laid it on his son
Isaac, and he himself carried the fire and the knife. So the two of them
walked on together. 7 Isaac said to his father Abraham, "Father!" And
he said, "Here I am, my son." He said, "The fire and the wood are here,
but where is the lamb for a burnt offering?" 8 Abraham said, "God
himself will provide the lamb for a burnt offering, my son." So the two
of them walked on together.
9 When they came to the place that God had shown him, Abraham built an altar there and laid the wood in order. He bound his son
Isaac, and laid him on the altar, on top of the wood. 10 Then Abraham
reached out his hand and took the knife to kill[c] his son. 11 But the angel
of the LORD called to him from heaven, and said, "Abraham, Abraham!" And he said, "Here I am." 12 He said, "Do not lay your hand on
the boy or do anything to him; for now I know that you fear God,
since you have not withheld your son, your only son, from me." 13 And
Abraham looked up and saw a ram, caught in a thicket by its horns.
Abraham went and took the ram and offered it up as a burnt offering instead of his son. 14 So Abraham called that place "The LORD will
provide";[d] as it is said to this day, "On the mount of the LORD it shall
be provided."[e]
15 The angel of the LORD called to Abraham a second time from
heaven, 16 and said, "By myself I have sworn, says the LORD: Because
you have done this, and have not withheld your son, your only son,
17 I will indeed bless you, and I will make your offspring as numerous

[a] Heb *He* [b] Or *the LORD, El Olam* [c] Or *to slaughter* [d] Or *will see;* Heb traditionally transliterated *Jehovah Jireh* [e] Or *he shall be seen*

22:1 God tested Abraham: The narrator informs readers, but not Abraham, that this is a test. God's purpose is not to kill Isaac but rather that God may know (22:12; see Deut 8:2) that the future can be entrusted to Abraham. Abraham's threefold attentive response, "Here I am," is rooted in his long-standing trust of God and highlights basic moments of the narrative (22:1, 7, 11). The test confirms a fact: Abraham trusts God wholeheartedly.

What, if anything, do you find troubling about this episode? What if someone attempted to do such a thing today?

22:2 your only son . . . Moriah: These words indirectly recall Abraham's loss of his other son, Ishmael (21:8-21 parallels chapter 22). The location of Moriah is uncertain, but it may refer to Jerusalem and is traditionally associated with the Temple Mount there (2 Chron 3:1).

22:2 a burnt offering: The offering needs to be placed within the context of the sacrificial system (Abraham intends to "worship," 22:5). It is not a command to murder. God's providing is a central feature of the text (22:8, 14).

22:16 Because you have done this: The original promises were made independent of Abraham's faith (12:1-3), and God's unconditional promises *create* his faith (15:5-6). So Abraham's faith here does not create the promises. God's promises will always remain intact, but Abraham could reject God and remove himself from the sphere of the promise. Human faithfulness is not an option; the promises are reiterated to a trusting Abraham.

Has God tested your faith? If so, how was it done and what was its effect?

What role has the near-sacrifice of Isaac played in Lutheran theological reflection? Abraham trusts God will keep the promise made to Abraham (that he will have a son and heir and many descendants), so Abraham can proceed in faith (22:8). He trusts that God will not fail to keep earlier promises regarding Isaac (17:9), though he does not know how God will work things out. In his *Lectures on Genesis*, Martin Luther colorfully expresses Abraham's faith this way: "Faith...has the power to kill death, to condemn hell, to be sin for sin, to be devil for the devil to such an extent that death is not death.... Of this Abraham is sure. He thinks: 'I am reducing my son to ashes. Nevertheless he is not dying. Indeed, those ashes will be my heir'" (*LW* 4:117). *Genesis 22*

22:20-24 Milcah also has borne children: This text, linked to 11:29, begins to make concrete God's promise of enduring family to Abraham. Rebekah is a grandniece of Abraham.

23:3-18 Hittites...Ephron: The Hittites probably were pre-Israelite peoples living in Canaan (27:46—28:1 seems to equate them with Canaanites). Ephron was the Hittite landowner with whom Abraham dealt.

23:9 Machpelah: A cave in southern Canaan near Mamre that became the burial place of Sarah and Abraham as well as Isaac, Rebekah, Jacob, and Leah. This purchase signals the beginning of Abraham's acquisition of the promised land of Canaan for Israel's descendants.

as the stars of heaven and as the sand that is on the seashore. And
your offspring shall possess the gate of their enemies, 18 and by your
offspring shall all the nations of the earth gain blessing for themselves,
because you have obeyed my voice." 19 So Abraham returned to his
young men, and they arose and went together to Beer-sheba; and
Abraham lived at Beer-sheba.

The Children of Nahor

20 Now after these things it was told Abraham, "Milcah also has
borne children, to your brother Nahor: 21 Uz the firstborn, Buz his
brother, Kemuel the father of Aram, 22 Chesed, Hazo, Pildash, Jidlaph,
and Bethuel." 23 Bethuel became the father of Rebekah. These eight
Milcah bore to Nahor, Abraham's brother. 24 Moreover, his concubine,
whose name was Reumah, bore Tebah, Gaham, Tahash, and Maacah.

Sarah's Death and Burial

23 Sarah lived one hundred twenty-seven years; this was the
length of Sarah's life. 2 And Sarah died at Kiriath-arba (that
is, Hebron) in the land of Canaan; and Abraham went in to mourn for
Sarah and to weep for her. 3 Abraham rose up from beside his dead,
and said to the Hittites, 4 "I am a stranger and an alien residing among
you; give me property among you for a burying place, so that I may
bury my dead out of my sight." 5 The Hittites answered Abraham,
6 "Hear us, my lord; you are a mighty prince among us. Bury your
dead in the choicest of our burial places; none of us will withhold
from you any burial ground for burying your dead." 7 Abraham rose
and bowed to the Hittites, the people of the land. 8 He said to them,
"If you are willing that I should bury my dead out of my sight, hear
me, and entreat for me Ephron son of Zohar, 9 so that he may give me
the cave of Machpelah, which he owns; it is at the end of his field. For
the full price let him give it to me in your presence as a possession for
a burying place." 10 Now Ephron was sitting among the Hittites; and
Ephron the Hittite answered Abraham in the hearing of the Hittites,
of all who went in at the gate of his city, 11 "No, my lord, hear me; I give
you the field, and I give you the cave that is in it; in the presence of
my people I give it to you; bury your dead." 12 Then Abraham bowed
down before the people of the land. 13 He said to Ephron in the hearing of the people of the land, "If you only will listen to me! I will give
the price of the field; accept it from me, so that I may bury my dead
there." 14 Ephron answered Abraham, 15 "My lord, listen to me; a piece
of land worth four hundred shekels of silver—what is that between
you and me? Bury your dead." 16 Abraham agreed with Ephron; and
Abraham weighed out for Ephron the silver that he had named in the
hearing of the Hittites, four hundred shekels of silver, according to the
weights current among the merchants.

17 So the field of Ephron in Machpelah, which was to the east of
Mamre, the field with the cave that was in it and all the trees that were
in the field, throughout its whole area, passed 18 to Abraham as a possession in the presence of the Hittites, in the presence of all who went
in at the gate of his city. 19 After this, Abraham buried Sarah his wife in
the cave of the field of Machpelah facing Mamre (that is, Hebron) in the
land of Canaan. 20 The field and the cave that is in it passed from the
Hittites into Abraham's possession as a burying place.

The Marriage of Isaac and Rebekah

24 Now Abraham was old, well advanced in years; and the
LORD had blessed Abraham in all things. 2 Abraham said
to his servant, the oldest of his house, who had charge of all that he
had, "Put your hand under my thigh 3 and I will make you swear by
the LORD, the God of heaven and earth, that you will not get a wife
for my son from the daughters of the Canaanites, among whom I
live, 4 but will go to my country and to my kindred and get a wife for
my son Isaac." 5 The servant said to him, "Perhaps the woman may
not be willing to follow me to this land; must I then take your son
back to the land from which you came?" 6 Abraham said to him, "See
to it that you do not take my son back there. 7 The LORD, the God of
heaven, who took me from my father's house and from the land of
my birth, and who spoke to me and swore to me, 'To your offspring
I will give this land,' he will send his angel before you, and you shall
take a wife for my son from there. 8 But if the woman is not willing
to follow you, then you will be free from this oath of mine; only you
must not take my son back there." 9 So the servant put his hand under
the thigh of Abraham his master and swore to him concerning this
matter.

10 Then the servant took ten of his master's camels and departed,
taking all kinds of choice gifts from his master; and he set out and
went to Aram-naharaim, to the city of Nahor. 11 He made the camels kneel down outside the city by the well of water; it was toward
evening, the time when women go out to draw water. 12 And he said,
"O LORD, God of my master Abraham, please grant me success today
and show steadfast love to my master Abraham. 13 I am standing here
by the spring of water, and the daughters of the townspeople are coming out to draw water. 14 Let the girl to whom I shall say, 'Please offer
your jar that I may drink,' and who shall say, 'Drink, and I will water
your camels'—let her be the one whom you have appointed for your
servant Isaac. By this I shall know that you have shown steadfast love
to my master."

15 Before he had finished speaking, there was Rebekah, who was
born to Bethuel son of Milcah, the wife of Nahor, Abraham's brother,
coming out with her water jar on her shoulder. 16 The girl was very fair

24:2 Under my thigh: Abraham, in commissioning his servant to find a wife for Isaac binds the servant by making him take an oath, which included placing his hand near the genitals, from which children of future generations would be produced.

24:10 Aram-naharaim…city of Nahor: The city of Nahor, Abraham's brother, is in Haran (11:31) near "Mesopotamian Aram" (southeastern Turkey). Abraham's relatives had remained in Haran after he set out for Canaan.

to look upon, a virgin, whom no man had known. She went down to the spring, filled her jar, and came up. [17]Then the servant ran to meet her and said, "Please let me sip a little water from your jar." [18]"Drink, my lord," she said, and quickly lowered her jar upon her hand and gave him a drink. [19]When she had finished giving him a drink, she said, "I will draw for your camels also, until they have finished drinking." [20]So she quickly emptied her jar into the trough and ran again to the well to draw, and she drew for all his camels. [21]The man gazed at her in silence to learn whether or not the LORD had made his journey successful.

24:21 made his journey successful: God's divine guidance is important in this story, evident in both the narrator's comments and in the servant's remarkable prayers. While success depends on God, note the numerous instances where human decisions and actions could further or frustrate God's plans (see 24:8, 41).

22 When the camels had finished drinking, the man took a gold nose-ring weighing a half shekel, and two bracelets for her arms weighing ten gold shekels, [23]and said, "Tell me whose daughter you are. Is there room in your father's house for us to spend the night?" [24]She said to him, "I am the daughter of Bethuel son of Milcah, whom she bore to Nahor." [25]She added, "We have plenty of straw and fodder and a place to spend the night." [26]The man bowed his head and worshiped the LORD [27]and said, "Blessed be the LORD, the God of my master Abraham, who has not forsaken his steadfast love and his faithfulness toward my master. As for me, the LORD has led me on the way to the house of my master's kin."

24:22 half shekel: The shekel here refers not to a coin but a weight (about half an ounce).

28 Then the girl ran and told her mother's household about these things. [29]Rebekah had a brother whose name was Laban; and Laban ran out to the man, to the spring. [30]As soon as he had seen the nose-ring, and the bracelets on his sister's arms, and when he heard the words of his sister Rebekah, "Thus the man spoke to me," he went to the man; and there he was, standing by the camels at the spring. [31]He said, "Come in, O blessed of the LORD. Why do you stand outside when I have prepared the house and a place for the camels?" [32]So the man came into the house; and Laban unloaded the camels, and gave him straw and fodder for the camels, and water to wash his feet and the feet of the men who were with him. [33]Then food was set before him to eat; but he said, "I will not eat until I have told my errand." He said, "Speak on."

24:29 Laban: Rebekah's brother, who assumes a prominent role in this story.

24:32-33 wash his feet…food was set before him: Common hospitality practices. Compare with Genesis 18:4-8.

34 So he said, "I am Abraham's servant. [35]The LORD has greatly blessed my master, and he has become wealthy; he has given him flocks and herds, silver and gold, male and female slaves, camels and donkeys. [36]And Sarah my master's wife bore a son to my master when she was old; and he has given him all that he has. [37]My master made me swear, saying, 'You shall not take a wife for my son from the daughters of the Canaanites, in whose land I live; [38]but you shall go to my father's house, to my kindred, and get a wife for my son.' [39]I said to my master, 'Perhaps the woman will not follow me.' [40]But he said to me, 'The LORD, before whom I walk, will send his angel with you and make your way successful. You shall get a wife for my son from my

kindred, from my father's house. [41]Then you will be free from my
oath, when you come to my kindred; even if they will not give her to
you, you will be free from my oath.'
42 "I came today to the spring, and said, 'O LORD, the God of
my master Abraham, if now you will only make successful the way I
am going! [43]I am standing here by the spring of water; let the young
woman who comes out to draw, to whom I shall say, "Please give me
a little water from your jar to drink," [44]and who will say to me, "Drink,
and I will draw for your camels also"—let her be the woman whom
the LORD has appointed for my master's son.'
45 "Before I had finished speaking in my heart, there was Rebekah coming out with her water jar on her shoulder; and she went
down to the spring, and drew. I said to her, 'Please let me drink.' [46]She
quickly let down her jar from her shoulder, and said, 'Drink, and I will
also water your camels.' So I drank, and she also watered the camels.
[47]Then I asked her, 'Whose daughter are you?' She said, 'The daughter
of Bethuel, Nahor's son, whom Milcah bore to him.' So I put the ring
on her nose, and the bracelets on her arms. [48]Then I bowed my head
and worshiped the LORD, and blessed the LORD, the God of my master Abraham, who had led me by the right way to obtain the daughter
of my master's kinsman for his son. [49]Now then, if you will deal loyally
and truly with my master, tell me; and if not, tell me, so that I may turn
either to the right hand or to the left."
50 Then Laban and Bethuel answered, "The thing comes from
the LORD; we cannot speak to you anything bad or good. [51]Look, Rebekah is before you, take her and go, and let her be the wife of your
master's son, as the LORD has spoken."
52 When Abraham's servant heard their words, he bowed himself
to the ground before the LORD. [53]And the servant brought out jewelry of silver and of gold, and garments, and gave them to Rebekah; he
also gave to her brother and to her mother costly ornaments. [54]Then
he and the men who were with him ate and drank, and they spent the
night there. When they rose in the morning, he said, "Send me back
to my master." [55]Her brother and her mother said, "Let the girl remain
with us a while, at least ten days; after that she may go." [56]But he said
to them, "Do not delay me, since the LORD has made my journey successful; let me go that I may go to my master." [57]They said, "We will
call the girl, and ask her." [58]And they called Rebekah, and said to her,
"Will you go with this man?" She said, "I will." [59]So they sent away
their sister Rebekah and her nurse along with Abraham's servant and
his men. [60]And they blessed Rebekah and said to her,

"May you, our sister, become
thousands of myriads;
may your offspring gain possession
of the gates of their foes."

[61]Then Rebekah and her maids rose up, mounted the camels, and followed the man; thus the servant took Rebekah, and went his way.

62 Now Isaac had come from[a] Beer-lahai-roi, and was settled in the Negeb. [63]Isaac went out in the evening to walk[b] in the field; and looking up, he saw camels coming. [64]And Rebekah looked up, and when she saw Isaac, she slipped quickly from the camel, [65]and said to the servant, "Who is the man over there, walking in the field to meet us?" The servant said, "It is my master." So she took her veil and covered herself. [66]And the servant told Isaac all the things that he had done. [67]Then Isaac brought her into his mother Sarah's tent. He took Rebekah, and she became his wife; and he loved her. So Isaac was comforted after his mother's death.

24:65 my master: This comment signals the transition from Abraham to Isaac, as does Rebekah's presence in "Sarah's tent."

Abraham Marries Keturah

25 Abraham took another wife, whose name was Keturah. [2]She bore him Zimran, Jokshan, Medan, Midian, Ishbak, and Shuah. [3]Jokshan was the father of Sheba and Dedan. The sons of Dedan were Asshurim, Letushim, and Leummim. [4]The sons of Midian were Ephah, Epher, Hanoch, Abida, and Eldaah. All these were the children of Keturah. [5]Abraham gave all he had to Isaac. [6]But to the sons of his concubines Abraham gave gifts, while he was still living, and he sent them away from his son Isaac, eastward to the east country.

25:1 Keturah…Midian: Keturah, Abraham's wife after Sarah's death, bore him six more sons, progenitors (meaning, "direct ancestors") of various Arabian groups. The most prominent of these is Midian (see 37:28, 36), the direct ancestor of Moses' wife, Zipporah (Exod 2:15-22). As with Ishmael, these sons are sent away with appropriate gifts, securing Isaac's line.

The Death of Abraham

7 This is the length of Abraham's life, one hundred seventy-five years. [8]Abraham breathed his last and died in a good old age, an old man and full of years, and was gathered to his people. [9]His sons Isaac and Ishmael buried him in the cave of Machpelah, in the field of Ephron son of Zohar the Hittite, east of Mamre, [10]the field that Abraham purchased from the Hittites. There Abraham was buried, with his wife Sarah. [11]After the death of Abraham God blessed his son Isaac. And Isaac settled at Beer-lahai-roi.

25:9 Isaac and Ishmael: Remarkably, Ishmael returns at the death of Abraham. He and Isaac bury their father next to Sarah.

What, if anything, is surprising about Ishmael's return for the burial of Abraham? What situations in the world today seem to call out for reconciliation and peace?

Ishmael's Descendants

12 These are the descendants of Ishmael, Abraham's son, whom Hagar the Egyptian, Sarah's slave-girl, bore to Abraham. [13]These are the names of the sons of Ishmael, named in the order of their birth: Nebaioth, the firstborn of Ishmael; and Kedar, Adbeel, Mibsam, [14]Mishma, Dumah, Massa, [15]Hadad, Tema, Jetur, Naphish, and Kedemah. [16]These are the sons of Ishmael and these are their names, by their villages and by their encampments, twelve princes according to their tribes. [17](This is the length of the life of Ishmael, one hundred

25:12-18 descendants of Ishmael: The many descendants of Ishmael (mirroring the twelve tribes of Israel), direct ancestors of various Arabian groups east and south of Canaan, testify to the fulfillment of God's promises. Ishmael too has a future that has been blessed by God.

[a] Syr Tg: Heb *from coming to* [b] Meaning of Heb word is uncertain

thirty-seven years; he breathed his last and died, and was gathered to
his people.) 18 They settled from Havilah to Shur, which is opposite
Egypt in the direction of Assyria; he settled down[a] alongside of[b] all
his people.

The Birth and Youth of Esau and Jacob

19 These are the descendants of Isaac, Abraham's son: Abraham
was the father of Isaac, 20 and Isaac was forty years old when he married Rebekah, daughter of Bethuel the Aramean of Paddan-aram, sister of Laban the Aramean. 21 Isaac prayed to the LORD for his wife,
because she was barren; and the LORD granted his prayer, and his
wife Rebekah conceived. 22 The children struggled together within
her; and she said, "If it is to be this way, why do I live?"[c] So she went to
inquire of the LORD. 23 And the LORD said to her,

"Two nations are in your womb,
 and two peoples born of you shall be divided;
the one shall be stronger than the other,
 the elder shall serve the younger."

24 When her time to give birth was at hand, there were twins in her
womb. 25 The first came out red, all his body like a hairy mantle; so
they named him Esau. 26 Afterward his brother came out, with his
hand gripping Esau's heel; so he was named Jacob.[d] Isaac was sixty
years old when she bore them.

27 When the boys grew up, Esau was a skillful hunter, a man of
the field, while Jacob was a quiet man, living in tents. 28 Isaac loved
Esau, because he was fond of game; but Rebekah loved Jacob.

Esau Sells His Birthright

29 Once when Jacob was cooking a stew, Esau came in from the
field, and he was famished. 30 Esau said to Jacob, "Let me eat some of
that red stuff, for I am famished!" (Therefore he was called Edom.[e])
31 Jacob said, "First sell me your birthright." 32 Esau said, "I am about
to die; of what use is a birthright to me?" 33 Jacob said, "Swear to me
first."[f] So he swore to him, and sold his birthright to Jacob. 34 Then Jacob gave Esau bread and lentil stew, and he ate and drank, and rose
and went his way. Thus Esau despised his birthright.

Isaac and Abimelech

26 Now there was a famine in the land, besides the former famine that had occurred in the days of Abraham. And Isaac
went to Gerar, to King Abimelech of the Philistines. 2 The LORD appeared to Isaac[g] and said, "Do not go down to Egypt; settle in the

25:20 Paddan-aram: A variation of Aram-naharaim (see 24:10).

25:22-23 went to inquire of the LORD...said: At Rebekah's request, the LORD *interprets* the struggle of the twins in her womb. The "two nations" refer to Edom and Israel, whose original ancestors are Esau and Jacob. Esau is the elder and probably the "stronger," but he will serve the weaker and younger Jacob, though that is not always the case (see the book of Obadiah). God's description anticipates but does not determine their later conflicted relationship; it establishes a certain *direction* for the future, but Rebekah's actions on behalf of Jacob help shape what occurs.

25:25-26 The Hebrew words for "red" and "hairy" play on the names Edom and Seir, where Esau settled. The name Jacob plays on the Hebrew words for "heel" and "supplant" (replace).

25:32-34 birthright: The birthright normally was the right of the eldest son. It entails the leadership position in the family and inheritance rights (see Deut 21:15-17).

---

[a] Heb *he fell* [b] Or *down in opposition to* [c] Syr: Meaning of Heb uncertain [d] That is *He takes by the heel* or *He supplants* [e] That is *Red* [f] Heb *today* [g] Heb *him*

land that I shall show you. [3]Reside in this land as an alien, and I will be with you, and will bless you; for to you and to your descendants I will give all these lands, and I will fulfill the oath that I swore to your father Abraham. [4]I will make your offspring as numerous as the stars of heaven, and will give to your offspring all these lands; and all the nations of the earth shall gain blessing for themselves through your offspring, [5]because Abraham obeyed my voice and kept my charge, my commandments, my statutes, and my laws."

6 So Isaac settled in Gerar. [7]When the men of the place asked him about his wife, he said, "She is my sister"; for he was afraid to say, "My wife," thinking, "or else the men of the place might kill me for the sake of Rebekah, because she is attractive in appearance." [8]When Isaac had been there a long time, King Abimelech of the Philistines looked out of a window and saw him fondling his wife Rebekah. [9]So Abimelech called for Isaac, and said, "So she is your wife! Why then did you say, 'She is my sister'?" Isaac said to him, "Because I thought I might die because of her." [10]Abimelech said, "What is this you have done to us? One of the people might easily have lain with your wife, and you would have brought guilt upon us." [11]So Abimelech warned all the people, saying, "Whoever touches this man or his wife shall be put to death."

12 Isaac sowed seed in that land, and in the same year reaped a hundredfold. The LORD blessed him, [13]and the man became rich; he prospered more and more until he became very wealthy. [14]He had possessions of flocks and herds, and a great household, so that the Philistines envied him. [15](Now the Philistines had stopped up and filled with earth all the wells that his father's servants had dug in the days of his father Abraham.) [16]And Abimelech said to Isaac, "Go away from us; you have become too powerful for us."

17 So Isaac departed from there and camped in the valley of Gerar and settled there. [18]Isaac dug again the wells of water that had been dug in the days of his father Abraham; for the Philistines had stopped them up after the death of Abraham; and he gave them the names that his father had given them. [19]But when Isaac's servants dug in the valley and found there a well of spring water, [20]the herders of Gerar quarreled with Isaac's herders, saying, "The water is ours." So he called the well Esek,[a] because they contended with him. [21]Then they dug another well, and they quarreled over that one also; so he called it Sitnah.[b] [22]He moved from there and dug another well, and they did not quarrel over it; so he called it Rehoboth,[c] saying, "Now the LORD has made room for us, and we shall be fruitful in the land."

23 From there he went up to Beer-sheba. [24]And that very night the LORD appeared to him and said, "I am the God of your father

[a] That is *Contention* [b] That is *Enmity* [c] That is *Broad places* or *Room*

26:5 Abraham obeyed my voice: God repeats the promise to Isaac (26:5, 24) because of *Abraham's* faithfulness, not Isaac's.

26:5 my laws: These terms are usually thought to refer to the law given to Moses and the Israelite people many years later at Sinai, so the reference here seems out of place. Yet they reinforce a claim that the law given at Sinai simply provides greater detail with respect to law already known in many cultures.

How have you received God's promises because of the faith of others who have come before you?

26:6 my sister: Isaac's experience mirrors that of Abraham (see 12:10-20).

26:8 Abimelech…Philistines: See the people in 20:1-18; 21:22-34.

26:12-33 Isaac…prospered…the LORD has been with you: Compare this to 21:22-34. Isaac is portrayed as an instrument of peace.

26:24 the God of your father: Through this personal title, God's promise is lifted up across the generations (see also 28:13).

Abraham; do not be afraid, for I am with you and will bless you and
make your offspring numerous for my servant Abraham's sake." [25]So
he built an altar there, called on the name of the LORD, and pitched
his tent there. And there Isaac's servants dug a well.

26 Then Abimelech went to him from Gerar, with Ahuzzath his
adviser and Phicol the commander of his army. [27]Isaac said to them,
"Why have you come to me, seeing that you hate me and have sent me
away from you?" [28]They said, "We see plainly that the LORD has been
with you; so we say, let there be an oath between you and us, and let
us make a covenant with you [29]so that you will do us no harm, just as
we have not touched you and have done to you nothing but good and
have sent you away in peace. You are now the blessed of the LORD."
[30]So he made them a feast, and they ate and drank. [31]In the morning
they rose early and exchanged oaths; and Isaac set them on their way,
and they departed from him in peace. [32]That same day Isaac's servants
came and told him about the well that they had dug, and said to him,
"We have found water!" [33]He called it Shibah;[a] therefore the name of
the city is Beer-sheba[b] to this day.

Esau's Hittite Wives

34 When Esau was forty years old, he married Judith daughter of
Beeri the Hittite, and Basemath daughter of Elon the Hittite; [35]and
they made life bitter for Isaac and Rebekah.

26:34-35; 27:46 Hittite women: Also called Canaanite in 28:1, 6-8. See also note on 23:3.

Isaac Blesses Jacob

27 When Isaac was old and his eyes were dim so that he could
not see, he called his elder son Esau and said to him, "My
son"; and he answered, "Here I am." [2]He said, "See, I am old; I do
not know the day of my death. [3]Now then, take your weapons, your
quiver and your bow, and go out to the field, and hunt game for me.
[4]Then prepare for me savory food, such as I like, and bring it to me to
eat, so that I may bless you before I die."

5 Now Rebekah was listening when Isaac spoke to his son Esau.
So when Esau went to the field to hunt for game and bring it, [6]Re-
bekah said to her son Jacob, "I heard your father say to your brother
Esau, [7]'Bring me game, and prepare for me savory food to eat, that I
may bless you before the LORD before I die.' [8]Now therefore, my son,
obey my word as I command you. [9]Go to the flock, and get me two
choice kids, so that I may prepare from them savory food for your
father, such as he likes; [10]and you shall take it to your father to eat, so
that he may bless you before he dies." [11]But Jacob said to his mother
Rebekah, "Look, my brother Esau is a hairy man, and I am a man of
smooth skin. [12]Perhaps my father will feel me, and I shall seem to be

27:4 bless you before I die: This departure blessing of the father to the son is not the birthright (27:36) nor equated with "the blessing of Abraham" (12:3). *God* gave the blessing to Isaac (26:3-4, 24), and Isaac can only *commend* Jacob to God (he does in 28:3-4).

---

[a] A word resembling the word for *oath* [b] That is *Well of the oath* or *Well of seven*

mocking him, and bring a curse on myself and not a blessing." [13]His
mother said to him, "Let your curse be on me, my son; only obey
my word, and go, get them for me." [14]So he went and got them and
brought them to his mother; and his mother prepared savory food,
such as his father loved. [15]Then Rebekah took the best garments of
her elder son Esau, which were with her in the house, and put them
on her younger son Jacob; [16]and she put the skins of the kids on his
hands and on the smooth part of his neck. [17]Then she handed the
savory food, and the bread that she had prepared, to her son Jacob.

18 So he went in to his father, and said, "My father"; and he said,
"Here I am; who are you, my son?" [19]Jacob said to his father, "I am
Esau your firstborn. I have done as you told me; now sit up and eat
of my game, so that you may bless me." [20]But Isaac said to his son,
"How is it that you have found it so quickly, my son?" He answered,
"Because the LORD your God granted me success." [21]Then Isaac said
to Jacob, "Come near, that I may feel you, my son, to know whether
you are really my son Esau or not." [22]So Jacob went up to his father
Isaac, who felt him and said, "The voice is Jacob's voice, but the hands
are the hands of Esau." [23]He did not recognize him, because his hands
were hairy like his brother Esau's hands; so he blessed him. [24]He said,
"Are you really my son Esau?" He answered, "I am." [25]Then he said,
"Bring it to me, that I may eat of my son's game and bless you." So he
brought it to him, and he ate; and he brought him wine, and he drank.
[26]Then his father Isaac said to him, "Come near and kiss me, my son."
[27]So he came near and kissed him; and he smelled the smell of his garments, and blessed him, and said,

"Ah, the smell of my son
  is like the smell of a field that the LORD has blessed.
28 May God give you of the dew of heaven,
  and of the fatness of the earth,
  and plenty of grain and wine.
29 Let peoples serve you,
  and nations bow down to you.
Be lord over your brothers,
  and may your mother's sons bow down to you.
Cursed be everyone who curses you,
  and blessed be everyone who blesses you!"

27:27-29 the LORD has blessed: Isaac's blessing of Jacob centers on fertility and dominion. Fertility refers to both animals and crops and dominion over some unnamed peoples. The plural refers to family members and descendants. Esau will have a prominent place among the nations. Compare the language of curse and blessing in 27:29 to 12:3.

Esau's Lost Blessing

30 As soon as Isaac had finished blessing Jacob, when Jacob had
scarcely gone out from the presence of his father Isaac, his brother
Esau came in from his hunting. [31]He also prepared savory food, and
brought it to his father. And he said to his father, "Let my father sit
up and eat of his son's game, so that you may bless me." [32]His father
Isaac said to him, "Who are you?" He answered, "I am your firstborn

son, Esau." 33 Then Isaac trembled violently, and said, "Who was it
then that hunted game and brought it to me, and I ate it all[a] before
you came, and I have blessed him?—yes, and blessed he shall be!"
34 When Esau heard his father's words, he cried out with an exceedingly great and bitter cry, and said to his father, "Bless me, me also, father!" 35 But he said, "Your brother came deceitfully, and he has taken
away your blessing." 36 Esau said, "Is he not rightly named Jacob?[b] For
he has supplanted me these two times. He took away my birthright;
and look, now he has taken away my blessing." Then he said, "Have
you not reserved a blessing for me?" 37 Isaac answered Esau, "I have
already made him your lord, and I have given him all his brothers as
servants, and with grain and wine I have sustained him. What then
can I do for you, my son?" 38 Esau said to his father, "Have you only
one blessing, father? Bless me, me also, father!" And Esau lifted up his
voice and wept.

39 Then his father Isaac answered him:

"See, away from[c] the fatness of the earth shall your home be,
and away from[d] the dew of heaven on high.

40 By your sword you shall live,
and you shall serve your brother;
but when you break loose,[e]
you shall break his yoke from your neck."

Jacob Escapes Esau's Fury

41 Now Esau hated Jacob because of the blessing with which his
father had blessed him, and Esau said to himself, "The days of mourning for my father are approaching; then I will kill my brother Jacob."
42 But the words of her elder son Esau were told to Rebekah; so she
sent and called her younger son Jacob and said to him, "Your brother
Esau is consoling himself by planning to kill you. 43 Now therefore, my
son, obey my voice; flee at once to my brother Laban in Haran, 44 and
stay with him a while, until your brother's fury turns away— 45 until
your brother's anger against you turns away, and he forgets what you
have done to him; then I will send, and bring you back from there.
Why should I lose both of you in one day?"

46 Then Rebekah said to Isaac, "I am weary of my life because
of the Hittite women. If Jacob marries one of the Hittite women such
as these, one of the women of the land, what good will my life be
to me?"

28 Then Isaac called Jacob and blessed him, and charged
him, "You shall not marry one of the Canaanite women.
2 Go at once to Paddan-aram to the house of Bethuel, your mother's

27:35-38 your blessing: Isaac's (or anyone's) blessing could be taken back if there were a conventional form by which that could be done. Here, Isaac's blessing of Jacob stands because Isaac was certain about what he did. Note that the curse could also be transferred (27:13).

27:39-40 break his yoke: Isaac responds to Esau's pleas with a secondary blessing. At the least, this blessing qualifies the blessing given to Jacob.

27:43 flee at once to...Haran: See note on 24:10.

28:1-9 Canaanite women...took Mahalath: Isaac sent Jacob to marry among relatives so that the main family line would continue and not be mixed with Canaanites.

---

[a] Cn: Heb *of all* [b] That is *He supplants* or *He takes by the heel* [c] Or *See, of* [d] Or *and of* [e] Meaning of Heb uncertain

father; and take as wife from there one of the daughters of Laban,
your mother's brother. 3 May God Almighty[a] bless you and make you
fruitful and numerous, that you may become a company of peoples.
4 May he give to you the blessing of Abraham, to you and to your offspring with you, so that you may take possession of the land where
you now live as an alien—land that God gave to Abraham." 5 Thus
Isaac sent Jacob away; and he went to Paddan-aram, to Laban son
of Bethuel the Aramean, the brother of Rebekah, Jacob's and Esau's
mother.

Esau Marries Ishmael's Daughter

6 Now Esau saw that Isaac had blessed Jacob and sent him away
to Paddan-aram to take a wife from there, and that as he blessed him
he charged him, "You shall not marry one of the Canaanite women,"
7 and that Jacob had obeyed his father and his mother and gone to
Paddan-aram. 8 So when Esau saw that the Canaanite women did
not please his father Isaac, 9 Esau went to Ishmael and took Mahalath
daughter of Abraham's son Ishmael, and sister of Nebaioth, to be his
wife in addition to the wives he had.

Jacob's Dream at Bethel

10 Jacob left Beer-sheba and went toward Haran. 11 He came to a
certain place and stayed there for the night, because the sun had set.
Taking one of the stones of the place, he put it under his head and
lay down in that place. 12 And he dreamed that there was a ladder[b] set
up on the earth, the top of it reaching to heaven; and the angels of
God were ascending and descending on it. 13 And the LORD stood beside him[c] and said, "I am the LORD, the God of Abraham your father
and the God of Isaac; the land on which you lie I will give to you and
to your offspring; 14 and your offspring shall be like the dust of the
earth, and you shall spread abroad to the west and to the east and to
the north and to the south; and all the families of the earth shall be
blessed[d] in you and in your offspring. 15 Know that I am with you and
will keep you wherever you go, and will bring you back to this land;
for I will not leave you until I have done what I have promised you."
16 Then Jacob woke from his sleep and said, "Surely the LORD is in this
place—and I did not know it!" 17 And he was afraid, and said, "How
awesome is this place! This is none other than the house of God, and
this is the gate of heaven."

18 So Jacob rose early in the morning, and he took the stone that
he had put under his head and set it up for a pillar and poured oil on
the top of it. 19 He called that place Bethel;[e] but the name of the city

28:12 ladder: Better translated "stairway," this feature of ancient temples linked the earthly world to the gods' dwelling on top of the tower. Priests were to stand by the stairway, acting as mediators (agents or negotiators) between heaven and earth. This text challenges that ritual world by claiming God's presence with Jacob without the need of any mediators. On dreams, see the note on 20:3.

28:13-15 I will give you…promised you: A series of eight promises, four of which stand in line with the "blessing of Abraham" (see 28:4); the other four are personal promises associated with his journey.

Think about God's promises to Jacob. How might they relate to your life?

28:17 house of God: The Hebrew word is *Bethel*, later an important city north of Jerusalem. Jacob poured oil on the stone to stain it for later ease in recognizing it.

---

[a] Traditional rendering of Heb *El Shaddai* [b] Or *stairway* or *ramp* [c] Or *stood above it* [d] Or *shall bless themselves* [e] That is *House of God*

was Luz at the first. [20]Then Jacob made a vow, saying, "If God will be
with me, and will keep me in this way that I go, and will give me bread
to eat and clothing to wear, [21]so that I come again to my father's house
in peace, then the LORD shall be my God, [22]and this stone, which I
have set up for a pillar, shall be God's house; and of all that you give
me I will surely give one-tenth to you."

28:20-22 If God will be with me: Jacob's vow should not be interpreted as bargaining, but as holding God accountable for promises made.

Jacob Meets Rachel

29 Then Jacob went on his journey, and came to the land of the
people of the east. [2]As he looked, he saw a well in the field
and three flocks of sheep lying there beside it; for out of that well the
flocks were watered. The stone on the well's mouth was large, [3]and
when all the flocks were gathered there, the shepherds would roll the
stone from the mouth of the well, and water the sheep, and put the
stone back in its place on the mouth of the well.

29:1 people of the east: People from desert regions northeast of Canaan (25:6).

29:3-10 the mouth of the well: Throughout the Bible, wells are important meeting places (for example, see John 4). This is not surprising given the fact that sources of water were so important to survival for people and animals in this arid region.

4 Jacob said to them, "My brothers, where do you come from?"
They said, "We are from Haran." [5]He said to them, "Do you know Laban son of Nahor?" They said, "We do." [6]He said to them, "Is it well
with him?" "Yes," they replied, "and here is his daughter Rachel, coming with the sheep." [7]He said, "Look, it is still broad daylight; it is not
time for the animals to be gathered together. Water the sheep, and
go, pasture them." [8]But they said, "We cannot until all the flocks are
gathered together, and the stone is rolled from the mouth of the well;
then we water the sheep."

29:5 Laban son of Nahor: See note on 24:29.

9 While he was still speaking with them, Rachel came with her
father's sheep; for she kept them. [10]Now when Jacob saw Rachel, the
daughter of his mother's brother Laban, and the sheep of his mother's
brother Laban, Jacob went up and rolled the stone from the well's
mouth, and watered the flock of his mother's brother Laban. [11]Then
Jacob kissed Rachel, and wept aloud. [12]And Jacob told Rachel that he
was her father's kinsman, and that he was Rebekah's son; and she ran
and told her father.

13 When Laban heard the news about his sister's son Jacob, he
ran to meet him; he embraced him and kissed him, and brought him
to his house. Jacob[a] told Laban all these things, [14]and Laban said to
him, "Surely you are my bone and my flesh!" And he stayed with him
a month.

Jacob Marries Laban's Daughters

15 Then Laban said to Jacob, "Because you are my kinsman, should
you therefore serve me for nothing? Tell me, what shall your wages
be?" [16]Now Laban had two daughters; the name of the elder was Leah,
and the name of the younger was Rachel. [17]Leah's eyes were lovely,[b]

[a] Heb *He* [b] Meaning of Heb uncertain

and Rachel was graceful and beautiful. 18 Jacob loved Rachel; so he
said, "I will serve you seven years for your younger daughter Rachel."
19 Laban said, "It is better that I give her to you than that I should give
her to any other man; stay with me." 20 So Jacob served seven years for
Rachel, and they seemed to him but a few days because of the love he
had for her.

21 Then Jacob said to Laban, "Give me my wife that I may go in
to her, for my time is completed." 22 So Laban gathered together all
the people of the place, and made a feast. 23 But in the evening he took
his daughter Leah and brought her to Jacob; and he went in to her.
24 (Laban gave his maid Zilpah to his daughter Leah to be her maid.)
25 When morning came, it was Leah! And Jacob said to Laban, "What
is this you have done to me? Did I not serve with you for Rachel?
Why then have you deceived me?" 26 Laban said, "This is not done
in our country—giving the younger before the firstborn. 27 Complete
the week of this one, and we will give you the other also in return for
serving me another seven years." 28 Jacob did so, and completed her
week; then Laban gave him his daughter Rachel as a wife. 29 (Laban
gave his maid Bilhah to his daughter Rachel to be her maid.) 30 So Jacob went in to Rachel also, and he loved Rachel more than Leah. He
served Laban[a] for another seven years.

31 When the LORD saw that Leah was unloved, he opened her
womb; but Rachel was barren. 32 Leah conceived and bore a son, and
she named him Reuben;[b] for she said, "Because the LORD has looked
on my affliction; surely now my husband will love me." 33 She conceived again and bore a son, and said, "Because the LORD has heard[c]
that I am hated, he has given me this son also"; and she named him
Simeon. 34 Again she conceived and bore a son, and said, "Now this
time my husband will be joined[d] to me, because I have borne him
three sons"; therefore he was named Levi. 35 She conceived again and
bore a son, and said, "This time I will praise[e] the LORD"; therefore she
named him Judah; then she ceased bearing.

30 When Rachel saw that she bore Jacob no children, she envied her sister; and she said to Jacob, "Give me children, or
I shall die!" 2 Jacob became very angry with Rachel and said, "Am I in
the place of God, who has withheld from you the fruit of the womb?"
3 Then she said, "Here is my maid Bilhah; go in to her, that she may
bear upon my knees and that I too may have children through her." 4 So
she gave him her maid Bilhah as a wife; and Jacob went in to her. 5 And
Bilhah conceived and bore Jacob a son. 6 Then Rachel said, "God has
judged me, and has also heard my voice and given me a son"; therefore she named him Dan.[f] 7 Rachel's maid Bilhah conceived again and
bore Jacob a second son. 8 Then Rachel said, "With mighty wrestlings

29:26-28 the younger before the firstborn...completed her week: Laban's statement about the rights of the older sister reminds the reader that Jacob has been tricked in a way that parallels his own earlier dealings with his older brother, Esau. The reference to "week" here is not certain but may refer to the seven-day period of the wedding feast.

29:31—30:24 opened her womb...named him Joseph: This section details the births of twelve of Jacob's thirteen children (except Benjamin, 35:18). Leah and Rachel name their children (and children of their slave-girls) out of their own experience, which includes theological reflection (see wordplays in NRSV footnotes). The only daughter (Dinah, 30:21) is given the briefest of notices (see Gen 34).

---

[a] Heb *him* [b] That is *See, a son* [c] Heb *shama* [d] Heb *lawah* [e] Heb *hodah* [f] That is *He judged*

I have wrestled[a] with my sister, and have prevailed"; so she named
him Naphtali.

9 When Leah saw that she had ceased bearing children, she
took her maid Zilpah and gave her to Jacob as a wife. 10Then Leah's
maid Zilpah bore Jacob a son. 11And Leah said, "Good fortune!" so
she named him Gad.[b] 12Leah's maid Zilpah bore Jacob a second son.
13And Leah said, "Happy am I! For the women will call me happy";
so she named him Asher.[c]

14 In the days of wheat harvest Reuben went and found mandrakes in the field, and brought them to his mother Leah. Then Rachel said to Leah, "Please give me some of your son's mandrakes."
15But she said to her, "Is it a small matter that you have taken away
my husband? Would you take away my son's mandrakes also?" Rachel
said, "Then he may lie with you tonight for your son's mandrakes."
16When Jacob came from the field in the evening, Leah went out to
meet him, and said, "You must come in to me; for I have hired you
with my son's mandrakes." So he lay with her that night. 17And God
heeded Leah, and she conceived and bore Jacob a fifth son. 18Leah
said, "God has given me my hire[d] because I gave my maid to my husband"; so she named him Issachar. 19And Leah conceived again, and
she bore Jacob a sixth son. 20Then Leah said, "God has endowed me
with a good dowry; now my husband will honor[e] me, because I have
borne him six sons"; so she named him Zebulun. 21Afterwards she
bore a daughter, and named her Dinah.

30:14-16 mandrakes: An herb thought to promote fertility. For all the mothers' God-talk, they take action themselves, hoping the herb will improve the chances of pregnancy.

22 Then God remembered Rachel, and God heeded her and
opened her womb. 23She conceived and bore a son, and said, "God
has taken away my reproach"; 24and she named him Joseph,[f] saying,
"May the LORD add to me another son!"

Jacob Prospers at Laban's Expense

25 When Rachel had borne Joseph, Jacob said to Laban, "Send
me away, that I may go to my own home and country. 26Give me my
wives and my children for whom I have served you, and let me go;
for you know very well the service I have given you." 27But Laban said
to him, "If you will allow me to say so, I have learned by divination
that the LORD has blessed me because of you; 28name your wages,
and I will give it." 29Jacob said to him, "You yourself know how I have
served you, and how your cattle have fared with me. 30For you had
little before I came, and it has increased abundantly; and the LORD
has blessed you wherever I turned. But now when shall I provide for
my own household also?" 31He said, "What shall I give you?" Jacob
said, "You shall not give me anything; if you will do this for me, I will
again feed your flock and keep it: 32let me pass through all your flock

30:27 divination: This refers to a method of (supposedly) discerning information regarding the wishes or desires of gods through many devices, such as examining the entrails of animals. Divination is later condemned in the Old Testament (see 2 Kgs 21:6).

---

[a] Heb *niphtal* [b] That is *Fortune* [c] That is *Happy* [d] Heb *sakar* [e] Heb *zabal* [f] That is *He adds*

today, removing from it every speckled and spotted sheep and every black lamb, and the spotted and speckled among the goats; and such shall be my wages. 33 So my honesty will answer for me later, when you come to look into my wages with you. Every one that is not speckled and spotted among the goats and black among the lambs, if found with me, shall be counted stolen." 34 Laban said, "Good! Let it be as you have said." 35 But that day Laban removed the male goats that were striped and spotted, and all the female goats that were speckled and spotted, every one that had white on it, and every lamb that was black, and put them in charge of his sons; 36 and he set a distance of three days' journey between himself and Jacob, while Jacob was pasturing the rest of Laban's flock.

30:37-42 fresh rods of poplar... peeled white streaks: Jacob's strategy (divinely suggested, 31:7-12) assumes that what the animals observe while mating will determine the coloration of their offspring. The effect is that Jacob's animals are stronger than Laban's.

37 Then Jacob took fresh rods of poplar and almond and plane, and peeled white streaks in them, exposing the white of the rods. 38 He set the rods that he had peeled in front of the flocks in the troughs, that is, the watering places, where the flocks came to drink. And since they bred when they came to drink, 39 the flocks bred in front of the rods, and so the flocks produced young that were striped, speckled, and spotted. 40 Jacob separated the lambs, and set the faces of the flocks toward the striped and the completely black animals in the flock of Laban; and he put his own droves apart, and did not put them with Laban's flock. 41 Whenever the stronger of the flock were breeding, Jacob laid the rods in the troughs before the eyes of the flock, that they might breed among the rods, 42 but for the feebler of the flock he did not lay them there; so the feebler were Laban's, and the stronger Jacob's. 43 Thus the man grew exceedingly rich, and had large flocks, and male and female slaves, and camels and donkeys.

Jacob Flees with Family and Flocks

31 Now Jacob heard that the sons of Laban were saying, "Jacob has taken all that was our father's; he has gained all this wealth from what belonged to our father." 2 And Jacob saw that Laban did not regard him as favorably as he did before. 3 Then the LORD said to Jacob, "Return to the land of your ancestors and to your kindred, and I will be with you." 4 So Jacob sent and called Rachel and Leah into the field where his flock was, 5 and said to them, "I see that your father does not regard me as favorably as he did before. But the God of my father has been with me. 6 You know that I have served your father with all my strength; 7 yet your father has cheated me and changed my wages ten times, but God did not permit him to harm me. 8 If he said, 'The speckled shall be your wages,' then all the flock bore speckled; and if he said, 'The striped shall be your wages,' then all the flock bore striped. 9 Thus God has taken away the livestock of your father, and given them to me.

10 "During the mating of the flock I once had a dream in which

I looked up and saw that the male goats that leaped upon the flock
were striped, speckled, and mottled. [11]Then the angel of God said to
me in the dream, 'Jacob,' and I said, 'Here I am!' [12]And he said, 'Look
up and see that all the goats that leap on the flock are striped, speckled, and mottled; for I have seen all that Laban is doing to you. [13]I am
the God of Bethel,[a] where you anointed a pillar and made a vow to
me. Now leave this land at once and return to the land of your birth.' "
[14]Then Rachel and Leah answered him, "Is there any portion or inheritance left to us in our father's house? [15]Are we not regarded by
him as foreigners? For he has sold us, and he has been using up the
money given for us. [16]All the property that God has taken away from
our father belongs to us and to our children; now then, do whatever
God has said to you."

17 So Jacob arose, and set his children and his wives on camels; [18]and he drove away all his livestock, all the property that he had
gained, the livestock in his possession that he had acquired in Paddan-
aram, to go to his father Isaac in the land of Canaan.

19 Now Laban had gone to shear his sheep, and Rachel stole her
father's household gods. [20]And Jacob deceived Laban the Aramean,
in that he did not tell him that he intended to flee. [21]So he fled with
all that he had; starting out he crossed the Euphrates,[b] and set his face
toward the hill country of Gilead.

Laban Overtakes Jacob

22 On the third day Laban was told that Jacob had fled. [23]So he
took his kinsfolk with him and pursued him for seven days until he
caught up with him in the hill country of Gilead. [24]But God came to
Laban the Aramean in a dream by night, and said to him, "Take heed
that you say not a word to Jacob, either good or bad."

25 Laban overtook Jacob. Now Jacob had pitched his tent in the
hill country, and Laban with his kinsfolk camped in the hill country
of Gilead. [26]Laban said to Jacob, "What have you done? You have deceived me, and carried away my daughters like captives of the sword.
[27]Why did you flee secretly and deceive me and not tell me? I would
have sent you away with mirth and songs, with tambourine and lyre.
[28]And why did you not permit me to kiss my sons and my daughters
farewell? What you have done is foolish. [29]It is in my power to do you
harm; but the God of your father spoke to me last night, saying, 'Take
heed that you speak to Jacob neither good nor bad.' [30]Even though you
had to go because you longed greatly for your father's house, why did
you steal my gods?" [31]Jacob answered Laban, "Because I was afraid,
for I thought that you would take your daughters from me by force.
[32]But anyone with whom you find your gods shall not live. In the

31:14-15 portion…belongs to us: This strong, public stand on the part of Jacob's wives against the abuse of their father is remarkable.

31:19 household gods: This refers to small human-shaped figurines (common in that world) that were symbols of Laban's authority in the household. They may have been tokens of inheritance rights, meaning the person who possessed them was thought to inherit the family property.

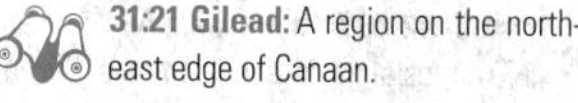

31:21 Gilead: A region on the northeast edge of Canaan.

---

[a] Cn: Meaning of Heb uncertain [b] Heb *the river*

presence of our kinsfolk, point out what I have that is yours, and take
it." Now Jacob did not know that Rachel had stolen the gods.[a]
33 So Laban went into Jacob's tent, and into Leah's tent, and into
the tent of the two maids, but he did not find them. And he went
out of Leah's tent, and entered Rachel's. 34 Now Rachel had taken the
household gods and put them in the camel's saddle, and sat on them.
Laban felt all about in the tent, but did not find them. 35 And she said
to her father, "Let not my lord be angry that I cannot rise before you,
for the way of women is upon me." So he searched, but did not find
the household gods.
36 Then Jacob became angry, and upbraided Laban. Jacob said
to Laban, "What is my offense? What is my sin, that you have hotly
pursued me? 37 Although you have felt about through all my goods,
what have you found of all your household goods? Set it here before
my kinsfolk and your kinsfolk, so that they may decide between us
two. 38 These twenty years I have been with you; your ewes and your
female goats have not miscarried, and I have not eaten the rams of
your flocks. 39 That which was torn by wild beasts I did not bring to
you; I bore the loss of it myself; of my hand you required it, whether
stolen by day or stolen by night. 40 It was like this with me: by day the
heat consumed me, and the cold by night, and my sleep fled from my
eyes. 41 These twenty years I have been in your house; I served you
fourteen years for your two daughters, and six years for your flock,
and you have changed my wages ten times. 42 If the God of my father, the God of Abraham and the Fear[b] of Isaac, had not been on
my side, surely now you would have sent me away empty-handed.
God saw my affliction and the labor of my hands, and rebuked you
last night."

Laban and Jacob Make a Covenant

43 Then Laban answered and said to Jacob, "The daughters are
my daughters, the children are my children, the flocks are my flocks,
and all that you see is mine. But what can I do today about these
daughters of mine, or about their children whom they have borne?
44 Come now, let us make a covenant, you and I; and let it be a witness between you and me." 45 So Jacob took a stone, and set it up as
a pillar. 46 And Jacob said to his kinsfolk, "Gather stones," and they
took stones, and made a heap; and they ate there by the heap. 47 Laban called it Jegar-sahadutha:[c] but Jacob called it Galeed.[d] 48 Laban
said, "This heap is a witness between you and me today." Therefore
he called it Galeed, 49 and the pillar[e] Mizpah,[f] for he said, "The LORD
watch between you and me, when we are absent one from the other.

---

[a] Heb *them* [b] Meaning of Heb uncertain [c] In Aramaic *The heap of witness* [d] In Hebrew *The heap of witness* [e] Compare Sam: MT lacks *the pillar* [f] That is *Watchpost*

31:35 way of women: This refers to her menstrual period.

31:42, 53 Fear of Isaac: An uncertain translation of a title for the God of Isaac (perhaps "Kinsman" of Isaac).

31:45-54 set it up as a pillar... offered a sacrifice: A pile of rocks was sometimes used as evidence of an agreement (see Josh 4, for example). To further seal the agreement, a sacrifice was offered. Sacrifices took many forms (see chart Offerings in Israel, p. 197).

31:47 Galeed: Probably a variation of Gilead (see 31:21).

31:49 Mizpah: The Gilead site of the Jacob/Laban covenant ("Mizpah Benediction") that God keep Jacob honest when Laban was not around to do so!

50 If you ill-treat my daughters, or if you take wives in addition to my
daughters, though no one else is with us, remember that God is witness between you and me."

51 Then Laban said to Jacob, "See this heap and see the pillar,
which I have set between you and me. 52 This heap is a witness, and
the pillar is a witness, that I will not pass beyond this heap to you,
and you will not pass beyond this heap and this pillar to me, for harm.
53 May the God of Abraham and the God of Nahor"—the God of their
father—"judge between us." So Jacob swore by the Fear[a] of his father
Isaac, 54 and Jacob offered a sacrifice on the height and called his kinsfolk to eat bread; and they ate bread and tarried all night in the hill
country.

55[b] Early in the morning Laban rose up, and kissed his grandchildren and his daughters and blessed them; then he departed and
returned home.

32 Jacob went on his way and the angels of God met him; 2 and
when Jacob saw them he said, "This is God's camp!" So he
called that place Mahanaim.[c]

Jacob Sends Presents to Appease Esau

3 Jacob sent messengers before him to his brother Esau in the
land of Seir, the country of Edom, 4 instructing them, "Thus you shall
say to my lord Esau: Thus says your servant Jacob, 'I have lived with
Laban as an alien, and stayed until now; 5 and I have oxen, donkeys,
flocks, male and female slaves; and I have sent to tell my lord, in order
that I may find favor in your sight.'"

6 The messengers returned to Jacob, saying, "We came to your
brother Esau, and he is coming to meet you, and four hundred men
are with him." 7 Then Jacob was greatly afraid and distressed; and he
divided the people that were with him, and the flocks and herds and
camels, into two companies, 8 thinking, "If Esau comes to the one
company and destroys it, then the company that is left will escape."

9 And Jacob said, "O God of my father Abraham and God of my
father Isaac, O LORD who said to me, 'Return to your country and to
your kindred, and I will do you good,' 10 I am not worthy of the least
of all the steadfast love and all the faithfulness that you have shown
to your servant, for with only my staff I crossed this Jordan; and now
I have become two companies. 11 Deliver me, please, from the hand
of my brother, from the hand of Esau, for I am afraid of him; he may
come and kill us all, the mothers with the children. 12 Yet you have
said, 'I will surely do you good, and make your offspring as the sand of
the sea, which cannot be counted because of their number.'"

13 So he spent that night there, and from what he had with him

32:1 angels: The Hebrew word is the same as the word for "messenger" in 32:3. Jacob "saw them," that is, human figures that he interprets as God's messengers accompanying him on his journey.

32:2 Mahanaim: The word means "two camps"; its location is uncertain. This anticipates the dividing of Jacob's family, flocks, and servants into two camps to meet Esau, one camp of angels for each of his companies (32:7, 10).

32:9-12 O God . . . you have said: Jacob's prayer has been interpreted as manipulative, but it need not be so; he claims God's earlier promises to him (28:13-15).

What, if anything, can be learned from the way Jacob approaches God in prayer?

---

[a] Meaning of Heb uncertain [b] Ch 32.1 in Heb [c] Here taken to mean *Two camps*

32:18-20 your servant…my lord: Jacob's referring to himself as "servant" and Esau as "lord" reverses earlier claims (25:23; 27:29) and serves the interests of reconciliation.

32:22 Jabbok: This is an eastern tributary of the Jordan River. Jacob was at or near the border of the promised land.

32:24 a man wrestled: Probably God appearing in human form, as suggested by both God (32:28) and Jacob (32:30; see also Hos 12:3-4). The *physical* wrestling is no game for either participant; it is a genuine match during which the man strikes Jacob, and Jacob holds on to the man (32:25-26). The concern about the dawn pertains to the issue of Jacob seeing God (32:30). It is not clear why God initiates the wrestling, but the new name suggests a concern for shaping and sharpening Jacob for what lies ahead. Intense wrestling will be characteristic of Israel's life with God through the centuries.

How has God wrestled with you? How have you wrestled with God?

How is the finite capable of the infinite? A key Lutheran theological principle is: The finite is capable of the infinite. This means that God comes to us through physical, tangible means. Though finite and created by human hands, the Bible itself contains God's Word for us. In the Sacrament of Holy Communion, the promises of God are given in and through the bread and wine. We talk of Jesus' body and blood being truly present through the Word of promise spoken, though the bread and wine do not change. We also speak of God becoming incarnate, real flesh and blood, in the person of Jesus. How might this principle help us to interpret Jacob's *actual* wrestling with God? *Genesis 32:22-32*

32:28 Israel: Probably meaning "he who strives with God." God gives this name to the father of the twelve tribes as a sign of his *success* (see also 35:10).

32:30-31 Peniel/Penuel: Meaning "the face of God," variants of the name Jacob gives to the place in view of his experience, seeing God and remaining alive (see 16:13).

33:2 last of all: Jacob places Rachel and Joseph in the least vulnerable position, which proves to be unnecessary in view of Esau's positive reception.

he took a present for his brother Esau, 14 two hundred female goats
and twenty male goats, two hundred ewes and twenty rams, 15 thirty
milch camels and their colts, forty cows and ten bulls, twenty female
donkeys and ten male donkeys. 16 These he delivered into the hand
of his servants, every drove by itself, and said to his servants, "Pass
on ahead of me, and put a space between drove and drove." 17 He instructed the foremost, "When Esau my brother meets you, and asks
you, 'To whom do you belong? Where are you going? And whose are
these ahead of you?' 18 then you shall say, 'They belong to your servant
Jacob; they are a present sent to my lord Esau; and moreover he is
behind us.'" 19 He likewise instructed the second and the third and all
who followed the droves, "You shall say the same thing to Esau when
you meet him, 20 and you shall say, 'Moreover your servant Jacob is
behind us.'" For he thought, "I may appease him with the present that
goes ahead of me, and afterwards I shall see his face; perhaps he will
accept me." 21 So the present passed on ahead of him; and he himself
spent that night in the camp.

Jacob Wrestles at Peniel

22 The same night he got up and took his two wives, his two
maids, and his eleven children, and crossed the ford of the Jabbok.
23 He took them and sent them across the stream, and likewise everything that he had. 24 Jacob was left alone; and a man wrestled with him
until daybreak. 25 When the man saw that he did not prevail against
Jacob, he struck him on the hip socket; and Jacob's hip was put out of
joint as he wrestled with him. 26 Then he said, "Let me go, for the day
is breaking." But Jacob said, "I will not let you go, unless you bless me."
27 So he said to him, "What is your name?" And he said, "Jacob." 28 Then
the man[a] said, "You shall no longer be called Jacob, but Israel,[b] for you
have striven with God and with humans,[c] and have prevailed." 29 Then
Jacob asked him, "Please tell me your name." But he said, "Why is it
that you ask my name?" And there he blessed him. 30 So Jacob called
the place Peniel,[d] saying, "For I have seen God face to face, and yet my
life is preserved." 31 The sun rose upon him as he passed Penuel, limping because of his hip. 32 Therefore to this day the Israelites do not eat
the thigh muscle that is on the hip socket, because he struck Jacob on
the hip socket at the thigh muscle.

Jacob and Esau Meet

33 Now Jacob looked up and saw Esau coming, and four hundred men with him. So he divided the children among Leah
and Rachel and the two maids. 2 He put the maids with their children

[a] Heb *he* [b] That is *The one who strives with God* or *God strives* [c] Or *with divine and human beings*
[d] That is *The face of God*

in front, then Leah with her children, and Rachel and Joseph last of
all. 3 He himself went on ahead of them, bowing himself to the ground
seven times, until he came near his brother.
4 But Esau ran to meet him, and embraced him, and fell on his
neck and kissed him, and they wept. 5 When Esau looked up and saw
the women and children, he said, "Who are these with you?" Jacob
said, "The children whom God has graciously given your servant."
6 Then the maids drew near, they and their children, and bowed down;
7 Leah likewise and her children drew near and bowed down; and finally Joseph and Rachel drew near, and they bowed down. 8 Esau said,
"What do you mean by all this company that I met?" Jacob answered,
"To find favor with my lord." 9 But Esau said, "I have enough, my
brother; keep what you have for yourself." 10 Jacob said, "No, please;
if I find favor with you, then accept my present from my hand; for
truly to see your face is like seeing the face of God—since you have
received me with such favor. 11 Please accept my gift that is brought to
you, because God has dealt graciously with me, and because I have
everything I want." So he urged him, and he took it.
12 Then Esau said, "Let us journey on our way, and I will go alongside you." 13 But Jacob said to him, "My lord knows that the children
are frail and that the flocks and herds, which are nursing, are a care to
me; and if they are overdriven for one day, all the flocks will die. 14 Let
my lord pass on ahead of his servant, and I will lead on slowly, according to the pace of the cattle that are before me and according to the
pace of the children, until I come to my lord in Seir."
15 So Esau said, "Let me leave with you some of the people who
are with me." But he said, "Why should my lord be so kind to me?"
16 So Esau returned that day on his way to Seir. 17 But Jacob journeyed
to Succoth,[a] and built himself a house, and made booths for his cattle;
therefore the place is called Succoth.

Jacob Reaches Shechem

18 Jacob came safely to the city of Shechem, which is in the land
of Canaan, on his way from Paddan-aram; and he camped before
the city. 19 And from the sons of Hamor, Shechem's father, he bought
for one hundred pieces of money[b] the plot of land on which he had
pitched his tent. 20 There he erected an altar and called it El-Elohe-
Israel.[c]

The Rape of Dinah

34 Now Dinah the daughter of Leah, whom she had borne to
Jacob, went out to visit the women of the region. 2 When
Shechem son of Hamor the Hivite, prince of the region, saw her,

[a] That is *Booths* [b] Heb *one hundred qesitah* [c] That is *God, the God of Israel*

33:10-11 the face of God: While showing the greatest respect to Esau, Jacob recalls God's graciousness in allowing him to see God's face and live (32:30).

33:14-17 to my lord in Seir: Jacob, still the trickster, misleads Esau in saying he will come to his home in Seir (Edom). Instead, he moves toward Canaan. Succoth is east of the Jordan valley. See Map 1, p. 2098.

33:18-19 Shechem: The name of a city in central Canaan and the name of the son of a leading citizen named Hamor, a Hivite (Canaanite).

33:20 El-Elohe-Israel: See the NRSV footnote *c*.

34:1-2 Dinah: Jacob's only daughter (30:21). She is raped by Shechem. The narrator does not give Dinah a voice, so we don't hear the story from her perspective.

34:3 loved the girl: Shechem's repeatedly expressed love for Dinah is not unusual in view of Israel's laws (see Deut 22:28-29). Dinah went to live in Shechem's house (34:26).

34:7 committed an outrage: Dinah's brothers' anger at the dishonor brought on the family moves to "deceitful" planning (34:13). They use the fact that Shechem is not circumcised as a ploy or excuse. That leads to unreasonable levels of violence against Shechem's family, spearheaded by Simeon and Levi, a move that Jacob condemns, not least for the terrible anger and cruelty involved (see 49:5-7).

How might this text, in which Dinah is silent, help us in the church talk about rape (and other forms of sexual abuse)?

he seized her and lay with her by force. 3And his soul was drawn to
Dinah daughter of Jacob; he loved the girl, and spoke tenderly to her.
4So Shechem spoke to his father Hamor, saying, "Get me this girl to
be my wife."

5 Now Jacob heard that Shechem[a] had defiled his daughter Dinah; but his sons were with his cattle in the field, so Jacob held his
peace until they came. 6And Hamor the father of Shechem went out
to Jacob to speak with him, 7just as the sons of Jacob came in from the
field. When they heard of it, the men were indignant and very angry,
because he had committed an outrage in Israel by lying with Jacob's
daughter, for such a thing ought not to be done.

8 But Hamor spoke with them, saying, "The heart of my son Shechem longs for your daughter; please give her to him in marriage.
9Make marriages with us; give your daughters to us, and take our
daughters for yourselves. 10You shall live with us; and the land shall
be open to you; live and trade in it, and get property in it." 11Shechem
also said to her father and to her brothers, "Let me find favor with
you, and whatever you say to me I will give. 12Put the marriage present
and gift as high as you like, and I will give whatever you ask me; only
give me the girl to be my wife."

13 The sons of Jacob answered Shechem and his father Hamor
deceitfully, because he had defiled their sister Dinah. 14They said to
them, "We cannot do this thing, to give our sister to one who is uncircumcised, for that would be a disgrace to us. 15Only on this condition
will we consent to you: that you will become as we are and every male
among you be circumcised. 16Then we will give our daughters to you,
and we will take your daughters for ourselves, and we will live among
you and become one people. 17But if you will not listen to us and be
circumcised, then we will take our daughter and be gone."

18 Their words pleased Hamor and Hamor's son Shechem.
19And the young man did not delay to do the thing, because he was
delighted with Jacob's daughter. Now he was the most honored of all
his family. 20So Hamor and his son Shechem came to the gate of their
city and spoke to the men of their city, saying, 21"These people are
friendly with us; let them live in the land and trade in it, for the land is
large enough for them; let us take their daughters in marriage, and let
us give them our daughters. 22Only on this condition will they agree
to live among us, to become one people: that every male among us be
circumcised as they are circumcised. 23Will not their livestock, their
property, and all their animals be ours? Only let us agree with them,
and they will live among us." 24And all who went out of the city gate
heeded Hamor and his son Shechem; and every male was circumcised, all who went out of the gate of his city.

---

[a] Heb *he*

Dinah's Brothers Avenge Their Sister

25 On the third day, when they were still in pain, two of the sons
of Jacob, Simeon and Levi, Dinah's brothers, took their swords and
came against the city unawares, and killed all the males. 26 They killed
Hamor and his son Shechem with the sword, and took Dinah out of
Shechem's house, and went away. 27 And the other sons of Jacob came
upon the slain, and plundered the city, because their sister had been
defiled. 28 They took their flocks and their herds, their donkeys, and
whatever was in the city and in the field. 29 All their wealth, all their
little ones and their wives, all that was in the houses, they captured
and made their prey. 30 Then Jacob said to Simeon and Levi, "You
have brought trouble on me by making me odious to the inhabitants
of the land, the Canaanites and the Perizzites; my numbers are few,
and if they gather themselves against me and attack me, I shall be destroyed, both I and my household." 31 But they said, "Should our sister
be treated like a whore?"

Jacob Returns to Bethel

35 God said to Jacob, "Arise, go up to Bethel, and settle there.
Make an altar there to the God who appeared to you when
you fled from your brother Esau." 2 So Jacob said to his household and
to all who were with him, "Put away the foreign gods that are among
you, and purify yourselves, and change your clothes; 3 then come, let
us go up to Bethel, that I may make an altar there to the God who answered me in the day of my distress and has been with me wherever I
have gone." 4 So they gave to Jacob all the foreign gods that they had,
and the rings that were in their ears; and Jacob hid them under the
oak that was near Shechem.

5 As they journeyed, a terror from God fell upon the cities all
around them, so that no one pursued them. 6 Jacob came to Luz (that
is, Bethel), which is in the land of Canaan, he and all the people who
were with him, 7 and there he built an altar and called the place El-
bethel,[a] because it was there that God had revealed himself to him
when he fled from his brother. 8 And Deborah, Rebekah's nurse, died,
and she was buried under an oak below Bethel. So it was called Allon-
bacuth.[b]

9 God appeared to Jacob again when he came from Paddan-aram,
and he blessed him. 10 God said to him, "Your name is Jacob; no longer
shall you be called Jacob, but Israel shall be your name." So he was
called Israel. 11 God said to him, "I am God Almighty:[c] be fruitful and
multiply; a nation and a company of nations shall come from you, and
kings shall spring from you. 12 The land that I gave to Abraham
and Isaac I will give to you, and I will give the land to your offspring

35:2-4 Put away the foreign gods: The command may refer to the household gods of 31:19. God commands Jacob to turn away from foreign gods in the same way God will later call the people of Israel to keep away from idolatrous practices (see Josh 24:14-15, 23).

35:5 terror from God: In view of Jacob's fears in 34:30, this may refer to a God-inspired fear in those who threatened Jacob and his family.

35:10-12 Israel shall be your name: Fulfilling God's command to go to Bethel, and with the action of getting rid of foreign idols still fresh in mind (35:1-4), God renames Jacob as Israel and extends the promises.

---

[a] That is *God of Bethel* [b] That is *Oak of weeping* [c] Traditional rendering of Heb *El Shaddai*

35:14-15 **set up a pillar...Bethel:** Jacob responds to God's repeated promises by setting up a place of remembrance and giving an offering. The oil likely was used to stain or color the stone so it could be recognized later. *Bethel* means "house of God."

How do our worship spaces ("houses of God") function as places of remembrance and offering? What place or places are especially holy to you and why?

35:16-20 Ephrath: This is another name for Bethlehem. Rachel died nearby while giving birth to Ben-oni/Benjamin (see NRSV footnotes *a, b*). The image of Rachel's weeping lives on to refer to the suffering of children in the fall of Jerusalem (Jer 31:15-17) and the slaughter of the innocents in Matthew 2:17-18.

36:1-43 the descendants...clans of Esau: This genealogy has numerous unidentifiable names. The remarkable growth and wealth of Esau's family confirms that Isaac's blessing in 27:39-40 had a positive end. Once again (see 25:12-18), the story pays detailed attention to the life of nonchosen peoples. God the Creator is at work bringing blessings independent of the chosen people, who descended from the family line of Esau's younger twin Jacob.

after you." [13]Then God went up from him at the place where he had
spoken with him. [14]Jacob set up a pillar in the place where he had spoken with him, a pillar of stone; and he poured out a drink offering on
it, and poured oil on it. [15]So Jacob called the place where God had
spoken with him Bethel.

The Birth of Benjamin and the Death of Rachel

16 Then they journeyed from Bethel; and when they were still
some distance from Ephrath, Rachel was in childbirth, and she had
hard labor. [17]When she was in her hard labor, the midwife said to her,
"Do not be afraid; for now you will have another son." [18]As her soul
was departing (for she died), she named him Ben-oni;[a] but his father
called him Benjamin.[b] [19]So Rachel died, and she was buried on the
way to Ephrath (that is, Bethlehem), [20]and Jacob set up a pillar at her
grave; it is the pillar of Rachel's tomb, which is there to this day. [21]Is-
rael journeyed on, and pitched his tent beyond the tower of Eder.

22 While Israel lived in that land, Reuben went and lay with Bilhah his father's concubine; and Israel heard of it.

Now the sons of Jacob were twelve. [23]The sons of Leah: Reuben
(Jacob's firstborn), Simeon, Levi, Judah, Issachar, and Zebulun. [24]The
sons of Rachel: Joseph and Benjamin. [25]The sons of Bilhah, Rachel's
maid: Dan and Naphtali. [26]The sons of Zilpah, Leah's maid: Gad and
Asher. These were the sons of Jacob who were born to him in Paddan-
aram.

The Death of Isaac

27 Jacob came to his father Isaac at Mamre, or Kiriath-arba (that
is, Hebron), where Abraham and Isaac had resided as aliens. [28]Now
the days of Isaac were one hundred eighty years. [29]And Isaac breathed
his last; he died and was gathered to his people, old and full of days;
and his sons Esau and Jacob buried him.

Esau's Descendants

36 These are the descendants of Esau (that is, Edom). [2]Esau
took his wives from the Canaanites: Adah daughter of Elon
the Hittite, Oholibamah daughter of Anah son[c] of Zibeon the Hivite,
[3]and Basemath, Ishmael's daughter, sister of Nebaioth. [4]Adah bore Eliphaz to Esau; Basemath bore Reuel; [5]and Oholibamah bore Jeush,
Jalam, and Korah. These are the sons of Esau who were born to him
in the land of Canaan.

6 Then Esau took his wives, his sons, his daughters, and all the
members of his household, his cattle, all his livestock, and all the
property he had acquired in the land of Canaan; and he moved to

---

[a] That is *Son of my sorrow* [b] That is *Son of the right hand* or *Son of the South* [c] Sam Gk Syr: Heb *daughter*

a land some distance from his brother Jacob. [7]For their possessions were too great for them to live together; the land where they were staying could not support them because of their livestock. [8]So Esau settled in the hill country of Seir; Esau is Edom.

9 These are the descendants of Esau, ancestor of the Edomites, in the hill country of Seir. [10]These are the names of Esau's sons: Eliphaz son of Adah the wife of Esau; Reuel, the son of Esau's wife Basemath. [11]The sons of Eliphaz were Teman, Omar, Zepho, Gatam, and Kenaz. [12](Timna was a concubine of Eliphaz, Esau's son; she bore Amalek to Eliphaz.) These were the sons of Adah, Esau's wife. [13]These were the sons of Reuel: Nahath, Zerah, Shammah, and Mizzah. These were the sons of Esau's wife, Basemath. [14]These were the sons of Esau's wife Oholibamah, daughter of Anah son[a] of Zibeon: she bore to Esau Jeush, Jalam, and Korah.

Clans and Kings of Edom

15 These are the clans[b] of the sons of Esau. The sons of Eliphaz the firstborn of Esau: the clans[b] Teman, Omar, Zepho, Kenaz, [16]Korah, Gatam, and Amalek; these are the clans[b] of Eliphaz in the land of Edom; they are the sons of Adah. [17]These are the sons of Esau's son Reuel: the clans[b] Nahath, Zerah, Shammah, and Mizzah; these are the clans[b] of Reuel in the land of Edom; they are the sons of Esau's wife Basemath. [18]These are the sons of Esau's wife Oholibamah: the clans[b] Jeush, Jalam, and Korah; these are the clans[b] born of Esau's wife Oholibamah, the daughter of Anah. [19]These are the sons of Esau (that is, Edom), and these are their clans.[b]

20 These are the sons of Seir the Horite, the inhabitants of the land: Lotan, Shobal, Zibeon, Anah, [21]Dishon, Ezer, and Dishan; these are the clans[b] of the Horites, the sons of Seir in the land of Edom. [22]The sons of Lotan were Hori and Heman; and Lotan's sister was Timna. [23]These are the sons of Shobal: Alvan, Manahath, Ebal, Shepho, and Onam. [24]These are the sons of Zibeon: Aiah and Anah; he is the Anah who found the springs[c] in the wilderness, as he pastured the donkeys of his father Zibeon. [25]These are the children of Anah: Dishon and Oholibamah daughter of Anah. [26]These are the sons of Dishon: Hemdan, Eshban, Ithran, and Cheran. [27]These are the sons of Ezer: Bilhan, Zaavan, and Akan. [28]These are the sons of Dishan: Uz and Aran. [29]These are the clans[b] of the Horites: the clans[b] Lotan, Shobal, Zibeon, Anah, [30]Dishon, Ezer, and Dishan; these are the clans[b] of the Horites, clan by clan[d] in the land of Seir.

31 These are the kings who reigned in the land of Edom, before any king reigned over the Israelites. [32]Bela son of Beor reigned in Edom, the name of his city being Dinhabah. [33]Bela died, and Jobab

---

[a] Gk Syr: Heb *daughter* [b] Or *chiefs* [c] Meaning of Heb uncertain [d] Or *chief by chief*

son of Zerah of Bozrah succeeded him as king. [34]Jobab died, and Husham of the land of the Temanites succeeded him as king. [35]Husham
died, and Hadad son of Bedad, who defeated Midian in the country of
Moab, succeeded him as king, the name of his city being Avith. [36]Ha-
dad died, and Samlah of Masrekah succeeded him as king. [37]Samlah
died, and Shaul of Rehoboth on the Euphrates succeeded him as king.
[38]Shaul died, and Baal-hanan son of Achbor succeeded him as king.
[39]Baal-hanan son of Achbor died, and Hadar succeeded him as
king, the name of his city being Pau; his wife's name was Mehetabel,
the daughter of Matred, daughter of Me-zahab.

40 These are the names of the clans[a] of Esau, according to their
families and their localities by their names: the clans[a] Timna, Alvah,
Jetheth, [41]Oholibamah, Elah, Pinon, [42]Kenaz, Teman, Mibzar, [43]Mag-
diel, and Iram; these are the clans[a] of Edom (that is, Esau, the father of
Edom), according to their settlements in the land that they held.

Joseph Dreams of Greatness

37:1 Jacob settled...alien: As Jacob's family grew and purchased or took over land, it began to look more like they were permanent settlers.

37:3 long robe with sleeves: Perhaps a striped coat (see NRSV footnote *a*). Clothing, often mentioned, suggests status (3:7, 21; 37:23, 32; 38:14, 19; 39:12; 41:14, 42).

37:5-11 a dream: The story contains three dream narratives, each with two dreams (see also 40:5-23; 41:1-36). This first narrative is often thought to prophesy later events regarding Joseph's authority (the sun and moon are his parents and the eleven stars his brothers), but this is only partially the case. Jacob never does bow before him, and Joseph will later deny that his dreams will continue to shape the future with his brothers (50:15-21).

37 Jacob settled in the land where his father had lived as an
alien, the land of Canaan. [2]This is the story of the family
of Jacob.

Joseph, being seventeen years old, was shepherding the flock with
his brothers; he was a helper to the sons of Bilhah and Zilpah, his
father's wives; and Joseph brought a bad report of them to their father. [3]Now Israel loved Joseph more than any other of his children,
because he was the son of his old age; and he had made him a long
robe with sleeves.[b] [4]But when his brothers saw that their father loved
him more than all his brothers, they hated him, and could not speak
peaceably to him.

5 Once Joseph had a dream, and when he told it to his brothers,
they hated him even more. [6]He said to them, "Listen to this dream
that I dreamed. [7]There we were, binding sheaves in the field. Suddenly
my sheaf rose and stood upright; then your sheaves gathered around
it, and bowed down to my sheaf." [8]His brothers said to him, "Are you
indeed to reign over us? Are you indeed to have dominion over us?"
So they hated him even more because of his dreams and his words.

9 He had another dream, and told it to his brothers, saying,
"Look, I have had another dream: the sun, the moon, and eleven
stars were bowing down to me." [10]But when he told it to his father
and to his brothers, his father rebuked him, and said to him, "What
kind of dream is this that you have had? Shall we indeed come, I and
your mother and your brothers, and bow to the ground before you?"
[11]So his brothers were jealous of him, but his father kept the matter
in mind.

---

[a] Or *chiefs* [b] Traditional rendering (compare Gk): *a coat of many colors;* meaning of Heb uncertain

Joseph Is Sold by His Brothers

12 Now his brothers went to pasture their father's flock near Shechem. 13And Israel said to Joseph, "Are not your brothers pasturing
the flock at Shechem? Come, I will send you to them." He answered,
"Here I am." 14So he said to him, "Go now, see if it is well with your
brothers and with the flock; and bring word back to me." So he sent
him from the valley of Hebron.
He came to Shechem, 15and a man found him wandering in the
fields; the man asked him, "What are you seeking?" 16"I am seeking
my brothers," he said; "tell me, please, where they are pasturing the
flock." 17The man said, "They have gone away, for I heard them say,
'Let us go to Dothan.'" So Joseph went after his brothers, and found
them at Dothan. 18They saw him from a distance, and before he came
near to them, they conspired to kill him. 19They said to one another,
"Here comes this dreamer. 20Come now, let us kill him and throw him
into one of the pits; then we shall say that a wild animal has devoured
him, and we shall see what will become of his dreams." 21But when
Reuben heard it, he delivered him out of their hands, saying, "Let us
not take his life." 22Reuben said to them, "Shed no blood; throw him
into this pit here in the wilderness, but lay no hand on him"—that he
might rescue him out of their hand and restore him to his father. 23So
when Joseph came to his brothers, they stripped him of his robe, the
long robe with sleeves[a] that he wore; 24and they took him and threw
him into a pit. The pit was empty; there was no water in it.
25 Then they sat down to eat; and looking up they saw a caravan
of Ishmaelites coming from Gilead, with their camels carrying gum,
balm, and resin, on their way to carry it down to Egypt. 26Then Judah said to his brothers, "What profit is it if we kill our brother and
conceal his blood? 27Come, let us sell him to the Ishmaelites, and not
lay our hands on him, for he is our brother, our own flesh." And his
brothers agreed. 28When some Midianite traders passed by, they drew
Joseph up, lifting him out of the pit, and sold him to the Ishmaelites
for twenty pieces of silver. And they took Joseph to Egypt.
29 When Reuben returned to the pit and saw that Joseph was
not in the pit, he tore his clothes. 30He returned to his brothers, and
said, "The boy is gone; and I, where can I turn?" 31Then they took
Joseph's robe, slaughtered a goat, and dipped the robe in the blood.
32They had the long robe with sleeves[a] taken to their father, and they
said, "This we have found; see now whether it is your son's robe or
not." 33He recognized it, and said, "It is my son's robe! A wild animal
has devoured him; Joseph is without doubt torn to pieces." 34Then
Jacob tore his garments, and put sackcloth on his loins, and mourned
for his son many days. 35All his sons and all his daughters sought to

[a] See note on 37.3

37:15 a man: Unidentified, could be a divine messenger.

37:17 Dothan: A town fifteen miles north of Shechem, even farther from home.

37:25, 28 Ishmaelites . . . Midianite: Both groups are said to sell Joseph to Egypt (37:36; 39:1; cf. 37:28); the story may be purposely ambiguous. The Ishmaelites were descendants of Abraham's son Ishmael and Hagar, the Egyptian servant woman (16:1-16). They likely were desert nomads and caravan traders. The Midianites were also descendants of Abraham and Keturah (25:1-2). The land of Midian was far to the south of Canaan and east of the Sinai Peninsula.

37:35 Sheol: This is the realm of all dead, a shadowy, silent existence—neither heaven nor hell (see also 42:38).

comfort him; but he refused to be comforted, and said, "No, I shall go
down to Sheol to my son, mourning." Thus his father bewailed him.
36 Meanwhile the Midianites had sold him in Egypt to Potiphar, one of
Pharaoh's officials, the captain of the guard.

Judah and Tamar

38 It happened at that time that Judah went down from his
brothers and settled near a certain Adullamite whose name
was Hirah. 2 There Judah saw the daughter of a certain Canaanite
whose name was Shua; he married her and went in to her. 3 She conceived and bore a son; and he named him Er. 4 Again she conceived
and bore a son whom she named Onan. 5 Yet again she bore a son, and
she named him Shelah. She[a] was in Chezib when she bore him. 6 Judah took a wife for Er his firstborn; her name was Tamar. 7 But Er, Judah's firstborn, was wicked in the sight of the LORD, and the LORD put
him to death. 8 Then Judah said to Onan, "Go in to your brother's wife
and perform the duty of a brother-in-law to her; raise up offspring
for your brother." 9 But since Onan knew that the offspring would not
be his, he spilled his semen on the ground whenever he went in to
his brother's wife, so that he would not give offspring to his brother.
10 What he did was displeasing in the sight of the LORD, and he put
him to death also. 11 Then Judah said to his daughter-in-law Tamar,
"Remain a widow in your father's house until my son Shelah grows
up"—for he feared that he too would die, like his brothers. So Tamar
went to live in her father's house.

12 In course of time the wife of Judah, Shua's daughter, died;
when Judah's time of mourning was over,[b] he went up to Timnah to
his sheepshearers, he and his friend Hirah the Adullamite. 13 When
Tamar was told, "Your father-in-law is going up to Timnah to shear
his sheep," 14 she put off her widow's garments, put on a veil, wrapped
herself up, and sat down at the entrance to Enaim, which is on the
road to Timnah. She saw that Shelah was grown up, yet she had not
been given to him in marriage. 15 When Judah saw her, he thought her
to be a prostitute, for she had covered her face. 16 He went over to her
at the roadside, and said, "Come, let me come in to you," for he did
not know that she was his daughter-in-law. She said, "What will you
give me, that you may come in to me?" 17 He answered, "I will send
you a kid from the flock." And she said, "Only if you give me a pledge,
until you send it." 18 He said, "What pledge shall I give you?" She replied, "Your signet and your cord, and the staff that is in your hand."
So he gave them to her, and went in to her, and she conceived by him.
19 Then she got up and went away, and taking off her veil she put on
the garments of her widowhood.

38:1 Adullamite: a Canaanite clan.

38:6 Tamar: The wife of Er, apparently a Canaanite, as was his mother, Shua (38:2). Jacob's sons begin to take wives from outside the family (see 41:45).

38:7, 10 the LORD put him to death: The deaths of both Er and Onan are described as death at the hands of God. This kind of action is uncommon in the Old Testament for individuals, but the key factor here is that the line leading to David is at risk. The narrator does not specify the means God uses. This language is used for Saul in 1 Chronicles 10:13-14, and we are told in 10:4 that Saul committed suicide.

38:8 the duty of a brother-in-law: This "duty" is known as the levirate law (Deut 25:5-10; Ruth 4). This law stated that a brother is obligated to marry the wife of his dead brother in order to carry on his brother's name (an heir for Er). Onan shirks his responsibility by refusing to let his semen enter her. (This refers to him stopping the act of intercourse, not masturbation.) Judah sends her home, where her future welfare is in jeopardy, rather than put his remaining son (Shelah) at risk. A resourceful Tamar takes the situation into her own hands in order to fulfill the law, even at the cost of her honor.

38:12, 14 Timnah…Enaim: Towns near Bethlehem.

38:18 signet…cord…staff: A seal (suspended on a neck cord) and a specially-marked staff are possessions of Judah that could readily be identified as his. The staff or walking stick may have had a unique family emblem or identifier carved into it. Asking for them was a clever move by Tamar since these items later prove that Judah is the father of her children (38:25).

[a] Gk: Heb *He* [b] Heb *when Judah was comforted*

20 When Judah sent the kid by his friend the Adullamite, to recover the pledge from the woman, he could not find her. [21]He asked the townspeople, "Where is the temple prostitute who was at Enaim by the wayside?" But they said, "No prostitute has been here." [22]So he returned to Judah, and said, "I have not found her; moreover the townspeople said, 'No prostitute has been here.'" [23]Judah replied, "Let her keep the things as her own, otherwise we will be laughed at; you see, I sent this kid, and you could not find her."

24 About three months later Judah was told, "Your daughter-in-law Tamar has played the whore; moreover she is pregnant as a result of whoredom." And Judah said, "Bring her out, and let her be burned." [25]As she was being brought out, she sent word to her father-in-law, "It was the owner of these who made me pregnant." And she said, "Take note, please, whose these are, the signet and the cord and the staff." [26]Then Judah acknowledged them and said, "She is more in the right than I, since I did not give her to my son Shelah." And he did not lie with her again.

27 When the time of her delivery came, there were twins in her womb. [28]While she was in labor, one put out a hand; and the midwife took and bound on his hand a crimson thread, saying, "This one came out first." [29]But just then he drew back his hand, and out came his brother; and she said, "What a breach you have made for yourself!" Therefore he was named Perez.[a] [30]Afterward his brother came out with the crimson thread on his hand; and he was named Zerah.[b]

Joseph and Potiphar's Wife

39 Now Joseph was taken down to Egypt, and Potiphar, an officer of Pharaoh, the captain of the guard, an Egyptian, bought him from the Ishmaelites who had brought him down there. [2]The LORD was with Joseph, and he became a successful man; he was in the house of his Egyptian master. [3]His master saw that the LORD was with him, and that the LORD caused all that he did to prosper in his hands. [4]So Joseph found favor in his sight and attended him; he made him overseer of his house and put him in charge of all that he had. [5]From the time that he made him overseer in his house and over all that he had, the LORD blessed the Egyptian's house for Joseph's sake; the blessing of the LORD was on all that he had, in house and field. [6]So he left all that he had in Joseph's charge; and, with him there, he had no concern for anything but the food that he ate.

Now Joseph was handsome and good-looking. [7]And after a time his master's wife cast her eyes on Joseph and said, "Lie with me." [8]But he refused and said to his master's wife, "Look, with me here, my master has no concern about anything in the house, and he has put

[a] That is *A breach* [b] That is *Brightness*; perhaps alluding to the crimson thread

38:21 temple prostitute: Prostitution was associated with idolatrous worship. Whether temple prostitution was actually part of the religious rituals of Israel's neighbors is a subject of debate. The people of the town indirectly witness to Tamar's integrity. They have not seen a prostitute.

38:26 She is more in the right than I: Judah uses the Hebrew word for "righteous," testifying to Tamar's doing justice to the law in a way he had not. Her resourceful commitment to justice and social responsibility stands as an important witness. (See also Jesus' breaking of Sabbath laws in Mark 2:23-28 for another instance of following a higher law).

38:29 Perez: The son of Judah and Tamar, who continues the line of promise all the way to David (Ruth 4:18) and Jesus (Matt 1:3).

How might this story help the church, which has so often neglected the topic of prostitution, be more straightforward in its speaking about this matter?

39:1 Pharaoh: This is a generic term for Egypt's king. Who this particular pharaoh may be is not clear.

39:2 The LORD was with Joseph: The nine references to God in this chapter strike the key theme. In his isolation from family and even in prison, God has not abandoned Joseph. God's presence is a more low-profile, behind-the-scenes presence than is common to this point in Genesis, but it is effective for good for both Joseph and those among whom he lives. God does not act alone but works in and through Joseph and his considerable political and administrative skills to bring blessings (see 39:5).

How would you speak about the presence of God in your life?

39:9 sin against God: Joseph resists the temptations of Potiphar's wife. That this sin is "against God" shows that God's will does not always get done in human life.

40:1 cupbearer: This probably refers to a trusted servant who was responsible for serving wine to Pharaoh or perhaps tasting it first to make sure it was drinkable and not poisoned.

everything that he has in my hand. [9]He is not greater in this house
than I am, nor has he kept back anything from me except yourself,
because you are his wife. How then could I do this great wickedness,
and sin against God?" [10]And although she spoke to Joseph day after
day, he would not consent to lie beside her or to be with her. [11]One
day, however, when he went into the house to do his work, and while
no one else was in the house, [12]she caught hold of his garment, saying,
"Lie with me!" But he left his garment in her hand, and fled and ran
outside. [13]When she saw that he had left his garment in her hand and
had fled outside, [14]she called out to the members of her household
and said to them, "See, my husband[a] has brought among us a Hebrew
to insult us! He came in to me to lie with me, and I cried out with a
loud voice; [15]and when he heard me raise my voice and cry out, he
left his garment beside me, and fled outside." [16]Then she kept his garment by her until his master came home, [17]and she told him the same
story, saying, "The Hebrew servant, whom you have brought among
us, came in to me to insult me; [18]but as soon as I raised my voice and
cried out, he left his garment beside me, and fled outside."

19 When his master heard the words that his wife spoke to him,
saying, "This is the way your servant treated me," he became enraged.
[20]And Joseph's master took him and put him into the prison, the
place where the king's prisoners were confined; he remained there in
prison. [21]But the LORD was with Joseph and showed him steadfast
love; he gave him favor in the sight of the chief jailer. [22]The chief jailer
committed to Joseph's care all the prisoners who were in the prison,
and whatever was done there, he was the one who did it. [23]The chief
jailer paid no heed to anything that was in Joseph's care, because
the LORD was with him; and whatever he did, the LORD made it
prosper.

The Dreams of Two Prisoners

40 Some time after this, the cupbearer of the king of Egypt
and his baker offended their lord the king of Egypt. [2]Pharaoh was angry with his two officers, the chief cupbearer and the chief
baker, [3]and he put them in custody in the house of the captain of the
guard, in the prison where Joseph was confined. [4]The captain of the
guard charged Joseph with them, and he waited on them; and they
continued for some time in custody. [5]One night they both dreamed—
the cupbearer and the baker of the king of Egypt, who were confined
in the prison—each his own dream, and each dream with its own
meaning. [6]When Joseph came to them in the morning, he saw that
they were troubled. [7]So he asked Pharaoh's officers, who were with
him in custody in his master's house, "Why are your faces downcast

[a] Heb *he*

today?” 8 They said to him, “We have had dreams, and there is no one
to interpret them.” And Joseph said to them, “Do not interpretations
belong to God? Please tell them to me.”

9 So the chief cupbearer told his dream to Joseph, and said to
him, “In my dream there was a vine before me, 10 and on the vine there
were three branches. As soon as it budded, its blossoms came out and
the clusters ripened into grapes. 11 Pharaoh’s cup was in my hand; and
I took the grapes and pressed them into Pharaoh’s cup, and placed the
cup in Pharaoh’s hand.” 12 Then Joseph said to him, “This is its interpretation: the three branches are three days; 13 within three days Pharaoh will lift up your head and restore you to your office; and you shall
place Pharaoh’s cup in his hand, just as you used to do when you were
his cupbearer. 14 But remember me when it is well with you; please do
me the kindness to make mention of me to Pharaoh, and so get me
out of this place. 15 For in fact I was stolen out of the land of the Hebrews; and here also I have done nothing that they should have put
me into the dungeon.”

16 When the chief baker saw that the interpretation was favorable, he said to Joseph, “I also had a dream: there were three cake baskets on my head, 17 and in the uppermost basket there were all sorts of
baked food for Pharaoh, but the birds were eating it out of the basket
on my head.” 18 And Joseph answered, “This is its interpretation: the
three baskets are three days; 19 within three days Pharaoh will lift up
your head—from you!—and hang you on a pole; and the birds will
eat the flesh from you.”

20 On the third day, which was Pharaoh’s birthday, he made a
feast for all his servants, and lifted up the head of the chief cupbearer
and the head of the chief baker among his servants. 21 He restored the
chief cupbearer to his cupbearing, and he placed the cup in Pharaoh’s
hand; 22 but the chief baker he hanged, just as Joseph had interpreted
to them. 23 Yet the chief cupbearer did not remember Joseph, but forgot him.

Joseph Interprets Pharaoh’s Dream

41 After two whole years, Pharaoh dreamed that he was standing by the Nile, 2 and there came up out of the Nile seven sleek
and fat cows, and they grazed in the reed grass. 3 Then seven other
cows, ugly and thin, came up out of the Nile after them, and stood by
the other cows on the bank of the Nile. 4 The ugly and thin cows ate up
the seven sleek and fat cows. And Pharaoh awoke. 5 Then he fell asleep
and dreamed a second time; seven ears of grain, plump and good,
were growing on one stalk. 6 Then seven ears, thin and blighted by the
east wind, sprouted after them. 7 The thin ears swallowed up the seven
plump and full ears. Pharaoh awoke, and it was a dream. 8 In the morning his spirit was troubled; so he sent and called for all the magicians

40:8 Do not interpretations belong to God?: The servant’s dreams are not said to come from God, but Joseph’s interpretation does (see 41:16). God works in and through the dreams of the nonchosen to develop the future of the chosen. While Joseph’s own dreams (37:5-9) resulted in his slavery, the dreams of others now become the means for his release from slavery.

Do you think God influences dreams? Have you ever experienced such dreams?

40:13-20 Pharaoh will lift up your head: This expression does double duty in these verses. It refers to a person’s status being elevated (40:13) and to beheading (40:19). Both of these senses appear in 40:20-22, where both dreams are realized. Notably, Joseph’s dream interpretation is crucial for the dreams themselves being realized; their fulfillment is not automatic.

40:14-15 remember me: Joseph speaks for the first time about his own experiences and, for all his reliance on God, he still expresses the need for *human* help, which is delayed (40:23; see 41:9-13).

41:1 the Nile: The Nile, the world’s second-longest river, floods yearly, leaving behind rich soil for planting crops. This annual cycle was so important to the fertility of the land and the constant food supply for Egypt’s people that it was worshiped as a god.

41:8 magicians . . . wise men: Pharaoh’s advisers included those who practiced magic tricks (see Exod 7:11-12) and wise men who claimed to be able to tell the future.

of Egypt and all its wise men. Pharaoh told them his dreams, but there
was no one who could interpret them to Pharaoh.

9 Then the chief cupbearer said to Pharaoh, "I remember my
faults today. 10 Once Pharaoh was angry with his servants, and put me
and the chief baker in custody in the house of the captain of the guard.
11 We dreamed on the same night, he and I, each having a dream with
its own meaning. 12 A young Hebrew was there with us, a servant
of the captain of the guard. When we told him, he interpreted our
dreams to us, giving an interpretation to each according to his dream.
13 As he interpreted to us, so it turned out; I was restored to my office,
and the baker was hanged."

14 Then Pharaoh sent for Joseph, and he was hurriedly brought
out of the dungeon. When he had shaved himself and changed his
clothes, he came in before Pharaoh. 15 And Pharaoh said to Joseph,
"I have had a dream, and there is no one who can interpret it. I have
heard it said of you that when you hear a dream you can interpret it."
16 Joseph answered Pharaoh, "It is not I; God will give Pharaoh a favorable answer." 17 Then Pharaoh said to Joseph, "In my dream I was
standing on the banks of the Nile; 18 and seven cows, fat and sleek,
came up out of the Nile and fed in the reed grass. 19 Then seven other
cows came up after them, poor, very ugly, and thin. Never had I seen
such ugly ones in all the land of Egypt. 20 The thin and ugly cows ate
up the first seven fat cows, 21 but when they had eaten them no one
would have known that they had done so, for they were still as ugly
as before. Then I awoke. 22 I fell asleep a second time[a] and I saw in my
dream seven ears of grain, full and good, growing on one stalk, 23 and
seven ears, withered, thin, and blighted by the east wind, sprouting
after them; 24 and the thin ears swallowed up the seven good ears. But
when I told it to the magicians, there was no one who could explain
it to me."

25 Then Joseph said to Pharaoh, "Pharaoh's dreams are one and
the same; God has revealed to Pharaoh what he is about to do. 26 The
seven good cows are seven years, and the seven good ears are seven
years; the dreams are one. 27 The seven lean and ugly cows that came
up after them are seven years, as are the seven empty ears blighted
by the east wind. They are seven years of famine. 28 It is as I told Pharaoh; God has shown to Pharaoh what he is about to do. 29 There will
come seven years of great plenty throughout all the land of Egypt.
30 After them there will arise seven years of famine, and all the plenty
will be forgotten in the land of Egypt; the famine will consume the
land. 31 The plenty will no longer be known in the land because of the
famine that will follow, for it will be very grievous. 32 And the doubling
of Pharaoh's dream means that the thing is fixed by God, and God will

[a] Gk Syr Vg: Heb lacks *I fell asleep a second time*

41:16 God will give Pharaoh a favorable answer: Note Joseph's confidence, even though he has not yet heard Pharaoh's dreams. God has given Joseph the insight to interpret dreams properly (see 40:8). Ironically, after hearing Joseph's dream interpretation (41:25-36), Pharaoh gets the theology right (41:38-39): Both God's leading *and* Joseph's wisdom and discernment are relevant. Activity in the world happens through both divine and human action. Yet, Joseph does not boast but gives the glory to God (note God as subject in 41:16, 25, 28).

41:32 the thing is fixed by God: God has firmly established the future to which the dreams point. Within that future human decisions will remain very important in the shape that developments take.

shortly bring it about. [33]Now therefore let Pharaoh select a man who is discerning and wise, and set him over the land of Egypt. [34]Let Pharaoh proceed to appoint overseers over the land, and take one-fifth of the produce of the land of Egypt during the seven plenteous years. [35]Let them gather all the food of these good years that are coming, and lay up grain under the authority of Pharaoh for food in the cities, and let them keep it. [36]That food shall be a reserve for the land against the seven years of famine that are to befall the land of Egypt, so that the land may not perish through the famine."

Joseph's Rise to Power

37 The proposal pleased Pharaoh and all his servants. [38]Pharaoh said to his servants, "Can we find anyone else like this—one in whom is the spirit of God?" [39]So Pharaoh said to Joseph, "Since God has shown you all this, there is no one so discerning and wise as you. [40]You shall be over my house, and all my people shall order themselves as you command; only with regard to the throne will I be greater than you." [41]And Pharaoh said to Joseph, "See, I have set you over all the land of Egypt." [42]Removing his signet ring from his hand, Pharaoh put it on Joseph's hand; he arrayed him in garments of fine linen, and put a gold chain around his neck. [43]He had him ride in the chariot of his second-in-command; and they cried out in front of him, "Bow the knee!"[a] Thus he set him over all the land of Egypt. [44]Moreover Pharaoh said to Joseph, "I am Pharaoh, and without your consent no one shall lift up hand or foot in all the land of Egypt." [45]Pharaoh gave Joseph the name Zaphenath-paneah; and he gave him Asenath daughter of Potiphera, priest of On, as his wife. Thus Joseph gained authority over the land of Egypt.

46 Joseph was thirty years old when he entered the service of Pharaoh king of Egypt. And Joseph went out from the presence of Pharaoh, and went through all the land of Egypt. [47]During the seven plenteous years the earth produced abundantly. [48]He gathered up all the food of the seven years when there was plenty[b] in the land of Egypt, and stored up food in the cities; he stored up in every city the food from the fields around it. [49]So Joseph stored up grain in such abundance—like the sand of the sea—that he stopped measuring it; it was beyond measure.

50 Before the years of famine came, Joseph had two sons, whom Asenath daughter of Potiphera, priest of On, bore to him. [51]Joseph named the firstborn Manasseh,[c] "For," he said, "God has made me forget all my hardship and all my father's house." [52]The second he named Ephraim,[d] "For God has made me fruitful in the land of my misfortunes."

41:38 one in whom is the spirit of God: Joseph has divinely given gifts suitable for the task at hand (see 41:16 and note).

41:42-43 signet ring…gold chain …chariot: The ring, fine linen clothing, and gold chain signify Joseph's authority, which comes directly from Pharaoh. No one would miss how Joseph's status had risen to the top of the highest level of Egyptian government.

41:45 Zaphenath-paneah: A new name for Joseph, to signify his new status. It may mean "God speaks and lives."

41:45 Asenath: The name of Joseph's Egyptian wife, the daughter of a priest of the sun god Re in the city of On, also known as Heliopolis (see Map 1, p. 2098).

41:50-52 Manasseh…Ephraim: Joseph's two sons, whose names summarize his recent experiences, namely God's preserving and prospering amid great hardship. The sons are two of the twelve tribes of Israel (see Gen 48).

---

[a] *Abrek,* apparently an Egyptian word similar in sound to the Hebrew word meaning *to kneel* [b] Sam Gk: MT *the seven years that were* [c] That is *Making to forget* [d] From a Hebrew word meaning *to be fruitful*

53 The seven years of plenty that prevailed in the land of Egypt
came to an end; 54 and the seven years of famine began to come, just as
Joseph had said. There was famine in every country, but throughout
the land of Egypt there was bread. 55 When all the land of Egypt was
famished, the people cried to Pharaoh for bread. Pharaoh said to all
the Egyptians, "Go to Joseph; what he says to you, do." 56 And since
the famine had spread over all the land, Joseph opened all the storehouses,[a] and sold to the Egyptians, for the famine was severe in the
land of Egypt. 57 Moreover, all the world came to Joseph in Egypt to
buy grain, because the famine became severe throughout the world.

Joseph's Brothers Go to Egypt

42 When Jacob learned that there was grain in Egypt, he said
to his sons, "Why do you keep looking at one another? 2 I
have heard," he said, "that there is grain in Egypt; go down and buy
grain for us there, that we may live and not die." 3 So ten of Joseph's
brothers went down to buy grain in Egypt. 4 But Jacob did not send
Joseph's brother Benjamin with his brothers, for he feared that harm
might come to him. 5 Thus the sons of Israel were among the other
people who came to buy grain, for the famine had reached the land
of Canaan.

6 Now Joseph was governor over the land; it was he who sold
to all the people of the land. And Joseph's brothers came and bowed
themselves before him with their faces to the ground. 7 When Joseph
saw his brothers, he recognized them, but he treated them like strangers and spoke harshly to them. "Where do you come from?" he said.
They said, "From the land of Canaan, to buy food." 8 Although Joseph
had recognized his brothers, they did not recognize him. 9 Joseph also
remembered the dreams that he had dreamed about them. He said
to them, "You are spies; you have come to see the nakedness of the
land!" 10 They said to him, "No, my lord; your servants have come to
buy food. 11 We are all sons of one man; we are honest men; your servants have never been spies." 12 But he said to them, "No, you have
come to see the nakedness of the land!" 13 They said, "We, your servants, are twelve brothers, the sons of a certain man in the land of
Canaan; the youngest, however, is now with our father, and one is no
more." 14 But Joseph said to them, "It is just as I have said to you; you
are spies! 15 Here is how you shall be tested: as Pharaoh lives, you shall
not leave this place unless your youngest brother comes here! 16 Let
one of you go and bring your brother, while the rest of you remain in
prison, in order that your words may be tested, whether there is truth
in you; or else, as Pharaoh lives, surely you are spies." 17 And he put
them all together in prison for three days.

---

[a] Gk Vg Compare Syr: Heb *opened all that was in* (or, *among*) *them*

41:57 all the world: Due to Joseph's political and economic wisdom, all from the known world, including Jacob's family (the subject of the next three chapters), can buy grain from Egypt for relief from the famine. The statement links this text to Genesis 12:3. Through Joseph's actions and leadership many are blessed.

42:6 bowed themselves: The brother's actions before Joseph are a partial fulfillment of Joseph's dream (37:5-9), which Joseph now remembers (42:9).

42:9, 12 nakedness of the land: This is a reference to Egypt's exposed borders. Turning the tables, Joseph exposes the brothers' defenselessness and tests their integrity. Have they changed or not? The brothers must be tested before reconciliation with them is possible.

42:13 one is no more: The brothers omit a role they had in Joseph's disappearance.

18 On the third day Joseph said to them, "Do this and you will
live, for I fear God: 19 if you are honest men, let one of your brothers
stay here where you are imprisoned. The rest of you shall go and carry
grain for the famine of your households, 20 and bring your youngest
brother to me. Thus your words will be verified, and you shall not die."
And they agreed to do so. 21 They said to one another, "Alas, we are
paying the penalty for what we did to our brother; we saw his anguish
when he pleaded with us, but we would not listen. That is why this anguish has come upon us." 22 Then Reuben answered them, "Did I not
tell you not to wrong the boy? But you would not listen. So now there
comes a reckoning for his blood." 23 They did not know that Joseph
understood them, since he spoke with them through an interpreter.
24 He turned away from them and wept; then he returned and spoke
to them. And he picked out Simeon and had him bound before their
eyes. 25 Joseph then gave orders to fill their bags with grain, to return
every man's money to his sack, and to give them provisions for their
journey. This was done for them.

42:21 anguish: Joseph's plan to hold back one of the brothers while the rest go to fetch Benjamin causes the brothers to think about Joseph. For the first time the brothers see what they have done from Joseph's perspective (his anguish) and unknowingly confess their crime. They are not aware that Joseph understands what they are saying.

42:24 wept: Joseph weeps several times in the story, signaling a new development in his relationship with his brothers and revealing his true feelings, which soften the harsh front he puts up (43:30; 45:1-2, 14-15; 46:29; 50:1, 17; see especially 45:1-2).

Joseph's Brothers Return to Canaan

26 They loaded their donkeys with their grain, and departed.
27 When one of them opened his sack to give his donkey fodder at the
lodging place, he saw his money at the top of the sack. 28 He said to his
brothers, "My money has been put back; here it is in my sack!" At this
they lost heart and turned trembling to one another, saying, "What is
this that God has done to us?"

29 When they came to their father Jacob in the land of Canaan,
they told him all that had happened to them, saying, 30 "The man, the
lord of the land, spoke harshly to us, and charged us with spying on
the land. 31 But we said to him, 'We are honest men, we are not spies.
32 We are twelve brothers, sons of our father; one is no more, and the
youngest is now with our father in the land of Canaan.' 33 Then the
man, the lord of the land, said to us, 'By this I shall know that you
are honest men: leave one of your brothers with me, take grain for
the famine of your households, and go your way. 34 Bring your youngest brother to me, and I shall know that you are not spies but honest
men. Then I will release your brother to you, and you may trade in
the land.'"

35 As they were emptying their sacks, there in each one's sack
was his bag of money. When they and their father saw their bundles
of money, they were dismayed. 36 And their father Jacob said to them,
"I am the one you have bereaved of children: Joseph is no more, and
Simeon is no more, and now you would take Benjamin. All this has
happened to me!" 37 Then Reuben said to his father, "You may kill my
two sons if I do not bring him back to you. Put him in my hands, and I
will bring him back to you." 38 But he said, "My son shall not go down

The family is intended to be a source of growth, protection, and comfort. But families can also be dysfunctional places of bitter rivalry and even abuse. In your experience, what is true about these statements? What does it mean that the earliest families described in Genesis were dysfunctional?

43:3 Judah: Judah is the chief spokesperson for the brothers through the balance of the story, risking his honor (43:8-9; 44:32). This narrative is also a story about Judah, who is the brother in the Davidic line (49:8-12).

43:11-12 choice fruits...double the money: Jacob arranges for the brothers to take back a variety of locally grown foods.

with you, for his brother is dead, and he alone is left. If harm should come to him on the journey that you are to make, you would bring down my gray hairs with sorrow to Sheol."

The Brothers Come Again, Bringing Benjamin

43 Now the famine was severe in the land. [2]And when they had
eaten up the grain that they had brought from Egypt, their
father said to them, "Go again, buy us a little more food." [3]But Judah
said to him, "The man solemnly warned us, saying, 'You shall not see
my face unless your brother is with you.' [4]If you will send our brother
with us, we will go down and buy you food; [5]but if you will not send
him, we will not go down, for the man said to us, 'You shall not see my
face, unless your brother is with you.'" [6]Israel said, "Why did you treat
me so badly as to tell the man that you had another brother?" [7]They
replied, "The man questioned us carefully about ourselves and our
kindred, saying, 'Is your father still alive? Have you another brother?'
What we told him was in answer to these questions. Could we in any
way know that he would say, 'Bring your brother down'?" [8]Then Judah said to his father Israel, "Send the boy with me, and let us be on
our way, so that we may live and not die—you and we and also our
little ones. [9]I myself will be surety for him; you can hold me accountable for him. If I do not bring him back to you and set him before you,
then let me bear the blame forever. [10]If we had not delayed, we would
now have returned twice."

11 Then their father Israel said to them, "If it must be so, then do
this: take some of the choice fruits of the land in your bags, and carry
them down as a present to the man—a little balm and a little honey,
gum, resin, pistachio nuts, and almonds. [12]Take double the money
with you. Carry back with you the money that was returned in the
top of your sacks; perhaps it was an oversight. [13]Take your brother
also, and be on your way again to the man; [14]may God Almighty[a]
grant you mercy before the man, so that he may send back your other
brother and Benjamin. As for me, if I am bereaved of my children, I
am bereaved." [15]So the men took the present, and they took double
the money with them, as well as Benjamin. Then they went on their
way down to Egypt, and stood before Joseph.

16 When Joseph saw Benjamin with them, he said to the steward
of his house, "Bring the men into the house, and slaughter an animal
and make ready, for the men are to dine with me at noon." [17]The man
did as Joseph said, and brought the men to Joseph's house. [18]Now the
men were afraid because they were brought to Joseph's house, and
they said, "It is because of the money, replaced in our sacks the first
time, that we have been brought in, so that he may have an opportu-

[a] Traditional rendering of Heb *El Shaddai*

nity to fall upon us, to make slaves of us and take our donkeys." [19]So they went up to the steward of Joseph's house and spoke with him at the entrance to the house. [20]They said, "Oh, my lord, we came down the first time to buy food; [21]and when we came to the lodging place we opened our sacks, and there was each one's money in the top of his sack, our money in full weight. So we have brought it back with us. [22]Moreover we have brought down with us additional money to buy food. We do not know who put our money in our sacks." [23]He replied, "Rest assured, do not be afraid; your God and the God of your father must have put treasure in your sacks for you; I received your money." Then he brought Simeon out to them. [24]When the steward[a] had brought the men into Joseph's house, and given them water, and they had washed their feet, and when he had given their donkeys fodder, [25]they made the present ready for Joseph's coming at noon, for they had heard that they would dine there.

26 When Joseph came home, they brought him the present that they had carried into the house, and bowed to the ground before him. [27]He inquired about their welfare, and said, "Is your father well, the old man of whom you spoke? Is he still alive?" [28]They said, "Your servant our father is well; he is still alive." And they bowed their heads and did obeisance. [29]Then he looked up and saw his brother Benjamin, his mother's son, and said, "Is this your youngest brother, of whom you spoke to me? God be gracious to you, my son!" [30]With that, Joseph hurried out, because he was overcome with affection for his brother, and he was about to weep. So he went into a private room and wept there. [31]Then he washed his face and came out; and controlling himself he said, "Serve the meal." [32]They served him by himself, and them by themselves, and the Egyptians who ate with him by themselves, because the Egyptians could not eat with the Hebrews, for that is an abomination to the Egyptians. [33]When they were seated before him, the firstborn according to his birthright and the youngest according to his youth, the men looked at one another in amazement. [34]Portions were taken to them from Joseph's table, but Benjamin's portion was five times as much as any of theirs. So they drank and were merry with him.

43:23 God...must have put treasure in your sacks: This Egyptian steward who is not part of God's chosen people offers a word of comfort and peace to the brothers and gives a theological interpretation. God did not directly place the money in their sacks (see 42:25), but this human action was in tune with God's purposes, so God was at work in this action (see 45:8).

43:26 bowed to the ground: The second fulfillment of Joseph's dream in 37:5-9.

43:32 an abomination to the Egyptians: Perhaps because of religious purity laws or cultural standards, Egyptians would not eat with Hebrews (see also Exod 8:26).

Joseph Detains Benjamin

44 Then he commanded the steward of his house, "Fill the men's sacks with food, as much as they can carry, and put each man's money in the top of his sack. [2]Put my cup, the silver cup, in the top of the sack of the youngest, with his money for the grain." And he did as Joseph told him. [3]As soon as the morning was light, the men were sent away with their donkeys. [4]When they had gone only

[a] Heb *the man*

44:5, 15 divination: See 30:27 and note.

a short distance from the city, Joseph said to his steward, "Go, follow
after the men; and when you overtake them, say to them, 'Why have
you returned evil for good? Why have you stolen my silver cup?[a] 5 Is it
not from this that my lord drinks? Does he not indeed use it for divination? You have done wrong in doing this.'"

6 When he overtook them, he repeated these words to them.
7 They said to him, "Why does my lord speak such words as these?
Far be it from your servants that they should do such a thing! 8 Look,
the money that we found at the top of our sacks, we brought back
to you from the land of Canaan; why then would we steal silver or
gold from your lord's house? 9 Should it be found with any one of your
servants, let him die; moreover the rest of us will become my lord's
slaves." 10 He said, "Even so; in accordance with your words, let it be:
he with whom it is found shall become my slave, but the rest of you
shall go free." 11 Then each one quickly lowered his sack to the ground,
and each opened his sack. 12 He searched, beginning with the eldest
and ending with the youngest; and the cup was found in Benjamin's
sack. 13 At this they tore their clothes. Then each one loaded his donkey, and they returned to the city.

44:13 tore their clothes: A common way of showing grief or despair.

14 Judah and his brothers came to Joseph's house while he was
still there; and they fell to the ground before him. 15 Joseph said to
them, "What deed is this that you have done? Do you not know that
one such as I can practice divination?" 16 And Judah said, "What can
we say to my lord? What can we speak? How can we clear ourselves?
God has found out the guilt of your servants; here we are then, my
lord's slaves, both we and also the one in whose possession the cup
has been found." 17 But he said, "Far be it from me that I should do
so! Only the one in whose possession the cup was found shall be my
slave; but as for you, go up in peace to your father."

44:16 God has found out: The brothers' treatment of Joseph has now come full circle ("my lord's slaves"). The brothers had confessed their guilt to one another (42:21), and now they confess it to Joseph. They use God language positively (compare with 42:28), bringing their guilt and God together, witnessing to God's activity to expose their guilt. To say that God has "found out" their guilt compresses the activity of both God and Joseph into a single action.

Judah Pleads for Benjamin's Release

18 Then Judah stepped up to him and said, "O my lord, let your
servant please speak a word in my lord's ears, and do not be angry
with your servant; for you are like Pharaoh himself. 19 My lord asked
his servants, saying, 'Have you a father or a brother?' 20 And we said
to my lord, 'We have a father, an old man, and a young brother, the
child of his old age. His brother is dead; he alone is left of his mother's
children, and his father loves him.' 21 Then you said to your servants,
'Bring him down to me, so that I may set my eyes on him.' 22 We said
to my lord, 'The boy cannot leave his father, for if he should leave his
father, his father would die.' 23 Then you said to your servants, 'Unless
your youngest brother comes down with you, you shall see my face
no more.' 24 When we went back to your servant my father we told

44:18-34 let your servant please speak: This gathering speech of Judah provides the turning point in the narrative (see 43:2). The emotional impact of his final remark prompts Joseph's response in Genesis 45.

45:1-2, 14-15 wept: See 42:24. Some reconciliation occurs between Joseph and his brothers at this point, but it is not complete until 50:15-21, where the brothers still have a lord/slave mentality and only there does Joseph deal with that issue. Notably, Joseph does not seek to shame his brothers (45:5). Instead, he sets aside his royal reputation and position and becomes fully vulnerable with his brothers.

---

[a] Gk Compare Vg: Heb lacks *Why have you stolen my silver cup?*

him the words of my lord. [25]And when our father said, 'Go again, buy
us a little food,' [26]we said, 'We cannot go down. Only if our youngest
brother goes with us, will we go down; for we cannot see the man's
face unless our youngest brother is with us.' [27]Then your servant my
father said to us, 'You know that my wife bore me two sons; [28]one left
me, and I said, Surely he has been torn to pieces; and I have never
seen him since. [29]If you take this one also from me, and harm comes
to him, you will bring down my gray hairs in sorrow to Sheol.' [30]Now
therefore, when I come to your servant my father and the boy is not
with us, then, as his life is bound up in the boy's life, [31]when he sees
that the boy is not with us, he will die; and your servants will bring
down the gray hairs of your servant our father with sorrow to Sheol.
[32]For your servant became surety for the boy to my father, saying, 'If I
do not bring him back to you, then I will bear the blame in the sight of
my father all my life.' [33]Now therefore, please let your servant remain
as a slave to my lord in place of the boy; and let the boy go back with
his brothers. [34]For how can I go back to my father if the boy is not with
me? I fear to see the suffering that would come upon my father."

Joseph Reveals Himself to His Brothers

45 Then Joseph could no longer control himself before all
those who stood by him, and he cried out, "Send everyone
away from me." So no one stayed with him when Joseph made himself known to his brothers. [2]And he wept so loudly that the Egyptians
heard it, and the household of Pharaoh heard it. [3]Joseph said to his
brothers, "I am Joseph. Is my father still alive?" But his brothers could
not answer him, so dismayed were they at his presence.

4 Then Joseph said to his brothers, "Come closer to me." And
they came closer. He said, "I am your brother, Joseph, whom you sold
into Egypt. [5]And now do not be distressed, or angry with yourselves,
because you sold me here; for God sent me before you to preserve
life. [6]For the famine has been in the land these two years; and there
are five more years in which there will be neither plowing nor harvest.
[7]God sent me before you to preserve for you a remnant on earth, and
to keep alive for you many survivors. [8]So it was not you who sent me
here, but God; he has made me a father to Pharaoh, and lord of all his
house and ruler over all the land of Egypt. [9]Hurry and go up to my
father and say to him, 'Thus says your son Joseph, God has made me
lord of all Egypt; come down to me, do not delay. [10]You shall settle in
the land of Goshen, and you shall be near me, you and your children
and your children's children, as well as your flocks, your herds, and all
that you have. [11]I will provide for you there—since there are five more
years of famine to come—so that you and your household, and all
that you have, will not come to poverty.' [12]And now your eyes and the
eyes of my brother Benjamin see that it is my own mouth that speaks

45:8 it was not you who sent me here, but God: This seems contradictory, but the force of it is similar to prior statements (see 41:16; 43:23; 44:16) that describe both human and divine activity to be at work, even if the decisive action is God's. In this context, God has, in effect, taken over what they, in fact, have done and used their evil (50:20) to bring about this good end. Their actions have *become* God's by being woven into God's life-giving purposes. Even more, *Pharaoh's* actions—elevating Joseph as ruler—have become God's! God's actions are independent of the brothers' repentance.

How is God at work in our lives to create faith? The story of Joseph and his brothers focuses on how God is present in their lives and actions. It is also clear from the story that human beings take action in concert with God to assure that God's purposes are carried out in the world. Regarding the creation of faith in our lives, Martin Luther made it clear in his explanation to the Third Article of the Apostles' Creed that faith is not something we do; it comes from God. Luther says: "I believe that by my own understanding or strength I cannot believe in Jesus Christ my Lord or come to him, but instead the Holy Spirit has called me through the gospel, enlightened me with his gifts, made me holy and kept me in the true faith." *Genesis 42–45*

45:5, 7 God sent me…to preserve life: An important theme in the Joseph story (see 46:30; 50:20). God's concern is life, both for this family and for the world (41:57).

45:7 a remnant on earth: Another Genesis theme, which can be traced back to the saving of the family of Noah (6:8) and on through the prophets (see Isaiah 6).

45:8 a father to Pharaoh: Meaning one whose policies protected Pharaoh.

45:10 the land of Goshen: A region in the northeastern Nile delta (nearest to Canaan), especially suitable for grazing animals, where Israelites are settled in Exodus. See Map 2, p. 2099.

to you. [13]You must tell my father how greatly I am honored in Egypt, and all that you have seen. Hurry and bring my father down here." [14]Then he fell upon his brother Benjamin's neck and wept, while Benjamin wept upon his neck. [15]And he kissed all his brothers and wept upon them; and after that his brothers talked with him.

16 When the report was heard in Pharaoh's house, "Joseph's brothers have come," Pharaoh and his servants were pleased. [17]Pharaoh said to Joseph, "Say to your brothers, 'Do this: load your animals and go back to the land of Canaan. [18]Take your father and your households and come to me, so that I may give you the best of the land of Egypt, and you may enjoy the fat of the land.' [19]You are further charged to say, 'Do this: take wagons from the land of Egypt for your little ones and for your wives, and bring your father, and come. [20]Give no thought to your possessions, for the best of all the land of Egypt is yours.' "

21 The sons of Israel did so. Joseph gave them wagons according to the instruction of Pharaoh, and he gave them provisions for the journey. [22]To each one of them he gave a set of garments; but to Benjamin he gave three hundred pieces of silver and five sets of garments. [23]To his father he sent the following: ten donkeys loaded with the good things of Egypt, and ten female donkeys loaded with grain, bread, and provision for his father on the journey. [24]Then he sent his brothers on their way, and as they were leaving he said to them, "Do not quarrel[a] along the way."

45:22 Benjamin: Joseph's only full brother receives special gifts.

25 So they went up out of Egypt and came to their father Jacob in the land of Canaan. [26]And they told him, "Joseph is still alive! He is even ruler over all the land of Egypt." He was stunned; he could not believe them. [27]But when they told him all the words of Joseph that he had said to them, and when he saw the wagons that Joseph had sent to carry him, the spirit of their father Jacob revived. [28]Israel said, "Enough! My son Joseph is still alive. I must go and see him before I die."

45:28 Enough! This phrase is shorthand for putting the past behind and getting on with new possibilities.

Jacob Brings His Whole Family to Egypt

46 When Israel set out on his journey with all that he had and came to Beer-sheba, he offered sacrifices to the God of his father Isaac. [2]God spoke to Israel in visions of the night, and said, "Jacob, Jacob." And he said, "Here I am." [3]Then he said, "I am God,[b] the God of your father; do not be afraid to go down to Egypt, for I will make of you a great nation there. [4]I myself will go down with you to Egypt, and I will also bring you up again; and Joseph's own hand shall close your eyes."

5 Then Jacob set out from Beer-sheba; and the sons of Israel car-

46:1-4 God spoke to Israel: God assures Jacob (Israel) and quiets his possible fear about going to Egypt. God will be present with Jacob and his family. Indeed, this will be a journey for *God* (46:4). God repeats the promise of a "great nation," which will happen in *Egypt* (46:3). The move from family to a people is now clearly in view and continues through the balance of Genesis.

[a] Or *be agitated* [b] Heb *the God*

ried their father Jacob, their little ones, and their wives, in the wagons that Pharaoh had sent to carry him. [6]They also took their livestock and the goods that they had acquired in the land of Canaan, and they came into Egypt, Jacob and all his offspring with him, [7]his sons, and his sons' sons with him, his daughters, and his sons' daughters; all his offspring he brought with him into Egypt.

8 Now these are the names of the Israelites, Jacob and his offspring, who came to Egypt. Reuben, Jacob's firstborn, [9]and the children of Reuben: Hanoch, Pallu, Hezron, and Carmi. [10]The children of Simeon: Jemuel, Jamin, Ohad, Jachin, Zohar, and Shaul,[a] the son of a Canaanite woman. [11]The children of Levi: Gershon, Kohath, and Merari. [12]The children of Judah: Er, Onan, Shelah, Perez, and Zerah (but Er and Onan died in the land of Canaan); and the children of Perez were Hezron and Hamul. [13]The children of Issachar: Tola, Puvah, Jashub,[b] and Shimron. [14]The children of Zebulun: Sered, Elon, and Jahleel [15](these are the sons of Leah, whom she bore to Jacob in Paddan-aram, together with his daughter Dinah; in all his sons and his daughters numbered thirty-three). [16]The children of Gad: Ziphion, Haggi, Shuni, Ezbon, Eri, Arodi, and Areli. [17]The children of Asher: Imnah, Ishvah, Ishvi, Beriah, and their sister Serah. The children of Beriah: Heber and Malchiel [18](these are the children of Zilpah, whom Laban gave to his daughter Leah; and these she bore to Jacob—sixteen persons). [19]The children of Jacob's wife Rachel: Joseph and Benjamin. [20]To Joseph in the land of Egypt were born Manasseh and Ephraim, whom Asenath daughter of Potiphera, priest of On, bore to him. [21]The children of Benjamin: Bela, Becher, Ashbel, Gera, Naaman, Ehi, Rosh, Muppim, Huppim, and Ard [22](these are the children of Rachel, who were born to Jacob—fourteen persons in all). [23]The children of Dan: Hashum.[c] [24]The children of Naphtali: Jahzeel, Guni, Jezer, and Shillem [25](these are the children of Bilhah, whom Laban gave to his daughter Rachel, and these she bore to Jacob—seven persons in all). [26]All the persons belonging to Jacob who came into Egypt, who were his own offspring, not including the wives of his sons, were sixty-six persons in all. [27]The children of Joseph, who were born to him in Egypt, were two; all the persons of the house of Jacob who came into Egypt were seventy.

Jacob Settles in Goshen

28 Israel[d] sent Judah ahead to Joseph to lead the way before him into Goshen. When they came to the land of Goshen, [29]Joseph made ready his chariot and went up to meet his father Israel in Goshen. He presented himself to him, fell on his neck, and wept on his neck a good while. [30]Israel said to Joseph, "I can die now, having seen for

46:7 his daughters: Includes Jacob's daughters-in-law (see 46:15; 37:35). The word "children" may also include grandchildren (46:22).

46:21 The children of Benjamin: This list of Jacob's descendants assumes a later time inasmuch as Benjamin was not yet married.

46:26-27 sixty-six persons...seventy: This list constitutes the family of Israel that is in place as Exodus begins (Exod 1:5). The numbers in 46:15, 18, 22, and 25 total seventy. The number sixty-six assumes that Er and Onan (46:12) and Joseph's sons never made the trip.

46:28 Goshen: see 45:10 and note.

46:29 wept: see 42:24; 45:1-2.

[a] Or *Saul* [b] Compare Sam Gk Num 26.24; 1 Chr 7.1: MT *Iob* [c] Gk: Heb *Hushim* [d] Heb *He*

myself that you are still alive." [31]Joseph said to his brothers and to his father's household, "I will go up and tell Pharaoh, and will say to him, 'My brothers and my father's household, who were in the land of Canaan, have come to me. [32]The men are shepherds, for they have been keepers of livestock; and they have brought their flocks, and their herds, and all that they have.' [33]When Pharaoh calls you, and says, 'What is your occupation?' [34]you shall say, 'Your servants have been keepers of livestock from our youth even until now, both we and our ancestors'—in order that you may settle in the land of Goshen, because all shepherds are abhorrent to the Egyptians."

46:34 all shepherds are abhorrent: This reference may be to foreign shepherds. To stress this point would assure that, given Joseph's position, Pharaoh would be pleased to have his family at some distance from the general Egyptian population. (This location also may make future escape from Egypt easier.)

47 So Joseph went and told Pharaoh, "My father and my brothers, with their flocks and herds and all that they possess, have come from the land of Canaan; they are now in the land of Goshen." [2]From among his brothers he took five men and presented them to Pharaoh. [3]Pharaoh said to his brothers, "What is your occupation?" And they said to Pharaoh, "Your servants are shepherds, as our ancestors were." [4]They said to Pharaoh, "We have come to reside as aliens in the land; for there is no pasture for your servants' flocks because the famine is severe in the land of Canaan. Now, we ask you, let your servants settle in the land of Goshen." [5]Then Pharaoh said to Joseph, "Your father and your brothers have come to you. [6]The land of Egypt is before you; settle your father and your brothers in the best part of the land; let them live in the land of Goshen; and if you know that there are capable men among them, put them in charge of my livestock."

7 Then Joseph brought in his father Jacob, and presented him before Pharaoh, and Jacob blessed Pharaoh. [8]Pharaoh said to Jacob, "How many are the years of your life?" [9]Jacob said to Pharaoh, "The years of my earthly sojourn are one hundred thirty; few and hard have been the years of my life. They do not compare with the years of the life of my ancestors during their long sojourn." [10]Then Jacob blessed Pharaoh, and went out from the presence of Pharaoh. [11]Joseph settled his father and his brothers, and granted them a holding in the land of Egypt, in the best part of the land, in the land of Rameses, as Pharaoh had instructed. [12]And Joseph provided his father, his brothers, and all his father's household with food, according to the number of their dependents.

47:7, 10 Jacob blessed Pharaoh: A recurring theme from 12:3.

47:11 land of Rameses: The land of Goshen. Rameses was a city in Egypt, perhaps named for a later Pharaoh who ruled Egypt at the time of the exodus (Exod 1:11).

The Famine in Egypt

13 Now there was no food in all the land, for the famine was very severe. The land of Egypt and the land of Canaan languished because of the famine. [14]Joseph collected all the money to be found in the land of Egypt and in the land of Canaan, in exchange for the grain that they bought; and Joseph brought the money into Pharaoh's house. [15]When the money from the land of Egypt and from the land of Canaan was spent, all the Egyptians came to Joseph, and said, "Give us

47:13-26 no food in the land… bought all the land: This episode seeks to show Joseph's administrative wisdom (see 41:46-57). Yet the harsh emergency measures of buying up all the land and making slaves of the people did concentrate power in the hands of Pharaoh. Under a less caring and compassionate leader, the Egyptians might not have been so pleased or eager to agree to Joseph's plan (47:25).

food! Why should we die before your eyes? For our money is gone."
[16]And Joseph answered, "Give me your livestock, and I will give you
food in exchange for your livestock, if your money is gone." [17]So they
brought their livestock to Joseph; and Joseph gave them food in exchange for the horses, the flocks, the herds, and the donkeys. That
year he supplied them with food in exchange for all their livestock.
[18]When that year was ended, they came to him the following year,
and said to him, "We can not hide from my lord that our money is all
spent; and the herds of cattle are my lord's. There is nothing left in the
sight of my lord but our bodies and our lands. [19]Shall we die before
your eyes, both we and our land? Buy us and our land in exchange
for food. We with our land will become slaves to Pharaoh; just give
us seed, so that we may live and not die, and that the land may not
become desolate."

20 So Joseph bought all the land of Egypt for Pharaoh. All the
Egyptians sold their fields, because the famine was severe upon them;
and the land became Pharaoh's. [21]As for the people, he made slaves
of them[a] from one end of Egypt to the other. [22]Only the land of the
priests he did not buy; for the priests had a fixed allowance from Pharaoh, and lived on the allowance that Pharaoh gave them; therefore
they did not sell their land. [23]Then Joseph said to the people, "Now
that I have this day bought you and your land for Pharaoh, here is seed
for you; sow the land. [24]And at the harvests you shall give one-fifth to
Pharaoh, and four-fifths shall be your own, as seed for the field and as
food for yourselves and your households, and as food for your little
ones." [25]They said, "You have saved our lives; may it please my lord,
we will be slaves to Pharaoh." [26]So Joseph made it a statute concerning
the land of Egypt, and it stands to this day, that Pharaoh should have
the fifth. The land of the priests alone did not become Pharaoh's.

The Last Days of Jacob

27 Thus Israel settled in the land of Egypt, in the region of Goshen; and they gained possessions in it, and were fruitful and multiplied exceedingly. [28]Jacob lived in the land of Egypt seventeen years;
so the days of Jacob, the years of his life, were one hundred forty-
seven years.

29 When the time of Israel's death drew near, he called his son
Joseph and said to him, "If I have found favor with you, put your hand
under my thigh and promise to deal loyally and truly with me. Do not
bury me in Egypt. [30]When I lie down with my ancestors, carry me out
of Egypt and bury me in their burial place." He answered, "I will do
as you have said." [31]And he said, "Swear to me"; and he swore to him.
Then Israel bowed himself on the head of his bed.

[a] Sam Gk Compare Vg: MT *He removed them to the cities*

Desperate times can call for desperate measures. How does that apply to modern leaders or governments? In your opinion, what is the proper role of the church and Christian individuals in setting or carrying out public policy?

47:27: in the land of Egypt: This summary verse emphasizes the growth of Israel in Egypt in fulfillment of the God's promise (35:11) and links it up with Exodus 1:7.

47:29 hand under my thigh: See 24:2 and note.

47:30 lie down with my ancestors...burial place: A way of describing death, not an afterlife. The burial place refers to the cave of Machpelah, where Jacob's ancestors were buried (see 23:9).

47:31 bowed himself: Showing an approval of the burial arrangements.

Jacob Blesses Joseph's Sons

48 After this Joseph was told, "Your father is ill." So he took
with him his two sons, Manasseh and Ephraim. [2]When
Jacob was told, "Your son Joseph has come to you," he[a] summoned
his strength and sat up in bed. [3]And Jacob said to Joseph, "God Almighty[b] appeared to me at Luz in the land of Canaan, and he blessed
me, [4]and said to me, 'I am going to make you fruitful and increase
your numbers; I will make of you a company of peoples, and will give
this land to your offspring after you for a perpetual holding.' [5]There-
fore your two sons, who were born to you in the land of Egypt before
I came to you in Egypt, are now mine; Ephraim and Manasseh shall
be mine, just as Reuben and Simeon are. [6]As for the offspring born to
you after them, they shall be yours. They shall be recorded under the
names of their brothers with regard to their inheritance. [7]For when
I came from Paddan, Rachel, alas, died in the land of Canaan on the
way, while there was still some distance to go to Ephrath; and I buried
her there on the way to Ephrath" (that is, Bethlehem).

8 When Israel saw Joseph's sons, he said, "Who are these?" [9]Jo-
seph said to his father, "They are my sons, whom God has given me
here." And he said, "Bring them to me, please, that I may bless them."
[10]Now the eyes of Israel were dim with age, and he could not see well.
So Joseph brought them near him; and he kissed them and embraced
them. [11]Israel said to Joseph, "I did not expect to see your face; and
here God has let me see your children also." [12]Then Joseph removed
them from his father's knees,[c] and he bowed himself with his face to
the earth. [13]Joseph took them both, Ephraim in his right hand toward
Israel's left, and Manasseh in his left hand toward Israel's right, and
brought them near him. [14]But Israel stretched out his right hand and
laid it on the head of Ephraim, who was the younger, and his left hand
on the head of Manasseh, crossing his hands, for Manasseh was the
firstborn. [15]He blessed Joseph, and said,

"The God before whom my ancestors Abraham and Isaac
walked,
the God who has been my shepherd all my life to this day,
16 the angel who has redeemed me from all harm, bless the boys;
and in them let my name be perpetuated, and the name of my
ancestors Abraham and Isaac;
and let them grow into a multitude on the earth."

17 When Joseph saw that his father laid his right hand on the
head of Ephraim, it displeased him; so he took his father's hand, to
remove it from Ephraim's head to Manasseh's head. [18]Joseph said to
his father, "Not so, my father! Since this one is the firstborn, put your
right hand on his head." [19]But his father refused, and said, "I know, my

48:5 Ephraim and Manasseh shall be mine: Jacob grants Joseph's two sons (grandchildren of his favorite wife, Rachel) full status as his own children. This explains their later status as Israelite tribes (in place of Joseph). Because the Levi tribe is not assigned territory, the number of tribes is kept at twelve.

48:7 Paddan…Ephrath: See 25:20; 35:16.

48:13-19 his right hand: Joseph places Manasseh on Jacob's right, the favored position, but Jacob crosses his hands (over Joseph's objection, 48:17-18) so his right hand is laid on Ephraim, giving him the favored position (again, the second born). Jacob blesses Joseph (which includes his sons) with a confessional statement regarding God's role in his life. Jacob blesses Manasseh similar to the way Abraham blessed Ishmael (17:20; 21:13). The growth of these two tribes is evident already in Num 26:28-37. Among Israel's leaders, Joshua and Samuel were descendants of Ephraim, while Gideon is a descendant of Manasseh.

---

[a] Heb *Israel* [b] Traditional rendering of Heb *El Shaddai* [c] Heb *from his knees*

son, I know; he also shall become a people, and he also shall be great. Nevertheless his younger brother shall be greater than he, and his offspring shall become a multitude of nations." [20]So he blessed them that day, saying,

"By you[a] Israel will invoke blessings, saying,
'God make you[a] like Ephraim and like Manasseh.'"

So he put Ephraim ahead of Manasseh. [21]Then Israel said to Joseph, "I am about to die, but God will be with you and will bring you again to the land of your ancestors. [22]I now give to you one portion[b] more than to your brothers, the portion[b] that I took from the hand of the Amorites with my sword and with my bow."

48:20 By you: "You" is singular. The first "you" refers to Joseph (see 48:15), and the second "you" refers to the one being blessed: may you be blessed as Joseph's two sons were.

48:22 one portion more: The elevation of Joseph's sons brings about an elevation of Joseph to the status of firstborn who, *in his sons,* receives the double inheritance of the firstborn (see Deut 21:15-17). The word "portion" is a play on the town of Shechem in Ephraim.

Jacob's Last Words to His Sons

49 Then Jacob called his sons, and said: "Gather around, that I may tell you what will happen to you in days to come.

2 Assemble and hear, O sons of Jacob;
listen to Israel your father.

3 Reuben, you are my firstborn,
my might and the first fruits of my vigor,
excelling in rank and excelling in power.
4 Unstable as water, you shall no longer excel
because you went up onto your father's bed;
then you defiled it—you[c] went up onto my couch!

5 Simeon and Levi are brothers;
weapons of violence are their swords.
6 May I never come into their council;
may I not be joined to their company—
for in their anger they killed men,
and at their whim they hamstrung oxen.
7 Cursed be their anger, for it is fierce,
and their wrath, for it is cruel!
I will divide them in Jacob,
and scatter them in Israel.

8 Judah, your brothers shall praise you;
your hand shall be on the neck of your enemies;
your father's sons shall bow down before you.
9 Judah is a lion's whelp;
from the prey, my son, you have gone up.
He crouches down, he stretches out like a lion,

49:1-28 that I may tell you what will happen: See the comparable poem in Deuteronomy 33:1-29. The poetry is difficult, and exact translations are often challenging (see the NRSV footnotes). The sayings come from various times and places, probably reflecting later tribal history in part. The poem includes curse and censure (49:4-7) and is not simply a blessing (49:28), but the overall perspective is positive. Judah (49:8-12) and Joseph (49:22-26) receive the most extensive and most positive blessings, reflecting their dominance in the narrative and in later tribal history.

49:3-4 your father's bed: See 35:22. The tribe of Reuben was later absorbed by the Moabites.

49:5-7 Simeon and Levi...weapons of violence: they are to be cursed based on their actions in avenging the rape of their sister Dinah (34:25-29). The dividing and scattering corresponds to Simeon being absorbed into Judah (Josh 19:9) and to Levi becoming the priestly family. The Levites were not assigned tribal territory (Num 18:20-24).

49:8-10 The scepter...Judah: The scepter was a staff that signified royal power. Judah's blessing contains a promise (especially 49:10) that anticipates the line of kings that would come from Judah's descendants, starting with David. Similar images are used in royal and messianic texts (see Num 24:17; "the Lion of the tribe of Judah," Rev 5:5).

---

[a] *you* here is singular in Heb [b] Or *mountain slope* (Heb *shekem,* a play on the name of the town and district of Shechem) [c] Gk Syr Tg: Heb *he*

49:10 tribute comes to him: This difficult text could be a reference to a unified Israel (Shiloh was a northern center) or, more likely, a person, whose rule (symbolized by the scepter/staff) will continue until a glorious and fertile future is assured (49:11-12).

49:13-21 Zebulun…Naphtali: See Map 3, pp. 2100-2101, for the location of the twelve tribes when they are later settled in the promised land.

49:22-26 Joseph…blessings: The six-fold use of "blessing" makes this segment about Joseph and his sons especially optimistic.

like a lioness—who dares rouse him up?
10 The scepter shall not depart from Judah,
nor the ruler's staff from between his feet,
until tribute comes to him;[a]
and the obedience of the peoples is his.
11 Binding his foal to the vine
and his donkey's colt to the choice vine,
he washes his garments in wine
and his robe in the blood of grapes;
12 his eyes are darker than wine,
and his teeth whiter than milk.

13 Zebulun shall settle at the shore of the sea;
he shall be a haven for ships,
and his border shall be at Sidon.

14 Issachar is a strong donkey,
lying down between the sheepfolds;
15 he saw that a resting place was good,
and that the land was pleasant;
so he bowed his shoulder to the burden,
and became a slave at forced labor.

16 Dan shall judge his people
as one of the tribes of Israel.
17 Dan shall be a snake by the roadside,
a viper along the path,
that bites the horse's heels
so that its rider falls backward.

18 I wait for your salvation, O LORD.

19 Gad shall be raided by raiders,
but he shall raid at their heels.

20 Asher's[b] food shall be rich,
and he shall provide royal delicacies.

21 Naphtali is a doe let loose
that bears lovely fawns.[a]

22 Joseph is a fruitful bough,
a fruitful bough by a spring;

---

[a] Or *until Shiloh comes* or *until he comes to Shiloh* or (with Syr) *until he comes to whom it belongs* [b] Gk Vg Syr: Heb *From Asher* [c] Or *that gives beautiful words*

his branches run over the wall.[a]
23 The archers fiercely attacked him;
they shot at him and pressed him hard.
24 Yet his bow remained taut,
and his arms[b] were made agile
by the hands of the Mighty One of Jacob,
by the name of the Shepherd, the Rock of Israel,
25 by the God of your father, who will help you,
by the Almighty[c] who will bless you
with blessings of heaven above,
blessings of the deep that lies beneath,
blessings of the breasts and of the womb.
26 The blessings of your father
are stronger than the blessings of the eternal mountains,
the bounties[d] of the everlasting hills;
may they be on the head of Joseph,
on the brow of him who was set apart from his brothers.

27 Benjamin is a ravenous wolf,
in the morning devouring the prey,
and at evening dividing the spoil."

28 All these are the twelve tribes of Israel, and this is what their father said to them when he blessed them, blessing each one of them with a suitable blessing.

Jacob's Death and Burial

29 Then he charged them, saying to them, "I am about to be gathered to my people. Bury me with my ancestors—in the cave in the
field of Ephron the Hittite, 30 in the cave in the field at Machpelah,
near Mamre, in the land of Canaan, in the field that Abraham bought
from Ephron the Hittite as a burial site. 31 There Abraham and his wife
Sarah were buried; there Isaac and his wife Rebekah were buried; and
there I buried Leah— 32 the field and the cave that is in it were purchased from the Hittites." 33 When Jacob ended his charge to his sons,
he drew up his feet into the bed, breathed his last, and was gathered
to his people.

49:29-33 This is a variation of 47:29-31, this time ending with Jacob's death.

50 Then Joseph threw himself on his father's face and wept
over him and kissed him. 2 Joseph commanded the physicians in his service to embalm his father. So the physicians embalmed
Israel; 3 they spent forty days in doing this, for that is the time required
for embalming. And the Egyptians wept for him seventy days.

50:1-14 physicians embalmed Israel: The mourning of the Egyptians for the Israelite Jacob is elaborate. This is especially remarkable, given the conflict to come in Exodus.

[a] Meaning of Heb uncertain [b] Heb *the arms of his hands* [c] Traditional rendering of Heb *Shaddai*
[d] Cn Compare Gk: Heb *of my progenitors to the boundaries*

4 When the days of weeping for him were past, Joseph addressed the household of Pharaoh, "If now I have found favor with you, please speak to Pharaoh as follows: 5My father made me swear an oath; he said, 'I am about to die. In the tomb that I hewed out for myself in the land of Canaan, there you shall bury me.' Now therefore let me go up, so that I may bury my father; then I will return." 6Pharaoh answered, "Go up, and bury your father, as he made you swear to do."

7 So Joseph went up to bury his father. With him went up all the servants of Pharaoh, the elders of his household, and all the elders of the land of Egypt, 8as well as all the household of Joseph, his brothers, and his father's household. Only their children, their flocks, and their herds were left in the land of Goshen. 9Both chariots and charioteers went up with him. It was a very great company. 10When they came to the threshing floor of Atad, which is beyond the Jordan, they held there a very great and sorrowful lamentation; and he observed a time of mourning for his father seven days. 11When the Canaanite inhabitants of the land saw the mourning on the threshing floor of Atad, they said, "This is a grievous mourning on the part of the Egyptians." Therefore the place was named Abel-mizraim;[a] it is beyond the Jordan. 12Thus his sons did for him as he had instructed them. 13They carried him to the land of Canaan and buried him in the cave of the field at Machpelah, the field near Mamre, which Abraham bought as a burial site from Ephron the Hittite. 14After he had buried his father, Joseph returned to Egypt with his brothers and all who had gone up with him to bury his father.

Joseph Forgives His Brothers

15 Realizing that their father was dead, Joseph's brothers said, "What if Joseph still bears a grudge against us and pays us back in full for all the wrong that we did to him?" 16So they approached[b] Joseph, saying, "Your father gave this instruction before he died, 17'Say to Joseph: I beg you, forgive the crime of your brothers and the wrong they did in harming you.' Now therefore please forgive the crime of the servants of the God of your father." Joseph wept when they spoke to him. 18Then his brothers also wept,[c] fell down before him, and said, "We are here as your slaves." 19But Joseph said to them, "Do not be afraid! Am I in the place of God? 20Even though you intended to do harm to me, God intended it for good, in order to preserve a numerous people, as he is doing today. 21So have no fear; I myself will provide for you and your little ones." In this way he reassured them, speaking kindly to them.

Joseph's Last Days and Death

22 So Joseph remained in Egypt, he and his father's household; and Joseph lived one hundred ten years. 23Joseph saw Ephraim's chil-

[a] That is *mourning* (or *meadow*) *of Egypt* [b] Gk Syr: Heb *they commanded* [c] Cn: Heb *also came*

50:11 Atad: an unknown site, aptly named Abel-mizraim ("mourning of Egypt").

50:16 Your father gave this instruction: This instruction is not recorded elsewhere. It could be a self-serving effort on the part of the brothers, who still remember the crime they have committed.

50:17 Joseph wept: See 42:24; 45:1-2.

50:18 his brothers . . . fell down before him: This gesture does not fulfill Joseph's dream of 37:7 (as it does in 42:6; 43:26; 44:14), for Joseph rejects their gesture and his status as "lord" over them.

50:19 Am I in the place of God? Joseph refers both to their request for forgiveness and to their offer to become slaves. Joseph is not God, so he will not be a Pharaoh to them; they will be servants of God alone. Also, Joseph rejects a guilt and forgiveness approach, leaving that matter to God.

50:20 you intended to do harm to me, God intended it for good: Joseph names the brothers' actions evil (see 44:4-5), but God has drawn their actions into God's larger purposes for goodness, and these have come to prevail (see at 45:4-8). Within their very evil plans, God has been working for good.

Sin and evil, even with all of their consequences, do not have the last word. With Joseph's words in 50:20 in mind, how have you experienced or witnessed God at work to bring good out of evil circumstances?

50:23 born on Joseph's knees: That is, claimed as his descendants.

dren of the third generation; the children of Machir son of Manasseh
were also born on Joseph's knees.

24 Then Joseph said to his brothers, "I am about to die; but God
will surely come to you, and bring you up out of this land to the land
that he swore to Abraham, to Isaac, and to Jacob." 25 So Joseph made
the Israelites swear, saying, "When God comes to you, you shall carry
up my bones from here." 26 And Joseph died, being one hundred ten
years old; he was embalmed and placed in a coffin in Egypt.

50:24 to the land: Joseph transmits the promises of God to all the brothers. Anticipating the exodus to come, he assures them that God will bring them up from Egypt to the land of promise.

Exodus 3:2

EXODUS

Background File

The title of the book of Exodus means "going out" (related to the English word "exit"). In the exodus story, God leads the Israelite people out of Egypt and out of slavery.

Based on all available evidence, the date of the exodus may have been 1250 B.C.E. Outside of the Bible, the first clear mention of a people called Israel in the land of Canaan appears in a list of Egyptian victories inscribed on a monument (known as the Merneptah stele) from the reign of Pharaoh Merneptah (1224-1200 B.C.E.), the son of Rameses II. This inscription suggests that Israelites had begun to settle in the land of Canaan shortly before this time.

What's the Story?

The book of Exodus has three main parts. In the first part (chapters 1-18), God hears the Israelites' cry for help in Egypt; remembers the covenant promise with Abraham, Isaac, and Jacob (2:23-24); and leads the people out of slavery. The Pharaoh or Egyptian king of the exodus period is never identified. However, Rameses—the name of a city built to store supplies for the Pharaoh—suggests that this person might have been Rameses II (around 1290-1224 B.C.E.). This king moved his capital to the delta region of the Nile River, near Goshen (where the Israelites lived). He engaged in huge construction projects requiring slave labor. Although there is no certain reference to the Israelites, Egyptian records from his reign report conflicts with foreign workers.

The second part of the book of Exodus (chapters 19-24) tells about Israel's new identity as God's covenant partner. The exodus out of Egypt shows God's lasting commitment to Israel. In turn, God calls for complete loyalty from the Israelites: "You shall have no other gods before me" (20:3). Through the Torah given by God on Mount Sinai, the people—already delivered and brought to God "on eagles' wings" (19:4)—receive a close and binding covenant relationship with the LORD. The Torah describes how the people of Israel are to live out their covenant relationship with God. While it includes various kinds of laws, the common translation of Torah as Moses' "law" is too narrow. The word "Torah" literally means the "teaching" about how the Israelites are to express undivided devotion to the God who has freed them from slavery. The Torah also teaches how to care for the weakest people in society and treat one another as fellow members of God's covenant community.

The final chapters of Exodus (chapters 25–31 and 35–40) include detailed instructions for constructing a movable place of worship (tabernacle), and worshiping in the wilderness. As the book ends, the Israelites have completed their work on the tabernacle. This work is very different from the slave labor the people carried out in Egypt! The people have moved from slavery under Pharaoh to freedom within their relationship with God. Remembering the way the LORD was with them in the wilderness would be especially meaningful later in their history, when the people of the southern kingdom of Judah would see the temple in Jerusalem destroyed (587 B.C.E.) and be forced to live far from their land.

What's the Message?

God acts in history to free a powerless people and bring them into a covenant relationship. This event reveals God's faithfulness to Israel and to Egypt and all other nations of the world as well. The exodus is so important that it is even used to help describe who God is: "I am the LORD your God, who brought you out of the land of Egypt, out of the house of slavery" (20:2). The people become the LORD's "treasured possession out of all the peoples," "a priestly kingdom," and "a holy nation" (19:5-6) and receive the Torah to show them how to live in relationship with this gracious and liberating God through the everyday activities of life.

The main purpose of the book of Exodus is to tell this story—a faith story of lasting significance. The exodus from Egypt is still celebrated every year in Jewish homes at the festival of Passover. Christian baptism draws on an image from Exodus of crossing through the waters of death to life. God's actions on behalf of the Israelite slaves continue to provide a way to understand human struggles for liberty and dignity throughout the course of history.

---

1 These are the names of the sons of Israel who came to Egypt with
Jacob, each with his household: 2 Reuben, Simeon, Levi, and Judah, 3 Issachar, Zebulun, and Benjamin, 4 Dan and Naphtali, Gad and
Asher. 5 The total number of people born to Jacob was seventy. Joseph
was already in Egypt. 6 Then Joseph died, and all his brothers, and that
whole generation. 7 But the Israelites were fruitful and prolific; they
multiplied and grew exceedingly strong, so that the land was filled
with them.

The Israelites Are Oppressed

8 Now a new king arose over Egypt, who did not know Joseph.
9 He said to his people, "Look, the Israelite people are more numerous and more powerful than we. 10 Come, let us deal shrewdly with
them, or they will increase and, in the event of war, join our enemies
and fight against us and escape from the land." 11 Therefore they set
taskmasters over them to oppress them with forced labor. They built
supply cities, Pithom and Rameses, for Pharaoh. 12 But the more they
were oppressed, the more they multiplied and spread, so that the

1:1-7 the sons of Israel: This connects Exodus to previous events in Genesis.

1:1 Israel: "Israel" is the new name given to Jacob after he struggles with God and receives a blessing. Israel is also the name of the people descended from Jacob.

1:1 came to Egypt with Jacob: Jacob's family came to Egypt to survive during a drought (Gen 46).

1:8 a new king: The identity of this king who does not recognize Joseph is not given.

1:11 Pharaoh: "Pharaoh" is a royal title meaning "great house" in Egyptian, but in Exodus it is used as a name. In ancient Egyptian thought the Pharaoh was a god. The true God's superiority over all other gods is an important theme in Exodus.

Egyptians came to dread the Israelites. 13The Egyptians became ruthless in imposing tasks on the Israelites, 14and made their lives bitter
with hard service in mortar and brick and in every kind of field labor.
They were ruthless in all the tasks that they imposed on them.
15 The king of Egypt said to the Hebrew midwives, one of whom
was named Shiphrah and the other Puah, 16"When you act as midwives to the Hebrew women, and see them on the birthstool, if it is a
boy, kill him; but if it is a girl, she shall live." 17But the midwives feared
God; they did not do as the king of Egypt commanded them, but they
let the boys live. 18So the king of Egypt summoned the midwives and
said to them, "Why have you done this, and allowed the boys to live?"
19The midwives said to Pharaoh, "Because the Hebrew women are not
like the Egyptian women; for they are vigorous and give birth before
the midwife comes to them." 20So God dealt well with the midwives;
and the people multiplied and became very strong. 21And because the
midwives feared God, he gave them families. 22Then Pharaoh commanded all his people, "Every boy that is born to the Hebrews[a] you
shall throw into the Nile, but you shall let every girl live."

Birth and Youth of Moses

2 Now a man from the house of Levi went and married a Levite
woman. 2The woman conceived and bore a son; and when she
saw that he was a fine baby, she hid him three months. 3When she
could hide him no longer she got a papyrus basket for him, and plastered it with bitumen and pitch; she put the child in it and placed it
among the reeds on the bank of the river. 4His sister stood at a distance, to see what would happen to him.
5 The daughter of Pharaoh came down to bathe at the river, while
her attendants walked beside the river. She saw the basket among the
reeds and sent her maid to bring it. 6When she opened it, she saw the
child. He was crying, and she took pity on him. "This must be one
of the Hebrews' children," she said. 7Then his sister said to Pharaoh's
daughter, "Shall I go and get you a nurse from the Hebrew women
to nurse the child for you?" 8Pharaoh's daughter said to her, "Yes." So
the girl went and called the child's mother. 9Pharaoh's daughter said
to her, "Take this child and nurse it for me, and I will give you your
wages." So the woman took the child and nursed it. 10When the child
grew up, she brought him to Pharaoh's daughter, and she took him as
her son. She named him Moses,[b] "because," she said, "I drew him out[c]
of the water."

Moses Flees to Midian

11 One day, after Moses had grown up, he went out to his people
and saw their forced labor. He saw an Egyptian beating a Hebrew, one

[a] Sam Gk Tg: Heb lacks *to the Hebrews* [b] Heb *Mosheh* [c] Heb *mashah*

1:14 hard service: Joseph introduced slavery in Egypt during the famine (Gen 47:20-26). Slavery in the book of Exodus involves forced labor, with large groups of slaves assigned to massive government projects.

1:15 Hebrew: This is another name for the Israelites. It is also the name of the language spoken by the Israelites and used over the centuries in Jewish study and worship as well as in present-day Israel.

1:16 if it is a boy: Because Israelites traced family lines and ethnicity through the father, killing the males would destroy them.

1:17 the midwives feared God: God is first mentioned in Exodus here, through the midwives' witness.

2:1 Levi: Levi was one of Jacob's twelve sons. His descendants were priests of Israel. Both of Moses' parents are from this priestly line.

2:2 she saw that he was a fine baby: This is literally "she saw that he was good," a reminder of God's delight in creation (Gen 1:4, 10, 12, 18, 21, 25, 31).

2:3 basket...reeds: The same word translated as "basket" is translated as "ark" in the story of Noah and the flood (Gen 6:14). The same word translated as "reeds" describes the Sea of Reeds, commonly translated as the "Red Sea" (10:19; 13:18; 15:4, 22; and 23:31).

2:3 on the bank of the river: Moses' mother obeys part of Pharaoh's order (1:22) when she places Moses on the bank of the Nile, but keeps him alive by hiding him.

2:4-10 sister: Miriam is the sister of Aaron and Moses (Num 26:59), a prophet (Exod 15:20), and leader of the exodus (Mic 6:4).

2:5-10 daughter of Pharaoh: A member of Pharaoh's own family saves Moses' life by adopting him.

of his kinsfolk. 12 He looked this way and that, and seeing no one he
killed the Egyptian and hid him in the sand. 13 When he went out the
next day, he saw two Hebrews fighting; and he said to the one who
was in the wrong, "Why do you strike your fellow Hebrew?" 14 He
answered, "Who made you a ruler and judge over us? Do you mean
to kill me as you killed the Egyptian?" Then Moses was afraid and
thought, "Surely the thing is known." 15 When Pharaoh heard of it, he
sought to kill Moses.
But Moses fled from Pharaoh. He settled in the land of Midian, and
sat down by a well. 16 The priest of Midian had seven daughters. They
came to draw water, and filled the troughs to water their father's flock.
17 But some shepherds came and drove them away. Moses got up and
came to their defense and watered their flock. 18 When they returned to
their father Reuel, he said, "How is it that you have come back so soon
today?" 19 They said, "An Egyptian helped us against the shepherds; he
even drew water for us and watered the flock." 20 He said to his daughters, "Where is he? Why did you leave the man? Invite him to break
bread." 21 Moses agreed to stay with the man, and he gave Moses his
daughter Zipporah in marriage. 22 She bore a son, and he named him
Gershom; for he said, "I have been an alien[a] residing in a foreign land."
23 After a long time the king of Egypt died. The Israelites groaned
under their slavery, and cried out. Out of the slavery their cry for help
rose up to God. 24 God heard their groaning, and God remembered
his covenant with Abraham, Isaac, and Jacob. 25 God looked upon the
Israelites, and God took notice of them.

Moses at the Burning Bush

3 Moses was keeping the flock of his father-in-law Jethro, the
priest of Midian; he led his flock beyond the wilderness, and
came to Horeb, the mountain of God. 2 There the angel of the LORD
appeared to him in a flame of fire out of a bush; he looked, and the
bush was blazing, yet it was not consumed. 3 Then Moses said, "I must
turn aside and look at this great sight, and see why the bush is not
burned up." 4 When the LORD saw that he had turned aside to see, God
called to him out of the bush, "Moses, Moses!" And he said, "Here I
am." 5 Then he said, "Come no closer! Remove the sandals from your
feet, for the place on which you are standing is holy ground." 6 He said
further, "I am the God of your father, the God of Abraham, the God
of Isaac, and the God of Jacob." And Moses hid his face, for he was
afraid to look at God.
7 Then the LORD said, "I have observed the misery of my people who are in Egypt; I have heard their cry on account of their
taskmasters. Indeed, I know their sufferings, 8 and I have come down

[a] Heb *ger*

2:10 Moses: "Moses" is part of an Egyptian name meaning "son of" a particular god. In Hebrew, Moses (MOW-sheh) means one who "draws out."

2:15 Midian: Midian was a desert region east of the Sinai Peninsula, possibly in southern Transjordan or northeastern Arabia (see Map 2, p. 2099). The Midianites were related to Israel, as descendants of Abraham's son by his wife Keturah (Gen 25:2).

2:15b-21 seven daughters...draw water: Moses meets his wife at a well, a common motif or pattern in the Bible (Gen 24:11; 29:2).

2:18 Reuel: Moses' priestly father-in-law is known most commonly by the name Jethro (3:1; 4:18; 18:1), and also Hobab (Judg 4:11). He recognizes what the God of Israel has done (18:1-11), provides leadership in worship (18:12), and makes positive contributions to the Israelites' legal system (18:13-27).

2:22 Gershom: The son of Moses and Zipporah is named Gershom, literally, a "foreigner there," referring to Moses' status in Midian.

2:24 God heard: God hears the Israelites cry out and remembers the covenant agreement with Abraham, Isaac, and Jacob (Gen 12:1-3; 15:1-21; 17:1-27; 26:2-5; 28:13-15; 48:3-4).

3:1 Horeb: This desert region and mountain where the Torah or teachings would be given to Israel is also called Sinai. (See Map 2, page 2099.)

3:2 bush: God appears to Moses from a mysterious bush with a flame that does not burn it up. Trees are connected with the worship of God in other passages. See the note on 25:31-40.

3:4 Moses, Moses!: The repeated call indicates urgency. (See Gen 22:11; 1 Sam 3:4).

3:5 holy ground: A place where God appears is often associated with a striking natural event. Moses is attracted to the sight of the burning bush, but shows respect by removing his shoes.

When have you experienced God's presence or felt that you were on holy ground?

3:10 **bring my people, the Israelites, out of Egypt:** These words will be repeated throughout Exodus. God will deliver the people from slavery and settle them in the land promised to their ancestors.

3:11 **Who am I?:** Moses objects to his call as God's prophet or messenger to Pharaoh and to the Israelites, to bring Israel out of Egypt. Other prophets shared Moses' feelings of unworthiness (Isa 6:5; Jer 1:6).

3:12: **I will be with you:** The main thing is not who the messenger is, but that God promises to be with him. "I will be with you" is a play of words on God's name, "I AM," revealed in 3:14.

3:12 **sign:** This sign will prove that God's promise is true: The Israelites will worship God at Horeb (Sinai) after they leave Egypt (chapters 19–24).

3:13 **What is his name?** Which god, among the many gods in the ancient Near East, is sending Moses to Pharaoh and Israel?

3:14 **I AM WHO I AM:** In Hebrew thought, names embody the essential character of a person or god. The Hebrew root of God's personal name, "YHWH" (3:15), means "to be," or, more accurately, "to be present" or "to encounter." "I AM WHO I AM" may also be translated "I will be present where I will be present." God's name expresses both freedom and availability. The promise "I will be with you" to Moses in 3:12 provides one interpretation of God's name, as does 33:19, where the name YHWH is announced along with the statement: "I will be gracious to whom I will be gracious, and will show mercy on whom I will show mercy."

3:15 **LORD:** God tells Moses the eternal name of the God of the ancestors, of the exodus, and of all future generations. In most English Bibles God's personal name appears as "LORD." This represents the four-letter name of God or YHWH. At one time this name was probably pronounced "Yahweh," but out of respect people stopped saying it. The title "LORD," in Hebrew *Adonai*, replaced the pronunciation of the divine name. The name Jehovah is a pronunciation of the consonants of YHWH using the vowels of Adonai.

to deliver them from the Egyptians, and to bring them up out of that
land to a good and broad land, a land flowing with milk and honey, to
the country of the Canaanites, the Hittites, the Amorites, the Perizzites, the Hivites, and the Jebusites. 9 The cry of the Israelites has now
come to me; I have also seen how the Egyptians oppress them. 10 So
come, I will send you to Pharaoh to bring my people, the Israelites,
out of Egypt." 11 But Moses said to God, "Who am I that I should go
to Pharaoh, and bring the Israelites out of Egypt?" 12 He said, "I will be
with you; and this shall be the sign for you that it is I who sent you:
when you have brought the people out of Egypt, you shall worship
God on this mountain."

The Divine Name Revealed

13 But Moses said to God, "If I come to the Israelites and say
to them, 'The God of your ancestors has sent me to you,' and they
ask me, 'What is his name?' what shall I say to them?" 14 God said to
Moses, "I AM WHO I AM."[a] He said further, "Thus you shall say to the
Israelites, 'I AM has sent me to you.'" 15 God also said to Moses, "Thus
you shall say to the Israelites, 'The LORD,[b] the God of your ancestors,
the God of Abraham, the God of Isaac, and the God of Jacob, has sent
me to you':

This is my name forever,
and this my title for all generations.

16 Go and assemble the elders of Israel, and say to them, 'The LORD,
the God of your ancestors, the God of Abraham, of Isaac, and of Jacob, has appeared to me, saying: I have given heed to you and to what
has been done to you in Egypt. 17 I declare that I will bring you up out
of the misery of Egypt, to the land of the Canaanites, the Hittites, the
Amorites, the Perizzites, the Hivites, and the Jebusites, a land flowing with milk and honey.' 18 They will listen to your voice; and you
and the elders of Israel shall go to the king of Egypt and say to him,
'The LORD, the God of the Hebrews, has met with us; let us now go
a three days' journey into the wilderness, so that we may sacrifice to
the LORD our God.' 19 I know, however, that the king of Egypt will not
let you go unless compelled by a mighty hand.[c] 20 So I will stretch out
my hand and strike Egypt with all my wonders that I will perform
in it; after that he will let you go. 21 I will bring this people into such
favor with the Egyptians that, when you go, you will not go empty-
handed; 22 each woman shall ask her neighbor and any woman living
in the neighbor's house for jewelry of silver and of gold, and clothing,
and you shall put them on your sons and on your daughters; and so
you shall plunder the Egyptians."

---

[a] Or *I AM WHAT I AM* or *I WILL BE WHAT I WILL BE* [b] The word "LORD" when spelled with capital letters stands for the divine name, *YHWH*, which is here connected with the verb *hayah*, "to be" [c] Gk Vg: Heb *no, not by a mighty hand*

Moses' Miraculous Power

4 Then Moses answered, "But suppose they do not believe me or listen to me, but say, 'The Lord did not appear to you.' " 2The Lord said to him, "What is that in your hand?" He said, "A staff." 3And he said, "Throw it on the ground." So he threw the staff on the ground, and it became a snake; and Moses drew back from it. 4Then the Lord said to Moses, "Reach out your hand, and seize it by the tail"—so he reached out his hand and grasped it, and it became a staff in his hand— 5"so that they may believe that the Lord, the God of their ancestors, the God of Abraham, the God of Isaac, and the God of Jacob, has appeared to you."

4:1 suppose they do not believe me: Moses is given three signs to convince the Israelites that he is God's messenger: his staff turns into a snake, his hand becomes leprous and is cured, and water becomes blood.

6 Again, the Lord said to him, "Put your hand inside your cloak." He put his hand into his cloak; and when he took it out, his hand was leprous,[a] as white as snow. 7Then God said, "Put your hand back into your cloak"—so he put his hand back into his cloak, and when he took it out, it was restored like the rest of his body— 8"If they will not believe you or heed the first sign, they may believe the second sign. 9If they will not believe even these two signs or heed you, you shall take some water from the Nile and pour it on the dry ground; and the water that you shall take from the Nile will become blood on the dry ground."

10 But Moses said to the Lord, "O my Lord, I have never been eloquent, neither in the past nor even now that you have spoken to your servant; but I am slow of speech and slow of tongue." 11Then the Lord said to him, "Who gives speech to mortals? Who makes them mute or deaf, seeing or blind? Is it not I, the Lord? 12Now go, and I will be with your mouth and teach you what you are to speak." 13But he said, "O my Lord, please send someone else." 14Then the anger of the Lord was kindled against Moses and he said, "What of your brother Aaron the Levite? I know that he can speak fluently; even now he is coming out to meet you, and when he sees you his heart will be glad. 15You shall speak to him and put the words in his mouth; and I will be with your mouth and with his mouth, and will teach you what you shall do. 16He indeed shall speak for you to the people; he shall serve as a mouth for you, and you shall serve as God for him. 17Take in your hand this staff, with which you shall perform the signs."

4:10 slow of speech: God gives speaking ability to humans and will teach Moses what to say.

4:13-14 send someone else: Moses' final objection raises God's anger.

4:14-16 your brother Aaron: Moses will speak to Aaron for God. In that way Moses will serve as God for him. Aaron will speak to the people for Moses, as Moses' spokesperson or messenger, which is the definition of a prophet (see 7:1).

Moses Returns to Egypt

18 Moses went back to his father-in-law Jethro and said to him, "Please let me go back to my kindred in Egypt and see whether they are still living." And Jethro said to Moses, "Go in peace." 19The Lord said to Moses in Midian, "Go back to Egypt; for all those who were seeking your life are dead." 20So Moses took his wife and his sons, put

[a] A term for several skin diseases; precise meaning uncertain

them on a donkey, and went back to the land of Egypt; and Moses
carried the staff of God in his hand.
21 And the LORD said to Moses, "When you go back to Egypt,
see that you perform before Pharaoh all the wonders that I have put
in your power; but I will harden his heart, so that he will not let the
people go. 22Then you shall say to Pharaoh, 'Thus says the LORD: Israel is my firstborn son. 23I said to you, "Let my son go that he may
worship me." But you refused to let him go; now I will kill your firstborn son.'"
24 On the way, at a place where they spent the night, the LORD
met him and tried to kill him. 25But Zipporah took a flint and cut off
her son's foreskin, and touched Moses'[a] feet with it, and said, "Truly
you are a bridegroom of blood to me!" 26So he let him alone. It was
then she said, "A bridegroom of blood by circumcision."
27 The LORD said to Aaron, "Go into the wilderness to meet
Moses." So he went; and he met him at the mountain of God and
kissed him. 28Moses told Aaron all the words of the LORD with which
he had sent him, and all the signs with which he had charged him.
29Then Moses and Aaron went and assembled all the elders of the
Israelites. 30Aaron spoke all the words that the LORD had spoken to
Moses, and performed the signs in the sight of the people. 31The people believed; and when they heard that the LORD had given heed to
the Israelites and that he had seen their misery, they bowed down and
worshiped.

Bricks without Straw

5 Afterward Moses and Aaron went to Pharaoh and said, "Thus
says the LORD, the God of Israel, 'Let my people go, so that they
may celebrate a festival to me in the wilderness.'" 2But Pharaoh said,
"Who is the LORD, that I should heed him and let Israel go? I do not
know the LORD, and I will not let Israel go." 3Then they said, "The
God of the Hebrews has revealed himself to us; let us go a three days'
journey into the wilderness to sacrifice to the LORD our God, or he
will fall upon us with pestilence or sword." 4But the king of Egypt said
to them, "Moses and Aaron, why are you taking the people away from
their work? Get to your labors!" 5Pharaoh continued, "Now they are
more numerous than the people of the land[b] and yet you want them
to stop working!" 6That same day Pharaoh commanded the taskmasters of the people, as well as their supervisors, 7"You shall no longer
give the people straw to make bricks, as before; let them go and gather
straw for themselves. 8But you shall require of them the same quantity
of bricks as they have made previously; do not diminish it, for they
are lazy; that is why they cry, 'Let us go and offer sacrifice to our God.'

[a] Heb *his* [b] Sam: Heb *The people of the land are now many*

4:21-23 I will harden his heart: God's control and human freedom are both essential beliefs in the story of the exodus. God is in complete control of all aspects of the exodus, even Pharaoh's decision to oppose God's message (7:2-6; 10:1-2). Yet, he is also portrayed in some places as hardening his own heart (8:15; 8:32), so human freedom and responsibility are also upheld.

To what extent are we responsible for our own decisions, and to what extent are our decisions based on factors such as social background, education, and experience that may be beyond our control?

4:24-26 bridegroom of blood: In this strange scene, Zipporah, Moses' Midianite wife, saves the life of Moses or their son (the Hebrew text is unclear) through the blood of circumcision. The power of blood to "turn away" death is seen also in the Passover narrative. See first note on 12:12-13.

4:25-26 circumcision: Circumcision, the ritual cutting of the male foreskin, is a sign of God's covenant with Abraham and his descendants (Gen 17:9-14).

4:27-31 Moses and Aaron: Aaron speaks the words and performs the signs that Moses tells him, confirming God's promise that Aaron would serve as Moses' spokesperson.

4:29 Israelites: The Israelites, descended from the sons of Israel, were also known as Hebrews in Egypt. The people would be called Jews, from the tribe of Judah, especially after the return from exile in Babylonia, beginning in 539 B.C.E.

5:1 Let my people go...celebrate a festival: The request to let the Israelites worship God for three days in the wilderness is related to the sign promised to Moses that the people would worship God at the holy mountain. It also serves as a ploy by the Israelites, as the underdogs in this situation, to gain Pharaoh's consent.

5:2 Who is LORD?: Pharaoh comes to know the answer to his own question through the coming plagues. God will be made known to Pharaoh and all of Egypt (14:4, 18), to the Israelites (14:31), and to all nations through these displays of power in nature and history.

9 Let heavier work be laid on them; then they will labor at it and pay no attention to deceptive words."

10 So the taskmasters and the supervisors of the people went out and said to the people, "Thus says Pharaoh, 'I will not give you straw. 11 Go and get straw yourselves, wherever you can find it; but your work will not be lessened in the least.'" 12 So the people scattered throughout the land of Egypt, to gather stubble for straw. 13 The taskmasters were urgent, saying, "Complete your work, the same daily assignment as when you were given straw." 14 And the supervisors of the Israelites, whom Pharaoh's taskmasters had set over them, were beaten, and were asked, "Why did you not finish the required quantity of bricks yesterday and today, as you did before?"

15 Then the Israelite supervisors came to Pharaoh and cried, "Why do you treat your servants like this? 16 No straw is given to your servants, yet they say to us, 'Make bricks!' Look how your servants are beaten! You are unjust to your own people."[a] 17 He said, "You are lazy, lazy; that is why you say, 'Let us go and sacrifice to the LORD.' 18 Go now, and work; for no straw shall be given you, but you shall still deliver the same number of bricks." 19 The Israelite supervisors saw that they were in trouble when they were told, "You shall not lessen your daily number of bricks." 20 As they left Pharaoh, they came upon Moses and Aaron who were waiting to meet them. 21 They said to them, "The LORD look upon you and judge! You have brought us into bad odor with Pharaoh and his officials, and have put a sword in their hand to kill us."

22 Then Moses turned again to the LORD and said, "O LORD, why have you mistreated this people? Why did you ever send me? 23 Since I first came to Pharaoh to speak in your name, he has mistreated this people, and you have done nothing at all to deliver your people."

Israel's Deliverance Assured

6 Then the LORD said to Moses, "Now you shall see what I will do to Pharaoh: Indeed, by a mighty hand he will let them go; by a mighty hand he will drive them out of his land."

2 God also spoke to Moses and said to him: "I am the LORD. 3 I appeared to Abraham, Isaac, and Jacob as God Almighty,[b] but by my name 'The LORD'[c] I did not make myself known to them. 4 I also established my covenant with them, to give them the land of Canaan, the land in which they resided as aliens. 5 I have also heard the groaning of the Israelites whom the Egyptians are holding as slaves, and I have remembered my covenant. 6 Say therefore to the Israelites, 'I am the LORD, and I will free you from the burdens of the Egyptians

[a] Gk Compare Syr Vg: Heb *beaten, and the sin of your people* [b] Traditional rendering of Heb *El Shaddai*
[c] Heb *YHWH*; see note at 3.15

5:13-16 Make bricks!: Already doing forced labor, the people now have to add a step to their work while making the same number of bricks each day. Straw added strength to these sun-dried bricks.

5:22-23 Why did you ever send me?: Moses sees his first encounter with Pharaoh as a failure.

6:2-13 Go and tell Pharaoh king of Egypt to let the Israelites go: God re-commissions Moses, confirming that he is a messenger between God, Pharaoh, and the people. Moses raises the same issues as he did at the burning bush: the people's disbelief and his ineffectiveness as speaker.

6:3 God Almighty: Israel's ancestors did not know God by the name LORD, but by *El Shaddai*, God almighty, or possibly "god of the mountains." *El Shaddai* was a family God to Abraham, Isaac, and Jacob. The LORD is made known by name to the entire people of Israel.

6:7 **my people...your God:** This expression points to the covenant relationship between God and Israel.

and deliver you from slavery to them. I will redeem you with an outstretched arm and with mighty acts of judgment. [7]I will take you as my people, and I will be your God. You shall know that I am the LORD your God, who has freed you from the burdens of the Egyptians. [8]I will bring you into the land that I swore to give to Abraham, Isaac, and Jacob; I will give it to you for a possession. I am the LORD.'" [9]Moses told this to the Israelites; but they would not listen to Moses, because of their broken spirit and their cruel slavery.

10 Then the LORD spoke to Moses, [11]"Go and tell Pharaoh king of Egypt to let the Israelites go out of his land." [12]But Moses spoke to the LORD, "The Israelites have not listened to me; how then shall Pharaoh listen to me, poor speaker that I am?"[a] [13]Thus the LORD spoke to Moses and Aaron, and gave them orders regarding the Israelites and Pharaoh king of Egypt, charging them to free the Israelites from the land of Egypt.

The Genealogy of Moses and Aaron

14 The following are the heads of their ancestral houses: the sons of Reuben, the firstborn of Israel: Hanoch, Pallu, Hezron, and Carmi; these are the families of Reuben. [15]The sons of Simeon: Jemuel, Jamin, Ohad, Jachin, Zohar, and Shaul,[b] the son of a Canaanite woman; these are the families of Simeon. [16]The following are the names of the sons of Levi according to their genealogies: Gershon,[c] Kohath, and Merari, and the length of Levi's life was one hundred thirty-seven years. [17]The sons of Gershon:[c] Libni and Shimei, by their families. [18]The sons of Kohath: Amram, Izhar, Hebron, and Uzziel, and the length of Kohath's life was one hundred thirty-three years. [19]The sons of Merari: Mahli and Mushi. These are the families of the Levites according to their genealogies. [20]Amram married Jochebed his father's sister and she bore him Aaron and Moses, and the length of Amram's life was one hundred thirty-seven years. [21]The sons of Izhar: Korah, Nepheg, and Zichri. [22]The sons of Uzziel: Mishael, Elzaphan, and Sithri. [23]Aaron married Elisheba, daughter of Amminadab and sister of Nahshon, and she bore him Nadab, Abihu, Eleazar, and Ithamar. [24]The sons of Korah: Assir, Elkanah, and Abiasaph; these are the families of the Korahites. [25]Aaron's son Eleazar married one of the daughters of Putiel, and she bore him Phinehas. These are the heads of the ancestral houses of the Levites by their families.

26 It was this same Aaron and Moses to whom the LORD said, "Bring the Israelites out of the land of Egypt, company by company." [27]It was they who spoke to Pharaoh king of Egypt to bring the Israelites out of Egypt, the same Moses and Aaron.

---

[a] Heb *me? I am uncircumcised of lips* [b] Or *Saul* [c] Also spelled *Gershom*; see 2.22

Moses and Aaron Obey God's Commands

28 On the day when the LORD spoke to Moses in the land of
Egypt, 29he said to him, "I am the LORD; tell Pharaoh king of Egypt all
that I am speaking to you." 30But Moses said in the LORD's presence,
"Since I am a poor speaker,[a] why would Pharaoh listen to me?"
7 The LORD said to Moses, "See, I have made you like God to
Pharaoh, and your brother Aaron shall be your prophet. 2You
shall speak all that I command you, and your brother Aaron shall tell
Pharaoh to let the Israelites go out of his land. 3But I will harden Pharaoh's heart, and I will multiply my signs and wonders in the land of
Egypt. 4When Pharaoh does not listen to you, I will lay my hand upon
Egypt and bring my people the Israelites, company by company, out
of the land of Egypt by great acts of judgment. 5The Egyptians shall
know that I am the LORD, when I stretch out my hand against Egypt
and bring the Israelites out from among them." 6Moses and Aaron did
so; they did just as the LORD commanded them. 7Moses was eighty
years old and Aaron eighty-three when they spoke to Pharaoh.

Aaron's Miraculous Rod

8 The LORD said to Moses and Aaron, 9"When Pharaoh says to
you, 'Perform a wonder,' then you shall say to Aaron, 'Take your staff
and throw it down before Pharaoh, and it will become a snake.'" 10So
Moses and Aaron went to Pharaoh and did as the LORD had commanded; Aaron threw down his staff before Pharaoh and his officials,
and it became a snake. 11Then Pharaoh summoned the wise men and
the sorcerers; and they also, the magicians of Egypt, did the same by
their secret arts. 12Each one threw down his staff, and they became
snakes; but Aaron's staff swallowed up theirs. 13Still Pharaoh's heart
was hardened, and he would not listen to them, as the LORD had
said.

The First Plague: Water Turned to Blood

14 Then the LORD said to Moses, "Pharaoh's heart is hardened;
he refuses to let the people go. 15Go to Pharaoh in the morning, as
he is going out to the water; stand by at the river bank to meet him,
and take in your hand the staff that was turned into a snake. 16Say
to him, 'The LORD, the God of the Hebrews, sent me to you to say,
"Let my people go, so that they may worship me in the wilderness."
But until now you have not listened. 17Thus says the LORD, "By this
you shall know that I am the LORD." See, with the staff that is in my
hand I will strike the water that is in the Nile, and it shall be turned to
blood. 18The fish in the river shall die, the river itself shall stink, and
the Egyptians shall be unable to drink water from the Nile.'" 19The

[a] Heb *am uncircumcised of lips*; see 6.12

7:1 God to Pharaoh: Moses will bring God's message to Pharaoh through Aaron, his prophet or spokesperson. See note on 4:14-16.

7:3-4 signs and wonders...great acts of judgment: Scientific theories have been proposed to show that many of the plagues could occur naturally in Egypt in a similar sequence. The biblical story, however, stresses that the plagues come from God and display God's power.

7:3-7 Pharaoh's heart: The hardening of Pharaoh's heart will lead to a display of power so that Egypt, Israel, and the nations will know God. See note on 4:21-23.

7:8-13 Perform a wonder: The magicians' snakes are eaten by Moses' snake—a sign of God's power. This begins a competition of sorts in Pharaoh's court, the wisdom of Egypt versus the wisdom of God.

7:14—12:32 I will plague your whole country: The ten plagues are generally listed as blood, frogs, gnats, flies, livestock, boils, hail, locusts, darkness, and death of firstborn sons. The plagues become more and more severe as Pharaoh continues to resist. See Psalm 77 and Psalm 105 for slightly different lists and sequences.

7:17-24 all the water in the river was turned into blood: Moses and Aaron follow God's command, and the Nile River turns to blood. The magicians of Egypt perform the same feat.

LORD said to Moses, "Say to Aaron, 'Take your staff and stretch out
your hand over the waters of Egypt—over its rivers, its canals, and its
ponds, and all its pools of water—so that they may become blood;
and there shall be blood throughout the whole land of Egypt, even in
vessels of wood and in vessels of stone.'"
20 Moses and Aaron did just as the LORD commanded. In the
sight of Pharaoh and of his officials he lifted up the staff and struck the
water in the river, and all the water in the river was turned into blood,
21 and the fish in the river died. The river stank so that the Egyptians
could not drink its water, and there was blood throughout the whole
land of Egypt. 22 But the magicians of Egypt did the same by their secret arts; so Pharaoh's heart remained hardened, and he would not
listen to them, as the LORD had said. 23 Pharaoh turned and went into
his house, and he did not take even this to heart. 24 And all the Egyptians had to dig along the Nile for water to drink, for they could not
drink the water of the river.
25 Seven days passed after the LORD had struck the Nile.

The Second Plague: Frogs

8:1-7 frogs: Moses and Aaron follow God's command, and frogs swarm everywhere. Again the magicians of Egypt perform the same feat.

8 [a] Then the LORD said to Moses, "Go to Pharaoh and say to him,
'Thus says the LORD: Let my people go, so that they may worship me. 2 If you refuse to let them go, I will plague your whole country with frogs. 3 The river shall swarm with frogs; they shall come up
into your palace, into your bedchamber and your bed, and into the
houses of your officials and of your people,[b] and into your ovens and
your kneading bowls. 4 The frogs shall come up on you and on your
people and on all your officials.'" 5[c] And the LORD said to Moses, "Say
to Aaron, 'Stretch out your hand with your staff over the rivers, the
canals, and the pools, and make frogs come up on the land of Egypt.'"
6 So Aaron stretched out his hand over the waters of Egypt; and the
frogs came up and covered the land of Egypt. 7 But the magicians
did the same by their secret arts, and brought frogs up on the land of
Egypt.
8 Then Pharaoh called Moses and Aaron, and said, "Pray to the
LORD to take away the frogs from me and my people, and I will let the
people go to sacrifice to the LORD." 9 Moses said to Pharaoh, "Kindly
tell me when I am to pray for you and for your officials and for your
people, that the frogs may be removed from you and your houses and
be left only in the Nile." 10 And he said, "Tomorrow." Moses said, "As
you say! So that you may know that there is no one like the LORD our
God, 11 the frogs shall leave you and your houses and your officials
and your people; they shall be left only in the Nile." 12 Then Moses
and Aaron went out from Pharaoh; and Moses cried out to the LORD

---

[a] Ch 7.26 in Heb [b] Gk: Heb *upon your people* [c] Ch 8.1 in Heb

The Ten Plagues on Egypt

Plague (Exodus Passage)	Result
Water to Blood (7:14-25)	The fish in the Nile died. The water smelled bad and was undrinkable. Pharaoh's heart hardened.
Frogs (8:1-15)	Dead frogs were found everywhere. The dead frogs were gathered into piles and "the land stank." Pharaoh's heart hardened.
Gnats (8:16-19)	Each dust particle became a gnat. Gnats were everywhere and on everyone. Pharaoh's heart hardened.
Flies (8:20-32)	Flies were everywhere. Pharaoh said he would let the people go if Moses removed the flies. The flies were removed, but Pharaoh's heart hardened.
Diseased Livestock (9:1-7)	All livestock belonging to Egyptians died. All livestock belonging to Israelites survived. Pharaoh's heart was hardened.
Boils (9:8-12)	Moses tossed soot in the air, which caused boils to break out on the skin of all Egyptians. The LORD hardened Pharaoh's heart.
Hail (9:13-35)	The worst hailstorm ever occurred. Pharaoh said he would let the people go if Moses stopped the hail. The hail stopped, but Pharaoh's heart hardened.
Locusts (10:1-20)	Locusts were everywhere. Pharaoh said he would let the people go if Moses removed the locusts. The locusts were removed, but the LORD hardened Pharaoh's heart.
Darkness (10:21-29)	Darkness covered Egypt for three days. Pharaoh said he would let the people go if Moses returned the daylight. The daylight returned, but the LORD hardened Pharaoh's heart.
Death of Firstborn Sons (11:1—12:32)	All the firstborn sons of Egyptians, including firstborn livestock, were killed. The first-born sons of the Israelites were not killed. Pharaoh let the people go.

concerning the frogs that he had brought upon Pharaoh.[a] 13And the
LORD did as Moses requested: the frogs died in the houses, the court-
yards, and the fields. 14And they gathered them together in heaps, and
the land stank. 15But when Pharaoh saw that there was a respite, he
hardened his heart, and would not listen to them, just as the LORD
had said.

The Third Plague: Gnats

16 Then the LORD said to Moses, "Say to Aaron, 'Stretch out
your staff and strike the dust of the earth, so that it may become gnats
throughout the whole land of Egypt.'" 17And they did so; Aaron
stretched out his hand with his staff and struck the dust of the earth,
and gnats came on humans and animals alike; all the dust of the
earth turned into gnats throughout the whole land of Egypt. 18The
magicians tried to produce gnats by their secret arts, but they could

8:16-19 gnats: Moses and Aaron follow God's command, and dust turns to gnats. The magicians of Egypt attempt to do this but fail.

[a] Or *frogs, as he had agreed with Pharaoh*

8:19 the finger of God!: The plagues are a display of power sent so that Egypt, Israel, and the nations will know God. The court magicians or wise men begin to recognize and testify to God's power, which exceeds their own. Pharaoh still has not recognized this power.

Do you believe God makes bad things happen to people? Do bad things happen to get people to change direction, to make God's power known in the world, or for other reasons?

8:20-32 swarms of flies: Flies swarm over the land of Egypt, but they do not appear in the land of Goshen (see Map 2, p. 2099), where the Israelites live.

not. There were gnats on both humans and animals. [19]And the magicians said to Pharaoh, "This is the finger of God!" But Pharaoh's heart
was hardened, and he would not listen to them, just as the LORD
had said.

The Fourth Plague: Flies

20 Then the LORD said to Moses, "Rise early in the morning and
present yourself before Pharaoh, as he goes out to the water, and say
to him, 'Thus says the LORD: Let my people go, so that they may worship me. [21]For if you will not let my people go, I will send swarms of
flies on you, your officials, and your people, and into your houses;
and the houses of the Egyptians shall be filled with swarms of flies;
so also the land where they live. [22]But on that day I will set apart the
land of Goshen, where my people live, so that no swarms of flies shall
be there, that you may know that I the LORD am in this land. [23]Thus
I will make a distinction[a] between my people and your people. This
sign shall appear tomorrow.'" [24]The LORD did so, and great swarms of
flies came into the house of Pharaoh and into his officials' houses; in
all of Egypt the land was ruined because of the flies.

25 Then Pharaoh summoned Moses and Aaron, and said, "Go,
sacrifice to your God within the land." [26]But Moses said, "It would not
be right to do so; for the sacrifices that we offer to the LORD our God
are offensive to the Egyptians. If we offer in the sight of the Egyptians
sacrifices that are offensive to them, will they not stone us? [27]We must
go a three days' journey into the wilderness and sacrifice to the LORD
our God as he commands us." [28]So Pharaoh said, "I will let you go to
sacrifice to the LORD your God in the wilderness, provided you do
not go very far away. Pray for me." [29]Then Moses said, "As soon as I
leave you, I will pray to the LORD that the swarms of flies may depart
tomorrow from Pharaoh, from his officials, and from his people; only
do not let Pharaoh again deal falsely by not letting the people go to
sacrifice to the LORD."

30 So Moses went out from Pharaoh and prayed to the LORD.
[31]And the LORD did as Moses asked: he removed the swarms of flies
from Pharaoh, from his officials, and from his people; not one remained. [32]But Pharaoh hardened his heart this time also, and would
not let the people go.

The Fifth Plague: Livestock Diseased

9:1-7 all the livestock of the Egyptians died: Livestock belonging to Egyptians dies, but livestock belonging to the Israelites is spared.

9 Then the LORD said to Moses, "Go to Pharaoh, and say to him,
'Thus says the LORD, the God of the Hebrews: Let my people go,
so that they may worship me. [2]For if you refuse to let them go and still
hold them, [3]the hand of the LORD will strike with a deadly pestilence
your livestock in the field: the horses, the donkeys, the camels, the

[a] Gk Vg: Heb *will set redemption*

herds, and the flocks. [4]But the LORD will make a distinction between
the livestock of Israel and the livestock of Egypt, so that nothing shall
die of all that belongs to the Israelites.'" [5]The LORD set a time, saying,
"Tomorrow the LORD will do this thing in the land." [6]And on the next
day the LORD did so; all the livestock of the Egyptians died, but of the
livestock of the Israelites not one died. [7]Pharaoh inquired and found
that not one of the livestock of the Israelites was dead. But the heart of
Pharaoh was hardened, and he would not let the people go.

The Sixth Plague: Boils

8 Then the LORD said to Moses and Aaron, "Take handfuls of
soot from the kiln, and let Moses throw it in the air in the sight of Pharaoh. [9]It shall become fine dust all over the land of Egypt, and shall
cause festering boils on humans and animals throughout the whole
land of Egypt." [10]So they took soot from the kiln, and stood before
Pharaoh, and Moses threw it in the air, and it caused festering boils on
humans and animals. [11]The magicians could not stand before Moses
because of the boils, for the boils afflicted the magicians as well as all
the Egyptians. [12]But the LORD hardened the heart of Pharaoh, and he
would not listen to them, just as the LORD had spoken to Moses.

9:8-12 festering boils: Infected sores appear on people, including the magicians, and even on animals.

The Seventh Plague: Thunder and Hail

13 Then the LORD said to Moses, "Rise up early in the morning
and present yourself before Pharaoh, and say to him, 'Thus says the
LORD, the God of the Hebrews: Let my people go, so that they may
worship me. [14]For this time I will send all my plagues upon you yourself, and upon your officials, and upon your people, so that you may
know that there is no one like me in all the earth. [15]For by now I could
have stretched out my hand and struck you and your people with pestilence, and you would have been cut off from the earth. [16]But this
is why I have let you live: to show you my power, and to make my
name resound through all the earth. [17]You are still exalting yourself
against my people, and will not let them go. [18]Tomorrow at this time
I will cause the heaviest hail to fall that has ever fallen in Egypt from
the day it was founded until now. [19]Send, therefore, and have your
livestock and everything that you have in the open field brought to
a secure place; every human or animal that is in the open field and is
not brought under shelter will die when the hail comes down upon
them.'" [20]Those officials of Pharaoh who feared the word of the LORD
hurried their slaves and livestock off to a secure place. [21]Those who
did not regard the word of the LORD left their slaves and livestock in
the open field.

9:13-27 the heaviest hail: Hail hits people, animals, and plants, but not in the land of Goshen, where the Israelites live.

22 The LORD said to Moses, "Stretch out your hand toward
heaven so that hail may fall on the whole land of Egypt, on humans
and animals and all the plants of the field in the land of Egypt." [23]Then

Moses stretched out his staff toward heaven, and the LORD sent thunder and hail, and fire came down on the earth. And the LORD rained hail on the land of Egypt; [24]there was hail with fire flashing continually in the midst of it, such heavy hail as had never fallen in all the land of Egypt since it became a nation. [25]The hail struck down everything that was in the open field throughout all the land of Egypt, both human and animal; the hail also struck down all the plants of the field, and shattered every tree in the field. [26]Only in the land of Goshen, where the Israelites were, there was no hail.

27 Then Pharaoh summoned Moses and Aaron, and said to them, "This time I have sinned; the LORD is in the right, and I and my people are in the wrong. [28]Pray to the LORD! Enough of God's thunder and hail! I will let you go; you need stay no longer." [29]Moses said to him, "As soon as I have gone out of the city, I will stretch out my hands to the LORD; the thunder will cease, and there will be no more hail, so that you may know that the earth is the LORD's. [30]But as for you and your officials, I know that you do not yet fear the LORD God." [31](Now the flax and the barley were ruined, for the barley was in the ear and the flax was in bud. [32]But the wheat and the spelt were not ruined, for they are late in coming up.) [33]So Moses left Pharaoh, went out of the city, and stretched out his hands to the LORD; then the thunder and the hail ceased, and the rain no longer poured down on the earth. [34]But when Pharaoh saw that the rain and the hail and the thunder had ceased, he sinned once more and hardened his heart, he and his officials. [35]So the heart of Pharaoh was hardened, and he would not let the Israelites go, just as the LORD had spoken through Moses.

The Eighth Plague: Locusts

10 Then the LORD said to Moses, "Go to Pharaoh; for I have hardened his heart and the heart of his officials, in order that I may show these signs of mine among them, [2]and that you may tell your children and grandchildren how I have made fools of the Egyptians and what signs I have done among them—so that you may know that I am the LORD."

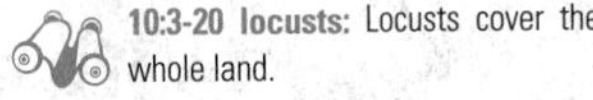

10:3-20 locusts: Locusts cover the whole land.

3 So Moses and Aaron went to Pharaoh, and said to him, "Thus says the LORD, the God of the Hebrews, 'How long will you refuse to humble yourself before me? Let my people go, so that they may worship me. [4]For if you refuse to let my people go, tomorrow I will bring locusts into your country. [5]They shall cover the surface of the land, so that no one will be able to see the land. They shall devour the last remnant left you after the hail, and they shall devour every tree of yours that grows in the field. [6]They shall fill your houses, and the houses of all your officials and of all the Egyptians—something that neither your parents nor your grandparents have seen, from the day they came on earth to this day.'" Then he turned and went out from Pharaoh.

7 Pharaoh's officials said to him, "How long shall this fellow be
a snare to us? Let the people go, so that they may worship the LORD
their God; do you not yet understand that Egypt is ruined?" 8So
Moses and Aaron were brought back to Pharaoh, and he said to them,
"Go, worship the LORD your God! But which ones are to go?" 9Moses
said, "We will go with our young and our old; we will go with our sons
and daughters and with our flocks and herds, because we have the
LORD's festival to celebrate." 10He said to them, "The LORD indeed
will be with you, if ever I let your little ones go with you! Plainly, you
have some evil purpose in mind. 11No, never! Your men may go and
worship the LORD, for that is what you are asking." And they were
driven out from Pharaoh's presence.

12 Then the LORD said to Moses, "Stretch out your hand over the
land of Egypt, so that the locusts may come upon it and eat every
plant in the land, all that the hail has left." 13So Moses stretched out his
staff over the land of Egypt, and the LORD brought an east wind upon
the land all that day and all that night; when morning came, the east
wind had brought the locusts. 14The locusts came upon all the land of
Egypt and settled on the whole country of Egypt, such a dense swarm
of locusts as had never been before, nor ever shall be again. 15They
covered the surface of the whole land, so that the land was black; and
they ate all the plants in the land and all the fruit of the trees that the
hail had left; nothing green was left, no tree, no plant in the field, in all
the land of Egypt. 16Pharaoh hurriedly summoned Moses and Aaron
and said, "I have sinned against the LORD your God, and against you.
17Do forgive my sin just this once, and pray to the LORD your God
that at the least he remove this deadly thing from me." 18So he went
out from Pharaoh and prayed to the LORD. 19The LORD changed the
wind into a very strong west wind, which lifted the locusts and drove
them into the Red Sea;[a] not a single locust was left in all the country
of Egypt. 20But the LORD hardened Pharaoh's heart, and he would not
let the Israelites go.

The Ninth Plague: Darkness

21 Then the LORD said to Moses, "Stretch out your hand toward heaven so that there may be darkness over the land of Egypt,
a darkness that can be felt." 22So Moses stretched out his hand toward heaven, and there was dense darkness in all the land of Egypt
for three days. 23People could not see one another, and for three days
they could not move from where they were; but all the Israelites had
light where they lived. 24Then Pharaoh summoned Moses, and said,
"Go, worship the LORD. Only your flocks and your herds shall remain
behind. Even your children may go with you." 25But Moses said, "You

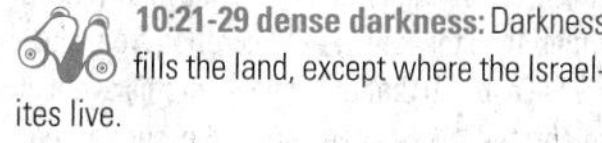
10:21-29 dense darkness: Darkness fills the land, except where the Israelites live.

[a] Or *Sea of Reeds*

must also let us have sacrifices and burnt offerings to sacrifice to the LORD our God. [26]Our livestock also must go with us; not a hoof shall be left behind, for we must choose some of them for the worship of the LORD our God, and we will not know what to use to worship the LORD until we arrive there." [27]But the LORD hardened Pharaoh's heart, and he was unwilling to let them go. [28]Then Pharaoh said to him, "Get away from me! Take care that you do not see my face again, for on the day you see my face you shall die." [29]Moses said, "Just as you say! I will never see your face again."

Warning of the Final Plague

11:1-10 one more plague: The LORD gives a warning about the tenth and final plague and hardens Pharaoh's heart.

Are natural disasters to be taken as signs from God? What message might we take from events like crop failures, floods, tornadoes, and droughts?

11 The LORD said to Moses, "I will bring one more plague upon Pharaoh and upon Egypt; afterwards he will let you go from here; indeed, when he lets you go, he will drive you away. [2]Tell the people that every man is to ask his neighbor and every woman is to ask her neighbor for objects of silver and gold." [3]The LORD gave the people favor in the sight of the Egyptians. Moreover, Moses himself was a man of great importance in the land of Egypt, in the sight of Pharaoh's officials and in the sight of the people.

4 Moses said, "Thus says the LORD: About midnight I will go out through Egypt. [5]Every firstborn in the land of Egypt shall die, from the firstborn of Pharaoh who sits on his throne to the firstborn of the female slave who is behind the handmill, and all the firstborn of the livestock. [6]Then there will be a loud cry throughout the whole land of Egypt, such as has never been or will ever be again. [7]But not a dog shall growl at any of the Israelites—not at people, not at animals—so that you may know that the LORD makes a distinction between Egypt and Israel. [8]Then all these officials of yours shall come down to me, and bow low to me, saying, 'Leave us, you and all the people who follow you.' After that I will leave." And in hot anger he left Pharaoh.

9 The LORD said to Moses, "Pharaoh will not listen to you, in order that my wonders may be multiplied in the land of Egypt." [10]Moses and Aaron performed all these wonders before Pharaoh; but the LORD hardened Pharaoh's heart, and he did not let the people of Israel go out of his land.

The First Passover Instituted

12:1-20 a day of remembrance for you: The Israelites receive instructions before the final plague arrives. Originally, there were two ancient festivals in the spring: *Pesah* or Passover, the spring festival for shepherds during the time when the lambs and kids are born (12:1-13), and *Matzot* or unleavened bread, a spring festival for farmers (12:14-20). These celebrations are combined and placed within the story of Israel's liberation from slavery in Egypt, so that the memory of this event is celebrated every year during the spring season. The festival of Passover continues to be celebrated in Jewish homes every year, mainly through the home *Seder*, which includes symbolic foods and a retelling of the exodus story. In the Gospel of John, Jesus is crucified on the day before Passover, when the Passover lambs were sacrificed, showing Jesus as the Passover lamb (John 19:14, 31). According to the other Gospels the Last Supper was a celebration of Passover (Mark 14:12-16; Matt 26:17-25; Luke 22:7-15).

12 The LORD said to Moses and Aaron in the land of Egypt: [2]This month shall mark for you the beginning of months; it shall be the first month of the year for you. [3]Tell the whole congregation of Israel that on the tenth of this month they are to take a lamb for each family, a lamb for each household. [4]If a household is too small for a whole lamb, it shall join its closest neighbor in obtaining one; the lamb shall be divided in proportion to the number of people who eat

of it. [5]Your lamb shall be without blemish, a year-old male; you may
take it from the sheep or from the goats. [6]You shall keep it until the
fourteenth day of this month; then the whole assembled congregation of Israel shall slaughter it at twilight. [7]They shall take some of the
blood and put it on the two doorposts and the lintel of the houses in
which they eat it. [8]They shall eat the lamb that same night; they shall
eat it roasted over the fire with unleavened bread and bitter herbs. [9]Do
not eat any of it raw or boiled in water, but roasted over the fire, with
its head, legs, and inner organs. [10]You shall let none of it remain until
the morning; anything that remains until the morning you shall burn.
[11]This is how you shall eat it: your loins girded, your sandals on your
feet, and your staff in your hand; and you shall eat it hurriedly. It is the
passover of the LORD. [12]For I will pass through the land of Egypt that
night, and I will strike down every firstborn in the land of Egypt, both
human beings and animals; on all the gods of Egypt I will execute
judgments: I am the LORD. [13]The blood shall be a sign for you on the
houses where you live: when I see the blood, I will pass over you, and
no plague shall destroy you when I strike the land of Egypt.

14 This day shall be a day of remembrance for you. You shall celebrate it as a festival to the LORD; throughout your generations you
shall observe it as a perpetual ordinance. [15]Seven days you shall eat
unleavened bread; on the first day you shall remove leaven from your
houses, for whoever eats leavened bread from the first day until the
seventh day shall be cut off from Israel. [16]On the first day you shall
hold a solemn assembly, and on the seventh day a solemn assembly;
no work shall be done on those days; only what everyone must eat,
that alone may be prepared by you. [17]You shall observe the festival
of unleavened bread, for on this very day I brought your companies
out of the land of Egypt: you shall observe this day throughout your
generations as a perpetual ordinance. [18]In the first month, from the
evening of the fourteenth day until the evening of the twenty-first day,
you shall eat unleavened bread. [19]For seven days no leaven shall be
found in your houses; for whoever eats what is leavened shall be cut
off from the congregation of Israel, whether an alien or a native of
the land. [20]You shall eat nothing leavened; in all your settlements you
shall eat unleavened bread.

21 Then Moses called all the elders of Israel and said to them,
"Go, select lambs for your families, and slaughter the passover lamb.
[22]Take a bunch of hyssop, dip it in the blood that is in the basin, and
touch the lintel and the two doorposts with the blood in the basin.
None of you shall go outside the door of your house until morning.
[23]For the LORD will pass through to strike down the Egyptians; when
he sees the blood on the lintel and on the two doorposts, the LORD
will pass over that door and will not allow the destroyer to enter your
houses to strike you down. [24]You shall observe this rite as a perpetual

12:12-13 The blood shall be a sign for you: The angel of death will "pass over" the Israelite homes marked with the blood of the lamb on the doorposts and beams, so the festival becomes known as Passover.

12:12-13 the houses where you live: Israelites and Egyptians appear to live in close proximity in this passage, while elsewhere, as in 8:22 and 9:26, they live apart.

12:21-23 the passover lamb: The blood of the Passover lamb has the power to turn away death. When the Jerusalem temple was destroyed in 70 C.E., the sacrifice of Passover lambs ceased, and Passover became a home festival.

ordinance for you and your children. [25]When you come to the land that the LORD will give you, as he has promised, you shall keep this observance. [26]And when your children ask you, 'What do you mean by this observance?' [27]you shall say, 'It is the passover sacrifice to the LORD, for he passed over the houses of the Israelites in Egypt, when he struck down the Egyptians but spared our houses.'" And the people bowed down and worshiped.

28 The Israelites went and did just as the LORD had commanded Moses and Aaron.

12:29-32 a loud cry in Egypt: Firstborn Egyptian sons die, including Pharaoh's son. Pharaoh tells Moses and Aaron to take the Israelites and leave the country.

12:33-34, 38-39 unleavened cakes: The Israelites leave so quickly that they cannot wait for bread dough to rise; therefore the exodus is remembered with eight days of eating unleavened bread, or matzah.

12:35-36 they plundered the Egyptians: Because God gives the Israelites favor in the eyes of the Egyptians, they leave with gold, silver, and clothing (see 3:21-22). In Deuteronomy the law states that a freed slave should not leave empty-handed but should be given financial resources to start a new life (Deut 15:13-14).

12:37 six hundred thousand men: This number is exaggerated to emphasize God's abundant blessings on the Israelites. This many men plus women and children would have totaled more than two million, more people than any nation had at the time.

12:38 a mixed crowd: The mixed multitude with the Israelites gives the people diversity and a more complex identity.

12:38 flocks and herds: Livestock meant wealth for people at the time. Livestock had been a sticking point with Pharaoh earlier in the story (10:24).

12:40 four hundred thirty years: Four hundred years in exile is predicted in Genesis 15:13. Exodus 6:16-20, however, portrays Moses as among the fourth generation of Israelites in Egypt, corresponding with Genesis 15:16, which predicts four generations (approximately 160 years). Different traditional chronologies are preserved side by side in the Bible.

12:42 a vigil to be kept for the LORD: The LORD kept watch through the night as the Israelites left Egypt. Now Israelites through all generations are to keep vigil to celebrate their flight from Egypt and liberation from slavery.

The Tenth Plague: Death of the Firstborn

29 At midnight the LORD struck down all the firstborn in the land of Egypt, from the firstborn of Pharaoh who sat on his throne to the firstborn of the prisoner who was in the dungeon, and all the firstborn of the livestock. [30]Pharaoh arose in the night, he and all his officials and all the Egyptians; and there was a loud cry in Egypt, for there was not a house without someone dead. [31]Then he summoned Moses and Aaron in the night, and said, "Rise up, go away from my people, both you and the Israelites! Go, worship the LORD, as you said. [32]Take your flocks and your herds, as you said, and be gone. And bring a blessing on me too!"

The Exodus: From Rameses to Succoth

33 The Egyptians urged the people to hasten their departure from the land, for they said, "We shall all be dead." [34]So the people took their dough before it was leavened, with their kneading bowls wrapped up in their cloaks on their shoulders. [35]The Israelites had done as Moses told them; they had asked the Egyptians for jewelry of silver and gold, and for clothing, [36]and the LORD had given the people favor in the sight of the Egyptians, so that they let them have what they asked. And so they plundered the Egyptians.

37 The Israelites journeyed from Rameses to Succoth, about six hundred thousand men on foot, besides children. [38]A mixed crowd also went up with them, and livestock in great numbers, both flocks and herds. [39]They baked unleavened cakes of the dough that they had brought out of Egypt; it was not leavened, because they were driven out of Egypt and could not wait, nor had they prepared any provisions for themselves.

40 The time that the Israelites had lived in Egypt was four hundred thirty years. [41]At the end of four hundred thirty years, on that very day, all the companies of the LORD went out from the land of Egypt. [42]That was for the LORD a night of vigil, to bring them out of the land of Egypt. That same night is a vigil to be kept for the LORD by all the Israelites throughout their generations.

Directions for the Passover

43 The LORD said to Moses and Aaron: This is the ordinance for
the passover: no foreigner shall eat of it, 44 but any slave who has been
purchased may eat of it after he has been circumcised; 45 no bound or
hired servant may eat of it. 46 It shall be eaten in one house; you shall
not take any of the animal outside the house, and you shall not break
any of its bones. 47 The whole congregation of Israel shall celebrate it.
48 If an alien who resides with you wants to celebrate the passover to
the LORD, all his males shall be circumcised; then he may draw near
to celebrate it; he shall be regarded as a native of the land. But no uncircumcised person shall eat of it; 49 there shall be one law for the native and for the alien who resides among you.

50 All the Israelites did just as the LORD had commanded Moses
and Aaron. 51 That very day the LORD brought the Israelites out of the
land of Egypt, company by company.

13 The LORD said to Moses: 2 Consecrate to me all the firstborn;
whatever is the first to open the womb among the Israelites,
of human beings and animals, is mine.

12:43—13:10 the ordinance for the passover: These additional instructions for Passover show the importance of remembering the exodus story during an annual celebration.

The Festival of Unleavened Bread

3 Moses said to the people, "Remember this day on which you
came out of Egypt, out of the house of slavery, because the LORD
brought you out from there by strength of hand; no leavened bread
shall be eaten. 4 Today, in the month of Abib, you are going out. 5 When
the LORD brings you into the land of the Canaanites, the Hittites, the
Amorites, the Hivites, and the Jebusites, which he swore to your ancestors to give you, a land flowing with milk and honey, you shall keep
this observance in this month. 6 Seven days you shall eat unleavened
bread, and on the seventh day there shall be a festival to the LORD.
7 Unleavened bread shall be eaten for seven days; no leavened bread
shall be seen in your possession, and no leaven shall be seen among
you in all your territory. 8 You shall tell your child on that day, 'It is
because of what the LORD did for me when I came out of Egypt.' 9 It
shall serve for you as a sign on your hand and as a reminder on your
forehead, so that the teaching of the LORD may be on your lips; for
with a strong hand the LORD brought you out of Egypt. 10 You shall
keep this ordinance at its proper time from year to year.

The Consecration of the Firstborn

11 "When the LORD has brought you into the land of the Canaanites, as he swore to you and your ancestors, and has given it to
you, 12 you shall set apart to the LORD all that first opens the womb.
All the firstborn of your livestock that are males shall be the LORD's.
13 But every firstborn donkey you shall redeem with a sheep; if you do

13:11-16 set apart to the LORD: The firstborn animals and sons belong to God and should be sacrificed or redeemed.

13:11-16 redeem: Another animal can redeem or take the place of a human firstborn in death. In Numbers firstborn children may be redeemed through the payment of five shekel weights of silver.

not redeem it, you must break its neck. Every firstborn male among your children you shall redeem. [14]When in the future your child asks you, 'What does this mean?' you shall answer, 'By strength of hand the LORD brought us out of Egypt, from the house of slavery. [15]When Pharaoh stubbornly refused to let us go, the LORD killed all the firstborn in the land of Egypt, from human firstborn to the firstborn of animals. Therefore I sacrifice to the LORD every male that first opens the womb, but every firstborn of my sons I redeem.' [16]It shall serve as a sign on your hand and as an emblem[a] on your forehead that by strength of hand the LORD brought us out of Egypt."

The Pillars of Cloud and Fire

17 When Pharaoh let the people go, God did not lead them by way of the land of the Philistines, although that was nearer; for God thought, "If the people face war, they may change their minds and return to Egypt." [18]So God led the people by the roundabout way of the wilderness toward the Red Sea.[b] The Israelites went up out of the land of Egypt prepared for battle. [19]And Moses took with him the bones of Joseph who had required a solemn oath of the Israelites, saying, "God will surely take notice of you, and then you must carry my bones with you from here." [20]They set out from Succoth, and camped at Etham, on the edge of the wilderness. [21]The LORD went in front of them in a pillar of cloud by day, to lead them along the way, and in a pillar of fire by night, to give them light, so that they might travel by day and by night. [22]Neither the pillar of cloud by day nor the pillar of fire by night left its place in front of the people.

Crossing the Red Sea

14 Then the LORD said to Moses: [2]Tell the Israelites to turn back and camp in front of Pi-hahiroth, between Migdol and the sea, in front of Baal-zephon; you shall camp opposite it, by the sea. [3]Pharaoh will say of the Israelites, "They are wandering aimlessly in the land; the wilderness has closed in on them." [4]I will harden Pharaoh's heart, and he will pursue them, so that I will gain glory for myself over Pharaoh and all his army; and the Egyptians shall know that I am the LORD. And they did so.

5 When the king of Egypt was told that the people had fled, the minds of Pharaoh and his officials were changed toward the people, and they said, "What have we done, letting Israel leave our service?" [6]So he had his chariot made ready, and took his army with him; [7]he took six hundred picked chariots and all the other chariots of Egypt with officers over all of them. [8]The LORD hardened the heart of Pharaoh king of Egypt and he pursued the Israelites, who were going out boldly. [9]The Egyptians pursued them, all Pharaoh's horses and chari-

13:17-18 land of the Philistines: The Philistines were a sea-people from the Aegean region (the modern day Greek islands), who invaded the northern coast of Egypt and were pushed back by Rameses III around 1200 B.C.E., approximately the same time the Israelites were entering the land of Canaan under Joshua. The Philistines moved east to settle in five cities, including Gaza, in the coastal region of Canaan. The region of Palestine was named after the Philistines by the Romans—after two wars with Jewish resistance fighters, ending in 70 and 135 C.E.—in an attempt to erase the memory of Jewish history from the land.

13:18 prepared for battle: This description contrasts with the hasty departure of the Israelites in 12:33-34, 39, in which there is no time to make any preparations.

13:19 the bones of Joseph: Moses takes Joseph's bones, connecting the exodus story with Joseph's last request (Gen 50:24-25). Joseph's bones are buried in Shechem (Josh 24:32), where Joshua renews the covenant between God and Israel after conquering the promised land.

13:21-22 pillar of cloud...pillar of fire: The presence of God, in pillars of cloud and fire, guides the Israelites day and night.

14:1-18: hardened the heart of Pharaoh: Pharaoh's heart is hardened, and he chases after the Israelites. See note on 4:21-23.

[a] Or *as a frontlet*; meaning of Heb uncertain [b] Or *Sea of Reeds*

ots, his chariot drivers and his army; they overtook them camped by
the sea, by Pi-hahiroth, in front of Baal-zephon.
10 As Pharaoh drew near, the Israelites looked back, and there
were the Egyptians advancing on them. In great fear the Israelites
cried out to the LORD. [11]They said to Moses, "Was it because there
were no graves in Egypt that you have taken us away to die in the wilderness? What have you done to us, bringing us out of Egypt? [12]Is
this not the very thing we told you in Egypt, 'Let us alone and let us
serve the Egyptians'? For it would have been better for us to serve
the Egyptians than to die in the wilderness." [13]But Moses said to the
people, "Do not be afraid, stand firm, and see the deliverance that the
LORD will accomplish for you today; for the Egyptians whom you see
today you shall never see again. [14]The LORD will fight for you, and you
have only to keep still."
15 Then the LORD said to Moses, "Why do you cry out to me? Tell
the Israelites to go forward. [16]But you lift up your staff, and stretch out
your hand over the sea and divide it, that the Israelites may go into the
sea on dry ground. [17]Then I will harden the hearts of the Egyptians so
that they will go in after them; and so I will gain glory for myself over
Pharaoh and all his army, his chariots, and his chariot drivers. [18]And
the Egyptians shall know that I am the LORD, when I have gained glory
for myself over Pharaoh, his chariots, and his chariot drivers."
19 The angel of God who was going before the Israelite army
moved and went behind them; and the pillar of cloud moved from
in front of them and took its place behind them. [20]It came between
the army of Egypt and the army of Israel. And so the cloud was there
with the darkness, and it lit up the night; one did not come near the
other all night.
21 Then Moses stretched out his hand over the sea. The LORD
drove the sea back by a strong east wind all night, and turned the sea
into dry land; and the waters were divided. [22]The Israelites went into
the sea on dry ground, the waters forming a wall for them on their
right and on their left. [23]The Egyptians pursued, and went into the sea
after them, all of Pharaoh's horses, chariots, and chariot drivers. [24]At
the morning watch the LORD in the pillar of fire and cloud looked
down upon the Egyptian army, and threw the Egyptian army into
panic. [25]He clogged[a] their chariot wheels so that they turned with
difficulty. The Egyptians said, "Let us flee from the Israelites, for the
LORD is fighting for them against Egypt."

The Pursuers Drowned

26 Then the LORD said to Moses, "Stretch out your hand over
the sea, so that the water may come back upon the Egyptians, upon

[a] Sam Gk Syr: MT *removed*

14:11 no graves in Egypt: There is wry humor in this question of the Israelites, who are afraid that Moses took them away from Egypt only to die elsewhere.

14:13-14 The LORD will fight for you: God will fight for Israel. This key statement about God corresponds with the portrayal of the divine warrior in Exodus 15.

14:17-18 I will gain glory: The Egyptians will know that God is the LORD. This is the goal of the exodus and the defeat of the powerful Egyptian army. God's action in history is aimed at Egypt as well as Israel.

14:21-25 The LORD drove the sea back: The exact location of the crossing of Reed Sea (Red Sea), traditionally the "Sea of Destruction," is not known, but it may have been at a shallow, reedy branch off the Nile River. This event is caused by nature through the east wind (14:21), by Moses (14:16, 21-22, 29), and by God (14:27; 15:1, 4, 8, 10-12, 21).

14:21-25 turned the sea into dry land: Notice the creation images in the crossing of the sea: water, wind, and dry land, similar to Genesis 1. This event is the creation, not of world, but of the people Israel in covenant relationship to God.

their chariots and chariot drivers." 27 So Moses stretched out his hand
over the sea, and at dawn the sea returned to its normal depth. As the
Egyptians fled before it, the LORD tossed the Egyptians into the sea.
28 The waters returned and covered the chariots and the chariot drivers, the entire army of Pharaoh that had followed them into the sea;
not one of them remained. 29 But the Israelites walked on dry ground
through the sea, the waters forming a wall for them on their right and
on their left.

30 Thus the LORD saved Israel that day from the Egyptians; and
Israel saw the Egyptians dead on the seashore. 31 Israel saw the great
work that the LORD did against the Egyptians. So the people feared
the LORD and believed in the LORD and in his servant Moses.

The Song of Moses

15:1-18 I will sing to the LORD: This Song of the Sea is an ancient poem with images from the Canaanite gods Baal and Anat. God's deliverance of the Israelites is not only spiritual and religious but also physical, national, and political.

15 Then Moses and the Israelites sang this song to the LORD:
"I will sing to the LORD, for he has triumphed gloriously;
horse and rider he has thrown into the sea.
2 The LORD is my strength and my might,[a]
and he has become my salvation;
this is my God, and I will praise him,
my father's God, and I will exalt him.
3 The LORD is a warrior;
the LORD is his name.

15:3 warrior: The LORD is a divine warrior without equal. This is one of the most common portrayals of the God of Israel. Others include God as king, judge, husband, and master.

4 "Pharaoh's chariots and his army he cast into the sea;
his picked officers were sunk in the Red Sea.[b]
5 The floods covered them;
they went down into the depths like a stone.
6 Your right hand, O LORD, glorious in power—
your right hand, O LORD, shattered the enemy.
7 In the greatness of your majesty you overthrew your adversaries;
you sent out your fury, it consumed them like stubble.
8 At the blast of your nostrils the waters piled up,
the floods stood up in a heap;
the deeps congealed in the heart of the sea.
9 The enemy said, 'I will pursue, I will overtake,
I will divide the spoil, my desire shall have its fill of them.
I will draw my sword, my hand shall destroy them.'
10 You blew with your wind, the sea covered them;
they sank like lead in the mighty waters.

15:11-12 Who is like you?: The gods of Egypt were no match for God. The LORD is incomparable.

11 "Who is like you, O LORD, among the gods?
Who is like you, majestic in holiness,

---

[a] Or *song* [b] Or *Sea of Reeds*

awesome in splendor, doing wonders?
12 You stretched out your right hand,
the earth swallowed them.

13 "In your steadfast love you led the people whom you redeemed;
you guided them by your strength to your holy abode.
14 The peoples heard, they trembled;
pangs seized the inhabitants of Philistia.
15 Then the chiefs of Edom were dismayed;
trembling seized the leaders of Moab;
all the inhabitants of Canaan melted away.
16 Terror and dread fell upon them;
by the might of your arm, they became still as a stone
until your people, O LORD, passed by,
until the people whom you acquired passed by.
17 You brought them in and planted them on the mountain of your own possession,
the place, O LORD, that you made your abode,
the sanctuary, O LORD, that your hands have established.
18 The LORD will reign forever and ever."

19 When the horses of Pharaoh with his chariots and his chariot
drivers went into the sea, the LORD brought back the waters of the sea
upon them; but the Israelites walked through the sea on dry ground.

The Song of Miriam

20 Then the prophet Miriam, Aaron's sister, took a tambourine in
her hand; and all the women went out after her with tambourines and
with dancing. 21 And Miriam sang to them:

"Sing to the LORD, for he has triumphed gloriously;
horse and rider he has thrown into the sea."

Bitter Water Made Sweet

22 Then Moses ordered Israel to set out from the Red Sea,[a] and
they went into the wilderness of Shur. They went three days in the
wilderness and found no water. 23 When they came to Marah, they
could not drink the water of Marah because it was bitter. That is why
it was called Marah.[b] 24 And the people complained against Moses,
saying, "What shall we drink?" 25 He cried out to the LORD; and the
LORD showed him a piece of wood;[c] he threw it into the water, and
the water became sweet.

There the LORD[d] made for them a statute and an ordinance and
there he put them to the test. 26 He said, "If you will listen carefully to
the voice of the LORD your God, and do what is right in his sight, and

15:13-18 to your holy abode: Israel's liberation from Egypt is not the final goal. The people will enter the land promised by God and will worship at God's mountain and sanctuary, where God reigns forever.

15:20-21 Miriam sang: In this "Song of Miriam," she and the women lead the crowd in song and dance. The mention of Miriam as a prophet is significant because men generally held the leadership positions and power in the culture of the time.

15:22—17:7 the people complained: During the time in the wilderness, the people complain, but God continues to provide for their needs in surprising ways.

15:22-27 the water became sweet: God provides water in the wilderness. *Marah* means "bitter" in Hebrew. For more on the theme of water, see also 17:1-7.

[a] Or *Sea of Reeds* [b] That is *Bitterness* [c] Or *a tree* [d] Heb *he*

give heed to his commandments and keep all his statutes, I will not
bring upon you any of the diseases that I brought upon the Egyptians;
for I am the LORD who heals you."

27 Then they came to Elim, where there were twelve springs of
water and seventy palm trees; and they camped there by the water.

Bread from Heaven

16 The whole congregation of the Israelites set out from Elim;
and Israel came to the wilderness of Sin, which is between
Elim and Sinai, on the fifteenth day of the second month after they
had departed from the land of Egypt. [2]The whole congregation of
the Israelites complained against Moses and Aaron in the wilderness.
[3]The Israelites said to them, "If only we had died by the hand of the
LORD in the land of Egypt, when we sat by the fleshpots and ate our
fill of bread; for you have brought us out into this wilderness to kill
this whole assembly with hunger."

4 Then the LORD said to Moses, "I am going to rain bread from
heaven for you, and each day the people shall go out and gather
enough for that day. In that way I will test them, whether they will
follow my instruction or not. [5]On the sixth day, when they prepare
what they bring in, it will be twice as much as they gather on other
days." [6]So Moses and Aaron said to all the Israelites, "In the evening
you shall know that it was the LORD who brought you out of the land
of Egypt, [7]and in the morning you shall see the glory of the LORD,
because he has heard your complaining against the LORD. For what
are we, that you complain against us?" [8]And Moses said, "When the
LORD gives you meat to eat in the evening and your fill of bread in
the morning, because the LORD has heard the complaining that you
utter against him—what are we? Your complaining is not against us
but against the LORD."

9 Then Moses said to Aaron, "Say to the whole congregation of
the Israelites, 'Draw near to the LORD, for he has heard your complaining.'" [10]And as Aaron spoke to the whole congregation of the Israelites, they looked toward the wilderness, and the glory of the LORD
appeared in the cloud. [11]The LORD spoke to Moses and said, [12]"I have
heard the complaining of the Israelites; say to them, 'At twilight you
shall eat meat, and in the morning you shall have your fill of bread;
then you shall know that I am the LORD your God.'"

13 In the evening quails came up and covered the camp; and in
the morning there was a layer of dew around the camp. [14]When the
layer of dew lifted, there on the surface of the wilderness was a fine
flaky substance, as fine as frost on the ground. [15]When the Israelites
saw it, they said to one another, "What is it?"[a] For they did not know

16:3 If only we had died: The people accuse Moses of bringing them into the wilderness to starve them to death.

16:4-36 bread from heaven: Bread rains down from heaven. The word "manna" comes from the Israelites' question, "What is it?" Dependence on this unfamiliar food taught the Israelites that "one does not live by bread alone, but by every word that comes from the mouth of the LORD" (Deut 8:3).

How does the vision of everyone in the manna story having enough to eat, with no hoarding and no hunger, contrast with the distribution of food in today's world?

16:6-13 meat to eat in the evening: God provides the Israelites with quail at night. (See Num 11:1-15, 18-25, 31-34.)

---

[a] Or *"It is manna"* (Heb *man hu,* see verse 31)

what it was. Moses said to them, "It is the bread that the LORD has
given you to eat. [16]This is what the LORD has commanded: 'Gather
as much of it as each of you needs, an omer to a person according to
the number of persons, all providing for those in their own tents.'"
[17]The Israelites did so, some gathering more, some less. [18]But when
they measured it with an omer, those who gathered much had nothing over, and those who gathered little had no shortage; they gathered
as much as each of them needed. [19]And Moses said to them, "Let no
one leave any of it over until morning." [20]But they did not listen to
Moses; some left part of it until morning, and it bred worms and became foul. And Moses was angry with them. [21]Morning by morning
they gathered it, as much as each needed; but when the sun grew hot,
it melted.

22 On the sixth day they gathered twice as much food, two
omers apiece. When all the leaders of the congregation came and told
Moses, [23]he said to them, "This is what the LORD has commanded:
'Tomorrow is a day of solemn rest, a holy sabbath to the LORD; bake
what you want to bake and boil what you want to boil, and all that is
left over put aside to be kept until morning.'" [24]So they put it aside until morning, as Moses commanded them; and it did not become foul,
and there were no worms in it. [25]Moses said, "Eat it today, for today
is a sabbath to the LORD; today you will not find it in the field. [26]Six
days you shall gather it; but on the seventh day, which is a sabbath,
there will be none."

27 On the seventh day some of the people went out to gather,
and they found none. [28]The LORD said to Moses, "How long will
you refuse to keep my commandments and instructions? [29]See!
The LORD has given you the sabbath, therefore on the sixth day he
gives you food for two days; each of you stay where you are; do not
leave your place on the seventh day." [30]So the people rested on the
seventh day.

31 The house of Israel called it manna; it was like coriander seed,
white, and the taste of it was like wafers made with honey. [32]Moses
said, "This is what the LORD has commanded: 'Let an omer of it be
kept throughout your generations, in order that they may see the
food with which I fed you in the wilderness, when I brought you out
of the land of Egypt.'" [33]And Moses said to Aaron, "Take a jar, and
put an omer of manna in it, and place it before the LORD, to be kept
throughout your generations." [34]As the LORD commanded Moses,
so Aaron placed it before the covenant,[a] for safekeeping. [35]The Israelites ate manna forty years, until they came to a habitable land; they
ate manna, until they came to the border of the land of Canaan. [36]An
omer is a tenth of an ephah.

16:22-30 the sabbath: The people receive enough food on the sixth day to last two days, so they can rest and worship on the seventh day, the Sabbath.

Does your week include "sabbath time," set aside for worship and rest, to recognize God's good creation?

---

[a] Or *treaty* or *testimony*; Heb *eduth*

17:1-7 Strike the rock, and water will come out of it: The people complain about having no water. Water flows from a rock at Meribah, a place name meaning "quarrel," after Moses strikes it with his staff (see also Num 20:2-13.)

When have you complained while going from a bad situation to one that may be much better? Why does this happen?

Water from the Rock

17 From the wilderness of Sin the whole congregation of the
Israelites journeyed by stages, as the LORD commanded.
They camped at Rephidim, but there was no water for the people to
drink. 2The people quarreled with Moses, and said, "Give us water
to drink." Moses said to them, "Why do you quarrel with me? Why
do you test the LORD?" 3But the people thirsted there for water; and
the people complained against Moses and said, "Why did you bring
us out of Egypt, to kill us and our children and livestock with thirst?"
4So Moses cried out to the LORD, "What shall I do with this people?
They are almost ready to stone me." 5The LORD said to Moses, "Go
on ahead of the people, and take some of the elders of Israel with you;
take in your hand the staff with which you struck the Nile, and go. 6I
will be standing there in front of you on the rock at Horeb. Strike the
rock, and water will come out of it, so that the people may drink."
Moses did so, in the sight of the elders of Israel. 7He called the place
Massah[a] and Meribah,[b] because the Israelites quarreled and tested
the LORD, saying, "Is the LORD among us or not?"

17:8-16 fight with Amalek: Amalek and his people attack the Israelites on their way to Sinai (see also Num 24:20; Deut 25:17-19). Amalekites continued to be enemies of the Israelites during, for example, the time of the kingdom of Israel under Saul (1 Sam 15) and the time of Esther and Mordecai (Esth 3:1).

Amalek Attacks Israel and Is Defeated

8 Then Amalek came and fought with Israel at Rephidim. 9Moses
said to Joshua, "Choose some men for us and go out, fight with Amalek. Tomorrow I will stand on the top of the hill with the staff of
God in my hand." 10So Joshua did as Moses told him, and fought with
Amalek, while Moses, Aaron, and Hur went up to the top of the hill.
11Whenever Moses held up his hand, Israel prevailed; and whenever
he lowered his hand, Amalek prevailed. 12But Moses' hands grew
weary; so they took a stone and put it under him, and he sat on it.
Aaron and Hur held up his hands, one on one side, and the other
on the other side; so his hands were steady until the sun set. 13And
Joshua defeated Amalek and his people with the sword.

14 Then the LORD said to Moses, "Write this as a reminder in a
book and recite it in the hearing of Joshua: I will utterly blot out the
remembrance of Amalek from under heaven." 15And Moses built an
altar and called it, The LORD is my banner. 16He said, "A hand upon
the banner of the LORD![c] The LORD will have war with Amalek from
generation to generation."

18:1-11 Jethro: Moses is reunited with his wife, two sons, and his father-in-law, Jethro. Jethro hears how God brought the Israelites out of slavery in Egypt, and recognizes Yahweh in these things.

Jethro's Advice

18 Jethro, the priest of Midian, Moses' father-in-law, heard of
all that God had done for Moses and for his people Israel,
how the LORD had brought Israel out of Egypt. 2After Moses had sent
away his wife Zipporah, his father-in-law Jethro took her back, 3along

---

[a] That is *Test* [b] That is *Quarrel* [c] Cn: Meaning of Heb uncertain

with her two sons. The name of the one was Gershom (for he said, "I
have been an alien[a] in a foreign land"), [4]and the name of the other,
Eliezer[b] (for he said, "The God of my father was my help, and delivered me from the sword of Pharaoh"). [5]Jethro, Moses' father-in-law,
came into the wilderness where Moses was encamped at the mountain of God, bringing Moses' sons and wife to him. [6]He sent word
to Moses, "I, your father-in-law Jethro, am coming to you, with your
wife and her two sons." [7]Moses went out to meet his father-in-law; he
bowed down and kissed him; each asked after the other's welfare, and
they went into the tent. [8]Then Moses told his father-in-law all that the
LORD had done to Pharaoh and to the Egyptians for Israel's sake, all
the hardship that had beset them on the way, and how the LORD had
delivered them. [9]Jethro rejoiced for all the good that the LORD had
done to Israel, in delivering them from the Egyptians.

10 Jethro said, "Blessed be the LORD, who has delivered you
from the Egyptians and from Pharaoh. [11]Now I know that the LORD
is greater than all gods, because he delivered the people from the
Egyptians,[c] when they dealt arrogantly with them." [12]And Jethro,
Moses' father-in-law, brought a burnt offering and sacrifices to God;
and Aaron came with all the elders of Israel to eat bread with Moses'
father-in-law in the presence of God.

13 The next day Moses sat as judge for the people, while the people stood around him from morning until evening. [14]When Moses' father-in-law saw all that he was doing for the people, he said, "What is
this that you are doing for the people? Why do you sit alone, while all
the people stand around you from morning until evening?" [15]Moses
said to his father-in-law, "Because the people come to me to inquire
of God. [16]When they have a dispute, they come to me and I decide
between one person and another, and I make known to them the
statutes and instructions of God." [17]Moses' father-in-law said to him,
"What you are doing is not good. [18]You will surely wear yourself out,
both you and these people with you. For the task is too heavy for you;
you cannot do it alone. [19]Now listen to me. I will give you counsel,
and God be with you! You should represent the people before God,
and you should bring their cases before God; [20]teach them the statutes and instructions and make known to them the way they are to
go and the things they are to do. [21]You should also look for able men
among all the people, men who fear God, are trustworthy, and hate
dishonest gain; set such men over them as officers over thousands,
hundreds, fifties, and tens. [22]Let them sit as judges for the people at all
times; let them bring every important case to you, but decide every
minor case themselves. So it will be easier for you, and they will bear

18:13-26 Moses sat as judge for the people: At Jethro's suggestion, a judicial system is set up to make rulings and settle disputes. This is a positive example of the influence of the larger surrounding culture on Israel.

How would you react if an individual or group from a different ethnic or religious background suggested a change to you or your congregation?

[a] Heb *ger* [b] Heb *Eli*, my God; *ezer*, help [c] The clause *because ... Egyptians* has been transposed from verse 10

19:1-2 Sinai: This is also known as Horeb (see Map 2, p. 2099).

How do Lutherans see God's law? The law that God reveals through Moses at Sinai is a gracious gift to the Israelites. It provides guidance on how to live in freedom as God's covenant people. The Israelites have just experienced God's deliverance from slavery in Egypt. At Sinai they receive a new identity when they accept the Torah as their way of life in relationship with God. *Exodus 19:4-5*

What is the priesthood of all believers? The Israelites are a "priestly kingdom and a holy nation"—a people set apart for a special calling to do God's work among the nations. In a similar way, as Christians we all share the work of worshiping God, serving our neighbors, and caring for God's good creation. *Exodus 19:6*

19:10-15 Go to the people and consecrate them: The people are consecrated or made pure during three days of preparation. Purity is not primarily related to dirt, health, sin, or guilt here. Rather, the people remove themselves from certain aspects of personal and communal life so that they can devote themselves to being in God's presence.

19:15 do not go near a woman: Moses is speaking to the men. In the Israelites' thinking, sexual relations would render both partners impure and unable to approach God until they washed in water and waited until the next day (Lev 15:18). The men of the community are told to abstain for a defined, short period of time in order to be available for God's appearance on the mountain.

19:16-25 thunder and lightning: God appears with a storm, volcano, earthquake, thunder, lightning, smoke, and fire, plus a trumpet blast and voice.

20:1—24:18 Then God spoke all these words: God gives the *Torah* or "teaching" at Sinai. In Judaism, Torah also refers to the first five books of Scripture (also called the Pentateuch). The meaning of Torah expands to include a living tradition of conduct and ethics, with ongoing interpretation for current situations. There is another version of the Commandments in Deuteronomy 5:6-21 and an alternate list of ritual commandments in Exodus 34. (See also Numbering the Ten Commandments, p. 154).

the burden with you. [23]If you do this, and God so commands you,
then you will be able to endure, and all these people will go to their
home in peace."

24 So Moses listened to his father-in-law and did all that he had
said. [25]Moses chose able men from all Israel and appointed them as
heads over the people, as officers over thousands, hundreds, fifties,
and tens. [26]And they judged the people at all times; hard cases they
brought to Moses, but any minor case they decided themselves.
[27]Then Moses let his father-in-law depart, and he went off to his own
country.

The Israelites Reach Mount Sinai

19 On the third new moon after the Israelites had gone out of the
land of Egypt, on that very day, they came into the wilderness
of Sinai. [2]They had journeyed from Rephidim, entered the wilderness
of Sinai, and camped in the wilderness; Israel camped there in front of
the mountain. [3]Then Moses went up to God; the LORD called to him
from the mountain, saying, "Thus you shall say to the house of Jacob,
and tell the Israelites: [4]You have seen what I did to the Egyptians, and
how I bore you on eagles' wings and brought you to myself. [5]Now
therefore, if you obey my voice and keep my covenant, you shall be
my treasured possession out of all the peoples. Indeed, the whole
earth is mine, [6]but you shall be for me a priestly kingdom and a holy
nation. These are the words that you shall speak to the Israelites."

7 So Moses came, summoned the elders of the people, and set before them all these words that the LORD had commanded him. [8]The
people all answered as one: "Everything that the LORD has spoken we
will do." Moses reported the words of the people to the LORD. [9]Then
the LORD said to Moses, "I am going to come to you in a dense cloud,
in order that the people may hear when I speak with you and so trust
you ever after."

The People Consecrated

When Moses had told the words of the people to the LORD, [10]the
LORD said to Moses: "Go to the people and consecrate them today
and tomorrow. Have them wash their clothes [11]and prepare for the
third day, because on the third day the LORD will come down upon
Mount Sinai in the sight of all the people. [12]You shall set limits for the
people all around, saying, 'Be careful not to go up the mountain or
to touch the edge of it. Any who touch the mountain shall be put to
death. [13]No hand shall touch them, but they shall be stoned or shot
with arrows;[a] whether animal or human being, they shall not live.'
When the trumpet sounds a long blast, they may go up on the moun-

[a] Heb lacks *with arrows*

tain.” 14 So Moses went down from the mountain to the people. He
consecrated the people, and they washed their clothes. 15 And he said
to the people, “Prepare for the third day; do not go near a woman.”
16 On the morning of the third day there was thunder and
lightning, as well as a thick cloud on the mountain, and a blast of
a trumpet so loud that all the people who were in the camp trembled. 17 Moses brought the people out of the camp to meet God. They
took their stand at the foot of the mountain. 18 Now Mount Sinai was
wrapped in smoke, because the LORD had descended upon it in fire;
the smoke went up like the smoke of a kiln, while the whole mountain shook violently. 19 As the blast of the trumpet grew louder and
louder, Moses would speak and God would answer him in thunder.
20 When the LORD descended upon Mount Sinai, to the top of the
mountain, the LORD summoned Moses to the top of the mountain,
and Moses went up. 21 Then the LORD said to Moses, “Go down and
warn the people not to break through to the LORD to look; otherwise many of them will perish. 22 Even the priests who approach the
LORD must consecrate themselves or the LORD will break out against
them.” 23 Moses said to the LORD, “The people are not permitted to
come up to Mount Sinai; for you yourself warned us, saying, ‘Set limits around the mountain and keep it holy.’ ” 24 The LORD said to him,
“Go down, and come up bringing Aaron with you; but do not let either the priests or the people break through to come up to the LORD;
otherwise he will break out against them.” 25 So Moses went down to
the people and told them.

The Ten Commandments

20 Then God spoke all these words:
2 I am the LORD your God, who brought you out of the
land of Egypt, out of the house of slavery; 3 you shall have no other
gods before[a] me.
4 You shall not make for yourself an idol, whether in the form of
anything that is in heaven above, or that is on the earth beneath, or
that is in the water under the earth. 5 You shall not bow down to them
or worship them; for I the LORD your God am a jealous God, punishing children for the iniquity of parents, to the third and the fourth
generation of those who reject me, 6 but showing steadfast love to the
thousandth generation[b] of those who love me and keep my commandments.
7 You shall not make wrongful use of the name of the LORD your
God, for the LORD will not acquit anyone who misuses his name.
8 Remember the sabbath day, and keep it holy. 9 Six days you
shall labor and do all your work. 10 But the seventh day is a sabbath

[a] Or *besides* [b] Or *to thousands*

20:1—24:18 covenant: The key event for the Israelites is the *covenant* God makes with them at Sinai (Horeb). A covenant is a binding agreement between two parties. By freeing the Israelite slaves, the LORD brings them into a new relationship as God's covenant people. The covenant at Sinai requires a way of life that reflects undivided loyalty to God and responsibility to other community members.

20:1—24:18 The LORD said to Moses: The Sinai covenant is patterned after political treaties in the ancient Near East between a suzerain, or powerful king, and a vassal, or weaker king.The suzerain promises good treatment and protection if the vassal is loyal and fulfils certain obligations. In Exodus, God is portrayed as the suzerain and Israel as the vassal.

What is the purpose of the Ten Commandments? The Ten Commandments give us the basics for faithful living in relationship to God and our neighbors. In his Small Catechism, Martin Luther expands these commandments from a series of statements—mainly about things we should not do—into a set of positive instructions for a Christian life of service to God and neighbor. Of the laws given at Sinai, Martin Luther believed that only those that agreed with natural law—meaning the moral sensibility imprinted on each human heart—were binding on Christians. All others were intended for a specific people, the Israelites, within their ancient time and culture. *Exodus 20:1—24:18*

20:2 I am the LORD your God: In Jewish tradition, this is the First Commandment. Receiving God's deliverance in the past provides motivation for worshiping the LORD and following the Commandments.

20:3 you shall have no other gods before me: "Before me" implies that other gods existed and Israel must not worship them.

20:4-6 You shall not make for yourself an idol: Human beings are the "image" and "likeness" of God on earth (Gen 1:26-27, 5:1-3; 9:6). They are prohibited from making and worshiping artistic representations of the divine in the form of any creature.

Numbering the Ten Commandments

In general, there are three traditional ways to number the Commandments.

	Jewish	Roman Catholic, Lutheran, Eastern Orthodox	Reformed, Anglican, other Protestant traditions
1	I am the Lord your God.	You shall have no other gods.	You shall have no other gods.
2	You shall have no other gods.	You shall not make wrongful use of the name of the Lord your God.	You shall not make for yourself a graven image.
3	You shall not take the name of the Lord your God in vain.	Remember the sabbath day, and keep it holy.	You shall not take the name of the Lord your God in vain.
4	Remember the sabbath day, to keep it holy.	Honor your father and your mother.	Remember the sabbath day, to keep it holy.
5	Honor your father and your mother.	You shall not murder.	Honor your father and your mother.
6	You shall not kill.	You shall not commit adultery.	You shall not kill.
7	You shall not commit adultery.	You shall not steal.	You shall not commit adultery.
8	You shall not steal.	You shall not bear false witness against your neighbor.	You shall not steal.
9	You shall not bear false witness against your neighbor.	You shall not covet your neighbor's house.	You shall not bear false witness against your neighbor.
10	You shall not covet your neighbor's wife; and you shall not desire anything that is your neighbor's.	You shall not covet your neighbor's wife, or male or female slave, or ox, or donkey, or anything that belongs to your neighbor.	You shall not covet your neighbor's wife; and you shall not desire anything that is your neighbor's.

The list used in Judaism begins with the declaration, "I am the Lord your God."

The list used by Roman Catholics, Lutherans, and Eastern Orthodox Christians comes from Augustine, a fifth-century bishop. Augustine placed the command against graven images (idols) under the first commandment and counted the material about coveting as two commandments.

The list used by the Reformed, Anglican, Presbyterian, Methodist, Baptist, and other traditions started with Origen and other early church leaders. It counts "You shall have no other gods" and "You shall not make for yourself a graven image" as two separate commandments.

to the LORD your God; you shall not do any work—you, your son or
your daughter, your male or female slave, your livestock, or the alien
resident in your towns. 11 For in six days the LORD made heaven and
earth, the sea, and all that is in them, but rested the seventh day; therefore the LORD blessed the sabbath day and consecrated it.
12 Honor your father and your mother, so that your days may be
long in the land that the LORD your God is giving you.
13 You shall not murder.[a]
14 You shall not commit adultery.
15 You shall not steal.
16 You shall not bear false witness against your neighbor.

20:13 You shall not murder: The word used for murder refers to intentional premeditated murder, not all killing.

20:15 You shall not steal: The Hebrew word for stealing includes kidnapping.

[a] Or *kill*

17 You shall not covet your neighbor's house; you shall not covet your neighbor's wife, or male or female slave, or ox, or donkey, or anything that belongs to your neighbor.

18 When all the people witnessed the thunder and lightning, the sound of the trumpet, and the mountain smoking, they were afraid[a] and trembled and stood at a distance, [19]and said to Moses, "You speak to us, and we will listen; but do not let God speak to us, or we will die." [20]Moses said to the people, "Do not be afraid; for God has come only to test you and to put the fear of him upon you so that you do not sin." [21]Then the people stood at a distance, while Moses drew near to the thick darkness where God was.

The Law concerning the Altar

22 The LORD said to Moses: Thus you shall say to the Israelites: "You have seen for yourselves that I spoke with you from heaven. [23]You shall not make gods of silver alongside me, nor shall you make for yourselves gods of gold. [24]You need make for me only an altar of earth and sacrifice on it your burnt offerings and your offerings of well-being, your sheep and your oxen; in every place where I cause my name to be remembered I will come to you and bless you. [25]But if you make for me an altar of stone, do not build it of hewn stones; for if you use a chisel upon it you profane it. [26]You shall not go up by steps to my altar, so that your nakedness may not be exposed on it."

The Law concerning Slaves

21 These are the ordinances that you shall set before them:

2 When you buy a male Hebrew slave, he shall serve six years, but in the seventh he shall go out a free person, without debt. [3]If he comes in single, he shall go out single; if he comes in married, then his wife shall go out with him. [4]If his master gives him a wife and she bears him sons or daughters, the wife and her children shall be her master's and he shall go out alone. [5]But if the slave declares, "I love my master, my wife, and my children; I will not go out a free person," [6]then his master shall bring him before God.[b] He shall be brought to the door or the doorpost; and his master shall pierce his ear with an awl; and he shall serve him for life.

7 When a man sells his daughter as a slave, she shall not go out as the male slaves do. [8]If she does not please her master, who designated her for himself, then he shall let her be redeemed; he shall have no right to sell her to a foreign people, since he has dealt unfairly with her. [9]If he designates her for his son, he shall deal with her as with a daughter. [10]If he takes another wife to himself, he shall not diminish the food, clothing, or marital rights of the first wife.[c] [11]And if he does

[a] Sam Gk Syr Vg: MT *they saw* [b] Or *to the judges* [c] Heb *of her*

20:17 You shall not covet: The word "covet" implies desiring something to the extent of trying to take possession, as in Exodus 34:24 and Joshua 7:21.

20:18-19 You speak to us: The people are afraid they will die if God speaks directly to them. They ask Moses to speak to them on behalf of God.

20:22—23:33 Thus you shall say: This is the Covenant Code, also known as the "book of the covenant" (24:7), the oldest collection of legal materials in the first five books of the Bible (or Pentateuch), dating from the early Israelite settlement in the land. Its family, community, criminal, and religious laws, as well as ethical instructions, show that all of life is part of the covenant relationship with Israel's God, Yahweh. It has similarities with the famous law code of Hammurabi, ruler of Babylon (1728–1686 B.C.E.).

20:22-26 an altar of earth: To worship God, altars made of earth and unhewn stones can be built and used for burnt offerings and offerings of well-being. Later on a whole sacrificial system would be put in place at the Jerusalem temple (see Leviticus). A burnt offering involved sacrificing an animal and offering it to God by burning the entire carcass, causing it to "go up" in smoke—the core meaning of the name of the sacrifice, *olah* in Hebrew. An offering of well-being, also known as the "peace offering," involved an animal sacrifice and a meal with family members and others in the covenant community. In ancient biblical times, before the temple in Jerusalem became the only site for sacrifices, all meat eaten by people was slaughtered in a sacrificial ritual such as the offering of well-being.

21:2-6, 20-21, 26-27 Hebrew slave: Male Hebrew slaves had certain rights, such as a limit of six years of service, unless they became permanent members of their masters' households. In Deuteronomy 15:12-18 the same rule is extended to female Hebrew slaves. The Covenant Code also includes consequences for injuring slaves.

not do these three things for her, she shall go out without debt, without payment of money.

The Law concerning Violence

12 Whoever strikes a person mortally shall be put to death. [13]If it was not premeditated, but came about by an act of God, then I will appoint for you a place to which the killer may flee. [14]But if someone willfully attacks and kills another by treachery, you shall take the killer from my altar for execution.

15 Whoever strikes father or mother shall be put to death.

16 Whoever kidnaps a person, whether that person has been sold or is still held in possession, shall be put to death.

17 Whoever curses father or mother shall be put to death.

18 When individuals quarrel and one strikes the other with a stone or fist so that the injured party, though not dead, is confined to bed, [19]but recovers and walks around outside with the help of a staff, then the assailant shall be free of liability, except to pay for the loss of time, and to arrange for full recovery.

20 When a slaveowner strikes a male or female slave with a rod and the slave dies immediately, the owner shall be punished. [21]But if the slave survives a day or two, there is no punishment; for the slave is the owner's property.

22 When people who are fighting injure a pregnant woman so that there is a miscarriage, and yet no further harm follows, the one responsible shall be fined what the woman's husband demands, paying as much as the judges determine. [23]If any harm follows, then you shall give life for life, [24]eye for eye, tooth for tooth, hand for hand, foot for foot, [25]burn for burn, wound for wound, stripe for stripe.

26 When a slaveowner strikes the eye of a male or female slave, destroying it, the owner shall let the slave go, a free person, to compensate for the eye. [27]If the owner knocks out a tooth of a male or female slave, the slave shall be let go, a free person, to compensate for the tooth.

Laws concerning Property

28 When an ox gores a man or a woman to death, the ox shall be stoned, and its flesh shall not be eaten; but the owner of the ox shall not be liable. [29]If the ox has been accustomed to gore in the past, and its owner has been warned but has not restrained it, and it kills a man or a woman, the ox shall be stoned, and its owner also shall be put to death. [30]If a ransom is imposed on the owner, then the owner shall pay whatever is imposed for the redemption of the victim's life. [31]If it gores a boy or a girl, the owner shall be dealt with according to this same rule. [32]If the ox gores a male or female slave, the owner shall pay to the slaveowner thirty shekels of silver, and the ox shall be stoned.

21:12-36 if someone willfully attacks and kills another: Assault, injury, murder, and manslaughter are distinguished from one another.

21:22-25 injure a pregnant woman: Special protections apply to people seen as weak and marginalized by society, including pregnant women, as well as non-Israelites, widows, and orphans (22:21-24; 23:9).

21:23-25 eye for eye, tooth for tooth: This is sometimes known as *lex talionis*, or "law of the talons," because of a mistaken view that it illustrates the cruelty of Old Testament law. Rather, it places limits on punishments, so that the severity of punishment does not go beyond the crime committed. This was a common ancient Near Eastern legal principle, also seen in the law code of Hammurabi.

21:26-27 slave…free person: Slaves who lose an eye or tooth due to abuse by their master are granted freedom. They were not just part of their master's financial gains and losses.

21:28-32 When an ox gores: This would be a topic of importance in a settled, agricultural society, such as the one depicted in the book of Judges. Hammurabi's law code has similar regulations.

33 If someone leaves a pit open, or digs a pit and does not cover
it, and an ox or a donkey falls into it, 34 the owner of the pit shall make
restitution, giving money to its owner, but keeping the dead animal.
35 If someone's ox hurts the ox of another, so that it dies, then
they shall sell the live ox and divide the price of it; and the dead animal they shall also divide. 36 But if it was known that the ox was accustomed to gore in the past, and its owner has not restrained it, the
owner shall restore ox for ox, but keep the dead animal.

21:33-36 If someone leaves a pit open: The laws given on Sinai include the welfare of animals.

Laws of Restitution

22[a] When someone steals an ox or a sheep, and slaughters it or
sells it, the thief shall pay five oxen for an ox, and four
sheep for a sheep.[b] The thief shall make restitution, but if unable to do
so, shall be sold for the theft. 4 When the animal, whether ox or donkey or sheep, is found alive in the thief's possession, the thief shall pay
double.
2[c] If a thief is found breaking in, and is beaten to death, no
bloodguilt is incurred; 3 but if it happens after sunrise, bloodguilt is
incurred.
5 When someone causes a field or vineyard to be grazed over, or
lets livestock loose to graze in someone else's field, restitution shall be
made from the best in the owner's field or vineyard.
6 When fire breaks out and catches in thorns so that the stacked
grain or the standing grain or the field is consumed, the one who
started the fire shall make full restitution.
7 When someone delivers to a neighbor money or goods for safekeeping, and they are stolen from the neighbor's house, then the thief,
if caught, shall pay double. 8 If the thief is not caught, the owner of the
house shall be brought before God,[d] to determine whether or not the
owner had laid hands on the neighbor's goods.
9 In any case of disputed ownership involving ox, donkey, sheep,
clothing, or any other loss, of which one party says, "This is mine,"
the case of both parties shall come before God;[d] the one whom God
condemns[e] shall pay double to the other.
10 When someone delivers to another a donkey, ox, sheep, or any
other animal for safekeeping, and it dies or is injured or is carried off,
without anyone seeing it, 11 an oath before the LORD shall decide between the two of them that the one has not laid hands on the property
of the other; the owner shall accept the oath, and no restitution shall
be made. 12 But if it was stolen, restitution shall be made to its owner.
13 If it was mangled by beasts, let it be brought as evidence; restitution
shall not be made for the mangled remains.

22:1-15 When someone steals: There is no capital punishment or imprisonment for crimes against property such as theft and arson, but restoration or payment (equaling several times the item's value) is required.

---

[a] Ch 21.37 in Heb [b] Verses 2, 3, and 4 rearranged thus: 3b, 4, 2, 3a [c] Ch 22.1 in Heb [d] Or *before the judges* [e] Or *the judges condemn*

14 When someone borrows an animal from another and it is injured or dies, the owner not being present, full restitution shall be
made. 15 If the owner was present, there shall be no restitution; if it
was hired, only the hiring fee is due.

Social and Religious Laws

16 When a man seduces a virgin who is not engaged to be married, and lies with her, he shall give the bride-price for her and make
her his wife. 17 But if her father refuses to give her to him, he shall pay
an amount equal to the bride-price for virgins.

18 You shall not permit a female sorcerer to live.

19 Whoever lies with an animal shall be put to death.

20 Whoever sacrifices to any god, other than the LORD alone,
shall be devoted to destruction.

22:21-25 You shall not wrong or oppress: These moral principles are the basis for some of the laws given at Sinai.

22:22-24 I will surely heed their cry: Special protections apply to people who are seen as weak and marginalized by society, including widows, orphans, and the poor, as well as pregnant women and non-Israelites (21:22-25; 22:21; 23:6, 9).

21 You shall not wrong or oppress a resident alien, for you were
aliens in the land of Egypt. 22 You shall not abuse any widow or orphan. 23 If you do abuse them, when they cry out to me, I will surely
heed their cry; 24 my wrath will burn, and I will kill you with the sword,
and your wives shall become widows and your children orphans.

25 If you lend money to my people, to the poor among you, you
shall not deal with them as a creditor; you shall not exact interest from
them. 26 If you take your neighbor's cloak in pawn, you shall restore it
before the sun goes down; 27 for it may be your neighbor's only clothing to use as cover; in what else shall that person sleep? And if your
neighbor cries out to me, I will listen, for I am compassionate.

28 You shall not revile God, or curse a leader of your people.

29 You shall not delay to make offerings from the fullness of your
harvest and from the outflow of your presses.[a]

The firstborn of your sons you shall give to me. 30 You shall do the
same with your oxen and with your sheep: seven days it shall remain
with its mother; on the eighth day you shall give it to me.

22:31 people consecrated to me: This is a principle for Jewish kosher (food) laws (see also 23:19b, the basis for separating milk and meat).

31 You shall be people consecrated to me; therefore you shall not
eat any meat that is mangled by beasts in the field; you shall throw it
to the dogs.

Justice for All

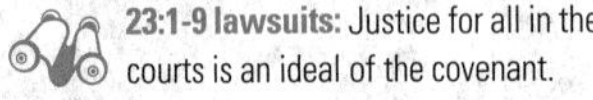
23:1-9 lawsuits: Justice for all in the courts is an ideal of the covenant.

23 You shall not spread a false report. You shall not join hands
with the wicked to act as a malicious witness. 2 You shall not
follow a majority in wrongdoing; when you bear witness in a lawsuit,
you shall not side with the majority so as to pervert justice; 3 nor shall
you be partial to the poor in a lawsuit.

4 When you come upon your enemy's ox or donkey going astray,
you shall bring it back.

[a] Meaning of Heb uncertain

5 When you see the donkey of one who hates you lying under its
burden and you would hold back from setting it free, you must help
to set it free.[a]
6 You shall not pervert the justice due to your poor in their lawsuits. 7 Keep far from a false charge, and do not kill the innocent and
those in the right, for I will not acquit the guilty. 8 You shall take no
bribe, for a bribe blinds the officials, and subverts the cause of those
who are in the right.
9 You shall not oppress a resident alien; you know the heart of an
alien, for you were aliens in the land of Egypt.

23:9 a resident alien: The experience of slavery in the foreign land of Egypt should help the Israelites understand those in a similar situation within their community.

Sabbatical Year and Sabbath

10 For six years you shall sow your land and gather in its yield;
11 but the seventh year you shall let it rest and lie fallow, so that the
poor of your people may eat; and what they leave the wild animals
may eat. You shall do the same with your vineyard, and with your olive orchard.
12 Six days you shall do your work, but on the seventh day you
shall rest, so that your ox and your donkey may have relief, and your
homeborn slave and the resident alien may be refreshed. 13 Be attentive to all that I have said to you. Do not invoke the names of other
gods; do not let them be heard on your lips.

23:10-12 seventh year...seventh day: The seventh year (or sabbatical year) and the seventh day of the week (or Sabbath) are set apart to provide food and rest for humans and animals alike.

The Annual Festivals

14 Three times in the year you shall hold a festival for me. 15 You
shall observe the festival of unleavened bread; as I commanded you,
you shall eat unleavened bread for seven days at the appointed time in
the month of Abib, for in it you came out of Egypt.
No one shall appear before me empty-handed.
16 You shall observe the festival of harvest, of the first fruits of
your labor, of what you sow in the field. You shall observe the festival
of ingathering at the end of the year, when you gather in from the field
the fruit of your labor. 17 Three times in the year all your males shall
appear before the Lord GOD.
18 You shall not offer the blood of my sacrifice with anything
leavened, or let the fat of my festival remain until the morning.
19 The choicest of the first fruits of your ground you shall bring
into the house of the LORD your God.
You shall not boil a kid in its mother's milk.

23:14-19 hold a festival: Israel will celebrate three agricultural festivals that come to be connected to events in Exodus: Unleavened Bread/Passover (the exodus from Egypt); the harvest festival, also known as Shavuot or Pentecost (the giving of the law at Sinai), and the festival of ingathering, also known as Sukkot or Booths (the wilderness wandering). See also Exodus 34:18-26.

The Conquest of Canaan Promised

20 I am going to send an angel in front of you, to guard you on the
way and to bring you to the place that I have prepared. 21 Be attentive

[a] Meaning of Heb uncertain

to him and listen to his voice; do not rebel against him, for he will not
pardon your transgression; for my name is in him.

22 But if you listen attentively to his voice and do all that I say,
then I will be an enemy to your enemies and a foe to your foes.

23 When my angel goes in front of you, and brings you to the
Amorites, the Hittites, the Perizzites, the Canaanites, the Hivites, and
the Jebusites, and I blot them out, 24 you shall not bow down to their
gods, or worship them, or follow their practices, but you shall utterly
demolish them and break their pillars in pieces. 25 You shall worship
the LORD your God, and I[a] will bless your bread and your water; and
I will take sickness away from among you. 26 No one shall miscarry or
be barren in your land; I will fulfill the number of your days. 27 I will
send my terror in front of you, and will throw into confusion all the
people against whom you shall come, and I will make all your enemies turn their backs to you. 28 And I will send the pestilence[b] in front
of you, which shall drive out the Hivites, the Canaanites, and the Hittites from before you. 29 I will not drive them out from before you in
one year, or the land would become desolate and the wild animals
would multiply against you. 30 Little by little I will drive them out from
before you, until you have increased and possess the land. 31 I will set
your borders from the Red Sea[c] to the sea of the Philistines, and from
the wilderness to the Euphrates; for I will hand over to you the inhabitants of the land, and you shall drive them out before you. 32 You shall
make no covenant with them and their gods. 33 They shall not live in
your land, or they will make you sin against me; for if you worship
their gods, it will surely be a snare to you.

The Blood of the Covenant

24 Then he said to Moses, "Come up to the LORD, you and
Aaron, Nadab, and Abihu, and seventy of the elders of Israel, and worship at a distance. 2 Moses alone shall come near the
LORD; but the others shall not come near, and the people shall not
come up with him."

3 Moses came and told the people all the words of the LORD and
all the ordinances; and all the people answered with one voice, and
said, "All the words that the LORD has spoken we will do." 4 And Moses
wrote down all the words of the LORD. He rose early in the morning,
and built an altar at the foot of the mountain, and set up twelve pillars,
corresponding to the twelve tribes of Israel. 5 He sent young men of
the people of Israel, who offered burnt offerings and sacrificed oxen
as offerings of well-being to the LORD. 6 Moses took half of the blood
and put it in basins, and half of the blood he dashed against the altar.
7 Then he took the book of the covenant, and read it in the hearing of

23:25-33 I will bless: Blessings and curses are part of the covenant. This follows a pattern also used in political treaties in the ancient Near East, in which a vassal, a weaker king, was rewarded for obeying the terms of a treaty and punished for disobeying a suzerain, a more powerful king (see World of the Bible note on chapters 20:1–24:18).

Does obedience to God's way lead to blessing? How do you explain why some people seem blessed while others suffer?

24:3-18 All the words that the LORD has spoken we will do: The people say "yes" to the covenant relationship with God and the way of life within the covenant community.

[a] Gk Vg: Heb *he* [b] Or *hornets*: Meaning of Heb uncertain [c] Or *Sea of Reeds*

the people; and they said, "All that the LORD has spoken we will do,
and we will be obedient." [8]Moses took the blood and dashed it on the
people, and said, "See the blood of the covenant that the LORD has
made with you in accordance with all these words."

On the Mountain with God

9 Then Moses and Aaron, Nadab, and Abihu, and seventy of the
elders of Israel went up, [10]and they saw the God of Israel. Under his
feet there was something like a pavement of sapphire stone, like the
very heaven for clearness. [11]God[a] did not lay his hand on the chief
men of the people of Israel; also they beheld God, and they ate and
drank.

12 The LORD said to Moses, "Come up to me on the mountain,
and wait there; and I will give you the tablets of stone, with the law
and the commandment, which I have written for their instruction."
[13]So Moses set out with his assistant Joshua, and Moses went up into
the mountain of God. [14]To the elders he had said, "Wait here for us,
until we come to you again; for Aaron and Hur are with you; whoever
has a dispute may go to them."

15 Then Moses went up on the mountain, and the cloud covered the mountain. [16]The glory of the LORD settled on Mount Sinai,
and the cloud covered it for six days; on the seventh day he called
to Moses out of the cloud. [17]Now the appearance of the glory of the
LORD was like a devouring fire on the top of the mountain in the sight
of the people of Israel. [18]Moses entered the cloud, and went up on
the mountain. Moses was on the mountain for forty days and forty
nights.

Offerings for the Tabernacle

25 The LORD said to Moses: [2]Tell the Israelites to take for me
an offering; from all whose hearts prompt them to give you
shall receive the offering for me. [3]This is the offering that you shall
receive from them: gold, silver, and bronze, [4]blue, purple, and crimson yarns and fine linen, goats' hair, [5]tanned rams' skins, fine leather,[b]
acacia wood, [6]oil for the lamps, spices for the anointing oil and for the
fragrant incense, [7]onyx stones and gems to be set in the ephod and for
the breastpiece. [8]And have them make me a sanctuary, so that I may
dwell among them. [9]In accordance with all that I show you concerning the pattern of the tabernacle and of all its furniture, so you shall
make it.

The Ark of the Covenant

10 They shall make an ark of acacia wood; it shall be two and a
half cubits long, a cubit and a half wide, and a cubit and a half high.

---

[a] Heb *He* [b] Meaning of Heb uncertain

25:1—31:18 make me a sanctuary: This begins a long block of material in Exodus 25—Numbers 10 that focuses on Israelite worship of God in the wilderness. In Mesopotamia and Egypt, gods reveal the blueprints for their temples. Here the LORD gives detailed instructions to Moses for a tabernacle, a word based on the Hebrew root "to dwell." It will be a dwelling place for the divine presence as the Israelites leave Mount Sinai (see 25:9; 26:30; 27:8) and a movable sanctuary for worship in the wilderness (29:42-46). The attention to construction details seems more appropriate for a later time, perhaps referring to the Temple of Solomon in Jerusalem or the restored Jerusalem temple after the exile to Persia.

Where do you experience God's presence more—in an elaborate or simple church building, or does it matter?

25:1-7 an offering: This freewill offering is a response to God's spirit stirring the hearts of the people to generous giving. Christian stewardship draws upon this concept.

25:1-9 the tabernacle: The tabernacle is to be constructed through freewill offerings from the people (see 35:4-9, 20-29; 36:3-7). The people give more than what is needed (36:5-7). An alternate tradition says a half-shekel was collected from each male twenty years or older (30:11-16; 38:21-31). Tithing, giving one-tenth of one's wealth or income, is yet another way the worship of God is supported (see Gen 14:20; 28:22; Deut 14:22-29; 26:12-15).

What do you think is the best way to support the church's mission, through freewill offerings, the collection of an equal amount from each person, tithing, or some other means? What works best for you?

25:10-22 make an ark: The ark of the covenant is a mobile shrine for God's presence in front of the people as they travel. (See artist's rendition, p. 162.) It is used in worship and for continuing revelations from God to Moses (see 37:1-9; 39:35; 40:3, 5, 20-21). David brings it to the newly captured city of Jerusalem, to introduce an old tradition into a city that previously had little connection to Israelite history and worship. The ark accompanies David as he flees from his son Absalom's rebellion. During Solomon's reign the ark is placed in the Holy of Holies during the dedication of the Jerusalem temple (1 Kgs 8). The ark is lost at some point, perhaps during the exile that begins in 587 B.C.E. (Jer 3:16).

Ark of the covenant (artist's rendition)

25:10 cubit: This is approximately eighteen to twenty-one inches (about forty-six to fifty-three centimeters).

25:17 mercy seat: This term comes from a Hebrew word meaning to "cover," which could refer to the "covering" or atoning of sins on the Day of Atonement (Lev 16:2-34), or simply to the cover on the top of the ark. It is made of pure gold because God's invisible presence dwells on and above the mercy seat, like on a throne.

25:18 cherubim: Winged creatures with animal bodies (either a bull or a lion) and human heads, cherubim were common in ancient Near Eastern artistic images. The cherubim (plural of cherub) serve as armrests or guardians for God's throne (see 1 Kgs 6:23-28; Ezek 1:4-28; 10:1-22; 41:18-20). God rides on a cherub in 2 Samuel 22:11 (see also Ps 18:10).

25:21-22 the covenant: Literally the "treaty" or "testimony," the covenant is the two tablets of stone inscribed with the Commandments that God gives Moses at Sinai (24:12; 31:18). These are set inside the ark as a sign of God's covenant relationship with the Israelites (40:20; see also Deut 31:24-26).

25:23-30 table . . . plates and dishes . . . flagons and bowls: These items represent the hospitality of a meal (see 26:35; 35:13; 39:36; 40:4, 22-23; 1 Kgs 7:48).

25:30 bread of the Presence: Loaves of holy bread were set out on the table every Sabbath (Lev 24:8; 1 Chr 9:32), as a sign of the twelve tribes' commitment to the covenant. This bread was eaten only by the priests (Lev 24:5-9; see also 1 Sam 21:1-6).

25:31-40 a lampstand: This seven-branched candelabra is known as a menorah, one of the oldest symbols of Judaism. The lampstand is also associated with the temple in Jerusalem (see 1 Kgs 7:49; Zech 4:1-14). Its plant-like features recall the burning bush, where God

11 You shall overlay it with pure gold, inside and outside you shall overlay it, and you shall make a molding of gold upon it all around. 12 You
shall cast four rings of gold for it and put them on its four feet, two
rings on the one side of it, and two rings on the other side. 13 You shall
make poles of acacia wood, and overlay them with gold. 14 And you
shall put the poles into the rings on the sides of the ark, by which to
carry the ark. 15 The poles shall remain in the rings of the ark; they
shall not be taken from it. 16 You shall put into the ark the covenant[a]
that I shall give you.

17 Then you shall make a mercy seat[b] of pure gold; two cubits
and a half shall be its length, and a cubit and a half its width. 18 You
shall make two cherubim of gold; you shall make them of hammered
work, at the two ends of the mercy seat.[c] 19 Make one cherub at the one
end, and one cherub at the other; of one piece with the mercy seat[c]
you shall make the cherubim at its two ends. 20 The cherubim shall
spread out their wings above, overshadowing the mercy seat[c] with
their wings. They shall face one to another; the faces of the cherubim
shall be turned toward the mercy seat.[c] 21 You shall put the mercy seat[c]
on the top of the ark; and in the ark you shall put the covenant[a] that I
shall give you. 22 There I will meet with you, and from above the mercy
seat,[c] from between the two cherubim that are on the ark of the covenant,[a] I will deliver to you all my commands for the Israelites.

The Table for the Bread of the Presence

23 You shall make a table of acacia wood, two cubits long, one
cubit wide, and a cubit and a half high. 24 You shall overlay it with pure
gold, and make a molding of gold around it. 25 You shall make around
it a rim a handbreadth wide, and a molding of gold around the rim.
26 You shall make for it four rings of gold, and fasten the rings to the
four corners at its four legs. 27 The rings that hold the poles used for
carrying the table shall be close to the rim. 28 You shall make the poles
of acacia wood, and overlay them with gold, and the table shall be carried with these. 29 You shall make its plates and dishes for incense, and
its flagons and bowls with which to pour drink offerings; you shall
make them of pure gold. 30 And you shall set the bread of the Presence
on the table before me always.

The Lampstand

31 You shall make a lampstand of pure gold. The base and the
shaft of the lampstand shall be made of hammered work; its cups, its
calyxes, and its petals shall be of one piece with it; 32 and there shall be
six branches going out of its sides, three branches of the lampstand
out of one side of it and three branches of the lampstand out of the

[a] Or *treaty*, or *testimony*; Heb *eduth* [b] Or *a cover* [c] Or *the cover*

other side of it; [33]three cups shaped like almond blossoms, each with calyx and petals, on one branch, and three cups shaped like almond blossoms, each with calyx and petals, on the other branch—so for the six branches going out of the lampstand. [34]On the lampstand itself there shall be four cups shaped like almond blossoms, each with its calyxes and petals. [35]There shall be a calyx of one piece with it under the first pair of branches, a calyx of one piece with it under the next pair of branches, and a calyx of one piece with it under the last pair of branches—so for the six branches that go out of the lampstand. [36]Their calyxes and their branches shall be of one piece with it, the whole of it one hammered piece of pure gold. [37]You shall make the seven lamps for it; and the lamps shall be set up so as to give light on the space in front of it. [38]Its snuffers and trays shall be of pure gold. [39]It, and all these utensils, shall be made from a talent of pure gold. [40]And see that you make them according to the pattern for them, which is being shown you on the mountain.

appeared to Moses (3:1-3; see also 26:35; 27:20-21; 37:17-24; 39:37; 40:4, 24-25).

The cherubim and lampstand are works of beauty and craftsmanship. What place does art have in the worship of God today?

The Tabernacle

26 Moreover you shall make the tabernacle with ten curtains of fine twisted linen, and blue, purple, and crimson yarns; you shall make them with cherubim skillfully worked into them. [2]The length of each curtain shall be twenty-eight cubits, and the width of each curtain four cubits; all the curtains shall be of the same size. [3]Five curtains shall be joined to one another; and the other five curtains shall be joined to one another. [4]You shall make loops of blue on the edge of the outermost curtain in the first set; and likewise you shall make loops on the edge of the outermost curtain in the second set. [5]You shall make fifty loops on the one curtain, and you shall make fifty loops on the edge of the curtain that is in the second set; the loops shall be opposite one another. [6]You shall make fifty clasps of gold, and join the curtains to one another with the clasps, so that the tabernacle may be one whole.

7 You shall also make curtains of goats' hair for a tent over the tabernacle; you shall make eleven curtains. [8]The length of each curtain shall be thirty cubits, and the width of each curtain four cubits; the eleven curtains shall be of the same size. [9]You shall join five curtains by themselves, and six curtains by themselves, and the sixth curtain you shall double over at the front of the tent. [10]You shall make fifty loops on the edge of the curtain that is outermost in one set, and fifty loops on the edge of the curtain that is outermost in the second set.

11 You shall make fifty clasps of bronze, and put the clasps into the loops, and join the tent together, so that it may be one whole. [12]The part that remains of the curtains of the tent, the half curtain that remains, shall hang over the back of the tabernacle. [13]The cubit on the one side, and the cubit on the other side, of what remains in the length

26:1-14 curtains: Four layers cover the tabernacle, including fine inner curtains of linen decorated with cherubim, sturdier goat hair curtains to form a tent, and two outer leather layers for waterproofing. The curtains are made in segments, for easy transport (see 36:8-19).

26:1 cherubim: See note on 25:18.

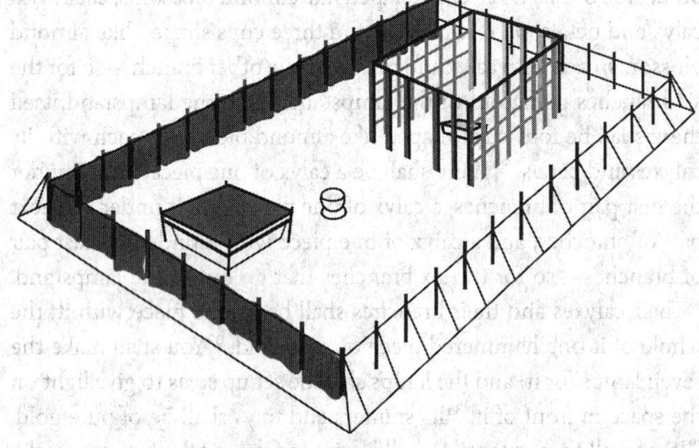

A view of the tabernacle showing its framework, the altar of burnt offering and the basin in the courtyard, and the curtain around the Holy of Holies.

of the curtains of the tent, shall hang over the sides of the tabernacle,
on this side and that side, to cover it. 14 You shall make for the tent a
covering of tanned rams' skins and an outer covering of fine leather.[a]

The Framework

26:15-30 frames: The framework of the tabernacle is made of detachable components for easy transport. The length of the tabernacle is placed on an east-west axis, with the opening to the east. Acacia wood was a hardwood from a desert tree.

15 You shall make upright frames of acacia wood for the tabernacle. 16 Ten cubits shall be the length of a frame, and a cubit and a half
the width of each frame. 17 There shall be two pegs in each frame to fit
the frames together; you shall make these for all the frames of the tabernacle. 18 You shall make the frames for the tabernacle: twenty frames
for the south side; 19 and you shall make forty bases of silver under the
twenty frames, two bases under the first frame for its two pegs, and
two bases under the next frame for its two pegs; 20 and for the second
side of the tabernacle, on the north side twenty frames, 21 and their
forty bases of silver, two bases under the first frame, and two bases
under the next frame; 22 and for the rear of the tabernacle westward
you shall make six frames. 23 You shall make two frames for corners of
the tabernacle in the rear; 24 they shall be separate beneath, but joined
at the top, at the first ring; it shall be the same with both of them; they
shall form the two corners. 25 And so there shall be eight frames, with
their bases of silver, sixteen bases; two bases under the first frame, and
two bases under the next frame.

26 You shall make bars of acacia wood, five for the frames of the
one side of the tabernacle, 27 and five bars for the frames of the other
side of the tabernacle, and five bars for the frames of the side of the tabernacle at the rear westward. 28 The middle bar, halfway up the frames,
shall pass through from end to end. 29 You shall overlay the frames with
gold, and shall make their rings of gold to hold the bars; and you shall
overlay the bars with gold. 30 Then you shall erect the tabernacle according to the plan for it that you were shown on the mountain.

[a] Meaning of Heb uncertain

The Curtain

31 You shall make a curtain of blue, purple, and crimson yarns, and of fine twisted linen; it shall be made with cherubim skillfully worked into it. [32]You shall hang it on four pillars of acacia overlaid with gold, which have hooks of gold and rest on four bases of silver. [33]You shall hang the curtain under the clasps, and bring the ark of the covenant[a] in there, within the curtain; and the curtain shall separate for you the holy place from the most holy. [34]You shall put the mercy seat[b] on the ark of the covenant[a] in the most holy place. [35]You shall set the table outside the curtain, and the lampstand on the south side of the tabernacle opposite the table; and you shall put the table on the north side.

36 You shall make a screen for the entrance of the tent, of blue, purple, and crimson yarns, and of fine twisted linen, embroidered with needlework. [37]You shall make for the screen five pillars of acacia, and overlay them with gold; their hooks shall be of gold, and you shall cast five bases of bronze for them.

26:31-34 the most holy: A curtain of material identical to the fine inner curtains (26:1) separates the Holy of Holies from the rest of the tabernacle. This western section of the tabernacle houses the ark of the covenant where God's presence dwells.

26:35-37 the table. . . the lampstand: These items are placed in the tabernacle outside the Holy of Holies. A screen on the eastern end separates the tabernacle from its courtyard.

The Altar of Burnt Offering

27 You shall make the altar of acacia wood, five cubits long and five cubits wide; the altar shall be square, and it shall be three cubits high. [2]You shall make horns for it on its four corners; its horns shall be of one piece with it, and you shall overlay it with bronze. [3]You shall make pots for it to receive its ashes, and shovels and basins and forks and firepans; you shall make all its utensils of bronze. [4]You shall also make for it a grating, a network of bronze; and on the net you shall make four bronze rings at its four corners. [5]You shall set it under the ledge of the altar so that the net shall extend halfway down the altar. [6]You shall make poles for the altar, poles of acacia wood, and overlay them with bronze; [7]the poles shall be put through the rings, so that the poles shall be on the two sides of the altar when it is carried. [8]You shall make it hollow, with boards. They shall be made just as you were shown on the mountain.

27:1-8 altar: A large altar and tools for burnt offerings (see 29:38-46) are to be set in the courtyard to the east of the tabernacle. The horns on the altar were projections on each corner of the altar, possibly representing God's strength (Num 23:22) or the animals sacrificed as burnt offerings.

The Court and Its Hangings

9 You shall make the court of the tabernacle. On the south side the court shall have hangings of fine twisted linen one hundred cubits long for that side; [10]its twenty pillars and their twenty bases shall be of bronze, but the hooks of the pillars and their bands shall be of silver. [11]Likewise for its length on the north side there shall be hangings one hundred cubits long, their pillars twenty and their bases twenty, of bronze, but the hooks of the pillars and their bands shall be of silver. [12]For the width of the court on the west side there shall be fifty cubits of hangings, with ten pillars and ten bases. [13]The width of the court on

27:9-19 court: The courtyard for the tabernacle will be 100 cubits long by 50 cubits wide or approximately 150 feet (45.72 meters) by 75 feet (22.86 meters), with an eastern entrance.

---

[a] Or *treaty*, or *testimony*; Heb *eduth* [b] Or *the cover*

the front to the east shall be fifty cubits. [14]There shall be fifteen cubits of hangings on the one side, with three pillars and three bases. [15]There shall be fifteen cubits of hangings on the other side, with three pillars and three bases. [16]For the gate of the court there shall be a screen twenty cubits long, of blue, purple, and crimson yarns, and of fine twisted linen, embroidered with needlework; it shall have four pillars and with them four bases. [17]All the pillars around the court shall be banded with silver; their hooks shall be of silver, and their bases of bronze. [18]The length of the court shall be one hundred cubits, the width fifty, and the height five cubits, with hangings of fine twisted linen and bases of bronze. [19]All the utensils of the tabernacle for every use, and all its pegs and all the pegs of the court, shall be of bronze.

The Oil for the Lamp

27:20-21 oil: Instructions are given for tending the lampstand (see 25:31-40).

20 You shall further command the Israelites to bring you pure oil of beaten olives for the light, so that a lamp may be set up to burn regularly. [21]In the tent of meeting, outside the curtain that is before the covenant,[a] Aaron and his sons shall tend it from evening to morning before the LORD. It shall be a perpetual ordinance to be observed throughout their generations by the Israelites.

Vestments for the Priesthood

28:1-43 sacred vestments: Special pieces of clothing would be worn by Aaron as high priest (see 29:5-6) and by his sons (see 29:8-9) when they entered the tabernacle or approached the altar. An ephod is the vest to be worn by the high priest when approaching God as a representative of Israel. The breastpiece is a square pocket worn over the ephod, set with rows of gems bearing the names of the twelve tribes of Israel. Urim and Thummim, placed in this pocket, are objects that were cast as lots to reach judgments (see 1 Sam 14:41).

28 Then bring near to you your brother Aaron, and his sons with him, from among the Israelites, to serve me as priests—Aaron and Aaron's sons, Nadab and Abihu, Eleazar and Ithamar. [2]You shall make sacred vestments for the glorious adornment of your brother Aaron. [3]And you shall speak to all who have ability, whom I have endowed with skill, that they make Aaron's vestments to consecrate him for my priesthood. [4]These are the vestments that they shall make: a breastpiece, an ephod, a robe, a checkered tunic, a turban, and a sash. When they make these sacred vestments for your brother Aaron and his sons to serve me as priests, [5]they shall use gold, blue, purple, and crimson yarns, and fine linen.

The Ephod

6 They shall make the ephod of gold, of blue, purple, and crimson yarns, and of fine twisted linen, skillfully worked. [7]It shall have two shoulder-pieces attached to its two edges, so that it may be joined together. [8]The decorated band on it shall be of the same workmanship and materials, of gold, of blue, purple, and crimson yarns, and of fine twisted linen. [9]You shall take two onyx stones, and engrave on them the names of the sons of Israel, [10]six of their names on the one stone, and the names of the remaining six on the other stone, in the order of their birth. [11]As a gem-cutter engraves signets, so you shall engrave

[a] Or *treaty*, or *testimony*; Heb *eduth*

the two stones with the names of the sons of Israel; you shall mount them in settings of gold filigree. [12]You shall set the two stones on the shoulder-pieces of the ephod, as stones of remembrance for the sons of Israel; and Aaron shall bear their names before the LORD on his two shoulders for remembrance. [13]You shall make settings of gold filigree, [14]and two chains of pure gold, twisted like cords; and you shall attach the corded chains to the settings.

The Breastplate

15 You shall make a breastpiece of judgment, in skilled work; you shall make it in the style of the ephod; of gold, of blue and purple and crimson yarns, and of fine twisted linen you shall make it. [16]It shall be square and doubled, a span in length and a span in width. [17]You shall set in it four rows of stones. A row of carnelian,[a] chrysolite, and emerald shall be the first row; [18]and the second row a turquoise, a sapphire,[b] and a moonstone; [19]and the third row a jacinth, an agate, and an amethyst; [20]and the fourth row a beryl, an onyx, and a jasper; they shall be set in gold filigree. [21]There shall be twelve stones with names corresponding to the names of the sons of Israel; they shall be like signets, each engraved with its name, for the twelve tribes. [22]You shall make for the breastpiece chains of pure gold, twisted like cords; [23]and you shall make for the breastpiece two rings of gold, and put the two rings on the two edges of the breastpiece. [24]You shall put the two cords of gold in the two rings at the edges of the breastpiece; [25]the two ends of the two cords you shall attach to the two settings, and so attach it in front to the shoulder-pieces of the ephod. [26]You shall make two rings of gold, and put them at the two ends of the breastpiece, on its inside edge next to the ephod. [27]You shall make two rings of gold, and attach them in front to the lower part of the two shoulder-pieces of the ephod, at its joining above the decorated band of the ephod. [28]The breastpiece shall be bound by its rings to the rings of the ephod with a blue cord, so that it may lie on the decorated band of the ephod, and so that the breastpiece shall not come loose from the ephod. [29]So Aaron shall bear the names of the sons of Israel in the breastpiece of judgment on his heart when he goes into the holy place, for a continual remembrance before the LORD. [30]In the breastpiece of judgment you shall put the Urim and the Thummim, and they shall be on Aaron's heart when he goes in before the LORD; thus Aaron shall bear the judgment of the Israelites on his heart before the LORD continually.

Other Priestly Vestments

31 You shall make the robe of the ephod all of blue. [32]It shall have an opening for the head in the middle of it, with a woven binding

[a] The identity of several of these stones is uncertain [b] Or *lapis lazuli*

around the opening, like the opening in a coat of mail,[a] so that it may
not be torn. 33 On its lower hem you shall make pomegranates of blue,
purple, and crimson yarns, all around the lower hem, with bells of
gold between them all around— 34 a golden bell and a pomegranate
alternating all around the lower hem of the robe. 35 Aaron shall wear
it when he ministers, and its sound shall be heard when he goes into
the holy place before the LORD, and when he comes out, so that he
may not die.

36 You shall make a rosette of pure gold, and engrave on it, like
the engraving of a signet, "Holy to the LORD." 37 You shall fasten it on
the turban with a blue cord; it shall be on the front of the turban. 38 It
shall be on Aaron's forehead, and Aaron shall take on himself any guilt
incurred in the holy offering that the Israelites consecrate as their sacred donations; it shall always be on his forehead, in order that they
may find favor before the LORD.

39 You shall make the checkered tunic of fine linen, and you shall
make a turban of fine linen, and you shall make a sash embroidered
with needlework.

40 For Aaron's sons you shall make tunics and sashes and headdresses; you shall make them for their glorious adornment. 41 You
shall put them on your brother Aaron, and on his sons with him, and
shall anoint them and ordain them and consecrate them, so that they
may serve me as priests. 42 You shall make for them linen undergarments to cover their naked flesh; they shall reach from the hips to the
thighs; 43 Aaron and his sons shall wear them when they go into the
tent of meeting, or when they come near the altar to minister in
the holy place; or they will bring guilt on themselves and die. This shall
be a perpetual ordinance for him and for his descendants after him.

28:41 ordain: This word literally means to "fill the hands" or hand over a responsibility.

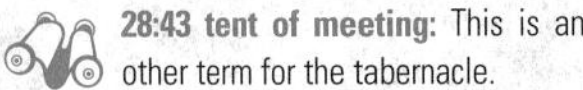

28:43 tent of meeting: This is another term for the tabernacle.

The Ordination of the Priests

29 Now this is what you shall do to them to consecrate them,
so that they may serve me as priests. Take one young bull
and two rams without blemish, 2 and unleavened bread, unleavened
cakes mixed with oil, and unleavened wafers spread with oil. You
shall make them of choice wheat flour. 3 You shall put them in one
basket and bring them in the basket, and bring the bull and the two
rams. 4 You shall bring Aaron and his sons to the entrance of the tent
of meeting, and wash them with water. 5 Then you shall take the vestments, and put on Aaron the tunic and the robe of the ephod, and the
ephod, and the breastpiece, and gird him with the decorated band of
the ephod; 6 and you shall set the turban on his head, and put the holy
diadem on the turban. 7 You shall take the anointing oil, and pour it
on his head and anoint him. 8 Then you shall bring his sons, and put
tunics on them, 9 and you shall gird them with sashes[b] and tie head-

29:1-37 ordain Aaron and his sons: These instructions for consecrating Aaron and his sons for priestly service to God include washing, installing, and anointing, followed by sacrifices of a bull and two rams. This ordain takes place in Leviticus 8–9.

29:9 ordination: See note on 28:41.

---

[a] Meaning of Heb uncertain [b] Gk: Heb *sashes, Aaron and his sons*

dresses on them; and the priesthood shall be theirs by a perpetual
ordinance. You shall then ordain Aaron and his sons.

10 You shall bring the bull in front of the tent of meeting. Aaron
and his sons shall lay their hands on the head of the bull, 11 and you
shall slaughter the bull before the LORD, at the entrance of the tent
of meeting, 12 and shall take some of the blood of the bull and put it
on the horns of the altar with your finger, and all the rest of the blood
you shall pour out at the base of the altar. 13 You shall take all the fat
that covers the entrails, and the appendage of the liver, and the two
kidneys with the fat that is on them, and turn them into smoke on the
altar. 14 But the flesh of the bull, and its skin, and its dung, you shall
burn with fire outside the camp; it is a sin offering.

15 Then you shall take one of the rams, and Aaron and his sons
shall lay their hands on the head of the ram, 16 and you shall slaughter
the ram, and shall take its blood and dash it against all sides of the
altar. 17 Then you shall cut the ram into its parts, and wash its entrails
and its legs, and put them with its parts and its head, 18 and turn the
whole ram into smoke on the altar; it is a burnt offering to the LORD;
it is a pleasing odor, an offering by fire to the LORD.

19 You shall take the other ram; and Aaron and his sons shall lay
their hands on the head of the ram, 20 and you shall slaughter the ram,
and take some of its blood and put it on the lobe of Aaron's right ear
and on the lobes of the right ears of his sons, and on the thumbs of
their right hands, and on the big toes of their right feet, and dash the
rest of the blood against all sides of the altar. 21 Then you shall take
some of the blood that is on the altar, and some of the anointing oil,
and sprinkle it on Aaron and his vestments and on his sons and his
sons' vestments with him; then he and his vestments shall be holy, as
well as his sons and his sons' vestments.

22 You shall also take the fat of the ram, the fat tail, the fat that
covers the entrails, the appendage of the liver, the two kidneys with
the fat that is on them, and the right thigh (for it is a ram of ordination), 23 and one loaf of bread, one cake of bread made with oil, and
one wafer, out of the basket of unleavened bread that is before the
LORD; 24 and you shall place all these on the palms of Aaron and on
the palms of his sons, and raise them as an elevation offering before
the LORD. 25 Then you shall take them from their hands, and turn
them into smoke on the altar on top of the burnt offering of pleasing
odor before the LORD; it is an offering by fire to the LORD.

26 You shall take the breast of the ram of Aaron's ordination and
raise it as an elevation offering before the LORD; and it shall be your
portion. 27 You shall consecrate the breast that was raised as an elevation offering and the thigh that was raised as an elevation offering
from the ram of ordination, from that which belonged to Aaron and
his sons. 28 These things shall be a perpetual ordinance for Aaron and

29:10-14 sin offering: A bull will be slaughtered for the cleansing and forgiveness of Aaron and his sons, and the cleansing of the altar (29:36-37), to purify them for holy service to God.

29:15-18 burnt offering: One ram is burnt whole as an offering by fire, after its blood is dashed against the altar.

29:19-31 ram of ordination: The blood of the second ram purifies Aaron, his sons, and their vestments, while select parts are presented to God and eaten by the priests as a well-being offering (Lev 3).

his sons from the Israelites, for this is an offering; and it shall be an
offering by the Israelites from their sacrifice of offerings of well-being,
their offering to the LORD.

29 The sacred vestments of Aaron shall be passed on to his sons
after him; they shall be anointed in them and ordained in them. [30]The
son who is priest in his place shall wear them seven days, when he
comes into the tent of meeting to minister in the holy place.

31 You shall take the ram of ordination, and boil its flesh in a
holy place; [32]and Aaron and his sons shall eat the flesh of the ram and
the bread that is in the basket, at the entrance of the tent of meeting.
[33]They themselves shall eat the food by which atonement is made, to
ordain and consecrate them, but no one else shall eat of them, because they are holy. [34]If any of the flesh for the ordination, or of the
bread, remains until the morning, then you shall burn the remainder
with fire; it shall not be eaten, because it is holy.

35 Thus you shall do to Aaron and to his sons, just as I have commanded you; through seven days you shall ordain them. [36]Also every
day you shall offer a bull as a sin offering for atonement. Also you shall
offer a sin offering for the altar, when you make atonement for it, and
shall anoint it, to consecrate it. [37]Seven days you shall make atonement for the altar, and consecrate it, and the altar shall be most holy;
whatever touches the altar shall become holy.

The Daily Offerings

29:38-45 lamb: Twice a day, a lamb is offered on the altar in the tabernacle courtyard, along with offerings of grain, oil, and wine, so that God may dwell among the Israelites and be their God.

38 Now this is what you shall offer on the altar: two lambs a year
old regularly each day. [39]One lamb you shall offer in the morning, and
the other lamb you shall offer in the evening; [40]and with the first lamb
one-tenth of a measure of choice flour mixed with one-fourth of a
hin of beaten oil, and one-fourth of a hin of wine for a drink offering.
[41]And the other lamb you shall offer in the evening, and shall offer
with it a grain offering and its drink offering, as in the morning, for
a pleasing odor, an offering by fire to the LORD. [42]It shall be a regular
burnt offering throughout your generations at the entrance of the tent
of meeting before the LORD, where I will meet with you, to speak to
you there. [43]I will meet with the Israelites there, and it shall be sanctified by my glory; [44]I will consecrate the tent of meeting and the altar;
Aaron also and his sons I will consecrate, to serve me as priests. [45]I
will dwell among the Israelites, and I will be their God. [46]And they
shall know that I am the LORD their God, who brought them out of
the land of Egypt that I might dwell among them; I am the LORD their
God.

29:43 glory: This refers to God's presence dwelling in the sanctuary.

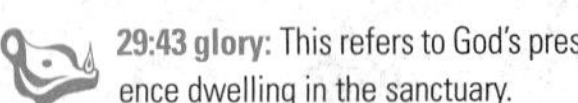

30:1-10 incense: Aaron will offer incense twice daily on a small altar outside the curtain separating the Holy of Holies. He will perform an atonement rite once a year, most likely on the day of Atonement (see Lev 16).

The Altar of Incense

30 You shall make an altar on which to offer incense; you shall
make it of acacia wood. [2]It shall be one cubit long, and one

cubit wide; it shall be square, and shall be two cubits high; its horns
shall be of one piece with it. 3You shall overlay it with pure gold, its
top, and its sides all around and its horns; and you shall make for it a
molding of gold all around. 4And you shall make two golden rings for
it; under its molding on two opposite sides of it you shall make them,
and they shall hold the poles with which to carry it. 5You shall make
the poles of acacia wood, and overlay them with gold. 6You shall place
it in front of the curtain that is above the ark of the covenant,[a] in front
of the mercy seat[b] that is over the covenant,[a] where I will meet with
you. 7Aaron shall offer fragrant incense on it; every morning when he
dresses the lamps he shall offer it, 8and when Aaron sets up the lamps
in the evening, he shall offer it, a regular incense offering before the
LORD throughout your generations. 9You shall not offer unholy incense on it, or a burnt offering, or a grain offering; and you shall not
pour a drink offering on it. 10Once a year Aaron shall perform the rite
of atonement on its horns. Throughout your generations he shall perform the atonement for it once a year with the blood of the atoning
sin offering. It is most holy to the LORD.

The Half Shekel for the Sanctuary

11 The LORD spoke to Moses: 12When you take a census of the
Israelites to register them, at registration all of them shall give a ransom for their lives to the LORD, so that no plague may come upon
them for being registered. 13This is what each one who is registered
shall give: half a shekel according to the shekel of the sanctuary (the
shekel is twenty gerahs), half a shekel as an offering to the LORD.
14Each one who is registered, from twenty years old and upward, shall
give the LORD's offering. 15The rich shall not give more, and the poor
shall not give less, than the half shekel, when you bring this offering
to the LORD to make atonement for your lives. 16You shall take the
atonement money from the Israelites and shall designate it for the service of the tent of meeting; before the LORD it will be a reminder to
the Israelites of the ransom given for your lives.

30:11-16 half a shekel: See note on 25:1-9. This offering from all males twenty years and older protected them from the harm associated with taking a census (see 2 Sam 24).

The Bronze Basin

17 The LORD spoke to Moses: 18You shall make a bronze basin
with a bronze stand for washing. You shall put it between the tent of
meeting and the altar, and you shall put water in it; 19with the water[c]
Aaron and his sons shall wash their hands and their feet. 20When
they go into the tent of meeting, or when they come near the altar
to minister, to make an offering by fire to the LORD, they shall wash
with water, so that they may not die. 21They shall wash their hands
and their feet, so that they may not die: it shall be a perpetual ordi-

30:17-21 bronze basin: Priests were required to do a ritual washing of hands and feet before serving in the tabernacle or at the altar.

[a] Or *treaty*, or *testimony*; Heb *eduth* [b] Or *the cover* [c] Heb *it*

nance for them, for him and for his descendants throughout their
generations.

The Anointing Oil and Incense

30:22-38 anointing oil: Instructions are given for preparing the holy oil used for anointing the tabernacle, furnishings, and priests, and for making the holy incense burned in the tabernacle.

22 The LORD spoke to Moses: [23]Take the finest spices: of liquid
myrrh five hundred shekels, and of sweet-smelling cinnamon half as
much, that is, two hundred fifty, and two hundred fifty of aromatic
cane, [24]and five hundred of cassia—measured by the sanctuary
shekel—and a hin of olive oil; [25]and you shall make of these a sacred
anointing oil blended as by the perfumer; it shall be a holy anointing
oil. [26]With it you shall anoint the tent of meeting and the ark of the
covenant,[a] [27]and the table and all its utensils, and the lampstand and
its utensils, and the altar of incense, [28]and the altar of burnt offering
with all its utensils, and the basin with its stand; [29]you shall consecrate them, so that they may be most holy; whatever touches them
will become holy. [30]You shall anoint Aaron and his sons, and consecrate them, in order that they may serve me as priests. [31]You shall say
to the Israelites, "This shall be my holy anointing oil throughout your
generations. [32]It shall not be used in any ordinary anointing of the
body, and you shall make no other like it in composition; it is holy,
and it shall be holy to you. [33]Whoever compounds any like it or whoever puts any of it on an unqualified person shall be cut off from the
people."

34 The LORD said to Moses: Take sweet spices, stacte, and on-
ycha, and galbanum, sweet spices with pure frankincense (an equal
part of each), [35]and make an incense blended as by the perfumer,
seasoned with salt, pure and holy; [36]and you shall beat some of it
into powder, and put part of it before the covenant[a] in the tent of
meeting where I shall meet with you; it shall be for you most holy.
[37]When you make incense according to this composition, you shall
not make it for yourselves; it shall be regarded by you as holy to the
LORD. [38]Whoever makes any like it to use as perfume shall be cut off
from the people.

Bezalel and Oholiab

31:1-11 the skillful: Bezalel (in Hebrew, "in the shade of God") and Oholiab (in Hebrew, "my tent is [my] father" (meaning God) are inspired and skilled artisans called by God to make all of the objects described in Exodus 25–30. The importance of the Jerusalem temple, located in the region of Judah, is foreshadowed in Bezalel, who comes from the tribe of Judah.

31 The LORD spoke to Moses: [2]See, I have called by name Bezalel son of Uri son of Hur, of the tribe of Judah: [3]and I have
filled him with divine spirit,[b] with ability, intelligence, and knowledge
in every kind of craft, [4]to devise artistic designs, to work in gold, silver, and bronze, [5]in cutting stones for setting, and in carving wood,
in every kind of craft. [6]Moreover, I have appointed with him Oholiab
son of Ahisamach, of the tribe of Dan; and I have given skill to all the
skillful, so that they may make all that I have commanded you: [7]the

[a] Or *treaty*, or *testimony*; Heb *eduth* [b] Or *with the spirit of God*

tent of meeting, and the ark of the covenant,[a] and the mercy seat[b] that
is on it, and all the furnishings of the tent, 8the table and its utensils,
and the pure lampstand with all its utensils, and the altar of incense,
9and the altar of burnt offering with all its utensils, and the basin with
its stand, 10and the finely worked vestments, the holy vestments for
the priest Aaron and the vestments of his sons, for their service as
priests, 11and the anointing oil and the fragrant incense for the holy
place. They shall do just as I have commanded you.

The Sabbath Law

12 The LORD said to Moses: 13You yourself are to speak to the
Israelites: "You shall keep my sabbaths, for this is a sign between me
and you throughout your generations, given in order that you may
know that I, the LORD, sanctify you. 14You shall keep the sabbath,
because it is holy for you; everyone who profanes it shall be put to
death; whoever does any work on it shall be cut off from among the
people. 15Six days shall work be done, but the seventh day is a sabbath of solemn rest, holy to the LORD; whoever does any work on the
sabbath day shall be put to death. 16Therefore the Israelites shall keep
the sabbath, observing the sabbath throughout their generations, as a
perpetual covenant. 17It is a sign forever between me and the people
of Israel that in six days the LORD made heaven and earth, and on the
seventh day he rested, and was refreshed."

The Two Tablets of the Covenant

18 When God[c] finished speaking with Moses on Mount Sinai,
he gave him the two tablets of the covenant,[a] tablets of stone, written
with the finger of God.

The Golden Calf

32 When the people saw that Moses delayed to come down
from the mountain, the people gathered around Aaron, and
said to him, "Come, make gods for us, who shall go before us; as for
this Moses, the man who brought us up out of the land of Egypt, we
do not know what has become of him." 2Aaron said to them, "Take off
the gold rings that are on the ears of your wives, your sons, and your
daughters, and bring them to me." 3So all the people took off the gold
rings from their ears, and brought them to Aaron. 4He took the gold
from them, formed it in a mold,[d] and cast an image of a calf; and they
said, "These are your gods, O Israel, who brought you up out of the
land of Egypt!" 5When Aaron saw this, he built an altar before it; and
Aaron made proclamation and said, "Tomorrow shall be a festival to

[a] Or *treaty*, or *testimony*; Heb *eduth* [b] Or *the cover* [c] Heb *he* [d] Or *fashioned it with a graving tool*; Meaning of Heb uncertain

31:12-17 sabbath: This holy day of rest is an eternal sign of the covenant between God and Israel, through which God sanctifies the people. See also 16:22-26; 20:8-11; 34:21; 35:1-2.

31:18 tablets of the covenant: These tablets contain the law and Commandments that God gives for Israel's instruction. See also 24:12.

32:1-35 image of a calf: The Israelites set up and worship another god at the foot of Mount Sinai, at the very moment Moses is receiving the Torah or law. This is the central sin in the Bible, according to the Jewish faith.

What "false gods" exist today? What gods do you worship?

32:4 These are your gods, O Israel, who brought you up out of the land of Egypt: Aaron falsely claims that other gods, not the LORD, freed the Israelites from slavery in Egypt. This episode foreshadows the time later when Jeroboam I, first king of the Northern Kingdom, sets up calves, probably representing the animal mounts of the invisible God Yahweh, at shrines at Bethel and Dan. He declares, "You have gone up to Jerusalem long enough. Here are your gods, O Israel, who brought you up out of the land of Egypt" (1 Kgs 12:28). Worship at these shrines is known after that as the "sin of Jeroboam."

the LORD." 6They rose early the next day, and offered burnt offerings and brought sacrifices of well-being; and the people sat down to eat and drink, and rose up to revel.

7 The LORD said to Moses, "Go down at once! Your people, whom you brought up out of the land of Egypt, have acted perversely; 8they have been quick to turn aside from the way that I commanded them; they have cast for themselves an image of a calf, and have worshiped it and sacrificed to it, and said, 'These are your gods, O Israel, who brought you up out of the land of Egypt!'" 9The LORD said to Moses, "I have seen this people, how stiff-necked they are. 10Now let me alone, so that my wrath may burn hot against them and I may consume them; and of you I will make a great nation."

11 But Moses implored the LORD his God, and said, "O LORD, why does your wrath burn hot against your people, whom you brought out of the land of Egypt with great power and with a mighty hand? 12Why should the Egyptians say, 'It was with evil intent that he brought them out to kill them in the mountains, and to consume them from the face of the earth'? Turn from your fierce wrath; change your mind and do not bring disaster on your people. 13Remember Abraham, Isaac, and Israel, your servants, how you swore to them by your own self, saying to them, 'I will multiply your descendants like the stars of heaven, and all this land that I have promised I will give to your descendants, and they shall inherit it forever.'" 14And the LORD changed his mind about the disaster that he planned to bring on his people.

15 Then Moses turned and went down from the mountain, carrying the two tablets of the covenant[a] in his hands, tablets that were written on both sides, written on the front and on the back. 16The tablets were the work of God, and the writing was the writing of God, engraved upon the tablets. 17When Joshua heard the noise of the people as they shouted, he said to Moses, "There is a noise of war in the camp." 18But he said,

"It is not the sound made by victors,
or the sound made by losers;
it is the sound of revelers that I hear."

19As soon as he came near the camp and saw the calf and the dancing, Moses' anger burned hot, and he threw the tablets from his hands and broke them at the foot of the mountain. 20He took the calf that they had made, burned it with fire, ground it to powder, scattered it on the water, and made the Israelites drink it.

21 Moses said to Aaron, "What did this people do to you that you have brought so great a sin upon them?" 22And Aaron said, "Do not let the anger of my lord burn hot; you know the people, that they are

32:7 Your people, whom you brought up: This statement puts distance between God and the Israelites, by holding Moses responsible for them.

32:11-14 Moses implored the LORD: Moses' role as a prophet includes being a mediator between God and the people (see also 32:30-32). Here Moses pleads with God on the Israelites' behalf. God's reputation is at stake, Moses claims, because other nations will say God led the people into the wilderness to kill them. (Earlier in Exodus, God says the purpose of the plagues is to show the LORD's power to Pharaoh, the rest of the Egyptians, and other nations, as well as to Israel.) Moses also appeals to God's faithfulness to the promises made to Abraham, Isaac, and Jacob, which would be broken if the people were wiped out.

32:15-20 threw the tablets: In his anger, Moses shatters the two tablets of the covenant, which contain the Commandments.

---

[a] Or *treaty*, or *testimony*; Heb *eduth*

bent on evil. 23 They said to me, 'Make us gods, who shall go before
us; as for this Moses, the man who brought us up out of the land of
Egypt, we do not know what has become of him.' 24 So I said to them,
'Whoever has gold, take it off'; so they gave it to me, and I threw it
into the fire, and out came this calf!"

25 When Moses saw that the people were running wild (for
Aaron had let them run wild, to the derision of their enemies), 26 then
Moses stood in the gate of the camp, and said, "Who is on the LORD's
side? Come to me!" And all the sons of Levi gathered around him.
27 He said to them, "Thus says the LORD, the God of Israel, 'Put your
sword on your side, each of you! Go back and forth from gate to gate
throughout the camp, and each of you kill your brother, your friend,
and your neighbor.'" 28 The sons of Levi did as Moses commanded,
and about three thousand of the people fell on that day. 29 Moses said,
"Today you have ordained yourselves[a] for the service of the LORD,
each one at the cost of a son or a brother, and so have brought a blessing on yourselves this day."

32:25-29 the people were running wild: The Levites remain loyal to Moses, who calls them to execute punishment. They kill three thousand Israelites before a plague breaks out (32:35).

30 On the next day Moses said to the people, "You have sinned a
great sin. But now I will go up to the LORD; perhaps I can make atonement for your sin." 31 So Moses returned to the LORD and said, "Alas,
this people has sinned a great sin; they have made for themselves gods
of gold. 32 But now, if you will only forgive their sin—but if not, blot
me out of the book that you have written." 33 But the LORD said to
Moses, "Whoever has sinned against me I will blot out of my book.
34 But now go, lead the people to the place about which I have spoken
to you; see, my angel shall go in front of you. Nevertheless, when the
day comes for punishment, I will punish them for their sin."

35 Then the LORD sent a plague on the people, because they
made the calf—the one that Aaron made.

The Command to Leave Sinai

33 The LORD said to Moses, "Go, leave this place, you and the
people whom you have brought up out of the land of Egypt,
and go to the land of which I swore to Abraham, Isaac, and Jacob,
saying, 'To your descendants I will give it.' 2 I will send an angel before
you, and I will drive out the Canaanites, the Amorites, the Hittites,
the Perizzites, the Hivites, and the Jebusites. 3 Go up to a land flowing
with milk and honey; but I will not go up among you, or I would consume you on the way, for you are a stiff-necked people."

33:1-3 Go, leave this place: God commands Moses and the people to leave Sinai and go to the land promised to Abraham, Isaac, and Jacob. God's presence will not be with them, because the LORD's anger (over the making of the golden calf) would destroy them.

4 When the people heard these harsh words, they mourned, and
no one put on ornaments. 5 For the LORD had said to Moses, "Say to
the Israelites, 'You are a stiff-necked people; if for a single moment I
should go up among you, I would consume you. So now take off your

---

[a] Gk Vg Compare Tg: Heb *Today ordain yourselves*

ornaments, and I will decide what to do to you.' " 6Therefore the Israelites stripped themselves of their ornaments, from Mount Horeb onward.

33:7-11 tent of meeting: This tent is used before the tabernacle is constructed. Here Moses speaks face to face with God, as with a friend (see also Num 12:8; Deut 34:10). In Exodus 34:29, a direct encounter with God is implied. A different tradition in 33:20-23 claims that no one can see God's face and live.

33:11 Joshua son of Nun: Joshua is Moses' assistant and would lead the people after Moses' death.

The Tent outside the Camp

7 Now Moses used to take the tent and pitch it outside the camp, far off from the camp; he called it the tent of meeting. And everyone who sought the LORD would go out to the tent of meeting, which was outside the camp. 8Whenever Moses went out to the tent, all the people would rise and stand, each of them, at the entrance of their tents and watch Moses until he had gone into the tent. 9When Moses entered the tent, the pillar of cloud would descend and stand at the entrance of the tent, and the LORD would speak with Moses. 10When all the people saw the pillar of cloud standing at the entrance of the tent, all the people would rise and bow down, all of them, at the entrance of their tent. 11Thus the LORD used to speak to Moses face to face, as one speaks to a friend. Then he would return to the camp; but his young assistant, Joshua son of Nun, would not leave the tent.

33:14 My presence will go with you: God promises to go with the people as they leave Sinai (see also 34:9, where Moses asks the LORD to go with the people).

33:18-19 Show me your glory: God's presence in a sanctuary or another place is sometimes described as a cloud or thick smoke. Moses asks to see God's glory, but is shown God's goodness. For God's name, see note on 3:14.

33:23 see my back: Moses is protected from the danger of full exposure to the LORD's presence.

Moses' Intercession

12 Moses said to the LORD, "See, you have said to me, 'Bring up this people'; but you have not let me know whom you will send with me. Yet you have said, 'I know you by name, and you have also found favor in my sight.' 13Now if I have found favor in your sight, show me your ways, so that I may know you and find favor in your sight. Consider too that this nation is your people." 14He said, "My presence will go with you, and I will give you rest." 15And he said to him, "If your presence will not go, do not carry us up from here. 16For how shall it be known that I have found favor in your sight, I and your people, unless you go with us? In this way, we shall be distinct, I and your people, from every people on the face of the earth."

17 The LORD said to Moses, "I will do the very thing that you have asked; for you have found favor in my sight, and I know you by name." 18Moses said, "Show me your glory, I pray." 19And he said, "I will make all my goodness pass before you, and will proclaim before you the name, 'The LORD';[a] and I will be gracious to whom I will be gracious, and will show mercy on whom I will show mercy. 20But," he said, "you cannot see my face; for no one shall see me and live." 21And the LORD continued, "See, there is a place by me where you shall stand on the rock; 22and while my glory passes by I will put you in a cleft of the rock, and I will cover you with my hand until I have passed by; 23then I will take away my hand, and you shall see my back; but my face shall not be seen."

[a] Heb *YHWH*; see note at 3.15

Moses Makes New Tablets

34

The LORD said to Moses, "Cut two tablets of stone like the former ones, and I will write on the tablets the words that were on the former tablets, which you broke. 2 Be ready in the morning, and come up in the morning to Mount Sinai and present yourself there to me, on the top of the mountain. 3 No one shall come up with you, and do not let anyone be seen throughout all the mountain; and do not let flocks or herds graze in front of that mountain." 4 So Moses cut two tablets of stone like the former ones; and he rose early in the morning and went up on Mount Sinai, as the LORD had commanded him, and took in his hand the two tablets of stone. 5 The LORD descended in the cloud and stood with him there, and proclaimed the name, "The LORD."[a] 6 The LORD passed before him, and proclaimed,

"The LORD, the LORD,
a God merciful and gracious,
slow to anger,
and abounding in steadfast love and faithfulness,
7 keeping steadfast love for the thousandth generation,[b]
forgiving iniquity and transgression and sin,
yet by no means clearing the guilty,
but visiting the iniquity of the parents
upon the children
and the children's children,
to the third and the fourth generation."

8 And Moses quickly bowed his head toward the earth, and worshiped. 9 He said, "If now I have found favor in your sight, O Lord, I pray, let the Lord go with us. Although this is a stiff-necked people, pardon our iniquity and our sin, and take us for your inheritance."

The Covenant Renewed

10 He said: I hereby make a covenant. Before all your people I will perform marvels, such as have not been performed in all the earth or in any nation; and all the people among whom you live shall see the work of the LORD; for it is an awesome thing that I will do with you.

11 Observe what I command you today. See, I will drive out before you the Amorites, the Canaanites, the Hittites, the Perizzites, the Hivites, and the Jebusites. 12 Take care not to make a covenant with the inhabitants of the land to which you are going, or it will become a snare among you. 13 You shall tear down their altars, break their pillars, and cut down their sacred poles[c] 14 (for you shall worship no other god, because the LORD, whose name is Jealous, is a jealous God). 15 You shall not make a covenant with the inhabitants of the land, for when they prostitute themselves to their gods and sacrifice to their

---

[a] Heb *YHWH*; see note at 3.15 [b] Or *for thousands* [c] Heb *Asherim*

34:1-28 I hereby make a covenant: God renews the covenant after the golden calf episode. This sets a precedent for renewing the covenant periodically, before Moses' death (Deut 29–30), in the next generation (twice, Josh 4–5, 24), during King Josiah's reform in the seventh century (2 Kgs 22–23), and after the exile to Babylonia (Neh 8–10).

34:1 two tablets of stone: The Ten Commandments, literally the "ten words" (Exod 34:28), would be written again, on new tablets.

34:5-7 proclaimed the name: The LORD declares God's name and character, with a description ("merciful and gracious, slow to anger") used many times in the Old Testament (Num 14:18; Neh 9:17; Pss 86:15; 103:8; 145:8; Joel 2:13; Jonah 4:2; Nah 1:3).

gods, someone among them will invite you, and you will eat of the
sacrifice. 16 And you will take wives from among their daughters for
your sons, and their daughters who prostitute themselves to their
gods will make your sons also prostitute themselves to their gods.

17 You shall not make cast idols.

18 You shall keep the festival of unleavened bread. Seven days you shall eat unleavened bread, as I commanded you, at the time appointed in the month of Abib; for in the month of Abib you came out from Egypt.

19 All that first opens the womb is mine, all your male[a] livestock,
the firstborn of cow and sheep. 20 The firstborn of a donkey you shall
redeem with a lamb, or if you will not redeem it you shall break its
neck. All the firstborn of your sons you shall redeem.

No one shall appear before me empty-handed.

21 Six days you shall work, but on the seventh day you shall rest;
even in plowing time and in harvest time you shall rest. 22 You shall
observe the festival of weeks, the first fruits of wheat harvest, and the
festival of ingathering at the turn of the year. 23 Three times in the year
all your males shall appear before the LORD God, the God of Israel.
24 For I will cast out nations before you, and enlarge your borders; no
one shall covet your land when you go up to appear before the LORD
your God three times in the year.

25 You shall not offer the blood of my sacrifice with leaven, and the sacrifice of the festival of the passover shall not be left until the morning.

26 The best of the first fruits of your ground you shall bring to the house of the LORD your God.

You shall not boil a kid in its mother's milk.

27 The LORD said to Moses: Write these words; in accordance
with these words I have made a covenant with you and with Israel.
28 He was there with the LORD forty days and forty nights; he neither
ate bread nor drank water. And he wrote on the tablets the words of
the covenant, the ten commandments.[b]

34:27-28 Write these words: These are "ten words" or ten commandments. Two versions of the Ten Commandments are presented in Exodus 20:1-17 and Deuteronomy 5:6-21 (with an additional set of ritual ten commandments presented in Exod 34:10-28).

The Shining Face of Moses

29 Moses came down from Mount Sinai. As he came down
from the mountain with the two tablets of the covenant[c] in his
hand, Moses did not know that the skin of his face shone because
he had been talking with God. 30 When Aaron and all the Israelites
saw Moses, the skin of his face was shining, and they were afraid to
come near him. 31 But Moses called to them; and Aaron and all the
leaders of the congregation returned to him, and Moses spoke with

34:29-35 the skin of his face shone: See note on 33:7-11. The people see God's glory through the reflection on Moses' face. The veil protects them, because even the reflected radiance is unbearable to look at.

[a] Gk Theodotion Vg Tg: Meaning of Heb uncertain [b] Heb *words* [c] Or *treaty*, or *testimony*; Heb *eduth*

them. 32 Afterward all the Israelites came near, and he gave them in commandment all that the LORD had spoken with him on Mount Sinai. 33 When Moses had finished speaking with them, he put a veil on his face; 34 but whenever Moses went in before the LORD to speak with him, he would take the veil off, until he came out; and when he came out, and told the Israelites what he had been commanded, 35 the Israelites would see the face of Moses, that the skin of his face was shining; and Moses would put the veil on his face again, until he went in to speak with him.

Sabbath Regulations

35 Moses assembled all the congregation of the Israelites and said to them: These are the things that the LORD has commanded you to do:

2 Six days shall work be done, but on the seventh day you shall have a holy sabbath of solemn rest to the LORD; whoever does any work on it shall be put to death. 3 You shall kindle no fire in all your dwellings on the sabbath day.

Preparations for Making the Tabernacle

4 Moses said to all the congregation of the Israelites: This is the thing that the LORD has commanded: 5 Take from among you an offering to the LORD; let whoever is of a generous heart bring the LORD's offering: gold, silver, and bronze; 6 blue, purple, and crimson yarns, and fine linen; goats' hair, 7 tanned rams' skins, and fine leather;[a] acacia wood, 8 oil for the light, spices for the anointing oil and for the fragrant incense, 9 and onyx stones and gems to be set in the ephod and the breastpiece.

10 All who are skillful among you shall come and make all that the LORD has commanded: the tabernacle, 11 its tent and its covering, its clasps and its frames, its bars, its pillars, and its bases; 12 the ark with its poles, the mercy seat,[b] and the curtain for the screen; 13 the table with its poles and all its utensils, and the bread of the Presence; 14 the lampstand also for the light, with its utensils and its lamps, and the oil for the light; 15 and the altar of incense, with its poles, and the anointing oil and the fragrant incense, and the screen for the entrance, the entrance of the tabernacle; 16 the altar of burnt offering, with its grating of bronze, its poles, and all its utensils, the basin with its stand; 17 the hangings of the court, its pillars and its bases, and the screen for the gate of the court; 18 the pegs of the tabernacle and the pegs of the court, and their cords; 19 the finely worked vestments for ministering in the holy place, the holy vestments for the priest Aaron, and the vestments of his sons, for their service as priests.

[a] Meaning of Heb uncertain [b] Or *the cover*

35:1—39:43 the things that the LORD has commanded you to do: The instructions in chapters 25–30 for the tabernacle, its furnishings, and the priestly vestments are now carried out.

35:1-3 sabbath: Moses teaches the people about the day of rest, the last topic revealed to him before the golden calf incident (31:12-17).

35:4-9, 20-29 the LORD's offering: Moses calls for a freewill offering for the construction of the tabernacle. See note on 25:1-9 (see also 36:3-7; 38:21-31).

35:5 generous heart: This is the opposite of Pharaoh's hardened heart (see also 35:21, 26).

35:10-19 make all that the LORD has commanded: Material goods and skilled labor are offered for making everything described in detail in chapters 25–30.

Offerings for the Tabernacle

35:21, 26 heart was stirred: This is the opposite of Pharaoh's hardened heart (see also 35:4).

35:22 gold objects: Giving gold objects for the tabernacle recalls jewelry given to make the golden calf (32:2-4), ornaments taken off as a symbol of repentance (33:4-6), and also Egyptian wealth taken during Exodus (11:2; 12:35), but here put to a proper use for the worship of God.

20 Then all the congregation of the Israelites withdrew from the presence of Moses. 21 And they came, everyone whose heart was stirred, and everyone whose spirit was willing, and brought the LORD's offering to be used for the tent of meeting, and for all its service, and for the sacred vestments. 22 So they came, both men and women; all who were of a willing heart brought brooches and earrings and signet rings and pendants, all sorts of gold objects, everyone bringing an offering of gold to the LORD. 23 And everyone who possessed blue or purple or crimson yarn or fine linen or goats' hair or tanned rams' skins or fine leather,[a] brought them. 24 Everyone who could make an offering of silver or bronze brought it as the LORD's offering; and everyone who possessed acacia wood of any use in the work, brought it. 25 All the skillful women spun with their hands, and brought what they had spun in blue and purple and crimson yarns and fine linen; 26 all the women whose hearts moved them to use their skill spun the goats' hair. 27 And the leaders brought onyx stones and gems to be set in the ephod and the breastpiece, 28 and spices and oil for the light, and for the anointing oil, and for the fragrant incense. 29 All the Israelite men and women whose hearts made them willing to bring anything for the work that the LORD had commanded by Moses to be done, brought it as a freewill offering to the LORD.

Bezalel and Oholiab

35:30—36:2 Bezalel... Oholiab: See note on 31:1-11.

30 Then Moses said to the Israelites: See, the LORD has called by name Bezalel son of Uri son of Hur, of the tribe of Judah; 31 he has filled him with divine spirit,[b] with skill, intelligence, and knowledge in every kind of craft, 32 to devise artistic designs, to work in gold, silver, and bronze, 33 in cutting stones for setting, and in carving wood, in every kind of craft. 34 And he has inspired him to teach, both him and Oholiab son of Ahisamach, of the tribe of Dan. 35 He has filled them with skill to do every kind of work done by an artisan or by a designer or by an embroiderer in blue, purple, and crimson yarns, and in fine linen, or by a weaver—by any sort of artisan or skilled designer.

36 Bezalel and Oholiab and every skillful one to whom the LORD has given skill and understanding to know how to do any work in the construction of the sanctuary shall work in accordance with all that the LORD has commanded.

36:3-7 freewill offerings: See note on 25:1-9 (see also 35:4-9, 20-29; 38:21-31). The response is so great that Moses has to command the people to stop bringing offerings.

2 Moses then called Bezalel and Oholiab and every skillful one to whom the LORD had given skill, everyone whose heart was stirred to come to do the work; 3 and they received from Moses all the freewill offerings that the Israelites had brought for doing the work on the sanctuary. They still kept bringing him freewill offerings every

---

[a] Meaning of Heb uncertain [b] Or *the spirit of God*

morning, [4]so that all the artisans who were doing every sort of task
on the sanctuary came, each from the task being performed, [5]and
said to Moses, "The people are bringing much more than enough
for doing the work that the LORD has commanded us to do." [6]So
Moses gave command, and word was proclaimed throughout the
camp: "No man or woman is to make anything else as an offering
for the sanctuary." So the people were restrained from bringing;
[7]for what they had already brought was more than enough to do all
the work.

Construction of the Tabernacle

8 All those with skill among the workers made the tabernacle
with ten curtains; they were made of fine twisted linen, and blue, purple, and crimson yarns, with cherubim skillfully worked into them.
[9]The length of each curtain was twenty-eight cubits, and the width of
each curtain four cubits; all the curtains were of the same size.

36:8-19 made the tabernacle: See note on 26:1-14. This account of the construction of the items described in chapters 25–30 follows a different order, in which the tabernacle is built before its furnishings.

10 He joined five curtains to one another, and the other five curtains he joined to one another. [11]He made loops of blue on the edge
of the outermost curtain of the first set; likewise he made them on the
edge of the outermost curtain of the second set; [12]he made fifty loops
on the one curtain, and he made fifty loops on the edge of the curtain that was in the second set; the loops were opposite one another.
[13]And he made fifty clasps of gold, and joined the curtains one to the
other with clasps; so the tabernacle was one whole.

14 He also made curtains of goats' hair for a tent over the tabernacle; he made eleven curtains. [15]The length of each curtain was thirty
cubits, and the width of each curtain four cubits; the eleven curtains
were of the same size. [16]He joined five curtains by themselves, and six
curtains by themselves. [17]He made fifty loops on the edge of the outermost curtain of the one set, and fifty loops on the edge of the other
connecting curtain. [18]He made fifty clasps of bronze to join the tent
together so that it might be one whole. [19]And he made for the tent a
covering of tanned rams' skins and an outer covering of fine leather.[a]

20 Then he made the upright frames for the tabernacle of acacia wood. [21]Ten cubits was the length of a frame, and a cubit and a
half the width of each frame. [22]Each frame had two pegs for fitting
together; he did this for all the frames of the tabernacle. [23]The frames
for the tabernacle he made in this way: twenty frames for the south
side; [24]and he made forty bases of silver under the twenty frames, two
bases under the first frame for its two pegs, and two bases under the
next frame for its two pegs. [25]For the second side of the tabernacle,
on the north side, he made twenty frames [26]and their forty bases of
silver, two bases under the first frame and two bases under the next

36:20-34 frames for the tabernacle: See note on 26:15-30.

[a] Meaning of Heb uncertain

frame. [27]For the rear of the tabernacle westward he made six frames. [28]He made two frames for corners of the tabernacle in the rear. [29]They were separate beneath, but joined at the top, at the first ring; he made two of them in this way, for the two corners. [30]There were eight frames with their bases of silver: sixteen bases, under every frame two bases.

31 He made bars of acacia wood, five for the frames of the one side of the tabernacle, [32]and five bars for the frames of the other side of the tabernacle, and five bars for the frames of the tabernacle at the rear westward. [33]He made the middle bar to pass through from end to end halfway up the frames. [34]And he overlaid the frames with gold, and made rings of gold for them to hold the bars, and overlaid the bars with gold.

36:35-38 curtain...with cherubim: See note on 26:31-34.

35 He made the curtain of blue, purple, and crimson yarns, and fine twisted linen, with cherubim skillfully worked into it. [36]For it he made four pillars of acacia, and overlaid them with gold; their hooks were of gold, and he cast for them four bases of silver. [37]He also made a screen for the entrance to the tent, of blue, purple, and crimson yarns, and fine twisted linen, embroidered with needlework; [38]and its five pillars with their hooks. He overlaid their capitals and their bases with gold, but their five bases were of bronze.

Making the Ark of the Covenant

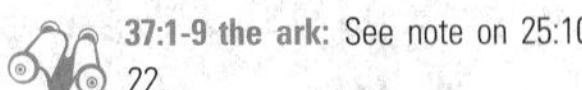

37:1-9 the ark: See note on 25:10-22.

37 Bezalel made the ark of acacia wood; it was two and a half cubits long, a cubit and a half wide, and a cubit and a half high. [2]He overlaid it with pure gold inside and outside, and made a molding of gold around it. [3]He cast for it four rings of gold for its four feet, two rings on its one side and two rings on its other side. [4]He made poles of acacia wood, and overlaid them with gold, [5]and put the poles into the rings on the sides of the ark, to carry the ark. [6]He made a mercy seat[a] of pure gold; two cubits and a half was its length, and a cubit and a half its width. [7]He made two cherubim of hammered gold; at the two ends of the mercy seat[b] he made them, [8]one cherub at the one end, and one cherub at the other end; of one piece with the mercy seat[b] he made the cherubim at its two ends. [9]The cherubim spread out their wings above, overshadowing the mercy seat[a] with their wings. They faced one another; the faces of the cherubim were turned toward the mercy seat.[b]

Making the Table for the Bread of the Presence

37:10-16 table...vessels: See note on 25:23-30.

10 He also made the table of acacia wood, two cubits long, one cubit wide, and a cubit and a half high. [11]He overlaid it with pure gold, and made a molding of gold around it. [12]He made around it a rim a handbreadth wide, and made a molding of gold around the rim. [13]He

[a] Or *a cover* [b] Or *the cover*

cast for it four rings of gold, and fastened the rings to the four corners at its four legs. [14]The rings that held the poles used for carrying the table were close to the rim. [15]He made the poles of acacia wood to carry the table, and overlaid them with gold. [16]And he made the vessels of pure gold that were to be on the table, its plates and dishes for incense, and its bowls and flagons with which to pour drink offerings.

Making the Lampstand

17 He also made the lampstand of pure gold. The base and the shaft of the lampstand were made of hammered work; its cups, its calyxes, and its petals were of one piece with it. [18]There were six branches going out of its sides, three branches of the lampstand out of one side of it and three branches of the lampstand out of the other side of it; [19]three cups shaped like almond blossoms, each with calyx and petals, on one branch, and three cups shaped like almond blossoms, each with calyx and petals, on the other branch—so for the six branches going out of the lampstand. [20]On the lampstand itself there were four cups shaped like almond blossoms, each with its calyxes and petals. [21]There was a calyx of one piece with it under the first pair of branches, a calyx of one piece with it under the next pair of branches, and a calyx of one piece with it under the last pair of branches. [22]Their calyxes and their branches were of one piece with it, the whole of it one hammered piece of pure gold. [23]He made its seven lamps and its snuffers and its trays of pure gold. [24]He made it and all its utensils of a talent of pure gold.

37:17-24 lampstand: See note on 25:31-40.

Making the Altar of Incense

25 He made the altar of incense of acacia wood, one cubit long, and one cubit wide; it was square, and was two cubits high; its horns were of one piece with it. [26]He overlaid it with pure gold, its top, and its sides all around, and its horns; and he made for it a molding of gold all around, [27]and made two golden rings for it under its molding, on two opposite sides of it, to hold the poles with which to carry it. [28]And he made the poles of acacia wood, and overlaid them with gold.

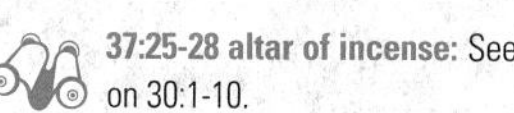
37:25-28 altar of incense: See note on 30:1-10.

Making the Anointing Oil and the Incense

29 He made the holy anointing oil also, and the pure fragrant incense, blended as by the perfumer.

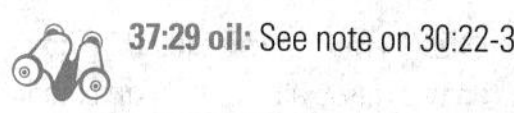
37:29 oil: See note on 30:22-38.

Making the Altar of Burnt Offering

38 He made the altar of burnt offering also of acacia wood; it was five cubits long, and five cubits wide; it was square, and three cubits high. [2]He made horns for it on its four corners; its horns were of one piece with it, and he overlaid it with bronze. [3]He made all the utensils of the altar, the pots, the shovels, the basins, the

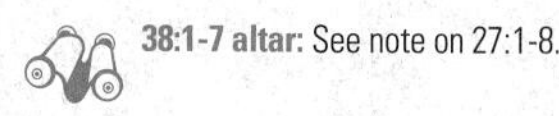
38:1-7 altar: See note on 27:1-8.

forks, and the firepans: all its utensils he made of bronze. 4 He made
for the altar a grating, a network of bronze, under its ledge, extending
halfway down. 5 He cast four rings on the four corners of the bronze
grating to hold the poles; 6 he made the poles of acacia wood, and
overlaid them with bronze. 7 And he put the poles through the rings
on the sides of the altar, to carry it with them; he made it hollow,
with boards.

38:8 basin: See note on 30:17-21.

8 He made the basin of bronze with its stand of bronze, from
the mirrors of the women who served at the entrance to the tent of
meeting.

Making the Court of the Tabernacle

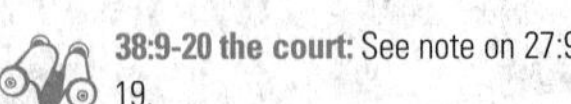

38:9-20 the court: See note on 27:9-19.

9 He made the court; for the south side the hangings of the court
were of fine twisted linen, one hundred cubits long; 10 its twenty pillars and their twenty bases were of bronze, but the hooks of the pillars and their bands were of silver. 11 For the north side there were
hangings one hundred cubits long; its twenty pillars and their twenty
bases were of bronze, but the hooks of the pillars and their bands were
of silver. 12 For the west side there were hangings fifty cubits long, with
ten pillars and ten bases; the hooks of the pillars and their bands were
of silver. 13 And for the front to the east, fifty cubits. 14 The hangings for
one side of the gate were fifteen cubits, with three pillars and three
bases. 15 And so for the other side; on each side of the gate of the court
were hangings of fifteen cubits, with three pillars and three bases. 16 All
the hangings around the court were of fine twisted linen. 17 The bases
for the pillars were of bronze, but the hooks of the pillars and their
bands were of silver; the overlaying of their capitals was also of silver,
and all the pillars of the court were banded with silver. 18 The screen
for the entrance to the court was embroidered with needlework in
blue, purple, and crimson yarns and fine twisted linen. It was twenty
cubits long and, along the width of it, five cubits high, corresponding
to the hangings of the court. 19 There were four pillars; their four bases
were of bronze, their hooks of silver, and the overlaying of their capitals and their bands of silver. 20 All the pegs for the tabernacle and for
the court all around were of bronze.

Materials of the Tabernacle

38:21-31 the tabernacle of the covenant: This is an inventory of materials used in construction of the tabernacle.

21 These are the records of the tabernacle, the tabernacle of the
covenant,[a] which were drawn up at the commandment of Moses, the
work of the Levites being under the direction of Ithamar son of the
priest Aaron. 22 Bezalel son of Uri son of Hur, of the tribe of Judah,
made all that the LORD commanded Moses; 23 and with him was Oholiab son of Ahisamach, of the tribe of Dan, engraver, designer, and embroiderer in blue, purple, and crimson yarns, and in fine linen.

[a] Or *treaty,* or *testimony;* Heb *eduth*

24 All the gold that was used for the work, in all the construction
of the sanctuary, the gold from the offering, was twenty-nine talents
and seven hundred thirty shekels, measured by the sanctuary shekel.
25 The silver from those of the congregation who were counted was
one hundred talents and one thousand seven hundred seventy-five
shekels, measured by the sanctuary shekel; 26 a beka a head (that is,
half a shekel, measured by the sanctuary shekel), for everyone who
was counted in the census, from twenty years old and upward, for six
hundred three thousand, five hundred fifty men. 27 The hundred talents of silver were for casting the bases of the sanctuary, and the bases
of the curtain; one hundred bases for the hundred talents, a talent for
a base. 28 Of the thousand seven hundred seventy-five shekels he made
hooks for the pillars, and overlaid their capitals and made bands for
them. 29 The bronze that was contributed was seventy talents, and two
thousand four hundred shekels; 30 with it he made the bases for the
entrance of the tent of meeting, the bronze altar and the bronze grating for it and all the utensils of the altar, 31 the bases all around the
court, and the bases of the gate of the court, all the pegs of the tabernacle, and all the pegs around the court.

38:25-26 half a shekel: Money collected from each male counted assumes the census described in 30:12-16 was already taken, but it was called for a month after the construction of the tabernacle (40:17; Num 1:1-3).

Making the Vestments for the Priesthood

39 Of the blue, purple, and crimson yarns they made finely
worked vestments, for ministering in the holy place; they
made the sacred vestments for Aaron; as the LORD had commanded
Moses.

39:1-31 vestments: See note on 28:1-43.

2 He made the ephod of gold, of blue, purple, and crimson yarns,
and of fine twisted linen. 3 Gold leaf was hammered out and cut into
threads to work into the blue, purple, and crimson yarns and into
the fine twisted linen, in skilled design. 4 They made for the ephod
shoulder-pieces, joined to it at its two edges. 5 The decorated band on
it was of the same materials and workmanship, of gold, of blue, purple, and crimson yarns, and of fine twisted linen; as the LORD had
commanded Moses.

6 The onyx stones were prepared, enclosed in settings of gold filigree and engraved like the engravings of a signet, according to the
names of the sons of Israel. 7 He set them on the shoulder-pieces of
the ephod, to be stones of remembrance for the sons of Israel; as the
LORD had commanded Moses.

8 He made the breastpiece, in skilled work, like the work of the
ephod, of gold, of blue, purple, and crimson yarns, and of fine twisted
linen. 9 It was square; the breastpiece was made double, a span in length
and a span in width when doubled. 10 They set in it four rows of stones.
A row of carnelian,[a] chrysolite, and emerald was the first row; 11 and

[a] The identification of several of these stones is uncertain

the second row, a turquoise, a sapphire,[a] and a moonstone; [12]and the third row, a jacinth, an agate, and an amethyst; [13]and the fourth row, a beryl, an onyx, and a jasper; they were enclosed in settings of gold filigree. [14]There were twelve stones with names corresponding to the names of the sons of Israel; they were like signets, each engraved with its name, for the twelve tribes. [15]They made on the breastpiece chains of pure gold, twisted like cords; [16]and they made two settings of gold filigree and two gold rings, and put the two rings on the two edges of the breastpiece; [17]and they put the two cords of gold in the two rings at the edges of the breastpiece. [18]Two ends of the two cords they had attached to the two settings of filigree; in this way they attached it in front to the shoulder-pieces of the ephod. [19]Then they made two rings of gold, and put them at the two ends of the breastpiece, on its inside edge next to the ephod. [20]They made two rings of gold, and attached them in front to the lower part of the two shoulder-pieces of the ephod, at its joining above the decorated band of the ephod. [21]They bound the breastpiece by its rings to the rings of the ephod with a blue cord, so that it should lie on the decorated band of the ephod, and that the breastpiece should not come loose from the ephod; as the LORD had commanded Moses.

22 He also made the robe of the ephod woven all of blue yarn; [23]and the opening of the robe in the middle of it was like the opening in a coat of mail,[b] with a binding around the opening, so that it might not be torn. [24]On the lower hem of the robe they made pomegranates of blue, purple, and crimson yarns, and of fine twisted linen. [25]They also made bells of pure gold, and put the bells between the pomegranates on the lower hem of the robe all around, between the pomegranates; [26]a bell and a pomegranate, a bell and a pomegranate all around on the lower hem of the robe for ministering; as the LORD had commanded Moses.

27 They also made the tunics, woven of fine linen, for Aaron and his sons, [28]and the turban of fine linen, and the headdresses of fine linen, and the linen undergarments of fine twisted linen, [29]and the sash of fine twisted linen, and of blue, purple, and crimson yarns, embroidered with needlework; as the LORD had commanded Moses.

30 They made the rosette of the holy diadem of pure gold, and wrote on it an inscription, like the engraving of a signet, "Holy to the LORD." [31]They tied to it a blue cord, to fasten it on the turban above; as the LORD had commanded Moses.

The Work Completed

39:32-43 all the work…was finished: The Israelites complete the work commanded by God through Moses, and bring everything to Moses. See Exodus 25–30 for detailed descriptions of the items listed here.

32 In this way all the work of the tabernacle of the tent of meeting was finished; the Israelites had done everything just as the LORD had

[a] Or *lapis lazuli* [b] Meaning of Heb uncertain

commanded Moses. [33]Then they brought the tabernacle to Moses,
the tent and all its utensils, its hooks, its frames, its bars, its pillars,
and its bases; [34]the covering of tanned rams' skins and the covering of
fine leather,[a] and the curtain for the screen; [35]the ark of the covenant[b]
with its poles and the mercy seat;[c] [36]the table with all its utensils, and
the bread of the Presence; [37]the pure lampstand with its lamps set on
it and all its utensils, and the oil for the light; [38]the golden altar, the
anointing oil and the fragrant incense, and the screen for the entrance
of the tent; [39]the bronze altar, and its grating of bronze, its poles, and
all its utensils; the basin with its stand; [40]the hangings of the court, its
pillars, and its bases, and the screen for the gate of the court, its cords,
and its pegs; and all the utensils for the service of the tabernacle, for
the tent of meeting; [41]the finely worked vestments for ministering in
the holy place, the sacred vestments for the priest Aaron, and the vestments
of his sons to serve as priests. [42]The Israelites had done all of the
work just as the LORD had commanded Moses. [43]When Moses saw
that they had done all the work just as the LORD had commanded,
he blessed them.

39:43 Moses...blessed them: Blessing is a theme in the Bible that is associated with the completion of creative work (see Gen 2:3).

The Tabernacle Erected and Its Equipment Installed

40 The LORD spoke to Moses: [2]On the first day of the first
month you shall set up the tabernacle of the tent of meet-
ing. [3]You shall put in it the ark of the covenant,[b] and you shall screen
the ark with the curtain. [4]You shall bring in the table, and arrange its
setting; and you shall bring in the lampstand, and set up its lamps.
[5]You shall put the golden altar for incense before the ark of the covenant,[a] and set up the screen for the entrance of the tabernacle. [6]You
shall set the altar of burnt offering before the entrance of the tabernacle of the tent of meeting, [7]and place the basin between the tent of
meeting and the altar, and put water in it. [8]You shall set up the court
all around, and hang up the screen for the gate of the court. [9]Then
you shall take the anointing oil, and anoint the tabernacle and all that
is in it, and consecrate it and all its furniture, so that it shall become
holy. [10]You shall also anoint the altar of burnt offering and all its utensils, and consecrate the altar, so that the altar shall be most holy. [11]You
shall also anoint the basin with its stand, and consecrate it. [12]Then
you shall bring Aaron and his sons to the entrance of the tent of meeting, and shall wash them with water, [13]and put on Aaron the sacred
vestments, and you shall anoint him and consecrate him, so that he
may serve me as priest. [14]You shall bring his sons also and put tunics
on them, [15]and anoint them, as you anointed their father, that they
may serve me as priests: and their anointing shall admit them to a
perpetual priesthood throughout all generations to come.

40:1-33 set up the tabernacle: Moses receives instructions, sets up the tabernacle with its furnishings and equipment, and prepares Aaron and his sons for their priestly role.

40:1, 17 first day of the first month: These words support themes of new year, temple, and creation. It is a little less than one year since the exodus from Egypt.

---

[a] Meaning of Heb uncertain [b] Or *treaty*, or *testimony*; Heb *eduth* [c] Or *the cover*

16 Moses did everything just as the LORD had commanded him.
17 In the first month in the second year, on the first day of the month,
the tabernacle was set up. 18 Moses set up the tabernacle; he laid its
bases, and set up its frames, and put in its poles, and raised up its pillars; 19 and he spread the tent over the tabernacle, and put the covering of the tent over it; as the LORD had commanded Moses. 20 He
took the covenant[a] and put it into the ark, and put the poles on the
ark, and set the mercy seat[b] above the ark; 21 and he brought the ark
into the tabernacle, and set up the curtain for screening, and screened
the ark of the covenant;[a] as the LORD had commanded Moses. 22 He
put the table in the tent of meeting, on the north side of the tabernacle, outside the curtain, 23 and set the bread in order on it before the
LORD; as the LORD had commanded Moses. 24 He put the lampstand
in the tent of meeting, opposite the table on the south side of the tabernacle, 25 and set up the lamps before the LORD; as the LORD had
commanded Moses. 26 He put the golden altar in the tent of meeting
before the curtain, 27 and offered fragrant incense on it; as the LORD
had commanded Moses. 28 He also put in place the screen for the entrance of the tabernacle. 29 He set the altar of burnt offering at the entrance of the tabernacle of the tent of meeting, and offered on it the
burnt offering and the grain offering as the LORD had commanded
Moses. 30 He set the basin between the tent of meeting and the altar,
and put water in it for washing, 31 with which Moses and Aaron and
his sons washed their hands and their feet. 32 When they went into the
tent of meeting, and when they approached the altar, they washed; as
the LORD had commanded Moses. 33 He set up the court around the
tabernacle and the altar, and put up the screen at the gate of the court.
So Moses finished the work.

40:33 finished: The same word is used here and in Genesis 2:1-2, at God's completion of creation.

The Cloud and the Glory

34 Then the cloud covered the tent of meeting, and the glory
of the LORD filled the tabernacle. 35 Moses was not able to enter the
tent of meeting because the cloud settled upon it, and the glory of the
LORD filled the tabernacle. 36 Whenever the cloud was taken up from
the tabernacle, the Israelites would set out on each stage of their journey; 37 but if the cloud was not taken up, then they did not set out until
the day that it was taken up. 38 For the cloud of the LORD was on the
tabernacle by day, and fire was in the cloud[c] by night, before the eyes
of all the house of Israel at each stage of their journey.

40:34-38 cloud: God's presence is in the tabernacle in a cloud as it was at the time of the exodus from Egypt, accompanying the Israelites.

40:34 the glory of the LORD: See note on 33:18-19. God is present in the tabernacle (see 1 Kgs 8, on God's presence in the temple).

---

[a] Or *treaty*, or *testimony*; Heb *eduth* [b] Or *the cover* [c] Heb *it*

Leviticus 24:2

LEVITICUS

Background File

The book's title comes from the Greek and Latin meaning "the book of the Levites." The Levites were the tribe of Israel assigned to be priests. Some Old Testament traditions trace the Levites' family line back to Moses' brother Aaron, who was Israel's first high priest (Exod 40:12-15). The Hebrew name for the book is *wayyiqra* (pronounced vay-yik-RAH), meaning "And he called." At the beginning of the book, God calls out to ("summons") Moses *from* the sacred tent of meeting, or tabernacle (1:1).

What's the Story?

Leviticus claims to contain the "statutes and ordinances and laws" that God gives to Israel through Moses. Israel was to order its festivals, worship, and community life as God's holy people according to these laws (Lev 26:46; 27:34). As God's chosen people, they were to live differently than their neighbors. Even though Leviticus 26:46 and 27:34 locate the action more generally "at Mount Sinai," the reader is invited to imagine the action as focused upon the Tent of Meeting. From there, God gives instructions directly to Moses while Israel is encamped at Mount Sinai (see Exod 19:1–20:21).

The Tent of Meeting had just recently been erected by Moses and the people at the foot of Mount Sinai (Exod 40:16-33). In those verses we discover that Aaron and the priests could now minister in the tabernacle, having been consecrated ("set apart") to do so. But Moses was no longer able to enter the sacred sanctuary, because its holiness made it off-limits even to Moses (Exod 40:30-38). In this tradition, the voice of God is amplified and directed to the ears of Moses alone, even though he cannot enter the sanctuary. Contrast this tradition of the Tent of Meeting with that of Exodus 33:7-11. There the tent, located outside the encampment, functions as the occasional meeting point of God and Moses. Why the difference? It is likely that the dominant tradition represented in Leviticus locates the tent at the center of the community where the Lord dwells in the midst of the people. In this tradition God's holy presence resides in the tabernacle, except when it is time to relocate on the journey toward the land of promise (Canaan).

The book of Leviticus is basically divided into two major sections. The first section (chapters 1–16) contains descriptions of offerings, rituals, laws, and rites. Some refer to these chapters as the Priestly Code, even though the instructions are not just for the priests, but apply to the people as well.

The second section includes the laws of Leviticus 17–26. These are often thought to be from an older collection of legal material referred to as the Holiness Code. Much of this material may have had its origins during the period of Israel's monarchy (1000–600 B.C.E.), prior to the Babylonian exile (597–539 B.C.E.). Most scholars, however, assume that the Holiness Code also reflects the setting, concerns, and theological assumptions of the community in the period after the exile. Leviticus can be outlined in the following way:

Israel's system of offerings and sacrifices (Lev 1:1—7:38). The first seven chapters concern the sacrificial rituals. These are understood to be sacramental in the sense that they bring together God's divine grace and human praise and thanksgiving.

The rites of ordination of Israel's priests (Lev 8:1—10:20. Chapters 8–10 present the story of the ordination of Aaron and his four sons. It is followed by the story of the misadventures of these same sons, Nadab and Abihu (10:1-7) and Eleazar and Ithamar (10:12-20).

Laws related to ritual purity (Lev 11:1—16:34): These chapters describe how Israel could maintain its worship life given the presence of "uncleanness" that is a normal part of humans living together. Community purity matters are addressed through laws and regulations, including which foods can properly be eaten (Lev 11) and how to deal with physical conditions such as those that involve blood, life, bodily emissions, wasting disease, or death. These life forces were considered so powerful that prolonged contact with them could cause contamination and make a person ritually unclean (Lev 12–15). This section ends with a description of the annual Day of Atonement when the high priest got rid of the impurity (the sins and unintended wrongdoing) of the people.

The laws known as the Holiness Code (Lev 17:1—26:46). This section includes additional regulations regarding proper sexual relations, penalties for violating holiness, the restrictions regarding the purity of priests, and laws related to offerings and special festivals. It concludes with a series of rewards and threats for obedience and disobedience.

Offerings and gifts dedicated to the LORD (Lev 27:1-34). This final section summarizes the rules regarding redemption of various offerings and gifts.

What's the Message?

The "statutes and ordinances and laws" that God gives to Moses have a clear purpose: Israel is commanded to maintain its identity as God's "holy" people. God's continued presence as the holy one in Israel's midst requires that the land not be contaminated by the effects of sin and uncleanness. Such contamination would eventually disgust the holy presence of God and force God's departure, insuring Israel's destruction (for example, see Ezek 8–11). To prevent such a disaster, Leviticus presents the *torah* ("guidance") for life surrounding God's holiness.

Throughout Israel's history, the threat is made that the land might become so polluted that it would "vomit" out God's people (20:22). Such uncleanness can endanger the community's holiness and be an offense to God. The final editors of the Holiness Code knew that this is precisely what happened when Israel was scattered among the nations in exile (26:33). In this late tradition, however, exile was not simply a period of divine punishment. It was also a period when the *land* would again "enjoy its sabbath years" (26:34) and heal from its wounds. The land would prepare to receive a repentant Jewish people back once again, for God would honor the covenant made with their ancestors, to whom God gave these laws and ordinances (26:34-45).

The book of Leviticus summons God's people of every generation to live lives that honor God, honor the worship of God, honor God's people, and honor the land/earth. Christians are called to honor God but not through the complex system of sacrifices described in Leviticus. Why? Because of Jesus' self-sacrifice for the sins of the world (Rom 3:23-26; Heb 10:8-10). He has replaced the high priest as our representative before God (Heb 4:14-16).

The Burnt Offering

1 The LORD summoned Moses and spoke to him from the tent of
meeting, saying: [2]Speak to the people of Israel and say to them:
When any of you bring an offering of livestock to the LORD, you shall
bring your offering from the herd or from the flock.
3 If the offering is a burnt offering from the herd, you shall offer a
male without blemish; you shall bring it to the entrance of the tent of
meeting, for acceptance in your behalf before the LORD. [4]You shall lay
your hand on the head of the burnt offering, and it shall be acceptable
in your behalf as atonement for you. [5]The bull shall be slaughtered
before the LORD; and Aaron's sons the priests shall offer the blood,
dashing the blood against all sides of the altar that is at the entrance
of the tent of meeting. [6]The burnt offering shall be flayed and cut up
into its parts. [7]The sons of the priest Aaron shall put fire on the altar
and arrange wood on the fire. [8]Aaron's sons the priests shall arrange
the parts, with the head and the suet, on the wood that is on the fire
on the altar; [9]but its entrails and its legs shall be washed with water.
Then the priest shall turn the whole into smoke on the altar as a burnt
offering, an offering by fire of pleasing odor to the LORD.
10 If your gift for a burnt offering is from the flock, from the
sheep or goats, your offering shall be a male without blemish. [11]It shall
be slaughtered on the north side of the altar before the LORD, and
Aaron's sons the priests shall dash its blood against all sides of the altar. [12]It shall be cut up into its parts, with its head and its suet, and the
priest shall arrange them on the wood that is on the fire on the altar;
[13]but the entrails and the legs shall be washed with water. Then the
priest shall offer the whole and turn it into smoke on the altar; it is a
burnt offering, an offering by fire of pleasing odor to the LORD.
14 If your offering to the LORD is a burnt offering of birds, you
shall choose your offering from turtledoves or pigeons. [15]The priest

1:1—7:38 Speak to the people of Israel: This section is presented as a long speech by God, who declares laws for various sacrifices. Leviticus 1–3 includes instructions regarding the three "all-purpose" sacrifices: burnt offerings, grain offerings, and the offerings of well-being. See chart Offerings in Israel, p. 197.

1:3-9 from the herd: These are listed in order from most to least costly: herd, flock, and fowl. The blood ritual was understood to cleanse the sanctuary from the contaminating effect of the people's sin since blood was understood to contain the very "life" of a living being (see 17:11).

1:3 burnt offering: The Hebrew term *ola* (oh-LAH) indicates that the offering goes "up" to God in smoke as a "pleasing odor" (see Gen 8:20-21).

1:3 without blemish: That is, in healthy condition; not those that were blind, lame, deformed, or otherwise ill (see 22:17-25; Mal 1:8, 13).

1:11 Aaron's sons the priests: At Mount Sinai, the LORD had commanded that Aaron and his sons be set apart (consecrated) to perform the duties of the priests.

shall bring it to the altar and wring off its head, and turn it into smoke
on the altar; and its blood shall be drained out against the side of the
altar. [16]He shall remove its crop with its contents[a] and throw it at the
east side of the altar, in the place for ashes. [17]He shall tear it open by
its wings without severing it. Then the priest shall turn it into smoke
on the altar, on the wood that is on the fire; it is a burnt offering, an
offering by fire of pleasing odor to the LORD.

Grain Offerings

2 When anyone presents a grain offering to the LORD, the offering shall be of choice flour; the worshiper shall pour oil on it,
and put frankincense on it, [2]and bring it to Aaron's sons the priests.
After taking from it a handful of the choice flour and oil, with all its
frankincense, the priest shall turn this token portion into smoke on
the altar, an offering by fire of pleasing odor to the LORD. [3]And what
is left of the grain offering shall be for Aaron and his sons, a most holy
part of the offerings by fire to the LORD.

4 When you present a grain offering baked in the oven, it shall
be of choice flour: unleavened cakes mixed with oil, or unleavened
wafers spread with oil. [5]If your offering is grain prepared on a griddle, it shall be of choice flour mixed with oil, unleavened; [6]break it
in pieces, and pour oil on it; it is a grain offering. [7]If your offering is
grain prepared in a pan, it shall be made of choice flour in oil. [8]You
shall bring to the LORD the grain offering that is prepared in any of
these ways; and when it is presented to the priest, he shall take it to
the altar. [9]The priest shall remove from the grain offering its token
portion and turn this into smoke on the altar, an offering by fire of
pleasing odor to the LORD. [10]And what is left of the grain offering
shall be for Aaron and his sons; it is a most holy part of the offerings
by fire to the LORD.

11 No grain offering that you bring to the LORD shall be made
with leaven, for you must not turn any leaven or honey into smoke
as an offering by fire to the LORD. [12]You may bring them to the LORD
as an offering of choice products, but they shall not be offered on the
altar for a pleasing odor. [13]You shall not omit from your grain offerings
the salt of the covenant with your God; with all your offerings you
shall offer salt.

14 If you bring a grain offering of first fruits to the LORD, you shall
bring as the grain offering of your first fruits coarse new grain from
fresh ears, parched with fire. [15]You shall add oil to it and lay frankincense on it; it is a grain offering. [16]And the priest shall turn a token
portion of it into smoke—some of the coarse grain and oil with all its
frankincense; it is an offering by fire to the LORD.

[a] Meaning of Heb uncertain

2:3 for Aaron and his sons, a most holy part: In some sacrifices a portion was reserved to be eaten by the priests and was designated particularly holy (see 5:14-16). Holiness was thought to be dangerously contagious and therefore had to be kept within the area of the holy.

What do you think about the idea that holiness had to be confined to holy spaces? Do you think that there are certain areas that are holy and others that are "common"? What or where is a holy place in your experience?

2:11 made with leaven...or honey: Though these items could be otherwise presented as an offering (7:13; 23:17), they were not to be burned on the altar (see also Exod 23:18; 34:25).

2:12-14 choice products...first fruits: God was to receive the best of the harvest, not the leftovers.

2:13 salt of the covenant: Salt was a purifying agent that made things "clean" and "holy" (Exod 30:35; 2 Kgs 2:19-21). It was apparently applied to newborns (Ezek 16:4) and symbolized the healing purity of God's covenant with Israel (Num 18:19; 2 Chr 13:5). It also reinforces the meal-like quality of these sacrifices.

2:15 frankincense: This white, gummy resin came from the wood of Boswellia shrubs. When burned, it gave off a sweet smell.

Offerings of Well-Being

3 If the offering is a sacrifice of well-being, if you offer an animal
of the herd, whether male or female, you shall offer one without
blemish before the LORD. [2]You shall lay your hand on the head of the
offering and slaughter it at the entrance of the tent of meeting; and
Aaron's sons the priests shall dash the blood against all sides of the
altar. [3]You shall offer from the sacrifice of well-being, as an offering
by fire to the LORD, the fat that covers the entrails and all the fat that
is around the entrails; [4]the two kidneys with the fat that is on them
at the loins, and the appendage of the liver, which he shall remove
with the kidneys. [5]Then Aaron's sons shall turn these into smoke on
the altar, with the burnt offering that is on the wood on the fire, as an
offering by fire of pleasing odor to the LORD.

6 If your offering for a sacrifice of well-being to the LORD is from
the flock, male or female, you shall offer one without blemish. [7]If you
present a sheep as your offering, you shall bring it before the LORD
[8]and lay your hand on the head of the offering. It shall be slaughtered before the tent of meeting, and Aaron's sons shall dash its blood
against all sides of the altar. [9]You shall present its fat from the sacrifice
of well-being, as an offering by fire to the LORD: the whole broad tail,
which shall be removed close to the backbone, the fat that covers the
entrails, and all the fat that is around the entrails; [10]the two kidneys
with the fat that is on them at the loins, and the appendage of the liver,
which you shall remove with the kidneys. [11]Then the priest shall turn
these into smoke on the altar as a food offering by fire to the LORD.

12 If your offering is a goat, you shall bring it before the LORD
[13]and lay your hand on its head; it shall be slaughtered before the tent
of meeting; and the sons of Aaron shall dash its blood against all sides
of the altar. [14]You shall present as your offering from it, as an offering
by fire to the LORD, the fat that covers the entrails, and all the fat that
is around the entrails; [15]the two kidneys with the fat that is on them at
the loins, and the appendage of the liver, which you shall remove with
the kidneys. [16]Then the priest shall turn these into smoke on the altar
as a food offering by fire for a pleasing odor.

All fat is the LORD's. [17]It shall be a perpetual statute throughout
your generations, in all your settlements: you must not eat any fat or
any blood.

Sin Offerings

4 The LORD spoke to Moses, saying, [2]Speak to the people of Israel, saying: When anyone sins unintentionally in any of the
LORD's commandments about things not to be done, and does any
one of them:

3 If it is the anointed priest who sins, thus bringing guilt on the

3:1-17 sacrifice of well-being: The *zebah* (ZEH-bach) sacrifice was different from the burnt offering because this sacrifice was eaten principally by those offering it as a festive, family-oriented celebration. Some of the fatty parts and important internal organs were burned for God's enjoyment (3:3-4; "all fat is the LORD'S," 3:16b).

Community and family celebrations were important for Israel (consider also what it meant to "offer a tithe" in Deuteronomy 14:22-26). What are your favorite family celebrations? What do you especially like about them? Why is eating together so important? Why is it important for the members of a congregation to eat together, especially around the Lord's Table?

3:17 you must not eat any fat or any blood: Meat had to be ritually slaughtered and the blood properly drained because of the powerful nature of blood (see 1:3-9 and note). Eating "with its blood" (19:26; Deut 12:23; 1 Sam 14:31-34) was considered a serious offense against life itself (Gen 9:4), as was eating fat (1 Sam 2:15-17; Ezek 34:3).

4:1—6:7 When anyone sins unintentionally: This section presents remedies for offenses that are committed unintentionally or unknowingly.

4:2 sins unintentionally: Ancient people recognized that accidents and unintentional offenses still carried severe consequences. Even if they were accidents, they still counted as sins that needed to be remedied for the sake of the community.

4:3 bringing guilt on the people: The series begins with the priest because he is the one who oversees these sacrificial rites and especially because his offense brings guilt not only on himself but on the entire community.

In our worship services we pray for forgiveness for our sins, "known and unknown" (*ELW*, p. 95). Can you think of offenses the community commits that might be either unknown or unintentional? Why are such sins especially troubling and dangerous?

people, he shall offer for the sin that he has committed a bull of the
herd without blemish as a sin offering to the LORD. [4]He shall bring the
bull to the entrance of the tent of meeting before the LORD and lay his
hand on the head of the bull; the bull shall be slaughtered before the
LORD. [5]The anointed priest shall take some of the blood of the bull and
bring it into the tent of meeting. [6]The priest shall dip his finger in the
blood and sprinkle some of the blood seven times before the LORD in
front of the curtain of the sanctuary. [7]The priest shall put some of the
blood on the horns of the altar of fragrant incense that is in the tent
of meeting before the LORD; and the rest of the blood of the bull he
shall pour out at the base of the altar of burnt offering, which is at the
entrance of the tent of meeting. [8]He shall remove all the fat from the
bull of sin offering: the fat that covers the entrails and all the fat that is
around the entrails; [9]the two kidneys with the fat that is on them at the
loins; and the appendage of the liver, which he shall remove with the
kidneys, [10]just as these are removed from the ox of the sacrifice of well-
being. The priest shall turn them into smoke upon the altar of burnt
offering. [11]But the skin of the bull and all its flesh, as well as its head, its
legs, its entrails, and its dung— [12]all the rest of the bull—he shall carry
out to a clean place outside the camp, to the ash heap, and shall burn it
on a wood fire; at the ash heap it shall be burned.

13 If the whole congregation of Israel errs unintentionally and the
matter escapes the notice of the assembly, and they do any one of the
things that by the LORD's commandments ought not to be done and
incur guilt; [14]when the sin that they have committed becomes known,
the assembly shall offer a bull of the herd for a sin offering and bring
it before the tent of meeting. [15]The elders of the congregation shall lay
their hands on the head of the bull before the LORD, and the bull shall
be slaughtered before the LORD. [16]The anointed priest shall bring
some of the blood of the bull into the tent of meeting, [17]and the priest
shall dip his finger in the blood and sprinkle it seven times before the
LORD, in front of the curtain. [18]He shall put some of the blood on the
horns of the altar that is before the LORD in the tent of meeting; and
the rest of the blood he shall pour out at the base of the altar of burnt
offering that is at the entrance of the tent of meeting. [19]He shall remove all its fat and turn it into smoke on the altar. [20]He shall do with
the bull just as is done with the bull of sin offering; he shall do the
same with this. The priest shall make atonement for them, and they
shall be forgiven. [21]He shall carry the bull outside the camp, and burn
it as he burned the first bull; it is the sin offering for the assembly.

22 When a ruler sins, doing unintentionally any one of all the
things that by commandments of the LORD his God ought not to be
done and incurs guilt, [23]once the sin that he has committed is made
known to him, he shall bring as his offering a male goat without blemish. [24]He shall lay his hand on the head of the goat; it shall be slaugh-

4:20 priest shall make atonement: The concept of atonement is mentioned often in Leviticus. Sins were considered to cause a person to be in debt to God or to other people. Atonement by performing sacrifices was the way such sin "debts" could be paid off. See also the note on 16:1-34.

4:25 horns of the altar: Ancient Israelite altars were made of worked stones that had smooth sides and simple horn-shaped protrusions at each of the four corners on the top. These "horns" had important symbolic functions, especially when one fled to a temple to seek "sanctuary" from danger (1 Kgs 1:50-53; 2:28-29).

tered at the spot where the burnt offering is slaughtered before the
LORD; it is a sin offering. 25 The priest shall take some of the blood of
the sin offering with his finger and put it on the horns of the altar of
burnt offering, and pour out the rest of its blood at the base of the altar of burnt offering. 26 All its fat he shall turn into smoke on the altar,
like the fat of the sacrifice of well-being. Thus the priest shall make
atonement on his behalf for his sin, and he shall be forgiven.

27 If anyone of the ordinary people among you sins unintentionally in doing any one of the things that by the LORD's commandments
ought not to be done and incurs guilt, 28 when the sin that you have
committed is made known to you, you shall bring a female goat without blemish as your offering, for the sin that you have committed. 29 You
shall lay your hand on the head of the sin offering; and the sin offering
shall be slaughtered at the place of the burnt offering. 30 The priest shall
take some of its blood with his finger and put it on the horns of the
altar of burnt offering, and he shall pour out the rest of its blood at the
base of the altar. 31 He shall remove all its fat, as the fat is removed from
the offering of well-being, and the priest shall turn it into smoke on
the altar for a pleasing odor to the LORD. Thus the priest shall make
atonement on your behalf, and you shall be forgiven.

32 If the offering you bring as a sin offering is a sheep, you shall
bring a female without blemish. 33 You shall lay your hand on the head
of the sin offering; and it shall be slaughtered as a sin offering at the
spot where the burnt offering is slaughtered. 34 The priest shall take
some of the blood of the sin offering with his finger and put it on the
horns of the altar of burnt offering, and pour out the rest of its blood
at the base of the altar. 35 You shall remove all its fat, as the fat of the
sheep is removed from the sacrifice of well-being, and the priest shall
turn it into smoke on the altar, with the offerings by fire to the LORD.
Thus the priest shall make atonement on your behalf for the sin that
you have committed, and you shall be forgiven.

5 When any of you sin in that you have heard a public adjuration
to testify and—though able to testify as one who has seen or
learned of the matter—do not speak up, you are subject to punishment. 2 Or when any of you touch any unclean thing—whether the
carcass of an unclean beast or the carcass of unclean livestock or the
carcass of an unclean swarming thing—and are unaware of it, you
have become unclean, and are guilty. 3 Or when you touch human
uncleanness—any uncleanness by which one can become unclean—
and are unaware of it, when you come to know it, you shall be guilty.
4 Or when any of you utter aloud a rash oath for a bad or a good purpose, whatever people utter in an oath, and are unaware of it, when
you come to know it, you shall in any of these be guilty. 5 When you
realize your guilt in any of these, you shall confess the sin that you
have committed. 6 And you shall bring to the LORD, as your penalty

4:35 You shall remove all its fat: The priest was directed to perform this job (see 4:19, 26, 31).

Why does the Lutheran church ordain pastors? Just as God commanded that priests be consecrated (set apart) to serve as priests for the Israelite people, so the Lutheran church and other Christian denominations ordain people to do specific ministries. According to the bylaws of the Evangelical Lutheran Church in America, "This church affirms the universal priesthood of all its baptized members" (7.11). But the ELCA also states: "...for the sake of the Gospel ministry entrusted to believers, God has instituted the office of ministry of Word and Sacrament" (7.21). This means that some are chosen to receive special training to do certain tasks, such as preaching, administering the sacraments, conducting public worship, and providing pastoral care (7.31.12). Calling people to do this ministry is not meant to keep nonordained people from participating fully, but it helps to provide a sense of order and to maintain sound teaching and preaching. *Leviticus 4:30-35*

What do you think would be most challenging about being a minister set aside to serve God? How are all people called to serve?

5:1-13 do not speak up: These verses present two categories of offenses that are particularly dangerous because they jeopardize the community in ways that can easily go undetected. The first and last (5:1, 4) relate to sworn oaths and perjury, offenses that undermine the legal system itself. The middle two offenses (5:2-3) relate to persons who have been contaminated by uncleanness but do not realize it.

5:3-13 uncleanness...make atonement: Many offenses could make someone ritually unclean. In order to become ritually clean again, people had to perform sacrifices. These verses specify the sacrifices required for atonement in certain cases. As in 1:14-17 poorer people could substitute birds. Note that some people could not afford even birds, so a small measure of flour, one-tenth of an *ephah,* could be substituted (5:11). In this case atonement (5:13) did not require a blood ritual. This illustrates how the sacrifice system itself was modified to accommodate the needs of the very poor.

for the sin that you have committed, a female from the flock, a sheep or a goat, as a sin offering; and the priest shall make atonement on your behalf for your sin.

7 But if you cannot afford a sheep, you shall bring to the LORD, as your penalty for the sin that you have committed, two turtledoves or two pigeons, one for a sin offering and the other for a burnt offering. [8]You shall bring them to the priest, who shall offer first the one for the sin offering, wringing its head at the nape without severing it. [9]He shall sprinkle some of the blood of the sin offering on the side of the altar, while the rest of the blood shall be drained out at the base of the altar; it is a sin offering. [10]And the second he shall offer for a burnt offering according to the regulation. Thus the priest shall make atonement on your behalf for the sin that you have committed, and you shall be forgiven.

11 But if you cannot afford two turtledoves or two pigeons, you shall bring as your offering for the sin that you have committed one-tenth of an ephah of choice flour for a sin offering; you shall not put oil on it or lay frankincense on it, for it is a sin offering. [12]You shall bring it to the priest, and the priest shall scoop up a handful of it as its memorial portion, and turn this into smoke on the altar, with the offerings by fire to the LORD; it is a sin offering. [13]Thus the priest shall make atonement on your behalf for whichever of these sins you have committed, and you shall be forgiven. Like the grain offering, the rest shall be for the priest.

Offerings with Restitution

5:15 commit a trespass...of the holy things: Encroachment by lay persons (those not chosen as priests) on items reserved for sanctuary use was considered trespassing. It was considered disastrous to the community if committed in secrecy, as was the case of Achan (Josh 7:1).

14 The LORD spoke to Moses, saying: [15]When any of you commit a trespass and sin unintentionally in any of the holy things of the LORD, you shall bring, as your guilt offering to the LORD, a ram without blemish from the flock, convertible into silver by the sanctuary shekel; it is a guilt offering. [16]And you shall make restitution for the holy thing in which you were remiss, and shall add one-fifth to it and give it to the priest. The priest shall make atonement on your behalf with the ram of the guilt offering, and you shall be forgiven.

17 If any of you sin without knowing it, doing any of the things that by the LORD's commandments ought not to be done, you have incurred guilt, and are subject to punishment. [18]You shall bring to the priest a ram without blemish from the flock, or the equivalent, as a guilt offering; and the priest shall make atonement on your behalf for the error that you committed unintentionally, and you shall be forgiven. [19]It is a guilt offering; you have incurred guilt before the LORD.

6:1-7 deceiving a neighbor: This section continues legislation regarding "trespass" against the LORD. Here the issue is stealing property from another in ways that again undermine the judicial system: lying, fraud, and giving false testimony.

6 [a] The LORD spoke to Moses, saying: [2]When any of you sin and commit a trespass against the LORD by deceiving a neigh-

[a] Ch 5.20 in Heb

Offerings in Israel

Leviticus describes the basic kinds of offerings or sacrifices that Israel's priests were to offer for the people.

Type of offering or sacrifice	Object to be sacrificed	Reason for the offering
Whole burnt offerings	Bull, male sheep or goat without blemish; a dove or pigeon for the poor The entire animal is to be burned on the altar.	• For atonement (forgiveness) of sins (1:1-4; 16:23-24). • To please and honor God with a pleasing odor (1:5-17; 6:8-13; 8:18-21).
Grain offerings	Wheat flour, olive oil and frankincense mixed together; bread baked without yeast or honey in loaves or wafers; salt At times offered along with burnt offerings or peace offerings.	• To please and honor God with a pleasing odor (2:1-16; 6:14-18). A portion kept as food for priests and families. • To honor God with "first fruits" as a way to acknowledge God as provider (2:14). • To celebrate the anointing of a priest. Entire offering burned and none eaten (6:19-23).
Offerings of well-being	Fat and certain inner organs from a bull, cow, sheep, or goat that has no blemish; various kinds of bread made without yeast	• To give thanks to God and ask for God's blessing. The leftover meat was to be kept and eaten by the priests (3:1-17; 7:11-36). • A votive offering in response to fulfilling a vow (7:16-18).
Purification offerings; Sometimes referred to as "sin" offerings	A young bull for the high priest and the whole nation; a male goat for a tribal leader; a female goat or lamb for ordinary people; two doves or pigeons for the poor; two pounds of fine flour for the very poor; two goats and a ram on Day of Atonement	• To ask God's forgiveness for sins committed; to make up for unintentional sins (4:1—5:1; 5:4-13; 6:24-30; 8:14-17). • To be purified after becoming ritually unclean (5:2-3; 12:1-8; 15:13-30). • To forgive the sins of all the people on the Day of Atonement. The scapegoat is sent away into the wilderness (16:2-22).
Guilt offerings or offerings of restitution	A ram that has nothing wrong with it, or the price of the ram; and, the guilty person is to pay back the value of what was stolen or destroyed plus an additional one-fifth.	• To make things right after cheating the LORD, or for unintentionally destroying something that belonged to the Lord (5:14-19). • To make up for intentionally or unintentionally robbing, cheating or injuring another person (6:1-7; 7:1-10).

bor in a matter of a deposit or a pledge, or by robbery, or if you have
defrauded a neighbor, [3]or have found something lost and lied about
it—if you swear falsely regarding any of the various things that one
may do and sin thereby— [4]when you have sinned and realize your
guilt, and would restore what you took by robbery or by fraud or the
deposit that was committed to you, or the lost thing that you found,
[5]or anything else about which you have sworn falsely, you shall repay the principal amount and shall add one-fifth to it. You shall pay it
to its owner when you realize your guilt. [6]And you shall bring to the
priest, as your guilt offering to the LORD, a ram without blemish from
the flock, or its equivalent, for a guilt offering. [7]The priest shall make
atonement on your behalf before the LORD, and you shall be forgiven
for any of the things that one may do and incur guilt thereby.

Instructions concerning Sacrifices

8[a] The LORD spoke to Moses, saying: [9]Command Aaron and his
sons, saying: This is the ritual of the burnt offering. The burnt offering itself shall remain on the hearth upon the altar all night until the
morning, while the fire on the altar shall be kept burning. [10]The priest
shall put on his linen vestments after putting on his linen undergarments next to his body; and he shall take up the ashes to which the
fire has reduced the burnt offering on the altar, and place them beside the altar. [11]Then he shall take off his vestments and put on other
garments, and carry the ashes out to a clean place outside the camp.
[12]The fire on the altar shall be kept burning; it shall not go out. Every
morning the priest shall add wood to it, lay out the burnt offering on
it, and turn into smoke the fat pieces of the offerings of well-being. [13]A
perpetual fire shall be kept burning on the altar; it shall not go out.

14 This is the ritual of the grain offering: The sons of Aaron shall
offer it before the LORD, in front of the altar. [15]They shall take from
it a handful of the choice flour and oil of the grain offering, with all
the frankincense that is on the offering, and they shall turn its memorial portion into smoke on the altar as a pleasing odor to the LORD.
[16]Aaron and his sons shall eat what is left of it; it shall be eaten as unleavened cakes in a holy place; in the court of the tent of meeting they
shall eat it. [17]It shall not be baked with leaven. I have given it as their
portion of my offerings by fire; it is most holy, like the sin offering and
the guilt offering. [18]Every male among the descendants of Aaron shall
eat of it, as their perpetual due throughout your generations, from the
LORD's offerings by fire; anything that touches them shall become
holy.

19 The LORD spoke to Moses, saying: [20]This is the offering that
Aaron and his sons shall offer to the LORD on the day when he is

[a] Ch 6.1 in Heb

6:4, 5 realize your guilt: In these cases the Hebrew verb *ašēm* (a-SHAME) must mean "admit your guilt" or "seek to remedy your guilt."

6:8—7:36 ritual of the burnt offering: This section contains instructions about how to perform the burnt offering and describes the priests' right to consume a designated portion of the sacrifices as payment due to them for their service.

6:11 he shall take off his vestments: Service at the altar placed the priests in contact with the potential lethal quality of God's holiness, requiring special precautions. Here the priest dresses back into his "street-clothing" to be worn in the "profane" or "common" realm of everyday living. Otherwise holiness would leak out and contaminate the common area of day-to-day life.

6:19-23 offering...shall not be eaten: A description of the priest's ordination grain offering. This anticipates the ordination of Aaron and his sons in Chapter 8.

anointed: one-tenth of an ephah of choice flour as a regular offering,
half of it in the morning and half in the evening. 21 It shall be made with
oil on a griddle; you shall bring it well soaked, as a grain offering of
baked[a] pieces, and you shall present it as a pleasing odor to the LORD.
22 And so the priest, anointed from among Aaron's descendants as a
successor, shall prepare it; it is the LORD's—a perpetual due—to be
turned entirely into smoke. 23 Every grain offering of a priest shall be
wholly burned; it shall not be eaten.

24 The LORD spoke to Moses, saying: 25 Speak to Aaron and his
sons, saying: This is the ritual of the sin offering. The sin offering shall
be slaughtered before the LORD at the spot where the burnt offering
is slaughtered; it is most holy. 26 The priest who offers it as a sin offering shall eat of it; it shall be eaten in a holy place, in the court of the
tent of meeting. 27 Whatever touches its flesh shall become holy; and
when any of its blood is spattered on a garment, you shall wash the
bespattered part in a holy place. 28 An earthen vessel in which it was
boiled shall be broken; but if it is boiled in a bronze vessel, that shall
be scoured and rinsed in water. 29 Every male among the priests shall
eat of it; it is most holy. 30 But no sin offering shall be eaten from which
any blood is brought into the tent of meeting for atonement in the
holy place; it shall be burned with fire.

7 This is the ritual of the guilt offering. It is most holy; 2 at the spot
where the burnt offering is slaughtered, they shall slaughter the
guilt offering, and its blood shall be dashed against all sides of the altar. 3 All its fat shall be offered: the broad tail, the fat that covers the
entrails, 4 the two kidneys with the fat that is on them at the loins, and
the appendage of the liver, which shall be removed with the kidneys.
5 The priest shall turn them into smoke on the altar as an offering by
fire to the LORD; it is a guilt offering. 6 Every male among the priests
shall eat of it; it shall be eaten in a holy place; it is most holy.

7 The guilt offering is like the sin offering, there is the same ritual
for them; the priest who makes atonement with it shall have it. 8 So,
too, the priest who offers anyone's burnt offering shall keep the skin of
the burnt offering that he has offered. 9 And every grain offering baked
in the oven, and all that is prepared in a pan or on a griddle, shall belong to the priest who offers it. 10 But every other grain offering, mixed
with oil or dry, shall belong to all the sons of Aaron equally.

Further Instructions

11 This is the ritual of the sacrifice of the offering of well-being
that one may offer to the LORD. 12 If you offer it for thanksgiving, you
shall offer with the thank offering unleavened cakes mixed with oil,
unleavened wafers spread with oil, and cakes of choice flour well

[a] Meaning of Heb uncertain

6:24 the ritual of the sin offering: Similar instructions are given concerning the need to guard and contain the holiness associated with sacrificial blood and with the cooking of sacrificial meat for priestly consumption.

6:30 blood is brought into the tent of meeting for atonement: The priests are not to eat the sin offerings for the anointed priests themselves (4:5-12) and the entire community (4:13-21). These were to be burned completely. This rule possibly was intended to prevent conflicts of interest regarding priestly revenue.

7:1-10 guilt offering: These rules regarding the guilt offering focus upon priestly rights of consumption. The priests are to receive equal portions.

7:11-36 offering of well-being: This concludes the section on sacrifice. The instructions for priestly consumption of the sacrifice of well-being include occasions of joyful thanksgiving (7:12-15) and the making of vows or offerings free of any obligation.

soaked in oil. [13]With your thanksgiving sacrifice of well-being you
shall bring your offering with cakes of leavened bread. [14]From this you
shall offer one cake from each offering, as a gift to the LORD; it shall
belong to the priest who dashes the blood of the offering of well-
being. [15]And the flesh of your thanksgiving sacrifice of well-being
shall be eaten on the day it is offered; you shall not leave any of it until
morning. [16]But if the sacrifice you offer is a votive offering or a freewill
offering, it shall be eaten on the day that you offer your sacrifice, and
what is left of it shall be eaten the next day; [17]but what is left of the
flesh of the sacrifice shall be burned up on the third day. [18]If any of the
flesh of your sacrifice of well-being is eaten on the third day, it shall
not be acceptable, nor shall it be credited to the one who offers it; it
shall be an abomination, and the one who eats of it shall incur guilt.

19 Flesh that touches any unclean thing shall not be eaten; it
shall be burned up. As for other flesh, all who are clean may eat such
flesh. [20]But those who eat flesh from the LORD's sacrifice of well-being
while in a state of uncleanness shall be cut off from their kin. [21]When
any one of you touches any unclean thing—human uncleanness or an
unclean animal or any unclean creature—and then eats flesh from the
LORD's sacrifice of well-being, you shall be cut off from your kin.

22 The LORD spoke to Moses, saying: [23]Speak to the people of
Israel, saying: You shall eat no fat of ox or sheep or goat. [24]The fat of
an animal that died or was torn by wild animals may be put to any
other use, but you must not eat it. [25]If any one of you eats the fat from
an animal of which an offering by fire may be made to the LORD, you
who eat it shall be cut off from your kin. [26]You must not eat any blood
whatever, either of bird or of animal, in any of your settlements. [27]Any
one of you who eats any blood shall be cut off from your kin.

28 The LORD spoke to Moses, saying: [29]Speak to the people of
Israel, saying: Any one of you who would offer to the LORD your
sacrifice of well-being must yourself bring to the LORD your offering from your sacrifice of well-being. [30]Your own hands shall bring
the LORD's offering by fire; you shall bring the fat with the breast,
so that the breast may be raised as an elevation offering before the
LORD. [31]The priest shall turn the fat into smoke on the altar, but the
breast shall belong to Aaron and his sons. [32]And the right thigh from
your sacrifices of well-being you shall give to the priest as an offering; [33]the one among the sons of Aaron who offers the blood and fat
of the offering of well-being shall have the right thigh for a portion.
[34]For I have taken the breast of the elevation offering, and the thigh
that is offered, from the people of Israel, from their sacrifices of well-
being, and have given them to Aaron the priest and to his sons, as a
perpetual due from the people of Israel. [35]This is the portion allotted
to Aaron and to his sons from the offerings made by fire to the LORD,
once they have been brought forward to serve the LORD as priests;

7:18 it shall not be acceptable… credited: If not "credited" to the worshiper, it was invalid for fulfilling the purpose for which it was offered. The same term is used of God "crediting" Abraham with righteousness because of his trust (Gen 15:6).

7:20 in a state of uncleanness: It was no moral offense to become contaminated by uncleanness. It happened often in the course of daily life. However, it had to be remedied—usually by ritual washing and by a period of waiting—before the person could again rejoin the community in its normal affairs. Uncleanness could contaminate the realm of the "common" or "profane" just as could "holiness." See chapters 11–15.

36these the LORD commanded to be given them, when he anointed
them, as a perpetual due from the people of Israel throughout their
generations.

37 This is the ritual of the burnt offering, the grain offering, the
sin offering, the guilt offering, the offering of ordination, and the sacrifice of well-being, 38which the LORD commanded Moses on Mount
Sinai, when he commanded the people of Israel to bring their offerings to the LORD, in the wilderness of Sinai.

The Rites of Ordination

8 The LORD spoke to Moses, saying: 2Take Aaron and his sons
with him, the vestments, the anointing oil, the bull of sin offering, the two rams, and the basket of unleavened bread; 3and assemble
the whole congregation at the entrance of the tent of meeting. 4And
Moses did as the LORD commanded him. When the congregation
was assembled at the entrance of the tent of meeting, 5Moses said
to the congregation, "This is what the LORD has commanded to be
done."

6 Then Moses brought Aaron and his sons forward, and washed
them with water. 7He put the tunic on him, fastened the sash around
him, clothed him with the robe, and put the ephod on him. He then
put the decorated band of the ephod around him, tying the ephod to
him with it. 8He placed the breastpiece on him, and in the breastpiece
he put the Urim and the Thummim. 9And he set the turban on his
head, and on the turban, in front, he set the golden ornament, the
holy crown, as the LORD commanded Moses.

10 Then Moses took the anointing oil and anointed the tabernacle and all that was in it, and consecrated them. 11He sprinkled some
of it on the altar seven times, and anointed the altar and all its utensils, and the basin and its base, to consecrate them. 12He poured some
of the anointing oil on Aaron's head and anointed him, to consecrate
him. 13And Moses brought forward Aaron's sons, and clothed them
with tunics, and fastened sashes around them, and tied headdresses
on them, as the LORD commanded Moses.

14 He led forward the bull of sin offering; and Aaron and his
sons laid their hands upon the head of the bull of sin offering, 15and it
was slaughtered. Moses took the blood and with his finger put some
on each of the horns of the altar, purifying the altar; then he poured
out the blood at the base of the altar. Thus he consecrated it, to make
atonement for it. 16Moses took all the fat that was around the entrails,
and the appendage of the liver, and the two kidneys with their fat, and
turned them into smoke on the altar. 17But the bull itself, its skin and
flesh and its dung, he burned with fire outside the camp, as the LORD
commanded Moses.

18 Then he brought forward the ram of burnt offering. Aaron and

8:1-2 Aaron and his sons . . . anointing oil: These verses open the second major unit in the book. Included are instructions and a story detailing the ordination and installation of Aaron and his sons as priests (chapters 8–9) as well as the misadventures of Aaron's sons (chapter 10). Anointing oil refers to olive oil that was poured on one's head as a sign that the person had been chosen (see also Exod 28:41; 29:7).

8:7-8 ephod . . . the Urim and the Thummim: See Exodus 28:6-29, 39:2-21, and the illustration on p. 166. The ephod was an outer garment worn by Israel's priests. One was made of plain linen, for the priest and there was another more elaborate embroidered one for the high priest. The ephods of Gideon and Micah were inappropriately worshiped (Judg 8:27; 17:5; 18:14-20). In 1 Samuel 23:8-12 and 30:7-8 the ephod is associated with ritual divination (foretelling events), likely through the use of sacred objects called Urim and Thummim. Since legal cases were sometimes determined by such priestly ritual actions (Exod 22:8-9), the ephod, Urim, and Thummim were associated with the breastpiece of *judgment* (Lev 8:8).

How do you think God's will and purposes are made known to us? What do you think are some signs or means by which God speaks to us? How do you best listen to what God has to say to you?

his sons laid their hands on the head of the ram, 19 and it was slaughtered. Moses dashed the blood against all sides of the altar. 20 The ram
was cut into its parts, and Moses turned into smoke the head and the
parts and the suet. 21 And after the entrails and the legs were washed
with water, Moses turned into smoke the whole ram on the altar;
it was a burnt offering for a pleasing odor, an offering by fire to the
LORD, as the LORD commanded Moses.

22 Then he brought forward the second ram, the ram of ordination. Aaron and his sons laid their hands on the head of the ram, 23 and
it was slaughtered. Moses took some of its blood and put it on the
lobe of Aaron's right ear and on the thumb of his right hand and on
the big toe of his right foot. 24 After Aaron's sons were brought forward, Moses put some of the blood on the lobes of their right ears
and on the thumbs of their right hands and on the big toes of their
right feet; and Moses dashed the rest of the blood against all sides of
the altar. 25 He took the fat—the broad tail, all the fat that was around
the entrails, the appendage of the liver, and the two kidneys with their
fat—and the right thigh. 26 From the basket of unleavened bread that
was before the LORD, he took one cake of unleavened bread, one cake
of bread with oil, and one wafer, and placed them on the fat and on
the right thigh. 27 He placed all these on the palms of Aaron and on the
palms of his sons, and raised them as an elevation offering before the
LORD. 28 Then Moses took them from their hands and turned them
into smoke on the altar with the burnt offering. This was an ordination offering for a pleasing odor, an offering by fire to the LORD.
29 Moses took the breast and raised it as an elevation offering before
the LORD; it was Moses' portion of the ram of ordination, as the
LORD commanded Moses.

30 Then Moses took some of the anointing oil and some of the
blood that was on the altar and sprinkled them on Aaron and his vestments, and also on his sons and their vestments. Thus he consecrated
Aaron and his vestments, and also his sons and their vestments.

31 And Moses said to Aaron and his sons, "Boil the flesh at the
entrance of the tent of meeting, and eat it there with the bread that
is in the basket of ordination offerings, as I was commanded, 'Aaron
and his sons shall eat it'; 32 and what remains of the flesh and the bread
you shall burn with fire. 33 You shall not go outside the entrance of the
tent of meeting for seven days, until the day when your period of ordination is completed. For it will take seven days to ordain you; 34 as
has been done today, the LORD has commanded to be done to make
atonement for you. 35 You shall remain at the entrance of the tent of
meeting day and night for seven days, keeping the LORD's charge so
that you do not die; for so I am commanded." 36 Aaron and his sons
did all the things that the LORD commanded through Moses.

8:22 the ram of ordination: The term here for ordination is *mill'im* [mil-oo-EEM]. It refers to "filling," as the full expression was to "fill the hand" (Exod 28:41; 29:9, 33, 35; Lev 8:33), perhaps a reference to placing something in the hand of the priest, such as is done in 8:27.

Aaron's Priesthood Inaugurated

9 On the eighth day Moses summoned Aaron and his sons and
the elders of Israel. [2]He said to Aaron, "Take a bull calf for a sin
offering and a ram for a burnt offering, without blemish, and offer
them before the LORD. [3]And say to the people of Israel, 'Take a male
goat for a sin offering; a calf and a lamb, yearlings without blemish,
for a burnt offering; [4]and an ox and a ram for an offering of well-being
to sacrifice before the LORD; and a grain offering mixed with oil. For
today the LORD will appear to you.' " [5]They brought what Moses commanded to the front of the tent of meeting; and the whole congregation drew near and stood before the LORD. [6]And Moses said, "This
is the thing that the LORD commanded you to do, so that the glory
of the LORD may appear to you." [7]Then Moses said to Aaron, "Draw
near to the altar and sacrifice your sin offering and your burnt offering, and make atonement for yourself and for the people; and sacrifice the offering of the people, and make atonement for them; as the
LORD has commanded."

8 Aaron drew near to the altar, and slaughtered the calf of the sin
offering, which was for himself. [9]The sons of Aaron presented the
blood to him, and he dipped his finger in the blood and put it on the
horns of the altar; and the rest of the blood he poured out at the base
of the altar. [10]But the fat, the kidneys, and the appendage of the liver
from the sin offering he turned into smoke on the altar, as the LORD
commanded Moses; [11]and the flesh and the skin he burned with fire
outside the camp.

12 Then he slaughtered the burnt offering. Aaron's sons brought
him the blood, and he dashed it against all sides of the altar. [13]And
they brought him the burnt offering piece by piece, and the head,
which he turned into smoke on the altar. [14]He washed the entrails
and the legs and, with the burnt offering, turned them into smoke
on the altar.

15 Next he presented the people's offering. He took the goat of
the sin offering that was for the people, and slaughtered it, and presented it as a sin offering like the first one. [16]He presented the burnt
offering, and sacrificed it according to regulation. [17]He presented the
grain offering, and, taking a handful of it, he turned it into smoke on
the altar, in addition to the burnt offering of the morning.

18 He slaughtered the ox and the ram as a sacrifice of well-being
for the people. Aaron's sons brought him the blood, which he dashed
against all sides of the altar, [19]and the fat of the ox and of the ram—the
broad tail, the fat that covers the entrails, the two kidneys and the fat
on them,[a] and the appendage of the liver. [20]They first laid the fat on
the breasts, and the fat was turned into smoke on the altar; [21]and the

9:1-24 Moses summoned Aaron: This section tells the story of the first sacrifices of Aaron and the priests. First Aaron sacrificed a sin offering to make atonement (see note on 4:20) for himself (9:8-11), then the burnt offering (9:12-14), then the sin offering to make atonement for the people (9:15), followed by their burnt offering and grain offering (9:16-17), and lastly the sacrifice of well-being (or "concluding sacrifice," 9:18-21).

---

[a] Gk: Heb *the broad tail, and that which covers, and the kidneys*

breasts and the right thigh Aaron raised as an elevation offering before the LORD, as Moses had commanded.

22 Aaron lifted his hands toward the people and blessed them; and he came down after sacrificing the sin offering, the burnt offering, and the offering of well-being. 23Moses and Aaron entered the tent of meeting, and then came out and blessed the people; and the glory of the LORD appeared to all the people. 24Fire came out from the LORD and consumed the burnt offering and the fat on the altar; and when all the people saw it, they shouted and fell on their faces.

Nadab and Abihu

10 Now Aaron's sons, Nadab and Abihu, each took his censer, put fire in it, and laid incense on it; and they offered unholy fire before the LORD, such as he had not commanded them. 2And fire came out from the presence of the LORD and consumed them, and they died before the LORD. 3Then Moses said to Aaron, "This is what the LORD meant when he said,

'Through those who are near me
  I will show myself holy,
and before all the people
  I will be glorified.' "

And Aaron was silent.

4 Moses summoned Mishael and Elzaphan, sons of Uzziel the uncle of Aaron, and said to them, "Come forward, and carry your kinsmen away from the front of the sanctuary to a place outside the camp." 5They came forward and carried them by their tunics out of the camp, as Moses had ordered. 6And Moses said to Aaron and to his sons Eleazar and Ithamar, "Do not dishevel your hair, and do not tear your vestments, or you will die and wrath will strike all the congregation; but your kindred, the whole house of Israel, may mourn the burning that the LORD has sent. 7You shall not go outside the entrance of the tent of meeting, or you will die; for the anointing oil of the LORD is on you." And they did as Moses had ordered.

8 And the LORD spoke to Aaron: 9Drink no wine or strong drink, neither you nor your sons, when you enter the tent of meeting, that you may not die; it is a statute forever throughout your generations. 10You are to distinguish between the holy and the common, and between the unclean and the clean; 11and you are to teach the people of Israel all the statutes that the LORD has spoken to them through Moses.

12 Moses spoke to Aaron and to his remaining sons, Eleazar and Ithamar: Take the grain offering that is left from the LORD's offerings by fire, and eat it unleavened beside the altar, for it is most holy; 13you shall eat it in a holy place, because it is your due and your sons' due, from the offerings by fire to the LORD; for so I am commanded.

9:22 Aaron . . . blessed them: Though no words are recorded here, Aaron's famous blessing, known as the Aaronic Benediction, is given in Numbers 6:24-26.

9:23-24 entered the tent of meeting . . . Fire came out: This additional report seems to be added to enhance this scene. Moses himself enters the tent of meeting with Aaron and joined with Aaron in blessing the people. The line "Fire came out from the LORD and consumed the burnt offering and the fat" conflicts with the rest of the story, suggesting that it was added later.

10:1 unholy fire: Probably better translated as "strange fire" (see Num 3:4 and 26:61). The Hebrew term translated as "unholy" is used of dangerous strangeness and can be used of lay persons in contrast to priests (see also Lev 22:10-13). But here Nadab and Abihu were sons of Aaron himself. Scholars debate why their incense fires were strange or prohibited. The connection with Leviticus 16:1 suggests that the two had entered the inner sanctum of the sanctuary improperly. That would explain the connection with fire coming out "from the presence of the LORD" (see below).

10:2 fire came out from the presence of the LORD and consumed: This is virtually identical to the line in 9:24 and perhaps accounts for why these two stories found their place next to one another in this material.

10:6 Do not dishevel your hair . . . do not tear your vestments: These were standard mourning rituals for the dead. Priests were not permitted to participate in such rites while in a state of holiness (21:10-12) because dead bodies were primary sources of uncleanness.

10:9 Drink no wine: Wine was commonly drunk, but it impaired judgment. Drinking wine while on duty could jeopardize the priest's ability to distinguish between holy and common, clean and unclean, and teaching divine instruction (10:10-11).

What do Lutherans believe about distinctions between "holy" and "common," "clean" and "unclean"? Martin Luther stressed in his writings that all people are "sinful" but yet "made righteous," so it

14 But the breast that is elevated and the thigh that is raised, you and
your sons and daughters as well may eat in any clean place; for they
have been assigned to you and your children from the sacrifices of
the offerings of well-being of the people of Israel. 15 The thigh that is
raised and the breast that is elevated they shall bring, together with
the offerings by fire of the fat, to raise for an elevation offering before
the LORD; they are to be your due and that of your children forever,
as the LORD has commanded.

16 Then Moses made inquiry about the goat of the sin offering,
and—it had already been burned! He was angry with Eleazar and
Ithamar, Aaron's remaining sons, and said, 17 "Why did you not eat
the sin offering in the sacred area? For it is most holy, and God[a] has
given it to you that you may remove the guilt of the congregation,
to make atonement on their behalf before the LORD. 18 Its blood was
not brought into the inner part of the sanctuary. You should certainly
have eaten it in the sanctuary, as I commanded." 19 And Aaron spoke
to Moses, "See, today they offered their sin offering and their burnt
offering before the LORD; and yet such things as these have befallen
me! If I had eaten the sin offering today, would it have been agreeable
to the LORD?" 20 And when Moses heard that, he agreed.

Clean and Unclean Foods

11 The LORD spoke to Moses and Aaron, saying to them: 2 Speak
to the people of Israel, saying:

From among all the land animals, these are the creatures that you
may eat. 3 Any animal that has divided hoofs and is cleft-footed and
chews the cud—such you may eat. 4 But among those that chew the
cud or have divided hoofs, you shall not eat the following: the camel,
for even though it chews the cud, it does not have divided hoofs; it
is unclean for you. 5 The rock badger, for even though it chews the
cud, it does not have divided hoofs; it is unclean for you. 6 The hare,
for even though it chews the cud, it does not have divided hoofs; it is
unclean for you. 7 The pig, for even though it has divided hoofs and is
cleft-footed, it does not chew the cud; it is unclean for you. 8 Of their
flesh you shall not eat, and their carcasses you shall not touch; they
are unclean for you.

9 These you may eat, of all that are in the waters. Everything in the
waters that has fins and scales, whether in the seas or in the streams—
such you may eat. 10 But anything in the seas or the streams that does
not have fins and scales, of the swarming creatures in the waters and
among all the other living creatures that are in the waters—they are
detestable to you 11 and detestable they shall remain. Of their flesh
you shall not eat, and their carcasses you shall regard as detestable.

[a] Heb *he*

is not helpful to imagine that anyone is only one or the other. We do not describe people as being ritually unclean, nor do we consider pastors to be more holy than anyone else. Also, God commands common things such as water and bread and wine to be used along with God's Word to make God's promises concrete in the sacraments of Baptism and Holy Communion. *Leviticus 10:10*

What, if anything, do you think might make people unclean in God's eyes?

10:16 goat of the sin offering: The first sin offering (9:8-11) was for Aaron, so it was not for priestly consumption (the flesh being burned along with the skin "outside the camp," 9:11). The second was "for the people" (9:15), and Aaron and his sons should have eaten their "holy portions" (24:9). Because they failed to do so, Moses was angry with them.

10:19 such things as these: Aaron protests that making their own sin offering did not bring any divine favor for Nadab and Abihu, so what difference would have been made by eating their portion of the people's sin offering? Moses finds this response appropriate.

11:1-47 the creatures that you may eat: This section focuses on the priestly task of distinguishing between clean and unclean (10:10; 11:47) by reviewing food that can and cannot be eaten. A popular theory today is that some animals are considered unclean because they are "out of place" in their environment.

11:7 The pig: See also Deuteronomy 14:8. Swine became the main symbol of the unclean animal (Isa 65:4; 66:3, 17; 1 Macc 1:47; 2 Macc 6:18; 7:1).

11:10 swarming creatures: The Hebrew term *sherets* (SHER-ets) indicates animals that move in ways that seem ill-adapted to their environment, such as water creatures that do not have fins and scales to move.

[12]Everything in the waters that does not have fins and scales is detestable to you.

13 These you shall regard as detestable among the birds. They
shall not be eaten; they are an abomination: the eagle, the vulture, the
osprey, [14]the buzzard, the kite of any kind; [15]every raven of any kind;
[16]the ostrich, the nighthawk, the sea gull, the hawk of any kind; [17]the
little owl, the cormorant, the great owl, [18]the water hen, the desert
owl,[a] the carrion vulture, [19]the stork, the heron of any kind, the hoopoe, and the bat.[b]

11:20 winged insects: This literally means "swarming winged things," namely animals that ought to fly but have legs for walking. Some in this category are equipped with legs for springing (locusts, grasshoppers), however, so they are not sufficiently "out of place" and can be eaten.

20 All winged insects that walk upon all fours are detestable to
you. [21]But among the winged insects that walk on all fours you may
eat those that have jointed legs above their feet, with which to leap on
the ground. [22]Of them you may eat: the locust according to its kind,
the bald locust according to its kind, the cricket according to its kind,
and the grasshopper according to its kind. [23]But all other winged insects that have four feet are detestable to you.

Unclean Animals

24 By these you shall become unclean; whoever touches the carcass of any of them shall be unclean until the evening, [25]and whoever
carries any part of the carcass of any of them shall wash his clothes and
be unclean until the evening. [26]Every animal that has divided hoofs
but is not cleft-footed or does not chew the cud is unclean for you;
everyone who touches one of them shall be unclean. [27]All that walk
on their paws, among the animals that walk on all fours, are unclean
for you; whoever touches the carcass of any of them shall be unclean
until the evening, [28]and the one who carries the carcass shall wash his
clothes and be unclean until the evening; they are unclean for you.

29 These are unclean for you among the creatures that swarm
upon the earth: the weasel, the mouse, the great lizard according to its
kind, [30]the gecko, the land crocodile, the lizard, the sand lizard, and the
chameleon. [31]These are unclean for you among all that swarm; whoever touches one of them when they are dead shall be unclean until
the evening. [32]And anything upon which any of them falls when they
are dead shall be unclean, whether an article of wood or cloth or skin
or sacking, any article that is used for any purpose; it shall be dipped
into water, and it shall be unclean until the evening, and then it shall be
clean. [33]And if any of them falls into any earthen vessel, all that is in it
shall be unclean, and you shall break the vessel. [34]Any food that could
be eaten shall be unclean if water from any such vessel comes upon
it; and any liquid that could be drunk shall be unclean if it was in any
such vessel. [35]Everything on which any part of the carcass falls shall be
unclean; whether an oven or stove, it shall be broken in pieces; they

---

[a] Or *pelican* [b] Identification of several of the birds in verses 13–19 is uncertain

are unclean, and shall remain unclean for you. 36 But a spring or a cistern holding water shall be clean, while whatever touches the carcass in it shall be unclean. 37 If any part of their carcass falls upon any seed set aside for sowing, it is clean; 38 but if water is put on the seed and any part of their carcass falls on it, it is unclean for you.

39 If an animal of which you may eat dies, anyone who touches its carcass shall be unclean until the evening. 40 Those who eat of its carcass shall wash their clothes and be unclean until the evening; and those who carry the carcass shall wash their clothes and be unclean until the evening.

41 All creatures that swarm upon the earth are detestable; they shall not be eaten. 42 Whatever moves on its belly, and whatever moves on all fours, or whatever has many feet, all the creatures that swarm upon the earth, you shall not eat; for they are detestable. 43 You shall not make yourselves detestable with any creature that swarms; you shall not defile yourselves with them, and so become unclean. 44 For I am the LORD your God; sanctify yourselves therefore, and be holy, for I am holy. You shall not defile yourselves with any swarming creature that moves on the earth. 45 For I am the LORD who brought you up from the land of Egypt, to be your God; you shall be holy, for I am holy.

46 This is the law pertaining to land animal and bird and every living creature that moves through the waters and every creature that swarms upon the earth, 47 to make a distinction between the unclean and the clean, and between the living creature that may be eaten and the living creature that may not be eaten.

11:39-40 animal…dies…shall be unclean: Touching the carcass of a dead animal made a person unclean for the remainder of the day. This required washing one's clothes and likely not touching others to avoid making them unclean as well.

Purification of Women after Childbirth

12 The LORD spoke to Moses, saying: 2 Speak to the people of Israel, saying:

If a woman conceives and bears a male child, she shall be ceremonially unclean seven days; as at the time of her menstruation, she shall be unclean. 3 On the eighth day the flesh of his foreskin shall be circumcised. 4 Her time of blood purification shall be thirty-three days; she shall not touch any holy thing, or come into the sanctuary, until the days of her purification are completed. 5 If she bears a female child, she shall be unclean two weeks, as in her menstruation; her time of blood purification shall be sixty-six days.

6 When the days of her purification are completed, whether for a son or for a daughter, she shall bring to the priest at the entrance of the tent of meeting a lamb in its first year for a burnt offering, and a pigeon or a turtledove for a sin offering. 7 He shall offer it before the LORD, and make atonement on her behalf; then she shall be clean from her flow of blood. This is the law for her who bears a child, male or female. 8 If she cannot afford a sheep, she shall take two turtledoves

12:1—15:33 ceremonially unclean: This section turns to issues of uncleanness encountered in daily life, especially in contexts of birth (12:1-8), wasting disease (13:1-14:57) and bodily discharges (15:1-33).

12:2 ceremonially unclean seven days: Bodily fluids and blood commonly accompany childbirth, making the birth mother ritually unclean. For seven days she must limit social contacts and can contaminate the "common" with "uncleanness." For another thirty-three days she can contaminate the "holy," so she cannot touch holy things or enter the sanctuary area. This extended period results from contact with the power of blood and the potent force of life-generation itself.

12:5 two weeks…sixty-six days: The time of blood purification is doubled for a mother of a female infant, perhaps because she has given birth to one who herself is a producer of life and of blood.

12:6 for a sin offering: The side effect of uncleanness associated with birth is "sin." This indicates that for ancient Israel the concept of sin was not simply connected to moral intent.

Do you think that sinners are necessarily bad people? What do we mean when we say that we are "in bondage to sin" (*LBW*, p. 56) or that we are "captive to sin and cannot free ourselves" (*ELW*, p. 95)? Can you think of some examples of people being trapped in a sinful situation or condition?

or two pigeons, one for a burnt offering and the other for a sin offering; and the priest shall make atonement on her behalf, and she shall be clean.

Leprosy, Varieties and Symptoms

13 The LORD spoke to Moses and Aaron, saying:
2 When a person has on the skin of his body a swelling or
an eruption or a spot, and it turns into a leprous[a] disease on the skin
of his body, he shall be brought to Aaron the priest or to one of his
sons the priests. 3 The priest shall examine the disease on the skin of
his body, and if the hair in the diseased area has turned white and
the disease appears to be deeper than the skin of his body, it is a leprous[a] disease; after the priest has examined him he shall pronounce
him ceremonially unclean. 4 But if the spot is white in the skin of his
body, and appears no deeper than the skin, and the hair in it has not
turned white, the priest shall confine the diseased person for seven
days. 5 The priest shall examine him on the seventh day, and if he sees
that the disease is checked and the disease has not spread in the skin,
then the priest shall confine him seven days more. 6 The priest shall
examine him again on the seventh day, and if the disease has abated
and the disease has not spread in the skin, the priest shall pronounce
him clean; it is only an eruption; and he shall wash his clothes, and
be clean. 7 But if the eruption spreads in the skin after he has shown
himself to the priest for his cleansing, he shall appear again before the
priest. 8 The priest shall make an examination, and if the eruption has
spread in the skin, the priest shall pronounce him unclean; it is a leprous[a] disease.

13:2 leprous disease: This term covers a number of skin conditions, most of which are not technically classified today as leprosy. Such conditions (fungus, mold, and mildew infestations) also affected clothing (13:47-59) and houses (14:34-53). The priest made the diagnosis as part of his task of distinguishing between clean and unclean (10:10; Luke 17:14).

9 When a person contracts a leprous[a] disease, he shall be brought
to the priest. 10 The priest shall make an examination, and if there is a
white swelling in the skin that has turned the hair white, and there is
quick raw flesh in the swelling, 11 it is a chronic leprous[a] disease in the
skin of his body. The priest shall pronounce him unclean; he shall not
confine him, for he is unclean. 12 But if the disease breaks out in the
skin, so that it covers all the skin of the diseased person from head
to foot, so far as the priest can see, 13 then the priest shall make an examination, and if the disease has covered all his body, he shall pronounce him clean of the disease; since it has all turned white, he is
clean. 14 But if raw flesh ever appears on him, he shall be unclean; 15 the
priest shall examine the raw flesh and pronounce him unclean. Raw
flesh is unclean, for it is a leprous[a] disease. 16 But if the raw flesh again
turns white, he shall come to the priest; 17 the priest shall examine
him, and if the disease has turned white, the priest shall pronounce
the diseased person clean. He is clean.

13:11 he shall not confine him: No quarantine period is required because the diagnosis is clear. He has leprosy. Other cases require quarantine for seven days, after which another examination is performed (13:5-6, 21, 26-28, 31-32).

13:14 raw flesh: Literally means "living flesh" and is regarded as the sign of active leprosy.

---

[a] A term for several skin diseases; precise meaning uncertain

18 When there is on the skin of one's body a boil that has healed, 19 and in the place of the boil there appears a white swelling or a reddish-white spot, it shall be shown to the priest. 20 The priest shall make an examination, and if it appears deeper than the skin and its hair has turned white, the priest shall pronounce him unclean; this is a leprous[a] disease, broken out in the boil. 21 But if the priest examines it and the hair on it is not white, nor is it deeper than the skin but has abated, the priest shall confine him seven days. 22 If it spreads in the skin, the priest shall pronounce him unclean; it is diseased. 23 But if the spot remains in one place and does not spread, it is the scar of the boil; the priest shall pronounce him clean.

24 Or, when the body has a burn on the skin and the raw flesh of the burn becomes a spot, reddish-white or white, 25 the priest shall examine it. If the hair in the spot has turned white and it appears deeper than the skin, it is a leprous[a] disease; it has broken out in the burn, and the priest shall pronounce him unclean. This is a leprous[a] disease. 26 But if the priest examines it and the hair in the spot is not white, and it is no deeper than the skin but has abated, the priest shall confine him seven days. 27 The priest shall examine him the seventh day; if it is spreading in the skin, the priest shall pronounce him unclean. This is a leprous[a] disease. 28 But if the spot remains in one place and does not spread in the skin but has abated, it is a swelling from the burn, and the priest shall pronounce him clean; for it is the scar of the burn.

29 When a man or woman has a disease on the head or in the beard, 30 the priest shall examine the disease. If it appears deeper than the skin and the hair in it is yellow and thin, the priest shall pronounce him unclean; it is an itch, a leprous[a] disease of the head or the beard. 31 If the priest examines the itching disease, and it appears no deeper than the skin and there is no black hair in it, the priest shall confine the person with the itching disease for seven days. 32 On the seventh day the priest shall examine the itch; if the itch has not spread, and there is no yellow hair in it, and the itch appears to be no deeper than the skin, 33 he shall shave, but the itch he shall not shave. The priest shall confine the person with the itch for seven days more. 34 On the seventh day the priest shall examine the itch; if the itch has not spread in the skin and it appears to be no deeper than the skin, the priest shall pronounce him clean. He shall wash his clothes and be clean. 35 But if the itch spreads in the skin after he was pronounced clean, 36 the priest shall examine him. If the itch has spread in the skin, the priest need not seek for the yellow hair; he is unclean. 37 But if in his eyes the itch is checked, and black hair has grown in it, the itch is healed, he is clean; and the priest shall pronounce him clean.

---

[a] A term for several skin diseases; precise meaning uncertain

38 When a man or a woman has spots on the skin of the body,
white spots, 39 the priest shall make an examination, and if the spots
on the skin of the body are of a dull white, it is a rash that has broken
out on the skin; he is clean.

40 If anyone loses the hair from his head, he is bald but he is clean.
41 If he loses the hair from his forehead and temples, he has baldness
of the forehead but he is clean. 42 But if there is on the bald head or the
bald forehead a reddish-white diseased spot, it is a leprous[a] disease
breaking out on his bald head or his bald forehead. 43 The priest shall
examine him; if the diseased swelling is reddish-white on his bald
head or on his bald forehead, which resembles a leprous[a] disease in
the skin of the body, 44 he is leprous,[a] he is unclean. The priest shall
pronounce him unclean; the disease is on his head.

13:45-46 torn clothes…be outside the camp: Describes the sad fate of those declared to be leprous. Marked by tattered clothing and a peculiar way of announcing their presence, they had to live apart from the rest of society ("outside the camp"). See also Numbers 5:2-3, 2 Chronicles 26:19-23.

13:48 in warp or woof: The "warp" refers to the threads that run lengthwise in a piece of fabric. The "woof" refers to the cloth and its texture. A stain caused by disease could not easily be washed out, so it was to be cut away.

45 The person who has the leprous[a] disease shall wear torn
clothes and let the hair of his head be disheveled; and he shall cover
his upper lip and cry out, "Unclean, unclean." 46 He shall remain unclean as long as he has the disease; he is unclean. He shall live alone;
his dwelling shall be outside the camp.

47 Concerning clothing: when a leprous[a] disease appears in it, in
woolen or linen cloth, 48 in warp or woof of linen or wool, or in a skin
or in anything made of skin, 49 if the disease shows greenish or reddish
in the garment, whether in warp or woof or in skin or in anything
made of skin, it is a leprous[a] disease and shall be shown to the priest.
50 The priest shall examine the disease, and put the diseased article
aside for seven days. 51 He shall examine the disease on the seventh
day. If the disease has spread in the cloth, in warp or woof, or in the
skin, whatever be the use of the skin, this is a spreading leprous[a] disease; it is unclean. 52 He shall burn the clothing, whether diseased in
warp or woof, woolen or linen, or anything of skin, for it is a spreading
leprous[a] disease; it shall be burned in fire.

53 If the priest makes an examination, and the disease has not
spread in the clothing, in warp or woof or in anything of skin, 54 the
priest shall command them to wash the article in which the disease
appears, and he shall put it aside seven days more. 55 The priest shall
examine the diseased article after it has been washed. If the diseased
spot has not changed color, though the disease has not spread, it is
unclean; you shall burn it in fire, whether the leprous[a] spot is on the
inside or on the outside.

56 If the priest makes an examination, and the disease has abated
after it is washed, he shall tear the spot out of the cloth, in warp or
woof, or out of skin. 57 If it appears again in the garment, in warp or
woof, or in anything of skin, it is spreading; you shall burn with fire
that in which the disease appears. 58 But the cloth, warp or woof, or

[a] A term for several skin diseases; precise meaning uncertain

anything of skin from which the disease disappears when you have
washed it, shall then be washed a second time, and it shall be clean.
59 This is the ritual for a leprous[a] disease in a cloth of wool or
linen, either in warp or woof, or in anything of skin, to decide whether
it is clean or unclean.

Purification of Lepers and Leprous Houses

14 The LORD spoke to Moses, saying: 2 This shall be the ritual
for the leprous[a] person at the time of his cleansing:
He shall be brought to the priest; 3 the priest shall go out of the
camp, and the priest shall make an examination. If the disease is
healed in the leprous[a] person, 4 the priest shall command that two
living clean birds and cedarwood and crimson yarn and hyssop be
brought for the one who is to be cleansed. 5 The priest shall command
that one of the birds be slaughtered over fresh water in an earthen vessel. 6 He shall take the living bird with the cedarwood and the crimson
yarn and the hyssop, and dip them and the living bird in the blood of
the bird that was slaughtered over the fresh water. 7 He shall sprinkle
it seven times upon the one who is to be cleansed of the leprous[a] disease; then he shall pronounce him clean, and he shall let the living
bird go into the open field. 8 The one who is to be cleansed shall wash
his clothes, and shave off all his hair, and bathe himself in water, and
he shall be clean. After that he shall come into the camp, but shall live
outside his tent seven days. 9 On the seventh day he shall shave all his
hair: of head, beard, eyebrows; he shall shave all his hair. Then he shall
wash his clothes, and bathe his body in water, and he shall be clean.
10 On the eighth day he shall take two male lambs without blemish, and one ewe lamb in its first year without blemish, and a grain
offering of three-tenths of an ephah of choice flour mixed with oil,
and one log[b] of oil. 11 The priest who cleanses shall set the person to be
cleansed, along with these things, before the LORD, at the entrance of
the tent of meeting. 12 The priest shall take one of the lambs, and offer
it as a guilt offering, along with the log[b] of oil, and raise them as an
elevation offering before the LORD. 13 He shall slaughter the lamb in
the place where the sin offering and the burnt offering are slaughtered
in the holy place; for the guilt offering, like the sin offering, belongs to
the priest: it is most holy. 14 The priest shall take some of the blood of
the guilt offering and put it on the lobe of the right ear of the one to
be cleansed, and on the thumb of the right hand, and on the big toe of
the right foot. 15 The priest shall take some of the log[b] of oil and pour it
into the palm of his own left hand, 16 and dip his right finger in the oil
that is in his left hand and sprinkle some oil with his finger seven times
before the LORD. 17 Some of the oil that remains in his hand the priest

14:2 the ritual...at the time of his cleansing: This ritual ceremony of cleansing was extensive. Even when clean, he cannot enter his home for seven days (14:8).

14:4 cedarwood...crimson yarn ...hyssop: It is not entirely clear why these items were used. The crimson yarn and the reddish cedar wood may have symbolized the life force of blood. The hyssop's stalk and leaves hold liquids well, so it may have been used to sprinkle liquids (see also Exod 12:22; Num 19:6, 17-18; Heb 9:19).

14:10 On the eighth day: There followed a second, even more complicated, ritual action involving the smearing of blood and oil on the right extremities of the person being cleansed (ear, thumb, and large toe; see also 8:22-24).

[a] A term for several skin diseases; precise meaning uncertain [b] A liquid measure

shall put on the lobe of the right ear of the one to be cleansed, and on
the thumb of the right hand, and on the big toe of the right foot, on
top of the blood of the guilt offering. 18 The rest of the oil that is in the
priest's hand he shall put on the head of the one to be cleansed. Then
the priest shall make atonement on his behalf before the LORD: 19 the
priest shall offer the sin offering, to make atonement for the one to be
cleansed from his uncleanness. Afterward he shall slaughter the burnt
offering; 20 and the priest shall offer the burnt offering and the grain
offering on the altar. Thus the priest shall make atonement on his behalf and he shall be clean.

14:21 But if he is poor: Options are provided for those who could not afford the full required payment. Otherwise the ritual acts remain much the same.

21 But if he is poor and cannot afford so much, he shall take one
male lamb for a guilt offering to be elevated, to make atonement on his
behalf, and one-tenth of an ephah of choice flour mixed with oil for a
grain offering and a log[a] of oil; 22 also two turtledoves or two pigeons,
such as he can afford, one for a sin offering and the other for a burnt
offering. 23 On the eighth day he shall bring them for his cleansing to
the priest, to the entrance of the tent of meeting, before the LORD;
24 and the priest shall take the lamb of the guilt offering and the log[a] of
oil, and the priest shall raise them as an elevation offering before the
LORD. 25 The priest shall slaughter the lamb of the guilt offering and
shall take some of the blood of the guilt offering, and put it on the
lobe of the right ear of the one to be cleansed, and on the thumb of the
right hand, and on the big toe of the right foot. 26 The priest shall pour
some of the oil into the palm of his own left hand, 27 and shall sprinkle
with his right finger some of the oil that is in his left hand seven times
before the LORD. 28 The priest shall put some of the oil that is in his
hand on the lobe of the right ear of the one to be cleansed, and on the
thumb of the right hand, and the big toe of the right foot, where the
blood of the guilt offering was placed. 29 The rest of the oil that is in
the priest's hand he shall put on the head of the one to be cleansed, to
make atonement on his behalf before the LORD. 30 And he shall offer,
of the turtledoves or pigeons such as he can afford, 31 one[b] for a sin
offering and the other for a burnt offering, along with a grain offering;
and the priest shall make atonement before the LORD on behalf of the
one being cleansed. 32 This is the ritual for the one who has a leprous[c]
disease, who cannot afford the offerings for his cleansing.

33 The LORD spoke to Moses and Aaron, saying:

14:34 When you come into the land of Canaan: A reminder of God's promise to Abraham and his descendants (see Gen 12:1-3; 15:18-21).

34 When you come into the land of Canaan, which I give you for
a possession, and I put a leprous[c] disease in a house in the land of your
possession, 35 the owner of the house shall come and tell the priest, saying, "There seems to me to be some sort of disease in my house." 36 The
priest shall command that they empty the house before the priest goes

---

[a] A liquid measure [b] Gk Syr: Heb *afford, 31 such as he can afford, one* [c] A term for several skin diseases; precise meaning uncertain

to examine the disease, or all that is in the house will become unclean;
and afterward the priest shall go in to inspect the house. [37]He shall examine the disease; if the disease is in the walls of the house with greenish or reddish spots, and if it appears to be deeper than the surface,
[38]the priest shall go outside to the door of the house and shut up the
house seven days. [39]The priest shall come again on the seventh day and
make an inspection; if the disease has spread in the walls of the house,
[40]the priest shall command that the stones in which the disease appears be taken out and thrown into an unclean place outside the city.
[41]He shall have the inside of the house scraped thoroughly, and the
plaster that is scraped off shall be dumped in an unclean place outside
the city. [42]They shall take other stones and put them in the place of
those stones, and take other plaster and plaster the house.

43 If the disease breaks out again in the house, after he has taken
out the stones and scraped the house and plastered it, [44]the priest shall
go and make inspection; if the disease has spread in the house, it is a
spreading leprous[a] disease in the house; it is unclean. [45]He shall have
the house torn down, its stones and timber and all the plaster of the
house, and taken outside the city to an unclean place. [46]All who enter
the house while it is shut up shall be unclean until the evening; [47]and
all who sleep in the house shall wash their clothes; and all who eat in
the house shall wash their clothes.

48 If the priest comes and makes an inspection, and the disease
has not spread in the house after the house was plastered, the priest
shall pronounce the house clean; the disease is healed. [49]For the
cleansing of the house he shall take two birds, with cedarwood and
crimson yarn and hyssop, [50]and shall slaughter one of the birds over
fresh water in an earthen vessel, [51]and shall take the cedarwood and
the hyssop and the crimson yarn, along with the living bird, and dip
them in the blood of the slaughtered bird and the fresh water, and
sprinkle the house seven times. [52]Thus he shall cleanse the house with
the blood of the bird, and with the fresh water, and with the living
bird, and with the cedarwood and hyssop and crimson yarn; [53]and he
shall let the living bird go out of the city into the open field; so he shall
make atonement for the house, and it shall be clean.

54 This is the ritual for any leprous[a] disease: for an itch, [55]for leprous[a] diseases in clothing and houses, [56]and for a swelling or an eruption or a spot, [57]to determine when it is unclean and when it is clean.
This is the ritual for leprous[a] diseases.

Concerning Bodily Discharges

15 The Lord spoke to Moses and Aaron, saying: [2]Speak to the
people of Israel and say to them:

[a] A term for several skin diseases; precise meaning uncertain

14:37 greenish or reddish spots: the language regarding the inspection of houses with leprosy and the ritual for cleansing them (14:48-53) are similar to those for humans and for clothing.

15:1-33 a discharge: This chapter concludes the section on ritual purification of uncleanness with instructions regarding bodily emissions. In Hebrew the word zab (ZAHB) refers to a person suffering such an emission. He or she was also quarantined from the community (Num 5:1-4; 2 Sam 3:29), because these bodily emissions were thought to be extremely contagious. The afflicted person was a primary source of uncleanness, requiring a seven-day period of quarantine following his "cleansing" (15:13-15). The regulations in 15:1-12 relate not to the *unclean person* him- or herself but rather to the person who has touched anything relating to the *unclean person.* Such secondary uncleanness required only a one-day quarantine.

15:3 his member: This literally means "his flesh." The reference here is likely to male genital problems. Again, such customs indicate that the concept of sin is not essentially connected to human willful intent or immoral actions.

When any man has a discharge from his member,[a] his discharge makes him ceremonially unclean. [3]The uncleanness of his discharge is this: whether his member[a] flows with his discharge, or his member[a] is stopped from discharging, it is uncleanness for him. [4]Every bed on which the one with the discharge lies shall be unclean; and everything on which he sits shall be unclean. [5]Anyone who touches his bed shall wash his clothes, and bathe in water, and be unclean until the evening. [6]All who sit on anything on which the one with the discharge has sat shall wash their clothes, and bathe in water, and be unclean until the evening. [7]All who touch the body of the one with the discharge shall wash their clothes, and bathe in water, and be unclean until the evening. [8]If the one with the discharge spits on persons who are clean, then they shall wash their clothes, and bathe in water, and be unclean until the evening. [9]Any saddle on which the one with the discharge rides shall be unclean. [10]All who touch anything that was under him shall be unclean until the evening, and all who carry such a thing shall wash their clothes, and bathe in water, and be unclean until the evening. [11]All those whom the one with the discharge touches without his having rinsed his hands in water shall wash their clothes, and bathe in water, and be unclean until the evening. [12]Any earthen vessel that the one with the discharge touches shall be broken; and every vessel of wood shall be rinsed in water.

13 When the one with a discharge is cleansed of his discharge, he shall count seven days for his cleansing; he shall wash his clothes and bathe his body in fresh water, and he shall be clean. [14]On the eighth day he shall take two turtledoves or two pigeons and come before the LORD to the entrance of the tent of meeting and give them to the priest. [15]The priest shall offer them, one for a sin offering and the other for a burnt offering; and the priest shall make atonement on his behalf before the LORD for his discharge.

15:16-18 emission of semen: Refers to natural secretions of semen. Because semen was considered the seed of life, it was thought to be potent and therefore producing "uncleanness." The husband and wife therefore had to remedy the uncleanness resulting from contact with semen. This is not because sexual activity was regarded as "dirty" but rather because it was regarded as mysteriously life-producing and involved extremely powerful forces requiring careful social controls.

In our modern scientific age, what, if any, mystery remains regarding conceiving and giving birth? What do you think of the idea that sexuality and sexual activity are powerful forces that require social controls? What role does the church play in this discussion?

16 If a man has an emission of semen, he shall bathe his whole body in water, and be unclean until the evening. [17]Everything made of cloth or of skin on which the semen falls shall be washed with water, and be unclean until the evening. [18]If a man lies with a woman and has an emission of semen, both of them shall bathe in water, and be unclean until the evening.

15:19-24 discharge of blood: These verses similarly recognize the powerful life-generating force associated with menstrual blood that also produced "uncleanness." For this reason, sexual activity with a woman during her menstrual cycle was discouraged (18:19; but see 15:24). See also the story of Laban and Rachel told in Genesis 31:34-35.

19 When a woman has a discharge of blood that is her regular discharge from her body, she shall be in her impurity for seven days, and whoever touches her shall be unclean until the evening. [20]Everything upon which she lies during her impurity shall be unclean; everything also upon which she sits shall be unclean. [21]Whoever touches her bed shall wash his clothes, and bathe in water, and be unclean until the evening. [22]Whoever touches anything upon which she sits shall

[a] Heb *flesh*

wash his clothes, and bathe in water, and be unclean until the evening; [23]whether it is the bed or anything upon which she sits, when he
touches it he shall be unclean until the evening. [24]If any man lies with
her, and her impurity falls on him, he shall be unclean seven days; and
every bed on which he lies shall be unclean.

25 If a woman has a discharge of blood for many days, not at the
time of her impurity, or if she has a discharge beyond the time of her
impurity, all the days of the discharge she shall continue in uncleanness; as in the days of her impurity, she shall be unclean. [26]Every bed
on which she lies during all the days of her discharge shall be treated
as the bed of her impurity; and everything on which she sits shall be
unclean, as in the uncleanness of her impurity. [27]Whoever touches
these things shall be unclean, and shall wash his clothes, and bathe
in water, and be unclean until the evening. [28]If she is cleansed of her
discharge, she shall count seven days, and after that she shall be clean.
[29]On the eighth day she shall take two turtledoves or two pigeons and
bring them to the priest at the entrance of the tent of meeting. [30]The
priest shall offer one for a sin offering and the other for a burnt offering; and the priest shall make atonement on her behalf before the
LORD for her unclean discharge.

31 Thus you shall keep the people of Israel separate from their
uncleanness, so that they do not die in their uncleanness by defiling
my tabernacle that is in their midst.

32 This is the ritual for those who have a discharge: for him who
has an emission of semen, becoming unclean thereby, [33]for her who is
in the infirmity of her period, for anyone, male or female, who has a
discharge, and for the man who lies with a woman who is unclean.

The Day of Atonement

16 The LORD spoke to Moses after the death of the two sons of
Aaron, when they drew near before the LORD and died. [2]The
LORD said to Moses:

Tell your brother Aaron not to come just at any time into the sanctuary inside the curtain before the mercy seat[a] that is upon the ark, or
he will die; for I appear in the cloud upon the mercy seat.[a] [3]Thus shall
Aaron come into the holy place: with a young bull for a sin offering
and a ram for a burnt offering. [4]He shall put on the holy linen tunic,
and shall have the linen undergarments next to his body, fasten the
linen sash, and wear the linen turban; these are the holy vestments.
He shall bathe his body in water, and then put them on. [5]He shall take
from the congregation of the people of Israel two male goats for a sin
offering, and one ram for a burnt offering.

6 Aaron shall offer the bull as a sin offering for himself, and shall

[a] Or *the cover*

15:25-30 beyond the time of her impurity: This concerns unnatural menstrual flow and is parallel to the instruction concerning unnatural male discharges (15:2-15).

16:1-34 shall make atonement: This chapter contains instructions for the annual Day of Atonement. Atonement was a daily ritual. Because some sins were unknown, unintended, or unacknowledged, the concern was that pollution would accumulate in the sacred sphere because of all the sins that had gone unnoticed. So the Day of Atonement was much like an annual cleansing of the sanctuary and community to rid them of such overlooked pollution. Atonement refers to the restoration of the broken relationship between God and sinful humanity. Christians have seen this ritual perfected in Christ's sacrifice on the cross (Heb 9:11-14).

16:1 after the death of the two sons of Aaron: See 10:2 above. This ritual continues the story from chapter 10. Aaron is warned to come into the inner sanctum of the sanctuary only on one specific day for this one particular ritual.

16:2 before the mercy seat: See Exodus 25:17-22. The word for this cover, *kapporet* (kap-POE-reth), connects it to atonement rituals on this Day of Atonement, which is celebrated in the Jewish tradition as *yom kippur* (yom kip-POOR).

make atonement for himself and for his house. 7 He shall take the two goats and set them before the LORD at the entrance of the tent of meeting; 8 and Aaron shall cast lots on the two goats, one lot for the LORD and the other lot for Azazel.[a] 9 Aaron shall present the goat on which the lot fell for the LORD, and offer it as a sin offering; 10 but the goat on which the lot fell for Azazel[a] shall be presented alive before the LORD to make atonement over it, that it may be sent away into the wilderness to Azazel.[a]

16:8 the other lot for Azazel: The term Azazel occurs only here, and it is not clear whether it refers to a "desert demon," as in later Jewish tradition, or means something like "for complete removal (of sin)." This second meaning is how it was understood in the early translation of the Hebrew Scriptures into Greek, called the Septuagint. See also 17:7.

11 Aaron shall present the bull as a sin offering for himself, and shall make atonement for himself and for his house; he shall slaughter the bull as a sin offering for himself. 12 He shall take a censer full of coals of fire from the altar before the LORD, and two handfuls of crushed sweet incense, and he shall bring it inside the curtain 13 and put the incense on the fire before the LORD, that the cloud of the incense may cover the mercy seat[b] that is upon the covenant,[c] or he will die. 14 He shall take some of the blood of the bull, and sprinkle it with his finger on the front of the mercy seat,[b] and before the mercy seat[b] he shall sprinkle the blood with his finger seven times.

15 He shall slaughter the goat of the sin offering that is for the people and bring its blood inside the curtain, and do with its blood as he did with the blood of the bull, sprinkling it upon the mercy seat[b] and before the mercy seat.[b] 16 Thus he shall make atonement for the sanctuary, because of the uncleannesses of the people of Israel, and because of their transgressions, all their sins; and so he shall do for the tent of meeting, which remains with them in the midst of their uncleannesses. 17 No one shall be in the tent of meeting from the time he enters to make atonement in the sanctuary until he comes out and has made atonement for himself and for his house and for all the assembly of Israel. 18 Then he shall go out to the altar that is before the LORD and make atonement on its behalf, and shall take some of the blood of the bull and of the blood of the goat, and put it on each of the horns of the altar. 19 He shall sprinkle some of the blood on it with his finger seven times, and cleanse it and hallow it from the uncleannesses of the people of Israel.

16:20-21 live goat…confess over it all the iniquities of the people: The high priest symbolically transfers the sins and uncleanness of the people to the goat, which is then released into the wilderness. The idea of the "scapegoat," one who takes the blame for another guilty party, comes from this ceremony.

20 When he has finished atoning for the holy place and the tent of meeting and the altar, he shall present the live goat. 21 Then Aaron shall lay both his hands on the head of the live goat, and confess over it all the iniquities of the people of Israel, and all their transgressions, all their sins, putting them on the head of the goat, and sending it away into the wilderness by means of someone designated for the task.[d] 22 The goat shall bear on itself all their iniquities to a barren region; and the goat shall be set free in the wilderness.

---

[a] Traditionally rendered *a scapegoat* [b] Or *the cover* [c] Or *treaty*, or *testament*; Heb *eduth* [d] Meaning of Heb uncertain

23 Then Aaron shall enter the tent of meeting, and shall take off
the linen vestments that he put on when he went into the holy place,
and shall leave them there. 24 He shall bathe his body in water in a holy
place, and put on his vestments; then he shall come out and offer his
burnt offering and the burnt offering of the people, making atonement for himself and for the people. 25 The fat of the sin offering he
shall turn into smoke on the altar. 26 The one who sets the goat free for
Azazel[a] shall wash his clothes and bathe his body in water, and afterward may come into the camp. 27 The bull of the sin offering and the
goat of the sin offering, whose blood was brought in to make atonement in the holy place, shall be taken outside the camp; their skin and
their flesh and their dung shall be consumed in fire. 28 The one who
burns them shall wash his clothes and bathe his body in water, and
afterward may come into the camp.

29 This shall be a statute to you forever: In the seventh month,
on the tenth day of the month, you shall deny yourselves,[b] and shall
do no work, neither the citizen nor the alien who resides among you.
30 For on this day atonement shall be made for you, to cleanse you;
from all your sins you shall be clean before the LORD. 31 It is a sabbath
of complete rest to you, and you shall deny yourselves;[b] it is a statute
forever. 32 The priest who is anointed and consecrated as priest in his
father's place shall make atonement, wearing the linen vestments, the
holy vestments. 33 He shall make atonement for the sanctuary, and he
shall make atonement for the tent of meeting and for the altar, and
he shall make atonement for the priests and for all the people of the
assembly. 34 This shall be an everlasting statute for you, to make atonement for the people of Israel once in the year for all their sins. And
Moses did as the LORD had commanded him.

The Slaughtering of Animals

17 The LORD spoke to Moses:
2 Speak to Aaron and his sons and to all the people of Israel
and say to them: This is what the LORD has commanded. 3 If anyone of
the house of Israel slaughters an ox or a lamb or a goat in the camp, or
slaughters it outside the camp, 4 and does not bring it to the entrance
of the tent of meeting, to present it as an offering to the LORD before
the tabernacle of the LORD, he shall be held guilty of bloodshed; he
has shed blood, and he shall be cut off from the people. 5 This is in order that the people of Israel may bring their sacrifices that they offer
in the open field, that they may bring them to the LORD, to the priest
at the entrance of the tent of meeting, and offer them as sacrifices of
well-being to the LORD. 6 The priest shall dash the blood against the
altar of the LORD at the entrance of the tent of meeting, and turn the

[a] Traditionally rendered *a scapegoat* [b] Or *shall fast*

16:29 Seventh month: The festival Day of Atonement falls in September or early October. The reference to the seventh month reflects a late custom used in this tradition, following the Babylonian calendar. Israel's earlier calendar began in the fall, so this would have been the first month in the earlier tradition. See the Jewish Festivals and Feasts chart, p. 227.

How do Lutherans relate the "blood of Christ" to the Day of Atonement? Like other Christians, Lutherans relate this scene from Leviticus and several other Bible passages to what Jesus did on the cross. We relate Jesus' suffering and death to the suffering servant described by the Old Testament prophet Isaiah (Isa 53:10). In Hebrews 10:11-14 Jesus is described as "a single sacrifice for sins." In Matthew 26:27-28 Jesus tells his disciples that the wine he shares with them "is my blood of the covenant, which is poured out for many for the forgiveness of sins." The word for atonement only appears once in the New Testament, in Romans 5:11, where it is translated as "reconciliation." A simple way to remember the meaning of atonement is by saying that in Jesus' death we are "at one" (reconciled) with God. *Leviticus 16:17-26*

Being reconciled with God can be described as being both once for all time and daily. How can this be?

17:1-16 If anyone...slaughters: These verses treat the unauthorized slaughter of animals. Added logically to this context is instruction about wild animals or birds taken in hunting. Because of the concern for draining blood immediately upon the animal's death, the eating of animals that were found dead, whether from natural causes or from attacks by other animals, was not permitted (17:15).

17:4 does not bring it to the entrance of the tent of meeting: Ancient custom regarded slaughter to be a sacred act requiring an altar (Exod 20:24; 1 Sam 14:31-35). A later custom allowed for slaughter to be a "secular" act of common daily life (Deut 12:15). The "priestly" tradition, reflected in Leviticus, again made slaughter a "sacral" act to be performed at the sanctuary in Jerusalem under priestly control.

17:7 goat-demons: This literally means "billy goats, bucks," the basic meaning of which is to "be hairy." Some references suggest, however, that these represented satyrs that were objects of idolatry and pagan worship (see Isa 13:21 and 34:14, where they are associated with "Lilith," often regarded as a night demon). See also 2 Chronicles 11:15.

fat into smoke as a pleasing odor to the LORD, [7]so that they may no
longer offer their sacrifices for goat-demons, to whom they prostitute
themselves. This shall be a statute forever to them throughout their
generations.
8 And say to them further: Anyone of the house of Israel or of the
aliens who reside among them who offers a burnt offering or sacrifice,
[9]and does not bring it to the entrance of the tent of meeting, to sacrifice it to the LORD, shall be cut off from the people.

Eating Blood Prohibited

10 If anyone of the house of Israel or of the aliens who reside
among them eats any blood, I will set my face against that person who
eats blood, and will cut that person off from the people. [11]For the life
of the flesh is in the blood; and I have given it to you for making atonement for your lives on the altar; for, as life, it is the blood that makes
atonement. [12]Therefore I have said to the people of Israel: No person
among you shall eat blood, nor shall any alien who resides among you
eat blood. [13]And anyone of the people of Israel, or of the aliens who
reside among them, who hunts down an animal or bird that may be
eaten shall pour out its blood and cover it with earth.
14 For the life of every creature—its blood is its life; therefore
I have said to the people of Israel: You shall not eat the blood of any
creature, for the life of every creature is its blood; whoever eats it shall
be cut off. [15]All persons, citizens or aliens, who eat what dies of itself
or what has been torn by wild animals, shall wash their clothes, and
bathe themselves in water, and be unclean until the evening; then
they shall be clean. [16]But if they do not wash themselves or bathe their
body, they shall bear their guilt.

17:12 alien: The *ger* [GAIR] held something like permanent guest-resident status. Unlike the "foreigner," the *alien* was the object of special social concern and often was included among other vulnerable members of the community who enjoyed special protection (19:33-34). However, they also bore the same responsibilities as full members of the community, as they do in this verse.

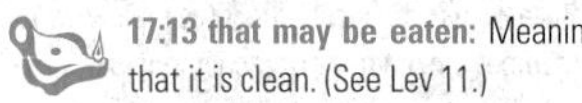

17:13 that may be eaten: Meaning that it is clean. (See Lev 11.)

Sexual Relations

18 The LORD spoke to Moses, saying:
2 Speak to the people of Israel and say to them: I am the
LORD your God. [3]You shall not do as they do in the land of Egypt,
where you lived, and you shall not do as they do in the land of Canaan, to which I am bringing you. You shall not follow their statutes.
[4]My ordinances you shall observe and my statutes you shall keep, following them: I am the LORD your God. [5]You shall keep my statutes
and my ordinances; by doing so one shall live: I am the LORD.
6 None of you shall approach anyone near of kin to uncover nakedness: I am the LORD. [7]You shall not uncover the nakedness of your
father, which is the nakedness of your mother; she is your mother,
you shall not uncover her nakedness. [8]You shall not uncover the nakedness of your father's wife; it is the nakedness of your father. [9]You
shall not uncover the nakedness of your sister, your father's daughter
or your mother's daughter, whether born at home or born abroad.

18:1-18 not do as... in the land of Canaan... nakedness: This section lists prohibited sexual relationships. Avoiding such behavior or practices was meant to set Israel apart from these neighbors and to keep Israel and its families free from this and other sexual uncleanness.

18:6 near of kin: Literally means "of his own flesh." Directed toward the male members of the family, this states the general principle and includes female relations within an extended family with multiple wives.

18:9 born abroad: Meaning "born outside," as opposed to being "born in the house." Perhaps it means born "outside the extended family" (*bet ab* [baith AHB], "father's house").

10 You shall not uncover the nakedness of your son's daughter or of
your daughter's daughter, for their nakedness is your own nakedness.
11 You shall not uncover the nakedness of your father's wife's daughter,
begotten by your father, since she is your sister. 12 You shall not uncover the nakedness of your father's sister; she is your father's flesh.
13 You shall not uncover the nakedness of your mother's sister, for she
is your mother's flesh. 14 You shall not uncover the nakedness of your
father's brother, that is, you shall not approach his wife; she is your
aunt. 15 You shall not uncover the nakedness of your daughter-in-law:
she is your son's wife; you shall not uncover her nakedness. 16 You shall
not uncover the nakedness of your brother's wife; it is your brother's
nakedness. 17 You shall not uncover the nakedness of a woman and her
daughter, and you shall not take[a] her son's daughter or her daughter's
daughter to uncover her nakedness; they are your[b] flesh; it is depravity. 18 And you shall not take[a] a woman as a rival to her sister, uncovering her nakedness while her sister is still alive.
19 You shall not approach a woman to uncover her nakedness
while she is in her menstrual uncleanness. 20 You shall not have sexual
relations with your kinsman's wife, and defile yourself with her. 21 You
shall not give any of your offspring to sacrifice them[c] to Molech, and
so profane the name of your God: I am the LORD. 22 You shall not lie
with a male as with a woman; it is an abomination. 23 You shall not
have sexual relations with any animal and defile yourself with it, nor
shall any woman give herself to an animal to have sexual relations
with it: it is perversion.
24 Do not defile yourselves in any of these ways, for by all these
practices the nations I am casting out before you have defiled themselves. 25 Thus the land became defiled; and I punished it for its iniquity, and the land vomited out its inhabitants. 26 But you shall keep my
statutes and my ordinances and commit none of these abominations,
either the citizen or the alien who resides among you 27 (for the inhabitants of the land, who were before you, committed all of these
abominations, and the land became defiled); 28 otherwise the land
will vomit you out for defiling it, as it vomited out the nation that was
before you. 29 For whoever commits any of these abominations shall
be cut off from their people. 30 So keep my charge not to commit any
of these abominations that were done before you, and not to defile
yourselves by them: I am the LORD your God.

Ritual and Moral Holiness

19 The LORD spoke to Moses, saying:
2 Speak to all the congregation of the people of Israel and
say to them: You shall be holy, for I the LORD your God am holy. 3 You

[a] Or *marry* [b] Gk: Heb lacks *your* [c] Heb *to pass them over*

18:16 nakedness of your brother's wife: An exception to this prohibition was the custom of "levirate marriage," in which a widow with no children might marry the brother of her dead husband to insure her social protection and inheritance rights (see Gen 38:8 and note; Deut 25:5-10).

18:19 menstrual uncleanness: See 15:19-24.

18:21 sacrifice them to Molech: Part of the offenses of the land of Canaan discussed here (18:3, 24-26). See 2 Kings 23:10 and Jeremiah 32:35, where infants were offered as a sacrifice to Molech by placing them in fire. Molech was either the patron god of Ammon (1 Kgs 11:7) or a mocking title for Baal (Jer 19:5; 32:35).

18:22-23 you shall not lie with: Prohibitions against sexual activity between men and between person and animal.

19:1-37 You shall be holy: This chapter presents a listing of instructions central to the concern for maintaining Israel's holiness in the presence of God's holiness (19:2). Holiness was to be maintained by being separated or set apart from the practices and religion of their non-Israelite neighbors. Some of these laws echo the fundamental tradition of the Ten Commandments (for example, 19:3-4, 11-13).

shall each revere your mother and father, and you shall keep my sabbaths: I am the LORD your God. 4 Do not turn to idols or make cast
images for yourselves: I am the LORD your God.
5 When you offer a sacrifice of well-being to the LORD, offer it in
such a way that it is acceptable in your behalf. 6 It shall be eaten on the
same day you offer it, or on the next day; and anything left over until
the third day shall be consumed in fire. 7 If it is eaten at all on the third
day, it is an abomination; it will not be acceptable. 8 All who eat it shall
be subject to punishment, because they have profaned what is holy to
the LORD; and any such person shall be cut off from the people.
9 When you reap the harvest of your land, you shall not reap to
the very edges of your field, or gather the gleanings of your harvest.
10 You shall not strip your vineyard bare, or gather the fallen grapes of
your vineyard; you shall leave them for the poor and the alien: I am
the LORD your God.
11 You shall not steal; you shall not deal falsely; and you shall not
lie to one another. 12 And you shall not swear falsely by my name, profaning the name of your God: I am the LORD.
13 You shall not defraud your neighbor; you shall not steal; and
you shall not keep for yourself the wages of a laborer until morning.
14 You shall not revile the deaf or put a stumbling block before the
blind; you shall fear your God: I am the LORD.
15 You shall not render an unjust judgment; you shall not be partial to the poor or defer to the great: with justice you shall judge your
neighbor. 16 You shall not go around as a slanderer[a] among your people, and you shall not profit by the blood[b] of your neighbor: I am the
LORD.
17 You shall not hate in your heart anyone of your kin; you shall
reprove your neighbor, or you will incur guilt yourself. 18 You shall not
take vengeance or bear a grudge against any of your people, but you
shall love your neighbor as yourself: I am the LORD.
19 You shall keep my statutes. You shall not let your animals breed
with a different kind; you shall not sow your field with two kinds of
seed; nor shall you put on a garment made of two different materials.
20 If a man has sexual relations with a woman who is a slave, designated for another man but not ransomed or given her freedom, an
inquiry shall be held. They shall not be put to death, since she has
not been freed; 21 but he shall bring a guilt offering for himself to the
LORD, at the entrance of the tent of meeting, a ram as guilt offering.
22 And the priest shall make atonement for him with the ram of guilt
offering before the LORD for his sin that he committed; and the sin he
committed shall be forgiven him.
23 When you come into the land and plant all kinds of trees for

[a] Meaning of Heb uncertain [b] Heb *stand against the blood*

19:9 gleanings of your harvest: Gleaning describes the activity of going over a field that has just been harvested in order to gather by hand any usable parts of the crop that remain. The custom of gleaning was important for the poor members of the community, including the resident alien (see Deut 24:21, which includes the widow and orphan). See also Ruth 2, where Ruth is an alien gleaning in the field of Boaz.

19:12 swear falsely: The reference here is to the swearing of oaths in legal cases, not to using swear words.

19:15 you shall not be partial to the poor: The legal system required absolute fairness that favored neither the powerful nor the weak. It insists that "justice is blind." We speak today of God's "preferential option for the poor," and in many ways the Bible supports God's special favor to the poor and disadvantaged. Legal disputes, however, require equal justice.

19:17-18 You shall not hate…you shall love your neighbor as yourself: This contrast is basic to Israel's sense of care for members of the community. Jesus calls it one of the most important commandments in the whole law (see Matt 19:19; 22:39; Mark 12:31; Luke 10:27).

How is the command to "love your neighbor as you love yourself" similar to the "golden rule" (Treat others as you would have them treat you)? How is it different? Luther called Christians to be "dutiful servants of all." What do you think this means? What do you think is the basis for treating other people with love and compassion?

19:19 different kind: This law expresses a concern for mixing things that by nature do not belong together. Three cases illustrate the principle: cross-breeding animals, mixing seed for planting, mixing materials in fabric for clothing. See Deuteronomy 22:9-11, which adds another illustration.

19:23 regard their fruit as forbidden: this literally means "regard it as uncircumcised." (For circumcision, see Gen 17:10 and note.) The language of uncircumcision runs throughout this particular law, perhaps because the fruit tree required pruning prior to full production.

food, then you shall regard their fruit as forbidden;[a] three years it shall
be forbidden[b] to you, it must not be eaten. 24 In the fourth year all their
fruit shall be set apart for rejoicing in the LORD. 25 But in the fifth year
you may eat of their fruit, that their yield may be increased for you: I
am the LORD your God.
26 You shall not eat anything with its blood. You shall not practice augury or witchcraft. 27 You shall not round off the hair on your
temples or mar the edges of your beard. 28 You shall not make any
gashes in your flesh for the dead or tattoo any marks upon you: I am
the LORD.
29 Do not profane your daughter by making her a prostitute, that
the land not become prostituted and full of depravity. 30 You shall keep
my sabbaths and reverence my sanctuary: I am the LORD.
31 Do not turn to mediums or wizards; do not seek them out, to
be defiled by them: I am the LORD your God.
32 You shall rise before the aged, and defer to the old; and you
shall fear your God: I am the LORD.
33 When an alien resides with you in your land, you shall not oppress the alien. 34 The alien who resides with you shall be to you as the
citizen among you; you shall love the alien as yourself, for you were
aliens in the land of Egypt: I am the LORD your God.
35 You shall not cheat in measuring length, weight, or quantity.
36 You shall have honest balances, honest weights, an honest ephah,
and an honest hin: I am the LORD your God, who brought you out
of the land of Egypt. 37 You shall keep all my statutes and all my ordinances, and observe them: I am the LORD.

19:26-31 augury or witchcraft...prostitute...wizards: *Augury* refers to various ways of foretelling the future, such as divination (see Gen 30:27 and note). See also the note on Leviticus 18:1-18. All forms of witchcraft or wizardry practiced by Canaanite neighbors were rejected. The reference in 19:27 to "rounding off" (or chopping off) the earlocks and mutilation of the beard seems, in connection with 19:28, to refer to typical funeral customs to mourn the dead (see Deut 14:1; Jer 7:29; Mic 1:16).

Why do you think tattoos or marking the body is rejected in Leviticus 19:28? What, if anything, does this mean for us today?

Penalties for Violations of Holiness

20 The LORD spoke to Moses, saying: 2 Say further to the people of Israel:
Any of the people of Israel, or of the aliens who reside in Israel, who
give any of their offspring to Molech shall be put to death; the people
of the land shall stone them to death. 3 I myself will set my face against
them, and will cut them off from the people, because they have given
of their offspring to Molech, defiling my sanctuary and profaning my
holy name. 4 And if the people of the land should ever close their eyes
to them, when they give of their offspring to Molech, and do not put
them to death, 5 I myself will set my face against them and against their
family, and will cut them off from among their people, them and all
who follow them in prostituting themselves to Molech.
6 If any turn to mediums and wizards, prostituting themselves
to them, I will set my face against them, and will cut them off from
the people. 7 Consecrate yourselves therefore, and be holy; for I am

20:2 Molech: See 18:21 and note.

20:5 cut them off from among their people: Literally means "cut him off," referring to the offender, not to the larger community. To be "cut off" may mean to be banned from the worshiping assembly, excluded from the community, shunned by society, or placed under divine curse, with the punishment left up to God.

[a] Heb *as their uncircumcision* [b] Heb *uncircumcision*

the Lord your God. 8 Keep my statutes, and observe them; I am the
Lord; I sanctify you. 9 All who curse father or mother shall be put to
death; having cursed father or mother, their blood is upon them.

10 If a man commits adultery with the wife of[a] his neighbor, both
the adulterer and the adulteress shall be put to death. 11 The man who
lies with his father's wife has uncovered his father's nakedness; both
of them shall be put to death; their blood is upon them. 12 If a man lies
with his daughter-in-law, both of them shall be put to death; they have
committed perversion, their blood is upon them. 13 If a man lies with
a male as with a woman, both of them have committed an abomination; they shall be put to death; their blood is upon them. 14 If a man
takes a wife and her mother also, it is depravity; they shall be burned
to death, both he and they, that there may be no depravity among
you. 15 If a man has sexual relations with an animal, he shall be put to
death; and you shall kill the animal. 16 If a woman approaches any animal and has sexual relations with it, you shall kill the woman and the
animal; they shall be put to death, their blood is upon them.

17 If a man takes his sister, a daughter of his father or a daughter
of his mother, and sees her nakedness, and she sees his nakedness, it
is a disgrace, and they shall be cut off in the sight of their people; he
has uncovered his sister's nakedness, he shall be subject to punishment. 18 If a man lies with a woman having her sickness and uncovers
her nakedness, he has laid bare her flow and she has laid bare her flow
of blood; both of them shall be cut off from their people. 19 You shall
not uncover the nakedness of your mother's sister or of your father's
sister, for that is to lay bare one's own flesh; they shall be subject to
punishment. 20 If a man lies with his uncle's wife, he has uncovered his
uncle's nakedness; they shall be subject to punishment; they shall die
childless. 21 If a man takes his brother's wife, it is impurity; he has uncovered his brother's nakedness; they shall be childless.

22 You shall keep all my statutes and all my ordinances, and observe them, so that the land to which I bring you to settle in may not
vomit you out. 23 You shall not follow the practices of the nation that
I am driving out before you. Because they did all these things, I abhorred them. 24 But I have said to you: You shall inherit their land, and
I will give it to you to possess, a land flowing with milk and honey. I
am the Lord your God; I have separated you from the peoples. 25 You
shall therefore make a distinction between the clean animal and the
unclean, and between the unclean bird and the clean; you shall not
bring abomination on yourselves by animal or by bird or by anything
with which the ground teems, which I have set apart for you to hold
unclean. 26 You shall be holy to me; for I the Lord am holy, and I have
separated you from the other peoples to be mine.

20:14 burned to death: An extremely unusual form of capital punishment in Israel. Compare to Joshua 7:15. In light of 21:1-6, this may mean that a body executed by stoning is to be burned to avoid the severe contamination caused by exposed bloody bruises (literally, "she shall be burned in fire"). See also Daniel 7:11. That may also be the implication here.

20:18 a woman having her sickness: Meaning "a woman feeling faint or ill," which characterizes the time of menstruation. See also Leviticus 12:2; 15:33, where the same term is used of a woman having "her period." Having a period was not looked upon as having a disease.

20:20 they shall die childless: This likely refers to being placed under a divine curse of barrenness, as in 20:21. See also Genesis 15:2; Jeremiah 22:30.

20:26 You shall be holy...separated: See the note at 19:1-37. Maintaining holiness required separation from things and people who were considered unclean.

---

[a] Heb repeats *if a man commits adultery with the wife of*

27 A man or a woman who is a medium or a wizard shall be put to death; they shall be stoned to death, their blood is upon them.

The Holiness of Priests

21 The LORD said to Moses: Speak to the priests, the sons of Aaron, and say to them:

No one shall defile himself for a dead person among his relatives,
[2]except for his nearest kin: his mother, his father, his son, his daughter, his brother; [3]likewise, for a virgin sister, close to him because she
has had no husband, he may defile himself for her. [4]But he shall not
defile himself as a husband among his people and so profane himself.
[5]They shall not make bald spots upon their heads, or shave off the
edges of their beards, or make any gashes in their flesh. [6]They shall be
holy to their God, and not profane the name of their God; for they offer the LORD's offerings by fire, the food of their God; therefore they
shall be holy. [7]They shall not marry a prostitute or a woman who has been defiled; neither shall they marry a woman divorced from her
husband. For they are holy to their God, [8]and you shall treat them as
holy, since they offer the food of your God; they shall be holy to you,
for I the LORD, I who sanctify you, am holy. [9]When the daughter of a
priest profanes herself through prostitution, she profanes her father; she shall be burned to death.

10 The priest who is exalted above his fellows, on whose head the anointing oil has been poured and who has been consecrated to wear
the vestments, shall not dishevel his hair, nor tear his vestments. [11]He
shall not go where there is a dead body; he shall not defile himself
even for his father or mother. [12]He shall not go outside the sanctuary
and thus profane the sanctuary of his God; for the consecration of the
anointing oil of his God is upon him: I am the LORD. [13]He shall marry
only a woman who is a virgin. [14]A widow, or a divorced woman, or a
woman who has been defiled, a prostitute, these he shall not marry.
He shall marry a virgin of his own kin, [15]that he may not profane his
offspring among his kin; for I am the LORD; I sanctify him.

16 The LORD spoke to Moses, saying: [17]Speak to Aaron and say:
No one of your offspring throughout their generations who has a
blemish may approach to offer the food of his God. [18]For no one who
has a blemish shall draw near, one who is blind or lame, or one who
has a mutilated face or a limb too long, [19]or one who has a broken
foot or a broken hand, [20]or a hunchback, or a dwarf, or a man with a
blemish in his eyes or an itching disease or scabs or crushed testicles.
[21]No descendant of Aaron the priest who has a blemish shall come
near to offer the LORD's offerings by fire; since he has a blemish, he
shall not come near to offer the food of his God. [22]He may eat the food
of his God, of the most holy as well as of the holy. [23]But he shall not
come near the curtain or approach the altar, because he has a blemish,

21:1-6 a dead person: This relates to contamination by dead bodies. On priestly restrictions, see 10:6 and 22:4.

21:5 bald spots: These are references to traditional mourning rituals for the dead. See 19:27-28.

21:12 profane the sanctuary: The opposite of holy is common, or "profane," the realm of normal life. The two had to be kept strictly separate.

21:16-24 your offspring... who has a blemish: Priests from Aaron's family ("your offspring") were excluded from their priestly service if they have certain significant bodily ailments or disabilities ("blemishes"). For the same reason, animals with similar ailments were excluded from being acceptable sacrifices. See 1:3; 22:17-25.

21:19 broken foot... broken hand: Since the other conditions are chronic or natural, the exclusion here must be of those with deformities.

What qualities do you look for in a worship leader? In your opinion, what sorts of qualities would disqualify a person from taking leadership roles? What skills do you possess that would make you a leader?

that he may not profane my sanctuaries; for I am the LORD; I sanctify them. [24]Thus Moses spoke to Aaron and to his sons and to all the people of Israel.

The Use of Holy Offerings

22:1-16 sacred donations: This section presents instructions regarding the eating of sacrificial food restricted to the priests to eat. These restrictions also had practical purposes. Since the priests from the Levite tradition served the worship and later the temple, they did not receive a share of the land like other Israelite tribes. They and their families relied on eating portions of the sacred offerings (see 2:3; 7:11-36; Num 8:20-24).

22:4 made unclean by a corpse: Dead bodies were regarded as particularly defiling, since death was regarded as the opposite of life (see 21:1, 11; Num 5:2; 6:6, 11; 9:6-12; 19:11-16). For "semen," see 15:16-18 and note.

22:8 died or was torn: Refers to an animal not properly slaughtered, so as to guarantee that the blood was appropriately disposed of. See 17:13-16.

22 The LORD spoke to Moses, saying: [2]Direct Aaron and his sons to deal carefully with the sacred donations of the people of Israel, which they dedicate to me, so that they may not profane my holy name; I am the LORD. [3]Say to them: If anyone among all your offspring throughout your generations comes near the sacred donations, which the people of Israel dedicate to the LORD, while he is in a state of uncleanness, that person shall be cut off from my presence: I am the LORD. [4]No one of Aaron's offspring who has a leprous[a] disease or suffers a discharge may eat of the sacred donations until he is clean. Whoever touches anything made unclean by a corpse or a man who has had an emission of semen, [5]and whoever touches any swarming thing by which he may be made unclean or any human being by whom he may be made unclean—whatever his uncleanness may be— [6]the person who touches any such shall be unclean until evening and shall not eat of the sacred donations unless he has washed his body in water. [7]When the sun sets he shall be clean; and afterward he may eat of the sacred donations, for they are his food. [8]That which died or was torn by wild animals he shall not eat, becoming unclean by it: I am the LORD. [9]They shall keep my charge, so that they may not incur guilt and die in the sanctuary[b] for having profaned it: I am the LORD; I sanctify them.

10 No lay person shall eat of the sacred donations. No bound or hired servant of the priest shall eat of the sacred donations; [11]but if a priest acquires anyone by purchase, the person may eat of them; and those that are born in his house may eat of his food. [12]If a priest's daughter marries a layman, she shall not eat of the offering of the sacred donations; [13]but if a priest's daughter is widowed or divorced, without offspring, and returns to her father's house, as in her youth, she may eat of her father's food. No lay person shall eat of it. [14]If a man eats of the sacred donation unintentionally, he shall add one-fifth of its value to it, and give the sacred donation to the priest. [15]No one shall profane the sacred donations of the people of Israel, which they offer to the LORD, [16]causing them to bear guilt requiring a guilt offering, by eating their sacred donations: for I am the LORD; I sanctify them.

Acceptable Offerings

22:17-26 offering...to be acceptable: Gives instructions concerning the disqualification of sacrificial animals, which had to be "perfect" (22:21), that is, unmarked by serious defect (see 1:3). These disqualifications largely mirror those for priests (see 21:17-23).

17 The LORD spoke to Moses, saying: [18]Speak to Aaron and his sons and all the people of Israel and say to them: When anyone of the

[a] A term for several skin diseases; precise meaning uncertain [b] Vg: Heb *incur guilt for it and die in it*

house of Israel or of the aliens residing in Israel presents an offering,
whether in payment of a vow or as a freewill offering that is offered
to the LORD as a burnt offering, [19]to be acceptable in your behalf it
shall be a male without blemish, of the cattle or the sheep or the goats.
[20]You shall not offer anything that has a blemish, for it will not be acceptable in your behalf.

21 When anyone offers a sacrifice of well-being to the LORD, in
fulfillment of a vow or as a freewill offering, from the herd or from the
flock, to be acceptable it must be perfect; there shall be no blemish in
it. [22]Anything blind, or injured, or maimed, or having a discharge or
an itch or scabs—these you shall not offer to the LORD or put any of
them on the altar as offerings by fire to the LORD. [23]An ox or a lamb
that has a limb too long or too short you may present for a freewill
offering; but it will not be accepted for a vow. [24]Any animal that has
its testicles bruised or crushed or torn or cut, you shall not offer to the
LORD; such you shall not do within your land, [25]nor shall you accept
any such animals from a foreigner to offer as food to your God; since
they are mutilated, with a blemish in them, they shall not be accepted
in your behalf.

26 The LORD spoke to Moses, saying: [27]When an ox or a sheep or
a goat is born, it shall remain seven days with its mother, and from the
eighth day on it shall be acceptable as the LORD's offering by fire. [28]But
you shall not slaughter, from the herd or the flock, an animal with its
young on the same day. [29]When you sacrifice a thanksgiving offering
to the LORD, you shall sacrifice it so that it may be acceptable in your
behalf. [30]It shall be eaten on the same day; you shall not leave any of it
until morning: I am the LORD.

31 Thus you shall keep my commandments and observe them:
I am the LORD. [32]You shall not profane my holy name, that I may be
sanctified among the people of Israel: I am the LORD; I sanctify you,
[33]I who brought you out of the land of Egypt to be your God: I am
the LORD.

22:28 an animal with its young: This law extends a humanitarian principle to animals, likely expressing the same concern as that found in the strange prohibition in Deuteronomy 14:22.

22:33 brought you out of…Egypt: A reminder of God's saving help in the time of the exodus and of the God's promise spoken at the giving of the Ten Commandments (see Exod 20:1-3).

Appointed Festivals

23 The LORD spoke to Moses, saying: [2]Speak to the people of
Israel and say to them: These are the appointed festivals of
the LORD that you shall proclaim as holy convocations, my appointed
festivals.

The Sabbath, Passover, and Unleavened Bread

3 Six days shall work be done; but the seventh day is a sabbath of
complete rest, a holy convocation; you shall do no work: it is a sabbath to the LORD throughout your settlements.

4 These are the appointed festivals of the LORD, the holy convocations, which you shall celebrate at the time appointed for them. [5]In

23:1-44 the appointed festivals of the LORD: Gives instructions concerning the Sabbath and the religious festivals to be celebrated throughout the year, in chronological order. Following the Sabbath (23:3), they are: the festivals of Passover and unleavened bread (23:4-8); first fruits (23:9-14); festival of weeks (23:15-21); new year (23:23-25); Day of Atonement (23:26-32); and festival of booths (23:33-43). (See also Exod 23:14-17; 34:18-24; Deut 16:1-17; and the chart Jewish Festivals and Feasts, p. 227.)

23:5-6 passover offering…festival of unleavened bread: The festival of unleavened bread (*maccoth* [mats-TSOTH]) was one of three pilgrimage festivals focused on the crops and harvests. Passover (*pasah* [PE-sach]) was a shepherd's ritual celebrated in the home. Eventually, Passover was centralized by the government and grew together with the festival of unleavened bread until they effectively became one festival. See Exodus 12:43—13:10.

the first month, on the fourteenth day of the month, at twilight,[a] there
shall be a passover offering to the LORD, 6and on the fifteenth day of
the same month is the festival of unleavened bread to the LORD;
seven days you shall eat unleavened bread. 7On the first day you shall
have a holy convocation; you shall not work at your occupations. 8For
seven days you shall present the LORD's offerings by fire; on the seventh day there shall be a holy convocation: you shall not work at your
occupations.

The Offering of First Fruits

9 The LORD spoke to Moses: 10Speak to the people of Israel and
say to them: When you enter the land that I am giving you and you
reap its harvest, you shall bring the sheaf of the first fruits of your
harvest to the priest. 11He shall raise the sheaf before the LORD, that
you may find acceptance; on the day after the sabbath the priest
shall raise it. 12On the day when you raise the sheaf, you shall offer a
lamb a year old, without blemish, as a burnt offering to the LORD.
13And the grain offering with it shall be two-tenths of an ephah of
choice flour mixed with oil, an offering by fire of pleasing odor to
the LORD; and the drink offering with it shall be of wine, one-fourth
of a hin. 14You shall eat no bread or parched grain or fresh ears until
that very day, until you have brought the offering of your God: it is
a statute forever throughout your generations in all your settlements.

The Festival of Weeks

15 And from the day after the sabbath, from the day on which
you bring the sheaf of the elevation offering, you shall count off seven
weeks; they shall be complete. 16You shall count until the day after
the seventh sabbath, fifty days; then you shall present an offering of
new grain to the LORD. 17You shall bring from your settlements two
loaves of bread as an elevation offering, each made of two-tenths of an
ephah; they shall be of choice flour, baked with leaven, as first fruits
to the LORD. 18You shall present with the bread seven lambs a year
old without blemish, one young bull, and two rams; they shall be a
burnt offering to the LORD, along with their grain offering and their
drink offerings, an offering by fire of pleasing odor to the LORD. 19You
shall also offer one male goat for a sin offering, and two male lambs
a year old as a sacrifice of well-being. 20The priest shall raise them
with the bread of the first fruits as an elevation offering before the
LORD, together with the two lambs; they shall be holy to the LORD
for the priest. 21On that same day you shall make proclamation; you
shall hold a holy convocation; you shall not work at your occupations.

23:16 fifty days: Pentecost ("fifty"), or the feast of weeks, is celebrated fifty days after the festival of unleavened bread and marks the conclusion of the wheat harvest. This was the second of the three great early pilgrimage festivals (Deut 16:16).

[a] Heb *between the two evenings*

Jewish Festivals and Feasts

Festival	Duration and Time of Year	Description	References
Feast of Trumpets (Rosh Hashanah)	One day in September/ October	Signals the beginning of the civil new year and festival year with the blowing of trumpets.	Lev 23:23-25 Num 29:1-6
Day of Atonement (Yom Kippur)	One day in September/ October	Expresses the people's sorrow for their sins through fasting (going without food) and sacrifices.	Exod 30:10; Lev 16:1-34, 23:26-32; Num 29:7-11
Feast of Booths or Tabernacles (Sukkot)	One week in September/ October	Remembers the forty years the people wandered in the wilderness before entering the promised land.	Lev 23:33-43; Num 29:12-39; Deut 16:13-15
Feast of Dedication or Festival of Lights (Hanukkah)	One week in November/ December /January	Celebrates the rededication of the temple by Judas Maccabeus in 164 B.C.E.	1 Maccabees 4:36-59* John 10:22
Feast of Purim or Esther	One day in February/March	Marks the rescue of the people from Haman's plot against the Jews in the time of Esther.	Esth 9:18-32
Passover and Feast of Unleavened Bread	One week in March/April	Recalls God's rescue of the people out of slavery in Egypt and includes thanksgiving for the barley harvest.	Exod 12:1-27; Lev 23:5-8
Feast of Weeks or Harvest (Pentecost)	One day in May/June (seven weeks after Passover)	Honors God's gift of the law at Mount Sinai and includes thanksgiving for the wheat harvest.	Exod 23:16, 34:22; Lev 23:15-21; Deut 16:9-12

*See "Different Canons of the Hebrew Bible (Old Testament)," pp. 28-29

This is a statute forever in all your settlements throughout your generations.

22 When you reap the harvest of your land, you shall not reap to the very edges of your field, or gather the gleanings of your harvest; you shall leave them for the poor and for the alien: I am the LORD your God.

The Festival of Trumpets

23 The LORD spoke to Moses, saying: [24]Speak to the people of Israel, saying: In the seventh month, on the first day of the month, you shall observe a day of complete rest, a holy convocation commemorated with trumpet blasts. [25]You shall not work at your occupations; and you shall present the LORD's offering by fire.

23:24 seventh month, on the first day of the month: On the "seventh month," see 16:29. See the reference in Exodus 34:22 to "the turn of the year."

The Day of Atonement

23:27 day of atonement: See Leviticus 16 and notes; also Numbers 29:7-11. This was not one of the early pilgrimage festivals, but became one of the most significant of Israel's holy days in later tradition.

26 The LORD spoke to Moses, saying: 27 Now, the tenth day of this seventh month is the day of atonement; it shall be a holy convocation for you: you shall deny yourselves[a] and present the LORD's offering by fire; 28 and you shall do no work during that entire day; for it is a day of atonement, to make atonement on your behalf before the LORD your God. 29 For anyone who does not practice self-denial[b] during that entire day shall be cut off from the people. 30 And anyone who does any work during that entire day, such a one I will destroy from the midst of the people. 31 You shall do no work: it is a statute forever throughout your generations in all your settlements. 32 It shall be to you a sabbath of complete rest, and you shall deny yourselves;[a] on the ninth day of the month at evening, from evening to evening you shall keep your sabbath.

The Festival of Booths

23:34 festival of booths: The feast of booths (*sukkot* [suk-KOTH]) was the last of the three early pilgrimage festivals, celebrating the "ingathering" of fruit in the fall. It came to be associated with the wilderness traditions, especially the remembrance of Israel living in "booths" (tents, 23:43) while wandering in the wilderness.

What festivals do we celebrate during the Christian year? Why do we celebrate them? How do the liturgical colors mark our church year? Which festivals are your favorites? Why?

33 The LORD spoke to Moses, saying: 34 Speak to the people of Israel, saying: On the fifteenth day of this seventh month, and lasting seven days, there shall be the festival of booths[c] to the LORD. 35 The first day shall be a holy convocation; you shall not work at your occupations. 36 Seven days you shall present the LORD's offerings by fire; on the eighth day you shall observe a holy convocation and present the LORD's offerings by fire; it is a solemn assembly; you shall not work at your occupations.

37 These are the appointed festivals of the LORD, which you shall celebrate as times of holy convocation, for presenting to the LORD offerings by fire—burnt offerings and grain offerings, sacrifices and drink offerings, each on its proper day— 38 apart from the sabbaths of the LORD, and apart from your gifts, and apart from all your votive offerings, and apart from all your freewill offerings, which you give to the LORD.

39 Now, the fifteenth day of the seventh month, when you have gathered in the produce of the land, you shall keep the festival of the LORD, lasting seven days; a complete rest on the first day, and a complete rest on the eighth day. 40 On the first day you shall take the fruit of majestic[d] trees, branches of palm trees, boughs of leafy trees, and willows of the brook; and you shall rejoice before the LORD your God for seven days. 41 You shall keep it as a festival to the LORD seven days in the year; you shall keep it in the seventh month as a statute forever throughout your generations. 42 You shall live in booths for seven days; all that are citizens in Israel shall live in booths, 43 so that your generations may know that I made the people of Israel live in booths when I brought them out of the land of Egypt: I am the LORD your God.

---

[a] Or *shall fast* [b] Or *does not fast* [c] Or *tabernacles*: Heb *succoth* [d] Meaning of Heb uncertain

44 Thus Moses declared to the people of Israel the appointed festivals of the LORD.

The Lamp

24 The LORD spoke to Moses, saying: 2 Command the people
of Israel to bring you pure oil of beaten olives for the lamp,
that a light may be kept burning regularly. 3 Aaron shall set it up in the
tent of meeting, outside the curtain of the covenant,[a] to burn from
evening to morning before the LORD regularly; it shall be a statute
forever throughout your generations. 4 He shall set up the lamps on
the lampstand of pure gold[b] before the LORD regularly.

The Bread for the Tabernacle

5 You shall take choice flour, and bake twelve loaves of it; two-
tenths of an ephah shall be in each loaf. 6 You shall place them in two
rows, six in a row, on the table of pure gold.[c] 7 You shall put pure frankincense with each row, to be a token offering for the bread, as an offering
by fire to the LORD. 8 Every sabbath day Aaron shall set them in order
before the LORD regularly as a commitment of the people of Israel, as
a covenant forever. 9 They shall be for Aaron and his descendants, who
shall eat them in a holy place, for they are most holy portions for him
from the offerings by fire to the LORD, a perpetual due.

Blasphemy and Its Punishment

10 A man whose mother was an Israelite and whose father was an
Egyptian came out among the people of Israel; and the Israelite woman's son and a certain Israelite began fighting in the camp. 11 The Israelite woman's son blasphemed the Name in a curse. And they brought
him to Moses—now his mother's name was Shelomith, daughter of
Dibri, of the tribe of Dan— 12 and they put him in custody, until the
decision of the LORD should be made clear to them.

13 The LORD said to Moses, saying: 14 Take the blasphemer outside the camp; and let all who were within hearing lay their hands on
his head, and let the whole congregation stone him. 15 And speak to
the people of Israel, saying: Anyone who curses God shall bear the
sin. 16 One who blasphemes the name of the LORD shall be put to
death; the whole congregation shall stone the blasphemer. Aliens as
well as citizens, when they blaspheme the Name, shall be put to death.
17 Anyone who kills a human being shall be put to death. 18 Anyone
who kills an animal shall make restitution for it, life for life. 19 Anyone
who maims another shall suffer the same injury in return: 20 fracture
for fracture, eye for eye, tooth for tooth; the injury inflicted is the injury to be suffered. 21 One who kills an animal shall make restitution

[a] Or *treaty*, or *testament*; Heb *eduth* [b] Heb *pure lampstand* [c] Heb *pure table*

24:1-9 pure oil of beaten olives… twelve loaves: The lamp is to be kept burning at all times in the sanctuary, and the loaves of sacrifice are to be set out each week. See Exodus 25:31-40, 27:20-21, and 37:17-24 for the *menorah* (lamp stand) and lamps, and Exodus 25:23-30 and 37:10-16 for the table.

24:11 blasphemed the Name in a curse: On the illegitimate use of God's holy name and the belittling of God, see Exodus 20:7 and 22:28. The punishment for a person who blasphemed the name of the LORD was death.

What does Luther's Small Catechism say about the wrongful use of God's name? The explanation to the Second Commandment states: "We are to fear and love God, so that we do not curse, swear, practice magic, lie, or deceive using God's name, but instead use that very name in every time of need to call on, pray to, praise, and give thanks to God." *Leviticus 24:11*

What's "wrong" with the wrongful use of God's name? What should or could be done about such wrongful use? For what purposes do people take an oath on the Bible or some other holy book, such as the Qur'an? What is "perjury," and why is it such a serious offense?

24:16 Aliens: See 17:12 and note. Aliens (non-Israelites), together with the Israelite, are subject to a common code of conduct (24:22).

24:17 kills: More specifically, "beats to death." This is not a general ban of all forms of killing but rather a specific ban of killing someone in a violent rage.

for it; but one who kills a human being shall be put to death. 22 You
shall have one law for the alien and for the citizen: for I am the LORD
your God. 23 Moses spoke thus to the people of Israel; and they took
the blasphemer outside the camp, and stoned him to death. The people of Israel did as the LORD had commanded Moses.

The Sabbatical Year

25 The LORD spoke to Moses on Mount Sinai, saying: 2 Speak
to the people of Israel and say to them: When you enter
the land that I am giving you, the land shall observe a sabbath for
the LORD. 3 Six years you shall sow your field, and six years you shall
prune your vineyard, and gather in their yield; 4 but in the seventh year
there shall be a sabbath of complete rest for the land, a sabbath for the
LORD: you shall not sow your field or prune your vineyard. 5 You shall
not reap the aftergrowth of your harvest or gather the grapes of your
unpruned vine: it shall be a year of complete rest for the land. 6 You
may eat what the land yields during its sabbath—you, your male and
female slaves, your hired and your bound laborers who live with you;
7 for your livestock also, and for the wild animals in your land all its
yield shall be for food.

The Year of Jubilee

8 You shall count off seven weeks[a] of years, seven times seven
years, so that the period of seven weeks of years gives forty-nine years.
9 Then you shall have the trumpet sounded loud; on the tenth day of
the seventh month—on the day of atonement—you shall have the
trumpet sounded throughout all your land. 10 And you shall hallow
the fiftieth year and you shall proclaim liberty throughout the land to
all its inhabitants. It shall be a jubilee for you: you shall return, every
one of you, to your property and every one of you to your family.
11 That fiftieth year shall be a jubilee for you: you shall not sow, or reap
the aftergrowth, or harvest the unpruned vines. 12 For it is a jubilee; it
shall be holy to you: you shall eat only what the field itself produces.

13 In this year of jubilee you shall return, every one of you, to
your property. 14 When you make a sale to your neighbor or buy from
your neighbor, you shall not cheat one another. 15 When you buy from
your neighbor, you shall pay only for the number of years since the
jubilee; the seller shall charge you only for the remaining crop years.
16 If the years are more, you shall increase the price, and if the years are
fewer, you shall diminish the price; for it is a certain number of harvests that are being sold to you. 17 You shall not cheat one another, but
you shall fear your God; for I am the LORD your God.

18 You shall observe my statutes and faithfully keep my or-

[a] Or *sabbaths*

25:1-55 observe a Sabbath . . . a jubilee: This chapter deals with the "sabbatical" year and the "jubilee" year. These were to be periods of "release," allowing the land to lie fallow (go unplanted) every seventh year and allowing for a return of all property (land) to the original owner or owner's family every fiftieth year.

25:1 on Mount Sinai: Or "at Mount Sinai," since it is not presumed that Moses is actually on the mountain.

Why do farmers let their land lie fallow on occasion? Why is this year referred to as a sabbath for the land, and how does it compare to the sabbath that we are to observe every week? What do you think about giving the land a year off as a way of caring for God's earth?

25:10 liberty: The Hebrew word *derôr* (de-ROHR) indicates a periodic "release" or "amnesty," a practice common in the ancient Near East. Such an amnesty might involve the release of one's slaves (Jer 34:8-17) or of prisoners (Isa 61:1). Here the release is regularized to every fiftieth year, when land ownership reverts back to the original owners (see Ezek 46:17).

25:10-13 jubilee: The Hebrew word *yobel* (yo-BAIL) means "ram's horn." The beginning of the year of release was signaled by the blast of the trumpet, made from a ram's horn (25:9).

dinances, so that you may live on the land securely. 19The land will
yield its fruit, and you will eat your fill and live on it securely. 20Should
you ask, "What shall we eat in the seventh year, if we may not sow
or gather in our crop?" 21I will order my blessing for you in the sixth
year, so that it will yield a crop for three years. 22When you sow in the
eighth year, you will be eating from the old crop; until the ninth year,
when its produce comes in, you shall eat the old. 23The land shall not
be sold in perpetuity, for the land is mine; with me you are but aliens
and tenants. 24Throughout the land that you hold, you shall provide
for the redemption of the land.

25 If anyone of your kin falls into difficulty and sells a piece of
property, then the next of kin shall come and redeem what the relative has sold. 26If the person has no one to redeem it, but then prospers and finds sufficient means to do so, 27the years since its sale shall
be computed and the difference shall be refunded to the person to
whom it was sold, and the property shall be returned. 28But if there are
not sufficient means to recover it, what was sold shall remain with the
purchaser until the year of jubilee; in the jubilee it shall be released,
and the property shall be returned.

29 If anyone sells a dwelling house in a walled city, it may be redeemed until a year has elapsed since its sale; the right of redemption shall be one year. 30If it is not redeemed before a full year has
elapsed, a house that is in a walled city shall pass in perpetuity to the
purchaser, throughout the generations; it shall not be released in the
jubilee. 31But houses in villages that have no walls around them shall
be classed as open country; they may be redeemed, and they shall be
released in the jubilee. 32As for the cities of the Levites, the Levites
shall forever have the right of redemption of the houses in the cities belonging to them. 33Such property as may be redeemed from the
Levites—houses sold in a city belonging to them—shall be released
in the jubilee; because the houses in the cities of the Levites are their
possession among the people of Israel. 34But the open land around
their cities may not be sold; for that is their possession for all time.

35 If any of your kin fall into difficulty and become dependent
on you,[a] you shall support them; they shall live with you as though
resident aliens. 36Do not take interest in advance or otherwise make
a profit from them, but fear your God; let them live with you. 37You
shall not lend them your money at interest taken in advance, or provide them food at a profit. 38I am the LORD your God, who brought
you out of the land of Egypt, to give you the land of Canaan, to be
your God.

39 If any who are dependent on you become so impoverished
that they sell themselves to you, you shall not make them serve as

[a] Meaning of Heb uncertain

25:23 the land is mine: This represents the primary theological view regarding land ownership. Israel and its land were regarded as God's "inheritance" and "portion" (Deut 32:9; Ps 33:12). God owned the land, and individuals were granted the right to live on it as "aliens and tenants."

How does the idea that "God owns the land" serve as a basis for our stewardship as Christians? What does it mean to be "stewards" of what God has given us?

25:24-25 redemption of the land: When ancestral property was in danger of falling out of family ownership, a family member could perform the duty of the "redeemer" (*go'ēl* [go-AIL]) and purchase the land to secure it for the family (see Jer 32:6-15).

25:35 your kin: Literally means "brother," "fellow Israelites." They are to be treated as resident aliens. That is, they are to be given the social protections given the vulnerable members of the community. See Exodus 22:25; Deuteronomy 23:19-20.

25:39-46 not make them serve as slaves: Slaves could be taken from among foreigners (25:44) and resident aliens (25:45), but fellow Israelites could never be considered as "servants" or "slaves" because they all were already considered to be servants or slaves of God. Contrast Exodus 21:1-6, which did envision "Hebrews" being reduced to the status of slavery, but which required a release after six years of service.

slaves. 40 They shall remain with you as hired or bound laborers. They shall serve with you until the year of the jubilee. 41 Then they and their children with them shall be free from your authority; they shall go back to their own family and return to their ancestral property. 42 For they are my servants, whom I brought out of the land of Egypt; they shall not be sold as slaves are sold. 43 You shall not rule over them with harshness, but shall fear your God. 44 As for the male and female slaves whom you may have, it is from the nations around you that you may acquire male and female slaves. 45 You may also acquire them from among the aliens residing with you, and from their families that are with you, who have been born in your land; and they may be your property. 46 You may keep them as a possession for your children after you, for them to inherit as property. These you may treat as slaves, but as for your fellow Israelites, no one shall rule over the other with harshness.

47 If resident aliens among you prosper, and if any of your kin fall into difficulty with one of them and sell themselves to an alien, or to a branch of the alien's family, 48 after they have sold themselves they shall have the right of redemption; one of their brothers may redeem them, 49 or their uncle or their uncle's son may redeem them, or anyone of their family who is of their own flesh may redeem them; or if they prosper they may redeem themselves. 50 They shall compute with the purchaser the total from the year when they sold themselves to the alien until the jubilee year; the price of the sale shall be applied to the number of years: the time they were with the owner shall be rated as the time of a hired laborer. 51 If many years remain, they shall pay for their redemption in proportion to the purchase price; 52 and if few years remain until the jubilee year, they shall compute thus: according to the years involved they shall make payment for their redemption. 53 As a laborer hired by the year they shall be under the alien's authority, who shall not, however, rule with harshness over them in your sight. 54 And if they have not been redeemed in any of these ways, they and their children with them shall go free in the jubilee year. 55 For to me the people of Israel are servants; they are my servants whom I brought out from the land of Egypt: I am the LORD your God.

Rewards for Obedience

26 You shall make for yourselves no idols and erect no carved images or pillars, and you shall not place figured stones in your land, to worship at them; for I am the LORD your God. 2 You shall keep my sabbaths and reverence my sanctuary: I am the LORD.

3 If you follow my statutes and keep my commandments and observe them faithfully, 4 I will give you your rains in their season, and the land shall yield its produce, and the trees of the field shall yield their fruit. 5 Your threshing shall overtake the vintage, and the vintage

25:47-55 sell themselves…laborer hired: These laws treat the situation in which Israelites sell themselves to a resident alien. Because they are in the service of aliens rather than fellow Israelites, they may be "redeemed" by a family member at any time.

26:1-45 You shall…I will…punish: This section originally formed the concluding blessings and curses associated with the Holiness Code (chapters 17–26). See Deuteronomy 28:1-46 for a similar listing.

26:1 pillars: The standing stone (*macceba* [mats-tsay-BAH]) represented male gods and was a common religious symbol in Israel, often the object of religious attack.

26:5 threshing shall overtake…vintage: Envisions such agricultural blessings that the harvest overwhelms the planting. On this theme, see also Amos 9:13.

shall overtake the sowing; you shall eat your bread to the full, and live
securely in your land. [6]And I will grant peace in the land, and you shall
lie down, and no one shall make you afraid; I will remove dangerous
animals from the land, and no sword shall go through your land. [7]You
shall give chase to your enemies, and they shall fall before you by the
sword. [8]Five of you shall give chase to a hundred, and a hundred of
you shall give chase to ten thousand; your enemies shall fall before
you by the sword. [9]I will look with favor upon you and make you fruitful and multiply you; and I will maintain my covenant with you. [10]You
shall eat old grain long stored, and you shall have to clear out the old
to make way for the new. [11]I will place my dwelling in your midst, and
I shall not abhor you. [12]And I will walk among you, and will be your
God, and you shall be my people. [13]I am the LORD your God who
brought you out of the land of Egypt, to be their slaves no more; I
have broken the bars of your yoke and made you walk erect.

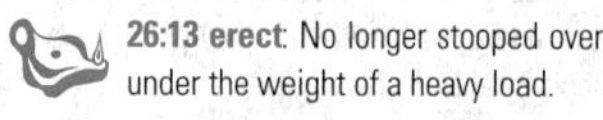

26:13 erect: No longer stooped over under the weight of a heavy load.

Penalties for Disobedience

14 But if you will not obey me, and do not observe all these commandments, [15]if you spurn my statutes, and abhor my ordinances, so
that you will not observe all my commandments, and you break my
covenant, [16]I in turn will do this to you: I will bring terror on you;
consumption and fever that waste the eyes and cause life to pine away.
You shall sow your seed in vain, for your enemies shall eat it. [17]I will set
my face against you, and you shall be struck down by your enemies;
your foes shall rule over you, and you shall flee though no one pursues
you. [18]And if in spite of this you will not obey me, I will continue to
punish you sevenfold for your sins. [19]I will break your proud glory,
and I will make your sky like iron and your earth like copper. [20]Your
strength shall be spent to no purpose: your land shall not yield its produce, and the trees of the land shall not yield their fruit.

26:18 sevenfold: This was considered the extreme upper limit of punishment, the standard definition of "vengeance." See also Genesis 4:15, 24; Proverbs 6:31.

26:19 like iron…like copper. Meaning the heavens will produce no rain, and the ground will be so hard it cannot be plowed and planted.

21 If you continue hostile to me, and will not obey me, I will
continue to plague you sevenfold for your sins. [22]I will let loose wild
animals against you, and they shall bereave you of your children and
destroy your livestock; they shall make you few in number, and your
roads shall be deserted.

23 If in spite of these punishments you have not turned back to
me, but continue hostile to me, [24]then I too will continue hostile to
you: I myself will strike you sevenfold for your sins. [25]I will bring the
sword against you, executing vengeance for the covenant; and if you
withdraw within your cities, I will send pestilence among you, and
you shall be delivered into enemy hands. [26]When I break your staff
of bread, ten women shall bake your bread in a single oven, and they
shall dole out your bread by weight; and though you eat, you shall not
be satisfied.

27 But if, despite this, you disobey me, and continue hostile to

me, 28 I will continue hostile to you in fury; I in turn will punish you
myself sevenfold for your sins. 29 You shall eat the flesh of your sons,
and you shall eat the flesh of your daughters. 30 I will destroy your high
places and cut down your incense altars; I will heap your carcasses
on the carcasses of your idols. I will abhor you. 31 I will lay your cities waste, will make your sanctuaries desolate, and I will not smell
your pleasing odors. 32 I will devastate the land, so that your enemies
who come to settle in it shall be appalled at it. 33 And you I will scatter
among the nations, and I will unsheathe the sword against you; your
land shall be a desolation, and your cities a waste.

34 Then the land shall enjoy[a] its sabbath years as long as it lies
desolate, while you are in the land of your enemies; then the land shall
rest, and enjoy[a] its sabbath years. 35 As long as it lies desolate, it shall
have the rest it did not have on your sabbaths when you were living
on it. 36 And as for those of you who survive, I will send faintness into
their hearts in the lands of their enemies; the sound of a driven leaf
shall put them to flight, and they shall flee as one flees from the sword,
and they shall fall though no one pursues. 37 They shall stumble over
one another, as if to escape a sword, though no one pursues; and you
shall have no power to stand against your enemies. 38 You shall perish
among the nations, and the land of your enemies shall devour you.
39 And those of you who survive shall languish in the land of your enemies because of their iniquities; also they shall languish because of
the iniquities of their ancestors.

40 But if they confess their iniquity and the iniquity of their ancestors, in that they committed treachery against me and, moreover, that
they continued hostile to me— 41 so that I, in turn, continued hostile
to them and brought them into the land of their enemies; if then their
uncircumcised heart is humbled and they make amends for their iniquity, 42 then will I remember my covenant with Jacob; I will remember
also my covenant with Isaac and also my covenant with Abraham, and
I will remember the land. 43 For the land shall be deserted by them, and
enjoy[a] its sabbath years by lying desolate without them, while they
shall make amends for their iniquity, because they dared to spurn my
ordinances, and they abhorred my statutes. 44 Yet for all that, when they
are in the land of their enemies, I will not spurn them, or abhor them
so as to destroy them utterly and break my covenant with them; for I
am the LORD their God; 45 but I will remember in their favor the covenant with their ancestors whom I brought out of the land of Egypt in
the sight of the nations, to be their God: I am the LORD.

46 These are the statutes and ordinances and laws that the LORD
established between himself and the people of Israel on Mount Sinai
through Moses.

[a] Or *make up for*

26:29 eat the flesh of your sons… daughters. A nightmare vision characteristic of siege warfare, when starvation is killing those trapped and surrounded, with no way to replenish the food supply. See 2 Kings 6:28-30.

26:34 its sabbath years: This ironic statement refers to the laws in 25:1-7. Israel's exile will provide a lengthy period for the land to lie fallow, to make up for the overlooked sabbath years.

Do you ever feel abandoned by God? Even Jesus did (Mark 15:34; Matt 27:46). Does God ever completely forget us, even when we stubbornly continue in our sin? How does God's promise to remember in 26:42 and 45 relate to God's promise following the flood (Gen 9:15)?

26:46 on Mount Sinai: Or "at Mount Sinai." See 25:1.

Votive Offerings

27 The LORD spoke to Moses, saying: 2Speak to the people of
Israel and say to them: When a person makes an explicit
vow to the LORD concerning the equivalent for a human being, 3the
equivalent for a male shall be: from twenty to sixty years of age the
equivalent shall be fifty shekels of silver by the sanctuary shekel. 4If
the person is a female, the equivalent is thirty shekels. 5If the age is
from five to twenty years of age, the equivalent is twenty shekels for
a male and ten shekels for a female. 6If the age is from one month to
five years, the equivalent for a male is five shekels of silver, and for a
female the equivalent is three shekels of silver. 7And if the person is
sixty years old or over, then the equivalent for a male is fifteen shekels,
and for a female ten shekels. 8If any cannot afford the equivalent, they
shall be brought before the priest and the priest shall assess them; the
priest shall assess them according to what each one making a vow can
afford.

9 If it concerns an animal that may be brought as an offering to
the LORD, any such that may be given to the LORD shall be holy. 10An-
other shall not be exchanged or substituted for it, either good for bad
or bad for good; and if one animal is substituted for another, both
that one and its substitute shall be holy. 11If it concerns any unclean
animal that may not be brought as an offering to the LORD, the animal shall be presented before the priest. 12The priest shall assess it:
whether good or bad, according to the assessment of the priest, so it
shall be. 13But if it is to be redeemed, one-fifth must be added to the
assessment.

14 If a person consecrates a house to the LORD, the priest shall assess it: whether good or bad, as the priest assesses it, so it shall stand.
15And if the one who consecrates the house wishes to redeem it, one-
fifth shall be added to its assessed value, and it shall revert to the original owner.

16 If a person consecrates to the LORD any inherited landholding, its assessment shall be in accordance with its seed requirements:
fifty shekels of silver to a homer of barley seed. 17If the person consecrates the field as of the year of jubilee, that assessment shall stand;
18but if the field is consecrated after the jubilee, the priest shall compute the price for it according to the years that remain until the year
of jubilee, and the assessment shall be reduced. 19And if the one who
consecrates the field wishes to redeem it, then one-fifth shall be added
to its assessed value, and it shall revert to the original owner; 20but if
the field is not redeemed, or if it has been sold to someone else, it
shall no longer be redeemable. 21But when the field is released in the
jubilee, it shall be holy to the LORD as a devoted field; it becomes
the priest's holding. 22If someone consecrates to the LORD a field that

27:1-33 vow…concerning…human being: This chapter concerns the redemption ("buying back") of persons or property promised to God in a religious vow. Though vows were not required and were even discouraged (Deut 23:22; Eccl 5:5; Prov 20:25), once made it was regarded as critically important to make good on one's vow (Num 30:2; Deut 23:21).

27:1 The equivalent for a human being: On vows involving persons, see Judges 11:30-31 (Jephthah and his daughter) and 1 Samuel 1:11, 28 (Hannah and Samuel). At a time of crisis, a person might vow to dedicate oneself or a family member to God in exchange for God's aid. If granted, the one taking the vow would have the option of redeeming it by paying an equivalent amount, based upon the gender and age of the person vowed (27:3-7). The same was true for vows involving animals (27:9-13), houses (27:14-15), and fields (27:16-25).

has been purchased, which is not a part of the inherited landholding,
23 the priest shall compute for it the proportionate assessment up to
the year of jubilee, and the assessment shall be paid as of that day, a
sacred donation to the LORD. 24 In the year of jubilee the field shall
return to the one from whom it was bought, whose holding the land
is. 25 All assessments shall be by the sanctuary shekel: twenty gerahs
shall make a shekel.

26 A firstling of animals, however, which as a firstling belongs to
the LORD, cannot be consecrated by anyone; whether ox or sheep, it
is the LORD's. 27 If it is an unclean animal, it shall be ransomed at its
assessment, with one-fifth added; if it is not redeemed, it shall be sold
at its assessment.

28 Nothing that a person owns that has been devoted to destruction for the LORD, be it human or animal, or inherited landholding,
may be sold or redeemed; every devoted thing is most holy to the
LORD. 29 No human beings who have been devoted to destruction can
be ransomed; they shall be put to death.

30 All tithes from the land, whether the seed from the ground or
the fruit from the tree, are the LORD's; they are holy to the LORD. 31 If
persons wish to redeem any of their tithes, they must add one-fifth to
them. 32 All tithes of herd and flock, every tenth one that passes under
the shepherd's staff, shall be holy to the LORD. 33 Let no one inquire
whether it is good or bad, or make substitution for it; if one makes
substitution for it, then both it and the substitute shall be holy and
cannot be redeemed.

34 These are the commandments that the LORD gave to Moses
for the people of Israel on Mount Sinai.

27:26 firstling belongs to the LORD: The first-born animals of the flocks belonged to God (Exod 34:19), just as the first harvested crops were to be presented to God (see Lev 2:12-14 and note).

27:28 devoted to destruction: Objects taken in warfare were often declared to be "devoted to God." The Hebrew word for these things was *herem* (KHE-ram) and therefore "holy" and lethally dangerous. The classic example is the story of Achan, who stole "devoted" items (Josh 7:1-26).

27:30-32 tithes: Refers to one-tenth of Israel's harvest and flocks, which were to be set aside (holy) for the LORD.

27:34 on Mount Sinai: Or "at Mount Sinai." See 25:1.

As you review Leviticus, what seems most "foreign" to Christian faith and practice? What seems useful and helps us better understand the Christian message?

Numbers 2:2

NUMBERS

Background File

The story of Numbers begins with organizing the people by counting those who can serve as soldiers to defend the people. This is how Numbers got its name in Greek, Latin, and English (in Hebrew Numbers is called "In the Wilderness," for the location of the opening scene). *Organization* is one of the themes of Numbers. There are a number of stories about organizing community worship and for war. Mostly, Numbers is the story of a journey full of unexpected events that happen as the people move from place to place in the desert wilderness as they make their way toward the promised land of Canaan.

What's the Story?

While known as one of the Five Books of Moses, Numbers was written hundreds of years after the time of Moses, after the division of Israel into two kingdoms. There is no single author for any of the first five books of the Bible (called the Torah or Pentateuch). The individual stories were written by at least three different communities. Based on their language and their particular way of describing the relationship between the Jewish people and God, they are known as the Yahwist (Y or J), Elohist (E), and Priestly (P) communities or traditions.

Numbers is really Exodus: Part Two. The Exodus story begins in Exodus, pauses for an extended sermon in Leviticus, and continues in Numbers. Many familiar stories about the Israelites wandering in the wilderness occur in Numbers: God's gifts of manna and quails, Israelite wandering and whining in the wilderness, sending of spies into Canaan, and God's guidance in a pillar of cloud and fire are just a few.

It is difficult to talk about *history* and the earliest stories in the Bible, because the ancient understanding of history was not the same as the modern understanding, especially with regard to dates and facts. And there is almost no evidence outside of the Bible that any of these events happened. That does not mean that they did not happen, but that the category of history does not easily apply to the early books. These books are founding stories for the people of Israel. (Think of the American founding stories surrounding the first Thanksgiving. It is a shared story for many who call the United States home, even if their own ancestors did not participate in that event.)

Because Numbers is made up of several unexpected events it is difficult to fit into an outline. Almost every chapter tells a different story. There are stories about famous Israelites like Moses, Miriam, and Aaron, and stories about non-Israelites like Balaam. There are instructions about serving God and living together in the wilderness and in the promised land. Each story has been preserved by first being passed down as an oral story, then written as separate stories and accounts, and finally edited into a whole. They were preserved because they reflected truth to those who spoke, heard, and wrote them. Some readers will relate more to some stories than to others.

The action in the book does take place generally at the camp at Sinai (1:1–10:10), journeying from Sinai to Moab (10:11–22:1), and at the Moab camp (22:2–36:13). Numbers ends in suspense on the brink of the Jordan, which is also the brink of the promised land.

What's the Message?

The message of Numbers may be found in the metaphor of the journey. The story of Israel's journey through the wilderness can be understood as a metaphor for the journey of a community (for example the passage of African Americans from slavery to freedom) or of an individual (perhaps going through a difficult period in her or his life). In each reading, whether individual or community, the traveler is not alone. God is with us. Each story in Numbers makes this point in one way or another. Numbers teaches how to follow God by waiting for God to lead. It also teaches that horrible things can happen to people, even with God in their midst. There can be conflict between individuals, families, and nations. There can be natural and ecological disaster. There can be individual criminal acts of violence, and war between peoples and nations, all in the presence of God dwelling among God's people. Many contemporary Christian readers may be unfamiliar with Numbers, but the authors and editors of the Bible use stories from Numbers about fifty times in *other* books of the Bible.

How do you reconcile faith or religious commitments with obligations to serve your nation, even in war?

1:5-15 From Rueben...Naphtali: The list of Israel's twelve tribes. See Genesis 49, and the notes at Genesis 48:5 (Joseph's sons) and Numbers 3:11-51 (Levites).

The First Census of Israel

1 The LORD spoke to Moses in the wilderness of Sinai, in the tent
of meeting, on the first day of the second month, in the second
year after they had come out of the land of Egypt, saying: 2 Take a census of the whole congregation of Israelites, in their clans, by ancestral
houses, according to the number of names, every male individually;
3 from twenty years old and upward, everyone in Israel able to go to
war. You and Aaron shall enroll them, company by company. 4 A man
from each tribe shall be with you, each man the head of his ancestral
house. 5 These are the names of the men who shall assist you:

From Reuben, Elizur son of Shedeur.
6 From Simeon, Shelumiel son of Zurishaddai.
7 From Judah, Nahshon son of Amminadab.
8 From Issachar, Nethanel son of Zuar.
9 From Zebulun, Eliab son of Helon.
10 From the sons of Joseph:

from Ephraim, Elishama son of Ammihud;
from Manasseh, Gamaliel son of Pedahzur.
11 From Benjamin, Abidan son of Gideoni.
12 From Dan, Ahiezer son of Ammishaddai.
13 From Asher, Pagiel son of Ochran.
14 From Gad, Eliasaph son of Deuel.
15 From Naphtali, Ahira son of Enan.
16 These were the ones chosen from the congregation, the leaders of
their ancestral tribes, the heads of the divisions of Israel.

17 Moses and Aaron took these men who had been designated
by name, 18 and on the first day of the second month they assembled
the whole congregation together. They registered themselves in their
clans, by their ancestral houses, according to the number of names
from twenty years old and upward, individually, 19 as the LORD commanded Moses. So he enrolled them in the wilderness of Sinai.

20 The descendants of Reuben, Israel's firstborn, their lineage,
in their clans, by their ancestral houses, according to the number of
names, individually, every male from twenty years old and upward,
everyone able to go to war: 21 those enrolled of the tribe of Reuben
were forty-six thousand five hundred.

22 The descendants of Simeon, their lineage, in their clans, by
their ancestral houses, those of them that were numbered, according
to the number of names, individually, every male from twenty years
old and upward, everyone able to go to war: 23 those enrolled of the
tribe of Simeon were fifty-nine thousand three hundred.

24 The descendants of Gad, their lineage, in their clans, by their
ancestral houses, according to the number of the names, from twenty
years old and upward, everyone able to go to war: 25 those enrolled of
the tribe of Gad were forty-five thousand six hundred fifty.

26 The descendants of Judah, their lineage, in their clans, by their
ancestral houses, according to the number of names, from twenty
years old and upward, everyone able to go to war: 27 those enrolled of
the tribe of Judah were seventy-four thousand six hundred.

28 The descendants of Issachar, their lineage, in their clans, by
their ancestral houses, according to the number of names, from
twenty years old and upward, everyone able to go to war: 29 those
enrolled of the tribe of Issachar were fifty-four thousand four
hundred.

30 The descendants of Zebulun, their lineage, in their clans, by
their ancestral houses, according to the number of names, from twenty
years old and upward, everyone able to go to war: 31 those enrolled of
the tribe of Zebulun were fifty-seven thousand four hundred.

32 The descendants of Joseph, namely, the descendants of
Ephraim, their lineage, in their clans, by their ancestral houses, according to the number of names, from twenty years old and upward,

everyone able to go to war: [33]those enrolled of the tribe of Ephraim
were forty thousand five hundred.

34 The descendants of Manasseh, their lineage, in their clans,
by their ancestral houses, according to the number of names, from
twenty years old and upward, everyone able to go to war: [35]those enrolled of the tribe of Manasseh were thirty-two thousand two hundred.

36 The descendants of Benjamin, their lineage, in their clans, by
their ancestral houses, according to the number of names, from twenty
years old and upward, everyone able to go to war: [37]those enrolled of
the tribe of Benjamin were thirty-five thousand four hundred.

38 The descendants of Dan, their lineage, in their clans, by their
ancestral houses, according to the number of names, from twenty
years old and upward, everyone able to go to war: [39]those enrolled of
the tribe of Dan were sixty-two thousand seven hundred.

40 The descendants of Asher, their lineage, in their clans, by their
ancestral houses, according to the number of names, from twenty
years old and upward, everyone able to go to war: [41]those enrolled of
the tribe of Asher were forty-one thousand five hundred.

42 The descendants of Naphtali, their lineage, in their clans, by
their ancestral houses, according to the number of names, from twenty
years old and upward, everyone able to go to war: [43]those enrolled of
the tribe of Naphtali were fifty-three thousand four hundred.

44 These are those who were enrolled, whom Moses and Aaron
enrolled with the help of the leaders of Israel, twelve men, each representing his ancestral house. [45]So the whole number of the Israelites,
by their ancestral houses, from twenty years old and upward, everyone able to go to war in Israel— [46]their whole number was six hundred three thousand five hundred fifty. [47]The Levites, however, were
not numbered by their ancestral tribe along with them.

1:47 Levites . . . were not numbered: The Levite men were to serve as priests, which included overseeing the tabernacle and the worship connected with it. In a sense, their role as priests made them exempt from being considered a military regiment.

48 The LORD had said to Moses: [49]Only the tribe of Levi you
shall not enroll, and you shall not take a census of them with the
other Israelites. [50]Rather you shall appoint the Levites over the tabernacle of the covenant,[a] and over all its equipment, and over all that
belongs to it; they are to carry the tabernacle and all its equipment,
and they shall tend it, and shall camp around the tabernacle. [51]When
the tabernacle is to set out, the Levites shall take it down; and when
the tabernacle is to be pitched, the Levites shall set it up. And any
outsider who comes near shall be put to death. [52]The other Israelites shall camp in their respective regimental camps, by companies;
[53]but the Levites shall camp around the tabernacle of the covenant,[a]
that there may be no wrath on the congregation of the Israelites; and
the Levites shall perform the guard duty of the tabernacle of the

[a] Or *treaty*, or *testimony*; Heb *eduth*

covenant.[a] [54]The Israelites did so; they did just as the LORD commanded Moses.

The Order of Encampment and Marching

2 The LORD spoke to Moses and Aaron, saying: [2]The Israelites shall camp each in their respective regiments, under ensigns by their ancestral houses; they shall camp facing the tent of meeting on every side. [3]Those to camp on the east side toward the sunrise shall be of the regimental encampment of Judah by companies. The leader of the people of Judah shall be Nahshon son of Amminadab, [4]with a company as enrolled of seventy-four thousand six hundred. [5]Those to camp next to him shall be the tribe of Issachar. The leader of the Issacharites shall be Nethanel son of Zuar, [6]with a company as enrolled of fifty-four thousand four hundred. [7]Then the tribe of Zebulun: The leader of the Zebulunites shall be Eliab son of Helon, [8]with a company as enrolled of fifty-seven thousand four hundred. [9]The total enrollment of the camp of Judah, by companies, is one hundred eighty-six thousand four hundred. They shall set out first on the march.

2:2 under ensigns by their ancestral houses: Likely refers to banners or flags that had unique designs representing each of the tribes.

10 On the south side shall be the regimental encampment of Reuben by companies. The leader of the Reubenites shall be Elizur son of Shedeur, [11]with a company as enrolled of forty-six thousand five hundred. [12]And those to camp next to him shall be the tribe of Simeon. The leader of the Simeonites shall be Shelumiel son of Zurishaddai, [13]with a company as enrolled of fifty-nine thousand three hundred. [14]Then the tribe of Gad: The leader of the Gadites shall be Eliasaph son of Reuel, [15]with a company as enrolled of forty-five thousand six hundred fifty. [16]The total enrollment of the camp of Reuben, by companies, is one hundred fifty-one thousand four hundred fifty. They shall set out second.

17 The tent of meeting, with the camp of the Levites, shall set out in the center of the camps; they shall set out just as they camp, each in position, by their regiments.

18 On the west side shall be the regimental encampment of Ephraim by companies. The leader of the people of Ephraim shall be Elishama son of Ammihud, [19]with a company as enrolled of forty thousand five hundred. [20]Next to him shall be the tribe of Manasseh. The leader of the people of Manasseh shall be Gamaliel son of Pedahzur, [21]with a company as enrolled of thirty-two thousand two hundred. [22]Then the tribe of Benjamin: The leader of the Benjaminites shall be Abidan son of Gideoni, [23]with a company as enrolled of thirty-five thousand four hundred. [24]The total enrollment of the camp of Ephraim, by companies, is one hundred eight thousand one hundred. They shall set out third on the march.

---

[a] Or *treaty*, or *testimony*; Heb *eduth*

25 On the north side shall be the regimental encampment of Dan
by companies. The leader of the Danites shall be Ahiezer son of Ammishaddai, [26]with a company as enrolled of sixty-two thousand seven
hundred. [27]Those to camp next to him shall be the tribe of Asher. The
leader of the Asherites shall be Pagiel son of Ochran, [28]with a company as enrolled of forty-one thousand five hundred. [29]Then the tribe
of Naphtali: The leader of the Naphtalites shall be Ahira son of Enan,
[30]with a company as enrolled of fifty-three thousand four hundred.
[31]The total enrollment of the camp of Dan is one hundred fifty-seven
thousand six hundred. They shall set out last, by companies.[a]

32 This was the enrollment of the Israelites by their ancestral
houses; the total enrollment in the camps by their companies was
six hundred three thousand five hundred fifty. [33]Just as the LORD had
commanded Moses, the Levites were not enrolled among the other
Israelites.

34 The Israelites did just as the LORD had commanded Moses:
They camped by regiments, and they set out the same way, everyone
by clans, according to ancestral houses.

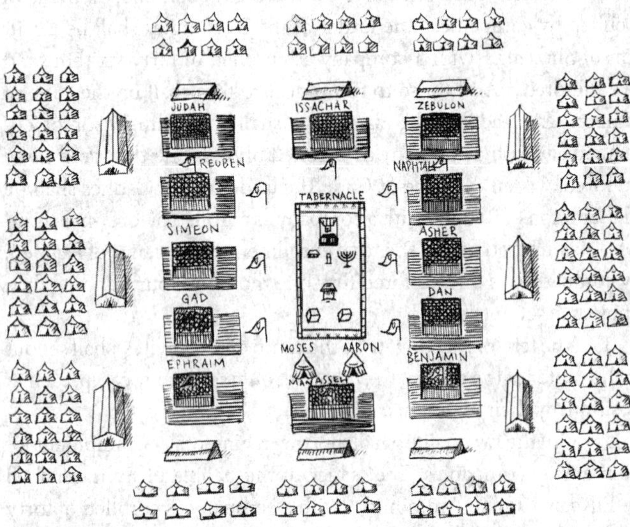

Israel's wilderness encampment around the central tabernacle *Numbers 2*

The Sons of Aaron

3

3 This is the lineage of Aaron and Moses at the time when the
LORD spoke with Moses on Mount Sinai. [2]These are the names
of the sons of Aaron: Nadab the firstborn, and Abihu, Eleazar, and
Ithamar; [3]these are the names of the sons of Aaron, the anointed
priests, whom he ordained to minister as priests. [4]Nadab and Abihu
died before the LORD when they offered unholy fire before the LORD

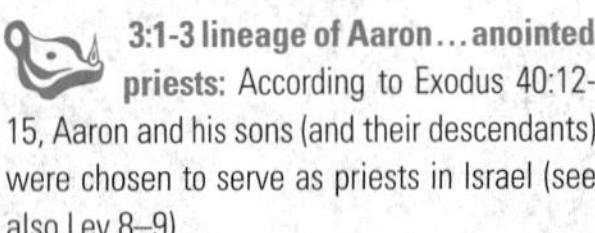

3:1-3 lineage of Aaron... anointed priests: According to Exodus 40:12-15, Aaron and his sons (and their descendants) were chosen to serve as priests in Israel (see also Lev 8–9).

3:4 Nadab and Abihu: See Leviticus 10 and note at Leviticus 10:1.

[a] Compare verses 9, 16, 24: Heb *by their regiments*

in the wilderness of Sinai, and they had no children. Eleazar and Ithamar served as priests in the lifetime of their father Aaron.

The Duties of the Levites

5 Then the LORD spoke to Moses, saying: [6]Bring the tribe of Levi
near, and set them before Aaron the priest, so that they may assist
him. [7]They shall perform duties for him and for the whole congregation in front of the tent of meeting, doing service at the tabernacle;
[8]they shall be in charge of all the furnishings of the tent of meeting,
and attend to the duties for the Israelites as they do service at the tabernacle. [9]You shall give the Levites to Aaron and his descendants; they
are unreservedly given to him from among the Israelites. [10]But you
shall make a register of Aaron and his descendants; it is they who shall
attend to the priesthood, and any outsider who comes near shall be
put to death.

11 Then the LORD spoke to Moses, saying: [12]I hereby accept the
Levites from among the Israelites as substitutes for all the firstborn
that open the womb among the Israelites. The Levites shall be mine,
[13]for all the firstborn are mine; when I killed all the firstborn in the
land of Egypt, I consecrated for my own all the firstborn in Israel,
both human and animal; they shall be mine. I am the LORD.

3:11-51 Levites: All of the Levites, male and female, belong to God. Later texts specify that female Levites receive privileges that are not given to other women, as long as they remain unmarried in the Levite community or marry other Levites. Numbers 3:45 specifies that the Levites are substitutes for *all* of the firstborn; this is repeated in 8:18. When the Levites are dedicated to God in the place of the firstborn in 8:18, the priest lays hands on them as though they were sacrificial animals. The remainder of this chapter continues the organization of the Levite tribe according to clans related to the sons of Levi: Gershon, Kohath, and Merari. Each clan had particular duties regarding the tabernacle (see 3:25-26, 29-31, 36-37).

A Census of the Levites

14 Then the LORD spoke to Moses in the wilderness of Sinai, saying: [15]Enroll the Levites by ancestral houses and by clans. You shall
enroll every male from a month old and upward. [16]So Moses enrolled
them according to the word of the LORD, as he was commanded.
[17]The following were the sons of Levi, by their names: Gershon, Kohath, and Merari. [18]These are the names of the sons of Gershon by
their clans: Libni and Shimei. [19]The sons of Kohath by their clans:
Amram, Izhar, Hebron, and Uzziel. [20]The sons of Merari by their
clans: Mahli and Mushi. These are the clans of the Levites, by their
ancestral houses.

21 To Gershon belonged the clan of the Libnites and the clan of
the Shimeites; these were the clans of the Gershonites. [22]Their enrollment, counting all the males from a month old and upward, was
seven thousand five hundred. [23]The clans of the Gershonites were to
camp behind the tabernacle on the west, [24]with Eliasaph son of Lael
as head of the ancestral house of the Gershonites. [25]The responsibility
of the sons of Gershon in the tent of meeting was to be the tabernacle,
the tent with its covering, the screen for the entrance of the tent of
meeting, [26]the hangings of the court, the screen for the entrance of the
court that is around the tabernacle and the altar, and its cords—all
the service pertaining to these.

27 To Kohath belonged the clan of the Amramites, the clan of the

Izharites, the clan of the Hebronites, and the clan of the Uzzielites; these are the clans of the Kohathites. 28 Counting all the males, from a month old and upward, there were eight thousand six hundred, attending to the duties of the sanctuary. 29 The clans of the Kohathites were to camp on the south side of the tabernacle, 30 with Elizaphan son of Uzziel as head of the ancestral house of the clans of the Kohathites. 31 Their responsibility was to be the ark, the table, the lampstand, the altars, the vessels of the sanctuary with which the priests minister, and the screen—all the service pertaining to these. 32 Eleazar son of Aaron the priest was to be chief over the leaders of the Levites, and to have oversight of those who had charge of the sanctuary.

33 To Merari belonged the clan of the Mahlites and the clan of the Mushites: these are the clans of Merari. 34 Their enrollment, counting all the males from a month old and upward, was six thousand two hundred. 35 The head of the ancestral house of the clans of Merari was Zuriel son of Abihail; they were to camp on the north side of the tabernacle. 36 The responsibility assigned to the sons of Merari was to be the frames of the tabernacle, the bars, the pillars, the bases, and all their accessories—all the service pertaining to these; 37 also the pillars of the court all around, with their bases and pegs and cords.

38 Those who were to camp in front of the tabernacle on the east—in front of the tent of meeting toward the east—were Moses and Aaron and Aaron's sons, having charge of the rites within the sanctuary, whatever had to be done for the Israelites; and any outsider who came near was to be put to death. 39 The total enrollment of the Levites whom Moses and Aaron enrolled at the commandment of the LORD, by their clans, all the males from a month old and upward, was twenty-two thousand.

The Redemption of the Firstborn

40 Then the LORD said to Moses: Enroll all the firstborn males of the Israelites, from a month old and upward, and count their names. 41 But you shall accept the Levites for me—I am the LORD—as substitutes for all the firstborn among the Israelites, and the livestock of the Levites as substitutes for all the firstborn among the livestock of the Israelites. 42 So Moses enrolled all the firstborn among the Israelites, as the LORD commanded him. 43 The total enrollment, all the firstborn males from a month old and upward, counting the number of names, was twenty-two thousand two hundred seventy-three.

44 Then the LORD spoke to Moses, saying: 45 Accept the Levites as substitutes for all the firstborn among the Israelites, and the livestock of the Levites as substitutes for their livestock; and the Levites shall be mine. I am the LORD. 46 As the price of redemption of the two hundred seventy-three of the firstborn of the Israelites, over and above the number of the Levites, 47 you shall accept five shekels apiece, reck-

3:43-47 price of redemption…five shekels apiece: The shekel was a unit of measure weighing between three and six ounces. The number of Levites enrolled was twenty-two thousand (see 3:39), while the number of firstborn in Israel was 22,273 (3:46). So the extra 273 had to be paid for.

4:1-4 Take a census: Israel is organizing itself again, this time for worship. Specifically, the family of Kohath, from the tribe of Levi, is being given the task of preparing the holy things in the desert sanctuary for travel. Kohath was Moses and Aaron's grandfather (Exod 6:16-20). In response to this move of God, the priestly families prepared the sacred space of the sanctuary and its sacred objects for the next leg of the journey. God provided detailed instructions on *how* to move

oning by the shekel of the sanctuary, a shekel of twenty gerahs. 48 Give
to Aaron and his sons the money by which the excess number of them
is redeemed. 49 So Moses took the redemption money from those who
were over and above those redeemed by the Levites; 50 from the firstborn of the Israelites he took the money, one thousand three hundred sixty-five shekels, reckoned by the shekel of the sanctuary; 51 and
Moses gave the redemption money to Aaron and his sons, according
to the word of the LORD, as the LORD had commanded Moses.

The Kohathites

4 The LORD spoke to Moses and Aaron, saying: 2 Take a census
of the Kohathites separate from the other Levites, by their clans
and their ancestral houses, 3 from thirty years old up to fifty years old,
all who qualify to do work relating to the tent of meeting. 4 The service
of the Kohathites relating to the tent of meeting concerns the most
holy things.

5 When the camp is to set out, Aaron and his sons shall go in and
take down the screening curtain, and cover the ark of the covenant[a]
with it; 6 then they shall put on it a covering of fine leather,[b] and spread
over that a cloth all of blue, and shall put its poles in place. 7 Over the
table of the bread of the Presence they shall spread a blue cloth, and
put on it the plates, the dishes for incense, the bowls, and the flagons
for the drink offering; the regular bread also shall be on it; 8 then they
shall spread over them a crimson cloth, and cover it with a covering
of fine leather,[b] and shall put its poles in place. 9 They shall take a blue
cloth, and cover the lampstand for the light, with its lamps, its snuffers, its trays, and all the vessels for oil with which it is supplied; 10 and
they shall put it with all its utensils in a covering of fine leather,[b] and
put it on the carrying frame. 11 Over the golden altar they shall spread
a blue cloth, and cover it with a covering of fine leather,[b] and shall put
its poles in place; 12 and they shall take all the utensils of the service
that are used in the sanctuary, and put them in a blue cloth, and cover
them with a covering of fine leather,[b] and put them on the carrying
frame. 13 They shall take away the ashes from the altar, and spread a
purple cloth over it; 14 and they shall put on it all the utensils of the
altar, which are used for the service there, the firepans, the forks, the
shovels, and the basins, all the utensils of the altar; and they shall
spread on it a covering of fine leather,[b] and shall put its poles in place.
15 When Aaron and his sons have finished covering the sanctuary and
all the furnishings of the sanctuary, as the camp sets out, after that
the Kohathites shall come to carry these, but they must not touch the
holy things, or they will die. These are the things of the tent of meeting that the Kohathites are to carry.

---

[a] Or *treaty*, or *testimony*; Heb *eduth*   [b] Meaning of Heb uncertain

God, for God was understood to be enthroned and riding on the chariot-throne of the ark of the covenant. The specific duties of the Kohathites are detailed in the verses that follow.

4:13 a purple cloth: In the ancient Near East, the color purple came from the murex snail. A little over six pounds of snail glands, roughly twelve thousand snails, were needed to dye one pound of wool. In ancient Israel purple was associated with aristocracy and especially with royalty. Purple was used in the garments of the high priest, who was decked out in royal splendor. Where did all of this purple come from in the wilderness? See Exodus 35:25-26. The ark and the altar of sacrifice were dressed in pure purple cloths. Of all of the sacred objects in the sanctuary only these two rated purple. They framed the most immediate, visible forms of the presence of God: the ark as the early parallel to the heavenly throne and the altar of sacrifice as the place where God heard prayer. The veil and the screening curtain protected humanity from the presence of God. The color purple signaled the presence of the holy in the objects dressed in royal robes.

How do you think of God being present in the world? In your life? How has this understanding changed over time?

4:13 take away the ashes: The old ashes from various offerings were removed from the altar to make room for new sacrifices. The burnt offering, or *'ola*, (OH-lah)—the origin of the word *holocaust*—was one that was entirely burnt on the altar, so its smoke—or better, its scent—was directed toward the heavenly realm. The peace offering led to a harmonious relationship between God and God's people, symbolizing a communion between them. It is also possible that the peacefulness (or wholeness or wellbeing) refers to a covenantal pact, either between God and humanity or simply between different peoples. Offerings of wellbeing include the thanksgiving sacrifice, the vowed sacrifice, and the freewill offering. The purification or sin offering both restored the sinner and made people and places clean in situations that have no relation to sin—for example, new mothers, the person suffering from a disease, the Nazirite who completes a vow, or the installation of a new altar. The basic feature of guilt offering is reparation; unlike other sacrifices, this offering could be converted into a monetary equivalent and simply paid. See also Leviticus and the chart Offerings in Israel, p. 197.

16 Eleazar son of Aaron the priest shall have charge of the oil
for the light, the fragrant incense, the regular grain offering, and the
anointing oil, the oversight of all the tabernacle and all that is in it, in
the sanctuary and in its utensils.
17 Then the LORD spoke to Moses and Aaron, saying: [18]You
must not let the tribe of the clans of the Kohathites be destroyed from
among the Levites. [19]This is how you must deal with them in order
that they may live and not die when they come near to the most holy
things: Aaron and his sons shall go in and assign each to a particular
task or burden. [20]But the Kohathites[a] must not go in to look on the
holy things even for a moment; otherwise they will die.

The Gershonites and Merarites

21 Then the LORD spoke to Moses, saying: [22]Take a census of
the Gershonites also, by their ancestral houses and by their clans;
[23]from thirty years old up to fifty years old you shall enroll them, all
who qualify to do work in the tent of meeting. [24]This is the service of
the clans of the Gershonites, in serving and bearing burdens: [25]They
shall carry the curtains of the tabernacle, and the tent of meeting
with its covering, and the outer covering of fine leather[b] that is on
top of it, and the screen for the entrance of the tent of meeting, [26]and
the hangings of the court, and the screen for the entrance of the gate
of the court that is around the tabernacle and the altar, and their
cords, and all the equipment for their service; and they shall do all
that needs to be done with regard to them. [27]All the service of the
Gershonites shall be at the command of Aaron and his sons, in all
that they are to carry, and in all that they have to do; and you shall
assign to their charge all that they are to carry. [28]This is the service
of the clans of the Gershonites relating to the tent of meeting, and
their responsibilities are to be under the oversight of Ithamar son of
Aaron the priest.
29 As for the Merarites, you shall enroll them by their clans and
their ancestral houses; [30]from thirty years old up to fifty years old you
shall enroll them, everyone who qualifies to do the work of the tent of
meeting. [31]This is what they are charged to carry, as the whole of their
service in the tent of meeting: the frames of the tabernacle, with its
bars, pillars, and bases, [32]and the pillars of the court all around with
their bases, pegs, and cords, with all their equipment and all their related service; and you shall assign by name the objects that they are
required to carry. [33]This is the service of the clans of the Merarites, the
whole of their service relating to the tent of meeting, under the hand
of Ithamar son of Aaron the priest.

---

[a] Heb *they* [b] Meaning of Heb uncertain

Census of the Levites

34 So Moses and Aaron and the leaders of the congregation enrolled the Kohathites, by their clans and their ancestral houses, 35 from
thirty years old up to fifty years old, everyone who qualified for work
relating to the tent of meeting; 36 and their enrollment by clans was
two thousand seven hundred fifty. 37 This was the enrollment of the
clans of the Kohathites, all who served at the tent of meeting, whom
Moses and Aaron enrolled according to the commandment of the
LORD by Moses.

38 The enrollment of the Gershonites, by their clans and their ancestral houses, 39 from thirty years old up to fifty years old, everyone
who qualified for work relating to the tent of meeting— 40 their enrollment by their clans and their ancestral houses was two thousand six
hundred thirty. 41 This was the enrollment of the clans of the Gershonites, all who served at the tent of meeting, whom Moses and Aaron
enrolled according to the commandment of the LORD.

42 The enrollment of the clans of the Merarites, by their clans
and their ancestral houses, 43 from thirty years old up to fifty years old,
everyone who qualified for work relating to the tent of meeting—
44 their enrollment by their clans was three thousand two hundred.
45 This is the enrollment of the clans of the Merarites, whom Moses
and Aaron enrolled according to the commandment of the LORD by
Moses.

46 All those who were enrolled of the Levites, whom Moses
and Aaron and the leaders of Israel enrolled, by their clans and their
ancestral houses, 47 from thirty years old up to fifty years old, everyone who qualified to do the work of service and the work of bearing
burdens relating to the tent of meeting, 48 their enrollment was eight
thousand five hundred eighty. 49 According to the commandment of
the LORD through Moses they were appointed to their several tasks
of serving or carrying; thus they were enrolled by him, as the LORD
commanded Moses.

Unclean Persons

5 The LORD spoke to Moses, saying: 2 Command the Israelites
to put out of the camp everyone who is leprous,[a] or has a discharge, and everyone who is unclean through contact with a corpse;
3 you shall put out both male and female, putting them outside the
camp; they must not defile their camp, where I dwell among them.
4 The Israelites did so, putting them outside the camp; as the LORD
had spoken to Moses, so the Israelites did.

[a] A term for several skin diseases; precise meaning uncertain

5:1-4 put out of the camp: The categories *clean* and *unclean* are confusing to many modern readers. They refer to whether or not one is ready to be in God's presence. While germs were not recognized in the ancient world, the general concept of infection, spreading disease from one person to another, was. Many of the rules about putting people out of the camp can be understood as matters of public health. These periods of quarantine were enforced to ensure that the entire camp did not succumb to disease or death. See Leviticus 12–15.

Confession and Restitution

5 The LORD spoke to Moses, saying: [6]Speak to the Israelites: When a man or a woman wrongs another, breaking faith with the LORD, that person incurs guilt [7]and shall confess the sin that has been committed. The person shall make full restitution for the wrong, adding one-fifth to it, and giving it to the one who was wronged. [8]If the injured party has no next of kin to whom restitution may be made for the wrong, the restitution for wrong shall go to the LORD for the priest, in addition to the ram of atonement with which atonement is made for the guilty party. [9]Among all the sacred donations of the Israelites, every gift that they bring to the priest shall be his. [10]The sacred donations of all are their own; whatever anyone gives to the priest shall be his.

Concerning an Unfaithful Wife

11 The LORD spoke to Moses, saying: [12]Speak to the Israelites and say to them: If any man's wife goes astray and is unfaithful to him, [13]if a man has had intercourse with her but it is hidden from her husband, so that she is undetected though she has defiled herself, and there is no witness against her since she was not caught in the act; [14]if a spirit of jealousy comes on him, and he is jealous of his wife who has defiled herself; or if a spirit of jealousy comes on him, and he is jealous of his wife, though she has not defiled herself; [15]then the man shall bring his wife to the priest. And he shall bring the offering required for her, one-tenth of an ephah of barley flour. He shall pour no oil on it and put no frankincense on it, for it is a grain offering of jealousy, a grain offering of remembrance, bringing iniquity to remembrance.

16 Then the priest shall bring her near, and set her before the LORD; [17]the priest shall take holy water in an earthen vessel, and take some of the dust that is on the floor of the tabernacle and put it into the water. [18]The priest shall set the woman before the LORD, dishevel the woman's hair, and place in her hands the grain offering of remembrance, which is the grain offering of jealousy. In his own hand the priest shall have the water of bitterness that brings the curse. [19]Then the priest shall make her take an oath, saying, "If no man has lain with you, if you have not turned aside to uncleanness while under your husband's authority, be immune to this water of bitterness that brings the curse. [20]But if you have gone astray while under your husband's authority, if you have defiled yourself and some man other than your husband has had intercourse with you," [21]—let the priest make the woman take the oath of the curse and say to the woman—"the LORD make you an execration and an oath among your people, when the LORD makes your uterus drop, your womb discharge; [22]now may this water that brings the curse enter your bowels and make your womb discharge, your uterus drop!" And the woman shall say, "Amen. Amen."

5:11-31 If any man's wife goes astray: This is an example of a text that is painful for many, particularly because it has been preserved as sacred Scripture. It serves as a reminder that the word of God is indeed present in Scripture, but that the words of God have been remembered and preserved by men living in a social world that favored men. This text deals only with accusations brought by the woman's husband; there was no remedy for women who suspected that their husbands were unfaithful to them. The ancient Israelites understood that sexual sins polluted the people and the land and that polluting the land resulted in being removed from it. While sin knows no gender, the Israelites believed that adultery was the most serious of women's crimes, though both partners received the same death sentence when there was no doubt of guilt.

In this case, since there is no witness, there is no proof and no death sentence. The jealous man is suspicious, rightly or wrongly. There was nothing the woman could do to defend herself. In fact, she had to agree to be cursed if she was guilty and trust God to invalidate the curse if she was innocent. The woman had to say "Amen" to her own cursing (5:22). In the Scriptures, to curse is to predict, wish, pray for, or cause trouble or disaster on a person or thing. The punishment here was to fit the crime. An essential part of the cursing ritual was the public humiliation of the accused. The woman who has received forbidden seed would be unable to bear seed—"her womb shall discharge" (5:27). Ultimately, the outcome was in God's hands. This is the only situation in the Hebrew Scriptures in which a supernatural witness was necessary to convict someone of a crime. And it should be remembered that suspected adultery (without a witness) could not be punished by death. Men could not lie about their wives just to get rid of them. Still, the accused woman had to go through this ordeal and had to trust that God vindicates the innocent and redeems the guilty. This text legitimizes male jealousy even as it offers limited protections to women—they cannot be stoned on mere suspicion.

23 Then the priest shall put these curses in writing, and wash
them off into the water of bitterness. [24]He shall make the woman drink
the water of bitterness that brings the curse, and the water that brings
the curse shall enter her and cause bitter pain. [25]The priest shall
take the grain offering of jealousy out of the woman's hand, and shall
elevate the grain offering before the LORD and bring it to the altar;
[26]and the priest shall take a handful of the grain offering, as its memorial portion, and turn it into smoke on the altar, and afterward shall
make the woman drink the water. [27]When he has made her drink the
water, then, if she has defiled herself and has been unfaithful to her
husband, the water that brings the curse shall enter into her and cause
bitter pain, and her womb shall discharge, her uterus drop, and the
woman shall become an execration among her people. [28]But if the
woman has not defiled herself and is clean, then she shall be immune
and be able to conceive children.

29 This is the law in cases of jealousy, when a wife, while under
her husband's authority, goes astray and defiles herself, [30]or when a
spirit of jealousy comes on a man and he is jealous of his wife; then he
shall set the woman before the LORD, and the priest shall apply this
entire law to her. [31]The man shall be free from iniquity, but the woman
shall bear her iniquity.

The Nazirites

6 The LORD spoke to Moses, saying: [2]Speak to the Israelites and
say to them: When either men or women make a special vow,
the vow of a nazirite,[a] to separate themselves to the LORD, [3]they shall
separate themselves from wine and strong drink; they shall drink no
wine vinegar or other vinegar, and shall not drink any grape juice or
eat grapes, fresh or dried. [4]All their days as nazirites[b] they shall eat
nothing that is produced by the grapevine, not even the seeds or the
skins.

5 All the days of their nazirite vow no razor shall come upon the
head; until the time is completed for which they separate themselves
to the LORD, they shall be holy; they shall let the locks of the head
grow long.

6 All the days that they separate themselves to the LORD they
shall not go near a corpse. [7]Even if their father or mother, brother or
sister, should die, they may not defile themselves; because their consecration to God is upon the head. [8]All their days as nazirites[b] they are
holy to the LORD.

9 If someone dies very suddenly nearby, defiling the consecrated
head, then they shall shave the head on the day of their cleansing;
on the seventh day they shall shave it. [10]On the eighth day they shall

6:1-8 the vow of a nazirite: Nazirites were ordinary women and men who made specific religious vows for specific periods or for their whole lives. During the course of the vow, the person displays holiness with uncut hair and by refraining from wine and the grapes from which wine is produced. (Other alcoholic beverages were not generally consumed in ancient Israel, making the prohibition against wine effectively a ban on all alcoholic beverages.) Samuel's involuntary, lifelong consecration (to be dedicated to God) made on his behalf by his mother, Hannah (1 Sam 1:11; 1:22), is generally understood as a Nazirite vow. Samson is also a Nazirite from birth. His mother not only makes the vow on his behalf, but she also takes the vow herself during her pregnancy as directed by a divine messenger (Judg 13:4). When Paul cuts his hair in Acts 18:18, he may have completed a Nazirite vow.

---

[a] That is *one separated* or *one consecrated* [b] That is *those separated* or *those consecrated*

bring two turtledoves or two young pigeons to the priest at the entrance of the tent of meeting, 11 and the priest shall offer one as a sin offering and the other as a burnt offering, and make atonement for them, because they incurred guilt by reason of the corpse. They shall sanctify the head that same day, 12 and separate themselves to the LORD for their days as nazirites,[a] and bring a male lamb a year old as a guilt offering. The former time shall be void, because the consecrated head was defiled.

13 This is the law for the nazirites[a] when the time of their consecration has been completed: they shall be brought to the entrance of the tent of meeting, 14 and they shall offer their gift to the LORD, one male lamb a year old without blemish as a burnt offering, one ewe lamb a year old without blemish as a sin offering, one ram without blemish as an offering of well-being, 15 and a basket of unleavened bread, cakes of choice flour mixed with oil and unleavened wafers spread with oil, with their grain offering and their drink offerings. 16 The priest shall present them before the LORD and offer their sin offering and burnt offering, 17 and shall offer the ram as a sacrifice of well-being to the LORD, with the basket of unleavened bread; the priest also shall make the accompanying grain offering and drink offering. 18 Then the nazirites[a] shall shave the consecrated head at the entrance of the tent of meeting, and shall take the hair from the consecrated head and put it on the fire under the sacrifice of well-being. 19 The priest shall take the shoulder of the ram, when it is boiled, and one unleavened cake out of the basket, and one unleavened wafer, and shall put them in the palms of the nazirites,[a] after they have shaved the consecrated head. 20 Then the priest shall elevate them as an elevation offering before the LORD; they are a holy portion for the priest, together with the breast that is elevated and the thigh that is offered. After that the nazirites[a] may drink wine.

21 This is the law for the nazirites[a] who take a vow. Their offering to the LORD must be in accordance with the nazirite[b] vow, apart from what else they can afford. In accordance with whatever vow they take, so they shall do, following the law for their consecration.

The Priestly Benediction

22 The LORD spoke to Moses, saying: 23 Speak to Aaron and his sons, saying, Thus you shall bless the Israelites: You shall say to them,

24 The LORD bless you and keep you;
25 the LORD make his face to shine upon you, and be gracious
to you;
26 the LORD lift up his countenance upon you, and give you
peace.

---

[a] That is *those separated* or *those consecrated* [b] That is *one separated* or *one consecrated*

6:22-26 you shall bless: This familiar blessing can be translated in each case as "the LORD *will*. . . ." While it is customary for those giving blessings today to say, "*May* the LORD," that form is not used here. The priests are empowered to speak on behalf of God, declaring God's blessing on God's people. There is a tradition that the priests would hold their hands up with their palms facing the people, their thumbs pointing to themselves, the first two fingers touching each other, and the last two fingers touching each other. This is still practiced in some Jewish congregations. (You may recognize the characteristic greeting of Mr. Spock from the StarTrek series. It is widely believed that the actor playing the neck-pinching, eyebrow-raising space officer brought Jewish tradition to bear on the character.)

6:27 put my name on the Israelites: Ancient peoples believed that there was great power in names, particularly in the names of gods. Some believed that if you knew the name of a person or a god, you had power over that person or god. Here the priests are being authorized to put God's name on God's people. God's name is bestowed in the blessing from 6:24-26.

6:27 LORD: God's name is a mystery. In Exodus, God told Moses that God's name is "I AM WHO I AM." God also uses the

27 So they shall put my name on the Israelites, and I will bless them.

Offerings of the Leaders

7 On the day when Moses had finished setting up the tabernacle, and had anointed and consecrated it with all its furnishings, and had anointed and consecrated the altar with all its utensils, 2 the leaders of Israel, heads of their ancestral houses, the leaders of the tribes, who were over those who were enrolled, made offerings. 3 They brought their offerings before the LORD, six covered wagons and twelve oxen, a wagon for every two of the leaders, and for each one an ox; they presented them before the tabernacle. 4 Then the LORD said to Moses: 5 Accept these from them, that they may be used in doing the service of the tent of meeting, and give them to the Levites, to each according to his service. 6 So Moses took the wagons and the oxen, and gave them to the Levites. 7 Two wagons and four oxen he gave to the Gershonites, according to their service; 8 and four wagons and eight oxen he gave to the Merarites, according to their service, under the direction of Ithamar son of Aaron the priest. 9 But to the Kohathites he gave none, because they were charged with the care of the holy things that had to be carried on the shoulders.

10 The leaders also presented offerings for the dedication of the altar at the time when it was anointed; the leaders presented their offering before the altar. 11 The LORD said to Moses: They shall present their offerings, one leader each day, for the dedication of the altar.

12 The one who presented his offering the first day was Nahshon son of Amminadab, of the tribe of Judah; 13 his offering was one silver plate weighing one hundred thirty shekels, one silver basin weighing seventy shekels, according to the shekel of the sanctuary, both of them full of choice flour mixed with oil for a grain offering; 14 one golden dish weighing ten shekels, full of incense; 15 one young bull, one ram, one male lamb a year old, for a burnt offering; 16 one male goat for a sin offering; 17 and for the sacrifice of well-being, two oxen, five rams, five male goats, and five male lambs a year old. This was the offering of Nahshon son of Amminadab.

18 On the second day Nethanel son of Zuar, the leader of Issachar, presented an offering; 19 he presented for his offering one silver plate weighing one hundred thirty shekels, one silver basin weighing seventy shekels, according to the shekel of the sanctuary, both of them full of choice flour mixed with oil for a grain offering; 20 one golden dish weighing ten shekels, full of incense; 21 one young bull, one ram, one male lamb a year old, as a burnt offering; 22 one male goat as a sin offering; 23 and for the sacrifice of well-being, two oxen, five rams, five male goats, and five male lambs a year old. This was the offering of Nethanel son of Zuar.

short form "I AM" in Exodus 3. But this is not used as God's name in the rest of the Scriptures. "The LORD" is used as God's name in many places, but *lord* is a title, not a name. So what then is God's name? The simple answer is that no one knows. In the Hebrew manuscripts from which the Old Testament is translated, four special letters, *YHWH*, represent the name of God. They do not actually *spell* a word, because they do not have their own vowels. Vowels from the word that means *lord* are combined with the consonants from God's name. The resulting word is not a real word and cannot be read or pronounced. (Imagine the consonants *BCDF* combined with the vowels *aei*.) This combined word was created so that Hebrew readers would just say *lord* instead of saying God's name. The four letters of God's name, *YHWH*, include letters from the verbs that mean "to be" or "to exist" in both the Hebrew and Aramaic languages, but it is not an exact match for a word in either language. Preserving the mystery of the divine name means that no one can manipulate God. Placing the name of God on the Israelites was understood to confer blessing, prosperity, and protection on them. In most Bible translations, *YHWH* is shown as LORD.

How can we honor God's name by being careful about how we use it or speak it? What do you think it means to "preserve the mystery of God's divine name"?

7:10 dedication of the altar: The seventh chapter of Numbers has eighty-nine verses, which emphasize that every family gave abundantly to supply their new place of worship. The Hebrew word for *dedication* is *chanukah* (CHA-nu-kah). The rededication of the altar by the Maccabean warriors (1 Macc 4:36-61) is celebrated to this day as the Jewish festival of Chanukah. Jesus celebrates Hanukah, called "the festival of the Dedication" in John 10:22. See also the chart Jewish Festivals and Feasts, p. 227.

7:13 silver plate weighing one hundred thirty shekels: See the note at 3:46-47 (shekel).

24 On the third day Eliab son of Helon, the leader of the Zebulunites: 25 his offering was one silver plate weighing one hundred
thirty shekels, one silver basin weighing seventy shekels, according
to the shekel of the sanctuary, both of them full of choice flour mixed
with oil for a grain offering; 26 one golden dish weighing ten shekels,
full of incense; 27 one young bull, one ram, one male lamb a year old,
for a burnt offering; 28 one male goat for a sin offering; 29 and for the
sacrifice of well-being, two oxen, five rams, five male goats, and five
male lambs a year old. This was the offering of Eliab son of Helon.

30 On the fourth day Elizur son of Shedeur, the leader of the
Reubenites: 31 his offering was one silver plate weighing one hundred
thirty shekels, one silver basin weighing seventy shekels, according to
the shekel of the sanctuary, both of them full of choice flour mixed
with oil for a grain offering; 32 one golden dish weighing ten shekels,
full of incense; 33 one young bull, one ram, one male lamb a year old,
for a burnt offering; 34 one male goat for a sin offering; 35 and for the
sacrifice of well-being, two oxen, five rams, five male goats, and five
male lambs a year old. This was the offering of Elizur son of Shedeur.

36 On the fifth day Shelumiel son of Zurishaddai, the leader of
the Simeonites: 37 his offering was one silver plate weighing one hundred thirty shekels, one silver basin weighing seventy shekels, according to the shekel of the sanctuary, both of them full of choice flour
mixed with oil for a grain offering; 38 one golden dish weighing ten
shekels, full of incense; 39 one young bull, one ram, one male lamb a
year old, for a burnt offering; 40 one male goat for a sin offering; 41 and
for the sacrifice of well-being, two oxen, five rams, five male goats, and
five male lambs a year old. This was the offering of Shelumiel son of
Zurishaddai.

42 On the sixth day Eliasaph son of Deuel, the leader of the Gadites: 43 his offering was one silver plate weighing one hundred thirty
shekels, one silver basin weighing seventy shekels, according to the
shekel of the sanctuary, both of them full of choice flour mixed with
oil for a grain offering; 44 one golden dish weighing ten shekels, full of
incense; 45 one young bull, one ram, one male lamb a year old, for a
burnt offering; 46 one male goat for a sin offering; 47 and for the sacrifice of well-being, two oxen, five rams, five male goats, and five male
lambs a year old. This was the offering of Eliasaph son of Deuel.

48 On the seventh day Elishama son of Ammihud, the leader of
the Ephraimites: 49 his offering was one silver plate weighing one hundred thirty shekels, one silver basin weighing seventy shekels, according to the shekel of the sanctuary, both of them full of choice flour
mixed with oil for a grain offering; 50 one golden dish weighing ten
shekels, full of incense; 51 one young bull, one ram, one male lamb a
year old, for a burnt offering; 52 one male goat for a sin offering; 53 and
for the sacrifice of well-being, two oxen, five rams, five male goats,

and five male lambs a year old. This was the offering of Elishama son
of Ammihud.
54 On the eighth day Gamaliel son of Pedahzur, the leader of the
Manassites: 55 his offering was one silver plate weighing one hundred
thirty shekels, one silver basin weighing seventy shekels, according to
the shekel of the sanctuary, both of them full of choice flour mixed
with oil for a grain offering; 56 one golden dish weighing ten shekels,
full of incense; 57 one young bull, one ram, one male lamb a year old,
for a burnt offering; 58 one male goat for a sin offering; 59 and for the
sacrifice of well-being, two oxen, five rams, five male goats, and five
male lambs a year old. This was the offering of Gamaliel son of Pedahzur.
60 On the ninth day Abidan son of Gideoni, the leader of the
Benjaminites: 61 his offering was one silver plate weighing one hundred thirty shekels, one silver basin weighing seventy shekels, according to the shekel of the sanctuary, both of them full of choice flour
mixed with oil for a grain offering; 62 one golden dish weighing ten
shekels, full of incense; 63 one young bull, one ram, one male lamb a
year old, for a burnt offering; 64 one male goat for a sin offering; 65 and
for the sacrifice of well-being, two oxen, five rams, five male goats,
and five male lambs a year old. This was the offering of Abidan son
of Gideoni.
66 On the tenth day Ahiezer son of Ammishaddai, the leader of
the Danites: 67 his offering was one silver plate weighing one hundred
thirty shekels, one silver basin weighing seventy shekels, according to
the shekel of the sanctuary, both of them full of choice flour mixed
with oil for a grain offering; 68 one golden dish weighing ten shekels,
full of incense; 69 one young bull, one ram, one male lamb a year old,
for a burnt offering; 70 one male goat for a sin offering; 71 and for the
sacrifice of well-being, two oxen, five rams, five male goats, and five
male lambs a year old. This was the offering of Ahiezer son of Ammishaddai.
72 On the eleventh day Pagiel son of Ochran, the leader of the
Asherites: 73 his offering was one silver plate weighing one hundred
thirty shekels, one silver basin weighing seventy shekels, according
to the shekel of the sanctuary, both of them full of choice flour mixed
with oil for a grain offering; 74 one golden dish weighing ten shekels,
full of incense; 75 one young bull, one ram, one male lamb a year old,
for a burnt offering; 76 one male goat for a sin offering; 77 and for the
sacrifice of well-being, two oxen, five rams, five male goats, and five
male lambs a year old. This was the offering of Pagiel son of Ochran.
78 On the twelfth day Ahira son of Enan, the leader of the Naphtalites: 79 his offering was one silver plate weighing one hundred thirty
shekels, one silver basin weighing seventy shekels, according to the
shekel of the sanctuary, both of them full of choice flour mixed with

oil for a grain offering; [80]one golden dish weighing ten shekels, full of
incense; [81]one young bull, one ram, one male lamb a year old, for a
burnt offering; [82]one male goat for a sin offering; [83]and for the sacrifice of well-being, two oxen, five rams, five male goats, and five male
lambs a year old. This was the offering of Ahira son of Enan.

84 This was the dedication offering for the altar, at the time when
it was anointed, from the leaders of Israel: twelve silver plates, twelve
silver basins, twelve golden dishes, [85]each silver plate weighing one
hundred thirty shekels and each basin seventy, all the silver of the
vessels two thousand four hundred shekels according to the shekel of
the sanctuary, [86]the twelve golden dishes, full of incense, weighing ten
shekels apiece according to the shekel of the sanctuary, all the gold of
the dishes being one hundred twenty shekels; [87]all the livestock for
the burnt offering twelve bulls, twelve rams, twelve male lambs a year
old, with their grain offering; and twelve male goats for a sin offering;
[88]and all the livestock for the sacrifice of well-being twenty-four bulls,
the rams sixty, the male goats sixty, the male lambs a year old sixty.
This was the dedication offering for the altar, after it was anointed.

89 When Moses went into the tent of meeting to speak with
the LORD,[a] he would hear the voice speaking to him from above the
mercy seat[b] that was on the ark of the covenant[c] from between the
two cherubim; thus it spoke to him.

The Seven Lamps

8:1-4 seven lamps…the lampstand: The lampstand or *menorah* (me-NO-rah) was an extremely important part of the worship space. It served a practical function, lighting the space. The lamp also held a great deal of religious symbolism. Its seven branches were understood by some to represent the tree of life from the Garden of Eden (see Gen 2:9).

8 The LORD spoke to Moses, saying: [2]Speak to Aaron and say to
him: When you set up the lamps, the seven lamps shall give light
in front of the lampstand. [3]Aaron did so; he set up its lamps to give
light in front of the lampstand, as the LORD had commanded Moses.
[4]Now this was how the lampstand was made, out of hammered work
of gold. From its base to its flowers, it was hammered work; according to the pattern that the LORD had shown Moses, so he made the
lampstand.

Consecration and Service of the Levites

8:5-13 shave their whole body: This is quite an ordination ritual! Needless to say, it is not practiced by anyone today. In these instructions, cleanliness is less about soap and water and more about smooth surfaces. They are only sprinkled with water in 8:7. This is a desert setting, so baths would have been extremely rare. That precious water being used to wash clothes makes this event truly special.

5 The LORD spoke to Moses, saying: [6]Take the Levites from
among the Israelites and cleanse them. [7]Thus you shall do to them, to
cleanse them: sprinkle the water of purification on them, have them
shave their whole body with a razor and wash their clothes, and so
cleanse themselves. [8]Then let them take a young bull and its grain
offering of choice flour mixed with oil, and you shall take another
young bull for a sin offering. [9]You shall bring the Levites before the
tent of meeting, and assemble the whole congregation of the Israelites. [10]When you bring the Levites before the LORD, the Israelites shall

[a] Heb *him* [b] Or *the cover* [c] Or *treaty*, or *testimony*; Heb *eduth*

lay their hands on the Levites, [11]and Aaron shall present the Levites
before the LORD as an elevation offering from the Israelites, that they
may do the service of the LORD. [12]The Levites shall lay their hands on
the heads of the bulls, and he shall offer the one for a sin offering and
the other for a burnt offering to the LORD, to make atonement for the
Levites. [13]Then you shall have the Levites stand before Aaron and his
sons, and you shall present them as an elevation offering to the LORD.

14 Thus you shall separate the Levites from among the other Israelites, and the Levites shall be mine. [15]Thereafter the Levites may go in
to do service at the tent of meeting, once you have cleansed them and
presented them as an elevation offering. [16]For they are unreservedly
given to me from among the Israelites; I have taken them for myself,
in place of all that open the womb, the firstborn of all the Israelites.
[17]For all the firstborn among the Israelites are mine, both human and
animal. On the day that I struck down all the firstborn in the land of
Egypt I consecrated them for myself, [18]but I have taken the Levites in
place of all the firstborn among the Israelites. [19]Moreover, I have given
the Levites as a gift to Aaron and his sons from among the Israelites,
to do the service for the Israelites at the tent of meeting, and to make
atonement for the Israelites, in order that there may be no plague
among the Israelites for coming too close to the sanctuary.

8:14-26 the Levites: The Levites are the members of the tribe of Levi. There were three major families in the tribe: Gershon, Kohath (the ancestor of the priests), and Merari. There were numerous sub-families of Levites; the family of Zadok would become one of the most famous during the time of the Israelite monarchy. In Numbers they are engaged in serving as priests. Once the temple is built in Jerusalem, most of them become unemployed because there is not enough work for the whole tribe in Jerusalem. That is why Deuteronomy (composed during the time of the Israelite Monarchy) lists Levites as vulnerable people who should be provided for by the community (See Deut 14:29; 16:11; 26:12.).

20 Moses and Aaron and the whole congregation of the Israelites did with the Levites accordingly; the Israelites did with the Levites just as the LORD had commanded Moses concerning them.
[21]The Levites purified themselves from sin and washed their clothes;
then Aaron presented them as an elevation offering before the LORD,
and Aaron made atonement for them to cleanse them. [22]Thereafter
the Levites went in to do their service in the tent of meeting in attendance on Aaron and his sons. As the LORD had commanded Moses
concerning the Levites, so they did with them.

23 The LORD spoke to Moses, saying: [24]This applies to the Levites: from twenty-five years old and upward they shall begin to do
duty in the service of the tent of meeting; [25]and from the age of fifty
years they shall retire from the duty of the service and serve no more.
[26]They may assist their brothers in the tent of meeting in carrying out
their duties, but they shall perform no service. Thus you shall do with
the Levites in assigning their duties.

The Passover at Sinai

9 The LORD spoke to Moses in the wilderness of Sinai, in the first
month of the second year after they had come out of the land
of Egypt, saying: [2]Let the Israelites keep the passover at its appointed
time. [3]On the fourteenth day of this month, at twilight,[a] you shall

9:1-14 Passover: These verses treat the unusual need for a "second Passover" for those who cannot observe the first because they were in a state of impurity or on a journey. These instructions expand on those that begin in Exodus 12 and continue in Exodus 34. In a special ruling, Moses tells such people to bring a passover offering one month later "according to all its statutes and all its regulations" and to eat it with unleavened bread and bitter herbs. Failure to participate in the Passover causes dire results; such persons were to be "cut off" (exiled) from the community (9:13).

[a] Heb *between the two evenings*

keep it at its appointed time; according to all its statutes and all its regulations you shall keep it. 4 So Moses told the Israelites that they should keep the passover. 5 They kept the passover in the first month, on the fourteenth day of the month, at twilight,[a] in the wilderness of Sinai. Just as the LORD had commanded Moses, so the Israelites did. 6 Now there were certain people who were unclean through touching a corpse, so that they could not keep the passover on that day. They came before Moses and Aaron on that day, 7 and said to him, "Although we are unclean through touching a corpse, why must we be kept from presenting the LORD's offering at its appointed time among the Israelites?" 8 Moses spoke to them, "Wait, so that I may hear what the LORD will command concerning you."

9 The LORD spoke to Moses, saying: 10 Speak to the Israelites, saying: Anyone of you or your descendants who is unclean through touching a corpse, or is away on a journey, shall still keep the passover to the LORD. 11 In the second month on the fourteenth day, at twilight,[a] they shall keep it; they shall eat it with unleavened bread and bitter herbs. 12 They shall leave none of it until morning, nor break a bone of it; according to all the statute for the passover they shall keep it. 13 But anyone who is clean and is not on a journey, and yet refrains from keeping the passover, shall be cut off from the people for not presenting the LORD's offering at its appointed time; such a one shall bear the consequences for the sin. 14 Any alien residing among you who wishes to keep the passover to the LORD shall do so according to the statute of the passover and according to its regulation; you shall have one statute for both the resident alien and the native.

The Cloud and the Fire

9:15-23 It was always so: Sometimes the Bible makes statements that if taken literally would be impossible to understand. Numbers 9:16 says that "it was always so" that whenever the pillars of cloud or fire moved, the people moved to follow God. But Ezekiel says that when God's cloud (called "the glory of the LORD") left the temple for the mountains, no one noticed (see Ezek 9:3; 10:4, 18-19; 11:22-23).

Since few people today claim to see a physical appearance of God, how can one know where God is at any one time? Is God moving? How do we know when God is leading?

15 On the day the tabernacle was set up, the cloud covered the tabernacle, the tent of the covenant;[b] and from evening until morning it was over the tabernacle, having the appearance of fire. 16 It was always so: the cloud covered it by day[c] and the appearance of fire by night. 17 Whenever the cloud lifted from over the tent, then the Israelites would set out; and in the place where the cloud settled down, there the Israelites would camp. 18 At the command of the LORD the Israelites would set out, and at the command of the LORD they would camp. As long as the cloud rested over the tabernacle, they would remain in camp. 19 Even when the cloud continued over the tabernacle many days, the Israelites would keep the charge of the LORD, and would not set out. 20 Sometimes the cloud would remain a few days over the tabernacle, and according to the command of the LORD they would remain in camp; then according to the command of the LORD they would set out. 21 Sometimes the cloud would remain from

---

[a] Heb *between the two evenings* [b] Or *treaty*, or *testimony*; Heb *eduth* [c] Gk Syr Vg: Heb lacks *by day*

evening until morning; and when the cloud lifted in the morning,
they would set out, or if it continued for a day and a night, when
the cloud lifted they would set out. [22]Whether it was two days, or a
month, or a longer time, that the cloud continued over the tabernacle,
resting upon it, the Israelites would remain in camp and would not
set out; but when it lifted they would set out. [23]At the command of
the LORD they would camp, and at the command of the LORD they
would set out. They kept the charge of the LORD, at the command of
the LORD by Moses.

The Silver Trumpets

10 The LORD spoke to Moses, saying: [2]Make two silver trumpets; you shall make them of hammered work; and you shall
use them for summoning the congregation, and for breaking camp.
[3]When both are blown, the whole congregation shall assemble before
you at the entrance of the tent of meeting. [4]But if only one is blown,
then the leaders, the heads of the tribes of Israel, shall assemble before you. [5]When you blow an alarm, the camps on the east side shall
set out; [6]when you blow a second alarm, the camps on the south side
shall set out. An alarm is to be blown whenever they are to set out.
[7]But when the assembly is to be gathered, you shall blow, but you
shall not sound an alarm. [8]The sons of Aaron, the priests, shall blow
the trumpets; this shall be a perpetual institution for you throughout
your generations. [9]When you go to war in your land against the adversary who oppresses you, you shall sound an alarm with the trumpets,
so that you may be remembered before the LORD your God and be
saved from your enemies. [10]Also on your days of rejoicing, at your
appointed festivals, and at the beginnings of your months, you shall
blow the trumpets over your burnt offerings and over your sacrifices
of well-being; they shall serve as a reminder on your behalf before the
LORD your God: I am the LORD your God.

10:1-10 trumpets: The silver trumpets that God commands the Israelites to make serve expected purposes, such as calling together the assembly and sounding the alarm. They also serve an unexpected purpose—like a reminder alarm on a watch or electronic calendar. The silver trumpets will *remind* (10:9) God to deliver the Israelites when they are in danger! They will also call God to pay attention to their sacrifices and cause God to remember the Israelites for their well-being. This does not sound like the *omniscient* (all-knowing), *omnipresent* (in every place) and *omnipotent* (all-powerful) God in whom many believe. That particular description, (the three *Os*), was developed by theologians long after the Bible was written. In the Bible itself, God is occasionally forgetful. (See Mal 3:16 where a scroll or book of remembrance is recorded so that God will not forget those who respect the holy name of God.)

Departure from Sinai

11 In the second year, in the second month, on the twentieth day
of the month, the cloud lifted from over the tabernacle of the covenant.[a] [12]Then the Israelites set out by stages from the wilderness of
Sinai, and the cloud settled down in the wilderness of Paran. [13]They
set out for the first time at the command of the LORD by Moses. [14]The
standard of the camp of Judah set out first, company by company, and
over the whole company was Nahshon son of Amminadab. [15]Over
the company of the tribe of Issachar was Nethanel son of Zuar; [16]and
over the company of the tribe of Zebulun was Eliab son of Helon.
17 Then the tabernacle was taken down, and the Gershonites and

10:11, 33-36 the cloud of the LORD: God's presence accompanied Israel in the form of a standing cloud or pillar of clouds by day and a tower of fire at night (9:15-23). In Exodus, the cloud and fire pillars led the Israelites (Exod 13:17-22). In Numbers, the cloud settles in Paran, and Moses calls out for God's leading presence. For the location of the wilderness of Paran, see Map 2, p. 2099.

[a] Or *treaty*, or *testimony*; Heb *eduth*

the Merarites, who carried the tabernacle, set out. [18]Next the standard
of the camp of Reuben set out, company by company; and over the
whole company was Elizur son of Shedeur. [19]Over the company of
the tribe of Simeon was Shelumiel son of Zurishaddai, [20]and over the
company of the tribe of Gad was Eliasaph son of Deuel.

21 Then the Kohathites, who carried the holy things, set out; and
the tabernacle was set up before their arrival. [22]Next the standard of
the Ephraimite camp set out, company by company, and over the
whole company was Elishama son of Ammihud. [23]Over the company
of the tribe of Manasseh was Gamaliel son of Pedahzur, [24]and over the
company of the tribe of Benjamin was Abidan son of Gideoni.

25 Then the standard of the camp of Dan, acting as the rear guard
of all the camps, set out, company by company, and over the whole
company was Ahiezer son of Ammishaddai. [26]Over the company of
the tribe of Asher was Pagiel son of Ochran, [27]and over the company
of the tribe of Naphtali was Ahira son of Enan. [28]This was the order of
march of the Israelites, company by company, when they set out.

29 Moses said to Hobab son of Reuel the Midianite, Moses' father-in-law, "We are setting out for the place of which the LORD said, 'I will
give it to you'; come with us, and we will treat you well; for the LORD
has promised good to Israel." [30]But he said to him, "I will not go, but
I will go back to my own land and to my kindred." [31]He said, "Do not
leave us, for you know where we should camp in the wilderness, and
you will serve as eyes for us. [32]Moreover, if you go with us, whatever
good the LORD does for us, the same we will do for you."

33 So they set out from the mount of the LORD three days' journey with the ark of the covenant of the LORD going before them three
days' journey, to seek out a resting place for them, [34]the cloud of the
LORD being over them by day when they set out from the camp.

35 Whenever the ark set out, Moses would say,

"Arise, O LORD, let your enemies be scattered,
and your foes flee before you."

[36]And whenever it came to rest, he would say,

"Return, O LORD of the ten thousand thousands of Israel."[a]

Complaining in the Desert

11 Now when the people complained in the hearing of the LORD
about their misfortunes, the LORD heard it and his anger was
kindled. Then the fire of the LORD burned against them, and consumed some outlying parts of the camp. [2]But the people cried out
to Moses; and Moses prayed to the LORD, and the fire abated. [3]So
that place was called Taberah,[b] because the fire of the LORD burned
against them.

[a] Meaning of Heb uncertain [b] That is *Burning*

11:1-9 the people complained: During their wilderness wanderings the new Israelite nation took the scenic route from Egypt to Canaan. Here in Numbers 11 they were almost back where they started, just about a hop, skip, and a jump from Egypt. In spite of God's faithful promises and covenant with them, the people were miserable and Egypt was starting to look good to them. It was just across the water. They missed the good old days in Egypt, even though the way it used to be was not good. Even though God gave them manna and quail, they wanted to go back to Egypt for boiled flesh and bread, and leeks and garlic. Some people are never satisfied! In anger, God set part of the camp on fire. Moses prayed and the fire was extinguished.

How do people understand (or even experience) God's anger today? Do you believe that prayer can produce miracles?

11:7 manna . . . like coriander seed: Coriander seeds came from a wild annual plant that grew in the region. The seeds were small, white, and spicy.

4 The rabble among them had a strong craving; and the Israelites
also wept again, and said, "If only we had meat to eat! [5]We remember the fish we used to eat in Egypt for nothing, the cucumbers, the
melons, the leeks, the onions, and the garlic; [6]but now our strength is
dried up, and there is nothing at all but this manna to look at."

7 Now the manna was like coriander seed, and its color was like
the color of gum resin. [8]The people went around and gathered it,
ground it in mills or beat it in mortars, then boiled it in pots and made
cakes of it; and the taste of it was like the taste of cakes baked with
oil. [9]When the dew fell on the camp in the night, the manna would
fall with it.

10 Moses heard the people weeping throughout their families, all
at the entrances of their tents. Then the LORD became very angry, and
Moses was displeased. [11]So Moses said to the LORD, "Why have you
treated your servant so badly? Why have I not found favor in your
sight, that you lay the burden of all this people on me? [12]Did I conceive all this people? Did I give birth to them, that you should say to
me, 'Carry them in your bosom, as a nurse carries a sucking child, to
the land that you promised on oath to their ancestors'? [13]Where am
I to get meat to give to all this people? For they come weeping to me
and say, 'Give us meat to eat!' [14]I am not able to carry all this people
alone, for they are too heavy for me. [15]If this is the way you are going
to treat me, put me to death at once—if I have found favor in your
sight—and do not let me see my misery."

The Seventy Elders

16 So the LORD said to Moses, "Gather for me seventy of the elders of Israel, whom you know to be the elders of the people and officers over them; bring them to the tent of meeting, and have them take
their place there with you. [17]I will come down and talk with you there;
and I will take some of the spirit that is on you and put it on them; and
they shall bear the burden of the people along with you so that you
will not bear it all by yourself. [18]And say to the people: Consecrate
yourselves for tomorrow, and you shall eat meat; for you have wailed
in the hearing of the LORD, saying, 'If only we had meat to eat! Surely
it was better for us in Egypt.' Therefore the LORD will give you meat,
and you shall eat. [19]You shall eat not only one day, or two days, or five
days, or ten days, or twenty days, [20]but for a whole month—until it
comes out of your nostrils and becomes loathsome to you—because
you have rejected the LORD who is among you, and have wailed before him, saying, 'Why did we ever leave Egypt?' " [21]But Moses said,
"The people I am with number six hundred thousand on foot; and
you say, 'I will give them meat, that they may eat for a whole month'!
[22]Are there enough flocks and herds to slaughter for them? Are there
enough fish in the sea to catch for them?" [23]The LORD said to Moses,

11:10-15 Did I conceive all this people?: The people's grumbling in the wilderness tests—and, one may argue, bests—the patience of God and Moses. Arguing that they had been fed a virtual banquet for free in Egypt—utterly discounting 430 years of slavery—the people craved meat, literally "craved a craving for flesh." Moses demands to know why God is treating him so badly. In his protest, Moses describes himself as a man trying to do a woman's job. Moses describes the LORD as the woman whose job Moses is forced to perform because she has abdicated her responsibilities.

Moses asks a series of rhetorical questions in 11:12-13: "Did I conceive all this people?" and "Did I give birth to them . . . ?" The unspoken answer is that *God* conceived and gave birth to Israel. In 11:15 Moses offers to quit as nanny of God's people, "If this is the way you [using a feminine form in Hebrew] are going to treat me, put me to death at once—if I have found favor in your sight—and do not let me see my misery."

What do you think of Moses' way of talking back to God? This is one of many places in which the Bible depicts God as Mother. Where else in the Bible can you find feminine images of God?

11:16-30 seventy elders: The seventy elders are respected persons in the community. They are often older persons or males. Here they are called to make their stand with Moses at the gateway to holiness. A human process (Moses) selects the leaders of the sacred community, but God equips them for service. Moses obeys God, selects the leaders, and God keeps God's word. The LORD came down into their midst (11:25). God's Spirit filled them, and for one moment they all prophesied. The form of this prophecy could have included speaking, singing, playing musical instruments, dancing, or collapsing into a mystical trance. Meanwhile, the people had been complaining again, this time about the bread of heaven, the manna that God had been raining down. They decided that the bread of freedom did not compare with the meat of slavery and that they wanted to go back to Egypt (11:18).

God decided to teach them a lesson. Essentially, God said, "You want meat? I'll give you meat. I'll give you meat until it's coming out of your noses!" Even Moses had a serious attitude. Look at how he spoke to God in 11:21-22. Not only does he doubt God; he is challenging and mocking God. God reminds Moses that there is no limit to God's power.

"Is the Lord's power limited?[a] Now you shall see whether my word
will come true for you or not."
24 So Moses went out and told the people the words of the
Lord; and he gathered seventy elders of the people, and placed them
all around the tent. 25 Then the Lord came down in the cloud and
spoke to him, and took some of the spirit that was on him and put
it on the seventy elders; and when the spirit rested upon them, they
prophesied. But they did not do so again.
26 Two men remained in the camp, one named Eldad, and the
other named Medad, and the spirit rested on them; they were among
those registered, but they had not gone out to the tent, and so they
prophesied in the camp. 27 And a young man ran and told Moses, "Eldad and Medad are prophesying in the camp." 28 And Joshua son of
Nun, the assistant of Moses, one of his chosen men,[b] said, "My lord
Moses, stop them!" 29 But Moses said to him, "Are you jealous for my
sake? Would that all the Lord's people were prophets, and that the
Lord would put his spirit on them!" 30 And Moses and the elders of
Israel returned to the camp.

The Quails

31 Then a wind went out from the Lord, and it brought quails
from the sea and let them fall beside the camp, about a day's journey
on this side and a day's journey on the other side, all around the camp,
about two cubits deep on the ground. 32 So the people worked all that
day and night and all the next day, gathering the quails; the least anyone gathered was ten homers; and they spread them out for themselves all around the camp. 33 But while the meat was still between
their teeth, before it was consumed, the anger of the Lord was kindled against the people, and the Lord struck the people with a very
great plague. 34 So that place was called Kibroth-hattaavah,[c] because
there they buried the people who had the craving. 35 From Kibroth-
hattaavah the people journeyed to Hazeroth.

Aaron and Miriam Jealous of Moses

12 While they were at Hazeroth, Miriam and Aaron spoke
against Moses because of the Cushite woman whom he had
married (for he had indeed married a Cushite woman); 2 and they
said, "Has the Lord spoken only through Moses? Has he not spoken
through us also?" And the Lord heard it. 3 Now the man Moses was
very humble,[d] more so than anyone else on the face of the earth. 4 Suddenly the Lord said to Moses, Aaron, and Miriam, "Come out, you
three, to the tent of meeting." So the three of them came out. 5 Then
the Lord came down in a pillar of cloud, and stood at the entrance of

[a] Heb *Lord's hand too short?* [b] Or *of Moses from his youth* [c] That is *Graves of craving* [d] Or *devout*

11:28-29 Stop them!: Moses shows that he is not jealous of the gifts of others, saying that all God's people should have gifts such as prophecy.

An ugly part of communal life, especially religious life, attempts to silence the voices of those who do not look or behave like someone who is speaking on behalf of God. Those doing the silencing imagine how God's spokespersons should look or behave. Perhaps they judge others on the basis of age, gender, sexual orientation, disabling condition, race, culture, or community. They may treat those not like themselves as if they could not possibly speak for God, and urge that they be stopped. How have you seen or experienced this? What would it look like if all of God's people spoke for God?

12:1-16 Miriam and Aaron spoke against Moses: The prophet Miriam is the older sister of Moses and Aaron. Like Moses, she is God's prophet (Exod 15:20-21), while Aaron is Moses' prophet (Exod 7:1). She and Aaron—the order of their names and the feminine singular verb in Hebrew shows that she led and Aaron followed—were concerned about Moses' marital situation and how that reflected on him as God's prophet or spokesperson. Moses has married a Nubian woman (the ancient land of Cush corresponds with contemporary Ethiopia, Sudan, and Nubia). They are upset because Moses had sent his first wife Zipporah and their two children away (Exod 18:2), and in spite of his father-in-law's attempt at a reconciliation (Exod 18:6), Moses has married someone else. Some scholars have thought that this story is about race and racism. But *race* is not used as a way to describe people in the Bible. The concept that people belong to different races was not developed until thousands of years after the last biblical book was written. In addition, because Israel and Canaan (now Palestine) are located on the land-bridge between Africa and Asia, ancient Israelites are known as *Afro-Asiatic*, meaning that they have both Asian and African ancestry. See Map 2, p. 2099.

This dispute is about whether Moses was *really* God's preferred prophet. God confirms Moses' status, and Miriam receives a skin disease (this biblical disease was not modern leprosy; the descriptions of it in Leviticus 14–15 do not include the loss of the body's extremities that characterizes contemporary leprosy). Because God leaves before Miriam is diseased in 12:10, it is not clear that God has done this to her. And because Aaron asks Moses for healing in 12:11, it is possible that

the tent, and called Aaron and Miriam; and they both came forward.
6 And he said, "Hear my words:
When there are prophets among you,
I the LORD make myself known to them in visions;
I speak to them in dreams.
7 Not so with my servant Moses;
he is entrusted with all my house.
8 With him I speak face to face— clearly, not in riddles;
and he beholds the form of the LORD.
Why then were you not afraid to speak against my servant Moses?"
9 And the anger of the LORD was kindled against them, and he departed.
10 When the cloud went away from over the tent, Miriam had become leprous,[a] as white as snow. And Aaron turned towards Miriam
and saw that she was leprous. 11 Then Aaron said to Moses, "Oh, my
lord, do not punish us[b] for a sin that we have so foolishly committed.
12 Do not let her be like one stillborn, whose flesh is half consumed
when it comes out of its mother's womb." 13 And Moses cried to the
LORD, "O God, please heal her." 14 But the LORD said to Moses, "If her
father had but spit in her face, would she not bear her shame for seven
days? Let her be shut out of the camp for seven days, and after that she
may be brought in again." 15 So Miriam was shut out of the camp for
seven days; and the people did not set out on the march until Miriam
had been brought in again. 16 After that the people set out from Hazeroth, and camped in the wilderness of Paran.

Spies Sent into Canaan

13 The LORD said to Moses, 2 "Send men to spy out the land of
Canaan, which I am giving to the Israelites; from each of their
ancestral tribes you shall send a man, every one a leader among them."
3 So Moses sent them from the wilderness of Paran, according to the
command of the LORD, all of them leading men among the Israelites.
4 These were their names: From the tribe of Reuben, Shammua son
of Zaccur; 5 from the tribe of Simeon, Shaphat son of Hori; 6 from the
tribe of Judah, Caleb son of Jephunneh; 7 from the tribe of Issachar,
Igal son of Joseph; 8 from the tribe of Ephraim, Hoshea son of Nun;
9 from the tribe of Benjamin, Palti son of Raphu; 10 from the tribe of
Zebulun, Gaddiel son of Sodi; 11 from the tribe of Joseph (that is, from
the tribe of Manasseh), Gaddi son of Susi; 12 from the tribe of Dan,
Ammiel son of Gemalli; 13 from the tribe of Asher, Sethur son of Michael; 14 from the tribe of Naphtali, Nahbi son of Vophsi; 15 from the
tribe of Gad, Geuel son of Machi. 16 These were the names of the men
whom Moses sent to spy out the land. And Moses changed the name
of Hoshea son of Nun to Joshua.

[a] A term for several skin diseases; precise meaning uncertain [b] Heb *do not lay sin upon us*

Moses has given her the disease that God once gave to him as a sign (Exod 4:6). Also, because Aaron says, "Do not punish us," it is likely that he had the disease as well. The Hebrew makes a stronger case for this, with Aaron saying "It is in me." Some rabbis who studied this text in the thousand years after it was completed read it this way. The chapter ends with only Miriam performing the ritual for healing. Because she is so beloved by her people, they refuse to travel without her (12:15).

Can you imagine a world without placing people into racial categories? How would you describe people if you did not use racial categories? How do you acknowledge and respect the difference between people?

13:1-15 spy out the land of Canaan: One of the most challenging aspects of the promised-land story is that God promised the Israelites an *occupied* land. Joshua (chapters 6–12) will claim that Israel conquered the Canaanites. The first two chapters of Judges will say that the Israelites and Canaanites lived in Canaan together.

13:16 Moses changed the name: Moses changes Joshua's name from Hoshea—meaning "Save!"—to *Yehoshua* [yeh-HOH-shoo-a] in Hebrew, which became Joshua in English (after passing through German), meaning "the LORD will save." The editors of the Hebrew Bible used this verse to explain why someone as old as Joshua would have a name that includes part of God's most holy name, revealed to Moses in Exodus 3:14. Joshua would have already been born and named when Moses met God on the mountain. And if no one except Moses' father-in-law knew the holy name, how did Joshua come to have it as part of his name? This story ties up all of those loose ends.

13:17-20 spy out the land...the people: See Map 2, p. 2099, for the location of places mentioned. One of the most difficult struggles of the current age is the struggle between Israel and Palestine. Some Jewish and Christian groups cite the Joshua tradition of the conquest of Canaan, saying that every Palestinian man, woman, and child should be forcibly removed from Israel/Palestine. Other Jewish and Christian communities are working for a resolution in which both peoples live in the land.

What do you think about the struggle between Israel and Palestine? What can be learned from reading the story of this struggle in the Bible?

17 Moses sent them to spy out the land of Canaan, and said to
them, "Go up there into the Negeb, and go up into the hill country,
18 and see what the land is like, and whether the people who live in it
are strong or weak, whether they are few or many, 19 and whether the
land they live in is good or bad, and whether the towns that they live
in are unwalled or fortified, 20 and whether the land is rich or poor, and
whether there are trees in it or not. Be bold, and bring some of the
fruit of the land." Now it was the season of the first ripe grapes.

21 So they went up and spied out the land from the wilderness
of Zin to Rehob, near Lebo-hamath. 22 They went up into the Negeb,
and came to Hebron; and Ahiman, Sheshai, and Talmai, the Anakites,
were there. (Hebron was built seven years before Zoan in Egypt.)
23 And they came to the Wadi Eshcol, and cut down from there a
branch with a single cluster of grapes, and they carried it on a pole between two of them. They also brought some pomegranates and figs.
24 That place was called the Wadi Eshcol,[a] because of the cluster that
the Israelites cut down from there.

The Report of the Spies

25 At the end of forty days they returned from spying out the
land. 26 And they came to Moses and Aaron and to all the congregation
of the Israelites in the wilderness of Paran, at Kadesh; they brought
back word to them and to all the congregation, and showed them the
fruit of the land. 27 And they told him, "We came to the land to which
you sent us; it flows with milk and honey, and this is its fruit. 28 Yet the
people who live in the land are strong, and the towns are fortified and
very large; and besides, we saw the descendants of Anak there. 29 The
Amalekites live in the land of the Negeb; the Hittites, the Jebusites,
and the Amorites live in the hill country; and the Canaanites live by
the sea, and along the Jordan."

30 But Caleb quieted the people before Moses, and said, "Let
us go up at once and occupy it, for we are well able to overcome it."
31 Then the men who had gone up with him said, "We are not able
to go up against this people, for they are stronger than we." 32 So they
brought to the Israelites an unfavorable report of the land that they
had spied out, saying, "The land that we have gone through as spies is
a land that devours its inhabitants; and all the people that we saw in
it are of great size. 33 There we saw the Nephilim (the Anakites come
from the Nephilim); and to ourselves we seemed like grasshoppers,
and so we seemed to them."

The People Rebel

14 Then all the congregation raised a loud cry, and the people
wept that night. 2 And all the Israelites complained against

[a] That is *Cluster*

14:3 booty: Finding this word in the Bible may raise some eyebrows or cause some giggling. At the times when most

Moses and Aaron; the whole congregation said to them, "Would that
we had died in the land of Egypt! Or would that we had died in this
wilderness! [3]Why is the LORD bringing us into this land to fall by the
sword? Our wives and our little ones will become booty; would it not
be better for us to go back to Egypt?" [4]So they said to one another,
"Let us choose a captain, and go back to Egypt."

5 Then Moses and Aaron fell on their faces before all the assembly of the congregation of the Israelites. [6]And Joshua son of Nun and
Caleb son of Jephunneh, who were among those who had spied out
the land, tore their clothes [7]and said to all the congregation of the Israelites, "The land that we went through as spies is an exceedingly good
land. [8]If the LORD is pleased with us, he will bring us into this land and
give it to us, a land that flows with milk and honey. [9]Only, do not rebel
against the LORD; and do not fear the people of the land, for they are
no more than bread for us; their protection is removed from them,
and the LORD is with us; do not fear them." [10]But the whole congregation threatened to stone them.

Then the glory of the LORD appeared at the tent of meeting to all
the Israelites. [11]And the LORD said to Moses, "How long will this people despise me? And how long will they refuse to believe in me, in
spite of all the signs that I have done among them? [12]I will strike them
with pestilence and disinherit them, and I will make of you a nation
greater and mightier than they."

Moses Intercedes for the People

13 But Moses said to the LORD, "Then the Egyptians will hear of
it, for in your might you brought up this people from among them,
[14]and they will tell the inhabitants of this land. They have heard that
you, O LORD, are in the midst of this people; for you, O LORD, are
seen face to face, and your cloud stands over them and you go in
front of them, in a pillar of cloud by day and in a pillar of fire by night.
[15]Now if you kill this people all at one time, then the nations who
have heard about you will say, [16]'It is because the LORD was not able
to bring this people into the land he swore to give them that he has
slaughtered them in the wilderness.' [17]And now, therefore, let the
power of the LORD be great in the way that you promised when you
spoke, saying,

18 'The LORD is slow to anger,
and abounding in steadfast love,
forgiving iniquity and transgression,
but by no means clearing the guilty,
visiting the iniquity of the parents
upon the children
to the third and the fourth generation.'

[19]Forgive the iniquity of this people according to the greatness of your

Bibles were first translated into English, *booty* meant *plunder*—cattle and other valuable possessions that were taken by force in armed conflict. In recent times, *booty* has come to mean certain parts of the human body, specifically, the front and back of the pelvis. The contemporary meaning is based in part on biblical stories like this. When women and children were captured in war or other conflicts, they were regarded as booty or plunder, in part because they were vulnerable to sexual abuse.

14:4 back to Egypt: The Israelite journey through the wilderness is punctuated by fits of complaining in Exodus 17 and Numbers 11. This time they are ready to fire Moses and choose someone who will take them back to Egypt. They would rather live in the familiar chains of slavery than the uncertainty of freedom.

Many people are like the Israelites, afraid of the responsibilities of liberation. They have been freed from abusive or destructive circumstances, but choose to return to what is familiar. Can you think of situations in which people choose the familiar over the freeing? Why do you think this happens?

14:5-25 the Egyptians will hear: When Moses and Aaron hear that the people are planning to go back to Egypt—with or without them—they fall on their faces in prayer. They begin to pray *before* God responds because they know what is coming. Joshua and Caleb tear their clothes—usually a sign of mourning, and occasionally a sign of frustration or helplessness. They beg the people not to go back to Egypt and are nearly stoned for their efforts. God appears in a cloud of glory and announces plans to inflict the Israelites with a contagious disease. Moses argues with God, using an interesting strategy—*shame*—specifically, a concern for God's reputation. Moses points out that God will not be able to keep this a secret. The Egyptians *will* find out about it. And they will say that the God of Israel was not powerful enough to deliver the people to the promised land and had to kill them all and try to bury the evidence in the desert. Moses has to *remind* God that God's self-description is "slow to anger."

14:19-20 I do forgive: The words of forgiveness, "forgive the iniquity of this people" (14:19) and "I do forgive" (14:20) are part of the prayer service of Jewish people on the most holy day of the Jewish calendar, the Day of Atonement. In this story, God forgives the people because Moses asks.

Now many people believe that anyone can ask God for forgiveness. What do you think the role of clergy is in the process of forgiveness?

What does Luther's Small Catechism teach about confession and forgiveness? Confession consists of two parts. One is that we confess our sins. The other is that we receive the absolution, that is, forgiveness, from the pastor as from God himself and by no means doubt but firmly believe that our sins are thereby forgiven before God in heaven. Luther found forgiveness so important that he counted it as one of the "marks of the church." If you want to find out where the church is, look for where people can forgive one another. We are able to forgive because God has first forgiven us. In the Apostles' Creed we express our belief in "the forgiveness of sins," meaning we trust that God does forgive us as promised. *Numbers 14:19-20*

steadfast love, just as you have pardoned this people, from Egypt even
until now."

20 Then the LORD said, "I do forgive, just as you have asked;
21 nevertheless—as I live, and as all the earth shall be filled with the
glory of the LORD— 22 none of the people who have seen my glory
and the signs that I did in Egypt and in the wilderness, and yet have
tested me these ten times and have not obeyed my voice, 23 shall see
the land that I swore to give to their ancestors; none of those who
despised me shall see it. 24 But my servant Caleb, because he has a different spirit and has followed me wholeheartedly, I will bring into the
land into which he went, and his descendants shall possess it. 25 Now,
since the Amalekites and the Canaanites live in the valleys, turn tomorrow and set out for the wilderness by the way to the Red Sea."[a]

An Attempted Invasion is Repulsed

26 And the LORD spoke to Moses and to Aaron, saying: 27 How
long shall this wicked congregation complain against me? I have heard
the complaints of the Israelites, which they complain against me. 28 Say
to them, "As I live," says the LORD, "I will do to you the very things I
heard you say: 29 your dead bodies shall fall in this very wilderness;
and of all your number, included in the census, from twenty years old
and upward, who have complained against me, 30 not one of you shall
come into the land in which I swore to settle you, except Caleb son
of Jephunneh and Joshua son of Nun. 31 But your little ones, who you
said would become booty, I will bring in, and they shall know the land
that you have despised. 32 But as for you, your dead bodies shall fall in
this wilderness. 33 And your children shall be shepherds in the wilderness for forty years, and shall suffer for your faithlessness, until the last
of your dead bodies lies in the wilderness. 34 According to the number
of the days in which you spied out the land, forty days, for every day a
year, you shall bear your iniquity, forty years, and you shall know my
displeasure." 35 I the LORD have spoken; surely I will do thus to all this
wicked congregation gathered together against me: in this wilderness
they shall come to a full end, and there they shall die.

36 And the men whom Moses sent to spy out the land, who
returned and made all the congregation complain against him by
bringing a bad report about the land— 37 the men who brought an
unfavorable report about the land died by a plague before the LORD.
38 But Joshua son of Nun and Caleb son of Jephunneh alone remained
alive, of those men who went to spy out the land.

39 When Moses told these words to all the Israelites, the people
mourned greatly. 40 They rose early in the morning and went up to the
heights of the hill country, saying, "Here we are. We will go up to the

[a] Or *Sea of Reeds*

place that the LORD has promised, for we have sinned.” 41 But Moses said, “Why do you continue to transgress the command of the LORD? That will not succeed. 42 Do not go up, for the LORD is not with you; do not let yourselves be struck down before your enemies. 43 For the Amalekites and the Canaanites will confront you there, and you shall fall by the sword; because you have turned back from following the LORD, the LORD will not be with you.” 44 But they presumed to go up to the heights of the hill country, even though the ark of the covenant of the LORD, and Moses, had not left the camp. 45 Then the Amalekites and the Canaanites who lived in that hill country came down and defeated them, pursuing them as far as Hormah.

Various Offerings

15 The LORD spoke to Moses, saying: 2 Speak to the Israelites and say to them: When you come into the land you are to inhabit, which I am giving you, 3 and you make an offering by fire to the LORD from the herd or from the flock—whether a burnt offering or a sacrifice, to fulfill a vow or as a freewill offering or at your appointed festivals—to make a pleasing odor for the LORD, 4 then whoever presents such an offering to the LORD shall present also a grain offering, one-tenth of an ephah of choice flour, mixed with one-fourth of a hin of oil. 5 Moreover, you shall offer one-fourth of a hin of wine as a drink offering with the burnt offering or the sacrifice, for each lamb. 6 For a ram, you shall offer a grain offering, two-tenths of an ephah of choice flour mixed with one-third of a hin of oil; 7 and as a drink offering you shall offer one-third of a hin of wine, a pleasing odor to the LORD. 8 When you offer a bull as a burnt offering or a sacrifice, to fulfill a vow or as an offering of well-being to the LORD, 9 then you shall present with the bull a grain offering, three-tenths of an ephah of choice flour, mixed with half a hin of oil, 10 and you shall present as a drink offering half a hin of wine, as an offering by fire, a pleasing odor to the LORD.

11 Thus it shall be done for each ox or ram, or for each of the male lambs or the kids. 12 According to the number that you offer, so you shall do with each and every one. 13 Every native Israelite shall do these things in this way, in presenting an offering by fire, a pleasing odor to the LORD. 14 An alien who lives with you, or who takes up permanent residence among you, and wishes to offer an offering by fire, a pleasing odor to the LORD, shall do as you do. 15 As for the assembly, there shall be for both you and the resident alien a single statute, a perpetual statute throughout your generations; you and the alien shall be alike before the LORD. 16 You and the alien who resides with you shall have the same law and the same ordinance.

17 The LORD spoke to Moses, saying: 18 Speak to the Israelites and say to them: After you come into the land to which I am bringing

15:1-16 make an offering by fire: The concept of offerings has changed significantly. In the ancient world, people believed they were *feeding* their God (or gods) with their offerings. The God of Israel was not believed to *eat* offerings but rather to greatly enjoy the smell. With animal sacrifices, this would have been the smell of fire-grilled meat (think *barbeque*). For grain sacrifices, the scent would have been something like the smell of baking bread. In 15:17-21 God receives baked bread, not just the raw ingredients.

you, [19]whenever you eat of the bread of the land, you shall present a donation to the LORD. [20]From your first batch of dough you shall present a loaf as a donation; you shall present it just as you present a donation from the threshing floor. [21]Throughout your generations you shall give to the LORD a donation from the first of your batch of dough.

15:22-31 if you unintentionally fail: Even unintentional sins needed to be atoned (paid for) through proper repentance. Verses 22-26 discuss unintentional communal sin; verses 27-31 discuss unintentional individual sin. In both cases, the priest makes atonement by sacrificing an animal on behalf of the guilty. Verses 30-31 make it clear that intentional sin (called "high-handed") cannot be forgiven. In these cases the guilty person is banished from the community without the possibility of being part of the community in the future.

22 But if you unintentionally fail to observe all these commandments that the LORD has spoken to Moses— [23]everything that the LORD has commanded you by Moses, from the day the LORD gave commandment and thereafter, throughout your generations— [24]then if it was done unintentionally without the knowledge of the congregation, the whole congregation shall offer one young bull for a burnt offering, a pleasing odor to the LORD, together with its grain offering and its drink offering, according to the ordinance, and one male goat for a sin offering. [25]The priest shall make atonement for all the congregation of the Israelites, and they shall be forgiven; it was unintentional, and they have brought their offering, an offering by fire to the LORD, and their sin offering before the LORD, for their error. [26]All the congregation of the Israelites shall be forgiven, as well as the aliens residing among them, because the whole people was involved in the error.

27 An individual who sins unintentionally shall present a female goat a year old for a sin offering. [28]And the priest shall make atonement before the LORD for the one who commits an error, when it is unintentional, to make atonement for the person, who then shall be forgiven. [29]For both the native among the Israelites and the alien residing among them—you shall have the same law for anyone who acts in error. [30]But whoever acts high-handedly, whether a native or an alien, affronts the LORD, and shall be cut off from among the people. [31]Because of having despised the word of the LORD and broken his commandment, such a person shall be utterly cut off and bear the guilt.

Penalty for Violating the Sabbath

32 When the Israelites were in the wilderness, they found a man gathering sticks on the sabbath day. [33]Those who found him gathering sticks brought him to Moses, Aaron, and to the whole congregation. [34]They put him in custody, because it was not clear what should be done to him. [35]Then the LORD said to Moses, "The man shall be put to death; all the congregation shall stone him outside the camp." [36]The whole congregation brought him outside the camp and stoned him to death, just as the LORD had commanded Moses.

15:37-41 make fringes: The Israelites are instructed to make fringes on edges and hems of their clothing so that they would look at them and recall all the commandments of God and observe them, and not follow the desires of their hearts and eyes. Women and men in the ancient Near Eastern countries surrounding Israel also wore this religious fringe.

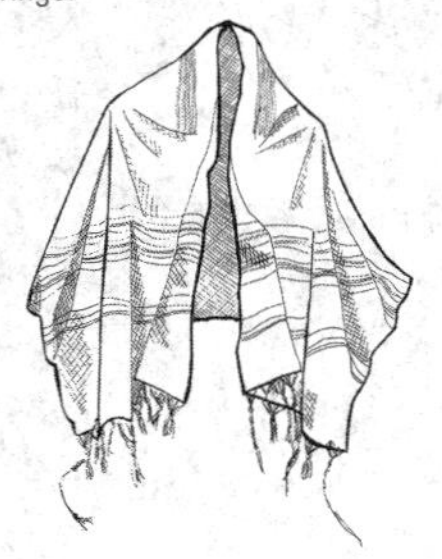

Fringes on Garments

37 The LORD said to Moses: [38]Speak to the Israelites, and tell them to make fringes on the corners of their garments throughout

their generations and to put a blue cord on the fringe at each corner.
39 You have the fringe so that, when you see it, you will remember all
the commandments of the LORD and do them, and not follow the lust
of your own heart and your own eyes. 40 So you shall remember and
do all my commandments, and you shall be holy to your God. 41 I am
the LORD your God, who brought you out of the land of Egypt, to be
your God: I am the LORD your God.

Revolt of Korah, Dathan, and Abiram

16 Now Korah son of Izhar son of Kohath son of Levi, along with
Dathan and Abiram sons of Eliab, and On son of Peleth—descendants of Reuben—took 2 two hundred fifty Israelite men, leaders
of the congregation, chosen from the assembly, well-known men,[a] and
they confronted Moses. 3 They assembled against Moses and against
Aaron, and said to them, "You have gone too far! All the congregation are holy, every one of them, and the LORD is among them. So
why then do you exalt yourselves above the assembly of the LORD?"
4 When Moses heard it, he fell on his face. 5 Then he said to Korah and
all his company, "In the morning the LORD will make known who is
his, and who is holy, and who will be allowed to approach him; the
one whom he will choose he will allow to approach him. 6 Do this:
take censers, Korah and all your[b] company, 7 and tomorrow put fire in
them, and lay incense on them before the LORD; and the man whom
the LORD chooses shall be the holy one. You Levites have gone too
far!" 8 Then Moses said to Korah, "Hear now, you Levites! 9 Is it too
little for you that the God of Israel has separated you from the congregation of Israel, to allow you to approach him in order to perform
the duties of the LORD's tabernacle, and to stand before the congregation and serve them? 10 He has allowed you to approach him, and all
your brother Levites with you; yet you seek the priesthood as well!
11 Therefore you and all your company have gathered together against
the LORD. What is Aaron that you rail against him?"

12 Moses sent for Dathan and Abiram sons of Eliab; but they
said, "We will not come! 13 Is it too little that you have brought us up
out of a land flowing with milk and honey to kill us in the wilderness,
that you must also lord it over us? 14 It is clear you have not brought us
into a land flowing with milk and honey, or given us an inheritance of
fields and vineyards. Would you put out the eyes of these men? We
will not come!"

15 Moses was very angry and said to the LORD, "Pay no attention to their offering. I have not taken one donkey from them, and I
have not harmed any one of them." 16 And Moses said to Korah, "As
for you and all your company, be present tomorrow before the LORD,

16:1-35 Korah: This story is usually referred to as "Korah's rebellion." But if you read the text closely, you'll see that Korah never utters a single word. There are some similarities between this story and Miriam and Aaron's complaint in chapter 12. In both cases people doubt that Moses alone speaks for God. In this story Korah has the same grandfather as Moses (Kohath) and so is his cousin, and he is a Levite authorized to serve in and around the desert sanctuary. He is not asking for anything, nor is anything being asked on his behalf. Dathan and Abiram are the other two ringleaders; they are from the tribe of Reuben and not authorized to serve in or around the tent of meeting. Reuben was Jacob's (Israel's) firstborn. The tribe of Reuben may have expected to have the most honorable assignment because ancient peoples in this part of the world held the firstborn in such high esteem. They rally 250 men to their cause. Their tribal identity is not known. Their charge is that Moses does not recognize the holiness of all the people of God and is essentially playing favorites. They do not seem to believe that *God* chose the Levites for divine service. (The notion that the Levites are *holier* than the rest of the people seems to contradict Exodus 19:6, "you shall be for me a priestly kingdom and a holy nation," repeated in 1 Peter 2:9.)

---

[a] Cn: Heb *and they confronted Moses, and two hundred fifty men . . . well-known men* [b] Heb *his*

you and they and Aaron; 17and let each one of you take his censer, and put incense on it, and each one of you present his censer before the LORD, two hundred fifty censers; you also, and Aaron, each his censer." 18So each man took his censer, and they put fire in the censers and laid incense on them, and they stood at the entrance of the tent of meeting with Moses and Aaron. 19Then Korah assembled the whole congregation against them at the entrance of the tent of meeting. And the glory of the LORD appeared to the whole congregation.

20 Then the LORD spoke to Moses and to Aaron, saying: 21Separate yourselves from this congregation, so that I may consume them in a moment. 22They fell on their faces, and said, "O God, the God of the spirits of all flesh, shall one person sin and you become angry with the whole congregation?"

23 And the LORD spoke to Moses, saying: 24Say to the congregation: Get away from the dwellings of Korah, Dathan, and Abiram. 25So Moses got up and went to Dathan and Abiram; the elders of Israel followed him. 26He said to the congregation, "Turn away from the tents of these wicked men, and touch nothing of theirs, or you will be swept away for all their sins." 27So they got away from the dwellings of Korah, Dathan, and Abiram; and Dathan and Abiram came out and stood at the entrance of their tents, together with their wives, their children, and their little ones. 28And Moses said, "This is how you shall know that the LORD has sent me to do all these works; it has not been of my own accord: 29If these people die a natural death, or if a natural fate comes on them, then the LORD has not sent me. 30But if the LORD creates something new, and the ground opens its mouth and swallows them up, with all that belongs to them, and they go down alive into Sheol, then you shall know that these men have despised the LORD."

16:27-33 with their wives, their children, and their little ones: Contemporary readers struggle with the morality of the ancient world, in which women and children seem to *belong* to their husbands and fathers and are regularly punished with the men in order to punish the men, without any thought for the innocence of the women and children. How do you differentiate the moral standards of the ancient and contemporary worlds? How do you determine which family patterns and behaviors in the Bible to imitate in your own life and family?

31 As soon as he finished speaking all these words, the ground under them was split apart. 32The earth opened its mouth and swallowed them up, along with their households—everyone who belonged to Korah and all their goods. 33So they with all that belonged to them went down alive into Sheol; the earth closed over them, and they perished from the midst of the assembly. 34All Israel around them fled at their outcry, for they said, "The earth will swallow us too!" 35And fire came out from the LORD and consumed the two hundred fifty men offering the incense.

36[a] Then the LORD spoke to Moses, saying: 37Tell Eleazar son of Aaron the priest to take the censers out of the blaze; then scatter the fire far and wide. 38For the censers of these sinners have become holy at the cost of their lives. Make them into hammered plates as a covering for the altar, for they presented them before the LORD and they

[a] Ch 17.1 in Heb

became holy. Thus they shall be a sign to the Israelites. 39 So Eleazar the priest took the bronze censers that had been presented by those who were burned; and they were hammered out as a covering for the altar— 40 a reminder to the Israelites that no outsider, who is not of the descendants of Aaron, shall approach to offer incense before the LORD, so as not to become like Korah and his company—just as the LORD had said to him through Moses.

41 On the next day, however, the whole congregation of the Israelites rebelled against Moses and against Aaron, saying, "You have killed the people of the LORD." 42 And when the congregation had assembled against them, Moses and Aaron turned toward the tent of meeting; the cloud had covered it and the glory of the LORD appeared. 43 Then Moses and Aaron came to the front of the tent of meeting, 44 and the LORD spoke to Moses, saying, 45 "Get away from this congregation, so that I may consume them in a moment." And they fell on their faces. 46 Moses said to Aaron, "Take your censer, put fire on it from the altar and lay incense on it, and carry it quickly to the congregation and make atonement for them. For wrath has gone out from the LORD; the plague has begun." 47 So Aaron took it as Moses had ordered, and ran into the middle of the assembly, where the plague had already begun among the people. He put on the incense, and made atonement for the people. 48 He stood between the dead and the living; and the plague was stopped. 49 Those who died by the plague were fourteen thousand seven hundred, besides those who died in the affair of Korah. 50 When the plague was stopped, Aaron returned to Moses at the entrance of the tent of meeting.

The Budding of Aaron's Rod

17 [a] The LORD spoke to Moses, saying: 2 Speak to the Israelites, and get twelve staffs from them, one for each ancestral house, from all the leaders of their ancestral houses. Write each man's name on his staff, 3 and write Aaron's name on the staff of Levi. For there shall be one staff for the head of each ancestral house. 4 Place them in the tent of meeting before the covenant,[b] where I meet with you. 5 And the staff of the man whom I choose shall sprout; thus I will put a stop to the complaints of the Israelites that they continually make against you. 6 Moses spoke to the Israelites; and all their leaders gave him staffs, one for each leader, according to their ancestral houses, twelve staffs; and the staff of Aaron was among theirs. 7 So Moses placed the staffs before the LORD in the tent of the covenant.[b]

8 When Moses went into the tent of the covenant[b] on the next day, the staff of Aaron for the house of Levi had sprouted. It put forth buds, produced blossoms, and bore ripe almonds. 9 Then Moses

17:1-11 twelve staffs: As a follow-up to the previous story, to demonstrate that God chose Aaron and his descendants for the priesthood, God caused Aaron's tribal staff to blossom like a living tree. Hebrews 9:4 claims that Aaron's staff was preserved in the ark of the covenant with the second set of tablets recording the Ten Commandments (Exod 34:1-4, 27).

[a] Ch 17.16 in Heb [b] Or *treaty*, or *testimony*; Heb *eduth*

brought out all the staffs from before the LORD to all the Israelites; and they looked, and each man took his staff. [10]And the LORD said to Moses, "Put back the staff of Aaron before the covenant,[a] to be kept as a warning to rebels, so that you may make an end of their complaints against me, or else they will die." [11]Moses did so; just as the LORD commanded him, so he did.

12 The Israelites said to Moses, "We are perishing; we are lost, all of us are lost! [13]Everyone who approaches the tabernacle of the LORD will die. Are we all to perish?"

18:1-7 of the tribe of Levi: See notes on 1:47 and 3:11-51. See also the introduction to Leviticus.

Responsibility of Priests and Levites

18 The LORD said to Aaron: You and your sons and your ancestral house with you shall bear responsibility for offenses connected with the sanctuary, while you and your sons alone shall bear responsibility for offenses connected with the priesthood. [2]So bring with you also your brothers of the tribe of Levi, your ancestral tribe, in order that they may be joined to you, and serve you while you and your sons with you are in front of the tent of the covenant.[a] [3]They shall perform duties for you and for the whole tent. But they must not approach either the utensils of the sanctuary or the altar, otherwise both they and you will die. [4]They are attached to you in order to perform the duties of the tent of meeting, for all the service of the tent; no outsider shall approach you. [5]You yourselves shall perform the duties of the sanctuary and the duties of the altar, so that wrath may never again come upon the Israelites. [6]It is I who now take your brother Levites from among the Israelites; they are now yours as a gift, dedicated to the LORD, to perform the service of the tent of meeting. [7]But you and your sons with you shall diligently perform your priestly duties in all that concerns the altar and the area behind the curtain. I give your priesthood as a gift;[b] any outsider who approaches shall be put to death.

18:8-32 This shall be yours: The *biblical* system for managing gifts to God is shocking to contemporary readers. What was not burned up on the altars or used to furnish the worship space was given to the clergy! The Levites are to receive a *tithe* (one-tenth) in return for their service in the tent of meeting (18:21). There were no institutional budget or infrastructure costs for worship space: no building, electricity, plumbing, health insurance, or pensions. The sanctuary was equipped with lamps, tables and curtains, but no chairs or pews.

The Priests' Portion

8 The LORD spoke to Aaron: I have given you charge of the offerings made to me, all the holy gifts of the Israelites; I have given them to you and your sons as a priestly portion due you in perpetuity. [9]This shall be yours from the most holy things, reserved from the fire: every offering of theirs that they render to me as a most holy thing, whether grain offering, sin offering, or guilt offering, shall belong to you and your sons. [10]As a most holy thing you shall eat it; every male may eat it; it shall be holy to you. [11]This also is yours: I have given to you, together with your sons and daughters, as a perpetual due, whatever is set aside from the gifts of all the elevation offerings of the Israelites;

---

[a] Or *treaty*, or *testimony*; Heb *eduth* [b] Heb *as a service of gift*

everyone who is clean in your house may eat them. [12]All the best of
the oil and all the best of the wine and of the grain, the choice produce
that they give to the Lord, I have given to you. [13]The first fruits of all
that is in their land, which they bring to the Lord, shall be yours;
everyone who is clean in your house may eat of it. [14]Every devoted
thing in Israel shall be yours. [15]The first issue of the womb of all creatures, human and animal, which is offered to the Lord, shall be yours;
but the firstborn of human beings you shall redeem, and the firstborn
of unclean animals you shall redeem. [16]Their redemption price, reckoned from one month of age, you shall fix at five shekels of silver, according to the shekel of the sanctuary (that is, twenty gerahs). [17]But
the firstborn of a cow, or the firstborn of a sheep, or the firstborn of a
goat, you shall not redeem; they are holy. You shall dash their blood
on the altar, and shall turn their fat into smoke as an offering by fire for
a pleasing odor to the Lord; [18]but their flesh shall be yours, just as the
breast that is elevated and as the right thigh are yours. [19]All the holy
offerings that the Israelites present to the Lord I have given to you,
together with your sons and daughters, as a perpetual due; it is a covenant of salt forever before the Lord for you and your descendants as
well. [20]Then the Lord said to Aaron: You shall have no allotment in
their land, nor shall you have any share among them; I am your share
and your possession among the Israelites.

21 To the Levites I have given every tithe in Israel for a possession
in return for the service that they perform, the service in the tent of
meeting. [22]From now on the Israelites shall no longer approach the
tent of meeting, or else they will incur guilt and die. [23]But the Levites
shall perform the service of the tent of meeting, and they shall bear
responsibility for their own offenses; it shall be a perpetual statute
throughout your generations. But among the Israelites they shall have
no allotment, [24]because I have given to the Levites as their portion the
tithe of the Israelites, which they set apart as an offering to the Lord.
Therefore I have said of them that they shall have no allotment among
the Israelites.

25 Then the Lord spoke to Moses, saying: [26]You shall speak to
the Levites, saying: When you receive from the Israelites the tithe
that I have given you from them for your portion, you shall set apart
an offering from it to the Lord, a tithe of the tithe. [27]It shall be reckoned to you as your gift, the same as the grain of the threshing floor
and the fullness of the wine press. [28]Thus you also shall set apart an
offering to the Lord from all the tithes that you receive from the Israelites; and from them you shall give the Lord's offering to the priest
Aaron. [29]Out of all the gifts to you, you shall set apart every offering
due to the Lord; the best of all of them is the part to be consecrated.
[30]Say also to them: When you have set apart the best of it, then the
rest shall be reckoned to the Levites as produce of the threshing floor,

and as produce of the wine press. [31]You may eat it in any place, you and your households; for it is your payment for your service in the tent of meeting. [32]You shall incur no guilt by reason of it, when you have offered the best of it. But you shall not profane the holy gifts of the Israelites, on pain of death.

Ceremony of the Red Heifer

19 The LORD spoke to Moses and Aaron, saying: [2]This is a statute of the law that the LORD has commanded: Tell the Israelites to bring you a red heifer without defect, in which there is no blemish and on which no yoke has been laid. [3]You shall give it to the priest Eleazar, and it shall be taken outside the camp and slaughtered in his presence. [4]The priest Eleazar shall take some of its blood with his finger and sprinkle it seven times towards the front of the tent of meeting. [5]Then the heifer shall be burned in his sight; its skin, its flesh, and its blood, with its dung, shall be burned. [6]The priest shall take cedarwood, hyssop, and crimson material, and throw them into the fire in which the heifer is burning. [7]Then the priest shall wash his clothes and bathe his body in water, and afterwards he may come into the camp; but the priest shall remain unclean until evening. [8]The one who burns the heifer[a] shall wash his clothes in water and bathe his body in water; he shall remain unclean until evening. [9]Then someone who is clean shall gather up the ashes of the heifer, and deposit them outside the camp in a clean place; and they shall be kept for the congregation of the Israelites for the water for cleansing. It is a purification offering. [10]The one who gathers the ashes of the heifer shall wash his clothes and be unclean until evening.

This shall be a perpetual statute for the Israelites and for the alien residing among them. [11]Those who touch the dead body of any human being shall be unclean seven days. [12]They shall purify themselves with the water on the third day and on the seventh day, and so be clean; but if they do not purify themselves on the third day and on the seventh day, they will not become clean. [13]All who touch a corpse, the body of a human being who has died, and do not purify themselves, defile the tabernacle of the LORD; such persons shall be cut off from Israel. Since water for cleansing was not dashed on them, they remain unclean; their uncleanness is still on them.

14 This is the law when someone dies in a tent: everyone who comes into the tent, and everyone who is in the tent, shall be unclean seven days. [15]And every open vessel with no cover fastened on it is unclean. [16]Whoever in the open field touches one who has been killed by a sword, or who has died naturally,[b] or a human bone, or a grave, shall be unclean seven days. [17]For the unclean they shall take some ashes

---

[a] Heb *it* [b] Heb lacks *naturally*

19:1-22 red heifer: One of the great mysteries of the Bible is just what sort of red cow is meant by this passage. The red heifer, a young cow that has not given birth, is wholly burned on the altar as part of a ritual to purify people who have touched or even just been near a dead body. It is not clear from the biblical text what shade of red or intensity of color is required or whether the entire cow must be red, without a single hair of another color. That latter understanding, requiring a pure red cow, has meant that the ritual restoring purity to persons who have contact with the dead has not been practiced since the destruction of the temple in Jerusalem during the time of the early Christian church. The lack of this purification ritual means that even if there were a restored temple in Jerusalem it could not be used, because no priests would be able to enter, having not been ritually purified from the deaths of people around them. Now this is something of an imaginative scenario.

The area where the remains of the temple stand are hotly contested between Israelis and Palestinians, with Jews, Muslims, and Christians from all over the world holding strong feelings about what should and should not happen on the Temple Mount. In addition, since contemporary Judaism is Rabbinic, meaning it follows the teachings and writing of the rabbis from the time of Nehemiah forward, most Jews do not seek a restored temple for religious reasons. Rabbinic Judaism grew out of ancient Israelite religion, particularly Second-Temple Judaism; it is structured around the first five books of the Bible and their interpretation, but does not seek to reproduce biblical Israelite religion. (The *Second Temple* was completed in 519 B.C.E. by Jews who returned to Israel after a period of forced exile in Babylonia; see Hag 1:1-14.)

of the burnt purification offering, and running water shall be added
in a vessel; [18]then a clean person shall take hyssop, dip it in the water,
and sprinkle it on the tent, on all the furnishings, on the persons who
were there, and on whoever touched the bone, the slain, the corpse,
or the grave. [19]The clean person shall sprinkle the unclean ones on the
third day and on the seventh day, thus purifying them on the seventh
day. Then they shall wash their clothes and bathe themselves in water,
and at evening they shall be clean. [20]Any who are unclean but do not
purify themselves, those persons shall be cut off from the assembly,
for they have defiled the sanctuary of the LORD. Since the water for
cleansing has not been dashed on them, they are unclean.

21 It shall be a perpetual statute for them. The one who sprinkles
the water for cleansing shall wash his clothes, and whoever touches
the water for cleansing shall be unclean until evening. [22]Whatever the
unclean person touches shall be unclean, and anyone who touches it
shall be unclean until evening.

The Waters of Meribah

20 The Israelites, the whole congregation, came into the wilderness of Zin in the first month, and the people stayed in
Kadesh. Miriam died there, and was buried there.

2 Now there was no water for the congregation; so they gathered
together against Moses and against Aaron. [3]The people quarreled
with Moses and said, "Would that we had died when our kindred
died before the LORD! [4]Why have you brought the assembly of the
LORD into this wilderness for us and our livestock to die here? [5]Why
have you brought us up out of Egypt, to bring us to this wretched
place? It is no place for grain, or figs, or vines, or pomegranates; and
there is no water to drink." [6]Then Moses and Aaron went away from
the assembly to the entrance of the tent of meeting; they fell on their
faces, and the glory of the LORD appeared to them. [7]The LORD spoke
to Moses, saying: [8]Take the staff, and assemble the congregation,
you and your brother Aaron, and command the rock before their
eyes to yield its water. Thus you shall bring water out of the rock for
them; thus you shall provide drink for the congregation and their
livestock.

9 So Moses took the staff from before the LORD, as he had commanded him. [10]Moses and Aaron gathered the assembly together before the rock, and he said to them, "Listen, you rebels, shall we bring
water for you out of this rock?" [11]Then Moses lifted up his hand and
struck the rock twice with his staff; water came out abundantly, and
the congregation and their livestock drank. [12]But the LORD said to
Moses and Aaron, "Because you did not trust in me, to show my holiness before the eyes of the Israelites, therefore you shall not bring this
assembly into the land that I have given them." [13]These are the waters

20:1 Miriam died: Miriam is one of the most important characters in the exodus story and one of the most important women in the Bible. She and her mother, Jochebed, along with the Hebrew midwives Shiprah and Puah and Pharaoh's daughter, saved Moses so that he would live to be used by God to save the people of Israel (see Exod 1:15-22 and 2:1-10). The deaths of very few women are recorded in the Bible. Those whose deaths are remembered were extremely important to their communities: Sarah in Genesis 23:2; Deborah, Rebekah's nurse, in Genesis 35:8; and Rachel in Genesis 35:18, (retold in Gen 48:7), are among the most well-known. Miriam's age at her death is difficult to estimate. Moses is eighty and Aaron is eighty-three when they began to demand the freedom of their people (Exod 7:7); Miriam is perhaps five, six, seven, or more years older than Moses. She is a mature woman when she leads the people through the Sea of Reeds; she is at least in her eighties, perhaps even in her nineties! Before her death, Miriam was one of three prophets who led Israel (Mic 6:4). As a prophet, she conducts the first religious musical performance in post-exodus Israel; she sang (chanted) and played the hand-drum (in Exod 15:20-21 her drum is misidentified as a tambourine). Most scholars believe that Miriam wrote and sang the entire song that makes up Exodus 15. The witness to her legacy is the great number of women who share her name in the New Testament, where it is translated as *Mary*. Women sharing her name are also found in ancient Palestinian Aramaic inscriptions, in the literature of the communities at Qumran who preserved the Dead Sea Scrolls, and in contemporary times.

20:2-13 Moses…struck the rock: In this story, God bans Moses and Aaron from entering the promised land because Moses, apparently in anger and frustration, strikes a rock with the staff God gave to work miracles. The major challenge to a straightforward reading of this passage is that it is a near duplicate of a passage in Exodus 17:1-7; both passages discuss the "waters of Meribah," or rebellion. The footnote translates the word as "quarrel." In the Exodus account God *tells* Moses to strike the rock, and Moses and Aaron are *not* banned from the promised land.

of Meribah,[a] where the people of Israel quarreled with the LORD, and
by which he showed his holiness.

Passage through Edom Refused

14 Moses sent messengers from Kadesh to the king of Edom,
"Thus says your brother Israel: You know all the adversity that has
befallen us: 15 how our ancestors went down to Egypt, and we lived in
Egypt a long time; and the Egyptians oppressed us and our ancestors;
16 and when we cried to the LORD, he heard our voice, and sent an angel and brought us out of Egypt; and here we are in Kadesh, a town
on the edge of your territory. 17 Now let us pass through your land. We
will not pass through field or vineyard, or drink water from any well;
we will go along the King's Highway, not turning aside to the right
hand or to the left until we have passed through your territory."
18 But Edom said to him, "You shall not pass through, or we will
come out with the sword against you." 19 The Israelites said to him,
"We will stay on the highway; and if we drink of your water, we and
our livestock, then we will pay for it. It is only a small matter; just let
us pass through on foot." 20 But he said, "You shall not pass through."
And Edom came out against them with a large force, heavily armed.
21 Thus Edom refused to give Israel passage through their territory; so
Israel turned away from them.

The Death of Aaron

22 They set out from Kadesh, and the Israelites, the whole congregation, came to Mount Hor. 23 Then the LORD said to Moses and
Aaron at Mount Hor, on the border of the land of Edom, 24 "Let Aaron
be gathered to his people. For he shall not enter the land that I have
given to the Israelites, because you rebelled against my command at
the waters of Meribah. 25 Take Aaron and his son Eleazar, and bring
them up Mount Hor; 26 strip Aaron of his vestments, and put them on
his son Eleazar. But Aaron shall be gathered to his people,[b] and shall
die there." 27 Moses did as the LORD had commanded; they went up
Mount Hor in the sight of the whole congregation. 28 Moses stripped
Aaron of his vestments, and put them on his son Eleazar; and Aaron
died there on the top of the mountain. Moses and Eleazar came down
from the mountain. 29 When all the congregation saw that Aaron had
died, all the house of Israel mourned for Aaron thirty days.

The Bronze Serpent

21 When the Canaanite, the king of Arad, who lived in the
Negeb, heard that Israel was coming by the way of Atharim,
he fought against Israel and took some of them captive. 2 Then Israel

[a] That is *Quarrel* [b] Heb lacks *to his people*

made a vow to the LORD and said, "If you will indeed give this people
into our hands, then we will utterly destroy their towns." 3 The LORD
listened to the voice of Israel, and handed over the Canaanites; and
they utterly destroyed them and their towns; so the place was called
Hormah.[a]

4 From Mount Hor they set out by the way to the Red Sea,[b] to go
around the land of Edom; but the people became impatient on the
way. 5 The people spoke against God and against Moses, "Why have
you brought us up out of Egypt to die in the wilderness? For there is
no food and no water, and we detest this miserable food." 6 Then the
LORD sent poisonous[c] serpents among the people, and they bit the
people, so that many Israelites died. 7 The people came to Moses and
said, "We have sinned by speaking against the LORD and against you;
pray to the LORD to take away the serpents from us." So Moses prayed
for the people. 8 And the LORD said to Moses, "Make a poisonous[c]
serpent, and set it on a pole; and everyone who is bitten shall look at it
and live." 9 So Moses made a serpent of bronze, and put it upon a pole;
and whenever a serpent bit someone, that person would look at the
serpent of bronze and live.

The Journey to Moab

10 The Israelites set out, and camped in Oboth. 11 They set out
from Oboth, and camped at Iye-abarim, in the wilderness bordering
Moab toward the sunrise. 12 From there they set out, and camped in
the Wadi Zered. 13 From there they set out, and camped on the other
side of the Arnon, in[d] the wilderness that extends from the boundary
of the Amorites; for the Arnon is the boundary of Moab, between
Moab and the Amorites. 14 Wherefore it is said in the Book of the Wars
of the LORD,

"Waheb in Suphah and the wadis.
The Arnon 15 and the slopes of the wadis
that extend to the seat of Ar,
and lie along the border of Moab."[e]

16 From there they continued to Beer;[f] that is the well of which
the LORD said to Moses, "Gather the people together, and I will give
them water." 17 Then Israel sang this song:

"Spring up, O well!—Sing to it!—
18 the well that the leaders sank,
that the nobles of the people dug,
with the scepter, with the staff."

From the wilderness to Mattanah, 19 from Mattanah to Nahaliel, from
Nahaliel to Bamoth, 20 and from Bamoth to the valley lying in the region of Moab by the top of Pisgah that overlooks the wasteland.[g]

21:4-9 a serpent of bronze: In yet another episode of grumbling, the Israelites become cranky in chapter 21. First, they complain about the lack of food—even though abundant manna and quail are available. Then they concede that they do, in fact, have food, but complain that it is not *really* food. God is not patient with the Israelites this time and sends poisonous fire-snakes to bite them. These fire-serpents in the wilderness burned in an interesting way: they are described using the same word that is used of the fiery beings that Isaiah saw in Isaiah 6:2 (*seraph* [SEH-raf], singular, or *seraphim* [seh-rah-PHEEM], plural). As a result of their repentance combined with Moses' prayers on their behalf, God forgave them but did not recall the fire-snakes. In verse 8, God told Moses to do something that seems strange to modern ears, something that reeks of magic, superstition, and idolatry. God told Moses to make a bronze fire-serpent and to place it on a pole and lift it up. And God told Moses to tell the people to look at the image he made. While the fire-serpents were swarming about their feet, the Israelites, to be healed, were to take their eyes off their very real problems and look only at an image of their problems. King Hezekiah destroyed the image in 2 Kings 18:1-4 because the Judeans began to worship the image and make offerings to it. Jesus makes reference to this story in John 3.

21:12-13 Wadi Zered...Arnon: A *wadi* is a stream or the narrow channel of a stream. Sometimes it is filled with water and sometimes it is dry. The exact location of Zered is unclear. For locations of Arnon and Moab, see Map 7, p. 2105.

21:14 the Book of the Wars of the LORD: Refers to documents that are lost or unknown.

---

[a] Heb *Destruction* [b] Or *Sea of Reeds* [c] Or *fiery;* Heb *seraphim* [d] Gk: Heb *which is in* [e] Meaning of Heb uncertain [f] That is *Well* [g] Or *Jeshimon*

King Sihon Defeated

21 Then Israel sent messengers to King Sihon of the Amorites,
saying, 22“Let me pass through your land; we will not turn aside into
field or vineyard; we will not drink the water of any well; we will go
by the King’s Highway until we have passed through your territory.”
23But Sihon would not allow Israel to pass through his territory. Sihon gathered all his people together, and went out against Israel to
the wilderness; he came to Jahaz, and fought against Israel. 24Israel put
him to the sword, and took possession of his land from the Arnon to
the Jabbok, as far as to the Ammonites; for the boundary of the Ammonites was strong. 25Israel took all these towns, and Israel settled in
all the towns of the Amorites, in Heshbon, and in all its villages. 26For
Heshbon was the city of King Sihon of the Amorites, who had fought
against the former king of Moab and captured all his land as far as the
Arnon. 27Therefore the ballad singers say,

“Come to Heshbon, let it be built;
  let the city of Sihon be established.
28 For fire came out from Heshbon,
  flame from the city of Sihon.
It devoured Ar of Moab,
  and swallowed up[a] the heights of the Arnon.
29 Woe to you, O Moab!
  You are undone, O people of Chemosh!
He has made his sons fugitives,
  and his daughters captives,
  to an Amorite king, Sihon.
30 So their posterity perished
  from Heshbon[b] to Dibon,
  and we laid waste until fire spread to Medeba.”[c]

31 Thus Israel settled in the land of the Amorites. 32Moses sent
to spy out Jazer; and they captured its villages, and dispossessed the
Amorites who were there.

21:31 land of the Amorites: Little is known about these people, though they are mentioned elsewhere (see Judg 1; 1 Sam 7:14; 1 Kgs 9:20-21).

King Og Defeated

33 Then they turned and went up the road to Bashan; and King
Og of Bashan came out against them, he and all his people, to battle
at Edrei. 34But the LORD said to Moses, “Do not be afraid of him;
for I have given him into your hand, with all his people, and all his
land. You shall do to him as you did to King Sihon of the Amorites,
who ruled in Heshbon.” 35So they killed him, his sons, and all his
people, until there was no survivor left; and they took possession of
his land.

---

[a] Gk: Heb *and the lords of* [b] Gk: Heb *we have shot at them; Heshbon has perished* [c] Compare Sam Gk: Meaning of MT uncertain

Balak Summons Balaam to Curse Israel

22 The Israelites set out, and camped in the plains of Moab
across the Jordan from Jericho. 2 Now Balak son of Zippor
saw all that Israel had done to the Amorites. 3 Moab was in great dread
of the people, because they were so numerous; Moab was overcome
with fear of the people of Israel. 4 And Moab said to the elders of Midian, "This horde will now lick up all that is around us, as an ox licks
up the grass of the field." Now Balak son of Zippor was king of Moab
at that time. 5 He sent messengers to Balaam son of Beor at Pethor,
which is on the Euphrates, in the land of Amaw,[a] to summon him, saying, "A people has come out of Egypt; they have spread over the face
of the earth, and they have settled next to me. 6 Come now, curse this
people for me, since they are stronger than I; perhaps I shall be able to
defeat them and drive them from the land; for I know that whomever
you bless is blessed, and whomever you curse is cursed."

7 So the elders of Moab and the elders of Midian departed with
the fees for divination in their hand; and they came to Balaam, and
gave him Balak's message. 8 He said to them, "Stay here tonight, and
I will bring back word to you, just as the LORD speaks to me"; so the
officials of Moab stayed with Balaam. 9 God came to Balaam and said,
"Who are these men with you?" 10 Balaam said to God, "King Balak
son of Zippor of Moab, has sent me this message: 11 'A people has
come out of Egypt and has spread over the face of the earth; now
come, curse them for me; perhaps I shall be able to fight against them
and drive them out.'" 12 God said to Balaam, "You shall not go with
them; you shall not curse the people, for they are blessed." 13 So Balaam rose in the morning, and said to the officials of Balak, "Go to
your own land, for the LORD has refused to let me go with you." 14 So
the officials of Moab rose and went to Balak, and said, "Balaam refuses to come with us."

15 Once again Balak sent officials, more numerous and more distinguished than these. 16 They came to Balaam and said to him, "Thus
says Balak son of Zippor: 'Do not let anything hinder you from coming to me; 17 for I will surely do you great honor, and whatever you say
to me I will do; come, curse this people for me.'" 18 But Balaam replied
to the servants of Balak, "Although Balak were to give me his house
full of silver and gold, I could not go beyond the command of the
LORD my God, to do less or more. 19 You remain here, as the others
did, so that I may learn what more the LORD may say to me." 20 That
night God came to Balaam and said to him, "If the men have come to
summon you, get up and go with them; but do only what I tell you to
do." 21 So Balaam got up in the morning, saddled his donkey, and went
with the officials of Moab.

---

[a] Or *land of his kinsfolk*

22:5 Balaam son of Beor: Balaam was a famous prophet at the time of the stories in Numbers and for quite some time afterward. He is the only prophet in the Bible who has stories preserved about him outside of the Bible. Some of Balaam's stories have been found on an ancient clay tablet dating to the time of the divided monarchy. Balaam's story shows that he knows the God of Israel very well, and he knows a number of different names for God—more than anyone else in the story. He describes himself as hearing the words of God, seeing visions of the Almighty, and obtaining knowledge from the Most High. Some readers are surprised to find that the spirit of God comes over Balaam and speaks through this foreign, non-Israelite, prophet.

22:20 God came to Balaam: One version of Balaam's story ends in 22:21. In it, God comes to Balaam, probably in a dream, and tells him to go with the people from Moab. God will tell Balaam what to say and do when he arrives at his destination. Another version of Balaam's story begins at 22:22. This is the story of Balaam and his talking donkey. In it God is angry that Balaam is going with the people from Moab. What is the source of this contradiction? These two stories originated in different circumstances. The larger story, chapters 22–24, without 22:22-35, is the earlier story. The donkey story was inserted later, in part to discredit Balaam, who was a hugely popular but *foreign* prophet. While the larger story makes clear that Balaam is a legitimate prophet through whom God speaks, acts, and blesses, the donkey story paints Balaam in an extremely bad light.

22:22 his adversary: One interesting aspect of the donkey story is its vocabulary. The single Hebrew word that is translated as "his adversary" literally means *his satan*. *Satan* is a Hebrew word that in its earliest form meant *adversary*, and not a specific evil being. Some readers are surprised to find that the first *satan* in the Bible is God's angel.

22:22 the angel of the Lord: The angel of the Lord is usually God in disguise. If you look closely at 22:32 and 22:35, the angel speaks God's words in the first person. In most stories, the Angel of the Lord switches between first and third person as though God forgets that God is in disguise. When modern people think about angels, they imagine wings, halos, and musical instruments. Those are medieval and renaissance ideas about angels. The English word *angel* comes from a similar Greek word, *angelos* [an-GHE-los]. But because the ancient Israelites did not have lasting contact with the Greek-speaking world until their Hebrew Scriptures, which we share in our Old Testament, were recorded and circulated, they had entirely different words and understandings.

The *cherubim* (see Gen 3:24) were usually sphinx-like creatures with wings and animal heads. When they had human heads and sometimes torsos, they had animal legs and were male and female. The pair on the ark of the covenant were said to be in such an intimate embrace that the great Jewish historians Philo and Josephus were scandalized by them and refused to describe them. The holiness of their union gave rise to the tradition of baby-faced cherubs. The second divine species are the *seraphim*, found in Isaiah 6. They are fire-creatures with six wings: one pair covering their faces, the second covering their legs—a delicate Semitic allusion to everything below the waist—and the third pair for flying. The third category are the *godlings*, or the *sons of God*. They are found only in Genesis 6:2, 4; Job 1:6 and 2:1. Some texts suggest they are the demoted gods of other peoples. Some suggest they are the heavenly host, the stars who wage war on behalf of God. Greek philosophy and theology refers to them as *angels*.

The fourth category, *messengers*, is the oldest. The Hebrew word for *messenger* can mean what is now called an *angel* or a regular human being serving as a messenger (see Gen 16:7; 32:3). God uses them to announce momentous births: Hagar the Egyptian is the first person on earth to whom God sends a divine messenger (Gen 16:11); God also sends them to the mother of Samson (Judg 13:3) and to Mary (Luke 1:26-31). There is some-

Balaam, the Donkey, and the Angel

22 God's anger was kindled because he was going, and the angel of
the Lord took his stand in the road as his adversary. Now he was riding on the donkey, and his two servants were with him. 23 The donkey
saw the angel of the Lord standing in the road, with a drawn sword in
his hand; so the donkey turned off the road, and went into the field;
and Balaam struck the donkey, to turn it back onto the road. 24 Then the
angel of the Lord stood in a narrow path between the vineyards, with
a wall on either side. 25 When the donkey saw the angel of the Lord,
it scraped against the wall, and scraped Balaam's foot against the wall;
so he struck it again. 26 Then the angel of the Lord went ahead, and
stood in a narrow place, where there was no way to turn either to the
right or to the left. 27 When the donkey saw the angel of the Lord, it lay
down under Balaam; and Balaam's anger was kindled, and he struck
the donkey with his staff. 28 Then the Lord opened the mouth of the
donkey, and it said to Balaam, "What have I done to you, that you have
struck me these three times?" 29 Balaam said to the donkey, "Because
you have made a fool of me! I wish I had a sword in my hand! I would
kill you right now!" 30 But the donkey said to Balaam, "Am I not your
donkey, which you have ridden all your life to this day? Have I been in
the habit of treating you this way?" And he said, "No."

31 Then the Lord opened the eyes of Balaam, and he saw the
angel of the Lord standing in the road, with his drawn sword in his
hand; and he bowed down, falling on his face. 32 The angel of the Lord
said to him, "Why have you struck your donkey these three times?
I have come out as an adversary, because your way is perverse[a] before me. 33 The donkey saw me, and turned away from me these three
times. If it had not turned away from me, surely just now I would have
killed you and let it live." 34 Then Balaam said to the angel of the Lord,
"I have sinned, for I did not know that you were standing in the road
to oppose me. Now therefore, if it is displeasing to you, I will return
home." 35 The angel of the Lord said to Balaam, "Go with the men;
but speak only what I tell you to speak." So Balaam went on with the
officials of Balak.

36 When Balak heard that Balaam had come, he went out to meet
him at Ir-moab, on the boundary formed by the Arnon, at the farthest point of the boundary. 37 Balak said to Balaam, "Did I not send to
summon you? Why did you not come to me? Am I not able to honor
you?" 38 Balaam said to Balak, "I have come to you now, but do I have
power to say just anything? The word God puts in my mouth, that is
what I must say." 39 Then Balaam went with Balak, and they came to
Kiriath-huzoth. 40 Balak sacrificed oxen and sheep, and sent them to
Balaam and to the officials who were with him.

---

[a] Meaning of Heb uncertain

Balaam's First Oracle

41 On the next day Balak took Balaam and brought him up
to Bamoth-baal; and from there he could see part of the people of
23 Israel.[a] 1Then Balaam said to Balak, "Build me seven altars
here, and prepare seven bulls and seven rams for me." 2Ba-
lak did as Balaam had said; and Balak and Balaam offered a bull and a
ram on each altar. 3Then Balaam said to Balak, "Stay here beside your
burnt offerings while I go aside. Perhaps the LORD will come to meet
me. Whatever he shows me I will tell you." And he went to a bare
height.

4 Then God met Balaam; and Balaam said to him, "I have arranged the seven altars, and have offered a bull and a ram on each
altar." 5The LORD put a word in Balaam's mouth, and said, "Return to
Balak, and this is what you must say." 6So he returned to Balak,[b] who
was standing beside his burnt offerings with all the officials of Moab.
7Then Balaam[c] uttered his oracle, saying:

"Balak has brought me from Aram,
    the king of Moab from the eastern mountains:
'Come, curse Jacob for me;
    Come, denounce Israel!'
8 How can I curse whom God has not cursed?
    How can I denounce those whom the LORD has not
        denounced?
9 For from the top of the crags I see him,
    from the hills I behold him.
Here is a people living alone,
    and not reckoning itself among the nations!
10 Who can count the dust of Jacob,
    or number the dust-cloud[d] of Israel?
Let me die the death of the upright,
    and let my end be like his!"

11 Then Balak said to Balaam, "What have you done to me? I
brought you to curse my enemies, but now you have done nothing
but bless them." 12He answered, "Must I not take care to say what the
LORD puts into my mouth?"

Balaam's Second Oracle

13 So Balak said to him, "Come with me to another place from
which you may see them; you shall see only part of them, and shall
not see them all; then curse them for me from there." 14So he took him
to the field of Zophim, to the top of Pisgah. He built seven altars, and
offered a bull and a ram on each altar. 15Balaam said to Balak, "Stand
here beside your burnt offerings, while I meet the LORD over there."

[a] Heb lacks *of Israel* [b] Heb *him* [c] Heb *he* [d] Or *fourth part*

thing else about the messenger-angels: they are the messengers that Jacob dreamed of in Genesis 28:12—they don't have wings! They need a ladder to go back and forth to and from heaven.

How do you understand angels? How do you think they work in the world?

[16]The LORD met Balaam, put a word into his mouth, and said, "Return to Balak, and this is what you shall say." [17]When he came to him, he was standing beside his burnt offerings with the officials of Moab. Balak said to him, "What has the LORD said?" [18]Then Balaam uttered his oracle, saying:

"Rise, Balak, and hear;
listen to me, O son of Zippor:
19 God is not a human being, that he should lie,
or a mortal, that he should change his mind.
Has he promised, and will he not do it?
Has he spoken, and will he not fulfill it?
20 See, I received a command to bless;
he has blessed, and I cannot revoke it.
21 He has not beheld misfortune in Jacob;
nor has he seen trouble in Israel.
The LORD their God is with them,
acclaimed as a king among them.
22 God, who brings them out of Egypt,
is like the horns of a wild ox for them.
23 Surely there is no enchantment against Jacob,
no divination against Israel;
now it shall be said of Jacob and Israel,
'See what God has done!'
24 Look, a people rising up like a lioness,
and rousing itself like a lion!
It does not lie down until it has eaten the prey
and drunk the blood of the slain."

25 Then Balak said to Balaam, "Do not curse them at all, and do not bless them at all." [26]But Balaam answered Balak, "Did I not tell you, 'Whatever the LORD says, that is what I must do'?"

27 So Balak said to Balaam, "Come now, I will take you to another place; perhaps it will please God that you may curse them for me from there." [28]So Balak took Balaam to the top of Peor, which overlooks the wasteland.[a] [29]Balaam said to Balak, "Build me seven altars here, and prepare seven bulls and seven rams for me." [30]So Balak did as Balaam had said, and offered a bull and a ram on each altar.

24:1-9 The oracle of Balaam: An "oracle" is a type of prophetic speech. Numbers 24 presents Balaam's prophetic technique in some detail. In each step he uses a different name for God, demonstrating his intimate familiarity with Israel's God: he hears the words of *El* ("God") and sees visions of *Shaddai* ("Almighty," 24:4). He obtains knowledge from *Elyon* ("the Most High," 24:16). Then he crouches down, but his vision is not impaired.

Balaam's Third Oracle

24 Now Balaam saw that it pleased the LORD to bless Israel, so he did not go, as at other times, to look for omens, but set his face toward the wilderness. [2]Balaam looked up and saw Israel camping tribe by tribe. Then the spirit of God came upon him, [3]and he uttered his oracle, saying:

[a] Or *overlooks Jeshimon*

"The oracle of Balaam son of Beor,
the oracle of the man whose eye is clear,[a]
4 the oracle of one who hears the words of God,
who sees the vision of the Almighty,[b]
who falls down, but with eyes uncovered:
5 how fair are your tents, O Jacob,
your encampments, O Israel!
6 Like palm groves that stretch far away,
like gardens beside a river,
like aloes that the LORD has planted,
like cedar trees beside the waters.
7 Water shall flow from his buckets,
and his seed shall have abundant water,
his king shall be higher than Agag,
and his kingdom shall be exalted.
8 God who brings him out of Egypt,
is like the horns of a wild ox for him;
he shall devour the nations that are his foes
and break their bones.
He shall strike with his arrows.[c]
9 He crouched, he lay down like a lion,
and like a lioness; who will rouse him up?
Blessed is everyone who blesses you,
and cursed is everyone who curses you."

10 Then Balak's anger was kindled against Balaam, and he struck
his hands together. Balak said to Balaam, "I summoned you to curse
my enemies, but instead you have blessed them these three times.
11 Now be off with you! Go home! I said, 'I will reward you richly,'
but the LORD has denied you any reward." 12 And Balaam said to Balak, "Did I not tell your messengers whom you sent to me, 13 'If Balak
should give me his house full of silver and gold, I would not be able
to go beyond the word of the LORD, to do either good or bad of my
own will; what the LORD says, that is what I will say'? 14 So now, I am
going to my people; let me advise you what this people will do to your
people in days to come."

Balaam's Fourth Oracle

15 So he uttered his oracle, saying:
"The oracle of Balaam son of Beor,
the oracle of the man whose eye is clear,[a]
16 the oracle of one who hears the words of God,
and knows the knowledge of the Most High,[d]

---

[a] Or *closed* or *open* [b] Traditional rendering of Heb *Shaddai* [c] Meaning of Heb uncertain
[d] Or *of Elyon*

who sees the vision of the Almighty,[a]
who falls down, but with his eyes uncovered:
17 I see him, but not now;
I behold him, but not near—
a star shall come out of Jacob,
and a scepter shall rise out of Israel;
it shall crush the borderlands[b] of Moab,
and the territory[c] of all the Shethites.
18 Edom will become a possession,
Seir a possession of its enemies,[d]
while Israel does valiantly.
19 One out of Jacob shall rule,
and destroy the survivors of Ir."

20 Then he looked on Amalek, and uttered his oracle, saying:

"First among the nations was Amalek,
but its end is to perish forever."

21 Then he looked on the Kenite, and uttered his oracle, saying:

"Enduring is your dwelling place,
and your nest is set in the rock;
22 yet Kain is destined for burning.
How long shall Asshur take you away captive?"

23 Again he uttered his oracle, saying:

"Alas, who shall live when God does this?
24 But ships shall come from Kittim
and shall afflict Asshur and Eber;
and he also shall perish forever."

25 Then Balaam got up and went back to his place, and Balak also went his way.

Worship of Baal of Peor

25:1-18 impale them: This is the beginning of one of the most violent and most disturbing stories in Numbers (it will continue in 31:1-20). In this story, intercultural intimate relationships with Moabite women lead to worship of other gods. In 25:4 God orders Moses to impale the leaders of the people in daylight as a sort of sacrificial offering, so that God will not destroy everyone. In 25:6, an Israelite man marries Cozbi, a local woman from a different place, Midian; he seems not to know about the death sentence. Just as he is introducing her to his family, Phineas, a priest and grandson of Aaron, stabs and kills both of them. God credits Phineas with saving the people.

What is a story like this doing in the Bible? It helps to remember that the stories in the beginning of the Bible were selected, written down,

25 While Israel was staying at Shittim, the people began to
have sexual relations with the women of Moab. 2 These invited the people to the sacrifices of their gods, and the people ate
and bowed down to their gods. 3 Thus Israel yoked itself to the Baal
of Peor, and the LORD's anger was kindled against Israel. 4 The LORD
said to Moses, "Take all the chiefs of the people, and impale them in
the sun before the LORD, in order that the fierce anger of the LORD
may turn away from Israel." 5 And Moses said to the judges of Israel,
"Each of you shall kill any of your people who have yoked themselves
to the Baal of Peor."

6 Just then one of the Israelites came and brought a Midianite
woman into his family, in the sight of Moses and in the sight of the

[a] Traditional rendering of Heb *Shaddai* [b] Or *forehead* [c] Some Mss read *skull* [d] Heb *Seir, its enemies, a possession*

whole congregation of the Israelites, while they were weeping at the
entrance of the tent of meeting. [7]When Phinehas son of Eleazar, son
of Aaron the priest, saw it, he got up and left the congregation. Taking
a spear in his hand, [8]he went after the Israelite man into the tent, and
pierced the two of them, the Israelite and the woman, through the
belly. So the plague was stopped among the people of Israel. [9]Never-
theless those that died by the plague were twenty-four thousand.
10 The LORD spoke to Moses, saying: [11]"Phinehas son of Eleazar,
son of Aaron the priest, has turned back my wrath from the Israelites
by manifesting such zeal among them on my behalf that in my jealousy I did not consume the Israelites. [12]Therefore say, 'I hereby grant
him my covenant of peace. [13]It shall be for him and for his descendants after him a covenant of perpetual priesthood, because he was
zealous for his God, and made atonement for the Israelites.' "
14 The name of the slain Israelite man, who was killed with the
Midianite woman, was Zimri son of Salu, head of an ancestral house
belonging to the Simeonites. [15]The name of the Midianite woman
who was killed was Cozbi daughter of Zur, who was the head of a
clan, an ancestral house in Midian.
16 The LORD said to Moses, [17]"Harass the Midianites, and defeat
them; [18]for they have harassed you by the trickery with which they deceived you in the affair of Peor, and in the affair of Cozbi, the daughter of a leader of Midian, their sister; she was killed on the day of the
plague that resulted from Peor."

A Census of the New Generation

26 After the plague the LORD said to Moses and to Eleazar son
of Aaron the priest, [2]"Take a census of the whole congregation of the Israelites, from twenty years old and upward, by their
ancestral houses, everyone in Israel able to go to war." [3]Moses and Eleazar the priest spoke with them in the plains of Moab by the Jordan
opposite Jericho, saying, [4]"Take a census of the people,[a] from twenty
years old and upward," as the LORD commanded Moses.
The Israelites, who came out of the land of Egypt, were:
5 Reuben, the firstborn of Israel. The descendants of Reuben:
of Hanoch, the clan of the Hanochites; of Pallu, the clan of the Pal-
luites; [6]of Hezron, the clan of the Hezronites; of Carmi, the clan of
the Carmites. [7]These are the clans of the Reubenites; the number of
those enrolled was forty-three thousand seven hundred thirty. [8]And
the descendants of Pallu: Eliab. [9]The descendants of Eliab: Nemuel,
Dathan, and Abiram. These are the same Dathan and Abiram, chosen
from the congregation, who rebelled against Moses and Aaron in the
company of Korah, when they rebelled against the LORD, [10]and the

[a] Heb lacks *take a census of the people*: Compare verse 2

and edited hundreds of years after the times they portray. At the time this story was shaped, the Israelites were wrestling with their invasion and defeat by foreigners who worshiped different gods. They looked for theological reasons to explain their defeat and deportation by the Babylonians and Assyrians and their occupation by the Persians. They concluded that all their troubles stemmed from their own worship of other gods and that it was all the fault of the foreign women who seduced them. Not surprisingly, a number of stories were shaped to make this point, and here even God is found to support this idea.

What are the dangers of blaming another country or ethnic group for the problems in your nation or community? What are the consequences for saying that God blames a nation or ethnic group for a particular disaster? What happens if you belong to a community that is blamed for all of the wrong done in another community?

earth opened its mouth and swallowed them up along with Korah,
when that company died, when the fire devoured two hundred fifty
men; and they became a warning. [11]Notwithstanding, the sons of Korah did not die.
12 The descendants of Simeon by their clans: of Nemuel, the clan
of the Nemuelites; of Jamin, the clan of the Jaminites; of Jachin, the
clan of the Jachinites; [13]of Zerah, the clan of the Zerahites; of Shaul,
the clan of the Shaulites.[a] [14]These are the clans of the Simeonites,
twenty-two thousand two hundred.
15 The children of Gad by their clans: of Zephon, the clan of the
Zephonites; of Haggi, the clan of the Haggites; of Shuni, the clan of
the Shunites; [16]of Ozni, the clan of the Oznites; of Eri, the clan of the
Erites; [17]of Arod, the clan of the Arodites; of Areli, the clan of the
Arelites. [18]These are the clans of the Gadites: the number of those enrolled was forty thousand five hundred.
19 The sons of Judah: Er and Onan; Er and Onan died in the land
of Canaan. [20]The descendants of Judah by their clans were: of Shelah, the clan of the Shelanites; of Perez, the clan of the Perezites; of
Zerah, the clan of the Zerahites. [21]The descendants of Perez were: of
Hezron, the clan of the Hezronites; of Hamul, the clan of the Hamul-
ites. [22]These are the clans of Judah: the number of those enrolled was
seventy-six thousand five hundred.
23 The descendants of Issachar by their clans: of Tola, the clan
of the Tolaites; of Puvah, the clan of the Punites; [24]of Jashub, the clan
of the Jashubites; of Shimron, the clan of the Shimronites. [25]These are
the clans of Issachar: sixty-four thousand three hundred enrolled.
26 The descendants of Zebulun by their clans: of Sered, the clan
of the Seredites; of Elon, the clan of the Elonites; of Jahleel, the clan of
the Jahleelites. [27]These are the clans of the Zebulunites; the number of
those enrolled was sixty thousand five hundred.
28 The sons of Joseph by their clans: Manasseh and Ephraim.
[29]The descendants of Manasseh: of Machir, the clan of the Machirites; and Machir was the father of Gilead; of Gilead, the clan of the
Gileadites. [30]These are the descendants of Gilead: of Iezer, the clan
of the Iezerites; of Helek, the clan of the Helekites; [31]and of Asriel,
the clan of the Asrielites; and of Shechem, the clan of the Shechem-
ites; [32]and of Shemida, the clan of the Shemidaites; and of Hepher,
the clan of the Hepherites. [33]Now Zelophehad son of Hepher had
no sons, but daughters: and the names of the daughters of Zelophehad were Mahlah, Noah, Hoglah, Milcah, and Tirzah. [34]These are the
clans of Manasseh; the number of those enrolled was fifty-two thousand seven hundred.
35 These are the descendants of Ephraim according to their clans:

---

[a] Or *Saul . . . Saulites*

of Shuthelah, the clan of the Shuthelahites; of Becher, the clan of the
Becherites; of Tahan, the clan of the Tahanites. [36]And these are the
descendants of Shuthelah: of Eran, the clan of the Eranites. [37]These
are the clans of the Ephraimites: the number of those enrolled was
thirty-two thousand five hundred. These are the descendants of Joseph by their clans.

38 The descendants of Benjamin by their clans: of Bela, the clan
of the Belaites; of Ashbel, the clan of the Ashbelites; of Ahiram, the
clan of the Ahiramites; [39]of Shephupham, the clan of the Shupham-
ites; of Hupham, the clan of the Huphamites. [40]And the sons of Bela
were Ard and Naaman: of Ard, the clan of the Ardites; of Naaman,
the clan of the Naamites. [41]These are the descendants of Benjamin by
their clans; the number of those enrolled was forty-five thousand six
hundred.

42 These are the descendants of Dan by their clans: of Shuham,
the clan of the Shuhamites. These are the clans of Dan by their clans.
[43]All the clans of the Shuhamites: sixty-four thousand four hundred
enrolled.

44 The descendants of Asher by their families: of Imnah, the clan
of the Imnites; of Ishvi, the clan of the Ishvites; of Beriah, the clan of
the Beriites. [45]Of the descendants of Beriah: of Heber, the clan of the
Heberites; of Malchiel, the clan of the Malchielites. [46]And the name of
the daughter of Asher was Serah. [47]These are the clans of the Asherites:
the number of those enrolled was fifty-three thousand four hundred.

48 The descendants of Naphtali by their clans: of Jahzeel, the clan
of the Jahzeelites; of Guni, the clan of the Gunites; [49]of Jezer, the clan
of the Jezerites; of Shillem, the clan of the Shillemites. [50]These are the
Naphtalites[a] by their clans: the number of those enrolled was forty-
five thousand four hundred.

51 This was the number of the Israelites enrolled: six hundred
and one thousand seven hundred thirty.

52 The LORD spoke to Moses, saying: [53]To these the land shall be
apportioned for inheritance according to the number of names. [54]To
a large tribe you shall give a large inheritance, and to a small tribe you
shall give a small inheritance; every tribe shall be given its inheritance
according to its enrollment. [55]But the land shall be apportioned by
lot; according to the names of their ancestral tribes they shall inherit.
[56]Their inheritance shall be apportioned according to lot between the
larger and the smaller.

57 This is the enrollment of the Levites by their clans: of Gershon, the clan of the Gershonites; of Kohath, the clan of the Kohathites; of Merari, the clan of the Merarites. [58]These are the clans of Levi:
the clan of the Libnites, the clan of the Hebronites, the clan of the

[a] Heb *clans of Naphtali*

Mahlites, the clan of the Mushites, the clan of the Korahites. Now Kohath was the father of Amram. [59]The name of Amram's wife was Jochebed daughter of Levi, who was born to Levi in Egypt; and she bore to Amram: Aaron, Moses, and their sister Miriam. [60]To Aaron were born Nadab, Abihu, Eleazar, and Ithamar. [61]But Nadab and Abihu died when they offered unholy fire before the LORD. [62]The number of those enrolled was twenty-three thousand, every male one month old and upward; for they were not enrolled among the Israelites because there was no allotment given to them among the Israelites.

63 These were those enrolled by Moses and Eleazar the priest, who enrolled the Israelites in the plains of Moab by the Jordan opposite Jericho. [64]Among these there was not one of those enrolled by Moses and Aaron the priest, who had enrolled the Israelites in the wilderness of Sinai. [65]For the LORD had said of them, "They shall die in the wilderness." Not one of them was left, except Caleb son of Jephunneh and Joshua son of Nun.

The Daughters of Zelophehad

27 Then the daughters of Zelophehad came forward. Zelophehad was son of Hepher son of Gilead son of Machir son of Manasseh son of Joseph, a member of the Manassite clans. The names of his daughters were: Mahlah, Noah, Hoglah, Milcah, and Tirzah. [2]They stood before Moses, Eleazar the priest, the leaders, and all the congregation, at the entrance of the tent of meeting, and they said, [3]"Our father died in the wilderness; he was not among the company of those who gathered themselves together against the LORD in the company of Korah, but died for his own sin; and he had no sons. [4]Why should the name of our father be taken away from his clan because he had no son? Give to us a possession among our father's brothers."

5 Moses brought their case before the LORD. [6]And the LORD spoke to Moses, saying: [7]The daughters of Zelophehad are right in what they are saying; you shall indeed let them possess an inheritance among their father's brothers and pass the inheritance of their father on to them. [8]You shall also say to the Israelites, "If a man dies, and has no son, then you shall pass his inheritance on to his daughter. [9]If he has no daughter, then you shall give his inheritance to his brothers. [10]If he has no brothers, then you shall give his inheritance to his father's brothers. [11]And if his father has no brothers, then you shall give his inheritance to the nearest kinsman of his clan, and he shall possess it. It shall be for the Israelites a statute and ordinance, as the LORD commanded Moses."

27:1-11 the daughters of Zelophehad: Numbers contains one of the most powerful stories about women's rights in the Bible. Their story is so important that they are mentioned in five different places: Numbers 26:33; 27:1-11; 36:1-12; Joshua 17:3-6; and 1 Chronicles 7:15. Numbers 26:28-33 gives a genealogy of the descendants of the African woman Asenath and Joseph. They became the parents of the two half-Egyptian, half-tribes of Israel, Ephraim and Manasseh. One of their tenth-generation sons, Zelophehad, fathered five daughters: Mahlah, Noah, Hoglah, Milcah, and Tirzah. They did not receive an inheritance in the promised land because Moses was only handing out land to men. Their father was dead, and they were not married. The daughters waited until everyone was at the worship center. The five women stand in the door of the sanctuary (27:2) and tell Moses to "Give to us a possession [land]" (27:4). God agrees, saying, "The daughters of Zelophehad are right; . . . you shall indeed let them possess an inheritance" (27:7). God changed the inheritance laws in the Torah for the daughters of Zelophehad, but nothing had changed. Moses did not give them an inheritance in the promised land. Their story continues in chapter 36.

Joshua Appointed Moses' Successor

12 The LORD said to Moses, "Go up this mountain of the Abarim range, and see the land that I have given to the Israelites. [13]When you

have seen it, you also shall be gathered to your people, as your brother Aaron was, 14 because you rebelled against my word in the wilderness of Zin when the congregation quarreled with me.[a] You did not show my holiness before their eyes at the waters." (These are the waters of Meribath-kadesh in the wilderness of Zin.) 15 Moses spoke to the LORD, saying, 16 "Let the LORD, the God of the spirits of all flesh, appoint someone over the congregation 17 who shall go out before them and come in before them, who shall lead them out and bring them in, so that the congregation of the LORD may not be like sheep without a shepherd." 18 So the LORD said to Moses, "Take Joshua son of Nun, a man in whom is the spirit, and lay your hand upon him; 19 have him stand before Eleazar the priest and all the congregation, and commission him in their sight. 20 You shall give him some of your authority, so that all the congregation of the Israelites may obey. 21 But he shall stand before Eleazar the priest, who shall inquire for him by the decision of the Urim before the LORD; at his word they shall go out, and at his word they shall come in, both he and all the Israelites with him, the whole congregation." 22 So Moses did as the LORD commanded him. He took Joshua and had him stand before Eleazar the priest and the whole congregation; 23 he laid his hands on him and commissioned him—as the LORD had directed through Moses.

Daily Offerings

28 The LORD spoke to Moses, saying: 2 Command the Israelites, and say to them: My offering, the food for my offerings by fire, my pleasing odor, you shall take care to offer to me at its appointed time. 3 And you shall say to them, This is the offering by fire that you shall offer to the LORD: two male lambs a year old without blemish, daily, as a regular offering. 4 One lamb you shall offer in the morning, and the other lamb you shall offer at twilight;[b] 5 also one-tenth of an ephah of choice flour for a grain offering, mixed with one-fourth of a hin of beaten oil. 6 It is a regular burnt offering, ordained at Mount Sinai for a pleasing odor, an offering by fire to the LORD. 7 Its drink offering shall be one-fourth of a hin for each lamb; in the sanctuary you shall pour out a drink offering of strong drink to the LORD. 8 The other lamb you shall offer at twilight[b] with a grain offering and a drink offering like the one in the morning; you shall offer it as an offering by fire, a pleasing odor to the LORD.

Sabbath Offerings

9 On the sabbath day: two male lambs a year old without blemish, and two-tenths of an ephah of choice flour for a grain offering, mixed with oil, and its drink offering— 10 this is the burnt offering for

[a] Heb lacks *with me* [b] Heb *between the two evenings*

27:14 did not show my holiness... at the waters: See Numbers 20:2-13 and note.

27:19-21 commission him... inquire... of the Urim: The high priest probably poured oil over Joshua's head as a sign that he would take over leadership of the Israelite people. What the Urim was is not certain, but it may have been a small carved stone worn in a pouch over the high priest's chest and under his breastplate (see Exod 28:29-30). The Urim and Thummim were apparently consulted to receive a message concerning God's will (see also Lev 8:7-8; Deut 33:8).

28:1-8 my offerings: See Leviticus 1–7 and the note at Num 4:13 (take away the ashes).

28:9-10 sabbath... offering: Observing the Sabbath was one of the Ten Commandments (see Exod 20:8-11; Deut 5:12-15).

every sabbath, in addition to the regular burnt offering and its drink
offering.

Monthly Offerings

11 At the beginnings of your months you shall offer a burnt offering to the LORD: two young bulls, one ram, seven male lambs a year
old without blemish; [12]also three-tenths of an ephah of choice flour
for a grain offering, mixed with oil, for each bull; and two-tenths
of choice flour for a grain offering, mixed with oil, for the one ram;
[13]and one-tenth of choice flour mixed with oil as a grain offering for
every lamb—a burnt offering of pleasing odor, an offering by fire to
the LORD. [14]Their drink offerings shall be half a hin of wine for a bull,
one-third of a hin for a ram, and one-fourth of a hin for a lamb. This is
the burnt offering of every month throughout the months of the year.
[15]And there shall be one male goat for a sin offering to the LORD; it
shall be offered in addition to the regular burnt offering and its drink
offering.

Offerings at Passover

16 On the fourteenth day of the first month there shall be a passover offering to the LORD. [17]And on the fifteenth day of this month is
a festival; seven days shall unleavened bread be eaten. [18]On the first
day there shall be a holy convocation. You shall not work at your occupations. [19]You shall offer an offering by fire, a burnt offering to the
LORD: two young bulls, one ram, and seven male lambs a year old; see
that they are without blemish. [20]Their grain offering shall be of choice
flour mixed with oil: three-tenths of an ephah shall you offer for a
bull, and two-tenths for a ram; [21]one-tenth shall you offer for each of
the seven lambs; [22]also one male goat for a sin offering, to make atonement for you. [23]You shall offer these in addition to the burnt offering
of the morning, which belongs to the regular burnt offering. [24]In the
same way you shall offer daily, for seven days, the food of an offering
by fire, a pleasing odor to the LORD; it shall be offered in addition to
the regular burnt offering and its drink offering. [25]And on the seventh
day you shall have a holy convocation; you shall not work at your occupations.

Offerings at the Festival of Weeks

26 On the day of the first fruits, when you offer a grain offering
of new grain to the LORD at your festival of weeks, you shall have a
holy convocation; you shall not work at your occupations. [27]You shall
offer a burnt offering, a pleasing odor to the LORD: two young bulls,
one ram, seven male lambs a year old. [28]Their grain offering shall
be of choice flour mixed with oil, three-tenths of an ephah for each
bull, two-tenths for one ram, [29]one-tenth for each of the seven lambs;

How and why do Lutherans continue to "observe the Sabbath"? In his explanation to the Third Commandment in the Small Catechism, Luther says: "We are to fear and love God, so that we do not despise preaching or God's word, but instead keep that word holy and gladly hear and learn it." Luther's focus was on the importance of setting aside time to gather to hear God's word preached. We also hear God's word of promise when we receive the Lord's Supper. Lutherans today generally follow a form of worship whose parts are drawn directly from the Bible. *Numbers 28:9-10*

28:16-25 passover offering...unleavened bread: The Festival of Passover was celebrated during the first spring month of the Jewish year. The Jewish calendar is a moon-based or lunar calendar. Two different calendars are represented in the Hebrew Bible. In this chapter, the new year begins in the spring, following the Babylonian practice. The Passover festival recalled the passover that preceded the Hebrew people's exodus from Egypt. Passover was to be followed immediately by the festival of unleavened bread. See Exodus 12:43—13:10.

28:26-31 festival of weeks: Celebrating the harvest of first fruits, this festival is celebrated fifty days after the festival of unleavened bread. It is also known as Pentecost.

30 with one male goat, to make atonement for you. 31 In addition to the
regular burnt offering with its grain offering, you shall offer them and
their drink offering. They shall be without blemish.

Offerings at the Festival of Trumpets

29 On the first day of the seventh month you shall have a holy
convocation; you shall not work at your occupations. It
is a day for you to blow the trumpets, 2 and you shall offer a burnt
offering, a pleasing odor to the LORD: one young bull, one ram, seven
male lambs a year old without blemish. 3 Their grain offering shall be
of choice flour mixed with oil, three-tenths of one ephah for the bull,
two-tenths for the ram, 4 and one-tenth for each of the seven lambs;
5 with one male goat for a sin offering, to make atonement for you.
6 These are in addition to the burnt offering of the new moon and
its grain offering, and the regular burnt offering and its grain offering, and their drink offerings, according to the ordinance for them, a
pleasing odor, an offering by fire to the LORD.

Offerings on the Day of Atonement

7 On the tenth day of this seventh month you shall have a holy
convocation, and deny yourselves;[a] you shall do no work. 8 You shall
offer a burnt offering to the LORD, a pleasing odor: one young bull,
one ram, seven male lambs a year old. They shall be without blemish. 9 Their grain offering shall be of choice flour mixed with oil, three-
tenths of an ephah for the bull, two-tenths for the one ram, 10 one-tenth
for each of the seven lambs; 11 with one male goat for a sin offering, in
addition to the sin offering of atonement, and the regular burnt offering and its grain offering, and their drink offerings.

Offerings at the Festival of Booths

12 On the fifteenth day of the seventh month you shall have a
holy convocation; you shall not work at your occupations. You shall
celebrate a festival to the LORD seven days. 13 You shall offer a burnt
offering, an offering by fire, a pleasing odor to the LORD: thirteen
young bulls, two rams, fourteen male lambs a year old. They shall be
without blemish. 14 Their grain offering shall be of choice flour mixed
with oil, three-tenths of an ephah for each of the thirteen bulls, two-
tenths for each of the two rams, 15 and one-tenth for each of the fourteen lambs; 16 also one male goat for a sin offering, in addition to the
regular burnt offering, its grain offering and its drink offering.

17 On the second day: twelve young bulls, two rams, fourteen
male lambs a year old without blemish, 18 with the grain offering and
the drink offerings for the bulls, for the rams, and for the lambs, as

[a] Or *and fast*

When do Lutherans and other Christians celebrate Pentecost? Christians celebrate Pentecost on the seventh Sunday after Easter because the Holy Spirit came to Jesus' disciples during the Jewish celebration of Festival of Weeks, or fifty days after the Passover that had immediately preceded Jesus' crucifixion and resurrection. Most Western Christians use a sun-based or solar calendar to calculate the dates of Easter and Pentecost. This can result in Christians and Jews observing Pentecost at different times. *Numbers 28:26-31*

29:1 blow the trumpets: The festival occurring on the first day of the seventh month celebrated the new year and is known as Rosh Hashanah, or "head of the year." Here the new year begins in the fall on the Hebrew calendar; this "second" new year (see note on 28:16-25) eventually became dominant.

29:11 offering of atonement: The festival Day of Atonement falls in September or early October. See Leviticus 16 and notes.

29:12-38 celebrate a festival...seven days: These verses describe the seven-day Festival of Booths, or Sukkot. One part of the festival called for the people to make booths or shelters out of tree branches and leaves. They were to live in the shelters to recall how they lived in such shelters in the wilderness after leaving Egypt.

prescribed in accordance with their number; [19]also one male goat for a sin offering, in addition to the regular burnt offering and its grain offering, and their drink offerings.

20 On the third day: eleven bulls, two rams, fourteen male lambs a year old without blemish, [21]with the grain offering and the drink offerings for the bulls, for the rams, and for the lambs, as prescribed in accordance with their number; [22]also one male goat for a sin offering, in addition to the regular burnt offering and its grain offering and its drink offering.

23 On the fourth day: ten bulls, two rams, fourteen male lambs a year old without blemish, [24]with the grain offering and the drink offerings for the bulls, for the rams, and for the lambs, as prescribed in accordance with their number; [25]also one male goat for a sin offering, in addition to the regular burnt offering, its grain offering and its drink offering.

26 On the fifth day: nine bulls, two rams, fourteen male lambs a year old without blemish, [27]with the grain offering and the drink offerings for the bulls, for the rams, and for the lambs, as prescribed in accordance with their number; [28]also one male goat for a sin offering, in addition to the regular burnt offering and its grain offering and its drink offering.

29 On the sixth day: eight bulls, two rams, fourteen male lambs a year old without blemish, [30]with the grain offering and the drink offerings for the bulls, for the rams, and for the lambs, as prescribed in accordance with their number; [31]also one male goat for a sin offering, in addition to the regular burnt offering, its grain offering, and its drink offerings.

32 On the seventh day: seven bulls, two rams, fourteen male lambs a year old without blemish, [33]with the grain offering and the drink offerings for the bulls, for the rams, and for the lambs, as prescribed in accordance with their number; [34]also one male goat for a sin offering, besides the regular burnt offering, its grain offering, and its drink offering.

35 On the eighth day you shall have a solemn assembly; you shall not work at your occupations. [36]You shall offer a burnt offering, an offering by fire, a pleasing odor to the LORD: one bull, one ram, seven male lambs a year old without blemish, [37]and the grain offering and the drink offerings for the bull, for the ram, and for the lambs, as prescribed in accordance with their number; [38]also one male goat for a sin offering, in addition to the regular burnt offering and its grain offering and its drink offering.

39 These you shall offer to the LORD at your appointed festivals, in addition to your votive offerings and your freewill offerings, as your burnt offerings, your grain offerings, your drink offerings, and your offerings of well-being.

40[a] So Moses told the Israelites everything just as the LORD had
commanded Moses.

Vows Made by Women

30 Then Moses said to the heads of the tribes of the Israelites: This is what the LORD has commanded. 2 When a
man makes a vow to the LORD, or swears an oath to bind himself by
a pledge, he shall not break his word; he shall do according to all that
proceeds out of his mouth.
3 When a woman makes a vow to the LORD, or binds herself by
a pledge, while within her father's house, in her youth, 4 and her father
hears of her vow or her pledge by which she has bound herself, and
says nothing to her; then all her vows shall stand, and any pledge by
which she has bound herself shall stand. 5 But if her father expresses
disapproval to her at the time that he hears of it, no vow of hers, and no
pledge by which she has bound herself, shall stand; and the LORD will
forgive her, because her father had expressed to her his disapproval.
6 If she marries, while obligated by her vows or any thoughtless
utterance of her lips by which she has bound herself, 7 and her husband hears of it and says nothing to her at the time that he hears, then
her vows shall stand, and her pledges by which she has bound herself shall stand. 8 But if, at the time that her husband hears of it, he
expresses disapproval to her, then he shall nullify the vow by which
she was obligated, or the thoughtless utterance of her lips, by which
she bound herself; and the LORD will forgive her. 9 (But every vow of
a widow or of a divorced woman, by which she has bound herself,
shall be binding upon her.) 10 And if she made a vow in her husband's
house, or bound herself by a pledge with an oath, 11 and her husband
heard it and said nothing to her, and did not express disapproval to
her, then all her vows shall stand, and any pledge by which she bound
herself shall stand. 12 But if her husband nullifies them at the time that
he hears them, then whatever proceeds out of her lips concerning her
vows, or concerning her pledge of herself, shall not stand. Her husband has nullified them, and the LORD will forgive her. 13 Any vow or
any binding oath to deny herself,[b] her husband may allow to stand,
or her husband may nullify. 14 But if her husband says nothing to her
from day to day,[c] then he validates all her vows, or all her pledges, by
which she is obligated; he has validated them, because he said nothing to her at the time that he heard of them. 15 But if he nullifies them
some time after he has heard of them, then he shall bear her guilt.
16 These are the statutes that the LORD commanded Moses concerning a husband and his wife, and a father and his daughter while
she is still young and in her father's house.

[a] Ch 30.1 in Heb [b] Or *to fast* [c] Or *from that day to the next*

30:3 when a woman makes a vow: Unlike the earlier account of Nazirite vows in chapter 6, now married women's vows can be cancelled by their fathers or husbands. Biblical scholars call this kind of change in the biblical text *secondary*, meaning that it represents a change in an earlier story.

Why do you think the story changed? Who benefits from the change? If a biblical practice changes once, can it change again? Why or why not?

War against Midian

31 The LORD spoke to Moses, saying, 2“Avenge the Israelites on
the Midianites; afterward you shall be gathered to your people.” 3So Moses said to the people, “Arm some of your number for the
war, so that they may go against Midian, to execute the LORD’s vengeance on Midian. 4You shall send a thousand from each of the tribes
of Israel to the war.” 5So out of the thousands of Israel, a thousand
from each tribe were conscripted, twelve thousand armed for battle.
6Moses sent them to the war, a thousand from each tribe, along with
Phinehas son of Eleazar the priest,[a] with the vessels of the sanctuary
and the trumpets for sounding the alarm in his hand. 7They did battle
against Midian, as the LORD had commanded Moses, and killed every
male. 8They killed the kings of Midian: Evi, Rekem, Zur, Hur, and
Reba, the five kings of Midian, in addition to others who were slain by
them; and they also killed Balaam son of Beor with the sword. 9The
Israelites took the women of Midian and their little ones captive; and
they took all their cattle, their flocks, and all their goods as booty. 10All
their towns where they had settled, and all their encampments, they
burned, 11but they took all the spoil and all the booty, both people
and animals. 12Then they brought the captives and the booty and the
spoil to Moses, to Eleazar the priest, and to the congregation of the
Israelites, at the camp on the plains of Moab by the Jordan at Jericho.

Return from the War

13 Moses, Eleazar the priest, and all the leaders of the congregation went to meet them outside the camp. 14Moses became angry with
the officers of the army, the commanders of thousands and the commanders of hundreds, who had come from service in the war. 15Moses
said to them, “Have you allowed all the women to live? 16These women
here, on Balaam’s advice, made the Israelites act treacherously against
the LORD in the affair of Peor, so that the plague came among the
congregation of the LORD. 17Now therefore, kill every male among
the little ones, and kill every woman who has known a man by sleeping with him. 18But all the young girls who have not known a man by
sleeping with him, keep alive for yourselves. 19Camp outside the camp
seven days; whoever of you has killed any person or touched a corpse,
purify yourselves and your captives on the third and on the seventh
day. 20You shall purify every garment, every article of skin, everything
made of goats’ hair, and every article of wood.”

21 Eleazar the priest said to the troops who had gone to battle:
“This is the statute of the law that the LORD has commanded Moses:
22gold, silver, bronze, iron, tin, and lead— 23everything that can withstand fire, shall be passed through fire, and it shall be clean. Never-

[a] Gk: Heb adds *to the war*

31:1-20 Avenge the Israelites: This story is supposed to be read as the second part of the violent narrative in chapter 25. They are not easily connected. For what are the Israelites seeking vengeance? The Israelites killed their own leaders who had freely entered into unions that were ultimately condemned. The Israelites killed the Midianite woman, Cozbi, simply for marrying into their community. In verse 8, the foreign prophet Balaam is blamed and killed, but he is not a Midianite. Yet now the Israelites slaughter the Midianite men, taking the women and girls captive. These captives are forced into marriages called *rape-marriages* by some scholars, because the women and girls have no choice (in other biblical marriages, women can choose whom to marry; see Gen 24:58). These unions are marriages because they are legitimate conjugal unions that produce children who are recognized as legitimate members of the Israelite community. Certain statutes were developed to offer limited protections to the abducted women and their children (Deut 21:14). The text presents these rape-marriages as Moses’ own notion, apart from God’s instruction. According to the text, the Israelites captured thirty-two thousand young girls. In Deuteronomy 20 and 21 the practice becomes standardized. There is an infamous story in Judges 21:10-23 in which Israelite men abduct Israelite women for rape-marriages (see also 2 Chr 28:8-15). And Ruth and her sister-in-law Orpah were similarly abducted; the Hebrew verb that describes their marriages literally means to *carry off.*

The story in 31:1-20 begs the question, if the *fault* was intercultural marriages, then why is the solution *forced* intercultural marriages? This practice endured and endures in today’s world because it is effective. It demoralizes the conquered, and when the children of these unions are counted as children of the victors, the forced impregnation simultaneously builds up the community of the victor while eradicating the community of the conquered. Forced impregnation is a tool of genocide. The modern world has seen it in Bosnia, Rwanda, and Darfur.

In what ways might people of faith respond to unjust situations in our communities, nation, or world?

theless it shall also be purified with the water for purification; and whatever cannot withstand fire, shall be passed through the water. 24You must wash your clothes on the seventh day, and you shall be clean; afterward you may come into the camp."

Disposition of Captives and Booty

25 The Lord spoke to Moses, saying, 26"You and Eleazar the priest and the heads of the ancestral houses of the congregation make an inventory of the booty captured, both human and animal. 27Divide the booty into two parts, between the warriors who went out to battle and all the congregation. 28From the share of the warriors who went out to battle, set aside as tribute for the Lord, one item out of every five hundred, whether persons, oxen, donkeys, sheep, or goats. 29Take it from their half and give it to Eleazar the priest as an offering to the Lord. 30But from the Israelites' half you shall take one out of every fifty, whether persons, oxen, donkeys, sheep, or goats—all the animals—and give them to the Levites who have charge of the tabernacle of the Lord."

31 Then Moses and Eleazar the priest did as the Lord had commanded Moses:

32 The booty remaining from the spoil that the troops had taken totaled six hundred seventy-five thousand sheep, 33seventy-two thousand oxen, 34sixty-one thousand donkeys, 35and thirty-two thousand persons in all, women who had not known a man by sleeping with him.

36 The half-share, the portion of those who had gone out to war, was in number three hundred thirty-seven thousand five hundred sheep and goats, 37and the Lord's tribute of sheep and goats was six hundred seventy-five. 38The oxen were thirty-six thousand, of which the Lord's tribute was seventy-two. 39The donkeys were thirty thousand five hundred, of which the Lord's tribute was sixty-one. 40The persons were sixteen thousand, of which the Lord's tribute was thirty-two persons. 41Moses gave the tribute, the offering for the Lord, to Eleazar the priest, as the Lord had commanded Moses.

42 As for the Israelites' half, which Moses separated from that of the troops, 43the congregation's half was three hundred thirty-seven thousand five hundred sheep and goats, 44thirty-six thousand oxen, 45thirty thousand five hundred donkeys, 46and sixteen thousand persons. 47From the Israelites' half Moses took one of every fifty, both of persons and of animals, and gave them to the Levites who had charge of the tabernacle of the Lord; as the Lord had commanded Moses.

48 Then the officers who were over the thousands of the army, the commanders of thousands and the commanders of hundreds, approached Moses, 49and said to Moses, "Your servants have counted the warriors who are under our command, and not one of us is missing.

[50]And we have brought the LORD's offering, what each of us found,
articles of gold, armlets and bracelets, signet rings, earrings, and pendants, to make atonement for ourselves before the LORD." [51]Moses
and Eleazar the priest received the gold from them, all in the form of
crafted articles. [52]And all the gold of the offering that they offered to
the LORD, from the commanders of thousands and the commanders
of hundreds, was sixteen thousand seven hundred fifty shekels. [53](The
troops had all taken plunder for themselves.) [54]So Moses and Eleazar
the priest received the gold from the commanders of thousands and
of hundreds, and brought it into the tent of meeting as a memorial for
the Israelites before the LORD.

Conquest and Division of Transjordan

32:1-32 do not make us cross the Jordan: Two of the twelve tribes, Reuben and Gad, decide that they do not want to go all the way to the promised land. They like the land they see around them. They see no need to cross the Jordan. They decide to stay put. This decision is given as the reason the Israelites are condemned to wander for forty years in the wilderness. This contradicts Numbers 14:32-36, in which the Israelites are condemned to wander for grumbling about land while the spies were exploring it. In 14:34, they are told that the forty-year sentence represents one year for each day of the spies' trip. In response to Moses' concern in verse 15 that the Israelites will be destroyed, the two tribes promise that they will help their relatives conquer the land, but their children will be safe on this side of the Jordan. Ironically, Moses is depending on their numbers—not just God's power—to keep the people safe in Canaan. The tribes of Reuben and Gad trust neither their numbers nor God's power to keep their families safe; they will keep out of harm's way by not allowing their women and children to cross the Jordan.

32 Now the Reubenites and the Gadites owned a very great
number of cattle. When they saw that the land of Jazer and
the land of Gilead was a good place for cattle, [2]the Gadites and the
Reubenites came and spoke to Moses, to Eleazar the priest, and to
the leaders of the congregation, saying, [3]"Ataroth, Dibon, Jazer, Nim-
rah, Heshbon, Elealeh, Sebam, Nebo, and Beon— [4]the land that the
LORD subdued before the congregation of Israel—is a land for cattle;
and your servants have cattle." [5]They continued, "If we have found
favor in your sight, let this land be given to your servants for a possession; do not make us cross the Jordan."

6 But Moses said to the Gadites and to the Reubenites, "Shall
your brothers go to war while you sit here? [7]Why will you discour-
age the hearts of the Israelites from going over into the land that the
LORD has given them? [8]Your fathers did this, when I sent them from
Kadesh-barnea to see the land. [9]When they went up to the Wadi
Eshcol and saw the land, they discouraged the hearts of the Israelites
from going into the land that the LORD had given them. [10]The LORD's
anger was kindled on that day and he swore, saying, [11]'Surely none of
the people who came up out of Egypt, from twenty years old and upward, shall see the land that I swore to give to Abraham, to Isaac, and
to Jacob, because they have not unreservedly followed me— [12]none
except Caleb son of Jephunneh the Kenizzite and Joshua son of Nun,
for they have unreservedly followed the LORD.' [13]And the LORD's anger was kindled against Israel, and he made them wander in the wilderness for forty years, until all the generation that had done evil in
the sight of the LORD had disappeared. [14]And now you, a brood of
sinners, have risen in place of your fathers, to increase the LORD's
fierce anger against Israel! [15]If you turn away from following him, he
will again abandon them in the wilderness; and you will destroy all
this people."

16 Then they came up to him and said, "We will build sheepfolds
here for our flocks, and towns for our little ones, [17]but we will take

up arms as a vanguard[a] before the Israelites, until we have brought
them to their place. Meanwhile our little ones will stay in the fortified
towns because of the inhabitants of the land. [18]We will not return to
our homes until all the Israelites have obtained their inheritance. [19]We
will not inherit with them on the other side of the Jordan and beyond,
because our inheritance has come to us on this side of the Jordan to
the east."

20 So Moses said to them, "If you do this—if you take up arms to
go before the LORD for the war, [21]and all those of you who bear arms
cross the Jordan before the LORD, until he has driven out his enemies
from before him [22]and the land is subdued before the LORD—then
after that you may return and be free of obligation to the LORD and to
Israel, and this land shall be your possession before the LORD. [23]But
if you do not do this, you have sinned against the LORD; and be sure
your sin will find you out. [24]Build towns for your little ones, and folds
for your flocks; but do what you have promised."

25 Then the Gadites and the Reubenites said to Moses, "Your
servants will do as my lord commands. [26]Our little ones, our wives,
our flocks, and all our livestock shall remain there in the towns of Gilead; [27]but your servants will cross over, everyone armed for war, to do
battle for the LORD, just as my lord orders."

28 So Moses gave command concerning them to Eleazar the
priest, to Joshua son of Nun, and to the heads of the ancestral houses
of the Israelite tribes. [29]And Moses said to them, "If the Gadites and
the Reubenites, everyone armed for battle before the LORD, will cross
over the Jordan with you and the land shall be subdued before you,
then you shall give them the land of Gilead for a possession; [30]but if
they will not cross over with you armed, they shall have possessions
among you in the land of Canaan." [31]The Gadites and the Reubenites
answered, "As the LORD has spoken to your servants, so we will do.
[32]We will cross over armed before the LORD into the land of Canaan,
but the possession of our inheritance shall remain with us on this side
of[b] the Jordan."

33 Moses gave to them—to the Gadites and to the Reubenites
and to the half-tribe of Manasseh son of Joseph—the kingdom of
King Sihon of the Amorites and the kingdom of King Og of Bashan,
the land and its towns, with the territories of the surrounding towns.
[34]And the Gadites rebuilt Dibon, Ataroth, Aroer, [35]Atroth-shophan,
Jazer, Jogbehah, [36]Beth-nimrah, and Beth-haran, fortified cities, and
folds for sheep. [37]And the Reubenites rebuilt Heshbon, Elealeh, Kiriathaim, [38]Nebo, and Baal-meon (some names being changed), and
Sibmah; and they gave names to the towns that they rebuilt. [39]The descendants of Machir son of Manasseh went to Gilead, captured it, and

---

[a] Cn: Heb *hurrying* [b] Heb *beyond*

dispossessed the Amorites who were there; 40 so Moses gave Gilead to Machir son of Manasseh, and he settled there. 41 Jair son of Manasseh went and captured their villages, and renamed them Havvoth-jair.[a] 42 And Nobah went and captured Kenath and its villages, and renamed it Nobah after himself.

The Stages of Israel's Journey from Egypt

33 These are the stages by which the Israelites went out of the land of Egypt in military formation under the leadership of Moses and Aaron. 2 Moses wrote down their starting points, stage by stage, by command of the LORD; and these are their stages according to their starting places. 3 They set out from Rameses in the first month, on the fifteenth day of the first month; on the day after the passover the Israelites went out boldly in the sight of all the Egyptians, 4 while the Egyptians were burying all their firstborn, whom the LORD had struck down among them. The LORD executed judgments even against their gods.

5 So the Israelites set out from Rameses, and camped at Succoth. 6 They set out from Succoth, and camped at Etham, which is on the edge of the wilderness. 7 They set out from Etham, and turned back to Pi-hahiroth, which faces Baal-zephon; and they camped before Migdol. 8 They set out from Pi-hahiroth, passed through the sea into the wilderness, went a three days' journey in the wilderness of Etham, and camped at Marah. 9 They set out from Marah and came to Elim; at Elim there were twelve springs of water and seventy palm trees, and they camped there. 10 They set out from Elim and camped by the Red Sea.[b] 11 They set out from the Red Sea[b] and camped in the wilderness of Sin. 12 They set out from the wilderness of Sin and camped at Dophkah. 13 They set out from Dophkah and camped at Alush. 14 They set out from Alush and camped at Rephidim, where there was no water for the people to drink. 15 They set out from Rephidim and camped in the wilderness of Sinai. 16 They set out from the wilderness of Sinai and camped at Kibroth-hattaavah. 17 They set out from Kibroth-hattaavah and camped at Hazeroth. 18 They set out from Hazeroth and camped at Rithmah. 19 They set out from Rithmah and camped at Rimmon-perez. 20 They set out from Rimmon-perez and camped at Libnah. 21 They set out from Libnah and camped at Rissah. 22 They set out from Rissah and camped at Kehelathah. 23 They set out from Kehelathah and camped at Mount Shepher. 24 They set out from Mount Shepher and camped at Haradah. 25 They set out from Haradah and camped at Makheloth. 26 They set out from Makheloth and camped at Tahath. 27 They set out from Tahath and camped at Terah. 28 They set out from Terah and camped at Mithkah. 29 They set

---

[a] That is *the villages of Jair* [b] Or *Sea of Reeds*

out from Mithkah and camped at Hashmonah. [30]They set out from
Hashmonah and camped at Moseroth. [31]They set out from Moseroth and camped at Bene-jaakan. [32]They set out from Bene-jaakan
and camped at Hor-haggidgad. [33]They set out from Hor-haggidgad
and camped at Jotbathah. [34]They set out from Jotbathah and camped
at Abronah. [35]They set out from Abronah and camped at Ezion-
geber. [36]They set out from Ezion-geber and camped in the wilderness
of Zin (that is, Kadesh). [37]They set out from Kadesh and camped at
Mount Hor, on the edge of the land of Edom.

38 Aaron the priest went up Mount Hor at the command of the
LORD and died there in the fortieth year after the Israelites had come
out of the land of Egypt, on the first day of the fifth month. [39]Aaron was
one hundred twenty-three years old when he died on Mount Hor.

40 The Canaanite, the king of Arad, who lived in the Negeb in the
land of Canaan, heard of the coming of the Israelites.

41 They set out from Mount Hor and camped at Zalmonah.
[42]They set out from Zalmonah and camped at Punon. [43]They set out
from Punon and camped at Oboth. [44]They set out from Oboth and
camped at Iye-abarim, in the territory of Moab. [45]They set out from
Iyim and camped at Dibon-gad. [46]They set out from Dibon-gad and
camped at Almon-diblathaim. [47]They set out from Almon-diblathaim
and camped in the mountains of Abarim, before Nebo. [48]They set out
from the mountains of Abarim and camped in the plains of Moab by
the Jordan at Jericho; [49]they camped by the Jordan from Beth-jeshimoth as far as Abel-shittim in the plains of Moab.

Directions for the Conquest of Canaan

50 In the plains of Moab by the Jordan at Jericho, the LORD spoke
to Moses, saying: [51]Speak to the Israelites, and say to them: When you
cross over the Jordan into the land of Canaan, [52]you shall drive out
all the inhabitants of the land from before you, destroy all their figured stones, destroy all their cast images, and demolish all their high
places. [53]You shall take possession of the land and settle in it, for I have
given you the land to possess. [54]You shall apportion the land by lot according to your clans; to a large one you shall give a large inheritance,
and to a small one you shall give a small inheritance; the inheritance
shall belong to the person on whom the lot falls; according to your
ancestral tribes you shall inherit. [55]But if you do not drive out the inhabitants of the land from before you, then those whom you let remain shall be as barbs in your eyes and thorns in your sides; they shall
trouble you in the land where you are settling. [56]And I will do to you
as I thought to do to them.

The Boundaries of the Land

34 The LORD spoke to Moses, saying: [2]Command the Israelites, and say to them: When you enter the land of Canaan

(this is the land that shall fall to you for an inheritance, the land of
Canaan, defined by its boundaries), 3 your south sector shall extend
from the wilderness of Zin along the side of Edom. Your southern
boundary shall begin from the end of the Dead Sea[a] on the east; 4 your
boundary shall turn south of the ascent of Akrabbim, and cross to Zin,
and its outer limit shall be south of Kadesh-barnea; then it shall go on
to Hazar-addar, and cross to Azmon; 5 the boundary shall turn from
Azmon to the Wadi of Egypt, and its termination shall be at the Sea.

6 For the western boundary, you shall have the Great Sea and its[b]
coast; this shall be your western boundary.

7 This shall be your northern boundary: from the Great Sea you
shall mark out your line to Mount Hor; 8 from Mount Hor you shall
mark it out to Lebo-hamath, and the outer limit of the boundary shall
be at Zedad; 9 then the boundary shall extend to Ziphron, and its end
shall be at Hazar-enan; this shall be your northern boundary.

10 You shall mark out your eastern boundary from Hazar-enan to
Shepham; 11 and the boundary shall continue down from Shepham to
Riblah on the east side of Ain; and the boundary shall go down, and
reach the eastern slope of the sea of Chinnereth; 12 and the boundary
shall go down to the Jordan, and its end shall be at the Dead Sea.[a] This
shall be your land with its boundaries all around.

13 Moses commanded the Israelites, saying: This is the land that
you shall inherit by lot, which the Lord has commanded to give to
the nine tribes and to the half-tribe; 14 for the tribe of the Reubenites
by their ancestral houses and the tribe of the Gadites by their ancestral houses have taken their inheritance, and also the half-tribe of Manasseh; 15 the two tribes and the half-tribe have taken their inheritance
beyond the Jordan at Jericho eastward, toward the sunrise.

Tribal Leaders

16 The Lord spoke to Moses, saying: 17 These are the names of
the men who shall apportion the land to you for inheritance: the
priest Eleazar and Joshua son of Nun. 18 You shall take one leader of
every tribe to apportion the land for inheritance. 19 These are the
names of the men: Of the tribe of Judah, Caleb son of Jephunneh.
20 Of the tribe of the Simeonites, Shemuel son of Ammihud. 21 Of the
tribe of Benjamin, Elidad son of Chislon. 22 Of the tribe of the Danites
a leader, Bukki son of Jogli. 23 Of the Josephites: of the tribe of the
Manassites a leader, Hanniel son of Ephod, 24 and of the tribe of the
Ephraimites a leader, Kemuel son of Shiphtan. 25 Of the tribe of
the Zebulunites a leader, Eli-zaphan son of Parnach. 26 Of the tribe of
the Issacharites a leader, Paltiel son of Azzan. 27 And of the tribe of the
Asherites a leader, Ahihud son of Shelomi. 28 Of the tribe of the Naph-

---

[a] Heb *Salt Sea* [b] Syr: Heb lacks *its*

talites a leader, Pedahel son of Ammihud. 29 These were the ones
whom the LORD commanded to apportion the inheritance for the
Israelites in the land of Canaan.

Cities for the Levites

35 In the plains of Moab by the Jordan at Jericho, the LORD
spoke to Moses, saying: 2 Command the Israelites to give,
from the inheritance that they possess, towns for the Levites to live
in; you shall also give to the Levites pasture lands surrounding the
towns. 3 The towns shall be theirs to live in, and their pasture lands
shall be for their cattle, for their livestock, and for all their animals.
4 The pasture lands of the towns, which you shall give to the Levites,
shall reach from the wall of the town outward a thousand cubits all
around. 5 You shall measure, outside the town, for the east side two
thousand cubits, for the south side two thousand cubits, for the west
side two thousand cubits, and for the north side two thousand cubits,
with the town in the middle; this shall belong to them as pasture land
for their towns.

6 The towns that you give to the Levites shall include the six cities of refuge, where you shall permit a slayer to flee, and in addition to
them you shall give forty-two towns. 7 The towns that you give to the
Levites shall total forty-eight, with their pasture lands. 8 And as for the
towns that you shall give from the possession of the Israelites, from
the larger tribes you shall take many, and from the smaller tribes you
shall take few; each, in proportion to the inheritance that it obtains,
shall give of its towns to the Levites.

Cities of Refuge

9 The LORD spoke to Moses, saying: 10 Speak to the Israelites,
and say to them: When you cross the Jordan into the land of Canaan,
11 then you shall select cities to be cities of refuge for you, so that a
slayer who kills a person without intent may flee there. 12 The cities
shall be for you a refuge from the avenger, so that the slayer may not
die until there is a trial before the congregation.

13 The cities that you designate shall be six cities of refuge for
you: 14 you shall designate three cities beyond the Jordan, and three
cities in the land of Canaan, to be cities of refuge. 15 These six cities
shall serve as refuge for the Israelites, for the resident or transient
alien among them, so that anyone who kills a person without intent
may flee there.

Concerning Murder and Blood Revenge

16 But anyone who strikes another with an iron object, and death
ensues, is a murderer; the murderer shall be put to death. 17 Or anyone who strikes another with a stone in hand that could cause death,

35:11 cities of refuge: Verses 9-34 make one of the few allowances for homicide in the Hebrew Scriptures. If someone kills in violation of the command (see Exod 20:13 and Deut 5:17, where the same Hebrew word for *kill* is used), it is possible for the killer to escape being killed in revenge by the victim's family. This is only possible if the killing was unintentional. Verse 16 makes clear that a person who intentionally kills another person should be put to death (35:30 modifies this instruction by requiring two witnesses to put someone to death). The same word for *kill* used in verse 11 is also used in verse 16; however, it is accompanied by the verb *to strike, to wound,* or, in older translations, *to smite.* It is crucial that the land not be polluted or defiled with blood because the God of Israel dwells in the land with them. In spite of not having a physical body, God's presence is so substantial that it is affected by what happens on the earth in which God dwells.

and death ensues, is a murderer; the murderer shall be put to death. [18]Or anyone who strikes another with a weapon of wood in hand that could cause death, and death ensues, is a murderer; the murderer shall be put to death. [19]The avenger of blood is the one who shall put the murderer to death; when they meet, the avenger of blood shall execute the sentence. [20]Likewise, if someone pushes another from hatred, or hurls something at another, lying in wait, and death ensues, [21]or in enmity strikes another with the hand, and death ensues, then the one who struck the blow shall be put to death; that person is a murderer; the avenger of blood shall put the murderer to death, when they meet.

22 But if someone pushes another suddenly without enmity, or hurls any object without lying in wait, [23]or, while handling any stone that could cause death, unintentionally[a] drops it on another and death ensues, though they were not enemies, and no harm was intended, [24]then the congregation shall judge between the slayer and the avenger of blood, in accordance with these ordinances; [25]and the congregation shall rescue the slayer from the avenger of blood. Then the congregation shall send the slayer back to the original city of refuge. The slayer shall live in it until the death of the high priest who was anointed with the holy oil. [26]But if the slayer shall at any time go outside the bounds of the original city of refuge, [27]and is found by the avenger of blood outside the bounds of the city of refuge, and is killed by the avenger, no bloodguilt shall be incurred. [28]For the slayer must remain in the city of refuge until the death of the high priest; but after the death of the high priest the slayer may return home.

29 These things shall be a statute and ordinance for you throughout your generations wherever you live.

30 If anyone kills another, the murderer shall be put to death on the evidence of witnesses; but no one shall be put to death on the testimony of a single witness. [31]Moreover you shall accept no ransom for the life of a murderer who is subject to the death penalty; a murderer must be put to death. [32]Nor shall you accept ransom for one who has fled to a city of refuge, enabling the fugitive to return to live in the land before the death of the high priest. [33]You shall not pollute the land in which you live; for blood pollutes the land, and no expiation can be made for the land, for the blood that is shed in it, except by the blood of the one who shed it. [34]You shall not defile the land in which you live, in which I also dwell; for I the Lord dwell among the Israelites.

Marriage of Female Heirs

36:1-12 the daughters of Zelophehad: This is the third account of Zelophehad's daughters. In Numbers 36, Moses continued to pass out the land and passed right over Mahlah, Noah, Hoglah, Milcah, and Tir-

36 The heads of the ancestral houses of the clans of the descendants of Gilead son of Machir son of Manasseh, of the

[a] Heb *without seeing*

Josephite clans, came forward and spoke in the presence of Moses and
the leaders, the heads of the ancestral houses of the Israelites; [2]they
said, "The LORD commanded my lord to give the land for inheritance
by lot to the Israelites; and my lord was commanded by the LORD to
give the inheritance of our brother Zelophehad to his daughters. [3]But
if they are married into another Israelite tribe, then their inheritance
will be taken from the inheritance of our ancestors and added to the
inheritance of the tribe into which they marry; so it will be taken away
from the allotted portion of our inheritance. [4]And when the jubilee of
the Israelites comes, then their inheritance will be added to the inheritance of the tribe into which they have married; and their inheritance
will be taken from the inheritance of our ancestral tribe."

5 Then Moses commanded the Israelites according to the word
of the LORD, saying, "The descendants of the tribe of Joseph are right
in what they are saying. [6]This is what the LORD commands concerning the daughters of Zelophehad, 'Let them marry whom they think
best; only it must be into a clan of their father's tribe that they are married, [7]so that no inheritance of the Israelites shall be transferred from
one tribe to another; for all Israelites shall retain the inheritance of
their ancestral tribes. [8]Every daughter who possesses an inheritance
in any tribe of the Israelites shall marry one from the clan of her father's tribe, so that all Israelites may continue to possess their ancestral inheritance. [9]No inheritance shall be transferred from one tribe
to another; for each of the tribes of the Israelites shall retain its own
inheritance.' "

10 The daughters of Zelophehad did as the LORD had commanded Moses. [11]Mahlah, Tirzah, Hoglah, Milcah, and Noah, the
daughters of Zelophehad, married sons of their father's brothers.
[12]They were married into the clans of the descendants of Manasseh
son of Joseph, and their inheritance remained in the tribe of their father's clan.

13 These are the commandments and the ordinances that the
LORD commanded through Moses to the Israelites in the plains of
Moab by the Jordan at Jericho.

zah, disobeying God's instructions in 27:7-11. Some of the men get together and explain to Moses why he can't do what God said. The daughters of Zelophehad might marry outside their father's tribe, one tribe would get more land than another, and then everybody would go around marrying fatherless daughters to get their land. Speaking in God's name Moses declares, "the descendants of the tribe of Joseph are right" (36:5).

God had said (in chapter 27) that "the daughters of Zelophehad are right . . . you shall indeed let them possess an inheritance." Now it seems that God's instructions have changed; there is now a restriction on the promise. Even though Zelophehad's daughters follow the revised instructions, Moses *still* does not give them the land as instructed by God. In Joshua 17, Moses has died and Joshua has succeeded him. Mahlah, Noah, Hoglah, Milcah, and Tirzah are again standing in the door of the sanctuary, demanding a piece of the promised land from Joshua in front of the priest Eleazar and all the leadership. They are standing there because Moses refused to obey God—again. Moses had already been told he would not live to see the promised land because of his earlier disobedience. He could not get himself into the promised land, but he could use the power he had left to keep the women out. They are standing there because Moses went to his grave holding their piece of the promised land clutched in his cold, dead hand. *They* are standing there because they refuse to give up. They are standing there because they believe God. Finally, in Joshua 17:4 they receive their inheritance.

Deuteronomy 6:8

DEUTERONOMY

Background File

The book of Deuteronomy takes the form of a series of speeches given by Moses to the people of Israel. He speaks just before the conquest of the promised land of Canaan. Faithful scribes and priests wrote the core of this book around 700–640 B.C.E. At that time the power of Assyria was causing a crisis of faith in Judah. The authors of Deuteronomy wanted the people to stay faithful to God. A shorter form of this book was found during repairs on the temple in the time of King Josiah (640–609 B.C.E.). Josiah then put the laws of Deuteronomy into effect (see 2 Kgs 22–23).

What's the Story?

You can read this book on two levels at the same time. On the one hand, Deuteronomy is a timeless theological book, meaning that it tells us about God and God's relationship with us and the world. The reader overhears Moses making God's law known to God's people before the conquest of the promised land. He wants to convince them to obey that law after they have entered the land. On the other hand, Deuteronomy grew out of a specific time in history. Its authors wrote for the people of Judah in the seventh century B.C.E. Chapters 18–23 in the book of 2 Kings describe this dangerous period. The Assyrian Empire had strengthened its control over Judah and appeared ready to destroy it. As a result, many people tried to mix loyalty to Yahweh, the God of Israel, with the worship of rival gods such as Baal. The popularity of Assyrian culture led others to adopt Assyrian religious practices. Small farmers and day laborers had fallen deeply into poverty and were sold into slavery because of their debts. To meet this crisis, the authors of Deuteronomy restated and revised older laws, particularly laws found in Exodus 20–23. They wanted to inspire readers to be loyal to God and obey God's law.

The theology, style, and language of Deuteronomy influenced the way other Old Testament books were written, particularly Joshua, 1 and 2 Kings, and Jeremiah.

Deuteronomy has five major sections:

- Moses reviews history from the time the people of Israel left Mount Horeb (Sinai) to their arrival in Moab, east of the Jordan River (chapters 1–4).

- Moses reminds the people of the Ten Commandments (chapter 5). Next he delivers a sermon to encourage the people to obey the law (chapters 6–11).

- Moses proclaims the law that the people of Israel are to follow in the land (chapters 12–26).

- Moses tells the people about the special relationship or covenant that God is making with them. Yet he also warns of punishment in the future if they disobey God (chapters 27–30).

- Moses recites two poems (chapters 32–33). The change of leadership from Moses to Joshua and the death of Moses (chapters 31, 34) prepare for the conquest of Canaan, recounted in the book of Joshua.

What's the Message?

This book calls for obedience to God's law because of the unique relationship God has brought about with the people of Israel.

Deuteronomy describes the covenant or mutual agreement that God has made with the people. God wants to be their God, and they will be God's people (29:12-13). God has chosen them (4:37-38; 7:6-8) and given them a fruitful land (6:10-11; 8:7-10; 11:7-12). As God's covenant people, they have a duty to obey God's law. Every new generation must learn about God's grace and God's law (6:7, 20-25). The people are to worship the true God alone (6:4-5) and eliminate the temptation to worship idols and other gods (7:1-5, 25-26; 12:29—13:18).

Deuteronomy seeks to remake Israel into a just and humane society. It promotes concern for the poor and underprivileged, including slaves, women, and foreigners (15:1-18). Fair justice is everyone's right. Judges, priests, and the king should work together to make sure there is social fairness and faithfulness to God (16:18—17:20).

Deuteronomy is about mutual love. God has expressed love by choosing Israel as a special people and freeing them from Egypt (7:7-8, 13; 10:15). The people are to love God in return and show their love by obeying God's law (6:5; 7:9; 10:12; 11:1, 13; 13:3; 30:6).

Deuteronomy calls for joyous worship that includes everyone. To make sure that the people of Israel worship only the true God and no other gods, Deuteronomy demands that they offer sacrifice and celebrate festivals in only one place (chapter 12). Earlier practice permitted sacrificial worship at many local altars scattered around the country (see Exod 20:24-25). Requiring that people offer sacrifice only at a single central holy place was a radical change. Festive worship is to include everybody, regardless of social class, age, or gender (12:12; 16:11, 14).

Deuteronomy offers a choice to everyone who reads it. This choice is between disobedience leading to death and faithful obedience leading to life (30:15-20). Deuteronomy urges its readers to "Choose life" (30:19). If Israel fails to obey, the forces of history will destroy it (6:13-15). However, fear is not the right reason to obey God's law. Israel is to obey out of love for God and neighbor (10:12-13, 19) and because God freed the people from slavery in Egypt (24:17-18, 22).

Events at Horeb Recalled

1 These are the words that Moses spoke to all Israel beyond the
Jordan—in the wilderness, on the plain opposite Suph, between
Paran and Tophel, Laban, Hazeroth, and Di-zahab. 2 (By the way of
Mount Seir it takes eleven days to reach Kadesh-barnea from Horeb.)
3 In the fortieth year, on the first day of the eleventh month, Moses
spoke to the Israelites just as the LORD had commanded him to speak
to them. 4 This was after he had defeated King Sihon of the Amorites,
who reigned in Heshbon, and King Og of Bashan, who reigned in
Ashtaroth and[a] in Edrei. 5 Beyond the Jordan in the land of Moab,
Moses undertook to expound this law as follows:

6 The LORD our God spoke to us at Horeb, saying, "You have
stayed long enough at this mountain. 7 Resume your journey, and go
into the hill country of the Amorites as well as into the neighboring
regions—the Arabah, the hill country, the Shephelah, the Negeb, and
the seacoast—the land of the Canaanites and the Lebanon, as far as
the great river, the river Euphrates. 8 See, I have set the land before
you; go in and take possession of the land that I[b] swore to your ancestors, to Abraham, to Isaac, and to Jacob, to give to them and to their
descendants after them."

Appointment of Tribal Leaders

9 At that time I said to you, "I am unable by myself to bear you.
10 The LORD your God has multiplied you, so that today you are as
numerous as the stars of heaven. 11 May the LORD, the God of your
ancestors, increase you a thousand times more and bless you, as he
has promised you! 12 But how can I bear the heavy burden of your disputes all by myself? 13 Choose for each of your tribes individuals who
are wise, discerning, and reputable to be your leaders." 14 You answered
me, "The plan you have proposed is a good one." 15 So I took the leaders of your tribes, wise and reputable individuals, and installed them
as leaders over you, commanders of thousands, commanders of
hundreds, commanders of fifties, commanders of tens, and officials,
throughout your tribes. 16 I charged your judges at that time: "Give the
members of your community a fair hearing, and judge rightly between
one person and another, whether citizen or resident alien. 17 You must
not be partial in judging: hear out the small and the great alike; you
shall not be intimidated by anyone, for the judgment is God's. Any
case that is too hard for you, bring to me, and I will hear it." 18 So I
charged you at that time with all the things that you should do.

Israel's Refusal to Enter the Land

19 Then, just as the LORD our God had ordered us, we set out
from Horeb and went through all that great and terrible wilderness

[a] Gk Syr Vg Compare Josh 12.4: Heb lacks *and* [b] Sam Gk: MT *the LORD*

1:1-8 These are the words: In chapters 1–3 Moses prepares the people to hear God's law. He reminds them of their past disobedience and God's constant grace. Soon they will invade the land that God has promised them. They will move westward from Moab across the Jordan River (see Map 2, p. 2099). Horeb is another name for Mount Sinai.

1:9-18 Choose...individuals who are wise: The population of Israel has grown. This has created too much work for Moses. To ease the situation, he designs a fair system of justice to handle disputes.

What do Lutherans say about God's relationship to government? In appointing human judges, Moses insists that fair judgment belongs to God (1:17). In the *Small Catechism*'s explanation of the Fourth Commandment, Martin Luther urges us to honor, serve, obey, love, and respect those whom God has set in authority over us. Luther also identified spiritual authority (of God) and temporal authority (of human government) as God's twofold way of ruling in the world. God works through the Holy Spirit to rule the hearts of believers; God works through civil authorities to order common life. See also Romans 13:1-7. *Deuteronomy 1:9-18*

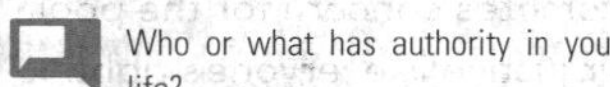

Who or what has authority in your life?

1:16 resident alien: God's law gave special protections to foreigners who lived inside Israel's territory. Deuteronomy teaches that orphans, widows, and resident aliens (often translated "sojourners") are people at risk who deserve special kindness (24:19-21; see Jer 7:6 and Mal 3:5).

1:19-45 You rebelled against the command of the LORD: Moses reminds the people how their lack of faith and foolish false confidence led to defeat. Numbers 13–14 recounts these events. Notice that Deuteronomy at first reveals only positive facts from the spies' report (compare 1:25 with 1:28). This makes Israel's refusal to attack even more shocking. Stories about giants called *Anakim* fueled their fears. All adults of that generation except Caleb and Joshua would have to die before conquest could begin again. To make matters worse, Israel then followed its lack of faith with an overconfident attack carried out against God's orders.

that you saw, on the way to the hill country of the Amorites, until we
reached Kadesh-barnea. [20]I said to you, "You have reached the hill
country of the Amorites, which the LORD our God is giving us. [21]See,
the LORD your God has given the land to you; go up, take possession,
as the LORD, the God of your ancestors, has promised you; do not
fear or be dismayed."

22 All of you came to me and said, "Let us send men ahead of us
to explore the land for us and bring back a report to us regarding the
route by which we should go up and the cities we will come to." [23]The
plan seemed good to me, and I selected twelve of you, one from each
tribe. [24]They set out and went up into the hill country, and when they
reached the Valley of Eshcol they spied it out [25]and gathered some
of the land's produce, which they brought down to us. They brought
back a report to us, and said, "It is a good land that the LORD our God
is giving us."

26 But you were unwilling to go up. You rebelled against the command of the LORD your God; [27]you grumbled in your tents and said,
"It is because the LORD hates us that he has brought us out of the
land of Egypt, to hand us over to the Amorites to destroy us. [28]Where
are we headed? Our kindred have made our hearts melt by reporting, 'The people are stronger and taller than we; the cities are large
and fortified up to heaven! We actually saw there the offspring of the
Anakim!' " [29]I said to you, "Have no dread or fear of them. [30]The LORD
your God, who goes before you, is the one who will fight for you,
just as he did for you in Egypt before your very eyes, [31]and in the wilderness, where you saw how the LORD your God carried you, just as
one carries a child, all the way that you traveled until you reached this
place. [32]But in spite of this, you have no trust in the LORD your God,
[33]who goes before you on the way to seek out a place for you to camp,
in fire by night, and in the cloud by day, to show you the route you
should take."

The Penalty for Israel's Rebellion

34 When the LORD heard your words, he was wrathful and
swore: [35]"Not one of these—not one of this evil generation—shall
see the good land that I swore to give to your ancestors, [36]except
Caleb son of Jephunneh. He shall see it, and to him and to his descendants I will give the land on which he set foot, because of his
complete fidelity to the LORD." [37]Even with me the LORD was angry
on your account, saying, "You also shall not enter there. [38]Joshua
son of Nun, your assistant, shall enter there; encourage him, for he
is the one who will secure Israel's possession of it. [39]And as for your
little ones, who you thought would become booty, your children,
who today do not yet know right from wrong, they shall enter there;
to them I will give it, and they shall take possession of it. [40]But as

for you, journey back into the wilderness, in the direction of the Red Sea."[a]

41 You answered me, "We have sinned against the LORD! We are ready to go up and fight, just as the LORD our God commanded us." So all of you strapped on your battle gear, and thought it easy to go up into the hill country. [42]The LORD said to me, "Say to them, 'Do not go up and do not fight, for I am not in the midst of you; otherwise you will be defeated by your enemies.' " [43]Although I told you, you would not listen. You rebelled against the command of the LORD and presumptuously went up into the hill country. [44]The Amorites who lived in that hill country then came out against you and chased you as bees do. They beat you down in Seir as far as Hormah. [45]When you returned and wept before the LORD, the LORD would neither heed your voice nor pay you any attention.

The Desert Years

1:46—3:7 Head north: The death of the disobedient generation (2:14-15) meant that conquest could begin. Notice that all credit for victory belongs to God (2:24-25, 31, 33, 36; 3:2).

46 After you had stayed at Kadesh as many days as you did,

2 [1]we journeyed back into the wilderness, in the direction of the Red Sea,[a] as the LORD had told me and skirted Mount Seir for many days. [2]Then the LORD said to me: [3]"You have been skirting this hill country long enough. Head north, [4]and charge the people as follows: You are about to pass through the territory of your kindred, the descendants of Esau, who live in Seir. They will be afraid of you, so, be very careful [5]not to engage in battle with them, for I will not give you even so much as a foot's length of their land, since I have given Mount Seir to Esau as a possession. [6]You shall purchase food from them for money, so that you may eat; and you shall also buy water from them for money, so that you may drink. [7]Surely the LORD your God has blessed you in all your undertakings; he knows your going through this great wilderness. These forty years the LORD your God has been with you; you have lacked nothing." [8]So we passed by our kin, the descendants of Esau who live in Seir, leaving behind the route of the Arabah, and leaving behind Elath and Ezion-geber.

When we had headed out along the route of the wilderness of Moab, [9]the LORD said to me: "Do not harass Moab or engage them in battle, for I will not give you any of its land as a possession, since I have given Ar as a possession to the descendants of Lot." [10](The Emim—a large and numerous people, as tall as the Anakim—had formerly inhabited it. [11]Like the Anakim, they are usually reckoned as Rephaim, though the Moabites call them Emim. [12]Moreover, the Horim had formerly inhabited Seir, but the descendants of Esau dispossessed them, destroying them and settling in their place, as Israel has done

---

[a] Or *Sea of Reeds*

in the land that the LORD gave them as a possession.) [13]"Now then, proceed to cross over the Wadi Zered."

So we crossed over the Wadi Zered. [14]And the length of time we had traveled from Kadesh-barnea until we crossed the Wadi Zered was thirty-eight years, until the entire generation of warriors had perished from the camp, as the LORD had sworn concerning them. [15]Indeed, the LORD's own hand was against them, to root them out from the camp, until all had perished.

16 Just as soon as all the warriors had died off from among the people, [17]the LORD spoke to me, saying, [18]"Today you are going to cross the boundary of Moab at Ar. [19]When you approach the frontier of the Ammonites, do not harass them or engage them in battle, for I will not give the land of the Ammonites to you as a possession, because I have given it to the descendants of Lot." [20](It also is usually reckoned as a land of Rephaim. Rephaim formerly inhabited it, though the Ammonites call them Zamzummim, [21]a strong and numerous people, as tall as the Anakim. But the LORD destroyed them from before the Ammonites so that they could dispossess them and settle in their place. [22]He did the same for the descendants of Esau, who live in Seir, by destroying the Horim before them so that they could dispossess them and settle in their place even to this day. [23]As for the Avvim, who had lived in settlements in the vicinity of Gaza, the Caphtorim, who came from Caphtor, destroyed them and settled in their place.) [24]"Proceed on your journey and cross the Wadi Arnon. See, I have handed over to you King Sihon the Amorite of Heshbon, and his land. Begin to take possession by engaging him in battle. [25]This day I will begin to put the dread and fear of you upon the peoples everywhere under heaven; when they hear report of you, they will tremble and be in anguish because of you."

Defeat of King Sihon

26 So I sent messengers from the wilderness of Kedemoth to King Sihon of Heshbon with the following terms of peace: [27]"If you let me pass through your land, I will travel only along the road; I will turn aside neither to the right nor to the left. [28]You shall sell me food for money, so that I may eat, and supply me water for money, so that I may drink. Only allow me to pass through on foot— [29]just as the descendants of Esau who live in Seir have done for me and likewise the Moabites who live in Ar—until I cross the Jordan into the land that the LORD our God is giving us." [30]But King Sihon of Heshbon was not willing to let us pass through, for the LORD your God had hardened his spirit and made his heart defiant in order to hand him over to you, as he has now done.

31 The LORD said to me, "See, I have begun to give Sihon and his land over to you. Begin now to take possession of his land." [32]So when

2:30 hardened his spirit: God prompted Sihon's defiance. God acted in a similar way with Pharaoh in the exodus story (see Exod 4:21; 7:3).

Sihon came out against us, he and all his people for battle at Jahaz,
33 the LORD our God gave him over to us; and we struck him down,
along with his offspring and all his people. 34 At that time we captured
all his towns, and in each town we utterly destroyed men, women, and
children. We left not a single survivor. 35 Only the livestock we kept
as spoil for ourselves, as well as the plunder of the towns that we had
captured. 36 From Aroer on the edge of the Wadi Arnon (including the
town that is in the wadi itself) as far as Gilead, there was no citadel
too high for us. The LORD our God gave everything to us. 37 You did
not encroach, however, on the land of the Ammonites, avoiding the
whole upper region of the Wadi Jabbok as well as the towns of the hill
country, just as[a] the LORD our God had charged.

Defeat of King Og

3 When we headed up the road to Bashan, King Og of Bashan
came out against us, he and all his people, for battle at Edrei.
2 The LORD said to me, "Do not fear him, for I have handed him over
to you, along with his people and his land. Do to him as you did to
King Sihon of the Amorites, who reigned in Heshbon." 3 So the LORD
our God also handed over to us King Og of Bashan and all his people.
We struck him down until not a single survivor was left. 4 At that time
we captured all his towns; there was no citadel that we did not take
from them—sixty towns, the whole region of Argob, the kingdom of
Og in Bashan. 5 All these were fortress towns with high walls, double gates, and bars, besides a great many villages. 6 And we utterly destroyed them, as we had done to King Sihon of Heshbon, in each city
utterly destroying men, women, and children. 7 But all the livestock
and the plunder of the towns we kept as spoil for ourselves.

3:8-17 we took from the two kings: The tribes of Reuben, Gad, and part of Manasseh settled the areas east of the Jordan River that had been ruled by kings Sihon and Og (see Map 3, pp. 2100-2101).

8 So at that time we took from the two kings of the Amorites the
land beyond the Jordan, from the Wadi Arnon to Mount Hermon
9 (the Sidonians call Hermon Sirion, while the Amorites call it Senir),
10 all the towns of the tableland, the whole of Gilead, and all of Bashan,
as far as Salecah and Edrei, towns of Og's kingdom in Bashan. 11 (Now
only King Og of Bashan was left of the remnant of the Rephaim. In
fact his bed, an iron bed, can still be seen in Rabbah of the Ammonites. By the common cubit it is nine cubits long and four cubits wide.)
12 As for the land that we took possession of at that time, I gave to the
Reubenites and Gadites the territory north of Aroer,[b] that is on the
edge of the Wadi Arnon, as well as half the hill country of Gilead with
its towns, 13 and I gave to the half-tribe of Manasseh the rest of Gilead and all of Bashan, Og's kingdom. (The whole region of Argob:
all that portion of Bashan used to be called a land of Rephaim; 14 Jair
the Manassite acquired the whole region of Argob as far as the border

[a] Gk Tg: Heb *and all* [b] Heb *territory from Aroer*

of the Geshurites and the Maacathites, and he named them—that is,
Bashan—after himself, Havvoth-jair,[a] as it is to this day.) 15 To Machir
I gave Gilead. 16 And to the Reubenites and the Gadites I gave the territory from Gilead as far as the Wadi Arnon, with the middle of the
wadi as a boundary, and up to the Jabbok, the wadi being boundary
of the Ammonites; 17 the Arabah also, with the Jordan and its banks,
from Chinnereth down to the sea of the Arabah, the Dead Sea,[b] with
the lower slopes of Pisgah on the east.

18 At that time, I charged you as follows: "Although the LORD
your God has given you this land to occupy, all your troops shall
cross over armed as the vanguard of your Israelite kin. 19 Only your
wives, your children, and your livestock—I know that you have much
livestock—shall stay behind in the towns that I have given to you.
20 When the LORD gives rest to your kindred, as to you, and they too
have occupied the land that the LORD your God is giving them beyond the Jordan, then each of you may return to the property that I
have given to you." 21 And I charged Joshua as well at that time, saying:
"Your own eyes have seen everything that the LORD your God has
done to these two kings; so the LORD will do to all the kingdoms into
which you are about to cross. 22 Do not fear them, for it is the LORD
your God who fights for you."

Moses Views Canaan from Pisgah

23 At that time, too, I entreated the LORD, saying: 24 "O Lord
GOD, you have only begun to show your servant your greatness and
your might; what god in heaven or on earth can perform deeds and
mighty acts like yours! 25 Let me cross over to see the good land beyond the Jordan, that good hill country and the Lebanon." 26 But the
LORD was angry with me on your account and would not heed me.
The LORD said to me, "Enough from you! Never speak to me of this
matter again! 27 Go up to the top of Pisgah and look around you to the
west, to the north, to the south, and to the east. Look well, for you
shall not cross over this Jordan. 28 But charge Joshua, and encourage
and strengthen him, because it is he who shall cross over at the head
of this people and who shall secure their possession of the land that
you will see." 29 So we remained in the valley opposite Beth-peor.

3:27 you shall not cross over: Deuteronomy never fully explains why God was angry with Moses (1:37; 4:21-22). Moses will view the land before he dies (chapter 34).

Moses Commands Obedience

4 So now, Israel, give heed to the statutes and ordinances that I
am teaching you to observe, so that you may live to enter and
occupy the land that the LORD, the God of your ancestors, is giving
you. 2 You must neither add anything to what I command you nor take
away anything from it, but keep the commandments of the LORD

4:1-4 give heed to the statutes and ordinances: Moses encourages obedience to the law he is about to teach (4:5, 14). Numbers 25:1-13 tells what happened with people who followed Baal of Peor (4:3).

[a] That is *Settlement of Jair* [b] Heb *Salt Sea*

your God with which I am charging you. 3You have seen for yourselves what the LORD did with regard to the Baal of Peor—how the
LORD your God destroyed from among you everyone who followed
the Baal of Peor, 4while those of you who held fast to the LORD your
God are all alive today.
5 See, just as the LORD my God has charged me, I now teach you
statutes and ordinances for you to observe in the land that you are
about to enter and occupy. 6You must observe them diligently, for this
will show your wisdom and discernment to the peoples, who, when
they hear all these statutes, will say, "Surely this great nation is a wise
and discerning people!" 7For what other great nation has a god so
near to it as the LORD our God is whenever we call to him? 8And what
other great nation has statutes and ordinances as just as this entire law
that I am setting before you today?

4:9 make them known: Israel is to teach each new generation about God's actions and God's word (see also 6:20-25; 11:19-21).

9 But take care and watch yourselves closely, so as neither to forget the things that your eyes have seen nor to let them slip from your
mind all the days of your life; make them known to your children and
your children's children— 10how you once stood before the LORD
your God at Horeb, when the LORD said to me, "Assemble the people
for me, and I will let them hear my words, so that they may learn to
fear me as long as they live on the earth, and may teach their children
so"; 11you approached and stood at the foot of the mountain while
the mountain was blazing up to the very heavens, shrouded in dark
clouds. 12Then the LORD spoke to you out of the fire. You heard the
sound of words but saw no form; there was only a voice. 13He declared

4:13, 23, 31 covenant: God has set up a special two-sided relationship with Israel called the "covenant." This covenant or mutual agreement means that God will keep promises. It also requires Israel to keep God's law. God first made the covenant at Mount Horeb (5:2-3). See Map 2, page 2099. For a summary of the covenant, turn to 26:16-19.

to you his covenant, which he charged you to observe, that is, the ten
commandments;[a] and he wrote them on two stone tablets. 14And the
LORD charged me at that time to teach you statutes and ordinances
for you to observe in the land that you are about to cross into and
occupy.
15 Since you saw no form when the LORD spoke to you at Horeb
out of the fire, take care and watch yourselves closely, 16so that you do
not act corruptly by making an idol for yourselves, in the form of any
figure—the likeness of male or female, 17the likeness of any animal
that is on the earth, the likeness of any winged bird that flies in the air,
18the likeness of anything that creeps on the ground, the likeness of
any fish that is in the water under the earth. 19And when you look up
to the heavens and see the sun, the moon, and the stars, all the host of
heaven, do not be led astray and bow down to them and serve them,
things that the LORD your God has allotted to all the peoples everywhere under heaven. 20But the LORD has taken you and brought you
out of the iron-smelter, out of Egypt, to become a people of his very
own possession, as you are now.

---

[a] Heb *the ten words*

21 The LORD was angry with me because of you, and he vowed
that I should not cross the Jordan and that I should not enter the good
land that the LORD your God is giving for your possession. 22 For I am
going to die in this land without crossing over the Jordan, but you
are going to cross over to take possession of that good land. 23 So be
careful not to forget the covenant that the LORD your God made with
you, and not to make for yourselves an idol in the form of anything
that the LORD your God has forbidden you. 24 For the LORD your God
is a devouring fire, a jealous God.

25 When you have had children and children's children, and become complacent in the land, if you act corruptly by making an idol in
the form of anything, thus doing what is evil in the sight of the LORD
your God, and provoking him to anger, 26 I call heaven and earth to
witness against you today that you will soon utterly perish from the
land that you are crossing the Jordan to occupy; you will not live long
on it, but will be utterly destroyed. 27 The LORD will scatter you among
the peoples; only a few of you will be left among the nations where
the LORD will lead you. 28 There you will serve other gods made by
human hands, objects of wood and stone that neither see, nor hear,
nor eat, nor smell. 29 From there you will seek the LORD your God,
and you will find him if you search after him with all your heart and
soul. 30 In your distress, when all these things have happened to you in
time to come, you will return to the LORD your God and heed him.
31 Because the LORD your God is a merciful God, he will neither abandon you nor destroy you; he will not forget the covenant with your
ancestors that he swore to them.

32 For ask now about former ages, long before your own, ever
since the day that God created human beings on the earth; ask from
one end of heaven to the other: has anything so great as this ever happened or has its like ever been heard of? 33 Has any people ever heard
the voice of a god speaking out of a fire, as you have heard, and lived?
34 Or has any god ever attempted to go and take a nation for himself
from the midst of another nation, by trials, by signs and wonders, by
war, by a mighty hand and an outstretched arm, and by terrifying displays of power, as the LORD your God did for you in Egypt before
your very eyes? 35 To you it was shown so that you would acknowledge
that the LORD is God; there is no other besides him. 36 From heaven
he made you hear his voice to discipline you. On earth he showed
you his great fire, while you heard his words coming out of the fire.
37 And because he loved your ancestors, he chose their descendants
after them. He brought you out of Egypt with his own presence, by
his great power, 38 driving out before you nations greater and mightier
than yourselves, to bring you in, giving you their land for a possession, as it is still today. 39 So acknowledge today and take to heart that
the LORD is God in heaven above and on the earth beneath; there

4:25-31 When you . . . become complacent: Worship of false gods would eventually lead to exile to a pagan country. These words address later readers who had suffered military defeat and been exiled to Babylon (see Map 1, page 2098). Deuteronomy urges those exiles to return to the LORD and to rely on a merciful God who would not forget the covenant.

4:32-40 has anything so great . . . ever happened? No other people know God as fully as Israel does. God spoke directly to them (5:4, 22). God brought them out of Egypt. God gave them the promised land of Canaan. Therefore, the people should confess that God is the only god and obey God's teachings given through Moses.

Why is it difficult to put God first in our lives?

is no other. [40]Keep his statutes and his commandments, which I am
commanding you today for your own well-being and that of your
descendants after you, so that you may long remain in the land that
the LORD your God is giving you for all time.

Cities of Refuge East of the Jordan

41 Then Moses set apart on the east side of the Jordan three
cities [42]to which a homicide could flee, someone who unintentionally kills another person, the two not having been at enmity before;
the homicide could flee to one of these cities and live: [43]Bezer in the
wilderness on the tableland belonging to the Reubenites, Ramoth in
Gilead belonging to the Gadites, and Golan in Bashan belonging to
the Manassites.

Transition to the Second Address

44 This is the law that Moses set before the Israelites. [45]These
are the decrees and the statutes and ordinances that Moses spoke to
the Israelites when they had come out of Egypt, [46]beyond the Jordan in the valley opposite Beth-peor, in the land of King Sihon of the
Amorites, who reigned at Heshbon, whom Moses and the Israelites
defeated when they came out of Egypt. [47]They occupied his land and
the land of King Og of Bashan, the two kings of the Amorites on the
eastern side of the Jordan: [48]from Aroer, which is on the edge of the
Wadi Arnon, as far as Mount Sirion[a] (that is, Hermon), [49]together
with all the Arabah on the east side of the Jordan as far as the Sea of
the Arabah, under the slopes of Pisgah.

The Ten Commandments

5 Moses convened all Israel, and said to them:
Hear, O Israel, the statutes and ordinances that I am addressing to you today; you shall learn them and observe them diligently.
[2]The LORD our God made a covenant with us at Horeb. [3]Not with
our ancestors did the LORD make this covenant, but with us, who are
all of us here alive today. [4]The LORD spoke with you face to face at
the mountain, out of the fire. [5](At that time I was standing between
the LORD and you to declare to you the words[b] of the LORD; for you
were afraid because of the fire and did not go up the mountain.) And
he said:

6 I am the LORD your God, who brought you out of the land of
Egypt, out of the house of slavery; [7]you shall have no other gods before[c] me.

8 You shall not make for yourself an idol, whether in the form
of anything that is in heaven above, or that is on the earth beneath,

[a] Syr: Heb *Sion* [b] Q Mss Sam Gk Syr Vg Tg: MT *word* [c] Or *besides*

5:2-3 a covenant with us at Horeb: Short commands and prohibitions sum up the covenant God makes with every new generation. Originally, the Ten Commandments related to the culture of ancient Israel. Yet Christians and Jews have always expanded and adapted these words to apply them to their own lives.

5:6-10 no other gods before me: God's self-identification as Israel's liberator encourages total loyalty. A ban of all idols extends this demand for absolute faithfulness. The Hebrew word translated "steadfast love" (5:10) means loyalty to the covenant. God shows steadfast love to thousands of generations of obedient believers. Notice how this statement of grace overwhelms the warning to any three or four generations who reject God (5:9).

What motivates us as we try to obey God's law? In the *Small Catechism*, Luther encourages us to obey each commandment because "We are to fear and love God." Doing the right thing grows out of faith. Luther explains each commandment from two points of view. We are not to do certain things that dishonor God or harm our neighbor. We are also to act in positive ways that protect and help others. See also Ephesians 2:8-10. *Deuteronomy 5:6-21*

or that is in the water under the earth. 9You shall not bow down to
them or worship them; for I the LORD your God am a jealous God,
punishing children for the iniquity of parents, to the third and fourth
generation of those who reject me, 10but showing steadfast love to
the thousandth generation[a] of those who love me and keep my commandments.
11 You shall not make wrongful use of the name of the LORD your
God, for the LORD will not acquit anyone who misuses his name.
12 Observe the sabbath day and keep it holy, as the LORD your
God commanded you. 13Six days you shall labor and do all your work.
14But the seventh day is a sabbath to the LORD your God; you shall
not do any work—you, or your son or your daughter, or your male or
female slave, or your ox or your donkey, or any of your livestock, or
the resident alien in your towns, so that your male and female slave
may rest as well as you. 15Remember that you were a slave in the land
of Egypt, and the LORD your God brought you out from there with a
mighty hand and an outstretched arm; therefore the LORD your God
commanded you to keep the sabbath day.
16 Honor your father and your mother, as the LORD your God
commanded you, so that your days may be long and that it may go
well with you in the land that the LORD your God is giving you.
17 You shall not murder.[b]
18 Neither shall you commit adultery.
19 Neither shall you steal.
20 Neither shall you bear false witness against your neighbor.
21 Neither shall you covet your neighbor's wife.
Neither shall you desire your neighbor's house, or field, or male
or female slave, or ox, or donkey, or anything that belongs to your
neighbor.

Moses the Mediator of God's Will

22 These words the LORD spoke with a loud voice to your whole
assembly at the mountain, out of the fire, the cloud, and the thick
darkness, and he added no more. He wrote them on two stone tablets,
and gave them to me. 23When you heard the voice out of the darkness,
while the mountain was burning with fire, you approached me, all the
heads of your tribes and your elders; 24and you said, "Look, the LORD
our God has shown us his glory and greatness, and we have heard
his voice out of the fire. Today we have seen that God may speak to
someone and the person may still live. 25So now why should we die?
For this great fire will consume us; if we hear the voice of the LORD
our God any longer, we shall die. 26For who is there of all flesh that has
heard the voice of the living God speaking out of fire, as we have, and

[a] Or *to thousands* [b] Or *kill*

5:11 wrongful use of the name of the LORD: According to the Second Commandment, no one is to use God's personal name, YHWH (often pronounced and written as "Yahweh" and translated as "the LORD"), to swear false oaths or do harmful magic.

5:12-15 Observe the sabbath: Contrast this with Exodus 20:8-11. Notice that Deuteronomy's version encourages rest on the Sabbath by referring to Israel's past slavery in Egypt. The point is equality and fairness. Let your children, slaves, and domestic animals enjoy rest on Saturday.

5:16-21 Honor your father and your mother... Neither shall you covet: These commands were meant to govern and protect relationships in the community. The Fourth Commandment (5:16) applied not just to young people but required that adult children respect and protect aged parents.

The Fifth Commandment (5:17) was not a ban on all killing. Israel practiced capital punishment, fought wars, and sacrificed animals. The commandment originally outlawed outright murder, causing death by carelessness, and killing someone in unlawful reprisal.

In ancient Israel, adultery (5:18) was limited to what a man or woman might do to violate the marriage rights of that woman's husband.

The Seventh Commandment (5:19) originally included kidnapping people as slaves (see 24:7).

Israel's legal system depended almost entirely on truthful witnesses (17:6; 19:15), so the Eighth Commandment (5:20) prohibited telling lies about others, especially when called to testify.

The Ninth and Tenth Commandments (5:21) move beyond outward behavior to prohibit envious *thoughts* (see Matt 5:21-22, 27-28). Compare 5:21 with Exodus 20:17. Notice that Deuteronomy reverses the order of "house" and "wife." This reversal removes the wife from a list of household assets. It treats her as a person in her own right.

How do the Ten Commandments continue to shape our lives of faith and our lives in the wider public community? If the Commandments provide good order and protection, why do we struggle to live by them?

5:27 Go near...Then tell us: Israel believed that to be too closely involved with God risked death. Moses serves as a go-between. He hears God's word and proclaims it (5:31).

remained alive? [27]Go near, you yourself, and hear all that the LORD our God will say. Then tell us everything that the LORD our God tells you, and we will listen and do it."

28 The LORD heard your words when you spoke to me, and the LORD said to me: "I have heard the words of this people, which they have spoken to you; they are right in all that they have spoken. [29]If only they had such a mind as this, to fear me and to keep all my commandments always, so that it might go well with them and with their children forever! [30]Go say to them, 'Return to your tents.' [31]But you, stand here by me, and I will tell you all the commandments, the statutes and the ordinances, that you shall teach them, so that they may do them in the land that I am giving them to possess." [32]You must therefore be careful to do as the LORD your God has commanded you; you shall not turn to the right or to the left. [33]You must follow exactly the path that the LORD your God has commanded you, so that you may live, and that it may go well with you, and that you may live long in the land that you are to possess.

The Great Commandment

6 Now this is the commandment—the statutes and the ordinances—that the LORD your God charged me to teach you to observe in the land that you are about to cross into and occupy, [2]so that you and your children and your children's children may fear the LORD your God all the days of your life, and keep all his decrees and his commandments that I am commanding you, so that your days may be long. [3]Hear therefore, O Israel, and observe them diligently, so that it may go well with you, and so that you may multiply greatly in a land flowing with milk and honey, as the LORD, the God of your ancestors, has promised you.

4 Hear, O Israel: The LORD is our God, the LORD alone.[a] [5]You shall love the LORD your God with all your heart, and with all your soul, and with all your might. [6]Keep these words that I am commanding you today in your heart. [7]Recite them to your children and talk about them when you are at home and when you are away, when you lie down and when you rise. [8]Bind them as a sign on your hand, fix them as an emblem[b] on your forehead, [9]and write them on the doorposts of your house and on your gates.

Caution against Disobedience

10 When the LORD your God has brought you into the land that he swore to your ancestors, to Abraham, to Isaac, and to Jacob, to give you—a land with fine, large cities that you did not build, [11]houses

6:4-5 You shall love the LORD your God: This is Israel's central confession of faith. God is perfect in power and oneness. Therefore God can demand Israel's love and loyalty (see Mark 12:28-30). These verses form a prayer called the *Shema* (from the Hebrew word meaning "hear"), recited by faithful Jews twice a day.

How would you sum up the core of your personal faith in a single sentence?

6:6-9: in your heart...talk about them...bind them...write them: The people of Israel are not just to say these words. They are to believe them deeply and personally. The words are to be made public so that they control every aspect of life.

6:10-15 do not forget the LORD: The people of Israel may become prosperous and self-satisfied in their wonderful land. They may forget that the land was a gracious gift from God. Then Israel might be tempted to worship the false gods of neighboring peoples.

[a] Or *The LORD our God is one LORD,* or *The LORD our God, the LORD is one,* or *The LORD is our God, the LORD is one* [b] Or *as a frontlet*

filled with all sorts of goods that you did not fill, hewn cisterns that you did not hew, vineyards and olive groves that you did not plant—and when you have eaten your fill, [12]take care that you do not forget the LORD, who brought you out of the land of Egypt, out of the house of slavery. [13]The LORD your God you shall fear; him you shall serve, and by his name alone you shall swear. [14]Do not follow other gods, any of the gods of the peoples who are all around you, [15]because the LORD your God, who is present with you, is a jealous God. The anger of the LORD your God would be kindled against you and he would destroy you from the face of the earth.

16 Do not put the LORD your God to the test, as you tested him at Massah. [17]You must diligently keep the commandments of the LORD your God, and his decrees, and his statutes that he has commanded you. [18]Do what is right and good in the sight of the LORD, so that it may go well with you, and so that you may go in and occupy the good land that the LORD swore to your ancestors to give you, [19]thrusting out all your enemies from before you, as the LORD has promised.

20 When your children ask you in time to come, "What is the meaning of the decrees and the statutes and the ordinances that the LORD our God has commanded you?" [21]then you shall say to your children, "We were Pharaoh's slaves in Egypt, but the LORD brought us out of Egypt with a mighty hand. [22]The LORD displayed before our eyes great and awesome signs and wonders against Egypt, against Pharaoh and all his household. [23]He brought us out from there in order to bring us in, to give us the land that he promised on oath to our ancestors. [24]Then the LORD commanded us to observe all these statutes, to fear the LORD our God, for our lasting good, so as to keep us alive, as is now the case. [25]If we diligently observe this entire commandment before the LORD our God, as he has commanded us, we will be in the right."

A Chosen People

7 When the LORD your God brings you into the land that you are about to enter and occupy, and he clears away many nations before you—the Hittites, the Girgashites, the Amorites, the Canaanites, the Perizzites, the Hivites, and the Jebusites, seven nations mightier and more numerous than you— [2]and when the LORD your God gives them over to you and you defeat them, then you must utterly destroy them. Make no covenant with them and show them no mercy. [3]Do not intermarry with them, giving your daughters to their sons or taking their daughters for your sons, [4]for that would turn away your children from following me, to serve other gods. Then the anger of the LORD would be kindled against you, and he would destroy you quickly. [5]But this is how you must deal with them: break down their altars, smash their pillars, hew

6:15 a jealous God: "Jealous" is better understood as "zealous." In human terms, God is passionately in love with Israel and so claims the people's total loyalty (5:9).

6:20-25 When your children ask: Educating the next generation is vital. Notice the repeated "we" and "us" in the expected response. This shows that each generation personally accepts the faith passed on to them.

7:2 utterly destroy: Modern readers are usually shocked by the demand that Israel wipe out the earlier population of the promised land (2:34; 20:16-18; see Josh 6.21). See the Bible Concepts notes at 20:1 and at 20:17.

7:3-4 Do not intermarry: This is not a matter of ethnic pride. Israel is to keep itself separate in order to remain loyal to God. Marriage would form social and religious relationships that might lead the Israelite partner to worship false gods.

down their sacred poles,[a] and burn their idols with fire. [6]For you are a people holy to the LORD your God; the LORD your God has chosen you out of all the peoples on earth to be his people, his treasured possession.

7 It was not because you were more numerous than any other people that the LORD set his heart on you and chose you—for you were the fewest of all peoples. [8]It was because the LORD loved you and kept the oath that he swore to your ancestors, that the LORD has brought you out with a mighty hand, and redeemed you from the house of slavery, from the hand of Pharaoh king of Egypt. [9]Know therefore that the LORD your God is God, the faithful God who maintains covenant loyalty with those who love him and keep his commandments, to a thousand generations, [10]and who repays in their own person those who reject him. He does not delay but repays in their own person those who reject him. [11]Therefore, observe diligently the commandment—the statutes and the ordinances—that I am commanding you today.

Blessings for Obedience

12 If you heed these ordinances, by diligently observing them, the LORD your God will maintain with you the covenant loyalty that he swore to your ancestors; [13]he will love you, bless you, and multiply you; he will bless the fruit of your womb and the fruit of your ground, your grain and your wine and your oil, the increase of your cattle and the issue of your flock, in the land that he swore to your ancestors to give you. [14]You shall be the most blessed of peoples, with neither sterility nor barrenness among you or your livestock. [15]The LORD will turn away from you every illness; all the dread diseases of Egypt that you experienced, he will not inflict on you, but he will lay them on all who hate you. [16]You shall devour all the peoples that the LORD your God is giving over to you, showing them no pity; you shall not serve their gods, for that would be a snare to you.

7:13-14 he will love you, bless you: The gods of the Canaanites supposedly granted agricultural productivity. God's promise of fruitfulness for Israel's families, fields, and flocks undercuts that claim.

17 If you say to yourself, "These nations are more numerous than I; how can I dispossess them?" [18]do not be afraid of them. Just remember what the LORD your God did to Pharaoh and to all Egypt, [19]the great trials that your eyes saw, the signs and wonders, the mighty hand and the outstretched arm by which the LORD your God brought you out. The LORD your God will do the same to all the peoples of whom you are afraid. [20]Moreover, the LORD your God will send the pestilence[b] against them, until even the survivors and the fugitives are destroyed. [21]Have no dread of them, for the LORD your God, who is present with you, is a great and awesome God. [22]The LORD your God will clear away these nations before you little by little; you will not be

7:18-19 Just remember: Remembering is a favorite theme of Deuteronomy. Remembering the exodus gives Israel the courage it needs to trust in God's protection and rely on God's help in the conquest (1:29-30; 20:4). Remembering this event also inspires obedience to God's law (10:19; 16:12; 24:17-18, 21-22).

Remember some of the good things God has done in your life. How does this help you love and obey God?

[a] Heb *Asherim* [b] Or *hornets*: Meaning of Heb uncertain

able to make a quick end of them, otherwise the wild animals would become too numerous for you. [23]But the LORD your God will give them over to you, and throw them into great panic, until they are destroyed. [24]He will hand their kings over to you and you shall blot out their name from under heaven; no one will be able to stand against you, until you have destroyed them. [25]The images of their gods you shall burn with fire. Do not covet the silver or the gold that is on them and take it for yourself, because you could be ensnared by it; for it is abhorrent to the LORD your God. [26]Do not bring an abhorrent thing into your house, or you will be set apart for destruction like it. You must utterly detest and abhor it, for it is set apart for destruction.

A Warning Not to Forget God in Prosperity

8 This entire commandment that I command you today you must diligently observe, so that you may live and increase, and go in and occupy the land that the LORD promised on oath to your ancestors. [2]Remember the long way that the LORD your God has led you these forty years in the wilderness, in order to humble you, testing you to know what was in your heart, whether or not you would keep his commandments. [3]He humbled you by letting you hunger, then by feeding you with manna, with which neither you nor your ancestors were acquainted, in order to make you understand that one does not live by bread alone, but by every word that comes from the mouth of the LORD.[a] [4]The clothes on your back did not wear out and your feet did not swell these forty years. [5]Know then in your heart that as a parent disciplines a child so the LORD your God disciplines you. [6]Therefore keep the commandments of the LORD your God, by walking in his ways and by fearing him. [7]For the LORD your God is bringing you into a good land, a land with flowing streams, with springs and underground waters welling up in valleys and hills, [8]a land of wheat and barley, of vines and fig trees and pomegranates, a land of olive trees and honey, [9]a land where you may eat bread without scarcity, where you will lack nothing, a land whose stones are iron and from whose hills you may mine copper. [10]You shall eat your fill and bless the LORD your God for the good land that he has given you.

11 Take care that you do not forget the LORD your God, by failing to keep his commandments, his ordinances, and his statutes, which I am commanding you today. [12]When you have eaten your fill and have built fine houses and live in them, [13]and when your herds and flocks have multiplied, and your silver and gold is multiplied, and all that you have is multiplied, [14]then do not exalt yourself, forgetting the LORD your God, who brought you out of the land of Egypt, out of the house of slavery, [15]who led you through the great and terrible

[a] Or *by anything that the LORD decrees*

8:3 not...by bread alone: Exodus 16 tells the story of manna, a food that appeared each morning when the Israelites wandered in the wilderness. Its lesson is that God's word is the true source of life. Remembering their wilderness experiences teaches Israel to keep God's law in their new land (8:2-4).

Where can we find God's word? Lutherans talk of God's word as coming to us in three ways. God speaks to us through the Bible, God's written Word. It is also active and present in the sermons we hear and in faithful words that Christians speak to each other. Finally, we speak of Jesus as God's Incarnate Word, meaning God's Word came to us in the flesh as a living human being. In his explanation of the Third Commandment, Luther encourages us to keep God's word "holy and gladly hear and learn it" *(SC).* See also Romans 10:14-17. *Deuteronomy 8:3*

8:11-18 do not forget...But remember: Forgetfulness and pride would put Israel's good life in the land in danger. The solution is to remember God's past saving deeds.

wilderness, an arid wasteland with poisonous[a] snakes and scorpions.
He made water flow for you from flint rock, [16]and fed you in the wilderness with manna that your ancestors did not know, to humble you
and to test you, and in the end to do you good. [17]Do not say to yourself, "My power and the might of my own hand have gotten me this
wealth." [18]But remember the LORD your God, for it is he who gives
you power to get wealth, so that he may confirm his covenant that he
swore to your ancestors, as he is doing today. [19]If you do forget the
LORD your God and follow other gods to serve and worship them,
I solemnly warn you today that you shall surely perish. [20]Like the nations that the LORD is destroying before you, so shall you perish, because you would not obey the voice of the LORD your God.

The Consequences of Rebelling against God

9 Hear, O Israel! You are about to cross the Jordan today, to go in
and dispossess nations larger and mightier than you, great cities, fortified to the heavens, [2]a strong and tall people, the offspring of
the Anakim, whom you know. You have heard it said of them, "Who
can stand up to the Anakim?" [3]Know then today that the LORD your
God is the one who crosses over before you as a devouring fire; he
will defeat them and subdue them before you, so that you may dispossess and destroy them quickly, as the LORD has promised you.

9:4-5 do not say to yourself: Do not be arrogant. Success in conquering the promised land does not mean that Israel is especially righteous. Instead, it points to the wickedness of the Canaanites and proves God's faithfulness.

4 When the LORD your God thrusts them out before you, do not
say to yourself, "It is because of my righteousness that the LORD has
brought me in to occupy this land"; it is rather because of the wickedness of these nations that the LORD is dispossessing them before
you. [5]It is not because of your righteousness or the uprightness of
your heart that you are going in to occupy their land; but because of
the wickedness of these nations the LORD your God is dispossessing
them before you, in order to fulfill the promise that the LORD made
on oath to your ancestors, to Abraham, to Isaac, and to Jacob.

9:7-24 how you provoked the LORD: These verses retell a story of betrayal. Moses reminds the people that they made an image of a golden calf for themselves while he was receiving the Commandments. Notice how the repeated phrase "you have been rebellious against the LORD" encloses this entire section (9:7 and 9:24). We are to read this as a single paragraph.

6 Know, then, that the LORD your God is not giving you this good
land to occupy because of your righteousness; for you are a stubborn
people. [7]Remember and do not forget how you provoked the LORD
your God to wrath in the wilderness; you have been rebellious against
the LORD from the day you came out of the land of Egypt until you
came to this place.

8 Even at Horeb you provoked the LORD to wrath, and the LORD
was so angry with you that he was ready to destroy you. [9]When I
went up the mountain to receive the stone tablets, the tablets of the
covenant that the LORD made with you, I remained on the mountain forty days and forty nights; I neither ate bread nor drank water.
[10]And the LORD gave me the two stone tablets written with the finger

---

[a] Or *fiery*; Heb *seraph*

of God; on them were all the words that the LORD had spoken to you
at the mountain out of the fire on the day of the assembly. 11 At the end
of forty days and forty nights the LORD gave me the two stone tablets, the tablets of the covenant. 12 Then the LORD said to me, "Get up,
go down quickly from here, for your people whom you have brought
from Egypt have acted corruptly. They have been quick to turn from
the way that I commanded them; they have cast an image for themselves." 13 Furthermore the LORD said to me, "I have seen that this people is indeed a stubborn people. 14 Let me alone that I may destroy
them and blot out their name from under heaven; and I will make of
you a nation mightier and more numerous than they."

15 So I turned and went down from the mountain, while the
mountain was ablaze; the two tablets of the covenant were in my two
hands. 16 Then I saw that you had indeed sinned against the LORD your
God, by casting for yourselves an image of a calf; you had been quick
to turn from the way that the LORD had commanded you. 17 So I took
hold of the two tablets and flung them from my two hands, smashing them before your eyes. 18 Then I lay prostrate before the LORD as
before, forty days and forty nights; I neither ate bread nor drank water, because of all the sin you had committed, provoking the LORD by
doing what was evil in his sight. 19 For I was afraid that the anger that
the LORD bore against you was so fierce that he would destroy you.
But the LORD listened to me that time also. 20 The LORD was so angry
with Aaron that he was ready to destroy him, but I interceded also on
behalf of Aaron at that same time. 21 Then I took the sinful thing you
had made, the calf, and burned it with fire and crushed it, grinding it
thoroughly, until it was reduced to dust; and I threw the dust of it into
the stream that runs down the mountain.

22 At Taberah also, and at Massah, and at Kibroth-hattaavah, you
provoked the LORD to wrath. 23 And when the LORD sent you from
Kadesh-barnea, saying, "Go up and occupy the land that I have given
you," you rebelled against the command of the LORD your God, neither trusting him nor obeying him. 24 You have been rebellious against
the LORD as long as he has[a] known you.

25 Throughout the forty days and forty nights that I lay prostrate
before the LORD when the LORD intended to destroy you, 26 I prayed
to the LORD and said, "Lord GOD, do not destroy the people who are
your very own possession, whom you redeemed in your greatness,
whom you brought out of Egypt with a mighty hand. 27 Remember
your servants, Abraham, Isaac, and Jacob; pay no attention to the
stubbornness of this people, their wickedness and their sin, 28 otherwise the land from which you have brought us might say, 'Because
the LORD was not able to bring them into the land that he promised

[a] Sam Gk: MT *I have*

9:12-14 your people whom you have brought: God proposes giving up on Israel. God offers to form a new chosen people from the descendants of Moses. Notice how God's words in 9:12 imply rejection: they are *your* people, Moses, not mine. "Let me alone" (9:14) indicates that Moses should not plead for Israel. Moses refuses to comply and prays for Israel anyway (9:18-19).

9:17 smashing: Breaking the stone tablets of the law indicates in a concrete way that God's covenant with Israel has been shattered.

9:22-24 Taberah...Massah...Kibroth-hattaavah: These incidents are reported in Numbers 11:1-3, Exodus 17:1-7, and Numbers 11:31-34. Deuteronomy 1:19-45 recounts Israel's rebellion at Kadesh-barnea (see Map 2, page 2099).

9:25—10:11 I prayed to the LORD: Notice that the phrase "forty days and forty nights" encloses this long section (9:25 and 10:10), which should be read as a single unit. Moses re-examines his act of intercession, described earlier in 9:18-19. Making a second set of tablets restores Israel to its original relationship with God (compare 10:1-4 with 9:10).

them, and because he hated them, he has brought them out to let them die in the wilderness.' 29 For they are the people of your very own possession, whom you brought out by your great power and by your outstretched arm."

The Second Pair of Tablets

10 At that time the LORD said to me, "Carve out two tablets of stone like the former ones, and come up to me on the mountain, and make an ark of wood. 2 I will write on the tablets the words that were on the former tablets, which you smashed, and you shall put them in the ark." 3 So I made an ark of acacia wood, cut two tablets of stone like the former ones, and went up the mountain with the two tablets in my hand. 4 Then he wrote on the tablets the same words as before, the ten commandments[a] that the LORD had spoken to you on the mountain out of the fire on the day of the assembly; and the LORD gave them to me. 5 So I turned and came down from the mountain, and put the tablets in the ark that I had made; and there they are, as the LORD commanded me.

6 (The Israelites journeyed from Beeroth-bene-jaakan[b] to Moserah. There Aaron died, and there he was buried; his son Eleazar succeeded him as priest. 7 From there they journeyed to Gudgodah, and from Gudgodah to Jotbathah, a land with flowing streams. 8 At that time the LORD set apart the tribe of Levi to carry the ark of the covenant of the LORD, to stand before the LORD to minister to him, and to bless in his name, to this day. 9 Therefore Levi has no allotment or inheritance with his kindred; the LORD is his inheritance, as the LORD your God promised him.)

10 I stayed on the mountain forty days and forty nights, as I had done the first time. And once again the LORD listened to me. The LORD was unwilling to destroy you. 11 The LORD said to me, "Get up, go on your journey at the head of the people, that they may go in and occupy the land that I swore to their ancestors to give them."

The Essence of the Law

12 So now, O Israel, what does the LORD your God require of you? Only to fear the LORD your God, to walk in all his ways, to love him, to serve the LORD your God with all your heart and with all your soul, 13 and to keep the commandments of the LORD your God[c] and his decrees that I am commanding you today, for your own well-being. 14 Although heaven and the heaven of heavens belong to the LORD your God, the earth with all that is in it, 15 yet the LORD set his heart in love on your ancestors alone and chose you, their descendants after them, out of all the peoples, as it is today. 16 Circumcise,

10:12 fear . . . love . . . serve: To fear is to be reverent and obedient (10:20). To love God is part of a mutual relationship that began with God's love for Israel's ancestors (10:15). Love leads to acts of justice for the needy and oppressed on the part of both God and Israel (10:18-19). To serve in this context is to worship.

10:16 Circumcise . . . the foreskin of your heart: Physical circumcision signified membership in the covenant community (see Gen 17:9-14 and note on Gen 17:10). It set Israel apart from other peoples. Moses calls for inward change and the removal of any obstacle to willing obedience (30:6; see Jer 4:4; 9:25).

---

[a] Heb *the ten words* [b] Or *the wells of the Bene-jaakan* [c] Q Ms Gk Syr: MT lacks *your God*

then, the foreskin of your heart, and do not be stubborn any longer.
[17]For the LORD your God is God of gods and Lord of lords, the great
God, mighty and awesome, who is not partial and takes no bribe,
[18]who executes justice for the orphan and the widow, and who loves
the strangers, providing them food and clothing. [19]You shall also love
the stranger, for you were strangers in the land of Egypt. [20]You shall
fear the LORD your God; him alone you shall worship; to him you
shall hold fast, and by his name you shall swear. [21]He is your praise;
he is your God, who has done for you these great and awesome things
that your own eyes have seen. [22]Your ancestors went down to Egypt
seventy persons; and now the LORD your God has made you as numerous as the stars in heaven.

Rewards for Obedience

11 You shall love the LORD your God, therefore, and keep his
charge, his decrees, his ordinances, and his commandments
always. [2]Remember today that it was not your children (who have
not known or seen the discipline of the LORD your God), but it is
you who must acknowledge his greatness, his mighty hand and his
outstretched arm, [3]his signs and his deeds that he did in Egypt to
Pharaoh, the king of Egypt, and to all his land; [4]what he did to the
Egyptian army, to their horses and chariots, how he made the water of the Red Sea[a] flow over them as they pursued you, so that the
LORD has destroyed them to this day; [5]what he did to you in the
wilderness, until you came to this place; [6]and what he did to Dathan
and Abiram, sons of Eliab son of Reuben, how in the midst of all Israel the earth opened its mouth and swallowed them up, along with
their households, their tents, and every living being in their company; [7]for it is your own eyes that have seen every great deed that
the LORD did.

8 Keep, then, this entire commandment that I am commanding
you today, so that you may have strength to go in and occupy the land
that you are crossing over to occupy, [9]and so that you may live long in
the land that the LORD swore to your ancestors to give them and to
their descendants, a land flowing with milk and honey. [10]For the land
that you are about to enter to occupy is not like the land of Egypt,
from which you have come, where you sow your seed and irrigate by
foot like a vegetable garden. [11]But the land that you are crossing over
to occupy is a land of hills and valleys, watered by rain from the sky,
[12]a land that the LORD your God looks after. The eyes of the LORD
your God are always on it, from the beginning of the year to the end
of the year.

13 If you will only heed his every commandment[b] that I am

11:2-7 Remember today: In chapter 11, Moses gives three reasons (see following note and note on 11:22-25) to obey God's law. The first is the memory of gracious things God has done for them, as well as situations in which God had to discipline them. Numbers 16 tells the story of Dathan and Abiram (11: 6).

11:8-12 the land: A second reason to obey is the bounty of the land. It does not rain much in Egypt. Egyptian farmers had to irrigate with foot-powered devices. In contrast, God's providence sends dependable water on Israel's land.

---

[a] Or *Sea of Reeds* [b] Compare Gk: Heb *my commandments*

11:14 early rain and the later rain: Showers fell in October and then in April.

What is providence? God provides us with daily bread and all we need to live healthy and happy lives. This comes from the bounty of the earth and human labor. Luther's explanation of the First Article of the Creed in the *Small Catechism* reminds us, "God daily and abundantly provides shoes and clothing, food and drink, house and farm, spouse and children, fields, livestock, and all property—along with all the necessities and nourishment for this body and life." See also Matthew 6:26-33. *Deuteronomy 11:13-15*

commanding you today—loving the LORD your God, and serving
him with all your heart and with all your soul— 14 then he[a] will give
the rain for your land in its season, the early rain and the later rain, and
you will gather in your grain, your wine, and your oil; 15 and he[a] will
give grass in your fields for your livestock, and you will eat your fill.
16 Take care, or you will be seduced into turning away, serving other
gods and worshiping them, 17 for then the anger of the LORD will be
kindled against you and he will shut up the heavens, so that there will
be no rain and the land will yield no fruit; then you will perish quickly
off the good land that the LORD is giving you.

18 You shall put these words of mine in your heart and soul,
and you shall bind them as a sign on your hand, and fix them as an
emblem[b] on your forehead. 19 Teach them to your children, talking
about them when you are at home and when you are away, when you
lie down and when you rise. 20 Write them on the doorposts of your
house and on your gates, 21 so that your days and the days of your children may be multiplied in the land that the LORD swore to your ancestors to give them, as long as the heavens are above the earth.

11:22-25 the LORD will drive out: God's promise of easy conquest offers a third reason to keep the law (see notes above at 11:2-7 and 11:8-12). Verse 24 points to territories eventually controlled or influenced by Solomon (1:7; see 1 Kgs 4:21, 24).

22 If you will diligently observe this entire commandment that
I am commanding you, loving the LORD your God, walking in all
his ways, and holding fast to him, 23 then the LORD will drive out all
these nations before you, and you will dispossess nations larger and
mightier than yourselves. 24 Every place on which you set foot shall
be yours; your territory shall extend from the wilderness to the Lebanon and from the River, the river Euphrates, to the Western Sea.
25 No one will be able to stand against you; the LORD your God will
put the fear and dread of you on all the land on which you set foot,
as he promised you.

11:26-28: a blessing and a curse: The stark choice between obedience leading to blessing and disobedience leading to curse is typical of Deuteronomy (30:15-20). Moses will wrap up his speech with a long list of blessings and curses in Deuteronomy 28.

26 See, I am setting before you today a blessing and a curse: 27 the
blessing, if you obey the commandments of the LORD your God that
I am commanding you today; 28 and the curse, if you do not obey the
commandments of the LORD your God, but turn from the way that
I am commanding you today, to follow other gods that you have not
known.

11:29 set the blessing: Deuteronomy 27 will give detailed instructions for this ceremony. Turn to Joshua 8:30-35 to read how Joshua carried this out.

29 When the LORD your God has brought you into the land that
you are entering to occupy, you shall set the blessing on Mount Gerizim and the curse on Mount Ebal. 30 As you know, they are beyond the
Jordan, some distance to the west, in the land of the Canaanites who
live in the Arabah, opposite Gilgal, beside the oak[c] of Moreh.

31 When you cross the Jordan to go in to occupy the land that the
LORD your God is giving you, and when you occupy it and live in it,
32 you must diligently observe all the statutes and ordinances that I am
setting before you today.

---

[a] Sam Gk Vg: MT *I* [b] Or *as a frontlet* [c] Gk Syr: Compare Gen 12.6; Heb *oaks* or *terebinths*

Pagan Shrines to Be Destroyed

12 These are the statutes and ordinances that you must diligently
observe in the land that the LORD, the God of your ancestors,
has given you to occupy all the days that you live on the earth.
2 You must demolish completely all the places where the nations
whom you are about to dispossess served their gods, on the mountain
heights, on the hills, and under every leafy tree. [3]Break down their altars, smash their pillars, burn their sacred poles[a] with fire, and hew
down the idols of their gods, and thus blot out their name from their
places. [4]You shall not worship the LORD your God in such ways. [5]But
you shall seek the place that the LORD your God will choose out of
all your tribes as his habitation to put his name there. You shall go
there, [6]bringing there your burnt offerings and your sacrifices, your
tithes and your donations, your votive gifts, your freewill offerings,
and the firstlings of your herds and flocks. [7]And you shall eat there
in the presence of the LORD your God, you and your households together, rejoicing in all the undertakings in which the LORD your God
has blessed you.
8 You shall not act as we are acting here today, all of us according
to our own desires, [9]for you have not yet come into the rest and the
possession that the LORD your God is giving you. [10]When you cross
over the Jordan and live in the land that the LORD your God is allot-
ting to you, and when he gives you rest from your enemies all around
so that you live in safety, [11]then you shall bring everything that I command you to the place that the LORD your God will choose as a dwelling for his name: your burnt offerings and your sacrifices, your tithes
and your donations, and all your choice votive gifts that you vow to
the LORD. [12]And you shall rejoice before the LORD your God, you
together with your sons and your daughters, your male and female
slaves, and the Levites who reside in your towns (since they have no
allotment or inheritance with you).

A Prescribed Place of Worship

13 Take care that you do not offer your burnt offerings at any
place you happen to see. [14]But only at the place that the LORD will
choose in one of your tribes—there you shall offer your burnt offerings and there you shall do everything I command you.
15 Yet whenever you desire you may slaughter and eat meat
within any of your towns, according to the blessing that the LORD
your God has given you; the unclean and the clean may eat of it, as
they would of gazelle or deer. [16]The blood, however, you must not
eat; you shall pour it out on the ground like water. [17]Nor may you eat
within your towns the tithe of your grain, your wine, and your oil, the

[a] Heb *Asherim*

12:1 These are the statutes: In chapters 6–11 Moses encouraged and inspired his listeners. Now he begins to proclaim God's law. This is a law for life in the promised land of Canaan. It begins by doing away with the worship of false gods and their symbols (12:2-3).

12:5 the place that the LORD your God will choose . . . to put his name there: Israel often practiced pagan worship at local worship sites. For this reason, Deuteronomy demands that Israel perform all sacrifices at only one place (12:6, 11, 13-14, 17, 26-27). God's unique name is present at that place (12:11, 21). This means that God has chosen and claimed it. The original readers identified this place as the temple in Jerusalem, although Deuteronomy never names it.

12:6 sacrifices: A sacrifice was a gift to God. Burnt offerings were burned completely on the altar. Most other sacrifices ended with a common meal in which worshipers shared the meat from the sacrificed animal (12:7). See also the chart "Offerings in Israel" (p. 197).

12:12 you shall rejoice: Israel's joyful worship assembly is to be inclusive. Everyone is to join in, regardless of gender, age, or social class (12:18-19).

How can we make worship life more joyful and inclusive?

12:15 within . . . your towns: Originally, all animal slaughter was a religious act. Centralizing the location for sacrifice meant that animals killed and eaten locally were no longer regarded as sacrifices. As a result, people could eat these animals, including people who were in a state of ritual uncleanness (12:21-22).

12:16 blood: The Old Testament considered blood dangerous and powerful. Blood could never be eaten. It had to be disposed of properly (12:23-25).

firstlings of your herds and your flocks, any of your votive gifts that
you vow, your freewill offerings, or your donations; 18 these you shall
eat in the presence of the LORD your God at the place that the LORD
your God will choose, you together with your son and your daughter,
your male and female slaves, and the Levites resident in your towns,
rejoicing in the presence of the LORD your God in all your undertakings. 19 Take care that you do not neglect the Levite as long as you live
in your land.

20 When the LORD your God enlarges your territory, as he has
promised you, and you say, "I am going to eat some meat," because
you wish to eat meat, you may eat meat whenever you have the desire.
21 If the place where the LORD your God will choose to put his name
is too far from you, and you slaughter as I have commanded you any
of your herd or flock that the LORD has given you, then you may eat
within your towns whenever you desire. 22 Indeed, just as gazelle or
deer is eaten, so you may eat it; the unclean and the clean alike may
eat it. 23 Only be sure that you do not eat the blood; for the blood is
the life, and you shall not eat the life with the meat. 24 Do not eat it;
you shall pour it out on the ground like water. 25 Do not eat it, so that
all may go well with you and your children after you, because you do
what is right in the sight of the LORD. 26 But the sacred donations that
are due from you, and your votive gifts, you shall bring to the place
that the LORD will choose. 27 You shall present your burnt offerings,
both the meat and the blood, on the altar of the LORD your God; the
blood of your other sacrifices shall be poured out beside[a] the altar of
the LORD your God, but the meat you may eat.

28 Be careful to obey all these words that I command you today,[b]
so that it may go well with you and with your children after you forever, because you will be doing what is good and right in the sight of
the LORD your God.

Warning against Idolatry

29 When the LORD your God has cut off before you the nations
whom you are about to enter to dispossess them, when you have
dispossessed them and live in their land, 30 take care that you are not
snared into imitating them, after they have been destroyed before
you: do not inquire concerning their gods, saying, "How did these nations worship their gods? I also want to do the same." 31 You must not
do the same for the LORD your God, because every abhorrent thing
that the LORD hates they have done for their gods. They would even
burn their sons and their daughters in the fire to their gods. 32[c] You
must diligently observe everything that I command you; do not add
to it or take anything from it.

[a] Or *on* [b] Gk Sam Syr: MT lacks *today* [c] Ch 13.1 in Heb

13 [a] If prophets or those who divine by dreams appear among you and promise you omens or portents, 2 and the omens or the portents declared by them take place, and they say, "Let us follow other gods" (whom you have not known) "and let us serve them," 3 you must not heed the words of those prophets or those who divine by dreams; for the LORD your God is testing you, to know whether you indeed love the LORD your God with all your heart and soul. 4 The LORD your God you shall follow, him alone you shall fear, his commandments you shall keep, his voice you shall obey, him you shall serve, and to him you shall hold fast. 5 But those prophets or those who divine by dreams shall be put to death for having spoken treason against the LORD your God—who brought you out of the land of Egypt and redeemed you from the house of slavery—to turn you from the way in which the LORD your God commanded you to walk. So you shall purge the evil from your midst.

6 If anyone secretly entices you—even if it is your brother, your father's son or[b] your mother's son, or your own son or daughter, or the wife you embrace, or your most intimate friend—saying, "Let us go worship other gods," whom neither you nor your ancestors have known, 7 any of the gods of the peoples that are around you, whether near you or far away from you, from one end of the earth to the other, 8 you must not yield to or heed any such persons. Show them no pity or compassion and do not shield them. 9 But you shall surely kill them; your own hand shall be first against them to execute them, and afterwards the hand of all the people. 10 Stone them to death for trying to turn you away from the LORD your God, who brought you out of the land of Egypt, out of the house of slavery. 11 Then all Israel shall hear and be afraid, and never again do any such wickedness.

12 If you hear it said about one of the towns that the LORD your God is giving you to live in, 13 that scoundrels from among you have gone out and led the inhabitants of the town astray, saying, "Let us go and worship other gods," whom you have not known, 14 then you shall inquire and make a thorough investigation. If the charge is established that such an abhorrent thing has been done among you, 15 you shall put the inhabitants of that town to the sword, utterly destroying it and everything in it—even putting its livestock to the sword. 16 All of its spoil you shall gather into its public square; then burn the town and all its spoil with fire, as a whole burnt offering to the LORD your God. It shall remain a perpetual ruin, never to be rebuilt. 17 Do not let anything devoted to destruction stick to your hand, so that the LORD may turn from his fierce anger and show you compassion, and in his compassion multiply you, as he swore to your ancestors, 18 if you obey the voice of the LORD your God by keeping all his commandments

[a] Ch 13.2 in Heb [b] Sam Gk Compare Tg: MT lacks *your father's son or*

13:1-18 Let us follow other gods: Israel was seriously tempted to worship idols and other gods. The laws of chapter 13 are harsh and rigid in order to reduce this danger. The people of Israel have a close relationship with the true God, who freed them from Egypt (13:5, 10). However, they have had no experience with other gods (13:2, 6, 13). Chapter 13 portrays three sources of temptation. First, the bogus teaching of false prophets (13:1-5) would be very tempting if backed up by omens and signs that come true (13:2; 18:22). Second, temptation could come secretly from a close relative (13:6-11). Third, an entire town might become a source of corruption (13:12-18).

What are false gods for us, and how may we avoid them? We may no longer be tempted like the people of Israel to worship Baal or other false gods of the Canaanites. Other idols, however, can take first place in our hearts. Anything or anyone we trust and love above all else is our god. The First Commandment instructs us to have no other gods and "to fear, love, and trust God above all things" *(SC:4).* See also Philippians 3:7-9. *Deuteronomy 13:1-18*

Do you agree with this statement: "Anything or anyone we trust and love above all else is our god"? Why or why not?

that I am commanding you today, doing what is right in the sight of the LORD your God.

Pagan Practices Forbidden

14:1 **lacerate...shave:** These expressions of grief were probably part of pagan worship.

14 You are children of the LORD your God. You must not lacerate yourselves or shave your forelocks for the dead. [2]For you are a people holy to the LORD your God; it is you the LORD has chosen out of all the peoples on earth to be his people, his treasured possession.

Clean and Unclean Foods

14:3 **You shall not eat:** An "abhorrent thing" damaged a person's relationship with God (7:25-26; 12:31). Old Testament law considered persons, objects, and foods to be either clean or unclean. This had nothing to do modern ideas about hygiene. People who became unclean were barred from worship and social contact. Usually uncleanness faded away on its own or could be removed by a ceremony. For New Testament teaching, see Matthew 15:10-20 and Acts 10:9-16. Deuteronomy's food law parallels Leviticus 11:2-23. It covers four categories: animals (14:4-8), fish (14:9-10), flying creatures (14:11-20), and carrion (14:21).

14:8 **pig:** Canaanite religion may have used swine as sacrifices. Another Canaanite religious practice may explain the ban on boiling a baby goat in its own mother's milk (14:21).

3 You shall not eat any abhorrent thing. [4]These are the animals you may eat: the ox, the sheep, the goat, [5]the deer, the gazelle, the roebuck, the wild goat, the ibex, the antelope, and the mountain-sheep. [6]Any animal that divides the hoof and has the hoof cleft in two, and chews the cud, among the animals, you may eat. [7]Yet of those that chew the cud or have the hoof cleft you shall not eat these: the camel, the hare, and the rock badger, because they chew the cud but do not divide the hoof; they are unclean for you. [8]And the pig, because it divides the hoof but does not chew the cud, is unclean for you. You shall not eat their meat, and you shall not touch their carcasses.

9 Of all that live in water you may eat these: whatever has fins and scales you may eat. [10]And whatever does not have fins and scales you shall not eat; it is unclean for you.

11 You may eat any clean birds. [12]But these are the ones that you shall not eat: the eagle, the vulture, the osprey, [13]the buzzard, the kite of any kind; [14]every raven of any kind; [15]the ostrich, the nighthawk, the sea gull, the hawk of any kind; [16]the little owl and the great owl, the water hen [17]and the desert owl,[a] the carrion vulture and the cormorant, [18]the stork, the heron of any kind; the hoopoe and the bat.[b] [19]And all winged insects are unclean for you; they shall not be eaten. [20]You may eat any clean winged creature.

21 You shall not eat anything that dies of itself; you may give it to aliens residing in your towns for them to eat, or you may sell it to a foreigner. For you are a people holy to the LORD your God.

You shall not boil a kid in its mother's milk.

Regulations concerning Tithes

14:22-23 **Set apart a tithe:** Each farmer is to take ten percent of the harvest and every firstborn male domestic animal to the central sanctuary to eat as a communal sacrificial meal.

22 Set apart a tithe of all the yield of your seed that is brought in yearly from the field. [23]In the presence of the LORD your God, in the place that he will choose as a dwelling for his name, you shall eat the tithe of your grain, your wine, and your oil, as well as the firstlings of your herd and flock, so that you may learn to fear the LORD your God

---

[a] Or *pelican* [b] Identification of several of the birds in verses 12–18 is uncertain

always. [24]But if, when the LORD your God has blessed you, the distance is so great that you are unable to transport it, because the place
where the LORD your God will choose to set his name is too far away
from you, [25]then you may turn it into money. With the money secure
in hand, go to the place that the LORD your God will choose; [26]spend
the money for whatever you wish—oxen, sheep, wine, strong drink,
or whatever you desire. And you shall eat there in the presence of the
LORD your God, you and your household rejoicing together. [27]As for
the Levites resident in your towns, do not neglect them, because they
have no allotment or inheritance with you.

28 Every third year you shall bring out the full tithe of your
produce for that year, and store it within your towns; [29]the Levites,
because they have no allotment or inheritance with you, as well as
the resident aliens, the orphans, and the widows in your towns, may
come and eat their fill so that the LORD your God may bless you in all
the work that you undertake.

Laws concerning the Sabbatical Year

15 Every seventh year you shall grant a remission of debts. [2]And
this is the manner of the remission: every creditor shall remit
the claim that is held against a neighbor, not exacting it of a neighbor
who is a member of the community, because the LORD's remission
has been proclaimed. [3]Of a foreigner you may exact it, but you must
remit your claim on whatever any member of your community owes
you. [4]There will, however, be no one in need among you, because the
LORD is sure to bless you in the land that the LORD your God is giving
you as a possession to occupy, [5]if only you will obey the LORD your
God by diligently observing this entire commandment that I command you today. [6]When the LORD your God has blessed you, as he
promised you, you will lend to many nations, but you will not borrow; you will rule over many nations, but they will not rule over you.

7 If there is among you anyone in need, a member of your community in any of your towns within the land that the LORD your
God is giving you, do not be hard-hearted or tight-fisted toward your
needy neighbor. [8]You should rather open your hand, willingly lending
enough to meet the need, whatever it may be. [9]Be careful that you do
not entertain a mean thought, thinking, "The seventh year, the year of
remission, is near," and therefore view your needy neighbor with hostility and give nothing; your neighbor might cry to the LORD against
you, and you would incur guilt. [10]Give liberally and be ungrudging
when you do so, for on this account the LORD your God will bless
you in all your work and in all that you undertake. [11]Since there will
never cease to be some in need on the earth, I therefore command
you, "Open your hand to the poor and needy neighbor in your land."

12 If a member of your community, whether a Hebrew man or a

14:24-26 the distance is so great: In the past, worshipers celebrated the tithe sacrifice at one of many nearby holy places. Using only one place for sacrifice required a new approach. Farmers living far from this location could convert the tithe of their crops into cash. Then they could use the cash to buy food and drink for a festive banquet at the central sanctuary.

14:28-29 Every third year: Every three years, Israelites are to store up a second ten percent to provide for people in need. This would be in the third and sixth year of the seven-year cycle described in 15:1-3.

15:1 Every seventh year: Reduction or remission of debts prevented people from falling into a permanent state of debt.

15:11 Open your hand: The Old Testament understood generous lending as helping the poor (15:9). The tragedy of poverty is unending but provides an opportunity for generosity (see Mark 14:7).

How would you answer someone who says that we should stop helping people who are poor because we can never get rid of poverty?

15:12-18 set that person free: This law revises Exodus 21:2-6. Israelites at that time could be sold into slavery to meet unpaid debts, but were released on the seventh year of service (not at the end of the seven-year cycle described in 15:1-11). The law expects kindness on the part of the slave owner (15:14). Memory of the exodus motivates obedience to this law (15:15). Deuteronomy is concerned to protect the rights of women. Therefore, it goes on to apply the law to the female slave also (15:17).

Hebrew woman, is sold[a] to you and works for you six years, in the seventh year you shall set that person free. [13]And when you send a male
slave[b] out from you a free person, you shall not send him out empty-
handed. [14]Provide liberally out of your flock, your threshing floor, and
your wine press, thus giving to him some of the bounty with which
the LORD your God has blessed you. [15]Remember that you were a
slave in the land of Egypt, and the LORD your God redeemed you;
for this reason I lay this command upon you today. [16]But if he says
to you, "I will not go out from you," because he loves you and your
household, since he is well off with you, [17]then you shall take an awl
and thrust it through his earlobe into the door, and he shall be your
slave[c] forever.

You shall do the same with regard to your female slave.[d]

18 Do not consider it a hardship when you send them out from
you free persons, because for six years they have given you services
worth the wages of hired laborers; and the LORD your God will bless
you in all that you do.

15:19-23 Every firstling male: A "firstling" was the oldest male offspring of a domestic animal mother. Its owner could gain no economic benefit from it. Instead, the owner sacrificed this animal at the central sanctuary. If the animal was too imperfect to sacrifice, it became an ordinary meal at home (12:15-16, 20-25). This law is a revision of Exodus 22:29-30.

The Firstborn of Livestock

19 Every firstling male born of your herd and flock you shall
consecrate to the LORD your God; you shall not do work with your
firstling ox nor shear the firstling of your flock. [20]You shall eat it, you
together with your household, in the presence of the LORD your God
year by year at the place that the LORD will choose. [21]But if it has any
defect—any serious defect, such as lameness or blindness—you shall
not sacrifice it to the LORD your God; [22]within your towns you may
eat it, the unclean and the clean alike, as you would a gazelle or deer.
[23]Its blood, however, you must not eat; you shall pour it out on the
ground like water.

16:1-8 Passover: Deuteronomy commands three joyous festivals at the central sanctuary. Adult males were required to make the trip (16:16), but all people were allowed to participate if they chose (16:11, 14). This law is a revision of Exodus 23:14-17. The earlier practice was to eat the Passover sacrifice locally (16:5). Now everyone will celebrate Passover in one place. This was what was new about King Josiah's Passover observance described in 2 Kings 23:21-23. Jews still followed this custom in the first century C.E. when Jesus shared Passover with his disciples in Jerusalem. After the Romans destroyed the temple in 70 C.E., Passover once more became a household celebration.

The Passover Reviewed

16 Observe the month[e] of Abib by keeping the passover to the
LORD your God, for in the month of Abib the LORD your
God brought you out of Egypt by night. [2]You shall offer the passover
sacrifice to the LORD your God, from the flock and the herd, at the
place that the LORD will choose as a dwelling for his name. [3]You must
not eat with it anything leavened. For seven days you shall eat unleavened bread with it—the bread of affliction—because you came
out of the land of Egypt in great haste, so that all the days of your life
you may remember the day of your departure from the land of Egypt.
[4]No leaven shall be seen with you in all your territory for seven days;
and none of the meat of what you slaughter on the evening of the first
day shall remain until morning. [5]You are not permitted to offer the

---

[a] Or *sells himself or herself* [b] Heb *him* [c] Or *bondman* [d] Or *bondwoman* [e] Or *new moon*

passover sacrifice within any of your towns that the LORD your God
is giving you. [6]But at the place that the LORD your God will choose as
a dwelling for his name, only there shall you offer the passover sacrifice, in the evening at sunset, the time of day when you departed from
Egypt. [7]You shall cook it and eat it at the place that the LORD your
God will choose; the next morning you may go back to your tents.
[8]For six days you shall continue to eat unleavened bread, and on the
seventh day there shall be a solemn assembly for the LORD your God,
when you shall do no work.

The Festival of Weeks Reviewed

9 You shall count seven weeks; begin to count the seven weeks
from the time the sickle is first put to the standing grain. [10]Then you
shall keep the festival of weeks to the LORD your God, contributing a
freewill offering in proportion to the blessing that you have received
from the LORD your God. [11]Rejoice before the LORD your God—you
and your sons and your daughters, your male and female slaves, the
Levites resident in your towns, as well as the strangers, the orphans,
and the widows who are among you—at the place that the LORD
your God will choose as a dwelling for his name. [12]Remember that
you were a slave in Egypt, and diligently observe these statutes.

16:9-12 seven weeks: Seven weeks later in early summer came the Festival of Weeks. Worship is an opportunity to include society's most vulnerable groups: strangers, orphans, and widows.

The Festival of Booths Reviewed

13 You shall keep the festival of booths[a] for seven days, when
you have gathered in the produce from your threshing floor and your
wine press. [14]Rejoice during your festival, you and your sons and
your daughters, your male and female slaves, as well as the Levites,
the strangers, the orphans, and the widows resident in your towns.
[15]Seven days you shall keep the festival to the LORD your God at the
place that the LORD will choose; for the LORD your God will bless
you in all your produce and in all your undertakings, and you shall
surely celebrate.

16 Three times a year all your males shall appear before the LORD
your God at the place that he will choose: at the festival of unleavened
bread, at the festival of weeks, and at the festival of booths.[a] They shall
not appear before the LORD empty-handed; [17]all shall give as they
are able, according to the blessing of the LORD your God that he has
given you.

16:13-15 booths: The autumn grape and olive harvest ended with the Festival of Booths. Deuteronomy emphasizes open participation and joy.

Municipal Judges and Officers

18 You shall appoint judges and officials throughout your tribes,
in all your towns that the LORD your God is giving you, and they shall
render just decisions for the people. [19]You must not distort justice;

16:18 You shall appoint: This is the start of a long section (16:18—18:22) that focuses on leaders: judges (16:18—17:13), the king (17:14-20), priests (18:1-8), and prophets (18:9-22).

16:19-20 only justice: Impartial justice is God's will, so bribes cannot be accepted.

[a] Or *tabernacles*; Heb *succoth*

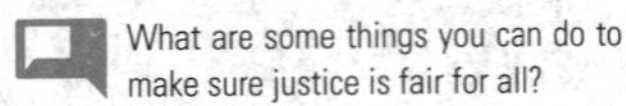
What are some things you can do to make sure justice is fair for all?

you must not show partiality; and you must not accept bribes, for a
bribe blinds the eyes of the wise and subverts the cause of those who
are in the right. [20]Justice, and only justice, you shall pursue, so that you
may live and occupy the land that the LORD your God is giving you.

Forbidden Forms of Worship

21 You shall not plant any tree as a sacred pole[a] beside the altar
that you make for the LORD your God; [22]nor shall you set up a stone
pillar—things that the LORD your God hates.

17 You must not sacrifice to the LORD your God an ox or a sheep
that has a defect, anything seriously wrong; for that is abhorrent to the LORD your God.

17:2-7 If there is found: A sample case illustrates fair legal procedures. True justice requires careful questioning and more than one eyewitness to a crime. Witnesses in a death penalty case must throw the first stones during the execution. By doing this, they confirm that they have spoken the truth (see John 8:7).

2 If there is found among you, in one of your towns that the LORD
your God is giving you, a man or woman who does what is evil in the
sight of the LORD your God, and transgresses his covenant [3]by going
to serve other gods and worshiping them—whether the sun or the
moon or any of the host of heaven, which I have forbidden— [4]and
if it is reported to you or you hear of it, and you make a thorough inquiry, and the charge is proved true that such an abhorrent thing has
occurred in Israel, [5]then you shall bring out to your gates that man
or that woman who has committed this crime and you shall stone
the man or woman to death. [6]On the evidence of two or three witnesses the death sentence shall be executed; a person must not be put
to death on the evidence of only one witness. [7]The hands of the witnesses shall be the first raised against the person to execute the death
penalty, and afterward the hands of all the people. So you shall purge
the evil from your midst.

Legal Decisions by Priests and Judges

8 If a judicial decision is too difficult for you to make between
one kind of bloodshed and another, one kind of legal right and another, or one kind of assault and another—any such matters of dispute in your towns—then you shall immediately go up to the place
that the LORD your God will choose, [9]where you shall consult with
the levitical priests and the judge who is in office in those days; they
shall announce to you the decision in the case. [10]Carry out exactly
the decision that they announce to you from the place that the LORD
will choose, diligently observing everything they instruct you. [11]You
must carry out fully the law that they interpret for you or the ruling
that they announce to you; do not turn aside from the decision that
they announce to you, either to the right or to the left. [12]As for anyone
who presumes to disobey the priest appointed to minister there to the
LORD your God, or the judge, that person shall die. So you shall purge

[a] Heb *Asherah*

the evil from Israel. [13]All the people will hear and be afraid, and will
not act presumptuously again.

Limitations of Royal Authority

14 When you have come into the land that the LORD your God
is giving you, and have taken possession of it and settled in it, and
you say, "I will set a king over me, like all the nations that are around
me," [15]you may indeed set over you a king whom the LORD your God
will choose. One of your own community you may set as king over
you; you are not permitted to put a foreigner over you, who is not of
your own community. [16]Even so, he must not acquire many horses
for himself, or return the people to Egypt in order to acquire more
horses, since the LORD has said to you, "You must never return that
way again." [17]And he must not acquire many wives for himself, or
else his heart will turn away; also silver and gold he must not acquire
in great quantity for himself. [18]When he has taken the throne of his
kingdom, he shall have a copy of this law written for him in the presence of the levitical priests. [19]It shall remain with him and he shall
read in it all the days of his life, so that he may learn to fear the LORD
his God, diligently observing all the words of this law and these statutes, [20]neither exalting himself above other members of the community nor turning aside from the commandment, either to the right
or to the left, so that he and his descendants may reign long over his
kingdom in Israel.

17:14-20 a king: Deuteronomy limits a king's authority and power. If the people have a king, he must be a fellow Israelite and follow God's law. Pomp, wealth, and military power (shown in the number of horses, for example) must be limited. Controlling the number of wives restricted a king's ability to form alliances by marrying into royal families in other lands. The king must obey the law (17:18-19). He would be on the same level as ordinary citizens (17:20). Contrast this description of an ideal king with King Solomon (see 1 Kgs 10-11).

Privileges of Priests and Levites

18 The levitical priests, the whole tribe of Levi, shall have no allotment or inheritance within Israel. They may eat the sacrifices that are the LORD's portion[a] [2]but they shall have no inheritance
among the other members of the community; the LORD is their inheritance, as he promised them.

3 This shall be the priests' due from the people, from those offering a sacrifice, whether an ox or a sheep: they shall give to the priest
the shoulder, the two jowls, and the stomach. [4]The first fruits of your
grain, your wine, and your oil, as well as the first of the fleece of your
sheep, you shall give him. [5]For the LORD your God has chosen Levi[b]
out of all your tribes, to stand and minister in the name of the LORD,
him and his sons for all time.

18:1-5 levitical priests: Unlike most of the Old Testament, Deuteronomy does not distinguish priests from other members of the tribe of Levi. The basic means of support for priests came from their share of the sacrifices.

6 If a Levite leaves any of your towns, from wherever he has
been residing in Israel, and comes to the place that the LORD will
choose (and he may come whenever he wishes), [7]then he may minister in the name of the LORD his God, like all his fellow-Levites
who stand to minister there before the LORD. [8]They shall have equal

18:6-8 he may come...he may minister: Shutting down neighborhood sanctuaries would reduce or eliminate the income of local priests. To offset this, any member of the Levi tribe who chooses to relocate to the central sanctuary will receive appointment as a priest and income there.

[a] Meaning of Heb uncertain [b] Heb *him*

portions to eat, even though they have income from the sale of family possessions.[a]

Child-Sacrifice, Divination, and Magic Prohibited

9 When you come into the land that the LORD your God is giving
you, you must not learn to imitate the abhorrent practices of those nations. 10 No one shall be found among you who makes a son or daughter pass through fire, or who practices divination, or is a soothsayer,
or an augur, or a sorcerer, 11 or one who casts spells, or who consults
ghosts or spirits, or who seeks oracles from the dead. 12 For whoever
does these things is abhorrent to the LORD; it is because of such abhorrent practices that the LORD your God is driving them out before
you. 13 You must remain completely loyal to the LORD your God. 14 Although these nations that you are about to dispossess do give heed
to soothsayers and diviners, as for you, the LORD your God does not
permit you to do so.

A New Prophet Like Moses

15 The LORD your God will raise up for you a prophet[b] like me
from among your own people; you shall heed such a prophet.[c] 16 This
is what you requested of the LORD your God at Horeb on the day of
the assembly when you said: "If I hear the voice of the LORD my God
any more, or ever again see this great fire, I will die." 17 Then the LORD
replied to me: "They are right in what they have said. 18 I will raise up
for them a prophet[b] like you from among their own people; I will
put my words in the mouth of the prophet,[d] who shall speak to them
everything that I command. 19 Anyone who does not heed the words
that the prophet[e] shall speak in my name, I myself will hold accountable. 20 But any prophet who speaks in the name of other gods, or who
presumes to speak in my name a word that I have not commanded the
prophet to speak—that prophet shall die." 21 You may say to yourself,
"How can we recognize a word that the LORD has not spoken?" 22 If a
prophet speaks in the name of the LORD but the thing does not take
place or prove true, it is a word that the LORD has not spoken. The
prophet has spoken it presumptuously; do not be frightened by it.

Laws concerning the Cities of Refuge

19 When the LORD your God has cut off the nations whose
land the LORD your God is giving you, and you have dispossessed them and settled in their towns and in their houses, 2 you shall
set apart three cities in the land that the LORD your God is giving you
to possess. 3 You shall calculate the distances[f] and divide into three

[a] Meaning of Heb uncertain [b] Or *prophets* [c] Or *such prophets* [d] Or *mouths of the prophets*
[e] Heb *he* [f] Or *prepare roads to them*

18:9-14 abhorrent practices: Israel must avoid Canaanite methods of divination (seeking answers from the world of gods and spirits). Instead, the people should remain loyal to God and to God's covenant or mutual agreement with them. Saul's meeting with a woman at Endor is an example of seeking oracles from the dead (18:11; see 1 Sam 28:6-19).

18:20-22 any prophet: It would be easy to disregard prophecy spoken in the name of a false god. Judging the truthfulness of a prophecy from someone who claims to speak in the name of the LORD would be more difficult. If a prophetic word or promised sign does not come true, it has not come from God (13:1-5).

How can we know whether someone who claims to speak for God is telling the truth?

19:1-7 set apart three cities: Although there was no formal punishment system in Israel, a member of the victim's family retaliated as punishment for murder. This person was the "avenger of blood" (19:6; see the story in 2 Sam 14:4-11). Before one sacrificial altar was established, someone who had killed another accidentally could find a place of safety or asylum by reaching one of the local altars (see Exod 21:13-14; 1 Kgs 1:50-53). To replace these local altars, new places of asylum had to be set up around the country. Moses has already set up three such cities east of the Jordan (4:41-43). Joshua would later establish three on the west side (see Josh 20). See Map 4, p. 2102.

regions the land that the LORD your God gives you as a possession, so
that any homicide can flee to one of them.
4 Now this is the case of a homicide who might flee there and live,
that is, someone who has killed another person unintentionally when
the two had not been at enmity before: 5 Suppose someone goes into
the forest with another to cut wood, and when one of them swings
the ax to cut down a tree, the head slips from the handle and strikes
the other person who then dies; the killer may flee to one of these
cities and live. 6 But if the distance is too great, the avenger of blood
in hot anger might pursue and overtake and put the killer to death,
although a death sentence was not deserved, since the two had not
been at enmity before. 7 Therefore I command you: You shall set apart
three cities.
8 If the LORD your God enlarges your territory, as he swore to
your ancestors—and he will give you all the land that he promised
your ancestors to give you, 9 provided you diligently observe this entire commandment that I command you today, by loving the LORD
your God and walking always in his ways—then you shall add three
more cities to these three, 10 so that the blood of an innocent person
may not be shed in the land that the LORD your God is giving you as
an inheritance, thereby bringing bloodguilt upon you.
11 But if someone at enmity with another lies in wait and attacks and takes the life of that person, and flees into one of these cities, 12 then the elders of the killer's city shall send to have the culprit
taken from there and handed over to the avenger of blood to be put
to death. 13 Show no pity; you shall purge the guilt of innocent blood
from Israel, so that it may go well with you.

19:11-12 lies in wait: This case of premeditated murder differs from the unintentional killing described by 19:4-6. The right of asylum does not apply to this person.

Property Boundaries

14 You must not move your neighbor's boundary marker, set up
by former generations, on the property that will be allotted to you in
the land that the LORD your God is giving you to possess.

19:14 boundary marker: Inherited land was a gift from God. It was possible to move a boundary line in secret (27:17) or by putting pressure on landowners who were poor, but Israel believed that the original family should always own the land.

Law concerning Witnesses

15 A single witness shall not suffice to convict a person of any
crime or wrongdoing in connection with any offense that may be
committed. Only on the evidence of two or three witnesses shall a
charge be sustained. 16 If a malicious witness comes forward to accuse
someone of wrongdoing, 17 then both parties to the dispute shall appear before the LORD, before the priests and the judges who are in
office in those days, 18 and the judges shall make a thorough inquiry. If
the witness is a false witness, having testified falsely against another,
19 then you shall do to the false witness just as the false witness had
meant to do to the other. So you shall purge the evil from your midst.
20 The rest shall hear and be afraid, and a crime such as this shall never

19:16-21 a malicious witness: The justice system depended almost entirely on eyewitnesses, so false testimony was sternly prohibited and punished. This law restates and expands Exodus 23:1, taking into account the central court established in 17:8-13.

again be committed among you. [21]Show no pity: life for life, eye for eye, tooth for tooth, hand for hand, foot for foot.

Rules of Warfare

20 When you go out to war against your enemies, and see horses and chariots, an army larger than your own, you shall not be afraid of them; for the LORD your God is with you, who brought you up from the land of Egypt. [2]Before you engage in battle, the priest shall come forward and speak to the troops, [3]and shall say to them: "Hear, O Israel! Today you are drawing near to do battle against your enemies. Do not lose heart, or be afraid, or panic, or be in dread of them; [4]for it is the LORD your God who goes with you, to fight for you against your enemies, to give you victory." [5]Then the officials shall address the troops, saying, "Has anyone built a new house but not dedicated it? He should go back to his house, or he might die in the battle and another dedicate it. [6]Has anyone planted a vineyard but not yet enjoyed its fruit? He should go back to his house, or he might die in the battle and another be first to enjoy its fruit. [7]Has anyone become engaged to a woman but not yet married her? He should go back to his house, or he might die in the battle and another marry her." [8]The officials shall continue to address the troops, saying, "Is anyone afraid or disheartened? He should go back to his house, or he might cause the heart of his comrades to melt like his own." [9]When the officials have finished addressing the troops, then the commanders shall take charge of them.

10 When you draw near to a town to fight against it, offer it terms of peace. [11]If it accepts your terms of peace and surrenders to you, then all the people in it shall serve you at forced labor. [12]If it does not submit to you peacefully, but makes war against you, then you shall besiege it; [13]and when the LORD your God gives it into your hand, you shall put all its males to the sword. [14]You may, however, take as your booty the women, the children, livestock, and everything else in the town, all its spoil. You may enjoy the spoil of your enemies, which the LORD your God has given you. [15]Thus you shall treat all the towns that are very far from you, which are not towns of the nations here. [16]But as for the towns of these peoples that the LORD your God is giving you as an inheritance, you must not let anything that breathes remain alive. [17]You shall annihilate them—the Hittites and the Amorites, the Canaanites and the Perizzites, the Hivites and the Jebusites—just as the LORD your God has commanded, [18]so that they may not teach you to do all the abhorrent things that they do for their gods, and you thus sin against the LORD your God.

19 If you besiege a town for a long time, making war against it in order to take it, you must not destroy its trees by wielding an ax against them. Although you may take food from them, you must not

20:1 war: The people of Israel believed that God fought on their side to conquer the promised land and defend them from their enemies. The phrase "holy war" is often used to describe this belief. Yet it is more accurate to say God acted as "Divine Warrior" (see Exod 15:3). God provided guidance and led heavenly armies. Israel's chief duty was to have faith in God's victorious power. Chapter 20 outlines the proper way to conduct the battles Israel was to fight together with God as Divine Warrior.

What should we do in a time of war? This is a tough question for Lutherans and all Christians. Jesus taught us to promote peace (see Matt 5:39), even though God sometimes commanded Israel to go to war in the Old Testament. Some Christians refuse to fight in any wars. Other Christians believe that defensive wars are sometimes a tragic necessity, and Christians may fight in such wars if commanded by their government. In this view, an unjust war or a war fought by an evil government puts Christians in a very difficult position. See also Romans 12:17-21. *Deuteronomy 20*

20:2-8 Before you engage in battle: Early Israel did not have a trained professional army. Instead, civilians joined together to fight. First, a priest encourages their faith. Then an official describes those who will be allowed not to fight. This is done to be fair to anyone who deserves to live long enough to enjoy some new venture. Releasing anyone who was afraid would prevent those people from spreading fear through the rest of the army.

20:10-15 terms of peace: Israel's plan of action depends on whether they are attacking a city farther away (20:15) or one within the borders of the promised land of Canaan (20:16-18). Cities outside the promised land are to be offered a way to surrender. Forced labor means people in a surrendering city will be required to work on public construction projects against their wills. If the city refuses to submit, the outcome is harsh. All adult males are to be killed, because they might threaten Israel's future security. Israel may make slaves of the women and children and plunder everything of value.

20:16 not let anything...remain alive: Things are different for a city inside the promised land. Its entire population and livestock must be wiped out. Joshua 1–12 describes the conquest of Canaan in similar ways.

cut them down. Are trees in the field human beings that they should come under siege from you? 20You may destroy only the trees that you know do not produce food; you may cut them down for use in building siegeworks against the town that makes war with you, until it falls.

Law concerning Murder by Persons Unknown

21 If, in the land that the LORD your God is giving you to possess, a body is found lying in open country, and it is not known who struck the person down, 2then your elders and your judges shall come out to measure the distances to the towns that are near the body. 3The elders of the town nearest the body shall take a heifer that has never been worked, one that has not pulled in the yoke; 4the elders of that town shall bring the heifer down to a wadi with running water, which is neither plowed nor sown, and shall break the heifer's neck there in the wadi. 5Then the priests, the sons of Levi, shall come forward, for the LORD your God has chosen them to minister to him and to pronounce blessings in the name of the LORD, and by their decision all cases of dispute and assault shall be settled. 6All the elders of that town nearest the body shall wash their hands over the heifer whose neck was broken in the wadi, 7and they shall declare: "Our hands did not shed this blood, nor were we witnesses to it. 8Absolve, O LORD, your people Israel, whom you redeemed; do not let the guilt of innocent blood remain in the midst of your people Israel." Then they will be absolved of bloodguilt. 9So you shall purge the guilt of innocent blood from your midst, because you must do what is right in the sight of the LORD.

Female Captives

10 When you go out to war against your enemies, and the LORD your God hands them over to you and you take them captive, 11suppose you see among the captives a beautiful woman whom you desire and want to marry, 12and so you bring her home to your house: she shall shave her head, pare her nails, 13discard her captive's garb, and shall remain in your house a full month, mourning for her father and mother; after that you may go in to her and be her husband, and she shall be your wife. 14But if you are not satisfied with her, you shall let her go free and not sell her for money. You must not treat her as a slave, since you have dishonored her.

The Right of the Firstborn

15 If a man has two wives, one of them loved and the other disliked, and if both the loved and the disliked have borne him sons, the firstborn being the son of the one who is disliked, 16then on the day when he wills his possessions to his sons, he is not permitted to treat

20:17 You shall annihilate them: Both materials taken and people captured in holy war were considered the property of God as Divine Warrior (see 20:1 and note). They were to be eliminated to prevent Israel from making use of captured goods and animals or the forced labor of the defeated people. This practice is often called the "ban." Many biblical scholars doubt that Israel ever actually followed this terrible custom. The ban also appears in 2:34; 3:6; 7:2, 26; 13:16-18.

20:19-20 its trees: The practice of not destroying trees during warfare would reduce devastation to the area's environment and economy.

21:1-9 a body is found: Israel believed that an unsolved murder created an unseen force that put the nearest community in danger (21:9). The death of a young cow and symbolic hand washing would remove this threat. The heifer is killed in a nonsacrificial way (21:4). The ceremony transfers the guilt to the animal. Running water (21:4) carries the guilt away.

21:10-14 take them captive…a beautiful woman: A woman captured in war would have no male relatives to protect her rights or negotiate her marriage. This law at least gives her time to grieve before marriage. It also protects her from becoming a slave later on. Their sexual relationship sets up the husband's responsibility to her. The woman seems to have no choice in the matter.

21:15-17 two wives: Perhaps a husband loves a second wife more than he loves his first wife, who is also mother to his oldest son. He must still give the oldest son his proper share of the inheritance. "Double portion" (21:17) means dividing the inheritance into shares equal to the number of sons plus one, then giving the oldest son two shares. Thus, the older of two sons would get two-thirds. The oldest of three sons would receive one-half (two-fourths), and so forth.

the son of the loved as the firstborn in preference to the son of the disliked, who is the firstborn. [17]He must acknowledge as firstborn the son of the one who is disliked, giving him a double portion[a] of all that he has; since he is the first issue of his virility, the right of the firstborn is his.

Rebellious Children

21:18-21 a stubborn and rebellious son: His behavior shames both father and mother. In fact, both parents must agree to take action. Punishment is both extreme and public in order to serve as an effective warning. Critics of Jesus echoed this passage when accusing him of being "a glutton and a drunkard" (see Matt 11:19).

18 If someone has a stubborn and rebellious son who will not obey his father and mother, who does not heed them when they discipline him, [19]then his father and his mother shall take hold of him and bring him out to the elders of his town at the gate of that place. [20]They shall say to the elders of his town, "This son of ours is stubborn and rebellious. He will not obey us. He is a glutton and a drunkard." [21]Then all the men of the town shall stone him to death. So you shall purge the evil from your midst; and all Israel will hear, and be afraid.

Miscellaneous Laws

21:22-23 you hang him on a tree: Israel's concept of clean and unclean meant that extended exposure of a hanged body would defile the land. Paul expands on this idea to illustrate the power of the cross (see Gal 3:13).

22 When someone is convicted of a crime punishable by death and is executed, and you hang him on a tree, [23]his corpse must not remain all night upon the tree; you shall bury him that same day, for anyone hung on a tree is under God's curse. You must not defile the land that the Lord your God is giving you for possession.

22:1-4 your neighbor's ox: These laws restate and revise Exodus 23:4-5. The Exodus version encourages the people to assist their enemies. Deuteronomy promotes giving help to neighbors, including those who are unknown.

22 You shall not watch your neighbor's ox or sheep straying away and ignore them; you shall take them back to their owner. [2]If the owner does not reside near you or you do not know who the owner is, you shall bring it to your own house, and it shall remain with you until the owner claims it; then you shall return it. [3]You shall do the same with a neighbor's donkey; you shall do the same with a neighbor's garment; and you shall do the same with anything else that your neighbor loses and you find. You may not withhold your help.

4 You shall not see your neighbor's donkey or ox fallen on the road and ignore it; you shall help to lift it up.

22:5 shall not wear: Gender roles were defined by the culture. Israel's concept of clean and unclean meant keeping these roles clear. This law may refer to forbidden religious practices.

5 A woman shall not wear a man's apparel, nor shall a man put on a woman's garment; for whoever does such things is abhorrent to the Lord your God.

22:6-7 a bird's nest: This environmentally sensitive law promotes conservation (compare this with 20:19-20) and respect for parents, even among animals. Compare this with the last sentence of 14:21.

6 If you come on a bird's nest, in any tree or on the ground, with fledglings or eggs, with the mother sitting on the fledglings or on the eggs, you shall not take the mother with the young. [7]Let the mother go, taking only the young for yourself, in order that it may go well with you and you may live long.

8 When you build a new house, you shall make a parapet for your

How does your faith make a difference in the way you treat animals and the environment?

[a] Heb *two-thirds*

roof; otherwise you might have bloodguilt on your house, if anyone
should fall from it.
9 You shall not sow your vineyard with a second kind of seed, or
the whole yield will have to be forfeited, both the crop that you have
sown and the yield of the vineyard itself.
10 You shall not plow with an ox and a donkey yoked together.
11 You shall not wear clothes made of wool and linen woven together.
12 You shall make tassels on the four corners of the cloak with
which you cover yourself.

Laws concerning Sexual Relations

13 Suppose a man marries a woman, but after going in to her, he
dislikes her 14 and makes up charges against her, slandering her by saying, "I married this woman; but when I lay with her, I did not find
evidence of her virginity." 15 The father of the young woman and her
mother shall then submit the evidence of the young woman's virginity
to the elders of the city at the gate. 16 The father of the young woman
shall say to the elders: "I gave my daughter in marriage to this man
but he dislikes her; 17 now he has made up charges against her, saying,
'I did not find evidence of your daughter's virginity.' But here is the
evidence of my daughter's virginity." Then they shall spread out the
cloth before the elders of the town. 18 The elders of that town shall take
the man and punish him; 19 they shall fine him one hundred shekels of
silver (which they shall give to the young woman's father) because he
has slandered a virgin of Israel. She shall remain his wife; he shall not
be permitted to divorce her as long as he lives.
20 If, however, this charge is true, that evidence of the young
woman's virginity was not found, 21 then they shall bring the young
woman out to the entrance of her father's house and the men of her
town shall stone her to death, because she committed a disgraceful
act in Israel by prostituting herself in her father's house. So you shall
purge the evil from your midst.
22 If a man is caught lying with the wife of another man, both
of them shall die, the man who lay with the woman as well as the
woman. So you shall purge the evil from Israel.
23 If there is a young woman, a virgin already engaged to be married, and a man meets her in the town and lies with her, 24 you shall
bring both of them to the gate of that town and stone them to death,
the young woman because she did not cry for help in the town and
the man because he violated his neighbor's wife. So you shall purge
the evil from your midst.
25 But if the man meets the engaged woman in the open country, and the man seizes her and lies with her, then only the man who
lay with her shall die. 26 You shall do nothing to the young woman;

22:9-11 You shall not sow…plow…wear: Israel's concept of clean and unclean meant that these mixtures caused impurity. They violated distinctions made in creation.

22:12 tassels: According to Numbers 15:38-40, these knotted threads reminded Israel to obey the law.

22:13-19 he dislikes her: Rather than simply divorcing his unwanted wife (24:1-4), the husband maliciously makes up lies against her. Evidence of virginity refers to a cloth showing blood from the first time the couple had intercourse. Israel conducted its legal business in the area around the gate. Compensation paid to the woman's father protects her reputation. A prohibition on divorce protects the woman from retaliation. Notice that her wishes in the matter are not taken into account.

22:20-21 if…true: "Disgraceful act" refers to shocking conduct, often sexual in nature, which violated Israel's core values.

22:22-29 If a man is caught: To understand these four legal cases, it is helpful to know some things about Israel's culture at this time. Society protected the rights of husbands and fathers (22:22, 24, 29) more than those of the women involved. Engagement (22:23) was legally the same as marriage. Paying money to the woman's father (22:29) would have carried out the custom of paying a "bride price" to a new wife's family. Prohibiting future divorce was a way of providing support and security for the woman.

the young woman has not committed an offense punishable by
death, because this case is like that of someone who attacks and
murders a neighbor. [27]Since he found her in the open country, the
engaged woman may have cried for help, but there was no one to
rescue her.

28 If a man meets a virgin who is not engaged, and seizes her and
lies with her, and they are caught in the act, [29]the man who lay with
her shall give fifty shekels of silver to the young woman's father, and
she shall become his wife. Because he violated her he shall not be permitted to divorce her as long as he lives.

22:30 his father's wife: Israelites lived together in large extended families. Forbidding marriage to the father's former wife (after divorce or death) protected family unity and honor.

30[a] A man shall not marry his father's wife, thereby violating his
father's rights.[b]

Those Excluded from the Assembly

23:1-4 the assembly of the LORD: When Israel gathered for worship, the notion of clean and unclean required keeping out anyone considered to be permanently impure. Those with physical abnormalities as well as children born out of an "illicit union" (perhaps incest) were believed to be unclean. The Ammonite and Moabite nations had a history of intentional hostility against Israel. They also supposedly originated from incestuous relationships (see Gen 19:30-38).

23 No one whose testicles are crushed or whose penis is cut off
shall be admitted to the assembly of the LORD.

2 Those born of an illicit union shall not be admitted to the assembly of the LORD. Even to the tenth generation, none of their descendants shall be admitted to the assembly of the LORD.

3 No Ammonite or Moabite shall be admitted to the assembly of
the LORD. Even to the tenth generation, none of their descendants
shall be admitted to the assembly of the LORD, [4]because they did not
meet you with food and water on your journey out of Egypt, and
because they hired against you Balaam son of Beor, from Pethor of
Mesopotamia, to curse you. [5](Yet the LORD your God refused to heed
Balaam; the LORD your God turned the curse into a blessing for you,
because the LORD your God loved you.) [6]You shall never promote
their welfare or their prosperity as long as you live.

7 You shall not abhor any of the Edomites, for they are your kin.
You shall not abhor any of the Egyptians, because you were an alien
residing in their land. [8]The children of the third generation that are
born to them may be admitted to the assembly of the LORD.

Sanitary, Ritual, and Humanitarian Precepts

9 When you are encamped against your enemies you shall guard
against any impropriety.

10 If one of you becomes unclean because of a nocturnal emission, then he shall go outside the camp; he must not come within the
camp. [11]When evening comes, he shall wash himself with water, and
when the sun has set, he may come back into the camp.

23:12-14 a designated area: Israel believed that God as Divine Warrior was present in the war camp. Therefore, ritual purity was essential.

12 You shall have a designated area outside the camp to which
you shall go. [13]With your utensils you shall have a trowel; when you
relieve yourself outside, you shall dig a hole with it and then cover

---

[a] Ch 23.1 in Heb [b] Heb *uncovering his father's skirt*

up your excrement. 14 Because the LORD your God travels along with your camp, to save you and to hand over your enemies to you, therefore your camp must be holy, so that he may not see anything indecent among you and turn away from you.

15 Slaves who have escaped to you from their owners shall not be given back to them. 16 They shall reside with you, in your midst, in any place they choose in any one of your towns, wherever they please; you shall not oppress them.

17 None of the daughters of Israel shall be a temple prostitute; none of the sons of Israel shall be a temple prostitute. 18 You shall not bring the fee of a prostitute or the wages of a male prostitute[a] into the house of the LORD your God in payment for any vow, for both of these are abhorrent to the LORD your God.

19 You shall not charge interest on loans to another Israelite, interest on money, interest on provisions, interest on anything that is lent. 20 On loans to a foreigner you may charge interest, but on loans to another Israelite you may not charge interest, so that the LORD your God may bless you in all your undertakings in the land that you are about to enter and possess.

21 If you make a vow to the LORD your God, do not postpone fulfilling it; for the LORD your God will surely require it of you, and you would incur guilt. 22 But if you refrain from vowing, you will not incur guilt. 23 Whatever your lips utter you must diligently perform, just as you have freely vowed to the LORD your God with your own mouth.

24 If you go into your neighbor's vineyard, you may eat your fill of grapes, as many as you wish, but you shall not put any in a container.

25 If you go into your neighbor's standing grain, you may pluck the ears with your hand, but you shall not put a sickle to your neighbor's standing grain.

Laws concerning Marriage and Divorce

24 Suppose a man enters into marriage with a woman, but she does not please him because he finds something objectionable about her, and so he writes her a certificate of divorce, puts it in her hand, and sends her out of his house; she then leaves his house 2 and goes off to become another man's wife. 3 Then suppose the second man dislikes her, writes her a bill of divorce, puts it in her hand, and sends her out of his house (or the second man who married her dies); 4 her first husband, who sent her away, is not permitted to take her again to be his wife after she has been defiled; for that would be abhorrent to the LORD, and you shall not bring guilt on the land that the LORD your God is giving you as a possession.

[a] Heb *a dog*

23:17 temple prostitute: The translation is probably incorrect. The Hebrew word describes banned female and male religious people of some kind, but they were not necessarily involved with sex.

23:18 fee . . . wages: To ensure ritual purity, obligations to the temple could not be paid with "dirty money" derived from prostitution.

23:19-20 interest on loans: Lending without charging interest was a way for wealthy Israelites to help poorer ones during hard times. This law restates Exodus 22:25.

23:24-25 your neighbor's vineyard . . . standing grain: The poor could gather leftover food from fields and orchards (24:19-22). See also Matthew 12:1-2. The law also protects landowners from those who might abuse this practice.

24:1-4 certificate of divorce: Only husbands could write a certificate of divorce. They could do so even for trivial reasons. Written proof of the divorce protected the woman by ensuring her right to remarry.

Miscellaneous Laws

5 When a man is newly married, he shall not go out with the army
or be charged with any related duty. He shall be free at home one year,
to be happy with the wife whom he has married.
6 No one shall take a mill or an upper millstone in pledge, for that
would be taking a life in pledge.
7 If someone is caught kidnaping another Israelite, enslaving or
selling the Israelite, then that kidnaper shall die. So you shall purge
the evil from your midst.
8 Guard against an outbreak of a leprous[a] skin disease by being
very careful; you shall carefully observe whatever the levitical priests
instruct you, just as I have commanded them. 9 Remember what the
LORD your God did to Miriam on your journey out of Egypt.
10 When you make your neighbor a loan of any kind, you shall
not go into the house to take the pledge. 11 You shall wait outside,
while the person to whom you are making the loan brings the pledge
out to you. 12 If the person is poor, you shall not sleep in the garment
given you as[b] the pledge. 13 You shall give the pledge back by sunset, so
that your neighbor may sleep in the cloak and bless you; and it will be
to your credit before the LORD your God.
14 You shall not withhold the wages of poor and needy laborers,
whether other Israelites or aliens who reside in your land in one of
your towns. 15 You shall pay them their wages daily before sunset, because they are poor and their livelihood depends on them; otherwise
they might cry to the LORD against you, and you would incur guilt.
16 Parents shall not be put to death for their children, nor shall
children be put to death for their parents; only for their own crimes
may persons be put to death.
17 You shall not deprive a resident alien or an orphan of justice;
you shall not take a widow's garment in pledge. 18 Remember that you
were a slave in Egypt and the LORD your God redeemed you from
there; therefore I command you to do this.
19 When you reap your harvest in your field and forget a sheaf in
the field, you shall not go back to get it; it shall be left for the alien, the
orphan, and the widow, so that the LORD your God may bless you in
all your undertakings. 20 When you beat your olive trees, do not strip
what is left; it shall be for the alien, the orphan, and the widow.
21 When you gather the grapes of your vineyard, do not glean
what is left; it shall be for the alien, the orphan, and the widow. 22 Remember that you were a slave in the land of Egypt; therefore I am
commanding you to do this.

25 Suppose two persons have a dispute and enter into litigation, and the judges decide between them, declaring one to

24:8-9 leprous skin disease: This phrase describes a number of skin ailments, not all as serious as what is called leprosy today. Numbers 12:10-15 describes Miriam's leprosy.

24:10-13 When you make your neighbor a loan: This set of laws protects the dignity of poor people who must provide collateral for a loan or have given up their collateral.

24:14-15 You shall not withhold: Employers must deal fairly with day laborers who live from hand to mouth. Matthew 20:1-15 reflects this situation.

24:19-21 When you reap: As a sort of "food bank," poor people had the right to gather whatever the harvesters left behind. The story of Ruth refers to this practice, called gleaning.

What does your church or community do to feed the hungry? What can you do to help?

[a] A term for several skin diseases; precise meaning uncertain [b] Heb lacks *the garment given you as*

be in the right and the other to be in the wrong. [2]If the one in the wrong deserves to be flogged, the judge shall make that person lie down and be beaten in his presence with the number of lashes proportionate to the offense. [3]Forty lashes may be given but not more; if more lashes than these are given, your neighbor will be degraded in your sight.

4 You shall not muzzle an ox while it is treading out the grain.

Levirate Marriage

5 When brothers reside together, and one of them dies and has no son, the wife of the deceased shall not be married outside the family to a stranger. Her husband's brother shall go in to her, taking her in marriage, and performing the duty of a husband's brother to her, [6]and the firstborn whom she bears shall succeed to the name of the deceased brother, so that his name may not be blotted out of Israel. [7]But if the man has no desire to marry his brother's widow, then his brother's widow shall go up to the elders at the gate and say, "My husband's brother refuses to perpetuate his brother's name in Israel; he will not perform the duty of a husband's brother to me." [8]Then the elders of his town shall summon him and speak to him. If he persists, saying, "I have no desire to marry her," [9]then his brother's wife shall go up to him in the presence of the elders, pull his sandal off his foot, spit in his face, and declare, "This is what is done to the man who does not build up his brother's house." [10]Throughout Israel his family shall be known as "the house of him whose sandal was pulled off."

Various Commands

11 If men get into a fight with one another, and the wife of one intervenes to rescue her husband from the grip of his opponent by reaching out and seizing his genitals, [12]you shall cut off her hand; show no pity.

13 You shall not have in your bag two kinds of weights, large and small. [14]You shall not have in your house two kinds of measures, large and small. [15]You shall have only a full and honest weight; you shall have only a full and honest measure, so that your days may be long in the land that the Lord your God is giving you. [16]For all who do such things, all who act dishonestly, are abhorrent to the Lord your God.

17 Remember what Amalek did to you on your journey out of Egypt, [18]how he attacked you on the way, when you were faint and weary, and struck down all who lagged behind you; he did not fear God. [19]Therefore when the Lord your God has given you rest from all your enemies on every hand, in the land that the Lord your God is giving you as an inheritance to possess, you shall blot out the remembrance of Amalek from under heaven; do not forget.

25:2-3 Forty lashes: The offender is punished appropriately, but he must not be humiliated by excessive brutality. It became the custom to stop at thirty-nine lashes in order to avoid breaking this law by mistake (see 2 Cor 11:24).

25:4 **You shall not muzzle an ox:** This law concerned the well-being of domestic animals.

25:5-10 Her husband's brother: The custom of a man's brother marrying his widow (called "levirate marriage") protected the rights of a deceased husband by insuring an heir to carry on his name. The law also protected the widow from poverty and childlessness. The surviving brother could refuse to perform this duty, but had to be prepared to endure public ridicule. The story of Ruth and the challenge to Jesus described in Luke 20:28-33 both refer to this practice.

25:13-16 two kinds of weights: Dishonesty in business would damage Israel's relationship with God (see Lev 19:35-36; Mic 6:10-11).

First Fruits and Tithes

26 When you have come into the land that the LORD your God
is giving you as an inheritance to possess, and you possess
it, and settle in it, [2]you shall take some of the first of all the fruit of the
ground, which you harvest from the land that the LORD your God is
giving you, and you shall put it in a basket and go to the place that
the LORD your God will choose as a dwelling for his name. [3]You shall
go to the priest who is in office at that time, and say to him, "Today I
declare to the LORD your God that I have come into the land that the
LORD swore to our ancestors to give us." [4]When the priest takes the
basket from your hand and sets it down before the altar of the LORD
your God, [5]you shall make this response before the LORD your God:
"A wandering Aramean was my ancestor; he went down into Egypt
and lived there as an alien, few in number, and there he became a great
nation, mighty and populous. [6]When the Egyptians treated us harshly
and afflicted us, by imposing hard labor on us, [7]we cried to the LORD,
the God of our ancestors; the LORD heard our voice and saw our affliction, our toil, and our oppression. [8]The LORD brought us out of Egypt
with a mighty hand and an outstretched arm, with a terrifying display
of power, and with signs and wonders; [9]and he brought us into this
place and gave us this land, a land flowing with milk and honey. [10]So
now I bring the first of the fruit of the ground that you, O LORD, have
given me." You shall set it down before the LORD your God and bow
down before the LORD your God. [11]Then you, together with the Levites and the aliens who reside among you, shall celebrate with all the
bounty that the LORD your God has given to you and to your house.

12 When you have finished paying all the tithe of your produce in
the third year (which is the year of the tithe), giving it to the Levites,
the aliens, the orphans, and the widows, so that they may eat their fill
within your towns, [13]then you shall say before the LORD your God: "I
have removed the sacred portion from the house, and I have given it
to the Levites, the resident aliens, the orphans, and the widows, in accordance with your entire commandment that you commanded me; I
have neither transgressed nor forgotten any of your commandments:
[14]I have not eaten of it while in mourning; I have not removed any of
it while I was unclean; and I have not offered any of it to the dead. I
have obeyed the LORD my God, doing just as you commanded me.
[15]Look down from your holy habitation, from heaven, and bless your
people Israel and the ground that you have given us, as you swore to
our ancestors—a land flowing with milk and honey."

Concluding Exhortation

16 This very day the LORD your God is commanding you to observe these statutes and ordinances; so observe them diligently with

26:5-9 A wandering Aramean: This prayer, which is also a statement of belief, reviews the history of God's saving acts. Farmers were to recite it during a thanksgiving ceremony as they gave a portion of their crops back to God. "Aramean" refers to Jacob, who spent much of his life in Aram (that is, Syria; see Gen 29–31). See Map 1, page 2098.

26:12-15 third year: This extra tithe was distributed to the poor (14:28-29). It was not eaten at the central sanctuary as the regular tithe was (14:22-23). Because this gift to the poor was a "sacred portion," contact with unclean persons or forbidden activities was prohibited (26:14).

26:16-19 This very day: "Today" refers to the day Moses spoke the words of Deuteronomy to Israel in the land of Moab (15:5; 19:9). The relationship between God and Israel is a covenant. Each party now agrees to abide by the principles of this covenant. God will be Israel's God. Israel will be God's treasured people (see Exod 6:7; 29:45-46; Jer 32:38; Hos 2:23), which means they will keep God's commandments.

all your heart and with all your soul. [17]Today you have obtained the
LORD's agreement: to be your God; and for you to walk in his ways,
to keep his statutes, his commandments, and his ordinances, and to
obey him. [18]Today the LORD has obtained your agreement: to be his
treasured people, as he promised you, and to keep his commandments; [19]for him to set you high above all nations that he has made,
in praise and in fame and in honor; and for you to be a people holy to
the LORD your God, as he promised.

The Inscribed Stones and Altar on Mount Ebal

27 Then Moses and the elders of Israel charged all the people as follows: Keep the entire commandment that I am
commanding you today. [2]On the day that you cross over the Jordan
into the land that the LORD your God is giving you, you shall set up
large stones and cover them with plaster. [3]You shall write on them all
the words of this law when you have crossed over, to enter the land
that the LORD your God is giving you, a land flowing with milk and
honey, as the LORD, the God of your ancestors, promised you. [4]So
when you have crossed over the Jordan, you shall set up these stones,
about which I am commanding you today, on Mount Ebal, and you
shall cover them with plaster. [5]And you shall build an altar there to
the LORD your God, an altar of stones on which you have not used an
iron tool. [6]You must build the altar of the LORD your God of unhewn[a]
stones. Then offer up burnt offerings on it to the LORD your God,
[7]make sacrifices of well-being, and eat them there, rejoicing before
the LORD your God. [8]You shall write on the stones all the words of
this law very clearly.
9 Then Moses and the levitical priests spoke to all Israel, saying:
Keep silence and hear, O Israel! This very day you have become the
people of the LORD your God. [10]Therefore obey the LORD your God,
observing his commandments and his statutes that I am commanding you today.

Twelve Curses

11 The same day Moses charged the people as follows: [12]When
you have crossed over the Jordan, these shall stand on Mount Gerizim for the blessing of the people: Simeon, Levi, Judah, Issachar, Joseph, and Benjamin. [13]And these shall stand on Mount Ebal for the
curse: Reuben, Gad, Asher, Zebulun, Dan, and Naphtali. [14]Then the
Levites shall declare in a loud voice to all the Israelites:
15 "Cursed be anyone who makes an idol or casts an image, anything abhorrent to the LORD, the work of an artisan, and sets it up in
secret." All the people shall respond, saying, "Amen!"

[a] Heb *whole*

How is the relationship between you and God like the relationship between God and the people of Israel?

27:2-8 On the day you cross over: The covenant will be formalized by a ceremony when Israel first enters the promised land (11:29; Josh 8:30-35). Mount Ebal and Mount Gerizim (27:12) stand to the north and south of Shechem (see Map 3, pp. 2100-2101). The stones in 27:8 are the ones referred to in 27:2-4, not the stones of the altar.

27:15-26 Cursed be...Amen!: In Old Testament times, curses were power-laden words that really brought danger to the person cursed. A solemn ceremony involving twelve curses will seal Israel's agreement to the covenant. By repeatedly saying, "Amen," the people publicly agree to avoid these behaviors. Most of these curses deal with actions committed secretly (27:24), situations that could not be controlled by disgrace or public outrage. A final summary curse motivates obedience to the entire law of Deuteronomy.

16 "Cursed be anyone who dishonors father or mother." All the people shall say, "Amen!"

17 "Cursed be anyone who moves a neighbor's boundary marker." All the people shall say, "Amen!"

18 "Cursed be anyone who misleads a blind person on the road." All the people shall say, "Amen!"

19 "Cursed be anyone who deprives the alien, the orphan, and the widow of justice." All the people shall say, "Amen!"

20 "Cursed be anyone who lies with his father's wife, because he has violated his father's rights."[a] All the people shall say, "Amen!"

21 "Cursed be anyone who lies with any animal." All the people shall say, "Amen!"

22 "Cursed be anyone who lies with his sister, whether the daughter of his father or the daughter of his mother." All the people shall say, "Amen!"

23 "Cursed be anyone who lies with his mother-in-law." All the people shall say, "Amen!"

24 "Cursed be anyone who strikes down a neighbor in secret." All the people shall say, "Amen!"

25 "Cursed be anyone who takes a bribe to shed innocent blood." All the people shall say, "Amen!"

26 "Cursed be anyone who does not uphold the words of this law by observing them." All the people shall say, "Amen!"

Blessings for Obedience

28:1-14 If you will only obey: Deuteronomy is similar to treaties in the ancient world that established agreements or covenants between nations. Those treaties closed with blessings upon those who abide by the agreement and curses against anyone who might violate it. Blessings were effective, powerful words that brought about well-being and prosperity. These blessings repeat themes of Israel's high status among the nations (28:1, 9-10, 13) and agricultural prosperity (28:4-5, 8, 11-12).

28 If you will only obey the LORD your God, by diligently observing all his commandments that I am commanding you today, the LORD your God will set you high above all the nations of the earth; [2]all these blessings shall come upon you and overtake you, if you obey the LORD your God:

3 Blessed shall you be in the city, and blessed shall you be in the field.

4 Blessed shall be the fruit of your womb, the fruit of your ground, and the fruit of your livestock, both the increase of your cattle and the issue of your flock.

5 Blessed shall be your basket and your kneading bowl.

6 Blessed shall you be when you come in, and blessed shall you be when you go out.

7 The LORD will cause your enemies who rise against you to be defeated before you; they shall come out against you one way, and flee before you seven ways. [8]The LORD will command the blessing upon you in your barns, and in all that you undertake; he will bless you in the land that the LORD your God is giving you. [9]The LORD will es-

[a] Heb *uncovered his father's skirt*

tablish you as his holy people, as he has sworn to you, if you keep the
commandments of the LORD your God and walk in his ways. [10]All
the peoples of the earth shall see that you are called by the name of
the LORD, and they shall be afraid of you. [11]The LORD will make you
abound in prosperity, in the fruit of your womb, in the fruit of your
livestock, and in the fruit of your ground in the land that the LORD
swore to your ancestors to give you. [12]The LORD will open for you his
rich storehouse, the heavens, to give the rain of your land in its season
and to bless all your undertakings. You will lend to many nations, but
you will not borrow. [13]The LORD will make you the head, and not the
tail; you shall be only at the top, and not at the bottom—if you obey
the commandments of the LORD your God, which I am commanding
you today, by diligently observing them, [14]and if you do not turn aside
from any of the words that I am commanding you today, either to the
right or to the left, following other gods to serve them.

Warnings against Disobedience

15 But if you will not obey the LORD your God by diligently observing all his commandments and decrees, which I am commanding you today, then all these curses shall come upon you and overtake you:

16 Cursed shall you be in the city, and cursed shall you be in the field.

17 Cursed shall be your basket and your kneading bowl.

18 Cursed shall be the fruit of your womb, the fruit of your ground, the increase of your cattle and the issue of your flock.

19 Cursed shall you be when you come in, and cursed shall you be when you go out.

20 The LORD will send upon you disaster, panic, and frustration
in everything you attempt to do, until you are destroyed and perish
quickly, on account of the evil of your deeds, because you have forsaken me. [21]The LORD will make the pestilence cling to you until it
has consumed you off the land that you are entering to possess. [22]The
LORD will afflict you with consumption, fever, inflammation, with fiery heat and drought, and with blight and mildew; they shall pursue
you until you perish. [23]The sky over your head shall be bronze, and the
earth under you iron. [24]The LORD will change the rain of your land
into powder, and only dust shall come down upon you from the sky
until you are destroyed.

25 The LORD will cause you to be defeated before your enemies;
you shall go out against them one way and flee before them seven
ways. You shall become an object of horror to all the kingdoms of the
earth. [26]Your corpses shall be food for every bird of the air and animal
of the earth, and there shall be no one to frighten them away. [27]The
LORD will afflict you with the boils of Egypt, with ulcers, scurvy, and

28:15-68 But if you will not obey: The curses divide into three sections: 28:15-46, 47-57, and 58-68. There are many more curses than blessings. This stresses the urgent need for the people to change their behavior. Notice that several curses correspond to the previous blessings: 28:16-19 to 28:3-6; 28:23-24 to 28:12; 28:25 to 28:7; 28:43-44 to 28:12-13. Notice that the curses in 28:47-57 treat Israel's disobedience as a fact and describe the horrors of invasion and siege. The third section of curses, 28:58-68, threatens a reversal of God's earlier saving acts.

itch, of which you cannot be healed. [28]The LORD will afflict you with madness, blindness, and confusion of mind; [29]you shall grope about at noon as blind people grope in darkness, but you shall be unable to find your way; and you shall be continually abused and robbed, without anyone to help. [30]You shall become engaged to a woman, but another man shall lie with her. You shall build a house, but not live in it. You shall plant a vineyard, but not enjoy its fruit. [31]Your ox shall be butchered before your eyes, but you shall not eat of it. Your donkey shall be stolen in front of you, and shall not be restored to you. Your sheep shall be given to your enemies, without anyone to help you. [32]Your sons and daughters shall be given to another people, while you look on; you will strain your eyes looking for them all day but be powerless to do anything. [33]A people whom you do not know shall eat up the fruit of your ground and of all your labors; you shall be continually abused and crushed, [34]and driven mad by the sight that your eyes shall see. [35]The LORD will strike you on the knees and on the legs with grievous boils of which you cannot be healed, from the sole of your foot to the crown of your head. [36]The LORD will bring you, and the king whom you set over you, to a nation that neither you nor your ancestors have known, where you shall serve other gods, of wood and stone. [37]You shall become an object of horror, a proverb, and a byword among all the peoples where the LORD will lead you.

38 You shall carry much seed into the field but shall gather little in, for the locust shall consume it. [39]You shall plant vineyards and dress them, but you shall neither drink the wine nor gather the grapes, for the worm shall eat them. [40]You shall have olive trees throughout all your territory, but you shall not anoint yourself with the oil, for your olives shall drop off. [41]You shall have sons and daughters, but they shall not remain yours, for they shall go into captivity. [42]All your trees and the fruit of your ground the cicada shall take over. [43]Aliens residing among you shall ascend above you higher and higher, while you shall descend lower and lower. [44]They shall lend to you but you shall not lend to them; they shall be the head and you shall be the tail.

45 All these curses shall come upon you, pursuing and overtaking you until you are destroyed, because you did not obey the LORD your God, by observing the commandments and the decrees that he commanded you. [46]They shall be among you and your descendants as a sign and a portent forever.

47 Because you did not serve the LORD your God joyfully and with gladness of heart for the abundance of everything, [48]therefore you shall serve your enemies whom the LORD will send against you, in hunger and thirst, in nakedness and lack of everything. He will put an iron yoke on your neck until he has destroyed you. [49]The LORD will bring a nation from far away, from the end of the earth, to swoop down on you like an eagle, a nation whose language you do not understand,

50 a grim-faced nation showing no respect to the old or favor to the
young. 51 It shall consume the fruit of your livestock and the fruit of
your ground until you are destroyed, leaving you neither grain, wine,
and oil, nor the increase of your cattle and the issue of your flock,
until it has made you perish. 52 It shall besiege you in all your towns
until your high and fortified walls, in which you trusted, come down
throughout your land; it shall besiege you in all your towns throughout the land that the LORD your God has given you. 53 In the desperate
straits to which the enemy siege reduces you, you will eat the fruit
of your womb, the flesh of your own sons and daughters whom the
LORD your God has given you. 54 Even the most refined and gentle of
men among you will begrudge food to his own brother, to the wife
whom he embraces, and to the last of his remaining children, 55 giving to none of them any of the flesh of his children whom he is eating, because nothing else remains to him, in the desperate straits to
which the enemy siege will reduce you in all your towns. 56 She who
is the most refined and gentle among you, so gentle and refined that
she does not venture to set the sole of her foot on the ground, will
begrudge food to the husband whom she embraces, to her own son,
and to her own daughter, 57 begrudging even the afterbirth that comes
out from between her thighs, and the children that she bears, because
she is eating them in secret for lack of anything else, in the desperate
straits to which the enemy siege will reduce you in your towns.

58 If you do not diligently observe all the words of this law that
are written in this book, fearing this glorious and awesome name, the
LORD your God, 59 then the LORD will overwhelm both you and your
offspring with severe and lasting afflictions and grievous and lasting
maladies. 60 He will bring back upon you all the diseases of Egypt, of
which you were in dread, and they shall cling to you. 61 Every other
malady and affliction, even though not recorded in the book of this
law, the LORD will inflict on you until you are destroyed. 62 Although
once you were as numerous as the stars in heaven, you shall be left few
in number, because you did not obey the LORD your God. 63 And just
as the LORD took delight in making you prosperous and numerous,
so the LORD will take delight in bringing you to ruin and destruction;
you shall be plucked off the land that you are entering to possess. 64 The
LORD will scatter you among all peoples, from one end of the earth
to the other; and there you shall serve other gods, of wood and stone,
which neither you nor your ancestors have known. 65 Among those
nations you shall find no ease, no resting place for the sole of your
foot. There the LORD will give you a trembling heart, failing eyes, and
a languishing spirit. 66 Your life shall hang in doubt before you; night
and day you shall be in dread, with no assurance of your life. 67 In the
morning you shall say, "If only it were evening!" and at evening you
shall say, "If only it were morning!"—because of the dread that your

heart shall feel and the sights that your eyes shall see. 68 The LORD
will bring you back in ships to Egypt, by a route that I promised you
would never see again; and there you shall offer yourselves for sale to
your enemies as male and female slaves, but there will be no buyer.

29 [a] These are the words of the covenant that the LORD com-
manded Moses to make with the Israelites in the land of
Moab, in addition to the covenant that he had made with them at
Horeb.

29:1 the words of the covenant... Moab...Horeb: God made a covenant with the previous generation at Horeb (5:2). Now this is renewed in the land of Moab, just before Israel crosses into its new land (1:5). See Map 2, page 2099.

The Covenant Renewed in Moab

2 [b] Moses summoned all Israel and said to them: You have seen
all that the LORD did before your eyes in the land of Egypt, to Pharaoh and to all his servants and to all his land, 3 the great trials that
your eyes saw, the signs, and those great wonders. 4 But to this day the
LORD has not given you a mind to understand, or eyes to see, or ears
to hear. 5 I have led you forty years in the wilderness. The clothes on
your back have not worn out, and the sandals on your feet have not
worn out; 6 you have not eaten bread, and you have not drunk wine or
strong drink—so that you may know that I am the LORD your God.
7 When you came to this place, King Sihon of Heshbon and King Og
of Bashan came out against us for battle, but we defeated them. 8 We
took their land and gave it as an inheritance to the Reubenites, the
Gadites, and the half-tribe of Manasseh. 9 Therefore diligently observe
the words of this covenant, in order that you may succeed[c] in everything that you do.

10 You stand assembled today, all of you, before the LORD your
God—the leaders of your tribes,[d] your elders, and your officials, all
the men of Israel, 11 your children, your women, and the aliens who
are in your camp, both those who cut your wood and those who
draw your water— 12 to enter into the covenant of the LORD your
God, sworn by an oath, which the LORD your God is making with
you today; 13 in order that he may establish you today as his people,
and that he may be your God, as he promised you and as he swore
to your ancestors, to Abraham, to Isaac, and to Jacob. 14 I am making
this covenant, sworn by an oath, not only with you who stand here
with us today before the LORD our God, 15 but also with those who
are not here with us today. 16 You know how we lived in the land of
Egypt, and how we came through the midst of the nations through
which you passed. 17 You have seen their detestable things, the filthy
idols of wood and stone, of silver and gold, that were among them. 18 It
may be that there is among you a man or woman, or a family or tribe,
whose heart is already turning away from the LORD our God to serve
the gods of those nations. It may be that there is among you a root

29:10-11 all of you: The covenant community includes males and females, all ages, and all social classes, including even foreigners who performed menial chores.

29:14-15 not only with you: Deuteronomy's readers, who lived many generations after Moses, are to see themselves as part of God's covenant community.

[a] Ch 28.69 in Heb [b] Ch 29.1 in Heb [c] Or *deal wisely* [d] Gk Syr: Heb *your leaders, your tribes*

sprouting poisonous and bitter growth. [19]All who hear the words of
this oath and bless themselves, thinking in their hearts, "We are safe
even though we go our own stubborn ways" (thus bringing disaster
on moist and dry alike)[a]— [20]the LORD will be unwilling to pardon
them, for the LORD's anger and passion will smoke against them. All
the curses written in this book will descend on them, and the LORD
will blot out their names from under heaven. [21]The LORD will single
them out from all the tribes of Israel for calamity, in accordance with
all the curses of the covenant written in this book of the law. [22]The
next generation, your children who rise up after you, as well as the
foreigner who comes from a distant country, will see the devastation
of that land and the afflictions with which the LORD has afflicted it—
[23]all its soil burned out by sulfur and salt, nothing planted, nothing
sprouting, unable to support any vegetation, like the destruction of
Sodom and Gomorrah, Admah and Zeboiim, which the LORD destroyed in his fierce anger— [24]they and indeed all the nations will
wonder, "Why has the LORD done thus to this land? What caused
this great display of anger?" [25]They will conclude, "It is because they
abandoned the covenant of the LORD, the God of their ancestors,
which he made with them when he brought them out of the land of
Egypt. [26]They turned and served other gods, worshiping them, gods
whom they had not known and whom he had not allotted to them;
[27]so the anger of the LORD was kindled against that land, bringing on
it every curse written in this book. [28]The LORD uprooted them from
their land in anger, fury, and great wrath, and cast them into another
land, as is now the case." [29]The secret things belong to the LORD our
God, but the revealed things belong to us and to our children forever,
to observe all the words of this law.

29:24-28 the nations will wonder: An imagined future conversation warns of the terrible destruction and exile that will take place if Israel violates God's covenant.

29:29 secret things: God's ways always remain a hidden mystery. But Israel is not to worry about such things. Israel's duty is plain: obey the words of the law that God has clearly revealed.

God's Fidelity Assured

30 When all these things have happened to you, the blessings
and the curses that I have set before you, if you call them
to mind among all the nations where the LORD your God has driven
you, [2]and return to the LORD your God, and you and your children
obey him with all your heart and with all your soul, just as I am commanding you today, [3]then the LORD your God will restore your fortunes and have compassion on you, gathering you again from all the
peoples among whom the LORD your God has scattered you. [4]Even
if you are exiled to the ends of the world,[b] from there the LORD your
God will gather you, and from there he will bring you back. [5]The
LORD your God will bring you into the land that your ancestors possessed, and you will possess it; he will make you more prosperous and
numerous than your ancestors.

30:1-5 When all these things have happened: Even their inevitable defeat and exile will not mean the end of Israel as God's people, if they ultimately repent (4:29-31).

[a] Meaning of Heb uncertain [b] Heb *of heaven*

30:6 circumcise your heart: Moses demanded this of Israel in 10:16. Yet in the end, God will do what Israel cannot and remove all obstacles to the people's heartfelt commitment. Love for God will become second nature.

6 Moreover, the LORD your God will circumcise your heart and
the heart of your descendants, so that you will love the LORD your
God with all your heart and with all your soul, in order that you may
live. 7 The LORD your God will put all these curses on your enemies
and on the adversaries who took advantage of you. 8 Then you shall
again obey the LORD, observing all his commandments that I am
commanding you today, 9 and the LORD your God will make you
abundantly prosperous in all your undertakings, in the fruit of your
body, in the fruit of your livestock, and in the fruit of your soil. For the
LORD will again take delight in prospering you, just as he delighted
in prospering your ancestors, 10 when you obey the LORD your God
by observing his commandments and decrees that are written in this
book of the law, because you turn to the LORD your God with all your
heart and with all your soul.

Exhortation to Choose Life

30:11-14 not too hard: In contrast to the proverbial impossibility of climbing up to heaven or the difficulty of crossing the sea, God's law is easy to understand and easy to carry out. In modern terms, the law is user-friendly. Paul reuses these words to speak of God's word and faith (Rom 10:6-8).

11 Surely, this commandment that I am commanding you today is
not too hard for you, nor is it too far away. 12 It is not in heaven, that you
should say, "Who will go up to heaven for us, and get it for us so that
we may hear it and observe it?" 13 Neither is it beyond the sea, that you
should say, "Who will cross to the other side of the sea for us, and get
it for us so that we may hear it and observe it?" 14 No, the word is very
near to you; it is in your mouth and in your heart for you to observe.

30:15-20 I have set before you: Israel's choice is clear-cut and uncomplicated. Choose life and prosperity or death and adversity. Obey and live, or disobey by worshiping false gods and perish. The only sensible option is to choose life (30:19).

What would it mean for you to "choose life" rather than death?

15 See, I have set before you today life and prosperity, death and
adversity. 16 If you obey the commandments of the LORD your God[a]
that I am commanding you today, by loving the LORD your God,
walking in his ways, and observing his commandments, decrees, and
ordinances, then you shall live and become numerous, and the LORD
your God will bless you in the land that you are entering to possess.
17 But if your heart turns away and you do not hear, but are led astray
to bow down to other gods and serve them, 18 I declare to you today
that you shall perish; you shall not live long in the land that you are
crossing the Jordan to enter and possess. 19 I call heaven and earth to
witness against you today that I have set before you life and death,
blessings and curses. Choose life so that you and your descendants
may live, 20 loving the LORD your God, obeying him, and holding fast
to him; for that means life to you and length of days, so that you may
live in the land that the LORD swore to give to your ancestors, to Abraham, to Isaac, and to Jacob.

Joshua Becomes Moses' Successor

31:1 When Moses had finished: After Moses' long speech proclaiming the law, the story carries on from where it left off in 3:23-29.

31 When Moses had finished speaking all[b] these words to all Israel, 2 he said to them: "I am now one hundred twenty years

[a] Gk: Heb lacks *If you obey the commandments of the LORD your God* [b] Q Ms Gk: MT *Moses went and spoke*

old. I am no longer able to get about, and the LORD has told me, 'You shall not cross over this Jordan.' [3]The LORD your God himself will cross over before you. He will destroy these nations before you, and you shall dispossess them. Joshua also will cross over before you, as the LORD promised. [4]The LORD will do to them as he did to Sihon and Og, the kings of the Amorites, and to their land, when he destroyed them. [5]The LORD will give them over to you and you shall deal with them in full accord with the command that I have given to you. [6]Be strong and bold; have no fear or dread of them, because it is the LORD your God who goes with you; he will not fail you or forsake you."

7 Then Moses summoned Joshua and said to him in the sight of all Israel: "Be strong and bold, for you are the one who will go with this people into the land that the LORD has sworn to their ancestors to give them; and you will put them in possession of it. [8]It is the LORD who goes before you. He will be with you; he will not fail you or forsake you. Do not fear or be dismayed."

The Law to Be Read Every Seventh Year

9 Then Moses wrote down this law, and gave it to the priests, the sons of Levi, who carried the ark of the covenant of the LORD, and to all the elders of Israel. [10]Moses commanded them: "Every seventh year, in the scheduled year of remission, during the festival of booths,[a] [11]when all Israel comes to appear before the LORD your God at the place that he will choose, you shall read this law before all Israel in their hearing. [12]Assemble the people—men, women, and children, as well as the aliens residing in your towns—so that they may hear and learn to fear the LORD your God and to observe diligently all the words of this law, [13]and so that their children, who have not known it, may hear and learn to fear the LORD your God, as long as you live in the land that you are crossing over the Jordan to possess."

31:10 year of remission: This is explained in 15:1-11. Deuteronomy 16:13-15 describes the Festival of Booths.

31:12-13 men, women, and children: The community that gathers to hear the reading of the law is inclusive. Everyone needs this opportunity to hear and learn.

Moses and Joshua Receive God's Charge

14 The LORD said to Moses, "Your time to die is near; call Joshua and present yourselves in the tent of meeting, so that I may commission him." So Moses and Joshua went and presented themselves in the tent of meeting, [15]and the LORD appeared at the tent in a pillar of cloud; the pillar of cloud stood at the entrance to the tent.

31:14 tent of meeting: God appeared in the tent of meeting from time to time to communicate with Israel (see Exod 33:7-11).

16 The LORD said to Moses, "Soon you will lie down with your ancestors. Then this people will begin to prostitute themselves to the foreign gods in their midst, the gods of the land into which they are going; they will forsake me, breaking my covenant that I have made with them. [17]My anger will be kindled against them in that day. I will

[a] Or *tabernacles*; Heb *succoth*

forsake them and hide my face from them; they will become easy prey, and many terrible troubles will come upon them. In that day they will say, 'Have not these troubles come upon us because our God is not in our midst?' [18]On that day I will surely hide my face on account of all the evil they have done by turning to other gods. [19]Now therefore write this song, and teach it to the Israelites; put it in their mouths, in order that this song may be a witness for me against the Israelites. [20]For when I have brought them into the land flowing with milk and honey, which I promised on oath to their ancestors, and they have eaten their fill and grown fat, they will turn to other gods and serve them, despising me and breaking my covenant. [21]And when many terrible troubles come upon them, this song will confront them as a witness, because it will not be lost from the mouths of their descendants. For I know what they are inclined to do even now, before I have brought them into the land that I promised them on oath." [22]That very day Moses wrote this song and taught it to the Israelites.

31:19 write this song: When Israel disobeys after the death of Moses, both the Song of Moses (32:1-43) and the book of the law (that is, Deuteronomy) will witness against them (31:21, 26). Israel is to learn the Song of Moses by heart.

23 Then the LORD commissioned Joshua son of Nun and said, "Be strong and bold, for you shall bring the Israelites into the land that I promised them; I will be with you."

24 When Moses had finished writing down in a book the words of this law to the very end, [25]Moses commanded the Levites who carried the ark of the covenant of the LORD, saying, [26]"Take this book of the law and put it beside the ark of the covenant of the LORD your God; let it remain there as a witness against you. [27]For I know well how rebellious and stubborn you are. If you already have been so rebellious toward the LORD while I am still alive among you, how much more after my death! [28]Assemble to me all the elders of your tribes and your officials, so that I may recite these words in their hearing and call heaven and earth to witness against them. [29]For I know that after my death you will surely act corruptly, turning aside from the way that I have commanded you. In time to come trouble will befall you, because you will do what is evil in the sight of the LORD, provoking him to anger through the work of your hands."

The Song of Moses

30 Then Moses recited the words of this song, to the very end, in the hearing of the whole assembly of Israel:

32 Give ear, O heavens, and I will speak;
let the earth hear the words of my mouth.
2 May my teaching drop like the rain,
my speech condense like the dew;
like gentle rain on grass,
like showers on new growth.
3 For I will proclaim the name of the LORD;
ascribe greatness to our God!

32:1-43 Give ear: In the Song of Moses, God uses the language of a lawsuit against Israel to accuse them of infidelity. God calls on the heavens and earth as witnesses to the charge. The Song has four stages: God chooses Israel (32:7-14), Israel disobeys (32:15-18), God punishes Israel by means of other nations (32:19-27), and God restores Israel by turning against those enemy nations (32:28-42).

4 The Rock, his work is perfect,
and all his ways are just.
A faithful God, without deceit,
just and upright is he;
5 yet his degenerate children have dealt falsely with him,[a]
a perverse and crooked generation.
6 Do you thus repay the LORD,
O foolish and senseless people?
Is not he your father, who created you,
who made you and established you?
7 Remember the days of old,
consider the years long past;
ask your father, and he will inform you;
your elders, and they will tell you.
8 When the Most High[b] apportioned the nations,
when he divided humankind,
he fixed the boundaries of the peoples
according to the number of the gods;[c]
9 the LORD's own portion was his people,
Jacob his allotted share.

10 He sustained[d] him in a desert land,
in a howling wilderness waste;
he shielded him, cared for him,
guarded him as the apple of his eye.
11 As an eagle stirs up its nest,
and hovers over its young;
as it spreads its wings, takes them up,
and bears them aloft on its pinions,
12 the LORD alone guided him;
no foreign god was with him.
13 He set him atop the heights of the land,
and fed him with[e] produce of the field;
he nursed him with honey from the crags,
with oil from flinty rock;
14 curds from the herd, and milk from the flock,
with fat of lambs and rams;
Bashan bulls and goats,
together with the choicest wheat—
you drank fine wine from the blood of grapes.
15 Jacob ate his fill;[f]

32:4 Rock: This is the main poetic image for God in the Song (32:15, 18, 30, 31). The Rock represents strength and protection.

What images of God from nature (like rock, wind, or fire) do you find meaningful?

32:8-9 the Most High apportioned: The story of the people of Israel begins with their election as God's special people. While dividing the nations among various lesser gods, God chose Israel as a personal possession.

32:15 grew fat: The second stage in the story is disobedience. Jeshurun is a poetic term for Israel. It means "the upright one" (33:5, 26).

[a] Meaning of Heb uncertain [b] Traditional rendering of Heb *Elyon* [c] Q Ms Compare Gk Tg: MT *the Israelites* [d] Sam Gk Compare Tg: MT *found* [e] Sam Gk Syr Tg: MT *he ate* [f] Q Mss Sam Gk: MT lacks *Jacob ate his fill*

Jeshurun grew fat, and kicked.
You grew fat, bloated, and gorged!
He abandoned God who made him,
and scoffed at the Rock of his salvation.
16 They made him jealous with strange gods,
with abhorrent things they provoked him.
17 They sacrificed to demons, not God,
to deities they had never known,
to new ones recently arrived,
whom your ancestors had not feared.
18 You were unmindful of the Rock that bore you;[a]
you forgot the God who gave you birth.

32:18 Rock that bore you: God is portrayed as a mother who gave birth to Israel (see Isa 49:15; 66:13).

32:19 spurned his sons and daughters: The third stage in the story is punishment at the hands of an enemy people.

19 The LORD saw it, and was jealous;[b]
he spurned[c] his sons and daughters.
20 He said: I will hide my face from them,
I will see what their end will be;
for they are a perverse generation,
children in whom there is no faithfulness.
21 They made me jealous with what is no god,
provoked me with their idols.
So I will make them jealous with what is no people,
provoke them with a foolish nation.
22 For a fire is kindled by my anger,
and burns to the depths of Sheol;
it devours the earth and its increase,
and sets on fire the foundations of the mountains.
23 I will heap disasters upon them,
spend my arrows against them:
24 wasting hunger,
burning consumption,
bitter pestilence.
The teeth of beasts I will send against them,
with venom of things crawling in the dust.
25 In the street the sword shall bereave,
and in the chambers terror,
for young man and woman alike,
nursing child and old gray head.
26 I thought to scatter them[d]
and blot out the memory of them from humankind;
27 but I feared provocation by the enemy,
for their adversaries might misunderstand

32:35 Vengeance is mine: The fourth stage of the song (32:28-42) is God's vindication and rescue of Israel. God's "vengeance" (also 32:41, 43) is not so much revenge or retribution, but a restoration of balance and justice.

[a] Or *that begot you* [b] Q Mss Gk: MT lacks *was jealous* [c] Cn: Heb *he spurned because of provocation*
[d] Gk: Meaning of Heb uncertain

and say, "Our hand is triumphant;
it was not the LORD who did all this."

28 They are a nation void of sense;
there is no understanding in them.
29 If they were wise, they would understand this;
they would discern what the end would be.
30 How could one have routed a thousand,
and two put a myriad to flight,
unless their Rock had sold them,
the LORD had given them up?
31 Indeed their rock is not like our Rock;
our enemies are fools.[a]
32 Their vine comes from the vinestock of Sodom,
from the vineyards of Gomorrah;
their grapes are grapes of poison,
their clusters are bitter;
33 their wine is the poison of serpents,
the cruel venom of asps.

34 Is not this laid up in store with me,
sealed up in my treasuries?
35 Vengeance is mine, and recompense,
for the time when their foot shall slip;
because the day of their calamity is at hand,
their doom comes swiftly.

36 Indeed the LORD will vindicate his people,
have compassion on his servants,
when he sees that their power is gone,
neither bond nor free remaining.
37 Then he will say: Where are their gods,
the rock in which they took refuge,
38 who ate the fat of their sacrifices,
and drank the wine of their libations?
Let them rise up and help you,
let them be your protection!

39 See now that I, even I, am he;
there is no god besides me.
I kill and I make alive;
I wound and I heal;
and no one can deliver from my hand.

[a] Gk: Meaning of Heb uncertain

40 For I lift up my hand to heaven,
and swear: As I live forever,
41 when I whet my flashing sword,
and my hand takes hold on judgment;
I will take vengeance on my adversaries,
and will repay those who hate me.
42 I will make my arrows drunk with blood,
and my sword shall devour flesh—
with the blood of the slain and the captives,
from the long-haired enemy.

43 Praise, O heavens,[a] his people,
worship him, all you gods![b]
For he will avenge the blood of his children,[c]
and take vengeance on his adversaries;
he will repay those who hate him,[b]
and cleanse the land for his people.[d]

44 Moses came and recited all the words of this song in the hearing of the people, he and Joshua[e] son of Nun. 45 When Moses had finished reciting all these words to all Israel, 46 he said to them: "Take to
heart all the words that I am giving in witness against you today; give
them as a command to your children, so that they may diligently observe all the words of this law. 47 This is no trifling matter for you, but
rather your very life; through it you may live long in the land that you
are crossing over the Jordan to possess."

Moses' Death Foretold

48 On that very day the LORD addressed Moses as follows: 49 "Ascend this mountain of the Abarim, Mount Nebo, which is in the land
of Moab, across from Jericho, and view the land of Canaan, which I
am giving to the Israelites for a possession; 50 you shall die there on
the mountain that you ascend and shall be gathered to your kin, as
your brother Aaron died on Mount Hor and was gathered to his kin;
51 because both of you broke faith with me among the Israelites at
the waters of Meribath-kadesh in the wilderness of Zin, by failing to
maintain my holiness among the Israelites. 52 Although you may view
the land from a distance, you shall not enter it—the land that I am
giving to the Israelites."

32:51 broke faith: Moses and Aaron sinned in some way while producing water from a rock at Meribath-kadesh (see Num 20:10-13, 24; 27:12-14).

33:1-29 This is the blessing: A second poem spoken by Moses concludes Deuteronomy. A description of God as Divine Warrior (33:1-5 and 33:26-29) surrounds a series of blessings on Israel's tribes (33:6-25).

33:2 the LORD came from Sinai: As Divine Warrior, God advances into battle from the southern wilderness. God leads an army of heavenly beings. For similar descriptions, see Judges 5:4-5 and Habakkuk 3:3-15.

Moses' Final Blessing on Israel

33 This is the blessing with which Moses, the man of God,
blessed the Israelites before his death. 2 He said:

[a] Q Ms Gk: MT *nations* [b] Q Ms Gk: MT lacks this line [c] Q Ms Gk: MT *his servants*
[d] Q Ms Sam Gk Vg: MT *his land his people* [e] Sam Gk Syr Vg: MT *Hoshea*

The LORD came from Sinai,
and dawned from Seir upon us;[a]
he shone forth from Mount Paran.
With him were myriads of holy ones;[b]
at his right, a host of his own.[c]
3 Indeed, O favorite among[d] peoples,
all his holy ones were in your charge;
they marched at your heels,
accepted direction from you.
4 Moses charged us with the law,
as a possession for the assembly of Jacob.
5 There arose a king in Jeshurun,
when the leaders of the people assembled—
the united tribes of Israel.

6 May Reuben live, and not die out,
even though his numbers are few.

7 And this he said of Judah:
O LORD, give heed to Judah,
and bring him to his people;
strengthen his hands for him,[e]
and be a help against his adversaries.

8 And of Levi he said:
Give to Levi[f] your Thummim,
and your Urim to your loyal one,
whom you tested at Massah,
with whom you contended at the waters of Meribah;
9 who said of his father and mother,
"I regard them not";
he ignored his kin,
and did not acknowledge his children.
For they observed your word,
and kept your covenant.
10 They teach Jacob your ordinances,
and Israel your law;
they place incense before you,
and whole burnt offerings on your altar.
11 Bless, O LORD, his substance,
and accept the work of his hands;

33:6-25 Reuben...Judah...Levi: Moses describes or blesses each tribe except Simeon. The tribe of Reuben has nearly vanished (33:6). For more on the loyalty of Levi, the tribe charged with priestly duties (33:8), see Exodus 17:1-7; 32:26-29; Numbers 20:1-13. "Thummin" and "Urim" were stones that served as lots to discover God's will. Ephraim and Manasseh, tribes descended from Joseph (33:13; 17), are praised for their military skill, using the image of an aggressive bull. Zebulun and Issachar (33:18-19) share a mountain holy place (Mount Tabor). They enjoy riches from the Mediterranean Sea and the Sea of Galilee. In Numbers 32:1-5, Gad (33:20-21) asked for rich territory east of the Jordan, choosing the best for himself. The image of dipping a foot in olive oil portrays the prosperity enjoyed by people in the tribe of Asher in their fertile territory (33:24). For tribal lands, see Map 3, pp. 2100-2101.

[a] Gk Syr Vg Compare Tg: Heb *upon them* [b] Cn Compare Gk Sam Syr Vg: MT *He came from Ribeboth-kodesh,* [c] Cn Compare Gk: meaning of Heb uncertain [d] Or *O lover of the* [e] Cn: Heb *with his hands he contended* [f] Q Ms Gk: MT lacks *Give to Levi*

crush the loins of his adversaries,
of those that hate him, so that they do not rise again.

12 Of Benjamin he said:
The beloved of the LORD rests in safety—
the High God[a] surrounds him all day long—
the beloved[b] rests between his shoulders.

13 And of Joseph he said:
Blessed by the LORD be his land,
with the choice gifts of heaven above,
and of the deep that lies beneath;
14 with the choice fruits of the sun,
and the rich yield of the months;
15 with the finest produce of the ancient mountains,
and the abundance of the everlasting hills;
16 with the choice gifts of the earth and its fullness,
and the favor of the one who dwells on Sinai.[c]
Let these come on the head of Joseph,
on the brow of the prince among his brothers.
17 A firstborn[d] bull—majesty is his!
His horns are the horns of a wild ox;
with them he gores the peoples,
driving them to[e] the ends of the earth;
such are the myriads of Ephraim,
such the thousands of Manasseh.

18 And of Zebulun he said:
Rejoice, Zebulun, in your going out;
and Issachar, in your tents.
19 They call peoples to the mountain;
there they offer the right sacrifices;
for they suck the affluence of the seas
and the hidden treasures of the sand.

20 And of Gad he said:
Blessed be the enlargement of Gad!
Gad lives like a lion;
he tears at arm and scalp.
21 He chose the best for himself,
for there a commander's allotment was reserved;
he came at the head of the people,

---

[a] Heb *above him* [b] Heb *he* [c] Cn: Heb *in the bush* [d] Q Ms Gk Syr Vg: MT *His firstborn*
[e] Cn: Heb *the peoples, together*

he executed the justice of the Lord,
and his ordinances for Israel.

22 And of Dan he said:
Dan is a lion's whelp
that leaps forth from Bashan.

23 And of Naphtali he said:
O Naphtali, sated with favor,
full of the blessing of the Lord,
possess the west and the south.

24 And of Asher he said:
Most blessed of sons be Asher;
may he be the favorite of his brothers,
and may he dip his foot in oil.
25 Your bars are iron and bronze;
and as your days, so is your strength.

26 There is none like God, O Jeshurun,
who rides through the heavens to your help,
majestic through the skies.
27 He subdues the ancient gods,[a]
shatters[b] the forces of old;[c]
he drove out the enemy before you,
and said, "Destroy!"
28 So Israel lives in safety,
untroubled is Jacob's abode[d]
in a land of grain and wine,
where the heavens drop down dew.
29 Happy are you, O Israel! Who is like you,
a people saved by the Lord,
the shield of your help,
and the sword of your triumph!
Your enemies shall come fawning to you,
and you shall tread on their backs.

Moses Dies and Is Buried in the Land of Moab

34 Then Moses went up from the plains of Moab to Mount
Nebo, to the top of Pisgah, which is opposite Jericho, and
the Lord showed him the whole land: Gilead as far as Dan, 2 all
Naphtali, the land of Ephraim and Manasseh, all the land of Judah as

34:1-4 Then Moses went up: The narrative picks up again after 32:52. Mount Nebo is at the northeast shore of the Dead Sea (see Map 2, page 2099). From there Moses surveys the promised land from north (Dan) to south (the Negeb). Deuteronomy never makes it entirely clear why Moses had to die outside the land (1:37; 4:21-22; 32:50-52).

[a] Or *The eternal God is a dwelling place* [b] Cn: Heb *from underneath* [c] Or *the everlasting arms*
[d] Or *fountain*

far as the Western Sea, [3]the Negeb, and the Plain—that is, the valley of Jericho, the city of palm trees—as far as Zoar. [4]The LORD said to him, "This is the land of which I swore to Abraham, to Isaac, and to Jacob, saying, 'I will give it to your descendants'; I have let you see it with your eyes, but you shall not cross over there." [5]Then Moses, the servant of the LORD, died there in the land of Moab, at the LORD's command. [6]He was buried in a valley in the land of Moab, opposite Beth-peor, but no one knows his burial place to this day. [7]Moses was one hundred twenty years old when he died; his sight was unimpaired and his vigor had not abated. [8]The Israelites wept for Moses in the plains of Moab thirty days; then the period of mourning for Moses was ended.

34:7 one hundred twenty years old: Long life was understood to be a reward for following God's will.

9 Joshua son of Nun was full of the spirit of wisdom, because Moses had laid his hands on him; and the Israelites obeyed him, doing as the LORD had commanded Moses.

10 Never since has there arisen a prophet in Israel like Moses, whom the LORD knew face to face. [11]He was unequaled for all the signs and wonders that the LORD sent him to perform in the land of Egypt, against Pharaoh and all his servants and his entire land, [12]and for all the mighty deeds and all the terrifying displays of power that Moses performed in the sight of all Israel.

34:10 a prophet . . . like Moses: God communicated to Moses directly ("face to face," 5:4). As the ideal prophet, Moses delivered God's message to the people (5:27) and pleaded with God for them (9:18-20, 25-29; 10:10).

HISTORICAL BOOKS

Joshua to Esther

Christians refer to the biblical books that follow Deuteronomy as the *Historical Books.* That name does not mean that other parts of the Old Testament are unconcerned with history. They are called Historical Books because they provide an account of the history of the Israelite people from the time of Israel's emergence in the promised land sometime in the thirteenth century B.C.E. down to the period when the Persians controlled Israel in the late fifth century B.C.E. (see the timeline on pp. 30-32).

Like modern historical accounts, the biblical writers gathered their information from various sources, both oral and written. For example, we discover references to lost books such as the Book of the Annals of the Kings of Israel (1 Kgs 14:19) or of Judah (1 Kgs 14:29), the Book of the Acts of Solomon (1 Kgs 11:41), and the written records of Samuel, Nathan, and Gad (1 Chr 29:29).

The biblical books are historical in the sense that they include historical data and draw upon historical records. But it is equally plain that they are not written simply to present historical facts. To the contrary, the events described are selected and told in ways that function much like sermons. This series of sermons proclaims the consequences of God's determination to have an ongoing and close relationship with the people of Israel.

The Deuteronomistic History

Deuteronomy, the final book of the Pentateuch, plays a pivotal role in this history. As the history unfolds in the books of Joshua through 2 Kings (excluding Ruth), Deuteronomy's basic claim is that those who obey the LORD will prosper and those who do not will suffer (Deut 11:26-32). Because this perspective of blessing and curse so fills the Historical Books, scholars have come to refer to the extended history as the "Deuteronomistic History" and its author (or multiple authors) as the "Deuteronomistic Historian." For that ancient historian, Deuteronomy was a theological lens that could be used to view the entire Israelite history. The northern nation of Israel, for example, was doomed to fall to Assyria because of the people's faithlessness (2 Kgs 17:7-18). Judah met a similar fate because of the misdeeds of Manasseh (2 Kgs 21:10-15). Of all Judah's kings only Asa (1 Kgs 15:11), Hezekiah (2 Kgs 18:3), and Josiah (2 Kgs 23:24-25) were judged worthy heirs of King David.

The Deuteronomistic History is thought to have been assembled first in the late seventh century B.C.E., during the optimistic time of King Josiah's religious reforms (2 Kgs 22–23). After Josiah's untimely death at Meggido (2 Kgs 23:29) and, later, the destruction of Jerusalem by Nebuchadnezzar of Babylon (2 Kgs 24–25), the history was revised to account for the new, disastrous situation. The last verses of 2 Kings give us an end date for the work, since it was the thirty-seventh year of King Jehoiachin's exile, about 760 B.C.E. (2 Kgs 25:27).

Other historical books

The Deuteronomistic History corresponds to the part of the biblical canon that Jews call the Former Prophets (see chart Different Canons of the Hebrew Bible (Old Testament), pp. 14-15). The other books labeled as Historical Books by Christians were all composed after the Babylonian Exile (586–539 B.C.E.), in a time when Israelites struggled to live faithfully under Persian rule. The books of Ezra, Nehemiah, and Esther, for example, include stories of Jewish interaction with the Persian court. The setting for the book of Ruth is the period of the judges (Ruth 1:1), so it is found after Judges in Christian Bibles. Ruth likely draws on older traditions, but the book appears to have been composed in the fifth century B.C.E. as a direct response to Ezra's demand that his peers divorce their non-Jewish wives (Ezra 10). Ruth, a foreigner, was the great grandmother of King David.

First and Second Chronicles were originally one book that concluded the Hebrew Scriptures. Already in the ancient Greek version, however, Chronicles was collected with Samuel and Kings, a tradition that persists in modern translations. Drawing much of its information from Kings, Chronicles recounts Israel's history from Adam to the Edict of Cyrus the Persian (539 B.C.E.). Beyond the Hebrew Scriptures, the history of the Jewish people is included in some of the books found in the Apocrypha or Deuterocanon, such as 1–4 Maccabees.

The present order of the Historical Books from Joshua to Esther presents a panoramic view of God's history with the Israelites. The settlement of the Promised Land and accounts of God's rule of Israel's tribes appears in Joshua and Judges. The rise of the monarchy and especially the rule of David occupy 1 and 2 Samuel. First Kings recalls the reign of Solomon and the construction of the temple in Jerusalem. The balance of Kings recounts the divided monarchy, leading to the defeat and destruction of the northern kingdom of Israel and, more than a century later, the southern kingdom of Judah. The books of Ezra and Nehemiah describe how God's people returned to Judah after the exile to rebuild the Jerusalem and the temple. Though the characters are many and the events are complex, it is clear in these historical books that God was at work directing the history of the people of Israel.

JOSHUA

Joshua 6:5

Background File

The book of Joshua describes the entry of God's people Israel into the promised land of Canaan after their time of wandering in the wilderness. The action in Joshua takes place sometime in the thirteenth century B.C.E., but the book was completed in its final form some centuries later, probably in the seventh century B.C.E.

What's the Story?

Joshua is part of a longer collected work known as the Deuteronomistic History (Deuteronomy–2 Kings). Joshua is listed as the first of the twelve Historical Books in the Old Testament, the books that start with Joshua and end with Esther. In the Hebrew Scriptures Joshua is part of what is called the Former Prophets (see chart Different Canons of the Hebrew Bible [Old Testament], pp. 28-29). Moses had led the people out of slavery in Egypt and through the wilderness to the border of the land God had promised them. Before Moses died, Joshua was chosen to lead people across the Jordan River into Canaan. But the story makes it clear that the LORD was the real leader. God had promised to give this land to Israel's ancestor Abraham (see Gen 12:1-3; 15:18-21; 17:8). This promise was repeated to Moses (Exod 3:7-8). The story in Joshua begins with God's command to "proceed to cross the Jordan, you and all this people, into the land that I am giving to them, to the Israelites" (1:2).

Joshua's own name, "the LORD saves," was a reminder that the LORD would lead and protect the people as they entered Canaan. Though Joshua 10:40 says that "Joshua defeated the whole land," it is clear that securing the land was not complete. Parts of the land remained uncaptured (13:2-6). Even so, God commanded Joshua to divide up the land among Israel's tribes (13:7—22:34). Finally, the aging Joshua called the people together to encourage them to renew their commitment to God. God had given them the land, and now the people were called to promise to worship and serve God only. So, the outline of the book has three main parts:

The conquest of the land (chapters 1–12)
The division of the land to some of the tribes (chapters 13–22)
The call to the people to repent and renew the covenant (chapters 23–24).

What's the Message?

The book reminded Israel that the promised land was a gift to them from the LORD. Keeping the land depended on the people being faithful to the LORD and living according to the LORD'S law. Joshua emphasizes Israel's faithfulness in his final speeches (23:1–24:28).

In the seventh century B.C.E., when the book of Joshua was likely finalized, the people of Judah were facing the threat of invasion by foreign powers. The people did turn away from God, so they were defeated by the Babylonians, who forced many of the people to leave their land. Joshua's promise at the end of the book—that their land would be returned when they again became faithful to God—was a comfort to those living in exile. The book of Joshua offered them hope. In exile, they were no longer ruled by God's anointed king, but they hoped that if they returned to God's covenant, or promise, God would return the promised land to them. For future generations, the book was a reminder that keeping the land depended on keeping their covenant promises with God.

The invasion described in Joshua is shockingly violent in places. Because the land and its cities were to be dedicated to God, this meant driving out and killing local people and taking or destroying their property. In spite of God's promise of this land, we may find it hard to understand why such violent means had to be used. The ongoing struggle over this land today is part of a long history. The books of Joshua and Judges offered Israel hope and encouraged faithfulness to God when the people faced threats from foreign invaders who wanted to take their land. Even in the days of Jesus, Joshua would have given courage to those in Israel who opposed the occupation by Rome.

After World War II and the Holocaust, a Jewish homeland was reestablished in Israel. The message of Joshua played out again in a new struggle. Today some Christians use Joshua to justify violent conquest in the name of God. Other Christians are challenged to understand this violence and seek peaceful solutions to struggles.

Martin Luther described the Bible as the cradle that holds Christ. We read the whole of Scripture and find meaning through Christ. The name *Jesus* is Greek for "Joshua." Though both their names mean "the LORD saves," the way Jesus saves the people of God seems to contrast starkly to Joshua's violent conquest.

Reading Joshua helps us understand what the people in Jesus' time expected of him. Many thought Jesus would be a king who came to defeat the Romans and take back the promised land. They expected Jesus to rule by force. But Jesus repeatedly shattered these expectations with his parables, teaching, and actions. Jesus brought a new kingdom without using force, so that God's kingdom could be open to all.

God's Commission to Joshua

1 After the death of Moses the servant of the LORD, the LORD spoke to Joshua son of Nun, Moses' assistant, saying, 2 "My servant Moses is dead. Now proceed to cross the Jordan, you and all this people, into the land that I am giving to them, to the Israelites. 3 Every place that the sole of your foot will tread upon I have given to you, as I promised to Moses. 4 From the wilderness and the Lebanon as far as the great river, the river Euphrates, all the land of the Hittites, to the Great Sea in the west shall be your territory. 5 No one shall be able to stand against you all the days of your life. As I was with Moses, so I will be with you; I will not fail you or forsake you. 6 Be strong and courageous; for you shall put this people in possession of the land that I swore to their ancestors to give them. 7 Only be strong and very courageous, being careful to act in accordance with all the law that my servant Moses commanded you; do not turn from it to the right hand or to the left, so that you may be successful wherever you go. 8 This book of the law shall not depart out of your mouth; you shall meditate on it day and night, so that you may be careful to act in accordance with all that is written in it. For then you shall make your way prosperous, and then you shall be successful. 9 I hereby command you: Be strong and courageous; do not be frightened or dismayed, for the LORD your God is with you wherever you go."

Preparations for the Invasion

10 Then Joshua commanded the officers of the people, 11 "Pass through the camp, and command the people: 'Prepare your provisions; for in three days you are to cross over the Jordan, to go in to take possession of the land that the LORD your God gives you to possess.'"

12 To the Reubenites, the Gadites, and the half-tribe of Manasseh Joshua said, 13 "Remember the word that Moses the servant of the LORD commanded you, saying, 'The LORD your God is providing you a place of rest, and will give you this land.' 14 Your wives, your little ones, and your livestock shall remain in the land that Moses gave you beyond the Jordan. But all the warriors among you shall cross over armed before your kindred and shall help them, 15 until the LORD gives rest to your kindred as well as to you, and they too take possession of the land that the LORD your God is giving them. Then you shall return to your own land and take possession of it, the land that Moses the servant of the LORD gave you beyond the Jordan to the east."

16 They answered Joshua: "All that you have commanded us we will do, and wherever you send us we will go. 17 Just as we obeyed Moses in all things, so we will obey you. Only may the LORD your

1:1-9 After the death of Moses... the LORD spoke to Joshua: Moses had led the people out of slavery in Egypt and through the wilderness for forty years. He also received God's laws and passed them on to the people during this time. These stories are described in the books of Exodus–Deuteronomy. Before Moses died he anointed Joshua with the laying on of hands (Deut 34:9). Now God commands Joshua to cross the Jordan River to possess all the land from the Euphrates River to the Mediterranean Sea. This land, which was also promised earlier to Moses (Exod 3:7-8), was larger than the land of Canaan. See Map 3, pp. 2100-2101. Joshua and the people are to be strong, to be courageous, and to follow all the laws that Moses commanded.

1:8 book of the law: This term probably refers to what is now part of Deuteronomy. The books of Deuteronomy–2 Kings (except Ruth) stress the law as central to Israel's faith. Many centuries after the time of Joshua, Ezra used the book of the law to rededicate the exiles who returned and rebuilt the temple in Jerusalem. The book of the law stresses ending the worship of other gods. It centralizes worship in Jerusalem. It also called for the people of Israel to marry among their own people and to take care to live according to the laws of God.

Some Christians argue that theirs should be a "Christian nation." What do you think this means? How do you believe Christians are called to live in nations with diverse religious (and nonreligious) people?

1:12-14 Reubenites...this land... beyond the Jordan: The twelve tribes of Israel were named for the twelve sons of Jacob (see Gen 35:23-26; 48:1—49:33). The tribes mentioned in these verses would eventually settle east of the Jordan River. But the warriors from those tribes were to enter Canaan and participate in securing the territory.

God be with you, as he was with Moses! 18 Whoever rebels against your orders and disobeys your words, whatever you command, shall be put to death. Only be strong and courageous."

Spies Sent to Jericho

2 Then Joshua son of Nun sent two men secretly from Shittim as spies, saying, "Go, view the land, especially Jericho." So they went, and entered the house of a prostitute whose name was Rahab, and spent the night there. 2 The king of Jericho was told, "Some Israelites have come here tonight to search out the land." 3 Then the king of Jericho sent orders to Rahab, "Bring out the men who have come to you, who entered your house, for they have come only to search out the whole land." 4 But the woman took the two men and hid them. Then she said, "True, the men came to me, but I did not know where they came from. 5 And when it was time to close the gate at dark, the men went out. Where the men went I do not know. Pursue them quickly, for you can overtake them." 6 She had, however, brought them up to the roof and hidden them with the stalks of flax that she had laid out on the roof. 7 So the men pursued them on the way to he Jordan as far as the fords. As soon as the pursuers had gone out, the gate was shut.

8 Before they went to sleep, she came up to them on the roof 9 and said to the men: "I know that the LORD has given you the land, and that dread of you has fallen on us, and that all the inhabitants of the land melt in fear before you. 10 For we have heard how the LORD dried up the water of the Red Sea[a] before you when you came out of Egypt, and what you did to the two kings of the Amorites that were beyond the Jordan, to Sihon and Og, whom you utterly destroyed. 11 As soon as we heard it, our hearts melted, and there was no courage left in any of us because of you. The LORD your God is indeed God in heaven above and on earth below. 12 Now then, since I have dealt kindly with you, swear to me by the LORD that you in turn will deal kindly with my family. Give me a sign of good faith 13 that you will spare my father and mother, my brothers and sisters, and all who belong to them, and deliver our lives from death." 14 The men said to her, "Our life for yours! If you do not tell this business of ours, then we will deal kindly and faithfully with you when the LORD gives us the land."

15 Then she let them down by a rope through the window, for her house was on the outer side of the city wall and she resided within the wall itself. 16 She said to them, "Go toward the hill country, so that the pursuers may not come upon you. Hide yourselves there three days, until the pursuers have returned; then afterward you may go your way." 17 The men said to her, "We will be released from this oath

2:1-2 Shittim...Jericho...The king: Shittim was located somewhere east of the Jordan River. Jericho was less than a ten-mile journey from the river. See Map 3, pp. 2100-2101. At the time of the story, Jericho was a small city of less than ten acres. Canaanite cities of the time were not connected by a central government. Each city had its own ruler.

2:1-24 entered the house of...Rahab: Rahab was a prostitute who hid Joshua's spies on the roof of her house, which was built into the outer wall of the city. She and her family avoided the destruction of Jericho because she provided shelter and helped the spies escape. Rahab and her family would later become part of the Israelite people (Josh 6:21-25).

2:10 dried up the water of the Red Sea...Sihon and Og: News had apparently spread about the miraculous way the Hebrews crossed the Red Sea (Exod 14) and about the Hebrew people's defeat of the Amorites (see Num 21:21-35).

[a] Or *Sea of Reeds*

that you have made us swear to you [18]if we invade the land and you
do not tie this crimson cord in the window through which you let us
down, and you do not gather into your house your father and mother,
your brothers, and all your family. [19]If any of you go out of the doors
of your house into the street, they shall be responsible for their own
death, and we shall be innocent; but if a hand is laid upon any who
are with you in the house, we shall bear the responsibility for their
death. [20]But if you tell this business of ours, then we shall be released
from this oath that you made us swear to you." [21]She said, "According
to your words, so be it." She sent them away and they departed. Then
she tied the crimson cord in the window.

22 They departed and went into the hill country and stayed there
three days, until the pursuers returned. The pursuers had searched all
along the way and found nothing. [23]Then the two men came down
again from the hill country. They crossed over, came to Joshua son
of Nun, and told him all that had happened to them. [24]They said to
Joshua, "Truly the LORD has given all the land into our hands; moreover all the inhabitants of the land melt in fear before us."

Israel Crosses the Jordan

3 Early in the morning Joshua rose and set out from Shittim with
all the Israelites, and they came to the Jordan. They camped
there before crossing over. [2]At the end of three days the officers went
through the camp [3]and commanded the people, "When you see the
ark of the covenant of the LORD your God being carried by the levitical priests, then you shall set out from your place. Follow it, [4]so that
you may know the way you should go, for you have not passed this
way before. Yet there shall be a space between you and it, a distance
of about two thousand cubits; do not come any nearer to it." [5]Then
Joshua said to the people, "Sanctify yourselves; for tomorrow the
LORD will do wonders among you." [6]To the priests Joshua said, "Take
up the ark of the covenant, and pass on in front of the people." So they
took up the ark of the covenant and went in front of the people.

7 The LORD said to Joshua, "This day I will begin to exalt you in
the sight of all Israel, so that they may know that I will be with you as
I was with Moses. [8]You are the one who shall command the priests
who bear the ark of the covenant, 'When you come to the edge of
the waters of the Jordan, you shall stand still in the Jordan.'" [9]Joshua
then said to the Israelites, "Draw near and hear the words of the LORD
your God." [10]Joshua said, "By this you shall know that among you is
the living God who without fail will drive out from before you the
Canaanites, Hittites, Hivites, Perizzites, Girgashites, Amorites, and
Jebusites: [11]the ark of the covenant of the Lord of all the earth is going
to pass before you into the Jordan. [12]So now select twelve men from
the tribes of Israel, one from each tribe. [13]When the soles of the feet

2:24 the LORD has given all the land into our hands: The spies sent by Joshua acknowledge that God is doing what God promised the Israelite people.

The author of Hebrews includes Rahab among the faithful (Heb 11:31). James says this Canaanite convert is "justified by works" when she welcomes the "messengers" of Joshua (Jas 2:25.) How is faith joined with works in your life?

3:1—4:24 they came to the Jordan…crossed over: Joshua led the tribes over the Jordan River (see Map 3, pp. 2100-2101) into the promised land, just as Moses led the people out of Egypt (Exod 14:1-31).

3:3 ark of the covenant: The ark of the covenant was a sacred box that contained the Ten Commandments and other holy items (see Exod 25:10-22). It was at the center of Israel's worship and was a sign of God's presence with them. The ark was to be carried out ahead of the people by the Levitical priests, as a sign that God was leading the way.

3:5 Sanctify yourselves: This refers to acts of worship, prayer, or sacrifice done in preparation for doing something in God's name. For example, see Deuteronomy 20:1-9; 1 Samuel 21:2-5, which talk of preparation for going into battle. The Jordan River crossing was to be a holy procession, led by God.

3:7 as I was with Moses: The LORD acts on the promise made in 1:5 and tells Joshua that the LORD will be with him.

3:10 Canaanites…Jebusites: This is a list of different peoples the Israelites would encounter in Canaan and surrounding lands. For example, the Jebusites controlled the area around Jerusalem when Israel's King David took over the city (2 Sam 5:6-9).

of the priests who bear the ark of the LORD, the Lord of all the earth,
rest in the waters of the Jordan, the waters of the Jordan flowing from
above shall be cut off; they shall stand in a single heap."
14 When the people set out from their tents to cross over the Jordan, the priests bearing the ark of the covenant were in front of the
people. [15]Now the Jordan overflows all its banks throughout the time
of harvest. So when those who bore the ark had come to the Jordan,
and the feet of the priests bearing the ark were dipped in the edge of
the water, [16]the waters flowing from above stood still, rising up in a single heap far off at Adam, the city that is beside Zarethan, while those
flowing toward the sea of the Arabah, the Dead Sea,[a] were wholly cut
off. Then the people crossed over opposite Jericho. [17]While all Israel
were crossing over on dry ground, the priests who bore the ark of the
covenant of the LORD stood on dry ground in the middle of the Jordan, until the entire nation finished crossing over the Jordan.

Twelve Stones Set Up at Gilgal

4 When the entire nation had finished crossing over the Jordan,
the LORD said to Joshua: [2]"Select twelve men from the people,
one from each tribe, [3]and command them, 'Take twelve stones from
here out of the middle of the Jordan, from the place where the priests'
feet stood, carry them over with you, and lay them down in the place
where you camp tonight.'" [4]Then Joshua summoned the twelve men
from the Israelites, whom he had appointed, one from each tribe.
[5]Joshua said to them, "Pass on before the ark of the LORD your God
into the middle of the Jordan, and each of you take up a stone on his
shoulder, one for each of the tribes of the Israelites, [6]so that this may
be a sign among you. When your children ask in time to come, 'What
do those stones mean to you?' [7]then you shall tell them that the waters of the Jordan were cut off in front of the ark of the covenant of the
LORD. When it crossed over the Jordan, the waters of the Jordan were
cut off. So these stones shall be to the Israelites a memorial forever."
8 The Israelites did as Joshua commanded. They took up twelve
stones out of the middle of the Jordan, according to the number of
the tribes of the Israelites, as the LORD told Joshua, carried them
over with them to the place where they camped, and laid them down
there. [9](Joshua set up twelve stones in the middle of the Jordan, in the
place where the feet of the priests bearing the ark of the covenant had
stood; and they are there to this day.)
10 The priests who bore the ark remained standing in the middle of the Jordan, until everything was finished that the LORD commanded Joshua to tell the people, according to all that Moses had
commanded Joshua. The people crossed over in haste. [11]As soon as

[a] Heb *Salt Sea*

3:16-17 the waters flowing from above stood still: When the priests stood in the water, the waters of the Jordan heaped up and did not flow. This is an echo of Moses' deeds (Exod 14:21-22). The city of Adam was to the north of Jericho.

4:6-7; 20-23 When your children ask: The issue is that children, or future generations, should know what the LORD has done for the people of God.

4:9, 20 twelve stones in the middle of the Jordan . . . Gilgal: Two monuments were set up to mark the crossing. Gilgal camp was about five miles northeast of Jericho (see Map 3, pp. 2100-2101). Gilgal was an important place of worship before Jerusalem became the main place of worship (see 1 Sam 11:15; 2 Sam 19:15).

When the Israelites crossed the Jordan River, a leader from each tribe carried a stone that became a symbol of the event. What symbols have you seen that proclaim that God's hand is mighty and that God is involved in our lives? How are these symbols explained to children or others? How is the cross our best symbol of God's mighty hand?

all the people had finished crossing over, the ark of the LORD, and
the priests, crossed over in front of the people. [12]The Reubenites, the
Gadites, and the half-tribe of Manasseh crossed over armed before
the Israelites, as Moses had ordered them. [13]About forty thousand
armed for war crossed over before the LORD to the plains of Jericho
for battle.

14 On that day the LORD exalted Joshua in the sight of all Israel;
and they stood in awe of him, as they had stood in awe of Moses, all
the days of his life.

15 The LORD said to Joshua, [16]"Command the priests who bear
the ark of the covenant,[a] to come up out of the Jordan." [17]Joshua therefore commanded the priests, "Come up out of the Jordan." [18]When
the priests bearing the ark of the covenant of the LORD came up from
the middle of the Jordan, and the soles of the priests' feet touched
dry ground, the waters of the Jordan returned to their place and overflowed all its banks, as before.

19 The people came up out of the Jordan on the tenth day of the
first month, and they camped in Gilgal on the east border of Jericho.
[20]Those twelve stones, which they had taken out of the Jordan, Joshua
set up in Gilgal, [21]saying to the Israelites, "When your children ask
their parents in time to come, 'What do these stones mean?' [22]then
you shall let your children know, 'Israel crossed over the Jordan here
on dry ground.' [23]For the LORD your God dried up the waters of the
Jordan for you until you crossed over, as the LORD your God did to
the Red Sea,[b] which he dried up for us until we crossed over, [24]so that
all the peoples of the earth may know that the hand of the LORD is
mighty, and so that you may fear the LORD your God forever."

The New Generation Circumcised

5 When all the kings of the Amorites beyond the Jordan to the
west, and all the kings of the Canaanites by the sea, heard that
the LORD had dried up the waters of the Jordan for the Israelites until
they had crossed over, their hearts melted, and there was no longer
any spirit in them, because of the Israelites.

2 At that time the LORD said to Joshua, "Make flint knives and
circumcise the Israelites a second time." [3]So Joshua made flint knives,
and circumcised the Israelites at Gibeath-haaraloth.[c] [4]This is the reason why Joshua circumcised them: all the males of the people who
came out of Egypt, all the warriors, had died during the journey
through the wilderness after they had come out of Egypt. [5]Although
all the people who came out had been circumcised, yet all the people
born on the journey through the wilderness after they had come out
of Egypt had not been circumcised. [6]For the Israelites traveled forty

5:2-12 circumcise the Israelites . . . kept the passover: God commanded that circumcision be a physical sign that Abraham's descendants were God's people (Gen 17:9-14). Passover celebrated the Hebrews' escape from slavery in Egypt (see Exod 12:43—13:10). This service of remembrance and circumcision marked Israel's entry into the promised land. These are key marks of Jewish identity to this day.

[a] Or *treaty*, or *testimony*; Heb *eduth* [b] Or *Sea of Reeds* [c] That is *the Hill of the Foreskins*

years in the wilderness, until all the nation, the warriors who came out of Egypt, perished, not having listened to the voice of the LORD. To them the LORD swore that he would not let them see the land that he had sworn to their ancestors to give us, a land flowing with milk and honey. 7 So it was their children, whom he raised up in their place, that Joshua circumcised; for they were uncircumcised, because they had not been circumcised on the way.

8 When the circumcising of all the nation was done, they remained in their places in the camp until they were healed. 9 The LORD said to Joshua, "Today I have rolled away from you the disgrace of Egypt." And so that place is called Gilgal[a] to this day.

The Passover at Gilgal

10 While the Israelites were camped in Gilgal they kept the passover in the evening on the fourteenth day of the month in the plains of Jericho. 11 On the day after the passover, on that very day, they ate the produce of the land, unleavened cakes and parched grain. 12 The manna ceased on the day they ate the produce of the land, and the Israelites no longer had manna; they ate the crops of the land of Canaan that year.

Joshua's Vision

13 Once when Joshua was by Jericho, he looked up and saw a man standing before him with a drawn sword in his hand. Joshua went to him and said to him, "Are you one of us, or one of our adversaries?" 14 He replied, "Neither; but as commander of the army of the LORD I have now come." And Joshua fell on his face to the earth and worshiped, and he said to him, "What do you command your servant, my lord?" 15 The commander of the army of the LORD said to Joshua, "Remove the sandals from your feet, for the place where you stand is holy." And Joshua did so.

Jericho Taken and Destroyed

6 Now Jericho was shut up inside and out because of the Israelites; no one came out and no one went in. 2 The LORD said to Joshua, "See, I have handed Jericho over to you, along with its king and soldiers. 3 You shall march around the city, all the warriors circling the city once. Thus you shall do for six days, 4 with seven priests bearing seven trumpets of rams' horns before the ark. On the seventh day you shall march around the city seven times, the priests blowing the trumpets. 5 When they make a long blast with the ram's horn, as soon as you hear the sound of the trumpet, then all the people shall shout with a great shout; and the wall of the city will fall down flat, and all

5:13-15 Joshua…looked up and saw a man standing before him: Joshua encounters God in a way similar to Moses (Exod 3:5). Joshua is told to remove his sandals, because he is in a holy place. This is out of respect for God.

The man with a drawn sword (5:13) is called commander of the army of the LORD. He insists he is neither an adversary nor an Israelite. In every war, people want to claim that God is on their side. What do you think of the idea that God takes sides in wars or conflicts?

6:3-6 march around the city… seven trumpets of rams' horns: Because the city was relatively small (see note on 2:1-2), marching around the city seven times in a day would not have been difficult. Trumpets made of hollowed out rams' horns are called *shofars*.

[a] Related to Heb *galal* to roll

the people shall charge straight ahead." [6]So Joshua son of Nun summoned the priests and said to them, "Take up the ark of the covenant,
and have seven priests carry seven trumpets of rams' horns in front of
the ark of the LORD." [7]To the people he said, "Go forward and march
around the city; have the armed men pass on before the ark of the
LORD."

8 As Joshua had commanded the people, the seven priests carrying the seven trumpets of rams' horns before the LORD went forward,
blowing the trumpets, with the ark of the covenant of the LORD following them. [9]And the armed men went before the priests who blew
the trumpets; the rear guard came after the ark, while the trumpets
blew continually. [10]To the people Joshua gave this command: "You
shall not shout or let your voice be heard, nor shall you utter a word,
until the day I tell you to shout. Then you shall shout." [11]So the ark of
the LORD went around the city, circling it once; and they came into
the camp, and spent the night in the camp.

12 Then Joshua rose early in the morning, and the priests took
up the ark of the LORD. [13]The seven priests carrying the seven trumpets of rams' horns before the ark of the LORD passed on, blowing the
trumpets continually. The armed men went before them, and the rear
guard came after the ark of the LORD, while the trumpets blew continually. [14]On the second day they marched around the city once and
then returned to the camp. They did this for six days.

15 On the seventh day they rose early, at dawn, and marched
around the city in the same manner seven times. It was only on that
day that they marched around the city seven times. [16]And at the seventh time, when the priests had blown the trumpets, Joshua said to
the people, "Shout! For the LORD has given you the city. [17]The city
and all that is in it shall be devoted to the LORD for destruction. Only
Rahab the prostitute and all who are with her in her house shall live
because she hid the messengers we sent. [18]As for you, keep away from
the things devoted to destruction, so as not to covet[a] and take any of
the devoted things and make the camp of Israel an object for destruction, bringing trouble upon it. [19]But all silver and gold, and vessels of
bronze and iron, are sacred to the LORD; they shall go into the treasury of the LORD." [20]So the people shouted, and the trumpets were
blown. As soon as the people heard the sound of the trumpets, they
raised a great shout, and the wall fell down flat; so the people charged
straight ahead into the city and captured it. [21]Then they devoted to
destruction by the edge of the sword all in the city, both men and
women, young and old, oxen, sheep, and donkeys.

22 Joshua said to the two men who had spied out the land, "Go
into the prostitute's house, and bring the woman out of it and all who

6:15-27 the LORD has given you the city . . . and the wall fell down flat: Jericho's destruction was complete. All the people (except Rahab's clan) were destroyed.

6:17-19 devoted to the LORD for destruction: The people are to take nothing that remains. Everything is to be *herem [KHE-rem]*, meaning set aside for God (see Lev 27:20-21, 28-29). Because they belonged to the LORD they were not for human use. Animals and booty were not always considered "devoted to God" (see Josh 8:2; 11:14), but everything in Jericho was.

[a] Gk: Heb *devote to destruction* Compare 7.21

belong to her, as you swore to her." 23 So the young men who had
been spies went in and brought Rahab out, along with her father, her
mother, her brothers, and all who belonged to her—they brought
all her kindred out—and set them outside the camp of Israel. 24 They
burned down the city, and everything in it; only the silver and gold,
and the vessels of bronze and iron, they put into the treasury of the
house of the LORD. 25 But Rahab the prostitute, with her family and
all who belonged to her, Joshua spared. Her family[a] has lived in Israel
ever since. For she hid the messengers whom Joshua sent to spy out
Jericho.

6:26 Cursed before the LORD...Jericho!: See 1 Kings 16:34, which reports that this curse was fulfilled. See also 2 Kings 2:19-22.

26 Joshua then pronounced this oath, saying,
"Cursed before the LORD be anyone who tries
to build this city—this Jericho!
At the cost of his firstborn he shall lay its foundation,
and at the cost of his youngest he shall set up its gates!"

27 So the LORD was with Joshua; and his fame was in all
the land.

The Sin of Achan and Its Punishment

7:1 Israelites broke faith...Achan ...took some of the devoted things: God judges all Israel for Achan's theft of some things that were considered "devoted to God (see 6:17-19 and note). The whole community is affected by the actions of a single person.

7:2-12 Joshua sent men...to Ai... Israelites are unable to stand: After Jericho, the next target was the city of Ai (see Map 3, pp. 2100-2101). But because Achan had stolen some of the devoted things at Jericho, Joshua's forces are defeated and demoralized.

7 But the Israelites broke faith in regard to the devoted things:
Achan son of Carmi son of Zabdi son of Zerah, of the tribe of
Judah, took some of the devoted things; and the anger of the LORD
burned against the Israelites.

2 Joshua sent men from Jericho to Ai, which is near Beth-aven,
east of Bethel, and said to them, "Go up and spy out the land." And the
men went up and spied out Ai. 3 Then they returned to Joshua and said
to him, "Not all the people need go up; about two or three thousand
men should go up and attack Ai. Since they are so few, do not make
the whole people toil up there." 4 So about three thousand of the people went up there; and they fled before the men of Ai. 5 The men of Ai
killed about thirty-six of them, chasing them from outside the gate as
far as Shebarim and killing them on the slope. The hearts of the people melted and turned to water.

6 Then Joshua tore his clothes, and fell to the ground on his face
before the ark of the LORD until the evening, he and the elders of Israel; and they put dust on their heads. 7 Joshua said, "Ah, Lord GOD!
Why have you brought this people across the Jordan at all, to hand
us over to the Amorites so as to destroy us? Would that we had been
content to settle beyond the Jordan! 8 O Lord, what can I say, now that
Israel has turned their backs to their enemies! 9 The Canaanites and
all the inhabitants of the land will hear of it, and surround us, and cut
off our name from the earth. Then what will you do for your great
name?"

---

[a] Heb *She*

10 The LORD said to Joshua, "Stand up! Why have you fallen upon your face? 11 Israel has sinned; they have transgressed my covenant that I imposed on them. They have taken some of the devoted things; they have stolen, they have acted deceitfully, and they have put them among their own belongings. 12 Therefore the Israelites are unable to stand before their enemies; they turn their backs to their enemies, because they have become a thing devoted for destruction themselves. I will be with you no more, unless you destroy the devoted things from among you. 13 Proceed to sanctify the people, and say, 'Sanctify yourselves for tomorrow; for thus says the LORD, the God of Israel, "There are devoted things among you, O Israel; you will be unable to stand before your enemies until you take away the devoted things from among you." 14 In the morning therefore you shall come forward tribe by tribe. The tribe that the LORD takes shall come near by clans, the clan that the LORD takes shall come near by households, and the household that the LORD takes shall come near one by one. 15 And the one who is taken as having the devoted things shall be burned with fire, together with all that he has, for having transgressed the covenant of the LORD, and for having done an outrageous thing in Israel.' "

16 So Joshua rose early in the morning, and brought Israel near tribe by tribe, and the tribe of Judah was taken. 17 He brought near the clans of Judah, and the clan of the Zerahites was taken; and he brought near the clan of the Zerahites, family by family,[a] and Zabdi was taken. 18 And he brought near his household one by one, and Achan son of Carmi son of Zabdi son of Zerah, of the tribe of Judah, was taken. 19 Then Joshua said to Achan, "My son, give glory to the LORD God of Israel and make confession to him. Tell me now what you have done; do not hide it from me." 20 And Achan answered Joshua, "It is true; I am the one who sinned against the LORD God of Israel. This is what I did: 21 when I saw among the spoil a beautiful mantle from Shinar, and two hundred shekels of silver, and a bar of gold weighing fifty shekels, then I coveted them and took them. They now lie hidden in the ground inside my tent, with the silver underneath."

22 So Joshua sent messengers, and they ran to the tent; and there it was, hidden in his tent with the silver underneath. 23 They took them out of the tent and brought them to Joshua and all the Israelites; and they spread them out before the LORD. 24 Then Joshua and all Israel with him took Achan son of Zerah, with the silver, the mantle, and the bar of gold, with his sons and daughters, with his oxen, donkeys, and sheep, and his tent and all that he had; and they brought them up to the Valley of Achor. 25 Joshua said, "Why did you bring trouble on us? The LORD is bringing trouble on you today." And all Israel stoned

---

[a] Mss Syr: MT *man by man*

7:13-26 sanctify the people...the LORD turned from his burning anger: Joshua's prayers do not stop God's judgment. The people could only be purified (sanctified) if the one who sinned confessed (7:20), the devoted things stolen were destroyed, and the sinner (Achan) punished by death (7:25). Only then would God forgive the people and stop being angry with them. A pile of stones marking Achan's burial place was located in the Valley of Achor, which means "trouble."

Achan's punishment for his sin appears to us to be severe. But the crime affected the relationship of all the people with God. Think about Jesus and what he did by dying on the cross. How does his action change the way we think about forgiveness?

him to death; they burned them with fire, cast stones on them, [26]and raised over him a great heap of stones that remains to this day. Then the LORD turned from his burning anger. Therefore that place to this day is called the Valley of Achor.[a]

Ai Captured by a Stratagem and Destroyed

8:1-2 go up now to Ai…its spoil and its livestock you may take as booty: Once the Achan situation is resolved, Joshua's forces can try again to take the city of Ai. This time the people are allowed to keep some of the goods and livestock they capture.

8 Then the LORD said to Joshua, "Do not fear or be dismayed; take all the fighting men with you, and go up now to Ai. See, I have handed over to you the king of Ai with his people, his city, and his land. [2]You shall do to Ai and its king as you did to Jericho and its king; only its spoil and its livestock you may take as booty for yourselves. Set an ambush against the city, behind it."

3 So Joshua and all the fighting men set out to go up against Ai. Joshua chose thirty thousand warriors and sent them out by night [4]with the command, "You shall lie in ambush against the city, behind it; do not go very far from the city, but all of you stay alert. [5]I and all the people who are with me will approach the city. When they come out against us, as before, we shall flee from them. [6]They will come out after us until we have drawn them away from the city; for they will say, 'They are fleeing from us, as before.' While we flee from them, [7]you shall rise up from the ambush and seize the city; for the LORD your God will give it into your hand. [8]And when you have taken the city, you shall set the city on fire, doing as the LORD has ordered; see, I have commanded you." [9]So Joshua sent them out; and they went to the place of ambush, and lay between Bethel and Ai, to the west of Ai; but Joshua spent that night in the camp.[b]

10 In the morning Joshua rose early and mustered the people, and went up, with the elders of Israel, before the people to Ai. [11]All the fighting men who were with him went up, and drew near before the city, and camped on the north side of Ai, with a ravine between them and Ai. [12]Taking about five thousand men, he set them in ambush between Bethel and Ai, to the west of the city. [13]So they stationed the forces, the main encampment that was north of the city and its rear guard west of the city. But Joshua spent that night in the valley. [14]When the king of Ai saw this, he and all his people, the inhabitants of the city, hurried out early in the morning to the meeting place facing the Arabah to meet Israel in battle; but he did not know that there was an ambush against him behind the city. [15]And Joshua and all Israel made a pretense of being beaten before them, and fled in the direction of the wilderness. [16]So all the people who were in the city were called together to pursue them, and as they pursued Joshua they were drawn away from the city. [17]There was not a man left in Ai or Bethel who did not go out after Israel; they left the city open, and pursued Israel.

---

[a] That is *Trouble* [b] Heb *among the people*

18 Then the LORD said to Joshua, "Stretch out the sword that is
in your hand toward Ai; for I will give it into your hand." And Joshua
stretched out the sword that was in his hand toward the city. [19]As soon
as he stretched out his hand, the troops in ambush rose quickly out
of their place and rushed forward. They entered the city, took it, and
at once set the city on fire. [20]So when the men of Ai looked back, the
smoke of the city was rising to the sky. They had no power to flee this
way or that, for the people who fled to the wilderness turned back
against the pursuers. [21]When Joshua and all Israel saw that the ambush had taken the city and that the smoke of the city was rising, then
they turned back and struck down the men of Ai. [22]And the others
came out from the city against them; so they were surrounded by Israelites, some on one side, and some on the other; and Israel struck
them down until no one was left who survived or escaped. [23]But the
king of Ai was taken alive and brought to Joshua.

24 When Israel had finished slaughtering all the inhabitants of
Ai in the open wilderness where they pursued them, and when all
of them to the very last had fallen by the edge of the sword, all Israel
returned to Ai, and attacked it with the edge of the sword. [25]The total
of those who fell that day, both men and women, was twelve thousand—all the people of Ai. [26]For Joshua did not draw back his hand,
with which he stretched out the sword, until he had utterly destroyed
all the inhabitants of Ai. [27]Only the livestock and the spoil of that city
Israel took as their booty, according to the word of the LORD that he
had issued to Joshua. [28]So Joshua burned Ai, and made it forever a
heap of ruins, as it is to this day. [29]And he hanged the king of Ai on a
tree until evening; and at sunset Joshua commanded, and they took
his body down from the tree, threw it down at the entrance of the gate
of the city, and raised over it a great heap of stones, which stands there
to this day.

8:24-25 slaughtering all the inhabitants of Ai…twelve thousand: Apparently the people of Ai were considered "devoted to God" (see 8:2 and note at 6:17-19) and so were to be killed. The large number killed has been questioned in light of archeological evidence at et-Tell dating to this period. At the time of Joshua's invasion, Ai was a small, unwalled city.

Joshua Renews the Covenant

30 Then Joshua built on Mount Ebal an altar to the LORD, the
God of Israel, [31]just as Moses the servant of the LORD had commanded the Israelites, as it is written in the book of the law of Moses,
"an altar of unhewn[a] stones, on which no iron tool has been used";
and they offered on it burnt offerings to the LORD, and sacrificed
offerings of well-being. [32]And there, in the presence of the Israelites,
Joshua[b] wrote on the stones a copy of the law of Moses, which he
had written. [33]All Israel, alien as well as citizen, with their elders and
officers and their judges, stood on opposite sides of the ark in front of
the levitical priests who carried the ark of the covenant of the LORD,
half of them in front of Mount Gerizim and half of them in front of

8:30-35 Joshua built on Mount Ebal an altar to the LORD: Joshua read the "book of the law" to the people (see note on 1:8). Both aliens and citizens were included in the gathering. Mount Ebal was located about twenty miles north of Ai. Moses had received instructions about the ceremony that was to take place at Ebal after the people crossed into Canaan (Deut 11:29-30; 27:2-8). Controlling the high land around Ebal made it easier to control the land below stretching toward Jerusalem.

[a] Heb *whole* [b] Heb *he*

Mount Ebal, as Moses the servant of the LORD had commanded at the first, that they should bless the people of Israel. 34 And afterward he read all the words of the law, blessings and curses, according to all that is written in the book of the law. 35 There was not a word of all that Moses commanded that Joshua did not read before all the assembly of Israel, and the women, and the little ones, and the aliens who resided among them.

The Gibeonites Save Themselves by Trickery

9 Now when all the kings who were beyond the Jordan in the hill country and in the lowland all along the coast of the Great Sea toward Lebanon—the Hittites, the Amorites, the Canaanites, the Perizzites, the Hivites, and the Jebusites—heard of this, 2 they gathered together with one accord to fight Joshua and Israel.

3 But when the inhabitants of Gibeon heard what Joshua had done to Jericho and to Ai, 4 they on their part acted with cunning: they went and prepared provisions,[a] and took worn-out sacks for their donkeys, and wineskins, worn-out and torn and mended, 5 with worn-out, patched sandals on their feet, and worn-out clothes; and all their provisions were dry and moldy. 6 They went to Joshua in the camp at Gilgal, and said to him and to the Israelites, "We have come from a far country; so now make a treaty with us." 7 But the Israelites said to the Hivites, "Perhaps you live among us; then how can we make a treaty with you?" 8 They said to Joshua, "We are your servants." And Joshua said to them, "Who are you? And where do you come from?" 9 They said to him, "Your servants have come from a very far country, because of the name of the LORD your God; for we have heard a report of him, of all that he did in Egypt, 10 and of all that he did to the two kings of the Amorites who were beyond the Jordan, King Sihon of Heshbon, and King Og of Bashan who lived in Ashtaroth. 11 So our elders and all the inhabitants of our country said to us, 'Take provisions in your hand for the journey; go to meet them, and say to them, "We are your servants; come now, make a treaty with us." ' 12 Here is our bread; it was still warm when we took it from our houses as our food for the journey, on the day we set out to come to you, but now, see, it is dry and moldy; 13 these wineskins were new when we filled them, and see, they are burst; and these garments and sandals of ours are worn out from the very long journey." 14 So the leaders[b] partook of their provisions, and did not ask direction from the LORD. 15 And Joshua made peace with them, guaranteeing their lives by a treaty; and the leaders of the congregation swore an oath to them.

16 But when three days had passed after they had made a treaty with them, they heard that they were their neighbors and were liv-

9:6 from a far country: Apparently Israel could make peace treaties with people who did not live in the land of Canaan.

9:14-15 the leaders…did not ask direction from the LORD: The Israelites made a treaty with the Gibeonites without asking the LORD for advice.

[a] Cn: Meaning of Heb uncertain [b] Gk: Heb *men*

ing among them. [17]So the Israelites set out and reached their cities
on the third day. Now their cities were Gibeon, Chephirah, Beeroth,
and Kiriath-jearim. [18]But the Israelites did not attack them, because
the leaders of the congregation had sworn to them by the LORD, the
God of Israel. Then all the congregation murmured against the leaders. [19]But all the leaders said to all the congregation, "We have sworn
to them by the LORD, the God of Israel, and now we must not touch
them. [20]This is what we will do to them: We will let them live, so that
wrath may not come upon us, because of the oath that we swore to
them." [21]The leaders said to them, "Let them live." So they became
hewers of wood and drawers of water for all the congregation, as the
leaders had decided concerning them.

22 Joshua summoned them, and said to them, "Why did you deceive us, saying, 'We are very far from you,' while in fact you are living among us? [23]Now therefore you are cursed, and some of you shall
always be slaves, hewers of wood and drawers of water for the house
of my God." [24]They answered Joshua, "Because it was told to your servants for a certainty that the LORD your God had commanded his
servant Moses to give you all the land, and to destroy all the inhabitants of the land before you; so we were in great fear for our lives
because of you, and did this thing. [25]And now we are in your hand:
do as it seems good and right in your sight to do to us." [26]This is what
he did for them: he saved them from the Israelites; and they did not
kill them. [27]But on that day Joshua made them hewers of wood and
drawers of water for the congregation and for the altar of the LORD, to
continue to this day, in the place that he should choose.

9:19-21 We have sworn to them: The Israelites had been tricked into making a treaty with the Gibeonites, who actually knew what had happened at Ai and Jericho (9:3). Even so, the treaty was not broken. In the Hebrew culture, the spoken word had power and once spoken was not taken back.

9:23-27 shall always be slaves... for the house of my God: The Gibeonites became servants, assisting those Israelite priests who took care of the house of God. At the time of Joshua the "house" was the tent carried from place to place. Later the house would be the temple built in Jerusalem. Verse 27 may imply that the Gibeonites were still serving as assistants in later times when book of Joshua was compiled (see introduction to Joshua).

The Sun Stands Still

10 When King Adoni-zedek of Jerusalem heard how Joshua
had taken Ai, and had utterly destroyed it, doing to Ai and its
king as he had done to Jericho and its king, and how the inhabitants
of Gibeon had made peace with Israel and were among them, [2]he[a] became greatly frightened, because Gibeon was a large city, like one of
the royal cities, and was larger than Ai, and all its men were warriors.
[3]So King Adoni-zedek of Jerusalem sent a message to King Hoham of
Hebron, to King Piram of Jarmuth, to King Japhia of Lachish, and to
King Debir of Eglon, saying, [4]"Come up and help me, and let us attack
Gibeon; for it has made peace with Joshua and with the Israelites."
[5]Then the five kings of the Amorites—the king of Jerusalem, the king
of Hebron, the king of Jarmuth, the king of Lachish, and the king of
Eglon—gathered their forces, and went up with all their armies and
camped against Gibeon, and made war against it.

6 And the Gibeonites sent to Joshua at the camp in Gilgal, saying,

10:1-5 King Adoni-zedek of Jerusalem...king of Eglon...against Gibeon: After hearing of Israel's victory at Ai and their peace treaty with Gibeon, five kings to the south decide to form an alliance to fight against Gibeon. Hebron had been an important location in the stories of Israel's ancestors Abraham and Sarah (see Gen 13:18; 18:1; 23:19). It would later be the place where David would be anointed king (2 Sam 2:1-5). Amorites is often used as another term for Canaanites.

---

[a] Heb *they*

“Do not abandon your servants; come up to us quickly, and save us,
and help us; for all the kings of the Amorites who live in the hill country are gathered against us.” 7 So Joshua went up from Gilgal, he and all
the fighting force with him, all the mighty warriors. 8 The LORD said
to Joshua, “Do not fear them, for I have handed them over to you;
not one of them shall stand before you.” 9 So Joshua came upon them
suddenly, having marched up all night from Gilgal. 10 And the LORD
threw them into a panic before Israel, who inflicted a great slaughter
on them at Gibeon, chased them by the way of the ascent of Beth-
horon, and struck them down as far as Azekah and Makkedah. 11 As
they fled before Israel, while they were going down the slope of Beth-
horon, the LORD threw down huge stones from heaven on them as far
as Azekah, and they died; there were more who died because of the
hailstones than the Israelites killed with the sword.

12 On the day when the LORD gave the Amorites over to the Israelites, Joshua spoke to the LORD; and he said in the sight of Israel,

“Sun, stand still at Gibeon,
and Moon, in the valley of Aijalon.”
13 And the sun stood still, and the moon stopped,
until the nation took vengeance on their enemies.

Is this not written in the Book of Jashar? The sun stopped in midheaven, and did not hurry to set for about a whole day. 14 There has
been no day like it before or since, when the LORD heeded a human
voice; for the LORD fought for Israel.

15 Then Joshua returned, and all Israel with him, to the camp at
Gilgal.

Five Kings Defeated

16 Meanwhile, these five kings fled and hid themselves in the
cave at Makkedah. 17 And it was told Joshua, “The five kings have
been found, hidden in the cave at Makkedah.” 18 Joshua said, “Roll
large stones against the mouth of the cave, and set men by it to guard
them; 19 but do not stay there yourselves; pursue your enemies, and
attack them from the rear. Do not let them enter their towns, for the
LORD your God has given them into your hand.” 20 When Joshua and
the Israelites had finished inflicting a very great slaughter on them,
until they were wiped out, and when the survivors had entered into
the fortified towns, 21 all the people returned safe to Joshua in the
camp at Makkedah; no one dared to speak[a] against any of the Israelites.

22 Then Joshua said, “Open the mouth of the cave, and bring
those five kings out to me from the cave.” 23 They did so, and brought
the five kings out to him from the cave, the king of Jerusalem, the king

[a] Heb *moved his tongue*

10:12-14 Sun, stand still ... Book of Jashar: The poetic text (also mentioned in 2 Sam 1:18) is from the Book of Jashar, apparently a collection of ancient war songs. It presents a powerful picture of God's day-long victory.

10:14 the LORD fought for Israel: God is behind Joshua's military victories and is keeping the promise made to him (1:5). This theme is sometimes referred to as the Divine Warrior tradition.

Joshua 10:12-14 speaks of Joshua commanding the sun and moon to stand still. We know today that the earth revolves around the sun. So we recognize that this passage is not to be read literally, as we might read an astronomy textbook. What difference does it make if we read this passage knowing it includes symbolic language? How does the symbolic language of the passage still reflect the faith of Israel? What meaning does it have for your own faith?

10:16-39 Makkedah ... Debir: After executing the five kings of the alliance at Makkedah cave (10:26), Joshua proceeded to lead deadly assaults on a series of towns. As before at Ai, all the people are killed (see the note on 6:17-19, "devoted to the LORD").

of Hebron, the king of Jarmuth, the king of Lachish, and the king of
Eglon. [24]When they brought the kings out to Joshua, Joshua summoned all the Israelites, and said to the chiefs of the warriors who had
gone with him, "Come near, put your feet on the necks of these kings."
Then they came near and put their feet on their necks. [25]And Joshua
said to them, "Do not be afraid or dismayed; be strong and courageous; for thus the LORD will do to all the enemies against whom you
fight." [26]Afterward Joshua struck them down and put them to death,
and he hung them on five trees. And they hung on the trees until evening. [27]At sunset Joshua commanded, and they took them down from
the trees and threw them into the cave where they had hidden themselves; they set large stones against the mouth of the cave, which remain to this very day.

28 Joshua took Makkedah on that day, and struck it and its king
with the edge of the sword; he utterly destroyed every person in it; he
left no one remaining. And he did to the king of Makkedah as he had
done to the king of Jericho.

29 Then Joshua passed on from Makkedah, and all Israel with
him, to Libnah, and fought against Libnah. [30]The LORD gave it also
and its king into the hand of Israel; and he struck it with the edge of
the sword, and every person in it; he left no one remaining in it; and
he did to its king as he had done to the king of Jericho.

31 Next Joshua passed on from Libnah, and all Israel with him, to
Lachish, and laid siege to it, and assaulted it. [32]The LORD gave Lachish
into the hand of Israel, and he took it on the second day, and struck
it with the edge of the sword, and every person in it, as he had done
to Libnah.

33 Then King Horam of Gezer came up to help Lachish; and
Joshua struck him and his people, leaving him no survivors.

34 From Lachish Joshua passed on with all Israel to Eglon; and
they laid siege to it, and assaulted it; [35]and they took it that day, and
struck it with the edge of the sword; and every person in it he utterly
destroyed that day, as he had done to Lachish.

36 Then Joshua went up with all Israel from Eglon to Hebron;
they assaulted it, [37]and took it, and struck it with the edge of the
sword, and its king and its towns, and every person in it; he left no
one remaining, just as he had done to Eglon, and utterly destroyed it
with every person in it.

38 Then Joshua, with all Israel, turned back to Debir and assaulted it, [39]and he took it with its king and all its towns; they struck
them with the edge of the sword, and utterly destroyed every person
in it; he left no one remaining; just as he had done to Hebron, and, as
he had done to Libnah and its king, so he did to Debir and its king.

40 So Joshua defeated the whole land, the hill country and the
Negeb and the lowland and the slopes, and all their kings; he left

10:40-41 Joshua defeated the whole land...to Gaza...Goshen: Joshua's victories here include much more land than is mentioned in the story so far. The Negeb is the desert region stretching southeast from Jerusalem all the way to the Sinai Peninsula. Gaza is the strip of land along the Mediterranean Sea (see Map 3, pp. 2100-2101). Goshen here is uncertain and not the land of Goshen in Egypt. The phrase "destroyed all that breathed" (see also 11:11, 14) is based on Deuteronomy 20:16. Joshua 13 makes it clear that at this point in the story, all these areas are not fully under Israel's control.

no one remaining, but utterly destroyed all that breathed, as the LORD God of Israel commanded. [41]And Joshua defeated them from Kadesh-barnea to Gaza, and all the country of Goshen, as far as Gibeon. [42]Joshua took all these kings and their land at one time, because the LORD God of Israel fought for Israel. [43]Then Joshua returned, and all Israel with him, to the camp at Gilgal.

The United Kings of Northern Canaan Defeated

11:1-23 When King Jabin…And the land had rest from war: This is a condensed version of the conquest of the northern part of Canaan. Hermon in the land of Mizpah refers to Mount Hermon. Controlling this high point made it easier to defeat enemies in the valleys below. These battles may have taken most of Joshua's lifetime. In 11:18 it says that "Joshua made war a long time."

11 When King Jabin of Hazor heard of this, he sent to King Jobab of Madon, to the king of Shimron, to the king of Achshaph, [2]and to the kings who were in the northern hill country, and in the Arabah south of Chinneroth, and in the lowland, and in Naphoth-dor on the west, [3]to the Canaanites in the east and the west, the Amorites, the Hittites, the Perizzites, and the Jebusites in the hill country, and the Hivites under Hermon in the land of Mizpah. [4]They came out, with all their troops, a great army, in number like the sand on the seashore, with very many horses and chariots. [5]All these kings joined their forces, and came and camped together at the waters of Merom, to fight with Israel.

6 And the LORD said to Joshua, "Do not be afraid of them, for tomorrow at this time I will hand over all of them, slain, to Israel; you shall hamstring their horses, and burn their chariots with fire." [7]So Joshua came suddenly upon them with all his fighting force, by the waters of Merom, and fell upon them. [8]And the LORD handed them over to Israel, who attacked them and chased them as far as Great Sidon and Misrephoth-maim, and eastward as far as the valley of Mizpeh. They struck them down, until they had left no one remaining. [9]And Joshua did to them as the LORD commanded him; he hamstrung their horses, and burned their chariots with fire.

11:9 hamstrung their horses…burned their chariots: Israel's armies fought as infantry until later (see 1 Kgs 10:26-29), so they did not capture the horses and chariots to use them.

10 Joshua turned back at that time, and took Hazor, and struck its king down with the sword. Before that time Hazor was the head of all those kingdoms. [11]And they put to the sword all who were in it, utterly destroying them; there was no one left who breathed, and he burned Hazor with fire. [12]And all the towns of those kings, and all their kings, Joshua took, and struck them with the edge of the sword, utterly destroying them, as Moses the servant of the LORD had commanded. [13]But Israel burned none of the towns that stood on mounds except Hazor, which Joshua did burn. [14]All the spoil of these towns, and the livestock, the Israelites took for their booty; but all the people they struck down with the edge of the sword, until they had destroyed them, and they did not leave any who breathed. [15]As the LORD had commanded his servant Moses, so Moses commanded Joshua, and so Joshua did; he left nothing undone of all that the LORD had commanded Moses.

Summary of Joshua's Conquests

16 So Joshua took all that land: the hill country and all the Negeb
and all the land of Goshen and the lowland and the Arabah and the
hill country of Israel and its lowland, 17 from Mount Halak, which rises
toward Seir, as far as Baal-gad in the valley of Lebanon below Mount
Hermon. He took all their kings, struck them down, and put them to
death. 18 Joshua made war a long time with all those kings. 19 There was
not a town that made peace with the Israelites, except the Hivites, the
inhabitants of Gibeon; all were taken in battle. 20 For it was the LORD's
doing to harden their hearts so that they would come against Israel
in battle, in order that they might be utterly destroyed, and might
receive no mercy, but be exterminated, just as the LORD had commanded Moses.

21 At that time Joshua came and wiped out the Anakim from the
hill country, from Hebron, from Debir, from Anab, and from all the
hill country of Judah, and from all the hill country of Israel; Joshua
utterly destroyed them with their towns. 22 None of the Anakim was
left in the land of the Israelites; some remained only in Gaza, in Gath,
and in Ashdod. 23 So Joshua took the whole land, according to all that
the LORD had spoken to Moses; and Joshua gave it for an inheritance
to Israel according to their tribal allotments. And the land had rest
from war.

The Kings Conquered by Moses

12 Now these are the kings of the land, whom the Israelites defeated, whose land they occupied beyond the Jordan toward
the east, from the Wadi Arnon to Mount Hermon, with all the Arabah eastward: 2 King Sihon of the Amorites who lived at Heshbon, and
ruled from Aroer, which is on the edge of the Wadi Arnon, and from
the middle of the valley as far as the river Jabbok, the boundary of the
Ammonites, that is, half of Gilead, 3 and the Arabah to the Sea of Chinneroth eastward, and in the direction of Beth-jeshimoth, to the sea of
the Arabah, the Dead Sea,[a] southward to the foot of the slopes of Pisgah; 4 and King Og[b] of Bashan, one of the last of the Rephaim, who lived
at Ashtaroth and at Edrei 5 and ruled over Mount Hermon and Salecah
and all Bashan to the boundary of the Geshurites and the Maacathites,
and over half of Gilead to the boundary of King Sihon of Heshbon.
6 Moses, the servant of the LORD, and the Israelites defeated them; and
Moses the servant of the LORD gave their land for a possession to the
Reubenites and the Gadites and the half-tribe of Manasseh.

The Kings Conquered by Joshua

7 The following are the kings of the land whom Joshua and the
Israelites defeated on the west side of the Jordan, from Baal-gad in the

---

[a] Heb *Salt Sea* [b] Gk: Heb *the boundary of King Og*

11:23 Joshua took the whole land…for an inheritance to Israel: This is the land God had promised in Genesis 12:7 and Exodus 32:13. The identity of the people of Israel is tied to the land.

This northern area that Joshua conquered is later known as Galilee, where Jesus was born and did most of his ministry. Joshua conquered it with military force. Jesus influenced and led the people without the use of force. How do these two different approaches (both involving God's direction) influence your thinking?

12:1-24 these are the kings of the land, whom the Israelites defeated: Moses had led the conquest east of the Jordan. Joshua led the western campaign. Wadi Arnon is a deep streambed that formed the border between northern Moab and an area claimed by Israel east of the Jordan. See Numbers 21:21-31 for the story of Sihon. Og is mentioned in Deuteronomy 3:1-13. He was described as being a large man who led the chariot warriors known as the Rephaim.

valley of Lebanon to Mount Halak, that rises toward Seir (and Joshua gave their land to the tribes of Israel as a possession according to their allotments, [8]in the hill country, in the lowland, in the Arabah, in the slopes, in the wilderness, and in the Negeb, the land of the Hittites, Amorites, Canaanites, Perizzites, Hivites, and Jebusites):

9	the king of Jericho	one
	the king of Ai, which is next to Bethel	one
10	the king of Jerusalem	one
	the king of Hebron	one
11	the king of Jarmuth	one
	the king of Lachish	one
12	the king of Eglon	one
	the king of Gezer	one
13	the king of Debir	one
	the king of Geder	one
14	the king of Hormah	one
	the king of Arad	one
15	the king of Libnah	one
	the king of Adullam	one
16	the king of Makkedah	one
	the king of Bethel	one
17	the king of Tappuah	one
	the king of Hepher	one
18	the king of Aphek	one
	the king of Lasharon	one
19	the king of Madon	one
	the king of Hazor	one
20	the king of Shimron-meron	one
	the king of Achshaph	one
21	the king of Taanach	one
	the king of Megiddo	one
22	the king of Kedesh	one
	the king of Jokneam in Carmel	one
23	the king of Dor in Naphath-dor	one
	the king of Goiim in Galilee,[a]	one
24	the king of Tirzah	one

thirty-one kings in all.

13:1—22:34 Now Joshua was old…and the LORD said to him: Although Joshua had not conquered all the land, the LORD told him to divide the land west of the Jordan River. Some of the area mentioned in 13:1-7, such as Lebanon, never came under Israel's control. The land of the Philistines (Gaza) was controlled only briefly during the time that kings David and Solomon ruled Israel. The land was divided among the tribes that are the descendants of Jacob's sons.

The Parts of Canaan Still Unconquered

13 Now Joshua was old and advanced in years; and the LORD
said to him, "You are old and advanced in years, and very
much of the land still remains to be possessed. [2]This is the land that
still remains: all the regions of the Philistines, and all those of the

[a] Gk: Heb *Gilgal*

Geshurites 3 (from the Shihor, which is east of Egypt, northward to the
boundary of Ekron, it is reckoned as Canaanite; there are five rulers of
the Philistines, those of Gaza, Ashdod, Ashkelon, Gath, and Ekron),
and those of the Avvim 4 in the south; all the land of the Canaanites,
and Mearah that belongs to the Sidonians, to Aphek, to the boundary
of the Amorites, 5 and the land of the Gebalites, and all Lebanon, toward the east, from Baal-gad below Mount Hermon to Lebo-hamath,
6 all the inhabitants of the hill country from Lebanon to Misrephoth-
maim, even all the Sidonians. I will myself drive them out from before
the Israelites; only allot the land to Israel for an inheritance, as I have
commanded you. 7 Now therefore divide this land for an inheritance
to the nine tribes and the half-tribe of Manasseh."

The Territory East of the Jordan

8 With the other half-tribe of Manasseh[a] the Reubenites and the
Gadites received their inheritance, which Moses gave them, beyond
the Jordan eastward, as Moses the servant of the LORD gave them:
9 from Aroer, which is on the edge of the Wadi Arnon, and the town
that is in the middle of the valley, and all the tableland from[b] Medeba as far as Dibon; 10 and all the cities of King Sihon of the Amorites,
who reigned in Heshbon, as far as the boundary of the Ammonites;
11 and Gilead, and the region of the Geshurites and Maacathites, and
all Mount Hermon, and all Bashan to Salecah; 12 all the kingdom of
Og in Bashan, who reigned in Ashtaroth and in Edrei (he alone was
left of the survivors of the Rephaim); these Moses had defeated and
driven out. 13 Yet the Israelites did not drive out the Geshurites or the
Maacathites; but Geshur and Maacath live within Israel to this day.
14 To the tribe of Levi alone Moses gave no inheritance; the
offerings by fire to the LORD God of Israel are their inheritance, as he
said to them.

The Territory of Reuben

15 Moses gave an inheritance to the tribe of the Reubenites according to their clans. 16 Their territory was from Aroer, which is on
the edge of the Wadi Arnon, and the town that is in the middle of
the valley, and all the tableland by Medeba; 17 with Heshbon, and all
its towns that are in the tableland; Dibon, and Bamoth-baal, and
Beth-baal-meon, 18 and Jahaz, and Kedemoth, and Mephaath, 19 and
Kiriathaim, and Sibmah, and Zereth-shahar on the hill of the valley,
20 and Beth-peor, and the slopes of Pisgah, and Beth-jeshimoth,
21 that is, all the towns of the tableland, and all the kingdom of King
Sihon of the Amorites, who reigned in Heshbon, whom Moses
defeated with the leaders of Midian, Evi and Rekem and Zur and

[a] Cn: Heb *With it* [b] Compare Gk: Heb lacks *from*

13:7 divide this land for an inheritance: In the times of the stories of Joshua and Judges, the people of Israel were a confederation of tribes. They were linked by the covenant with Moses. The nine and one-half tribes include those mentioned in 15:1—19:48. Manasseh and Ephraim were the sons of Joseph (and grandsons of Jacob). Each of them received a tribal share of land (see Gen 48:1-6). They each needed to have land to make the number twelve, since the descendants of Jacob's son Levi did not receive tribal land (see Deut 18:1-8 and the note on Josh 13:14; 14:3 below).

13:8-31 other half-tribe of Manasseh...Gadites: Half of the Manasseh tribe got tribal land east of the Jordan and the other half received tribal land west of the Jordan (see 17:1-13). See Map 4, p. 2102, which shows the lands given to Israel's tribes. Bashan (13:30) is the area now known as the Golan Heights.

13:14, 33; 14:3 tribe of Levi: The tribe of Levi received no tribal land. All Levites had the right to be priests. Ordinary Israelites could sacrifice at occasional altars. Only Levites were allowed to sacrifice in the temple. Their inheritance was "the offerings by fire to the LORD God of Israel." The Levites received a portion of the offerings the people brought to the temple for sacrifice. But in chapter 21 the Levites claim that God promised them cities and land for their cattle.

Hur and Reba, as princes of Sihon, who lived in the land. [22]Along
with the rest of those they put to death, the Israelites also put to the
sword Balaam son of Beor, who practiced divination. [23]And the border of the Reubenites was the Jordan and its banks. This was the
inheritance of the Reubenites according to their families with their
towns and villages.

The Territory of Gad

24 Moses gave an inheritance also to the tribe of the Gadites, according to their families. [25]Their territory was Jazer, and all the towns
of Gilead, and half the land of the Ammonites, to Aroer, which is
east of Rabbah, [26]and from Heshbon to Ramath-mizpeh and Beto-
nim, and from Mahanaim to the territory of Debir,[a] [27]and in the valley
Beth-haram, Beth-nimrah, Succoth, and Zaphon, the rest of the kingdom of King Sihon of Heshbon, the Jordan and its banks, as far as
the lower end of the Sea of Chinnereth, eastward beyond the Jordan.
[28]This is the inheritance of the Gadites according to their clans, with
their towns and villages.

The Territory of the Half-Tribe of Manasseh (East)

29 Moses gave an inheritance to the half-tribe of Manasseh; it
was allotted to the half-tribe of the Manassites according to their families. [30]Their territory extended from Mahanaim, through all Bashan,
the whole kingdom of King Og of Bashan, and all the settlements of
Jair, which are in Bashan, sixty towns, [31]and half of Gilead, and Ashtaroth, and Edrei, the towns of the kingdom of Og in Bashan; these
were allotted to the people of Machir son of Manasseh according to
their clans—for half the Machirites.

32 These are the inheritances that Moses distributed in the plains
of Moab, beyond the Jordan east of Jericho. [33]But to the tribe of Levi
Moses gave no inheritance; the LORD God of Israel is their inheritance, as he said to them.

The Distribution of Territory West of the Jordan

14 These are the inheritances that the Israelites received in the
land of Canaan, which the priest Eleazar, and Joshua son of
Nun, and the heads of the families of the tribes of the Israelites distributed to them. [2]Their inheritance was by lot, as the LORD had commanded Moses for the nine and one-half tribes. [3]For Moses had given
an inheritance to the two and one-half tribes beyond the Jordan; but
to the Levites he gave no inheritance among them. [4]For the people
of Joseph were two tribes, Manasseh and Ephraim; and no portion
was given to the Levites in the land, but only towns to live in, with

14:1-2 the priest Eleazar…Their inheritance was by lot: See Numbers 27:18-23, where Eleazar the priest lays his hands on Joshua to show that Joshua was the leader chosen to follow Moses. Eleazar also was the keeper of the sacred lots, the Urim and Thummim. These lots were marked sticks or stones used to determine God's will. Like rolling dice, these lots were by chance, but it was assumed God controlled the outcome. The lands were assigned by using the sacred lots.

[a] Gk Syr Vg: Heb *Lidebir*

their pasture lands for their flocks and herds. 5 The Israelites did as the
LORD commanded Moses; they allotted the land.

Hebron Allotted to Caleb

6 Then the people of Judah came to Joshua at Gilgal; and Caleb son of Jephunneh the Kenizzite said to him, "You know what the
LORD said to Moses the man of God in Kadesh-barnea concerning
you and me. 7 I was forty years old when Moses the servant of the
LORD sent me from Kadesh-barnea to spy out the land; and I brought
him an honest report. 8 But my companions who went up with me
made the heart of the people melt; yet I wholeheartedly followed
the LORD my God. 9 And Moses swore on that day, saying, 'Surely
the land on which your foot has trodden shall be an inheritance for
you and your children forever, because you have wholeheartedly followed the LORD my God.' 10 And now, as you see, the LORD has kept
me alive, as he said, these forty-five years since the time that the LORD
spoke this word to Moses, while Israel was journeying through the
wilderness; and here I am today, eighty-five years old. 11 I am still as
strong today as I was on the day that Moses sent me; my strength now
is as my strength was then, for war, and for going and coming. 12 So
now give me this hill country of which the LORD spoke on that day;
for you heard on that day how the Anakim were there, with great fortified cities; it may be that the LORD will be with me, and I shall drive
them out, as the LORD said."

13 Then Joshua blessed him, and gave Hebron to Caleb son of
Jephunneh for an inheritance. 14 So Hebron became the inheritance of
Caleb son of Jephunneh the Kenizzite to this day, because he whole-
heartedly followed the LORD, the God of Israel. 15 Now the name of
Hebron formerly was Kiriath-arba;[a] this Arba was[b] the greatest man
among the Anakim. And the land had rest from war.

14:6 people of Judah...Caleb: The tribe of Judah received prime land based on being given a place of honor when Jacob blessed his sons (Gen 49:8-10). King David would later come from the Judah tribe. Caleb makes a case for receiving land in the Judah territory based on his role as one of the spies who entered Canaan and encouraged the people to enter the land. He was one of only two from his entire generation allowed to enter the promised land (see Num 13–14).

14:15 And the land had rest from war. Perhaps this anticipates the completing of Caleb's occupation. Chapter 15 describes additional conflict.

We often do not think about the effect of war on the land itself. How do you think our call to care for the earth can guide our thinking about war?

The Territory of Judah

15 The lot for the tribe of the people of Judah according to their
families reached southward to the boundary of Edom, to the
wilderness of Zin at the farthest south. 2 And their south boundary ran
from the end of the Dead Sea,[c] from the bay that faces southward; 3 it
goes out southward of the ascent of Akrabbim, passes along to Zin,
and goes up south of Kadesh-barnea, along by Hezron, up to Addar,
makes a turn to Karka, 4 passes along to Azmon, goes out by the Wadi
of Egypt, and comes to its end at the sea. This shall be your south
boundary. 5 And the east boundary is the Dead Sea,[c] to the mouth of
the Jordan. And the boundary on the north side runs from the bay
of the sea at the mouth of the Jordan; 6 and the boundary goes up to

15:1-63 Judah: This tribe occupied important land and towns stretching east to west in the mid-southern part of the land. Included in this territory was Jerusalem, which was not captured until the time of David (2 Sam 5:6-9). Still later, after the united kingdom of Israel divided into two kingdoms, Judah was the primary territory in the south.

[a] That is *the city of Arba* [b] Heb lacks *this Arba was* [c] Heb *Salt Sea*

Beth-hoglah, and passes along north of Beth-arabah; and the boundary goes up to the Stone of Bohan, Reuben's son; 7 and the boundary goes up to Debir from the Valley of Achor, and so northward, turning toward Gilgal, which is opposite the ascent of Adummim, which is on the south side of the valley; and the boundary passes along to the waters of En-shemesh, and ends at En-rogel; 8 then the boundary goes up by the valley of the son of Hinnom at the southern slope of the Jebusites (that is, Jerusalem); and the boundary goes up to the top of the mountain that lies over against the valley of Hinnom, on the west, at the northern end of the valley of Rephaim; 9 then the boundary extends from the top of the mountain to the spring of the Waters of Nephtoah, and from there to the towns of Mount Ephron; then the boundary bends around to Baalah (that is, Kiriath-jearim); 10 and the boundary circles west of Baalah to Mount Seir, passes along to the northern slope of Mount Jearim (that is, Chesalon), and goes down to Beth-shemesh, and passes along by Timnah; 11 the boundary goes out to the slope of the hill north of Ekron, then the boundary bends around to Shikkeron, and passes along to Mount Baalah, and goes out to Jabneel; then the boundary comes to an end at the sea. 12 And the west boundary was the Mediterranean with its coast. This is the boundary surrounding the people of Judah according to their families.

Caleb Occupies His Portion

13 According to the commandment of the LORD to Joshua, he gave to Caleb son of Jephunneh a portion among the people of Judah, Kiriath-arba,[a] that is, Hebron (Arba was the father of Anak). 14 And Caleb drove out from there the three sons of Anak: Sheshai, Ahiman, and Talmai, the descendants of Anak. 15 From there he went up against the inhabitants of Debir; now the name of Debir formerly was Kiriath-sepher. 16 And Caleb said, "Whoever attacks Kiriath-sepher and takes it, to him I will give my daughter Achsah as wife." 17 Othniel son of Kenaz, the brother of Caleb, took it; and he gave him his daughter Achsah as wife. 18 When she came to him, she urged him to ask her father for a field. As she dismounted from her donkey, Caleb said to her, "What do you wish?" 19 She said to him, "Give me a present; since you have set me in the land of the Negeb, give me springs of water as well." So Caleb gave her the upper springs and the lower springs.

The Towns of Judah

20 This is the inheritance of the tribe of the people of Judah according to their families. 21 The towns belonging to the tribe of the people of Judah in the extreme south, toward the boundary of Edom,

15:16-19 I will give my daughter Achsah as wife…gave her the upper springs: Caleb gives his daughter to Othniel for conquering a city in Caleb's territory. In turn his daughter Achsah asked for her own property. Othniel was later chosen to be one of Israel's judges (Judg 3:7-11).

Some weddings today still include the question "Who gives this woman to be married to this man?" What do you think about using this tradition from the days when parents determined who their daughters would marry?

[a] That is *the city of Arba*

were Kabzeel, Eder, Jagur, [22]Kinah, Dimonah, Adadah, [23]Kedesh,
Hazor, Ithnan, [24]Ziph, Telem, Bealoth, [25]Hazor-hadattah, Kerioth-
hezron (that is, Hazor), [26]Amam, Shema, Moladah, [27]Hazar-gaddah,
Heshmon, Beth-pelet, [28]Hazar-shual, Beer-sheba, Biziothiah, [29]Ba-
alah, Iim, Ezem, [30]Eltolad, Chesil, Hormah, [31]Ziklag, Madmannah,
Sansannah, [32]Lebaoth, Shilhim, Ain, and Rimmon: in all, twenty-nine
towns, with their villages.

33 And in the lowland, Eshtaol, Zorah, Ashnah, [34]Zanoah, En-
gannim, Tappuah, Enam, [35]Jarmuth, Adullam, Socoh, Azekah, [36]Sha-
araim, Adithaim, Gederah, Gederothaim: fourteen towns with their
villages.

37 Zenan, Hadashah, Migdal-gad, [38]Dilan, Mizpeh, Jokthe-el,
[39]Lachish, Bozkath, Eglon, [40]Cabbon, Lahmam, Chitlish, [41]Gederoth,
Beth-dagon, Naamah, and Makkedah: sixteen towns with their villages.

42 Libnah, Ether, Ashan, [43]Iphtah, Ashnah, Nezib, [44]Keilah,
Achzib, and Mareshah: nine towns with their villages.

45 Ekron, with its dependencies and its villages; [46]from Ekron to
the sea, all that were near Ashdod, with their villages.

47 Ashdod, its towns and its villages; Gaza, its towns and its villages; to the Wadi of Egypt, and the Great Sea with its coast.

48 And in the hill country, Shamir, Jattir, Socoh, [49]Dannah,
Kiriath-sannah (that is, Debir), [50]Anab, Eshtemoh, Anim, [51]Goshen,
Holon, and Giloh: eleven towns with their villages.

52 Arab, Dumah, Eshan, [53]Janim, Beth-tappuah, Aphekah,
[54]Humtah, Kiriath-arba (that is, Hebron), and Zior: nine towns with
their villages.

55 Maon, Carmel, Ziph, Juttah, [56]Jezreel, Jokdeam, Zanoah,
[57]Kain, Gibeah, and Timnah: ten towns with their villages.

58 Halhul, Beth-zur, Gedor, [59]Maarath, Beth-anoth, and Eltekon:
six towns with their villages.

60 Kiriath-baal (that is, Kiriath-jearim) and Rabbah: two towns
with their villages.

61 In the wilderness, Beth-arabah, Middin, Secacah, [62]Nibshan,
the City of Salt, and En-gedi: six towns with their villages.

63 But the people of Judah could not drive out the Jebusites, the
inhabitants of Jerusalem; so the Jebusites live with the people of Judah in Jerusalem to this day.

The Territory of Ephraim

16 The allotment of the Josephites went from the Jordan by
Jericho, east of the waters of Jericho, into the wilderness, going up from Jericho into the hill country to Bethel; [2]then going from
Bethel to Luz, it passes along to Ataroth, the territory of the Archites;
[3]then it goes down westward to the territory of the Japhletites, as

16:1-10 the Josephites…Manasseh and Ephraim: Manasseh and Ephraim were the sons of Joseph, so in a sense the Joseph tribe received a double share of tribal land (see the note on 13:7).

far as the territory of Lower Beth-horon, then to Gezer, and it ends at the sea.

4 The Josephites—Manasseh and Ephraim—received their inheritance.

5 The territory of the Ephraimites by their families was as follows: the boundary of their inheritance on the east was Ataroth-addar as far as Upper Beth-horon, 6 and the boundary goes from there to the sea; on the north is Michmethath; then on the east the boundary makes a turn toward Taanath-shiloh, and passes along beyond it on the east to Janoah, 7 then it goes down from Janoah to Ataroth and to Naarah, and touches Jericho, ending at the Jordan. 8 From Tappuah the boundary goes westward to the Wadi Kanah, and ends at the sea. Such is the inheritance of the tribe of the Ephraimites by their families, 9 together with the towns that were set apart for the Ephraimites within the inheritance of the Manassites, all those towns with their villages. 10 They did not, however, drive out the Canaanites who lived in Gezer: so the Canaanites have lived within Ephraim to this day but have been made to do forced labor.

16:10 did not...drive out the Canaanites: The Canaanites were not completely driven out. They were kept for slave labor. As in 9:23-27, the phrase "to this day" suggests that the material was compiled at a later time. See also 17:13.

The Other Half-Tribe of Manasseh (West)

17:1-13 tribe of Manasseh...firstborn of Joseph: A portion of the Manasseh tribe was given land west of the Jordan River. This included land given to the daughters of Zelophehad, who had received land based on their appeal to Moses (see Num 27:1-11; 36:1-12). This land in the north balanced the land Caleb received in the south by special treatment (see the note on 14:6).

17 Then allotment was made to the tribe of Manasseh, for he was the firstborn of Joseph. To Machir the firstborn of Manasseh, the father of Gilead, were allotted Gilead and Bashan, because he was a warrior. 2 And allotments were made to the rest of the tribe of Manasseh, by their families, Abiezer, Helek, Asriel, Shechem, Hepher, and Shemida; these were the male descendants of Manasseh son of Joseph, by their families.

3 Now Zelophehad son of Hepher son of Gilead son of Machir son of Manasseh had no sons, but only daughters; and these are the names of his daughters: Mahlah, Noah, Hoglah, Milcah, and Tirzah. 4 They came before the priest Eleazar and Joshua son of Nun and the leaders, and said, "The LORD commanded Moses to give us an inheritance along with our male kin." So according to the commandment of the LORD he gave them an inheritance among the kinsmen of their father. 5 Thus there fell to Manasseh ten portions, besides the land of Gilead and Bashan, which is on the other side of the Jordan, 6 because the daughters of Manasseh received an inheritance along with his sons. The land of Gilead was allotted to the rest of the Manassites.

7 The territory of Manasseh reached from Asher to Michmethath, which is east of Shechem; then the boundary goes along southward to the inhabitants of En-tappuah. 8 The land of Tappuah belonged to Manasseh, but the town of Tappuah on the boundary of Manasseh belonged to the Ephraimites. 9 Then the boundary went down to the Wadi Kanah. The towns here, to the south of the wadi, among the towns of Manasseh, belong to Ephraim. Then the boundary of Ma-

nasseh goes along the north side of the wadi and ends at the sea. 10 The
land to the south is Ephraim's and that to the north is Manasseh's,
with the sea forming its boundary; on the north Asher is reached,
and on the east Issachar. 11 Within Issachar and Asher, Manasseh had
Beth-shean and its villages, Ibleam and its villages, the inhabitants of
Dor and its villages, the inhabitants of En-dor and its villages, the inhabitants of Taanach and its villages, and the inhabitants of Megiddo
and its villages (the third is Naphath).[a] 12 Yet the Manassites could not
take possession of those towns; but the Canaanites continued to live
in that land. 13 But when the Israelites grew strong, they put the Canaanites to forced labor, but did not utterly drive them out.

The Tribe of Joseph Protests

14 The tribe of Joseph spoke to Joshua, saying, "Why have you
given me but one lot and one portion as an inheritance, since we are
a numerous people, whom all along the LORD has blessed?" 15 And
Joshua said to them, "If you are a numerous people, go up to the forest, and clear ground there for yourselves in the land of the Perizzites
and the Rephaim, since the hill country of Ephraim is too narrow for
you." 16 The tribe of Joseph said, "The hill country is not enough for us;
yet all the Canaanites who live in the plain have chariots of iron, both
those in Beth-shean and its villages and those in the Valley of Jezreel."
17 Then Joshua said to the house of Joseph, to Ephraim and Manasseh,
"You are indeed a numerous people, and have great power; you shall
not have one lot only, 18 but the hill country shall be yours, for though
it is a forest, you shall clear it and possess it to its farthest borders; for
you shall drive out the Canaanites, though they have chariots of iron,
and though they are strong."

The Territories of the Remaining Tribes

18 Then the whole congregation of the Israelites assembled at
Shiloh, and set up the tent of meeting there. The land lay subdued before them.

2 There remained among the Israelites seven tribes whose inheritance had not yet been apportioned. 3 So Joshua said to the Israelites,
"How long will you be slack about going in and taking possession of
the land that the LORD, the God of your ancestors, has given you?
4 Provide three men from each tribe, and I will send them out that
they may begin to go throughout the land, writing a description of it
with a view to their inheritances. Then come back to me. 5 They shall
divide it into seven portions, Judah continuing in its territory on the
south, and the house of Joseph in their territory on the north. 6 You
shall describe the land in seven divisions and bring the description

[a] Meaning of Heb uncertain

17:14-18 Why have you given me but one lot: Not everyone was happy with their territory. Joseph's tribe complained that their portion would not support their large numbers.

18:1 tent of meeting...Shiloh: The tent of meeting is also called the tabernacle. It was Israel's place of worship. It is described in detail in Exodus 25–27. The tent of meeting was packed up and carried by the priests of Israel as the people journeyed from place to place (Num 4:1-49). See also note on 3:3.

Shiloh now replaced the Gilgal camp as the gathering place of the tribes. It was where the tent of meeting, God's dwelling place among them, would be set up. Shiloh was only about twenty miles north of Jerusalem, the eventual location for the tent of meeting—and the temple that would be built in the time of King Solomon. Years later, Shiloh was abandoned by God because the people worshiped idols there (Jer 7:12; Ps 78:56-72).

18:6 I will cast lots for you here before the LORD our God: It is not clear exactly how Joshua "cast lots." The lots decided the allotments for the remaining seven tribes. See also the note at 14:1-2. In the New Testament, Jesus' disciples cast lots to choose a replacement for Judas (Acts 1:26). As in the distribution of land by lot centuries earlier, this use of lots was not gambling but was seen as a way to leave the decision in God's hands.

Today governments sponsor lotteries. The word *lot* can be seen in lottery. Gambling games that use the luck of the draw are called games of chance. What difference is there between gambling and lotteries, and the casting of lots described in the Bible?

18:7 Levites have no portion among you: See the note on 13:7.

18:11-28: Benjamin: The tribe descended from the youngest son of Jacob and Rachel (Gen 35:16-18). Saul, Israel's first king, came from the tribe of Benjamin (1 Sam 9:21). Their territory included many of the towns initially defeated in Joshua 2–9.

here to me; and I will cast lots for you here before the LORD our God. [7]The Levites have no portion among you, for the priesthood of the LORD is their heritage; and Gad and Reuben and the half-tribe of Manasseh have received their inheritance beyond the Jordan eastward, which Moses the servant of the LORD gave them."

8 So the men started on their way; and Joshua charged those who went to write the description of the land, saying, "Go throughout the land and write a description of it, and come back to me; and I will cast lots for you here before the LORD in Shiloh." [9]So the men went and traversed the land and set down in a book a description of it by towns in seven divisions; then they came back to Joshua in the camp at Shiloh, [10]and Joshua cast lots for them in Shiloh before the LORD; and there Joshua apportioned the land to the Israelites, to each a portion.

The Territory of Benjamin

11 The lot of the tribe of Benjamin according to its families came up, and the territory allotted to it fell between the tribe of Judah and the tribe of Joseph. [12]On the north side their boundary began at the Jordan; then the boundary goes up to the slope of Jericho on the north, then up through the hill country westward; and it ends at the wilderness of Beth-aven. [13]From there the boundary passes along southward in the direction of Luz, to the slope of Luz (that is, Bethel), then the boundary goes down to Ataroth-addar, on the mountain that lies south of Lower Beth-horon. [14]Then the boundary goes in another direction, turning on the western side southward from the mountain that lies to the south, opposite Beth-horon, and it ends at Kiriath-baal (that is, Kiriath-jearim), a town belonging to the tribe of Judah. This forms the western side. [15]The southern side begins at the outskirts of Kiriath-jearim; and the boundary goes from there to Ephron,[a] to the spring of the Waters of Nephtoah; [16]then the boundary goes down to the border of the mountain that overlooks the valley of the son of Hinnom, which is at the north end of the valley of Rephaim; and it then goes down the valley of Hinnom, south of the slope of the Jebusites, and downward to En-rogel; [17]then it bends in a northerly direction going on to En-shemesh, and from there goes to Geliloth, which is opposite the ascent of Adummim; then it goes down to the Stone of Bohan, Reuben's son; [18]and passing on to the north of the slope of Beth-arabah[b] it goes down to the Arabah; [19]then the boundary passes on to the north of the slope of Beth-hoglah; and the boundary ends at the northern bay of the Dead Sea,[c] at the south end of the Jordan: this is the southern border. [20]The Jordan forms its boundary on the eastern side. This is the inheritance of the tribe of Benjamin, according to its families, boundary by boundary all around.

---

[a] Cn See 15.9. Heb *westward* [b] Gk: Heb *to the slope over against the Arabah* [c] Heb *Salt Sea*

21 Now the towns of the tribe of Benjamin according to their
families were Jericho, Beth-hoglah, Emek-keziz, [22]Beth-arabah, Zemaraim, Bethel, [23]Avvim, Parah, Ophrah, [24]Chephar-ammoni, Ophni,
and Geba—twelve towns with their villages: [25]Gibeon, Ramah, Beeroth, [26]Mizpeh, Chephirah, Mozah, [27]Rekem, Irpeel, Taralah, [28]Zela,
Haeleph, Jebus[a] (that is, Jerusalem), Gibeah[b] and Kiriath-jearim[c]—
fourteen towns with their villages. This is the inheritance of the tribe
of Benjamin according to its families.

The Territory of Simeon

19 The second lot came out for Simeon, for the tribe of Simeon, according to its families; its inheritance lay within the
inheritance of the tribe of Judah. [2]It had for its inheritance Beer-
sheba, Sheba, Moladah, [3]Hazar-shual, Balah, Ezem, [4]Eltolad, Bethul,
Hormah, [5]Ziklag, Beth-marcaboth, Hazar-susah, [6]Beth-lebaoth, and
Sharuhen—thirteen towns with their villages; [7]Ain, Rimmon, Ether,
and Ashan—four towns with their villages; [8]together with all the
villages all around these towns as far as Baalath-beer, Ramah of the
Negeb. This was the inheritance of the tribe of Simeon according to
its families. [9]The inheritance of the tribe of Simeon formed part of the
territory of Judah; because the portion of the tribe of Judah was too
large for them, the tribe of Simeon obtained an inheritance within
their inheritance.

19:1-48 Simeon...Dan: Tribal lands assigned to the last six tribes stretched from the south (Simeon) to the north (Asher and Naphtali). Simeon apparently shared part of the large Judah territory. The Issachar tribe's land included the Jezreel Valley, a fertile area that was often fought over. The Asher tribe in the north came close to the Phoenician cities of Tyre and Sidon. In later times King Hiram of Tyre provided Solomon with valuable cedar and cypress wood for the building of the temple in Jerusalem (1 Kgs 5:1-11).

The Territory of Zebulun

10 The third lot came up for the tribe of Zebulun, according
to its families. The boundary of its inheritance reached as far as Sarid; [11]then its boundary goes up westward, and on to Maralah, and
touches Dabbesheth, then the wadi that is east of Jokneam; [12]from Sarid it goes in the other direction eastward toward the sunrise to the
boundary of Chisloth-tabor; from there it goes to Daberath, then up
to Japhia; [13]from there it passes along on the east toward the sunrise to
Gath-hepher, to Eth-kazin, and going on to Rimmon it bends toward
Neah; [14]then on the north the boundary makes a turn to Hannathon,
and it ends at the valley of Iphtah-el; [15]and Kattath, Nahalal, Shimron,
Idalah, and Bethlehem—twelve towns with their villages. [16]This is the
inheritance of the tribe of Zebulun, according to its families—these
towns with their villages.

The Territory of Issachar

17 The fourth lot came out for Issachar, for the tribe of Issachar,
according to its families. [18]Its territory included Jezreel, Chesulloth,
Shunem, [19]Hapharaim, Shion, Anaharath, [20]Rabbith, Kishion, Ebez,

---

[a] Gk Syr Vg: Heb *the Jebusite* [b] Heb *Gibeath* [c] Gk: Heb *Kiriath*

[21]Remeth, En-gannim, En-haddah, Beth-pazzez; [22]the boundary also touches Tabor, Shahazumah, and Beth-shemesh, and its boundary ends at the Jordan—sixteen towns with their villages. [23]This is the inheritance of the tribe of Issachar, according to its families—the towns with their villages.

The Territory of Asher

24 The fifth lot came out for the tribe of Asher according to its families. [25]Its boundary included Helkath, Hali, Beten, Achshaph, [26]Allammelech, Amad, and Mishal; on the west it touches Carmel and Shihor-libnath, [27]then it turns eastward, goes to Beth-dagon, and touches Zebulun and the valley of Iphtah-el northward to Beth-emek and Neiel; then it continues in the north to Cabul, [28]Ebron, Rehob, Hammon, Kanah, as far as Great Sidon; [29]then the boundary turns to Ramah, reaching to the fortified city of Tyre; then the boundary turns to Hosah, and it ends at the sea; Mahalab,[a] Achzib, [30]Ummah, Aphek, and Rehob—twenty-two towns with their villages. [31]This is the inheritance of the tribe of Asher according to its families—these towns with their villages.

The Territory of Naphtali

32 The sixth lot came out for the tribe of Naphtali, for the tribe of Naphtali, according to its families. [33]And its boundary ran from Heleph, from the oak in Zaanannim, and Adami-nekeb, and Jabneel, as far as Lakkum; and it ended at the Jordan; [34]then the boundary turns westward to Aznoth-tabor, and goes from there to Hukkok, touching Zebulun at the south, and Asher on the west, and Judah on the east at the Jordan. [35]The fortified towns are Ziddim, Zer, Hammath, Rakkath, Chinnereth, [36]Adamah, Ramah, Hazor, [37]Kedesh, Edrei, En-hazor, [38]Iron, Migdal-el, Horem, Beth-anath, and Beth-shemesh—nineteen towns with their villages. [39]This is the inheritance of the tribe of Naphtali according to its families—the towns with their villages.

The Territory of Dan

40 The seventh lot came out for the tribe of Dan, according to its families. [41]The territory of its inheritance included Zorah, Eshtaol, Ir-shemesh, [42]Shaalabbin, Aijalon, Ithlah, [43]Elon, Timnah, Ekron, [44]Eltekeh, Gibbethon, Baalath, [45]Jehud, Bene-berak, Gath-rimmon, [46]Me-jarkon, and Rakkon at the border opposite Joppa. [47]When the territory of the Danites was lost to them, the Danites went up and fought against Leshem, and after capturing it and putting it to the sword, they took possession of it and settled in it, calling Leshem,

---

[a] Cn Compare Gk: Heb *Mehebel*

Dan, after their ancestor Dan. 48 This is the inheritance of the tribe of
Dan, according to their families—these towns with their villages.

Joshua's Inheritance

49 When they had finished distributing the several territories
of the land as inheritances, the Israelites gave an inheritance among
them to Joshua son of Nun. 50 By command of the LORD they gave
him the town that he asked for, Timnath-serah in the hill country of
Ephraim; he rebuilt the town, and settled in it.

51 These are the inheritances that the priest Eleazar and Joshua
son of Nun and the heads of the families of the tribes of the Israelites
distributed by lot at Shiloh before the LORD, at the entrance of the
tent of meeting. So they finished dividing the land.

The Cities of Refuge

20 Then the LORD spoke to Joshua, saying, 2 "Say to the Israelites, 'Appoint the cities of refuge, of which I spoke to
you through Moses, 3 so that anyone who kills a person without intent or by mistake may flee there; they shall be for you a refuge from
the avenger of blood. 4 The slayer shall flee to one of these cities and
shall stand at the entrance of the gate of the city, and explain the case
to the elders of that city; then the fugitive shall be taken into the city,
and given a place, and shall remain with them. 5 And if the avenger
of blood is in pursuit, they shall not give up the slayer, because the
neighbor was killed by mistake, there having been no enmity between
them before. 6 The slayer shall remain in that city until there is a trial
before the congregation, until the death of the one who is high priest
at the time: then the slayer may return home, to the town in which
the deed was done.' "

7 So they set apart Kedesh in Galilee in the hill country of Naphtali, and Shechem in the hill country of Ephraim, and Kiriath-arba
(that is, Hebron) in the hill country of Judah. 8 And beyond the Jordan
east of Jericho, they appointed Bezer in the wilderness on the tableland, from the tribe of Reuben, and Ramoth in Gilead, from the tribe
of Gad, and Golan in Bashan, from the tribe of Manasseh. 9 These
were the cities designated for all the Israelites, and for the aliens residing among them, that anyone who killed a person without intent
could flee there, so as not to die by the hand of the avenger of blood,
until there was a trial before the congregation.

Cities Allotted to the Levites

21 Then the heads of the families of the Levites came to the
priest Eleazar and to Joshua son of Nun and to the heads of
the families of the tribes of the Israelites; 2 they said to them at Shiloh
in the land of Canaan, "The LORD commanded through Moses that

19:49-50 gave an inheritance...to Joshua: Joshua received the town of Timnath-serah, located about fifteen miles southwest of Shechem. In Hebrew Timnath-serah means "leftover portion." See also 24:30.

20:2 Appoint the cities of refuge: Revenge was common for murder. This was true even for accidental murder and manslaughter. Both Numbers 35:9-28 and Deuteronomy 19:1-13 give directions to Moses for refuge cities. If innocent murderers reached those cities they were safe from revenge. But they were not free. They could not leave until the high priest died. There were six cities, three on each side of the Jordan. They were spaced evenly—north, middle, and south. This gave those who fled an opportunity to reach them. If they did not, the avenger (see below) could kill them.

20:3 the avenger of blood: This verse limits blood feuds. Extreme revenge was forbidden. The law of Moses called for punishment that fit the crime (Deut 19:15-21; Exod 21:23-25; Lev 24:19-21). A clan could choose a close male relative (an avenger) to find and kill a person who had killed a member of the clan (Num 35:16-19).

In the Sermon on the Mount, Jesus overrules even this limited type of vengeance (Matt 5:38-42). When whites in South Africa lost power, Nelson Mandela's black government forgave them. They set up reconciliation hearings. The crimes of the white power system were not ignored, but those who confessed were forgiven. In what ways are Christians called to go beyond revenge today? Who might you need to forgive?

21:1-42 families of the Levites...be given towns: Though the Levites were not to receive a particular tribal land (see note on 13:7), Moses was commanded to set up cities for the Levites (see Num 35:1-8). Joshua cast lots for the towns for the Levites. With the towns came pastures for the cattle that provided the Levites with food, income, and sacrifices. The Levites served as priests and were scattered among the tribes. The cities were assigned to the three Levite clans (Kohathites, Gershonites, and Merarites), as well as the descendants of Aaron, the high priest and brother of Moses. The descendants of Aaron were from the Kohathite clan, and they received thirteen towns in the tribal areas in the south.

we be given towns to live in, along with their pasture lands for our
livestock.” 3 So by command of the LORD the Israelites gave to the Levites the following towns and pasture lands out of their inheritance.

4 The lot came out for the families of the Kohathites. So those
Levites who were descendants of Aaron the priest received by lot thirteen towns from the tribes of Judah, Simeon, and Benjamin.

5 The rest of the Kohathites received by lot ten towns from the
families of the tribe of Ephraim, from the tribe of Dan, and the half-
tribe of Manasseh.

6 The Gershonites received by lot thirteen towns from the families of the tribe of Issachar, from the tribe of Asher, from the tribe of
Naphtali, and from the half-tribe of Manasseh in Bashan.

7 The Merarites according to their families received twelve towns
from the tribe of Reuben, the tribe of Gad, and the tribe of Zebulun.

8 These towns and their pasture lands the Israelites gave by lot to
the Levites, as the LORD had commanded through Moses.

9 Out of the tribe of Judah and the tribe of Simeon they gave the
following towns mentioned by name, 10 which went to the descendants of Aaron, one of the families of the Kohathites who belonged to
the Levites, since the lot fell to them first. 11 They gave them Kiriath-
arba (Arba being the father of Anak), that is Hebron, in the hill country of Judah, along with the pasture lands around it. 12 But the fields of
the town and its villages had been given to Caleb son of Jephunneh
as his holding.

13 To the descendants of Aaron the priest they gave Hebron,
the city of refuge for the slayer, with its pasture lands, Libnah with
its pasture lands, 14 Jattir with its pasture lands, Eshtemoa with its
pasture lands, 15 Holon with its pasture lands, Debir with its pasture
lands, 16 Ain with its pasture lands, Juttah with its pasture lands, and
Beth-shemesh with its pasture lands—nine towns out of these two
tribes. 17 Out of the tribe of Benjamin: Gibeon with its pasture lands,
Geba with its pasture lands, 18 Anathoth with its pasture lands, and
Almon with its pasture lands—four towns. 19 The towns of the descendants of Aaron—the priests—were thirteen in all, with their
pasture lands.

20 As to the rest of the Kohathites belonging to the Kohathite
families of the Levites, the towns allotted to them were out of the
tribe of Ephraim. 21 To them were given Shechem, the city of refuge
for the slayer, with its pasture lands in the hill country of Ephraim, Gezer with its pasture lands, 22 Kibzaim with its pasture lands, and Beth-
horon with its pasture lands—four towns. 23 Out of the tribe of Dan:
Elteke with its pasture lands, Gibbethon with its pasture lands, 24 Aijalon with its pasture lands, Gath-rimmon with its pasture lands—four
towns. 25 Out of the half-tribe of Manasseh: Taanach with its pasture
lands, and Gath-rimmon with its pasture lands—two towns. 26 The

towns of the families of the rest of the Kohathites were ten in all, with
their pasture lands.

27 To the Gershonites, one of the families of the Levites, were
given out of the half-tribe of Manasseh, Golan in Bashan with its
pasture lands, the city of refuge for the slayer, and Beeshterah with
its pasture lands—two towns. 28 Out of the tribe of Issachar: Kishion with its pasture lands, Daberath with its pasture lands, 29 Jarmuth
with its pasture lands, En-gannim with its pasture lands—four towns.
30 Out of the tribe of Asher: Mishal with its pasture lands, Abdon with
its pasture lands, 31 Helkath with its pasture lands, and Rehob with
its pasture lands—four towns. 32 Out of the tribe of Naphtali: Kedesh in Galilee with its pasture lands, the city of refuge for the slayer,
Hammoth-dor with its pasture lands, and Kartan with its pasture
lands—three towns. 33 The towns of the several families of the Gershonites were in all thirteen, with their pasture lands.

34 To the rest of the Levites—the Merarite families—were given
out of the tribe of Zebulun: Jokneam with its pasture lands, Kartah
with its pasture lands, 35 Dimnah with its pasture lands, Nahalal with
its pasture lands—four towns. 36 Out of the tribe of Reuben: Bezer
with its pasture lands, Jahzah with its pasture lands, 37 Kedemoth with
its pasture lands, and Mephaath with its pasture lands—four towns.
38 Out of the tribe of Gad: Ramoth in Gilead with its pasture lands, the
city of refuge for the slayer, Mahanaim with its pasture lands, 39 Heshbon with its pasture lands, Jazer with its pasture lands—four towns
in all. 40 As for the towns of the several Merarite families, that is, the
remainder of the families of the Levites, those allotted to them were
twelve in all.

41 The towns of the Levites within the holdings of the Israelites
were in all forty-eight towns with their pasture lands. 42 Each of these
towns had its pasture lands around it; so it was with all these towns.

43 Thus the LORD gave to Israel all the land that he swore to their
ancestors that he would give them; and having taken possession of it,
they settled there. 44 And the LORD gave them rest on every side just
as he had sworn to their ancestors; not one of all their enemies had
withstood them, for the LORD had given all their enemies into their
hands. 45 Not one of all the good promises that the LORD had made to
the house of Israel had failed; all came to pass.

21:43-45 the LORD gave to Israel all the land...all came to pass: This summary emphasizes the fulfillment of God's promises to Israel's ancestors. The statement that all their enemies had been given into their hands and that everything is under control is optimistic, especially in light of the beginning of the book of Judges, which opens shortly after Joshua's death.

The Eastern Tribes Return to Their Territory

22 Then Joshua summoned the Reubenites, the Gadites, and
the half-tribe of Manasseh, 2 and said to them, "You have
observed all that Moses the servant of the LORD commanded you,
and have obeyed me in all that I have commanded you; 3 you have not
forsaken your kindred these many days, down to this day, but have
been careful to keep the charge of the LORD your God. 4 And now the

22:1-6 Then Joshua summoned the Reubenites: The lands to the west had been taken, so Joshua summoned two and one-half tribes to return to the east. This ended the dividing of the lands. This was the way kings divided land for their allies.

Lord your God has given rest to your kindred, as he promised them;
therefore turn and go to your tents in the land where your possession
lies, which Moses the servant of the Lord gave you on the other side
of the Jordan. 5 Take good care to observe the commandment and instruction that Moses the servant of the Lord commanded you, to
love the Lord your God, to walk in all his ways, to keep his commandments, and to hold fast to him, and to serve him with all your
heart and with all your soul." 6 So Joshua blessed them and sent them
away, and they went to their tents.

7 Now to the one half of the tribe of Manasseh Moses had given
a possession in Bashan; but to the other half Joshua had given a possession beside their fellow Israelites in the land west of the Jordan.
And when Joshua sent them away to their tents and blessed them,
8 he said to them, "Go back to your tents with much wealth, and with
very much livestock, with silver, gold, bronze, and iron, and with a
great quantity of clothing; divide the spoil of your enemies with your
kindred." 9 So the Reubenites and the Gadites and the half-tribe of
Manasseh returned home, parting from the Israelites at Shiloh, which
is in the land of Canaan, to go to the land of Gilead, their own land of
which they had taken possession by command of the Lord through
Moses.

A Memorial Altar East of the Jordan

22:10-20 When they came to the region: The eastern tribes built an altar on their side of the Jordan. Most altars were for sacrifices, but the western tribes feared this altar was for idols. They recall Peor, where the idol Baal was worshiped (Num 23:28-30; 25:1-5).

10 When they came to the region[a] near the Jordan that lies in the
land of Canaan, the Reubenites and the Gadites and the half-tribe of
Manasseh built there an altar by the Jordan, an altar of great size. 11 The
Israelites heard that the Reubenites and the Gadites and the half-tribe
of Manasseh had built an altar at the frontier of the land of Canaan, in
the region[a] near the Jordan, on the side that belongs to the Israelites.
12 And when the people of Israel heard of it, the whole assembly of the
Israelites gathered at Shiloh, to make war against them.

13 Then the Israelites sent the priest Phinehas son of Eleazar to
the Reubenites and the Gadites and the half-tribe of Manasseh, in the
land of Gilead, 14 and with him ten chiefs, one from each of the tribal
families of Israel, every one of them the head of a family among the
clans of Israel. 15 They came to the Reubenites, the Gadites, and the
half-tribe of Manasseh, in the land of Gilead, and they said to them,
16 "Thus says the whole congregation of the Lord, 'What is this treachery that you have committed against the God of Israel in turning away
today from following the Lord, by building yourselves an altar today
in rebellion against the Lord? 17 Have we not had enough of the sin
at Peor from which even yet we have not cleansed ourselves, and for
which a plague came upon the congregation of the Lord, 18 that you

[a] Or *to Geliloth*

must turn away today from following the LORD! If you rebel against
the LORD today, he will be angry with the whole congregation of Israel tomorrow. 19 But now, if your land is unclean, cross over into the
LORD's land where the LORD's tabernacle now stands, and take for
yourselves a possession among us; only do not rebel against the LORD,
or rebel against us[a] by building yourselves an altar other than the altar
of the LORD our God. 20 Did not Achan son of Zerah break faith in the
matter of the devoted things, and wrath fell upon all the congregation
of Israel? And he did not perish alone for his iniquity!' "

21 Then the Reubenites, the Gadites, and the half-tribe of Manasseh said in answer to the heads of the families of Israel, 22 "The
LORD, God of gods! The LORD, God of gods! He knows; and let Israel itself know! If it was in rebellion or in breach of faith toward the
LORD, do not spare us today 23 for building an altar to turn away from
following the LORD; or if we did so to offer burnt offerings or grain
offerings or offerings of well-being on it, may the LORD himself take
vengeance. 24 No! We did it from fear that in time to come your children might say to our children, 'What have you to do with the LORD,
the God of Israel? 25 For the LORD has made the Jordan a boundary
between us and you, you Reubenites and Gadites; you have no portion in the LORD.' So your children might make our children cease to
worship the LORD. 26 Therefore we said, 'Let us now build an altar, not
for burnt offering, nor for sacrifice, 27 but to be a witness between us
and you, and between the generations after us, that we do perform the
service of the LORD in his presence with our burnt offerings and sacrifices and offerings of well-being; so that your children may never say
to our children in time to come, "You have no portion in the LORD." '
28 And we thought, If this should be said to us or to our descendants in
time to come, we could say, 'Look at this copy of the altar of the LORD,
which our ancestors made, not for burnt offerings, nor for sacrifice,
but to be a witness between us and you.' 29 Far be it from us that we
should rebel against the LORD, and turn away this day from following
the LORD by building an altar for burnt offering, grain offering, or
sacrifice, other than the altar of the LORD our God that stands before
his tabernacle!"

22:21-34 the [tribes] said in answer...an altar...to be a witness: The eastern tribes said the altar was a copy of the one at Shiloh. It was not for sacrifice but a witness that they worship the LORD. This kept the peace between the eastern and western tribes.

30 When the priest Phinehas and the chiefs of the congregation,
the heads of the families of Israel who were with him, heard the words
that the Reubenites and the Gadites and the Manassites spoke, they
were satisfied. 31 The priest Phinehas son of Eleazar said to the Reubenites and the Gadites and the Manassites, "Today we know that the
LORD is among us, because you have not committed this treachery
against the LORD; now you have saved the Israelites from the hand
of the LORD."

---

[a] Or *make rebels of us*

32 Then the priest Phinehas son of Eleazar and the chiefs returned from the Reubenites and the Gadites in the land of Gilead to
the land of Canaan, to the Israelites, and brought back word to them.
33 The report pleased the Israelites; and the Israelites blessed God and
spoke no more of making war against them, to destroy the land where
the Reubenites and the Gadites were settled. 34 The Reubenites and
the Gadites called the altar Witness;[a] "For," said they, "it is a witness
between us that the LORD is God."

Joshua Exhorts the People

23:1-16 A long time afterward… Joshua summoned all Israel: Joshua's farewell speech echoes Moses' speech (Deut 29–30). It warns against turning to other gods. It promises blessings for keeping faith with the LORD. At the time of Josiah (2 Kgs 23) the themes of both speeches undergirded the return to the covenant.

23 A long time afterward, when the LORD had given rest to
Israel from all their enemies all around, and Joshua was
old and well advanced in years, 2 Joshua summoned all Israel, their
elders and heads, their judges and officers, and said to them, "I am
now old and well advanced in years; 3 and you have seen all that the
LORD your God has done to all these nations for your sake, for it is
the LORD your God who has fought for you. 4 I have allotted to you
as an inheritance for your tribes those nations that remain, along
with all the nations that I have already cut off, from the Jordan to
the Great Sea in the west. 5 The LORD your God will push them back
before you, and drive them out of your sight; and you shall possess
their land, as the LORD your God promised you. 6 Therefore be very
steadfast to observe and do all that is written in the book of the law
of Moses, turning aside from it neither to the right nor to the left, 7 so
that you may not be mixed with these nations left here among you,
or make mention of the names of their gods, or swear by them, or
serve them, or bow yourselves down to them, 8 but hold fast to the
LORD your God, as you have done to this day. 9 For the LORD has
driven out before you great and strong nations; and as for you, no
one has been able to withstand you to this day. 10 One of you puts to
flight a thousand, since it is the LORD your God who fights for you, as
he promised you. 11 Be very careful, therefore, to love the LORD your
God. 12 For if you turn back, and join the survivors of these nations
left here among you, and intermarry with them, so that you marry
their women and they yours, 13 know assuredly that the LORD your
God will not continue to drive out these nations before you; but they
shall be a snare and a trap for you, a scourge on your sides, and thorns
in your eyes, until you perish from this good land that the LORD your
God has given you.

23:12-13 if you… intermarry with them: Marrying outside the Israelite people was seen as a threat to the security of the land. God would not continue to help the Israelites drive out the Canaanites. Instead, the people of the land would become a trap for them, meaning they might begin to worship the idols and gods worshiped by those non-Israelites. Centuries after the time of Joshua, the banning of intermarriage became part of the renewal led by Ezra (see Ezra 9:1-4; Neh 13:23-25).

14 "And now I am about to go the way of all the earth, and you
know in your hearts and souls, all of you, that not one thing has failed
of all the good things that the LORD your God promised concerning
you; all have come to pass for you, not one of them has failed. 15 But

[a] Cn Compare Syr: Heb lacks *Witness*

just as all the good things that the LORD your God promised concerning you have been fulfilled for you, so the LORD will bring upon you
all the bad things, until he has destroyed you from this good land that
the LORD your God has given you. 16If you transgress the covenant
of the LORD your God, which he enjoined on you, and go and serve
other gods and bow down to them, then the anger of the LORD will be
kindled against you, and you shall perish quickly from the good land
that he has given to you."

The Tribes Renew the Covenant

24 Then Joshua gathered all the tribes of Israel to Shechem,
and summoned the elders, the heads, the judges, and the
officers of Israel; and they presented themselves before God. 2And
Joshua said to all the people, "Thus says the LORD, the God of Israel:
Long ago your ancestors—Terah and his sons Abraham and Nahor—
lived beyond the Euphrates and served other gods. 3Then I took your
father Abraham from beyond the River and led him through all the
land of Canaan and made his offspring many. I gave him Isaac; 4and
to Isaac I gave Jacob and Esau. I gave Esau the hill country of Seir to
possess, but Jacob and his children went down to Egypt. 5Then I sent
Moses and Aaron, and I plagued Egypt with what I did in its midst;
and afterwards I brought you out. 6When I brought your ancestors
out of Egypt, you came to the sea; and the Egyptians pursued your
ancestors with chariots and horsemen to the Red Sea.[a] 7When they
cried out to the LORD, he put darkness between you and the Egyptians, and made the sea come upon them and cover them; and your
eyes saw what I did to Egypt. Afterwards you lived in the wilderness a
long time. 8Then I brought you to the land of the Amorites, who lived
on the other side of the Jordan; they fought with you, and I handed
them over to you, and you took possession of their land, and I destroyed them before you. 9Then King Balak son of Zippor of Moab,
set out to fight against Israel. He sent and invited Balaam son of Beor
to curse you, 10but I would not listen to Balaam; therefore he blessed
you; so I rescued you out of his hand. 11When you went over the Jordan and came to Jericho, the citizens of Jericho fought against you,
and also the Amorites, the Perizzites, the Canaanites, the Hittites, the
Girgashites, the Hivites, and the Jebusites; and I handed them over to
you. 12I sent the hornet[b] ahead of you, which drove out before you the
two kings of the Amorites; it was not by your sword or by your bow.
13I gave you a land on which you had not labored, and towns that you
had not built, and you live in them; you eat the fruit of vineyards and
oliveyards that you did not plant.
14 "Now therefore revere the LORD, and serve him in sincerity

[a] Or *Sea of Reeds* [b] Meaning of Heb uncertain

24:1-27 Joshua gathered all the tribes: Joshua gathered the tribes and called them to renew their covenant or agreement with the LORD. Covenants were treaties between kings and the people they ruled. This renewal uses some parts of the covenant form. After finishing the renewal of the covenant, Joshua sent the people home to their inheritances.

24:2 Thus says the LORD: Joshua uses a phrase spoken by prophets of God. His speech to the people is like the ones delivered by the prophets, who often called the people to worship God alone and turn away from their disloyal or evil ways.

24:2-13 Long ago your ancestors: The people are reminded of God's history with them. God made them a people and took them out of slavery in Egypt. God defeated their enemies and gave them the land, the towns they have not yet built, and the fruit they have yet to plant.

24:14-15 revere the LORD: Joshua gives the people a choice. They must serve and follow only the LORD and put away any other gods, or choose whom they will serve. This suggests that some of the people *were* already using idols. At the time the book of Joshua was compiled, it was an even greater problem.

and in faithfulness; put away the gods that your ancestors served
beyond the River and in Egypt, and serve the LORD. 15 Now if you are
unwilling to serve the LORD, choose this day whom you will serve,
whether the gods your ancestors served in the region beyond the
River or the gods of the Amorites in whose land you are living; but as
for me and my household, we will serve the LORD."

16 Then the people answered, "Far be it from us that we should
forsake the LORD to serve other gods; 17 for it is the LORD our God
who brought us and our ancestors up from the land of Egypt, out of
the house of slavery, and who did those great signs in our sight. He
protected us along all the way that we went, and among all the peoples through whom we passed; 18 and the LORD drove out before us
all the peoples, the Amorites who lived in the land. Therefore we also
will serve the LORD, for he is our God."

19 But Joshua said to the people, "You cannot serve the LORD,
for he is a holy God. He is a jealous God; he will not forgive your
transgressions or your sins. 20 If you forsake the LORD and serve foreign gods, then he will turn and do you harm, and consume you, after
having done you good." 21 And the people said to Joshua, "No, we will
serve the LORD!" 22 Then Joshua said to the people, "You are witnesses
against yourselves that you have chosen the LORD, to serve him." And
they said, "We are witnesses." 23 He said, "Then put away the foreign
gods that are among you, and incline your hearts to the LORD, the
God of Israel." 24 The people said to Joshua, "The LORD our God we
will serve, and him we will obey." 25 So Joshua made a covenant with
the people that day, and made statutes and ordinances for them at
Shechem. 26 Joshua wrote these words in the book of the law of God;
and he took a large stone, and set it up there under the oak in the
sanctuary of the LORD. 27 Joshua said to all the people, "See, this stone
shall be a witness against us; for it has heard all the words of the LORD
that he spoke to us; therefore it shall be a witness against you, if you
deal falsely with your God." 28 So Joshua sent the people away to their
inheritances.

Death of Joshua and Eleazar

29 After these things Joshua son of Nun, the servant of the LORD,
died, being one hundred ten years old. 30 They buried him in his own
inheritance at Timnath-serah, which is in the hill country of Ephraim,
north of Mount Gaash.

31 Israel served the LORD all the days of Joshua, and all the days
of the elders who outlived Joshua and had known all the work that the
LORD did for Israel.

32 The bones of Joseph, which the Israelites had brought up
from Egypt, were buried at Shechem, in the portion of ground that
Jacob had bought from the children of Hamor, the father of Shechem,

24:19 You cannot serve the LORD: Joshua presses the people to see just how committed they are. For those generations of Israelites who had seen the destruction that came from turning away from God to follow other gods, this dialogue between Joshua and the people would have been a strong reminder of the difficult reality: the people of Israel did turn away from following God and God's law.

Joshua reminded the people that they might be tempted to worship or serve other gods. Why is it difficult to serve God only? In what ways might you be serving other gods? What gods are they? How are you challenged by Joshua's words to be committed to serving God?

24:22, 26-27 You are witnesses against yourselves: The people are witnesses. A large stone is set up in the sanctuary of the LORD. Kings put such stones in sanctuaries of conquered countries, and they were used to make treaties official.

24:25-26 the book of the law of God: See Joshua 1:8 and the note.

24:29-33 Joshua . . . Eleazar: Joshua was buried in the town he was given as a reward for his service (see 19:49-50). The bones of Joseph had been brought up out of Egypt (see Gen 50:24-25; Exod 13:19). They are buried at Shechem. The mention of Eleazar at the end of Joshua (as well as several other times in the second half of the book) ties the events of Joshua to Deuteronomy and events that occur in the first five books of the Bible.

for one hundred pieces of money;[a] it became an inheritance of the
descendants of Joseph.

33 Eleazar son of Aaron died; and they buried him at Gibeah, the
town of his son Phinehas, which had been given him in the hill country of Ephraim.

Who has died that you think about? How do they continue to help in your faith and life?

[a] Heb *one hundred qesitah*

Judges 7:20

JUDGES

Background File

The book of Judges is a collection of stories about some of the heroes from the early days of God's people, between about 1200 and 1020 B.C.E. These heroes or leaders were called "judges." The tales were told in families and clans, in villages and in towns. Finally the stories were written down, collected, arranged, and new material was added to them. The book was put together when the people were in exile in Babylon, between 587 and 539 B.C.E.

What's the Story?

Judges tells the story of God's people after the exodus from Egypt (Exodus), the wandering in the wilderness (Numbers), and the invasion of Canaan, or the promised land (Joshua). For about two hundred years the people lived in the land without a king, under the leadership of individuals called judges. The book tells about twelve of them. Some called "minor judges" are mentioned only briefly: Shamgar, Tola, Jair, Ibzan, Elon, and Abdon. Longer stories are told about the others.

What sort of people were these judges? During the frontier time in North America (in the United States referred to as the "wild west"), independent leaders or heroes such as Buffalo Bill, Annie Oakley, and Davey Crockett stepped into leadership roles when needed. These were mostly young people doing wild and crazy things to help others in trouble. God's people, Israel, also had its wild and crazy heroes, especially in the early years in the land. Legends grew up around some of these heroes or judges. There was Samson, the strongman, who picked up a donkey's jawbone one day and went on a rampage, killing a thousand of Israel's enemies (15:14-17). There was Deborah, who led an army of thousands to drive out the evil Canaanites who were harassing her people (chapters 4–5). And there were the seven hundred left-handed marksmen who could sling a stone at a hair and not miss (20:16)! There are many stories about these superheroes in the Bible. And every one of them received his or her superpower from God. Since they lived in the area that even today is called the West Bank (the land west of the Jordan River), we could talk about the Bible's tales from the "wild, wild West Bank."

Judges can be outlined this way:

The world of the judges (1:1–3:6)

Enemies remain in the land (chapter 1)

The pattern for understanding the stories (2:1–3:6)

Stories about the judges (3:7–16:31)

Othniel, Ehud, and Shamgar (3:7-31)

Deborah (4–5)

Gideon (6–8)

Tola and Jair (10:1-5)

Jephthah (11:1–12:7)

Ibzan, Elon, and Abdon (12:8-15)

Samson (13–16)

The slide into chaos (17–21)

Idol worshipers (17–18)

Abuse, murder, fire, and chaos (19–21)

What's the Message?

The book of Judges was created for the people who were in exile in Babylon between 587 and 539 B.C.E. These were dark days for God's people, when they had little freedom and little reason to hope. These old stories were retold and reshaped to speak to people in sad times. The stories in Judges say to the exiles, "You are here because of your sins. But time after time, God heard the prayers of your ancestors when they were in trouble and helped them by sending deliverers. Now it is time for you to pray to God for help! Let's hope that in God's amazing grace, God will help once again!"

What message might Judges have for today? First, God may be working out God's purposes in all sorts of unexpected ways, through all kinds of unexpected people. Who would have thought that the muscle-bound Samson with his pranks, jokes, and outrageous behavior was God's instrument for that time? Second, even though darkness and despair may tempt people to give up on God, time and again God sent a deliverer in answer to people's prayers. The good news is that God has sent a deliverer for us, Jesus Christ. The promise is that because of Christ's death and resurrection we have hope for everlasting life. It's a story about grace, and it's amazing.

Israel's Failure to Complete the Conquest of Canaan

1 After the death of Joshua, the Israelites inquired of the LORD,
"Who shall go up first for us against the Canaanites, to fight
against them?" 2 The LORD said, "Judah shall go up. I hereby give the
land into his hand." 3 Judah said to his brother Simeon, "Come up
with me into the territory allotted to me, that we may fight against the
Canaanites; then I too will go with you into the territory allotted to
you." So Simeon went with him. 4 Then Judah went up and the LORD

1:1 After the death of Joshua: Before he died, the great leader Moses had passed on the leadership of Israel's tribes to Joshua (see Num 27:12-23). But at the time Joshua died, he did not appoint a leader to take his place (Josh 24:29-31).

The time between the death of Joshua and Israel's first king is called the "period of the judges" and extends from around 1200 to 1020 B.C.E. LORD (notice the capital letters) is the name of God. LORD is how the translation of the Hebrew name *Yahweh* (YAH-way) appears in this Bible. The Canaanites lived in the land to the west of the Jordan River before the Israelites arrived (see Map 3, pp. 2100-2101).While the book of Joshua gives the impression that the Israelites had totally conquered the land God had promised them, Judges says that there were still pockets of enemies who fought against them. God created all peoples of the world, and the Bible makes clear that "God so loved the world" (see John 3:16), including the Canaanites. But the Bible also says that Yahweh, the true God, was opposed to the worship of any other gods (see Exod 20:3-4). And the Canaanites worshiped gods named Baal and Astarte. The problem was with their religion.

1:2-36 Judah shall go up: The tribe of Judah is the leader in fighting against the enemies (1:2, 8, 10, 19). But not all the stories are ones of success. The tribes of Manasseh, Ephraim, Zebulun, Asher, Naphtali, and Dan did not drive out the Canaanites and other enemies. The stage is being set. The people of Israel are in enemy-held territory. They have no great leader like Moses or Joshua.

gave the Canaanites and the Perizzites into their hand; and they defeated ten thousand of them at Bezek. 5 They came upon Adoni-bezek at Bezek, and fought against him, and defeated the Canaanites and the Perizzites. 6 Adoni-bezek fled; but they pursued him, and caught him, and cut off his thumbs and big toes. 7 Adoni-bezek said, "Seventy kings with their thumbs and big toes cut off used to pick up scraps under my table; as I have done, so God has paid me back." They brought him to Jerusalem, and he died there.

8 Then the people of Judah fought against Jerusalem and took it. They put it to the sword and set the city on fire. 9 Afterward the people of Judah went down to fight against the Canaanites who lived in the hill country, in the Negeb, and in the lowland. 10 Judah went against the Canaanites who lived in Hebron (the name of Hebron was formerly Kiriath-arba); and they defeated Sheshai and Ahiman and Talmai.

11 From there they went against the inhabitants of Debir (the name of Debir was formerly Kiriath-sepher). 12 Then Caleb said, "Whoever attacks Kiriath-sepher and takes it, I will give him my daughter Achsah as wife." 13 And Othniel son of Kenaz, Caleb's younger brother, took it; and he gave him his daughter Achsah as wife. 14 When she came to him, she urged him to ask her father for a field. As she dismounted from her donkey, Caleb said to her, "What do you wish?" 15 She said to him, "Give me a present; since you have set me in the land of the Negeb, give me also Gulloth-mayim."[a] So Caleb gave her Upper Gulloth and Lower Gulloth.

16 The descendants of Hobab[b] the Kenite, Moses' father-in-law, went up with the people of Judah from the city of palms into the wilderness of Judah, which lies in the Negeb near Arad. Then they went and settled with the Amalekites.[c] 17 Judah went with his brother Simeon, and they defeated the Canaanites who inhabited Zephath, and devoted it to destruction. So the city was called Hormah. 18 Judah took Gaza with its territory, Ashkelon with its territory, and Ekron with its territory. 19 The LORD was with Judah, and he took possession of the hill country, but could not drive out the inhabitants of the plain, because they had chariots of iron. 20 Hebron was given to Caleb, as Moses had said; and he drove out from it the three sons of Anak. 21 But the Benjaminites did not drive out the Jebusites who lived in Jerusalem; so the Jebusites have lived in Jerusalem among the Benjaminites to this day.

22 The house of Joseph also went up against Bethel; and the LORD was with them. 23 The house of Joseph sent out spies to Bethel (the name of the city was formerly Luz). 24 When the spies saw a man coming out of the city, they said to him, "Show us the

[a] That is *Basins of Water* [b] Gk: Heb lacks *Hobab* [c] See 1 Sam 15.6: Heb *people*

way into the city, and we will deal kindly with you." 25 So he showed
them the way into the city; and they put the city to the sword, but
they let the man and all his family go. 26 So the man went to the land
of the Hittites and built a city, and named it Luz; that is its name
to this day.

27 Manasseh did not drive out the inhabitants of Beth-shean and
its villages, or Taanach and its villages, or the inhabitants of Dor and
its villages, or the inhabitants of Ibleam and its villages, or the inhabitants of Megiddo and its villages; but the Canaanites continued to
live in that land. 28 When Israel grew strong, they put the Canaanites
to forced labor, but did not in fact drive them out.

29 And Ephraim did not drive out the Canaanites who lived in
Gezer; but the Canaanites lived among them in Gezer.

30 Zebulun did not drive out the inhabitants of Kitron, or the inhabitants of Nahalol; but the Canaanites lived among them, and became subject to forced labor.

31 Asher did not drive out the inhabitants of Acco, or the inhabitants of Sidon, or of Ahlab, or of Achzib, or of Helbah, or of Aphik, or
of Rehob; 32 but the Asherites lived among the Canaanites, the inhabitants of the land; for they did not drive them out.

33 Naphtali did not drive out the inhabitants of Beth-shemesh,
or the inhabitants of Beth-anath, but lived among the Canaanites, the
inhabitants of the land; nevertheless the inhabitants of Beth-shemesh
and of Beth-anath became subject to forced labor for them.

34 The Amorites pressed the Danites back into the hill country;
they did not allow them to come down to the plain. 35 The Amorites
continued to live in Har-heres, in Aijalon, and in Shaalbim, but the
hand of the house of Joseph rested heavily on them, and they became
subject to forced labor. 36 The border of the Amorites ran from the ascent of Akrabbim, from Sela and upward.

Israel's Disobedience

2 Now the angel of the LORD went up from Gilgal to Bochim, and
said, "I brought you up from Egypt, and brought you into the
land that I had promised to your ancestors. I said, 'I will never break
my covenant with you. 2 For your part, do not make a covenant with
the inhabitants of this land; tear down their altars.' But you have not
obeyed my command. See what you have done! 3 So now I say, I will
not drive them out before you; but they shall become adversaries[a] to
you, and their gods shall be a snare to you." 4 When the angel of the
LORD spoke these words to all the Israelites, the people lifted up their
voices and wept. 5 So they named that place Bochim,[b] and there they
sacrificed to the LORD.

[a] OL Vg Compare Gk: Heb *sides* [b] That is *Weepers*

2:1-5 But you have not obeyed my command: The people of Israel were supposed to love and serve only the LORD, Yahweh, their God. But they have been switching religions, and the LORD is giving up on them. So they wept and were sorry for their disloyalty. Will the LORD give them another chance? The story continues.

Death of Joshua

6 When Joshua dismissed the people, the Israelites all went
to their own inheritances to take possession of the land. [7]The people worshiped the LORD all the days of Joshua, and all the days of
the elders who outlived Joshua, who had seen all the great work that
the LORD had done for Israel. [8]Joshua son of Nun, the servant of the
LORD, died at the age of one hundred ten years. [9]So they buried him
within the bounds of his inheritance in Timnath-heres, in the hill
country of Ephraim, north of Mount Gaash. [10]Moreover, that whole
generation was gathered to their ancestors, and another generation
grew up after them, who did not know the LORD or the work that he
had done for Israel.

Israel's Unfaithfulness

11 Then the Israelites did what was evil in the sight of the LORD
and worshiped the Baals; [12]and they abandoned the LORD, the God
of their ancestors, who had brought them out of the land of Egypt;
they followed other gods, from among the gods of the peoples who
were all around them, and bowed down to them; and they provoked
the LORD to anger. [13]They abandoned the LORD, and worshiped Baal
and the Astartes. [14]So the anger of the LORD was kindled against Israel, and he gave them over to plunderers who plundered them, and
he sold them into the power of their enemies all around, so that they
could no longer withstand their enemies. [15]Whenever they marched
out, the hand of the LORD was against them to bring misfortune, as
the LORD had warned them and sworn to them; and they were in
great distress.

16 Then the LORD raised up judges, who delivered them out of
the power of those who plundered them. [17]Yet they did not listen
even to their judges; for they lusted after other gods and bowed down
to them. They soon turned aside from the way in which their ancestors had walked, who had obeyed the commandments of the LORD;
they did not follow their example. [18]Whenever the LORD raised up
judges for them, the LORD was with the judge, and he delivered them
from the hand of their enemies all the days of the judge; for the LORD
would be moved to pity by their groaning because of those who persecuted and oppressed them. [19]But whenever the judge died, they
would relapse and behave worse than their ancestors, following other
gods, worshiping them and bowing down to them. They would not
drop any of their practices or their stubborn ways. [20]So the anger of
the LORD was kindled against Israel; and he said, "Because this people have transgressed my covenant that I commanded their ancestors,
and have not obeyed my voice, [21]I will no longer drive out before them
any of the nations that Joshua left when he died." [22]In order to test

2:11-23 the Israelites did what was evil...the LORD raised up judges, who delivered them: The stories that follow fit into a pattern.

1. *The people do what is evil,* switching religions, worshiping Baal and Astarte (2:11-13).
2. *The LORD gives up on them, and enemies attack* (2:14-15).
3. *The people cry to the LORD for help* (2:18, which refers to the people's "groaning"; see also 3:9, 15).
4. *The LORD raises up a judge who delivers them* (2:16). Eventually the people switch religions again, and the four-step pattern is repeated. There is a positive note to this pattern. Even though the people sin time and again, the LORD sends a deliverer to rescue them. The New Testament is the story about God sending a deliverer one more time, Jesus the Messiah.

In what way does this pattern also reflect what happens in our lives as Christians? From what do you need to be delivered or rescued? Where do you turn for help? How can Jesus deliver or rescue you?

Who is Jesus, according to Luther's Small Catechism? The Second Article of the Apostles' Creed says Jesus is "God's only son, our Lord." The explanation says Jesus "has freed me from all sins, from death, and from the power of the devil." It goes on to say that Jesus delivers God's people "in order that I may belong to him, live under him in his kingdom, and serve him in eternal righteousness, innocence, and blessedness...." *Judges 2:11-18*

Israel, whether or not they would take care to walk in the way of the
LORD as their ancestors did, [23]the LORD had left those nations, not
driving them out at once, and had not handed them over to Joshua.

Nations Remaining in the Land

3 Now these are the nations that the LORD left to test all those
in Israel who had no experience of any war in Canaan [2](it was
only that successive generations of Israelites might know war, to teach
those who had no experience of it before): [3]the five lords of the Philistines, and all the Canaanites, and the Sidonians, and the Hivites
who lived on Mount Lebanon, from Mount Baal-hermon as far as
Lebo-hamath. [4]They were for the testing of Israel, to know whether
Israel would obey the commandments of the LORD, which he commanded their ancestors by Moses. [5]So the Israelites lived among the
Canaanites, the Hittites, the Amorites, the Perizzites, the Hivites, and
the Jebusites; [6]and they took their daughters as wives for themselves,
and their own daughters they gave to their sons; and they worshiped
their gods.

Othniel

7 The Israelites did what was evil in the sight of the LORD, forgetting the LORD their God, and worshiping the Baals and the Asherahs.
[8]Therefore the anger of the LORD was kindled against Israel, and he
sold them into the hand of King Cushan-rishathaim of Aram-naharaim; and the Israelites served Cushan-rishathaim eight years. [9]But
when the Israelites cried out to the LORD, the LORD raised up a deliverer for the Israelites, who delivered them, Othniel son of Kenaz,
Caleb's younger brother. [10]The spirit of the LORD came upon him,
and he judged Israel; he went out to war, and the LORD gave King
Cushan-rishathaim of Aram into his hand; and his hand prevailed
over Cushan-rishathaim. [11]So the land had rest forty years. Then Othniel son of Kenaz died.

Ehud

12 The Israelites again did what was evil in the sight of the LORD;
and the LORD strengthened King Eglon of Moab against Israel, because they had done what was evil in the sight of the LORD. [13]In alliance with the Ammonites and the Amalekites, he went and defeated
Israel; and they took possession of the city of palms. [14]So the Israelites
served King Eglon of Moab eighteen years.

15 But when the Israelites cried out to the LORD, the LORD raised
up for them a deliverer, Ehud son of Gera, the Benjaminite, a left-
handed man. The Israelites sent tribute by him to King Eglon of Moab.
[16]Ehud made for himself a sword with two edges, a cubit in length;
and he fastened it on his right thigh under his clothes. [17]Then he

What does it mean for you to call Jesus the Messiah, or the Christ?

3:7-11 Othniel: The four-step pattern is clear (see note on 2:11-23). The people do evil, forgetting the LORD and worshiping other gods (3:7). The LORD gives up on them, and enemies attack (3:8). The people cry to the LORD for help (3:9). God rescues them through a deliverer, Othniel (3:9).

3:10 The spirit of the LORD: The spirit comes upon these judges, and they receive power (also 6:34; 11:29; 14:6). In his final words to his disciples Jesus promises them that "you will receive power when the Holy Spirit has come upon you" (Acts 1:8). The coming of the Spirit can mean the gift of power to lead an army, to kill a lion (14:6), or to witness throughout the world.

In what ways has the Holy Spirit brought power to your life?

What does the Small Catechism say about the Holy Spirit? The explanation to the Third Article of the Apostles' Creed says that "daily in this Christian church the Holy Spirit abundantly forgives all sins—mine and those of all believers." *Judges 3:10*

3:11 So the land had rest: After this time of war there are forty years of peace. Peace also follows the work of the judges Ehud (3:30), Deborah (5:31), and Gideon (8:28)—but then the situation begins to get worse.

3:12-30 Ehud: The four-step pattern (see note on 2:11-23) appears again. The people do evil (3:12). Enemies attack (3:12). The people cry to the LORD for help (3:15). The LORD sends a deliverer, Ehud (3:15-30). The king was taken by surprise when Ehud, who was left-handed, reached for his weapon on his right side. There were lots of left-handers in the tribe of Benjamin (see 20:16)! The Israelite listeners must have had a good laugh when they heard of this obese enemy king (3:17) who had been taken out by an Israelite spy and was found locked in his bathroom! Ten thousand (3:29) is probably better translated "ten units," each of perhaps a dozen or so men.

presented the tribute to King Eglon of Moab. Now Eglon was a very
fat man. 18 When Ehud had finished presenting the tribute, he sent the
people who carried the tribute on their way. 19 But he himself turned
back at the sculptured stones near Gilgal, and said, "I have a secret
message for you, O king." So the king said,[a] "Silence!" and all his attendants went out from his presence. 20 Ehud came to him, while he
was sitting alone in his cool roof chamber, and said, "I have a message
from God for you." So he rose from his seat. 21 Then Ehud reached
with his left hand, took the sword from his right thigh, and thrust it
into Eglon's[b] belly; 22 the hilt also went in after the blade, and the fat
closed over the blade, for he did not draw the sword out of his belly;
and the dirt came out.[c] 23 Then Ehud went out into the vestibule,[d] and
closed the doors of the roof chamber on him, and locked them.

24 After he had gone, the servants came. When they saw that the
doors of the roof chamber were locked, they thought, "He must be
relieving himself[e] in the cool chamber." 25 So they waited until they
were embarrassed. When he still did not open the doors of the roof
chamber, they took the key and opened them. There was their lord
lying dead on the floor.

26 Ehud escaped while they delayed, and passed beyond the
sculptured stones, and escaped to Seirah. 27 When he arrived, he
sounded the trumpet in the hill country of Ephraim; and the Israelites
went down with him from the hill country, having him at their head.
28 He said to them, "Follow after me; for the LORD has given your enemies the Moabites into your hand." So they went down after him, and
seized the fords of the Jordan against the Moabites, and allowed no
one to cross over. 29 At that time they killed about ten thousand of the
Moabites, all strong, able-bodied men; no one escaped. 30 So Moab
was subdued that day under the hand of Israel. And the land had rest
eighty years.

Shamgar

31 After him came Shamgar son of Anath, who killed six hundred
of the Philistines with an oxgoad. He too delivered Israel.

Deborah and Barak

4 The Israelites again did what was evil in the sight of the LORD,
after Ehud died. 2 So the LORD sold them into the hand of King
Jabin of Canaan, who reigned in Hazor; the commander of his army
was Sisera, who lived in Harosheth-ha-goiim. 3 Then the Israelites
cried out to the LORD for help; for he had nine hundred chariots of
iron, and had oppressed the Israelites cruelly twenty years.

---

[a] Heb *he said* [b] Heb *his* [c] With Tg Vg: Meaning of Heb uncertain [d] Meaning of Heb uncertain
[e] Heb *covering his feet*

3:31 Shamgar: The Philistines came across the Mediterranean from the area of Greece and settled in five cities on the coast: Ashdod, Ashkelon, Ekron, Gath, and Gaza (see Map 3, pp. 2100-2101).

4:1-24 Deborah: This story takes place in the northern part of Canaan (see Map 3, pp. 2100-2101). Bethel is north of Jerusalem in the territory of Ephraim. Tabor is in the north, just southwest of the Sea of Chinnereth (Galilee), on the northern edge of the plain of Esdraelon. Israel as a whole nation battles the Canaanites.

The typical elements of the pattern (see note on 2:11-23) are present. The Israelites sin, the Canaanites take over, the Israelites cry for help (4:1-3), and the LORD sends a deliverer (4:4—5:31). Deborah first appears going about the duties of a judge, settling legal cases (4:4-5). The Israelite armies under the leadership of both Barak and Deborah defeat the Canaanites, commanded by Sisera. The writer gives the LORD credit for the victory (4:6-16). Sisera runs away and finds refuge in the tent of Jael, wife of a Kenite. While some Kenites were on the side of the Canaanites (4:17), Jael was not. She invites the commander in for a drink and a rest. When he has dozed off, she kills him with a hammer. In the writer's view, God was working through the actions of Deborah, Jael, and Barak (4:17-24).

4 At that time Deborah, a prophetess, wife of Lappidoth, was
judging Israel. 5She used to sit under the palm of Deborah between
Ramah and Bethel in the hill country of Ephraim; and the Israelites
came up to her for judgment. 6She sent and summoned Barak son of
Abinoam from Kedesh in Naphtali, and said to him, "The LORD, the
God of Israel, commands you, 'Go, take position at Mount Tabor,
bringing ten thousand from the tribe of Naphtali and the tribe of Zebulun. 7I will draw out Sisera, the general of Jabin's army, to meet you
by the Wadi Kishon with his chariots and his troops; and I will give
him into your hand.'" 8Barak said to her, "If you will go with me, I will
go; but if you will not go with me, I will not go." 9And she said, "I
will surely go with you; nevertheless, the road on which you are going
will not lead to your glory, for the LORD will sell Sisera into the hand
of a woman." Then Deborah got up and went with Barak to Kedesh.
10Barak summoned Zebulun and Naphtali to Kedesh; and ten thousand warriors went up behind him; and Deborah went up with him.

11 Now Heber the Kenite had separated from the other Kenites,[a]
that is, the descendants of Hobab the father-in-law of Moses, and had
encamped as far away as Elon-bezaanannim, which is near Kedesh.

12 When Sisera was told that Barak son of Abinoam had gone up
to Mount Tabor, 13Sisera called out all his chariots, nine hundred chariots of iron, and all the troops who were with him, from Harosheth-
ha-goiim to the Wadi Kishon. 14Then Deborah said to Barak, "Up!
For this is the day on which the LORD has given Sisera into your hand.
The LORD is indeed going out before you." So Barak went down from
Mount Tabor with ten thousand warriors following him. 15And the
LORD threw Sisera and all his chariots and all his army into a panic[b]
before Barak; Sisera got down from his chariot and fled away on
foot, 16while Barak pursued the chariots and the army to Harosheth-
ha-goiim. All the army of Sisera fell by the sword; no one was left.

17 Now Sisera had fled away on foot to the tent of Jael wife of
Heber the Kenite; for there was peace between King Jabin of Hazor
and the clan of Heber the Kenite. 18Jael came out to meet Sisera, and
said to him, "Turn aside, my lord, turn aside to me; have no fear." So
he turned aside to her into the tent, and she covered him with a rug.
19Then he said to her, "Please give me a little water to drink; for I am
thirsty." So she opened a skin of milk and gave him a drink and covered him. 20He said to her, "Stand at the entrance of the tent, and if
anybody comes and asks you, 'Is anyone here?' say, 'No.'" 21But Jael
wife of Heber took a tent peg, and took a hammer in her hand, and
went softly to him and drove the peg into his temple, until it went
down into the ground—he was lying fast asleep from weariness—
and he died. 22Then, as Barak came in pursuit of Sisera, Jael went out

---

[a]Heb *from the Kain* [b]Heb adds *to the sword*; compare verse 16

to meet him, and said to him, "Come, and I will show you the man whom you are seeking." So he went into her tent; and there was Sisera lying dead, with the tent peg in his temple.

23 So on that day God subdued King Jabin of Canaan before the Israelites. 24 Then the hand of the Israelites bore harder and harder on King Jabin of Canaan, until they destroyed King Jabin of Canaan.

The Song of Deborah

5 Then Deborah and Barak son of Abinoam sang on that day, saying:

2 "When locks are long in Israel,
when the people offer themselves willingly—
bless[a] the LORD!

3 "Hear, O kings; give ear, O princes;
to the LORD I will sing,
I will make melody to the LORD, the God of Israel.

4 "LORD, when you went out from Seir,
when you marched from the region of Edom,
the earth trembled,
and the heavens poured,
the clouds indeed poured water.
5 The mountains quaked before the LORD, the One of Sinai,
before the LORD, the God of Israel.

6 "In the days of Shamgar son of Anath,
in the days of Jael, caravans ceased
and travelers kept to the byways.
7 The peasantry prospered in Israel,
they grew fat on plunder,
because you arose, Deborah,
arose as a mother in Israel.
8 When new gods were chosen,
then war was in the gates.
Was shield or spear to be seen
among forty thousand in Israel?
9 My heart goes out to the commanders of Israel
who offered themselves willingly among the people.
Bless the LORD.

10 "Tell of it, you who ride on white donkeys,
you who sit on rich carpets[b]

5:1-31 Then Deborah...sang: This is a poetic account of the events in chapter 4. The LORD is pictured as charging from Edom, south of the Dead Sea, into the northern lands amid storm and earthquake (5:4-5). Forty thousand (5:8) probably means forty military units (see note on 3:12-30). A picture of how stories were told in ancient Israel is seen in 5:10-11. Travelers rest at a watering place and musicians sing victory songs like this one. The song describes the victory as a cosmic event, with even the stars and a flood fighting for Israel (5:19-23). The song ends with the moving scene of a worried Canaanite mother waiting for a son who will never return (5:28-31). Now there will be only a forty-year period of peace (5:31), in contrast to the eighty years after the time of Ehud. As the stories of the judges go on, things are getting worse.

Judges describes God as being very active in Israel's history. For example, see 4:9, 15, and 23. What do you make of God's activity? How might we talk about how God is active in the world in our time?

---

[a] Or *You who offer yourselves willingly among the people, bless* [b] Meaning of Heb uncertain

and you who walk by the way.
11 To the sound of musicians[a] at the watering places,
there they repeat the triumphs of the LORD,
the triumphs of his peasantry in Israel.

"Then down to the gates marched the people of the LORD.

12 "Awake, awake, Deborah!
Awake, awake, utter a song!
Arise, Barak, lead away your captives,
O son of Abinoam.
13 Then down marched the remnant of the noble;
the people of the LORD marched down for him[b] against the mighty.
14 From Ephraim they set out[c] into the valley,[d]
following you, Benjamin, with your kin;
from Machir marched down the commanders,
and from Zebulun those who bear the marshal's staff;
15 the chiefs of Issachar came with Deborah,
and Issachar faithful to Barak;
into the valley they rushed out at his heels.
Among the clans of Reuben
there were great searchings of heart.
16 Why did you tarry among the sheepfolds,
to hear the piping for the flocks?
Among the clans of Reuben
there were great searchings of heart.
17 Gilead stayed beyond the Jordan;
and Dan, why did he abide with the ships?
Asher sat still at the coast of the sea,
settling down by his landings.
18 Zebulun is a people that scorned death;
Naphtali too, on the heights of the field.

19 "The kings came, they fought;
then fought the kings of Canaan,
at Taanach, by the waters of Megiddo;
they got no spoils of silver.
20 The stars fought from heaven,
from their courses they fought against Sisera.
21 The torrent Kishon swept them away,

---

[a] Meaning of Heb uncertain [b] Gk: Heb *me* [c] Cn: Heb *From Ephraim their root* [d] Gk: Heb *in Amalek*

the onrushing torrent, the torrent Kishon.
March on, my soul, with might!

22 "Then loud beat the horses' hoofs
with the galloping, galloping of his steeds.

23 "Curse Meroz, says the angel of the LORD,
curse bitterly its inhabitants,
because they did not come to the help of the LORD,
to the help of the LORD against the mighty.

24 "Most blessed of women be Jael,
the wife of Heber the Kenite,
of tent-dwelling women most blessed.
25 He asked water and she gave him milk,
she brought him curds in a lordly bowl.
26 She put her hand to the tent peg
and her right hand to the workmen's mallet;
she struck Sisera a blow,
she crushed his head,
she shattered and pierced his temple.
27 He sank, he fell,
he lay still at her feet;
at her feet he sank, he fell;
where he sank, there he fell dead.

28 "Out of the window she peered,
the mother of Sisera gazed[a] through the lattice:
'Why is his chariot so long in coming?
Why tarry the hoofbeats of his chariots?'
29 Her wisest ladies make answer,
indeed, she answers the question herself:
30 'Are they not finding and dividing the spoil?—
A girl or two for every man;
spoil of dyed stuffs for Sisera,
spoil of dyed stuffs embroidered,
two pieces of dyed work embroidered for my neck as spoil?'

31 "So perish all your enemies, O LORD!
But may your friends be like the sun as it rises in its might."

And the land had rest forty years.

---

[a] Gk Compare Tg: Heb *exclaimed*

The Midianite Oppression

6 The Israelites did what was evil in the sight of the LORD, and
the LORD gave them into the hand of Midian seven years. [2]The
hand of Midian prevailed over Israel; and because of Midian the Israelites provided for themselves hiding places in the mountains, caves
and strongholds. [3]For whenever the Israelites put in seed, the Midianites and the Amalekites and the people of the east would come
up against them. [4]They would encamp against them and destroy the
produce of the land, as far as the neighborhood of Gaza, and leave
no sustenance in Israel, and no sheep or ox or donkey. [5]For they and
their livestock would come up, and they would even bring their tents,
as thick as locusts; neither they nor their camels could be counted; so
they wasted the land as they came in. [6]Thus Israel was greatly impoverished because of Midian; and the Israelites cried out to the LORD
for help.

7 When the Israelites cried to the LORD on account of the Midianites, [8]the LORD sent a prophet to the Israelites; and he said to them,
"Thus says the LORD, the God of Israel: I led you up from Egypt, and
brought you out of the house of slavery; [9]and I delivered you from the
hand of the Egyptians, and from the hand of all who oppressed you,
and drove them out before you, and gave you their land; [10]and I said
to you, 'I am the LORD your God; you shall not pay reverence to the
gods of the Amorites, in whose land you live.' But you have not given
heed to my voice."

The Call of Gideon

11 Now the angel of the LORD came and sat under the oak at
Ophrah, which belonged to Joash the Abiezrite, as his son Gideon
was beating out wheat in the wine press, to hide it from the Midianites. [12]The angel of the LORD appeared to him and said to him, "The
LORD is with you, you mighty warrior." [13]Gideon answered him,
"But sir, if the LORD is with us, why then has all this happened to us?
And where are all his wonderful deeds that our ancestors recounted
to us, saying, 'Did not the LORD bring us up from Egypt?' But now the
LORD has cast us off, and given us into the hand of Midian." [14]Then
the LORD turned to him and said, "Go in this might of yours and deliver Israel from the hand of Midian; I hereby commission you." [15]He
responded, "But sir, how can I deliver Israel? My clan is the weakest in
Manasseh, and I am the least in my family." [16]The LORD said to him,
"But I will be with you, and you shall strike down the Midianites,
every one of them." [17]Then he said to him, "If now I have found favor
with you, then show me a sign that it is you who speak with me. [18]Do
not depart from here until I come to you, and bring out my present,
and set it before you." And he said, "I will stay until you return."

6:1—8:35 Gideon: The story fits the pattern (see note on 2:11-23), with the people doing evil (6:1a), the LORD giving them over to enemies (6:1b-6a), the people crying to the LORD for help (6:6b), and the LORD sending a deliverer (6:11—8:35). The desert tribes of Midianites and Amalekites, mounted on camels, regularly swept down upon the Israelites, destroying crops and animals. Ophrah is located near Shechem, midway between the Sea of Chinnereth and the Dead Sea (see Map 3, pp. 2100-2101). Because he is fearful, Gideon does his work in hiding, cowering down in a pit used for treading grapes. When someone greets him, saying, "The LORD is with you," Gideon doubts that this is so. He thinks he is being greeted by an ordinary person, but this turns out to be a messenger or angel (the Hebrew word means messenger) from the LORD. The messenger (now called "the LORD" in 6:16) tells Gideon to go and rescue his people. When Gideon is afraid and objects, the messenger promises that the LORD will be with him. After getting a sign as a guarantee that this message is from the LORD, Gideon builds an altar and tears down another once used for the worship of Baal (6:19-32). The spirit of the LORD comes upon him, and the fearful farm lad sounds the trumpet and bravely begins to gather an army to fight the Midianites (6:33-40).

Most of us would not be tempted to build an idol and worship it. But idols don't have to be made of stone or wood. What kinds of things, activities, or concerns could become "gods" in your life?

6:16 I will be with you: This promise from the LORD runs through the Bible and continues to be used in the church today. God promised Isaac, "I am *with* you" (see Gen 26:24), and the LORD was *with* Joseph in prison (see Gen 39:2, 3, 21, 23). God promised Moses, "I will be *with* you" (see Exod 3:12), and promised the reluctant Jeremiah the same (see Jer 1:8). When Paul was fearful about his missionary work, the LORD said in a dream, "Do not be afraid . . . for I am *with* you" (Acts 18:9-10). One of the names given to Jesus was *Emmanuel,* which means "God is *with* us" (Matt 1:23). Jesus promised that he would be *with* the disciples always (see Matt 28:20). Psalm 23 promises "for you are *with* me." The promise of God's *with-ness* is a promise of God's care and help.

Why do we use the greeting "The Lord be with you" in worship? This greeting used in worship services is followed by the response "and also *with* you." The worship leader gives this blessing to the congregation, often before a prayer. The response returns the blessing to the leader, giving the message "We're in this together." *Judges 6:16*

6:19 unleavened cakes: Refers to bread made without yeast, so it did not rise.

6:25 altar of Baal: Baal was the Canaanite god of fertility, apparently worshiped by Gideon's family and others in Israel. It is possible that ancient readers may have seen the humor in this situation: Gideon used his father's second-best bull to pull down the altar.

19 So Gideon went into his house and prepared a kid, and unleavened cakes from an ephah of flour; the meat he put in a basket, and
the broth he put in a pot, and brought them to him under the oak and
presented them. 20 The angel of God said to him, "Take the meat
and the unleavened cakes, and put them on this rock, and pour out
the broth." And he did so. 21 Then the angel of the LORD reached out
the tip of the staff that was in his hand, and touched the meat and the
unleavened cakes; and fire sprang up from the rock and consumed
the meat and the unleavened cakes; and the angel of the LORD vanished from his sight. 22 Then Gideon perceived that it was the angel of
the LORD; and Gideon said, "Help me, Lord GOD! For I have seen the
angel of the LORD face to face." 23 But the LORD said to him, "Peace
be to you; do not fear, you shall not die." 24 Then Gideon built an altar
there to the LORD, and called it, The LORD is peace. To this day it still
stands at Ophrah, which belongs to the Abiezrites.

25 That night the LORD said to him, "Take your father's bull, the
second bull seven years old, and pull down the altar of Baal that belongs to your father, and cut down the sacred pole[a] that is beside it;
26 and build an altar to the LORD your God on the top of the stronghold here, in proper order; then take the second bull, and offer it as
a burnt offering with the wood of the sacred pole[a] that you shall cut
down." 27 So Gideon took ten of his servants, and did as the LORD had
told him; but because he was too afraid of his family and the townspeople to do it by day, he did it by night.

Gideon Destroys the Altar of Baal

28 When the townspeople rose early in the morning, the altar of
Baal was broken down, and the sacred pole[a] beside it was cut down,
and the second bull was offered on the altar that had been built. 29 So
they said to one another, "Who has done this?" After searching and
inquiring, they were told, "Gideon son of Joash did it." 30 Then the
townspeople said to Joash, "Bring out your son, so that he may die,
for he has pulled down the altar of Baal and cut down the sacred pole[a]
beside it." 31 But Joash said to all who were arrayed against him, "Will
you contend for Baal? Or will you defend his cause? Whoever contends for him shall be put to death by morning. If he is a god, let him
contend for himself, because his altar has been pulled down." 32 Therefore on that day Gideon[b] was called Jerubbaal, that is to say, "Let Baal
contend against him," because he pulled down his altar.

33 Then all the Midianites and the Amalekites and the people of
the east came together, and crossing the Jordan they encamped in the
Valley of Jezreel. 34 But the spirit of the LORD took possession of Gideon; and he sounded the trumpet, and the Abiezrites were called out

---

[a] Heb *Asherah* [b] Heb *he*

to follow him. [35]He sent messengers throughout all Manasseh, and
they too were called out to follow him. He also sent messengers to
Asher, Zebulun, and Naphtali, and they went up to meet them.

The Sign of the Fleece

36 Then Gideon said to God, "In order to see whether you will
deliver Israel by my hand, as you have said, [37]I am going to lay a fleece
of wool on the threshing floor; if there is dew on the fleece alone, and
it is dry on all the ground, then I shall know that you will deliver Israel
by my hand, as you have said." [38]And it was so. When he rose early
next morning and squeezed the fleece, he wrung enough dew from
the fleece to fill a bowl with water. [39]Then Gideon said to God, "Do
not let your anger burn against me, let me speak one more time; let
me, please, make trial with the fleece just once more; let it be dry only
on the fleece, and on all the ground let there be dew." [40]And God did
so that night. It was dry on the fleece only, and on all the ground there
was dew.

Gideon Surprises and Routs the Midianites

7 Then Jerubbaal (that is, Gideon) and all the troops that were
with him rose early and encamped beside the spring of Harod;
and the camp of Midian was north of them, below[a] the hill of Moreh,
in the valley.

2 The LORD said to Gideon, "The troops with you are too many
for me to give the Midianites into their hand. Israel would only take
the credit away from me, saying, 'My own hand has delivered me.'
[3]Now therefore proclaim this in the hearing of the troops, 'Whoever
is fearful and trembling, let him return home.'" Thus Gideon sifted
them out;[b] twenty-two thousand returned, and ten thousand remained.

4 Then the LORD said to Gideon, "The troops are still too many;
take them down to the water and I will sift them out for you there.
When I say, 'This one shall go with you,' he shall go with you; and
when I say, 'This one shall not go with you,' he shall not go." [5]So he
brought the troops down to the water; and the LORD said to Gideon,
"All those who lap the water with their tongues, as a dog laps, you
shall put to one side; all those who kneel down to drink, putting their
hands to their mouths,[c] you shall put to the other side." [6]The number
of those that lapped was three hundred; but all the rest of the troops
knelt down to drink water. [7]Then the LORD said to Gideon, "With the
three hundred that lapped I will deliver you, and give the Midianites
into your hand. Let all the others go to their homes." [8]So he took the

7:1-8 all the troops: The massive army is cut down to an elite fighting force. Notice that the LORD is behind everything that happens here. Those who have any fear are allowed to go home, leaving only about one-third of the original number of troops. Gideon continues to reduce the numbers. He picked three hundred soldiers who would not put their faces down into the stream but took water in cupped hands, lapping it like a dog with eyes raised, keeping watch for enemies. Gideon is going to mount a surprise attack! The soldiers must have spent a good deal of time drilling, learning how to handle the trumpets, the torches, and the jars.

7:1-25 The LORD said to Gideon: God is involved in the story and should get the credit for the victory (7:2). But God's victory does not rule out using an elite army and clever military tactics. God works through human beings, in this case through Gideon. The soldiers cry, "A sword for the LORD *and for Gideon!*" (7:20). The story spells out the meaning of God's promise to Gideon, "I will be with you" (6:16), and this promise points to the meaning of the story for us.

---

[a]Heb *from* [b]Cn: Heb *home, and depart from Mount Gilead'"* [c]Heb places the words *putting their hands to their mouths* after the word *lapped* in verse 6

jars of the troops from their hands,[a] and their trumpets; and he sent
all the rest of Israel back to their own tents, but retained the three hundred. The camp of Midian was below him in the valley.
9 That same night the LORD said to him, "Get up, attack the
camp; for I have given it into your hand. 10 But if you fear to attack, go
down to the camp with your servant Purah; 11 and you shall hear what
they say, and afterward your hands shall be strengthened to attack the
camp." Then he went down with his servant Purah to the outposts
of the armed men that were in the camp. 12 The Midianites and the
Amalekites and all the people of the east lay along the valley as thick
as locusts; and their camels were without number, countless as the
sand on the seashore. 13 When Gideon arrived, there was a man telling
a dream to his comrade; and he said, "I had a dream, and in it a cake
of barley bread tumbled into the camp of Midian, and came to the
tent, and struck it so that it fell; it turned upside down, and the tent
collapsed." 14 And his comrade answered, "This is no other than the
sword of Gideon son of Joash, a man of Israel; into his hand God has
given Midian and all the army."
15 When Gideon heard the telling of the dream and its interpretation, he worshiped; and he returned to the camp of Israel, and said,
"Get up; for the LORD has given the army of Midian into your hand."
16 After he divided the three hundred men into three companies, and
put trumpets into the hands of all of them, and empty jars, with torches
inside the jars, 17 he said to them, "Look at me, and do the same; when I
come to the outskirts of the camp, do as I do. 18 When I blow the trumpet, I and all who are with me, then you also blow the trumpets around
the whole camp, and shout, 'For the LORD and for Gideon!' "
19 So Gideon and the hundred who were with him came to the
outskirts of the camp at the beginning of the middle watch, when
they had just set the watch; and they blew the trumpets and smashed
the jars that were in their hands. 20 So the three companies blew the
trumpets and broke the jars, holding in their left hands the torches,
and in their right hands the trumpets to blow; and they cried, "A
sword for the LORD and for Gideon!" 21 Every man stood in his place
all around the camp, and all the men in camp ran; they cried out and
fled. 22 When they blew the three hundred trumpets, the LORD set
every man's sword against his fellow and against all the army; and the
army fled as far as Beth-shittah toward Zererah,[b] as far as the border
of Abel-meholah, by Tabbath. 23 And the men of Israel were called out
from Naphtali and from Asher and from all Manasseh, and they pursued after the Midianites.
24 Then Gideon sent messengers throughout all the hill country
of Ephraim, saying, "Come down against the Midianites and seize the

7:9-14 Get up...you shall hear what they say: The LORD sends Gideon and a friend on a dangerous spy mission, sneaking into the enemy camp at night. When Gideon overhears a soldier predicting the Midianite defeat, he is encouraged.

7:15-25 Get up; for the LORD has given the army of Midian into your hand: Gideon says a prayer, then rallies the troops, telling them victory is theirs (7:15). Note the tactics: The attack comes at night, at the time of the change of the guard (7:19). Gideon uses what today's military would call psychological warfare. The sounds of the trumpets, the smashing of the jars, the shouting of the soldiers, and the sudden light of the torches setting fires frightened the sleeping Midianites so that they stumbled over one another and ran away. The story speeds up. Gideon calls in reinforcements from other tribes, who help defeat the Midianites, whose leaders are executed (7:23-25).

Reflect on the promise "for *you* are with me" in Psalm 23:4. Note that these words are no longer speaking *about* God as a shepherd, but are addressed to God as *you*. How can this psalm help when you or others are facing a crisis?

[a] Cn: Heb *So the people took provisions in their hands* [b] Another reading is *Zeredah*

Judges in Israel

Judge	Opponent(s)	Reference
Othniel	Cushan-rishathaim of Aram	3:7-11
Ehud	King Eglon of Moab	3:12-30
Shamgar	Philistines	3:31
Deborah/Barak	Jabin, king of Canaan, and his general Sisera	4–5, which include the "Song of Deborah"
Gideon	Midianites	6–8
Abimelech	His seventy brothers	9
Tola		10:1-2
Jair		10:3-5
Jephthah	Ammonites	10:6–12:7
Ibzan		12:8-10
Elon		12:11-12
Abdon		12:13-15
Samson	Philistines	13–16

waters against them, as far as Beth-barah, and also the Jordan." So all
the men of Ephraim were called out, and they seized the waters as far
as Beth-barah, and also the Jordan. 25 They captured the two captains
of Midian, Oreb and Zeeb; they killed Oreb at the rock of Oreb, and
Zeeb they killed at the wine press of Zeeb, as they pursued the Midianites. They brought the heads of Oreb and Zeeb to Gideon beyond
the Jordan.

Gideon's Triumph and Vengeance

8 Then the Ephraimites said to him, "What have you done to us,
not to call us when you went to fight against the Midianites?"
And they upbraided him violently. 2 So he said to them, "What have I
done now in comparison with you? Is not the gleaning of the grapes
of Ephraim better than the vintage of Abiezer? 3 God has given into
your hands the captains of Midian, Oreb and Zeeb; what have I been
able to do in comparison with you?" When he said this, their anger
against him subsided.

4 Then Gideon came to the Jordan and crossed over, he and the
three hundred who were with him, exhausted and famished.[a] 5 So he
said to the people of Succoth, "Please give some loaves of bread to

[a] Gk: Heb *pursuing*

8:1-35 Then Gideon came to the Jordan and crossed over: The Gideon of the story in chapters 6 and 7 appears as humble, hesitant, but then trusting in God. The young farmer proves to be a person through whom God could work to rescue God's people. Moreover, Gideon recognizes that the LORD is the real ruler of the people (8:23). But in chapter 8 things start to fall apart. The slide into sinfulness picks up speed. No longer do we hear of God directing Gideon's actions. Acting on his own, Gideon is out to get revenge on a variety of peoples (8:4-21). Acting against God's commandment (Exod 20:4-6), Gideon even constructs an idol to which the people bow down. Finally, after Gideon's death, the people of Israel slip back into the worship of Baal and forget about the LORD their God (8:33-35). As Judges continues, the people slide further and further into sinfulness and worship of other gods.

my followers, for they are exhausted, and I am pursuing Zebah and Zalmunna, the kings of Midian." [6]But the officials of Succoth said, "Do you already have in your possession the hands of Zebah and Zalmunna, that we should give bread to your army?" [7]Gideon replied, "Well then, when the LORD has given Zebah and Zalmunna into my hand, I will trample your flesh on the thorns of the wilderness and on briers." [8]From there he went up to Penuel, and made the same request of them; and the people of Penuel answered him as the people of Succoth had answered. [9]So he said to the people of Penuel, "When I come back victorious, I will break down this tower."

10 Now Zebah and Zalmunna were in Karkor with their army, about fifteen thousand men, all who were left of all the army of the people of the east; for one hundred twenty thousand men bearing arms had fallen. [11]So Gideon went up by the caravan route east of Nobah and Jogbehah, and attacked the army; for the army was off its guard. [12]Zebah and Zalmunna fled; and he pursued them and took the two kings of Midian, Zebah and Zalmunna, and threw all the army into a panic.

13 When Gideon son of Joash returned from the battle by the ascent of Heres, [14]he caught a young man, one of the people of Succoth, and questioned him; and he listed for him the officials and elders of Succoth, seventy-seven people. [15]Then he came to the people of Succoth, and said, "Here are Zebah and Zalmunna, about whom you taunted me, saying, 'Do you already have in your possession the hands of Zebah and Zalmunna, that we should give bread to your troops who are exhausted?' " [16]So he took the elders of the city and he took thorns of the wilderness and briers and with them he trampled[a] the people of Succoth. [17]He also broke down the tower of Penuel, and killed the men of the city.

18 Then he said to Zebah and Zalmunna, "What about the men whom you killed at Tabor?" They answered, "As you are, so were they, every one of them; they resembled the sons of a king." [19]And he replied, "They were my brothers, the sons of my mother; as the LORD lives, if you had saved them alive, I would not kill you." [20]So he said to Jether his firstborn, "Go kill them!" But the boy did not draw his sword, for he was afraid, because he was still a boy. [21]Then Zebah and Zalmunna said, "You come and kill us; for as the man is, so is his strength." So Gideon proceeded to kill Zebah and Zalmunna; and he took the crescents that were on the necks of their camels.

Gideon's Idolatry

22 Then the Israelites said to Gideon, "Rule over us, you and your son and your grandson also; for you have delivered us out of the hand

---

[a] With verse 7, Compare Gk: Heb *he taught*

of Midian." 23 Gideon said to them, "I will not rule over you, and my
son will not rule over you; the LORD will rule over you." 24 Then Gideon said to them, "Let me make a request of you; each of you give me
an earring he has taken as booty." (For the enemy[a] had golden earrings, because they were Ishmaelites.) 25 "We will willingly give them,"
they answered. So they spread a garment, and each threw into it an
earring he had taken as booty. 26 The weight of the golden earrings
that he requested was one thousand seven hundred shekels of gold
(apart from the crescents and the pendants and the purple garments
worn by the kings of Midian, and the collars that were on the necks
of their camels). 27 Gideon made an ephod of it and put it in his town,
in Ophrah; and all Israel prostituted themselves to it there, and it became a snare to Gideon and to his family. 28 So Midian was subdued
before the Israelites, and they lifted up their heads no more. So the
land had rest forty years in the days of Gideon.

Death of Gideon

29 Jerubbaal son of Joash went to live in his own house. 30 Now
Gideon had seventy sons, his own offspring, for he had many wives.
31 His concubine who was in Shechem also bore him a son, and he
named him Abimelech. 32 Then Gideon son of Joash died at a good
old age, and was buried in the tomb of his father Joash at Ophrah of
the Abiezrites.

33 As soon as Gideon died, the Israelites relapsed and prostituted
themselves with the Baals, making Baal-berith their god. 34 The Israelites did not remember the LORD their God, who had rescued them
from the hand of all their enemies on every side; 35 and they did not
exhibit loyalty to the house of Jerubbaal (that is, Gideon) in return for
all the good that he had done to Israel.

8:30-31 many wives...concubine: At this time Israelite men could have as many wives as they wished and could support. The concubine who bore him a son was the kind of wife who was legally bound to the husband but did not have the full rights of a primary wife.

8:33 Baal-berith: In Hebrew this name means "Lord of the Covenant" or "Covenant Baal." See note on 9:45-46.

Abimelech Attempts to Establish a Monarchy

9 Now Abimelech son of Jerubbaal went to Shechem to his mother's kinsfolk and said to them and to the whole clan of his mother's family, 2 "Say in the hearing of all the lords of Shechem, 'Which
is better for you, that all seventy of the sons of Jerubbaal rule over
you, or that one rule over you?' Remember also that I am your bone
and your flesh." 3 So his mother's kinsfolk spoke all these words on
his behalf in the hearing of all the lords of Shechem; and their hearts
inclined to follow Abimelech, for they said, "He is our brother." 4 They
gave him seventy pieces of silver out of the temple of Baal-berith with
which Abimelech hired worthless and reckless fellows, who followed
him. 5 He went to his father's house at Ophrah, and killed his brothers the sons of Jerubbaal, seventy men, on one stone; but Jotham, the

9:1-57 Abimelech ruled over Israel three years: This chapter tells of the first failed attempt to establish a king over Israel. The people of Israel have fallen back into Baal worship (8:33-35). The story begins with a horrible act. Abimelech, one of Gideon's sons with Jerubbaal (9:1), whose family was from Shechem, kills seventy of his brothers, making himself king (9:1-6). Jotham, the youngest brother survives and tells a story, identifying Abimelech as a worthless ruler and pronouncing a curse on the people who made him king and on Abimelech himself (9:7-21). The rest of the chapter tells how the curse works out, ending up with Abimelech being killed by a woman who crushed his skull with a millstone (9:22-57).

[a] Heb *they*

youngest son of Jerubbaal, survived, for he hid himself. [6]Then all the lords of Shechem and all Beth-millo came together, and they went and made Abimelech king, by the oak of the pillar[a] at Shechem.

The Parable of the Trees

9:7-15: The trees once went out to anoint a king: The story is a reminder of the important fact that the Bible contains a variety of literary forms. This story is a *fable*, a story that is not true-to-life but makes a point. The stories that Jesus told were *parables*, also true-to-life stories that made a point. Biblical materials need to be interpreted according to the type of literature they represent. For example, no one should argue on the basis of this *fable* that the Bible teaches that there was once a time when trees, vines, and bushes could speak to one another.

7 When it was told to Jotham, he went and stood on the top of Mount Gerizim, and cried aloud and said to them, "Listen to me, you lords of Shechem, so that God may listen to you.

8 The trees once went out
to anoint a king over themselves.
So they said to the olive tree,
'Reign over us.'
9 The olive tree answered them,
'Shall I stop producing my rich oil
by which gods and mortals are honored,
and go to sway over the trees?'
10 Then the trees said to the fig tree,
'You come and reign over us.'
11 But the fig tree answered them,
'Shall I stop producing my sweetness
and my delicious fruit,
and go to sway over the trees?'
12 Then the trees said to the vine,
'You come and reign over us.'
13 But the vine said to them,
'Shall I stop producing my wine
that cheers gods and mortals,
and go to sway over the trees?'
14 So all the trees said to the bramble,
'You come and reign over us.'
15 And the bramble said to the trees,
'If in good faith you are anointing me king over you,
then come and take refuge in my shade;
but if not, let fire come out of the bramble
and devour the cedars of Lebanon.'

16 "Now therefore, if you acted in good faith and honor when
you made Abimelech king, and if you have dealt well with Jerubbaal
and his house, and have done to him as his actions deserved— [17]for
my father fought for you, and risked his life, and rescued you from
the hand of Midian; [18]but you have risen up against my father's house
this day, and have killed his sons, seventy men on one stone, and have
made Abimelech, the son of his slave woman, king over the lords of
Shechem, because he is your kinsman— [19]if, I say, you have acted in

[a] Cn: Meaning of Heb uncertain

good faith and honor with Jerubbaal and with his house this day, then
rejoice in Abimelech, and let him also rejoice in you; 20 but if not, let
fire come out from Abimelech, and devour the lords of Shechem, and
Beth-millo; and let fire come out from the lords of Shechem, and from
Beth-millo, and devour Abimelech." 21 Then Jotham ran away and fled,
going to Beer, where he remained for fear of his brother Abimelech.

The Downfall of Abimelech

22 Abimelech ruled over Israel three years. 23 But God sent an evil
spirit between Abimelech and the lords of Shechem; and the lords of
Shechem dealt treacherously with Abimelech. 24 This happened so that
the violence done to the seventy sons of Jerubbaal might be avenged[a]
and their blood be laid on their brother Abimelech, who killed them,
and on the lords of Shechem, who strengthened his hands to kill his
brothers. 25 So, out of hostility to him, the lords of Shechem set ambushes on the mountain tops. They robbed all who passed by them
along that way; and it was reported to Abimelech.

26 When Gaal son of Ebed moved into Shechem with his kinsfolk, the lords of Shechem put confidence in him. 27 They went out
into the field and gathered the grapes from their vineyards, trod them,
and celebrated. Then they went into the temple of their god, ate and
drank, and ridiculed Abimelech. 28 Gaal son of Ebed said, "Who is
Abimelech, and who are we of Shechem, that we should serve him?
Did not the son of Jerubbaal and Zebul his officer serve the men of
Hamor father of Shechem? Why then should we serve him? 29 If only
this people were under my command! Then I would remove Abimelech; I would say[b] to him, 'Increase your army, and come out.' "

30 When Zebul the ruler of the city heard the words of Gaal son
of Ebed, his anger was kindled. 31 He sent messengers to Abimelech at
Arumah,[c] saying, "Look, Gaal son of Ebed and his kinsfolk have come
to Shechem, and they are stirring up[d] the city against you. 32 Now
therefore, go by night, you and the troops that are with you, and lie in
wait in the fields. 33 Then early in the morning, as soon as the sun rises,
get up and rush on the city; and when he and the troops that are with
him come out against you, you may deal with them as best you can."

34 So Abimelech and all the troops with him got up by night and
lay in wait against Shechem in four companies. 35 When Gaal son of
Ebed went out and stood in the entrance of the gate of the city, Abimelech and the troops with him rose from the ambush. 36 And when
Gaal saw them, he said to Zebul, "Look, people are coming down
from the mountain tops!" And Zebul said to him, "The shadows on
the mountains look like people to you." 37 Gaal spoke again and said,
"Look, people are coming down from Tabbur-erez, and one company

9:22 lords of Shechem: Shechem was an important city in the tribal territory of Manasseh (see Map 3, pp. 2100-2101).

---

[a] Heb *might come* [b] Gk: Heb *and he said* [c] Cn See 9.41. Heb *Tormah* [d] Cn: Heb *are besieging*

is coming from the direction of Elon-meonenim."[a] [38]Then Zebul said
to him, "Where is your boast[b] now, you who said, 'Who is Abimelech, that we should serve him?' Are not these the troops you made
light of? Go out now and fight with them." [39]So Gaal went out at the
head of the lords of Shechem, and fought with Abimelech. [40]Abime-
lech chased him, and he fled before him. Many fell wounded, up to
the entrance of the gate. [41]So Abimelech resided at Arumah; and Zebul drove out Gaal and his kinsfolk, so that they could not live on at
Shechem.

42 On the following day the people went out into the fields.
When Abimelech was told, [43]he took his troops and divided them
into three companies, and lay in wait in the fields. When he looked
and saw the people coming out of the city, he rose against them and
killed them. [44]Abimelech and the company that was[c] with him rushed
forward and stood at the entrance of the gate of the city, while the
two companies rushed on all who were in the fields and killed them.
[45]Abimelech fought against the city all that day; he took the city, and
killed the people that were in it; and he razed the city and sowed it
with salt.

9:45-46 sowed it with salt...Tower of Shechem...temple of El-berith: Throwing salt may have been part of a curse ceremony. The tower probably refers to a tall building that served as a look-out and fortress. The leaders (lords) tried to hide in the temple honoring *El-berith,* a Canaanite god whose name means "God of the Covenant." This god was also known as Baal-berith (see 8:33).

46 When all the lords of the Tower of Shechem heard of it, they
entered the stronghold of the temple of El-berith. [47]Abimelech was
told that all the lords of the Tower of Shechem were gathered together.
[48]So Abimelech went up to Mount Zalmon, he and all the troops that
were with him. Abimelech took an ax in his hand, cut down a bundle of brushwood, and took it up and laid it on his shoulder. Then he
said to the troops with him, "What you have seen me do, do quickly,
as I have done." [49]So every one of the troops cut down a bundle and
following Abimelech put it against the stronghold, and they set the
stronghold on fire over them, so that all the people of the Tower of
Shechem also died, about a thousand men and women.

50 Then Abimelech went to Thebez, and encamped against Thebez, and took it. [51]But there was a strong tower within the city, and
all the men and women and all the lords of the city fled to it and shut
themselves in; and they went to the roof of the tower. [52]Abimelech
came to the tower, and fought against it, and came near to the entrance of the tower to burn it with fire. [53]But a certain woman threw
an upper millstone on Abimelech's head, and crushed his skull. [54]Im-
mediately he called to the young man who carried his armor and said
to him, "Draw your sword and kill me, so people will not say about
me, 'A woman killed him.'" So the young man thrust him through,
and he died. [55]When the Israelites saw that Abimelech was dead, they
all went home. [56]Thus God repaid Abimelech for the crime he committed against his father in killing his seventy brothers; [57]and God

[a] That is *Diviners' Oak* [b] Heb *mouth* [c] Vg and some Gk Mss: Heb *companies that were*

also made all the wickedness of the people of Shechem fall back on
their heads, and on them came the curse of Jotham son of Jerubbaal.

Tola and Jair

10 After Abimelech, Tola son of Puah son of Dodo, a man of
Issachar, who lived at Shamir in the hill country of Ephraim,
rose to deliver Israel. 2 He judged Israel twenty-three years. Then he
died, and was buried at Shamir.

3 After him came Jair the Gileadite, who judged Israel twenty-two
years. 4 He had thirty sons who rode on thirty donkeys; and they had
thirty towns, which are in the land of Gilead, and are called Havvoth-
jair to this day. 5 Jair died, and was buried in Kamon.

Oppression by the Ammonites

6 The Israelites again did what was evil in the sight of the LORD,
worshiping the Baals and the Astartes, the gods of Aram, the gods of
Sidon, the gods of Moab, the gods of the Ammonites, and the gods of
the Philistines. Thus they abandoned the LORD, and did not worship
him. 7 So the anger of the LORD was kindled against Israel, and he sold
them into the hand of the Philistines and into the hand of the Ammonites, 8 and they crushed and oppressed the Israelites that year. For
eighteen years they oppressed all the Israelites that were beyond the
Jordan in the land of the Amorites, which is in Gilead. 9 The Ammonites also crossed the Jordan to fight against Judah and against Benjamin
and against the house of Ephraim; so that Israel was greatly distressed.

10 So the Israelites cried to the LORD, saying, "We have sinned
against you, because we have abandoned our God and have worshiped the Baals." 11 And the LORD said to the Israelites, "Did I not
deliver you[a] from the Egyptians and from the Amorites, from the
Ammonites and from the Philistines? 12 The Sidonians also, and the
Amalekites, and the Maonites, oppressed you; and you cried to
me, and I delivered you out of their hand. 13 Yet you have abandoned
me and worshiped other gods; therefore I will deliver you no more.
14 Go and cry to the gods whom you have chosen; let them deliver you
in the time of your distress." 15 And the Israelites said to the LORD,
"We have sinned; do to us whatever seems good to you; but deliver us
this day!" 16 So they put away the foreign gods from among them and
worshiped the LORD; and he could no longer bear to see Israel suffer.

17 Then the Ammonites were called to arms, and they encamped
in Gilead; and the Israelites came together, and they encamped at
Mizpah. 18 The commanders of the people of Gilead said to one another, "Who will begin the fight against the Ammonites? He shall be
head over all the inhabitants of Gilead."

[a] Heb lacks *Did I not deliver you*

10:6-18 The Israelites again did what was evil: The familiar pattern recurs (see note on 2:11-23), this time intensified. The "did evil" element now lists seven specific wrongdoings (10:6). The "anger of the LORD" element lists attacks from the west (Philistines) and the east (Ammonites, who lived east of the Jordan), so that Israel was "greatly distressed" (10:7-9). The "cried to the LORD" element now includes a double confession of sin (10:10, 15) as well as a cry for help (10:15) and a genuine repentance and turning back to the LORD (10:16a). Now the LORD is pictured as suffering, along with Israel. One senses that the LORD is about to come to the aid of the people one more time (10:16b). The people's sin is great, but God's love is greater still! Here is a hint of good news in the midst of all the suffering and bloodshed.

Read the words (or recall them from memory) of the hymn "Amazing Grace, How Sweet the Sound" (ELW 779). What is meant by *grace*, and why is it so amazing?

Jephthah

11 Now Jephthah the Gileadite, the son of a prostitute, was a mighty warrior. Gilead was the father of Jephthah. 2Gilead's wife also bore him sons; and when his wife's sons grew up, they drove Jephthah away, saying to him, "You shall not inherit anything in our father's house; for you are the son of another woman." 3Then Jephthah fled from his brothers and lived in the land of Tob. Outlaws collected around Jephthah and went raiding with him.

4 After a time the Ammonites made war against Israel. 5And when the Ammonites made war against Israel, the elders of Gilead went to bring Jephthah from the land of Tob. 6They said to Jephthah, "Come and be our commander, so that we may fight with the Ammonites." 7But Jephthah said to the elders of Gilead, "Are you not the very ones who rejected me and drove me out of my father's house? So why do you come to me now when you are in trouble?" 8The elders of Gilead said to Jephthah, "Nevertheless, we have now turned back to you, so that you may go with us and fight with the Ammonites, and become head over us, over all the inhabitants of Gilead." 9Jephthah said to the elders of Gilead, "If you bring me home again to fight with the Ammonites, and the LORD gives them over to me, I will be your head." 10And the elders of Gilead said to Jephthah, "The LORD will be witness between us; we will surely do as you say." 11So Jephthah went with the elders of Gilead, and the people made him head and commander over them; and Jephthah spoke all his words before the LORD at Mizpah.

12 Then Jephthah sent messengers to the king of the Ammonites and said, "What is there between you and me, that you have come to me to fight against my land?" 13The king of the Ammonites answered the messengers of Jephthah, "Because Israel, on coming from Egypt, took away my land from the Arnon to the Jabbok and to the Jordan; now therefore restore it peaceably." 14Once again Jephthah sent messengers to the king of the Ammonites 15and said to him: "Thus says Jephthah: Israel did not take away the land of Moab or the land of the Ammonites, 16but when they came up from Egypt, Israel went through the wilderness to the Red Sea[a] and came to Kadesh. 17Israel then sent messengers to the king of Edom, saying, 'Let us pass through your land'; but the king of Edom would not listen. They also sent to the king of Moab, but he would not consent. So Israel remained at Kadesh. 18Then they journeyed through the wilderness, went around the land of Edom and the land of Moab, arrived on the east side of the land of Moab, and camped on the other side of the Arnon. They did not enter the territory of Moab, for the Arnon was the boundary of Moab. 19Israel then sent messengers to King Sihon

[a] Or *Sea of Reeds*

11:1-40 Jephthah…was a mighty warrior: Gilead was Israelite territory, on the east side of the Jordan, between the Arnon and Jabbok Rivers (see Map 7, p. 2105). Jephthah came from a difficult family background. His mother was a prostitute. His brothers chased him out, and he fell in with a crowd of outlaws. When the Ammonites continue to harass the people of Gilead they begged him to be their leader because they knew he was a tough fighter (11:1-11). Jephthah agrees to take the leadership position and begins by trying to solve the problem through diplomacy (11:12-28). When negotiations fail, empowered by the spirit of the LORD, Jephthah defeats the Ammonites (11:29-33). But Jephthah makes a foolish vow and apparently ends up sacrificing his daughter (11:34-40). This is a difficult text to understand. Why didn't God intervene as God did in the case of Isaac's near sacrifice (see Gen 22)? Does the story intend to teach later readers not to make foolish vows? Does 11:39 hint that the daughter was not really killed? Or is this a further example of the downward spiral of Israel at this time?

11:12-28 Jephthah sent messengers: The account of "message sending" here is important for understanding the role of the prophets in the Old Testament. The expression "Thus says Jephthah" (11:15) introduces the message. The "I" that the messenger speaks is that of the message sender (11:27). The messenger is more like a modern ambassador than a postman; he has a good deal of freedom in shaping the message (11:15-27). The messenger provides a model for understanding the Old Testament prophets, who typically begin a message with "Thus says the LORD" (see Amos 1:3, 6, 9). The "I" of the prophetic messenger is the "I" of God, the message sender (Amos 1:3, 4, and continuing), and the prophet has freedom in the formulation of the message.

of the Amorites, king of Heshbon; and Israel said to him, 'Let us pass
through your land to our country.' [20]But Sihon did not trust Israel to
pass through his territory; so Sihon gathered all his people together,
and encamped at Jahaz, and fought with Israel. [21]Then the LORD, the
God of Israel, gave Sihon and all his people into the hand of Israel,
and they defeated them; so Israel occupied all the land of the Amorites, who inhabited that country. [22]They occupied all the territory of
the Amorites from the Arnon to the Jabbok and from the wilderness
to the Jordan. [23]So now the LORD, the God of Israel, has conquered
the Amorites for the benefit of his people Israel. Do you intend to take
their place? [24]Should you not possess what your god Chemosh gives
you to possess? And should we not be the ones to possess everything
that the LORD our God has conquered for our benefit? [25]Now are you
any better than King Balak son of Zippor of Moab? Did he ever enter
into conflict with Israel, or did he ever go to war with them? [26]While
Israel lived in Heshbon and its villages, and in Aroer and its villages,
and in all the towns that are along the Arnon, three hundred years,
why did you not recover them within that time? [27]It is not I who have
sinned against you, but you are the one who does me wrong by making war on me. Let the LORD, who is judge, decide today for the Israelites or for the Ammonites." [28]But the king of the Ammonites did not
heed the message that Jephthah sent him.

Jephthah's Vow

29 Then the spirit of the LORD came upon Jephthah, and he
passed through Gilead and Manasseh. He passed on to Mizpah of
Gilead, and from Mizpah of Gilead he passed on to the Ammonites.
[30]And Jephthah made a vow to the LORD, and said, "If you will give
the Ammonites into my hand, [31]then whoever comes out of the doors
of my house to meet me, when I return victorious from the Ammonites, shall be the LORD's, to be offered up by me as a burnt offering."
[32]So Jephthah crossed over to the Ammonites to fight against them;
and the LORD gave them into his hand. [33]He inflicted a massive defeat
on them from Aroer to the neighborhood of Minnith, twenty towns,
and as far as Abel-keramim. So the Ammonites were subdued before
the people of Israel.

Jephthah's Daughter

34 Then Jephthah came to his home at Mizpah; and there was his
daughter coming out to meet him with timbrels and with dancing.
She was his only child; he had no son or daughter except her. [35]When
he saw her, he tore his clothes, and said, "Alas, my daughter! You have
brought me very low; you have become the cause of great trouble
to me. For I have opened my mouth to the LORD, and I cannot take
back my vow." [36]She said to him, "My father, if you have opened your

Many parts of the Bible are difficult to understand. The story about Jephthah and his daughter is one of them. Often it is best to say "I don't understand this!" rather than trying to fake an explanation. There are plenty of parts of the Bible that we *do* understand. What messages of the Bible are clear and understandable to you? Are there other passages that are particularly difficult for you?

mouth to the LORD, do to me according to what has gone out of your mouth, now that the LORD has given you vengeance against your enemies, the Ammonites." 37 And she said to her father, "Let this thing be done for me: Grant me two months, so that I may go and wander[a] on the mountains, and bewail my virginity, my companions and I." 38 "Go," he said and sent her away for two months. So she departed, she and her companions, and bewailed her virginity on the mountains. 39 At the end of two months, she returned to her father, who did with her according to the vow he had made. She had never slept with a man. So there arose an Israelite custom that 40 for four days every year the daughters of Israel would go out to lament the daughter of Jephthah the Gileadite.

Intertribal Dissension

12 The men of Ephraim were called to arms, and they crossed to Zaphon and said to Jephthah, "Why did you cross over to fight against the Ammonites, and did not call us to go with you? We will burn your house down over you!" 2 Jephthah said to them, "My people and I were engaged in conflict with the Ammonites who oppressed us[b] severely. But when I called you, you did not deliver me from their hand. 3 When I saw that you would not deliver me, I took my life in my hand, and crossed over against the Ammonites, and the LORD gave them into my hand. Why then have you come up to me this day, to fight against me?" 4 Then Jephthah gathered all the men of Gilead and fought with Ephraim; and the men of Gilead defeated Ephraim, because they said, "You are fugitives from Ephraim, you Gileadites—in the heart of Ephraim and Manasseh."[c] 5 Then the Gileadites took the fords of the Jordan against the Ephraimites. Whenever one of the fugitives of Ephraim said, "Let me go over," the men of Gilead would say to him, "Are you an Ephraimite?" When he said, "No," 6 they said to him, "Then say Shibboleth," and he said, "Sibboleth," for he could not pronounce it right. Then they seized him and killed him at the fords of the Jordan. Forty-two thousand of the Ephraimites fell at that time.

7 Jephthah judged Israel six years. Then Jephthah the Gileadite died, and was buried in his town in Gilead.[d]

Ibzan, Elon, and Abdon

8 After him Ibzan of Bethlehem judged Israel. 9 He had thirty sons. He gave his thirty daughters in marriage outside his clan and brought in thirty young women from outside for his sons. He judged Israel seven years. 10 Then Ibzan died, and was buried at Bethlehem.

---

[a] Cn: Heb *go down* [b] Gk OL, Syr H: Heb lacks *who oppressed us* [c] Meaning of Heb uncertain: Gk omits *because . . . Manasseh* [d] Gk: Heb *in the towns of Gilead*

11 After him Elon the Zebulunite judged Israel; and he judged
Israel ten years. 12Then Elon the Zebulunite died, and was buried at
Aijalon in the land of Zebulun.
13 After him Abdon son of Hillel the Pirathonite judged Israel.
14He had forty sons and thirty grandsons, who rode on seventy donkeys; he judged Israel eight years. 15Then Abdon son of Hillel the Pirathonite died, and was buried at Pirathon in the land of Ephraim, in
the hill country of the Amalekites.

The Birth of Samson

13 The Israelites again did what was evil in the sight of the LORD,
and the LORD gave them into the hand of the Philistines forty
years.
2 There was a certain man of Zorah, of the tribe of the Danites,
whose name was Manoah. His wife was barren, having borne no children. 3And the angel of the LORD appeared to the woman and said
to her, "Although you are barren, having borne no children, you shall
conceive and bear a son. 4Now be careful not to drink wine or strong
drink, or to eat anything unclean, 5for you shall conceive and bear a
son. No razor is to come on his head, for the boy shall be a nazirite[a] to
God from birth. It is he who shall begin to deliver Israel from the hand
of the Philistines." 6Then the woman came and told her husband,
"A man of God came to me, and his appearance was like that of an
angel[b] of God, most awe-inspiring; I did not ask him where he came
from, and he did not tell me his name; 7but he said to me, 'You shall
conceive and bear a son. So then drink no wine or strong drink, and
eat nothing unclean, for the boy shall be a nazirite[c] to God from birth
to the day of his death.' "
8 Then Manoah entreated the LORD, and said, "O LORD, I pray,
let the man of God whom you sent come to us again and teach us
what we are to do concerning the boy who will be born." 9God listened to Manoah, and the angel of God came again to the woman as
she sat in the field; but her husband Manoah was not with her. 10So
the woman ran quickly and told her husband, "The man who came
to me the other day has appeared to me." 11Manoah got up and followed his wife, and came to the man and said to him, "Are you the
man who spoke to this woman?" And he said, "I am." 12Then Manoah
said, "Now when your words come true, what is to be the boy's rule
of life; what is he to do?" 13The angel of the LORD said to Manoah,
"Let the woman give heed to all that I said to her. 14She may not eat of
anything that comes from the vine. She is not to drink wine or strong
drink, or eat any unclean thing. She is to observe everything that I
commanded her."

---

[a] That is *one separated* or *one consecrated* [b] Or *the angel* [c] That is *one separated* or *one consecrated*

13:1—16:31 The Israelites again did what was evil: These stories take place along the border with the Philistines (see Map 3, pp. 2100-2101). Here the first two elements of the pattern (see 2:11-23) appear. The people do evil (13:1a); the Philistines rule over them for forty years (13:1b). The third element is missing, and the fourth element here is the story about Samson, who is given extraordinary strength when the spirit of the LORD comes upon him (14:6, 19; 15:14). He judges Israel for twenty years (15:20; 16:31).

13:2-25 His wife was barren.... The woman bore a son, and named him Samson: Zorah was about twenty miles west of Jerusalem, on the border between Dan and Judah (see Map 3, pp. 2100-2101). Manoah's wife stars in this story. A visitor appears to her, and when he leaves she suspects there is something special about him (13:6). The visitor appears to her a second time (13:8-9). Apparently this visitor looked like an ordinary person. Manoah doesn't realize who the visitor is until his dramatic exit (13:20). A *nazirite* (13:5) was a person who vowed not to drink wine and not to cut his hair (see Num 6:1-21). The boy is not to have his hair cut, and the woman is asked to follow some nazirite practices during the time of her pregnancy (13:4-5). When the visitor finally leaves, Manoah and his wife are convinced that he was an angel. A son is born, the LORD blesses him, and the spirit of the LORD begins to work in him (13:24).

13:1-25 the angel of the LORD appeared: This chapter teaches something about angels. The Hebrew word *malak,* here translated "angel," is also the word used for a human messenger, as in Genesis 32:3. Messengers of God may appear in everyday life. It may be that humans don't recognize them as such until they have left. The "spirit of the LORD" here is just beginning to stir, and it is associated with physical power (14:6, 19). The reference "the boy grew" is a reminder of what is said about Jesus (see Luke 2:52 and related NRSV footnote).

15 Manoah said to the angel of the LORD, "Allow us to detain you, and prepare a kid for you." 16 The angel of the LORD said to Manoah, "If you detain me, I will not eat your food; but if you want to prepare a burnt offering, then offer it to the LORD." (For Manoah did not know that he was the angel of the LORD.) 17 Then Manoah said to the angel of the LORD, "What is your name, so that we may honor you when your words come true?" 18 But the angel of the LORD said to him, "Why do you ask my name? It is too wonderful."

19 So Manoah took the kid with the grain offering, and offered it on the rock to the LORD, to him who works[a] wonders.[b] 20 When the flame went up toward heaven from the altar, the angel of the LORD ascended in the flame of the altar while Manoah and his wife looked on; and they fell on their faces to the ground. 21 The angel of the LORD did not appear again to Manoah and his wife. Then Manoah realized that it was the angel of the LORD. 22 And Manoah said to his wife, "We shall surely die, for we have seen God." 23 But his wife said to him, "If the LORD had meant to kill us, he would not have accepted a burnt offering and a grain offering at our hands, or shown us all these things, or now announced to us such things as these."

24 The woman bore a son, and named him Samson. The boy grew, and the LORD blessed him. 25 The spirit of the LORD began to stir him in Mahaneh-dan, between Zorah and Eshtaol.

Samson's Marriage

14 Once Samson went down to Timnah, and at Timnah he saw a Philistine woman. 2 Then he came up, and told his father and mother, "I saw a Philistine woman at Timnah; now get her for me as my wife." 3 But his father and mother said to him, "Is there not a woman among your kin, or among all our[c] people, that you must go to take a wife from the uncircumcised Philistines?" But Samson said to his father, "Get her for me, because she pleases me." 4 His father and mother did not know that this was from the LORD; for he was seeking a pretext to act against the Philistines. At that time the Philistines had dominion over Israel.

5 Then Samson went down with his father and mother to Timnah. When he came to the vineyards of Timnah, suddenly a young lion roared at him. 6 The spirit of the LORD rushed on him, and he tore the lion apart barehanded as one might tear apart a kid. But he did not tell his father or his mother what he had done. 7 Then he went down and talked with the woman, and she pleased Samson. 8 After a while he returned to marry her, and he turned aside to see the carcass of the lion, and there was a swarm of bees in the body of the lion, and honey. 9 He scraped it out into his hands, and went on, eating as he

[a] Gk Vg: Heb *and working* [b] Heb *wonders, while Manoah and his wife looked on* [c] Cn: Heb *my*

What is an angel? Martin Luther's morning and evening prayers both end with a reference to angels: "Let your holy angel be with me, so that the wicked foe may have no power over me. Amen *(SC:37)*." An angel may take the form of a human messenger from God, or may refer to God's unseen presence and protection. *Judges 13:3-18*

In Genesis 24 the angel is unseen but guiding and protecting. What does this biblical story tell us about angels in our own time and lives? How have you been aware of angels working in your life?

14:1-20 Samson went down to Timnah...he returned to marry her: Timnah was located between Ekron and Beth-shemesh (see Map 3, pp. 2100-2101). While troubling to his parents (see Deut 7:3), Samson's desire to marry outside his own tradition is declared to be part of God's plan (14:4). When the spirit of the LORD comes upon Samson, he is given great power (14:6). He sees the woman, likes what he sees, and marries her. Samson is a betting man and adds to the fun at the wedding party with a spontaneously composed riddle (14:10-14). His wife nags him for the answer to the riddle and then gives away the answer. Samson responds with a clever rhyme in Hebrew. *Today's English Version* of the Bible translates it nicely: "If you hadn't been plowing with my cow, you wouldn't know the answer now." The spirit again empowers Samson and he goes to Ashkelon, one of the five Philistine cities (see Map 3, pp. 2100-2101). He kills thirty Philistines, takes their suits, and pays off his bet. The wedding is broken up and Samson goes home.

went. When he came to his father and mother, he gave some to them, and they ate it. But he did not tell them that he had taken the honey from the carcass of the lion.

10 His father went down to the woman, and Samson made a feast there as the young men were accustomed to do. [11]When the people saw him, they brought thirty companions to be with him. [12]Samson said to them, "Let me now put a riddle to you. If you can explain it to me within the seven days of the feast, and find it out, then I will give you thirty linen garments and thirty festal garments. [13]But if you cannot explain it to me, then you shall give me thirty linen garments and thirty festal garments." So they said to him, "Ask your riddle; let us hear it." [14]He said to them,

"Out of the eater came something to eat.
Out of the strong came something sweet."

But for three days they could not explain the riddle.

15 On the fourth[a] day they said to Samson's wife, "Coax your husband to explain the riddle to us, or we will burn you and your father's house with fire. Have you invited us here to impoverish us?" [16]So Samson's wife wept before him, saying, "You hate me; you do not really love me. You have asked a riddle of my people, but you have not explained it to me." He said to her, "Look, I have not told my father or my mother. Why should I tell you?" [17]She wept before him the seven days that their feast lasted; and because she nagged him, on the seventh day he told her. Then she explained the riddle to her people. [18]The men of the town said to him on the seventh day before the sun went down,

"What is sweeter than honey?
What is stronger than a lion?"

And he said to them,

"If you had not plowed with my heifer,
you would not have found out my riddle."

[19]Then the spirit of the LORD rushed on him, and he went down to Ashkelon. He killed thirty men of the town, took their spoil, and gave the festal garments to those who had explained the riddle. In hot anger he went back to his father's house. [20]And Samson's wife was given to his companion, who had been his best man.

Samson Defeats the Philistines

15 After a while, at the time of the wheat harvest, Samson went to visit his wife, bringing along a kid. He said, "I want to go into my wife's room." But her father would not allow him to go in. [2]Her father said, "I was sure that you had rejected her; so I gave her to your companion. Is not her younger sister prettier than she? Why not

---

[a] Gk Syr: Heb *seventh*

15:1-20 Samson went and caught three hundred foxes: Samson's father-in-law had understandably given up on Samson and tried to settle things by giving him his wife's prettier younger sister. Samson escalates the whole incident into a typical Philistine trick and plays a prank with the foxes. He ties flaming torches to their tails and lets them run through the fields. Once again, when the spirit of the LORD rushes on him Samson is a superman, using a donkey's jawbone as a weapon. In Samson's song he gives himself credit for the victory (15:16). Then, in acute personal distress, he prays, gives God the credit, and God rescues him again (15:18-20).

take her instead?" 3 Samson said to them, "This time, when I do mischief to the Philistines, I will be without blame." 4 So Samson went and
caught three hundred foxes, and took some torches; and he turned
the foxes[a] tail to tail, and put a torch between each pair of tails. 5 When
he had set fire to the torches, he let the foxes go into the standing grain
of the Philistines, and burned up the shocks and the standing grain, as
well as the vineyards and[b] olive groves. 6 Then the Philistines asked,
"Who has done this?" And they said, "Samson, the son-in-law of the
Timnite, because he has taken Samson's wife and given her to his
companion." So the Philistines came up, and burned her and her father. 7 Samson said to them, "If this is what you do, I swear I will not
stop until I have taken revenge on you." 8 He struck them down hip
and thigh with great slaughter; and he went down and stayed in the
cleft of the rock of Etam.

9 Then the Philistines came up and encamped in Judah, and
made a raid on Lehi. 10 The men of Judah said, "Why have you come
up against us?" They said, "We have come up to bind Samson, to do to
him as he did to us." 11 Then three thousand men of Judah went down
to the cleft of the rock of Etam, and they said to Samson, "Do you not
know that the Philistines are rulers over us? What then have you done
to us?" He replied, "As they did to me, so I have done to them." 12 They
said to him, "We have come down to bind you, so that we may give
you into the hands of the Philistines." Samson answered them, "Swear
to me that you yourselves will not attack me." 13 They said to him, "No,
we will only bind you and give you into their hands; we will not kill
you." So they bound him with two new ropes, and brought him up
from the rock.

14 When he came to Lehi, the Philistines came shouting to meet
him; and the spirit of the LORD rushed on him, and the ropes that
were on his arms became like flax that has caught fire, and his bonds
melted off his hands. 15 Then he found a fresh jawbone of a donkey,
reached down and took it, and with it he killed a thousand men.
16 And Samson said,

"With the jawbone of a donkey,
    heaps upon heaps,
with the jawbone of a donkey
    I have slain a thousand men."

17 When he had finished speaking, he threw away the jawbone; and
that place was called Ramath-lehi.[c]

18 By then he was very thirsty, and he called on the LORD, saying,
"You have granted this great victory by the hand of your servant. Am
I now to die of thirst, and fall into the hands of the uncircumcised?"
19 So God split open the hollow place that is at Lehi, and water came

16:1-31 he fell in love with a woman...whose name was Delilah: This superhero story takes place in Gaza, one of the five Philistine cities. After playing around with a prostitute until midnight, the mighty Samson grabs the huge city-gate assembly and carries it uphill to Hebron, some forty miles distant. Again a new chapter begins with a woman in Samson's life. His new girlfriend can be bribed. Worn out by her constant nagging, Samson reveals to her the secret of his strength: his hair. She lovingly holds his head in her lap, then calls in a barber, who cuts off his flowing locks. His strength is gone, his

---

[a] Heb *them*   [b] Gk Tg Vg: Heb lacks *and*   [c] That is *The Hill of the Jawbone*

from it. When he drank, his spirit returned, and he revived. Therefore it was named En-hakkore,[a] which is at Lehi to this day. 20 And he
judged Israel in the days of the Philistines twenty years.

Samson and Delilah

16 Once Samson went to Gaza, where he saw a prostitute and
went in to her. 2 The Gazites were told,[b] "Samson has come
here." So they circled around and lay in wait for him all night at the
city gate. They kept quiet all night, thinking, "Let us wait until the
light of the morning; then we will kill him." 3 But Samson lay only until midnight. Then at midnight he rose up, took hold of the doors of
the city gate and the two posts, pulled them up, bar and all, put them
on his shoulders, and carried them to the top of the hill that is in front
of Hebron.

4 After this he fell in love with a woman in the valley of Sorek,
whose name was Delilah. 5 The lords of the Philistines came to her
and said to her, "Coax him, and find out what makes his strength so
great, and how we may overpower him, so that we may bind him in
order to subdue him; and we will each give you eleven hundred pieces
of silver." 6 So Delilah said to Samson, "Please tell me what makes your
strength so great, and how you could be bound, so that one could
subdue you." 7 Samson said to her, "If they bind me with seven fresh
bowstrings that are not dried out, then I shall become weak, and be
like anyone else." 8 Then the lords of the Philistines brought her seven
fresh bowstrings that had not dried out, and she bound him with
them. 9 While men were lying in wait in an inner chamber, she said
to him, "The Philistines are upon you, Samson!" But he snapped the
bowstrings, as a strand of fiber snaps when it touches the fire. So the
secret of his strength was not known.

10 Then Delilah said to Samson, "You have mocked me and told
me lies; please tell me how you could be bound." 11 He said to her, "If
they bind me with new ropes that have not been used, then I shall
become weak, and be like anyone else." 12 So Delilah took new ropes
and bound him with them, and said to him, "The Philistines are upon
you, Samson!" (The men lying in wait were in an inner chamber.) But
he snapped the ropes off his arms like a thread.

13 Then Delilah said to Samson, "Until now you have mocked
me and told me lies; tell me how you could be bound." He said to her,
"If you weave the seven locks of my head with the web and make it
tight with the pin, then I shall become weak, and be like anyone else."
14 So while he slept, Delilah took the seven locks of his head and wove
them into the web,[c] and made them tight with the pin. Then she said

---

[a] That is *The Spring of the One who Called* [b] Gk: Heb lacks *were told* [c] Compare Gk: in verses 13–14, Heb lacks *and make it tight . . . into the web*

eyes are put out, and Samson is put to work grinding at the prison mill. But eventually his hair grows back. Finally, at a festival where the Philistines are celebrating their god, they call in Samson so that they can make fun of him. Samson prays one more prayer, gives a mighty push, and pulls down the whole temple of Dagon, the Philistines' chief god. With this act Samson takes his own life and the lives of thousands of Philistines (16:23-31).

13:1—16:31 The boy grew, and the LORD blessed him: The author of Judges is a theologian, always trying to point out what these stories have to teach about God and God's relationship to people. God blessed Samson, and God's spirit was directing him, even his pranks and riddles (13:24-25; 14:4). No doubt the hearers of these stories cheered when they heard how their hero had embarrassed and defeated the hated Philistines.

These stories were retold in early Christian preaching. The sermon in Hebrews 11 tells about some of the great heroes of the faith, including Abraham, Isaac, Jacob, and Moses. Had there been more time, says the preacher, the sermon would also have told about Gideon, Barak, Jephthah—and Samson (Hebrews 11:32). What fun it would be to know what the preacher would have said about these judges.

What can these stories mean for our own time? First, we cannot take Samson as a good example—since much of what he did was not exemplary. But God used Samson as he was—betting, playing pranks, and womanizing. God uses people the way they are, not the way they ought to be. Second, these stories can remind us to make room in our lives and in our churches for the spontaneous and unplanned, the bold deed, the daring act. "The [Spirit] blows where it chooses," says the New Testament (see John 3:8), and in the case of Samson, the Spirit blew him into a series of most remarkable adventures (13:25; 14:6, 19; 15:14). Finally, these stories suggest that we should not be too quick to judge or dismiss the unusual person from the company of God's people. No doubt many of us would be uncomfortable with Samson as a member of our congregation. He was a jokester, a gambler, and had an inclination to the bawdy. Yet he is remembered in company with Abraham and Isaac, Moses and David. If God could use a person like Samson, then who knows what sort of person God might be using now? Like people of Samson's time, we might be surprised.

What do you think of the idea that God uses people the way they are, not the way they ought to be?

to him, "The Philistines are upon you, Samson!" But he awoke from his sleep, and pulled away the pin, the loom, and the web.

15 Then she said to him, "How can you say, 'I love you,' when your heart is not with me? You have mocked me three times now and have not told me what makes your strength so great." 16 Finally, after she had nagged him with her words day after day, and pestered him, he was tired to death. 17 So he told her his whole secret, and said to her, "A razor has never come upon my head; for I have been a nazirite[a] to God from my mother's womb. If my head were shaved, then my strength would leave me; I would become weak, and be like anyone else."

18 When Delilah realized that he had told her his whole secret, she sent and called the lords of the Philistines, saying, "This time come up, for he has told his whole secret to me." Then the lords of the Philistines came up to her, and brought the money in their hands. 19 She let him fall asleep on her lap; and she called a man, and had him shave off the seven locks of his head. He began to weaken,[b] and his strength left him. 20 Then she said, "The Philistines are upon you, Samson!" When he awoke from his sleep, he thought, "I will go out as at other times, and shake myself free." But he did not know that the LORD had left him. 21 So the Philistines seized him and gouged out his eyes. They brought him down to Gaza and bound him with bronze shackles; and he ground at the mill in the prison. 22 But the hair of his head began to grow again after it had been shaved.

Samson's Death

23 Now the lords of the Philistines gathered to offer a great sacrifice to their god Dagon, and to rejoice; for they said, "Our god has given Samson our enemy into our hand." 24 When the people saw him, they praised their god; for they said, "Our god has given our enemy into our hand, the ravager of our country, who has killed many of us." 25 And when their hearts were merry, they said, "Call Samson, and let him entertain us." So they called Samson out of the prison, and he performed for them. They made him stand between the pillars; 26 and Samson said to the attendant who held him by the hand, "Let me feel the pillars on which the house rests, so that I may lean against them." 27 Now the house was full of men and women; all the lords of the Philistines were there, and on the roof there were about three thousand men and women, who looked on while Samson performed.

28 Then Samson called to the LORD and said, "Lord GOD, remember me and strengthen me only this once, O God, so that with this one act of revenge I may pay back the Philistines for my two eyes."[c] 29 And Samson grasped the two middle pillars on which the

---

[a] That is *one separated* or *one consecrated* [b] Gk: Heb *She began to torment him* [c] Or *so that I may be avenged upon the Philistines for one of my two eyes*

house rested, and he leaned his weight against them, his right hand on
the one and his left hand on the other. 30 Then Samson said, "Let me
die with the Philistines." He strained with all his might; and the house
fell on the lords and all the people who were in it. So those he killed
at his death were more than those he had killed during his life. 31 Then
his brothers and all his family came down and took him and brought
him up and buried him between Zorah and Eshtaol in the tomb of his
father Manoah. He had judged Israel twenty years.

Micah and the Levite

17 There was a man in the hill country of Ephraim whose name
was Micah. 2 He said to his mother, "The eleven hundred
pieces of silver that were taken from you, about which you uttered
a curse, and even spoke it in my hearing,—that silver is in my possession; I took it; but now I will return it to you."[a] And his mother
said, "May my son be blessed by the LORD!" 3 Then he returned the
eleven hundred pieces of silver to his mother; and his mother said, "I
consecrate the silver to the LORD from my hand for my son, to make
an idol of cast metal." 4 So when he returned the money to his mother,
his mother took two hundred pieces of silver, and gave it to the silversmith, who made it into an idol of cast metal; and it was in the house
of Micah. 5 This man Micah had a shrine, and he made an ephod and
teraphim, and installed one of his sons, who became his priest. 6 In
those days there was no king in Israel; all the people did what was
right in their own eyes.

7 Now there was a young man of Bethlehem in Judah, of the clan
of Judah. He was a Levite residing there. 8 This man left the town of
Bethlehem in Judah, to live wherever he could find a place. He came
to the house of Micah in the hill country of Ephraim to carry on his
work.[b] 9 Micah said to him, "From where do you come?" He replied,
"I am a Levite of Bethlehem in Judah, and I am going to live wherever
I can find a place." 10 Then Micah said to him, "Stay with me, and be to
me a father and a priest, and I will give you ten pieces of silver a year,
a set of clothes, and your living."[c] 11 The Levite agreed to stay with the
man; and the young man became to him like one of his sons. 12 So
Micah installed the Levite, and the young man became his priest, and
was in the house of Micah. 13 Then Micah said, "Now I know that the
LORD will prosper me, because the Levite has become my priest."

The Migration of Dan

18 In those days there was no king in Israel. And in those days
the tribe of the Danites was seeking for itself a territory to

---

[a] The words *but now I will return it to you* are transposed from the end of verse 3 in Heb [b] Or *Ephraim, continuing his journey* [c] Heb *living, and the Levite went*

17:1-13 There was a man…whose name was Micah: The theme for this third part of Judges, "the slide into chaos," is sounded in 17:6 and 21:25. Things are falling apart. This Micah (not to be confused with the prophet Micah) is a thief who had robbed his mother. Since ten pieces of silver was a year's salary (17:10), eleven hundred pieces was a huge amount. Micah also was an idol worshiper, a practice forbidden by covenant law (Exod 20:4-6; Deut 5:8-10; 27:15). The members of the tribe of Levi served as clergy throughout Israel. Micah hires one of them as his personal chaplain, hoping this will make the LORD favor him (17:13). Stealing, idol worship, and trying to control God are all evidence of a falling away from true religion.

17:5 ephod: Originally a priestly vestment (Exod 28:1-14) that could become an object of worship (Judg 8:27). See also the note at Lev 8:7-8 and the illustration on p. 166. Here, Micah takes it upon himself to appoint his son as a priest and creates priestly clothing so he can play the part. The ephod Gideon made (8:27) resulted in improper worship.

17:5 teraphim: *Teraphim* (a plural form) refers to a personal idol or idols, perhaps used to help interpret God's will (see also Gen 31:19; 1 Sam 19:13; Hos 3:4-5).

18:1-31 the tribe of the Danites: The Danites did not have their own territory and were looking for a place to settle. Spies from Dan stopped by Micah's house, then visited nearby Laish and reported back that it would be easy to capture (18:7-10). They returned with an army, took Micah's idol, hired his personal chaplain, burned Laish, and renamed it Dan. They set up their captured idol for their own worship. The slide into sin continues (18:27-31).

live in; for until then no territory among the tribes of Israel had been
allotted to them. 2 So the Danites sent five valiant men from the whole
number of their clan, from Zorah and from Eshtaol, to spy out the
land and to explore it; and they said to them, "Go, explore the land."
When they came to the hill country of Ephraim, to the house of Micah, they stayed there. 3 While they were at Micah's house, they recognized the voice of the young Levite; so they went over and asked him,
"Who brought you here? What are you doing in this place? What is
your business here?" 4 He said to them, "Micah did such and such for
me, and he hired me, and I have become his priest." 5 Then they said
to him, "Inquire of God that we may know whether the mission we
are undertaking will succeed." 6 The priest replied, "Go in peace. The
mission you are on is under the eye of the LORD."

7 The five men went on, and when they came to Laish, they observed the people who were there living securely, after the manner of
the Sidonians, quiet and unsuspecting, lacking[a] nothing on earth, and
possessing wealth.[b] Furthermore, they were far from the Sidonians
and had no dealings with Aram.[c] 8 When they came to their kinsfolk
at Zorah and Eshtaol, they said to them, "What do you report?" 9 They
said, "Come, let us go up against them; for we have seen the land, and
it is very good. Will you do nothing? Do not be slow to go, but enter
in and possess the land. 10 When you go, you will come to an unsuspecting people. The land is broad—God has indeed given it into your
hands—a place where there is no lack of anything on earth."

11 Six hundred men of the Danite clan, armed with weapons of
war, set out from Zorah and Eshtaol, 12 and went up and encamped at
Kiriath-jearim in Judah. On this account that place is called Mahaneh-
dan[d] to this day; it is west of Kiriath-jearim. 13 From there they passed
on to the hill country of Ephraim, and came to the house of Micah.

14 Then the five men who had gone to spy out the land (that is,
Laish) said to their comrades, "Do you know that in these buildings
there are an ephod, teraphim, and an idol of cast metal? Now therefore consider what you will do." 15 So they turned in that direction and
came to the house of the young Levite, at the home of Micah, and
greeted him. 16 While the six hundred men of the Danites, armed with
their weapons of war, stood by the entrance of the gate, 17 the five men
who had gone to spy out the land proceeded to enter and take the
idol of cast metal, the ephod, and the teraphim.[e] The priest was standing by the entrance of the gate with the six hundred men armed with
weapons of war. 18 When the men went into Micah's house and took
the idol of cast metal, the ephod, and the teraphim, the priest said to
them, "What are you doing?" 19 They said to him, "Keep quiet! Put

---

[a] Cn Compare 18.10: Meaning of Heb uncertain [b] Meaning of Heb uncertain [c] Symmachus: Heb *with anyone* [d] That is *Camp of Dan* [e] Compare 17.4, 5; 18.14: Heb *teraphim and the cast metal*

your hand over your mouth, and come with us, and be to us a father and a priest. Is it better for you to be priest to the house of one person, or to be priest to a tribe and clan in Israel?" [20]Then the priest accepted the offer. He took the ephod, the teraphim, and the idol, and went along with the people.

21 So they resumed their journey, putting the little ones, the livestock, and the goods in front of them. [22]When they were some distance from the home of Micah, the men who were in the houses near Micah's house were called out, and they overtook the Danites. [23]They shouted to the Danites, who turned around and said to Micah, "What is the matter that you come with such a company?" [24]He replied, "You take my gods that I made, and the priest, and go away, and what have I left? How then can you ask me, 'What is the matter?' " [25]And the Danites said to him, "You had better not let your voice be heard among us or else hot-tempered fellows will attack you, and you will lose your life and the lives of your household." [26]Then the Danites went their way. When Micah saw that they were too strong for him, he turned and went back to his home.

The Danites Settle in Laish

27 The Danites, having taken what Micah had made, and the priest who belonged to him, came to Laish, to a people quiet and unsuspecting, put them to the sword, and burned down the city. [28]There was no deliverer, because it was far from Sidon and they had no dealings with Aram.[a] It was in the valley that belongs to Beth-rehob. They rebuilt the city, and lived in it. [29]They named the city Dan, after their ancestor Dan, who was born to Israel; but the name of the city was formerly Laish. [30]Then the Danites set up the idol for themselves. Jonathan son of Gershom, son of Moses,[b] and his sons were priests to the tribe of the Danites until the time the land went into captivity. [31]So they maintained as their own Micah's idol that he had made, as long as the house of God was at Shiloh.

The Levite's Concubine

19 In those days, when there was no king in Israel, a certain Levite, residing in the remote parts of the hill country of Ephraim, took to himself a concubine from Bethlehem in Judah. [2]But his concubine became angry with[c] him, and she went away from him to her father's house at Bethlehem in Judah, and was there some four months. [3]Then her husband set out after her, to speak tenderly to her and bring her back. He had with him his servant and a couple of donkeys. When he reached[d] her father's house, the girl's father saw him

[a] Cn Compare verse 7: Heb *with anyone* [b] Another reading is *son of Manasseh* [c] Gk OL: Heb *prostituted herself against* [d] Gk: Heb *she brought him to*

19:1-9 no king in Israel: This phrase again emphasizes the disorder in society (17:6; 18:1). It sets the stage for the story of Israel's getting a king, which will be told in the books of Samuel, which follow.

19:1-30 no king in Israel . . . a perverse lot, surrounded the house: This grisly story about gang rape, murder, and mutilation is difficult to understand. In some settings it could well be skipped over. It raises many questions. Why did the man offer this gang of ruffians his daughter? Why would he offer them the woman staying as a guest in his house? Why would the Levite offer his wife to this bunch? Why did no one let her in the house when she tried to get in? Why this horrible butchering of the corpse? It just shows how bad the situation in Israel had become. In a society where such gangs of hoodlums are on the loose, stable government is badly needed. Maybe the story is a political ad for installing a king.

19:2 concubine: See the note at 8:30-31.

19:3-9 spend the night: The repeated invitation to "spend the night" emphasizes the hospitality of the host.

and came with joy to meet him. 4 His father-in-law, the girl's father, made him stay, and he remained with him three days; so they ate and drank, and he[a] stayed there. 5 On the fourth day they got up early in the morning, and he prepared to go; but the girl's father said to his son-in-law, "Fortify yourself with a bit of food, and after that you may go." 6 So the two men sat and ate and drank together; and the girl's father said to the man, "Why not spend the night and enjoy yourself?" 7 When the man got up to go, his father-in-law kept urging him until he spent the night there again. 8 On the fifth day he got up early in the morning to leave; and the girl's father said, "Fortify yourself." So they lingered[b] until the day declined, and the two of them ate and drank.[c] 9 When the man with his concubine and his servant got up to leave, his father-in-law, the girl's father, said to him, "Look, the day has worn on until it is almost evening. Spend the night. See, the day has drawn to a close. Spend the night here and enjoy yourself. Tomorrow you can get up early in the morning for your journey, and go home."

10 But the man would not spend the night; he got up and departed, and arrived opposite Jebus (that is, Jerusalem). He had with him a couple of saddled donkeys, and his concubine was with him. 11 When they were near Jebus, the day was far spent, and the servant said to his master, "Come now, let us turn aside to this city of the Jebusites, and spend the night in it." 12 But his master said to him, "We will not turn aside into a city of foreigners, who do not belong to the people of Israel; but we will continue on to Gibeah." 13 Then he said to his servant, "Come, let us try to reach one of these places, and spend the night at Gibeah or at Ramah." 14 So they passed on and went their way; and the sun went down on them near Gibeah, which belongs to Benjamin. 15 They turned aside there, to go in and spend the night at Gibeah. He went in and sat down in the open square of the city, but no one took them in to spend the night.

19:10-30 no one took them in to spend the night: Offering hospitality to travelers was an important aspect of this ancient culture. People usually considered it their duty to invite travelers to spend the night. No one offers the travelers hospitality in Gibeah, in the territory of Benjamin. Finally an old man, originally from Ephraim, takes them in (19:16-20).

Not all parts of the Bible are G-rated, suitable for family devotions. This is one of them. Can you think of others? How do you feel about the Bible when you read stories like these? How do you feel when you hear such violent and inhumane actions in today's world? What can persons of faith do to respond?

16 Then at evening there was an old man coming from his work in the field. The man was from the hill country of Ephraim, and he was residing in Gibeah. (The people of the place were Benjaminites.) 17 When the old man looked up and saw the wayfarer in the open square of the city, he said, "Where are you going and where do you come from?" 18 He answered him, "We are passing from Bethlehem in Judah to the remote parts of the hill country of Ephraim, from which I come. I went to Bethlehem in Judah; and I am going to my home.[d] Nobody has offered to take me in. 19 We your servants have straw and fodder for our donkeys, with bread and wine for me and the woman and the young man along with us. We need nothing more." 20 The old man said, "Peace be to you. I will care for all your wants; only do not

---

[a] Compare verse 7 and Gk: Heb *they* [b] Cn: Heb *Linger* [c] Gk: Heb lacks *and drank*
[d] Gk Compare 19.29. Heb *to the house of the* LORD

spend the night in the square." 21 So he brought him into his house,
and fed the donkeys; they washed their feet, and ate and drank.

Gibeah's Crime

22 While they were enjoying themselves, the men of the city,
a perverse lot, surrounded the house, and started pounding on the
door. They said to the old man, the master of the house, "Bring out
the man who came into your house, so that we may have intercourse
with him." 23 And the man, the master of the house, went out to them
and said to them, "No, my brothers, do not act so wickedly. Since this
man is my guest, do not do this vile thing. 24 Here are my virgin daughter and his concubine; let me bring them out now. Ravish them and
do whatever you want to them; but against this man do not do such a
vile thing." 25 But the men would not listen to him. So the man seized
his concubine, and put her out to them. They wantonly raped her, and
abused her all through the night until the morning. And as the dawn
began to break, they let her go. 26 As morning appeared, the woman
came and fell down at the door of the man's house where her master
was, until it was light.

27 In the morning her master got up, opened the doors of the
house, and when he went out to go on his way, there was his concubine lying at the door of the house, with her hands on the threshold.
28 "Get up," he said to her, "we are going." But there was no answer.
Then he put her on the donkey; and the man set out for his home.
29 When he had entered his house, he took a knife, and grasping his
concubine he cut her into twelve pieces, limb by limb, and sent her
throughout all the territory of Israel. 30 Then he commanded the men
whom he sent, saying, "Thus shall you say to all the Israelites, 'Has
such a thing ever happened[a] since the day that the Israelites came up
from the land of Egypt until this day? Consider it, take counsel, and
speak out.' "

The Other Tribes Attack Benjamin

20 Then all the Israelites came out, from Dan to Beer-sheba,
including the land of Gilead, and the congregation assembled in one body before the LORD at Mizpah. 2 The chiefs of all the
people, of all the tribes of Israel, presented themselves in the assembly of the people of God, four hundred thousand foot-soldiers bearing arms. 3 (Now the Benjaminites heard that the people of Israel had
gone up to Mizpah.) And the Israelites said, "Tell us, how did this
criminal act come about?" 4 The Levite, the husband of the woman
who was murdered, answered, "I came to Gibeah that belongs to Benjamin, I and my concubine, to spend the night. 5 The lords of Gibeah

20:1-7 Dan to Beer-sheba: This means all Israel, from north to south. Mizpah is about eight miles north of Jerusalem (see Map 3, pp. 2100-2101). The Levite tells of the horrible act of violence committed by the men of Benjamin, spinning his story a bit in his own favor. In such a lawless time, this crime widens into civil war among Israel's tribes.

[a] Compare Gk: Heb 30 *And all who saw it said, "Such a thing has not happened or been seen*

rose up against me, and surrounded the house at night. They intended
to kill me, and they raped my concubine until she died. 6 Then I took
my concubine and cut her into pieces, and sent her throughout the
whole extent of Israel's territory; for they have committed a vile outrage in Israel. 7 So now, you Israelites, all of you, give your advice and
counsel here."

20:8-17 We will go up against it by lot: Answers to questions put to God were often determined by casting lots. Small stones or pieces of wood were used. This method was similar to rolling dice, flipping a coin, or drawing straws, and it was believed that God was behind the answer given by the lots. Ten percent of the men will provide provisions in this war against the people of Benjamin (20:8-11). The elite corps of seven hundred left-handed men with slingshots must have been an impressive bunch (20:16).

8 All the people got up as one, saying, "We will not any of us go to
our tents, nor will any of us return to our houses. 9 But now this is what
we will do to Gibeah: we will go up[a] against it by lot. 10 We will take ten
men of a hundred throughout all the tribes of Israel, and a hundred of
a thousand, and a thousand of ten thousand, to bring provisions for
the troops, who are going to repay[b] Gibeah of Benjamin for all the disgrace that they have done in Israel." 11 So all the men of Israel gathered
against the city, united as one.

12 The tribes of Israel sent men through all the tribe of Benjamin,
saying, "What crime is this that has been committed among you?
13 Now then, hand over those scoundrels in Gibeah, so that we may put
them to death, and purge the evil from Israel." But the Benjaminites
would not listen to their kinsfolk, the Israelites. 14 The Benjaminites
came together out of the towns to Gibeah, to go out to battle against
the Israelites. 15 On that day the Benjaminites mustered twenty-
six thousand armed men from their towns, besides the inhabitants
of Gibeah. 16 Of all this force, there were seven hundred picked men
who were left-handed; every one could sling a stone at a hair, and not
miss. 17 And the Israelites, apart from Benjamin, mustered four hundred thousand armed men, all of them warriors.

18 The Israelites proceeded to go up to Bethel, where they inquired of God, "Which of us shall go up first to battle against the Benjaminites?" And the LORD answered, "Judah shall go up first."

20:20 The Israelites went out to battle against Benjamin: The Benjaminites win the first two battles (20:18-25). The Israelites hold a service of sacrifice and prayer at nearby Bethel (see Map 3, pp. 2100-2101), and the priests there assure them that the LORD will help them win the next battle.

Tricking the Benjaminites into thinking they were running away, the Israelite troops draw them out of the city of Gibeah. Then the Benjaminites are ambushed, and the defenseless city is destroyed and burned. The warfare and chaos is going from bad to worse.

19 Then the Israelites got up in the morning, and encamped
against Gibeah. 20 The Israelites went out to battle against Benjamin;
and the Israelites drew up the battle line against them at Gibeah. 21 The
Benjaminites came out of Gibeah, and struck down on that day twenty-two thousand of the Israelites. 23[c] The Israelites went up and wept
before the LORD until the evening; and they inquired of the LORD,
"Shall we again draw near to battle against our kinsfolk the Benjaminites?" And the LORD said, "Go up against them." 22 The Israelites took
courage, and again formed the battle line in the same place where they
had formed it on the first day.

24 So the Israelites advanced against the Benjaminites the second day. 25 Benjamin moved out against them from Gibeah the second day, and struck down eighteen thousand of the Israelites, all of

---

[a] Gk: Heb lacks *we will go up* [b] Compare Gk: Meaning of Heb uncertain [c] Verses 22 and 23 are transposed

them armed men. 26 Then all the Israelites, the whole army, went back
to Bethel and wept, sitting there before the LORD; they fasted that day
until evening. Then they offered burnt offerings and sacrifices of well-
being before the LORD. 27 And the Israelites inquired of the LORD (for
the ark of the covenant of God was there in those days, 28 and Phinehas son of Eleazar, son of Aaron, ministered before it in those days),
saying, "Shall we go out once more to battle against our kinsfolk the
Benjaminites, or shall we desist?" The LORD answered, "Go up, for
tomorrow I will give them into your hand."

29 So Israel stationed men in ambush around Gibeah. 30 Then
the Israelites went up against the Benjaminites on the third day, and
set themselves in array against Gibeah, as before. 31 When the Benjaminites went out against the army, they were drawn away from the
city. As before they began to inflict casualties on the troops, along
the main roads, one of which goes up to Bethel and the other to Gibeah, as well as in the open country, killing about thirty men of Israel. 32 The Benjaminites thought, "They are being routed before us,
as previously." But the Israelites said, "Let us retreat and draw them
away from the city toward the roads." 33 The main body of the Israelites drew back its battle line to Baal-tamar, while those Israelites
who were in ambush rushed out of their place west[a] of Geba. 34 There
came against Gibeah ten thousand picked men out of all Israel, and
the battle was fierce. But the Benjaminites did not realize that disaster was close upon them.

35 The LORD defeated Benjamin before Israel; and the Israelites
destroyed twenty-five thousand one hundred men of Benjamin that
day, all of them armed.

36 Then the Benjaminites saw that they were defeated.[b]

The Israelites gave ground to Benjamin, because they trusted to
the troops in ambush that they had stationed against Gibeah. 37 The
troops in ambush rushed quickly upon Gibeah. Then they put the
whole city to the sword. 38 Now the agreement between the main
body of Israel and the men in ambush was that when they sent up a
cloud of smoke out of the city 39 the main body of Israel should turn
in battle. But Benjamin had begun to inflict casualties on the Israelites, killing about thirty of them; so they thought, "Surely they are defeated before us, as in the first battle." 40 But when the cloud, a column
of smoke, began to rise out of the city, the Benjaminites looked behind them—and there was the whole city going up in smoke toward
the sky! 41 Then the main body of Israel turned, and the Benjaminites were dismayed, for they saw that disaster was close upon them.
42 Therefore they turned away from the Israelites in the direction of
the wilderness; but the battle overtook them, and those who came

---

[a] Gk Vg: Heb *in the plain* [b] *This sentence is continued by verse 45.*

21:1-12 No one of us shall give his daughter in marriage to Benjamin: The tribe of Benjamin is now facing extinction because the Israelites had wiped out most of them in warfare (20:48). Six hundred men had escaped, and now they needed wives. Remembering that the people from Jabesh-Gilead had not provided troops for the war against Benjamin, the other tribes decide to pay them back by destroying their city. They do, taking four hundred unmarried young women as captives to provide wives for some of the Benjaminites.

21:1-25 all the people did what was right in their own eyes: Chapters 17–21 report how things got worse and worse for the people of Israel. These stories show what can happen in a society when the Ten Commandments are broken, with no honoring of God (idol worship) and no regard for other people (robbery, rape, murder, and warfare). Allowing all to do their own thing (21:25) leads to decline, disintegration, and chaos.

out of the city[a] were slaughtering them in between.[b] 43 Cutting down[c] the Benjaminites, they pursued them from Nohah[d] and trod them down as far as a place east of Gibeah. 44 Eighteen thousand Benjaminites fell, all of them courageous fighters. 45 When they turned and fled toward the wilderness to the rock of Rimmon, five thousand of them were cut down on the main roads, and they were pursued as far as Gidom, and two thousand of them were slain. 46 So all who fell that day of Benjamin were twenty-five thousand arms-bearing men, all of them courageous fighters. 47 But six hundred turned and fled toward the wilderness to the rock of Rimmon, and remained at the rock of Rimmon for four months. 48 Meanwhile, the Israelites turned back against the Benjaminites, and put them to the sword—the city, the people, the animals, and all that remained. Also the remaining towns they set on fire.

The Benjaminites Saved from Extinction

21 Now the Israelites had sworn at Mizpah, "No one of us shall give his daughter in marriage to Benjamin." 2 And the people came to Bethel, and sat there until evening before God, and they lifted up their voices and wept bitterly. 3 They said, "O LORD, the God of Israel, why has it come to pass that today there should be one tribe lacking in Israel?" 4 On the next day, the people got up early, and built an altar there, and offered burnt offerings and sacrifices of well-being. 5 Then the Israelites said, "Which of all the tribes of Israel did not come up in the assembly to the LORD?" For a solemn oath had been taken concerning whoever did not come up to the LORD to Mizpah, saying, "That one shall be put to death." 6 But the Israelites had compassion for Benjamin their kin, and said, "One tribe is cut off from Israel this day. 7 What shall we do for wives for those who are left, since we have sworn by the LORD that we will not give them any of our daughters as wives?"

8 Then they said, "Is there anyone from the tribes of Israel who did not come up to the LORD to Mizpah?" It turned out that no one from Jabesh-gilead had come to the camp, to the assembly. 9 For when the roll was called among the people, not one of the inhabitants of Jabesh-gilead was there. 10 So the congregation sent twelve thousand soldiers there and commanded them, "Go, put the inhabitants of Jabesh-gilead to the sword, including the women and the little ones. 11 This is what you shall do; every male and every woman that has lain with a male you shall devote to destruction." 12 And they found among the inhabitants of Jabesh-gilead four hundred young virgins who had never slept with a man and brought them to the camp at Shiloh, which is in the land of Canaan.

---

[a] Compare Vg and some Gk Mss: Heb *cities* [b] Compare Syr: Meaning of Heb uncertain [c] Gk: Heb *Surrounding* [e] Gk: Heb *pursued them at their resting place*

13 Then the whole congregation sent word to the Benjaminites
who were at the rock of Rimmon, and proclaimed peace to them.
14 Benjamin returned at that time; and they gave them the women
whom they had saved alive of the women of Jabesh-gilead; but they
did not suffice for them.

15 The people had compassion on Benjamin because the LORD
had made a breach in the tribes of Israel. 16 So the elders of the congregation said, "What shall we do for wives for those who are left, since
there are no women left in Benjamin?" 17 And they said, "There must
be heirs for the survivors of Benjamin, in order that a tribe may not be
blotted out from Israel. 18 Yet we cannot give any of our daughters to
them as wives." For the Israelites had sworn, "Cursed be anyone who
gives a wife to Benjamin." 19 So they said, "Look, the yearly festival of
the LORD is taking place at Shiloh, which is north of Bethel, on the
east of the highway that goes up from Bethel to Shechem, and south
of Lebonah." 20 And they instructed the Benjaminites, saying, "Go and
lie in wait in the vineyards, 21 and watch; when the young women of
Shiloh come out to dance in the dances, then come out of the vineyards and each of you carry off a wife for himself from the young
women of Shiloh, and go to the land of Benjamin. 22 Then if their fathers or their brothers come to complain to us, we will say to them,
'Be generous and allow us to have them; because we did not capture
in battle a wife for each man. But neither did you incur guilt by giving
your daughters to them.' " 23 The Benjaminites did so; they took wives
for each of them from the dancers whom they abducted. Then they
went and returned to their territory, and rebuilt the towns, and lived
in them. 24 So the Israelites departed from there at that time by tribes
and families, and they went out from there to their own territories.

25 In those days there was no king in Israel; all the people did
what was right in their own eyes.

21:13-25 What shall we do for wives for those who are left?: There were still two hundred Benjaminites who needed wives. So the Israelites decided to abduct some young women at Shiloh, where a festival was being held. They interrupt the dancing, capture the women, and take them home. Hardly the right thing to do—but the concluding verse in the book is a reminder that "In those days there was no king in Israel; all the people did what was right in their own eyes" (21:25).

The biblical story does not end on this discouraging note. In Ruth, the next book of the Bible, there is a story about godly people in a small village who care for one another. Then we hear that God still cares enough to send kings and prophets to these people (the books of Samuel and Kings and prophets). And God cares enough to hear their prayers and praises (Psalms). The New Testament will pick up the story, telling about God sending to the whole world a Savior—Christ the Lord. Such continuing, caring love of God is called grace, and it is amazing.

What do you find particularly difficult or challenging about the book of Judges? What do you find hopeful? Based on what you know about other parts of the Bible, where do the stories found in this book seem to fit into the whole?

Ruth 1:22

RUTH

Background File

The book of Ruth is a bridge between the unruly end of the period of the judges (see Judg 21:25) and the beginning of the kingdom ruled by David and his descendants. The author might have been a village teacher, such as a priest or a wise woman, who told ancestral stories to instruct and inspire the people.

What's the Story?

The book is set in the village of Bethlehem, in Judah. It gives us a picture of village life, including farming practices and how the city elders gathered at the village gate to make decisions. Ruth may have been written as early as the time of David (1000 B.C.E.) to tell the story of his foreign grandmother. But probably it was written much later, after folks people returned from the exile in Babylon. Folks then were suspicious of foreign women (see Ezra 9–10 and Neh 13), and the book of Ruth would have encouraged them to be more open.

The book of Ruth moves from famine and death at the beginning to harvest and finally birth at the end. Naomi goes with her family to the enemy country of Moab because there is a famine in Israel. Her sons marry Moabite women, Orpah and Ruth. Naomi's husband and sons die. She returns home to Bethlehem. Ruth, who pledges her loyalty to Naomi and to the God of Israel, returns with her. While working in the fields, Ruth meets Boaz, Naomi's relative. Even though Ruth comes from an enemy people, Boaz realizes that she is loyal and worthy. He marries her to preserve the line of Naomi's family. Ruth is blessed by the whole village of Bethlehem. Boaz and Ruth give birth to a baby, Obed, who becomes the grandfather of King David. The whole nation is blessed because of the loyalty of this devoted widow, this good man, and this foreign woman, Ruth.

What's the Message?

The book tells a wonderful story about three of Israel's ancestors—Naomi, a widow; Ruth, her foreign daughter-in-law; and Boaz, a wealthy farmer. Through acts of loyalty, generosity, and commitment, these three make possible the birth of King David's grandfather. They pave the way for the birth of

Jesus. Martin Luther frequently mentions Ruth as an example that Gentiles (non-Jews) are included in the promises of God. He highlights her inclusion in the birth line of Jesus in Matthew 1, along with the foreigners Tamar and Rahab.

Ruth's story also helps us think about how ordinary people—including widows, farmers, and foreign women—can change the course of history for the better by acting out of loyalty and love. The book invites us to open up the idea of family to include everyone. God does not act directly in the book. Rather, we see God acting indirectly through the interactions between people and in the many blessings that are scattered throughout the book.

Elimelech's Family Goes to Moab

1 In the days when the judges ruled, there was a famine in the land,
and a certain man of Bethlehem in Judah went to live in the country of Moab, he and his wife and two sons. 2 The name of the man was
Elimelech and the name of his wife Naomi, and the names of his two
sons were Mahlon and Chilion; they were Ephrathites from Bethlehem in Judah. They went into the country of Moab and remained
there. 3 But Elimelech, the husband of Naomi, died, and she was left
with her two sons. 4 These took Moabite wives; the name of the one
was Orpah and the name of the other Ruth. When they had lived
there about ten years, 5 both Mahlon and Chilion also died, so that
the woman was left without her two sons and her husband.

Naomi and Her Moabite Daughters-in-Law

6 Then she started to return with her daughters-in-law from the
country of Moab, for she had heard in the country of Moab that the
LORD had considered his people and given them food. 7 So she set out
from the place where she had been living, she and her two daughters-
in-law, and they went on their way to go back to the land of Judah.
8 But Naomi said to her two daughters-in-law, "Go back each of you
to your mother's house. May the LORD deal kindly with you, as you
have dealt with the dead and with me. 9 The LORD grant that you may
find security, each of you in the house of your husband." Then she
kissed them, and they wept aloud. 10 They said to her, "No, we will
return with you to your people." 11 But Naomi said, "Turn back, my
daughters, why will you go with me? Do I still have sons in my womb
that they may become your husbands? 12 Turn back, my daughters, go
your way, for I am too old to have a husband. Even if I thought there
was hope for me, even if I should have a husband tonight and bear
sons, 13 would you then wait until they were grown? Would you then
refrain from marrying? No, my daughters, it has been far more bitter
for me than for you, because the hand of the LORD has turned against

1:1-4 Moab: This country was one of Israel's most hated enemies (see Num 21–33; Neh 13:1-3).

How do you feel when people from your country live in nations that might be considered enemies or marry people from them?

1:3 Naomi: She is a widow. Widows in Israel, like orphans, resident aliens (travelers), and the poor, often need protection and care.

Notice the many family terms used in 1:1-8. Who counts as family?

1:8 May the LORD deal kindly with you: This is the first of seven blessings in the book.

How does God act in the ways we bless one another?

1:11 that they may become your husbands?: In Israel, a living brother must marry the wife of his dead brother, so that the property and name of the brother and the family is not lost. The formal name for this was "levirate marriage" (see Deut 25:5-10).

Ruth's speech about loyalty (1:16-17) is often used at weddings. How do you think about it differently when you know it was said to a mother-in-law by her foreign daughter-in-law?

me." 14 Then they wept aloud again. Orpah kissed her mother-in-law,
but Ruth clung to her.

15 So she said, "See, your sister-in-law has gone back to her people and to her gods; return after your sister-in-law." 16 But Ruth said,

"Do not press me to leave you
  or to turn back from following you!
Where you go, I will go;
  where you lodge, I will lodge;
your people shall be my people,
  and your God my God.
17 Where you die, I will die—
  there will I be buried.
May the LORD do thus and so to me,
  and more as well,
if even death parts me from you!"

18 When Naomi saw that she was determined to go with her, she said
no more to her.

19 So the two of them went on until they came to Bethlehem.
When they came to Bethlehem, the whole town was stirred because
of them; and the women said, "Is this Naomi?" 20 She said to them,

"Call me no longer Naomi,[a]
  call me Mara,[b]
  for the Almighty[c] has dealt bitterly with me.
21 I went away full,
  but the LORD has brought me back empty;
why call me Naomi
  when the LORD has dealt harshly with[d] me,
  and the Almighty[c] has brought calamity upon me?"

22 So Naomi returned together with Ruth the Moabite, her
daughter-in-law, who came back with her from the country of Moab.
They came to Bethlehem at the beginning of the barley harvest.

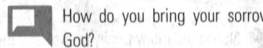

1:20 Mara: Naomi renames herself *Mara*, which means "bitter." Naomi's lament is like laments in Psalms and Job. Through a lament, people can faithfully bring their sorrow to God.

How do you bring your sorrows to God?

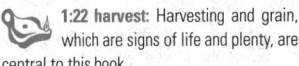

1:22 harvest: Harvesting and grain, which are signs of life and plenty, are central to this book.

Ruth Meets Boaz

2 Now Naomi had a kinsman on her husband's side, a prominent
rich man, of the family of Elimelech, whose name was Boaz.
2 And Ruth the Moabite said to Naomi, "Let me go to the field and
glean among the ears of grain, behind someone in whose sight I may
find favor." She said to her, "Go, my daughter." 3 So she went. She came
and gleaned in the field behind the reapers. As it happened, she came
to the part of the field belonging to Boaz, who was of the family of
Elimelech. 4 Just then Boaz came from Bethlehem. He said to the
reapers, "The LORD be with you." They answered, "The LORD bless
you." 5 Then Boaz said to his servant who was in charge of the reapers,

2:2 glean: *Gleaning* refers to collecting leftover grain in the field. In ancient Israel it was a way of providing for the poor (see Lev 19:9-10; 23:22; Deut 24:21). Gleaning was part of Israel's legal welfare system.

In 2:4-16 notice Boaz's relationships with both his workers and the poor foreign widow. How do his actions help us understand how wealthy community leaders can show loyalty and compassion?

[a] That is *Pleasant* [b] That is *Bitter* [c] Traditional rendering of Heb *Shaddai* [d] Or *has testified against*

“To whom does this young woman belong?” 6The servant who was in
charge of the reapers answered, “She is the Moabite who came back
with Naomi from the country of Moab. 7She said, ‘Please, let me glean
and gather among the sheaves behind the reapers.’ So she came, and
she has been on her feet from early this morning until now, without
resting even for a moment.”[a]

8 Then Boaz said to Ruth, “Now listen, my daughter, do not go
to glean in another field or leave this one, but keep close to my young
women. 9Keep your eyes on the field that is being reaped, and follow
behind them. I have ordered the young men not to bother you. If you
get thirsty, go to the vessels and drink from what the young men have
drawn.” 10Then she fell prostrate, with her face to the ground, and said
to him, “Why have I found favor in your sight, that you should take
notice of me, when I am a foreigner?” 11But Boaz answered her, “All
that you have done for your mother-in-law since the death of your husband has been fully told me, and how you left your father and mother
and your native land and came to a people that you did not know before. 12May the LORD reward you for your deeds, and may you have a
full reward from the LORD, the God of Israel, under whose wings you
have come for refuge!” 13Then she said, “May I continue to find favor
in your sight, my lord, for you have comforted me and spoken kindly
to your servant, even though I am not one of your servants.”

14 At mealtime Boaz said to her, “Come here, and eat some of
this bread, and dip your morsel in the sour wine.” So she sat beside
the reapers, and he heaped up for her some parched grain. She ate
until she was satisfied, and she had some left over. 15When she got up
to glean, Boaz instructed his young men, “Let her glean even among
the standing sheaves, and do not reproach her. 16You must also pull
out some handfuls for her from the bundles, and leave them for her to
glean, and do not rebuke her.”

17 So she gleaned in the field until evening. Then she beat out
what she had gleaned, and it was about an ephah of barley. 18She picked
it up and came into the town, and her mother-in-law saw how much
she had gleaned. Then she took out and gave her what was left over
after she herself had been satisfied. 19Her mother-in-law said to her,
“Where did you glean today? And where have you worked? Blessed
be the man who took notice of you.” So she told her mother-in-law
with whom she had worked, and said, “The name of the man with
whom I worked today is Boaz.” 20Then Naomi said to her daughter-
in-law, “Blessed be he by the LORD, whose kindness has not forsaken
the living or the dead!” Naomi also said to her, “The man is a relative
of ours, one of our nearest kin.”[b] 21Then Ruth the Moabite said, “He
even said to me, ‘Stay close by my servants, until they have finished all

2:17 ephah: An ephah is about two-thirds of a bushel.

2:20 nearest kin: Naomi’s lament (1:20-21) turns to blessing. The “nearest kin” in ancient Israel was called a *go’el* (go-ALE), a word that also means “redeemer.” In the final two chapters, *go’el*, as both noun and verb (to redeem), occurs twenty-one times.

What is Naomi’s role in this story (see 3:1-6), and what does she teach us about widows?

[a] Compare Gk Vg: Meaning of Heb uncertain [b] Or *one with the right to redeem*

my harvest.'" 22 Naomi said to Ruth, her daughter-in-law, "It is better,
my daughter, that you go out with his young women, otherwise you
might be bothered in another field." 23 So she stayed close to the young
women of Boaz, gleaning until the end of the barley and wheat harvests; and she lived with her mother-in-law.

Ruth and Boaz at the Threshing Floor

3 Naomi her mother-in-law said to her, "My daughter, I need
to seek some security for you, so that it may be well with you.
2 Now here is our kinsman Boaz, with whose young women you have
been working. See, he is winnowing barley tonight at the threshing
floor. 3 Now wash and anoint yourself, and put on your best clothes
and go down to the threshing floor; but do not make yourself known
to the man until he has finished eating and drinking. 4 When he lies
down, observe the place where he lies; then, go and uncover his feet
and lie down; and he will tell you what to do." 5 She said to her, "All
that you tell me I will do."

6 So she went down to the threshing floor and did just as her
mother-in-law had instructed her. 7 When Boaz had eaten and drunk,
and he was in a contented mood, he went to lie down at the end of the
heap of grain. Then she came stealthily and uncovered his feet, and lay
down. 8 At midnight the man was startled, and turned over, and there,
lying at his feet, was a woman! 9 He said, "Who are you?" And she
answered, "I am Ruth, your servant; spread your cloak over your servant, for you are next-of-kin."[a] 10 He said, "May you be blessed by the
LORD, my daughter; this last instance of your loyalty is better than the
first; you have not gone after young men, whether poor or rich. 11 And
now, my daughter, do not be afraid, I will do for you all that you ask,
for all the assembly of my people know that you are a worthy woman.
12 But now, though it is true that I am a near kinsman, there is another
kinsman more closely related than I. 13 Remain this night, and in the
morning, if he will act as next-of-kin[a] for you, good; let him do it. If he
is not willing to act as next-of-kin[a] for you, then, as the LORD lives, I
will act as next-of-kin[a] for you. Lie down until the morning."

14 So she lay at his feet until morning, but got up before one person could recognize another; for he said, "It must not be known that
the woman came to the threshing floor." 15 Then he said, "Bring the
cloak you are wearing and hold it out." So she held it, and he measured
out six measures of barley, and put it on her back; then he went into
the city. 16 She came to her mother-in-law, who said, "How did things
go with you,[b] my daughter?" Then she told her all that the man had
done for her, 17 saying, "He gave me these six measures of barley, for he
said, 'Do not go back to your mother-in-law empty-handed.'" 18 She

3:2 threshing floor: This large recessed area is where the men of the city winnowed the wheat and barley. In this process they separated the grains from the chaff by beating the stalks on the floor. Sometimes oxen were used to help separate the grain. The straw and chaff were tossed into the air so wind would blow them away, leaving heavier grain to fall to the recessed floor. Most reputable women would not go there

3:4 go and uncover his feet: In Hebrew the word for foot is often used to refer to a man's sexual organ, and thus the original hearers of this story would have heard a double meaning. Ruth is making a bold move by lying next to Boaz.

What do you think of Ruth's actions? What difference does the context of the story, God's purposes, or any other factor have on your response?

3:9 cloak: The word for cloak is the same word as God's "wings" in 2:12.

3:11 you are a worthy woman: The same Hebrew word *hayil* (HA-yil) is used to describe Ruth as being "worthy" and Boaz as a "prominent rich man" (2:1). As readers we hear that they share the same qualities and so would make a good match. The term is also used in Prov 31:10-13 to describe a "capable" wife.

3:15 six measures of barley: This might have been the marriage price.

[a] Or *one with the right to redeem* [b] Or *"Who are you,*

replied, "Wait, my daughter, until you learn how the matter turns out,
for the man will not rest, but will settle the matter today."

The Marriage of Boaz and Ruth

4 No sooner had Boaz gone up to the gate and sat down there
than the next-of-kin,[a] of whom Boaz had spoken, came passing
by. So Boaz said, "Come over, friend; sit down here." And he went
over and sat down. 2 Then Boaz took ten men of the elders of the city,
and said, "Sit down here"; so they sat down. 3 He then said to the next-
of-kin,[a] "Naomi, who has come back from the country of Moab, is
selling the parcel of land that belonged to our kinsman Elimelech. 4 So
I thought I would tell you of it, and say: Buy it in the presence of those
sitting here, and in the presence of the elders of my people. If you will
redeem it, redeem it; but if you will not, tell me, so that I may know;
for there is no one prior to you to redeem it, and I come after you." So
he said, "I will redeem it." 5 Then Boaz said, "The day you acquire the
field from the hand of Naomi, you are also acquiring Ruth[b] the Moabite, the widow of the dead man, to maintain the dead man's name
on his inheritance." 6 At this, the next-of-kin[a] said, "I cannot redeem it
for myself without damaging my own inheritance. Take my right of
redemption yourself, for I cannot redeem it."

7 Now this was the custom in former times in Israel concerning
redeeming and exchanging: to confirm a transaction, the one took
off a sandal and gave it to the other; this was the manner of attest-
ing in Israel. 8 So when the next-of-kin[a] said to Boaz, "Acquire it for
yourself," he took off his sandal. 9 Then Boaz said to the elders and all
the people, "Today you are witnesses that I have acquired from the
hand of Naomi all that belonged to Elimelech and all that belonged
to Chilion and Mahlon. 10 I have also acquired Ruth the Moabite, the
wife of Mahlon, to be my wife, to maintain the dead man's name on
his inheritance, in order that the name of the dead may not be cut
off from his kindred and from the gate of his native place; today you
are witnesses." 11 Then all the people who were at the gate, along with
the elders, said, "We are witnesses. May the LORD make the woman
who is coming into your house like Rachel and Leah, who together
built up the house of Israel. May you produce children in Ephrathah
and bestow a name in Bethlehem; 12 and, through the children that
the LORD will give you by this young woman, may your house be like
the house of Perez, whom Tamar bore to Judah."

The Genealogy of David

13 So Boaz took Ruth and she became his wife. When they came
together, the LORD made her conceive, and she bore a son. 14 Then

[a] Or *one with the right to redeem* [b] OL Vg: Heb *from the hand of Naomi and from Ruth*

4:1 gate: This is where legal business was done, like a courthouse.

4:1-3 next-of-kin: Boaz uses the lure of property and wealth to tempt the nearest next-of kin. He then cleverly includes marriage to a foreign woman as part of that person's responsibility. The next-of-kin never gets a name and also misses his chance to be part of the family line of David and Jesus.

4:5 acquiring Ruth...to maintain the dead man's name on his inheritance: An early form of levirate marriage called for a brother to marry the widow of a deceased brother (see Deut 25:5-10). Boaz is not a brother, and neither is the next-of-kin. Still, Boaz is trying to protect the interests of Naomi and Ruth in the same way the levirate marriage law was intended to provide protection.

How do we describe the first use of the Law? Laws stand behind a number of the references in this book (see 2:2, gleaning; 4:5, levirate marriage). God's law functions in our lives in several ways. The first use (civil or political use) is the law as all people experience it in their communal life. Its purpose is to establish justice, preserve peace, set boundaries to evil doing, and protect those in society who are marginal and vulnerable. When we hear these references as the first use of the law, we know that following these laws is good and helps to insure an ordered and just society. *Ruth 4:5*

4:8 took off his sandal: The sandal reminds us of the law in Deuteronomy 25:5-10 and referenced in 1:11 (see note).

Ruth, the Moabite woman, is compared to the matriarchs of Israel (4:11-12). As you think about your own community of faith or church, who are or were the matriarchs and patriarchs, the founding core? How did they shape the community? How have newcomers and people from other countries also shaped the community?

the women said to Naomi, "Blessed be the LORD, who has not left
you this day without next-of-kin;[a] and may his name be renowned in
Israel! 15 He shall be to you a restorer of life and a nourisher of your old
age; for your daughter-in-law who loves you, who is more to you than
seven sons, has borne him." 16 Then Naomi took the child and laid him
in her bosom, and became his nurse. 17 The women of the neighborhood gave him a name, saying, "A son has been born to Naomi." They
named him Obed; he became the father of Jesse, the father of David.
18 Now these are the descendants of Perez: Perez became the
father of Hezron, 19 Hezron of Ram, Ram of Amminadab, 20 Amminadab of Nahshon, Nahshon of Salmon, 21 Salmon of Boaz, Boaz of
Obed, 22 Obed of Jesse, and Jesse of David.

[a] Or *one with the right to redeem*

4:14-16 He shall be to you a restorer of life: This final blessing is stunning. Rather than saying Ruth is important because she has a son, the child is given importance because Ruth is his mother. The child is now the *go'el*, next-of-kin, and redeemer (see note on 2:20).

4:16-17 became his nurse: Naomi symbolically becomes the child's nurse and mother. Her family, whose members had died, now continues and lives.

4:18-22 Now these are the descendants: The final verses tie the book both to David and to Jesus (see Matt 1:3-6).

How do the final verses of Ruth point us to Christ? On the marriage of Moabite Ruth and Israelite Boaz, Luther says it was a union of Gentile and Israelite blood, so that Ruth the Moabitess also became the mother of Christ. This union shows how God is not only the God of the Jews but also the God of the Gentiles. See also the note at Matthew 1:1-17. *Ruth 4:18-22*

1 Samuel 10:1

1 SAMUEL

Background File

Exactly who wrote 1 Samuel is unclear. Scholars believe that the book comes from the hand of many different people with varying points of view about Samuel, Saul, David, and the monarchy. One view is favorable toward the idea of monarchy, while another view seems suspicious of it. The material was collected and edited in stages, with perhaps the largest part coming some time after the northern kingdom of Israel fell to the Assyrians in 721 B.C.E.

What's the Story?

The books of 1 and 2 Samuel tell of a time of great change in Israel's history. Israel had been a loose confederation of twelve tribes based in rural hill country. The book of Judges describes this well. In 1 Samuel we see a shift beginning. The people of Israel demand a king, and the monarchy is born. Israel rallies around their king, begins to defeat their enemies, and takes their cities. They are on their way to becoming a more unified state and greater political power. Following 1 and 2 Samuel, 1 Kings will present a more complete picture of this centralized power in the city of Jerusalem, beginning with the reign of Solomon.

There are four key people in this story: Hannah, Samuel, King Saul, and King David. Running over and through the lives of these people of faith is the work of God on behalf of God's people Israel. It is God who gives the barren, faithful Hannah a child; calls Samuel to be both priest and prophet; has Samuel anoint Saul king and gifts Saul with the power of the Spirit; rejects Saul as a failed king; and sends Samuel to anoint David as king, and then rescues David from Saul's jealous anger. Important conversations happen throughout the book. Pay close attention to what the main characters say to one another. Watch for additional meaningful encounters with Eli, Goliath, Jonathan, Michal, and Abigail.

Take note of the key places where this dramatic history of God's people is played out, such as the tent of meeting, where the ark of the covenant and *ephod* are present. Note how God is present there to choose and direct. Other important settings are the countryside, the battlefield, and the wilderness of Judah. Here God's people are threatened and tested. The Philistines are an ongoing danger, but a greater danger is the people's lack of trust in God.

Originally in the Hebrew Scriptures, the Samuel material was one book. The Hebrew text was not well preserved, so 1 Samuel, as we have it, is based on the Greek translation of that text. In that translation the book had been divided into two. First Samuel can be outlined this way:

The rise of Samuel (chapters 1-7)
The rule of Saul (8-15)
The rise of David (16-31)

The story of King David's reign will be the main subject of 2 Samuel.

What's the Message?

The message of 1 Samuel comes to God's people as they struggled to settle in the promised land. They were loosely organized and ill-equipped to deal with their iron-armed enemies. Out of their fear and lack of trust in God, they asked for a king. The book of 1 Samuel shows us where such fear and lack of trust lead and how a faithful God works to save God's people.

The key themes of the book are shown in the lives of its main characters. Samuel's leadership as priest and prophet (chapters 1-7) is a model of trust in God and absolute obedience to the commands of God. He sets the standard and tone for the entire book. When the people demand a king, God chooses Saul (8-15). This tall, strong warrior is faithful at first but he soon fails to listen and obey God's every command. The rest of Saul's story is a tragic tale of a great king who falls into despair and cuts himself off from his family and God. Despair and alienation, instead of trust and obedience, define his rule. As Saul fails, God has Samuel anoint David. In contrast to Saul, David personifies trust in Israel's God and successfully defends his people against their enemies (16-31).

The original hearers of 1 Samuel would see both the advantages and the limitations of having a king. They and their leaders would be challenged to listen to God above all and respond in obedience. This is also an important message for God's people in any time or place. No king or leader, no military, no voice of the people, no person or thing is as dependable and faithful as God. All, and especially leaders, are called to place their trust in God and follow God's leading. God alone is worthy. Only God can save.

Samuel's Birth and Dedication

1 There was a certain man of Ramathaim, a Zuphite[a] from the hill
country of Ephraim, whose name was Elkanah son of Jeroham
son of Elihu son of Tohu son of Zuph, an Ephraimite. 2 He had two
wives; the name of the one was Hannah, and the name of the other
Peninnah. Peninnah had children, but Hannah had no children.
3 Now this man used to go up year by year from his town to worship and to sacrifice to the LORD of hosts at Shiloh, where the two

[a] Compare Gk and 1 Chr 6.35–36: Heb *Ramathaim-zophim*

1:1-28 Hannah had no children: Hannah's childlessness is a great sorrow and disgrace, as it would be for any woman of her time. Like Hannah, God's people, Israel, are in sorrow and trouble because they are a poor nation, have corrupt leaders, and are threatened by the Philistines (see 1 Sam 2:12-26, and 4–7).

1:1-3 Elkanah son of Jeroham: Elkanah is from a respected family that faithfully worships at Shiloh, an important cen-

sons of Eli, Hophni and Phinehas, were priests of the LORD. 4 On the
day when Elkanah sacrificed, he would give portions to his wife Peninnah and to all her sons and daughters; 5 but to Hannah he gave a
double portion,[a] because he loved her, though the LORD had closed
her womb. 6 Her rival used to provoke her severely, to irritate her, because the LORD had closed her womb. 7 So it went on year by year; as
often as she went up to the house of the LORD, she used to provoke
her. Therefore Hannah wept and would not eat. 8 Her husband Elkanah said to her, "Hannah, why do you weep? Why do you not eat?
Why is your heart sad? Am I not more to you than ten sons?"

9 After they had eaten and drunk at Shiloh, Hannah rose and presented herself before the LORD.[b] Now Eli the priest was sitting on the
seat beside the doorpost of the temple of the LORD. 10 She was deeply
distressed and prayed to the LORD, and wept bitterly. 11 She made this
vow: "O LORD of hosts, if only you will look on the misery of your
servant, and remember me, and not forget your servant, but will give
to your servant a male child, then I will set him before you as a nazirite[c] until the day of his death. He shall drink neither wine nor intoxi-
cants,[d] and no razor shall touch his head."

12 As she continued praying before the LORD, Eli observed her
mouth. 13 Hannah was praying silently; only her lips moved, but her
voice was not heard; therefore Eli thought she was drunk. 14 So Eli
said to her, "How long will you make a drunken spectacle of yourself?
Put away your wine." 15 But Hannah answered, "No, my lord, I am a
woman deeply troubled; I have drunk neither wine nor strong drink,
but I have been pouring out my soul before the LORD. 16 Do not regard your servant as a worthless woman, for I have been speaking out
of my great anxiety and vexation all this time." 17 Then Eli answered,
"Go in peace; the God of Israel grant the petition you have made to
him." 18 And she said, "Let your servant find favor in your sight." Then
the woman went to her quarters,[e] ate and drank with her husband,[f]
and her countenance was sad no longer.[g]

19 They rose early in the morning and worshiped before the
LORD; then they went back to their house at Ramah. Elkanah knew
his wife Hannah, and the LORD remembered her. 20 In due time Hannah conceived and bore a son. She named him Samuel, for she said, "I
have asked him of the LORD."

21 The man Elkanah and all his household went up to offer to the
LORD the yearly sacrifice, and to pay his vow. 22 But Hannah did not
go up, for she said to her husband, "As soon as the child is weaned, I
will bring him, that he may appear in the presence of the LORD, and

---

[a] Syr: Meaning of Heb uncertain [b] Gk: Heb lacks *and presented herself before the LORD* [c] That is *one separated* or *one consecrated* [d] Cn Compare Gk Q Ms 1.22: MT *then I will give him to the LORD all the days of his life* [e] Gk: Heb *went her way* [f] Gk: Heb lacks *and drank with her husband* [g] Gk: Meaning of Heb uncertain

ter of worship in Israel's history. Samuel is born of faithful parents and ancestors.

1:9-18 Hannah rose and presented herself before the LORD: Hannah's prayer, vow, and trust model the faith God desires. Throughout 1 Samuel, God will call for such faith from all of Israel (7:3-6) and from its kings, Saul (9:15-17) and David (16:12-13).

1:19—2:10 Hannah . . . bore a son . . . and said, "My heart exults in the LORD": Hannah's song celebrates that God remembered her. God's saving action is at the center of this song and the entire life of Israel. Just as God has given Hannah help, so will God help Israel. Hundreds of years later another young woman, Mary, mother of Jesus, will sing such a song. She will rejoice in God's faithfulness, shown in the coming birth of Jesus (See Luke 1:46-55).

1:21-28 he is given to the LORD: God heard Hannah's prayer and answered it with the birth of Samuel. Now Elkanah and Hannah faithfully honor Hannah's vow. In place of sorrow and disgrace there is now gratitude, obedience, and praise. God seeks this same response from all Israel.

How can we as individuals and the church model the faith and obedience of Elkanah and Hannah? Where can we join in God's work to give strength and dignity to those in distress?

remain there forever; I will offer him as a nazirite[a] for all time."[b] 23Her
husband Elkanah said to her, "Do what seems best to you, wait until you have weaned him; only—may the LORD establish his word."[c]
So the woman remained and nursed her son, until she weaned him.
24When she had weaned him, she took him up with her, along with a
three-year-old bull,[d] an ephah of flour, and a skin of wine. She brought
him to the house of the LORD at Shiloh; and the child was young.
25Then they slaughtered the bull, and they brought the child to Eli.
26And she said, "Oh, my lord! As you live, my lord, I am the woman
who was standing here in your presence, praying to the LORD. 27For
this child I prayed; and the LORD has granted me the petition that I
made to him. 28Therefore I have lent him to the LORD; as long as he
lives, he is given to the LORD."

She left him there for[e] the LORD.

Hannah's Prayer

2 Hannah prayed and said,
"My heart exults in the LORD;
my strength is exalted in my God.[f]
My mouth derides my enemies,
because I rejoice in my[g] victory.

2 "There is no Holy One like the LORD,
no one besides you;
there is no Rock like our God.
3 Talk no more so very proudly,
let not arrogance come from your mouth;
for the LORD is a God of knowledge,
and by him actions are weighed.
4 The bows of the mighty are broken,
but the feeble gird on strength.
5 Those who were full have hired themselves out for bread,
but those who were hungry are fat with spoil.
The barren has borne seven,
but she who has many children is forlorn.
6 The LORD kills and brings to life;
he brings down to Sheol and raises up.
7 The LORD makes poor and makes rich;
he brings low, he also exalts.
8 He raises up the poor from the dust;
he lifts the needy from the ash heap,

2:1, 10 my strength: Strength means to receive worth, dignity, status, power, and well-being.

2:3 a God of knowledge: God not only understands but also acts and makes things happen.

2:3 let not arrogance: Arrogance and pride have been problems for God's people from the very beginning (see Gen 3) and continue to be even with Israel's greatest king, David (2 Sam 11).

How is Hannah's prayer a model for us? In faith Hannah brings her need to God, and in faith she trusts God to hear and answer. Luther writes about this in the Large Catechism as he discusses the last petition of the Lord's Prayer: "And deliver us from evil. Amen." He points out that God wants us to pray about everything that affects our bodily welfare but, then, to pray "Amen." We are not to doubt that our prayers are heard and granted by our merciful God. *1 Samuel 2:1-10*

2:8-10 He raises up the poor: God acts to help the poor and needy, both now and through future kings. First Samuel is a story of God at work, as God has been before (See Deut 10:14, 17-18), to remember those in need, and to save the people. Any chosen leaders (Eli, Samuel) or kings (Saul, David) are to serve these same purposes.

[a] That is *one separated* or *one consecrated* [b] Cn Compare Q Ms: MT lacks *I will offer him as a nazirite for all time* [c] MT: Q Ms Gk Compare Syr *that which goes out of your mouth* [d] Q Ms Gk Syr: MT *three bulls* [e] Gk (Compare Q Ms) and Gk at 2.11: MT *And he* (that is, Elkanah) *worshiped there before the LORD* [f] Gk: Heb *the LORD* [g] Q Ms: MT *your*

to make them sit with princes
and inherit a seat of honor.[a]
For the pillars of the earth are the LORD's,
and on them he has set the world.

9 "He will guard the feet of his faithful ones,
but the wicked shall be cut off in darkness;
for not by might does one prevail.
10 The LORD! His adversaries shall be shattered;
the Most High[b] will thunder in heaven.
The LORD will judge the ends of the earth;
he will give strength to his king,
and exalt the power of his anointed."

Eli's Wicked Sons

11 Then Elkanah went home to Ramah, while the boy remained
to minister to the LORD, in the presence of the priest Eli.
12 Now the sons of Eli were scoundrels; they had no regard for
the LORD 13 or for the duties of the priests to the people. When anyone offered sacrifice, the priest's servant would come, while the meat
was boiling, with a three-pronged fork in his hand, 14 and he would
thrust it into the pan, or kettle, or caldron, or pot; all that the fork
brought up the priest would take for himself.[c] This is what they did
at Shiloh to all the Israelites who came there. 15 Moreover, before the
fat was burned, the priest's servant would come and say to the one
who was sacrificing, "Give meat for the priest to roast; for he will not
accept boiled meat from you, but only raw." 16 And if the man said to
him, "Let them burn the fat first, and then take whatever you wish,"
he would say, "No, you must give it now; if not, I will take it by force."
17 Thus the sin of the young men was very great in the sight of the
LORD; for they treated the offerings of the LORD with contempt.

2:12-26 sons of Eli were scoundrels: God continues to be busy bringing up faithful and obedient leaders for Israel. Where Eli and his sons fail (2:22-25), Samuel succeeds. Again and again in Israel's history God calls servants to serve God's good purposes. For example, see David (1 Sam 10:1), Solomon (1 Kgs 3:5-14), Isaiah (Isa 6), Jeremiah (Jer Jer 1:4-10), and Ezekiel (Ezek 2:1—3:11).

2:17 they treated the offerings... with contempt: Eli's sons put themselves in God's place by demanding the meat before it is boiled and offered to God. They do not honor their priestly calling (see also Lev 7:31-38; Deut 18:3).

The Child Samuel at Shiloh

18 Samuel was ministering before the LORD, a boy wearing a linen
ephod. 19 His mother used to make for him a little robe and take it to
him each year, when she went up with her husband to offer the yearly
sacrifice. 20 Then Eli would bless Elkanah and his wife, and say, "May
the LORD repay[d] you with children by this woman for the gift that she
made to[e] the LORD"; and then they would return to their home.
21 And[f] the LORD took note of Hannah; she conceived and bore
three sons and two daughters. And the boy Samuel grew up in the
presence of the LORD.

2:18 a linen ephod: Israel's priests worn a simple linen outer garment known as an ephod, while the high priest's ephod was more elaborate and embroidered (see illustration, p. 166). Samuel's white linen garment is simple, perhaps just an apron, but wearing it is a sign of his priestly call to serve God in the temple.

[a] Gk (Compare Q Ms) adds *He grants the vow of the one who vows, and blesses the years of the just* [b] Cn Heb *against him he* [c] Gk Syr Vg: Heb *with it* [d] Q Ms Gk: MT *give* [e] Q Ms Gk: MT *for the petition that she asked of* [f] Q Ms Gk: MT *When*

Prophecy against Eli's Household

22 Now Eli was very old. He heard all that his sons were doing to all Israel, and how they lay with the women who served at the entrance to the tent of meeting. 23 He said to them, "Why do you do such things? For I hear of your evil dealings from all these people. 24 No, my sons; it is not a good report that I hear the people of the LORD spreading abroad. 25 If one person sins against another, someone can intercede for the sinner with the LORD;[a] but if someone sins against the LORD, who can make intercession?" But they would not listen to the voice of their father; for it was the will of the LORD to kill them.

26 Now the boy Samuel continued to grow both in stature and in favor with the LORD and with the people.

27 A man of God came to Eli and said to him, "Thus the LORD has said, 'I revealed[b] myself to the family of your ancestor in Egypt when they were slaves[c] to the house of Pharaoh. 28 I chose him out of all the tribes of Israel to be my priest, to go up to my altar, to offer incense, to wear an ephod before me; and I gave to the family of your ancestor all my offerings by fire from the people of Israel. 29 Why then look with greedy eye[d] at my sacrifices and my offerings that I commanded, and honor your sons more than me by fattening yourselves on the choicest parts of every offering of my people Israel?' 30 Therefore the LORD the God of Israel declares: 'I promised that your family and the family of your ancestor should go in and out before me forever'; but now the LORD declares: 'Far be it from me; for those who honor me I will honor, and those who despise me shall be treated with contempt. 31 See, a time is coming when I will cut off your strength and the strength of your ancestor's family, so that no one in your family will live to old age. 32 Then in distress you will look with greedy eye[e] on all the prosperity that shall be bestowed upon Israel; and no one in your family shall ever live to old age. 33 The only one of you whom I shall not cut off from my altar shall be spared to weep out his[f] eyes and grieve his[g] heart; all the members of your household shall die by the sword.[h] 34 The fate of your two sons, Hophni and Phinehas, shall be the sign to you—both of them shall die on the same day. 35 I will raise up for myself a faithful priest, who shall do according to what is in my heart and in my mind. I will build him a sure house, and he shall go in and out before my anointed one forever. 36 Everyone who is left in your family shall come to implore him for a piece of silver or a loaf of bread, and shall say, Please put me in one of the priest's places, that I may eat a morsel of bread.'"

---

[a] Gk Compare Q Ms: MT *another, God will mediate for him* [b] Gk Tg Syr: Heb *Did I reveal* [c] Q Ms Gk: MT lacks *slaves* [d] Q Ms Gk: MT *then kick* [e] Q Ms Gk: MT *will kick* [f] Q Ms Gk: MT *your* [g] Q Ms Gk: Heb *your* [h] Q Ms See Gk: MT *die like mortals*

Samuel's Calling and Prophetic Activity

3 Now the boy Samuel was ministering to the LORD under Eli. The word of the LORD was rare in those days; visions were not widespread.

2 At that time Eli, whose eyesight had begun to grow dim so that he could not see, was lying down in his room; [3]the lamp of God had not yet gone out, and Samuel was lying down in the temple of the LORD, where the ark of God was. [4]Then the LORD called, "Samuel! Samuel!"[a] and he said, "Here I am!" [5]and ran to Eli, and said, "Here I am, for you called me." But he said, "I did not call; lie down again." So he went and lay down. [6]The LORD called again, "Samuel!" Samuel got up and went to Eli, and said, "Here I am, for you called me." But he said, "I did not call, my son; lie down again." [7]Now Samuel did not yet know the LORD, and the word of the LORD had not yet been revealed to him. [8]The LORD called Samuel again, a third time. And he got up and went to Eli, and said, "Here I am, for you called me." Then Eli perceived that the LORD was calling the boy. [9]Therefore Eli said to Samuel, "Go, lie down; and if he calls you, you shall say, 'Speak, LORD, for your servant is listening.'" So Samuel went and lay down in his place.

10 Now the LORD came and stood there, calling as before, "Samuel! Samuel!" And Samuel said, "Speak, for your servant is listening." [11]Then the LORD said to Samuel, "See, I am about to do something in Israel that will make both ears of anyone who hears of it tingle. [12]On that day I will fulfill against Eli all that I have spoken concerning his house, from beginning to end. [13]For I have told him that I am about to punish his house forever, for the iniquity that he knew, because his sons were blaspheming God,[b] and he did not restrain them. [14]Therefore I swear to the house of Eli that the iniquity of Eli's house shall not be expiated by sacrifice or offering forever."

15 Samuel lay there until morning; then he opened the doors of the house of the LORD. Samuel was afraid to tell the vision to Eli. [16]But Eli called Samuel and said, "Samuel, my son." He said, "Here I am." [17]Eli said, "What was it that he told you? Do not hide it from me. May God do so to you and more also, if you hide anything from me of all that he told you." [18]So Samuel told him everything and hid nothing from him. Then he said, "It is the LORD; let him do what seems good to him."

19 As Samuel grew up, the LORD was with him and let none of his words fall to the ground. [20]And all Israel from Dan to Beersheba knew that Samuel was a trustworthy prophet of the LORD. [21]The LORD continued to appear at Shiloh, for the LORD revealed

[a] Q Ms Gk See 3.10: MT *the LORD called Samuel* [b] Another reading is *for themselves*

3:1-17 Speak, for your servant is listening: Samuel listens and so will serve as God's priest, prophet, and kingmaker as God leads Israel in a new direction. All this is by God's gracious call and blessing and not by human effort or plan.

3:18 let him do what seems good: Eli is a model of faith and obedience. He accepts the will of the LORD even though his own house will fall. This same kind of faith will be shown by Samuel (1 Sam 8) and much later by the young woman Mary after she hears the angel Gabriel's announcement (Luke 1:38).

3:19-20 let none of his words fall: Samuel's words will be effective because they are from God. The whole nation of Israel is listening.

Listening is essential in our relationship with God. Samuel listens and obeys God. Jesus calls us to listen (Matt 13:43). Later, the book of Revelation will repeat this call to the church (Rev 2:7, 11; 3:6, 13). How do you listen for God? Have you ever experienced anything like Samuel's call from God?

4:1-3 Philistines: These hard-fighting coastal people had been Israel's enemies for two hundred years. Equipped with iron weapons they will continue to fight Israel for another three hundred years. For the area where they primarily lived, see Map 3, pp 2100-2101.

4:5 the ark of the covenant: This box measured about four feet long and two feet deep and wide (Exod 25:10). The ark served as God's throne and was the center of Israel's worship. It contains three important things: the tables of the law given at Sinai, a jar of manna from the wilderness journey, and Aaron's rod that budded (see Num 17). The ark and its contents carry God's saving presence and power in Israel.

4 himself to Samuel at Shiloh by the word of the LORD. 1 And the word of Samuel came to all Israel.

The Ark of God Captured

In those days the Philistines mustered for war against Israel,[a] and Israel went out to battle against them;[b] they encamped at Ebenezer, and the Philistines encamped at Aphek. 2 The Philistines drew up in line against Israel, and when the battle was joined,[c] Israel was defeated by the Philistines, who killed about four thousand men on the field of battle. 3 When the troops came to the camp, the elders of Israel said, "Why has the LORD put us to rout today before the Philistines? Let us bring the ark of the covenant of the LORD here from Shiloh, so that he may come among us and save us from the power of our enemies." 4 So the people sent to Shiloh, and brought from there the ark of the covenant of the LORD of hosts, who is enthroned on the cherubim. The two sons of Eli, Hophni and Phinehas, were there with the ark of the covenant of God.

5 When the ark of the covenant of the LORD came into the camp, all Israel gave a mighty shout, so that the earth resounded. 6 When the Philistines heard the noise of the shouting, they said, "What does this great shouting in the camp of the Hebrews mean?" When they learned that the ark of the LORD had come to the camp, 7 the Philistines were afraid; for they said, "Gods have[d] come into the camp." They also said, "Woe to us! For nothing like this has happened before. 8 Woe to us! Who can deliver us from the power of these mighty gods? These are the gods who struck the Egyptians with every sort of plague in the wilderness. 9 Take courage, and be men, O Philistines, in order not to become slaves to the Hebrews as they have been to you; be men and fight."

10 So the Philistines fought; Israel was defeated, and they fled, everyone to his home. There was a very great slaughter, for there fell of Israel thirty thousand foot soldiers. 11 The ark of God was captured; and the two sons of Eli, Hophni and Phinehas, died.

Death of Eli

12 A man of Benjamin ran from the battle line, and came to Shiloh the same day, with his clothes torn and with earth upon his head. 13 When he arrived, Eli was sitting upon his seat by the road watching, for his heart trembled for the ark of God. When the man came into the city and told the news, all the city cried out. 14 When Eli heard the sound of the outcry, he said, "What is this uproar?" Then the man came quickly and told Eli. 15 Now Eli was ninety-eight years old and

---

[a] Gk: Heb lacks *In those days the Philistines mustered for war against Israel* [b] Gk: Heb *against the Philistines* [c] Meaning of Heb uncertain [d] Or *A god has*

his eyes were set, so that he could not see. 16 The man said to Eli, "I
have just come from the battle; I fled from the battle today." He said,
"How did it go, my son?" 17 The messenger replied, "Israel has fled before the Philistines, and there has also been a great slaughter among
the troops; your two sons also, Hophni and Phinehas, are dead, and
the ark of God has been captured." 18 When he mentioned the ark of
God, Eli[a] fell over backward from his seat by the side of the gate; and
his neck was broken and he died, for he was an old man, and heavy.
He had judged Israel forty years.

19 Now his daughter-in-law, the wife of Phinehas, was pregnant,
about to give birth. When she heard the news that the ark of God was
captured, and that her father-in-law and her husband were dead, she
bowed and gave birth; for her labor pains overwhelmed her. 20 As she
was about to die, the women attending her said to her, "Do not be
afraid, for you have borne a son." But she did not answer or give heed.
21 She named the child Ichabod, meaning, "The glory has departed
from Israel," because the ark of God had been captured and because
of her father-in-law and her husband. 22 She said, "The glory has departed from Israel, for the ark of God has been captured."

4:18 Eli fell over backward...and he died: The news of the capture of the ark shocks Eli more than the death of his two corrupt sons. He had devoted his life to the ark and now all seems lost. Eli and Israel are humiliated.

The Philistines and the Ark

5 When the Philistines captured the ark of God, they brought it
from Ebenezer to Ashdod; 2 then the Philistines took the ark of
God and brought it into the house of Dagon and placed it beside Dagon. 3 When the people of Ashdod rose early the next day, there was
Dagon, fallen on his face to the ground before the ark of the LORD.
So they took Dagon and put him back in his place. 4 But when they
rose early on the next morning, Dagon had fallen on his face to the
ground before the ark of the LORD, and the head of Dagon and both
his hands were lying cut off upon the threshold; only the trunk of[b]
Dagon was left to him. 5 This is why the priests of Dagon and all who
enter the house of Dagon do not step on the threshold of Dagon in
Ashdod to this day.

6 The hand of the LORD was heavy upon the people of Ashdod,
and he terrified and struck them with tumors, both in Ashdod and
in its territory. 7 And when the inhabitants of Ashdod saw how things
were, they said, "The ark of the God of Israel must not remain with
us; for his hand is heavy on us and on our god Dagon." 8 So they sent
and gathered together all the lords of the Philistines, and said, "What
shall we do with the ark of the God of Israel?" The inhabitants of Gath
replied, "Let the ark of God be moved on to us."[c] So they moved the
ark of the God of Israel to Gath.[d] 9 But after they had brought it to

5:1-12 the hand of God: The Philistine god, Dagon, is a lightweight. True power is close at hand in the God of Israel, who alone is worthy of trust and worship. Here is an important lesson for the Philistines, Israel, and all of God's people. This is the stuff of faith: to reject false gods and love God with all one's heart, soul, mind, and strength (Mark 12:29-30).

5:6, 11 heavy: God's power is not defeated but is glorious ("heavy") in the defeat of Dagon and the Philistines.

---

[a] Heb *he* [b] Heb lacks *the trunk of* [c] Gk Compare Q Ms: MT *They answered, "Let the ark of the God of Israel be brought around to Gath."* [d] Gk: Heb lacks *to Gath*

Gath,[a] the hand of the LORD was against the city, causing a very great
panic; he struck the inhabitants of the city, both young and old, so
that tumors broke out on them. 10 So they sent the ark of the God of
Israel[b] to Ekron. But when the ark of God came to Ekron, the people
of Ekron cried out, "Why[c] have they brought around to us[d] the ark of
the God of Israel to kill us[d] and our[e] people?" 11 They sent therefore
and gathered together all the lords of the Philistines, and said, "Send
away the ark of the God of Israel, and let it return to its own place,
that it may not kill us and our people." For there was a deathly panic[f]
throughout the whole city. The hand of God was very heavy there;
12 those who did not die were stricken with tumors, and the cry of the
city went up to heaven.

The Ark Returned to Israel

6 The ark of the LORD was in the country of the Philistines seven
months. 2 Then the Philistines called for the priests and the diviners and said, "What shall we do with the ark of the LORD? Tell us
what we should send with it to its place." 3 They said, "If you send away
the ark of the God of Israel, do not send it empty, but by all means
return him a guilt offering. Then you will be healed and will be ransomed;[g] will not his hand then turn from you?" 4 And they said, "What
is the guilt offering that we shall return to him?" They answered, "Five
gold tumors and five gold mice, according to the number of the lords
of the Philistines; for the same plague was upon all of you and upon
your lords. 5 So you must make images of your tumors and images of
your mice that ravage the land, and give glory to the God of Israel;
perhaps he will lighten his hand on you and your gods and your land.
6 Why should you harden your hearts as the Egyptians and Pharaoh
hardened their hearts? After he had made fools of them, did they not
let the people go, and they departed? 7 Now then, get ready a new cart
and two milch cows that have never borne a yoke, and yoke the cows
to the cart, but take their calves home, away from them. 8 Take the ark
of the LORD and place it on the cart, and put in a box at its side the figures of gold, which you are returning to him as a guilt offering. Then
send it off, and let it go its way. 9 And watch; if it goes up on the way to
its own land, to Beth-shemesh, then it is he who has done us this great
harm; but if not, then we shall know that it is not his hand that struck
us; it happened to us by chance."

10 The men did so; they took two milch cows and yoked them
to the cart, and shut up their calves at home. 11 They put the ark of
the LORD on the cart, and the box with the gold mice and the images
of their tumors. 12 The cows went straight in the direction of Beth-

6:10-21 the Philistines have returned the ark: God cannot be stopped and brings the ark back to Israel. Even when things seem hopeless, God is able to do a new thing. We see this later as God returns the exiles in Babylon to their homeland (Isaiah 40) and when God raises Jesus from the dead and proclaims forgiveness of sins (Luke 24:44-47).

---

[a] Q Ms: MT lacks *to Gath* [b] Q Ms Gk: MT lacks *of Israel* [c] Q Ms Gk: MT lacks *Why* [d] Heb *me* [e] Heb *my* [f] Q Ms reads *a panic from the LORD* [g] Q Ms Gk: MT *and it will be known to you*

shemesh along one highway, lowing as they went; they turned neither
to the right nor to the left, and the lords of the Philistines went after
them as far as the border of Beth-shemesh.

13 Now the people of Beth-shemesh were reaping their wheat
harvest in the valley. When they looked up and saw the ark, they went
with rejoicing to meet it.[a] 14 The cart came into the field of Joshua of
Beth-shemesh, and stopped there. A large stone was there; so they
split up the wood of the cart and offered the cows as a burnt offering
to the LORD. 15 The Levites took down the ark of the LORD and the box
that was beside it, in which were the gold objects, and set them upon
the large stone. Then the people of Beth-shemesh offered burnt offerings and presented sacrifices on that day to the LORD. 16 When the five
lords of the Philistines saw it, they returned that day to Ekron.

17 These are the gold tumors, which the Philistines returned as
a guilt offering to the LORD: one for Ashdod, one for Gaza, one for
Ashkelon, one for Gath, one for Ekron; 18 also the gold mice, according to the number of all the cities of the Philistines belonging to the
five lords, both fortified cities and unwalled villages. The great stone,
beside which they set down the ark of the LORD, is a witness to this
day in the field of Joshua of Beth-shemesh.

The Ark at Kiriath-jearim

19 The descendants of Jeconiah did not rejoice with the people of
Beth-shemesh when they greeted[b] the ark of the LORD; and he killed
seventy men of them.[c] The people mourned because the LORD had
made a great slaughter among the people. 20 Then the people of Beth-
shemesh said, "Who is able to stand before the LORD, this holy God?
To whom shall he go so that we may be rid of him?" 21 So they sent
messengers to the inhabitants of Kiriath-jearim, saying, "The Philis-
7 tines have returned the ark of the LORD. Come down and take
it up to you." 1 And the people of Kiriath-jearim came and took
up the ark of the LORD, and brought it to the house of Abinadab on
the hill. They consecrated his son, Eleazar, to have charge of the ark
of the LORD.

2 From the day that the ark was lodged at Kiriath-jearim, a long
time passed, some twenty years, and all the house of Israel lamented[d]
after the LORD.

Samuel as Judge

3 Then Samuel said to all the house of Israel, "If you are returning to the LORD with all your heart, then put away the foreign gods
and the Astartes from among you. Direct your heart to the LORD, and

6:15 Levites took down the ark: Only the men from the tribe of Levi were allowed to touch the ark, as part of their duties as priests for Israel.

6:19 greeted the ark . . . LORD . . . killed seventy men: See NRSV footnotes b and c. Apparently men of the village looked into the ark. This was considered a severe act of disrespect toward God. (See also 2 Sam 6:6-7.)

7:1-4 And the people . . . served the LORD only: The return of the ark is a sign of God's presence, and Samuel is God's spokesperson, calling the people back to trust and obedience.

7:3-11: put away the Baals: Like other leaders before him (Moses, Joshua), Samuel calls the people to admit their sins and turn to God. Their turning away from all false gods is absolutely necessary.

---

[a] Gk: Heb *rejoiced to see it* [b] Gk: Heb *And he killed some of the people of Beth-shemesh, because they looked into* [c] Heb *killed seventy men, fifty thousand men* [d] Meaning of Heb uncertain

serve him only, and he will deliver you out of the hand of the Philistines." 4So Israel put away the Baals and the Astartes, and they served the LORD only.

5 Then Samuel said, "Gather all Israel at Mizpah, and I will pray to the LORD for you." 6So they gathered at Mizpah, and drew water and poured it out before the LORD. They fasted that day, and said, "We have sinned against the LORD." And Samuel judged the people of Israel at Mizpah.

7 When the Philistines heard that the people of Israel had gathered at Mizpah, the lords of the Philistines went up against Israel. And when the people of Israel heard of it they were afraid of the Philistines. 8The people of Israel said to Samuel, "Do not cease to cry out to the LORD our God for us, and pray that he may save us from the hand of the Philistines." 9So Samuel took a sucking lamb and offered it as a whole burnt offering to the LORD; Samuel cried out to the LORD for Israel, and the LORD answered him. 10As Samuel was offering up the burnt offering, the Philistines drew near to attack Israel; but the LORD thundered with a mighty voice that day against the Philistines and threw them into confusion; and they were routed before Israel. 11And the men of Israel went out of Mizpah and pursued the Philistines, and struck them down as far as beyond Beth-car.

12 Then Samuel took a stone and set it up between Mizpah and Jeshanah,[a] and named it Ebenezer;[b] for he said, "Thus far the LORD has helped us." 13So the Philistines were subdued and did not again enter the territory of Israel; the hand of the LORD was against the Philistines all the days of Samuel. 14The towns that the Philistines had taken from Israel were restored to Israel, from Ekron to Gath; and Israel recovered their territory from the hand of the Philistines. There was peace also between Israel and the Amorites.

15 Samuel judged Israel all the days of his life. 16He went on a circuit year by year to Bethel, Gilgal, and Mizpah; and he judged Israel in all these places. 17Then he would come back to Ramah, for his home was there; he administered justice there to Israel, and built there an altar to the LORD.

Israel Demands a King

8 When Samuel became old, he made his sons judges over Israel. 2The name of his firstborn son was Joel, and the name of his second, Abijah; they were judges in Beer-sheba. 3Yet his sons did not follow in his ways, but turned aside after gain; they took bribes and perverted justice.

4 Then all the elders of Israel gathered together and came to Samuel at Ramah, 5and said to him, "You are old and your sons do not fol-

7:8: Do not cease to cry out: To cry out to God for deliverance is basic to a faith relationship with God. The pattern of crying out in prayer and receiving an answer from God was modeled in Hannah's prayer (1 Sam 2) and occurs often in Israel's history (see especially Judges).

When have you cried out to God? How, when, or where has God answered?

7:12-17 Ebenezer: Samuel and the people recognize that only God has saved them. *Ebenezer* means "stone of the helper."

8:1-5 a king to govern us: This is a huge change for Israel and marks the end of the leadership of judges appointed by God.

---

[a] Gk Syr: Heb *Shen* [b] That is *Stone of Help*

low in your ways; appoint for us, then, a king to govern us, like other
nations." [6]But the thing displeased Samuel when they said, "Give us
a king to govern us." Samuel prayed to the LORD, [7]and the LORD said
to Samuel, "Listen to the voice of the people in all that they say to
you; for they have not rejected you, but they have rejected me from
being king over them. [8]Just as they have done to me,[a] from the day I
brought them up out of Egypt to this day, forsaking me and serving
other gods, so also they are doing to you. [9]Now then, listen to their
voice; only—you shall solemnly warn them, and show them the ways
of the king who shall reign over them."

10 So Samuel reported all the words of the LORD to the people
who were asking him for a king. [11]He said, "These will be the ways of
the king who will reign over you: he will take your sons and appoint
them to his chariots and to be his horsemen, and to run before his
chariots; [12]and he will appoint for himself commanders of thousands
and commanders of fifties, and some to plow his ground and to reap
his harvest, and to make his implements of war and the equipment of
his chariots. [13]He will take your daughters to be perfumers and cooks
and bakers. [14]He will take the best of your fields and vineyards and
olive orchards and give them to his courtiers. [15]He will take one-tenth
of your grain and of your vineyards and give it to his officers and his
courtiers. [16]He will take your male and female slaves, and the best of
your cattle[b] and donkeys, and put them to his work. [17]He will take
one-tenth of your flocks, and you shall be his slaves. [18]And in that
day you will cry out because of your king, whom you have chosen for
yourselves; but the LORD will not answer you in that day."

Israel's Request for a King Granted

19 But the people refused to listen to the voice of Samuel; they
said, "No! but we are determined to have a king over us, [20]so that we
also may be like other nations, and that our king may govern us and go
out before us and fight our battles." [21]When Samuel had heard all the
words of the people, he repeated them in the ears of the LORD. [22]The
LORD said to Samuel, "Listen to their voice and set a king over them."
Samuel then said to the people of Israel, "Each of you return home."

Saul Chosen to Be King

9 There was a man of Benjamin whose name was Kish son of
Abiel son of Zeror son of Becorath son of Aphiah, a Benjaminite, a man of wealth. [2]He had a son whose name was Saul, a
handsome young man. There was not a man among the people of
Israel more handsome than he; he stood head and shoulders above
everyone else.

[a] Gk: Heb lacks *to me* [b] Gk: Heb *young men*

8:7: They have rejected me: Having a king comes about because of the people's lack of trust in God.

8:10-18 Samuel reported: This is one of the longest speeches in the Old Testament against kingship and the abuse of public power.

8:11 take: This word occurs often in Samuel's warning about a king. A king will take much away, which is exactly the opposite of God who acts to bless.

8:19-22 the people refused to listen: Here we go again! The people seek safety in someone else besides God. This time it is a king. God does not approve but does agree to the request.

What does Israel's cry-answer pattern mean for our daily lives? In his Small Catechism Luther talks about what baptism means for daily living. In baptism our sinful self dies and we are raised up in Christ to a new life. This becomes a pattern for our daily lives. Each day we are to cry out to God, admitting our sins and our need. In response to this cry and confession God answers us with Jesus Christ, forgiving us and raising us up to a new life in him. As Israel learned long ago under Samuel's leadership, crying to the Lord is a sign of faith, and God will answer. *1 Samuel 8:4-22*

9:1-2 handsome: Saul's handsome good looks and towering height are assumed to be a sign of God's favor.

In your opinion, what difference do physical attributes make regarding choosing people for certain jobs or even leadership roles? What, in your opinion, makes a good leader?

9:3-6 my father will . . . worry about us: Saul obeys his father's orders and faithfully searches for some lost donkeys. He'll need this same obedient humility as king.

9:11 girls coming out to draw water: Towns were often built near a water source, such as a stream. Women usually had the job of getting water for their families.

9:13 bless the sacrifice: One of Samuel's jobs as priest is to bless the meat for the sacrifice before it can be eaten.

9:16 my people: The true reason God provides a king is to save the people from the Philistines, rather than to satisfy their desire for a king like those of other nations.

9:17 the Lord told him, "Here is the man": The people want a king, but the choice is God's alone.

3 Now the donkeys of Kish, Saul's father, had strayed. So Kish said
to his son Saul, "Take one of the boys with you; go and look for the
donkeys." 4 He passed through the hill country of Ephraim and passed
through the land of Shalishah, but they did not find them. And they
passed through the land of Shaalim, but they were not there. Then
he passed through the land of Benjamin, but they did not find them.
5 When they came to the land of Zuph, Saul said to the boy who
was with him, "Let us turn back, or my father will stop worrying about
the donkeys and worry about us." 6 But he said to him, "There is a man
of God in this town; he is a man held in honor. Whatever he says always comes true. Let us go there now; perhaps he will tell us about
the journey on which we have set out." 7 Then Saul replied to the boy,
"But if we go, what can we bring the man? For the bread in our sacks
is gone, and there is no present to bring to the man of God. What have
we?" 8 The boy answered Saul again, "Here, I have with me a quarter
shekel of silver; I will give it to the man of God, to tell us our way."
9 (Formerly in Israel, anyone who went to inquire of God would say,
"Come, let us go to the seer"; for the one who is now called a prophet
was formerly called a seer.) 10 Saul said to the boy, "Good; come, let us
go." So they went to the town where the man of God was.
11 As they went up the hill to the town, they met some girls coming out to draw water, and said to them, "Is the seer here?" 12 They
answered, "Yes, there he is just ahead of you. Hurry; he has come
just now to the town, because the people have a sacrifice today at the
shrine. 13 As soon as you enter the town, you will find him, before he
goes up to the shrine to eat. For the people will not eat until he comes,
since he must bless the sacrifice; afterward those eat who are invited.
Now go up, for you will meet him immediately." 14 So they went up to
the town. As they were entering the town, they saw Samuel coming
out toward them on his way up to the shrine.
15 Now the day before Saul came, the Lord had revealed to Samuel: 16 "Tomorrow about this time I will send to you a man from the
land of Benjamin, and you shall anoint him to be ruler over my people
Israel. He shall save my people from the hand of the Philistines; for I
have seen the suffering of[a] my people, because their outcry has come
to me." 17 When Samuel saw Saul, the Lord told him, "Here is the
man of whom I spoke to you. He it is who shall rule over my people."
18 Then Saul approached Samuel inside the gate, and said, "Tell me,
please, where is the house of the seer?" 19 Samuel answered Saul, "I am
the seer; go up before me to the shrine, for today you shall eat with
me, and in the morning I will let you go and will tell you all that is on
your mind. 20 As for your donkeys that were lost three days ago, give no
further thought to them, for they have been found. And on whom is

[a] Gk: Heb lacks *the suffering of*

all Israel's desire fixed, if not on you and on all your ancestral house?"
21 Saul answered, "I am only a Benjaminite, from the least of the tribes
of Israel, and my family is the humblest of all the families of the tribe
of Benjamin. Why then have you spoken to me in this way?"
22 Then Samuel took Saul and his servant-boy and brought them
into the hall, and gave them a place at the head of those who had been
invited, of whom there were about thirty. 23 And Samuel said to the
cook, "Bring the portion I gave you, the one I asked you to put aside."
24 The cook took up the thigh and what went with it[a] and set them before Saul. Samuel said, "See, what was kept is set before you. Eat; for
it is set[b] before you at the appointed time, so that you might eat with
the guests."[c]
So Saul ate with Samuel that day. 25 When they came down from
the shrine into the town, a bed was spread for Saul[d] on the roof, and
he lay down to sleep.[e] 26 Then at the break of dawn[f] Samuel called to
Saul upon the roof, "Get up, so that I may send you on your way." Saul
got up, and both he and Samuel went out into the street.

Samuel Anoints Saul

27 As they were going down to the outskirts of the town, Samuel
said to Saul, "Tell the boy to go on before us, and when he has passed
on, stop here yourself for a while, that I may make known to you the
10 word of God." 1 Samuel took a vial of oil and poured it on
his head, and kissed him; he said, "The LORD has anointed
you ruler over his people Israel. You shall reign over the people of
the LORD and you will save them from the hand of their enemies all
around. Now this shall be the sign to you that the LORD has anointed
you ruler[g] over his heritage: 2 When you depart from me today you
will meet two men by Rachel's tomb in the territory of Benjamin at
Zelzah; they will say to you, 'The donkeys that you went to seek are
found, and now your father has stopped worrying about them and is
worrying about you, saying: What shall I do about my son?' 3 Then
you shall go on from there further and come to the oak of Tabor;
three men going up to God at Bethel will meet you there, one carrying three kids, another carrying three loaves of bread, and another
carrying a skin of wine. 4 They will greet you and give you two loaves
of bread, which you shall accept from them. 5 After that you shall
come to Gibeath-elohim,[h] at the place where the Philistine garrison
is; there, as you come to the town, you will meet a band of prophets
coming down from the shrine with harp, tambourine, flute, and lyre
playing in front of them; they will be in a prophetic frenzy. 6 Then the

[a] Meaning of Heb uncertain [b] Q Ms Gk: MT *it was kept* [c] Cn: Heb *it was kept for you, saying, I have invited the people* [d] Gk: Heb *and he spoke with Saul* [e] Gk: Heb lacks *and he lay down to sleep* [f] Gk: Heb *and they arose early and at break of dawn* [g] Gk: Heb lacks *over his people Israel. You shall . . . anointed you ruler* [h] Or *the Hill of God*

9:21 I am only a Benjaminite: Saul is not thinking about being a king; he's only after some lost donkeys! The tribe of Benjamin is the smallest of the twelve tribes and not highly respected.

10:1-8 took a vial of oil . . . anointed: Samuel takes a small clay flask filled with special olive oil to anoint Saul. A recipe for anointing oil is given in Exodus 30:22-25, and it includes myrrh and cinnamon. Samuel's kiss is a sign of God's blessing.

10:1 The LORD has anointed you: When Samuel pours oil over Saul's head, Saul receives God's Spirit and holiness and is set apart for special leadership. In the Bible priests (Exod 29:7) and prophets (1 Kgs 19:16) are anointed. Jesus Christ will be called the Messiah, which means "anointed one" (see Luke 2:11).

spirit of the Lord will possess you, and you will be in a prophetic frenzy along with them and be turned into a different person. 7 Now when these signs meet you, do whatever you see fit to do, for God is with you. 8 And you shall go down to Gilgal ahead of me; then I will come down to you to present burnt offerings and offer sacrifices of well-being. Seven days you shall wait, until I come to you and show you what you shall do."

Saul Prophesies

9 As he turned away to leave Samuel, God gave him another heart; and all these signs were fulfilled that day. 10 When they were going from there[a] to Gibeah,[b] a band of prophets met him; and the spirit of God possessed him, and he fell into a prophetic frenzy along with them. 11 When all who knew him before saw how he prophesied with the prophets, the people said to one another, "What has come over the son of Kish? Is Saul also among the prophets?" 12 A man of the place answered, "And who is their father?" Therefore it became a proverb, "Is Saul also among the prophets?" 13 When his prophetic frenzy had ended, he went home.[c]

10:9 another heart: God fills Saul with new power and freedom. Now he can lead Israel in new directions. Later God will give a new heart and spirit to the people in exile in Babylon (see Ezek 36:26). God gives a new heart to strengthen, restore, and save us.

10:10 the spirit of God possessed him: Clearly God is in charge! God's spirit seizes Saul and fills him—to the surprise of Saul and others. God's spirit will continue to be active in choosing and empowering people of God's own choosing: Mary (see Luke 1:35), Jesus (see Luke 4:18), and the church at Pentecost (see Acts 2:4).

14 Saul's uncle said to him and to the boy, "Where did you go?" And he replied, "To seek the donkeys; and when we saw they were not to be found, we went to Samuel." 15 Saul's uncle said, "Tell me what Samuel said to you." 16 Saul said to his uncle, "He told us that the donkeys had been found." But about the matter of the kingship, of which Samuel had spoken, he did not tell him anything.

Saul Proclaimed King

17 Samuel summoned the people to the Lord at Mizpah 18 and said to them,[d] "Thus says the Lord, the God of Israel, 'I brought up Israel out of Egypt, and I rescued you from the hand of the Egyptians and from the hand of all the kingdoms that were oppressing you.' 19 But today you have rejected your God, who saves you from all your calamities and your distresses; and you have said, 'No! but set a king over us.' Now therefore present yourselves before the Lord by your tribes and by your clans."

10:17 Mizpah: Earlier, Samuel gathered Israel here to repent and turn to God (7:6). Using the words of a prophet messenger, "Thus says the Lord," he reminds the people how God rescued them from Egypt.

20 Then Samuel brought all the tribes of Israel near, and the tribe of Benjamin was taken by lot. 21 He brought the tribe of Benjamin near by its families, and the family of the Matrites was taken by lot. Finally he brought the family of the Matrites near man by man,[e] and Saul the son of Kish was taken by lot. But when they sought him, he could not be found. 22 So they inquired again of the Lord, "Did the man come here?"[f] and the Lord said, "See, he has hidden himself among

---

[a] Gk: Heb *they came there* [b] Or *the hill* [c] Cn: Heb *he came to the shrine* [d] Heb *to the people of Israel*
[e] Gk: Heb lacks *Finally . . . man by man* [f] Gk: Heb *Is there yet a man to come here?*

the baggage." 23 Then they ran and brought him from there. When he
took his stand among the people, he was head and shoulders taller
than any of them. 24 Samuel said to all the people, "Do you see the one
whom the LORD has chosen? There is no one like him among all the
people." And all the people shouted, "Long live the king!"
25 Samuel told the people the rights and duties of the kingship;
and he wrote them in a book and laid it up before the LORD. Then
Samuel sent all the people back to their homes. 26 Saul also went to his
home at Gibeah, and with him went warriors whose hearts God had
touched. 27 But some worthless fellows said, "How can this man save
us?" They despised him and brought him no present. But he held his
peace.

Now Nahash, king of the Ammonites, had been grievously oppressing the Gadites and the Reubenites. He would gouge out the right eye of each of them and would not grant Israel a deliverer. No one was left of the Israelites across the Jordan whose right eye Nahash, king of the Ammonites, had not gouged out. But there were seven thousand men who had escaped from the Ammonites and had entered Jabesh-gilead.[a]

10:24 no one like him: Clearly Saul is specially chosen. Only Moses (see Deut 34:10-11) and Joshua (2 Kgs 23:25) are described like this.

10:27 How can this man save us?: All is not well! Even though God has clearly chosen Saul to be king, some refuse to follow him. God acts to save the people, but their unbelief is still a problem. The same can be said for us (see Luke 1:20, 4:29, 20:15, and 23:35).

Saul Defeats the Ammonites

11 About a month later,[b] Nahash the Ammonite went up and besieged Jabesh-gilead; and all the men of Jabesh said to Nahash,
"Make a treaty with us, and we will serve you." 2 But Nahash the Ammonite said to them, "On this condition I will make a treaty with you,
namely that I gouge out everyone's right eye, and thus put disgrace
upon all Israel." 3 The elders of Jabesh said to him, "Give us seven days'
respite that we may send messengers through all the territory of Israel.
Then, if there is no one to save us, we will give ourselves up to you."
4 When the messengers came to Gibeah of Saul, they reported the
matter in the hearing of the people; and all the people wept aloud.
5 Now Saul was coming from the field behind the oxen; and Saul
said, "What is the matter with the people, that they are weeping?" So
they told him the message from the inhabitants of Jabesh. 6 And the
spirit of God came upon Saul in power when he heard these words,
and his anger was greatly kindled. 7 He took a yoke of oxen, and cut
them in pieces and sent them throughout all the territory of Israel by
messengers, saying, "Whoever does not come out after Saul and Samuel, so shall it be done to his oxen!" Then the dread of the LORD fell
upon the people, and they came out as one. 8 When he mustered them
at Bezek, those from Israel were three hundred thousand, and those
from Judah seventy[c] thousand. 9 They said to the messengers who

11:1-3 Nahash the Ammonite: Nahash means "the snake" and that fits this brutal leader perfectly. Nahash doesn't want to make a true treaty that would give some protection in trade for loyalty. He wants to torture and humiliate the Israelites. According to Genesis 19:30-36, the Ammonites are related to the Israelites, but they later become a threat to Israel (see Judg 11:1-5).

11:5-6 the spirit of God came upon Saul: Saul returned to farming until God's spirit moved him to anger over the treatment of the people of Jabesh-gilead. God is always concerned about the oppressed, and so moves others to act boldly: Moses, the prophet Isaiah, and Jesus (See Exod 2:23—3:8; Isa 61:1; Luke 4:18-19).

11:7 cut them in pieces: The pieces of oxen give the clear message that those who do not now answer the call to war may suffer the same fate as the oxen (Judg 21:8-10).

---

[a] Q Ms Compare Josephus, *Antiquities* VI.v.1 (68-71): MT lacks *Now Nahash . . . entered Jabesh-gilead.*
[b] Q Ms Gk: MT lacks *About a month later* [c] Q Ms Gk: MT *thirty*

had come, "Thus shall you say to the inhabitants of Jabesh-gilead:
'Tomorrow, by the time the sun is hot, you shall have deliverance.'"
When the messengers came and told the inhabitants of Jabesh, they
rejoiced. [10]So the inhabitants of Jabesh said, "Tomorrow we will give
ourselves up to you, and you may do to us whatever seems good to
you." [11]The next day Saul put the people in three companies. At the
morning watch they came into the camp and cut down the Ammonites until the heat of the day; and those who survived were scattered,
so that no two of them were left together.

12 The people said to Samuel, "Who is it that said, 'Shall Saul
reign over us?' Give them to us so that we may put them to death."
[13]But Saul said, "No one shall be put to death this day, for today the
LORD has brought deliverance to Israel."

14 Samuel said to the people, "Come, let us go to Gilgal and there
renew the kingship." [15]So all the people went to Gilgal, and there they
made Saul king before the LORD in Gilgal. There they sacrificed offerings of well-being before the LORD, and there Saul and all the Israelites rejoiced greatly.

Samuel's Farewell Address

12 Samuel said to all Israel, "I have listened to you in all that you
have said to me, and have set a king over you. [2]See, it is the
king who leads you now; I am old and gray, but my sons are with you.
I have led you from my youth until this day. [3]Here I am; testify against
me before the LORD and before his anointed. Whose ox have I taken?
Or whose donkey have I taken? Or whom have I defrauded? Whom
have I oppressed? Or from whose hand have I taken a bribe to blind
my eyes with it? Testify against me[a] and I will restore it to you." [4]They
said, "You have not defrauded us or oppressed us or taken anything
from the hand of anyone." [5]He said to them, "The LORD is witness
against you, and his anointed is witness this day, that you have not
found anything in my hand." And they said, "He is witness."

6 Samuel said to the people, "The LORD is witness, who[b] appointed Moses and Aaron and brought your ancestors up out of the
land of Egypt. [7]Now therefore take your stand, so that I may enter
into judgment with you before the LORD, and I will declare to you[c]
all the saving deeds of the LORD that he performed for you and for
your ancestors. [8]When Jacob went into Egypt and the Egyptians oppressed them,[d] then your ancestors cried to the LORD and the LORD
sent Moses and Aaron, who brought forth your ancestors out of
Egypt, and settled them in this place. [9]But they forgot the LORD their
God; and he sold them into the hand of Sisera, commander of the

11:12-13 the LORD has brought deliverance: This is God's victory! Saul, like judges before him (Judg 2:11-16), simply serves God's plan to save Israel. The word *save* (or deliverance) comes up often in connection with Saul (10:27, 11:3, 9, 12, and 13), but God is the power behind him. Saul knows this and refuses to overstep his power and seek revenge on those who doubted him.

11:15 Saul and all the Israelites rejoiced greatly: Saul's bold military move pays off. Offerings of well-being are a community meal in God's presence. Animal parts are offered to God, and what is leftover provides a meal for all.

12:1 Samuel said to all Israel: It's time to be clear. Samuel speaks to all the people as he has done in the past (1 Sam 7:5, 8:4, 10:17, 11:14) and as Moses (Exod 19:7) and Joshua (Josh 24:1) have done before him. He clearly points out that he has not taken anything from them as their leader (12:1-5), that God has been faithful to Israel in troubled times (12:6-8), and that Israel has not been faithful (12:9-11).

12:7-11 all the saving deeds of the LORD: Israel has a long history of forgetting all that God has done for it. The book of Judges describes this well. In spite of such faithlessness, God remains faithful and rescues them.

[a] Gk: Heb lacks *Testify against me* [b] Gk: Heb lacks *is witness, who* [c] Gk: Heb lacks *and I will declare to you* [d] Gk: Heb lacks *and the Egyptians oppressed them*

army of King Jabin of[a] Hazor, and into the hand of the Philistines,
and into the hand of the king of Moab; and they fought against them.
10 Then they cried to the LORD, and said, 'We have sinned, because we
have forsaken the LORD, and have served the Baals and the Astartes;
but now rescue us out of the hand of our enemies, and we will serve
you.' 11 And the LORD sent Jerubbaal and Barak,[b] and Jephthah, and
Samson,[c] and rescued you out of the hand of your enemies on every
side; and you lived in safety. 12 But when you saw that King Nahash of
the Ammonites came against you, you said to me, 'No, but a king shall
reign over us,' though the LORD your God was your king. 13 See, here
is the king whom you have chosen, for whom you have asked; see, the
LORD has set a king over you. 14 If you will fear the LORD and serve
him and heed his voice and not rebel against the commandment of
the LORD, and if both you and the king who reigns over you will follow the LORD your God, it will be well; 15 but if you will not heed the
voice of the LORD, but rebel against the commandment of the LORD,
then the hand of the LORD will be against you and your king.[d] 16 Now
therefore take your stand and see this great thing that the LORD will
do before your eyes. 17 Is it not the wheat harvest today? I will call
upon the LORD, that he may send thunder and rain; and you shall
know and see that the wickedness that you have done in the sight of
the LORD is great in demanding a king for yourselves." 18 So Samuel
called upon the LORD, and the LORD sent thunder and rain that day;
and all the people greatly feared the LORD and Samuel.

12:14-15 If you will fear the LORD... then: Everything and nothing has changed for Israel. They now have a monarchy, but their king and people are still in covenant with God. The *if-then* is covenant language (Deut 28), telling of both blessings and curses. Samuel tells it like it is: Israel, including its king, is still called to listen to and obey God. Here the word *fear* means to respect or to regard with awe, not simply to be afraid.

19 All the people said to Samuel, "Pray to the LORD your God
for your servants, so that we may not die; for we have added to all our
sins the evil of demanding a king for ourselves." 20 And Samuel said to
the people, "Do not be afraid; you have done all this evil, yet do not
turn aside from following the LORD, but serve the LORD with all your
heart; 21 and do not turn aside after useless things that cannot profit or
save, for they are useless. 22 For the LORD will not cast away his people, for his great name's sake, because it has pleased the LORD to make
you a people for himself. 23 Moreover as for me, far be it from me that
I should sin against the LORD by ceasing to pray for you; and I will
instruct you in the good and the right way. 24 Only fear the LORD, and
serve him faithfully with all your heart; for consider what great things
he has done for you. 25 But if you still do wickedly, you shall be swept
away, both you and your king."

12:21 useless things: Probably a reference to worshiping idols that had no power to save (see Exod 20:3-6; Deut 5:8-10).

Saul's Unlawful Sacrifice

13 Saul was . . .[e] years old when he began to reign; and he
reigned . . . and two[f] years over Israel.

13:1 Saul... began to reign: Saul is the first of Israel's twenty-three kings. His rule lasted about twenty years, from about 1020–1000 B.C.E. Israel will be ruled by kings for just under 450 years.

[a] Gk: Heb lacks *King Jabin of* [b] Gk Syr: Heb *Bedan* [c] Gk: Heb *Samuel* [d] Gk: Heb *and your ancestors*
[e] The number is lacking in the Heb text (the verse is lacking in the Septuagint). [f] *Two* is not the entire number; something has dropped out.

13:2 Michmash: This mountain village is only a few miles from Geba (also Gibeah). These two cities were separated by a deep ravine, making this a narrow and important pass from the Jordan Valley to the Ephraimite hills.

13:5 The Philistines mustered to fight: Can Saul be obedient to the LORD in this fearful time? No. Out of desperation he tries to be both priest and king by making the offering (see 13:9).

13:13-14 done foolishly...established your kingdom...forever: Saul's time runs out. Saul's kingship, or any king in Israel, is always subject to the LORD and the LORD's prophet. The relationship between kingship and obedience to the LORD is an ongoing theme in 1 and 2 Samuel.

The future kings of Israel would have come from Saul's family. But Saul overstepped the commands of God by offering sacrifice, a task that only members of the priestly tribe of Levi were allowed to do. His "foolish" action meant his family would not be chosen to provide future kings for Israel.

13:14 after his own heart: The LORD is free to select a new king. This is the first clear sign that David is to be the next king.

2 Saul chose three thousand out of Israel; two thousand were
with Saul in Michmash and the hill country of Bethel, and a thousand
were with Jonathan in Gibeah of Benjamin; the rest of the people he
sent home to their tents. [3]Jonathan defeated the garrison of the Philistines that was at Geba; and the Philistines heard of it. And Saul blew
the trumpet throughout all the land, saying, "Let the Hebrews hear!"
[4]When all Israel heard that Saul had defeated the garrison of the Philistines, and also that Israel had become odious to the Philistines, the
people were called out to join Saul at Gilgal.

5 The Philistines mustered to fight with Israel, thirty thousand
chariots, and six thousand horsemen, and troops like the sand on the
seashore in multitude; they came up and encamped at Michmash, to
the east of Beth-aven. [6]When the Israelites saw that they were in distress (for the troops were hard pressed), the people hid themselves in
caves and in holes and in rocks and in tombs and in cisterns. [7]Some
Hebrews crossed the Jordan to the land of Gad and Gilead. Saul was
still at Gilgal, and all the people followed him trembling.

8 He waited seven days, the time appointed by Samuel; but Samuel did not come to Gilgal, and the people began to slip away from
Saul.[a] [9]So Saul said, "Bring the burnt offering here to me, and the
offerings of well-being." And he offered the burnt offering. [10]As soon
as he had finished offering the burnt offering, Samuel arrived; and
Saul went out to meet him and salute him. [11]Samuel said, "What have
you done?" Saul replied, "When I saw that the people were slipping
away from me, and that you did not come within the days appointed,
and that the Philistines were mustering at Michmash, [12]I said, 'Now
the Philistines will come down upon me at Gilgal, and I have not
entreated the favor of the LORD'; so I forced myself, and offered the
burnt offering." [13]Samuel said to Saul, "You have done foolishly; you
have not kept the commandment of the LORD your God, which he
commanded you. The LORD would have established your kingdom
over Israel forever, [14]but now your kingdom will not continue; the
LORD has sought out a man after his own heart; and the LORD has
appointed him to be ruler over his people, because you have not kept
what the LORD commanded you." [15]And Samuel left and went on
his way from Gilgal.[b] The rest of the people followed Saul to join the
army; they went up from Gilgal toward Gibeah of Benjamin.[c]

Preparations for Battle

Saul counted the people who were present with him, about six
hundred men. [16]Saul, his son Jonathan, and the people who were
present with them stayed in Geba of Benjamin; but the Philistines
encamped at Michmash. [17]And raiders came out of the camp of the

---

[a] Heb *him* [b] Gk: Heb *went up from Gilgal to Gibeah of Benjamin* [c] Gk: Heb lacks *The rest . . . of Benjamin*

Philistines in three companies; one company turned toward Ophrah,
to the land of Shual, 18 another company turned toward Beth-horon,
and another company turned toward the mountain[a] that looks down
upon the valley of Zeboim toward the wilderness.
19 Now there was no smith to be found throughout all the land of
Israel; for the Philistines said, "The Hebrews must not make swords
or spears for themselves"; 20 so all the Israelites went down to the Philistines to sharpen their plowshares, mattocks, axes, or sickles;[b] 21 The
charge was two-thirds of a shekel[c] for the plowshares and for the mattocks, and one-third of a shekel for sharpening the axes and for setting
the goads.[d] 22 So on the day of the battle neither sword nor spear was
to be found in the possession of any of the people with Saul and Jonathan; but Saul and his son Jonathan had them.

Jonathan Surprises and Routs the Philistines

23 Now a garrison of the Philistines had gone out to the pass of
14 Michmash. 1 One day Jonathan son of Saul said to the young
man who carried his armor, "Come, let us go over to the Philistine garrison on the other side." But he did not tell his father. 2 Saul
was staying in the outskirts of Gibeah under the pomegranate tree
that is at Migron; the troops that were with him were about six hundred men, 3 along with Ahijah son of Ahitub, Ichabod's brother, son
of Phinehas son of Eli, the priest of the LORD in Shiloh, carrying an
ephod. Now the people did not know that Jonathan had gone. 4 In the
pass,[e] by which Jonathan tried to go over to the Philistine garrison,
there was a rocky crag on one side and a rocky crag on the other; the
name of the one was Bozez, and the name of the other Seneh. 5 One
crag rose on the north in front of Michmash, and the other on the
south in front of Geba.
6 Jonathan said to the young man who carried his armor, "Come,
let us go over to the garrison of these uncircumcised; it may be that
the LORD will act for us; for nothing can hinder the LORD from saving
by many or by few." 7 His armor-bearer said to him, "Do all that your
mind inclines to.[f] I am with you; as your mind is, so is mine."[g] 8 Then
Jonathan said, "Now we will cross over to those men and will show
ourselves to them. 9 If they say to us, 'Wait until we come to you,' then
we will stand still in our place, and we will not go up to them. 10 But if
they say, 'Come up to us,' then we will go up; for the LORD has given
them into our hand. That will be the sign for us." 11 So both of them
showed themselves to the garrison of the Philistines; and the Philistines said, "Look, Hebrews are coming out of the holes where they
have hidden themselves." 12 The men of the garrison hailed Jonathan

[a] Cn Compare Gk: Heb *toward the border* [b] Gk: Heb *plowshare* [c] Heb *was a pim* [d] Cn: Meaning of Heb uncertain [e] Heb *Between the passes* [f] Gk: Heb *Do all that is in your mind. Turn* [g] Gk: Heb lacks *so is mine*

14:1-15 it may be that the LORD will act for us: Jonathan is the model of a believing warrior who relies on God (see 14:6, 10, 12).

14:3 carrying an ephod: In this story, the ephod is not a priestly garment (see the note on 2:18). Rather it is a container that likely holds some kind of dice, sticks, or pebbles, thrown to determine a "yes" or "no" answer from God. See also 23:6.

14:4 Bozez...Seneh: These dangerous outcroppings are well named: Slippery One and Thorny One.

14:6 these uncircumcised: Refers to non-Israelite men, since the men of Israel were to be circumcised according to God's ancient covenant with Abraham (see Gen 17:9-14).

and his armor-bearer, saying, "Come up to us, and we will show you something." Jonathan said to his armor-bearer, "Come up after me; for the LORD has given them into the hand of Israel." 13 Then Jonathan climbed up on his hands and feet, with his armor-bearer following after him. The Philistines[a] fell before Jonathan, and his armor-bearer, coming after him, killed them. 14 In that first slaughter Jonathan and his armor-bearer killed about twenty men within an area about half a furrow long in an acre[b] of land. 15 There was a panic in the camp, in the field, and among all the people; the garrison and even the raiders trembled; the earth quaked; and it became a very great panic.

14:15 There was a panic in the camp: Panic and confusion are the work of the LORD and lead to victory (see 14:20-23). How else could such an ill-equipped people like Israel triumph?

16 Saul's lookouts in Gibeah of Benjamin were watching as the multitude was surging back and forth.[c] 17 Then Saul said to the troops that were with him, "Call the roll and see who has gone from us." When they had called the roll, Jonathan and his armor-bearer were not there. 18 Saul said to Ahijah, "Bring the ark[d] of God here." For at that time the ark[d] of God went with the Israelites. 19 While Saul was talking to the priest, the tumult in the camp of the Philistines increased more and more; and Saul said to the priest, "Withdraw your hand." 20 Then Saul and all the people who were with him rallied and went into the battle; and every sword was against the other, so that there was very great confusion. 21 Now the Hebrews who previously had been with the Philistines and had gone up with them into the camp turned and joined the Israelites who were with Saul and Jonathan. 22 Likewise, when all the Israelites who had gone into hiding in the hill country of Ephraim heard that the Philistines were fleeing, they too followed closely after them in the battle. 23 So the LORD gave Israel the victory that day.

The battle passed beyond Beth-aven, and the troops with Saul numbered altogether about ten thousand men. The battle spread out over the hill country of Ephraim.

Saul's Rash Oath

24 Now Saul committed a very rash act on that day.[e] He had laid an oath on the troops, saying, "Cursed be anyone who eats food before it is evening and I have been avenged on my enemies." So none of the troops tasted food. 25 All the troops[f] came upon a honeycomb; and there was honey on the ground. 26 When the troops came upon the honeycomb, the honey was dripping out; but they did not put their hands to their mouths, for they feared the oath. 27 But Jonathan had not heard his father charge the troops with the oath; so he extended the staff that was in his hand, and dipped the tip of it in the honeycomb, and put his hand to his mouth; and his eyes brightened. 28 Then

14:24 a very rash act: Saul blunders along! This is an act out of ignorance and carelessness, without considering the consequences.

14:24-46 Saul…Jonathan: In contrast to Jonathan's heroism and trust in God, Saul is rash, distanced from God and the people (see 14:41, 45). Saul can act religiously (see 14:24, 35, 37, 39), but his action does not seem based on faithful obedience to God's command. God called for obedience from both king and people (see 12:14). None of Israel's twenty-three kings will fulfill this calling completely. Only Jesus Christ will fully humble himself and be obedient; obedient even to the point of death (see Phil 2:6-8).

---

[a] Heb *They* [b] Heb *yoke* [c] Gk: Heb *they went and there* [d] Gk *the ephod* [e] Gk: Heb *The Israelites were distressed that day* [f] Heb *land*

one of the soldiers said, “Your father strictly charged the troops with an oath, saying, ‘Cursed be anyone who eats food this day.’ And so the troops are faint.” 29 Then Jonathan said, “My father has troubled the land; see how my eyes have brightened because I tasted a little of this honey. 30 How much better if today the troops had eaten freely of the spoil taken from their enemies; for now the slaughter among the Philistines has not been great.”

31 After they had struck down the Philistines that day from Michmash to Aijalon, the troops were very faint; 32 so the troops flew upon the spoil, and took sheep and oxen and calves, and slaughtered them on the ground; and the troops ate them with the blood. 33 Then it was reported to Saul, “Look, the troops are sinning against the LORD by eating with the blood.” And he said, “You have dealt treacherously; roll a large stone before me here.”[a] 34 Saul said, “Disperse yourselves among the troops, and say to them, ‘Let all bring their oxen or their sheep, and slaughter them here, and eat; and do not sin against the LORD by eating with the blood.’ ” So all of the troops brought their oxen with them that night, and slaughtered them there. 35 And Saul built an altar to the LORD; it was the first altar that he built to the LORD.

14:33 troops are sinning…eating with the blood: Even though the troops had honored Saul’s request to not eat (fast) until after the battle, they were so hungry after a long day of fighting that they quickly started eating the meat of the slaughtered animals without first draining the blood. According to the law, the blood was to be drained from butchered animals before they were cooked and eaten (Gen 9:4; Lev 17:10-13; Deut 12:23-24). Blood was considered sacred because it carried the life force itself.

Jonathan in Danger of Death

36 Then Saul said, “Let us go down after the Philistines by night and despoil them until the morning light; let us not leave one of them.” They said, “Do whatever seems good to you.” But the priest said, “Let us draw near to God here.” 37 So Saul inquired of God, “Shall I go down after the Philistines? Will you give them into the hand of Israel?” But he did not answer him that day. 38 Saul said, “Come here, all you leaders of the people; and let us find out how this sin has arisen today. 39 For as the LORD lives who saves Israel, even if it is in my son Jonathan, he shall surely die!” But there was no one among all the people who answered him. 40 He said to all Israel, “You shall be on one side, and I and my son Jonathan will be on the other side.” The people said to Saul, “Do what seems good to you.” 41 Then Saul said, “O LORD God of Israel, why have you not answered your servant today? If this guilt is in me or in my son Jonathan, O LORD God of Israel, give Urim; but if this guilt is in your people Israel,[b] give Thummim.” And Jonathan and Saul were indicated by the lot, but the people were cleared. 42 Then Saul said, “Cast the lot between me and my son Jonathan.” And Jonathan was taken.

43 Then Saul said to Jonathan, “Tell me what you have done.” Jonathan told him, “I tasted a little honey with the tip of the staff that was in my hand; here I am, I will die.” 44 Saul said, “God do so to me

---

[a] Gk: Heb *me this day* [b] Vg Compare Gk: Heb *41 Saul said to the LORD, the God of Israel*

and more also; you shall surely die, Jonathan!" [45]Then the people said
to Saul, "Shall Jonathan die, who has accomplished this great victory
in Israel? Far from it! As the LORD lives, not one hair of his head shall
fall to the ground; for he has worked with God today." So the people
ransomed Jonathan, and he did not die. [46]Then Saul withdrew from
pursuing the Philistines; and the Philistines went to their own place.

Saul's Continuing Wars

47 When Saul had taken the kingship over Israel, he fought
against all his enemies on every side—against Moab, against the Ammonites, against Edom, against the kings of Zobah, and against the
Philistines; wherever he turned he routed them. [48]He did valiantly,
and struck down the Amalekites, and rescued Israel out of the hands
of those who plundered them.

49 Now the sons of Saul were Jonathan, Ishvi, and Malchishua;
and the names of his two daughters were these: the name of the firstborn was Merab, and the name of the younger, Michal. [50]The name of
Saul's wife was Ahinoam daughter of Ahimaaz. And the name of the
commander of his army was Abner son of Ner, Saul's uncle; [51]Kish was
the father of Saul, and Ner the father of Abner was the son of Abiel.

52 There was hard fighting against the Philistines all the days of
Saul; and when Saul saw any strong or valiant warrior, he took him
into his service.

Saul Defeats the Amalekites but Spares Their King

15 Samuel said to Saul, "The LORD sent me to anoint you king
over his people Israel; now therefore listen to the words of
the LORD. [2]Thus says the LORD of hosts, 'I will punish the Amalekites
for what they did in opposing the Israelites when they came up out of
Egypt. [3]Now go and attack Amalek, and utterly destroy all that they
have; do not spare them, but kill both man and woman, child and infant, ox and sheep, camel and donkey.'"

4 So Saul summoned the people, and numbered them in Telaim,
two hundred thousand foot soldiers, and ten thousand soldiers of Judah. [5]Saul came to the city of the Amalekites and lay in wait in the valley. [6]Saul said to the Kenites, "Go! Leave! Withdraw from among the
Amalekites, or I will destroy you with them; for you showed kindness
to all the people of Israel when they came up out of Egypt." So the
Kenites withdrew from the Amalekites. [7]Saul defeated the Amalekites, from Havilah as far as Shur, which is east of Egypt. [8]He took King
Agag of the Amalekites alive, but utterly destroyed all the people with
the edge of the sword. [9]Saul and the people spared Agag, and the best
of the sheep and of the cattle and of the fatlings, and the lambs, and
all that was valuable, and would not utterly destroy them; all that was
despised and worthless they utterly destroyed.

14:48 He did valiantly: This tells us that Saul gained power, wealth, and new land for Israel. Saul's kingship has the outward appearance of great success.

15:1 The LORD sent me: Samuel speaks and acts for the LORD, and Saul should not forget it! Now is Saul's time to listen to (obey) God's commands.

15:2 I will punish the Amalekites: Saul is to repay these people for their attack on Israel in the wilderness (see Exod 17:8-16). Later Moses reminds Israel that, when they are settled, their duty is to destroy this people (see Deut 25:17-19).

15:3 utterly destroy: The complete destruction of the Amalekites is a kind of religious sacrifice or devotion on the part of Israel. This command was central to the idea of holy war fought by Israel against enemies who worshiped other gods or opposed God's people.

What do you think of the idea that war can be justified on the grounds of being done in the name of God? What examples of this do you see today? What do you think of God's commanding Israel to utterly destroy their enemies?

15:9 Saul and the people spared Agag: Here is Saul's basic failure as king. He lacks complete trust in and obedience to God's command.

Saul Rejected as King

10 The word of the LORD came to Samuel: [11]"I regret that I made
Saul king, for he has turned back from following me, and has not car-
ried out my commands." Samuel was angry; and he cried out to the
LORD all night. [12]Samuel rose early in the morning to meet Saul, and
Samuel was told, "Saul went to Carmel, where he set up a monument
for himself, and on returning he passed on down to Gilgal." [13]When
Samuel came to Saul, Saul said to him, "May you be blessed by the
LORD; I have carried out the command of the LORD." [14]But Samuel
said, "What then is this bleating of sheep in my ears, and the lowing
of cattle that I hear?" [15]Saul said, "They have brought them from the
Amalekites; for the people spared the best of the sheep and the cattle, to sacrifice to the LORD your God; but the rest we have utterly
destroyed." [16]Then Samuel said to Saul, "Stop! I will tell you what the
LORD said to me last night." He replied, "Speak."

17 Samuel said, "Though you are little in your own eyes, are you
not the head of the tribes of Israel? The LORD anointed you king over
Israel. [18]And the LORD sent you on a mission, and said, 'Go, utterly
destroy the sinners, the Amalekites, and fight against them until they
are consumed.' [19]Why then did you not obey the voice of the LORD?
Why did you swoop down on the spoil, and do what was evil in the
sight of the LORD?" [20]Saul said to Samuel, "I have obeyed the voice of
the LORD, I have gone on the mission on which the LORD sent me, I
have brought Agag the king of Amalek, and I have utterly destroyed
the Amalekites. [21]But from the spoil the people took sheep and cattle,
the best of the things devoted to destruction, to sacrifice to the LORD
your God in Gilgal." [22]And Samuel said,

"Has the LORD as great delight in burnt offerings and sacrifices,
as in obedience to the voice of the LORD?
Surely, to obey is better than sacrifice,
and to heed than the fat of rams.
23 For rebellion is no less a sin than divination,
and stubbornness is like iniquity and idolatry.
Because you have rejected the word of the LORD,
he has also rejected you from being king."

24 Saul said to Samuel, "I have sinned; for I have transgressed
the commandment of the LORD and your words, because I feared
the people and obeyed their voice. [25]Now therefore, I pray, pardon
my sin, and return with me, so that I may worship the LORD." [26]Sam-
uel said to Saul, "I will not return with you; for you have rejected the
word of the LORD, and the LORD has rejected you from being king
over Israel." [27]As Samuel turned to go away, Saul caught hold of the
hem of his robe, and it tore. [28]And Samuel said to him, "The LORD has
torn the kingdom of Israel from you this very day, and has given it to a

15:15 they have brought them: Saul blames the people. Shifting blame to avoid responsibility is an old game, one played in the Garden of Eden (see Gen 3:12). Saul distances himself from God by saying *your* God instead of *my* God.

15:21 things devoted to destruction, to sacrifice: A certain portion of the captured spoils were to be sacrificed to God, and so destroyed.

15:22 Surely, to obey is better than sacrifice: Religious practices are hollow without obedience to God. Other prophets will accuse Israel of this same hypocrisy (see Hos 6:6; Amos 5:21-24; Isa 1:10-17).

neighbor of yours, who is better than you. 29 Moreover the Glory of Israel will not recant[a] or change his mind; for he is not a mortal, that he
should change his mind." 30 Then Saul[b] said, "I have sinned; yet honor
me now before the elders of my people and before Israel, and return
with me, so that I may worship the LORD your God." 31 So Samuel
turned back after Saul; and Saul worshiped the LORD.
32 Then Samuel said, "Bring Agag king of the Amalekites here to
me." And Agag came to him haltingly.[c] Agag said, "Surely this is the
bitterness of death."[d] 33 But Samuel said,

"As your sword has made women childless,
so your mother shall be childless among women."

And Samuel hewed Agag in pieces before the LORD in Gilgal.
34 Then Samuel went to Ramah; and Saul went up to his house
in Gibeah of Saul. 35 Samuel did not see Saul again until the day of his
death, but Samuel grieved over Saul. And the LORD was sorry that he
had made Saul king over Israel.

David Anointed as King

16 The LORD said to Samuel, "How long will you grieve over
Saul? I have rejected him from being king over Israel. Fill
your horn with oil and set out; I will send you to Jesse the Bethlehemite, for I have provided for myself a king among his sons." 2 Samuel
said, "How can I go? If Saul hears of it, he will kill me." And the LORD
said, "Take a heifer with you, and say, 'I have come to sacrifice to the
LORD.' 3 Invite Jesse to the sacrifice, and I will show you what you
shall do; and you shall anoint for me the one whom I name to you."
4 Samuel did what the LORD commanded, and came to Bethlehem.
The elders of the city came to meet him trembling, and said, "Do you
come peaceably?" 5 He said, "Peaceably; I have come to sacrifice to the
LORD; sanctify yourselves and come with me to the sacrifice." And he
sanctified Jesse and his sons and invited them to the sacrifice.
6 When they came, he looked on Eliab and thought, "Surely the
LORD's anointed is now before the LORD."[e] 7 But the LORD said to
Samuel, "Do not look on his appearance or on the height of his stature, because I have rejected him; for the LORD does not see as mortals
see; they look on the outward appearance, but the LORD looks on
the heart." 8 Then Jesse called Abinadab, and made him pass before
Samuel. He said, "Neither has the LORD chosen this one." 9 Then Jesse
made Shammah pass by. And he said, "Neither has the LORD chosen
this one." 10 Jesse made seven of his sons pass before Samuel, and Samuel said to Jesse, "The LORD has not chosen any of these." 11 Samuel
said to Jesse, "Are all your sons here?" And he said, "There remains yet

---

[a] Q Ms Gk: MT *deceive* [b] Heb *he* [c] Cn Compare Gk: Meaning of Heb uncertain [d] Q Ms Gk: MT *Surely the bitterness of death is past* [e] Heb *him*

15:34 Samuel grieved over Saul: Saul's kingship is rejected and regretted by God. The stage is now set for the rise of a new king, David.

16:1 Fill your horn with oil: God commands Samuel to take a horn flask to anoint a new king. In 1 Kings 1:39 Zadok anoints Solomon in a similar way. See the note on 10:1-8 (vial of oil).

16:7 the LORD looks on the heart: God sees what we cannot. The heart is a place of loyalty and faith (1 Sam 7:3; 10:9).

16:11 but he is keeping the sheep: How can a lowly shepherd boy be king? By God's command! David's youth and inexperience point to the power of God leading him. Later the apostle Paul will point to God's power in choosing the weak to do God's work (see 1 Cor 1:27-28).

the youngest, but he is keeping the sheep." And Samuel said to Jesse, "Send and bring him; for we will not sit down until he comes here." [12]He sent and brought him in. Now he was ruddy, and had beautiful eyes, and was handsome. The LORD said, "Rise and anoint him; for this is the one." [13]Then Samuel took the horn of oil, and anointed him in the presence of his brothers; and the spirit of the LORD came mightily upon David from that day forward. Samuel then set out and went to Ramah.

16:13 the spirit of the LORD came mightily upon David: What makes this young shepherd boy so capable? God's spirit does. God's spirit has been active since the beginning (see Gen 1:1). More than a story of Saul and David, this is a story of the working of God's spirit to save God's people and all creation.

David Plays the Lyre for Saul

14 Now the spirit of the LORD departed from Saul, and an evil spirit from the LORD tormented him. [15]And Saul's servants said to him, "See now, an evil spirit from God is tormenting you. [16]Let our lord now command the servants who attend you to look for someone who is skillful in playing the lyre; and when the evil spirit from God is upon you, he will play it, and you will feel better." [17]So Saul said to his servants, "Provide for me someone who can play well, and bring him to me." [18]One of the young men answered, "I have seen a son of Jesse the Bethlehemite who is skillful in playing, a man of valor, a warrior, prudent in speech, and a man of good presence; and the LORD is with him." [19]So Saul sent messengers to Jesse, and said, "Send me your son David who is with the sheep." [20]Jesse took a donkey loaded with bread, a skin of wine, and a kid, and sent them by his son David to Saul. [21]And David came to Saul, and entered his service. Saul loved him greatly, and he became his armor-bearer. [22]Saul sent to Jesse, saying, "Let David remain in my service, for he has found favor in my sight." [23]And whenever the evil spirit from God came upon Saul, David took the lyre and played it with his hand, and Saul would be relieved and feel better, and the evil spirit would depart from him.

16:14 the spirit of the LORD departed from Saul: This doesn't seem right to us. However, the writers of this book understand God to be the source of the spirit, whether good or bad. This is God's judgment on Saul. Still there is comfort for Saul from God: David's music.

David and Goliath

17 Now the Philistines gathered their armies for battle; they were gathered at Socoh, which belongs to Judah, and encamped between Socoh and Azekah, in Ephes-dammim. [2]Saul and the Israelites gathered and encamped in the valley of Elah, and formed ranks against the Philistines. [3]The Philistines stood on the mountain on the one side, and Israel stood on the mountain on the other side, with a valley between them. [4]And there came out from the camp of the Philistines a champion named Goliath, of Gath, whose height was six[a] cubits and a span. [5]He had a helmet of bronze on his head, and he was armed with a coat of mail; the weight of the coat was five thousand shekels of bronze. [6]He had greaves of bronze on his legs and a javelin of bronze slung between his shoulders. [7]The shaft of his spear was like

17:4 Goliath: Here is the ultimate warrior. Goliath's height is estimated to be seven to ten feet tall.

[a] MT: Q Ms Gk *four*

a weaver's beam, and his spear's head weighed six hundred shekels of
iron; and his shield-bearer went before him. 8He stood and shouted
to the ranks of Israel, "Why have you come out to draw up for battle?
Am I not a Philistine, and are you not servants of Saul? Choose a man
for yourselves, and let him come down to me. 9If he is able to fight
with me and kill me, then we will be your servants; but if I prevail
against him and kill him, then you shall be our servants and serve us."
10And the Philistine said, "Today I defy the ranks of Israel! Give me
a man, that we may fight together." 11When Saul and all Israel heard
these words of the Philistine, they were dismayed and greatly afraid.

12 Now David was the son of an Ephrathite of Bethlehem in Judah, named Jesse, who had eight sons. In the days of Saul the man was
already old and advanced in years.[a] 13The three eldest sons of Jesse
had followed Saul to the battle; the names of his three sons who went
to the battle were Eliab the firstborn, and next to him Abinadab, and
the third Shammah. 14David was the youngest; the three eldest followed Saul, 15but David went back and forth from Saul to feed his
father's sheep at Bethlehem. 16For forty days the Philistine came forward and took his stand, morning and evening.

17 Jesse said to his son David, "Take for your brothers an ephah
of this parched grain and these ten loaves, and carry them quickly to
the camp to your brothers; 18also take these ten cheeses to the commander of their thousand. See how your brothers fare, and bring
some token from them."

19 Now Saul, and they, and all the men of Israel, were in the valley of Elah, fighting with the Philistines. 20David rose early in the
morning, left the sheep with a keeper, took the provisions, and went
as Jesse had commanded him. He came to the encampment as the
army was going forth to the battle line, shouting the war cry. 21Israel
and the Philistines drew up for battle, army against army. 22David left
the things in charge of the keeper of the baggage, ran to the ranks,
and went and greeted his brothers. 23As he talked with them, the
champion, the Philistine of Gath, Goliath by name, came up out of
the ranks of the Philistines, and spoke the same words as before. And
David heard him.

24 All the Israelites, when they saw the man, fled from him and
were very much afraid. 25The Israelites said, "Have you seen this man
who has come up? Surely he has come up to defy Israel. The king will
greatly enrich the man who kills him, and will give him his daughter
and make his family free in Israel." 26David said to the men who stood
by him, "What shall be done for the man who kills this Philistine, and
takes away the reproach from Israel? For who is this uncircumcised
Philistine that he should defy the armies of the living God?" 27The

17:26 who is this…that he should defy…the living God?: Here's the main question of our story. The title "living God" stresses that Israel's God is alive and well, ready to defend and save the people. David trusts this living God.

---

[a] Gk Syr: Heb *among men*

people answered him in the same way, "So shall it be done for the man
who kills him."
28 His eldest brother Eliab heard him talking to the men; and Eliab's anger was kindled against David. He said, "Why have you come
down? With whom have you left those few sheep in the wilderness? I
know your presumption and the evil of your heart; for you have come
down just to see the battle." 29 David said, "What have I done now? It
was only a question." 30 He turned away from him toward another and
spoke in the same way; and the people answered him again as before.
31 When the words that David spoke were heard, they repeated
them before Saul; and he sent for him. 32 David said to Saul, "Let no
one's heart fail because of him; your servant will go and fight with this
Philistine." 33 Saul said to David, "You are not able to go against this
Philistine to fight with him; for you are just a boy, and he has been a
warrior from his youth." 34 But David said to Saul, "Your servant used
to keep sheep for his father; and whenever a lion or a bear came, and
took a lamb from the flock, 35 I went after it and struck it down, rescuing the lamb from its mouth; and if it turned against me, I would catch
it by the jaw, strike it down, and kill it. 36 Your servant has killed both
lions and bears; and this uncircumcised Philistine shall be like one of
them, since he has defied the armies of the living God." 37 David said,
"The LORD, who saved me from the paw of the lion and from the paw
of the bear, will save me from the hand of this Philistine." So Saul said
to David, "Go, and may the LORD be with you!"
38 Saul clothed David with his armor; he put a bronze helmet on
his head and clothed him with a coat of mail. 39 David strapped Saul's
sword over the armor, and he tried in vain to walk, for he was not used
to them. Then David said to Saul, "I cannot walk with these; for I am
not used to them." So David removed them. 40 Then he took his staff in
his hand, and chose five smooth stones from the wadi, and put them
in his shepherd's bag, in the pouch; his sling was in his hand, and he
drew near to the Philistine.
41 The Philistine came on and drew near to David, with his
shield-bearer in front of him. 42 When the Philistine looked and saw
David, he disdained him, for he was only a youth, ruddy and handsome in appearance. 43 The Philistine said to David, "Am I a dog, that
you come to me with sticks?" And the Philistine cursed David by his
gods. 44 The Philistine said to David, "Come to me, and I will give your
flesh to the birds of the air and to the wild animals of the field." 45 But
David said to the Philistine, "You come to me with sword and spear
and javelin; but I come to you in the name of the LORD of hosts, the
God of the armies of Israel, whom you have defied. 46 This very day
the LORD will deliver you into my hand, and I will strike you down
and cut off your head; and I will give the dead bodies of the Philistine
army this very day to the birds of the air and to the wild animals of

17:45-47 the LORD does not save by sword and spear: Goliath is no match for David, just as the Philistines are no match for Israel. Deliverance will never be found in anything or anyone but God, and David knows this.

17:50 David prevailed: David, fueled by God's spirit, is victorious. Later this same spirit will empower early Christians in the face of great danger (see Acts 4:1-13).

17:58 Whose son are you, young man?: Earlier Saul knew David, but now he does not. Why? As stories of David were collected and recorded, they would be combined and sometimes seem disjointed and inconsistent. The biblical writer was more interested in showing how God was at work in David than in giving a smooth, seamless account.

What does the Augsburg Confession say about the work of God's Spirit upon the heart? The Augsburg Confession, a kind of mission statement for the Reformation churches published in 1531, turns to the great theologian Augustine in its discussion of faith, the Spirit, and good works in Article 20. Augustine understood faith to be confidence in God and the grace of God for us. It is because of the Holy Spirit, who is given through faith, that our hearts are moved to do good works. Without God's Holy Spirit our heart is too weak to do what God commands. *1 Samuel 17:45*

What do you think of the idea that good works flow from God's grace? How has the Holy Spirit been at work in your heart, giving you David-like courage and trust to do God's loving will?

18:1 Jonathan was bound to . . . David: These two become inseparable and are so devoted that their very well-being is tied together. This same kind of devotion describes Jacob's relationship with his youngest son, Benjamin (see Gen 44:30-31).

18:3 Jonathan made a covenant with David: These two are kindred spirits. Their friendship is about a covenant or promise of steadfast love and loyalty to each other. First, this is about personal affection. Jonathan will warn David about his father's murderous plans (19:2). He will ask David to keep this covenant to his descendants (20:14-15), and he will remain faithful to David in the name of the LORD (20:42). Second, this covenant is also political. Jonathan gives his princely robe and armor to David (18:4). This is a striking move that gives David princely standing and a claim to the throne. Later Jonathan will oppose his kingly father in his hunt for David and deliberately deceive him (20:28-29).

the earth, so that all the earth may know that there is a God in Israel,
47 and that all this assembly may know that the LORD does not save by
sword and spear; for the battle is the LORD's and he will give you into
our hand."

48 When the Philistine drew nearer to meet David, David ran
quickly toward the battle line to meet the Philistine. 49 David put his
hand in his bag, took out a stone, slung it, and struck the Philistine on
his forehead; the stone sank into his forehead, and he fell face down
on the ground.

50 So David prevailed over the Philistine with a sling and a stone,
striking down the Philistine and killing him; there was no sword in
David's hand. 51 Then David ran and stood over the Philistine; he
grasped his sword, drew it out of its sheath, and killed him; then he
cut off his head with it.

When the Philistines saw that their champion was dead, they
fled. 52 The troops of Israel and Judah rose up with a shout and pursued the Philistines as far as Gath[a] and the gates of Ekron, so that the
wounded Philistines fell on the way from Shaaraim as far as Gath and
Ekron. 53 The Israelites came back from chasing the Philistines, and
they plundered their camp. 54 David took the head of the Philistine
and brought it to Jerusalem; but he put his armor in his tent.

55 When Saul saw David go out against the Philistine, he said to
Abner, the commander of the army, "Abner, whose son is this young
man?" Abner said, "As your soul lives, O king, I do not know." 56 The
king said, "Inquire whose son the stripling is." 57 On David's return
from killing the Philistine, Abner took him and brought him before
Saul, with the head of the Philistine in his hand. 58 Saul said to him,
"Whose son are you, young man?" And David answered, "I am the
son of your servant Jesse the Bethlehemite."

Jonathan's Covenant with David

18 When David[b] had finished speaking to Saul, the soul of Jonathan was bound to the soul of David, and Jonathan loved him
as his own soul. 2 Saul took him that day and would not let him return
to his father's house. 3 Then Jonathan made a covenant with David,
because he loved him as his own soul. 4 Jonathan stripped himself of
the robe that he was wearing, and gave it to David, and his armor, and
even his sword and his bow and his belt. 5 David went out and was successful wherever Saul sent him; as a result, Saul set him over the army.
And all the people, even the servants of Saul, approved.

6 As they were coming home, when David returned from killing
the Philistine, the women came out of all the towns of Israel, singing
and dancing, to meet King Saul, with tambourines, with songs of joy,

[a] Gk Syr: Heb *Gai* [b] Heb *he*

and with musical instruments.[a] 7And the women sang to one another
as they made merry,

"Saul has killed his thousands,
and David his ten thousands."

8Saul was very angry, for this saying displeased him. He said, "They
have ascribed to David ten thousands, and to me they have ascribed
thousands; what more can he have but the kingdom?" 9So Saul eyed
David from that day on.

Saul Tries to Kill David

10 The next day an evil spirit from God rushed upon Saul, and
he raved within his house, while David was playing the lyre, as he did
day by day. Saul had his spear in his hand; 11and Saul threw the spear,
for he thought, "I will pin David to the wall." But David eluded him
twice.

12 Saul was afraid of David, because the LORD was with him but
had departed from Saul. 13So Saul removed him from his presence,
and made him a commander of a thousand; and David marched out
and came in, leading the army. 14David had success in all his undertakings; for the LORD was with him. 15When Saul saw that he had
great success, he stood in awe of him. 16But all Israel and Judah loved
David; for it was he who marched out and came in leading them.

David Marries Michal

17 Then Saul said to David, "Here is my elder daughter Merab;
I will give her to you as a wife; only be valiant for me and fight the
LORD's battles." For Saul thought, "I will not raise a hand against him;
let the Philistines deal with him." 18David said to Saul, "Who am I
and who are my kinsfolk, my father's family in Israel, that I should be
son-in-law to the king?" 19But at the time when Saul's daughter Merab
should have been given to David, she was given to Adriel the Meholathite as a wife.

20 Now Saul's daughter Michal loved David. Saul was told, and
the thing pleased him. 21Saul thought, "Let me give her to him that
she may be a snare for him and that the hand of the Philistines may
be against him." Therefore Saul said to David a second time,[b] "You
shall now be my son-in-law." 22Saul commanded his servants, "Speak
to David in private and say, 'See, the king is delighted with you, and all
his servants love you; now then, become the king's son-in-law.'" 23So
Saul's servants reported these words to David in private. And David
said, "Does it seem to you a little thing to become the king's son-in-
law, seeing that I am a poor man and of no repute?" 24The servants
of Saul told him, "This is what David said." 25Then Saul said, "Thus

18:7 Saul has killed his thousands: The women dance in long lines, stepping back and forth as they sing. Their poetic expression of thousands and ten thousands is not meant to offend Saul. His fear and jealousy get the best of him. His deep anger toward and suspicion of David grows through the next two chapters.

18:12 the LORD was with him: David cannot lose! Several times in chapters 18–20 we read of God's presence and power with David (18:14, 28; 19:5) and protection of David from Saul (19:20-24). The LORD is determined to have David as king and Saul cannot stop the LORD. God's purpose is greater than any human plan or power.

18:20 Michal loved David: David inspires love almost wherever he goes. This love is both affection and loyalty. Later Michal will deceive her father in order to save David's life (19:17). Love for David comes up many times in chapters 18–20: Jonathan, Michal, the people (18:16), the servants in Saul's court (18:22), and Samuel.

---

[a] Or *triangles*, or *three-stringed instruments* [b] Heb *by two*

shall you say to David, 'The king desires no marriage present except
a hundred foreskins of the Philistines, that he may be avenged on the
king's enemies.'" Now Saul planned to make David fall by the hand
of the Philistines. 26When his servants told David these words, David
was well pleased to be the king's son-in-law. Before the time had
expired, 27David rose and went, along with his men, and killed one
hundred[a] of the Philistines; and David brought their foreskins, which
were given in full number to the king, that he might become the king's
son-in-law. Saul gave him his daughter Michal as a wife. 28But when
Saul realized that the LORD was with David, and that Saul's daughter
Michal loved him, 29Saul was still more afraid of David. So Saul was
David's enemy from that time forward.

30 Then the commanders of the Philistines came out to battle;
and as often as they came out, David had more success than all the
servants of Saul, so that his fame became very great.

Jonathan Intercedes for David

19 Saul spoke with his son Jonathan and with all his servants
about killing David. But Saul's son Jonathan took great delight in David. 2Jonathan told David, "My father Saul is trying to kill
you; therefore be on guard tomorrow morning; stay in a secret place
and hide yourself. 3I will go out and stand beside my father in the field
where you are, and I will speak to my father about you; if I learn anything I will tell you." 4Jonathan spoke well of David to his father Saul,
saying to him, "The king should not sin against his servant David,
because he has not sinned against you, and because his deeds have
been of good service to you; 5for he took his life in his hand when he
attacked the Philistine, and the LORD brought about a great victory
for all Israel. You saw it, and rejoiced; why then will you sin against an
innocent person by killing David without cause?" 6Saul heeded the
voice of Jonathan; Saul swore, "As the LORD lives, he shall not be put
to death." 7So Jonathan called David and related all these things to
him. Jonathan then brought David to Saul, and he was in his presence
as before.

Michal Helps David Escape from Saul

8 Again there was war, and David went out to fight the Philistines. He launched a heavy attack on them, so that they fled before
him. 9Then an evil spirit from the LORD came upon Saul, as he sat in
his house with his spear in his hand, while David was playing music.
10Saul sought to pin David to the wall with the spear; but he eluded
Saul, so that he struck the spear into the wall. David fled and escaped
that night.

19:9 an evil spirit from the LORD: This is emotional illness. Saul is now so unstable that he gives in to jealous suspicion and fear. He publicly announces his plan to kill David (19:1).

[a] Gk Compare 2 Sam 3.14: Heb *two hundred*

11 Saul sent messengers to David's house to keep watch over him, planning to kill him in the morning. David's wife Michal told him, "If you do not save your life tonight, tomorrow you will be killed." 12 So Michal let David down through the window; he fled away and escaped. 13 Michal took an idol[a] and laid it on the bed; she put a net[b] of goats' hair on its head, and covered it with the clothes. 14 When Saul sent messengers to take David, she said, "He is sick." 15 Then Saul sent the messengers to see David for themselves. He said, "Bring him up to me in the bed, that I may kill him." 16 When the messengers came in, the idol[c] was in the bed, with the covering[b] of goats' hair on its head. 17 Saul said to Michal, "Why have you deceived me like this, and let my enemy go, so that he has escaped?" Michal answered Saul, "He said to me, 'Let me go; why should I kill you?' "

David Joins Samuel in Ramah

18 Now David fled and escaped; he came to Samuel at Ramah, and told him all that Saul had done to him. He and Samuel went and settled at Naioth. 19 Saul was told, "David is at Naioth in Ramah." 20 Then Saul sent messengers to take David. When they saw the company of the prophets in a frenzy, with Samuel standing in charge of[b] them, the spirit of God came upon the messengers of Saul, and they also fell into a prophetic frenzy. 21 When Saul was told, he sent other messengers, and they also fell into a frenzy. Saul sent messengers again the third time, and they also fell into a frenzy. 22 Then he himself went to Ramah. He came to the great well that is in Secu;[d] he asked, "Where are Samuel and David?" And someone said, "They are at Naioth in Ramah." 23 He went there, toward Naioth in Ramah; and the spirit of God came upon him. As he was going, he fell into a prophetic frenzy, until he came to Naioth in Ramah. 24 He too stripped off his clothes, and he too fell into a frenzy before Samuel. He lay naked all that day and all that night. Therefore it is said, "Is Saul also among the prophets?"

The Friendship of David and Jonathan

20 David fled from Naioth in Ramah. He came before Jonathan and said, "What have I done? What is my guilt? And what is my sin against your father that he is trying to take my life?" 2 He said to him, "Far from it! You shall not die. My father does nothing either great or small without disclosing it to me; and why should my father hide this from me? Never!" 3 But David also swore, "Your father knows well that you like me; and he thinks, 'Do not let Jonathan know this, or he will be grieved.' But truly, as the LORD lives and as you yourself live, there is but a step between me and death." 4 Then

[a] Heb *took the teraphim* [b] Meaning of Heb uncertain [c] Heb *the teraphim* [d] Gk reads *to the well of the threshing floor on the bare height*

19:24 Is Saul also among the prophets?: Earlier Saul was seized by the spirit as he began his reign with a new heart from God (10:9-13). Now God comes again with the spirit, but this time it is to protect David and end Saul's reign. Both Saul's beginning and ending are in God's hands.

20:1 what is my sin?: David is not to blame, and the writer of this dramatic story wants us to know it.

Jonathan said to David, "Whatever you say, I will do for you." 5 David
said to Jonathan, "Tomorrow is the new moon, and I should not fail
to sit with the king at the meal; but let me go, so that I may hide in the
field until the third evening. 6 If your father misses me at all, then say,
'David earnestly asked leave of me to run to Bethlehem his city; for
there is a yearly sacrifice there for all the family.' 7 If he says, 'Good!' it
will be well with your servant; but if he is angry, then know that evil
has been determined by him. 8 Therefore deal kindly with your servant, for you have brought your servant into a sacred covenant[a] with
you. But if there is guilt in me, kill me yourself; why should you bring
me to your father?" 9 Jonathan said, "Far be it from you! If I knew that
it was decided by my father that evil should come upon you, would I
not tell you?" 10 Then David said to Jonathan, "Who will tell me if your
father answers you harshly?" 11 Jonathan replied to David, "Come, let
us go out into the field." So they both went out into the field.

12 Jonathan said to David, "By the LORD, the God of Israel!
When I have sounded out my father, about this time tomorrow, or on
the third day, if he is well disposed toward David, shall I not then send
and disclose it to you? 13 But if my father intends to do you harm, the
LORD do so to Jonathan, and more also, if I do not disclose it to you,
and send you away, so that you may go in safety. May the LORD be
with you, as he has been with my father. 14 If I am still alive, show me
the faithful love of the LORD; but if I die,[b] 15 never cut off your faithful
love from my house, even if the LORD were to cut off every one of the
enemies of David from the face of the earth." 16 Thus Jonathan made
a covenant with the house of David, saying, "May the LORD seek out
the enemies of David." 17 Jonathan made David swear again by his love
for him; for he loved him as he loved his own life.

20:15 never cut off your faithful love: Jonathan looks ahead. Saul is rejected by God as king, and there is no future for his descendants. Soon Saul will try to kill him. Jonathan needs David's promise that his heirs will not be destroyed once David rules. David keeps this promise in 2 Samuel 9:1, 7.

18 Jonathan said to him, "Tomorrow is the new moon; you will
be missed, because your place will be empty. 19 On the day after tomorrow, you shall go a long way down; go to the place where you
hid yourself earlier, and remain beside the stone there.[b] 20 I will shoot
three arrows to the side of it, as though I shot at a mark. 21 Then I will
send the boy, saying, 'Go, find the arrows.' If I say to the boy, 'Look,
the arrows are on this side of you, collect them,' then you are to come,
for, as the LORD lives, it is safe for you and there is no danger. 22 But if I
say to the young man, 'Look, the arrows are beyond you,' then go; for
the LORD has sent you away. 23 As for the matter about which you and
I have spoken, the LORD is witness[c] between you and me forever."

24 So David hid himself in the field. When the new moon came,
the king sat at the feast to eat. 25 The king sat upon his seat, as at other
times, upon the seat by the wall. Jonathan stood, while Abner sat by
Saul's side; but David's place was empty.

---

[a] Heb *a covenant of the LORD* [b] Meaning of Heb uncertain [c] Gk: Heb lacks *witness*

26 Saul did not say anything that day; for he thought, "Something
has befallen him; he is not clean, surely he is not clean." 27 But on the
second day, the day after the new moon, David's place was empty. And
Saul said to his son Jonathan, "Why has the son of Jesse not come to
the feast, either yesterday or today?" 28 Jonathan answered Saul, "David earnestly asked leave of me to go to Bethlehem; 29 he said, 'Let
me go; for our family is holding a sacrifice in the city, and my brother
has commanded me to be there. So now, if I have found favor in your
sight, let me get away, and see my brothers.' For this reason he has not
come to the king's table."

30 Then Saul's anger was kindled against Jonathan. He said to
him, "You son of a perverse, rebellious woman! Do I not know that
you have chosen the son of Jesse to your own shame, and to the
shame of your mother's nakedness? 31 For as long as the son of Jesse
lives upon the earth, neither you nor your kingdom shall be established. Now send and bring him to me, for he shall surely die." 32 Then
Jonathan answered his father Saul, "Why should he be put to death?
What has he done?" 33 But Saul threw his spear at him to strike him;
so Jonathan knew that it was the decision of his father to put David to
death. 34 Jonathan rose from the table in fierce anger and ate no food
on the second day of the month, for he was grieved for David, and
because his father had disgraced him.

35 In the morning Jonathan went out into the field to the appointment with David, and with him was a little boy. 36 He said to the boy,
"Run and find the arrows that I shoot." As the boy ran, he shot an arrow beyond him. 37 When the boy came to the place where Jonathan's
arrow had fallen, Jonathan called after the boy and said, "Is the arrow
not beyond you?" 38 Jonathan called after the boy, "Hurry, be quick,
do not linger." So Jonathan's boy gathered up the arrows and came
to his master. 39 But the boy knew nothing; only Jonathan and David
knew the arrangement. 40 Jonathan gave his weapons to the boy and
said to him, "Go and carry them to the city." 41 As soon as the boy had
gone, David rose from beside the stone heap[a] and prostrated himself
with his face to the ground. He bowed three times, and they kissed
each other, and wept with each other; David wept the more.[b] 42 Then
Jonathan said to David, "Go in peace, since both of us have sworn in
the name of the LORD, saying, 'The LORD shall be between me and
you, and between my descendants and your descendants, forever.'"
He got up and left; and Jonathan went into the city.[c]

David and the Holy Bread

21[d] David came to Nob to the priest Ahimelech. Ahimelech
came trembling to meet David, and said to him, "Why are

[a] Gk: Heb *from beside the south* [b] Vg: Meaning of Heb uncertain [c] This sentence is 21.1 in Heb
[d] Ch 21.2 in Heb

20:42 Go in peace: In trouble and tragedy Jonathan and David honor their covenant relationship and are strengthened by it. Jonathan is a model of faith as he remains loyal to David as God's chosen one, even though he will suffer great personal and political loss because of his friendship with David.

21:1 David came to Nob: David travels only about a mile away to seek food and weapons from this large city of priests. Nob is near Anathoth (see Isa 10:32; Neh 11:32), which places it between Gibeah (Saul's hometown) and Jerusalem.

you alone, and no one with you?" 2David said to the priest Ahimelech, "The king has charged me with a matter, and said to me, 'No
one must know anything of the matter about which I send you, and
with which I have charged you.' I have made an appointment[a] with
the young men for such and such a place. 3Now then, what have you
at hand? Give me five loaves of bread, or whatever is here." 4The priest
answered David, "I have no ordinary bread at hand, only holy bread—
provided that the young men have kept themselves from women."
5David answered the priest, "Indeed women have been kept from us
as always when I go on an expedition; the vessels of the young men
are holy even when it is a common journey; how much more today
will their vessels be holy?" 6So the priest gave him the holy bread; for
there was no bread there except the bread of the Presence, which is
removed from before the LORD, to be replaced by hot bread on the
day it is taken away.

7 Now a certain man of the servants of Saul was there that day,
detained before the LORD; his name was Doeg the Edomite, the chief
of Saul's shepherds.

8 David said to Ahimelech, "Is there no spear or sword here with
you? I did not bring my sword or my weapons with me, because the
king's business required haste." 9The priest said, "The sword of Goliath the Philistine, whom you killed in the valley of Elah, is here
wrapped in a cloth behind the ephod; if you will take that, take it, for
there is none here except that one." David said, "There is none like it;
give it to me."

David Flees to Gath

10 David rose and fled that day from Saul; he went to King Achish
of Gath. 11The servants of Achish said to him, "Is this not David the
king of the land? Did they not sing to one another of him in dances,

'Saul has killed his thousands,
and David his ten thousands'?"

12David took these words to heart and was very much afraid of King
Achish of Gath. 13So he changed his behavior before them; he pretended to be mad when in their presence.[b] He scratched marks on
the doors of the gate, and let his spittle run down his beard. 14Achish
said to his servants, "Look, you see the man is mad; why then have
you brought him to me? 15Do I lack madmen, that you have brought
this fellow to play the madman in my presence? Shall this fellow come
into my house?"

David and His Followers at Adullam

22 David left there and escaped to the cave of Adullam; when
his brothers and all his father's house heard of it, they went

[a] Q Ms Vg Compare Gk: Meaning of MT uncertain [b] Heb *in their hands*

21:4 only holy bread: This is sacred bread—twelve cakes of pure wheat flour arranged in rows (see Lev 24:1-9; 1 Chr 9:32). Only the priests were allowed to eat the sacred bread (Lev 24:5-9), but Ahimelech made an exception, provided David and his men had not had sexual relations with the women. Having sex was something that could exclude someone temporarily from worship or taking part in a sacred meal (see Exod 19:15; Lev 15:18).

What do think of the idea that the law tried to separate sacred things (such as the bread) from everyday use? What do you consider sacred? Why?

21:9 sword of Goliath: Here's a reminder of David's earlier victory against incredible odds (17:41-49). God is with him now, just as God was then. David will triumph.

21:12 King Achish of Gath: David enters enemy territory, perhaps hoping to hide out and work as a soldier for this Philistine king. He must use his wits and pretend insanity when he is recognized. God will be with David in this flight into the wilderness, which lasts through the end of 1 Samuel. God protects those who run from danger; for example, Israel in its flight from Egypt and Joseph, Mary, and baby Jesus in their flight from Herod.

down there to him. 2 Everyone who was in distress, and everyone who
was in debt, and everyone who was discontented gathered to him;
and he became captain over them. Those who were with him numbered about four hundred.

3 David went from there to Mizpeh of Moab. He said to the king
of Moab, "Please let my father and mother come[a] to you, until I know
what God will do for me." 4 He left them with the king of Moab, and
they stayed with him all the time that David was in the stronghold.
5 Then the prophet Gad said to David, "Do not remain in the stronghold; leave, and go into the land of Judah." So David left, and went
into the forest of Hereth.

Saul Slaughters the Priests at Nob

6 Saul heard that David and those who were with him had been
located. Saul was sitting at Gibeah, under the tamarisk tree on the
height, with his spear in his hand, and all his servants were standing
around him. 7 Saul said to his servants who stood around him, "Hear
now, you Benjaminites; will the son of Jesse give every one of you
fields and vineyards, will he make you all commanders of thousands
and commanders of hundreds? 8 Is that why all of you have conspired
against me? No one discloses to me when my son makes a league with
the son of Jesse, none of you is sorry for me or discloses to me that my
son has stirred up my servant against me, to lie in wait, as he is doing
today." 9 Doeg the Edomite, who was in charge of Saul's servants, answered, "I saw the son of Jesse coming to Nob, to Ahimelech son of
Ahitub; 10 he inquired of the LORD for him, gave him provisions, and
gave him the sword of Goliath the Philistine."

11 The king sent for the priest Ahimelech son of Ahitub and for
all his father's house, the priests who were at Nob; and all of them
came to the king. 12 Saul said, "Listen now, son of Ahitub." He answered, "Here I am, my lord." 13 Saul said to him, "Why have you conspired against me, you and the son of Jesse, by giving him bread and
a sword, and by inquiring of God for him, so that he has risen against
me, to lie in wait, as he is doing today?"

14 Then Ahimelech answered the king, "Who among all your servants is so faithful as David? He is the king's son-in-law, and is quick[b]
to do your bidding, and is honored in your house. 15 Is today the first
time that I have inquired of God for him? By no means! Do not let the
king impute anything to his servant or to any member of my father's
house; for your servant has known nothing of all this, much or little." 16 The king said, "You shall surely die, Ahimelech, you and all your
father's house." 17 The king said to the guard who stood around him,
"Turn and kill the priests of the LORD, because their hand also is with

22:2 discontented gathered to him: This conflict is bigger than Saul and David. It is also between the landless and the landholders (22:7) and between David in the south (Judah) and Saul in the north (Israel). God gives David an unlikely army, but God is good at raising up the lowly (2:4-8).

22:9 Doeg the Edomite: Here's an enemy and an outsider. He has no right to speak in this assembly. Edomites and Israel had long been enemies (see Num 20:18-20). The fact that Saul listens to Doeg and allows him to massacre the priests (descendants of Eli; 1 Sam 2) shows that Saul is insane with fear and jealousy.

[a] Syr Vg: Heb *come out* [b] Heb *and turns aside*

David; they knew that he fled, and did not disclose it to me." But the
servants of the king would not raise their hand to attack the priests of
the LORD. 18 Then the king said to Doeg, "You, Doeg, turn and attack
the priests." Doeg the Edomite turned and attacked the priests; on
that day he killed eighty-five who wore the linen ephod. 19 Nob, the
city of the priests, he put to the sword; men and women, children and
infants, oxen, donkeys, and sheep, he put to the sword.

20 But one of the sons of Ahimelech son of Ahitub, named Abiathar, escaped and fled after David. 21 Abiathar told David that Saul had
killed the priests of the LORD. 22 David said to Abiathar, "I knew on
that day, when Doeg the Edomite was there, that he would surely tell
Saul. I am responsible[a] for the lives of all your father's house. 23 Stay
with me, and do not be afraid; for the one who seeks my life seeks
your life; you will be safe with me."

David Saves the City of Keilah

23 Now they told David, "The Philistines are fighting against
Keilah, and are robbing the threshing floors." 2 David inquired of the LORD, "Shall I go and attack these Philistines?" The
LORD said to David, "Go and attack the Philistines and save Keilah."
3 But David's men said to him, "Look, we are afraid here in Judah; how
much more then if we go to Keilah against the armies of the Philistines?" 4 Then David inquired of the LORD again. The LORD answered
him, "Yes, go down to Keilah; for I will give the Philistines into your
hand." 5 So David and his men went to Keilah, fought with the Philistines, brought away their livestock, and dealt them a heavy defeat.
Thus David rescued the inhabitants of Keilah.

6 When Abiathar son of Ahimelech fled to David at Keilah, he
came down with an ephod in his hand. 7 Now it was told Saul that David had come to Keilah. And Saul said, "God has given[b] him into my
hand; for he has shut himself in by entering a town that has gates and
bars." 8 Saul summoned all the people to war, to go down to Keilah, to
besiege David and his men. 9 When David learned that Saul was plotting evil against him, he said to the priest Abiathar, "Bring the ephod
here." 10 David said, "O LORD, the God of Israel, your servant has heard
that Saul seeks to come to Keilah, to destroy the city on my account.
11 And now, will[c] Saul come down as your servant has heard? O LORD,
the God of Israel, I beseech you, tell your servant." The LORD said,
"He will come down." 12 Then David said, "Will the men of Keilah surrender me and my men into the hand of Saul?" The LORD said, "They
will surrender you." 13 Then David and his men, who were about six
hundred, set out and left Keilah; they wandered wherever they could

22:19 he put to the sword: Doeg wipes out all of Nob. Saul would not obey God and do this to the Amalekites (15:9), but he will do it to his own people. In both cases, Saul does what he wants rather than obey God and serve God's people.

22:20 Abiathar: This priest of God will be with David while he is on the run (23:6, 9; 30:7), but Saul has no priests left. Saul has cut himself off from God. Both Abiathar and the prophet Gad (22:5) are signs of God's presence with David.

23:6 ephod: See the note on 14:3 (ephod). Abiathar, God's priest, represents God's presence with David.

23:2-10 David inquired of the LORD: David is a model of faith as he depends on God. He will not act without God's direction. Like Samuel before him (7:8) he prays in times of danger, admitting his need of God.

[a] Gk Vg: Meaning of Heb uncertain [b] Gk Tg: Heb *made a stranger of* [c] Q Ms Compare Gk: MT *Will the men of Keilah surrender me into his hand? Will*

go. When Saul was told that David had escaped from Keilah, he gave up the expedition. [14]David remained in the strongholds in the wilderness, in the hill country of the Wilderness of Ziph. Saul sought him every day, but the LORD[a] did not give him into his hand.

23:14 Ziph: Run for the hills! This city is some twelve miles southeast of Keilah. It sits high on a ridge in the Judean hills (see Josh 15:55).

David Eludes Saul in the Wilderness

15 David was in the Wilderness of Ziph at Horesh when he learned that[b] Saul had come out to seek his life. [16]Saul's son Jonathan set out and came to David at Horesh; there he strengthened his hand through the LORD.[c] [17]He said to him, "Do not be afraid; for the hand of my father Saul shall not find you; you shall be king over Israel, and I shall be second to you; my father Saul also knows that this is so." [18]Then the two of them made a covenant before the LORD; David remained at Horesh, and Jonathan went home.

23:16 he strengthened his hand through the LORD: Jonathan encourages David at this last meeting between the two. He keeps his pledge of support made before God in their covenant (20:16).

19 Then some Ziphites went up to Saul at Gibeah and said, "David is hiding among us in the strongholds of Horesh, on the hill of Hachilah, which is south of Jeshimon. [20]Now, O king, whenever you wish to come down, do so; and our part will be to surrender him into the king's hand." [21]Saul said, "May you be blessed by the LORD for showing me compassion! [22]Go and make sure once more; find out exactly where he is, and who has seen him there; for I am told that he is very cunning. [23]Look around and learn all the hiding places where he lurks, and come back to me with sure information. Then I will go with you; and if he is in the land, I will search him out among all the thousands of Judah." [24]So they set out and went to Ziph ahead of Saul.

David and his men were in the wilderness of Maon, in the Arabah to the south of Jeshimon. [25]Saul and his men went to search for him. When David was told, he went down to the rock and stayed in the wilderness of Maon. When Saul heard that, he pursued David into the wilderness of Maon. [26]Saul went on one side of the mountain, and David and his men on the other side of the mountain. David was hurrying to get away from Saul, while Saul and his men were closing in on David and his men to capture them. [27]Then a messenger came to Saul, saying, "Hurry and come; for the Philistines have made a raid on the land." [28]So Saul stopped pursuing David, and went against the Philistines; therefore that place was called the Rock of Escape.[d] [29][e]David then went up from there, and lived in the strongholds of En-gedi.

23:26 closing in on David: Saul's men, who outnumber David's forces five to one, are coming at David from both sides, and David's defeat seems certain. The Philistines threaten Israel, and Saul must leave. God saves David at the last minute.

David Spares Saul's Life

24 When Saul returned from following the Philistines, he was told, "David is in the wilderness of En-gedi." [2]Then Saul took three thousand chosen men out of all Israel, and went to look for

24:1 En-gedi: An important, spring-fed oasis on the west shore of the Dead Sea. See Map 3, pp. 2100-2101.

---

[a] Q Ms Gk: MT *God* [b] Or *saw that* [c] Compare Q Ms Gk: MT *God* [d] Or *Rock of Division;* meaning of Heb uncertain [e] Ch 24.1 in Heb

David and his men in the direction of the Rocks of the Wild Goats.
[3]He came to the sheepfolds beside the road, where there was a cave;
and Saul went in to relieve himself.[a] Now David and his men were
sitting in the innermost parts of the cave. [4]The men of David said to
him, "Here is the day of which the LORD said to you, 'I will give your
enemy into your hand, and you shall do to him as it seems good to
you.'" Then David went and stealthily cut off a corner of Saul's cloak.
[5]Afterward David was stricken to the heart because he had cut off a
corner of Saul's cloak. [6]He said to his men, "The LORD forbid that
I should do this thing to my lord, the LORD's anointed, to raise my
hand against him; for he is the LORD's anointed." [7]So David scolded
his men severely and did not permit them to attack Saul. Then Saul
got up and left the cave, and went on his way.

8 Afterwards David also rose up and went out of the cave and
called after Saul, "My lord the king!" When Saul looked behind him,
David bowed with his face to the ground, and did obeisance. [9]David
said to Saul, "Why do you listen to the words of those who say, 'David
seeks to do you harm'? [10]This very day your eyes have seen how the
LORD gave you into my hand in the cave; and some urged me to kill
you, but I spared[b] you. I said, 'I will not raise my hand against my lord;
for he is the LORD's anointed.' [11]See, my father, see the corner of your
cloak in my hand; for by the fact that I cut off the corner of your cloak,
and did not kill you, you may know for certain that there is no wrong
or treason in my hands. I have not sinned against you, though you
are hunting me to take my life. [12]May the LORD judge between me
and you! May the LORD avenge me on you; but my hand shall not be
against you. [13]As the ancient proverb says, 'Out of the wicked comes
forth wickedness'; but my hand shall not be against you. [14]Against
whom has the king of Israel come out? Whom do you pursue? A dead
dog? A single flea? [15]May the LORD therefore be judge, and give sentence between me and you. May he see to it, and plead my cause, and
vindicate me against you."

16 When David had finished speaking these words to Saul, Saul
said, "Is this your voice, my son David?" Saul lifted up his voice and
wept. [17]He said to David, "You are more righteous than I; for you have
repaid me good, whereas I have repaid you evil. [18]Today you have explained how you have dealt well with me, in that you did not kill me
when the LORD put me into your hands. [19]For who has ever found
an enemy, and sent the enemy safely away? So may the LORD reward
you with good for what you have done to me this day. [20]Now I know
that you shall surely be king, and that the kingdom of Israel shall be
established in your hand. [21]Swear to me therefore by the LORD that
you will not cut off my descendants after me, and that you will not

24:5 David was stricken to the heart: How easy it would have been for David to kill Saul in the cave. David resists out of obedience to God, who had anointed Saul. This is the kind of faithful king God wants (12:14). The king and people are not to take matters into their own hands, but rather to obey God. Later Jesus Christ will embody such faithful obedience (see Phil 2:8).

When have you been tempted to take matters into your own hands? How did your faith guide you?

24:8-22 David also rose up and... called after Saul: David's speech (24: 8-15) and Saul's reply (24:16-21) sum up the story of their relationship. David's innocence is clear (24:11), and Saul faces his own evil (24:17).

24:18 the LORD put me into your hands: Saul finally faces the truth. He sees that God wants David to be king. God's purpose is accomplished in spite of Saul's blindness. Saul's words witness to the steady working of God to complete God's plan for David and all God's people. It is God, not Saul or David, who is in charge here and whose plan will prevail.

---

[a] Heb *to cover his feet* [b] Gk Syr Tg Vg: Heb *it* (my eye) *spared*

wipe out my name from my father's house." [22]So David swore this to
Saul. Then Saul went home; but David and his men went up to the
stronghold.

Death of Samuel

25 Now Samuel died; and all Israel assembled and mourned
for him. They buried him at his home in Ramah.
Then David got up and went down to the wilderness of Paran.

David and the Wife of Nabal

2 There was a man in Maon, whose property was in Carmel.
The man was very rich; he had three thousand sheep and a thousand
goats. He was shearing his sheep in Carmel. [3]Now the name of the
man was Nabal, and the name of his wife Abigail. The woman was
clever and beautiful, but the man was surly and mean; he was a Caleb-
ite. [4]David heard in the wilderness that Nabal was shearing his sheep.
[5]So David sent ten young men; and David said to the young men, "Go
up to Carmel, and go to Nabal, and greet him in my name. [6]Thus you
shall salute him: 'Peace be to you, and peace be to your house, and
peace be to all that you have. [7]I hear that you have shearers; now your
shepherds have been with us, and we did them no harm, and they
missed nothing, all the time they were in Carmel. [8]Ask your young
men, and they will tell you. Therefore let my young men find favor in
your sight; for we have come on a feast day. Please give whatever you
have at hand to your servants and to your son David.' "

9 When David's young men came, they said all this to Nabal in the
name of David; and then they waited. [10]But Nabal answered David's
servants, "Who is David? Who is the son of Jesse? There are many servants today who are breaking away from their masters. [11]Shall I take
my bread and my water and the meat that I have butchered for my
shearers, and give it to men who come from I do not know where?"
[12]So David's young men turned away, and came back and told him all
this. [13]David said to his men, "Every man strap on his sword!" And
every one of them strapped on his sword; David also strapped on his
sword; and about four hundred men went up after David, while two
hundred remained with the baggage.

14 But one of the young men told Abigail, Nabal's wife, "David
sent messengers out of the wilderness to salute our master; and he
shouted insults at them. [15]Yet the men were very good to us, and we
suffered no harm, and we never missed anything when we were in the
fields, as long as we were with them; [16]they were a wall to us both by
night and by day, all the while we were with them keeping the sheep.
[17]Now therefore know this and consider what you should do; for evil
has been decided against our master and against all his house; he is so
ill-natured that no one can speak to him."

25:3 Nabal...Abigail: Nabal mean "fool." He may be rich, but he has no wisdom about God and his neighbor. Abigail means "my father is joy." Just the opposite of her husband, she wisely honors David, saves him from doing violence (25:26), saves the lives of her own people (25:22), and sees God's hand in this meeting (25:28).

25:8 a feast day: Food is often given to needy neighbors at a time of harvest and celebration. David and his men are needy but have not tried to take Nabal's sheep while they camped near him. They have even protected Nabal's herds from others who would rob him (25:15-16).

25:10 Who is David?: Nabal implies that David is no more than a runaway slave. This is a deep insult that makes David's harsh reaction more understandable.

25:18 Abigail hurried: Abigail does what Nabal should have done for David's army of about four hundred. The parched grain amounts to about five bushels of roasted wheat or barley.

18 Then Abigail hurried and took two hundred loaves, two skins of wine, five sheep ready dressed, five measures of parched grain, one hundred clusters of raisins, and two hundred cakes of figs. She loaded them on donkeys [19]and said to her young men, "Go on ahead of me; I am coming after you." But she did not tell her husband Nabal. [20]As she rode on the donkey and came down under cover of the mountain, David and his men came down toward her; and she met them. [21]Now David had said, "Surely it was in vain that I protected all that this fellow has in the wilderness, so that nothing was missed of all that belonged to him; but he has returned me evil for good. [22]God do so to David[a] and more also, if by morning I leave so much as one male of all who belong to him."

23 When Abigail saw David, she hurried and alighted from the donkey, and fell before David on her face, bowing to the ground. [24]She fell at his feet and said, "Upon me alone, my lord, be the guilt; please let your servant speak in your ears, and hear the words of your servant. [25]My lord, do not take seriously this ill-natured fellow, Nabal; for as his name is, so is he; Nabal[b] is his name, and folly is with him; but I, your servant, did not see the young men of my lord, whom you sent.

25:28-31 a sure house: Abigail prophetically speaks of God's promise to establish David's line and throne forever (see 2 Sam 7:16). She calls David to kingly behavior, self-control regarding Nabal, and total reliance on God. Vengeance belongs to God alone. David must not overstep his bounds.

25:29 the bundle of the living: This is a heavenly book listing all living people (see Ps 69:28). Later it is used in reference to judgment and afterlife (see Dan 12:1; Rev 3:5).

26 "Now then, my lord, as the LORD lives, and as you yourself live, since the LORD has restrained you from bloodguilt and from taking vengeance with your own hand, now let your enemies and those who seek to do evil to my lord be like Nabal. [27]And now let this present that your servant has brought to my lord be given to the young men who follow my lord. [28]Please forgive the trespass of your servant; for the LORD will certainly make my lord a sure house, because my lord is fighting the battles of the LORD; and evil shall not be found in you so long as you live. [29]If anyone should rise up to pursue you and to seek your life, the life of my lord shall be bound in the bundle of the living under the care of the LORD your God; but the lives of your enemies he shall sling out as from the hollow of a sling. [30]When the LORD has done to my lord according to all the good that he has spoken concerning you, and has appointed you prince over Israel, [31]my lord shall have no cause of grief, or pangs of conscience, for having shed blood without cause or for having saved himself. And when the LORD has dealt well with my lord, then remember your servant."

32 David said to Abigail, "Blessed be the LORD, the God of Israel, who sent you to meet me today! [33]Blessed be your good sense, and blessed be you, who have kept me today from bloodguilt and from avenging myself by my own hand! [34]For as surely as the LORD the God of Israel lives, who has restrained me from hurting you, unless you had hurried and come to meet me, truly by morning there would not have been left to Nabal so much as one male." [35]Then David re-

---

[a] Gk Compare Syr: Heb *the enemies of David* [b] That is *Fool*

ceived from her hand what she had brought him; he said to her, "Go
up to your house in peace; see, I have heeded your voice, and I have
granted your petition."

36 Abigail came to Nabal; he was holding a feast in his house, like
the feast of a king. Nabal's heart was merry within him, for he was
very drunk; so she told him nothing at all until the morning light. 37 In
the morning, when the wine had gone out of Nabal, his wife told him
these things, and his heart died within him; he became like a stone.
38 About ten days later the LORD struck Nabal, and he died.

39 When David heard that Nabal was dead, he said, "Blessed be
the LORD who has judged the case of Nabal's insult to me, and has
kept back his servant from evil; the LORD has returned the evildoing
of Nabal upon his own head." Then David sent and wooed Abigail, to
make her his wife. 40 When David's servants came to Abigail at Carmel, they said to her, "David has sent us to you to take you to him as
his wife." 41 She rose and bowed down, with her face to the ground,
and said, "Your servant is a slave to wash the feet of the servants of
my lord." 42 Abigail got up hurriedly and rode away on a donkey; her
five maids attended her. She went after the messengers of David and
became his wife.

43 David also married Ahinoam of Jezreel; both of them became
his wives. 44 Saul had given his daughter Michal, David's wife, to Palti
son of Laish, who was from Gallim.

David Spares Saul's Life a Second Time

26 Then the Ziphites came to Saul at Gibeah, saying, "David
is in hiding on the hill of Hachilah, which is opposite Jeshimon."[a] 2 So Saul rose and went down to the Wilderness of Ziph, with
three thousand chosen men of Israel, to seek David in the Wilderness
of Ziph. 3 Saul encamped on the hill of Hachilah, which is opposite
Jeshimon[a] beside the road. But David remained in the wilderness.
When he learned that Saul had come after him into the wilderness,
4 David sent out spies, and learned that Saul had indeed arrived. 5 Then
David set out and came to the place where Saul had encamped;
and David saw the place where Saul lay, with Abner son of Ner, the
commander of his army. Saul was lying within the encampment,
while the army was encamped around him.

6 Then David said to Ahimelech the Hittite, and to Joab's brother
Abishai son of Zeruiah, "Who will go down with me into the camp to
Saul?" Abishai said, "I will go down with you." 7 So David and Abishai
went to the army by night; there Saul lay sleeping within the encampment, with his spear stuck in the ground at his head; and Abner and
the army lay around him. 8 Abishai said to David, "God has given

26:5-25 David…Saul: This last meeting between these two ends with David innocent (25:18) and with a bright future (25:25) and Saul guilty (25:21) and his power diminished (25:23).

26:7 his spear: Saul has tried to kill or "pin" David before (see 18:11; 19:10). He has also tried this with his own son Jonathan (see 20:33). Now the tables are turned. Abishai, David's nephew, is ready to pin Saul. David stops him. Later Jesus will also reject such violent revenge (see Matt 5:38-42).

[a] Or *opposite the wasteland*

your enemy into your hand today; now therefore let me pin him to
the ground with one stroke of the spear; I will not strike him twice."
[9]But David said to Abishai, "Do not destroy him; for who can raise
his hand against the LORD's anointed, and be guiltless?" [10]David said,
"As the LORD lives, the LORD will strike him down; or his day will
come to die; or he will go down into battle and perish. [11]The LORD
forbid that I should raise my hand against the LORD's anointed; but
now take the spear that is at his head, and the water jar, and let us go."
[12]So David took the spear that was at Saul's head and the water jar, and
they went away. No one saw it, or knew it, nor did anyone awake; for
they were all asleep, because a deep sleep from the LORD had fallen
upon them.

26:12 deep sleep from the LORD: God continues to defend David. Such a divine sleep came to Adam, Abram, and faithless leaders (see Gen 2:21; 15:12; Isa 29:10).

13 Then David went over to the other side, and stood on top of a
hill far away, with a great distance between them. [14]David called to the
army and to Abner son of Ner, saying, "Abner! Will you not answer?"
Then Abner replied, "Who are you that calls to the king?" [15]David
said to Abner, "Are you not a man? Who is like you in Israel? Why
then have you not kept watch over your lord the king? For one of the
people came in to destroy your lord the king. [16]This thing that you
have done is not good. As the LORD lives, you deserve to die, because
you have not kept watch over your lord, the LORD's anointed. See
now, where is the king's spear, or the water jar that was at his head?"

17 Saul recognized David's voice, and said, "Is this your voice,
my son David?" David said, "It is my voice, my lord, O king." [18]And
he added, "Why does my lord pursue his servant? For what have I
done? What guilt is on my hands? [19]Now therefore let my lord the
king hear the words of his servant. If it is the LORD who has stirred
you up against me, may he accept an offering; but if it is mortals, may
they be cursed before the LORD, for they have driven me out today
from my share in the heritage of the LORD, saying, 'Go, serve other
gods.' [20]Now therefore, do not let my blood fall to the ground, away
from the presence of the LORD; for the king of Israel has come out to
seek a single flea, like one who hunts a partridge in the mountains."

21 Then Saul said, "I have done wrong; come back, my son
David, for I will never harm you again, because my life was precious
in your sight today; I have been a fool, and have made a great mistake."
[22]David replied, "Here is the spear, O king! Let one of the young men
come over and get it. [23]The LORD rewards everyone for his righteousness and his faithfulness; for the LORD gave you into my hand today,
but I would not raise my hand against the LORD's anointed. [24]As your
life was precious today in my sight, so may my life be precious in the
sight of the LORD, and may he rescue me from all tribulation." [25]Then
Saul said to David, "Blessed be you, my son David! You will do many
things and will succeed in them." So David went his way, and Saul
returned to his place.

David Serves King Achish of Gath

27 David said in his heart, "I shall now perish one day by the
hand of Saul; there is nothing better for me than to escape
to the land of the Philistines; then Saul will despair of seeking me any
longer within the borders of Israel, and I shall escape out of his hand."
2 So David set out and went over, he and the six hundred men who
were with him, to King Achish son of Maoch of Gath. 3 David stayed
with Achish at Gath, he and his troops, every man with his household, and David with his two wives, Ahinoam of Jezreel, and Abigail
of Carmel, Nabal's widow. 4 When Saul was told that David had fled to
Gath, he no longer sought for him.

5 Then David said to Achish, "If I have found favor in your sight,
let a place be given me in one of the country towns, so that I may live
there; for why should your servant live in the royal city with you?" 6 So
that day Achish gave him Ziklag; therefore Ziklag has belonged to the
kings of Judah to this day. 7 The length of time that David lived in the
country of the Philistines was one year and four months.

8 Now David and his men went up and made raids on the Geshurites, the Girzites, and the Amalekites; for these were the landed settlements from Telam[a] on the way to Shur and on to the land of Egypt.
9 David struck the land, leaving neither man nor woman alive, but
took away the sheep, the oxen, the donkeys, the camels, and the clothing, and came back to Achish. 10 When Achish asked, "Against whom[b]
have you made a raid today?" David would say, "Against the Negeb of
Judah," or "Against the Negeb of the Jerahmeelites," or, "Against the
Negeb of the Kenites." 11 David left neither man nor woman alive to
be brought back to Gath, thinking, "They might tell about us, and say,
'David has done so and so.'" Such was his practice all the time he lived
in the country of the Philistines. 12 Achish trusted David, thinking,
"He has made himself utterly abhorrent to his people Israel; therefore
he shall always be my servant."

28 In those days the Philistines gathered their forces for war,
to fight against Israel. Achish said to David, "You know, of
course, that you and your men are to go out with me in the army."
2 David said to Achish, "Very well, then you shall know what your servant can do." Achish said to David, "Very well, I will make you my
bodyguard for life."

Saul Consults a Medium

3 Now Samuel had died, and all Israel had mourned for him and
buried him in Ramah, his own city. Saul had expelled the mediums
and the wizards from the land. 4 The Philistines assembled, and came
and encamped at Shunem. Saul gathered all Israel, and they encamped

27:1 to the land of the Philistines: What a risk David takes. Achish and his people are sworn enemies of Israel. Anyone who sides with them is a traitor. David resorts to doing this because he must escape Saul. But David remains a loyal Israelite and is able to deceive Achish and help Israel by defeating some of its longtime enemies (27:8).

27:6 Achish gave him Ziklag: What irony. This pagan king and his people provide for the anointed king of Israel. God continues to work in surprising ways to accomplish God's saving purposes. Elsewhere in the Bible, God uses Pharaoh's daughter, Cyrus of Persia, and Caesar Augustus to accomplish God's saving plan (see Exod 2:5-10; Isa 45:13; Luke 2:1-4).

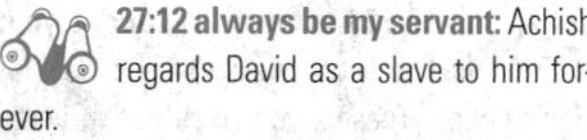

27:12 always be my servant: Achish regards David as a slave to him forever.

28:1 go out with me in the army: What a tight spot for David. Now it looks like he'll have to either fight his own people or be discovered as a traitor to Achish. The compiler of this history leaves us in suspense about the outcome until 29:3.

[a] Compare Gk 15.4: Heb *from of old* [b] Q Ms Gk Vg: MT lacks *whom*

28:5-14 his heart trembled greatly: Saul no longer acts as a king and faithful servant of God. He is fearful and desperate.

28:7-14 a medium at Endor: Seeking the dead in the underworld is forbidden in Israel (see Deut 18:9-12). Earlier Saul opposed this (28:3). Later Israel will see this as one of Saul's worst sins (1 Chr 10:13). Saul's violation of the First Commandment (see Deut 5:6-7) reveals his despair and complete failure as king.

28:14 Samuel: Samuel represents everything that is right and faithful. His robe is a sign of his special status, and its meaning is not lost on Saul. Just as Saul heard before when he clung to Samuel's robe (15:27), he will hear again the message that all is lost. Consulting a medium has not led to any new revelation from God.

28:17-19 the LORD has done to you: Samuel five times reminds Saul of God's action. These three verses bring home the main points of this chapter: Saul is judged faithless and disobedient, rejected as king, and his fate is sealed. God has spoken and acted; there is no greater power than Israel's God.

28:21-23 listen: Listening comes up four times here and implies trust and obedience. Earlier, Saul did not listen (15:1-10) and now we see fully how it has ruined him.

at Gilboa. 5When Saul saw the army of the Philistines, he was afraid,
and his heart trembled greatly. 6When Saul inquired of the LORD, the
LORD did not answer him, not by dreams, or by Urim, or by prophets.
7Then Saul said to his servants, "Seek out for me a woman who is a
medium, so that I may go to her and inquire of her." His servants said
to him, "There is a medium at Endor."

8 So Saul disguised himself and put on other clothes and went
there, he and two men with him. They came to the woman by night.
And he said, "Consult a spirit for me, and bring up for me the one
whom I name to you." 9The woman said to him, "Surely you know
what Saul has done, how he has cut off the mediums and the wizards
from the land. Why then are you laying a snare for my life to bring
about my death?" 10But Saul swore to her by the LORD, "As the LORD
lives, no punishment shall come upon you for this thing." 11Then the
woman said, "Whom shall I bring up for you?" He answered, "Bring
up Samuel for me." 12When the woman saw Samuel, she cried out
with a loud voice; and the woman said to Saul, "Why have you deceived me? You are Saul!" 13The king said to her, "Have no fear; what
do you see?" The woman said to Saul, "I see a divine being[a] coming
up out of the ground." 14He said to her, "What is his appearance?"
She said, "An old man is coming up; he is wrapped in a robe." So Saul
knew that it was Samuel, and he bowed with his face to the ground,
and did obeisance.

15 Then Samuel said to Saul, "Why have you disturbed me by
bringing me up?" Saul answered, "I am in great distress, for the Philistines are warring against me, and God has turned away from me and
answers me no more, either by prophets or by dreams; so I have summoned you to tell me what I should do." 16Samuel said, "Why then do
you ask me, since the LORD has turned from you and become your
enemy? 17The LORD has done to you just as he spoke by me; for the
LORD has torn the kingdom out of your hand, and given it to your
neighbor, David. 18Because you did not obey the voice of the LORD,
and did not carry out his fierce wrath against Amalek, therefore the
LORD has done this thing to you today. 19Moreover the LORD will
give Israel along with you into the hands of the Philistines; and tomorrow you and your sons shall be with me; the LORD will also give
the army of Israel into the hands of the Philistines."

20 Immediately Saul fell full length on the ground, filled with fear
because of the words of Samuel; and there was no strength in him,
for he had eaten nothing all day and all night. 21The woman came to
Saul, and when she saw that he was terrified, she said to him, "Your
servant has listened to you; I have taken my life in my hand, and have
listened to what you have said to me. 22Now therefore, you also lis-

---

[a] Or *a god*; or *gods*

ten to your servant; let me set a morsel of bread before you. Eat, that you may have strength when you go on your way." 23He refused, and said, "I will not eat." But his servants, together with the woman, urged him; and he listened to their words. So he got up from the ground and sat on the bed. 24Now the woman had a fatted calf in the house. She quickly slaughtered it, and she took flour, kneaded it, and baked unleavened cakes. 25She put them before Saul and his servants, and they ate. Then they rose and went away that night.

The Philistines Reject David

29 Now the Philistines gathered all their forces at Aphek, while the Israelites were encamped by the fountain that is in Jezreel. 2As the lords of the Philistines were passing on by hundreds and by thousands, and David and his men were passing on in the rear with Achish, 3the commanders of the Philistines said, "What are these Hebrews doing here?" Achish said to the commanders of the Philistines, "Is this not David, the servant of King Saul of Israel, who has been with me now for days and years? Since he deserted to me I have found no fault in him to this day." 4But the commanders of the Philistines were angry with him; and the commanders of the Philistines said to him, "Send the man back, so that he may return to the place that you have assigned to him; he shall not go down with us to battle, or else he may become an adversary to us in the battle. For how could this fellow reconcile himself to his lord? Would it not be with the heads of the men here? 5Is this not David, of whom they sing to one another in dances,

'Saul has killed his thousands,
  and David his ten thousands'?"

6 Then Achish called David and said to him, "As the LORD lives, you have been honest, and to me it seems right that you should march out and in with me in the campaign; for I have found nothing wrong in you from the day of your coming to me until today. Nevertheless the lords do not approve of you. 7So go back now; and go peaceably; do nothing to displease the lords of the Philistines." 8David said to Achish, "But what have I done? What have you found in your servant from the day I entered your service until now, that I should not go and fight against the enemies of my lord the king?" 9Achish replied to David, "I know that you are as blameless in my sight as an angel of God; nevertheless, the commanders of the Philistines have said, 'He shall not go up with us to the battle.' 10Now then rise early in the morning, you and the servants of your lord who came with you, and go to the place that I appointed for you. As for the evil report, do not take it to heart, for you have done well before me.[a] Start early in the morning,

[a] Gk: Heb lacks *and go to the place . . . done well before me*

What does Luther's Large Catechism say about Saul and his downfall? In his discussion of the First Commandment, Luther points to Saul as a great king, chosen by God, who turned from God and placed all his confidence in his crown and power. Luther encourages us all to learn the First Commandment well so that we see that God will not tolerate our trust in anything but God. Other lords or idols may last for a while, as Saul's success lasted for a time, but finally they will end in nothing. *1 Samuel 28:3-20*

Where or in whom do we look for safety and success? How might these become false gods and eventually lead us to nothing?

29:3 Hebrews: The Philistine commanders insult David and his men when they use this term. They imply that they are uncivilized scavengers who threaten their property and well-being.

29:3-7 Is this not David, the servant of King Saul: Both Achish and his commanders put the focus on David as a true Israelite. Without meaning to do it, they point to his solid connection to God's people (29:5) and spare him from having to go into battle against his own people.

29:10 you have done well before me: Unbelievable. David is on good terms with everyone in this complicated situation. It's not luck; it is God's quiet, hidden work on behalf of this anointed king. No wonder Israel loved David and the stories about him so much. His blessing and success represented their blessing and success.

and leave as soon as you have light." [11]So David set out with his men
early in the morning, to return to the land of the Philistines. But the
Philistines went up to Jezreel.

David Avenges the Destruction of Ziklag

30 Now when David and his men came to Ziklag on the third
day, the Amalekites had made a raid on the Negeb and on
Ziklag. They had attacked Ziklag, burned it down, [2]and taken captive
the women and all[a] who were in it, both small and great; they killed
none of them, but carried them off, and went their way. [3]When David
and his men came to the city, they found it burned down, and their
wives and sons and daughters taken captive. [4]Then David and the
people who were with him raised their voices and wept, until they
had no more strength to weep. [5]David's two wives also had been taken
captive, Ahinoam of Jezreel, and Abigail the widow of Nabal of Carmel. [6]David was in great danger; for the people spoke of stoning him,
because all the people were bitter in spirit for their sons and daughters. But David strengthened himself in the LORD his God.

7 David said to the priest Abiathar son of Ahimelech, "Bring me
the ephod." So Abiathar brought the ephod to David. [8]David inquired
of the LORD, "Shall I pursue this band? Shall I overtake them?" He
answered him, "Pursue; for you shall surely overtake and shall surely
rescue." [9]So David set out, he and the six hundred men who were with
him. They came to the Wadi Besor, where those stayed who were left
behind. [10]But David went on with the pursuit, he and four hundred
men; two hundred stayed behind, too exhausted to cross the Wadi
Besor.

11 In the open country they found an Egyptian, and brought him
to David. They gave him bread and he ate; they gave him water to
drink; [12]they also gave him a piece of fig cake and two clusters of raisins. When he had eaten, his spirit revived; for he had not eaten bread
or drunk water for three days and three nights. [13]Then David said to
him, "To whom do you belong? Where are you from?" He said, "I
am a young man of Egypt, servant to an Amalekite. My master left
me behind because I fell sick three days ago. [14]We had made a raid on
the Negeb of the Cherethites and on that which belongs to Judah and
on the Negeb of Caleb; and we burned Ziklag down." [15]David said to
him, "Will you take me down to this raiding party?" He said, "Swear
to me by God that you will not kill me, or hand me over to my master,
and I will take you down to them."

16 When he had taken him down, they were spread out all over
the ground, eating and drinking and dancing, because of the great
amount of spoil they had taken from the land of the Philistines and

[a] Gk: Heb lacks *and all*

30:6 great danger . . . strengthened himself in the LORD: "Danger" here is better translated "greatly distressed." David and his men have lost town, property, and loved ones. Most likely the Amalekites will sell the women and children to be slaves. Earlier Saul was also greatly distressed (28:15), but unlike him, David turns to God for direction and receives it. David seeks encouragement and direction by asking God what to do, by listening to God (30:8), then acting in obedience to God (30:9). It took great leadership and resolve to set out after the Amalekites, since David's men would be exhausted after a three-day march from Aphek to Ziklag, about sixty miles.

30:8 you shall surely overtake and shall surely rescue: God speaks absolutely of certain victory. David is a model of faith as he trusts this word and bases his plan and action on it.

30:9 Wadi Besor: Literally, this is "valley of good news." It is about fifteen miles from Ziklag. Later (30:24) the troops, who were left behind in this valley, will hear some very good news from David.

30:11 they found an Egyptian: God provides a guide. His own people left him to die, but David's troops show kindness and generosity.

30:14 Negeb: This refers to the dry land area that extended from Beersheba south and east to the desert. See Map 5, p. 2103.

from the land of Judah. 17David attacked them from twilight until the
evening of the next day. Not one of them escaped, except four hundred young men, who mounted camels and fled. 18David recovered
all that the Amalekites had taken; and David rescued his two wives.
19Nothing was missing, whether small or great, sons or daughters,
spoil or anything that had been taken; David brought back everything.
20David also captured all the flocks and herds, which were driven
ahead of the other cattle; people said, "This is David's spoil."

21 Then David came to the two hundred men who had been too
exhausted to follow David, and who had been left at the Wadi Besor.
They went out to meet David and to meet the people who were with
him. When David drew near to the people he saluted them. 22Then
all the corrupt and worthless fellows among the men who had gone
with David said, "Because they did not go with us, we will not give
them any of the spoil that we have recovered, except that each man
may take his wife and children, and leave." 23But David said, "You shall
not do so, my brothers, with what the LORD has given us; he has preserved us and handed over to us the raiding party that attacked us.
24Who would listen to you in this matter? For the share of the one
who goes down into the battle shall be the same as the share of the
one who stays by the baggage; they shall share alike." 25From that day
forward he made it a statute and an ordinance for Israel; it continues
to the present day.

26 When David came to Ziklag, he sent part of the spoil to his
friends, the elders of Judah, saying, "Here is a present for you from
the spoil of the enemies of the LORD"; 27it was for those in Bethel,
in Ramoth of the Negeb, in Jattir, 28in Aroer, in Siphmoth, in Eshtemoa, 29in Racal, in the towns of the Jerahmeelites, in the towns of the
Kenites, 30in Hormah, in Bor-ashan, in Athach, 31in Hebron, all the
places where David and his men had roamed.

30:24 they shall share alike: God has been generous. David is generous. This is kingly behavior—justice and equality for the whole community. Such generosity is God's will. Jesus' parable of the workers in the vineyard will stress the generosity of God toward all in the community (see Matt 20:1-16).

The Death of Saul and His Sons

31 Now the Philistines fought against Israel; and the men of Israel fled before the Philistines, and many fell[a] on Mount Gilboa. 2The Philistines overtook Saul and his sons; and the Philistines
killed Jonathan and Abinadab and Malchishua, the sons of Saul. 3The
battle pressed hard upon Saul; the archers found him, and he was
badly wounded by them. 4Then Saul said to his armor-bearer, "Draw
your sword and thrust me through with it, so that these uncircumcised may not come and thrust me through, and make sport of me."
But his armor-bearer was unwilling; for he was terrified. So Saul took
his own sword and fell upon it. 5When his armor-bearer saw that Saul

31:2 the Philistines overtook Saul: Samuel predicted this defeat and death (13:14; 15:28; 28:19).

31:4 So Saul took his own sword: Saul dies heroically. He entered this battle under the weight of a death sentence, then sees his sons killed, and continues to battle the Philistines until his end.

---

[a] Heb *and they fell slain*

31:9 the houses of their idols: The Philistines see this as a military and a religious victory. In their eyes the defeat of Saul is also a defeat of Israel's God. Later David will defeat the Philistines and their gods (see 2 Sam 5:19-21).

31:11 the inhabitants of Jabesh-gilead: Saul is regarded as a mighty deliverer by these people. Early in his kingship he saved them from the brutal, eye-gouging Ammonite Nahash (11:1-15).

31:13 under the tamarisk tree: Cremation was unusual in Israel, but the bodies are badly mutilated and decomposed. Burning keeps the bones intact for burial under this sacred tree. Saul's life ends in honor.

Consider again the main characters in this story—Hannah, Eli, Samuel, Saul, Jonathan, and David. What role does faith play for each? The book focuses a good deal on leadership. What qualities do you look for in a leader?

was dead, he also fell upon his sword and died with him. [6]So Saul and
his three sons and his armor-bearer and all his men died together on
the same day. [7]When the men of Israel who were on the other side of
the valley and those beyond the Jordan saw that the men of Israel had
fled and that Saul and his sons were dead, they forsook their towns
and fled; and the Philistines came and occupied them.

8 The next day, when the Philistines came to strip the dead, they
found Saul and his three sons fallen on Mount Gilboa. [9]They cut off
his head, stripped off his armor, and sent messengers throughout
the land of the Philistines to carry the good news to the houses of
their idols and to the people. [10]They put his armor in the temple of
Astarte;[a] and they fastened his body to the wall of Beth-shan. [11]But
when the inhabitants of Jabesh-gilead heard what the Philistines had
done to Saul, [12]all the valiant men set out, traveled all night long, and
took the body of Saul and the bodies of his sons from the wall of Beth-
shan. They came to Jabesh and burned them there. [13]Then they took
their bones and buried them under the tamarisk tree in Jabesh, and
fasted seven days.

[a] Heb plural

2 Samuel 7:13

2 SAMUEL

Background File

Regarding the authorship of 2 Samuel, see the introduction to 1 Samuel. Initially 1 and 2 Samuel were a single book. After the books were later translated in Greek, they became divided into two books (see chart Different Canons of the Hebrew Bible [Old Testament], pp. 28-29). Scholars hold that this book, like 1 Samuel, comes from many sources with different points of view about David and his kingship. The material was collected and edited in stages, with perhaps the largest part of it coming some time after the northern kingdom of Israel fell to the Assyrians in 721 B.C.E.

What's the Story?

The book of 2 Samuel tells of David coming to the throne, his reign, and then the conflicts in his own family and in Israel. It closes with four chapters of added material telling of David's leadership during times of famine and plague, including a long psalm of praise that celebrates David's kingship and testifies to God's faithfulness.

There are three key people in 2 Samuel: Saul, Nathan, and David. Although Saul is dead, his backers remain loyal and cause trouble for David almost to the end of the book (2 Sam 20). Nathan serves as prophet and priest to David and speaks a powerful and unique parable of judgment to him (2 Sam 12). David is considered the greatest king in Israel's history because of his great courage in battle and his even more remarkable trust in God. Even as a sinner under severe judgment, David impresses us with his humble confession and absolute reliance on God's steadfast love. It is God's unconditional, everlasting covenant with David and his house that is the high point of this book (2 Sam 7). God, sometimes seen but often not, is the center of this story. Watch for the times when God works in and through the words and actions of people such as Abner, Joab, and Abishai; Bathsheba and Uriah; Absalom, Shimei, the wise woman of Abel, and Rizpah.

Jerusalem is the key place in this dramatic history of David's kingship. David captures this Jebusite city, makes it his capital and the home of the ark. So many central events take place here: Nathan's announcement of the covenant, the Bathsheba and Uriah tragedy, Nathan's pronouncement of God's judgment, and Absalom's betrayal. The battlefield is also important, as it shows Israel's dominance of the region. The sword used both on the battlefield and between individuals makes many places the location of betrayal and violence.

Second Samuel can be outlined as follows:

- The question of Saul's successor (chapters 1–4)
- King David (5–8)
- David's troubled reign (9–20)
- Collected memories of David (21–24)

The story of David's death is found in 1 Kings.

What's the Message?

The purpose of 2 Samuel is to witness to God's faithful dealing with the chosen people, Israel. Whether in exile or returned to their homeland, the people of Israel hear again in these stories the promise of God's unconditional steadfast love for them. The covenant with David and his house is a foundation of their hope in God for salvation, no matter what comes their way.

The book of 2 Samuel puts David center stage in this drama of faith and life. It shows him to be the legitimate successor to Saul. He is blameless for the political violence around him, and he is the one God empowers to protect and rule Israel. But David is hardly perfect. Royal power does corrupt, as the prophet Samuel warned in 1 Samuel 8. Treachery, violence, a military buildup, and family power struggles are all parts of David's story. Most telling is his arranged murder of the loyal Uriah, to cover up David's adultery. This is David at his worst, but, more importantly, it is God at God's best. David is punished by God, but the unconditional covenant holds. God will not be stopped by human sin; God's steadfast love continues.

The story of David and Israel is our story too. Life is complex—a confusing mix of political, cultural, and personal events and tragedies. How are we to be faithful in the face of this? Reading David's story helps us enter into the conversation about this call to live faithfully in a troubled world. It also points us to the often hidden presence of God in our lives and our world. God is involved in all of life—political, cultural, and personal. God acts in life, bringing commands and judgment, but even more bringing faithful, renewing, steadfast love.

David Mourns for Saul and Jonathan

1:1 After the death of Saul: Originally 1 and 2 Samuel was one long book. It was later divided at the point of Saul's death.

1:1 Amalekites…Ziklag: This nomadic tribe, native to the desert area of south Judah, is a longtime enemy of Israel (see 1 Sam 30:1-6; Exod 17:8-16; Deut 25:17-19). Achish, the Philistine king of Gath, had granted David the city of Ziklag (see 1 Sam 27:5-6).

1 After the death of Saul, when David had returned from defeating the Amalekites, David remained two days in Ziklag. [2]On the
third day, a man came from Saul's camp, with his clothes torn and
dirt on his head. When he came to David, he fell to the ground and
did obeisance. [3]David said to him, "Where have you come from?"
He said to him, "I have escaped from the camp of Israel." [4]David said
to him, "How did things go? Tell me!" He answered, "The army fled
from the battle, but also many of the army fell and died; and Saul and
his son Jonathan also died." [5]Then David asked the young man who
was reporting to him, "How do you know that Saul and his son Jonathan died?" [6]The young man reporting to him said, "I happened to

be on Mount Gilboa; and there was Saul leaning on his spear, while
the chariots and the horsemen drew close to him. 7 When he looked
behind him, he saw me, and called to me. I answered, 'Here sir.' 8 And
he said to me, 'Who are you?' I answered him, 'I am an Amalekite.'
9 He said to me, 'Come, stand over me and kill me; for convulsions
have seized me, and yet my life still lingers.' 10 So I stood over him, and
killed him, for I knew that he could not live after he had fallen. I took
the crown that was on his head and the armlet that was on his arm,
and I have brought them here to my lord."

11 Then David took hold of his clothes and tore them; and all the
men who were with him did the same. 12 They mourned and wept, and
fasted until evening for Saul and for his son Jonathan, and for the army
of the LORD and for the house of Israel, because they had fallen by
the sword. 13 David said to the young man who had reported to him,
"Where do you come from?" He answered, "I am the son of a resident
alien, an Amalekite." 14 David said to him, "Were you not afraid to lift
your hand to destroy the LORD's anointed?" 15 Then David called one
of the young men and said, "Come here and strike him down." So he
struck him down and he died. 16 David said to him, "Your blood be
on your head; for your own mouth has testified against you, saying,
'I have killed the LORD's anointed.' "

17 David intoned this lamentation over Saul and his son Jonathan. 18 (He ordered that The Song of the Bow[a] be taught to the people of Judah; it is written in the Book of Jashar.) He said:

19 Your glory, O Israel, lies slain upon your high places!
How the mighty have fallen!
20 Tell it not in Gath,
proclaim it not in the streets of Ashkelon;
or the daughters of the Philistines will rejoice,
the daughters of the uncircumcised will exult.

21 You mountains of Gilboa,
let there be no dew or rain upon you,
nor bounteous fields![b]
For there the shield of the mighty was defiled,
the shield of Saul, anointed with oil no more.

22 From the blood of the slain,
from the fat of the mighty,
the bow of Jonathan did not turn back,
nor the sword of Saul return empty.

23 Saul and Jonathan, beloved and lovely!
In life and in death they were not divided;

[a] Heb *that The Bow* [b] Meaning of Heb uncertain

1:4-13 How did things go?: The Amalekite tells a slightly different story from the one in 1 Samuel 31. This one, written later, shows the Amalekite to be lying about killing Saul, perhaps hoping to receive a reward.

1:12 they mourned and wept: Samuel secretly anointed David as the new king long before this (see 1 Sam 16:13). David is a picture of innocence and loyalty, putting aside any personal ambition to the throne and any thoughts of revenge. This is the kind of king God wants for God's people, now and in the future (see 1 Sam 12:14-15; Phil 2:6-8).

1:16 Your blood be on your head: To kill God's anointed king is a great sin against God and one David has carefully avoided (see 1 Sam 24:6-7; 26:11-12). This Amalekite has put himself in the place of God by killing Saul. Only God chooses Israel's king (see 1 Sam 9:17; 16:1).

1:17 David intoned this lamentation: David voices passionate words of grief on behalf of all Israel. To voice such grief in songs of lament is part of Israel's faith relationship with God. See also the book of Lamentations.

1:19 How the mighty have fallen!: David sings this grief-filled phrase three times (1:19, 25, 27) and helps all Israel grieve Saul and their defeat by the Philistines. It takes the courage of faith to sing so honestly. Israel finds a pathway to hope in its lament psalms (see Pss 22:1, 22-31; 61; 64; 69).

How is lament, expressed either privately or publicly, a pathway of hope for you?

1:20 the Philistines will rejoice: They do rejoice (see 1 Sam 31:9). Israel despises these aggressive, hard-fighting, and well-equipped coastal people. They have been enemies for two hundred years and will continue to be so for many more.

1:23 beloved and lovely!: It could read: "loved and devoted." David sings of Saul in these glowing terms, even though Saul hated him and was trying to kill him (see 1 Sam 19:1). Jonathan and David shared deep love and loyalty (see 1 Sam 18:1).

they were swifter than eagles,
they were stronger than lions.

24 O daughters of Israel, weep over Saul,
who clothed you with crimson, in luxury,
who put ornaments of gold on your apparel.

25 How the mighty have fallen
in the midst of the battle!

Jonathan lies slain upon your high places.
26 I am distressed for you, my brother Jonathan;
greatly beloved were you to me;
your love to me was wonderful,
passing the love of women.

27 How the mighty have fallen,
and the weapons of war perished!

David Anointed King of Judah

2 After this David inquired of the LORD, "Shall I go up into any
of the cities of Judah?" The LORD said to him, "Go up." David
said, "To which shall I go up?" He said, "To Hebron." 2 So David went
up there, along with his two wives, Ahinoam of Jezreel, and Abigail
the widow of Nabal of Carmel. 3 David brought up the men who were
with him, every one with his household; and they settled in the towns
of Hebron. 4 Then the people of Judah came, and there they anointed
David king over the house of Judah.

When they told David, "It was the people of Jabesh-gilead who
buried Saul," 5 David sent messengers to the people of Jabesh-gilead,
and said to them, "May you be blessed by the LORD, because you
showed this loyalty to Saul your lord, and buried him! 6 Now may the
LORD show steadfast love and faithfulness to you! And I too will reward you because you have done this thing. 7 Therefore let your hands
be strong, and be valiant; for Saul your lord is dead, and the house of
Judah has anointed me king over them."

Ishbaal King of Israel

8 But Abner son of Ner, commander of Saul's army, had taken
Ishbaal[a] son of Saul, and brought him over to Mahanaim. 9 He made
him king over Gilead, the Ashurites, Jezreel, Ephraim, Benjamin, and
over all Israel. 10 Ishbaal,[a] Saul's son, was forty years old when he began

[a] Gk Compare 1 Chr 8.33; 9.39: Heb *Ish-bosheth*, "man of shame"

2:1 inquired: Dice, pebbles, or sticks, held in a special box, were thrown to determine a *yes* or *no* answer from God (see note at 1 Sam 14:3).

2:1 David inquired of the LORD: David continues to be obedient to God (see 1 Sam 23:2-10). Listening is crucial to leadership. Saul did not listen, and it was his undoing (see 1 Sam 15:10). Later, Jesus will call us to listen (see Matt 13:43), and so will the early church (see Rev 2:7, 11; 3:6, 13).

2:3 they settled in the towns of Hebron: Everyone goes to Hebron, showing that this is a permanent move in response to God's direction. Hebron, about nineteen miles southwest of Jerusalem, is a powerful city in the center of Judah and is where Sarah and Abraham are buried. See Map 5, p. 2103.

2:4 they anointed David king: This seems to be a popular, political move by the people, with no mention of priestly involvement (see 1 Sam 16:13).

2:5 the people of Jabesh-gilead: Earlier Saul had saved them from the brutal Nahash (see 1 Sam 11:1-11). In return, at great risk to themselves, they gave Saul a decent burial (see 1 Sam 31).

to reign over Israel, and he reigned two years. But the house of Judah followed David. [11]The time that David was king in Hebron over the house of Judah was seven years and six months.

The Battle of Gibeon

12 Abner son of Ner, and the servants of Ishbaal[a] son of Saul, went out from Mahanaim to Gibeon. [13]Joab son of Zeruiah, and the servants of David, went out and met them at the pool of Gibeon. One group sat on one side of the pool, while the other sat on the other side of the pool. [14]Abner said to Joab, "Let the young men come forward and have a contest before us." Joab said, "Let them come forward." [15]So they came forward and were counted as they passed by, twelve for Benjamin and Ishbaal[a] son of Saul, and twelve of the servants of David. [16]Each grasped his opponent by the head, and thrust his sword in his opponent's side; so they fell down together. Therefore that place was called Helkath-hazzurim,[b] which is at Gibeon. [17]The battle was very fierce that day; and Abner and the men of Israel were beaten by the servants of David.

18 The three sons of Zeruiah were there, Joab, Abishai, and Asahel. Now Asahel was as swift of foot as a wild gazelle. [19]Asahel pursued Abner, turning neither to the right nor to the left as he followed him. [20]Then Abner looked back and said, "Is it you, Asahel?" He answered, "Yes, it is." [21]Abner said to him, "Turn to your right or to your left, and seize one of the young men, and take his spoil." But Asahel would not turn away from following him. [22]Abner said again to Asahel, "Turn away from following me; why should I strike you to the ground? How then could I show my face to your brother Joab?" [23]But he refused to turn away. So Abner struck him in the stomach with the butt of his spear, so that the spear came out at his back. He fell there, and died where he lay. And all those who came to the place where Asahel had fallen and died, stood still.

2:23-24 Asahel . . . Joab . . . Abishai: Leaders in David's army, these reckless, bloodthirsty nephews are sons of David's sister, Zeruiah (2 Sam 2:18; 1 Chr 2:16).

24 But Joab and Abishai pursued Abner. As the sun was going down they came to the hill of Ammah, which lies before Giah on the way to the wilderness of Gibeon. [25]The Benjaminites rallied around Abner and formed a single band; they took their stand on the top of a hill. [26]Then Abner called to Joab, "Is the sword to keep devouring forever? Do you not know that the end will be bitter? How long will it be before you order your people to turn from the pursuit of their kinsmen?" [27]Joab said, "As God lives, if you had not spoken, the people would have continued to pursue their kinsmen, not stopping until morning." [28]Joab sounded the trumpet and all the people stopped; they no longer pursued Israel or engaged in battle any further.

2:26 Is the sword to keep devouring forever?: Abner's words signal that the road to a new king will be bloody. War begins, in contrast to David's peaceful offer of friendship (2:4-7). Jesus will later shed his own blood to save God's people and order his followers to put away their swords (see Matt 26:52).

29 Abner and his men traveled all that night through the Arabah;

[a] Gk Compare 1 Chr 8.33; 9.39: Heb *Ish-bosheth*, "man of shame" [b] That is *Field of Sword-edges*

they crossed the Jordan, and, marching the whole forenoon,[a] they came to Mahanaim. [30]Joab returned from the pursuit of Abner; and when he had gathered all the people together, there were missing of David's servants nineteen men besides Asahel. [31]But the servants of David had killed of Benjamin three hundred sixty of Abner's men. [32]They took up Asahel and buried him in the tomb of his father, which was at Bethlehem. Joab and his men marched all night, and the day broke upon them at Hebron.

Abner Defects to David

3:1 David grew stronger and stronger: This civil war will last more than seven years, but David is God's chosen one. This was foreseen by Saul, his son Jonathan, and Abigail (see 1 Sam 23:17; 24:20; 25:28; 26:25). Even the Saul-supporting Abner sees this (3:18).

3:2-5 Amnon…Absalom…Adonijah: Each of these will betray their father (see 13:20-22; 15:7-10; 1 Kgs 1:5-10). A much younger son, Solomon, will succeed David (see 1 Kgs 2:12).

3:7 Rizpah: This slave woman bore Saul two sons, giving her importance in the household (see 21:8). Abner's intimate relationship with her is an open defiance to Ishbaal's political power.

3 There was a long war between the house of Saul and the house of David; David grew stronger and stronger, while the house of Saul became weaker and weaker.

2 Sons were born to David at Hebron: his firstborn was Amnon, of Ahinoam of Jezreel; [3]his second, Chileab, of Abigail the widow of Nabal of Carmel; the third, Absalom son of Maacah, daughter of King Talmai of Geshur; [4]the fourth, Adonijah son of Haggith; the fifth, Shephatiah son of Abital; [5]and the sixth, Ithream, of David's wife Eglah. These were born to David in Hebron.

6 While there was war between the house of Saul and the house of David, Abner was making himself strong in the house of Saul. [7]Now Saul had a concubine whose name was Rizpah daughter of Aiah. And Ishbaal[b] said to Abner, "Why have you gone in to my father's concubine?" [8]The words of Ishbaal[c] made Abner very angry; he said, "Am I a dog's head for Judah? Today I keep showing loyalty to the house of your father Saul, to his brothers, and to his friends, and have not given you into the hand of David; and yet you charge me now with a crime concerning this woman. [9]So may God do to Abner and so may he add to it! For just what the LORD has sworn to David, that will I accomplish for him, [10]to transfer the kingdom from the house of Saul, and set up the throne of David over Israel and over Judah, from Dan to Beer-sheba." [11]And Ishbaal[b] could not answer Abner another word, because he feared him.

12 Abner sent messengers to David at Hebron,[d] saying, "To whom does the land belong? Make your covenant with me, and I will give you my support to bring all Israel over to you." [13]He said, "Good; I will make a covenant with you. But one thing I require of you: you shall never appear in my presence unless you bring Saul's daughter Michal when you come to see me." [14]Then David sent messengers to Saul's son Ishbaal,[e] saying, "Give me my wife Michal, to whom I became engaged at the price of one hundred foreskins of the Philistines." [15]Ishbaal[e] sent and took her from her husband Paltiel the son of

---

[a] Meaning of Heb uncertain [b] Heb *And he* [c] Gk Compare 1 Chr 8.33; 9.39: Heb *Ish-bosheth*, "man of shame" [d] Gk: Heb *where he was* [e] Heb *Ish-bosheth*

Laish. [16]But her husband went with her, weeping as he walked behind
her all the way to Bahurim. Then Abner said to him, "Go back home!"
So he went back.

17 Abner sent word to the elders of Israel, saying, "For some time
past you have been seeking David as king over you. [18]Now then bring
it about; for the LORD has promised David: Through my servant David I will save my people Israel from the hand of the Philistines, and
from all their enemies." [19]Abner also spoke directly to the Benjaminites; then Abner went to tell David at Hebron all that Israel and the
whole house of Benjamin were ready to do.

20 When Abner came with twenty men to David at Hebron,
David made a feast for Abner and the men who were with him. [21]Ab-
ner said to David, "Let me go and rally all Israel to my lord the king,
in order that they may make a covenant with you, and that you may
reign over all that your heart desires." So David dismissed Abner, and
he went away in peace.

Abner Is Killed by Joab

22 Just then the servants of David arrived with Joab from a raid,
bringing much spoil with them. But Abner was not with David at Hebron, for David[a] had dismissed him, and he had gone away in peace.
[23]When Joab and all the army that was with him came, it was told
Joab, "Abner son of Ner came to the king, and he has dismissed him,
and he has gone away in peace." [24]Then Joab went to the king and said,
"What have you done? Abner came to you; why did you dismiss him,
so that he got away? [25]You know that Abner son of Ner came to deceive you, and to learn your comings and goings and to learn all that
you are doing."

26 When Joab came out from David's presence, he sent messengers after Abner, and they brought him back from the cistern of Sirah;
but David did not know about it. [27]When Abner returned to Hebron,
Joab took him aside in the gateway to speak with him privately, and
there he stabbed him in the stomach. So he died for shedding[b] the
blood of Asahel, Joab's[c] brother. [28]Afterward, when David heard of
it, he said, "I and my kingdom are forever guiltless before the LORD
for the blood of Abner son of Ner. [29]May the guilt[d] fall on the head of
Joab, and on all his father's house; and may the house of Joab never
be without one who has a discharge, or who is leprous,[e] or who holds
a spindle, or who falls by the sword, or who lacks food!" [30]So Joab
and his brother Abishai murdered Abner because he had killed their
brother Asahel in the battle at Gibeon.

31 Then David said to Joab and to all the people who were with

---

[a] Heb *he* [b] Heb lacks *shedding* [c] Heb *his* [d] Heb *May it* [e] A term for several skin diseases; precise meaning uncertain

3:26 but David did not know: David makes peace with Abner (3:21), and the compiler of 2 Samuel emphasizes David's innocence in his death (3:28) and in the death of Ishbaal (4:9-11). Israel will continue hoping for a king of peace (see Isa 52) and finally receive him in Jesus Christ (see John 20:19-21).

3:29 May the guilt fall on the head of Joab: David's hands are clean. He is not guilty of shedding innocent or royal blood. He wants no part of such bloodguilt (see 1 Sam 24:12; 25:33; 26:18). The blood of those murdered will cry out to God (see Gen 4:10). Later, Judas will despair because of his bloodguilt (see Matt 27:4, 6).

3:31 King David: This is the first time we hear this formal title for David. It is used as David mourns Abner's death, showing that this kingship comes at great cost.

him, "Tear your clothes, and put on sackcloth, and mourn over
Abner." And King David followed the bier. 32 They buried Abner at
Hebron. The king lifted up his voice and wept at the grave of Abner,
and all the people wept. 33 The king lamented for Abner, saying,

"Should Abner die as a fool dies?
34 Your hands were not bound,
your feet were not fettered;
as one falls before the wicked
you have fallen."

And all the people wept over him again. 35 Then all the people came
to persuade David to eat something while it was still day; but David
swore, saying, "So may God do to me, and more, if I taste bread or
anything else before the sun goes down!" 36 All the people took notice of it, and it pleased them; just as everything the king did pleased
all the people. 37 So all the people and all Israel understood that day
that the king had no part in the killing of Abner son of Ner. 38 And the
king said to his servants, "Do you not know that a prince and a great
man has fallen this day in Israel? 39 Today I am powerless, even though
anointed king; these men, the sons of Zeruiah, are too violent for me.
The LORD pay back the one who does wickedly in accordance with
his wickedness!"

Ishbaal Assassinated

4:1 Ishbaal…feared him: After Abner's death the weak Ishbaal's courage fails, which literally means "his hands hung loose."

4 When Saul's son Ishbaal[a] heard that Abner had died at Hebron,
his courage failed, and all Israel was dismayed. 2 Saul's son had
two captains of raiding bands; the name of the one was Baanah, and
the name of the other Rechab. They were sons of Rimmon a Benjaminite from Beeroth—for Beeroth is considered to belong to Benjamin. 3 (Now the people of Beeroth had fled to Gittaim and are there as
resident aliens to this day).

4 Saul's son Jonathan had a son who was crippled in his feet. He
was five years old when the news about Saul and Jonathan came from
Jezreel. His nurse picked him up and fled; and, in her haste to flee,
it happened that he fell and became lame. His name was Mephibosheth.[b]

5 Now the sons of Rimmon the Beerothite, Rechab and Baanah,
set out, and about the heat of the day they came to the house of Ishbaal,[c] while he was taking his noonday rest. 6 They came inside the
house as though to take wheat, and they struck him in the stomach;
then Rechab and his brother Baanah escaped.[d] 7 Now they had come
into the house while he was lying on his couch in his bedchamber;
they attacked him, killed him, and beheaded him. Then they took his

---

[a] Heb lacks *Ishbaal* [b] In 1 Chr 8.34 and 9.40, *Merib-baal* [c] Heb *Ish-bosheth* [d] Meaning of Heb of verse 6 uncertain

head and traveled by way of the Arabah all night long. [8]They brought
the head of Ishbaal[a] to David at Hebron and said to the king, "Here
is the head of Ishbaal,[a] son of Saul, your enemy, who sought your life;
the LORD has avenged my lord the king this day on Saul and on his
offspring."
9 David answered Rechab and his brother Baanah, the sons of
Rimmon the Beerothite, "As the LORD lives, who has redeemed my
life out of every adversity, [10]when the one who told me, 'See, Saul is
dead,' thought he was bringing good news, I seized him and killed him
at Ziklag—this was the reward I gave him for his news. [11]How much
more then, when wicked men have killed a righteous man on his bed
in his own house! And now shall I not require his blood at your hand,
and destroy you from the earth?" [12]So David commanded the young
men, and they killed them; they cut off their hands and feet, and hung
their bodies beside the pool at Hebron. But the head of Ishbaal[a] they
took and buried in the tomb of Abner at Hebron.

David Anointed King of All Israel

5 Then all the tribes of Israel came to David at Hebron, and said,
"Look, we are your bone and flesh. [2]For some time, while Saul
was king over us, it was you who led out Israel and brought it in. The
LORD said to you: It is you who shall be shepherd of my people Israel,
you who shall be ruler over Israel." [3]So all the elders of Israel came to
the king at Hebron; and King David made a covenant with them at
Hebron before the LORD, and they anointed David king over Israel.
[4]David was thirty years old when he began to reign, and he reigned
forty years. [5]At Hebron he reigned over Judah seven years and six
months; and at Jerusalem he reigned over all Israel and Judah thirty-
three years.

Jerusalem Made Capital of the United Kingdom

6 The king and his men marched to Jerusalem against the Jebusites, the inhabitants of the land, who said to David, "You will not
come in here, even the blind and the lame will turn you back"—
thinking, "David cannot come in here." [7]Nevertheless David took the
stronghold of Zion, which is now the city of David. [8]David had said
on that day, "Whoever would strike down the Jebusites, let him get up
the water shaft to attack the lame and the blind, those whom David
hates."[b] Therefore it is said, "The blind and the lame shall not come
into the house." [9]David occupied the stronghold, and named it the
city of David. David built the city all around from the Millo inward.
[10]And David became greater and greater, for the LORD, the God of
hosts, was with him.

---

[a] Heb *Ish-bosheth* [b] Another reading is *those who hate David*

4:8 the head of Ishbaal: Rechab and Baanah have misunderstood David and God. There will be no reward for murder. David acted likewise when the Amalekite claimed to have murdered King Saul (see 1:14-16). David is above such brutal power grabbing.

4:9 As the LORD lives: David knows that his survival is due to God alone, and he will act according to God's word. Joab, Rechab and Baanah have gone their own way with their thirst for revenge and murder. Later, Jesus will make God's way clear when he teaches love of enemies and the great commandment to love God and neighbor (see Matt 5:38-48; 22:34-40).

5:2 shepherd of my people Israel: By God's design, the shepherd boy becomes the shepherd king (see 1 Sam 16:1-13). He is to care for and serve the community. Israel will often look for such a shepherd (see Ps 23; Isa 40:11; Jer 23:3-4; Ezek 34 and 37:24). Jesus will fulfill this role (John 10:11).

5:3 they anointed David king: This is David's third anointing (see 1 Sam 16; 2 Sam 2:1-4). God's promise is fulfilled, and Israel is a united kingdom. The balance of power has changed, and the Philistines will try to reassert themselves (5:17).

5:6 The king and his men marched to Jerusalem: This is the ideal capital, located on a defensible hill and centrally located in the kingdom. See Map 5, p. 2103.

5:6-8 the blind and the lame: Scholars debate the meaning of these verses because of unclear language and sources. Perhaps David is crudely biased against the lame and blind, or perhaps he is encouraging his men to kill the Jebusites rather than mutilate or blind them.

5:11 King Hiram of Tyre: Hiram generously provided valuable wood from cedar trees. He reigned long and successfully in Tyre, the Iron Age capital of the Phoenicians, who lived in the narrow coastal area bordered by the Lebanon Mountains on the east and the Mediterranean Sea on the west. The visit from Hiram's messengers marks Israel's entry into status among the nations. Later this will prove to be Israel's downfall (see Isa 2:5-8; Jer 22:13-17).

11 King Hiram of Tyre sent messengers to David, along with cedar trees, and carpenters and masons who built David a house. 12 David then perceived that the LORD had established him king over Israel, and that he had exalted his kingdom for the sake of his people Israel.

13 In Jerusalem, after he came from Hebron, David took more concubines and wives; and more sons and daughters were born to David. 14 These are the names of those who were born to him in Jerusalem: Shammua, Shobab, Nathan, Solomon, 15 Ibhar, Elishua, Nepheg, Japhia, 16 Elishama, Eliada, and Eliphelet.

Philistine Attack Repulsed

5:19, 23 David inquired of the LORD: David is still obedient and faithful. Defeating the Philistines is the job of God's anointed (see 1 Sam 9:16).

17 When the Philistines heard that David had been anointed king over Israel, all the Philistines went up in search of David; but David heard about it and went down to the stronghold. 18 Now the Philistines had come and spread out in the valley of Rephaim. 19 David inquired of the LORD, "Shall I go up against the Philistines? Will you give them into my hand?" The LORD said to David, "Go up; for I will certainly give the Philistines into your hand." 20 So David came to Baal-perazim, and David defeated them there. He said, "The LORD has burst forth against[a] my enemies before me, like a bursting flood." Therefore that place is called Baal-perazim.[b] 21 The Philistines abandoned their idols there, and David and his men carried them away.

22 Once again the Philistines came up, and were spread out in the valley of Rephaim. 23 When David inquired of the LORD, he said, "You shall not go up; go around to their rear, and come upon them opposite the balsam trees. 24 When you hear the sound of marching in the tops of the balsam trees, then be on the alert; for then the LORD has gone out before you to strike down the army of the Philistines." 25 David did just as the LORD had commanded him; and he struck down the Philistines from Geba all the way to Gezer.

David Brings the Ark to Jerusalem

6:2 the ark of God: This portable box is God's throne and a sign of God's powerful presence with Israel (see Exod 25:10-16; 1 Sam 4:4-5). David puts the focus on the kingship of God, rather than his own, by bringing the ark to Jerusalem.

6 David again gathered all the chosen men of Israel, thirty thousand. 2 David and all the people with him set out and went from Baale-judah, to bring up from there the ark of God, which is called by the name of the LORD of hosts who is enthroned on the cherubim. 3 They carried the ark of God on a new cart, and brought it out of the house of Abinadab, which was on the hill. Uzzah and Ahio,[c] the sons of Abinadab, were driving the new cart 4 with the ark of God;[d] and Ahio[c] went in front of the ark. 5 David and all the house of Israel were dancing before the LORD with all their might, with songs[e] and lyres and harps and tambourines and castanets and cymbals.

---

[a] Heb *paraz* [b] That is *LORD of Bursting Forth* [c] Or *and his brother* [d] Compare Gk: Heb *and brought it out of the house of Abinadab, which was on the hill with the ark of God* [e] Q Ms Gk 1 Chr 13.8: Heb *fir trees*

6 When they came to the threshing floor of Nacon, Uzzah reached out his hand to the ark of God and took hold of it, for the oxen shook it. [7]The anger of the LORD was kindled against Uzzah; and God struck him there because he reached out his hand to the ark;[a] and he died there beside the ark of God. [8]David was angry because the LORD had burst forth with an outburst upon Uzzah; so that place is called Perez-uzzah,[b] to this day. [9]David was afraid of the LORD that day; he said, "How can the ark of the LORD come into my care?" [10]So David was unwilling to take the ark of the LORD into his care in the city of David; instead David took it to the house of Obed-edom the Gittite. [11]The ark of the LORD remained in the house of Obed-edom the Gittite three months; and the LORD blessed Obed-edom and all his household.

12 It was told King David, "The LORD has blessed the household of Obed-edom and all that belongs to him, because of the ark of God." So David went and brought up the ark of God from the house of Obed-edom to the city of David with rejoicing; [13]and when those who bore the ark of the LORD had gone six paces, he sacrificed an ox and a fatling. [14]David danced before the LORD with all his might; David was girded with a linen ephod. [15]So David and all the house of Israel brought up the ark of the LORD with shouting, and with the sound of the trumpet.

16 As the ark of the LORD came into the city of David, Michal daughter of Saul looked out of the window, and saw King David leaping and dancing before the LORD; and she despised him in her heart.

17 They brought in the ark of the LORD, and set it in its place, inside the tent that David had pitched for it; and David offered burnt offerings and offerings of well-being before the LORD. [18]When David had finished offering the burnt offerings and the offerings of well-being, he blessed the people in the name of the LORD of hosts, [19]and distributed food among all the people, the whole multitude of Israel, both men and women, to each a cake of bread, a portion of meat,[c] and a cake of raisins. Then all the people went back to their homes.

20 David returned to bless his household. But Michal the daughter of Saul came out to meet David, and said, "How the king of Israel honored himself today, uncovering himself today before the eyes of his servants' maids, as any vulgar fellow might shamelessly uncover himself!" [21]David said to Michal, "It was before the LORD, who chose me in place of your father and all his household, to appoint me as prince over Israel, the people of the LORD, that I have danced before the LORD. [22]I will make myself yet more contemptible than this, and I will be abased in my own eyes; but by the maids of whom you have

6:6-7 Uzzah...took hold of it: The holy ark was not to be touched. Uzzah tries to protect God when the oxen shake the ark. It is God who protects Uzzah and all of Israel, so Uzzah didn't need to touch the ark.

6:9 David was afraid: The power of God impresses David in a fresh way and keeps him humble.

6:12 to the city of David with rejoicing: It's all coming together! The ark symbolizes God's presence, and God is Israel's past, present, and future strength. Now it is housed in Jerusalem, making David's rule totally legitimate and secure.

6:16 King David leaping and dancing before the LORD: David loses himself in praise of God, an act of humble worship.

6:20 vulgar fellow: This is not just a family disagreement. Michal represents the old house of Saul that is critical of David. David represents the new direction God is taking Israel.

6:22 I shall be held in honor: David humbles himself before God, worshiping wholeheartedly (6:14). God exalts him as the new leader of Israel. Hannah sang about this at the birth of Samuel (see 1 Sam 2:7-8). Jesus speaks of humility and exaltation (see Matt 18:4; 23:12; Luke 14:11).

---

[a] 1 Chr 13.10 Compare Q Ms: Meaning of Heb uncertain [b] That is *Bursting Out Against Uzzah*
[c] Vg: Meaning of Heb uncertain

7:1-3 **Now when the king:** David moves on to his next project—an expensive cedar temple for the Ark. Nathan, in his first appearance, approves the plan.

7:4-7 **Thus says the Lord:** This phrase signals prophetic speech. God's freedom and authority are reasserted (see also Ps 127:1; Exod 33:19; Ezek 12:25).

7:11 **I will give you rest:** Rest is God's gift. Both Moses and Joshua spoke of rest in the land that God would provide (see Deut 12:9-10; Josh 21:43-45). Solomon will point to the temple as a place of rest provided by God (1 Kgs 8:56). Jesus will give rest to all who come to him (see Matt 11:28).

7:11 **the Lord will make you a house:** God is the one truly in charge (see 1 Sam 16). The house God gives is a family or dynasty.

7:13 **forever:** This appears eight times in this chapter. God speaks it three times (7:13, 16), and David boldly claims it five times (7:24-29). It stresses the permanence of David's house and God's promise. In Luke 1, both and Mary and Zechariah will sing of God's promise being fulfilled in Jesus.

7:15 **but I will not take my steadfast love from him:** God's love and promise will continue, unconditionally, for David and his descendants, in spite of their sin. There will be punishment for sin, but they will not be cut off. This is one of the most important statements in the Old Testament and the beginning of ancient Israel's hope for a messiah or savior. The apostle Paul writes of God's unconditional love shown in Jesus Christ (see Rom 3:28; Gal 2:16-21).

7:18-21 **Then King David...sat before the Lord:** David sits in humility before the ark. His plans for a temple are exchanged for God's plan. Such humility and obedience have been David's strengths. Jesus taught his disciples to pray with humility before God (see Matt 6:9-10).

spoken, by them I shall be held in honor." [23]And Michal the daughter
of Saul had no child to the day of her death.

God's Covenant with David

7 Now when the king was settled in his house, and the LORD had
given him rest from all his enemies around him, [2]the king said to
the prophet Nathan, "See now, I am living in a house of cedar, but the
ark of God stays in a tent." [3]Nathan said to the king, "Go, do all that
you have in mind; for the LORD is with you."

4 But that same night the word of the LORD came to Nathan:
[5]Go and tell my servant David: Thus says the LORD: Are you the one
to build me a house to live in? [6]I have not lived in a house since the
day I brought up the people of Israel from Egypt to this day, but I
have been moving about in a tent and a tabernacle. [7]Wherever I have
moved about among all the people of Israel, did I ever speak a word
with any of the tribal leaders[a] of Israel, whom I commanded to shepherd my people Israel, saying, "Why have you not built me a house of
cedar?" [8]Now therefore thus you shall say to my servant David: Thus
says the LORD of hosts: I took you from the pasture, from following
the sheep to be prince over my people Israel; [9]and I have been with
you wherever you went, and have cut off all your enemies from before
you; and I will make for you a great name, like the name of the great
ones of the earth. [10]And I will appoint a place for my people Israel and
will plant them, so that they may live in their own place, and be disturbed no more; and evildoers shall afflict them no more, as formerly,
[11]from the time that I appointed judges over my people Israel; and I
will give you rest from all your enemies. Moreover the LORD declares
to you that the LORD will make you a house. [12]When your days are
fulfilled and you lie down with your ancestors, I will raise up your offspring after you, who shall come forth from your body, and I will establish his kingdom. [13]He shall build a house for my name, and I will
establish the throne of his kingdom forever. [14]I will be a father to him,
and he shall be a son to me. When he commits iniquity, I will punish
him with a rod such as mortals use, with blows inflicted by human
beings. [15]But I will not take[b] my steadfast love from him, as I took it
from Saul, whom I put away from before you. [16]Your house and your
kingdom shall be made sure forever before me;[c] your throne shall be
established forever. [17]In accordance with all these words and with all
this vision, Nathan spoke to David.

David's Prayer

18 Then King David went in and sat before the LORD, and said,
"Who am I, O Lord GOD, and what is my house, that you have brought

[a] Or *any of the tribes* [b] Gk Syr Vg 1 Chr 17.13: Heb *shall not depart* [c] Gk Heb Mss: MT *before you;* Compare 2 Sam 7.26, 29

me thus far? 19 And yet this was a small thing in your eyes, O Lord
GOD; you have spoken also of your servant's house for a great while
to come. May this be instruction for the people,[a] O Lord GOD! 20 And
what more can David say to you? For you know your servant, O Lord
GOD! 21 Because of your promise, and according to your own heart,
you have wrought all this greatness, so that your servant may know it.
22 Therefore you are great, O LORD God; for there is no one like you,
and there is no God besides you, according to all that we have heard
with our ears. 23 Who is like your people, like Israel? Is there another[b]
nation on earth whose God went to redeem it as a people, and to
make a name for himself, doing great and awesome things for them,[c]
by driving out[d] before his people nations and their gods?[e] 24 And you
established your people Israel for yourself to be your people forever;
and you, O LORD, became their God. 25 And now, O LORD God, as
for the word that you have spoken concerning your servant and concerning his house, confirm it forever; do as you have promised. 26 Thus
your name will be magnified forever in the saying, 'The LORD of hosts
is God over Israel'; and the house of your servant David will be established before you. 27 For you, O LORD of hosts, the God of Israel, have
made this revelation to your servant, saying, 'I will build you a house';
therefore your servant has found courage to pray this prayer to you.
28 And now, O Lord GOD, you are God, and your words are true, and
you have promised this good thing to your servant; 29 now therefore
may it please you to bless the house of your servant, so that it may
continue forever before you; for you, O Lord GOD, have spoken, and
with your blessing shall the house of your servant be blessed forever."

David's Wars

8 Some time afterward, David attacked the Philistines and subdued them; David took Metheg-ammah out of the hand of the
Philistines.

2 He also defeated the Moabites and, making them lie down on
the ground, measured them off with a cord; he measured two lengths
of cord for those who were to be put to death, and one length[f] for
those who were to be spared. And the Moabites became servants to
David and brought tribute.

3 David also struck down King Hadadezer son of Rehob of
Zobah, as he went to restore his monument[g] at the river Euphrates. 4 David took from him one thousand seven hundred horsemen,
and twenty thousand foot soldiers. David hamstrung all the chariot
horses, but left enough for a hundred chariots. 5 When the Arameans
of Damascus came to help King Hadadezer of Zobah, David killed

When in your life have you exchanged your plans for God's plans? How can we know what God intends for our lives?

7:22-24 you are great: Praise follows humility. It is only because of God's saving work that David and Israel are secure. People of faith recognize this. Hannah also does, and she sets the tone for both 1 and 2 Samuel (see 1 Sam 2:7-8). The prophet Samuel reminds Israel of this (see 1 Sam 12:6-11). Moses and Solomon do the same (see Deut 29:10-16; 1 Kgs 8:22-26).

7:25 And now, O LORD God: "And now" language is used to state a demand based on the preceding argument (7:18-24). This is bold, but David's demands are based on God's plan and promise rather than on his own.

8:1-12 David attacked: By waging war, David expands Israel's borders in all directions. He defeats six nations, including Moab, which had once given him refuge (see 1 Sam 22:3-5).

---

[a] Meaning of Heb uncertain [b] Gk: Heb *one* [c] Heb *you* [d] Gk 1 Chr 17.21: Heb *for your land*
[e] Cn: Heb *before your people, whom you redeemed for yourself from Egypt, nations and its gods* [f] Heb *one full length* [g] Compare 1 Sam 15.12 and 2 Sam 18.18

twenty-two thousand men of the Arameans. 6 Then David put garrisons among the Arameans of Damascus; and the Arameans became servants to David and brought tribute. The LORD gave victory to David wherever he went. 7 David took the gold shields that were carried by the servants of Hadadezer, and brought them to Jerusalem. 8 From Betah and from Berothai, towns of Hadadezer, King David took a great amount of bronze.

9 When King Toi of Hamath heard that David had defeated the whole army of Hadadezer, 10 Toi sent his son Joram to King David, to greet him and to congratulate him because he had fought against Hadadezer and defeated him. Now Hadadezer had often been at war with Toi. Joram brought with him articles of silver, gold, and bronze; 11 these also King David dedicated to the LORD, together with the silver and gold that he dedicated from all the nations he subdued, 12 from Edom, Moab, the Ammonites, the Philistines, Amalek, and from the spoil of King Hadadezer son of Rehob of Zobah.

13 David won a name for himself. When he returned, he killed eighteen thousand Edomites[a] in the Valley of Salt. 14 He put garrisons in Edom; throughout all Edom he put garrisons, and all the Edomites became David's servants. And the LORD gave victory to David wherever he went.

David's Officers

15 So David reigned over all Israel; and David administered justice and equity to all his people. 16 Joab son of Zeruiah was over the army; Jehoshaphat son of Ahilud was recorder; 17 Zadok son of Ahitub and Ahimelech son of Abiathar were priests; Seraiah was secretary; 18 Benaiah son of Jehoiada was over[b] the Cherethites and the Pelethites; and David's sons were priests.

David's Kindness to Mephibosheth

9 David asked, "Is there still anyone left of the house of Saul to whom I may show kindness for Jonathan's sake?" 2 Now there was a servant of the house of Saul whose name was Ziba, and he was summoned to David. The king said to him, "Are you Ziba?" And he said, "At your service!" 3 The king said, "Is there anyone remaining of the house of Saul to whom I may show the kindness of God?" Ziba said to the king, "There remains a son of Jonathan; he is crippled in his feet." 4 The king said to him, "Where is he?" Ziba said to the king, "He is in the house of Machir son of Ammiel, at Lo-debar." 5 Then King David sent and brought him from the house of Machir son of Ammiel, at Lo-debar. 6 Mephibosheth[c] son of Jonathan son of Saul came to David, and

---

[a] Gk: Heb *returned from striking down eighteen thousand Arameans* [b] Syr Tg Vg 20.23; 1 Chr 18.17: Heb lacks *was over* [c] Or *Merib-baal*: See 4.4 note

8:13 a name for himself: This could also mean that David built a monument to himself, celebrating his victory. His empire stretches from the Euphrates River to the borders of Egypt (see 1 Kgs 4:21). See Map 5, p. 2103.

8:14 the LORD gave victory to David: God is the reason for David's success. God has proven to be faithful since David was anointed (see 1 Sam 16:13; 17:37).

8:15 David administered justice and equity: This is what Israel's king is to do (see 1 Sam 12:14-15; Ps 72:1-4; Isa 9:7; Jer 22:15-16). But 2 Samuel 9–20 will show us another side of David: human weakness, hurt, and conflict.

8:16-17 Joab...Zadok...Abiathar: Joab, nephew of David, continues to command throughout David's reign. Abiathar, descendant of the priest Eli, survived Saul's massacre and then served David (see 1 Sam 22:6-23; 23:6-13; 30:7-8). Zadok took full title to the priesthood after David's death and Abiathar's banishment (see 1 Kgs 2:26-35).

8:18 Cherethites and the Pelethites: These royal bodyguards are mercenary soldiers. They may date back to David's days in the Philistine city of Ziklag (see 1 Sam 27–31).

9:1 Is there still anyone left: It seems that much of Saul's house is dead. This verse may have originally been part of the story of the execution of Saul's sons (see 21:1-14). The compiler has placed this story of Mephibosheth here so that we may hear of David's loyal love (kindness) early in his kingship and be aware of David's faithful behavior before all the trouble begins.

9:1 kindness: This is faithful, loyal love. Often it is translated as "steadfast love" in the Old Testament and "favor" or "grace" in the New Testament. God has promised such love to David's house (see 7:15), and David owes it to Jonathan's house (see 1 Sam 20:14-17, 42).

9:6 Mephibosheth: This son of Jonathan was crippled at age five and will continue to depend on David for support (see 4:4; 19:24-30).

fell on his face and did obeisance. David said, "Mephibosheth!"[a] He
answered, "I am your servant." 7 David said to him, "Do not be afraid,
for I will show you kindness for the sake of your father Jonathan; I will
restore to you all the land of your grandfather Saul, and you yourself
shall eat at my table always." 8 He did obeisance and said, "What is your
servant, that you should look upon a dead dog such as I?"
9 Then the king summoned Saul's servant Ziba, and said to him,
"All that belonged to Saul and to all his house I have given to your
master's grandson. 10 You and your sons and your servants shall till
the land for him, and shall bring in the produce, so that your master's grandson may have food to eat; but your master's grandson
Mephibosheth[a] shall always eat at my table." Now Ziba had fifteen
sons and twenty servants. 11 Then Ziba said to the king, "According
to all that my lord the king commands his servant, so your servant
will do." Mephibosheth[a] ate at David's[b] table, like one of the king's
sons. 12 Mephibosheth[a] had a young son whose name was Mica. And
all who lived in Ziba's house became Mephibosheth's[a] servants. 13 Mephibosheth[a] lived in Jerusalem, for he always ate at the king's table.
Now he was lame in both his feet.

The Ammonites and Arameans Are Defeated

10 Some time afterward, the king of the Ammonites died, and
his son Hanun succeeded him. 2 David said, "I will deal loyally with Hanun son of Nahash, just as his father dealt loyally with me."
So David sent envoys to console him concerning his father. When David's envoys came into the land of the Ammonites, 3 the princes of the
Ammonites said to their lord Hanun, "Do you really think that David is honoring your father just because he has sent messengers with
condolences to you? Has not David sent his envoys to you to search
the city, to spy it out, and to overthrow it?" 4 So Hanun seized David's
envoys, shaved off half the beard of each, cut off their garments in the
middle at their hips, and sent them away. 5 When David was told, he
sent to meet them, for the men were greatly ashamed. The king said,
"Remain at Jericho until your beards have grown, and then return."
6 When the Ammonites saw that they had become odious to
David, the Ammonites sent and hired the Arameans of Beth-rehob
and the Arameans of Zobah, twenty thousand foot soldiers, as well as
the king of Maacah, one thousand men, and the men of Tob, twelve
thousand men. 7 When David heard of it, he sent Joab and all the army
with the warriors. 8 The Ammonites came out and drew up in battle
array at the entrance of the gate; but the Arameans of Zobah and of
Rehob, and the men of Tob and Maacah, were by themselves in the
open country.

[a] Or *Merib-baal*: See 4.4 note [b] Gk: Heb *my*

9:7 Do not be afraid: Loyal love and kindness erase dishonor and fear. These words of reassurance and promise will be heard from angels and from Jesus (see Mark 4:40; 6:50; 16:6; Luke 1:13, 30; 2:10).

9:8 dead dog: Mephibosheth greatly humbles himself as truly insignificant before David.

9:10 always eat at my table: David grants royal protection and favor (see 2 Kgs 25:27-29). Loyal love (9:1) involves restoration of property and dignity.

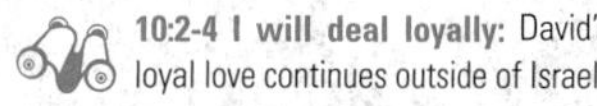
10:2-4 I will deal loyally: David's loyal love continues outside of Israel.

10:4 shaved off half the beard: This was meant to cause extreme humiliation and loss of pride (see Isa 15:2; Jer 41:5; 48:37). David's loyal love is rejected.

10:6 the Ammonites: Both Israel and the Ammonites are growing regional powers and bound to clash over control (see 11:1; 12:26-31).

9 When Joab saw that the battle was set against him both in front and in the rear, he chose some of the picked men of Israel, and arrayed them against the Arameans; 10 the rest of his men he put in the charge of his brother Abishai, and he arrayed them against the Ammonites. 11 He said, "If the Arameans are too strong for me, then you shall help me; but if the Ammonites are too strong for you, then I will come and help you. 12 Be strong, and let us be courageous for the sake of our people, and for the cities of our God; and may the LORD do what seems good to him." 13 So Joab and the people who were with him moved forward into battle against the Arameans; and they fled before him. 14 When the Ammonites saw that the Arameans fled, they likewise fled before Abishai, and entered the city. Then Joab returned from fighting against the Ammonites, and came to Jerusalem.

15 But when the Arameans saw that they had been defeated by Israel, they gathered themselves together. 16 Hadadezer sent and brought out the Arameans who were beyond the Euphrates; and they came to Helam, with Shobach the commander of the army of Hadadezer at their head. 17 When it was told David, he gathered all Israel together, and crossed the Jordan, and came to Helam. The Arameans arrayed themselves against David and fought with him. 18 The Arameans fled before Israel; and David killed of the Arameans seven hundred chariot teams, and forty thousand horsemen,[a] and wounded Shobach the commander of their army, so that he died there. 19 When all the kings who were servants of Hadadezer saw that they had been defeated by Israel, they made peace with Israel, and became subject to them. So the Arameans were afraid to help the Ammonites any more.

David Commits Adultery with Bathsheba

11 In the spring of the year, the time when kings go out to battle, David sent Joab with his officers and all Israel with him; they ravaged the Ammonites, and besieged Rabbah. But David remained at Jerusalem.

2 It happened, late one afternoon, when David rose from his couch and was walking about on the roof of the king's house, that he saw from the roof a woman bathing; the woman was very beautiful. 3 David sent someone to inquire about the woman. It was reported, "This is Bathsheba daughter of Eliam, the wife of Uriah the Hittite." 4 So David sent messengers to get her, and she came to him, and he lay with her. (Now she was purifying herself after her period.) Then she returned to her house. 5 The woman conceived; and she sent and told David, "I am pregnant."

6 So David sent word to Joab, "Send me Uriah the Hittite." And

10:12 may the LORD do what seems good: Joab's words are like a call to holy war (see Deut 20:3-4). He knows that Israel is outnumbered and their future is on the line. Israel's eventual victory shows that God is at work behind the scenes in this complicated political and military situation.

10:19 they made peace with Israel: First Joab checked the Arameans and Ammonites (10:6-15). Then, in a second battle, David defeats them (10:15-19). The Ammonite capital, modern day Amman, Jordan, will finally fall (see 12:26).

11:1 But David remained in Jerusalem: The story turns from military victories (chapters 5–10) to personal tragedy (12–20). While others fight his battles, David is tested at home and fails.

11:1—12:1 David sent someone: David exercises his royal power as he *sends* many people in many directions to serve his tragic purposes: Joab, Uriah, and messengers to Bathsheba. Finally, David's sending is cut off when God *sends* Nathan to him.

[a] 1 Chr 19.18 and some Gk Mss read *foot soldiers*

Joab sent Uriah to David. [7]When Uriah came to him, David asked how Joab and the people fared, and how the war was going. [8]Then David said to Uriah, "Go down to your house, and wash your feet." Uriah went out of the king's house, and there followed him a present from the king. [9]But Uriah slept at the entrance of the king's house with all the servants of his lord, and did not go down to his house. [10]When they told David, "Uriah did not go down to his house," David said to Uriah, "You have just come from a journey. Why did you not go down to your house?" [11]Uriah said to David, "The ark and Israel and Judah remain in booths;[a] and my lord Joab and the servants of my lord are camping in the open field; shall I then go to my house, to eat and to drink, and to lie with my wife? As you live, and as your soul lives, I will not do such a thing." [12]Then David said to Uriah, "Remain here today also, and tomorrow I will send you back." So Uriah remained in Jerusalem that day. On the next day, [13]David invited him to eat and drink in his presence and made him drunk; and in the evening he went out to lie on his couch with the servants of his lord, but he did not go down to his house.

11:9 But Uriah...did not go down to his house: Soldiers were not to enjoy the comforts of home and spouse in times of battle (see Deut 23:10-11; Lev 15:16-18). Uriah, whose name means "God is my light," proves more faithful and disciplined than the lustful King David.

David Has Uriah Killed

14 In the morning David wrote a letter to Joab, and sent it by the hand of Uriah. [15]In the letter he wrote, "Set Uriah in the forefront of the hardest fighting, and then draw back from him, so that he may be struck down and die." [16]As Joab was besieging the city, he assigned Uriah to the place where he knew there were valiant warriors. [17]The men of the city came out and fought with Joab; and some of the servants of David among the people fell. Uriah the Hittite was killed as well. [18]Then Joab sent and told David all the news about the fighting; [19]and he instructed the messenger, "When you have finished telling the king all the news about the fighting, [20]then, if the king's anger rises, and if he says to you, 'Why did you go so near the city to fight? Did you not know that they would shoot from the wall? [21]Who killed Abimelech son of Jerubbaal?[b] Did not a woman throw an upper millstone on him from the wall, so that he died at Thebez? Why did you go so near the wall?' then you shall say, 'Your servant Uriah the Hittite is dead too.' "

11:15 Set Uriah in the forefront of the hardest fighting: King David sees, wants, and takes. Samuel had warned Israel that a king would act selfishly and unjustly (see 1 Sam 8:10-18). God appointed kings to serve the welfare of God's people (see 1 Sam 9:16; Ps 72). Now God does the sending. The prophet Nathan stops David in his tracks, and David responds in humble confession and worship (12:13, 20).

22 So the messenger went, and came and told David all that Joab had sent him to tell. [23]The messenger said to David, "The men gained an advantage over us, and came out against us in the field; but we drove them back to the entrance of the gate. [24]Then the archers shot at your servants from the wall; some of the king's servants are dead; and your servant Uriah the Hittite is dead also." [25]David said to the messenger, "Thus you shall say to Joab, 'Do not let this matter trouble

---

[a] Or *at Succoth* [b] Gk Syr Judg 7.1: Heb *Jerubbesheth*

you, for the sword devours now one and now another; press your attack on the city, and overthrow it.' And encourage him."
26 When the wife of Uriah heard that her husband was dead, she
made lamentation for him. [27]When the mourning was over, David
sent and brought her to his house, and she became his wife, and bore
him a son.

Nathan Condemns David

12 But the thing that David had done displeased the LORD, [1]and
the LORD sent Nathan to David. He came to him, and said to
him, "There were two men in a certain city, the one rich and the other
poor. [2]The rich man had very many flocks and herds; [3]but the poor
man had nothing but one little ewe lamb, which he had bought. He
brought it up, and it grew up with him and with his children; it used
to eat of his meager fare, and drink from his cup, and lie in his bosom,
and it was like a daughter to him. [4]Now there came a traveler to the
rich man, and he was loath to take one of his own flock or herd to
prepare for the wayfarer who had come to him, but he took the poor
man's lamb, and prepared that for the guest who had come to him."
[5]Then David's anger was greatly kindled against the man. He said to
Nathan, "As the LORD lives, the man who has done this deserves to
die; [6]he shall restore the lamb fourfold, because he did this thing, and
because he had no pity."
7 Nathan said to David, "You are the man! Thus says the LORD,
the God of Israel: I anointed you king over Israel, and I rescued you
from the hand of Saul; [8]I gave you your master's house, and your
master's wives into your bosom, and gave you the house of Israel
and of Judah; and if that had been too little, I would have added as
much more. [9]Why have you despised the word of the LORD, to do
what is evil in his sight? You have struck down Uriah the Hittite with
the sword, and have taken his wife to be your wife, and have killed
him with the sword of the Ammonites. [10]Now therefore the sword
shall never depart from your house, for you have despised me, and
have taken the wife of Uriah the Hittite to be your wife. [11]Thus says
the LORD: I will raise up trouble against you from within your own
house; and I will take your wives before your eyes, and give them to
your neighbor, and he shall lie with your wives in the sight of this very
sun. [12]For you did it secretly; but I will do this thing before all Israel,
and before the sun." [13]David said to Nathan, "I have sinned against the
LORD." Nathan said to David, "Now the LORD has put away your sin;
you shall not die. [14]Nevertheless, because by this deed you have utterly scorned the LORD,[a] the child that is born to you shall die." [15]Then
Nathan went to his house.

12:1 and the LORD sent Nathan to David: David's abuse of power is over. Now he must listen to God and admit that he is one who takes (12:4-6) instead of gives.

12:7-8 You are the man! This is new and daring prophetic speech. Nathan uses the messenger formula: "Thus says the LORD." Four times we read "I," stressing how much *God* has given to David.

12:9 why have you despised the word of the LORD: David is guilty of coveting, adultery, and murder, prohibited by three of the Ten Commandments. He thought he was above God's law. But God is still in charge, and David will be punished. This is in keeping with the covenant between God and David's house (see 7:14-17).

12:10 the sword shall never depart from your house: How true this will be. Three of David's sons will die violently: Amnon, Absalom, and Adonijah (see 13:28-29, 18:14-15; 1 Kgs 2:23-25). Earlier David had lightly dismissed the work of the sword (11:25). His arrogance now comes back to haunt him.

12:13 I have sinned against the LORD: There is yet hope. Now that David's arrogance is broken, it is replaced with humble confession. He resubmits himself to God, God's rule, and God's mercy. This is the stuff of faith (see Pss 51; 102; 130; 143).

What are the two parts of repentance? The Augsburg Confession, Article 12, says that the two parts are contrition and faith. Contrition is the painful awareness of our sin. Faith trusts that our sin is forgiven on account of Christ. Luther and the reformers wrote that faith receives forgiveness, trusting God's gift of peace through Christ (see Rom 5:1). *2 Samuel 12:13*

12:13 Now the LORD has put away your sin: God is faithful. The covenant relationship holds (see 7:16). Although the consequences of David's sin are tragic, God is at work for good. A promising sign is the birth of Solomon, whose name means "peace." His God-given name, Jedediah, means "beloved of the LORD," and shows that God's blessing will continue through Solomon for the welfare of Israel (see 1 Kgs 3:10-14).

---

[a] Ancient scribal tradition: Compare 1 Sam 25.22 note: Heb *scorned the enemies of the LORD*

Bathsheba's Child Dies

The LORD struck the child that Uriah's wife bore to David, and
it became very ill. [16]David therefore pleaded with God for the child;
David fasted, and went in and lay all night on the ground. [17]The elders
of his house stood beside him, urging him to rise from the ground;
but he would not, nor did he eat food with them. [18]On the seventh
day the child died. And the servants of David were afraid to tell him
that the child was dead; for they said, "While the child was still alive,
we spoke to him, and he did not listen to us; how then can we tell him
the child is dead? He may do himself some harm." [19]But when David
saw that his servants were whispering together, he perceived that the
child was dead; and David said to his servants, "Is the child dead?"
They said, "He is dead."

20 Then David rose from the ground, washed, anointed himself,
and changed his clothes. He went into the house of the LORD, and
worshiped; he then went to his own house; and when he asked, they
set food before him and he ate. [21]Then his servants said to him, "What
is this thing that you have done? You fasted and wept for the child
while it was alive; but when the child died, you rose and ate food."
[22]He said, "While the child was still alive, I fasted and wept; for I said,
'Who knows? The LORD may be gracious to me, and the child may
live.' [23]But now he is dead; why should I fast? Can I bring him back
again? I shall go to him, but he will not return to me."

David found repentance difficult, but it led to renewal. How has this also been true for you? Is one part of repentance more difficult for you than the other? Why?

Solomon Is Born

24 Then David consoled his wife Bathsheba, and went to her, and
lay with her; and she bore a son, and he named him Solomon. The
LORD loved him, [25]and sent a message by the prophet Nathan; so he
named him Jedidiah,[a] because of the LORD.

The Ammonites Crushed

26 Now Joab fought against Rabbah of the Ammonites, and
took the royal city. [27]Joab sent messengers to David, and said, "I have
fought against Rabbah; moreover, I have taken the water city. [28]Now,
then, gather the rest of the people together, and encamp against the
city, and take it; or I myself will take the city, and it will be called by
my name." [29]So David gathered all the people together and went to
Rabbah, and fought against it and took it. [30]He took the crown of Milcom[b] from his head; the weight of it was a talent of gold, and in it was
a precious stone; and it was placed on David's head. He also brought
forth the spoil of the city, a very great amount. [31]He brought out the
people who were in it, and set them to work with saws and iron picks
and iron axes, or sent them to the brickworks. Thus he did to all the

12:30 He took the crown of Milcom: Milcom is the national god of the Ammonites.

[a] That is *Beloved of the* LORD [b] Gk See 1 Kings 11.5, 33: Heb *their kings*

cities of the Ammonites. Then David and all the people returned to
Jerusalem.

Amnon and Tamar

13 Some time passed. David's son Absalom had a beautiful sister
whose name was Tamar; and David's son Amnon fell in love
with her. [2]Amnon was so tormented that he made himself ill because
of his sister Tamar, for she was a virgin and it seemed impossible to
Amnon to do anything to her. [3]But Amnon had a friend whose name
was Jonadab, the son of David's brother Shimeah; and Jonadab was a
very crafty man. [4]He said to him, "O son of the king, why are you so
haggard morning after morning? Will you not tell me?" Amnon said
to him, "I love Tamar, my brother Absalom's sister." [5]Jonadab said to
him, "Lie down on your bed, and pretend to be ill; and when your father comes to see you, say to him, 'Let my sister Tamar come and give
me something to eat, and prepare the food in my sight, so that I may
see it and eat it from her hand.'" [6]So Amnon lay down, and pretended
to be ill; and when the king came to see him, Amnon said to the king,
"Please let my sister Tamar come and make a couple of cakes in my
sight, so that I may eat from her hand."

7 Then David sent home to Tamar, saying, "Go to your brother
Amnon's house, and prepare food for him." [8]So Tamar went to her
brother Amnon's house, where he was lying down. She took dough,
kneaded it, made cakes in his sight, and baked the cakes. [9]Then she
took the pan and set them[a] out before him, but he refused to eat. Amnon said, "Send out everyone from me." So everyone went out from
him. [10]Then Amnon said to Tamar, "Bring the food into the chamber,
so that I may eat from your hand." So Tamar took the cakes she had
made, and brought them into the chamber to Amnon her brother.
[11]But when she brought them near him to eat, he took hold of her, and
said to her, "Come, lie with me, my sister." [12]She answered him, "No,
my brother, do not force me; for such a thing is not done in Israel; do
not do anything so vile! [13]As for me, where could I carry my shame?
And as for you, you would be as one of the scoundrels in Israel. Now
therefore, I beg you, speak to the king; for he will not withhold me
from you." [14]But he would not listen to her; and being stronger than
she, he forced her and lay with her.

15 Then Amnon was seized with a very great loathing for her;
indeed, his loathing was even greater than the lust he had felt for
her. Amnon said to her, "Get out!" [16]But she said to him, "No, my
brother;[b] for this wrong in sending me away is greater than the other
that you did to me." But he would not listen to her. [17]He called the
young man who served him and said, "Put this woman out of my

[a] Heb *and poured* [a] Cn Compare Gk Vg: Meaning of Heb uncertain

13:1 Tamar: This daughter of David and Maacah is Amnon's half-sister. She speaks the most wisdom in chapters 13–14, but Amnon will not listen (see 13:12-14).

13:6 so Amnon...pretended to be ill: David's own family members draw him unknowingly into the plot to rape Tamar, fulfilling Nathan's words that David's own house will be troubled (see 12:11).

13:14 he forced her: This act is humiliating and pure self-indulgence on Amnon's part. It violates Israel's law (see Lev 18:9, 11; Deut 27:22). Sending Tamar away (13:15-16) only increases the wrong. Several years of suffering results (see 13:23, 38; 14:28). Tamar's *desolation* (13:20) will become Israel's as fighting breaks out.

13:14 he would not listen to her: Listening is a mark of character and faith. David listened to Abigail and was saved from bloodguilt (see 1 Sam 25:23-35). Samuel and Saul listened to God and obeyed (see 1 Sam 3:10; 12:14-15). Jesus calls us to listen (see Matt 13:43), just as earlier congregations were called to listen (see Rev 2:7, 11; 3:6, 13).

presence, and bolt the door after her." 18 (Now she was wearing a long
robe with sleeves; for this is how the virgin daughters of the king were
clothed in earlier times.[a]) So his servant put her out, and bolted the
door after her. 19 But Tamar put ashes on her head, and tore the long
robe that she was wearing; she put her hand on her head, and went
away, crying aloud as she went.

20 Her brother Absalom said to her, "Has Amnon your brother
been with you? Be quiet for now, my sister; he is your brother; do
not take this to heart." So Tamar remained, a desolate woman, in
her brother Absalom's house. 21 When King David heard of all these
things, he became very angry, but he would not punish his son Amnon, because he loved him, for he was his firstborn.[b] 22 But Absalom
spoke to Amnon neither good nor bad; for Absalom hated Amnon,
because he had raped his sister Tamar.

Absalom Avenges the Violation of His Sister

23 After two full years Absalom had sheepshearers at Baal-hazor,
which is near Ephraim, and Absalom invited all the king's sons. 24 Absalom came to the king, and said, "Your servant has sheepshearers;
will the king and his servants please go with your servant?" 25 But the
king said to Absalom, "No, my son, let us not all go, or else we will
be burdensome to you." He pressed him, but he would not go but
gave him his blessing. 26 Then Absalom said, "If not, please let my
brother Amnon go with us." The king said to him, "Why should he
go with you?" 27 But Absalom pressed him until he let Amnon and all
the king's sons go with him. Absalom made a feast like a king's feast.[c]
28 Then Absalom commanded his servants, "Watch when Amnon's
heart is merry with wine, and when I say to you, 'Strike Amnon,' then
kill him. Do not be afraid; have I not myself commanded you? Be
courageous and valiant." 29 So the servants of Absalom did to Amnon
as Absalom had commanded. Then all the king's sons rose, and each
mounted his mule and fled.

30 While they were on the way, the report came to David that
Absalom had killed all the king's sons, and not one of them was left.
31 The king rose, tore his garments, and lay on the ground; and all his
servants who were standing by tore their garments. 32 But Jonadab, the
son of David's brother Shimeah, said, "Let not my lord suppose that
they have killed all the young men the king's sons; Amnon alone is
dead. This has been determined by Absalom from the day Amnon[d]
raped his sister Tamar. 33 Now therefore, do not let my lord the king
take it to heart, as if all the king's sons were dead; for Amnon alone
is dead."

13:21 he would not punish his son Amnon: David fails to obey God's commandments as Israel's king should (see 1 Sam 12:14). He lets Amnon off the hook, ignores Tamar's plight, and later will not hold Absalom responsible for Amnon's murder (see 2 Sam 14:33). Instead he offers this violent, ambitious man shelter in Jerusalem. He puts personal concern above God's law and the welfare of Israel.

13:27-39 Absalom made a feast: Sheep-shearing calls for feasting (see 1 Sam 25:8) but Absalom uses it to avenge Tamar and put himself first in line for David's throne. For now, he flees to his grandparents for safety (13:37). Later he will try to overthrow David (see 2 Sam 15:6-12).

---

[a] Cn: Heb *were clothed in robes* [b] Q Ms Gk: MT lacks *but he would not punish . . . firstborn*
[c] Gk Compare Q Ms: MT lacks *Absalom made a feast like a king's feast* [d] Heb *he*

34 But Absalom fled. When the young man who kept watch
looked up, he saw many people coming from the Horonaim road[a] by
the side of the mountain. [35]Jonadab said to the king, "See, the king's
sons have come; as your servant said, so it has come about." [36]As
soon as he had finished speaking, the king's sons arrived, and raised
their voices and wept; and the king and all his servants also wept very
bitterly.

37 But Absalom fled, and went to Talmai son of Ammihud, king
of Geshur. David mourned for his son day after day. [38]Absalom, having fled to Geshur, stayed there three years. [39]And the heart of[b] the
king went out, yearning for Absalom; for he was now consoled over
the death of Amnon.

Absalom Returns to Jerusalem

14:2 a wise woman: This woman is wise only in persuasive speech. Her story is false, and she uses flattery (14:17, 20) to get David to swear to protect a guilty son (14:11). David must then honor his own oath and allow the guilty Absalom to come home (14:21).

14 Now Joab son of Zeruiah perceived that the king's mind was
on Absalom. [2]Joab sent to Tekoa and brought from there
a wise woman. He said to her, "Pretend to be a mourner; put on
mourning garments, do not anoint yourself with oil, but behave like
a woman who has been mourning many days for the dead. [3]Go to
the king and speak to him as follows." And Joab put the words into
her mouth.

4 When the woman of Tekoa came to the king, she fell on her
face to the ground and did obeisance, and said, "Help, O king!" [5]The
king asked her, "What is your trouble?" She answered, "Alas, I am a
widow; my husband is dead. [6]Your servant had two sons, and they
fought with one another in the field; there was no one to part them,
and one struck the other and killed him. [7]Now the whole family has
risen against your servant. They say, 'Give up the man who struck
his brother, so that we may kill him for the life of his brother whom
he murdered, even if we destroy the heir as well.' Thus they would
quench my one remaining ember, and leave to my husband neither
name nor remnant on the face of the earth."

8 Then the king said to the woman, "Go to your house, and I will
give orders concerning you." [9]The woman of Tekoa said to the king,
"On me be the guilt, my lord the king, and on my father's house; let
the king and his throne be guiltless." [10]The king said, "If anyone says
anything to you, bring him to me, and he shall never touch you again."
[11]Then she said, "Please, may the king keep the LORD your God in
mind, so that the avenger of blood may kill no more, and my son not
be destroyed." He said, "As the LORD lives, not one hair of your son
shall fall to the ground."

12 Then the woman said, "Please let your servant speak a word
to my lord the king." He said, "Speak." [13]The woman said, "Why then

---

[a] Cn Compare Gk: Heb *the road behind him* [b] Q Ms Gk: MT *And David*

have you planned such a thing against the people of God? For in giving this decision the king convicts himself, inasmuch as the king does
not bring his banished one home again. 14 We must all die; we are like
water spilled on the ground, which cannot be gathered up. But God
will not take away a life; he will devise plans so as not to keep an outcast banished forever from his presence.[a] 15 Now I have come to say
this to my lord the king because the people have made me afraid; your
servant thought, 'I will speak to the king; it may be that the king will
perform the request of his servant. 16 For the king will hear, and deliver
his servant from the hand of the man who would cut both me and my
son off from the heritage of God.' 17 Your servant thought, 'The word
of my lord the king will set me at rest'; for my lord the king is like
the angel of God, discerning good and evil. The LORD your God be
with you!"

18 Then the king answered the woman, "Do not withhold from
me anything I ask you." The woman said, "Let my lord the king speak."
19 The king said, "Is the hand of Joab with you in all this?" The woman
answered and said, "As surely as you live, my lord the king, one cannot turn right or left from anything that my lord the king has said. For
it was your servant Joab who commanded me; it was he who put all
these words into the mouth of your servant. 20 In order to change the
course of affairs your servant Joab did this. But my lord has wisdom
like the wisdom of the angel of God to know all things that are on
the earth."

21 Then the king said to Joab, "Very well, I grant this; go, bring
back the young man Absalom." 22 Joab prostrated himself with his face
to the ground and did obeisance, and blessed the king; and Joab said,
"Today your servant knows that I have found favor in your sight, my
lord the king, in that the king has granted the request of his servant."
23 So Joab set off, went to Geshur, and brought Absalom to Jerusalem.
24 The king said, "Let him go to his own house; he is not to come into
my presence." So Absalom went to his own house, and did not come
into the king's presence.

David Forgives Absalom

25 Now in all Israel there was no one to be praised so much for
his beauty as Absalom; from the sole of his foot to the crown of his
head there was no blemish in him. 26 When he cut the hair of his head
(for at the end of every year he used to cut it; when it was heavy on
him, he cut it), he weighed the hair of his head, two hundred shekels
by the king's weight. 27 There were born to Absalom three sons, and
one daughter whose name was Tamar; she was a beautiful woman.

28 So Absalom lived two full years in Jerusalem, without coming

14:25 his beauty: Like David, Absalom is very handsome and able to steal the hearts of many (15:6). His hair is remarkable but also a factor in his death (18:9). Earlier, God warned about using beauty as a mark of a good king (1 Sam 16:7).

[a] Meaning of Heb uncertain

into the king's presence. [29]Then Absalom sent for Joab to send him to the king; but Joab would not come to him. He sent a second time, but Joab would not come. [30]Then he said to his servants, "Look, Joab's field is next to mine, and he has barley there; go and set it on fire." So Absalom's servants set the field on fire. [31]Then Joab rose and went to Absalom at his house, and said to him, "Why have your servants set my field on fire?" [32]Absalom answered Joab, "Look, I sent word to you: Come here, that I may send you to the king with the question, 'Why have I come from Geshur? It would be better for me to be there still.' Now let me go into the king's presence; if there is guilt in me, let him kill me!" [33]Then Joab went to the king and told him; and he summoned Absalom. So he came to the king and prostrated himself with his face to the ground before the king; and the king kissed Absalom.

14:33 the king kissed Absalom: David's kiss is a public act of welcome, forgiveness, and pardon.

Absalom Usurps the Throne

15 After this Absalom got himself a chariot and horses, and fifty men to run ahead of him. [2]Absalom used to rise early and stand beside the road into the gate; and when anyone brought a suit before the king for judgment, Absalom would call out and say, "From what city are you?" When the person said, "Your servant is of such and such a tribe in Israel," [3]Absalom would say, "See, your claims are good and right; but there is no one deputed by the king to hear you." [4]Absalom said moreover, "If only I were judge in the land! Then all who had a suit or cause might come to me, and I would give them justice." [5]Whenever people came near to do obeisance to him, he would put out his hand and take hold of them, and kiss them. [6]Thus Absalom did to every Israelite who came to the king for judgment; so Absalom stole the hearts of the people of Israel.

15:1-12 Absalom got himself a chariot and horses: This is how royalty travels. Absalom steals the hearts, the minds, and the will of the people. He provides justice at the gate of the palace when David does not. All ambition and little faith, he uses a religious ceremony at Hebron to have himself declared king (15:4-13).

7 At the end of four[a] years Absalom said to the king, "Please let me go to Hebron and pay the vow that I have made to the LORD. [8]For your servant made a vow while I lived at Geshur in Aram: If the LORD will indeed bring me back to Jerusalem, then I will worship the LORD in Hebron."[b] [9]The king said to him, "Go in peace." So he got up, and went to Hebron. [10]But Absalom sent secret messengers throughout all the tribes of Israel, saying, "As soon as you hear the sound of the trumpet, then shout: Absalom has become king at Hebron!" [11]Two hundred men from Jerusalem went with Absalom; they were invited guests, and they went in their innocence, knowing nothing of the matter. [12]While Absalom was offering the sacrifices, he sent for[c] Ahithophel the Gilonite, David's counselor, from his city Giloh. The conspiracy grew in strength, and the people with Absalom kept increasing.

15:12 Ahithopel: This name suggests foolishness, perhaps an answer to David's prayer in 15:31.

---

[a] Gk Syr: Heb *forty* [b] Gk Mss: Heb lacks *in Hebron* [c] Or *he sent*

David Flees from Jerusalem

13 A messenger came to David, saying, "The hearts of the Israelites have gone after Absalom." [14]Then David said to all his officials who
were with him at Jerusalem, "Get up! Let us flee, or there will be no
escape for us from Absalom. Hurry, or he will soon overtake us, and
bring disaster down upon us, and attack the city with the edge of the
sword." [15]The king's officials said to the king, "Your servants are ready
to do whatever our lord the king decides." [16]So the king left, followed
by all his household, except ten concubines whom he left behind to
look after the house. [17]The king left, followed by all the people; and
they stopped at the last house. [18]All his officials passed by him; and all
the Cherethites, and all the Pelethites, and all the six hundred Gittites
who had followed him from Gath, passed on before the king.

19 Then the king said to Ittai the Gittite, "Why are you also coming with us? Go back, and stay with the king; for you are a foreigner,
and also an exile from your home. [20]You came only yesterday, and
shall I today make you wander about with us, while I go wherever
I can? Go back, and take your kinsfolk with you; and may the LORD
show[a] steadfast love and faithfulness to you." [21]But Ittai answered the
king, "As the LORD lives, and as my lord the king lives, wherever my
lord the king may be, whether for death or for life, there also your
servant will be." [22]David said to Ittai, "Go then, march on." So Ittai the
Gittite marched on, with all his men and all the little ones who were
with him. [23]The whole country wept aloud as all the people passed
by; the king crossed the Wadi Kidron, and all the people moved on
toward the wilderness.

24 Abiathar came up, and Zadok also, with all the Levites, carrying the ark of the covenant of God. They set down the ark of God,
until the people had all passed out of the city. [25]Then the king said to
Zadok, "Carry the ark of God back into the city. If I find favor in the
eyes of the LORD, he will bring me back and let me see both it and
the place where it stays. [26]But if he says, 'I take no pleasure in you,'
here I am, let him do to me what seems good to him." [27]The king also
said to the priest Zadok, "Look,[b] go back to the city in peace, you and
Abiathar,[c] with your two sons, Ahimaaz your son, and Jonathan son
of Abiathar. [28]See, I will wait at the fords of the wilderness until word
comes from you to inform me." [29]So Zadok and Abiathar carried the
ark of God back to Jerusalem, and they remained there.

30 But David went up the ascent of the Mount of Olives, weeping
as he went, with his head covered and walking barefoot; and all the
people who were with him covered their heads and went up, weeping as they went. [31]David was told that Ahithophel was among the

15:14-18 Let us flee: Absalom has the popular backing of the people; David has his bodyguard, the Cherethites and Pelethites, and paid mercenaries. The Philistine Gittites follow out of loyalty. This is a twenty-six mile trek to the Jordan River.

15:20 steadfast love and faithfulness: God has promised this, and David relies on it in his journey to the Jordan (see also 7:15). He refuses to test God by bringing the ark to protect himself (15:25-26). He humbly prays and worships on the Mount of Olives (15:30-32). He even hears God's voice in the curses of Shimei (16:10-11). In this time of extreme danger, David continues to hope in God (16:12). This is like the faithful Samuel who, long ago, courageously worshiped and prayed with the Philistine army bearing down on Israel (1 Sam 7:7-10). Later, Jesus will go to the Mount of Olives to pray in time of danger and betrayal and will trust in God alone (Matt 26:30-39).

---

[a] Gk Compare 2.6: Heb lacks *may the LORD show* [b] Gk: Heb *Are you a seer* or *Do you see?* [c] Cn: Heb lacks *and Abiathar*

conspirators with Absalom. And David said, "O LORD, I pray you,
turn the counsel of Ahithophel into foolishness."

Hushai Becomes David's Spy

32 When David came to the summit, where God was worshiped,
Hushai the Archite came to meet him with his coat torn and earth
on his head. 33 David said to him, "If you go on with me, you will be
a burden to me. 34 But if you return to the city and say to Absalom, 'I
will be your servant, O king; as I have been your father's servant in
time past, so now I will be your servant,' then you will defeat for me
the counsel of Ahithophel. 35 The priests Zadok and Abiathar will be
with you there. So whatever you hear from the king's house, tell it to
the priests Zadok and Abiathar. 36 Their two sons are with them there,
Zadok's son Ahimaaz and Abiathar's son Jonathan; and by them you
shall report to me everything you hear." 37 So Hushai, David's friend,
came into the city, just as Absalom was entering Jerusalem.

David's Adversaries

16 When David had passed a little beyond the summit, Ziba the
servant of Mephibosheth[a] met him, with a couple of donkeys
saddled, carrying two hundred loaves of bread, one hundred bunches
of raisins, one hundred of summer fruits, and one skin of wine. 2 The
king said to Ziba, "Why have you brought these?" Ziba answered,
"The donkeys are for the king's household to ride, the bread and
summer fruit for the young men to eat, and the wine is for those to
drink who faint in the wilderness." 3 The king said, "And where is your
master's son?" Ziba said to the king, "He remains in Jerusalem; for he
said, 'Today the house of Israel will give me back my grandfather's
kingdom.'" 4 Then the king said to Ziba, "All that belonged to Mephibosheth[a] is now yours." Ziba said, "I do obeisance; let me find favor in
your sight, my lord the king."

Shimei Curses David

5 When King David came to Bahurim, a man of the family of the
house of Saul came out whose name was Shimei son of Gera; he came
out cursing. 6 He threw stones at David and at all the servants of King
David; now all the people and all the warriors were on his right and
on his left. 7 Shimei shouted while he cursed, "Out! Out! Murderer!
Scoundrel! 8 The LORD has avenged on all of you the blood of the
house of Saul, in whose place you have reigned; and the LORD has
given the kingdom into the hand of your son Absalom. See, disaster
has overtaken you; for you are a man of blood."
9 Then Abishai son of Zeruiah said to the king, "Why should this

15:37 Hushai, David's friend: This means more than a pal. Hushai is a trusted adviser and high ranking military officer.

16:1-4 Ziba: Ziba looks out for himself. His gifts are lavish and his story doubtful. Later Mephibosheth will disagree (see 19:27-29).

16:5-8 Shimei: He is just one of many still loyal to Saul's household. David's enemies hold him responsible for the deaths of Abner, Ishbaal, and perhaps Uriah (see 3:26-27; 4:5-8; 11:14-15). Shimei's words remind us of Nathan's judgment: trouble in David's house and his wives taken by another (see 12:11). Absalom fulfills Nathan's warnings (16:22).

16:9 Abishai: This loyal nephew of David is quick to kill. He and his brother Joab represent what is rash and violent in this monarchy (see 1 Sam 26:9-11; 2 Sam 18:9-15).

[a] Or *Merib-baal*: See 4.4 note

dead dog curse my lord the king? Let me go over and take off his
head." 10But the king said, "What have I to do with you, you sons of
Zeruiah? If he is cursing because the LORD has said to him, 'Curse
David,' who then shall say, 'Why have you done so?' " 11David said
to Abishai and to all his servants, "My own son seeks my life; how
much more now may this Benjaminite! Let him alone, and let him
curse; for the LORD has bidden him. 12It may be that the LORD will
look on my distress,[a] and the LORD will repay me with good for this
cursing of me today." 13So David and his men went on the road, while
Shimei went along on the hillside opposite him and cursed as he
went, throwing stones and flinging dust at him. 14The king and all
the people who were with him arrived weary at the Jordan;[b] and
there he refreshed himself.

The Counsel of Ahithophel

15 Now Absalom and all the Israelites[c] came to Jerusalem; Ahithophel was with him. 16When Hushai the Archite, David's friend, came
to Absalom, Hushai said to Absalom, "Long live the king! Long live
the king!" 17Absalom said to Hushai, "Is this your loyalty to your
friend? Why did you not go with your friend?" 18Hushai said to Absalom, "No; but the one whom the LORD and this people and all
the Israelites have chosen, his I will be, and with him I will remain.
19Moreover, whom should I serve? Should it not be his son? Just as I
have served your father, so I will serve you."

20 Then Absalom said to Ahithophel, "Give us your counsel;
what shall we do?" 21Ahithophel said to Absalom, "Go in to your father's concubines, the ones he has left to look after the house; and
all Israel will hear that you have made yourself odious to your father,
and the hands of all who are with you will be strengthened." 22So they
pitched a tent for Absalom upon the roof; and Absalom went in to his
father's concubines in the sight of all Israel. 23Now in those days the
counsel that Ahithophel gave was as if one consulted the oracle[d] of
God; so all the counsel of Ahithophel was esteemed, both by David
and by Absalom.

17 Moreover Ahithophel said to Absalom, "Let me choose
twelve thousand men, and I will set out and pursue David tonight. 2I will come upon him while he is weary and discouraged, and
throw him into a panic; and all the people who are with him will flee.
I will strike down only the king, 3and I will bring all the people back
to you as a bride comes home to her husband. You seek the life of only
one man,[e] and all the people will be at peace." 4The advice pleased Absalom and all the elders of Israel.

17:1-4 I will…pursue David tonight: Ahithophel's plan is a good one. It intends to be swift, have few casualties, and cause little disruption of Israel's life.

[a] Gk Vg: Heb *iniquity* [b] Gk: Heb lacks *at the Jordan* [c] Gk: Heb *all the people, the men of Israel*
[d] Heb *word* [e] Gk: Heb *like the return of the whole (is) the man whom you seek*

The Counsel of Hushai

5 Then Absalom said, “Call Hushai the Archite also, and let us
hear too what he has to say.” 6When Hushai came to Absalom, Absalom said to him, “This is what Ahithophel has said; shall we do as
he advises? If not, you tell us.” 7Then Hushai said to Absalom, “This
time the counsel that Ahithophel has given is not good.” 8Hushai
continued, “You know that your father and his men are warriors, and
that they are enraged, like a bear robbed of her cubs in the field. Besides, your father is expert in war; he will not spend the night with
the troops. 9Even now he has hidden himself in one of the pits, or in
some other place. And when some of our troops[a] fall at the first attack, whoever hears it will say, ‘There has been a slaughter among the
troops who follow Absalom.’ 10Then even the valiant warrior, whose
heart is like the heart of a lion, will utterly melt with fear; for all Israel
knows that your father is a warrior, and that those who are with him
are valiant warriors. 11But my counsel is that all Israel be gathered to
you, from Dan to Beer-sheba, like the sand by the sea for multitude,
and that you go to battle in person. 12So we shall come upon him in
whatever place he may be found, and we shall light on him as the dew
falls on the ground; and he will not survive, nor will any of those with
him. 13If he withdraws into a city, then all Israel will bring ropes to that
city, and we shall drag it into the valley, until not even a pebble is to be
found there.” 14Absalom and all the men of Israel said, “The counsel of
Hushai the Archite is better than the counsel of Ahithophel.” For the
LORD had ordained to defeat the good counsel of Ahithophel, so that
the LORD might bring ruin on Absalom.

17:7-13 the counsel that Ahithophel has given is not good: Hushai is being ambiguous again (see 16:16). He pretends to care about Absalom, but he really means that Ahithophel's plan is not good for David. To buy David time, Hushai lays out a grand plan with an all-Israelite draft (17:11) and much killing (17:12). He plays up David's experience (17:8-9) and strength (17:10), implying that Absalom needs more time to prepare for battle.

17:14 For the LORD had ordained: Why is Hushai's grand plan accepted over Ahithophel's superior one? God is quietly at work behind the scenes to protect David, the anointed king. Hushai is God's effective agent in this battle for leadership. God will keep God's promise to David and his house (see 7:10-17).

Hushai Warns David to Escape

15 Then Hushai said to the priests Zadok and Abiathar, “Thus
and so did Ahithophel counsel Absalom and the elders of Israel; and
thus and so I have counseled. 16Therefore send quickly and tell David,
‘Do not lodge tonight at the fords of the wilderness, but by all means
cross over; otherwise the king and all the people who are with him
will be swallowed up.’ ” 17Jonathan and Ahimaaz were waiting at En-
rogel; a servant-girl used to go and tell them, and they would go and
tell King David; for they could not risk being seen entering the city.
18But a boy saw them, and told Absalom; so both of them went away
quickly, and came to the house of a man at Bahurim, who had a well
in his courtyard; and they went down into it. 19The man's wife took a
covering, stretched it over the well's mouth, and spread out grain on
it; and nothing was known of it. 20When Absalom's servants came to
the woman at the house, they said, “Where are Ahimaaz and Jonathan?” The woman said to them, “They have crossed over the brook[b]

17:20 The woman said: Michal also lied to protect David (see 1 Sam 19:17). God works through others to continue to protect the anointed king.

---

[a] Gk Mss: Heb *some of them* [b] Meaning of Heb uncertain

of water." And when they had searched and could not find them, they
returned to Jerusalem.

21 After they had gone, the men came up out of the well, and
went and told King David. They said to David, "Go and cross the
water quickly; for thus and so has Ahithophel counseled against you."
22 So David and all the people who were with him set out and crossed
the Jordan; by daybreak not one was left who had not crossed the
Jordan.

23 When Ahithophel saw that his counsel was not followed, he
saddled his donkey and went off home to his own city. He set his
house in order, and hanged himself; he died and was buried in the
tomb of his father.

24 Then David came to Mahanaim, while Absalom crossed the
Jordan with all the men of Israel. 25 Now Absalom had set Amasa over
the army in the place of Joab. Amasa was the son of a man named Ithra
the Ishmaelite,[a] who had married Abigal daughter of Nahash, sister
of Zeruiah, Joab's mother. 26 The Israelites and Absalom encamped in
the land of Gilead.

17:25 Amasa: This cousin of Joab will later serve in David's army (see 19:13).

27 When David came to Mahanaim, Shobi son of Nahash from
Rabbah of the Ammonites, and Machir son of Ammiel from Lo-debar, and Barzillai the Gileadite from Rogelim, 28 brought beds, basins,
and earthen vessels, wheat, barley, meal, parched grain, beans and lentils,[b] 29 honey and curds, sheep, and cheese from the herd, for David
and the people with him to eat; for they said, "The troops are hungry
and weary and thirsty in the wilderness."

17:27 Mahanaim: This was Saul's son Ishbaal's well-fortified capital. Several non-Israelite leaders support David here.

The Defeat and Death of Absalom

18 Then David mustered the men who were with him, and set
over them commanders of thousands and commanders of
hundreds. 2 And David divided the army into three groups:[c] one third
under the command of Joab, one third under the command of Abishai
son of Zeruiah, Joab's brother, and one third under the command of
Ittai the Gittite. The king said to the men, "I myself will also go out
with you." 3 But the men said, "You shall not go out. For if we flee, they
will not care about us. If half of us die, they will not care about us. But
you are worth ten thousand of us;[d] therefore it is better that you send
us help from the city." 4 The king said to them, "Whatever seems best
to you I will do." So the king stood at the side of the gate, while all the
army marched out by hundreds and by thousands. 5 The king ordered
Joab and Abishai and Ittai, saying, "Deal gently for my sake with the
young man Absalom." And all the people heard when the king gave
orders to all the commanders concerning Absalom.

18:1-8 David mustered the men: Hushai bought David time to reorganize, strategize, and pick the place of battle. This is wooded hill country with dense underbrush and dangerous, rocky terrain. David asks officers and army to "deal gently," or protect, Absalom (18:5).

---

[a] 1 Chr 2.17: Heb *Israelite* [b] Heb *and lentils and parched grain* [c] Gk: Heb *sent forth the army* [d] Gk Vg Symmachus: Heb *for now there are ten thousand such as we*

6 So the army went out into the field against Israel; and the battle was fought in the forest of Ephraim. 7 The men of Israel were defeated there by the servants of David, and the slaughter there was great on that day, twenty thousand men. 8 The battle spread over the face of all the country; and the forest claimed more victims that day than the sword.

18:9-18 between heaven and earth: A mule is a royal mount. Absalom's head is caught in the branches of an oak, and the mule continues on. His hair, seen as a mark of beauty and strength, leads to his helplessness and death (see 14:26). He hangs between life and death.

9 Absalom happened to meet the servants of David. Absalom was riding on his mule, and the mule went under the thick branches of a great oak. His head caught fast in the oak, and he was left hanging[a] between heaven and earth, while the mule that was under him went on. 10 A man saw it, and told Joab, "I saw Absalom hanging in an oak." 11 Joab said to the man who told him, "What, you saw him! Why then did you not strike him there to the ground? I would have been glad to give you ten pieces of silver and a belt." 12 But the man said to Joab, "Even if I felt in my hand the weight of a thousand pieces of silver, I would not raise my hand against the king's son; for in our hearing the king commanded you and Abishai and Ittai, saying: For my sake protect the young man Absalom! 13 On the other hand, if I had dealt treacherously against his life[b] (and there is nothing hidden from the king), then you yourself would have stood aloof." 14 Joab said, "I will not waste time like this with you." He took three spears in his hand, and thrust them into the heart of Absalom, while he was still alive in the oak. 15 And ten young men, Joab's armor-bearers, surrounded Absalom and struck him, and killed him.

18:17 a very great heap of stones: Joab violates David's command not to harm Absalom, then he violates Absalom himself. This is a shameful, brutal burial (see Josh 7:25-26; 8:29).

16 Then Joab sounded the trumpet, and the troops came back from pursuing Israel, for Joab restrained the troops. 17 They took Absalom, threw him into a great pit in the forest, and raised over him a very great heap of stones. Meanwhile all the Israelites fled to their homes. 18 Now Absalom in his lifetime had taken and set up for himself a pillar that is in the King's Valley, for he said, "I have no son to keep my name in remembrance"; he called the pillar by his own name. It is called Absalom's Monument to this day.

David Hears of Absalom's Death

19 Then Ahimaaz son of Zadok said, "Let me run, and carry tidings to the king that the LORD has delivered him from the power of his enemies." 20 Joab said to him, "You are not to carry tidings today; you may carry tidings another day, but today you shall not do so, because the king's son is dead." 21 Then Joab said to a Cushite, "Go, tell the king what you have seen." The Cushite bowed before Joab, and ran. 22 Then Ahimaaz son of Zadok said again to Joab, "Come what may, let me also run after the Cushite." And Joab said, "Why will you run, my son, seeing that you have no reward[c] for the tidings?" 23 "Come what may,"

---

[a] Gk Syr Tg: Heb *was put* [b] Another reading is *at the risk of my life* [c] Meaning of Heb uncertain

he said, "I will run." So he said to him, "Run." Then Ahimaaz ran by
the way of the Plain, and outran the Cushite.

24 Now David was sitting between the two gates. The sentinel
went up to the roof of the gate by the wall, and when he looked up,
he saw a man running alone. 25 The sentinel shouted and told the king.
The king said, "If he is alone, there are tidings in his mouth." He kept
coming, and drew near. 26 Then the sentinel saw another man running;
and the sentinel called to the gatekeeper and said, "See, another man
running alone!" The king said, "He also is bringing tidings." 27 The sentinel said, "I think the running of the first one is like the running of
Ahimaaz son of Zadok." The king said, "He is a good man, and comes
with good tidings."

28 Then Ahimaaz cried out to the king, "All is well!" He prostrated himself before the king with his face to the ground, and said,
"Blessed be the LORD your God, who has delivered up the men who
raised their hand against my lord the king." 29 The king said, "Is it well
with the young man Absalom?" Ahimaaz answered, "When Joab sent
your servant,[a] I saw a great tumult, but I do not know what it was."
30 The king said, "Turn aside, and stand here." So he turned aside, and
stood still.

31 Then the Cushite came; and the Cushite said, "Good tidings
for my lord the king! For the LORD has vindicated you this day, delivering you from the power of all who rose up against you." 32 The king
said to the Cushite, "Is it well with the young man Absalom?" The
Cushite answered, "May the enemies of my lord the king, and all who
rise up to do you harm, be like that young man."

David Mourns for Absalom

33[b] The king was deeply moved, and went up to the chamber
over the gate, and wept; and as he went, he said, "O my son Absalom,
my son, my son Absalom! Would I had died instead of you, O Absalom, my son, my son!"

19 It was told Joab, "The king is weeping and mourning for Absalom." 2 So the victory that day was turned into mourning
for all the troops; for the troops heard that day, "The king is grieving
for his son." 3 The troops stole into the city that day as soldiers steal in
who are ashamed when they flee in battle. 4 The king covered his face,
and the king cried with a loud voice, "O my son Absalom, O Absalom, my son, my son!" 5 Then Joab came into the house to the king,
and said, "Today you have covered with shame the faces of all your
officers who have saved your life today, and the lives of your sons and
your daughters, and the lives of your wives and your concubines, 6 for
love of those who hate you and for hatred of those who love you. You

18:33 O my son Absalom: David is in deep, unchecked grief. His troubled relationship with this second-born son costs him dearly, both personally and publicly (see 14:28-33). Once he would not even see Absalom, but now he repeatedly calls him "my son."

19:1-8 Joab: This reckless, violent commander and nephew of David is very practical. He confronts David, the grieving father, to force him back into his kingly role, and so saves the kingdom.

[a] Heb *the king's servant, your servant* [b] Ch 19.1 in Heb

have made it clear today that commanders and officers are nothing to you; for I perceive that if Absalom were alive and all of us were dead today, then you would be pleased. 7 So go out at once and speak kindly to your servants; for I swear by the LORD, if you do not go, not a man will stay with you this night; and this will be worse for you than any disaster that has come upon you from your youth until now." 8 Then the king got up and took his seat in the gate. The troops were all told, "See, the king is sitting in the gate"; and all the troops came before the king.

David Recalled to Jerusalem

Meanwhile, all the Israelites had fled to their homes. 9 All the people were disputing throughout all the tribes of Israel, saying, "The king delivered us from the hand of our enemies, and saved us from the hand of the Philistines; and now he has fled out of the land because of Absalom. 10 But Absalom, whom we anointed over us, is dead in battle. Now therefore why do you say nothing about bringing the king back?"

19:11-30 King David sent: Back in action, David is a merciful victor and eager to mend fences to keep Israel united. Amasa and Shimei, from Judah and allies of the Saul party, are welcomed and forgiven. David mediates the dispute between Ziba and Mephibosheth and manages to keep his covenant promise to Jonathan and Saul (see 1 Sam 20:14-17; 24:21-22).

11 King David sent this message to the priests Zadok and Abiathar, "Say to the elders of Judah, 'Why should you be the last to bring the king back to his house? The talk of all Israel has come to the king.[a] 12 You are my kin, you are my bone and my flesh; why then should you be the last to bring back the king?' 13 And say to Amasa, 'Are you not my bone and my flesh? So may God do to me, and more, if you are not the commander of my army from now on, in place of Joab.' " 14 Amasa[b] swayed the hearts of all the people of Judah as one, and they sent word to the king, "Return, both you and all your servants." 15 So the king came back to the Jordan; and Judah came to Gilgal to meet the king and to bring him over the Jordan.

16 Shimei son of Gera, the Benjaminite, from Bahurim, hurried to come down with the people of Judah to meet King David; 17 with him were a thousand people from Benjamin. And Ziba, the servant of the house of Saul, with his fifteen sons and his twenty servants, rushed down to the Jordan ahead of the king, 18 while the crossing was taking place,[c] to bring over the king's household, and to do his pleasure.

David's Mercy to Shimei

Shimei son of Gera fell down before the king, as he was about to cross the Jordan, 19 and said to the king, "May my lord not hold me guilty or remember how your servant did wrong on the day my lord the king left Jerusalem; may the king not bear it in mind. 20 For your servant knows that I have sinned; therefore, see, I have come this day, the first of all the house of Joseph to come down to meet my lord

---

[a] Gk: Heb *to the king, to his house* [b] Heb *He* [c] Cn: Heb *the ford crossed*

the king." 21 Abishai son of Zeruiah answered, "Shall not Shimei be put to death for this, because he cursed the LORD's anointed?" 22 But David said, "What have I to do with you, you sons of Zeruiah, that you should today become an adversary to me? Shall anyone be put to death in Israel this day? For do I not know that I am this day king over Israel?" 23 The king said to Shimei, "You shall not die." And the king gave him his oath.

David and Mephibosheth Meet

24 Mephibosheth[a] grandson of Saul came down to meet the king; he had not taken care of his feet, or trimmed his beard, or washed his clothes, from the day the king left until the day he came back in safety. 25 When he came from Jerusalem to meet the king, the king said to him, "Why did you not go with me, Mephibosheth?"[a] 26 He answered, "My lord, O king, my servant deceived me; for your servant said to him, 'Saddle a donkey for me,[b] so that I may ride on it and go with the king.' For your servant is lame. 27 He has slandered your servant to my lord the king. But my lord the king is like the angel of God; do therefore what seems good to you. 28 For all my father's house were doomed to death before my lord the king; but you set your servant among those who eat at your table. What further right have I, then, to appeal to the king?" 29 The king said to him, "Why speak any more of your affairs? I have decided: you and Ziba shall divide the land." 30 Mephibosheth[a] said to the king, "Let him take it all, since my lord the king has arrived home safely."

David's Kindness to Barzillai

31 Now Barzillai the Gileadite had come down from Rogelim; he went on with the king to the Jordan, to escort him over the Jordan. 32 Barzillai was a very aged man, eighty years old. He had provided the king with food while he stayed at Mahanaim, for he was a very wealthy man. 33 The king said to Barzillai, "Come over with me, and I will provide for you in Jerusalem at my side." 34 But Barzillai said to the king, "How many years have I still to live, that I should go up with the king to Jerusalem? 35 Today I am eighty years old; can I discern what is pleasant and what is not? Can your servant taste what he eats or what he drinks? Can I still listen to the voice of singing men and singing women? Why then should your servant be an added burden to my lord the king? 36 Your servant will go a little way over the Jordan with the king. Why should the king recompense me with such a reward? 37 Please let your servant return, so that I may die in my own town, near the graves of my father and my mother. But here is your servant Chimham; let him go over with my lord the king; and do for

19:31 Barzillai: David is eager to have this non-Israelite, or Barzillai's sons, in his government. He will remember Barzillai's loyalty on his deathbed (see 1 Kgs 2:7).

---

[a] Or *Merib-baal*: See 4.4 note [b] Gk Syr Vg: Heb *said, 'I will saddle a donkey for myself*

him whatever seems good to you." [38]The king answered, "Chimham shall go over with me, and I will do for him whatever seems good to you; and all that you desire of me I will do for you." [39]Then all the people crossed over the Jordan, and the king crossed over; the king kissed Barzillai and blessed him, and he returned to his own home. [40]The king went on to Gilgal, and Chimham went on with him; all the people of Judah, and also half the people of Israel, brought the king on his way.

41 Then all the people of Israel came to the king, and said to him, "Why have our kindred the people of Judah stolen you away, and brought the king and his household over the Jordan, and all David's men with him?" [42]All the people of Judah answered the people of Israel, "Because the king is near of kin to us. Why then are you angry over this matter? Have we eaten at all at the king's expense? Or has he given us any gift?" [43]But the people of Israel answered the people of Judah, "We have ten shares in the king, and in David also we have more than you. Why then did you despise us? Were we not the first to speak of bringing back our king?" But the words of the people of Judah were fiercer than the words of the people of Israel.

19:43 the words of the people of Judah were fiercer: This civil war gives new life and power to old rivalries between Israel (north) and Judah (south). David's kingdom is in danger of splitting up.

The Rebellion of Sheba

20:1 a Benjaminite: This northern tribe, loyal to Saul, has been unhappy with David (see 1 Sam 9:1-2; 2 Sam 16:5-8).

20:1 Everyone to your tents: This is a call to desert David's army and return home.

20 Now a scoundrel named Sheba son of Bichri, a Benjaminite, happened to be there. He sounded the trumpet and cried out,

"We have no portion in David,
no share in the son of Jesse!
Everyone to your tents, O Israel!"

[2]So all the people of Israel withdrew from David and followed Sheba son of Bichri; but the people of Judah followed their king steadfastly from the Jordan to Jerusalem.

20:3 the ten concubines: David had followed the practice of having several women as wives (concubines). This verse seems to be a comment on the fact that his son Absalom had sex with David's concubines earlier (16:21-22). This would have been humiliating for David, but it is not clear that this is the reason David had the concubines put under guard and never again had sexual relations with any of them. Perhaps he didn't trust them or didn't want to have additional sons by them who might betray him.

3 David came to his house at Jerusalem; and the king took the ten concubines whom he had left to look after the house, and put them in a house under guard, and provided for them, but did not go in to them. So they were shut up until the day of their death, living as if in widowhood.

4 Then the king said to Amasa, "Call the men of Judah together to me within three days, and be here yourself." [5]So Amasa went to summon Judah; but he delayed beyond the set time that had been appointed him. [6]David said to Abishai, "Now Sheba son of Bichri will do us more harm than Absalom; take your lord's servants and pursue him, or he will find fortified cities for himself, and escape from us." [7]Joab's men went out after him, along with the Cherethites, the Pelethites, and all the warriors; they went out from Jerusalem to pursue Sheba son of Bichri. [8]When they were at the large stone that is in Gibeon, Amasa came to meet them. Now Joab was wearing a soldier's

garment and over it was a belt with a sword in its sheath fastened at
his waist; as he went forward it fell out. 9 Joab said to Amasa, "Is it well
with you, my brother?" And Joab took Amasa by the beard with his
right hand to kiss him. 10 But Amasa did not notice the sword in Joab's
hand; Joab struck him in the belly so that his entrails poured out on
the ground, and he died. He did not strike a second blow.

Then Joab and his brother Abishai pursued Sheba son of Bichri.
11 And one of Joab's men took his stand by Amasa, and said, "Whoever
favors Joab, and whoever is for David, let him follow Joab." 12 Amasa
lay wallowing in his blood on the highway, and the man saw that all
the people were stopping. Since he saw that all who came by him were
stopping, he carried Amasa from the highway into a field, and threw a
garment over him. 13 Once he was removed from the highway, all the
people went on after Joab to pursue Sheba son of Bichri.

20:9 Joab took Amasa by the beard: It is traditional to greet a fellow officer with a kiss. Later, Joab will pay for his crimes (see 1 Kgs 2:5-6, 31-34).

14 Sheba[a] passed through all the tribes of Israel to Abel of Beth-
maacah;[b] and all the Bichrites[c] assembled, and followed him inside.
15 Joab's forces[d] came and besieged him in Abel of Beth-maacah; they
threw up a siege ramp against the city, and it stood against the rampart. Joab's forces were battering the wall to break it down. 16 Then a
wise woman called from the city, "Listen! Listen! Tell Joab, 'Come
here, I want to speak to you.'" 17 He came near her; and the woman
said, "Are you Joab?" He answered, "I am." Then she said to him,
"Listen to the words of your servant." He answered, "I am listening."
18 Then she said, "They used to say in the old days, 'Let them inquire
at Abel'; and so they would settle a matter. 19 I am one of those who
are peaceable and faithful in Israel; you seek to destroy a city that
is a mother in Israel; why will you swallow up the heritage of the
LORD?" 20 Joab answered, "Far be it from me, far be it, that I should
swallow up or destroy! 21 That is not the case! But a man of the hill
country of Ephraim, called Sheba son of Bichri, has lifted up his hand
against King David; give him up alone, and I will withdraw from the
city." The woman said to Joab, "His head shall be thrown over the
wall to you." 22 Then the woman went to all the people with her wise
plan. And they cut off the head of Sheba son of Bichri, and threw it
out to Joab. So he blew the trumpet, and they dispersed from the
city, and all went to their homes, while Joab returned to Jerusalem to
the king.

20:16-22 a wise woman called: Wise means skilled in persuasive speech. This woman's words of peace, respect for Israel's heritage, and the welfare of the people are a direct contrast to Joab's ruthless plans to destroy this northern city. Samuel warned that a king would create large armies and take much from the people (see 1 Sam 8:10-12). It is surprising that in this chapter dominated by war and killing, the wise woman's words of peace win out. God is working behind the scenes.

23 Now Joab was in command of all the army of Israel;[e] Benaiah
son of Jehoiada was in command of the Cherethites and the Pelethites;
24 Adoram was in charge of the forced labor; Jehoshaphat son of Ahilud was the recorder; 25 Sheva was secretary; Zadok and Abiathar were
priests; 26 and Ira the Jairite was also David's priest.

20:23-26 in command: David is in control (see 2 Sam 8:15-18). But, it is costly. A large army and forced labor spell danger for the welfare of Israel. Samuel warned of this (1 Sam 8:15-18).

---

[a] Heb *He* [b] Compare 20.15: Heb *and Beth-maacah* [c] Compare Gk Vg: Heb *Berites* [d] Heb *They*
[e] Cn: Heb *Joab to all the army, Israel*

21:1-22 Now there was a famine: This inserted material was collected from many different sources. It is loosely related to the chapters around it.

21:1 bloodguilt on Saul: There is no evidence of Saul killing these resident aliens of Israel. Some believe that he may have violated a long-held treaty with the Gibeonites (see Josh 9:3-27).

21:9 they impaled them on the mountain: The exact form of execution is not clear, but it may have been hanging or perhaps crucifixion. The main point was that the bodies were to be displayed publicly before God and the eyes of others.

21:10-14 Then Rizpah: She is center stage in this brutal story. Her protection of the bodies shows grief, steadfast devotion and love—godly behavior. This influences David to honor the bones of Saul, Jonathan, and the slain sons. Other women, such as Abigail and the two wise women, have been voices of peace and compassion in David's life (see 1 Sam 25:25-31; 2 Sam 14:1-17; 20:16-19). They join together to call for mercy in personal and public matters. Note that God's gift of rain comes in response to Rizpah's public devotion and David's honoring those who were killed.

David Avenges the Gibeonites

21 Now there was a famine in the days of David for three years, year after year; and David inquired of the LORD. The LORD said, “There is bloodguilt on Saul and on his house, because he put the Gibeonites to death.” [2]So the king called the Gibeonites and spoke to them. (Now the Gibeonites were not of the people of Israel, but of the remnant of the Amorites; although the people of Israel had sworn to spare them, Saul had tried to wipe them out in his zeal for the people of Israel and Judah.) [3]David said to the Gibeonites, “What shall I do for you? How shall I make expiation, that you may bless the heritage of the LORD?” [4]The Gibeonites said to him, “It is not a matter of silver or gold between us and Saul or his house; neither is it for us to put anyone to death in Israel.” He said, “What do you say that I should do for you?” [5]They said to the king, “The man who consumed us and planned to destroy us, so that we should have no place in all the territory of Israel— [6]let seven of his sons be handed over to us, and we will impale them before the LORD at Gibeon on the mountain of the LORD.”[a] The king said, “I will hand them over.”

7 But the king spared Mephibosheth,[b] the son of Saul's son Jonathan, because of the oath of the LORD that was between them, between David and Jonathan son of Saul. [8]The king took the two sons of Rizpah daughter of Aiah, whom she bore to Saul, Armoni and Mephibosheth;[b] and the five sons of Merab[c] daughter of Saul, whom she bore to Adriel son of Barzillai the Meholathite; [9]he gave them into the hands of the Gibeonites, and they impaled them on the mountain before the LORD. The seven of them perished together. They were put to death in the first days of harvest, at the beginning of barley harvest.

10 Then Rizpah the daughter of Aiah took sackcloth, and spread it on a rock for herself, from the beginning of harvest until rain fell on them from the heavens; she did not allow the birds of the air to come on the bodies[d] by day, or the wild animals by night. [11]When David was told what Rizpah daughter of Aiah, the concubine of Saul, had done, [12]David went and took the bones of Saul and the bones of his son Jonathan from the people of Jabesh-gilead, who had stolen them from the public square of Beth-shan, where the Philistines had hung them up, on the day the Philistines killed Saul on Gilboa. [13]He brought up from there the bones of Saul and the bones of his son Jonathan; and they gathered the bones of those who had been impaled. [14]They buried the bones of Saul and of his son Jonathan in the land of Benjamin in Zela, in the tomb of his father Kish; they did all that the king commanded. After that, God heeded supplications for the land.

---

[a] Cn Compare Gk and 21.9: Heb *at Gibeah of Saul, the chosen of the LORD* [b] Or *Merib-baal*: See 4.4 note
[c] Two Heb Mss Syr Compare Gk: MT *Michal* [d] Heb *them*

Exploits of David's Men

15 The Philistines went to war again with Israel, and David went
down together with his servants. They fought against the Philistines,
and David grew weary. [16]Ishbi-benob, one of the descendants of the
giants, whose spear weighed three hundred shekels of bronze, and
who was fitted out with new weapons,[a] said he would kill David. [17]But
Abishai son of Zeruiah came to his aid, and attacked the Philistine
and killed him. Then David's men swore to him, "You shall not go
out with us to battle any longer, so that you do not quench the lamp
of Israel."

18 After this a battle took place with the Philistines, at Gob; then
Sibbecai the Hushathite killed Saph, who was one of the descendants
of the giants. [19]Then there was another battle with the Philistines at
Gob; and Elhanan son of Jaare-oregim, the Bethlehemite, killed Goliath the Gittite, the shaft of whose spear was like a weaver's beam.
[20]There was again war at Gath, where there was a man of great size,
who had six fingers on each hand, and six toes on each foot, twenty-
four in number; he too was descended from the giants. [21]When he
taunted Israel, Jonathan son of David's brother Shimei, killed him.
[22]These four were descended from the giants in Gath; they fell by the
hands of David and his servants.

21:15-22 The Philistines went to war again: This story is probably connected with early Philistine wars (see 5:17-25). This is a rare description of David as weary and needy.

21:19 Goliath: This probably is the same Goliath of 1 Samuel 17:23.

David's Song of Thanksgiving

22 David spoke to the LORD the words of this song on the day
when the LORD delivered him from the hand of all his enemies, and from the hand of Saul. [2]He said:

The LORD is my rock, my fortress, and my deliverer,
3 my God, my rock, in whom I take refuge,
my shield and the horn of my salvation,
my stronghold and my refuge,
my savior; you save me from violence.
4 I call upon the LORD, who is worthy to be praised,
and I am saved from my enemies.

5 For the waves of death encompassed me,
the torrents of perdition assailed me;
6 the cords of Sheol entangled me,
the snares of death confronted me.

7 In my distress I called upon the LORD;
to my God I called.
From his temple he heard my voice,
and my cry came to his ears.

22:1-51 David spoke to the LORD: This psalm of deliverance sounds two main themes: deliverance by God and the gratitude of David and Israel. Like Psalm 18, it is attributed to David and used in worship.

22:7 he heard my voice: David and Israel faithfully cried to God for help (see 1 Sam 1:10-17, 20). God faithfully answered (see 1 Sam 7:8-10; 12:18-21).

[a] Heb *was belted anew*

8 Then the earth reeled and rocked;
the foundations of the heavens trembled
and quaked, because he was angry.
9 Smoke went up from his nostrils,
and devouring fire from his mouth;
glowing coals flamed forth from him.
10 He bowed the heavens, and came down;
thick darkness was under his feet.
11 He rode on a cherub, and flew;
he was seen upon the wings of the wind.
12 He made darkness around him a canopy,
thick clouds, a gathering of water.
13 Out of the brightness before him
coals of fire flamed forth.
14 The LORD thundered from heaven;
the Most High uttered his voice.
15 He sent out arrows, and scattered them
—lightning, and routed them.
16 Then the channels of the sea were seen,
the foundations of the world were laid bare
at the rebuke of the LORD,
at the blast of the breath of his nostrils.

17 He reached from on high, he took me,
he drew me out of mighty waters.
18 He delivered me from my strong enemy,
from those who hated me;
for they were too mighty for me.
19 They came upon me in the day of my calamity,
but the LORD was my stay.
20 He brought me out into a broad place;
he delivered me, because he delighted in me.

22:18 He delivered me: Verses 8-20 use striking images of God to point to God's bold and powerful rescue of David and Israel. We find similar language elsewhere (see Exod 15; Pss 68; 74; 80; 114). Only God is more powerful than the danger and chaos in our world (see Gen 1; Mark 4:35-41).

22:21-28 The LORD rewarded me: Given David's sin against Bathsheba and Uriah, these verses highlight God's grace more than David's purity (see 2 Sam 11–12).

21 The LORD rewarded me according to my righteousness;
according to the cleanness of my hands he
recompensed me.
22 For I have kept the ways of the LORD,
and have not wickedly departed from my God.
23 For all his ordinances were before me,
and from his statutes I did not turn aside.
24 I was blameless before him,
and I kept myself from guilt.
25 Therefore the LORD has recompensed me according to my
righteousness,
according to my cleanness in his sight.

26 With the loyal you show yourself loyal;
with the blameless you show yourself blameless;
27 with the pure you show yourself pure,
and with the crooked you show yourself perverse.
28 You deliver a humble people,
but your eyes are upon the haughty to bring them down.
29 Indeed, you are my lamp, O LORD,
the LORD lightens my darkness.
30 By you I can crush a troop,
and by my God I can leap over a wall.
31 This God—his way is perfect;
the promise of the LORD proves true;
he is a shield for all who take refuge in him.

22:31 This God: David emphasizes that God is the source of his salvation (22:31, 33, 48).

32 For who is God, but the LORD?
And who is a rock, except our God?
33 The God who has girded me with strength[a]
has opened wide my path.[b]
34 He made my[c] feet like the feet of deer,
and set me secure on the heights.
35 He trains my hands for war,
so that my arms can bend a bow of bronze.
36 You have given me the shield of your salvation,
and your help[d] has made me great.
37 You have made me stride freely,
and my feet do not slip;
38 I pursued my enemies and destroyed them,
and did not turn back until they were consumed.
39 I consumed them; I struck them down, so that they did not rise;
they fell under my feet.
40 For you girded me with strength for the battle;
you made my assailants sink under me.
41 You made my enemies turn their backs to me,
those who hated me, and I destroyed them.
42 They looked, but there was no one to save them;
they cried to the LORD, but he did not answer them.
43 I beat them fine like the dust of the earth,
I crushed them and stamped them down like the mire of the streets.

22:33-46 The God who has girded me: God equipped David for battle and gave the nations over into his rule.

44 You delivered me from strife with the peoples;[e]
you kept me as the head of the nations;

---

[a] Q Ms Gk Syr Vg Compare Ps 18.32: MT *God is my strong refuge* [b] Meaning of Heb uncertain
[c] Another reading is *his* [d] Q Ms: MT *your answering* [e] Gk: Heb *from strife with my people*

22:47-51 The Lord lives! David expresses faith, gratitude, and joy, (as Hannah did) for God's deliverance and new life (see 1 Sam 2:1-10). God will give such gifts through Jesus (see John 10:10; 20:31; Luke 24:46-48).

What does it mean that God is both judge and merciful deliverer, and what does Luther's Large Catechism say about this? In the Conclusion to the Ten Commandments Luther writes that God takes the commandments very seriously and punishes those who break them. But greater than this is God's mercy and blessing for all who love and obey God. David sinned and was punished. David also threw himself on the mercy of God and was delivered. God's steadfast love saved David in spite of his sin. *2 Samuel 22:1-51*

How is God both judge and merciful deliverer for you?

23:1-7 the last words of David: This psalm partners with the one in 2 Samuel 22 and continues to summarize David's life as king. It and Hannah's song are like bookends for 1 and 2 Samuel (see 1 Sam 2:1-10).

23:1 the anointed: David is chosen by God and not self-made. Jesus Christ is also called God's "anointed" (see Luke 1:32, 2:11).

23:2-3 The spirit of the Lord: David is spirit-made to rule in obedience to God and for the welfare of the people. Jesus is Spirit-led to bring good news to the people (see Luke 4:1, 14-19).

23:5-7 an everlasting covenant: David is God-held in spite of everything (see 7:8-17). God's love is long-term (see Gen 9:16, 17:1-8; Isa 54:9-10). Such steadfast love comes through Jesus Christ (see John 3:16; Rom 5:6-11).

people whom I had not known served me.
45 Foreigners came cringing to me;
as soon as they heard of me, they obeyed me.
46 Foreigners lost heart,
and came trembling out of their strongholds.

47 The LORD lives! Blessed be my rock,
and exalted be my God, the rock of my salvation,
48 the God who gave me vengeance
and brought down peoples under me,
49 who brought me out from my enemies;
you exalted me above my adversaries,
you delivered me from the violent.

50 For this I will extol you, O LORD, among the nations,
and sing praises to your name.
51 He is a tower of salvation for his king,
and shows steadfast love to his anointed,
to David and his descendants forever.

The Last Words of David

23 Now these are the last words of David:
The oracle of David, son of Jesse,
the oracle of the man whom God exalted,[a]
the anointed of the God of Jacob,
the favorite of the Strong One of Israel:

2 The spirit of the LORD speaks through me,
his word is upon my tongue.
3 The God of Israel has spoken,
the Rock of Israel has said to me:
One who rules over people justly,
ruling in the fear of God,
4 is like the light of morning,
like the sun rising on a cloudless morning,
gleaming from the rain on the grassy land.

5 Is not my house like this with God?
For he has made with me an everlasting covenant,
ordered in all things and secure.
Will he not cause to prosper
all my help and my desire?

[a] Q Ms: MT *who was raised on high*

6 But the godless are[a] all like thorns that are thrown away;
for they cannot be picked up with the hand;
7 to touch them one uses an iron bar
or the shaft of a spear.
And they are entirely consumed in fire on the spot.[b]

David's Mighty Men

8 These are the names of the warriors whom David had: Josheb-
basshebeth a Tahchemonite; he was chief of the Three;[c] he wielded
his spear[d] against eight hundred whom he killed at one time.

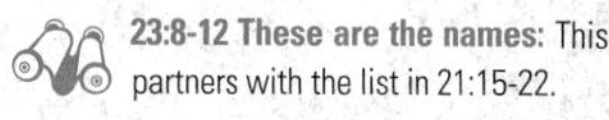

23:8-12 These are the names: This partners with the list in 21:15-22.

9 Next to him among the three warriors was Eleazar son of Dodo
son of Ahohi. He was with David when they defied the Philistines
who were gathered there for battle. The Israelites withdrew, 10 but he
stood his ground. He struck down the Philistines until his arm grew
weary, though his hand clung to the sword. The LORD brought about
a great victory that day. Then the people came back to him—but only
to strip the dead.
11 Next to him was Shammah son of Agee, the Hararite. The Philistines gathered together at Lehi, where there was a plot of ground
full of lentils; and the army fled from the Philistines. 12 But he took his
stand in the middle of the plot, defended it, and killed the Philistines;
and the LORD brought about a great victory.
13 Towards the beginning of harvest three of the thirty[e] chiefs
went down to join David at the cave of Adullam, while a band of Philistines was encamped in the valley of Rephaim. 14 David was then in
the stronghold; and the garrison of the Philistines was then at Bethlehem. 15 David said longingly, "O that someone would give me water to
drink from the well of Bethlehem that is by the gate!" 16 Then the three
warriors broke through the camp of the Philistines, drew water from
the well of Bethlehem that was by the gate, and brought it to David.
But he would not drink of it; he poured it out to the LORD, 17 for he
said, "The LORD forbid that I should do this. Can I drink the blood of
the men who went at the risk of their lives?" Therefore he would not
drink it. The three warriors did these things.

23:13-17 David: He inspires great loyalty among his soldiers. He sees the water as sacred because of their risk, and he humbly pours it on the ground in honor of their action (see 1 Chr 11:15-19).

18 Now Abishai son of Zeruiah, the brother of Joab, was chief of
the Thirty.[f] With his spear he fought against three hundred men and
killed them, and won a name beside the Three. 19 He was the most renowned of the Thirty,[g] and became their commander; but he did not
attain to the Three.

23:18-39 the Thirty: Four prominent names appear: Abishai, Benaiah, Asahel and Uriah. All are major players in David's life (see 2:18-23; 8:18; 11:6-21). Joab, often David's commander, is missing from the list.

20 Benaiah son of Jehoiada was a valiant warrior[h] from Kabzeel,
a doer of great deeds; he struck down two sons of Ariel[i] of Moab. He

[a] Heb *But worthlessness* [b] Heb *in sitting* [c] Gk Vg Compare 1 Chr 11.11: Meaning of Heb uncertain [d] 1 Chr 11.11: Meaning of Heb uncertain [e] Heb adds *head* [f] Two Heb Mss Syr: MT *Three* [g] Syr Compare 1 Chr 11.25: Heb *Was he the most renowned of the Three?* [h] Another reading is *the son of Ish-hai* [i] Gk: Heb lacks *sons of*

also went down and killed a lion in a pit on a day when snow had
fallen. 21 And he killed an Egyptian, a handsome man. The Egyptian
had a spear in his hand; but Benaiah went against him with a staff,
snatched the spear out of the Egyptian's hand, and killed him with his
own spear. 22 Such were the things Benaiah son of Jehoiada did, and
won a name beside the three warriors. 23 He was renowned among
the Thirty, but he did not attain to the Three. And David put him in
charge of his bodyguard.

24 Among the Thirty were Asahel brother of Joab; Elhanan son
of Dodo of Bethlehem; 25 Shammah of Harod; Elika of Harod; 26 Helez the Paltite; Ira son of Ikkesh of Tekoa; 27 Abiezer of Anathoth;
Mebunnai the Hushathite; 28 Zalmon the Ahohite; Maharai of Netophah; 29 Heleb son of Baanah of Netophah; Ittai son of Ribai of Gibeah of the Benjaminites; 30 Benaiah of Pirathon; Hiddai of the torrents
of Gaash; 31 Abi-albon the Arbathite; Azmaveth of Bahurim; 32 Eliahba
of Shaalbon; the sons of Jashen: Jonathan 33 son of[a] Shammah the Hararite; Ahiam son of Sharar the Hararite; 34 Eliphelet son of Ahasbai
of Maacah; Eliam son of Ahithophel the Gilonite; 35 Hezro[b] of Carmel; Paarai the Arbite; 36 Igal son of Nathan of Zobah; Bani the Gad-
ite; 37 Zelek the Ammonite; Naharai of Beeroth, the armor-bearer of
Joab son of Zeruiah; 38 Ira the Ithrite; Gareb the Ithrite; 39 Uriah the
Hittite—thirty-seven in all.

David's Census of Israel and Judah

24:1-9 Again the anger of the Lord: King David must deal with another crisis and seek the welfare of his people (see 21:1-14).

24:3 But why: A census only builds David's kingly power; it doesn't serve God's purposes. Samuel warned of this kingly abuse of power (see 1 Sam 8:10-18). Done wrongly a census can result in a plague (see Exod 30:12).

24 Again the anger of the Lord was kindled against Israel, and
he incited David against them, saying, "Go, count the people of Israel and Judah." 2 So the king said to Joab and the commanders
of the army,[c] who were with him, "Go through all the tribes of Israel,
from Dan to Beer-sheba, and take a census of the people, so that I
may know how many there are." 3 But Joab said to the king, "May the
Lord your God increase the number of the people a hundredfold,
while the eyes of my lord the king can still see it! But why does my
lord the king want to do this?" 4 But the king's word prevailed against
Joab and the commanders of the army. So Joab and the commanders
of the army went out from the presence of the king to take a census of
the people of Israel. 5 They crossed the Jordan, and began from[d] Aroer
and from the city that is in the middle of the valley, toward Gad and
on to Jazer. 6 Then they came to Gilead, and to Kadesh in the land of
the Hittites;[e] and they came to Dan, and from Dan[f] they went around
to Sidon, 7 and came to the fortress of Tyre and to all the cities of the
Hivites and Canaanites; and they went out to the Negeb of Judah at
Beer-sheba. 8 So when they had gone through all the land, they came

---

[a] Gk: Heb lacks *son of* [b] Another reading is *Hezrai* [c] 1 Chr 21.2 Gk: Heb *to Joab the commander of the army* [d] Gk Mss: Heb *encamped in Aroer south of* [e] Gk: Heb *to the land of Tahtim-hodshi* [f] Cn Compare Gk: Heb *they came to Dan-jaan and*

back to Jerusalem at the end of nine months and twenty days. [9]Joab
reported to the king the number of those who had been recorded: in
Israel there were eight hundred thousand soldiers able to draw the
sword, and those of Judah were five hundred thousand.

Judgment on David's Sin

10 But afterward, David was stricken to the heart because he had
numbered the people. David said to the LORD, "I have sinned greatly
in what I have done. But now, O LORD, I pray you, take away the guilt
of your servant; for I have done very foolishly." [11]When David rose in
the morning, the word of the LORD came to the prophet Gad, David's
seer, saying, [12]"Go and say to David: Thus says the LORD: Three
things I offer[a] you; choose one of them, and I will do it to you." [13]So
Gad came to David and told him; he asked him, "Shall three[b] years
of famine come to you on your land? Or will you flee three months
before your foes while they pursue you? Or shall there be three days'
pestilence in your land? Now consider, and decide what answer I shall
return to the one who sent me." [14]Then David said to Gad, "I am in
great distress; let us fall into the hand of the LORD, for his mercy is
great; but let me not fall into human hands."

15 So the LORD sent a pestilence on Israel from that morning until the appointed time; and seventy thousand of the people died, from
Dan to Beer-sheba. [16]But when the angel stretched out his hand toward Jerusalem to destroy it, the LORD relented concerning the evil,
and said to the angel who was bringing destruction among the people, "It is enough; now stay your hand." The angel of the LORD was
then by the threshing floor of Araunah the Jebusite. [17]When David
saw the angel who was destroying the people, he said to the LORD, "I
alone have sinned, and I alone have done wickedly; but these sheep,
what have they done? Let your hand, I pray, be against me and against
my father's house."

24:14 let us fall into the hand of the LORD: David knows that only God can be trusted for mercy (see 12:13, 20; 16:12). Confession is an act of faith (see Luke 18:9-14). David's need and prayer echo Hannah's at the beginning of the books of Samuel (see 1 Sam 1:9-16).

24:16 the angel: God's messenger or destroyer (see Exod 12:23).

24:16 stay your hand: No explanation is given for God's mercy; God acts beyond our reason and understanding. But God keeps covenantal steadfast love (see 7:14-15).

David's Altar on the Threshing Floor

18 That day Gad came to David and said to him, "Go up and
erect an altar to the LORD on the threshing floor of Araunah the Jebusite." [19]Following Gad's instructions, David went up, as the LORD had
commanded. [20]When Araunah looked down, he saw the king and his
servants coming toward him; and Araunah went out and prostrated
himself before the king with his face to the ground. [21]Araunah said,
"Why has my lord the king come to his servant?" David said, "To buy
the threshing floor from you in order to build an altar to the LORD,
so that the plague may be averted from the people." [22]Then Araunah
said to David, "Let my lord the king take and offer up what seems

24:18 erect an altar . . . on the threshing floor of Araunah: David's purchase of Araunah's threshing floor to offer sacrifice is important because it is later said to be the site of Solomon's temple (see 1 Chr 22:1; 2 Chr 3:1).

---

[a] Or *hold over* [b] 1 Chr 21.12 Gk: Heb *seven*

good to him; here are the oxen for the burnt offering, and the threshing sledges and the yokes of the oxen for the wood. 23 All this, O king,
Araunah gives to the king." And Araunah said to the king, "May the
LORD your God respond favorably to you."
24 But the king said to Araunah, "No, but I will buy them from
you for a price; I will not offer burnt offerings to the LORD my God
that cost me nothing." So David bought the threshing floor and the
oxen for fifty shekels of silver. 25 David built there an altar to the LORD,
and offered burnt offerings and offerings of well-being. So the LORD
answered his supplication for the land, and the plague was averted
from Israel.

24:25 offerings of well-being: These sacrifices were eaten principally by those offering them. Some of the fatty parts and important internal organs were burned for God's enjoyment.

God hears David's prayers on behalf of the people and the plague does not come upon the people. What has been your experience with praying for others, or having others pray for your well-being?

1 Kings 6:2

1 KINGS

Background File

Every historian writes with a distinct viewpoint. This perspective guides the historian in selecting materials to include in an account and in identifying the significance of the story. The author of the book of Kings is a historian influenced by the religious viewpoint and language of the book of Deuteronomy. In fact, most modern scholars believe that the long story of the people of Israel in the promised land—recounted in Joshua, Judges, and the books of Samuel and Kings—is written from this perspective. This story is called the Deuteronomistic History.

What's the Story?

The Deuteronomistic History is primarily the story of a kingdom or monarchy—the united monarchy of David and Solomon, and then the divided monarchy (see Kings of Judah and Israel, p. 545). The northern kingdom (Israel) and the southern kingdom (Judah) made up the divided monarchy. Israel was destroyed by Assyria in 722 B.C.E. Judah lasted until Babylon destroyed Jerusalem and the temple in 587 B.C.E. and Jews were driven into exile. The historical account was probably written in its present form in the mid-sixth century, after the northern and southern kingdoms had both fallen. It offers an explanation for the downfall of the kingdoms: the people had more than one sanctuary and more than one God. While there are numerous references to the people's sins, the focus in Kings is on the few rulers who stayed true to God's law and the many kings in both kingdoms who did not.

To cover nearly four hundred years of history, the author of Kings had to be very selective. For example, the biggest and most important battle that Israel fought was at Qarqar in Syria in 853 B.C.E., known to us from Assyrian records. Yet this battle is not even mentioned in Kings, probably because it did not contribute to the point the writer was trying to make.

In Jewish tradition, the two books of Kings are considered to be a single unit, and they have the following outline:

The death of David and the beginning of Solomon's reign (1 Kings 1–2)
Solomon's reign (3–11)
The kings of Israel and Judah, ending with the capture of Samaria (1 Kings 12—2 Kings 17)
The final kings of Judah, ending with the destruction of Jerusalem (2 Kings 18–25)

The first two chapters of Kings may continue a document, begun in 2 Samuel 9–20, that describes how David's sons struggled to succeed him. Amnon, Absalom, and Adonijah lose out in their quest for the throne. Solomon emerges the winner.

The high point and centerpiece of Solomon's reign, described in the second part of the outline above, is the construction and dedication of the temple in Jerusalem. But this section ends by telling about Solomon's many wives, his unfaithfulness to God, and his worship of other gods.

The third part of Kings goes back and forth between the northern and the southern kings, beginning with Jeroboam I in the north. The best kings by far after David and Solomon were Hezekiah and Josiah of Judah. The worst king in the north was Ahab, whose wife, Jezebel, is also criticized. The worst king in the south was Manasseh. For more on the third and fourth parts of the historical account, see 2 Kings.

The writer of Kings uses major events and the reigns of kings to mark time. Scholars do not all agree on how this system translates into exact years. In this Bible, the study notes for 1 and 2 Kings use the dates offered by Gershon Galil in *The Chronology of the Kings of Israel & Judah* (Leiden: Brill, 1996).

What's the Message?

The book of Kings continues to discuss two critical issues raised in Deuteronomy: the proposal that sacrificial worship should be conducted only in the temple in Jerusalem, and the belief that Israel should worship only one God. In addition, it explores the promise to David (2 Sam 7) that accompanies Israel through its history.

Clearly, the author of Kings wants to say that what happened to the two kingdoms can be explained by the people's behavior, as demonstrated especially by their kings. The downfalls of these kingdoms show the power of God's judgmental word; they do not show God's weakness. But the writer also underscores the importance of repentance, of turning away from evil and toward God. The overall story line in Kings says only that Israel sinned and was punished. What if Israel in its exile were to cry out to or turn to the LORD? Would they be delivered? Kings leaves us with questions like these, but also assures us that God's promise to David—and to us all—is still alive.

Kings of Judah and Israel

United Kingdom

Saul 1030-1010 B.C.E. • David 1010-970 B.C.E. • Solomon 970-922 B.C.E.

Divided Kingdom

Judah		Israel	
Rehoboam	922–915	Jeroboam	922–901
Abijah (Abijam)	915–913	Nadab	901–900
		Baasha	900–877
Asa	913–873	Elah	877–876
		Zimri	876
		Omride Era	
		Omri	876–869
Jehoshaphat	873–849	Ahab	869–850
		Ahaziah	850–849
Jehoram	849–843	Jehoram	849–843
Ahaziah	843–842		
		Jehu Dynasty	
		Jehu	843–815
Athaliah	842–837		
Joash	837–800		
		Jehoahaz	815–802
Amaziah	800–783	Jehoash	802–786
Uzziah (Azariah)	783–742	Jeroboam II	786–746
		Assyrian Intervention	
Jotham	742–735	Zechariah	746–745
		Shallum	745
		Menahem	745–737
		Pekahiah	737–736
Ahaz	735–727 or 715	Pekah	736–732
		Hoshea	732–722
Hezekiah	727 or 715–687		
		Fall of Samaria	**722**
Manasseh	687–642		
Amon	642–640		
Josiah	640–609		
Jehoahaz	609		
Jehoiachim	609–598		
Jehoiachin	598–597		
First capture of Jerusalem by Babylonians	597		
Zedekiah	597–586		
Destruction of Jerusalem	**586**		

1:1-4 Abishag: The story of King David begins in 1 Samuel 16. The first two chapters of Kings continue the story of David's sons struggling to succeed him, which begins in 2 Samuel 9 (this story is called the Succession Narrative or Court History of David). This strange incident with Abishag may have been a test to see whether David is still competent to rule.

1:5-27 Adonijah . . . exalted himself: Adonijah, David's oldest surviving son, sees David's weakness and tries to seize the kingship for himself. Joab, David's general, and Abiathar, one of David's high priests, support him. Following the prophet Nathan's advice, Bathsheba, the mother of Solomon (2 Sam 12:24), reminds David of his oath to make his son Solomon his successor, and informs him of Adonijah's attempt to seize the throne.

The Struggle for the Succession

1 King David was old and advanced in years; and although they
covered him with clothes, he could not get warm. 2 So his servants
said to him, "Let a young virgin be sought for my lord the king, and let
her wait on the king, and be his attendant; let her lie in your bosom, so
that my lord the king may be warm." 3 So they searched for a beautiful
girl throughout all the territory of Israel, and found Abishag the Shunammite, and brought her to the king. 4 The girl was very beautiful.
She became the king's attendant and served him, but the king did not
know her sexually.

5 Now Adonijah son of Haggith exalted himself, saying, "I will be
king"; he prepared for himself chariots and horsemen, and fifty men
to run before him. 6 His father had never at any time displeased him by
asking, "Why have you done thus and so?" He was also a very handsome man, and he was born next after Absalom. 7 He conferred with
Joab son of Zeruiah and with the priest Abiathar, and they supported
Adonijah. 8 But the priest Zadok, and Benaiah son of Jehoiada, and
the prophet Nathan, and Shimei, and Rei, and David's own warriors
did not side with Adonijah.

9 Adonijah sacrificed sheep, oxen, and fatted cattle by the stone
Zoheleth, which is beside En-rogel, and he invited all his brothers,
the king's sons, and all the royal officials of Judah, 10 but he did not
invite the prophet Nathan or Benaiah or the warriors or his brother
Solomon.

11 Then Nathan said to Bathsheba, Solomon's mother, "Have
you not heard that Adonijah son of Haggith has become king and our
lord David does not know it? 12 Now therefore come, let me give you
advice, so that you may save your own life and the life of your son
Solomon. 13 Go in at once to King David, and say to him, 'Did you not,
my lord the king, swear to your servant, saying: Your son Solomon
shall succeed me as king, and he shall sit on my throne? Why then
is Adonijah king?' 14 Then while you are still there speaking with the
king, I will come in after you and confirm your words."

15 So Bathsheba went to the king in his room. The king was very
old; Abishag the Shunammite was attending the king. 16 Bathsheba
bowed and did obeisance to the king, and the king said, "What do
you wish?" 17 She said to him, "My lord, you swore to your servant
by the LORD your God, saying: Your son Solomon shall succeed me
as king, and he shall sit on my throne. 18 But now suddenly Adonijah has become king, though you, my lord the king, do not know it.
19 He has sacrificed oxen, fatted cattle, and sheep in abundance, and
has invited all the children of the king, the priest Abiathar, and Joab
the commander of the army; but your servant Solomon he has not
invited. 20 But you, my lord the king—the eyes of all Israel are on you

to tell them who shall sit on the throne of my lord the king after him.
[21]Otherwise it will come to pass, when my lord the king sleeps with
his ancestors, that my son Solomon and I will be counted offenders."

22 While she was still speaking with the king, the prophet Nathan
came in. [23]The king was told, "Here is the prophet Nathan." When he
came in before the king, he did obeisance to the king, with his face
to the ground. [24]Nathan said, "My lord the king, have you said, 'Adonijah shall succeed me as king, and he shall sit on my throne'? [25]For
today he has gone down and has sacrificed oxen, fatted cattle, and
sheep in abundance, and has invited all the king's children, Joab the
commander[a] of the army, and the priest Abiathar, who are now eating
and drinking before him, and saying, 'Long live King Adonijah!' [26]But
he did not invite me, your servant, and the priest Zadok, and Benaiah son of Jehoiada, and your servant Solomon. [27]Has this thing been
brought about by my lord the king and you have not let your servants
know who should sit on the throne of my lord the king after him?"

The Accession of Solomon

28 King David answered, "Summon Bathsheba to me." So she
came into the king's presence, and stood before the king. [29]The king
swore, saying, "As the LORD lives, who has saved my life from every
adversity, [30]as I swore to you by the LORD, the God of Israel, 'Your
son Solomon shall succeed me as king, and he shall sit on my throne
in my place,' so will I do this day." [31]Then Bathsheba bowed with her
face to the ground, and did obeisance to the king, and said, "May my
lord King David live forever!"

32 King David said, "Summon to me the priest Zadok, the
prophet Nathan, and Benaiah son of Jehoiada." When they came before the king, [33]the king said to them, "Take with you the servants of
your lord, and have my son Solomon ride on my own mule, and bring
him down to Gihon. [34]There let the priest Zadok and the prophet
Nathan anoint him king over Israel; then blow the trumpet, and say,
'Long live King Solomon!' [35]You shall go up following him. Let him
enter and sit on my throne; he shall be king in my place; for I have
appointed him to be ruler over Israel and over Judah." [36]Benaiah son
of Jehoiada answered the king, "Amen! May the LORD, the God of
my lord the king, so ordain. [37]As the LORD has been with my lord the
king, so may he be with Solomon, and make his throne greater than
the throne of my lord King David."

38 So the priest Zadok, the prophet Nathan, and Benaiah son of
Jehoiada, and the Cherethites and the Pelethites, went down and had
Solomon ride on King David's mule, and led him to Gihon. [39]There
the priest Zadok took the horn of oil from the tent and anointed

1:28-40 Solomon shall succeed me: David instructs Zadok, another high priest, the prophet Nathan, and Benaiah, who is to become Solomon's chief general, to make Solomon king. They take him on a mule (see 2 Sam 13:29; 18:9; Zech 9:9) to the spring of Gihon, a sacred site, just east of the City of David (see Map 6, p. 2104), where Zadok anoints Solomon as king and all the people celebrate.

---

[a] Gk: Heb *the commanders*

Solomon. Then they blew the trumpet, and all the people said, "Long
live King Solomon!" 40And all the people went up following him,
playing on pipes and rejoicing with great joy, so that the earth quaked
at their noise.

1:41-48 Why is the city in an uproar?: Adonijah hears the celebration and a messenger informs him that Solomon has been made king at David's command. David thanks God for making one of his heirs king and keeping the promise (2 Sam 7:12).

1:49-53 Adonijah is afraid of King Solomon: By trying to make himself king, Adonijah could be accused of treason or disloyalty to Solomon. He goes to the altar, a place of safety or asylum (see Exod 21:13-14; 1 Kgs 2:28-35). Solomon grants him a conditional pardon (1:52), receives Adonijah's pledge of allegiance, and sends him home (but see 2:13-25).

41 Adonijah and all the guests who were with him heard it as they
finished feasting. When Joab heard the sound of the trumpet, he said,
"Why is the city in an uproar?" 42While he was still speaking, Jonathan son of the priest Abiathar arrived. Adonijah said, "Come in, for
you are a worthy man and surely you bring good news." 43Jonathan
answered Adonijah, "No, for our lord King David has made Solomon
king; 44the king has sent with him the priest Zadok, the prophet Nathan, and Benaiah son of Jehoiada, and the Cherethites and the Pelethites; and they had him ride on the king's mule; 45the priest Zadok
and the prophet Nathan have anointed him king at Gihon; and they
have gone up from there rejoicing, so that the city is in an uproar. This
is the noise that you heard. 46Solomon now sits on the royal throne.
47Moreover the king's servants came to congratulate our lord King
David, saying, 'May God make the name of Solomon more famous
than yours, and make his throne greater than your throne.' The king
bowed in worship on the bed 48and went on to pray thus, 'Blessed be
the LORD, the God of Israel, who today has granted one of my offspring[a] to sit on my throne and permitted me to witness it.' "

49 Then all the guests of Adonijah got up trembling and went
their own ways. 50Adonijah, fearing Solomon, got up and went to
grasp the horns of the altar. 51Solomon was informed, "Adonijah is
afraid of King Solomon; see, he has laid hold of the horns of the altar,
saying, 'Let King Solomon swear to me first that he will not kill his
servant with the sword.' " 52So Solomon responded, "If he proves to
be a worthy man, not one of his hairs shall fall to the ground; but if
wickedness is found in him, he shall die." 53Then King Solomon sent
to have him brought down from the altar. He came to do obeisance to
King Solomon; and Solomon said to him, "Go home."

David's Instruction to Solomon

2:1-4 keep the charge of the LORD: David urges Solomon to keep the law of Moses and promises him prosperity if he obeys. The LORD's promise to David that his kingship would last forever (2 Sam 7:12-16) depended on the faithfulness of those who followed him. The conditional nature of this promise is typical of the historical account in Joshua, Judges, and the books of Samuel and Kings.

2 When David's time to die drew near, he charged his son Solomon, saying: 2"I am about to go the way of all the earth. Be
strong, be courageous, 3and keep the charge of the LORD your God,
walking in his ways and keeping his statutes, his commandments, his
ordinances, and his testimonies, as it is written in the law of Moses,
so that you may prosper in all that you do and wherever you turn.
4Then the LORD will establish his word that he spoke concerning me:
'If your heirs take heed to their way, to walk before me in faithfulness
with all their heart and with all their soul, there shall not fail you a
successor on the throne of Israel.'

---

[a] Gk: Heb *one*

5 "Moreover you know also what Joab son of Zeruiah did to me,
how he dealt with the two commanders of the armies of Israel, Abner son of Ner, and Amasa son of Jether, whom he murdered, retaliat-
ing in time of peace for blood that had been shed in war, and putting
the blood of war on the belt around his waist, and on the sandals on
his feet. 6Act therefore according to your wisdom, but do not let his
gray head go down to Sheol in peace. 7Deal loyally, however, with the
sons of Barzillai the Gileadite, and let them be among those who eat
at your table; for with such loyalty they met me when I fled from your
brother Absalom. 8There is also with you Shimei son of Gera, the
Benjaminite from Bahurim, who cursed me with a terrible curse on
the day when I went to Mahanaim; but when he came down to meet
me at the Jordan, I swore to him by the LORD, 'I will not put you to
death with the sword.' 9Therefore do not hold him guiltless, for you
are a wise man; you will know what you ought to do to him, and you
must bring his gray head down with blood to Sheol."

Death of David

10 Then David slept with his ancestors, and was buried in the city
of David. 11The time that David reigned over Israel was forty years; he
reigned seven years in Hebron, and thirty-three years in Jerusalem.
12So Solomon sat on the throne of his father David; and his kingdom
was firmly established.

Solomon Consolidates His Reign

13 Then Adonijah son of Haggith came to Bathsheba, Solomon's
mother. She asked, "Do you come peaceably?" He said, "Peaceably."
14Then he said, "May I have a word with you?" She said, "Go on."
15He said, "You know that the kingdom was mine, and that all Israel
expected me to reign; however, the kingdom has turned about and
become my brother's, for it was his from the LORD. 16And now I have
one request to make of you; do not refuse me." She said to him, "Go
on." 17He said, "Please ask King Solomon—he will not refuse you—
to give me Abishag the Shunammite as my wife." 18Bathsheba said,
"Very well; I will speak to the king on your behalf."

19 So Bathsheba went to King Solomon, to speak to him on behalf of Adonijah. The king rose to meet her, and bowed down to her;
then he sat on his throne, and had a throne brought for the king's
mother, and she sat on his right. 20Then she said, "I have one small
request to make of you; do not refuse me." And the king said to her,
"Make your request, my mother; for I will not refuse you." 21She said,
"Let Abishag the Shunammite be given to your brother Adonijah as
his wife." 22King Solomon answered his mother, "And why do you ask
Abishag the Shunammite for Adonijah? Ask for him the kingdom as
well! For he is my elder brother; ask not only for him but also for the

2:5-9 you know also what Joab… did to me: David urges Solomon not to repeat the mistakes he made by letting guilty people go unpunished. Joab, who was involved in Adonijah's plot to become king, had also killed rival army leaders Abner (2 Sam 3:22-30) and Amasa (2 Sam 17:25; 19:11-15; 20:4-10). David instructs Solomon not to let Joab die as a peaceful old man. David instructs Solomon to be hospitable to the sons of Barzillai, who provided David with food when he fled from Absalom (2 Sam 17:27-29; 19:31-40). David claims that Shimei, who cursed David during Absalom's revolt and had been pardoned by David, should suffer the same fate as Joab (2 Sam 16:5-13; 19:16-23).

2:6-9 Sheol: Sheol in the Old Testament is not a place of punishment—it is the place where all the dead go.

David's last words to Solomon are about punishment and hospitality. What do you think about this?

2:10-12 David slept with his ancestors: David's reign lasts forty years. The first seven years are spent in Hebron, nineteen miles south of Jerusalem (see Map 5, p. 2103). Solomon immediately succeeds his father as king.

2:13-25 the kingdom was mine: Bathsheba, Solomon's mother, brings Adonijah's request to marry Abishag. The king defers to Bathsheba, which may indicate the power she has in palace politics. Solomon considers the request a capital crime (possibly an attempt to displace him as king) and orders Adonijah's execution.

priest Abiathar and for Joab son of Zeruiah!" 23 Then King Solomon swore by the LORD, "So may God do to me, and more also, for Adonijah has devised this scheme at the risk of his life! 24 Now therefore as the LORD lives, who has established me and placed me on the throne of my father David, and who has made me a house as he promised, today Adonijah shall be put to death." 25 So King Solomon sent Benaiah son of Jehoiada; he struck him down, and he died.

2:26-27 Solomon banished Abiathar: Solomon sends the high priest, Abiathar, who was involved in Adonijah's quest for the throne, into exile in Anathoth. The priest's association with the ark of the covenant (which held the stone tablets of the Ten Commandments) may have saved him from a death sentence, but his banishment fulfills an earlier announcement about Eli's descendants (1 Sam 2:27-36).

26 The king said to the priest Abiathar, "Go to Anathoth, to your estate; for you deserve death. But I will not at this time put you to death, because you carried the ark of the Lord GOD before my father David, and because you shared in all the hardships my father endured." 27 So Solomon banished Abiathar from being priest to the LORD, thus fulfilling the word of the LORD that he had spoken concerning the house of Eli in Shiloh.

2:28-35 Joab fled: Joab, sensing he also is in danger, seeks asylum or refuge in the tent of the LORD. But Solomon orders Benaiah to kill Joab because of his violence against Abner and Amasa. Solomon rewards Benaiah by placing him over the army as Joab's replacement.

28 When the news came to Joab—for Joab had supported Adonijah though he had not supported Absalom—Joab fled to the tent of the LORD and grasped the horns of the altar. 29 When it was told King Solomon, "Joab has fled to the tent of the LORD and now is beside the altar," Solomon sent Benaiah son of Jehoiada, saying, "Go, strike him down." 30 So Benaiah came to the tent of the LORD and said to him, "The king commands, 'Come out.'" But he said, "No, I will die here." Then Benaiah brought the king word again, saying, "Thus said Joab, and thus he answered me." 31 The king replied to him, "Do as he has said, strike him down and bury him; and thus take away from me and from my father's house the guilt for the blood that Joab shed without cause. 32 The LORD will bring back his bloody deeds on his own head, because, without the knowledge of my father David, he attacked and killed with the sword two men more righteous and better than himself, Abner son of Ner, commander of the army of Israel, and Amasa son of Jether, commander of the army of Judah. 33 So shall their blood come back on the head of Joab and on the head of his descendants forever; but to David, and to his descendants, and to his house, and to his throne, there shall be peace from the LORD forevermore." 34 Then Benaiah son of Jehoiada went up and struck him down and killed him; and he was buried at his own house near the wilderness. 35 The king put Benaiah son of Jehoiada over the army in his place, and the king put the priest Zadok in the place of Abiathar.

2:36-46 the king sent and summoned Shimei: Solomon puts Shimei under house arrest in Jerusalem, but when Shimei goes to Gath in search of his runaway slaves, Solomon orders Benaiah to execute him. Verse 46 notes that Solomon's actions have solidified his hold on kingship.

36 Then the king sent and summoned Shimei, and said to him, "Build yourself a house in Jerusalem, and live there, and do not go out from there to any place whatever. 37 For on the day you go out, and cross the Wadi Kidron, know for certain that you shall die; your blood shall be on your own head." 38 And Shimei said to the king, "The sentence is fair; as my lord the king has said, so will your servant do." So Shimei lived in Jerusalem many days.

39 But it happened at the end of three years that two of Shimei's

slaves ran away to King Achish son of Maacah of Gath. When it was
told Shimei, "Your slaves are in Gath," [40]Shimei arose and saddled a
donkey, and went to Achish in Gath, to search for his slaves; Shimei
went and brought his slaves from Gath. [41]When Solomon was told
that Shimei had gone from Jerusalem to Gath and returned, [42]the king
sent and summoned Shimei, and said to him, "Did I not make you
swear by the LORD, and solemnly adjure you, saying, 'Know for certain that on the day you go out and go to any place whatever, you shall
die'? And you said to me, 'The sentence is fair; I accept.' [43]Why then
have you not kept your oath to the LORD and the commandment
with which I charged you?" [44]The king also said to Shimei, "You know
in your own heart all the evil that you did to my father David; so the
LORD will bring back your evil on your own head. [45]But King Solomon shall be blessed, and the throne of David shall be established
before the LORD forever." [46]Then the king commanded Benaiah son
of Jehoiada; and he went out and struck him down, and he died.

So the kingdom was established in the hand of Solomon.

Solomon's Prayer for Wisdom

3 Solomon made a marriage alliance with Pharaoh king of Egypt;
he took Pharaoh's daughter and brought her into the city of David, until he had finished building his own house and the house of the
LORD and the wall around Jerusalem. [2]The people were sacrificing at
the high places, however, because no house had yet been built for the
name of the LORD.

3 Solomon loved the LORD, walking in the statutes of his father
David; only, he sacrificed and offered incense at the high places. [4]The
king went to Gibeon to sacrifice there, for that was the principal high
place; Solomon used to offer a thousand burnt offerings on that altar. [5]At Gibeon the LORD appeared to Solomon in a dream by night;
and God said, "Ask what I should give you." [6]And Solomon said, "You
have shown great and steadfast love to your servant my father David,
because he walked before you in faithfulness, in righteousness, and
in uprightness of heart toward you; and you have kept for him this
great and steadfast love, and have given him a son to sit on his throne
today. [7]And now, O LORD my God, you have made your servant king
in place of my father David, although I am only a little child; I do not
know how to go out or come in. [8]And your servant is in the midst of
the people whom you have chosen, a great people, so numerous they
cannot be numbered or counted. [9]Give your servant therefore an
understanding mind to govern your people, able to discern between
good and evil; for who can govern this your great people?"

10 It pleased the Lord that Solomon had asked this. [11]God said
to him, "Because you have asked this, and have not asked for yourself
long life or riches, or for the life of your enemies, but have asked for

3:1-2 high places: High places were places of worship outside Jerusalem that often fostered worship of other gods in addition to the LORD. Solomon's many marriages with foreign women would lead to his falling away from the faith (chapter 11).

3:3-15 a wise and discerning mind: Solomon acknowledges God's steadfast love toward David. Solomon admits he is young and his job enormous. The LORD is pleased that Solomon asks for wisdom and not for riches, long life, or military victory. God grants him riches and honor as well. The promise in 3:14 is again conditional (see note on 2:1-4).

If you could ask God for anything, what would it be?

yourself understanding to discern what is right, [12]I now do according to your word. Indeed I give you a wise and discerning mind; no one like you has been before you and no one like you shall arise after you. [13]I give you also what you have not asked, both riches and honor all your life; no other king shall compare with you. [14]If you will walk in my ways, keeping my statutes and my commandments, as your father David walked, then I will lengthen your life."

15 Then Solomon awoke; it had been a dream. He came to Jerusalem where he stood before the ark of the covenant of the LORD. He offered up burnt offerings and offerings of well-being, and provided a feast for all his servants.

Solomon's Wisdom in Judgment

3:16-28 the wisdom of God was in him: Two prostitutes argue over whose son is dead and whose son is alive. This situation indicates that kings were expected to hand out justice. When Solomon threatens to split the child in two, the real mother is willing to give up her son rather than have him killed. Solomon's wisdom in this matter leads to justice and public acclaim.

16 Later, two women who were prostitutes came to the king and stood before him. [17]The one woman said, "Please, my lord, this woman and I live in the same house; and I gave birth while she was in the house. [18]Then on the third day after I gave birth, this woman also gave birth. We were together; there was no one else with us in the house, only the two of us were in the house. [19]Then this woman's son died in the night, because she lay on him. [20]She got up in the middle of the night and took my son from beside me while your servant slept. She laid him at her breast, and laid her dead son at my breast. [21]When I rose in the morning to nurse my son, I saw that he was dead; but when I looked at him closely in the morning, clearly it was not the son I had borne." [22]But the other woman said, "No, the living son is mine, and the dead son is yours." The first said, "No, the dead son is yours, and the living son is mine." So they argued before the king.

23 Then the king said, "The one says, 'This is my son that is alive, and your son is dead'; while the other says, 'Not so! Your son is dead, and my son is the living one.' " [24]So the king said, "Bring me a sword," and they brought a sword before the king. [25]The king said, "Divide the living boy in two; then give half to the one, and half to the other." [26]But the woman whose son was alive said to the king—because compassion for her son burned within her—""Please, my lord, give her the living boy; certainly do not kill him!" The other said, "It shall be neither mine nor yours; divide it." [27]Then the king responded: "Give the first woman the living boy; do not kill him. She is his mother." [28]All Israel heard of the judgment that the king had rendered; and they stood in awe of the king, because they perceived that the wisdom of God was in him, to execute justice.

4:1-19 these were his high officials: The list of officials shows Solomon's administrative wisdom and the growing complexity of his kingdom. The twelve administrative districts are limited to the northern part of the kingdom, although one official is appointed in Judah. Each of the twelve districts provides food for the king for one month a year. This form of taxation may also be an attempt to break up the old system of twelve tribes.

Solomon's Administrative Officers

4 King Solomon was king over all Israel, [2]and these were his high officials: Azariah son of Zadok was the priest; [3]Elihoreph and Ahijah sons of Shisha were secretaries; Jehoshaphat son of Ahilud

was recorder; [4]Benaiah son of Jehoiada was in command of the army;
Zadok and Abiathar were priests; [5]Azariah son of Nathan was over
the officials; Zabud son of Nathan was priest and king's friend; [6]Ahi-
shar was in charge of the palace; and Adoniram son of Abda was in
charge of the forced labor.

7 Solomon had twelve officials over all Israel, who provided food
for the king and his household; each one had to make provision for
one month in the year. [8]These were their names: Ben-hur, in the hill
country of Ephraim; [9]Ben-deker, in Makaz, Shaalbim, Beth-shemesh,
and Elon-beth-hanan; [10]Ben-hesed, in Arubboth (to him belonged
Socoh and all the land of Hepher); [11]Ben-abinadab, in all Naphath-
dor (he had Taphath, Solomon's daughter, as his wife); [12]Baana son
of Ahilud, in Taanach, Megiddo, and all Beth-shean, which is beside
Zarethan below Jezreel, and from Beth-shean to Abel-meholah, as far
as the other side of Jokmeam; [13]Ben-geber, in Ramoth-gilead (he had
the villages of Jair son of Manasseh, which are in Gilead, and he had
the region of Argob, which is in Bashan, sixty great cities with walls
and bronze bars); [14]Ahinadab son of Iddo, in Mahanaim; [15]Ahim-
aaz, in Naphtali (he had taken Basemath, Solomon's daughter, as his
wife); [16]Baana son of Hushai, in Asher and Bealoth; [17]Jehoshaphat
son of Paruah, in Issachar; [18]Shimei son of Ela, in Benjamin; [19]Geber
son of Uri, in the land of Gilead, the country of King Sihon of the
Amorites and of King Og of Bashan. And there was one official in the
land of Judah.

Magnificence of Solomon's Rule

20 Judah and Israel were as numerous as the sand by the sea; they
ate and drank and were happy. [21] [a]Solomon was sovereign over all the
kingdoms from the Euphrates to the land of the Philistines, even to
the border of Egypt; they brought tribute and served Solomon all the
days of his life.

22 Solomon's provision for one day was thirty cors of choice
flour, and sixty cors of meal, [23]ten fat oxen, and twenty pasture-fed
cattle, one hundred sheep, besides deer, gazelles, roebucks, and fatted
fowl. [24]For he had dominion over all the region west of the Euphrates
from Tiphsah to Gaza, over all the kings west of the Euphrates; and
he had peace on all sides. [25]During Solomon's lifetime Judah and Israel lived in safety, from Dan even to Beer-sheba, all of them under
their vines and fig trees. [26]Solomon also had forty thousand stalls of
horses for his chariots, and twelve thousand horsemen. [27]Those officials supplied provisions for King Solomon and for all who came
to King Solomon's table, each one in his month; they let nothing be
lacking. [28]They also brought to the required place barley and straw for
the horses and swift steeds, each according to his charge.

4:20-28 Solomon was sovereign: The author of Kings exaggerates in describing the great size of Solomon's kingdom (see Map 5, p. 2103), but this is seen as fulfillment of God's promise (Gen 12:2; 13:14-17; 15:18-21; 22:17; 32:12; Deut 1:7-8). The list of food for one day indicates the size of the royal court. By the end of Solomon's reign, the peace and safety of the kingdom described here would diminish (see chapter 11).

---

[a] Ch 5.1 in Heb

Fame of Solomon's Wisdom

29 God gave Solomon very great wisdom, discernment, and
breadth of understanding as vast as the sand on the seashore, 30 so that
Solomon's wisdom surpassed the wisdom of all the people of the east,
and all the wisdom of Egypt. 31 He was wiser than anyone else, wiser
than Ethan the Ezrahite, and Heman, Calcol, and Darda, children
of Mahol; his fame spread throughout all the surrounding nations.
32 He composed three thousand proverbs, and his songs numbered a
thousand and five. 33 He would speak of trees, from the cedar that is in
the Lebanon to the hyssop that grows in the wall; he would speak of
animals, and birds, and reptiles, and fish. 34 People came from all the
nations to hear the wisdom of Solomon; they came from all the kings
of the earth who had heard of his wisdom.

Preparations and Materials for the Temple

5 [a] Now King Hiram of Tyre sent his servants to Solomon, when
he heard that they had anointed him king in place of his father;
for Hiram had always been a friend to David. 2 Solomon sent word to
Hiram, saying, 3 "You know that my father David could not build a
house for the name of the LORD his God because of the warfare with
which his enemies surrounded him, until the LORD put them under
the soles of his feet.[b] 4 But now the LORD my God has given me rest
on every side; there is neither adversary nor misfortune. 5 So I intend
to build a house for the name of the LORD my God, as the LORD said
to my father David, 'Your son, whom I will set on your throne in your
place, shall build the house for my name.' 6 Therefore command that
cedars from the Lebanon be cut for me. My servants will join your
servants, and I will give you whatever wages you set for your servants;
for you know that there is no one among us who knows how to cut
timber like the Sidonians."

7 When Hiram heard the words of Solomon, he rejoiced greatly,
and said, "Blessed be the LORD today, who has given to David a wise
son to be over this great people." 8 Hiram sent word to Solomon, "I
have heard the message that you have sent to me; I will fulfill all
your needs in the matter of cedar and cypress timber. 9 My servants
shall bring it down to the sea from the Lebanon; I will make it into
rafts to go by sea to the place you indicate. I will have them broken up there for you to take away. And you shall meet my needs by
providing food for my household." 10 So Hiram supplied Solomon's
every need for timber of cedar and cypress. 11 Solomon in turn gave
Hiram twenty thousand cors of wheat as food for his household,
and twenty cors of fine oil. Solomon gave this to Hiram year by year.
12 So the LORD gave Solomon wisdom, as he promised him. There

[a] Ch 5.15 in Heb [b] Gk Tg Vg: Heb *my feet* or *his feet*

4:29-34 breadth of understanding: Solomon gains an international reputation for wisdom. He is a writer and composer as well. (Although in the past Solomon was believed to be the author of such biblical books as Proverbs, Ecclesiastes, and Song of Solomon, scholars now believe those books were written centuries later.)

5:1-6 a house for the name of the LORD: Solomon appeals to his father's ally, King Hiram, to provide lumber for building the temple in Jerusalem. According to Solomon, David could not build the temple because he was too busy with foreign wars, although that is not mentioned in 2 Samuel 7. Now that God has granted Solomon peace on every side, the building effort is seen as a fulfillment of Nathan's prophecy about a house for the LORD.

5:2-5 the name of the LORD: The name of the LORD would have been pronounced "Yahweh" (YAH-way) in ancient times. Because of the sacredness of this name, Jews for more than two thousand years have substituted the Hebrew word for "LORD" in place of the name.

5:7-12 Hiram... rejoiced greatly: King Hiram rejoices when he hears that Solomon is king and even offers a prayer of thanksgiving to the God of Israel. He agrees to ship cedar and cypress lumber by sea to Solomon, in exchange for a lavish payment of wheat and fine oil. A cor of wheat was about 14 bushels (approximately 493 liters). A cor of oil would be 35 to 60 gallons (133 to 228 liters). This treaty relationship is seen as another example of Solomon's God-given wisdom.

was peace between Hiram and Solomon; and the two of them made a treaty.

13 King Solomon conscripted forced labor out of all Israel; the
levy numbered thirty thousand men. [14]He sent them to the Lebanon,
ten thousand a month in shifts; they would be a month in the Lebanon and two months at home; Adoniram was in charge of the forced
labor. [15]Solomon also had seventy thousand laborers and eighty
thousand stonecutters in the hill country, [16]besides Solomon's three
thousand three hundred supervisors who were over the work, having charge of the people who did the work. [17]At the king's command,
they quarried out great, costly stones in order to lay the foundation of
the house with dressed stones. [18]So Solomon's builders and Hiram's
builders and the Gebalites did the stonecutting and prepared the timber and the stone to build the house.

5:13-18 King Solomon conscripted forced labor: Ancient kings often imposed work projects on average citizens. Solomon's project in Lebanon requires crews of forced laborers, who spend one month abroad harvesting wood and two months at home. Adoniram is in charge of these forced laborers (see 2 Sam 20:24; 1 Kgs 4:6). More than 150,000 people are employed to gather stones for the temple. These massive efforts indicate the magnificence of Solomon's temple, but also foreshadow a future complaint about the extraordinary burden he imposed on the people (1 Kgs 12:4).

Solomon Builds the Temple

6 In the four hundred eightieth year after the Israelites came out of the land of Egypt, in the fourth year of Solomon's reign over Israel, in the month of Ziv, which is the second month, he began to
build the house of the LORD. [2]The house that King Solomon built for
the LORD was sixty cubits long, twenty cubits wide, and thirty cubits
high. [3]The vestibule in front of the nave of the house was twenty cubits wide, across the width of the house. Its depth was ten cubits in
front of the house. [4]For the house he made windows with recessed
frames.[a] [5]He also built a structure against the wall of the house, running around the walls of the house, both the nave and the inner sanctuary; and he made side chambers all around. [6]The lowest story[b] was
five cubits wide, the middle one was six cubits wide, and the third
was seven cubits wide; for around the outside of the house he made

6:1 the four hundred eightieth year: The fourth year of Solomon is 966 B.C.E. The month of Ziv corresponds to April–May in our calendar. The reference to the four hundred eightieth year is unexplained.

6:2-10 The house that King Solomon built: Many features of Solomon's temple correspond to temples discovered by archeologists in Syria. Solomon's temple was 90 feet (27.4 meters) long, 30 feet (9.1 meters) wide, and 45 feet (13.7 meters) high. It faced east and was divided into three rooms.

[a] Gk: Meaning of Heb uncertain [b] Gk: Heb *structure*

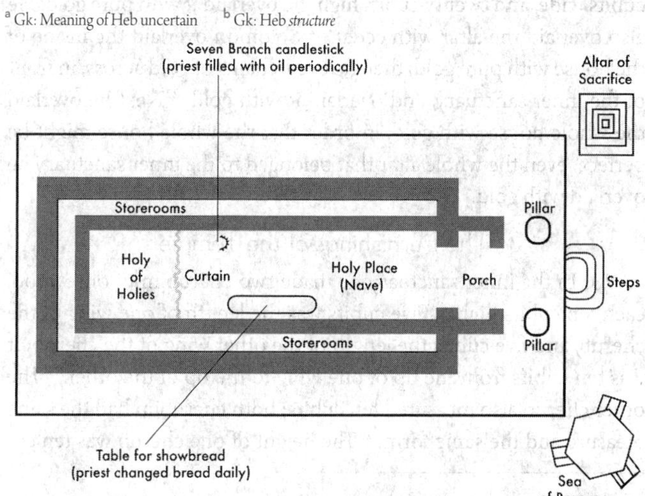

offsets on the wall in order that the supporting beams should not be
inserted into the walls of the house.

7 The house was built with stone finished at the quarry, so that
neither hammer nor ax nor any tool of iron was heard in the temple
while it was being built.

8 The entrance for the middle story was on the south side of the
house: one went up by winding stairs to the middle story, and from
the middle story to the third. [9]So he built the house, and finished it;
he roofed the house with beams and planks of cedar. [10]He built the
structure against the whole house, each story[a] five cubits high, and it
was joined to the house with timbers of cedar.

11 Now the word of the LORD came to Solomon, [12]"Concerning
this house that you are building, if you will walk in my statutes, obey
my ordinances, and keep all my commandments by walking in them,
then I will establish my promise with you, which I made to your father David. [13]I will dwell among the children of Israel, and will not
forsake my people Israel."

14 So Solomon built the house, and finished it. [15]He lined the
walls of the house on the inside with boards of cedar; from the floor
of the house to the rafters of the ceiling, he covered them on the inside with wood; and he covered the floor of the house with boards of
cypress. [16]He built twenty cubits of the rear of the house with boards
of cedar from the floor to the rafters, and he built this within as an inner sanctuary, as the most holy place. [17]The house, that is, the nave in
front of the inner sanctuary, was forty cubits long. [18]The cedar within
the house had carvings of gourds and open flowers; all was cedar, no
stone was seen. [19]The inner sanctuary he prepared in the innermost
part of the house, to set there the ark of the covenant of the LORD.
[20]The interior of the inner sanctuary was twenty cubits long, twenty
cubits wide, and twenty cubits high; he overlaid it with pure gold. He
also overlaid the altar with cedar.[b] [21]Solomon overlaid the inside of
the house with pure gold, then he drew chains of gold across, in front
of the inner sanctuary, and overlaid it with gold. [22]Next he overlaid
the whole house with gold, in order that the whole house might be
perfect; even the whole altar that belonged to the inner sanctuary he
overlaid with gold.

The Furnishings of the Temple

23 In the inner sanctuary he made two cherubim of olivewood,
each ten cubits high. [24]Five cubits was the length of one wing of the
cherub, and five cubits the length of the other wing of the cherub; it
was ten cubits from the tip of one wing to the tip of the other. [25]The
other cherub also measured ten cubits; both cherubim had the same
measure and the same form. [26]The height of one cherub was ten cu-

[a] Heb lacks *each story* [b] Meaning of Heb uncertain

6:11-13 walk in my statutes: Like the promise to David (1 Kgs 2:4), the LORD's promise to dwell among God's people in the temple depends upon the king keeping the commandments. By the time the book of Kings was written, the kings and the people had disobeyed God's commandments, and the temple had been destroyed by the Babylonians. Other passages in the Old Testament speak of God dwelling in Jerusalem (Pss 68:16 and 135:21).

6:14-22 the ark of the covenant: David brought the ark of the covenant to Jerusalem and placed it in a tent (2 Sam 6). The ark housed the Ten Commandments, and people believed the LORD sat invisibly on the cherubim on top of it. (Cherubim were winged lions, with human faces.) Solomon places the ark of the covenant in the inner sanctuary of the temple.

6:23-38 the inner sanctuary: The inner sanctuary, or holy of holies, is cubic in shape—thirty feet or 9.144 meters in each direction (6:20). The temple and inner sanctuary are built with the finest materials and decorated with carved engravings and gold overlays. The construction of the temple takes seven years.

bits, and so was that of the other cherub. [27]He put the cherubim in the
innermost part of the house; the wings of the cherubim were spread
out so that a wing of one was touching the one wall, and a wing of the
other cherub was touching the other wall; their other wings toward
the center of the house were touching wing to wing. [28]He also overlaid the cherubim with gold.

29 He carved the walls of the house all around about with carved
engravings of cherubim, palm trees, and open flowers, in the inner
and outer rooms. [30]The floor of the house he overlaid with gold, in the
inner and outer rooms.

31 For the entrance to the inner sanctuary he made doors of
olivewood; the lintel and the doorposts were five-sided.[a] [32]He covered the two doors of olivewood with carvings of cherubim, palm
trees, and open flowers; he overlaid them with gold, and spread gold
on the cherubim and on the palm trees.

33 So also he made for the entrance to the nave doorposts of
olivewood, four-sided each, [34]and two doors of cypress wood; the
two leaves of the one door were folding, and the two leaves of the
other door were folding. [35]He carved cherubim, palm trees, and open
flowers, overlaying them with gold evenly applied upon the carved
work. [36]He built the inner court with three courses of dressed stone
to one course of cedar beams.

37 In the fourth year the foundation of the house of the LORD was
laid, in the month of Ziv. [38]In the eleventh year, in the month of Bul,
which is the eighth month, the house was finished in all its parts, and
according to all its specifications. He was seven years in building it.

Solomon's Palace and Other Buildings

7 Solomon was building his own house thirteen years, and he finished his entire house.

2 He built the House of the Forest of the Lebanon one hundred
cubits long, fifty cubits wide, and thirty cubits high, built on four rows
of cedar pillars, with cedar beams on the pillars. [3]It was roofed with
cedar on the forty-five rafters, fifteen in each row, which were on the
pillars. [4]There were window frames in the three rows, facing each
other in the three rows. [5]All the doorways and doorposts had four-
sided frames, opposite, facing each other in the three rows.

6 He made the Hall of Pillars fifty cubits long and thirty cubits
wide. There was a porch in front with pillars, and a canopy in front
of them.

7 He made the Hall of the Throne where he was to pronounce
judgment, the Hall of Justice, covered with cedar from floor to floor.

8 His own house where he would reside, in the other court
back of the hall, was of the same construction. Solomon also made

[b] Meaning of Heb uncertain

7:1-12 Solomon was building his own house: The building of Solomon's palace takes almost twice as long as the building of the temple. This may be a not so subtle evaluation of the king's priorities. "The House of the Forest of the Lebanon" (7:2) got its name either from its cedar wood, imported from Phoenicia, or from pillars that resembled a forest. "Where he was to pronounce judgment" (7:7) indicates that the king exercised certain judicial powers (see 1 Kgs 3:16-28). In addition to his palace, Solomon builds a similar house for Pharaoh's daughter (1 Kgs 7:8).

Looking at elegance and the latest conveniences, how do our homes compare to our places of worship?

a house like this hall for Pharaoh's daughter, whom he had taken in marriage.

9 All these were made of costly stones, cut according to measure, sawed with saws, back and front, from the foundation to the coping, and from outside to the great court. 10 The foundation was of costly stones, huge stones, stones of eight and ten cubits. 11 There were costly stones above, cut to measure, and cedarwood. 12 The great court had three courses of dressed stone to one layer of cedar beams all around; so had the inner court of the house of the LORD, and the vestibule of the house.

Products of Hiram the Bronzeworker

7:13-47 Hiram from Tyre: Solomon brings in a man named Hiram to create various items of bronze (this is not King Hiram of Tyre, who supplied Solomon with lumber). This Hiram's mother was a member of the Naphtali tribe. The pillars Hiram fashioned stand in front of the temple. Their names, Jachin and Boaz, may be abbreviations for blessings on the dynasty of David and Solomon. The exact function of the bronze sea (7:23) is unknown, although 2 Chronicles 4:6 suggests it was for purifying the priests. It held eleven thousand gallons (41,627 liters) of water. The sea stood on the backs of twelve oxen, representing the twelve tribes of Israel. All these bronze items were cast in clay molds in the towns of Succoth and Zarethan, near the Jabbok River, just across the river Jordan.

13 Now King Solomon invited and received Hiram from Tyre.
14 He was the son of a widow of the tribe of Naphtali, whose father, a man of Tyre, had been an artisan in bronze; he was full of skill, intelligence, and knowledge in working bronze. He came to King Solomon, and did all his work.

15 He cast two pillars of bronze. Eighteen cubits was the height of the one, and a cord of twelve cubits would encircle it; the second pil-
lar was the same.[a] 16 He also made two capitals of molten bronze, to set on the tops of the pillars; the height of the one capital was five cubits, and the height of the other capital was five cubits. 17 There were nets of checker work with wreaths of chain work for the capitals on the tops of the pillars; seven[b] for the one capital, and seven[b] for the other capital.
18 He made the columns with two rows around each latticework to cover the capitals that were above the pomegranates; he did the same with the other capital. 19 Now the capitals that were on the tops of the pillars in the vestibule were of lily-work, four cubits high. 20 The capitals were on the two pillars and also above the rounded projection that was beside the latticework; there were two hundred pomegranates in rows all around; and so with the other capital. 21 He set up the pillars at the vestibule of the temple; he set up the pillar on the south and called it Jachin; and he set up the pillar on the north and called it Boaz. 22 On the tops of the pillars was lily-work. Thus the work of the pillars was finished.

23 Then he made the molten sea; it was round, ten cubits from brim to brim, and five cubits high. A line of thirty cubits would encircle it completely. 24 Under its brim were panels all around it, each of ten cubits, surrounding the sea; there were two rows of panels, cast when it was cast. 25 It stood on twelve oxen, three facing north, three facing west, three facing south, and three facing east; the sea was set on them. The hindquarters of each were toward the inside. 26 Its thickness was a handbreadth; its brim was made like the brim of a cup, like the flower of a lily; it held two thousand baths.[c]

---

[a] Cn: Heb *and a cord of twelve cubits encircled the second pillar*; Compare Jer 52.21 [b] Heb: Gk *a net*
[c] A Heb measure of volume

27 He also made the ten stands of bronze; each stand was four
cubits long, four cubits wide, and three cubits high. [28]This was the
construction of the stands: they had borders; the borders were
within the frames; [29]on the borders that were set in the frames were
lions, oxen, and cherubim. On the frames, both above and below the
lions and oxen, there were wreaths of beveled work. [30]Each stand had
four bronze wheels and axles of bronze; at the four corners were supports for a basin. The supports were cast with wreaths at the side
of each. [31]Its opening was within the crown whose height was one
cubit; its opening was round, as a pedestal is made; it was a cubit
and a half wide. At its opening there were carvings; its borders were
four-sided, not round. [32]The four wheels were underneath the borders; the axles of the wheels were in the stands; and the height of a
wheel was a cubit and a half. [33]The wheels were made like a chariot
wheel; their axles, their rims, their spokes, and their hubs were all
cast. [34]There were four supports at the four corners of each stand; the
supports were of one piece with the stands. [35]On the top of the stand
there was a round band half a cubit high; on the top of the stand, its
stays and its borders were of one piece with it. [36]On the surfaces of
its stays and on its borders he carved cherubim, lions, and palm trees,
where each had space, with wreaths all around. [37]In this way he made
the ten stands; all of them were cast alike, with the same size and the
same form.

38 He made ten basins of bronze; each basin held forty baths,[a]
each basin measured four cubits; there was a basin for each of the ten
stands. [39]He set five of the stands on the south side of the house, and
five on the north side of the house; he set the sea on the southeast
corner of the house.

40 Hiram also made the pots, the shovels, and the basins. So Hiram finished all the work that he did for King Solomon on the house
of the Lord: [41]the two pillars, the two bowls of the capitals that were
on the tops of the pillars, the two latticeworks to cover the two bowls
of the capitals that were on the tops of the pillars; [42]the four hundred
pomegranates for the two latticeworks, two rows of pomegranates for
each latticework, to cover the two bowls of the capitals that were on
the pillars; [43]the ten stands, the ten basins on the stands; [44]the one sea,
and the twelve oxen underneath the sea.

45 The pots, the shovels, and the basins, all these vessels that
Hiram made for King Solomon for the house of the Lord were of
burnished bronze. [46]In the plain of the Jordan the king cast them, in
the clay ground between Succoth and Zarethan. [47]Solomon left all the
vessels unweighed, because there were so many of them; the weight
of the bronze was not determined.

---

[a] A Heb measure of volume

7:48-51 all the vessels that were in the house of the LORD: Several items in these paragraphs resemble tabernacle furnishings (Exod 25:23-40; 30:1-10). The "bread of the Presence" was placed fresh in the sanctuary on each Sabbath day and consisted of twelve loaves of bread. It was used in the temple and eaten by the priests afterwards. Objects David dedicated to the LORD are mentioned in 2 Samuel 8:9-12 and 1 Chronicles 29:1-5.

48 So Solomon made all the vessels that were in the house of the
LORD: the golden altar, the golden table for the bread of the Presence,
49 the lampstands of pure gold, five on the south side and five on the
north, in front of the inner sanctuary; the flowers, the lamps, and the
tongs, of gold; 50 the cups, snuffers, basins, dishes for incense, and firepans, of pure gold; the sockets for the doors of the innermost part of
the house, the most holy place, and for the doors of the nave of the
temple, of gold.

51 Thus all the work that King Solomon did on the house of the
LORD was finished. Solomon brought in the things that his father
David had dedicated, the silver, the gold, and the vessels, and stored
them in the treasuries of the house of the LORD.

Dedication of the Temple

8:1-13 All the people of Israel assembled: The dedication of the temple took place in the fall (September–October). Bringing the ark of the covenant and the tent of meeting into the temple shows the link between the new temple and Israel's former way of worshiping. (Worship practices were established at Mount Sinai, here called by its alternate name, Horeb.) The "city of David," or Zion, was located south of the temple. The poles of the ark could be seen in the "holy place," where the priests served, but not outside the temple. The ark of the covenant housed the Ten Commandments, which were part of the covenant the LORD had made with Israel after the exodus. Once the priests emerged from the temple, a cloud filled the temple (8:10). This cloud and the references to the "glory of the LORD" indicate God's presence.

8 Then Solomon assembled the elders of Israel and all the heads
of the tribes, the leaders of the ancestral houses of the Israelites,
before King Solomon in Jerusalem, to bring up the ark of the covenant
of the LORD out of the city of David, which is Zion. 2 All the people
of Israel assembled to King Solomon at the festival in the month Eth-
anim, which is the seventh month. 3 And all the elders of Israel came,
and the priests carried the ark. 4 So they brought up the ark of the
LORD, the tent of meeting, and all the holy vessels that were in the
tent; the priests and the Levites brought them up. 5 King Solomon and
all the congregation of Israel, who had assembled before him, were
with him before the ark, sacrificing so many sheep and oxen that they
could not be counted or numbered. 6 Then the priests brought the ark
of the covenant of the LORD to its place, in the inner sanctuary of the
house, in the most holy place, underneath the wings of the cherubim.
7 For the cherubim spread out their wings over the place of the ark, so
that the cherubim made a covering above the ark and its poles. 8 The
poles were so long that the ends of the poles were seen from the holy
place in front of the inner sanctuary; but they could not be seen from

outside; they are there to this day. [9]There was nothing in the ark except the two tablets of stone that Moses had placed there at Horeb,
where the LORD made a covenant with the Israelites, when they came
out of the land of Egypt. [10]And when the priests came out of the holy
place, a cloud filled the house of the LORD, [11]so that the priests could
not stand to minister because of the cloud; for the glory of the LORD
filled the house of the LORD.

12 Then Solomon said,

"The LORD has said that he would dwell in thick darkness.
13 I have built you an exalted house,
 a place for you to dwell in forever."

Solomon's Speech

14 Then the king turned around and blessed all the assembly of
Israel, while all the assembly of Israel stood. [15]He said, "Blessed be
the LORD, the God of Israel, who with his hand has fulfilled what
he promised with his mouth to my father David, saying, [16]'Since the
day that I brought my people Israel out of Egypt, I have not chosen a
city from any of the tribes of Israel in which to build a house, that my
name might be there; but I chose David to be over my people Israel.'
[17]My father David had it in mind to build a house for the name of
the LORD, the God of Israel. [18]But the LORD said to my father David,
'You did well to consider building a house for my name; [19]neverthe-
less you shall not build the house, but your son who shall be born to
you shall build the house for my name.' [20]Now the LORD has upheld
the promise that he made; for I have risen in the place of my father
David; I sit on the throne of Israel, as the LORD promised, and have
built the house for the name of the LORD, the God of Israel. [21]There
I have provided a place for the ark, in which is the covenant of the
LORD that he made with our ancestors when he brought them out of
the land of Egypt."

8:14-21 the king...blessed all the assembly: Solomon tells the history of David's plan to build a temple and how the LORD had affirmed it, but decided that the temple would only be built by David's son. Solomon had succeeded his father, David, and built the temple, as the LORD had promised. The reference to "a house for the name of the LORD" (8:17) is typical of the historical account in Joshua, Judges, and the books of Samuel and Kings. God did not dwell in the temple, but God's name did.

Solomon's Prayer of Dedication

22 Then Solomon stood before the altar of the LORD in the presence of all the assembly of Israel, and spread out his hands to heaven.
[23]He said, "O LORD, God of Israel, there is no God like you in heaven
above or on earth beneath, keeping covenant and steadfast love for
your servants who walk before you with all their heart, [24]the covenant
that you kept for your servant my father David as you declared to him;
you promised with your mouth and have this day fulfilled with your
hand. [25]Therefore, O LORD, God of Israel, keep for your servant my
father David that which you promised him, saying, 'There shall never
fail you a successor before me to sit on the throne of Israel, if only
your children look to their way, to walk before me as you have walked
before me.' [26]Therefore, O God of Israel, let your word be confirmed,
which you promised to your servant my father David.

8:22-45 Solomon ...spread out his hands to heaven: Solomon prays and describes God's incomparable goodness, seen especially in keeping the promise to David that his heirs would always be kings. After asking God to listen to Israel's prayers, Solomon describes seven times when the people sinned, prayed toward this temple, and then were forgiven by God: 8:31-32; 33-34; 35-36; 37-40; 41-43; 44-45; and 46-53. The sins of the people might lead to defeat in war, drought, or famine, but if they people pray toward this place and turn from their sins, Solomon asks God to hear, forgive, and guide them into a new way of life. Verses 41-43 display a warm welcome to foreigners who might come to the temple. Solomon expresses the hope that the nations will trust in the LORD just as Israel does.

27 "But will God indeed dwell on the earth? Even heaven and the
highest heaven cannot contain you, much less this house that I have
built! 28 Regard your servant's prayer and his plea, O LORD my God,
heeding the cry and the prayer that your servant prays to you today;
29 that your eyes may be open night and day toward this house, the
place of which you said, My name shall be there,' that you may heed
the prayer that your servant prays toward this place. 30 Hear the plea
of your servant and of your people Israel when they pray toward this
place; O hear in heaven your dwelling place; heed and forgive.

31 "If someone sins against a neighbor and is given an oath to
swear, and comes and swears before your altar in this house, 32 then
hear in heaven, and act, and judge your servants, condemning the
guilty by bringing their conduct on their own head, and vindicating
the righteous by rewarding them according to their righteousness.

33 "When your people Israel, having sinned against you, are defeated before an enemy but turn again to you, confess your name, pray
and plead with you in this house, 34 then hear in heaven, forgive the sin
of your people Israel, and bring them again to the land that you gave
to their ancestors.

35 "When heaven is shut up and there is no rain because they
have sinned against you, and then they pray toward this place, confess
your name, and turn from their sin, because you punish[a] them, 36 then
hear in heaven, and forgive the sin of your servants, your people
Israel, when you teach them the good way in which they should walk;
and grant rain on your land, which you have given to your people as
an inheritance.

37 "If there is famine in the land, if there is plague, blight, mildew, locust, or caterpillar; if their enemy besieges them in any[b] of
their cities; whatever plague, whatever sickness there is; 38 whatever
prayer, whatever plea there is from any individual or from all your
people Israel, all knowing the afflictions of their own hearts so that
they stretch out their hands toward this house; 39 then hear in heaven
your dwelling place, forgive, act, and render to all whose hearts you
know—according to all their ways, for only you know what is in every
human heart— 40 so that they may fear you all the days that they live
in the land that you gave to our ancestors.

41 "Likewise when a foreigner, who is not of your people Israel,
comes from a distant land because of your name 42—for they shall
hear of your great name, your mighty hand, and your outstretched
arm—when a foreigner comes and prays toward this house, 43 then
hear in heaven your dwelling place, and do according to all that
the foreigner calls to you, so that all the peoples of the earth may
know your name and fear you, as do your people Israel, and so that

---

[a] Or *when you answer* [b] Gk Syr: Heb *in the land*

they may know that your name has been invoked on this house that
I have built.
44 "If your people go out to battle against their enemy, by whatever way you shall send them, and they pray to the LORD toward the
city that you have chosen and the house that I have built for your
name, [45]then hear in heaven their prayer and their plea, and maintain
their cause.
46 "If they sin against you—for there is no one who does not
sin—and you are angry with them and give them to an enemy, so that
they are carried away captive to the land of the enemy, far off or near;
[47]yet if they come to their senses in the land to which they have been
taken captive, and repent, and plead with you in the land of their captors, saying, 'We have sinned, and have done wrong; we have acted
wickedly'; [48]if they repent with all their heart and soul in the land of
their enemies, who took them captive, and pray to you toward their
land, which you gave to their ancestors, the city that you have chosen,
and the house that I have built for your name; [49]then hear in heaven
your dwelling place their prayer and their plea, maintain their cause
[50]and forgive your people who have sinned against you, and all their
transgressions that they have committed against you; and grant them
compassion in the sight of their captors, so that they may have compassion on them [51](for they are your people and heritage, which you
brought out of Egypt, from the midst of the iron-smelter). [52]Let your
eyes be open to the plea of your servant, and to the plea of your people Israel, listening to them whenever they call to you. [53]For you have
separated them from among all the peoples of the earth, to be your
heritage, just as you promised through Moses, your servant, when
you brought our ancestors out of Egypt, O Lord GOD."

8:46-53 they are your people and heritage: Solomon describes the situation Israel would experience in exile, almost four hundred years after the temple dedication. If these exiles repent, pray, and confess their sins, Solomon prays that God will hear, forgive, and make their captors show compassion on them. Finally, Solomon describes God's commitment to the people of Israel at the time of the exodus (8:51-52).

Solomon's prayer includes a reminder of God's promise to Israel. Who do you think needs this reminder most—God, Solomon, or the people?

Solomon Blesses the Assembly

54 Now when Solomon finished offering all this prayer and this
plea to the LORD, he arose from facing the altar of the LORD, where
he had knelt with hands outstretched toward heaven; [55]he stood and
blessed all the assembly of Israel with a loud voice:
56 "Blessed be the LORD, who has given rest to his people Israel according to all that he promised; not one word has failed of all
his good promise, which he spoke through his servant Moses. [57]The
LORD our God be with us, as he was with our ancestors; may he not
leave us or abandon us, [58]but incline our hearts to him, to walk in all
his ways, and to keep his commandments, his statutes, and his ordinances, which he commanded our ancestors. [59]Let these words of
mine, with which I pleaded before the LORD, be near to the LORD
our God day and night, and may he maintain the cause of his servant
and the cause of his people Israel, as each day requires; [60]so that all
the peoples of the earth may know that the LORD is God; there is

8:54-61 he stood and blessed all the assembly: Rest refers to God's gift of the land, a promise that had now been completely fulfilled. Solomon urges the people to obey the law and devote themselves to God. The wording here is typical of the historical account in Joshua, Judges, and the books of Samuel and Kings.

no other. [61]Therefore devote yourselves completely to the LORD our God, walking in his statutes and keeping his commandments, as at this day."

Solomon Offers Sacrifices

8:62-66 the king…offered sacrifice: The number of Solomon's sacrifices is astronomical, showing great joy and thanksgiving over completing the temple. At the end of the seven-day festival, the people from the entire land of Israel go home in great joy because of God's goodness to David, to Solomon, and to them.

62 Then the king, and all Israel with him, offered sacrifice before the LORD. [63]Solomon offered as sacrifices of well-being to the LORD twenty-two thousand oxen and one hundred twenty thousand sheep. So the king and all the people of Israel dedicated the house of the LORD. [64]The same day the king consecrated the middle of the court that was in front of the house of the LORD; for there he offered the burnt offerings and the grain offerings and the fat pieces of the sacrifices of well-being, because the bronze altar that was before the LORD was too small to receive the burnt offerings and the grain offerings and the fat pieces of the sacrifices of well-being.

65 So Solomon held the festival at that time, and all Israel with him—a great assembly, people from Lebo-hamath to the Wadi of Egypt—before the LORD our God, seven days.[a] [66]On the eighth day he sent the people away; and they blessed the king, and went to their tents, joyful and in good spirits because of all the goodness that the LORD had shown to his servant David and to his people Israel.

God Appears Again to Solomon

9:1-9 The LORD appeared to Solomon a second time: The LORD approves of the temple and indicates that if Solomon lives with integrity, his dynasty will last forever. By the end of his reign, however, Solomon would not live up to these expectations (chapter 11). Verses 6-9 threaten the nation with exile and the temple with destruction if Solomon and his descendants do not follow the LORD.

9 When Solomon had finished building the house of the LORD and the king's house and all that Solomon desired to build, [2]the LORD appeared to Solomon a second time, as he had appeared to him at Gibeon. [3]The LORD said to him, "I have heard your prayer and your plea, which you made before me; I have consecrated this house that you have built, and put my name there forever; my eyes and my heart will be there for all time. [4]As for you, if you will walk before me, as David your father walked, with integrity of heart and uprightness, doing according to all that I have commanded you, and keeping my statutes and my ordinances, [5]then I will establish your royal throne over Israel forever, as I promised your father David, saying, 'There shall not fail you a successor on the throne of Israel.'

6 "If you turn aside from following me, you or your children, and do not keep my commandments and my statutes that I have set before you, but go and serve other gods and worship them, [7]then I will cut Israel off from the land that I have given them; and the house that I have consecrated for my name I will cast out of my sight; and Israel will become a proverb and a taunt among all peoples. [8]This house will become a heap of ruins;[b] everyone passing by it will be astonished, and will hiss; and they will say, 'Why has the LORD done such a thing to this land and to this house?' [9]Then they will say, 'Because they have

[a] Compare Gk: Heb *seven days and seven days, fourteen days* [b] Syr Old Latin: Heb *will become high*

forsaken the Lord their God, who brought their ancestors out of the
land of Egypt, and embraced other gods, worshiping them and serving them; therefore the Lord has brought this disaster upon them.' "
10 At the end of twenty years, in which Solomon had built the
two houses, the house of the Lord and the king's house, 11 King Hiram of Tyre having supplied Solomon with cedar and cypress timber
and gold, as much as he desired, King Solomon gave to Hiram twenty
cities in the land of Galilee. 12 But when Hiram came from Tyre to
see the cities that Solomon had given him, they did not please him.
13 Therefore he said, "What kind of cities are these that you have given
me, my brother?" So they are called the land of Cabul[a] to this day.
14 But Hiram had sent to the king one hundred twenty talents of gold.

9:10-14 King Solomon gave to Hiram twenty cities: Solomon had paid for the building materials supplied by King Hiram of Tyre (1 Kgs 5:9-11). He also sold twenty cities in Galilee to Hiram, perhaps to build up his treasury, but Hiram was displeased with these cities for some reason. According to 2 Chronicles 8:2, Hiram (here, Huram) gave these cities back to Solomon. The amount paid for these cities by Hiram is about eight thousand pounds (3.6 metric tons) of gold.

Other Acts of Solomon

15 This is the account of the forced labor that King Solomon conscripted to build the house of the Lord and his own house, the Millo
and the wall of Jerusalem, Hazor, Megiddo, Gezer 16 (Pharaoh king of
Egypt had gone up and captured Gezer and burned it down, had killed
the Canaanites who lived in the city, and had given it as dowry to his
daughter, Solomon's wife; 17 so Solomon rebuilt Gezer), Lower Beth-
horon, 18 Baalath, Tamar in the wilderness, within the land, 19 as well
as all of Solomon's storage cities, the cities for his chariots, the cities
for his cavalry, and whatever Solomon desired to build, in Jerusalem,
in Lebanon, and in all the land of his dominion. 20 All the people who
were left of the Amorites, the Hittites, the Perizzites, the Hivites, and
the Jebusites, who were not of the people of Israel— 21 their descendants who were still left in the land, whom the Israelites were unable
to destroy completely—these Solomon conscripted for slave labor,
and so they are to this day. 22 But of the Israelites Solomon made no
slaves; they were the soldiers, they were his officials, his commanders,
his captains, and the commanders of his chariotry and cavalry.
23 These were the chief officers who were over Solomon's work:
five hundred fifty, who had charge of the people who carried on
the work.
24 But Pharaoh's daughter went up from the city of David to her
own house that Solomon had built for her; then he built the Millo.
25 Three times a year Solomon used to offer up burnt offerings
and sacrifices of well-being on the altar that he built for the Lord,
offering incense[b] before the Lord. So he completed the house.

9:15-25 Hazor, Megiddo, Gezer: Archaeologists have found city gates of similar architecture in Hazor, Megiddo, and Gezer (see Map 5, p. 2103). Solomon used forced labor for work on these cities, including survivors of people who lived in the land before the Israelites. An unnamed Pharaoh gave Solomon the city of Gezer as his daughter's dowry (money or possessions given to a groom by the bride or bride's family). She moves into a house Solomon has built for her.

Solomon's Commercial Activity

26 King Solomon built a fleet of ships at Ezion-geber, which is
near Eloth on the shore of the Red Sea,[c] in the land of Edom. 27 Hiram
sent his servants with the fleet, sailors who were familiar with the sea,

9:26-28 a fleet of ships: Solomon and Hiram engage in a very profitable joint sea venture.

---

[a] Perhaps meaning *a land good for nothing* [b] Gk: Heb *offering incense with it that was* [c] Or *Sea of Reeds*

together with the servants of Solomon. 28 They went to Ophir, and imported from there four hundred twenty talents of gold, which they
delivered to King Solomon.

Visit of the Queen of Sheba

10:1-13 the queen of Sheba: This story demonstrates the great political power of Solomon. The Queen of Sheba probably came from the region of the modern country of Yemen. She may have planned to set up trade routes with Solomon. She is amazed at Solomon's wisdom, wealth, and lavish lifestyle and gives the credit for his success to the LORD. She gives Solomon eight thousand pounds (3.6 metric tons) of gold, just as Hiram had done (9:14).

10 When the queen of Sheba heard of the fame of Solomon
(fame due to[a] the name of the LORD), she came to test him
with hard questions. 2 She came to Jerusalem with a very great retinue, with camels bearing spices, and very much gold, and precious
stones; and when she came to Solomon, she told him all that was on
her mind. 3 Solomon answered all her questions; there was nothing
hidden from the king that he could not explain to her. 4 When the
queen of Sheba had observed all the wisdom of Solomon, the house
that he had built, 5 the food of his table, the seating of his officials, and
the attendance of his servants, their clothing, his valets, and his burnt
offerings that he offered at the house of the LORD, there was no more
spirit in her.

6 So she said to the king, "The report was true that I heard in my
own land of your accomplishments and of your wisdom, 7 but I did
not believe the reports until I came and my own eyes had seen it. Not
even half had been told me; your wisdom and prosperity far surpass
the report that I had heard. 8 Happy are your wives![b] Happy are these
your servants, who continually attend you and hear your wisdom!
9 Blessed be the LORD your God, who has delighted in you and set
you on the throne of Israel! Because the LORD loved Israel forever,
he has made you king to execute justice and righteousness." 10 Then
she gave the king one hundred twenty talents of gold, a great quantity
of spices, and precious stones; never again did spices come in such
quantity as that which the queen of Sheba gave to King Solomon.

11 Moreover, the fleet of Hiram, which carried gold from Ophir,
brought from Ophir a great quantity of almug wood and precious
stones. 12 From the almug wood the king made supports for the house
of the LORD, and for the king's house, lyres also and harps for the singers; no such almug wood has come or been seen to this day.

13 Meanwhile King Solomon gave to the queen of Sheba every
desire that she expressed, as well as what he gave her out of Solomon's
royal bounty. Then she returned to her own land, with her servants.

10:14-29 The weight of gold that came to Solomon: The Bible presents Solomon as a very wealthy king, receiving more than five tons (4.5 metric tons) of gold a year in personal income. He has a lavish throne, golden drinking vessels, an enormously successful shipping venture with Hiram, international attention, and gifts from people throughout the world. Because of him, silver is said to be as common as stones in Jerusalem.

14 The weight of gold that came to Solomon in one year was six
hundred sixty-six talents of gold, 15 besides that which came from
the traders and from the business of the merchants, and from all the
kings of Arabia and the governors of the land. 16 King Solomon made
two hundred large shields of beaten gold; six hundred shekels of
gold went into each large shield. 17 He made three hundred shields of
beaten gold; three minas of gold went into each shield; and the king

---

[a] Meaning of Heb uncertain [b] Gk Syr: Heb *men*

put them in the House of the Forest of Lebanon. 18 The king also made
a great ivory throne, and overlaid it with the finest gold. 19 The throne
had six steps. The top of the throne was rounded in the back, and on
each side of the seat were arm rests and two lions standing beside the
arm rests, 20 while twelve lions were standing, one on each end of a
step on the six steps. Nothing like it was ever made in any kingdom.
21 All King Solomon's drinking vessels were of gold, and all the vessels
of the House of the Forest of Lebanon were of pure gold; none were
of silver—it was not considered as anything in the days of Solomon.
22 For the king had a fleet of ships of Tarshish at sea with the fleet of
Hiram. Once every three years the fleet of ships of Tarshish used to
come bringing gold, silver, ivory, apes, and peacocks.[a]

23 Thus King Solomon excelled all the kings of the earth in riches
and in wisdom. 24 The whole earth sought the presence of Solomon
to hear his wisdom, which God had put into his mind. 25 Every one of
them brought a present, objects of silver and gold, garments, weaponry, spices, horses, and mules, so much year by year.

26 Solomon gathered together chariots and horses; he had fourteen hundred chariots and twelve thousand horses, which he stationed in the chariot cities and with the king in Jerusalem. 27 The king
made silver as common in Jerusalem as stones, and he made cedars
as numerous as the sycamores of the Shephelah. 28 Solomon's import
of horses was from Egypt and Kue, and the king's traders received
them from Kue at a price. 29 A chariot could be imported from Egypt
for six hundred shekels of silver, and a horse for one hundred fifty; so
through the king's traders they were exported to all the kings of the
Hittites and the kings of Aram.

Solomon's Errors

11 King Solomon loved many foreign women along with the
daughter of Pharaoh: Moabite, Ammonite, Edomite, Sidonian,
and Hittite women, 2 from the nations concerning which the LORD
had said to the Israelites, "You shall not enter into marriage with
them, neither shall they with you; for they will surely incline your
heart to follow their gods"; Solomon clung to these in love. 3 Among
his wives were seven hundred princesses and three hundred concubines; and his wives turned away his heart. 4 For when Solomon was
old, his wives turned away his heart after other gods; and his heart
was not true to the LORD his God, as was the heart of his father David. 5 For Solomon followed Astarte the goddess of the Sidonians, and
Milcom the abomination of the Ammonites. 6 So Solomon did what
was evil in the sight of the LORD, and did not completely follow the
LORD, as his father David had done. 7 Then Solomon built a high place

11:1-13 King Solomon loved many foreign women: Solomon's many wives follow other gods, so he builds a number of sanctuaries for these gods east of Jerusalem and ignores God's warnings about worshiping other gods. The LORD tells Solomon that his kingdom will be divided because he has not kept the covenant, but for his father David's sake, this will not happen until after he dies, during his son Rehoboam's lifetime (chapter 12).

[a] Or *baboons*

for Chemosh the abomination of Moab, and for Molech the abomination of the Ammonites, on the mountain east of Jerusalem. 8 He did
the same for all his foreign wives, who offered incense and sacrificed
to their gods.

9 Then the LORD was angry with Solomon, because his heart had
turned away from the LORD, the God of Israel, who had appeared to
him twice, 10 and had commanded him concerning this matter, that he
should not follow other gods; but he did not observe what the LORD
commanded. 11 Therefore the LORD said to Solomon, "Since this has
been your mind and you have not kept my covenant and my statutes
that I have commanded you, I will surely tear the kingdom from you
and give it to your servant. 12 Yet for the sake of your father David I will
not do it in your lifetime; I will tear it out of the hand of your son. 13 I
will not, however, tear away the entire kingdom; I will give one tribe
to your son, for the sake of my servant David and for the sake of Jerusalem, which I have chosen."

Adversaries of Solomon

14 Then the LORD raised up an adversary against Solomon, Hadad the Edomite; he was of the royal house in Edom. 15 For when
David was in Edom, and Joab the commander of the army went up
to bury the dead, he killed every male in Edom 16 (for Joab and all Israel remained there six months, until he had eliminated every male in
Edom); 17 but Hadad fled to Egypt with some Edomites who were servants of his father. He was a young boy at that time. 18 They set out from
Midian and came to Paran; they took people with them from Paran
and came to Egypt, to Pharaoh king of Egypt, who gave him a house,
assigned him an allowance of food, and gave him land. 19 Hadad found
great favor in the sight of Pharaoh, so that he gave him his sister-in-law
for a wife, the sister of Queen Tahpenes. 20 The sister of Tahpenes gave
birth by him to his son Genubath, whom Tahpenes weaned in Pharaoh's house; Genubath was in Pharaoh's house among the children
of Pharaoh. 21 When Hadad heard in Egypt that David slept with his
ancestors and that Joab the commander of the army was dead, Hadad
said to Pharaoh, "Let me depart, that I may go to my own country."
22 But Pharaoh said to him, "What do you lack with me that you now
seek to go to your own country?" And he said, "No, do let me go."

23 God raised up another adversary against Solomon,[a] Rezon
son of Eliada, who had fled from his master, King Hadadezer of Zobah. 24 He gathered followers around him and became leader of a marauding band, after the slaughter by David; they went to Damascus,
settled there, and made him king in Damascus. 25 He was an adversary
of Israel all the days of Solomon, making trouble as Hadad did; he
despised Israel and reigned over Aram.

11:14-40 the LORD raised up an adversary against Solomon: Joab's violence against the Edomites during David's reign led a man named Hadad to turn to Egypt for assistance. Hadad gains such favor in Egypt that Pharaoh gives him his sister-in-law for a wife. When Hadad hears about David and Joab's deaths, he goes home to Edom, despite Pharaoh's objections. Another of Solomon's enemies is an Aramean named Rezon, but the biggest threat is Jeroboam, the son of Nebat, who had been an official under Solomon. The prophet Ahijah, from the ancient sanctuary of Shiloh (see 1 Sam 1–3), promises that Jeroboam will rule over ten Israelite tribes, with only Judah, and perhaps Benjamin, left for David's descendants. Solomon's kingdom will break up after his death, because he has worshiped other gods from Sidon, Moab, and Ammon. There will be a lamp for David, however (11:36; see also 1 Kgs 15:4; 2 Kgs 8:19). Jeroboam is promised an everlasting kingdom if he follows God's commandments. When Solomon hears this prophecy, he tries to kill Jeroboam. Jeroboam flees to Egypt and stays with Shishak, who is identified with Pharaoh Shoshenq I of Egypt (931–910 B.C.E.; see 1 Kgs 14:25-26).

[a] Heb *him*

Jeroboam's Rebellion

26 Jeroboam son of Nebat, an Ephraimite of Zeredah, a servant
of Solomon, whose mother's name was Zeruah, a widow, rebelled
against the king. 27The following was the reason he rebelled against
the king. Solomon built the Millo, and closed up the gap in the wall[a]
of the city of his father David. 28The man Jeroboam was very able,
and when Solomon saw that the young man was industrious he gave
him charge over all the forced labor of the house of Joseph. 29About
that time, when Jeroboam was leaving Jerusalem, the prophet Ahijah the Shilonite found him on the road. Ahijah had clothed himself
with a new garment. The two of them were alone in the open country
30when Ahijah laid hold of the new garment he was wearing and tore
it into twelve pieces. 31He then said to Jeroboam: Take for yourself
ten pieces; for thus says the LORD, the God of Israel, "See, I am about
to tear the kingdom from the hand of Solomon, and will give you ten
tribes. 32One tribe will remain his, for the sake of my servant David
and for the sake of Jerusalem, the city that I have chosen out of all
the tribes of Israel. 33This is because he has[b] forsaken me, worshiped
Astarte the goddess of the Sidonians, Chemosh the god of Moab, and
Milcom the god of the Ammonites, and has[b] not walked in my ways,
doing what is right in my sight and keeping my statutes and my ordinances, as his father David did. 34Nevertheless I will not take the
whole kingdom away from him but will make him ruler all the days
of his life, for the sake of my servant David whom I chose and who
did keep my commandments and my statutes; 35but I will take the
kingdom away from his son and give it to you—that is, the ten tribes.
36Yet to his son I will give one tribe, so that my servant David may
always have a lamp before me in Jerusalem, the city where I have chosen to put my name. 37I will take you, and you shall reign over all that
your soul desires; you shall be king over Israel. 38If you will listen to
all that I command you, walk in my ways, and do what is right in my
sight by keeping my statutes and my commandments, as David my
servant did, I will be with you, and will build you an enduring house,
as I built for David, and I will give Israel to you. 39For this reason I will
punish the descendants of David, but not forever." 40Solomon sought
therefore to kill Jeroboam; but Jeroboam promptly fled to Egypt,
to King Shishak of Egypt, and remained in Egypt until the death of
Solomon.

Death of Solomon

41 Now the rest of the acts of Solomon, all that he did as well as
his wisdom, are they not written in the Book of the Acts of Solomon?
42The time that Solomon reigned in Jerusalem over all Israel was forty

11:41-43 Solomon slept with his ancestors: Solomon dies, and his son Rehoboam becomes king. "The Book of the Acts of Solomon" is the first reference to original documents containing more information about a given reign. Unfortunately, none of these documents has survived.

[a] Heb lacks *in the wall* [b] Gk Syr Vg: Heb *they have*

years. 43 Solomon slept with his ancestors and was buried in the city of
his father David; and his son Rehoboam succeeded him.

The Northern Tribes Secede

12:1-19 Rehoboam reigned over the Israelites...in the towns of Judah: Rehoboam (931–914 B.C.E.) travels north from Jerusalem to Shechem to be made king. Jeroboam also shows up for this assembly, and the northern tribes demand that Rehoboam reduce the taxes and the forced labor that his father Solomon had imposed. A group of elders urge Rehoboam to be lenient, but a group of young men advise him to respond harshly and tell the people that he will be much tougher than his father. This strategy causes a split in the kingdom, fulfilling the prophecy of Ahijah. The ten northern tribes split off and form the northern kingdom, sometimes known as Ephraim. Rehoboam remained king of the much smaller kingdom of Judah (see Map 7, p. 2105). Rehoboam sends Adoram, who is in charge of forced labor, to enforce his will on the northern tribes, but Adoram is stoned to death, and Rehoboam flees to Jerusalem.

12 Rehoboam went to Shechem, for all Israel had come to Shechem to make him king. 2 When Jeroboam son of Nebat heard
of it (for he was still in Egypt, where he had fled from King Solomon),
then Jeroboam returned from[a] Egypt. 3 And they sent and called him;
and Jeroboam and all the assembly of Israel came and said to Rehoboam, 4 "Your father made our yoke heavy. Now therefore lighten the
hard service of your father and his heavy yoke that he placed on us,
and we will serve you." 5 He said to them, "Go away for three days,
then come again to me." So the people went away.

6 Then King Rehoboam took counsel with the older men who
had attended his father Solomon while he was still alive, saying, "How
do you advise me to answer this people?" 7 They answered him, "If
you will be a servant to this people today and serve them, and speak
good words to them when you answer them, then they will be your
servants forever." 8 But he disregarded the advice that the older men
gave him, and consulted with the young men who had grown up with
him and now attended him. 9 He said to them, "What do you advise
that we answer this people who have said to me, 'Lighten the yoke
that your father put on us'?" 10 The young men who had grown up
with him said to him, "Thus you should say to this people who spoke
to you, 'Your father made our yoke heavy, but you must lighten it for
us'; thus you should say to them, 'My little finger is thicker than my
father's loins. 11 Now, whereas my father laid on you a heavy yoke, I
will add to your yoke. My father disciplined you with whips, but I will
discipline you with scorpions.'"

12 So Jeroboam and all the people came to Rehoboam the third
day, as the king had said, "Come to me again the third day." 13 The king
answered the people harshly. He disregarded the advice that the older
men had given him 14 and spoke to them according to the advice of the
young men, "My father made your yoke heavy, but I will add to your
yoke; my father disciplined you with whips, but I will discipline you
with scorpions." 15 So the king did not listen to the people, because it
was a turn of affairs brought about by the LORD that he might fulfill
his word, which the LORD had spoken by Ahijah the Shilonite to Jeroboam son of Nebat.

16 When all Israel saw that the king would not listen to them, the
people answered the king,

"What share do we have in David?
 We have no inheritance in the son of Jesse.

---

[a] Gk Vg Compare 2 Chr 10.2: Heb *lived in*

To your tents, O Israel!
Look now to your own house, O David."
So Israel went away to their tents. [17]But Rehoboam reigned over the
Israelites who were living in the towns of Judah. [18]When King Re-
hoboam sent Adoram, who was taskmaster over the forced labor, all
Israel stoned him to death. King Rehoboam then hurriedly mounted
his chariot to flee to Jerusalem. [19]So Israel has been in rebellion against
the house of David to this day.

First Dynasty: Jeroboam Reigns over Israel

20 When all Israel heard that Jeroboam had returned, they sent
and called him to the assembly and made him king over all Israel.
There was no one who followed the house of David, except the tribe
of Judah alone.
21 When Rehoboam came to Jerusalem, he assembled all the
house of Judah and the tribe of Benjamin, one hundred eighty thousand chosen troops to fight against the house of Israel, to restore the
kingdom to Rehoboam son of Solomon. [22]But the word of God came
to Shemaiah the man of God: [23]Say to King Rehoboam of Judah, son
of Solomon, and to all the house of Judah and Benjamin, and to the
rest of the people, [24]"Thus says the LORD, You shall not go up or fight
against your kindred the people of Israel. Let everyone go home, for
this thing is from me." So they heeded the word of the LORD and went
home again, according to the word of the LORD.

12:20-24 You shall not...fight against your kindred: The assembly at Shechem installs Jeroboam (931–909 B.C.E.) as king (see 11:26-40). Rehoboam tries to take the northern kingdom by force. However, a prophet named Shemaiah delivers a message from the LORD not allowing this attack, and the king sends his large army home.

Jeroboam's Golden Calves

25 Then Jeroboam built Shechem in the hill country of Ephraim,
and resided there; he went out from there and built Penuel. [26]Then
Jeroboam said to himself, "Now the kingdom may well revert to the
house of David. [27]If this people continues to go up to offer sacrifices in
the house of the LORD at Jerusalem, the heart of this people will turn
again to their master, King Rehoboam of Judah; they will kill me and
return to King Rehoboam of Judah." [28]So the king took counsel, and
made two calves of gold. He said to the people,[a] "You have gone up
to Jerusalem long enough. Here are your gods, O Israel, who brought
you up out of the land of Egypt." [29]He set one in Bethel, and the other
he put in Dan. [30]And this thing became a sin, for the people went to
worship before the one at Bethel and before the other as far as Dan.[b]
[31]He also made houses[c] on high places, and appointed priests from
among all the people, who were not Levites. [32]Jeroboam appointed a
festival on the fifteenth day of the eighth month like the festival that
was in Judah, and he offered sacrifices on the altar; so he did in Bethel,

12:25-33 Here are your gods, O Israel: Jeroboam moves his capital from Shechem to Penuel, east of the Jordan (see Map 7, p. 2105), where Jacob wrestled with God (Gen 32:22-32). God's law said there was to be only one place for sacrifice. Jeroboam, however, evidently fears that if the people make pilgrimages to Jerusalem, they might also decide to reunite politically with the southern kingdom, so he sets up sanctuaries at Bethel and Dan, on the southern and northern borders of his kingdom. Through the rest of 1 and 2 Kings the sanctuaries at Bethel and Dan become known as the sin that Jeroboam made Israel to sin.

---

[a] Gk: Heb *to them* [b] Compare Gk: Heb *went to the one as far as Dan* [c] Gk Vg Compare 13.32: Heb *a house*

sacrificing to the calves that he had made. And he placed in Bethel the
priests of the high places that he had made. 33 He went up to the altar
that he had made in Bethel on the fifteenth day in the eighth month,
in the month that he alone had devised; he appointed a festival for the
people of Israel, and he went up to the altar to offer incense.

A Man of God from Judah

13 While Jeroboam was standing by the altar to offer incense, a
man of God came out of Judah by the word of the LORD to
Bethel 2 and proclaimed against the altar by the word of the LORD,
and said, "O altar, altar, thus says the LORD: 'A son shall be born to
the house of David, Josiah by name; and he shall sacrifice on you the
priests of the high places who offer incense on you, and human bones
shall be burned on you.'" 3 He gave a sign the same day, saying, "This is
the sign that the LORD has spoken: 'The altar shall be torn down, and
the ashes that are on it shall be poured out.'" 4 When the king heard
what the man of God cried out against the altar at Bethel, Jeroboam
stretched out his hand from the altar, saying, "Seize him!" But the
hand that he stretched out against him withered so that he could not
draw it back to himself. 5 The altar also was torn down, and the ashes
poured out from the altar, according to the sign that the man of God
had given by the word of the LORD. 6 The king said to the man of God,
"Entreat now the favor of the LORD your God, and pray for me, so
that my hand may be restored to me." So the man of God entreated
the LORD; and the king's hand was restored to him, and became as it
was before. 7 Then the king said to the man of God, "Come home with
me and dine, and I will give you a gift." 8 But the man of God said to
the king, "If you give me half your kingdom, I will not go in with you;
nor will I eat food or drink water in this place. 9 For thus I was commanded by the word of the LORD: You shall not eat food, or drink
water, or return by the way that you came." 10 So he went another way,
and did not return by the way that he had come to Bethel.

11 Now there lived an old prophet in Bethel. One of his sons
came and told him all that the man of God had done that day in
Bethel; the words also that he had spoken to the king, they told to
their father. 12 Their father said to them, "Which way did he go?" And
his sons showed him the way that the man of God who came from
Judah had gone. 13 Then he said to his sons, "Saddle a donkey for me."
So they saddled a donkey for him, and he mounted it. 14 He went after
the man of God, and found him sitting under an oak tree. He said to
him, "Are you the man of God who came from Judah?" He answered,
"I am." 15 Then he said to him, "Come home with me and eat some
food." 16 But he said, "I cannot return with you, or go in with you; nor
will I eat food or drink water with you in this place; 17 for it was said
to me by the word of the LORD: You shall not eat food or drink water

13:1-10 a man of God came out of Judah: A "man of God" is another name for a prophet. This man tells Jeroboam that someday a Judean king by the name of Josiah will kill the priests serving at Bethel and tear down the altar. This prophecy was fulfilled three centuries later (2 Kgs 23:15-18). Jeroboam wants the man of God arrested, but the hand he stretches out against the man becomes lame. The healing of the king's hand demonstrates the power of the man of God's words.

13:11-32 an old prophet in Bethel: An unnamed prophet in Bethel hears about the incident with the man of God and decides to deceive him. He invites the man of God to dinner, but the man of God declines, because the LORD has told him not to eat or drink anything. Then the old prophet lies to the man of God and tells him he has received a message through an angel to provide a meal for the man of God. Perhaps the fact that the old prophet has not received the oracle directly from God is an indication that the message is not from God. During dinner the old prophet receives another message, condemning the man of God to death. The man of God goes on his way, but is met by a lion that kills him. The lion does not harm the donkey or eat the man of God, however, signaling that this event is supernatural. When the old prophet hears about this, he buries the man of God in his own tomb. The old prophet instructs his disciples (here called his sons) to bury him someday in the same tomb and announces that the prophecy against Bethel and the other high places will be fulfilled.

there, or return by the way that you came.” 18 Then the other[a] said to
him, “I also am a prophet as you are, and an angel spoke to me by the
word of the LORD: Bring him back with you into your house so that
he may eat food and drink water.” But he was deceiving him. 19 Then
the man of God[a] went back with him, and ate food and drank water
in his house.

20 As they were sitting at the table, the word of the LORD came
to the prophet who had brought him back; 21 and he proclaimed to
the man of God who came from Judah, “Thus says the LORD: Because you have disobeyed the word of the LORD, and have not kept
the commandment that the LORD your God commanded you, 22 but
have come back and have eaten food and drunk water in the place of
which he said to you, ‘Eat no food, and drink no water,’ your body
shall not come to your ancestral tomb.” 23 After the man of God[a] had
eaten food and had drunk, they saddled for him a donkey belonging
to the prophet who had brought him back. 24 Then as he went away, a
lion met him on the road and killed him. His body was thrown in the
road, and the donkey stood beside it; the lion also stood beside the
body. 25 People passed by and saw the body thrown in the road, with
the lion standing by the body. And they came and told it in the town
where the old prophet lived.

26 When the prophet who had brought him back from the way
heard of it, he said, “It is the man of God who disobeyed the word of
the LORD; therefore the LORD has given him to the lion, which has
torn him and killed him according to the word that the LORD spoke
to him.” 27 Then he said to his sons, “Saddle a donkey for me.” So they
saddled one, 28 and he went and found the body thrown in the road,
with the donkey and the lion standing beside the body. The lion had
not eaten the body or attacked the donkey. 29 The prophet took up
the body of the man of God, laid it on the donkey, and brought it
back to the city,[b] to mourn and to bury him. 30 He laid the body in his
own grave; and they mourned over him, saying, “Alas, my brother!”
31 After he had buried him, he said to his sons, “When I die, bury
me in the grave in which the man of God is buried; lay my bones
beside his bones. 32 For the saying that he proclaimed by the word
of the LORD against the altar in Bethel, and against all the houses
of the high places that are in the cities of Samaria, shall surely come
to pass.”

33 Even after this event Jeroboam did not turn from his evil way,
but made priests for the high places again from among all the people; any who wanted to be priests he consecrated for the high places.
34 This matter became sin to the house of Jeroboam, so as to cut it off
and to destroy it from the face of the earth.

13:33-34 Jeroboam did not turn from his evil way: Even after his confrontation with the man of God, Jeroboam continues in his unfaithful ways by appointing priests for the high places. The “house of Jeroboam” refers to his family line.

---

[a] Heb *he* [b] Gk: Heb *he came to the town of the old prophet*

14:1-18 Abijah son of Jeroboam fell sick: His son's serious illness causes Jeroboam to send his wife to the prophet Ahijah, who earlier had prophesied that Jeroboam would be king (11:29-39). She goes in disguise, but the blind prophet knows who she is because of a message from the LORD. Ahijah invites her in and delivers a devastating message about the fate of her husband and his family. In addition, Israel will be sent in exile to Assyria ("beyond the Euphrates"), because the people had made "sacred poles," indicating worship of the goddess Asherah. The capital of Israel had been moved to Tirzah. The prophecy about Jeroboam's son came true as the woman returned home. The prophecy about the exile to Assyria was delayed for almost two centuries.

Judgment on the House of Jeroboam

14 At that time Abijah son of Jeroboam fell sick. 2 Jeroboam said
to his wife, "Go, disguise yourself, so that it will not be known
that you are the wife of Jeroboam, and go to Shiloh; for the prophet
Ahijah is there, who said of me that I should be king over this people.
3 Take with you ten loaves, some cakes, and a jar of honey, and go to
him; he will tell you what shall happen to the child."

4 Jeroboam's wife did so; she set out and went to Shiloh, and
came to the house of Ahijah. Now Ahijah could not see, for his eyes
were dim because of his age. 5 But the LORD said to Ahijah, "The wife
of Jeroboam is coming to inquire of you concerning her son; for he is
sick. Thus and thus you shall say to her."

When she came, she pretended to be another woman. 6 But when
Ahijah heard the sound of her feet, as she came in at the door, he said,
"Come in, wife of Jeroboam; why do you pretend to be another? For I
am charged with heavy tidings for you. 7 Go, tell Jeroboam, 'Thus says
the LORD, the God of Israel: Because I exalted you from among the
people, made you leader over my people Israel, 8 and tore the kingdom
away from the house of David to give it to you; yet you have not been
like my servant David, who kept my commandments and followed
me with all his heart, doing only that which was right in my sight,
9 but you have done evil above all those who were before you and have
gone and made for yourself other gods, and cast images, provoking
me to anger, and have thrust me behind your back; 10 therefore, I will
bring evil upon the house of Jeroboam. I will cut off from Jeroboam
every male, both bond and free in Israel, and will consume the house
of Jeroboam, just as one burns up dung until it is all gone. 11 Anyone
belonging to Jeroboam who dies in the city, the dogs shall eat; and
anyone who dies in the open country, the birds of the air shall eat; for
the LORD has spoken.' 12 Therefore set out, go to your house. When
your feet enter the city, the child shall die. 13 All Israel shall mourn for
him and bury him; for he alone of Jeroboam's family shall come to the
grave, because in him there is found something pleasing to the LORD,
the God of Israel, in the house of Jeroboam. 14 Moreover the LORD
will raise up for himself a king over Israel, who shall cut off the house
of Jeroboam today, even right now![a]

15 "The LORD will strike Israel, as a reed is shaken in the water;
he will root up Israel out of this good land that he gave to their ancestors, and scatter them beyond the Euphrates, because they have made
their sacred poles,[b] provoking the LORD to anger. 16 He will give Israel
up because of the sins of Jeroboam, which he sinned and which he
caused Israel to commit."

17 Then Jeroboam's wife got up and went away, and she came to

---

[b] Meaning of Heb uncertain [b] Heb *Asherim*

Tirzah. As she came to the threshold of the house, the child died. 18 All
Israel buried him and mourned for him, according to the word of the
Lord, which he spoke by his servant the prophet Ahijah.

Death of Jeroboam

19 Now the rest of the acts of Jeroboam, how he warred and how
he reigned, are written in the Book of the Annals of the Kings of Israel.
20 The time that Jeroboam reigned was twenty-two years; then he slept
with his ancestors, and his son Nadab succeeded him.

14:19-20 [Jeroboam] slept with his ancestors: Jeroboam dies after a twenty-two year reign. His son Nadab (909–908 B.C.E.) becomes king.

Rehoboam Reigns over Judah

21 Now Rehoboam son of Solomon reigned in Judah. Rehoboam was forty-one years old when he began to reign, and he reigned
seventeen years in Jerusalem, the city that the Lord had chosen out
of all the tribes of Israel, to put his name there. His mother's name was
Naamah the Ammonite. 22 Judah did what was evil in the sight of the
Lord; they provoked him to jealousy with their sins that they committed, more than all that their ancestors had done. 23 For they also
built for themselves high places, pillars, and sacred poles[a] on every
high hill and under every green tree; 24 there were also male temple
prostitutes in the land. They committed all the abominations of the
nations that the Lord drove out before the people of Israel.

25 In the fifth year of King Rehoboam, King Shishak of Egypt
came up against Jerusalem; 26 he took away the treasures of the house
of the Lord and the treasures of the king's house; he took everything.
He also took away all the shields of gold that Solomon had made;
27 so King Rehoboam made shields of bronze instead, and committed them to the hands of the officers of the guard, who kept the door
of the king's house. 28 As often as the king went into the house of the
Lord, the guard carried them and brought them back to the guardroom.

29 Now the rest of the acts of Rehoboam, and all that he did, are
they not written in the Book of the Annals of the Kings of Judah?
30 There was war between Rehoboam and Jeroboam continually. 31 Rehoboam slept with his ancestors and was buried with his ancestors in
the city of David. His mother's name was Naamah the Ammonite.
His son Abijam succeeded him.

14:21-29 Rehoboam son of Solomon reigned in Judah: Jerusalem is identified as the place where the Lord chooses to put the Lord's name (see Deut 12:5). Judah is criticized for its high places (3:2), standing stones (often associated with the worship of Baal), and sacred poles (see 14:15). The term translated "male temple prostitutes" in 14:24 should be understood only as consecrated individuals. The attack by King Shishak is also reported in Egyptian sources. As a consequence of the people's idolatry, Shishak takes goods and treasures from the temple and the palace. Rehoboam can only replace the golden shields, which had been part of the temple liturgy, with bronze shields. Rehoboam's mother was an Ammonite and one of Solomon's many foreign wives. Abijam (914–911 B.C.E.) succeeds Rehoboam as king of Judah.

Abijam Reigns over Judah: Idolatry and War

15 Now in the eighteenth year of King Jeroboam son of Nebat,
Abijam began to reign over Judah. 2 He reigned for three years
in Jerusalem. His mother's name was Maacah daughter of Abishalom.
3 He committed all the sins that his father did before him; his heart

15:1-8 Abijam … reigned for three years: Verse 1 links the kings of the south (Abijam) and the north (Jeroboam). Abijam is not true to God, but the Lord shows mercy on him by permitting his son to succeed him for David's sake. War with the north continues throughout Abijam's reign. He dies and Asa (911–870 B.C.E.) succeeds him.

---

[a] Heb *Asherim*

was not true to the LORD his God, like the heart of his father David. [4]Nevertheless for David's sake the LORD his God gave him a lamp in Jerusalem, setting up his son after him, and establishing Jerusalem; [5]because David did what was right in the sight of the LORD, and did not turn aside from anything that he commanded him all the days of his life, except in the matter of Uriah the Hittite. [6]The war begun between Rehoboam and Jeroboam continued all the days of his life. [7]The rest of the acts of Abijam, and all that he did, are they not written in the Book of the Annals of the Kings of Judah? There was war between Abijam and Jeroboam. [8]Abijam slept with his ancestors, and they buried him in the city of David. Then his son Asa succeeded him.

Asa Reigns over Judah

15:9-15 Asa was true to the LORD: Asa follows in the pious ways of David and gets rid of many signs of the worship of other gods. He even demotes his mother, because she made an image for the goddess Asherah. Although Asa does not get rid of the high places, he is generous in his contributions to the temple.

9 In the twentieth year of King Jeroboam of Israel, Asa began to reign over Judah; [10]he reigned forty-one years in Jerusalem. His mother's name was Maacah daughter of Abishalom. [11]Asa did what was right in the sight of the LORD, as his father David had done. [12]He put away the male temple prostitutes out of the land, and removed all the idols that his ancestors had made. [13]He also removed his mother Maacah from being queen mother, because she had made an abominable image for Asherah; Asa cut down her image and burned it at the Wadi Kidron. [14]But the high places were not taken away. Nevertheless the heart of Asa was true to the LORD all his days. [15]He brought into the house of the LORD the votive gifts of his father and his own votive gifts—silver, gold, and utensils.

Alliance with Aram against Israel

15:16-24 war between Asa and King Baasha of Israel: The war between Judah and Israel continues. The northern king, Baasha (908–885 B.C.E.), fortifies Ramah, about five miles north of Jerusalem, to protect his borders (see Map 7, p. 2105). Asa sends temple and palace treasures as a tribute or bribe to King Ben-hadad of Damascus and proposes that they form an alliance. This proposal requires Ben-hadad to break off his alliance with Baasha, which he does. He also attacks a number of cities in northern Israel, forcing Baasha to stop his aggressive actions against Judah. Asa brings in forced labor to take materials from Baasha's building projects in Ramah and use them for construction in the towns of Geba and Mizpah.

16 There was war between Asa and King Baasha of Israel all their days. [17]King Baasha of Israel went up against Judah, and built Ramah, to prevent anyone from going out or coming in to King Asa of Judah. [18]Then Asa took all the silver and the gold that were left in the treasures of the house of the LORD and the treasures of the king's house, and gave them into the hands of his servants. King Asa sent them to King Ben-hadad son of Tabrimmon son of Hezion of Aram, who resided in Damascus, saying, [19]"Let there be an alliance between me and you, like that between my father and your father: I am sending you a present of silver and gold; go, break your alliance with King Baasha of Israel, so that he may withdraw from me." [20]Ben-hadad listened to King Asa, and sent the commanders of his armies against the cities of Israel. He conquered Ijon, Dan, Abel-beth-maacah, and all Chinneroth, with all the land of Naphtali. [21]When Baasha heard of it, he stopped building Ramah and lived in Tirzah. [22]Then King Asa made a proclamation to all Judah, none was exempt: they carried away the stones of Ramah and its timber, with which Baasha had been building; with them King Asa built Geba of Benjamin and Mizpah. [23]Now

the rest of all the acts of Asa, all his power, all that he did, and the cities that he built, are they not written in the Book of the Annals of the Kings of Judah? But in his old age he was diseased in his feet. 24 Then Asa slept with his ancestors, and was buried with his ancestors in the city of his father David; his son Jehoshaphat succeeded him.

Nadab Reigns over Israel

25 Nadab son of Jeroboam began to reign over Israel in the second year of King Asa of Judah; he reigned over Israel two years. 26 He did what was evil in the sight of the LORD, walking in the way of his ancestor and in the sin that he caused Israel to commit.

27 Baasha son of Ahijah, of the house of Issachar, conspired against him; and Baasha struck him down at Gibbethon, which belonged to the Philistines; for Nadab and all Israel were laying siege to Gibbethon. 28 So Baasha killed Nadab[a] in the third year of King Asa of Judah, and succeeded him. 29 As soon as he was king, he killed all the house of Jeroboam; he left to the house of Jeroboam not one that breathed, until he had destroyed it, according to the word of the LORD that he spoke by his servant Ahijah the Shilonite— 30 because of the sins of Jeroboam that he committed and that he caused Israel to commit, and because of the anger to which he provoked the LORD, the God of Israel.

15:25-34 Baasha killed Nadab: The northern king, Nadab, follows in his father Jeroboam's evil ways. Baasha assassinates him, becomes king himself, and destroys Nadab's royal household, which fulfills Ahijah's prophecy (14:10-11). The second dynasty in northern Israel begins with Baasha, who continues Jeroboam's evil ways.

31 Now the rest of the acts of Nadab, and all that he did, are they not written in the Book of the Annals of the Kings of Israel? 32 There was war between Asa and King Baasha of Israel all their days.

Second Dynasty: Baasha Reigns over Israel

33 In the third year of King Asa of Judah, Baasha son of Ahijah began to reign over all Israel at Tirzah; he reigned twenty-four years. 34 He did what was evil in the sight of the LORD, walking in the way of Jeroboam and in the sin that he caused Israel to commit.

16 The word of the LORD came to Jehu son of Hanani against Baasha, saying, 2 "Since I exalted you out of the dust and made you leader over my people Israel, and you have walked in the way of Jeroboam, and have caused my people Israel to sin, provoking me to anger with their sins, 3 therefore, I will consume Baasha and his house, and I will make your house like the house of Jeroboam son of Nebat. 4 Anyone belonging to Baasha who dies in the city the dogs shall eat; and anyone of his who dies in the field the birds of the air shall eat."

16:1-7 the word of the LORD... against Baasha: The prophet Jehu delivers God's message that because Baasha continues the evil ways of Jeroboam, his dynasty will suffer the same fate as Jeroboam's (see 14:10-11). Jehu also delivers a message against Jehoshaphat (2 Chr 19:2-3). In verse 7 Baasha is also criticized for destroying the dynasty of Jeroboam. Baasha dies and his son Elah (885–884 B.C.E.) succeeds him.

5 Now the rest of the acts of Baasha, what he did, and his power, are they not written in the Book of the Annals of the Kings of Israel? 6 Baasha slept with his ancestors, and was buried at Tirzah; and his son Elah succeeded him. 7 Moreover the word of the LORD came by the prophet Jehu son of Hanani against Baasha and his house, both

[a] Heb *him*

because of all the evil that he did in the sight of the LORD, provoking him to anger with the work of his hands, in being like the house of Jeroboam, and also because he destroyed it.

Elah Reigns over Israel

16:8-14 Elah son of Baasha began to reign over Israel: Elah's brief and evil reign ends in his assassination by Zimri, one of the officers in his army. Zimri immediately kills all the survivors in Baasha's family, fulfilling Jehu's prophecy (16:1-4).

8 In the twenty-sixth year of King Asa of Judah, Elah son of Baasha began to reign over Israel in Tirzah; he reigned two years. [9]But his servant Zimri, commander of half his chariots, conspired against him. When he was at Tirzah, drinking himself drunk in the house of Arza, who was in charge of the palace at Tirzah, [10]Zimri came in and struck him down and killed him, in the twenty-seventh year of King Asa of Judah, and succeeded him.

11 When he began to reign, as soon as he had seated himself on his throne, he killed all the house of Baasha; he did not leave him a single male of his kindred or his friends. [12]Thus Zimri destroyed all the house of Baasha, according to the word of the LORD, which he spoke against Baasha by the prophet Jehu— [13]because of all the sins of Baasha and the sins of his son Elah that they committed, and that they caused Israel to commit, provoking the LORD God of Israel to anger with their idols. [14]Now the rest of the acts of Elah, and all that he did, are they not written in the Book of the Annals of the Kings of Israel?

Third Dynasty: Zimri Reigns over Israel

16:15-20 Zimri reigned seven days: Zimri's reign lasts only seven days in 884 B.C.E. After hearing the news of Elah's assassination, "all Israel," or at least a segment of the army, makes Omri (884–874 B.C.E.) king instead. Omri immediately attacks Zimri at his capital in Tirzah, and the panicked king burns down the palace with himself inside.

15 In the twenty-seventh year of King Asa of Judah, Zimri reigned seven days in Tirzah. Now the troops were encamped against Gibbethon, which belonged to the Philistines, [16]and the troops who were encamped heard it said, "Zimri has conspired, and he has killed the king"; therefore all Israel made Omri, the commander of the army, king over Israel that day in the camp. [17]So Omri went up from Gibbethon, and all Israel with him, and they besieged Tirzah. [18]When Zimri saw that the city was taken, he went into the citadel of the king's house; he burned down the king's house over himself with fire, and died— [19]because of the sins that he committed, doing evil in the sight of the LORD, walking in the way of Jeroboam, and for the sin that he committed, causing Israel to sin. [20]Now the rest of the acts of Zimri, and the conspiracy that he made, are they not written in the Book of the Annals of the Kings of Israel?

Fourth Dynasty: Omri Reigns over Israel

16:21-23 Omri became king: A short civil war breaks out, with half the people following Omri and the other half following Tibni. "So Tibni died" may be another way here of saying that he was killed.

21 Then the people of Israel were divided into two parts; half of the people followed Tibni son of Ginath, to make him king, and half followed Omri. [22]But the people who followed Omri overcame the people who followed Tibni son of Ginath; so Tibni died, and Omri became king. [23]In the thirty-first year of King Asa of Judah, Omri began to reign over Israel; he reigned for twelve years, six of them in Tirzah.

Samaria the New Capital

24 He bought the hill of Samaria from Shemer for two talents of
silver; he fortified the hill, and called the city that he built, Samaria,
after the name of Shemer, the owner of the hill.
25 Omri did what was evil in the sight of the LORD; he did more
evil than all who were before him. 26For he walked in all the way of Jeroboam son of Nebat, and in the sins that he caused Israel to commit,
provoking the LORD, the God of Israel, to anger by their idols. 27Now
the rest of the acts of Omri that he did, and the power that he showed,
are they not written in the Book of the Annals of the Kings of Israel?
28Omri slept with his ancestors, and was buried in Samaria; his son
Ahab succeeded him.

16:24-28 Omri did what was evil in the sight of the LORD: Omri moves the capital to the beautiful and strategically located site of Samaria (see Map 7, p. 2105), and it remains there until the defeat of Israel by the Assyrians in 722 B.C.E. Although the writer of Kings says Omri continued in the sins of Jeroboam, his dynasty is one of the most important in northern Israel. Other sources indicate that Omri gained a military victory in the country of Moab in Transjordan, and the Assyrians referred to northern Israel as the "land of Omri" long after his death.

Ahab Reigns over Israel

29 In the thirty-eighth year of King Asa of Judah, Ahab son of
Omri began to reign over Israel; Ahab son of Omri reigned over Israel
in Samaria twenty-two years. 30Ahab son of Omri did evil in the sight
of the LORD more than all who were before him.

Ahab Marries Jezebel and Worships Baal

31 And as if it had been a light thing for him to walk in the sins of
Jeroboam son of Nebat, he took as his wife Jezebel daughter of King
Ethbaal of the Sidonians, and went and served Baal, and worshiped
him. 32He erected an altar for Baal in the house of Baal, which he built
in Samaria. 33Ahab also made a sacred pole.[a] Ahab did more to provoke the anger of the LORD, the God of Israel, than had all the kings of
Israel who were before him. 34In his days Hiel of Bethel built Jericho;
he laid its foundation at the cost of Abiram his firstborn, and set up its
gates at the cost of his youngest son Segub, according to the word of
the LORD, which he spoke by Joshua son of Nun.

16:29-34 Ahab son of Omri did evil in the sight of the LORD: The reign of Ahab (873–852 B.C.E.), along with many stories about the prophet Elijah, will continue through the rest of 1 Kings. Ahab, the most severely criticized king of the north, married a Phoenician princess named Jezebel. This marriage may have solidified Israel's relationship to Phoenicia, its powerful neighbor to the northwest. Ahab built a temple for the storm god Baal and set up a sacred pole for the fertility goddess Asherah. The sad fate of Hiel's sons fulfills a prophecy from Joshua (Josh 6:26).

Elijah Predicts a Drought

17 Now Elijah the Tishbite, of Tishbe[b] in Gilead, said to Ahab,
"As the LORD the God of Israel lives, before whom I stand,
there shall be neither dew nor rain these years, except by my word."
2The word of the LORD came to him, saying, 3"Go from here and turn
eastward, and hide yourself by the Wadi Cherith, which is east of the
Jordan. 4You shall drink from the wadi, and I have commanded the
ravens to feed you there." 5So he went and did according to the word
of the LORD; he went and lived by the Wadi Cherith, which is east of
the Jordan. 6The ravens brought him bread and meat in the morning,
and bread and meat in the evening; and he drank from the wadi. 7But
after a while the wadi dried up, because there was no rain in the land.

17:1-7 Elijah: Throughout Ahab's reign he is in constant conflict with Elijah, who says there is only one God (see Exod 20:2-6). Elijah is a prophet, someone who receives a word from the LORD and passes it on to a third party. Elijah tells Ahab there will be a severe drought because of his sins. Elijah suffers from the drought as well, and finds temporary relief at a brook in Transjordan, where ravens bring him food in the morning and evening.

---

[a] Heb *Asherah* [b] Gk: Heb *of the settlers*

The Widow of Zarephath

17:8-16 Go now to Zarephath: Elijah seeks refuge with a widow in Phoenicia (see Map 7, p. 2105). She is down to her last flour and oil when Elijah asks her to bake him some bread. He promises that a miracle will take place—the jar of flour and jug of oil will not be empty until the LORD sends rain again. This promise proves to be true. A similar story appears in 2 Kings 4:1-7.

Why should we thank God for our food?

8 Then the word of the LORD came to him, saying, [9]"Go now to
Zarephath, which belongs to Sidon, and live there; for I have commanded a widow there to feed you." [10]So he set out and went to Zarephath. When he came to the gate of the town, a widow was there
gathering sticks; he called to her and said, "Bring me a little water in
a vessel, so that I may drink." [11]As she was going to bring it, he called
to her and said, "Bring me a morsel of bread in your hand." [12]But she
said, "As the LORD your God lives, I have nothing baked, only a handful of meal in a jar, and a little oil in a jug; I am now gathering a couple
of sticks, so that I may go home and prepare it for myself and my son,
that we may eat it, and die." [13]Elijah said to her, "Do not be afraid; go
and do as you have said; but first make me a little cake of it and bring
it to me, and afterwards make something for yourself and your son.
[14]For thus says the LORD the God of Israel: The jar of meal will not
be emptied and the jug of oil will not fail until the day that the LORD
sends rain on the earth." [15]She went and did as Elijah said, so that she
as well as he and her household ate for many days. [16]The jar of meal
was not emptied, neither did the jug of oil fail, according to the word
of the LORD that he spoke by Elijah.

Elijah Revives the Widow's Son

17:17-24 the son of the woman… became ill: The widow's son becomes sick and dies, and the woman blames Elijah for his death. But when Elijah prays, the boy is revived. This miracle demonstrates the LORD's power over life and death. The widow acknowledges that Elijah is a man of God and that the LORD's word is true.

17 After this the son of the woman, the mistress of the house,
became ill; his illness was so severe that there was no breath left in
him. [18]She then said to Elijah, "What have you against me, O man of
God? You have come to me to bring my sin to remembrance, and to
cause the death of my son!" [19]But he said to her, "Give me your son."
He took him from her bosom, carried him up into the upper chamber where he was lodging, and laid him on his own bed. [20]He cried
out to the LORD, "O LORD my God, have you brought calamity even
upon the widow with whom I am staying, by killing her son?" [21]Then
he stretched himself upon the child three times, and cried out to the
LORD, "O LORD my God, let this child's life come into him again."
[22]The LORD listened to the voice of Elijah; the life of the child came
into him again, and he revived. [23]Elijah took the child, brought him
down from the upper chamber into the house, and gave him to his
mother; then Elijah said, "See, your son is alive." [24]So the woman said
to Elijah, "Now I know that you are a man of God, and that the word
of the LORD in your mouth is truth."

Elijah's Message to Ahab

18:1-19 troubler of Israel?: Obadiah, Ahab's chief of staff, is faithful to the LORD and had hid one hundred of the LORD's prophets when their lives were threatened by Ahab. When Elijah meets Ahab, the king calls him a "troubler of Israel." Elijah responds that Ahab is the real troubler of Israel because of his disobedience and Baal worship. Elijah challenges Ahab's four hundred fifty prophets of Baal and four hundred prophets of Asherah to a contest on Mount Carmel to see which God—the LORD or Baal—is able to send rain.

18 After many days the word of the LORD came to Elijah, in the
third year of the drought,[a] saying, "Go, present yourself to

[a] Heb lacks *of the drought*

Ahab; I will send rain on the earth." [2]So Elijah went to present himself to Ahab. The famine was severe in Samaria. [3]Ahab summoned Obadiah, who was in charge of the palace. (Now Obadiah revered the LORD greatly; [4]when Jezebel was killing off the prophets of the LORD, Obadiah took a hundred prophets, hid them fifty to a cave, and provided them with bread and water.) [5]Then Ahab said to Obadiah, "Go through the land to all the springs of water and to all the wadis; perhaps we may find grass to keep the horses and mules alive, and not lose some of the animals." [6]So they divided the land between them to pass through it; Ahab went in one direction by himself, and Obadiah went in another direction by himself.

7 As Obadiah was on the way, Elijah met him; Obadiah recognized him, fell on his face, and said, "Is it you, my lord Elijah?" [8]He answered him, "It is I. Go, tell your lord that Elijah is here." [9]And he said, "How have I sinned, that you would hand your servant over to Ahab, to kill me? [10]As the LORD your God lives, there is no nation or kingdom to which my lord has not sent to seek you; and when they would say, 'He is not here,' he would require an oath of the kingdom or nation, that they had not found you. [11]But now you say, 'Go, tell your lord that Elijah is here.' [12]As soon as I have gone from you, the spirit of the LORD will carry you I know not where; so, when I come and tell Ahab and he cannot find you, he will kill me, although I your servant have revered the LORD from my youth. [13]Has it not been told my lord what I did when Jezebel killed the prophets of the LORD, how I hid a hundred of the LORD's prophets fifty to a cave, and provided them with bread and water? [14]Yet now you say, 'Go, tell your lord that Elijah is here'; he will surely kill me." [15]Elijah said, "As the LORD of hosts lives, before whom I stand, I will surely show myself to him today." [16]So Obadiah went to meet Ahab, and told him; and Ahab went to meet Elijah.

17 When Ahab saw Elijah, Ahab said to him, "Is it you, you troubler of Israel?" [18]He answered, "I have not troubled Israel; but you have, and your father's house, because you have forsaken the commandments of the LORD and followed the Baals. [19]Now therefore have all Israel assemble for me at Mount Carmel, with the four hundred fifty prophets of Baal and the four hundred prophets of Asherah, who eat at Jezebel's table."

Elijah's Triumph over the Priests of Baal

20 So Ahab sent to all the Israelites, and assembled the prophets at Mount Carmel. [21]Elijah then came near to all the people, and said, "How long will you go limping with two different opinions? If the LORD is God, follow him; but if Baal, then follow him." The people did not answer him a word. [22]Then Elijah said to the people, "I, even I only, am left a prophet of the LORD; but Baal's prophets number four

18:20-40 the god who answers by fire is indeed God: The Baal prophets go first in this contest and call on their god all morning. Elijah mocks their efforts, suggesting that their god is meditating, on a trip (Baal went to the underworld during the dry season), or even asleep. The Baal prophets increase their efforts, cutting themselves as a kind of magic or mourning rite. This lasts almost until sunset, the time of "the offering of the oblation." Elijah builds his own altar of twelve stones, symbolic of the twelve tribes of Israel, and has the people thoroughly soak the altar with water three times. Lightning from Yahweh burns up the sacrifice and dries up all the water that had been poured over the altar. The people are convinced that the LORD is God. Elijah orders the execution of all the prophets of Baal.

Does passion for faith ever go too far? What do you make of Elijah's execution of the false prophets?

hundred fifty. 23 Let two bulls be given to us; let them choose one bull for themselves, cut it in pieces, and lay it on the wood, but put no fire to it; I will prepare the other bull and lay it on the wood, but put no fire to it. 24 Then you call on the name of your god and I will call on the name of the LORD; the god who answers by fire is indeed God." All the people answered, "Well spoken!" 25 Then Elijah said to the prophets of Baal, "Choose for yourselves one bull and prepare it first, for you are many; then call on the name of your god, but put no fire to it." 26 So they took the bull that was given them, prepared it, and called on the name of Baal from morning until noon, crying, "O Baal, answer us!" But there was no voice, and no answer. They limped about the altar that they had made. 27 At noon Elijah mocked them, saying, "Cry aloud! Surely he is a god; either he is meditating, or he has wandered away, or he is on a journey, or perhaps he is asleep and must be awakened." 28 Then they cried aloud and, as was their custom, they cut themselves with swords and lances until the blood gushed out over them. 29 As midday passed, they raved on until the time of the offering of the oblation, but there was no voice, no answer, and no response.

30 Then Elijah said to all the people, "Come closer to me"; and all the people came closer to him. First he repaired the altar of the LORD that had been thrown down; 31 Elijah took twelve stones, according to the number of the tribes of the sons of Jacob, to whom the word of the LORD came, saying, "Israel shall be your name"; 32 with the stones he built an altar in the name of the LORD. Then he made a trench around the altar, large enough to contain two measures of seed. 33 Next he put the wood in order, cut the bull in pieces, and laid it on the wood. He said, "Fill four jars with water and pour it on the burnt offering and on the wood." 34 Then he said, "Do it a second time"; and they did it a second time. Again he said, "Do it a third time"; and they did it a third time, 35 so that the water ran all around the altar, and filled the trench also with water.

36 At the time of the offering of the oblation, the prophet Elijah came near and said, "O LORD, God of Abraham, Isaac, and Israel, let it be known this day that you are God in Israel, that I am your servant, and that I have done all these things at your bidding. 37 Answer me, O LORD, answer me, so that this people may know that you, O LORD, are God, and that you have turned their hearts back." 38 Then the fire of the LORD fell and consumed the burnt offering, the wood, the stones, and the dust, and even licked up the water that was in the trench. 39 When all the people saw it, they fell on their faces and said, "The LORD indeed is God; the LORD indeed is God." 40 Elijah said to them, "Seize the prophets of Baal; do not let one of them escape." Then they seized them; and Elijah brought them down to the Wadi Kishon, and killed them there.

The Drought Ends

41 Elijah said to Ahab, "Go up, eat and drink; for there is a sound of rushing rain." [42]So Ahab went up to eat and to drink. Elijah went up to the top of Carmel; there he bowed himself down upon the earth and put his face between his knees. [43]He said to his servant, "Go up now, look toward the sea." He went up and looked, and said, "There is nothing." Then he said, "Go again seven times." [44]At the seventh time he said, "Look, a little cloud no bigger than a person's hand is rising out of the sea." Then he said, "Go say to Ahab, 'Harness your chariot and go down before the rain stops you.' " [45]In a little while the heavens grew black with clouds and wind; there was a heavy rain. Ahab rode off and went to Jezreel. [46]But the hand of the LORD was on Elijah; he girded up his loins and ran in front of Ahab to the entrance of Jezreel.

18:41-45 a sound of rushing rain: Elijah starts a ritual apparently meant to ask for rain or to find out when rain is coming. After seven trips to a mountain peak to look out over the Mediterranean Sea, a servant spots a small cloud. Elijah tells Ahab to hurry to his alternate palace at Jezreel, some seventeen miles away. Because the hand of the LORD is on him, Elijah is able to run and beat Ahab's chariot to Jezreel.

Elijah Flees from Jezebel

19 Ahab told Jezebel all that Elijah had done, and how he had killed all the prophets with the sword. [2]Then Jezebel sent a messenger to Elijah, saying, "So may the gods do to me, and more also, if I do not make your life like the life of one of them by this time tomorrow." [3]Then he was afraid; he got up and fled for his life, and came to Beer-sheba, which belongs to Judah; he left his servant there.

4 But he himself went a day's journey into the wilderness, and came and sat down under a solitary broom tree. He asked that he might die: "It is enough; now, O LORD, take away my life, for I am no better than my ancestors." [5]Then he lay down under the broom tree and fell asleep. Suddenly an angel touched him and said to him, "Get up and eat." [6]He looked, and there at his head was a cake baked on hot stones, and a jar of water. He ate and drank, and lay down again. [7]The angel of the LORD came a second time, touched him, and said, "Get up and eat, otherwise the journey will be too much for you." [8]He got up, and ate and drank; then he went in the strength of that food forty days and forty nights to Horeb the mount of God. [9]At that place he came to a cave, and spent the night there.

Then the word of the LORD came to him, saying, "What are you doing here, Elijah?" [10]He answered, "I have been very zealous for the LORD, the God of hosts; for the Israelites have forsaken your covenant, thrown down your altars, and killed your prophets with the sword. I alone am left, and they are seeking my life, to take it away."

19:1-10 he got up and fled for his life: Ahab's wife, Jezebel, threatens to kill Elijah, just as he executed the prophets of Baal. Elijah flees far south, to Beer-sheba, on the southern border of Judah (see Map 7, p. 2105). When he falls asleep, an angel wakes him twice and feeds him in preparation for a long journey. His trip of forty days and nights takes him to Horeb (Sinai), where he spends the night in a cave. When the LORD asks him what he is doing, he says he is the last faithful believer—and now people want to kill him as well!

Elijah Meets God at Horeb

11 He said, "Go out and stand on the mountain before the LORD, for the LORD is about to pass by." Now there was a great wind, so strong that it was splitting mountains and breaking rocks

19:11-18 a sound of sheer silence: Strong winds, earthquake, and fire often accompany God's appearances in the Old Testament. They happen here too, but the LORD is not in any of them. The only thing Elijah experiences is "sheer silence." Elijah complains about his solitary and dangerous mission—and the LORD gives him three new assignments: anointing Hazael as king over Aram (done by Elisha in 2 Kgs 8:7-15), Jehu as king over Israel (also done by Elisha through one of his disciples in 2 Kgs 9), and Elisha as his successor. These three people will outdo one another in violence, and many people will die, but there still will be seven thousand people who have not worshiped Baal. Elijah is not the last believer after all.

in pieces before the LORD, but the LORD was not in the wind; and after the wind an earthquake, but the LORD was not in the earthquake; [12]and after the earthquake a fire, but the LORD was not in the fire; and after the fire a sound of sheer silence. [13]When Elijah heard it, he wrapped his face in his mantle and went out and stood at the entrance of the cave. Then there came a voice to him that said, "What are you doing here, Elijah?" [14]He answered, "I have been very zealous for the LORD, the God of hosts; for the Israelites have forsaken your covenant, thrown down your altars, and killed your prophets with the sword. I alone am left, and they are seeking my life, to take it away." [15]Then the LORD said to him, "Go, return on your way to the wilderness of Damascus; when you arrive, you shall anoint Hazael as king over Aram. [16]Also you shall anoint Jehu son of Nimshi as king over Israel; and you shall anoint Elisha son of Shaphat of Abel-meholah as prophet in your place. [17]Whoever escapes from the sword of Hazael, Jehu shall kill; and whoever escapes from the sword of Jehu, Elisha shall kill. [18]Yet I will leave seven thousand in Israel, all the knees that have not bowed to Baal, and every mouth that has not kissed him."

Elisha Becomes Elijah's Disciple

19:19-21 I will follow you: Elijah seeks out Elisha as his successor and throws his cloak over him (see 2 Kgs 2:13). Elisha was evidently a well-to-do farmer, plowing with twelve yoke of oxen, but the number twelve may also symbolize the twelve tribes of Israel. Elisha wants to kiss his parents goodbye, but Elijah takes this as a sign of halfheartedness. Elisha then slaughters the oxen, cooks the meat, and distributes it to the people. He becomes Elijah's ardent disciple. (See a similar incident in Luke 9:57-62.)

19 So he set out from there, and found Elisha son of Shaphat, who was plowing. There were twelve yoke of oxen ahead of him, and he was with the twelfth. Elijah passed by him and threw his mantle over him. [20]He left the oxen, ran after Elijah, and said, "Let me kiss my father and my mother, and then I will follow you." Then Elijah[a] said to him, "Go back again; for what have I done to you?" [21]He returned from following him, took the yoke of oxen, and slaughtered them; using the equipment from the oxen, he boiled their flesh, and gave it to the people, and they ate. Then he set out and followed Elijah, and became his servant.

Ahab's Wars with the Arameans

20:1-12 King Ben-hadad of Aram gathered all his army together: In this battle against the Arameans (Syrians), Ben-hadad seems to have the upper hand. He first demands silver and gold and the king's wives and children, and Ahab agrees. His second demand (20:5-6) would allow the Arameans to take whatever they want from the palace. After consulting with the elders, Ahab rejects this. Ben-hadad, somewhat drunk, orders his men to their battle positions.

20 King Ben-hadad of Aram gathered all his army together; thirty-two kings were with him, along with horses and chariots. He marched against Samaria, laid siege to it, and attacked it. [2]Then he sent messengers into the city to King Ahab of Israel, and said to him: "Thus says Ben-hadad: [3]Your silver and gold are mine; your fairest wives and children also are mine." [4]The king of Israel answered, "As you say, my lord, O king, I am yours, and all that I have." [5]The messengers came again and said: "Thus says Ben-hadad: I sent to you, saying, 'Deliver to me your silver and gold, your wives and children'; [6]nevertheless I will send my servants to you tomorrow

[a] Heb *he*

about this time, and they shall search your house and the houses
of your servants, and lay hands on whatever pleases them,[a] and take
it away."
7 Then the king of Israel called all the elders of the land, and said,
"Look now! See how this man is seeking trouble; for he sent to me for
my wives, my children, my silver, and my gold; and I did not refuse
him." [8]Then all the elders and all the people said to him, "Do not listen or consent." [9]So he said to the messengers of Ben-hadad, "Tell my
lord the king: All that you first demanded of your servant I will do;
but this thing I cannot do." The messengers left and brought him word
again. [10]Ben-hadad sent to him and said, "The gods do so to me, and
more also, if the dust of Samaria will provide a handful for each of the
people who follow me." [11]The king of Israel answered, "Tell him: One
who puts on armor should not brag like one who takes it off." [12]When
Ben-hadad heard this message—now he had been drinking with the
kings in the booths—he said to his men, "Take your positions!" And
they took their positions against the city.

Prophetic Opposition to Ahab

13 Then a certain prophet came up to King Ahab of Israel and
said, "Thus says the LORD, Have you seen all this great multitude?
Look, I will give it into your hand today; and you shall know that
I am the LORD." [14]Ahab said, "By whom?" He said, "Thus says the
LORD, By the young men who serve the district governors." Then
he said, "Who shall begin the battle?" He answered, "You." [15]Then
he mustered the young men who served the district governors, two
hundred thirty-two; after them he mustered all the people of Israel,
seven thousand.
16 They went out at noon, while Ben-hadad was drinking himself drunk in the booths, he and the thirty-two kings allied with him.
[17]The young men who served the district governors went out first.
Ben-hadad had sent out scouts,[b] and they reported to him, "Men have
come out from Samaria." [18]He said, "If they have come out for peace,
take them alive; if they have come out for war, take them alive."
19 But these had already come out of the city: the young men
who served the district governors, and the army that followed them.
[20]Each killed his man; the Arameans fled and Israel pursued them, but
King Ben-hadad of Aram escaped on a horse with the cavalry. [21]The
king of Israel went out, attacked the horses and chariots, and defeated
the Arameans with a great slaughter.
22 Then the prophet approached the king of Israel and said to
him, "Come, strengthen yourself, and consider well what you have to
do; for in the spring the king of Aram will come up against you."

20:13-22 a certain prophet came up to King Ahab: Elijah and other prophets normally opposed Ahab, but in this case an unnamed prophet encourages Ahab for the battle. Ben-hadad and the kings allied with him continue their drinking bout. The army of Israel is successful, and Ben-hadad flees with his cavalry. The anonymous prophet urges Ahab to get ready for a second attack in the spring (see 2 Sam 11:1).

[a] Gk Syr Vg: Heb *you* [b] Heb lacks *scouts*

20:23-34 In the spring Ben-hadad mustered the Arameans: The Arameans change their military strategy, thinking that the LORD is a god of the hills and not of the plains. Ahab, again with a prophet's support, wins an overwhelming victory: one hundred thousand Arameans are killed in battle and an additional twenty-seven thousand are crushed by a wall that falls in the city of Aphek. The Arameans again change their strategy and appeal to Ahab's compassion. Ben-hadad agrees to give back towns taken from Israel by his father and to give Israel rights to conduct business in Damascus. Ahab, persuaded by these offers, lets Ben-hadad get away.

The Arameans Are Defeated

23 The servants of the king of Aram said to him, "Their gods are gods of the hills, and so they were stronger than we; but let us fight against them in the plain, and surely we shall be stronger than they. 24 Also do this: remove the kings, each from his post, and put commanders in place of them; 25 and muster an army like the army that you have lost, horse for horse, and chariot for chariot; then we will fight against them in the plain, and surely we shall be stronger than they." He heeded their voice, and did so.

26 In the spring Ben-hadad mustered the Arameans and went up to Aphek to fight against Israel. 27 After the Israelites had been mustered and provisioned, they went out to engage them; the people of Israel encamped opposite them like two little flocks of goats, while the Arameans filled the country. 28 A man of God approached and said to the king of Israel, "Thus says the LORD: Because the Arameans have said, 'The LORD is a god of the hills but he is not a god of the valleys,' therefore I will give all this great multitude into your hand, and you shall know that I am the LORD." 29 They encamped opposite one another seven days. Then on the seventh day the battle began; the Israelites killed one hundred thousand Aramean foot soldiers in one day. 30 The rest fled into the city of Aphek; and the wall fell on twenty-seven thousand men that were left.

Ben-hadad also fled, and entered the city to hide. 31 His servants said to him, "Look, we have heard that the kings of the house of Israel are merciful kings; let us put sackcloth around our waists and ropes on our heads, and go out to the king of Israel; perhaps he will spare your life." 32 So they tied sackcloth around their waists, put ropes on their heads, went to the king of Israel, and said, "Your servant Ben-hadad says, 'Please let me live.'" And he said, "Is he still alive? He is my brother." 33 Now the men were watching for an omen; they quickly took it up from him and said, "Yes, Ben-hadad is your brother." Then he said, "Go and bring him." So Ben-hadad came out to him; and he had him come up into the chariot. 34 Ben-hadad[a] said to him, "I will restore the towns that my father took from your father; and you may establish bazaars for yourself in Damascus, as my father did in Samaria." The king of Israel responded,[b] "I will let you go on those terms." So he made a treaty with him and let him go.

20:35-43 you have not obeyed the voice of the LORD: An unnamed prophet asks a man to hit him, but the man refuses and is killed by a lion. A second man hits the prophet and wounds him. The prophet disguises himself but eventually confronts Ahab for letting Ben-hadad get away. Ben-hadad should have been killed, according to the rules of holy war, and since he was not, Ahab and his people will suffer the consequences. As Ahab interprets the prophet's words, he condemns himself, much as David did when confronted by Nathan (see 2 Sam 12:1-12).

A Prophet Condemns Ahab

35 At the command of the LORD a certain member of a company of prophets[c] said to another, "Strike me!" But the man refused to strike him. 36 Then he said to him, "Because you have not obeyed the voice of the LORD, as soon as you have left me, a lion will kill

[a] Heb *He* [b] Heb lacks *The king of Israel responded* [c] Heb *of the sons of the prophets*

you." And when he had left him, a lion met him and killed him. 37 Then he found another man and said, "Strike me!" So the man hit him, striking and wounding him. 38 Then the prophet departed, and waited for the king along the road, disguising himself with a bandage over his eyes. 39 As the king passed by, he cried to the king and said, "Your servant went out into the thick of the battle; then a soldier turned and brought a man to me, and said, 'Guard this man; if he is missing, your life shall be given for his life, or else you shall pay a talent of silver.' 40 While your servant was busy here and there, he was gone." The king of Israel said to him, "So shall your judgment be; you yourself have decided it." 41 Then he quickly took the bandage away from his eyes. The king of Israel recognized him as one of the prophets. 42 Then he said to him, "Thus says the LORD, 'Because you have let the man go whom I had devoted to destruction, therefore your life shall be for his life, and your people for his people.' " 43 The king of Israel set out toward home, resentful and sullen, and came to Samaria.

Naboth's Vineyard

21 Later the following events took place: Naboth the Jezreelite had a vineyard in Jezreel, beside the palace of King Ahab of Samaria. 2 And Ahab said to Naboth, "Give me your vineyard, so that I may have it for a vegetable garden, because it is near my house; I will give you a better vineyard for it; or, if it seems good to you, I will give you its value in money." 3 But Naboth said to Ahab, "The LORD forbid that I should give you my ancestral inheritance." 4 Ahab went home resentful and sullen because of what Naboth the Jezreelite had said to him; for he had said, "I will not give you my ancestral inheritance." He lay down on his bed, turned away his face, and would not eat.

5 His wife Jezebel came to him and said, "Why are you so depressed that you will not eat?" 6 He said to her, "Because I spoke to Naboth the Jezreelite and said to him, 'Give me your vineyard for money; or else, if you prefer, I will give you another vineyard for it'; but he answered, 'I will not give you my vineyard.' " 7 His wife Jezebel said to him, "Do you now govern Israel? Get up, eat some food, and be cheerful; I will give you the vineyard of Naboth the Jezreelite."

8 So she wrote letters in Ahab's name and sealed them with his seal; she sent the letters to the elders and the nobles who lived with Naboth in his city. 9 She wrote in the letters, "Proclaim a fast, and seat Naboth at the head of the assembly; 10 seat two scoundrels opposite him, and have them bring a charge against him, saying, 'You have cursed God and the king.' Then take him out, and stone him to death." 11 The men of his city, the elders and the nobles who lived in his city, did as Jezebel had sent word to them. Just as it was written in the letters that she had sent to them, 12 they proclaimed a fast and seated

21:1-7 Naboth the Jezreelite had a vineyard: King Ahab wants to acquire Naboth's vineyard and offers him a reasonable price. Naboth, however, refuses to sell the land he inherited from his ancestors. Ahab pouts over this, but Jezebel urges him to use the full powers of kingship and offers to help him get the vineyard.

21:8-16 she wrote letters in Ahab's name: Jezebel writes letters to get people to make false accusations against Naboth. People willingly join this plot, and two false witnesses claim that Naboth has cursed God and the king. Naboth is convicted and immediately executed. Jezebel urges Ahab to immediately take possession of Naboth's vineyard.

Naboth at the head of the assembly. [13]The two scoundrels came in
and sat opposite him; and the scoundrels brought a charge against
Naboth, in the presence of the people, saying, "Naboth cursed God
and the king." So they took him outside the city, and stoned him to
death. [14]Then they sent to Jezebel, saying, "Naboth has been stoned;
he is dead."

15 As soon as Jezebel heard that Naboth had been stoned and
was dead, Jezebel said to Ahab, "Go, take possession of the vineyard
of Naboth the Jezreelite, which he refused to give you for money; for
Naboth is not alive, but dead." [16]As soon as Ahab heard that Naboth
was dead, Ahab set out to go down to the vineyard of Naboth the Jezreelite, to take possession of it.

Elijah Pronounces God's Sentence

21:17-29 Have you killed, and also taken possession?: Sent by the LORD, Elijah brings a message of judgment to Ahab: He will be killed at the exact spot that Naboth was, and his dynasty will meet a violent end, like the dynasties of Jeroboam and Baasha. For her role in the plot, Jezebel is also condemned to a violent death. Verses 25-26 underscore the wickedness of Ahab. Ahab, however, has a change of heart and repents, and the punishment of his family line is delayed to his son's generation (see 2 Sam 12:13-14 and 2 Kgs 22:11-20). The prophecy against Ahab's dynasty is fulfilled in 2 Kings 10:17, and the one against Jezebel finds fulfillment in 2 Kings 9:30-37. Ahab meets his own fate in 1 Kings 22.

17 Then the word of the LORD came to Elijah the Tishbite, saying:
[18]Go down to meet King Ahab of Israel, who rules[a] in Samaria; he is
now in the vineyard of Naboth, where he has gone to take possession.
[19]You shall say to him, "Thus says the LORD: Have you killed, and also
taken possession?" You shall say to him, "Thus says the LORD: In the
place where dogs licked up the blood of Naboth, dogs will also lick
up your blood."

20 Ahab said to Elijah, "Have you found me, O my enemy?" He
answered, "I have found you. Because you have sold yourself to do
what is evil in the sight of the LORD, [21]I will bring disaster on you;
I will consume you, and will cut off from Ahab every male, bond or
free, in Israel; [22]and I will make your house like the house of Jeroboam
son of Nebat, and like the house of Baasha son of Ahijah, because you
have provoked me to anger and have caused Israel to sin. [23]Also concerning Jezebel the LORD said, 'The dogs shall eat Jezebel within the
bounds of Jezreel.' [24]Anyone belonging to Ahab who dies in the city
the dogs shall eat; and anyone of his who dies in the open country the
birds of the air shall eat."

25 (Indeed, there was no one like Ahab, who sold himself to do
what was evil in the sight of the LORD, urged on by his wife Jezebel.
[26]He acted most abominably in going after idols, as the Amorites had
done, whom the LORD drove out before the Israelites.)

27 When Ahab heard those words, he tore his clothes and put
sackcloth over his bare flesh; he fasted, lay in the sackcloth, and went
about dejectedly. [28]Then the word of the LORD came to Elijah the
Tishbite: [29]"Have you seen how Ahab has humbled himself before
me? Because he has humbled himself before me, I will not bring the
disaster in his days; but in his son's days I will bring the disaster on
his house."

---

[a] Heb *who is*

Joint Campaign with Judah against Aram

22 For three years Aram and Israel continued without war.
2But in the third year King Jehoshaphat of Judah came
down to the king of Israel. 3The king of Israel said to his servants, "Do
you know that Ramoth-gilead belongs to us, yet we are doing nothing
to take it out of the hand of the king of Aram?" 4He said to Jehoshaphat, "Will you go with me to battle at Ramoth-gilead?" Jehoshaphat
replied to the king of Israel, "I am as you are; my people are your people, my horses are your horses."
5 But Jehoshaphat also said to the king of Israel, "Inquire first for
the word of the LORD." 6Then the king of Israel gathered the prophets
together, about four hundred of them, and said to them, "Shall I go to
battle against Ramoth-gilead, or shall I refrain?" They said, "Go up;
for the LORD will give it into the hand of the king." 7But Jehoshaphat
said, "Is there no other prophet of the LORD here of whom we may inquire?" 8The king of Israel said to Jehoshaphat, "There is still one other
by whom we may inquire of the LORD, Micaiah son of Imlah; but I hate
him, for he never prophesies anything favorable about me, but only disaster." Jehoshaphat said, "Let the king not say such a thing." 9Then the
king of Israel summoned an officer and said, "Bring quickly Micaiah
son of Imlah." 10Now the king of Israel and King Jehoshaphat of Judah
were sitting on their thrones, arrayed in their robes, at the threshing
floor at the entrance of the gate of Samaria; and all the prophets were
prophesying before them. 11Zedekiah son of Chenaanah made for
himself horns of iron, and he said, "Thus says the LORD: With these
you shall gore the Arameans until they are destroyed." 12All the prophets were prophesying the same and saying, "Go up to Ramoth-gilead
and triumph; the LORD will give it into the hand of the king."

Micaiah Predicts Failure

13 The messenger who had gone to summon Micaiah said to
him, "Look, the words of the prophets with one accord are favorable
to the king; let your word be like the word of one of them, and speak
favorably." 14But Micaiah said, "As the LORD lives, whatever the LORD
says to me, that I will speak."
15 When he had come to the king, the king said to him, "Micaiah, shall we go to Ramoth-gilead to battle, or shall we refrain?" He
answered him, "Go up and triumph; the LORD will give it into the
hand of the king." 16But the king said to him, "How many times must
I make you swear to tell me nothing but the truth in the name of the
LORD?" 17Then Micaiah[a] said, "I saw all Israel scattered on the mountains, like sheep that have no shepherd; and the LORD said, 'These
have no master; let each one go home in peace.'" 18The king of Israel

[a] Heb *he*

22:1-12 my people are your people, my horses are your horses: The alliance of Jehoshaphat (Judah) and Ahab (Israel) is a striking new development, but Jehoshaphat (870–845 B.C.E.) insists that they get Yahweh's consent, which was necessary according to the rules of holy war. Four hundred prophets give their approval, but because they are all employed by Ahab, Jehoshaphat pushes for another opinion. Ahab mentions the prophet Micaiah, who has never given him a favorable message.

22:13-28 whatever the LORD says to me, that I will speak: Micaiah's advice supports that of the four hundred prophets at first, but Ahab realizes he is not telling the truth. Micaiah then adds that he sees all Israel scattered, as if they have no shepherd (in other words, no king). Ahab puts Micaiah in prison until the army comes back victorious (in peace). Micaiah replies that if Ahab comes back in peace, the LORD has not spoken through him.

said to Jehoshaphat, "Did I not tell you that he would not prophesy anything favorable about me, but only disaster?"

19 Then Micaiah[a] said, "Therefore hear the word of the LORD: I saw the LORD sitting on his throne, with all the host of heaven standing beside him to the right and to the left of him. 20 And the LORD said, 'Who will entice Ahab, so that he may go up and fall at Ramoth-gilead?' Then one said one thing, and another said another, 21 until a spirit came forward and stood before the LORD, saying, 'I will entice him.' 22 'How?' the LORD asked him. He replied, 'I will go out and be a lying spirit in the mouth of all his prophets.' Then the LORD[a] said, 'You are to entice him, and you shall succeed; go out and do it.' 23 So you see, the LORD has put a lying spirit in the mouth of all these your prophets; the LORD has decreed disaster for you."

24 Then Zedekiah son of Chenaanah came up to Micaiah, slapped him on the cheek, and said, "Which way did the spirit of the LORD pass from me to speak to you?" 25 Micaiah replied, "You will find out on that day when you go in to hide in an inner chamber." 26 The king of Israel then ordered, "Take Micaiah, and return him to Amon the governor of the city and to Joash the king's son, 27 and say, 'Thus says the king: Put this fellow in prison, and feed him on reduced rations of bread and water until I come in peace.'" 28 Micaiah said, "If you return in peace, the LORD has not spoken by me." And he said, "Hear, you peoples, all of you!"

Defeat and Death of Ahab

22:29-40 the king of Israel and King Jehoshaphat of Judah went up to Ramoth-gilead: Ahab uses a disguise but Jehoshaphat fights in his royal robes. The Arameans, ordered to attack the king directly, initially target Jehoshaphat. When they realize he is not Ahab, they turn away, but one of them accidentally shoots Ahab with an arrow. He is propped up in his chariot until sunset to fool the enemy, but then he dies. The army scatters and goes home, and Micaiah's prophecy is fulfilled. The "ivory house" indicates the wealth and power exercised by Ahab. His son Ahaziah (843–842 B.C.E.) succeeds him.

29 So the king of Israel and King Jehoshaphat of Judah went up to Ramoth-gilead. 30 The king of Israel said to Jehoshaphat, "I will disguise myself and go into battle, but you wear your robes." So the king of Israel disguised himself and went into battle. 31 Now the king of Aram had commanded the thirty-two captains of his chariots, "Fight with no one small or great, but only with the king of Israel." 32 When the captains of the chariots saw Jehoshaphat, they said, "It is surely the king of Israel." So they turned to fight against him; and Jehoshaphat cried out. 33 When the captains of the chariots saw that it was not the king of Israel, they turned back from pursuing him. 34 But a certain man drew his bow and unknowingly struck the king of Israel between the scale armor and the breastplate; so he said to the driver of his chariot, "Turn around, and carry me out of the battle, for I am wounded." 35 The battle grew hot that day, and the king was propped up in his chariot facing the Arameans, until at evening he died; the blood from the wound had flowed into the bottom of the chariot. 36 Then about sunset a shout went through the army, "Every man to his city, and every man to his country!"

---

[a] Heb *he*

37 So the king died, and was brought to Samaria; they buried the
king in Samaria. 38 They washed the chariot by the pool of Samaria;
the dogs licked up his blood, and the prostitutes washed themselves
in it,[a] according to the word of the LORD that he had spoken. 39 Now
the rest of the acts of Ahab, and all that he did, and the ivory house
that he built, and all the cities that he built, are they not written in the
Book of the Annals of the Kings of Israel? 40 So Ahab slept with his
ancestors; and his son Ahaziah succeeded him.

Jehoshaphat Reigns over Judah

41 Jehoshaphat son of Asa began to reign over Judah in the fourth
year of King Ahab of Israel. 42 Jehoshaphat was thirty-five years old
when he began to reign, and he reigned twenty-five years in Jerusalem. His mother's name was Azubah daughter of Shilhi. 43 He walked
in all the way of his father Asa; he did not turn aside from it, doing
what was right in the sight of the LORD; yet the high places were not
taken away, and the people still sacrificed and offered incense on the
high places. 44 Jehoshaphat also made peace with the king of Israel.
45 Now the rest of the acts of Jehoshaphat, and his power that he
showed, and how he waged war, are they not written in the Book of
the Annals of the Kings of Judah? 46 The remnant of the male temple
prostitutes who were still in the land in the days of his father Asa, he
exterminated.
47 There was no king in Edom; a deputy was king. 48 Jehoshaphat
made ships of the Tarshish type to go to Ophir for gold; but they did
not go, for the ships were wrecked at Ezion-geber. 49 Then Ahaziah son
of Ahab said to Jehoshaphat, "Let my servants go with your servants
in the ships," but Jehoshaphat was not willing. 50 Jehoshaphat slept
with his ancestors and was buried with his ancestors in the city of his
father David; his son Jehoram succeeded him.

22:41-50 Jehoshaphat . . . reigned twenty-five years in Jerusalem: Jehoshaphat follows in the faithful footsteps of his father, Asa, but does not get rid of the high places. He tries to arrange a trading expedition to Ophir, but his ships are wrecked. Jehoshaphat also declines a joint trading venture with Ahaziah of northern Israel. He dies and is buried in Jerusalem. His son Jehoram (851–842 B.C.E.) succeeds him.

Ahaziah Reigns over Israel

51 Ahaziah son of Ahab began to reign over Israel in Samaria in
the seventeenth year of King Jehoshaphat of Judah; he reigned two
years over Israel. 52 He did what was evil in the sight of the LORD, and
walked in the way of his father and mother, and in the way of Jeroboam son of Nebat, who caused Israel to sin. 53 He served Baal and
worshiped him; he provoked the LORD, the God of Israel, to anger,
just as his father had done.

22:51-53 Ahaziah . . . did what was evil in the sight of the LORD: Ahaziah (852–851 B.C.E.) is compared to his parents, Ahab and Jezebel, and to Jeroboam.

[a] Heb lacks *in it*

2 Kings 22:8

2 KINGS

Background File

In Jewish tradition, 1 and 2 Kings are considered to be one book with one author. This author is a historian influenced by the religious viewpoint and language of the book of Deuteronomy. In fact, most modern scholars believe that Joshua, Judges, and the books of Samuel and Kings are *all* written from this perspective.

What's the Story?

The book of Kings has the following outline:

The death of David and the beginning of Solomon's reign (1 Kings 1–2)
Solomon's reign (1 Kings 3–11)
The kings of Israel (northern kingdom) and Judah (southern kingdom), ending with the capture of Samaria (1 Kings 12—2 Kings 17)
The final kings of Judah, ending with the destruction of Jerusalem (2 Kings 18–25)

The book of 2 Kings continues the story of the northern and southern kings, describing both kingdoms in a given era. The fourth part of Kings—2 Kings 18–25— recounts the last century and a half of the history of Judah (southern kingdom).

The writer of Kings uses major events and the reigns of kings to mark time. Scholars do not all agree on how this system translates into years. The study notes for 1 and 2 Kings use the dates offered by Gershon Galil in *The Chronology of the Kings of Israel & Judah* (Leiden: Brill, 1996).

What's the Message?

Like 1 Kings, the book of 2 Kings looks at two critical issues raised in Deuteronomy: the proposal that sacrificial worship should be conducted only in the temple in Jerusalem, and the belief that Israel should worship only one God. In addition, 2 Kings explores the promise to David (2 Samuel 7) that accompanies Israel through its history. With the release of Jehoiachin from prison (in the last verses of 2 Kings), this promise is still alive.

Elijah Denounces Ahaziah

1 After the death of Ahab, Moab rebelled against Israel.
2 Ahaziah had fallen through the lattice in his upper chamber in
Samaria, and lay injured; so he sent messengers, telling them, "Go,
inquire of Baal-zebub, the god of Ekron, whether I shall recover from
this injury." 3But the angel of the LORD said to Elijah the Tishbite,
"Get up, go to meet the messengers of the king of Samaria, and say to
them, 'Is it because there is no God in Israel that you are going to inquire of Baal-zebub, the god of Ekron?' 4Now therefore thus says the
LORD, 'You shall not leave the bed to which you have gone, but you
shall surely die.' " So Elijah went.
5 The messengers returned to the king, who said to them, "Why
have you returned?" 6They answered him, "There came a man to meet
us, who said to us, 'Go back to the king who sent you, and say to him:
Thus says the LORD: Is it because there is no God in Israel that you
are sending to inquire of Baal-zebub, the god of Ekron? Therefore you
shall not leave the bed to which you have gone, but shall surely die.' "
7He said to them, "What sort of man was he who came to meet you
and told you these things?" 8They answered him, "A hairy man, with a
leather belt around his waist." He said, "It is Elijah the Tishbite."
9 Then the king sent to him a captain of fifty with his fifty men.
He went up to Elijah, who was sitting on the top of a hill, and said to
him, "O man of God, the king says, 'Come down.' " 10But Elijah answered the captain of fifty, "If I am a man of God, let fire come down
from heaven and consume you and your fifty." Then fire came down
from heaven, and consumed him and his fifty.
11 Again the king sent to him another captain of fifty with his
fifty. He went up[a] and said to him, "O man of God, this is the king's
order: Come down quickly!" 12But Elijah answered them, "If I am a
man of God, let fire come down from heaven and consume you and
your fifty." Then the fire of God came down from heaven and consumed him and his fifty.
13 Again the king sent the captain of a third fifty with his fifty.
So the third captain of fifty went up, and came and fell on his knees
before Elijah, and entreated him, "O man of God, please let my life,
and the life of these fifty servants of yours, be precious in your sight.
14Look, fire came down from heaven and consumed the two former
captains of fifty men with their fifties; but now let my life be precious
in your sight." 15Then the angel of the LORD said to Elijah, "Go down
with him; do not be afraid of him." So he set out and went down with
him to the king, 16and said to him, "Thus says the LORD: Because you
have sent messengers to inquire of Baal-zebub, the god of Ekron,—is
it because there is no God in Israel to inquire of his word?—therefore

[a] Gk Compare verses 9, 13: Heb *He answered*

1:1-16 you shall surely die: King Ahaziah (852–851 B.C.E.) is seriously injured in a fall and sends a delegation to ask the god of the Philistine city of Ekron whether he will recover. This god's name is probably Baal zebul (prince Baal), but here he is given the tongue-in-cheek name Baal zebub, meaning "lord of the flies." Elijah intercepts the group going to Ekron and sends them back with the message that Ahaziah will die from his injury. The king sends a series of fifty men to arrest Elijah, but in each case Elijah calls down fire from heaven to kill them. The captain of the third group pleads for his life and the lives of his men. Instructed by an angel, Elijah spares this group and delivers a death sentence to the king in person.

you shall not leave the bed to which you have gone, but you shall
surely die."

1:17-18 So he died: Ahaziah dies, as Elijah had prophesied, and his brother Jehoram (851–842 B.C.E.) becomes king.

Death of Ahaziah

17 So he died according to the word of the LORD that Elijah had
spoken. His brother,[a] Jehoram succeeded him as king in the second
year of King Jehoram son of Jehoshaphat of Judah, because Ahaziah
had no son. [18]Now the rest of the acts of Ahaziah that he did, are they
not written in the Book of the Annals of the Kings of Israel?

2:1-12 Elijah ascended in a whirlwind into heaven: Elisha follows Elijah on his final trip, even though Elijah encourages him to stay put and other prophets tell him his master is about to leave. Elijah uses his "mantle" or cloak to part the Jordan River, reenacting earlier miracles by Joshua (Josh 4:7-17) and Moses (Exod 14:21-22). Elisha asks for a double portion of Elijah's spirit, as if he were Elijah's firstborn son (Deut 21:15-17), and calls him "Father." Elijah is swept up to heaven with a "chariot of fire" and "horses of fire" in a whirlwind—all signs of divine intervention. Elisha calls after Elijah: "The chariots of Israel and its horsemen!," indicating Elijah's important role as the agent of holy war. When Elijah disappears, Elisha rips his clothes in mourning.

Elijah Ascends to Heaven

2 Now when the LORD was about to take Elijah up to heaven by
a whirlwind, Elijah and Elisha were on their way from Gilgal.
[2]Elijah said to Elisha, "Stay here; for the LORD has sent me as far as
Bethel." But Elisha said, "As the LORD lives, and as you yourself live,
I will not leave you." So they went down to Bethel. [3]The company of
prophets[b] who were in Bethel came out to Elisha, and said to him,
"Do you know that today the LORD will take your master away from
you?" And he said, "Yes, I know; keep silent."

4 Elijah said to him, "Elisha, stay here; for the LORD has sent me
to Jericho." But he said, "As the LORD lives, and as you yourself live,
I will not leave you." So they came to Jericho. [5]The company of prophets[b] who were at Jericho drew near to Elisha, and said to him, "Do you
know that today the LORD will take your master away from you?" And
he answered, "Yes, I know; be silent."

6 Then Elijah said to him, "Stay here; for the LORD has sent me to
the Jordan." But he said, "As the LORD lives, and as you yourself live,
I will not leave you." So the two of them went on. [7]Fifty men of the
company of prophets[b] also went, and stood at some distance from
them, as they both were standing by the Jordan. [8]Then Elijah took his
mantle and rolled it up, and struck the water; the water was parted to
the one side and to the other, until the two of them crossed on dry
ground.

9 When they had crossed, Elijah said to Elisha, "Tell me what I
may do for you, before I am taken from you." Elisha said, "Please let
me inherit a double share of your spirit." [10]He responded, "You have
asked a hard thing; yet, if you see me as I am being taken from you,
it will be granted you; if not, it will not." [11]As they continued walking
and talking, a chariot of fire and horses of fire separated the two of
them, and Elijah ascended in a whirlwind into heaven. [12]Elisha kept
watching and crying out, "Father, father! The chariots of Israel and its
horsemen!" But when he could no longer see him, he grasped his own
clothes and tore them in two pieces.

---

[a] Gk Syr: Heb lacks *His brother* [b] Heb *sons of the prophets*

Elisha Succeeds Elijah

13 He picked up the mantle of Elijah that had fallen from him,
and went back and stood on the bank of the Jordan. 14 He took the
mantle of Elijah that had fallen from him, and struck the water, saying, "Where is the LORD, the God of Elijah?" When he had struck
the water, the water was parted to the one side and to the other, and
Elisha went over.

15 When the company of prophets[a] who were at Jericho saw
him at a distance, they declared, "The spirit of Elijah rests on Elisha."
They came to meet him and bowed to the ground before him. 16 They
said to him, "See now, we have fifty strong men among your servants;
please let them go and seek your master; it may be that the spirit of the
LORD has caught him up and thrown him down on some mountain
or into some valley." He responded, "No, do not send them." 17 But
when they urged him until he was ashamed, he said, "Send them." So
they sent fifty men who searched for three days but did not find him.
18 When they came back to him (he had remained at Jericho), he said
to them, "Did I not say to you, Do not go?"

Elisha Performs Miracles

19 Now the people of the city said to Elisha, "The location of this
city is good, as my lord sees; but the water is bad, and the land is unfruitful." 20 He said, "Bring me a new bowl, and put salt in it." So they
brought it to him. 21 Then he went to the spring of water and threw
the salt into it, and said, "Thus says the LORD, I have made this water
wholesome; from now on neither death nor miscarriage shall come
from it." 22 So the water has been wholesome to this day, according to
the word that Elisha spoke.

23 He went up from there to Bethel; and while he was going up on
the way, some small boys came out of the city and jeered at him, saying,
"Go away, baldhead! Go away, baldhead!" 24 When he turned around
and saw them, he cursed them in the name of the LORD. Then two she-
bears came out of the woods and mauled forty-two of the boys. 25 From
there he went on to Mount Carmel, and then returned to Samaria.

Jehoram Reigns over Israel

3 In the eighteenth year of King Jehoshaphat of Judah, Jehoram
son of Ahab became king over Israel in Samaria; he reigned
twelve years. 2 He did what was evil in the sight of the LORD, though
not like his father and mother, for he removed the pillar of Baal that
his father had made. 3 Nevertheless he clung to the sin of Jeroboam
son of Nebat, which he caused Israel to commit; he did not depart
from it.

[a] Heb *sons of the prophets*

2:13-18 He picked up the mantle of Elijah: Elisha picks up Elijah's cloak and uses it to miraculously part the waters of the Jordan River, just as Elijah had done. The group of fifty prophets at Jericho recognizes that Elisha has the spirit of the LORD. They urge Elisha to authorize a search in case Elijah has been thrown down on a mountain or in a valley. At first Elisha refuses, but then he authorizes the search. As he suspects, the search for Elijah is unsuccessful.

2:14 the water was parted to the one side and to the other: Miracles in the Bible cluster around three important eras: events leading up to the exodus out of Egypt, the Elijah and Elisha stories, and the life of Jesus and the early church. In the stories of Elisha, miracles demonstrate his authority as prophet and also show divine compassion in providing abundant food, healing people from illnesses, and even raising people from the dead.

2:19-22 made this water wholesome: When the people of Jericho complain about contaminated water, Elisha miraculously cleanses it by throwing salt into a spring.

2:23-25 some small boys . . . jeered at him: Elisha moved on toward Bethel, the site of a sanctuary built by King Jeroboam. When small boys mock his bald head, he calls down a curse on them. Elisha's prophetic authority is clear, even though the punishment seems excessive. Elisha goes on to Mount Carmel, the scene of Elijah's victory over the prophets of Baal (1 Kings 18:17-40), then turns back to the kingdom's capital at Samaria.

3:1-3 Jehoram son of Ahab became king over Israel: The timing of the start of Jehoram's twelve-year reign in 3:1 does not agree with the timing given in 1:17. Jehoram continues Jeroboam's sin of offering sacrifices at Dan and Bethel, instead of only at Jerusalem. In one improvement, however, Jehoram gets rid of the standing stone dedicated to the god Baal.

3:4-27 the king of Moab rebelled against the king of Israel: Mesha, the king of Moab, is known from a Moabite stone discovered in the nineteenth century. He had a successful business trading animals with Israel, but he rebelled when Ahab, Jehoram's father, died. Jehoram joins forces with King Jehoshaphat of Judah, and they decide to attack Moab from the south through Edom (see Map 7, p. 2105). The king of Edom joins the battle too. When the army runs out of water, the three kings go to Elisha to hear from the LORD. Elisha agrees to help them only because of his respect for Jehoshaphat; he puts Jehoram in the same category as Ahab and Jezebel, who had resorted to the prophets of Baal and Asherah. The LORD fills a dry stream bed with water, and Elisha promises victory to the three kings. When the Moabites see the sun's glare off the new water, they believe it is blood and conclude that the armies of the three kings have killed one another. They rush out to steal what they can, but the Israelite army beats them soundly, claims many pieces of land, and destroys the countryside. The king of Moab tries to break through the side of the battle line defended by Edom, but fails. In desperation he offers his son as a sacrifice to his god on the city wall. Great wrath comes to the Israelites, possibly from the god of Moab, and they return home.

War with Moab

4 Now King Mesha of Moab was a sheep breeder, who used to deliver to the king of Israel one hundred thousand lambs, and the wool of
one hundred thousand rams. [5]But when Ahab died, the king of Moab
rebelled against the king of Israel. [6]So King Jehoram marched out of
Samaria at that time and mustered all Israel. [7]As he went he sent word
to King Jehoshaphat of Judah, "The king of Moab has rebelled against
me; will you go with me to battle against Moab?" He answered, "I
will; I am with you, my people are your people, my horses are your
horses." [8]Then he asked, "By which way shall we march?" Jehoram answered, "By the way of the wilderness of Edom."

9 So the king of Israel, the king of Judah, and the king of Edom
set out; and when they had made a roundabout march of seven days,
there was no water for the army or for the animals that were with
them. [10]Then the king of Israel said, "Alas! The LORD has summoned
us, three kings, only to be handed over to Moab." [11]But Jehoshaphat
said, "Is there no prophet of the LORD here, through whom we may
inquire of the LORD?" Then one of the servants of the king of Israel
answered, "Elisha son of Shaphat, who used to pour water on the
hands of Elijah, is here." [12]Jehoshaphat said, "The word of the LORD is
with him." So the king of Israel and Jehoshaphat and the king of Edom
went down to him.

13 Elisha said to the king of Israel, "What have I to do with you?
Go to your father's prophets or to your mother's." But the king of Israel
said to him, "No; it is the LORD who has summoned us, three kings,
only to be handed over to Moab." [14]Elisha said, "As the LORD of hosts
lives, whom I serve, were it not that I have regard for King Jehoshaphat of Judah, I would give you neither a look nor a glance. [15]But get
me a musician." And then, while the musician was playing, the power
of the LORD came on him. [16]And he said, "Thus says the LORD, 'I will
make this wadi full of pools.' [17]For thus says the LORD, 'You shall see
neither wind nor rain, but the wadi shall be filled with water, so that
you shall drink, you, your cattle, and your animals.' [18]This is only a
trifle in the sight of the LORD, for he will also hand Moab over to you.
[19]You shall conquer every fortified city and every choice city; every
good tree you shall fell, all springs of water you shall stop up, and
every good piece of land you shall ruin with stones." [20]The next day,
about the time of the morning offering, suddenly water began to flow
from the direction of Edom, until the country was filled with water.

21 When all the Moabites heard that the kings had come up to
fight against them, all who were able to put on armor, from the youngest to the oldest, were called out and were drawn up at the frontier.
[22]When they rose early in the morning, and the sun shone upon the
water, the Moabites saw the water opposite them as red as blood.
[23]They said, "This is blood; the kings must have fought together, and

killed one another. Now then, Moab, to the spoil!" 24 But when they
came to the camp of Israel, the Israelites rose up and attacked the Moabites, who fled before them; as they entered Moab they continued
the attack.[a] 25 The cities they overturned, and on every good piece
of land everyone threw a stone, until it was covered; every spring of
water they stopped up, and every good tree they felled. Only at Kir-
hareseth did the stone walls remain, until the slingers surrounded and
attacked it. 26 When the king of Moab saw that the battle was going
against him, he took with him seven hundred swordsmen to break
through, opposite the king of Edom; but they could not. 27 Then he
took his firstborn son who was to succeed him, and offered him as a
burnt offering on the wall. And great wrath came upon Israel, so they
withdrew from him and returned to their own land.

Elisha and the Widow's Oil

4 Now the wife of a member of the company of prophets[b] cried
to Elisha, "Your servant my husband is dead; and you know that
your servant feared the LORD, but a creditor has come to take my two
children as slaves." 2 Elisha said to her, "What shall I do for you? Tell
me, what do you have in the house?" She answered, "Your servant
has nothing in the house, except a jar of oil." 3 He said, "Go outside,
borrow vessels from all your neighbors, empty vessels and not just a
few. 4 Then go in, and shut the door behind you and your children, and
start pouring into all these vessels; when each is full, set it aside." 5 So
she left him and shut the door behind her and her children; they kept
bringing vessels to her, and she kept pouring. 6 When the vessels were
full, she said to her son, "Bring me another vessel." But he said to her,
"There are no more." Then the oil stopped flowing. 7 She came and
told the man of God, and he said, "Go sell the oil and pay your debts,
and you and your children can live on the rest."

Elisha Raises the Shunammite's Son

8 One day Elisha was passing through Shunem, where a wealthy
woman lived, who urged him to have a meal. So whenever he passed
that way, he would stop there for a meal. 9 She said to her husband,
"Look, I am sure that this man who regularly passes our way is a holy
man of God. 10 Let us make a small roof chamber with walls, and put
there for him a bed, a table, a chair, and a lamp, so that he can stay
there whenever he comes to us."

11 One day when he came there, he went up to the chamber and
lay down there. 12 He said to his servant Gehazi, "Call the Shunammite
woman." When he had called her, she stood before him. 13 He said to
him, "Say to her, Since you have taken all this trouble for us, what may

---

[a] Compare Gk Syr: Meaning of Heb uncertain [b] Heb *the sons of the prophets*

4:1-7 a jar of oil: A widow of one of the prophets accompanying Elisha accumulates a heavy debt, and those she owes threaten to turn her children into slaves. All she has left is a little cooking oil. Elisha tells her to borrow as many containers from her neighbors as possible and begin pouring oil into them. She does this until all the containers are full. Then Elisha tells her to sell all the oil, pay off her debts, and live on the rest of the money. This story resembles the story about Elijah and the widow of Zarephath in 1 Kings 17:8-16.

4:8-37 the Shunammite woman: Elisha regularly visited a wealthy woman in the town of Shunem in the Jezreel valley (see Map 7, p. 2105), and she and her husband built a special guest room for Elisha on the second floor of their house. She refuses Elisha's offer to contact various government officials on her behalf, and Elisha's servant Gehazi informs him that the woman has no son and her husband is old. Elisha promises her she will have a son, and the child is born in due time. After a few years the child joins a threshing crew, complains about a severe headache, possibly from sunstroke, and dies a few hours later in his mother's arms. She tells her husband she wants to visit Elisha, but he does not understand the reason for the visit (apparently he does not know about the child's death). Leaving the child in Elisha's room, the woman rides off to meet Elisha at Mount Carmel. At first she denies to Gehazi that anything is wrong. Elisha sends Gehazi ahead to lay his staff on the child, but there is no response. When Elisha arrives, he goes into his room, prays, stretches himself over the child, and walks back and forth in the room. Finally the boy opens his eyes. Elisha presents the child to the mother, who honors Elisha and leaves. A similar story about the prophet Elijah appears in 1 Kings 17:17-24.

be done for you? Would you have a word spoken on your behalf to the
king or to the commander of the army?" She answered, "I live among
my own people." [14]He said, "What then may be done for her?" Gehazi
answered, "Well, she has no son, and her husband is old." [15]He said,
"Call her." When he had called her, she stood at the door. [16]He said,
"At this season, in due time, you shall embrace a son." She replied,
"No, my lord, O man of God; do not deceive your servant."

17 The woman conceived and bore a son at that season, in due
time, as Elisha had declared to her.

18 When the child was older, he went out one day to his father
among the reapers. [19]He complained to his father, "Oh, my head, my
head!" The father said to his servant, "Carry him to his mother." [20]He
carried him and brought him to his mother; the child sat on her lap
until noon, and he died. [21]She went up and laid him on the bed of the
man of God, closed the door on him, and left. [22]Then she called to
her husband, and said, "Send me one of the servants and one of the
donkeys, so that I may quickly go to the man of God and come back
again." [23]He said, "Why go to him today? It is neither new moon nor
sabbath." She said, "It will be all right." [24]Then she saddled the donkey
and said to her servant, "Urge the animal on; do not hold back for
me unless I tell you." [25]So she set out, and came to the man of God at
Mount Carmel.

When the man of God saw her coming, he said to Gehazi his servant, "Look, there is the Shunammite woman; [26]run at once to meet
her, and say to her, Are you all right? Is your husband all right? Is the
child all right?" She answered, "It is all right." [27]When she came to the
man of God at the mountain, she caught hold of his feet. Gehazi approached to push her away. But the man of God said, "Let her alone,
for she is in bitter distress; the Lord has hidden it from me and has
not told me." [28]Then she said, "Did I ask my lord for a son? Did I not
say, Do not mislead me?" [29]He said to Gehazi, "Gird up your loins,
and take my staff in your hand, and go. If you meet anyone, give no
greeting, and if anyone greets you, do not answer; and lay my staff
on the face of the child." [30]Then the mother of the child said, "As the
Lord lives, and as you yourself live, I will not leave without you." So
he rose up and followed her. [31]Gehazi went on ahead and laid the staff
on the face of the child, but there was no sound or sign of life. He
came back to meet him and told him, "The child has not awakened."

32 When Elisha came into the house, he saw the child lying
dead on his bed. [33]So he went in and closed the door on the two of
them, and prayed to the Lord. [34]Then he got up on the bed[a] and lay
upon the child, putting his mouth upon his mouth, his eyes upon his
eyes, and his hands upon his hands; and while he lay bent over him,

---

[a] Heb lacks *on the bed*

the flesh of the child became warm. 35 He got down, walked once to
and fro in the room, then got up again and bent over him; the child
sneezed seven times, and the child opened his eyes. 36 Elisha[a] summoned Gehazi and said, "Call the Shunammite woman." So he called
her. When she came to him, he said, "Take your son." 37 She came and
fell at his feet, bowing to the ground; then she took her son and left.

Elisha Purifies the Pot of Stew

38 When Elisha returned to Gilgal, there was a famine in the land.
As the company of prophets was[b] sitting before him, he said to his servant, "Put the large pot on, and make some stew for the company of
prophets."[c] 39 One of them went out into the field to gather herbs; he
found a wild vine and gathered from it a lapful of wild gourds, and
came and cut them up into the pot of stew, not knowing what they
were. 40 They served some for the men to eat. But while they were eating the stew, they cried out, "O man of God, there is death in the pot!"
They could not eat it. 41 He said, "Then bring some flour." He threw it
into the pot, and said, "Serve the people and let them eat." And there
was nothing harmful in the pot.

Elisha Feeds One Hundred Men

42 A man came from Baal-shalishah, bringing food from the first
fruits to the man of God: twenty loaves of barley and fresh ears of
grain in his sack. Elisha said, "Give it to the people and let them eat."
43 But his servant said, "How can I set this before a hundred people?"
So he repeated, "Give it to the people and let them eat, for thus says
the LORD, 'They shall eat and have some left.' " 44 He set it before them,
they ate, and had some left, according to the word of the LORD.

The Healing of Naaman

5 Naaman, commander of the army of the king of Aram, was a
great man and in high favor with his master, because by him the
LORD had given victory to Aram. The man, though a mighty warrior,
suffered from leprosy.[d] 2 Now the Arameans on one of their raids had
taken a young girl captive from the land of Israel, and she served Naaman's wife. 3 She said to her mistress, "If only my lord were with the
prophet who is in Samaria! He would cure him of his leprosy."[d] 4 So
Naaman[a] went in and told his lord just what the girl from the land of
Israel had said. 5 And the king of Aram said, "Go then, and I will send
along a letter to the king of Israel."

He went, taking with him ten talents of silver, six thousand shekels
of gold, and ten sets of garments. 6 He brought the letter to the king

[a] Heb *he* [b] Heb *sons of the prophets were* [c] Heb *sons of the prophets* [d] A term for several skin diseases; precise meaning uncertain

4:38-41 make some stew for the company of prophets: Elisha visits a band of prophets at Gilgal during a famine. While he is teaching them, Elisha suggests that they make some stew. One of the prophets unknowingly cuts up a poisonous plant into the stew. When Elisha throws flour in the pot, the stew becomes safe.

4:42-44 they ate, and had some left: In this miracle story, Elisha multiplies twenty loaves of bread so that they feed one hundred people, with some left over, demonstrating the power of the word of the LORD. Compare this with some of the feeding stories in the ministry of Jesus (Matt 14:13-21; 15:32-38; Mark 8:1-10).

5:1-19 Naaman, commander of the army of the king of Aram: Naaman, an important person in Aram, suffered from a severe skin disease, although what is called leprosy in the Bible is probably not the disease known today as leprosy. At least one of Naaman's victories comes because of the LORD's help. An unnamed Israelite girl, a prisoner of war, recommends that Naaman see the prophet Elisha in Samaria. Armed with a letter from his king and an enormous amount of money, Naaman approaches an unnamed king of Israel, who says he is unable to help and thinks Naaman is picking a fight. Elisha hears about this and invites Naaman to visit him. Without meeting with Naaman, Elisha sends instructions for him to bathe seven times in the Jordan river and be healed. Naaman is miffed with this because he sees nothing special about the river, but his servants convince him to try it—and it works. Naaman returns to Elisha with thanksgiving, confesses that the God of Israel is the only God, and urges Elisha to accept a gift from him. Eventually Naaman takes two loads of dirt back to Aram so that he can worship the LORD at home on a piece of Israelite land. He asks for Elisha's permission and the LORD's pardon to accompany his supervisor to the temple of Rimmon, another name for the god Hadad, often identified with Baal.

Based on the story of Naaman, how would you define faith?

of Israel, which read, "When this letter reaches you, know that I have
sent to you my servant Naaman, that you may cure him of his leprosy."[a] 7 When the king of Israel read the letter, he tore his clothes and
said, "Am I God, to give death or life, that this man sends word to me
to cure a man of his leprosy?[a] Just look and see how he is trying to
pick a quarrel with me."

8 But when Elisha the man of God heard that the king of Israel
had torn his clothes, he sent a message to the king, "Why have you
torn your clothes? Let him come to me, that he may learn that there
is a prophet in Israel." 9 So Naaman came with his horses and chariots,
and halted at the entrance of Elisha's house. 10 Elisha sent a messenger
to him, saying, "Go, wash in the Jordan seven times, and your flesh
shall be restored and you shall be clean." 11 But Naaman became angry
and went away, saying, "I thought that for me he would surely come
out, and stand and call on the name of the LORD his God, and would
wave his hand over the spot, and cure the leprosy![a] 12 Are not Abana[b]
and Pharpar, the rivers of Damascus, better than all the waters of Israel? Could I not wash in them, and be clean?" He turned and went
away in a rage. 13 But his servants approached and said to him, "Father, if the prophet had commanded you to do something difficult,
would you not have done it? How much more, when all he said to you
was, 'Wash, and be clean'?" 14 So he went down and immersed himself
seven times in the Jordan, according to the word of the man of God;
his flesh was restored like the flesh of a young boy, and he was clean.

15 Then he returned to the man of God, he and all his company;
he came and stood before him and said, "Now I know that there is no
God in all the earth except in Israel; please accept a present from your
servant." 16 But he said, "As the LORD lives, whom I serve, I will accept
nothing!" He urged him to accept, but he refused. 17 Then Naaman
said, "If not, please let two mule-loads of earth be given to your servant; for your servant will no longer offer burnt offering or sacrifice to
any god except the LORD. 18 But may the LORD pardon your servant
on one count: when my master goes into the house of Rimmon to
worship there, leaning on my arm, and I bow down in the house of
Rimmon, when I do bow down in the house of Rimmon, may the
LORD pardon your servant on this one count." 19 He said to him, "Go
in peace."

5:19b-27 Gehazi went after Naaman: Gehazi, Elisha's servant, goes after Naaman and tells him a lie about two unexpected visitors and his need for money and clothes for the visitors. Naaman gladly gives these items. When Gehazi returns to Elisha, he lies again, saying he has not been away. Elisha says Naaman's skin disease will cling to Gehazi and his family forever. This story contrasts Gehazi's greed with Elisha's selflessness and demonstrates Elisha's miraculous ability to travel "in spirit."

Gehazi's Greed

But when Naaman had gone from him a short distance, 20 Gehazi,
the servant of Elisha the man of God, thought, "My master has let that
Aramean Naaman off too lightly by not accepting from him what he
offered. As the LORD lives, I will run after him and get something out
of him." 21 So Gehazi went after Naaman. When Naaman saw some-

[a] A term for several skin diseases; precise meaning uncertain [b] Another reading is *Amana*

one running after him, he jumped down from the chariot to meet him and said, "Is everything all right?" 22 He replied, "Yes, but my master has sent me to say, 'Two members of a company of prophets[a] have just come to me from the hill country of Ephraim; please give them a talent of silver and two changes of clothing.'" 23 Naaman said, "Please accept two talents." He urged him, and tied up two talents of silver in two bags, with two changes of clothing, and gave them to two of his servants, who carried them in front of Gehazi.[b] 24 When he came to the citadel, he took the bags[c] from them, and stored them inside; he dismissed the men, and they left.

25 He went in and stood before his master; and Elisha said to him, "Where have you been, Gehazi?" He answered, "Your servant has not gone anywhere at all." 26 But he said to him, "Did I not go with you in spirit when someone left his chariot to meet you? Is this a time to accept money and to accept clothing, olive orchards and vineyards, sheep and oxen, and male and female slaves? 27 Therefore the leprosy[d] of Naaman shall cling to you, and to your descendants forever." So he left his presence leprous,[d] as white as snow.

The Miracle of the Ax Head

6 Now the company of prophets[a] said to Elisha, "As you see, the place where we live under your charge is too small for us. 2 Let us go to the Jordan, and let us collect logs there, one for each of us, and build a place there for us to live." He answered, "Do so." 3 Then one of them said, "Please come with your servants." And he answered, "I will." 4 So he went with them. When they came to the Jordan, they cut down trees. 5 But as one was felling a log, his ax head fell into the water; he cried out, "Alas, master! It was borrowed." 6 Then the man of God said, "Where did it fall?" When he showed him the place, he cut off a stick, and threw it in there, and made the iron float. 7 He said, "Pick it up." So he reached out his hand and took it.

6:1-7 he . . . made the iron float: The prophets with Elisha decide they need bigger places to live. As they chop down trees, an ax head flies off and sinks in the Jordan River. This was cause for alarm, because the ax belonged to someone else. Elisha throws a stick in the Jordan, and miraculously the ax head floats.

The Aramean Attack Is Thwarted

8 Once when the king of Aram was at war with Israel, he took counsel with his officers. He said, "At such and such a place shall be my camp." 9 But the man of God sent word to the king of Israel, "Take care not to pass this place, because the Arameans are going down there." 10 The king of Israel sent word to the place of which the man of God spoke. More than once or twice he warned such a place[e] so that it was on the alert.

11 The mind of the king of Aram was greatly perturbed because of this; he called his officers and said to them, "Now tell me who among

6:8-23 the man of God sent word to the king of Israel: Elisha performs a series of miracles to help the Israelite army avoid a dangerous confrontation with the Arameans. Elisha is even able to hear what the Aramean king says in his bedroom! The Aramean king tries to arrest Elisha in Dothan, ten miles north of Samaria. When the city is surrounded by the enemy army, Elisha prays that his servant's eyes be opened to see God's horses and chariots of fire defending the city. Men try to seize Elisha, but he prays that they be blinded and leads them into the capital city of Samaria. The LORD then opens the men's eyes. When the king wonders what he should do, Elisha suggests that the men be served a banquet. This hospitality ends the Aramean raids, at least temporarily.

---

[a] Heb *sons of the prophets* [b] Heb *him* [c] Heb lacks *the bags* [d] A term for several skin diseases; precise meaning uncertain [e] Heb *warned it*

us sides with the king of Israel?" [12]Then one of his officers said, "No one, my lord king. It is Elisha, the prophet in Israel, who tells the king of Israel the words that you speak in your bedchamber." [13]He said, "Go and find where he is; I will send and seize him." He was told, "He is in Dothan." [14]So he sent horses and chariots there and a great army; they came by night, and surrounded the city.

15 When an attendant of the man of God rose early in the morning and went out, an army with horses and chariots was all around the city. His servant said, "Alas, master! What shall we do?" [16]He replied, "Do not be afraid, for there are more with us than there are with them." [17]Then Elisha prayed: "O LORD, please open his eyes that he may see." So the LORD opened the eyes of the servant, and he saw; the mountain was full of horses and chariots of fire all around Elisha. [18]When the Arameans[a] came down against him, Elisha prayed to the LORD, and said, "Strike this people, please, with blindness." So he struck them with blindness as Elisha had asked. [19]Elisha said to them, "This is not the way, and this is not the city; follow me, and I will bring you to the man whom you seek." And he led them to Samaria.

20 As soon as they entered Samaria, Elisha said, "O LORD, open the eyes of these men so that they may see." The LORD opened their eyes, and they saw that they were inside Samaria. [21]When the king of Israel saw them he said to Elisha, "Father, shall I kill them? Shall I kill them?" [22]He answered, "No! Did you capture with your sword and your bow those whom you want to kill? Set food and water before them so that they may eat and drink; and let them go to their master." [23]So he prepared for them a great feast; after they ate and drank, he sent them on their way, and they went to their master. And the Arameans no longer came raiding into the land of Israel.

Ben-hadad's Siege of Samaria

6:24-7:2 King Ben-hadad... marched against Samaria and laid siege to it: During a siege of Samaria, the lack of food becomes so terrible that two women agree to eat their sons. The second woman goes back on the deal. The king of Israel mourns the situation and puts the blame on Elisha. Elisha refuses to speak with the king's messenger, but does speak with the king himself, who now blames his troubles on the LORD. Elisha promises relief the next day (compare the prices in 7:1 with those in 6:25). A captain of the king says this is impossible, but Elisha assures him that the promise is true, even if the captain will not benefit from it.

24 Some time later King Ben-hadad of Aram mustered his entire army; he marched against Samaria and laid siege to it. [25]As the siege continued, famine in Samaria became so great that a donkey's head was sold for eighty shekels of silver, and one-fourth of a kab of dove's dung for five shekels of silver. [26]Now as the king of Israel was walking on the city wall, a woman cried out to him, "Help, my lord king!" [27]He said, "No! Let the LORD help you. How can I help you? From the threshing floor or from the wine press?" [28]But then the king asked her, "What is your complaint?" She answered, "This woman said to me, 'Give up your son; we will eat him today, and we will eat my son tomorrow.' [29]So we cooked my son and ate him. The next day I said to her, 'Give up your son and we will eat him.' But she has hidden her son." [30]When the king heard the words of the woman he tore his

[a] Heb *they*

clothes—now since he was walking on the city wall, the people could
see that he had sackcloth on his body underneath— 31and he said,
"So may God do to me, and more, if the head of Elisha son of Shaphat stays on his shoulders today." 32So he dispatched a man from his
presence.

Now Elisha was sitting in his house, and the elders were sitting
with him. Before the messenger arrived, Elisha said to the elders, "Are
you aware that this murderer has sent someone to take off my head?
When the messenger comes, see that you shut the door and hold it
closed against him. Is not the sound of his master's feet behind him?"
33While he was still speaking with them, the king[a] came down to him
and said, "This trouble is from the LORD! Why should I hope in the
7 LORD any longer?" 1But Elisha said, "Hear the word of the
LORD: thus says the LORD, Tomorrow about this time a measure of choice meal shall be sold for a shekel, and two measures of
barley for a shekel, at the gate of Samaria." 2Then the captain on
whose hand the king leaned said to the man of God, "Even if the
LORD were to make windows in the sky, could such a thing happen?"
But he said, "You shall see it with your own eyes, but you shall not
eat from it."

The Arameans Flee

3 Now there were four leprous[b] men outside the city gate, who
said to one another, "Why should we sit here until we die? 4If we say,
'Let us enter the city,' the famine is in the city, and we shall die there;
but if we sit here, we shall also die. Therefore, let us desert to the Aramean camp; if they spare our lives, we shall live; and if they kill us, we
shall but die." 5So they arose at twilight to go to the Aramean camp;
but when they came to the edge of the Aramean camp, there was no
one there at all. 6For the Lord had caused the Aramean army to hear
the sound of chariots, and of horses, the sound of a great army, so
that they said to one another, "The king of Israel has hired the kings
of the Hittites and the kings of Egypt to fight against us." 7So they fled
away in the twilight and abandoned their tents, their horses, and their
donkeys leaving the camp just as it was, and fled for their lives. 8When
these leprous[b] men had come to the edge of the camp, they went into
a tent, ate and drank, carried off silver, gold, and clothing, and went
and hid them. Then they came back, entered another tent, carried off
things from it, and went and hid them.

9 Then they said to one another, "What we are doing is wrong.
This is a day of good news; if we are silent and wait until the morning
light, we will be found guilty; therefore let us go and tell the king's
household." 10So they came and called to the gatekeepers of the city,

7:3-20 let us desert to the Aramean camp: Four men with a serious skin disease decide to go over to the Arameans' side rather than die in the famine in the city. The Arameans, however, had fled. When the LORD made them hear the sounds of chariots and horses, they thought Israel had hired other nations against them. The four men find the Aramean camp deserted and loot several tents until, stricken with guilt, they decide to tell this good news to people in the city. The Israelite king thinks the empty enemy camp is a trick, sends a delegation to check it out, and discovers the report is true. Everyone goes out to pillage the camp, and in their haste they trample to death the captain who had doubted Elisha's word. This fulfills both the good news and the bad news announced by Elisha in 7:1-2.

---

[a] See 7.2: Heb *messenger* [b] A term for several skin diseases; precise meaning uncertain

and told them, "We went to the Aramean camp, but there was no one
to be seen or heard there, nothing but the horses tied, the donkeys
tied, and the tents as they were." 11 Then the gatekeepers called out and
proclaimed it to the king's household. 12 The king got up in the night,
and said to his servants, "I will tell you what the Arameans have prepared against us. They know that we are starving; so they have left the
camp to hide themselves in the open country, thinking, 'When they
come out of the city, we shall take them alive and get into the city.' "
13 One of his servants said, "Let some men take five of the remaining
horses, since those left here will suffer the fate of the whole multitude of Israel that have perished already;[a] let us send and find out."
14 So they took two mounted men, and the king sent them after the
Aramean army, saying, "Go and find out." 15 So they went after them
as far as the Jordan; the whole way was littered with garments and
equipment that the Arameans had thrown away in their haste. So the
messengers returned, and told the king.

16 Then the people went out, and plundered the camp of the Arameans. So a measure of choice meal was sold for a shekel, and two
measures of barley for a shekel, according to the word of the LORD.
17 Now the king had appointed the captain on whose hand he leaned
to have charge of the gate; the people trampled him to death in the
gate, just as the man of God had said when the king came down to
him. 18 For when the man of God had said to the king, "Two measures
of barley shall be sold for a shekel, and a measure of choice meal for a
shekel, about this time tomorrow in the gate of Samaria," 19 the captain
had answered the man of God, "Even if the LORD were to make windows in the sky, could such a thing happen?" And he had answered,
"You shall see it with your own eyes, but you shall not eat from it."
20 It did indeed happen to him; the people trampled him to death in
the gate.

The Shunammite Woman's Land Restored

8 Now Elisha had said to the woman whose son he had restored
to life, "Get up and go with your household, and settle wherever
you can; for the LORD has called for a famine, and it will come on the
land for seven years." 2 So the woman got up and did according to the
word of the man of God; she went with her household and settled in
the land of the Philistines seven years. 3 At the end of the seven years,
when the woman returned from the land of the Philistines, she set
out to appeal to the king for her house and her land. 4 Now the king
was talking with Gehazi the servant of the man of God, saying, "Tell
me all the great things that Elisha has done." 5 While he was telling
the king how Elisha had restored a dead person to life, the woman
whose son he had restored to life appealed to the king for her house

8:1-6 she set out to appeal to the king for her house and her land: The woman whose son had been raised had gone into exile at Elisha's instruction during a famine and had to appeal to regain her property when she returned. Just as she approaches the king, Elisha's servant Gehazi is telling the king how Elisha raised the woman's son. The king agrees to her request and restores her land. It is not clear whether Gehazi has been restored to his former position and cured of his leprosy (5:25-27) or whether this story is out of chronological order—that is, it occurs before Gehazi seeks a payoff from Naaman (5:19b-24).

[a] Compare Gk Syr Vg: Meaning of Heb uncertain

and her land. Gehazi said, "My lord king, here is the woman, and here
is her son whom Elisha restored to life." 6When the king questioned
the woman, she told him. So the king appointed an official for her,
saying, "Restore all that was hers, together with all the revenue of the
fields from the day that she left the land until now."

Death of Ben-hadad

7 Elisha went to Damascus while King Ben-hadad of Aram was
ill. When it was told him, "The man of God has come here," 8the king
said to Hazael, "Take a present with you and go to meet the man of
God. Inquire of the LORD through him, whether I shall recover from
this illness." 9So Hazael went to meet him, taking a present with him,
all kinds of goods of Damascus, forty camel loads. When he entered
and stood before him, he said, "Your son King Ben-hadad of Aram
has sent me to you, saying, 'Shall I recover from this illness?' " 10Eli-
sha said to him, "Go, say to him, 'You shall certainly recover'; but the
LORD has shown me that he shall certainly die." 11He fixed his gaze
and stared at him, until he was ashamed. Then the man of God wept.
12Hazael asked, "Why does my lord weep?" He answered, "Because
I know the evil that you will do to the people of Israel; you will set
their fortresses on fire, you will kill their young men with the sword,
dash in pieces their little ones, and rip up their pregnant women."
13Hazael said, "What is your servant, who is a mere dog, that he
should do this great thing?" Elisha answered, "The LORD has shown
me that you are to be king over Aram." 14Then he left Elisha, and
went to his master Ben-hadad,[a] who said to him, "What did Elisha
say to you?" And he answered, "He told me that you would certainly
recover." 15But the next day he took the bed-cover and dipped it in
water and spread it over the king's face, until he died. And Hazael
succeeded him.

8:7-15 King Ben-hadad of Aram was ill: King Ben-hadad becomes ill and sends his servant Hazael to Elisha to ask if he will recover. Elisha gives a double answer: Ben-hadad will recover from the illness but will die anyway. Elisha stares at Hazael and then cries because of all the harm Hazael will do to Israel as the king of Aram. The next day Hazael shares only the first part of the message with Ben-hadad and then suffocates him. Elijah had been commanded to anoint Hazael (1 Kgs 19:15) as Aram's king.

Jehoram Reigns over Judah

16 In the fifth year of King Joram son of Ahab of Israel,[b] Jehoram
son of King Jehoshaphat of Judah began to reign. 17He was thirty-two
years old when he became king, and he reigned eight years in Jerusalem. 18He walked in the way of the kings of Israel, as the house of
Ahab had done, for the daughter of Ahab was his wife. He did what
was evil in the sight of the LORD. 19Yet the LORD would not destroy
Judah, for the sake of his servant David, since he had promised to give
a lamp to him and to his descendants forever.

20 In his days Edom revolted against the rule of Judah, and set up
a king of their own. 21Then Joram crossed over to Zair with all his chariots. He set out by night and attacked the Edomites and their chariot

8:16-24 Jehoram…reigned eight years in Jerusalem: Jehoram (852–843 B.C.E.) succeeds his father, Jehoshaphat, and follows the evil ways of the kings of Israel, since he is married to Athaliah, who is either the daughter of Omri or granddaughter of Ahab (in verse 18 the word *daughter* could also be translated *granddaughter*). Nevertheless, the LORD preserves Judah for King David's sake. Jehoram also faces revolts from Edom and the city of Libnah, near the Philistines. His son Ahaziah (843–842 B.C.E.) succeeds him.

[a] Heb lacks *Ben-hadad* [b] Gk Syr: Heb adds *Jehoshaphat being king of Judah,*

commanders who had surrounded him;[a] but his army fled home. 22 So Edom has been in revolt against the rule of Judah to this day. Libnah also revolted at the same time. 23 Now the rest of the acts of Joram, and all that he did, are they not written in the Book of the Annals of the Kings of Judah? 24 So Joram slept with his ancestors, and was buried with them in the city of David; his son Ahaziah succeeded him.

Ahaziah Reigns over Judah

8:25-29 Ahaziah . . . began to reign: Ahaziah continues in the evil ways of his father. In a joint military adventure with Joram of northern Israel, Joram is wounded and taken to the palace at Jezreel. Ahaziah makes a fateful sick call there.

25 In the twelfth year of King Joram son of Ahab of Israel, Ahaziah son of King Jehoram of Judah began to reign. 26 Ahaziah was twenty-two years old when he began to reign; he reigned one year in Jerusalem. His mother's name was Athaliah, a granddaughter of King Omri of Israel. 27 He also walked in the way of the house of Ahab, doing what was evil in the sight of the LORD, as the house of Ahab had done, for he was son-in-law to the house of Ahab.

28 He went with Joram son of Ahab to wage war against King Hazael of Aram at Ramoth-gilead, where the Arameans wounded Joram. 29 King Joram returned to be healed in Jezreel of the wounds that the Arameans had inflicted on him at Ramah, when he fought against King Hazael of Aram. King Ahaziah son of Jehoram of Judah went down to see Joram son of Ahab in Jezreel, because he was wounded.

Anointing of Jehu

9:1-13 Jehu is king: Elisha sends a prophet to take aside the military officer Jehu and secretly anoint him as king (this assignment was also given to Elijah in 1 Kgs 19:16). The young prophet does this and commands Jehu to destroy the whole household of Ahab as punishment for all the prophets killed under the orders of Jezebel, Ahab's wife. This family line will suffer the same fate as those of Jeroboam and Baasha, other kings who did what was evil. Jehu returns to the other officers and at first denies that anything has happened. When he tells the officers the truth, they all hail him as king.

9 Then the prophet Elisha called a member of the company of prophets[b] and said to him, "Gird up your loins; take this flask of oil in your hand, and go to Ramoth-gilead. 2 When you arrive, look there for Jehu son of Jehoshaphat, son of Nimshi; go in and get him to leave his companions, and take him into an inner chamber. 3 Then take the flask of oil, pour it on his head, and say, 'Thus says the LORD: I anoint you king over Israel.' Then open the door and flee; do not linger."

4 So the young man, the young prophet, went to Ramoth-gilead. 5 He arrived while the commanders of the army were in council, and he announced, "I have a message for you, commander." "For which one of us?" asked Jehu. "For you, commander." 6 So Jehu[c] got up and went inside; the young man poured the oil on his head, saying to him, "Thus says the LORD the God of Israel: I anoint you king over the people of the LORD, over Israel. 7 You shall strike down the house of your master Ahab, so that I may avenge on Jezebel the blood of my servants the prophets, and the blood of all the servants of the LORD. 8 For the whole house of Ahab shall perish; I will cut off from Ahab every male, bond or free, in Israel. 9 I will make the house of Ahab like the house of Jeroboam son of Nebat, and like the house of Baasha son

---

[a] Meaning of Heb uncertain [b] Heb *sons of the prophets* [c] Heb *he*

of Ahijah. 10The dogs shall eat Jezebel in the territory of Jezreel, and
no one shall bury her." Then he opened the door and fled.
11 When Jehu came back to his master's officers, they said to him,
"Is everything all right? Why did that madman come to you?" He answered them, "You know the sort and how they babble." 12They said,
"Liar! Come on, tell us!" So he said, "This is just what he said to me:
'Thus says the LORD, I anoint you king over Israel.'" 13Then hurriedly
they all took their cloaks and spread them for him on the bare[a] steps;
and they blew the trumpet, and proclaimed, "Jehu is king."

Joram of Israel Killed

14 Thus Jehu son of Jehoshaphat son of Nimshi conspired against
Joram. Joram with all Israel had been on guard at Ramoth-gilead
against King Hazael of Aram; 15but King Joram had returned to be
healed in Jezreel of the wounds that the Arameans had inflicted on
him, when he fought against King Hazael of Aram. So Jehu said, "If
this is your wish, then let no one slip out of the city to go and tell the
news in Jezreel." 16Then Jehu mounted his chariot and went to Jezreel,
where Joram was lying ill. King Ahaziah of Judah had come down to
visit Joram.
17 In Jezreel, the sentinel standing on the tower spied the company of Jehu arriving, and said, "I see a company." Joram said, "Take
a horseman; send him to meet them, and let him say, 'Is it peace?'"
18So the horseman went to meet him; he said, "Thus says the king, 'Is
it peace?'" Jehu responded, "What have you to do with peace? Fall in
behind me." The sentinel reported, saying, "The messenger reached
them, but he is not coming back." 19Then he sent out a second horseman, who came to them and said, "Thus says the king, 'Is it peace?'"
Jehu answered, "What have you to do with peace? Fall in behind me."
20Again the sentinel reported, "He reached them, but he is not coming back. It looks like the driving of Jehu son of Nimshi; for he drives
like a maniac."
21 Joram said, "Get ready." And they got his chariot ready. Then
King Joram of Israel and King Ahaziah of Judah set out, each in his
chariot, and went to meet Jehu; they met him at the property of
Naboth the Jezreelite. 22When Joram saw Jehu, he said, "Is it peace,
Jehu?" He answered, "What peace can there be, so long as the many
whoredoms and sorceries of your mother Jezebel continue?" 23Then
Joram reined about and fled, saying to Ahaziah, "Treason, Ahaziah!"
24Jehu drew his bow with all his strength, and shot Joram between
the shoulders, so that the arrow pierced his heart; and he sank in his
chariot. 25Jehu said to his aide Bidkar, "Lift him out, and throw him on
the plot of ground belonging to Naboth the Jezreelite; for remember,

[a] Meaning of Heb uncertain

9:14-24 Jehu drew his bow . . . and shot Joram: Jehu begins a march against the city of Jezreel and persuades messengers who had been sent by that city's sentinel (or lookout) to join his group. The lookout recognizes Jehu by his furious chariot driving. King Joram of Israel and King Ahaziah of Judah go out in their chariots to meet Jehu, who rejects their offer of peace and reprimands Joram for the sins of his mother, Jezebel. Joram attempts to flee, but Jehu shoots him dead with an arrow.

9:25-26 in accordance with the word of the LORD: The author of Kings often notes how a word spoken by a prophet is later fulfilled. These events give authority to the prophets, who frequently warn the people of the north and south that they need to change their ways. Here Joram's body is thrown onto Naboth's vineyard, fulfilling a prophecy made by Elijah (1 Kgs 21:19-22).

when you and I rode side by side behind his father Ahab how the LORD uttered this oracle against him: 26‘For the blood of Naboth and for the blood of his children that I saw yesterday, says the LORD, I swear I will repay you on this very plot of ground.’ Now therefore lift him out and throw him on the plot of ground, in accordance with the word of the LORD.”

Ahaziah of Judah Killed

9:27-29 King Ahaziah of Judah: Jehu's men also shoot Ahaziah, who flees to Megiddo and dies. His officers carry him to Jerusalem for burial.

27 When King Ahaziah of Judah saw this, he fled in the direction of Beth-haggan. Jehu pursued him, saying, “Shoot him also!” And they shot him[a] in the chariot at the ascent to Gur, which is by Ibleam. Then he fled to Megiddo, and died there. 28His officers carried him in a chariot to Jerusalem, and buried him in his tomb with his ancestors in the city of David.

29 In the eleventh year of Joram son of Ahab, Ahaziah began to reign over Judah.

Jezebel's Violent Death

9:30-37 dogs shall eat the flesh of Jezebel: As Jehu enters Jezreel, Jezebel taunts him by comparing him to Zimri, the assassin of Elah, who reigned for seven days (1 Kgs 16:8-14). Jezebel is thrown out a window and is trampled by horses. Jehu orders that Jezebel be buried because she was a king's daughter, but dogs have already eaten her flesh, fulfilling Elijah's prophecy (1 Kgs 21:23).

30 When Jehu came to Jezreel, Jezebel heard of it; she painted her eyes, and adorned her head, and looked out of the window. 31As Jehu entered the gate, she said, “Is it peace, Zimri, murderer of your master?” 32He looked up to the window and said, “Who is on my side? Who?” Two or three eunuchs looked out at him. 33He said, “Throw her down.” So they threw her down; some of her blood spattered on the wall and on the horses, which trampled on her. 34Then he went in and ate and drank; he said, “See to that cursed woman and bury her; for she is a king's daughter.” 35But when they went to bury her, they found no more of her than the skull and the feet and the palms of her hands. 36When they came back and told him, he said, “This is the word of the LORD, which he spoke by his servant Elijah the Tishbite, ‘In the territory of Jezreel the dogs shall eat the flesh of Jezebel; 37the corpse of Jezebel shall be like dung on the field in the territory of Jezreel, so that no one can say, This is Jezebel.’ ”

Massacre of Ahab's Descendants

10:1-17 he killed all who were left to Ahab: This gruesome account tells of Jehu's “zeal for the LORD,” which can only be described as fanatical. Jehu takes responsibility for the killings of all the king's sons, seeing this as a fulfillment of Elijah's word (1 Kgs 21:21-22, 24). He also kills forty-two relatives of the southern king, Ahaziah, and all the relatives and supporters of Ahab in Samaria. He invites Jehonadab son of Rechab to ride in the chariot with him. The Rechabites were also fanatical worshipers of the LORD. They considered all aspects of Canaanite culture corrupt (see Jer 35).

10 Now Ahab had seventy sons in Samaria. So Jehu wrote letters and sent them to Samaria, to the rulers of Jezreel,[b] to the elders, and to the guardians of the sons of[c] Ahab, saying, 2“Since your master's sons are with you and you have at your disposal chariots and horses, a fortified city, and weapons, 3select the son of your master who is the best qualified, set him on his father's throne, and fight for your master's house.” 4But they were utterly terrified and said, “Look,

---

[a] Syr Vg Compare Gk: Heb lacks *and they shot him* [b] Or *of the city*; Vg Compare Gk [c] Gk: Heb lacks *of the sons of*

two kings could not withstand him; how then can we stand?" [5]So the steward of the palace, and the governor of the city, along with the elders and the guardians, sent word to Jehu: "We are your servants; we will do anything you say. We will not make anyone king; do whatever you think right." [6]Then he wrote them a second letter, saying, "If you are on my side, and if you are ready to obey me, take the heads of your master's sons and come to me at Jezreel tomorrow at this time." Now the king's sons, seventy persons, were with the leaders of the city, who were charged with their upbringing. [7]When the letter reached them, they took the king's sons and killed them, seventy persons; they put their heads in baskets and sent them to him at Jezreel. [8]When the messenger came and told him, "They have brought the heads of the king's sons," he said, "Lay them in two heaps at the entrance of the gate until the morning." [9]Then in the morning when he went out, he stood and said to all the people, "You are innocent. It was I who conspired against my master and killed him; but who struck down all these? [10]Know then that there shall fall to the earth nothing of the word of the LORD, which the LORD spoke concerning the house of Ahab; for the LORD has done what he said through his servant Elijah." [11]So Jehu killed all who were left of the house of Ahab in Jezreel, all his leaders, close friends, and priests, until he left him no survivor.

12 Then he set out and went to Samaria. On the way, when he was at Beth-eked of the Shepherds, [13]Jehu met relatives of King Ahaziah of Judah and said, "Who are you?" They answered, "We are kin of Ahaziah; we have come down to visit the royal princes and the sons of the queen mother." [14]He said, "Take them alive." They took them alive, and slaughtered them at the pit of Beth-eked, forty-two in all; he spared none of them.

15 When he left there, he met Jehonadab son of Rechab coming to meet him; he greeted him, and said to him, "Is your heart as true to mine as mine is to yours?"[a] Jehonadab answered, "It is." Jehu said,[b] "If it is, give me your hand." So he gave him his hand. Jehu took him up with him into the chariot. [16]He said, "Come with me, and see my zeal for the LORD." So he[c] had him ride in his chariot. [17]When he came to Samaria, he killed all who were left to Ahab in Samaria, until he had wiped them out, according to the word of the LORD that he spoke to Elijah.

Slaughter of Worshipers of Baal

18 Then Jehu assembled all the people and said to them, "Ahab offered Baal small service; but Jehu will offer much more. [19]Now therefore summon to me all the prophets of Baal, all his worshipers, and all his priests; let none be missing, for I have a great sacrifice to offer to Baal; whoever is missing shall not live." But Jehu was acting with

10:18-31 Jehu wiped out Baal from Israel: Jehu pretends to be a Baal worshiper and invites all other Baal worshipers to a sacrifice at Baal's temple. He gives a burnt offering, but then orders all the Baal worshipers killed. He destroys a standing stone dedicated to Baal and turns Baal's temple into a toilet. For his zeal, Jehu is promised that his descendants to the fourth generation will serve as kings, but he is criticized for keeping golden calves at Bethel and Dan. The word of the LORD to the prophet Hosea speaks of Jehu's excessive zeal and violence (Hos 1:4).

[a] Gk: Heb *Is it right with your heart, as my heart is with your heart?* [b] Gk: Heb lacks *Jehu said* [c] Gk Syr Tg: Heb *they*

How should we look at people of other faith traditions?

cunning in order to destroy the worshipers of Baal. [20]Jehu decreed,
"Sanctify a solemn assembly for Baal." So they proclaimed it. [21]Jehu
sent word throughout all Israel; all the worshipers of Baal came, so
that there was no one left who did not come. They entered the temple of Baal, until the temple of Baal was filled from wall to wall. [22]He
said to the keeper of the wardrobe, "Bring out the vestments for all
the worshipers of Baal." So he brought out the vestments for them.
[23]Then Jehu entered the temple of Baal with Jehonadab son of Rechab; he said to the worshipers of Baal, "Search and see that there is
no worshiper of the LORD here among you, but only worshipers of
Baal." [24]Then they proceeded to offer sacrifices and burnt offerings.

Now Jehu had stationed eighty men outside, saying, "Whoever
allows any of those to escape whom I deliver into your hands shall
forfeit his life." [25]As soon as he had finished presenting the burnt
offering, Jehu said to the guards and to the officers, "Come in and kill
them; let no one escape." So they put them to the sword. The guards
and the officers threw them out, and then went into the citadel of the
temple of Baal. [26]They brought out the pillar[a] that was in the temple
of Baal, and burned it. [27]Then they demolished the pillar of Baal, and
destroyed the temple of Baal, and made it a latrine to this day.

28 Thus Jehu wiped out Baal from Israel. [29]But Jehu did not turn
aside from the sins of Jeroboam son of Nebat, which he caused Israel
to commit—the golden calves that were in Bethel and in Dan. [30]The
LORD said to Jehu, "Because you have done well in carrying out what
I consider right, and in accordance with all that was in my heart have
dealt with the house of Ahab, your sons of the fourth generation shall
sit on the throne of Israel." [31]But Jehu was not careful to follow the law
of the LORD the God of Israel with all his heart; he did not turn from
the sins of Jeroboam, which he caused Israel to commit.

Death of Jehu

10:32-36 Jehu slept with his ancestors: During Jehu's reign, King Hazael and the Arameans begin to reduce Israel's territory. Jehu's son Jehoahaz (819–804 B.C.E.) succeeds him.

32 In those days the LORD began to trim off parts of Israel. Hazael
defeated them throughout the territory of Israel: [33]from the Jordan
eastward, all the land of Gilead, the Gadites, the Reubenites, and the
Manassites, from Aroer, which is by the Wadi Arnon, that is, Gilead
and Bashan. [34]Now the rest of the acts of Jehu, all that he did, and all
his power, are they not written in the Book of the Annals of the Kings
of Israel? [35]So Jehu slept with his ancestors, and they buried him in Samaria. His son Jehoahaz succeeded him. [36]The time that Jehu reigned
over Israel in Samaria was twenty-eight years.

Athaliah Reigns over Judah

11:1-3 Athaliah . . . set about to destroy all the royal family: Athaliah (842–835 B.C.E.), King Ahaziah's mother, tries to kill off all the royal descendants in Judea to secure her place on the throne, but Ahaziah's sister, Jehosheba, puts Ahaziah's son Joash and his nurse in a secret room in the temple. Joash stays there six years.

11 Now when Athaliah, Ahaziah's mother, saw that her son was
dead, she set about to destroy all the royal family. [2]But Jehosh-

---

[a] Gk Vg Syr Tg: Heb *pillars*

eba, King Joram's daughter, Ahaziah's sister, took Joash son of Ahaziah, and stole him away from among the king's children who were
about to be killed; she put[a] him and his nurse in a bedroom. Thus
she[b] hid him from Athaliah, so that he was not killed; 3 he remained
with her six years, hidden in the house of the LORD, while Athaliah
reigned over the land.

Jehoiada Anoints the Child Joash

4 But in the seventh year Jehoiada summoned the captains of the
Carites and of the guards and had them come to him in the house of
the LORD. He made a covenant with them and put them under oath in
the house of the LORD; then he showed them the king's son. 5 He commanded them, "This is what you are to do: one-third of you, those who
go off duty on the sabbath and guard the king's house 6 (another third
being at the gate Sur and a third at the gate behind the guards), shall
guard the palace; 7 and your two divisions that come on duty in force
on the sabbath and guard the house of the LORD[c] 8 shall surround the
king, each with weapons in hand; and whoever approaches the ranks
is to be killed. Be with the king in his comings and goings."
9 The captains did according to all that the priest Jehoiada commanded; each brought his men who were to go off duty on the sabbath, with those who were to come on duty on the sabbath, and
came to the priest Jehoiada. 10 The priest delivered to the captains
the spears and shields that had been King David's, which were in the
house of the LORD; 11 the guards stood, every man with his weapons
in his hand, from the south side of the house to the north side of the
house, around the altar and the house, to guard the king on every side.
12 Then he brought out the king's son, put the crown on him, and gave
him the covenant;[d] they proclaimed him king, and anointed him;
they clapped their hands and shouted, "Long live the king!"

Death of Athaliah

13 When Athaliah heard the noise of the guard and of the people, she went into the house of the LORD to the people; 14 when she
looked, there was the king standing by the pillar, according to custom, with the captains and the trumpeters beside the king, and all
the people of the land rejoicing and blowing trumpets. Athaliah tore
her clothes and cried, "Treason! Treason!" 15 Then the priest Jehoiada
commanded the captains who were set over the army, "Bring her out
between the ranks, and kill with the sword anyone who follows her."
For the priest said, "Let her not be killed in the house of the LORD."
16 So they laid hands on her; she went through the horses' entrance to
the king's house, and there she was put to death.

---

[a] With 2 Chr 22.11: Heb lacks *she put* [b] Gk Syr Vg Compare 2 Chr 22.11: Heb *they* [c] Heb *the LORD to the king* [d] Or *treaty* or *testimony*; Heb *eduth*

11:4-12 Then he brought out the king's son: The priest Jehoiada takes the lead in ousting Athaliah and anointing Joash (835–802 B.C.E.) as her successor. According to tradition, the weapons he supplies to supporters were kept in the temple and had belonged to David (see 2 Sam 8:7). Jehoiada puts the crown on seven-year-old Joash (also called Jehoash) and anoints him, and the people hail him as king.

11:13-21 Jehoash was seven years old when he began to reign: Athaliah comes to the temple because of the commotion. The "people of the land" were wealthy landowners with a great deal of political influence (21:23-24; 23:30; Jer 1:18; 34:19-20; 37:2). Jehoiada orders Athaliah removed from the temple, and she is killed in the palace. Jehoiada makes a covenant between the LORD and the king and the people, and also between the king and the people. The people of the land destroy the temple of Baal and execute its priest. Jehoiada then leads the boy king to his throne in the palace.

11:17 Jehoiada made a covenant: Scholars believe that the covenant or agreement between God and the Israelites was renewed from time to time over the years. Renewing the covenant at this point is particularly important because of the disruption during Athaliah's reign.

12:1-16 Jehoash did what was right in the sight of the Lord: Guided by the priest Jehoiada, the young king Jehoash pleases God, although he does not remove the controversial places of sacrifice in Bethel and Dan. He begins a plan to use various taxes and contributions to repair the temple, but nothing has begun as late as his twenty-third year. The priests hesitate to use the money usually given for their own support for temple repairs. Jehoash places a chest near the altar to receive new contributions, and the king's secretary and the high priest count the money and hand it over to the temple overseers, who pay the construction workers.

17 Jehoiada made a covenant between the LORD and the king
and people, that they should be the LORD's people; also between
the king and the people. 18 Then all the people of the land went to the
house of Baal, and tore it down; his altars and his images they broke
in pieces, and they killed Mattan, the priest of Baal, before the altars.
The priest posted guards over the house of the LORD. 19 He took the
captains, the Carites, the guards, and all the people of the land; then
they brought the king down from the house of the LORD, marching
through the gate of the guards to the king's house. He took his seat on
the throne of the kings. 20 So all the people of the land rejoiced; and
the city was quiet after Athaliah had been killed with the sword at the
king's house.

21[a] Jehoash[b] was seven years old when he began to reign.

The Temple Repaired

12 In the seventh year of Jehu, Jehoash began to reign; he reigned
forty years in Jerusalem. His mother's name was Zibiah of
Beer-sheba. 2 Jehoash did what was right in the sight of the LORD all
his days, because the priest Jehoiada instructed him. 3 Nevertheless
the high places were not taken away; the people continued to sacrifice and make offerings on the high places.

4 Jehoash said to the priests, "All the money offered as sacred
donations that is brought into the house of the LORD, the money
for which each person is assessed—the money from the assessment
of persons—and the money from the voluntary offerings brought
into the house of the LORD, 5 let the priests receive from each of the
donors; and let them repair the house wherever any need of repairs is
discovered." 6 But by the twenty-third year of King Jehoash the priests
had made no repairs on the house. 7 Therefore King Jehoash summoned the priest Jehoiada with the other priests and said to them,
"Why are you not repairing the house? Now therefore do not accept
any more money from your donors but hand it over for the repair of
the house." 8 So the priests agreed that they would neither accept more
money from the people nor repair the house.

9 Then the priest Jehoiada took a chest, made a hole in its lid, and
set it beside the altar on the right side as one entered the house of the
LORD; the priests who guarded the threshold put in it all the money
that was brought into the house of the LORD. 10 Whenever they saw
that there was a great deal of money in the chest, the king's secretary
and the high priest went up, counted the money that was found in
the house of the LORD, and tied it up in bags. 11 They would give the
money that was weighed out into the hands of the workers who had
the oversight of the house of the LORD; then they paid it out to the

[a] Ch 12.1 in Heb [b] Another spelling is *Joash*; see verse 19

carpenters and the builders who worked on the house of the Lord,
[12]to the masons and the stonecutters, as well as to buy timber and
quarried stone for making repairs on the house of the Lord, as well as
for any outlay for repairs of the house. [13]But for the house of the Lord
no basins of silver, snuffers, bowls, trumpets, or any vessels of gold, or
of silver, were made from the money that was brought into the house
of the Lord, [14]for that was given to the workers who were repairing
the house of the Lord with it. [15]They did not ask an accounting from
those into whose hand they delivered the money to pay out to the
workers, for they dealt honestly. [16]The money from the guilt offerings
and the money from the sin offerings was not brought into the house
of the Lord; it belonged to the priests.

Hazael Threatens Jerusalem

17 At that time King Hazael of Aram went up, fought against
Gath, and took it. But when Hazael set his face to go up against Jerusalem, [18]King Jehoash of Judah took all the votive gifts that Jehoshaphat, Jehoram, and Ahaziah, his ancestors, the kings of Judah, had
dedicated, as well as his own votive gifts, all the gold that was found
in the treasuries of the house of the Lord and of the king's house,
and sent these to King Hazael of Aram. Then Hazael withdrew from
Jerusalem.

12:17-18 Hazael withdrew from Jerusalem: The Aramean king makes a raid on Gath, a Philistine city, and prepares to attack Jerusalem (see Map 7, p. 2105). But Hazael calls off the attack when Jehoash takes gifts donated to the temple and sends them to him (see 1 Kgs 15:18; 2 Kgs 18:15).

Death of Joash

19 Now the rest of the acts of Joash, and all that he did, are they
not written in the Book of the Annals of the Kings of Judah? [20]His
servants arose, devised a conspiracy, and killed Joash in the house
of Millo, on the way that goes down to Silla. [21]It was Jozacar son of
Shimeath and Jehozabad son of Shomer, his servants, who struck him
down, so that he died. He was buried with his ancestors in the city of
David; then his son Amaziah succeeded him.

12:19-21 His servants arose . . . and killed Joash: For reasons not given here, Joash (spelled Jehoash in earlier verses) is killed by members of his staff. According to 2 Chronicles 24:25-27 this happened because Joash killed the son of the high priest. Amaziah (805–776 B.C.E.), Joash's son, replaces him.

Jehoahaz Reigns over Israel

13 In the twenty-third year of King Joash son of Ahaziah of Judah, Jehoahaz son of Jehu began to reign over Israel in Samaria; he reigned seventeen years. [2]He did what was evil in the sight
of the Lord, and followed the sins of Jeroboam son of Nebat, which
he caused Israel to sin; he did not depart from them. [3]The anger of the
Lord was kindled against Israel, so that he gave them repeatedly into
the hand of King Hazael of Aram, then into the hand of Ben-hadad
son of Hazael. [4]But Jehoahaz entreated the Lord, and the Lord
heeded him; for he saw the oppression of Israel, how the king of Aram
oppressed them. [5]Therefore the Lord gave Israel a savior, so that they
escaped from the hand of the Arameans; and the people of Israel lived
in their homes as formerly. [6]Nevertheless they did not depart from

13:1-9 Jehoahaz . . . began to reign over Israel: Because of the wickedness of Jehoahaz (819–804 B.C.E.), Hazael and his son Ben-hadad defeat Israel several times. Jehoahaz prays and the Lord answers his prayer out of compassion. The (military) savior who relieves Israel is not identified by name. The army maintained by Jehoahaz is small compared to other accounts in Kings. Jehoahaz is succeeded by his son Jehoash (805–790 B.C.E.) as king of Israel (not to be confused with Joash/Jehoash, son of Ahaziah, who was king of Judah (835–802 B.C.E.).

13:3-5 the Lord heeded him: This sequence of punishment, prayer, and deliverance is common in the book of Judges.

the sins of the house of Jeroboam, which he caused Israel to sin, but
walked[a] in them; the sacred pole[b] also remained in Samaria. 7 So Jehoahaz was left with an army of not more than fifty horsemen, ten chariots and ten thousand footmen; for the king of Aram had destroyed
them and made them like the dust at threshing. 8 Now the rest of the
acts of Jehoahaz and all that he did, including his might, are they not
written in the Book of the Annals of the Kings of Israel? 9 So Jehoahaz
slept with his ancestors, and they buried him in Samaria; then his son
Joash succeeded him.

Jehoash Reigns over Israel

13:10-13 Jehoash son of Jehoahaz began to reign over Israel: The author of Kings provides no information on Jehoash, except that he continued the sin of Jeroboam I. Jehoash is succeeded by his son Jeroboam II (790–750 B.C.E.).

10 In the thirty-seventh year of King Joash of Judah, Jehoash son
of Jehoahaz began to reign over Israel in Samaria; he reigned sixteen
years. 11 He also did what was evil in the sight of the LORD; he did not
depart from all the sins of Jeroboam son of Nebat, which he caused
Israel to sin, but he walked in them. 12 Now the rest of the acts of Joash, and all that he did, as well as the might with which he fought
against King Amaziah of Judah, are they not written in the Book of
the Annals of the Kings of Israel? 13 So Joash slept with his ancestors,
and Jeroboam sat upon his throne; Joash was buried in Samaria with
the kings of Israel.

Death of Elisha

13:14-21 So Elisha died: King Joash visits Elisha on his deathbed and says the same thing about Elisha that Elisha had said about Elijah: "My father, my father! The chariots of Israel and its horsemen!" (see 2:12). Elisha has the king shoot an arrow out the window, symbolizing the LORD's victory over Aram. Elisha also commands Joash to strike the ground with the arrows, and he does this three times. Elisha, however, says the king should have struck the ground more times to gain a total victory over Aram. When a dead man is thrown into Elisha's grave, he touches the bones of Elisha and comes back to life. This shows that Elisha's miraculous powers continued even after his death (see also 4:32-35).

14 Now when Elisha had fallen sick with the illness of which he
was to die, King Joash of Israel went down to him, and wept before
him, crying, "My father, my father! The chariots of Israel and its horsemen!" 15 Elisha said to him, "Take a bow and arrows"; so he took a bow
and arrows. 16 Then he said to the king of Israel, "Draw the bow"; and
he drew it. Elisha laid his hands on the king's hands. 17 Then he said,
"Open the window eastward"; and he opened it. Elisha said, "Shoot";
and he shot. Then he said, "The LORD's arrow of victory, the arrow of
victory over Aram! For you shall fight the Arameans in Aphek until
you have made an end of them." 18 He continued, "Take the arrows";
and he took them. He said to the king of Israel, "Strike the ground
with them"; he struck three times, and stopped. 19 Then the man of
God was angry with him, and said, "You should have struck five or six
times; then you would have struck down Aram until you had made an
end of it, but now you will strike down Aram only three times."

20 So Elisha died, and they buried him. Now bands of Moabites
used to invade the land in the spring of the year. 21 As a man was being
buried, a marauding band was seen and the man was thrown into the
grave of Elisha; as soon as the man touched the bones of Elisha, he
came to life and stood on his feet.

---

[a] Gk Syr Tg Vg: Heb *he walked* [b] Heb *Asherah*

Israel Recaptures Cities from Aram

22 Now King Hazael of Aram oppressed Israel all the days of Jehoahaz. 23 But the LORD was gracious to them and had compassion
on them; he turned toward them, because of his covenant with Abraham, Isaac, and Jacob, and would not destroy them; nor has he banished them from his presence until now.

24 When King Hazael of Aram died, his son Ben-hadad succeeded
him. 25 Then Jehoash son of Jehoahaz took again from Ben-hadad son
of Hazael the towns that he had taken from his father Jehoahaz in war.
Three times Joash defeated him and recovered the towns of Israel.

13:22-25 Joash defeated him and recovered the towns of Israel: During the reign of Jehoahaz (see 13:1-9), King Hazael of Aram prevails over Israel, but the LORD had compassion on the people because of the covenant with Abraham, Isaac, and Jacob. After Hazael's death, Jehoash defeats Hazael's son Ben-hadad three times and recovers the towns Israel had lost.

Amaziah Reigns over Judah

14 In the second year of King Joash son of Joahaz of Israel, King
Amaziah son of Joash of Judah, began to reign. 2 He was twenty-
five years old when he began to reign, and he reigned twenty-nine
years in Jerusalem. His mother's name was Jehoaddin of Jerusalem.
3 He did what was right in the sight of the LORD, yet not like his ancestor David; in all things he did as his father Joash had done. 4 But the
high places were not removed; the people still sacrificed and made
offerings on the high places. 5 As soon as the royal power was firmly in
his hand he killed his servants who had murdered his father the king.
6 But he did not put to death the children of the murderers; according
to what is written in the book of the law of Moses, where the LORD
commanded, "The parents shall not be put to death for the children,
or the children be put to death for the parents; but all shall be put to
death for their own sins."

7 He killed ten thousand Edomites in the Valley of Salt and took
Sela by storm; he called it Jokthe-el, which is its name to this day.

14:1-7 In the second year of King Joash...of Israel, King Amaziah...of Judah, began to reign: Amaziah (805–776 B.C.E.) is given mild praise but does not live up to the standards of David or remove the high places. He executes the murderers of his father, Joash, but not their children, following a law given in Deuteronomy 24:16 (see also Jer 31:29-30; Ezek 18:2-4, 20). Amaziah also defeats the Edomites, as David had done (2 Sam 8:13).

8 Then Amaziah sent messengers to King Jehoash son of Jehoahaz, son of Jehu, of Israel, saying, "Come, let us look one another in
the face." 9 King Jehoash of Israel sent word to King Amaziah of Judah,
"A thornbush on Lebanon sent to a cedar on Lebanon, saying, 'Give
your daughter to my son for a wife'; but a wild animal of Lebanon
passed by and trampled down the thornbush. 10 You have indeed defeated Edom, and your heart has lifted you up. Be content with your
glory, and stay at home; for why should you provoke trouble so that
you fall, you and Judah with you?"

11 But Amaziah would not listen. So King Jehoash of Israel went
up; he and King Amaziah of Judah faced one another in battle at
Beth-shemesh, which belongs to Judah. 12 Judah was defeated by Israel; everyone fled home. 13 King Jehoash of Israel captured King Amaziah of Judah son of Jehoash, son of Ahaziah, at Beth-shemesh; he
came to Jerusalem, and broke down the wall of Jerusalem from the
Ephraim Gate to the Corner Gate, a distance of four hundred cubits.
14 He seized all the gold and silver, and all the vessels that were found

14:8-22 look one another in the face: Jehoash sees Amaziah's invitation to do this as a hostile act. Jehoash responds with a dismissive story (14:9) and a sharp rebuke (14:10). When they face one another in battle, Jehoash wins a clear victory, captures Amaziah, inflicts severe damage on Jerusalem, loots the temple and palace treasuries, and takes some hostages. The death notice for Jehoash in verses 15-16 repeats what is written in 13:12-13. Amaziah reigns fifteen more years after Jehoash's death. A conspiracy leads to his assassination in Lachish, some thirty miles southwest of Jerusalem (see Map 7, p. 2105). Azariah (also known as Uzziah; 788–736 B.C.E.), Amaziah's son, is installed as king by the people. He rebuilds Elath on the northern coast of the Gulf of Aqabah, implying that he effectively controlled Edom.

in the house of the LORD and in the treasuries of the king's house, as well as hostages; then he returned to Samaria.

15 Now the rest of the acts that Jehoash did, his might, and how he fought with King Amaziah of Judah, are they not written in the Book of the Annals of the Kings of Israel? [16]Jehoash slept with his ancestors, and was buried in Samaria with the kings of Israel; then his son Jeroboam succeeded him.

17 King Amaziah son of Joash of Judah lived fifteen years after the death of King Jehoash son of Jehoahaz of Israel. [18]Now the rest of the deeds of Amaziah, are they not written in the Book of the Annals of the Kings of Judah? [19]They made a conspiracy against him in Jerusalem, and he fled to Lachish. But they sent after him to Lachish, and killed him there. [20]They brought him on horses; he was buried in Jerusalem with his ancestors in the city of David. [21]All the people of Judah took Azariah, who was sixteen years old, and made him king to succeed his father Amaziah. [22]He rebuilt Elath and restored it to Judah, after King Amaziah[a] slept with his ancestors.

Jeroboam II Reigns over Israel

23 In the fifteenth year of King Amaziah son of Joash of Judah, King Jeroboam son of Joash of Israel began to reign in Samaria; he reigned forty-one years. [24]He did what was evil in the sight of the LORD; he did not depart from all the sins of Jeroboam son of Nebat, which he caused Israel to sin. [25]He restored the border of Israel from Lebo-hamath as far as the Sea of the Arabah, according to the word of the LORD, the God of Israel, which he spoke by his servant Jonah son of Amittai, the prophet, who was from Gath-hepher. [26]For the LORD saw that the distress of Israel was very bitter; there was no one left, bond or free, and no one to help Israel. [27]But the LORD had not said that he would blot out the name of Israel from under heaven, so he saved them by the hand of Jeroboam son of Joash.

28 Now the rest of the acts of Jeroboam, and all that he did, and his might, how he fought, and how he recovered for Israel Damascus and Hamath, which had belonged to Judah, are they not written in the Book of the Annals of the Kings of Israel? [29]Jeroboam slept with his ancestors, the kings of Israel; his son Zechariah succeeded him.

Azariah Reigns over Judah

15 In the twenty-seventh year of King Jeroboam of Israel King Azariah son of Amaziah of Judah began to reign. [2]He was sixteen years old when he began to reign, and he reigned fifty-two years in Jerusalem. His mother's name was Jecoliah of Jerusalem. [3]He did what was right in the sight of the LORD, just as his father Amaziah had

[a] Heb *the king*

14:23-29 Jeroboam…began to reign: Little information is provided for the king known as Jeroboam II (790–750 B.C.E.), despite the fact that he has a long and prosperous reign. Prosperity was unevenly distributed, however, as the prophet Amos makes clear. The author of Kings includes the standard accusation that Jeroboam II continues in the sins of Jeroboam I. He is successful in expanding the borders of Israel, and this success is supported by a word of the LORD from the prophet Jonah. (The book of Jonah itself was written much later.) Compassion leads the LORD to intervene on behalf of the north—indicating a positive outlook on the north that is rare in Kings. Jeroboam's expansion into the area of Aram (Damascus and Hamath) is made possible because the Assyrians had curbed Aramean power. Jeroboam II dies peacefully, despite a threat of a violent death (Amos 7:11).

15:1-7 King Azariah…of Judah began to reign: Azariah's long reign (788–736 B.C.E.), roughly at the same time as Jeroboam II in the north (790–750 B.C.E.), also is described briefly. He too is given mild praise but continues the practice of sacrifices at Bethel and Dan. The LORD strikes Azariah with leprosy (some kind of skin disease), but no reason is given for this punishment (see 2 Chr 26:16-20). Because of Azariah's sickness, his son Jotham (758–742 B.C.E.) and grandson Ahaz (742–726 B.C.E.) rule with him. The prophet Isaiah is called by God in the year that Azariah/Uzziah dies (Isa 6:1).

done. 4 Nevertheless the high places were not taken away; the people still sacrificed and made offerings on the high places. 5 The LORD
struck the king, so that he was leprous[a] to the day of his death, and
lived in a separate house. Jotham the king's son was in charge of the
palace, governing the people of the land. 6 Now the rest of the acts of
Azariah, and all that he did, are they not written in the Book of the
Annals of the Kings of Judah? 7 Azariah slept with his ancestors; they
buried him with his ancestors in the city of David; his son Jotham
succeeded him.

Zechariah Reigns over Israel

8 In the thirty-eighth year of King Azariah of Judah, Zechariah
son of Jeroboam reigned over Israel in Samaria six months. 9 He did
what was evil in the sight of the LORD, as his ancestors had done.
He did not depart from the sins of Jeroboam son of Nebat, which he
caused Israel to sin. 10 Shallum son of Jabesh conspired against him,
and struck him down in public and killed him, and reigned in place
of him. 11 Now the rest of the deeds of Zechariah are written in the
Book of the Annals of the Kings of Israel. 12 This was the promise of
the LORD that he gave to Jehu, "Your sons shall sit on the throne of
Israel to the fourth generation." And so it happened.

15:8-12 Zechariah... reigned over Israel in Samaria six months: In his very short reign, Zechariah (750 B.C.E.) continues the sins of his ancestors. He is assassinated by Shallum, bringing the dynasty of Jehu to an end in the fourth generation, fulfilling the word of the LORD (2 Kgs 10:30).

Shallum Reigns over Israel

13 Shallum son of Jabesh began to reign in the thirty-ninth year
of King Uzziah of Judah; he reigned one month in Samaria. 14 Then
Menahem son of Gadi came up from Tirzah and came to Samaria;
he struck down Shallum son of Jabesh in Samaria and killed him; he
reigned in place of him. 15 Now the rest of the deeds of Shallum, including the conspiracy that he made, are written in the Book of the
Annals of the Kings of Israel. 16 At that time Menahem sacked Tiphsah, all who were in it and its territory from Tirzah on; because they
did not open it to him, he sacked it. He ripped open all the pregnant
women in it.

15:13-16 Shallum...reigned one month in Samaria: Shallum (749 B.C.E.) rules only a month until he too is assassinated, and the writer of Kings does not bother to evaluate him. His successor, Menahem (749–738 B.C.E.), brutally attacks Tiphsah (this location is unknown). The violence against pregnant women is only mentioned elsewhere in the Bible in talking about foreign armies (2 Kgs 8:12; Hos 13:16; Amos 1:13).

Menahem Reigns over Israel

17 In the thirty-ninth year of King Azariah of Judah, Menahem
son of Gadi began to reign over Israel; he reigned ten years in Samaria.
18 He did what was evil in the sight of the LORD; he did not depart
all his days from any of the sins of Jeroboam son of Nebat, which he
caused Israel to sin. 19 King Pul of Assyria came against the land; Menahem gave Pul a thousand talents of silver, so that he might help him
confirm his hold on the royal power. 20 Menahem exacted the money
from Israel, that is, from all the wealthy, fifty shekels of silver from
each one, to give to the king of Assyria. So the king of Assyria turned

15:17-22 Menahem...began to reign over Israel: Menahem does "what was evil in the sight of the LORD"—that is, continues in the sins of Jeroboam I, making sacrifices at Bethel and Dan. King Pul of Assyria is Tiglath-pilezer III (745—727 B.C.E.). With money raised by imposing a tax on each person, Menahem pays Pul an enormous bribe so that he will support his claim to the throne. Menahem dies peacefully and is succeeded by his son Pekahiah (738–736 B.C.E.).

[a] A term for several skin diseases; precise meaning uncertain

back, and did not stay there in the land. 21 Now the rest of the deeds
of Menahem, and all that he did, are they not written in the Book of
the Annals of the Kings of Israel? 22 Menahem slept with his ancestors,
and his son Pekahiah succeeded him.

Pekahiah Reigns over Israel

15:23-26 Pekahiah...reigned two years: Pekahiah also continues the sins of Jeroboam I. He is assassinated by Pekah, an army officer, who succeeds him.

23 In the fiftieth year of King Azariah of Judah, Pekahiah son of
Menahem began to reign over Israel in Samaria; he reigned two years.
24 He did what was evil in the sight of the LORD; he did not turn away
from the sins of Jeroboam son of Nebat, which he caused Israel to
sin. 25 Pekah son of Remaliah, his captain, conspired against him with
fifty of the Gileadites, and attacked him in Samaria, in the citadel of
the palace along with Argob and Arieh; he killed him, and reigned in
place of him. 26 Now the rest of the deeds of Pekahiah, and all that he
did, are written in the Book of the Annals of the Kings of Israel.

Pekah Reigns over Israel

15:27-31 Pekah...reigned twenty years: Pekah loses a significant amount of territory to the growing power of the Assyrians under Tiglath-pilezer III. His reign seems to have begun in 736 B.C.E., so the twenty years assigned to him in 15:27 is puzzling. Pekah's reign ends in 732 B.C.E. when he is assassinated by Hoshea, the last king of Israel.

27 In the fifty-second year of King Azariah of Judah, Pekah son
of Remaliah began to reign over Israel in Samaria; he reigned twenty
years. 28 He did what was evil in the sight of the LORD; he did not depart from the sins of Jeroboam son of Nebat, which he caused Israel
to sin.

29 In the days of King Pekah of Israel, King Tiglath-pileser of Assyria came and captured Ijon, Abel-beth-maacah, Janoah, Kedesh,
Hazor, Gilead, and Galilee, all the land of Naphtali; and he carried the
people captive to Assyria. 30 Then Hoshea son of Elah made a conspiracy against Pekah son of Remaliah, attacked him, and killed him; he
reigned in place of him, in the twentieth year of Jotham son of Uzziah.
31 Now the rest of the acts of Pekah, and all that he did, are written in
the Book of the Annals of the Kings of Israel.

Jotham Reigns over Judah

15:32-37 King Jotham...of Judah began to reign: Jotham (758–742 B.C.E.) rules with his father, Azariah/Uzziah, and precedes him in death. He receives mild praise but is criticized for allowing the high places to continue. During his reign a gate is built by the temple and war against Aram and Israel begins (see note on 16:1-20).

32 In the second year of King Pekah son of Remaliah of Israel,
King Jotham son of Uzziah of Judah began to reign. 33 He was twenty-
five years old when he began to reign and reigned sixteen years in
Jerusalem. His mother's name was Jerusha daughter of Zadok. 34 He
did what was right in the sight of the LORD, just as his father Uzziah
had done. 35 Nevertheless the high places were not removed; the people still sacrificed and made offerings on the high places. He built the
upper gate of the house of the LORD. 36 Now the rest of the acts of
Jotham, and all that he did, are they not written in the Book of the
Annals of the Kings of Judah? 37 In those days the LORD began to send
King Rezin of Aram and Pekah son of Remaliah against Judah. 38 Jotham slept with his ancestors, and was buried with his ancestors in the
city of David, his ancestor; his son Ahaz succeeded him.

Ahaz Reigns over Judah

16 In the seventeenth year of Pekah son of Remaliah, King Ahaz
son of Jotham of Judah began to reign. 2 Ahaz was twenty
years old when he began to reign; he reigned sixteen years in Jerusalem. He did not do what was right in the sight of the LORD his God, as
his ancestor David had done, 3 but he walked in the way of the kings of
Israel. He even made his son pass through fire, according to the abominable practices of the nations whom the LORD drove out before the
people of Israel. 4 He sacrificed and made offerings on the high places,
on the hills, and under every green tree.

5 Then King Rezin of Aram and King Pekah son of Remaliah
of Israel came up to wage war on Jerusalem; they besieged Ahaz but
could not conquer him. 6 At that time the king of Edom[a] recovered
Elath for Edom,[b] and drove the Judeans from Elath; and the Edomites
came to Elath, where they live to this day. 7 Ahaz sent messengers to
King Tiglath-pileser of Assyria, saying, "I am your servant and your
son. Come up, and rescue me from the hand of the king of Aram and
from the hand of the king of Israel, who are attacking me." 8 Ahaz also
took the silver and gold found in the house of the LORD and in the
treasures of the king's house, and sent a present to the king of Assyria.
9 The king of Assyria listened to him; the king of Assyria marched up
against Damascus, and took it, carrying its people captive to Kir; then
he killed Rezin.

10 When King Ahaz went to Damascus to meet King Tiglath-
pileser of Assyria, he saw the altar that was at Damascus. King Ahaz
sent to the priest Uriah a model of the altar, and its pattern, exact in all
its details. 11 The priest Uriah built the altar; in accordance with all that
King Ahaz had sent from Damascus, just so did the priest Uriah build
it, before King Ahaz arrived from Damascus. 12 When the king came
from Damascus, the king viewed the altar. Then the king drew near to
the altar, went up on it, 13 and offered his burnt offering and his grain
offering, poured his drink offering, and dashed the blood of his offerings of well-being against the altar. 14 The bronze altar that was before
the LORD he removed from the front of the house, from the place
between his altar and the house of the LORD, and put it on the north
side of his altar. 15 King Ahaz commanded the priest Uriah, saying,
"Upon the great altar offer the morning burnt offering, and the evening grain offering, and the king's burnt offering, and his grain offering, with the burnt offering of all the people of the land, their grain
offering, and their drink offering; then dash against it all the blood of
the burnt offering, and all the blood of the sacrifice; but the bronze
altar shall be for me to inquire by." 16 The priest Uriah did everything
that King Ahaz commanded.

[a] Cn: Heb *King Rezin of Aram* [b] Cn: Heb *Aram*

16:1-20 King Ahaz...of Judah began to reign: Ahaz (742–726 B.C.E.) succeeds his father, Jotham, and reigns with his grandfather until Azariah/Uzziah's death in 736 B.C.E. The writer of Kings judges Ahaz harshly and notes that he is the first king since Solomon to have worshiped personally at the high places. The reference to making his son "pass through fire" (16:3) may indicate worship of the god Molech and child sacrifice. (Molech worship and child sacrifice are condemned in Deut 18:9-14; Lev 18:21; 20:2-5; Jer 7:31; 19:5; 32:35.) King Rezin of Aram and King Pekah of Israel apparently wanted to replace Ahaz with another king and bring Judah into a coalition against Assyria. This war is also referred to in Hosea and Isaiah (Isa 7:1—8:10) and is known as the Syro-Ephraimitic war. Edom seizes this opportunity to revolt. Against the advice of the prophet Isaiah, Ahaz sends a bribe to Tiglath-pileser III of Assyria, hoping for some relief from Rezin and Pekah. Tiglath-pileser obliges by attacking Damascus, killing Rezin, and sending some people into exile. Ahaz goes to Damascus to meet Tiglath-pileser and while there sends back to the priest Uriah plans for an altar he admires there (16:10). Ahaz worships at this altar (dedicated to another god?) in Damascus (compare with 1 Kgs 8:63; 12:32) and constructs a copy in Jerusalem, which displaces the bronze altar in the temple. Ahaz tells Uriah how to use the new altar, while he himself uses the bronze altar to look into the future. Ahaz also makes several alterations in the temple in order to please the king of Assyria. He dies peacefully and is succeeded by his son Hezekiah.

17 Then King Ahaz cut off the frames of the stands, and removed
the laver from them; he removed the sea from the bronze oxen that
were under it, and put it on a pediment of stone. [18]The covered portal
for use on the sabbath that had been built inside the palace, and the
outer entrance for the king he removed from[a] the house of the LORD.
He did this because of the king of Assyria. [19]Now the rest of the acts of
Ahaz that he did, are they not written in the Book of the Annals of the
Kings of Judah? [20]Ahaz slept with his ancestors, and was buried with
his ancestors in the city of David; his son Hezekiah succeeded him.

Hoshea Reigns over Israel

17 In the twelfth year of King Ahaz of Judah, Hoshea son of Elah
began to reign in Samaria over Israel; he reigned nine years.
[2]He did what was evil in the sight of the LORD, yet not like the kings
of Israel who were before him. [3]King Shalmaneser of Assyria came up
against him; Hoshea became his vassal, and paid him tribute. [4]But the
king of Assyria found treachery in Hoshea; for he had sent messengers to King So of Egypt, and offered no tribute to the king of Assyria,
as he had done year by year; therefore the king of Assyria confined
him and imprisoned him.

17:1-6 Hoshea ... began to reign in Samaria over Israel: Hoshea (732–722 B.C.E.) is criticized for his evil ways, which were different than those who ruled before him. (Strangely, the author does not here mention the sins of Jeroboam I.) In 17:1 the years of Hoshea's reign are connected to Ahaz, while in 15:30 they are linked to Jotham. Hoshea places himself under the protection of King Shalmaneser V of Assyria (727–722 B.C.E.) and pays him tribute. But when he conspires with Egypt and withholds his annual tribute, the Assyrian king imprisons him. After a three-year siege, Samaria falls to Sargon II of Assyria. Many Israelite leaders are carried off into exile in Assyria.

Israel Carried Captive to Assyria

5 Then the king of Assyria invaded all the land and came to Samaria; for three years he besieged it. [6]In the ninth year of Hoshea the
king of Assyria captured Samaria; he carried the Israelites away to
Assyria. He placed them in Halah, on the Habor, the river of Gozan,
and in the cities of the Medes.
7 This occurred because the people of Israel had sinned against
the LORD their God, who had brought them up out of the land of
Egypt from under the hand of Pharaoh king of Egypt. They had worshiped other gods [8]and walked in the customs of the nations whom
the LORD drove out before the people of Israel, and in the customs
that the kings of Israel had introduced.[b] [9]The people of Israel secretly
did things that were not right against the LORD their God. They built
for themselves high places at all their towns, from watchtower to fortified city; [10]they set up for themselves pillars and sacred poles[c] on
every high hill and under every green tree; [11]there they made offerings on all the high places, as the nations did whom the LORD carried away before them. They did wicked things, provoking the LORD
to anger; [12]they served idols, of which the LORD had said to them,
"You shall not do this." [13]Yet the LORD warned Israel and Judah by
every prophet and every seer, saying, "Turn from your evil ways and
keep my commandments and my statutes, in accordance with all the

17:7-23 the people of Israel had sinned against the LORD their God: This is a sermon that offers an explanation for the fall of Israel and the exile: The people had sinned against the God of the exodus by worshiping other gods. The high places of sacrifice, standing stones, and sacred poles (for the god Asherim) are also criticized. The people had acted like the earlier inhabitants of the land. They had turned their backs on the covenant God made with them at Mount Sinai with the law, even though God had warned them through the prophets, calling them to repent and keep the commandments. They had set up the inappropriate sanctuaries at Dan and Bethel, where God's presence was indicated by golden calves (this was Jeroboam's sin, which was continued by many kings).

[a] Cn: Heb lacks *from* [b] Meaning of Heb uncertain [c] Heb *Asherim*

law that I commanded your ancestors and that I sent to you by my
servants the prophets." [14]They would not listen but were stubborn, as
their ancestors had been, who did not believe in the LORD their God.
[15]They despised his statutes, and his covenant that he made with their
ancestors, and the warnings that he gave them. They went after false
idols and became false; they followed the nations that were around
them, concerning whom the LORD had commanded them that they
should not do as they did. [16]They rejected all the commandments
of the LORD their God and made for themselves cast images of two
calves; they made a sacred pole,[a] worshiped all the host of heaven, and
served Baal. [17]They made their sons and their daughters pass through
fire; they used divination and augury; and they sold themselves to do
evil in the sight of the LORD, provoking him to anger. [18]Therefore the
LORD was very angry with Israel and removed them out of his sight;
none was left but the tribe of Judah alone.

17:18 none was left but the tribe of Judah alone: This implies that the whole population goes into exile, but historically Assyrians exiled only the upper classes.

19 Judah also did not keep the commandments of the LORD
their God but walked in the customs that Israel had introduced. [20]The
LORD rejected all the descendants of Israel; he punished them and
gave them into the hand of plunderers, until he had banished them
from his presence.

21 When he had torn Israel from the house of David, they made
Jeroboam son of Nebat king. Jeroboam drove Israel from following
the LORD and made them commit great sin. [22]The people of Israel
continued in all the sins that Jeroboam committed; they did not depart from them [23]until the LORD removed Israel out of his sight, as he
had foretold through all his servants the prophets. So Israel was exiled
from their own land to Assyria until this day.

Assyria Resettles Samaria

24 The king of Assyria brought people from Babylon, Cuthah,
Avva, Hamath, and Sepharvaim, and placed them in the cities of Samaria in place of the people of Israel; they took possession of Samaria,
and settled in its cities. [25]When they first settled there, they did not
worship the LORD; therefore the LORD sent lions among them, which
killed some of them. [26]So the king of Assyria was told, "The nations
that you have carried away and placed in the cities of Samaria do not
know the law of the god of the land; therefore he has sent lions among
them; they are killing them, because they do not know the law of the
god of the land." [27]Then the king of Assyria commanded, "Send there
one of the priests whom you carried away from there; let him[b] go and
live there, and teach them the law of the god of the land." [28]So one of
the priests whom they had carried away from Samaria came and lived
in Bethel; he taught them how they should worship the LORD.

17:24-41 The king of Assyria brought people . . . and placed them in the cities of Samaria in place of the people of Israel: The Assyrians take leaders into exile and replace them with a new population from Mesopotamia. These newcomers did not worship the LORD, so they were punished by lions. To remedy this situation, the king of Assyria sends back one of the exiled priests, who goes to the old sanctuary of Bethel and teaches proper worship. The new population, however, worships both the gods they knew from their homelands and the LORD.

---

[a] Heb *Asherah* [b] Syr Vg: Heb *them*

29 But every nation still made gods of its own and put them in the shrines of the high places that the people of Samaria had made, every nation in the cities in which they lived; [30]the people of Babylon made Succoth-benoth, the people of Cuth made Nergal, the people of Hamath made Ashima; [31]the Avvites made Nibhaz and Tartak; the Sepharvites burned their children in the fire to Adrammelech and Anammelech, the gods of Sepharvaim. [32]They also worshiped the LORD and appointed from among themselves all sorts of people as priests of the high places, who sacrificed for them in the shrines of the high places. [33]So they worshiped the LORD but also served their own gods, after the manner of the nations from among whom they had been carried away. [34]To this day they continue to practice their former customs.

17:34-41 They do not worship the LORD: The critique from the writer of Kings in 17:34-41 deals primarily with what we would call the First Commandment.

They do not worship the LORD and they do not follow the statutes or the ordinances or the law or the commandment that the LORD commanded the children of Jacob, whom he named Israel. [35]The LORD had made a covenant with them and commanded them, "You shall not worship other gods or bow yourselves to them or serve them or sacrifice to them, [36]but you shall worship the LORD, who brought you out of the land of Egypt with great power and with an outstretched arm; you shall bow yourselves to him, and to him you shall sacrifice. [37]The statutes and the ordinances and the law and the commandment that he wrote for you, you shall always be careful to observe. You shall not worship other gods; [38]you shall not forget the covenant that I have made with you. You shall not worship other gods, [39]but you shall worship the LORD your God; he will deliver you out of the hand of all your enemies." [40]They would not listen, however, but they continued to practice their former custom.

41 So these nations worshiped the LORD, but also served their carved images; to this day their children and their children's children continue to do as their ancestors did.

Hezekiah's Reign over Judah

18:1-12 Hezekiah ... began to reign: Hezekiah (726–697 B.C.E.; others date him to 715-687) ranks high among the kings here, comparable to David. He removes the high places and worship objects that were seen as inappropriate, including Nehushtan, a copy of the brazen serpent from the wilderness period (Num 21:4-9), which people were worshiping. His perfect obedience and the fact that the LORD is with him lead to rebellion against the Assyrian king and military success against the Philistines. Verses 9-12 repeat the earlier account of the Assyrian capture of Samaria (see 17:5-6).

18 In the third year of King Hoshea son of Elah of Israel, Hezekiah son of King Ahaz of Judah began to reign. [2]He was twenty-five years old when he began to reign; he reigned twenty-nine years in Jerusalem. His mother's name was Abi daughter of Zechariah. [3]He did what was right in the sight of the LORD just as his ancestor David had done. [4]He removed the high places, broke down the pillars, and cut down the sacred pole.[a] He broke in pieces the bronze serpent that Moses had made, for until those days the people of Israel had made offerings to it; it was called Nehushtan. [5]He trusted in the LORD the God of Israel; so that there was no one like him among all the kings of Judah after him, or among those who

---

[a] Heb *Asherah*

were before him. [6]For he held fast to the LORD; he did not depart
from following him but kept the commandments that the LORD
commanded Moses. [7]The LORD was with him; wherever he went,
he prospered. He rebelled against the king of Assyria and would not
serve him. [8]He attacked the Philistines as far as Gaza and its territory,
from watchtower to fortified city.

9 In the fourth year of King Hezekiah, which was the seventh year
of King Hoshea son of Elah of Israel, King Shalmaneser of Assyria
came up against Samaria, besieged it, [10]and at the end of three years,
took it. In the sixth year of Hezekiah, which was the ninth year of King
Hoshea of Israel, Samaria was taken. [11]The king of Assyria carried the
Israelites away to Assyria, settled them in Halah, on the Habor, the
river of Gozan, and in the cities of the Medes, [12]because they did
not obey the voice of the LORD their God but transgressed his covenant—all that Moses the servant of the LORD had commanded; they
neither listened nor obeyed.

Sennacherib Invades Judah

13 In the fourteenth year of King Hezekiah, King Sennacherib
of Assyria came up against all the fortified cities of Judah and captured them. [14]King Hezekiah of Judah sent to the king of Assyria at
Lachish, saying, "I have done wrong; withdraw from me; whatever
you impose on me I will bear." The king of Assyria demanded of King
Hezekiah of Judah three hundred talents of silver and thirty talents of
gold. [15]Hezekiah gave him all the silver that was found in the house
of the LORD and in the treasuries of the king's house. [16]At that time
Hezekiah stripped the gold from the doors of the temple of the LORD,
and from the doorposts that King Hezekiah of Judah had overlaid and
gave it to the king of Assyria. [17]The king of Assyria sent the Tartan, the
Rabsaris, and the Rabshakeh with a great army from Lachish to King
Hezekiah at Jerusalem. They went up and came to Jerusalem. When
they arrived, they came and stood by the conduit of the upper pool,
which is on the highway to the Fuller's Field. [18]When they called for
the king, there came out to them Eliakim son of Hilkiah, who was
in charge of the palace, and Shebnah the secretary, and Joah son of
Asaph, the recorder.

19 The Rabshakeh said to them, "Say to Hezekiah: Thus says the
great king, the king of Assyria: On what do you base this confidence
of yours? [20]Do you think that mere words are strategy and power for
war? On whom do you now rely, that you have rebelled against me?
[21]See, you are relying now on Egypt, that broken reed of a staff, which
will pierce the hand of anyone who leans on it. Such is Pharaoh king
of Egypt to all who rely on him. [22]But if you say to me, 'We rely on the
LORD our God,' is it not he whose high places and altars Hezekiah has
removed, saying to Judah and to Jerusalem, 'You shall worship before

18:13-16 King Sennacherib of Assyria came up against all the fortified cities of Judah and captured them: The Assyrian king Sennacherib (705–681 B.C.E.) invaded Palestine in his third campaign and reported on it in his royal records. Images of his siege of Lachish have been excavated in Nineveh, and biblical accounts similar to 2 Kings 18–19 are preserved in Isaiah 36–37 and 2 Chronicles 32. Despite this abundant evidence, there are many unanswered questions about Sennacherib's campaign against Judah. According to these verses, which are most similar to Assyrian records, Hezekiah was forced to hand over a large payment from the resources of the temple and the palace.

18:17-37 Make your peace with me: The Rabshakeh, an official who was normally responsible for running the royal court, casts doubt on Judah's self image and the reliability of Egypt as an ally. If the people place their confidence in the LORD, the Rabshakeh says, they should keep in mind that Hezekiah has been tearing down the LORD's altars. (Of course, the writer of Kings says Hezekiah only destroyed places and objects for the worship of *other* gods.) The Rabshakeh also claims that the LORD sent the Assyrians to destroy Judah. He refuses to speak in Aramaic, which only Hezekiah's officials can understand, and speaks directly to the common people in Hebrew. He tells them that the king of Assyria offers land and prosperity to any who will come over to his side. He challenges the power of the LORD to withstand the Assyrian king, since the other gods of the region have been totally unsuccessful in resisting Sennacherib's advances. Though the people are silent because of the king's orders, Hezekiah's officials report to him in deep mourning.

this altar in Jerusalem'? 23 Come now, make a wager with my master
the king of Assyria: I will give you two thousand horses, if you are
able on your part to set riders on them. 24 How then can you repulse a
single captain among the least of my master's servants, when you rely
on Egypt for chariots and for horsemen? 25 Moreover, is it without the
LORD that I have come up against this place to destroy it? The LORD
said to me, Go up against this land, and destroy it."

26 Then Eliakim son of Hilkiah, and Shebnah, and Joah said to
the Rabshakeh, "Please speak to your servants in the Aramaic language, for we understand it; do not speak to us in the language of
Judah within the hearing of the people who are on the wall." 27 But
the Rabshakeh said to them, "Has my master sent me to speak these
words to your master and to you, and not to the people sitting on the
wall, who are doomed with you to eat their own dung and to drink
their own urine?"

28 Then the Rabshakeh stood and called out in a loud voice in
the language of Judah, "Hear the word of the great king, the king of
Assyria! 29 Thus says the king: 'Do not let Hezekiah deceive you, for
he will not be able to deliver you out of my hand. 30 Do not let Hezekiah make you rely on the LORD by saying, The LORD will surely
deliver us, and this city will not be given into the hand of the king
of Assyria.' 31 Do not listen to Hezekiah; for thus says the king of Assyria: 'Make your peace with me and come out to me; then every one
of you will eat from your own vine and your own fig tree, and drink
water from your own cistern, 32 until I come and take you away to a
land like your own land, a land of grain and wine, a land of bread and
vineyards, a land of olive oil and honey, that you may live and not die.
Do not listen to Hezekiah when he misleads you by saying, The LORD
will deliver us. 33 Has any of the gods of the nations ever delivered its
land out of the hand of the king of Assyria? 34 Where are the gods of
Hamath and Arpad? Where are the gods of Sepharvaim, Hena, and
Ivvah? Have they delivered Samaria out of my hand? 35 Who among
all the gods of the countries have delivered their countries out of my
hand, that the LORD should deliver Jerusalem out of my hand?'"

36 But the people were silent and answered him not a word, for
the king's command was, "Do not answer him." 37 Then Eliakim son
of Hilkiah, who was in charge of the palace, and Shebna the secretary, and Joah son of Asaph, the recorder, came to Hezekiah with their
clothes torn and told him the words of the Rabshakeh.

19:1-7 lift up your prayer: Hezekiah goes to the temple and sends a delegation to tell the prophet Isaiah that the Rabshakeh has mocked the LORD. The words in 19:3 indicate that now is the time for deliverance, but the people by themselves cannot achieve it. Isaiah tells Hezekiah that Sennacherib will hear a rumor requiring him to return home, where he will die.

Hezekiah Consults Isaiah

19 When King Hezekiah heard it, he tore his clothes, covered
himself with sackcloth, and went into the house of the LORD.
2 And he sent Eliakim, who was in charge of the palace, and Shebna
the secretary, and the senior priests, covered with sackcloth, to the

prophet Isaiah son of Amoz. [3]They said to him, "Thus says Hezekiah,
This day is a day of distress, of rebuke, and of disgrace; children have
come to the birth, and there is no strength to bring them forth. [4]It may
be that the LORD your God heard all the words of the Rabshakeh,
whom his master the king of Assyria has sent to mock the living God,
and will rebuke the words that the LORD your God has heard; therefore lift up your prayer for the remnant that is left." [5]When the servants of King Hezekiah came to Isaiah, [6]Isaiah said to them, "Say to
your master, 'Thus says the LORD: Do not be afraid because of the
words that you have heard, with which the servants of the king of Assyria have reviled me. [7]I myself will put a spirit in him, so that he shall
hear a rumor and return to his own land; I will cause him to fall by the
sword in his own land.' "

Sennacherib's Threat

8 The Rabshakeh returned, and found the king of Assyria fighting against Libnah; for he had heard that the king had left Lachish.
[9]When the king[a] heard concerning King Tirhakah of Ethiopia,[b] "See,
he has set out to fight against you," he sent messengers again to Hezekiah, saying, [10]"Thus shall you speak to King Hezekiah of Judah: Do
not let your God on whom you rely deceive you by promising that
Jerusalem will not be given into the hand of the king of Assyria. [11]See,
you have heard what the kings of Assyria have done to all lands, destroying them utterly. Shall you be delivered? [12]Have the gods of the
nations delivered them, the nations that my predecessors destroyed,
Gozan, Haran, Rezeph, and the people of Eden who were in Telassar?
[13]Where is the king of Hamath, the king of Arpad, the king of the city
of Sepharvaim, the king of Hena, or the king of Ivvah?"

19:8-13 he sent messengers again to Hezekiah: The Rabshakeh left, but Sennacherib again sent messengers to remind Hezekiah that the gods of neighboring nations had not been able to defend people from him and therefore Judah should not trust its God to help either.

Hezekiah's Prayer

14 Hezekiah received the letter from the hand of the messengers
and read it; then Hezekiah went up to the house of the LORD and
spread it before the LORD. [15]And Hezekiah prayed before the LORD,
and said: "O LORD the God of Israel, who are enthroned above the
cherubim, you are God, you alone, of all the kingdoms of the earth;
you have made heaven and earth. [16]Incline your ear, O LORD, and
hear; open your eyes, O LORD, and see; hear the words of Sennacherib, which he has sent to mock the living God. [17]Truly, O LORD, the
kings of Assyria have laid waste the nations and their lands, [18]and have
hurled their gods into the fire, though they were no gods but the work
of human hands—wood and stone—and so they were destroyed.
[19]So now, O LORD our God, save us, I pray you, from his hand, so
that all the kingdoms of the earth may know that you, O LORD, are
God alone."

19:14-19 Hezekiah prayed before the LORD: In response to the messengers, Hezekiah goes to the temple and prays directly to God, rather than seeking help through the prophet Isaiah. Hezekiah points out that the Assyrians have mocked God and overpowered other nations and their gods, but adds that these gods were only idols made of wood and stone. Hezekiah prays for deliverance which will also enhance the LORD's reputation everywhere.

---

[a] Heb *he* [b] Or *Nubia;* Heb *Cush*

19:20-34 I have heard your prayer to me: Isaiah assures Hezekiah that God has heard his prayer and disapproves of the Assyrians' mockery. The great personal and military accomplishments of the Assyrians, Isaiah says, were planned by the LORD long ago, at the beginning of the world, and the LORD will turn around Sennacherib like a stubborn animal and drag him back to Assyria (see Isa 10:12-19; 14:24-27). Isaiah also offers Judah a sign. For the next two years they will eat from grain that grows without cultivation. By the third year their crops will be productive, and the people will be firmly planted and highly successful in the land. The LORD's zeal would assure that these promises would come true. The LORD would defend Jerusalem, and Sennacherib would never shoot an arrow into the city. This would happen for the LORD's sake and for King David's sake.

In times of crisis, what is the appropriate balance between trusting in military power and relying on the Lord's help?

20 Then Isaiah son of Amoz sent to Hezekiah, saying, "Thus says
the LORD, the God of Israel: I have heard your prayer to me about
King Sennacherib of Assyria. 21 This is the word that the LORD has
spoken concerning him:

She despises you, she scorns you—
virgin daughter Zion;
she tosses her head—behind your back,
daughter Jerusalem.

22 "Whom have you mocked and reviled?
Against whom have you raised your voice
and haughtily lifted your eyes?
Against the Holy One of Israel!
23 By your messengers you have mocked the Lord,
and you have said, 'With my many chariots
I have gone up the heights of the mountains,
to the far recesses of Lebanon;
I felled its tallest cedars,
its choicest cypresses;
I entered its farthest retreat,
its densest forest.
24 I dug wells
and drank foreign waters,
I dried up with the sole of my foot
all the streams of Egypt.'

25 "Have you not heard
that I determined it long ago?
I planned from days of old
what now I bring to pass,
that you should make fortified cities
crash into heaps of ruins,
26 while their inhabitants, shorn of strength,
are dismayed and confounded;
they have become like plants of the field
and like tender grass,
like grass on the housetops,
blighted before it is grown.

27 "But I know your rising[a] and your sitting,
your going out and coming in,
and your raging against me.
28 Because you have raged against me
and your arrogance has come to my ears,

---

[a] Gk Compare Isa 37.27 Q Ms: MT lacks *rising*

I will put my hook in your nose
and my bit in your mouth;
I will turn you back on the way
by which you came.

29 "And this shall be the sign for you: This year you shall eat what
grows of itself, and in the second year what springs from that; then
in the third year sow, reap, plant vineyards, and eat their fruit. 30 The
surviving remnant of the house of Judah shall again take root
downward, and bear fruit upward; 31 for from Jerusalem a remnant
shall go out, and from Mount Zion a band of survivors. The zeal of
the LORD of hosts will do this.
32 "Therefore thus says the LORD concerning the king of Assyria:
He shall not come into this city, shoot an arrow there, come before it
with a shield, or cast up a siege ramp against it. 33 By the way that he
came, by the same he shall return; he shall not come into this city, says
the LORD. 34 For I will defend this city to save it, for my own sake and
for the sake of my servant David."

Sennacherib's Defeat and Death

35 That very night the angel of the LORD set out and struck down
one hundred eighty-five thousand in the camp of the Assyrians; when
morning dawned, they were all dead bodies. 36 Then King Sennacherib of Assyria left, went home, and lived at Nineveh. 37 As he was worshiping in the house of his god Nisroch, his sons Adrammelech and
Sharezer killed him with the sword, and they escaped into the land of
Ararat. His son Esar-haddon succeeded him.

Hezekiah's Illness

20 In those days Hezekiah became sick and was at the point
of death. The prophet Isaiah son of Amoz came to him,
and said to him, "Thus says the LORD: Set your house in order, for
you shall die; you shall not recover." 2 Then Hezekiah turned his face
to the wall and prayed to the LORD: 3 "Remember now, O LORD, I
implore you, how I have walked before you in faithfulness with a
whole heart, and have done what is good in your sight." Hezekiah
wept bitterly. 4 Before Isaiah had gone out of the middle court, the
word of the LORD came to him: 5 "Turn back, and say to Hezekiah
prince of my people, Thus says the LORD, the God of your ancestor
David: I have heard your prayer, I have seen your tears; indeed, I will
heal you; on the third day you shall go up to the house of the LORD.
6 I will add fifteen years to your life. I will deliver you and this city
out of the hand of the king of Assyria; I will defend this city for my
own sake and for my servant David's sake." 7 Then Isaiah said, "Bring
a lump of figs. Let them take it and apply it to the boil, so that he may
recover."

19:35-37 King Sennacherib of Assyria left: An angel kills 185,000 Assyrians, forcing Sennacherib to flee home. Twenty years later two of Sennacherib's sons assassinate him in his temple. This implies that Sennacherib's god was unable to protect him, even as Sennacherib charged that the LORD would be unable to protect Judah. In his records, Sennacherib himself claimed that he took two hundred thousand Judeans captive and received much tribute from Solomon. Modern historians conclude that Hezekiah did not defeat Sennacherib, but the fact that Sennacherib nowhere claims that he took Jerusalem shows that it is easy to overestimate his success.

20:1-11 Hezekiah became sick: Hezekiah becomes deathly sick, and Isaiah tells him that he will not recover. Hezekiah prays fervently, reminding God how he has lived faithfully and expressing his deep grief. The LORD instructs Isaiah to tell Hezekiah he will recover in three days and live fifteen more years, and Hezekiah and Jerusalem will be delivered from the Assyrians. Isaiah orders that a mixture of figs be applied to Hezekiah's boil. Hezekiah asks for a sign that this will result in a cure, and Isaiah says that if the shadow on the sundial moves backwards by ten intervals—contrary to its usual motion—Hezekiah will be cured. Isaiah prays for this to happen, and it does.

20:12-19 King Merodach-baladan... of Babylon sent envoys: Merodach-baladan was ruler in Babylon 722–710 B.C.E. and again 704–703, so this incident would have taken place before Sennacherib's invasion. Merodach-baladan may have been seeking good trading relations with Judah or a defensive treaty against the Assyrians. Hezekiah shows all his treasures to representatives of the Babylonian ruler. Isaiah reprimands him for this show of pride and prophesies that the Babylonians will someday take all these treasures and some of Hezekiah's descendants to their country. Hezekiah takes an optimistic view of Isaiah's words: At least there will be peace and security in his lifetime.

20:20-21 Hezekiah slept with his ancestors: Hezekiah carves a tunnel about seventeen hundred feet (approximately 518 meters) through limestone to bring water into Jerusalem during a siege. Hezekiah's tunnel still exists today (see Map 6, p. 2104). Hezekiah dies, and Manasseh succeeds him.

21:1-18 Manasseh... did what was evil in the sight of the LORD: The writer of Kings gives the strongest criticism to Ahab and Jezebel in the north (Israel) and to Manasseh (697–642 B.C.E.) in the south (Judah). Manasseh reverses the reforms of his father, returns to the practices of his grandfather Ahaz (16:2-4), and erects altars for Baal. "Altars for all the host of heaven" refers to worship of the stars, and "made his son pass through fire" to child sacrifice (16:3). Manasseh even installs a carved image of the god Asherah in the Jerusalem temple. The promise to David and Solomon had been conditional, according to verses 21:10-12 (see 1 Kgs 9:3-9), and clearly Manasseh is completely unfaithful. Under his rule, the people commit more sins than the pre-Israelite inhabitants of the land (see Deut 12:29-31), and his sins are the same ones that led to the destruction of the northern kingdom (17:7-18). Because of Manasseh's grievous sins, an unnamed group of prophets announces that Jerusalem will be destroyed just as Samaria has been. After Samaria's defeat, Judah became the "remnant of [God's] heritage" (21:14). "Manasseh shed very much innocent blood" puts the blame for unspecified acts of violence on the king, who also leads Judah into false worship. Manasseh serves as king longer than anyone else in either kingdom. A more positive view of Manasseh is presented in Chronicles, including a midlife conversion (2 Chr 33:1-20).

8 Hezekiah said to Isaiah, "What shall be the sign that the LORD
will heal me, and that I shall go up to the house of the LORD on the
third day?" 9 Isaiah said, "This is the sign to you from the LORD, that
the LORD will do the thing that he has promised: the shadow has now
advanced ten intervals; shall it retreat ten intervals?" 10 Hezekiah answered, "It is normal for the shadow to lengthen ten intervals; rather
let the shadow retreat ten intervals." 11 The prophet Isaiah cried to the
LORD; and he brought the shadow back the ten intervals, by which
the sun[a] had declined on the dial of Ahaz.

Envoys from Babylon

12 At that time King Merodach-baladan son of Baladan of Babylon sent envoys with letters and a present to Hezekiah, for he had
heard that Hezekiah had been sick. 13 Hezekiah welcomed them;[b] he
showed them all his treasure house, the silver, the gold, the spices, the
precious oil, his armory, all that was found in his storehouses; there
was nothing in his house or in all his realm that Hezekiah did not
show them. 14 Then the prophet Isaiah came to King Hezekiah, and
said to him, "What did these men say? From where did they come to
you?" Hezekiah answered, "They have come from a far country, from
Babylon." 15 He said, "What have they seen in your house?" Hezekiah
answered, "They have seen all that is in my house; there is nothing in
my storehouses that I did not show them."

16 Then Isaiah said to Hezekiah, "Hear the word of the LORD:
17 Days are coming when all that is in your house, and that which your
ancestors have stored up until this day, shall be carried to Babylon;
nothing shall be left, says the LORD. 18 Some of your own sons who are
born to you shall be taken away; they shall be eunuchs in the palace
of the king of Babylon." 19 Then Hezekiah said to Isaiah, "The word of
the LORD that you have spoken is good." For he thought, "Why not, if
there will be peace and security in my days?"

Death of Hezekiah

20 The rest of the deeds of Hezekiah, all his power, how he made
the pool and the conduit and brought water into the city, are they not
written in the Book of the Annals of the Kings of Judah? 21 Hezekiah
slept with his ancestors; and his son Manasseh succeeded him.

Manasseh Reigns over Judah

21 Manasseh was twelve years old when he began to reign; he
reigned fifty-five years in Jerusalem. His mother's name was
Hephzibah. 2 He did what was evil in the sight of the LORD, following the abominable practices of the nations that the LORD drove out

---

[a] Syr See Isa 38.8 and Tg: Heb *it* [b] Gk Vg Syr: Heb *When Hezekiah heard about them*

before the people of Israel. [3]For he rebuilt the high places that his father Hezekiah had destroyed; he erected altars for Baal, made a sacred pole,[a] as King Ahab of Israel had done, worshiped all the host of
heaven, and served them. [4]He built altars in the house of the LORD, of
which the LORD had said, "In Jerusalem I will put my name." [5]He built
altars for all the host of heaven in the two courts of the house of the
LORD. [6]He made his son pass through fire; he practiced soothsaying
and augury, and dealt with mediums and with wizards. He did much
evil in the sight of the LORD, provoking him to anger. [7]The carved
image of Asherah that he had made he set in the house of which the
LORD said to David and to his son Solomon, "In this house, and in Jerusalem, which I have chosen out of all the tribes of Israel, I will put my
name forever; [8]I will not cause the feet of Israel to wander any more
out of the land that I gave to their ancestors, if only they will be careful
to do according to all that I have commanded them, and according to
all the law that my servant Moses commanded them." [9]But they did
not listen; Manasseh misled them to do more evil than the nations
had done that the LORD destroyed before the people of Israel.

10 The LORD said by his servants the prophets, [11]"Because King
Manasseh of Judah has committed these abominations, has done
things more wicked than all that the Amorites did, who were before
him, and has caused Judah also to sin with his idols; [12]therefore thus
says the LORD, the God of Israel, I am bringing upon Jerusalem and
Judah such evil that the ears of everyone who hears of it will tingle.
[13]I will stretch over Jerusalem the measuring line for Samaria, and the
plummet for the house of Ahab; I will wipe Jerusalem as one wipes
a dish, wiping it and turning it upside down. [14]I will cast off the remnant of my heritage, and give them into the hand of their enemies;
they shall become a prey and a spoil to all their enemies, [15]because
they have done what is evil in my sight and have provoked me to anger, since the day their ancestors came out of Egypt, even to this day."

16 Moreover Manasseh shed very much innocent blood, until
he had filled Jerusalem from one end to another, besides the sin that
he caused Judah to sin so that they did what was evil in the sight of
the LORD.

17 Now the rest of the acts of Manasseh, all that he did, and the
sin that he committed, are they not written in the Book of the Annals of the Kings of Judah? [18]Manasseh slept with his ancestors, and
was buried in the garden of his house, in the garden of Uzza. His son
Amon succeeded him.

Amon Reigns over Judah

19 Amon was twenty-two years old when he began to reign; he
reigned two years in Jerusalem. His mother's name was Meshullemeth

[a] Heb *Asherah*

21:19-26 Amon...reigned two years in Jerusalem: Amon (642–640 B.C.E.) continues the bad practices of his father, Manasseh. His servants assassinate him, but the people of the land execute the assassins and install his son Josiah in his place. Amon and his father are buried in the garden of Uzza (21:18, 26).

daughter of Haruz of Jotbah. [20]He did what was evil in the sight of the
LORD, as his father Manasseh had done. [21]He walked in all the way in
which his father walked, served the idols that his father served, and
worshiped them; [22]he abandoned the LORD, the God of his ancestors,
and did not walk in the way of the LORD. [23]The servants of Amon conspired against him, and killed the king in his house. [24]But the people
of the land killed all those who had conspired against King Amon,
and the people of the land made his son Josiah king in place of him.
[25]Now the rest of the acts of Amon that he did, are they not written in
the Book of the Annals of the Kings of Judah? [26]He was buried in his
tomb in the garden of Uzza; then his son Josiah succeeded him.

22:1-20 I have found the book of the law: Josiah (640–609 B.C.E.) returns to the practices of his great-grandfather, Hezekiah. There is no king like him, earlier or later (23:25; see the same statement about Hezekiah in 18:5). Josiah sends the secretary Shaphan to the temple to account for contributions and how they are being used for temple repairs. The high priest surprises Shaphan with the news that he has found "the book of the law," which most modern scholars believe was an early version of the book of Deuteronomy. Shaphan reports back to Josiah about the contributions and the discovery of the book. After Shaphan reads this book for the king, Josiah tears his clothes in mourning, probably because of the threatened curses in Deuteronomy 28, and tells his staff to ask the LORD about the book and its curses. The staff members go to the prophetess Huldah, who gives them a message from the LORD: Because of the worship of other gods, Jerusalem and its people will suffer disaster. Because of his obvious sorrow and repentance, Josiah will die peacefully or at least before the final judgment on Jerusalem. Actually, Josiah died a violent death (23:28-30).

Josiah Reigns over Judah

22 Josiah was eight years old when he began to reign; he
reigned thirty-one years in Jerusalem. His mother's name
was Jedidah daughter of Adaiah of Bozkath. [2]He did what was right in
the sight of the LORD, and walked in all the way of his father David; he
did not turn aside to the right or to the left.

Hilkiah Finds the Book of the Law

3 In the eighteenth year of King Josiah, the king sent Shaphan
son of Azaliah, son of Meshullam, the secretary, to the house of the
LORD, saying, [4]"Go up to the high priest Hilkiah, and have him count
the entire sum of the money that has been brought into the house
of the LORD, which the keepers of the threshold have collected from
the people; [5]let it be given into the hand of the workers who have the
oversight of the house of the LORD; let them give it to the workers
who are at the house of the LORD, repairing the house, [6]that is, to the
carpenters, to the builders, to the masons; and let them use it to buy
timber and quarried stone to repair the house. [7]But no accounting
shall be asked from them for the money that is delivered into their
hand, for they deal honestly."

8 The high priest Hilkiah said to Shaphan the secretary, "I have
found the book of the law in the house of the LORD." When Hilkiah
gave the book to Shaphan, he read it. [9]Then Shaphan the secretary
came to the king, and reported to the king, "Your servants have emptied out the money that was found in the house, and have delivered it
into the hand of the workers who have oversight of the house of the
LORD." [10]Shaphan the secretary informed the king, "The priest Hilkiah has given me a book." Shaphan then read it aloud to the king.

11 When the king heard the words of the book of the law, he tore
his clothes. [12]Then the king commanded the priest Hilkiah, Ahikam
son of Shaphan, Achbor son of Micaiah, Shaphan the secretary, and
the king's servant Asaiah, saying, [13]"Go, inquire of the LORD for me,
for the people, and for all Judah, concerning the words of this book

that has been found; for great is the wrath of the LORD that is kindled
against us, because our ancestors did not obey the words of this book,
to do according to all that is written concerning us."
14 So the priest Hilkiah, Ahikam, Achbor, Shaphan, and Asaiah
went to the prophetess Huldah the wife of Shallum son of Tikvah, son
of Harhas, keeper of the wardrobe; she resided in Jerusalem in the
Second Quarter, where they consulted her. 15 She declared to them,
"Thus says the LORD, the God of Israel: Tell the man who sent you
to me, 16 Thus says the LORD, I will indeed bring disaster on this place
and on its inhabitants—all the words of the book that the king of
Judah has read. 17 Because they have abandoned me and have made
offerings to other gods, so that they have provoked me to anger with
all the work of their hands, therefore my wrath will be kindled against
this place, and it will not be quenched. 18 But as to the king of Judah,
who sent you to inquire of the LORD, thus shall you say to him, Thus
says the LORD, the God of Israel: Regarding the words that you have
heard, 19 because your heart was penitent, and you humbled yourself
before the LORD, when you heard how I spoke against this place, and
against its inhabitants, that they should become a desolation and a
curse, and because you have torn your clothes and wept before me, I
also have heard you, says the LORD. 20 Therefore, I will gather you to
your ancestors, and you shall be gathered to your grave in peace; your
eyes shall not see all the disaster that I will bring on this place." They
took the message back to the king.

Josiah's Reformation

23 Then the king directed that all the elders of Judah and Jerusalem should be gathered to him. 2 The king went up to the
house of the LORD, and with him went all the people of Judah, all the
inhabitants of Jerusalem, the priests, the prophets, and all the people, both small and great; he read in their hearing all the words of the
book of the covenant that had been found in the house of the LORD.
3 The king stood by the pillar and made a covenant before the LORD,
to follow the LORD, keeping his commandments, his decrees, and his
statutes, with all his heart and all his soul, to perform the words of
this covenant that were written in this book. All the people joined in
the covenant.
4 The king commanded the high priest Hilkiah, the priests of the
second order, and the guardians of the threshold, to bring out of the
temple of the LORD all the vessels made for Baal, for Asherah, and for
all the host of heaven; he burned them outside Jerusalem in the fields
of the Kidron, and carried their ashes to Bethel. 5 He deposed the idolatrous priests whom the kings of Judah had ordained to make offerings in the high places at the cities of Judah and around Jerusalem;
those also who made offerings to Baal, to the sun, the moon, the

23:1-20 The king…made a covenant before the LORD: Josiah leads all the people to the temple, where the "book of the covenant" (earlier called the book of the law) is read. One of the main provisions of the book of Deuteronomy is that sacrifices can only be made at one place, which is implicitly Jerusalem. The king makes a covenant to follow all the stipulations of the book, and all the people agree. Josiah cleanses the temple of items used to worship the gods Baal and Asherah, throws out priests at the high places throughout Judah, and defiles those sanctuaries. The fact that the priests of the high places do not come to Jerusalem seems to contradict more lenient instructions in Deuteronomy 18:6-8. Josiah breaks down the houses of the sacred individuals (not prostitutes, as translated here; see note on 1 Kings 14:21-29), where women made weavings for the goddess Asherah. He also defiles the sanctuaries for the gods of Solomon's many wives by scattering human bones on them. Then Josiah goes north and defiles the sanctuary at Bethel, one of two illegitimate sanctuaries that Jeroboam I had established. This fulfills the prophecy that "the man of God" had uttered in 1 Kings 13. While other bones from tombs are used to defile that altar, Josiah lets the bones of the man of God rest in peace, as well as the prophet buried with him. Josiah removes other high places in Samaria and kills the priests who serve them.

constellations, and all the host of the heavens. 6 He brought out the image of[a] Asherah from the house of the LORD, outside Jerusalem, to the Wadi Kidron, burned it at the Wadi Kidron, beat it to dust and threw the dust of it upon the graves of the common people. 7 He broke down the houses of the male temple prostitutes that were in the house of the LORD, where the women did weaving for Asherah. 8 He brought all the priests out of the towns of Judah, and defiled the high places where the priests had made offerings, from Geba to Beer-sheba; he broke down the high places of the gates that were at the entrance of the gate of Joshua the governor of the city, which were on the left at the gate of the city. 9 The priests of the high places, however, did not come up to the altar of the LORD in Jerusalem, but ate unleavened bread among their kindred. 10 He defiled Topheth, which is in the valley of Ben-hinnom, so that no one would make a son or a daughter pass through fire as an offering to Molech. 11 He removed the horses that the kings of Judah had dedicated to the sun, at the entrance to the house of the LORD, by the chamber of the eunuch Nathan-melech, which was in the precincts;[b] then he burned the chariots of the sun with fire. 12 The altars on the roof of the upper chamber of Ahaz, which the kings of Judah had made, and the altars that Manasseh had made in the two courts of the house of the LORD, he pulled down from there and broke in pieces, and threw the rubble into the Wadi Kidron. 13 The king defiled the high places that were east of Jerusalem, to the south of the Mount of Destruction, which King Solomon of Israel had built for Astarte the abomination of the Sidonians, for Chemosh the abomination of Moab, and for Milcom the abomination of the Ammonites. 14 He broke the pillars in pieces, cut down the sacred poles,[c] and covered the sites with human bones.

15 Moreover, the altar at Bethel, the high place erected by Jeroboam son of Nebat, who caused Israel to sin—he pulled down that altar along with the high place. He burned the high place, crushing it to dust; he also burned the sacred pole.[c] 16 As Josiah turned, he saw the tombs there on the mount; and he sent and took the bones out of the tombs, and burned them on the altar, and defiled it, according to the word of the LORD that the man of God proclaimed,[d] when Jeroboam stood by the altar at the festival; he turned and looked up at the tomb of the man of God who had predicted these things. 17 Then he said, "What is that monument that I see?" The people of the city told him, "It is the tomb of the man of God who came from Judah and predicted these things that you have done against the altar at Bethel." 18 He said, "Let him rest; let no one move his bones." So they let his bones alone, with the bones of the prophet who came out of Samaria.

---

[a] Heb lacks *image of* [b] Meaning of Heb uncertain [c] Heb *Asherim* [d] Gk: Heb *proclaimed, who had predicted these things*

[19]Moreover, Josiah removed all the shrines of the high places that
were in the towns of Samaria, which kings of Israel had made, provoking the LORD to anger; he did to them just as he had done at Bethel.
[20]He slaughtered on the altars all the priests of the high places who
were there, and burned human bones on them. Then he returned to
Jerusalem.

The Passover Celebrated

21 The king commanded all the people, "Keep the passover to
the LORD your God as prescribed in this book of the covenant." [22]No
such passover had been kept since the days of the judges who judged
Israel, even during all the days of the kings of Israel and of the kings
of Judah; [23]but in the eighteenth year of King Josiah this passover was
kept to the LORD in Jerusalem.

24 Moreover Josiah put away the mediums, wizards, teraphim,[a]
idols, and all the abominations that were seen in the land of Judah
and in Jerusalem, so that he established the words of the law that were
written in the book that the priest Hilkiah had found in the house of
the LORD. [25]Before him there was no king like him, who turned to the
LORD with all his heart, with all his soul, and with all his might, according to all the law of Moses; nor did any like him arise after him.

23:21-25 Keep the passover: Josiah orders a passover observance as prescribed in the book of the covenant. According to Deuteronomy 16:5-6, Passover was to be held at the central sanctuary and not in homes. The last time such a Passover had been held was during the conquest of the land (Josh 5:10-11).

26 Still the LORD did not turn from the fierceness of his great
wrath, by which his anger was kindled against Judah, because of all
the provocations with which Manasseh had provoked him. [27]The
LORD said, "I will remove Judah also out of my sight, as I have removed Israel; and I will reject this city that I have chosen, Jerusalem,
and the house of which I said, My name shall be there."

23:26-27 the Lord did not turn from the fierceness of his great wrath: Despite the wonderful deeds of Josiah, Judah will be destroyed, because Manasseh's evil deeds outweigh the merits of Josiah (see 21:10-15).

Josiah Dies in Battle

28 Now the rest of the acts of Josiah, and all that he did, are they
not written in the Book of the Annals of the Kings of Judah? [29]In his
days Pharaoh Neco king of Egypt went up to the king of Assyria to
the river Euphrates. King Josiah went to meet him; but when Pharaoh
Neco met him at Megiddo, he killed him. [30]His servants carried him
dead in a chariot from Megiddo, brought him to Jerusalem, and buried him in his own tomb. The people of the land took Jehoahaz son of
Josiah, anointed him, and made him king in place of his father.

23:28-30 Pharaoh Neco…killed [King Josiah]: Neco comes to the throne of Egypt in 610 B.C.E. He is on his way to Mesopotamia to prop up the remnants of Assyria as a buffer against the Neo-Babylonian Empire. Why Josiah meets Neco and why Neco kills him is not clear. "The people of the land" (see note on 11:13-21) make Jehoahaz king.

Reign and Captivity of Jehoahaz

31 Jehoahaz was twenty-three years old when he began to reign;
he reigned three months in Jerusalem. His mother's name was Hamutal daughter of Jeremiah of Libnah. [32]He did what was evil in the sight
of the LORD, just as his ancestors had done. [33]Pharaoh Neco confined
him at Riblah in the land of Hamath, so that he might not reign in

23:31-35 Jehoahaz…reigned three months in Jerusalem: The short reign of Jehoahaz in 609 B.C.E. is sharply criticized, as are all the reigns after Josiah. Pharaoh Neco overthrows him, takes him to Egypt, and installs in his place his brother Eliakim, and changes Eliakim's name to Jehoiakim. Jehoiakim imposes taxes on the people of the land to pay tribute to Neco.

[a] Or *household gods*

Jerusalem, and imposed tribute on the land of one hundred talents of silver and a talent of gold. [34]Pharaoh Neco made Eliakim son of Josiah king in place of his father Josiah, and changed his name to Jehoiakim. But he took Jehoahaz away; he came to Egypt, and died there. [35]Jehoiakim gave the silver and the gold to Pharaoh, but he taxed the land in order to meet Pharaoh's demand for money. He exacted the silver and the gold from the people of the land, from all according to their assessment, to give it to Pharaoh Neco.

Jehoiakim Reigns over Judah

23:36—24:7 Jehoiakim . . . began to reign: Jehoiakim (609–598 B.C.E.) is sharply criticized, and the prophet Jeremiah becomes his bitter opponent. In the meantime Nebuchadnezzar (605–562 B.C.E.) becomes ruler of the Neo-Babylonian Empire, and Jehoiakim foolishly rebels against him. Jehoiakim endures multiple attacks from nearby nations that are considered judgments by the LORD because of the sins of Manasseh.

36 Jehoiakim was twenty-five years old when he began to reign; he reigned eleven years in Jerusalem. His mother's name was Zebidah daughter of Pedaiah of Rumah. [37]He did what was evil in the sight of the LORD, just as all his ancestors had done.

Judah Overrun by Enemies

24 In his days King Nebuchadnezzar of Babylon came up; Jehoiakim became his servant for three years; then he turned and rebelled against him. [2]The LORD sent against him bands of the Chaldeans, bands of the Arameans, bands of the Moabites, and bands of the Ammonites; he sent them against Judah to destroy it, according to the word of the LORD that he spoke by his servants the prophets. [3]Surely this came upon Judah at the command of the LORD, to remove them out of his sight, for the sins of Manasseh, for all that he had committed, [4]and also for the innocent blood that he had shed; for he filled Jerusalem with innocent blood, and the LORD was not willing to pardon. [5]Now the rest of the deeds of Jehoiakim, and all that he did, are they not written in the Book of the Annals of the Kings of Judah? [6]So Jehoiakim slept with his ancestors; then his son Jehoiachin succeeded him. [7]The king of Egypt did not come again out of his land, for the king of Babylon had taken over all that belonged to the king of Egypt from the Wadi of Egypt to the River Euphrates.

Reign and Captivity of Jehoiachin

24:8-12 Jehoiachin . . . began to reign: Jehoiachin (598–597 B.C.E.) rules for three months. In 597 B.C.E. the Babylonians attack Jerusalem and take Jehoiachin as a prisoner. He spends the next thirty-five years in a Babylonian prison (see 25:27-30).

8 Jehoiachin was eighteen years old when he began to reign; he reigned three months in Jerusalem. His mother's name was Nehushta daughter of Elnathan of Jerusalem. [9]He did what was evil in the sight of the LORD, just as his father had done.

10 At that time the servants of King Nebuchadnezzar of Babylon came up to Jerusalem, and the city was besieged. [11]King Nebuchadnezzar of Babylon came to the city, while his servants were besieging it; [12]King Jehoiachin of Judah gave himself up to the king of Babylon, himself, his mother, his servants, his officers, and his palace officials. The king of Babylon took him prisoner in the eighth year of his reign.

Capture of Jerusalem

13 He carried off all the treasures of the house of the LORD, and
the treasures of the king's house; he cut in pieces all the vessels of gold
in the temple of the LORD, which King Solomon of Israel had made,
all this as the LORD had foretold. [14]He carried away all Jerusalem, all
the officials, all the warriors, ten thousand captives, all the artisans
and the smiths; no one remained, except the poorest people of the
land. [15]He carried away Jehoiachin to Babylon; the king's mother, the
king's wives, his officials, and the elite of the land, he took into captivity from Jerusalem to Babylon. [16]The king of Babylon brought captive
to Babylon all the men of valor, seven thousand, the artisans and the
smiths, one thousand, all of them strong and fit for war. [17]The king of
Babylon made Mattaniah, Jehoiachin's uncle, king in his place, and
changed his name to Zedekiah.

24:13-17 He carried away all Jerusalem: Nebuchadnezzar takes away much of Jerusalem's wealth, in fulfillment of prophecy (see 20:12-21). He exiles about ten thousand elite citizens in 597 B.C.E., including seven thousand soldiers and one thousand artisans. Nebuchadnezzar makes Mattaniah, a son of Josiah, king and changes his name to Zedekiah.

Zedekiah Reigns over Judah

18 Zedekiah was twenty-one years old when he began to reign;
he reigned eleven years in Jerusalem. His mother's name was Hamutal daughter of Jeremiah of Libnah. [19]He did what was evil in the sight
of the LORD, just as Jehoiakim had done. [20]Indeed, Jerusalem and Judah so angered the LORD that he expelled them from his presence.

24:18—25:7 Zedekiah...began to reign: Zedekiah (597–586 B.C.E.) foolishly rebels against Nebuchadnezzar, seeking an alliance with Egypt and leading the Babylonian king to lay siege to Jerusalem. When the city wall is breached in July of 586, the king and his soldiers try to escape, but the Babylonian army overtakes them near Jericho. Zedekiah is taken to Riblah in Syria, where his sons are murdered and his eyes poked out, so that his last sight is the murder of his sons. Then he is taken to exile in Babylon.

The Fall and Captivity of Judah

25 Zedekiah rebelled against the king of Babylon. [1]And in the
ninth year of his reign, in the tenth month, on the tenth
day of the month, King Nebuchadnezzar of Babylon came with all
his army against Jerusalem, and laid siege to it; they built siegeworks
against it all around. [2]So the city was besieged until the eleventh year
of King Zedekiah. [3]On the ninth day of the fourth month the famine
became so severe in the city that there was no food for the people
of the land. [4]Then a breach was made in the city wall;[a] the king with
all the soldiers fled[b] by night by the way of the gate between the two
walls, by the king's garden, though the Chaldeans were all around
the city. They went in the direction of the Arabah. [5]But the army of
the Chaldeans pursued the king, and overtook him in the plains of
Jericho; all his army was scattered, deserting him. [6]Then they captured the king and brought him up to the king of Babylon at Riblah,
who passed sentence on him. [7]They slaughtered the sons of Zedekiah before his eyes, then put out the eyes of Zedekiah; they bound
him in fetters and took him to Babylon.

8 In the fifth month, on the seventh day of the month—which
was the nineteenth year of King Nebuchadnezzar, king of Babylon—
Nebuzaradan, the captain of the bodyguard, a servant of the king of

25:8-21 Judah went into exile out of its land: In their final attack on Jerusalem, the Babylonians destroy the temple and tear down the walls of the city. Additional elite citizens are taken into exile. Only the poorest people are left. Details of the *destruction* of the temple in 25:13-17 link to details of the *building* of the temple (see 1 Kgs 7:15-50). The high priest Seraiah and other officials are taken to Riblah, where they are killed.

[a] Heb lacks *wall* [b] Gk Compare Jer 39.4; 52.7: Heb lacks *the king* and lacks *fled*

Babylon, came to Jerusalem. [9]He burned the house of the LORD, the king's house, and all the houses of Jerusalem; every great house he burned down. [10]All the army of the Chaldeans who were with the captain of the guard broke down the walls around Jerusalem. [11]Nebuzaradan the captain of the guard carried into exile the rest of the people who were left in the city and the deserters who had defected to the king of Babylon—all the rest of the population. [12]But the captain of the guard left some of the poorest people of the land to be vinedressers and tillers of the soil.

13 The bronze pillars that were in the house of the LORD, as well as the stands and the bronze sea that were in the house of the LORD, the Chaldeans broke in pieces, and carried the bronze to Babylon. [14]They took away the pots, the shovels, the snuffers, the dishes for incense, and all the bronze vessels used in the temple service, [15]as well as the firepans and the basins. What was made of gold the captain of the guard took away for the gold, and what was made of silver, for the silver. [16]As for the two pillars, the one sea, and the stands, which Solomon had made for the house of the LORD, the bronze of all these vessels was beyond weighing. [17]The height of the one pillar was eighteen cubits, and on it was a bronze capital; the height of the capital was three cubits; latticework and pomegranates, all of bronze, were on the capital all around. The second pillar had the same, with the latticework.

18 The captain of the guard took the chief priest Seraiah, the second priest Zephaniah, and the three guardians of the threshold; [19]from the city he took an officer who had been in command of the soldiers, and five men of the king's council who were found in the city; the secretary who was the commander of the army who mustered the people of the land; and sixty men of the people of the land who were found in the city. [20]Nebuzaradan the captain of the guard took them, and brought them to the king of Babylon at Riblah. [21]The king of Babylon struck them down and put them to death at Riblah in the land of Hamath. So Judah went into exile out of its land.

Gedaliah Made Governor of Judah

22 He appointed Gedaliah son of Ahikam son of Shaphan as governor over the people who remained in the land of Judah, whom King Nebuchadnezzar of Babylon had left. [23]Now when all the captains of the forces and their men heard that the king of Babylon had appointed Gedaliah as governor, they came with their men to Gedaliah at Mizpah, namely, Ishmael son of Nethaniah, Johanan son of Kareah, Seraiah son of Tanhumeth the Netophathite, and Jaazaniah son of the Maacathite. [24]Gedaliah swore to them and their men, saying, "Do not be afraid because of the Chaldean officials; live in the land, serve the king of Babylon, and it shall be well with you." [25]But in the seventh

25:22-26 appointed Gedaliah . . . as governor over the people who remained: Gedaliah, the grandson of Shaphan (22:3) and the son of Ahikam (22:12; Jer 26:24) becomes governor and sets up his headquarters at Mizpah, about eight miles north of Jerusalem. After a few months in office he is assassinated by Ishmael and ten other men. Many of the remaining people flee to Egypt at this point, taking the prophet Jeremiah with them (Jer 43–44).

month, Ishmael son of Nethaniah son of Elishama, of the royal family, came with ten men; they struck down Gedaliah so that he died,
along with the Judeans and Chaldeans who were with him at Mizpah.
26 Then all the people, high and low,[a] and the captains of the forces set
out and went to Egypt; for they were afraid of the Chaldeans.

Jehoiachin Released from Prison

27 In the thirty-seventh year of the exile of King Jehoiachin of
Judah, in the twelfth month, on the twenty-seventh day of the month,
King Evil-merodach of Babylon, in the year that he began to reign,
released King Jehoiachin of Judah from prison; 28 he spoke kindly to
him, and gave him a seat above the other seats of the kings who were
with him in Babylon. 29 So Jehoiachin put aside his prison clothes.
Every day of his life he dined regularly in the king's presence. 30 For his
allowance, a regular allowance was given him by the king, a portion
every day, as long as he lived.

---

[a] Or *young and old*

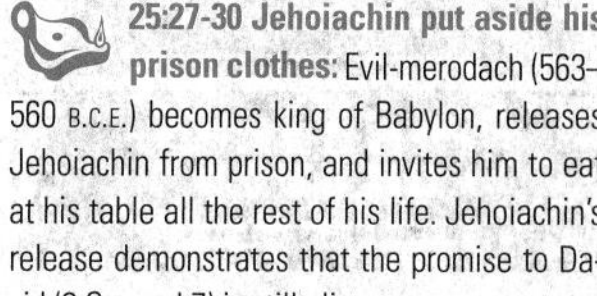

25:27-30 Jehoiachin put aside his prison clothes: Evil-merodach (563–560 B.C.E.) becomes king of Babylon, releases Jehoiachin from prison, and invites him to eat at his table all the rest of his life. Jehoiachin's release demonstrates that the promise to David (2 Samuel 7) is still alive.

What is the basis for faith and hope? The writer of the books of Samuel and Kings emphasizes God's promise to David in 2 Samuel 7 and highlights that promise once more in the final paragraph in the book of Kings. Lutherans recognize that faith and hope are based not on our words or actions but solely on God's promise to us. *2 Kings 25:29-30*

1 Chronicles 16:1

1 CHRONICLES

Background File

The two books now known as 1 and 2 Chronicles were originally a single writing titled *The Book of the Events of the Days.* They were written in Jerusalem by an anonymous author called the Chronicler sometime in the Persian period (539-332 B.C.E.). They were for the Israelites after they returned from exile in Babylon.

What's the Story?

The historical background for 1 Chronicles can be traced to the restored community of Yehud (Judah), a province in the Persian Empire. The Jewish people there had returned from exile at different times with Zerubbabel (see Ezra 1-6, 538 B.C.E.), Ezra (see Ezra 7-10, 458 B.C.E.), and Nehemiah (see Neh 1-13, 445 B.C.E.). See the introductions to Ezra and Nehemiah for additional background.

After seventy years of captivity the people had many questions. The collected history found in Joshua through 1-2 Kings had answered the exiles' questions: "Why are we here? Has God abandoned us?" The Chronicler helped his community deal with their relationship to the past and their path to the future: "Are we still the people of God? What do God's promises to David mean for us today?" The people of the Chronicler's community are now in Jerusalem, having returned from exile in Babylon.

First Chronicles falls into two major sections. The first traces the history of God's people from Adam through Israel's return from exile (chapters 1-9). The second presents the reign of David (9:35—29:30). Note especially how the listing of tribes in the first main section follows a pattern.

Israel's family tree (1:1—9:34)

- From Adam to Israel (Jacob) (1:1—2:2)
- The tribes of Israel (2:3—9:1)
    - Royal Judah (2:3—4:23)
    - Northern tribes east of Jordan (4:24—5:26)
    - Priestly Levi (6:1-81)
    - Northern tribes west of Jordan (7:1-40)
    - Royal Benjamin (8:1—9:2)
- The inhabitants of Jerusalem (9:3-34)

The reign of David (9:35–29:30)

- God rejects Saul as king (9:35–10:14)
- All Israel recognizes David as king (11:1–12:40)
- David brings the ark to Jerusalem (13:1–16:43)
- God's promise to David (17:1-27)
- David's wars (18:1–20:8)
- David prepares for the construction of the temple (21:1–29:30)

The family tree that begins 1 Chronicles is designed to help the Chronicler's community see that God's promises still applied to them. The lists of names connect the Chronicler's generation with their ancestors going all the way back to Adam.

The people were already familiar with the story of David from 2 Samuel. The Chronicler retells the story in a new way that omits many of the negative incidents of David's life, such as his adultery with Bathsheba; David's arranging the death of her husband, Uriah; Nathan's scolding of the king (2 Sam 12); and David's physical weakness at the end of his life (1 Kgs 1-2). By emphasizing David's care of the ark of the covenant, establishment of worship, and preparations for the building of the temple, David is presented as a model of faithful obedience and devotion to God.

What's the Message?

Three themes run through 1 Chronicles. First, there is a concern to connect the community in Jerusalem with its historical, geographical, and religious roots. The historical and geographical aspects of this concern appear in the long family tree at the beginning of 1 Chronicles. The central presence of the temple, prepared for by David and constructed by Solomon, also links the people with their religious heritage.

Second, recent scholarship recognizes an inclusive concern here for "all Israel," that is, all twelve tribes, both north and south. A more narrow concern for the tribes of Judah and Benjamin had often been the focus in the past. Now, every turning point in the story is marked by the enthusiastic and unanimous participation of "all Israel." This phrase occurs forty times in Chronicles, usually in direct contrast to the books of Samuel.

Third, God's promise that a descendant of David will always sit upon the throne of Israel also appears frequently. But notice in Chronicles that it is God who reigns, not David. In fact, everything depends upon God. David's desire to build the temple must wait for God's way and God's timetable. God will first build a house for David and choose the temple builder. Biblical accounts of Israel's history written in earlier times emphasized God's choice of "Israel" and "the place which the LORD has chosen." In contrast, Chronicles emphasizes God's choice of David and his family, Jerusalem and the temple, and the priests and Levites. These divine choices and God's rejection of Saul and his family confirm God's choice of David and his heirs.

Two key promises of God form the central message of the books of 1 and 2 Chronicles—God's promise to David (1 Chr 17:3-15) and God's promise of forgiveness to Solomon (2 Chr 7:11-22).

From Adam to Abraham

1:1—9:44 Adam…Saul : The first nine chapters of Chronicles are a family tree that traces Israel's roots back to Adam.

1:1—2:2 Adam…sons of Israel: Information from family trees in Genesis 5; 10–11; 25; and 35–36 is arranged so that the branch leading to Israel is presented last, stressing God's choice.

1 Adam, Seth, Enosh; 2 Kenan, Mahalalel, Jared; 3 Enoch, Methuselah, Lamech; 4 Noah, Shem, Ham, and Japheth.

5 The descendants of Japheth: Gomer, Magog, Madai, Javan,
Tubal, Meshech, and Tiras. 6 The descendants of Gomer: Ashkenaz,
Diphath,[a] and Togarmah. 7 The descendants of Javan: Elishah, Tar-
shish, Kittim, and Rodanim.[b]

8 The descendants of Ham: Cush, Egypt, Put, and Canaan. 9 The
descendants of Cush: Seba, Havilah, Sabta, Raama, and Sabteca.
The descendants of Raamah: Sheba and Dedan. 10 Cush became the
father of Nimrod; he was the first to be a mighty one on the earth.

11 Egypt became the father of Ludim, Anamim, Lehabim, Naphtuhim, 12 Pathrusim, Casluhim, and Caphtorim, from whom the
Philistines come.[c]

13 Canaan became the father of Sidon his firstborn, and Heth,
14 and the Jebusites, the Amorites, the Girgashites, 15 the Hivites, the Arkites, the Sinites, 16 the Arvadites, the Zemarites, and the Hamathites.

17 The descendants of Shem: Elam, Asshur, Arpachshad, Lud,
Aram, Uz, Hul, Gether, and Meshech.[d] 18 Arpachshad became the
father of Shelah; and Shelah became the father of Eber. 19 To Eber
were born two sons: the name of the one was Peleg (for in his days
the earth was divided), and the name of his brother Joktan. 20 Joktan became the father of Almodad, Sheleph, Hazarmaveth, Jerah,
21 Hadoram, Uzal, Diklah, 22 Ebal, Abimael, Sheba, 23 Ophir, Havilah,
and Jobab; all these were the descendants of Joktan.

24 Shem, Arpachshad, Shelah; 25 Eber, Peleg, Reu; 26 Serug, Nahor, Terah; 27 Abram, that is, Abraham.

From Abraham to Jacob

1:28-34 The sons of Abraham: The descendants of Abraham are traced through their mothers, with the primary line (Isaac) again presented last.

28 The sons of Abraham: Isaac and Ishmael. 29 These are their
genealogies: the firstborn of Ishmael, Nebaioth; and Kedar, Adbeel,
Mibsam, 30 Mishma, Dumah, Massa, Hadad, Tema, 31 Jetur, Naphish,
and Kedemah. These are the sons of Ishmael. 32 The sons of Keturah,
Abraham's concubine: she bore Zimran, Jokshan, Medan, Midian,
Ishbak, and Shuah. The sons of Jokshan: Sheba and Dedan. 33 The
sons of Midian: Ephah, Epher, Hanoch, Abida, and Eldaah. All these
were the descendants of Keturah.

1:35-54 The sons of Esau: The pattern of presenting the secondary line (Esau) first continues.

34 Abraham became the father of Isaac. The sons of Isaac: Esau
and Israel. 35 The sons of Esau: Eliphaz, Reuel, Jeush, Jalam, and Korah. 36 The sons of Eliphaz: Teman, Omar, Zephi, Gatam, Kenaz,
Timna, and Amalek. 37 The sons of Reuel: Nahath, Zerah, Shammah,
and Mizzah.

---

[a] Gen 10.3 *Ripath*; See Gk Vg [b] Gen 10.4 *Dodanim*; See Syr Vg [c] Heb *Casluhim, from which the Philistines come, Caphtorim*; See Am 9.7, Jer 47.4 [d] *Mash* in Gen 10.23

38 The sons of Seir: Lotan, Shobal, Zibeon, Anah, Dishon, Ezer,
and Dishan. 39 The sons of Lotan: Hori and Homam; and Lotan's sister was Timna. 40 The sons of Shobal: Alian, Manahath, Ebal, Shephi,
and Onam. The sons of Zibeon: Aiah and Anah. 41 The sons of Anah:
Dishon. The sons of Dishon: Hamran, Eshban, Ithran, and Cheran.
42 The sons of Ezer: Bilhan, Zaavan, and Jaakan.[a] The sons of Dishan:[b]
Uz and Aran.

43 These are the kings who reigned in the land of Edom before
any king reigned over the Israelites: Bela son of Beor, whose city was
called Dinhabah. 44 When Bela died, Jobab son of Zerah of Bozrah
succeeded him. 45 When Jobab died, Husham of the land of the Temanites succeeded him. 46 When Husham died, Hadad son of Bedad,
who defeated Midian in the country of Moab, succeeded him; and the
name of his city was Avith. 47 When Hadad died, Samlah of Masrekah
succeeded him. 48 When Samlah died, Shaul[c] of Rehoboth on the Euphrates succeeded him. 49 When Shaul[c] died, Baal-hanan son of Achbor succeeded him. 50 When Baal-hanan died, Hadad succeeded him;
the name of his city was Pai, and his wife's name Mehetabel daughter
of Matred, daughter of Me-zahab. 51 And Hadad died.

The clans[d] of Edom were: clans[d] Timna, Aliah,[e] Jetheth, 52 Oholibamah, Elah, Pinon, 53 Kenaz, Teman, Mibzar, 54 Magdiel, and Iram;
these are the clans[d] of Edom.

The Sons of Israel and the Descendants of Judah

2 These are the sons of Israel: Reuben, Simeon, Levi, Judah, Issachar, Zebulun, 2 Dan, Joseph, Benjamin, Naphtali, Gad, and
Asher. 3 The sons of Judah: Er, Onan, and Shelah; these three the
Canaanite woman Bath-shua bore to him. Now Er, Judah's firstborn,
was wicked in the sight of the LORD, and he put him to death. 4 His
daughter-in-law Tamar also bore him Perez and Zerah. Judah had five
sons in all.

5 The sons of Perez: Hezron and Hamul. 6 The sons of Zerah:
Zimri, Ethan, Heman, Calcol, and Dara,[f] five in all. 7 The sons of
Carmi: Achar, the troubler of Israel, who transgressed in the matter of
the devoted thing; 8 and Ethan's son was Azariah.

9 The sons of Hezron, who were born to him: Jerahmeel, Ram,
and Chelubai. 10 Ram became the father of Amminadab, and Amminadab became the father of Nahshon, prince of the sons of Judah.
11 Nahshon became the father of Salma, Salma of Boaz, 12 Boaz of
Obed, Obed of Jesse. 13 Jesse became the father of Eliab his firstborn,
Abinadab the second, Shimea the third, 14 Nethanel the fourth, Rad-
dai the fifth, 15 Ozem the sixth, David the seventh; 16 and their sisters

---

[a] Or *and Akan*; See Gen 36.27 [b] See 1.38: Heb *Dishon* [c] Or *Saul* [d] Or *chiefs* [e] Or *Alvah*; See Gen 36.40 [f] Or *Darda*; Compare Syr Tg some Gk Mss; See 1 Kings 4.31

2:1-2 the sons of Israel: The Chronicler always refers to Jacob as "Israel." By including Levi and Joseph, the chronicler presents a full listing of Israel's sons and concern for all Israel.

2:3–9:1 So all Israel was enrolled by genealogies: See the outline of this section in the introduction (p. 638). Notice how the arrangement of these lists forms a pattern that emphasizes the tribes of Judah, Benjamin, and Levi. These had supported David when the other tribes broke away (922 B.C.E.). These three tribes became the Chronicler's community.

The royal tribe of Judah (2:3—4:23) comes first, because "a ruler [David, see 11:2; 17:7] came from him" (5:2). Benjamin, an ancestor of King Saul, balances the royal claim at the end (8:1-40). The priestly tribe of Levi anchors the middle (6:1-81). The family trees of the northern tribes east of the Jordan River (5:1-26) have been placed between Judah and Levi to balance the northern tribes of the Jordan's western bank, which are placed between Levi and Benjamin (7:1-40). This careful arrangement emphasizes the royal tribes of Judah and Benjamin and the priestly tribe of Levi. It also introduces the Chronicler's primary concerns of king and Israel's religion life. The inclusion of the northern tribes indicates a concern for all Israel. See Map 4, p. 2102.

2:3—4:23 the sons of Judah: The names listed in this section come from the tribe of Judah. The pattern of presenting secondary lines first is reversed. Judah, born fourth among the sons of Israel (2:1), appears first. The list falls into five parts. At the center is David's clan, the family of Hezron (2:9—3:24). Framing this are Judah's twin sons Perez and Zerah (2:5-8; 4:1-20). The divided presentation of Shelah's descendants surrounds the whole (2:3-4; 4:21-23).

2:3-4 these three the Canaanite woman: Judah's first three sons were born to Judah's Canaanite wife, "the daughter of Shua" (not Bath-shua as in NRSV; see Gen 38). Er angered God and was put to death. Judah's two other sons, Perez and Zerah, were the product of an incestuous relationship with his daughter-in-law, Tamar. God's judgment is seen in the killing of Er, but God works grace through the ill-conceived line of Perez. David, and even Jesus (Matt 1:3), will come from this line, suggesting that God can bring good even out of human sin.

were Zeruiah and Abigail. The sons of Zeruiah: Abishai, Joab, and Asahel, three. [17]Abigail bore Amasa, and the father of Amasa was Jether the Ishmaelite.

18 Caleb son of Hezron had children by his wife Azubah, and by Jerioth; these were her sons: Jesher, Shobab, and Ardon. [19]When Azubah died, Caleb married Ephrath, who bore him Hur. [20]Hur became the father of Uri, and Uri became the father of Bezalel.

21 Afterward Hezron went in to the daughter of Machir father of Gilead, whom he married when he was sixty years old; and she bore him Segub; [22]and Segub became the father of Jair, who had twenty-three towns in the land of Gilead. [23]But Geshur and Aram took from them Havvoth-jair, Kenath and its villages, sixty towns. All these were descendants of Machir, father of Gilead. [24]After the death of Hezron, in Caleb-ephrathah, Abijah wife of Hezron bore him Ashhur, father of Tekoa.

25 The sons of Jerahmeel, the firstborn of Hezron: Ram his firstborn, Bunah, Oren, Ozem, and Ahijah. [26]Jerahmeel also had another wife, whose name was Atarah; she was the mother of Onam. [27]The sons of Ram, the firstborn of Jerahmeel: Maaz, Jamin, and Eker. [28]The sons of Onam: Shammai and Jada. The sons of Shammai: Nadab and Abishur. [29]The name of Abishur's wife was Abihail, and she bore him Ahban and Molid. [30]The sons of Nadab: Seled and Appaim; and Seled died childless. [31]The son[a] of Appaim: Ishi. The son[a] of Ishi: Sheshan. The son[a] of Sheshan: Ahlai. [32]The sons of Jada, Shammai's brother: Jether and Jonathan; and Jether died childless. [33]The sons of Jonathan: Peleth and Zaza. These were the descendants of Jerahmeel. [34]Now Sheshan had no sons, only daughters; but Sheshan had an Egyptian slave, whose name was Jarha. [35]So Sheshan gave his daughter in marriage to his slave Jarha; and she bore him Attai. [36]Attai became the father of Nathan, and Nathan of Zabad. [37]Zabad became the father of Ephlal, and Ephlal of Obed. [38]Obed became the father of Jehu, and Jehu of Azariah. [39]Azariah became the father of Helez, and Helez of Eleasah. [40]Eleasah became the father of Sismai, and Sismai of Shallum. [41]Shallum became the father of Jekamiah, and Jekamiah of Elishama.

42 The sons of Caleb brother of Jerahmeel: Mesha[b] his firstborn, who was father of Ziph. The sons of Mareshah father of Hebron. [43]The sons of Hebron: Korah, Tappuah, Rekem, and Shema. [44]Shema became father of Raham, father of Jorkeam; and Rekem became the father of Shammai. [45]The son of Shammai: Maon; and Maon was the father of Beth-zur. [46]Ephah also, Caleb's concubine, bore Haran, Moza, and Gazez; and Haran became the father of Gazez. [47]The sons of Jahdai: Regem, Jotham, Geshan, Pelet, Ephah, and Shaaph. [48]Ma-

---

[a] Heb *sons* [b] Gk reads *Mareshah*

acah, Caleb's concubine, bore Sheber and Tirhanah. [49]She also bore Shaaph father of Madmannah, Sheva father of Machbenah and father of Gibea; and the daughter of Caleb was Achsah. [50]These were the descendants of Caleb.

The sons[a] of Hur the firstborn of Ephrathah: Shobal father of Kiriath-jearim, [51]Salma father of Bethlehem, and Hareph father of Beth-gader. [52]Shobal father of Kiriath-jearim had other sons: Haroeh, half of the Menuhoth. [53]And the families of Kiriath-jearim: the Ithrites, the Puthites, the Shumathites, and the Mishraites; from these came the Zorathites and the Eshtaolites. [54]The sons of Salma: Bethlehem, the Netophathites, Atroth-beth-joab, and half of the Manahathites, the Zorites. [55]The families also of the scribes that lived at Jabez: the Tirathites, the Shimeathites, and the Sucathites. These are the Kenites who came from Hammath, father of the house of Rechab.

Descendants of David and Solomon

3 These are the sons of David who were born to him in Hebron: the firstborn Amnon, by Ahinoam the Jezreelite; the second Daniel, by Abigail the Carmelite; [2]the third Absalom, son of Maacah, daughter of King Talmai of Geshur; the fourth Adonijah, son of Haggith; [3]the fifth Shephatiah, by Abital; the sixth Ithream, by his wife Eglah; [4]six were born to him in Hebron, where he reigned for seven years and six months. And he reigned thirty-three years in Jerusalem. [5]These were born to him in Jerusalem: Shimea, Shobab, Nathan, and Solomon, four by Bath-shua, daughter of Ammiel; [6]then Ibhar, Elishama, Eliphelet, [7]Nogah, Nepheg, Japhia, [8]Elishama, Eliada, and Eliphelet, nine. [9]All these were David's sons, besides the sons of the concubines; and Tamar was their sister.

10 The descendants of Solomon: Rehoboam, Abijah his son, Asa his son, Jehoshaphat his son, [11]Joram his son, Ahaziah his son, Joash his son, [12]Amaziah his son, Azariah his son, Jotham his son, [13]Ahaz his son, Hezekiah his son, Manasseh his son, [14]Amon his son, Josiah his son. [15]The sons of Josiah: Johanan the firstborn, the second Jehoiakim, the third Zedekiah, the fourth Shallum. [16]The descendants of Jehoiakim: Jeconiah his son, Zedekiah his son; [17]and the sons of Jeconiah, the captive: Shealtiel his son, [18]Malchiram, Pedaiah, Shenazzar, Jekamiah, Hoshama, and Nedabiah; [19]The sons of Pedaiah: Zerubbabel and Shimei; and the sons of Zerubbabel: Meshullam and Hananiah, and Shelomith was their sister; [20]and Hashubah, Ohel, Berechiah, Hasadiah, and Jushab-hesed, five. [21]The sons of Hananiah: Pelatiah and Jeshaiah, his son[b] Rephaiah, his son[b] Arnan, his son[b] Obadiah, his son[b] Shecaniah. [22]The son[c] of Shecaniah: Shemaiah. And the sons of Shemaiah: Hattush, Igal, Bariah, Neariah, and Shaphat, six. [23]The

3:1-24 sons of David: The family of David appears at the center of the arrangement of Judah's family tree.

3:1-9 sons of David: This is the most complete listing in the Old Testament of David's immediate family.

3:10-16 Solomon…Zedekiah: This is a complete listing of the kings of Judah. Ahab's daughter Athaliah, who had illegally seized the throne (2 Kgs 11:1-3), is intentionally omitted.

3:19 Zerubbabel: Zerubbabel was the first governor of the Persian province of Yehud (Judah) after the exile. As a descendant of David, he establishes continuity with the Chronicler's community.

---

[a] Gk Vg: Heb *son* [b] Gk Compare Syr Vg: Heb *sons of* [c] Heb *sons*

sons of Neariah: Elioenai, Hizkiah, and Azrikam, three. 24 The sons of
Elioenai: Hodaviah, Eliashib, Pelaiah, Akkub, Johanan, Delaiah, and
Anani, seven.

Descendants of Judah

4 The sons of Judah: Perez, Hezron, Carmi, Hur, and Shobal.
2 Reaiah son of Shobal became the father of Jahath, and Jahath
became the father of Ahumai and Lahad. These were the families of
the Zorathites. 3 These were the sons[a] of Etam: Jezreel, Ishma, and
Idbash; and the name of their sister was Hazzelelponi, 4 and Penuel
was the father of Gedor, and Ezer the father of Hushah. These were
the sons of Hur, the firstborn of Ephrathah, the father of Bethlehem.
5 Ashhur father of Tekoa had two wives, Helah and Naarah; 6 Naarah
bore him Ahuzzam, Hepher, Temeni, and Haahashtari.[b] These were
the sons of Naarah. 7 The sons of Helah: Zereth, Izhar,[c] and Eth-
nan. 8 Koz became the father of Anub, Zobebah, and the families of
Aharhel son of Harum. 9 Jabez was honored more than his brothers;
and his mother named him Jabez, saying, "Because I bore him in
pain." 10 Jabez called on the God of Israel, saying, "Oh that you would
bless me and enlarge my border, and that your hand might be with
me, and that you would keep me from hurt and harm!" And God
granted what he asked. 11 Chelub the brother of Shuhah became the
father of Mehir, who was the father of Eshton. 12 Eshton became the
father of Beth-rapha, Paseah, and Tehinnah the father of Ir-nahash.
These are the men of Recah. 13 The sons of Kenaz: Othniel and Seraiah; and the sons of Othniel: Hathath and Meonothai.[d] 14 Meonothai
became the father of Ophrah; and Seraiah became the father of Joab
father of Ge-harashim,[e] so-called because they were artisans. 15 The
sons of Caleb son of Jephunneh: Iru, Elah, and Naam; and the son[f]
of Elah: Kenaz. 16 The sons of Jehallelel: Ziph, Ziphah, Tiria, and As-
arel. 17 The sons of Ezrah: Jether, Mered, Epher, and Jalon. These are
the sons of Bithiah, daughter of Pharaoh, whom Mered married;[g]
and she conceived and bore[h] Miriam, Shammai, and Ishbah father
of Eshtemoa. 18 And his Judean wife bore Jered father of Gedor, Heber father of Soco, and Jekuthiel father of Zanoah. 19 The sons of the
wife of Hodiah, the sister of Naham, were the fathers of Keilah the
Garmite and Eshtemoa the Maacathite. 20 The sons of Shimon: Amnon, Rinnah, Ben-hanan, and Tilon. The sons of Ishi: Zoheth and
Ben-zoheth. 21 The sons of Shelah son of Judah: Er father of Lecah,
Laadah father of Mareshah, and the families of the guild of linen
workers at Beth-ashbea; 22 and Jokim, and the men of Cozeba, and
Joash, and Saraph, who married into Moab but returned to Lehem[i]

[a] Gk Compare Vg: Heb *the father* [b] Or *Ahashtari* [c] Another reading is *Zohar* [d] Gk Vg: Heb lacks *and Meonothai* [e] That is *Valley of artisans* [f] Heb *sons* [g] The clause: *These are . . . married* is transposed from verse 18 [h] Heb lacks *and bore* [i] Vg Compare Gk: Heb *and Jashubi-lahem*

4:9-10 Jabez called on the God of Israel: In Hebrew, *Jabez* sounds like "pain." Since one's name was thought to influence one's life, his prayer was an attempt to undo this negative suggestion. God's positive response is the first reference to the Chronicler's belief that God rewards or punishes in a fair way. Those who act in evil ways or are unfaithful receive punishment. Those who are good or faithful are rewarded.

The text doesn't say exactly why God granted Jabez's prayer request. In your experience, how are prayers answered? How has God answered your prayers?

(now the records[a] are ancient). 23 These were the potters and inhabitants of Netaim and Gederah; they lived there with the king in his
service.

Descendants of Simeon

24 The sons of Simeon: Nemuel, Jamin, Jarib, Zerah, Shaul;[b]
25 Shallum was his son, Mibsam his son, Mishma his son. 26 The
sons of Mishma: Hammuel his son, Zaccur his son, Shimei his son.
27 Shimei had sixteen sons and six daughters; but his brothers did not
have many children, nor did all their family multiply like the Judeans.
28 They lived in Beer-sheba, Moladah, Hazar-shual, 29 Bilhah, Ezem,
Tolad, 30 Bethuel, Hormah, Ziklag, 31 Beth-marcaboth, Hazar-susim,
Beth-biri, and Shaaraim. These were their towns until David became king. 32 And their villages were Etam, Ain, Rimmon, Tochen,
and Ashan, five towns, 33 along with all their villages that were around
these towns as far as Baal. These were their settlements. And they kept
a genealogical record.
34 Meshobab, Jamlech, Joshah son of Amaziah, 35 Joel, Jehu son of
Joshibiah son of Seraiah son of Asiel, 36 Elioenai, Jaakobah, Jeshoha-
iah, Asaiah, Adiel, Jesimiel, Benaiah, 37 Ziza son of Shiphi son of Allon
son of Jedaiah son of Shimri son of Shemaiah— 38 these mentioned
by name were leaders in their families, and their clans increased
greatly. 39 They journeyed to the entrance of Gedor, to the east side
of the valley, to seek pasture for their flocks, 40 where they found rich,
good pasture, and the land was very broad, quiet, and peaceful; for
the former inhabitants there belonged to Ham. 41 These, registered
by name, came in the days of King Hezekiah of Judah, and attacked
their tents and the Meunim who were found there, and exterminated
them to this day, and settled in their place, because there was pasture
there for their flocks. 42 And some of them, five hundred men of the
Simeonites, went to Mount Seir, having as their leaders Pelatiah, Neariah, Rephaiah, and Uzziel, sons of Ishi; 43 they destroyed the remnant of the Amalekites that had escaped, and they have lived there to
this day.

Descendants of Reuben

5 The sons of Reuben the firstborn of Israel. (He was the firstborn, but because he defiled his father's bed his birthright was
given to the sons of Joseph son of Israel, so that he is not enrolled
in the genealogy according to the birthright; 2 though Judah became
prominent among his brothers and a ruler came from him, yet the
birthright belonged to Joseph.) 3 The sons of Reuben, the firstborn
of Israel: Hanoch, Pallu, Hezron, and Carmi. 4 The sons of Joel:

[a] Or *matters*   [b] Or *Saul*

5:1-26 Reuben . . . Gad . . . Manasseh: The tribes of Reuben (5:1-10), Gad (5:11-22), and the half-tribe of Manasseh (5:23-26) are located on the eastern bank of the Jordan River and represent the northern tribes defeated by Assyria in 721 B.C.E. The Chronicler sees them as one (compare 5:18, 26). See Map 4, p. 2102.

5:1 the firstborn of Israel: The firstborn son inherited two-thirds of the property and became the leader of the family (Deut 21:15-17). Reuben's privilege was transferred to the sons of Joseph (Ephraim and Manasseh) because of his incest with Bilhah, Joseph's concubine (see Gen 35:22; 49:3-4).

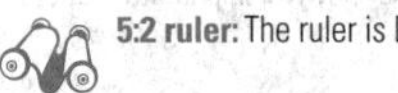

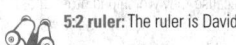

5:2 ruler: The ruler is David.

5:6 Tilgath-pilneser: Another spelling of Tiglath-pileser III, the Assyrian king (744–727 B.C.E.). The exile of Beerah took place in 733 B.C.E.

Shemaiah his son, Gog his son, Shimei his son, [5]Micah his son, Reaiah his son, Baal his son, [6]Beerah his son, whom King Tilgath-pilneser of Assyria carried away into exile; he was a chieftain of the Reubenites. [7]And his kindred by their families, when the genealogy of their generations was reckoned: the chief, Jeiel, and Zechariah, [8]and Bela son of Azaz, son of Shema, son of Joel, who lived in Aroer, as far as Nebo and Baal-meon. [9]He also lived to the east as far as the beginning of the desert this side of the Euphrates, because their cattle had multiplied in the land of Gilead. [10]And in the days of Saul they made war on the Hagrites, who fell by their hand; and they lived in their tents throughout all the region east of Gilead.

Descendants of Gad

11 The sons of Gad lived beside them in the land of Bashan as far as Salecah: [12]Joel the chief, Shapham the second, Janai, and Shaphat in Bashan. [13]And their kindred according to their clans: Michael, Meshullam, Sheba, Jorai, Jacan, Zia, and Eber, seven. [14]These were the sons of Abihail son of Huri, son of Jaroah, son of Gilead, son of Michael, son of Jeshishai, son of Jahdo, son of Buz; [15]Ahi son of Abdiel, son of Guni, was chief in their clan; [16]and they lived in Gilead, in Bashan and in its towns, and in all the pasture lands of Sharon to their limits. [17]All of these were enrolled by genealogies in the days of King Jotham of Judah, and in the days of King Jeroboam of Israel.

5:18-22 valiant warriors…made war: The exaggerated numbers in these verses portray the battle as a holy war in which God grants victory to those who demonstrate their faith through prayer. This belief in God's retributive justice (rewarding faith and punishing sin) is a major theme in Chronicles.

18 The Reubenites, the Gadites, and the half-tribe of Manasseh had valiant warriors, who carried shield and sword, and drew the bow, expert in war, forty-four thousand seven hundred sixty, ready for service. [19]They made war on the Hagrites, Jetur, Naphish, and Nodab; [20]and when they received help against them, the Hagrites and all who were with them were given into their hands, for they cried to God in the battle, and he granted their entreaty because they trusted in him. [21]They captured their livestock: fifty thousand of their camels, two hundred fifty thousand sheep, two thousand donkeys, and one hundred thousand captives. [22]Many fell slain, because the war was of God. And they lived in their territory until the exile.

5:22 until the exile: This refers to the exile that occurred when the Assyrians deported people from the northern tribes of Israel in 722 B.C.E.

The Half-Tribe of Manasseh

23 The members of the half-tribe of Manasseh lived in the land; they were very numerous from Bashan to Baal-hermon, Senir, and Mount Hermon. [24]These were the heads of their clans: Epher,[a] Ishi, Eliel, Azriel, Jeremiah, Hodaviah, and Jahdiel, mighty warriors, famous men, heads of their clans. [25]But they transgressed against the God of their ancestors, and prostituted themselves to the gods of the peoples of the land, whom God had destroyed before them. [26]So the God of

5:25-26 they transgressed…God …carried them away: God hands out the justice the people deserve. They are defeated in battle and handed over to the Assyrians because they worshiped other gods.

---

[a] Gk Vg: Heb *and Epher*

Israel stirred up the spirit of King Pul of Assyria, the spirit of King Tilgath-pilneser of Assyria, and he carried them away, namely, the Reubenites, the Gadites, and the half-tribe of Manasseh, and brought them to Halah, Habor, Hara, and the river Gozan, to this day.

Descendants of Levi

6 [a] The sons of Levi: Gershom,[b] Kohath, and Merari. 2 The sons of Kohath: Amram, Izhar, Hebron, and Uzziel. 3 The children of Amram: Aaron, Moses, and Miriam. The sons of Aaron: Nadab, Abihu, Eleazar, and Ithamar. 4 Eleazar became the father of Phinehas, Phinehas of Abishua, 5 Abishua of Bukki, Bukki of Uzzi, 6 Uzzi of Zerahiah, Zerahiah of Meraioth, 7 Meraioth of Amariah, Amariah of Ahitub, 8 Ahitub of Zadok, Zadok of Ahimaaz, 9 Ahimaaz of Azariah, Azariah of Johanan, 10 and Johanan of Azariah (it was he who served as priest in the house that Solomon built in Jerusalem). 11 Azariah became the father of Amariah, Amariah of Ahitub, 12 Ahitub of Zadok, Zadok of Shallum, 13 Shallum of Hilkiah, Hilkiah of Azariah, 14 Azariah of Seraiah, Seraiah of Jehozadak; 15 and Jehozadak went into exile when the LORD sent Judah and Jerusalem into exile by the hand of Nebuchadnezzar.

16 [c] The sons of Levi: Gershom, Kohath, and Merari. 17 These are the names of the sons of Gershom: Libni and Shimei. 18 The sons of Kohath: Amram, Izhar, Hebron, and Uzziel. 19 The sons of Merari: Mahli and Mushi. These are the clans of the Levites according to their ancestry. 20 Of Gershom: Libni his son, Jahath his son, Zimmah his son, 21 Joah his son, Iddo his son, Zerah his son, Jeatherai his son. 22 The sons of Kohath: Amminadab his son, Korah his son, Assir his son, 23 Elkanah his son, Ebiasaph his son, Assir his son, 24 Tahath his son, Uriel his son, Uzziah his son, and Shaul his son. 25 The sons of Elkanah: Amasai and Ahimoth, 26 Elkanah his son, Zophai his son, Nahath his son, 27 Eliab his son, Jeroham his son, Elkanah his son. 28 The sons of Samuel: Joel[d] his firstborn, the second Abijah.[e] 29 The sons of Merari: Mahli, Libni his son, Shimei his son, Uzzah his son, 30 Shimea his son, Haggiah his son, and Asaiah his son.

Musicians Appointed by David

31 These are the men whom David put in charge of the service of song in the house of the LORD, after the ark came to rest there. 32 They ministered with song before the tabernacle of the tent of meeting, until Solomon had built the house of the LORD in Jerusalem; and they performed their service in due order. 33 These are the men who served; and their sons were: Of the Kohathites: Heman, the singer,

[a] Ch 5.27 in Heb [b] Heb *Gershon*, variant of *Gershom*; See 6.16 [c] Ch 6.1 in Heb [d] Gk Syr Compare verse 33 and 1 Sam 8.2: Heb lacks *Joel* [e] Heb reads *Vashni, and Abijah* for *the second Abijah*, taking *the second* as a proper name

6:1-81 sons of Levi: Notice how the Chronicler indicates the importance of the priests by the length and the central location of their family tree within the arrangement of the tribal listings. In Chronicles, the descendants of Aaron were the priests, the rest of the tribe of Levi were Levites, who fulfilled lesser roles in the temple. According to the Chronicler, David organized the Levites, even though the temple was built later by Solomon.

6:1-15 sons of Aaron: The list is not complete. Eli (1 Sam 2:27-36), Jehoiada (2 Chr 22:11), Uriah (2 Kgs 16:10-16), and at least two other Azariahs (2 Chr 26:20; 31:10-13) are missing. The high priesthood was hereditary and for life after Jeshua (see Ezra 3:8). It is clear from Ezekiel 40–48 that there were no high priests before the exile. This, of course, complicates the reported earlier history.

6:4 Phinehas: Phinehas' decisive action in a religious crisis earned God's promise that his descendants would always be priests (Num 25:1-13).

6:8 Zadok: When Abiathar supported Adonijah rather than Solomon for king, Solomon made Zadok the high priest, restoring the high priesthood to the line of Phinehas (see 1 Kgs 1:5—2:35). God had promised that Phineas' descendants would always be priests (Num 25:11-13).

6:13 Hilkiah: When Hilkiah, the high priest, found the book of the law in the temple, Judah's King Josiah was persuaded to carry out the religious reforms of 622 B.C.E. (2 Chr 34:14-21; 2 Kgs 22:8-13).

6:16-48 the Levites: The Levites descended from Levi serve as priests in Israel. The descendants of Moses' brother Aaron are also priests, and they are distinct from Levites. The three central Levitical branches were Gershom (6:17, 20-21), Kohath (6:18, 22-28), and Merari (6:19, 29-30). The duties of these Levite clans are described in detail in Numbers 4:1—5:31.

son of Joel, son of Samuel, [34]son of Elkanah, son of Jeroham, son of Eliel, son of Toah, [35]son of Zuph, son of Elkanah, son of Mahath, son of Amasai, [36]son of Elkanah, son of Joel, son of Azariah, son of Zephaniah, [37]son of Tahath, son of Assir, son of Ebiasaph, son of Korah, [38]son of Izhar, son of Kohath, son of Levi, son of Israel; [39]and his brother Asaph, who stood on his right, namely, Asaph son of Berechiah, son of Shimea, [40]son of Michael, son of Baaseiah, son of Malchijah, [41]son of Ethni, son of Zerah, son of Adaiah, [42]son of Ethan, son of Zimmah, son of Shimei, [43]son of Jahath, son of Gershom, son of Levi. [44]On the left were their kindred the sons of Merari: Ethan son of Kishi, son of Abdi, son of Malluch, [45]son of Hashabiah, son of Amaziah, son of Hilkiah, [46]son of Amzi, son of Bani, son of Shemer, [47]son of Mahli, son of Mushi, son of Merari, son of Levi; [48]and their kindred the Levites were appointed for all the service of the tabernacle of the house of God.

49 But Aaron and his sons made offerings on the altar of burnt offering and on the altar of incense, doing all the work of the most holy place, to make atonement for Israel, according to all that Moses the servant of God had commanded. [50]These are the sons of Aaron: Eleazar his son, Phinehas his son, Abishua his son, [51]Bukki his son, Uzzi his son, Zerahiah his son, [52]Meraioth his son, Amariah his son, Ahitub his son, [53]Zadok his son, Ahimaaz his son.

Settlements of the Levites

54 These are their dwelling places according to their settlements within their borders: to the sons of Aaron of the families of Kohathites—for the lot fell to them first— [55]to them they gave Hebron in the land of Judah and its surrounding pasture lands, [56]but the fields of the city and its villages they gave to Caleb son of Jephunneh. [57]To the sons of Aaron they gave the cities of refuge: Hebron, Libnah with its pasture lands, Jattir, Eshtemoa with its pasture lands, [58]Hilen[a] with its pasture lands, Debir with its pasture lands, [59]Ashan with its pasture lands, and Beth-shemesh with its pasture lands. [60]From the tribe of Benjamin, Geba with its pasture lands, Alemeth with its pasture lands, and Anathoth with its pasture lands. All their towns throughout their families were thirteen.

61 To the rest of the Kohathites were given by lot out of the family of the tribe, out of the half-tribe, the half of Manasseh, ten towns. [62]To the Gershomites according to their families were allotted thirteen towns out of the tribes of Issachar, Asher, Naphtali, and Manasseh in Bashan. [63]To the Merarites according to their families were allotted twelve towns out of the tribes of Reuben, Gad, and Zebulun. [64]So the people of Israel gave the Levites the towns with their pasture

6:49-53 Aaron and his sons: The priestly line (6:1-15) resumes and provides a framework around the information about the Levites (6:16-48). Their duties are listed, including leading in music and providing security as gatekeepers (chapters 25–26), teaching and administration among the people (9:26), and even prophesying (25:2-3). These are to be distinguished from the duties of the priests, who alone could make offerings (Exod 27:1-8), burn incense (Exod 30:1-10), and make atonement, or the covering of people's sins before God (Lev 4:31; 16:1-34).

6:54-81 dwelling places…the sons of Aaron: The tribe of Levi received these towns and the surrounding pasturelands instead of a share of the land of Canaan (Deut 10:9). The Levites did not possess them, but they received special privileges and property rights within them (Lev 25:32-34). This stressed God's ownership of the land and God's promise to provide for the Levites.

---

[a] Other readings *Hilez, Holon*; See Josh 21.15

lands. 65 They also gave them by lot out of the tribes of Judah, Simeon,
and Benjamin these towns that are mentioned by name.

66 And some of the families of the sons of Kohath had towns of
their territory out of the tribe of Ephraim. 67 They were given the cities of refuge: Shechem with its pasture lands in the hill country of
Ephraim, Gezer with its pasture lands, 68 Jokmeam with its pasture
lands, Beth-horon with its pasture lands, 69 Aijalon with its pasture
lands, Gath-rimmon with its pasture lands; 70 and out of the half-tribe
of Manasseh, Aner with its pasture lands, and Bileam with its pasture
lands, for the rest of the families of the Kohathites.

71 To the Gershomites: out of the half-tribe of Manasseh: Golan
in Bashan with its pasture lands and Ashtaroth with its pasture lands;
72 and out of the tribe of Issachar: Kedesh with its pasture lands, Daberath[a] with its pasture lands, 73 Ramoth with its pasture lands, and
Anem with its pasture lands; 74 out of the tribe of Asher: Mashal with
its pasture lands, Abdon with its pasture lands, 75 Hukok with its pasture lands, and Rehob with its pasture lands; 76 and out of the tribe of
Naphtali: Kedesh in Galilee with its pasture lands, Hammon with its
pasture lands, and Kiriathaim with its pasture lands. 77 To the rest of
the Merarites out of the tribe of Zebulun: Rimmono with its pasture
lands, Tabor with its pasture lands, 78 and across the Jordan from
Jericho, on the east side of the Jordan, out of the tribe of Reuben:
Bezer in the steppe with its pasture lands, Jahzah with its pasture
lands, 79 Kedemoth with its pasture lands, and Mephaath with its pasture lands; 80 and out of the tribe of Gad: Ramoth in Gilead with its
pasture lands, Mahanaim with its pasture lands, 81 Heshbon with its
pasture lands, and Jazer with its pasture lands.

Descendants of Issachar

7 The sons[b] of Issachar: Tola, Puah, Jashub, and Shimron, four.
2 The sons of Tola: Uzzi, Rephaiah, Jeriel, Jahmai, Ibsam, and
Shemuel, heads of their ancestral houses, namely of Tola, mighty
warriors of their generations, their number in the days of David being
twenty-two thousand six hundred. 3 The son[c] of Uzzi: Izrahiah. And
the sons of Izrahiah: Michael, Obadiah, Joel, and Isshiah, five, all of
them chiefs; 4 and along with them, by their generations, according
to their ancestral houses, were units of the fighting force, thirty-six
thousand, for they had many wives and sons. 5 Their kindred belonging to all the families of Issachar were in all eighty-seven thousand
mighty warriors, enrolled by genealogy.

Descendants of Benjamin

6 The sons of Benjamin: Bela, Becher, and Jediael, three. 7 The
sons of Bela: Ezbon, Uzzi, Uzziel, Jerimoth, and Iri, five, heads of

---

[a] Or *Dobrath* [b] Syr Compare Vg: Heb *And to the sons* [c] Heb *sons*

7:1-40 sons of Issachar...Ulla: These lists are drawn from military lists in the time of David (see the numerical data in 7:2, 4, 5, 7, 9, 11). They complete the tribal genealogies begun in 2:1. These northern tribes west of the Jordan balance the northern tribes east of the Jordan in chapter 5. See Map 4, p. 2102.

7:1 Issachar: The fifth son of Jacob and Leah (Gen 30:16-18).

7:6 Benjamin: The youngest son of Jacob and Rachel (Gen 35:16-18). Benjamin's descendants are listed again in 1 Chronicles 8.

ancestral houses, mighty warriors; and their enrollment by genealogies was twenty-two thousand thirty-four. 8 The sons of Becher: Zemirah, Joash, Eliezer, Elioenai, Omri, Jeremoth, Abijah, Anathoth, and Alemeth. All these were the sons of Becher; 9 and their enrollment by genealogies, according to their generations, as heads of their ancestral houses, mighty warriors, was twenty thousand two hundred. 10 The sons of Jediael: Bilhan. And the sons of Bilhan: Jeush, Benjamin, Ehud, Chenaanah, Zethan, Tarshish, and Ahishahar. 11 All these were the sons of Jediael according to the heads of their ancestral houses, mighty warriors, seventeen thousand two hundred, ready for service in war. 12 And Shuppim and Huppim were the sons of Ir, Hushim the son[a] of Aher.

Descendants of Naphtali

7:13 Naphtali: The son of Jacob and Rachel's servant Bilhah (Gen 30:1-8).

13 The descendants of Naphtali: Jahziel, Guni, Jezer, and Shallum, the descendants of Bilhah.

Descendants of Manasseh

7:14, 20 Manasseh . . . Ephraim: Manasseh and Ephraim were the sons of Jacob's son Joseph. Each of their families received a share of the land in Canaan (Gen 48:5-6). Since the family of Levi would not receive tribal land (see note at 6:54-81), these grandsons of Jacob both need to inherit land to keep the tribes at the number twelve.

14 The sons of Manasseh: Asriel, whom his Aramean concubine bore; she bore Machir the father of Gilead. 15 And Machir took a wife for Huppim and for Shuppim. The name of his sister was Maacah. And the name of the second was Zelophehad; and Zelophehad had daughters. 16 Maacah the wife of Machir bore a son, and she named him Peresh; the name of his brother was Sheresh; and his sons were Ulam and Rekem. 17 The son[a] of Ulam: Bedan. These were the sons of Gilead son of Machir, son of Manasseh. 18 And his sister Hammolecheth bore Ishhod, Abiezer, and Mahlah. 19 The sons of Shemida were Ahian, Shechem, Likhi, and Aniam.

Descendants of Ephraim

20 The sons of Ephraim: Shuthelah, and Bered his son, Tahath his son, Eleadah his son, Tahath his son, 21 Zabad his son, Shuthelah his son, and Ezer and Elead. Now the people of Gath, who were born in the land, killed them, because they came down to raid their cattle. 22 And their father Ephraim mourned many days, and his brothers came to comfort him. 23 Ephraim[b] went in to his wife, and she conceived and bore a son; and he named him Beriah, because disaster[c] had befallen his house. 24 His daughter was Sheerah, who built both Lower and Upper Beth-horon, and Uzzen-sheerah. 25 Rephah was his son, Resheph his son, Telah his son, Tahan his son, 26 Ladan his son, Ammihud his son, Elishama his son, 27 Nun[d] his son, Joshua his son. 28 Their possessions and settlements were Bethel and its towns, and eastward Naaran, and westward Gezer and its towns, Shechem

---

[a] Heb *sons* [b] Heb *He* [c] Heb *beraah* [d] Here spelled *Non*; see Ex 33.11

and its towns, as far as Ayyah and its towns; 29 also along the borders
of the Manassites, Beth-shean and its towns, Taanach and its towns,
Megiddo and its towns, Dor and its towns. In these lived the sons of
Joseph son of Israel.

Descendants of Asher

30 The sons of Asher: Imnah, Ishvah, Ishvi, Beriah, and their
sister Serah. 31 The sons of Beriah: Heber and Malchiel, who was the
father of Birzaith. 32 Heber became the father of Japhlet, Shomer, Hotham, and their sister Shua. 33 The sons of Japhlet: Pasach, Bimhal, and
Ashvath. These are the sons of Japhlet. 34 The sons of Shemer: Ahi,
Rohgah, Hubbah, and Aram. 35 The sons of Helem[a] his brother: Zophah, Imna, Shelesh, and Amal. 36 The sons of Zophah: Suah, Harne-
pher, Shual, Beri, Imrah, 37 Bezer, Hod, Shamma, Shilshah, Ithran, and
Beera. 38 The sons of Jether: Jephunneh, Pispa, and Ara. 39 The sons
of Ulla: Arah, Hanniel, and Rizia. 40 All of these were men of Asher,
heads of ancestral houses, select mighty warriors, chief of the princes.
Their number enrolled by genealogies, for service in war, was twenty-
six thousand men.

7:30 Asher: The second son of Jacob and Zilpah, servant of his wife, Leah (Gen 30:9-13).

Descendants of Benjamin

8 Benjamin became the father of Bela his firstborn, Ashbel the
second, Aharah the third, 2 Nohah the fourth, and Rapha the
fifth. 3 And Bela had sons: Addar, Gera, Abihud,[b] 4 Abishua, Naaman,
Ahoah, 5 Gera, Shephuphan, and Huram. 6 These are the sons of Ehud
(they were heads of ancestral houses of the inhabitants of Geba, and
they were carried into exile to Manahath): 7 Naaman,[c] Ahijah, and
Gera, that is, Heglam,[d] who became the father of Uzza and Ahihud.
8 And Shaharaim had sons in the country of Moab after he had sent
away his wives Hushim and Baara. 9 He had sons by his wife Hodesh:
Jobab, Zibia, Mesha, Malcam, 10 Jeuz, Sachia, and Mirmah. These were
his sons, heads of ancestral houses. 11 He also had sons by Hushim:
Abitub and Elpaal. 12 The sons of Elpaal: Eber, Misham, and Shemed,
who built Ono and Lod with its towns, 13 and Beriah and Shema (they
were heads of ancestral houses of the inhabitants of Aijalon, who put
to flight the inhabitants of Gath); 14 and Ahio, Shashak, and Jeremoth.
15 Zebadiah, Arad, Eder, 16 Michael, Ishpah, and Joha were sons of Beriah. 17 Zebadiah, Meshullam, Hizki, Heber, 18 Ishmerai, Izliah, and
Jobab were the sons of Elpaal. 19 Jakim, Zichri, Zabdi, 20 Elienai, Zillethai, Eliel, 21 Adaiah, Beraiah, and Shimrath were the sons of Shimei.
22 Ishpan, Eber, Eliel, 23 Abdon, Zichri, Hanan, 24 Hananiah, Elam, An-
thothijah, 25 Iphdeiah, and Penuel were the sons of Shashak. 26 Sham-
sherai, Shehariah, Athaliah, 27 Jaareshiah, Elijah, and Zichri were the

8:1-40 Benjamin: This branch differs from other family trees of Benjamin (Gen 46:21; Num 26:38-40; 1 Chr 7:6-11). The tribe of Benjamin receives special attention because Saul, Israel's first king, was a Benjaminite (8:33-40). Even though Saul was Israel's first king, his family lists appear here in chapter 8, while King David's family lists appear earlier, in chapter 3.

[a] Or *Hotham*; see 7.32 [b] Or *father of Ehud*; see 8.6 [c] Heb *and Naaman* [d] Or *he carried them into exile*

sons of Jeroham. 28 These were the heads of ancestral houses, according to their generations, chiefs. These lived in Jerusalem.

29 Jeiel[a] the father of Gibeon lived in Gibeon, and the name of his wife was Maacah. 30 His firstborn son: Abdon, then Zur, Kish, Baal,[b] Nadab, 31 Gedor, Ahio, Zecher, 32 and Mikloth, who became the father of Shimeah. Now these also lived opposite their kindred in Jerusalem, with their kindred. 33 Ner became the father of Kish, Kish of Saul,[c] Saul[c] of Jonathan, Malchishua, Abinadab, and Esh-baal; 34 and the son of Jonathan was Merib-baal; and Merib-baal became the father of Micah. 35 The sons of Micah: Pithon, Melech, Tarea, and Ahaz. 36 Ahaz became the father of Jehoaddah; and Jehoaddah became the father of Alemeth, Azmaveth, and Zimri; Zimri became the father of Moza. 37 Moza became the father of Binea; Raphah was his son, Eleasah his son, Azel his son. 38 Azel had six sons, and these are their names: Azrikam, Bocheru, Ishmael, Sheariah, Obadiah, and Hanan; all these were the sons of Azel. 39 The sons of his brother Eshek: Ulam his firstborn, Jeush the second, and Eliphelet the third. 40 The sons of Ulam were mighty warriors, archers, having many children and grandchildren, one hundred fifty. All these were Benjaminites.

9 So all Israel was enrolled by genealogies; and these are written in the Book of the Kings of Israel. And Judah was taken into exile in Babylon because of their unfaithfulness. 2 Now the first to live again in their possessions in their towns were Israelites, priests, Levites, and temple servants.

Inhabitants of Jerusalem after the Exile

3 And some of the people of Judah, Benjamin, Ephraim, and Manasseh lived in Jerusalem: 4 Uthai son of Ammihud, son of Omri, son of Imri, son of Bani, from the sons of Perez son of Judah. 5 And of the Shilonites: Asaiah the firstborn, and his sons. 6 Of the sons of Zerah: Jeuel and their kin, six hundred ninety. 7 Of the Benjaminites: Sallu son of Meshullam, son of Hodaviah, son of Hassenuah, 8 Ibneiah son of Jeroham, Elah son of Uzzi, son of Michri, and Meshullam son of Shephatiah, son of Reuel, son of Ibnijah; 9 and their kindred according to their generations, nine hundred fifty-six. All these were heads of families according to their ancestral houses.

Priestly Families

10 Of the priests: Jedaiah, Jehoiarib, Jachin, 11 and Azariah son of Hilkiah, son of Meshullam, son of Zadok, son of Meraioth, son of Ahitub, the chief officer of the house of God; 12 and Adaiah son of Jeroham, son of Pashhur, son of Malchijah, and Maasai son of Adiel, son of Jahzerah, son of Meshullam, son of Meshillemith, son of

[a] Compare 9.35: Heb lacks *Jeiel* [b] Gk Ms adds *Ner*; Compare 8.33 and 9.36 [c] Or *Shaul*

9:1 all Israel was enrolled–: This summary concludes the family tree of the tribes of ancient Israel (1 Chr 1–8). The unity of the people (all Israel), the exile of the people to Babylon, and its cause (the people's unfaithfulness) will continue as major themes.

9:1 all Israel: The unity of all the tribes of Israel is an important theme in Chronicles, as seen in their united support for David's kingship (chapter 12) and the building of Solomon's temple (chapters 28–29). Later, Judah's King Hezekiah will call for a united response in worship (2 Chr 30).

How might the Chronicler's vision of the unity of all God's people guide your thinking about efforts to eliminate social, racial, ethnic, and religious tensions? Is unity in the church important? If so, why?

9:2-34 some of the people... lived in Jerusalem: Chronicles only mentions the resettlement that followed the exile in this list of those who returned from Babylon. The Chronicler wants his community to see themselves as part of the people he has just described in the family trees (1–8). These lists also are concerned with the status of the inhabitants, listed in four groups: Israelite common or lay people (9:3-9), priests (9:10-13), and Levites (9:14-34), which includes the fourth group, the gatekeepers and temple guards. Notice that the lay people, the Israelites, are listed before the clergy.

Immer; [13]besides their kindred, heads of their ancestral houses, one
thousand seven hundred sixty, qualified for the work of the service of
the house of God.

Levitical Families

14 Of the Levites: Shemaiah son of Hasshub, son of Azrikam, son
of Hashabiah, of the sons of Merari; [15]and Bakbakkar, Heresh, Galal,
and Mattaniah son of Mica, son of Zichri, son of Asaph; [16]and Obadiah son of Shemaiah, son of Galal, son of Jeduthun, and Berechiah
son of Asa, son of Elkanah, who lived in the villages of the Netophathites.

17 The gatekeepers were: Shallum, Akkub, Talmon, Ahiman;
and their kindred Shallum was the chief, [18]stationed previously in the
king's gate on the east side. These were the gatekeepers of the camp
of the Levites. [19]Shallum son of Kore, son of Ebiasaph, son of Korah,
and his kindred of his ancestral house, the Korahites, were in charge
of the work of the service, guardians of the thresholds of the tent, as
their ancestors had been in charge of the camp of the LORD, guardians of the entrance. [20]And Phinehas son of Eleazar was chief over
them in former times; the LORD was with him. [21]Zechariah son of
Meshelemiah was gatekeeper at the entrance of the tent of meeting.
[22]All these, who were chosen as gatekeepers at the thresholds, were
two hundred twelve. They were enrolled by genealogies in their villages. David and the seer Samuel established them in their office of
trust. [23]So they and their descendants were in charge of the gates of
the house of the LORD, that is, the house of the tent, as guards. [24]The
gatekeepers were on the four sides, east, west, north, and south; [25]and
their kindred who were in their villages were obliged to come in every
seven days, in turn, to be with them; [26]for the four chief gatekeepers,
who were Levites, were in charge of the chambers and the treasures of
the house of God. [27]And they would spend the night near the house
of God; for on them lay the duty of watching, and they had charge of
opening it every morning.

28 Some of them had charge of the utensils of service, for they
were required to count them when they were brought in and taken
out. [29]Others of them were appointed over the furniture, and over all
the holy utensils, also over the choice flour, the wine, the oil, the incense, and the spices. [30]Others, of the sons of the priests, prepared the
mixing of the spices, [31]and Mattithiah, one of the Levites, the firstborn of Shallum the Korahite, was in charge of making the flat cakes.
[32]Also some of their kindred of the Kohathites had charge of the rows
of bread, to prepare them for each sabbath.

33 Now these are the singers, the heads of ancestral houses of the
Levites, living in the chambers of the temple free from other service,
for they were on duty day and night. [34]These were heads of ancestral

9:18-27 king's gate on the east side…house of God: The exact location of this gate in Jerusalem is unclear. The Levite gatekeepers or guards kept watch over entrances to the city and at the entrances to the sacred tent or temple. The guards were divided into three shifts and covered twenty-four stations (see 1 Chr 26:16-18).

9:28-32 utensils of service…rows of bread: Some of the Levites were in charge of the plates, pans, and altar where sacrifices were prepared and then offered in worship of God. Some had special responsibility for making the bread that was used in offering and later eaten by the priests (see Lev 2:2-7). On each Sabbath, twelve loaves of fresh bread, representing the twelve tribes of Israel, were to be placed on the altar in the temple (see Lev 24:5-9).

houses of the Levites, according to their generations; these leaders lived in Jerusalem.

The Family of King Saul

35 In Gibeon lived the father of Gibeon, Jeiel, and the name of his wife was Maacah. [36]His firstborn son was Abdon, then Zur, Kish, Baal, Ner, Nadab, [37]Gedor, Ahio, Zechariah, and Mikloth; [38]and Mikloth became the father of Shimeam; and these also lived opposite their kindred in Jerusalem, with their kindred. [39]Ner became the father of Kish, Kish of Saul, Saul of Jonathan, Malchishua, Abinadab, and Esh-baal; [40]and the son of Jonathan was Merib-baal; and Merib-baal became the father of Micah. [41]The sons of Micah: Pithon, Melech, Tahrea, and Ahaz;[a] [42]and Ahaz became the father of Jarah, and Jarah of Alemeth, Azmaveth, and Zimri; and Zimri became the father of Moza. [43]Moza became the father of Binea; and Rephaiah was his son, Eleasah his son, Azel his son. [44]Azel had six sons, and these are their names: Azrikam, Bocheru, Ishmael, Sheariah, Obadiah, and Hanan; these were the sons of Azel.

Death of Saul and His Sons

10 Now the Philistines fought against Israel; and the men of Israel fled before the Philistines, and fell slain on Mount Gilboa. [2]The Philistines overtook Saul and his sons; and the Philistines killed Jonathan and Abinadab and Malchishua, sons of Saul. [3]The battle pressed hard on Saul; and the archers found him, and he was wounded by the archers. [4]Then Saul said to his armor-bearer, "Draw your sword, and thrust me through with it, so that these uncircumcised may not come and make sport of me." But his armor-bearer was unwilling, for he was terrified. So Saul took his own sword and fell on it. [5]When his armor-bearer saw that Saul was dead, he also fell on his sword and died. [6]Thus Saul died; he and his three sons and all his house died together. [7]When all the men of Israel who were in the valley saw that the army[b] had fled and that Saul and his sons were dead, they abandoned their towns and fled; and the Philistines came and occupied them.

8 The next day when the Philistines came to strip the dead, they found Saul and his sons fallen on Mount Gilboa. [9]They stripped him and took his head and his armor, and sent messengers throughout the land of the Philistines to carry the good news to their idols and to the people. [10]They put his armor in the temple of their gods, and fastened his head in the temple of Dagon. [11]But when all Jabesh-gilead heard everything that the Philistines had done to Saul, [12]all the valiant warriors got up and took away the body of Saul and the bodies of his sons,

[a] Compare 8.35: Heb lacks *and Ahaz* [b] Heb *they*

10:1-14 The Philistines overtook Saul . . . Saul was dead: The story of Saul, Israel's first king, took up twenty-three chapters in the earlier history (1 Sam 8–31). Chronicles is only interested in Saul's death at the hands of the Philistines. This is because Saul functions as a negative example for the Chronicler's portrayal of David and Solomon. The Chronicler begins his narrative of David's reign with a picture of Saul losing the land because of unfaithfulness. David and Solomon will keep the land due to their faithfulness to the LORD and especially to their support of proper worship in the temple.

10:1-14 the LORD . . . turned the kingdom over to David: The last section of 1 Chronicles (10–29) focuses on the reign of King David. The Chronicler presents the reigns of David and Solomon as an ideal time in which God's will for Israel was realized. Their separate reigns are portrayed as a single, united monarchy by paralleling their individual stories in ways that complement each other. David prepares for the building of the temple and Solomon builds it. See the outline on p. 639 for the sections of 1 Chronicles that relate to David's reign.

Why is faith important in justification? The principle of justification by faith is important to Lutherans and other Christians. To be justified means to be made right with God. In 1 Chronicles, we read that "Saul died for his unfaithfulness" (10:13). He did not seek guidance from the LORD. In his discussion of repentance, Melanchthon (a theologian of Luther's time) uses Saul's unfaithfulness as an example of someone whose regret was useless apart from faith (*Apology* 12:36). *1 Chronicles 10:13-14*

and brought them to Jabesh. Then they buried their bones under the
oak in Jabesh, and fasted seven days.
13 So Saul died for his unfaithfulness; he was unfaithful to the
LORD in that he did not keep the command of the LORD; moreover,
he had consulted a medium, seeking guidance, [14]and did not seek
guidance from the LORD. Therefore the LORD[a] put him to death and
turned the kingdom over to David son of Jesse.

David Anointed King of All Israel

11 Then all Israel gathered together to David at Hebron and said,
"See, we are your bone and flesh. [2]For some time now, even
while Saul was king, it was you who commanded the army of Israel.
The LORD your God said to you: It is you who shall be shepherd of
my people Israel, you who shall be ruler over my people Israel." [3]So all
the elders of Israel came to the king at Hebron, and David made a covenant with them at Hebron before the LORD. And they anointed David king over Israel, according to the word of the LORD by Samuel.

Jerusalem Captured

4 David and all Israel marched to Jerusalem, that is Jebus, where
the Jebusites were, the inhabitants of the land. [5]The inhabitants of Jebus said to David, "You will not come in here." Nevertheless David
took the stronghold of Zion, now the city of David. [6]David had said,
"Whoever attacks the Jebusites first shall be chief and commander."
And Joab son of Zeruiah went up first, so he became chief. [7]David resided in the stronghold; therefore it was called the city of David. [8]He
built the city all around, from the Millo in complete circuit; and Joab
repaired the rest of the city. [9]And David became greater and greater,
for the LORD of hosts was with him.

David's Mighty Men and Their Exploits

10 Now these are the chiefs of David's warriors, who gave him
strong support in his kingdom, together with all Israel, to make him
king, according to the word of the LORD concerning Israel. [11]This
is an account of David's mighty warriors: Jashobeam, son of Hachmoni,[b] was chief of the Three;[c] he wielded his spear against three hundred whom he killed at one time.
12 And next to him among the three warriors was Eleazar son of
Dodo, the Ahohite. [13]He was with David at Pas-dammim when the
Philistines were gathered there for battle. There was a plot of ground
full of barley. Now the people had fled from the Philistines, [14]but he
and David took their stand in the middle of the plot, defended it, and
killed the Philistines; and the LORD saved them by a great victory.

---

[a] Heb *he* [b] Or *a Hachmonite* [c] Compare 2 Sam 23.8: Heb *Thirty* or *captains*

10:13-14 the LORD put him to death and turned the kingdom over to David: These verses, not found in Samuel, set the stage for the rest of Chronicles. Saul's "unfaithfulness" results in his death at the hand of the Philistine archers. The same unfaithfulness had resulted in exile for Judah (9:1) and the northern tribes (5:25-26). In 5:25 the Hebrew word is translated as "transgressed." Note that the LORD is the subject of the phrase "put him to death." God was responsible for Saul's death as well as for David's rise.

What do you think of the idea that God directly caused the death of unfaithful Saul? How does this fit with your image of God? In general, do you believe that God causes bad things and good things to happen in the world? In your life?

11:1—12:40 all Israel gathered... to make David king: In this section a circular pattern of various lists points to the unity of all Israel and their immediate recognition of David as their king. An outer framework describing David's anointing at Hebron (11:1-3; 12:38-40) encloses lists of military personnel in attendance (11:10-47; 12:23-37). An inner framework of David's forces stationed at Ziklag (12:1-7; 12:19-22) frames those who were at the stronghold (12:8-18). These chapters present David (and later, Solomon,) as kings who faithfully seek God, unlike Saul.

11:1-3 anointed David king over Israel: The process of pouring olive oil on the head of a prophet, priest, or king to show that the person had been chosen and dedicated as a leader was called "anointing." The Greek word *Christ* and the Hebrew word *Messiah* mean "the anointed one." In 2 Samuel David is anointed separately by Judah (2 Sam 2:4) and Israel (2 Sam 5:3). Chronicles stresses David's acceptance by a united Israel.

11:4-9 David...marched to Jerusalem: David's first task as leader of a united Israel is to capture Jebus, a neutral city that became Jerusalem, David's political and religious capital. See Map 5, p. 2103.

11:19 Can I drink the blood of these men?: The story in 11:15-19 reveals David's respect for God's law. Since the warriors had risked their lives to get the water, it represented the lifeblood of the warriors. To drink blood was forbidden in ancient Israel (Lev 17:10-16).

15 Three of the thirty chiefs went down to the rock to David at the cave of Adullam, while the army of Philistines was encamped in the valley of Rephaim. [16]David was then in the stronghold; and the garrison of the Philistines was then at Bethlehem. [17]David said longingly, "O that someone would give me water to drink from the well of Bethlehem that is by the gate!" [18]Then the Three broke through the camp of the Philistines, and drew water from the well of Bethlehem that was by the gate, and they brought it to David. But David would not drink of it; he poured it out to the LORD, [19]and said, "My God forbid that I should do this. Can I drink the blood of these men? For at the risk of their lives they brought it." Therefore he would not drink it. The three warriors did these things.

20 Now Abishai,[a] the brother of Joab, was chief of the Thirty.[b] With his spear he fought against three hundred and killed them, and won a name beside the Three. [21]He was the most renowned[c] of the Thirty,[b] and became their commander; but he did not attain to the Three.

22 Benaiah son of Jehoiada was a valiant man[d] of Kabzeel, a doer of great deeds; he struck down two sons of[e] Ariel of Moab. He also went down and killed a lion in a pit on a day when snow had fallen. [23]And he killed an Egyptian, a man of great stature, five cubits tall. The Egyptian had in his hand a spear like a weaver's beam; but Benaiah went against him with a staff, snatched the spear out of the Egyptian's hand, and killed him with his own spear. [24]Such were the things Benaiah son of Jehoiada did, and he won a name beside the three warriors. [25]He was renowned among the Thirty, but he did not attain to the Three. And David put him in charge of his bodyguard.

26 The warriors of the armies were Asahel brother of Joab, Elhanan son of Dodo of Bethlehem, [27]Shammoth of Harod,[f] Helez the Pelonite, [28]Ira son of Ikkesh of Tekoa, Abiezer of Anathoth, [29]Sibbecai the Hushathite, Ilai the Ahohite, [30]Maharai of Netophah, Heled son of Baanah of Netophah, [31]Ithai son of Ribai of Gibeah of the Benjaminites, Benaiah of Pirathon, [32]Hurai of the wadis of Gaash, Abiel the Arbathite, [33]Azmaveth of Baharum, Eliahba of Shaalbon, [34]Hashem[g] the Gizonite, Jonathan son of Shagee the Hararite, [35]Ahiam son of Sachar the Hararite, Eliphal son of Ur, [36]Hepher the Mecherathite, Ahijah the Pelonite, [37]Hezro of Carmel, Naarai son of Ezbai, [38]Joel the brother of Nathan, Mibhar son of Hagri, [39]Zelek the Ammonite, Naharai of Beeroth, the armor-bearer of Joab son of Zeruiah, [40]Ira the Ithrite, Gareb the Ithrite, [41]Uriah the Hittite, Zabad son of Ahlai, [42]Adina son of Shiza the Reubenite, a leader of the Reubenites, and thirty with him, [43]Hanan son of Maacah, and Josh-

[a] Gk Vg Tg Compare 2 Sam 23.18: Heb *Abshai* [b] Syr: Heb *Three* [c] Compare 2 Sam 23.19: Heb *more renowned among the two* [d] Syr: Heb *the son of a valiant man* [e] See 2 Sam 23.20: Heb lacks *sons of* [f] Compare 2 Sam 23.25: Heb *the Harorite* [g] Compare Gk and 2 Sam 23.32: Heb *the sons of Hashem*

aphat the Mithnite, [44]Uzzia the Ashterathite, Shama and Jeiel sons of Hotham the Aroerite, [45]Jediael son of Shimri, and his brother Joha the Tizite, [46]Eliel the Mahavite, and Jeribai and Joshaviah sons of Elnaam, and Ithmah the Moabite, [47]Eliel, and Obed, and Jaasiel the Mezobaite.

David's Followers in the Wilderness

12 The following are those who came to David at Ziklag, while he could not move about freely because of Saul son of Kish; they were among the mighty warriors who helped him in war. [2]They were archers, and could shoot arrows and sling stones with either the right hand or the left; they were Benjaminites, Saul's kindred. [3]The chief was Ahiezer, then Joash, both sons of Shemaah of Gibeah; also Jeziel and Pelet sons of Azmaveth; Beracah, Jehu of Anathoth, [4]Ishmaiah of Gibeon, a warrior among the Thirty and a leader over the Thirty; Jeremiah,[a] Jahaziel, Johanan, Jozabad of Gederah, [5]Eluzai,[b] Jerimoth, Bealiah, Shemariah, Shephatiah the Haruphite; [6]Elkanah, Isshiah, Azarel, Joezer, and Jashobeam, the Korahites; [7]and Joelah and Zebadiah, sons of Jeroham of Gedor.

8 From the Gadites there went over to David at the stronghold in the wilderness mighty and experienced warriors, expert with shield and spear, whose faces were like the faces of lions, and who were swift as gazelles on the mountains: [9]Ezer the chief, Obadiah second, Eliab third, [10]Mishmannah fourth, Jeremiah fifth, [11]Attai sixth, Eliel seventh, [12]Johanan eighth, Elzabad ninth, [13]Jeremiah tenth, Machbannai eleventh. [14]These Gadites were officers of the army, the least equal to a hundred and the greatest to a thousand. [15]These are the men who crossed the Jordan in the first month, when it was overflowing all its banks, and put to flight all those in the valleys, to the east and to the west.

16 Some Benjaminites and Judahites came to the stronghold to David. [17]David went out to meet them and said to them, "If you have come to me in friendship, to help me, then my heart will be knit to you; but if you have come to betray me to my adversaries, though my hands have done no wrong, then may the God of our ancestors see and give judgment." [18]Then the spirit came upon Amasai, chief of the Thirty, and he said,

"We are yours, O David;
and with you, O son of Jesse!
Peace, peace to you,
and peace to the one who helps you!
For your God is the one who helps you."

[a] Heb verse 5 [b] Heb verse 6

12:1-7 Ziklag: David hid from Saul and set up a command center here for his partnership with the Philistines (1 Sam 27). Chronicles uses flashbacks to show all Israel's early support of David. Even Benjamin, King Saul's own tribe, had abandoned him for David.

12:8-18 stronghold in the wilderness: The story flashes back again to David's days as a soldier of fortune in the wilderness (1 Sam 23–26), where warriors from the northern tribe of Gad join others from Benjamin and Judah.

12:18 peace: This familiar translation of *shalom* is inadequate. *Prosperity* and *success* are closer, but fall short of the emphasis on the wholeness, unity, and integrity that the prophet Amasai wishes for the people.

What would change in your life if you thought of peace as more than the absence of war? In what way does your life need peace?

12:18 the one who helps: God is the true source of help, who will bring David victory (12:1, 17, 18, 19, 21, 22).

Then David received them, and made them officers of his troops.
19 Some of the Manassites deserted to David when he came with
the Philistines for the battle against Saul. (Yet he did not help them,
for the rulers of the Philistines took counsel and sent him away, saying, "He will desert to his master Saul at the cost of our heads.") [20]As
he went to Ziklag these Manassites deserted to him: Adnah, Jozabad,
Jediael, Michael, Jozabad, Elihu, and Zillethai, chiefs of the thousands
in Manasseh. [21]They helped David against the band of raiders,[a] for
they were all warriors and commanders in the army. [22]Indeed from
day to day people kept coming to David to help him, until there was a
great army, like an army of God.

David's Army at Hebron

23 These are the numbers of the divisions of the armed troops
who came to David in Hebron to turn the kingdom of Saul over to
him, according to the word of the LORD. [24]The people of Judah bearing shield and spear numbered six thousand eight hundred armed
troops. [25]Of the Simeonites, mighty warriors, seven thousand one
hundred. [26]Of the Levites four thousand six hundred. [27]Jehoiada,
leader of the house of Aaron, and with him three thousand seven
hundred. [28]Zadok, a young warrior, and twenty-two commanders
from his own ancestral house. [29]Of the Benjaminites, the kindred of
Saul, three thousand, of whom the majority had continued to keep
their allegiance to the house of Saul. [30]Of the Ephraimites, twenty
thousand eight hundred, mighty warriors, notables in their ancestral
houses. [31]Of the half-tribe of Manasseh, eighteen thousand, who were
expressly named to come and make David king. [32]Of Issachar, those
who had understanding of the times, to know what Israel ought to
do, two hundred chiefs, and all their kindred under their command.
[33]Of Zebulun, fifty thousand seasoned troops, equipped for battle
with all the weapons of war, to help David[b] with singleness of purpose. [34]Of Naphtali, a thousand commanders, with whom there were
thirty-seven thousand armed with shield and spear. [35]Of the Danites,
twenty-eight thousand six hundred equipped for battle. [36]Of Asher,
forty thousand seasoned troops ready for battle. [37]Of the Reubenites
and Gadites and the half-tribe of Manasseh from beyond the Jordan,
one hundred twenty thousand armed with all the weapons of war.
38 All these, warriors arrayed in battle order, came to Hebron
with full intent to make David king over all Israel; likewise all the rest
of Israel were of a single mind to make David king. [39]They were there
with David for three days, eating and drinking, for their kindred had
provided for them. [40]And also their neighbors, from as far away as
Issachar and Zebulun and Naphtali, came bringing food on donkeys,

[a] Or *as officers of his troops* [b] Gk: Heb lacks *David*

12:19-37 an army of God: The huge numbers (340,822) of northern troops that join the army of God (12:22) emphasize all Israel's enthusiastic support for David. Compare to 2 Sam 6:1, where Israel's army numbers thirty thousand.

12:38 were of a single mind: Once again, Chronicles emphasizes the unanimous choice of David as king. In Hebrew, decisions were thought to be made in the heart, not the mind, as in the literal Hebrew expression "with a whole [or complete] heart."

12:40 joy: In Chronicles, joy accompanies significant religious events. Examples include the appointment of the liturgical singers (1 Chr 15:16), Solomon's coronation (1 Chr 29:9, 17, 22), the contributions for Joash's repair of the temple (2 Chr 24:10), and especially Hezekiah's reforms (2 Chr 29:30, 36; 30:21, 23, 25, 26).

13:1—16:43 let us bring again the ark of our God to us: As his first act as king, David tries to bring the ark, the symbol of God's presence, from Kiriath-jearim to his new capital, Jerusalem. The description of these two attempts to bring the ark to Jerusalem presents seeking God as another of the Chronicler's key themes.

What is meant by "seeking the Lord"? What ways of seeking the Lord work best for you?

13:3 ark: The ark was the symbol of God's presence among the people, serving as God's throne, and containing the

camels, mules, and oxen—abundant provisions of meal, cakes of
figs, clusters of raisins, wine, oil, oxen, and sheep, for there was joy in
Israel.

The Ark Brought from Kiriath-jearim

13 David consulted with the commanders of the thousands and
of the hundreds, with every leader. 2David said to the whole
assembly of Israel, "If it seems good to you, and if it is the will of the
LORD our God, let us send abroad to our kindred who remain in all
the land of Israel, including the priests and Levites in the cities that
have pasture lands, that they may come together to us. 3Then let us
bring again the ark of our God to us; for we did not turn to it in the
days of Saul." 4The whole assembly agreed to do so, for the thing
pleased all the people.

5 So David assembled all Israel from the Shihor of Egypt to Lebo-
hamath, to bring the ark of God from Kiriath-jearim. 6And David and
all Israel went up to Baalah, that is, to Kiriath-jearim, which belongs
to Judah, to bring up from there the ark of God, the LORD, who is enthroned on the cherubim, which is called by his[a] name. 7They carried
the ark of God on a new cart, from the house of Abinadab, and Uzzah
and Ahio[b] were driving the cart. 8David and all Israel were dancing
before God with all their might, with song and lyres and harps and
tambourines and cymbals and trumpets.

9 When they came to the threshing floor of Chidon, Uzzah put
out his hand to hold the ark, for the oxen shook it. 10The anger of the
LORD was kindled against Uzzah; he struck him down because he put
out his hand to the ark; and he died there before God. 11David was
angry because the LORD had burst out against Uzzah; so that place is
called Perez-uzzah[c] to this day. 12David was afraid of God that day; he
said, "How can I bring the ark of God into my care?" 13So David did
not take the ark into his care into the city of David; he took it instead
to the house of Obed-edom the Gittite. 14The ark of God remained
with the household of Obed-edom in his house three months, and
the LORD blessed the household of Obed-edom and all that he had.

David Established at Jerusalem

14 King Hiram of Tyre sent messengers to David, along with
cedar logs, and masons and carpenters to build a house for
him. 2David then perceived that the LORD had established him as
king over Israel, and that his kingdom was highly exalted for the sake
of his people Israel.

3 David took more wives in Jerusalem, and David became the
father of more sons and daughters. 4These are the names of the chil-

[a] Heb lacks *his* [b] Or *and his brother* [c] That is *Bursting Out Against Uzzah*

stone tablets of the covenant, the Ten Commandments (Exod 25:10-22).

13:1-14 David did not take the ark into his care: David's first attempt to take the ark fails. Saul's neglect of the ark (1 Chr 13:3) led to his death, and he became a model of "exile." In contrast, David models faithful obedience to Israel's institutions with his active concern for God and the religious duties that such concern requires.

What religious duties does God require of you?

13:9-14 struck him down because he put out his hand to the ark: Uzzah accidentally ruins David's first attempt to transfer the ark by trying to steady it. No one can touch the ark, only the Levites can carry it, and they must do so by means of poles slipped through rings on the side of the ark (Num 4:14-15). Uzzah's death, despite his good intentions, seems unfair to modern readers, but the Chronicler intends to show the seriousness of Israel's religious rules or rituals.

14:1-17 LORD had established him as king over Israel: David is successful in Jerusalem because of the LORD (14:2, 17). The Chronicler often shows God's approval with fame, children, and military victory. David receives these blessings because he has faithfully taken care of the ark. His good example is in contrast to Saul's bad example (1 Chr 10). David's kingdom is secured (14:2); Saul's had been taken away (10:14). David's house increased (14:3-7); Saul's was eliminated (10:6). David sought God (14:10, 14); Saul had not (10:13-14). David defeats the Philistines who had defeated Saul and burns their gods; Saul's head was presented to those Philistine gods (14:12; 10:8-10).

14:1-2 his kingdom was highly exalted: The first sign of David's blessing is a foreign king sending building materials to build the house (the royal palace).

14:1 Tyre: Tyre was an important Mediterranean seaport in Phoenicia (see Map 5, p. 2103). The trade routes necessary for that seaport's financial success were controlled by Israel.

14:3-7 sons and daughters: The second sign of blessing comes in the large family born to David in Jerusalem.

dren whom he had in Jerusalem: Shammua, Shobab, and Nathan;
Solomon, 5 Ibhar, Elishua, and Elpelet; 6 Nogah, Nepheg, and Japhia;
7 Elishama, Beeliada, and Eliphelet.

Defeat of the Philistines

8 When the Philistines heard that David had been anointed king
over all Israel, all the Philistines went up in search of David; and David heard of it and went out against them. 9 Now the Philistines had
come and made a raid in the valley of Rephaim. 10 David inquired of
God, "Shall I go up against the Philistines? Will you give them into
my hand?" The LORD said to him, "Go up, and I will give them into
your hand." 11 So he went up to Baal-perazim, and David defeated
them there. David said, "God has burst out[a] against my enemies by
my hand, like a bursting flood." Therefore that place is called Baal-
perazim.[b] 12 They abandoned their gods there, and at David's command they were burned.
13 Once again the Philistines made a raid in the valley. 14 When
David again inquired of God, God said to him, "You shall not go up
after them; go around and come on them opposite the balsam trees.
15 When you hear the sound of marching in the tops of the balsam
trees, then go out to battle; for God has gone out before you to strike
down the army of the Philistines." 16 David did as God had commanded him, and they struck down the Philistine army from Gibeon
to Gezer. 17 The fame of David went out into all lands, and the LORD
brought the fear of him on all nations.

14:8-17 went out against them… struck down the Philistine army: David's defeat of the Philistines is a third sign of blessing. By placing David's success after his care for the ark, the Chronicler presents fame, children, and military victory as rewards for David's faithfulness.

God helped deliver David from his enemies. From what enemy or enemies do you need deliverance? How have you ever experienced God delivering you?

The Ark Brought to Jerusalem

15 David[c] built houses for himself in the city of David, and he
prepared a place for the ark of God and pitched a tent for it.
2 Then David commanded that no one but the Levites were to carry
the ark of God, for the LORD had chosen them to carry the ark of
the LORD and to minister to him forever. 3 David assembled all Israel
in Jerusalem to bring up the ark of the LORD to its place, which he
had prepared for it. 4 Then David gathered together the descendants
of Aaron and the Levites: 5 of the sons of Kohath, Uriel the chief, with
one hundred twenty of his kindred; 6 of the sons of Merari, Asaiah
the chief, with two hundred twenty of his kindred; 7 of the sons of
Gershom, Joel the chief, with one hundred thirty of his kindred; 8 of
the sons of Elizaphan, Shemaiah the chief, with two hundred of his
kindred; 9 of the sons of Hebron, Eliel the chief, with eighty of his kindred; 10 of the sons of Uzziel, Amminadab the chief, with one hundred
twelve of his kindred.
11 David summoned the priests Zadok and Abiathar, and the

15:1—16:3 he prepared a place for the ark…the ark of the covenant of the LORD came to the city of David: Military success gave David the confidence to try to bring the ark to Jerusalem again. This time he follows the guidelines prescribed by Moses. Not following those guidelines had cost Uzzah his life (13:6-10).

15:1 tent: Not the tabernacle, which would still be in Gibeon (16:39).

15:2, 12-15 Levites: This time, David is careful to follow scripture; only Levites carry the ark as Moses had commanded (15:15; Deut 10:8).

---

[a] Heb *paraz* [b] That is *Lord of Bursting Out* [c] Heb *He*

Levites Uriel, Asaiah, Joel, Shemaiah, Eliel, and Amminadab. [12]He
said to them, "You are the heads of families of the Levites; sanctify
yourselves, you and your kindred, so that you may bring up the ark
of the LORD, the God of Israel, to the place that I have prepared for it.
[13]Because you did not carry it the first time,[a] the LORD our God burst
out against us, because we did not give it proper care." [14]So the priests
and the Levites sanctified themselves to bring up the ark of the LORD,
the God of Israel. [15]And the Levites carried the ark of God on their
shoulders with the poles, as Moses had commanded according to the
word of the LORD.

16 David also commanded the chiefs of the Levites to appoint
their kindred as the singers to play on musical instruments, on harps
and lyres and cymbals, to raise loud sounds of joy. [17]So the Levites
appointed Heman son of Joel; and of his kindred Asaph son of Berechiah; and of the sons of Merari, their kindred, Ethan son of Kushaiah;
[18]and with them their kindred of the second order, Zechariah, Jaaziel,
Shemiramoth, Jehiel, Unni, Eliab, Benaiah, Maaseiah, Mattithiah,
Eliphelehu, and Mikneiah, and the gatekeepers Obed-edom and Jeiel.
[19]The singers Heman, Asaph, and Ethan were to sound bronze cymbals; [20]Zechariah, Aziel, Shemiramoth, Jehiel, Unni, Eliab, Maaseiah,
and Benaiah were to play harps according to Alamoth; [21]but Mattithiah, Eliphelehu, Mikneiah, Obed-edom, Jeiel, and Azaziah were to
lead with lyres according to the Sheminith. [22]Chenaniah, leader of the
Levites in music, was to direct the music, for he understood it. [23]Ber-
echiah and Elkanah were to be gatekeepers for the ark. [24]Shebaniah,
Joshaphat, Nethanel, Amasai, Zechariah, Benaiah, and Eliezer, the
priests, were to blow the trumpets before the ark of God. Obed-edom
and Jehiah also were to be gatekeepers for the ark.

25 So David and the elders of Israel, and the commanders of the
thousands, went to bring up the ark of the covenant of the LORD from
the house of Obed-edom with rejoicing. [26]And because God helped
the Levites who were carrying the ark of the covenant of the LORD,
they sacrificed seven bulls and seven rams. [27]David was clothed with
a robe of fine linen, as also were all the Levites who were carrying
the ark, and the singers, and Chenaniah the leader of the music of
the singers; and David wore a linen ephod. [28]So all Israel brought
up the ark of the covenant of the LORD with shouting, to the sound
of the horn, trumpets, and cymbals, and made loud music on harps
and lyres.

29 As the ark of the covenant of the LORD came to the city of
David, Michal daughter of Saul looked out of the window, and saw
King David leaping and dancing; and she despised him in her heart.

15:12 sanctify yourselves: The priests would prepare themselves for their holy task by bathing, washing their clothes, and not having sex.

15:16-24 singers: The Levites will bring the ark into Jerusalem in a liturgical procession.

15:25-26 Levites: In the older history, David sacrifices an ox and a fatling (2 Sam 6:13). Here, the Levites perform this task and the number of sacrificial animals is increased to seven bulls and seven rams, as a thanksgiving offering. The Chronicler may also want to avoid the suggestion that David functioned as a priest.

15:27 ephod: Notice that in the beginning of the verse David and the Levites are clothed in fine linen. The ephod was a linen garment only worn by the priest. The ephod David wore at the end of the verse is either a different garment or has been added to the text from 2 Sam 6:14. For more on the ephod, see the note at Exod 28:1-43.

15:29 Michal daughter of Saul: Michal was one of David's wives. Her hatred of David recalls her father's neglect of the ark that led to his death (1 Chr 10).

The Ark Placed in the Tent

[a] Meaning of Heb uncertain

16:1-3 burnt offerings and the offerings of well-being: In a burnt offering the whole animal was burned on the altar, releasing a pleasing odor for God to smell. Offerings of well being were made to ask for God's blessing. See also Leviticus 3:1-17.

16:4-43 David first appointed the singing of praises: The ark narrative concludes with worship. The appointment of worship and ceremonial personnel (16:4-6, 37-42) frames a hymn of praise made up of Pss 105:1-15 (16:8-22); 96:1b-13a (16:23-33); and 106:1, 47-48 (16:34-36).

16:4-7 to invoke, to thank, and to praise: David charges the Levites with these functions because sacrifice could only take place at Gibeon until the dedication of the temple (16:29-30).

16:12 remember the wonderful works: Demonstrations of God's past faithfulness include delivering them from slavery in Egypt (Exod 2–15), providing for them in the wilderness (Exod 15–17), giving them the law at Mount Sinai (Exod 19–24), and helping them occupy the land of Canaan (Joshua 4–23).

16:16 covenant: God's promise of the land of Canaan to Abraham, Isaac, and Jacob (Gen 12:7; 26:3; 28:13).

16 They brought in the ark of God, and set it inside the tent that
David had pitched for it; and they offered burnt offerings and
offerings of well-being before God. 2 When David had finished offering the burnt offerings and the offerings of well-being, he blessed the
people in the name of the LORD; 3 and he distributed to every person
in Israel—man and woman alike—to each a loaf of bread, a portion
of meat,[a] and a cake of raisins.

4 He appointed certain of the Levites as ministers before the ark
of the LORD, to invoke, to thank, and to praise the LORD, the God
of Israel. 5 Asaph was the chief, and second to him Zechariah, Jeiel,
Shemiramoth, Jehiel, Mattithiah, Eliab, Benaiah, Obed-edom, and Jeiel, with harps and lyres; Asaph was to sound the cymbals, 6 and the
priests Benaiah and Jahaziel were to blow trumpets regularly, before
the ark of the covenant of God.

David's Psalm of Thanksgiving

7 Then on that day David first appointed the singing of praises to
the LORD by Asaph and his kindred.

8 O give thanks to the LORD, call on his name,
make known his deeds among the peoples.
9 Sing to him, sing praises to him,
tell of all his wonderful works.
10 Glory in his holy name;
let the hearts of those who seek the LORD rejoice.
11 Seek the LORD and his strength,
seek his presence continually.
12 Remember the wonderful works he has done,
his miracles, and the judgments he uttered,
13 O offspring of his servant Israel,[b]
children of Jacob, his chosen ones.

14 He is the LORD our God;
his judgments are in all the earth.
15 Remember his covenant forever,
the word that he commanded, for a thousand generations,
16 the covenant that he made with Abraham,
his sworn promise to Isaac,
17 which he confirmed to Jacob as a statute,
to Israel as an everlasting covenant,
18 saying, "To you I will give the land of Canaan
as your portion for an inheritance."

[a] Compare Gk Syr Vg: Meaning of Heb uncertain [b] Another reading is *Abraham* (compare Ps 105.6)

19 When they were few in number,
of little account, and strangers in the land,[a]
20 wandering from nation to nation,
from one kingdom to another people,
21 he allowed no one to oppress them;
he rebuked kings on their account,
22 saying, "Do not touch my anointed ones;
do my prophets no harm."

23 Sing to the LORD, all the earth.
Tell of his salvation from day to day.
24 Declare his glory among the nations,
his marvelous works among all the peoples.
25 For great is the LORD, and greatly to be praised;
he is to be revered above all gods.
26 For all the gods of the peoples are idols,
but the LORD made the heavens.
27 Honor and majesty are before him;
strength and joy are in his place.

28 Ascribe to the LORD, O families of the peoples,
ascribe to the LORD glory and strength.
29 Ascribe to the LORD the glory due his name;
bring an offering, and come before him.
Worship the LORD in holy splendor;
30 tremble before him, all the earth.
The world is firmly established; it shall never be moved.
31 Let the heavens be glad, and let the earth rejoice,
and let them say among the nations, "The LORD is king!"
32 Let the sea roar, and all that fills it;
let the field exult, and everything in it.
33 Then shall the trees of the forest sing for joy
before the LORD, for he comes to judge the earth.
34 O give thanks to the LORD, for he is good;
for his steadfast love endures forever.

35 Say also:
"Save us, O God of our salvation,
and gather and rescue us from among the nations,
that we may give thanks to your holy name,
and glory in your praise.
36 Blessed be the LORD, the God of Israel,
from everlasting to everlasting."
Then all the people said "Amen!" and praised the LORD.

16:31-33 the LORD is king: The announcement of God's rule over the gods of other nations would reassure the post-exile community under Persian rule that God is in control.

16:35 God of our salvation…rescue us: This reference, added to Ps 106:47, directly applies the promises of the psalm to its hearers.

What can you do to make your worship life more meaningful?

---

[a] Heb *in it*

Regular Worship Maintained

37 David left Asaph and his kinsfolk there before the ark of the covenant of the LORD to minister regularly before the ark as each day required, 38 and also Obed-edom and his[a] sixty-eight kinsfolk; while Obed-edom son of Jeduthun and Hosah were to be gatekeepers. 39 And he left the priest Zadok and his kindred the priests before the tabernacle of the LORD in the high place that was at Gibeon, 40 to offer burnt offerings to the LORD on the altar of burnt offering regularly, morning and evening, according to all that is written in the law of the LORD that he commanded Israel. 41 With them were Heman and Jeduthun, and the rest of those chosen and expressly named to render thanks to the LORD, for his steadfast love endures forever. 42 Heman and Jeduthun had with them trumpets and cymbals for the music, and instruments for sacred song. The sons of Jeduthun were appointed to the gate.

43 Then all the people departed to their homes, and David went home to bless his household.

God's Covenant with David

17 Now when David settled in his house, David said to the prophet Nathan, "I am living in a house of cedar, but the ark of the covenant of the LORD is under a tent." 2 Nathan said to David, "Do all that you have in mind, for God is with you."

3 But that same night the word of the LORD came to Nathan, saying: 4 Go and tell my servant David: Thus says the LORD: You shall not build me a house to live in. 5 For I have not lived in a house since the day I brought out Israel to this very day, but I have lived in a tent and a tabernacle.[b] 6 Wherever I have moved about among all Israel, did I ever speak a word with any of the judges of Israel, whom I commanded to shepherd my people, saying, Why have you not built me a house of cedar? 7 Now therefore thus you shall say to my servant David: Thus says the LORD of hosts: I took you from the pasture, from following the sheep, to be ruler over my people Israel; 8 and I have been with you wherever you went, and have cut off all your enemies before you; and I will make for you a name, like the name of the great ones of the earth. 9 I will appoint a place for my people Israel, and will plant them, so that they may live in their own place, and be disturbed no more; and evildoers shall wear them down no more, as they did formerly, 10 from the time that I appointed judges over my people Israel; and I will subdue all your enemies.

Moreover I declare to you that the LORD will build you a house. 11 When your days are fulfilled to go to be with your ancestors, I will raise up your offspring after you, one of your own sons, and I will

17:1-27 God is with you: God's promise to David that a member of his family would always rule Israel and God's promise to Solomon of forgiveness for those who repent (2 Chr 7:12-22) are the most important parts of the Chronicler's message.

17:1-2 the ark...is under a tent: David desires to build a house for the ark. Notice that Nathan agrees with David's wish. Nathan is acting as an adviser here, not a prophet, since he has not consulted God. His bad advice will be corrected in the following verses, after God speaks to him.

17:3-15 house: The prophet Nathan makes use of three separate meanings of the word *house* in Hebrew to make three points. House can mean "palace" (17:1), "temple" (17:4), or "dynasty" (17:10b, 14). David may not build a house (temple) for God (17:4), but God will build a house (dynasty) for David (17:10). One of that house (dynasty)—meaning one of David's descendants—will build a house (the temple) for the LORD (17:12a). Someone from David's house (descendants) will rule Israel forever (17:12b).

17:10 subdue: See 2 Samuel 7:11, "and I will give you rest." In Chronicles, Solomon is associated with rest, David with war. David cannot build the temple, because he has shed blood in war (22:8). In Deuteronomy 12:9-11 the people are to gather at one central sanctuary after God gives them "rest." That sanctuary was built by Solomon, whose name may mean "peaceful" and who will receive "rest" from God (see note at 22:9).

17:14 my house and in my kingdom: Instead of "your house and your kingdom" (as in 2 Sam 7:16), the Chronicler uses the word *my*. In 2 Samuel "your house" means David's descendants; here "my house" means God's house, that is, the temple. The Chronicler stresses the understanding that God, not David, rules (see also 28:5-6; 29:23; 2 Chr 1:11; 9:8; 13:4-8).

---

[a] Gk Syr Vg: Heb *their* [b] Gk 2 Sam 7.6: Heb *but I have been from tent to tent and from tabernacle*

establish his kingdom. [12]He shall build a house for me, and I will establish his throne forever. [13]I will be a father to him, and he shall be a son to me. I will not take my steadfast love from him, as I took it from him who was before you, [14]but I will confirm him in my house and in my kingdom forever, and his throne shall be established forever. [15]In accordance with all these words and all this vision, Nathan spoke to David.

David's Prayer

16 Then King David went in and sat before the LORD, and said, "Who am I, O LORD God, and what is my house, that you have brought me thus far? [17]And even this was a small thing in your sight, O God; you have also spoken of your servant's house for a great while to come. You regard me as someone of high rank,[a] O LORD God! [18]And what more can David say to you for honoring your servant? You know your servant. [19]For your servant's sake, O LORD, and according to your own heart, you have done all these great deeds, making known all these great things. [20]There is no one like you, O LORD, and there is no God besides you, according to all that we have heard with our ears. [21]Who is like your people Israel, one nation on the earth whom God went to redeem to be his people, making for yourself a name for great and terrible things, in driving out nations before your people whom you redeemed from Egypt? [22]And you made your people Israel to be your people forever; and you, O LORD, became their God.

23 "And now, O LORD, as for the word that you have spoken concerning your servant and concerning his house, let it be established forever, and do as you have promised. [24]Thus your name will be established and magnified forever in the saying, 'The LORD of hosts, the God of Israel, is Israel's God'; and the house of your servant David will be established in your presence. [25]For you, my God, have revealed to your servant that you will build a house for him; therefore your servant has found it possible to pray before you. [26]And now, O LORD, you are God, and you have promised this good thing to your servant; [27]therefore may it please you to bless the house of your servant, that it may continue forever before you. For you, O LORD, have blessed and are blessed[b] forever."

David's Kingdom Established and Extended

18 Some time afterward, David attacked the Philistines and subdued them; he took Gath and its villages from the Philistines.

2 He defeated Moab, and the Moabites became subject to David and brought tribute.

[a] Meaning of Heb uncertain [b] Or *and it is blessed*

What dreams do you have that probably are not going to happen? How does David's experience help you?

17:16-27 David...sat before the LORD: David accepts God's task with a model prayer containing thanksgiving, praise, and petition. Sitting was an unusual posture for prayer. Perhaps David knelt and sat on his heels.

17:16-19 Who am I...that you have brought me thus far: David thanks God for present help and the promise that someone from his family would always rule Israel.

17:16 my house: David's family (17:17, 23, 24, 27).

17:20-22 There is no one like you: David praises God for what God has done in the past, especially the exodus. From now on in Chronicles, the covenant will be based upon God's promise to David, not on the exodus.

17:23-27 And now, O LORD...may it please you: The prayer ends with a request that God would do in the future as God had promised.

When you pray, do you usually thank God, praise God, or ask God to help you?

18:1—20:8 David attacked...fell by the hand of David: The Chronicler stresses David's empire-building that links God's promise (1 Chr 17) with David's preparations for building the temple (1 Chr 21–29). In contrast, the book of 2 Samuel is concerned with David's increasing inability to govern his personal life: David's adultery with Bathsheba (2 Sam 11–12), the incest and murder of Amnon (2 Sam 13), and the rebellions of his sons Absalom and Sheba (2 Sam 15–20).

18:1-17 David attacked...the LORD gave victory to David: David's defeat of the Philistines in the west (18:1), Moab in the east (18:2), Zobah (18:3-4), Damascus to the north (18:5-6), and Edom in the south (18:12-13) fulfills God's promise to subdue all David's enemies (1 Chr 17:10). It is ironic that these victories, given by God (18:6, 13b), prevent David from building the temple (22:8-9). See Map 5, p. 2103.

3 David also struck down King Hadadezer of Zobah, toward Hamath,[a] as he went to set up a monument at the river Euphrates. 4 David took from him one thousand chariots, seven thousand cavalry, and twenty thousand foot soldiers. David hamstrung all the chariot horses, but left one hundred of them. 5 When the Arameans of Damascus came to help King Hadadezer of Zobah, David killed twenty-two thousand Arameans. 6 Then David put garrisons[b] in Aram of Damascus; and the Arameans became subject to David, and brought tribute. The LORD gave victory to David wherever he went. 7 David took the gold shields that were carried by the servants of Hadadezer, and brought them to Jerusalem. 8 From Tibhath and from Cun, cities of Hadadezer, David took a vast quantity of bronze; with it Solomon made the bronze sea and the pillars and the vessels of bronze.

18:6, 13 garrisons: Garrisons were forts or armies stationed on borders for defense.

9 When King Tou of Hamath heard that David had defeated the whole army of King Hadadezer of Zobah, 10 he sent his son Hadoram to King David, to greet him and to congratulate him, because he had fought against Hadadezer and defeated him. Now Hadadezer had often been at war with Tou. He sent all sorts of articles of gold, of silver, and of bronze; 11 these also King David dedicated to the LORD, together with the silver and gold that he had carried off from all the nations, from Edom, Moab, the Ammonites, the Philistines, and Amalek.

18:11 dedicated to the LORD: The spoils of war will be used to finance the building of the temple. Even David's wars play a role in the Chronicler's main theme, the building of the temple.

12 Abishai son of Zeruiah killed eighteen thousand Edomites in the Valley of Salt. 13 He put garrisons in Edom; and all the Edomites became subject to David. And the LORD gave victory to David wherever he went.

David's Administration

14 So David reigned over all Israel; and he administered justice and equity to all his people. 15 Joab son of Zeruiah was over the army; Jehoshaphat son of Ahilud was recorder; 16 Zadok son of Ahitub and Ahimelech son of Abiathar were priests; Shavsha was secretary; 17 Benaiah son of Jehoiada was over the Cherethites and the Pelethites; and David's sons were the chief officials in the service of the king.

18:14-17 administered justice: David's administration may be modeled on that of Egypt and indicates that the kingdom will be marked by justice.

Defeat of the Ammonites and Arameans

19 Some time afterward, King Nahash of the Ammonites died, and his son succeeded him. 2 David said, "I will deal loyally with Hanun son of Nahash, for his father dealt loyally with me." So David sent messengers to console him concerning his father. When David's servants came to Hanun in the land of the Ammonites, to console him, 3 the officials of the Ammonites said to Hanun, "Do you think, because David has sent consolers to you, that he is honoring your

19:1—20:3 Ammonites...Arameans: The Chronicler uses this battle report to illustrate the expansion of David's rule. This war forms the background for David's adultery with Bathsheba and murder of her husband, Uriah the Hittite (2 Sam 10–12), which the Chronicler omits. The Ammonites were said to be descendants of Lot's sons (Gen 19:30-38). They often battled with Israel (see Judg 10:11-18; 1 Sam 14:47-48; Jer 49:1-6). The Arameans likely refers to tribal groups to the north and northeast of Israel, in areas of present-day Syria.

[a] Meaning of Heb uncertain [b] Gk Vg 2 Sam 8.6 Compare Syr: Heb lacks *garrisons*

father? Have not his servants come to you to search and to overthrow and to spy out the land?" [4]So Hanun seized David's servants, shaved them, cut off their garments in the middle at their hips, and sent them away; [5]and they departed. When David was told about the men, he sent messengers to them, for they felt greatly humiliated. The king said, "Remain at Jericho until your beards have grown, and then return."

6 When the Ammonites saw that they had made themselves odious to David, Hanun and the Ammonites sent a thousand talents of silver to hire chariots and cavalry from Mesopotamia, from Aram-maacah and from Zobah. [7]They hired thirty-two thousand chariots and the king of Maacah with his army, who came and camped before Medeba. And the Ammonites were mustered from their cities and came to battle. [8]When David heard of it, he sent Joab and all the army of the warriors. [9]The Ammonites came out and drew up in battle array at the entrance of the city, and the kings who had come were by themselves in the open country.

10 When Joab saw that the line of battle was set against him both in front and in the rear, he chose some of the picked men of Israel and arrayed them against the Arameans; [11]the rest of his troops he put in the charge of his brother Abishai, and they were arrayed against the Ammonites. [12]He said, "If the Arameans are too strong for me, then you shall help me; but if the Ammonites are too strong for you, then I will help you. [13]Be strong, and let us be courageous for our people and for the cities of our God; and may the LORD do what seems good to him." [14]So Joab and the troops who were with him advanced toward the Arameans for battle; and they fled before him. [15]When the Ammonites saw that the Arameans fled, they likewise fled before Abishai, Joab's brother, and entered the city. Then Joab came to Jerusalem.

16 But when the Arameans saw that they had been defeated by Israel, they sent messengers and brought out the Arameans who were beyond the Euphrates, with Shophach the commander of the army of Hadadezer at their head. [17]When David was informed, he gathered all Israel together, crossed the Jordan, came to them, and drew up his forces against them. When David set the battle in array against the Arameans, they fought with him. [18]The Arameans fled before Israel; and David killed seven thousand Aramean charioteers and forty thousand foot soldiers, and also killed Shophach the commander of their army. [19]When the servants of Hadadezer saw that they had been defeated by Israel, they made peace with David, and became subject to him. So the Arameans were not willing to help the Ammonites any more.

Siege and Capture of Rabbah

20 In the spring of the year, the time when kings go out to battle, Joab led out the army, ravaged the country of the Ammonites, and came and besieged Rabbah. But David remained at

19:4 shaved them…cut off their garments: Shaving a prisoner's beard and exposing his private parts was intended to humiliate him.

19:5 Remain at Jericho: An important city on the trade routes from the east to Canaan. See Map 4, p. 2102.

19:13-15 may the LORD do what seems good: Joab, the commander of David's army, trusts in God and is rewarded with military victory.

Jerusalem. Joab attacked Rabbah, and overthrew it. [2]David took the
crown of Milcom[a] from his head; he found that it weighed a talent of
gold, and in it was a precious stone; and it was placed on David's head.
He also brought out the booty of the city, a very great amount. [3]He
brought out the people who were in it, and set them to work[b] with
saws and iron picks and axes.[c] Thus David did to all the cities of the
Ammonites. Then David and all the people returned to Jerusalem.

Exploits against the Philistines

4 After this, war broke out with the Philistines at Gezer; then
Sibbecai the Hushathite killed Sippai, who was one of the descendants of the giants; and the Philistines were subdued. [5]Again there
was war with the Philistines; and Elhanan son of Jair killed Lahmi
the brother of Goliath the Gittite, the shaft of whose spear was like a
weaver's beam. [6]Again there was war at Gath, where there was a man
of great size, who had six fingers on each hand, and six toes on each
foot, twenty-four in number; he also was descended from the giants.
[7]When he taunted Israel, Jonathan son of Shimea, David's brother,
killed him. [8]These were descended from the giants in Gath; they fell
by the hand of David and his servants.

20:4-8 giants: In the wars against the Philistines, David and his armies fought against "giant" warriors, including Goliath and the six-fingered man from Gath. These giant men were probably descended from a group famous for their large size (see also Josh 12:4; Deut 2:10-11, 20-21).

The Census and Plague

21 Satan stood up against Israel, and incited David to count the
people of Israel. [2]So David said to Joab and the commanders
of the army, "Go, number Israel, from Beer-sheba to Dan, and bring
me a report, so that I may know their number." [3]But Joab said, "May
the LORD increase the number of his people a hundredfold! Are
they not, my lord the king, all of them my lord's servants? Why then
should my lord require this? Why should he bring guilt on Israel?"
[4]But the king's word prevailed against Joab. So Joab departed and
went throughout all Israel, and came back to Jerusalem. [5]Joab gave the
total count of the people to David. In all Israel there were one million
one hundred thousand men who drew the sword, and in Judah four
hundred seventy thousand who drew the sword. [6]But he did not include Levi and Benjamin in the numbering, for the king's command
was abhorrent to Joab.

7 But God was displeased with this thing, and he struck Israel.
[8]David said to God, "I have sinned greatly in that I have done this
thing. But now, I pray you, take away the guilt of your servant; for I
have done very foolishly." [9]The LORD spoke to Gad, David's seer, saying, [10]"Go and say to David, 'Thus says the LORD: Three things I offer
you; choose one of them, so that I may do it to you.'" [11]So Gad came
to David and said to him, "Thus says the LORD, 'Take your choice:

21:1-8 Satan...incited David....I have sinned: The story of David's census of the people is very different from that in 2 Samuel 24. Satan—merely an enemy, not the devil—causes David to count the people (21:1), not "the anger of the LORD" (2 Sam 24:1). Joab's blaming of David (21:3b) and his disgust (21:6) increase David's guilt. When God struck Israel, David is moved to repentance (21:8). The Chronicler does not go so far as to say God allowed this situation. The census itself may not have been sinful. It may have been David's trust in numbers rather than in God or that David's restructuring of Israel for taxes went against the ancient traditions. The Chronicler does not say.

21:2 from Beer-sheba to Dan: This included all of Israel, from the north to the south.

21:2—29:30 "Go, number Israel... David...reigned over all Israel: In this final major section of 1 Chronicles, David completes his preparation for the temple by planning its construction (21–22; 28–29) and organizing the people who will run it (23–27).

---

[a] Gk Vg See 1 Kings 11.5, 33: MT *of their king* [b] Compare 2 Sam 12.31: Heb *and he sawed*
[c] Compare 2 Sam 12.31: Heb *saws*

12 either three years of famine; or three months of devastation by your
foes, while the sword of your enemies overtakes you; or three days of
the sword of the LORD, pestilence on the land, and the angel of the
LORD destroying throughout all the territory of Israel.' Now decide
what answer I shall return to the one who sent me." 13 Then David said
to Gad, "I am in great distress; let me fall into the hand of the LORD,
for his mercy is very great; but let me not fall into human hands."

14 So the LORD sent a pestilence on Israel; and seventy thousand persons fell in Israel. 15 And God sent an angel to Jerusalem to
destroy it; but when he was about to destroy it, the LORD took note
and relented concerning the calamity; he said to the destroying angel,
"Enough! Stay your hand." The angel of the LORD was then standing by the threshing floor of Ornan the Jebusite. 16 David looked up
and saw the angel of the LORD standing between earth and heaven,
and in his hand a drawn sword stretched out over Jerusalem. Then
David and the elders, clothed in sackcloth, fell on their faces. 17 And
David said to God, "Was it not I who gave the command to count
the people? It is I who have sinned and done very wickedly. But these
sheep, what have they done? Let your hand, I pray, O LORD my God,
be against me and against my father's house; but do not let your people be plagued!"

David's Altar and Sacrifice

18 Then the angel of the LORD commanded Gad to tell David
that he should go up and erect an altar to the LORD on the threshing
floor of Ornan the Jebusite. 19 So David went up following Gad's instructions, which he had spoken in the name of the LORD. 20 Ornan
turned and saw the angel; and while his four sons who were with him
hid themselves, Ornan continued to thresh wheat. 21 As David came to
Ornan, Ornan looked and saw David; he went out from the threshing
floor, and did obeisance to David with his face to the ground. 22 David
said to Ornan, "Give me the site of the threshing floor that I may build
on it an altar to the LORD—give it to me at its full price—so that the
plague may be averted from the people." 23 Then Ornan said to David,
"Take it; and let my lord the king do what seems good to him; see,
I present the oxen for burnt offerings, and the threshing sledges for
the wood, and the wheat for a grain offering. I give it all." 24 But King
David said to Ornan, "No; I will buy them for the full price. I will
not take for the LORD what is yours, nor offer burnt offerings that
cost me nothing." 25 So David paid Ornan six hundred shekels of gold
by weight for the site. 26 David built there an altar to the LORD and
presented burnt offerings and offerings of well-being. He called upon
the LORD, and he answered him with fire from heaven on the altar of
burnt offering. 27 Then the LORD commanded the angel, and he put
his sword back into its sheath.

21:18—22:1 erect an altar . . . Here shall be the house of the LORD: David pays six hundred shekels of gold for the threshing floor of Ornan ("Araunah" in 2 Sam 24:18) as the site of the future temple (21:25). Compare this to the fifty shekels of silver David reportedly paid for the threshing floor and the oxen in 2 Samuel 24:24.

Finally, God answers David's prayer with fire from heaven (21:26; also see 2 Chr 7:1; Lev 9:24; Judg 6:21; 1 Kgs 18:38). These differences suggest that the Chronicler's story emphasizes David's repentance and God's forgiveness (21:15-27), rather than David's sin and God's judgment (21:1-14). The new ending to the story (21:26b—22:1) reveals the primary purpose: the connection between this place of reconciliation and forgiveness and the site of the future temple.

When are you tempted to trust in your own strength rather than lean upon God?

The Place Chosen for the Temple

28 At that time, when David saw that the LORD had answered
him at the threshing floor of Ornan the Jebusite, he made his sacrifices there. 29For the tabernacle of the LORD, which Moses had made
in the wilderness, and the altar of burnt offering were at that time in
the high place at Gibeon; 30but David could not go before it to inquire
22 of God, for he was afraid of the sword of the angel of the
LORD. 1Then David said, "Here shall be the house of the
LORD God and here the altar of burnt offering for Israel."

David Prepares to Build the Temple

2 David gave orders to gather together the aliens who were residing in the land of Israel, and he set stonecutters to prepare dressed
stones for building the house of God. 3David also provided great
stores of iron for nails for the doors of the gates and for clamps, as
well as bronze in quantities beyond weighing, 4and cedar logs without number—for the Sidonians and Tyrians brought great quantities
of cedar to David. 5For David said, "My son Solomon is young and
inexperienced, and the house that is to be built for the LORD must be
exceedingly magnificent, famous and glorified throughout all lands; I
will therefore make preparation for it." So David provided materials in
great quantity before his death.

David's Charge to Solomon and the Leaders

6 Then he called for his son Solomon and charged him to build a
house for the LORD, the God of Israel. 7David said to Solomon, "My
son, I had planned to build a house to the name of the LORD my God.
8But the word of the LORD came to me, saying, 'You have shed much
blood and have waged great wars; you shall not build a house to my
name, because you have shed so much blood in my sight on the earth.
9See, a son shall be born to you; he shall be a man of peace. I will
give him peace from all his enemies on every side; for his name shall
be Solomon,[a] and I will give peace[b] and quiet to Israel in his days.
10He shall build a house for my name. He shall be a son to me, and
I will be a father to him, and I will establish his royal throne in Israel
forever.' 11Now, my son, the LORD be with you, so that you may succeed in building the house of the LORD your God, as he has spoken
concerning you. 12Only, may the LORD grant you discretion and understanding, so that when he gives you charge over Israel you may
keep the law of the LORD your God. 13Then you will prosper if you
are careful to observe the statutes and the ordinances that the LORD
commanded Moses for Israel. Be strong and of good courage. Do
not be afraid or dismayed. 14With great pains I have provided for the

[a] Heb *Shelomoh* [b] Heb *shalom*

22:5 young and inexperienced: This is not necessarily a comment about Solomon's youth; it also justifies David's preparations. God chose Solomon to build the temple, not David (1 Chr 17:11-12). David's task was to prepare for its construction. David needs Solomon to build, and Solomon needs David to plan.

How does the church benefit from people receiving different gifts from God? In what ways are different tasks or roles important? Are you more of a planner or a builder?

22:6-10 charged him: David's wars had disqualified him from building the temple, but God had promised that one of David's "offspring" would build the temple (17:11). David now reveals that Solomon is the one who will fulfill that promise.

22:9 man of peace...I will give him peace: These phrases are better translated "man of rest" and "I will give him rest." In Deuteronomy God gives the people "rest" in the land before the people gather in the central sanctuary (Deut 12:8-14). David cannot build the temple because of his wars (22:8; 28:3). Solomon fulfills God's promise of a son who would build the temple (17:11-14), but only after the necessary condition of God's gift of "rest" for the land is met. Thus, God gives Solomon the name that will characterize his reign: "Solomon" sounds like "shalom" (22:9b).

22:11-16 Now, my son: Just as Moses made Joshua his successor (Deut 31; Josh 1), David assigns Solomon the task of building the temple. Both stories include a promise of God's presence (22:11, 16; Deut 31:6, 8, 23; Josh 1:5, 9), a description of the task (22:11; Deut 31:7; Josh 1:6), and words of encouragement (22:13; Deut 31:7, 8, 23; Josh 1:6-9).

22:12-13 discretion and understanding: Solomon receives this wisdom from God (2 Chr 1:7-12). Part of that wisdom involves obeying God's law. David tells Solomon he will succeed as long as he does so.

house of the LORD one hundred thousand talents of gold, one million talents of silver, and bronze and iron beyond weighing, for there
is so much of it; timber and stone too I have provided. To these you
must add more. [15]You have an abundance of workers: stonecutters,
masons, carpenters, and all kinds of artisans without number, skilled
in working [16]gold, silver, bronze, and iron. Now begin the work, and
the LORD be with you."

17 David also commanded all the leaders of Israel to help his son
Solomon, saying, [18]"Is not the LORD your God with you? Has he not
given you peace on every side? For he has delivered the inhabitants
of the land into my hand; and the land is subdued before the LORD
and his people. [19]Now set your mind and heart to seek the LORD your
God. Go and build the sanctuary of the LORD God so that the ark of
the covenant of the LORD and the holy vessels of God may be brought
into a house built for the name of the LORD."

Families of the Levites and Their Functions

23 When David was old and full of days, he made his son Solomon king over Israel.

2 David assembled all the leaders of Israel and the priests and
the Levites. [3]The Levites, thirty years old and upward, were counted,
and the total was thirty-eight thousand. [4]"Twenty-four thousand of
these," David said, "shall have charge of the work in the house of the
LORD, six thousand shall be officers and judges, [5]four thousand gatekeepers, and four thousand shall offer praises to the LORD with the
instruments that I have made for praise." [6]And David organized them
in divisions corresponding to the sons of Levi: Gershon,[a] Kohath,
and Merari.

7 The sons of Gershon[b] were Ladan and Shimei. [8]The sons of Ladan: Jehiel the chief, Zetham, and Joel, three. [9]The sons of Shimei:
Shelomoth, Haziel, and Haran, three. These were the heads of families of Ladan. [10]And the sons of Shimei: Jahath, Zina, Jeush, and Beriah. These four were the sons of Shimei. [11]Jahath was the chief, and
Zizah the second; but Jeush and Beriah did not have many sons, so
they were enrolled as a single family.

12 The sons of Kohath: Amram, Izhar, Hebron, and Uzziel, four.
[13]The sons of Amram: Aaron and Moses. Aaron was set apart to consecrate the most holy things, so that he and his sons forever should
make offerings before the LORD, and minister to him and pronounce
blessings in his name forever; [14]but as for Moses the man of God,
his sons were to be reckoned among the tribe of Levi. [15]The sons of
Moses: Gershom and Eliezer. [16]The sons of Gershom: Shebuel the
chief. [17]The sons of Eliezer: Rehabiah the chief; Eliezer had no other

22:18 peace: A better translation is "rest" (see note at 22:9).

22:19 seek the LORD: Here meaning "obedience to God," demonstrated by building the temple.

23:1 old and full of days: The similar descriptions of Abraham as "full of years" (Gen 25:8) and Isaac and Job as "full of days" (Gen 35:29; Job 42:17) suggest honor, not weakness.

23:1 made his son Solomon king: The orderly succession contrasts sharply with the scheming reported in 1 Kings 1–2. David transfers an organized administrative system to Solomon as the climax of his reign.

23:2—27:34 David assembled all the leaders: In this section, the Chronicler uses more lists to describe David's organization of Israel.

23:3 thirty years old: The youngest age for priests varies in the Old Testament: thirty years (Num 4:3, 23, 30, and here); twenty years (23:24, 27; 2 Chr 31:17; and Ezra 3:8); and twenty-five years (Num 8:24). At times the shortage of priests may have required a lowering of this requirement.

---

[a] Or *Gershom*; See 1 Chr 6.1, note, and 23.15 [b] Vg Compare Gk Syr: Heb *to the Gershonite*

sons, but the sons of Rehabiah were very numerous. [18]The sons of Izhar: Shelomith the chief. [19]The sons of Hebron: Jeriah the chief, Amariah the second, Jahaziel the third, and Jekameam the fourth. [20]The sons of Uzziel: Micah the chief and Isshiah the second.

21 The sons of Merari: Mahli and Mushi. The sons of Mahli: Eleazar and Kish. [22]Eleazar died having no sons, but only daughters; their kindred, the sons of Kish, married them. [23]The sons of Mushi: Mahli, Eder, and Jeremoth, three.

24 These were the sons of Levi by their ancestral houses, the heads of families as they were enrolled according to the number of the names of the individuals from twenty years old and upward who were to do the work for the service of the house of the LORD. [25]For David said, "The LORD, the God of Israel, has given rest to his people; and he resides in Jerusalem forever. [26]And so the Levites no longer need to carry the tabernacle or any of the things for its service"— [27]for according to the last words of David these were the number of the Levites from twenty years old and upward— [28]"but their duty shall be to assist the descendants of Aaron for the service of the house of the LORD, having the care of the courts and the chambers, the cleansing of all that is holy, and any work for the service of the house of God; [29]to assist also with the rows of bread, the choice flour for the grain offering, the wafers of unleavened bread, the baked offering, the offering mixed with oil, and all measures of quantity or size. [30]And they shall stand every morning, thanking and praising the LORD, and likewise at evening, [31]and whenever burnt offerings are offered to the LORD on sabbaths, new moons, and appointed festivals, according to the number required of them, regularly before the LORD. [32]Thus they shall keep charge of the tent of meeting and the sanctuary, and shall attend the descendants of Aaron, their kindred, for the service of the house of the LORD."

Divisions of the Priests

24 The divisions of the descendants of Aaron were these. The sons of Aaron: Nadab, Abihu, Eleazar, and Ithamar. [2]But Nadab and Abihu died before their father, and had no sons; so Eleazar and Ithamar became the priests. [3]Along with Zadok of the sons of Eleazar, and Ahimelech of the sons of Ithamar, David organized them according to the appointed duties in their service. [4]Since more chief men were found among the sons of Eleazar than among the sons of Ithamar, they organized them under sixteen heads of ancestral houses of the sons of Eleazar, and eight of the sons of Ithamar. [5]They organized them by lot, all alike, for there were officers of the sanctuary and officers of God among both the sons of Eleazar and the sons of Ithamar. [6]The scribe Shemaiah son of Nethanel, a Levite, recorded them in the presence of the king, and the officers, and Zadok the priest, and

23:25-26 resides in Jerusalem forever...carry the tabernacle: The building of the temple in Jerusalem would mean that Israel's God would have a permanent dwelling place. Up to this time, the tabernacle had been a tent of meeting that was dismantled and moved from place to place by the Levites (see Exod 25:1—27:21; Num 3:5—4:49).

23:31 new moons, and appointed festivals: For a summary of Israel's festivals, see Jewish Festivals and Feasts, p. 227.

24:1-19 The divisions of the descendants of Aaron: The primary priestly families of Aaron's sons Eleazar and Ithamar (24:1-6) are listed before David divides the priesthood into twenty-four divisions. This division actually took place much later, in the Chronicler's community.

24:5 by lot: The divisions took place by lot, but not by chance (see Prov 16:33). Casting lots, similar to throwing dice, was often used to determine God's will (1 Sam 10:21; Jonah 1:7; Prov 18:18). The tribes received their holdings in the promised land by casting lots (Josh 14:2).

Ahimelech son of Abiathar, and the heads of ancestral houses of the priests and of the Levites; one ancestral house being chosen for Eleazar and one chosen for Ithamar.

7 The first lot fell to Jehoiarib, the second to Jedaiah, [8]the third to Harim, the fourth to Seorim, [9]the fifth to Malchijah, the sixth to Mijamin, [10]the seventh to Hakkoz, the eighth to Abijah, [11]the ninth to Jeshua, the tenth to Shecaniah, [12]the eleventh to Eliashib, the twelfth to Jakim, [13]the thirteenth to Huppah, the fourteenth to Jeshebeab, [14]the fifteenth to Bilgah, the sixteenth to Immer, [15]the seventeenth to Hezir, the eighteenth to Happizzez, [16]the nineteenth to Pethahiah, the twentieth to Jehezkel, [17]the twenty-first to Jachin, the twenty-second to Gamul, [18]the twenty-third to Delaiah, the twenty-fourth to Maaziah. [19]These had as their appointed duty in their service to enter the house of the LORD according to the procedure established for them by their ancestor Aaron, as the LORD God of Israel had commanded him.

24:10 Abijah: Zechariah, the father of John the Baptist, was a descendant of Abijah (see Luke 1:5).

Other Levites

20 And of the rest of the sons of Levi: of the sons of Amram, Shubael; of the sons of Shubael, Jehdeiah. [21]Of Rehabiah: of the sons of Rehabiah, Isshiah the chief. [22]Of the Izharites, Shelomoth; of the sons of Shelomoth, Jahath. [23]The sons of Hebron:[a] Jeriah the chief,[b] Amariah the second, Jahaziel the third, Jekameam the fourth. [24]The sons of Uzziel, Micah; of the sons of Micah, Shamir. [25]The brother of Micah, Isshiah; of the sons of Isshiah, Zechariah. [26]The sons of Merari: Mahli and Mushi. The sons of Jaaziah: Beno.[c] [27]The sons of Merari: of Jaaziah, Beno,[c] Shoham, Zaccur, and Ibri. [28]Of Mahli: Eleazar, who had no sons. [29]Of Kish, the sons of Kish: Jerahmeel. [30]The sons of Mushi: Mahli, Eder, and Jerimoth. These were the sons of the Levites according to their ancestral houses. [31]These also cast lots corresponding to their kindred, the descendants of Aaron, in the presence of King David, Zadok, Ahimelech, and the heads of ancestral houses of the priests and of the Levites, the chief as well as the youngest brother.

The Temple Musicians

25 David and the officers of the army also set apart for the service the sons of Asaph, and of Heman, and of Jeduthun, who should prophesy with lyres, harps, and cymbals. The list of those who did the work and of their duties was: [2]Of the sons of Asaph: Zaccur, Joseph, Nethaniah, and Asarelah, sons of Asaph, under the direction of Asaph, who prophesied under the direction of the king. [3]Of Jeduthun, the sons of Jeduthun: Gedaliah, Zeri, Jeshaiah, Shimei,[d]

25:1-31 set apart for the service: David divides the musicians into twenty-four divisions of twelve musicians each. As in 1 Chronicles 15–16, the musicians are Levites from the three families of Asaph (four divisions, 25:2), Jeduthan (six divisions, 25:3), and Heman (fourteen divisions, 25:4-5).

25:1-3 prophesy: The musicians are seen as prophets who announce God's word.

---

[a] See 23.19: Heb lacks *Hebron* [b] See 23.19: Heb lacks *the chief* [c] Or *his son*: Meaning of Heb uncertain [d] One Ms: Gk: MT lacks *Shimei*

Hashabiah, and Mattithiah, six, under the direction of their father
Jeduthun, who prophesied with the lyre in thanksgiving and praise
to the LORD. 4 Of Heman, the sons of Heman: Bukkiah, Mattaniah,
Uzziel, Shebuel, and Jerimoth, Hananiah, Hanani, Eliathah, Giddalti,
and Romamti-ezer, Joshbekashah, Mallothi, Hothir, Mahazioth. 5 All
these were the sons of Heman the king's seer, according to the promise of God to exalt him; for God had given Heman fourteen sons and
three daughters. 6 They were all under the direction of their father for
the music in the house of the LORD with cymbals, harps, and lyres
for the service of the house of God. Asaph, Jeduthun, and Heman
were under the order of the king. 7 They and their kindred, who were
trained in singing to the LORD, all of whom were skillful, numbered
two hundred eighty-eight. 8 And they cast lots for their duties, small
and great, teacher and pupil alike.

9 The first lot fell for Asaph to Joseph; the second to Gedaliah, to
him and his brothers and his sons, twelve; 10 the third to Zaccur, his
sons and his brothers, twelve; 11 the fourth to Izri, his sons and his
brothers, twelve; 12 the fifth to Nethaniah, his sons and his brothers,
twelve; 13 the sixth to Bukkiah, his sons and his brothers, twelve; 14 the
seventh to Jesarelah,[a] his sons and his brothers, twelve; 15 the eighth to
Jeshaiah, his sons and his brothers, twelve; 16 the ninth to Mattaniah,
his sons and his brothers, twelve; 17 the tenth to Shimei, his sons and
his brothers, twelve; 18 the eleventh to Azarel, his sons and his brothers, twelve; 19 the twelfth to Hashabiah, his sons and his brothers,
twelve; 20 to the thirteenth, Shubael, his sons and his brothers, twelve;
21 to the fourteenth, Mattithiah, his sons and his brothers, twelve; 22 to
the fifteenth, to Jeremoth, his sons and his brothers, twelve; 23 to the
sixteenth, to Hananiah, his sons and his brothers, twelve; 24 to the seventeenth, to Joshbekashah, his sons and his brothers, twelve; 25 to the
eighteenth, to Hanani, his sons and his brothers, twelve; 26 to the nineteenth, to Mallothi, his sons and his brothers, twelve; 27 to the twentieth, to Eliathah, his sons and his brothers, twelve; 28 to the twenty-first,
to Hothir, his sons and his brothers, twelve; 29 to the twenty-second,
to Giddalti, his sons and his brothers, twelve; 30 to the twenty-third, to
Mahazioth, his sons and his brothers, twelve; 31 to the twenty-fourth,
to Romamti-ezer, his sons and his brothers, twelve.

The Gatekeepers

26:1-32 gatekeepers . . . officers: These lists of gatekeepers (26:1-19) and other officials (26:20-32) indicate the thoroughness of David's organization. In addition to guarding the gates and storehouses, the Levites were in charge of the treasuries of the house of God and the gifts dedicated to God. Those gifts included booty won in battle (26:20, 27).

26 As for the divisions of the gatekeepers: of the Korahites,
Meshelemiah son of Kore, of the sons of Asaph. 2 Meshelemiah had sons: Zechariah the firstborn, Jediael the second, Zebadiah
the third, Jathniel the fourth, 3 Elam the fifth, Jehohanan the sixth, Eliehoenai the seventh. 4 Obed-edom had sons: Shemaiah the firstborn,

[a] Or *Asarelah*; see 25.2

Jehozabad the second, Joah the third, Sachar the fourth, Nethanel the fifth, [5]Ammiel the sixth, Issachar the seventh, Peullethai the eighth; for God blessed him. [6]Also to his son Shemaiah sons were born who exercised authority in their ancestral houses, for they were men of great ability. [7]The sons of Shemaiah: Othni, Rephael, Obed, and Elzabad, whose brothers were able men, Elihu and Semachiah. [8]All these, sons of Obed-edom with their sons and brothers, were able men qualified for the service; sixty-two of Obed-edom. [9]Meshelemiah had sons and brothers, able men, eighteen. [10]Hosah, of the sons of Merari, had sons: Shimri the chief (for though he was not the firstborn, his father made him chief), [11]Hilkiah the second, Tebaliah the third, Zechariah the fourth: all the sons and brothers of Hosah totaled thirteen.

12 These divisions of the gatekeepers, corresponding to their leaders, had duties, just as their kindred did, ministering in the house of the LORD; [13]and they cast lots by ancestral houses, small and great alike, for their gates. [14]The lot for the east fell to Shelemiah. They cast lots also for his son Zechariah, a prudent counselor, and his lot came out for the north. [15]Obed-edom's came out for the south, and to his sons was allotted the storehouse. [16]For Shuppim and Hosah it came out for the west, at the gate of Shallecheth on the ascending road. Guard corresponded to guard. [17]On the east there were six Levites each day,[a] on the north four each day, on the south four each day, as well as two and two at the storehouse; [18]and for the colonnade[b] on the west there were four at the road and two at the colonnade.[b] [19]These were the divisions of the gatekeepers among the Korahites and the sons of Merari.

26:14-17 lot for the east...west: The main gates to the temple area faced in all four directions. The divisions of gatekeepers cast lots to determine which gate each would guard. See the illustration of the temple on p. 555.

The Treasurers, Officers, and Judges

20 And of the Levites, Ahijah had charge of the treasuries of the house of God and the treasuries of the dedicated gifts. [21]The sons of Ladan, the sons of the Gershonites belonging to Ladan, the heads of families belonging to Ladan the Gershonite: Jehieli.[c]

22 The sons of Jehieli, Zetham and his brother Joel, were in charge of the treasuries of the house of the LORD. [23]Of the Amramites, the Izharites, the Hebronites, and the Uzzielites: [24]Shebuel son of Gershom, son of Moses, was chief officer in charge of the treasuries. [25]His brothers: from Eliezer were his son Rehabiah, his son Jeshaiah, his son Joram, his son Zichri, and his son Shelomoth. [26]This Shelomoth and his brothers were in charge of all the treasuries of the dedicated gifts that King David, and the heads of families, and the officers of the thousands and the hundreds, and the commanders of the army, had dedicated. [27]From booty won in battles they dedicated gifts for the maintenance of the house of the LORD. [28]Also all that Samuel the seer,

26:28 Samuel the seer...Saul...Abner: Samuel served Israel as a priest, prophet, and judge. He anointed both Saul to be Israel's first king. Abner's father Ner was also the father of Saul's father Kish and so was King Saul's uncle (1 Chr 8:33) and an honored general (see 1 Sam 14:49-51).

---

[a] Gk: Heb lacks *each day* [b] Heb *parbar*: meaning uncertain [c] The Hebrew text of verse 21 is confused

and Saul son of Kish, and Abner son of Ner, and Joab son of Zeruiah had dedicated—all dedicated gifts were in the care of Shelomoth[a] and his brothers.

29 Of the Izharites, Chenaniah and his sons were appointed to outside duties for Israel, as officers and judges. [30]Of the Hebronites, Hashabiah and his brothers, one thousand seven hundred men of ability, had the oversight of Israel west of the Jordan for all the work of the LORD and for the service of the king. [31]Of the Hebronites, Jerijah was chief of the Hebronites. (In the fortieth year of David's reign search was made, of whatever genealogy or family, and men of great ability among them were found at Jazer in Gilead.) [32]King David appointed him and his brothers, two thousand seven hundred men of ability, heads of families, to have the oversight of the Reubenites, the Gadites, and the half-tribe of the Manassites for everything pertaining to God and for the affairs of the king.

The Military Divisions

27:1-34 list of the people of Israel: Four lists of civil officials in David's administration are described. Two are national: the army (27:1-15) and the tribal leaders (27:16-22). Two are royal: the treasury (27:25-31) and David's personal advisers (27:32-34).

27:1-15 concerning the divisions: The army of Israel had twelve divisions of twenty-four thousand men each. The commanders of each division are listed here and are also named in the lists of David's warriors (1 Chr 11:11-14, 20-47).

27 This is the list of the people of Israel, the heads of families, the commanders of the thousands and the hundreds, and their officers who served the king in all matters concerning the divisions that came and went, month after month throughout the year, each division numbering twenty-four thousand:

2 Jashobeam son of Zabdiel was in charge of the first division in the first month; in his division were twenty-four thousand. [3]He was a descendant of Perez, and was chief of all the commanders of the army for the first month. [4]Dodai the Ahohite was in charge of the division of the second month; Mikloth was the chief officer of his division. In his division were twenty-four thousand. [5]The third commander, for the third month, was Benaiah son of the priest Jehoiada, as chief; in his division were twenty-four thousand. [6]This is the Benaiah who was a mighty man of the Thirty and in command of the Thirty; his son Ammizabad was in charge of his division.[b] [7]Asahel brother of Joab was fourth, for the fourth month, and his son Zebadiah after him; in his division were twenty-four thousand. [8]The fifth commander, for the fifth month, was Shamhuth, the Izrahite; in his division were twenty-four thousand. [9]Sixth, for the sixth month, was Ira son of Ikkesh the Tekoite; in his division were twenty-four thousand. [10]Seventh, for the seventh month, was Helez the Pelonite, of the Ephraimites; in his division were twenty-four thousand. [11]Eighth, for the eighth month, was Sibbecai the Hushathite, of the Zerahites; in his division were twenty-four thousand. [12]Ninth, for the ninth month, was Abiezer of Anathoth, a Benjaminite; in his division were twenty-four thousand. [13]Tenth, for the tenth month, was Maharai of Netophah, of the

---

[a] Gk Compare 26.28: Heb *Shelomith* [b] Gk Vg: Heb *Ammizabad was his division*

Zerahites; in his division were twenty-four thousand. 14 Eleventh, for
the eleventh month, was Benaiah of Pirathon, of the Ephraimites; in
his division were twenty-four thousand. 15 Twelfth, for the twelfth
month, was Heldai the Netophathite, of Othniel; in his division were
twenty-four thousand.

Leaders of Tribes

16 Over the tribes of Israel, for the Reubenites, Eliezer son of
Zichri was chief officer; for the Simeonites, Shephatiah son of Maacah; 17 for Levi, Hashabiah son of Kemuel; for Aaron, Zadok; 18 for
Judah, Elihu, one of David's brothers; for Issachar, Omri son of Michael; 19 for Zebulun, Ishmaiah son of Obadiah; for Naphtali, Jerimoth son of Azriel; 20 for the Ephraimites, Hoshea son of Azaziah; for
the half-tribe of Manasseh, Joel son of Pedaiah; 21 for the half-tribe of
Manasseh in Gilead, Iddo son of Zechariah; for Benjamin, Jaasiel son
of Abner; 22 for Dan, Azarel son of Jeroham. These were the leaders of
the tribes of Israel. 23 David did not count those below twenty years
of age, for the LORD had promised to make Israel as numerous as the
stars of heaven. 24 Joab son of Zeruiah began to count them, but did
not finish; yet wrath came upon Israel for this, and the number was
not entered into the account of the Annals of King David.

Other Civic Officials

25 Over the king's treasuries was Azmaveth son of Adiel. Over
the treasuries in the country, in the cities, in the villages and in the
towers, was Jonathan son of Uzziah. 26 Over those who did the work of
the field, tilling the soil, was Ezri son of Chelub. 27 Over the vineyards
was Shimei the Ramathite. Over the produce of the vineyards for the
wine cellars was Zabdi the Shiphmite. 28 Over the olive and sycamore
trees in the Shephelah was Baal-hanan the Gederite. Over the stores
of oil was Joash. 29 Over the herds that pastured in Sharon was Shitrai
the Sharonite. Over the herds in the valleys was Shaphat son of Ad-
lai. 30 Over the camels was Obil the Ishmaelite. Over the donkeys was
Jehdeiah the Meronothite. Over the flocks was Jaziz the Hagrite. 31 All
these were stewards of King David's property.

32 Jonathan, David's uncle, was a counselor, being a man of understanding and a scribe; Jehiel son of Hachmoni attended the king's
sons. 33 Ahithophel was the king's counselor, and Hushai the Archite
was the king's friend. 34 After Ahithophel came Jehoiada son of Benaiah, and Abiathar. Joab was commander of the king's army.

Solomon Instructed to Build the Temple

28 David assembled at Jerusalem all the officials of Israel, the
officials of the tribes, the officers of the divisions that served
the king, the commanders of the thousands, the commanders of the

28:1—29:25 It is your son Solomon who shall build my house: David turns the kingdom over to Solomon. The temple is still the main focus of the Chronicler's presentation, and worship will be more important than political matters.

hundreds, the stewards of all the property and cattle of the king and
his sons, together with the palace officials, the mighty warriors, and
all the warriors. 2 Then King David rose to his feet and said: "Hear me,
my brothers and my people. I had planned to build a house of rest for
the ark of the covenant of the LORD, for the footstool of our God; and
I made preparations for building. 3 But God said to me, 'You shall not
build a house for my name, for you are a warrior and have shed blood.'
4 Yet the LORD God of Israel chose me from all my ancestral house to
be king over Israel forever; for he chose Judah as leader, and in the
house of Judah my father's house, and among my father's sons he took
delight in making me king over all Israel. 5 And of all my sons, for the
LORD has given me many, he has chosen my son Solomon to sit upon
the throne of the kingdom of the LORD over Israel. 6 He said to me, 'It
is your son Solomon who shall build my house and my courts, for I
have chosen him to be a son to me, and I will be a father to him. 7 I will
establish his kingdom forever if he continues resolute in keeping my
commandments and my ordinances, as he is today.' 8 Now therefore in
the sight of all Israel, the assembly of the LORD, and in the hearing of
our God, observe and search out all the commandments of the LORD
your God; that you may possess this good land, and leave it for an inheritance to your children after you forever.

9 "And you, my son Solomon, know the God of your father, and
serve him with single mind and willing heart; for the LORD searches
every mind, and understands every plan and thought. If you seek him,
he will be found by you; but if you forsake him, he will abandon you
forever. 10 Take heed now, for the LORD has chosen you to build a
house as the sanctuary; be strong, and act."

11 Then David gave his son Solomon the plan of the vestibule of
the temple, and of its houses, its treasuries, its upper rooms, and its
inner chambers, and of the room for the mercy seat;[a] 12 and the plan of
all that he had in mind: for the courts of the house of the LORD, all the
surrounding chambers, the treasuries of the house of God, and the
treasuries for dedicated gifts; 13 for the divisions of the priests and of
the Levites, and all the work of the service in the house of the LORD;
for all the vessels for the service in the house of the LORD, 14 the weight
of gold for all golden vessels for each service, the weight of silver vessels for each service, 15 the weight of the golden lampstands and their
lamps, the weight of gold for each lampstand and its lamps, the weight
of silver for a lampstand and its lamps, according to the use of each in
the service, 16 the weight of gold for each table for the rows of bread,
the silver for the silver tables, 17 and pure gold for the forks, the basins,
and the cups; for the golden bowls and the weight of each; for the
silver bowls and the weight of each; 18 for the altar of incense made of

[a] Or *the cover*

28:2-3 house: God rejected David's offer to build the house (the temple) because David as a warrior had shed blood (22:7-9).

Have you ever felt that your best efforts or work were rejected or passed over? What makes such experiences especially difficult? How do you see God at work in such moments?

28:4-5 house: God's choice of Solomon begins a different house, the dynasty of David (see also 22:9-10).

28:6 chosen: Chronicles alone speaks of Solomon's election by God (22:10; 28:5, 10), in order to stress that the reigns of David and Solomon are united.

28:8-10 If: Both the people and now Solomon are reminded that God's promise depends on their faithful obedience.

28:11-21 the plan of the vestibule of the temple: David has little advice about political leadership. He is more concerned with the importance of worship, as his transfer of the temple plans to Solomon shows.

28:11-12 plan: David's preparations for the temple are modeled upon Moses and the tabernacle (Exod 25:9, 40; 26:30) and Ezekiel and the ideal temple (Ezek 40–48). All three projects are divinely revealed. The Hebrew word for the plan (28:11, 12, 18, 19) is used for the tabernacle in Exodus 25:9, 40 and is similar to one used in Ezekiel 43:10.

28:13b-18 vessels: After the exile, the temple vessels became powerful symbols of continuity from David's planning of worship to the construction of the temple by Solomon in 2 Chronicles 4:6, the destruction of the temple in 2 Chronicles 36:18, and its restoration in Ezra 1:7-11 and 8:24-34.

In 28:20, David comforts and encourages his son Solomon by reminding him that their LORD God will be with him and not forsake him, especially during the time when Solomon will complete the temple. What is the most encouraging word about God that you have heard, and who gave it to you? What encouraging word would you want to pass on to someone else, such as a friend or children?

refined gold, and its weight; also his plan for the golden chariot of the
cherubim that spread their wings and covered the ark of the covenant
of the LORD.
19 "All this, in writing at the LORD's direction, he made clear to
me—the plan of all the works."
20 David said further to his son Solomon, "Be strong and of good
courage, and act. Do not be afraid or dismayed; for the LORD God,
my God, is with you. He will not fail you or forsake you, until all the
work for the service of the house of the LORD is finished. 21 Here are
the divisions of the priests and the Levites for all the service of the
house of God; and with you in all the work will be every volunteer
who has skill for any kind of service; also the officers and all the people will be wholly at your command."

Offerings for Building the Temple

29 King David said to the whole assembly, "My son Solomon,
whom alone God has chosen, is young and inexperienced,
and the work is great; for the temple[a] will not be for mortals but for
the LORD God. 2 So I have provided for the house of my God, so far
as I was able, the gold for the things of gold, the silver for the things of
silver, and the bronze for the things of bronze, the iron for the things
of iron, and wood for the things of wood, besides great quantities of
onyx and stones for setting, antimony, colored stones, all sorts of precious stones, and marble in abundance. 3 Moreover, in addition to all
that I have provided for the holy house, I have a treasure of my own
of gold and silver, and because of my devotion to the house of my
God I give it to the house of my God: 4 three thousand talents of gold,
of the gold of Ophir, and seven thousand talents of refined silver, for
overlaying the walls of the house, 5 and for all the work to be done by
artisans, gold for the things of gold and silver for the things of silver.
Who then will offer willingly, consecrating themselves today to the
LORD?"
6 Then the leaders of ancestral houses made their freewill offerings, as did also the leaders of the tribes, the commanders of the
thousands and of the hundreds, and the officers over the king's work.
7 They gave for the service of the house of God five thousand talents
and ten thousand darics of gold, ten thousand talents of silver, eighteen thousand talents of bronze, and one hundred thousand talents
of iron. 8 Whoever had precious stones gave them to the treasury of
the house of the LORD, into the care of Jehiel the Gershonite. 9 Then
the people rejoiced because these had given willingly, for with single
mind they had offered freely to the LORD; King David also rejoiced
greatly.

[a] Heb *fortress*

29:1-9 King David said: Once again, the Chronicler compares and contrasts Moses' preparations for the tabernacle (Exod 25–31; 35–40) with David's preparations for the temple.

29:1 God has chosen: Solomon is designated as God's chosen only in Chronicles (1 Chr 22:10; 28:5, 10).

29:1 temple: This Persian word meaning "fortress" only occurs in late passages in the Old Testament (29:19).

29:2 gold…silver…bronze…precious stones…marble: Notice that David asked for the same materials for the construction of the temple that Moses requested for the tabernacle (Exod 35:4-9, 20-29). Iron was unknown in Moses' day.

29:3 I give it to the house of my God: Unlike Moses, David contributes generously.

29:4 three thousand talents: The huge amounts, literally hundreds of tons of gold and silver, proclaim the magnificence of the temple and the attention to detail in David's preparations.

29:5 Who then will offer willingly: Like Moses (Exod 25:1-7; 35:4-9, 20-29), David seeks contributions from the people so that they too may take part in the preparations for the temple.

29:5 consecrating themselves: This is literally "fill his hand," descriptive of the ordination of priests (Exod 28:41). Only Chronicles describes lay people (non-priests) this way (2 Chr 29:31).

What is the priesthood of all believers? One aspect of this principle developed by Martin Luther would emphasize that all the baptized are to live their lives as a living sacrifice before God. Specifically, in Luther's day, he encouraged all people of faith, not just priests, to care for the poor among them. When David calls on the people to participate in the preparations for the temple, he is asking them to witness to their faith and uses terminology elsewhere reserved for priests (29:5, 20-21). *1 Chronicles 29:1-5*

29:6-9 five thousand talents: Huge amounts demonstrate the people's faithful response, again recalling Moses' appeal for the tabernacle (Exod 35:4-9).

David's Praise to God

10 Then David blessed the LORD in the presence of all the assembly; David said: "Blessed are you, O LORD, the God of our ancestor
Israel, forever and ever. 11 Yours, O LORD, are the greatness, the power,
the glory, the victory, and the majesty; for all that is in the heavens and
on the earth is yours; yours is the kingdom, O LORD, and you are exalted as head above all. 12 Riches and honor come from you, and you
rule over all. In your hand are power and might; and it is in your hand
to make great and to give strength to all. 13 And now, our God, we give
thanks to you and praise your glorious name.

14 "But who am I, and what is my people, that we should be able
to make this freewill offering? For all things come from you, and of
your own have we given you. 15 For we are aliens and transients before you, as were all our ancestors; our days on the earth are like a
shadow, and there is no hope. 16 O LORD our God, all this abundance
that we have provided for building you a house for your holy name
comes from your hand and is all your own. 17 I know, my God, that
you search the heart, and take pleasure in uprightness; in the uprightness of my heart I have freely offered all these things, and now I have
seen your people, who are present here, offering freely and joyously to
you. 18 O LORD, the God of Abraham, Isaac, and Israel, our ancestors,
keep forever such purposes and thoughts in the hearts of your people,
and direct their hearts toward you. 19 Grant to my son Solomon that
with single mind he may keep your commandments, your decrees,
and your statutes, performing all of them, and that he may build the
temple[a] for which I have made provision."

20 Then David said to the whole assembly, "Bless the LORD your
God." And all the assembly blessed the LORD, the God of their ancestors, and bowed their heads and prostrated themselves before the LORD
and the king. 21 On the next day they offered sacrifices and burnt offerings to the LORD, a thousand bulls, a thousand rams, and a thousand
lambs, with their libations, and sacrifices in abundance for all Israel;
22 and they ate and drank before the LORD on that day with great joy.

Solomon Anointed King

They made David's son Solomon king a second time; they anointed
him as the LORD's prince, and Zadok as priest. 23 Then Solomon sat
on the throne of the LORD, succeeding his father David as king; he
prospered, and all Israel obeyed him. 24 All the leaders and the mighty
warriors, and also all the sons of King David, pledged their allegiance
to King Solomon. 25 The LORD highly exalted Solomon in the sight of
all Israel, and bestowed upon him such royal majesty as had not been
on any king before him in Israel.

[a] Heb *fortress*

29:10-19 David blessed the LORD . . . David said: David's preparations end, as they had begun (17:16-27), with a prayer containing the basic elements of worship: praise of God's rule over them (29:10-12); thanksgiving for the people's offering, emphasizing that everything comes from God (29:13-17); and prayers for God's continued presence (29:18-19).

Why do Lutherans end the Lord's Prayer with a doxology? The doxology is "For the kingdom, the power, and the glory are yours, now and forever. Amen." It is used in most Protestant versions, and it is based upon 1 Chronicles 29:11-12. While Luther included it in his German translation of Matthew 6:13, he omitted it in worship, following the Roman Catholic practice of his day. *1 Chronicles 29:10-11*

29:20-25 all Israel: Solomon's coronation frames David's reign as a whole by repeating the themes of David's rise to power (10:1—12:40), especially the "all Israel" theme found in 29:21, 23, and 25 (also see 11:1-3; 12:38-40).

29:24 pledged their allegiance to King Solomon: In 1 Kings 1—2 the end of David's reign is marked by the murderous plots and schemes of David's sons as they try to take the throne by force. This book ends with the orderly transfer of power from David to Solomon that marks their reign as a unity intended by God.

Summary of David's Reign

26 Thus David son of Jesse reigned over all Israel. 27 The period
that he reigned over Israel was forty years; he reigned seven years in
Hebron, and thirty-three years in Jerusalem. 28 He died in a good old
age, full of days, riches, and honor; and his son Solomon succeeded
him. 29 Now the acts of King David, from first to last, are written in the
records of the seer Samuel, and in the records of the prophet Nathan,
and in the records of the seer Gad, 30 with accounts of all his rule and
his might and of the events that befell him and Israel and all the kingdoms of the earth.

29:27 forty years: Probably 1010–970 B.C.E.

Israel's history in the time of David and Solomon is described differently by the Chronicler, who authored 1 and 2 Chronicles, and by editors who put together collected history that included 1 and 2 Samuel and 1 and 2 Kings. What do you make of these differences? How can different reports of the same events help us better understand those events?

2 Chronicles 36:19

2 CHRONICLES

Background File

The two books now known as 1 and 2 Chronicles were originally a single writing titled *The Book of the Events of the Days.* They were written in Jerusalem by an anonymous author called "the Chronicler" sometime in the Persian period (539–332 B.C.E.). They address the questions and concerns of the Israelites after they returned from exile in Babylon and rebuilt their community around God's law.

What's the Story?

The historical background for 2 Chronicles can be traced to the restored community of Yehud (Judah), a province in the Persian Empire. The Jewish people there had returned from exile with Zerubbabel (Ezra 1–6, 538 B.C.E.), Ezra (Ezra 7–10, 458 B.C.E.), and Nehemiah (Neh 1–13, 445 B.C.E.) See the introductions to those books for additional background.

After seventy years of captivity in Babylon, the people needed to hear the reassuring words that God's plan for them was not affected by the fall of Jerusalem, the destruction of the temple, or their seventy-year captivity in Babylon. The tragedies they had experienced were just another stage in the accomplishment of God's purposes for them. Now was the time to reestablish worship as a faithful response to the God who had brought them home. Second Chronicles falls into three major sections. The book can be outlined in the following way.

Solomon (1:1—9:31)
- Solomon's wisdom and wealth (1:1-17)
- First preparations for the temple (2:1-18)
- Temple construction (3:1—5:1)
- Temple dedication (5:2—7:22)
- Completion of the temple (8:1-16)
- Solomon's wisdom and wealth (8:17—9:31)

The divided monarchy (10:1—28:27)
- The northern tribes rebel (10:1—11:4)
- Kings of Judah (11:5—28:27)

The reunited monarchy (29:1–36:23)

- Hezekiah's reform (29:1–32:33)
- Manasseh and Amon (33:1-25)
- Josiah's reform (34:1–35:27)
- Exile, return, and restoration (36:1-23)

The first section, the story of Solomon, completes the presentation of the united monarchy begun in 1 Chronicles. There David prepares for the building of the temple, and Solomon finishes the project.

The second section retells the story of the divided monarchy following the rebellion of the northern tribes in 922 B.C.E. The Chronicler records only the history of the southern kings of Judah (not the northern kings of Israel). The Chronicler evaluates how closely their reigns live up to the ideal presented in the reigns of David and Solomon.

The third section, the reunited monarchy, covers the time from the destruction of the northern kingdom of Israel by Assyria in 722 B.C.E. to end of the exile of the people of Judah to Babylon in 586 B.C.E. The religious reforms of Hezekiah (chapters 29–32) and Josiah (chapters 34–35) are especially important. Hezekiah is a king in the tradition of David and Solomon. He restores the idea of "all Israel" that is reunited and worshiping in Jerusalem under a descendant of King David. Finally, King Cyrus of Persia declares the end of the exile and encourages the people to return to their homeland and rebuild their temple (36:22-23).

What's the Message?

Three themes run through 2 Chronicles, in addition to those discussed in the introduction to 1 Chronicles. The most important of these is the temple. Construction of the temple in Jerusalem dominates the story of Solomon, who was chosen to follow David as king for the temple's construction. The temple is now the home of the ark of the covenant and connects the people to the religious institutions of their ancestors. When the northern tribes broke away from Judah in 922 B.C.E., Abijah said their abandonment of the temple and its priesthood was their offense or wrongdoing (2 Chr 13:8-12). The other kings of Judah are evaluated primarily on their faithfulness in supporting proper worship at the temple. Hezekiah and Josiah are especially praised in this regard.

Second, the theme of retributive justice is important here, as it was in 1–2 Kings. Retributive justice is the idea that obedience leads to blessing and disobedience leads to judgment (faith is rewarded and sin is punished). But the concept is not always illustrated in an expected way. On several occasions judgment does *not* take place, because the guilty parties have humbled themselves and repented in response to a warning by a prophet (for example, 2 Chr 12:5-8; 15:1-15).

Third, God's promise of a dynasty to David (1 Chr 17:3-15) is now joined by God's promise of forgiveness to Solomon (2 Chr 7:11-22). These two divine promises form the theological backbone of Chronicles. In 2 Chronicles 7:14 God promises Solomon that "If my people . . . humble themselves, pray, seek my face, and turn from their wicked ways, . . . I . . . will forgive their sin and heal their land."

Solomon Requests Wisdom

1 Solomon son of David established himself in his kingdom; the
LORD his God was with him and made him exceedingly great.
2 Solomon summoned all Israel, the commanders of the thousands and of the hundreds, the judges, and all the leaders of all Israel, the heads of families. [3]Then Solomon, and the whole assembly
with him, went to the high place that was at Gibeon; for God's tent
of meeting, which Moses the servant of the LORD had made in the
wilderness, was there. [4](But David had brought the ark of God up
from Kiriath-jearim to the place that David had prepared for it; for
he had pitched a tent for it in Jerusalem.) [5]Moreover the bronze altar
that Bezalel son of Uri, son of Hur, had made, was there in front of
the tabernacle of the LORD. And Solomon and the assembly inquired
at it. [6]Solomon went up there to the bronze altar before the LORD,
which was at the tent of meeting, and offered a thousand burnt offerings on it.
7 That night God appeared to Solomon, and said to him, "Ask
what I should give you." [8]Solomon said to God, "You have shown
great and steadfast love to my father David, and have made me succeed him as king. [9]O LORD God, let your promise to my father David
now be fulfilled, for you have made me king over a people as numerous as the dust of the earth. [10]Give me now wisdom and knowledge to
go out and come in before this people, for who can rule this great people of yours?" [11]God answered Solomon, "Because this was in your
heart, and you have not asked for possessions, wealth, honor, or the
life of those who hate you, and have not even asked for long life, but
have asked for wisdom and knowledge for yourself that you may rule
my people over whom I have made you king, [12]wisdom and knowledge are granted to you. I will also give you riches, possessions, and
honor, such as none of the kings had who were before you, and none
after you shall have the like." [13]So Solomon came from[a] the high place
at Gibeon, from the tent of meeting, to Jerusalem. And he reigned
over Israel.

Solomon's Military and Commercial Activity

14 Solomon gathered together chariots and horses; he had fourteen hundred chariots and twelve thousand horses, which he stationed
in the chariot cities and with the king in Jerusalem. [15]The king made
silver and gold as common in Jerusalem as stone, and he made cedar as plentiful as the sycamore of the Shephelah. [16]Solomon's horses
were imported from Egypt and Kue; the king's traders received them
from Kue at the prevailing price. [17]They imported from Egypt, and
then exported, a chariot for six hundred shekels of silver, and a horse

What is *simul justus et peccator*? Lutherans believe that we are all justified and sinful at the same time and always in need of renewal and sanctification. The presence of sin in even the "holiest" of Judah's kings, who are blessed by God, witnesses to the truth of this insight. *2 Chronicles 1:1*

1:1-17 Solomon: Solomon's reign begins with worship (1:2-6), wisdom (1:7-13), and wealth (1:14-17).

1:2-6 Solomon summoned all Israel…for God's tent of meeting: Solomon is introduced as a pious king who shows deep respect for God and is devoted to worship. He leads all Israel in worship at the tent of meeting, also called the tabernacle. The presence of the tent of meeting (Lev 17:8-9) in Gibeon makes Gibeon the only legitimate site for sacrifice before the temple is constructed in Jerusalem.

1:7-13 God appeared to Solomon, and said…wisdom and knowledge are granted to you: Solomon's prayer for wisdom fulfills David's request (1 Chr 22:12). The wisdom he receives (1:12) equips him to build the temple.

When God gives Solomon an opportunity to ask for something, Solomon asks for wisdom and knowledge to rule God's people. What would you ask God for?

1:14-17 Solomon gathered together chariots and horses…The king made silver and gold…common: The gathering of Solomon's wealth before the construction of the temple instead of at the end of his reign, as in 1 Kings 10:26-29, fulfills God's promise of wealth (1:12b). It also shows God is providing for the building of the temple.

---

[a] Gk Vg: Heb *to*

for one hundred fifty; so through them these were exported to all the
kings of the Hittites and the kings of Aram.

Preparations for Building the Temple

2 [a] Solomon decided to build a temple for the name of the LORD,
and a royal palace for himself. 2[b] Solomon conscripted seventy
thousand laborers and eighty thousand stonecutters in the hill country, with three thousand six hundred to oversee them.

Alliance with Huram of Tyre

3 Solomon sent word to King Huram of Tyre: "Once you dealt
with my father David and sent him cedar to build himself a house to
live in. 4 I am now about to build a house for the name of the LORD
my God and dedicate it to him for offering fragrant incense before
him, and for the regular offering of the rows of bread, and for burnt
offerings morning and evening, on the sabbaths and the new moons
and the appointed festivals of the LORD our God, as ordained forever
for Israel. 5 The house that I am about to build will be great, for our
God is greater than other gods. 6 But who is able to build him a house,
since heaven, even highest heaven, cannot contain him? Who am I to
build a house for him, except as a place to make offerings before him?
7 So now send me an artisan skilled to work in gold, silver, bronze, and
iron, and in purple, crimson, and blue fabrics, trained also in engraving, to join the skilled workers who are with me in Judah and Jerusalem, whom my father David provided. 8 Send me also cedar, cypress,
and algum timber from Lebanon, for I know that your servants are
skilled in cutting Lebanon timber. My servants will work with your
servants 9 to prepare timber for me in abundance, for the house I am
about to build will be great and wonderful. 10 I will provide for your
servants, those who cut the timber, twenty thousand cors of crushed
wheat, twenty thousand cors of barley, twenty thousand baths[c] of
wine, and twenty thousand baths of oil."

11 Then King Huram of Tyre answered in a letter that he sent to
Solomon, "Because the LORD loves his people he has made you king
over them." 12 Huram also said, "Blessed be the LORD God of Israel,
who made heaven and earth, who has given King David a wise son,
endowed with discretion and understanding, who will build a temple
for the LORD, and a royal palace for himself.

13 "I have dispatched Huram-abi, a skilled artisan, endowed with
understanding, 14 the son of one of the Danite women, his father a
Tyrian. He is trained to work in gold, silver, bronze, iron, stone, and
wood, and in purple, blue, and crimson fabrics and fine linen, and to
do all sorts of engraving and execute any design that may be assigned

---

[a] Ch 1.18 in Heb [b] Ch 2.1 in Heb [c] A Hebrew measure of volume

2:1-18 King Huram of Tyre: Solomon, the chosen temple builder (1 Chr 22:10), is in complete control of the temple project. This is in contrast to the story told about Solomon and Huram (named Hiram in Kings) in Kings.

2:3 Solomon sent word: Solomon, not Hiram (1 Kgs 5:1), begins the correspondence and sets the price for the timber (2:10).

2:4-6 cannot contain him: The temple is a place of worship, but God is too great to be contained by it (7:12).

2:13-14 Huram-abi: The skills of Huram-abi are like those of Bezalel and Oholiab, who built the wilderness tabernacle (Exod 31:1-11; Exod 35:30-35). This suggests that the temple is a second tabernacle.

Solomon asks for help in building the temple because his servants cannot do all the work. How can you help further God's work in the world today?

him, with your artisans, the artisans of my lord, your father David.
[15]Now, as for the wheat, barley, oil, and wine, of which my lord has
spoken, let him send them to his servants. [16]We will cut whatever
timber you need from Lebanon, and bring it to you as rafts by sea to
Joppa; you will take it up to Jerusalem."

2:17 census of all the aliens: Israelites cannot work as slaves (Lev 25:39-45) to build the temple.

17 Then Solomon took a census of all the aliens who were residing in the land of Israel, after the census that his father David had
taken; and there were found to be one hundred fifty-three thousand
six hundred. [18]Seventy thousand of them he assigned as laborers,
eighty thousand as stonecutters in the hill country, and three thousand six hundred as overseers to make the people work.

Solomon Builds the Temple

3:1—5:1 Solomon began to build the house of the Lord: The description of building the temple here is shorter than the similar story in 1 Kings 6–7. This is to emphasize worship over architecture. The temple is a symbol of God's presence, but it cannot contain God.

3:1-2 Moriah: The Chronicler connects David's designation of the temple site (1 Chr 22:1) with Moriah, the site of Abraham's obedience (see Gen 22:2, 14), rather than the exodus (1 Kgs 6:1). In Chronicles God's covenant promise with David is more important than the covenant with Moses.

3 Solomon began to build the house of the LORD in Jerusalem on
Mount Moriah, where the LORD had appeared to his father David, at the place that David had designated, on the threshing floor of
Ornan the Jebusite. [2]He began to build on the second day of the second month of the fourth year of his reign. [3]These are Solomon's measurements[a] for building the house of God: the length, in cubits of the
old standard, was sixty cubits, and the width twenty cubits. [4]The vestibule in front of the nave of the house was twenty cubits long, across
the width of the house;[b] and its height was one hundred twenty cubits. He overlaid it on the inside with pure gold. [5]The nave he lined
with cypress, covered it with fine gold, and made palms and chains on
it. [6]He adorned the house with settings of precious stones. The gold
was gold from Parvaim. [7]So he lined the house with gold—its beams,
its thresholds, its walls, and its doors; and he carved cherubim on
the walls.

8 He made the most holy place; its length, corresponding to the
width of the house, was twenty cubits, and its width was twenty cubits; he overlaid it with six hundred talents of fine gold. [9]The weight
of the nails was fifty shekels of gold. He overlaid the upper chambers
with gold.

10 In the most holy place he made two carved cherubim and
overlaid[c] them with gold. [11]The wings of the cherubim together extended twenty cubits: one wing of the one, five cubits long, touched
the wall of the house, and its other wing, five cubits long, touched
the wing of the other cherub; [12]and of this cherub, one wing, five cubits long, touched the wall of the house, and the other wing, also five
cubits long, was joined to the wing of the first cherub. [13]The wings
of these cherubim extended twenty cubits; the cherubim[d] stood on
their feet, facing the nave. [14]And Solomon[e] made the curtain of blue

---

[a] Syr: Heb *foundations* [b] Compare 1 Kings 6.3: Meaning of Heb uncertain [c] Heb *they overlaid*
[d] Heb *they* [e] Heb *he*

and purple and crimson fabrics and fine linen, and worked cherubim
into it.
15 In front of the house he made two pillars thirty-five cubits
high, with a capital of five cubits on the top of each. [16]He made encircling[a] chains and put them on the tops of the pillars; and he made one
hundred pomegranates, and put them on the chains. [17]He set up the
pillars in front of the temple, one on the right, the other on the left;
the one on the right he called Jachin, and the one on the left, Boaz.

Furnishings of the Temple

4 He made an altar of bronze, twenty cubits long, twenty cubits
wide, and ten cubits high. [2]Then he made the molten sea; it
was round, ten cubits from rim to rim, and five cubits high. A line
of thirty cubits would encircle it completely. [3]Under it were panels
all around, each of ten cubits, surrounding the sea; there were two
rows of panels, cast when it was cast. [4]It stood on twelve oxen, three
facing north, three facing west, three facing south, and three facing
east; the sea was set on them. The hindquarters of each were toward the inside. [5]Its thickness was a handbreadth; its rim was made
like the rim of a cup, like the flower of a lily; it held three thousand
baths.[b] [6]He also made ten basins in which to wash, and set five
on the right side, and five on the left. In these they were to rinse
what was used for the burnt offering. The sea was for the priests to
wash in.
7 He made ten golden lampstands as prescribed, and set them in
the temple, five on the south side and five on the north. [8]He also made
ten tables and placed them in the temple, five on the right side and
five on the left. And he made one hundred basins of gold. [9]He made
the court of the priests, and the great court, and doors for the court;
he overlaid their doors with bronze. [10]He set the sea at the southeast
corner of the house.
11 And Huram made the pots, the shovels, and the basins. Thus
Huram finished the work that he did for King Solomon on the house
of God: [12]the two pillars, the bowls, and the two capitals on the top
of the pillars; and the two latticeworks to cover the two bowls of the
capitals that were on the top of the pillars; [13]the four hundred pomegranates for the two latticeworks, two rows of pomegranates for each
latticework, to cover the two bowls of the capitals that were on the pillars. [14]He made the stands, the basins on the stands, [15]the one sea, and
the twelve oxen underneath it. [16]The pots, the shovels, the forks, and
all the equipment for these Huram-abi made of burnished bronze for
King Solomon for the house of the LORD. [17]In the plain of the Jordan
the king cast them, in the clay ground between Succoth and Zeredah.

[a] Cn: Heb *in the inner sanctuary* [b] A Hebrew measure of volume

4:1—5:1 the golden altar...the work...for the house of the LORD: Chronicles is more concerned with the temple furnishings as a sign of God's glory and blessing of Israel than descriptions of the building's architecture or construction.

The furnishings in a church help provide an environment for worship. Visualize yourself in your place of worship. What furnishings help set an environment for worship for you?

4:2-6 molten sea: The use of the "molten sea" is uncertain. It may have symbolized the Babylonian chaos monster or "the deep" in the creation story (Gen 1:2). The claim in 4:6b is that it was used for priestly cleansing. The dimensions are either approximate or refer to the inside rim. The twelve oxen that support it are in four groups of three, with each group facing a different direction. Together, the oxen may symbolize the twelve tribes of Israel.

18 Solomon made all these things in great quantities, so that the weight of the bronze was not determined.

19 So Solomon made all the things that were in the house of God: the golden altar, the tables for the bread of the Presence, 20 the lampstands and their lamps of pure gold to burn before the inner sanctuary, as prescribed; 21 the flowers, the lamps, and the tongs, of purest gold; 22 the snuffers, basins, ladles, and firepans, of pure gold. As for the entrance to the temple: the inner doors to the most holy place and the doors of the nave of the temple were of gold.

5 Thus all the work that Solomon did for the house of the LORD was finished. Solomon brought in the things that his father David had dedicated, and stored the silver, the gold, and all the vessels in the treasuries of the house of God.

The Ark Brought into the Temple

2 Then Solomon assembled the elders of Israel and all the heads of the tribes, the leaders of the ancestral houses of the people of Israel, in Jerusalem, to bring up the ark of the covenant of the LORD out of the city of David, which is Zion. 3 And all the Israelites assembled before the king at the festival that is in the seventh month. 4 And all the elders of Israel came, and the Levites carried the ark. 5 So they brought up the ark, the tent of meeting, and all the holy vessels that were in the tent; the priests and the Levites brought them up. 6 King Solomon and all the congregation of Israel, who had assembled before him, were before the ark, sacrificing so many sheep and oxen that they could not be numbered or counted. 7 Then the priests brought the ark of the covenant of the LORD to its place, in the inner sanctuary of the house, in the most holy place, underneath the wings of the cherubim. 8 For the cherubim spread out their wings over the place of the ark, so that the cherubim made a covering above the ark and its poles. 9 The poles were so long that the ends of the poles were seen from the holy place in front of the inner sanctuary; but they could not be seen from outside; they are there to this day. 10 There was nothing in the ark except the two tablets that Moses put there at Horeb, where the LORD made a covenant[a] with the people of Israel after they came out of Egypt.

11 Now when the priests came out of the holy place (for all the priests who were present had sanctified themselves, without regard to their divisions), 12 all the levitical singers, Asaph, Heman, and Jeduthun, their sons and kindred, arrayed in fine linen, with cymbals, harps, and lyres, stood east of the altar with one hundred twenty priests who were trumpeters. 13 It was the duty of the trumpeters and singers to make themselves heard in unison in praise and thanksgiv-

[a] Heb lacks *a covenant*

5:1 the work that Solomon did for the house of the LORD was finished: The Hebrew word for "was finished" sounds like Solomon's name.

In addition to formal places of worship, you can meet with God in other places. Describe your favorite place to meet with God.

5:1 Solomon . . . David: Notice how both Solomon and David are mentioned. Chronicles understands the temple project as the combined work of both.

5:2—7:22 Solomon assembled the elders: The dedication of the temple has five distinct sections: a liturgical procession bringing the ark into the temple (5:2—6:2); Solomon's speech to the assembly (6:3-11); Solomon's prayer (6:12-42); sacrifices (7:1-11); and God's response (7:12-22).

5:2—6:2 bring up the ark of the covenant: When Solomon brings the ark of the covenant into the sanctuary, he does things similar to what David did when he brought the ark to Jerusalem (1 Chr 13–16). Both occur at national assemblies (1 Chr 13:1-5; 15:3; 2 Chr 5:2-3); sacrifices are offered during the procession and installation (1 Chr 15:26; 16:1; 2 Chr 5:6); there is musical accompaniment (1 Chr 13:8; 15:16-28; 2 Chr 5:12-13); and a blessing is given by the king (1 Chr 16:1-3; 2 Chr 6:3). In both, the Levites carry the ark (1 Chr 15:2, 11-15; 2 Chr 5:4) and sing "For he is good, for his steadfast love endures forever" (1 Chr 16:34; 2 Chr 5:13). The temple is filled with a cloud (5:13-14) indicating God's presence and acceptance (6:1-2). This also occurred when the tabernacle was dedicated by Moses (Exod 40:34-38).

6:10 fulfilled his promise: God's promises to David (1 Chr 17:10-14) were fulfilled when Solomon became king and built the temple.

ing to the LORD, and when the song was raised, with trumpets and
cymbals and other musical instruments, in praise to the LORD,

"For he is good,
    for his steadfast love endures forever,"

the house, the house of the LORD, was filled with a cloud, 14 so that the
priests could not stand to minister because of the cloud; for the glory
of the LORD filled the house of God.

Dedication of the Temple

6 Then Solomon said, "The LORD has said that he would reside
in thick darkness. 2 I have built you an exalted house, a place for
you to reside in forever."

3 Then the king turned around and blessed all the assembly of
Israel, while all the assembly of Israel stood. 4 And he said, "Blessed be
the LORD, the God of Israel, who with his hand has fulfilled what he
promised with his mouth to my father David, saying, 5 'Since the day
that I brought my people out of the land of Egypt, I have not chosen
a city from any of the tribes of Israel in which to build a house, so
that my name might be there, and I chose no one as ruler over my
people Israel; 6 but I have chosen Jerusalem in order that my name
may be there, and I have chosen David to be over my people Israel.'
7 My father David had it in mind to build a house for the name of the
LORD, the God of Israel. 8 But the LORD said to my father David, 'You
did well to consider building a house for my name; 9 nevertheless you
shall not build the house, but your son who shall be born to you shall
build the house for my name.' 10 Now the LORD has fulfilled his promise that he made; for I have succeeded my father David, and sit on the
throne of Israel, as the LORD promised, and have built the house for
the name of the LORD, the God of Israel. 11 There I have set the ark, in
which is the covenant of the LORD that he made with the people of
Israel."

6:11 with the people of Israel: 1 Kings 8:21 refers to the exodus. In Chronicles, God's covenant with David is more important than the exodus.

Solomon's Prayer of Dedication

12 Then Solomon[a] stood before the altar of the LORD in the presence of the whole assembly of Israel, and spread out his hands. 13 Solomon had made a bronze platform five cubits long, five cubits wide,
and three cubits high, and had set it in the court; and he stood on it.
Then he knelt on his knees in the presence of the whole assembly of
Israel, and spread out his hands toward heaven. 14 He said, "O LORD,
God of Israel, there is no God like you, in heaven or on earth, keeping
covenant in steadfast love with your servants who walk before you
with all their heart— 15 you who have kept for your servant, my father David, what you promised to him. Indeed, you promised with

As Solomon prays, he kneels and spreads his hands toward heaven. What posture or position do you take when you pray? What does your prayer posture say about you?

6:14-17 a successor: Solomon prays that someone from David's family would always be king of Israel, as God had promised David (1 Chr 17:12).

[a] Heb *he*

your mouth and this day have fulfilled with your hand. [16]Therefore,
O LORD, God of Israel, keep for your servant, my father David, that
which you promised him, saying, 'There shall never fail you a successor before me to sit on the throne of Israel, if only your children keep
to their way, to walk in my law as you have walked before me.' [17]There-
fore, O LORD, God of Israel, let your word be confirmed, which you
promised to your servant David.

6:18-21 heaven...cannot contain you: God's presence is not limited. The temple does not contain God; it is the place where prayer is offered. Solomon asks that God will hear the many prayers that will be offered in and towards the temple (chapters 10–36).

18 "But will God indeed reside with mortals on earth? Even
heaven and the highest heaven cannot contain you, how much less
this house that I have built! [19]Regard your servant's prayer and his
plea, O LORD my God, heeding the cry and the prayer that your servant prays to you. [20]May your eyes be open day and night toward this
house, the place where you promised to set your name, and may you
heed the prayer that your servant prays toward this place. [21]And hear
the plea of your servant and of your people Israel, when they pray toward this place; may you hear from heaven your dwelling place; hear
and forgive.

22 "If someone sins against another and is required to take an
oath and comes and swears before your altar in this house, [23]may
you hear from heaven, and act, and judge your servants, repaying the
guilty by bringing their conduct on their own head, and vindicating
those who are in the right by rewarding them in accordance with their
righteousness.

24 "When your people Israel, having sinned against you, are defeated before an enemy but turn again to you, confess your name, pray
and plead with you in this house, [25]may you hear from heaven, and
forgive the sin of your people Israel, and bring them again to the land
that you gave to them and to their ancestors.

26 "When heaven is shut up and there is no rain because they
have sinned against you, and then they pray toward this place, confess
your name, and turn from their sin, because you punish them, [27]may
you hear in heaven, forgive the sin of your servants, your people Israel, when you teach them the good way in which they should walk;
and send down rain upon your land, which you have given to your
people as an inheritance.

28 "If there is famine in the land, if there is plague, blight, mildew,
locust, or caterpillar; if their enemies besiege them in any of the settlements of the lands; whatever suffering, whatever sickness there is;
[29]whatever prayer, whatever plea from any individual or from all your
people Israel, all knowing their own suffering and their own sorrows
so that they stretch out their hands toward this house; [30]may you hear
from heaven, your dwelling place, forgive, and render to all whose
heart you know, according to all their ways, for only you know the
human heart. [31]Thus may they fear you and walk in your ways all the
days that they live in the land that you gave to our ancestors.

6:30 render to all...according to all their ways: This refers to the Chronicler's concept of retributive justice that will frequently appear. Retributive justice is the idea that obedience leads to blessing and disobedience leads to judgment (faithfulness is rewarded and sin is punished).

32 “Likewise when foreigners, who are not of your people Israel, come from a distant land because of your great name, and your
mighty hand, and your outstretched arm, when they come and pray
toward this house, 33 may you hear from heaven your dwelling place,
and do whatever the foreigners ask of you, in order that all the peoples
of the earth may know your name and fear you, as do your people Israel, and that they may know that your name has been invoked on this
house that I have built.

34 “If your people go out to battle against their enemies, by whatever way you shall send them, and they pray to you toward this city
that you have chosen and the house that I have built for your name,
35 then hear from heaven their prayer and their plea, and maintain
their cause.

36 “If they sin against you—for there is no one who does not
sin—and you are angry with them and give them to an enemy, so that
they are carried away captive to a land far or near; 37 then if they come
to their senses in the land to which they have been taken captive, and
repent, and plead with you in the land of their captivity, saying, ‘We
have sinned, and have done wrong; we have acted wickedly’; 38 if they
repent with all their heart and soul in the land of their captivity, to
which they were taken captive, and pray toward their land, which you
gave to their ancestors, the city that you have chosen, and the house
that I have built for your name, 39 then hear from heaven your dwelling place their prayer and their pleas, maintain their cause and forgive
your people who have sinned against you. 40 Now, O my God, let your
eyes be open and your ears attentive to prayer from this place.

41 “Now rise up, O LORD God, and go to your resting place,
you and the ark of your might.
Let your priests, O LORD God, be clothed with salvation,
and let your faithful rejoice in your goodness.
42 O LORD God, do not reject your anointed one.
Remember your steadfast love for your servant David.”

6:41-42 ark…David: The prayer ends with David and the ark (see Ps 132:8-10), not Moses and the exodus as in 1 Kgs 8:51-53. (See note on 6:11.)

Solomon Dedicates the Temple

7 When Solomon had ended his prayer, fire came down from
heaven and consumed the burnt offering and the sacrifices;
and the glory of the LORD filled the temple. 2 The priests could not
enter the house of the LORD, because the glory of the LORD filled
the LORD’s house. 3 When all the people of Israel saw the fire come
down and the glory of the LORD on the temple, they bowed down on
the pavement with their faces to the ground, and worshiped and gave
thanks to the LORD, saying,

“For he is good,
for his steadfast love endures forever.”

4 Then the king and all the people offered sacrifice before the

7:1-3 fire came down from heaven: The fire from heaven is evidence of God’s acceptance of David and Solomon’s combined work on the temple. God’s presence in fire from heaven also is evident in the wilderness sacrifices (Lev 9:24), Elijah’s triumph over the prophets of Baal (1 Kgs 18:38), and the designation of the temple site (1 Chr 21:26).

LORD. 5King Solomon offered as a sacrifice twenty-two thousand oxen and one hundred twenty thousand sheep. So the king and all the people dedicated the house of God. 6The priests stood at their posts; the Levites also, with the instruments for music to the LORD that King David had made for giving thanks to the LORD—for his steadfast love endures forever—whenever David offered praises by their ministry. Opposite them the priests sounded trumpets; and all Israel stood.

7 Solomon consecrated the middle of the court that was in front of the house of the LORD; for there he offered the burnt offerings and the fat of the offerings of well-being because the bronze altar Solomon had made could not hold the burnt offering and the grain offering and the fat parts.

8 At that time Solomon held the festival for seven days, and all Israel with him, a very great congregation, from Lebo-hamath to the Wadi of Egypt. 9On the eighth day they held a solemn assembly; for they had observed the dedication of the altar seven days and the festival seven days. 10On the twenty-third day of the seventh month he sent the people away to their homes, joyful and in good spirits because of the goodness that the LORD had shown to David and to Solomon and to his people Israel.

7:9-10 joyful: The celebration lasts two weeks and is marked by joy. Hezekiah's Passover will be described in a similar way (2 Chr 30:23).

11 Thus Solomon finished the house of the LORD and the king's house; all that Solomon had planned to do in the house of the LORD and in his own house he successfully accomplished.

God's Second Appearance to Solomon

12 Then the LORD appeared to Solomon in the night and said to him: "I have heard your prayer, and have chosen this place for myself as a house of sacrifice. 13When I shut up the heavens so that there is no rain, or command the locust to devour the land, or send pestilence among my people, 14if my people who are called by my name humble themselves, pray, seek my face, and turn from their wicked ways, then I will hear from heaven, and will forgive their sin and heal their land. 15Now my eyes will be open and my ears attentive to the prayer that is made in this place. 16For now I have chosen and consecrated this house so that my name may be there forever; my eyes and my heart will be there for all time. 17As for you, if you walk before me, as your father David walked, doing according to all that I have commanded you and keeping my statutes and my ordinances, 18then I will establish your royal throne, as I made covenant with your father David saying, 'You shall never lack a successor to rule over Israel.'

7:14 humble themselves, pray, seek my face, and turn from their wicked ways: These four verbs or actions describe what the Chronicler means by repentance. The concept of repentance balances the theme of retributive justice (see note on 6:30) as the story continues. Repentance is the confessing of one's sins in order to receive forgiveness. God's promise of forgiveness and God's promise that one of David's descendants will rule Israel (1 Chr 17) are the heart of the Chronicler's message.

19 "But if you[a] turn aside and forsake my statutes and my commandments that I have set before you, and go and serve other gods

[a] The word *you* in this verse is plural

and worship them, [20]then I will pluck you[a] up from the land that I
have given you;[a] and this house, which I have consecrated for my
name, I will cast out of my sight, and will make it a proverb and a
byword among all peoples. [21]And regarding this house, now exalted,
everyone passing by will be astonished, and say, 'Why has the LORD
done such a thing to this land and to this house?' [22]Then they will say,
'Because they abandoned the LORD the God of their ancestors who
brought them out of the land of Egypt, and they adopted other gods,
and worshiped them and served them; therefore he has brought all
this calamity upon them.'"

Various Activities of Solomon

8 At the end of twenty years, during which Solomon had built the
house of the LORD and his own house, [2]Solomon rebuilt the
cities that Huram had given to him, and settled the people of Israel
in them.

3 Solomon went to Hamath-zobah, and captured it. [4]He built
Tadmor in the wilderness and all the storage towns that he built in
Hamath. [5]He also built Upper Beth-horon and Lower Beth-horon,
fortified cities, with walls, gates, and bars, [6]and Baalath, as well as
all Solomon's storage towns, and all the towns for his chariots, the
towns for his cavalry, and whatever Solomon desired to build, in
Jerusalem, in Lebanon, and in all the land of his dominion. [7]All the
people who were left of the Hittites, the Amorites, the Perizzites, the
Hivites, and the Jebusites, who were not of Israel, [8]from their descendants who were still left in the land, whom the people of Israel had
not destroyed—these Solomon conscripted for forced labor, as is still
the case today. [9]But of the people of Israel Solomon made no slaves
for his work; they were soldiers, and his officers, the commanders
of his chariotry and cavalry. [10]These were the chief officers of King
Solomon, two hundred fifty of them, who exercised authority over
the people.

11 Solomon brought Pharaoh's daughter from the city of David
to the house that he had built for her, for he said, "My wife shall not
live in the house of King David of Israel, for the places to which the
ark of the LORD has come are holy."

12 Then Solomon offered up burnt offerings to the LORD on the
altar of the LORD that he had built in front of the vestibule, [13]as the
duty of each day required, offering according to the commandment
of Moses for the sabbaths, the new moons, and the three annual festivals—the festival of unleavened bread, the festival of weeks, and the
festival of booths. [14]According to the ordinance of his father David, he
appointed the divisions of the priests for their service, and the Levites

[a] Heb *them*

What does repentance look like? Luther, in the first of his famous *Ninety-five Theses* maintained that "the entire life of believers be one of repentance." In Chronicles, repentance is literally a "turning around," changing the direction of one's life to conform to God's intention. In the most important verse of 2 Chronicles, God promises to forgive the sin of those who "humble themselves, pray, seek my face, and turn from their wicked ways." *2 Chronicles 7:14*

8:1-16 Solomon...accomplished: In Chronicles Solomon's building projects indicate God's favor.

8:2 cities that Huram had given to him: Solomon gives the cities to Hiram in 1 Kings 9:11. In Chronicles, the situation is reversed. Huram gives the cities to Solomon, which glorifies Solomon.

8:3 captured it: Solomon's only military campaign. The city is unknown. While military victory is a sign of God's favor, Solomon is supposedly a "man of peace" (1 Chr 22:9).

for their offices of praise and ministry alongside the priests as the duty
of each day required, and the gatekeepers in their divisions for the
several gates; for so David the man of God had commanded. 15 They
did not turn away from what the king had commanded the priests and
Levites regarding anything at all, or regarding the treasuries.

16 Thus all the work of Solomon was accomplished from[a] the day
the foundation of the house of the LORD was laid until the house of
the LORD was finished completely.

17 Then Solomon went to Ezion-geber and Eloth on the shore
of the sea, in the land of Edom. 18 Huram sent him, in the care of his
servants, ships and servants familiar with the sea. They went to Ophir,
together with the servants of Solomon, and imported from there four
hundred fifty talents of gold and brought it to King Solomon.

8:17—9:31 Then Solomon...slept with his ancestors: Solomon's story ends as it began (1:1-17), with Solomon's wisdom, wealth, and fame fulfilling God's promise (1:12).

8:17-18 Huram sent him: Huram provides the ships and capital, not Solomon as in 1 Kings 9:26-28. Solomon is glorified at Huram's expense.

8:17 the sea: The Red Sea (see Map 2, p. 2099).

Visit of the Queen of Sheba

9 When the queen of Sheba heard of the fame of Solomon, she
came to Jerusalem to test him with hard questions, having a
very great retinue and camels bearing spices and very much gold and
precious stones. When she came to Solomon, she discussed with him
all that was on her mind. 2 Solomon answered all her questions; there
was nothing hidden from Solomon that he could not explain to her.
3 When the queen of Sheba had observed the wisdom of Solomon,
the house that he had built, 4 the food of his table, the seating of his
officials, and the attendance of his servants, and their clothing, his valets, and their clothing, and his burnt offerings[b] that he offered at the
house of the LORD, there was no more spirit left in her.

5 So she said to the king, "The report was true that I heard in my
own land of your accomplishments and of your wisdom, 6 but I did
not believe the[c] reports until I came and my own eyes saw it. Not even
half of the greatness of your wisdom had been told to me; you far surpass the report that I had heard. 7 Happy are your people! Happy are
these your servants, who continually attend you and hear your wisdom! 8 Blessed be the LORD your God, who has delighted in you and
set you on his throne as king for the LORD your God. Because your
God loved Israel and would establish them forever, he has made you
king over them, that you may execute justice and righteousness."
9 Then she gave the king one hundred twenty talents of gold, a very
great quantity of spices, and precious stones: there were no spices
such as those that the queen of Sheba gave to King Solomon.

10 Moreover the servants of Huram and the servants of Solomon
who brought gold from Ophir brought algum wood and precious
stones. 11 From the algum wood, the king made steps[d] for the house of

9:5-6 The report was true...of your wisdom: The queen of Sheba (modern Yemen) praises Solomon's wisdom.

9:8 his throne: Refers to "the throne of Israel" (1 Kgs 10:9). In Chronicles, God rules Israel. The Chronicler's community was ruled by God even without a human king on the throne.

9:9 one hundred twenty talents: At seventy-five pounds per talent, this is four and one-half tons.

---

[a] Gk Syr Vg: Heb *to* [b] Gk Syr Vg 1 Kings 10.5: Heb *ascent* [c] Heb *their* [d] Gk Vg: Meaning of Heb uncertain

the LORD and for the king's house, lyres also and harps for the singers;
there never was seen the like of them before in the land of Judah.
12 Meanwhile King Solomon granted the queen of Sheba every
desire that she expressed, well beyond what she had brought to the
king. Then she returned to her own land, with her servants.

Solomon's Great Wealth

13 The weight of gold that came to Solomon in one year was six
hundred sixty-six talents of gold, [14]besides that which the traders
and merchants brought; and all the kings of Arabia and the governors of the land brought gold and silver to Solomon. [15]King Solomon
made two hundred large shields of beaten gold; six hundred shekels
of beaten gold went into each large shield. [16]He made three hundred
shields of beaten gold; three hundred shekels of gold went into each
shield; and the king put them in the House of the Forest of Lebanon.
[17]The king also made a great ivory throne, and overlaid it with pure
gold. [18]The throne had six steps and a footstool of gold, which were
attached to the throne, and on each side of the seat were arm rests
and two lions standing beside the arm rests, [19]while twelve lions were
standing, one on each end of a step on the six steps. The like of it was
never made in any kingdom. [20]All King Solomon's drinking vessels
were of gold, and all the vessels of the House of the Forest of Lebanon
were of pure gold; silver was not considered as anything in the days
of Solomon. [21]For the king's ships went to Tarshish with the servants
of Huram; once every three years the ships of Tarshish used to come
bringing gold, silver, ivory, apes, and peacocks.[a]
22 Thus King Solomon excelled all the kings of the earth in
riches and in wisdom. [23]All the kings of the earth sought the presence of Solomon to hear his wisdom, which God had put into his
mind. [24]Every one of them brought a present, objects of silver and
gold, garments, weaponry, spices, horses, and mules, so much year
by year. [25]Solomon had four thousand stalls for horses and chariots,
and twelve thousand horses, which he stationed in the chariot cities
and with the king in Jerusalem. [26]He ruled over all the kings from the
Euphrates to the land of the Philistines, and to the border of Egypt.
[27]The king made silver as common in Jerusalem as stone, and cedar as
plentiful as the sycamore of the Shephelah. [28]Horses were imported
for Solomon from Egypt and from all lands.

Death of Solomon

29 Now the rest of the acts of Solomon, from first to last, are they
not written in the history of the prophet Nathan, and in the prophecy
of Ahijah the Shilonite, and in the visions of the seer Iddo concerning

9:13-28 the weight of gold that came to Solomon: Solomon's wealth and fame brings honor from all the kings of the earth.

Solomon's accomplishments, his wealth, and his fame contribute to his greatness in the eyes of others as well as God. What do you think greatness is? What do you think greatness is in God's eyes?

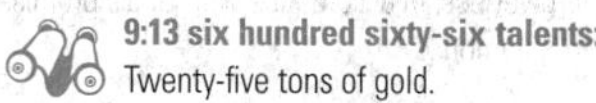

9:13 six hundred sixty-six talents: Twenty-five tons of gold.

9:26 he ruled over all: To emphasize his greatness, Solomon's unfaithfulness at the end of his reign (1 Kgs 11:1-13; 33-40) is replaced with a statement of his authority from 1 Kings 4:21.

[a] Or *baboons*

Jeroboam son of Nebat? 30Solomon reigned in Jerusalem over all Israel forty years. 31Solomon slept with his ancestors and was buried in
the city of his father David; and his son Rehoboam succeeded him.

The Revolt against Rehoboam

10 Rehoboam went to Shechem, for all Israel had come to Shechem to make him king. 2When Jeroboam son of Nebat
heard of it (for he was in Egypt, where he had fled from King Solomon), then Jeroboam returned from Egypt. 3They sent and called
him; and Jeroboam and all Israel came and said to Rehoboam, 4"Your
father made our yoke heavy. Now therefore lighten the hard service
of your father and his heavy yoke that he placed on us, and we will
serve you." 5He said to them, "Come to me again in three days." So the
people went away.
6 Then King Rehoboam took counsel with the older men who
had attended his father Solomon while he was still alive, saying, "How
do you advise me to answer this people?" 7They answered him, "If you
will be kind to this people and please them, and speak good words to
them, then they will be your servants forever." 8But he rejected the
advice that the older men gave him, and consulted the young men
who had grown up with him and now attended him. 9He said to them,
"What do you advise that we answer this people who have said to me,
'Lighten the yoke that your father put on us'?" 10The young men who
had grown up with him said to him, "Thus should you speak to the
people who said to you, 'Your father made our yoke heavy, but you
must lighten it for us'; tell them, 'My little finger is thicker than my
father's loins. 11Now, whereas my father laid on you a heavy yoke, I
will add to your yoke. My father disciplined you with whips, but I will
discipline you with scorpions.' "
12 So Jeroboam and all the people came to Rehoboam the third
day, as the king had said, "Come to me again the third day." 13The king
answered them harshly. King Rehoboam rejected the advice of the
older men; 14he spoke to them in accordance with the advice of the
young men, "My father made your yoke heavy, but I will add to it;
my father disciplined you with whips, but I will discipline you with
scorpions." 15So the king did not listen to the people, because it was
a turn of affairs brought about by God so that the LORD might fulfill
his word, which he had spoken by Ahijah the Shilonite to Jeroboam
son of Nebat.
16 When all Israel saw that the king would not listen to them, the
people answered the king,

"What share do we have in David?
    We have no inheritance in the son of Jesse.
Each of you to your tents, O Israel!
    Look now to your own house, O David."

10:1—28:27 Rehoboam went to Shechem, for all Israel had come... to make him king: The divided monarchy begins under Rehoboam. The Chronicler's focus upon the southern kingdom of Judah means that references to the north are scattered. Kings are measured against David and Solomon (see, for example, 7:10; 11:17; 35:4). Obedient kings enjoy wealth, military victory, "rest," building projects, and large families. Disobedient kings endure punishment, military defeat, and illness. A host of otherwise unknown prophets who point to these failures also hold out the possibility of repentance and forgiveness, in accordance with God's promise to Solomon (7:14).

10:1—12:16 Rehoboam: Rehoboam is the first king to follow the ideal reigns of David and Solomon. He represents the three patterns that will dominate the following stories: sin brings failure (10:1—11:4), obedience brings success (11:5-23), and repentance brings deliverance (12:1-16).

10:1—11:4 Rehoboam...in rebellion against the house of David: This text illustrates the first pattern: sin brings failure. The earlier history, told in 1 Kings, blamed the division of the kingdom on Solomon's sin (1 Kgs 11). The Chronicler, however, omitted this material in his story of Solomon. In 2 Chronicles, Solomon's "heavy yoke" (10:4, 9-11, 14), Jeroboam's rebellion (10:19), and Rehoboam's failure to take advice (10:6-8, 13) are all responsible for the division of the kingdom. Sin brings failure.

10:4, 9-11, 14 heavy yoke: Solomon taxed the people and forced them to work on his projects, according to 1 Kings 5:6-18; 11:28, though the Chronicler denies this (2:17-18; 8:7-10).

10:15 brought about by God: While Solomon, Jeroboam, and Rehoboam are blamed for the division of the kingdom, it would not have happened apart from God's activity that fulfilled God's judgment upon Jeroboam (1 Kings 11:29-39). In 1 Kings the division is due to God's will. The Chronicler agrees in this verse, but assigns some of the blame to Solomon, Jeroboam, and Rehoboam.

So all Israel departed to their tents. 17But Rehoboam reigned over the
people of Israel who were living in the cities of Judah. 18When King
Rehoboam sent Hadoram, who was taskmaster over the forced labor,
the people of Israel stoned him to death. King Rehoboam hurriedly
mounted his chariot to flee to Jerusalem. 19So Israel has been in rebellion against the house of David to this day.

Judah and Benjamin Fortified

11 When Rehoboam came to Jerusalem, he assembled one hundred eighty thousand chosen troops of the house of Judah and
Benjamin to fight against Israel, to restore the kingdom to Rehoboam.
2But the word of the LORD came to Shemaiah the man of God: 3Say
to King Rehoboam of Judah, son of Solomon, and to all Israel in Judah and Benjamin, 4"Thus says the LORD: You shall not go up or fight
against your kindred. Let everyone return home, for this thing is from
me." So they heeded the word of the LORD and turned back from the
expedition against Jeroboam.
5 Rehoboam resided in Jerusalem, and he built cities for defense in Judah. 6He built up Bethlehem, Etam, Tekoa, 7Beth-zur,
Soco, Adullam, 8Gath, Mareshah, Ziph, 9Adoraim, Lachish, Azekah,
10Zorah, Aijalon, and Hebron, fortified cities that are in Judah and in
Benjamin. 11He made the fortresses strong, and put commanders in
them, and stores of food, oil, and wine. 12He also put large shields and
spears in all the cities, and made them very strong. So he held Judah
and Benjamin.

11:5-23 Rehoboam…walked for three years in the way of David and Solomon: This text illustrates the second pattern: faithful obedience brings success. Rehoboam's fortifications are introduced in the story before Shishak's coming invasion (12:1-12) to portray Rehoboam as an obedient king who prospers. God rewards Rehoboam's faithful obedience with three years of prosperity and blessing (11:17).

Priests and Levites Support Rehoboam

13 The priests and the Levites who were in all Israel presented
themselves to him from all their territories. 14The Levites had left
their common lands and their holdings and had come to Judah and
Jerusalem, because Jeroboam and his sons had prevented them from
serving as priests of the LORD, 15and had appointed his own priests
for the high places, and for the goat-demons, and for the calves that
he had made. 16Those who had set their hearts to seek the LORD God
of Israel came after them from all the tribes of Israel to Jerusalem to
sacrifice to the LORD, the God of their ancestors. 17They strengthened
the kingdom of Judah, and for three years they made Rehoboam son
of Solomon secure, for they walked for three years in the way of David
and Solomon.

Rehoboam's Marriages

18 Rehoboam took as his wife Mahalath daughter of Jerimoth
son of David, and of Abihail daughter of Eliab son of Jesse. 19She
bore him sons: Jeush, Shemariah, and Zaham. 20After her he took
Maacah daughter of Absalom, who bore him Abijah, Attai, Ziza, and

Shelomith. 21 Rehoboam loved Maacah daughter of Absalom more than all his other wives and concubines (he took eighteen wives and sixty concubines, and became the father of twenty-eight sons and sixty daughters). 22 Rehoboam appointed Abijah son of Maacah as chief prince among his brothers, for he intended to make him king. 23 He dealt wisely, and distributed some of his sons through all the districts of Judah and Benjamin, in all the fortified cities; he gave them abundant provisions, and found many wives for them.

Egypt Attacks Judah

12 When the rule of Rehoboam was established and he grew strong, he abandoned the law of the LORD, he and all Israel with him. 2 In the fifth year of King Rehoboam, because they had been unfaithful to the LORD, King Shishak of Egypt came up against Jerusalem 3 with twelve hundred chariots and sixty thousand cavalry. A countless army came with him from Egypt—Libyans, Sukkiim, and Ethiopians.[a] 4 He took the fortified cities of Judah and came as far as Jerusalem. 5 Then the prophet Shemaiah came to Rehoboam and to the officers of Judah, who had gathered at Jerusalem because of Shishak, and said to them, "Thus says the LORD: You abandoned me, so I have abandoned you to the hand of Shishak." 6 Then the officers of Israel and the king humbled themselves and said, "The LORD is in the right." 7 When the LORD saw that they humbled themselves, the word of the LORD came to Shemaiah, saying: "They have humbled themselves; I will not destroy them, but I will grant them some deliverance, and my wrath shall not be poured out on Jerusalem by the hand of Shishak. 8 Nevertheless they shall be his servants, so that they may know the difference between serving me and serving the kingdoms of other lands."

9 So King Shishak of Egypt came up against Jerusalem; he took away the treasures of the house of the LORD and the treasures of the king's house; he took everything. He also took away the shields of gold that Solomon had made; 10 but King Rehoboam made in place of them shields of bronze, and committed them to the hands of the officers of the guard, who kept the door of the king's house. 11 Whenever the king went into the house of the LORD, the guard would come along bearing them, and would then bring them back to the guardroom. 12 Because he humbled himself the wrath of the LORD turned from him, so as not to destroy them completely; moreover, conditions were good in Judah.

Death of Rehoboam

13 So King Rehoboam established himself in Jerusalem and reigned. Rehoboam was forty-one years old when he began to reign;

[a] Or *Nubians;* Heb *Cushites*

11:21 loved Maacah: Rehoboam's love for Maacah explains why Maacah's son Abijah becomes king (11:22), even though he is not the eldest.

11:21 twenty-eight sons and sixty daughters: Large families are a sign of God's favor, as are building projects.

12:1-16 Rehoboam...abandoned the law of the LORD...Because he humbled himself the wrath of the LORD turned from him: This text illustrates the third pattern: repentance brings deliverance. The invasion of Judah by Shishak of Egypt (945–925 B.C.E.) is blamed on the sin of Rehoboam and all Israel (12:1-2, 5). But when they repent in response to the prophet's warning, God spares them (12:6-7, 12).

12:6-7 humbled themselves: In response to Shemaiah the prophet, Rehoboam and the leaders repent. This is the first fulfillment of God's promise to Solomon (7:14).

Repentance is turning away from sin and turning back to God and God's promise of forgiveness. Repentance is something that can be done every day. What role does repentance play in your life? How does it feel for you to be a forgiven sinner?

he reigned seventeen years in Jerusalem, the city that the LORD had
chosen out of all the tribes of Israel to put his name there. His mother's name was Naamah the Ammonite. 14He did evil, for he did not set
his heart to seek the LORD.
15 Now the acts of Rehoboam, from first to last, are they not written in the records of the prophet Shemaiah and of the seer Iddo, recorded by genealogy? There were continual wars between Rehoboam
and Jeroboam. 16Rehoboam slept with his ancestors and was buried
in the city of David; and his son Abijah succeeded him.

Abijah Reigns over Judah

13 In the eighteenth year of King Jeroboam, Abijah began to
reign over Judah. 2He reigned for three years in Jerusalem.
His mother's name was Micaiah daughter of Uriel of Gibeah.
Now there was war between Abijah and Jeroboam. 3Abijah engaged in battle, having an army of valiant warriors, four hundred thousand picked men; and Jeroboam drew up his line of battle against him
with eight hundred thousand picked mighty warriors. 4Then Abijah
stood on the slope of Mount Zemaraim that is in the hill country of
Ephraim, and said, "Listen to me, Jeroboam and all Israel! 5Do you
not know that the LORD God of Israel gave the kingship over Israel
forever to David and his sons by a covenant of salt? 6Yet Jeroboam
son of Nebat, a servant of Solomon son of David, rose up and rebelled
against his lord; 7and certain worthless scoundrels gathered around
him and defied Rehoboam son of Solomon, when Rehoboam was
young and irresolute and could not withstand them.
8 "And now you think that you can withstand the kingdom of
the LORD in the hand of the sons of David, because you are a great
multitude and have with you the golden calves that Jeroboam made
as gods for you. 9Have you not driven out the priests of the LORD, the
descendants of Aaron, and the Levites, and made priests for yourselves like the peoples of other lands? Whoever comes to be consecrated with a young bull or seven rams becomes a priest of what are
no gods. 10But as for us, the LORD is our God, and we have not abandoned him. We have priests ministering to the LORD who are descendants of Aaron, and Levites for their service. 11They offer to the
LORD every morning and every evening burnt offerings and fragrant
incense, set out the rows of bread on the table of pure gold, and care
for the golden lampstand so that its lamps may burn every evening;
for we keep the charge of the LORD our God, but you have abandoned him. 12See, God is with us at our head, and his priests have
their battle trumpets to sound the call to battle against you. O Israelites, do not fight against the LORD, the God of your ancestors; for
you cannot succeed."
13 Jeroboam had sent an ambush around to come on them from

13:1—14:1 Abijah began to reign . . . Asa succeeded him: Reliance upon God links the reigns of Abijah and Asa. (The word *rely* is used only in the reigns of Abijah and Asa (13:18; 14:11; 16:7, 8). Although Abijah is praised here for his clear expression of the faith, 1 Kings 15:3-6 condemns him.

13:3 four hundred thousand . . . eight hundred thousand: The huge numbers and two-to-one odds against Judah are the basis of the claim that God is the source of Abijah's victory (13:15).

13:4-12 Abijah stood . . . and said: Abijah's speech presents three of the Chronicler's theological themes: the reign of David and his descendants, Israel's religious and worship life, and "all Israel" (see the introductions to 1 and 2 Chronicles).

13:5-8a the LORD . . . gave the kingship over Israel forever to David and his sons: God promised David that someone from his family would always sit on the throne of Israel (1 Chr 17:12, 14).

13:5 covenant of salt: Salt's ability to preserve food illustrates the eternal nature of God's promises and loyalty (Lev 2:13; Num 18:19).

13:6-7 young and irresolute: The Chronicler explains away Rehoboam's guilt for the division of the monarchy. He was actually forty-one years of age at the time (12:13).

13:8b-12 the LORD is our God . . . O Israelites, do not fight against the LORD: Abijah pleads for reunification under one God and one king. He says that with a faithful king on the throne (a descendant of David) and proper worship in the temple, there is no reason for the north to continue in their rebellion. Abijah invites the north to return, restoring the unity lost in the division of 922 B.C.E. Later Hezekiah will offer a similar invitation following the north's fall to Assyria in 722 B.C.E. (2 Chr 30:6-9).

13:14-18 They cried out to the Lord... people of Judah prevailed, because they relied on the Lord: God defeated Jeroboam and the Israelites. The people of Judah relied on God, as seen in the people's prayer and the priests' trumpets, and God delivered them from defeat.

The people of Judah relied upon God. Besides God, upon what things or people do you most rely? What is the difference between relying on God and on others?

13:19—14:1 cities... wives... rest: Territory (13:19), many wives and children (13:21), and rest (14:1) indicate God's favor.

14:2—16:14 Asa: The theme of reliance upon God, introduced in Abijah's reign (13:1—14:1), continues. Asa's reign, like that of Rehoboam, divides into two periods, illustrating the blessings of faithful obedience (14:2—15:19) and the results of unfaithfulness (16:1-14).

14:1—16:14 seek: Two terms, each meaning "seek," appear nine times in these chapters. The first, *darash* [dah-RAHSH], appears at 14:4, twice at 14:7, 15:2, 12, 13, and 16:12. The second, *biqqesh* [bi-QEHSH], appears at 15:4, 15. Seeking the Lord, meaning faithful obedience, is a key element of the Chronicler's theology.

14:2—15:19 Asa did what was good: The report of Asa's religious reforms in 1 Kings 15:9-15 is expanded in 2 Chronicles to emphasize blessing as the reward of faithful obedience.

14:6a fortified cities: Building projects and fortifications are signs of God's favor.

14:6b-7 peace... peace: The word *peace* means "rest" (Deut 12:10; 1 Chr 22:8-10) and is a characteristic of blessing in Chronicles. The other occurrences of "rest" in this chapter (14:1b, 5, 6a) are a different Hebrew word.

14:8 army: Asa's army of 580,000 warriors is a final indication of blessing.

14:9-15 Asa cried to the Lord his God: When invaded by Ethiopia (modern Sudan and Ethiopia), Asa relies upon God and is delivered from the enemy.

behind; thus his troops[a] were in front of Judah, and the ambush was
behind them. 14 When Judah turned, the battle was in front of them
and behind them. They cried out to the Lord, and the priests blew
the trumpets. 15 Then the people of Judah raised the battle shout. And
when the people of Judah shouted, God defeated Jeroboam and all
Israel before Abijah and Judah. 16 The Israelites fled before Judah, and
God gave them into their hands. 17 Abijah and his army defeated them
with great slaughter; five hundred thousand picked men of Israel fell
slain. 18 Thus the Israelites were subdued at that time, and the people of Judah prevailed, because they relied on the Lord, the God of
their ancestors. 19 Abijah pursued Jeroboam, and took cities from him:
Bethel with its villages and Jeshanah with its villages and Ephron[b]
with its villages. 20 Jeroboam did not recover his power in the days of
Abijah; the Lord struck him down, and he died. 21 But Abijah grew
strong. He took fourteen wives, and became the father of twenty-two
sons and sixteen daughters. 22 The rest of the acts of Abijah, his behavior and his deeds, are written in the story of the prophet Iddo.

Asa Reigns

14 [c] So Abijah slept with his ancestors, and they buried him in
the city of David. His son Asa succeeded him. In his days
the land had rest for ten years. 2[d] Asa did what was good and right
in the sight of the Lord his God. 3 He took away the foreign altars
and the high places, broke down the pillars, hewed down the sacred
poles,[e] 4 and commanded Judah to seek the Lord, the God of their
ancestors, and to keep the law and the commandment. 5 He also removed from all the cities of Judah the high places and the incense
altars. And the kingdom had rest under him. 6 He built fortified cities in Judah while the land had rest. He had no war in those years,
for the Lord gave him peace. 7 He said to Judah, "Let us build these
cities, and surround them with walls and towers, gates and bars; the
land is still ours because we have sought the Lord our God; we have
sought him, and he has given us peace on every side." So they built
and prospered. 8 Asa had an army of three hundred thousand from
Judah, armed with large shields and spears, and two hundred eighty
thousand troops from Benjamin who carried shields and drew bows;
all these were mighty warriors.

Ethiopian Invasion Repulsed

9 Zerah the Ethiopian[f] came out against them with an army of
a million men and three hundred chariots, and came as far as Mareshah. 10 Asa went out to meet him, and they drew up their lines

---

[a] Heb *they* [b] Another reading is *Ephrain* [c] Ch 13.23 in Heb [d] Ch 14.1 in Heb [e] Heb *Asherim*
[f] Or *Nubian*; Heb *Cushite*

of battle in the valley of Zephathah at Mareshah. 11 Asa cried to the
LORD his God, "O LORD, there is no difference for you between
helping the mighty and the weak. Help us, O LORD our God, for
we rely on you, and in your name we have come against this multitude. O LORD, you are our God; let no mortal prevail against you."
12 So the LORD defeated the Ethiopians[a] before Asa and before Judah, and the Ethiopians[a] fled. 13 Asa and the army with him pursued
them as far as Gerar, and the Ethiopians[a] fell until no one remained
alive; for they were broken before the LORD and his army. The people of Judah[b] carried away a great quantity of booty. 14 They defeated
all the cities around Gerar, for the fear of the LORD was on them.
They plundered all the cities; for there was much plunder in them.
15 They also attacked the tents of those who had livestock,[c] and carried away sheep and goats in abundance, and camels. Then they returned to Jerusalem.

15 The spirit of God came upon Azariah son of Oded. 2 He went
out to meet Asa and said to him, "Hear me, Asa, and all Judah
and Benjamin: The LORD is with you, while you are with him. If you
seek him, he will be found by you, but if you abandon him, he will
abandon you. 3 For a long time Israel was without the true God, and
without a teaching priest, and without law; 4 but when in their distress
they turned to the LORD, the God of Israel, and sought him, he was
found by them. 5 In those times it was not safe for anyone to go or
come, for great disturbances afflicted all the inhabitants of the lands.
6 They were broken in pieces, nation against nation and city against
city, for God troubled them with every sort of distress. 7 But you, take
courage! Do not let your hands be weak, for your work shall be rewarded."

8 When Asa heard these words, the prophecy of Azariah son of
Oded,[d] he took courage, and put away the abominable idols from all
the land of Judah and Benjamin and from the towns that he had taken
in the hill country of Ephraim. He repaired the altar of the LORD that
was in front of the vestibule of the house of the LORD.[e] 9 He gathered
all Judah and Benjamin, and those from Ephraim, Manasseh, and
Simeon who were residing as aliens with them, for great numbers had
deserted to him from Israel when they saw that the LORD his God was
with him. 10 They were gathered at Jerusalem in the third month of the
fifteenth year of the reign of Asa. 11 They sacrificed to the LORD on
that day, from the booty that they had brought, seven hundred oxen
and seven thousand sheep. 12 They entered into a covenant to seek the
LORD, the God of their ancestors, with all their heart and with all their
soul. 13 Whoever would not seek the LORD, the God of Israel, should

---

[a] Or *Nubians*; Heb *Cushites* [b] Heb *They* [c] Meaning of Heb uncertain [d] Compare Syr Vg: Heb *the prophecy, the prophet Obed* [e] Heb *the vestibule of the LORD*

14:9 a million: The huge numbers also indicate that Asa is outnumbered two-to-one, as was his father, Abijah (13:3).

14:11 rely: Asa's reliance upon God mirrors that of his father, Abijah (13:18), in the second appearance of this key term (see note on 13:1—14:1).

14:12 the LORD defeated: God answers Asa's prayer as promised to Solomon (2 Chr 6:34-35).

Both Abijah and Asa take on armies much larger than theirs. That might indicate risk-taking to us. What does God's defeat of larger armies say about risk-taking?

15:1-7 Azariah...went out to meet Asa and said to him: The Chronicler has written several addresses or speeches and had them spoken by otherwise unknown prophets to illustrate the concepts of retributive justice and repentance (see notes for 6:30 and 7:14). These speeches sound more like sermons on biblical themes than typical prophetic speeches. Azariah's speech begins with a statement of faith that the LORD will be with them as long as they remain faithful (15:2b). Then he recalls Israel's past (the time of the Judges) to show the effects of both faithful and unfaithful responses (15:3-6). Finally he quotes Jeremiah 31:16 and Zephaniah 3:16, to urge Asa to complete his religious reform (15:7), which Asa does (15:8-9).

15:8-9 When Asa heard these words...he gathered...those from Ephraim, Manasseh: By including the northern tribes of Ephraim and Manasseh, the Chronicler demonstrates his concern for the unity of all Israel. Jehoshaphat, Hezekiah, and Josiah also will include the north in their reforms.

Azariah's sermon influenced Asa's behavior. In what ways has a sermon changed your behavior or your life?

be put to death, whether young or old, man or woman. 14They took
an oath to the LORD with a loud voice, and with shouting, and with
trumpets, and with horns. 15All Judah rejoiced over the oath; for they
had sworn with all their heart, and had sought him with their whole
desire, and he was found by them, and the LORD gave them rest all
around.

16 King Asa even removed his mother Maacah from being queen
mother because she had made an abominable image for Asherah. Asa
cut down her image, crushed it, and burned it at the Wadi Kidron.
17But the high places were not taken out of Israel. Nevertheless the
heart of Asa was true all his days. 18He brought into the house of God
the votive gifts of his father and his own votive gifts—silver, gold, and
utensils. 19And there was no more war until the thirty-fifth year of the
reign of Asa.

15:17 Israel: The northern kingdom.

Alliance with Aram Condemned

16 In the thirty-sixth year of the reign of Asa, King Baasha of
Israel went up against Judah, and built Ramah, to prevent
anyone from going out or coming into the territory of[a] King Asa of
Judah. 2Then Asa took silver and gold from the treasures of the house
of the LORD and the king's house, and sent them to King Ben-hadad
of Aram, who resided in Damascus, saying, 3"Let there be an alliance
between me and you, like that between my father and your father; I
am sending to you silver and gold; go, break your alliance with King
Baasha of Israel, so that he may withdraw from me." 4Ben-hadad listened to King Asa, and sent the commanders of his armies against
the cities of Israel. They conquered Ijon, Dan, Abel-maim, and all the
store-cities of Naphtali. 5When Baasha heard of it, he stopped building Ramah, and let his work cease. 6Then King Asa brought all Judah, and they carried away the stones of Ramah and its timber, with
which Baasha had been building, and with them he built up Geba and
Mizpah.

16:1-14 Then Asa took silver and gold…an alliance between me and you: This text describes Asa's negative period. Notice how this time is described as a reversal of Asa's positive period. Instead of "relying" upon God (13:18; 14:11), he now "relies" upon a foreign alliance with Ben-hadad of Syria (16:7). Foreign alliances signify unfaithfulness in Chronicles.

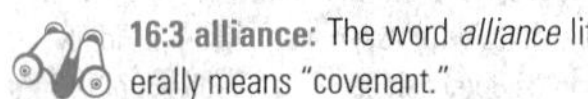

16:3 alliance: The word *alliance* literally means "covenant."

7 At that time the seer Hanani came to King Asa of Judah, and
said to him, "Because you relied on the king of Aram, and did not rely
on the LORD your God, the army of the king of Aram has escaped
you. 8Were not the Ethiopians[b] and the Libyans a huge army with exceedingly many chariots and cavalry? Yet because you relied on the
LORD, he gave them into your hand. 9For the eyes of the LORD range
throughout the entire earth, to strengthen those whose heart is true
to him. You have done foolishly in this; for from now on you will have
wars." 10Then Asa was angry with the seer, and put him in the stocks,
in prison, for he was in a rage with him because of this. And Asa inflicted cruelties on some of the people at the same time.

16:7-10 seer: Another name for a prophet. Here, Hanani states the theological opinion of the Chronicler: If Asa had "relied" on the LORD, he would not have been defeated.

[a] Heb lacks *the territory of* [b] Or *Nubians*; Heb *Cushites*

Asa's Disease and Death

11 The acts of Asa, from first to last, are written in the Book of the
Kings of Judah and Israel. [12]In the thirty-ninth year of his reign Asa
was diseased in his feet, and his disease became severe; yet even in his
disease he did not seek the LORD, but sought help from physicians.
[13]Then Asa slept with his ancestors, dying in the forty-first year of his
reign. [14]They buried him in the tomb that he had hewn out for himself
in the city of David. They laid him on a bier that had been filled with
various kinds of spices prepared by the perfumer's art; and they made
a very great fire in his honor.

16:11-14 Asa...sought help from physicians: Asa does not "seek the LORD" for help but instead seeks help from doctors. This is ironic, since Asa's name means "May [God] heal."

Jehoshaphat's Reign

17 His son Jehoshaphat succeeded him, and strengthened himself against Israel. [2]He placed forces in all the fortified cities
of Judah, and set garrisons in the land of Judah, and in the cities of
Ephraim that his father Asa had taken. [3]The LORD was with Jehoshaphat, because he walked in the earlier ways of his father;[a] he did not
seek the Baals, [4]but sought the God of his father and walked in his
commandments, and not according to the ways of Israel. [5]Therefore
the LORD established the kingdom in his hand. All Judah brought
tribute to Jehoshaphat, and he had great riches and honor. [6]His heart
was courageous in the ways of the LORD; and furthermore he removed the high places and the sacred poles[b] from Judah.
7 In the third year of his reign he sent his officials, Ben-hail, Obadiah, Zechariah, Nethanel, and Micaiah, to teach in the cities of Judah. [8]With them were the Levites, Shemaiah, Nethaniah, Zebadiah,
Asahel, Shemiramoth, Jehonathan, Adonijah, Tobijah, and Tob-
adonijah; and with these Levites, the priests Elishama and Jehoram.
[9]They taught in Judah, having the book of the law of the LORD with
them; they went around through all the cities of Judah and taught
among the people.
10 The fear of the LORD fell on all the kingdoms of the lands
around Judah, and they did not make war against Jehoshaphat.
[11]Some of the Philistines brought Jehoshaphat presents, and silver for
tribute; and the Arabs also brought him seven thousand seven hundred rams and seven thousand seven hundred male goats. [12]Jehosh-
aphat grew steadily greater. He built fortresses and storage cities in
Judah. [13]He carried out great works in the cities of Judah. He had soldiers, mighty warriors, in Jerusalem. [14]This was the muster of them by
ancestral houses: Of Judah, the commanders of the thousands: Adnah the commander, with three hundred thousand mighty warriors,
[15]and next to him Jehohanan the commander, with two hundred
eighty thousand, [16]and next to him Amasiah son of Zichri, a volunteer

17:1—21:1 Jehoshaphat: Jehoshaphat's reign is covered in ten verses of 1 Kings (22:41-50), compared to four *chapters* in 2 Chronicles. The Chronicler uses Jehoshaphat to illustrate key elements of his theology: seeking the LORD (17:4), removing idols (17:6, and teaching God's law. Signs of God's favor—building projects, honor, wealth, rest, and victory in battle—open and close the description of his reign (chapters 17 and 20). Nevertheless, Jehoshaphat is condemned by the prophet Jehu (19:1-2) and punished (20:37) for his alliance with the northern kings Ahab and Ahaziah.

17:1-19 Jehoshaphat...sought the God of his father: Jehoshaphat's reign opens positively. His piety or faithfulness contrasts with the "ways of Israel" (17:4). In addition, sixteen princes, priests, and Levites form a traveling group of teachers charged with instructing the people in the book of the law (17:9; 19:4-11).

[a] Another reading is *his father David* [b] Heb *Asherim*

for the service of the LORD, with two hundred thousand mighty warriors. [17]Of Benjamin: Eliada, a mighty warrior, with two hundred thousand armed with bow and shield, [18]and next to him Jehozabad with one hundred eighty thousand armed for war. [19]These were in the service of the king, besides those whom the king had placed in the fortified cities throughout all Judah.

Micaiah Predicts Failure

18 Now Jehoshaphat had great riches and honor; and he made a marriage alliance with Ahab. [2]After some years he went down to Ahab in Samaria. Ahab slaughtered an abundance of sheep and oxen for him and for the people who were with him, and induced him to go up against Ramoth-gilead. [3]King Ahab of Israel said to King Jehoshaphat of Judah, "Will you go with me to Ramoth-gilead?" He answered him, "I am with you, my people are your people. We will be with you in the war."

4 But Jehoshaphat also said to the king of Israel, "Inquire first for the word of the LORD." [5]Then the king of Israel gathered the prophets together, four hundred of them, and said to them, "Shall we go to battle against Ramoth-gilead, or shall I refrain?" They said, "Go up; for God will give it into the hand of the king." [6]But Jehoshaphat said, "Is there no other prophet of the LORD here of whom we may inquire?" [7]The king of Israel said to Jehoshaphat, "There is still one other by whom we may inquire of the LORD, Micaiah son of Imlah; but I hate him, for he never prophesies anything favorable about me, but only disaster." Jehoshaphat said, "Let the king not say such a thing." [8]Then the king of Israel summoned an officer and said, "Bring quickly Micaiah son of Imlah." [9]Now the king of Israel and King Jehoshaphat of Judah were sitting on their thrones, arrayed in their robes; and they were sitting at the threshing floor at the entrance of the gate of Samaria; and all the prophets were prophesying before them. [10]Zedekiah son of Chenaanah made for himself horns of iron, and he said, "Thus says the LORD: With these you shall gore the Arameans until they are destroyed." [11]All the prophets were prophesying the same and saying, "Go up to Ramoth-gilead and triumph; the LORD will give it into the hand of the king."

12 The messenger who had gone to summon Micaiah said to him, "Look, the words of the prophets with one accord are favorable to the king; let your word be like the word of one of them, and speak favorably." [13]But Micaiah said, "As the LORD lives, whatever my God says, that I will speak."

14 When he had come to the king, the king said to him, "Micaiah, shall we go to Ramoth-gilead to battle, or shall I refrain?" He answered, "Go up and triumph; they will be given into your hand." [15]But the king said to him, "How many times must I make you swear to tell

18:1—19:3 Jehoshaphat...war: The prophet Micaiah warns against the dangers of foreign alliances. Chronicles adds a new introduction (18:1-2) and conclusion (19:1-3) to the story told in 1 Kings 22.

18:1-2 marriage alliance: Kings often strengthened their position through marriage alliances. The marriage between Athaliah, the daughter of Ahab, Israel's king, and Jehoram, Jehoshaphat's son (2 Kgs 8:18; 2 Chr 21:6), was unnecessary, since Jehoshaphat was already wealthy and honored (18:1). The alliance had destructive consequences: military defeat, the undoing of Jehoshaphat's reforms, the spread of Baal worship, and the near elimination of David's line (22:10-12).

18:2 Samaria: The capital of Israel, forty miles north of Jerusalem, was built on a hill 300 feet above the surrounding plain (see Map 7, p. 2105).

18:4-27 Micaiah: Jehoshaphat does not follow the good advice of this true prophet, who has stood in the heavenly council (Jer 23:22). Instead Jehoshaphat follows the self-serving assurances of the four hundred court prophets and goes to war (18:28-29).

me nothing but the truth in the name of the LORD?" [16]Then Micaiah[a] said, "I saw all Israel scattered on the mountains, like sheep without a shepherd; and the LORD said, 'These have no master; let each one go home in peace.'" [17]The king of Israel said to Jehoshaphat, "Did I not tell you that he would not prophesy anything favorable about me, but only disaster?"

18 Then Micaiah[a] said, "Therefore hear the word of the LORD: I saw the LORD sitting on his throne, with all the host of heaven standing to the right and to the left of him. [19]And the LORD said, 'Who will entice King Ahab of Israel, so that he may go up and fall at Ramoth-gilead?' Then one said one thing, and another said another, [20]until a spirit came forward and stood before the LORD, saying, 'I will entice him.' The LORD asked him, 'How?' [21]He replied, 'I will go out and be a lying spirit in the mouth of all his prophets.' Then the LORD[a] said, 'You are to entice him, and you shall succeed; go out and do it.' [22]So you see, the LORD has put a lying spirit in the mouth of these your prophets; the LORD has decreed disaster for you."

18:20-22 lying spirit: The lying spirit sent by God deceives no one, since it is sent to those who are covering up the truth.

18:28-34 disguise: Ahab pretends to be Jehoshaphat and fools the Arameans, but God protects Jehoshaphat from their arrows, one of which strikes Ahab, who later dies.

23 Then Zedekiah son of Chenaanah came up to Micaiah, slapped him on the cheek, and said, "Which way did the spirit of the LORD pass from me to speak to you?" [24]Micaiah replied, "You will find out on that day when you go in to hide in an inner chamber." [25]The king of Israel then ordered, "Take Micaiah, and return him to Amon the governor of the city and to Joash the king's son; [26]and say, 'Thus says the king: Put this fellow in prison, and feed him on reduced rations of bread and water until I return in peace.'" [27]Micaiah said, "If you return in peace, the LORD has not spoken by me." And he said, "Hear, you peoples, all of you!"

Defeat and Death of Ahab

28 So the king of Israel and King Jehoshaphat of Judah went up to Ramoth-gilead. [29]The king of Israel said to Jehoshaphat, "I will disguise myself and go into battle, but you wear your robes." So the king of Israel disguised himself, and they went into battle. [30]Now the king of Aram had commanded the captains of his chariots, "Fight with no one small or great, but only with the king of Israel." [31]When the captains of the chariots saw Jehoshaphat, they said, "It is the king of Israel." So they turned to fight against him; and Jehoshaphat cried out, and the LORD helped him. God drew them away from him, [32]for when the captains of the chariots saw that it was not the king of Israel, they turned back from pursuing him. [33]But a certain man drew his bow and unknowingly struck the king of Israel between the scale armor and the breastplate; so he said to the driver of his chariot, "Turn around, and carry me out of the battle, for I am wounded." [34]The battle grew

---

[a] Heb *he*

hot that day, and the king of Israel propped himself up in his chariot
facing the Arameans until evening; then at sunset he died.

19:1-3 Jehu: Jehu is another prophet who condemns Jehoshaphat's disregard of Micaiah's advice (19:2), but the king's earlier faithful obedience (19:3) saves his life.

Jehoshaphat destroyed "the sacred poles" or shrines to worship foreign gods (14:3). What have you had to destroy or turn away from in order to seek and be faithful to God?

19:4-11 Jehoshaphat... appointed judges: Jehoshaphat's judicial reform only appears in the history told in Chronicles, and not in Kings. (A judicial reform is appropriate for one whose name means "may the LORD judge.") The king responds to Jehu's warning (19:2-3) by creating a system of judges in the outlying areas and a court of appeals in Jerusalem. The system is similar to the one described in Deuteronomy 17:8-13, except now there is a division into spiritual and secular areas ("matters of the LORD" and the "king's matters," 19:11). The reforms are a return to God's rule, not a political plot (19:7).

19 King Jehoshaphat of Judah returned in safety to his house in
Jerusalem. 2 Jehu son of Hanani the seer went out to meet him
and said to King Jehoshaphat, "Should you help the wicked and love
those who hate the LORD? Because of this, wrath has gone out against
you from the LORD. 3 Nevertheless, some good is found in you, for
you destroyed the sacred poles[a] out of the land, and have set your
heart to seek God."

The Reforms of Jehoshaphat

4 Jehoshaphat resided at Jerusalem; then he went out again
among the people, from Beer-sheba to the hill country of Ephraim,
and brought them back to the LORD, the God of their ancestors. 5 He
appointed judges in the land in all the fortified cities of Judah, city by
city, 6 and said to the judges, "Consider what you are doing, for you
judge not on behalf of human beings but on the LORD's behalf; he is
with you in giving judgment. 7 Now, let the fear of the LORD be upon
you; take care what you do, for there is no perversion of justice with
the LORD our God, or partiality, or taking of bribes."

8 Moreover in Jerusalem Jehoshaphat appointed certain Levites
and priests and heads of families of Israel, to give judgment for the
LORD and to decide disputed cases. They had their seat at Jerusalem.
9 He charged them: "This is how you shall act: in the fear of the LORD,
in faithfulness, and with your whole heart; 10 whenever a case comes
to you from your kindred who live in their cities, concerning bloodshed, law or commandment, statutes or ordinances, then you shall
instruct them, so that they may not incur guilt before the LORD and
wrath may not come on you and your kindred. Do so, and you will
not incur guilt. 11 See, Amariah the chief priest is over you in all matters of the LORD; and Zebadiah son of Ishmael, the governor of the
house of Judah, in all the king's matters; and the Levites will serve you
as officers. Deal courageously, and may the LORD be with the good!"

20:1-30 Ammonites... came against Jehoshaphat for battle: This is the focus of the Chronicler's account of the divided monarchy (2 Chr 10–28). Notice how the effectiveness of faith is illustrated in three sections: Jehoshaphat's prayer (20:5-13), God's response (20:14-19), and the story of the battle itself (20:20-27). Verses 1-4 and 28-30 frame these three sections, contrasting Jehoshaphat's fear (20:3) with the fear of God that overcame Israel's enemies (20:29). "Stand" is the key term. The first and third sections begin with the phrase "Jehoshaphat stood" (20:5, 20b). All three sections include "stand" in a key statement that recalls a significant moment from Israel's past (20:9, 17, 20). The story as a whole encourages those in need to seek the LORD in prayer.

Invasion from the East

20 After this the Moabites and Ammonites, and with them
some of the Meunites,[b] came against Jehoshaphat for battle. 2 Messengers[c] came and told Jehoshaphat, "A great multitude is
coming against you from Edom,[d] from beyond the sea; already they
are at Hazazon-tamar" (that is, En-gedi). 3 Jehoshaphat was afraid; he
set himself to seek the LORD, and proclaimed a fast throughout all
Judah. 4 Judah assembled to seek help from the LORD; from all the
towns of Judah they came to seek the LORD.

---

[a] Heb *Asheroth* [b] Compare 26.7: Heb *Ammonites* [c] Heb *They* [d] One Ms: MT *Aram*

Jehoshaphat's Prayer and Victory

5 Jehoshaphat stood in the assembly of Judah and Jerusalem, in
the house of the LORD, before the new court, [6]and said, "O LORD,
God of our ancestors, are you not God in heaven? Do you not rule
over all the kingdoms of the nations? In your hand are power and
might, so that no one is able to withstand you. [7]Did you not, O our
God, drive out the inhabitants of this land before your people Israel, and give it forever to the descendants of your friend Abraham?
[8]They have lived in it, and in it have built you a sanctuary for your
name, saying, [9]'If disaster comes upon us, the sword, judgment,[a] or
pestilence, or famine, we will stand before this house, and before
you, for your name is in this house, and cry to you in our distress,
and you will hear and save.' [10]See now, the people of Ammon, Moab,
and Mount Seir, whom you would not let Israel invade when they
came from the land of Egypt, and whom they avoided and did not
destroy— [11]they reward us by coming to drive us out of your possession that you have given us to inherit. [12]O our God, will you not execute judgment upon them? For we are powerless against this great
multitude that is coming against us. We do not know what to do, but
our eyes are on you."

13 Meanwhile all Judah stood before the LORD, with their little
ones, their wives, and their children. [14]Then the spirit of the LORD
came upon Jahaziel son of Zechariah, son of Benaiah, son of Jeiel, son
of Mattaniah, a Levite of the sons of Asaph, in the middle of the assembly. [15]He said, "Listen, all Judah and inhabitants of Jerusalem, and
King Jehoshaphat: Thus says the LORD to you: 'Do not fear or be dismayed at this great multitude; for the battle is not yours but God's.
[16]Tomorrow go down against them; they will come up by the ascent
of Ziz; you will find them at the end of the valley, before the wilderness of Jeruel. [17]This battle is not for you to fight; take your position,
stand still, and see the victory of the LORD on your behalf, O Judah
and Jerusalem.' Do not fear or be dismayed; tomorrow go out against
them, and the LORD will be with you."

18 Then Jehoshaphat bowed down with his face to the ground,
and all Judah and the inhabitants of Jerusalem fell down before the
LORD, worshiping the LORD. [19]And the Levites, of the Kohathites and
the Korahites, stood up to praise the LORD, the God of Israel, with a
very loud voice.

20 They rose early in the morning and went out into the wilderness of Tekoa; and as they went out, Jehoshaphat stood and said, "Listen to me, O Judah and inhabitants of Jerusalem! Believe in the LORD
your God and you will be established; believe his prophets." [21]When
he had taken counsel with the people, he appointed those who were

---

[a] Or *the sword of judgment*

How has praying to God helped you in time of need?

20:5-13 Jehoshaphat stood . . . in the house of the LORD . . . and cry to you in our distress: This key statement (20:9) recalls Solomon's prayer at the dedication of the temple (2 Chr 6:20, 28-30; see also 7:13-15) and shows our human dependence upon God.

20:14-19 stand still, and see the victory of the LORD: This key statement (20:17) advises the people to follow Moses' instructions at the Red Sea (Exod 14:13).

20:20-27 attacked the inhabitants: "Attacked" literally means "stood against" (20:23). The confusion that caused the enemies to destroy each other when "the Ammonites and Moab attacked the inhabitants of Mount Seir" recalls a similar situation in Gideon's day (Judg 7:15-23).

20:20 Believe in the LORD your God and you will be established: The Chronicler's community had been opposed by the descendants of these same peoples (20:1; Neh 2:19; 4:1-3, 7-9; 6:1-4; 13). They are encouraged by Jehoshaphat's positive message, which is a restatement of Isaiah 7:9.

20:20 believe his prophets: The following additional phrase comes after these words in the Hebrew text: "and you will be successful." This phrase is omitted in the NRSV text and should be restored.

to sing to the LORD and praise him in holy splendor, as they went before the army, saying,

"Give thanks to the LORD,
for his steadfast love endures forever."

22 As they began to sing and praise, the LORD set an ambush against
the Ammonites, Moab, and Mount Seir, who had come against Judah,
so that they were routed. 23 For the Ammonites and Moab attacked
the inhabitants of Mount Seir, destroying them utterly; and when
they had made an end of the inhabitants of Seir, they all helped to
destroy one another.

24 When Judah came to the watchtower of the wilderness, they
looked toward the multitude; they were corpses lying on the ground;
no one had escaped. 25 When Jehoshaphat and his people came to
take the booty from them, they found livestock[a] in great numbers,
goods, clothing, and precious things, which they took for themselves
until they could carry no more. They spent three days taking the
booty, because of its abundance. 26 On the fourth day they assembled
in the Valley of Beracah, for there they blessed the LORD; therefore
that place has been called the Valley of Beracah[b] to this day. 27 Then
all the people of Judah and Jerusalem, with Jehoshaphat at their head,
returned to Jerusalem with joy, for the LORD had enabled them to
rejoice over their enemies. 28 They came to Jerusalem, with harps and
lyres and trumpets, to the house of the LORD. 29 The fear of God came
on all the kingdoms of the countries when they heard that the LORD
had fought against the enemies of Israel. 30 And the realm of Jehoshaphat was quiet, for his God gave him rest all around.

The End of Jehoshaphat's Reign

31 So Jehoshaphat reigned over Judah. He was thirty-five years
old when he began to reign; he reigned twenty-five years in Jerusalem. His mother's name was Azubah daughter of Shilhi. 32 He walked
in the way of his father Asa and did not turn aside from it, doing what
was right in the sight of the LORD. 33 Yet the high places were not removed; the people had not yet set their hearts upon the God of their
ancestors.

34 Now the rest of the acts of Jehoshaphat, from first to last, are
written in the Annals of Jehu son of Hanani, which are recorded in the
Book of the Kings of Israel.

35 After this King Jehoshaphat of Judah joined with King Ahaziah of Israel, who did wickedly. 36 He joined him in building ships
to go to Tarshish; they built the ships in Ezion-geber. 37 Then Eliezer
son of Dodavahu of Mareshah prophesied against Jehoshaphat, saying, "Because you have joined with Ahaziah, the LORD will destroy

---

[a] Gk: Heb *among them* [b] That is *Blessing*

what you have made." And the ships were wrecked and were not able to go to Tarshish.

Jehoram's Reign

21 Jehoshaphat slept with his ancestors and was buried with his ancestors in the city of David; his son Jehoram succeeded him. 2He had brothers, the sons of Jehoshaphat: Azariah, Jehiel, Zechariah, Azariah, Michael, and Shephatiah; all these were the sons of King Jehoshaphat of Judah.[a] 3Their father gave them many gifts, of silver, gold, and valuable possessions, together with fortified cities in Judah; but he gave the kingdom to Jehoram, because he was the firstborn. 4When Jehoram had ascended the throne of his father and was established, he put all his brothers to the sword, and also some of the officials of Israel. 5Jehoram was thirty-two years old when he began to reign; he reigned eight years in Jerusalem. 6He walked in the way of the kings of Israel, as the house of Ahab had done; for the daughter of Ahab was his wife. He did what was evil in the sight of the LORD. 7Yet the LORD would not destroy the house of David because of the covenant that he had made with David, and since he had promised to give a lamp to him and to his descendants forever.

Revolt of Edom

8 In his days Edom revolted against the rule of Judah and set up a king of their own. 9Then Jehoram crossed over with his commanders and all his chariots. He set out by night and attacked the Edomites, who had surrounded him and his chariot commanders. 10So Edom has been in revolt against the rule of Judah to this day. At that time Libnah also revolted against his rule, because he had forsaken the LORD, the God of his ancestors.

Elijah's Letter

11 Moreover he made high places in the hill country of Judah, and led the inhabitants of Jerusalem into unfaithfulness, and made Judah go astray. 12A letter came to him from the prophet Elijah, saying: "Thus says the LORD, the God of your father David: Because you have not walked in the ways of your father Jehoshaphat or in the ways of King Asa of Judah, 13but have walked in the way of the kings of Israel, and have led Judah and the inhabitants of Jerusalem into unfaithfulness, as the house of Ahab led Israel into unfaithfulness, and because you also have killed your brothers, members of your father's house, who were better than yourself, 14see, the LORD will bring a great plague on your people, your children, your wives, and all your possessions, 15and you yourself will have a severe sickness with a disease

21:2—22:1 [Jehoram] had brothers…but [Jehoshaphat] gave the kingdom to Jehoram, because he was the firstborn:[Jehoram is the first king to be presented in a totally negative way. His reign is the first of three in which the dynasty of David is threatened with extinction. Jehoram's sin was trying to preserve his own interests to the point of taking the lives of others.

21:8-11, 16-20 The LORD aroused …struck him in his bowels: Jehoram's gruesome death and the death of his wife and children shows God's retributive justice at work. The rebellion of Edom and the attack by the Philistines also are evidence of Jehoram getting what he brought upon himself by murdering his own brothers (21:4) and leading the people into unfaithfulness (21:11).

21:6-7, 18-19 He did what was evil in the sight of the LORD: Jehoram is judged three times. First is the Chronicler's matter-of-fact theological judgment of Jehoram that he did what was evil (21:6-7). Second is God's gruesome judgment in striking Jehoram with disease (21:18-19a). And third is the strange judgment of the people who "made no fire in his honor" and denied this wicked king the burial rites of his ancestors (21:19b).

21:12-15 A letter came to him from the prophet Elijah: Elijah's judgment announces a plague for the people and disease for the king. God brings these about in the paired rebellions that frame the letter.

[a] Gk Syr: Heb *Israel*

of your bowels, until your bowels come out, day after day, because of
the disease."
16 The LORD aroused against Jehoram the anger of the Philistines and of the Arabs who are near the Ethiopians.[a] 17They came up
against Judah, invaded it, and carried away all the possessions they
found that belonged to the king's house, along with his sons and his
wives, so that no son was left to him except Jehoahaz, his youngest
son.

21:17 Jehoahaz: Jehoram's only positive contribution was preserving David's line in the life of Jehoahaz.

Disease and Death of Jehoram

18 After all this the LORD struck him in his bowels with an incurable disease. 19In course of time, at the end of two years, his bowels
came out because of the disease, and he died in great agony. His people made no fire in his honor, like the fires made for his ancestors.
20He was thirty-two years old when he began to reign; he reigned
eight years in Jerusalem. He departed with no one's regret. They buried him in the city of David, but not in the tombs of the kings.

Ahaziah's Reign

22 The inhabitants of Jerusalem made his youngest son Ahaziah king as his successor; for the troops who came with the
Arabs to the camp had killed all the older sons. So Ahaziah son of
Jehoram reigned as king of Judah. 2Ahaziah was forty-two years old
when he began to reign; he reigned one year in Jerusalem. His mother's name was Athaliah, a granddaughter of Omri. 3He also walked in
the ways of the house of Ahab, for his mother was his counselor in
doing wickedly. 4He did what was evil in the sight of the LORD, as the
house of Ahab had done; for after the death of his father they were his
counselors, to his ruin. 5He even followed their advice, and went with
Jehoram son of King Ahab of Israel to make war against King Hazael
of Aram at Ramoth-gilead. The Arameans wounded Joram, 6and he
returned to be healed in Jezreel of the wounds that he had received
at Ramah, when he fought King Hazael of Aram. And Ahaziah son of
King Jehoram of Judah went down to see Joram son of Ahab in Jezreel, because he was sick.
7 But it was ordained by God that the downfall of Ahaziah should
come about through his going to visit Joram. For when he came there
he went out with Jehoram to meet Jehu son of Nimshi, whom the
LORD had anointed to destroy the house of Ahab. 8When Jehu was
executing judgment on the house of Ahab, he met the officials of Judah and the sons of Ahaziah's brothers, who attended Ahaziah, and
he killed them. 9He searched for Ahaziah, who was captured while
hiding in Samaria and was brought to Jehu, and put to death. They

22:2-9 Ahaziah: Although Ahaziah was misled by Ahab's family and continued his father's unfaithfulness, he is judged for his own sin.

22:2 forty-two: Ahaziah was probably twenty-two. He cannot be forty-two if his father died at forty (21:20).

22:7-9a ordained by God: The Chronicler attributes to God Ahaziah's death with the rest of the house of Ahab in Jehu's bloody coup (2 Kgs 8:28—10:31).

22:9b no one able to rule: This phrase literally means "strong enough." God's promise to David (1 Chr 17:12) is threatened when Ahaziah dies without an heir.

[a] Or *Nubians*; Heb *Cushites*

buried him, for they said, "He is the grandson of Jehoshaphat, who sought the LORD with all his heart." And the house of Ahaziah had no one able to rule the kingdom.

Athaliah Seizes the Throne

10 Now when Athaliah, Ahaziah's mother, saw that her son was dead, she set about to destroy all the royal family of the house of Judah. 11 But Jehoshabeath, the king's daughter, took Joash son of Ahaziah, and stole him away from among the king's children who were about to be killed; she put him and his nurse in a bedroom. Thus Jehoshabeath, daughter of King Jehoram and wife of the priest Jehoiada—because she was a sister of Ahaziah—hid him from Athaliah, so that she did not kill him; 12 he remained with them six years, hidden in the house of God, while Athaliah reigned over the land.

23 But in the seventh year Jehoiada took courage, and entered into a compact with the commanders of the hundreds, Azariah son of Jeroham, Ishmael son of Jehohanan, Azariah son of Obed, Maaseiah son of Adaiah, and Elishaphat son of Zichri. 2 They went around through Judah and gathered the Levites from all the towns of Judah, and the heads of families of Israel, and they came to Jerusalem. 3 Then the whole assembly made a covenant with the king in the house of God. Jehoiada[a] said to them, "Here is the king's son! Let him reign, as the LORD promised concerning the sons of David. 4 This is what you are to do: one-third of you, priests and Levites, who come on duty on the sabbath, shall be gatekeepers, 5 one-third shall be at the king's house, and one-third at the Gate of the Foundation; and all the people shall be in the courts of the house of the LORD. 6 Do not let anyone enter the house of the LORD except the priests and ministering Levites; they may enter, for they are holy, but all the other[b] people shall observe the instructions of the LORD. 7 The Levites shall surround the king, each with his weapons in his hand; and whoever enters the house shall be killed. Stay with the king in his comings and goings."

Joash Crowned King

8 The Levites and all Judah did according to all that the priest Jehoiada commanded; each brought his men, who were to come on duty on the sabbath, with those who were to go off duty on the sabbath; for the priest Jehoiada did not dismiss the divisions. 9 The priest Jehoiada delivered to the captains the spears and the large and small shields that had been King David's, which were in the house of God; 10 and he set all the people as a guard for the king, everyone with weapon in hand, from the south side of the house to the north side of

[a] Heb *He* [b] Heb lacks *other*

22:10—23:21 Athaliah: She is Israel's only ruling queen. This break in the dynasty or line of David is the final consequence of Jehoshaphat's alliance with Ahab. The Chronicler indicates the illegitimacy of her reign by omitting the royal formulas that introduce and conclude the accounts of all the kings of Israel and Judah.

22:10-12 Jehoshabeath: Little Joash is saved by the wife of Jehoiada, the priest. The duel between Athaliah and Jehoshabeath contrasts calculating evil with a brave attempt to protect the child who represents God's promise to David (1 Chr 17:12).

23:1-15 Jehoiada took courage . . . they put [Athaliah] to death: The Chronicler adds information to the account in 2 Kings 11. The priests and Levites lead the attack rather than the royal bodyguard, and the threat to the line of David is emphasized. Jehoiada's preparation (23:1-7) is followed by the crowning of Joash (23:8-11) and the assassination of Athaliah (23:12-15).

23:1 compact: This Hebrew word is usually translated "covenant" (*bryt*). But it may be a mistake for "house/temple" (*byt*). If so, the group "entered the temple."

the house, around the altar and the house. 11 Then he brought out the
king's son, put the crown on him, and gave him the covenant;[a] they
proclaimed him king, and Jehoiada and his sons anointed him; and
they shouted, "Long live the king!"

Athaliah Murdered

12 When Athaliah heard the noise of the people running and
praising the king, she went into the house of the LORD to the people;
13 and when she looked, there was the king standing by his pillar at the
entrance, and the captains and the trumpeters beside the king, and all
the people of the land rejoicing and blowing trumpets, and the singers with their musical instruments leading in the celebration. Athaliah
tore her clothes, and cried, "Treason! Treason!" 14 Then the priest Jehoiada brought out the captains who were set over the army, saying
to them, "Bring her out between the ranks; anyone who follows her is
to be put to the sword." For the priest said, "Do not put her to death
in the house of the LORD." 15 So they laid hands on her; she went into
the entrance of the Horse Gate of the king's house, and there they put
her to death.

16 Jehoiada made a covenant between himself and all the people and the king that they should be the LORD's people. 17 Then all
the people went to the house of Baal, and tore it down; his altars and
his images they broke in pieces, and they killed Mattan, the priest of
Baal, in front of the altars. 18 Jehoiada assigned the care of the house of
the LORD to the levitical priests whom David had organized to be in
charge of the house of the LORD, to offer burnt offerings to the LORD,
as it is written in the law of Moses, with rejoicing and with singing,
according to the order of David. 19 He stationed the gatekeepers at the
gates of the house of the LORD so that no one should enter who was
in any way unclean. 20 And he took the captains, the nobles, the governors of the people, and all the people of the land, and they brought
the king down from the house of the LORD, marching through the
upper gate to the king's house. They set the king on the royal throne.
21 So all the people of the land rejoiced, and the city was quiet after
Athaliah had been killed with the sword.

Joash Repairs the Temple

24 Joash was seven years old when he began to reign; he
reigned forty years in Jerusalem; his mother's name was
Zibiah of Beer-sheba. 2 Joash did what was right in the sight of the
LORD all the days of the priest Jehoiada. 3 Jehoiada got two wives for
him, and he became the father of sons and daughters.

4 Some time afterward Joash decided to restore the house of the

[a] Or *treaty*, or *testimony*; Heb *eduth*

23:16-21 covenant: The people agree to restore worship of the LORD alone and destroy everything connected with Baal (23:16-17). They restore the temple to David's specifications (23:18-19), and place the young king on the throne (23:20-21).

23:16 himself and all the people and the king: Jehoiada's inclusion as a partner in making the covenant reflects the expanded role of the high priest in the community of those who returned from exile in Babylon. Only the people and God are partners in 2 Kings 11:17.

24:1-27 Joash: The Chronicler explains the inconsistency between Joash's positive evaluation in 2 Kings 12:2 and his violent death in 2 Kings 12:20-21 by returning to the pattern of faithfulness (blessing) and unfaithfulness (punishment). Joash served in faithful obedience to God under the guidance of Jehoiada (24:1-14), but he fell into disobedience and sin after the death of the faithful priest (24:17-27).

24:1-14 Joash...did what was right in the sight of the LORD: In Joash's faithful period, he repairs the temple using money from a tax that Moses introduced for the tabernacle (Exod 30:12-16; 38:25-26) and later was used by David and Solomon for the construction of the temple (1 Chr 29:1-9). The people's joyful generosity also recalls both those events (Exod 36:4-7; 1 Chr 29:9).

24:4 restore: Probably not ritual cleaning to remove the remains of Baal worship, but structural repair necessary after 130 years of use.

LORD. 5He assembled the priests and the Levites and said to them,
"Go out to the cities of Judah and gather money from all Israel to repair the house of your God, year by year; and see that you act quickly."
But the Levites did not act quickly. 6So the king summoned Jehoiada
the chief, and said to him, "Why have you not required the Levites
to bring in from Judah and Jerusalem the tax levied by Moses, the
servant of the LORD, on[a] the congregation of Israel for the tent of the
covenant?"[b] 7For the children of Athaliah, that wicked woman, had
broken into the house of God, and had even used all the dedicated
things of the house of the LORD for the Baals.

8 So the king gave command, and they made a chest, and set it
outside the gate of the house of the LORD. 9A proclamation was made
throughout Judah and Jerusalem to bring in for the LORD the tax that
Moses the servant of God laid on Israel in the wilderness. 10All the
leaders and all the people rejoiced and brought their tax and dropped
it into the chest until it was full. 11Whenever the chest was brought to
the king's officers by the Levites, when they saw that there was a large
amount of money in it, the king's secretary and the officer of the chief
priest would come and empty the chest and take it and return it to its
place. So they did day after day, and collected money in abundance.
12The king and Jehoiada gave it to those who had charge of the work
of the house of the LORD, and they hired masons and carpenters to
restore the house of the LORD, and also workers in iron and bronze
to repair the house of the LORD. 13So those who were engaged in the
work labored, and the repairing went forward at their hands, and they
restored the house of God to its proper condition and strengthened
it. 14When they had finished, they brought the rest of the money to
the king and Jehoiada, and with it were made utensils for the house
of the LORD, utensils for the service and for the burnt offerings, and
ladles, and vessels of gold and silver. They offered burnt offerings in
the house of the LORD regularly all the days of Jehoiada.

Apostasy of Joash

15 But Jehoiada grew old and full of days, and died; he was one
hundred thirty years old at his death. 16And they buried him in the
city of David among the kings, because he had done good in Israel,
and for God and his house.

17 Now after the death of Jehoiada the officials of Judah came
and did obeisance to the king; then the king listened to them. 18They
abandoned the house of the LORD, the God of their ancestors, and
served the sacred poles[c] and the idols. And wrath came upon Judah
and Jerusalem for this guilt of theirs. 19Yet he sent prophets among
them to bring them back to the LORD; they testified against them, but
they would not listen.

[a] Compare Vg: Heb *and* [b] Or *treaty*, or *testimony*; Heb *eduth* [c] Heb *Asherim*

24:15-16 Jehoiada . . . died: Although not mentioned in 2 Kings, Jehoiada's death separates the two periods of Joash's reign. Jehoiada kept the young king faithful (24:2). Without his influence, however, the king repeats the sins of his ancestors (24:17-27). The priest's faithful service is rewarded with long life and burial in the royal tombs, an honor denied to king Joash (24:25).

Jehoiada had significant influence over King Joash and helped him remain faithful to God. Think about your life. Who has been a supportive presence for you? How has that person helped you be faithful to God?

24:17-27 after the death of Jehoiada . . . They abandoned the house of the LORD: Without Jehoiada to guide him, Joash becomes one of Judah's worst kings, worshiping the sacred poles and idols of Baal.

24:20-24 Zechariah: Jehoiada's son Zechariah warns Joash. The beginning of his warning recalls Moses' similar warning in the wilderness (Num 14:41). The end fulfills Azariah's warning to Asa (2 Chr 15:2b) that if Asa abandons God, God will abandon him. When Joash ignores Zechariah's warning and executes him (24:21), God's judgment comes through the army of Aram (24:23-24) and assassination (24:25-27).

20 Then the spirit of God took possession of[a] Zechariah son
of the priest Jehoiada; he stood above the people and said to them,
"Thus says God: Why do you transgress the commandments of the
LORD, so that you cannot prosper? Because you have forsaken the
LORD, he has also forsaken you." [21]But they conspired against him,
and by command of the king they stoned him to death in the court of
the house of the LORD. [22]King Joash did not remember the kindness
that Jehoiada, Zechariah's father, had shown him, but killed his son.
As he was dying, he said, "May the LORD see and avenge!"

Death of Joash

24:24 the LORD: Defeat by a smaller army indicates God's retributive justice (Joash is punished for his unfaithfulness).

24:25 because of the blood of the son of the priest: Zechariah's dying request for retributive justice, "May the LORD see and avenge!" (24:22) is granted when the king's servants assassinate Joash.

23 At the end of the year the army of Aram came up against Joash.
They came to Judah and Jerusalem, and destroyed all the officials of
the people from among them, and sent all the booty they took to the
king of Damascus. [24]Although the army of Aram had come with few
men, the LORD delivered into their hand a very great army, because
they had abandoned the LORD, the God of their ancestors. Thus they
executed judgment on Joash.

25 When they had withdrawn, leaving him severely wounded, his
servants conspired against him because of the blood of the son[b] of
the priest Jehoiada, and they killed him on his bed. So he died; and
they buried him in the city of David, but they did not bury him in
the tombs of the kings. [26]Those who conspired against him were Zabad son of Shimeath the Ammonite, and Jehozabad son of Shimrith
the Moabite. [27]Accounts of his sons, and of the many oracles against
him, and of the rebuilding[c] of the house of God are written in the
Commentary on the Book of the Kings. And his son Amaziah succeeded him.

Reign of Amaziah

25:1—26:2 Amaziah: As in the account of Joash, the reign of Joash's son Amaziah is divided into a faithful (25:1-13) period and an unfaithful one (25:14-28). His reign also will end in conspiracy and assassination.

25:1-13 Amaziah…did what was right in the sight of the LORD: Amaziah's "faithful" period is half-hearted at best. But he did follow Deuteronomy 24:16 by showing leniency (25:4), and he abandoned his foreign alliances in response to a warning by a prophet sent by God (25:10).

25:2 yet not with a true heart: This additional phrase tones down the evaluation that Amaziah "did what was right in the sight of the LORD," as does the omission of "like his ancestor David" from 2 Kings 14:3. Amaziah's problem was compromise. Just *knowing* what is right is not sufficient. Proper attitude is also important.

25 Amaziah was twenty-five years old when he began to reign,
and he reigned twenty-nine years in Jerusalem. His mother's
name was Jehoaddan of Jerusalem. [2]He did what was right in the sight
of the LORD, yet not with a true heart. [3]As soon as the royal power
was firmly in his hand he killed his servants who had murdered his
father the king. [4]But he did not put their children to death, according
to what is written in the law, in the book of Moses, where the LORD
commanded, "The parents shall not be put to death for the children,
or the children be put to death for the parents; but all shall be put to
death for their own sins."

Slaughter of the Edomites

5 Amaziah assembled the people of Judah, and set them by ancestral houses under commanders of the thousands and of the hun-

[a] Heb *clothed itself with* [b] Gk Vg: Heb *sons* [c] Heb *founding*

dreds for all Judah and Benjamin. He mustered those twenty years old and upward, and found that they were three hundred thousand picked troops fit for war, able to handle spear and shield. [6]He also hired one hundred thousand mighty warriors from Israel for one hundred talents of silver. [7]But a man of God came to him and said, "O king, do not let the army of Israel go with you, for the LORD is not with Israel—all these Ephraimites. [8]Rather, go by yourself and act; be strong in battle, or God will fling you down before the enemy; for God has power to help or to overthrow." [9]Amaziah said to the man of God, "But what shall we do about the hundred talents that I have given to the army of Israel?" The man of God answered, "The LORD is able to give you much more than this." [10]Then Amaziah discharged the army that had come to him from Ephraim, letting them go home again. But they became very angry with Judah, and returned home in fierce anger.

11 Amaziah took courage, and led out his people; he went to the Valley of Salt, and struck down ten thousand men of Seir. [12]The people of Judah captured another ten thousand alive, took them to the top of Sela, and threw them down from the top of Sela, so that all of them were dashed to pieces. [13]But the men of the army whom Amaziah sent back, not letting them go with him to battle, fell on the cities of Judah from Samaria to Beth-horon; they killed three thousand people in them, and took much booty.

14 Now after Amaziah came from the slaughter of the Edomites, he brought the gods of the people of Seir, set them up as his gods, and worshiped them, making offerings to them. [15]The LORD was angry with Amaziah and sent to him a prophet, who said to him, "Why have you resorted to a people's gods who could not deliver their own people from your hand?" [16]But as he was speaking the king[a] said to him, "Have we made you a royal counselor? Stop! Why should you be put to death?" So the prophet stopped, but said, "I know that God has determined to destroy you, because you have done this and have not listened to my advice."

Israel Defeats Judah

17 Then King Amaziah of Judah took counsel and sent to King Joash son of Jehoahaz son of Jehu of Israel, saying, "Come, let us look one another in the face." [18]King Joash of Israel sent word to King Amaziah of Judah, "A thornbush on Lebanon sent to a cedar on Lebanon, saying, 'Give your daughter to my son for a wife'; but a wild animal of Lebanon passed by and trampled down the thornbush. [19]You say, 'See, I have defeated Edom,' and your heart has lifted you up in boastfulness. Now stay at home; why should you provoke trouble so that you fall, you and Judah with you?"

[a] Heb *he*

25:7-9 man of God: An unknown prophet warns about foreign alliance (13:4-12; 16:1-9; 19:1-11; 22:1-7). In response, Amaziah dismisses the army (25:10-13).

25:14-28 Amaziah…brought the gods of the people of Seir: The faithless period of Amaziah's reign concerns war with the north.

25:15-16 prophet: One more nameless prophet announces God's retributive justice.

25:17-19 A thornbush…a cedar: Joash, the northern king, tells Amaziah a strange fable indicating that arrogance leads to disaster.

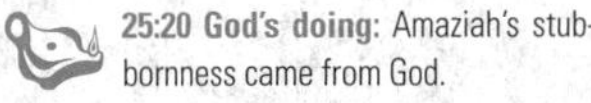
25:20 God's doing: Amaziah's stubbornness came from God.

20 But Amaziah would not listen—it was God's doing, in order
to hand them over, because they had sought the gods of Edom. [21]So
King Joash of Israel went up; he and King Amaziah of Judah faced one
another in battle at Beth-shemesh, which belongs to Judah. [22]Judah
was defeated by Israel; everyone fled home. [23]King Joash of Israel captured King Amaziah of Judah, son of Joash, son of Ahaziah, at Beth-
shemesh; he brought him to Jerusalem, and broke down the wall of
Jerusalem from the Ephraim Gate to the Corner Gate, a distance of
four hundred cubits. [24]He seized all the gold and silver, and all the
vessels that were found in the house of God, and Obed-edom with
them; he seized also the treasuries of the king's house, also hostages;
then he returned to Samaria.

Death of Amaziah

25 King Amaziah son of Joash of Judah, lived fifteen years after
the death of King Joash son of Jehoahaz of Israel. [26]Now the rest of
the deeds of Amaziah, from first to last, are they not written in the
Book of the Kings of Judah and Israel? [27]From the time that Amaziah
turned away from the LORD they made a conspiracy against him in
Jerusalem, and he fled to Lachish. But they sent after him to Lachish,
and killed him there. [28]They brought him back on horses; he was buried with his ancestors in the city of David.

25:27 From the time that Amaziah turned away from the LORD: The conspiracy to assassinate Amaziah was in response to his idolatry (25:14, 20).

Reign of Uzziah

26 Then all the people of Judah took Uzziah, who was sixteen
years old, and made him king to succeed his father Amaziah. [2]He rebuilt Eloth and restored it to Judah, after the king slept
with his ancestors. [3]Uzziah was sixteen years old when he began to
reign, and he reigned fifty-two years in Jerusalem. His mother's name
was Jecoliah of Jerusalem. [4]He did what was right in the sight of the
LORD, just as his father Amaziah had done. [5]He set himself to seek
God in the days of Zechariah, who instructed him in the fear of God;
and as long as he sought the LORD, God made him prosper.

26:3-23 Uzziah: Known as Azariah in Kings, the Chronicler may wish to avoid confusion with Azariah the priest (26:17, 20). As with his father, Amaziah, and grandfather, Joash, Uzziah's reign is divided into two periods, the first faithful, the second not.

26:5-15 He set himself to seek God: At first Uzziah sought the LORD and prospered. This was his faithful period.

26:4 He did what was right: The omission of Uzziah's failure to remove the local shrines strengthens this positive verdict from 2 Kings 15:3-4.

6 He went out and made war against the Philistines, and broke
down the wall of Gath and the wall of Jabneh and the wall of Ashdod;
he built cities in the territory of Ashdod and elsewhere among the
Philistines. [7]God helped him against the Philistines, against the Arabs
who lived in Gur-baal, and against the Meunites. [8]The Ammonites
paid tribute to Uzziah, and his fame spread even to the border of
Egypt, for he became very strong. [9]Moreover Uzziah built towers in
Jerusalem at the Corner Gate, at the Valley Gate, and at the Angle,
and fortified them. [10]He built towers in the wilderness and hewed out
many cisterns, for he had large herds, both in the Shephelah and in
the plain, and he had farmers and vinedressers in the hills and in the
fertile lands, for he loved the soil. [11]Moreover Uzziah had an army of

26:6-15 God helped him: Success in war and fame (26:6-8, 16), building projects (26:9-10), and military might (26:11-15) are signs of God's favor.

soldiers, fit for war, in divisions according to the numbers in the muster made by the secretary Jeiel and the officer Maaseiah, under the
direction of Hananiah, one of the king's commanders. 12 The whole
number of the heads of ancestral houses of mighty warriors was two
thousand six hundred. 13 Under their command was an army of three
hundred seven thousand five hundred, who could make war with
mighty power, to help the king against the enemy. 14 Uzziah provided
for all the army the shields, spears, helmets, coats of mail, bows, and
stones for slinging. 15 In Jerusalem he set up machines, invented by
skilled workers, on the towers and the corners for shooting arrows
and large stones. And his fame spread far, for he was marvelously
helped until he became strong.

Pride and Apostasy

16 But when he had become strong he grew proud, to his destruction. For he was false to the LORD his God, and entered the temple of
the LORD to make offering on the altar of incense. 17 But the priest
Azariah went in after him, with eighty priests of the LORD who were
men of valor; 18 they withstood King Uzziah, and said to him, "It is
not for you, Uzziah, to make offering to the LORD, but for the priests
the descendants of Aaron, who are consecrated to make offering. Go
out of the sanctuary; for you have done wrong, and it will bring you
no honor from the LORD God." 19 Then Uzziah was angry. Now he
had a censer in his hand to make offering, and when he became angry with the priests a leprous[a] disease broke out on his forehead, in
the presence of the priests in the house of the LORD, by the altar of
incense. 20 When the chief priest Azariah, and all the priests, looked
at him, he was leprous[a] in his forehead. They hurried him out, and he
himself hurried to get out, because the LORD had struck him. 21 King
Uzziah was leprous[a] to the day of his death, and being leprous[a] lived
in a separate house, for he was excluded from the house of the LORD.
His son Jotham was in charge of the palace of the king, governing the
people of the land.
22 Now the rest of the acts of Uzziah, from first to last, the
prophet Isaiah son of Amoz wrote. 23 Uzziah slept with his ancestors;
they buried him near his ancestors in the burial field that belonged to
the kings, for they said, "He is leprous."[a] His son Jotham succeeded
him.

Reign of Jotham

27 Jotham was twenty-five years old when he began to reign; he
reigned sixteen years in Jerusalem. His mother's name was
Jerushah daughter of Zadok. 2 He did what was right in the sight of the

[a] A term for several skin diseases; precise meaning uncertain

26:16-21 But when he had become strong he grew proud: This is Uzziah's faithless period. To explain the leprosy that struck the king later in life (2 Kgs 15:5), a second period of unfaithfulness, similar to those of Amaziah and Joash, appears (26:16-21).

26:16 grew proud: Pride was the source of Amaziah's downfall as well (25:19). In Uzziah's case, he dared to offer incense, an activity that was only to be done by the priests (Num 16:40).

Pride can be thought of as an inflated sense of self-esteem. How can pride affect your relationship with God?

26:17-18 Azariah: Azariah, a priest, functions as a prophet and rebukes or reprimands Uzziah.

26:20-21 the LORD had struck him: Uzziah's leprosy, though not what we call leprosy, was a serious skin condition that made him ritually unclean and prevented him from ruling and from participating in worship. God's judgment on Uzziah for his failure to repent is immediate.

26:23 buried him near his ancestors: Because of his leprosy Uzziah was not buried in the royal cemetery.

27:1-9 Jotham: Jotham's brief account is the first completely positive report since Abijah. Through comparisons with Uzziah, his good but flawed father, and Ahaz, his totally wicked son, the Chronicler shows that heredity is not the only factor in faith or in behavior.

27:2 Jotham...did not invade the temple: Unlike Uzziah, his father (26:16-20), Jotham did not invade the temple. The Chronicler praises Jotham for not entering the temple ("invade" is a bit strong) to assume priestly functions.

Lord just as his father Uzziah had done—only he did not invade the temple of the Lord. But the people still followed corrupt practices. 3He built the upper gate of the house of the Lord, and did extensive building on the wall of Ophel. 4Moreover he built cities in the hill country of Judah, and forts and towers on the wooded hills. 5He fought with the king of the Ammonites and prevailed against them. The Ammonites gave him that year one hundred talents of silver, ten thousand cors of wheat and ten thousand of barley. The Ammonites paid him the same amount in the second and the third years. 6So Jotham became strong because he ordered his ways before the Lord his God. 7Now the rest of the acts of Jotham, and all his wars and his ways, are written in the Book of the Kings of Israel and Judah. 8He was twenty-five years old when he began to reign; he reigned sixteen years in Jerusalem. 9Jotham slept with his ancestors, and they buried him in the city of David; and his son Ahaz succeeded him.

27:3-4 He built: Like Uzziah, Jotham engages in building projects, a sign of God's favor.

27:6 ordered his ways before the Lord: Jotham's success is credited to his faithful obedience. Chronicles omits his failure to remove the local shrines (2 Kgs 15:35).

Reign of Ahaz

28 Ahaz was twenty years old when he began to reign; he reigned sixteen years in Jerusalem. He did not do what was right in the sight of the Lord, as his ancestor David had done, 2but he walked in the ways of the kings of Israel. He even made cast images for the Baals; 3and he made offerings in the valley of the son of Hinnom, and made his sons pass through fire, according to the abominable practices of the nations whom the Lord drove out before the people of Israel. 4He sacrificed and made offerings on the high places, on the hills, and under every green tree.

28:1-27 Ahaz: In 2 Kings, Manasseh is the worst king in the history of Judah. In Chronicles, however, that distinction belongs to Ahaz. The Chronicler ends his account of the divided monarchy (10:1—28:27) by comparing the unfaithfulness of Ahaz with the unfaithfulness of the northern kingdom at the beginning of the divided monarchy. Abijah's speech (2 Chr 13:4-12) still sets the agenda, but it is Ahaz, not Jeroboam of the northern kingdom, who is unfaithful. Ahaz makes idols and worships foreign gods (28:2, 10-16, 23) as had Jeroboam (13:8-9), closes the temple doors (28:24), and extinguishes the lamps and stops the sacrifices (29:7). The reversal of Israel and Judah also is depicted. Israel was defeated in Abijah's day (13:18); now Judah suffers defeat (28:19). Judah listened to and obeyed the prophet Shemaiah with regard to Israel (11:1-4). Now Israel obeys another prophet, Oded, with regard to Judah (28:9). Judah has fallen to Israel's level of unfaithfulness at the time of the division.

Aram and Israel Defeat Judah

5 Therefore the Lord his God gave him into the hand of the king of Aram, who defeated him and took captive a great number of his people and brought them to Damascus. He was also given into the hand of the king of Israel, who defeated him with great slaughter. 6Pekah son of Remaliah killed one hundred twenty thousand in Judah in one day, all of them valiant warriors, because they had abandoned the Lord, the God of their ancestors. 7And Zichri, a mighty warrior of Ephraim, killed the king's son Maaseiah, Azrikam the commander of the palace, and Elkanah the next in authority to the king.

28:5 God gave him into the hand of: *God* defeats Ahaz, using both Aram (Syria) and Israel (Ephraim) in separate battles. In Kings, these separate battles are seen as one (2 Kgs 16:5-6).

Intervention of Oded

8 The people of Israel took captive two hundred thousand of their kin, women, sons, and daughters; they also took much booty from them and brought the booty to Samaria. 9But a prophet of the Lord was there, whose name was Oded; he went out to meet the army that came to Samaria, and said to them, "Because the Lord, the God of your ancestors, was angry with Judah, he gave them into

your hand, but you have killed them in a rage that has reached up to heaven. [10]Now you intend to subjugate the people of Judah and Jerusalem, male and female, as your slaves. But what have you except sins against the LORD your God? [11]Now hear me, and send back the captives whom you have taken from your kindred, for the fierce wrath of the LORD is upon you." [12]Moreover, certain chiefs of the Ephraimites, Azariah son of Johanan, Berechiah son of Meshillemoth, Jehizkiah son of Shallum, and Amasa son of Hadlai, stood up against those who were coming from the war, [13]and said to them, "You shall not bring the captives in here, for you propose to bring on us guilt against the LORD in addition to our present sins and guilt. For our guilt is already great, and there is fierce wrath against Israel." [14]So the warriors left the captives and the booty before the officials and all the assembly. [15]Then those who were mentioned by name got up and took the captives, and with the booty they clothed all that were naked among them; they clothed them, gave them sandals, provided them with food and drink, and anointed them; and carrying all the feeble among them on donkeys, they brought them to their kindred at Jericho, the city of palm trees. Then they returned to Samaria.

28:12-13 chiefs: Literally "heads" of groups of people, not the king. The inclusion of "all Israel" is stressed throughout Chronicles. Reunification of the north and the south is now possible with the elimination of the evil northern kings. Their confession of guilt follows the accusations of Abijah's address (13:4-12), and this contributes to the reversal of north and south at the beginning and end of the divided monarchy.

Assyria Refuses to Help Judah

16 At that time King Ahaz sent to the king[a] of Assyria for help. [17]For the Edomites had again invaded and defeated Judah, and carried away captives. [18]And the Philistines had made raids on the cities in the Shephelah and the Negeb of Judah, and had taken Beth-shemesh, Aijalon, Gederoth, Soco with its villages, Timnah with its villages, and Gimzo with its villages; and they settled there. [19]For the LORD brought Judah low because of King Ahaz of Israel, for he had behaved without restraint in Judah and had been faithless to the LORD. [20]So King Tilgath-pilneser of Assyria came against him, and oppressed him instead of strengthening him. [21]For Ahaz plundered the house of the LORD and the houses of the king and of the officials, and gave tribute to the king of Assyria; but it did not help him.

28:16-27 King Ahaz…had been faithless: Faithlessness, Ahaz's basic flaw (28:19, 22), also caused the fall of the north in 1 Chronicles 5:25-26, Judah's exile to Babylon in 2 Chronicles 36:14-18, and Saul's "exile" (1 Chr 10:13).

Apostasy and Death of Ahaz

22 In the time of his distress he became yet more faithless to the LORD—this same King Ahaz. [23]For he sacrificed to the gods of Damascus, which had defeated him, and said, "Because the gods of the kings of Aram helped them, I will sacrifice to them so that they may help me." But they were the ruin of him, and of all Israel. [24]Ahaz gathered together the utensils of the house of God, and cut in pieces the utensils of the house of God. He shut up the doors of the house of the LORD and made himself altars in every corner of Jerusalem. [25]In

28:24 shut up the doors: In Chronicles, the temple is central. Closing the temple, therefore, becomes Ahab's greatest offense. Hezekiah will set things right (29:3).

[a] Gk Syr Vg Compare 2 Kings 16.7: Heb *kings*

every city of Judah he made high places to make offerings to other
gods, provoking to anger the LORD, the God of his ancestors. [26]Now
the rest of his acts and all his ways, from first to last, are written in the
Book of the Kings of Judah and Israel. [27]Ahaz slept with his ancestors,
and they buried him in the city, in Jerusalem; but they did not bring
him into the tombs of the kings of Israel. His son Hezekiah succeeded
him.

Reign of Hezekiah

29 Hezekiah began to reign when he was twenty-five years old;
he reigned twenty-nine years in Jerusalem. His mother's
name was Abijah daughter of Zechariah. [2]He did what was right in
the sight of the LORD, just as his ancestor David had done.

The Temple Cleansed

3 In the first year of his reign, in the first month, he opened the
doors of the house of the LORD and repaired them. [4]He brought in
the priests and the Levites and assembled them in the square on the
east. [5]He said to them, "Listen to me, Levites! Sanctify yourselves,
and sanctify the house of the LORD, the God of your ancestors, and
carry out the filth from the holy place. [6]For our ancestors have been
unfaithful and have done what was evil in the sight of the LORD our
God; they have forsaken him, and have turned away their faces from
the dwelling of the LORD, and turned their backs. [7]They also shut the
doors of the vestibule and put out the lamps, and have not offered
incense or made burnt offerings in the holy place to the God of Israel.
[8]Therefore the wrath of the LORD came upon Judah and Jerusalem,
and he has made them an object of horror, of astonishment, and of
hissing, as you see with your own eyes. [9]Our fathers have fallen by the
sword and our sons and our daughters and our wives are in captivity
for this. [10]Now it is in my heart to make a covenant with the LORD,
the God of Israel, so that his fierce anger may turn away from us. [11]My
sons, do not now be negligent, for the LORD has chosen you to stand
in his presence to minister to him, and to be his ministers and make
offerings to him."

12 Then the Levites arose, Mahath son of Amasai, and Joel son
of Azariah, of the sons of the Kohathites; and of the sons of Merari,
Kish son of Abdi, and Azariah son of Jehallelel; and of the Gershonites, Joah son of Zimmah, and Eden son of Joah; [13]and of the sons of
Elizaphan, Shimri and Jeuel; and of the sons of Asaph, Zechariah and
Mattaniah; [14]and of the sons of Heman, Jehuel and Shimei; and of the
sons of Jeduthun, Shemaiah and Uzziel. [15]They gathered their brothers, sanctified themselves, and went in as the king had commanded,
by the words of the LORD, to cleanse the house of the LORD. [16]The
priests went into the inner part of the house of the LORD to cleanse

29:1—36:23 Hezekiah sent word to all Israel and Judah: In the introduction (1 Chr 1–9) and the time of the united monarchy of David and Solomon (1 Chr 10—2 Chr 9), "all Israel" was seen as a people united under a Davidic king and worshiping in the Jerusalem temple. But the third section of Chronicles saw "all Israel" as a divided monarchy (2 Chr 10—28). In this final section, Assyria's defeat of the north (2 Chr 30:6) and the faithlessness of Ahaz (28:6, 24-25) completely reverse that situation and lead to Hezekiah's reunification.

29:1—32:33 Hezekiah: Judah's worst king is followed by its best—Hezekiah. In Chronicles, Hezekiah is a second David *and* Solomon who restores the ideal of the united monarchy with regard to the temple (29:1-36), Passover (30:1—31:1), and regular worship (31:2-21). Sennacherib's invasion (32:1-23) and a summary of his reign (32:24-32) closes the account.

29:1-36 Hezekiah began to reign: Hezekiah's reform, stage one. By unlocking the doors of the temple, Hezekiah symbolically restored relationship with God and reversed the sin of Ahaz, who had "shut up the doors of the house of the LORD" (28:24).

29:5 filth: The word refers to neglect, not idolatry, since the temple had been closed.

29:6-10 unfaithful…forsaken him…covenant: Hezekiah's explanation uses the Chronicler's theological vocabulary to stress Ahaz's neglect of the temple as neglect of God.

it, and they brought out all the unclean things that they found in the
temple of the LORD into the court of the house of the LORD; and the
Levites took them and carried them out to the Wadi Kidron. 17 They
began to sanctify on the first day of the first month, and on the eighth
day of the month they came to the vestibule of the LORD; then for
eight days they sanctified the house of the LORD, and on the sixteenth
day of the first month they finished. 18 Then they went inside to King
Hezekiah and said, "We have cleansed all the house of the LORD, the
altar of burnt offering and all its utensils, and the table for the rows of
bread and all its utensils. 19 All the utensils that King Ahaz repudiated
during his reign when he was faithless, we have made ready and sanctified; see, they are in front of the altar of the LORD."

Temple Worship Restored

20 Then King Hezekiah rose early, assembled the officials of the
city, and went up to the house of the LORD. 21 They brought seven
bulls, seven rams, seven lambs, and seven male goats for a sin offering
for the kingdom and for the sanctuary and for Judah. He commanded
the priests the descendants of Aaron to offer them on the altar of the
LORD. 22 So they slaughtered the bulls, and the priests received the
blood and dashed it against the altar; they slaughtered the rams and
their blood was dashed against the altar; they also slaughtered the
lambs and their blood was dashed against the altar. 23 Then the male
goats for the sin offering were brought to the king and the assembly;
they laid their hands on them, 24 and the priests slaughtered them and
made a sin offering with their blood at the altar, to make atonement
for all Israel. For the king commanded that the burnt offering and the
sin offering should be made for all Israel.

25 He stationed the Levites in the house of the LORD with cymbals, harps, and lyres, according to the commandment of David and
of Gad the king's seer and of the prophet Nathan, for the commandment was from the LORD through his prophets. 26 The Levites stood
with the instruments of David, and the priests with the trumpets.
27 Then Hezekiah commanded that the burnt offering be offered on
the altar. When the burnt offering began, the song to the LORD began
also, and the trumpets, accompanied by the instruments of King David of Israel. 28 The whole assembly worshiped, the singers sang, and
the trumpeters sounded; all this continued until the burnt offering
was finished. 29 When the offering was finished, the king and all who
were present with him bowed down and worshiped. 30 King Hezekiah
and the officials commanded the Levites to sing praises to the LORD
with the words of David and of the seer Asaph. They sang praises with
gladness, and they bowed down and worshiped.

31 Then Hezekiah said, "You have now consecrated yourselves
to the LORD; come near, bring sacrifices and thank offerings to the

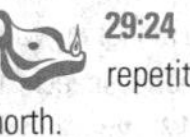

29:24 all Israel…all Israel: The repetition highlights concern for the north.

29:25-30 according to the commandment of David: Hezekiah restores sacrifice and worship under the Levites' musical leadership, recalling David's installation of the ark of the covenant (1 Chr 15:16) and Solomon's dedication of the temple (7:6).

29:31 burnt offerings: Totally consumed by the fire, these offerings symbolize a complete self-giving of the people who willingly exceed Hezekiah's request. They had done the same in response to David's plea for self-giving (1 Chr 29:17-18).

house of the LORD." The assembly brought sacrifices and thank offerings; and all who were of a willing heart brought burnt offerings. 32 The number of the burnt offerings that the assembly brought was seventy bulls, one hundred rams, and two hundred lambs; all these were for a burnt offering to the LORD. 33 The consecrated offerings were six hundred bulls and three thousand sheep. 34 But the priests were too few and could not skin all the burnt offerings, so, until other priests had sanctified themselves, their kindred, the Levites, helped them until the work was finished—for the Levites were more conscientious[a] than the priests in sanctifying themselves. 35 Besides the great number of burnt offerings there was the fat of the offerings of well-being, and there were the drink offerings for the burnt offerings. Thus the service of the house of the LORD was restored. 36 And Hezekiah and all the people rejoiced because of what God had done for the people; for the thing had come about suddenly.

The Great Passover

30 Hezekiah sent word to all Israel and Judah, and wrote letters also to Ephraim and Manasseh, that they should come to the house of the LORD at Jerusalem, to keep the passover to the LORD the God of Israel. 2 For the king and his officials and all the assembly in Jerusalem had taken counsel to keep the passover in the second month 3 (for they could not keep it at its proper time because the priests had not sanctified themselves in sufficient number, nor had the people assembled in Jerusalem). 4 The plan seemed right to the king and all the assembly. 5 So they decreed to make a proclamation throughout all Israel, from Beer-sheba to Dan, that the people should come and keep the passover to the LORD the God of Israel, at Jerusalem; for they had not kept it in great numbers as prescribed. 6 So couriers went throughout all Israel and Judah with letters from the king and his officials, as the king had commanded, saying, "O people of Israel, return to the LORD, the God of Abraham, Isaac, and Israel, so that he may turn again to the remnant of you who have escaped from the hand of the kings of Assyria. 7 Do not be like your ancestors and your kindred, who were faithless to the LORD God of their ancestors, so that he made them a desolation, as you see. 8 Do not now be stiff-necked as your ancestors were, but yield yourselves to the LORD and come to his sanctuary, which he has sanctified forever, and serve the LORD your God, so that his fierce anger may turn away from you. 9 For as you return to the LORD, your kindred and your children will find compassion with their captors, and return to this land. For the LORD your God is gracious and merciful, and will not turn away his face from you, if you return to him."

30:1—31:1 Hezekiah sent word: Hezekiah's reform, stage two. Passover usually recalls Israel's deliverance from Egypt. Here, Hezekiah uses the festival to reunite the nation in worship.

30:1-12 passover: Hezekiah's invitation to all Israel and Judah (30:1) from Beer-sheba to Dan (30:5) to celebrate Passover frames the period of the divided monarchy with calls to repentance. As in Abijah's speech at the time of the division (13:4-12), the Chronicler refuses to exclude the north but rather recognizes them as fellow believers worthy of being welcomed in the name of the LORD.

30:2 second month: Passover is celebrated in the first month of the Hebrew calendar. An ancient tradition allowed a delay for those who were unclean or absent (Num 9:9-11).

30:6-9 escaped from…Assyria: Hezekiah calls for all Israel and Judah to repent and heal the division of the nation following the Assyrian destruction of the northern kings.

30:9 return: Notice that the word *return* is repeated three times. This verb also means "repent."

---

[a] Heb *upright in heart*

10 So the couriers went from city to city through the country of Ephraim and Manasseh, and as far as Zebulun; but they laughed them to scorn, and mocked them. 11 Only a few from Asher, Manasseh, and Zebulun humbled themselves and came to Jerusalem. 12 The hand of God was also on Judah to give them one heart to do what the king and the officials commanded by the word of the LORD.

13 Many people came together in Jerusalem to keep the festival of unleavened bread in the second month, a very large assembly. 14 They set to work and removed the altars that were in Jerusalem, and all the altars for offering incense they took away and threw into the Wadi Kidron. 15 They slaughtered the passover lamb on the fourteenth day of the second month. The priests and the Levites were ashamed, and they sanctified themselves and brought burnt offerings into the house of the LORD. 16 They took their accustomed posts according to the law of Moses the man of God; the priests dashed the blood that they received[a] from the hands of the Levites. 17 For there were many in the assembly who had not sanctified themselves; therefore the Levites had to slaughter the passover lamb for everyone who was not clean, to make it holy to the LORD. 18 For a multitude of the people, many of them from Ephraim, Manasseh, Issachar, and Zebulun, had not cleansed themselves, yet they ate the passover otherwise than as prescribed. But Hezekiah prayed for them, saying, "The good LORD pardon all 19 who set their hearts to seek God, the LORD the God of their ancestors, even though not in accordance with the sanctuary's rules of cleanness." 20 The LORD heard Hezekiah, and healed the people. 21 The people of Israel who were present at Jerusalem kept the festival of unleavened bread seven days with great gladness; and the Levites and the priests praised the LORD day by day, accompanied by loud instruments for the LORD. 22 Hezekiah spoke encouragingly to all the Levites who showed good skill in the service of the LORD. So the people ate the food of the festival for seven days, sacrificing offerings of well-being and giving thanks to the LORD the God of their ancestors.

23 Then the whole assembly agreed together to keep the festival for another seven days; so they kept it for another seven days with gladness. 24 For King Hezekiah of Judah gave the assembly a thousand bulls and seven thousand sheep for offerings, and the officials gave the assembly a thousand bulls and ten thousand sheep. The priests sanctified themselves in great numbers. 25 The whole assembly of Judah, the priests and the Levites, and the whole assembly that came out of Israel, and the resident aliens who came out of the land of Israel, and the resident aliens who lived in Judah, rejoiced. 26 There was great joy in Jerusalem, for since the time of Solomon son of King David of

30:13—31:1 festival of unleavened bread: This was a separate agricultural festival that was joined to Passover when the people were in exile. With the nation healed, the Chronicler describes Hezekiah's Great Passover.

30:13-14 Many people…set to work: The priests had cleansed the temple (29:16); now the people cleanse the city.

30:18-20 Hezekiah prayed for them: Hezekiah follows God's instructions to Solomon (7:14) and prayed for those who had not properly prepared themselves for the Passover but participated anyway.

30:23 another seven days: The fourteen-day celebration mirrored Solomon's feast of dedication (7:8-10).

---

[a] Heb lacks *that they received*

Israel there had been nothing like this in Jerusalem. [27]Then the priests
and the Levites stood up and blessed the people, and their voice was
heard; their prayer came to his holy dwelling in heaven.

Pagan Shrines Destroyed

31 Now when all this was finished, all Israel who were present
went out to the cities of Judah and broke down the pillars,
hewed down the sacred poles,[a] and pulled down the high places and
the altars throughout all Judah and Benjamin, and in Ephraim and
Manasseh, until they had destroyed them all. Then all the people of
Israel returned to their cities, all to their individual properties.

2 Hezekiah appointed the divisions of the priests and of the Levites, division by division, everyone according to his service, the
priests and the Levites, for burnt offerings and offerings of well-being,
to minister in the gates of the camp of the LORD and to give thanks
and praise. [3]The contribution of the king from his own possessions
was for the burnt offerings: the burnt offerings of morning and evening, and the burnt offerings for the sabbaths, the new moons, and
the appointed festivals, as it is written in the law of the LORD. [4]He
commanded the people who lived in Jerusalem to give the portion
due to the priests and the Levites, so that they might devote themselves to the law of the LORD. [5]As soon as the word spread, the people
of Israel gave in abundance the first fruits of grain, wine, oil, honey,
and of all the produce of the field; and they brought in abundantly the
tithe of everything. [6]The people of Israel and Judah who lived in
the cities of Judah also brought in the tithe of cattle and sheep, and the
tithe of the dedicated things that had been consecrated to the LORD
their God, and laid them in heaps. [7]In the third month they began to
pile up the heaps, and finished them in the seventh month. [8]When
Hezekiah and the officials came and saw the heaps, they blessed the
LORD and his people Israel. [9]Hezekiah questioned the priests and
the Levites about the heaps. [10]The chief priest Azariah, who was of the
house of Zadok, answered him, "Since they began to bring the contributions into the house of the LORD, we have had enough to eat and
have plenty to spare; for the LORD has blessed his people, so that we
have this great supply left over."

Reorganization of Priests and Levites

11 Then Hezekiah commanded them to prepare store-chambers
in the house of the LORD; and they prepared them. [12]Faithfully they
brought in the contributions, the tithes and the dedicated things.
The chief officer in charge of them was Conaniah the Levite, with
his brother Shimei as second; [13]while Jehiel, Azaziah, Nahath, Asa-

[a] Heb *Asherim*

31:1 Ephraim and Manasseh: The removal of symbols of idolatry spread out to include the north.

31:2-21 Hezekiah...undertook in the service of the house of God: Hezekiah's reform, stage three. Regular worship is restored.

31:2-4 appointed: The appointment of worship leaders, provision of sacrificial animals, and arrangements for financial support restores what David began (1 Chr 23–26; 29:3) and Solomon expanded (2 Chr 8:12-16).

31:5-10 the people...gave in abundance: Their generosity recalls contributions to Moses' tabernacle (Exod 36:2-7) and David's temple (1 Chr 29:1-9).

31:10 the LORD has blessed: The chief priest states the positive side of the Chronicler's concept of retributive justice (faithfulness is rewarded).

31:11-19 store-chambers: Hezekiah makes arrangements for the storage (31:11-13) and distribution (31:14-19) of the contributions.

hel, Jerimoth, Jozabad, Eliel, Ismachiah, Mahath, and Benaiah were overseers assisting Conaniah and his brother Shimei, by the appointment of King Hezekiah and of Azariah the chief officer of the house of God. [14]Kore son of Imnah the Levite, keeper of the east gate, was in charge of the freewill offerings to God, to apportion the contribution reserved for the LORD and the most holy offerings. [15]Eden, Miniamin, Jeshua, Shemaiah, Amariah, and Shecaniah were faithfully assisting him in the cities of the priests, to distribute the portions to their kindred, old and young alike, by divisions, [16]except those enrolled by genealogy, males from three years old and upwards, all who entered the house of the LORD as the duty of each day required, for their service according to their offices, by their divisions. [17]The enrollment of the priests was according to their ancestral houses; that of the Levites from twenty years old and upwards was according to their offices, by their divisions. [18]The priests were enrolled with all their little children, their wives, their sons, and their daughters, the whole multitude; for they were faithful in keeping themselves holy. [19]And for the descendants of Aaron, the priests, who were in the fields of common land belonging to their towns, town by town, the people designated by name were to distribute portions to every male among the priests and to everyone among the Levites who was enrolled.

20 Hezekiah did this throughout all Judah; he did what was good and right and faithful before the LORD his God. [21]And every work that he undertook in the service of the house of God, and in accordance with the law and the commandments, to seek his God, he did with all his heart; and he prospered.

Sennacherib's Invasion

32 After these things and these acts of faithfulness, King Sennacherib of Assyria came and invaded Judah and encamped against the fortified cities, thinking to win them for himself. [2]When Hezekiah saw that Sennacherib had come and intended to fight against Jerusalem, [3]he planned with his officers and his warriors to stop the flow of the springs that were outside the city; and they helped him. [4]A great many people were gathered, and they stopped all the springs and the wadi that flowed through the land, saying, "Why should the Assyrian kings come and find water in abundance?" [5]Hezekiah[a] set to work resolutely and built up the entire wall that was broken down, and raised towers on it,[b] and outside it he built another wall; he also strengthened the Millo in the city of David, and made weapons and shields in abundance. [6]He appointed combat commanders over the people, and gathered them together to him in the square at the gate of the city and spoke encouragingly to them, saying, [7]"Be strong and of

[a] Heb *He* [b] Vg: Heb *and raised on the towers*

32:1-33 Hezekiah...planned with his officers: Chronicles omits Hezekiah's surrender, trust in foreign alliances, stripping of the temple, and most of Isaiah's leadership from 2 Kings 18–20 and Isaiah 38–39. Instead, Sennacherib's invasion is framed by statements of success (31:20-21; 32:30) and suggests that victory and success are the reward of faithfulness.

32:1-23 King Sennacherib of Assyria came and invaded: Hezekiah's trust in foreign alliances, surrender to Sennacherib, payment of tribute, and stripping of the temple, emphasized in the other versions of his reign (2 Kgs 18–20; Isa 38–39) are left out to highlight the effectiveness of Hezekiah's prayer.

32:2-6a planned: Hezekiah's methodical preparations for war, including building projects, fortifications, and large armies, indicate God's approval. Closing the springs around the city cut off the enemy's water supply, while a hidden tunnel from the Gihon supplied Jerusalem. This tunnel can still be seen in Jerusalem today.

32:6b-8 spoke encouragingly: Hezekiah's inspiring words express complete trust in God's victory, as had the similar words of David, Asa, and Jehoshaphat before battle (1 Chr 22:13; 2 Chr 14:11; 19:5-7; 20:15-17, 20). "Be strong" is a play on Hezekiah's name, "May the LORD strengthen."

good courage. Do not be afraid or dismayed before the king of Assyria
and all the horde that is with him; for there is one greater with us than
with him. [8]With him is an arm of flesh; but with us is the LORD our
God, to help us and to fight our battles." The people were encouraged
by the words of King Hezekiah of Judah.
9 After this, while King Sennacherib of Assyria was at Lachish
with all his forces, he sent his servants to Jerusalem to King Hezekiah
of Judah and to all the people of Judah that were in Jerusalem, saying,
[10]"Thus says King Sennacherib of Assyria: On what are you relying,
that you undergo the siege of Jerusalem? [11]Is not Hezekiah misleading you, handing you over to die by famine and by thirst, when he
tells you, 'The LORD our God will save us from the hand of the king
of Assyria'? [12]Was it not this same Hezekiah who took away his high
places and his altars and commanded Judah and Jerusalem, saying,
'Before one altar you shall worship, and upon it you shall make your
offerings'? [13]Do you not know what I and my ancestors have done to
all the peoples of other lands? Were the gods of the nations of those
lands at all able to save their lands out of my hand? [14]Who among all
the gods of those nations that my ancestors utterly destroyed was able
to save his people from my hand, that your God should be able to save
you from my hand? [15]Now therefore do not let Hezekiah deceive you
or mislead you in this fashion, and do not believe him, for no god of
any nation or kingdom has been able to save his people from my hand
or from the hand of my ancestors. How much less will your God save
you out of my hand!"
16 His servants said still more against the Lord GOD and against
his servant Hezekiah. [17]He also wrote letters to throw contempt on
the LORD the God of Israel and to speak against him, saying, "Just as
the gods of the nations in other lands did not rescue their people from
my hands, so the God of Hezekiah will not rescue his people from my
hand." [18]They shouted it with a loud voice in the language of Judah to
the people of Jerusalem who were on the wall, to frighten and terrify
them, in order that they might take the city. [19]They spoke of the God
of Jerusalem as if he were like the gods of the peoples of the earth,
which are the work of human hands.

Sennacherib's Defeat and Death

20 Then King Hezekiah and the prophet Isaiah son of Amoz
prayed because of this and cried to heaven. [21]And the LORD sent an
angel who cut off all the mighty warriors and commanders and officers in the camp of the king of Assyria. So he returned in disgrace
to his own land. When he came into the house of his god, some of
his own sons struck him down there with the sword. [22]So the LORD
saved Hezekiah and the inhabitants of Jerusalem from the hand of
King Sennacherib of Assyria and from the hand of all his enemies;

32:9-19 Hezekiah...took away his high places and his altars: In his message to the people of Judah, Sennacherib mistakenly thought Hezekiah had removed places to worship the LORD when he destroyed the local shrines, and that God would be displeased with Hezekiah.

32:20-23 Hezekiah and...Isaiah...prayed: The prayers of Isaiah and Hezekiah are answered. Elsewhere, Hezekiah asks Isaiah to pray (2 Kgs 19:4; Isa 37:4). Hezekiah is portrayed as a second Solomon because he is a person of prayer, rest, tribute, and fame (1 Chr 22:8-10; 2 Chr 9:23-24).

In a crisis Hezekiah and Isaiah prayed. What do you focus on when you are in a crisis, the problem or God? Why?

he gave them rest[a] on every side. 23 Many brought gifts to the LORD in
Jerusalem and precious things to King Hezekiah of Judah, so that he
was exalted in the sight of all nations from that time onward.

Hezekiah's Sickness

24 In those days Hezekiah became sick and was at the point of
death. He prayed to the LORD, and he answered him and gave him a
sign. 25 But Hezekiah did not respond according to the benefit done
to him, for his heart was proud. Therefore wrath came upon him and
upon Judah and Jerusalem. 26 Then Hezekiah humbled himself for the
pride of his heart, both he and the inhabitants of Jerusalem, so that
the wrath of the LORD did not come upon them in the days of Hezekiah.

Hezekiah's Prosperity and Achievements

27 Hezekiah had very great riches and honor; and he made for
himself treasuries for silver, for gold, for precious stones, for spices,
for shields, and for all kinds of costly objects; 28 storehouses also for
the yield of grain, wine, and oil; and stalls for all kinds of cattle, and
sheepfolds.[b] 29 He likewise provided cities for himself, and flocks and
herds in abundance; for God had given him very great possessions.
30 This same Hezekiah closed the upper outlet of the waters of Gihon
and directed them down to the west side of the city of David. Hezekiah prospered in all his works. 31 So also in the matter of the envoys
of the officials of Babylon, who had been sent to him to inquire about
the sign that had been done in the land, God left him to himself, in
order to test him and to know all that was in his heart.

32 Now the rest of the acts of Hezekiah, and his good deeds, are
written in the vision of the prophet Isaiah son of Amoz in the Book
of the Kings of Judah and Israel. 33 Hezekiah slept with his ancestors,
and they buried him on the ascent to the tombs of the descendants of
David; and all Judah and the inhabitants of Jerusalem did him honor
at his death. His son Manasseh succeeded him.

Reign of Manasseh

33 Manasseh was twelve years old when he began to reign; he
reigned fifty-five years in Jerusalem. 2 He did what was evil
in the sight of the LORD, according to the abominable practices of the
nations whom the LORD drove out before the people of Israel. 3 For
he rebuilt the high places that his father Hezekiah had pulled down,
and erected altars to the Baals, made sacred poles,[c] worshiped all the
host of heaven, and served them. 4 He built altars in the house of the
LORD, of which the LORD had said, "In Jerusalem shall my name be
forever." 5 He built altars for all the host of heaven in the two courts

[a] Gk Vg: Heb *guided them* [b] Gk Vg: Heb *flocks for folds* [c] Heb *Asheroth*

32:24-26 his heart was proud…wrath…humbled himself: Hezekiah's pride in his miraculous healing results in God's wrath. Unlike Asa (16:12) and Uzziah (26:16-21), however, Hezekiah humbles himself (see God's promise to Solomon in 7:14) and delays the judgment to a later date.

32:27-33 Hezekiah had very great riches and honor: At the end of his reign, this ideal king is praised with the usual signs of blessing: wealth, building projects, and prosperity.

33:1-20 Manasseh: Elsewhere, Manasseh is the worst of Judah's kings, totally unrepentant and responsible for the Babylonian exile (2 Kgs 21:11-16; 24:3-4; Jer 15:4). Chronicles, however, blames the exile on the unfaithfulness of the people, not Manasseh (36:14-17). Manasseh is an example of someone who suffered divine punishment (33:11) for his sins (33:2-9) but who repented, changed his ways, and received forgiveness (33:12-19; 7:14).

33:1 fifty-five years: The length of Manasseh's reign, the longest of any king in Judah, may account for the Chronicler's positive portrayal. Length of reign, however, is not a sign of blessing elsewhere in Chronicles.

33:3 made sacred poles, worshiped all the host of heaven: Manasseh worshiped Canaanite deities and gods associated with the zodiac, forbidden in Deuteronomy 4:19; 17:3.

of the house of the LORD. [6]He made his son pass through fire in the valley of the son of Hinnom, practiced soothsaying and augury and sorcery, and dealt with mediums and with wizards. He did much evil in the sight of the LORD, provoking him to anger. [7]The carved image of the idol that he had made he set in the house of God, of which God said to David and to his son Solomon, "In this house, and in Jerusalem, which I have chosen out of all the tribes of Israel, I will put my name forever; [8]I will never again remove the feet of Israel from the land that I appointed for your ancestors, if only they will be careful to do all that I have commanded them, all the law, the statutes, and the ordinances given through Moses." [9]Manasseh misled Judah and the inhabitants of Jerusalem, so that they did more evil than the nations whom the LORD had destroyed before the people of Israel.

Manasseh Restored after Repentance

10 The LORD spoke to Manasseh and to his people, but they gave no heed. [11]Therefore the LORD brought against them the commanders of the army of the king of Assyria, who took Manasseh captive in manacles, bound him with fetters, and brought him to Babylon. [12]While he was in distress he entreated the favor of the LORD his God and humbled himself greatly before the God of his ancestors. [13]He prayed to him, and God received his entreaty, heard his plea, and restored him again to Jerusalem and to his kingdom. Then Manasseh knew that the LORD indeed was God.

14 Afterward he built an outer wall for the city of David west of Gihon, in the valley, reaching the entrance at the Fish Gate; he carried it around Ophel, and raised it to a very great height. He also put commanders of the army in all the fortified cities in Judah. [15]He took away the foreign gods and the idol from the house of the LORD, and all the altars that he had built on the mountain of the house of the LORD and in Jerusalem, and he threw them out of the city. [16]He also restored the altar of the LORD and offered on it sacrifices of well-being and of thanksgiving; and he commanded Judah to serve the LORD the God of Israel. [17]The people, however, still sacrificed at the high places, but only to the LORD their God.

Death of Manasseh

18 Now the rest of the acts of Manasseh, his prayer to his God, and the words of the seers who spoke to him in the name of the LORD God of Israel, these are in the Annals of the Kings of Israel. [19]His prayer, and how God received his entreaty, all his sin and his faithlessness, the sites on which he built high places and set up the sacred poles[a] and the images, before he humbled himself, these are written in

33:11 Babylon: Manasseh's exile foreshadows the later exile of Judah. Babylon as a destination is strange but not impossible, and helps the foreshadowing.

33:12-13 humbled himself: Manasseh's unexpected repentance and restoration illustrates God's promise to Solomon (7:14), perhaps the major theme of these books. The Chronicler has presented other kings with faithful and unfaithful periods, but only Manasseh moves from negative to positive.

33:14-16 Afterward he built: Building programs are a frequent sign of blessing (11:5; 14:6-7; 17:12; 27:3-4; 34:10-13), as are strong armies (11:1; 14:8; 25:5; 26:9-10). In the reforms, Manasseh destroys the objects he introduced for idol worship in 33:2-9 and restores the worship of God.

Manasseh responded to God's forgiveness by destroying objects for idol worship, and he began to worship God. How do you respond to God's forgiveness?

33:17 at the high places: The reform is incomplete, since the people still sacrifice at the local shrines.

[a] Heb *Asherim*

the records of the seers.[a] 20 So Manasseh slept with his ancestors, and they buried him in his house. His son Amon succeeded him.

Amon's Reign and Death

21 Amon was twenty-two years old when he began to reign; he reigned two years in Jerusalem. 22 He did what was evil in the sight of the LORD, as his father Manasseh had done. Amon sacrificed to all the images that his father Manasseh had made, and served them. 23 He did not humble himself before the LORD, as his father Manasseh had humbled himself, but this Amon incurred more and more guilt. 24 His servants conspired against him and killed him in his house. 25 But the people of the land killed all those who had conspired against King Amon; and the people of the land made his son Josiah king to succeed him.

Reign of Josiah

34 Josiah was eight years old when he began to reign; he reigned thirty-one years in Jerusalem. 2 He did what was right in the sight of the LORD, and walked in the ways of his ancestor David; he did not turn aside to the right or to the left. 3 For in the eighth year of his reign, while he was still a boy, he began to seek the God of his ancestor David, and in the twelfth year he began to purge Judah and Jerusalem of the high places, the sacred poles,[b] and the carved and the cast images. 4 In his presence they pulled down the altars of the Baals; he demolished the incense altars that stood above them. He broke down the sacred poles[b] and the carved and the cast images; he made dust of them and scattered it over the graves of those who had sacrificed to them. 5 He also burned the bones of the priests on their altars, and purged Judah and Jerusalem. 6 In the towns of Manasseh, Ephraim, and Simeon, and as far as Naphtali, in their ruins[c] all around, 7 he broke down the altars, beat the sacred poles[b] and the images into powder, and demolished all the incense altars throughout all the land of Israel. Then he returned to Jerusalem.

Discovery of the Book of the Law

8 In the eighteenth year of his reign, when he had purged the land and the house, he sent Shaphan son of Azaliah, Maaseiah the governor of the city, and Joah son of Joahaz, the recorder, to repair the house of the LORD his God. 9 They came to the high priest Hilkiah and delivered the money that had been brought into the house of God, which the Levites, the keepers of the threshold, had collected from Manasseh and Ephraim and from all the remnant of Israel and from all Judah and Benjamin and from the inhabitants of Jerusalem.

[a] One Ms Gk: MT *of Hozai* [b] Heb *Asherim* [c] Meaning of Heb uncertain

33:21-35 Amon: Manasseh's reforms are reversed by Amon's short but disastrous reign. Notice the lack of burial notice.

34:1—36:1 Josiah: In the book of 2 Kings, Josiah is Judah's greatest king, because of his reforms (2 Kgs 22:1—23:30). The Chronicler's portrayal of Josiah is more restrained. Hezekiah is the great reformer. Josiah merely repeats some of Hezekiah's reforms, and many of Josiah's reforms in 2 Kings are carried out by the *people* in 2 Chronicles. The sequence of events is also different. In 2 Kings 22, Josiah's reforms and repair of the temple appear as a single response to the discovery of the book of the law in Josiah's eighteenth year. In 2 Chronicles, however, the reform begins with Josiah seeking God in the eighth year of his reign (34:3a) and continues through his twelfth (34:3b) and eighteenth years (34:8).

34:1-7 he began to purge Judah and Jerusalem: Josiah tears down the sacred poles and idols put up in the land to honor Baal, but he is not given credit for purifying the temple. The Chronicler gives credit to Manasseh for the temple's restoration (33:15-16).

34:6 Manasseh, Ephraim, and Simeon, and as far as Naphtali: Josiah's reform includes areas of the northern kingdom reclaimed from Assyria, reuniting all Israel under a descendant of King David.

34:8-13 repair the house of the LORD his God: Similar to 2 Kings 22:3-6, but emphasizing the contributions of the Levites and the "remnant of Israel."

[10]They delivered it to the workers who had the oversight of the house
of the LORD, and the workers who were working in the house of the
LORD gave it for repairing and restoring the house. [11]They gave it to
the carpenters and the builders to buy quarried stone, and timber for
binders, and beams for the buildings that the kings of Judah had let
go to ruin. [12]The people did the work faithfully. Over them were appointed the Levites Jahath and Obadiah, of the sons of Merari, along
with Zechariah and Meshullam, of the sons of the Kohathites, to have
oversight. Other Levites, all skillful with instruments of music, [13]were
over the burden bearers and directed all who did work in every kind
of service; and some of the Levites were scribes, and officials, and
gatekeepers.

14 While they were bringing out the money that had been brought
into the house of the LORD, the priest Hilkiah found the book of the
law of the LORD given through Moses. [15]Hilkiah said to the secretary
Shaphan, "I have found the book of the law in the house of the LORD";
and Hilkiah gave the book to Shaphan. [16]Shaphan brought the book
to the king, and further reported to the king, "All that was committed
to your servants they are doing. [17]They have emptied out the money
that was found in the house of the LORD and have delivered it into
the hand of the overseers and the workers." [18]The secretary Shaphan
informed the king, "The priest Hilkiah has given me a book." Shaphan
then read it aloud to the king.

19 When the king heard the words of the law he tore his clothes.
[20]Then the king commanded Hilkiah, Ahikam son of Shaphan, Abdon son of Micah, the secretary Shaphan, and the king's servant Asaiah: [21]"Go, inquire of the LORD for me and for those who are left in
Israel and in Judah, concerning the words of the book that has been
found; for the wrath of the LORD that is poured out on us is great,
because our ancestors did not keep the word of the LORD, to act in
accordance with all that is written in this book."

The Prophet Huldah Consulted

22 So Hilkiah and those whom the king had sent went to the
prophet Huldah, the wife of Shallum son of Tokhath son of Hasrah,
keeper of the wardrobe (who lived in Jerusalem in the Second Quarter) and spoke to her to that effect. [23]She declared to them, "Thus says
the LORD, the God of Israel: Tell the man who sent you to me, [24]Thus
says the LORD: I will indeed bring disaster upon this place and upon
its inhabitants, all the curses that are written in the book that was read
before the king of Judah. [25]Because they have forsaken me and have
made offerings to other gods, so that they have provoked me to anger
with all the works of their hands, my wrath will be poured out on this
place and will not be quenched. [26]But as to the king of Judah, who sent
you to inquire of the LORD, thus shall you say to him: Thus says the

34:14-21 found the book of the law of the LORD given through Moses: The "book of the law" that Hilkiah found during the temple repairs (2 Kgs 22:8) was the core of the book of Deuteronomy. The Chronicler's longer title may indicate that the book is the Pentateuch (the name for the first five books of the Hebrew Scriptures: Genesis–Deuteronomy).

34:19 tore his clothes: Josiah's reaction to what was in the book was a common way of showing grief (Job 1:20).

34:22-25 the prophet Huldah: A female prophet announces Jerusalem's destruction.

34:26-28 the king of Judah...to your grave in peace: Josiah will die a natural death without witnessing the destruction of Jerusalem, despite his death in battle (35:23-24).

LORD, the God of Israel: Regarding the words that you have heard,
[27]because your heart was penitent and you humbled yourself before
God when you heard his words against this place and its inhabitants,
and you have humbled yourself before me, and have torn your clothes
and wept before me, I also have heard you, says the LORD. [28]I will
gather you to your ancestors and you shall be gathered to your grave
in peace; your eyes shall not see all the disaster that I will bring on this
place and its inhabitants." They took the message back to the king.

The Covenant Renewed

29 Then the king sent word and gathered together all the elders
of Judah and Jerusalem. [30]The king went up to the house of the LORD,
with all the people of Judah, the inhabitants of Jerusalem, the priests
and the Levites, all the people both great and small; he read in their
hearing all the words of the book of the covenant that had been found
in the house of the LORD. [31]The king stood in his place and made a
covenant before the LORD, to follow the LORD, keeping his commandments, his decrees, and his statutes, with all his heart and all his
soul, to perform the words of the covenant that were written in this
book. [32]Then he made all who were present in Jerusalem and in Benjamin pledge themselves to it. And the inhabitants of Jerusalem acted
according to the covenant of God, the God of their ancestors. [33]Josiah
took away all the abominations from all the territory that belonged
to the people of Israel, and made all who were in Israel worship the
LORD their God. All his days they did not turn away from following
the LORD the God of their ancestors.

Celebration of the Passover

35 Josiah kept a passover to the LORD in Jerusalem; they
slaughtered the passover lamb on the fourteenth day of the
first month. [2]He appointed the priests to their offices and encouraged them in the service of the house of the LORD. [3]He said to the
Levites who taught all Israel and who were holy to the LORD, "Put the
holy ark in the house that Solomon son of David, king of Israel, built;
you need no longer carry it on your shoulders. Now serve the LORD
your God and his people Israel. [4]Make preparations by your ancestral houses by your divisions, following the written directions of King
David of Israel and the written directions of his son Solomon. [5]Take
position in the holy place according to the groupings of the ancestral
houses of your kindred the people, and let there be Levites for each
division of an ancestral house.[a] [6]Slaughter the passover lamb, sanctify
yourselves, and on behalf of your kindred make preparations, acting
according to the word of the LORD by Moses."

---

[a] Meaning of Heb uncertain

Huldah warned the people of upcoming destruction. Who helps you see things in your life that you need to avoid?

34:29-32 The king sent word and gathered together...made a covenant: Josiah renews the covenant. This leads to the reforms described in 2 Kings 23:4-10. In 2 Chronicles these reforms have already occurred (34:3-7).

What does *sola scriptura* mean? Sola scriptura or "scripture alone" means that the Bible is the governing principle in matters of faith and life. Nowhere in 2 Chronicles is this more clearly seen than in Josiah's reforms, based entirely upon the teaching of Deuteronomy, found in the temple (2 Chr 34:29-33). *2 Chronicles 34:31*

35:1-19 Josiah kept a passover: The Chronicler expands the role of the Levites to include teaching, bearing the ark, and the slaughter of sacrificial animals (35:3-4) and mentions the presence of all Israel (35:17-18).

7 Then Josiah contributed to the people, as passover offerings for all that were present, lambs and kids from the flock to the number of thirty thousand, and three thousand bulls; these were from the king's possessions. [8]His officials contributed willingly to the people, to the priests, and to the Levites. Hilkiah, Zechariah, and Jehiel, the chief officers of the house of God, gave to the priests for the passover offerings two thousand six hundred lambs and kids and three hundred bulls. [9]Conaniah also, and his brothers Shemaiah and Nethanel, and Hashabiah and Jeiel and Jozabad, the chiefs of the Levites, gave to the Levites for the passover offerings five thousand lambs and kids and five hundred bulls.

10 When the service had been prepared for, the priests stood in their place, and the Levites in their divisions according to the king's command. [11]They slaughtered the passover lamb, and the priests dashed the blood that they received[a] from them, while the Levites did the skinning. [12]They set aside the burnt offerings so that they might distribute them according to the groupings of the ancestral houses of the people, to offer to the LORD, as it is written in the book of Moses. And they did the same with the bulls. [13]They roasted the passover lamb with fire according to the ordinance; and they boiled the holy offerings in pots, in caldrons, and in pans, and carried them quickly to all the people. [14]Afterward they made preparations for themselves and for the priests, because the priests the descendants of Aaron were occupied in offering the burnt offerings and the fat parts until night; so the Levites made preparations for themselves and for the priests, the descendants of Aaron. [15]The singers, the descendants of Asaph, were in their place according to the command of David, and Asaph, and Heman, and the king's seer Jeduthun. The gatekeepers were at each gate; they did not need to interrupt their service, for their kindred the Levites made preparations for them.

16 So all the service of the LORD was prepared that day, to keep the passover and to offer burnt offerings on the altar of the LORD, according to the command of King Josiah. [17]The people of Israel who were present kept the passover at that time, and the festival of unleavened bread seven days. [18]No passover like it had been kept in Israel since the days of the prophet Samuel; none of the kings of Israel had kept such a passover as was kept by Josiah, by the priests and the Levites, by all Judah and Israel who were present, and by the inhabitants of Jerusalem. [19]In the eighteenth year of the reign of Josiah this passover was kept.

35:20—36:1 Josiah . . . died: Josiah dies because he fails to obey a prophetic word from God delivered in a pharaoh's request for safe passage.

Josiah died unexpectedly (35:22-24). What do you want to do before you die?

Defeat by Pharaoh Neco and Death of Josiah

20 After all this, when Josiah had set the temple in order, King Neco of Egypt went up to fight at Carchemish on the Euphrates, and

[a] Heb lacks *that they received*

Josiah went out against him. 21 But Neco[a] sent envoys to him, saying,
"What have I to do with you, king of Judah? I am not coming against
you today, but against the house with which I am at war; and God has
commanded me to hurry. Cease opposing God, who is with me, so
that he will not destroy you." 22 But Josiah would not turn away from
him, but disguised himself in order to fight with him. He did not listen to the words of Neco from the mouth of God, but joined battle
in the plain of Megiddo. 23 The archers shot King Josiah; and the king
said to his servants, "Take me away, for I am badly wounded." 24 So his
servants took him out of the chariot and carried him in his second
chariot[b] and brought him to Jerusalem. There he died, and was buried
in the tombs of his ancestors. All Judah and Jerusalem mourned for
Josiah. 25 Jeremiah also uttered a lament for Josiah, and all the singing
men and singing women have spoken of Josiah in their laments to this
day. They made these a custom in Israel; they are recorded in the Laments. 26 Now the rest of the acts of Josiah and his faithful deeds in
accordance with what is written in the law of the LORD, 27 and his acts,
first and last, are written in the Book of the Kings of Israel and Judah.

Reign of Jehoahaz

36 The people of the land took Jehoahaz son of Josiah and
made him king to succeed his father in Jerusalem. 2 Jehoahaz
was twenty-three years old when he began to reign; he reigned three
months in Jerusalem. 3 Then the king of Egypt deposed him in Jerusalem and laid on the land a tribute of one hundred talents of silver and
one talent of gold. 4 The king of Egypt made his brother Eliakim king
over Judah and Jerusalem, and changed his name to Jehoiakim; but
Neco took his brother Jehoahaz and carried him to Egypt.

36:2-21 Jehoahaz…Eliakim…Zedekiah: Josiah is followed by three sons (and one grandson, Jehoiachin). These are Judah's last kings. The Chronicler quickly foreshadows the coming disaster for Israel in the personal "exile" of each of these kings. Repeated references to "doing evil" (36:5, 9, 12), deportation (36:3, 4, 6, 10), and loss of temple vessels (36:7, 10, 18, 19) point to the cause.

36:4 Eliakim…Jehoiakim: The king of Egypt, Pharaoh Neco (610–595 B.C.E.) changed Eliakim's name to Jehoiakim to make a show of his power. Eliakim/Jehoiakim is older than Jehoahaz, whom he replaced.

Reign and Captivity of Jehoiakim

5 Jehoiakim was twenty-five years old when he began to reign; he
reigned eleven years in Jerusalem. He did what was evil in the sight of
the LORD his God. 6 Against him King Nebuchadnezzar of Babylon
came up, and bound him with fetters to take him to Babylon. 7 Nebuchadnezzar also carried some of the vessels of the house of the LORD
to Babylon and put them in his palace in Babylon. 8 Now the rest of
the acts of Jehoiakim, and the abominations that he did, and what was
found against him, are written in the Book of the Kings of Israel and
Judah; and his son Jehoiachin succeeded him.

36:6 Nebuchadnezzar: Nebuchadnezzar II ruled Babylon (605–562 B.C.E.).

Reign and Captivity of Jehoiachin

9 Jehoiachin was eight years old when he began to reign; he
reigned three months and ten days in Jerusalem. He did what was evil

36:9 eight years old: He probably was eighteen (2 Kgs 24:8).

[a] Heb *he* [b] Or *the chariot of his deputy*

in the sight of the LORD. [10]In the spring of the year King Nebuchadnezzar sent and brought him to Babylon, along with the precious vessels of the house of the LORD, and made his brother Zedekiah king
over Judah and Jerusalem.

Reign of Zedekiah

36:11-21 Zedekiah...exile in Babylon: The pattern of the king being defeated and the temple vessels being robbed concludes with Judah's final destruction and exile under Zedekiah (586 B.C.E.).

11 Zedekiah was twenty-one years old when he began to reign;
he reigned eleven years in Jerusalem. [12]He did what was evil in the
sight of the LORD his God. He did not humble himself before the
prophet Jeremiah who spoke from the mouth of the LORD. [13]He also
rebelled against King Nebuchadnezzar, who had made him swear by
God; he stiffened his neck and hardened his heart against turning
to the LORD, the God of Israel. [14]All the leading priests and the people also were exceedingly unfaithful, following all the abominations
of the nations; and they polluted the house of the LORD that he had
consecrated in Jerusalem.

36:14 unfaithful: The people's lack of faith, seen in the genealogies of Israel (1 Chr 5:25-26) and Judah (1 Chr 9:1), Saul (1 Chr 10:13), and throughout Chronicles, reaches its high point here.

The Fall of Jerusalem

36:15-21 the wrath of the LORD... became so great: In 2 Kings the exile is blamed on Manasseh's sins (21:10-15), not the failure of the kings and the people to listen to and obey the prophets (36:15-16).

15 The LORD, the God of their ancestors, sent persistently to
them by his messengers, because he had compassion on his people
and on his dwelling place; [16]but they kept mocking the messengers
of God, despising his words, and scoffing at his prophets, until the
wrath of the LORD against his people became so great that there was
no remedy.

36:17-19 all: The total destruction of the temple, the city, and the exile of all the people to Babylon is emphasized by repeating the word *all* five times.

36:17 therefore he: God, not Babylon, brought the exile.

17 Therefore he brought up against them the king of the Chaldeans, who killed their youths with the sword in the house of their
sanctuary, and had no compassion on young man or young woman,
the aged or the feeble; he gave them all into his hand. [18]All the vessels
of the house of God, large and small, and the treasures of the house
of the LORD, and the treasures of the king and of his officials, all these
he brought to Babylon. [19]They burned the house of God, broke down
the wall of Jerusalem, burned all its palaces with fire, and destroyed
all its precious vessels. [20]He took into exile in Babylon those who had
escaped from the sword, and they became servants to him and to his
sons until the establishment of the kingdom of Persia, [21]to fulfill the
word of the LORD by the mouth of Jeremiah, until the land had made
up for its sabbaths. All the days that it lay desolate it kept sabbath, to
fulfill seventy years.

36:21 seventy years: The exile is limited to seventy years (Jer 25:11-12; 29:10) so the land may experience Sabbath rest, making up for 490 (7 times 70) years of neglect (Lev 26:34-39).

Cyrus Proclaims Liberty for the Exiles

36:22-23 In the first year of King Cyrus: These verses are nearly identical to Ezra 1:1-3a. Cyrus, who ruled Persia from 539 to 530 B.C.E., reverses the situation for the people in exile and allows those who want to go back to Judah to return and rebuild the temple in Jerusalem. In this invitation is an echo of a key theme of Chronicles: repent and return to the LORD.

22 In the first year of King Cyrus of Persia, in fulfillment of the
word of the LORD spoken by Jeremiah, the LORD stirred up the spirit
of King Cyrus of Persia so that he sent a herald throughout all his kingdom and also declared in a written edict: [23]"Thus says King Cyrus of

Persia: The LORD, the God of heaven, has given me all the kingdoms of the earth, and he has charged me to build him a house at Jerusalem, which is in Judah. Whoever is among you of all his people, may the LORD his God be with him! Let him go up."

Ezra 6:16

EZRA

Background File

Ezra-Nehemiah was one book in Hebrew until the fifteenth century. It is closely related to the book of 1-2 Chronicles. Many scholars suggest that both Ezra-Nehemiah and 1-2 Chronicles are theological-historical narratives from the priestly/Levitical school of thought in the time of the Second Temple (515 B.C.E.-70 C.E.). The author representing this school is sometimes referred to as "the Chronicler." Other recent scholarship suggests that Ezra-Nehemiah had its own distinct author. This person or group used sources including first-person accounts usually referred to as, respectively, the Ezra Memoir and the Nehemiah Memoir, letters in Aramaic as well as lists and narratives in Hebrew. The Ezra-Nehemiah book was probably completed by about 400 B.C.E. Its audience would have been Jews who returned from the Babylonian exile (sometime after 539 B.C.E.). Exiles who came back to Jerusalem and the surrounding area were settling among those Jews who had never left the Holy Land. These exiles also began setting themselves apart from the non-Jewish, especially Samaritan, population.

What's the Story?

The first temple built by Israel's King Solomon had been destroyed along with Jerusalem in 586 B.C.E. by the Babylonians, who took many of the Hebrew people into exile. In 539, Cyrus the Persian defeated Babylon and allowed the exiles to return to Jerusalem to build the second temple. There are three phases in the narrative of Ezra-Nehemiah: the initial return and rebuilding of the temple; the work of Ezra in establishing the Torah as the "constitution" of Second Temple Judaism; and the work of Nehemiah in rebuilding the walls of Jerusalem. Here is a summary of the first two phases:

Ezra 1-6: God's people return from exile

Cyrus' decree and the people's departure
The list of those who returned
The altar is rebuilt in Jerusalem, and the foundation for the temple is laid
Local residents oppose rebuilding the temple and Jerusalem
Building of the temple resumes, with continued opposition from locals
The decree of Darius, temple completed, and worship restored to Jerusalem

Ezra 7–10: The work of Ezra

The priest Ezra brings a second group of exiles to Jerusalem
Listing of exiles who returned and their arrival in Jerusalem
Marriage to people outside the faith threatens the restoration of the community
Drastic measures are taken to protect the faith of the worshiping community

What's the Message?

As with 1–2 Chronicles (as well as 1–2 Kings in its different way) Ezra-Nehemiah is a "theological history." While it is interested in providing historical facts, it is equally interested in assigning *meaning* to the events. The Greek book of 1 Esdras, found in the collection of books known as the Apocrypha, arranges many of the stories found in Ezra-Nehemiah in different ways. Given the custom of monarchs and priests to reuse the same names in successive generations and of our author's tendency to compress history for theological reasons, we are not even certain whether Ezra or Nehemiah came to Jerusalem first or whether their missions overlapped. The author has used his sources to present a theological narrative demonstrating that the temple, the Torah (the Law), and the distinctiveness of the Jewish people are of principal importance in Second Temple Judaism. For Christians today, these books teach us about the centrality of regular worship with the community of faith, the importance of the Bible for instructing us in our faith, and the necessity of living "holy" lives—*in* the world but not *of* the world. Ezra, the person, could be called a "pastor of the priesthood of all believers." He offers a model for those called to the ordained ministry: leader, priest, and teacher of the worshiping community.

End of the Babylonian Captivity

1 In the first year of King Cyrus of Persia, in order that the word
of the Lord by the mouth of Jeremiah might be accomplished,
the Lord stirred up the spirit of King Cyrus of Persia so that he sent
a herald throughout all his kingdom, and also in a written edict declared:
2 "Thus says King Cyrus of Persia: The Lord, the God of heaven,
has given me all the kingdoms of the earth, and he has charged me to
build him a house at Jerusalem in Judah. [3]Any of those among you
who are of his people—may their God be with them!—are now permitted to go up to Jerusalem in Judah, and rebuild the house of the
Lord, the God of Israel—he is the God who is in Jerusalem; [4]and let
all survivors, in whatever place they reside, be assisted by the people
of their place with silver and gold, with goods and with animals, besides freewill offerings for the house of God in Jerusalem."
5 The heads of the families of Judah and Benjamin, and the
priests and the Levites—everyone whose spirit God had stirred—
got ready to go up and rebuild the house of the Lord in Jerusalem.

1:1 first year of King Cyrus: It was 539 B.C.E. Unlike the Assyrians and Babylonians before him, Cyrus believed a happy empire was a united one, and so he allowed the various nations to practice their own religions.

1:1 word of the Lord…might be accomplished: See Jeremiah 29:10. This is not merely the fulfillment of prophecy but the working out of God's dynamic word in the world.

1:1 the Lord stirred up the spirit: Cyrus does not act out of his own initiative. God stirs him to act, even as before the exile God had stirred up foreign powers against Israel for judgment (see 1 Chr 5:26; 2 Chr 21:16). Likewise, not all the Jews return to Jerusalem, but only those "whose spirit God had stirred" (1:5).

How and for what purpose(s) does God stir the spirits of people today?

[6]All their neighbors aided them with silver vessels, with gold, with goods, with animals, and with valuable gifts, besides all that was freely offered. [7]King Cyrus himself brought out the vessels of the house of the LORD that Nebuchadnezzar had carried away from Jerusalem and placed in the house of his gods. [8]King Cyrus of Persia had them released into the charge of Mithredath the treasurer, who counted them out to Sheshbazzar the prince of Judah. [9]And this was the inventory: gold basins, thirty; silver basins, one thousand; knives,[a] twenty-nine; [10]gold bowls, thirty; other silver bowls, four hundred ten; other vessels, one thousand; [11]the total of the gold and silver vessels was five thousand four hundred. All these Sheshbazzar brought up, when the exiles were brought up from Babylonia to Jerusalem.

List of the Returned Exiles

2 Now these were the people of the province who came from those captive exiles whom King Nebuchadnezzar of Babylon had carried captive to Babylonia; they returned to Jerusalem and Judah, all to their own towns. [2]They came with Zerubbabel, Jeshua, Nehemiah, Seraiah, Reelaiah, Mordecai, Bilshan, Mispar, Bigvai, Rehum, and Baanah.

The number of the Israelite people: [3]the descendants of Parosh, two thousand one hundred seventy-two. [4]Of Shephatiah, three hundred seventy-two. [5]Of Arah, seven hundred seventy-five. [6]Of Pahath-moab, namely the descendants of Jeshua and Joab, two thousand eight hundred twelve. [7]Of Elam, one thousand two hundred fifty-four. [8]Of Zattu, nine hundred forty-five. [9]Of Zaccai, seven hundred sixty. [10]Of Bani, six hundred forty-two. [11]Of Bebai, six hundred twenty-three. [12]Of Azgad, one thousand two hundred twenty-two. [13]Of Adonikam, six hundred sixty-six. [14]Of Bigvai, two thousand fifty-six. [15]Of Adin, four hundred fifty-four. [16]Of Ater, namely of Hezekiah, ninety-eight. [17]Of Bezai, three hundred twenty-three. [18]Of Jorah, one hundred twelve. [19]Of Hashum, two hundred twenty-three. [20]Of Gibbar, ninety-five. [21]Of Bethlehem, one hundred twenty-three. [22]The people of Netophah, fifty-six. [23]Of Anathoth, one hundred twenty-eight. [24]The descendants of Azmaveth, forty-two. [25]Of Kiriatharim, Chephirah, and Beeroth, seven hundred forty-three. [26]Of Ramah and Geba, six hundred twenty-one. [27]The people of Michmas, one hundred twenty-two. [28]Of Bethel and Ai, two hundred twenty-three. [29]The descendants of Nebo, fifty-two. [30]Of Magbish, one hundred fifty-six. [31]Of the other Elam, one thousand two hundred fifty-four. [32]Of Harim, three hundred twenty. [33]Of Lod, Hadid, and Ono, seven hundred twenty-five. [34]Of Jericho, three hundred forty-five. [35]Of Senaah, three thousand six hundred thirty.

---

[a] Vg: Meaning of Heb uncertain

1:2 The LORD...has given me...build...a house: Cyrus is not a worshiper of the LORD but speaks to Jewish ears. While the Assyrians and Babylonians had moved conquered peoples out of their homelands, the Persian leader Cyrus attempts to win the loyalty of displaced peoples by allowing them to return home and rebuild their place of worship.

1:7-8 Sheshbazzar: Little else is known about this governor of Judah appointed by Cyrus.

1:9-11 bowls...vessels: These were removed from the temple in Jerusalem by the Babylonians and carried away to Babylonia (2 Chr 36:18). Now Cyrus is allowing them out of the Babylonian treasury, so they can return with the Jewish people to Jerusalem.

2:1 Now these were the people: The families and towns relate to what had been the territories of Judah and Benjamin at the end of the First Temple period (see 1:5). They would comprise the Persian province of Yehud for much of the Second Temple period. This chapter (with 3:1) is repeated, with some minor differences, in Nehemiah 7:6—8:1. This shows that the author is using historical sources for theological purposes. The numbers in the list are too large for the initial return; they represent the total number of returnees over successive years, to demonstrate for the audience of the text the enthusiastic way the Jews renewed their homeland.

2:2 Zerubbabel, Jeshua: Both are well-known from the books of Haggai and Zechariah as, respectively, the governor and high priest who supervised the building of the second temple.

36 The priests: the descendants of Jedaiah, of the house of Jeshua, nine hundred seventy-three. [37]Of Immer, one thousand fifty-two. [38]Of Pashhur, one thousand two hundred forty-seven. [39]Of Harim, one thousand seventeen.

40 The Levites: the descendants of Jeshua and Kadmiel, of the descendants of Hodaviah, seventy-four. [41]The singers: the descendants of Asaph, one hundred twenty-eight. [42]The descendants of the gatekeepers: of Shallum, of Ater, of Talmon, of Akkub, of Hatita, and of Shobai, in all one hundred thirty-nine.

43 The temple servants: the descendants of Ziha, Hasupha, Tabbaoth, [44]Keros, Siaha, Padon, [45]Lebanah, Hagabah, Akkub, [46]Hagab, Shamlai, Hanan, [47]Giddel, Gahar, Reaiah, [48]Rezin, Nekoda, Gazzam, [49]Uzza, Paseah, Besai, [50]Asnah, Meunim, Nephisim, [51]Bakbuk, Hakupha, Harhur, [52]Bazluth, Mehida, Harsha, [53]Barkos, Sisera, Temah, [54]Neziah, and Hatipha.

55 The descendants of Solomon's servants: Sotai, Hassophereth, Peruda, [56]Jaalah, Darkon, Giddel, [57]Shephatiah, Hattil, Pochereth-hazzebaim, and Ami.

58 All the temple servants and the descendants of Solomon's servants were three hundred ninety-two.

59 The following were those who came up from Tel-melah, Tel-harsha, Cherub, Addan, and Immer, though they could not prove their families or their descent, whether they belonged to Israel: [60]the descendants of Delaiah, Tobiah, and Nekoda, six hundred fifty-two. [61]Also, of the descendants of the priests: the descendants of Habaiah, Hakkoz, and Barzillai (who had married one of the daughters of Barzillai the Gileadite, and was called by their name). [62]These looked for their entries in the genealogical records, but they were not found there, and so they were excluded from the priesthood as unclean; [63]the governor told them that they were not to partake of the most holy food, until there should be a priest to consult Urim and Thummim.

64 The whole assembly together was forty-two thousand three hundred sixty, [65]besides their male and female servants, of whom there were seven thousand three hundred thirty-seven; and they had two hundred male and female singers. [66]They had seven hundred thirty-six horses, two hundred forty-five mules, [67]four hundred thirty-five camels, and six thousand seven hundred twenty donkeys.

68 As soon as they came to the house of the LORD in Jerusalem, some of the heads of families made freewill offerings for the house of God, to erect it on its site. [69]According to their resources they gave to the building fund sixty-one thousand darics of gold, five thousand minas of silver, and one hundred priestly robes.

70 The priests, the Levites, and some of the people lived in

2:36, 40 The priests . . . The Levites: The list begins with the lay people and then proceeds to the priests, who alone were ordained to preside at the temple in Jerusalem. The Levites were of priestly descent and were assigned to the offices designated in the list as inherited from First Temple times. The Levites were descended from the family of the first high priest Aaron, brother of Moses, (Exod 40:12-15; Num 18:21-32).

2:63 Urim and Thummim: Exactly what these sacred lots were is not certain, but they may have been a small carved stones worn in a pouch over the high priest's chest and under his breastplate (see Exod 28:29-30). The Urim and Thummim were apparently consulted to receive a message concerning God's will. See also Lev 8:7-8; Deut 33:8.

Jerusalem and its vicinity;[a] and the singers, the gatekeepers, and the
temple servants lived in their towns, and all Israel in their towns.

Worship Restored at Jerusalem

3 When the seventh month came, and the Israelites were in the
towns, the people gathered together in Jerusalem. 2 Then Jeshua
son of Jozadak, with his fellow priests, and Zerubbabel son of Shealtiel with his kin set out to build the altar of the God of Israel, to
offer burnt offerings on it, as prescribed in the law of Moses the man
of God. 3 They set up the altar on its foundation, because they were
in dread of the neighboring peoples, and they offered burnt offerings
upon it to the LORD, morning and evening. 4 And they kept the festival of booths,[b] as prescribed, and offered the daily burnt offerings by
number according to the ordinance, as required for each day, 5 and after that the regular burnt offerings, the offerings at the new moon and
at all the sacred festivals of the LORD, and the offerings of everyone
who made a freewill offering to the LORD. 6 From the first day of the
seventh month they began to offer burnt offerings to the LORD. But
the foundation of the temple of the LORD was not yet laid. 7 So they
gave money to the masons and the carpenters, and food, drink, and
oil to the Sidonians and the Tyrians to bring cedar trees from Lebanon to the sea, to Joppa, according to the grant that they had from
King Cyrus of Persia.

Foundation Laid for the Temple

8 In the second year after their arrival at the house of God at Jerusalem, in the second month, Zerubbabel son of Shealtiel and Jeshua
son of Jozadak made a beginning, together with the rest of their people, the priests and the Levites and all who had come to Jerusalem
from the captivity. They appointed the Levites, from twenty years old
and upward, to have the oversight of the work on the house of the
LORD. 9 And Jeshua with his sons and his kin, and Kadmiel and his
sons, Binnui and Hodaviah[c] along with the sons of Henadad, the Levites, their sons and kin, together took charge of the workers in the
house of God.

10 When the builders laid the foundation of the temple of the
LORD, the priests in their vestments were stationed to praise the
LORD with trumpets, and the Levites, the sons of Asaph, with cymbals, according to the directions of King David of Israel; 11 and they
sang responsively, praising and giving thanks to the LORD,

"For he is good,
for his steadfast love endures forever toward Israel."

---

[a] 1 Esdras 5.46: Heb lacks *lived in Jerusalem and its vicinity* [b] Or *tabernacles*; Heb *succoth* [c] Compare 2.40; Neh 7.43; 1 Esdras 5.58: Heb *sons of Judah*

3:2 Then Jeshua son of Jozadak...and Zerubbabel: Jozadak (sometimes Jehozadak) was high priest when Judah was taken into exile (see 1 Chr 6:15), so Jeshua—the Aramaic spelling of the Hebrew Joshua, found in the books of Haggai and Zechariah—continues in this office. Zerubbabel is of the dynasty of King David but disappears mysteriously from the narrative here, in Haggai, and in Zechariah 1–8. Was Persia perhaps uncomfortable with his royal blood?

3:2 Zerubbabel: He is from the line of rulers who come from the family of King David. Zerubbabel is the first and last of the Davidic—meaning "messianic"—rulers to lead Judah during the Second Temple period. "Messiah" simply means "anointed king" in the Old Testament, and the lack of such a figure in the postexilic period gives rise to "messianic hope" for the ideal Messiah who will come in the future.

3:9 Jeshua: A Levite, not the priest above in 3:2. Note the division of duties assigned in the chapter to priests and Levites.

Think about "workers in the house of God" today. What makes this work so important? How do you see yourself involved in such work?

3:10-11 praise the LORD with trumpets: This is a major theme of 1–2 Chronicles. Ezra–Nehemiah espouses the joyful praise of God in worship and liturgy.

What was Martin Luther's view of music and its role in worship? Luther's view is that music and the word of God were meant for each other from the creation, both in proclamation and praise, and that music with the word is an instrument of the Spirit

And all the people responded with a great shout when they praised
the LORD, because the foundation of the house of the LORD was
laid. 12But many of the priests and Levites and heads of families, old
people who had seen the first house on its foundations, wept with a
loud voice when they saw this house, though many shouted aloud for
joy, 13so that the people could not distinguish the sound of the joyful
shout from the sound of the people's weeping, for the people shouted
so loudly that the sound was heard far away.

Resistance to Rebuilding the Temple

4 When the adversaries of Judah and Benjamin heard that the
returned exiles were building a temple to the LORD, the God
of Israel, 2they approached Zerubbabel and the heads of families and
said to them, "Let us build with you, for we worship your God as you
do, and we have been sacrificing to him ever since the days of King
Esar-haddon of Assyria who brought us here." 3But Zerubbabel,
Jeshua, and the rest of the heads of families in Israel said to them,
"You shall have no part with us in building a house to our God; but
we alone will build to the LORD, the God of Israel, as King Cyrus of
Persia has commanded us."
4 Then the people of the land discouraged the people of Judah,
and made them afraid to build, 5and they bribed officials to frustrate
their plan throughout the reign of King Cyrus of Persia and until the
reign of King Darius of Persia.

Rebuilding of Jerusalem Opposed

6 In the reign of Ahasuerus, in his accession year, they wrote an
accusation against the inhabitants of Judah and Jerusalem.
7 And in the days of Artaxerxes, Bishlam and Mithredath and Tabeel and the rest of their associates wrote to King Artaxerxes of Persia;
the letter was written in Aramaic and translated.[a] 8Rehum the royal
deputy and Shimshai the scribe wrote a letter against Jerusalem to
King Artaxerxes as follows 9(then Rehum the royal deputy, Shimshai
the scribe, and the rest of their associates, the judges, the envoys, the
officials, the Persians, the people of Erech, the Babylonians, the people of Susa, that is, the Elamites, 10and the rest of the nations whom
the great and noble Osnappar deported and settled in the cities of Samaria and in the rest of the province Beyond the River wrote—and
now 11this is a copy of the letter that they sent):
"To King Artaxerxes: Your servants, the people of the province Beyond the River, send greeting. And now 12may it be known to the king
that the Jews who came up from you to us have gone to Jerusalem.

[a] Heb adds *in Aramaic*, indicating that 4.8-6.18 is in Aramaic. Another interpretation is *The letter was written in the Aramaic script and set forth in the Aramaic language*

for writing the word on the human heart. In one of his writings, Luther taught that "next to the Word of God, music deserves the highest praise" (*LW* 53:323). Luther himself was a composer of hymns, such as "A Mighty Fortress Is Our God." Following the lead of Luther and others, Lutherans have always emphasized music as an essential part of our worship and spirituality. *Ezra 3:10-11*

4:1 the adversaries of Judah and Benjamin: We have been prepared for this by mention of the "dread of the neighboring peoples" (3:3), who would have heard the shouts of the Jews (3:13) as threatening to their status in the empire. Here "adversaries" refers to people of Samaria who had been captured by Assyria and forced to settle in the area after the Assyrians conquered the northern kingdom of Israel in 721 B.C.E. (4:2).

4:3 You shall have no part with us . . . we alone will build: The returning exiles feel they have been tested by fire and have been given a mission that cannot be compromised, a theme to which our author will return.

For you, what aspect of faith and religion cannot be compromised? Why?

4:4 people of the land: This includes Judeans who did not go into exile in Babylon.

4:5 Cyrus . . . Darius: Ruled 539–530 and 522–486 B.C.E., respectively.

4:6 Ahasuerus: Another name for Xerxes (ruled 486–465 B.C.E.).

4:7 Artaxerxes: He ruled 465–424 B.C.E. Verses 6-23 are out of chronological order and deal with opposition to rebuilding the walls of Jerusalem. They are placed here by the author to stress the ongoing tension between the returning Jews and the local inhabitants. Verse 24 brings us back to the time of 4:5.

4:10 Osnappar: Another name for Asshurbanipal (669–630 B.C.E.).

4:10, 16: the province Beyond the River: Meaning the lands west of the Euphrates River, including Jerusalem and the surrounding area. See Map 10, p. 2107.

They are rebuilding that rebellious and wicked city; they are finishing the walls and repairing the foundations. 13 Now may it be known
to the king that, if this city is rebuilt and the walls finished, they will
not pay tribute, custom, or toll, and the royal revenue will be reduced.
14 Now because we share the salt of the palace and it is not fitting for
us to witness the king's dishonor, therefore we send and inform the
king, 15 so that a search may be made in the annals of your ancestors.
You will discover in the annals that this is a rebellious city, hurtful to
kings and provinces, and that sedition was stirred up in it from long
ago. On that account this city was laid waste. 16 We make known to the
king that, if this city is rebuilt and its walls finished, you will then have
no possession in the province Beyond the River."

17 The king sent an answer: "To Rehum the royal deputy and
Shimshai the scribe and the rest of their associates who live in Samaria and in the rest of the province Beyond the River, greeting. And
now 18 the letter that you sent to us has been read in translation before
me. 19 So I made a decree, and someone searched and discovered that
this city has risen against kings from long ago, and that rebellion and
sedition have been made in it. 20 Jerusalem has had mighty kings who
ruled over the whole province Beyond the River, to whom tribute,
custom, and toll were paid. 21 Therefore issue an order that these people be made to cease, and that this city not be rebuilt, until I make
a decree. 22 Moreover, take care not to be slack in this matter; why
should damage grow to the hurt of the king?"

23 Then when the copy of King Artaxerxes' letter was read before
Rehum and the scribe Shimshai and their associates, they hurried to
the Jews in Jerusalem and by force and power made them cease. 24 At
that time the work on the house of God in Jerusalem stopped and
was discontinued until the second year of the reign of King Darius
of Persia.

4:24 work on the house of God… stopped: The story of the rebuilding of the temple resumes from 4:5. Work resumed in the second year of King Darius' reign, 520 B.C.E.

Restoration of the Temple Resumed

5 Now the prophets, Haggai[a] and Zechariah son of Iddo, prophesied to the Jews who were in Judah and Jerusalem, in the name
of the God of Israel who was over them. 2 Then Zerubbabel son of
Shealtiel and Jeshua son of Jozadak set out to rebuild the house of
God in Jerusalem; and with them were the prophets of God, helping
them.

3 At the same time Tattenai the governor of the province Beyond
the River and Shethar-bozenai and their associates came to them and
spoke to them thus, "Who gave you a decree to build this house and
to finish this structure?" 4 They[b] also asked them this, "What are the
names of the men who are building this building?" 5 But the eye of

5:1 Haggai and Zechariah: The messages of these prophets can be found in the books bearing their name. They urged the people to resume and complete the rebuilding of the temple. The rebuilding of the temple 520–515 B.C.E. emphasized the importance of regular, corporate worship among God's people.

5:3 Tattenai: The new emerging province of Yehud is diminishing his rule and authority as governor.

[a] Aram adds *the prophet* [b] Gk Syr: Aram *We*

their God was upon the elders of the Jews, and they did not stop them
until a report reached Darius and then answer was returned by letter
in reply to it.
6 The copy of the letter that Tattenai the governor of the province Beyond the River and Shethar-bozenai and his associates the envoys who were in the province Beyond the River sent to King Darius;
7they sent him a report, in which was written as follows: "To Darius
the king, all peace! 8May it be known to the king that we went to the
province of Judah, to the house of the great God. It is being built of
hewn stone, and timber is laid in the walls; this work is being done diligently and prospers in their hands. 9Then we spoke to those elders and
asked them, 'Who gave you a decree to build this house and to finish
this structure?' 10We also asked them their names, for your information, so that we might write down the names of the men at their head.
11This was their reply to us: 'We are the servants of the God of heaven
and earth, and we are rebuilding the house that was built many years
ago, which a great king of Israel built and finished. 12But because our
ancestors had angered the God of heaven, he gave them into the hand
of King Nebuchadnezzar of Babylon, the Chaldean, who destroyed
this house and carried away the people to Babylonia. 13However, King
Cyrus of Babylon, in the first year of his reign, made a decree that this
house of God should be rebuilt. 14Moreover, the gold and silver vessels of the house of God, which Nebuchadnezzar had taken out of
the temple in Jerusalem and had brought into the temple of Babylon,
these King Cyrus took out of the temple of Babylon, and they were
delivered to a man named Sheshbazzar, whom he had made governor.
15He said to him, "Take these vessels; go and put them in the temple in
Jerusalem, and let the house of God be rebuilt on its site." 16Then this
Sheshbazzar came and laid the foundations of the house of God in Jerusalem; and from that time until now it has been under construction,
and it is not yet finished.' 17And now, if it seems good to the king, have
a search made in the royal archives there in Babylon, to see whether
a decree was issued by King Cyrus for the rebuilding of this house of
God in Jerusalem. Let the king send us his pleasure in this matter."

5:11 great king of Israel: Refers to Israel's King Solomon, who was responsible for building the first temple in Jerusalem (see 1 Kgs 5–6).

The Decree of Darius

6 Then King Darius made a decree, and they searched the archives
where the documents were stored in Babylon. 2But it was in Ecbatana, the capital in the province of Media, that a scroll was found on
which this was written: "A record. 3In the first year of his reign, King
Cyrus issued a decree: Concerning the house of God at Jerusalem, let
the house be rebuilt, the place where sacrifices are offered and burnt
offerings are brought;[a] its height shall be sixty cubits and its width

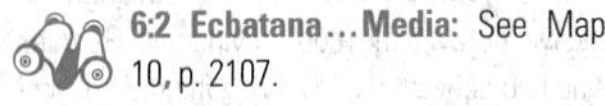
6:2 Ecbatana…Media: See Map 10, p. 2107.

[a] Meaning of Aram uncertain

sixty cubits, 4 with three courses of hewn stones and one course of
timber; let the cost be paid from the royal treasury. 5 Moreover, let the
gold and silver vessels of the house of God, which Nebuchadnezzar
took out of the temple in Jerusalem and brought to Babylon, be restored and brought back to the temple in Jerusalem, each to its place;
you shall put them in the house of God."

6 "Now you, Tattenai, governor of the province Beyond the
River, Shethar-bozenai, and you, their associates, the envoys in the
province Beyond the River, keep away; 7 let the work on this house
of God alone; let the governor of the Jews and the elders of the Jews
rebuild this house of God on its site. 8 Moreover I make a decree regarding what you shall do for these elders of the Jews for the rebuilding of this house of God: the cost is to be paid to these people, in full
and without delay, from the royal revenue, the tribute of the province Beyond the River. 9 Whatever is needed—young bulls, rams,
or sheep for burnt offerings to the God of heaven, wheat, salt, wine,
or oil, as the priests in Jerusalem require—let that be given to them
day by day without fail, 10 so that they may offer pleasing sacrifices
to the God of heaven, and pray for the life of the king and his children. 11 Furthermore I decree that if anyone alters this edict, a beam
shall be pulled out of the house of the perpetrator, who then shall be
impaled on it. The house shall be made a dunghill. 12 May the God
who has established his name there overthrow any king or people
that shall put forth a hand to alter this, or to destroy this house of
God in Jerusalem. I, Darius, make a decree; let it be done with all
diligence."

Completion and Dedication of the Temple

13 Then, according to the word sent by King Darius, Tattenai,
the governor of the province Beyond the River, Shethar-bozenai, and
their associates did with all diligence what King Darius had ordered.
14 So the elders of the Jews built and prospered, through the prophesying of the prophet Haggai and Zechariah son of Iddo. They finished their building by command of the God of Israel and by decree
of Cyrus, Darius, and King Artaxerxes of Persia; 15 and this house was
finished on the third day of the month of Adar, in the sixth year of the
reign of King Darius.

16 The people of Israel, the priests and the Levites, and the rest
of the returned exiles, celebrated the dedication of this house of God
with joy. 17 They offered at the dedication of this house of God one
hundred bulls, two hundred rams, four hundred lambs, and as a sin
offering for all Israel, twelve male goats, according to the number of
the tribes of Israel. 18 Then they set the priests in their divisions and
the Levites in their courses for the service of God at Jerusalem, as it is
written in the book of Moses.

6:10, 16 may offer pleasing sacrifices to the God of heaven...celebrated the dedication of this house of God with joy: These offerings were intended to send sweet-smelling aromas up to God. This was the way of Old Testament worship. Christ's sacrifice on the cross replaced animal sacrifice, and we continue the practice of joyful temple worship through the celebration of the Eucharist.

6:10 pray for the life of the king: The Persian monarch had an ulterior motive for financing the temple rebuilding.

6:12 God who has established his name there: The name of God represents the divine presence. One cannot overestimate the importance of the temple on Mount Zion in Jerusalem as the symbol of God's intimate presence on earth.

6:14 Artaxerxes: He rules fifty years later, but his mention here reminds the reader that he too will support the temple (see 7:12-26).

6:17 twelve male goats: Even though only the tribes of Judah, Benjamin, and Levi are present, the past sin of all Israel is "paid for" through the sin offering, and the new Israel is reborn.

6:19 On the fourteenth day: In the original text, the international language of correspondence, Aramaic, has been used, beginning at 4:8. In this verse the author returns to Hebrew to describe Passover. The first month of Israel's calendar is Nisan. Passover celebrated God's deliverance of the people from slavery in Egypt (see Exod 12:23-25).

6:21 and also by all who had joined them: This is a strikingly inclusive note in the book. Evidently, Gentiles who had converted and Jews who did not participate in the exile but have rededicated themselves to the faith are welcomed into the worshiping community.

6:22 king of Assyria: The reference is really to the Persian monarch, as Assyria had now been taken over by Persia. The reference to Assyria recalls the horrible way that kingdom had treated God's people.

The Passover Celebrated

19 On the fourteenth day of the first month the returned exiles
kept the passover. [20]For both the priests and the Levites had purified
themselves; all of them were clean. So they killed the passover lamb
for all the returned exiles, for their fellow priests, and for themselves.
[21]It was eaten by the people of Israel who had returned from exile, and
also by all who had joined them and separated themselves from the
pollutions of the nations of the land to worship the LORD, the God
of Israel. [22]With joy they celebrated the festival of unleavened bread
seven days; for the LORD had made them joyful, and had turned the
heart of the king of Assyria to them, so that he aided them in the work
on the house of God, the God of Israel.

The Coming and Work of Ezra

7 After this, in the reign of King Artaxerxes of Persia, Ezra son of
Seraiah, son of Azariah, son of Hilkiah, [2]son of Shallum, son of
Zadok, son of Ahitub, [3]son of Amariah, son of Azariah, son of Meraioth, [4]son of Zerahiah, son of Uzzi, son of Bukki, [5]son of Abishua, son
of Phinehas, son of Eleazar, son of the chief priest Aaron— [6]this Ezra
went up from Babylonia. He was a scribe skilled in the law of Moses
that the LORD the God of Israel had given; and the king granted him
all that he asked, for the hand of the LORD his God was upon him.

7 Some of the people of Israel, and some of the priests and Levites, the singers and gatekeepers, and the temple servants also went
up to Jerusalem, in the seventh year of King Artaxerxes. [8]They came
to Jerusalem in the fifth month, which was in the seventh year of the
king. [9]On the first day of the first month the journey up from Babylon
was begun, and on the first day of the fifth month he came to Jerusalem, for the gracious hand of his God was upon him. [10]For Ezra had
set his heart to study the law of the LORD, and to do it, and to teach
the statutes and ordinances in Israel.

The Letter of Artaxerxes to Ezra

11 This is a copy of the letter that King Artaxerxes gave to the
priest Ezra, the scribe, a scholar of the text of the commandments of
the LORD and his statutes for Israel: [12]"Artaxerxes, king of kings, to
the priest Ezra, the scribe of the law of the God of heaven: Peace.[a]
And now [13]I decree that any of the people of Israel or their priests
or Levites in my kingdom who freely offers to go to Jerusalem may
go with you. [14]For you are sent by the king and his seven counselors
to make inquiries about Judah and Jerusalem according to the law of
your God, which is in your hand, [15]and also to convey the silver and
gold that the king and his counselors have freely offered to the God

[a] Syr Vg 1 Esdras 8.9: Aram *Perfect*

7:1 After this: It is fifty-eight years later as Ezra starts this essential second phase of the postexilic period. He is often called "the father of Judaism," because he takes an ill-defined and rather chaotic group in Jerusalem and transforms it into a community based on the "Teaching,"—in Hebrew, the Torah. Also called the Pentateuch, these first five books of the Bible had been collected and edited by the priestly community in Babylon. Ezra was part of that community.

7:2-5 Zadok...Aaron: This genealogy establishes Ezra's priestly pedigree. Only descendants of Aaron through the line of Zadok could preside at the temple in Jerusalem. One of Ezra's jobs was that of priest.

7:6 scribe skilled in the law of Moses: The "law of Moses" (in English) represents the Hebrew *Torah*, better translated "Teaching." That it is "of Moses" means that it stems from his original teachings as they developed through the centuries. The title "scribe" here indicates that Ezra was also an expert in the law and in reading and writing. During the exile, the duties of the scribes included copying, editing, studying, and teaching the Hebrew Scriptures.

7:6, 9, 28 hand of the LORD his God was upon him: This is repeated three times, the Hebrew number of completeness.

7:7 people of Israel: The laity are mentioned first, followed by the clergy and other ministers.

What special roles do lay members, pastors, and lay ministers have in the church today? What roles do they share in common? What aspect of your church do you celebrate or prize most highly? Why?

7:7 the seventh year of King Artaxerxes: See the note on 4:7. If this refers to Artaxerxes I, the year is 458 B.C.E.

7:9 journey...was begun: April 8, 458 B.C.E. , arriving in Jerusalem August 4, 458.

7:11 This is a copy: The letter (7:12-26) is in Aramaic, the language used in the Persian Empire for official communications.

of Israel, whose dwelling is in Jerusalem, [16]with all the silver and gold that you shall find in the whole province of Babylonia, and with the freewill offerings of the people and the priests, given willingly for the house of their God in Jerusalem. [17]With this money, then, you shall with all diligence buy bulls, rams, and lambs, and their grain offerings and their drink offerings, and you shall offer them on the altar of the house of your God in Jerusalem. [18]Whatever seems good to you and your colleagues to do with the rest of the silver and gold, you may do, according to the will of your God. [19]The vessels that have been given you for the service of the house of your God, you shall deliver before the God of Jerusalem. [20]And whatever else is required for the house of your God, which you are responsible for providing, you may provide out of the king's treasury.

21 "I, King Artaxerxes, decree to all the treasurers in the province Beyond the River: Whatever the priest Ezra, the scribe of the law of the God of heaven, requires of you, let it be done with all diligence, [22]up to one hundred talents of silver, one hundred cors of wheat, one hundred baths[a] of wine, one hundred baths[a] of oil, and unlimited salt. [23]Whatever is commanded by the God of heaven, let it be done with zeal for the house of the God of heaven, or wrath will come upon the realm of the king and his heirs. [24]We also notify you that it shall not be lawful to impose tribute, custom, or toll on any of the priests, the Levites, the singers, the doorkeepers, the temple servants, or other servants of this house of God.

25 "And you, Ezra, according to the God-given wisdom you possess, appoint magistrates and judges who may judge all the people in the province Beyond the River who know the laws of your God; and you shall teach those who do not know them. [26]All who will not obey the law of your God and the law of the king, let judgment be strictly executed on them, whether for death or for banishment or for confiscation of their goods or for imprisonment."

27 Blessed be the LORD, the God of our ancestors, who put such a thing as this into the heart of the king to glorify the house of the LORD in Jerusalem, [28]and who extended to me steadfast love before the king and his counselors, and before all the king's mighty officers. I took courage, for the hand of the LORD my God was upon me, and I gathered leaders from Israel to go up with me.

Heads of Families Who Returned with Ezra

8:1 These are their family heads: The total includes 1,513 men. With women and children the group numbered about 5,000. There are twelve lay families, symbolizing all the tribes of Israel (see 8:24, where twelve priests serve the same function).

8 These are their family heads, and this is the genealogy of those who went up with me from Babylonia, in the reign of King Artaxerxes: [2]Of the descendants of Phinehas, Gershom. Of Ithamar, Daniel. Of David, Hattush, [3]of the descendants of Shecaniah. Of Pa-

[a] A Heb measure of volume

rosh, Zechariah, with whom were registered one hundred fifty males.
4 Of the descendants of Pahath-moab, Eliehoenai son of Zerahiah, and
with him two hundred males. 5 Of the descendants of Zattu,[a] Shecaniah son of Jahaziel, and with him three hundred males. 6 Of the descendants of Adin, Ebed son of Jonathan, and with him fifty males.
7 Of the descendants of Elam, Jeshaiah son of Athaliah, and with him
seventy males. 8 Of the descendants of Shephatiah, Zebadiah son of
Michael, and with him eighty males. 9 Of the descendants of Joab,
Obadiah son of Jehiel, and with him two hundred eighteen males.
10 Of the descendants of Bani,[b] Shelomith son of Josiphiah, and with
him one hundred sixty males. 11 Of the descendants of Bebai, Zechariah son of Bebai, and with him twenty-eight males. 12 Of the descendants of Azgad, Johanan son of Hakkatan, and with him one hundred
ten males. 13 Of the descendants of Adonikam, those who came later,
their names being Eliphelet, Jeuel, and Shemaiah, and with them sixty
males. 14 Of the descendants of Bigvai, Uthai and Zaccur, and with
them seventy males.

Servants for the Temple

15 I gathered them by the river that runs to Ahava, and there we
camped three days. As I reviewed the people and the priests, I found
there none of the descendants of Levi. 16 Then I sent for Eliezer, Ariel,
Shemaiah, Elnathan, Jarib, Elnathan, Nathan, Zechariah, and Meshullam, who were leaders, and for Joiarib and Elnathan, who were wise,
17 and sent them to Iddo, the leader at the place called Casiphia, telling them what to say to Iddo and his colleagues the temple servants
at Casiphia, namely, to send us ministers for the house of our God.
18 Since the gracious hand of our God was upon us, they brought us a
man of discretion, of the descendants of Mahli son of Levi son of Israel, namely Sherebiah, with his sons and kin, eighteen; 19 also Hashabiah and with him Jeshaiah of the descendants of Merari, with his kin
and their sons, twenty; 20 besides two hundred twenty of the temple
servants, whom David and his officials had set apart to attend the Levites. These were all mentioned by name.

Fasting and Prayer for Protection

21 Then I proclaimed a fast there, at the river Ahava, that we
might deny ourselves[c] before our God, to seek from him a safe journey for ourselves, our children, and all our possessions. 22 For I was
ashamed to ask the king for a band of soldiers and cavalry to protect
us against the enemy on our way, since we had told the king that the
hand of our God is gracious to all who seek him, but his power and his
wrath are against all who forsake him. 23 So we fasted and petitioned
our God for this, and he listened to our entreaty.

8:15 Ahava...Levi: A town or place in Babylonia whose exact location is unknown. Why no Levites were among the returnees is not certain. Perhaps they preferred to stay in Babylon, where they may have had greater status or importance than they expected to have if they returned to Jerusalem.

8:17 send us ministers for the house of our God: God needs many types of ministers to serve the community of faith.

8:23 So we fasted and petitioned our God: Ezra and the group prepare for the difficult-yet-exciting journey with fasting and prayer. Fasting was done to honor God or to show sorrow for disobeying God.

[a] Gk 1 Esdras 8.32: Heb lacks *of Zattu* [b] Gk 1 Esdras 8.36: Heb lacks *Bani* [c] Or *might fast*

Consider the role prayer and fasting play in your life and faith journey. How important are they? Would you like to them to play a bigger role? If so, how might that happen?

8:25-30 And I weighed out...the silver...vessels: These offerings for the temple are of more value than those brought by the original group of returning exiles (Ezra 1:9-11). This punctuated the importance of this second stage of the development of Jewish life in the Second Temple period initiated by Ezra.

Gifts for the Temple

24 Then I set apart twelve of the leading priests: Sherebiah, Hashabiah, and ten of their kin with them. 25 And I weighed out to them
the silver and the gold and the vessels, the offering for the house of
our God that the king, his counselors, his lords, and all Israel there
present had offered; 26 I weighed out into their hand six hundred fifty
talents of silver, and one hundred silver vessels worth . . . talents,[a] and
one hundred talents of gold, 27 twenty gold bowls worth a thousand
darics, and two vessels of fine polished bronze as precious as gold.
28 And I said to them, "You are holy to the LORD, and the vessels are
holy; and the silver and the gold are a freewill offering to the LORD,
the God of your ancestors. 29 Guard them and keep them until you
weigh them before the chief priests and the Levites and the heads of
families in Israel at Jerusalem, within the chambers of the house of the
LORD." 30 So the priests and the Levites took over the silver, the gold,
and the vessels as they were weighed out, to bring them to Jerusalem,
to the house of our God.

The Return to Jerusalem

31 Then we left the river Ahava on the twelfth day of the first
month, to go to Jerusalem; the hand of our God was upon us, and he
delivered us from the hand of the enemy and from ambushes along
the way. 32 We came to Jerusalem and remained there three days. 33 On
the fourth day, within the house of our God, the silver, the gold,
and the vessels were weighed into the hands of the priest Meremoth
son of Uriah, and with him was Eleazar son of Phinehas, and with
them were the Levites, Jozabad son of Jeshua and Noadiah son of Binnui. 34 The total was counted and weighed, and the weight of everything was recorded.

35 At that time those who had come from captivity, the returned
exiles, offered burnt offerings to the God of Israel, twelve bulls for
all Israel, ninety-six rams, seventy-seven lambs, and as a sin offering
twelve male goats; all this was a burnt offering to the LORD. 36 They
also delivered the king's commissions to the king's satraps and to the
governors of the province Beyond the River; and they supported the
people and the house of God.

8:35 offered burnt offerings: The number twelve, for all Israel, continues to be important: twelve bulls, ninety-six (eight times twelve) rams, seventy-two (six times twelve) lambs. The Greek translation of 1 Esdras uses the number seventy-two, a natural multiple of twelve, and this may be more likely than the number seventy-seven that appears in this verse.

Denunciation of Mixed Marriages

9 After these things had been done, the officials approached
me and said, "The people of Israel, the priests, and the Levites
have not separated themselves from the peoples of the lands with
their abominations, from the Canaanites, the Hittites, the Perizzites,
the Jebusites, the Ammonites, the Moabites, the Egyptians, and the

9:1 The people of Israel, the priests, and the Levites have not separated themselves: The exiles who have returned home and rebuilt the temple have not set themselves apart as different and distinct from the worldly society and culture around them. This is a difficult concept for us today. On the one hand, we are to be "in the world" and agents of its salvation. On the other hand, can we be "of the world" and still carry out our mission?

In what ways are you, as a baptized child of God, in the world but not *of* the world? How important do you believe it is for Christians to separate or distinguish themselves from the world we live in? Why?

[a] The number of talents is lacking

Amorites. [2]For they have taken some of their daughters as wives for
themselves and for their sons. Thus the holy seed has mixed itself with
the peoples of the lands, and in this faithlessness the officials and leaders have led the way." [3]When I heard this, I tore my garment and my
mantle, and pulled hair from my head and beard, and sat appalled.
[4]Then all who trembled at the words of the God of Israel, because of
the faithlessness of the returned exiles, gathered around me while I
sat appalled until the evening sacrifice.

Ezra's Prayer

5 At the evening sacrifice I got up from my fasting, with my garments and my mantle torn, and fell on my knees, spread out my hands
to the LORD my God, [6]and said,
"O my God, I am too ashamed and embarrassed to lift my face to
you, my God, for our iniquities have risen higher than our heads, and
our guilt has mounted up to the heavens. [7]From the days of our ancestors to this day we have been deep in guilt, and for our iniquities we,
our kings, and our priests have been handed over to the kings of the
lands, to the sword, to captivity, to plundering, and to utter shame, as
is now the case. [8]But now for a brief moment favor has been shown
by the LORD our God, who has left us a remnant, and given us a stake
in his holy place, in order that he[a] may brighten our eyes and grant us
a little sustenance in our slavery. [9]For we are slaves; yet our God has
not forsaken us in our slavery, but has extended to us his steadfast love
before the kings of Persia, to give us new life to set up the house of our
God, to repair its ruins, and to give us a wall in Judea and Jerusalem.
10 "And now, our God, what shall we say after this? For we have
forsaken your commandments, [11]which you commanded by your
servants the prophets, saying, 'The land that you are entering to possess is a land unclean with the pollutions of the peoples of the lands,
with their abominations. They have filled it from end to end with their
uncleanness. [12]Therefore do not give your daughters to their sons,
neither take their daughters for your sons, and never seek their peace
or prosperity, so that you may be strong and eat the good of the land
and leave it for an inheritance to your children forever.' [13]After all that
has come upon us for our evil deeds and for our great guilt, seeing that
you, our God, have punished us less than our iniquities deserved and
have given us such a remnant as this, [14]shall we break your commandments again and intermarry with the peoples who practice these
abominations? Would you not be angry with us until you destroy us
without remnant or survivor? [15]O LORD, God of Israel, you are just,
but we have escaped as a remnant, as is now the case. Here we are before you in our guilt, though no one can face you because of this."

[a] Heb *our God*

9:2 For they have taken some of their daughters as wives: One particular way the problem described in 9:1 has been visible is through intermarriage with non-Jewish women. Most surprising is the fact that some of Israel's leaders and officials have led the way in this practice.

9:2 holy seed: "Holy" means set apart as different.

As God's people, how do you think we are called to be "holy"?

9:3 I tore my garment...pulled hair: These were common gestures of extreme sorrow or mourning.

What is Christian marriage? Marriage is a holy and permanent union instituted by God and affirmed by Jesus. In choosing a life partner, his or her commitment to the faith and life of the church will be of extreme importance (see Mark 10:7-8). The statement on marriage in *Evangelical Lutheran Worship* (p. 286) is:

Marriage is a gift of God, intended for the joy and mutual strength of those who enter it and for the well-being of the whole human family. God created us male and female and blessed humankind with the gifts of companionship, the capacity to love, and the care and nurture of children. Jesus affirmed the covenant of marriage and revealed God's own self-giving love on the cross. The Holy Spirit helps those who are united in marriage to be living signs of God's grace, love, and faithfulness. *Ezra 9:1-4*

9:11 abominations...uncleanness: Those who returned to Jerusalem and Judah in several waves after the exile were often poor and had no land. This made them especially vulnerable in times of drought (see Hag 1). Some may have seen marriage to non-Jews as a way to have a better, more financially stable life. Whatever the reasons, intermarriage introduced the problem of worshiping other gods. This is likely the kind of "abomination" Ezra and other Second Temple priests spoke out against. Maintaining God's covenant relationship with the people of Israel could only be assured by keeping God's chosen race pure. Israel was chosen by a holy God (Lev 19:2) and set apart for God (Deut 7:6) as God's servants (Isa 43:1) and to be a light to the nations (Gen 12:1-3; Isa 42:6).

The People's Response

10 While Ezra prayed and made confession, weeping and
throwing himself down before the house of God, a very
great assembly of men, women, and children gathered to him out of
Israel; the people also wept bitterly. 2 Shecaniah son of Jehiel, of the
descendants of Elam, addressed Ezra, saying, "We have broken faith
with our God and have married foreign women from the peoples of
the land, but even now there is hope for Israel in spite of this. 3 So now
let us make a covenant with our God to send away all these wives and
their children, according to the counsel of my lord and of those who
tremble at the commandment of our God; and let it be done according to the law. 4 Take action, for it is your duty, and we are with you; be
strong, and do it." 5 Then Ezra stood up and made the leading priests,
the Levites, and all Israel swear that they would do as had been said.
So they swore.

Foreign Wives and Their Children Rejected

6 Then Ezra withdrew from before the house of God, and went to
the chamber of Jehohanan son of Eliashib, where he spent the night.[a]
He did not eat bread or drink water, for he was mourning over the
faithlessness of the exiles. 7 They made a proclamation throughout Judah and Jerusalem to all the returned exiles that they should assemble
at Jerusalem, 8 and that if any did not come within three days, by order
of the officials and the elders all their property should be forfeited,
and they themselves banned from the congregation of the exiles.

9 Then all the people of Judah and Benjamin assembled at Jerusalem within the three days; it was the ninth month, on the twentieth
day of the month. All the people sat in the open square before the
house of God, trembling because of this matter and because of the
heavy rain. 10 Then Ezra the priest stood up and said to them, "You
have trespassed and married foreign women, and so increased the
guilt of Israel. 11 Now make confession to the LORD the God of your
ancestors, and do his will; separate yourselves from the peoples of the
land and from the foreign wives." 12 Then all the assembly answered
with a loud voice, "It is so; we must do as you have said. 13 But the
people are many, and it is a time of heavy rain; we cannot stand in
the open. Nor is this a task for one day or for two, for many of us have
transgressed in this matter. 14 Let our officials represent the whole assembly, and let all in our towns who have taken foreign wives come at
appointed times, and with them the elders and judges of every town,
until the fierce wrath of our God on this account is averted from us."
15 Only Jonathan son of Asahel and Jahzeiah son of Tikvah opposed
this, and Meshullam and Shabbethai the Levites supported them.

[a] 1 Esdras 9.2: Heb *where he went*

10:2 We have broken faith with our God: See note on 9:11. This is a difficult chapter. The issue is where the line is drawn between being an inclusive community and yet exclusive of those opposed to the faith and ethics of the people of God. To be true to the dynamic Word of God (see note on 1:1 and "word") we must give this chapter two interpretations. On the one hand, the foreign wives represent the practice of following other gods that had sent the people into exile in the first place. The action of Ezra's community may have preserved biblical religion so that it could birth Judaism and Christianity. But from a humanitarian point of view this action is cruel and was opposed by the prophet Malachi (see Mal 2:14-16).

10:2-3 send away all these wives ...according to the law: This appears especially cruel to modern ears. The Old Testament laws allowed men to divorce wives for various reasons, and wives had little protection. Here, even the usual laws are suspended in an attempt to maintain purity. The "law" mentioned in 10:3 is not the Torah, since it did not forbid marriage to foreign wives. Rather, it likely refers to law established by Ezra (see also Neh 8–10). Jesus tweaked Old Testament notions of divorce by declaring that it is never God's will. Paul's counsel agrees with Malachi. (See also Mark 10:9-12; 1 Cor 7:10-16.)

16 Then the returned exiles did so. Ezra the priest selected men,[a]
heads of families, according to their families, each of them designated
by name. On the first day of the tenth month they sat down to examine the matter. [17]By the first day of the first month they had come to
the end of all the men who had married foreign women.

18 There were found of the descendants of the priests who had
married foreign women, of the descendants of Jeshua son of Jozadak and his brothers: Maaseiah, Eliezer, Jarib, and Gedaliah. [19]They
pledged themselves to send away their wives, and their guilt offering
was a ram of the flock for their guilt. [20]Of the descendants of Immer:
Hanani and Zebadiah. [21]Of the descendants of Harim: Maaseiah, Elijah, Shemaiah, Jehiel, and Uzziah. [22]Of the descendants of Pashhur:
Elioenai, Maaseiah, Ishmael, Nethanel, Jozabad, and Elasah.

23 Of the Levites: Jozabad, Shimei, Kelaiah (that is, Kelita), Pethahiah, Judah, and Eliezer. [24]Of the singers: Eliashib. Of the gatekeepers: Shallum, Telem, and Uri.

25 And of Israel: of the descendants of Parosh: Ramiah, Izziah,
Malchijah, Mijamin, Eleazar, Hashabiah,[b] and Benaiah. [26]Of the descendants of Elam: Mattaniah, Zechariah, Jehiel, Abdi, Jeremoth, and
Elijah. [27]Of the descendants of Zattu: Elioenai, Eliashib, Mattaniah,
Jeremoth, Zabad, and Aziza. [28]Of the descendants of Bebai: Jehohanan, Hananiah, Zabbai, and Athlai. [29]Of the descendants of Bani:
Meshullam, Malluch, Adaiah, Jashub, Sheal, and Jeremoth. [30]Of the
descendants of Pahath-moab: Adna, Chelal, Benaiah, Maaseiah, Mat-
taniah, Bezalel, Binnui, and Manasseh. [31]Of the descendants of Harim: Eliezer, Isshijah, Malchijah, Shemaiah, Shimeon, [32]Benjamin,
Malluch, and Shemariah. [33]Of the descendants of Hashum: Mattenai, Mattattah, Zabad, Eliphelet, Jeremai, Manasseh, and Shimei. [34]Of
the descendants of Bani: Maadai, Amram, Uel, [35]Benaiah, Bedeiah,
Cheluhi, [36]Vaniah, Meremoth, Eliashib, [37]Mattaniah, Mattenai, and
Jaasu. [38]Of the descendants of Binnui:[c] Shimei, [39]Shelemiah, Nathan,
Adaiah, [40]Machnadebai, Shashai, Sharai, [41]Azarel, Shelemiah, Shemariah, [42]Shallum, Amariah, and Joseph. [43]Of the descendants of Nebo:
Jeiel, Mattithiah, Zabad, Zebina, Jaddai, Joel, and Benaiah. [44]All these
had married foreign women, and they sent them away with their
children.[d]

10:18-44 who married foreign women: Only 110 men, less than 1 percent of the total, actually divorced.

What influences, both inside and outside our communities of faith, threaten your relationship with God? What, if anything, can be learned from the situation faced by Ezra and the exiled community that returned to Jerusalem?

---

[a] 1 Esdras 9.16: Syr: Heb *And there were selected Ezra,* [b] 1 Esdras 9.26 Gk: Heb *Malchijah* [c] Gk: Heb *Bani, Binnui* [d] 1 Esdras 9.36; meaning of Heb uncertain

Nehemiah 6:15

NEHEMIAH

Background File

Nehemiah, along with Ezra, was originally one book (see the introduction to the book of Ezra, p. 736). It continues and fills out the story of the Jewish people who returned to Jerusalem following a time of exile in Babylonia.

What's the Story?

Nehemiah presents what may be called "phase three" of the Jews' return to Judah from the Babylonian exile. This phase centers on rebuilding the wall around Jerusalem. The rebuilt walls provided protection from hostile forces in the region and made a visible statement of the permanence of the Jewish presence and authority in the Persian province of Yehud (Judah). And what about Ezra's role in the book? Some scholars think it odd that Ezra would have waited thirteen years to read the Torah to the community, and so they would place the account of this event in Nehemiah 8 immediately following Ezra 8. The same scholars would doubt that Ezra and Nehemiah lived and provided leadership during the same period. However, there is no evidence that Ezra somehow evaporated, and the unfinished Torah (Book of the Law) that he brought with him from Babylon would have needed continued work by him and his priestly colleagues in Jerusalem. Therefore the sequence of events following the chapter by chapter story line of the present book and assumed in the notes, while not certain, is not unreasonable.

1 Nehemiah, at the court of the king of Persia, learns of the Jews' situation in Jerusalem
2 He arrives in Jerusalem
3 He starts repair of the wall and its gates
4 Local non-Jewish leaders object
5 Nehemiah enacts social reform
6 Enemy opposition continues
7 List of those who returned
8 Ezra reads the Torah
9 Confession
10 The "firm agreement"
11 Population of Jerusalem and surrounding towns

12 Priests and Levites; the great dedication of the city wall liturgy
13 Separation from foreigners and Sabbath reforms

What's the Message?

Nehemiah was a trusted servant to Persian King Artaxerxes and had achieved a high ranking in the Persian court. His negotiating skills and ability to lead others becomes clear as he supervises the effort to rebuild the walls and gates of Jerusalem, the holy city of his people. Nehemiah is a perfect example of Luther's concept of *ora et labora*, "pray and work." He offers a model for those called to various lay vocations and the life of faith: trust in God and work out your vocation using your skills and gifts. His refrain of "remember my good works" is not boasting, but rather a statement of living out his holy calling.

Nehemiah Prays for His People

1 The words of Nehemiah son of Hacaliah. In the month of Chislev,
in the twentieth year, while I was in Susa the capital, [2]one of my
brothers, Hanani, came with certain men from Judah; and I asked
them about the Jews that survived, those who had escaped the captivity, and about Jerusalem. [3]They replied, "The survivors there in the
province who escaped captivity are in great trouble and shame; the
wall of Jerusalem is broken down, and its gates have been destroyed
by fire."
4 When I heard these words I sat down and wept, and mourned for
days, fasting and praying before the God of heaven. [5]I said, "O LORD
God of heaven, the great and awesome God who keeps covenant and
steadfast love with those who love him and keep his commandments;
[6]let your ear be attentive and your eyes open to hear the prayer of your
servant that I now pray before you day and night for your servants, the
people of Israel, confessing the sins of the people of Israel, which we
have sinned against you. Both I and my family have sinned. [7]We have
offended you deeply, failing to keep the commandments, the statutes,
and the ordinances that you commanded your servant Moses. [8]Re-
member the word that you commanded your servant Moses, 'If you
are unfaithful, I will scatter you among the peoples; [9]but if you return
to me and keep my commandments and do them, though your outcasts are under the farthest skies, I will gather them from there and
bring them to the place at which I have chosen to establish my name.'
[10]They are your servants and your people, whom you redeemed by
your great power and your strong hand. [11]O Lord, let your ear be attentive to the prayer of your servant, and to the prayer of your servants who delight in revering your name. Give success to your servant
today, and grant him mercy in the sight of this man!"

At the time, I was cupbearer to the king.

1:1 in the twentieth year, while I was in Susa: We meet Nehemiah, a very dedicated lay person, in Persia during the reign of Artaxerxes I (465–424 B.C.E.), in Susa, at the king's winter palace. See Map 10, p. 2107.

1:1 month of Chislev: The ninth month of the Hebrew calendar (mid-November to mid-December).

1:3 who escaped captivity: Nehemiah hears reports from Jews who had returned to Jerusalem from captivity in Babylonia in various waves (see the introduction to Ezra and Ezra 1–2.

1:8-9 Remember the word: Nehemiah refers to many biblical passages in order to recall why the Hebrews are in exile and to express their hope of return to Jerusalem to rebuild. For example, see Leviticus 26:27-45; Deuteronomy 4:25-31; 30:1-4.

1:11 cupbearer to the king: Nehemiah had the job of selecting and tasting the king's wine to make sure it was good and not poisoned. In such a role he had frequent access to the monarch.

Confession is a very important part of Nehemiah's prayer life as he begins this mission God will be sending him on. What role does confession play in your prayer life? In what way can confession enable us to move forward in our lives?

Nehemiah Sent to Judah

2 In the month of Nisan, in the twentieth year of King Artaxerxes,
when wine was served him, I carried the wine and gave it to the
king. Now, I had never been sad in his presence before. [2]So the king
said to me, "Why is your face sad, since you are not sick? This can
only be sadness of the heart." Then I was very much afraid. [3]I said
to the king, "May the king live forever! Why should my face not be
sad, when the city, the place of my ancestors' graves, lies waste, and its
gates have been destroyed by fire?" [4]Then the king said to me, "What
do you request?" So I prayed to the God of heaven. [5]Then I said to
the king, "If it pleases the king, and if your servant has found favor
with you, I ask that you send me to Judah, to the city of my ancestors' graves, so that I may rebuild it." [6]The king said to me (the queen
also was sitting beside him), "How long will you be gone, and when
will you return?" So it pleased the king to send me, and I set him a
date. [7]Then I said to the king, "If it pleases the king, let letters be given
me to the governors of the province Beyond the River, that they may
grant me passage until I arrive in Judah; [8]and a letter to Asaph, the
keeper of the king's forest, directing him to give me timber to make
beams for the gates of the temple fortress, and for the wall of the city,
and for the house that I shall occupy." And the king granted me what I
asked, for the gracious hand of my God was upon me.

9 Then I came to the governors of the province Beyond the River,
and gave them the king's letters. Now the king had sent officers of the
army and cavalry with me. [10]When Sanballat the Horonite and Tobiah the Ammonite official heard this, it displeased them greatly that
someone had come to seek the welfare of the people of Israel.

Nehemiah's Inspection of the Walls

11 So I came to Jerusalem and was there for three days. [12]Then I
got up during the night, I and a few men with me; I told no one what
my God had put into my heart to do for Jerusalem. The only animal
I took was the animal I rode. [13]I went out by night by the Valley Gate
past the Dragon's Spring and to the Dung Gate, and I inspected the
walls of Jerusalem that had been broken down and its gates that had
been destroyed by fire. [14]Then I went on to the Fountain Gate and to
the King's Pool; but there was no place for the animal I was riding to
continue. [15]So I went up by way of the valley by night and inspected
the wall. Then I turned back and entered by the Valley Gate, and so
returned. [16]The officials did not know where I had gone or what I was
doing; I had not yet told the Jews, the priests, the nobles, the officials,
and the rest that were to do the work.

Decision to Restore the Walls

17 Then I said to them, "You see the trouble we are in, how Jeru-

2:4 So I prayed to the God of heaven: Instead of just depending on his own intellect, Nehemiah precedes his request to the king with prayer to God.

Why pray? Why not just act? Luther was fond of saying, "Since I am so busy today I will spend more time in prayer." He knew that prayer is essential to getting done what needs to be done. Prayer is central to our life on earth with God, and if we neglect it we will actually accomplish less. *Nehemiah 2:4, 8b*

2:7 province Beyond the River: This was the western Persian satrapy (imperial administrative district), the most western province of which was Yehud (Judah).

2:8 for the gracious hand of my God was upon me: There is a clear sense throughout the book that God is working in and through the life of Nehemiah (see also 2:12, 20).

2:10 Sanballat...Tobiah: These were the governors of Samaria, north of Judah, and Ammon, east across the Jordan River. During the Jewish absence they had grown used to considering Jerusalem as part of the territory under their control. They consider Nehemiah's activity a threat to their authority and influence.

2:13-15 I went out by night: Nehemiah exits the city on the west side and proceeds counterclockwise past the Tyropoeon (or Central) Valley and the old City of David in the south, on to the Kidron Valley on the east (with the Temple Mount on his left and the Mount of Olives on his right), almost to the northern side of the city. When the destruction was so great that his animal could not continue walking, he returned by the way he had come. See the map of Jerusalem in Nehemiah's time, p. 755.

salem lies in ruins with its gates burned. Come, let us rebuild the wall
of Jerusalem, so that we may no longer suffer disgrace." 18 I told them
that the hand of my God had been gracious upon me, and also the
words that the king had spoken to me. Then they said, "Let us start
building!" So they committed themselves to the common good. 19 But
when Sanballat the Horonite and Tobiah the Ammonite official, and
Geshem the Arab heard of it, they mocked and ridiculed us, saying,
"What is this that you are doing? Are you rebelling against the king?"
20 Then I replied to them, "The God of heaven is the one who will give
us success, and we his servants are going to start building; but you
have no share or claim or historic right in Jerusalem."

Organization of the Work

3 Then the high priest Eliashib set to work with his fellow priests
and rebuilt the Sheep Gate. They consecrated it and set up its
doors; they consecrated it as far as the Tower of the Hundred and as
far as the Tower of Hananel. 2 And the men of Jericho built next to
him. And next to them[a] Zaccur son of Imri built.
3 The sons of Hassenaah built the Fish Gate; they laid its beams
and set up its doors, its bolts, and its bars. 4 Next to them Meremoth
son of Uriah son of Hakkoz made repairs. Next to them Meshullam
son of Berechiah son of Meshezabel made repairs. Next to them

[a] Heb *him*

2:19 Sanballat...Geshem: See note on 2:10. The Persians allowed Geshem to rule over a large number of Arab tribes located south and east of Judah.

3:1 Sheep Gate...consecrated it: It seems that virtually the entire Jewish population, including priests, Levites, and lay persons from Jerusalem and the surrounding districts, joined in the work of rebuilding the city and its protective wall. The Sheep Gate was at the northeast corner of the city, near the New Testament Pool of Bethesda (John 5:2), the Crusader Church of St. Anne, and what is today called the Lion or St. Stephan's Gate. The consecration ceremony probably included prayers to bless the sections of wall rebuilt and dedicate them to God.

3:3-6 Fish Gate...Old Gate: The ongoing description of the building and repair proceeds in a counterclockwise direction to the northwest corner of the city, which due to its vastly reduced population was even smaller than Solomon's Jerusalem. While today the walls of the Old City of Jerusalem extend far to the north and west, Nehemiah's Jerusalem included only the City of David and the Temple Mount. The Fish Gate was presumably in the area of the city's fish markets.

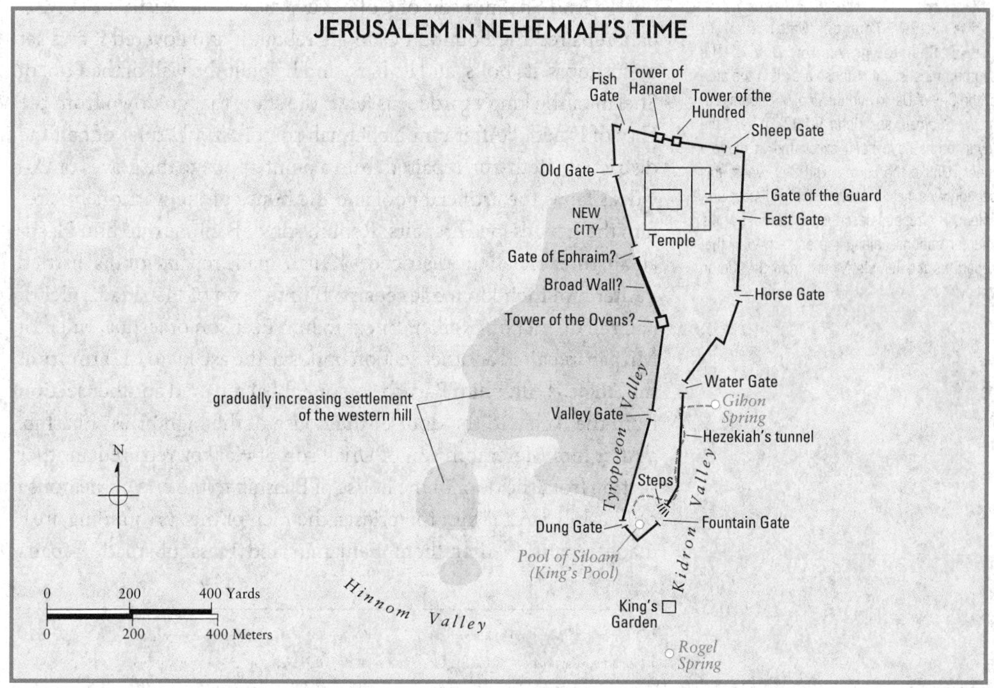

Zadok son of Baana made repairs. 5 Next to them the Tekoites made
repairs; but their nobles would not put their shoulders to the work of
their Lord.[a]

6 Joiada son of Paseah and Meshullam son of Besodeiah repaired
the Old Gate; they laid its beams and set up its doors, its bolts, and its
bars. 7 Next to them repairs were made by Melatiah the Gibeonite and
Jadon the Meronothite—the men of Gibeon and of Mizpah—who
were under the jurisdiction of[b] the governor of the province Beyond
the River. 8 Next to them Uzziel son of Harhaiah, one of the goldsmiths, made repairs. Next to him Hananiah, one of the perfumers,
made repairs; and they restored Jerusalem as far as the Broad Wall.
9 Next to them Rephaiah son of Hur, ruler of half the district of[c] Jerusalem, made repairs. 10 Next to them Jedaiah son of Harumaph made
repairs opposite his house; and next to him Hattush son of Hashabneiah made repairs. 11 Malchijah son of Harim and Hasshub son of
Pahath-moab repaired another section and the Tower of the Ovens.
12 Next to him Shallum son of Hallohesh, ruler of half the district of[c]
Jerusalem, made repairs, he and his daughters.

3:11 Tower of the Ovens: It was located in the area of baking and/or pottery making.

13 Hanun and the inhabitants of Zanoah repaired the Valley
Gate; they rebuilt it and set up its doors, its bolts, and its bars, and
repaired a thousand cubits of the wall, as far as the Dung Gate.

14 Malchijah son of Rechab, ruler of the district of[d] Beth-
haccherem, repaired the Dung Gate; he rebuilt it and set up its doors,
its bolts, and its bars.

3:14 Dung Gate: So called because it was the exit point for waste from the required sacrifices on the nearby Temple Mount.

15 And Shallum son of Col-hozeh, ruler of the district of[d] Mizpah, repaired the Fountain Gate; he rebuilt it and covered it and set
up its doors, its bolts, and its bars; and he built the wall of the Pool of
Shelah of the king's garden, as far as the stairs that go down from the
City of David. 16 After him Nehemiah son of Azbuk, ruler of half the
district of[c] Beth-zur, repaired from a point opposite the graves of David, as far as the artificial pool and the house of the warriors. 17 After
him the Levites made repairs: Rehum son of Bani; next to him Hashabiah, ruler of half the district of[c] Keilah, made repairs for his district.
18 After him their kin made repairs: Binnui,[e] son of Henadad, ruler of
half the district of[c] Keilah; 19 next to him Ezer son of Jeshua, ruler[f] of
Mizpah, repaired another section opposite the ascent to the armory at
the Angle. 20 After him Baruch son of Zabbai repaired another section
from the Angle to the door of the house of the high priest Eliashib.
21 After him Meremoth son of Uriah son of Hakkoz repaired another
section from the door of the house of Eliashib to the end of the house
of Eliashib. 22 After him the priests, the men of the surrounding area,
made repairs. 23 After them Benjamin and Hasshub made repairs

3:15-16 Fountain Gate…Pool of Shelah…graves of David: The southernmost section, these are all in the area of the City of David and the Pool of Siloam (Hebrew, *Sheloah*, see John 9:1-12), where the royal tombs have been excavated in modern times. Unlike the current Old City walls, this section was included within the walls of Jerusalem. The repairs described in the rest of the chapter continue along the eastern wall that separates the Temple Mount from the Kidron Valley.

---

[a] Or *lords* [a] Meaning of Heb uncertain [c] Or *supervisor of half the portion assigned to* [d] Or *supervisor of the portion assigned to* [e] Gk Syr Compare verse 24, 10.9: Heb *Bavvai* [f] Or *supervisor*

opposite their house. After them Azariah son of Maaseiah son of Ananiah made repairs beside his own house. 24 After him Binnui son of
Henadad repaired another section, from the house of Azariah to the
Angle and to the corner. 25 Palal son of Uzai repaired opposite the Angle and the tower projecting from the upper house of the king at the
court of the guard. After him Pedaiah son of Parosh 26 and the temple
servants living[a] on Ophel made repairs up to a point opposite the Water Gate on the east and the projecting tower. 27 After him the Tekoites
repaired another section opposite the great projecting tower as far as
the wall of Ophel.

28 Above the Horse Gate the priests made repairs, each one opposite his own house. 29 After them Zadok son of Immer made repairs
opposite his own house. After him Shemaiah son of Shecaniah, the
keeper of the East Gate, made repairs. 30 After him Hananiah son of
Shelemiah and Hanun sixth son of Zalaph repaired another section.
After him Meshullam son of Berechiah made repairs opposite his living quarters. 31 After him Malchijah, one of the goldsmiths, made repairs as far as the house of the temple servants and of the merchants,
opposite the Muster Gate,[b] and to the upper room of the corner.
32 And between the upper room of the corner and the Sheep Gate the
goldsmiths and the merchants made repairs.

Hostile Plots Thwarted

4[c] Now when Sanballat heard that we were building the wall, he
was angry and greatly enraged, and he mocked the Jews. 2 He
said in the presence of his associates and of the army of Samaria,
"What are these feeble Jews doing? Will they restore things? Will
they sacrifice? Will they finish it in a day? Will they revive the stones
out of the heaps of rubbish—and burned ones at that?" 3 Tobiah the
Ammonite was beside him, and he said, "That stone wall they are
building—any fox going up on it would break it down!" 4 Hear, O our
God, for we are despised; turn their taunt back on their own heads,
and give them over as plunder in a land of captivity. 5 Do not cover
their guilt, and do not let their sin be blotted out from your sight; for
they have hurled insults in the face of the builders.

6 So we rebuilt the wall, and all the wall was joined together to
half its height; for the people had a mind to work.

7[d] But when Sanballat and Tobiah and the Arabs and the Ammonites and the Ashdodites heard that the repairing of the walls
of Jerusalem was going forward and the gaps were beginning to be
closed, they were very angry, 8 and all plotted together to come and
fight against Jerusalem and to cause confusion in it. 9 So we prayed to
our God, and set a guard as a protection against them day and night.

---

[a] Cn: Heb *were living* [b] Or *Hammiphkad Gate* [c] Ch 3.33 in Heb [d] Ch 4.1 in Heb

4:4-5 Hear, O our God: Nehemiah prays. In light of the threat of the Samaritans from the north and the Ammonites from the west, he puts his faith in God.

4:6 for the people had a mind to work: The rebuilding of Jerusalem will ultimately be successful, because God is behind the project and the people are committed to working for God.

What major challenges do the people of God need to address today? How can we put ourselves and our resources to work to do what needs to be done?

4:7 Arabs...Ashdodites: Geshem, leader of the Arabs in the south, has been mentioned already in 2:19 as part of the alliance against the Jews, and now they are joined by Ashdod in the west. In other words, the enemies of Nehemiah encircle Judah and Jerusalem.

10 But Judah said, “The strength of the burden bearers is failing,
and there is too much rubbish so that we are unable to work on the
wall.” 11 And our enemies said, “They will not know or see anything
before we come upon them and kill them and stop the work.” 12 When
the Jews who lived near them came, they said to us ten times, “From
all the places where they live[a] they will come up against us.”[b] 13 So in
the lowest parts of the space behind the wall, in open places, I stationed the people according to their families,[c] with their swords, their
spears, and their bows. 14 After I looked these things over, I stood up
and said to the nobles and the officials and the rest of the people, “Do
not be afraid of them. Remember the LORD, who is great and awesome, and fight for your kin, your sons, your daughters, your wives,
and your homes.”

15 When our enemies heard that their plot was known to us,
and that God had frustrated it, we all returned to the wall, each to his
work. 16 From that day on, half of my servants worked on construction, and half held the spears, shields, bows, and body-armor; and the
leaders posted themselves behind the whole house of Judah, 17 who
were building the wall. The burden bearers carried their loads in such
a way that each labored on the work with one hand and with the other
held a weapon. 18 And each of the builders had his sword strapped at
his side while he built. The man who sounded the trumpet was beside
me. 19 And I said to the nobles, the officials, and the rest of the people,
“The work is great and widely spread out, and we are separated far
from one another on the wall. 20 Rally to us wherever you hear the
sound of the trumpet. Our God will fight for us.”

4:20 sound of the trumpet: Probably refers to a ram's horn *(shofar).*

21 So we labored at the work, and half of them held the spears
from break of dawn until the stars came out. 22 I also said to the people at that time, “Let every man and his servant pass the night inside
Jerusalem, so that they may be a guard for us by night and may labor
by day.” 23 So neither I nor my brothers nor my servants nor the men
of the guard who followed me ever took off our clothes; each kept his
weapon in his right hand.[d]

Nehemiah Deals with Oppression

5 Now there was a great outcry of the people and of their wives
against their Jewish kin. 2 For there were those who said, “With
our sons and our daughters, we are many; we must get grain, so that
we may eat and stay alive.” 3 There were also those who said, “We are
having to pledge our fields, our vineyards, and our houses in order to
get grain during the famine.” 4 And there were those who said, “We are
having to borrow money on our fields and vineyards to pay the king's

5:1-5 Now there was a great outcry: The Jews who had been taken into exile were from the upper and middle classes, while those who remained behind in Judah were from the lower classes who depended on the land for sustenance. The latter were helping with the rebuilding of Jerusalem, meaning that the women and children had to run the farms. Their economic difficulties included pledging the labor of their children to pay for food, pledging their property to pay debts, and borrowing money to pay the Persian tax.

[a] Cn: Heb *you return* [b] Compare Gk Syr: Meaning of Heb uncertain [c] Meaning of Heb uncertain
[d] Cn: Heb *each his weapon the water*

tax. 5 Now our flesh is the same as that of our kindred; our children are
the same as their children; and yet we are forcing our sons and daughters to be slaves, and some of our daughters have been ravished; we
are powerless, and our fields and vineyards now belong to others."
6 I was very angry when I heard their outcry and these complaints. 7 After thinking it over, I brought charges against the nobles
and the officials; I said to them, "You are all taking interest from your
own people." And I called a great assembly to deal with them, 8 and
said to them, "As far as we were able, we have bought back our Jewish
kindred who had been sold to other nations; but now you are selling
your own kin, who must then be bought back by us!" They were silent, and could not find a word to say. 9 So I said, "The thing that you
are doing is not good. Should you not walk in the fear of our God,
to prevent the taunts of the nations our enemies? 10 Moreover I and
my brothers and my servants are lending them money and grain. Let
us stop this taking of interest. 11 Restore to them, this very day, their
fields, their vineyards, their olive orchards, and their houses, and the
interest on money, grain, wine, and oil that you have been exacting
from them." 12 Then they said, "We will restore everything and demand nothing more from them. We will do as you say." And I called
the priests, and made them take an oath to do as they had promised.
13 I also shook out the fold of my garment and said, "So may God shake
out everyone from house and from property who does not perform
this promise. Thus may they be shaken out and emptied." And all the
assembly said, "Amen," and praised the LORD. And the people did as
they had promised.

The Generosity of Nehemiah

14 Moreover from the time that I was appointed to be their governor in the land of Judah, from the twentieth year to the thirty-second year of King Artaxerxes, twelve years, neither I nor my brothers
ate the food allowance of the governor. 15 The former governors who
were before me laid heavy burdens on the people, and took food and
wine from them, besides forty shekels of silver. Even their servants
lorded it over the people. But I did not do so, because of the fear of
God. 16 Indeed, I devoted myself to the work on this wall, and acquired no land; and all my servants were gathered there for the work.
17 Moreover there were at my table one hundred fifty people, Jews and
officials, besides those who came to us from the nations around us.
18 Now that which was prepared for one day was one ox and six choice
sheep; also fowls were prepared for me, and every ten days skins of
wine in abundance; yet with all this I did not demand the food allowance of the governor, because of the heavy burden of labor on the
people. 19 Remember for my good, O my God, all that I have done for
this people.

5:6-7 taking interest from your own people: The Hebrew text actually refers to seizing the pledges for the loans mentioned above from fellow Jews in need, not charging interest (see note on 5:11).

5:11 and the interest on money: The Law (Torah) forbids charging interest on loans to poor people (see Exod 22:25; Lev 25:35-37; Deut 23:19-20). But taking a guarantee was acceptable (see Deut 24:10-13). Even Nehemiah lent money and grain without charging interest (5:10).

Many people today are in need and require help. How can people of faith address these needs?

What positive viewpoint does Luther take in his explanation to the Seventh Commandment—"You shall not steal"? "We are to fear and love God, so that we neither take our neighbors' money or property nor acquire them by using shoddy merchandise or crooked deals, but instead help them to improve and protect their property and income *(SC:7)*." *Nehemiah 5:6-13*

5:13 I also shook out the fold of my garment: This action is like those done by prophets from the First Temple period, before the time of the exile. Prophecy is declining in the Second Temple period. Nehemiah is not a prophet, but he is one of the first laypersons to live the example of a prophetic life.

What do you think it means to live a prophetic life (based on the teachings of the prophets)?

5:14 I was appointed to be their governor: His appointment covered the years 445–433 B.C.E.

How can civil servants (people who work in the government) serve God today?

5:15 fear of God: This is a technical term in Hebrew meaning reverence for and total faith in the Lord.

5:19 Remember: This prayer is repeated as a sort of doxology through Nehemiah's memoir (see also 13:14, 22, 31). It may have originally been part of his report to Artaxerxes, the king who had supported him in his work.

Intrigues of Enemies Foiled

6 Now when it was reported to Sanballat and Tobiah and to Geshem the Arab and to the rest of our enemies that I had built the wall and that there was no gap left in it (though up to that time I had not set up the doors in the gates), 2 Sanballat and Geshem sent to me, saying, "Come and let us meet together in one of the villages in the plain of Ono." But they intended to do me harm. 3 So I sent messengers to them, saying, "I am doing a great work and I cannot come down. Why should the work stop while I leave it to come down to you?" 4 They sent to me four times in this way, and I answered them in the same manner. 5 In the same way Sanballat for the fifth time sent his servant to me with an open letter in his hand. 6 In it was written, "It is reported among the nations—and Geshem[a] also says it—that you and the Jews intend to rebel; that is why you are building the wall; and according to this report you wish to become their king. 7 You have also set up prophets to proclaim in Jerusalem concerning you, 'There is a king in Judah!' And now it will be reported to the king according to these words. So come, therefore, and let us confer together." 8 Then I sent to him, saying, "No such things as you say have been done; you are inventing them out of your own mind" 9 —for they all wanted to frighten us, thinking, "Their hands will drop from the work, and it will not be done." But now, O God, strengthen my hands.

10 One day when I went into the house of Shemaiah son of Delaiah son of Mehetabel, who was confined to his house, he said, "Let us meet together in the house of God, within the temple, and let us close the doors of the temple, for they are coming to kill you; indeed, tonight they are coming to kill you." 11 But I said, "Should a man like me run away? Would a man like me go into the temple to save his life? I will not go in!" 12 Then I perceived and saw that God had not sent him at all, but he had pronounced the prophecy against me because Tobiah and Sanballat had hired him. 13 He was hired for this purpose, to intimidate me and make me sin by acting in this way, and so they could give me a bad name, in order to taunt me. 14 Remember Tobiah and Sanballat, O my God, according to these things that they did, and also the prophetess Noadiah and the rest of the prophets who wanted to make me afraid.

The Wall Completed

15 So the wall was finished on the twenty-fifth day of the month Elul, in fifty-two days. 16 And when all our enemies heard of it, all the nations around us were afraid[b] and fell greatly in their own esteem; for they perceived that this work had been accomplished with the help of our God. 17 Moreover in those days the nobles of Judah sent many let-

[a] Heb *Gashmu* [b] Another reading is *saw*

6:7 There is a king in Judah!: Persia would not allow the people of Israel to set up a king over Judah. That is not Nehemiah's intent.

6:9 But now, O God, strengthen my hands: Nehemiah provides us a good example of the phrase that Luther practiced as well: *ora et labora*, "pray and work."

6:10-14 Shemaiah…Noadiah: In addition to authentic prophets who speak the word of God to the contemporary situation, there were "prophets for hire," such as these two, ready to lie for pay.

6:15 wall was finished…in fifty-two days: For a wall estimated to be three feet thick, the job was completed in a relatively short time.

6:17 nobles of Judah sent many letters to Tobiah: We learned in 3:5 that the noblemen of Tekoa "would not put their shoulders to the work," and even some of those who had joined in the rebuilding of the wall had previously developed economic, political, and family ties with Nehemiah's enemies.

ters to Tobiah, and Tobiah's letters came to them. [18]For many in Judah
were bound by oath to him, because he was the son-in-law of Shecaniah son of Arah: and his son Jehohanan had married the daughter of
Meshullam son of Berechiah. [19]Also they spoke of his good deeds in
my presence, and reported my words to him. And Tobiah sent letters
to intimidate me.

7 Now when the wall had been built and I had set up the doors,
and the gatekeepers, the singers, and the Levites had been appointed, [2]I gave my brother Hanani charge over Jerusalem, along with
Hananiah the commander of the citadel—for he was a faithful man
and feared God more than many. [3]And I said to them, "The gates of Jerusalem are not to be opened until the sun is hot; while the gatekeepers[a] are still standing guard, let them shut and bar the doors. Appoint
guards from among the inhabitants of Jerusalem, some at their watch
posts, and others before their own houses." [4]The city was wide and
large, but the people within it were few and no houses had been built.

Lists of the Returned Exiles

5 Then my God put it into my mind to assemble the nobles and
the officials and the people to be enrolled by genealogy. And I found
the book of the genealogy of those who were the first to come back,
and I found the following written in it:

6 These are the people of the province who came up out of the
captivity of those exiles whom King Nebuchadnezzar of Babylon
had carried into exile; they returned to Jerusalem and Judah, each to
his town. [7]They came with Zerubbabel, Jeshua, Nehemiah, Azariah,
Raamiah, Nahamani, Mordecai, Bilshan, Mispereth, Bigvai, Nehum,
Baanah.

The number of the Israelite people: [8]the descendants of Parosh,
two thousand one hundred seventy-two. [9]Of Shephatiah, three hundred seventy-two. [10]Of Arah, six hundred fifty-two. [11]Of Pahath-moab,
namely the descendants of Jeshua and Joab, two thousand eight hundred eighteen. [12]Of Elam, one thousand two hundred fifty-four. [13]Of
Zattu, eight hundred forty-five. [14]Of Zaccai, seven hundred sixty. [15]Of
Binnui, six hundred forty-eight. [16]Of Bebai, six hundred twenty-eight.
[17]Of Azgad, two thousand three hundred twenty-two. [18]Of Adonikam,
six hundred sixty-seven. [19]Of Bigvai, two thousand sixty-seven. [20]Of
Adin, six hundred fifty-five. [21]Of Ater, namely of Hezekiah, ninety-
eight. [22]Of Hashum, three hundred twenty-eight. [23]Of Bezai, three
hundred twenty-four. [24]Of Hariph, one hundred twelve. [25]Of Gibeon, ninety-five. [26]The people of Bethlehem and Netophah, one hundred eighty-eight. [27]Of Anathoth, one hundred twenty-eight. [28]Of
Beth-azmaveth, forty-two. [29]Of Kiriath-jearim, Chephirah, and

7:1 the gatekeepers, the singers, and the Levites: The gatekeepers appointed here are secular guards at the city gates. The other kind of gatekeeper often mentioned in the Bible in liturgical texts was stationed with the singers and Levites at the temple, which was also surrounded by a smaller wall with gates (see 7:43-45). A scribe copying this text has confused the temple gatekeepers with the secular gatekeepers and mistakenly added the words "the singers, and the Levites."

7:2 Hanani...Hananiah: Hanani is the short form of the name Nananiah, as, for example, Micah is short for Micaiah. A later scribe copying the text mistook them for two different men; but they are one and the same. Nehemiah appointed his brother, known popularly as Hanani, to be the military commander over Jerusalem, stationed at the city fortress, or citadel.

7:4-5 the people within it were few... God put it into my mind to assemble the...people: The following genealogical list is repeated from Ezra 2 (see notes at Ezra 2:1; 2:36, 40). As explained in the note on Ezra 2:1, the list comprises the total number of returnees over successive years. Its placement here may indicate that Nehemiah intended to use it and the assembly to help repopulate Jerusalem. It also prepares the reader to envision the vast audience that would listen to Ezra's reading of the Torah in the next chapter.

[a] Heb *while they*

Beeroth, seven hundred forty-three. 30 Of Ramah and Geba, six hundred twenty-one. 31 Of Michmas, one hundred twenty-two. 32 Of Bethel and Ai, one hundred twenty-three. 33 Of the other Nebo, fifty-two. 34 The descendants of the other Elam, one thousand two hundred fifty-four. 35 Of Harim, three hundred twenty. 36 Of Jericho, three hundred forty-five. 37 Of Lod, Hadid, and Ono, seven hundred twenty-one. 38 Of Senaah, three thousand nine hundred thirty.

7:39, 43, 46 priests...Levites...temple servants: See note at Ezra 2:36, 40 (priests and Levites). The "temple servants" here may refer to Levites who were not considered fit to do anything but cleaning in the temple, because they followed other gods.

39 The priests: the descendants of Jedaiah, namely the house of Jeshua, nine hundred seventy-three. 40 Of Immer, one thousand fifty-two. 41 Of Pashhur, one thousand two hundred forty-seven. 42 Of Harim, one thousand seventeen.

43 The Levites: the descendants of Jeshua, namely of Kadmiel of the descendants of Hodevah, seventy-four. 44 The singers: the descendants of Asaph, one hundred forty-eight. 45 The gatekeepers: the descendants of Shallum, of Ater, of Talmon, of Akkub, of Hatita, of Shobai, one hundred thirty-eight.

46 The temple servants: the descendants of Ziha, of Hasupha, of Tabbaoth, 47 of Keros, of Sia, of Padon, 48 of Lebana, of Hagaba, of Shalmai, 49 of Hanan, of Giddel, of Gahar, 50 of Reaiah, of Rezin, of Nekoda, 51 of Gazzam, of Uzza, of Paseah, 52 of Besai, of Meunim, of Nephushesim, 53 of Bakbuk, of Hakupha, of Harhur, 54 of Bazlith, of Mehida, of Harsha, 55 of Barkos, of Sisera, of Temah, 56 of Neziah, of Hatipha.

57 The descendants of Solomon's servants: of Sotai, of Sophereth, of Perida, 58 of Jaala, of Darkon, of Giddel, 59 of Shephatiah, of Hattil, of Pochereth-hazzebaim, of Amon.

60 All the temple servants and the descendants of Solomon's servants were three hundred ninety-two.

61 The following were those who came up from Tel-melah, Telharsha, Cherub, Addon, and Immer, but they could not prove their ancestral houses or their descent, whether they belonged to Israel: 62 the descendants of Delaiah, of Tobiah, of Nekoda, six hundred forty-two. 63 Also, of the priests: the descendants of Hobaiah, of Hakkoz, of Barzillai (who had married one of the daughters of Barzillai the Gileadite and was called by their name). 64 These sought their registration among those enrolled in the genealogies, but it was not found there, so they were excluded from the priesthood as unclean; 65 the governor told them that they were not to partake of the most holy food, until a priest with Urim and Thummim should come.

7:65 Urim and Thummim: See the note on Ezra 2:63. The use of these sacred lots may have signaled a return to an earlier time in Israel's history when the lots were used as a way to get messages from God.

66 The whole assembly together was forty-two thousand three hundred sixty, 67 besides their male and female slaves, of whom there were seven thousand three hundred thirty-seven; and they had two hundred forty-five singers, male and female. 68 They had seven hundred thirty-six horses, two hundred forty-five mules,[a] 69 four hundred

[a] Ezra 2.66 and the margins of some Hebrew Mss: MT lacks *They had . . . forty-five mules*

thirty-five camels, and six thousand seven hundred twenty donkeys.
70 Now some of the heads of ancestral houses contributed to the
work. The governor gave to the treasury one thousand darics of gold,
fifty basins, and five hundred thirty priestly robes. 71And some of the
heads of ancestral houses gave into the building fund twenty thousand darics of gold and two thousand two hundred minas of silver.
72And what the rest of the people gave was twenty thousand darics of
gold, two thousand minas of silver, and sixty-seven priestly robes.
73 So the priests, the Levites, the gatekeepers, the singers, some of
the people, the temple servants, and all Israel settled in their towns.

Ezra Summons the People to Obey the Law

8 When the seventh month came—the people of Israel being settled in their towns—1all the people gathered together into the
square before the Water Gate. They told the scribe Ezra to bring
the book of the law of Moses, which the LORD had given to Israel.
2Accordingly, the priest Ezra brought the law before the assembly,
both men and women and all who could hear with understanding.
This was on the first day of the seventh month. 3He read from it facing
the square before the Water Gate from early morning until midday, in
the presence of the men and the women and those who could understand; and the ears of all the people were attentive to the book of the
law. 4The scribe Ezra stood on a wooden platform that had been made
for the purpose; and beside him stood Mattithiah, Shema, Anaiah,
Uriah, Hilkiah, and Maaseiah on his right hand; and Pedaiah, Mishael, Malchijah, Hashum, Hash-baddanah, Zechariah, and Meshullam
on his left hand. 5And Ezra opened the book in the sight of all the people, for he was standing above all the people; and when he opened it,
all the people stood up. 6Then Ezra blessed the LORD, the great God,
and all the people answered, "Amen, Amen," lifting up their hands.
Then they bowed their heads and worshiped the LORD with their
faces to the ground. 7Also Jeshua, Bani, Sherebiah, Jamin, Akkub,
Shabbethai, Hodiah, Maaseiah, Kelita, Azariah, Jozabad, Hanan, Pelaiah, the Levites,[a] helped the people to understand the law, while the
people remained in their places. 8So they read from the book, from
the law of God, with interpretation. They gave the sense, so that the
people understood the reading.
9 And Nehemiah, who was the governor, and Ezra the priest and
scribe, and the Levites who taught the people said to all the people,
"This day is holy to the LORD your God; do not mourn or weep." For
all the people wept when they heard the words of the law. 10Then he
said to them, "Go your way, eat the fat and drink sweet wine and send
portions of them to those for whom nothing is prepared, for this day

[a] 1 Esdras 9.48 Vg: Heb *and the Levites*

7:71 darics of gold…minas of silver: The daric was thick gold coin that pictured King Darius of Persia. The mina was weight used to measure silver and gold. The exact amount of gold and weight of silver here is not clear.

8:1 Water Gate: Located near the southeast corner of the Temple Mount.

8:1 scribe Ezra to bring book of the law of Moses: The book Ezra brought is better called "the Teaching of Moses," that is, the Torah or Pentateuch (the Five Scrolls), the first five books of the Old Testament. It is called "of Moses" not because he wrote all of it but because he was Israel's first great teacher, and the Torah is the logical expansion of his teachings over the centuries. During the Babylonian exile, Ezra and other priests had been collecting and editing the Torah, and it is this version or parts of it that Ezra reads. Minor discrepancies of practice indicate that Ezra's was not the final version we have but very close to it. See also the note on Ezra 7:6.

8:7 the Levites, helped the people to understand: The Levites were the traditional teachers (see Deut 33:10; 2 Chr 17:7-9; 35:3) of God's Word. As Ezra read the Torah, the Levites moved among the people and helped them interpret it and apply it to their lives.

What teachers have been especially helpful to you in understanding and applying God's word? What makes a skilled teacher of God's word? What laypersons in your congregation have such skills?

Why is interpreting the Bible important to Lutherans? "For the most part, Lutherans are more interested in *understanding* the Bible than they are in *defending* it. We don't think we have to *prove* the Bible is the Word of God—we just believe it is the word of God, and then we focus on asking, 'What *does* God have to say to us?'" *(OBF: 22) Nehemiah 8:8*

is holy to our LORD; and do not be grieved, for the joy of the LORD is your strength." 11 So the Levites stilled all the people, saying, "Be quiet, for this day is holy; do not be grieved." 12 And all the people went their way to eat and drink and to send portions and to make great rejoicing, because they had understood the words that were declared to them.

The Festival of Booths Celebrated

13 On the second day the heads of ancestral houses of all the people, with the priests and the Levites, came together to the scribe Ezra in order to study the words of the law. 14 And they found it written in the law, which the LORD had commanded by Moses, that the people of Israel should live in booths[a] during the festival of the seventh month, 15 and that they should publish and proclaim in all their towns and in Jerusalem as follows, "Go out to the hills and bring branches of olive, wild olive, myrtle, palm, and other leafy trees to make booths,[a] as it is written." 16 So the people went out and brought them, and made booths[a] for themselves, each on the roofs of their houses, and in their courts and in the courts of the house of God, and in the square at the Water Gate and in the square at the Gate of Ephraim. 17 And all the assembly of those who had returned from the captivity made booths[a] and lived in them; for from the days of Jeshua son of Nun to that day the people of Israel had not done so. And there was very great rejoicing. 18 And day by day, from the first day to the last day, he read from the book of the law of God. They kept the festival seven days; and on the eighth day there was a solemn assembly, according to the ordinance.

National Confession

9 Now on the twenty-fourth day of this month the people of Israel were assembled with fasting and in sackcloth, and with earth on their heads.[b] 2 Then those of Israelite descent separated themselves from all foreigners, and stood and confessed their sins and the iniquities of their ancestors. 3 They stood up in their place and read from the book of the law of the LORD their God for a fourth part of the day, and for another fourth they made confession and worshiped the LORD their God. 4 Then Jeshua, Bani, Kadmiel, Shebaniah, Bunni, Sherebiah, Bani, and Chenani stood on the stairs of the Levites and cried out with a loud voice to the LORD their God. 5 Then the Levites, Jeshua, Kadmiel, Bani, Hashabneiah, Sherebiah, Hodiah, Shebaniah, and Pethahiah, said, "Stand up and bless the LORD your God from everlasting to everlasting. Blessed be your glorious name, which is exalted above all blessing and praise."

---

[a] Or *tabernacles*; Heb *succoth* [b] Heb *on them*

8:16 on the roofs of their houses: Homes in the Holy Land tend to have flat roofs that serve as patios for outdoor living.

8:15-17 made booths…from the days of Jeshua…had not done so: The Festival of Booths was to be a yearly festival celebrated on the fifteenth day of the seventh month (Tishri). The festival was a time of remembering how their ancestors wandered in the wilderness after escaping from Egypt (see Lev 23:33-43; Num 29:12-38). Apparently, since the time of Joshua they had not observed the festival in this way, eating under temporary structures of four poles holding up a ceiling of branches.

9:1-2 fasting and in sackcloth, and with earth on their heads: After first hearing and receiving God's word with joy, the people turn to mourning rites and confession, because the law has showed them their sin. These rites included going without food, wearing rough clothing, and putting dirt on their heads and bodies.

How is confession of sins connected to Luther's understanding of the second use of the law? The second or theological use of the law is at work in our relationship with God. It reveals to us just how hopelessly we fail to fulfill the law. Because we know we cannot fulfill the law, it drives us to Christ and his mercy. *Nehemiah 9:1-2*

9:4-5 Levites: As today, lay ministers lead the congregation in song, prayer, and blessing.

6 And Ezra said:[a] "You are the LORD, you alone; you have made
heaven, the heaven of heavens, with all their host, the earth and all
that is on it, the seas and all that is in them. To all of them you give
life, and the host of heaven worships you. 7 You are the LORD, the God
who chose Abram and brought him out of Ur of the Chaldeans and
gave him the name Abraham; 8 and you found his heart faithful before you, and made with him a covenant to give to his descendants
the land of the Canaanite, the Hittite, the Amorite, the Perizzite, the
Jebusite, and the Girgashite; and you have fulfilled your promise, for
you are righteous.

9 "And you saw the distress of our ancestors in Egypt and heard
their cry at the Red Sea.[b] 10 You performed signs and wonders against
Pharaoh and all his servants and all the people of his land, for you
knew that they acted insolently against our ancestors. You made a
name for yourself, which remains to this day. 11 And you divided the
sea before them, so that they passed through the sea on dry land, but
you threw their pursuers into the depths, like a stone into mighty waters. 12 Moreover, you led them by day with a pillar of cloud, and by
night with a pillar of fire, to give them light on the way in which they
should go. 13 You came down also upon Mount Sinai, and spoke with
them from heaven, and gave them right ordinances and true laws,
good statutes and commandments, 14 and you made known your holy
sabbath to them and gave them commandments and statutes and a
law through your servant Moses. 15 For their hunger you gave them
bread from heaven, and for their thirst you brought water for them
out of the rock, and you told them to go in to possess the land that
you swore to give them.

16 "But they and our ancestors acted presumptuously and stiffened their necks and did not obey your commandments; 17 they
refused to obey, and were not mindful of the wonders that you performed among them; but they stiffened their necks and determined
to return to their slavery in Egypt. But you are a God ready to forgive,
gracious and merciful, slow to anger and abounding in steadfast love,
and you did not forsake them. 18 Even when they had cast an image of
a calf for themselves and said, 'This is your God who brought you up
out of Egypt,' and had committed great blasphemies, 19 you in your
great mercies did not forsake them in the wilderness; the pillar of
cloud that led them in the way did not leave them by day, nor the
pillar of fire by night that gave them light on the way by which they
should go. 20 You gave your good spirit to instruct them, and did not
withhold your manna from their mouths, and gave them water for
their thirst. 21 Forty years you sustained them in the wilderness so that
they lacked nothing; their clothes did not wear out and their feet did

[a] Gk: Heb lacks *And Ezra said* [b] Or *Sea of Reeds*

9:6-31 You are the LORD, you alone: This magnificent prayer begins with the Hebrew *Shema*, which means "listen" or "hear"(see Deut 6:4-5 and note), the most holy creed of Judaism and central to the Torah newly proclaimed by Ezra. What follows could fit into the Christian liturgy of Holy Communion. The first section (9:6-15) is a recital of God's salvation history on the part of Israel, which is reminiscent of our Eucharistic Prayer. The latter section (9:16-31) is a confession, which ends in an assurance of God's graciousness and mercy.

9:14 holy sabbath: The lifting up of the Sabbath is typical of Second Temple Judaism. The Sabbath day was to be a day of rest from work (see 10:31; 13:15-22; Isa 56:1-8). It is a gift from God to God's people: a time for rest and renewal and the worship of our Creator, Redeemer, and Sustainer.

Christians moved the Sabbath from Saturday to Sunday in order to celebrate every week Jesus Christ's resurrection from the dead. How do you "Remember the Sabbath Day to keep it holy"?

9:17 gracious and merciful: This is quoting Exodus 34:6, which became a sort of creed in Second Temple Judaism (see also Joel 2:13; Jonah 4:2; Ps 145:8).

not swell. [22]And you gave them kingdoms and peoples, and allotted to them every corner,[a] so they took possession of the land of King Sihon of Heshbon and the land of King Og of Bashan. [23]You multiplied their descendants like the stars of heaven, and brought them into the land that you had told their ancestors to enter and possess. [24]So the descendants went in and possessed the land, and you subdued before them the inhabitants of the land, the Canaanites, and gave them into their hands, with their kings and the peoples of the land, to do with them as they pleased. [25]And they captured fortress cities and a rich land, and took possession of houses filled with all sorts of goods, hewn cisterns, vineyards, olive orchards, and fruit trees in abundance; so they ate, and were filled and became fat, and delighted themselves in your great goodness.

26 "Nevertheless they were disobedient and rebelled against you and cast your law behind their backs and killed your prophets, who had warned them in order to turn them back to you, and they committed great blasphemies. [27]Therefore you gave them into the hands of their enemies, who made them suffer. Then in the time of their suffering they cried out to you and you heard them from heaven, and according to your great mercies you gave them saviors who saved them from the hands of their enemies. [28]But after they had rest, they again did evil before you, and you abandoned them to the hands of their enemies, so that they had dominion over them; yet when they turned and cried to you, you heard from heaven, and many times you rescued them according to your mercies. [29]And you warned them in order to turn them back to your law. Yet they acted presumptuously and did not obey your commandments, but sinned against your ordinances, by the observance of which a person shall live. They turned a stubborn shoulder and stiffened their neck and would not obey. [30]Many years you were patient with them, and warned them by your spirit through your prophets; yet they would not listen. Therefore you handed them over to the peoples of the lands. [31]Nevertheless, in your great mercies you did not make an end of them or forsake them, for you are a gracious and merciful God.

32 "Now therefore, our God—the great and mighty and awesome God, keeping covenant and steadfast love—do not treat lightly all the hardship that has come upon us, upon our kings, our officials, our priests, our prophets, our ancestors, and all your people, since the time of the kings of Assyria until today. [33]You have been just in all that has come upon us, for you have dealt faithfully and we have acted wickedly; [34]our kings, our officials, our priests, and our ancestors have not kept your law or heeded the commandments and the warnings that you gave them. [35]Even in their own kingdom, and in the great

9:36 slaves: Meaning that they are Persian subjects.

9:38 firm agreement: Or "faithful promise" to obey the Torah.

[a] Meaning of Heb uncertain

goodness you bestowed on them, and in the large and rich land that
you set before them, they did not serve you and did not turn from
their wicked works. [36]Here we are, slaves to this day—slaves in the
land that you gave to our ancestors to enjoy its fruit and its good gifts.
[37]Its rich yield goes to the kings whom you have set over us because of
our sins; they have power also over our bodies and over our livestock
at their pleasure, and we are in great distress."

Those Who Signed the Covenant

38[a] Because of all this we make a firm agreement in writing, and
on that sealed document are inscribed the names of our officials, our
Levites, and our priests.

10[b] Upon the sealed document are the names of Nehemiah
the governor, son of Hacaliah, and Zedekiah; [2]Seraiah, Azariah, Jeremiah, [3]Pashhur, Amariah, Malchijah, [4]Hattush, Shebaniah,
Malluch, [5]Harim, Meremoth, Obadiah, [6]Daniel, Ginnethon, Baruch,
[7]Meshullam, Abijah, Mijamin, [8]Maaziah, Bilgai, Shemaiah; these are
the priests. [9]And the Levites: Jeshua son of Azaniah, Binnui of the
sons of Henadad, Kadmiel; [10]and their associates, Shebaniah, Hodiah, Kelita, Pelaiah, Hanan, [11]Mica, Rehob, Hashabiah, [12]Zaccur,
Sherebiah, Shebaniah, [13]Hodiah, Bani, Beninu. [14]The leaders of the
people: Parosh, Pahath-moab, Elam, Zattu, Bani, [15]Bunni, Azgad,
Bebai, [16]Adonijah, Bigvai, Adin, [17]Ater, Hezekiah, Azzur, [18]Hodiah,
Hashum, Bezai, [19]Hariph, Anathoth, Nebai, [20]Magpiash, Meshullam, Hezir, [21]Meshezabel, Zadok, Jaddua, [22]Pelatiah, Hanan, Anaiah,
[23]Hoshea, Hananiah, Hasshub, [24]Hallohesh, Pilha, Shobek, [25]Rehum,
Hashabnah, Maaseiah, [26]Ahiah, Hanan, Anan, [27]Malluch, Harim, and
Baanah.

Summary of the Covenant

28 The rest of the people, the priests, the Levites, the gatekeepers, the singers, the temple servants, and all who have separated themselves from the peoples of the lands to adhere to the law of God, their
wives, their sons, their daughters, all who have knowledge and understanding, [29]join with their kin, their nobles, and enter into a curse and
an oath to walk in God's law, which was given by Moses the servant
of God, and to observe and do all the commandments of the LORD
our Lord and his ordinances and his statutes. [30]We will not give our
daughters to the peoples of the land or take their daughters for our
sons; [31]and if the peoples of the land bring in merchandise or any
grain on the sabbath day to sell, we will not buy it from them on the
sabbath or on a holy day; and we will forego the crops of the seventh
year and the exaction of every debt.

---

[a] Ch 10.1 in Heb [b] Ch 10.2 in Heb

10:28-29 The rest of the people…all who have separated themselves: Those who did not sign the *firm agreement* pledge themselves to it by a curse and an oath. Part of the agreement was to separate themselves from the neighboring peoples who did not worship Israel's God.

10:29 walk in God's law: Better understood as "walk in God's Torah" or "follow God's teaching." Since Torah means "instruction for life," and Jesus is the Word of God (see John 1:14) and the New Moses who fulfills the Torah and helps us know how to live it (see Matt 5–7), the teachings of Jesus are also Torah for us. Baptism is our "firm agreement" to live by the teaching of God.

How does the Affirmation of Baptism rite address our Christian commitment to live out our baptism? Those who have been baptized are asked:
Do you intend to continue in the covenant God made with you in holy baptism:
- to live among God's faithful people,
- to hear the word of God and share in the Lord's supper,
- to proclaim the good news of God in Christ through word and deed,
- to serve all people, following the example of Jesus, and
- to strive for justice and peace in all the earth? (*ELW: 237) Nehemiah 10:28-39*

Compare the oath to walk in God's law (Neh 10:29) to the promises in the rite of Affirmation of Baptism. How do they seem to be similar? How do you think they are different?

10:30 peoples of the land: Non-Jews; the problem of intermarriage is dealt with in Ezra 9–10 and Nehemiah 13:1-3, 23-31.

10:31 sabbath: The concept of keeping the Sabbath is expanded to include refraining from buying and selling (see 13:15-22). It is typical of Second Temple Judaism to gradually explain in more detail how the various laws of the Torah are to be obeyed.

10:31 we will forego: Land lies fallow, meaning not planted with crops (see Exod 23:10-11) and debts are forgiven (see Exod 21:2-6) in the seventh year.

32 We also lay on ourselves the obligation to charge ourselves
yearly one-third of a shekel for the service of the house of our God:
33 for the rows of bread, the regular grain offering, the regular burnt
offering, the sabbaths, the new moons, the appointed festivals, the sacred donations, and the sin offerings to make atonement for Israel,
and for all the work of the house of our God. 34 We have also cast lots
among the priests, the Levites, and the people, for the wood offering,
to bring it into the house of our God, by ancestral houses, at appointed
times, year by year, to burn on the altar of the LORD our God, as it is
written in the law. 35 We obligate ourselves to bring the first fruits of
our soil and the first fruits of all fruit of every tree, year by year, to
the house of the LORD; 36 also to bring to the house of our God, to
the priests who minister in the house of our God, the firstborn of our
sons and of our livestock, as it is written in the law, and the firstlings
of our herds and of our flocks; 37 and to bring the first of our dough,
and our contributions, the fruit of every tree, the wine and the oil, to
the priests, to the chambers of the house of our God; and to bring
to the Levites the tithes from our soil, for it is the Levites who collect
the tithes in all our rural towns. 38 And the priest, the descendant of
Aaron, shall be with the Levites when the Levites receive the tithes;
and the Levites shall bring up a tithe of the tithes to the house of our
God, to the chambers of the storehouse. 39 For the people of Israel and
the sons of Levi shall bring the contribution of grain, wine, and oil to
the storerooms where the vessels of the sanctuary are, and where the
priests that minister, and the gatekeepers and the singers are. We will
not neglect the house of our God.

10:34 wood offering: An innovation to ensure that the altar at the temple was always aflame.

10:35-37 We obligate ourselves to bring the first fruits…tithes: The offering of first things was a way to acknowledge with thankfulness that all comes from God and thereby support the ministry of God's house. A tithe is 10 percent.

How do you offer your first fruits and tithes to God's house?

Population of the City Increased

11 Now the leaders of the people lived in Jerusalem; and the rest
of the people cast lots to bring one out of ten to live in the holy
city Jerusalem, while nine-tenths remained in the other towns. 2 And
the people blessed all those who willingly offered to live in Jerusalem.

3 These are the leaders of the province who lived in Jerusalem;
but in the towns of Judah all lived on their property in their towns: Israel, the priests, the Levites, the temple servants, and the descendants
of Solomon's servants. 4 And in Jerusalem lived some of the Judahites
and of the Benjaminites. Of the Judahites: Athaiah son of Uzziah son
of Zechariah son of Amariah son of Shephatiah son of Mahalalel, of
the descendants of Perez; 5 and Maaseiah son of Baruch son of Col-
hozeh son of Hazaiah son of Adaiah son of Joiarib son of Zechariah
son of the Shilonite. 6 All the descendants of Perez who lived in Jerusalem were four hundred sixty-eight valiant warriors.

7 And these are the Benjaminites: Sallu son of Meshullam son of
Joed son of Pedaiah son of Kolaiah son of Maaseiah son of Ithiel son

11:3-24 These are the leaders of the province who lived in Jerusalem: We return to the issue of the repopulation of the restored city, mentioned earlier in 7:4-5. The list begins with lay leaders and proceeds to priests and other ministers (see also 1 Chr 9:2-16).

of Jeshaiah. [8]And his brothers[a] Gabbai, Sallai: nine hundred twenty-eight. [9]Joel son of Zichri was their overseer; and Judah son of Hassenuah was second in charge of the city.

10 Of the priests: Jedaiah son of Joiarib, Jachin, [11]Seraiah son of Hilkiah son of Meshullam son of Zadok son of Meraioth son of Ahitub, officer of the house of God, [12]and their associates who did the work of the house, eight hundred twenty-two; and Adaiah son of Jeroham son of Pelaliah son of Amzi son of Zechariah son of Pashhur son of Malchijah, [13]and his associates, heads of ancestral houses, two hundred forty-two; and Amashsai son of Azarel son of Ahzai son of Meshillemoth son of Immer, [14]and their associates, valiant warriors, one hundred twenty-eight; their overseer was Zabdiel son of Haggedolim.

15 And of the Levites: Shemaiah son of Hasshub son of Azrikam son of Hashabiah son of Bunni; [16]and Shabbethai and Jozabad, of the leaders of the Levites, who were over the outside work of the house of God; [17]and Mattaniah son of Mica son of Zabdi son of Asaph, who was the leader to begin the thanksgiving in prayer, and Bakbukiah, the second among his associates; and Abda son of Shammua son of Galal son of Jeduthun. [18]All the Levites in the holy city were two hundred eighty-four.

19 The gatekeepers, Akkub, Talmon and their associates, who kept watch at the gates, were one hundred seventy-two. [20]And the rest of Israel, and of the priests and the Levites, were in all the towns of Judah, all of them in their inheritance. [21]But the temple servants lived on Ophel; and Ziha and Gishpa were over the temple servants.

22 The overseer of the Levites in Jerusalem was Uzzi son of Bani son of Hashabiah son of Mattaniah son of Mica, of the descendants of Asaph, the singers, in charge of the work of the house of God. [23]For there was a command from the king concerning them, and a settled provision for the singers, as was required every day. [24]And Pethahiah son of Meshezabel, of the descendants of Zerah son of Judah, was at the king's hand in all matters concerning the people.

Villages outside Jerusalem

25 And as for the villages, with their fields, some of the people of Judah lived in Kiriath-arba and its villages, and in Dibon and its villages, and in Jekabzeel and its villages, [26]and in Jeshua and in Moladah and Beth-pelet, [27]in Hazar-shual, in Beer-sheba and its villages, [28]in Ziklag, in Meconah and its villages, [29]in En-rimmon, in Zorah, in Jarmuth, [30]Zanoah, Adullam, and their villages, Lachish and its fields, and Azekah and its villages. So they camped from Beer-sheba to the valley of Hinnom. [31]The people of Benjamin also lived from Geba

[a] Gk Mss: Heb *And after him*

11:20 inheritance: Meaning family property.

11:21 Ophel: Rather, *the* Ophel, the hill just below and south of the Temple Mount, where they would be nearby but outside the sacred precincts.

11:22 Asaph: A family responsible for authoring Psalms 50 and 73–83.

11:25-36 And as for the villages: The list of those families settling outside Jerusalem in the traditional territories of Judah and Benjamin (see Josh 15:20-63). The territory described is larger than the Persian province of Yehud (Judah).

Imagine how the people felt who returned to their family properties after having been exiled for a generation or more. Think of individuals or peoples who may long to be restored in various ways. How can God's faithful people help those in such circumstances?

onward, at Michmash, Aija, Bethel and its villages, [32]Anathoth, Nob, Ananiah, [33]Hazor, Ramah, Gittaim, [34]Hadid, Zeboim, Neballat, [35]Lod, and Ono, the valley of artisans. [36]And certain divisions of the Levites in Judah were joined to Benjamin.

A List of Priests and Levites

12 These are the priests and the Levites who came up with Zerubbabel son of Shealtiel, and Jeshua: Seraiah, Jeremiah, Ezra, [2]Amariah, Malluch, Hattush, [3]Shecaniah, Rehum, Meremoth, [4]Iddo, Ginnethoi, Abijah, [5]Mijamin, Maadiah, Bilgah, [6]Shemaiah, Joiarib, Jedaiah, [7]Sallu, Amok, Hilkiah, Jedaiah. These were the leaders of the priests and of their associates in the days of Jeshua.

8 And the Levites: Jeshua, Binnui, Kadmiel, Sherebiah, Judah, and Mattaniah, who with his associates was in charge of the songs of thanksgiving. [9]And Bakbukiah and Unno their associates stood opposite them in the service. [10]Jeshua was the father of Joiakim, Joiakim the father of Eliashib, Eliashib the father of Joiada, [11]Joiada the father of Jonathan, and Jonathan the father of Jaddua.

12 In the days of Joiakim the priests, heads of ancestral houses, were: of Seraiah, Meraiah; of Jeremiah, Hananiah; [13]of Ezra, Meshullam; of Amariah, Jehohanan; [14]of Malluchi, Jonathan; of Shebaniah, Joseph; [15]of Harim, Adna; of Meraioth, Helkai; [16]of Iddo, Zechariah; of Ginnethon, Meshullam; [17]of Abijah, Zichri; of Miniamin, of Moadiah, Piltai; [18]of Bilgah, Shammua; of Shemaiah, Jehonathan; [19]of Joiarib, Mattenai; of Jedaiah, Uzzi; [20]of Sallai, Kallai; of Amok, Eber; [21]of Hilkiah, Hashabiah; of Jedaiah, Nethanel.

22 As for the Levites, in the days of Eliashib, Joiada, Johanan, and Jaddua, there were recorded the heads of ancestral houses; also the priests until the reign of Darius the Persian. [23]The Levites, heads of ancestral houses, were recorded in the Book of the Annals until the days of Johanan son of Eliashib. [24]And the leaders of the Levites: Hashabiah, Sherebiah, and Jeshua son of Kadmiel, with their associates over against them, to praise and to give thanks, according to the commandment of David the man of God, section opposite to section. [25]Mattaniah, Bakbukiah, Obadiah, Meshullam, Talmon, and Akkub were gatekeepers standing guard at the storehouses of the gates. [26]These were in the days of Joiakim son of Jeshua son of Jozadak, and in the days of the governor Nehemiah and of the priest Ezra, the scribe.

Dedication of the City Wall

27 Now at the dedication of the wall of Jerusalem they sought out the Levites in all their places, to bring them to Jerusalem to celebrate the dedication with rejoicing, with thanksgivings and with singing, with cymbals, harps, and lyres. [28]The companies of the singers gath-

12:1-7 Zerubbabel...Jeshua: The original governor and high priest who led the initial return of the Jews from exile (see Ezra 2:1-2, 36-39). Listed here are the priestly families from the time of Joiakim, son of Jeshua (see 12:12-21). The author of Ezra-Nehemiah wants to bring his book to a close by uniting the Second Temple priesthood with the returnees, cementing the connection with the First Temple period. See note on Ezra 2:1.

12:10-11 Jeshua was the father of Joiakim: The NRSV is misleading. These verses form a separate paragraph from 12:8-9 and concern not the Levites but rather list the high priestly line in the Second Temple period: Joiakim during the time of Ezra's work, Eliashib and Joiada during Nehemiah's governorship.

12:22 in the days of: Again the NRSV is misleading. "In the days of Eliashib . . ." repeats the list of high priests from 12:10-11 above. Johanan is an alternative spelling of Jonathan (12:11). Darius the Persian would be king Darius III, a contemporary of Alexander the Great.

12:26 in the days of the governor Nehemiah and...Ezra: As mentioned in the introductions to Ezra and Nehemiah, historical difficulties and the theological nature of Ezra-Nehemiah make it difficult to determine who came first or whether their ministries overlapped.

12:27 Now at the dedication of the wall of Jerusalem: As in 1–2 Chronicles and Ezra, the Levites lead the people in joyful worship, with singing accompanied by many musical instruments. This is a festive occasion indeed, the climax of the book of Ezra-Nehemiah, with the processions including the priests and the governor, Nehemiah.

ered together from the circuit around Jerusalem and from the villages
of the Netophathites; 29 also from Beth-gilgal and from the region of
Geba and Azmaveth; for the singers had built for themselves villages
around Jerusalem. 30 And the priests and the Levites purified themselves; and they purified the people and the gates and the wall.

31 Then I brought the leaders of Judah up onto the wall, and appointed two great companies that gave thanks and went in procession. One went to the right on the wall to the Dung Gate; 32 and after
them went Hoshaiah and half the officials of Judah, 33 and Azariah,
Ezra, Meshullam, 34 Judah, Benjamin, Shemaiah, and Jeremiah, 35 and
some of the young priests with trumpets: Zechariah son of Jonathan
son of Shemaiah son of Mattaniah son of Micaiah son of Zaccur son
of Asaph; 36 and his kindred, Shemaiah, Azarel, Milalai, Gilalai, Maai,
Nethanel, Judah, and Hanani, with the musical instruments of David
the man of God; and the scribe Ezra went in front of them. 37 At the
Fountain Gate, in front of them, they went straight up by the stairs of
the city of David, at the ascent of the wall, above the house of David,
to the Water Gate on the east.

38 The other company of those who gave thanks went to the
left,[a] and I followed them with half of the people on the wall, above
the Tower of the Ovens, to the Broad Wall, 39 and above the Gate of
Ephraim, and by the Old Gate, and by the Fish Gate and the Tower
of Hananel and the Tower of the Hundred, to the Sheep Gate; and
they came to a halt at the Gate of the Guard. 40 So both companies of
those who gave thanks stood in the house of God, and I and half of
the officials with me; 41 and the priests Eliakim, Maaseiah, Miniamin,
Micaiah, Elioenai, Zechariah, and Hananiah, with trumpets; 42 and
Maaseiah, Shemaiah, Eleazar, Uzzi, Jehohanan, Malchijah, Elam, and
Ezer. And the singers sang with Jezrahiah as their leader. 43 They offered great sacrifices that day and rejoiced, for God had made them
rejoice with great joy; the women and children also rejoiced. The joy
of Jerusalem was heard far away.

Temple Responsibilities

44 On that day men were appointed over the chambers for the stores,
the contributions, the first fruits, and the tithes, to gather into them
the portions required by the law for the priests and for the Levites
from the fields belonging to the towns; for Judah rejoiced over the
priests and the Levites who ministered. 45 They performed the service of their God and the service of purification, as did the singers
and the gatekeepers, according to the command of David and his son
Solomon. 46 For in the days of David and Asaph long ago there was a
leader of the singers, and there were songs of praise and thanksgiving

[a] Cn: Heb *opposite*

Does your church ever "pull out all the stops" with a procession and many acolytes? If so, when and why? How does this enrich your faith and worship life?

12:43 The joy of Jerusalem was heard far away: No longer is the sound filled with the ominous fear of their neighbors, and it is not mixed with weeping as at the original dedication of the Second Temple foundation when the exiles first returned from Babylon (see Ezra 3:3, 13).

to God. [47]In the days of Zerubbabel and in the days of Nehemiah all
Israel gave the daily portions for the singers and the gatekeepers. They
set apart that which was for the Levites; and the Levites set apart that
which was for the descendants of Aaron.

Foreigners Separated from Israel

13:1 no Ammonite or Moabite: See Deuteronomy 23:3-6. For a more inclusive view see the book of Ruth.

13 On that day they read from the book of Moses in the hearing
of the people; and in it was found written that no Ammonite
or Moabite should ever enter the assembly of God, [2]because they did
not meet the Israelites with bread and water, but hired Balaam against
them to curse them—yet our God turned the curse into a blessing.
[3]When the people heard the law, they separated from Israel all those
of foreign descent.

The Reforms of Nehemiah

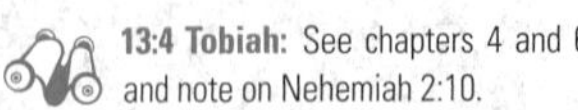

13:4 Tobiah: See chapters 4 and 6, and note on Nehemiah 2:10.

13:6 thirty-second year: 433 B.C.E.

4 Now before this, the priest Eliashib, who was appointed over
the chambers of the house of our God, and who was related to Tobiah, [5]prepared for Tobiah a large room where they had previously
put the grain offering, the frankincense, the vessels, and the tithes of
grain, wine, and oil, which were given by commandment to the Levites, singers, and gatekeepers, and the contributions for the priests.
[6]While this was taking place I was not in Jerusalem, for in the thirty-
second year of King Artaxerxes of Babylon I went to the king. After
some time I asked leave of the king [7]and returned to Jerusalem. I then
discovered the wrong that Eliashib had done on behalf of Tobiah, preparing a room for him in the courts of the house of God. [8]And I was
very angry, and I threw all the household furniture of Tobiah out of
the room. [9]Then I gave orders and they cleansed the chambers, and I
brought back the vessels of the house of God, with the grain offering
and the frankincense.

10 I also found out that the portions of the Levites had not been
given to them; so that the Levites and the singers, who had conducted
the service, had gone back to their fields. [11]So I remonstrated with the
officials and said, "Why is the house of God forsaken?" And I gathered
them together and set them in their stations. [12]Then all Judah brought
the tithe of the grain, wine, and oil into the storehouses. [13]And I appointed as treasurers over the storehouses the priest Shelemiah, the
scribe Zadok, and Pedaiah of the Levites, and as their assistant Hanan
son of Zaccur son of Mattaniah, for they were considered faithful; and
their duty was to distribute to their associates. [14]Remember me, O my
God, concerning this, and do not wipe out my good deeds that I have
done for the house of my God and for his service.

Sabbath Reforms Begun

13:15-31 In those days: This is about Sabbath reform and the problem of mixed marriages. See notes on 10:31 and Ezra 9–10.

15 In those days I saw in Judah people treading wine presses on
the sabbath, and bringing in heaps of grain and loading them on don-

keys; and also wine, grapes, figs, and all kinds of burdens, which they
brought into Jerusalem on the sabbath day; and I warned them at that
time against selling food. [16]Tyrians also, who lived in the city, brought
in fish and all kinds of merchandise and sold them on the sabbath to
the people of Judah, and in Jerusalem. [17]Then I remonstrated with the
nobles of Judah and said to them, "What is this evil thing that you are
doing, profaning the sabbath day? [18]Did not your ancestors act in this
way, and did not our God bring all this disaster on us and on this city?
Yet you bring more wrath on Israel by profaning the sabbath."

19 When it began to be dark at the gates of Jerusalem before the
sabbath, I commanded that the doors should be shut and gave orders that they should not be opened until after the sabbath. And I set
some of my servants over the gates, to prevent any burden from being
brought in on the sabbath day. [20]Then the merchants and sellers of
all kinds of merchandise spent the night outside Jerusalem once or
twice. [21]But I warned them and said to them, "Why do you spend the
night in front of the wall? If you do so again, I will lay hands on you."
From that time on they did not come on the sabbath. [22]And I commanded the Levites that they should purify themselves and come and
guard the gates, to keep the sabbath day holy. Remember this also in
my favor, O my God, and spare me according to the greatness of your
steadfast love.

Mixed Marriages Condemned

23 In those days also I saw Jews who had married women of Ashdod, Ammon, and Moab; [24]and half of their children spoke the language of Ashdod, and they could not speak the language of Judah,
but spoke the language of various peoples. [25]And I contended with
them and cursed them and beat some of them and pulled out their
hair; and I made them take an oath in the name of God, saying, "You
shall not give your daughters to their sons, or take their daughters for
your sons or for yourselves. [26]Did not King Solomon of Israel sin on
account of such women? Among the many nations there was no king
like him, and he was beloved by his God, and God made him king
over all Israel; nevertheless, foreign women made even him to sin.
[27]Shall we then listen to you and do all this great evil and act treacherously against our God by marrying foreign women?"

28 And one of the sons of Jehoiada, son of the high priest Eliashib, was the son-in-law of Sanballat the Horonite; I chased him away
from me. [29]Remember them, O my God, because they have defiled
the priesthood, the covenant of the priests and the Levites.

30 Thus I cleansed them from everything foreign, and I established the duties of the priests and Levites, each in his work; [31]and I
provided for the wood offering, at appointed times, and for the first
fruits. Remember me, O my God, for good.

Ezra and Nehemiah were important leaders in the reform of Israel's faith and life. Centuries later, Martin Luther and others led the way in a reformation of the church. What, if anything, do you think needs reform in the church today? Why?

Esther 9:29-31

ESTHER

Background File

The book of Esther is set in the city of Susa, the winter capital of the Persian Empire. This empire formed when Cyrus brought together the kingdoms of Persia and Media and then defeated the Babylonians in 539 B.C.E. Centered in modern Iran, the Persian Empire eventually reached as far west as northern Greece and as far east as India, before it was conquered by Alexander the Great in 330 B.C.E.

The Persian Empire included a great variety of peoples. Many had been resettled far from their homelands after their nations were conquered by the Assyrians and the Babylonians. This included Jews who were taken from their homeland when the Babylonian king Nebuchadnezzar attacked Jerusalem in 597 B.C.E., then destroyed the city in 587.

The book of Esther uses Persian terms and includes features from the lands, leadership, languages, and royal luxury of the Persian Empire.

What's the Story?

The book of Esther is a comic tale of inept leadership, huge egos, devious plans, unusual events, laugh-out-loud silliness, and startling reversals. It has a festive side and a deadly side. Through a series of banquets and royal decrees, the queen is replaced, the king's chief official rises and falls, and the Jewish people of the kingdom are condemned to death and then raised to power. The book of Esther also introduces the Jewish festival of Purim.

Esther is best read aloud, with others, and with much laughter. When Esther is read publicly, listeners are encouraged to make noise and drown out the name of the "villain" Haman each time it is spoken.

What's the Message?

Like some TV comedies, the book of Esther exaggerates familiar human attitudes and behaviors. People can recognize themselves in the story. The humor exposes foolish thoughts, harmful policies, and human weaknesses.

No features of Jewish faith and life are mentioned in Esther, and there is no direct mention of God. The Jews live scattered among other peoples (3:8). They are subjects of a non-Jewish king and become targets for destruction in a scheme brought to the king by his highest official, Haman. Mordecai's confidence in "relief and deliverance" (4:14) can only rest in God.

Martin Luther once said he wished the book of Esther "did not exist at all," yet the assurance of deliverance and bold service to the neighbor are Lutheran themes. Like Mordecai, we can be confident that God is our deliverer. Like Esther, we can choose to seek deliverance for others.

King Ahasuerus Deposes Queen Vashti

1 This happened in the days of Ahasuerus, the same Ahasuerus
who ruled over one hundred twenty-seven provinces from India to Ethiopia.[a] 2In those days when King Ahasuerus sat on his royal
throne in the citadel of Susa, 3in the third year of his reign, he gave
a banquet for all his officials and ministers. The army of Persia and
Media and the nobles and governors of the provinces were present,
4while he displayed the great wealth of his kingdom and the splendor and pomp of his majesty for many days, one hundred eighty days
in all.

5 When these days were completed, the king gave for all the people present in the citadel of Susa, both great and small, a banquet
lasting for seven days, in the court of the garden of the king's palace.
6There were white cotton curtains and blue hangings tied with cords
of fine linen and purple to silver rings[b] and marble pillars. There were
couches of gold and silver on a mosaic pavement of porphyry, marble,
mother-of-pearl, and colored stones. 7Drinks were served in golden
goblets, goblets of different kinds, and the royal wine was lavished according to the bounty of the king. 8Drinking was by flagons, without
restraint; for the king had given orders to all the officials of his palace
to do as each one desired. 9Furthermore, Queen Vashti gave a banquet for the women in the palace of King Ahasuerus.

10 On the seventh day, when the king was merry with wine, he
commanded Mehuman, Biztha, Harbona, Bigtha and Abagtha, Ze-
thar and Carkas, the seven eunuchs who attended him, 11to bring
Queen Vashti before the king, wearing the royal crown, in order to
show the peoples and the officials her beauty; for she was fair to behold. 12But Queen Vashti refused to come at the king's command
conveyed by the eunuchs. At this the king was enraged, and his anger
burned within him.

13 Then the king consulted the sages who knew the laws[c] (for

1:1 Ahasuerus: No king named Ahasuerus is known. In Ezra 4:6 "Ahasuerus" likely refers to Xerxes I (486–465 B.C.E.).

1:10-22 Queen Vashti refused to come at the king's command: No one in the king's inner circle asks why the king wants to show off the queen's beauty or why the queen refuses. The advisers tell the king to decree that Vashti—who refused to come this time—can never come before the king again.

1:12 eunuchs: In the ancient world, eunuchs were among the senior and most trusted officials serving the king.

---

[a] Or *Nubia;* Heb *Cush* [b] Or *rods* [c] Cn: Heb *times*

this was the king's procedure toward all who were versed in law and
custom, [14]and those next to him were Carshena, Shethar, Admatha,
Tarshish, Meres, Marsena, and Memucan, the seven officials of Persia
and Media, who had access to the king, and sat first in the kingdom):
[15]"According to the law, what is to be done to Queen Vashti because
she has not performed the command of King Ahasuerus conveyed by
the eunuchs?" [16]Then Memucan said in the presence of the king and
the officials, "Not only has Queen Vashti done wrong to the king, but
also to all the officials and all the peoples who are in all the provinces
of King Ahasuerus. [17]For this deed of the queen will be made known
to all women, causing them to look with contempt on their husbands,
since they will say, 'King Ahasuerus commanded Queen Vashti to be
brought before him, and she did not come.' [18]This very day the noble ladies of Persia and Media who have heard of the queen's behavior will rebel against[a] the king's officials, and there will be no end of
contempt and wrath! [19]If it pleases the king, let a royal order go out
from him, and let it be written among the laws of the Persians and the
Medes so that it may not be altered, that Vashti is never again to come
before King Ahasuerus; and let the king give her royal position to another who is better than she. [20]So when the decree made by the king
is proclaimed throughout all his kingdom, vast as it is, all women will
give honor to their husbands, high and low alike."
21 This advice pleased the king and the officials, and the king did
as Memucan proposed; [22]he sent letters to all the royal provinces, to
every province in its own script and to every people in its own language, declaring that every man should be master in his own house.[b]

Esther Becomes Queen

2 After these things, when the anger of King Ahasuerus had abated, he remembered Vashti and what she had done and what had
been decreed against her. [2]Then the king's servants who attended him
said, "Let beautiful young virgins be sought out for the king. [3]And let
the king appoint commissioners in all the provinces of his kingdom
to gather all the beautiful young virgins to the harem in the citadel of
Susa under custody of Hegai, the king's eunuch, who is in charge of
the women; let their cosmetic treatments be given them. [4]And let the
girl who pleases the king be queen instead of Vashti." This pleased the
king, and he did so.
5 Now there was a Jew in the citadel of Susa whose name was
Mordecai son of Jair son of Shimei son of Kish, a Benjaminite. [6]Kish[c]
had been carried away from Jerusalem among the captives carried
away with King Jeconiah of Judah, whom King Nebuchadnezzar of
Babylon had carried away. [7]Mordecai[d] had brought up Hadassah, that

[a] Cn: Heb *will tell* [b] Heb adds *and speak according to the language of his people* [c] Heb *a Benjaminite* [6]*who*
[d] Heb *He*

1:18 no end of contempt: Persian queens may have been involved in government matters, but Vashti would have to have enormous influence, and the king very little respect, to cause this much trouble!

1:21 This advice pleased the king: What pleases the king (and what later pleases Haman) is not always wise or good.

1:22 every people in its own language: This suggests a kingdom of very diverse people.

2:2 Let beautiful young virgins be sought out: This is not the way a match for a king was usually found in the ancient world. The background and abilities of each woman, and the alliances that might be made if she were queen, would have been considered.

2:3 the harem: The Hebrew phrase here is "the house of women." *Harem* can refer to a women's residence. Unlike the description here, women were in charge of harems, the residents were active in royal business and politics, and they were not all wives or concubines.

2:6 among the captives carried away: When the Persians defeated the Babylonians, they helped many Jews who had been taken from their land return home (see Ezra). Other Jews remained in their new lands. Those Jews were likely the earliest audience for the Esther story.

is Esther, his cousin, for she had neither father nor mother; the girl was fair and beautiful, and when her father and her mother died, Mordecai adopted her as his own daughter. [8]So when the king's order and his edict were proclaimed, and when many young women were gathered in the citadel of Susa in custody of Hegai, Esther also was taken into the king's palace and put in custody of Hegai, who had charge of the women. [9]The girl pleased him and won his favor, and he quickly provided her with her cosmetic treatments and her portion of food, and with seven chosen maids from the king's palace, and advanced her and her maids to the best place in the harem. [10]Esther did not reveal her people or kindred, for Mordecai had charged her not to tell. [11]Every day Mordecai would walk around in front of the court of the harem, to learn how Esther was and how she fared.

12 The turn came for each girl to go in to King Ahasuerus, after being twelve months under the regulations for the women, since this was the regular period of their cosmetic treatment, six months with oil of myrrh and six months with perfumes and cosmetics for women. [13]When the girl went in to the king she was given whatever she asked for to take with her from the harem to the king's palace. [14]In the evening she went in; then in the morning she came back to the second harem in custody of Shaashgaz, the king's eunuch, who was in charge of the concubines; she did not go in to the king again, unless the king delighted in her and she was summoned by name.

15 When the turn came for Esther daughter of Abihail the uncle of Mordecai, who had adopted her as his own daughter, to go in to the king, she asked for nothing except what Hegai the king's eunuch, who had charge of the women, advised. Now Esther was admired by all who saw her. [16]When Esther was taken to King Ahasuerus in his royal palace in the tenth month, which is the month of Tebeth, in the seventh year of his reign, [17]the king loved Esther more than all the other women; of all the virgins she won his favor and devotion, so that he set the royal crown on her head and made her queen instead of Vashti. [18]Then the king gave a great banquet to all his officials and ministers—""Esther's banquet." He also granted a holiday[a] to the provinces, and gave gifts with royal liberality.

Mordecai Discovers a Plot

19 When the virgins were being gathered together,[b] Mordecai was sitting at the king's gate. [20]Now Esther had not revealed her kindred or her people, as Mordecai had charged her; for Esther obeyed Mordecai just as when she was brought up by him. [21]In those days, while Mordecai was sitting at the king's gate, Bigthan and Teresh, two of the king's eunuchs, who guarded the threshold, became angry

2:10 did not reveal her people or kindred: No reason is given for Mordecai's instructions to Esther, and it is not clear how she would conceal these things. There appears to be no disadvantage to being Jewish until later on when Haman gets angry.

When do you conceal your Christian identity? When do you reveal it? What would you do if your faith led you into danger?

[a] Or *an amnesty* [b] Heb adds *a second time*

and conspired to assassinate[a] King Ahasuerus. [22]But the matter came to the knowledge of Mordecai, and he told it to Queen Esther, and Esther told the king in the name of Mordecai. [23]When the affair was investigated and found to be so, both the men were hanged on the gallows. It was recorded in the book of the annals in the presence of the king.

Haman Undertakes to Destroy the Jews

3 After these things King Ahasuerus promoted Haman son of Hammedatha the Agagite, and advanced him and set his seat above all the officials who were with him. [2]And all the king's servants who were at the king's gate bowed down and did obeisance to Haman; for the king had so commanded concerning him. But Mordecai did not bow down or do obeisance. [3]Then the king's servants who were at the king's gate said to Mordecai, "Why do you disobey the king's command?" [4]When they spoke to him day after day and he would not listen to them, they told Haman, in order to see whether Mordecai's words would avail; for he had told them that he was a Jew. [5]When Haman saw that Mordecai did not bow down or do obeisance to him, Haman was infuriated. [6]But he thought it beneath him to lay hands on Mordecai alone. So, having been told who Mordecai's people were, Haman plotted to destroy all the Jews, the people of Mordecai, throughout the whole kingdom of Ahasuerus.

7 In the first month, which is the month of Nisan, in the twelfth year of King Ahasuerus, they cast Pur—which means "the lot"—before Haman for the day and for the month, and the lot fell on the thirteenth day[b] of the twelfth month, which is the month of Adar. [8]Then Haman said to King Ahasuerus, "There is a certain people scattered and separated among the peoples in all the provinces of your kingdom; their laws are different from those of every other people, and they do not keep the king's laws, so that it is not appropriate for the king to tolerate them. [9]If it pleases the king, let a decree be issued for their destruction, and I will pay ten thousand talents of silver into the hands of those who have charge of the king's business, so that they may put it into the king's treasuries." [10]So the king took his signet ring from his hand and gave it to Haman son of Hammedatha the Agagite, the enemy of the Jews. [11]The king said to Haman, "The money is given to you, and the people as well, to do with them as it seems good to you."

12 Then the king's secretaries were summoned on the thirteenth day of the first month, and an edict, according to all that Haman commanded, was written to the king's satraps and to the governors over all the provinces and to the officials of all the peoples, to every province

2:22 the matter came to the knowledge of Mordecai: The report of the plot to kill the king seems out of place, especially since it is followed by Haman's promotion, but the details are important later.

3:1 son of Hammedatha the Agagite: Haman descends from the Amalekites, who attacked the Israelites leaving Egypt (Exod 17:8-15; Deut 25:17-19) and were later defeated by King Saul (1 Sam 15). Mordecai is one of Saul's descendants (2:5; 1 Sam 9:1-2).

3:4 for he had told them that he was a Jew: There is no indication that Mordecai refuses to bow down to Haman because he is a Jew, or that other Jews act similarly, but Haman decides to destroy everyone who is a Jew.

Think about ways people have been targeted because of features such as gender, religion, skin color, language, or ethnic heritage. What reasons have been given for this kind of targeting?

3:8-9 their destruction: Haman's words are vague and unclear. He talks about "a certain people" who "do not keep the king's laws" and asks for "their destruction," but he never mentions who these people are, and the king does not ask.

3:9 ten thousand talents of silver: This was an extremely large amount of money.

3:12 an edict, according to all that Haman commanded: The decree to destroy the Jews is now prepared in great detail, in contrast to Haman's vague words earlier (3:8-9).

[a] Heb *to lay hands on* [b] Cn Compare Gk and verse 13 below: Heb *the twelfth month*

in its own script and every people in its own language; it was written
in the name of King Ahasuerus and sealed with the king's ring. 13 Letters were sent by couriers to all the king's provinces, giving orders to
destroy, to kill, and to annihilate all Jews, young and old, women and
children, in one day, the thirteenth day of the twelfth month, which is
the month of Adar, and to plunder their goods. 14 A copy of the document was to be issued as a decree in every province by proclamation,
calling on all the peoples to be ready for that day. 15 The couriers went
quickly by order of the king, and the decree was issued in the citadel
of Susa. The king and Haman sat down to drink; but the city of Susa
was thrown into confusion.

Esther Agrees to Help the Jews

4 When Mordecai learned all that had been done, Mordecai tore
his clothes and put on sackcloth and ashes, and went through
the city, wailing with a loud and bitter cry; 2 he went up to the entrance of the king's gate, for no one might enter the king's gate clothed
with sackcloth. 3 In every province, wherever the king's command and
his decree came, there was great mourning among the Jews, with fasting and weeping and lamenting, and most of them lay in sackcloth
and ashes.

4 When Esther's maids and her eunuchs came and told her, the
queen was deeply distressed; she sent garments to clothe Mordecai,
so that he might take off his sackcloth; but he would not accept them.
5 Then Esther called for Hathach, one of the king's eunuchs, who had
been appointed to attend her, and ordered him to go to Mordecai to
learn what was happening and why. 6 Hathach went out to Mordecai
in the open square of the city in front of the king's gate, 7 and Mordecai
told him all that had happened to him, and the exact sum of money
that Haman had promised to pay into the king's treasuries for the destruction of the Jews. 8 Mordecai also gave him a copy of the written
decree issued in Susa for their destruction, that he might show it to
Esther, explain it to her, and charge her to go to the king to make supplication to him and entreat him for her people.

9 Hathach went and told Esther what Mordecai had said. 10 Then
Esther spoke to Hathach and gave him a message for Mordecai, saying, 11 "All the king's servants and the people of the king's provinces
know that if any man or woman goes to the king inside the inner court
without being called, there is but one law—all alike are to be put to
death. Only if the king holds out the golden scepter to someone, may
that person live. I myself have not been called to come in to the king
for thirty days." 12 When they told Mordecai what Esther had said,
13 Mordecai told them to reply to Esther, "Do not think that in the
king's palace you will escape any more than all the other Jews. 14 For
if you keep silence at such a time as this, relief and deliverance will

4:3 fasting: Fasting is a voluntary decision not to eat or drink (or both) for a period of time. It can be a way of expressing grief (see 1 Sam 31:13; 2 Sam 3:35) or of preparing for a difficult task (see Ezra 8:21-23; Luke 4:1-4). Mordecai is in grief over the king's decree. Esther fasts to prepare to approach the king.

How do Lutherans understand vocation? Vocation is the special calling of each person to serve God and neighbor through every role and relationship in the family, workplace, faith community, and neighborhood. In reminding her that she is a Jew, a family member, and a member of the royal house, Mordecai calls Esther to serve others through those roles and relationships. *Esther 4:13-14*

What are your roles and relationships? How might you be called to serve others through them?

rise for the Jews from another quarter, but you and your father's family will perish. Who knows? Perhaps you have come to royal dignity
for just such a time as this." 15 Then Esther said in reply to Mordecai,
16 "Go, gather all the Jews to be found in Susa, and hold a fast on my
behalf, and neither eat nor drink for three days, night or day. I and my
maids will also fast as you do. After that I will go to the king, though it
is against the law; and if I perish, I perish." 17 Mordecai then went away
and did everything as Esther had ordered him.

4:16 I will go to the king, though it is against the law: The book of Esther makes fun of those who think the society will fall apart when a woman makes choices (1:13-22). It honors Esther, who chooses to go where she is not invited and put her life on the line to save others.

Esther's Banquet

5 On the third day Esther put on her royal robes and stood in the
inner court of the king's palace, opposite the king's hall. The
king was sitting on his royal throne inside the palace opposite the entrance to the palace. 2 As soon as the king saw Queen Esther standing
in the court, she won his favor and he held out to her the golden scepter that was in his hand. Then Esther approached and touched the
top of the scepter. 3 The king said to her, "What is it, Queen Esther?
What is your request? It shall be given you, even to the half of my
kingdom." 4 Then Esther said, "If it pleases the king, let the king and
Haman come today to a banquet that I have prepared for the king."
5 Then the king said, "Bring Haman quickly, so that we may do as Esther desires." So the king and Haman came to the banquet that Esther
had prepared. 6 While they were drinking wine, the king said to Esther, "What is your petition? It shall be granted you. And what is your
request? Even to the half of my kingdom, it shall be fulfilled." 7 Then
Esther said, "This is my petition and request: 8 If I have won the king's
favor, and if it pleases the king to grant my petition and fulfill my request, let the king and Haman come tomorrow to the banquet that I
will prepare for them, and then I will do as the king has said."

Haman Plans to Have Mordecai Hanged

9 Haman went out that day happy and in good spirits. But when
Haman saw Mordecai in the king's gate, and observed that he neither
rose nor trembled before him, he was infuriated with Mordecai; 10 nevertheless Haman restrained himself and went home. Then he sent and
called for his friends and his wife Zeresh, 11 and Haman recounted to
them the splendor of his riches, the number of his sons, all the pro-
motions with which the king had honored him, and how he had advanced him above the officials and the ministers of the king. 12 Haman
added, "Even Queen Esther let no one but myself come with the king
to the banquet that she prepared. Tomorrow also I am invited by her,
together with the king. 13 Yet all this does me no good so long as I see
the Jew Mordecai sitting at the king's gate." 14 Then his wife Zeresh and
all his friends said to him, "Let a gallows fifty cubits high be made, and
in the morning tell the king to have Mordecai hanged on it; then go

5:9-19 he was infuriated: When Mordecai again doesn't bow down to him, Haman is so consumed with anger that he plans to hang the man the next morning. When Cain let his disappointment and anger take control, he murdered his brother Abel (Gen 4).

5:14 fifty cubits: A basic cubit is the length of a forearm, about 18–20 inches or .5 meter, making the gallows built by Haman about 75 feet (22.86 meters) tall!

with the king to the banquet in good spirits." This advice pleased Haman, and he had the gallows made.

The King Honors Mordecai

6 On that night the king could not sleep, and he gave orders to bring the book of records, the annals, and they were read to the king. 2 It was found written how Mordecai had told about Bigthana and Teresh, two of the king's eunuchs, who guarded the threshold, and who had conspired to assassinate[a] King Ahasuerus. 3 Then the king said, "What honor or distinction has been bestowed on Mordecai for this?" The king's servants who attended him said, "Nothing has been done for him." 4 The king said, "Who is in the court?" Now Haman had just entered the outer court of the king's palace to speak to the king about having Mordecai hanged on the gallows that he had prepared for him. 5 So the king's servants told him, "Haman is there, standing in the court." The king said, "Let him come in." 6 So Haman came in, and the king said to him, "What shall be done for the man whom the king wishes to honor?" Haman said to himself, "Whom would the king wish to honor more than me?" 7 So Haman said to the king, "For the man whom the king wishes to honor, 8 let royal robes be brought, which the king has worn, and a horse that the king has ridden, with a royal crown on its head. 9 Let the robes and the horse be handed over to one of the king's most noble officials; let him[b] robe the man whom the king wishes to honor, and let him[b] conduct the man on horseback through the open square of the city, proclaiming before him: 'Thus shall it be done for the man whom the king wishes to honor.' " 10 Then the king said to Haman, "Quickly, take the robes and the horse, as you have said, and do so to the Jew Mordecai who sits at the king's gate. Leave out nothing that you have mentioned." 11 So Haman took the robes and the horse and robed Mordecai and led him riding through the open square of the city, proclaiming, "Thus shall it be done for the man whom the king wishes to honor."

12 Then Mordecai returned to the king's gate, but Haman hurried to his house, mourning and with his head covered. 13 When Haman told his wife Zeresh and all his friends everything that had happened to him, his advisers and his wife Zeresh said to him, "If Mordecai, before whom your downfall has begun, is of the Jewish people, you will not prevail against him, but will surely fall before him."

Haman's Downfall and Mordecai's Advancement

14 While they were still talking with him, the king's eunuchs arrived and hurried Haman off to the banquet that Esther had prepared.

---

[a] Heb *to lay hands on* [b] Heb *them*

6:1-3 What honor or distinction has been bestowed on Mordecai for this?: The king has trouble sleeping, so he reads the record of his own reign and wonders whether anything was done for the person who saved his life. This episode is comic, full of coincidences—and well-timed, because it interrupts Haman's plan to have Mordecai hanged that day.

6:10 the Jew Mordecai: The king is clearly aware that Mordecai is a Jew, but acts as if he does not know about the decree to destroy the Jews.

6:11 the man whom the king wishes to honor: Honor is a recurring theme in Esther 5 and 6. One dimension of honor relates to status, praise, and respect (see Deut 26:19; Judg 13:17; 1 Cor 12:20-26); another is loyal action (see 1 Sam 2:30; Exod 20:12; John 12:26).

7:3-4 this damage to the king: Esther does not say why her life is threatened or who her people are. She indirectly refers to the money Haman offered the king (3:9, 11) and to the decree to destroy the Jews (3:13). She says these things are harmful to the king!

The king asks, "Who has presumed to do this?" Is he unaware of what has been happening? Is he harmless, easily misled, or is he guilty of evil?

7:8 Will he even assault the queen ...in my own house?: Haman throws himself upon Esther to beg for mercy and is accused of sexual assault.

7:9 Hang him on that: Haman is hanged for a crime he did not actually commit, on the gallows he built for Mordecai.

7 [1]So the king and Haman went in to feast with Queen Esther. [2]On the second day, as they were drinking wine, the king again said to Esther, "What is your petition, Queen Esther? It shall be granted you. And what is your request? Even to the half of my kingdom, it shall be fulfilled." [3]Then Queen Esther answered, "If I have won your favor, O king, and if it pleases the king, let my life be given me—that is my petition—and the lives of my people—that is my request. [4]For we have been sold, I and my people, to be destroyed, to be killed, and to be annihilated. If we had been sold merely as slaves, men and women, I would have held my peace; but no enemy can compensate for this damage to the king."[a] [5]Then King Ahasuerus said to Queen Esther, "Who is he, and where is he, who has presumed to do this?" [6]Esther said, "A foe and enemy, this wicked Haman!" Then Haman was terrified before the king and the queen. [7]The king rose from the feast in wrath and went into the palace garden, but Haman stayed to beg his life from Queen Esther, for he saw that the king had determined to destroy him. [8]When the king returned from the palace garden to the banquet hall, Haman had thrown himself on the couch where Esther was reclining; and the king said, "Will he even assault the queen in my presence, in my own house?" As the words left the mouth of the king, they covered Haman's face. [9]Then Harbona, one of the eunuchs in attendance on the king, said, "Look, the very gallows that Haman has prepared for Mordecai, whose word saved the king, stands at Haman's house, fifty cubits high." And the king said, "Hang him on that." [10]So they hanged Haman on the gallows that he had prepared for Mordecai. Then the anger of the king abated.

Esther Saves the Jews

8 On that day King Ahasuerus gave to Queen Esther the house of Haman, the enemy of the Jews; and Mordecai came before the king, for Esther had told what he was to her. [2]Then the king took off his signet ring, which he had taken from Haman, and gave it to Mordecai. So Esther set Mordecai over the house of Haman.

3 Then Esther spoke again to the king; she fell at his feet, weeping and pleading with him to avert the evil design of Haman the Agagite and the plot that he had devised against the Jews. [4]The king held out the golden scepter to Esther, [5]and Esther rose and stood before the king. She said, "If it pleases the king, and if I have won his favor, and if the thing seems right before the king, and I have his approval, let an order be written to revoke the letters devised by Haman son of Hammedatha the Agagite, which he wrote giving orders to destroy the Jews who are in all the provinces of the king. [6]For how can I bear to see the calamity that is coming on my people? Or how can I bear

[a] Meaning of Heb uncertain

to see the destruction of my kindred?" 7Then King Ahasuerus said to Queen Esther and to the Jew Mordecai, "See, I have given Esther the house of Haman, and they have hanged him on the gallows, because he plotted to lay hands on the Jews. 8You may write as you please with regard to the Jews, in the name of the king, and seal it with the king's ring; for an edict written in the name of the king and sealed with the king's ring cannot be revoked."

9 The king's secretaries were summoned at that time, in the third month, which is the month of Sivan, on the twenty-third day; and an edict was written, according to all that Mordecai commanded, to the Jews and to the satraps and the governors and the officials of the provinces from India to Ethiopia,[a] one hundred twenty-seven provinces, to every province in its own script and to every people in its own language, and also to the Jews in their script and their language. 10He wrote letters in the name of King Ahasuerus, sealed them with the king's ring, and sent them by mounted couriers riding on fast steeds bred from the royal herd.[b] 11By these letters the king allowed the Jews who were in every city to assemble and defend their lives, to destroy, to kill, and to annihilate any armed force of any people or province that might attack them, with their children and women, and to plunder their goods 12on a single day throughout all the provinces of King Ahasuerus, on the thirteenth day of the twelfth month, which is the month of Adar. 13A copy of the writ was to be issued as a decree in every province and published to all peoples, and the Jews were to be ready on that day to take revenge on their enemies. 14So the couriers, mounted on their swift royal steeds, hurried out, urged by the king's command. The decree was issued in the citadel of Susa.

15 Then Mordecai went out from the presence of the king, wearing royal robes of blue and white, with a great golden crown and a mantle of fine linen and purple, while the city of Susa shouted and rejoiced. 16For the Jews there was light and gladness, joy and honor. 17In every province and in every city, wherever the king's command and his edict came, there was gladness and joy among the Jews, a festival and a holiday. Furthermore, many of the peoples of the country professed to be Jews, because the fear of the Jews had fallen upon them.

8:8 cannot be revoked: The system of Persian laws prevented random, unpredictable rulings, but there is no evidence that laws could not be changed.

8:10-14 He wrote letters: Mordecai's decree copies the language and tone of the one composed by Haman, but it permits the Jews to defend themselves on the day of attack.

Destruction of the Enemies of the Jews

9 Now in the twelfth month, which is the month of Adar, on the thirteenth day, when the king's command and edict were about to be executed, on the very day when the enemies of the Jews hoped to gain power over them, but which had been changed to a day when the Jews would gain power over their foes, 2the Jews gathered in their cities throughout all the provinces of King Ahasuerus to lay hands on

---

[a]Or *Nubia;* Heb *Cush* [b] Meaning of Heb uncertain

those who had sought their ruin; and no one could withstand them, because the fear of them had fallen upon all peoples. [3]All the officials of the provinces, the satraps and the governors, and the royal officials were supporting the Jews, because the fear of Mordecai had fallen upon them. [4]For Mordecai was powerful in the king's house, and his fame spread throughout all the provinces as the man Mordecai grew more and more powerful. [5]So the Jews struck down all their enemies with the sword, slaughtering, and destroying them, and did as they pleased to those who hated them. [6]In the citadel of Susa the Jews killed and destroyed five hundred people. [7]They killed Parshandatha, Dalphon, Aspatha, [8]Poratha, Adalia, Aridatha, [9]Parmashta, Arisai, Aridai, Vaizatha, [10]the ten sons of Haman son of Hammedatha, the enemy of the Jews; but they did not touch the plunder.

11 That very day the number of those killed in the citadel of Susa was reported to the king. [12]The king said to Queen Esther, "In the citadel of Susa the Jews have killed five hundred people and also the ten sons of Haman. What have they done in the rest of the king's provinces? Now what is your petition? It shall be granted you. And what further is your request? It shall be fulfilled." [13]Esther said, "If it pleases the king, let the Jews who are in Susa be allowed tomorrow also to do according to this day's edict, and let the ten sons of Haman be hanged on the gallows." [14]So the king commanded this to be done; a decree was issued in Susa, and the ten sons of Haman were hanged. [15]The Jews who were in Susa gathered also on the fourteenth day of the month of Adar and they killed three hundred persons in Susa; but they did not touch the plunder.

16 Now the other Jews who were in the king's provinces also gathered to defend their lives, and gained relief from their enemies, and killed seventy-five thousand of those who hated them; but they laid no hands on the plunder. [17]This was on the thirteenth day of the month of Adar, and on the fourteenth day they rested and made that a day of feasting and gladness.

The Feast of Purim Inaugurated

18 But the Jews who were in Susa gathered on the thirteenth day and on the fourteenth, and rested on the fifteenth day, making that a day of feasting and gladness. [19]Therefore the Jews of the villages, who live in the open towns, hold the fourteenth day of the month of Adar as a day for gladness and feasting, a holiday on which they send gifts of food to one another.

20 Mordecai recorded these things, and sent letters to all the Jews who were in all the provinces of King Ahasuerus, both near and far, [21]enjoining them that they should keep the fourteenth day of the month Adar and also the fifteenth day of the same month, year by year, [22]as the days on which the Jews gained relief from their enemies,

9:3 royal officials were supporting the Jews: The king's officials hear about Mordecai's power, and all of them now support the Jews. What takes place is the opposite of what Haman wanted.

9:12 what further is your request?: It is not clear why the king offers and why Esther requests an additional day of killing and the hanging of Haman's sons, or why so many citizens follow Haman's decree.

9:16 relief from their enemies: While Haman's decree (3:13) targeted Jews, their "enemies" are not a group identified by religion, nationality, or language.

9:16 they laid no hands on the plunder: The repeated note about the Jews not taking stolen goods (9:10, 15) indicates that they seek "relief from their enemies," not their neighbors' possessions.

9:22 presents to the poor: The Jews celebrate relief from their enemies partly by providing relief to people in need.

and as the month that had been turned for them from sorrow into
gladness and from mourning into a holiday; that they should make
them days of feasting and gladness, days for sending gifts of food to
one another and presents to the poor. 23 So the Jews adopted as a custom what they had begun to do, as Mordecai had written to them.

24 Haman son of Hammedatha the Agagite, the enemy of all
the Jews, had plotted against the Jews to destroy them, and had cast
Pur—that is "the lot"—to crush and destroy them; 25 but when Esther
came before the king, he gave orders in writing that the wicked plot
that he had devised against the Jews should come upon his own head,
and that he and his sons should be hanged on the gallows. 26 Therefore these days are called Purim, from the word Pur. Thus because
of all that was written in this letter, and of what they had faced in this
matter, and of what had happened to them, 27 the Jews established and
accepted as a custom for themselves and their descendants and all
who joined them, that without fail they would continue to observe
these two days every year, as it was written and at the time appointed.
28 These days should be remembered and kept throughout every generation, in every family, province, and city; and these days of Purim
should never fall into disuse among the Jews, nor should the com-
memoration of these days cease among their descendants.

29 Queen Esther daughter of Abihail, along with the Jew Mordecai, gave full written authority, confirming this second letter about
Purim. 30 Letters were sent wishing peace and security to all the Jews,
to the one hundred twenty-seven provinces of the kingdom of Ahasuerus, 31 and giving orders that these days of Purim should be observed
at their appointed seasons, as the Jew Mordecai and Queen Esther
enjoined on the Jews, just as they had laid down for themselves and
for their descendants regulations concerning their fasts and their lamentations. 32 The command of Queen Esther fixed these practices of
Purim, and it was recorded in writing.

10 King Ahasuerus laid tribute on the land and on the islands
of the sea. 2 All the acts of his power and might, and the full
account of the high honor of Mordecai, to which the king advanced
him, are they not written in the annals of the kings of Media and Persia? 3 For Mordecai the Jew was next in rank to King Ahasuerus, and
he was powerful among the Jews and popular with his many kindred,
for he sought the good of his people and interceded for the welfare of
all his descendants.

9:32 The command of Queen Esther fixed these practices of Purim: Two days of feasting and gladness will be celebrated each year by the Jews.

10:2 the high honor of Mordecai: Mordecai provides an example of a Jew finding favor and providing superior leadership in a non-Jewish court.

The end of the book does not mention Vashti or Esther. Why should Vashti be remembered? How is Esther an example of faith?

WISDOM AND POETRY BOOKS

Job to Song of Solomon

Following the Historical Books, the next major division in the Christian Old Testament includes a set of writings that are predominantly poetry and practical wisdom. They include Job, Psalms, Proverbs, Ecclesiastes, and the Song of Solomon. Of course, poetry is present in many other biblical books, including the Prophetic Books where prophetic speeches called oracles are usually delivered in Hebrew verse. But the books that make up the Writings are defined in part by what they are **not**. They are not part of the Pentateuch, the Historical Books, or the Prophets. In the Hebrew Bible, these and six other books (Ruth, Lamentations, Esther, Daniel, Ezra-Nehemiah and 1-2 Chronicles) are collected in the third and concluding section and called the Writings (see chart Different Canons of the Hebrew Bible, pp. 28-29).

Several of these books are associated with Israel's King Solomon (Prov 1:1; 25:1; Eccl 1:1; Song 1:1), because of his renowned personal wisdom and skill as an author (1 Kgs 4:29-34). A close reading, however, shows that not all of these writings claim Solomon's authorship (Prov 22:17–23:11; 24:23-24; 30:1; 31:1, 11). Other books in this section are judged to have been written much later than the time of Solomon, based on criteria such as grammar and vocabulary. Nevertheless, and in the same way that Moses became linked to the entire Pentateuch and David was linked to the book of Psalms, Solomon came to be associated with poetic works and especially with practical wisdom.

Wisdom Literature

Scholars classify three of these books, Job, Proverbs, and Ecclesiastes, as Wisdom literature. Two other books collected in the Apocrypha (or Deuterocanon), Sirach and the Wisdom of Solomon, are also considered part of the wisdom tradition. The theological views of these books vary considerably, although all wrestle with problems of living faithfully in the real world.

Generally speaking, wisdom thinking is rooted in creation. The wise teachers (sages) developed their advice from observations of nature and society. Lessons could be learned from ants (Prov 6:6-8) or lazy farmers (Prov 24:30-34) since, it was assumed, God had created an orderly world in which people usually got the reward or punishment they earned. Individuals were considered able to make wise choices in life, and they were summoned by the sages to do so.

The confident worldview so firmly set forth in Proverbs came under suspicion in Job with that book's scrutiny of undeserved suffering. Ecclesiastes was even less confident in the human ability to discover wisdom or meaning in life; its author advises readers simply to enjoy the vain life they have been given (Eccl 2:24; 9:7-8).

Although Wisdom thinking is sometimes thought to be more "secular" than the rest of the Bible, it appears that Wisdom simply assumes faith in the LORD and reliance on God's law. True wisdom is a gift of God (Prov 2:6-7), which originates in the fear of the LORD (Prov 1:7; 9:10; Job 28:28; Sir 1:14). Of course, to speak of the "fear of the LORD" does not mean dread, but rather worshipful awe and respect, such as Luther had in mind in his explanation of the Commandments in the Small Catechism ("We are to fear and love God, so that . . .").

The Psalms

The Psalms consist of 150 poems, mostly addressed to God and evidently sung as a part of worship. Like hymns in a modern hymnal, these poems were written by many people over centuries, although they were collected and given their present order during the Second Temple period (sometime after 515 B.C.E.). The psalms are arranged into five "books" (Pss 1–41, 42–72, 73–89, 90–106, 107–150), likely in imitation of the five books of the Pentateuch. This feature also reflects an increasing appreciation of the Psalms as authoritative scripture among Jews and early Christians (Luke 24:44). But beyond that, determining the date when individual psalms were written remains a challenge to biblical scholars.

The name Psalms is derived from a Greek word meaning "songs of praise." That title is based on the Hebrew title for the book: The Book of Praises. This name is ironic, given that psalms of sadness or mourning (laments) of individuals and of the community occupy a full third of the Psalms. Lament psalms are important, however, since they provide a worshipful voice for believers who find themselves in pain or distress. Laments help remind communities of faith that God is present to save precisely in such times.

Beyond laments, there are also songs of thanksgiving, hymns, royal psalms (likely used in coronation festivals), psalms celebrating God's protection of Zion or praising God as king, and "Psalms of Ascent," sung as believers traveled to Jerusalem. Finally, a few psalms reflect wisdom theology, because they aim to instruct believers or to reflect on human mortality (Pss 1, 37, 112, 128). For more on psalm types, see the chart, pp. 849-850.

The Song of Solomon

The Song of Solomon, also known as the Song of Songs, celebrates human love. The book consists mostly of love poems between a man and a woman. Jewish and Christian traditions have long seen in these poems an allegory of God's love for God's people.

Job 2:8

JOB

Background File

The author of the book of Job is unknown. He was likely a Jew writing to other Jews, because he quotes from other biblical books and refers to God as Yahweh. Yahweh is the divine name revealed to Israel and written in English as LORD. The date of the book's composition is debated. Most scholars place it in the Babylonian exile (sixth century B.C.E. or later).

What's the Story?

The book of Job is the story of a good, innocent man who suffers terrible loss. Everything he has is destroyed: his wealth, his beloved children, and his health. Three friends come to comfort him and offer reasons for Job's misfortunes, but Job will have none of it. He protests his innocence, he yells, he dares God to answer him. At the end of the book, God does indeed answer him, with a vision of creation in all its glory.

The book of Job should not be read as history. Rather, it should be read as a meditation on the problem of undeserved suffering. It explores questions such as: "Why do the innocent suffer?" "Where is God in my suffering?" "What kind of world is this?" These questions are as old as the Bible and as new as today's newspaper.

The story can be outlined in the following way:

Introduction (chapters 1–2). The book introduces Job, a righteous man—meaning he is in right relationship with God. God and the Satan talk about Job. The Satan argues that Job is righteous only because he gets rewarded for *being* righteous. God allows the Satan to test Job two times, by destroying his property, children, and health. Job responds piously, with respect for God, both times. Job's three friends, Eliphaz, Bildad, and Zophar, come to comfort him.

Dialogue (chapters 3–28). After an initial prayer of sadness and anger (lament) by Job, he and his three friends argue about the reasons for his suffering. The friends claim that Job must have done something wrong to deserve such suffering. Job protests that he is innocent and calls on God to go to court with him, to answer him directly. The dialogue ends with a poem about the search for wisdom.

Job's final defense (chapters 29-31). Job offers a final defense of himself. He takes a long oath of innocence and calls on God to answer him.

Elihu's Speech (chapters 32-37). Elihu, a young man, enters the story and offers his own explanations for Job's suffering, which are not significantly different from the explanations of the friends.

God's speeches (chapters 38-41). The LORD answers Job out of a whirlwind. God takes Job on a tour of the cosmos, or universe, describing to him the heavens, the earth, the sea, the wild animals, and the mythological creatures Behemoth and Leviathan. All the while, God asks Job questions, such as "Do you know?" "Were you there?" "Are you able?" Job responds with silence.

Conclusion (chapter 42). Job responds a second time to God's speeches, this time acknowledging that he spoke of things he didn't know. God chastises Job's three friends and commends Job. God blesses Job with more children and restores Job's fortunes, granting him a long life.

What's the Message?

Job is a complicated book, because it addresses a very difficult question: "Why do the innocent suffer?" Perhaps the author of Job knew there was no final answer to that question and that's why he incorporates so many different "voices" in his story. Even God does not answer the question directly. Instead, God speaks about creation. The book of Job does claim certain things about suffering, about God, and about the world.

Suffering is not always the result of sin. There was widespread belief in the ancient world that suffering was punishment for sin. The friends of Job hold this belief, repeatedly accusing Job of sin and calling for him to repent. Job maintains his innocence. His suffering is not the result of sin, and his friends' accusations only add to his suffering.

Prayer (including lament) is the proper response to suffering. The book of Job teaches its readers about the power of prayer. Job is the only human being in the book who speaks to God directly. The friends talk *about* God, but they never speak *to* God. In the end, Job is commended for speaking to God (42:7-8). Job's speaking most often takes the form of lament—an honest cry of anger and anguish to God. The Old Testament claims that lament is a faithful response to suffering (see also Pss 13; 22; 74).

God cares for the good creation God has made and takes delight in it. At the end of the book, God takes Job on a grand tour of the cosmos. God does not speak of Job's suffering, but instead takes Job's focus off himself and helps him see the world around him. The world, as God describes it, is a good, ordered creation, but it is also given a certain freedom. God takes delight in the wildest of creatures—the sea, the wild animals, Leviathan. God cares for them as God also cares for Job. In the face of his suffering, Job is invited to see and delight in the world God has created. Job is invited to live in it with the same freedom God gives all God's creatures. In spite of his great suffering, Job accepts that invitation and chooses to live and to love again.

The book of Job is a profound meditation on the mystery of suffering. It invites new questions and new interpretations from every generation of readers. Most importantly, it invites its readers into an encounter with God, the God of life who created and sustains the world in love and who, through the cross of Christ, enters fully into the suffering of that world and redeems it.

Job and His Family

1 There was once a man in the land of Uz whose name was Job. That
man was blameless and upright, one who feared God and turned
away from evil. 2 There were born to him seven sons and three daughters. 3 He had seven thousand sheep, three thousand camels, five hundred yoke of oxen, five hundred donkeys, and very many servants; so
that this man was the greatest of all the people of the east. 4 His sons
used to go and hold feasts in one another's houses in turn; and they
would send and invite their three sisters to eat and drink with them.
5 And when the feast days had run their course, Job would send and
sanctify them, and he would rise early in the morning and offer burnt
offerings according to the number of them all; for Job said, "It may be
that my children have sinned, and cursed God in their hearts." This is
what Job always did.

Attack on Job's Character

6 One day the heavenly beings[a] came to present themselves before the LORD, and Satan[b] also came among them. 7 The LORD said
to Satan,[b] "Where have you come from?" Satan[b] answered the LORD,
"From going to and fro on the earth, and from walking up and down
on it." 8 The LORD said to Satan,[b] "Have you considered my servant
Job? There is no one like him on the earth, a blameless and upright
man who fears God and turns away from evil." 9 Then Satan[b] answered
the LORD, "Does Job fear God for nothing? 10 Have you not put a
fence around him and his house and all that he has, on every side?
You have blessed the work of his hands, and his possessions have increased in the land. 11 But stretch out your hand now, and touch all
that he has, and he will curse you to your face." 12 The LORD said to
Satan,[b] "Very well, all that he has is in your power; only do not stretch
out your hand against him!" So Satan[b] went out from the presence
of the LORD.

[a] Heb *sons of God* [b] Or *the Accuser;* Heb *ha-satan*

1:1-5 Job…was blameless and upright: Job is mentioned once in the Old Testament as an example of a very righteous man (Ezek 14:12-20) and once in the New Testament, (James 5:11), as an example of patience or endurance. The latter reference is striking, as the Job we encounter in the core of this book (chapters 3–41) is anything but patient! Many biblical scholars think that the story about Job may have been taken from an older folktale that the author of Job used as the framework for his book. It's possible that Job is not a historical figure but a folktale hero used by the author of the book to "set up" the problem of undeserved suffering.

1:1 land of Uz: The location of Uz is unknown. The name appears as a personal name in genealogies in Genesis (Gen 10:23; 22:21; 36:28) and is associated with the land of Edom in Lamentations 4:21. Job is not described as an Israelite but as the "greatest of all the people of the east" (1:3).

1:6 heavenly beings: Also called the "sons of God," they are heavenly beings or angels that attend God in God's court. (For other biblical images of this heavenly court, see 1 Kgs 22:19; Pss 82:1; 89:5-8; Isa 6:1-3; and Dan 7:9-10.)

1:6 Satan: "Satan" here is a title, not a proper name. The Hebrew text says "*the* Satan." This is not the same figure as the devil. Instead, the Satan in Job is best understood as something like a prosecuting attorney, someone who is given the task of investigating wrongdoing and bringing it to God's attention. The word *satan* in Hebrew means "accuser" or "adversary."

Job Loses Property and Children

13 One day when his sons and daughters were eating and drinking wine in the eldest brother's house, [14]a messenger came to Job and
said, "The oxen were plowing and the donkeys were feeding beside
them, [15]and the Sabeans fell on them and carried them off, and killed
the servants with the edge of the sword; I alone have escaped to tell
you." [16]While he was still speaking, another came and said, "The fire
of God fell from heaven and burned up the sheep and the servants,
and consumed them; I alone have escaped to tell you." [17]While he was
still speaking, another came and said, "The Chaldeans formed three
columns, made a raid on the camels and carried them off, and killed
the servants with the edge of the sword; I alone have escaped to tell
you." [18]While he was still speaking, another came and said, "Your sons
and daughters were eating and drinking wine in their eldest brother's
house, [19]and suddenly a great wind came across the desert, struck the
four corners of the house, and it fell on the young people, and they are
dead; I alone have escaped to tell you."

20 Then Job arose, tore his robe, shaved his head, and fell on the
ground and worshiped. [21]He said, "Naked I came from my mother's
womb, and naked shall I return there; the LORD gave, and the LORD
has taken away; blessed be the name of the LORD."

22 In all this Job did not sin or charge God with wrongdoing.

Attack on Job's Health

2 One day the heavenly beings[a] came to present themselves before the LORD, and Satan[b] also came among them to present
himself before the LORD. [2]The LORD said to Satan,[b] "Where have you
come from?" Satan[b] answered the LORD, "From going to and fro on
the earth, and from walking up and down on it." [3]The LORD said to
Satan,[b] "Have you considered my servant Job? There is no one like
him on the earth, a blameless and upright man who fears God and
turns away from evil. He still persists in his integrity, although you
incited me against him, to destroy him for no reason." [4]Then Satan[b]
answered the LORD, "Skin for skin! All that people have they will give
to save their lives.[c] [5]But stretch out your hand now and touch his bone
and his flesh, and he will curse you to your face." [6]The LORD said to
Satan,[b] "Very well, he is in your power; only spare his life."

7 So Satan[b] went out from the presence of the LORD, and inflicted loathsome sores on Job from the sole of his foot to the crown of
his head. [8]Job[d] took a potsherd with which to scrape himself, and sat
among the ashes.

9 Then his wife said to him, "Do you still persist in your integrity?

---

[a] Heb *sons of God* [b] Or *the Accuser;* Heb *ha-satan* [c] Or *All that the man has he will give for his life*
[d] Heb *He*

1:9-10 Does Job fear God for nothing?: The book of Job is filled with questions. The questions the Satan asks in these verses set into motion the whole story. The Satan accuses Job of self-interest. According to the Satan, Job believes in God and obeys God only because of what Job gets out of it. If God takes away all the blessings, Job will curse God.

What do you think of the Satan's question? Can you love God for who God is and not for what you get out of the relationship?

1:13—2:10 One day...In all this Job did not sin with his lips: The narrator does not spend much time describing the disasters that befall Job. The narrator is more interested in how Job will respond. Job's response takes up the next twenty-nine chapters of the book. This prologue sets up the problem of undeserved suffering—that will be the topic of the rest of the book.

1:21 [Job] said: Job responds to the loss of his children by using the language of birth. He will not return to the womb of his mother but rather to the "womb" of "Mother Earth," or the grave. Described in the language of maternal care, this return to the womb is not necessarily something to be feared.

Job is stripped naked of what helps to give a person identity—family and possessions. Exposed and vulnerable, he still continues to trust in the God who gave him life in the first place: "The LORD gave, and the LORD has taken away; blessed be the name of the LORD."

Try to put yourself in Job's place. How would you react to such terrible losses? What would you say to God?

2:9-10 But [Job] said: Job's first response to his losses is remarkable: "Blessed be the name of the LORD." His wife, who shares in the loss of wealth and children, is more bitter: "Curse God, and die!" Job's second response is a question, not a statement, and it does not include any praise of God: "Shall we receive the good at the hand of God, and not receive the bad?" This is a hint of the accusations Job will soon throw at God.

2:11-13 **Job's three friends… comfort him:** The actions of Job's three friends—tearing their clothes and putting dust on their heads—was a ritual for expressing grief in the ancient world. They sit with him in silence for seven days. Such a custom is still practiced today in Jewish homes. The immediate family of a deceased person "sits shiva" (*shiva* is from the Hebrew word for "seven") for seven days after the funeral, staying together in one house and receiving visits from those who would comfort them.

What would you do if you were Job's friend? How would you care for someone who had experienced such suffering?

What does the concept "theology of the cross" mean? Martin Luther said that a theologian of the cross knows a God hidden in suffering and knows God through the cross of Christ. He wrote, "God can be found only in suffering and the cross" (*Heidelberg Disputation*, thesis 21). When we suffer, or when we walk with those who suffer, we may encounter God. *Job 2:11-13*

3:1—27:23 After this Job opened his mouth: The core of the book is dialogue between Job and his three friends. The dialogue has three cycles (chapters 3–14; 15–21; and 22–27). In each cycle, the friends speak to Job in the same order: first Eliphaz, then Bildad, then Zophar, and Job responds to each of them in turn. The last cycle of the dialogue breaks down and the friends are silenced.

3:1-26 Job opened his mouth and cursed: Notice the difference between chapters 1–2 and chapter 3. In chapter 3 Job is anything but patient! He curses the day of his birth and wishes for death, so that his suffering might end. Job repeats this death wish later in the book (7:15-16; 10:18-19). As the book continues, however, Job stops wishing for death and starts wishing for justice. Eventually he wants to go to court with God so that things can be settled.

3:3-10 Let the day perish: Modern commentators Michael Fishbane and Norman Habel have noted that Job uses the language of creation from Genesis 1 to curse the day of his birth. God says, "Let there be light" (Gen 1:3). Using the same Hebrew verb, Job says, "Let that day be darkness!" (3:4). The seven days of creation in Genesis 1 end in the rest of Sabbath; Job's curse on creation ends in

Curse[a] God, and die." [10]But he said to her, "You speak as any foolish
woman would speak. Shall we receive the good at the hand of God,
and not receive the bad?" In all this Job did not sin with his lips.

Job's Three Friends

11 Now when Job's three friends heard of all these troubles that
had come upon him, each of them set out from his home—Eliphaz
the Temanite, Bildad the Shuhite, and Zophar the Naamathite. They
met together to go and console and comfort him. [12]When they saw
him from a distance, they did not recognize him, and they raised their
voices and wept aloud; they tore their robes and threw dust in the air
upon their heads. [13]They sat with him on the ground seven days and
seven nights, and no one spoke a word to him, for they saw that his
suffering was very great.

Job Curses the Day He Was Born

3 After this Job opened his mouth and cursed the day of his birth.
[2]Job said:

3 "Let the day perish in which I was born,
and the night that said,
'A man-child is conceived.'
4 Let that day be darkness!
May God above not seek it,
or light shine on it.
5 Let gloom and deep darkness claim it.
Let clouds settle upon it;
let the blackness of the day terrify it.
6 That night—let thick darkness seize it!
let it not rejoice among the days of the year;
let it not come into the number of the months.
7 Yes, let that night be barren;
let no joyful cry be heard[b] in it.
8 Let those curse it who curse the Sea,[c]
those who are skilled to rouse up Leviathan.
9 Let the stars of its dawn be dark;
let it hope for light, but have none;
may it not see the eyelids of the morning—
10 because it did not shut the doors of my mother's womb,
and hide trouble from my eyes.

11 "Why did I not die at birth,
come forth from the womb and expire?
12 Why were there knees to receive me,

---

[a] Heb *Bless* [b] Heb *come* [c] Cn: Heb *day*

or breasts for me to suck?
13 Now I would be lying down and quiet;
I would be asleep; then I would be at rest
14 with kings and counselors of the earth
who rebuild ruins for themselves,
15 or with princes who have gold,
who fill their houses with silver.
16 Or why was I not buried like a stillborn child,
like an infant that never sees the light?
17 There the wicked cease from troubling,
and there the weary are at rest.
18 There the prisoners are at ease together;
they do not hear the voice of the taskmaster.
19 The small and the great are there,
and the slaves are free from their masters.

20 "Why is light given to one in misery,
and life to the bitter in soul,
21 who long for death, but it does not come,
and dig for it more than for hidden treasures;
22 who rejoice exceedingly,
and are glad when they find the grave?
23 Why is light given to one who cannot see the way,
whom God has fenced in?
24 For my sighing comes like[a] my bread,
and my groanings are poured out like water.
25 Truly the thing that I fear comes upon me,
and what I dread befalls me.
26 I am not at ease, nor am I quiet;
I have no rest; but trouble comes."

Eliphaz Speaks: Job Has Sinned

4 Then Eliphaz the Temanite answered:
2 "If one ventures a word with you, will you be offended?
But who can keep from speaking?
3 See, you have instructed many;
you have strengthened the weak hands.
4 Your words have supported those who were stumbling,
and you have made firm the feeble knees.
5 But now it has come to you, and you are impatient;
it touches you, and you are dismayed.
6 Is not your fear of God your confidence,
and the integrity of your ways your hope?

[a] Heb *before*

the rest of death (3:13-19). There seems to be a deliberate undoing of creation in Job's first lament. He wishes to plunge the whole world into the chaos his life has become.

3:8 the Sea…Leviathan: The sea was a symbol of chaos in the ancient world. Many ancient Near Eastern cultures had some story of the gods defeating the sea or the sea monster in order to establish creation. This sea monster (or dragon) was itself a symbol of chaos and was known by various names: Rahab, Lotan, Leviathan. Leviathan is described at greater length in the speeches of God at the end of Job. (See Isa 27:1 and Pss 74:14; 104:26 for other references to Leviathan.)

4:1—5:27 Eliphaz the Temanite answered: Eliphaz, the first of Job's three friends, speaks in response to Job's lament. He begins gently, reminding Job that Job himself had encouraged those who were suffering (4:1-6). He seeks to comfort and encourage Job. Note that Eliphaz's tone will change over the course of the dialogue. He resorts to harsher language, until by the end he is accusing Job of all sorts of wrongdoing (22:5-11).

4:7-11 who that was innocent ever perished?: Much of what Eliphaz and the other friends say to Job sounds like the traditional wisdom of the ancient world. Indeed, much of what they say sounds like other parts of the Old Testament (compare 5:17-26 to Prov 3:11-12 and Ps 91). Several passages in the Old Testament point to a belief in retributive justice, the belief that sinners will be punished and the righteous will be rewarded (Deut 28:1, 15; Prov 2:20-22; 3:33). Job's friends certainly hold to this belief. They reason that Job is suffering because he must have done something sinful to deserve it. Job himself argues against such an understanding of the world and protests that he is innocent. Readers know that Job is correct; he has done nothing to deserve his suffering. The whole book of Job can be understood as an argument against the doctrine of retributive justice.

4:12-21 visions of the night: Eliphaz speaks of a vision he had, in which he is told that no human being can be righteous before God. If angels aren't pure, how can humans be? Similar sentiments are expressed later by Job's friends (15:14-16; 25:1-6).

What does it mean to be *simul justus et peccator* (at the same time righteous and a sinner)? Eliphaz claims that no one can be righteous before God. Because human beings are subject to death and corruption, they cannot be pure before Almighty God. Luther would not disagree with Eliphaz about the sinfulness of humanity. He knew that human beings are sinners. But Luther also held to a firm understanding that those who believe in Christ are justified by grace through faith. So Christians are *at the same time* sinful (by human nature) and righteous (through faith in Christ). They do not earn this righteousness, as Job argues in chapters 29-31. Instead, it is a gift of God. *Job 4:17-21*

7 "Think now, who that was innocent ever perished?
Or where were the upright cut off?
8 As I have seen, those who plow iniquity
and sow trouble reap the same.
9 By the breath of God they perish,
and by the blast of his anger they are consumed.
10 The roar of the lion, the voice of the fierce lion,
and the teeth of the young lions are broken.
11 The strong lion perishes for lack of prey,
and the whelps of the lioness are scattered.

12 "Now a word came stealing to me,
my ear received the whisper of it.
13 Amid thoughts from visions of the night,
when deep sleep falls on mortals,
14 dread came upon me, and trembling,
which made all my bones shake.
15 A spirit glided past my face;
the hair of my flesh bristled.
16 It stood still,
but I could not discern its appearance.
A form was before my eyes;
there was silence, then I heard a voice:
17 'Can mortals be righteous before[a] God?
Can human beings be pure before[a] their Maker?
18 Even in his servants he puts no trust,
and his angels he charges with error;
19 how much more those who live in houses of clay,
whose foundation is in the dust,
who are crushed like a moth.
20 Between morning and evening they are destroyed;
they perish forever without any regarding it.
21 Their tent-cord is plucked up within them,
and they die devoid of wisdom.'

Job Is Corrected by God

5 "Call now; is there anyone who will answer you?
To which of the holy ones will you turn?
2 Surely vexation kills the fool,
and jealousy slays the simple.
3 I have seen fools taking root,
but suddenly I cursed their dwelling.
4 Their children are far from safety,

[a] Or *more than*

they are crushed in the gate,
and there is no one to deliver them.
5 The hungry eat their harvest,
and they take it even out of the thorns;[a]
and the thirsty[b] pant after their wealth.
6 For misery does not come from the earth,
nor does trouble sprout from the ground;
7 but human beings are born to trouble
just as sparks[c] fly upward.

8 "As for me, I would seek God,
and to God I would commit my cause.
9 He does great things and unsearchable,
marvelous things without number.
10 He gives rain on the earth
and sends waters on the fields;
11 he sets on high those who are lowly,
and those who mourn are lifted to safety.
12 He frustrates the devices of the crafty,
so that their hands achieve no success.
13 He takes the wise in their own craftiness;
and the schemes of the wily are brought to a quick end.
14 They meet with darkness in the daytime,
and grope at noonday as in the night.
15 But he saves the needy from the sword of their mouth,
from the hand of the mighty.
16 So the poor have hope,
and injustice shuts its mouth.

17 "How happy is the one whom God reproves;
therefore do not despise the discipline of the Almighty.[d]
18 For he wounds, but he binds up;
he strikes, but his hands heal.
19 He will deliver you from six troubles;
in seven no harm shall touch you.
20 In famine he will redeem you from death,
and in war from the power of the sword.
21 You shall be hidden from the scourge of the tongue,
and shall not fear destruction when it comes.
22 At destruction and famine you shall laugh,
and shall not fear the wild animals of the earth.
23 For you shall be in league with the stones of the field,

---

[a] Meaning of Heb uncertain [b] Aquila Symmachus Syr Vg: Heb *snare* [c] Or *birds*; Heb *sons of Resheph*
[d] Traditional rendering of Heb *Shaddai*

and the wild animals shall be at peace with you.
24 You shall know that your tent is safe,
you shall inspect your fold and miss nothing.
25 You shall know that your descendants will be many,
and your offspring like the grass of the earth.
26 You shall come to your grave in ripe old age,
as a shock of grain comes up to the threshing floor in its season.
27 See, we have searched this out; it is true.
Hear, and know it for yourself."

Job Replies: My Complaint Is Just

6 Then Job answered:
2 "O that my vexation were weighed,
and all my calamity laid in the balances!
3 For then it would be heavier than the sand of the sea;
therefore my words have been rash.
4 For the arrows of the Almighty[a] are in me;
my spirit drinks their poison;
the terrors of God are arrayed against me.
5 Does the wild ass bray over its grass,
or the ox low over its fodder?
6 Can that which is tasteless be eaten without salt,
or is there any flavor in the juice of mallows?[b]
7 My appetite refuses to touch them;
they are like food that is loathsome to me.[b]

8 "O that I might have my request,
and that God would grant my desire;
9 that it would please God to crush me,
that he would let loose his hand and cut me off!
10 This would be my consolation;
I would even exult[b] in unrelenting pain;
for I have not denied the words of the Holy One.
11 What is my strength, that I should wait?
And what is my end, that I should be patient?
12 Is my strength the strength of stones,
or is my flesh bronze?
13 In truth I have no help in me,
and any resource is driven from me.

14 "Those who withhold[c] kindness from a friend
forsake the fear of the Almighty.[a]

6:14-21 My companions: Job compares his friends to a "torrent-bed" or a wadi, a geographical feature common in the Near East. Wadis are streambeds that run with water in the rainy season but dry up in the heat of summer. Job had looked to his friends for comfort but is as disappointed in them as a traveler is in a dry streambed.

[a] Traditional rendering of Heb *Shaddai* [b] Meaning of Heb uncertain [c] Syr Vg Compare Tg: Meaning of Heb uncertain

15 My companions are treacherous like a torrent-bed,
like freshets that pass away,
16 that run dark with ice,
turbid with melting snow.
17 In time of heat they disappear;
when it is hot, they vanish from their place.
18 The caravans turn aside from their course;
they go up into the waste, and perish.
19 The caravans of Tema look,
the travelers of Sheba hope.
20 They are disappointed because they were confident;
they come there and are confounded.
21 Such you have now become to me;[a]
you see my calamity, and are afraid.
22 Have I said, 'Make me a gift'?
Or, 'From your wealth offer a bribe for me'?
23 Or, 'Save me from an opponent's hand'?
Or, 'Ransom me from the hand of oppressors'?

24 "Teach me, and I will be silent;
make me understand how I have gone wrong.
25 How forceful are honest words!
But your reproof, what does it reprove?
26 Do you think that you can reprove words,
as if the speech of the desperate were wind?
27 You would even cast lots over the orphan,
and bargain over your friend.

28 "But now, be pleased to look at me;
for I will not lie to your face.
29 Turn, I pray, let no wrong be done.
Turn now, my vindication is at stake.
30 Is there any wrong on my tongue?
Cannot my taste discern calamity?

Job: My Suffering Is without End

7 "Do not human beings have a hard service on earth,
and are not their days like the days of a laborer?
2 Like a slave who longs for the shadow,
and like laborers who look for their wages,
3 so I am allotted months of emptiness,
and nights of misery are apportioned to me.

[a] Cn Compare Gk Syr: Meaning of Heb uncertain

[4] When I lie down I say, 'When shall I rise?'
But the night is long,
and I am full of tossing until dawn.
[5] My flesh is clothed with worms and dirt;
my skin hardens, then breaks out again.
[6] My days are swifter than a weaver's shuttle,
and come to their end without hope.[a]

7:7-10 Sheol: Job believes that he is close to death. Sheol is the name Israelites gave to the grave or the underworld. It wasn't "hell" so much as a dark, silent, confined place from which there was no return. Outside of the book of Daniel, there is little evidence in the Old Testament of a belief in resurrection or in an afterlife. Later in Job however, there are hints of such a hope (14:13-17; 19:25-27).

[7] "Remember that my life is a breath;
my eye will never again see good.
[8] The eye that beholds me will see me no more;
while your eyes are upon me, I shall be gone.
[9] As the cloud fades and vanishes,
so those who go down to Sheol do not come up;
[10] they return no more to their houses,
nor do their places know them any more.

7:7-21 I will not restrain my mouth: In 7:7 and continuing until the end of the chapter, Job speaks directly to God for the first time. (In chapter 6, Job is still speaking to his friends with the plural form of "you." Now he uses the singular "you," speaking to God.) Throughout the rest of the book, Job will alternate between speaking to his friends and speaking to God. His friends, though they advise him to pray, never speak to God directly.

[11] "Therefore I will not restrain my mouth;
I will speak in the anguish of my spirit;
I will complain in the bitterness of my soul.
[12] Am I the Sea, or the Dragon,
that you set a guard over me?
[13] When I say, 'My bed will comfort me,
my couch will ease my complaint,'
[14] then you scare me with dreams
and terrify me with visions,
[15] so that I would choose strangling
and death rather than this body.
[16] I loathe my life; I would not live forever.
Let me alone, for my days are a breath.
[17] What are human beings, that you make so much of them,
that you set your mind on them,
[18] visit them every morning,
test them every moment?
[19] Will you not look away from me for a while,
let me alone until I swallow my spittle?
[20] If I sin, what do I do to you, you watcher of humanity?
Why have you made me your target?
Why have I become a burden to you?
[21] Why do you not pardon my transgression
and take away my iniquity?
For now I shall lie in the earth;
you will seek me, but I shall not be."

7:17-21 What are human beings: Job quotes Psalm 8:4, "What are human beings that you are mindful of them, mortals that you care for them?" Job asks the same question—"What are human beings…?"—but his answer is different from the writer of the psalm. The psalmist says, "Yet you have made them a little lower than God, and crowned them with glory and honor" (Ps 8:5). By contrast, Job says, "Will you not look away from me for a while, let me alone until I swallow my spittle?" (7:19). The psalmist, echoing the creation account in Genesis 1, says that God values humanity highly and gives them dominion over the rest of the world. In contrast, Job believes that God watches humanity like a hawk, waiting for them to sin so that God can punish them. Job believes that God is particularly concerned with *him*, treating him like the sea, a force of chaos (7:12).

[a] Or *as the thread runs out*

Bildad Speaks: Job Should Repent

How would you answer Job's question, "What are human beings?"

8 Then Bildad the Shuhite answered:
2 "How long will you say these things,
and the words of your mouth be a great wind?
3 Does God pervert justice?
Or does the Almighty[a] pervert the right?
4 If your children sinned against him,
he delivered them into the power of their transgression.
5 If you will seek God
and make supplication to the Almighty,[a]
6 if you are pure and upright,
surely then he will rouse himself for you
and restore to you your rightful place.
7 Though your beginning was small,
your latter days will be very great.

8 "For inquire now of bygone generations,
and consider what their ancestors have found;
9 for we are but of yesterday, and we know nothing,
for our days on earth are but a shadow.
10 Will they not teach you and tell you
and utter words out of their understanding?

11 "Can papyrus grow where there is no marsh?
Can reeds flourish where there is no water?
12 While yet in flower and not cut down,
they wither before any other plant.
13 Such are the paths of all who forget God;
the hope of the godless shall perish.
14 Their confidence is gossamer,
a spider's house their trust.
15 If one leans against its house, it will not stand;
if one lays hold of it, it will not endure.
16 The wicked thrive[b] before the sun,
and their shoots spread over the garden.
17 Their roots twine around the stoneheap;
they live among the rocks.[c]
18 If they are destroyed from their place,
then it will deny them, saying, 'I have never seen you.'
19 See, these are their happy ways,[d]
and out of the earth still others will spring.

---

[a] Traditional rendering of Heb *Shaddai* [b] Heb *He thrives* [c] Gk Vg: Meaning of Heb uncertain
[d] Meaning of Heb uncertain

20 "See, God will not reject a blameless person,
nor take the hand of evildoers.
21 He will yet fill your mouth with laughter,
and your lips with shouts of joy.
22 Those who hate you will be clothed with shame,
and the tent of the wicked will be no more."

Job Replies: There Is No Mediator

9 Then Job answered:
2 "Indeed I know that this is so;
but how can a mortal be just before God?
3 If one wished to contend with him,
one could not answer him once in a thousand.
4 He is wise in heart, and mighty in strength
—who has resisted him, and succeeded?—
5 he who removes mountains, and they do not know it,
when he overturns them in his anger;
6 who shakes the earth out of its place,
and its pillars tremble;
7 who commands the sun, and it does not rise;
who seals up the stars;
8 who alone stretched out the heavens
and trampled the waves of the Sea;[a]
9 who made the Bear and Orion,
the Pleiades and the chambers of the south;
10 who does great things beyond understanding,
and marvelous things without number.
11 Look, he passes by me, and I do not see him;
he moves on, but I do not perceive him.
12 He snatches away; who can stop him?
Who will say to him, 'What are you doing?'

13 "God will not turn back his anger;
the helpers of Rahab bowed beneath him.
14 How then can I answer him,
choosing my words with him?
15 Though I am innocent, I cannot answer him;
I must appeal for mercy to my accuser.[b]
16 If I summoned him and he answered me,
I do not believe that he would listen to my voice.
17 For he crushes me with a tempest,
and multiplies my wounds without cause;

9:1-24 Job answered: Job acknowledges that God is the all-powerful creator of the world. He confesses that God "does great things beyond understanding, and marvelous things without number" (9:10). But his description of God's activity is a picture of an unpredictable and even cruel God, one who overturns mountains in anger (9:5), stops the sun from rising (9:7), destroys the innocent and the wicked together (9:22), and gives the earth to the wicked (9: 2). See Job's speech at 12:7-25 for a similar description of God's unpredictability. God's speeches at the end of the book will provide a different vision of God's activity in creation.

9:1-3, 13-35 If one wished to contend with him…for I know I am not what I am thought to be: Job begins to speak of his desire for a trial with God. Because of God's immense power, Job does not think he would get a fair hearing. Still, he wishes for his time in court to defend his innocence.

---

[a] Or *trampled the back of the sea dragon* [b] Or *for my right*

18 he will not let me get my breath,
but fills me with bitterness.
19 If it is a contest of strength, he is the strong one!
If it is a matter of justice, who can summon him?[a]
20 Though I am innocent, my own mouth would condemn me;
though I am blameless, he would prove me perverse.
21 I am blameless; I do not know myself;
I loathe my life.
22 It is all one; therefore I say,
he destroys both the blameless and the wicked.
23 When disaster brings sudden death,
he mocks at the calamity[b] of the innocent.
24 The earth is given into the hand of the wicked;
he covers the eyes of its judges—
if it is not he, who then is it?

25 "My days are swifter than a runner;
they flee away, they see no good.
26 They go by like skiffs of reed,
like an eagle swooping on the prey.
27 If I say, 'I will forget my complaint;
I will put off my sad countenance and be of good cheer,'
28 I become afraid of all my suffering,
for I know you will not hold me innocent.
29 I shall be condemned;
why then do I labor in vain?
30 If I wash myself with soap
and cleanse my hands with lye,
31 yet you will plunge me into filth,
and my own clothes will abhor me.
32 For he is not a mortal, as I am, that I might answer him,
that we should come to trial together.
33 There is no umpire[c] between us,
who might lay his hand on us both.
34 If he would take his rod away from me,
and not let dread of him terrify me,
35 then I would speak without fear of him,
for I know I am not what I am thought to be.[d]

Job: I Loathe My Life

10 "I loathe my life;
I will give free utterance to my complaint;

---

[a] Compare Gk: Heb *me* [b] Meaning of Heb uncertain [c] Another reading is *Would that there were an umpire* [d] Cn: Heb *for I am not so in myself*

I will speak in the bitterness of my soul.
2 I will say to God, Do not condemn me;
let me know why you contend against me.
3 Does it seem good to you to oppress,
to despise the work of your hands
and favor the schemes of the wicked?
4 Do you have eyes of flesh?
Do you see as humans see?
5 Are your days like the days of mortals,
or your years like human years,
6 that you seek out my iniquity
and search for my sin,
7 although you know that I am not guilty,
and there is no one to deliver out of your hand?
8 Your hands fashioned and made me;
and now you turn and destroy me.[a]
9 Remember that you fashioned me like clay;
and will you turn me to dust again?
10 Did you not pour me out like milk
and curdle me like cheese?
11 You clothed me with skin and flesh,
and knit me together with bones and sinews.
12 You have granted me life and steadfast love,
and your care has preserved my spirit.
13 Yet these things you hid in your heart;
I know that this was your purpose.
14 If I sin, you watch me,
and do not acquit me of my iniquity.
15 If I am wicked, woe to me!
If I am righteous, I cannot lift up my head,
for I am filled with disgrace
and look upon my affliction.
16 Bold as a lion you hunt me;
you repeat your exploits against me.
17 You renew your witnesses against me,
and increase your vexation toward me;
you bring fresh troops against me.[b]

18 "Why did you bring me forth from the womb?
Would that I had died before any eye had seen me,
19 and were as though I had not been,
carried from the womb to the grave.

[a] Cn Compare Gk Syr: Heb *made me together all around, and you destroy me* [b] Cn Compare Gk: Heb *toward me; changes and a troop are with me*

10:8-17 Your hands fashioned and made me; and now you turn and destroy me: There are two pictures of God in Job's speech. Job acknowledges God as his maker, even saying that God has given him life and "steadfast love" (10:12). But he also accuses God of destroying him, of hunting him like a lion (10:8, 16). Like the writer of Psalm 22, Job appeals to God's mercy while at the same time accusing God. Both of these texts are examples of lament, a form of prayer that allows the speaker to complain to God honestly while never "letting go" of God.

Have you ever complained to God or been angry with God? If so, how did you feel after expressing it?

What does Luther mean when he speaks of God as both hidden and revealed? Job paints different pictures of God, sometimes in the same passage. He doesn't understand why God is afflicting him, especially since he has experienced God's love and faithfulness in the past. In a similar way, Martin Luther spoke of God as both "hidden" and "revealed." In this life, we cannot know fully God's ways or workings. God cannot be fully comprehended, and often God's work in our lives and in the world is hidden. Nevertheless, God chooses to be revealed in Jesus Christ. In Christ, we can know the essence of the hidden God and trust God's love for us, even (or especially) in times when we suffer. *Job 10:8-17*

20 Are not the days of my life few?[a]
Let me alone, that I may find a little comfort[b]
21 before I go, never to return,
to the land of gloom and deep darkness,
22 the land of gloom[c] and chaos,
where light is like darkness."

Zophar Speaks: Job's Guilt Deserves Punishment

11 Then Zophar the Naamathite answered:
2 "Should a multitude of words go unanswered,
and should one full of talk be vindicated?
3 Should your babble put others to silence,
and when you mock, shall no one shame you?
4 For you say, 'My conduct[d] is pure,
and I am clean in God's[e] sight.'
5 But O that God would speak,
and open his lips to you,
6 and that he would tell you the secrets of wisdom!
For wisdom is many-sided.[f]
Know then that God exacts of you less than your guilt deserves.

7 "Can you find out the deep things of God?
Can you find out the limit of the Almighty?[g]
8 It is higher than heaven[h]—what can you do?
Deeper than Sheol—what can you know?
9 Its measure is longer than the earth,
and broader than the sea.
10 If he passes through, and imprisons,
and assembles for judgment, who can hinder him?
11 For he knows those who are worthless;
when he sees iniquity, will he not consider it?
12 But a stupid person will get understanding,
when a wild ass is born human.[f]

13 "If you direct your heart rightly,
you will stretch out your hands toward him.
14 If iniquity is in your hand, put it far away,
and do not let wickedness reside in your tents.
15 Surely then you will lift up your face without blemish;
you will be secure, and will not fear.
16 You will forget your misery;
you will remember it as waters that have passed away.

---

[a] Cn Compare Gk Syr: Heb *Are not my days few? Let him cease!* [b] Heb *that I may brighten up a little*
[c] Heb *gloom as darkness, deep darkness* [d] Gk: Heb *teaching* [e] Heb *your* [f] Meaning of Heb uncertain
[g] Traditional rendering of Heb *Shaddai* [h] Heb *The heights of heaven*

17 And your life will be brighter than the noonday;
its darkness will be like the morning.
18 And you will have confidence, because there is hope;
you will be protected[a] and take your rest in safety.
19 You will lie down, and no one will make you afraid;
many will entreat your favor.
20 But the eyes of the wicked will fail;
all way of escape will be lost to them,
and their hope is to breathe their last."

Job Replies: I Am a Laughingstock

12 Then Job answered:
2 "No doubt you are the people,
and wisdom will die with you.
3 But I have understanding as well as you;
I am not inferior to you.
Who does not know such things as these?
4 I am a laughingstock to my friends;
I, who called upon God and he answered me,
a just and blameless man, I am a laughingstock.
5 Those at ease have contempt for misfortune,[b]
but it is ready for those whose feet are unstable.
6 The tents of robbers are at peace,
and those who provoke God are secure,
who bring their god in their hands.[c]

7 "But ask the animals, and they will teach you;
the birds of the air, and they will tell you;
8 ask the plants of the earth,[d] and they will teach you;
and the fish of the sea will declare to you.
9 Who among all these does not know
that the hand of the LORD has done this?
10 In his hand is the life of every living thing
and the breath of every human being.
11 Does not the ear test words
as the palate tastes food?
12 Is wisdom with the aged,
and understanding in length of days?

13 "With God[e] are wisdom and strength;
he has counsel and understanding.
14 If he tears down, no one can rebuild;

---

[a] Or *you will look around* [b] Meaning of Heb uncertain [c] Or *whom God brought forth by his hand;* Meaning of Heb uncertain [d] Or *speak to the earth* [e] Heb *him*

if he shuts someone in, no one can open up.
15 If he withholds the waters, they dry up;
if he sends them out, they overwhelm the land.
16 With him are strength and wisdom;
the deceived and the deceiver are his.
17 He leads counselors away stripped,
and makes fools of judges.
18 He looses the sash of kings,
and binds a waistcloth on their loins.
19 He leads priests away stripped,
and overthrows the mighty.
20 He deprives of speech those who are trusted,
and takes away the discernment of the elders.
21 He pours contempt on princes,
and looses the belt of the strong.
22 He uncovers the deeps out of darkness,
and brings deep darkness to light.
23 He makes nations great, then destroys them;
he enlarges nations, then leads them away.
24 He strips understanding from the leaders[a] of the earth,
and makes them wander in a pathless waste.
25 They grope in the dark without light;
he makes them stagger like a drunkard.

13 "Look, my eye has seen all this,
my ear has heard and understood it.
2 What you know, I also know;
I am not inferior to you.
3 But I would speak to the Almighty,[b]
and I desire to argue my case with God.
4 As for you, you whitewash with lies;
all of you are worthless physicians.
5 If you would only keep silent,
that would be your wisdom!
6 Hear now my reasoning,
and listen to the pleadings of my lips.
7 Will you speak falsely for God,
and speak deceitfully for him?
8 Will you show partiality toward him,
will you plead the case for God?
9 Will it be well with you when he searches you out?
Or can you deceive him, as one person deceives another?
10 He will surely rebuke you

13:7-19 Will you speak falsely for God…I shall be vindicated: Job defends himself against his friends' accusations of sin (see chapter 11). Job accuses his friends of speaking falsely for God and argues that God will rebuke them for it. This comes true at the end of the book (42:7-8). Job continues to use the language of the courtroom as he defends himself (13:17-19).

[a] Heb adds *of the people* [b] Traditional rendering of Heb *Shaddai*

if in secret you show partiality.
11 Will not his majesty terrify you,
and the dread of him fall upon you?
12 Your maxims are proverbs of ashes,
your defenses are defenses of clay.

13 "Let me have silence, and I will speak,
and let come on me what may.
14 I will take my flesh in my teeth,
and put my life in my hand.[a]
15 See, he will kill me; I have no hope;[b]
but I will defend my ways to his face.
16 This will be my salvation,
that the godless shall not come before him.
17 Listen carefully to my words,
and let my declaration be in your ears.
18 I have indeed prepared my case;
I know that I shall be vindicated.
19 Who is there that will contend with me?
For then I would be silent and die.

Job's Despondent Prayer

20 Only grant two things to me,
then I will not hide myself from your face:
21 withdraw your hand far from me,
and do not let dread of you terrify me.
22 Then call, and I will answer;
or let me speak, and you reply to me.
23 How many are my iniquities and my sins?
Make me know my transgression and my sin.
24 Why do you hide your face,
and count me as your enemy?
25 Will you frighten a windblown leaf
and pursue dry chaff?
26 For you write bitter things against me,
and make me reap[c] the iniquities of my youth.
27 You put my feet in the stocks,
and watch all my paths;
you set a bound to the soles of my feet.
28 One wastes away like a rotten thing,
like a garment that is moth-eaten.

14 "A mortal, born of woman, few of days and full of trouble,
2 comes up like a flower and withers,

14:1-2 A mortal…does not last: Job uses a common biblical image or picture to speak of human mortality. Human beings are like flowers of the field or blades of grass, which quickly die (for similar images, see Pss 37:2; 102:11; 103:15; Isa 40:6-7; 51:12). Job uses the image to argue that God should not be overly concerned with him. God should leave him alone so that he might enjoy his brief time on earth.

[a] Gk: Heb *Why should I take… in my hand?* [b] Or *Though he kill me, yet I will trust in him* [c] Heb *inherit*

flees like a shadow and does not last.
3 Do you fix your eyes on such a one?
Do you bring me into judgment with you?
4 Who can bring a clean thing out of an unclean?
No one can.
5 Since their days are determined,
and the number of their months is known to you,
and you have appointed the bounds that they cannot pass,
6 look away from them, and desist,[a]
that they may enjoy, like laborers, their days.

7 "For there is hope for a tree,
if it is cut down, that it will sprout again,
and that its shoots will not cease.
8 Though its root grows old in the earth,
and its stump dies in the ground,
9 yet at the scent of water it will bud
and put forth branches like a young plant.
10 But mortals die, and are laid low;
humans expire, and where are they?
11 As waters fail from a lake,
and a river wastes away and dries up,
12 so mortals lie down and do not rise again;
until the heavens are no more, they will not awake
or be roused out of their sleep.
13 O that you would hide me in Sheol,
that you would conceal me until your wrath is past,
that you would appoint me a set time, and remember me!
14 If mortals die, will they live again?
All the days of my service I would wait
until my release should come.
15 You would call, and I would answer you;
you would long for the work of your hands.
16 For then you would not[b] number my steps,
you would not keep watch over my sin;
17 my transgression would be sealed up in a bag,
and you would cover over my iniquity.

18 "But the mountain falls and crumbles away,
and the rock is removed from its place;
19 the waters wear away the stones;
the torrents wash away the soil of the earth;
so you destroy the hope of mortals.

14:13-17 hide me in Sheol: At the same time Job is accusing God, he again appeals to what he has known of God in the past. Job appeals to God's mercy and love for him. Job wants to be hidden in Sheol, the underworld, until God's anger has passed. Then "you would call, and I would answer you; you would long for the work of your hands" (14:15). In the midst of lament, Job speaks sometimes of hope (19:25-27).

---

[a] Cn: Heb *that they may desist* [b] Syr: Heb lacks *not*

[20] You prevail forever against them, and they pass away;
you change their countenance, and send them away.
[21] Their children come to honor, and they do not know it;
they are brought low, and it goes unnoticed.
[22] They feel only the pain of their own bodies,
and mourn only for themselves."

Eliphaz Speaks: Job Undermines Religion

15:1—21:34 Then Eliphaz . . .answered: Eliphaz's second speech marks the beginning of the second cycle of the dialogue. All the participants grow angrier in this cycle. Job is angry because his friends accuse him of sin when he knows he is innocent. The friends are angry because Job is refusing to repent of his sins, which (they think) he must have done to deserve the suffering he endures.

15 Then Eliphaz the Temanite answered:
[2] "Should the wise answer with windy knowledge,
and fill themselves with the east wind?
[3] Should they argue in unprofitable talk,
or in words with which they can do no good?
[4] But you are doing away with the fear of God,
and hindering meditation before God.
[5] For your iniquity teaches your mouth,
and you choose the tongue of the crafty.
[6] Your own mouth condemns you, and not I;
your own lips testify against you.

[7] "Are you the firstborn of the human race?
Were you brought forth before the hills?
[8] Have you listened in the council of God?
And do you limit wisdom to yourself?
[9] What do you know that we do not know?
What do you understand that is not clear to us?
[10] The gray-haired and the aged are on our side,
those older than your father.
[11] Are the consolations of God too small for you,
or the word that deals gently with you?
[12] Why does your heart carry you away,
and why do your eyes flash,[a]
[13] so that you turn your spirit against God,
and let such words go out of your mouth?
[14] What are mortals, that they can be clean?
Or those born of woman, that they can be righteous?
[15] God puts no trust even in his holy ones,
and the heavens are not clean in his sight;
[16] how much less one who is abominable and corrupt,
one who drinks iniquity like water!

[17] "I will show you; listen to me;
what I have seen I will declare—

---

[a] Meaning of Heb uncertain

18 what sages have told,
and their ancestors have not hidden,
19 to whom alone the land was given,
and no stranger passed among them.
20 The wicked writhe in pain all their days,
through all the years that are laid up for the ruthless.
21 Terrifying sounds are in their ears;
in prosperity the destroyer will come upon them.
22 They despair of returning from darkness,
and they are destined for the sword.
23 They wander abroad for bread, saying, 'Where is it?'
They know that a day of darkness is ready at hand;
24 distress and anguish terrify them;
they prevail against them, like a king prepared for battle.
25 Because they stretched out their hands against God,
and bid defiance to the Almighty,[a]
26 running stubbornly against him
with a thick-bossed shield;
27 because they have covered their faces with their fat,
and gathered fat upon their loins,
28 they will live in desolate cities,
in houses that no one should inhabit,
houses destined to become heaps of ruins;
29 they will not be rich, and their wealth will not endure,
nor will they strike root in the earth;[b]
30 they will not escape from darkness;
the flame will dry up their shoots,
and their blossom[c] will be swept away[d] by the wind.
31 Let them not trust in emptiness, deceiving themselves;
for emptiness will be their recompense.
32 It will be paid in full before their time,
and their branch will not be green.
33 They will shake off their unripe grape, like the vine,
and cast off their blossoms, like the olive tree.
34 For the company of the godless is barren,
and fire consumes the tents of bribery.
35 They conceive mischief and bring forth evil
and their heart prepares deceit."

Job Reaffirms His Innocence

16 Then Job answered:
2 "I have heard many such things;

---

[a] Traditional rendering of Heb *Shaddai* [b] Vg: Meaning of Heb uncertain [c] Gk: Heb *mouth*
[d] Cn: Heb *will depart*

miserable comforters are you all.
3 Have windy words no limit?
Or what provokes you that you keep on talking?
4 I also could talk as you do,
if you were in my place;
I could join words together against you,
and shake my head at you.
5 I could encourage you with my mouth,
and the solace of my lips would assuage your pain.

6 "If I speak, my pain is not assuaged,
and if I forbear, how much of it leaves me?
7 Surely now God has worn me out;
he has[a] made desolate all my company.
8 And he has[a] shriveled me up,
which is a witness against me;
my leanness has risen up against me,
and it testifies to my face.
9 He has torn me in his wrath, and hated me;
he has gnashed his teeth at me;
my adversary sharpens his eyes against me.
10 They have gaped at me with their mouths;
they have struck me insolently on the cheek;
they mass themselves together against me.
11 God gives me up to the ungodly,
and casts me into the hands of the wicked.
12 I was at ease, and he broke me in two;
he seized me by the neck and dashed me to pieces;
he set me up as his target;
13 his archers surround me.
He slashes open my kidneys, and shows no mercy;
he pours out my gall on the ground.
14 He bursts upon me again and again;
he rushes at me like a warrior.
15 I have sewed sackcloth upon my skin,
and have laid my strength in the dust.
16 My face is red with weeping,
and deep darkness is on my eyelids,
17 though there is no violence in my hands,
and my prayer is pure.

18 "O earth, do not cover my blood;
let my outcry find no resting place.

16:7-14 God has worn me out: Job's description of God is of a warrior, one who attacks his enemies and destroys them. Similar images of God as divine warrior, fighting against the forces of chaos and evil, are found elsewhere in the Bible (see Ps 74:12-14; Exod 15:3-10). Job is not evil, and he is bitter that God seems to be treating him as if he were evil.

16:18-19 O earth, do not cover my blood.... my witness is in heaven: Job uses the image of innocent blood crying out for justice against the one who spilled it. In the same way, Abel's blood cries out to God after his brother Cain kills him (Gen 4:10). The identity of Job's heavenly witness is unclear. It could be his blood itself, or it could be a heavenly being, perhaps even God. This daring hope for a witness or redeemer is made more explicit in 19:25.

[a] Heb *you have*

[19] Even now, in fact, my witness is in heaven,
and he that vouches for me is on high.
[20] My friends scorn me;
my eye pours out tears to God,
[21] that he would maintain the right of a mortal with God,
as[a] one does for a neighbor.
[22] For when a few years have come,
I shall go the way from which I shall not return.

Job Prays for Relief

17 My spirit is broken, my days are extinct,
the grave is ready for me.
[2] Surely there are mockers around me,
and my eye dwells on their provocation.

[3] "Lay down a pledge for me with yourself;
who is there that will give surety for me?
[4] Since you have closed their minds to understanding,
therefore you will not let them triumph.
[5] Those who denounce friends for reward—
the eyes of their children will fail.

[6] "He has made me a byword of the peoples,
and I am one before whom people spit.
[7] My eye has grown dim from grief,
and all my members are like a shadow.
[8] The upright are appalled at this,
and the innocent stir themselves up against the godless.
[9] Yet the righteous hold to their way,
and they that have clean hands grow stronger and stronger.
[10] But you, come back now, all of you,
and I shall not find a sensible person among you.
[11] My days are past, my plans are broken off,
the desires of my heart.
[12] They make night into day;
'The light,' they say, 'is near to the darkness.'[b]
[13] If I look for Sheol as my house,
if I spread my couch in darkness,
[14] if I say to the Pit, 'You are my father,'
and to the worm, 'My mother,' or 'My sister,'
[15] where then is my hope?
Who will see my hope?

---

[a] Syr Vg Tg: Heb *and* [b] Meaning of Heb uncertain

[16] Will it go down to the bars of Sheol?
Shall we descend together into the dust?"

Bildad Speaks: God Punishes the Wicked

18 Then Bildad the Shuhite answered:
[2] "How long will you hunt for words?
Consider, and then we shall speak.
[3] Why are we counted as cattle?
Why are we stupid in your sight?
[4] You who tear yourself in your anger—
shall the earth be forsaken because of you,
or the rock be removed out of its place?

18:5-21 Surely the light of the wicked is put out: Bildad angrily responds to Job and asserts that the wicked will be punished for their wickedness. Their skin will be consumed by disease (18:13); their possessions will be lost (18:15); and their children will be no more (18:19). All of these calamities, of course, are what Job is experiencing. Bildad is explicitly identifying Job as one of the "wicked" here. He no longer holds out any hope of repentance to Job, as he did in his first speech (8:5-7). He is angry that Job is not listening to him and his friends (18:2-3).

[5] "Surely the light of the wicked is put out,
and the flame of their fire does not shine.
[6] The light is dark in their tent,
and the lamp above them is put out.
[7] Their strong steps are shortened,
and their own schemes throw them down.
[8] For they are thrust into a net by their own feet,
and they walk into a pitfall.
[9] A trap seizes them by the heel;
a snare lays hold of them.
[10] A rope is hid for them in the ground,
a trap for them in the path.
[11] Terrors frighten them on every side,
and chase them at their heels.
[12] Their strength is consumed by hunger,[a]
and calamity is ready for their stumbling.
[13] By disease their skin is consumed,[b]
the firstborn of Death consumes their limbs.
[14] They are torn from the tent in which they trusted,
and are brought to the king of terrors.
[15] In their tents nothing remains;
sulfur is scattered upon their habitations.
[16] Their roots dry up beneath,
and their branches wither above.
[17] Their memory perishes from the earth,
and they have no name in the street.
[18] They are thrust from light into darkness,
and driven out of the world.
[19] They have no offspring or descendant among their people,
and no survivor where they used to live.

---

[a] Or *Disaster is hungry for them* [b] Cn: Heb *It consumes the limbs of his skin*

20 They of the west are appalled at their fate,
and horror seizes those of the east.
21 Surely such are the dwellings of the ungodly,
such is the place of those who do not know God."

Job Replies: I Know That My Redeemer Lives

19 Then Job answered:
2 "How long will you torment me,
and break me in pieces with words?
3 These ten times you have cast reproach upon me;
are you not ashamed to wrong me?
4 And even if it is true that I have erred,
my error remains with me.
5 If indeed you magnify yourselves against me,
and make my humiliation an argument against me,
6 know then that God has put me in the wrong,
and closed his net around me.
7 Even when I cry out, 'Violence!' I am not answered;
I call aloud, but there is no justice.
8 He has walled up my way so that I cannot pass,
and he has set darkness upon my paths.
9 He has stripped my glory from me,
and taken the crown from my head.
10 He breaks me down on every side, and I am gone,
he has uprooted my hope like a tree.
11 He has kindled his wrath against me,
and counts me as his adversary.
12 His troops come on together;
they have thrown up siegeworks[a] against me,
and encamp around my tent.

13 "He has put my family far from me,
and my acquaintances are wholly estranged from me.
14 My relatives and my close friends have failed me;
15 the guests in my house have forgotten me;
my serving girls count me as a stranger;
I have become an alien in their eyes.
16 I call to my servant, but he gives me no answer;
I must myself plead with him.
17 My breath is repulsive to my wife;
I am loathsome to my own family.
18 Even young children despise me;
when I rise, they talk against me.

19:5-6 an argument against me… God has put me in the wrong: Job responds to Bildad's argument that God is punishing Job because he has sinned. His friends' accusations only serve to make his humiliation greater. He also says explicitly that God is the one who has brought this suffering on him.

[a] Cn: Heb *their way*

[19] All my intimate friends abhor me,
and those whom I loved have turned against me.
[20] My bones cling to my skin and to my flesh,
and I have escaped by the skin of my teeth.
[21] Have pity on me, have pity on me, O you my friends,
for the hand of God has touched me!
[22] Why do you, like God, pursue me,
never satisfied with my flesh?

[23] "O that my words were written down!
O that they were inscribed in a book!
[24] O that with an iron pen and with lead
they were engraved on a rock forever!
[25] For I know that my Redeemer[a] lives,
and that at the last he[b] will stand upon the earth;[c]
[26] and after my skin has been thus destroyed,
then in[d] my flesh I shall see God,[e]
[27] whom I shall see on my side,[f]
and my eyes shall behold, and not another.
My heart faints within me!
[28] If you say, 'How we will persecute him!'
and, 'The root of the matter is found in him';
[29] be afraid of the sword,
for wrath brings the punishment of the sword,
so that you may know there is a judgment."

Zophar Speaks: Wickedness Receives Just Retribution

20 Then Zophar the Naamathite answered:
[2] "Pay attention! My thoughts urge me to answer,
because of the agitation within me.
[3] I hear censure that insults me,
and a spirit beyond my understanding answers me.
[4] Do you not know this from of old,
ever since mortals were placed on earth,
[5] that the exulting of the wicked is short,
and the joy of the godless is but for a moment?
[6] Even though they mount up high as the heavens,
and their head reaches to the clouds,
[7] they will perish forever like their own dung;
those who have seen them will say, 'Where are they?'
[8] They will fly away like a dream, and not be found;
they will be chased away like a vision of the night.

[a] Or *Vindicator* [b] Or *that he the Last* [c] Heb *dust* [d] Or *without* [e] Meaning of Heb of this verse uncertain [f] Or *for myself*

19:23-27 O that my words were written down!: Probably the most famous passage from the book, Job 19:25 declares, "I know that my Redeemer lives." The Hebrew word here translated "redeemer" means a close relative responsible for "redeeming" a person who has had to sell himself or his land to pay a debt (see Lev 25). The redeemer redeems by buying back the person or land. George Frideric Handel, in his oratorio *Messiah,* uses this verse from Job to speak about the resurrection of Jesus, but the identity of the redeemer in this passage is unclear. Is the redeemer a heavenly being? A human being? God? In any case, the passage speaks of hope rising out of Job's despair.

What does the Small Catechism say about Jesus and redemption? In his explanation to the Second Article of the Apostles' Creed, Luther says: "He [Jesus] has redeemed me, a lost and condemned human being. He has purchased and freed me from all sins, from death, and from the power of the devil, not with gold or silver but with his holy, precious blood and with his innocent suffering and death" (*SC*:15). *Job 19:25*

What difference does it make to know Jesus redeems you from sin? How can or do you respond to such news?

20:1—21:34 Zophar answered… Then Job answered: Zophar continues to claim that the wicked will be punished by God, while Job argues that the wicked are not punished. Indeed, Job says, the wicked prosper. They enjoy wealth and children and long life, even while they mock God (21:14-15).

Do you agree with Zophar or with Job? Do the wicked prosper in this world?

9 The eye that saw them will see them no more,
nor will their place behold them any longer.
10 Their children will seek the favor of the poor,
and their hands will give back their wealth.
11 Their bodies, once full of youth,
will lie down in the dust with them.

12 "Though wickedness is sweet in their mouth,
though they hide it under their tongues,
13 though they are loath to let it go,
and hold it in their mouths,
14 yet their food is turned in their stomachs;
it is the venom of asps within them.
15 They swallow down riches and vomit them up again;
God casts them out of their bellies.
16 They will suck the poison of asps;
the tongue of a viper will kill them.
17 They will not look on the rivers,
the streams flowing with honey and curds.
18 They will give back the fruit of their toil,
and will not swallow it down;
from the profit of their trading
they will get no enjoyment.
19 For they have crushed and abandoned the poor,
they have seized a house that they did not build.

20 "They knew no quiet in their bellies;
in their greed they let nothing escape.
21 There was nothing left after they had eaten;
therefore their prosperity will not endure.
22 In full sufficiency they will be in distress;
all the force of misery will come upon them.
23 To fill their belly to the full
God[a] will send his fierce anger into them,
and rain it upon them as their food.[b]
24 They will flee from an iron weapon;
a bronze arrow will strike them through.
25 It is drawn forth and comes out of their body,
and the glittering point comes out of their gall;
terrors come upon them.
26 Utter darkness is laid up for their treasures;
a fire fanned by no one will devour them;
what is left in their tent will be consumed.

20:17 streams flowing with honey and curds: This is similar to the description of the land God promised to the Hebrew people (Exod 3:16-17). This could have been a painful reminder of Israel's own sins, which had earlier led to them being defeated and taken into exile, away from their promised land.

[a] Heb *he* [b] Cn: Meaning of Heb uncertain

27 The heavens will reveal their iniquity,
and the earth will rise up against them.
28 The possessions of their house will be carried away,
dragged off in the day of God's[a] wrath.
29 This is the portion of the wicked from God,
the heritage decreed for them by God."

Job Replies: The Wicked Often Go Unpunished

21 Then Job answered:
2 "Listen carefully to my words,
and let this be your consolation.
3 Bear with me, and I will speak;
then after I have spoken, mock on.
4 As for me, is my complaint addressed to mortals?
Why should I not be impatient?
5 Look at me, and be appalled,
and lay your hand upon your mouth.
6 When I think of it I am dismayed,
and shuddering seizes my flesh.
7 Why do the wicked live on,
reach old age, and grow mighty in power?
8 Their children are established in their presence,
and their offspring before their eyes.
9 Their houses are safe from fear,
and no rod of God is upon them.
10 Their bull breeds without fail;
their cow calves and never miscarries.
11 They send out their little ones like a flock,
and their children dance around.
12 They sing to the tambourine and the lyre,
and rejoice to the sound of the pipe.
13 They spend their days in prosperity,
and in peace they go down to Sheol.
14 They say to God, 'Leave us alone!
We do not desire to know your ways.
15 What is the Almighty,[b] that we should serve him?
And what profit do we get if we pray to him?'
16 Is not their prosperity indeed their own achievement?[c]
The plans of the wicked are repugnant to me.

17 "How often is the lamp of the wicked put out?
How often does calamity come upon them?
How often does God[d] distribute pains in his anger?

---

[a] Heb *his* [b] Traditional rendering of Heb *Shaddai* [c] Heb *in their hand* [d] Heb *he*

18 How often are they like straw before the wind,
and like chaff that the storm carries away?
19 You say, 'God stores up their iniquity for their children.'
Let it be paid back to them, so that they may know it.
20 Let their own eyes see their destruction,
and let them drink of the wrath of the Almighty.[a]
21 For what do they care for their household after them,
when the number of their months is cut off?
22 Will any teach God knowledge,
seeing that he judges those that are on high?
23 One dies in full prosperity,
being wholly at ease and secure,
24 his loins full of milk
and the marrow of his bones moist.
25 Another dies in bitterness of soul,
never having tasted of good.
26 They lie down alike in the dust,
and the worms cover them.

27 "Oh, I know your thoughts,
and your schemes to wrong me.
28 For you say, 'Where is the house of the prince?
Where is the tent in which the wicked lived?'
29 Have you not asked those who travel the roads,
and do you not accept their testimony,
30 that the wicked are spared in the day of calamity,
and are rescued in the day of wrath?
31 Who declares their way to their face,
and who repays them for what they have done?
32 When they are carried to the grave,
a watch is kept over their tomb.
33 The clods of the valley are sweet to them;
everyone will follow after,
and those who went before are innumerable.
34 How then will you comfort me with empty nothings?
There is nothing left of your answers but falsehood."

Eliphaz Speaks: Job's Wickedness Is Great

22 Then Eliphaz the Temanite answered:
2 "Can a mortal be of use to God?
Can even the wisest be of service to him?
3 Is it any pleasure to the Almighty[a] if you are righteous,
or is it gain to him if you make your ways blameless?

[a] Traditional rendering of Heb *Shaddai*

21:20 drink of the wrath of the Almighty: A common phrase for receiving God's punishment (see also Ps 60:3; Isa 51:22; Rev 14:10; 16:19).

22:1—27:23 Eliphaz: Eliphaz's third speech begins the third and final cycle of the dialogue. Communication between Job and his friends breaks down. Bildad has only a short speech (25:1-6), and Zophar does not speak at all. Job argues in his speech (27:7-23) that God will punish the wicked, which sounds a lot like his friends' earlier speeches (see Zophar's speech in chapter 20). Some scholars argue that this final speech of Job's in chapter 27 was originally Zophar's. Others claim that Job is mocking Zophar and the other friends by saying what he knows they will say. In either case, the dialogue breaks down, the friends are silenced, and Job has the last word.

22:1-30 Then Eliphaz...answered: Notice the difference between Eliphaz's first speech, in chapters 4–5, and this last one. Eliphaz had begun gently, praising Job's work on behalf of those who suffered (4:1-6). Now, in this last speech, however, Eliphaz criticizes Job for all kinds of sins. According to Eliphaz, Job has taken clothing from the poor and withheld food and water from the hungry and thirsty (22:5-9). Like the other friends, Eliphaz continues to believe that Job suffers because he must have sinned in some way. Job has consistently defended his innocence, so Eliphaz is left to imagine the sins that Job must have committed. He calls on Job to repent (22:21-30).

4 Is it for your piety that he reproves you,
and enters into judgment with you?
5 Is not your wickedness great?
There is no end to your iniquities.
6 For you have exacted pledges from your family for no reason,
and stripped the naked of their clothing.
7 You have given no water to the weary to drink,
and you have withheld bread from the hungry.
8 The powerful possess the land,
and the favored live in it.
9 You have sent widows away empty-handed,
and the arms of the orphans you have crushed.[a]
10 Therefore snares are around you,
and sudden terror overwhelms you,
11 or darkness so that you cannot see;
a flood of water covers you.

22:12-14 God high in the heavens?…walks on the dome of heaven: Ancient people thought of the sky as being a bowl-like dome set over a flat earth. The mountains were said to hold up the sky (Job 9:5-10). The dome held back the flood of water or snow, which came through the dome when God opened windows in the sky (Gen 7:11-12; Ps 78:23).

12 "Is not God high in the heavens?
See the highest stars, how lofty they are!
13 Therefore you say, 'What does God know?
Can he judge through the deep darkness?
14 Thick clouds enwrap him, so that he does not see,
and he walks on the dome of heaven.'
15 Will you keep to the old way
that the wicked have trod?
16 They were snatched away before their time;
their foundation was washed away by a flood.
17 They said to God, 'Leave us alone,'
and 'What can the Almighty[b] do to us?'[c]
18 Yet he filled their houses with good things—
but the plans of the wicked are repugnant to me.
19 The righteous see it and are glad;
the innocent laugh them to scorn,
20 saying, 'Surely our adversaries are cut off,
and what they left, the fire has consumed.'

21 "Agree with God,[d] and be at peace;
in this way good will come to you.
22 Receive instruction from his mouth,
and lay up his words in your heart.
23 If you return to the Almighty,[b] you will be restored,
if you remove unrighteousness from your tents,

22:23 you will be restored: Eliphaz suggests that Job will get his wealth back if he returns to God by admitting his sins.

[a] Gk Syr Tg Vg: Heb *were crushed* [b] Traditional rendering of Heb *Shaddai* [c] Gk Syr: Heb *them*
[d] Heb *him*

[24] if you treat gold like dust,
and gold of Ophir like the stones of the torrent-bed,
[25] and if the Almighty[a] is your gold
and your precious silver,
[26] then you will delight yourself in the Almighty,[a]
and lift up your face to God.
[27] You will pray to him, and he will hear you,
and you will pay your vows.
[28] You will decide on a matter, and it will be established for you,
and light will shine on your ways.
[29] When others are humiliated, you say it is pride;
for he saves the humble.
[30] He will deliver even those who are guilty;
they will escape because of the cleanness of your hands."[b]

Job Replies: My Complaint Is Bitter

23 Then Job answered:
[2] "Today also my complaint is bitter;[c]
his[d] hand is heavy despite my groaning.
[3] Oh, that I knew where I might find him,
that I might come even to his dwelling!
[4] I would lay my case before him,
and fill my mouth with arguments.
[5] I would learn what he would answer me,
and understand what he would say to me.
[6] Would he contend with me in the greatness of his power?
No; but he would give heed to me.
[7] There an upright person could reason with him,
and I should be acquitted forever by my judge.

[8] "If I go forward, he is not there;
or backward, I cannot perceive him;
[9] on the left he hides, and I cannot behold him;
I turn[e] to the right, but I cannot see him.
[10] But he knows the way that I take;
when he has tested me, I shall come out like gold.
[11] My foot has held fast to his steps;
I have kept his way and have not turned aside.
[12] I have not departed from the commandment of his lips;
I have treasured in[f] my bosom the words of his mouth.
[13] But he stands alone and who can dissuade him?
What he desires, that he does.

23:4-7 lay my case before him . . . be acquitted forever: Job argues that if he could just get a hearing with God, he knows he would be found innocent.

---

[a] Traditional rendering of Heb *Shaddai* [b] Meaning of Heb uncertain [c] Syr Vg Tg: Heb *rebellious*
[d] Gk Syr: Heb *my* [e] Syr Vg: Heb *he turns* [f] Gk Vg: Heb *from*

14 For he will complete what he appoints for me;
and many such things are in his mind.
15 Therefore I am terrified at his presence;
when I consider, I am in dread of him.
16 God has made my heart faint;
the Almighty[a] has terrified me;
17 If only I could vanish in darkness,
and thick darkness would cover my face![b]

Job Complains of Violence on the Earth

24 "Why are times not kept by the Almighty,[a]
and why do those who know him never see his days?
2 The wicked[c] remove landmarks;
they seize flocks and pasture them.
3 They drive away the donkey of the orphan;
they take the widow's ox for a pledge.
4 They thrust the needy off the road;
the poor of the earth all hide themselves.
5 Like wild asses in the desert
they go out to their toil,
scavenging in the wasteland
food for their young.
6 They reap in a field not their own
and they glean in the vineyard of the wicked.
7 They lie all night naked, without clothing,
and have no covering in the cold.
8 They are wet with the rain of the mountains,
and cling to the rock for want of shelter.

9 "There are those who snatch the orphan child from the breast,
and take as a pledge the infant of the poor.
10 They go about naked, without clothing;
though hungry, they carry the sheaves;
11 between their terraces[d] they press out oil;
they tread the wine presses, but suffer thirst.
12 From the city the dying groan,
and the throat of the wounded cries for help;
yet God pays no attention to their prayer.

13 "There are those who rebel against the light,
who are not acquainted with its ways,
and do not stay in its paths.

24:2 wicked remove landmarks: One of the many unjust things the wicked do is removing stones or other objects used to define a person's land. This was a serious crime under Israel's law (Deut 27:14-26), because it amounted to stealing property.

24:5-6 scavenging...reap in a field not their own: It was the custom in Israel to leave some stalks of grain in the field for poor people, especially widows, orphans and foreigners, to gather and eat for free (see Lev 19:9-10; Deut 24:19-22; Ruth 2:1-3).

24:9 take as a pledge the infant of the poor: The evil practice of kidnapping an infant from someone who owed money as a guarantee of the loan was forbidden by law and punishable by death (Deut 24:7). In the case of the poor, children were the primary source of future income and well-being.

---

[a] Traditional rendering of Heb *Shaddai* [b] Or *But I am not destroyed by the darkness; he has concealed the thick darkness from me* [c] Gk: Heb *they* [d] Meaning of Heb uncertain

14 The murderer rises at dusk
to kill the poor and needy,
and in the night is like a thief.
15 The eye of the adulterer also waits for the twilight,
saying, 'No eye will see me';
and he disguises his face.
16 In the dark they dig through houses;
by day they shut themselves up;
they do not know the light.
17 For deep darkness is morning to all of them;
for they are friends with the terrors of deep darkness.

18 "Swift are they on the face of the waters;
their portion in the land is cursed;
no treader turns toward their vineyards.
19 Drought and heat snatch away the snow waters;
so does Sheol those who have sinned.
20 The womb forgets them;
the worm finds them sweet;
they are no longer remembered;
so wickedness is broken like a tree.

21 "They harm[a] the childless woman,
and do no good to the widow.
22 Yet God[b] prolongs the life of the mighty by his power;
they rise up when they despair of life.
23 He gives them security, and they are supported;
his eyes are upon their ways.
24 They are exalted a little while, and then are gone;
they wither and fade like the mallow;[c]
they are cut off like the heads of grain.
25 If it is not so, who will prove me a liar,
and show that there is nothing in what I say?"

Bildad Speaks: How Can a Mortal Be Righteous Before God?

25 Then Bildad the Shuhite answered:
2 "Dominion and fear are with God;[d]
he makes peace in his high heaven.
3 Is there any number to his armies?
Upon whom does his light not arise?
4 How then can a mortal be righteous before God?
How can one born of woman be pure?

[a] Gk Tg: Heb *feed on* or *associate with* [b] Heb *he* [c] Gk: Heb *like all others* [d] Heb *him*

24:19 Sheol: See the note on 7:7-10.

25:4 righteous before God?: Bildad asks how any human being, including Job, who is described in 1:1 as "blameless and upright," can be righteous before God, the ultimate judge. For similar sentiments, see the comments by Eliphaz at 4:12-21 and 15:14-16.

How would you answer Bildad's questions in 25:4?

26:5-14 The shades below tremble...the thunder of his power: Job's hymn-like response seems to carry on Bildad's comments about God in 25:1-6. Because it seems a bit out of place in Job's mouth at this point, some scholars have suggested that this section really belongs to Bildad's speech. It should be noted, however, that Job has said similar things already about God's power in creation in 9:1-13.

26:12 Rahab: Like Leviathan, Rahab is a name for the sea monster of ancient legend, or for the sea itself. See note on 3:8.

27:1-6 As God lives...I hold fast my righteousness: Job will not give up his defense. He maintains he is innocent. For him to admit otherwise would be a lie.

5 If even the moon is not bright
and the stars are not pure in his sight,
6 how much less a mortal, who is a maggot,
and a human being, who is a worm!"

Job Replies: God's Majesty Is Unsearchable

26 Then Job answered:
2 "How you have helped one who has no power!
How you have assisted the arm that has no strength!
3 How you have counseled one who has no wisdom,
and given much good advice!
4 With whose help have you uttered words,
and whose spirit has come forth from you?
5 The shades below tremble,
the waters and their inhabitants.
6 Sheol is naked before God,
and Abaddon has no covering.
7 He stretches out Zaphon[a] over the void,
and hangs the earth upon nothing.
8 He binds up the waters in his thick clouds,
and the cloud is not torn open by them.
9 He covers the face of the full moon,
and spreads over it his cloud.
10 He has described a circle on the face of the waters,
at the boundary between light and darkness.
11 The pillars of heaven tremble,
and are astounded at his rebuke.
12 By his power he stilled the Sea;
by his understanding he struck down Rahab.
13 By his wind the heavens were made fair;
his hand pierced the fleeing serpent.
14 These are indeed but the outskirts of his ways;
and how small a whisper do we hear of him!
But the thunder of his power who can understand?"

Job Maintains His Integrity

27 Job again took up his discourse and said:
2 "As God lives, who has taken away my right,
and the Almighty,[b] who has made my soul bitter,
3 as long as my breath is in me
and the spirit of God is in my nostrils,
4 my lips will not speak falsehood,
and my tongue will not utter deceit.

---

[a] Or *the North* [b] Traditional rendering of Heb *Shaddai*

5 Far be it from me to say that you are right;
until I die I will not put away my integrity from me.
6 I hold fast my righteousness, and will not let it go;
my heart does not reproach me for any of my days.

7 "May my enemy be like the wicked,
and may my opponent be like the unrighteous.
8 For what is the hope of the godless when God cuts them off,
when God takes away their lives?
9 Will God hear their cry
when trouble comes upon them?
10 Will they take delight in the Almighty?[a]
Will they call upon God at all times?
11 I will teach you concerning the hand of God;
that which is with the Almighty[a] I will not conceal.
12 All of you have seen it yourselves;
why then have you become altogether vain?

13 "This is the portion of the wicked with God,
and the heritage that oppressors receive from the Almighty:[a]
14 If their children are multiplied, it is for the sword;
and their offspring have not enough to eat.
15 Those who survive them the pestilence buries,
and their widows make no lamentation.
16 Though they heap up silver like dust,
and pile up clothing like clay—
17 they may pile it up, but the just will wear it,
and the innocent will divide the silver.
18 They build their houses like nests,
like booths made by sentinels of the vineyard.
19 They go to bed with wealth, but will do so no more;
they open their eyes, and it is gone.
20 Terrors overtake them like a flood;
in the night a whirlwind carries them off.
21 The east wind lifts them up and they are gone;
it sweeps them out of their place.
22 It[b] hurls at them without pity;
they flee from its[c] power in headlong flight.
23 It[b] claps its[c] hands at them,
and hisses at them from its[c] place.

Interlude: Where Wisdom Is Found

28 "Surely there is a mine for silver,
and a place for gold to be refined.

[a] Traditional rendering of Heb *Shaddai* [b] Or *He* (that is God) [c] Or *his*

27:7-23 May my enemy be like the wicked...Terrors overtake them: Some scholars argue that this final speech of Job's in chapter 27 was originally Zophar's, partly because he does not have a third speech as do Bildad and Eliphaz.

28:1-28 But where shall wisdom be found?: This speech does not sound like Job's earlier speeches. It is not angry. Instead, it is a meditation on the difficulty of finding wisdom. Wisdom is a major subject of other books in the Old Testament, especially Proverbs, and was understood in ancient Israel as something to be sought in order to live a good life. Job's three friends often sound like wisdom teachers. Perhaps Job uses this poem on wisdom to make the point that in spite of the many things they have said to him, they have not obtained wisdom. The final verse of the chapter declares that only those who fear the LORD and turn away from evil can obtain wisdom (compare Prov 1:7; 9:10). It is Job himself who is described as one who "feared God and turned away from evil" (1:1).

2 Iron is taken out of the earth,
and copper is smelted from ore.
3 Miners put[a] an end to darkness,
and search out to the farthest bound
the ore in gloom and deep darkness.
4 They open shafts in a valley away from human habitation;
they are forgotten by travelers,
they sway suspended, remote from people.
5 As for the earth, out of it comes bread;
but underneath it is turned up as by fire.
6 Its stones are the place of sapphires,[b]
and its dust contains gold.

7 "That path no bird of prey knows,
and the falcon's eye has not seen it.
8 The proud wild animals have not trodden it;
the lion has not passed over it.

28:9-19 put their hand to flinty rock…chrysolite of Ethiopia: Job compares searching for wisdom to various kinds of mining for precious metals and gems. Mining is a difficult process, but searching for wisdom is even more challenging.

9 "They put their hand to the flinty rock,
and overturn mountains by the roots.
10 They cut out channels in the rocks,
and their eyes see every precious thing.
11 The sources of the rivers they probe;[c]
hidden things they bring to light.

12 "But where shall wisdom be found?
And where is the place of understanding?
13 Mortals do not know the way to it,[d]
and it is not found in the land of the living.
14 The deep says, 'It is not in me,'
and the sea says, 'It is not with me.'
15 It cannot be gotten for gold,
and silver cannot be weighed out as its price.
16 It cannot be valued in the gold of Ophir,
in precious onyx or sapphire.[b]
17 Gold and glass cannot equal it,
nor can it be exchanged for jewels of fine gold.
18 No mention shall be made of coral or of crystal;
the price of wisdom is above pearls.
19 The chrysolite of Ethiopia[e] cannot compare with it,
nor can it be valued in pure gold.

20 "Where then does wisdom come from?
And where is the place of understanding?

---

[a] Heb *He puts* [b] Or *lapis lazuli* [c] Gk Vg: Heb *bind* [d] Gk: Heb *its price* [e] Or *Nubia;* Heb *Cush*

21 It is hidden from the eyes of all living,
and concealed from the birds of the air.
22 Abaddon and Death say,
'We have heard a rumor of it with our ears.'

23 "God understands the way to it,
and he knows its place.
24 For he looks to the ends of the earth,
and sees everything under the heavens.
25 When he gave to the wind its weight,
and apportioned out the waters by measure;
26 when he made a decree for the rain,
and a way for the thunderbolt;
27 then he saw it and declared it;
he established it, and searched it out.
28 And he said to humankind,
'Truly, the fear of the Lord, that is wisdom;
and to depart from evil is understanding.' "

Job Finishes His Defense

29 Job again took up his discourse and said:
2 "O that I were as in the months of old,
as in the days when God watched over me;
3 when his lamp shone over my head,
and by his light I walked through darkness;
4 when I was in my prime,
when the friendship of God was upon my tent;
5 when the Almighty[a] was still with me,
when my children were around me;
6 when my steps were washed with milk,
and the rock poured out for me streams of oil!
7 When I went out to the gate of the city,
when I took my seat in the square,
8 the young men saw me and withdrew,
and the aged rose up and stood;
9 the nobles refrained from talking,
and laid their hands on their mouths;
10 the voices of princes were hushed,
and their tongues stuck to the roof of their mouths.
11 When the ear heard, it commended me,
and when the eye saw, it approved;
12 because I delivered the poor who cried,
and the orphan who had no helper.

[a] Traditional rendering of Heb *Shaddai*

28:28 the fear of the Lord, that is wisdom: "Fear" is not to be equated with terror, but rather awe and respect. This is a common way of describing wisdom in the Old Testament (see also Job 37:24; Ps 111:10; Prov 1:7; 9:10).

29:1—31:40 Job again took up his discourse: These three chapters are Job's final defense of himself. In chapter 29 he recalls what his life was like before he was afflicted. He was the center of his social world, helper of the poor, and leader of the elders. His companions waited eagerly for his words, and he was like a king among his troops (29:25). In chapter 30 he laments his current situation. He has become an object of scorn and ridicule. Even the outcasts of society mock him. God has cast him into the mud, and he has become "like dust and ashes" (30:19). Finally, in chapter 31, Job takes a long oath. He lists a number of sins and swears that he has not committed them. Then, using the language of a court of law, he calls on God, his accuser, to answer him (31:35-37).

29:7-10 I went out to the gate of the city…voices of princes were hushed: In the ancient world the city gate was the place where important business was discussed and transacted (for example, see Ruth 4:1-12). Job had been so important that the most powerful people were silent when he spoke during town meetings.

29:12-16 I delivered the poor…father to the needy: Job's listing of the many ways he helped the needy is a direct response to Eliphaz's earlier charges against him (22:3-11).

Have you ever been "made sport of" (30:1) or mocked (30:9) by others? How were you able to endure this treatment?

13 The blessing of the wretched came upon me,
and I caused the widow's heart to sing for joy.
14 I put on righteousness, and it clothed me;
my justice was like a robe and a turban.
15 I was eyes to the blind,
and feet to the lame.
16 I was a father to the needy,
and I championed the cause of the stranger.
17 I broke the fangs of the unrighteous,
and made them drop their prey from their teeth.
18 Then I thought, 'I shall die in my nest,
and I shall multiply my days like the phoenix;[a]
19 my roots spread out to the waters,
with the dew all night on my branches;
20 my glory was fresh with me,
and my bow ever new in my hand.'

21 "They listened to me, and waited,
and kept silence for my counsel.
22 After I spoke they did not speak again,
and my word dropped upon them like dew.[b]
23 They waited for me as for the rain;
they opened their mouths as for the spring rain.
24 I smiled on them when they had no confidence;
and the light of my countenance they did not extinguish.[c]
25 I chose their way, and sat as chief,
and I lived like a king among his troops,
like one who comforts mourners.

30

"But now they make sport of me,
those who are younger than I,
whose fathers I would have disdained
to set with the dogs of my flock.
2 What could I gain from the strength of their hands?
All their vigor is gone.
3 Through want and hard hunger
they gnaw the dry and desolate ground,
4 they pick mallow and the leaves of bushes,
and to warm themselves the roots of broom.
5 They are driven out from society;
people shout after them as after a thief.
6 In the gullies of wadis they must live,
in holes in the ground, and in the rocks.

---

[a] Or *like sand* [b] Heb lacks *like dew* [c] Meaning of Heb uncertain

7 Among the bushes they bray;
under the nettles they huddle together.
8 A senseless, disreputable brood,
they have been whipped out of the land.

9 "And now they mock me in song;
I am a byword to them.
10 They abhor me, they keep aloof from me;
they do not hesitate to spit at the sight of me.
11 Because God has loosed my bowstring and humbled me,
they have cast off restraint in my presence.
12 On my right hand the rabble rise up;
they send me sprawling,
and build roads for my ruin.
13 They break up my path,
they promote my calamity;
no one restrains[a] them.
14 As through a wide breach they come;
amid the crash they roll on.
15 Terrors are turned upon me;
my honor is pursued as by the wind,
and my prosperity has passed away like a cloud.

16 "And now my soul is poured out within me;
days of affliction have taken hold of me.
17 The night racks my bones,
and the pain that gnaws me takes no rest.
18 With violence he seizes my garment;[b]
he grasps me by[c] the collar of my tunic.
19 He has cast me into the mire,
and I have become like dust and ashes.
20 I cry to you and you do not answer me;
I stand, and you merely look at me.
21 You have turned cruel to me;
with the might of your hand you persecute me.
22 You lift me up on the wind, you make me ride on it,
and you toss me about in the roar of the storm.
23 I know that you will bring me to death,
and to the house appointed for all living.

24 "Surely one does not turn against the needy,[d]
when in disaster they cry for help.[e]

30:11 God has loosed my bowstring: The archer's bow and arrow were symbols of power and strength. God has made Job's former power and status useless.

---

[a] Cn: Heb *helps* [b] Gk: Heb *my garment is disfigured* [c] Heb *like* [d] Heb *ruin* [e] Cn: Meaning of Heb uncertain

25 Did I not weep for those whose day was hard?
Was not my soul grieved for the poor?
26 But when I looked for good, evil came;
and when I waited for light, darkness came.
27 My inward parts are in turmoil, and are never still;
days of affliction come to meet me.
28 I go about in sunless gloom;
I stand up in the assembly and cry for help.
29 I am a brother of jackals,
and a companion of ostriches.
30 My skin turns black and falls from me,
and my bones burn with heat.
31 My lyre is turned to mourning,
and my pipe to the voice of those who weep.

30:29 brother of jackals: These desert animals known for their distinctive howl were considered scavengers and pests, especially to those who owned herds of goats and sheep.

31 "I have made a covenant with my eyes;
how then could I look upon a virgin?
2 What would be my portion from God above,
and my heritage from the Almighty[a] on high?
3 Does not calamity befall the unrighteous,
and disaster the workers of iniquity?
4 Does he not see my ways,
and number all my steps?

5 "If I have walked with falsehood,
and my foot has hurried to deceit—
6 let me be weighed in a just balance,
and let God know my integrity!—
7 if my step has turned aside from the way,
and my heart has followed my eyes,
and if any spot has clung to my hands;
8 then let me sow, and another eat;
and let what grows for me be rooted out.

9 "If my heart has been enticed by a woman,
and I have lain in wait at my neighbor's door;
10 then let my wife grind for another,
and let other men kneel over her.
11 For that would be a heinous crime;
that would be a criminal offense;
12 for that would be a fire consuming down to
Abaddon,
and it would burn to the root all my harvest.

31:1-40 I have made a covenant with my eyes . . . if I have . . . caused the death of its owners: Job tries to think of as many ways he might have broken God's laws as he can—from looking with lust at a virgin or other women to taking advantage of the poor to stealing land and killing the landowner. If he had acted in some of these ways, he would deserve the punishment he has gotten. But this chapter is one long oath that he has not done any of these things.

What is works righteousness? Martin Luther and other reformers argued against the concept of "works righteousness," the belief that human beings can obtain salvation through doing good works. Luther taught that salvation is a free gift of God through faith in Jesus Christ. Good works are the "fruit" of that salvation, what we do in thankful response to God's free gift of grace. Job here is arguing that his good works should have earned him something better than the suffering he is enduring, a common belief in his day—and in our own. *Job 31*

[a] Traditional rendering of Heb *Shaddai*

13 “If I have rejected the cause of my male or female slaves,
when they brought a complaint against me;
14 what then shall I do when God rises up?
When he makes inquiry, what shall I answer him?
15 Did not he who made me in the womb make them?
And did not one fashion us in the womb?

16 “If I have withheld anything that the poor desired,
or have caused the eyes of the widow to fail,
17 or have eaten my morsel alone,
and the orphan has not eaten from it—
18 for from my youth I reared the orphan[a] like a father,
and from my mother’s womb I guided the widow[b]—
19 if I have seen anyone perish for lack of clothing,
or a poor person without covering,
20 whose loins have not blessed me,
and who was not warmed with the fleece of my sheep;
21 if I have raised my hand against the orphan,
because I saw I had supporters at the gate;
22 then let my shoulder blade fall from my shoulder,
and let my arm be broken from its socket.
23 For I was in terror of calamity from God,
and I could not have faced his majesty.

24 “If I have made gold my trust,
or called fine gold my confidence;
25 if I have rejoiced because my wealth was great,
or because my hand had gotten much;
26 if I have looked at the sun[c] when it shone,
or the moon moving in splendor,
27 and my heart has been secretly enticed,
and my mouth has kissed my hand;
28 this also would be an iniquity to be punished by the judges,
for I should have been false to God above.

29 “If I have rejoiced at the ruin of those who hated me,
or exulted when evil overtook them—
30 I have not let my mouth sin
by asking for their lives with a curse—
31 if those of my tent ever said,
‘O that we might be sated with his flesh!’[d]—
32 the stranger has not lodged in the street;
I have opened my doors to the traveler—

---

[a] Heb *him* [b] Heb *her* [c] Heb *the light* [d] Meaning of Heb uncertain

33 if I have concealed my transgressions as others do,[a]
by hiding my iniquity in my bosom,
34 because I stood in great fear of the multitude,
and the contempt of families terrified me,
so that I kept silence, and did not go out of doors—
35 O that I had one to hear me!
(Here is my signature! Let the Almighty[b] answer me!)
O that I had the indictment written by my adversary!
36 Surely I would carry it on my shoulder;
I would bind it on me like a crown;
37 I would give him an account of all my steps;
like a prince I would approach him.

38 "If my land has cried out against me,
and its furrows have wept together;
39 if I have eaten its yield without payment,
and caused the death of its owners;
40 let thorns grow instead of wheat,
and foul weeds instead of barley."

The words of Job are ended.

Elihu Rebukes Job's Friends

32:1—37:24 Then Elihu…became angry: These six chapters contain the speech of Elihu, a young man who has been listening to the dialogue and has grown impatient with Job and his three friends. He quotes earlier portions of their speeches and offers his own opinions about why Job suffers. Much of what he says has already been said. The last portion of Elihu's speech (36:24—37:24) seems to anticipate the speeches of God by describing God's work in creation. Elihu does not appear before or after these chapters. For this reason, many scholars think these chapters are a late addition to the original book of Job.

32:2 Elihu…the Buzite: His name means "he is my God." Elihu may have been a descendant of Buz, the nephew of Abraham (Gen 22:2-23). The territory of Buz is mentioned along with the land of Tema in Jeremiah 25:23-24.

32 So these three men ceased to answer Job, because he was
righteous in his own eyes. 2 Then Elihu son of Barachel the
Buzite, of the family of Ram, became angry. He was angry at Job because he justified himself rather than God; 3 he was angry also at Job's
three friends because they had found no answer, though they had declared Job to be in the wrong.[c] 4 Now Elihu had waited to speak to Job,
because they were older than he. 5 But when Elihu saw that there was
no answer in the mouths of these three men, he became angry.
6 Elihu son of Barachel the Buzite answered:
"I am young in years,
and you are aged;
therefore I was timid and afraid
to declare my opinion to you.
7 I said, 'Let days speak,
and many years teach wisdom.'
8 But truly it is the spirit in a mortal,
the breath of the Almighty,[b] that makes for understanding.
9 It is not the old[d] that are wise,
nor the aged that understand what is right.

---

[a] Or *as Adam did* [b] Traditional rendering of Heb *Shaddai* [c] Another ancient tradition reads *answer, and had put God in the wrong* [d] Gk Syr Vg: Heb *many*

10 Therefore I say, 'Listen to me;
let me also declare my opinion.'

11 "See, I waited for your words,
I listened for your wise sayings,
while you searched out what to say.
12 I gave you my attention,
but there was in fact no one that confuted Job,
no one among you that answered his words.
13 Yet do not say, 'We have found wisdom;
God may vanquish him, not a human.'
14 He has not directed his words against me,
and I will not answer him with your speeches.

15 "They are dismayed, they answer no more;
they have not a word to say.
16 And am I to wait, because they do not speak,
because they stand there, and answer no more?
17 I also will give my answer;
I also will declare my opinion.
18 For I am full of words;
the spirit within me constrains me.
19 My heart is indeed like wine that has no vent;
like new wineskins, it is ready to burst.
20 I must speak, so that I may find relief;
I must open my lips and answer.
21 I will not show partiality to any person
or use flattery toward anyone.
22 For I do not know how to flatter—
or my Maker would soon put an end to me!

Elihu Rebukes Job

33 "But now, hear my speech, O Job,
and listen to all my words.
2 See, I open my mouth;
the tongue in my mouth speaks.
3 My words declare the uprightness of my heart,
and what my lips know they speak sincerely.
4 The spirit of God has made me,
and the breath of the Almighty[a] gives me life.
5 Answer me, if you can;
set your words in order before me; take your stand.
6 See, before God I am as you are;

32:19 My heart is . . . like wine that has no vent: As juice ferments into wine it produces a gas that stretches wineskins. Wineskins that don't have any natural venting or that are new can burst from the pressure.

33:6 formed from a piece of clay: A reference to the story that God created the first humans from dirt (Gen 2:7).

[a] Traditional rendering of Heb *Shaddai*

I too was formed from a piece of clay.
7 No fear of me need terrify you;
my pressure will not be heavy on you.

8 "Surely, you have spoken in my hearing,
and I have heard the sound of your words.
9 You say, 'I am clean, without transgression;
I am pure, and there is no iniquity in me.
10 Look, he finds occasions against me,
he counts me as his enemy;
11 he puts my feet in the stocks,
and watches all my paths.'

12 "But in this you are not right. I will answer you:
God is greater than any mortal.
13 Why do you contend against him,
saying, 'He will answer none of my[a] words'?
14 For God speaks in one way,
and in two, though people do not perceive it.
15 In a dream, in a vision of the night,
when deep sleep falls on mortals,
while they slumber on their beds,
16 then he opens their ears,
and terrifies them with warnings,
17 that he may turn them aside from their deeds,
and keep them from pride,
18 to spare their souls from the Pit,
their lives from traversing the River.
19 They are also chastened with pain upon their beds,
and with continual strife in their bones,
20 so that their lives loathe bread,
and their appetites dainty food.
21 Their flesh is so wasted away that it cannot be seen;
and their bones, once invisible, now stick out.
22 Their souls draw near the Pit,
and their lives to those who bring death.
23 Then, if there should be for one of them an angel,
a mediator, one of a thousand,
one who declares a person upright,
24 and he is gracious to that person, and says,
'Deliver him from going down into the Pit;
I have found a ransom;
25 let his flesh become fresh with youth;

33:23 an angel, a mediator: Elihu suggests that if an angel or mediator does come to a person's defense before God, that person can be redeemed (33:26, 28).

[a] Compare Gk: Heb *his*

let him return to the days of his youthful vigor';
26 then he prays to God, and is accepted by him,
he comes into his presence with joy,
and God[a] repays him for his righteousness.
27 That person sings to others and says,
'I sinned, and perverted what was right,
and it was not paid back to me.
28 He has redeemed my soul from going down to the Pit,
and my life shall see the light.'

29 "God indeed does all these things,
twice, three times, with mortals,
30 to bring back their souls from the Pit,
so that they may see the light of life.[b]
31 Pay heed, Job, listen to me;
be silent, and I will speak.
32 If you have anything to say, answer me;
speak, for I desire to justify you.
33 If not, listen to me;
be silent, and I will teach you wisdom."

Elihu Proclaims God's Justice

34 Then Elihu continued and said:
2 "Hear my words, you wise men,
and give ear to me, you who know;
3 for the ear tests words
as the palate tastes food.
4 Let us choose what is right;
let us determine among ourselves what is good.
5 For Job has said, 'I am innocent,
and God has taken away my right;
6 in spite of being right I am counted a liar;
my wound is incurable, though I am without transgression.'
7 Who is there like Job,
who drinks up scoffing like water,
8 who goes in company with evildoers
and walks with the wicked?
9 For he has said, 'It profits one nothing
to take delight in God.'

10 "Therefore, hear me, you who have sense,
far be it from God that he should do wickedness,
and from the Almighty[c] that he should do wrong.

[a] Heb *he* [b] Syr: Heb *to be lighted with the light of life* [c] Traditional rendering of Heb *Shaddai*

33:29-30 God indeed does all these things…bring back their souls from the Pit: Elihu suggests that God is willing to redeem those who have done wrong and save them from the Pit, or the world of the dead.

34:9 It profits one nothing to take delight in God: Elihu scolds Job for his attitude, which seems to question, "What's the use of trying to do what God wants?" (see 9:20-24). But, like the other friends, he doesn't take into account how badly Job is suffering.

How can pain or suffering cause us to lose our perspective or to give up? Has such a thing ever happened to you or someone you know?

[11] For according to their deeds he will repay them,
and according to their ways he will make it befall them.
[12] Of a truth, God will not do wickedly,
and the Almighty[a] will not pervert justice.
[13] Who gave him charge over the earth
and who laid on him[b] the whole world?
[14] If he should take back his spirit[c] to himself,
and gather to himself his breath,
[15] all flesh would perish together,
and all mortals return to dust.

[16] "If you have understanding, hear this;
listen to what I say.
[17] Shall one who hates justice govern?
Will you condemn one who is righteous and mighty,
[18] who says to a king, 'You scoundrel!'
and to princes, 'You wicked men!';
[19] who shows no partiality to nobles,
nor regards the rich more than the poor,
for they are all the work of his hands?
[20] In a moment they die;
at midnight the people are shaken and pass away,
and the mighty are taken away by no human hand.

[21] "For his eyes are upon the ways of mortals,
and he sees all their steps.
[22] There is no gloom or deep darkness
where evildoers may hide themselves.
[23] For he has not appointed a time[d] for anyone
to go before God in judgment.
[24] He shatters the mighty without investigation,
and sets others in their place.
[25] Thus, knowing their works,
he overturns them in the night, and they are crushed.
[26] He strikes them for their wickedness
while others look on,
[27] because they turned aside from following him,
and had no regard for any of his ways,
[28] so that they caused the cry of the poor to come to him,
and he heard the cry of the afflicted—
[29] When he is quiet, who can condemn?
When he hides his face, who can behold him,
whether it be a nation or an individual?—

34:17 Will you condemn one who is…mighty: Elihu suggests Job, or any human being, has no right to question God, who always acts justly.

What do you think about the idea that God always acts justly? Is Elihu correct to suggest that God's ways cannot be questioned? Why or why not?

---

[a] Traditional rendering of Heb *Shaddai* [b] Heb lacks *on him* [c] Heb *his heart his spirit* [d] Cn: Heb *yet*

30 so that the godless should not reign,
or those who ensnare the people.

31 "For has anyone said to God,
'I have endured punishment; I will not offend any more;
32 teach me what I do not see;
if I have done iniquity, I will do it no more'?
33 Will he then pay back to suit you,
because you reject it?
For you must choose, and not I;
therefore declare what you know.[a]
34 Those who have sense will say to me,
and the wise who hear me will say,
35 'Job speaks without knowledge,
his words are without insight.'
36 Would that Job were tried to the limit,
because his answers are those of the wicked.
37 For he adds rebellion to his sin;
he claps his hands among us,
and multiplies his words against God."

Elihu Condemns Self-Righteousness

35 Elihu continued and said:
2 "Do you think this to be just?
You say, 'I am in the right before God.'
3 If you ask, 'What advantage have I?
How am I better off than if I had sinned?'
4 I will answer you
and your friends with you.
5 Look at the heavens and see;
observe the clouds, which are higher than you.
6 If you have sinned, what do you accomplish against him?
And if your transgressions are multiplied, what do you do to him?
7 If you are righteous, what do you give to him;
or what does he receive from your hand?
8 Your wickedness affects others like you,
and your righteousness, other human beings.

9 "Because of the multitude of oppressions people cry out;
they call for help because of the arm of the mighty.
10 But no one says, 'Where is God my Maker,

35:9-16 people cry out…empty talk: Elihu accuses Job and others of empty prayers if they question God's motives or treatment and don't acknowledge their own sins.

[a] Meaning of Heb of verses 29–33 uncertain

who gives strength in the night,
11 who teaches us more than the animals of the earth,
and makes us wiser than the birds of the air?'
12 There they cry out, but he does not answer,
because of the pride of evildoers.
13 Surely God does not hear an empty cry,
nor does the Almighty[a] regard it.
14 How much less when you say that you do not see him,
that the case is before him, and you are waiting for him!
15 And now, because his anger does not punish,
and he does not greatly heed transgression,[b]
16 Job opens his mouth in empty talk,
he multiplies words without knowledge."

Elihu Exalts God's Goodness

36 Elihu continued and said:
2 "Bear with me a little, and I will show you,
for I have yet something to say on God's behalf.
3 I will bring my knowledge from far away,
and ascribe righteousness to my Maker.
4 For truly my words are not false;
one who is perfect in knowledge is with you.

5 "Surely God is mighty and does not despise any;
he is mighty in strength of understanding.
6 He does not keep the wicked alive,
but gives the afflicted their right.
7 He does not withdraw his eyes from the righteous,
but with kings on the throne
he sets them forever, and they are exalted.
8 And if they are bound in fetters
and caught in the cords of affliction,
9 then he declares to them their work
and their transgressions, that they are behaving
arrogantly.
10 He opens their ears to instruction,
and commands that they return from iniquity.
11 If they listen, and serve him,
they complete their days in prosperity,
and their years in pleasantness.
12 But if they do not listen, they shall perish by the sword,
and die without knowledge.

36:6-7 wicked…righteous: Elihu returns to a common theme. God punishes the wicked and takes care of the righteous. The implication is that Job must have acted in a wicked way. That's why he is being punished.

---

[a] Traditional rendering of Heb *Shaddai* [b] Theodotion Symmachus Compare Vg: Meaning of Heb uncertain

13 “The godless in heart cherish anger;
they do not cry for help when he binds them.
14 They die in their youth,
and their life ends in shame.[a]
15 He delivers the afflicted by their affliction,
and opens their ear by adversity.
16 He also allured you out of distress
into a broad place where there was no constraint,
and what was set on your table was full of fatness.

17 “But you are obsessed with the case of the wicked;
judgment and justice seize you.
18 Beware that wrath does not entice you into scoffing,
and do not let the greatness of the ransom turn you aside.
19 Will your cry avail to keep you from distress,
or will all the force of your strength?
20 Do not long for the night,
when peoples are cut off in their place.
21 Beware! Do not turn to iniquity;
because of that you have been tried by affliction.
22 See, God is exalted in his power;
who is a teacher like him?
23 Who has prescribed for him his way,
or who can say, ‘You have done wrong’?

Elihu Proclaims God’s Majesty

24 “Remember to extol his work,
of which mortals have sung.
25 All people have looked on it;
everyone watches it from far away.
26 Surely God is great, and we do not know him;
the number of his years is unsearchable.
27 For he draws up the drops of water;
he distills[b] his mist in rain,
28 which the skies pour down
and drop upon mortals abundantly.
29 Can anyone understand the spreading of the clouds,
the thunderings of his pavilion?
30 See, he scatters his lightning around him
and covers the roots of the sea.
31 For by these he governs peoples;
he gives food in abundance.
32 He covers his hands with the lightning,

36:15-18 opens their ear by adversity...wrath does not entice you into scoffing: Now Elihu suggests to Job that his troubles and afflictions are given by God as a way of opening his ears and helping Job see a way toward being restored again. He cautions Job not to scoff at or turn away from the adversity, but to embrace it as God’s way of teaching Job.

What do you think of the idea that adversity can be seen in a positive way? How can difficult times make us stronger?

36:26—37:14 God is great...consider the wondrous works of God: In this section Elihu describes how God controls all the forces of nature. So, how can Job question such a powerful force?

---

[a] Heb *ends among the temple prostitutes* [b] Cn: Heb *they distill*

and commands it to strike the mark.
33 Its crashing[a] tells about him;
he is jealous[a] with anger against iniquity.

37 "At this also my heart trembles,
and leaps out of its place.
2 Listen, listen to the thunder of his voice
and the rumbling that comes from his mouth.
3 Under the whole heaven he lets it loose,
and his lightning to the corners of the earth.
4 After it his voice roars;
he thunders with his majestic voice
and he does not restrain the lightnings[b] when his voice is heard.
5 God thunders wondrously with his voice;
he does great things that we cannot comprehend.
6 For to the snow he says, 'Fall on the earth';
and the shower of rain, his heavy shower of rain,
7 serves as a sign on everyone's hand,
so that all whom he has made may know it.[c]
8 Then the animals go into their lairs
and remain in their dens.
9 From its chamber comes the whirlwind,
and cold from the scattering winds.
10 By the breath of God ice is given,
and the broad waters are frozen fast.
11 He loads the thick cloud with moisture;
the clouds scatter his lightning.
12 They turn round and round by his guidance,
to accomplish all that he commands them
on the face of the habitable world.
13 Whether for correction, or for his land,
or for love, he causes it to happen.

14 "Hear this, O Job;
stop and consider the wondrous works of God.
15 Do you know how God lays his command upon them,
and causes the lightning of his cloud to shine?
16 Do you know the balancings of the clouds,
the wondrous works of the one whose knowledge is perfect,
17 you whose garments are hot
when the earth is still because of the south wind?
18 Can you, like him, spread out the skies,

37:23-24 The Almighty—we cannot find him.... who are wise in their own conceit: Eliphaz says that God will not pay attention to those who think they are wise but are only deceiving themselves, especially those who think they know better than God. Of course, immediately after these verses, God speaks to Job, not to Job's friends. Such an event seems to vindicate the innocent sufferer.

[a] Meaning of Heb uncertain [b] Heb *them* [c] Meaning of Heb of verse 7 uncertain

hard as a molten mirror?
19 Teach us what we shall say to him;
we cannot draw up our case because of darkness.
20 Should he be told that I want to speak?
Did anyone ever wish to be swallowed up?
21 Now, no one can look on the light
when it is bright in the skies,
when the wind has passed and cleared them.
22 Out of the north comes golden splendor;
around God is awesome majesty.
23 The Almighty[a]—we cannot find him;
he is great in power and justice,
and abundant righteousness he will not violate.
24 Therefore mortals fear him;
he does not regard any who are wise in their own conceit."

The LORD Answers Job

38 Then the LORD answered Job out of the whirlwind:
2"Who is this that darkens counsel by words without knowledge?
3 Gird up your loins like a man,
I will question you, and you shall declare to me.

4 "Where were you when I laid the foundation of the earth?
Tell me, if you have understanding.
5 Who determined its measurements—surely you know!
Or who stretched the line upon it?
6 On what were its bases sunk,
or who laid its cornerstone
7 when the morning stars sang together
and all the heavenly beings[b] shouted for joy?

8 "Or who shut in the sea with doors
when it burst out from the womb?—
9 when I made the clouds its garment,
and thick darkness its swaddling band,
10 and prescribed bounds for it,
and set bars and doors,
11 and said, 'Thus far shall you come, and no farther,
and here shall your proud waves be stopped'?

12 "Have you commanded the morning since your days began,
and caused the dawn to know its place,

[a] Traditional rendering of Heb *Shaddai* [b] Heb *sons of God*

38:1—41:34 the LORD answered Job: After all the human participants have had their say, God finally speaks. God does not address Job's suffering directly or tell Job about the wager with the Satan. God appears to Job in a "whirlwind" and takes Job on a verbal tour of the cosmos. God begins by describing the establishment of the earth and the birth of the sea. God then talks about the whole cosmos, including constellations and meteorological forces. God describes a number of wild animals. Finally, after a brief response from Job, God describes two mythological creatures, Behemoth and Leviathan. Throughout the speeches, God asks Job questions such as, "Were you there?" "Can you?" "Do you know?" The answer, of course, is *no*—because Job is a human being, not God.

38:7 stars sang together…heavenly beings shouted: This is a description of the beginning of creation. The morning stars and the heavenly beings shout for joy to see God's good creation established. The rest of the divine speeches will continue to describe God's obvious delight and pride in that beautiful creation. God, in a sense, reestablishes creation here, after Job has tried to undo creation in his first lament (chapter 3). Job wanted the stars to be darkened (3:9); but here they sing for joy.

Describe your favorite outdoor place. Why is it your favorite place? How do you see God's hand at work in making it?

38:8-11 the sea…burst out from the womb: In the ancient Near East the sea was a symbol and force of chaos. There are many stories in ancient Mesopotamian and Canaanite literature about the gods' defeat of the sea at the beginning of time. It was thought that a defeat of the sea needed to happen before creation could be established (see note on 3:8). Here, in the divine speeches, God doesn't defeat the sea. Instead, God is the midwife who attends the birth of the sea. The sea is not so much a force of chaos as it is a rambunctious infant who needs to be restrained so that it doesn't hurt itself or others. It is a strikingly positive image, compared to the negative portrayal of the sea in other ancient Near Eastern literature. God makes sure the sea has a place in creation, though God also establishes boundaries for it (38:11), so that it does not overrun the rest of creation.

13 so that it might take hold of the skirts of the earth,
and the wicked be shaken out of it?
14 It is changed like clay under the seal,
and it is dyed[a] like a garment.
15 Light is withheld from the wicked,
and their uplifted arm is broken.

16 "Have you entered into the springs of the sea,
or walked in the recesses of the deep?
17 Have the gates of death been revealed to you,
or have you seen the gates of deep darkness?
18 Have you comprehended the expanse of the earth?
Declare, if you know all this.

19 "Where is the way to the dwelling of light,
and where is the place of darkness,
20 that you may take it to its territory
and that you may discern the paths to its home?
21 Surely you know, for you were born then,
and the number of your days is great!

22 "Have you entered the storehouses of the snow,
or have you seen the storehouses of the hail,
23 which I have reserved for the time of trouble,
for the day of battle and war?
24 What is the way to the place where the light is distributed,
or where the east wind is scattered upon the earth?

38:25-27 Who has cut a channel for the torrents of rain...to make the ground put forth grass?: Human beings are almost completely absent from the divine speeches. God is said to send rain on land where no human being lives, to sprout grass that no human being will ever see. God takes Job's focus off himself and expands Job's vision of the world to include places and creatures he never imagined. In these speeches of God human beings are not the most important creatures in the world, though God cares for them as God cares for the rest of God's creatures (38:39-41). To care for the wilderness, God is generous with rain, the most precious resource in an arid climate.

25 "Who has cut a channel for the torrents of rain,
and a way for the thunderbolt,
26 to bring rain on a land where no one lives,
on the desert, which is empty of human life,
27 to satisfy the waste and desolate land,
and to make the ground put forth grass?

28 "Has the rain a father,
or who has begotten the drops of dew?
29 From whose womb did the ice come forth,
and who has given birth to the hoarfrost of heaven?
30 The waters become hard like stone,
and the face of the deep is frozen.

31 "Can you bind the chains of the Pleiades,
or loose the cords of Orion?

[a] Cn: Heb *and they stand forth*

32 Can you lead forth the Mazzaroth in their season,
or can you guide the Bear with its children?
33 Do you know the ordinances of the heavens?
Can you establish their rule on the earth?

34 "Can you lift up your voice to the clouds,
so that a flood of waters may cover you?
35 Can you send forth lightnings, so that they may go
and say to you, 'Here we are'?
36 Who has put wisdom in the inward parts,[a]
or given understanding to the mind?[a]
37 Who has the wisdom to number the clouds?
Or who can tilt the waterskins of the heavens,
38 when the dust runs into a mass
and the clods cling together?

39 "Can you hunt the prey for the lion,
or satisfy the appetite of the young lions,
40 when they crouch in their dens,
or lie in wait in their covert?
41 Who provides for the raven its prey,
when its young ones cry to God,
and wander about for lack of food?

39 "Do you know when the mountain goats give birth?
Do you observe the calving of the deer?
2 Can you number the months that they fulfill,
and do you know the time when they give birth,
3 when they crouch to give birth to their offspring,
and are delivered of their young?
4 Their young ones become strong, they grow up in the open;
they go forth, and do not return to them.

5 "Who has let the wild ass go free?
Who has loosed the bonds of the swift ass,
6 to which I have given the steppe for its home,
the salt land for its dwelling place?
7 It scorns the tumult of the city;
it does not hear the shouts of the driver.
8 It ranges the mountains as its pasture,
and it searches after every green thing.

9 "Is the wild ox willing to serve you?
Will it spend the night at your crib?

[a] Meaning of Heb uncertain

39:5-12 Who has let the wild ass go free?…Is the wild ox willing to serve you?: God describes two creatures that cannot be tamed by human beings. The wild ass laughs at the "tumult of the city" and "does not hear the shouts of the driver." The wild ox will not consent to plowing the fields or bringing in the harvest. Unlike their domestic cousins, many of which Job had owned (1:3), the wild donkey and the wild ox are of no use to human beings and will not serve them. Like the rest of the animals in the divine speeches, they are free, wild creatures.

10 Can you tie it in the furrow with ropes,
or will it harrow the valleys after you?
11 Will you depend on it because its strength is great,
and will you hand over your labor to it?
12 Do you have faith in it that it will return,
and bring your grain to your threshing floor?[a]

13 "The ostrich's wings flap wildly,
though its pinions lack plumage.[b]
14 For it leaves its eggs to the earth,
and lets them be warmed on the ground,
15 forgetting that a foot may crush them,
and that a wild animal may trample them.
16 It deals cruelly with its young, as if they were not its own;
though its labor should be in vain, yet it has no fear;
17 because God has made it forget wisdom,
and given it no share in understanding.
18 When it spreads its plumes aloft,[b]
it laughs at the horse and its rider.

39:19-25 Do you give the horse its might?: The war horse seems to be the one exception to the rule in the divine speeches. It does serve humanity; it has a human rider. Nevertheless, this animal, too, is wild. It rejoices in battle and facilitates the killing of human beings by other human beings.

19 "Do you give the horse its might?
Do you clothe its neck with mane?
20 Do you make it leap like the locust?
Its majestic snorting is terrible.
21 It paws[c] violently, exults mightily;
it goes out to meet the weapons.
22 It laughs at fear, and is not dismayed;
it does not turn back from the sword.
23 Upon it rattle the quiver,
the flashing spear, and the javelin.
24 With fierceness and rage it swallows the ground;
it cannot stand still at the sound of the trumpet.
25 When the trumpet sounds, it says 'Aha!'
From a distance it smells the battle,
the thunder of the captains, and the shouting.

26 "Is it by your wisdom that the hawk soars,
and spreads its wings toward the south?
27 Is it at your command that the eagle mounts up
and makes its nest on high?
28 It lives on the rock and makes its home
in the fastness of the rocky crag.
29 From there it spies the prey;

---

[a] Heb *your grain and your threshing floor* [b] Meaning of Heb uncertain [c] Gk Syr Vg: Heb *they dig*

its eyes see it from far away.
30 Its young ones suck up blood;
and where the slain are, there it is."

40 And the LORD said to Job:
2 "Shall a faultfinder contend with the Almighty?[a]
Anyone who argues with God must respond."

40:1-5 Job answered the LORD: God demands a response from Job, but Job says he cannot respond. He is small and God is big; what can he say? (See note on 42:1-6 for Job's second response.)

Job's Response to God

3 Then Job answered the LORD:
4 "See, I am of small account; what shall I answer you?
I lay my hand on my mouth.
5 I have spoken once, and I will not answer;
twice, but will proceed no further."

God's Challenge to Job

6 Then the LORD answered Job out of the whirlwind:
7 "Gird up your loins like a man;
I will question you, and you declare to me.
8 Will you even put me in the wrong?
Will you condemn me that you may be justified?
9 Have you an arm like God,
and can you thunder with a voice like his?

40:6-14 Then the LORD answered Job: This is the only part of the divine speeches that seems to directly address some of Job's concern with justice. "Will you put me in the wrong?" says God. "Will you condemn me that you may be justified?" This is what Job attempted to do with his desire to go to court with God. God then challenges Job to take on God's attributes and defeat the wicked. Being only human, Job cannot accept the challenge.

10 "Deck yourself with majesty and dignity;
clothe yourself with glory and splendor.
11 Pour out the overflowings of your anger,
and look on all who are proud, and abase them.
12 Look on all who are proud, and bring them low;
tread down the wicked where they stand.
13 Hide them all in the dust together;
bind their faces in the world below.[b]
14 Then I will also acknowledge to you
that your own right hand can give you victory.

15 "Look at Behemoth,
which I made just as I made you;
it eats grass like an ox.
16 Its strength is in its loins,
and its power in the muscles of its belly.
17 It makes its tail stiff like a cedar;
the sinews of its thighs are knit together.
18 Its bones are tubes of bronze,
its limbs like bars of iron.

40:15-24 Look at Behemoth: Behemoth is a strong land animal living in or near water. It is a creature that seems to share some characteristics with the hippopotamus, but Behemoth is more than a mere animal. Its strength is that of bronze and iron (40:18), and it is "the first of the great acts of God" (40:19), created at the beginning of the world. (See Prov 8:22 for a similar description of Woman Wisdom.) God made Behemoth just as God made Job, implying something of an equality between the two (40:15). Job cannot master Behemoth.

[a] Traditional rendering of Heb *Shaddai* [b] Heb *the hidden place*

19 "It is the first of the great acts of God—
only its Maker can approach it with the sword.
20 For the mountains yield food for it
where all the wild animals play.
21 Under the lotus plants it lies,
in the covert of the reeds and in the marsh.
22 The lotus trees cover it for shade;
the willows of the wadi surround it.
23 Even if the river is turbulent, it is not frightened;
it is confident though Jordan rushes against its mouth.
24 Can one take it with hooks[a]
or pierce its nose with a snare?

41 [b] "Can you draw out Leviathan[c] with a fishhook,
or press down its tongue with a cord?
2 Can you put a rope in its nose,
or pierce its jaw with a hook?
3 Will it make many supplications to you?
Will it speak soft words to you?
4 Will it make a covenant with you
to be taken as your servant forever?
5 Will you play with it as with a bird,
or will you put it on leash for your girls?
6 Will traders bargain over it?
Will they divide it up among the merchants?
7 Can you fill its skin with harpoons,
or its head with fishing spears?
8 Lay hands on it;
think of the battle; you will not do it again!
9[d] Any hope of capturing it[e] will be disappointed;
were not even the gods[f] overwhelmed at the sight of it?
10 No one is so fierce as to dare to stir it up.
Who can stand before it?[g]
11 Who can confront it[g] and be safe?[h]
—under the whole heaven, who?[i]

12 "I will not keep silence concerning its limbs,
or its mighty strength, or its splendid frame.
13 Who can strip off its outer garment?
Who can penetrate its double coat of mail?[j]
14 Who can open the doors of its face?
There is terror all around its teeth.

41:1-34 Can you draw out Leviathan: The last and longest description in the divine speeches is saved for Leviathan, the mythological sea dragon. Leviathan bears some resemblance to the crocodile but, like Behemoth, it is a primordial or ancient creature. Leviathan, like the sea it inhabits, was a symbol of chaos in the ancient Near East. (See Ps 74:14 and Isa 27:1 for descriptions of God's defeat of Leviathan.)

In the divine speeches (as in Ps 104:26), Leviathan is described in positive terms as part of God's good creation. God takes delight and pride in Leviathan's strength and body (41:12-32). God challenges Job to make use of Leviathan. Will the sea dragon be his servant (41:4)? Will Job take him as a pet (41:5)? Will merchants divide up his body for food or other uses (41:6)? All the ways in which human beings use animals are ridiculous when applied to Leviathan, that fiercest of creatures. Indeed, God names him "king" over all proud beings on earth (41:33-34). As with the sea, God gives Leviathan a place in creation while also maintaining control over Leviathan, so that he cannot overrun the rest of creation. God establishes order in creation, but it is an order including creatures that are wild and potentially dangerous to humanity. Nevertheless, they are part of a good creation, and God delights in their beauty and wildness.

[a] Cn: Heb *in his eyes* [b] Ch 40.25 in Heb [c] Or *the crocodile* [d] Ch 41.1 in Heb [e] Heb *of it* [f] Cn Compare Symmachus Syr: Heb *one is* [g] Heb *me* [h] Gk: Heb *that I shall repay* [i] Heb *to me* [j] Gk: Heb *bridle*

15 Its back[a] is made of shields in rows,
shut up closely as with a seal.
16 One is so near to another
that no air can come between them.
17 They are joined one to another;
they clasp each other and cannot be separated.
18 Its sneezes flash forth light,
and its eyes are like the eyelids of the dawn.
19 From its mouth go flaming torches;
sparks of fire leap out.
20 Out of its nostrils comes smoke,
as from a boiling pot and burning rushes.
21 Its breath kindles coals,
and a flame comes out of its mouth.
22 In its neck abides strength,
and terror dances before it.
23 The folds of its flesh cling together;
it is firmly cast and immovable.
24 Its heart is as hard as stone,
as hard as the lower millstone.
25 When it raises itself up the gods are afraid;
at the crashing they are beside themselves.
26 Though the sword reaches it, it does not avail,
nor does the spear, the dart, or the javelin.
27 It counts iron as straw,
and bronze as rotten wood.
28 The arrow cannot make it flee;
slingstones, for it, are turned to chaff.
29 Clubs are counted as chaff;
it laughs at the rattle of javelins.
30 Its underparts are like sharp potsherds;
it spreads itself like a threshing sledge on the mire.
31 It makes the deep boil like a pot;
it makes the sea like a pot of ointment.
32 It leaves a shining wake behind it;
one would think the deep to be white-haired.
33 On earth it has no equal,
a creature without fear.
34 It surveys everything that is lofty;
it is king over all that are proud."

Job Is Humbled and Satisfied

42 Then Job answered the LORD:
2 "I know that you can do all things,

[a] Cn Compare Gk Vg: Heb *pride*

42:1-6 Then Job answered the LORD: Quoting God's words (42:3a, 4), Job acknowledges God's power and his own lack of understanding. Job also says he has seen God, something he had hoped for earlier in his life (19:26).

Verse 6 can be translated various ways. In the Hebrew there is no object for the first verb, which means "despise" or "reject," so the translator has to supply an object (perhaps "my words;" see 42:3). There is also disagreement over whether the phrase "dust and ashes" should be understood literally or symbolically. In support of the symbolic meaning, when the phrase "dust and ashes" occurs elsewhere in the Bible (Gen 18:27; Job 30:19), it seems to refer to human mortality. The last translation issue has to do with the second verb, which can mean either "repent" or "change one's mind" (see Jonah 3:10 for the same verb).

For the reasons discussed above, this verse might be better translated, "Therefore I recant and change my mind about humanity." Such a translation would fit in well with what Job has learned from the divine speeches. Contrary to what Job had thought before, humanity is not the center of God's creation. Nevertheless, human beings are recipients of God's care, along with the rest of the creatures God loves.

and that no purpose of yours can be thwarted.
3 'Who is this that hides counsel without knowledge?'
Therefore I have uttered what I did not understand,
things too wonderful for me, which I did not know.
4 'Hear, and I will speak;
I will question you, and you declare to me.'
5 I had heard of you by the hearing of the ear,
but now my eye sees you;
6 therefore I despise myself,
and repent in dust and ashes."

Job's Friends Are Humiliated

7 After the LORD had spoken these words to Job, the LORD said
to Eliphaz the Temanite: "My wrath is kindled against you and against
your two friends; for you have not spoken of me what is right, as my
servant Job has. 8 Now therefore take seven bulls and seven rams, and
go to my servant Job, and offer up for yourselves a burnt offering; and
my servant Job shall pray for you, for I will accept his prayer not to
deal with you according to your folly; for you have not spoken of me
what is right, as my servant Job has done." 9 So Eliphaz the Temanite and Bildad the Shuhite and Zophar the Naamathite went and did
what the LORD had told them; and the LORD accepted Job's prayer.

Job's Fortunes Are Restored Twofold

10 And the LORD restored the fortunes of Job when he had
prayed for his friends; and the LORD gave Job twice as much as he
had before. 11 Then there came to him all his brothers and sisters and
all who had known him before, and they ate bread with him in his
house; they showed him sympathy and comforted him for all the evil
that the LORD had brought upon him; and each of them gave him a
piece of money[a] and a gold ring. 12 The LORD blessed the latter days
of Job more than his beginning; and he had fourteen thousand sheep,
six thousand camels, a thousand yoke of oxen, and a thousand donkeys. 13 He also had seven sons and three daughters. 14 He named the
first Jemimah, the second Keziah, and the third Keren-happuch. 15 In
all the land there were no women so beautiful as Job's daughters; and
their father gave them an inheritance along with their brothers. 16 After this Job lived one hundred and forty years, and saw his children,
and his children's children, four generations. 17 And Job died, old and
full of days.

[a] Heb *a qesitah*

42:7-8 you have not spoken of me what is right, as my servant Job has done: God speaks to Job's friends and rebukes them, as Job predicted God would do (13:7-12). God says two times, "you have not spoken of me what is right, as my servant Job has done." The phrase also can be translated, "you have not spoken *to* me rightly, as my servant Job has done." In the many speeches of the friends, they have never once spoken directly *to* God or offered prayers for their suffering friend. On the other hand, Job has spoken increasingly *to* God, rather than just *about* God. For his prayers and honest lament, Job is praised. God instructs him to offer sacrifices for his friends and to pray for them, and God accepts Job's prayer.

42:10-17 the LORD restored the fortunes of Job: The book ends by describing what becomes of Job. God restores Job's fortunes. Job and his wife have more children. Their daughters are the most beautiful women in the land. Job gives them names to match their beauty: Jemimah (Dove), Keziah (Cinnamon), and Keren-happuch (Horn-of-Eye-shadow). He also gives them an inheritance along with their brothers, a rare practice in ancient Israel. According to commentator Ellen F. Davis, it seems that Job has learned from God how to appreciate beauty and how to give his children the freedom God gives all his creatures. After all his suffering, Job's life ends on a note of joy and hope. Job chooses, even at the risk of more suffering, to live again and to love again. His choice bears fruit. Job, like the faithful patriarchs before him (see note on 1:1-5), lives a long life and sees his children and his grandchildren grow up. Then he dies, "old and full of days."

What does the story of Job seem to say about how God can be approached in prayer?

Psalm 119:105

PSALMS

Background File

The book of Psalms (also called the Psalter) contains one hundred-fifty prayers, songs, liturgies, and poems that are divided into five smaller books:

Book I (Psalms 1–41)
Book II (Psalms 42–72)
Book III (Psalms 73–89)
Book IV (Psalms 90–106)
Book V (Psalms 107–150)

Within these smaller books, there are other divisions, such as the "Songs of Ascent" (Psalms 120–134).

The psalms were composed by many different authors, who are not identified. Some psalms include a *superscription* (writing or printing that appears above or to the side) such as "of David" or "of Asaph." These terms do not mean that David or Asaph wrote these psalms, but that the poem or song is associated with them in some manner.

The superscriptions were not originally included in the psalms. They were added at a later date and often include terms with unknown meanings, such as "with stringed instruments" (Ps 4), "for the flutes" (Ps 5), "according to The Sheminith" (Pss 6, 12), "A Shiggaion" (Ps 7), "according to The Gittith" (Ps 8), and "according to Muth-labben" (Ps 9). These may have been musical instructions for the singing of these psalms. The term *selah,* which occurs seventy-one times in the book of Psalms (and three times in Habakkuk 3), is also unknown. Many scholars believe this term was also a musical or liturgical notation.

What's the Story?

The Hebrew name for the book of Psalms is *Tehillim,* which literally means "praises." The book is a collection of material used by individuals, communities, and kings. This includes a wide variety of psalms:

Prayers for help
Hymns of praise

Liturgies
Instructional psalms
Songs of thanksgiving
Royal psalms
Trust psalms
Acrostic poems
Festival psalms
Historical psalms

The chart on the next two pages provides more information on each type of psalm.

What's the Message?

Martin Luther wrote that the book of Psalms "might well be called a little Bible. In it is comprehended most beautifully and briefly everything that is in the entire Bible. It is really a fine enchiridion or handbook. In fact, I have a notion that the Holy Spirit wanted to take the trouble himself to compile a short Bible and book of examples of all Christendom or all saints, so that anyone who could not read the whole Bible would here have anyway almost an entire summary of it, comprised in one little book" (*LW* 35:254). By this Luther obviously did not mean that the Psalms teach Christian beliefs, since they were all written before the time of Christ. Rather, Luther was referring to the fact that the Psalms explore the highs and lows of the life of faith. They sing with joy and trust from the mountaintop moments and cry out with pain "out of the depths" (Ps 130:1). The Psalms weep with those who suffer, laugh with those who celebrate, and teach all of us about the long journey of faith.

Types of Psalms

Prayers for help	
Individual 3, 4, 5, 6, 7, 9/10, 13, 17, 22, 26, 28, 31, 35, 36, 38, 39, 42/43, 51, 54, 55, 56, 57, 58, 59, 61, 64, 69, 70, 71, 77, 86, 88, 89, 90, 94, 102, 109, 120, 130, 139, 140, 141, 142, 143, 144	Individual prayers for help, sometimes called laments, were prayed by individuals in crisis. These pleas for help generally include several elements: • a call to be heard • complaints about God's absence, the person's suffering, and oppressors • pleas for help (the most important part of a prayer for help) • statements of trust in God • promises to praise God after the crisis is past The specific crisis in the psalm usually cannot be identified, perhaps so that individuals of every generation could pray these prayers as their own. Penitential and imprecatory psalms are two sub-categories of individual prayers for help. Penitential psalms (6, 32, 38, 51, 102, 130, 143) were identified by the Western church as prayers for individuals who want to ask God for forgiveness. Imprecatory psalms (36, 69, 109, 137, 139) ask God to rescue the person who is praying and also to punish evildoers.
Communal 44, 60, 67, 74, 79, 80, 82, 83, 85, 108, 123, 126, 137	Communal prayers for help, or communal laments, are the prayers of a community or nation in crisis.

Hymns of praise	
8, 33, 47, 48, 65, 66, 67, 68, 76, 84, 87, 89, 93, 96, 97, 98, 99, 100, 103, 104, 105, 111, 112, 113, 114, 117, 135, 145, 146, 147, 148, 149, 150	Hymns of praise give witness to God's love and grace through a call to praise ("Praise the Lord") and reasons for praise ("for the Lord . . ."). These songs were composed for community worship.
Creation psalms 8, 19, 104, 139	Creation psalms are hymns that praise God as creator of heaven and earth.
Enthronement 47, 93, 95, 96, 97, 99	Enthronement hymns specifically praise God as "king." Originally they may have been sung at a festival celebrating the Lord as the universal king.
Songs of Zion 46, 48, 76, 84, 87, 122	Songs of Zion praise God for choosing to "dwell" (or causing God's "name" to dwell) in the Jerusalem temple. They also celebrate God's promise to protect Jerusalem and to remain faithful to David's descendants.

Liturgies	
2, 12, 15, 24, 50, 81, 82, 85, 91, 95, 107, 115, 118, 121, 124, 129, 132, 134, 136	Liturgies were usually composed for more than one person to perform (with various people speaking different parts) and often for some specific purpose (such as to enter the temple, request God's help, or thank God). A priest or another leader of the people probably spoke at least part of many of these psalms.

Instructional psalms	
1, 14, 19, 37, 41, 49, 53, 62, 73, 90, 119, 127, 128, 133	Instructional psalms often include comparisons between the righteous and unrighteous, the wise and the fool, or God's way and the world's way. Also known as Wisdom psalms, they were written to teach the community. Many other psalms include significant teaching (see 25, 91, and 94), and Christians read all the psalms as instruction. The three psalms that focus specifically on God's Law (1, 19, and 119) are also called Torah Psalms.

Songs of thanksgiving	
Individual 30, 32, 34, 40, 57, 66, 92, 116, 138	Individual songs of thanksgiving praise God for help given to a person during a crisis. Individuals would pray for God's help and promise to praise God afterward (see "Prayers for help—Individual"). They would thank God in the worshiping community, where their praise could build up the faith of others.
Communal 66, 75, 107	Communal songs of thanksgiving praise God for help given to a community during a crisis. The community sings these songs after passing through a difficult time, such as war, famine, or plague.

Royal psalms	
2, 18, 20, 21, 45, 72, 89, 101, 110, 132, 144	Royal psalms were composed for specific events in the king's life, such as his coronation (2) or wedding (45). Other psalms celebrate the king as one of God's servants, or were specifically designed for the king to pray or sing as the leader of the people (18, 20, and 21). Royal psalms were preserved even after kings no longer ruled Israel, because they maintained God's promise that one day the Messiah, the ideal king, would come.

Trust psalms	
11, 16, 23, 27, 46, 52, 63, 121, 125, 129, 131	Trust psalms express faith and confidence in God amid great difficulties, threats, and dangers.

Acrostic poems	
9/10, 25, 34, 37, 111, 112, 119, 145	Acrostic poems are written so that particular letters follow a pattern, sometimes spelling out words or phrases. The book of Psalms contains eight acrostic poems, in which each line or section begins with a succeeding letter of the Hebrew alphabet.

Festival psalms	
50, 81, 95	Festival psalms were composed for use at one or more of Israel's three annual festivals.

Historical psalms	
78, 105, 106	Historical psalms tell a portion of Israel's history to give witness to God's faithfulness as shown in history.

BOOK I

(Psalms 1–41)

PSALM 1
The Two Ways

1 Happy are those
 who do not follow the advice of the wicked,
or take the path that sinners tread,
 or sit in the seat of scoffers;
2 but their delight is in the law of the LORD,
 and on his law they meditate day and night.
3 They are like trees
 planted by streams of water,
which yield their fruit in its season,
 and their leaves do not wither.
In all that they do, they prosper.

4 The wicked are not so,
 but are like chaff that the wind drives away.
5 Therefore the wicked will not stand in the judgment,
 nor sinners in the congregation of the righteous;
6 for the LORD watches over the way of the righteous,
 but the way of the wicked will perish.

PSALM 2
God's Promise to His Anointed

1 Why do the nations conspire,
 and the peoples plot in vain?
2 The kings of the earth set themselves,
 and the rulers take counsel together,
 against the LORD and his anointed, saying,
3 "Let us burst their bonds asunder,
 and cast their cords from us."

4 He who sits in the heavens laughs;
 the LORD has them in derision.
5 Then he will speak to them in his wrath,
 and terrify them in his fury, saying,
6 "I have set my king on Zion, my holy hill."

7 I will tell of the decree of the LORD:
He said to me, "You are my son;
 today I have begotten you.
8 Ask of me, and I will make the nations your heritage,
 and the ends of the earth your possession.

Psalm 1: An instructional psalm (see Types of Psalms, pp. 849-850) about the way of God and the way of the wicked, (see note on 25:4-5).

1:1 Happy: This word does not refer to an emotion but to the public reputation of those who live an enviable or desirable life. The "wicked," "sinners," and "scoffers" are those who actively oppose God's will and refuse to follow God's instruction.

1:2 law: The Hebrew word *torah* (TOE-rah), which can be translated as "instruction," does not carry the negative connotations of the word "law." The term refers to the Bible's instruction in the way of faith and to the Bible as a whole, which is God's Word.

What is God's law? Martin Luther taught that God's law is good and has two uses. The first use teaches us how to live in this world. The second use reminds us that nobody is perfect and that we all need God's forgiveness. *Psalm 1:2*

Those who delight in God's law are like trees that provide fruit (1:3). Why is a fruitful tree a good image for the life of faith?

1:5 the judgment: This does not refer to the final judgment at Christ's second coming, but to times of crisis when past actions catch up with people. "The righteous" actively seek to love God and follow God's will. They are not sinless but are committed to God, God's world, and God's people.

Psalm 2: A royal psalm and liturgy (see Types of Psalms, pp. 849-850), probably composed for the king's coronation.

2:2 his anointed: The Hebrew word *meshiach* (Muh-SHEE-ack) refers to the anointed king. (Anointing involved pouring oil on a person's head to designate him as king.) When rule by kings failed, people believed God would keep this promise by sending the Messiah.

2:7 my son: God will consider the human king as God's son. God ruled the people through the king.

2:8 nations: God's promise to the king echoes God's promise to Abraham (see Gen 12:1-3).

9 You shall break them with a rod of iron,
and dash them in pieces like a potter's vessel."

10 Now therefore, O kings, be wise;
be warned, O rulers of the earth.
11 Serve the LORD with fear,
with trembling 12kiss his feet,[a]
or he will be angry, and you will perish in the way;
for his wrath is quickly kindled.

Happy are all who take refuge in him.

PSALM 3
Trust in God under Adversity

A Psalm of David, when he fled from his son Absalom.

1 O LORD, how many are my foes!
Many are rising against me;
2 many are saying to me,
"There is no help for you[b] in God." *Selah*

3 But you, O LORD, are a shield around me,
my glory, and the one who lifts up my head.
4 I cry aloud to the LORD,
and he answers me from his holy hill. *Selah*

5 I lie down and sleep;
I wake again, for the LORD sustains me.
6 I am not afraid of ten thousands of people
who have set themselves against me all around.

7 Rise up, O LORD!
Deliver me, O my God!
For you strike all my enemies on the cheek;
you break the teeth of the wicked.

8 Deliverance belongs to the LORD;
may your blessing be on your people! *Selah*

PSALM 4
Confident Plea for Deliverance from Enemies

To the leader: with stringed instruments. A Psalm of David.

1 Answer me when I call, O God of my right!

---

[a] Cn: Meaning of Heb of verses 11b and 12a is uncertain [b] Syr: Heb *him*

2:11 Happy: See note on 1:1.

2:11 refuge: A central concept in the Psalms is that humans can take refuge in God during times of danger (see 5:11). To take refuge in God is to cling to God in times of trouble, trust in God's protection, and seek to follow God's way. It is like the wings of a bird spread to protect (see 91:1-2).

Psalm 3: A prayer for help (see Types of Psalms, pp. 849-850) from a person pursued by enemies.

3:2 There is no help for you in God: One of the defining characteristics of the wicked is that they deny God's power to deliver them from evil. They often even assume that God does not see evil or hear the prayers of sufferers.

3:2 Selah: The meaning is unclear, but most likely this involves directions for someone leading worship.

3:4 I cry aloud . . . he answers: The psalmist or writer believes that God hears prayers and answers the faithful when they cry out. The temple in Jerusalem is God's *holy hill. Selah*: see note on 3:2.

When have you experienced God's love so powerfully that you felt you didn't need to fear anything?

3:7-8 Deliver me: The psalmist asks for rescue from threatening situations. Deliverance is one of the marks of God's reign.

Psalm 4: A prayer for help (see Types of Psalms, pp. 849-850) from a person challenged by people who do not worship the LORD.

4:1 God of my right: The psalmist prays with confidence because the LORD is committed to just or "right" social order, and the psalmist has been persecuted unjustly. Rescue is pictured as being provided with space to live.

You gave me room when I was in distress.
Be gracious to me, and hear my prayer.

2 How long, you people, shall my honor suffer shame?
How long will you love vain words, and seek after lies? *Selah*
3 But know that the LORD has set apart the faithful for himself;
the LORD hears when I call to him.

4 When you are disturbed,[a] do not sin;
ponder it on your beds, and be silent. *Selah*
5 Offer right sacrifices,
and put your trust in the LORD.

6 There are many who say, "O that we might see some good!
Let the light of your face shine on us, O LORD!"
7 You have put gladness in my heart
more than when their grain and wine abound.

8 I will both lie down and sleep in peace;
for you alone, O LORD, make me lie down in safety.

PSALM 5

Trust in God for Deliverance from Enemies

To the leader: for the flutes. A Psalm of David.

1 Give ear to my words, O LORD;
give heed to my sighing.
2 Listen to the sound of my cry,
my King and my God,
for to you I pray.
3 O LORD, in the morning you hear my voice;
in the morning I plead my case to you, and watch.

4 For you are not a God who delights in wickedness;
evil will not sojourn with you.
5 The boastful will not stand before your eyes;
you hate all evildoers.
6 You destroy those who speak lies;
the LORD abhors the bloodthirsty and deceitful.

7 But I, through the abundance of your steadfast love,
will enter your house,
I will bow down toward your holy temple
in awe of you.

[a] Or *are angry*

4:2 seek after lies: The wicked worship false gods and also speak lies about the psalmist. Regarding *Selah,* see note on 3:2.

4:4-5, 7 right sacrifices: Israel's neighbors made sacrifices to fertility gods, whom they believed provided grain and wine (see Hos 7:14; 9:1-3). The psalmist or writer teaches that true joy is found in worshiping the LORD alone.

What does it mean to trust in the LORD? According to Martin Luther, to trust in God is to reach out to God with all your heart and arrange your life accordingly. Luther also said, "True faith . . . does not allow itself to be torn away from Christ" (*LW* 32:239). *Psalm 4:5*

What things keep you awake with worry during the night? What would give you peace?

Psalm 5: A prayer for help (see Types of Psalms, pp. 849-850).

5:3 in the morning: Morning was a figure of speech for God's deliverance arriving like the sun, driving away darkness (see 46:5, Isa 33:2).

5:4-7 not a God who delights in wickedness: God's character is the basis for the psalmist's prayer. It is God's nature to reject the evil behavior of those who are threatening and to remain faithful to the psalmist, who is in need.

[8] Lead me, O LORD, in your righteousness
because of my enemies;
make your way straight before me.

[9] For there is no truth in their mouths;
their hearts are destruction;
their throats are open graves;
they flatter with their tongues.
[10] Make them bear their guilt, O God;
let them fall by their own counsels;
because of their many transgressions cast them out,
for they have rebelled against you.

5:11 take refuge in you: See Bible Concepts note on 2:11.

[11] But let all who take refuge in you rejoice;
let them ever sing for joy.
Spread your protection over them,
so that those who love your name may exult in you.
[12] For you bless the righteous, O LORD;
you cover them with favor as with a shield.

Psalm 6: A prayer for help from a person who is ill, and a penitential psalm (see Types of Psalms, pp. 849-850).

PSALM 6

Prayer for Recovery from Grave Illness

To the leader: with stringed instruments; according to The Sheminith. A Psalm of David.

[1] O LORD, do not rebuke me in your anger,
or discipline me in your wrath.
[2] Be gracious to me, O LORD, for I am languishing;
O LORD, heal me, for my bones are shaking with terror.
[3] My soul also is struck with terror,
while you, O LORD—how long?

[4] Turn, O LORD, save my life;
deliver me for the sake of your steadfast love.
[5] For in death there is no remembrance of you;
in Sheol who can give you praise?

[6] I am weary with my moaning;
every night I flood my bed with tears;
I drench my couch with my weeping.
[7] My eyes waste away because of grief;
they grow weak because of all my foes.

[8] Depart from me, all you workers of evil,
for the LORD has heard the sound of my weeping.
[9] The LORD has heard my supplication;

6:1 anger…wrath: Many people in the ancient world assumed that an illness or other crisis was an indication that God was punishing a sin. Jesus later ruled out this viewpoint (see John 9:1-3). This prayer is still real, even though one of the psalmist's assumptions seems to be mistaken.

6:2 languishing: The psalmist is desperately ill (see also 6:6-7).

6:3 how long?: Not knowing how long it might last makes suffering worse, while knowing this might give reason for hope (see 74:9).

6:5 Sheol: Sometimes translated "the Pit," *Sheol* is the dwelling place of the dead. Many people in ancient times believed that there was existence after death, but that no relationship with God continued, and so there was no praise or worship. The psalmist is not bargaining with God here, but promising to praise God after deliverance.

6:9 The LORD has heard: The psalmist has confidence that God will answer the prayer. It may be that a priest or prophet listened in on the prayer and then announced that God had accepted the prayer (see Hannah and Eli in 1 Sam 1:9-17). Or the psalmist may see things differently after praying.

the Lord accepts my prayer.
10 All my enemies shall be ashamed and struck with terror;
they shall turn back, and in a moment be put to shame.

PSALM 7

Plea for Help against Persecutors

A Shiggaion of David, which he sang to the Lord concerning Cush, a Benjaminite.

1 O Lord my God, in you I take refuge;
save me from all my pursuers, and deliver me,
2 or like a lion they will tear me apart;
they will drag me away, with no one to rescue.

3 O Lord my God, if I have done this,
if there is wrong in my hands,
4 if I have repaid my ally with harm
or plundered my foe without cause,
5 then let the enemy pursue and overtake me,
trample my life to the ground,
and lay my soul in the dust. *Selah*

6 Rise up, O Lord, in your anger;
lift yourself up against the fury of my enemies;
awake, O my God;[a] you have appointed a judgment.
7 Let the assembly of the peoples be gathered around you,
and over it take your seat[b] on high.
8 The Lord judges the peoples;
judge me, O Lord, according to my righteousness
and according to the integrity that is in me.

9 O let the evil of the wicked come to an end,
but establish the righteous,
you who test the minds and hearts,
O righteous God.
10 God is my shield,
who saves the upright in heart.
11 God is a righteous judge,
and a God who has indignation every day.

12 If one does not repent, God[c] will whet his sword;
he has bent and strung his bow;
13 he has prepared his deadly weapons,
making his arrows fiery shafts.

6:10 shame: The ancient world was very conscious of the values of honor and shame. For God to "side with" a person's cause is the ultimate source of honor, but for God to side against a person's cause is the ultimate source of shame.

Psalm 7: A prayer for help (see Types of Psalms, pp. 849-850) from a person falsely accused.

7:1 refuge: See Bible Concepts note on 2:11.

7:2 no one to rescue: If God does not help the psalmist, there will be no help, because all human help has disappeared.

7:3-5 if I have done this: The psalmist does not claim to be innocent of all sin, but only of the particular accusation from the enemies.

7:5 Selah: See note on 3:2.

7:6-11 The Lord judges: A basic biblical image of God is judge. Here the psalmist claims to have been falsely accused and calls on God to make a fair ruling in this particular crisis. The psalmist is not referring to the final judgment.

What do you do when you feel you are being treated very unfairly by someone?

[a] Or *awake for me* [b] Cn: Heb *return* [c] Heb *he*

7:15-16 fall into the hole that they have made: A common theme in the Old Testament is that the plots of the wicked (see note on 1:1) will ultimately hurt them (see Prov 1:8-19). This teaching does not deny that the wicked may also harm others, but assures the righteous that there are consequences to taking the way of the wicked.

Psalm 8: A hymn of praise and a creation psalm (see Types of Psalms, pp. 849-850).

8:1, 9 O Lord: The psalm opens and closes with praise of God as creator.

8:1-6 above the heavens...your heavens...a little lower than God... crowned them...hands...feet: This hymn artistically describes creation by starting at the top and looking steadily down toward the bottom, where humans are to exercise godly care for everything "under their feet."

8:2 out of the mouths of babes...to silence: The meaning of this phrase is not clear.

8:4-5 what are human beings?...a little lower than God: Struck by the vastness of creation (8:3), the psalmist wonders why God would care for a human being. God values humans enough to give them a meaningful role within God's mission—to care for creation. This is similar to the "image of God" in Genesis 1:26-28.

8:6 dominion: This is a concept borrowed from the realm of royalty. God makes human beings the royalty of creation and gives them the responsibility for caring for creation.

Psalms 9 and 10: Many ancient translations consider these as one psalm. Together they form one lengthy acrostic poem and prayer for help (see Types of Psalms, pp. 849-850).

9:1 wonderful deeds: The Bible teaches that the Lord's love has been made known through a history of "wonderful deeds" (also translated as "wondrous works," "marvels," "miracles," and "great wonders"). These refer to many types of actions (such as creating, providing food, and delivering from evil) for many different people (humanity as a whole, the nation of Israel, individuals, and so on).

14 See how they conceive evil,
and are pregnant with mischief,
and bring forth lies.
15 They make a pit, digging it out,
and fall into the hole that they have made.
16 Their mischief returns upon their own heads,
and on their own heads their violence descends.

17 I will give to the Lord the thanks due to his righteousness,
and sing praise to the name of the Lord, the Most High.

PSALM 8
Divine Majesty and Human Dignity

To the leader: according to The Gittith. A Psalm of David.

1 O Lord, our Sovereign,
how majestic is your name in all the earth!

You have set your glory above the heavens.
2 Out of the mouths of babes and infants
you have founded a bulwark because of your foes,
to silence the enemy and the avenger.

3 When I look at your heavens, the work of your fingers,
the moon and the stars that you have established;
4 what are human beings that you are mindful of them,
mortals[a] that you care for them?

5 Yet you have made them a little lower than God,[b]
and crowned them with glory and honor.
6 You have given them dominion over the works of your hands;
you have put all things under their feet,
7 all sheep and oxen,
and also the beasts of the field,
8 the birds of the air, and the fish of the sea,
whatever passes along the paths of the seas.

9 O Lord, our Sovereign,
how majestic is your name in all the earth!

PSALM 9
God's Power and Justice

To the leader: according to Muth-labben. A Psalm of David.

1 I will give thanks to the Lord with my whole heart;

---

[a] Heb *ben adam*, lit. *son of man* [b] Or *than the divine beings* or *angels*: Heb *elohim*

I will tell of all your wonderful deeds.
2 I will be glad and exult in you;
I will sing praise to your name, O Most High.

3 When my enemies turned back,
they stumbled and perished before you.
4 For you have maintained my just cause;
you have sat on the throne giving righteous judgment.

5 You have rebuked the nations, you have destroyed the wicked;
you have blotted out their name forever and ever.
6 The enemies have vanished in everlasting ruins;
their cities you have rooted out;
the very memory of them has perished.

7 But the LORD sits enthroned forever,
he has established his throne for judgment.
8 He judges the world with righteousness;
he judges the peoples with equity.

9 The LORD is a stronghold for the oppressed,
a stronghold in times of trouble.
10 And those who know your name put their trust in you,
for you, O LORD, have not forsaken those who seek you.

11 Sing praises to the LORD, who dwells in Zion.
Declare his deeds among the peoples.
12 For he who avenges blood is mindful of them;
he does not forget the cry of the afflicted.

13 Be gracious to me, O LORD.
See what I suffer from those who hate me;
you are the one who lifts me up from the gates of death,
14 so that I may recount all your praises,
and, in the gates of daughter Zion,
rejoice in your deliverance.

15 The nations have sunk in the pit that they made;
in the net that they hid has their own foot been caught.
16 The LORD has made himself known, he has executed judgment;
the wicked are snared in the work of their own hands.
Higgaion. Selah

17 The wicked shall depart to Sheol,
all the nations that forget God.

9:7-9 judges the world: See note on 7:6-11.

9:7, 11 the LORD sits enthroned ...dwells in Zion: The LORD is present in heaven and in the temple on Mount Zion. The heavenly and earthly realms overlap in the temple.

9:13-14 Be gracious to me: The psalmist asks for God's grace (in the form of rescue or deliverance) and promises to praise God afterward.

9:15-18 The LORD has made himself known: The psalmist trusts that, in spite of the present reality, God's faithfulness will be made known.

[18] For the needy shall not always be forgotten,
nor the hope of the poor perish forever.

9:19—10:1 **Why?:** The psalmist begs God to act quickly, and expresses pain through agonizing questions.

[19] Rise up, O LORD! Do not let mortals prevail;
let the nations be judged before you.
[20] Put them in fear, O LORD;
let the nations know that they are only human. *Selah*

PSALM 10

Prayer for Deliverance from Enemies

[1] Why, O LORD, do you stand far off?
Why do you hide yourself in times of trouble?

10:2-4 the wicked: See note on 1:1.

[2] In arrogance the wicked persecute the poor—
let them be caught in the schemes they have devised.

[3] For the wicked boast of the desires of their heart,
those greedy for gain curse and renounce the LORD.

10:4, 11, 13 the wicked say: See Bible Concepts note on 3:2.

[4] In the pride of their countenance the wicked say, "God will not
seek it out";
all their thoughts are, "There is no God."

[5] Their ways prosper at all times;
your judgments are on high, out of their sight;
as for their foes, they scoff at them.
[6] They think in their heart, "We shall not be moved;
throughout all generations we shall not meet adversity."

[7] Their mouths are filled with cursing and deceit and oppression;
under their tongues are mischief and iniquity.
[8] They sit in ambush in the villages;
in hiding places they murder the innocent.

Their eyes stealthily watch for the helpless;
[9] they lurk in secret like a lion in its covert;
they lurk that they may seize the poor;
they seize the poor and drag them off in their net.

[10] They stoop, they crouch,
and the helpless fall by their might.
[11] They think in their heart, "God has forgotten,
he has hidden his face, he will never see it."

[12] Rise up, O LORD; O God, lift up your hand;
do not forget the oppressed.
[13] Why do the wicked renounce God,
and say in their hearts, "You will not call us to account"?

14 But you do see! Indeed you note trouble and grief,
that you may take it into your hands;
the helpless commit themselves to you;
you have been the helper of the orphan.

15 Break the arm of the wicked and evildoers;
seek out their wickedness until you find none.
16 The LORD is king forever and ever;
the nations shall perish from his land.

17 O LORD, you will hear the desire of the meek;
you will strengthen their heart, you will incline your ear
18 to do justice for the orphan and the oppressed,
so that those from earth may strike terror no more.[a]

10:14-15 But you do see!: The wicked act defiantly because they believe God does not "see" evil deeds (10:11) or look for wickedness (10:4). The psalmist, however, states that God does see and asks God to "seek out their wickedness." The psalmist commits life, actions, and fate to God's faithfulness.

How is it possible to continue to trust in God amid desperate situations?

PSALM 11
Song of Trust in God

To the leader. Of David.

1 In the LORD I take refuge; how can you say to me,
"Flee like a bird to the mountains;[b]
2 for look, the wicked bend the bow,
they have fitted their arrow to the string,
to shoot in the dark at the upright in heart.
3 If the foundations are destroyed,
what can the righteous do?"

4 The LORD is in his holy temple;
the LORD's throne is in heaven.
His eyes behold, his gaze examines humankind.
5 The LORD tests the righteous and the wicked,
and his soul hates the lover of violence.
6 On the wicked he will rain coals of fire and sulfur;
a scorching wind shall be the portion of their cup.
7 For the LORD is righteous;
he loves righteous deeds;
the upright shall behold his face.

Psalm 11: A trust psalm (see Types of Psalms, pp. 849-850) by a person who is overwhelmed.

11:1 in the LORD I take refuge: See Bible Concepts note on 2:11.

11:3 what can the righteous do?: The psalmist quotes the words of well-meaning advisers who tell the psalmist to run away, because they believe the righteous (see note on 1:5) are powerless in the face of evil.

11:4-7 The LORD is in his holy temple: The psalmist refuses to flee the current location, because God is located in heaven and rules over the earth.

PSALM 12
Plea for Help in Evil Times

To the leader: according to The Sheminith. A Psalm of David.

1 Help, O LORD, for there is no longer anyone who is godly;
the faithful have disappeared from humankind.

Psalm 12: A liturgy based on a prayer for help (see Types of Psalms, pp. 849-850). Various people probably spoke different parts of the psalm.

12:1-4 Help: The psalmist or writer asks for rescue from the wicked. The words of the wicked indicate that they do whatever they want because they answer to no one.

---

[a] Meaning of Heb uncertain [b] Gk Syr Jerome Tg: Heb *flee to your mountain, O bird*

12:5-6 I will now rise up: These words of promise, probably spoken to the psalmist by a priest, indicate that because God has seen the suffering of the poor, God will act.

12:6 The promises of the Lord: Although the term translated as "promises" here literally means "words" in Hebrew, the translation reflects the biblical teaching that God works through promises and always keeps promises. If these words were spoken to the psalmist by a priest, they demonstrate a minister's calling to proclaim God's promises to God's people.

Psalm 13: A prayer for help (see Types of Psalms, pp. 849-850) by a person in severe crisis.

13:1-2 How long?: See note on 6:3. The psalmist expresses anguish by questioning God. The questions have three dimensions: "I," "you," and "they" (the enemy).

What questions do you have for God?

13:3-4 Consider and answer me: The psalmist asks for rescue. This request has three dimensions—"I," "you," and "they"—matching the questions in 13:1-2.

13:5 steadfast love: The concept that most briefly and clearly sums up God's character is "steadfast love," based on the Hebrew term *chesed* (KHESS-uhd). This term describes the character of one who keeps promises, proves faithful, establishes justice, and defends the vulnerable. (See Ruth 3:10, where Ruth shows steadfast love).

Psalm 14: An instructional psalm (see Types of Psalms, pp. 849-850) that teaches the foolishness of those who reject God's ways. It is repeated almost word for word in Psalm 53.

14:1 Fools say: The fool is a typical character in Israel's tradition of teachings or "wisdom." Fools reject God's ways and stubbornly refuse to learn from personal experience or godly instruction. They doubt that God has the power to act on earth (see note on the wicked at 3:2).

14:1, 3 no one who does good: There is a connection between not believing in God and not doing good. The two often—but not always—go together.

2 They utter lies to each other;
with flattering lips and a double heart they speak.

3 May the Lord cut off all flattering lips,
the tongue that makes great boasts,
4 those who say, "With our tongues we will prevail;
our lips are our own—who is our master?"

5 "Because the poor are despoiled, because the needy groan,
I will now rise up," says the Lord;
"I will place them in the safety for which they long."
6 The promises of the Lord are promises that are pure,
silver refined in a furnace on the ground,
purified seven times.

7 You, O Lord, will protect us;
you will guard us from this generation forever.
8 On every side the wicked prowl,
as vileness is exalted among humankind.

PSALM 13

Prayer for Deliverance from Enemies

To the leader. A Psalm of David.

1 How long, O Lord? Will you forget me forever?
How long will you hide your face from me?
2 How long must I bear pain[a] in my soul,
and have sorrow in my heart all day long?
How long shall my enemy be exalted over me?

3 Consider and answer me, O Lord my God!
Give light to my eyes, or I will sleep the sleep of death,
4 and my enemy will say, "I have prevailed";
my foes will rejoice because I am shaken.

5 But I trusted in your steadfast love;
my heart shall rejoice in your salvation.
6 I will sing to the Lord,
because he has dealt bountifully with me.

PSALM 14

Denunciation of Godlessness

To the leader. Of David.

1 Fools say in their hearts, "There is no God."

---

[a] Syr: Heb *hold counsels*

They are corrupt, they do abominable deeds;
there is no one who does good.

2 The LORD looks down from heaven on humankind
to see if there are any who are wise,
who seek after God.

14:2 The LORD looks: The assertion that the LORD sifts hearts to weigh whether people are wise proves that the fools' statement in 14:1 is false.

Why is it wise to believe in God?

3 They have all gone astray, they are all alike perverse;
there is no one who does good,
no, not one.

4 Have they no knowledge, all the evildoers
who eat up my people as they eat bread,
and do not call upon the LORD?

14:4 knowledge: In the biblical view, there is no distinction between thought and action. To know something is to do it. To do evil, then, is to lack knowledge of God and God's ways. Priests and prophets were responsible for teaching knowledge to God's people so that the people would be able to follow God's ways (see Hos 4:4-6).

5 There they shall be in great terror,
for God is with the company of the righteous.
6 You would confound the plans of the poor,
but the LORD is their refuge.

7 O that deliverance for Israel would come from Zion!
When the LORD restores the fortunes of his people,
Jacob will rejoice; Israel will be glad.

PSALM 15
Who Shall Abide in God's Sanctuary?

A Psalm of David.

Psalm 15: A liturgy (see Types of Psalms, pp. 849-850) for entering the temple.

1 O LORD, who may abide in your tent?
Who may dwell on your holy hill?

15:1 who may abide in your tent?: "Tent" and "holy hill" are terms for the temple and its surroundings on Mount Zion. Verse 1 asks God who may enter the temple. The rest of the psalm offers an answer, probably spoken by a priest.

2 Those who walk blamelessly, and do what is right,
and speak the truth from their heart;
3 who do not slander with their tongue,
and do no evil to their friends,
nor take up a reproach against their neighbors;
4 in whose eyes the wicked are despised,
but who honor those who fear the LORD;
who stand by their oath even to their hurt;
5 who do not lend money at interest,
and do not take a bribe against the innocent.

Those who do these things shall never be moved.

15:2-5 Those who walk blamelessly: What is surprising here is that the requirements for entering into God's presence are based on how people treat others, not on ritual preparations (see Num 19:10-22; Lev 21:10-24). Those who love their neighbors "even to their [own] hurt" may enter. A special concern is placed on sins of the tongue and sins with finances. (See also note on 6:10.)

How do you prepare to enter into God's presence?

Psalm 16: A trust psalm (see Types of Psalms, pp. 849-850) in which the psalmist declares faith in the LORD.

16:1 refuge: See Bible Concepts note on 2:11.

16:2 I say: This declaration of faith emphasizes the difference between the psalmist and the enemies.

16:3-4 Those who choose another god: The translation of these verses is uncertain, but it is clear that the psalmist is surrounded by people who worship false gods in disturbing and dangerous ways.

16:5-6 a goodly heritage: The psalmist is a priest who delights in his calling. "Cup" symbolizes ritual acts of thanksgiving (116:13). Portion, lot, and boundary lines refer to God's distribution of the land among the people. The priestly tribe of Levi was given no land. The LORD (18:20) and offerings to the LORD (Lev 6:9-10) were their portion.

16:7-11 my heart is glad...my body also rests secure: Bodily images are used to describe the psalmist's love for and trust in God.

Psalm 17: A prayer for help (see Types of Psalms, pp. 849-850) from a person overwhelmed by enemies.

17:3, 15 by night...when I awake: Night is often a time for prayer, and morning often a time for deliverance (5:3). The psalmist may have prayed all night in the temple or when it was impossible to fall asleep.

17:1-5 Hear a just cause: The psalmist claims to be innocent—not morally perfect, but innocent of doing anything to cause the immediate crisis. The psalmist believes the LORD is just and will not let an innocent person suffer.

PSALM 16

Song of Trust and Security in God

A Miktam of David.

1 Protect me, O God, for in you I take refuge.
2 I say to the LORD, "You are my Lord;
I have no good apart from you."[a]

3 As for the holy ones in the land, they are the noble,
in whom is all my delight.

4 Those who choose another god multiply their sorrows;[b]
their drink offerings of blood I will not pour out
or take their names upon my lips.

5 The LORD is my chosen portion and my cup;
you hold my lot.
6 The boundary lines have fallen for me in pleasant places;
I have a goodly heritage.

7 I bless the LORD who gives me counsel;
in the night also my heart instructs me.
8 I keep the LORD always before me;
because he is at my right hand, I shall not be moved.

9 Therefore my heart is glad, and my soul rejoices;
my body also rests secure.
10 For you do not give me up to Sheol,
or let your faithful one see the Pit.

11 You show me the path of life.
In your presence there is fullness of joy;
in your right hand are pleasures forevermore.

PSALM 17

Prayer for Deliverance from Persecutors

A Prayer of David.

1 Hear a just cause, O LORD; attend to my cry;
give ear to my prayer from lips free of deceit.
2 From you let my vindication come;
let your eyes see the right.

3 If you try my heart, if you visit me by night,
if you test me, you will find no wickedness in me;

---

[a] Jerome Tg: Meaning of Heb uncertain [b] Cn: Meaning of Heb uncertain

my mouth does not transgress.
4 As for what others do, by the word of your lips
I have avoided the ways of the violent.
5 My steps have held fast to your paths;
my feet have not slipped.

6 I call upon you, for you will answer me, O God;
incline your ear to me, hear my words.
7 Wondrously show your steadfast love,
O savior of those who seek refuge
from their adversaries at your right hand.

8 Guard me as the apple of the eye;
hide me in the shadow of your wings,
9 from the wicked who despoil me,
my deadly enemies who surround me.
10 They close their hearts to pity;
with their mouths they speak arrogantly.
11 They track me down;[a] now they surround me;
they set their eyes to cast me to the ground.
12 They are like a lion eager to tear,
like a young lion lurking in ambush.

13 Rise up, O LORD, confront them, overthrow them!
By your sword deliver my life from the wicked,
14 from mortals—by your hand, O LORD—
from mortals whose portion in life is in this world.
May their bellies be filled with what you have stored up for them;
may their children have more than enough;
may they leave something over to their little ones.

15 As for me, I shall behold your face in righteousness;
when I awake I shall be satisfied, beholding your likeness.

17:6-7 Wondrously show your steadfast love: Trusting in God's character, the psalmist calls upon God confidently. For "wondrously show," see note on 9:1. For "steadfast love," see note on 13:5.

17:9-14 They are like a lion: The psalmist is helpless against the enemies, who are portrayed as prowling predators. Rather than their bellies being filled with the psalmist, the prayer is that the enemies might be filled with what has been "stored up for them."

PSALM 18

Royal Thanksgiving for Victory

To the leader. A Psalm of David the servant of the LORD, who addressed the words of this song to the LORD on the day when the LORD delivered him from the hand of all his enemies, and from the hand of Saul. He said:

1 I love you, O LORD, my strength.
2 The LORD is my rock, my fortress, and my deliverer,
my God, my rock in whom I take refuge,
my shield, and the horn of my salvation, my stronghold.

Psalm 18: A royal psalm (see Types of Psalms, pp. 849-850) of thanksgiving. An almost identical poem appears in 2 Samuel 22.

18:1-3 I call upon the LORD: The opening verses offer praise because of what God has done.

[a] One Ms Compare Syr: MT *Our steps*

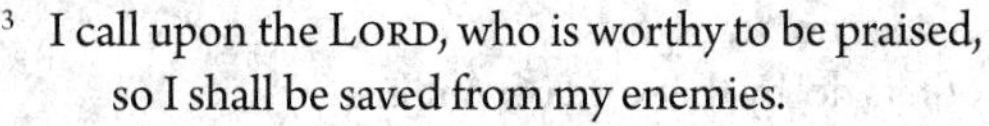

3 I call upon the LORD, who is worthy to be praised,
so I shall be saved from my enemies.

18:4-6 The cords of death: The psalmist almost died.

4 The cords of death encompassed me;
the torrents of perdition assailed me;
5 the cords of Sheol entangled me;
the snares of death confronted me.

6 In my distress I called upon the LORD;
to my God I cried for help.
From his temple he heard my voice,
and my cry to him reached his ears.

18:7-19 Then the earth reeled and rocked: The image of a thunderstorm depicts God's coming to earth. God's coming disturbs the normal rhythms of earth, and nature's powerful forces are hints of God's power. The psalmist experienced God's saving help as similar to this.

When have you experienced God's saving help? What was it like?

7 Then the earth reeled and rocked;
the foundations also of the mountains trembled
and quaked, because he was angry.
8 Smoke went up from his nostrils,
and devouring fire from his mouth;
glowing coals flamed forth from him.
9 He bowed the heavens, and came down;
thick darkness was under his feet.
10 He rode on a cherub, and flew;
he came swiftly upon the wings of the wind.
11 He made darkness his covering around him,
his canopy thick clouds dark with water.
12 Out of the brightness before him
there broke through his clouds
hailstones and coals of fire.
13 The LORD also thundered in the heavens,
and the Most High uttered his voice.[a]
14 And he sent out his arrows, and scattered them;
he flashed forth lightnings, and routed them.
15 Then the channels of the sea were seen,
and the foundations of the world were laid bare
at your rebuke, O LORD,
at the blast of the breath of your nostrils.

16 He reached down from on high, he took me;
he drew me out of mighty waters.
17 He delivered me from my strong enemy,
and from those who hated me;
for they were too mighty for me.
18 They confronted me in the day of my calamity;

[a] Gk See 2 Sam 22.14: Heb adds *hailstones and coals of fire*

but the LORD was my support.
19 He brought me out into a broad place;
he delivered me, because he delighted in me.

20 The LORD rewarded me according to my righteousness;
according to the cleanness of my hands he recompensed me.
21 For I have kept the ways of the LORD,
and have not wickedly departed from my God.
22 For all his ordinances were before me,
and his statutes I did not put away from me.
23 I was blameless before him,
and I kept myself from guilt.
24 Therefore the LORD has recompensed me according to my
righteousness,
according to the cleanness of my hands in his sight.

25 With the loyal you show yourself loyal;
with the blameless you show yourself blameless;
26 with the pure you show yourself pure;
and with the crooked you show yourself perverse.
27 For you deliver a humble people,
but the haughty eyes you bring down.
28 It is you who light my lamp;
the LORD, my God, lights up my darkness.
29 By you I can crush a troop,
and by my God I can leap over a wall.
30 This God—his way is perfect;
the promise of the LORD proves true;
he is a shield for all who take refuge in him.

31 For who is God except the LORD?
And who is a rock besides our God?—
32 the God who girded me with strength,
and made my way safe.
33 He made my feet like the feet of a deer,
and set me secure on the heights.
34 He trains my hands for war,
so that my arms can bend a bow of bronze.
35 You have given me the shield of your salvation,
and your right hand has supported me;
your help[a] has made me great.
36 You gave me a wide place for my steps under me,
and my feet did not slip.

18:30 the promise of the LORD proves true: See note on 12:6.

18:31-42 who is God except the LORD?: The psalmist declares faith in the LORD, claiming that the LORD alone is God. The LORD has proved this by delivering the psalmist and defeating the enemies.

[a] Or *gentleness*

[37] I pursued my enemies and overtook them;
and did not turn back until they were consumed.
[38] I struck them down, so that they were not able to rise;
they fell under my feet.
[39] For you girded me with strength for the battle;
you made my assailants sink under me.
[40] You made my enemies turn their backs to me,
and those who hated me I destroyed.
[41] They cried for help, but there was no one to save them;
they cried to the LORD, but he did not answer them.
[42] I beat them fine, like dust before the wind;
I cast them out like the mire of the streets.

[43] You delivered me from strife with the peoples;[a]
you made me head of the nations;
people whom I had not known served me.
[44] As soon as they heard of me they obeyed me;
foreigners came cringing to me.
[45] Foreigners lost heart,
and came trembling out of their strongholds.

18:46-50 The LORD lives!: The psalm ends with a shout of praise. To praise God is not to flatter God, but to tell others what God has done. The phrase "the LORD lives" may be translated as "living God" or "God of life." God provides for life by delivering people from the threat of death.

[46] The LORD lives! Blessed be my rock,
and exalted be the God of my salvation,
[47] the God who gave me vengeance
and subdued peoples under me;
[48] who delivered me from my enemies;
indeed, you exalted me above my adversaries;
you delivered me from the violent.

[49] For this I will extol you, O LORD, among the nations,
and sing praises to your name.
[50] Great triumphs he gives to his king,
and shows steadfast love to his anointed,
to David and his descendants forever.

Psalm 19: A creation psalm and instructional psalm (see Types of Psalms, pp. 849-850).

PSALM 19
God's Glory in Creation and the Law

To the leader. A Psalm of David.

19:1-4 their voice is not heard; yet their voice goes out: Creation praises its Creator using speech and words that humans cannot understand, and yet in some mysterious way humans do indeed overhear creation's praise of God.

When have you sensed that creation was praising God?

[1] The heavens are telling the glory of God;
and the firmament[b] proclaims his handiwork.
[2] Day to day pours forth speech,
and night to night declares knowledge.
[3] There is no speech, nor are there words;
their voice is not heard;

---

[a] Gk Tg: Heb *people* [b] Or *dome*

4 yet their voice[a] goes out through all the earth,
and their words to the end of the world.

In the heavens[b] he has set a tent for the sun,
5 which comes out like a bridegroom from his wedding canopy,
and like a strong man runs its course with joy.
6 Its rising is from the end of the heavens,
and its circuit to the end of them;
and nothing is hid from its heat.

7 The law of the LORD is perfect,
reviving the soul;
the decrees of the LORD are sure,
making wise the simple;
8 the precepts of the LORD are right,
rejoicing the heart;
the commandment of the LORD is clear,
enlightening the eyes;
9 the fear of the LORD is pure,
enduring forever;
the ordinances of the LORD are true
and righteous altogether.
10 More to be desired are they than gold,
even much fine gold;
sweeter also than honey,
and drippings of the honeycomb.

11 Moreover by them is your servant warned;
in keeping them there is great reward.
12 But who can detect their errors?
Clear me from hidden faults.
13 Keep back your servant also from the insolent;[c]
do not let them have dominion over me.
Then I shall be blameless,
and innocent of great transgression.

14 Let the words of my mouth and the meditation of my heart
be acceptable to you,
O LORD, my rock and my redeemer.

PSALM 20

Prayer for Victory

To the leader. A Psalm of David.

1 The LORD answer you in the day of trouble!

[a] Gk Jerome Compare Syr: Heb *line* [b] Heb *In them* [c] Or *from proud thoughts*

19:7-10 The law of the LORD: Law, decrees, precepts, commandment, fear, and ordinances are all words for the "instruction" of the LORD (see note on 1:2). This passage describes what they are ("perfect," "sure," and so on) and what they do (revive the soul, make simple people wise, and so on). God's glory is shown in creation (19:1-6) and in the *torah* (19:7-10), two of God's greatest works.

19:11-12 by them is your servant warned: God's law works in two ways. First, it teaches us how to live in the world. Second, the law warns. It shows us where we have failed to keep the law and teaches us to ask for forgiveness (see Lutheran Perspectives note on 1:2).

19:14 Let the words of my mouth: This closing prayer teaches us how to pray. We ask that our words and thoughts will be acceptable to God.

Psalm 20: A royal psalm (see Types of Psalms, pp. 849-850).

20:1-5 May the LORD fulfill all your petitions: The first five verses of this psalm were spoken by a priest or by the community to the king, perhaps before battle or at a worship service that highlighted the king's military leadership for symbolic reasons. The welfare of the people often depends on the welfare of its leaders, so the people pray for the king.

When and how do you pray for your leaders?

The name of the God of Jacob protect you!
2 May he send you help from the sanctuary,
and give you support from Zion.
3 May he remember all your offerings,
and regard with favor your burnt sacrifices. *Selah*

4 May he grant you your heart's desire,
and fulfill all your plans.
5 May we shout for joy over your victory,
and in the name of our God set up our banners.
May the LORD fulfill all your petitions.

20:6-8 Some take pride in chariots: A priest continues the prayer, emphasizing that the people do not trust in the military power of the king, God's anointed one (see note on 2:2), but in the promises of God.

20:7 the name of the LORD: God revealed the name "The LORD" (Hebrew: *YHWH*) in Exodus 3:13-15. God gave the people this name as part of the relationship established with them, so that they could call upon God in troubled times and praise God. God's name was understood to dwell in the temple, making it the place above all others where the people could call on God's name in prayer and praise.

6 Now I know that the LORD will help his anointed;
he will answer him from his holy heaven
with mighty victories by his right hand.
7 Some take pride in chariots, and some in horses,
but our pride is in the name of the LORD our God.
8 They will collapse and fall,
but we shall rise and stand upright.

9 Give victory to the king, O LORD;
answer us when we call.[a]

PSALM 21
Thanksgiving for Victory

To the leader. A Psalm of David.

Psalm 21: A royal psalm (see Types of Psalms, pp. 849-850) of thanksgiving and praise.

21:1-6 In your strength the king rejoices: The psalm thanks God for many blessings that the LORD has showered on the king. If Psalm 20 is a prayer before a crisis, Psalm 21 may be a corresponding prayer after God rescued the people from the crisis.

1 In your strength the king rejoices, O LORD,
and in your help how greatly he exults!
2 You have given him his heart's desire,
and have not withheld the request of his lips. *Selah*
3 For you meet him with rich blessings;
you set a crown of fine gold on his head.
4 He asked you for life; you gave it to him—
length of days forever and ever.
5 His glory is great through your help;
splendor and majesty you bestow on him.
6 You bestow on him blessings forever;
you make him glad with the joy of your presence.
7 For the king trusts in the LORD,
and through the steadfast love of the Most High he shall not be moved.

21:7 For the king trusts in the LORD: The king does not trust in his own power, but in God's steadfast love (see note on 13:5).

21:8-13 we will sing and praise your power: It is unclear whether these verses are directed to the king or to God. If directed to the king, they are words of promise about God's ongoing blessings on the king. If directed to God, they are words of trust in God's ongoing protection. Either way, the community trusts in God's continuing faithfulness.

8 Your hand will find out all your enemies;
your right hand will find out those who hate you.

[a] Gk: Heb *give victory, O LORD; let the King answer us when we call*

[9] You will make them like a fiery furnace
when you appear.
The LORD will swallow them up in his wrath,
and fire will consume them.
[10] You will destroy their offspring from the earth,
and their children from among humankind.
[11] If they plan evil against you,
if they devise mischief, they will not succeed.
[12] For you will put them to flight;
you will aim at their faces with your bows.

[13] Be exalted, O LORD, in your strength!
We will sing and praise your power.

PSALM 22

Plea for Deliverance from Suffering and Hostility

To the leader: according to The Deer of the Dawn. A Psalm of David.

[1] My God, my God, why have you forsaken me?
Why are you so far from helping me, from the words of my groaning?
[2] O my God, I cry by day, but you do not answer;
and by night, but find no rest.

[3] Yet you are holy,
enthroned on the praises of Israel.
[4] In you our ancestors trusted;
they trusted, and you delivered them.
[5] To you they cried, and were saved;
in you they trusted, and were not put to shame.

[6] But I am a worm, and not human;
scorned by others, and despised by the people.
[7] All who see me mock at me;
they make mouths at me, they shake their heads;
[8] "Commit your cause to the LORD; let him deliver—
let him rescue the one in whom he delights!"

[9] Yet it was you who took me from the womb;
you kept me safe on my mother's breast.
[10] On you I was cast from my birth,
and since my mother bore me you have been my God.
[11] Do not be far from me,
for trouble is near
and there is no one to help.

Psalm 22: A prayer for help (see Types of Psalms, pp. 849-850) from a person in a severe crisis.

22:1 My God, My God, why have you forsaken me?: A desperate cry for help, Christ spoke these words while dying on the cross (see Matt 27:46; Mark 15:34).

22:3-5 In you our ancestors trusted: Although in a severe crisis, the psalmist remembers God's past deliverance of the people and finds hope in that. God is pictured as enthroned on Israel's praise, emphasizing that praise is a part of our relationship with God. See note on *shame* at 6:10.

22:6-8 I am a worm, and not human: The psalmist experiences the current crisis and the enemies' words as dehumanizing.

22:9-11 you kept me safe on my mother's breast: God was faithful through the love and care of the psalmist's mother. Remembering this, the psalmist again asks for God's help.

22:12-21 strong bulls…roaring lion…dogs are all around…power of the dog…mouth of the lion…horns of the wild oxen: The images of the enemies as devouring predators emphasizes the dehumanizing and desperate situation the psalmist is in. The description of the psalmist's physical condition in 22:14-15 and 16b-17 shows that death is very near.

Times of intense illness or suffering can make one feel less than human; have you or a loved one experienced such a time?

22:22-31 I will tell of your name: Perhaps a priest has spoken a word of promise or forgiveness to the psalmist, or perhaps during the act of praying the psalmist's trust in God was restored. What is clear is that the psalmist trusts in God's faithfulness, and so the psalm closes by celebrating God's goodness.

In difficult times, what can change your pleas for help into words of praise?

12 Many bulls encircle me,
strong bulls of Bashan surround me;
13 they open wide their mouths at me,
like a ravening and roaring lion.

14 I am poured out like water,
and all my bones are out of joint;
my heart is like wax;
it is melted within my breast;
15 my mouth[a] is dried up like a potsherd,
and my tongue sticks to my jaws;
you lay me in the dust of death.

16 For dogs are all around me;
a company of evildoers encircles me.
My hands and feet have shriveled;[b]
17 I can count all my bones.
They stare and gloat over me;
18 they divide my clothes among themselves,
and for my clothing they cast lots.

19 But you, O LORD, do not be far away!
O my help, come quickly to my aid!
20 Deliver my soul from the sword,
my life[c] from the power of the dog!
21 Save me from the mouth of the lion!

From the horns of the wild oxen you have rescued[d] me.
22 I will tell of your name to my brothers and sisters;[e]
in the midst of the congregation I will praise you:
23 You who fear the LORD, praise him!
All you offspring of Jacob, glorify him;
stand in awe of him, all you offspring of Israel!
24 For he did not despise or abhor
the affliction of the afflicted;
he did not hide his face from me,[f]
but heard when I[g] cried to him.

25 From you comes my praise in the great congregation;
my vows I will pay before those who fear him.
26 The poor[h] shall eat and be satisfied;
those who seek him shall praise the LORD.
May your hearts live forever!

---

[a] Cn: Heb *strength* [b] Meaning of Heb uncertain [c] Heb *my only one* [d] Heb *answered*
[e] Or *kindred* [f] Heb *him* [g] Heb *he* [h] Or *afflicted*

27 All the ends of the earth shall remember
and turn to the LORD;
and all the families of the nations
shall worship before him.[a]
28 For dominion belongs to the LORD,
and he rules over the nations.

29 To him,[b] indeed, shall all who sleep in[c] the earth bow
down;
before him shall bow all who go down to the dust,
and I shall live for him.[d]
30 Posterity will serve him;
future generations will be told about the Lord,
31 and[e] proclaim his deliverance to a people yet unborn,
saying that he has done it.

PSALM 23
The Divine Shepherd

A Psalm of David.

1 The LORD is my shepherd, I shall not want.
2 He makes me lie down in green pastures;
he leads me beside still waters;[f]
3 he restores my soul.[g]
He leads me in right paths[h]
for his name's sake.

4 Even though I walk through the darkest valley,[i]
I fear no evil;
for you are with me;
your rod and your staff—
they comfort me.

5 You prepare a table before me
in the presence of my enemies;
you anoint my head with oil;
my cup overflows.
6 Surely[j] goodness and mercy[k] shall follow me
all the days of my life,
and I shall dwell in the house of the LORD
my whole life long.[l]

Psalm 23: A trust psalm (see Types of Psalms, pp. 849-850).

23:1 The LORD is my shepherd: The shepherd is an image of the king (see 1 Kgs 22:17-18; Jer 23:1; Ezek 34:1-2). God is pictured here as the shepherd king who cares for faithful followers. "Shall not want" is better translated as "shall not be in need."

23:3 in right paths for his name's sake: The phrase "right paths" has a double meaning—"safe paths" and also "morally right ways." "For his name's sake:" See note on 20:7.

23:4 for you are with me: There are many reasons to fear, but the psalmist has confidence because God is present. The rod and staff are images for God's guidance. A rod defends the sheep from predators, and a staff keeps the sheep from straying.

23:5 You prepare a table: The feast is an image for God's actions (see Luke 14:7-24). God gives honor by feasting and welcoming the psalmist while enemies are present.

23:6 shall follow: This can also be translated as "shall pursue." In many psalms, enemies pursue the psalmist. Here God's goodness and mercy also pursue. They actively chase down and "capture" the psalmist.

---

[a] Gk Syr Jerome: Heb *you* [b] Cn: Heb *They have eaten and* [c] Cn: Heb *all the fat ones* [d] Compare Gk Syr Vg: Heb *and he who cannot keep himself alive* [e] Compare Gk: Heb *it will be told about the Lord to the generation, [31]they will come and* [f] Heb *waters of rest* [g] Or *life* [h] Or *paths of righteousness* [i] Or *the valley of the shadow of death* [j] Or *Only* [k] Or *kindness* [l] Heb *for length of days*

Psalm 24: A liturgy (see Types of Psalms, pp. 849-850) for entering the temple.

24:1-2 The earth is the LORD's: The psalm declares that God is creator of the world and everything in it.

24:3-6 Who shall ascend the hill of the LORD?: The hill and holy place refer to God's temple, the point of contact between heaven and earth. Those who are clean can enter. This is not a ritual cleanness (see Num 19:10-22; Lev 21:10-24) but a moral cleanness.

24:7-10 Who is the King of glory?: Just as worshipers come to enter God's space, the LORD comes to enter human space. Verses 3-6 asked, "Who can enter God's space?" Now verses 7-10 ask, "Who is God who comes to enter our space?" The congregation answers: "The LORD of hosts," the creator (24:1-2) of all.

Psalm 25: An acrostic poem (see Types of Psalms, pp. 849-850) that focuses on God's teaching and forgiveness.

25:1-3, 20 shame: The psalmist expresses trust that God will grant honor to the righteous and shame (see note on 6:10) to the enemies.

25:4-5, 8-10, 12 your ways: The ways, paths, and instruction of the LORD make up a central concept in the psalms. These ways are part of the covenant relationship with God (see note on 25:14). They guide us through life's dangers, help us find refuge, and show us how to live in a relationship with God. They are available to all who want to learn them.

What part of living in a relationship with God gives you the most joy?

PSALM 24

Entrance into the Temple

Of David. A Psalm.

1 The earth is the LORD's and all that is in it,
the world, and those who live in it;
2 for he has founded it on the seas,
and established it on the rivers.

3 Who shall ascend the hill of the LORD?
And who shall stand in his holy place?
4 Those who have clean hands and pure hearts,
who do not lift up their souls to what is false,
and do not swear deceitfully.
5 They will receive blessing from the LORD,
and vindication from the God of their salvation.
6 Such is the company of those who seek him,
who seek the face of the God of Jacob.[a] *Selah*

7 Lift up your heads, O gates!
and be lifted up, O ancient doors!
that the King of glory may come in.
8 Who is the King of glory?
The LORD, strong and mighty,
the LORD, mighty in battle.
9 Lift up your heads, O gates!
and be lifted up, O ancient doors!
that the King of glory may come in.
10 Who is this King of glory?
The LORD of hosts,
he is the King of glory. *Selah*

PSALM 25

Prayer for Guidance and for Deliverance

Of David.

1 To you, O LORD, I lift up my soul.
2 O my God, in you I trust;
do not let me be put to shame;
do not let my enemies exult over me.
3 Do not let those who wait for you be put to shame;
let them be ashamed who are wantonly treacherous.

4 Make me to know your ways, O LORD;
teach me your paths.

---

[a] Gk Syr: Heb *your face, O Jacob*

[5] Lead me in your truth, and teach me,
for you are the God of my salvation;
for you I wait all day long.

[6] Be mindful of your mercy, O LORD, and of your steadfast love,
for they have been from of old.
[7] Do not remember the sins of my youth or my transgressions;
according to your steadfast love remember me,
for your goodness' sake, O LORD!

[8] Good and upright is the LORD;
therefore he instructs sinners in the way.
[9] He leads the humble in what is right,
and teaches the humble his way.
[10] All the paths of the LORD are steadfast love and faithfulness,
for those who keep his covenant and his decrees.

[11] For your name's sake, O LORD,
pardon my guilt, for it is great.
[12] Who are they that fear the LORD?
He will teach them the way that they should choose.

[13] They will abide in prosperity,
and their children shall possess the land.
[14] The friendship of the LORD is for those who fear him,
and he makes his covenant known to them.
[15] My eyes are ever toward the LORD,
for he will pluck my feet out of the net.

[16] Turn to me and be gracious to me,
for I am lonely and afflicted.
[17] Relieve the troubles of my heart,
and bring me[a] out of my distress.
[18] Consider my affliction and my trouble,
and forgive all my sins.

[19] Consider how many are my foes,
and with what violent hatred they hate me.
[20] O guard my life, and deliver me;
do not let me be put to shame, for I take refuge in you.
[21] May integrity and uprightness preserve me,
for I wait for you.

25:14 covenant: One of the main themes in the Bible is *covenant*, which is an exchange of promises. Here covenant refers to the relationships God establishes with the community and with individuals in the community. God promises to remain faithful to the people, and God expects the people to keep God's laws.

25:16 I am lonely: Loneliness is one of the afflictions we experience because of our sinfulness. God's presence and God's community heal loneliness.

25:7, 11, 17-18 forgive all my sins: The psalmist does not have one particular sin in mind, but knows that receiving the promise of forgiveness continually is a key part of the ongoing relationship with God.

---

[a] Or *The troubles of my heart are enlarged; bring me*

22 Redeem Israel, O God,
out of all its troubles.

PSALM 26
Plea for Justice and Declaration of Righteousness
Of David.

1 Vindicate me, O LORD,
for I have walked in my integrity,
and I have trusted in the LORD without wavering.
2 Prove me, O LORD, and try me;
test my heart and mind.
3 For your steadfast love is before my eyes,
and I walk in faithfulness to you.[a]

4 I do not sit with the worthless,
nor do I consort with hypocrites;
5 I hate the company of evildoers,
and will not sit with the wicked.

6 I wash my hands in innocence,
and go around your altar, O LORD,
7 singing aloud a song of thanksgiving,
and telling all your wondrous deeds.

8 O LORD, I love the house in which you dwell,
and the place where your glory abides.
9 Do not sweep me away with sinners,
nor my life with the bloodthirsty,
10 those in whose hands are evil devices,
and whose right hands are full of bribes.

11 But as for me, I walk in my integrity;
redeem me, and be gracious to me.
12 My foot stands on level ground;
in the great congregation I will bless the LORD.

PSALM 27
Triumphant Song of Confidence
Of David.

1 The LORD is my light and my salvation;
whom shall I fear?
The LORD is the stronghold[b] of my life;
of whom shall I be afraid?

[a] Or *in your faithfulness* [b] Or *refuge*

Psalm 26: A prayer for help (see Types of Psalms, pp. 849-850) from a person who claims innocence and wants to be rescued by God.

26:1, 3, 11 Vindicate me…for I have walked in my integrity: The psalm opens and closes with the writer's claim to have walked in integrity, which is an image for someone who has lived a good life of faith. The psalmist also asks God to consider the present situation and provide deliverance.

26:4-5 will not sit with the wicked: The psalmist does not claim moral perfection, but claims not to have done anything to deserve such a desperate situation.

26:6-8 I wash my hands: These verses may refer to a ritual in which people washed their hands as a way of declaring their innocence. Those with "clean hands" (24:4) may enter God's house.

26:7, 12 in the great congregation I will bless the LORD: The psalmist praises God as a way of telling the community about God's faithfulness. Receiving forgiveness from God involves being received back into good standing in the community.

Psalm 27: A trust psalm (see Types of Psalms, pp. 849-850) that also asks God for rescue.

27:1-3 The LORD is my light: Strong threats have put the psalmist in danger, but God is present as light, salvation, and stronghold. This gives the psalmist confidence in spite of the situation. God's presence makes it possible to face danger.

2 When evildoers assail me
to devour my flesh—
my adversaries and foes—
they shall stumble and fall.

3 Though an army encamp against me,
my heart shall not fear;
though war rise up against me,
yet I will be confident.

4 One thing I asked of the LORD,
that will I seek after:
to live in the house of the LORD
all the days of my life,
to behold the beauty of the LORD,
and to inquire in his temple.

27:4 to live in the house of the LORD: To constantly return to God's house helps to sustain the relationship with God and show that this is the central relationship of the psalmist's life.

Who or what do you seek in your life?

5 For he will hide me in his shelter
in the day of trouble;
he will conceal me under the cover of his tent;
he will set me high on a rock.

6 Now my head is lifted up
above my enemies all around me,
and I will offer in his tent
sacrifices with shouts of joy;
I will sing and make melody to the LORD.

7 Hear, O LORD, when I cry aloud,
be gracious to me and answer me!
8 "Come," my heart says, "seek his face!"
Your face, LORD, do I seek.
9 Do not hide your face from me.

Do not turn your servant away in anger,
you who have been my help.
Do not cast me off, do not forsake me,
O God of my salvation!
10 If my father and mother forsake me,
the LORD will take me up.

27:10 father and mother: The psalmist describes God's faithfulness as even greater than the faithfulness of parents to a child.

11 Teach me your way, O LORD,
and lead me on a level path
because of my enemies.
12 Do not give me up to the will of my adversaries,

27:11 your way: See note on 25:4-5.

for false witnesses have risen against me,
and they are breathing out violence.

13 I believe that I shall see the goodness of the LORD
in the land of the living.
14 Wait for the LORD;
be strong, and let your heart take courage;
wait for the LORD!

27:14 Wait for the LORD: To wait for the LORD is to maintain hope that God's deliverance will arrive, and also refrain from going one's own way.

PSALM 28

Prayer for Help and Thanksgiving for It

Of David.

Psalm 28: A prayer for help (see Types of Psalms, pp. 849-850) from a person within a hostile community.

28:1-2 if you are silent: The psalmist pleads for an end to God's silence, or death will come. See note on Pit/Sheol at 6:5.

1 To you, O LORD, I call;
my rock, do not refuse to hear me,
for if you are silent to me,
I shall be like those who go down to the Pit.
2 Hear the voice of my supplication,
as I cry to you for help,
as I lift up my hands
toward your most holy sanctuary.[a]

28:3 with the wicked: The psalmist is in crisis and perhaps fears being included in God's judgment on a community of wicked people.

3 Do not drag me away with the wicked,
with those who are workers of evil,
who speak peace with their neighbors,
while mischief is in their hearts.
4 Repay them according to their work,
and according to the evil of their deeds;
repay them according to the work of their hands;
render them their due reward.
5 Because they do not regard the works of the LORD,
or the work of his hands,
he will break them down and build them up no more.

28:4-5 Repay them according to their work: A fundamental theme in this psalm is work. The works of the LORD may refer to any number of God's actions, including God's judgment, which the wicked do not fear. The psalmist asks God to work to repay the wicked for their evil work.

6 Blessed be the LORD,
for he has heard the sound of my pleadings.
7 The LORD is my strength and my shield;
in him my heart trusts;
so I am helped, and my heart exults,
and with my song I give thanks to him.

8 The LORD is the strength of his people;
he is the saving refuge of his anointed.
9 O save your people, and bless your heritage;
be their shepherd, and carry them forever.

28:6-9 with my song I give thanks: The psalmist responds to being rescued by praising God so that others may learn of the deliverance available to all. Many images are used here for God: strength, shield, saving refuge, and shepherd. See note on anointed at 2:2.

[a] Heb *your innermost sanctuary*

PSALM 29

The Voice of God in a Great Storm

A Psalm of David.

1 Ascribe to the LORD, O heavenly beings,[a]
ascribe to the LORD glory and strength.
2 Ascribe to the LORD the glory of his name;
worship the LORD in holy splendor.

3 The voice of the LORD is over the waters;
the God of glory thunders,
the LORD, over mighty waters.
4 The voice of the LORD is powerful;
the voice of the LORD is full of majesty.

5 The voice of the LORD breaks the cedars;
the LORD breaks the cedars of Lebanon.
6 He makes Lebanon skip like a calf,
and Sirion like a young wild ox.

7 The voice of the LORD flashes forth flames of fire.
8 The voice of the LORD shakes the wilderness;
the LORD shakes the wilderness of Kadesh.

9 The voice of the LORD causes the oaks to whirl,[b]
and strips the forest bare;
and in his temple all say, "Glory!"

10 The LORD sits enthroned over the flood;
the LORD sits enthroned as king forever.
11 May the LORD give strength to his people!
May the LORD bless his people with peace!

Psalm 29: A hymn of praise (see Types of Psalms, pp. 849-850) celebrating God's glory in nature.

29:1-2 heavenly beings: Both the Old and New Testaments portray certain "heavenly beings" as hostile to God's reign. Here the psalmist poetically calls on the heavenly beings to praise God and recognize God's rule.

29:3-9 The voice of the LORD: This passage compares God's coming to the coming of a thunderstorm (see note on 18:7-19). God's glory is mysterious and powerful, like a storm. The storm's coming, like God's coming, disrupts the normal patterns of creation.

29:10-11 The LORD sits enthroned over the flood: The flood represents forces of chaos, which God has subdued in the process of giving order to creation.

The Bible does not worship creation as divine, but worships the LORD as God of creation. How do we honor God as creator today?

PSALM 30

Thanksgiving for Recovery from Grave Illness

A Psalm. A Song at the dedication of the temple. Of David.

1 I will extol you, O LORD, for you have drawn me up,
and did not let my foes rejoice over me.
2 O LORD my God, I cried to you for help,
and you have healed me.
3 O LORD, you brought up my soul from Sheol,
restored me to life from among those gone down to the Pit.[c]

4 Sing praises to the LORD, O you his faithful ones,
and give thanks to his holy name.

Psalm 30: A song of thanksgiving (see Types of Psalms, pp. 849-850) by a person God has rescued from a crisis.

30:1-5 you have healed me: The psalmist praises God for rescue from a near-death crisis. See note on Sheol/Pit at 6:5.

---

[a] Heb *sons of gods* [b] Or *causes the deer to calve* [c] Or *that I should not go down to the Pit*

30:5 anger is but for a moment; his favor is for a lifetime: God's faithfulness and love are far more enduring than God's anger, which only exists to bring about changes in sinful human behavior.

30:6-10 To you, O Lord, I cried: The psalmist tells about the past crisis and rescue, first by quoting the arrogant attitude that caused the trouble ("I shall never be moved"), and then by quoting the prayer that God answered ("Hear, O Lord, and be gracious").

30:11-12 mourning into dancing: The metaphor of exchanging the attitudes and clothes of repentance for those of joy symbolizes the Lord's transforming grace.

The psalmist now dances and cannot remain silent. When has your joy in the Lord overflowed like this?

Psalm 31: A prayer for help from a person who has severe pain but profound trust in God. It changes into a song of thankgiving (see Types of Psalms, pp. 849-850).

31:1-5 my rock and my fortress: The opening plea for help emphasizes God's protecting power. See notes on refuge (2:11), shame (6:10), and the Lord's name (20:7).

31:5 Into your hand I commit my spirit: Jesus quoted these words while dying on the cross (Luke 23:46), which indicates this psalmist is near death.

5 For his anger is but for a moment;
his favor is for a lifetime.
Weeping may linger for the night,
but joy comes with the morning.

6 As for me, I said in my prosperity,
"I shall never be moved."
7 By your favor, O Lord,
you had established me as a strong mountain;
you hid your face;
I was dismayed.

8 To you, O Lord, I cried,
and to the Lord I made supplication:
9 "What profit is there in my death,
if I go down to the Pit?
Will the dust praise you?
Will it tell of your faithfulness?
10 Hear, O Lord, and be gracious to me!
O Lord, be my helper!"

11 You have turned my mourning into dancing;
you have taken off my sackcloth
and clothed me with joy,
12 so that my soul[a] may praise you and not be silent.
O Lord my God, I will give thanks to you forever.

PSALM 31

Prayer and Praise for Deliverance from Enemies

To the leader. A Psalm of David.

1 In you, O Lord, I seek refuge;
do not let me ever be put to shame;
in your righteousness deliver me.
2 Incline your ear to me;
rescue me speedily.
Be a rock of refuge for me,
a strong fortress to save me.

3 You are indeed my rock and my fortress;
for your name's sake lead me and guide me,
4 take me out of the net that is hidden for me,
for you are my refuge.
5 Into your hand I commit my spirit;
you have redeemed me, O Lord, faithful God.

[a] Heb *that glory*

6 You hate[a] those who pay regard to worthless idols,
but I trust in the LORD.
7 I will exult and rejoice in your steadfast love,
because you have seen my affliction;
you have taken heed of my adversities,
8 and have not delivered me into the hand of the enemy;
you have set my feet in a broad place.

9 Be gracious to me, O LORD, for I am in distress;
my eye wastes away from grief,
my soul and body also.
10 For my life is spent with sorrow,
and my years with sighing;
my strength fails because of my misery,[b]
and my bones waste away.

11 I am the scorn of all my adversaries,
a horror[c] to my neighbors,
an object of dread to my acquaintances;
those who see me in the street flee from me.
12 I have passed out of mind like one who is dead;
I have become like a broken vessel.
13 For I hear the whispering of many—
terror all around!—
as they scheme together against me,
as they plot to take my life.

14 But I trust in you, O LORD;
I say, "You are my God."
15 My times are in your hand;
deliver me from the hand of my enemies and persecutors.
16 Let your face shine upon your servant;
save me in your steadfast love.
17 Do not let me be put to shame, O LORD,
for I call on you;
let the wicked be put to shame;
let them go dumbfounded to Sheol.
18 Let the lying lips be stilled
that speak insolently against the righteous
with pride and contempt.

19 O how abundant is your goodness
that you have laid up for those who fear you,

31:9-13 I am in distress: The central section of the psalm is filled with images of the psalmist's distress, which emphasize physical pain as well as social isolation and threat.

31:6-8, 14-15, 19-20 how abundant is your goodness: In spite of the desperate physical and social crisis, the psalmist still boldly declares faith in God's steadfast love (see note on 13:5) and goodness.

[a] One Heb Ms Gk Syr Jerome: MT *I hate* [b] Gk Syr: Heb *my iniquity* [c] Cn: Heb *exceedingly*

and accomplished for those who take refuge in you,
in the sight of everyone!
20 In the shelter of your presence you hide them
from human plots;
you hold them safe under your shelter
from contentious tongues.

21 Blessed be the LORD,
for he has wondrously shown his steadfast love to me
when I was beset as a city under siege.
22 I had said in my alarm,
"I am driven far[a] from your sight."
But you heard my supplications
when I cried out to you for help.

23 Love the LORD, all you his saints.
The LORD preserves the faithful,
but abundantly repays the one who acts haughtily.
24 Be strong, and let your heart take courage,
all you who wait for the LORD.

PSALM 32

The Joy of Forgiveness

Of David. A Maskil.

1 Happy are those whose transgression is forgiven,
whose sin is covered.
2 Happy are those to whom the LORD imputes no iniquity,
and in whose spirit there is no deceit.

3 While I kept silence, my body wasted away
through my groaning all day long.
4 For day and night your hand was heavy upon me;
my strength was dried up[b] as by the heat of summer. *Selah*

5 Then I acknowledged my sin to you,
and I did not hide my iniquity;
I said, "I will confess my transgressions to the LORD,"
and you forgave the guilt of my sin. *Selah*

6 Therefore let all who are faithful
offer prayer to you;
at a time of distress,[c] the rush of mighty waters
shall not reach them.

31:21-24 Blessed be the LORD: A song of thanksgiving ends this psalm, with the writer telling about the past crisis and calling for praise and trust in God. Wait for the LORD: see note at 27:14.

Psalm 32: A song of thanksgiving and a penitential psalm (see Types of Psalms, pp. 849-850).

32:1-2 Happy are those: This opening section of praise takes the form of "happy are" statements (see note on 1:1), celebrating the joy of forgiveness.

32:3-5 Then I acknowledged my sin: In a past crisis the psalmist at first "kept silence" and did not confess or acknowledge sin. This may have happened during an illness—many at this time assumed illness was the result of some sin (see note on 6:1). Then the psalmist confessed sin, received forgiveness, and was restored.

How important is it to confess our sins and receive forgiveness? Confession and forgiveness are necessary and ongoing gifts in our relationships with God and one another. Martin Luther taught that part of the Christian life is "daily sorrow for sin," knowing that, in baptism, God promises forgiveness of sins. When we remember this promise, "daily a new person is to come forth and rise up to live before God" (*SC*:30). *Psalm 32:3-5*

How can confession and forgiveness be gifts to your relationship with God or another person?

32:6-11 Be glad in the LORD: The psalmist praises God and offers instruction to the community. Because the purpose of praise is to offer testimony about God, praise and instruction are very similar. The horse and mule most likely refer to the psalmist's previously stubborn silence (verse 3).

[a] Another reading is *cut off* [b] Meaning of Heb uncertain [c] Cn: Heb *at a time of finding only*

7 You are a hiding place for me;
you preserve me from trouble;
you surround me with glad cries of deliverance. *Selah*

8 I will instruct you and teach you the way you should go;
I will counsel you with my eye upon you.
9 Do not be like a horse or a mule, without understanding,
whose temper must be curbed with bit and bridle,
else it will not stay near you.

10 Many are the torments of the wicked,
but steadfast love surrounds those who trust in the LORD.
11 Be glad in the LORD and rejoice, O righteous,
and shout for joy, all you upright in heart.

PSALM 33

The Greatness and Goodness of God

1 Rejoice in the LORD, O you righteous.
Praise befits the upright.
2 Praise the LORD with the lyre;
make melody to him with the harp of ten strings.
3 Sing to him a new song;
play skillfully on the strings, with loud shouts.

4 For the word of the LORD is upright,
and all his work is done in faithfulness.
5 He loves righteousness and justice;
the earth is full of the steadfast love of the LORD.

6 By the word of the LORD the heavens were made,
and all their host by the breath of his mouth.
7 He gathered the waters of the sea as in a bottle;
he put the deeps in storehouses.

8 Let all the earth fear the LORD;
let all the inhabitants of the world stand in awe of him.
9 For he spoke, and it came to be;
he commanded, and it stood firm.

10 The LORD brings the counsel of the nations to nothing;
he frustrates the plans of the peoples.
11 The counsel of the LORD stands forever,
the thoughts of his heart to all generations.
12 Happy is the nation whose God is the LORD,
the people whom he has chosen as his heritage.

Psalm 33: A hymn of praise (see Types of Psalms, pp. 849-850) that celebrates the word of God.

33:1-3 Rejoice: The opening call to praise is not just a call to make music, but to do so with skill and passion, as a fitting response to God's gracious actions.

33:4-11 word of the LORD: This is the central concept in the psalm. God's word is the main feature of worship. When the faithful praise, they speak God's word and join in the work God does through the word—creating, promising, and instructing. God's word also undoes the plots of the wicked.

Psalm 33:10 says, "The LORD . . . frustrates the plans of the peoples." Has the LORD ever frustrated your plans in a way that turned out better for you? What happened?

33:12-22 Our soul waits for the LORD: True hope lies in the LORD's steadfast love (see note on 13:5). It is tempting to trust in earthly comforts, but at best they are only the means for deliverance. True hope rests in God, the source of deliverance.

[13] The LORD looks down from heaven;
he sees all humankind.
[14] From where he sits enthroned he watches
all the inhabitants of the earth—
[15] he who fashions the hearts of them all,
and observes all their deeds.
[16] A king is not saved by his great army;
a warrior is not delivered by his great strength.
[17] The war horse is a vain hope for victory,
and by its great might it cannot save.

[18] Truly the eye of the LORD is on those who fear him,
on those who hope in his steadfast love,
[19] to deliver their soul from death,
and to keep them alive in famine.

[20] Our soul waits for the LORD;
he is our help and shield.
[21] Our heart is glad in him,
because we trust in his holy name.
[22] Let your steadfast love, O LORD, be upon us,
even as we hope in you.

Psalm 34: A song of thanksgiving that is also an acrostic poem (see Types of Psalms, pp. 849-850).

PSALM 34

Praise for Deliverance from Trouble

Of David, when he feigned madness before Abimelech, so that he drove him out, and he went away.

1 I will bless the LORD at all times;
his praise shall continually be in my mouth.
2 My soul makes its boast in the LORD;
let the humble hear and be glad.
3 O magnify the LORD with me,
and let us exalt his name together.

34:3 magnify the LORD with me: The psalmist or writer has passed through a time of crisis (34:4-6) and now calls on the community to join in thankful praise. Times of distress tend to isolate those who suffer, while times of joy bring communities back together. When we celebrate with those God has delivered, we build up the community.

4 I sought the LORD, and he answered me,
and delivered me from all my fears.
5 Look to him, and be radiant;
so your[a] faces shall never be ashamed.
6 This poor soul cried, and was heard by the LORD,
and was saved from every trouble.
7 The angel of the LORD encamps
around those who fear him, and delivers them.
8 O taste and see that the LORD is good;

34:8 taste and see that the LORD is good: This may be a reference to a sacrificial meal celebrated as part of the ritual of thanksgiving (see Num 15:2-5). Others may have shared in such meals as a way to recognize what God had done for a person.

[a] Gk Syr Jerome: Heb *their*

happy are those who take refuge in him.
9 O fear the LORD, you his holy ones,
for those who fear him have no want.
10 The young lions suffer want and hunger,
but those who seek the LORD lack no good thing.

11 Come, O children, listen to me;
I will teach you the fear of the LORD.
12 Which of you desires life,
and covets many days to enjoy good?
13 Keep your tongue from evil,
and your lips from speaking deceit.
14 Depart from evil, and do good;
seek peace, and pursue it.

15 The eyes of the LORD are on the righteous,
and his ears are open to their cry.
16 The face of the LORD is against evildoers,
to cut off the remembrance of them from the earth.
17 When the righteous cry for help, the LORD hears,
and rescues them from all their troubles.
18 The LORD is near to the brokenhearted,
and saves the crushed in spirit.

19 Many are the afflictions of the righteous,
but the LORD rescues them from them all.
20 He keeps all their bones;
not one of them will be broken.
21 Evil brings death to the wicked,
and those who hate the righteous will be condemned.
22 The LORD redeems the life of his servants;
none of those who take refuge in him will be
condemned.

PSALM 35

Prayer for Deliverance from Enemies

Of David.

1 Contend, O LORD, with those who contend with me;
fight against those who fight against me!
2 Take hold of shield and buckler,
and rise up to help me!
3 Draw the spear and javelin
against my pursuers;
say to my soul,
"I am your salvation."

34:9-11 I will teach you the fear of the LORD: The phrase "fear the LORD" is common in Israel's teachings and writings. This term sums up a proper relationship with God—worship, love, obey, and revere God. The psalmist contrasts fear of earthly things and fear of God, the proper one to "fear" (often translated as "revere").

34:15-19 The eyes of the LORD are on the righteous: The psalm balances the protection that God promises to those who fear God with the realities of life. Those who follow God are not immune from suffering, but God provides strength and promises to them.

How do God's promises help you during difficult times?

Psalm 35: A prayer for help (see Types of Psalms, pp. 849-850) that includes pleas for rescue from evildoers.

35:1-8 fight against those who fight against me!: Many psalms include a "double wish"—that God would rescue the suffering person and also defeat those causing the suffering. However, these would not be seen as two separate wishes by the psalmist, who would have assumed at the time that the only way to be rescued was for the evildoers to be defeated.

4 Let them be put to shame and dishonor
who seek after my life.
Let them be turned back and confounded
who devise evil against me.
5 Let them be like chaff before the wind,
with the angel of the LORD driving them on.
6 Let their way be dark and slippery,
with the angel of the LORD pursuing them.

7 For without cause they hid their net[a] for me;
without cause they dug a pit[b] for my life.
8 Let ruin come on them unawares.
And let the net that they hid ensnare them;
let them fall in it—to their ruin.

35:9-10 my soul shall rejoice: The psalmist promises to praise God after being rescued. This is not bargaining for help, but a promise to spread the good news that God helps those who suffer.

9 Then my soul shall rejoice in the LORD,
exulting in his deliverance.
10 All my bones shall say,
"O LORD, who is like you?
You deliver the weak
from those too strong for them,
the weak and needy from those who despoil
them."

35:11-16 They repay me evil for good: The psalm uses many metaphors for the evildoers' behavior, but exactly what they have done is uncertain. It is clear that they take joy in another's downfall and do not return the psalmist's kindness.

11 Malicious witnesses rise up;
they ask me about things I do not know.
12 They repay me evil for good;
my soul is forlorn.
13 But as for me, when they were sick,
I wore sackcloth;
I afflicted myself with fasting.
I prayed with head bowed[c] on my bosom,
14 as though I grieved for a friend or a brother;
I went about as one who laments for a mother,
bowed down and in mourning.

15 But at my stumbling they gathered in glee,
they gathered together against me;
ruffians whom I did not know
tore at me without ceasing;
16 they impiously mocked more and more,[d]
gnashing at me with their teeth.

---

[a] Heb *a pit, their net* [b] The word *pit* is transposed from the preceding line [c] Or *My prayer turned back*
[d] Cn Compare Gk: Heb *like the profanest of mockers of a cake*

17 How long, O LORD, will you look on?
Rescue me from their ravages,
my life from the lions!
18 Then I will thank you in the great congregation;
in the mighty throng I will praise you.

19 Do not let my treacherous enemies rejoice over me,
or those who hate me without cause wink the eye.
20 For they do not speak peace,
but they conceive deceitful words
against those who are quiet in the land.
21 They open wide their mouths against me;
they say, "Aha, Aha,
our eyes have seen it."

22 You have seen, O LORD; do not be silent!
O Lord, do not be far from me!
23 Wake up! Bestir yourself for my defense,
for my cause, my God and my Lord!
24 Vindicate me, O LORD, my God,
according to your righteousness,
and do not let them rejoice over me.
25 Do not let them say to themselves,
"Aha, we have our heart's desire."
Do not let them say, "We have swallowed you[a] up."

26 Let all those who rejoice at my calamity
be put to shame and confusion;
let those who exalt themselves against me
be clothed with shame and dishonor.

27 Let those who desire my vindication
shout for joy and be glad,
and say evermore,
"Great is the LORD,
who delights in the welfare of his servant."
28 Then my tongue shall tell of your righteousness
and of your praise all day long.

PSALM 36
Human Wickedness and Divine Goodness

To the leader. Of David, the servant of the LORD.

1 Transgression speaks to the wicked

[a] Heb *him*

35:17 How long?: See note on 6:3. Faced with betrayal, the psalmist turns to God.

35:18-25 You have seen, O LORD, do not be silent!: The concept of speech is important in the psalm. God is silent while the enemies lie and speak maliciously. The psalmist promises to praise God. Most of all, the psalmist wants God to break the silence and say, "I am your salvation" (35:3).

When have you wanted God to break the silence? What happened?

35:26-28 say evermore, "Great is the LORD": The theme of speech continues. The psalmist appeals to the community to "shout for joy" to the LORD, in contrast to those who "rejoice at my calamity." The psalm ends with another promise to praise God and a request for the community to say, "Great is the LORD."

Psalm 36: A prayer for help (see Types of Psalms, pp. 849-850) that meditates on the character of the wicked and the character of God.

36:1-4 there is no fear of God before their eyes: Instead of the usual complaint about the wicked, this prayer for help begins with a meditation about them. The key characteristic of the wicked is that they have no fear of God (see note on 34:9-11). They imagine that they govern their own lives, refusing to acknowledge God's higher power and purpose.

deep in their hearts;
there is no fear of God
before their eyes.
2 For they flatter themselves in their own eyes
that their iniquity cannot be found out and hated.
3 The words of their mouths are mischief and deceit;
they have ceased to act wisely and do good.
4 They plot mischief while on their beds;
they are set on a way that is not good;
they do not reject evil.

5 Your steadfast love, O LORD, extends to the heavens,
your faithfulness to the clouds.
6 Your righteousness is like the mighty mountains,
your judgments are like the great deep;
you save humans and animals alike, O LORD.

7 How precious is your steadfast love, O God!
All people may take refuge in the shadow of your wings.
8 They feast on the abundance of your house,
and you give them drink from the river of your delights.
9 For with you is the fountain of life;
in your light we see light.

10 O continue your steadfast love to those who know you,
and your salvation to the upright of heart!
11 Do not let the foot of the arrogant tread on me,
or the hand of the wicked drive me away.
12 There the evildoers lie prostrate;
they are thrust down, unable to rise.

PSALM 37

Exhortation to Patience and Trust

Of David.

1 Do not fret because of the wicked;
do not be envious of wrongdoers,
2 for they will soon fade like the grass,
and wither like the green herb.

3 Trust in the LORD, and do good;
so you will live in the land, and enjoy security.
4 Take delight in the LORD,
and he will give you the desires of your heart.

5 Commit your way to the LORD;
trust in him, and he will act.

36:5-6 your steadfast love: Teachings and writings in Israel's wisdom tradition normally contrast the wicked with the righteous, but this psalm contrasts the wicked with God. This is fitting, because the wicked think they rule their own lives. The prayer describes God's character with a series of natural images—a reminder that God is creator of all.

36:7 refuge: See note on 2:11.

36:7-8 shadow of your wings… abundance of your house…river of your delights: These images most likely refer to the temple, where the cherubim's wings were a symbol of protection (Exod 37:7-9). Blessings from the temple were compared to a flowing river (see 46:4).

36:9 the fountain of life; in your light we see light: Perhaps a reference to the lamp in the temple (Lev 24:1-4), but even more an image for God's guiding and saving power (27:1; 119:105; John 9:5).

Light can dispel darkness, reveal hidden traps, and shine as a beacon for travelers. How is God a light in your life?

36:10-12 continue your steadfast love: On the basis of God's character, the psalmist now asks God to defeat the wicked.

Psalm 37: An instructional psalm that appears as an acrostic poem (see Types of Psalms, pp. 849-850), written from the perspective of a community elder (37:25).

37:5 Commit your way to the LORD: The psalm calls us to trust that following God's way is the best course in life and that God's plans and purposes will win the day. To *commit* to the LORD means entrusting our entire lives to God and refusing to do evil acts for short-term gain.

6 He will make your vindication shine like the light,
and the justice of your cause like the noonday.

7 Be still before the LORD, and wait patiently for him;
do not fret over those who prosper in their way,
over those who carry out evil devices.

8 Refrain from anger, and forsake wrath.
Do not fret—it leads only to evil.
9 For the wicked shall be cut off,
but those who wait for the LORD shall inherit the land.

10 Yet a little while, and the wicked will be no more;
though you look diligently for their place, they will not be there.
11 But the meek shall inherit the land,
and delight themselves in abundant prosperity.

12 The wicked plot against the righteous,
and gnash their teeth at them;
13 but the LORD laughs at the wicked,
for he sees that their day is coming.

14 The wicked draw the sword and bend their bows
to bring down the poor and needy,
to kill those who walk uprightly;
15 their sword shall enter their own heart,
and their bows shall be broken.

16 Better is a little that the righteous person has
than the abundance of many wicked.
17 For the arms of the wicked shall be broken,
but the LORD upholds the righteous.

18 The LORD knows the days of the blameless,
and their heritage will abide forever;
19 they are not put to shame in evil times,
in the days of famine they have abundance.

20 But the wicked perish,
and the enemies of the LORD are like the glory of the pastures;
they vanish—like smoke they vanish away.

21 The wicked borrow, and do not pay back,
but the righteous are generous and keep giving;

37:7-8, 12 Do not fret: The psalm warns against the temptation to become obsessed with the success of "those who prosper in their way" (37:7). Such obsessing can lead to unhappiness and evil deeds. The success of the wicked is short-lived, "they will soon fade like the grass" (37:2).

37:3, 9, 11, 22, 29, 34 the land: God promised Abram's descendants a blessing and land (Gen 12:1-3). Although this promise seems to be in danger many times in the Old Testament, God keeps the promise in the long run. To live in the land is to trust in God's promise in the long run, to have an identity and place, and to know that God's promises to Abraham are still being kept for you.

22 for those blessed by the LORD shall inherit the land,
but those cursed by him shall be cut off.

23 Our steps[a] are made firm by the LORD,
when he delights in our[b] way;
24 though we stumble,[c] we[d] shall not fall headlong,
for the LORD holds us[e] by the hand.

37:25-28 I have been young, and now am old: The elder psalmist has experienced God's faithfulness across many years and knows that God keeps promises—even though at times that may be hard to see. The promise that the children of the righteous will not go hungry is not absolute. Rather, it is an assurance that in the long run God is faithful. It is also a call for the people of God to care for and share with the hungry.

25 I have been young, and now am old,
yet I have not seen the righteous forsaken
or their children begging bread.
26 They are ever giving liberally and lending,
and their children become a blessing.

27 Depart from evil, and do good;
so you shall abide forever.
28 For the LORD loves justice;
he will not forsake his faithful ones.

The righteous shall be kept safe forever,
but the children of the wicked shall be cut off.
29 The righteous shall inherit the land,
and live in it forever.

30 The mouths of the righteous utter wisdom,
and their tongues speak justice.
31 The law of their God is in their hearts;
their steps do not slip.

32 The wicked watch for the righteous,
and seek to kill them.
33 The LORD will not abandon them to their power,
or let them be condemned when they are brought to trial.

37:34-40 Wait for the LORD, and keep to his way: Regarding "wait for the LORD," see note on 27:14. The image in verses 35-36—of the wicked towering like a tall tree one instant, but then being gone the next—reinforces the message of the psalm: trust in God, live for the long haul, and take refuge in God (see note on 2:11).

34 Wait for the LORD, and keep to his way,
and he will exalt you to inherit the land;
you will look on the destruction of the wicked.

35 I have seen the wicked oppressing,
and towering like a cedar of Lebanon.[f]
36 Again I[g] passed by, and they were no more;
though I sought them, they could not be found.

---

[a] Heb *A man's steps* [b] Heb *his* [c] Heb *he stumbles* [d] Heb *he* [e] Heb *him* [f] Gk: Meaning of Heb uncertain [g] Gk Syr Jerome: Heb *he*

37 Mark the blameless, and behold the upright,
for there is posterity for the peaceable.
38 But transgressors shall be altogether destroyed;
the posterity of the wicked shall be cut off.

39 The salvation of the righteous is from the LORD;
he is their refuge in the time of trouble.
40 The LORD helps them and rescues them;
he rescues them from the wicked, and saves them,
because they take refuge in him.

PSALM 38

A Penitent Sufferer's Plea for Healing

A Psalm of David, for the memorial offering.

1 O LORD, do not rebuke me in your anger,
or discipline me in your wrath.
2 For your arrows have sunk into me,
and your hand has come down on me.

3 There is no soundness in my flesh
because of your indignation;
there is no health in my bones
because of my sin.
4 For my iniquities have gone over my head;
they weigh like a burden too heavy for me.

5 My wounds grow foul and fester
because of my foolishness;
6 I am utterly bowed down and prostrate;
all day long I go around mourning.
7 For my loins are filled with burning,
and there is no soundness in my flesh.
8 I am utterly spent and crushed;
I groan because of the tumult of my heart.

9 O Lord, all my longing is known to you;
my sighing is not hidden from you.
10 My heart throbs, my strength fails me;
as for the light of my eyes—it also has gone from me.
11 My friends and companions stand aloof from my affliction,
and my neighbors stand far off.

12 Those who seek my life lay their snares;
those who seek to hurt me speak of ruin,
and meditate treachery all day long.

Psalm 38: A prayer for help and a penitential psalm (see Types of Psalms, pp. 849-850).

38:1-4 do not rebuke me in your anger: The psalmist believes that illness is God's punishment for sin (see note on 6:1). Jesus rejected this common belief (see John 9:1-3), but sometimes there are consequences for breaking God's law. This psalm claims that we can turn to God in times like these.

38:5-10 my strength fails me: The psalmist is gravely ill. This description of personal suffering reflects the teaching that God cares about human suffering, even the suffering of those who have brought it on themselves.

38:11-12 My friends and companions stand aloof from my affliction: Perhaps the community saw the psalmist's illness as punishment or even rejection by God (see Job 4).

[13] But I am like the deaf, I do not hear;
like the mute, who cannot speak.
[14] Truly, I am like one who does not hear,
and in whose mouth is no retort.

38:15-16 it is for you, O Lord, that I wait: See note on 37:34-40.

The psalmist waits for the Lord, even though the taunts of enemies make the waiting difficult. What makes waiting for and trusting in the Lord difficult for you?

38:17-22 Do not forsake me, O Lord: The psalmist's appeal to God reflects the teaching that confessing sin and hearing God's promise of forgiveness are necessary parts of the ongoing life of faith.

[15] But it is for you, O Lord, that I wait;
it is you, O Lord my God, who will answer.
[16] For I pray, "Only do not let them rejoice over me,
those who boast against me when my foot slips."

[17] For I am ready to fall,
and my pain is ever with me.
[18] I confess my iniquity;
I am sorry for my sin.
[19] Those who are my foes without cause[a] are mighty,
and many are those who hate me wrongfully.
[20] Those who render me evil for good
are my adversaries because I follow after good.

[21] Do not forsake me, O Lord;
O my God, do not be far from me;
[22] make haste to help me,
O Lord, my salvation.

Psalm 39: A prayer for help (see Types of Psalms, pp. 849-850).

39:1-3 then I spoke with my tongue: The psalmist was in distress, but hoped that God would reward silence. Then the psalmist complained to God.

39:4-7 Lord, let me know my end: The psalmist has learned that life is brief and we cannot know how long life or health will last (see also 90:9-12).

PSALM 39

Prayer for Wisdom and Forgiveness

To the leader: to Jeduthun. A Psalm of David.

[1] I said, "I will guard my ways
that I may not sin with my tongue;
I will keep a muzzle on my mouth
as long as the wicked are in my presence."
[2] I was silent and still;
I held my peace to no avail;
my distress grew worse,
[3] my heart became hot within me.
While I mused, the fire burned;
then I spoke with my tongue:

[4] "Lord, let me know my end,
and what is the measure of my days;
let me know how fleeting my life is.
[5] You have made my days a few handbreadths,
and my lifetime is as nothing in your sight.

---

[a] Q Ms: MT *my living foes*

Surely everyone stands as a mere breath. *Selah*
6 Surely everyone goes about like a shadow.
Surely for nothing they are in turmoil;
they heap up, and do not know who will gather.

7 "And now, O Lord, what do I wait for?
My hope is in you.
8 Deliver me from all my transgressions.
Do not make me the scorn of the fool.
9 I am silent; I do not open my mouth,
for it is you who have done it.
10 Remove your stroke from me;
I am worn down by the blows[a] of your hand.

11 "You chastise mortals
in punishment for sin,
consuming like a moth what is dear to them;
surely everyone is a mere breath. *Selah*

12 "Hear my prayer, O LORD,
and give ear to my cry;
do not hold your peace at my tears.
For I am your passing guest,
an alien, like all my forebears.
13 Turn your gaze away from me, that I may smile again,
before I depart and am no more."

PSALM 40

Thanksgiving for Deliverance and Prayer for Help

To the leader. Of David. A Psalm.

1 I waited patiently for the LORD;
he inclined to me and heard my cry.
2 He drew me up from the desolate pit,[b]
out of the miry bog,
and set my feet upon a rock,
making my steps secure.
3 He put a new song in my mouth,
a song of praise to our God.
Many will see and fear,
and put their trust in the LORD.

4 Happy are those who make
the LORD their trust,

39:8-12 Deliver me from all my transgressions: The psalmist confesses sins (see note on 38:17-22), vows to be silent and wait for God, and then begs God to not be silent.

39:12 I am your passing guest, an alien, like all my forebears: The word translated here as "alien" could be "wanderer." The psalmist finds a place in Israel's history, which is the story of those "wandering" through life with God (see Deut 26:5-10). The only permanent home God's people know is God.

Psalm 40: A song of thanksgiving that leads into a renewed prayer for help (see Types of Psalms, pp. 849-850).

40:1-3 He drew me up from the desolate pit: The psalm begins with a description of a crisis and God's deliverance. The image of feet sinking into a soggy swamp and then being set on firm rock portrays this. A "new song" is a term for a song of praise to God, sung after being rescued. The new song in this case is Psalm 40, especially verses 3-5.

---

[a] Heb *hostility* [b] Cn: Heb *pit of tumult*

who do not turn to the proud,
to those who go astray after false gods.

5 You have multiplied, O LORD my God,
your wondrous deeds and your thoughts toward us;
none can compare with you.
Were I to proclaim and tell of them,
they would be more than can be counted.

40:6 Sacrifice and offering: Four different types of offerings are mentioned. It was customary for a person to make a sacrifice as part of the ritual of thanksgiving for God's help (see note on 34:8). But what God truly desires is obedience (40:8; see also Mic 6:6-8), repentance (51:16-17), and praise that teaches and inspires others (69:30-32).

40:7 Here I am: Verse 7 can also be translated: "Here I am; I bring a scroll that tells what happened to me." The scroll is the psalmist's testimony of praise that describes the crisis and deliverance.

40:9-10 I have not hidden your saving help within my heart: To praise God and tell others what God has done is a necessary part of the life of faith. In the Old Testament era, worship included times for people to give testimony to what God had done for them.

What has God done for you that you can tell others to build up their faith?

40:11-17 Do not, O LORD, withhold your mercy from me: The psalmist did not hold back the news about what God had done and here asks God not to hold back mercy. The rest of the psalm is a renewed prayer for help. God's saving help is not a one-time experience, but something that is required again and again throughout life.

6 Sacrifice and offering you do not desire,
but you have given me an open ear.[a]
Burnt offering and sin offering
you have not required.
7 Then I said, "Here I am;
in the scroll of the book it is written of me.[b]
8 I delight to do your will, O my God;
your law is within my heart."

9 I have told the glad news of deliverance
in the great congregation;
see, I have not restrained my lips,
as you know, O LORD.
10 I have not hidden your saving help within my heart,
I have spoken of your faithfulness and your salvation;
I have not concealed your steadfast love and your faithfulness
from the great congregation.

11 Do not, O LORD, withhold
your mercy from me;
let your steadfast love and your faithfulness
keep me safe forever.
12 For evils have encompassed me
without number;
my iniquities have overtaken me,
until I cannot see;
they are more than the hairs of my head,
and my heart fails me.

13 Be pleased, O LORD, to deliver me;
O LORD, make haste to help me.
14 Let all those be put to shame and confusion
who seek to snatch away my life;
let those be turned back and brought to dishonor
who desire my hurt.

---

[a] Heb *ears you have dug for me* [b] Meaning of Heb uncertain

15 Let those be appalled because of their shame
who say to me, "Aha, Aha!"

16 But may all who seek you
rejoice and be glad in you;
may those who love your salvation
say continually, "Great is the LORD!"
17 As for me, I am poor and needy,
but the Lord takes thought for me.
You are my help and my deliverer;
do not delay, O my God.

PSALM 41

Assurance of God's Help and a Plea for Healing

To the leader. A Psalm of David.

1 Happy are those who consider the poor;[a]
the LORD delivers them in the day of trouble.
2 The LORD protects them and keeps them alive;
they are called happy in the land.
You do not give them up to the will of their enemies.
3 The LORD sustains them on their sickbed;
in their illness you heal all their infirmities.[b]

4 As for me, I said, "O LORD, be gracious to me;
heal me, for I have sinned against you."
5 My enemies wonder in malice
when I will die, and my name perish.
6 And when they come to see me, they utter empty words,
while their hearts gather mischief;
when they go out, they tell it abroad.
7 All who hate me whisper together about me;
they imagine the worst for me.

8 They think that a deadly thing has fastened on me,
that I will not rise again from where I lie.
9 Even my bosom friend in whom I trusted,
who ate of my bread, has lifted the heel against me.
10 But you, O LORD, be gracious to me,
and raise me up, that I may repay them.

11 By this I know that you are pleased with me;
because my enemy has not triumphed over me.
12 But you have upheld me because of my integrity,
and set me in your presence forever.

---

[a] Or *weak* [b] Heb *you change all his bed*

Psalm 41: An instructional psalm (see Types of Psalms, pp. 849-850) from a person who has come through a time of crisis.

41:1 Happy are those: See note on 1:1.The enviable or desirable life is pictured in what might be a surprising way—as those who consider the poor. In the Bible, however, this is not surprising. The emphasis on caring for the poor fits within God's desire for a just world.

41:3 The LORD sustains them on their sickbed: God sustained the psalmist through an illness. Now the psalmist teaches others as a way of thanking God.

41:4 I have sinned: See note on 38:17-22.

41:9-10 Even my bosom friend in whom I trusted: Similar to Job's friends (see Job 4), the psalmist's friends interpret the illness as a sign of God's rejection. This kind of treatment might be expected from enemies, but from friends it is a severe blow. The psalmist turns to God: "But you, O LORD, be gracious to me."

41:11 By this I know that you are pleased with me: This may also be translated "that you delight in me." God has shown honor to the psalmist through healing (on honor and shame, see note on 6:10).

41:13 Blessed be the LORD: This verse is not actually part of Psalm 41. It is the closing word of praise at the end of Book I of the Psalms.

Psalms 42–43: A prayer for help (see Types of Psalms, pp. 849-850), from a person who has been exiled from God's presence in the temple. Although numbered as separate psalms, they together form one poem, as indicated by the refrain that occurs three times (42:5-6a; 42:11; 43:5).

42:1-3 As a deer longs for flowing streams: Water is a key image in this prayer. The psalmist thirsts for God's quenching presence, but has only tears for food or drink.

42:3, 10 Where is your God? The psalmist was forced into exile and ridiculed by enemies after the Israelites suffered a defeat. The taunt, "Where is your God?" (see also 79:10; 115:2; Joel 2:17; Mic 7:10) reflects the ancient belief that a battle between two nations was also a battle between their gods. A defeat meant that the losing nation's god had been defeated as well.

42:4 These things I remember: The psalmist or writer is a priest living in exile. In prayers for help, memories of the past often bring encouragement, but here they have the opposite effect. As memories of water might torment a thirsting person, the memories of leading God's people in worship torment the priest.

42:5, 11; 43:5 Why are you cast down, O my soul?: The Hebrew word *nephesh* (NE-fesh) is often translated as "soul," but it does not mean soul in the sense of an eternal, spiritual part of a human being. Rather, it means "most essential being," "inner self," or "the real me." The psalmist, who may be wrestling with personal doubt and despair, tries to stir up hope in God instead (see note on 103:1-5).

42:6 I remember you from the land of Jordan: The psalmist admits feeling cast down and remembers God. This time, memories bring encouragement. The psalmist, who may be exiled from God's presence in the temple, still has "his song . . . a prayer to the God of my life."

13 Blessed be the LORD, the God of Israel,
from everlasting to everlasting.
Amen and Amen.

BOOK II

(Psalms 42–72)

PSALM 42

Longing for God and His Help in Distress

To the leader. A Maskil of the Korahites.

1 As a deer longs for flowing streams,
so my soul longs for you, O God.
2 My soul thirsts for God,
for the living God.
When shall I come and behold
the face of God?
3 My tears have been my food
day and night,
while people say to me continually,
"Where is your God?"

4 These things I remember,
as I pour out my soul:
how I went with the throng,[a]
and led them in procession to the house of God,
with glad shouts and songs of thanksgiving,
a multitude keeping festival.
5 Why are you cast down, O my soul,
and why are you disquieted within me?
Hope in God; for I shall again praise him,
my help 6 and my God.

My soul is cast down within me;
therefore I remember you
from the land of Jordan and of Hermon,
from Mount Mizar.
7 Deep calls to deep
at the thunder of your cataracts;
all your waves and your billows
have gone over me.
8 By day the LORD commands his steadfast love,
and at night his song is with me,
a prayer to the God of my life.

[a] Meaning of Heb uncertain

9 I say to God, my rock,
"Why have you forgotten me?
Why must I walk about mournfully
because the enemy oppresses me?"
10 As with a deadly wound in my body,
my adversaries taunt me,
while they say to me continually,
"Where is your God?"

11 Why are you cast down, O my soul,
and why are you disquieted within me?
Hope in God; for I shall again praise him,
my help and my God.

PSALM 43

Prayer to God in Time of Trouble

1 Vindicate me, O God, and defend my cause
against an ungodly people;
from those who are deceitful and unjust
deliver me!
2 For you are the God in whom I take refuge;
why have you cast me off?
Why must I walk about mournfully
because of the oppression of the enemy?

3 O send out your light and your truth;
let them lead me;
let them bring me to your holy hill
and to your dwelling.
4 Then I will go to the altar of God,
to God my exceeding joy;
and I will praise you with the harp,
O God, my God.

5 Why are you cast down, O my soul,
and why are you disquieted within me?
Hope in God; for I shall again praise him,
my help and my God.

PSALM 44

National Lament and Prayer for Help

To the leader. Of the Korahites. A Maskil.

1 We have heard with our ears, O God,
our ancestors have told us,
what deeds you performed in their days,

What memories and stories are helpful to you when you feel "cast down"?

42:9 Why have you forgotten me?: Remembering has both depressed and encouraged the psalmist, who now asks to be remembered by God.

43:1-2 defend my cause against an ungodly people: It is not clear who the oppressors are, but it is clear that they keep the psalmist away from God's presence in the temple and taunt the psalmist's faith in God.

43:3-4 send out your light and your truth: The light may be a reference to a lamp used in temple processions. The psalmist begs to be restored to God's presence and once again lead praise and worship in the temple.

Psalm 44: A prayer for help (see Types of Psalms, pp. 849-850) from a community.

44:1-3 our ancestors have told us: People in the community listened to the testimony of those who came before them, who believed that the nation was victorious—not because of military power—but because of God's faithfulness. By beginning the psalm in this way, the community calls on God to show faithfulness again.

in the days of old:
2 you with your own hand drove out the nations,
but them you planted;
you afflicted the peoples,
but them you set free;
3 for not by their own sword did they win the land,
nor did their own arm give them victory;
but your right hand, and your arm,
and the light of your countenance,
for you delighted in them.

44:4-8 we will give thanks to your name forever: A representative, perhaps the king, speaks on behalf of the people to express their continuing trust in God's guidance and deliverance—and not in their own military power.

4 You are my King and my God;
you command[a] victories for Jacob.
5 Through you we push down our foes;
through your name we tread down our assailants.
6 For not in my bow do I trust,
nor can my sword save me.
7 But you have saved us from our foes,
and have put to confusion those who hate us.
8 In God we have boasted continually,
and we will give thanks to your name forever. *Selah*

44:9-12 you have rejected us: The people's representative expresses the community's pain and suffering.

9 Yet you have rejected us and abased us,
and have not gone out with our armies.
10 You made us turn back from the foe,
and our enemies have gotten spoil.
11 You have made us like sheep for slaughter,
and have scattered us among the nations.
12 You have sold your people for a trifle,
demanding no high price for them.

44:13-16 You have made us the taunt: Enemies taunt the community with words such as "Where is your God?" (see note on 42:3).

13 You have made us the taunt of our neighbors,
the derision and scorn of those around us.
14 You have made us a byword among the nations,
a laughingstock[b] among the peoples.
15 All day long my disgrace is before me,
and shame has covered my face
16 at the words of the taunters and revilers,
at the sight of the enemy and the avenger.

44:17-22 yet we have not forgotten you: The spokesperson expresses the people's ongoing faith in God, saying the people have not and will not forget God. This is both a claim of innocence and a cry for God to remember the promises God has made (see Exod 2:23-25).

17 All this has come upon us,
yet we have not forgotten you,
or been false to your covenant.

---

[a] Gk Syr: Heb *You are my King, O God; command* [b] Heb *a shaking of the head*

18 Our heart has not turned back,
nor have our steps departed from your way,
19 yet you have broken us in the haunt of jackals,
and covered us with deep darkness.

20 If we had forgotten the name of our God,
or spread out our hands to a strange god,
21 would not God discover this?
For he knows the secrets of the heart.
22 Because of you we are being killed all day long,
and accounted as sheep for the slaughter.

23 Rouse yourself! Why do you sleep, O Lord?
Awake, do not cast us off forever!
24 Why do you hide your face?
Why do you forget our affliction and oppression?
25 For we sink down to the dust;
our bodies cling to the ground.
26 Rise up, come to our help.
Redeem us for the sake of your steadfast love.

44:23-25 Rouse yourself!: The psalm ends with fierce calls for God to act. The statement that God has forgotten the people stands out against earlier references to the people not forgetting God. The community's appeal is based on God's steadfast love (see note on 13:5).

PSALM 45
Ode for a Royal Wedding

To the leader: according to Lilies. Of the Korahites. A Maskil. A love song.

1 My heart overflows with a goodly theme;
I address my verses to the king;
my tongue is like the pen of a ready scribe.

2 You are the most handsome of men;
grace is poured upon your lips;
therefore God has blessed you forever.
3 Gird your sword on your thigh, O mighty one,
in your glory and majesty.

4 In your majesty ride on victoriously
for the cause of truth and to defend[a] the right;
let your right hand teach you dread deeds.
5 Your arrows are sharp
in the heart of the king's enemies;
the peoples fall under you.

6 Your throne, O God,[b] endures forever and ever.
Your royal scepter is a scepter of equity;

Psalm 45: A royal psalm (see Types of Psalms, pp. 849-850), probably composed for the king's wedding.

45:1 the king: In ancient Israel, government and religion were united. The king was seen as a channel for God to bless the people with military security (45:3, 5), fairness and equity (45:4, 6), and righteousness (45:7). The king was also a channel for God to connect with the people and keep the promises of land, descendants, and identity (45:16-17). Israel's human kings did not live up to God's standards, and the kingdom eventually failed. This and other royal psalms were preserved as a promise that God would one day send the perfect king.

---

[a] Cn: Heb *and the meekness of* [b] Or *Your throne is a throne of God, it*

45:7 God, your God, has anointed you: See note on 2:2.

45:10-15 Hear, O daughter: These words are for the king's bride, who was most likely a foreign king's daughter.

Psalm 46: A trust psalm from a community and a song of Zion (see Types of Psalms, pp. 849-850). The psalm has three stanzas (46:1-3; 4-6; 8-10), with a refrain occurring after the second and third stanzas (46:7, 11).

What role does music play in Lutheran tradition? Music and singing are vital parts of the Lutheran tradition. Martin Luther himself wrote many hymns. For example, Psalm 46 inspired Luther to write the hymn "A Mighty Fortress." *Psalm 46*

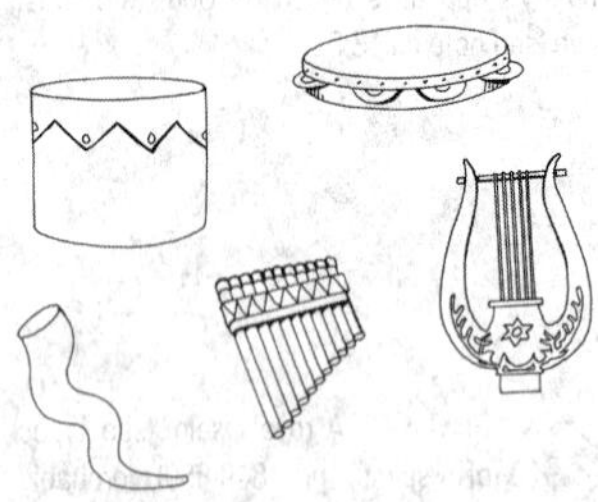

What songs or hymns comfort, inspire, or cheer you?

46:1-3 Therefore we will not fear, though the earth should change: Many dangers and threats surround the community. This first stanza describes the threat that comes from cosmic forces of chaos.

46:4 There is a river whose streams make glad the city of God: The river is a poetic image that shows God's presence in the temple as the source of God's abundance and blessing (see Ezek 47; Rev 22:1-2).

46:5 God is in the midst of the city; it shall not be moved: The temple was considered God's earthly dwelling (see note on 84:1). God's presence offered protection and blessing to the city and its residents.

46:6 The nations are in an uproar: This second stanza portrays the threats that human powers pose to God's people and describes the deliverance God offers in the face of cosmic threats.

7 you love righteousness and hate wickedness.
Therefore God, your God, has anointed you
with the oil of gladness beyond your companions;
8 your robes are all fragrant with myrrh and aloes and cassia.
From ivory palaces stringed instruments make you glad;
9 daughters of kings are among your ladies of honor;
at your right hand stands the queen in gold of Ophir.

10 Hear, O daughter, consider and incline your ear;
forget your people and your father's house,
11 and the king will desire your beauty.
Since he is your lord, bow to him;
12 the people[a] of Tyre will seek your favor with gifts,
the richest of the people 13 with all kinds of wealth.

The princess is decked in her chamber with gold-woven robes;[b]
14 in many-colored robes she is led to the king;
behind her the virgins, her companions, follow.
15 With joy and gladness they are led along
as they enter the palace of the king.

16 In the place of ancestors you, O king,[c] shall have sons;
you will make them princes in all the earth.
17 I will cause your name to be celebrated in all generations;
therefore the peoples will praise you forever and ever.

PSALM 46

God's Defense of His City and People

To the leader. Of the Korahites. According to Alamoth. A Song.

1 God is our refuge and strength,
a very present[d] help in trouble.
2 Therefore we will not fear, though the earth should change,
though the mountains shake in the heart of the sea;
3 though its waters roar and foam,
though the mountains tremble with its tumult. *Selah*

4 There is a river whose streams make glad the city of God,
the holy habitation of the Most High.
5 God is in the midst of the city;[e] it shall not be moved;
God will help it when the morning dawns.
6 The nations are in an uproar, the kingdoms totter;
he utters his voice, the earth melts.

---

[a] Heb *daughter* [b] Or *people.* [13]*All glorious is the princess within, gold embroidery is her clothing* [c] Heb lacks *O king* [d] Or *well proved* [e] Heb *of it*

7 The LORD of hosts is with us;
the God of Jacob is our refuge.[a] *Selah*

8 Come, behold the works of the LORD;
see what desolations he has brought on the earth.
9 He makes wars cease to the end of the earth;
he breaks the bow, and shatters the spear;
he burns the shields with fire.
10 "Be still, and know that I am God!
I am exalted among the nations,
I am exalted in the earth."
11 The LORD of hosts is with us;
the God of Jacob is our refuge.[a] *Selah*

PSALM 47

God's Rule over the Nations

To the leader. Of the Korahites. A Psalm.

1 Clap your hands, all you peoples;
shout to God with loud songs of joy.
2 For the LORD, the Most High, is awesome,
a great king over all the earth.
3 He subdued peoples under us,
and nations under our feet.
4 He chose our heritage for us,
the pride of Jacob whom he loves. *Selah*

5 God has gone up with a shout,
the LORD with the sound of a trumpet.
6 Sing praises to God, sing praises;
sing praises to our King, sing praises.
7 For God is the king of all the earth;
sing praises with a psalm.[b]

8 God is king over the nations;
God sits on his holy throne.
9 The princes of the peoples gather
as the people of the God of Abraham.
For the shields of the earth belong to God;
he is highly exalted.

PSALM 48

The Glory and Strength of Zion

A Song. A Psalm of the Korahites.

1 Great is the LORD and greatly to be praised

[a] Or *fortress* [b] Heb *Maskil*

46:7, 11 The LORD of hosts is with us; the God of Jacob is our refuge: This refrain may have been spoken by the congregation. It expresses the trust that because of God's presence, the people need not be afraid, in spite of cosmic and earthly threats.

46:8-9 Come, behold the works of the LORD: In this third stanza, the LORD delivers the people from earthly threats by destroying the weapons of war.

46:10 I am exalted among the nations, I am exalted in the earth: God's promise is spoken, most likely by a worship leader: God is more powerful than threats posed by human powers (46:6, 9) or cosmic powers (46:2-3). The concluding refrain expresses the people's trust in God's promise.

Psalm 47: A hymn of praise and an enthronement psalm (see Types of Psalms, pp. 849-850).

47:1-4 Clap your hands: This call for praise is followed by reasons for praise. The chief reason is God's rule over all creation, especially shown in giving the land ("heritage") to the people.

47:5 God has gone up with a shout: This refers to a liturgical action, probably bringing the ark of the covenant into the temple. The ark was a movable shrine that held the tablets of the Ten Commandments.

47:6-9 Sing praises: This passage restates a call for praise and reasons for praise, again emphasizing God's rule over creation, especially shown in God's faithfulness to promises made to Abraham.

Psalm 48: A hymn of praise and a song of Zion (see Types of Psalms, pp. 849-850).

48:1 Mount Zion: Zion, a name for Jerusalem, and specifically for the temple area, was considered God's dwelling, the place in which God's *name* dwelt. God promised to be with the people, to protect them and the city, and to remain faithful to the kings in David's line who ruled there. "In the far north" is a poetic reference to Mount Zaphon (the Hebrew word *zaphon* means north in Hebrew), the mythological dwelling place of the gods. Zion, then, is the point of contact between heaven and earth.

in the city of our God.
His holy mountain, [2]beautiful in elevation,
is the joy of all the earth,
Mount Zion, in the far north,
the city of the great King.
3 Within its citadels God
has shown himself a sure defense.

4 Then the kings assembled,
they came on together.
5 As soon as they saw it, they were astounded;
they were in panic, they took to flight;
6 trembling took hold of them there,
pains as of a woman in labor,
7 as when an east wind shatters
the ships of Tarshish.
8 As we have heard, so have we seen
in the city of the LORD of hosts,
in the city of our God,
which God establishes forever. *Selah*

9 We ponder your steadfast love, O God,
in the midst of your temple.
10 Your name, O God, like your praise,
reaches to the ends of the earth.
Your right hand is filled with victory.
11 Let Mount Zion be glad,
let the towns[a] of Judah rejoice
because of your judgments.

12 Walk about Zion, go all around it,
count its towers,
13 consider well its ramparts;
go through its citadels,
that you may tell the next generation
14 that this is God,
our God forever and ever.
He will be our guide forever.

48:4-8 they were astounded: This probably does not refer to a literal gathering of kings, but it does portray the proper reaction of humans when they encounter God's faithfulness.

48:9-14 Let Mount Zion be glad: The city is a place that embodies God's steadfast love. It provides identity for the people, so that the psalmist calls on "Mount Zion" and "the towns of Judah" to rejoice.

48:12-14 Walk about Zion: The city was almost seen as a physical sign of God's faithfulness. God was present "in the midst of the city" (46:5), so that the psalmist could even write, "this is God"—meaning that it was a sign of God's love and commitment to the people.

What are some real, concrete signs of God's faithfulness and commitment to you?

Psalm 49: An instructional psalm (see Types of Psalms, pp. 849-850), with an introduction (49:1-4) and two stanzas (49:5-11; 13-19), each of which ends with a refrain (49:12, 20).

49:1-4 low and high, rich and poor: The opening verses speak to all humanity—from the wealthy and powerful to the poor and lowly. God's word makes all humans equal, since it makes human wisdom foolish and offers God's wisdom even to fools (see 1 Cor 1:18-31).

PSALM 49

The Folly of Trust in Riches

To the leader. Of the Korahites. A Psalm.

1 Hear this, all you peoples;

[a] Heb *daughters*

give ear, all inhabitants of the world,
2 both low and high,
rich and poor together.
3 My mouth shall speak wisdom;
the meditation of my heart shall be understanding.
4 I will incline my ear to a proverb;
I will solve my riddle to the music of the harp.

5 Why should I fear in times of trouble,
when the iniquity of my persecutors surrounds me,
6 those who trust in their wealth
and boast of the abundance of their riches?
7 Truly, no ransom avails for one's life,[a]
there is no price one can give to God for it.
8 For the ransom of life is costly,
and can never suffice,
9 that one should live on forever
and never see the grave.[b]

10 When we look at the wise, they die;
fool and dolt perish together
and leave their wealth to others.
11 Their graves[c] are their homes forever,
their dwelling places to all generations,
though they named lands their own.
12 Mortals cannot abide in their pomp;
they are like the animals that perish.

13 Such is the fate of the foolhardy,
the end of those[d] who are pleased with their lot. *Selah*
14 Like sheep they are appointed for Sheol;
Death shall be their shepherd;
straight to the grave they descend,[e]
and their form shall waste away;
Sheol shall be their home.[f]
15 But God will ransom my soul from the power of Sheol,
for he will receive me. *Selah*

16 Do not be afraid when some become rich,
when the wealth of their houses increases.
17 For when they die they will carry nothing away;
their wealth will not go down after them.

---

[a] Another reading is *no one can ransom a brother* [b] Heb *the pit* [c] Gk Syr Compare Tg: Heb *their inward (thought)* [d] Tg: Heb *after them* [e] Cn: Heb *the upright shall have dominion over them in the morning* [f] Meaning of Heb uncertain

Do you find it comforting or threatening to hear that God's word makes all human beings equal?

49:5-11 Why should I fear in times of trouble: God's people should not fear when others prosper or succeed, because their success is brief. Instead God's people should trust in the one, eternal God.

49:7-8, 15 ransom: To ransom means to rescue someone from a debt by paying a price (Exod 34:20; Num 18:17). No amount of earthly wealth will release a person from the debt owed to death. Only God can "ransom" a human life "from the power of Sheol" (see note on 6:5). In Mark 10:45, Jesus says that he came "to give his life a ransom for many."

49:12, 20 Mortals cannot abide in their pomp: This psalm refrain emphasizes that all human life and accomplishments come to an end, reinforcing the central message of the psalm—not to fear when the wicked prosper, but to trust in the eternal God.

49:13-19 Death shall be their shepherd: Death will rule over those who foolishly place their trust in earthly things (on the image of the shepherd, see Ps 23).

18 Though in their lifetime they count themselves happy
—for you are praised when you do well for yourself—
19 they[a] will go to the company of their ancestors,
who will never again see the light.
20 Mortals cannot abide in their pomp;
they are like the animals that perish.

Psalm 50: A liturgy and festival psalm (see Types of Psalms, pp. 849-850), probably composed for use during one of Israel's three annual festivals (see Exod 23:14-19).

50:1-3 The mighty one, God the Lord, speaks: The worship service celebrates God's arrival in power to speak to the earth. God encounters us and speaks to us in worship through God's Word. The references to God shining forth and a devouring fire and mighty tempest poetically describe the fact that God's arrival upsets the normal rhythms of life on earth.

50:4-6 who made a covenant with me by sacrifice!…God himself is judge: See note on covenant at 25:14 and the note on God as judge at 7:6-11. God confronts the people for failing to live up to their obligations under the covenant.

50:7-23 Hear, O my people: God challenges and admonishes the people—probably through a priest or the king—because they have not lived up to their side of the relationship.

50:8-15 Offer to God a sacrifice of thanksgiving: Animal sacrifice played a major part in the annual festivals celebrated by Israel, but sacrifice does nothing for God, since all creation belongs to God (24:1). Rather, God wants the people to offer songs of thanksgiving and prayers for help.

PSALM 50
The Acceptable Sacrifice

A Psalm of Asaph.

1 The mighty one, God the LORD,
speaks and summons the earth
from the rising of the sun to its setting.
2 Out of Zion, the perfection of beauty,
God shines forth.

3 Our God comes and does not keep silence,
before him is a devouring fire,
and a mighty tempest all around him.
4 He calls to the heavens above
and to the earth, that he may judge his people:
5 "Gather to me my faithful ones,
who made a covenant with me by sacrifice!"
6 The heavens declare his righteousness,
for God himself is judge. *Selah*

7 "Hear, O my people, and I will speak,
O Israel, I will testify against you.
I am God, your God.
8 Not for your sacrifices do I rebuke you;
your burnt offerings are continually before me.
9 I will not accept a bull from your house,
or goats from your folds.
10 For every wild animal of the forest is mine,
the cattle on a thousand hills.
11 I know all the birds of the air,[b]
and all that moves in the field is mine.

12 "If I were hungry, I would not tell you,
for the world and all that is in it is mine.
13 Do I eat the flesh of bulls,
or drink the blood of goats?
14 Offer to God a sacrifice of thanksgiving,[c]

---

[a] Cn: Heb *you* [b] Gk Syr Tg: Heb *mountains* [c] Or *make thanksgiving your sacrifice to God*

and pay your vows to the Most High.
15 Call on me in the day of trouble;
I will deliver you, and you shall glorify me."

16 But to the wicked God says:
"What right have you to recite my statutes,
or take my covenant on your lips?
17 For you hate discipline,
and you cast my words behind you.
18 You make friends with a thief when you see one,
and you keep company with adulterers.

19 "You give your mouth free rein for evil,
and your tongue frames deceit.
20 You sit and speak against your kin;
you slander your own mother's child.
21 These things you have done and I have been silent;
you thought that I was one just like yourself.
But now I rebuke you, and lay the charge before you.

22 "Mark this, then, you who forget God,
or I will tear you apart, and there will be no one to deliver.
23 Those who bring thanksgiving as their sacrifice honor me;
to those who go the right way[a]
I will show the salvation of God."

50:18-20 You make friends with a thief...you keep company with adulterers...you sit and speak against your kin: This refers to the commandments against stealing, adultery, and bearing false witness against the neighbor (see Exod 20:14-16). Instead of sacrifice, God wants us to love our neighbors by keeping God's law.

PSALM 51

Prayer for Cleansing and Pardon

To the leader. A Psalm of David, when the prophet Nathan came to him, after he had gone in to Bathsheba.

1 Have mercy on me, O God,
according to your steadfast love;
according to your abundant mercy
blot out my transgressions.
2 Wash me thoroughly from my iniquity,
and cleanse me from my sin.

3 For I know my transgressions,
and my sin is ever before me.
4 Against you, you alone, have I sinned,
and done what is evil in your sight,
so that you are justified in your sentence
and blameless when you pass judgment.

Psalm 51: A prayer for help and a penitential psalm (see Types of Psalms, pp. 849-850). The title that relates the psalm to an event in David's life (see 2 Sam 12:1-15) is not an original part of the psalm, but indicates the type of situation in which this prayer might be used.

51:1-2 my transgressions...my iniquity...my sin: The psalmist or writer uses three different words for the same thing, emphasizing the magnitude of personal sin. The request for forgiveness is based solely on God's mercy and character, not on anything the psalmist can do.

51:4 Against you, you alone, have I sinned: Sin often harms other humans (see 2 Sam 11), but this emphasizes that *God* is deeply affected when humans harm one another.

[a] Heb *who set a way*

51:5 I was born guilty, a sinner when my mother conceived me: This does not mean that sin is passed on to people through their mothers, but that all humans enter into a fallen world and share in the fallen condition.

51:7-9 Purge me with hyssop: This may be a reference to a cleansing ceremony (see Lev 14:2-9). The sinner cannot cleanse him or herself; only God can do that.

51:10-12 Create in me a clean heart: The psalmist asks for forgiveness, using the image of being re-created with a new heart and a new spirit. Being forgiven is like being created afresh by the Creator (see 2 Cor 5:17). It is a joyful experience.

When has forgiving or being forgiven brought you joy?

51:15 O Lord, open my lips, and my mouth will declare your praise: The image of being re-created continues, as the sinner promises to praise God if God will grant forgiveness.

51:16-17 The sacrifice acceptable to God is... a broken and contrite heart: Repentance, prayers for help, praise, justice, and loving the neighbor (see 50:8-15; Mic 6:6-8)—not sacrifice—are essential parts of our relationship with God.

51:18-19 you will delight in right sacrifices: Right sacrifices are those that God accepts and desires. These verses were probably added to the psalm later, to emphasize that offerings and sacrifices were still part of the life of faith.

Psalm 52: A trust psalm (see Types of Psalms, pp. 849-850), written during or after a personal crisis.

52:1-5 he will uproot you from the land of the living: The psalmist addresses someone who has plotted evil against others in spite of God's faithfulness. (The end of 52:1 could be translated "The steadfast love of God endures all day!") This person may have falsely accused or threatened the psalmist.

5 Indeed, I was born guilty,
a sinner when my mother conceived me.

6 You desire truth in the inward being;[a]
therefore teach me wisdom in my secret heart.
7 Purge me with hyssop, and I shall be clean;
wash me, and I shall be whiter than snow.
8 Let me hear joy and gladness;
let the bones that you have crushed rejoice.
9 Hide your face from my sins,
and blot out all my iniquities.

10 Create in me a clean heart, O God,
and put a new and right[b] spirit within me.
11 Do not cast me away from your presence,
and do not take your holy spirit from me.
12 Restore to me the joy of your salvation,
and sustain in me a willing[c] spirit.

13 Then I will teach transgressors your ways,
and sinners will return to you.
14 Deliver me from bloodshed, O God,
O God of my salvation,
and my tongue will sing aloud of your deliverance.

15 O Lord, open my lips,
and my mouth will declare your praise.
16 For you have no delight in sacrifice;
if I were to give a burnt offering, you would not be pleased.
17 The sacrifice acceptable to God[d] is a broken spirit;
a broken and contrite heart, O God, you will not despise.

18 Do good to Zion in your good pleasure;
rebuild the walls of Jerusalem,
19 then you will delight in right sacrifices,
in burnt offerings and whole burnt offerings;
then bulls will be offered on your altar.

PSALM 52
Judgment on the Deceitful

To the leader. A Maskil of David, when Doeg the Edomite came to Saul and said to him, "David has come to the house of Ahimelech."

1 Why do you boast, O mighty one,

---

[a] Meaning of Heb uncertain [b] Or *steadfast* [c] Or *generous* [d] Or *My sacrifice, O God,*

of mischief done against the godly?[a]
All day long [2]you are plotting destruction.
Your tongue is like a sharp razor,
you worker of treachery.
3 You love evil more than good,
and lying more than speaking the truth. *Selah*
4 You love all words that devour,
O deceitful tongue.

5 But God will break you down forever;
he will snatch and tear you from your tent;
he will uproot you from the land of the living. *Selah*
6 The righteous will see, and fear,
and will laugh at the evildoer,[b] saying,
7 "See the one who would not take
refuge in God,
but trusted in abundant riches,
and sought refuge in wealth!"[c]

8 But I am like a green olive tree
in the house of God.
I trust in the steadfast love of God
forever and ever.
9 I will thank you forever,
because of what you have done.
In the presence of the faithful
I will proclaim[d] your name, for it is good.

52:6-7 The righteous will see, and fear: The psalmist expresses trust that the community will see the psalmist's rescue and join in praising God (see 40:3).

52:8-9 I trust in the steadfast love of God: The wicked trust in earthly wealth, but the psalmist trusts in eternal God. To proclaim God's good name means to trust that God keeps promises (see note on 20:7).

PSALM 53

Denunciation of Godlessness

To the leader: according to Mahalath. A Maskil of David.

1 Fools say in their hearts, "There is no God."
They are corrupt, they commit abominable acts;
there is no one who does good.

2 God looks down from heaven on humankind
to see if there are any who are wise,
who seek after God.

3 They have all fallen away, they are all alike perverse;
there is no one who does good,
no, not one.

Psalm 53: See notes on Psalm 14, which is identical to Psalm 53, except for minor differences.

[a] Cn Compare Syr: Heb *the kindness of God* [b] Heb *him* [c] Syr Tg: Heb *in his destruction* [d] Cn: Heb *wait for*

4 Have they no knowledge, those evildoers,
who eat up my people as they eat bread,
and do not call upon God?

5 There they shall be in great terror,
in terror such as has not been.
For God will scatter the bones of the ungodly;[a]
they will be put to shame,[b] for God has rejected them.

6 O that deliverance for Israel would come from Zion!
When God restores the fortunes of his people,
Jacob will rejoice; Israel will be glad.

Psalm 54: A prayer for help (see Types of Psalms, pp. 849-850) from a person in a dire crisis.

54:1-3 Save me…vindicate me… Hear my prayer…give ear: These four pleas indicate the urgency of the sufferer's cry for help. The ruthless are violent and disregard God's presence and law.

54:4-7 But surely, God is my helper: Unlike the ruthless, the psalmist trusts that God will provide rescue. See note on God's name at 20:7.

PSALM 54

Prayer for Vindication

To the leader: with stringed instruments. A Maskil of David, when the Ziphites went and told Saul, "David is in hiding among us."

1 Save me, O God, by your name,
and vindicate me by your might.
2 Hear my prayer, O God;
give ear to the words of my mouth.

3 For the insolent have risen against me,
the ruthless seek my life;
they do not set God before them. *Selah*

4 But surely, God is my helper;
the Lord is the upholder of[c] my life.
5 He will repay my enemies for their evil.
In your faithfulness, put an end to them.

6 With a freewill offering I will sacrifice to you;
I will give thanks to your name, O LORD, for it is good.
7 For he has delivered me from every trouble,
and my eye has looked in triumph on my enemies.

Psalm 55: A prayer for help (see Types of Psalms, pp. 849-850) from a person who has been betrayed by a friend.

55:1-3 Give ear to my prayer: The psalmist turns to God because of a violent threat from those who intend evil.

PSALM 55

Complaint about a Friend's Treachery

To the leader: with stringed instruments. A Maskil of David.

1 Give ear to my prayer, O God;
do not hide yourself from my supplication.

---

[a] Cn Compare Gk Syr: Heb *him who encamps against you* [b] Gk: Heb *you have put (them) to shame*
[c] Gk Syr Jerome: Heb *is of those who uphold* or *is with those who uphold*

2 Attend to me, and answer me;
I am troubled in my complaint.
I am distraught 3 by the noise of the enemy,
because of the clamor of the wicked.
For they bring[a] trouble upon me,
and in anger they cherish enmity against me.

4 My heart is in anguish within me,
the terrors of death have fallen upon me.
5 Fear and trembling come upon me,
and horror overwhelms me.
6 And I say, "O that I had wings like a dove!
I would fly away and be at rest;
7 truly, I would flee far away;
I would lodge in the wilderness; *Selah*
8 I would hurry to find a shelter for myself
from the raging wind and tempest."

9 Confuse, O Lord, confound their speech;
for I see violence and strife in the city.
10 Day and night they go around it
on its walls,
and iniquity and trouble are within it;
11 ruin is in its midst;
oppression and fraud
do not depart from its marketplace.

12 It is not enemies who taunt me—
I could bear that;
it is not adversaries who deal insolently with me—
I could hide from them.
13 But it is you, my equal,
my companion, my familiar friend,
14 with whom I kept pleasant company;
we walked in the house of God with the throng.
15 Let death come upon them;
let them go down alive to Sheol;
for evil is in their homes and in their hearts.

16 But I call upon God,
and the LORD will save me.
17 Evening and morning and at noon
I utter my complaint and moan,

55:4-8 O that I had wings like a dove!: The psalmist is terrified, like a dove seeking shelter amid a raging storm.

55:9-11 violence and strife in the city…oppression and fraud: The psalmist sees the enemies as violence and strife stalking the city day and night like soldiers, iniquity and trouble living in the city like citizens, and oppression and fraud doing business in the city.

55:12-14 it is you, my equal, my companion, my familiar friend: The psalmist describes the deep pain of being betrayed by a friend—even worse, by a fellow worshiper of God. The psalmist and the betrayer may have been fellow priests in the temple.

55:17 Evening and morning and at noon I utter my complaint: These times of day may give poetic balance to the description of "violence and strife" stalking the city "day and night" (55:9-10), but they may also refer to times when priests made ritual offerings to God in the temple.

[a] Cn Compare Gk: Heb *they cause to totter*

and he will hear my voice.
18 He will redeem me unharmed
from the battle that I wage,
for many are arrayed against me.
19 God, who is enthroned from of old, *Selah*
will hear, and will humble them—
because they do not change,
and do not fear God.

55:20-21 My companion...violated a covenant with me: The psalmist again describes the pain of a friend's betrayal. A covenant is a mutual sharing of obligations, such as between spouses, friends, nations, and so on (see note on 25:14).

20 My companion laid hands on a friend
and violated a covenant with me[a]
21 with speech smoother than butter,
but with a heart set on war;
with words that were softer than oil,
but in fact were drawn swords.

55:22-23 Cast your burden on the LORD: The psalmist declares that those who turn to God in prayer can trust in the LORD's faithfulness.

22 Cast your burden[b] on the LORD,
and he will sustain you;
he will never permit
the righteous to be moved.

23 But you, O God, will cast them down
into the lowest pit;
the bloodthirsty and treacherous
shall not live out half their days.
But I will trust in you.

Psalm 56: A prayer for help (see Types of Psalms, pp. 849-850) that also expresses trust in God. A refrain occurs in verses 4 and 10-11.

PSALM 56

Trust in God under Persecution

To the leader: according to The Dove on Far-off Terebinths. Of David. A Miktam, when the Philistines seized him in Gath.

56:3 when I am afraid, I put my trust in you: Because there are real reasons to fear, the psalmist's trust in God offers real hope and comfort.

56:4, 10-11 In God, whose word I praise, in God I trust: This refrain identifies the main reason for trusting God—God's word. This is often translated in the Psalms as "God's promise." The psalmist can trust because God has promised to remain faithful.

1 Be gracious to me, O God, for people trample on me;
all day long foes oppress me;
2 my enemies trample on me all day long,
for many fight against me.
O Most High, 3 when I am afraid,
I put my trust in you.
4 In God, whose word I praise,
in God I trust; I am not afraid;
what can flesh do to me?

5 All day long they seek to injure my cause;
all their thoughts are against me for evil.

---

[a] Heb lacks *with me* [b] Or *Cast what he has given you*

6 They stir up strife, they lurk,
they watch my steps.
As they hoped to have my life,
7 so repay[a] them for their crime;
in wrath cast down the peoples, O God!

8 You have kept count of my tossings;
put my tears in your bottle.
Are they not in your record?
9 Then my enemies will retreat
in the day when I call.
This I know, that[b] God is for me.
10 In God, whose word I praise,
in the LORD, whose word I praise,
11 in God I trust; I am not afraid.
What can a mere mortal do to me?

12 My vows to you I must perform, O God;
I will render thank offerings to you.
13 For you have delivered my soul from death,
and my feet from falling,
so that I may walk before God
in the light of life.

PSALM 57

Praise and Assurance under Persecution

To the leader: Do Not Destroy. Of David. A Miktam, when he fled from Saul, in the cave.

1 Be merciful to me, O God, be merciful to me,
for in you my soul takes refuge;
in the shadow of your wings I will take refuge,
until the destroying storms pass by.
2 I cry to God Most High,
to God who fulfills his purpose for me.
3 He will send from heaven and save me,
he will put to shame those who trample on me. *Selah*
God will send forth his steadfast love and his faithfulness.

4 I lie down among lions
that greedily devour[c] human prey;
their teeth are spears and arrows,
their tongues sharp swords.

[a] Cn: Heb *rescue* [b] Or *because* [c] Cn: Heb *are aflame for*

56:8 You have kept count of my tossings; put my tears in your bottle: The image of God keeping a record of how many times a person tosses and turns at night, saving each tear in a bottle, shows the permanence of the relationship and the importance God places on each individual.

56:13 you have delivered…my feet from falling, so that I may walk before God: The image of feet not stumbling but walking before God shows that our love for God is a response to what God has done for us. Because God has freely called and forgiven us, we love God and walk in God's light.

Psalm 57: A prayer for help that becomes a song of thanksgiving (see Types of Psalms, pp. 849-850). The psalm has two stanzas (57:1-4; 6-10), with a refrain occurring after each (57:5, 11).

57:1 Be merciful to me, O God: The psalmist turns to God as refuge (see note on 2:11). "In the shadow of your wings" refers to the inner sanctuary of the temple, where the wings of two carved cherubim spread out in an image of protection (see 1 Kgs 6:23-28). People could seek protection in the temple from persecutors (see also 91:1).

57:2-3 his purpose for me: *Purpose* here does not mean that God has planned out each moment of our lives, but that God will be the ultimate author of the purpose and end of our lives—the enemy will not. The psalmist portrays God's steadfast love and faithfulness as physical beings sent out by God to rescue the lowly.

57:4-6 I lie down among lions: The enemies are described as predators, emphasizing the psalmist's lowliness.

57:5 Be exalted, O God, above the heavens: The psalm's refrain calls on God to be exalted, which expresses the writer's confidence that God is faithful and will provide rescue. God is described as high above the heavens, an intentional contrast with the writer's lowly condition.

57:6 my soul was bowed down: See note on soul at 42:5. Because God is exalted on high (57:5), the psalmist was rescued from the lowly crisis.

57:7-11 Awake, O harp and lyre! I will awake the dawn: Often in prayers for help, the psalmist calls on God to awake (see 44:23). The morning is a metaphor for God's help arriving (see 5:3; 30:5). Because God's help has come, the psalmist calls on those with musical gifts and promises to awaken the dawn with song. The poetic theme of high and low continues with a description of God's steadfast love and in the closing refrain (57:10-11).

Psalm 58: A prayer for help that asks God to destroy evildoers (see Types of Psalms, pp. 849-850).

58:1-2 Do you indeed decree what is right, you gods?: This can also be translated "Do you truly speak what is right, O mighty ones?" (see NRSV footnote *a*). If this is the case, the psalm begins by addressing corrupt judges. If not, the psalm begins by addressing the false gods of Israel's neighbors.

58:6-11 The righteous will rejoice when they see vengeance done: See notes on the righteous and the wicked at 1:1 and 1:5. The psalmist prays for deliverance from evil, believing that can only happen if God will defeat the wicked. This prayer's passion for the enemy's defeat reflects the real situation of an ancient community that was suffering at the hands of others. The psalmist asks God to set things right (see Rom 12:19).

5 Be exalted, O God, above the heavens.
Let your glory be over all the earth.

6 They set a net for my steps;
my soul was bowed down.
They dug a pit in my path,
but they have fallen into it themselves. *Selah*
7 My heart is steadfast, O God,
my heart is steadfast.
I will sing and make melody.
8 Awake, my soul!
Awake, O harp and lyre!
I will awake the dawn.
9 I will give thanks to you, O Lord, among the peoples;
I will sing praises to you among the nations.
10 For your steadfast love is as high as the heavens;
your faithfulness extends to the clouds.

11 Be exalted, O God, above the heavens.
Let your glory be over all the earth.

PSALM 58
Prayer for Vengeance

To the leader: Do Not Destroy. Of David. A Miktam.

1 Do you indeed decree what is right, you gods?[a]
Do you judge people fairly?
2 No, in your hearts you devise wrongs;
your hands deal out violence on earth.

3 The wicked go astray from the womb;
they err from their birth, speaking lies.
4 They have venom like the venom of a serpent,
like the deaf adder that stops its ear,
5 so that it does not hear the voice of charmers
or of the cunning enchanter.

6 O God, break the teeth in their mouths;
tear out the fangs of the young lions, O LORD!
7 Let them vanish like water that runs away;
like grass let them be trodden down[b] and wither.
8 Let them be like the snail that dissolves into slime;
like the untimely birth that never sees the sun.
9 Sooner than your pots can feel the heat of thorns,
whether green or ablaze, may he sweep them away!

[a] Or *mighty lords* [b] Cn: Meaning of Heb uncertain

10 The righteous will rejoice when they see vengeance done;
they will bathe their feet in the blood of the wicked.
11 People will say, "Surely there is a reward for the righteous;
surely there is a God who judges on earth."

PSALM 59

Prayer for Deliverance from Enemies

To the leader: Do Not Destroy. Of David. A Miktam, when Saul ordered his house to be watched in order to kill him.

1 Deliver me from my enemies, O my God;
protect me from those who rise up against me.
2 Deliver me from those who work evil;
from the bloodthirsty save me.

3 Even now they lie in wait for my life;
the mighty stir up strife against me.
For no transgression or sin of mine, O LORD,
4 for no fault of mine, they run and make ready.

Rouse yourself, come to my help and see!
5 You, LORD God of hosts, are God of Israel.
Awake to punish all the nations;
spare none of those who treacherously plot evil. *Selah*

6 Each evening they come back,
howling like dogs
and prowling about the city.
7 There they are, bellowing with their mouths,
with sharp words[a] on their lips—
for "Who," they think,[b] "will hear us?"

8 But you laugh at them, O LORD;
you hold all the nations in derision.
9 O my strength, I will watch for you;
for you, O God, are my fortress.
10 My God in his steadfast love will meet me;
my God will let me look in triumph on my enemies.

11 Do not kill them, or my people may forget;
make them totter by your power, and bring them down,
O Lord, our shield.
12 For the sin of their mouths, the words of their lips,
let them be trapped in their pride.

---

[a] Heb *with swords* [b] Heb lacks *they think*

Psalm 59: A prayer for help (see Types of Psalms, pp. 849-850) in three stanzas (59:1-5, 7-13, 15-17), with a refrain between the stanzas (59:6, 14). The speaker of the psalm may be the king or another leader, praying on behalf of the people.

59:1-5 Deliver me from my enemies: The speaker has done nothing to cause or invite persecution and begs for rescue.

59:6, 14 Each evening they come back, howling like dogs: The psalm's refrain portrays the enemies as a pack of vicious dogs. The howling of these "dogs" indicates that they act violently because they do not believe God can or will hold them accountable (59:7). The dogs may symbolize nations that attacked Israel.

59:10 My God in his steadfast love will meet me: God is faithful and will not abandon those who suffer at the hands of evildoers.

59:11-13 Then it will be known to the ends of the earth that God rules over Jacob: This expresses the desire for people inside and outside of Israel to know God.

For the cursing and lies that they utter,
13 consume them in wrath;
consume them until they are no more.
Then it will be known to the ends of the earth
that God rules over Jacob. *Selah*

14 Each evening they come back,
howling like dogs
and prowling about the city.
15 They roam about for food,
and growl if they do not get their fill.

16 But I will sing of your might;
I will sing aloud of your steadfast love in the morning.
For you have been a fortress for me
and a refuge in the day of my distress.
17 O my strength, I will sing praises to you,
for you, O God, are my fortress,
the God who shows me steadfast love.

59:16-17 I will sing aloud of your steadfast love in the morning: The evildoers howl each evening, but the psalmist sings of God's faithfulness in the morning. The psalmist promises to remain in relationship with God and trusts that God's faithfulness will prevail.

PSALM 60

Prayer for National Victory after Defeat

To the leader: according to the Lily of the Covenant. A Miktam of David; for instruction; when he struggled with Aram-naharaim and with Aram-zobah, and when Joab on his return killed twelve thousand Edomites in the Valley of Salt.

1 O God, you have rejected us, broken our defenses;
you have been angry; now restore us!
2 You have caused the land to quake; you have torn it open;
repair the cracks in it, for it is tottering.
3 You have made your people suffer hard things;
you have given us wine to drink that made us reel.

4 You have set up a banner for those who fear you,
to rally to it out of bowshot.[a] *Selah*
5 Give victory with your right hand, and answer us,[b]
so that those whom you love may be rescued.

6 God has promised in his sanctuary:[c]
"With exultation I will divide up Shechem,
and portion out the Vale of Succoth.
7 Gilead is mine, and Manasseh is mine;
Ephraim is my helmet;
Judah is my scepter.

Psalm 60: A prayer for help from a community (see Types of Psalms, pp. 849-850).

60:1-5 O God, you have rejected us: The community complains that God has abandoned them and asks for rescue. This prayer may have been prayed after a particular military crisis, or perhaps was used annually as a liturgy that described the people's ongoing need for God's help.

60:6 God has promised in his sanctuary: The basis of the prayer is God's promise (see note on 12:6). The people base their hope on God's character as one who keeps promises, rather than on their own character or deeds.

60:6-8 Shechem...Gilead...Manasseh...Ephraim...Judah: The promise of God includes places inside the promised land (Shechem, Manasseh, Ephraim, Judah) and outside it (Moab, Edom, Philistia). God's promise of the land was one of the foundational promises to the people (see Gen 12:1-3). Through the land the people received identity as Israelites, nourishment, protection, and relationship with God. If the people lost the land, they were in danger of losing their identity and their relationship with God.

[a] Gk Syr Jerome: Heb *because of the truth* [b] Another reading is *me* [c] Or *by his holiness*

8 Moab is my washbasin;
on Edom I hurl my shoe;
over Philistia I shout in triumph."

9 Who will bring me to the fortified city?
Who will lead me to Edom?
10 Have you not rejected us, O God?
You do not go out, O God, with our armies.
11 O grant us help against the foe,
for human help is worthless.
12 With God we shall do valiantly;
it is he who will tread down our foes.

PSALM 61

Assurance of God's Protection

To the leader: with stringed instruments. Of David.

1 Hear my cry, O God;
listen to my prayer.
2 From the end of the earth I call to you,
when my heart is faint.

Lead me to the rock
that is higher than I;
3 for you are my refuge,
a strong tower against the enemy.

4 Let me abide in your tent forever,
find refuge under the shelter of your wings. *Selah*
5 For you, O God, have heard my vows;
you have given me the heritage of those who fear your name.

6 Prolong the life of the king;
may his years endure to all generations!
7 May he be enthroned forever before God;
appoint steadfast love and faithfulness to watch over him!

8 So I will always sing praises to your name,
as I pay my vows day after day.

PSALM 62

Song of Trust in God Alone

To the leader: according to Jeduthun. A Psalm of David.

1 For God alone my soul waits in silence;
from him comes my salvation.

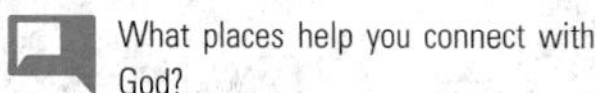
What places help you connect with God?

60:12 With God we shall do valiantly: The prayer ends with a statement of the people's faith in God's continued love and guidance.

Psalm 61: A prayer for help from an individual (see Types of Psalms, pp. 849-850).

61:2 From the end of the earth I call to you: The psalmist may have been stranded far from the temple, but most likely this is a metaphor for feeling distant from God. Because God's help has not arrived yet, the psalmist poetically describes the situation as being at the end of the earth.

61:2b-5: the rock... your tent... under the shelter of your wings... the heritage: The psalmist asks for guidance back to God's presence in the temple, here described as a rock or refuge (see note on 2:11), tent, and heritage (a term for the land as a whole). The temple symbolizes the active presence of God that the psalmist desires.

61:6-7 Prolong the life of the king: The prayer for the king reflects the reality that the health of a people's government directly affects the people. God's steadfast love and faithfulness watch over the king. This emphasizes that God's character and actions are inseparable.

Psalm 62: An instructional psalm (see Types of Psalms, pp. 849-850) about trust in the face of threats. The psalm has two sections (62:1-4, 5-12), each beginning with a refrain (62:1-2, 5-6).

62:1-2, 5-6 For God alone my soul waits in silence: This refrain emphasizes trust in God. Because God is the only one able to deliver, the psalmist hopes and trusts only in God and is confident of God's protection.

2 He alone is my rock and my salvation,
my fortress; I shall never be shaken.

62:3 you batter your victim: The wicked and others of weak character prey on the weak (a leaning wall, a tottering fence) at the same time as they dream of bringing down the strong.

3 How long will you assail a person,
will you batter your victim, all of you,
as you would a leaning wall, a tottering fence?
4 Their only plan is to bring down a person of prominence.
They take pleasure in falsehood;
they bless with their mouths,
but inwardly they curse. *Selah*

5 For God alone my soul waits in silence,
for my hope is from him.
6 He alone is my rock and my salvation,
my fortress; I shall not be shaken.
7 On God rests my deliverance and my honor;
my mighty rock, my refuge is in God.

62:8-9 Trust in him at all times, O people: The psalmist pauses in the midst of a deep crisis to instruct others to trust in God. Those who experience crisis often gain fresh insights into God's ways—insights that can be shared with others. Those who are successful and unsuccessful, according to earthly measures, are all equal in the sight of God.

8 Trust in him at all times, O people;
pour out your heart before him;
God is a refuge for us. *Selah*

9 Those of low estate are but a breath,
those of high estate are a delusion;
in the balances they go up;
they are together lighter than a breath.
10 Put no confidence in extortion,
and set no vain hopes on robbery;
if riches increase, do not set your heart on them.

62:10 if riches increase, do not set your heart on them: To trust in God alone (62:1) means to refuse to trust in other things, such as wealth.

Who or what do you trust?

11 Once God has spoken;
twice have I heard this:
that power belongs to God,
12 and steadfast love belongs to you, O Lord.
For you repay to all
according to their work.

Psalm 63: A trust psalm (see Types of Psalms, pp. 849-850) that includes longing for God's presence.

63:1-2 I seek you, my soul thirsts for you: To "seek" implies a search for something that has been lost. In this case, the psalmist recalls being close to God in the temple and wants to return to that feeling of closeness. The common human experience of thirst gives an image of this longing for God.

PSALM 63

Comfort and Assurance in God's Presence

A Psalm of David, when he was in the Wilderness of Judah.

1 O God, you are my God, I seek you,
my soul thirsts for you;
my flesh faints for you,
as in a dry and weary land where there is no water.
2 So I have looked upon you in the sanctuary,

beholding your power and glory.
3 Because your steadfast love is better than life,
my lips will praise you.
4 So I will bless you as long as I live;
I will lift up my hands and call on your name.

5 My soul is satisfied as with a rich feast,[a]
and my mouth praises you with joyful lips
6 when I think of you on my bed,
and meditate on you in the watches of the night;
7 for you have been my help,
and in the shadow of your wings I sing for joy.
8 My soul clings to you;
your right hand upholds me.

9 But those who seek to destroy my life
shall go down into the depths of the earth;
10 they shall be given over to the power of the sword,
they shall be prey for jackals.
11 But the king shall rejoice in God;
all who swear by him shall exult,
for the mouths of liars will be stopped.

PSALM 64

Prayer for Protection from Enemies

To the leader. A Psalm of David.

1 Hear my voice, O God, in my complaint;
preserve my life from the dread enemy.
2 Hide me from the secret plots of the wicked,
from the scheming of evildoers,
3 who whet their tongues like swords,
who aim bitter words like arrows,
4 shooting from ambush at the blameless;
they shoot suddenly and without fear.
5 They hold fast to their evil purpose;
they talk of laying snares secretly,
thinking, "Who can see us?[b]
6 Who can search out our crimes?[c]
We have thought out a cunningly conceived plot."
For the human heart and mind are deep.

7 But God will shoot his arrow at them;
they will be wounded suddenly.

[a] Heb *with fat and fatness* [b] Syr: Heb *them* [c] Cn: Heb *They search out crimes*

63:3 your steadfast love is better than life: After experiencing God's love, the psalmist cannot imagine life without it.

63:5 My soul is satisfied as with a rich feast: The common human experience of having hunger satisfied describes the joy of God's presence. The same mouth satisfied by food now sings for joy about God's love. "My soul" means "my inmost self" (see note on 42:5).

When you are extremely hungry or thirsty, all you can think about is food and drink. When have you been hungry or thirsty for God?

63:11 the king shall rejoice: See note on 61:6-7.

Psalm 64: A prayer for help (see Types of Psalms, pp. 849-850) from a person overwhelmed by threats.

64:2-4 Hide me from the secret plots of the wicked: The psalmist wants protection from those who wait to ambush innocent travelers. "Bitter words" refer to the plots and beliefs of the enemies, quoted in verses 5-6.

64:5-6 Who can see us?: The enemies' words are typical (see Bible Concepts note on 3:2) and show unity of thought and action. Because they think they will not be seen or caught, they feel free to make harmful plots.

64:7-8 But God will shoot his arrow at them: The wicked shoot arrows at the innocent during an ambush (64:4), but God's arrows will find the wicked. They say that God does not see their evil deeds, but God hears their evil words and will stop their plots.

64:9 everyone will fear; they will tell what God has brought about: See note on fearing God, at 34:9-11. The enemies say God will not see, but God hears their words, and in the end all will see and tell about God's deeds.

What signs of God's love and faithfulness have you seen in your life?

Psalm 65: A hymn of praise (see Types of Psalms, pp. 849-850) celebrating the sustaining power of God, especially through the fruits of creation.

65:1-2 Praise is due you: The psalmist gives praise for God's gracious acts of answering prayer and granting forgiveness. We do not praise God for God's benefit, but for our own. Praise is a form of teaching and witness—it lets others know about the joy of living in relationship with God.

65:6-8 you established the mountains: God's act of creation is praised. God creates order and also defeats the powers of chaos, to create a hospitable space for life.

65:9-10 you visit the earth and water it: God is not a distant, far-off God, but visits the earth and continues creating and providing for life into the present.

8 Because of their tongue he will bring them to ruin;[a]
all who see them will shake with horror.
9 Then everyone will fear;
they will tell what God has brought about,
and ponder what he has done.

10 Let the righteous rejoice in the LORD
and take refuge in him.
Let all the upright in heart glory.

PSALM 65

Thanksgiving for Earth's Bounty

To the leader. A Psalm of David. A Song.

1 Praise is due to you,
O God, in Zion;
and to you shall vows be performed,
2 O you who answer prayer!
To you all flesh shall come.
3 When deeds of iniquity overwhelm us,
you forgive our transgressions.
4 Happy are those whom you choose and bring near
to live in your courts.
We shall be satisfied with the goodness of your house,
your holy temple.

5 By awesome deeds you answer us with deliverance,
O God of our salvation;
you are the hope of all the ends of the earth
and of the farthest seas.
6 By your[b] strength you established the mountains;
you are girded with might.
7 You silence the roaring of the seas,
the roaring of their waves,
the tumult of the peoples.
8 Those who live at earth's farthest bounds are awed by your signs;
you make the gateways of the morning and the evening shout for joy.

9 You visit the earth and water it,
you greatly enrich it;
the river of God is full of water;
you provide the people with grain,

---

[a] Cn: Heb *They will bring him to ruin, their tongue being against them* [b] Gk Jerome: Heb *his*

for so you have prepared it.
10 You water its furrows abundantly,
settling its ridges,
softening it with showers,
and blessing its growth.
11 You crown the year with your bounty;
your wagon tracks overflow with richness.
12 The pastures of the wilderness overflow,
the hills gird themselves with joy,
13 the meadows clothe themselves with flocks,
the valleys deck themselves with grain,
they shout and sing together for joy.

PSALM 66

Praise for God's Goodness to Israel

To the leader. A Song. A Psalm.

1 Make a joyful noise to God, all the earth;
2 sing the glory of his name;
give to him glorious praise.
3 Say to God, "How awesome are your deeds!
Because of your great power, your enemies cringe before you.
4 All the earth worships you;
they sing praises to you,
sing praises to your name." *Selah*

5 Come and see what God has done:
he is awesome in his deeds among mortals.
6 He turned the sea into dry land;
they passed through the river on foot.
There we rejoiced in him,
7 who rules by his might forever,
whose eyes keep watch on the nations—
let the rebellious not exalt themselves. *Selah*

8 Bless our God, O peoples,
let the sound of his praise be heard,
9 who has kept us among the living,
and has not let our feet slip.
10 For you, O God, have tested us;
you have tried us as silver is tried.
11 You brought us into the net;
you laid burdens on our backs;
12 you let people ride over our heads;

65:11-13 You crown the year with your bounty: God joyfully dresses creation at harvest time with crown, robes, and ornaments—signs that God cares for creation and takes joy in each year.

What is your favorite season? What hints of God's love do you see in nature at this time of year?

Psalm 66: A psalm that includes elements of a hymn of praise (66:1-7), a community's song of thanksgiving (66:8-12), and an individual's song of thanksgiving (66:13-20; see Types of Psalms, pp. 849-850).

66:1-4 Make a joyful noise to God, all the earth: The opening call to praise imagines the entire world joining in praise of Israel's God.

66:5 Come and see what God has done: To come is to enter into a relationship with God. It is to learn to know God, to learn the story of God's loving actions, such as bringing the Israelites out of slavery in Egypt and through the Red Sea (66:6), and to learn to follow God's path.

66:8-12 Bless our God, O peoples...you have tried us as silver is tried: To bless is to praise God. The image of the people being tested like silver comes from the refining process. God has been at work through the people's trials and tribulations, to refine and perfect them. God provided the land ("a spacious place") for the people.

we went through fire and through water;
yet you have brought us out to a spacious place.[a]

66:13-15 I will come into your house: The psalmist comes anew into the relationship with God, sharing a testimony of what God has done and offering gifts as signs of the ongoing relationship with God. Regarding sacrifice, see note on 50:8-15.

13 I will come into your house with burnt offerings;
I will pay you my vows,
14 those that my lips uttered
and my mouth promised when I was in trouble.
15 I will offer to you burnt offerings of fatlings,
with the smoke of the sacrifice of rams;
I will make an offering of bulls and goats. *Selah*

66:16-19 Come and hear, all of you who fear God: The psalmist renews the call for the community to enter into relationship with God. To fear God is to be in proper relationship with the Lord (see note on 34:9-11).

16 Come and hear, all you who fear God,
and I will tell what he has done for me.
17 I cried aloud to him,
and he was extolled with my tongue.
18 If I had cherished iniquity in my heart,
the Lord would not have listened.
19 But truly God has listened;
he has given heed to the words of my prayer.

66:20 Blessed be God: The psalm ends with another call for the people to praise God, this time because of what God has done for the psalmist. To be a part of God's people is to praise and thank God, not just for the goodness we experience personally, but also for what God does for others.

20 Blessed be God,
because he has not rejected my prayer
or removed his steadfast love from me.

Psalm 67: A prayer for help, asking for God's blessing, and a hymn of praise (see Types of Psalms, pp. 849-850).

PSALM 67
The Nations Called to Praise God

To the leader: with stringed instruments. A Psalm. A Song.

67:1-2 May God be gracious to us…that your way may be known upon earth: The psalm opens with a prayer for blessing, similar to the priestly blessing in Numbers 6:24-26 that still is spoken at the end of many Christian worship services. God's blessing is for the purpose of God's mission—so that God's ways may be known throughout the earth.

1 May God be gracious to us and bless us
and make his face to shine upon us, *Selah*
2 that your way may be known upon earth,
your saving power among all nations.
3 Let the peoples praise you, O God;
let all the peoples praise you.

67:3, 5 Let the peoples praise you, O God: This song refrain calls all people to praise the Lord, indicating that God's mission has reached the ends of the earth.

67:4 for you judge the peoples with equity and guide the nations: God's justice and guidance are central aspects of God's mission to the entire earth. Because of these, the earth is to praise God. On God as judge, see note on 7:6-11.

4 Let the nations be glad and sing for joy,
for you judge the peoples with equity
and guide the nations upon earth. *Selah*
5 Let the peoples praise you, O God;
let all the peoples praise you.

67:6-7 May God continue to bless us: God's blessings are not just in the past, they continue in the fruit of creation and ongoing provisions for the people.

6 The earth has yielded its increase;
God, our God, has blessed us.
7 May God continue to bless us;
let all the ends of the earth revere him.

[a] Cn Compare Gk Syr Jerome Tg: Heb *to a saturation*

PSALM 68

Praise and Thanksgiving

To the leader. Of David. A Psalm. A Song.

1 Let God rise up, let his enemies be scattered;
let those who hate him flee before him.
2 As smoke is driven away, so drive them away;
as wax melts before the fire,
let the wicked perish before God.
3 But let the righteous be joyful;
let them exult before God;
let them be jubilant with joy.

4 Sing to God, sing praises to his name;
lift up a song to him who rides upon the clouds[a]—
his name is the LORD—
be exultant before him.

5 Father of orphans and protector of widows
is God in his holy habitation.
6 God gives the desolate a home to live in;
he leads out the prisoners to prosperity,
but the rebellious live in a parched land.

7 O God, when you went out before your people,
when you marched through the wilderness, *Selah*
8 the earth quaked, the heavens poured down rain
at the presence of God, the God of Sinai,
at the presence of God, the God of Israel.
9 Rain in abundance, O God, you showered abroad;
you restored your heritage when it languished;
10 your flock found a dwelling in it;
in your goodness, O God, you provided for the needy.

11 The Lord gives the command;
great is the company of those[b] who bore the tidings:
12 "The kings of the armies, they flee, they flee!"
The women at home divide the spoil,
13 though they stay among the sheepfolds—
the wings of a dove covered with silver,
its pinions with green gold.
14 When the Almighty[c] scattered kings there,
snow fell on Zalmon.

[a] Or *cast up a highway for him who rides through the deserts* [b] Or *company of the women* [c] Traditional rendering of Heb *Shaddai*

Psalm 68: A hymn of praise (see Types of Psalms, pp. 849-850) that is one of the oldest psalms. It celebrates the revealing of God's will and presence to Israel, often combining descriptions of God's actions for Israel with descriptions of God's glory revealed in nature.

68:1-3 Let God rise up, let his enemies be scattered: These words are a prayer for God's guidance. They were spoken when the ark of the covenant was carried in front of the people (Num 10:35). See note on ark at 47:5. God is revealed in God's guidance, which includes acts of victory and rescue.

68:4-6 a song to him who rides upon the clouds: This brief hymn of praise pictures God riding the chariot of a storm to perform acts of mercy for the lowly and rescue for the oppressed.

68:7-10 you went out before your people...Rain in abundance, O God, you showered: God has been revealed in guiding the Israelites through the wilderness, giving the law at Mount Sinai (see Exod 19–20) and providing rain and harvest. On the image of God revealed in a storm, see note on 18:7-19.

68:11-14 The kings of the armies, they flee: God gave the people the land by defeating the kings of Canaan (see Judg 5). God's presence in this victory is paired with God's glory in a snowstorm.

68:15-20 Why do you look with envy, O many-peaked mountain, at the mount that God desired for his abode: God is revealed in his choice of Zion (Jerusalem) as a dwelling place (see note on 48:1). The unknown mountain Bashan is asked why it envies Zion. The meaning of verses 17-18 is uncertain, but they may describe God's arrival at Zion.

68:24-27 Your solemn processions are seen: God has been revealed in the rescue of former captives, who march victoriously into God's presence.

68:28-35 Summon your might, O God: This is a final call for God to provide victory for the people, and for the people to praise God. For rider in the heavens, see note on 68:4-6. The sanctuary in the temple is important throughout the psalm. It is God's heavenly dwelling and the temple, the point of contact between heaven and earth.

15 O mighty mountain, mountain of Bashan;
O many-peaked mountain, mountain of Bashan!
16 Why do you look with envy, O many-peaked mountain,
at the mount that God desired for his abode,
where the LORD will reside forever?

17 With mighty chariotry, twice ten thousand,
thousands upon thousands,
the Lord came from Sinai into the holy place.[a]
18 You ascended the high mount,
leading captives in your train
and receiving gifts from people,
even from those who rebel against the LORD God's abiding there.
19 Blessed be the Lord,
who daily bears us up;
God is our salvation. *Selah*
20 Our God is a God of salvation,
and to GOD, the Lord, belongs escape from death.

21 But God will shatter the heads of his enemies,
the hairy crown of those who walk in their guilty ways.
22 The Lord said,
"I will bring them back from Bashan,
I will bring them back from the depths of the sea,
23 so that you may bathe[b] your feet in blood,
so that the tongues of your dogs may have their share from the foe."

24 Your solemn processions are seen,[c] O God,
the processions of my God, my King, into the sanctuary—
25 the singers in front, the musicians last,
between them girls playing tambourines:
26 "Bless God in the great congregation,
the LORD, O you who are of Israel's fountain!"
27 There is Benjamin, the least of them, in the lead,
the princes of Judah in a body,
the princes of Zebulun, the princes of Naphtali.

28 Summon your might, O God;
show your strength, O God, as you have done for us before.
29 Because of your temple at Jerusalem
kings bear gifts to you.

---

[a] Cn: Heb *The Lord among them Sinai in the holy* (place) [b] Gk Syr Tg: Heb *shatter* [c] Or *have been seen*

30 Rebuke the wild animals that live among the reeds,
the herd of bulls with the calves of the peoples.
Trample[a] under foot those who lust after tribute;
scatter the peoples who delight in war.[b]
31 Let bronze be brought from Egypt;
let Ethiopia[c] hasten to stretch out its hands to God.

32 Sing to God, O kingdoms of the earth;
sing praises to the Lord, *Selah*
33 O rider in the heavens, the ancient heavens;
listen, he sends out his voice, his mighty voice.
34 Ascribe power to God,
whose majesty is over Israel;
and whose power is in the skies.
35 Awesome is God in his[d] sanctuary,
the God of Israel;
he gives power and strength to his people.

Blessed be God!

PSALM 69

Prayer for Deliverance from Persecution

To the leader: according to Lilies. Of David.

1 Save me, O God,
for the waters have come up to my neck.
2 I sink in deep mire,
where there is no foothold;
I have come into deep waters,
and the flood sweeps over me.
3 I am weary with my crying;
my throat is parched.
My eyes grow dim
with waiting for my God.

4 More in number than the hairs of my head
are those who hate me without cause;
many are those who would destroy me,
my enemies who accuse me falsely.
What I did not steal
must I now restore?
5 O God, you know my folly;
the wrongs I have done are not hidden from you.

Psalm 69: A prayer for help (see Types of Psalms, pp. 849-850) from a person overwhelmed by violent enemies.

69:1-4 the waters have come up to my neck…I sink: The terrifying image of drowning depicts the psalmist's crisis (see also 69:15). In the ancient world, this symbolism was especially powerful. Water, sea, and flood symbolized the forces of chaos that opposed the LORD's orderly creation. To be caught in those forces was to be in desperate need. The psalmist's human tormenters are also described, showing a connection between human evil and natural evil.

69:5 the wrongs I have done are not hidden from you: The psalmist admits faults, but also claims not to deserve to suffer.

---

[a] Cn: Heb *Trampling* [b] Meaning of Heb of verse 30 is uncertain [c] Or *Nubia;* Heb *Cush*
[d] Gk: Heb *from your*

69:6-8 Do not let those who hope in you be put to shame: On honor and shame, see note on 6:10. The psalmist is viewed with shame because of loyalty to God, and asks God to provide honor in return. See also 69:19: "my shame and dishonor."

69:10-12 When I humbled my soul with fasting, they insulted me: The life and actions of faith often look silly to the world, as Paul also realizes in 1 Corinthians 1:18-31.

Has anyone ever made fun of you or misunderstood you because of your faith in God? How has this affected you?

69:13-18 At an acceptable time, O God…make haste to answer me: Although the prayer is for speedy and decisive rescue by God, the psalmist also trusts that God's timing will be the right timing.

6 Do not let those who hope in you be put to shame because of me,
O Lord God of hosts;
do not let those who seek you be dishonored because of me,
O God of Israel.
7 It is for your sake that I have borne reproach,
that shame has covered my face.
8 I have become a stranger to my kindred,
an alien to my mother's children.

9 It is zeal for your house that has consumed me;
the insults of those who insult you have fallen on me.
10 When I humbled my soul with fasting,[a]
they insulted me for doing so.
11 When I made sackcloth my clothing,
I became a byword to them.
12 I am the subject of gossip for those who sit in the gate,
and the drunkards make songs about me.

13 But as for me, my prayer is to you, O Lord.
At an acceptable time, O God,
in the abundance of your steadfast love, answer me.
With your faithful help 14 rescue me
from sinking in the mire;
let me be delivered from my enemies
and from the deep waters.
15 Do not let the flood sweep over me,
or the deep swallow me up,
or the Pit close its mouth over me.

16 Answer me, O Lord, for your steadfast love is good;
according to your abundant mercy, turn to me.
17 Do not hide your face from your servant,
for I am in distress—make haste to answer me.
18 Draw near to me, redeem me,
set me free because of my enemies.

19 You know the insults I receive,
and my shame and dishonor;
my foes are all known to you.
20 Insults have broken my heart,
so that I am in despair.
I looked for pity, but there was none;
and for comforters, but I found none.

---

[a] Gk Syr: Heb *I wept, with fasting my soul,* or *I made my soul mourn with fasting*

21 They gave me poison for food,
and for my thirst they gave me vinegar to drink.

22 Let their table be a trap for them,
a snare for their allies.
23 Let their eyes be darkened so that they cannot see,
and make their loins tremble continually.
24 Pour out your indignation upon them,
and let your burning anger overtake them.
25 May their camp be a desolation;
let no one live in their tents.
26 For they persecute those whom you have struck down,
and those whom you have wounded, they attack still
more.[a]
27 Add guilt to their guilt;
may they have no acquittal from you.
28 Let them be blotted out of the book of the living;
let them not be enrolled among the righteous.
29 But I am lowly and in pain;
let your salvation, O God, protect me.

30 I will praise the name of God with a song;
I will magnify him with thanksgiving.
31 This will please the LORD more than an ox
or a bull with horns and hoofs.
32 Let the oppressed see it and be glad;
you who seek God, let your hearts revive.
33 For the LORD hears the needy,
and does not despise his own that are in bonds.

34 Let heaven and earth praise him,
the seas and everything that moves in them.
35 For God will save Zion
and rebuild the cities of Judah;
and his servants shall live[b] there and possess it;
36 the children of his servants shall inherit it,
and those who love his name shall live in it.

PSALM 70

Prayer for Deliverance from Enemies

To the leader. Of David, for the memorial offering.

1 Be pleased, O God, to deliver me.
O LORD, make haste to help me!

[a] Gk Syr: Heb *recount the pain of* [b] Syr: Heb *and they shall live*

69:21-22 Let their table be a trap for them: The imagery here is typical of Israel's wisdom tradition of teachings and writings, in which evildoers are often caught in the very traps they lay for others. The psalmist prays for this sort of rescue.

69:28 Let them be blotted out of the book of the living: The image of a book in which God records names was even more powerful in an ancient, mostly illiterate culture. It shows God's commitment to creating and maintaining a just and loving world.

69:30-32 Let the oppressed see it and be glad: Praise moves God's mission forward, as those who are oppressed find hope and people come to know and seek God. This praise is more pleasing to God than offerings or sacrifices (see note on 50:8-15).

69:34 Let heaven and earth praise him: In verses 1-2, the psalmist uses the image of drowning to describe the urgency of the crisis. In a surprising twist, the psalmist here calls even on the seas—the forces of chaos—to join in praising God.

Psalm 70: A prayer for help (see Types of Psalms, pp. 849-850). This prayer also appears in Psalm 40:13-17.

70:1-3 Let those be put to shame and confusion who seek my life: The prayer contrasts two types of people—those who seek to kill the psalmist and those who seek God. The psalmist asks God for honor and rescue. See note on 6:10.

[2] Let those be put to shame and confusion
who seek my life.
Let those be turned back and brought to dishonor
who desire to hurt me.
[3] Let those who say, "Aha, Aha!"
turn back because of their shame.

[4] Let all who seek you
rejoice and be glad in you.
Let those who love your salvation
say evermore, "God is great!"
[5] But I am poor and needy;
hasten to me, O God!
You are my help and my deliverer;
O LORD, do not delay!

70:4-5 Let all who seek you rejoice and be glad: The people who seek God celebrate when God raises up one who is lowly or rescues one who is oppressed.

When have you rejoiced over something God did for another person?

PSALM 71

Prayer for Lifelong Protection and Help

Psalm 71: A prayer for help (see Types of Psalms, pp. 849-850) from an elderly person.

71:1-4 In you, O LORD, I take refuge: To take refuge in God is to actively seek God's help and trust in God (see note on 2:11).

[1] In you, O LORD, I take refuge;
let me never be put to shame.
[2] In your righteousness deliver me and rescue me;
incline your ear to me and save me.
[3] Be to me a rock of refuge,
a strong fortress,[a] to save me,
for you are my rock and my fortress.

[4] Rescue me, O my God, from the hand of the wicked,
from the grasp of the unjust and cruel.
[5] For you, O Lord, are my hope,
my trust, O LORD, from my youth.
[6] Upon you I have leaned from my birth;
it was you who took me from my mother's womb.
My praise is continually of you.

71:5-21 Do not cast me off in the time of old age: This is the prayer of an elderly person who completely turns to God and leaves this poem as instruction for "all the generations to come" (71:18).). This person is now more vulnerable to enemy attacks and has few friends left to help (71:11). But during a long life the sufferer has come to trust in God's help, even though this help is often times hard to see (71:20).

[7] I have been like a portent to many,
but you are my strong refuge.
[8] My mouth is filled with your praise,
and with your glory all day long.
[9] Do not cast me off in the time of old age;
do not forsake me when my strength is spent.
[10] For my enemies speak concerning me,
and those who watch for my life consult together.
[11] They say, "Pursue and seize that person

---

[a] Gk Compare 31.3: Heb *to come continually you have commanded*

whom God has forsaken,
for there is no one to deliver."

12 O God, do not be far from me;
O my God, make haste to help me!
13 Let my accusers be put to shame and consumed;
let those who seek to hurt me
be covered with scorn and disgrace.
14 But I will hope continually,
and will praise you yet more and more.
15 My mouth will tell of your righteous acts,
of your deeds of salvation all day long,
though their number is past my knowledge.
16 I will come praising the mighty deeds of the Lord GOD,
I will praise your righteousness, yours alone.

17 O God, from my youth you have taught me,
and I still proclaim your wondrous deeds.
18 So even to old age and gray hairs,
O God, do not forsake me,
until I proclaim your might
to all the generations to come.[a]
Your power 19 and your righteousness, O God,
reach the high heavens.

You who have done great things,
O God, who is like you?
20 You who have made me see many troubles and calamities
will revive me again;
from the depths of the earth
you will bring me up again.
21 You will increase my honor,
and comfort me once again.

22 I will also praise you with the harp
for your faithfulness, O my God;
I will sing praises to you with the lyre,
O Holy One of Israel.
23 My lips will shout for joy
when I sing praises to you;
my soul also, which you have rescued.
24 All day long my tongue will talk of your righteous help,
for those who tried to do me harm
have been put to shame, and disgraced.

71:21, 24: You will increase my honor: The psalmist's trust reflects God's commandment to honor fathers and mothers (Exod 20:12).

In what ways have elderly people blessed your life?

71:22-24 I will also praise you: The psalmist is confident of God's rescue and praises God's faithfulness and help.

[a] Gk Compare Syr: Heb *to a generation, to all that come*

Psalm 72: A royal psalm (see Types of Psalms, pp. 849-850), asking God's blessings for the king.

72:1 Give the king your justice, O God, and your righteousness: On the role of the king, see note on Psalm 45:1. As God's representative, the king is expected to rule in light of God's will, with righteousness and justice.

72:4, 12-14 May he defend the cause of the poor of the people, give deliverance to the needy, and crush the oppressor: God's will for the people includes protection for the poor and needy—especially from oppressors.

72:15-16 May there be abundance of grain in the land: Prayers for the king's health and the land's harvest reflect the fact that although people often cannot control the weather or the quality of their government, these factors have a significant impact on their daily lives. Good government and plentiful harvests are blessings from God.

PSALM 72

Prayer for Guidance and Support for the King

Of Solomon.

1 Give the king your justice, O God,
and your righteousness to a king's son.
2 May he judge your people with righteousness,
and your poor with justice.
3 May the mountains yield prosperity for the people,
and the hills, in righteousness.
4 May he defend the cause of the poor of the people,
give deliverance to the needy,
and crush the oppressor.

5 May he live[a] while the sun endures,
and as long as the moon, throughout all generations.
6 May he be like rain that falls on the mown grass,
like showers that water the earth.
7 In his days may righteousness flourish
and peace abound, until the moon is no more.

8 May he have dominion from sea to sea,
and from the River to the ends of the earth.
9 May his foes[b] bow down before him,
and his enemies lick the dust.
10 May the kings of Tarshish and of the isles
render him tribute,
may the kings of Sheba and Seba
bring gifts.
11 May all kings fall down before him,
all nations give him service.

12 For he delivers the needy when they call,
the poor and those who have no helper.
13 He has pity on the weak and the needy,
and saves the lives of the needy.
14 From oppression and violence he redeems their life;
and precious is their blood in his sight.

15 Long may he live!
May gold of Sheba be given to him.
May prayer be made for him continually,
and blessings invoked for him all day long.
16 May there be abundance of grain in the land;

---

[a] Gk: Heb *may they fear you* [b] Cn: Heb *those who live in the wilderness*

may it wave on the tops of the mountains;
may its fruit be like Lebanon;
and may people blossom in the cities
like the grass of the field.
17 May his name endure forever,
his fame continue as long as the sun.
May all nations be blessed in him;[a]
may they pronounce him happy.

18 Blessed be the LORD, the God of Israel,
who alone does wondrous things.
19 Blessed be his glorious name forever;
may his glory fill the whole earth.
Amen and Amen.

20 The prayers of David son of Jesse are ended.

72:17 May all the nations be blessed in him: Israel's kings did not live up to God's ideal, and the kingdom failed. The royal psalms were preserved, however, as part of God's promise that one day the perfect king—the Messiah—would come and would bless not just Israel but all nations.

72:18-20 Blessed be the LORD: Verses 18-19 are not part of Psalm 72 but a song of praise or doxology that concludes Book II of the Psalms. Verse 20 is an editorial note stating that the major group of "Psalms of David" ends here.

BOOK III

(Psalms 73–89)

PSALM 73

Plea for Relief from Oppressors

A Psalm of Asaph.

1 Truly God is good to the upright,[b]
to those who are pure in heart.
2 But as for me, my feet had almost stumbled;
my steps had nearly slipped.
3 For I was envious of the arrogant;
I saw the prosperity of the wicked.

4 For they have no pain;
their bodies are sound and sleek.
5 They are not in trouble as others are;
they are not plagued like other people.
6 Therefore pride is their necklace;
violence covers them like a garment.
7 Their eyes swell out with fatness;
their hearts overflow with follies.
8 They scoff and speak with malice;
loftily they threaten oppression.
9 They set their mouths against heaven,
and their tongues range over the earth.

Psalm 73: An instructional psalm (see Types of Psalms, pp. 849-850) by a person tempted to leave God's path.

73:1 Truly God is good to the upright: The rest of the psalm describes how the psalmist reaches the point where it is possible to say this.

73:2-14 But as for me, my feet had almost stumbled: The psalmist recalls a time when joining those who reject God's ways seemed like a good idea. The wicked seem to prosper ("They are not in trouble as others are"), while those who attempt to follow God's ways seem to suffer. On the words of the wicked in verse 11, see Bible Concepts note on 3:2.

When has it seemed to you that a life of faith might be all for nothing (73:13)?

[a] Or *bless themselves by him* [b] Or *good to Israel*

[10] Therefore the people turn and praise them,[a]
and find no fault in them.[b]
[11] And they say, "How can God know?
Is there knowledge in the Most High?"
[12] Such are the wicked;
always at ease, they increase in riches.
[13] All in vain I have kept my heart clean
and washed my hands in innocence.
[14] For all day long I have been plagued,
and am punished every morning.

73:15 If I had said, "I will talk on in this way," I would have been untrue to the circle of your children: The psalmist describes the point of no return and the commitment to remain part of God's family.

73:17 until I went into the sanctuary of God: This is the turning point of the poem. Although confused about whether to give up on God's ways, the psalmist still goes to God's house and experiences God and God's will in a fresh way. Exactly what happened is not clear, but the psalmist realized that although God's way is not always the easiest one, it is the true and best way.

73:21-26 God is the strength of my heart: Even though the psalmist's faithfulness to God wavered, God's faithfulness to the psalmist was rock-solid. See note on shame/honor at 6:10. See note on portion at 16:5-6.

[15] If I had said, "I will talk on in this way,"
I would have been untrue to the circle of your children.
[16] But when I thought how to understand this,
it seemed to me a wearisome task,
[17] until I went into the sanctuary of God;
then I perceived their end.
[18] Truly you set them in slippery places;
you make them fall to ruin.
[19] How they are destroyed in a moment,
swept away utterly by terrors!
[20] They are[c] like a dream when one awakes;
on awaking you despise their phantoms.

[21] When my soul was embittered,
when I was pricked in heart,
[22] I was stupid and ignorant;
I was like a brute beast toward you.
[23] Nevertheless I am continually with you;
you hold my right hand.
[24] You guide me with your counsel,
and afterward you will receive me with honor.[d]
[25] Whom have I in heaven but you?
And there is nothing on earth that I desire other than you.
[26] My flesh and my heart may fail,
but God is the strength[e] of my heart and my portion forever.

[27] Indeed, those who are far from you will perish;
you put an end to those who are false to you.
[28] But for me it is good to be near God;
I have made the Lord GOD my refuge,
to tell of all your works.

---

[a] Cn: Heb *his people return here* [b] Cn: Heb *abundant waters are drained by them* [c] Cn: Heb *Lord*
[d] Or *to glory* [e] Heb *rock*

PSALM 74

Plea for Help in Time of National Humiliation

A Maskil of Asaph.

1 O God, why do you cast us off forever?
Why does your anger smoke against the sheep of your pasture?
2 Remember your congregation, which you acquired long ago,
which you redeemed to be the tribe of your heritage.
Remember Mount Zion, where you came to dwell.
3 Direct your steps to the perpetual ruins;
the enemy has destroyed everything in the sanctuary.

4 Your foes have roared within your holy place;
they set up their emblems there.
5 At the upper entrance they hacked
the wooden trellis with axes.[a]
6 And then, with hatchets and hammers,
they smashed all its carved work.
7 They set your sanctuary on fire;
they desecrated the dwelling place of your name,
bringing it to the ground.
8 They said to themselves, "We will utterly subdue them";
they burned all the meeting places of God in the land.

9 We do not see our emblems;
there is no longer any prophet,
and there is no one among us who knows how long.
10 How long, O God, is the foe to scoff?
Is the enemy to revile your name forever?
11 Why do you hold back your hand;
why do you keep your hand in[b] your bosom?

12 Yet God my King is from of old,
working salvation in the earth.
13 You divided the sea by your might;
you broke the heads of the dragons in the waters.
14 You crushed the heads of Leviathan;
you gave him as food[c] for the creatures of the wilderness.
15 You cut openings for springs and torrents;
you dried up ever-flowing streams.
16 Yours is the day, yours also the night;
you established the luminaries[d] and the sun.

Psalm 74: A prayer for help (see Types of Psalms, pp. 849-850) from a community after a national defeat, such as the destruction of the temple in 587 B.C.E.

74:1-2 Remember your congregation: The psalmist reminds God that the people are "the sheep of your pasture," "your congregation, which you acquired," and "the tribe of your heritage." The psalmist also insists that God "remember" (see also 74:18, 22), meaning that the future will depend on God keeping the promises of the covenant (74:20). See note on covenant at 25:14.

74:3-11 the enemy has destroyed everything in the sanctuary...We do not see our emblems; there is no longer any prophet: The psalmist describes the sacking of God's house, most likely a reference to the Babylonian destruction of Jerusalem in 587 B.C.E. "Emblems" here should be translated as "signs," referring to signs the prophets would give as to God's will (see Isa 7:10-17).

74:12-17 Yet God my King is from of old, working salvation in the earth: In the face of national defeat, the poem recalls God's faithful acts of creation, which emphasize that God is ruler of all the universe.

Which of God's actions are most helpful for you to remember when you are in crisis?

---

[a] Cn Compare Gk Syr: Meaning of Heb uncertain [b] Cn: Heb *do you consume your right hand from*
[c] Heb *food for the people* [d] Or *moon;* Heb *light*

[17] You have fixed all the bounds of the earth;
you made summer and winter.

[18] Remember this, O LORD, how the enemy scoffs,
and an impious people reviles your name.
[19] Do not deliver the soul of your dove to the wild animals;
do not forget the life of your poor forever.

74:20-23 Have regard for your covenant: The psalm places all hope for the future in God's pattern of keeping promises.

[20] Have regard for your[a] covenant,
for the dark places of the land are full of the haunts of violence.
[21] Do not let the downtrodden be put to shame;
let the poor and needy praise your name.
[22] Rise up, O God, plead your cause;
remember how the impious scoff at you all day long.
[23] Do not forget the clamor of your foes,
the uproar of your adversaries that goes up continually.

PSALM 75

Thanksgiving for God's Wondrous Deeds

To the leader: Do Not Destroy. A Psalm of Asaph. A Song.

Psalm 75: A song of thanksgiving (see Types of Psalms, pp. 849-850) from a community that God has rescued.

75:1 your name is near: God's name (see note on 20:7) dwells in the temple.

[1] We give thanks to you, O God;
we give thanks; your name is near.
People tell of your wondrous deeds.

75:2-5 At the set time that I appoint I will judge with equity: God acts according to God's timeline, not ours. To "judge" refers here to God's interventions within history, such as rescuing the Israelites from slavery in Egypt. In light of God's actions, humans should be humble and not arrogant.

[2] At the set time that I appoint
I will judge with equity.
[3] When the earth totters, with all its inhabitants,
it is I who keep its pillars steady. *Selah*
[4] I say to the boastful, "Do not boast,"
and to the wicked, "Do not lift up your horn;
[5] do not lift up your horn on high,
or speak with insolent neck."

75:8 in the hand of the LORD there is a cup: The cup is an image of God's judgment (see Isa 51:17; Rev 14:10), signaling that God is preparing defeat for those who are so proud and arrogant that they oppress the poor and needy.

[6] For not from the east or from the west
and not from the wilderness comes lifting up;
[7] but it is God who executes judgment,
putting down one and lifting up another.
[8] For in the hand of the LORD there is a cup
with foaming wine, well mixed;
he will pour a draught from it,
and all the wicked of the earth
shall drain it down to the dregs.

75:9-10 I will rejoice...the horns of the wicked...the horns of the righteous: A worship leader sings confidently on behalf of the people. The horn is a symbol of status—the wicked shall be humbled and the lowly shall be honored (see note on 6:10).

[9] But I will rejoice[b] forever;
I will sing praises to the God of Jacob.

---

[a] Gk Syr: Heb *the* [b] Gk: Heb *declare*

10 All the horns of the wicked I will cut off,
but the horns of the righteous shall be exalted.

PSALM 76
Israel's God—Judge of All the Earth

To the leader: with stringed instruments. A Psalm of Asaph. A Song.

1 In Judah God is known,
his name is great in Israel.
2 His abode has been established in Salem,
his dwelling place in Zion.
3 There he broke the flashing arrows,
the shield, the sword, and the weapons of war. *Selah*

4 Glorious are you, more majestic
than the everlasting mountains.[a]
5 The stouthearted were stripped of their spoil;
they sank into sleep;
none of the troops
was able to lift a hand.
6 At your rebuke, O God of Jacob,
both rider and horse lay stunned.

7 But you indeed are awesome!
Who can stand before you
when once your anger is roused?
8 From the heavens you uttered judgment;
the earth feared and was still
9 when God rose up to establish judgment,
to save all the oppressed of the earth. *Selah*

10 Human wrath serves only to praise you,
when you bind the last bit of your[b] wrath around you.
11 Make vows to the LORD your God, and perform them;
let all who are around him bring gifts
to the one who is awesome,
12 who cuts off the spirit of princes,
who inspires fear in the kings of the earth.

PSALM 77
God's Mighty Deeds Recalled

To the leader: according to Jeduthun. Of Asaph. A Psalm.

1 I cry aloud to God,

[a] Gk: Heb *the mountains of prey* [b] Heb lacks *your*

Psalm 76: A hymn of praise and a song of Zion (see Types of Psalms, pp. 849-850). The psalm may have been written after a specific experience of God's deliverance, such as God's rescue of Jerusalem in 701 B.C.E., or it may reflect the long history of God's many saving actions.

76:1-2 In Judah God is known . . . his dwelling place in Zion: The temple was God's dwelling place, the point of contact between heaven and earth (see note on 9:7, 11).

76:3-12 God rose up to establish judgment, to save all the oppressed of the earth: God creates peace (see 46:9) and judges the earth. These two actions are connected, because God's love of peace and rescue of the oppressed of the earth requires that God stand against evil and evil deeds.

Psalm 77: A prayer for help (see Types of Psalms, pp. 849-850), in which memory and remembering play a key role.

77:1-4 You keep my eyelids from closing: The psalmist is in a deep crisis. The cause is unclear—which means that people in many different situations can pray this prayer. The psalmist describes staying awake all night—praying, suffering, and waiting on God.

aloud to God, that he may hear me.
2 In the day of my trouble I seek the Lord;
in the night my hand is stretched out without wearying;
my soul refuses to be comforted.
3 I think of God, and I moan;
I meditate, and my spirit faints. *Selah*

4 You keep my eyelids from closing;
I am so troubled that I cannot speak.
5 I consider the days of old,
and remember the years of long ago.
6 I commune[a] with my heart in the night;
I meditate and search my spirit:[b]
7 "Will the Lord spurn forever,
and never again be favorable?
8 Has his steadfast love ceased forever?
Are his promises at an end for all time?
9 Has God forgotten to be gracious?
Has he in anger shut up his compassion?" *Selah*
10 And I say, "It is my grief
that the right hand of the Most High has changed."

11 I will call to mind the deeds of the LORD;
I will remember your wonders of old.
12 I will meditate on all your work,
and muse on your mighty deeds.
13 Your way, O God, is holy.
What god is so great as our God?
14 You are the God who works wonders;
you have displayed your might among the peoples.
15 With your strong arm you redeemed your people,
the descendants of Jacob and Joseph. *Selah*

16 When the waters saw you, O God,
when the waters saw you, they were afraid;
the very deep trembled.
17 The clouds poured out water;
the skies thundered;
your arrows flashed on every side.
18 The crash of your thunder was in the whirlwind;
your lightnings lit up the world;
the earth trembled and shook.
19 Your way was through the sea,

77:5-10 I consider the days of old, and remember the years: Lying awake, the psalmist's mind races from memory to memory, trying to understand why the LORD, who was so gracious in the past, seems too distant in the present. These memories lead the psalmist first to wonder if God has forgotten, and then to conclude that God's mind has changed.

77:11-20 Your way was through the sea, your path, through the mighty waters; yet your footprints were unseen: The psalmist remembers the exodus of the Israelites out of Egypt (see Exod 1–15) and realizes that although God's footprints are often unseen, God is still active.

Recall a time when you felt God was not there—but later came to realize God was present all along.

---

[a] Gk Syr: Heb *My music* [b] Syr Jerome: Heb *my spirit searches*

your path, through the mighty waters;
yet your footprints were unseen.
20 You led your people like a flock
by the hand of Moses and Aaron.

PSALM 78
God's Goodness and Israel's Ingratitude

A Maskil of Asaph.

1 Give ear, O my people, to my teaching;
incline your ears to the words of my mouth.
2 I will open my mouth in a parable;
I will utter dark sayings from of old,
3 things that we have heard and known,
that our ancestors have told us.
4 We will not hide them from their children;
we will tell to the coming generation
the glorious deeds of the LORD, and his might,
and the wonders that he has done.

5 He established a decree in Jacob,
and appointed a law in Israel,
which he commanded our ancestors
to teach to their children;
6 that the next generation might know them,
the children yet unborn,
and rise up and tell them to their children,
7 so that they should set their hope in God,
and not forget the works of God,
but keep his commandments;
8 and that they should not be like their ancestors,
a stubborn and rebellious generation,
a generation whose heart was not steadfast,
whose spirit was not faithful to God.

9 The Ephraimites, armed with[a] the bow,
turned back on the day of battle.
10 They did not keep God's covenant,
but refused to walk according to his law.
11 They forgot what he had done,
and the miracles that he had shown them.
12 In the sight of their ancestors he worked marvels
in the land of Egypt, in the fields of Zoan.
13 He divided the sea and let them pass through it,
and made the waters stand like a heap.

[a] Heb *armed with shooting*

Psalm 78: A historical psalm (see Types of Psalms, pp. 849-850) that tells Israel's story in order to teach future generations to know the LORD and the LORD's ways.

78:1-6 Give ear, O my people, to my teaching…that the next generation might know: The psalm tells Israel's story from the exodus (78:42-51), through the wilderness wanderings (78:9-41), to the time of the settlement of the land and through King David (78:52-72). This is the story of God's faithfulness to the people, in spite of the people's unfaithfulness to God.

Stories about the past teach us who we are. Recall a story about your ancestors, your country, or your faith community that helps you know who you are.

78:11 They forgot what he had done: One of the main ways of being unfaithful to God is to forget God. The people forgot God, but God "remembered that they were but flesh" and had mercy on them (78:39).

14 In the daytime he led them with a cloud,
and all night long with a fiery light.
15 He split rocks open in the wilderness,
and gave them drink abundantly as from the deep.
16 He made streams come out of the rock,
and caused waters to flow down like rivers.

17 Yet they sinned still more against him,
rebelling against the Most High in the desert.
18 They tested God in their heart
by demanding the food they craved.
19 They spoke against God, saying,
"Can God spread a table in the wilderness?
20 Even though he struck the rock so that water gushed out
and torrents overflowed,
can he also give bread,
or provide meat for his people?"

21 Therefore, when the LORD heard, he was full of rage;
a fire was kindled against Jacob,
his anger mounted against Israel,
22 because they had no faith in God,
and did not trust his saving power.
23 Yet he commanded the skies above,
and opened the doors of heaven;
24 he rained down on them manna to eat,
and gave them the grain of heaven.
25 Mortals ate of the bread of angels;
he sent them food in abundance.
26 He caused the east wind to blow in the heavens,
and by his power he led out the south wind;
27 he rained flesh upon them like dust,
winged birds like the sand of the seas;
28 he let them fall within their camp,
all around their dwellings.
29 And they ate and were well filled,
for he gave them what they craved.
30 But before they had satisfied their craving,
while the food was still in their mouths,
31 the anger of God rose against them
and he killed the strongest of them,
and laid low the flower of Israel.

32 In spite of all this they still sinned;
they did not believe in his wonders.

78:18 They tested God: Another way of being unfaithful is to test God (see also 78:41, 56), which means to try to force God to act in a certain manner rather than to trust that God's ways are good. In spite of putting God to the test, God remained faithful and provided for the people.

78:22 they had no faith in God: Another way of being unfaithful is to not trust in God (see also 78:32, 37), which can result in failing to follow God's ways—even though these ways are best for our neighbors and ourselves. In spite of this, God continued to love, guide, and provide for the people.

33 So he made their days vanish like a breath,
and their years in terror.
34 When he killed them, they sought for him;
they repented and sought God earnestly.
35 They remembered that God was their rock,
the Most High God their redeemer.
36 But they flattered him with their mouths;
they lied to him with their tongues.
37 Their heart was not steadfast toward him;
they were not true to his covenant.
38 Yet he, being compassionate,
forgave their iniquity,
and did not destroy them;
often he restrained his anger,
and did not stir up all his wrath.
39 He remembered that they were but flesh,
a wind that passes and does not come again.
40 How often they rebelled against him in the wilderness
and grieved him in the desert!
41 They tested God again and again,
and provoked the Holy One of Israel.
42 They did not keep in mind his power,
or the day when he redeemed them from the foe;
43 when he displayed his signs in Egypt,
and his miracles in the fields of Zoan.
44 He turned their rivers to blood,
so that they could not drink of their streams.
45 He sent among them swarms of flies, which devoured them,
and frogs, which destroyed them.
46 He gave their crops to the caterpillar,
and the fruit of their labor to the locust.
47 He destroyed their vines with hail,
and their sycamores with frost.
48 He gave over their cattle to the hail,
and their flocks to thunderbolts.
49 He let loose on them his fierce anger,
wrath, indignation, and distress,
a company of destroying angels.
50 He made a path for his anger;
he did not spare them from death,
but gave their lives over to the plague.
51 He struck all the firstborn in Egypt,
the first issue of their strength in the tents of Ham.
52 Then he led out his people like sheep,
and guided them in the wilderness like a flock.

53 He led them in safety, so that they were not afraid;
but the sea overwhelmed their enemies.
54 And he brought them to his holy hill,
to the mountain that his right hand had won.
55 He drove out nations before them;
he apportioned them for a possession
and settled the tribes of Israel in their tents.

78:56 They did not observe his decrees: The people did not observe God's law, such as the Ten Commandments (see Exod 20), and worshiped at the "high places" (78:58) or worshiped other gods. God rejected the northern kingdom (78:59, 67), but did not reject the people as a whole (see 78:68-72).

56 Yet they tested the Most High God,
and rebelled against him.
They did not observe his decrees,
57 but turned away and were faithless like their ancestors;
they twisted like a treacherous bow.
58 For they provoked him to anger with their high places;
they moved him to jealousy with their idols.
59 When God heard, he was full of wrath,
and he utterly rejected Israel.
60 He abandoned his dwelling at Shiloh,
the tent where he dwelt among mortals,
61 and delivered his power to captivity,
his glory to the hand of the foe.
62 He gave his people to the sword,
and vented his wrath on his heritage.
63 Fire devoured their young men,
and their girls had no marriage song.
64 Their priests fell by the sword,
and their widows made no lamentation.
65 Then the Lord awoke as from sleep,
like a warrior shouting because of wine.
66 He put his adversaries to rout;
he put them to everlasting disgrace.

67 He rejected the tent of Joseph,
he did not choose the tribe of Ephraim;
68 but he chose the tribe of Judah,
Mount Zion, which he loves.
69 He built his sanctuary like the high heavens,
like the earth, which he has founded forever.
70 He chose his servant David,
and took him from the sheepfolds;
71 from tending the nursing ewes he brought him
to be the shepherd of his people Jacob,
of Israel, his inheritance.
72 With upright heart he tended them,
and guided them with skillful hand.

PSALM 79
Plea for Mercy for Jerusalem

A Psalm of Asaph.

1 O God, the nations have come into your inheritance;
they have defiled your holy temple;
they have laid Jerusalem in ruins.
2 They have given the bodies of your servants
to the birds of the air for food,
the flesh of your faithful to the wild animals of the earth.
3 They have poured out their blood like water
all around Jerusalem,
and there was no one to bury them.
4 We have become a taunt to our neighbors,
mocked and derided by those around us.

5 How long, O LORD? Will you be angry forever?
Will your jealous wrath burn like fire?
6 Pour out your anger on the nations
that do not know you,
and on the kingdoms
that do not call on your name.
7 For they have devoured Jacob
and laid waste his habitation.

8 Do not remember against us the iniquities of our
ancestors;
let your compassion come speedily to meet us,
for we are brought very low.
9 Help us, O God of our salvation,
for the glory of your name;
deliver us, and forgive our sins,
for your name's sake.
10 Why should the nations say,
"Where is their God?"
Let the avenging of the outpoured blood of your servants
be known among the nations before our eyes.

11 Let the groans of the prisoners come before you;
according to your great power preserve those doomed
to die.
12 Return sevenfold into the bosom of our neighbors
the taunts with which they taunted you, O Lord!
13 Then we your people, the flock of your pasture,
will give thanks to you forever;
from generation to generation we will recount your praise.

Psalm 79: A prayer for help (see Types of Psalms, pp. 849-850) from a community in the midst of a national crisis.

79:1-4 the nations have come into your inheritance…We have become a taunt: The psalm begins with the community crying out to God because the nations have destroyed God's temple and mistreated the land ("your inheritance"). The victorious enemy (probably the Babylonians, who destroyed Jerusalem in 587 B.C.E.) taunts the defeated people (see 79:10).

79:5-10 How long, O LORD?…Why should the nations say, "Where is their God?": The people ask God to restore them to their land by rescuing them from defeat. See notes on "How long" at 6:3, "Where is their God?" at 42:3, and God's name at 20:7.

79:6 Pour out your anger: Anger is not the opposite of love. In fact, God shows love by being angry at those who cause God's people to suffer. God's anger is temporary, while God's love is permanent.

When has your love for someone caused you to be angry? What made your anger fade?

79:11-13 Let the groans of the prisoners come before you: God knows the pain of those who suffer (see Exod 2:23-25) and is moved to rescue them. The rescued people, described here as God's flock, give thanks.

Psalm 80: A prayer for help (see Types of Psalms, pp. 849-850) from a community. This prayer has three stanzas (80:1-2; 4-6; 8-18) with a refrain between each stanza (80:3, 7, 19).

80:1-2 Give ear, O Shepherd of Israel: The title "shepherd of Israel" occurs only here in the Bible, although God is often described as a royal shepherd (see note on 23:1). The people ask for rescue.

80:3, 7, 19 Restore us…let your face shine: The people beg God to restore them. This restoration might include their health, security, prosperity, and faith. "Let your face shine" is a request for blessing (see Num 6:25) and a way God's power is shown (67:1-2).

Describe a time when you saw someone's face and felt overwhelming joy. How is experiencing God's love like that?

80:4-6 how long will you be angry with your people's prayers?: God is angry because the people prayed for blessing even though they oppressed their neighbors and lived unjustly (see Isa 1:12-17).

80:8-13 You brought a vine out of Egypt: God's people are often described as a vine or vineyard (see Isa 5:1-7). The image expresses the care that God has shown Israel in the past and also the threat to the people in the present crisis.

80:14-18 give us life, and we will call on your name: The people ask God to turn away from judgment and rescue them. To "give life" here means to rescue the people from danger.

PSALM 80

Prayer for Israel's Restoration

To the leader: on Lilies, a Covenant. Of Asaph. A Psalm.

1 Give ear, O Shepherd of Israel,
you who lead Joseph like a flock!
You who are enthroned upon the cherubim, shine forth
2 before Ephraim and Benjamin and Manasseh.
Stir up your might,
and come to save us!

3 Restore us, O God;
let your face shine, that we may be saved.

4 O LORD God of hosts,
how long will you be angry with your people's prayers?
5 You have fed them with the bread of tears,
and given them tears to drink in full measure.
6 You make us the scorn[a] of our neighbors;
our enemies laugh among themselves.

7 Restore us, O God of hosts;
let your face shine, that we may be saved.

8 You brought a vine out of Egypt;
you drove out the nations and planted it.
9 You cleared the ground for it;
it took deep root and filled the land.
10 The mountains were covered with its shade,
the mighty cedars with its branches;
11 it sent out its branches to the sea,
and its shoots to the River.
12 Why then have you broken down its walls,
so that all who pass along the way pluck its fruit?
13 The boar from the forest ravages it,
and all that move in the field feed on it.

14 Turn again, O God of hosts;
look down from heaven, and see;
have regard for this vine,
15 the stock that your right hand planted.[b]
16 They have burned it with fire, they have cut it down;[c]
may they perish at the rebuke of your countenance.

---

[a] Syr: Heb *strife* [b] Heb adds from verse 17 *and upon the one whom you made strong for yourself*
[c] Cn: Heb *it is cut down*

[17] But let your hand be upon the one at your right hand,
the one whom you made strong for yourself.
[18] Then we will never turn back from you;
give us life, and we will call on your name.

[19] Restore us, O LORD God of hosts;
let your face shine, that we may be saved.

PSALM 81

God's Appeal to Stubborn Israel

To the leader: according to The Gittith. Of Asaph.

[1] Sing aloud to God our strength;
shout for joy to the God of Jacob.
[2] Raise a song, sound the tambourine,
the sweet lyre with the harp.
[3] Blow the trumpet at the new moon,
at the full moon, on our festal day.
[4] For it is a statute for Israel,
an ordinance of the God of Jacob.
[5] He made it a decree in Joseph,
when he went out over[a] the land of Egypt.

I hear a voice I had not known:
[6] "I relieved your[b] shoulder of the burden;
your[b] hands were freed from the basket.
[7] In distress you called, and I rescued you;
I answered you in the secret place of thunder;
I tested you at the waters of Meribah. *Selah*
[8] Hear, O my people, while I admonish you;
O Israel, if you would but listen to me!
[9] There shall be no strange god among you;
you shall not bow down to a foreign god.
[10] I am the LORD your God,
who brought you up out of the land of Egypt.
Open your mouth wide and I will fill it.

[11] "But my people did not listen to my voice;
Israel would not submit to me.
[12] So I gave them over to their stubborn hearts,
to follow their own counsels.
[13] O that my people would listen to me,
that Israel would walk in my ways!
[14] Then I would quickly subdue their enemies,

Psalm 81: A liturgy and festival psalm (see Types of Psalms, pp. 849-850), probably composed for use during one of Israel's three annual festivals.

81:1-5a He made it a decree: The three joyful festival celebrations (see Exod 23:14-19) were tied to times of planting and harvest.

81:5b-16 : But my people did not listen . . . I would feed you with the finest of the wheat: In the festival celebration, the people were reminded of what God had done for them in the past, encouraged to thank God for current blessings, and told to change their ways and become faithful to God.

How would you react if you were told in a Christmas or Easter worship service that you have failed to obey God fully and must change your ways?

81:9-10 There shall be no strange god among you: This refers to the First Commandment (see Exod 20:1-3).

---

[a] Or *against* [b] Heb *his*

and turn my hand against their foes.
15 Those who hate the LORD would cringe before him,
and their doom would last forever.
16 I would feed you[a] with the finest of the wheat,
and with honey from the rock I would satisfy you."

PSALM 82
A Plea for Justice

A Psalm of Asaph.

Psalm 82: A liturgy that becomes a community prayer for help (see Types of Psalms, pp. 849-850), asking God to judge the earth.

82:1 the divine council: This refers to the heavenly assembly of beings (such as angels) that surround the one God. The Bible describes God as discussing and deliberating with these beings (see Gen 1:26; 1 Kgs 22:19-23; Isa 6:6-8), but makes it clear that only the LORD is God.

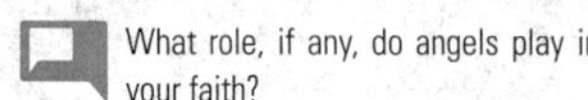

What role, if any, do angels play in your faith?

82:1-8 How long will you judge unjustly: This liturgy portrays God as judging other heavenly beings and condemning them to die like humans, because they have not acted justly, as God desires. Part of the message here is that human rulers must also act justly, or God will end their rule. The psalm ends with a cry for God to establish justice throughout all the earth.

1 God has taken his place in the divine council;
in the midst of the gods he holds judgment:
2 "How long will you judge unjustly
and show partiality to the wicked? *Selah*
3 Give justice to the weak and the orphan;
maintain the right of the lowly and the destitute.
4 Rescue the weak and the needy;
deliver them from the hand of the wicked."

5 They have neither knowledge nor understanding,
they walk around in darkness;
all the foundations of the earth are shaken.

6 I say, "You are gods,
children of the Most High, all of you;
7 nevertheless, you shall die like mortals,
and fall like any prince."[b]

8 Rise up, O God, judge the earth;
for all the nations belong to you!

PSALM 83
Prayer for Judgment on Israel's Foes

A Song. A Psalm of Asaph.

Psalm 83: A prayer for help (see Types of Psalms, pp. 849-850) from a community, most likely written for repeated use in the temple.

83:2 Even now your enemies are in tumult: The enemies of God and God's people are always working against God's will. Only with God's help can the people survive.

1 O God, do not keep silence;
do not hold your peace or be still, O God!
2 Even now your enemies are in tumult;
those who hate you have raised their heads.
3 They lay crafty plans against your people;
they consult together against those you protect.
4 They say, "Come, let us wipe them out as a nation;
let the name of Israel be remembered no more."
5 They conspire with one accord;

---

[a] Cn Compare verse 16b: Heb *he would feed him* [b] Or *fall as one man, O princes*

against you they make a covenant—
6 the tents of Edom and the Ishmaelites,
Moab and the Hagrites,
7 Gebal and Ammon and Amalek,
Philistia with the inhabitants of Tyre;
8 Assyria also has joined them;
they are the strong arm of the children of Lot. *Selah*

9 Do to them as you did to Midian,
as to Sisera and Jabin at the Wadi Kishon,
10 who were destroyed at En-dor,
who became dung for the ground.
11 Make their nobles like Oreb and Zeeb,
all their princes like Zebah and Zalmunna,
12 who said, "Let us take the pastures of God
for our own possession."

13 O my God, make them like whirling dust,[a]
like chaff before the wind.
14 As fire consumes the forest,
as the flame sets the mountains ablaze,
15 so pursue them with your tempest
and terrify them with your hurricane.
16 Fill their faces with shame,
so that they may seek your name, O LORD.
17 Let them be put to shame and dismayed forever;
let them perish in disgrace.
18 Let them know that you alone,
whose name is the LORD,
are the Most High over all the earth.

PSALM 84

The Joy of Worship in the Temple

To the leader: according to The Gittith. Of the Korahites. A Psalm.

1 How lovely is your dwelling place,
O LORD of hosts!
2 My soul longs, indeed it faints
for the courts of the LORD;
my heart and my flesh sing for joy
to the living God.

3 Even the sparrow finds a home,
and the swallow a nest for herself,

[a] Or *a tumbleweed*

83:6-8 Edom...the Ishmaelites, Moab and the Hagrites: There is no known time when all these nations simultaneously threatened Israel. For this reason, some scholars believe that this psalm was used annually in the temple. The reference to these nations shows that the enemies of God are always working against God's will.

83:9-18 Let them know that you alone, whose name is the LORD, are the Most High: God has a history of faithfully rescuing the people from threats. The people pray for and trust in God's continuing faithfulness. The evil intention of the nations that "the name of Israel be remembered no more" (83:4) is contrasted with the people's trust that God's name will be known through God's acts of faithfulness.

Psalm 84: A hymn of praise and a song of Zion (see Types of Psalms, pp. 849-850), most likely sung by travelers on their way to celebrate in the temple.

84:1 your dwelling place: The temple in Jerusalem was the house of God—the dwelling place of the LORD. The Israelites believed that God dwells in heaven (115:3) and is also present everywhere (see 139:7-10). The temple was seen as the closest point of contact between the heavenly and earthly realms—the place where the two realms overlap, and where God "dwells."

How do Lutherans understand God "dwelling" in physical, concrete things? Lutherans believe that God's grace, favor, and blessing flow out to us through the "means of grace"—earthly things like the water in Baptism and the bread and wine of Holy Communion. The temple in Jerusalem worked in a similar way for the Israelites. Through this earthly channel, God's grace, favor, and blessing flowed out for Israel and for the entire world (Isa 2:1-4). *Psalm 84:1*

84:3 Even the sparrow finds a home: The hospitality and spiritual rest offered by God is symbolized in this image. Even a vulnerable and insignificant bird is welcome in God's house.

where she may lay her young,
at your altars, O LORD of hosts,
my King and my God.
4 Happy are those who live in your house,
ever singing your praise. *Selah*

5 Happy are those whose strength is in you,
in whose heart are the highways to Zion.[a]
6 As they go through the valley of Baca
they make it a place of springs;
the early rain also covers it with pools.
7 They go from strength to strength;
the God of gods will be seen in Zion.

8 O LORD God of hosts, hear my prayer;
give ear, O God of Jacob! *Selah*
9 Behold our shield, O God;
look on the face of your anointed.

10 For a day in your courts is better
than a thousand elsewhere.
I would rather be a doorkeeper in the house of my God
than live in the tents of wickedness.
11 For the LORD God is a sun and shield;
he bestows favor and honor.
No good thing does the LORD withhold
from those who walk uprightly.
12 O LORD of hosts,
happy is everyone who trusts in you.

84:6-7 As they go through the valley of Baca they make it a place of springs…the God of gods will be seen in Zion: The location of the valley of Baca is unknown, but it seems to have been a dry area. As the worshipers come and go from the temple, they spread God's blessings throughout the land.

84:10 For a day in your courts is better than a thousand elsewhere: God's courts would be the outer, open-air part of the temple buildings, the only part of the temple where most people were allowed. The term "doorkeeper" means something like "one who waits outside." The least of God's blessings are greater than the best that one can receive from the wicked.

PSALM 85

Prayer for the Restoration of God's Favor

To the leader. Of the Korahites. A Psalm.

1 LORD, you were favorable to your land;
you restored the fortunes of Jacob.
2 You forgave the iniquity of your people;
you pardoned all their sin. *Selah*
3 You withdrew all your wrath;
you turned from your hot anger.

4 Restore us again, O God of our salvation,
and put away your indignation toward us.
5 Will you be angry with us forever?

Psalm 85: A liturgy and prayer for help (see Types of Psalms, pp. 849-850) in which the community asks for restoration.

85:1 LORD, you were favorable to your land; you restored the fortunes of Jacob: The people recall God's past actions of forgiving and restoring.

85:4 Restore us again, O God: The people ask God to forgive and restore them.

[a] Heb lacks *to Zion*

Will you prolong your anger to all generations?
6 Will you not revive us again,
so that your people may rejoice in you?
7 Show us your steadfast love, O LORD,
and grant us your salvation.

8 Let me hear what God the LORD will speak,
for he will speak peace to his people,
to his faithful, to those who turn to him in their hearts.[a]
9 Surely his salvation is at hand for those who fear him,
that his glory may dwell in our land.

10 Steadfast love and faithfulness will meet;
righteousness and peace will kiss each other.
11 Faithfulness will spring up from the ground,
and righteousness will look down from the sky.
12 The LORD will give what is good,
and our land will yield its increase.
13 Righteousness will go before him,
and will make a path for his steps.

PSALM 86

Supplication for Help against Enemies

A Prayer of David.

1 Incline your ear, O LORD, and answer me,
for I am poor and needy.
2 Preserve my life, for I am devoted to you;
save your servant who trusts in you.
You are my God; 3be gracious to me, O Lord,
for to you do I cry all day long.
4 Gladden the soul of your servant,
for to you, O Lord, I lift up my soul.
5 For you, O Lord, are good and forgiving,
abounding in steadfast love to all who call on you.
6 Give ear, O LORD, to my prayer;
listen to my cry of supplication.
7 In the day of my trouble I call on you,
for you will answer me.

8 There is none like you among the gods, O Lord,
nor are there any works like yours.
9 All the nations you have made shall come
and bow down before you, O Lord,

[a] Gk: Heb *but let them not turn back to folly*

85:7 Show us your steadfast love: The people cannot save themselves. Rescue must come from God, and it is a sign of God's love. See note on God's steadfast love at 13:5.

85:10-13 Steadfast love and faithfulness will meet: The psalm ends with words of promise. "Steadfast love," "faithfulness," "righteousness," and "peace" are all terms for God's character. Here they appear as creatures that come together to fulfill God's will.

Psalm 86: An individual's prayer for help (see Types of Psalms, pp. 849-850) in three stanzas (86:1-7; 8-13; 14-17).

86:1-7 I am poor and needy... you, O LORD, are good and forgiving: The psalmist has no one else to turn to in this crisis other than God. The prayer contrasts the psalmist's situation ("I am poor and needy") with God's nature ("you... are good").

Has there ever been a time when it seemed that no one but God could help you? What happened?

86:8-13 For great is your steadfast love toward me: The psalmist gives praise for who God is, which makes God unlike any other being. This is summed up in the statement about God's steadfast love (see note on 13:5).

and shall glorify your name.
10 For you are great and do wondrous things;
you alone are God.
11 Teach me your way, O LORD,
that I may walk in your truth;
give me an undivided heart to revere your name.
12 I give thanks to you, O Lord my God, with my whole heart,
and I will glorify your name forever.
13 For great is your steadfast love toward me;
you have delivered my soul from the depths of Sheol.

86:14-17 Show me a sign of your favor: The prayer ends with new appeals for rescue. This stanza focuses on the threats the psalmist faces. The core of the psalmist's faith is stated in the middle of the stanza: "you, O LORD, are a God merciful and gracious, slow to anger and abounding in steadfast love and faithfulness."

14 O God, the insolent rise up against me;
a band of ruffians seeks my life,
and they do not set you before them.
15 But you, O Lord, are a God merciful and gracious,
slow to anger and abounding in steadfast love and faithfulness.
16 Turn to me and be gracious to me;
give your strength to your servant;
save the child of your serving girl.
17 Show me a sign of your favor,
so that those who hate me may see it and be put to shame,
because you, LORD, have helped me and comforted me.

Psalm 87: A hymn of praise and a song of Zion (see Types of Psalms, pp. 849-850).

87:1-3 Glorious things are spoken of you, O city of God: The song praises Jerusalem because it is God's dwelling place (see note on 84:1). By speaking poetically to the city, the psalmist emphasizes that the city is a channel of God's grace and blessing.

87:4-7 Among those who know me I mention Rahab and Babylon: The meaning of these verses is unclear. The locations mentioned in verse 4 praise those born in Jerusalem, which may be a poetic way of celebrating the joy and blessing of living under God's protection.

PSALM 87

The Joy of Living in Zion

Of the Korahites. A Psalm. A Song.

1 On the holy mount stands the city he founded;
2 the LORD loves the gates of Zion
more than all the dwellings of Jacob.
3 Glorious things are spoken of you,
O city of God. *Selah*

4 Among those who know me I mention Rahab and Babylon;
Philistia too, and Tyre, with Ethiopia[a]—
"This one was born there," they say.

5 And of Zion it shall be said,
"This one and that one were born in it";
for the Most High himself will establish it.
6 The LORD records, as he registers the peoples,
"This one was born there." *Selah*

7 Singers and dancers alike say,
"All my springs are in you."

---

[a] Or *Nubia;* Heb *Cush*

PSALM 88
Prayer for Help in Despondency

A Song. A Psalm of the Korahites. To the leader: according to Mahalath Leannoth. A Maskil of Heman the Ezrahite.

1 O LORD, God of my salvation,
when, at night, I cry out in your presence,
2 let my prayer come before you;
incline your ear to my cry.

3 For my soul is full of troubles,
and my life draws near to Sheol.
4 I am counted among those who go down to the Pit;
I am like those who have no help,
5 like those forsaken among the dead,
like the slain that lie in the grave,
like those whom you remember no more,
for they are cut off from your hand.
6 You have put me in the depths of the Pit,
in the regions dark and deep.
7 Your wrath lies heavy upon me,
and you overwhelm me with all your waves. *Selah*

8 You have caused my companions to shun me;
you have made me a thing of horror to them.
I am shut in so that I cannot escape;
9 my eye grows dim through sorrow.
Every day I call on you, O LORD;
I spread out my hands to you.
10 Do you work wonders for the dead?
Do the shades rise up to praise you? *Selah*
11 Is your steadfast love declared in the grave,
or your faithfulness in Abaddon?
12 Are your wonders known in the darkness,
or your saving help in the land of forgetfulness?

13 But I, O LORD, cry out to you;
in the morning my prayer comes before you.
14 O LORD, why do you cast me off?
Why do you hide your face from me?
15 Wretched and close to death from my youth up,
I suffer your terrors; I am desperate.[a]
16 Your wrath has swept over me;
your dread assaults destroy me.
17 They surround me like a flood all day long;

[a] Meaning of Heb uncertain

Psalm 88: An individual's prayer for help (see Types of Psalms, pp. 849-850). This psalm, the most dark and desperate of all, has three similar parts.

88:1-9a O LORD, God of my salvation, when, at night, I cry out in your presence…my eye grows dim: In the first part of the prayer, the sufferer cries out to the LORD at night and complains that "my eye grows dim." The situation is so dire that death draws near.

88:9b-12 Every day I call on you, O LORD: In the second part of the prayer, the sufferer cries out to the LORD in the day. This person has no hope for a relationship with God beyond death (88:12).

88:13-18 But I, O LORD, cry out to you; in the morning my prayer comes before you…you hide your face: In the third part of the prayer, the sufferer cries out to the LORD "in the morning." The morning is usually the time of deliverance in the psalms (see 30:5; 143:8), but here it only brings more despair. The last line of the psalm can also be translated "my companion is darkness"—a statement about the person's utter isolation.

When might a prayer like Psalm 88 be helpful to you?

from all sides they close in on me.
18 You have caused friend and neighbor to shun me;
my companions are in darkness.

PSALM 89
God's Covenant with David

A Maskil of Ethan the Ezrahite.

1 I will sing of your steadfast love, O LORD,[a] forever;
with my mouth I will proclaim your faithfulness to all
generations.
2 I declare that your steadfast love is established forever;
your faithfulness is as firm as the heavens.

3 You said, "I have made a covenant with my chosen one,
I have sworn to my servant David:
4 'I will establish your descendants forever,
and build your throne for all generations.'" *Selah*

5 Let the heavens praise your wonders, O LORD,
your faithfulness in the assembly of the holy ones.
6 For who in the skies can be compared to the LORD?
Who among the heavenly beings is like the LORD,
7 a God feared in the council of the holy ones,
great and awesome[b] above all that are around him?
8 O LORD God of hosts,
who is as mighty as you, O LORD?
Your faithfulness surrounds you.
9 You rule the raging of the sea;
when its waves rise, you still them.
10 You crushed Rahab like a carcass;
you scattered your enemies with your mighty arm.
11 The heavens are yours, the earth also is yours;
the world and all that is in it—you have founded them.
12 The north and the south[c]—you created them;
Tabor and Hermon joyously praise your name.
13 You have a mighty arm;
strong is your hand, high your right hand.
14 Righteousness and justice are the foundation of your throne;
steadfast love and faithfulness go before you.
15 Happy are the people who know the festal shout,
who walk, O LORD, in the light of your countenance;
16 they exult in your name all day long,
and extol[d] your righteousness.

Psalm 89: A royal psalm that begins as a hymn of praise in verses 1-37 and changes into a prayer for help in verses 38-51 (see Types of Psalms, pp. 849-850). Regarding the king, see note on 45:1. The psalm complains about the fall of the line of David as kings. Some scholars believe it was placed at the end of the Book III in Psalms to signal that the rule by kings was a failure, but God would remain faithful to Israel.

89:1-4 I will sing of your steadfast love, O LORD, forever . . . I have sworn to my servant David: "I will establish your descendants forever": The song emphasizes the word "forever." The psalmist sings forever because of God's promise to King David that one of his descendants would forever rule over God's people (see 2 Sam 7:1-17).

89:5-18 Let the heavens praise your wonders. . . . Righteousness and justice are the foundation of your throne: God has established the universe by creating the world and ordering the powers of chaos. The earthly rule of Israel's king is based on the rule of God as king of all creation.

---

[a] Gk: Heb *the steadfast love of the LORD* [b] Gk Syr: Heb *greatly awesome* [c] Or *Zaphon and Yamin*
[d] Cn: Heb *are exalted in*

[17] For you are the glory of their strength;
by your favor our horn is exalted.
[18] For our shield belongs to the LORD,
our king to the Holy One of Israel.

[19] Then you spoke in a vision to your faithful one, and said:
"I have set the crown[a] on one who is mighty,
I have exalted one chosen from the people.
[20] I have found my servant David;
with my holy oil I have anointed him;
[21] my hand shall always remain with him;
my arm also shall strengthen him.
[22] The enemy shall not outwit him,
the wicked shall not humble him.
[23] I will crush his foes before him
and strike down those who hate him.
[24] My faithfulness and steadfast love shall be with him;
and in my name his horn shall be exalted.
[25] I will set his hand on the sea
and his right hand on the rivers.
[26] He shall cry to me, 'You are my Father,
my God, and the Rock of my salvation!'
[27] I will make him the firstborn,
the highest of the kings of the earth.
[28] Forever I will keep my steadfast love for him,
and my covenant with him will stand firm.
[29] I will establish his line forever,
and his throne as long as the heavens endure.
[30] If his children forsake my law
and do not walk according to my ordinances,
[31] if they violate my statutes
and do not keep my commandments,
[32] then I will punish their transgression with the rod
and their iniquity with scourges;
[33] but I will not remove from him my steadfast love,
or be false to my faithfulness.
[34] I will not violate my covenant,
or alter the word that went forth from my lips.
[35] Once and for all I have sworn by my holiness;
I will not lie to David.
[36] His line shall continue forever,
and his throne endure before me like the sun.
[37] It shall be established forever like the moon,
an enduring witness in the skies." *Selah*

89:19-37 "I have found my servant David…I will establish his line forever: The song praises God's promise to secure the line of David forever. If the kings broke God's law, they would be disciplined (89:31-32) but would not be permanently rejected (89:33-34).

[a] Cn: Heb *help*

89:38-45 You have renounced the covenant with your servant: This may be the most direct complaint in all of the psalms. In verse 33, God promises never to violate the promise, but here the psalmist says that is exactly what God has done. This raises the psalm's basic question: Is God faithful to God's promises?

38 But now you have spurned and rejected him;
you are full of wrath against your anointed.
39 You have renounced the covenant with your servant;
you have defiled his crown in the dust.
40 You have broken through all his walls;
you have laid his strongholds in ruins.
41 All who pass by plunder him;
he has become the scorn of his neighbors.
42 You have exalted the right hand of his foes;
you have made all his enemies rejoice.
43 Moreover, you have turned back the edge of his sword,
and you have not supported him in battle.
44 You have removed the scepter from his hand,[a]
and hurled his throne to the ground.
45 You have cut short the days of his youth;
you have covered him with shame. *Selah*

46 How long, O LORD? Will you hide yourself forever?
How long will your wrath burn like fire?
47 Remember how short my time is—[b]
for what vanity you have created all mortals!
48 Who can live and never see death?
Who can escape the power of Sheol? *Selah*

89:47-51 Remember, O LORD, how your servant is taunted: These words are either the request of the king to be restored or of an individual speaking on behalf of the king. The final answer to human suffering will come from God. The psalmist hopes God will remember that humans cannot save themselves and, as a result, remember to keep God's promises.

49 Lord, where is your steadfast love of old,
which by your faithfulness you swore to David?
50 Remember, O Lord, how your servant is taunted;
how I bear in my bosom the insults of the peoples,[c]
51 with which your enemies taunt, O LORD,
with which they taunted the footsteps of your anointed.

89:52 Blessed be the LORD: This verse was not originally part of Psalm 89. It is a song of praise or doxology that concludes Book III of the Psalms.

52 Blessed be the LORD forever.
Amen and Amen.

BOOK IV

(Psalms 90–106)

PSALM 90

God's Eternity and Human Frailty

A Prayer of Moses, the man of God.

Psalm 90: A prayer for help and instructional psalm (see Types of Psalms, pp. 849-850). The poem contrasts the eternity of God with the shortness of human life.

90:1-2 LORD, you have been our dwelling place in all generations…from everlasting to everlasting you are God: The image of God as the eternal home of Israel emphasizes God's hospitality and immortality.

1 Lord, you have been our dwelling place[d]
in all generations.

[a] Cn: Heb *removed his cleanness* [b] Meaning of Heb uncertain [c] Cn: Heb *bosom all of many peoples*
[d] Another reading is *our refuge*

2 Before the mountains were brought forth,
or ever you had formed the earth and the world,
from everlasting to everlasting you are God.

3 You turn us[a] back to dust,
and say, "Turn back, you mortals."
4 For a thousand years in your sight
are like yesterday when it is past,
or like a watch in the night.

5 You sweep them away; they are like a dream,
like grass that is renewed in the morning;
6 in the morning it flourishes and is renewed;
in the evening it fades and withers.

7 For we are consumed by your anger;
by your wrath we are overwhelmed.
8 You have set our iniquities before you,
our secret sins in the light of your countenance.

9 For all our days pass away under your wrath;
our years come to an end[b] like a sigh.
10 The days of our life are seventy years,
or perhaps eighty, if we are strong;
even then their span[c] is only toil and trouble;
they are soon gone, and we fly away.

11 Who considers the power of your anger?
Your wrath is as great as the fear that is due you.
12 So teach us to count our days
that we may gain a wise heart.

13 Turn, O Lord! How long?
Have compassion on your servants!
14 Satisfy us in the morning with your steadfast love,
so that we may rejoice and be glad all our days.
15 Make us glad as many days as you have afflicted us,
and as many years as we have seen evil.
16 Let your work be manifest to your servants,
and your glorious power to their children.
17 Let the favor of the Lord our God be upon us,
and prosper for us the work of our hands—
O prosper the work of our hands!

---

[a] Heb *humankind* [b] Syr: Heb *we bring our years to an end* [c] Cn Compare Gk Syr Jerome Tg: Heb *pride*

90:3-10 our years come to an end: Using words related to time—years, yesterday, morning, evening, days—the prayer complains and teaches about the shortness of human life. The statement that "we are consumed by your anger" may reflect the teaching that death is a judgment for sin (see Rom 6:23).

90:12 So teach us to count our days that we may gain a wise heart: In light of the shortness of human life, the psalmist asks God to grant a "wise heart." The phrase occurs in the Bible only here, but it seems to mean the wisdom to see what God is up to in the world and to find a place in God's story.

90:17 prosper for us the work of our hands: The prayer ends by holding up the value of daily work. Our daily work—no matter what it is—is important to God.

What is the Lutheran understanding of vocation? Every baptized person has a vocation or special calling to serve God and neighbor. Any job or career is holy when a Christian carries it out as part of this calling. The daily work of vocation can happen in a workplace, but it can happen in the home, school, church, community, and world as well. Vocation can include being a father, mother, sister, brother, friend, student, co-worker, boss, and so on. *Psalm 90:17*

The psalmist prays about daily work. What joys and concerns from your daily work (whatever it may be) could you include in your prayers?

PSALM 91

Assurance of God's Protection

Psalm 91: A liturgy (see Types of Psalms, pp. 849-850), with strong teaching elements. This psalm also reflects on the image of God as refuge.

91:1 You who live in the shelter of the Most High, who abide in the shadow of the Almighty: See note on 57:1.

91:2 say to the LORD, "My refuge . . . in whom I trust": The liturgy instructs us to say these words as a way of entering into God's protective care. See Bible Concepts note on refuge at 2:11.

91:3-13 Because you have made the LORD your refuge . . . no evil shall befall you: Using various images, the psalmist offers more reasons why a person can trust in God's protection. These poetic images should not be used to suggest that believers will not face the consequences of risky actions, or that Christians are immune from all evil.

What image for God's love and care speaks most powerfully to you?

91:14-16 Those who love me, I will deliver . . . and show them my salvation: In these final verses, God speaks words of promise. In the liturgy, these words were most likely spoken by a priest.

1 You who live in the shelter of the Most High,
who abide in the shadow of the Almighty,[a]
2 will say to the LORD, "My refuge and my fortress;
my God, in whom I trust."
3 For he will deliver you from the snare of the fowler
and from the deadly pestilence;
4 he will cover you with his pinions,
and under his wings you will find refuge;
his faithfulness is a shield and buckler.
5 You will not fear the terror of the night,
or the arrow that flies by day,
6 or the pestilence that stalks in darkness,
or the destruction that wastes at noonday.

7 A thousand may fall at your side,
ten thousand at your right hand,
but it will not come near you.
8 You will only look with your eyes
and see the punishment of the wicked.

9 Because you have made the LORD your refuge,[b]
the Most High your dwelling place,
10 no evil shall befall you,
no scourge come near your tent.

11 For he will command his angels concerning you
to guard you in all your ways.
12 On their hands they will bear you up,
so that you will not dash your foot against a stone.
13 You will tread on the lion and the adder,
the young lion and the serpent you will trample under foot.

14 Those who love me, I will deliver;
I will protect those who know my name.
15 When they call to me, I will answer them;
I will be with them in trouble,
I will rescue them and honor them.
16 With long life I will satisfy them,
and show them my salvation.

---

[a] Traditional rendering of Heb *Shaddai* [b] Cn: Heb *Because you, LORD, are my refuge; you have made*

PSALM 92
Thanksgiving for Vindication
A Psalm. A Song for the Sabbath Day.

1 It is good to give thanks to the LORD,
to sing praises to your name, O Most High;
2 to declare your steadfast love in the morning,
and your faithfulness by night,
3 to the music of the lute and the harp,
to the melody of the lyre.
4 For you, O LORD, have made me glad by your work;
at the works of your hands I sing for joy.

5 How great are your works, O LORD!
Your thoughts are very deep!
6 The dullard cannot know,
the stupid cannot understand this:
7 though the wicked sprout like grass
and all evildoers flourish,
they are doomed to destruction forever,
8 but you, O LORD, are on high forever.
9 For your enemies, O LORD,
for your enemies shall perish;
all evildoers shall be scattered.

10 But you have exalted my horn like that of the wild ox;
you have poured over me[a] fresh oil.
11 My eyes have seen the downfall of my enemies;
my ears have heard the doom of my evil assailants.

12 The righteous flourish like the palm tree,
and grow like a cedar in Lebanon.
13 They are planted in the house of the LORD;
they flourish in the courts of our God.
14 In old age they still produce fruit;
they are always green and full of sap,
15 showing that the LORD is upright;
he is my rock, and there is no unrighteousness in him.

PSALM 93
The Majesty of God's Rule

1 The LORD is king, he is robed in majesty;
the LORD is robed, he is girded with strength.
He has established the world; it shall never be moved;

[a] Syr: Meaning of Heb uncertain

Psalm 92: A song of thanksgiving (see Types of Psalms, pp. 849-850) by a person God has rescued from a crisis. This song also has strong instructional elements.

92:1-4 It is good to give thanks to the LORD: The song opens with a call to praise God in the morning and the evening. Praise is not just for worship. Our entire lives should be lived in praise. The works of God's hands are everything from creation (see Psalm 8) to guidance through life (see Psalm 139).

92:5-9 Your thoughts are very deep!: Those who ignore God's will often seem to succeed and prosper quickly, but it is better to live for the long run, trusting that God is good and God's ways are best.

92:10 you have exalted my horn…you have poured over me fresh oil: In the ancient world these were images of honor (see note on 6:10). God will grant honor to those the world often puts to shame—those who are poor, oppressed, and mocked.

92:14-15 In old age they still produce fruit: The image of a tree that still gives fruit in old age fits those who follow God's ways. They do not live for the short term, but trust in God for the long run.

Name someone you know who has trusted in God for the long run. What can you learn from this person?

What makes a person righteous in God's sight? If we are left to ourselves, we are not righteous, or made right with God. Righteousness is not something inside of us, but something that God does for us. God gives us Christ's righteousness, and that makes us righteous. *Psalm 92:12-15*

Psalm 93: A hymn of praise that is also an enthronement psalm (see Types of Psalms, pp. 849-850).

93:1 The LORD is king: This declaration of faith, similar to the Easter announcement that "Christ is risen," announces that God's kingship was established long ago and also that God is at work right now, constantly reestablishing God's gracious rule. God does not rule like human kings, who use power and glorify themselves in ways we can see. God is a king who suffers on a cross, whose rule is hidden from our sight.

93:2-5 you are from everlasting. . . Your decrees are very sure: Because God always was and always will be, God's instruction and laws are trustworthy.

Psalm 94: A prayer for help (see Types of Psalms, pp. 849-850) from a person oppressed by enemies. It also offers instruction.

94:1 God of vengeance: Some people having mistakenly said that the Old Testament describes a God of vengeance and the New Testament a God of love. The God of both Testaments is the same God, who loves all of creation. This God sometimes gets angry with those who cause the suffering of others. Individuals, however, should leave revenge to God (see Rom 12:14-21).

94:7-11 The LORD knows our thoughts: The wicked ignore God's will because they believe God does not know and cannot do anything about evil deeds. This prayer, however, states that God knows, cares, and will do something about evil actions.

94:12 Happy are those whom you discipline, O LORD: Few people enjoy being disciplined, but discipline from God is in our long-term best interests.

2 your throne is established from of old;
you are from everlasting.

3 The floods have lifted up, O LORD,
the floods have lifted up their voice;
the floods lift up their roaring.
4 More majestic than the thunders of mighty waters,
more majestic than the waves[a] of the sea,
majestic on high is the LORD!

5 Your decrees are very sure;
holiness befits your house,
O LORD, forevermore.

PSALM 94

God the Avenger of the Righteous

1 O LORD, you God of vengeance,
you God of vengeance, shine forth!
2 Rise up, O judge of the earth;
give to the proud what they deserve!
3 O LORD, how long shall the wicked,
how long shall the wicked exult?

4 They pour out their arrogant words;
all the evildoers boast.
5 They crush your people, O LORD,
and afflict your heritage.
6 They kill the widow and the stranger,
they murder the orphan,
7 and they say, "The LORD does not see;
the God of Jacob does not perceive."

8 Understand, O dullest of the people;
fools, when will you be wise?
9 He who planted the ear, does he not hear?
He who formed the eye, does he not see?
10 He who disciplines the nations,
he who teaches knowledge to humankind,
does he not chastise?
11 The LORD knows our thoughts,[b]
that they are but an empty breath.

12 Happy are those whom you discipline, O LORD,
and whom you teach out of your law,

[a] Cn: Heb *majestic are the waves* [b] Heb *the thoughts of humankind*

13 giving them respite from days of trouble,
until a pit is dug for the wicked.
14 For the LORD will not forsake his people;
he will not abandon his heritage;
15 for justice will return to the righteous,
and all the upright in heart will follow it.

16 Who rises up for me against the wicked?
Who stands up for me against evildoers?
17 If the LORD had not been my help,
my soul would soon have lived in the land of silence.
18 When I thought, "My foot is slipping,"
your steadfast love, O LORD, held me up.
19 When the cares of my heart are many,
your consolations cheer my soul.
20 Can wicked rulers be allied with you,
those who contrive mischief by statute?
21 They band together against the life of the righteous,
and condemn the innocent to death.
22 But the LORD has become my stronghold,
and my God the rock of my refuge.
23 He will repay them for their iniquity
and wipe them out for their wickedness;
the LORD our God will wipe them out.

PSALM 95

A Call to Worship and Obedience

1 O come, let us sing to the LORD;
let us make a joyful noise to the rock of our salvation!
2 Let us come into his presence with thanksgiving;
let us make a joyful noise to him with songs of praise!
3 For the LORD is a great God,
and a great King above all gods.
4 In his hand are the depths of the earth;
the heights of the mountains are his also.
5 The sea is his, for he made it,
and the dry land, which his hands have formed.

6 O come, let us worship and bow down,
let us kneel before the LORD, our Maker!
7 For he is our God,
and we are the people of his pasture,
and the sheep of his hand.

O that today you would listen to his voice!
8 Do not harden your hearts, as at Meribah,

94:14 the LORD will not forsake his people: This is the psalm's central confession or declaration of trust—that God will be faithful.

94:17-19 When the cares of my heart are many, your consolations cheer my soul: Just as God has provided help in the past, the psalmist trusts that God will do so again. In moments of despair, the "consolations" that God has provided in the past can provide encouragement and renewed hope.

Psalm 95: An enthronement psalm, a liturgy, and a festival psalm (see Types of Psalms, pp. 849-850), probably composed for one of Israel's three annual festivals (see also Pss 50, 81).

95:1-5 The sea is his, for he made it: God's rule over the universe was established in creation. God constantly renews and refreshes creation, thus maintaining God's rule. See note on king at 93:1.

95:7 he is our God, and we are the people of his pasture: God's rule is not just based on God's power, but on God's faithful care for the people.

95:7-11 O that today you would listen: We are warned not to test God or stubbornly refuse God's will. Even when God disciplines (see 94:12) a person or even a whole generation, however, God still remains faithful.

as on the day at Massah in the wilderness,
9 when your ancestors tested me,
and put me to the proof, though they had seen my work.
10 For forty years I loathed that generation
and said, "They are a people whose hearts go astray,
and they do not regard my ways."
11 Therefore in my anger I swore,
"They shall not enter my rest."

PSALM 96

Praise to God Who Comes in Judgment

Psalm 96: A hymn of praise that is also an enthronement psalm (see Types of Psalms, pp. 849-850).

1 O sing to the LORD a new song;
sing to the LORD, all the earth.
2 Sing to the LORD, bless his name;
tell of his salvation from day to day.
3 Declare his glory among the nations,
his marvelous works among all the peoples.
4 For great is the LORD, and greatly to be praised;
he is to be revered above all gods.
5 For all the gods of the peoples are idols,
but the LORD made the heavens.
6 Honor and majesty are before him;
strength and beauty are in his sanctuary.

96:1-9 O sing to the LORD...tell of his salvation from day to day: We do not praise God because God needs our praise or to flatter God, but to "tell of his salvation." We spread the good news about what God has done, how God is "for us" no matter what (see Rom 8:38-39), and what God has promised. Praise is how we come into God's presence (see 95:2). Praise says, "God is good! I am going to live in God's goodness."

What is your favorite Christian hymn or song? What does it say about God? What good news does it teach?

7 Ascribe to the LORD, O families of the peoples,
ascribe to the LORD glory and strength.
8 Ascribe to the LORD the glory due his name;
bring an offering, and come into his courts.
9 Worship the LORD in holy splendor;
tremble before him, all the earth.

96:10 Say among the nations, "The LORD is king!" See note on 93:1.

10 Say among the nations, "The LORD is king!
The world is firmly established; it shall never be moved.
He will judge the peoples with equity."
11 Let the heavens be glad, and let the earth rejoice;
let the sea roar, and all that fills it;
12 let the field exult, and everything in it.
Then shall all the trees of the forest sing for joy
13 before the LORD; for he is coming,
for he is coming to judge the earth.
He will judge the world with righteousness,
and the peoples with his truth.

96:13 he is coming to judge the earth: God enters into history to save the oppressed, rescue the downtrodden, and forgive sinners.

PSALM 97

The Glory of God's Reign

1 The LORD is king! Let the earth rejoice;
let the many coastlands be glad!
2 Clouds and thick darkness are all around him;
righteousness and justice are the foundation of his throne.
3 Fire goes before him,
and consumes his adversaries on every side.
4 His lightnings light up the world;
the earth sees and trembles.
5 The mountains melt like wax before the LORD,
before the Lord of all the earth.

6 The heavens proclaim his righteousness;
and all the peoples behold his glory.
7 All worshipers of images are put to shame,
those who make their boast in worthless idols;
all gods bow down before him.
8 Zion hears and is glad,
and the towns[a] of Judah rejoice,
because of your judgments, O God.
9 For you, O LORD, are most high over all the earth;
you are exalted far above all gods.

10 The LORD loves those who hate[b] evil;
he guards the lives of his faithful;
he rescues them from the hand of the wicked.
11 Light dawns[c] for the righteous,
and joy for the upright in heart.
12 Rejoice in the LORD, O you righteous,
and give thanks to his holy name!

Psalm 97: A hymn of praise that is also an enthronement psalm (see Types of Psalms, pp. 849-850).

97:1 The LORD is king!: See note on 93:1.

97:1-5 Clouds and thick darkness are all around him...The mountains melt like wax before the LORD: God is depicted as coming to the people in a thunderstorm, showing that the LORD's presence is as mysterious, invisible, and unsettling as a storm. God's presence amazes us and puts earthly powers in their place.

97:6-7 The heavens proclaim his righteousness: "The heavens" refer to the skies, in which the storm thunders and flashes in testimony to the power of the creator, and also the heavenly kingdom, in which God lives and rules. Other things that we worship—such as money, power, career—exist only on earth and cannot save us.

97:8 Zion hears and is glad: Zion is the city of God, referring to Jerusalem. It hears the thunderstorm, but more importantly, it hears the message that God is king—and it rejoices in that good news.

97:11 Light dawns for the righteous, and joy for the upright in heart: God's presence is as real as light that comes after a storm.

PSALM 98

Praise the Judge of the World

A Psalm.

1 O sing to the LORD a new song,
for he has done marvelous things.
His right hand and his holy arm
have gotten him victory.
2 The LORD has made known his victory;
he has revealed his vindication in the sight of the nations.
3 He has remembered his steadfast love and faithfulness
to the house of Israel.

Psalm 98: A hymn of praise (see Types of Psalms, pp. 849-850) in three stanzas (98:1-3, 4-6, 7-9).

98:1-3 O sing to the LORD a new song: The hymn starts with a call to praise. See note on "new song" at 40:1-3. By delivering Israel from some national crisis, God's character has been revealed as "steadfast love and faithfulness."

---

[a] Heb *daughters* [b] Cn: Heb *You who love the LORD hate* [c] Gk Syr Jerome: Heb *is sown*

All the ends of the earth have seen
the victory of our God.

98:4-6 Make a joyful noise to the LORD, all the earth: The call for "all the earth" to praise God means that *all people* are invited to join in telling the good news of what God has done.

4 Make a joyful noise to the LORD, all the earth;
break forth into joyous song and sing praises.
5 Sing praises to the LORD with the lyre,
with the lyre and the sound of melody.
6 With trumpets and the sound of the horn
make a joyful noise before the King, the LORD.

98:7-9 Let the sea roar…for he is coming to judge the earth: The sea and the floods symbolize the forces of chaos that resist God's will. Here the psalmist calls even on these forces to praise the LORD and acknowledge God's gracious kingship.

7 Let the sea roar, and all that fills it;
the world and those who live in it.
8 Let the floods clap their hands;
let the hills sing together for joy
9 at the presence of the LORD, for he is coming
to judge the earth.
He will judge the world with righteousness,
and the peoples with equity.

PSALM 99

Praise to God for His Holiness

Psalm 99: A hymn of praise that is also an enthronement psalm (see Types of Psalms, pp. 849-850).

99:1 The LORD is king: See note on 93:1.

1 The LORD is king; let the peoples tremble!
He sits enthroned upon the cherubim; let the earth quake!
2 The LORD is great in Zion;
he is exalted over all the peoples.
3 Let them praise your great and awesome name.
Holy is he!
4 Mighty King,[a] lover of justice,
you have established equity;
you have executed justice
and righteousness in Jacob.
5 Extol the LORD our God;
worship at his footstool.
Holy is he!

99:4 Mighty King, lover of justice, you have established equity: God's kingship is not based just in God's power, but by what God does with power. God establishes justice, fairness, and righteousness among God's people ("in Jacob") and God's mission is to spread this throughout the world.

6 Moses and Aaron were among his priests,
Samuel also was among those who called on his name.
They cried to the LORD, and he answered them.
7 He spoke to them in the pillar of cloud;
they kept his decrees,
and the statutes that he gave them.

99:6-8 They cried to the LORD, and he answered them: The relationship between God and God's people is one of faithfulness. God proves faithful to us by actions such as answering our cries, giving us laws to live by, and forgiving us. We are asked to be faithful by praying and keeping the law.

8 O LORD our God, you answered them;
you were a forgiving God to them,

[a] Cn: Heb *And a king's strength*

but an avenger of their wrongdoings.
9 Extol the LORD our God,
and worship at his holy mountain;
for the LORD our God is holy.

PSALM 100
All Lands Summoned to Praise God

A Psalm of thanksgiving.

1 Make a joyful noise to the LORD, all the earth.
2 Worship the LORD with gladness;
come into his presence with singing.

3 Know that the LORD is God.
It is he that made us, and we are his;[a]
we are his people, and the sheep of his pasture.

4 Enter his gates with thanksgiving,
and his courts with praise.
Give thanks to him, bless his name.

5 For the LORD is good;
his steadfast love endures forever,
and his faithfulness to all generations.

PSALM 101
A Sovereign's Pledge of Integrity and Justice

Of David. A Psalm.

1 I will sing of loyalty and of justice;
to you, O LORD, I will sing.
2 I will study the way that is blameless.
When shall I attain it?

I will walk with integrity of heart
within my house;
3 I will not set before my eyes
anything that is base.

I hate the work of those who fall away;
it shall not cling to me.
4 Perverseness of heart shall be far from me;
I will know nothing of evil.

---

[a] Another reading is *and not we ourselves*

Psalm 100: A hymn of praise (see Types of Psalms, pp. 849-850).

100:1 Make a joyful noise to the LORD: On praise, see note on 96:1-9. Praise is to be joyful and filled with gladness, because it is a response to what God has done for us.

100:3 Know that the LORD is God: To "know" God goes beyond what we can know with our minds. It also means to obey and follow (see Hos 4:1-4). To "know" God is to internalize in your whole body that God is your LORD.

What has happened in your life to help you want to *know* God, and not just know some things *about* God?

100:4 gates...courts: The temple buildings; see note on 84:1.

Psalm 101: A royal psalm (see Types of Psalms, pp. 849-850), in which the king makes a commitment to rule with justice.

101:1-7 I will sing of loyalty and of justice: The singer is apparently the king, because he commits himself to actions that fit best with a king of Israel. Israel's kings failed to live up to the ideals expressed in this song, but the poem was preserved as a promise of the ideal king that God would send—Jesus the Christ.

5 One who secretly slanders a neighbor
I will destroy.
A haughty look and an arrogant heart
I will not tolerate.

6 I will look with favor on the faithful in the land,
so that they may live with me;
whoever walks in the way that is blameless
shall minister to me.

7 No one who practices deceit
shall remain in my house;
no one who utters lies
shall continue in my presence.

8 Morning by morning I will destroy
all the wicked in the land,
cutting off all evildoers
from the city of the LORD.

101:8 the city of the LORD: God chose Jerusalem as God's dwelling place and promised to protect it. In response to this protection, God expected justice and righteousness from the people of the city.

PSALM 102

Prayer to the Eternal King for Help

A prayer of one afflicted, when faint and pleading before the LORD.

1 Hear my prayer, O LORD;
let my cry come to you.
2 Do not hide your face from me
in the day of my distress.
Incline your ear to me;
answer me speedily in the day when I call.

3 For my days pass away like smoke,
and my bones burn like a furnace.
4 My heart is stricken and withered like grass;
I am too wasted to eat my bread.
5 Because of my loud groaning
my bones cling to my skin.
6 I am like an owl of the wilderness,
like a little owl of the waste places.
7 I lie awake;
I am like a lonely bird on the housetop.
8 All day long my enemies taunt me;
those who deride me use my name for a curse.
9 For I eat ashes like bread,
and mingle tears with my drink,
10 because of your indignation and anger;

Psalm 102: A prayer for help and a penitential psalm (see Types of Psalms, pp. 849-850).

A prayer of one afflicted, when faint and pleading before the LORD: This superscription (see introduction) was not an original part of the psalm, but was added for later readers. It signals that this—and all the psalms—are available for others to pray in similar situations.

102:3 For my days pass away: The prayer contrasts "my days" (102:3, 11, 23, 24; "my life" in 102:24 is "my days" in Hebrew) with "you whose years" and "your years" (102:24, 27). In light of how short human life is, relying on the eternal God is a wise course (see 102:26-27).

102:6-7 I am like an owl…I lie awake; I am like a lonely bird on the housetop: This is a touching image of isolation. The psalmist prays at night, but feels as lonely as an owl hooting in the desert.

When you have been at your loneliest and lowest points, what thoughts and memories comforted you?

for you have lifted me up and thrown me aside.
11 My days are like an evening shadow;
I wither away like grass.

12 But you, O Lord, are enthroned forever;
your name endures to all generations.
13 You will rise up and have compassion on Zion,
for it is time to favor it;
the appointed time has come.
14 For your servants hold its stones dear,
and have pity on its dust.
15 The nations will fear the name of the Lord,
and all the kings of the earth your glory.
16 For the Lord will build up Zion;
he will appear in his glory.
17 He will regard the prayer of the destitute,
and will not despise their prayer.

18 Let this be recorded for a generation to come,
so that a people yet unborn may praise the Lord:
19 that he looked down from his holy height,
from heaven the Lord looked at the earth,
20 to hear the groans of the prisoners,
to set free those who were doomed to die;
21 so that the name of the Lord may be declared in Zion,
and his praise in Jerusalem,
22 when peoples gather together,
and kingdoms, to worship the Lord.

23 He has broken my strength in midcourse;
he has shortened my days.
24 "O my God," I say, "do not take me away
at the midpoint of my life,
you whose years endure
throughout all generations."

25 Long ago you laid the foundation of the earth,
and the heavens are the work of your hands.
26 They will perish, but you endure;
they will all wear out like a garment.
You change them like clothing, and they pass away;
27 but you are the same, and your years have no end.
28 The children of your servants shall live secure;
their offspring shall be established in your
presence.

102:17 He will regard the prayer of the destitute: The psalmist is convinced that God will hear and answer the prayers of the needy.

102:18-22 Let this be recorded for a generation to come: Even amid great suffering, the psalmist left these words of testimony so that in the future people might know of God's goodness.

Psalm 103: A hymn of praise (see Types of Psalms, pp. 849-850) that focuses on God's acts of deliverance.

103:1-5 soul: See note on 42:5. Here, the psalmist says, "Come on, self, praise God for what God has done for you: God forgives, heals, rescues, satisfies, and renews!"

103:6-19 The LORD works vindication and justice for all who are oppressed: The psalmist praises God so that other people will know God's benefits: God rescues the oppressed, gives the law, shows compassion, is gracious, and forgives.

103:8-10 The LORD is merciful and gracious, slow to anger: These verses summarize who God is for us.

PSALM 103

Thanksgiving for God's Goodness

Of David.

1 Bless the LORD, O my soul,
and all that is within me,
bless his holy name.
2 Bless the LORD, O my soul,
and do not forget all his benefits—
3 who forgives all your iniquity,
who heals all your diseases,
4 who redeems your life from the Pit,
who crowns you with steadfast love and mercy,
5 who satisfies you with good as long as you live[a]
so that your youth is renewed like the eagle's.

6 The LORD works vindication
and justice for all who are oppressed.
7 He made known his ways to Moses,
his acts to the people of Israel.
8 The LORD is merciful and gracious,
slow to anger and abounding in steadfast love.
9 He will not always accuse,
nor will he keep his anger forever.
10 He does not deal with us according to our sins,
nor repay us according to our iniquities.
11 For as the heavens are high above the earth,
so great is his steadfast love toward those who fear him;
12 as far as the east is from the west,
so far he removes our transgressions from us.
13 As a father has compassion for his children,
so the LORD has compassion for those who fear him.
14 For he knows how we were made;
he remembers that we are dust.

15 As for mortals, their days are like grass;
they flourish like a flower of the field;
16 for the wind passes over it, and it is gone,
and its place knows it no more.
17 But the steadfast love of the LORD is from everlasting to everlasting
on those who fear him,
and his righteousness to children's children,
18 to those who keep his covenant
and remember to do his commandments.

---

[a] Meaning of Heb uncertain

19 The LORD has established his throne in the heavens,
and his kingdom rules over all.
20 Bless the LORD, O you his angels,
you mighty ones who do his bidding,
obedient to his spoken word.
21 Bless the LORD, all his hosts,
his ministers that do his will.
22 Bless the LORD, all his works,
in all places of his dominion.
Bless the LORD, O my soul.

PSALM 104
God the Creator and Provider

1 Bless the LORD, O my soul.
O LORD my God, you are very great.
You are clothed with honor and majesty,
2 wrapped in light as with a garment.
You stretch out the heavens like a tent,
3 you set the beams of your[a] chambers on the waters,
you make the clouds your[a] chariot,
you ride on the wings of the wind,
4 you make the winds your[a] messengers,
fire and flame your[a] ministers.

5 You set the earth on its foundations,
so that it shall never be shaken.
6 You cover it with the deep as with a garment;
the waters stood above the mountains.
7 At your rebuke they flee;
at the sound of your thunder they take to flight.
8 They rose up to the mountains, ran down to the valleys
to the place that you appointed for them.
9 You set a boundary that they may not pass,
so that they might not again cover the earth.

10 You make springs gush forth in the valleys;
they flow between the hills,
11 giving drink to every wild animal;
the wild asses quench their thirst.
12 By the streams[b] the birds of the air have their habitation;
they sing among the branches.
13 From your lofty abode you water the mountains;
the earth is satisfied with the fruit of your work.

Psalm 104: A hymn of praise and creation psalm (see Types of Psalms, pp. 849-850).

104:1 Bless the LORD, O my soul: See note on 42:5.

104:1-35 O LORD my God, you are very great: God's creating activity plays a key role throughout the psalms. God's kingship is based in God's work of creation. Similarly, God's lordship over the community of Israel and individuals of faith is based in part on God's providing through creation.

104:2-4 You stretch out the heavens: The psalm follows an order for creation similar to Genesis 1. First, God creates the heavens (see Gen 1:1-5).

104:5-9 You set the earth on its foundations...You cover it with the deep: After creating the heavens, God creates the earth and the sea (see Gen 1:6-10).

104:10-22: You make springs gush forth...giving drink to every wild animal: After creating the earth, God creates plants and animals and the means to sustain them (see Gen 1:11-12, 20-25).

[a] Heb *his* [b] Heb *By them*

14 You cause the grass to grow for the cattle,
and plants for people to use,[a]
to bring forth food from the earth,
15 and wine to gladden the human heart,
oil to make the face shine,
and bread to strengthen the human heart.
16 The trees of the LORD are watered abundantly,
the cedars of Lebanon that he planted.
17 In them the birds build their nests;
the stork has its home in the fir trees.
18 The high mountains are for the wild goats;
the rocks are a refuge for the coneys.
19 You have made the moon to mark the seasons;
the sun knows its time for setting.
20 You make darkness, and it is night,
when all the animals of the forest come creeping out.
21 The young lions roar for their prey,
seeking their food from God.
22 When the sun rises, they withdraw
and lie down in their dens.
23 People go out to their work
and to their labor until the evening.

24 O LORD, how manifold are your works!
In wisdom you have made them all;
the earth is full of your creatures.
25 Yonder is the sea, great and wide,
creeping things innumerable are there,
living things both small and great.
26 There go the ships,
and Leviathan that you formed to sport in it.

27 These all look to you
to give them their food in due season;
28 when you give to them, they gather it up;
when you open your hand, they are filled with good things.
29 When you hide your face, they are dismayed;
when you take away their breath, they die
and return to their dust.
30 When you send forth your spirit,[b] they are created;
and you renew the face of the ground.

31 May the glory of the LORD endure forever;
may the LORD rejoice in his works—

[a] Or *to cultivate* [b] Or *your breath*

104:23 People go out to their work and to their labor until the evening: Human beings are the crown of God's creation (see Gen 1:26-27; Ps 8). Work is a special aspect of human life, but there are rhythms to work—we rest at night and also on the Sabbath (see Gen 2:2-3).

104:24-26 In wisdom you have made them all: The world was formed by God through wisdom. To investigate God's creation using science is a part of the life of faith, because it is God's world.

104:26 Leviathan that you formed to sport in it: This can also be translated as "whom you made in order to laugh at it." God delights in creation. Laughter and joy are part of God's creative order.

32 who looks on the earth and it trembles,
who touches the mountains and they smoke.
33 I will sing to the LORD as long as I live;
I will sing praise to my God while I have being.
34 May my meditation be pleasing to him,
for I rejoice in the LORD.
35 Let sinners be consumed from the earth,
and let the wicked be no more.
Bless the LORD, O my soul.
Praise the LORD!

104:34 May my meditation be pleasing to him, for I rejoice in the LORD: Similar to the ending of Psalm 19, the psalmist dedicates this song of praise to God's glory.

PSALM 105
God's Faithfulness to Israel

1 O give thanks to the LORD, call on his name,
make known his deeds among the peoples.
2 Sing to him, sing praises to him;
tell of all his wonderful works.
3 Glory in his holy name;
let the hearts of those who seek the LORD rejoice.
4 Seek the LORD and his strength;
seek his presence continually.
5 Remember the wonderful works he has done,
his miracles, and the judgments he has uttered,
6 O offspring of his servant Abraham,[a]
children of Jacob, his chosen ones.

7 He is the LORD our God;
his judgments are in all the earth.
8 He is mindful of his covenant forever,
of the word that he commanded, for a thousand generations,
9 the covenant that he made with Abraham,
his sworn promise to Isaac,
10 which he confirmed to Jacob as a statute,
to Israel as an everlasting covenant,
11 saying, "To you I will give the land of Canaan
as your portion for an inheritance."

12 When they were few in number,
of little account, and strangers in it,
13 wandering from nation to nation,
from one kingdom to another people,
14 he allowed no one to oppress them;
he rebuked kings on their account,

Psalm 105: A historical psalm and hymn of praise (see Types of Psalms, pp. 849-850) that tells the story of God rescuing the Israelites from slavery in Egypt as the history of God keeping promises.

105:1 O give thanks to the LORD: The psalmist sings the history of God's actions on behalf of the people, combining praise with history.

105:4-5 Seek the LORD and his strength...Remember the wonderful works he has done: To seek God is to put God first in your life. Remembering what God has done in the past draws us closer to God and motivates us to seek God.

105:8 He is mindful of his covenant forever, of the word that he commanded, for a thousand generations: A *covenant* is an exchange of promises. Even though we are unable to be fully faithful to our promises, God's faithfulness is perfect and lasts forever. Verses 9-11 recall God's promises to Abraham (see Gen 12:1-3).

105:9 his sworn promise: God's promises are the key concept in this psalm. The Hebrew word translated as *promise* here occurs as "promise," "word," and "what he had said" in verses 8, 19, 28, and 42. The Bible teaches that one of the basic ways that God works is through promises—and promises can only be received by believing them. A promise depends on the character of the one making the promise. God's character is faithful, so God keeps promises.

[a] Another reading is *Israel* (compare 1 Chr 16.13)

[15] saying, "Do not touch my anointed ones;
do my prophets no harm."

[16] When he summoned famine against the land,
and broke every staff of bread,
[17] he had sent a man ahead of them,
Joseph, who was sold as a slave.
[18] His feet were hurt with fetters,
his neck was put in a collar of iron;
[19] until what he had said came to pass,
the word of the LORD kept testing him.
[20] The king sent and released him;
the ruler of the peoples set him free.
[21] He made him lord of his house,
and ruler of all his possessions,
[22] to instruct[a] his officials at his pleasure,
and to teach his elders wisdom.

[23] Then Israel came to Egypt;
Jacob lived as an alien in the land of Ham.
[24] And the LORD made his people very fruitful,
and made them stronger than their foes,
[25] whose hearts he then turned to hate his people,
to deal craftily with his servants.

105:26-39 He sent his servants Moses, and Aaron: God was faithful to the people when they suffered in slavery in Egypt. Working through humans and in other ways, God brought the people out of Egypt.

[26] He sent his servant Moses,
and Aaron whom he had chosen.
[27] They performed his signs among them,
and miracles in the land of Ham.
[28] He sent darkness, and made the land dark;
they rebelled[b] against his words.
[29] He turned their waters into blood,
and caused their fish to die.
[30] Their land swarmed with frogs,
even in the chambers of their kings.
[31] He spoke, and there came swarms of flies,
and gnats throughout their country.
[32] He gave them hail for rain,
and lightning that flashed through their land.
[33] He struck their vines and fig trees,
and shattered the trees of their country.
[34] He spoke, and the locusts came,
and young locusts without number;

---

[a] Gk Syr Jerome: Heb *to bind* [b] Cn Compare Gk Syr: Heb *they did not rebel*

35 they devoured all the vegetation in their land,
and ate up the fruit of their ground.
36 He struck down all the firstborn in their land,
the first issue of all their strength.

37 Then he brought Israel[a] out with silver and gold,
and there was no one among their tribes who stumbled.
38 Egypt was glad when they departed,
for dread of them had fallen upon it.
39 He spread a cloud for a covering,
and fire to give light by night.
40 They asked, and he brought quails,
and gave them food from heaven in abundance.
41 He opened the rock, and water gushed out;
it flowed through the desert like a river.
42 For he remembered his holy promise,
and Abraham, his servant.

43 So he brought his people out with joy,
his chosen ones with singing.
44 He gave them the lands of the nations,
and they took possession of the wealth of the peoples,
45 that they might keep his statutes
and observe his laws.
Praise the LORD!

PSALM 106
A Confession of Israel's Sins

1 Praise the LORD!
O give thanks to the LORD, for he is good;
for his steadfast love endures forever.
2 Who can utter the mighty doings of the LORD,
or declare all his praise?
3 Happy are those who observe justice,
who do righteousness at all times.

4 Remember me, O LORD, when you show favor to your people;
help me when you deliver them;
5 that I may see the prosperity of your chosen ones,
that I may rejoice in the gladness of your nation,
that I may glory in your heritage.

6 Both we and our ancestors have sinned;
we have committed iniquity, have done wickedly.

[a] Heb *them*

105:40-44 he brought quails, and gave them food: In the desert, God faithfully provided and brought the people through the dry lands into the promised land.

105:45 that they might keep his statutes and observe his laws: One of the ways God provides for us is by giving us laws to live by, such as the Ten Commandments. We love our neighbor by keeping God's commandments: not stealing, not killing, and so on. See notes on 1:2; 19:11-12.

Stories tell not just what happened to us, but reveal who we are. What story from your family or church family's life reveals something important about who you are?

Psalm 106: A historical psalm (see Types of Psalms, pp. 849-850) that tells Israel's story as the history of people rebelling against God.

106:1 O give thanks to the LORD: The psalmist sings the history of God's actions on behalf of the people, combining praise with history.

106:4 Remember me, O LORD: Although it begins with praise, this is also a prayer for help (see 106:4-5, 47). The emphasis on the people's constant sin and rebellion may have influenced the psalmist to ask for forgiveness and help.

106:6 Both we and our ancestors have sinned: The stories about the past are our stories. They tell us who we are. When this psalm tells the story about past sins, it is a reminder that we sin too. And as the people in the past needed God's forgiveness, so do we.

106:7-39 they did not remember…but rebelled: The long story of the people's sins against God reflects on the meaning of the First Commandment: You shall have no other gods. The psalm explores the many ways people disobeyed the commandment, but it also shows the way that rebellion gets worse and worse, until finally the people sacrificed children to the false gods they worshiped.

This psalm describes many ways in which people disobey the First Commandment. Which of these ways are most tempting for you?

7 Our ancestors, when they were in Egypt,
did not consider your wonderful works;
they did not remember the abundance of your steadfast love,
but rebelled against the Most High[a] at the Red Sea.[b]
8 Yet he saved them for his name's sake,
so that he might make known his mighty power.
9 He rebuked the Red Sea,[b] and it became dry;
he led them through the deep as through a desert.
10 So he saved them from the hand of the foe,
and delivered them from the hand of the enemy.
11 The waters covered their adversaries;
not one of them was left.
12 Then they believed his words;
they sang his praise.

13 But they soon forgot his works;
they did not wait for his counsel.
14 But they had a wanton craving in the wilderness,
and put God to the test in the desert;
15 he gave them what they asked,
but sent a wasting disease among them.

16 They were jealous of Moses in the camp,
and of Aaron, the holy one of the LORD.
17 The earth opened and swallowed up Dathan,
and covered the faction of Abiram.
18 Fire also broke out in their company;
the flame burned up the wicked.

19 They made a calf at Horeb
and worshiped a cast image.
20 They exchanged the glory of God[c]
for the image of an ox that eats grass.
21 They forgot God, their Savior,
who had done great things in Egypt,
22 wondrous works in the land of Ham,
and awesome deeds by the Red Sea.[b]
23 Therefore he said he would destroy them—
had not Moses, his chosen one,
stood in the breach before him,
to turn away his wrath from destroying them.

---

[a] Cn Compare 78.17, 56: Heb *rebelled at the sea* [b] Or *Sea of Reeds* [c] Compare Gk Mss: Heb *exchanged their glory*

24 Then they despised the pleasant land,
having no faith in his promise.
25 They grumbled in their tents,
and did not obey the voice of the LORD.
26 Therefore he raised his hand and swore to them
that he would make them fall in the wilderness,
27 and would disperse[a] their descendants among the nations,
scattering them over the lands.

28 Then they attached themselves to the Baal of Peor,
and ate sacrifices offered to the dead;
29 they provoked the LORD to anger with their deeds,
and a plague broke out among them.
30 Then Phinehas stood up and interceded,
and the plague was stopped.
31 And that has been reckoned to him as righteousness
from generation to generation forever.

32 They angered the LORD[b] at the waters of Meribah,
and it went ill with Moses on their account;
33 for they made his spirit bitter,
and he spoke words that were rash.

34 They did not destroy the peoples,
as the LORD commanded them,
35 but they mingled with the nations
and learned to do as they did.
36 They served their idols,
which became a snare to them.
37 They sacrificed their sons
and their daughters to the demons;
38 they poured out innocent blood,
the blood of their sons and daughters,
whom they sacrificed to the idols of Canaan;
and the land was polluted with blood.
39 Thus they became unclean by their acts,
and prostituted themselves in their doings.

40 Then the anger of the LORD was kindled against his people,
and he abhorred his heritage;
41 he gave them into the hand of the nations,
so that those who hated them ruled over them.
42 Their enemies oppressed them,

---

[a] Syr Compare Ezek 20.23: Heb *cause to fall* [b] Heb *him*

and they were brought into subjection under their power.

43 Many times he delivered them,
but they were rebellious in their purposes,
and were brought low through their iniquity.

44 Nevertheless he regarded their distress
when he heard their cry.

106:45 For their sake he remembered his covenant, and showed compassion: Even though the people forgot God and rebelled, God proved faithful by remembering the covenant promises and showing mercy.

45 For their sake he remembered his covenant,
and showed compassion according to the abundance of his steadfast love.

46 He caused them to be pitied
by all who held them captive.

47 Save us, O LORD our God,
and gather us from among the nations,
that we may give thanks to your holy name
and glory in your praise.

106:48 Blessed be the LORD: This verse is not an original part of this psalm. It is the doxology or song of praise that concludes Book IV of the Psalms.

48 Blessed be the LORD, the God of Israel,
from everlasting to everlasting.
And let all the people say, "Amen."
Praise the LORD!

BOOK V

(Psalms 107–150)

PSALM 107

Thanksgiving for Deliverance from Many Troubles

Psalm 107: A liturgy and community song of thanksgiving (see Types of Psalms, pp. 849-850). The song has an introduction (107:1-3), four parallel stanzas (107:4-9, 10-16, 17-22, 23-32), and a conclusion (107:33-43).

107:1-3 O give thanks to the LORD: This is a call to praise God for God's many acts of rescuing people from troubled situations, such as the rescue of the people from Egypt, Babylon, and other crises.

107:4-9 he satisfies the thirsty: Stanza one describes God's rescue of those lost in the desert and dying of thirst. God's characteristic act of satisfying the thirsty is emphasized.

1 O give thanks to the LORD, for he is good;
for his steadfast love endures forever.

2 Let the redeemed of the LORD say so,
those he redeemed from trouble

3 and gathered in from the lands,
from the east and from the west,
from the north and from the south.[a]

4 Some wandered in desert wastes,
finding no way to an inhabited town;

5 hungry and thirsty,
their soul fainted within them.

6 Then they cried to the LORD in their trouble,
and he delivered them from their distress;

7 he led them by a straight way,

[a] Cn: Heb *sea*

until they reached an inhabited town.
8 Let them thank the LORD for his steadfast love,
for his wonderful works to humankind.
9 For he satisfies the thirsty,
and the hungry he fills with good things.

10 Some sat in darkness and in gloom,
prisoners in misery and in irons,
11 for they had rebelled against the words of God,
and spurned the counsel of the Most High.
12 Their hearts were bowed down with hard labor;
they fell down, with no one to help.
13 Then they cried to the LORD in their trouble,
and he saved them from their distress;
14 he brought them out of darkness and gloom,
and broke their bonds asunder.
15 Let them thank the LORD for his steadfast love,
for his wonderful works to humankind.
16 For he shatters the doors of bronze,
and cuts in two the bars of iron.

107:10-16 he shatters the doors of bronze: Stanza two describes God's rescue of those suffering in prison. God's characteristic act of shattering prisons is emphasized.

17 Some were sick[a] through their sinful ways,
and because of their iniquities endured affliction;
18 they loathed any kind of food,
and they drew near to the gates of death.
19 Then they cried to the LORD in their trouble,
and he saved them from their distress;
20 he sent out his word and healed them,
and delivered them from destruction.
21 Let them thank the LORD for his steadfast love,
for his wonderful works to humankind.
22 And let them offer thanksgiving sacrifices,
and tell of his deeds with songs of joy.

107:17-22 he saved them from their distress: Stanza three describes God's healing of the sick. The connection of illness with personal sin reflects the ancient belief that illness was often a judgment for sin. Jesus rejects this interpretation (John 9:1-5).

23 Some went down to the sea in ships,
doing business on the mighty waters;
24 they saw the deeds of the LORD,
his wondrous works in the deep.
25 For he commanded and raised the stormy wind,
which lifted up the waves of the sea.
26 They mounted up to heaven, they went down to the depths;
their courage melted away in their calamity;
27 they reeled and staggered like drunkards,

107:23-32 Some went down to the sea in ships…he brought them out from their distress: Stanza four describes God's rescue of those caught in a storm at sea.

[a] Cn: Heb *fools*

and were at their wits' end.
28 Then they cried to the LORD in their trouble,
and he brought them out from their distress;
29 he made the storm be still,
and the waves of the sea were hushed.
30 Then they were glad because they had quiet,
and he brought them to their desired haven.
31 Let them thank the LORD for his steadfast love,
for his wonderful works to humankind.
32 Let them extol him in the congregation of the people,
and praise him in the assembly of the elders.

33 He turns rivers into a desert,
springs of water into thirsty ground,
34 a fruitful land into a salty waste,
because of the wickedness of its inhabitants.
35 He turns a desert into pools of water,
a parched land into springs of water.
36 And there he lets the hungry live,
and they establish a town to live in;
37 they sow fields, and plant vineyards,
and get a fruitful yield.
38 By his blessing they multiply greatly,
and he does not let their cattle decrease.

39 When they are diminished and brought low
through oppression, trouble, and sorrow,
40 he pours contempt on princes
and makes them wander in trackless wastes;
41 but he raises up the needy out of distress,
and makes their families like flocks.
42 The upright see it and are glad;
and all wickedness stops its mouth.
43 Let those who are wise give heed to these things,
and consider the steadfast love of the LORD.

107:33-43 consider the steadfast love of the LORD: As emphasized throughout this psalm, the LORD is a God of steadfast love (see note on 13:5). This steadfast love is revealed in God's characteristic actions of providing the fruits of creation for the starving (107:33-38) and of overturning the oppressive structures of human sin (107:39-43). Those who are wise will learn about who God is by reflecting on the history of God's loving actions.

PSALM 108

Praise and Prayer for Victory

A Song. A Psalm of David.

1 My heart is steadfast, O God, my heart is steadfast;[a]
I will sing and make melody.
Awake, my soul![b]
2 Awake, O harp and lyre!

Psalm 108: A community prayer for help (see Types of Psalms, pp. 849-850). This poem is formed from segments of two other psalms (57:7-11; 60:5-12).

108:1-4 Awake, O harp and lyre! I will awake the dawn: The metaphor of a solid heart expresses the psalmist's confidence in God. Often in prayers for help, the psalmist calls on God to awake (see 44:23) and the morning is a metaphor for God's help arriving (see 5:3; 30:5). Here, because God's help has come, the psalmist poetically calls on music to awake and promises to awaken the dawn with song.

[a] Heb Mss Gk Syr: MT lacks *my heart is steadfast* [b] Compare 57.8: Heb *also my soul*

I will awake the dawn.
3 I will give thanks to you, O LORD, among the peoples,
and I will sing praises to you among the nations.
4 For your steadfast love is higher than the heavens,
and your faithfulness reaches to the clouds.

5 Be exalted, O God, above the heavens,
and let your glory be over all the earth.
6 Give victory with your right hand, and answer me,
so that those whom you love may be rescued.

7 God has promised in his sanctuary:[a]
"With exultation I will divide up Shechem,
and portion out the Vale of Succoth.
8 Gilead is mine; Manasseh is mine;
Ephraim is my helmet;
Judah is my scepter.
9 Moab is my washbasin;
on Edom I hurl my shoe;
over Philistia I shout in triumph."

10 Who will bring me to the fortified city?
Who will lead me to Edom?
11 Have you not rejected us, O God?
You do not go out, O God, with our armies.
12 O grant us help against the foe,
for human help is worthless.
13 With God we shall do valiantly;
it is he who will tread down our foes.

PSALM 109

Prayer for Vindication and Vengeance

To the leader. Of David. A Psalm.

1 Do not be silent, O God of my praise.
2 For wicked and deceitful mouths are opened against me,
speaking against me with lying tongues.
3 They beset me with words of hate,
and attack me without cause.
4 In return for my love they accuse me,
even while I make prayer for them.[b]
5 So they reward me evil for good,
and hatred for my love.

108:7 God has promised in his sanctuary: The basis of the prayer is God's promise (see note on 12:6). The people base their hope on God, whose character is to keep promises, rather than on their own character or deeds.

108:7-9 Shechem...Gilead...Manasseh...Ephraim...Judah: See note on 60:6-8.

108:12-13 With God we shall do valiantly: The prayer ends with a statement of the people's faith in God's continued love and guidance. This confidence is based on past experiences of rescue and on God's promise.

Psalm 109: A prayer for help (see Types of Psalms, pp. 849-850) from a person who may have been falsely accused.

109:1-6 Do not be silent, O God of my praise. For wicked and deceitful mouths are opened against me: This prayer is all about speech. The wicked (see note on 1:1) tell lies. The psalmist praises God. God is silent, but the psalmist trusts that God will speak out—meaning act.

---

[a] Or *by his holiness* [b] Syr: Heb *I prayer*

109:6-19 They say, "Appoint a wicked man against him": Although the words "They say" are not present in Hebrew, the content of these verses indicates that they are the lying speech of the wicked. The complete corruption of the wicked is indicated by their desire for the psalmist's wife and children to suffer (109:9-10).

109:20-31 May that be the reward of my accusers from the LORD: In the Old Testament, the violence that one intends to do to another is often the penalty one receives. Similarly, evildoers often end up ensnared in the very traps that they lay for others. That is the prayer of the psalmist.

Have you had a time when false accusations were made against you? How did you respond? How was God present in that event?

6 They say,[a] "Appoint a wicked man against him;
let an accuser stand on his right.
7 When he is tried, let him be found guilty;
let his prayer be counted as sin.
8 May his days be few;
may another seize his position.
9 May his children be orphans,
and his wife a widow.
10 May his children wander about and beg;
may they be driven out of[b] the ruins they inhabit.
11 May the creditor seize all that he has;
may strangers plunder the fruits of his toil.
12 May there be no one to do him a kindness,
nor anyone to pity his orphaned children.
13 May his posterity be cut off;
may his name be blotted out in the second generation.
14 May the iniquity of his father[c] be remembered before the
LORD,
and do not let the sin of his mother be blotted out.
15 Let them be before the LORD continually,
and may his[d] memory be cut off from the earth.
16 For he did not remember to show kindness,
but pursued the poor and needy
and the brokenhearted to their death.
17 He loved to curse; let curses come on him.
He did not like blessing; may it be far from him.
18 He clothed himself with cursing as his coat,
may it soak into his body like water,
like oil into his bones.
19 May it be like a garment that he wraps around himself,
like a belt that he wears every day."

20 May that be the reward of my accusers from the LORD,
of those who speak evil against my life.
21 But you, O LORD my Lord,
act on my behalf for your name's sake;
because your steadfast love is good, deliver me.
22 For I am poor and needy,
and my heart is pierced within me.
23 I am gone like a shadow at evening;
I am shaken off like a locust.
24 My knees are weak through fasting;
my body has become gaunt.

[a] Heb lacks *They say* [b] Gk: Heb *and seek* [c] Cn: Heb *fathers* [d] Gk: Heb *their*

25 I am an object of scorn to my accusers;
when they see me, they shake their heads.

26 Help me, O LORD my God!
Save me according to your steadfast love.
27 Let them know that this is your hand;
you, O LORD, have done it.
28 Let them curse, but you will bless.
Let my assailants be put to shame;[a] may your servant be glad.
29 May my accusers be clothed with dishonor;
may they be wrapped in their own shame as in a mantle.
30 With my mouth I will give great thanks to the LORD;
I will praise him in the midst of the throng.
31 For he stands at the right hand of the needy,
to save them from those who would condemn them to death.

PSALM 110

Assurance of Victory for God's Priest-King

Of David. A Psalm.

1 The LORD says to my lord,
"Sit at my right hand
until I make your enemies your footstool."

2 The LORD sends out from Zion
your mighty scepter.
Rule in the midst of your foes.
3 Your people will offer themselves willingly
on the day you lead your forces
on the holy mountains.[b]
From the womb of the morning,
like dew, your youth[c] will come to you.
4 The LORD has sworn and will not change his mind,
"You are a priest forever according to the order of
Melchizedek."[d]

5 The Lord is at your right hand;
he will shatter kings on the day of his wrath.
6 He will execute judgment among the nations,
filling them with corpses;
he will shatter heads
over the wide earth.
7 He will drink from the stream by the path;
therefore he will lift up his head.

[a] Gk: Heb *They have risen up and have been put to shame* [b] Another reading is *in holy splendor* [c] Cn: Heb *the dew of your youth* [d] Or *forever, a rightful king by my edict*

Psalm 110: A royal psalm (see Types of Psalms, pp. 849-850) that may have been performed at a king's coronation. The meaning of parts of the psalm is unclear.

110:1 The LORD says to my lord... until I make your enemies your footstool: This promise from God to the king is related to the king's role as the people's military leader.

110:4 The LORD has sworn... You are a priest forever according to the order of Melchizedek: This promise from God to the king is related to the king's role as the people's spiritual leader (for more on Melchizedek, see Gen 14:17-20).

PSALM 111
Praise for God's Wonderful Works

1 Praise the LORD!
I will give thanks to the LORD with my whole heart,
in the company of the upright, in the congregation.
2 Great are the works of the LORD,
studied by all who delight in them.
3 Full of honor and majesty is his work,
and his righteousness endures forever.
4 He has gained renown by his wonderful deeds;
the LORD is gracious and merciful.
5 He provides food for those who fear him;
he is ever mindful of his covenant.
6 He has shown his people the power of his works,
in giving them the heritage of the nations.
7 The works of his hands are faithful and just;
all his precepts are trustworthy.
8 They are established forever and ever,
to be performed with faithfulness and uprightness.
9 He sent redemption to his people;
he has commanded his covenant forever.
Holy and awesome is his name.
10 The fear of the LORD is the beginning of wisdom;
all those who practice it[a] have a good understanding.
His praise endures forever.

Psalm 111: A hymn of praise and acrostic poem (see Types of Psalms, pp. 849-850), explaining God's role in the relationship with humans.

111:2 Great are the works of the LORD, studied by all who delight in them: We tell about God's works when we praise God, so that others might learn to know God and God's ways.

111:4-5 the LORD is gracious and merciful. He provides food...he is ever mindful of his covenant: God's grace comes in the forms of mercy (forgiveness) and blessing (the fruits of harvest). Both of these gifts are signs that God keeps the promises God has made in the covenant with the people.

111:7 all his precepts are trustworthy: God's commandments are good. We keep them because they are good, not simply because God has ordered us to do so.

111:10 The fear of the LORD: See note on 34:9-11.

PSALM 112
Blessings of the Righteous

1 Praise the LORD!
Happy are those who fear the LORD,
who greatly delight in his commandments.
2 Their descendants will be mighty in the land;
the generation of the upright will be blessed.
3 Wealth and riches are in their houses,
and their righteousness endures forever.
4 They rise in the darkness as a light for the upright;
they are gracious, merciful, and righteous.
5 It is well with those who deal generously and lend,
who conduct their affairs with justice.
6 For the righteous will never be moved;
they will be remembered forever.
7 They are not afraid of evil tidings;
their hearts are firm, secure in the LORD.

Psalm 112: A hymn of praise and acrostic poem (see Types of Psalms, pp. 849-850) about human responsibility in the relationship between God and people.

112:1 those who fear the LORD: See note on 34:9-11. The psalm can be understood as an extended reflection on what it means to fear the LORD.

112:4-9 those who deal generously and lend, who conduct their affairs with justice: Similar to Jesus' teaching that disciples are the light of the world (Matt 5:14), the psalm teaches that following God's law is the way to love your neighbor.

Keeping God's commandments benefits us, but the real point of keeping the law is to benefit our neighbor. When has someone else keeping God's law been a blessing to you?

[a] Gk Syr: Heb *them*

8 Their hearts are steady, they will not be afraid;
in the end they will look in triumph on their foes.
9 They have distributed freely, they have given to the poor;
their righteousness endures forever;
their horn is exalted in honor.
10 The wicked see it and are angry;
they gnash their teeth and melt away;
the desire of the wicked comes to nothing.

PSALM 113
God the Helper of the Needy

1 Praise the LORD!
Praise, O servants of the LORD;
praise the name of the LORD.

2 Blessed be the name of the LORD
from this time on and forevermore.
3 From the rising of the sun to its setting
the name of the LORD is to be praised.
4 The LORD is high above all nations,
and his glory above the heavens.

5 Who is like the LORD our God,
who is seated on high,
6 who looks far down
on the heavens and the earth?
7 He raises the poor from the dust,
and lifts the needy from the ash heap,
8 to make them sit with princes,
with the princes of his people.
9 He gives the barren woman a home,
making her the joyous mother of children.
Praise the LORD!

Psalm 113: A hymn of praise (see Types of Psalms, pp. 849-850). In Jewish tradition, Psalms 113–118 are the Egyptian *Hallel* ("praise"). The first two are sung on Passover before the meal, the last four are sung after the meal.

113:3 From the rising of the sun to its setting: This means to praise God all day, and everywhere (because the sun rises in the east and sets in the west).

113:4-7 The LORD is high above... He raises the poor from the dust: The song playfully shows God on high, looking down to the lowest places in human life, and raising up the lowly.

113:5-9 seated on high...to make them sit with princes...gives the barren woman a home: The same Hebrew word (*yashab* [YA-shav]) can be translated as "seated," "make them sit," and "gives...a home." When God comes down to earth and mixes in human life, God gives God's qualities (to be seated in glory) to humans (giving them honor and a place).

PSALM 114
God's Wonders at the Exodus

1 When Israel went out from Egypt,
the house of Jacob from a people of strange language,
2 Judah became God's[a] sanctuary,
Israel his dominion.

3 The sea looked and fled;
Jordan turned back.

Psalm 114: A hymn of praise (see Types of Psalms, pp. 849-850) in four stanzas (114:1-2, 3-4, 5-6, 7-8).

114:1-4 When Israel went out from Egypt: The first two stanzas of the song celebrate God's rescue of Israel from Egypt, including the entry into the promised land.

[a] Heb *his*

114:5-8 Why is it, O sea, that you flee?...Tremble, O earth, at the presence of the Lord: The song addresses the sea, the Jordan River, mountains, hills, and the earth—but it is really directed at worshipers. If the land itself obeys and responds to God, shouldn't mere humans also show awe and obedience in God's presence?

When the psalm talks about the land responding to God's presence, this is a poetic way to talk about people responding to God. How has God touched the land you live in or come from, and also touched you through it?

Psalm 115: A liturgy of praise and trust (see Types of Psalms, pp. 849-850).

115:1-2 to your name give glory ...Why should the nations say, "Where is their God?": For "name," see note on 20:7. For "Where is their God?" see note on 42:3. The rest of the psalm offers an answer to this question.

115:3-8 Our God is in the heavens: Although the taunt "Where is their God?" is not meant to be answered, the psalm dares to do just that. It compares the true God, who is in heaven and who acts, with the idols of earth, which are made of earth and cannot act.

115:9-11 O Israel, trust in the Lord!: Verse 8 comments on the foolishness of trusting in idols. Now a brief liturgy begins, urging Israel to trust in God, because true help can only come from God.

115:9-13 Israel...house of Aaron... You who fear the Lord: "Israel" refers to all the lay people present in worship, "House of Aaron" refers to the priests present in worship, and those "who fear the Lord" refers to non-Israelites who worship the Lord but have not yet fully joined the people.

115:12-18 The Lord has been mindful...But we will bless the Lord: The liturgy ends with a series of extravagant promises: the Lord will bless and protect the people, who in response praise God. The reference to God being in heaven and humans on earth in verse 16 brings the psalm full circle (see 115:3).

4 The mountains skipped like rams,
the hills like lambs.

5 Why is it, O sea, that you flee?
O Jordan, that you turn back?
6 O mountains, that you skip like rams?
O hills, like lambs?

7 Tremble, O earth, at the presence of the Lord,
at the presence of the God of Jacob,
8 who turns the rock into a pool of water,
the flint into a spring of water.

PSALM 115

The Impotence of Idols and the Greatness of God

1 Not to us, O Lord, not to us, but to your name give glory,
for the sake of your steadfast love and your faithfulness.
2 Why should the nations say,
"Where is their God?"

3 Our God is in the heavens;
he does whatever he pleases.
4 Their idols are silver and gold,
the work of human hands.
5 They have mouths, but do not speak;
eyes, but do not see.
6 They have ears, but do not hear;
noses, but do not smell.
7 They have hands, but do not feel;
feet, but do not walk;
they make no sound in their throats.
8 Those who make them are like them;
so are all who trust in them.

9 O Israel, trust in the Lord!
He is their help and their shield.
10 O house of Aaron, trust in the Lord!
He is their help and their shield.
11 You who fear the Lord, trust in the Lord!
He is their help and their shield.

12 The Lord has been mindful of us; he will bless us;
he will bless the house of Israel;
he will bless the house of Aaron;
13 he will bless those who fear the Lord,
both small and great.

14 May the LORD give you increase,
both you and your children.
15 May you be blessed by the LORD,
who made heaven and earth.

16 The heavens are the LORD's heavens,
but the earth he has given to human beings.
17 The dead do not praise the LORD,
nor do any that go down into silence.
18 But we will bless the LORD
from this time on and forevermore.
Praise the LORD!

PSALM 116

Thanksgiving for Recovery from Illness

1 I love the LORD, because he has heard
my voice and my supplications.
2 Because he inclined his ear to me,
therefore I will call on him as long as I live.
3 The snares of death encompassed me;
the pangs of Sheol laid hold on me;
I suffered distress and anguish.
4 Then I called on the name of the LORD:
"O LORD, I pray, save my life!"

5 Gracious is the LORD, and righteous;
our God is merciful.
6 The LORD protects the simple;
when I was brought low, he saved me.
7 Return, O my soul, to your rest,
for the LORD has dealt bountifully with you.

8 For you have delivered my soul from death,
my eyes from tears,
my feet from stumbling.
9 I walk before the LORD
in the land of the living.
10 I kept my faith, even when I said,
"I am greatly afflicted";
11 I said in my consternation,
"Everyone is a liar."

12 What shall I return to the LORD
for all his bounty to me?
13 I will lift up the cup of salvation

Psalm 116: A song of thanksgiving (see Types of Psalms, pp. 849-850) following a grave illness or a similar crisis.

116:1-3 I love the LORD, because he has heard my voice: The psalmist praises God for rescue from a severe crisis.

116:4-11 I called on the name of the LORD: In the depths of the crisis, turning to God in prayer was the key moment that turned things around.

116:13 I will lift up the cup of salvation: The cup of salvation probably refers to a meal of celebration (see Lev 7:11-18) in which a person rescued from crisis could thank God and be welcomed back into the community. The community welcomes someone back by listening to the person praise God and acknowledging that God was the rescuer.

Has there been a time when a personal crisis kept you or someone you know from attending worship? What happened to make it possible to return to worship?

and call on the name of the LORD,
14 I will pay my vows to the LORD
in the presence of all his people.
15 Precious in the sight of the LORD
is the death of his faithful ones.
16 O LORD, I am your servant;
I am your servant, the child of your serving girl.
You have loosed my bonds.
17 I will offer to you a thanksgiving sacrifice
and call on the name of the LORD.
18 I will pay my vows to the LORD
in the presence of all his people,
19 in the courts of the house of the LORD,
in your midst, O Jerusalem.
Praise the LORD!

116:15 Precious in the sight: This verse can also be translated "Grievous in the sight of the LORD is the death of his faithful ones."

PSALM 117
Universal Call to Worship

1 Praise the LORD, all you nations!
Extol him, all you peoples!
2 For great is his steadfast love toward us,
and the faithfulness of the LORD endures forever.
Praise the LORD!

Psalm 117: A hymn of praise (see Types of Psalms, pp. 849-850).

117:1-2 For great is his steadfast love...the faithfulness of the LORD endures forever: This shortest of all the psalms gets right to the heart of the good news about God: God is faithful and loving.

If you were to boil down the good news about God into a few words, what would they be?

PSALM 118
A Song of Victory

1 O give thanks to the LORD, for he is good;
his steadfast love endures forever!

2 Let Israel say,
"His steadfast love endures forever."
3 Let the house of Aaron say,
"His steadfast love endures forever."
4 Let those who fear the LORD say,
"His steadfast love endures forever."

5 Out of my distress I called on the LORD;
the LORD answered me and set me in a broad
place.
6 With the LORD on my side I do not fear.
What can mortals do to me?
7 The LORD is on my side to help me;
I shall look in triumph on those who hate me.
8 It is better to take refuge in the LORD

Psalm 118: A liturgy of thanksgiving (see Types of Psalms, pp. 849-850) by a person who has passed through a severe crisis.

118:1-4 O give thanks to the LORD: See note on 136:1.

118:2-4 Israel...house of Aaron...those who fear the LORD: See note on 115:9-13. The psalmist calls on all at worship to join in thanking God for rescuing them.

118:5-13 Out of my distress I called on the LORD: The psalmist recalls the perilous crisis and God's help. In the middle of these verses, the psalmist offers instruction to others about the life of faith. Especially powerful is the teaching that it is better to trust in God than in earthly forms of refuge (118:8-9).

than to put confidence in mortals.
9 It is better to take refuge in the LORD
than to put confidence in princes.

10 All nations surrounded me;
in the name of the LORD I cut them off!
11 They surrounded me, surrounded me on every side;
in the name of the LORD I cut them off!
12 They surrounded me like bees;
they blazed[a] like a fire of thorns;
in the name of the LORD I cut them off!
13 I was pushed hard,[b] so that I was falling,
but the LORD helped me.
14 The LORD is my strength and my might;
he has become my salvation.

15 There are glad songs of victory in the tents of the
righteous:
"The right hand of the LORD does valiantly;
16 the right hand of the LORD is exalted;
the right hand of the LORD does valiantly."
17 I shall not die, but I shall live,
and recount the deeds of the LORD.
18 The LORD has punished me severely,
but he did not give me over to death.

19 Open to me the gates of righteousness,
that I may enter through them
and give thanks to the LORD.

20 This is the gate of the LORD;
the righteous shall enter through it.

21 I thank you that you have answered me
and have become my salvation.
22 The stone that the builders rejected
has become the chief cornerstone.
23 This is the LORD's doing;
it is marvelous in our eyes.
24 This is the day that the LORD has made;
let us rejoice and be glad in it.[c]
25 Save us, we beseech you, O LORD!
O LORD, we beseech you, give us success!

---

[a] Gk: Heb *were extinguished* [b] Gk Syr Jerome: Heb *You pushed me hard* [c] Or *in him*

118:19-20 Open to me the gates of righteousness: These verses probably indicate a liturgical entry into the temple and surrounding area (see also 118:26-27 for further evidence of this kind of action in the song). Illnesses and other crises often lead to isolation, so part of thanking God included rejoining the community of God's people.

118:24 This is the day: This verse can also be translated: "This is the day that the LORD has acted, let us rejoice and be glad in him!" This does not celebrate the creation of a new day as much as it celebrates the fact that the Creator of all things has rescued the psalmist from a crisis.

Tell about a time when you experienced God's help in a powerful way. Did you praise or thank God for this help?

[26] Blessed is the one who comes in the name of the LORD.[a]
We bless you from the house of the LORD.
[27] The LORD is God,
and he has given us light.
Bind the festal procession with branches,
up to the horns of the altar.[b]

118:28 You are my God: The mere fact of God's existence is important, but God's existence means even more to a person who shares a relationship with the LORD. Having experienced God's help, the psalmist celebrates this personal relationship.

[28] You are my God, and I will give thanks to you;
you are my God, I will extol you.

[29] O give thanks to the LORD, for he is good,
for his steadfast love endures forever.

PSALM 119
The Glories of God's Law

Psalm 119: An instructional psalm celebrating God's law (see note on 1:2) and an acrostic poem (see Types of Psalms, pp. 849-850). The poem has twenty-two stanzas, each beginning with a different letter of the Hebrew alphabet. Each stanza has eight lines, and all eight in each stanza begin with the same letter (in Hebrew). The central theme of the psalm is God's law or instruction. This theme is emphasized by the repetition of nine words for God's instruction: law, decrees, ways, precepts, statutes, commandments, ordinances, word, and promise. The basic message of the psalm is summarized in 119:97: "Oh, how I love your law! It is my meditation all day long."

119:1-8 Happy: See note on 1:1. The enviable life is found among those who keep God's law.

[1] Happy are those whose way is blameless,
who walk in the law of the LORD.
[2] Happy are those who keep his decrees,
who seek him with their whole heart,
[3] who also do no wrong,
but walk in his ways.
[4] You have commanded your precepts
to be kept diligently.
[5] O that my ways may be steadfast
in keeping your statutes!
[6] Then I shall not be put to shame,
having my eyes fixed on all your commandments.
[7] I will praise you with an upright heart,
when I learn your righteous ordinances.
[8] I will observe your statutes;
do not utterly forsake me.

119:9-16 How can young people keep their way pure?: God's law is especially recommended to young people for study.

[9] How can young people keep their way pure?
By guarding it according to your word.
[10] With my whole heart I seek you;
do not let me stray from your commandments.
[11] I treasure your word in my heart,
so that I may not sin against you.
[12] Blessed are you, O LORD;
teach me your statutes.
[13] With my lips I declare
all the ordinances of your mouth.
[14] I delight in the way of your decrees

[a] Or *Blessed in the name of the LORD is the one who comes* [b] Meaning of Heb uncertain

as much as in all riches.
15 I will meditate on your precepts,
and fix my eyes on your ways.
16 I will delight in your statutes;
I will not forget your word.

17 Deal bountifully with your servant,
so that I may live and observe your word.
18 Open my eyes, so that I may behold
wondrous things out of your law.
19 I live as an alien in the land;
do not hide your commandments from me.
20 My soul is consumed with longing
for your ordinances at all times.
21 You rebuke the insolent, accursed ones,
who wander from your commandments;
22 take away from me their scorn and contempt,
for I have kept your decrees.
23 Even though princes sit plotting against me,
your servant will meditate on your statutes.
24 Your decrees are my delight,
they are my counselors.

119:17-24 Deal bountifully with your servant: The psalmist asks for God's help in keeping the law and protection from those who do not.

25 My soul clings to the dust;
revive me according to your word.
26 When I told of my ways, you answered me;
teach me your statutes.
27 Make me understand the way of your precepts,
and I will meditate on your wondrous works.
28 My soul melts away for sorrow;
strengthen me according to your word.
29 Put false ways far from me;
and graciously teach me your law.
30 I have chosen the way of faithfulness;
I set your ordinances before me.
31 I cling to your decrees, O Lord;
let me not be put to shame.
32 I run the way of your commandments,
for you enlarge my understanding.

119:25-32 revive me according to your word: God's word brings rescue and new life.

33 Teach me, O Lord, the way of your statutes,
and I will observe it to the end.
34 Give me understanding, that I may keep your law
and observe it with my whole heart.
35 Lead me in the path of your commandments,

119:33-40 Teach me, O Lord, the way: Following God's ways requires prayer and willingness to learn throughout our lives.

for I delight in it.

36 Turn my heart to your decrees,
and not to selfish gain.
37 Turn my eyes from looking at vanities;
give me life in your ways.
38 Confirm to your servant your promise,
which is for those who fear you.
39 Turn away the disgrace that I dread,
for your ordinances are good.
40 See, I have longed for your precepts;
in your righteousness give me life.

119:41-48 Let your steadfast love come to me: God's word is a means of grace. It is a channel for God's steadfast loves to come to sinners and a form of refuge from evildoers.

41 Let your steadfast love come to me, O Lord,
your salvation according to your promise.
42 Then I shall have an answer for those who taunt me,
for I trust in your word.
43 Do not take the word of truth utterly out of my mouth,
for my hope is in your ordinances.
44 I will keep your law continually,
forever and ever.
45 I shall walk at liberty,
for I have sought your precepts.
46 I will also speak of your decrees before kings,
and shall not be put to shame;
47 I find my delight in your commandments,
because I love them.
48 I revere your commandments, which I love,
and I will meditate on your statutes.

119:49-56 Remember your word: This is a prayer for help and an expression of trust, because God keeps God's word.

49 Remember your word to your servant,
in which you have made me hope.
50 This is my comfort in my distress,
that your promise gives me life.
51 The arrogant utterly deride me,
but I do not turn away from your law.
52 When I think of your ordinances from of old,
I take comfort, O Lord.
53 Hot indignation seizes me because of the wicked,
those who forsake your law.
54 Your statutes have been my songs
wherever I make my home.
55 I remember your name in the night, O Lord,
and keep your law.
56 This blessing has fallen to me,
for I have kept your precepts.

57 The LORD is my portion;
I promise to keep your words.
58 I implore your favor with all my heart;
be gracious to me according to your promise.
59 When I think of your ways,
I turn my feet to your decrees;
60 I hurry and do not delay
to keep your commandments.
61 Though the cords of the wicked ensnare me,
I do not forget your law.
62 At midnight I rise to praise you,
because of your righteous ordinances.
63 I am a companion of all who fear you,
of those who keep your precepts.
64 The earth, O LORD, is full of your steadfast love;
teach me your statutes.

65 You have dealt well with your servant,
O LORD, according to your word.
66 Teach me good judgment and knowledge,
for I believe in your commandments.
67 Before I was humbled I went astray,
but now I keep your word.
68 You are good and do good;
teach me your statutes.
69 The arrogant smear me with lies,
but with my whole heart I keep your precepts.
70 Their hearts are fat and gross,
but I delight in your law.
71 It is good for me that I was humbled,
so that I might learn your statutes.
72 The law of your mouth is better to me
than thousands of gold and silver pieces.

73 Your hands have made and fashioned me;
give me understanding that I may learn your commandments.
74 Those who fear you shall see me and rejoice,
because I have hoped in your word.
75 I know, O LORD, that your judgments are right,
and that in faithfulness you have humbled me.
76 Let your steadfast love become my comfort
according to your promise to your servant.
77 Let your mercy come to me, that I may live;
for your law is my delight.
78 Let the arrogant be put to shame,

119:57-64 The LORD is my portion: For "portion," see note on 16:5-6. This stanza indicates the psalmist may have been a priest, dedicating a life to God's service and word.

119:65-72 You have dealt well with your servant: The psalmist is God's "servant," indicating humility and obedience. The experience of being humbled is necessary, so that one might approach God's law with an open spirit.

119:73-80 Your hands have made and fashioned me: The psalmist renews the prayer for God's understanding, guidance, and deliverance.

because they have subverted me with guile;
as for me, I will meditate on your precepts.
79 Let those who fear you turn to me,
so that they may know your decrees.
80 May my heart be blameless in your statutes,
so that I may not be put to shame.

119:81-88 My soul languishes for your salvation: In prayers for help, the sufferer often promises to praise God after being rescued. Here the person promises to study the law in response to rescue.

81 My soul languishes for your salvation;
I hope in your word.
82 My eyes fail with watching for your promise;
I ask, "When will you comfort me?"
83 For I have become like a wineskin in the smoke,
yet I have not forgotten your statutes.
84 How long must your servant endure?
When will you judge those who persecute me?
85 The arrogant have dug pitfalls for me;
they flout your law.
86 All your commandments are enduring;
I am persecuted without cause; help me!
87 They have almost made an end of me on earth;
but I have not forsaken your precepts.
88 In your steadfast love spare my life,
so that I may keep the decrees of your mouth.

119:89-96 The Lord exists forever: This is a vow to be devoted to God's word, which is eternal like God is.

89 The Lord exists forever;
your word is firmly fixed in heaven.
90 Your faithfulness endures to all generations;
you have established the earth, and it stands fast.
91 By your appointment they stand today,
for all things are your servants.
92 If your law had not been my delight,
I would have perished in my misery.
93 I will never forget your precepts,
for by them you have given me life.
94 I am yours; save me,
for I have sought your precepts.
95 The wicked lie in wait to destroy me,
but I consider your decrees.
96 I have seen a limit to all perfection,
but your commandment is exceedingly broad.

119:97-104 Oh, how I love your law!: This expression of love for God's law is based on the power and goodness of God's word.

97 Oh, how I love your law!
It is my meditation all day long.
98 Your commandment makes me wiser than my enemies,
for it is always with me.

[99] I have more understanding than all my teachers,
for your decrees are my meditation.
[100] I understand more than the aged,
for I keep your precepts.
[101] I hold back my feet from every evil way,
in order to keep your word.
[102] I do not turn away from your ordinances,
for you have taught me.
[103] How sweet are your words to my taste,
sweeter than honey to my mouth!
[104] Through your precepts I get understanding;
therefore I hate every false way.

[105] Your word is a lamp to my feet
and a light to my path.
[106] I have sworn an oath and confirmed it,
to observe your righteous ordinances.
[107] I am severely afflicted;
give me life, O LORD, according to your word.
[108] Accept my offerings of praise, O LORD,
and teach me your ordinances.
[109] I hold my life in my hand continually,
but I do not forget your law.
[110] The wicked have laid a snare for me,
but I do not stray from your precepts.
[111] Your decrees are my heritage forever;
they are the joy of my heart.
[112] I incline my heart to perform your statutes
forever, to the end.

119:105-112 Your word is a lamp to my feet: God's word provides guidance away from evil and toward what is good.

How has God's word been like a light in your life?

[113] I hate the double-minded,
but I love your law.
[114] You are my hiding place and my shield;
I hope in your word.
[115] Go away from me, you evildoers,
that I may keep the commandments of my God.
[116] Uphold me according to your promise, that I may live,
and let me not be put to shame in my hope.
[117] Hold me up, that I may be safe
and have regard for your statutes continually.
[118] You spurn all who go astray from your statutes;
for their cunning is in vain.
[119] All the wicked of the earth you count as dross;
therefore I love your decrees.
[120] My flesh trembles for fear of you,
and I am afraid of your judgments.

119:113-120 I hate the double-minded, but I love your law: Dedication to God's law requires rejecting ungodly standards of goodness.

119:121-128 I have done what is just and right: The psalmist again asks for rescue, describes a crisis, and promises to live faithfully.

121 I have done what is just and right;
do not leave me to my oppressors.
122 Guarantee your servant's well-being;
do not let the godless oppress me.
123 My eyes fail from watching for your salvation,
and for the fulfillment of your righteous promise.
124 Deal with your servant according to your steadfast love,
and teach me your statutes.
125 I am your servant; give me understanding,
so that I may know your decrees.
126 It is time for the LORD to act,
for your law has been broken.
127 Truly I love your commandments
more than gold, more than fine gold.
128 Truly I direct my steps by all your precepts;[a]
I hate every false way.

119:129-136 Your decrees are wonderful: The psalmist praises God's word and asks for protection.

129 Your decrees are wonderful;
therefore my soul keeps them.
130 The unfolding of your words gives light;
it imparts understanding to the simple.
131 With open mouth I pant,
because I long for your commandments.
132 Turn to me and be gracious to me,
as is your custom toward those who love your name.
133 Keep my steps steady according to your promise,
and never let iniquity have dominion over me.
134 Redeem me from human oppression,
that I may keep your precepts.
135 Make your face shine upon your servant,
and teach me your statutes.
136 My eyes shed streams of tears
because your law is not kept.

119:137-144 You are righteous, O LORD: God's righteousness and faithfulness are revealed in God's word and teaching.

137 You are righteous, O LORD,
and your judgments are right.
138 You have appointed your decrees in righteousness
and in all faithfulness.
139 My zeal consumes me
because my foes forget your words.
140 Your promise is well tried,
and your servant loves it.
141 I am small and despised,

---

[a] Gk Jerome: Meaning of Heb uncertain

yet I do not forget your precepts.
142 Your righteousness is an everlasting righteousness,
and your law is the truth.
143 Trouble and anguish have come upon me,
but your commandments are my delight.
144 Your decrees are righteous forever;
give me understanding that I may live.

145 With my whole heart I cry; answer me, O LORD.
I will keep your statutes.
146 I cry to you; save me,
that I may observe your decrees.
147 I rise before dawn and cry for help;
I put my hope in your words.
148 My eyes are awake before each watch of the night,
that I may meditate on your promise.
149 In your steadfast love hear my voice;
O LORD, in your justice preserve my life.
150 Those who persecute me with evil purpose draw near;
they are far from your law.
151 Yet you are near, O LORD,
and all your commandments are true.
152 Long ago I learned from your decrees
that you have established them forever.

119:145-152 With my whole heart I cry: Again the psalmist asks for rescue and promises to keep the law.

153 Look on my misery and rescue me,
for I do not forget your law.
154 Plead my cause and redeem me;
give me life according to your promise.
155 Salvation is far from the wicked,
for they do not seek your statutes.
156 Great is your mercy, O LORD;
give me life according to your justice.
157 Many are my persecutors and my adversaries,
yet I do not swerve from your decrees.
158 I look at the faithless with disgust,
because they do not keep your commands.
159 Consider how I love your precepts;
preserve my life according to your steadfast love.
160 The sum of your word is truth;
and every one of your righteous ordinances endures forever.

119:153-160 Look on my misery and rescue me: This is another appeal for rescue, based on God's justice.

161 Princes persecute me without cause,
but my heart stands in awe of your words.
162 I rejoice at your word

119:161-168 Princes persecute me without cause: The psalmist's devotion to God's word results in persecution.

like one who finds great spoil.

163 I hate and abhor falsehood,
but I love your law.

164 Seven times a day I praise you
for your righteous ordinances.

165 Great peace have those who love your law;
nothing can make them stumble.

166 I hope for your salvation, O LORD,
and I fulfill your commandments.

167 My soul keeps your decrees;
I love them exceedingly.

168 I keep your precepts and decrees,
for all my ways are before you.

119:169-176 Let my cry come before you: This is a final appeal for God's rescue.

169 Let my cry come before you, O LORD;
give me understanding according to your word.

170 Let my supplication come before you;
deliver me according to your promise.

171 My lips will pour forth praise,
because you teach me your statutes.

172 My tongue will sing of your promise,
for all your commandments are right.

173 Let your hand be ready to help me,
for I have chosen your precepts.

174 I long for your salvation, O LORD,
and your law is my delight.

175 Let me live that I may praise you,
and let your ordinances help me.

176 I have gone astray like a lost sheep; seek out your servant,
for I do not forget your commandments.

PSALM 120

Prayer for Deliverance from Slanderers

A Song of Ascents.

Psalms 120–134: These are called "Songs of Ascents." The meaning of this title is debated, but many scholars believe these psalms were collected for believers to use on the way to celebrate a festival in Jerusalem.

Psalm 120: A prayer for help (see Types of Psalms, pp. 849-850) from a person forced to live a distance from the temple.

120:2-3 Deliver me, O LORD, from lying lips, from a deceitful tongue: The tormenters' lies may be about the psalmist's God (see note on 42:3).

1 In my distress I cry to the LORD,
that he may answer me:

2 "Deliver me, O LORD,
from lying lips,
from a deceitful tongue."

3 What shall be given to you?
And what more shall be done to you,
you deceitful tongue?

4 A warrior's sharp arrows,
with glowing coals of the broom tree!

5 Woe is me, that I am an alien in Meshech,
that I must live among the tents of Kedar.
6 Too long have I had my dwelling
among those who hate peace.
7 I am for peace;
but when I speak,
they are for war.

120:5-7 I am an alien in Meshech…among the tents of Kedar: The psalmist feels separated from God. Meshech (in Asia Minor near the Black Sea) and Kedar (in the Arabian peninsula) are not near each other.

When have you felt "homesick" for God or God's people? How did you make it through that time?

PSALM 121
Assurance of God's Protection

A Song of Ascents.

1 I lift up my eyes to the hills—
from where will my help come?
2 My help comes from the LORD,
who made heaven and earth.

3 He will not let your foot be moved;
he who keeps you will not slumber.
4 He who keeps Israel
will neither slumber nor sleep.

5 The LORD is your keeper;
the LORD is your shade at your right hand.
6 The sun shall not strike you by day,
nor the moon by night.

7 The LORD will keep you from all evil;
he will keep your life.
8 The LORD will keep
your going out and your coming in
from this time on and forevermore.

Psalm 121: A liturgy and a trust psalm (see Types of Psalms, pp. 849-850) that promises protection for a journey.

121:1-2 from where will my help come? My help comes from the LORD: The psalm starts with a question, and the rest of the psalm gives an answer: Saving help does not come from the hills, but from the LORD, who is Creator of the hills, heaven, and earth.

121:3-8 The LORD is your keeper: Six times in verses 3-8, the poem promises that the LORD will "keep" the psalmist from evil. This term means to "watch over," as a guard protects a city at night (see 127:1; 130:6), a fitting image for the LORD's guidance, for the LORD protects us through this life and into the next.

When have you needed God's protection? At what time of life do you think we need God's protection the most?

PSALM 122
Song of Praise and Prayer for Jerusalem

A Song of Ascents. Of David.

1 I was glad when they said to me,
"Let us go to the house of the LORD!"
2 Our feet are standing
within your gates, O Jerusalem.

3 Jerusalem—built as a city
that is bound firmly together.
4 To it the tribes go up,
the tribes of the LORD,

Psalm 122: A song of Zion (see Types of Psalms, pp. 849-850).

122:1-2 I was glad when they said to me: This verse is often used to call people to worship. It expresses the joy of coming into God's presence. See note on Jerusalem at 84:1.

122:3-5 the tribes go up…as was decreed for Israel: Israelites were commanded to make a pilgrimage to Jerusalem (see Exod 23:14-19). Judgment happens there, because it was the role of the king to resolve disputes and issue judgments.

as was decreed for Israel,
to give thanks to the name of the LORD.
5 For there the thrones for judgment were set up,
the thrones of the house of David.

6 Pray for the peace of Jerusalem:
"May they prosper who love you.
7 Peace be within your walls,
and security within your towers."
8 For the sake of my relatives and friends
I will say, "Peace be within you."
9 For the sake of the house of the LORD our God,
I will seek your good.

122:7 Peace be within your walls: The song speaks to Jerusalem, which is here a poetic reference to God, because God's blessings of peace and security come out of Jerusalem for the whole world (see Isa 2:1-4).

Is there a place where you feel closer to God? Why or why not?

PSALM 123
Supplication for Mercy

A Song of Ascents.

Psalm 123: A community prayer for help (see Types of Psalms, pp. 849-850) in two stanzas (123:1-2; 3-4).

123:1-2 To you I lift up my eyes: The repeated image of eyes emphasizes the community's humble need for God's mercy.

1 To you I lift up my eyes,
O you who are enthroned in the heavens!
2 As the eyes of servants
look to the hand of their master,
as the eyes of a maid
to the hand of her mistress,
so our eyes look to the LORD our God,
until he has mercy upon us.

123:3-4 Have mercy upon us: The second stanza picks up where the first stanza left off, with an appeal for God's mercy. This stanza emphasizes the arrogance of those who oppress the community.

3 Have mercy upon us, O LORD, have mercy upon us,
for we have had more than enough of contempt.
4 Our soul has had more than its fill
of the scorn of those who are at ease,
of the contempt of the proud.

PSALM 124
Thanksgiving for Israel's Deliverance

A Song of Ascents. Of David.

Psalm 124: A liturgy of thanksgiving (see Types of Psalms, pp. 849-850).

124:1-5 If it had not been the LORD who was on our side: A worship leader speaks this phrase, and then the community repeats it (124:2). The phrase tells a fundamental truth about Israel's faith: If God had not been for Israel—in Egypt, in the wilderness, in the land, in drought, during the exile—Israel would have been "swallowed." This is also the church's story. The church's history is the story of God preserving it from external dangers and from its own sins.

1 If it had not been the LORD who was on our side
—let Israel now say—
2 if it had not been the LORD who was on our side,
when our enemies attacked us,
3 then they would have swallowed us up alive,
when their anger was kindled against us;
4 then the flood would have swept us away,
the torrent would have gone over us;
5 then over us would have gone
the raging waters.

6 Blessed be the LORD,
who has not given us
as prey to their teeth.
7 We have escaped like a bird
from the snare of the fowlers;
the snare is broken,
and we have escaped.

8 Our help is in the name of the LORD,
who made heaven and earth.

PSALM 125
The Security of God's People
A Song of Ascents.

1 Those who trust in the LORD are like Mount Zion,
which cannot be moved, but abides forever.
2 As the mountains surround Jerusalem,
so the LORD surrounds his people,
from this time on and forevermore.
3 For the scepter of wickedness shall not rest
on the land allotted to the righteous,
so that the righteous might not stretch out
their hands to do wrong.
4 Do good, O LORD, to those who are good,
and to those who are upright in their hearts.
5 But those who turn aside to their own crooked ways
the LORD will lead away with evildoers.
Peace be upon Israel!

PSALM 126
A Harvest of Joy
A Song of Ascents.

1 When the LORD restored the fortunes of Zion,[a]
we were like those who dream.
2 Then our mouth was filled with laughter,
and our tongue with shouts of joy;
then it was said among the nations,
"The LORD has done great things for them."
3 The LORD has done great things for us,
and we rejoiced.

4 Restore our fortunes, O LORD,
like the watercourses in the Negeb.

[a] Or *brought back those who returned to Zion*

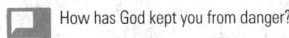

How has God kept you from danger?

Psalm 125: A trust psalm from the community (see Types of Psalms, pp. 849-850).

125:1-3 Those who trust in the LORD are like Mount Zion…the scepter of wickedness shall not rest on the land: The scepter is a symbol of human rulers, indicating that the psalm may have been written during a time of oppression. The psalm expresses trust that oppressors will pass away and those who trust in God will remain, even as Mount Zion remains.

Psalm 126: A community prayer for help (see Types of Psalms, pp. 849-850).

126:1-3 When the LORD restored the fortunes of Zion…then it was said among the nations: The psalm probably refers to the return of the exiles from Babylon, when the LORD restored the people to the land. Normally in the psalms, the nations taunt the Israelites and their God (see note on 42:3, 10), but in a surprising turn, here the nations praise God for what God has done for them.

126:4-6 Restore our fortunes: This is a prayer for continued restoration, especially through the fruits of creation. The Negeb is the desert, here pictured as flowing with rain.

5 May those who sow in tears
reap with shouts of joy.
6 Those who go out weeping,
bearing the seed for sowing,
shall come home with shouts of joy,
carrying their sheaves.

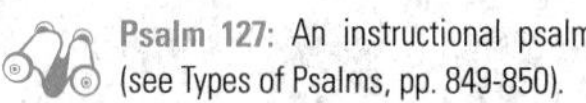

Psalm 127: An instructional psalm (see Types of Psalms, pp. 849-850).

127:1-5 Unless the Lord builds the house: The word *house* can mean a home, a temple, or family. This poem plays on all three meanings, teaching that human effort (to build cities, families, and so on) is useless without God's blessing.

Do you take time each day to ask for God to bless the work of your hands, heart, and mind? Why or why not?

PSALM 127

God's Blessings in the Home

A Song of Ascents. Of Solomon.

1 Unless the Lord builds the house,
those who build it labor in vain.
Unless the Lord guards the city,
the guard keeps watch in vain.
2 It is in vain that you rise up early
and go late to rest,
eating the bread of anxious toil;
for he gives sleep to his beloved.[a]

3 Sons are indeed a heritage from the Lord,
the fruit of the womb a reward.
4 Like arrows in the hand of a warrior
are the sons of one's youth.
5 Happy is the man who has
his quiver full of them.
He shall not be put to shame
when he speaks with his enemies in the gate.

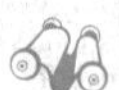

Psalm 128: An instructional psalm (see Types of Psalms, pp. 849-850).

128:1 who fears the Lord: See note on 34:9-11.

128:3 Your wife shall be like a fruitful vine: In the ancient world, security and honor (see note on 6:10) came from having children.

PSALM 128

The Happy Home of the Faithful

A Song of Ascents.

1 Happy is everyone who fears the Lord,
who walks in his ways.
2 You shall eat the fruit of the labor of your hands;
you shall be happy, and it shall go well with you.

3 Your wife will be like a fruitful vine
within your house;
your children will be like olive shoots
around your table.
4 Thus shall the man be blessed
who fears the Lord.

---

[a] Or *for he provides for his beloved during sleep*

[5] The LORD bless you from Zion.
May you see the prosperity of Jerusalem
all the days of your life.
[6] May you see your children's children.
Peace be upon Israel!

PSALM 129
Prayer for the Downfall of Israel's Enemies

A Song of Ascents.

[1] "Often have they attacked me from my youth"
—let Israel now say—
[2] "often have they attacked me from my youth,
yet they have not prevailed against me.
[3] The plowers plowed on my back;
they made their furrows long."
[4] The LORD is righteous;
he has cut the cords of the wicked.
[5] May all who hate Zion
be put to shame and turned backward.
[6] Let them be like the grass on the housetops
that withers before it grows up,
[7] with which reapers do not fill their hands
or binders of sheaves their arms,
[8] while those who pass by do not say,
"The blessing of the LORD be upon you!
We bless you in the name of the LORD!"

PSALM 130
Waiting for Divine Redemption

A Song of Ascents.

[1] Out of the depths I cry to you, O LORD.
[2] Lord, hear my voice!
Let your ears be attentive
to the voice of my supplications!

[3] If you, O LORD, should mark iniquities,
Lord, who could stand?
[4] But there is forgiveness with you,
so that you may be revered.

[5] I wait for the LORD, my soul waits,
and in his word I hope;
[6] my soul waits for the Lord
more than those who watch for the morning,
more than those who watch for the morning.

128:5 The LORD bless you from Zion. May you see the prosperity of Jerusalem: We seek God's blessings for ourselves and extend them to others.

Psalm 129: A liturgy and trust psalm (see Types of Psalms, pp. 849-850).

129:1-2 Often have they attacked me from my youth: A worship leader says this phrase, and then the community repeats it (129:2). It speaks to Israel's constant persecution, but also to God's faithfulness.

129:5-8 May all: This can also be translated, "All who hate Zion will be put to shame and turned back. They will be like grass on the housetops." Those who curse Israel actually bring curses back upon themselves (see Gen 12:1-3). Instead of gathering an abundant harvest, they will be like dried-up grass. Blessings multiply the more they are shared.

We are called to live in the abundance of God's creation, trusting that God will continue to provide. When has sharing God's blessings with others actually increased your blessings?

Psalm 130: A prayer for help from a person who has sinned, and a penitential psalm (see Types of Psalms, pp. 849-850).

130:1 Out of the depths: The depths (see 69:1-4) are an image of extreme crisis, connected with the view from mythology that the watery floods represent chaos.

130:3-4 If you, O LORD, should mark iniquities: This is a confession of sins, although it is not directly stated. God's gracious and forgiving nature is the reason God is to be feared (translated "revered" in NRSV; see note on 34:9-11).

130:5-6 I wait for the LORD . . . more than those who watch for the morning: Morning symbolizes hope and renewal (30:5). Like guards who wait for morning, the sinner waits for the good news of God's forgiveness. (Regarding "wait for the LORD," see note on 27:14.)

Tell about a time when you were forgiven.

Psalm 131: A trust psalm (see Types of Psalms, pp. 849-850) from an individual.

131:1 my heart is not lifted up, my eyes are not raised too high: The psalmist approaches God with humility and with confidence that God will hear the prayer.

131:2 my soul is like the weaned child that is with me: This may indicate that a woman originally prayed this psalm. Although troubled, the psalmist finds security and comfort in God's presence, like a sleeping child with its mother.

Psalm 132: A royal psalm and liturgy (see Types of Psalms, pp. 849-850), celebrating the arrival of the ark of the covenant (see note on 47:5) in Jerusalem (see 2 Sam 6).

132:1-10 O LORD, remember in David's favor: The psalm tells how King David brought the ark of the covenant to Jerusalem. David's son Solomon later built the temple, which became the home for the ark and for God.

7 O Israel, hope in the LORD!
For with the LORD there is steadfast love,
and with him is great power to redeem.
8 It is he who will redeem Israel
from all its iniquities.

PSALM 131
Song of Quiet Trust

A Song of Ascents. Of David.

1 O LORD, my heart is not lifted up,
my eyes are not raised too high;
I do not occupy myself with things
too great and too marvelous for me.
2 But I have calmed and quieted my soul,
like a weaned child with its mother;
my soul is like the weaned child that is with me.[a]

3 O Israel, hope in the LORD
from this time on and forevermore.

PSALM 132
The Eternal Dwelling of God in Zion

A Song of Ascents.

1 O LORD, remember in David's favor
all the hardships he endured;
2 how he swore to the LORD
and vowed to the Mighty One of Jacob,
3 "I will not enter my house
or get into my bed;
4 I will not give sleep to my eyes
or slumber to my eyelids,
5 until I find a place for the LORD,
a dwelling place for the Mighty One of Jacob."

6 We heard of it in Ephrathah;
we found it in the fields of Jaar.
7 "Let us go to his dwelling place;
let us worship at his footstool."

8 Rise up, O LORD, and go to your resting place,
you and the ark of your might.
9 Let your priests be clothed with righteousness,

---

[a] Or *my soul within me is like a weaned child*

and let your faithful shout for joy.
10 For your servant David's sake
do not turn away the face of your anointed one.

11 The LORD swore to David a sure oath
from which he will not turn back:
"One of the sons of your body
I will set on your throne.
12 If your sons keep my covenant
and my decrees that I shall teach them,
their sons also, forevermore,
shall sit on your throne."

13 For the LORD has chosen Zion;
he has desired it for his habitation:
14 "This is my resting place forever;
here I will reside, for I have desired it.
15 I will abundantly bless its provisions;
I will satisfy its poor with bread.
16 Its priests I will clothe with salvation,
and its faithful will shout for joy.
17 There I will cause a horn to sprout up for David;
I have prepared a lamp for my anointed one.
18 His enemies I will clothe with disgrace,
but on him, his crown will gleam."

PSALM 133
The Blessedness of Unity

A Song of Ascents.

1 How very good and pleasant it is
when kindred live together in unity!
2 It is like the precious oil on the head,
running down upon the beard,
on the beard of Aaron,
running down over the collar of his robes.
3 It is like the dew of Hermon,
which falls on the mountains of Zion.
For there the LORD ordained his blessing,
life forevermore.

PSALM 134
Praise in the Night

A Song of Ascents.

1 Come, bless the LORD, all you servants of the LORD,
who stand by night in the house of the LORD!

132:11-18 The LORD swore to David a sure oath…For the LORD has chosen Zion…I will abundantly bless: God chose David's descendants to be kings and Jerusalem to be God's dwelling place, for the sake of blessing the people. The people, in turn, were blessed in order to be a blessing to the world (see Gen 12:1-3).

As individuals and as a community, we are blessed for the sake of the world. What happens when we forget that we are blessed to be a blessing?

Psalm 133 An instructional psalm (see Types of Psalms, pp. 849-850) about the unity of God's people.

133:1 How very good and pleasant it is when kindred live together in unity: "Kindred" refers to the entire people of God. Often in the Old Testament and throughout history, God's people have not been united.

133:2-3 like the precious oil: To anoint a guest, by pouring oil on the person's head, was to show hospitality and welcome. To anoint a priest, such as Aaron, was to set him aside as one who blesses others. Both acts are represented here—the poem portrays a people who show hospitality and who are a blessing to others.

When have you felt truly welcome? How can God's people offer this sense of welcome?

Psalm 134: A liturgy (see Types of Psalms, pp. 849-850) of praise and blessing.

134:1-3 Come, bless the LORD… May the LORD…bless you from Zion: To "bless" can mean both to praise and to offer blessings. In worship, we come to praise God and God comes to bless us. We sing, pray, read, talk, and give, but the real actor is God—God comes, blesses, forgives, and speaks to us.

What is one powerful worship experience that you have had?

2 Lift up your hands to the holy place,
and bless the LORD.

3 May the LORD, maker of heaven and earth,
bless you from Zion.

Psalm 135: A hymn of praise (see Types of Psalms, pp. 849-850) celebrating God's faithfulness.

135:1-3 Praise the LORD!: The song starts with a repeated call to praise.

135:4 For the LORD has chosen Jacob: God chose Israel to be a priestly nation—one that is blessed in order to bless all the other nations (see Gen 12:1-3; Exod 19:5-6).

135:7 He it is who makes the clouds rise: God's faithfulness is also seen in creation.

135:8-11 He it was who: These verses summarize God's actions for Israel during the exodus from Egypt, wandering in the wilderness, and settlement of the land.

135:13 Your name: See note on 20:7.

PSALM 135
Praise for God's Goodness and Might

1 Praise the LORD!
Praise the name of the LORD;
give praise, O servants of the LORD,
2 you that stand in the house of the LORD,
in the courts of the house of our God.
3 Praise the LORD, for the LORD is good;
sing to his name, for he is gracious.
4 For the LORD has chosen Jacob for himself,
Israel as his own possession.

5 For I know that the LORD is great;
our Lord is above all gods.
6 Whatever the LORD pleases he does,
in heaven and on earth,
in the seas and all deeps.
7 He it is who makes the clouds rise at the end of the earth;
he makes lightnings for the rain
and brings out the wind from his storehouses.

8 He it was who struck down the firstborn of Egypt,
both human beings and animals;
9 he sent signs and wonders
into your midst, O Egypt,
against Pharaoh and all his servants.
10 He struck down many nations
and killed mighty kings—
11 Sihon, king of the Amorites,
and Og, king of Bashan,
and all the kingdoms of Canaan—
12 and gave their land as a heritage,
a heritage to his people Israel.

13 Your name, O LORD, endures forever,
your renown, O LORD, throughout all ages.
14 For the LORD will vindicate his people,
and have compassion on his servants.

15 The idols of the nations are silver and gold,
the work of human hands.
16 They have mouths, but they do not speak;
they have eyes, but they do not see;
17 they have ears, but they do not hear,
and there is no breath in their mouths.
18 Those who make them
and all who trust them
shall become like them.

19 O house of Israel, bless the LORD!
O house of Aaron, bless the LORD!
20 O house of Levi, bless the LORD!
You that fear the LORD, bless the LORD!
21 Blessed be the LORD from Zion,
he who resides in Jerusalem.
Praise the LORD!

PSALM 136

God's Work in Creation and in History

1 O give thanks to the LORD, for he is good,
for his steadfast love endures forever.
2 O give thanks to the God of gods,
for his steadfast love endures forever.
3 O give thanks to the Lord of lords,
for his steadfast love endures forever;

4 who alone does great wonders,
for his steadfast love endures forever;
5 who by understanding made the heavens,
for his steadfast love endures forever;
6 who spread out the earth on the waters,
for his steadfast love endures forever;
7 who made the great lights,
for his steadfast love endures forever;
8 the sun to rule over the day,
for his steadfast love endures forever;
9 the moon and stars to rule over the night,
for his steadfast love endures forever;

10 who struck Egypt through their firstborn,
for his steadfast love endures forever;
11 and brought Israel out from among them,
for his steadfast love endures forever;
12 with a strong hand and an outstretched arm,

135:15-18 The idols of the nations: It is foolish to trust in anything other than the living God.

135:19-21 bless the LORD!: The song ends with a repeated call to bless the LORD, which mirrors the way the song starts.

Psalm 136: A liturgy (see Types of Psalms, pp. 849-850) celebrating God's faithfulness, as shown in creation and Israel's history.

136:1 for his steadfast love endures forever: The major claim about God in the book of Psalms is that God is faithful and God's steadfast love is permanent (see notes on 13:5 and 117:1-2). Each verse of this liturgy names something God has done and responds with this declaration or confession of faith.

136:4-9 who alone does great wonders: This stanza of the liturgy praises God's faithfulness in creation.

136:10-24 who struck Egypt: These verses praise God's faithfulness in choosing and saving Israel.

Write, say, or sing your own liturgy of praise, listing what the LORD has done for you and your loved ones, and responding after each item with "for God's steadfast love endures forever."

for his steadfast love endures forever;
13 who divided the Red Sea[a] in two,
for his steadfast love endures forever;
14 and made Israel pass through the midst of it,
for his steadfast love endures forever;
15 but overthrew Pharaoh and his army in the Red Sea,[a]
for his steadfast love endures forever;
16 who led his people through the wilderness,
for his steadfast love endures forever;
17 who struck down great kings,
for his steadfast love endures forever;
18 and killed famous kings,
for his steadfast love endures forever;
19 Sihon, king of the Amorites,
for his steadfast love endures forever;
20 and Og, king of Bashan,
for his steadfast love endures forever;
21 and gave their land as a heritage,
for his steadfast love endures forever;
22 a heritage to his servant Israel,
for his steadfast love endures forever.

23 It is he who remembered us in our low estate,
for his steadfast love endures forever;
24 and rescued us from our foes,
for his steadfast love endures forever;
25 who gives food to all flesh,
for his steadfast love endures forever.

26 O give thanks to the God of heaven,
for his steadfast love endures forever.

Psalm 137: A community prayer for help (see Types of Psalms, pp. 849-850).

137:1-3 By the rivers of Babylon: This song was composed during the people's exile in Babylon. Tormentors taunted the psalmist, who was a temple musician, mockingly asking for a "song of Zion" (see Types of Psalms, pp. 849-850).

PSALM 137

Lament over the Destruction of Jerusalem

1 By the rivers of Babylon—
there we sat down and there we wept
when we remembered Zion.
2 On the willows[b] there
we hung up our harps.
3 For there our captors
asked us for songs,
and our tormentors asked for mirth, saying,
"Sing us one of the songs of Zion!"

[a] Or *Sea of Reeds* [b] Or *poplars*

⁴ How could we sing the LORD's song
in a foreign land?
⁵ If I forget you, O Jerusalem,
let my right hand wither!
⁶ Let my tongue cling to the roof of my mouth,
if I do not remember you,
if I do not set Jerusalem
above my highest joy.

⁷ Remember, O LORD, against the Edomites
the day of Jerusalem's fall,
how they said, "Tear it down! Tear it down!
Down to its foundations!"
⁸ O daughter Babylon, you devastator![a]
Happy shall they be who pay you back
what you have done to us!
⁹ Happy shall they be who take your little ones
and dash them against the rock!

PSALM 138
Thanksgiving and Praise
Of David.

¹ I give you thanks, O LORD, with my whole heart;
before the gods I sing your praise;
² I bow down toward your holy temple
and give thanks to your name for your steadfast love and your faithfulness;
for you have exalted your name and your word
above everything.[b]
³ On the day I called, you answered me,
you increased my strength of soul.[c]

⁴ All the kings of the earth shall praise you, O LORD,
for they have heard the words of your mouth.
⁵ They shall sing of the ways of the LORD,
for great is the glory of the LORD.
⁶ For though the LORD is high, he regards the lowly;
but the haughty he perceives from far away.

⁷ Though I walk in the midst of trouble,
you preserve me against the wrath of my enemies;
you stretch out your hand,

137:4-6 How could we sing the LORD's song in a foreign land?: In despair over being separated from Jerusalem, the musician asks, "How could we sing?" Yet, ironically, the psalm is a song that expresses hope and promises not to forget Jerusalem.

137:8-9 O daughter Babylon: The extreme desire for revenge is troubling, but it is a burden we can turn over to the LORD, leaving vengeance in God's hands (see note on 58:6-11).

Have you ever given feelings of anger or bitterness to God in prayer? How would this help?

Psalm 138: A song of thanksgiving (see Types of Psalms, pp. 849-850) that responds to God's saving help.

138:1 before the gods: See note on 82:1.

138:2 you have exalted your name and your word: God has kept a promise (a word), and that has exalted God's name.

138:6 though the LORD is high, he regards the lowly: It is God's nature to care about the downtrodden and oppressed, and to raise them up (see 113:5-9). The world may look down on these people, but God loves and is faithful to all.

[a] Or *you who are devastated* [b] Cn: Heb *you have exalted your word above all your name* [c] Syr Compare Gk Tg: Heb *you made me arrogant in my soul with strength*

138:8 The Lord will fulfill his purpose for me: The psalmist trusts that God's guidance and protection will continue.

and your right hand delivers me.
8 The Lord will fulfill his purpose for me;
your steadfast love, O Lord, endures forever.
Do not forsake the work of your hands.

Psalm 139: A prayer for help and a creation psalm (see Types of Psalms, pp. 849-850) in four stanzas (139:1-6; 7-12; 13-18; 19-24).

139:1-6 you have searched me and known me: The first stanza is about God's knowledge. God knows all about us, intimately and completely.

PSALM 139

The Inescapable God

To the leader. Of David. A Psalm.

1 O Lord, you have searched me and known me.
2 You know when I sit down and when I rise up;
you discern my thoughts from far away.
3 You search out my path and my lying down,
and are acquainted with all my ways.
4 Even before a word is on my tongue,
O Lord, you know it completely.
5 You hem me in, behind and before,
and lay your hand upon me.
6 Such knowledge is too wonderful for me;
it is so high that I cannot attain it.

139:7-12 Where can I go from your spirit?: The second stanza is about God's presence. Using beautiful poetic language, the psalm claims that there is no place, time, or situation that can separate us from God (see Rom 8:38-39).

7 Where can I go from your spirit?
Or where can I flee from your presence?
8 If I ascend to heaven, you are there;
if I make my bed in Sheol, you are there.
9 If I take the wings of the morning
and settle at the farthest limits of the sea,
10 even there your hand shall lead me,
and your right hand shall hold me fast.
11 If I say, "Surely the darkness shall cover me,
and the light around me become night,"
12 even the darkness is not dark to you;
the night is as bright as the day,
for darkness is as light to you.

139:13-18 it was you who formed my inward parts: The third stanza is about God the Creator. God's wisdom surpasses all our attempts to understand it, and with this wisdom God formed us. To be "fearfully and wonderfully made" means that every human being is a unique and marvelous act of God's creation. God knows our past and our future.

We are not mere accidents of nature, but loving creations of the Creator. What difference does this make to you?

13 For it was you who formed my inward parts;
you knit me together in my mother's womb.
14 I praise you, for I am fearfully and wonderfully made.
Wonderful are your works;
that I know very well.
15 My frame was not hidden from you,
when I was being made in secret,
intricately woven in the depths of the earth.
16 Your eyes beheld my unformed substance.
In your book were written
all the days that were formed for me,

when none of them as yet existed.
17 How weighty to me are your thoughts, O God!
How vast is the sum of them!
18 I try to count them—they are more than the sand;
I come to the end[a]—I am still with you.

19 O that you would kill the wicked, O God,
and that the bloodthirsty would depart from me—
20 those who speak of you maliciously,
and lift themselves up against you for evil![b]
21 Do I not hate those who hate you, O LORD?
And do I not loathe those who rise up against you?
22 I hate them with perfect hatred;
I count them my enemies.
23 Search me, O God, and know my heart;
test me and know my thoughts.
24 See if there is any wicked[c] way in me,
and lead me in the way everlasting.[d]

139:19-24 O that you would kill the wicked...Search me, O God, and know my heart: The psalmist begs God, who searches and knows all people (139:1), to investigate and prove that the accusations of the wicked are false. Regarding the prayer for vengeance, see note on 58:6-11.

PSALM 140

Prayer for Deliverance from Enemies

To the leader. A Psalm of David.

1 Deliver me, O LORD, from evildoers;
protect me from those who are violent,
2 who plan evil things in their minds
and stir up wars continually.
3 They make their tongue sharp as a snake's,
and under their lips is the venom of vipers. *Selah*

4 Guard me, O LORD, from the hands of the wicked;
protect me from the violent
who have planned my downfall.
5 The arrogant have hidden a trap for me,
and with cords they have spread a net,[e]
along the road they have set snares for me. *Selah*

6 I say to the LORD, "You are my God;
give ear, O LORD, to the voice of my supplications."
7 O LORD, my Lord, my strong deliverer,
you have covered my head in the day of battle.
8 Do not grant, O LORD, the desires of the wicked;
do not further their evil plot.[f] *Selah*

Psalm 140: A prayer for help (see Types of Psalms, pp. 849-850) from a person oppressed by evildoers.

140:1-5 The arrogant have hidden a trap for me: The evildoers place themselves above God's law, so they feel free to harm others.

140:6 I say to the LORD, "You are my God": To have faith in God is to trust God in the face of danger. The psalmist humbly submits to God's love and God's law.

---

[a] Or *I awake* [b] Cn: Meaning of Heb uncertain [c] Heb *hurtful* [d] Or *the ancient way.* Compare Jer 6.16 [e] Or *they have spread cords as a net* [f] Heb adds *they are exalted*

[9] Those who surround me lift up their heads;[a]
let the mischief of their lips overwhelm them!
[10] Let burning coals fall on them!
Let them be flung into pits, no more to rise!
[11] Do not let the slanderer be established in the land;
let evil speedily hunt down the violent!

[12] I know that the LORD maintains the cause of the needy,
and executes justice for the poor.
[13] Surely the righteous shall give thanks to your name;
the upright shall live in your presence.

140:11 Do not let the slanderer: The "slanderer" is literally "a man of the tongue" in Hebrew. This is one who speaks against God (see note on 3:2 about the wicked), not necessarily one who falsely accuses.

140:12 I know that the LORD maintains the cause of the needy: Even under oppression, the psalmist trusts in God's saving help.

Psalm 141: A prayer for help (see Types of Psalms, pp. 849-850) and an evening prayer from a person separated from the temple.

PSALM 141

Prayer for Preservation from Evil

A Psalm of David.

[1] I call upon you, O LORD; come quickly to me;
give ear to my voice when I call to you.
[2] Let my prayer be counted as incense before you,
and the lifting up of my hands as an evening sacrifice.

[3] Set a guard over my mouth, O LORD;
keep watch over the door of my lips.
[4] Do not turn my heart to any evil,
to busy myself with wicked deeds
in company with those who work iniquity;
do not let me eat of their delicacies.

[5] Let the righteous strike me;
let the faithful correct me.
Never let the oil of the wicked anoint my head,[b]
for my prayer is continually[c] against their wicked deeds.
[6] When they are given over to those who shall condemn them,
then they shall learn that my words were pleasant.
[7] Like a rock that one breaks apart and shatters on the land,
so shall their bones be strewn at the mouth of Sheol.[d]

[8] But my eyes are turned toward you, O GOD, my Lord;
in you I seek refuge; do not leave me defenseless.
[9] Keep me from the trap that they have laid for me,
and from the snares of evildoers.

141:2 incense: Incense was offered with the evening sacrifice (see Exod 30:8; 29:38-42). The psalmist may have been unable to offer incense and so asks that the prayer be accepted instead.

141:3-4 Set a guard over my mouth: The psalmist asks God for help against the temptation to pursue harmful paths. We cannot walk in God's ways without God's help.

141:8 my eyes are turned toward you: The psalmist turns toward heaven, humbly submitting to God's love and care. On the wicked falling into their own trap, see note on 7:15-16.

---

[a] Cn Compare Gk: Heb *those who surround me are uplifted in head;* Heb divides verses 8 and 9 differently
[b] Gk: Meaning of Heb uncertain [c] Cn: Heb *for continually and my prayer* [d] Meaning of Heb of verses 5–7 is uncertain

10 Let the wicked fall into their own nets,
while I alone escape.

PSALM 142

Prayer for Deliverance from Persecutors

A Maskil of David. When he was in the cave. A Prayer.

1 With my voice I cry to the LORD;
with my voice I make supplication to the LORD.
2 I pour out my complaint before him;
I tell my trouble before him.
3 When my spirit is faint,
you know my way.

In the path where I walk
they have hidden a trap for me.
4 Look on my right hand and see—
there is no one who takes notice of me;
no refuge remains to me;
no one cares for me.

5 I cry to you, O LORD;
I say, "You are my refuge,
my portion in the land of the living."
6 Give heed to my cry,
for I am brought very low.

Save me from my persecutors,
for they are too strong for me.
7 Bring me out of prison,
so that I may give thanks to your name.
The righteous will surround me,
for you will deal bountifully with me.

Psalm 142: A prayer for help (see Types of Psalms, pp. 849-850) from an individual.

142:1 I cry to the LORD: A key term in the prayer is "cry," which expresses desperation, but also trust—because the psalmist cries *to God.*

142:4-5 I say, "You are my refuge": Regarding "refuge," see note on 2:11. Because no source of help or comfort exists on earth, the psalmist turns to the only hope left—God.

You do not have to wait to turn to God only after you exhaust all other options. But when this is the case, you can always turn to the LORD. When have you been so overwhelmed that you gave up and asked for help?

PSALM 143

Prayer for Deliverance from Enemies

A Psalm of David.

1 Hear my prayer, O LORD;
give ear to my supplications in your faithfulness;
answer me in your righteousness.
2 Do not enter into judgment with your servant,
for no one living is righteous before you.

3 For the enemy has pursued me,
crushing my life to the ground,

Psalm 143: A prayer for help and a penitential psalm (see Types of Psalms, pp. 849-850) that is also a morning prayer.

143:2 for no one living is righteous before you: In the psalms, sufferers often proclaim that they are innocent of specific charges (see 139:19-24). Here the psalmist confesses sin and recognizes that nobody is sinless or perfectly righteous before God (see Rom 3:23).

making me sit in darkness like those long dead.
4 Therefore my spirit faints within me;
my heart within me is appalled.

143:5 I remember the days of old: The psalmist draws hope from remembering what God has done for the people.

5 I remember the days of old,
I think about all your deeds,
I meditate on the works of your hands.
6 I stretch out my hands to you;
my soul thirsts for you like a parched land. *Selah*

7 Answer me quickly, O LORD;
my spirit fails.
Do not hide your face from me,
or I shall be like those who go down to the Pit.
8 Let me hear of your steadfast love in the morning,
for in you I put my trust.
Teach me the way I should go,
for to you I lift up my soul.

9 Save me, O LORD, from my enemies;
I have fled to you for refuge.[a]
10 Teach me to do your will,
for you are my God.
Let your good spirit lead me
on a level path.

143:11-12 For your name's sake: Not because of anything that the psalmist has done—but only because of God's righteousness and steadfast love—there is hope for forgiveness.

Our relationship with God depends on who God is, not what we do. Why is this good news for you?

11 For your name's sake, O LORD, preserve my life.
In your righteousness bring me out of trouble.
12 In your steadfast love cut off my enemies,
and destroy all my adversaries,
for I am your servant.

Psalm 144: A royal psalm and prayer for help (see Types of Psalms, pp. 849-850), probably used before battle.

144:1-2 Blessed be the LORD, my rock: The king praises God and asks for God's protection in war.

PSALM 144

Prayer for National Deliverance and Security

Of David.

1 Blessed be the LORD, my rock,
who trains my hands for war, and my fingers for battle;
2 my rock[b] and my fortress,
my stronghold and my deliverer,
my shield, in whom I take refuge,
who subdues the peoples[c] under me.

---

[a] One Heb Ms Gk: MT *to you I have hidden* [b] With 18.2 and 2 Sam 22.2: Heb *my steadfast love*
[c] Heb Mss Syr Aquila Jerome: MT *my people*

3 O LORD, what are human beings that you regard them,
or mortals that you think of them?
4 They are like a breath;
their days are like a passing shadow.

5 Bow your heavens, O LORD, and come down;
touch the mountains so that they smoke.
6 Make the lightning flash and scatter them;
send out your arrows and rout them.
7 Stretch out your hand from on high;
set me free and rescue me from the mighty waters,
from the hand of aliens,
8 whose mouths speak lies,
and whose right hands are false.

9 I will sing a new song to you, O God;
upon a ten-stringed harp I will play to you,
10 the one who gives victory to kings,
who rescues his servant David.
11 Rescue me from the cruel sword,
and deliver me from the hand of aliens,
whose mouths speak lies,
and whose right hands are false.

12 May our sons in their youth
be like plants full grown,
our daughters like corner pillars,
cut for the building of a palace.
13 May our barns be filled,
with produce of every kind;
may our sheep increase by thousands,
by tens of thousands in our fields,
14 and may our cattle be heavy with young.
May there be no breach in the walls,[a] no exile,
and no cry of distress in our streets.

15 Happy are the people to whom such blessings fall;
happy are the people whose God is the LORD.

PSALM 145

The Greatness and the Goodness of God

Praise. Of David.

1 I will extol you, my God and King,

144:3 O LORD, what are human beings that you regard them: This verse is similar to 8:4 in recognizing human weakness, but here this acknowledgement leads the king to pray for God's saving help.

144:12-15 happy are the people whose God is the LORD: The king does not pray primarily for himself, but for the people he leads. Because of the responsibility that he has for the people, the king asks for God's blessing.

Who depends on you? What requests will you include in your prayers, on behalf of these people?

Psalm 145: A hymn of praise that is also an acrostic poem (see Types of Psalms, pp. 849-850).

[a] Heb lacks *in the walls*

and bless your name forever and ever.
2 Every day I will bless you,
and praise your name forever and ever.
3 Great is the LORD, and greatly to be praised;
his greatness is unsearchable.

145:4 One generation shall laud your works to another: The purpose of praise is not to flatter God, but to bear witness to God's deeds, so that others may know God and be in relationship with God (see note on 96:1-9).

4 One generation shall laud your works to another,
and shall declare your mighty acts.
5 On the glorious splendor of your majesty,
and on your wondrous works, I will meditate.
6 The might of your awesome deeds shall be proclaimed,
and I will declare your greatness.
7 They shall celebrate the fame of your abundant goodness,
and shall sing aloud of your righteousness.

145:8-9 The LORD is gracious and merciful: These verses are like a creed or statement of faith. Similar to the ancient creed in Exodus 34:6, they state the heart of Israel's faith: God is gracious and merciful, abounding in steadfast love. See also 145:13.

8 The LORD is gracious and merciful,
slow to anger and abounding in steadfast love.
9 The LORD is good to all,
and his compassion is over all that he has made.

10 All your works shall give thanks to you, O LORD,
and all your faithful shall bless you.
11 They shall speak of the glory of your kingdom,
and tell of your power,
12 to make known to all people your[a] mighty deeds,
and the glorious splendor of your[b] kingdom.
13 Your kingdom is an everlasting kingdom,
and your dominion endures throughout all generations.

The LORD is faithful in all his words,
and gracious in all his deeds.[c]
14 The LORD upholds all who are falling,
and raises up all who are bowed down.

145:15-16 The eyes of all look to you: These verses ask for God's blessing and give thanks to God. (Martin Luther suggested using them as a table prayer.)

Before meals, some people use memorized or written prayers, while others pray in their own words. What sort of table prayer works best for you?

145:18 The LORD is near to all who call on him: God's name is given to us so that we might call on God in times of need and in times of thanksgiving.

15 The eyes of all look to you,
and you give them their food in due season.
16 You open your hand,
satisfying the desire of every living thing.
17 The LORD is just in all his ways,
and kind in all his doings.
18 The LORD is near to all who call on him,
to all who call on him in truth.
19 He fulfills the desire of all who fear him;
he also hears their cry, and saves them.

---

[a] Gk Jerome Syr: Heb *his* [b] Heb *his* [c] These two lines supplied by Q Ms Gk Syr

20 The LORD watches over all who love him,
but all the wicked he will destroy.

21 My mouth will speak the praise of the LORD,
and all flesh will bless his holy name forever and ever.

PSALM 146
Praise for God's Help

1 Praise the LORD!
Praise the LORD, O my soul!
2 I will praise the LORD as long as I live;
I will sing praises to my God all my life long.

3 Do not put your trust in princes,
in mortals, in whom there is no help.
4 When their breath departs, they return to the earth;
on that very day their plans perish.

5 Happy are those whose help is the God of Jacob,
whose hope is in the LORD their God,
6 who made heaven and earth,
the sea, and all that is in them;
who keeps faith forever;
7 who executes justice for the oppressed;
who gives food to the hungry.

The LORD sets the prisoners free;
8 the LORD opens the eyes of the blind.
The LORD lifts up those who are bowed down;
the LORD loves the righteous.
9 The LORD watches over the strangers;
he upholds the orphan and the widow,
but the way of the wicked he brings to ruin.

10 The LORD will reign forever,
your God, O Zion, for all generations.
Praise the LORD!

PSALM 147
Praise for God's Care for Jerusalem

1 Praise the LORD!
How good it is to sing praises to our God;

Psalm 146: A hymn of praise (see Types of Psalms, pp. 849-850).

146:1 Praise the LORD, O my soul!: Regarding "soul," see note on 42:5.

146:3 Do not put your trust in princes: The song praises God and teaches that only God is worthy of our ultimate trust and faith.

146:6-7 who made heaven and earth...who executes justice for the oppressed: Two of the ways that God's faithfulness is made known are through creation and through the justice God works to establish on earth.

One way God works to establish justice is by building communities of faith based on God's Word. How is your community of faith sharing in this mission?

How does God work? God does not work the way we might expect. It is God's nature to work by turning the ways of this world upside down, for example, by setting prisoners free. As Luther wrote: "True Christian religion does not begin at the highest as all other religions do, but at the lowest. Therefore whenever you are concerned to think and act about your salvation, you must put away all speculations about the Majesty, all thoughts of works, traditions, and philosophy—indeed, of the Law of God itself. And you must run directly to the manger and the mother's womb, embrace this Infant and Virgin's Child in your arms, and look at Him—born, being nursed, growing up, going about in human society, teaching, dying, rising again, ascending above all the heavens, and having authority over all things" (*LW* 26:30). *Psalm 146:7b-9*

Psalm 147: A hymn of praise (see Types of Psalms, pp. 849-850) in three stanzas (147:1-6, 7-11, 12-20). Each stanza calls for and gives reasons for praise.

147:1-6 Praise the LORD!...The LORD lifts up the downtrodden: Praise is called for because God works by turning the normal patterns of the sinful world upside down.

for he is gracious, and a song of praise is fitting.
2 The LORD builds up Jerusalem;
he gathers the outcasts of Israel.
3 He heals the brokenhearted,
and binds up their wounds.
4 He determines the number of the stars;
he gives to all of them their names.
5 Great is our Lord, and abundant in power;
his understanding is beyond measure.
6 The LORD lifts up the downtrodden;
he casts the wicked to the ground.

7 Sing to the LORD with thanksgiving;
make melody to our God on the lyre.
8 He covers the heavens with clouds,
prepares rain for the earth,
makes grass grow on the hills.
9 He gives to the animals their food,
and to the young ravens when they cry.
10 His delight is not in the strength of the horse,
nor his pleasure in the speed of a runner;[a]
11 but the LORD takes pleasure in those who fear him,
in those who hope in his steadfast love.

12 Praise the LORD, O Jerusalem!
Praise your God, O Zion!
13 For he strengthens the bars of your gates;
he blesses your children within you.
14 He grants peace[b] within your borders;
he fills you with the finest of wheat.
15 He sends out his command to the earth;
his word runs swiftly.
16 He gives snow like wool;
he scatters frost like ashes.
17 He hurls down hail like crumbs—
who can stand before his cold?
18 He sends out his word, and melts them;
he makes his wind blow, and the waters flow.
19 He declares his word to Jacob,
his statutes and ordinances to Israel.
20 He has not dealt thus with any other nation;
they do not know his ordinances.
Praise the LORD!

147:7-11 Sing to the LORD...He covers the heavens with clouds: Praise is called for because God is at work through creation, providing and caring for humans and animals (see also 147:14-18).

147:12-20 Praise the LORD...He grants peace within your borders...He declares his word to Jacob: Praise is called for because God is at work through God's people, creating a just and fair world.

When you look at our world, what is the number-one reason you see for praising God?

[a] Heb *legs of a person* [b] Or *prosperity*

PSALM 148

Praise for God's Universal Glory

Psalm 148: A hymn of praise (see Types of Psalms, pp. 849-850).

148:1-10 Praise the LORD!...Praise him, sun and moon: This song is an extended call for praise. Heavenly and earthly creations are all called on to praise God, indicating the universal nature of God's rule and complete joy and enthusiasm in the song's praise.

1 Praise the LORD!
Praise the LORD from the heavens;
praise him in the heights!
2 Praise him, all his angels;
praise him, all his host!

3 Praise him, sun and moon;
praise him, all you shining stars!
4 Praise him, you highest heavens,
and you waters above the heavens!

5 Let them praise the name of the LORD,
for he commanded and they were created.
6 He established them forever and ever;
he fixed their bounds, which cannot be passed.[a]

7 Praise the LORD from the earth,
you sea monsters and all deeps,
8 fire and hail, snow and frost,
stormy wind fulfilling his command!

9 Mountains and all hills,
fruit trees and all cedars!
10 Wild animals and all cattle,
creeping things and flying birds!

148:11-14 Kings of the earth and all peoples...He has raised up a horn for his people: The entire earth is called to praise God, because of what God has done by choosing Israel. Israel was chosen and blessed in order to be a blessing for all the other nations.

11 Kings of the earth and all peoples,
princes and all rulers of the earth!
12 Young men and women alike,
old and young together!

13 Let them praise the name of the LORD,
for his name alone is exalted;
his glory is above earth and heaven.
14 He has raised up a horn for his people,
praise for all his faithful,
for the people of Israel who are close to him.
Praise the LORD!

PSALM 149

Praise for God's Goodness to Israel

Psalm 149: A hymn of praise (see Types of Psalms, pp. 849-850).

149:1 Sing to the LORD a new song: For "new song," see note on 40:1-3.

1 Praise the LORD!

[a] Or *he set a law that cannot pass away*

Sing to the LORD a new song,
his praise in the assembly of the faithful.
2 Let Israel be glad in its Maker;
let the children of Zion rejoice in their King.
3 Let them praise his name with dancing,
making melody to him with tambourine and lyre.
4 For the LORD takes pleasure in his people;
he adorns the humble with victory.
5 Let the faithful exult in glory;
let them sing for joy on their couches.
6 Let the high praises of God be in their throats
and two-edged swords in their hands,
7 to execute vengeance on the nations
and punishment on the peoples,
8 to bind their kings with fetters
and their nobles with chains of iron,
9 to execute on them the judgment decreed.
This is glory for all his faithful ones.
Praise the LORD!

149:3-4 Let them praise his name with dancing . . . For the LORD takes pleasure in his people: Praising God is not a certain action in a certain place at a certain time. Praising God includes and encompasses our entire lives. Praise includes the joy of sharing our lives with God, and the joy God takes from being present in our lives.

All of life is about praising God. What are some ways you will praise God?

PSALM 150

Praise for God's Surpassing Greatness

1 Praise the LORD!
Praise God in his sanctuary;
praise him in his mighty firmament![a]
2 Praise him for his mighty deeds;
praise him according to his surpassing greatness!

3 Praise him with trumpet sound;
praise him with lute and harp!
4 Praise him with tambourine and dance;
praise him with strings and pipe!
5 Praise him with clanging cymbals;
praise him with loud clashing cymbals!
6 Let everything that breathes praise the LORD!
Praise the LORD!

Psalm 150: A hymn of praise (see Types of Psalms, pp. 849-850). This final doxology or song of praise closes the book of Psalms.

150:1-6 Praise the LORD! . . . Let everything that breathes praise the LORD!: In this extended call to praise, "everything that breathes" is called to praise the LORD.

[a] Or *dome*

PROVERBS

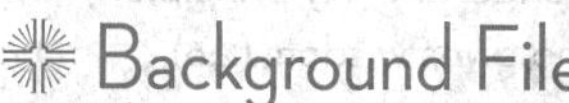

Proverbs 9:1

Background File

Like other "wisdom" books such as Song of Solomon and Ecclesiastes, Proverbs has traditionally been connected with King Solomon of Israel. While some sayings may go back to Solomon's time or beyond, Proverbs probably includes wisdom instructions collected over several centuries in Israel and from other cultures. Scholars generally agree that Proverbs in its present form dates to about the fourth century B.C.E.

What's the Story?

In the ancient world, wisdom was popular among intellectuals from Babylon to Egypt. Sages or wise persons would reflect on life and condense their wisdom into brief sayings. Israel's wisdom instructors would welcome a profound saying from Egypt or Mesopotamia. The sayings in Proverbs make no mention of the great events that shaped Israel's history. In this way, Proverbs seems to contrast with the teachings of Israel that centered on the Torah, or Teaching, found in the first five books of the Hebrew Scriptures (Genesis–Deuteronomy). Wisdom seems to have a more secular tone, because it observes life as it is and instructs people how to make the best of it. Like our "how to succeed" books, collections of wisdom sayings offered instructions for successful living.

Still, Proverbs does have a theological accent. It emphasizes "fear of the LORD" as the essential foundation for true wisdom. The "good life" builds on the foundation of Israel's religion. Israel's wisdom aims to help people develop a balanced life with proper relations to self, others, society, and God.

The wisdom sayings of Proverbs probably came to be used with other wisdom teachings in schools or by tutors. Those schools were open to young boys, so the teachings often focus on helping young men live successful and sensible lives. This is why sexual imagery and advice also slants toward males. In this way the sayings reflect an ancient patriarchal society. But it is clear that wisdom is to be honored and followed by all—boys and girls, women and men.

Overall, Proverbs can be outlined this way:

The worth of wisdom (1:1–9:18)
First collection of Solomon (10:1–22:16)

Sayings of the wise (22:17–24:34)
Second collection of Solomon, copied by Hezekiah's officials (25:1–29:27)
An Appendix (30:1–31:31)
The words of Agur (30:1-33)
The words of Lemuel (31:1-9)
The ideal wife (31:10-31)

What's the Message?

The Prologue (1:2-7) introduces the purpose of the book's many proverbs. In short, the proverbs provide practical insights and instruction about right living and wise dealing. The emphasis is on teaching knowledge and good sense ("prudence") to the young. All this is presented under the key principle: the beginning of knowledge or wisdom is "fear of the LORD" (1:7), the one who gives wisdom (2:6). Here, the word *fear* means awe or respect.

The wisdom sayings in Proverbs present knowledge gained through life experience in a rather uncomplicated way. Those who are wise understand that meaningful life includes treating others with fairness and justice, working hard, being loyal and humble, controlling one's emotions, respecting parents and others in authority, and helping the poor and needy. Wise persons make choices that lead to health, wealth, and happiness. On the other hand, foolish persons make poor choices that lead to discontent and punishment. For modern readers, the wisdom of Proverbs may seem to oversimplify the complexities of life. First, it divides people too neatly into two groups: the wise, who are righteous, and the fools, who are wicked and lost because they reject wisdom. Second, Proverbs assumes that people automatically get what they deserve. The wise will prosper and enjoy a long, rich life. Fools will suffer and fall. But we recognize that in a sinful world good folks often experience suffering while the wicked sometimes prosper.

Wisdom is celebrated in chapters 1–9 for its special character. For example, wisdom is described in feminine terms (1:20; 3:13-18). There is no evidence that Wisdom was regarded as a goddess in either Israel or Canaan, but it is likely that portraying Wisdom as a female was influenced by similar descriptions of the feminine gods of Israel's neighbors, such as Egypt. This does not mean Wisdom was considered a goddess herself. She is connected directly to God from the very beginning of creation (8:22-31). And the LORD founded the earth "by wisdom" (3:19-20). It's important to keep this strong positive view of female wisdom in mind when reading about the "loose woman," a figure representing those things that tempt youth to make poor choices (see 2:16-19; 5:3-6; 7:4-27). In fact, the reader is encouraged to stick with Wisdom as a sister or friend, to avoid the dangerous one (7:4).

In the New Testament, all the treasures of wisdom and knowledge are said to be hidden in Jesus Christ (Col 2:2-3). The Apostle Paul speaks of the message of the cross of Christ as being foolishness to those who think they are wise (1 Cor 1:18-31). Jesus, he says, "became for us wisdom from God" (1:30), and it is God's Holy Spirit that helps us comprehend this true wisdom from God (1 Cor 2:6-16). As Christian readers of the Bible, we read the wise sayings of Proverbs with our eyes also on this gospel message about Jesus and his cross, and we listen carefully to Jesus' teachings. As Lutherans, we also believe that it is not our good works that make us right with God. Rather, we are made right by God's grace through faith in Christ Jesus.

1

The proverbs of Solomon son of David, king of Israel:

Prologue

2 For learning about wisdom and instruction,
for understanding words of insight,
3 for gaining instruction in wise dealing,
righteousness, justice, and equity;
4 to teach shrewdness to the simple,
knowledge and prudence to the young—
5 let the wise also hear and gain in learning,
and the discerning acquire skill,
6 to understand a proverb and a figure,
the words of the wise and their riddles.

7 The fear of the LORD is the beginning of knowledge;
fools despise wisdom and instruction.

Warnings against Evil Companions

8 Hear, my child, your father's instruction,
and do not reject your mother's teaching;
9 for they are a fair garland for your head,
and pendants for your neck.
10 My child, if sinners entice you,
do not consent.
11 If they say, "Come with us, let us lie in wait for blood;
let us wantonly ambush the innocent;
12 like Sheol let us swallow them alive
and whole, like those who go down to the Pit.
13 We shall find all kinds of costly things;
we shall fill our houses with booty.
14 Throw in your lot among us;
we will all have one purse"—
15 my child, do not walk in their way,
keep your foot from their paths;
16 for their feet run to evil,
and they hurry to shed blood.
17 For in vain is the net baited
while the bird is looking on;
18 yet they lie in wait—to kill themselves!
and set an ambush—for their own lives!
19 Such is the end[a] of all who are greedy for gain;
it takes away the life of its possessors.

[a] Gk: Heb *are the ways*

1:1 the proverbs of Solomon: For more about what a proverb is, see the chart Types of Proverbs, p. 1018. Israel celebrated Solomon for his wisdom (see 1 Kgs 3:3-28, 4:29-34). Later wisdom collections used his name. Wisdom collections were sometimes named for rulers in the ancient world. Wise rulers were said to be those who ruled with justice and honesty (1 Kgs 3:9-12; Prov 8:12-16).

1:3 gaining instruction in wise dealing...equity: A wise person works for justice and fairness in dealing with others. This idea was supported by both Israel's law and by the message of the prophets.

1:7 The fear of the LORD: The phrase means respecting and honoring God and living according to God's commands. See also the note on 19:23.

1:8 your father's instruction... mother's teaching: "Father" could also mean a teacher in a classroom. Wisdom is passed on to the young from older generations. Wisdom is to be worn like a crown of flowers or a necklace. Compare this to Deuteronomy 6:8-9, which encourages God's teachings to be worn in leather pouches tied to one's arm or forehead.

1:11-14 If they say...lie in wait: The temptation is to join a criminal gang that robs. The lure of bad companions tempted youth then as now.

1:12 Sheol...the Pit: This is the dark underground world of the dead, a shadowy place of isolation, but not what Christians would consider hell.

The Call of Wisdom

1:20 Wisdom cries out . . . at the entrance of the city gates: The word "wisdom" is feminine in both Greek and Hebrew. Here wisdom appears as a woman. (See also 8:1-36 and 9:1-6.) Later writings spoke of wisdom as an expression of God. Paul called Jesus "the wisdom of God" (1 Cor 1:24). The gate of the city was the primary city meeting place where important matters were discussed and decided.

1:22 O simple ones: The "simple" are not yet instructed in wisdom but willing to learn. "Fools" and "scoffers" reject the pursuit of wisdom.

20 Wisdom cries out in the street;
in the squares she raises her voice.
21 At the busiest corner she cries out;
at the entrance of the city gates she speaks:
22 "How long, O simple ones, will you love being simple?
How long will scoffers delight in their scoffing
and fools hate knowledge?
23 Give heed to my reproof;
I will pour out my thoughts to you;
I will make my words known to you.
24 Because I have called and you refused,
have stretched out my hand and no one heeded,
25 and because you have ignored all my counsel
and would have none of my reproof,
26 I also will laugh at your calamity;
I will mock when panic strikes you,
27 when panic strikes you like a storm,
and your calamity comes like a whirlwind,
when distress and anguish come upon you.
28 Then they will call upon me, but I will not answer;
they will seek me diligently, but will not find me.
29 Because they hated knowledge
and did not choose the fear of the LORD,
30 would have none of my counsel,
and despised all my reproof,
31 therefore they shall eat the fruit of their way
and be sated with their own devices.
32 For waywardness kills the simple,
and the complacency of fools destroys them;
33 but those who listen to me will be secure
and will live at ease, without dread of disaster."

1:31 eat the fruit of their way: Another way of saying that people's actions (fruits) will determine how they are judged. Jesus used a similar proverb when he taught that "each tree is known by its own fruit" (Luke 6:44).

How would you describe a wise person, someone filled with wisdom?

The Value of Wisdom

2:1-22 My child: In Hebrew, this poem has twenty-two lines, the number of letters in the Hebrew alphabet.

2:2 inclining your heart: In ancient Hebrew thought, the heart, rather than the brain, guided a person's intentions. Wise Solomon asked for an "understanding mind" or, literally, "a listening heart" (1 Kgs 3:9).

2 My child, if you accept my words
and treasure up my commandments within you,
2 making your ear attentive to wisdom
and inclining your heart to understanding;
3 if you indeed cry out for insight,
and raise your voice for understanding;
4 if you seek it like silver,
and search for it as for hidden treasures—
5 then you will understand the fear of the LORD
and find the knowledge of God.

[6] For the LORD gives wisdom;
from his mouth come knowledge and understanding;
[7] he stores up sound wisdom for the upright;
he is a shield to those who walk blamelessly,
[8] guarding the paths of justice
and preserving the way of his faithful ones.
[9] Then you will understand righteousness and justice
and equity, every good path;
[10] for wisdom will come into your heart,
and knowledge will be pleasant to your soul;
[11] prudence will watch over you;
and understanding will guard you.
[12] It will save you from the way of evil,
from those who speak perversely,
[13] who forsake the paths of uprightness
to walk in the ways of darkness,
[14] who rejoice in doing evil
and delight in the perverseness of evil;
[15] those whose paths are crooked,
and who are devious in their ways.

[16] You will be saved from the loose[a] woman,
from the adulteress with her smooth words,
[17] who forsakes the partner of her youth
and forgets her sacred covenant;
[18] for her way[b] leads down to death,
and her paths to the shades;
[19] those who go to her never come back,
nor do they regain the paths of life.

[20] Therefore walk in the way of the good,
and keep to the paths of the just.
[21] For the upright will abide in the land,
and the innocent will remain in it;
[22] but the wicked will be cut off from the land,
and the treacherous will be rooted out of it.

Admonition to Trust and Honor God

3 My child, do not forget my teaching,
but let your heart keep my commandments;
[2] for length of days and years of life
and abundant welfare they will give you.

[a] Heb *strange* [b] Cn: Heb *house*

2:6 For the LORD: God is the source of true wisdom. Seeking wisdom (2:4) leads to understanding how God wants persons to live in this world.

What are you seeking most to understand about God? How do you seek God's wisdom?

2:10-11 for wisdom will come into your heart: Wisdom should guide one's thoughts and actions as naturally as breathing. By taking wisdom to heart, a person will have a constant guard over mind and soul.

2:16 loose woman: This "strange" (see NRSV footnote *a*) woman can be understood in two ways. The term can refer to a smooth-talking woman who may tempt a young man sexually. But the more important meaning is more symbolic. Just as Wisdom is described as a woman who can provide peace and well-being if followed (3:13-18), this loose woman stands for the opposite. Following her leads to destruction. This same image of adultery was used to describe Israel's unfaithfulness to God when its people worshiped other gods (Hos 1:2).

2:17 sacred covenant: Refers to marriage. Faithfulness in marriage is a sacred obligation (see Mal 2:14-15).

3:1-2 My child: The Fourth Commandment also promises a long life for those who honor their parents (Exod 20:12; Deut 5:16).

3 Do not let loyalty and faithfulness forsake you;
bind them around your neck,
write them on the tablet of your heart.
4 So you will find favor and good repute
in the sight of God and of people.

5 Trust in the LORD with all your heart,
and do not rely on your own insight.
6 In all your ways acknowledge him,
and he will make straight your paths.
7 Do not be wise in your own eyes;
fear the LORD, and turn away from evil.
8 It will be a healing for your flesh
and a refreshment for your body.

9 Honor the LORD with your substance
and with the first fruits of all your produce;
10 then your barns will be filled with plenty,
and your vats will be bursting with wine.

11 My child, do not despise the LORD's discipline
or be weary of his reproof,
12 for the LORD reproves the one he loves,
as a father the son in whom he delights.

The True Wealth

13 Happy are those who find wisdom,
and those who get understanding,
14 for her income is better than silver,
and her revenue better than gold.
15 She is more precious than jewels,
and nothing you desire can compare with her.
16 Long life is in her right hand;
in her left hand are riches and honor.
17 Her ways are ways of pleasantness,
and all her paths are peace.
18 She is a tree of life to those who lay hold of her;
those who hold her fast are called happy.

God's Wisdom in Creation

19 The LORD by wisdom founded the earth;
by understanding he established the heavens;
20 by his knowledge the deeps broke open,
and the clouds drop down the dew.

3:5 Trust in the LORD with all your heart: This verse echoes the great commandment in Deuteronomy 6:5 to love the LORD with heart, soul, and mind. This kind of trust is contrasted with trusting one's own insight.

Why do Lutherans speak of the importance of trust in our relationship with God? Trust and faith are closely related. Faith comes from God, just as Proverbs says that wisdom comes from God. Even though God's wisdom may be perfect, human beings cannot live according to this wisdom in a perfect way. We all sin and fall short of the glory of God (Rom 3:23), so we can't save ourselves by our own actions or by trusting in our own wisdom. We are made right with God by trust (faith) in Jesus Christ, the one God sent to save us by grace (Rom 3:24). *Proverbs 3:5*

3:11-12 do not despise: God's discipline can refer to suffering and misfortune. This suggestion that God does discipline may have been meant to balance the teaching in Proverbs that health and prosperity always come to those who seek wisdom. These verses suggest that this kind of discipline can be a good thing. See also Jeremiah 9:7; Hebrews 12:5-7.

What do you think of the idea that God disciplines and corrects us? When, if ever, have you experienced this?

3:13 Happy are those: Jesus used this typical way of expressing wisdom teachings in the Beatitudes (Matt 5:3-11; Luke 6:20-22).

3:18 She is a tree of life: Compare this to Psalm 1:3, which describes those who follow God's law as trees planted by streams of water. In the Bible, the tree of life image symbolizes well-being and God's abundance (see also Gen 2:9; Ezek 47:12; Rev 2:7; 22:2).

3:19 The LORD by wisdom: Wisdom is also useful to God. She was involved in creation (see also 8:22-36 and the note on 8:22-24).

The True Security

21 My child, do not let these escape from your sight:
keep sound wisdom and prudence,
22 and they will be life for your soul
and adornment for your neck.
23 Then you will walk on your way securely
and your foot will not stumble.
24 If you sit down,[a] you will not be afraid;
when you lie down, your sleep will be sweet.
25 Do not be afraid of sudden panic,
or of the storm that strikes the wicked;
26 for the LORD will be your confidence
and will keep your foot from being caught.

27 Do not withhold good from those to whom it is due,[b]
when it is in your power to do it.
28 Do not say to your neighbor, "Go, and come again,
tomorrow I will give it"—when you have it with
you.
29 Do not plan harm against your neighbor
who lives trustingly beside you.
30 Do not quarrel with anyone without cause,
when no harm has been done to you.
31 Do not envy the violent
and do not choose any of their ways;
32 for the perverse are an abomination to the LORD,
but the upright are in his confidence.
33 The LORD's curse is on the house of the wicked,
but he blesses the abode of the righteous.
34 Toward the scorners he is scornful,
but to the humble he shows favor.
35 The wise will inherit honor,
but stubborn fools, disgrace.

Parental Advice

4 Listen, children, to a father's instruction,
and be attentive, that you may gain[c] insight;
2 for I give you good precepts:
do not forsake my teaching.
3 When I was a son with my father,
tender, and my mother's favorite,
4 he taught me, and said to me,
"Let your heart hold fast my words;

[a] Gk: Heb *lie down* [b] Heb *from its owners* [c] Heb *know*

3:27-31 Do not withhold ... envy: These commands follow the form of the Ten Commandments and describe some ways to deal rightly with others. (Compare to Exod 20:12-17, which covers right dealings with others.)

3:33-35 The LORD's curse ... blesses: The "curse" here is like the kind of curse related to God's judgment on those who abandon God's commands (see Deut 27:11-26). The LORD blesses and stands on the side of the righteous, humble, and wise. Such persons "inherit honor," the respect of both God and right-thinking people.

What helps you most to keep your life focused on the right track?

4:1-27 Listen ... hear ... be attentive: This chapter praises wisdom in three short essays (1-9, 10-19, and 20-27). Each begins with an invitation to hear.

4:1-4 Listen, children: Fathers (parents) and teachers pass on wisdom. "Insight" means understanding how to live in right relationship to God, self, and others.

Types of Proverbs

In the original Hebrew, the sayings in Proverbs use all kinds of literary devices such as puns, repeated consonant or vowel sounds, numbered lists, and rhyming. Some of these are captured in English translation, while many are not. One characteristic of Hebrew poetry is captured well and appears in many passages in Proverbs. This characteristic called parallelism refers to how Hebrew poetry rhymes with thoughts rather than sounds. This parallelism works in three main ways (see examples 1-3 below). Proverbs are also expressed in other ways, including comparisons (metaphors) and descriptive lists.

Type of Proverb	Examples
1. Meaning repeated: The second line expresses the same thought as the first but in different words.	A good name is to be chosen rather than great riches, and favor is better than silver or gold. (22:1)
2. Meaning contrasted: The second line contrasts with the first. This is the most common form in Proverbs.	A wise child makes a glad father, but a foolish child is a mother's grief. (10:1)
3. Meaning developed: The second line advances the thought of the first line in some way without direct agreement or disagreement.	Train children in the right way, And when old, they will not stray. (22:6)
4. Single statement: These proverbs don't use any form of parallel. They are short, simple statements of truth or warning.	The wicked accept a concealed bribe to pervert the ways of justice. (17:23)
5. Metaphors: Some proverbs use striking images that compare one thing or person to another. These are called "metaphors."	A word fitly spoken is like apples of gold in a setting of silver. (25:11)
6. Descriptive List: A series of answers follows a statement based on an unspoken question. Often the pattern is three plus one as in the example.	Three things are stately in their stride; four are stately in their gait: the lion, which is mightiest among wild animals and does not turn back before any; the strutting rooster, the he-goat, and a king striding before his people. (30:29-31)
7. "If...then" statements The second part explains the consequences of doing or not doing something.	If you indeed cry out for insight, and raise your voice for understanding; if you seek it like silver, and search for it as for hidden treasures— then you will understand the fear of the LORD and find the knowledge of God. (2:3-5)

keep my commandments, and live.
5 Get wisdom; get insight: do not forget, nor turn away
from the words of my mouth.
6 Do not forsake her, and she will keep you;
love her, and she will guard you.
7 The beginning of wisdom is this: Get wisdom,
and whatever else you get, get insight.
8 Prize her highly, and she will exalt you;
she will honor you if you embrace her.

4:7 The beginning: Compare to 1:7. The sense is, seek wisdom at any cost; it is that valuable.

9 She will place on your head a fair garland;
she will bestow on you a beautiful crown."

4:9 She will place: The image may suggest marriage. At marriage, the groom wore a crown (Song 3:11).

Admonition to Keep to the Right Path

10 Hear, my child, and accept my words,
that the years of your life may be many.
11 I have taught you the way of wisdom;
I have led you in the paths of uprightness.
12 When you walk, your step will not be hampered;
and if you run, you will not stumble.
13 Keep hold of instruction; do not let go;
guard her, for she is your life.
14 Do not enter the path of the wicked,
and do not walk in the way of evildoers.
15 Avoid it; do not go on it;
turn away from it and pass on.
16 For they cannot sleep unless they have done wrong;
they are robbed of sleep unless they have made someone
stumble.
17 For they eat the bread of wickedness
and drink the wine of violence.
18 But the path of the righteous is like the light of dawn,
which shines brighter and brighter until full day.
19 The way of the wicked is like deep darkness;
they do not know what they stumble over.

4:18-19 But the path: The image of two mutually exclusive paths—righteous/evil, light/dark—also occurs in the New Testament (John 3:19-21, 1 John 2:10-11). Compare also to Psalm 119:105, which describes God's word as a "light to my path."

20 My child, be attentive to my words;
incline your ear to my sayings.
21 Do not let them escape from your sight;
keep them within your heart.
22 For they are life to those who find them,
and healing to all their flesh.
23 Keep your heart with all vigilance,
for from it flow the springs of life.
24 Put away from you crooked speech,
and put devious talk far from you.

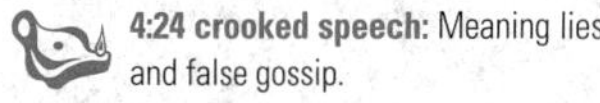

4:24 crooked speech: Meaning lies and false gossip.

25 Let your eyes look directly forward,
and your gaze be straight before you.
26 Keep straight the path of your feet,
and all your ways will be sure.
27 Do not swerve to the right or to the left;
turn your foot away from evil.

Warning against Impurity and Infidelity

5 My child, be attentive to my wisdom;
incline your ear to my understanding,

5:3-14 a loose woman...Sheol: See the notes on 2:16 (loose woman) and 1:12 (Sheol).

5:7-14 And now, my child: Deuteronomy 22:22 sets death as the punishment for adultery. But here the punishment is loss of honor and a potential lawsuit.

5:15-19 Drink water from your own cistern: These verses compare one's wife to woman wisdom. Being faithful to a wife is like being faithful to wisdom. The sexual imagery was perhaps meant to appeal to young (male) students. The language resembles the love poetry in Song of Solomon. Also see 23:26-28.

5:21-23 For human ways: "Folly" means the rejection of wisdom. Folly is equated with "iniquities," or sins against the LORD. Wisdom leads to a disciplined moral life.

2 so that you may hold on to prudence,
and your lips may guard knowledge.
3 For the lips of a loose[a] woman drip honey,
and her speech is smoother than oil;
4 but in the end she is bitter as wormwood,
sharp as a two-edged sword.
5 Her feet go down to death;
her steps follow the path to Sheol.
6 She does not keep straight to the path of life;
her ways wander, and she does not know it.

7 And now, my child,[b] listen to me,
and do not depart from the words of my mouth.
8 Keep your way far from her,
and do not go near the door of her house;
9 or you will give your honor to others,
and your years to the merciless,
10 and strangers will take their fill of your wealth,
and your labors will go to the house of an alien;
11 and at the end of your life you will groan,
when your flesh and body are consumed,
12 and you say, "Oh, how I hated discipline,
and my heart despised reproof!
13 I did not listen to the voice of my teachers
or incline my ear to my instructors.
14 Now I am at the point of utter ruin
in the public assembly."

15 Drink water from your own cistern,
flowing water from your own well.
16 Should your springs be scattered abroad,
streams of water in the streets?
17 Let them be for yourself alone,
and not for sharing with strangers.
18 Let your fountain be blessed,
and rejoice in the wife of your youth,
19 a lovely deer, a graceful doe.
May her breasts satisfy you at all times;
may you be intoxicated always by her love.
20 Why should you be intoxicated, my son, by another woman
and embrace the bosom of an adulteress?
21 For human ways are under the eyes of the LORD,
and he examines all their paths.

[a] Heb *strange* [b] Gk Vg: Heb *children*

22 The iniquities of the wicked ensnare them,
and they are caught in the toils of their sin.
23 They die for lack of discipline,
and because of their great folly they are lost.

Practical Admonitions

6 My child, if you have given your pledge to your neighbor,
if you have bound yourself to another,[a]
2 you are snared by the utterance of your lips,[b]
caught by the words of your mouth.
3 So do this, my child, and save yourself,
for you have come into your neighbor's power:
go, hurry,[c] and plead with your neighbor.
4 Give your eyes no sleep
and your eyelids no slumber;
5 save yourself like a gazelle from the hunter,[d]
like a bird from the hand of the fowler.

6:1-5 given your pledge: Be wise in your financial affairs. "Pledge" means co-signing another's loan. This is dangerous, because persons who do this may end up owing the money or even becoming the lender's servant. Wisdom prefers simply to give money to the needy (see 11:25 and 14:21).

6 Go to the ant, you lazybones;
consider its ways, and be wise.
7 Without having any chief
or officer or ruler,
8 it prepares its food in summer,
and gathers its sustenance in harvest.
9 How long will you lie there, O lazybones?
When will you rise from your sleep?
10 A little sleep, a little slumber,
a little folding of the hands to rest,
11 and poverty will come upon you like a robber,
and want, like an armed warrior.

6:6-11 Go to the ant: A moral lesson drawn from nature. Employers hate laziness (see 10:26).

12 A scoundrel and a villain
goes around with crooked speech,
13 winking the eyes, shuffling the feet,
pointing the fingers,
14 with perverted mind devising evil,
continually sowing discord;
15 on such a one calamity will descend suddenly;
in a moment, damage beyond repair.

16 There are six things that the LORD hates,
seven that are an abomination to him:
17 haughty eyes, a lying tongue,

6:16-19 There are six things: An example of a numerical proverb (see the chart Types of Proverbs, p. 1018). This particular one uses a pattern of a number plus one.

[a] Or *a stranger* [b] Cn Compare Gk Syr: Heb *the words of your mouth* [c] Or *humble yourself*
[d] Cn: Heb *from the hand*

and hands that shed innocent blood,
18 a heart that devises wicked plans,
feet that hurry to run to evil,
19 a lying witness who testifies falsely,
and one who sows discord in a family.

20 My child, keep your father's commandment,
and do not forsake your mother's teaching.
21 Bind them upon your heart always;
tie them around your neck.
22 When you walk, they[a] will lead you;
when you lie down, they[a] will watch over you;
and when you awake, they[a] will talk with you.
23 For the commandment is a lamp and the teaching a light,
and the reproofs of discipline are the way of life,
24 to preserve you from the wife of another,[b]
from the smooth tongue of the adulteress.
25 Do not desire her beauty in your heart,
and do not let her capture you with her eyelashes;
26 for a prostitute's fee is only a loaf of bread,[c]
but the wife of another stalks a man's very life.
27 Can fire be carried in the bosom
without burning one's clothes?
28 Or can one walk on hot coals
without scorching the feet?
29 So is he who sleeps with his neighbor's wife;
no one who touches her will go unpunished.
30 Thieves are not despised who steal only
to satisfy their appetite when they are hungry.
31 Yet if they are caught, they will pay sevenfold;
they will forfeit all the goods of their house.
32 But he who commits adultery has no sense;
he who does it destroys himself.
33 He will get wounds and dishonor,
and his disgrace will not be wiped away.
34 For jealousy arouses a husband's fury,
and he shows no restraint when he takes revenge.
35 He will accept no compensation,
and refuses a bribe no matter how great.

6:21-22: Bind them…tie them…when you awake: Wisdom teaching here compares to the way God's commands are to be kept close day and night. They were even to be put in small leather pouches and tied to the forehead or arm (see Deut 6:4-9).

6:26-35 wife of another stalks…jealousy arouses a husband's fury: Several images warn of the dangers of adultery. Adultery destroys the family solidarity and harmony that supports a sound society. See also the note on 5:7-14.

The False Attractions of Adultery

7 My child, keep my words
and store up my commandments with you;

7:1-3 keep my words…write them on the tablet of your heart: This chapter begins and ends with classroom-style teachings. Verses 2-3 echo Deuteronomy 6:8-9 (see also note on 6:21-22).

[a] Heb *it* [b] Gk: MT *the evil woman* [c] Cn Compare Gk Syr Vg Tg: Heb *for because of a harlot to a piece of bread*

2 keep my commandments and live,
keep my teachings as the apple of your eye;
3 bind them on your fingers,
write them on the tablet of your heart.
4 Say to wisdom, "You are my sister,"
and call insight your intimate friend,
5 that they may keep you from the loose[a] woman,
from the adulteress with her smooth words.

6 For at the window of my house
I looked out through my lattice,
7 and I saw among the simple ones,
I observed among the youths,
a young man without sense,
8 passing along the street near her corner,
taking the road to her house
9 in the twilight, in the evening,
at the time of night and darkness.

10 Then a woman comes toward him,
decked out like a prostitute, wily of heart.[b]
11 She is loud and wayward;
her feet do not stay at home;
12 now in the street, now in the squares,
and at every corner she lies in wait.
13 She seizes him and kisses him,
and with impudent face she says to him:
14 "I had to offer sacrifices,
and today I have paid my vows;
15 so now I have come out to meet you,
to seek you eagerly, and I have found you!
16 I have decked my couch with coverings,
colored spreads of Egyptian linen;
17 I have perfumed my bed with myrrh,
aloes, and cinnamon.
18 Come, let us take our fill of love until morning;
let us delight ourselves with love.
19 For my husband is not at home;
he has gone on a long journey.
20 He took a bag of money with him;
he will not come home until full moon."

21 With much seductive speech she persuades him;
with her smooth talk she compels him.

[a] Heb *strange* [b] Meaning of Heb uncertain

7:4-5 wisdom, "You are my sister" ...keep you from the loose woman: The Hebrew word translated as sister may also refer to the more intimate relationship of a wife. Keeping a close relationship with wisdom will keep one from chasing after the loose woman, which can have both symbolic and actual meaning (see note on 2:16). The adulteress can stand for all things that tempt us away from right living. But the following passage also clearly warns about the seductive danger of having sex with someone else's spouse. In certain cases, the laws of Israel said this could be punishable by death (Lev 20:10).

7:14 offer sacrifices...paid my vows: Likely refers to the meat that was saved after a portion of it had been sacrificed (see Lev 7:11-21; Jer 7:21). Perhaps the leftover food was meant to be set out as a feast.

7:16-17 Egyptian linen...myrrh: These exotic imported items were expensive and may show that the woman was wealthy.

7:21-23 With much seductive speech: The young man falls for her allure. He doesn't think about the price he will pay. Wisdom encourages measuring the consequences before acting—look before you leap!

If you are asked, "Why would God care about how we behave sexually," how would you answer? What most influences your response?

22 Right away he follows her,
and goes like an ox to the slaughter,
or bounds like a stag toward the trap[a]
23 until an arrow pierces its entrails.
He is like a bird rushing into a snare,
not knowing that it will cost him his life.

24 And now, my children, listen to me,
and be attentive to the words of my mouth.
25 Do not let your hearts turn aside to her ways;
do not stray into her paths.
26 For many are those she has laid low,
and numerous are her victims.
27 Her house is the way to Sheol,
going down to the chambers of death.

7:27 Her house is the way to Sheol: "Sheol" is the state after death. It is an empty, shadowy world. The ideas of resurrection and life after death had not yet fully developed. The dangers of adultery are described as life-threatening.

The Gifts of Wisdom

8 Does not wisdom call,
and does not understanding raise her voice?
2 On the heights, beside the way,
at the crossroads she takes her stand;
3 beside the gates in front of the town,
at the entrance of the portals she cries out:
4 "To you, O people, I call,
and my cry is to all that live.
5 O simple ones, learn prudence;
acquire intelligence, you who lack it.
6 Hear, for I will speak noble things,
and from my lips will come what is right;
7 for my mouth will utter truth;
wickedness is an abomination to my lips.
8 All the words of my mouth are righteous;
there is nothing twisted or crooked in them.
9 They are all straight to one who understands
and right to those who find knowledge.
10 Take my instruction instead of silver,
and knowledge rather than choice gold;
11 for wisdom is better than jewels,
and all that you may desire cannot compare with her.
12 I, wisdom, live with prudence,[b]
and I attain knowledge and discretion.
13 The fear of the LORD is hatred of evil.
Pride and arrogance and the way of evil

8:1—9:18 Does not wisdom call... raise her voice: Again, woman wisdom speaks (see note on 1:20). These two chapters present the most exalted teaching in Proverbs about wisdom.

8:2-3 On the heights...at the crossroads...gates: Woman wisdom cries out in all the most important meeting places—on high places where worship often takes place, on the major intersections where travelers and traders meet and do business, and the city gate where important town discussions take place. Wisdom invites the public to come in. Wisdom is available to all who seek it. Job 28:12-13 offers the opposite view.

8:6-31 I will speak: Woman wisdom speaks about her worth (8:6-11); her authority (8:12-16); her rewards (8:17-21); and her creation by God at the beginning of time (8:22-31).

8:13 fear of the LORD is hatred of evil: Compare this to 1:7. Knowledge gained from God's wisdom is opposed to evil.

[a] Cn Compare Gk: Meaning of Heb uncertain [b] Meaning of Heb uncertain

and perverted speech I hate.
14 I have good advice and sound wisdom;
I have insight, I have strength.
15 By me kings reign,
and rulers decree what is just;
16 by me rulers rule,
and nobles, all who govern rightly.
17 I love those who love me,
and those who seek me diligently find me.
18 Riches and honor are with me,
enduring wealth and prosperity.
19 My fruit is better than gold, even fine gold,
and my yield than choice silver.
20 I walk in the way of righteousness,
along the paths of justice,
21 endowing with wealth those who love me,
and filling their treasuries.

Wisdom's Part in Creation

22 The LORD created me at the beginning[a] of his work,[b]
the first of his acts of long ago.
23 Ages ago I was set up,
at the first, before the beginning of the earth.
24 When there were no depths I was brought forth,
when there were no springs abounding with water.
25 Before the mountains had been shaped,
before the hills, I was brought forth—
26 when he had not yet made earth and fields,[c]
or the world's first bits of soil.
27 When he established the heavens, I was there,
when he drew a circle on the face of the deep,
28 when he made firm the skies above,
when he established the fountains of the deep,
29 when he assigned to the sea its limit,
so that the waters might not transgress his
command,
when he marked out the foundations of the earth,
30 then I was beside him, like a master worker;[d]
and I was daily his[e] delight,
rejoicing before him always,
31 rejoicing in his inhabited world
and delighting in the human race.

[a] Or *me as the beginning* [b] Heb *way* [c] Meaning of Heb uncertain [d] Another reading is *little child*
[e] Gk: Heb lacks *his*

8:19 My fruit: See note on 1:31.

8:22-24 The LORD created me at the beginning: The exact meaning of this phrase is uncertain. See NRSV footnotes *a* and *b*. Was wisdom the first created thing given birth, "brought forth" in 8:24, before everything else existed? That may be implied. "Created" here can also be translated as "possessed" or "acquired." Whatever the exact meaning, it is clear that wisdom was with God from the beginning of God's creation.

What do Lutherans and other Christians believe about the nature of Jesus? Proverbs 8:22-24 played a part in debates in the early church about the nature of Jesus and his relationship to God. Using 1 Corinthians 1:24, which refers to Jesus as the "wisdom of God," a man named Arius argued that Jesus, like wisdom, was the first created thing. As a created being, he could not be equal to God. Another church leader, Athanasius, translated the Proverbs passage differently. He spoke of wisdom as being the head of creation and born from God as a child is born from one's parent. This understanding was accepted by the church and appears in the phrase we recite in the Nicene Creed: "We believe in one Lord, Jesus Christ, . . . true God from true God, begotten, not made, of one being with the Father; through him all things were made." See also John 1:1-3, which describes Jesus as the Word, who was with God and was God from the beginning. *Proverbs 8:22-24*

8:30 master worker: The alternate translation, "little child," fits the birth image in 8:22-24.

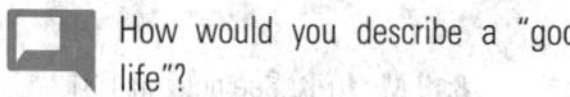

8:35 finds life: This refers not to eternal life but a full, rich life on earth.

How would you describe a "good life"?

9:1-6, 13-18 Wisdom has built her house…foolish woman is loud: Wisdom (9:1-6) and foolishness (9:13-18) are again presented as a women inviting all who will hear to come to their houses and eat with them.

9:1 seven pillars: This could refer to the mythical foundations of the earth or pillars around the interior courtyard of a fancy house.

9:2-3 She also has set her table: Wisdom invites seekers to an elegant banquet.

9:5-6 Come, eat: This invitation resembles that of Jesus in Matthew 11:28-30.

9:7-12 Whoever corrects: These maxims (wise sayings) interrupt the invitations being given by woman wisdom and the foolish woman. They may be a later addition.

9:10 fear of the LORD: See the note on 1:7.

9:13-15 The foolish woman: In contrast to Wisdom, the foolish woman is pictured as a prostitute selling herself to a passerby.

32 "And now, my children, listen to me:
happy are those who keep my ways.
33 Hear instruction and be wise,
and do not neglect it.
34 Happy is the one who listens to me,
watching daily at my gates,
waiting beside my doors.
35 For whoever finds me finds life
and obtains favor from the LORD;
36 but those who miss me injure themselves;
all who hate me love death."

Wisdom's Feast

9 Wisdom has built her house,
she has hewn her seven pillars.
2 She has slaughtered her animals, she has mixed her wine,
she has also set her table.
3 She has sent out her servant-girls, she calls
from the highest places in the town,
4 "You that are simple, turn in here!"
To those without sense she says,
5 "Come, eat of my bread
and drink of the wine I have mixed.
6 Lay aside immaturity,[a] and live,
and walk in the way of insight."

General Maxims

7 Whoever corrects a scoffer wins abuse;
whoever rebukes the wicked gets hurt.
8 A scoffer who is rebuked will only hate you;
the wise, when rebuked, will love you.
9 Give instruction[b] to the wise, and they will become wiser still;
teach the righteous and they will gain in learning.
10 The fear of the LORD is the beginning of wisdom,
and the knowledge of the Holy One is insight.
11 For by me your days will be multiplied,
and years will be added to your life.
12 If you are wise, you are wise for yourself;
if you scoff, you alone will bear it.

Folly's Invitation and Promise

13 The foolish woman is loud;
she is ignorant and knows nothing.

---

[a] Or *simpleness* [b] Heb lacks *instruction*

14 She sits at the door of her house,
on a seat at the high places of the town,
15 calling to those who pass by,
who are going straight on their way,
16 "You who are simple, turn in here!"
And to those without sense she says,
17 "Stolen water is sweet,
and bread eaten in secret is pleasant."
18 But they do not know that the dead[a] are there,
that her guests are in the depths of Sheol.

Wise Sayings of Solomon

10 The proverbs of Solomon.

A wise child makes a glad father,
but a foolish child is a mother's grief.
2 Treasures gained by wickedness do not profit,
but righteousness delivers from death.
3 The LORD does not let the righteous go hungry,
but he thwarts the craving of the wicked.
4 A slack hand causes poverty,
but the hand of the diligent makes rich.
5 A child who gathers in summer is prudent,
but a child who sleeps in harvest brings shame.
6 Blessings are on the head of the righteous,
but the mouth of the wicked conceals violence.
7 The memory of the righteous is a blessing,
but the name of the wicked will rot.
8 The wise of heart will heed commandments,
but a babbling fool will come to ruin.
9 Whoever walks in integrity walks securely,
but whoever follows perverse ways will be found out.
10 Whoever winks the eye causes trouble,
but the one who rebukes boldly makes peace.[b]
11 The mouth of the righteous is a fountain of life,
but the mouth of the wicked conceals violence.
12 Hatred stirs up strife,
but love covers all offenses.
13 On the lips of one who has understanding wisdom is found,
but a rod is for the back of one who lacks sense.
14 The wise lay up knowledge,
but the babbling of a fool brings ruin near.
15 The wealth of the rich is their fortress;

[a] Heb *shades* [b] Gk: Heb *but a babbling fool will come to ruin*

9:17-18 Stolen water: The foolish woman's banquet may look good, but it is stolen and leads to death. Compare this to the benefit that comes to those who are wise and fear the LORD (9:10-11).

10:1—22:16 The proverbs of Solomon: This collection of proverbs, attributed to Solomon, consists of two-line sayings on a wide variety of topics. These sayings summarize human experience and were the content of wisdom instruction. While they reflect their times and culture, many still make sense. In the first part of the section (10:1—15:33) most of these proverbs use opposite parallelism. The first line states a positive idea, while the second line presents a contrasting negative. See the chart Types of Proverbs, p. 1018.

10:4 slack hand causes poverty: Several proverbs criticize laziness and poor work habits (6:6-11; 13:4; 28:19). Here is an example of how the message of proverbs can overstate a theme. Working hard and doing our best is always a good thing, and hard work often pays off. But many people who live in circumstances of poverty work very hard. It is certainly not true that poverty is always directly related to poor work habits. Many factors influence poverty as well as good fortune and success.

What factors influence poverty or wealth? What role can people of faith play in helping those who face challenges such as poverty, hunger, or lack of safe drinking water?

10:8-14 babbling fool: How we talk, when we talk, and what we say can show us to be foolish or wise.

What characteristics would you use to define appropriate speech or talk?

10:15 The wealth of the rich: An observation that the rich have it over the poor. But wisdom embraces justice and knows the limits of wealth (see 11:4 and 18:11).

the poverty of the poor is their ruin.
16 The wage of the righteous leads to life,
the gain of the wicked to sin.
17 Whoever heeds instruction is on the path to life,
but one who rejects a rebuke goes astray.
18 Lying lips conceal hatred,
and whoever utters slander is a fool.
19 When words are many, transgression is not lacking,
but the prudent are restrained in speech.
20 The tongue of the righteous is choice silver;
the mind of the wicked is of little worth.
21 The lips of the righteous feed many,
but fools die for lack of sense.
22 The blessing of the LORD makes rich,
and he adds no sorrow with it.[a]
23 Doing wrong is like sport to a fool,
but wise conduct is pleasure to a person of understanding.
24 What the wicked dread will come upon them,
but the desire of the righteous will be granted.
25 When the tempest passes, the wicked are no more,
but the righteous are established forever.
26 Like vinegar to the teeth, and smoke to the eyes,
so are the lazy to their employers.
27 The fear of the LORD prolongs life,
but the years of the wicked will be short.
28 The hope of the righteous ends in gladness,
but the expectation of the wicked comes to nothing.
29 The way of the LORD is a stronghold for the upright,
but destruction for evildoers.
30 The righteous will never be removed,
but the wicked will not remain in the land.
31 The mouth of the righteous brings forth wisdom,
but the perverse tongue will be cut off.
32 The lips of the righteous know what is acceptable,
but the mouth of the wicked what is perverse.

11 A false balance is an abomination to the LORD,
but an accurate weight is his delight.
2 When pride comes, then comes disgrace;
but wisdom is with the humble.
3 The integrity of the upright guides them,
but the crookedness of the treacherous destroys them.
4 Riches do not profit in the day of wrath,
but righteousness delivers from death.

[a] Or *and toil adds nothing to it*

10:26 Like vinegar…so are the lazy: Wisdom schools trained young men as hardworking bureaucrats in the royal court. Here is a strong reminder about being a good employee who works hard.

10:27 The fear of the LORD: An early death was thought to be punishment for sin or moral failure.

Does right living always bring long life and blessings? Living a just and caring life is in itself a blessing. But God makes the sun rise on both the evil and the good (Matt 5:44-45). Lutherans realize that living God's way does not always bring prosperity in a sinful world. Good people sometimes suffer for doing good, as Jesus did (Mark 8:34-36). *Proverbs 10:27-30*

11:1 A false balance: Fair dealings in the marketplace are basic to God's justice (see Lev 19:35-37; Amos 8:4-6). Some merchants or traders cheated customers by using incorrect balances when weighing grain or other goods.

5 The righteousness of the blameless keeps their ways straight,
but the wicked fall by their own wickedness.
6 The righteousness of the upright saves them,
but the treacherous are taken captive by their schemes.
7 When the wicked die, their hope perishes,
and the expectation of the godless comes to nothing.
8 The righteous are delivered from trouble,
and the wicked get into it instead.
9 With their mouths the godless would destroy their neighbors,
but by knowledge the righteous are delivered.
10 When it goes well with the righteous, the city rejoices;
and when the wicked perish, there is jubilation.
11 By the blessing of the upright a city is exalted,
but it is overthrown by the mouth of the wicked.
12 Whoever belittles another lacks sense,
but an intelligent person remains silent.
13 A gossip goes about telling secrets,
but one who is trustworthy in spirit keeps a confidence.
14 Where there is no guidance, a nation[a] falls,
but in an abundance of counselors there is safety.
15 To guarantee loans for a stranger brings trouble,
but there is safety in refusing to do so.
16 A gracious woman gets honor,
but she who hates virtue is covered with shame.[b]
The timid become destitute,[c]
but the aggressive gain riches.
17 Those who are kind reward themselves,
but the cruel do themselves harm.
18 The wicked earn no real gain,
but those who sow righteousness get a true reward.
19 Whoever is steadfast in righteousness will live,
but whoever pursues evil will die.
20 Crooked minds are an abomination to the LORD,
but those of blameless ways are his delight.
21 Be assured, the wicked will not go unpunished,
but those who are righteous will escape.
22 Like a gold ring in a pig's snout
is a beautiful woman without good sense.
23 The desire of the righteous ends only in good;
the expectation of the wicked in wrath.
24 Some give freely, yet grow all the richer;
others withhold what is due, and only suffer want.
25 A generous person will be enriched,

[a] Or *an army* [b] Compare Gk Syr: Heb lacks *but she . . . shame* [c] Gk: Heb lacks *The timid . . . destitute*

11:13 A gossip: The proper use of language and speech is a theme running through Proverbs. See 12:6, 18; 21:6; 25:18. Compare James 1:26 and 3:5b-12.

How can you use words to build others up rather than putting them down?

11:14 Where there is no guidance: Wisdom teaches careful listening to God and to wise advisers (see 12:15). Those who lead nations especially need good counselors.

11:22 Like a gold ring: Women of the time wore nose rings as jewelry (see Ezek 16:11-12). Inner character counts more than outer beauty (see 31:30).

11:24-26 Some give freely . . . will be enriched: These three verses urge generosity and sharing. Verse 24 points up a paradox or unexpected truth about generosity: those who give will receive more in return. Compare this to Jesus' words in Luke 6:38.

What do you think about this idea that generosity and giving freely result in blessings for both the giver and the receiver? How have you experienced this?

and one who gives water will get water.
26 The people curse those who hold back grain,
but a blessing is on the head of those who sell it.
27 Whoever diligently seeks good seeks favor,
but evil comes to the one who searches for it.
28 Those who trust in their riches will wither,[a]
but the righteous will flourish like green leaves.
29 Those who trouble their households will inherit wind,
and the fool will be servant to the wise.
30 The fruit of the righteous is a tree of life,
but violence[b] takes lives away.
31 If the righteous are repaid on earth,
how much more the wicked and the sinner!

12 Whoever loves discipline loves knowledge,
but those who hate to be rebuked are stupid.
2 The good obtain favor from the LORD,
but those who devise evil he condemns.
3 No one finds security by wickedness,
but the root of the righteous will never be moved.
4 A good wife is the crown of her husband,
but she who brings shame is like rottenness in his bones.

12:4 A good wife: Young men were the original audience for wisdom teachers. Thus, marriage advice is slanted toward choosing and supporting wives rather than husbands. In ancient Hebrew society a man's reputation and standing in the community were affected by the actions of his wife and children. See also 31:10-31.

5 The thoughts of the righteous are just;
the advice of the wicked is treacherous.
6 The words of the wicked are a deadly ambush,
but the speech of the upright delivers them.
7 The wicked are overthrown and are no more,
but the house of the righteous will stand.
8 One is commended for good sense,
but a perverse mind is despised.
9 Better to be despised and have a servant,
than to be self-important and lack food.
10 The righteous know the needs of their animals,
but the mercy of the wicked is cruel.
11 Those who till their land will have plenty of food,
but those who follow worthless pursuits have no sense.
12 The wicked covet the proceeds of wickedness,[c]
but the root of the righteous bears fruit.

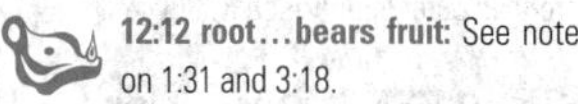
12:12 root...bears fruit: See notes on 1:31 and 3:18.

13 The evil are ensnared by the transgression of their lips,
but the righteous escape from trouble.
14 From the fruit of the mouth one is filled with good things,
and manual labor has its reward.
15 Fools think their own way is right,
but the wise listen to advice.

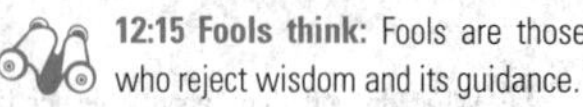
12:15 Fools think: Fools are those who reject wisdom and its guidance.

---

[a] Cn: Heb *fall* [b] Cn Compare Gk Syr: Heb *a wise man* [c] Or *covet the catch of the wicked*

16 Fools show their anger at once,
but the prudent ignore an insult.
17 Whoever speaks the truth gives honest evidence,
but a false witness speaks deceitfully.
18 Rash words are like sword thrusts,
but the tongue of the wise brings healing.
19 Truthful lips endure forever,
but a lying tongue lasts only a moment.
20 Deceit is in the mind of those who plan evil,
but those who counsel peace have joy.
21 No harm happens to the righteous,
but the wicked are filled with trouble.
22 Lying lips are an abomination to the LORD,
but those who act faithfully are his delight.
23 One who is clever conceals knowledge,
but the mind of a fool[a] broadcasts folly.
24 The hand of the diligent will rule,
while the lazy will be put to forced labor.
25 Anxiety weighs down the human heart,
but a good word cheers it up.
26 The righteous gives good advice to friends,[b]
but the way of the wicked leads astray.
27 The lazy do not roast[c] their game,
but the diligent obtain precious wealth.[c]
28 In the path of righteousness there is life,
in walking its path there is no death.

13 A wise child loves discipline,[d]
but a scoffer does not listen to rebuke.
2 From the fruit of their words good persons eat good things,
but the desire of the treacherous is for wrongdoing.
3 Those who guard their mouths preserve their lives;
those who open wide their lips come to ruin.
4 The appetite of the lazy craves, and gets nothing,
while the appetite of the diligent is richly supplied.
5 The righteous hate falsehood,
but the wicked act shamefully and disgracefully.
6 Righteousness guards one whose way is upright,
but sin overthrows the wicked.
7 Some pretend to be rich, yet have nothing;
others pretend to be poor, yet have great wealth.
8 Wealth is a ransom for a person's life,
but the poor get no threats.

12:16 Fools show their anger: Wise people keep cool and exercise restraint—good advice for impetuous young men and women.

12:23 One who is clever: Keep your own counsel. For young workers in the royal court a slip of the tongue or withholding important information could be fatal.

12:28 In the path of righteousness: "Life" means the good life on earth, not eternal life. See the note on 7:27. Walking on the path of righteousness means living the right way according to wisdom. See also the note on 4:18-19.

13:2 From the fruit: Good words bring good outcomes. Speech has power. See the notes on 1:31 (fruits) and 11:13 (gossip).

13:7 Some pretend: This proverb may contrast what truly is with what appears to be. The rich may really be poor in spirit, while the poor may actually be rich in nonmaterial blessings.

---

[a] Heb *the heart of fools* [b] Syr: Meaning of Heb uncertain [c] Meaning of Heb uncertain [d] Cn:Heb *A wise child the discipline of his father*

13:11 Wealth hastily gotten: Slow and steady wins the race. Get-rich-quick schemes are questionable.

13:12 Hope deferred: An observation from life. Gaining our desires does energize us.

13:14 fountain of life: Compare this to Jesus' words in John 4:10-14, where Jesus speaks of himself as life-giving water that gushes up to eternal life.

13:20 Whoever walks: You are known by and heavily influenced by the company you keep.

How do the people you spend your time with influence you? How do your interests and values affect your choice of friends and associates?

13:24 Those who spare the rod: This reflects a culture that endorsed physical discipline. (Compare Eph 6:4.)

14:1 The wise woman: The text refers to a human woman rather than woman wisdom (see 31:10-31). "House" is a metaphor for household and family (see 24:3-4).

9 The light of the righteous rejoices,
but the lamp of the wicked goes out.
10 By insolence the heedless make strife,
but wisdom is with those who take advice.
11 Wealth hastily gotten[a] will dwindle,
but those who gather little by little will increase it.
12 Hope deferred makes the heart sick,
but a desire fulfilled is a tree of life.
13 Those who despise the word bring destruction on themselves,
but those who respect the commandment will be rewarded.
14 The teaching of the wise is a fountain of life,
so that one may avoid the snares of death.
15 Good sense wins favor,
but the way of the faithless is their ruin.[b]
16 The clever do all things intelligently,
but the fool displays folly.
17 A bad messenger brings trouble,
but a faithful envoy, healing.
18 Poverty and disgrace are for the one who ignores instruction,
but one who heeds reproof is honored.
19 A desire realized is sweet to the soul,
but to turn away from evil is an abomination to fools.
20 Whoever walks with the wise becomes wise,
but the companion of fools suffers harm.
21 Misfortune pursues sinners,
but prosperity rewards the righteous.
22 The good leave an inheritance to their children's children,
but the sinner's wealth is laid up for the righteous.
23 The field of the poor may yield much food,
but it is swept away through injustice.
24 Those who spare the rod hate their children,
but those who love them are diligent to discipline them.
25 The righteous have enough to satisfy their appetite,
but the belly of the wicked is empty.

14 The wise woman[c] builds her house,
but the foolish tears it down with her own hands.
2 Those who walk uprightly fear the LORD,
but one who is devious in conduct despises him.
3 The talk of fools is a rod for their backs,[d]
but the lips of the wise preserve them.
4 Where there are no oxen, there is no grain;
abundant crops come by the strength of the ox.

---

[a] Gk Vg: Heb *from vanity* [b] Cn Compare Gk Syr Vg Tg: Heb *is enduring* [c] Heb *Wisdom of women*
[d] Cn: Heb *a rod of pride*

5 A faithful witness does not lie,
but a false witness breathes out lies.
6 A scoffer seeks wisdom in vain,
but knowledge is easy for one who understands.
7 Leave the presence of a fool,
for there you do not find words of knowledge.
8 It is the wisdom of the clever to understand where they go,
but the folly of fools misleads.
9 Fools mock at the guilt offering,[a]
but the upright enjoy God's favor.
10 The heart knows its own bitterness,
and no stranger shares its joy.
11 The house of the wicked is destroyed,
but the tent of the upright flourishes.
12 There is a way that seems right to a person,
but its end is the way to death.[b]
13 Even in laughter the heart is sad,
and the end of joy is grief.
14 The perverse get what their ways deserve,
and the good, what their deeds deserve.[c]
15 The simple believe everything,
but the clever consider their steps.
16 The wise are cautious and turn away from evil,
but the fool throws off restraint and is careless.
17 One who is quick-tempered acts foolishly,
and the schemer is hated.
18 The simple are adorned with[d] folly,
but the clever are crowned with knowledge.
19 The evil bow down before the good,
the wicked at the gates of the righteous.
20 The poor are disliked even by their neighbors,
but the rich have many friends.
21 Those who despise their neighbors are sinners,
but happy are those who are kind to the poor.
22 Do they not err that plan evil?
Those who plan good find loyalty and faithfulness.
23 In all toil there is profit,
but mere talk leads only to poverty.
24 The crown of the wise is their wisdom,[e]
but folly is the garland[f] of fools.
25 A truthful witness saves lives,
but one who utters lies is a betrayer.

[a] Meaning of Heb uncertain [b] Heb *ways of death* [c] Cn: Heb *from upon him* [d] Or *inherit*
[e] Cn Compare Gk: Heb *riches* [f] Cn: Heb *is the folly*

14:6 A scoffer seeks: Those who won't work to gain wisdom seek it in vain. Those who understand the need for concentration and discipline find the search easier. (Compare Matt 11:29-30.)

14:10 The heart knows: This is an observation about human isolation. No person can completely know, or be known by, another person (except God; see note on 15:3).

How can you make best use of times when you are alone or feel isolated?

14:20-21 The poor...kind to the poor: Verse 20 states a sad reality that is often true even today. Those who are materially rich may get plenty of attention and respect, while those who have less may be ignored or even disliked. Verse 21 balances this situation by reminding the wise that being kind to the poor leads to happiness (see also 14:31).

14:26 In the fear of: The verse implies responsibility of parents to pass this key wisdom on to their children.

14:28 glory of the king: The fate of a nation's ruler is tied to what happens to the people. If the people are destroyed or defeated, the same happens to the ruler.

15:3 The eyes of the LORD: A metaphor that means God knows all things, including the human heart. See also Hebrews 4:13 and Psalms 103:14; 139:23.

15:8 The sacrifice…prayer: Worship does not substitute for right living. The sacrifices and worship of those who treat others unjustly are considered hollow and meaningless (see Amos 5:21-24). This echoes the message of other prophets as well (see Hos 6:6 and Mic 6:8).

26 In the fear of the LORD one has strong confidence,
and one's children will have a refuge.
27 The fear of the LORD is a fountain of life,
so that one may avoid the snares of death.
28 The glory of a king is a multitude of people;
without people a prince is ruined.
29 Whoever is slow to anger has great understanding,
but one who has a hasty temper exalts folly.
30 A tranquil mind gives life to the flesh,
but passion makes the bones rot.
31 Those who oppress the poor insult their Maker,
but those who are kind to the needy honor him.
32 The wicked are overthrown by their evildoing,
but the righteous find a refuge in their integrity.[a]
33 Wisdom is at home in the mind of one who has understanding,
but it is not[b] known in the heart of fools.
34 Righteousness exalts a nation,
but sin is a reproach to any people.
35 A servant who deals wisely has the king's favor,
but his wrath falls on one who acts shamefully.

15 A soft answer turns away wrath,
but a harsh word stirs up anger.
2 The tongue of the wise dispenses knowledge,[c]
but the mouths of fools pour out folly.
3 The eyes of the LORD are in every place,
keeping watch on the evil and the good.
4 A gentle tongue is a tree of life,
but perverseness in it breaks the spirit.
5 A fool despises a parent's instruction,
but the one who heeds admonition is prudent.
6 In the house of the righteous there is much treasure,
but trouble befalls the income of the wicked.
7 The lips of the wise spread knowledge;
not so the minds of fools.
8 The sacrifice of the wicked is an abomination to the LORD,
but the prayer of the upright is his delight.
9 The way of the wicked is an abomination to the LORD,
but he loves the one who pursues righteousness.
10 There is severe discipline for one who forsakes the way,
but one who hates a rebuke will die.
11 Sheol and Abaddon lie open before the LORD,
how much more human hearts!
12 Scoffers do not like to be rebuked;

[a] Gk Syr: Heb *in their death* [b] Gk Syr: Heb lacks *not* [c] Cn: Heb *makes knowledge good*

they will not go to the wise.
13 A glad heart makes a cheerful countenance,
but by sorrow of heart the spirit is broken.
14 The mind of one who has understanding seeks knowledge,
but the mouths of fools feed on folly.
15 All the days of the poor are hard,
but a cheerful heart has a continual feast.
16 Better is a little with the fear of the LORD
than great treasure and trouble with it.
17 Better is a dinner of vegetables where love is
than a fatted ox and hatred with it.
18 Those who are hot-tempered stir up strife,
but those who are slow to anger calm contention.
19 The way of the lazy is overgrown with thorns,
but the path of the upright is a level highway.
20 A wise child makes a glad father,
but the foolish despise their mothers.
21 Folly is a joy to one who has no sense,
but a person of understanding walks straight ahead.
22 Without counsel, plans go wrong,
but with many advisers they succeed.
23 To make an apt answer is a joy to anyone,
and a word in season, how good it is!
24 For the wise the path of life leads upward,
in order to avoid Sheol below.
25 The LORD tears down the house of the proud,
but maintains the widow's boundaries.
26 Evil plans are an abomination to the LORD,
but gracious words are pure.
27 Those who are greedy for unjust gain make trouble for their households,
but those who hate bribes will live.
28 The mind of the righteous ponders how to answer,
but the mouth of the wicked pours out evil.
29 The LORD is far from the wicked,
but he hears the prayer of the righteous.
30 The light of the eyes rejoices the heart,
and good news refreshes the body.
31 The ear that heeds wholesome admonition
will lodge among the wise.
32 Those who ignore instruction despise themselves,
but those who heed admonition gain understanding.
33 The fear of the LORD is instruction in wisdom,
and humility goes before honor.

15:13 but by sorrow: See 17:22. "Spirit" here refers to our inner energy and drive. It describes depression.

A friend tells you, "I am really feeling down." What would you suggest? If you face depression, where do you turn for help?

15:16-17 Better is: These two sayings shift to the "better this than that" form of proverb. Jesus used a variation of this form called "lesser to greater." (See Matt 7:9-11 for an example.)

15:25 the widow's boundaries: Care for widows, often helpless in the ancient world, was a trademark of biblical justice. God is especially concerned for widows and orphans (see Deut 10:17-18; 24:17-22, Isa 1:16-17). Stealing property by moving a boundary marker was forbidden by God's law (see Deut 19:14; Job 24:2-8; Prov 22:28).

16:1-9 The plans of the mind belong to mortals…Lord directs the steps: These verses deal with God's all-powerful direction of human affairs. God's control over what happens in life is a common theme in the wisdom literature of the Old Testament (see also Prov 19:21; Ecc 3:11-15; 8:6). Even the wicked serve God's purposes (16:4) Still, human intelligence plays an important role (16:9), but it can be mistaken (16:25).

The image of God as one who directs everything that happens is different than the image of God who allows the creation and created ones to act freely. What do you think of these two images? How do you think of God's role in guiding your life or influencing the affairs of the world?

16:10-15 Inspired decisions…throne is established by righteousness: The ideal ruler is viewed as one who follows God's leading, especially in making judgments. Righteous actions are based on God's justice. Wise folk keep on the good side of power (16:14-15). See also Romans 13:1-4.

16:11 Honest balances: See the note on 11:1.

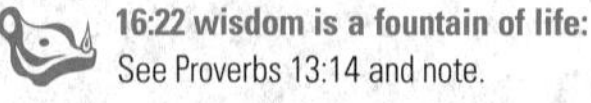

16:22 wisdom is a fountain of life: See Proverbs 13:14 and note.

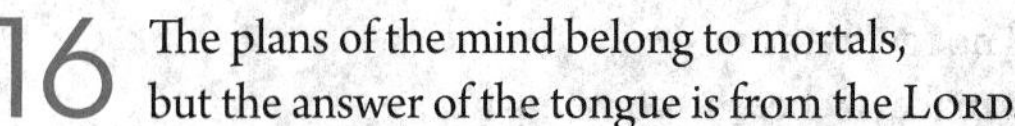

16 The plans of the mind belong to mortals,
but the answer of the tongue is from the Lord.
2 All one's ways may be pure in one's own eyes,
but the Lord weighs the spirit.
3 Commit your work to the Lord,
and your plans will be established.
4 The Lord has made everything for its purpose,
even the wicked for the day of trouble.
5 All those who are arrogant are an abomination to the Lord;
be assured, they will not go unpunished.
6 By loyalty and faithfulness iniquity is atoned for,
and by the fear of the Lord one avoids evil.
7 When the ways of people please the Lord,
he causes even their enemies to be at peace with them.
8 Better is a little with righteousness
than large income with injustice.
9 The human mind plans the way,
but the Lord directs the steps.
10 Inspired decisions are on the lips of a king;
his mouth does not sin in judgment.
11 Honest balances and scales are the Lord's;
all the weights in the bag are his work.
12 It is an abomination to kings to do evil,
for the throne is established by righteousness.
13 Righteous lips are the delight of a king,
and he loves those who speak what is right.
14 A king's wrath is a messenger of death,
and whoever is wise will appease it.
15 In the light of a king's face there is life,
and his favor is like the clouds that bring the spring rain.
16 How much better to get wisdom than gold!
To get understanding is to be chosen rather than silver.
17 The highway of the upright avoids evil;
those who guard their way preserve their lives.
18 Pride goes before destruction,
and a haughty spirit before a fall.
19 It is better to be of a lowly spirit among the poor
than to divide the spoil with the proud.
20 Those who are attentive to a matter will prosper,
and happy are those who trust in the Lord.
21 The wise of heart is called perceptive,
and pleasant speech increases persuasiveness.
22 Wisdom is a fountain of life to one who has it,
but folly is the punishment of fools.
23 The mind of the wise makes their speech judicious,

and adds persuasiveness to their lips.
24 Pleasant words are like a honeycomb,
sweetness to the soul and health to the body.
25 Sometimes there is a way that seems to be right,
but in the end it is the way to death.
26 The appetite of workers works for them;
their hunger urges them on.
27 Scoundrels concoct evil,
and their speech is like a scorching fire.
28 A perverse person spreads strife,
and a whisperer separates close friends.
29 The violent entice their neighbors,
and lead them in a way that is not good.
30 One who winks the eyes plans[a] perverse things;
one who compresses the lips brings evil to pass.
31 Gray hair is a crown of glory;
it is gained in a righteous life.
32 One who is slow to anger is better than the mighty,
and one whose temper is controlled than one who captures
a city.
33 The lot is cast into the lap,
but the decision is the LORD's alone.

17 Better is a dry morsel with quiet
than a house full of feasting with strife.
2 A slave who deals wisely will rule over a child who acts
shamefully,
and will share the inheritance as one of the family.
3 The crucible is for silver, and the furnace is for gold,
but the LORD tests the heart.
4 An evildoer listens to wicked lips;
and a liar gives heed to a mischievous tongue.
5 Those who mock the poor insult their Maker;
those who are glad at calamity will not go unpunished.
6 Grandchildren are the crown of the aged,
and the glory of children is their parents.
7 Fine speech is not becoming to a fool;
still less is false speech to a ruler.[b]
8 A bribe is like a magic stone in the eyes of those who give it;
wherever they turn they prosper.
9 One who forgives an affront fosters friendship,
but one who dwells on disputes will alienate a friend.
10 A rebuke strikes deeper into a discerning person
than a hundred blows into a fool.

16:26 The appetite: This is an observation rather than a moral statement, as are 10:15 and 13:12.

16:31 Gray hair is a crown of glory: Since it was thought that wise, righteous living brought longevity, gray hair would mark a good person.

16:33 lot is cast: Lots were like dice. They were used to make decisions. The people thought that God directed the outcome of the toss, so God really decided. See Proverbs 18:18; 1 Chronicles 25:8; Acts 1:26.

17:3 crucible…furnace: Precious metals such as gold and silver were purified by being heated in heat-resistant containers such as a crucible or furnace. This process burned away impurities within the melted gold or silver. This image of refining is compared to the LORD's testing of the human heart (see also Isa 1:25; Ezek 22:18-22; Zech 13:9).

17:5 Those who mock: Insulting the poor is offensive to God, who cares for all people and pays special attention to the poor, widows, and orphans. See also 14:31.

17:8 A bribe is like a magic stone: This is a morally neutral observation about the power of bribes, but 17:23 condemns bribery. See Deuteronomy 10:17.

17:9 One who forgives: Holding grudges destroys social harmony, so forgiveness is important. See Matthew 18:24-35 and Colossians 3:13.

[a] Gk Syr Vg Tg: Heb *to plan* [b] Or *a noble person*

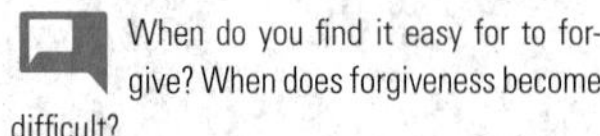

When do you find it easy for to forgive? When does forgiveness become difficult?

[11] Evil people seek only rebellion,
but a cruel messenger will be sent against them.
[12] Better to meet a she-bear robbed of its cubs
than to confront a fool immersed in folly.
[13] Evil will not depart from the house
of one who returns evil for good.
[14] The beginning of strife is like letting out water;
so stop before the quarrel breaks out.
[15] One who justifies the wicked and one who condemns the righteous
are both alike an abomination to the LORD.
[16] Why should fools have a price in hand
to buy wisdom, when they have no mind to learn?

17:17 A friend loves: Friends and family ideally provide unwavering support.

17:18 pledge: See the note on 6:1-5.

[17] A friend loves at all times,
and kinsfolk are born to share adversity.
[18] It is senseless to give a pledge,
to become surety for a neighbor.
[19] One who loves transgression loves strife;
one who builds a high threshold invites broken bones.
[20] The crooked of mind do not prosper,
and the perverse of tongue fall into calamity.
[21] The one who begets a fool gets trouble;
the parent of a fool has no joy.
[22] A cheerful heart is a good medicine,
but a downcast spirit dries up the bones.
[23] The wicked accept a concealed bribe
to pervert the ways of justice.
[24] The discerning person looks to wisdom,
but the eyes of a fool to the ends of the earth.
[25] Foolish children are a grief to their father
and bitterness to her who bore them.
[26] To impose a fine on the innocent is not right,
or to flog the noble for their integrity.

17:27-28 One who spares: Here is more advice on proper use of language, suggesting that the less said, the better.

18:1-2 The one who: Only fools forsake the community, for that is where wisdom and understanding thrive. Also see 27:17.

[27] One who spares words is knowledgeable;
one who is cool in spirit has understanding.
[28] Even fools who keep silent are considered wise;
when they close their lips, they are deemed intelligent.

18 The one who lives alone is self-indulgent,
showing contempt for all who have sound judgment.[a]
[2] A fool takes no pleasure in understanding,
but only in expressing personal opinion.
[3] When wickedness comes, contempt comes also;
and with dishonor comes disgrace.

---

[a] Meaning of Heb uncertain

4 The words of the mouth are deep waters;
the fountain of wisdom is a gushing stream.
5 It is not right to be partial to the guilty,
or to subvert the innocent in judgment.
6 A fool's lips bring strife,
and a fool's mouth invites a flogging.
7 The mouths of fools are their ruin,
and their lips a snare to themselves.
8 The words of a whisperer are like delicious morsels;
they go down into the inner parts of the body.
9 One who is slack in work
is close kin to a vandal.
10 The name of the LORD is a strong tower;
the righteous run into it and are safe.
11 The wealth of the rich is their strong city;
in their imagination it is like a high wall.
12 Before destruction one's heart is haughty,
but humility goes before honor.
13 If one gives answer before hearing,
it is folly and shame.
14 The human spirit will endure sickness;
but a broken spirit—who can bear?
15 An intelligent mind acquires knowledge,
and the ear of the wise seeks knowledge.
16 A gift opens doors;
it gives access to the great.
17 The one who first states a case seems right,
until the other comes and cross-examines.
18 Casting the lot puts an end to disputes
and decides between powerful contenders.
19 An ally offended is stronger than a city;[a]
such quarreling is like the bars of a castle.
20 From the fruit of the mouth one's stomach is satisfied;
the yield of the lips brings satisfaction.
21 Death and life are in the power of the tongue,
and those who love it will eat its fruits.
22 He who finds a wife finds a good thing,
and obtains favor from the LORD.
23 The poor use entreaties,
but the rich answer roughly.
24 Some[b] friends play at friendship[c]
but a true friend sticks closer than one's nearest kin.

18:8 The words of the whisperer: Gossip is delicious to hear and easily digested, so it becomes part of us. That makes it especially dangerous (see 16:28).

Luther said in his explanation to the Eighth Commandment that instead of spreading rumors about people, we should "interpret everything they do in the best possible light (*SC*:8)." If you took his words with absolute seriousness, what difference would it make in your life?

18:15 the ear: This comes from an oral culture, where people learn by listening. Verse 13 also encourages careful listening, and verse 17 urges listening to both sides of an argument.

18:18 Casting the lot: See the note on 16:33.

18:22 He who finds a wife: God as Creator supports ordinary life, including marriage. Also see 19:14 and the note on 12:4.

---

[a] Gk Syr Vg Tg: Meaning of Heb uncertain [b] Syr Tg: Heb *A man of* [c] Cn Compare Syr Vg Tg: Meaning of Heb uncertain

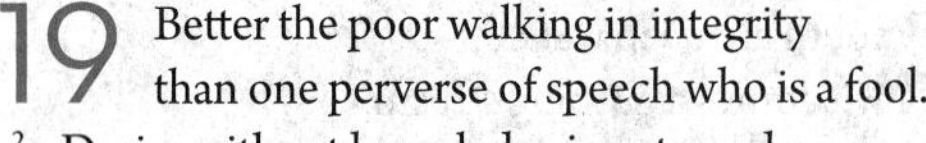

19 Better the poor walking in integrity
than one perverse of speech who is a fool.
2 Desire without knowledge is not good,
and one who moves too hurriedly misses the way.
3 One's own folly leads to ruin,
yet the heart rages against the LORD.
4 Wealth brings many friends,
but the poor are left friendless.
5 A false witness will not go unpunished,
and a liar will not escape.
6 Many seek the favor of the generous,
and everyone is a friend to a giver of gifts.
7 If the poor are hated even by their kin,
how much more are they shunned by their friends!
When they call after them, they are not there.[a]
8 To get wisdom is to love oneself;
to keep understanding is to prosper.
9 A false witness will not go unpunished,
and the liar will perish.
10 It is not fitting for a fool to live in luxury,
much less for a slave to rule over princes.
11 Those with good sense are slow to anger,
and it is their glory to overlook an offense.
12 A king's anger is like the growling of a lion,
but his favor is like dew on the grass.
13 A stupid child is ruin to a father,
and a wife's quarreling is a continual dripping of rain.
14 House and wealth are inherited from parents,
but a prudent wife is from the LORD.
15 Laziness brings on deep sleep;
an idle person will suffer hunger.
16 Those who keep the commandment will live;
those who are heedless of their ways will die.
17 Whoever is kind to the poor lends to the LORD,
and will be repaid in full.
18 Discipline your children while there is hope;
do not set your heart on their destruction.
19 A violent tempered person will pay the penalty;
if you effect a rescue, you will only have to do it again.[a]
20 Listen to advice and accept instruction,
that you may gain wisdom for the future.
21 The human mind may devise many plans,
but it is the purpose of the LORD that will be established.

19:4 Wealth brings many friends: See the note on 14:20-21.

19:10 It is not fitting: Since wisdom taught that the wise prosper and fools suffer, prosperous fools were an embarrassment.

19:13-14 A stupid child: Wisdom's desire for harmonious relationships included family life. Young people were urged to listen to parents and elders and to choose one's wife with care. Also see 19:18-27; 20:20; 21:9; and note on 18:22.

[a] Meaning of Heb uncertain

22 What is desirable in a person is loyalty,
and it is better to be poor than a liar.
23 The fear of the LORD is life indeed;
filled with it one rests secure
and suffers no harm.
24 The lazy person buries a hand in the dish,
and will not even bring it back to the mouth.
25 Strike a scoffer, and the simple will learn prudence;
reprove the intelligent, and they will gain knowledge.
26 Those who do violence to their father and chase away their mother
are children who cause shame and bring reproach.
27 Cease straying, my child, from the words of knowledge,
in order that you may hear instruction.
28 A worthless witness mocks at justice,
and the mouth of the wicked devours iniquity.
29 Condemnation is ready for scoffers,
and flogging for the backs of fools.

20 Wine is a mocker, strong drink a brawler,
and whoever is led astray by it is not wise.
2 The dread anger of a king is like the growling of a lion;
anyone who provokes him to anger forfeits life itself.
3 It is honorable to refrain from strife,
but every fool is quick to quarrel.
4 The lazy person does not plow in season;
harvest comes, and there is nothing to be found.
5 The purposes in the human mind are like deep water,
but the intelligent will draw them out.
6 Many proclaim themselves loyal,
but who can find one worthy of trust?
7 The righteous walk in integrity—
happy are the children who follow them!
8 A king who sits on the throne of judgment
winnows all evil with his eyes.
9 Who can say, "I have made my heart clean;
I am pure from my sin"?
10 Diverse weights and diverse measures
are both alike an abomination to the LORD.
11 Even children make themselves known by their acts,
by whether what they do is pure and right.
12 The hearing ear and the seeing eye—
the LORD has made them both.
13 Do not love sleep, or else you will come to poverty;
open your eyes, and you will have plenty of bread.
14 "Bad, bad," says the buyer,

19:23 The fear of the LORD: This phrase occurs at least thirteen times in Proverbs. Proper faith and right living for the people of Israel flow from this understanding. Wisdom enhances and develops the promises of religion, and it begins with a proper regard for the ways and requirements of the LORD. See note on 1:7.

20:1 Wine is a mocker: This criticizes wine for practical rather than moral reasons. Drinking too much wine can cause one to lose discipline and self-control. See 5:15-23 and compare Leviticus 10:8-11.

20:9 made my heart clean...am pure from my sin: This is the only reference in Proverbs to universal human sinfulness. Also see Psalm 51:5.

Why do we confess our sins in worship? The confession of sins in our worship is based on a passage from 1 John 1:8-10, which begins by saying, "If we say we have no sin, we deceive ourselves, and the truth is not in us." We believe that all people are sinful and need God's gracious forgiveness in order to be in right relationship with God and with our neighbors. That is why we confess our sins. As the confession goes on to say, "If we confess our sins, [God] who is faithful and just will forgive our sins and cleanse us from all unrighteousness." *Proverbs 20:9*

20:14 Bad, bad: When haggling in the marketplace, a buyer would intentionally question the quality of the goods to get a lower price. Later, the buyer would boast of his bargain.

then goes away and boasts.

15 There is gold, and abundance of costly stones;
but the lips informed by knowledge are a precious jewel.

16 Take the garment of one who has given surety for a stranger;
seize the pledge given as surety for foreigners.

17 Bread gained by deceit is sweet,
but afterward the mouth will be full of gravel.

18 Plans are established by taking advice;
wage war by following wise guidance.

20:19 A gossip reveals: In the royal court, keeping secrets was very important.

19 A gossip reveals secrets;
therefore do not associate with a babbler.

20 If you curse father or mother,
your lamp will go out in utter darkness.

21 An estate quickly acquired in the beginning
will not be blessed in the end.

22 Do not say, "I will repay evil";
wait for the LORD, and he will help you.

23 Differing weights are an abomination to the LORD,
and false scales are not good.

20:24-25 All our steps: Verse 24 proclaims the supreme authority of God. Because making a vow before God is so sacred, verse 25 urges caution making a vow to God that one might later regret. Proper reflection should come first. (See Eccl 5:1-6.)

24 All our steps are ordered by the LORD;
how then can we understand our own ways?

25 It is a snare for one to say rashly, "It is holy,"
and begin to reflect only after making a vow.

26 A wise king winnows the wicked,
and drives the wheel over them.

20:27 The human spirit: The human spirit, seen here as a gift from the LORD, resembles our idea of conscience.

When do you think it is important to keep secrets? When is it dangerous or harmful?

27 The human spirit is the lamp of the LORD,
searching every inmost part.

28 Loyalty and faithfulness preserve the king,
and his throne is upheld by righteousness.[a]

29 The glory of youths is their strength,
but the beauty of the aged is their gray hair.

30 Blows that wound cleanse away evil;
beatings make clean the innermost parts.

21:1 the king's heart is a stream: God guides the actions of rulers (see note at 16:10-15).

21:2 All deeds: This is an observation about self-deception. We can fool ourselves, but we can't fool God. See 21:27; compare to Psalm 44:21 and Revelation 2:23.

21:3 To do righteousness: See note on 15:8.

21

The king's heart is a stream of water in the hand of the LORD;
he turns it wherever he will.

2 All deeds are right in the sight of the doer,
but the LORD weighs the heart.

3 To do righteousness and justice
is more acceptable to the LORD than sacrifice.

4 Haughty eyes and a proud heart—
the lamp of the wicked—are sin.

5 The plans of the diligent lead surely to abundance,

[a] Gk: Heb *loyalty*

but everyone who is hasty comes only to want.

6 The getting of treasures by a lying tongue
is a fleeting vapor and a snare[a] of death.

7 The violence of the wicked will sweep them away,
because they refuse to do what is just.

8 The way of the guilty is crooked,
but the conduct of the pure is right.

9 It is better to live in a corner of the housetop
than in a house shared with a contentious wife.

10 The souls of the wicked desire evil;
their neighbors find no mercy in their eyes.

11 When a scoffer is punished, the simple become wiser;
when the wise are instructed, they increase in knowledge.

12 The Righteous One observes the house of the wicked;
he casts the wicked down to ruin.

13 If you close your ear to the cry of the poor,
you will cry out and not be heard.

14 A gift in secret averts anger;
and a concealed bribe in the bosom, strong wrath.

15 When justice is done, it is a joy to the righteous,
but dismay to evildoers.

16 Whoever wanders from the way of understanding
will rest in the assembly of the dead.

17 Whoever loves pleasure will suffer want;
whoever loves wine and oil will not be rich.

18 The wicked is a ransom for the righteous,
and the faithless for the upright.

19 It is better to live in a desert land
than with a contentious and fretful wife.

20 Precious treasure remains[b] in the house of the wise,
but the fool devours it.

21 Whoever pursues righteousness and kindness
will find life[c] and honor.

22 One wise person went up against a city of warriors
and brought down the stronghold in which they trusted.

23 To watch over mouth and tongue
is to keep out of trouble.

24 The proud, haughty person, named "Scoffer,"
acts with arrogant pride.

25 The craving of the lazy person is fatal,
for lazy hands refuse to labor.

26 All day long the wicked covet,[d]

---

[a] Gk: Heb *seekers* [b] Gk: Heb *and oil* [c] Gk: Heb *life and righteousness* [d] Gk: Heb *all day long one covets covetously*

21:9 It is better: See note on 15:16-17.

21:12 The Righteous One: This likely refers to God as judge of the wicked. It is sometimes translated as "just man."

21:13 If you close your ear . . . of the poor: Those who ignore charity for the poor will receive the same treatment when they are in need. Also see 21:26.

21:17 Whoever loves pleasure: The life that loves or strives after only personal pleasure is a wasted life. In the New Testament, the parable of the prodigal son (Luke 15:11-32) shows this in a dramatic way. Wisdom teachings guided the young to see success in life as more than material success or achieving personal pleasure.

What do you think of the idea that making personal pleasure the highest priority in life can take away from having a full life?

21:26 the righteous give and do not hold back: The wise person is generous. See 21:13 and the note on 11:24-26.

but the righteous give and do not hold back.
27 The sacrifice of the wicked is an abomination;
how much more when brought with evil intent.
28 A false witness will perish,
but a good listener will testify successfully.
29 The wicked put on a bold face,
but the upright give thought to[a] their ways.
30 No wisdom, no understanding, no counsel,
can avail against the LORD.
31 The horse is made ready for the day of battle,
but the victory belongs to the LORD.

22 A good name is to be chosen rather than great riches,
and favor is better than silver or gold.
2 The rich and the poor have this in common:
the LORD is the maker of them all.
3 The clever see danger and hide;
but the simple go on, and suffer for it.
4 The reward for humility and fear of the LORD
is riches and honor and life.
5 Thorns and snares are in the way of the perverse;
the cautious will keep far from them.
6 Train children in the right way,
and when old, they will not stray.
7 The rich rule over the poor,
and the borrower is the slave of the lender.
8 Whoever sows injustice will reap calamity,
and the rod of anger will fail.
9 Those who are generous are blessed,
for they share their bread with the poor.
10 Drive out a scoffer, and strife goes out;
quarreling and abuse will cease.
11 Those who love a pure heart and are gracious in speech
will have the king as a friend.
12 The eyes of the LORD keep watch over knowledge,
but he overthrows the words of the faithless.
13 The lazy person says, "There is a lion outside!
I shall be killed in the streets!"
14 The mouth of a loose[b] woman is a deep pit;
he with whom the LORD is angry falls into it.
15 Folly is bound up in the heart of a boy,
but the rod of discipline drives it far away.
16 Oppressing the poor in order to enrich oneself,
and giving to the rich, will lead only to loss.

[a] Another reading is *establish* [b] Heb *strange*

21:30-31 No wisdom . . . victory belongs to the LORD: Human wisdom is no match and no replacement for God's wisdom. No matter what plans human beings put together, including battle plans, victory comes from God alone. See also Isaiah 8:9-10.

22:2 The rich and the poor: Students of wisdom were drawn from the wealthy classes. This proverb reminds them that the poor are also God's children.

22:6 Train children: This oft-quoted (and optimistic) proverb emphasizes the importance of early foundations.

Who provided or who provides you with clear direction in your life? If you are looking for such guidance, where can you find it?

22:7-9 The rich rule: The rich have an advantage over the poor, so the rich are urged to give generously towards the poor (22:9). Caring for the poor is a matter of justice (22:8). See note on 22:2 and compare 22:16.

22:14 The mouth of a loose woman: See the notes on 2:16 and 7:4-5.

Sayings of the Wise

17 The words of the wise:

Incline your ear and hear my words,[a]
and apply your mind to my teaching;
18 for it will be pleasant if you keep them within you,
if all of them are ready on your lips.
19 So that your trust may be in the LORD,
I have made them known to you today—yes, to you.
20 Have I not written for you thirty sayings
of admonition and knowledge,
21 to show you what is right and true,
so that you may give a true answer to those who sent you?

22:17—24:34 The words of the wise: Often called "The Thirty Sayings" (see 22:20). Part of this section (22:17—23:12) closely parallels an Egyptian wisdom collection called "Instruction of Amenemope," which was divided into thirty sections or "houses." Most sayings in this section address the reader directly by use of "you."

22 Do not rob the poor because they are poor,
or crush the afflicted at the gate;
23 for the LORD pleads their cause
and despoils of life those who despoil them.
24 Make no friends with those given to anger,
and do not associate with hotheads,
25 or you may learn their ways
and entangle yourself in a snare.
26 Do not be one of those who give pledges,
who become surety for debts.
27 If you have nothing with which to pay,
why should your bed be taken from under you?
28 Do not remove the ancient landmark
that your ancestors set up.
29 Do you see those who are skillful in their work?
They will serve kings;
they will not serve common people.

22:22-23 Do not rob: The Egyptian saying closely resembles 22:22, but the Israelite sage adds a point about God's intentions in 21:23.

22:28 the ancient landmark: Refers to markers that formed property lines. Because the gift of land was a sacred gift of God, these were not to be moved. See 23:10 and the note on 15:25.

23 When you sit down to eat with a ruler,
observe carefully what[b] is before you,
2 and put a knife to your throat
if you have a big appetite.
3 Do not desire the ruler's[c] delicacies,
for they are deceptive food.
4 Do not wear yourself out to get rich;
be wise enough to desist.
5 When your eyes light upon it, it is gone;
for suddenly it takes wings to itself,
flying like an eagle toward heaven.

23:4-5 Do not wear yourself out: This proverb cautions against spending too much effort on seeking riches, because they can suddenly disappear.

---

[a] Cn Compare Gk: Heb *Incline your ear, and hear the words of the wise* [b] Or *who* [c] Heb *his*

6 Do not eat the bread of the stingy;
do not desire their delicacies;
7 for like a hair in the throat, so are they.[a]
"Eat and drink!" they say to you;
but they do not mean it.
8 You will vomit up the little you have eaten,
and you will waste your pleasant words.
9 Do not speak in the hearing of a fool,
who will only despise the wisdom of your words.
10 Do not remove an ancient landmark
or encroach on the fields of orphans,
11 for their redeemer is strong;
he will plead their cause against you.
12 Apply your mind to instruction
and your ear to words of knowledge.
13 Do not withhold discipline from your children;
if you beat them with a rod, they will not die.
14 If you beat them with the rod,
you will save their lives from Sheol.
15 My child, if your heart is wise,
my heart too will be glad.
16 My soul will rejoice
when your lips speak what is right.
17 Do not let your heart envy sinners,
but always continue in the fear of the LORD.
18 Surely there is a future,
and your hope will not be cut off.

19 Hear, my child, and be wise,
and direct your mind in the way.
20 Do not be among winebibbers,
or among gluttonous eaters of meat;
21 for the drunkard and the glutton will come to poverty,
and drowsiness will clothe them with rags.

22 Listen to your father who begot you,
and do not despise your mother when she is old.
23 Buy truth, and do not sell it;
buy wisdom, instruction, and understanding.
24 The father of the righteous will greatly rejoice;
he who begets a wise son will be glad in him.
25 Let your father and mother be glad;
let her who bore you rejoice.

23:11 their redeemer is strong: Another reference to God's concern for orphans. See the note on 15:25.

23:13-14 Do not withhold discipline...beat them: See also 13:24. Strong physical punishment was considered one way to keep children from bad behavior and poor choices that could lead even to Sheol (see the note on 1:12).

23:22 Listen to your father...do not despise your mother: Wise persons bring honor to parents. In ancient culture, disgracing parents brought great shame.

[a] Meaning of Heb uncertain

26 My child, give me your heart,
and let your eyes observe[a] my ways.
27 For a prostitute is a deep pit;
an adulteress[b] is a narrow well.
28 She lies in wait like a robber
and increases the number of the faithless.

29 Who has woe? Who has sorrow?
Who has strife? Who has complaining?
Who has wounds without cause?
Who has redness of eyes?
30 Those who linger late over wine,
those who keep trying mixed wines.
31 Do not look at wine when it is red,
when it sparkles in the cup
and goes down smoothly.
32 At the last it bites like a serpent,
and stings like an adder.
33 Your eyes will see strange things,
and your mind utter perverse things.
34 You will be like one who lies down in the midst of the sea,
like one who lies on the top of a mast.[c]
35 "They struck me," you will say,[d] "but I was not hurt;
they beat me, but I did not feel it.
When shall I awake?
I will seek another drink."

24 Do not envy the wicked,
nor desire to be with them;
2 for their minds devise violence,
and their lips talk of mischief.

3 By wisdom a house is built,
and by understanding it is established;
4 by knowledge the rooms are filled
with all precious and pleasant riches.
5 Wise warriors are mightier than strong ones,[e]
and those who have knowledge than those who have
strength;
6 for by wise guidance you can wage your war,
and in abundance of counselors there is victory.
7 Wisdom is too high for fools;
in the gate they do not open their mouths.

23:26-28 My child: More on unwise sexual behavior. See also the note on the "loose woman" at 2:16.

23:29-35 Who has woe?: A powerful picture of the dangers of getting drunk. Verse 35 expressively describes the compulsive drinker. Also see 23:19-21.

24:3 By wisdom a house is built: A true home is built on wise teaching, and those who live in it benefit. Compare this image to woman wisdom who builds a house (9:1).

[a] Another reading is *delight in* [b] Heb *an alien woman* [c] Meaning of Heb uncertain [d] Gk Syr Vg Tg: Heb lacks *you will say* [e] Gk Compare Syr Tg: Heb *A wise man is strength*

24:10-12 If you faint…"we did not know": Holding back help from those in need or pleading ignorance are not excuses when it comes to helping those in need. God will strictly hold you to account.

What do you do when you discover a friend was dealing with a real problem and you didn't notice the signs of struggle, so you didn't help?

24:13 honey: An image for wisdom. In Psalm 19:10, God's law is more desirable than honey or gold.

24:19-20 Do not fret because of evildoers: In reality, fools and evildoers often prospered. This and similar verses declare a common theme in Proverbs that in the end these evil ones will fail.

24:23 These also: An editorial comment introducing an appendix to this collection (24:23b-34).

8 Whoever plans to do evil
will be called a mischief-maker.
9 The devising of folly is sin,
and the scoffer is an abomination to all.

10 If you faint in the day of adversity,
your strength being small;
11 if you hold back from rescuing those taken away to death,
those who go staggering to the slaughter;
12 if you say, "Look, we did not know this"—
does not he who weighs the heart perceive it?
Does not he who keeps watch over your soul know it?
And will he not repay all according to their deeds?

13 My child, eat honey, for it is good,
and the drippings of the honeycomb are sweet to your taste.
14 Know that wisdom is such to your soul;
if you find it, you will find a future,
and your hope will not be cut off.

15 Do not lie in wait like an outlaw against the home of the
righteous;
do no violence to the place where the righteous live;
16 for though they fall seven times, they will rise again;
but the wicked are overthrown by calamity.

17 Do not rejoice when your enemies fall,
and do not let your heart be glad when they stumble,
18 or else the LORD will see it and be displeased,
and turn away his anger from them.

19 Do not fret because of evildoers.
Do not envy the wicked;
20 for the evil have no future;
the lamp of the wicked will go out.

21 My child, fear the LORD and the king,
and do not disobey either of them;[a]
22 for disaster comes from them suddenly,
and who knows the ruin that both can bring?

Further Sayings of the Wise

23 These also are sayings of the wise:

[a] Gk: Heb *do not associate with those who change*

Partiality in judging is not good.
24 Whoever says to the wicked, "You are innocent,"
will be cursed by peoples, abhorred by nations;
25 but those who rebuke the wicked will have delight,
and a good blessing will come upon them.
26 One who gives an honest answer
gives a kiss on the lips.

27 Prepare your work outside,
get everything ready for you in the field;
and after that build your house.

28 Do not be a witness against your neighbor without cause,
and do not deceive with your lips.
29 Do not say, "I will do to others as they have done to me;
I will pay them back for what they have done."

30 I passed by the field of one who was lazy,
by the vineyard of a stupid person;
31 and see, it was all overgrown with thorns;
the ground was covered with nettles,
and its stone wall was broken down.
32 Then I saw and considered it;
I looked and received instruction.
33 A little sleep, a little slumber,
a little folding of the hands to rest,
34 and poverty will come upon you like a robber,
and want, like an armed warrior.

Further Wise Sayings of Solomon

25 These are other proverbs of Solomon that the officials of King Hezekiah of Judah copied.

2 It is the glory of God to conceal things,
but the glory of kings is to search things out.
3 Like the heavens for height, like the earth for depth,
so the mind of kings is unsearchable.
4 Take away the dross from the silver,
and the smith has material for a vessel;
5 take away the wicked from the presence of the king,
and his throne will be established in righteousness.
6 Do not put yourself forward in the king's presence
or stand in the place of the great;
7 for it is better to be told, "Come up here,"
than to be put lower in the presence of a noble.

24:29 pay them back: This proverb warns against taking revenge when someone hurts us in some way. Compare this to Jesus' words in Matthew 5:38-41.

24:30-34 I passed by...poverty will come upon you: More advice to avoid laziness. See also 6:6-11 and the note on 10:4.

25:1—29:27 other proverbs of Solomon...officials of King Hezekiah...copied: See the note on 1:1. King Hezekiah (715–687 B.C.E.) ruled Judah about two hundred years after the time of Solomon. Hezekiah helped lead a time of religious renewal in the country (see 2 Kgs 18:1-7). His prosperous reign probably stimulated cultural and literary activity, including interest in the older wisdom sayings, which he had others copy and edit in his royal court. See 2 Kings 18–20.

25:6-7 Do not put yourself forward: Jesus taught this wisdom in one of his parables (see Luke 14:7-11).

25:7-10 do not hastily bring into court: Strive to avoid lawsuits in court. Instead, deal directly with your neighbor. See Matthew 5:25.

What do you think of the idea of trying to settle disputes directly with someone, rather than taking the dispute to court? What are the advantages and disadvantages of each?

What your eyes have seen
8 do not hastily bring into court;
for[a] what will you do in the end,
when your neighbor puts you to shame?
9 Argue your case with your neighbor directly,
and do not disclose another's secret;
10 or else someone who hears you will bring shame upon you,
and your ill repute will have no end.

11 A word fitly spoken
is like apples of gold in a setting of silver.
12 Like a gold ring or an ornament of gold
is a wise rebuke to a listening ear.
13 Like the cold of snow in the time of harvest
are faithful messengers to those who send them;
they refresh the spirit of their masters.
14 Like clouds and wind without rain
is one who boasts of a gift never given.
15 With patience a ruler may be persuaded,
and a soft tongue can break bones.
16 If you have found honey, eat only enough for you,
or else, having too much, you will vomit it.
17 Let your foot be seldom in your neighbor's house,
otherwise the neighbor will become weary of you and hate you.
18 Like a war club, a sword, or a sharp arrow
is one who bears false witness against a neighbor.
19 Like a bad tooth or a lame foot
is trust in a faithless person in time of trouble.
20 Like vinegar on a wound[b]
is one who sings songs to a heavy heart.
Like a moth in clothing or a worm in wood,
sorrow gnaws at the human heart.[c]
21 If your enemies are hungry, give them bread to eat;
and if they are thirsty, give them water to drink;
22 for you will heap coals of fire on their heads,
and the LORD will reward you.
23 The north wind produces rain,
and a backbiting tongue, angry looks.
24 It is better to live in a corner of the housetop
than in a house shared with a contentious wife.
25 Like cold water to a thirsty soul,

25:16-17 If you have: Don't make too much of a good thing. Don't take advantage of friendships. Also see 25:27.

25:21-22 If your enemies are hungry: Being kind to an enemy is preferred to getting revenge (see also the note on 24:29). This passage is quoted by Paul in Romans 12:20. Compare Matthew 5:43-48 and Luke 6:27-36.

How do you deal with people who hurt you in some way?

---

[a] Cn: Heb *or else* [b] Gk: Heb *Like one who takes off a garment on a cold day, like vinegar on lye* [c] Gk Syr Tg: Heb lacks *Like a moth . . . human heart*

so is good news from a far country.
26 Like a muddied spring or a polluted fountain
are the righteous who give way before the wicked.
27 It is not good to eat much honey,
or to seek honor on top of honor.
28 Like a city breached, without walls,
is one who lacks self-control.

25:28 self-control: Self-control, an essential virtue of the wise, is a major theme in wisdom teaching.

What role does self-control play in your development as a disciple?

26

Like snow in summer or rain in harvest,
so honor is not fitting for a fool.
2 Like a sparrow in its flitting, like a swallow in its flying,
an undeserved curse goes nowhere.
3 A whip for the horse, a bridle for the donkey,
and a rod for the back of fools.
4 Do not answer fools according to their folly,
or you will be a fool yourself.
5 Answer fools according to their folly,
or they will be wise in their own eyes.
6 It is like cutting off one's foot and drinking down violence,
to send a message by a fool.
7 The legs of a disabled person hang limp;
so does a proverb in the mouth of a fool.
8 It is like binding a stone in a sling
to give honor to a fool.
9 Like a thornbush brandished by the hand of a drunkard
is a proverb in the mouth of a fool.
10 Like an archer who wounds everybody
is one who hires a passing fool or drunkard.[a]
11 Like a dog that returns to its vomit
is a fool who reverts to his folly.
12 Do you see persons wise in their own eyes?
There is more hope for fools than for them.
13 The lazy person says, "There is a lion in the road!
There is a lion in the streets!"
14 As a door turns on its hinges,
so does a lazy person in bed.
15 The lazy person buries a hand in the dish,
and is too tired to bring it back to the mouth.
16 The lazy person is wiser in self-esteem
than seven who can answer discreetly.
17 Like somebody who takes a passing dog by the ears
is one who meddles in the quarrel of another.
18 Like a maniac who shoots deadly firebrands and arrows,
19 so is one who deceives a neighbor

26:1-12 Like snow in summer: Here are a number of sayings about dealing with fools who reject wisdom. Verses 4 and 5 suggest that there are times to ignore fools and times to challenge them.

26:8-9 binding a stone in a sling: Tying or binding a stone in the pocket of a slingshot would keep the stone from flying when shot and it would come back and hit the shooter.

26:13-16 The lazy person: Sayings put together in a humorous sequence: The sluggard sees a lion in the streets but cannot get out of bed. His tossing and turning makes him too tired to eat. Yet he still thinks himself wiser than seven who have common sense. The sayings appear independently at 19:24; 22:13; and 26:13, 15.

26:17 takes a passing dog by the ears: Clearly, this is a dangerous situation. So this proverb cautions to mind your own business.

26:18-20 Like a maniac: Be careful about joking around.

[a] Meaning of Heb uncertain

and says, "I am only joking!"
20 For lack of wood the fire goes out,
and where there is no whisperer, quarreling ceases.
21 As charcoal is to hot embers and wood to fire,
so is a quarrelsome person for kindling strife.
22 The words of a whisperer are like delicious morsels;
they go down into the inner parts of the body.
23 Like the glaze[a] covering an earthen vessel
are smooth[b] lips with an evil heart.
24 An enemy dissembles in speaking
while harboring deceit within;
25 when an enemy speaks graciously, do not believe it,
for there are seven abominations concealed within;
26 though hatred is covered with guile,
the enemy's wickedness will be exposed in the assembly.
27 Whoever digs a pit will fall into it,
and a stone will come back on the one who starts it rolling.
28 A lying tongue hates its victims,
and a flattering mouth works ruin.

27 Do not boast about tomorrow,
for you do not know what a day may bring.
2 Let another praise you, and not your own mouth—
a stranger, and not your own lips.
3 A stone is heavy, and sand is weighty,
but a fool's provocation is heavier than both.
4 Wrath is cruel, anger is overwhelming,
but who is able to stand before jealousy?
5 Better is open rebuke
than hidden love.
6 Well meant are the wounds a friend inflicts,
but profuse are the kisses of an enemy.
7 The sated appetite spurns honey,
but to a ravenous appetite even the bitter is sweet.
8 Like a bird that strays from its nest
is one who strays from home.
9 Perfume and incense make the heart glad,
but the soul is torn by trouble.[c]
10 Do not forsake your friend or the friend of your parent;
do not go to the house of your kindred in the day of your calamity.
Better is a neighbor who is nearby
than kindred who are far away.

27:1 Do not boast…Let another praise you: Living for the present is important, because we don't know what tomorrow will bring. Boasting about plans or future actions can be risky. And it is better if others boast about you. Also see Matthew 6:34.

Why do you think boasting is discouraged? Why is it better if others praise you instead of you praising yourself?

27:5 Better is open rebuke…kisses of an enemy: Love must be active, not hidden. Relationships may call for frank "tough love."

Would you rather a friend tell you the truth, even if it hurt? Why?

27:10 Do not forsake: The middle line ("Better is a neighbor…") does not seem to fit. The last line complements the meaning of the first.

---

[a] Cn: Heb *silver of dross* [b] Gk: Heb *burning* [c] Gk: Heb *the sweetness of a friend is better than one's own counsel*

11 Be wise, my child, and make my heart glad,
so that I may answer whoever reproaches me.
12 The clever see danger and hide;
but the simple go on, and suffer for it.
13 Take the garment of one who has given surety for a stranger;
seize the pledge given as surety for foreigners.[a]
14 Whoever blesses a neighbor with a loud voice,
rising early in the morning,
will be counted as cursing.
15 A continual dripping on a rainy day
and a contentious wife are alike;
16 to restrain her is to restrain the wind
or to grasp oil in the right hand.[b]
17 Iron sharpens iron,
and one person sharpens the wits[c] of another.
18 Anyone who tends a fig tree will eat its fruit,
and anyone who takes care of a master will be honored.
19 Just as water reflects the face,
so one human heart reflects another.
20 Sheol and Abaddon are never satisfied,
and human eyes are never satisfied.
21 The crucible is for silver, and the furnace is for gold,
so a person is tested[d] by being praised.
22 Crush a fool in a mortar with a pestle
along with crushed grain,
but the folly will not be driven out.

23 Know well the condition of your flocks,
and give attention to your herds;
24 for riches do not last forever,
nor a crown for all generations.
25 When the grass is gone, and new growth appears,
and the herbage of the mountains is gathered,
26 the lambs will provide your clothing,
and the goats the price of a field;
27 there will be enough goats' milk for your food,
for the food of your household
and nourishment for your servant-girls.

28 The wicked flee when no one pursues,
but the righteous are as bold as a lion.
2 When a land rebels
it has many rulers;

27:13 Take the garment…seize the pledge: This may refer to getting some item as a guarantee to offset a loan, since loans were considered risky business.

27:15-16 A continual dripping: Choose wisely, for you can't reshape your spouse after marriage. Even though this passage names "wife," the same can be said of a contentious husband.

27:17 Iron sharpens: Two heads are better than one. We learn and grow by interacting with others.

27:20 Sheol and Abaddon: See the note on 1:12 (Sheol). Abbadon is a Hebrew word that refers to Sheol or the grave. See also Job 28:22; 31:12. In Revelation 9:11, Abaddon is called the angel of the bottomless pit, the ruler of the underworld.

28:1—29:27 The wicked flee … but the righteous are as bold: These sayings are close in form to those in chapters 10–16. Most use opposite parallelism (see the chart Types of Proverbs, p. 1018). A number of sayings deal with governmental administration. These were likely intended to teach young men destined for civil service.

---

[a] Vg and 20.16: Heb *for a foreign woman* [b] Meaning of Heb uncertain [c] Heb *face* [d] Heb lacks *is tested*

but with an intelligent ruler
there is lasting order.[a]

28:3 A ruler: A good ruler gives priority to aiding the poor. See also Psalm 72:1-4, 12-14; and Proverbs 28:15.

28:6 Better to be poor: Wisdom builds character. It is worthwhile even if it does not bring the prosperity it promises.

28:8 One who augments wealth by exorbitant interest: In Israel lending at interest was forbidden (see Exod 22:25).

28:13 conceals transgressions… confesses: Hiding wrongdoings or trying to cover up evil actions will eventually lead to loss. But confessing these wrongs provides an opportunity for a second chance, for receiving God's mercy. See 20:9 and note on confession there.

28:21 To show partiality: An enduring justice problem: Uphold the law, but consider extenuating circumstances.

3 A ruler[b] who oppresses the poor
is a beating rain that leaves no food.
4 Those who forsake the law praise the wicked,
but those who keep the law struggle against them.
5 The evil do not understand justice,
but those who seek the LORD understand it completely.
6 Better to be poor and walk in integrity
than to be crooked in one's ways even though rich.
7 Those who keep the law are wise children,
but companions of gluttons shame their parents.
8 One who augments wealth by exorbitant interest
gathers it for another who is kind to the poor.
9 When one will not listen to the law,
even one's prayers are an abomination.
10 Those who mislead the upright into evil ways
will fall into pits of their own making,
but the blameless will have a goodly inheritance.
11 The rich is wise in self-esteem,
but an intelligent poor person sees through the pose.
12 When the righteous triumph, there is great glory,
but when the wicked prevail, people go into hiding.
13 No one who conceals transgressions will prosper,
but one who confesses and forsakes them will obtain mercy.
14 Happy is the one who is never without fear,
but one who is hard-hearted will fall into calamity.
15 Like a roaring lion or a charging bear
is a wicked ruler over a poor people.
16 A ruler who lacks understanding is a cruel oppressor;
but one who hates unjust gain will enjoy a long life.
17 If someone is burdened with the blood of another,
let that killer be a fugitive until death;
let no one offer assistance.
18 One who walks in integrity will be safe,
but whoever follows crooked ways will fall into the Pit.[c]
19 Anyone who tills the land will have plenty of bread,
but one who follows worthless pursuits will have plenty of
poverty.
20 The faithful will abound with blessings,
but one who is in a hurry to be rich will not go unpunished.
21 To show partiality is not good—
yet for a piece of bread a person may do wrong.

---

[a] Meaning of Heb uncertain [b] Cn: Heb *A poor person* [c] Syr: Heb *fall all at once*

22 The miser is in a hurry to get rich
and does not know that loss is sure to come.
23 Whoever rebukes a person will afterward find more favor
than one who flatters with the tongue.
24 Anyone who robs father or mother
and says, "That is no crime,"
is partner to a thug.
25 The greedy person stirs up strife,
but whoever trusts in the LORD will be enriched.
26 Those who trust in their own wits are fools;
but those who walk in wisdom come through safely.
27 Whoever gives to the poor will lack nothing,
but one who turns a blind eye will get many a curse.
28 When the wicked prevail, people go into hiding;
but when they perish, the righteous increase.

29 One who is often reproved, yet remains stubborn,
will suddenly be broken beyond healing.
2 When the righteous are in authority, the people rejoice;
but when the wicked rule, the people groan.
3 A child who loves wisdom makes a parent glad,
but to keep company with prostitutes is to squander one's substance.
4 By justice a king gives stability to the land,
but one who makes heavy exactions ruins it.
5 Whoever flatters a neighbor
is spreading a net for the neighbor's feet.
6 In the transgression of the evil there is a snare,
but the righteous sing and rejoice.
7 The righteous know the rights of the poor;
the wicked have no such understanding.
8 Scoffers set a city aflame,
but the wise turn away wrath.
9 If the wise go to law with fools,
there is ranting and ridicule without relief.
10 The bloodthirsty hate the blameless,
and they seek the life of the upright.
11 A fool gives full vent to anger,
but the wise quietly holds it back.
12 If a ruler listens to falsehood,
all his officials will be wicked.
13 The poor and the oppressor have this in common:
the LORD gives light to the eyes of both.
14 If a king judges the poor with equity,
his throne will be established forever.
15 The rod and reproof give wisdom,

28:27 Whoever gives to the poor: See the notes on 14:20-21 and 22:7-9.

29:2, 4, 12, 14, 16 When the righteous are in authority…king judges the poor with equity: A number of proverbs detail how good rulers make for happy people. People rejoice when rulers rule fairly (29:2; see also 1 Kgs 12:4, 12-15), don't overburden their people (29:4), set a good example for others (29:12), and take care of the poor (29:14). A wicked administration is doomed (29:16).

29:3 A child who loves wisdom: More caution to young men about sexual misadventures. See chapters 7 and 9 and the note on 19:13-14.

but a mother is disgraced by a neglected child.
16 When the wicked are in authority, transgression
increases,
but the righteous will look upon their downfall.
17 Discipline your children, and they will give you rest;
they will give delight to your heart.
18 Where there is no prophecy, the people cast off restraint,
but happy are those who keep the law.
19 By mere words servants are not disciplined,
for though they understand, they will not give heed.
20 Do you see someone who is hasty in speech?
There is more hope for a fool than for anyone like that.
21 A slave pampered from childhood
will come to a bad end.[a]
22 One given to anger stirs up strife,
and the hothead causes much transgression.
23 A person's pride will bring humiliation,
but one who is lowly in spirit will obtain honor.
24 To be a partner of a thief is to hate one's own life;
one hears the victim's curse, but discloses nothing.[b]
25 The fear of others[c] lays a snare,
but one who trusts in the LORD is secure.
26 Many seek the favor of a ruler,
but it is from the LORD that one gets justice.
27 The unjust are an abomination to the righteous,
but the upright are an abomination to the wicked.

29:20 Do you see: Careful, thoughtful, measured speech was the signature of a wise person. See 10:19; 17:27-28; James 1:19.

29:26 from the LORD: Though people seek favorable treatment from rulers, ultimately God is in charge of justice.

Sayings of Agur

30 The words of Agur son of Jakeh. An oracle. Thus says the
man: I am weary, O God,
I am weary, O God. How can I prevail?[d]
2 Surely I am too stupid to be human;
I do not have human understanding.
3 I have not learned wisdom,
nor have I knowledge of the holy ones.[e]
4 Who has ascended to heaven and come down?
Who has gathered the wind in the hollow of the hand?
Who has wrapped up the waters in a garment?
Who has established all the ends of the earth?
What is the person's name?
And what is the name of the person's child?
Surely you know!

30:1—31:31 The words of Agur: The final two chapters form an appendix or miscellaneous collection named for unknown persons, Agur (chapter 30) and King Lemuel's mother (chapter 31).

30:2-4 Surely I am: Divine wisdom exceeds human wisdom. We cannot reach God by human wisdom (see Isa 40:18-26). The unspoken answer to the riddle in 30:4 is God.

---

[a] Vg: Meaning of Heb uncertain [b] Meaning of Heb uncertain [c] Or *human fear* [d] Or *I am spent.* Meaning of Heb uncertain [e] Or *Holy One*

5 Every word of God proves true;
he is a shield to those who take refuge in him.
6 Do not add to his words,
or else he will rebuke you, and you will be found a liar.

7 Two things I ask of you;
do not deny them to me before I die:
8 Remove far from me falsehood and lying;
give me neither poverty nor riches;
feed me with the food that I need,
9 or I shall be full, and deny you,
and say, "Who is the LORD?"
or I shall be poor, and steal,
and profane the name of my God.

10 Do not slander a servant to a master,
or the servant will curse you, and you will be held guilty.

11 There are those who curse their fathers
and do not bless their mothers.
12 There are those who are pure in their own eyes
yet are not cleansed of their filthiness.
13 There are those—how lofty are their eyes,
how high their eyelids lift!—
14 there are those whose teeth are swords,
whose teeth are knives,
to devour the poor from off the earth,
the needy from among mortals.

15 The leech[a] has two daughters;
"Give, give," they cry.
Three things are never satisfied;
four never say, "Enough":
16 Sheol, the barren womb,
the earth ever thirsty for water,
and the fire that never says, "Enough."[a]

17 The eye that mocks a father
and scorns to obey a mother
will be pecked out by the ravens of the valley
and eaten by the vultures.

18 Three things are too wonderful for me;
four I do not understand:

[a] Meaning of Heb uncertain

30:5-6 Every word of God proves true: God's words reveal who God is (see Isa 40:27-31). See Revelation 22:18-19 for another warning about adding to or subtracting from God's words.

30:7-9 Two things: A prayer for an honest, balanced life. Compare the request for God to "feed me" (30:8) to Matthew 6:11 and Luke 11:3. This whole section (30:2-9) could be read together as the prayer of a pious person.

30:15-16 four never say "Enough": A numerical proverb that has the pattern of three plus one things. Based on observations from life, they explore the mysteries of creation. See also 30:18-31 for more examples. In this list, Sheol, the place of the dead, never is satisfied and continues to receive those who die. A woman who cannot have children may continue to long for the possibility. The earth and its inhabitants need water to survive. Fires keep burning as long as they have fuel.

The list in 30:18-19 names four things the writer calls "too wonderful for me." As you think about your life and experiences, what would you add to this list? Why?

19 the way of an eagle in the sky,
the way of a snake on a rock,
the way of a ship on the high seas,
and the way of a man with a girl.

20 This is the way of an adulteress:
she eats, and wipes her mouth,
and says, "I have done no wrong."

21 Under three things the earth trembles;
under four it cannot bear up:
22 a slave when he becomes king,
and a fool when glutted with food;
23 an unloved woman when she gets a husband,
and a maid when she succeeds her mistress.

24 Four things on earth are small,
yet they are exceedingly wise:
25 the ants are a people without strength,
yet they provide their food in the summer;
26 the badgers are a people without power,
yet they make their homes in the rocks;
27 the locusts have no king,
yet all of them march in rank;
28 the lizard[a] can be grasped in the hand,
yet it is found in kings' palaces.

29 Three things are stately in their stride;
four are stately in their gait:
30 the lion, which is mightiest among wild animals
and does not turn back before any;
31 the strutting rooster,[b] the he-goat,
and a king striding before[c] his people.

32 If you have been foolish, exalting yourself,
or if you have been devising evil,
put your hand on your mouth.
33 For as pressing milk produces curds,
and pressing the nose produces blood,
so pressing anger produces strife.

The Teaching of King Lemuel's Mother

31 The words of King Lemuel. An oracle that his mother taught him:

---

[a] Or *spider* [b] Gk Syr Tg Compare Vg: Meaning of Heb uncertain [c] Meaning of Heb uncertain

2 No, my son! No, son of my womb!
No, son of my vows!
3 Do not give your strength to women,
your ways to those who destroy kings.
4 It is not for kings, O Lemuel,
it is not for kings to drink wine,
or for rulers to desire[a] strong drink;
5 or else they will drink and forget what has been decreed,
and will pervert the rights of all the afflicted.
6 Give strong drink to one who is perishing,
and wine to those in bitter distress;
7 let them drink and forget their poverty,
and remember their misery no more.
8 Speak out for those who cannot speak,
for the rights of all the destitute.[b]
9 Speak out, judge righteously,
defend the rights of the poor and needy.

Ode to a Capable Wife

10 A capable wife who can find?
She is far more precious than jewels.
11 The heart of her husband trusts in her,
and he will have no lack of gain.
12 She does him good, and not harm,
all the days of her life.
13 She seeks wool and flax,
and works with willing hands.
14 She is like the ships of the merchant,
she brings her food from far away.
15 She rises while it is still night
and provides food for her household
and tasks for her servant-girls.
16 She considers a field and buys it;
with the fruit of her hands she plants a vineyard.
17 She girds herself with strength,
and makes her arms strong.
18 She perceives that her merchandise is profitable.
Her lamp does not go out at night.
19 She puts her hands to the distaff,
and her hands hold the spindle.
20 She opens her hand to the poor,
and reaches out her hands to the needy.
21 She is not afraid for her household when it snows,

[a] Cn: Heb *where* [b] Heb *all children of passing away*

31:2-9 No, my son!: Advice of the queen mother to her royal son includes being honorable and disciplined in relationships with women (31:3), being sober (31:4-7), and defending the poor (31:8-9).

31:6 Give strong drink: This verse became the motto of guilds of women who gave wine mixed with drugs to criminals being executed, to ease their pain. See John 19:28-30; Matthew 27:34.

31:10-31 A capable wife: This is an alphabetical acrostic where each line begins with a successive letter of the Hebrew alphabet. We can read this as a picture of the ideal woman who embodies in human form the virtues of woman wisdom (chapters 8–9). Not only does this ideal wife provide for her family's personal needs, she is a business person, making independent, wise financial decisions (31:16, 22, 24) and supports the needy (31:20).

31:15 her servant-girls: This woman enjoys an upper-class life.

31:17 She girds herself: Military terms suggesting a strong protective role.

for all her household are clothed in crimson.
22 She makes herself coverings;
her clothing is fine linen and purple.
23 Her husband is known in the city gates,
taking his seat among the elders of the land.
24 She makes linen garments and sells them;
she supplies the merchant with sashes.
25 Strength and dignity are her clothing,
and she laughs at the time to come.
26 She opens her mouth with wisdom,
and the teaching of kindness is on her tongue.
27 She looks well to the ways of her household,
and does not eat the bread of idleness.
28 Her children rise up and call her happy;
her husband too, and he praises her:
29 "Many women have done excellently,
but you surpass them all."
30 Charm is deceitful, and beauty is vain,
but a woman who fears the LORD is to be praised.
31 Give her a share in the fruit of her hands,
and let her works praise her in the city gates.

31:30 who fears the LORD: A reference back to Proverbs 1:7 closes the book. This woman embodies wisdom (31:26), and wisdom trumps mere beauty.

What strikes you about the description of this capable woman, written more than two thousand years ago? What themes or proverbs in this book ring especially true today? Why?

Ecclesiastes 3:1-8

ECCLESIASTES

Background File

The book of Ecclesiastes is one of the latest books in the Old Testament to be written—possibly only three or four hundred years before the birth of Jesus. Its story is told from the perspective of an old king or wise person, identified in the book as "the Teacher." Traditionally, this teacher was identified as Solomon, the wisest of Israel's kings.

What's the Story?

Ecclesiastes is written as a personal memoir, a story of one's personal experience. The teacher looks back over his life and shares with his readers the many things he has learned. He has found that striving after riches, pleasure, success, and even wisdom is like chasing after the wind. Such striving brings frustration rather than fulfillment or meaning.

The teacher shares both advice and reflections about life. He often repeats key phases such as "all is vanity and a chasing after wind" (1:14), references to deeds, toiling, and nothing new "under the sun" (1:3, 9, 14; 2:11, 17) and "eat and drink and find enjoyment in all the toil" (5:18). Ecclesiastes includes two stirring poems (3:1-8; 12:1-8). After the first, "For everything there is a season," the teacher laments that though there is a time for everything, we humans cannot know when they are. The second poem uses many metaphors to describe what it feels like to be old. The book ends with a concluding speech that tells everyone to fear God and keep the commandments.

Ecclesiastes is read in the Jewish community during the feast of Sukkoth—also called the Festival of Booths, or Tabernacles, or Ingathering (see Lev 23:39-43; Num 29:12-39; Deut 16:13-15). This festival occurs in the fall of the year and celebrates God's care for the people of Israel as they wandered in the wilderness. The festival celebrates God's care and the joy that can be found in life, even life that is fragile and unpredictable.

What's the Message?

The teacher's reflections include a number of themes:

Becoming very rich or very smart or having fun all the time does not lead to a meaningful life.

We are all going to die, so no one is finally better than anyone else.

We cannot know what God has in store for the future, and this is very frustrating when we want to make plans.

The world is not fair; the good do not always get rewarded and the bad do not always get punished.

We should all find times to enjoy the work and life God has given to us.

Like Job, the teacher is skeptical about traditional answers.

The book helps us understand that realism and skepticism are an important part of faith. Some readers think the book is cynical and depressing, reflecting a crisis of faith. But Ecclesiastes can be read as uplifting. The teacher concludes that once people discover that they cannot find meaning on their own, then they can leave such matters to God and learn to find pleasure in the simple living of life.

Martin Luther said Ecclesiastes was "a very beautiful and useful book . . . which on many counts deserves to be in everyone's hands and to be familiar to everyone" (*LW* 15:4, 7). For Luther the purpose and aim of the book was clear—that we be content with the word and work of God, take pleasure in the gifts God has given, and not strive for that which one cannot have. Luther understood the book to describe accurately the sin of always wanting more than we can have or need, of wanting to control everything, and finally of not trusting God.

1:1 the Teacher, the son of David, king in Jerusalem: The teacher is *Qoheleth,* the Hebrew name of the book. It perhaps means someone who speaks to the assembly, so Luther translated this as "the Preacher." Though connected with Solomon, it is likely the book was written long after his time (see introduction).

1:2 Vanity: In Ecclesiastes the word *vanity* is repeated thirty-eight times. It means "meaninglessness" or "emptiness." The Hebrew word *hebel* [HE-bel] is literally "vapor" or "mist," suggesting something that has little substance and disappears quickly.

Reflections of a Royal Philosopher

1 The words of the Teacher,[a] the son of David, king in Jerusalem.
2 Vanity of vanities, says the Teacher,[a]
vanity of vanities! All is vanity.
3 What do people gain from all the toil
at which they toil under the sun?
4 A generation goes, and a generation comes,
but the earth remains forever.
5 The sun rises and the sun goes down,
and hurries to the place where it rises.
6 The wind blows to the south,
and goes around to the north;
round and round goes the wind,
and on its circuits the wind returns.

[a] Heb *Qoheleth,* traditionally rendered *Preacher*

7 All streams run to the sea,
but the sea is not full;
to the place where the streams flow,
there they continue to flow.
8 All things[a] are wearisome;
more than one can express;
the eye is not satisfied with seeing,
or the ear filled with hearing.
9 What has been is what will be,
and what has been done is what will be done;
there is nothing new under the sun.
10 Is there a thing of which it is said,
"See, this is new"?
It has already been,
in the ages before us.
11 The people of long ago are not remembered,
nor will there be any remembrance
of people yet to come
by those who come after them.

The Futility of Seeking Wisdom

12 I, the Teacher,[b] when king over Israel in Jerusalem, 13applied
my mind to seek and to search out by wisdom all that is done under
heaven; it is an unhappy business that God has given to human beings
to be busy with. 14I saw all the deeds that are done under the sun; and
see, all is vanity and a chasing after wind.[c]
15 What is crooked cannot be made straight,
and what is lacking cannot be counted.
16 I said to myself, "I have acquired great wisdom, surpassing all
who were over Jerusalem before me; and my mind has had great experience of wisdom and knowledge." 17And I applied my mind to know
wisdom and to know madness and folly. I perceived that this also is
but a chasing after wind.[c]
18 For in much wisdom is much vexation,
and those who increase knowledge increase sorrow.

The Futility of Self-Indulgence

2 I said to myself, "Come now, I will make a test of pleasure; enjoy
yourself." But again, this also was vanity. 2I said of laughter, "It
is mad," and of pleasure, "What use is it?" 3I searched with my mind
how to cheer my body with wine—my mind still guiding me with
wisdom—and how to lay hold on folly, until I might see what was

How does Luther interpret the phrase "there is nothing new under the sun"? Luther notes that while God certainly does new things, people remain sinful, unable to do anything truly new "under the sun"—that is, in this world. *Ecclesiastes 1:9*

Do you agree with the teacher about how the world is? Why or why not?

1:14-15 a chasing after wind... What is crooked cannot be made straight: People cannot straighten out what God has bent (3:14; 7:13). The unchangeable nature of the world seems to offer little hope and little encouragement to try to change things.

Have you ever felt a sense of hopelessness or wondered what use there is in trying? If so, how did you deal with these feelings?

2:1-11 I will make a test of pleasure...made great works...I became great: Using Solomon as a prime example, the teacher speaks of trying to find meaning through pleasure-seeking, building and accumulating great wealth, and gaining a big reputation. Nothing brought meaning.

[a] Or *words* [b] Heb *Qoheleth,* traditionally rendered *Preacher* [c] Or *a feeding on wind.* See Hos 12.1

good for mortals to do under heaven during the few days of their life.
4 I made great works; I built houses and planted vineyards for myself;
5 I made myself gardens and parks, and planted in them all kinds of
fruit trees. 6 I made myself pools from which to water the forest of
growing trees. 7 I bought male and female slaves, and had slaves who
were born in my house; I also had great possessions of herds and
flocks, more than any who had been before me in Jerusalem. 8 I also
gathered for myself silver and gold and the treasure of kings and of
the provinces; I got singers, both men and women, and delights of the
flesh, and many concubines.[a]

9 So I became great and surpassed all who were before me in
Jerusalem; also my wisdom remained with me. 10 Whatever my eyes
desired I did not keep from them; I kept my heart from no pleasure,
for my heart found pleasure in all my toil, and this was my reward for
all my toil. 11 Then I considered all that my hands had done and the
toil I had spent in doing it, and again, all was vanity and a chasing after
wind,[b] and there was nothing to be gained under the sun.

Wisdom and Joy Given to One Who Pleases God

In 2:12-17 the teacher speaks of wisdom in two opposite ways. He compares wisdom to light and folly to darkness. But then he calls wisdom into question. What do you think about pursuing wisdom?

12 So I turned to consider wisdom and madness and folly; for
what can the one do who comes after the king? Only what has already been done. 13 Then I saw that wisdom excels folly as light excels
darkness.

14 The wise have eyes in their head,
but fools walk in darkness.

Yet I perceived that the same fate befalls all of them. 15 Then I said
to myself, "What happens to the fool will happen to me also; why then
have I been so very wise?" And I said to myself that this also is vanity.
16 For there is no enduring remembrance of the wise or of fools, seeing
that in the days to come all will have been long forgotten. How can the
wise die just like fools? 17 So I hated life, because what is done under the
sun was grievous to me; for all is vanity and a chasing after wind.[b]

18 I hated all my toil in which I had toiled under the sun, seeing
that I must leave it to those who come after me 19—and who knows
whether they will be wise or foolish? Yet they will be master of all for
which I toiled and used my wisdom under the sun. This also is vanity.
20 So I turned and gave my heart up to despair concerning all the toil
of my labors under the sun, 21 because sometimes one who has toiled
with wisdom and knowledge and skill must leave all to be enjoyed
by another who did not toil for it. This also is vanity and a great evil.
22 What do mortals get from all the toil and strain with which they toil
under the sun? 23 For all their days are full of pain, and their work is a
vexation; even at night their minds do not rest. This also is vanity.

---

[a] Meaning of Heb uncertain [b] Or *a feeding on wind.* See Hos 12.1

24 There is nothing better for mortals than to eat and drink, and
find enjoyment in their toil. This also, I saw, is from the hand of God;
25 for apart from him[a] who can eat or who can have enjoyment? 26 For
to the one who pleases him God gives wisdom and knowledge and
joy; but to the sinner he gives the work of gathering and heaping, only
to give to one who pleases God. This also is vanity and a chasing after
wind.[b]

Everything Has Its Time

3 For everything there is a season, and a time for every matter under heaven:

2 a time to be born, and a time to die;
a time to plant, and a time to pluck up what is planted;
3 a time to kill, and a time to heal;
a time to break down, and a time to build up;
4 a time to weep, and a time to laugh;
a time to mourn, and a time to dance;
5 a time to throw away stones, and a time to gather stones together;
a time to embrace, and a time to refrain from embracing;
6 a time to seek, and a time to lose;
a time to keep, and a time to throw away;
7 a time to tear, and a time to sew;
a time to keep silence, and a time to speak;
8 a time to love, and a time to hate;
a time for war, and a time for peace.

The God-Given Task

9 What gain have the workers from their toil? 10 I have seen the
business that God has given to everyone to be busy with. 11 He has
made everything suitable for its time; moreover he has put a sense of
past and future into their minds, yet they cannot find out what God
has done from the beginning to the end. 12 I know that there is nothing
better for them than to be happy and enjoy themselves as long as they
live; 13 moreover, it is God's gift that all should eat and drink and take
pleasure in all their toil. 14 I know that whatever God does endures
forever; nothing can be added to it, nor anything taken from it; God
has done this, so that all should stand in awe before him. 15 That which
is, already has been; that which is to be, already is; and God seeks out
what has gone by.[c]

Judgment and the Future Belong to God

16 Moreover I saw under the sun that in the place of justice, wickedness was there, and in the place of righteousness, wickedness was

---

[a] Gk Syr: Heb *apart from me* [b] Or *a feeding on wind.* See Hos 12.1 [c] Heb *what is pursued*

2:24-26 eat and drink, and find enjoyment in their toil: This is the first of seven times the teacher speaks highly of enjoying life (see also 3:12; 3:22; 5:18; 8:15; 9:7-9; 11:9—12:1).

3:1-8 For everything there is a season...a time: All of life is summarized by the phrases grouped in two sets of seven opposites. Seven was considered a number symbolizing completeness.

Ecclesiastes 3:1-8 is the most familiar passage in the book. Where have you heard them? *How* do you hear them—as hopeful or depressing? Why?

3:11 they cannot find out what God has done: Note that even though the teacher says there is a time for everything, he also says we cannot know what God is up to. We may not be able to discern the times.

3:16-22 in the place of justice, wickedness was there: Throughout the Old Testament, God's concern for justice comes through, and God's people are called to treat others with justice and righteousness (see Exod 23:6; Ps 33:5; Prov 21:15; Amos 5:15, 24). Here the teacher simply says that both the unjust (wicked) and the just (righteous) will be judged and face death. Death is final, with no idea of an afterlife. Also, death is the great equalizer, because everyone will die.

there as well. [17]I said in my heart, God will judge the righteous and
the wicked, for he has appointed a time for every matter, and for every
work. [18]I said in my heart with regard to human beings that God is
testing them to show that they are but animals. [19]For the fate of humans and the fate of animals is the same; as one dies, so dies the other.
They all have the same breath, and humans have no advantage over
the animals; for all is vanity. [20]All go to one place; all are from the dust,
and all turn to dust again. [21]Who knows whether the human spirit
goes upward and the spirit of animals goes downward to the earth?
[22]So I saw that there is nothing better than that all should enjoy their
work, for that is their lot; who can bring them to see what will be after
them?

3:20 All go to one place: Probably refers to Sheol, the dark place of the dead.

How does thinking about death help us think about how we should live our lives?

4 Again I saw all the oppressions that are practiced under the
sun. Look, the tears of the oppressed—with no one to comfort
them! On the side of their oppressors there was power—with no one
to comfort them. [2]And I thought the dead, who have already died,
more fortunate than the living, who are still alive; [3]but better than
both is the one who has not yet been, and has not seen the evil deeds
that are done under the sun.

4:1-3 I saw all the oppressions... better...the one who has not yet been: The teacher sees oppression leading to horrible suffering. People are better off not being born at all if it means having go through such horrible suffering.

4 Then I saw that all toil and all skill in work come from one person's envy of another. This also is vanity and a chasing after wind.[a]

5 Fools fold their hands
and consume their own flesh.

6 Better is a handful with quiet
than two handfuls with toil,
and a chasing after wind.[a]

7 Again, I saw vanity under the sun: [8]the case of solitary individuals, without sons or brothers; yet there is no end to all their toil, and
their eyes are never satisfied with riches. "For whom am I toiling,"
they ask, "and depriving myself of pleasure?" This also is vanity and
an unhappy business.

The Value of a Friend

9 Two are better than one, because they have a good reward for
their toil. [10]For if they fall, one will lift up the other; but woe to one
who is alone and falls and does not have another to help. [11]Again, if
two lie together, they keep warm; but how can one keep warm alone?
[12]And though one might prevail against another, two will withstand
one. A threefold cord is not quickly broken.

4:9-12 Two are better than one: The teacher suggests that those who share life's toils, or who toil for the sake of another, find life more meaningful.

13 Better is a poor but wise youth than an old but foolish king,
who will no longer take advice. [14]One can indeed come out of prison
to reign, even though born poor in the kingdom. [15]I saw all the living
who, moving about under the sun, follow that[b] youth who replaced

4:13-16 Better is a poor but wise youth: A form of wisdom saying that reverses normal expectations (see also 10:5-7; Prov 17:2; 20:29).

---

[a] Or *a feeding on wind.* See Hos 12.1 [b] Heb *the second*

the king;[a] [16]there was no end to all those people whom he led. Yet those who come later will not rejoice in him. Surely this also is vanity and a chasing after wind.[b]

Reverence, Humility, and Contentment

5 [c] Guard your steps when you go to the house of God; to draw near to listen is better than the sacrifice offered by fools; for they do not know how to keep from doing evil.[d] [2] [e]Never be rash with your mouth, nor let your heart be quick to utter a word before God, for God is in heaven, and you upon earth; therefore let your words be few.

3 For dreams come with many cares, and a fool's voice with many words.

4 When you make a vow to God, do not delay fulfilling it; for he has no pleasure in fools. Fulfill what you vow. [5]It is better that you should not vow than that you should vow and not fulfill it. [6]Do not let your mouth lead you into sin, and do not say before the messenger that it was a mistake; why should God be angry at your words, and destroy the work of your hands?

7 With many dreams come vanities and a multitude of words;[f] but fear God.

8 If you see in a province the oppression of the poor and the violation of justice and right, do not be amazed at the matter; for the high official is watched by a higher, and there are yet higher ones over them. [9]But all things considered, this is an advantage for a land: a king for a plowed field.[f]

10 The lover of money will not be satisfied with money; nor the lover of wealth, with gain. This also is vanity.

11 When goods increase, those who eat them increase; and what gain has their owner but to see them with his eyes?

12 Sweet is the sleep of laborers, whether they eat little or much; but the surfeit of the rich will not let them sleep.

13 There is a grievous ill that I have seen under the sun: riches were kept by their owners to their hurt, [14]and those riches were lost in a bad venture; though they are parents of children, they have nothing in their hands. [15]As they came from their mother's womb, so they shall go again, naked as they came; they shall take nothing for their toil, which they may carry away with their hands. [16]This also is a grievous ill: just as they came, so shall they go; and what gain do they have from toiling for the wind? [17]Besides, all their days they eat in darkness, in much vexation and sickness and resentment.

18 This is what I have seen to be good: it is fitting to eat and drink

---

[a] Heb *him* [b] Or *a feeding on wind.* See Hos 12.1 [c] Ch 4.17 in Heb [d] Cn: Heb *they do not know how to do evil* [e] Ch 5.1 in Heb [f] Meaning of Heb uncertain

5:1 to listen is better than the sacrifice offered by fools: To listen to (obey) God and live according to God's law is more important than offering sacrifices, especially those offered by those who are not sincere (see also Isa 1:11-17).

The teacher has a good deal to say about money not buying happiness (5:10-12). How does this insight speak to us?

5:4-5 When you make a vow: Making a vow was considered a sacred promise. The writer says it is better not to make a vow at all, if you don't intend to or can't keep it.

5:8-9 violation of justice...high official is watched by a higher: This probably means that the poor cannot expect to receive just treatment from government officials who only look out for their own interests and support one another's policies.

How does Luther reflect on Ecclesiastes' view of riches? Referring to the book's author as King Solomon, Luther says this about the passage on riches: "Solomon does not condemn riches, nor does he forbid that we acquire riches or food or drink. But he calls these things gifts of God in order to teach us to put down our anxieties; then we shall wait for all of these things from God by faith and when God wills shall surrender them with patience.... Therefore riches are not to be rejected. Nor are they granted to us by God for the purpose of our rejecting them or abstaining from them, but rather so that we use them and distribute them to the poor. This statement is the interpreter of the entire book: Solomon intends to forbid vain anxieties, so that we may happily enjoy the things that are present and not care at all about the things that are in the future, lest we permit the present moment, our moment, to slip away" (*LW* 15:93). *Ecclesiastes 5:18-20*

How do you respond to Luther's comments above about riches, the use of riches, enjoying life? How have these words been true for you?

and find enjoyment in all the toil with which one toils under the sun
the few days of the life God gives us; for this is our lot. 19Likewise all
to whom God gives wealth and possessions and whom he enables to
enjoy them, and to accept their lot and find enjoyment in their toil—
this is the gift of God. 20For they will scarcely brood over the days of
their lives, because God keeps them occupied with the joy of their
hearts.

The Frustration of Desires

6 There is an evil that I have seen under the sun, and it lies heavy
upon humankind: 2those to whom God gives wealth, possessions, and honor, so that they lack nothing of all that they desire, yet
God does not enable them to enjoy these things, but a stranger enjoys
them. This is vanity; it is a grievous ill. 3A man may beget a hundred
children, and live many years; but however many are the days of his
years, if he does not enjoy life's good things, or has no burial, I say that
a stillborn child is better off than he. 4For it comes into vanity and
goes into darkness, and in darkness its name is covered; 5moreover it
has not seen the sun or known anything; yet it finds rest rather than
he. 6Even though he should live a thousand years twice over, yet enjoy
no good—do not all go to one place?

7 All human toil is for the mouth, yet the appetite is not satisfied.
8For what advantage have the wise over fools? And what do the poor
have who know how to conduct themselves before the living? 9Better
is the sight of the eyes than the wandering of desire; this also is vanity
and a chasing after wind.[a]

10 Whatever has come to be has already been named, and it is
known what human beings are, and that they are not able to dispute
with those who are stronger. 11The more words, the more vanity, so
how is one the better? 12For who knows what is good for mortals while
they live the few days of their vain life, which they pass like a shadow?
For who can tell them what will be after them under the sun?

A Disillusioned View of Life

7 A good name is better than precious ointment,
and the day of death, than the day of birth.
2 It is better to go to the house of mourning
than to go to the house of feasting;
for this is the end of everyone,
and the living will lay it to heart.
3 Sorrow is better than laughter,
for by sadness of countenance the heart is made glad.
4 The heart of the wise is in the house of mourning;

[a] Or *a feeding on wind.* See Hos 12.1

6:3 beget a hundred children... has no burial: In ancient Israel, having many children was considered a great blessing. Not receiving a proper burial was considered a great disgrace. Just as distressing is having wealth that cannot be enjoyed or having wealth that cannot be passed on to heirs (see also 2:18-21).

7:1-13 A good name is better... Consider the work of God: This series of ancient proverbs focuses on what may seem like contradictions. Mourning is better than feasting; sorrow is better than laughter; the end is better than the beginning. It concludes with the traditional view of wisdom—that it is as good as an inheritance and gives life to those who have it (see Prov 3:13-15; 16:16).

but the heart of fools is in the house of mirth.
5 It is better to hear the rebuke of the wise
than to hear the song of fools.
6 For like the crackling of thorns under a pot,
so is the laughter of fools;
this also is vanity.
7 Surely oppression makes the wise foolish,
and a bribe corrupts the heart.
8 Better is the end of a thing than its beginning;
the patient in spirit are better than the proud in spirit.
9 Do not be quick to anger,
for anger lodges in the bosom of fools.
10 Do not say, "Why were the former days better than these?"
For it is not from wisdom that you ask this.
11 Wisdom is as good as an inheritance,
an advantage to those who see the sun.
12 For the protection of wisdom is like the protection of money,
and the advantage of knowledge is that wisdom gives life to
the one who possesses it.
13 Consider the work of God;
who can make straight what he has made crooked?

14 In the day of prosperity be joyful, and in the day of adversity consider; God has made the one as well as the other, so that mortals may not find out anything that will come after them.

The Riddles of Life

15 In my vain life I have seen everything; there are righteous people who perish in their righteousness, and there are wicked people
who prolong their life in their evildoing. 16 Do not be too righteous,
and do not act too wise; why should you destroy yourself? 17 Do not
be too wicked, and do not be a fool; why should you die before your
time? 18 It is good that you should take hold of the one, without letting
go of the other; for the one who fears God shall succeed with both.

19 Wisdom gives strength to the wise more than ten rulers that are in a city.

20 Surely there is no one on earth so righteous as to do good without ever sinning.

21 Do not give heed to everything that people say, or you may
hear your servant cursing you; 22 your heart knows that many times
you have yourself cursed others.

23 All this I have tested by wisdom; I said, "I will be wise," but it
was far from me. 24 That which is, is far off, and deep, very deep; who
can find it out? 25 I turned my mind to know and to search out and
to seek wisdom and the sum of things, and to know that wickedness
is folly and that foolishness is madness. 26 I found more bitter than

7:15 righteous people…wicked people: Like Job, the teacher learns from experience that the good are not always rewarded and the bad are not always punished.

7:26-29 the woman who is a trap: The woman is described as in Proverbs (7:5-27; 9:13-18; 22:14). The tempting figure is a woman, likely because the teacher was speaking primarily to young men.

Men and women of all ages need to be aware of the ways they are tempted to manipulate one another. If the "woman who is a trap" stands for *anything* that tempts you to disobey God, what are the traps in your life?

death the woman who is a trap, whose heart is snares and nets, whose
hands are fetters; one who pleases God escapes her, but the sinner is
taken by her. 27 See, this is what I found, says the Teacher,[a] adding one
thing to another to find the sum, 28 which my mind has sought repeatedly, but I have not found. One man among a thousand I found, but
a woman among all these I have not found. 29 See, this alone I found,
that God made human beings straightforward, but they have devised
many schemes.

Obey the King and Enjoy Yourself

8 Who is like the wise man?
And who knows the interpretation of a thing?
Wisdom makes one's face shine,
and the hardness of one's countenance is changed.

2 Keep[b] the king's command because of your sacred oath. 3 Do
not be terrified; go from his presence, do not delay when the matter is unpleasant, for he does whatever he pleases. 4 For the word of
the king is powerful, and who can say to him, "What are you doing?"
5 Whoever obeys a command will meet no harm, and the wise mind
will know the time and way. 6 For every matter has its time and way, although the troubles of mortals lie heavy upon them. 7 Indeed, they do
not know what is to be, for who can tell them how it will be? 8 No one
has power over the wind[c] to restrain the wind,[c] or power over the day
of death; there is no discharge from the battle, nor does wickedness
deliver those who practice it. 9 All this I observed, applying my mind
to all that is done under the sun, while one person exercises authority
over another to the other's hurt.

God's Ways Are Inscrutable

8:10-14 wicked . . . were praised in the city: The teacher is distressed that the world is unfair (also 7:15; 9:11-12).

What are your expectations about reward and punishment in this world? What if your expectations are not met?

10 Then I saw the wicked buried; they used to go in and out of
the holy place, and were praised in the city where they had done
such things.[d] This also is vanity. 11 Because sentence against an evil
deed is not executed speedily, the human heart is fully set to do evil.
12 Though sinners do evil a hundred times and prolong their lives, yet I
know that it will be well with those who fear God, because they stand
in fear before him, 13 but it will not be well with the wicked, neither
will they prolong their days like a shadow, because they do not stand
in fear before God.

14 There is a vanity that takes place on earth, that there are righteous people who are treated according to the conduct of the wicked,
and there are wicked people who are treated according to the conduct
of the righteous. I said that this also is vanity. 15 So I commend enjoyment, for there is nothing better for people under the sun than to eat,

[a] *Qoheleth*, traditionally rendered *Preacher* [b] Heb *I keep* [c] Or *breath* [d] Meaning of Heb uncertain

and drink, and enjoy themselves, for this will go with them in their toil through the days of life that God gives them under the sun.

16 When I applied my mind to know wisdom, and to see the business that is done on earth, how one's eyes see sleep neither day nor night, [17]then I saw all the work of God, that no one can find out what is happening under the sun. However much they may toil in seeking, they will not find it out; even though those who are wise claim to know, they cannot find it out.

Take Life as It Comes

9 All this I laid to heart, examining it all, how the righteous and the wise and their deeds are in the hand of God; whether it is love or hate one does not know. Everything that confronts them [2]is vanity,[a] since the same fate comes to all, to the righteous and the wicked, to the good and the evil,[b] to the clean and the unclean, to those who sacrifice and those who do not sacrifice. As are the good, so are the sinners; those who swear are like those who shun an oath. [3]This is an evil in all that happens under the sun, that the same fate comes to everyone. Moreover, the hearts of all are full of evil; madness is in their hearts while they live, and after that they go to the dead. [4]But whoever is joined with all the living has hope, for a living dog is better than a dead lion. [5]The living know that they will die, but the dead know nothing; they have no more reward, and even the memory of them is lost. [6]Their love and their hate and their envy have already perished; never again will they have any share in all that happens under the sun.

7 Go, eat your bread with enjoyment, and drink your wine with a merry heart; for God has long ago approved what you do. [8]Let your garments always be white; do not let oil be lacking on your head. [9]Enjoy life with the wife whom you love, all the days of your vain life that are given you under the sun, because that is your portion in life and in your toil at which you toil under the sun. [10]Whatever your hand finds to do, do with your might; for there is no work or thought or knowledge or wisdom in Sheol, to which you are going.

11 Again I saw that under the sun the race is not to the swift, nor the battle to the strong, nor bread to the wise, nor riches to the intelligent, nor favor to the skillful; but time and chance happen to them all. [12]For no one can anticipate the time of disaster. Like fish taken in a cruel net, and like birds caught in a snare, so mortals are snared at a time of calamity, when it suddenly falls upon them.

Wisdom Superior to Folly

13 I have also seen this example of wisdom under the sun, and it seemed great to me. [14]There was a little city with few people in it.

[a] Syr Compare Gk: Heb *Everything that confronts them* [2]*is everything* [b] Gk Syr Vg: Heb lacks *and the evil*

8:16-17 When I applied my mind . . . I saw all the work of God: These verses clearly state the human frustration of not being able to know what God is up to and what the future will be.

What about trying to seek God? We have a hard time accepting our human limitations. We would like to be like God, knowing good and evil. See the temptation of the serpent in Genesis 3:4. Luther was against the notion that we could work our way back into relationship with God: nothing we can do can rectify that relationship or mend that break. This drives the Christian to despair, as it did Luther. His entire theology was a search for an answer to the question: How can I find a gracious God? The answer is not a doctrine, a spiritual practice, or a self-help book. The answer is a *person*: Christ, the righteousness of God. Luther discovered that the gracious God had already found him. There was nothing left to do but say "Yes!" *Ecclesiastes 8:16-17*

9:1-12 their deeds are in the hand of God: All people experience the same fate (death) in the end, righteous and wicked alike. So enjoy life, because when life ends, these things cannot be enjoyed in Sheol (9:10), the dark place of the dead.

9:2 clean and the unclean, to those who sacrifice: The "clean" refers to those who are ritually clean according to laws of Israel (see Lev 11–16). Offering proper sacrifices was considered a religious obligation. The teacher is not saying that being ritually clean or making proper sacrifices is worthless and should not be done, but rather that in the end even those who have been religious will die.

What do you think the teacher means by saying that "the race is not to the swift, nor the battle to the strong," in 9:11?

9:13-18 this example of wisdom: See also 4:13-16. The teacher uses stories (which might be called parables) and proverbs to illustrate his points. He observes well and invites the reader into his observations. Often he commends certain behaviors based on these observations or simply draws a conclusion. Many centuries later, Jesus will use parables and proverbs in a similar fashion to teach his followers.

A great king came against it and besieged it, building great siegeworks
against it. [15]Now there was found in it a poor wise man, and he by his
wisdom delivered the city. Yet no one remembered that poor man.
[16]So I said, "Wisdom is better than might; yet the poor man's wisdom
is despised, and his words are not heeded."

17 The quiet words of the wise are more to be heeded
than the shouting of a ruler among fools.
18 Wisdom is better than weapons of war,
but one bungler destroys much good.

Miscellaneous Observations

10:1—11:6 so a little folly outweighs wisdom: This is a series of proverbs like those found in the book of Proverbs (see chart Types of Proverbs, p. 1018).

10:2 heart of the wise inclines to the right: The heart was considered the place where a person's will and intentions came from. The "right" hand symbolizes the place of strength and wisdom.

10:6-7 folly is set in many high places…princes walking on foot: Sometimes the expected social order is mixed up (also 10:16-17). This theme is taken up in other places (see Prov 26:1), sometimes as a consequence of God's judgment (Isa 3:4-5).

10 Dead flies make the perfumer's ointment give off a foul odor;
so a little folly outweighs wisdom and honor.
2 The heart of the wise inclines to the right,
but the heart of a fool to the left.
3 Even when fools walk on the road, they lack sense,
and show to everyone that they are fools.
4 If the anger of the ruler rises against you, do not leave your post,
for calmness will undo great offenses.

5 There is an evil that I have seen under the sun, as great an error
as if it proceeded from the ruler: [6]folly is set in many high places, and
the rich sit in a low place. [7]I have seen slaves on horseback, and princes
walking on foot like slaves.

8 Whoever digs a pit will fall into it;
and whoever breaks through a wall will be bitten by a snake.
9 Whoever quarries stones will be hurt by them;
and whoever splits logs will be endangered by them.
10 If the iron is blunt, and one does not whet the edge,
then more strength must be exerted;
but wisdom helps one to succeed.
11 If the snake bites before it is charmed,
there is no advantage in a charmer.

12 Words spoken by the wise bring them favor,
but the lips of fools consume them.
13 The words of their mouths begin in foolishness,
and their talk ends in wicked madness;
14 yet fools talk on and on.
No one knows what is to happen,
and who can tell anyone what the future holds?
15 The toil of fools wears them out,
for they do not even know the way to town.

16 Alas for you, O land, when your king is a servant,[a]
and your princes feast in the morning!
17 Happy are you, O land, when your king is a nobleman,
and your princes feast at the proper time—
for strength, and not for drunkenness!
18 Through sloth the roof sinks in,
and through indolence the house leaks.
19 Feasts are made for laughter;
wine gladdens life,
and money meets every need.
20 Do not curse the king, even in your thoughts,
or curse the rich, even in your bedroom;
for a bird of the air may carry your voice,
or some winged creature tell the matter.

The Value of Diligence

11 Send out your bread upon the waters,
for after many days you will get it back.
2 Divide your means seven ways, or even eight,
for you do not know what disaster may happen on earth.
3 When clouds are full,
they empty rain on the earth;
whether a tree falls to the south or to the north,
in the place where the tree falls, there it will lie.
4 Whoever observes the wind will not sow;
and whoever regards the clouds will not reap.

5 Just as you do not know how the breath comes to the bones in
the mother's womb, so you do not know the work of God, who makes
everything.

6 In the morning sow your seed, and at evening do not let your
hands be idle; for you do not know which will prosper, this or that, or
whether both alike will be good.

11:1 Send out your bread upon the waters: Even though this verse is often quoted, its meaning is obscure. Perhaps it means that if we are generous, we will ultimately get back what we give.

Youth and Old Age

7 Light is sweet, and it is pleasant for the eyes to see the sun.

8 Even those who live many years should rejoice in them all; yet
let them remember that the days of darkness will be many. All that
comes is vanity.

9 Rejoice, young man, while you are young, and let your heart
cheer you in the days of your youth. Follow the inclination of your
heart and the desire of your eyes, but know that for all these things
God will bring you into judgment.

11:9 God will bring you into judgment: See note on 3:16-22.

---

[a] Or *a child*

10 Banish anxiety from your mind, and put away pain from your
body; for youth and the dawn of life are vanity.

12 Remember your creator in the days of your youth, before the
days of trouble come, and the years draw near when you will
say, "I have no pleasure in them"; 2before the sun and the light and
the moon and the stars are darkened and the clouds return with[a] the
rain; 3in the day when the guards of the house tremble, and the strong
men are bent, and the women who grind cease working because they
are few, and those who look through the windows see dimly; 4when
the doors on the street are shut, and the sound of the grinding is low,
and one rises up at the sound of a bird, and all the daughters of song
are brought low; 5when one is afraid of heights, and terrors are in the
road; the almond tree blossoms, the grasshopper drags itself along[b]
and desire fails; because all must go to their eternal home, and the
mourners will go about the streets; 6before the silver cord is snapped,[c]
and the golden bowl is broken, and the pitcher is broken at the fountain, and the wheel broken at the cistern, 7and the dust returns to the
earth as it was, and the breath[d] returns to God who gave it. 8Vanity of
vanities, says the Teacher;[e] all is vanity.

Epilogue

9 Besides being wise, the Teacher[e] also taught the people knowledge, weighing and studying and arranging many proverbs. 10The
Teacher[e] sought to find pleasing words, and he wrote words of truth
plainly.

11 The sayings of the wise are like goads, and like nails firmly
fixed are the collected sayings that are given by one shepherd.[f] 12Of
anything beyond these, my child, beware. Of making many books
there is no end, and much study is a weariness of the flesh.

13 The end of the matter; all has been heard. Fear God, and keep
his commandments; for that is the whole duty of everyone. 14For God
will bring every deed into judgment, including[g] every secret thing,
whether good or evil.

---

[a] Or *after*; Heb *'ahar* [b] Or *is a burden* [c] Syr Vg Compare Gk: Heb *is removed* [d] Or *the spirit*
[e] *Qoheleth*, traditionally rendered *Preacher* [f] Meaning of Heb uncertain [g] Or *into the judgment on*

12:1-8 Remember…the days of your youth: In this poem about growing old, each image may represent a different part of the body, such as "strong men" being one's back, and the "women who grind" being teeth.

What do the images in the poem (12:1-8) bring to your mind or imagination?

12:9-14 the Teacher also taught: The final verses look back, approve, and summarize the words of the teacher.

12:13 Fear God, and keep his commandments: "Fear" means to respect and honor God. Proper faith and right living for the people of Israel flowed from this understanding. Wisdom enhances and develops the promises of religion, and it begins with a proper regard for the ways and requirements of the LORD (see also Prov 1:7; 3:7; 19:23).

In your experience, what aspect of what the teacher says in Ecclesiastes seems most "true" to you? Why? How do these "true things" intersect with faith, especially Christian faith?

Song of Solomon 8:6

SONG OF SOLOMON

Background File

The author of this book is unknown. The language indicates that it was written in the fourth or third century B.C.E., some six hundred years after King Solomon. The book's strong female character and voice suggest that the author may have been a woman. Mothers are mentioned rather than fathers (3:4), and the woman speaks more than the man.

What's the Story?

Song of Solomon consists of a series of love poems between two lovers. The poems don't tell a story that has an ending, but move back and forth in a celebration of physical love and desire. The lovers express delight in each other's body when they are together. They long for each other when they are apart. They tease and admire each other and boast to others of their lover's charms. Each lover uses sensuous images from nature and the human world to describe the other's body. The book concludes with claims about the power and value of love.

The book can be outlined as follows:

Title (1:1)
Introduction to the female lover (1:2-6)
Mutual longing (1:7–2:7)
Springtime of love (2:8-17)
Nighttime search for the beloved (3:1-5)
Solomon's wedding party (3:6-11)
The woman's beauty described and praised (4:1–5:1)
Dialogue between the woman and her friends, the daughters of Jerusalem (5:2–6:3)
Mutual praise of the beauty of the lovers (6:4-12)
Dialogues between the two lovers (6:13–8:4)
Love's power affirmed (8:5-14)

What's the Message?

Like Esther, Song of Solomon is unusual in the Old Testament in that it never mentions God or religious practices. It also gives us glimpses into the feelings and everyday lives of ordinary people, and it may be in the Bible for that reason.

Song of Solomon is about the beauty and power of human physical love. It affirms the goodness of creation, human bodies, and sexuality. Song of Solomon also acknowledges that relationships are a struggle and hard work. They cannot be built only on mutual attraction but must include conversation, commitment, faithfulness, and respect. The book claims that love is as strong as death (8:6) and precious beyond all wealth.

Later interpreters of this book saw these love poems as symbolic of the love between God and God's people. The claims about human love take on deeper, fuller meanings when applied to God's love for us. Song of Solomon is best read at two levels, celebrating both human and divine love.

What is meant by reading the Bible for its plain meaning, and why is that important? During Martin Luther's time, people sometimes used allegorical or spiritual interpretations to find hidden meanings in Scripture. These allegories were used to give the story symbolic rather than literal (factual) meaning. This meant that people often interpreted the Bible to mean what they wanted it to mean. Martin Luther argued that the Bible both accuses us of our sin and teaches us of God's love. The Bible is to be interpreted according to its plain, literal meaning unless it is clear that figurative (symbolic) language is being used. Luther said that Song of Solomon used figurative language to thank God for Solomon's rule over Israel, which brought peace and happiness. Although the words are about human love, they can also be interpreted to be about God's love for God's people. Since Luther, many Lutherans have balanced literal and symbolic readings of this book, seeing in human love hints of the fullness and perfection of God's love. *Song of Solomon 1*

1:1 The Song of Songs, which is Solomon's: This title is to be understood as "the best song." While Solomon is mentioned in the book (1:5, 3:7, 9, 11), it comes from a much later time. The book was probably named after Solomon because he had so many wives (1 Kgs 11:3) and composed songs (1 Kgs 4:32). Solomon followed David as king of Israel. He was responsible for building the first

1 The Song of Songs, which is Solomon's.

Colloquy of Bride and Friends

2 Let him kiss me with the kisses of his mouth!
For your love is better than wine,
3 your anointing oils are fragrant,
your name is perfume poured out;
therefore the maidens love you.
4 Draw me after you, let us make haste.
The king has brought me into his chambers.
We will exult and rejoice in you;
we will extol your love more than wine;
rightly do they love you.

5 I am black and beautiful,
O daughters of Jerusalem,
like the tents of Kedar,
like the curtains of Solomon.
6 Do not gaze at me because I am dark,
because the sun has gazed on me.
My mother's sons were angry with me;
they made me keeper of the vineyards,
but my own vineyard I have not kept!
7 Tell me, you whom my soul loves,
where you pasture your flock,
where you make it lie down at noon;

for why should I be like one who is veiled
beside the flocks of your companions?

8 If you do not know,
O fairest among women,
follow the tracks of the flock,
and pasture your kids
beside the shepherds' tents.

Colloquy of Bridegroom, Friends, and Bride

9 I compare you, my love,
to a mare among Pharaoh's chariots.
10 Your cheeks are comely with ornaments,
your neck with strings of jewels.
11 We will make you ornaments of gold,
studded with silver.

12 While the king was on his couch,
my nard gave forth its fragrance.
13 My beloved is to me a bag of myrrh
that lies between my breasts.
14 My beloved is to me a cluster of henna blossoms
in the vineyards of En-gedi.

15 Ah, you are beautiful, my love;
ah, you are beautiful;
your eyes are doves.
16 Ah, you are beautiful, my beloved,
truly lovely.
Our couch is green;
17 the beams of our house are cedar,
our rafters[a] are pine.

2 I am a rose[b] of Sharon,
a lily of the valleys.

2 As a lily among brambles,
so is my love among maidens.

3 As an apple tree among the trees of the wood,
so is my beloved among young men.
With great delight I sat in his shadow,
and his fruit was sweet to my taste.

[a] Meaning of Heb uncertain [b] Heb *crocus*

temple in Jerusalem (1 Kgs 5–8), and he was known for being very wise (see also 1 Kgs 3:5-28; Prov 1:1; Eccl 1:1).

1:5 black and beautiful: The woman's skin is dark from being exposed to the sun, not because of her ethnic background. The woman claims her own sense of beauty, because fair skin was valued. *Kedar* is the name of a Bedouin tribe known for its wealth and means "dark."

1:6 vineyards . . . I have not kept: Vineyards are symbols both of Israel (Isa 5:1-7) and female sexuality. The woman's reference to not keeping her own vineyard may refer to her virginity, or it may be tied to her reference to her skin. Perhaps working out in the vineyards has left her skin not only darker but dried out and rough, not her normal soft skin and fair complexion.

1:7 pasture your flock: The male lover is described as a shepherd, an image also used to describe God (Ps 23).

1:6-7 vineyards . . . pasture your flock: These images were common in ancient love poetry and may be symbolic. Their use here allows scholars to see this song as a love song between God and God's people. God is sometimes described as the nation of Israel's husband (Isa 62:4-5; Hos 1–2).

How does it feel to think about your relationship with God in terms of lover and beloved?

1:12-14 nard . . . myrrh . . . henna: Nard is a sweet-smelling ointment made from the spikenard plant. Myrrh was fragrant gum or resin from several shrubs used in making perfume. Henna flowers are strongly scented.

1:14 En-gedi: An oasis on the western shore of the Dead Sea. See Map 3, pp. 2100-2101. Its running water and green plants stood out from the surrounding desert.

2:1-17 I am a rose . . . my beloved is mine and I am his: The mutual signs of desire, love, and worth reflect part of God's plan for creation. The physical body and its sexuality were declared good (Gen 1:27, 31). Men and women are created for mutual relationships, not control by one over the other. Such control reflects the way sin ruined God's creation (Gen 3:16).

What qualities do you feel are most important in a loving relationship? Do the same qualities apply to your loving relationships with different people? What about your relationship with God?

2:7 do not stir up or awaken love until it is ready!: This verse (repeated in 3:5 and 8:4) suggests that mutual love is a strong power and more than physical desire or short-term feelings. When love is ready, then it can be enjoyed.

2:11 winter is past…rain is over: Winter is the rainy season in this region of the world.

4 He brought me to the banqueting house,
and his intention toward me was love.
5 Sustain me with raisins,
refresh me with apples;
for I am faint with love.
6 O that his left hand were under my head,
and that his right hand embraced me!
7 I adjure you, O daughters of Jerusalem,
by the gazelles or the wild does:
do not stir up or awaken love
until it is ready!

Springtime Rhapsody

8 The voice of my beloved!
Look, he comes,
leaping upon the mountains,
bounding over the hills.
9 My beloved is like a gazelle
or a young stag.
Look, there he stands
behind our wall,
gazing in at the windows,
looking through the lattice.
10 My beloved speaks and says to me:
"Arise, my love, my fair one,
and come away;
11 for now the winter is past,
the rain is over and gone.
12 The flowers appear on the earth;
the time of singing has come,
and the voice of the turtledove
is heard in our land.
13 The fig tree puts forth its figs,
and the vines are in blossom;
they give forth fragrance.
Arise, my love, my fair one,
and come away.
14 O my dove, in the clefts of the rock,
in the covert of the cliff,
let me see your face,
let me hear your voice;
for your voice is sweet,
and your face is lovely.
15 Catch us the foxes,
the little foxes,

that ruin the vineyards--
for our vineyards are in blossom."

16 My beloved is mine and I am his;
he pastures his flock among the lilies.
17 Until the day breathes
and the shadows flee,
turn, my beloved, be like a gazelle
or a young stag on the cleft mountains.[a]

Love's Dream

3 Upon my bed at night
I sought him whom my soul loves;
I sought him, but found him not;
I called him, but he gave no answer.[b]
2 "I will rise now and go about the city,
in the streets and in the squares;
I will seek him whom my soul loves."
I sought him, but found him not.
3 The sentinels found me,
as they went about in the city.
"Have you seen him whom my soul loves?"
4 Scarcely had I passed them,
when I found him whom my soul loves.
I held him, and would not let him go
until I brought him into my mother's house,
and into the chamber of her that conceived me.
5 I adjure you, O daughters of Jerusalem,
by the gazelles or the wild does:
do not stir up or awaken love
until it is ready!

The Groom and His Party Approach

6 What is that coming up from the wilderness,
like a column of smoke,
perfumed with myrrh and frankincense,
with all the fragrant powders of the merchant?
7 Look, it is the litter of Solomon!
Around it are sixty mighty men
of the mighty men of Israel,
8 all equipped with swords
and expert in war,
each with his sword at his thigh
because of alarms by night.

3:1, 2, 3, 4 whom my soul loves: The repeated refrain shows the powerful life-giving force of love.

3:4 mother's house: In ancient Israel the normal term would be father's house. This term is found only in Song of Solomon and the book of Ruth, two books that are primarily about women.

3:6-11 What is that coming up from the wilderness…litter: Refers to the strange procession of King Solomon. It contains the only reference to weddings or marriage in the entire book. The "litter" is a hand-held carriage (palanquin) where a king sat. A group of carriers using poles attached to the sides hoisted and moved the carriage. The man and woman do not live together, must search for each other even at night, and go to the woman's mother's house, rather than the man's or their own house. The woman is also despised for her relationship to the man (8:1). These images and the lack of marital imagery have led many scholars to believe the lovers in the book are unmarried.

[a] Or *on the mountains of Bether;* meaning of Heb uncertain [b] Gk: Heb lacks this line

9 King Solomon made himself a palanquin
from the wood of Lebanon.
10 He made its posts of silver,
its back of gold, its seat of purple;
its interior was inlaid with love.[a]
Daughters of Jerusalem,
11 come out.
Look, O daughters of Zion,
at King Solomon,
at the crown with which his mother crowned him
on the day of his wedding,
on the day of the gladness of his heart.

The Bride's Beauty Extolled

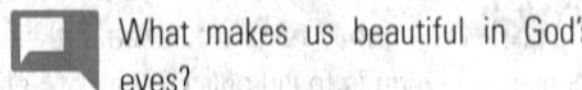

4:1-15 how beautiful you are: Ancient love poetry often has a description of the lover's beauty. Some of these images, such as "Your neck is like the tower of David" (4:4), sound strange or unfamiliar today, but they are meant to present a picture of beauty. Such comparisons are typical of this type of love song and are always complimentary. Most of these images involve different senses and have sexual overtones.

What makes us beautiful in God's eyes?

4 How beautiful you are, my love,
how very beautiful!
Your eyes are doves
behind your veil.
Your hair is like a flock of goats,
moving down the slopes of Gilead.
2 Your teeth are like a flock of shorn ewes
that have come up from the washing,
all of which bear twins,
and not one among them is bereaved.
3 Your lips are like a crimson thread,
and your mouth is lovely.
Your cheeks are like halves of a pomegranate
behind your veil.
4 Your neck is like the tower of David,
built in courses;
on it hang a thousand bucklers,
all of them shields of warriors.
5 Your two breasts are like two fawns,
twins of a gazelle,
that feed among the lilies.
6 Until the day breathes
and the shadows flee,
I will hasten to the mountain of myrrh
and the hill of frankincense.
7 You are altogether beautiful, my love;
there is no flaw in you.
8 Come with me from Lebanon, my bride;
come with me from Lebanon.

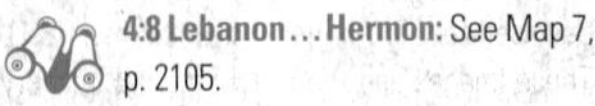

4:8 Lebanon . . . Hermon: See Map 7, p. 2105.

[a] Meaning of Heb uncertain

Depart[a] from the peak of Amana,
from the peak of Senir and Hermon,
from the dens of lions,
from the mountains of leopards.

9 You have ravished my heart, my sister, my bride,
you have ravished my heart with a glance of your eyes,
with one jewel of your necklace.
10 How sweet is your love, my sister, my bride!
how much better is your love than wine,
and the fragrance of your oils than any spice!
11 Your lips distill nectar, my bride;
honey and milk are under your tongue;
the scent of your garments is like the scent of Lebanon.
12 A garden locked is my sister, my bride,
a garden locked, a fountain sealed.
13 Your channel[b] is an orchard of pomegranates
with all choicest fruits,
henna with nard,
14 nard and saffron, calamus and cinnamon,
with all trees of frankincense,
myrrh and aloes,
with all chief spices--
15 a garden fountain, a well of living water,
and flowing streams from Lebanon.

16 Awake, O north wind,
and come, O south wind!
Blow upon my garden
that its fragrance may be wafted abroad.
Let my beloved come to his garden,
and eat its choicest fruits.

5 I come to my garden, my sister, my bride;
I gather my myrrh with my spice,
I eat my honeycomb with my honey,
I drink my wine with my milk.

Eat, friends, drink,
and be drunk with love.

Another Dream

2 I slept, but my heart was awake.
Listen! my beloved is knocking.

[a] Or *Look* [b] Meaning of Heb uncertain

4:9 my heart, my sister, my bride: These are terms of endearment and not to be taken literally.

4:11 scent of Lebanon: Probably referring to the fragrant cedar trees that grew there.

4:14 saffron, calamus...frankincense: Saffron probably refers to the blue-flowered saffron crocus. Part of the flower is used to make yellow dye that is used in cooking and perfume. Calamus refers to a long-stemmed reed or cane used to make sweet-smelling oil. Frankincense was made by crushing a certain gummy resin into powder. It was used in various oils and burned to give off fragrant smoke.

5:2-8 I slept, but my heart was awake...I sought him, but did not find him: The woman describes how she delayed opening the door for her lover because it was too much trouble. She then rushes through Jerusalem searching for her lover. She is breaking several social conventions. Women were not to be out at night alone or to talk to strange men. The guards beat her for defying social custom.

What is it like to search for God's presence and not find it? Have you ever ignored your relationship with God because it was too much trouble?

"Open to me, my sister, my love,
my dove, my perfect one;
for my head is wet with dew,
my locks with the drops of the night."
3 I had put off my garment;
how could I put it on again?
I had bathed my feet;
how could I soil them?
4 My beloved thrust his hand into the opening,
and my inmost being yearned for him.
5 I arose to open to my beloved,
and my hands dripped with myrrh,
my fingers with liquid myrrh,
upon the handles of the bolt.
6 I opened to my beloved,
but my beloved had turned and was gone.
My soul failed me when he spoke.
I sought him, but did not find him;
I called him, but he gave no answer.
7 Making their rounds in the city
the sentinels found me;
they beat me, they wounded me,
they took away my mantle,
those sentinels of the walls.
8 I adjure you, O daughters of Jerusalem,
if you find my beloved,
tell him this:
I am faint with love.

Colloquy of Friends and Bride

9 What is your beloved more than another beloved,
O fairest among women?
What is your beloved more than another beloved,
that you thus adjure us?

5:10-16 gold…sapphires: The use of precious metals to describe the man suggests wealth and dignity.

10 My beloved is all radiant and ruddy,
distinguished among ten thousand.
11 His head is the finest gold;
his locks are wavy,
black as a raven.
12 His eyes are like doves
beside springs of water,
bathed in milk,
fitly set.[a]

[a] Meaning of Heb uncertain

13 His cheeks are like beds of spices,
yielding fragrance.
His lips are lilies,
distilling liquid myrrh.
14 His arms are rounded gold,
set with jewels.
His body is ivory work,[a]
encrusted with sapphires.[b]
15 His legs are alabaster columns,
set upon bases of gold.
His appearance is like Lebanon,
choice as the cedars.
16 His speech is most sweet,
and he is altogether desirable.
This is my beloved and this is my friend,
O daughters of Jerusalem.

6 Where has your beloved gone,
O fairest among women?
Which way has your beloved turned,
that we may seek him with you?

2 My beloved has gone down to his garden,
to the beds of spices,
to pasture his flock in the gardens,
and to gather lilies.
3 I am my beloved's and my beloved is mine;
he pastures his flock among the lilies.

The Bride's Matchless Beauty

4 You are beautiful as Tirzah, my love,
comely as Jerusalem,
terrible as an army with banners.
5 Turn away your eyes from me,
for they overwhelm me!
Your hair is like a flock of goats,
moving down the slopes of Gilead.
6 Your teeth are like a flock of ewes,
that have come up from the washing;
all of them bear twins,
and not one among them is bereaved.
7 Your cheeks are like halves of a pomegranate
behind your veil.

6:4 Jerusalem . . . Tirzah: Jerusalem was Israel's capital city and the location of the temple. King Jeroboam lived in Tirzah, in the northern kingdom, after the united kingdom split into two (1 Kgs 14:17; 16:23-24).

[a] Meaning of Heb uncertain [b] Heb *lapis lazuli*

8 There are sixty queens and eighty concubines,
and maidens without number.
9 My dove, my perfect one, is the only one,
the darling of her mother,
flawless to her that bore her.
The maidens saw her and called her happy;
the queens and concubines also, and they praised her.
10 "Who is this that looks forth like the dawn,
fair as the moon, bright as the sun,
terrible as an army with banners?"

11 I went down to the nut orchard,
to look at the blossoms of the valley,
to see whether the vines had budded,
whether the pomegranates were in bloom.
12 Before I was aware, my fancy set me
in a chariot beside my prince.[a]

6:13 look upon the Shulammite, as upon a dance before two armies: A confusing phrase. The idea is that the woman will turn around so that others may look at her. *Shulammite* may be a feminine form of the name *Solomon.* It is unclear what the dance of the two camps refers to. The phrase may mean that the woman refuses to put on a show for others.

13[b] Return, return, O Shulammite!
Return, return, that we may look upon you.

Why should you look upon the Shulammite,
as upon a dance before two armies?[c]

Expressions of Praise

7 How graceful are your feet in sandals,
O queenly maiden!
Your rounded thighs are like jewels,
the work of a master hand.
2 Your navel is a rounded bowl
that never lacks mixed wine.
Your belly is a heap of wheat,
encircled with lilies.
3 Your two breasts are like two fawns,
twins of a gazelle.
4 Your neck is like an ivory tower.
Your eyes are pools in Heshbon,
by the gate of Bath-rabbim.
Your nose is like a tower of Lebanon,
overlooking Damascus.
5 Your head crowns you like Carmel,

7:4-5 Heshbon . . . Bath-rabbim . . . Lebanon . . . Damascus . . . Carmel: These place names draw images of royalty, majesty, and fertility.

[a] Cn: Meaning of Heb uncertain [b] Ch 7.1 in Heb [c] Or *dance of Mahanaim*

and your flowing locks are like purple;
a king is held captive in the tresses.[a]

6 How fair and pleasant you are,
O loved one, delectable maiden![b]
7 You are stately[c] as a palm tree,
and your breasts are like its clusters.
8 I say I will climb the palm tree
and lay hold of its branches.
O may your breasts be like clusters of the vine,
and the scent of your breath like apples,
9 and your kisses[d] like the best wine
that goes down[e] smoothly,
gliding over lips and teeth.[f]

10 I am my beloved's,
and his desire is for me.
11 Come, my beloved,
let us go forth into the fields,
and lodge in the villages;
12 let us go out early to the vineyards,
and see whether the vines have budded,
whether the grape blossoms have opened
and the pomegranates are in bloom.
There I will give you my love.
13 The mandrakes give forth fragrance,
and over our doors are all choice fruits,
new as well as old,
which I have laid up for you, O my beloved.
8 O that you were like a brother to me,
who nursed at my mother's breast!
If I met you outside, I would kiss you,
and no one would despise me.
2 I would lead you and bring you
into the house of my mother,
and into the chamber of the one who bore me.[g]
I would give you spiced wine to drink,
the juice of my pomegranates.
3 O that his left hand were under my head,
and that his right hand embraced me!
4 I adjure you, O daughters of Jerusalem,

7:13 mandrakes: The flowers, fruit, and root of this plant were used in medicines. They were also thought to increase sexual powers (see Gen 30:14-16).

---

[a] Meaning of Heb uncertain [b] Syr: Heb *in delights* [c] Heb *This your stature is* [d] Heb *palate* [e] Heb *down for my lover* [f] Gk Syr Vg: Heb *lips of sleepers* [g] Gk Syr: Heb *my mother; she (or you) will teach me*

do not stir up or awaken love
until it is ready!

Homecoming

5 Who is that coming up from the wilderness,
leaning upon her beloved?

Under the apple tree I awakened you.
There your mother was in labor with you;
there she who bore you was in labor.

8:6 Set me as a seal upon your heart: A seal was an inscribed ring or piece of jewelry used to leave a stamp to show ownership or authority. A seal shows public recognition of the relationship. To be sealed upon the heart shows the closeness of the couple.

8:6 love is strong as death, passion fierce as the grave: The high point of the book. Love is a power as undeniable and relentless as death.

8:6-7 love…passion: Ancient Israelites understood that there were several different types of love. There is passionate love, physical love, deep love between friends (1 Sam 18:3), and God's love for God's people (1 Kgs 10:9).

The prophet Isaiah describes God as a bridegroom rejoicing over the bride, meaning the people of Israel (Isa 62:5). Christians sometimes describe the church as the bride of Jesus. Why are such images used to describe God's relationship with the people of God? In what way do you find such descriptions helpful, or not?

6 Set me as a seal upon your heart,
as a seal upon your arm;
for love is strong as death,
passion fierce as the grave.
Its flashes are flashes of fire,
a raging flame.
7 Many waters cannot quench love,
neither can floods drown it.
If one offered for love
all the wealth of one's house,
it would be utterly scorned.

8 We have a little sister,
and she has no breasts.
What shall we do for our sister,
on the day when she is spoken for?
9 If she is a wall,
we will build upon her a battlement of silver;
but if she is a door,
we will enclose her with boards of cedar.
10 I was a wall,
and my breasts were like towers;
then I was in his eyes
as one who brings[a] peace.
11 Solomon had a vineyard at Baal-hamon;
he entrusted the vineyard to keepers;
each one was to bring for its fruit a thousand pieces of silver.
12 My vineyard, my very own, is for myself;
you, O Solomon, may have the thousand,
and the keepers of the fruit two hundred!

---

[a] Or *finds*

13 O you who dwell in the gardens,
my companions are listening for your voice;
let me hear it.

14 Make haste, my beloved,
and be like a gazelle
or a young stag
upon the mountains of spices!

PROPHETS

Isaiah to Malachi

In most English translations of the Bible, about one-third of the pages are books associated with named prophets. The amount of space dedicated to preserving the words of ancient prophets—not to mention the stories about prophets found in the Historical Books—testifies to the important role prophets played in the life of ancient Israel.

In the Bible, prophets and prophecy appear with the rise of Israel's kings. Early on, prophets anointed kings by pouring oil on their heads. This action had the effect of giving their reigns authority and a sense of being legal (see 1 Sam 9:16; 16:12). More important, the prophets spoke the word of the LORD to the king. The prophetic word provided the LORD's check on the king's otherwise absolute power. The stories of Nathan, Elijah, Elisha, Micaiah, and other prophets in the Historical Books testify to the several ways prophets interacted with kings, either as personal advisers or as opponents.

Beginning in the eighth century B.C.E., the prophets began to address the Israelite people at large. The words of prophets, together with stories from their lives and historical narratives, were assembled and preserved. It is this collection plus a few other books that make up the part of the Old Testament that Christians call the Prophetic Books.

The order of the Prophetic Books in the Bible is not chronological. The longer books come first (Isaiah, Jeremiah, and Ezekiel). These are followed by the twelve Minor Prophets, also known as the Book of the Twelve. In the Christian Bible, two other books have been included with the prophets. The book of Lamentations appears after Jeremiah, because Jeremiah was at one time mistakenly thought to be its author. Daniel is also erroneously counted as one of the Prophetic Books. Daniel was actually written later in the second century B.C.E. and belongs among the type of literature known as apocalyptic. Neither Daniel nor Lamentations is found among the Prophets in the Hebrew Bible, these books are instead included among the Writings.

The prophets and history

The collection of Prophetic Books represents the words of many prophets ranging from the eighth down to the fifth centuries B.C.E. Some of the historical developments during this period included the fall of Israel, the destruction of Jerusalem, the exile, and the return from the exile. The prophets were given a timely word from God about these events. It is important to understand the historical circumstances behind these events in order to better understand the messages of the prophets. The introductions to each prophetic book in this study Bible will help the reader in this regard (see also the charts of prophets and kings, pp. 1089 and 545).

While biblical scholars are generally agreed on the dates and events of the prophets' activities, there are some controversies about individual passages. Unlike the Historical Books, the prophetic speeches (oracles) are not arranged in chronological order. Also, except for Ezekiel, the prophets' sayings are not dated. That means it can be challenging to figure out which specific event the prophet may be describing. The difficulties are increased by the fact that, as the prophetic works were passed down, they were added to by later prophets and faithful disciples. A clear example of how prophetic books were edited occurs in the book of Isaiah. Chapters 1–39 are mostly from the eighth-century B.C.E. prophet Isaiah, while chapters 40–66 originated in the last decades of the sixth century. In those latter chapters, a prophet offered comfort to a people who had experienced the destruction of Jerusalem (586 B.C.E.) many decades earlier.

The message of the prophets

Although the prophets addressed varied situations, it is useful to make a few general observations about their messages. First, the prophets called their listeners to return to a faithful relationship with God, especially as that was defined by the covenant (laws) of Moses. Often, the prophetic message included a specific call for rulers to repent from unjust social practices that allowed for the oppression and economic exploitation of the poor. The prophets had an ability to imagine the world not as it was

Prophets

Major Prophets		Minor Prophets	
1st Isaiah	740 B.C.E.	Amos	775 B.C.E.
Jeremiah	620 B.C.E.	Hosea	770 B.C.E.
Ezekiel	590 B.C.E.	Micah	738 B.C.E.
2nd Isaiah (chapters 40-55)	550 B.C.E.	Zephaniah	640 B.C.E.
3rd Isaiah (chapters 56-66)	490 B.C.E.	Nahum	636 B.C.E.
Daniel	Prior to 164 B.C.E.	Habakkuk	630 B.C.E.
		Jonah	After 612 B.C.E.
		Haggai	520 B.C.E.
		1st Zechariah (chapters 1-8)	520 B.C.E.
		Obadiah	440 B.C.E.
		Joel	430 B.C.E.
		Malachi	425 B.C.E.
		2nd Zechariah (chapters 9-14)	350 B.C.E. ?

but as God would have it be. They called their listeners to share that vision. The prophets also warned that ignoring God's will and vision for the world would lead to divine anger, judgment, and punishment. Finally, when God's judgment came, the prophets held forth the promise that angry judgment was not God's final word. God would bring about a new beginning for God's people.

The prophets were not fortune tellers or predictors of future events. Rather, they addressed circumstances of their own day, not events centuries or millennia in the future. When the prophets did speak about future events, they described their hearers' own near future. The prophetic books are relevant not because they "predicted" things that would take place in the New Testament or in our own day. Instead, as the word of God, the prophetic books address each generation of believers anew. Prophecies are fulfilled—that is, "filled full" of new meaning—as the Holy Spirit guides believers to understand what is God's will for individuals and communities of faith today.

ISAIAH

Isaiah 11:1

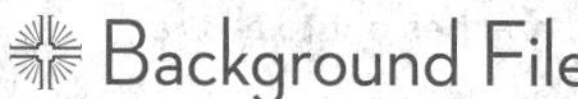

Background File

The book of Isaiah contains some of most well-known passages in the Bible. In its chapters can be found the promise of a coming Prince of Peace (9:6-7) and the description of God's suffering Servant (49:1-6; 50:1-11; 52:13—53:12). But Isaiah is a complex book, written and compiled by several prophets and editors over a long and important period of Israel's history. The story covered in Isaiah stretches from 742 B.C.E. all the way down to the time after 538 B.C.E. when many of God's people returned to Judah after a time of exile in Babylon.

What's the Story?

What makes the book of Isaiah so complex? Here is an overview. Much of the first part of Isaiah (chapters 1–33) is attributed to Isaiah son of Amoz, who preached in Judah from about 742 to 700 B.C.E. He is sometimes called First Isaiah or Isaiah of Jerusalem. Chapters 34–39 probably date to a later time. The second major portion of the book (chapters 40–55) dates from the time when God's people had been taken away from their homeland to live in exile in Babylonia (587 to 538 B.C.E.). The writer of this section is an unnamed prophet sometimes called Second Isaiah or Isaiah of Babylon. Chapters 56–66, dated in the period after many of the people returned from exile after538 B.C.E., are sometimes called Third Isaiah, but these chapters are probably not the work of a single writer. See also the chart Prophets, p. 1089.

The material called First Isaiah takes place amid conflicts among Israel, Judah, Syria, and Assyria, especially the Syro-Ephraimite war. Years earlier, the united kingdom of Israel had split into two kingdoms—Judah in the south and Israel in the north. Even though both kingdoms were made up of Israel's tribes, they were in almost constant conflict over theological and social issues. At the time of First Isaiah Syria and the northern kingdom, Israel (also known as Ephraim), attacked Judah, perhaps in an attempt to remove King Ahaz (735–715 B.C.E.) and force Judah to join a coalition against the expanding kingdom of Assyria. Assyria briefly came to the aid of Judah, conquering Damascus (Syria) in 732 B.C.E. and then attacking Israel. Assyria destroyed Samaria, the capital of Israel, in 722/721 B.C.E., bringing the northern kingdom to an end. Judah, the southern kingdom, remained independent but came under the control of the Assyrian Empire.

Later, King Hezekiah revolted against Sennacherib, the Assyrian king (about 705–701 B.C.E.) and sought an alliance with Egypt (Isa 30:15b, 18; 31:1). Sennacherib was defeated and Jerusalem was spared (Isa 37:36-38).

The second part of Isaiah takes place about one hundred years later. Assyria's power had diminished and; Babylon had become the great power. The Babylonians destroyed Jerusalem and took many of its people captive in 597 and 587 B.C.E. In that situation, a new prophet (Second Isaiah) brought words of comfort, promising that God would free the exiles (chapters 40-55). These promises were realized in 538 B.C.E., when the Persian ruler Cyrus captured Babylon. He allowed exiles to return and rebuild Jerusalem and the temple, and to restart their lives. This new life in Jerusalem forms the background of the final part of the book of Isaiah (chapters 56-66).

In all these events, Israel and Judah were caught between the great powers of the day, Egypt to the south and west, Assyria and Babylon to the north and east. Against that background, the task of the prophetic voices in the book of Isaiah was to announce to people what God was doing with and for them in these events. For the prophets, history is not merely a stage for human actors but is the arena where God guides, warns, challenges, and liberates God's chosen people and reaches out to all the peoples of the world.

Throughout the tumultuous history behind the first part of the book, the two kingdoms of God's people sought political advantage in one way or another. But Isaiah called upon them to recognize that the only real advantage for such politically insignificant states was their reliance on the promises and protection of God. Later, Second Isaiah reminded the people that Babylon's destruction of Jerusalem was the consequence of human sin, but now God was at work in Cyrus the Persian to set the people free. And in the servant of the LORD, God was bringing salvation to the entire world. Finally, in the last part of the book (chapters 56-66), the people of Israel, back in Jerusalem, hear again God's promises of renewal and restoration. They are also reminded of God's demand that they practice justice toward one another. The chapters contain words of judgment against the nations as well as calls to reach out to them with God's offer of salvation.

What's the Message?

Isaiah is the longest and perhaps most important of the prophetic books, offering the full range of God's prophetic message: terrifying words of judgment and comforting words of promise. Isaiah portrays God as the powerful Creator, like no other, and also the gentlest comforter, like an earthly lover or mother. The New Testament quotes Isaiah more than any other prophet, especially its proclamation of hope for a coming messiah (see chapters 2, 9, and 11) and its introduction of the servant of God. This servant's faithfulness will bring suffering, but God will give him as a light to the nations for the salvation of all.

Throughout the various sections of Isaiah one key theme shines through: God has a "plan" or "purpose" (see the notes) that makes history more than a series of random events. The fierce judgment of the first part of the book (especially in chapter 6) is reversed in the second part (chapters 35; 40-55), not because that earlier message is rejected but because the judgment is seen as having done its cleansing work. God can now bring the comfort God desires for the people of Judah (chapter 40). Despite this broad, overall movement from judgment to freedom, elements of warning and promise occur in all three major parts of the book, bringing to each generation and to the present reader the prophetic voice of warning, challenge, and comfort.

1 The vision of Isaiah son of Amoz, which he saw concerning Judah and Jerusalem in the days of Uzziah, Jotham, Ahaz, and Hezekiah, kings of Judah.

The Wickedness of Judah

2 Hear, O heavens, and listen, O earth;
for the LORD has spoken:
I reared children and brought them up,
but they have rebelled against me.
3 The ox knows its owner,
and the donkey its master's crib;
but Israel does not know,
my people do not understand.

4 Ah, sinful nation,
people laden with iniquity,
offspring who do evil,
children who deal corruptly,
who have forsaken the LORD,
who have despised the Holy One of Israel,
who are utterly estranged!

5 Why do you seek further beatings?
Why do you continue to rebel?
The whole head is sick,
and the whole heart faint.
6 From the sole of the foot even to the head,
there is no soundness in it,
but bruises and sores
and bleeding wounds;
they have not been drained, or bound up,
or softened with oil.

7 Your country lies desolate,
your cities are burned with fire;
in your very presence
aliens devour your land;
it is desolate, as overthrown by foreigners.
8 And daughter Zion is left
like a booth in a vineyard,
like a shelter in a cucumber field,
like a besieged city.
9 If the LORD of hosts
had not left us a few survivors,
we would have been like Sodom,
and become like Gomorrah.

1:1 the vision of Isaiah: This brief summary (called a superscription) introduces the first part of the book (chapters 1–33). It contains the preaching of Isaiah of Jerusalem (sometimes called First Isaiah) from perhaps 742 to about 700 B.C.E.

1:2 they have rebelled: The book of Isaiah begins and ends with the same Hebrew phrase: "rebelled against me," see 66:24. The prophet's message is given in order to turn God's children away from their rebellion, so that the terrible consequences of sin will not come into effect (1:27-31).

1:2-20 you come to appear before me . . . I am weary: This "word of the Lord," addressed sarcastically to God's people as the "rulers of Sodom" and "people of Gomorrah" (names used in the Bible to designate wickedness; see Gen 18–19), is a strong word of judgment. Isaiah, like the other eighth-century prophets (Amos, Hosea, Micah), sharply criticized the people of Israel and Judah for hypocritical worship (1:10-15) and their lack of concern for the oppressed, the orphan, and the widow (1:16-17), those easily marginalized and forgotten by an affluent society.

Many interpreters describe this section as reading like a lawsuit in which God calls the heavens and the earth (1:2) as witnesses in a trial. God accuses and judges a people found guilty in a fair and open hearing (compare Mic 6:1-8). But listen also to the tone of the text. God's sadness comes through in phrases that are common in the lament psalms of the Bible. A lament is a prayerful cry to God that comes from personal sadness or pain. Here, God despairs that Israel has "forsaken" the Lord (1:4; see also Ps 22:1). And God repeats the pleading question of "why" Israel continues to rebel (1: 5; also Pss 10:13; 44:24). With God's lament, the book offers, at the outset, a surprising vision of God's tears, through which all of the judgments to come should be read.

1:3 The ox . . . donkey: Unlike Israel, the ox and donkey know their owner and their master's crib or feeding trough. Here in Isaiah and in Christian art, the faithful animals serve as role models for God's people.

1:4 the Holy One of Israel: A favorite title for God in Isaiah, used here twenty-five times (and only six times elsewhere in the Bible) to describe Israel's great and awe-inspiring God. In spite of being the Holy One, God comes to redeem and save the people (43:14) and to love them (43:3-4).

What does Luther say about Isaiah? In his preface to the book of Isaiah, Martin Luther recognizes the importance of knowing the historical background of the book and of recognizing its quite different parts. He observes, however, that readers can best discover for themselves the value of the book through their own reading of it, rather than by hearing him or others talk about the book. "The book is truly full of living, comforting, tender sayings for all poor consciences and miserable, disturbed hearts. There are also plenty of words of threatening and terror in it against the stubborn, proud hardheads—if that may be of any help." (*LW* 35:273-278) *Isaiah 1:1-17*

1:18-20 sins . . . like snow: As part of God's warning against continuing in rebellion, these words are meant conditionally: "if you are willing and obedient," your sins may become "like snow." At this point in the book, the matter is still open and the outcome uncertain. What will the people choose—obedience or destruction?

10 Hear the word of the LORD,
you rulers of Sodom!
Listen to the teaching of our God,
you people of Gomorrah!
11 What to me is the multitude of your sacrifices?
says the LORD;
I have had enough of burnt offerings of rams
and the fat of fed beasts;
I do not delight in the blood of bulls,
or of lambs, or of goats.

12 When you come to appear before me,[a]
who asked this from your hand?
Trample my courts no more;
13 bringing offerings is futile;
incense is an abomination to me.
New moon and sabbath and calling of convocation—
I cannot endure solemn assemblies with iniquity.
14 Your new moons and your appointed festivals
my soul hates;
they have become a burden to me,
I am weary of bearing them.
15 When you stretch out your hands,
I will hide my eyes from you;
even though you make many prayers,
I will not listen;
your hands are full of blood.
16 Wash yourselves; make yourselves clean;
remove the evil of your doings
from before my eyes;
cease to do evil,
17 learn to do good;
seek justice,
rescue the oppressed,
defend the orphan,
plead for the widow.

18 Come now, let us argue it out,
says the LORD:
though your sins are like scarlet,
they shall be like snow;
though they are red like crimson,
they shall become like wool.

[a] Or *see my face*

19 If you are willing and obedient,
you shall eat the good of the land;
20 but if you refuse and rebel,
you shall be devoured by the sword;
for the mouth of the LORD has spoken.

The Degenerate City

21 How the faithful city
has become a whore!
She that was full of justice,
righteousness lodged in her—
but now murderers!
22 Your silver has become dross,
your wine is mixed with water.
23 Your princes are rebels
and companions of thieves.
Everyone loves a bribe
and runs after gifts.
They do not defend the orphan,
and the widow's cause does not come before them.

24 Therefore says the Sovereign, the LORD of hosts, the Mighty One
of Israel:
Ah, I will pour out my wrath on my enemies,
and avenge myself on my foes!
25 I will turn my hand against you;
I will smelt away your dross as with lye
and remove all your alloy.
26 And I will restore your judges as at the first,
and your counselors as at the beginning.
Afterward you shall be called the city of righteousness,
the faithful city.

27 Zion shall be redeemed by justice,
and those in her who repent, by righteousness.
28 But rebels and sinners shall be destroyed together,
and those who forsake the LORD shall be consumed.
29 For you shall be ashamed of the oaks
in which you delighted;
and you shall blush for the gardens
that you have chosen.
30 For you shall be like an oak
whose leaf withers,
and like a garden without water.
31 The strong shall become like tinder,

How can sins be made white? With the prophets, Lutheran theology recognizes the terrible consequences of sin and therefore the need for proclaiming God's warning law. In Christ, the promise of forgiveness becomes certain, however. In his Isaiah lectures, Martin Luther comments on 1:18: "Though your sins are in the highest degree deserving of punishments and death, they will be worthy of righteousness and faith; and though they are worms, they will not bite you" (*LW* 16:20). *Isaiah 1:18*

Consider God's call to return, to be willing and obedient. Do you hear this as threat or promise, as a harsh warning or a new opportunity?

and their work[a] like a spark;
they and their work shall burn together,
with no one to quench them.

The Future House of God

2 The word that Isaiah son of Amoz saw concerning Judah and Jerusalem.

2 In days to come
the mountain of the LORD's house
shall be established as the highest of the mountains,
and shall be raised above the hills;
all the nations shall stream to it.
3 Many peoples shall come and say,
"Come, let us go up to the mountain of the LORD,
to the house of the God of Jacob;
that he may teach us his ways
and that we may walk in his paths."
For out of Zion shall go forth instruction,
and the word of the LORD from Jerusalem.
4 He shall judge between the nations,
and shall arbitrate for many peoples;
they shall beat their swords into plowshares,
and their spears into pruning hooks;
nation shall not lift up sword against nation,
neither shall they learn war any more.

Judgment Pronounced on Arrogance

5 O house of Jacob,
come, let us walk
in the light of the LORD!
6 For you have forsaken the ways of[b] your people,
O house of Jacob.
Indeed they are full of diviners[c] from the east
and of soothsayers like the Philistines,
and they clasp hands with foreigners.
7 Their land is filled with silver and gold,
and there is no end to their treasures;
their land is filled with horses,
and there is no end to their chariots.
8 Their land is filled with idols;
they bow down to the work of their hands,
to what their own fingers have made.

[a] Or *its makers* [b] Heb lacks *the ways of* [c] Cn: Heb lacks *of diviners*

2:1 Judah and Jerusalem: This brief introduction apparently applies to chapters 2–4 or 2–5. These chapters may have once been a separate collection of prophetic speeches (called "oracles") to the people of the southern kingdom of Judah. Before addressing the foreign nations (13:1), the prophet speaks words of hope and warning to God's chosen people.

2:2-4 swords into plowshares: Interspersed throughout the dark words of judgment that characterize the first part of the book are several radiant promises of hope (see 9:2-7; 11:1-9). "In days to come," that is, when God is made fully known, the nations will come to God's mountain to hear God's teaching, and peace will be established at last. The Zion tradition that points to the importance of Mount Zion in Jerusalem as the center for Israel's worship informs this text. God's mountain will in that day become so elevated and so brilliant that it will attract the nations, who will recognize God as Lord and put away their weapons (see Ps 48:1-2; Mic 4:1-3). Jesus builds on this tradition when he calls his followers the "light of the world" and a "city built on a hill" (Matt 5:14; see also Isa 60:1-3).

2:5-6 come, let us walk: Isaiah uses the coming of the nations (2:2-4) as a role model for God's people. Just as the nations will come to walk in God's ways and paths (1:3), Jacob (another name for Israel)—who has forsaken God's ways—is urged to come and "walk in the light of the LORD!" God's mercy extends to all, and God's people are not exempt from the need to repent and return.

2:6-22 the pride of everyone shall be humbled: The Bible speaks frequently of the reversal of all things that occurs when God appears: the high are brought low, the poor are exalted (see 1 Sam 2:7; Luke 1:52-53). Here the emphasis is on the humbling of the proud and arrogant, including both Israel (2:6) and the nations (2:13-16). The pride of idolatry that places things, images, and self above God is condemned here. Such idolatry will be brought to nothing on the day when "the LORD alone will be exalted (2:17).

9 And so people are humbled,
and everyone is brought low—
do not forgive them!
10 Enter into the rock,
and hide in the dust
from the terror of the LORD,
and from the glory of his majesty.
11 The haughty eyes of people shall be brought low,
and the pride of everyone shall be humbled;
and the LORD alone will be exalted on that day.
12 For the LORD of hosts has a day
against all that is proud and lofty,
against all that is lifted up and high;[a]
13 against all the cedars of Lebanon,
lofty and lifted up;
and against all the oaks of Bashan;
14 against all the high mountains,
and against all the lofty hills;
15 against every high tower,
and against every fortified wall;
16 against all the ships of Tarshish,
and against all the beautiful craft.[b]
17 The haughtiness of people shall be humbled,
and the pride of everyone shall be brought low;
and the LORD alone will be exalted on that day.
18 The idols shall utterly pass away.
19 Enter the caves of the rocks
and the holes of the ground,
from the terror of the LORD,
and from the glory of his majesty,
when he rises to terrify the earth.
20 On that day people will throw away
to the moles and to the bats
their idols of silver and their idols of gold,
which they made for themselves to worship,
21 to enter the caverns of the rocks
and the clefts in the crags,
from the terror of the LORD,
and from the glory of his majesty,
when he rises to terrify the earth.
22 Turn away from mortals,
who have only breath in their nostrils,
for of what account are they?

[a] Cn Compare Gk: Heb *low* [b] Compare Gk: Meaning of Heb uncertain

2:12 the LORD of hosts has a day: This refers to a theme, common in the writings of the prophets, called the "day of the LORD." It describes the time when God will come at last to judge the earth and make all things right (for example, see Isa 13:6; Jer 46:10; Ezek 30:3; Joel 2:31; Amos 5:18-20; Obad 15; Zeph 1:14; Mal 4:5).

2:17 pride: The English proverb "Pride goes before a fall" is based on Proverbs 16:18: "Pride goes before destruction, and a haughty spirit before a fall." Throughout the Bible, "pride" is included among the greatest of human faults (Mark 7:22). Not surprisingly, it emerges in early Christian teaching as chief among the "seven deadly sins." In Christian tradition, pride has frequently been seen as the flaw that led to the human fall into sin (Gen 3). This does not refer to appropriate pride in legitimate accomplishments or in faithful others. The Bible praises those examples (4:2; 2 Cor 7:4; Gal 6:4; Heb 3:6). But this text speaks of the pride that puts self before everything and everyone else, even before God. That kind of pride makes impossible the basic human vocation to love God and serve the neighbor. Jesus demonstrates and encourages the opposite of this destructive pride: the childlike humility (Matt 18:4) that gives support to the other (Matt 11:29). In the Bible, destructive pride is humbled (2:17) and true humility exalted (Matt 23:12).

How can both pride and humility be positive and negative? When is pride especially destructive?

3 For now the Sovereign, the LORD of hosts,
is taking away from Jerusalem and from Judah
support and staff—
all support of bread,
and all support of water—
2 warrior and soldier,
judge and prophet,
diviner and elder,
3 captain of fifty
and dignitary,
counselor and skillful magician
and expert enchanter.
4 And I will make boys their princes,
and babes shall rule over them.
5 The people will be oppressed,
everyone by another
and everyone by a neighbor;
the youth will be insolent to the elder,
and the base to the honorable.

6 Someone will even seize a relative,
a member of the clan, saying,
"You have a cloak;
you shall be our leader,
and this heap of ruins
shall be under your rule."
7 But the other will cry out on that day, saying,
"I will not be a healer;
in my house there is neither bread nor cloak;
you shall not make me
leader of the people."
8 For Jerusalem has stumbled
and Judah has fallen,
because their speech and their deeds are against the LORD,
defying his glorious presence.

9 The look on their faces bears witness against them;
they proclaim their sin like Sodom,
they do not hide it.
Woe to them!
For they have brought evil on themselves.
10 Tell the innocent how fortunate they are,
for they shall eat the fruit of their labors.
11 Woe to the guilty! How unfortunate they are,
for what their hands have done shall be done to them.

12 My people—children are their oppressors,
and women rule over them.
O my people, your leaders mislead you,
and confuse the course of your paths.

13 The LORD rises to argue his case;
he stands to judge the peoples.
14 The LORD enters into judgment
with the elders and princes of his people:
It is you who have devoured the vineyard;
the spoil of the poor is in your houses.
15 What do you mean by crushing my people,
by grinding the face of the poor? says the Lord GOD of hosts.

16 The LORD said:
Because the daughters of Zion are haughty
and walk with outstretched necks,
glancing wantonly with their eyes,
mincing along as they go,
tinkling with their feet;
17 the Lord will afflict with scabs
the heads of the daughters of Zion,
and the LORD will lay bare their secret parts.

18 In that day the Lord will take away the finery of the anklets, the
headbands, and the crescents; 19 the pendants, the bracelets, and the
scarfs; 20 the headdresses, the armlets, the sashes, the perfume boxes,
and the amulets; 21 the signet rings and nose rings; 22 the festal robes,
the mantles, the cloaks, and the handbags; 23 the garments of gauze,
the linen garments, the turbans, and the veils.
24 Instead of perfume there will be a stench;
and instead of a sash, a rope;
and instead of well-set hair, baldness;
and instead of a rich robe, a binding of sackcloth;
instead of beauty, shame.[a]
25 Your men shall fall by the sword
and your warriors in battle.
26 And her gates shall lament and mourn;
ravaged, she shall sit upon the ground.
4 Seven women shall take hold of one man in that day, saying,
"We will eat our own bread and wear our own clothes;
just let us be called by your name;
take away our disgrace."

[a] Q Ms: MT lacks *shame*

3:13—4:1 The LORD rises to argue his case: Here again, God brings a lawsuit against the leaders of the people for failing in their fundamental duty: to ensure justice for all and to care for those in need. Instead, the men are found "grinding the face of the poor" (3:15), and the wealthy women are recognized by the "tinkling" of their fine anklets and the scent of their perfumes (3:16-23). Wealth itself is not the enemy, but abusing wealth crushes the poor rather than sharing with them. The description of the rich clothing and accessories here calls attention to the affluence of eighth-century Judah and Jerusalem. Because many of the people have misused this wealth, the leading men and women alike will suffer the consequences (3:24—4:1).

4:2-6 the branch of the LORD shall be beautiful...over all the glory: In contrast to the words of warning just before, the prophet provides an image of hope. Jerusalem will be purified and restored, living under the protection of God. As in Exodus 13:21-22, God appears as a cloud by day and fire by night, providing shade and shelter for God's people (25:4; Ps 121:5-8).

4:3 Whoever is left in Zion: Whoever remains in Jerusalem will be called holy. Isaiah builds on the theme of the "remnant" found throughout the Bible. Though God's judgment must sometimes be fierce, it will never destroy everything, since its only purpose is to promote new life and permit new beginnings. Thus, a "remnant" will always remain, whether in the flood (Gen 7:23), in the great famine (Gen 45:7), or now in the destruction of the kingdoms of Israel (4:2; 10:20-23; see Mic 2:12) and Judah (4:3; 37:31-32). God's pledge always to preserve a remnant is so important to Isaiah that it becomes the name of one of his sons: Shear-jashub ("a remnant shall return," 7:3).

5:1-7 a vineyard: The prophet uses the form of a love-song to create a parable that makes the hearers accuse themselves for their own failures. The song was no doubt actually sung, inviting the listeners to appreciate first the loving care of the owner for his vineyard and then his disappointment when it yields wild grapes that are bitter and sour, unusable. They would agree that the only remedy is radical: total destruction of the old to make way for a new beginning. Finally, they are condemned as they hear that they themselves are the unproductive vineyard. (For more examples, see 27:2-6; Ps 80:8-13; Jer 2:21; 12:10-11; Ezek 19:10-14).

The prophet Nathan's story (parable) accusing King David of his sin works the same way (2 Sam 12:1-15). From the vineyard, God expects "justice" (Hebrew *mishpat* [mish-PAHT]) but gets "bloodshed" (*mispach* [mis-PACH]) instead. God expects "righteousness" (*tsedaqah* [tse-dah-QAH]), but hears the "cry" (*tse'aqah* [tse-'ah-QAH]) of those made to suffer injustice. The wordplays add to the effect of the song.

What kind of "vineyard" describes your life?

The Future Glory of the Survivors in Zion

2 On that day the branch of the LORD shall be beautiful and glorious, and the fruit of the land shall be the pride and glory of the survivors of Israel. 3 Whoever is left in Zion and remains in Jerusalem will
be called holy, everyone who has been recorded for life in Jerusalem,
4 once the Lord has washed away the filth of the daughters of Zion
and cleansed the bloodstains of Jerusalem from its midst by a spirit of
judgment and by a spirit of burning. 5 Then the LORD will create over
the whole site of Mount Zion and over its places of assembly a cloud
by day and smoke and the shining of a flaming fire by night. Indeed
over all the glory there will be a canopy. 6 It will serve as a pavilion, a
shade by day from the heat, and a refuge and a shelter from the storm
and rain.

The Song of the Unfruitful Vineyard

5 Let me sing for my beloved
my love-song concerning his vineyard:
My beloved had a vineyard
on a very fertile hill.
2 He dug it and cleared it of stones,
and planted it with choice vines;
he built a watchtower in the midst of it,
and hewed out a wine vat in it;
he expected it to yield grapes,
but it yielded wild grapes.

3 And now, inhabitants of Jerusalem
and people of Judah,
judge between me
and my vineyard.
4 What more was there to do for my vineyard
that I have not done in it?
When I expected it to yield grapes,
why did it yield wild grapes?

5 And now I will tell you
what I will do to my vineyard.
I will remove its hedge,
and it shall be devoured;
I will break down its wall,
and it shall be trampled down.
6 I will make it a waste;
it shall not be pruned or hoed,
and it shall be overgrown with briers and thorns;

I will also command the clouds
that they rain no rain upon it.

7 For the vineyard of the LORD of hosts
is the house of Israel,
and the people of Judah
are his pleasant planting;
he expected justice,
but saw bloodshed;
righteousness,
but heard a cry!

Social Injustice Denounced

8 Ah, you who join house to house,
who add field to field,
until there is room for no one but you,
and you are left to live alone
in the midst of the land!
9 The LORD of hosts has sworn in my hearing:
Surely many houses shall be desolate,
large and beautiful houses, without inhabitant.
10 For ten acres of vineyard shall yield but one bath,
and a homer of seed shall yield a mere ephah.[a]

11 Ah, you who rise early in the morning
in pursuit of strong drink,
who linger in the evening
to be inflamed by wine,
12 whose feasts consist of lyre and harp,
tambourine and flute and wine,
but who do not regard the deeds of the LORD,
or see the work of his hands!
13 Therefore my people go into exile without knowledge;
their nobles are dying of hunger,
and their multitude is parched with thirst.

14 Therefore Sheol has enlarged its appetite
and opened its mouth beyond measure;
the nobility of Jerusalem[b] and her multitude go down,
her throng and all who exult in her.
15 People are bowed down, everyone is brought low,
and the eyes of the haughty are humbled.
16 But the LORD of hosts is exalted by justice,

[a] The Heb *bath, homer,* and *ephah* are measures of quantity [b] Heb *her nobility*

5:8-24 Ah, you who: The oracles in this series are introduced with "Ah" (Hebrew *hoy*), also variously translated "Alas," "Woe," "Oh," or "Ha!" The interjection is used twenty-one times in Isaiah, but much less frequently in other prophets. It almost always introduces a word of divine judgment (but see 55:1). As in 1:2-20, the message is one of mournful bewilderment that people would do such self-destructive things. Here the oracles condemn taking property at the expense of others (5:8-10); drunkenness (5:11-13, 22); scoffing at the God's work (5:18-19); confusing good and evil (5:20); conceit (5:21); and taking bribes (5:23). Of all these, the first is perhaps the most serious. The land had been distributed among the tribes to provide equally and adequately for all (see Josh 13:1—19:51). Among other practices, the laws of the Jubilee year and the right of the redemption of property (Lev 25:8-55) were put in place to prevent anyone from losing their land for all time (Lev 25:23). But now the wealthy and powerful threatened to disinherit the poor, with disastrous economic, social, and even theological consequences. They would lose not only their livelihood but also their share of the land of promise.

Despite the great differences between that world and our own, what might we learn from this biblical ideal of the Jubilee year as we think about our economic policies and issues of justice today?

and the Holy God shows himself holy by righteousness.
17 Then the lambs shall graze as in their pasture,
fatlings and kids[a] shall feed among the ruins.

18 Ah, you who drag iniquity along with cords of falsehood,
who drag sin along as with cart ropes,
19 who say, "Let him make haste,
let him speed his work
that we may see it;
let the plan of the Holy One of Israel hasten to fulfillment,
that we may know it!"
20 Ah, you who call evil good
and good evil,
who put darkness for light
and light for darkness,
who put bitter for sweet
and sweet for bitter!
21 Ah, you who are wise in your own eyes,
and shrewd in your own sight!
22 Ah, you who are heroes in drinking wine
and valiant at mixing drink,
23 who acquit the guilty for a bribe,
and deprive the innocent of their rights!

Foreign Invasion Predicted

24 Therefore, as the tongue of fire devours the stubble,
and as dry grass sinks down in the flame,
so their root will become rotten,
and their blossom go up like dust;
for they have rejected the instruction of the LORD of hosts,
and have despised the word of the Holy One of Israel.

25 Therefore the anger of the LORD was kindled against his people,
and he stretched out his hand against them and struck them;
the mountains quaked,
and their corpses were like refuse
in the streets.
For all this his anger has not turned away,
and his hand is stretched out still.

26 He will raise a signal for a nation far away,
and whistle for a people at the ends of the earth;
Here they come, swiftly, speedily!

---

[a] Cn Compare Gk: Heb *aliens*

27 None of them is weary, none stumbles,
none slumbers or sleeps,
not a loincloth is loose,
not a sandal-thong broken;
28 their arrows are sharp,
all their bows bent,
their horses' hoofs seem like flint,
and their wheels like the whirlwind.
29 Their roaring is like a lion,
like young lions they roar;
they growl and seize their prey,
they carry it off, and no one can rescue.
30 They will roar over it on that day,
like the roaring of the sea.
And if one look to the land—
only darkness and distress;
and the light grows dark with clouds.

A Vision of God in the Temple

6 In the year that King Uzziah died, I saw the Lord sitting on a
throne, high and lofty; and the hem of his robe filled the temple. 2 Seraphs were in attendance above him; each had six wings: with
two they covered their faces, and with two they covered their feet, and
with two they flew. 3 And one called to another and said:

"Holy, holy, holy is the LORD of hosts;
the whole earth is full of his glory."

4 The pivots[a] on the thresholds shook at the voices of those who called,
and the house filled with smoke. 5 And I said: "Woe is me! I am lost,
for I am a man of unclean lips, and I live among a people of unclean
lips; yet my eyes have seen the King, the LORD of hosts!"
6 Then one of the seraphs flew to me, holding a live coal that had
been taken from the altar with a pair of tongs. 7 The seraph[b] touched
my mouth with it and said: "Now that this has touched your lips,
your guilt has departed and your sin is blotted out." 8 Then I heard the
voice of the Lord saying, "Whom shall I send, and who will go for
us?" And I said, "Here am I; send me!" 9 And he said, "Go and say to
this people:

'Keep listening, but do not comprehend;
keep looking, but do not understand.'
10 Make the mind of this people dull,
and stop their ears,
and shut their eyes,
so that they may not look with their eyes,

[a] Meaning of Heb uncertain [b] Heb *He*

6:1-13 I saw the LORD sitting on a throne: Chapters 6 through 8 introduce the call of the prophet himself. Isaiah's call vision occurs "in the year that King Uzziah died," variously dated from 742 to 736 B.C.E. Isaiah has a vision of God—or at least of God's robe, so large that the hem fills the temple. That sight alone gave Isaiah great fear, for no one could see God and live (Exod 33:20). The seraphs, too, must protect their faces and cover themselves in God's presence. (The seraphs were heavenly beings, apparently in the form of winged snakes. Note that the same root, *seraph*, is used to describe the serpents in Num 21:8; Isa 14:29; 30:6). Their song ("Holy, holy, holy") becomes the never-ending song of heaven in Revelation 4:8.

Isaiah's "unclean lips" (6:5) are not so much a personal failing as a condition of separation from God that he shares with all humanity ("a people of unclean lips"). His lips are cleansed with a burning coal from the altar that prepares him to serve as God's spokesperson. Isaiah's answer to God's "Whom shall I send?" is "Here I am," a common response of those addressed by God throughout the Bible, from Abraham (Gen 22:1) to Jacob (Gen 31:11), to Moses (Exod 3:4), to Samuel (1 Sam 3:4), to Mary, the mother of Jesus (Luke 1:38). The message given to Isaiah is one of the most difficult in the Bible. His message will cause hearers to "not look with their eyes" or "listen with their ears," with the result that they will not "turn and be healed" (6:10). Generally, the prophetic warning is given to make the hearers turn and repent so that the judgment does not happen (Jonah 3:4-10), but in Isaiah's day it was too late. The judgment was unavoidable and would come inevitably, until cities were laid waste and the land was utterly desolate (6:11). This judgment came eventually both to Israel and Judah, as they were destroyed by Assyria and Babylon, respectively, in 722 B.C.E. and 587 B.C.E.

6:9 Go and say to this people: God commissions Isaiah to "go and say" (Isa 6:9). This is a double command repeated often in the Bible (Exod 6:10-11; 2 Sam 7:4-5; Jonah 3:2; see also Matt 11:4; Acts 5:20). Both parts are essential to the work of the prophet: obediently to go where and when God calls (the context) and faithfully to speak what God says (the text). These two things coming together comprise the word of the Lord. God's word is not an abstract or timeless truth but a particular message for a specific time and place. In the Bible these particular messages are then reinterpreted and heard anew in other times and places as well.

When have you sensed or heard God's call to go and do or say something? What do you think of the idea that the ancient message of the Bible can come alive in a new way for people today? How does that happen?

7:1-9 you and your son Shear-jashub: The setting is the Syro-Ephraimite war (735–732 B.C.E.). The northern kingdom of Israel (Ephraim) joined with Syria to attack Judah. Israel wanted support in its battle against Assyria in the north, so it desired to set up a puppet king in Judah's capital, Jerusalem, as an ally. King Ahaz of Judah dangerously turned to Assyria for assistance (see 2 Kgs 16). In response to this move Isaiah urges reliance on God. This will be the only thing strong enough to resist the threat (7:9). The symbolic name of Isaiah's son Shear-jashub ("a remnant shall remain") is first confirmed here in God's promise that the coalition of Syria and Ephraim will fail (7:7-9). But the name also contains the implied warning that only a remnant of the northern kingdom will remain when Assyria turns against them.

What does the warning in 7:9—"If you do not stand firm in faith, you shall not stand at all"—mean to you?

and listen with their ears,
and comprehend with their minds,
and turn and be healed."
11 Then I said, "How long, O Lord?" And he said:
"Until cities lie waste
without inhabitant,
and houses without people,
and the land is utterly desolate;
12 until the LORD sends everyone far away,
and vast is the emptiness in the midst of the land.
13 Even if a tenth part remain in it,
it will be burned again,
like a terebinth or an oak
whose stump remains standing
when it is felled."[a]
The holy seed is its stump.

Isaiah Reassures King Ahaz

7 In the days of Ahaz son of Jotham son of Uzziah, king of Judah,
King Rezin of Aram and King Pekah son of Remaliah of Israel
went up to attack Jerusalem, but could not mount an attack against
it. 2When the house of David heard that Aram had allied itself with
Ephraim, the heart of Ahaz[b] and the heart of his people shook as the
trees of the forest shake before the wind.
3 Then the LORD said to Isaiah, Go out to meet Ahaz, you and
your son Shear-jashub,[c] at the end of the conduit of the upper pool on
the highway to the Fuller's Field, 4and say to him, Take heed, be quiet,
do not fear, and do not let your heart be faint because of these two
smoldering stumps of firebrands, because of the fierce anger of Rezin
and Aram and the son of Remaliah. 5Because Aram—with Ephraim
and the son of Remaliah—has plotted evil against you, saying, 6Let
us go up against Judah and cut off Jerusalem[d] and conquer it for ourselves and make the son of Tabeel king in it; 7therefore thus says the
Lord GOD:
It shall not stand,
and it shall not come to pass.
8 For the head of Aram is Damascus,
and the head of Damascus is Rezin.
(Within sixty-five years Ephraim will be shattered, no longer a
people.)
9 The head of Ephraim is Samaria,
and the head of Samaria is the son of Remaliah.
If you do not stand firm in faith,
you shall not stand at all.

---

[a] Meaning of Heb uncertain [b] Heb *his heart* [c] That is *A remnant shall return* [d] Heb *cut it off*

Isaiah Gives Ahaz the Sign of Immanuel

10 Again the LORD spoke to Ahaz, saying, 11Ask a sign of the
LORD your God; let it be deep as Sheol or high as heaven. 12But Ahaz
said, I will not ask, and I will not put the LORD to the test. 13Then Isaiah[a] said: "Hear then, O house of David! Is it too little for you to weary
mortals, that you weary my God also? 14Therefore the Lord himself
will give you a sign. Look, the young woman[b] is with child and shall
bear a son, and shall name him Immanuel.[c] 15He shall eat curds and
honey by the time he knows how to refuse the evil and choose the
good. 16For before the child knows how to refuse the evil and choose
the good, the land before whose two kings you are in dread will be
deserted. 17The LORD will bring on you and on your people and on
your ancestral house such days as have not come since the day that
Ephraim departed from Judah—the king of Assyria."
18 On that day the LORD will whistle for the fly that is at the
sources of the streams of Egypt, and for the bee that is in the land of
Assyria. 19And they will all come and settle in the steep ravines, and
in the clefts of the rocks, and on all the thornbushes, and on all the
pastures.
20 On that day the Lord will shave with a razor hired beyond the
River—with the king of Assyria—the head and the hair of the feet,
and it will take off the beard as well.
21 On that day one will keep alive a young cow and two sheep,
22and will eat curds because of the abundance of milk that they give;
for everyone that is left in the land shall eat curds and honey.
23 On that day every place where there used to be a thousand
vines, worth a thousand shekels of silver, will become briers and
thorns. 24With bow and arrows one will go there, for all the land will
be briers and thorns; 25and as for all the hills that used to be hoed with
a hoe, you will not go there for fear of briers and thorns; but they will
become a place where cattle are let loose and where sheep tread.

Isaiah's Son a Sign of the Assyrian Invasion

8 Then the LORD said to me, Take a large tablet and write on it
in common characters, "Belonging to Maher-shalal-hash-baz,"[d]
2and have it attested[e] for me by reliable witnesses, the priest Uriah
and Zechariah son of Jeberechiah. 3And I went to the prophetess, and
she conceived and bore a son. Then the LORD said to me, Name him
Maher-shalal-hash-baz; 4for before the child knows how to call "My
father" or "My mother," the wealth of Damascus and the spoil of Samaria will be carried away by the king of Assyria.
5 The LORD spoke to me again: 6Because this people has refused

[a] Heb *he* [b] Gk *the virgin* [c] That is *God is with us* [d] That is *The spoil speeds, the prey hastens* [e] Q Ms Gk Syr: MT *and I caused to be attested*

7:10-17 name him Immanuel: Refusal to seek a sign is often viewed positively in the Bible (Deut 6:16; Matt 4:7). Here, when the sign is offered directly by God, Ahaz's rejection is an act of little faith. But God will give the sign anyway: a child soon to be born will be given the symbolic name Immanuel ("God is with us"). And before the child is perhaps two years old the threat from Ephraim and Syria will be gone (7:16). Unhappily, though, the threat from Assyria will grow (7:17). The sign of God's presence brings both good news and bad, as God both rescues and judges. The Greek version of the Hebrew Scriptures, called the Septuagint, translated the term "young woman" (Hebrew *'almah* ['al-MAH]) as "virgin." This enabled a New Testament writer to use this promise to point to Mary's virgin conception of Jesus (Matt 1:23).

7:14 give you a sign: When the Bible refers to the fulfillment of Old Testament texts in New Testament events, the historical sense of the Old Testament text is often strikingly reinterpreted. With the words of Isaiah that happens several times—here, for example, with the Immanuel sign applied to Jesus; and again with the application of the voice "in the wilderness" (40:3) to John the Baptist (Mark 1:3-4). In both these cases, the different emphasis comes in part because the New Testament's writers relied heavily on the Septuagint, the Greek translation of the Old Testament. More than that, however, the New Testament uses the Old not so much as literal proof of the New Testament fulfillment, but as a living word of God that can serve as the basis for a new "sermon" or new proclamation of what the God of Israel is doing now in the life of Jesus and his followers.

8:1-4 Name him Maher-shalal-hash-baz: Again, the birth of a child to Isaiah and his wife becomes the occasion for a symbolic name: Ma-HER-sha-LAL-hash-baz ("the spoil speeds, the prey hastens")—again, an ominous one. Within a year, both Syria and the northern kingdom (Samaria) will fall to the Assyrians. The similarity between this sign and the Immanuel sign suggests to some that Immanuel too might have been a son of Isaiah. Although there were women prophets in Israel, such as Miriam (Exod 15:20), Deborah (Judg 4:4), Huldah (2 Kgs 22:14),; and Noadiah (Neh 6:14), here "prophetess" seems to mean simply Isaiah's wife.

the waters of Shiloah that flow gently, and melt in fear before[a] Rezin
and the son of Remaliah; 7 therefore, the Lord is bringing up against
it the mighty flood waters of the River, the king of Assyria and all his
glory; it will rise above all its channels and overflow all its banks; 8 it
will sweep on into Judah as a flood, and, pouring over, it will reach up
to the neck; and its outspread wings will fill the breadth of your land,
O Immanuel.

9 Band together, you peoples, and be dismayed;
listen, all you far countries;
gird yourselves and be dismayed;
gird yourselves and be dismayed!
10 Take counsel together, but it shall be brought to naught;
speak a word, but it will not stand,
for God is with us.[b]

11 For the LORD spoke thus to me while his hand was strong
upon me, and warned me not to walk in the way of this people, saying: 12 Do not call conspiracy all that this people calls conspiracy, and
do not fear what it fears, or be in dread. 13 But the LORD of hosts, him
you shall regard as holy; let him be your fear, and let him be your
dread. 14 He will become a sanctuary, a stone one strikes against; for
both houses of Israel he will become a rock one stumbles over—a
trap and a snare for the inhabitants of Jerusalem. 15 And many among
them shall stumble; they shall fall and be broken; they shall be snared
and taken.

8:11-22 Bind up the testimony, seal the teaching: Security is to be found in God alone, not in human alliances and conspiracies (8:11-15). This becomes a central message of Isaiah (30:1-5; 31:1-3). To ensure the survival of the prophet's message, his disciples seal it for safekeeping. God's word will prevail over the counterclaims of soothsayers and diviners (8:19), those who attempted to tell the future by various methods. Some have suggested that Isaiah's disciples may have played a role in the formation of the book of Isaiah. Later, Isaiah of the exile identifies himself or God's servant also as a "disciple" (one of "those who are taught," 50:4).

Disciples of Isaiah

16 Bind up the testimony, seal the teaching among my disciples.
17 I will wait for the LORD, who is hiding his face from the house of Jacob, and I will hope in him. 18 See, I and the children whom the LORD
has given me are signs and portents in Israel from the LORD of hosts,
who dwells on Mount Zion. 19 Now if people say to you, "Consult the
ghosts and the familiar spirits that chirp and mutter; should not a
people consult their gods, the dead on behalf of the living, 20 for teaching and for instruction?" surely, those who speak like this will have no
dawn! 21 They will pass through the land,[c] greatly distressed and hungry; when they are hungry, they will be enraged and will curse[d] their
king and their gods. They will turn their faces upward, 22 or they will
look to the earth, but will see only distress and darkness, the gloom of
anguish; and they will be thrust into thick darkness.[e]

The Righteous Reign of the Coming King

9 [f] But there will be no gloom for those who were in anguish. In the
former time he brought into contempt the land of Zebulun and

[a] Cn: Meaning of Heb uncertain [b] Heb *immanu el* [c] Heb *it* [d] Or *curse by* [e] Meaning of Heb uncertain [f] Ch 8.23 in Heb

the land of Naphtali, but in the latter time he will make glorious the
way of the sea, the land beyond the Jordan, Galilee of the nations.

2[a] The people who walked in darkness
have seen a great light;
those who lived in a land of deep darkness—
on them light has shined.
3 You have multiplied the nation,
you have increased its joy;
they rejoice before you
as with joy at the harvest,
as people exult when dividing plunder.
4 For the yoke of their burden,
and the bar across their shoulders,
the rod of their oppressor,
you have broken as on the day of Midian.
5 For all the boots of the tramping warriors
and all the garments rolled in blood
shall be burned as fuel for the fire.
6 For a child has been born for us,
a son given to us;
authority rests upon his shoulders;
and he is named
Wonderful Counselor, Mighty God,
Everlasting Father, Prince of Peace.
7 His authority shall grow continually,
and there shall be endless peace
for the throne of David and his kingdom.
He will establish and uphold it
with justice and with righteousness
from this time onward and forevermore.
The zeal of the LORD of hosts will do this.

9:2-7 a great light...a child has been born for us: The voice of promise breaks through again, this time announcing the coming of a new king in the line of David (see 2 Sam 7:12-13). This may originally have referred to the birth of King Hezekiah, though now it describes the ideal Davidic ruler or messiah, awaited by Israel. Typically, the fullest sign of the messiah's reign will be "endless peace" (9:4-7). The titles "Wonderful Counselor, Mighty God, Everlasting Father, Prince of Peace" were names given to the king at his coronation.

Judgment on Arrogance and Oppression

8 The Lord sent a word against Jacob,
and it fell on Israel;
9 and all the people knew it—
Ephraim and the inhabitants of Samaria—
but in pride and arrogance of heart they said:
10 "The bricks have fallen,
but we will build with dressed stones;
the sycamores have been cut down,
but we will put cedars in their place."
11 So the LORD raised adversaries[b] against them,

9:8—10:4 the LORD raised adversaries...his anger has not turned away: Unlike the coming age of peace (9:2-7), the present time is characterized by conflict and wickedness.

[a] Ch 9.1 in Heb [b] Cn: Heb *the adversaries of Rezin*

and stirred up their enemies,
12 the Arameans on the east and the Philistines on the west,
and they devoured Israel with open mouth.
For all this his anger has not turned away;
his hand is stretched out still.

13 The people did not turn to him who struck them,
or seek the LORD of hosts.
14 So the LORD cut off from Israel head and tail,
palm branch and reed in one day—
15 elders and dignitaries are the head,
and prophets who teach lies are the tail;
16 for those who led this people led them astray,
and those who were led by them were left in confusion.
17 That is why the Lord did not have pity on[a] their young people,
or compassion on their orphans and widows;
for everyone was godless and an evildoer,
and every mouth spoke folly.
For all this his anger has not turned away;
his hand is stretched out still.

18 For wickedness burned like a fire,
consuming briers and thorns;
it kindled the thickets of the forest,
and they swirled upward in a column of smoke.
19 Through the wrath of the LORD of hosts
the land was burned,
and the people became like fuel for the fire;
no one spared another.
20 They gorged on the right, but still were hungry,
and they devoured on the left, but were not satisfied;
they devoured the flesh of their own kindred;[b]
21 Manasseh devoured Ephraim, and Ephraim Manasseh,
and together they were against Judah.
For all this his anger has not turned away;
his hand is stretched out still.

10 Ah, you who make iniquitous decrees,
who write oppressive statutes,
2 to turn aside the needy from justice
and to rob the poor of my people of their right,
that widows may be your spoil,
and that you may make the orphans your prey!

---

[a] Q Ms: MT *rejoice over* [b] Or *arm*

3 What will you do on the day of punishment,
in the calamity that will come from far away?
To whom will you flee for help,
and where will you leave your wealth,
4 so as not to crouch among the prisoners
or fall among the slain?
For all this his anger has not turned away;
his hand is stretched out still.

Arrogant Assyria Also Judged

5 Ah, Assyria, the rod of my anger—
the club in their hands is my fury!
6 Against a godless nation I send him,
and against the people of my wrath I command him,
to take spoil and seize plunder,
and to tread them down like the mire of the streets.
7 But this is not what he intends,
nor does he have this in mind;
but it is in his heart to destroy,
and to cut off nations not a few.
8 For he says:
"Are not my commanders all kings?
9 Is not Calno like Carchemish?
Is not Hamath like Arpad?
Is not Samaria like Damascus?
10 As my hand has reached to the kingdoms of the idols
whose images were greater than those of Jerusalem and Samaria,
11 shall I not do to Jerusalem and her idols
what I have done to Samaria and her images?"

12 When the Lord has finished all his work on Mount Zion and
on Jerusalem, he[a] will punish the arrogant boasting of the king of Assyria and his haughty pride. 13 For he says:
"By the strength of my hand I have done it,
and by my wisdom, for I have understanding;
I have removed the boundaries of peoples,
and have plundered their treasures;
like a bull I have brought down those who sat on thrones.
14 My hand has found, like a nest,
the wealth of the peoples;
and as one gathers eggs that have been forsaken,
so I have gathered all the earth;

10:5-19 Ah, Assyria: Probably because of the important role of Assyria in the history behind these early chapters, it is singled out here for judgment. It is mentioned again more briefly among the oracles against foreign nations that follow in chapters 13–23 (see 14:24-27). Assyria was meant to serve as God's tool of judgment against Israel, but Assyria chose to take its destruction much too far (10:7-11). For this arrogance, God judges Assyria harshly. Babylon is judged for similar arrogance in chapter 47.

[a] Heb *I*

and there was none that moved a wing,
or opened its mouth, or chirped."

15 Shall the ax vaunt itself over the one who wields it,
or the saw magnify itself against the one who handles it?
As if a rod should raise the one who lifts it up,
or as if a staff should lift the one who is not wood!
16 Therefore the Sovereign, the LORD of hosts,
will send wasting sickness among his stout warriors,
and under his glory a burning will be kindled,
like the burning of fire.
17 The light of Israel will become a fire,
and his Holy One a flame;
and it will burn and devour
his thorns and briers in one day.
18 The glory of his forest and his fruitful land
the LORD will destroy, both soul and body,
and it will be as when an invalid wastes away.
19 The remnant of the trees of his forest will be so few
that a child can write them down.

The Repentant Remnant of Israel

20 On that day the remnant of Israel and the survivors of the
house of Jacob will no more lean on the one who struck them, but
will lean on the LORD, the Holy One of Israel, in truth. 21 A remnant
will return, the remnant of Jacob, to the mighty God. 22 For though
your people Israel were like the sand of the sea, only a remnant of
them will return. Destruction is decreed, overflowing with righteousness. 23 For the Lord GOD of hosts will make a full end, as decreed, in
all the earth.[a]

24 Therefore thus says the Lord GOD of hosts: O my people, who
live in Zion, do not be afraid of the Assyrians when they beat you with
a rod and lift up their staff against you as the Egyptians did. 25 For in
a very little while my indignation will come to an end, and my anger
will be directed to their destruction. 26 The LORD of hosts will wield a
whip against them, as when he struck Midian at the rock of Oreb; his
staff will be over the sea, and he will lift it as he did in Egypt. 27 On that
day his burden will be removed from your shoulder, and his yoke will
be destroyed from your neck.

He has gone up from Rimmon,[b]
28 he has come to Aiath;
he has passed through Migron,

---

[a] Or *land* [b] Cn: Heb *and his yoke from your neck, and a yoke will be destroyed because of fatness*

at Michmash he stores his baggage;
29 they have crossed over the pass,
at Geba they lodge for the night;
Ramah trembles,
Gibeah of Saul has fled.
30 Cry aloud, O daughter Gallim!
Listen, O Laishah!
Answer her, O Anathoth!
31 Madmenah is in flight,
the inhabitants of Gebim flee for safety.
32 This very day he will halt at Nob,
he will shake his fist
at the mount of daughter Zion,
the hill of Jerusalem.

33 Look, the Sovereign, the LORD of hosts,
will lop the boughs with terrifying power;
the tallest trees will be cut down,
and the lofty will be brought low.
34 He will hack down the thickets of the forest with an ax,
and Lebanon with its majestic trees[a] will fall.

The Peaceful Kingdom

11 A shoot shall come out from the stump of Jesse,
and a branch shall grow out of his roots.
2 The spirit of the LORD shall rest on him,
the spirit of wisdom and understanding,
the spirit of counsel and might,
the spirit of knowledge and the fear of the LORD.
3 His delight shall be in the fear of the LORD.

He shall not judge by what his eyes see,
or decide by what his ears hear;
4 but with righteousness he shall judge the poor,
and decide with equity for the meek of the earth;
he shall strike the earth with the rod of his mouth,
and with the breath of his lips he shall kill the wicked.
5 Righteousness shall be the belt around his waist,
and faithfulness the belt around his loins.

6 The wolf shall live with the lamb,
the leopard shall lie down with the kid,
the calf and the lion and the fatling together,

11:1-9 A shoot shall come out from the stump of Jesse...They will not hurt or destroy: Though now only a lowly "stump," the family tree of Jesse (David's father) will grow and flourish, producing a new messianic king. "The spirit of the LORD shall rest on him," just as it had come to rest on David (1 Sam 16:13) and as it will come later to the servant of God (42:1; 48:16; 61:1) and to all Israel (44:3). The king will wear "righteousness" and "faithfulness" (11:4-5), similar to the armor of God in 59:16-17. Even the violence inherent in nature itself is transformed. Not only do the prey and the predators live in peace, so do the child and the snake. In God's coming kingdom the curse of sin itself is overcome (see Gen 3:14-15).

[a] Cn Compare Gk Vg: Heb *with a majestic one*

and a little child shall lead them.
7 The cow and the bear shall graze,
their young shall lie down together;
and the lion shall eat straw like the ox.
8 The nursing child shall play over the hole of the asp,
and the weaned child shall put its hand on the adder's den.
9 They will not hurt or destroy
on all my holy mountain;
for the earth will be full of the knowledge of the LORD
as the waters cover the sea.

Return of the Remnant of Israel and Judah

10 On that day the root of Jesse shall stand as a signal to the
peoples; the nations shall inquire of him, and his dwelling shall be
glorious.
11 On that day the Lord will extend his hand yet a second time
to recover the remnant that is left of his people, from Assyria, from
Egypt, from Pathros, from Ethiopia,[a] from Elam, from Shinar, from
Hamath, and from the coastlands of the sea.
12 He will raise a signal for the nations,
and will assemble the outcasts of Israel,
and gather the dispersed of Judah
from the four corners of the earth.
13 The jealousy of Ephraim shall depart,
the hostility of Judah shall be cut off;
Ephraim shall not be jealous of Judah,
and Judah shall not be hostile towards Ephraim.
14 But they shall swoop down on the backs of the Philistines in the west,
together they shall plunder the people of the east.
They shall put forth their hand against Edom and Moab,
and the Ammonites shall obey them.
15 And the LORD will utterly destroy
the tongue of the sea of Egypt;
and will wave his hand over the River
with his scorching wind;
and will split it into seven channels,
and make a way to cross on foot;
16 so there shall be a highway from Assyria
for the remnant that is left of his people,
as there was for Israel
when they came up from the land of Egypt.

---

[a] Or *Nubia;* Heb *Cush*

Thanksgiving and Praise

12 You will say in that day:
I will give thanks to you, O LORD,
for though you were angry with me,
your anger turned away,
and you comforted me.

2 Surely God is my salvation;
I will trust, and will not be afraid,
for the LORD GOD[a] is my strength and my might;
he has become my salvation.

3 With joy you will draw water from the wells of salvation. 4 And
you will say in that day:
Give thanks to the LORD,
call on his name;
make known his deeds among the nations;
proclaim that his name is exalted.

5 Sing praises to the LORD, for he has done gloriously;
let this be known[b] in all the earth.
6 Shout aloud and sing for joy, O royal[c] Zion,
for great in your midst is the Holy One of Israel.

Proclamation against Babylon

13 The oracle concerning Babylon that Isaiah son of Amoz saw.
2 On a bare hill raise a signal,
cry aloud to them;
wave the hand for them to enter
the gates of the nobles.
3 I myself have commanded my consecrated ones,
have summoned my warriors, my proudly exulting ones,
to execute my anger.

4 Listen, a tumult on the mountains
as of a great multitude!
Listen, an uproar of kingdoms,
of nations gathering together!
The LORD of hosts is mustering
an army for battle.
5 They come from a distant land,
from the end of the heavens,

[a] Heb *for Yah, the LORD* [b] Or *this is made known* [c] Or *O inhabitant of*

12:1-6 I will give thanks to you, O LORD: This section of the book closes with traditional songs of praise (doxologies). This may reflect a structuring of the book for liturgical reading or for its use in worship.

13:1—23:18 The oracle concerning Babylon . . . Tyre: These words of judgment on the surrounding nations make clear that Yahweh (YAH-wey), the God of Israel, is not merely a national God but is LORD of the entire world. All nations fall under God's rule and are subject to God's judgment, just as, also in this book, the nations are invited to share in God's teaching (2:3) and in God's salvation (45:22).

13:1-22 oracle concerning Babylon: Throughout biblical history Babylon emerges again and again as an enemy of God's people and God's work. This oracle (prophetic speech) may date from a later period (perhaps sixth century B.C.E.) when Babylon, not Assyria, was the major world power (see chapter 47). Even so, a less-powerful Babylon was also involved in the events of the eighth century described in Isaiah.

the LORD and the weapons of his indignation,
to destroy the whole earth.

6 Wail, for the day of the LORD is near;
it will come like destruction from the Almighty![a]
7 Therefore all hands will be feeble,
and every human heart will melt,
8 and they will be dismayed.
Pangs and agony will seize them;
they will be in anguish like a woman in labor.
They will look aghast at one another;
their faces will be aflame.
9 See, the day of the LORD comes,
cruel, with wrath and fierce anger,
to make the earth a desolation,
and to destroy its sinners from it.
10 For the stars of the heavens and their constellations
will not give their light;
the sun will be dark at its rising,
and the moon will not shed its light.
11 I will punish the world for its evil,
and the wicked for their iniquity;
I will put an end to the pride of the arrogant,
and lay low the insolence of tyrants.
12 I will make mortals more rare than fine gold,
and humans than the gold of Ophir.
13 Therefore I will make the heavens tremble,
and the earth will be shaken out of its place,
at the wrath of the LORD of hosts
in the day of his fierce anger.
14 Like a hunted gazelle,
or like sheep with no one to gather them,
all will turn to their own people,
and all will flee to their own lands.
15 Whoever is found will be thrust through,
and whoever is caught will fall by the sword.
16 Their infants will be dashed to pieces
before their eyes;
their houses will be plundered,
and their wives ravished.
17 See, I am stirring up the Medes against them,
who have no regard for silver
and do not delight in gold.

[a] Traditional rendering of Heb *Shaddai*

18 Their bows will slaughter the young men;
they will have no mercy on the fruit of the womb;
their eyes will not pity children.
19 And Babylon, the glory of kingdoms,
the splendor and pride of the Chaldeans,
will be like Sodom and Gomorrah
when God overthrew them.
20 It will never be inhabited
or lived in for all generations;
Arabs will not pitch their tents there,
shepherds will not make their flocks lie down there.
21 But wild animals will lie down there,
and its houses will be full of howling creatures;
there ostriches will live,
and there goat-demons will dance.
22 Hyenas will cry in its towers,
and jackals in the pleasant palaces;
its time is close at hand,
and its days will not be prolonged.

Restoration of Judah

14 But the LORD will have compassion on Jacob and will again
choose Israel, and will set them in their own land; and aliens
will join them and attach themselves to the house of Jacob. 2 And the
nations will take them and bring them to their place, and the house of
Israel will possess the nations[a] as male and female slaves in the LORD's
land; they will take captive those who were their captors, and rule
over those who oppressed them.

Downfall of the King of Babylon

3 When the LORD has given you rest from your pain and turmoil
and the hard service with which you were made to serve, 4 you will
take up this taunt against the king of Babylon:
How the oppressor has ceased!
How his insolence[b] has ceased!
5 The LORD has broken the staff of the wicked,
the scepter of rulers,
6 that struck down the peoples in wrath
with unceasing blows,
that ruled the nations in anger
with unrelenting persecution.
7 The whole earth is at rest and quiet;
they break forth into singing.

14:3-23 this taunt against the king of Babylon: The judgment of Babylon continues with this song mocking its king. Once high and mighty, the king is now laid low. Once pretending even to be a god ("Day Star, son of Dawn" are names of gods in Canaanite myth), now the king is sent off to Sheol, the realm of the dead. "Day Star" is "Lucifer" in Latin. With that connection this fall of Lucifer was later associated with the fall of Satan described by Jesus (Luke 10:18). Here even the cedar trees of Lebanon rejoice over the destruction of the tyrant king (14:8), since ancient rulers cut the large trees to build their palaces and temples (including Solomon; see 1 Kgs 5:6).

[a] Heb *them* [b] Q Ms Compare Gk Syr Vg: Meaning of MT uncertain

8 The cypresses exult over you,
the cedars of Lebanon, saying,
"Since you were laid low,
no one comes to cut us down."
9 Sheol beneath is stirred up
to meet you when you come;
it rouses the shades to greet you,
all who were leaders of the earth;
it raises from their thrones
all who were kings of the nations.
10 All of them will speak
and say to you:
"You too have become as weak as we!
You have become like us!"
11 Your pomp is brought down to Sheol,
and the sound of your harps;
maggots are the bed beneath you,
and worms are your covering.

12 How you are fallen from heaven,
O Day Star, son of Dawn!
How you are cut down to the ground,
you who laid the nations low!
13 You said in your heart,
"I will ascend to heaven;
I will raise my throne
above the stars of God;
I will sit on the mount of assembly
on the heights of Zaphon;[a]
14 I will ascend to the tops of the clouds,
I will make myself like the Most High."
15 But you are brought down to Sheol,
to the depths of the Pit.
16 Those who see you will stare at you,
and ponder over you:
"Is this the man who made the earth tremble,
who shook kingdoms,
17 who made the world like a desert
and overthrew its cities,
who would not let his prisoners go home?"
18 All the kings of the nations lie in glory,
each in his own tomb;
19 but you are cast out, away from your grave,

[a] Or *assembly in the far north*

like loathsome carrion,[a]
clothed with the dead, those pierced by the sword,
who go down to the stones of the Pit,
like a corpse trampled underfoot.
20 You will not be joined with them in burial,
because you have destroyed your land,
you have killed your people.

May the descendants of evildoers
nevermore be named!
21 Prepare slaughter for his sons
because of the guilt of their father.[b]
Let them never rise to possess the earth
or cover the face of the world with cities.

22 I will rise up against them, says the LORD of hosts, and will cut
off from Babylon name and remnant, offspring and posterity, says the
LORD. 23 And I will make it a possession of the hedgehog, and pools
of water, and I will sweep it with the broom of destruction, says the
LORD of hosts.

An Oracle concerning Assyria

24 The LORD of hosts has sworn:
As I have designed,
so shall it be;
and as I have planned,
so shall it come to pass:
25 I will break the Assyrian in my land,
and on my mountains trample him under foot;
his yoke shall be removed from them,
and his burden from their shoulders.
26 This is the plan that is planned
concerning the whole earth;
and this is the hand that is stretched out
over all the nations.
27 For the LORD of hosts has planned,
and who will annul it?
His hand is stretched out,
and who will turn it back?

An Oracle concerning Philistia

28 In the year that King Ahaz died this oracle came:

29 Do not rejoice, all you Philistines,

---

[a] Cn Compare Gk: Heb *like a loathed branch* [b] Syr Compare Gk: Heb *fathers*

14:24-27 I will break the Assyrian: See the introduction to Isaiah and the note on 10:5-19.

14:28-32 you Philistines: The Philistines were constant enemies of Israel (for example, see Judg 13:5; 1 Sam 4:1; 23:1; 2 Sam 3:18). In an oracle dated about 715 B.C.E. ("the year that King Ahaz died"), the Philistines too fall under God's judgment. The dating shows that these oracles against the nations are not random but refer to peoples involved in the events of Isaiah's time.

that the rod that struck you is broken,
for from the root of the snake will come forth an adder,
and its fruit will be a flying fiery serpent.
30 The firstborn of the poor will graze,
and the needy lie down in safety;
but I will make your root die of famine,
and your remnant I[a] will kill.
31 Wail, O gate; cry, O city;
melt in fear, O Philistia, all of you!
For smoke comes out of the north,
and there is no straggler in its ranks.

32 What will one answer the messengers of the nation?
"The LORD has founded Zion,
and the needy among his people
will find refuge in her."

An Oracle concerning Moab

15:1—16:14 oracle concerning Moab: Moab, east of the Dead Sea, had been an occasional enemy of Israel at least since its king had hired Balaam to curse God's people during their wilderness trek from Egypt (Num 23:7). Dibon, Nebo, and Medeba (15:2) and Heshbon and Elealeh (15:4) were ancient cities of Moab. See Maps 4 and 5, pp. 2102-2103. Moabite refugees come to Judah seeking asylum, and the king of Judah is encouraged to give shelter (16:1-5). Even so, the lament prayers of Moab will not help them erase their pride, and they will be devastated (16:12-14).

15:3 sackcloth: This is coarse wool cloth worn to show grief or sorrow for doing wrong.

15 An oracle concerning Moab.

Because Ar is laid waste in a night,
Moab is undone;
because Kir is laid waste in a night,
Moab is undone.
2 Dibon[b] has gone up to the temple,
to the high places to weep;
over Nebo and over Medeba
Moab wails.
On every head is baldness,
every beard is shorn;
3 in the streets they bind on sackcloth;
on the housetops and in the squares
everyone wails and melts in tears.
4 Heshbon and Elealeh cry out,
their voices are heard as far as Jahaz;
therefore the loins of Moab quiver;[c]
his soul trembles.
5 My heart cries out for Moab;
his fugitives flee to Zoar,
to Eglath-shelishiyah.
For at the ascent of Luhith

---

[a] Q Ms Vg: MT *he* [b] Cn: Heb *the house and Dibon* [c] Cn Compare Gk Syr: Heb *the armed men of Moab cry aloud*

they go up weeping;
on the road to Horonaim
they raise a cry of destruction;
6 the waters of Nimrim
are a desolation;
the grass is withered, the new growth fails,
the verdure is no more.
7 Therefore the abundance they have gained
and what they have laid up
they carry away
over the Wadi of the Willows.
8 For a cry has gone
around the land of Moab;
the wailing reaches to Eglaim,
the wailing reaches to Beer-elim.
9 For the waters of Dibon[a] are full of blood;
yet I will bring upon Dibon[a] even more—
a lion for those of Moab who escape,
for the remnant of the land.

16 Send lambs
to the ruler of the land,
from Sela, by way of the desert,
to the mount of daughter Zion.
2 Like fluttering birds,
like scattered nestlings,
so are the daughters of Moab
at the fords of the Arnon.
3 "Give counsel,
grant justice;
make your shade like night
at the height of noon;
hide the outcasts,
do not betray the fugitive;
4 let the outcasts of Moab
settle among you;
be a refuge to them
from the destroyer."

When the oppressor is no more,
and destruction has ceased,
and marauders have vanished from the land,
5 then a throne shall be established in steadfast love
in the tent of David,

16:5 tent of David: A reference to a future ruler descended from the family of David, who will rule Moab in justice.

---

[a] Q Ms Vg Compare Syr: MT *Dimon*

and on it shall sit in faithfulness
a ruler who seeks justice
and is swift to do what is right.

6 We have heard of the pride of Moab
—how proud he is!—
of his arrogance, his pride, and his insolence;
his boasts are false.
7 Therefore let Moab wail,
let everyone wail for Moab.
Mourn, utterly stricken,
for the raisin cakes of Kir-hareseth.

16:8-10 vines of Sibmah: The vineyards of this Moabite city known for its grape vines and winemaking will dry up.

8 For the fields of Heshbon languish,
and the vines of Sibmah,
whose clusters once made drunk
the lords of the nations,
reached to Jazer
and strayed to the desert;
their shoots once spread abroad
and crossed over the sea.
9 Therefore I weep with the weeping of Jazer
for the vines of Sibmah;
I drench you with my tears,
O Heshbon and Elealeh;
for the shout over your fruit harvest
and your grain harvest has ceased.
10 Joy and gladness are taken away
from the fruitful field;
and in the vineyards no songs are sung,
no shouts are raised;
no treader treads out wine in the presses;
the vintage-shout is hushed.[a]
11 Therefore my heart throbs like a harp for Moab,
and my very soul for Kir-heres.

12 When Moab presents himself, when he wearies himself upon the high place, when he comes to his sanctuary to pray, he will not prevail.

13 This was the word that the LORD spoke concerning Moab in the past. 14 But now the LORD says, In three years, like the years of a hired worker, the glory of Moab will be brought into contempt, in spite of all its great multitude; and those who survive will be very few and feeble.

---

[a] Gk: Heb *I have hushed*

An Oracle concerning Damascus

17 An oracle concerning Damascus.

See, Damascus will cease to be a city,
and will become a heap of ruins.
2 Her towns will be deserted forever;[a]
they will be places for flocks,
which will lie down, and no one will make them afraid.
3 The fortress will disappear from Ephraim,
and the kingdom from Damascus;
and the remnant of Aram will be
like the glory of the children of Israel,
says the LORD of hosts.

4 On that day
the glory of Jacob will be brought low,
and the fat of his flesh will grow lean.
5 And it shall be as when reapers gather standing grain
and their arms harvest the ears,
and as when one gleans the ears of grain
in the Valley of Rephaim.
6 Gleanings will be left in it,
as when an olive tree is beaten—
two or three berries
in the top of the highest bough,
four or five
on the branches of a fruit tree,
says the LORD God of Israel.

7 On that day people will regard their Maker, and their eyes will
look to the Holy One of Israel; 8 they will not have regard for the altars, the work of their hands, and they will not look to what their own
fingers have made, either the sacred poles[b] or the altars of incense.
9 On that day their strong cities will be like the deserted places
of the Hivites and the Amorites,[c] which they deserted because of the
children of Israel, and there will be desolation.

10 For you have forgotten the God of your salvation,
and have not remembered the Rock of your refuge;
therefore, though you plant pleasant plants
and set out slips of an alien god,
11 though you make them grow on the day that you plant them,

[a] Cn Compare Gk: Heb *the cities of Aroer are deserted* [b] Heb *Asherim* [c] Cn Compare Gk: Heb *places of the wood and the highest bough*

17:1-6 oracle concerning Damascus: During the time of Isaiah, Damascus, capital of Syria to the north, had been in an alliance with Ephraim (the northern kingdom of Israel) against Judah. Because of this alliance, "the glory of Jacob [Israel] will be brought low" (17:4), along with its Syrian allies.

17:7-8 their eyes will look to the Holy One of Israel...not look to what their own fingers have made: This refers to the people of Israel creating idols as objects of their worship. Because of what happens to Syria, the people will again return to worshiping God alone.

and make them blossom in the morning that you sow;
yet the harvest will flee away
in a day of grief and incurable pain.

12 Ah, the thunder of many peoples,
they thunder like the thundering of the sea!
Ah, the roar of nations,
they roar like the roaring of mighty waters!
13 The nations roar like the roaring of many waters,
but he will rebuke them, and they will flee far away,
chased like chaff on the mountains before the wind
and whirling dust before the storm.
14 At evening time, lo, terror!
Before morning, they are no more.
This is the fate of those who despoil us,
and the lot of those who plunder us.

An Oracle concerning Ethiopia

18 Ah, land of whirring wings
beyond the rivers of Ethiopia,[a]
2 sending ambassadors by the Nile
in vessels of papyrus on the waters!
Go, you swift messengers,
to a nation tall and smooth,
to a people feared near and far,
a nation mighty and conquering,
whose land the rivers divide.

3 All you inhabitants of the world,
you who live on the earth,
when a signal is raised on the mountains, look!
When a trumpet is blown, listen!
4 For thus the LORD said to me:
I will quietly look from my dwelling
like clear heat in sunshine,
like a cloud of dew in the heat of harvest.
5 For before the harvest, when the blossom is over
and the flower becomes a ripening grape,
he will cut off the shoots with pruning hooks,
and the spreading branches he will hew away.
6 They shall all be left
to the birds of prey of the mountains
and to the animals of the earth.

18:1—19:17 beyond the rivers of Ethiopia . . . oracle concerning Egypt: Egypt had been a symbol of bondage to Israel since the time of Moses. Here, these two oracles may reflect the conquest of Ethiopia and Egypt by the king of Assyria (about 713–711 B.C.E.; see 20:1-6).

18:2 a nation tall and smooth: The black Ethiopian warriors were taller than most and clean-shaven.

[a] Or *Nubia*; Heb *Cush*

And the birds of prey will summer on them,
and all the animals of the earth will winter on them.

7 At that time gifts will be brought to the LORD of hosts from[a] a people tall and smooth, from a people feared near and far, a nation mighty and conquering, whose land the rivers divide, to Mount Zion, the place of the name of the LORD of hosts.

An Oracle concerning Egypt

19 An oracle concerning Egypt.

See, the LORD is riding on a swift cloud
and comes to Egypt;
the idols of Egypt will tremble at his presence,
and the heart of the Egyptians will melt within them.
2 I will stir up Egyptians against Egyptians,
and they will fight, one against the other,
neighbor against neighbor,
city against city, kingdom against kingdom;
3 the spirit of the Egyptians within them will be emptied out,
and I will confound their plans;
they will consult the idols and the spirits of the dead
and the ghosts and the familiar spirits;
4 I will deliver the Egyptians
into the hand of a hard master;
a fierce king will rule over them,
says the Sovereign, the LORD of hosts.

5 The waters of the Nile will be dried up,
and the river will be parched and dry;
6 its canals will become foul,
and the branches of Egypt's Nile will diminish and dry up,
reeds and rushes will rot away.
7 There will be bare places by the Nile,
on the brink of the Nile;
and all that is sown by the Nile will dry up,
be driven away, and be no more.
8 Those who fish will mourn;
all who cast hooks in the Nile will lament,
and those who spread nets on the water will languish.
9 The workers in flax will be in despair,
and the carders and those at the loom will grow pale.

19:5-8 waters of the Nile will be dried up: The Nile River was the primary source of water in Egypt. Its yearly floods made the ground fertile. Even the plentiful fish supply in the river will diminish.

[a] Q Ms Gk Vg: MT *of*

10 Its weavers will be dismayed,
and all who work for wages will be grieved.

11 The princes of Zoan are utterly foolish;
the wise counselors of Pharaoh give stupid counsel.
How can you say to Pharaoh,
"I am one of the sages,
a descendant of ancient kings"?
12 Where now are your sages?
Let them tell you and make known
what the LORD of hosts has planned against Egypt.
13 The princes of Zoan have become fools,
and the princes of Memphis are deluded;
those who are the cornerstones of its tribes
have led Egypt astray.
14 The LORD has poured into them[a]
a spirit of confusion;
and they have made Egypt stagger in all its doings
as a drunkard staggers around in vomit.
15 Neither head nor tail, palm branch or reed,
will be able to do anything for Egypt.

16 On that day the Egyptians will be like women, and tremble
with fear before the hand that the LORD of hosts raises against them.
17 And the land of Judah will become a terror to the Egyptians; everyone to whom it is mentioned will fear because of the plan that the
LORD of hosts is planning against them.

Egypt, Assyria, and Israel Blessed

19:18-24 Blessed be Egypt...and Assyria...and Israel: In a remarkable turn of events, an altar to Israel's God will put up in Egypt, and the language of Canaan (probably meaning the Hebrew dialect) will be spoken in five of its cities. Assyria and Israel will join in worshiping the LORD, who will in turn bless these nations.

18 On that day there will be five cities in the land of Egypt that
speak the language of Canaan and swear allegiance to the LORD of
hosts. One of these will be called the City of the Sun.
19 On that day there will be an altar to the LORD in the center
of the land of Egypt, and a pillar to the LORD at its border. 20 It will
be a sign and a witness to the LORD of hosts in the land of Egypt;
when they cry to the LORD because of oppressors, he will send them a
savior, and will defend and deliver them. 21 The LORD will make himself known to the Egyptians; and the Egyptians will know the LORD
on that day, and will worship with sacrifice and burnt offering, and
they will make vows to the LORD and perform them. 22 The LORD will
strike Egypt, striking and healing; they will return to the LORD, and
he will listen to their supplications and heal them.
23 On that day there will be a highway from Egypt to Assyria,

[a] Gk Compare Tg: Heb *it*

and the Assyrian will come into Egypt, and the Egyptian into Assyria, and the Egyptians will worship with the Assyrians.

24 On that day Israel will be the third with Egypt and Assyria,
a blessing in the midst of the earth, 25 whom the LORD of hosts has
blessed, saying, "Blessed be Egypt my people, and Assyria the work
of my hands, and Israel my heritage."

Isaiah Dramatizes the Conquest of Egypt and Ethiopia

20 In the year that the commander-in-chief, who was sent by
King Sargon of Assyria, came to Ashdod and fought against
it and took it— 2 at that time the LORD had spoken to Isaiah son of
Amoz, saying, "Go, and loose the sackcloth from your loins and take
your sandals off your feet," and he had done so, walking naked and
barefoot. 3 Then the LORD said, "Just as my servant Isaiah has walked
naked and barefoot for three years as a sign and a portent against
Egypt and Ethiopia,[a] 4 so shall the king of Assyria lead away the Egyptians as captives and the Ethiopians[b] as exiles, both the young and
the old, naked and barefoot, with buttocks uncovered, to the shame
of Egypt. 5 And they shall be dismayed and confounded because of
Ethiopia[a] their hope and of Egypt their boast. 6 In that day the inhabitants of this coastland will say, 'See, this is what has happened to those
in whom we hoped and to whom we fled for help and deliverance
from the king of Assyria! And we, how shall we escape?'"

20:1-6 Isaiah has walked naked: In addition to their words, the prophets of Israel frequently engaged in symbolic actions to imprint their message on the viewers' minds and hearts. Here, Isaiah walked naked and barefoot for three years to illustrate the captivity of Egypt and Ethiopia, who would be humiliated with nakedness as prisoners of Assyria. The primary audience for the prophet's bizarre activity would, of course, be the people of Judah. They should have seen in Isaiah's actions the futility of relying on the neighboring powers rather than on God. The prophet Jeremiah wore a yoke to symbolize Israel's coming slavery to Babylon (Jer 27:2-22).

Oracles concerning Babylon, Edom, and Arabia

21 The oracle concerning the wilderness of the sea.

As whirlwinds in the Negeb sweep on,
it comes from the desert,
from a terrible land.
2 A stern vision is told to me;
the betrayer betrays,
and the destroyer destroys.
Go up, O Elam,
lay siege, O Media;
all the sighing she has caused
I bring to an end.
3 Therefore my loins are filled with anguish;
pangs have seized me,
like the pangs of a woman in labor;
I am bowed down so that I cannot hear,
I am dismayed so that I cannot see.
4 My mind reels, horror has appalled me;

21:1-16 oracle concerning the wilderness of the sea...Dumah... desert plain: Again, as in chapters 13–14, Babylon will fall (21:1-10). Now other peoples living in the Arabian desert region are also included (21:11-17). Dumah in the northern Arabian desert was invaded and robbed by the Assyrian general Sennacherib's forces. Another desert nomadic group, the Dedanites, are mentioned in Ezekiel 25:13.

[a] Or *Nubia;* Heb *Cush* [b] Or *Nubians;* Heb *Cushites*

the twilight I longed for
has been turned for me into trembling.
5 They prepare the table,
they spread the rugs,
they eat, they drink.
Rise up, commanders,
oil the shield!
6 For thus the Lord said to me:
"Go, post a lookout,
let him announce what he sees.
7 When he sees riders, horsemen in pairs,
riders on donkeys, riders on camels,
let him listen diligently,
very diligently."
8 Then the watcher[a] called out:
"Upon a watchtower I stand, O Lord,
continually by day,
and at my post I am stationed
throughout the night.
9 Look, there they come, riders,
horsemen in pairs!"
Then he responded,
"Fallen, fallen is Babylon;
and all the images of her gods
lie shattered on the ground."
10 O my threshed and winnowed one,
what I have heard from the LORD of hosts,
the God of Israel, I announce to you.

11 The oracle concerning Dumah.

One is calling to me from Seir,
"Sentinel, what of the night?
Sentinel, what of the night?"
12 The sentinel says:
"Morning comes, and also the night.
If you will inquire, inquire;
come back again."

13 The oracle concerning the desert plain.

In the scrub of the desert plain you will lodge,
O caravans of Dedanites.

---

[a] Q Ms: MT *a lion*

14 Bring water to the thirsty,
meet the fugitive with bread,
O inhabitants of the land of Tema.
15 For they have fled from the swords,
from the drawn sword,
from the bent bow,
and from the stress of battle.

16 For thus the Lord said to me: Within a year, according to the
years of a hired worker, all the glory of Kedar will come to an end;
17 and the remaining bows of Kedar's warriors will be few; for the
LORD, the God of Israel, has spoken.

A Warning of Destruction of Jerusalem

22 The oracle concerning the valley of vision.

What do you mean that you have gone up,
all of you, to the housetops,
2 you that are full of shoutings,
tumultuous city, exultant town?
Your slain are not slain by the sword,
nor are they dead in battle.
3 Your rulers have all fled together;
they were captured without the use of a bow.[a]
All of you who were found were captured,
though they had fled far away.[b]
4 Therefore I said:
Look away from me,
let me weep bitter tears;
do not try to comfort me
for the destruction of my beloved people.

5 For the Lord GOD of hosts has a day
of tumult and trampling and confusion
in the valley of vision,
a battering down of walls
and a cry for help to the mountains.
6 Elam bore the quiver
with chariots and cavalry,[c]
and Kir uncovered the shield.
7 Your choicest valleys were full of chariots,
and the cavalry took their stand at the gates.
8 He has taken away the covering of Judah.

[a] Or *without their bows* [b] Gk Syr Vg: Heb *fled from far away* [c] Meaning of Heb uncertain

22:1-14 oracle…this iniquity will not be forgiven you until you die: Jerusalem is not exempt from divine judgment. The oracle is even sharper for being placed here among the words against the foreign nations. Though the people of Judah are God's "beloved people" (22:4), their disobedience and lack of faith put them into the same category as the nations in the surrounding chapters that do not know God at all. The oracle refers to the time of the Assyrian invasions, perhaps King Sennacherib's siege of Jerusalem in 701 B.C.E., which resulted in his departure before succeeding in destroying the city. This was viewed by Judah as divine rescue (37:36-38). The prophet weeps for the city and for the people's disobedience. (22:4; 24:16; see also Jer 12:1-6; Lam 1:9, 16, 17, 21). Isaiah sees the coming destruction as the day of the LORD (22:5), that is, God's final judgment (see the note on 2:12). Typically for Isaiah, the prophet accuses the people of making every preparation for defense except the one that could save them: turning to God (22: 8-11; see the note on 8:11-22). The "House of the Forest" refers to Solomon's royal armory (1 Kgs 7:2; 10:17). "Collected the waters" may refer to Hezekiah's excavations to bring water into the city, now known as the Siloam tunnel (2 Kgs 20:20).

On that day you looked to the weapons of the House of the Forest,
9 and you saw that there were many breaches in the city of David, and
you collected the waters of the lower pool. 10 You counted the houses
of Jerusalem, and you broke down the houses to fortify the wall. 11 You
made a reservoir between the two walls for the water of the old pool.
But you did not look to him who did it, or have regard for him who
planned it long ago.

12 In that day the Lord GOD of hosts
called to weeping and mourning,
to baldness and putting on sackcloth;
13 but instead there was joy and festivity,
killing oxen and slaughtering sheep,
eating meat and drinking wine.
"Let us eat and drink,
for tomorrow we die."
14 The LORD of hosts has revealed himself in my ears:
Surely this iniquity will not be forgiven you until you die,
says the Lord GOD of hosts.

Denunciation of Self-Seeking Officials

15 Thus says the Lord GOD of hosts: Come, go to this steward, to
Shebna, who is master of the household, and say to him: 16 What right
do you have here? Who are your relatives here, that you have cut out
a tomb here for yourself, cutting a tomb on the height, and carving a
habitation for yourself in the rock? 17 The LORD is about to hurl you
away violently, my fellow. He will seize firm hold on you, 18 whirl
you round and round, and throw you like a ball into a wide land; there
you shall die, and there your splendid chariots shall lie, O you disgrace to your master's house! 19 I will thrust you from your office, and
you will be pulled down from your post.

20 On that day I will call my servant Eliakim son of Hilkiah,
21 and will clothe him with your robe and bind your sash on him. I
will commit your authority to his hand, and he shall be a father to
the inhabitants of Jerusalem and to the house of Judah. 22 I will place
on his shoulder the key of the house of David; he shall open, and no
one shall shut; he shall shut, and no one shall open. 23 I will fasten him
like a peg in a secure place, and he will become a throne of honor to
his ancestral house. 24 And they will hang on him the whole weight of
his ancestral house, the offspring and issue, every small vessel, from
the cups to all the flagons. 25 On that day, says the LORD of hosts, the
peg that was fastened in a secure place will give way; it will be cut
down and fall, and the load that was on it will perish, for the LORD
has spoken.

22:15-25 go to this steward, to Shebna…Eliakim: The judgment also includes Shebna, Hezekiah's chief steward, who will be removed from office for his arrogance and replaced by Eliakim (see 36:3; 37:2, where Eliakim does seem to have the higher rank). Eliakim was in charge of the royal household, which remained in the hands of David's descendants. Even though he was firmly in place like a tent peg stuck in the ground, he would also fall (22:22-24).

An Oracle concerning Tyre

23 The oracle concerning Tyre.

Wail, O ships of Tarshish,
for your fortress is destroyed.[a]
When they came in from Cyprus
they learned of it.
2 Be still, O inhabitants of the coast,
O merchants of Sidon,
your messengers crossed over the sea[b]
3 and were on the mighty waters;
your revenue was the grain of Shihor,
the harvest of the Nile;
you were the merchant of the nations.
4 Be ashamed, O Sidon, for the sea has spoken,
the fortress of the sea, saying:
"I have neither labored nor given birth,
I have neither reared young men
nor brought up young women."
5 When the report comes to Egypt,
they will be in anguish over the report about Tyre.
6 Cross over to Tarshish—
wail, O inhabitants of the coast!
7 Is this your exultant city
whose origin is from days of old,
whose feet carried her
to settle far away?
8 Who has planned this
against Tyre, the bestower of crowns,
whose merchants were princes,
whose traders were the honored of the earth?
9 The LORD of hosts has planned it—
to defile the pride of all glory,
to shame all the honored of the earth.
10 Cross over to your own land,
O ships of[c] Tarshish;
this is a harbor[d] no more.
11 He has stretched out his hand over the sea,
he has shaken the kingdoms;
the LORD has given command concerning Canaan
to destroy its fortresses.
12 He said:

23:1-18 oracle concerning Tyre: The lament of the "ships of Tarshish" (23:1) points to the importance of Tyre as a major Phoenician seaport and trading center in Lebanon. Tarshish was probably a trading colony in the western Mediterranean Sea (see Jonah 1:3). The colonies wail because the home port is to be destroyed. The oracle may describe one of the Assyrian attacks on Phoenicia, by Tilglath-pileser III in 734 B.C.E. or Sennacherib in 701 B.C.E.

23:2 Sidon: Another city on the Mediterranean coast of Lebanon. See Map 7, p. 2105.

[a] Cn Compare verse 14: Heb *for it is destroyed, without houses* [b] Q Ms: MT *crossing over the sea, they replenished you* [c] Cn Compare Gk: Heb *like the Nile, daughter* [d] Cn: Heb *restraint*

You will exult no longer,
O oppressed virgin daughter Sidon;
rise, cross over to Cyprus—
even there you will have no rest.

23:13 land of the Chaldeans!: This is another name for Babylonia and may refer to an attack about one hundred years later when the Babylonians were invading Lebanon and Canaan. This section (23:13-18) may have been added at the time of Babylonia's rise to power.

24:1—27:13 judgment of the earth: These chapters are frequently called the Isaiah Apocalypse because they refer to the kind of universal judgment often found in later apocalyptic literature (see the note below) They are generally regarded as being written later than other parts of the book of Isaiah, though they pick up themes common to the eighth-century prophet.

24:1—27:13 the Lord is about to lay waste the earth...on that day a great trumpet will be blown: Prophecy and apocalyptic literature are related but not the same. Biblical prophecy, although often sweeping in its vision, is generally linked to historical times and places, usually in the present or near future. It provides a theological interpretation of actual events. Apocalyptic literature, while always addressed to the needs of a historical audience, moves to cosmic themes and often refers to things seemingly impossible in history as we know it. For example, in these chapters of Isaiah, the total often refers to things seemingly impossible in history as we know it—for example, in these chapters of Isaiah, the total devastation of the earth (24:3-4), the involvement of sun and moon (24:23), the end of death (25:8; 26:19), and the destruction of heavenly being (24:21) and mythic monsters (27:1). Apocalyptic literature became even more recognizable in biblical books such as Daniel (chapters 7–12) and Revelation.

24:5 earth lies polluted: When people break God's laws which are designed to promote life and community, "the earth lies polluted under its inhabitants." The book of Isaiah frequently includes such "environmental-impact statements," noting both the negative effects on the earth of human wickedness (as here, for example) and the positive effects of God's gracious intervention (14:8; 35:1-7).

13 Look at the land of the Chaldeans! This is the people; it was
not Assyria. They destined Tyre for wild animals. They erected their
siege towers, they tore down her palaces, they made her a ruin.[a]
14 Wail, O ships of Tarshish,
for your fortress is destroyed.
15 From that day Tyre will be forgotten for seventy years, the lifetime
of one king. At the end of seventy years, it will happen to Tyre as in
the song about the prostitute:
16 Take a harp,
go about the city,
you forgotten prostitute!
Make sweet melody,
sing many songs,
that you may be remembered.
17 At the end of seventy years, the Lord will visit Tyre, and she will
return to her trade, and will prostitute herself with all the kingdoms
of the world on the face of the earth. 18 Her merchandise and her
wages will be dedicated to the Lord; her profits[b] will not be stored
or hoarded, but her merchandise will supply abundant food and fine
clothing for those who live in the presence of the Lord.

Impending Judgment on the Earth

24 Now the Lord is about to lay waste the earth and make it
desolate,
and he will twist its surface and scatter its inhabitants.
2 And it shall be, as with the people, so with the priest;
as with the slave, so with his master;
as with the maid, so with her mistress;
as with the buyer, so with the seller;
as with the lender, so with the borrower;
as with the creditor, so with the debtor.
3 The earth shall be utterly laid waste and utterly despoiled;
for the Lord has spoken this word.

4 The earth dries up and withers,
the world languishes and withers;
the heavens languish together with the earth.
5 The earth lies polluted

[a] Meaning of Heb uncertain [b] Heb *it*

under its inhabitants;
for they have transgressed laws,
violated the statutes,
broken the everlasting covenant.
6 Therefore a curse devours the earth,
and its inhabitants suffer for their guilt;
therefore the inhabitants of the earth dwindled,
and few people are left.
7 The wine dries up,
the vine languishes,
all the merry-hearted sigh.
8 The mirth of the timbrels is stilled,
the noise of the jubilant has ceased,
the mirth of the lyre is stilled.
9 No longer do they drink wine with singing;
strong drink is bitter to those who drink it.
10 The city of chaos is broken down,
every house is shut up so that no one can enter.
11 There is an outcry in the streets for lack of wine;
all joy has reached its eventide;
the gladness of the earth is banished.
12 Desolation is left in the city,
the gates are battered into ruins.
13 For thus it shall be on the earth
and among the nations,
as when an olive tree is beaten,
as at the gleaning when the grape harvest is ended.

14 They lift up their voices, they sing for joy;
they shout from the west over the majesty of the LORD.
15 Therefore in the east give glory to the LORD;
in the coastlands of the sea glorify the name of the LORD, the God of Israel.
16 From the ends of the earth we hear songs of praise,
of glory to the Righteous One.
But I say, I pine away,
I pine away. Woe is me!
For the treacherous deal treacherously,
the treacherous deal very treacherously.

17 Terror, and the pit, and the snare
are upon you, O inhabitant of the earth!
18 Whoever flees at the sound of the terror
shall fall into the pit;
and whoever climbs out of the pit

In your experience how do people pollute not only the earth's environment but also their various personal and community relationships? Where do you see God's gracious activity at work?

shall be caught in the snare.
For the windows of heaven are opened,
and the foundations of the earth tremble.
19 The earth is utterly broken,
the earth is torn asunder,
the earth is violently shaken.
20 The earth staggers like a drunkard,
it sways like a hut;
its transgression lies heavy upon it,
and it falls, and will not rise again.

21 On that day the LORD will punish
the host of heaven in heaven,
and on earth the kings of the earth.
22 They will be gathered together
like prisoners in a pit;
they will be shut up in a prison,
and after many days they will be punished.
23 Then the moon will be abashed,
and the sun ashamed;
for the LORD of hosts will reign
on Mount Zion and in Jerusalem,
and before his elders he will manifest his glory.

Praise for Deliverance from Oppression

25 O LORD, you are my God;
I will exalt you, I will praise your name;
for you have done wonderful things,
plans formed of old, faithful and sure.
2 For you have made the city a heap,
the fortified city a ruin;
the palace of aliens is a city no more,
it will never be rebuilt.
3 Therefore strong peoples will glorify you;
cities of ruthless nations will fear you.
4 For you have been a refuge to the poor,
a refuge to the needy in their distress,
a shelter from the rainstorm and a shade from the heat.
When the blast of the ruthless was like a winter rainstorm,
5 the noise of aliens like heat in a dry place,
you subdued the heat with the shade of clouds;
the song of the ruthless was stilled.

6 On this mountain the LORD of hosts will make for all peoples
a feast of rich food, a feast of well-aged wines,

25:1-5 my God; I will exalt you: This psalm praises God for overturning the powerful (25:2) and becoming "a refuge to the poor"—a strong and recurrent theme of the eighth-century prophets. Typically for Isaiah, this is all done according to God's "plans formed of old." For Isaiah, God works according to plan (the same Hebrew term is used in this way also in 5:19; 14:26; 19:17; 46:10-11; but see 30:1). The point is not that events are predetermined, since human actions in the book have real effect, both positively (6:8) and negatively (7:12). But neither does God act randomly or without purpose. As we learn here, God's plan involves putting a stop to the wicked and caring for the oppressed.

25:6-10 On this mountain the LORD...will make...a feast: "This mountain" is Mount Zion (see note at 2:2-4), where God will provide a banquet "for all peoples." The heavenly banquet derives from the communal meal celebrated as part of Israel's sacrificial worship (see Deut 14:22-29; 1 Sam 9:13; see also the banquet on Mount Sinai, Exod 24:9-11). This banquet becomes an important feature in the messianic kingdom (Matt 22:1-10; Luke 14:15-24). The banquet includes the finest food and wines, a fitting accompaniment to the amazing promise that God finally "will swallow up death forever" (see 1 Cor 15:54).

of rich food filled with marrow, of well-aged wines strained
clear.
7 And he will destroy on this mountain
the shroud that is cast over all peoples,
the sheet that is spread over all nations;
8 he will swallow up death forever.
Then the Lord GOD will wipe away the tears from all faces,
and the disgrace of his people he will take away from all the
earth,
for the LORD has spoken.
9 It will be said on that day,
Lo, this is our God; we have waited for him, so that he might
save us.
This is the LORD for whom we have waited;
let us be glad and rejoice in his salvation.
10 For the hand of the LORD will rest on this mountain.

The Moabites shall be trodden down in their place
as straw is trodden down in a dung-pit.
11 Though they spread out their hands in the midst of it,
as swimmers spread out their hands to swim,
their pride will be laid low despite the struggle[a] of their hands.
12 The high fortifications of his walls will be brought down,
laid low, cast to the ground, even to the dust.

Judah's Song of Victory

26 On that day this song will be sung in the land of Judah:
We have a strong city;
he sets up victory
like walls and bulwarks.
2 Open the gates,
so that the righteous nation that keeps faith
may enter in.
3 Those of steadfast mind you keep in peace—
in peace because they trust in you.
4 Trust in the LORD forever,
for in the LORD GOD[b]
you have an everlasting rock.
5 For he has brought low
the inhabitants of the height;
the lofty city he lays low.
He lays it low to the ground,
casts it to the dust.

[a] Meaning of Heb uncertain [b] Heb *in Yah, the LORD*

26:1-19 this song will be sung… Your dead shall live: The community sings a praise song of victory (26:1-6) and a song of lament (26:7-19). Both are similar to psalms in the Bible that were used in worship processions (see Pss 15; 24; 118) or in community laments (Pss 44; 74). This means that these verses may have been developed from a worship setting, or they may have been written to be sung or spoken in worship. "He has brought low the inhabitants of the height" (26:5) recites again the great transformation that occurs when God's judgment is shown "on that day" (26:1; see notes on 2:6-22; 2:12).

In the phrase "O Just One" (26:7) the term for "just" is *yashar* [ya-SHAR], usually translated "upright." Most often, faithful Israelites are termed "upright" (including especially Job; Job 1:1). But "upright" is also a significant characteristic of God (Deut 32:4; Pss 25:8; 92:15). Only here, apparently, is the term used as a direct title or name of God. With the announcement that "your dead shall live" (26:19), the prophet makes one of the rare Old Testament promises of resurrection. The common Old Testament view was that death brought the end of all meaningful life. The feeling was that if a person could no longer praise God, there was no life worthy of the name (38:18; Pss 6:5; 88:10-12; Job 10:21-22). Occasionally, however, the Old Testament writers recognized the possibility of God's breakthrough even into Sheol, the realm of the dead, to bring new life (Pss 16:10; 139:8; Ezek 37:1-14; and later, Dan 12:2-3). Even if the language is meant to be symbolic, these references indicate a growing notion that not even death can defeat God's loving care for Israel.

6 The foot tramples it,
the feet of the poor,
the steps of the needy.

7 The way of the righteous is level;
O Just One, you make smooth the path of the righteous.
8 In the path of your judgments,
O LORD, we wait for you;
your name and your renown
are the soul's desire.
9 My soul yearns for you in the night,
my spirit within me earnestly seeks you.
For when your judgments are in the earth,
the inhabitants of the world learn righteousness.
10 If favor is shown to the wicked,
they do not learn righteousness;
in the land of uprightness they deal perversely
and do not see the majesty of the LORD.
11 O LORD, your hand is lifted up,
but they do not see it.
Let them see your zeal for your people, and be ashamed.
Let the fire for your adversaries consume them.
12 O LORD, you will ordain peace for us,
for indeed, all that we have done, you have done for us.
13 O LORD our God,
other lords besides you have ruled over us,
but we acknowledge your name alone.
14 The dead do not live;
shades do not rise—
because you have punished and destroyed them,
and wiped out all memory of them.
15 But you have increased the nation, O LORD,
you have increased the nation; you are glorified;
you have enlarged all the borders of the land.

16 O LORD, in distress they sought you,
they poured out a prayer[a]
when your chastening was on them.
17 Like a woman with child,
who writhes and cries out in her pangs
when she is near her time,
so were we because of you, O LORD;
18 we were with child, we writhed,

[a] Meaning of Heb uncertain

but we gave birth only to wind.
We have won no victories on earth,
and no one is born to inhabit the world.
19 Your dead shall live, their corpses[a] shall rise.
O dwellers in the dust, awake and sing for joy!
For your dew is a radiant dew,
and the earth will give birth to those long dead.[b]

20 Come, my people, enter your chambers,
and shut your doors behind you;
hide yourselves for a little while
until the wrath is past.
21 For the LORD comes out from his place
to punish the inhabitants of the earth for their iniquity;
the earth will disclose the blood shed on it,
and will no longer cover its slain.

Israel's Redemption

27 On that day the LORD with his cruel and great and strong sword will punish Leviathan the fleeing serpent, Leviathan the twisting serpent, and he will kill the dragon that is in the sea.

2 On that day:
A pleasant vineyard, sing about it!
3 I, the LORD, am its keeper;
every moment I water it.
I guard it night and day
so that no one can harm it;
4 I have no wrath.
If it gives me thorns and briers,
I will march to battle against it.
I will burn it up.
5 Or else let it cling to me for protection,
let it make peace with me,
let it make peace with me.

6 In days to come[c] Jacob shall take root,
Israel shall blossom and put forth shoots,
and fill the whole world with fruit.

7 Has he struck them down as he struck down those who struck them?
Or have they been killed as their killers were killed?

[a]Cn Compare Syr Tg: Heb *my corpse* [b]Heb *to the shades* [c]Heb *Those to come*

27:2-6 A pleasant vineyard: A repeat of the song of the vineyard in Isaiah 5:1-7, now in a new key. The earlier song was a love song gone sour that became a word of harsh judgment. Here the Lord keeps and watches over the vineyard "so that no one can harm it" (27:3). Translation issues here are difficult, but the sense seems to be that even if thorns and briers appear (27:4), God will turn against them to root them out rather than turning against the vineyard as a whole.

Is the vineyard parable law or gospel? Lutheran theology speaks often of the need to distinguish properly between law and gospel, that is, between God's word of judgment and God's word of promise. The point is not that one is right and one is wrong, but rather that the church must not confuse one with the other. The law challenges, the gospel saves. People are not saved through the law, nor must they do good works to achieve the gospel's promise of salvation. The two versions of the song of the vineyard in Isaiah demonstrate, in Lutheran terms, both law (5:1-7) and gospel (27:2-6). God challenges the people to repentance in the first; God promises care and protection in the second. The task of the prophet originally and of the interpreter now is to address the right version to the right people at the right time—to afflict the comfortable and comfort the afflicted. *Isaiah 27:2-6*

8 By expulsion,[a] by exile you struggled against them;
with his fierce blast he removed them in the day of the east wind.
9 Therefore by this the guilt of Jacob will be expiated,
and this will be the full fruit of the removal of his sin:
when he makes all the stones of the altars
like chalkstones crushed to pieces,
no sacred poles[b] or incense altars will remain standing.
10 For the fortified city is solitary,
a habitation deserted and forsaken, like the wilderness;
the calves graze there,
there they lie down, and strip its branches.
11 When its boughs are dry, they are broken;
women come and make a fire of them.
For this is a people without understanding;
therefore he that made them will not have compassion on them,
he that formed them will show them no favor.

12 On that day the LORD will thresh from the channel of the Euphrates to the Wadi of Egypt, and you will be gathered one by one,
O people of Israel. 13 And on that day a great trumpet will be blown,
and those who were lost in the land of Assyria and those who were
driven out to the land of Egypt will come and worship the LORD on
the holy mountain at Jerusalem.

28:1-15 the drunkards of Ephraim ... scoffers who rule this people in Jerusalem: The rulers, priests, and prophets of both Israel (Ephraim) and Judah, who should lead and protect, are condemned for their corruption. The "drunkards of Ephraim ... bloated with rich food" (28:1) and whose "tables are covered with filthy vomit" (28:8) provide a striking contrast to God's banquet of rich food and fine wine "for all peoples" (25:6). The "garland ... of Ephraim" probably refers to the walls of Israel's capital city, Samaria, which eventually fell to the Assyrians. The repeated phrase "precept upon precept, line upon line, ... here a little" (28:10, 13) refers to the mocking way Judah's leaders responded to Isaiah's prophecies. In a modern sense, it was like they were saying his words sounded to them like "Blah, blah, blah." But their actions and attitude are sealing their fate (28:15).

Judgment on Corrupt Rulers, Priests, and Prophets

28 Ah, the proud garland of the drunkards of Ephraim,
and the fading flower of its glorious beauty,
which is on the head of those bloated with rich food, of those overcome with wine!
2 See, the Lord has one who is mighty and strong;
like a storm of hail, a destroying tempest,
like a storm of mighty, overflowing waters;
with his hand he will hurl them down to the earth.
3 Trampled under foot will be
the proud garland of the drunkards of Ephraim.
4 And the fading flower of its glorious beauty,
which is on the head of those bloated with rich food,
will be like a first-ripe fig before the summer;
whoever sees it, eats it up
as soon as it comes to hand.

[a] Meaning of Heb uncertain [b] Heb *Asherim*

5 In that day the LORD of hosts will be a garland of glory,
and a diadem of beauty, to the remnant of his people;
6 and a spirit of justice to the one who sits in judgment,
and strength to those who turn back the battle at the gate.

7 These also reel with wine
and stagger with strong drink;
the priest and the prophet reel with strong drink,
they are confused with wine,
they stagger with strong drink;
they err in vision,
they stumble in giving judgment.
8 All tables are covered with filthy vomit;
no place is clean.

9 "Whom will he teach knowledge,
and to whom will he explain the message?
Those who are weaned from milk,
those taken from the breast?
10 For it is precept upon precept, precept upon precept,
line upon line, line upon line,
here a little, there a little."[a]

11 Truly, with stammering lip
and with alien tongue
he will speak to this people,
12 to whom he has said,
"This is rest;
give rest to the weary;
and this is repose";
yet they would not hear.
13 Therefore the word of the LORD will be to them,
"Precept upon precept, precept upon precept,
line upon line, line upon line,
here a little, there a little;"[a]
in order that they may go, and fall backward,
and be broken, and snared, and taken.

14 Therefore hear the word of the LORD, you scoffers
who rule this people in Jerusalem.
15 Because you have said, "We have made a covenant with death,
and with Sheol we have an agreement;
when the overwhelming scourge passes through

---

[a] Meaning of Heb of this verse uncertain

it will not come to us;
for we have made lies our refuge,
and in falsehood we have taken shelter";
16 therefore thus says the Lord GOD,
See, I am laying in Zion a foundation stone,
a tested stone,
a precious cornerstone, a sure foundation:
"One who trusts will not panic."
17 And I will make justice the line,
and righteousness the plummet;
hail will sweep away the refuge of lies,
and waters will overwhelm the shelter.
18 Then your covenant with death will be annulled,
and your agreement with Sheol will not stand;
when the overwhelming scourge passes through
you will be beaten down by it.
19 As often as it passes through, it will take you;
for morning by morning it will pass through,
by day and by night;
and it will be sheer terror to understand the message.
20 For the bed is too short to stretch oneself on it,
and the covering too narrow to wrap oneself in it.
21 For the LORD will rise up as on Mount Perazim,
he will rage as in the valley of Gibeon
to do his deed—strange is his deed!—
and to work his work—alien is his work!
22 Now therefore do not scoff,
or your bonds will be made stronger;
for I have heard a decree of destruction
from the Lord GOD of hosts upon the whole land.

28:16-17 I am laying in Zion a foundation stone...justice the line: God or God's messenger will be like a foundation stone (a place of safety) or stumbling block. Justice and righteousness will be used to measure who is part of God's foundation. The line and plummet (plumb line) was used to check the straightness of a wall. New Testament writers referred to Jesus as this stone or stumbling block (Matt 21:42; Acts 4:11; 1 Pet 2:6-8).

23 Listen, and hear my voice;
Pay attention, and hear my speech.
24 Do those who plow for sowing plow continually?
Do they continually open and harrow their ground?
25 When they have leveled its surface,
do they not scatter dill, sow cummin,
and plant wheat in rows
and barley in its proper place,
and spelt as the border?
26 For they are well instructed;
their God teaches them.

27 Dill is not threshed with a threshing sledge,
nor is a cart wheel rolled over cummin;

28:23-29 those who plow for sowing: Like the farmer who carefully tills and plants, God, too, carefully measures the divine judgment. God brings only the amount of plowing and harvesting necessary to promote life without causing final destruction. This is why God is "wonderful in counsel, and excellent in wisdom" (28:29).

but dill is beaten out with a stick,
and cummin with a rod.
28 Grain is crushed for bread,
but one does not thresh it forever;
one drives the cart wheel and horses over it,
but does not pulverize it.
29 This also comes from the LORD of hosts;
he is wonderful in counsel,
and excellent in wisdom.

The Siege of Jerusalem

29 Ah, Ariel, Ariel,
the city where David encamped!
Add year to year;
let the festivals run their round.
2 Yet I will distress Ariel,
and there shall be moaning and lamentation,
and Jerusalem[a] shall be to me like an Ariel.[b]
3 And like David[c] I will encamp against you;
I will besiege you with towers
and raise siegeworks against you.
4 Then deep from the earth you shall speak,
from low in the dust your words shall come;
your voice shall come from the ground like the voice of a ghost,
and your speech shall whisper out of the dust.

5 But the multitude of your foes[d] shall be like small dust,
and the multitude of tyrants like flying chaff.
And in an instant, suddenly,
6 you will be visited by the LORD of hosts
with thunder and earthquake and great noise,
with whirlwind and tempest, and the flame of a devouring fire.
7 And the multitude of all the nations that fight against Ariel,
all that fight against her and her stronghold, and who distress her,
shall be like a dream, a vision of the night.
8 Just as when a hungry person dreams of eating
and wakes up still hungry,
or a thirsty person dreams of drinking
and wakes up faint, still thirsty,

29:1-16 the city where David encamped…You turned things upside down!: Ariel means "lion of God" or "altar hearth" (see Ezek 43:15). It is meant to be a poetic name for Jerusalem, which King David made the capital of united Israel. These verses probably describe the siege of Jerusalem by the Assyrian armies in 701 B.C.E. If Ariel is an altar hearth, it means Jerusalem will burn as a hearth does. For the prophet, the destruction of Jerusalem is not Assyria's work but God's, as punishment for Jerusalem's disobedience. Judah cannot recognize God's work because even the prophets are figuratively blind and drunk (29:9); no one remains who can read or understand God's word (see also 6:9-10). Jesus quotes 29:13 in Matthew 15:8-9 and Mark 7:6-7.

---

[a] Heb *she* [b] Probable meaning, *altar hearth*; compare Ezek 43.15 [c] Gk: Meaning of Heb uncertain
[d] Cn: Heb *strangers*

so shall the multitude of all the nations be
that fight against Mount Zion.

9 Stupefy yourselves and be in a stupor,
blind yourselves and be blind!
Be drunk, but not from wine;
stagger, but not from strong drink!
10 For the LORD has poured out upon you
a spirit of deep sleep;
he has closed your eyes, you prophets,
and covered your heads, you seers.

11 The vision of all this has become for you like the words of a
sealed document. If it is given to those who can read, with the command, "Read this," they say, "We cannot, for it is sealed." 12 And if it
is given to those who cannot read, saying, "Read this," they say, "We
cannot read."

13 The Lord said:
Because these people draw near with their mouths
and honor me with their lips,
while their hearts are far from me,
and their worship of me is a human commandment learned by
rote;
14 so I will again do
amazing things with this people,
shocking and amazing.
The wisdom of their wise shall perish,
and the discernment of the discerning shall be hidden.

15 Ha! You who hide a plan too deep for the LORD,
whose deeds are in the dark,
and who say, "Who sees us? Who knows us?"
16 You turn things upside down!
Shall the potter be regarded as the clay?
Shall the thing made say of its maker,
"He did not make me";
or the thing formed say of the one who formed it,
"He has no understanding"?

29:17-24 Shall not Lebanon... become a fruitful field... those who err in spirit will come to understanding: Despite Jerusalem's failures, God will turn things around, so that now the deaf shall hear the words of God (28:18) and the neediest people will again have justice (29:19). As always, God's judgment is only a momentary prelude to God's everlasting mercy (see also 54:7-8).

Hope for the Future

17 Shall not Lebanon in a very little while
become a fruitful field,
and the fruitful field be regarded as a forest?
18 On that day the deaf shall hear
the words of a scroll,

and out of their gloom and darkness
the eyes of the blind shall see.
19 The meek shall obtain fresh joy in the LORD,
and the neediest people shall exult in the Holy One of Israel.
20 For the tyrant shall be no more,
and the scoffer shall cease to be;
all those alert to do evil shall be cut off—
21 those who cause a person to lose a lawsuit,
who set a trap for the arbiter in the gate,
and without grounds deny justice to the one in the right.

22 Therefore thus says the LORD, who redeemed Abraham, concerning the house of Jacob:
No longer shall Jacob be ashamed,
no longer shall his face grow pale.
23 For when he sees his children,
the work of my hands, in his midst,
they will sanctify my name;
they will sanctify the Holy One of Jacob,
and will stand in awe of the God of Israel.
24 And those who err in spirit will come to understanding,
and those who grumble will accept instruction.

The Futility of Reliance on Egypt

30 Oh, rebellious children, says the LORD,
who carry out a plan, but not mine;
who make an alliance, but against my will,
adding sin to sin;
2 who set out to go down to Egypt
without asking for my counsel,
to take refuge in the protection of Pharaoh,
and to seek shelter in the shadow of Egypt;
3 Therefore the protection of Pharaoh shall become your shame,
and the shelter in the shadow of Egypt your humiliation.
4 For though his officials are at Zoan
and his envoys reach Hanes,
5 everyone comes to shame
through a people that cannot profit them,
that brings neither help nor profit,
but shame and disgrace.

6 An oracle concerning the animals of the Negeb.
Through a land of trouble and distress,
of lioness and roaring[a] lion,

30:1-7 Oh, rebellious children... who set out to go down to Egypt: In the years prior to 701 B.C.E., Judah had sought help from Egypt against the threat from Assyria—trying to pit one superpower against another. Such plans, says God, are "not mine" (30:1). See also the note on 25:1-5. The alliance with Egypt is seen as having a lack of faith in God. Egypt is described as being powerless to help Judah. It is like the motionless sea monster Rahab (30:7), the mythological creature that God killed in the creation of the world (see Isa 51:9-10; Job 26:12-13; Ps 89:9-10).

[a] Cn: Heb *from them*

of viper and flying serpent,
they carry their riches on the backs of donkeys,
and their treasures on the humps of camels,
to a people that cannot profit them.
7 For Egypt's help is worthless and empty,
therefore I have called her,
"Rahab who sits still."[a]

A Rebellious People

30:8-17 write it before them on a tablet…as a witness forever: God commands that the prophet's words be gathered "in a book" to serve "as a witness forever" against God's faithless people. Now they refuse to hear the truth, demanding only "smooth things" (30:10), even if these are not true. But future generations will be able to read the prophet's words and know the reason for the present destruction. Again, Isaiah repeats the familiar theme that there is no security in arms and horses (30:16), but only in "returning and rest" (30:15), allowing God to be God.

What kinds of things might be the "smooth things" we would prefer to hear, rather than God's word?

8 Go now, write it before them on a tablet,
and inscribe it in a book,
so that it may be for the time to come
as a witness forever.
9 For they are a rebellious people,
faithless children,
children who will not hear
the instruction of the LORD;
10 who say to the seers, "Do not see";
and to the prophets, "Do not prophesy to us what is right;
speak to us smooth things,
prophesy illusions,
11 leave the way, turn aside from the path,
let us hear no more about the Holy One of Israel."
12 Therefore thus says the Holy One of Israel:
Because you reject this word,
and put your trust in oppression and deceit,
and rely on them;
13 therefore this iniquity shall become for you
like a break in a high wall, bulging out, and about to collapse,
whose crash comes suddenly, in an instant;
14 its breaking is like that of a potter's vessel
that is smashed so ruthlessly
that among its fragments not a sherd is found
for taking fire from the hearth,
or dipping water out of the cistern.

15 For thus said the Lord GOD, the Holy One of Israel:
In returning and rest you shall be saved;
in quietness and in trust shall be your strength.
But you refused 16 and said,
"No! We will flee upon horses"—
therefore you shall flee!
and, "We will ride upon swift steeds"—

[a] Meaning of Heb uncertain

therefore your pursuers shall be swift!
17 A thousand shall flee at the threat of one,
at the threat of five you shall flee,
until you are left
like a flagstaff on the top of a mountain,
like a signal on a hill.

God's Promise to Zion

18 Therefore the LORD waits to be gracious to you;
therefore he will rise up to show mercy to you.
For the LORD is a God of justice;
blessed are all those who wait for him.

19 Truly, O people in Zion, inhabitants of Jerusalem, you shall
weep no more. He will surely be gracious to you at the sound of your
cry; when he hears it, he will answer you. 20 Though the Lord may give
you the bread of adversity and the water of affliction, yet your Teacher
will not hide himself any more, but your eyes shall see your Teacher.
21 And when you turn to the right or when you turn to the left, your
ears shall hear a word behind you, saying, "This is the way; walk in it."
22 Then you will defile your silver-covered idols and your gold-plated
images. You will scatter them like filthy rags; you will say to them,
"Away with you!"

23 He will give rain for the seed with which you sow the ground,
and grain, the produce of the ground, which will be rich and plenteous. On that day your cattle will graze in broad pastures; 24 and the
oxen and donkeys that till the ground will eat silage, which has been
winnowed with shovel and fork. 25 On every lofty mountain and
every high hill there will be brooks running with water—on a day of
the great slaughter, when the towers fall. 26 Moreover the light of the
moon will be like the light of the sun, and the light of the sun will
be sevenfold, like the light of seven days, on the day when the LORD
binds up the injuries of his people, and heals the wounds inflicted by
his blow.

30:18-26 a God of justice: Despite the disobedience of the people, "the LORD waits to be gracious" and will restore Jerusalem (Zion) with abundance. As in the time of the exodus, when God heard the people's cry, God will answer (30:19; see also Exod 2:23-25; 3:7-9). The people will throw away their foreign idols like dirty rags (30:22), the land will grow rich crops, and God will heal the wounds that have come from earlier judgments against them (30:26).

Judgment on Assyria

27 See, the name of the LORD comes from far away,
burning with his anger, and in thick rising smoke;[a]
his lips are full of indignation,
and his tongue is like a devouring fire;
28 his breath is like an overflowing stream
that reaches up to the neck—
to sift the nations with the sieve of destruction,
and to place on the jaws of the peoples a bridle that leads
them astray.

[a] Meaning of Heb uncertain

29 You shall have a song as in the night when a holy festival is kept; and gladness of heart, as when one sets out to the sound of the flute to go to the mountain of the LORD, to the Rock of Israel. [30] And the LORD will cause his majestic voice to be heard and the descending blow of his arm to be seen, in furious anger and a flame of devouring fire, with a cloudburst and tempest and hailstones. [31] The Assyrian will be terror-stricken at the voice of the LORD, when he strikes with his rod. [32] And every stroke of the staff of punishment that the LORD lays upon him will be to the sound of timbrels and lyres; battling with brandished arm he will fight with him. [33] For his burning place[a] has long been prepared; truly it is made ready for the king,[b] its pyre made deep and wide, with fire and wood in abundance; the breath of the LORD, like a stream of sulfur, kindles it.

31:1-3 The Egyptians are human, and not God: The prophet repeats the theme that reliance on military power will not save them (8:11-22; 30:1-5).

In several places, Isaiah condemns God's people for relying on military strength rather than consulting the Lord (31:1-3; 30:1-5; 8:11-22). Do you think this applies to Christians today? Why or why not?

Alliance with Egypt Is Futile

31 Alas for those who go down to Egypt for help
and who rely on horses,
who trust in chariots because they are many
and in horsemen because they are very strong,
but do not look to the Holy One of Israel
or consult the LORD!
2 Yet he too is wise and brings disaster;
he does not call back his words,
but will rise against the house of the evildoers,
and against the helpers of those who work iniquity.
3 The Egyptians are human, and not God;
their horses are flesh, and not spirit.
When the LORD stretches out his hand,
the helper will stumble, and the one helped will fall,
and they will all perish together.

4 For thus the LORD said to me,
As a lion or a young lion growls over its prey,
and—when a band of shepherds is called out against it—
is not terrified by their shouting
or daunted at their noise,
so the LORD of hosts will come down
to fight upon Mount Zion and upon its hill.
5 Like birds hovering overhead, so the LORD of hosts
will protect Jerusalem;
he will protect and deliver it,
he will spare and rescue it.

---

[a] Or *Topheth* [b] Or *Molech*

6 Turn back to him whom you[a] have deeply betrayed, O people
of Israel. 7 For on that day all of you shall throw away your idols of silver and idols of gold, which your hands have sinfully made for you.
8 "Then the Assyrian shall fall by a sword, not of mortals;
and a sword, not of humans, shall devour him;
he shall flee from the sword,
and his young men shall be put to forced labor.
9 His rock shall pass away in terror,
and his officers desert the standard in panic,"
says the LORD, whose fire is in Zion,
and whose furnace is in Jerusalem.

Government with Justice Predicted

32 See, a king will reign in righteousness,
and princes will rule with justice.
2 Each will be like a hiding place from the wind,
a covert from the tempest,
like streams of water in a dry place,
like the shade of a great rock in a weary land.
3 Then the eyes of those who have sight will not be closed,
and the ears of those who have hearing will listen.
4 The minds of the rash will have good judgment,
and the tongues of stammerers will speak readily and
distinctly.
5 A fool will no longer be called noble,
nor a villain said to be honorable.
6 For fools speak folly,
and their minds plot iniquity:
to practice ungodliness,
to utter error concerning the LORD,
to leave the craving of the hungry unsatisfied,
and to deprive the thirsty of drink.
7 The villainies of villains are evil;
they devise wicked devices
to ruin the poor with lying words,
even when the plea of the needy is right.
8 But those who are noble plan noble things,
and by noble things they stand.

Complacent Women Warned of Disaster

9 Rise up, you women who are at ease, hear my voice;
you complacent daughters, listen to my speech.

[a] Heb *they*

32:1-8 a king will reign in righteousness…justice: Again the book changes from a message of judgment to one of hope. The poem in 32:1-8 looks for the coming messianic king who "will reign in righteousness." Anticipating the promises of chapters 35 and 40–55, the prophet announces a reversal of the judgment of 6:9-10. In the coming kingdom eyes and ears will be open, minds and tongues will be set free. People will treat one another fairly and stand for noble things (32:7-8).

32:9-20 Tremble…you complacent ones: The time of renewal is not yet. Wealthy and complacent women (and men) will be overthrown and "the fruit harvest will not come" (32:10)—that is, not "until a spirit from on high is poured out on us" (32:15; see also11:2; 42:1; 61:1). Then, in God's new kingdom, everything is transformed, people and nature alike. (Here, the forest and the city stand for places of danger.)

10 In little more than a year
you will shudder, you complacent ones;
for the vintage will fail,
the fruit harvest will not come.
11 Tremble, you women who are at ease,
shudder, you complacent ones;
strip, and make yourselves bare,
and put sackcloth on your loins.
12 Beat your breasts for the pleasant fields,
for the fruitful vine,
13 for the soil of my people
growing up in thorns and briers;
yes, for all the joyous houses
in the jubilant city.
14 For the palace will be forsaken,
the populous city deserted;
the hill and the watchtower
will become dens forever,
the joy of wild asses,
a pasture for flocks;
15 until a spirit from on high is poured out on us,
and the wilderness becomes a fruitful field,
and the fruitful field is deemed a forest.

The Peace of God's Reign

16 Then justice will dwell in the wilderness,
and righteousness abide in the fruitful field.
17 The effect of righteousness will be peace,
and the result of righteousness, quietness and trust forever.
18 My people will abide in a peaceful habitation,
in secure dwellings, and in quiet resting places.
19 The forest will disappear completely,[a]
and the city will be utterly laid low.
20 Happy will you be who sow beside every stream,
who let the ox and the donkey range freely.

A Prophecy of Deliverance from Foes

33 Ah, you destroyer,
who yourself have not been destroyed;
you treacherous one,
with whom no one has dealt treacherously!
When you have ceased to destroy,
you will be destroyed;

[a] Cn: Heb *And it will hail when the forest comes down*

33:1-16 Ah, you destroyer…you will be destroyed: The "destroyer" is causing great harm to God's people. The destroyer (Babylon in 21:9) is not named here. In First Isaiah's time, it would have been Assyria; in the exile period, it would have been Babylon (either could be the original setting of this passage). In either case, God's presence is said to be in Zion (Jerusalem). The unnamed destroyer can be heard to be any enemy attacking the people of God, including "sinners in Zion" itself. Against any such enemy, God responds with a promise to arise and protect God's own (33:10-12).

and when you have stopped dealing treacherously,
you will be dealt with treacherously.

2 O LORD, be gracious to us; we wait for you.
Be our arm every morning,
our salvation in the time of trouble.
3 At the sound of tumult, peoples fled;
before your majesty, nations scattered.
4 Spoil was gathered as the caterpillar gathers;
as locusts leap, they leaped[a] upon it.
5 The LORD is exalted, he dwells on high;
he filled Zion with justice and righteousness;
6 he will be the stability of your times,
abundance of salvation, wisdom, and knowledge;
the fear of the LORD is Zion's treasure.[b]

7 Listen! the valiant[a] cry in the streets;
the envoys of peace weep bitterly.
8 The highways are deserted,
travelers have quit the road.
The treaty is broken,
its oaths[c] are despised,
its obligation[d] is disregarded.
9 The land mourns and languishes;
Lebanon is confounded and withers away;
Sharon is like a desert;
and Bashan and Carmel shake off their leaves.

10 "Now I will arise," says the LORD,
"now I will lift myself up;
now I will be exalted.
11 You conceive chaff, you bring forth stubble;
your breath is a fire that will consume you.
12 And the peoples will be as if burned to lime,
like thorns cut down, that are burned in the fire."

13 Hear, you who are far away, what I have done;
and you who are near, acknowledge my might.
14 The sinners in Zion are afraid;
trembling has seized the godless:
"Who among us can live with the devouring fire?
Who among us can live with everlasting flames?"

---

[a] Meaning of Heb uncertain [b] Heb *his treasure;* meaning of Heb uncertain [c] Q Ms: MT *cities*
[d] Or *everyone*

15 Those who walk righteously and speak uprightly,
who despise the gain of oppression,
who wave away a bribe instead of accepting it,
who stop their ears from hearing of bloodshed
and shut their eyes from looking on evil,
16 they will live on the heights;
their refuge will be the fortresses of rocks;
their food will be supplied, their water assured.

The Land of the Majestic King

33:17-24 Your eyes will see the king in his beauty...the LORD is our king: When God rules as king, the former terror will seem like just a bad dream (33:18-20).

How do you hear the promise of 33:17-22? How do we properly hear this word addressed to us?

17 Your eyes will see the king in his beauty;
they will behold a land that stretches far away.
18 Your mind will muse on the terror:
"Where is the one who counted?
Where is the one who weighed the tribute?
Where is the one who counted the towers?"
19 No longer will you see the insolent people,
the people of an obscure speech that you cannot comprehend,
stammering in a language that you cannot understand.
20 Look on Zion, the city of our appointed festivals!
Your eyes will see Jerusalem,
a quiet habitation, an immovable tent,
whose stakes will never be pulled up,
and none of whose ropes will be broken.
21 But there the LORD in majesty will be for us
a place of broad rivers and streams,
where no galley with oars can go,
nor stately ship can pass.
22 For the LORD is our judge, the LORD is our ruler,
the LORD is our king; he will save us.

23 Your rigging hangs loose;
it cannot hold the mast firm in its place,
or keep the sail spread out.

Then prey and spoil in abundance will be divided;
even the lame will fall to plundering.
24 And no inhabitant will say, "I am sick";
the people who live there will be forgiven their iniquity.

34:1—35:10 Draw near, O nations, to hear: These two chapters are seen by most scholars as stemming from the exile or post-exile periods (see the introduction to Isaiah). They are placed here to begin a transition to the second part of the book of Isaiah. God's coming transformation will involve both total judgment of the wicked (chapter 34) and final salvation for the redeemed (chapter 35).

34:1-17 the LORD is enraged against all the nations: In this fierce description of God's judgment of the nations (especially Edom), God is pictured as the divine warrior swinging a sword against the enemy (34:5-7; see also 59:15b-19; 63:1-6; Exod 15:3). As in other prophetic books (see Jer 46:10 and Ezek 39:17-20), this passage describes God's destruction of the enemy as a ritual sacrifice. Vengeance against the enemy turns out to be vindication for God's people, who are set free from their bondage to a wicked regime (34:8).

Judgment on the Nations

34 Draw near, O nations, to hear;
O peoples, give heed!
Let the earth hear, and all that fills it;
the world, and all that comes from it.

2 For the LORD is enraged against all the nations,
and furious against all their hordes;
he has doomed them, has given them over for slaughter.
3 Their slain shall be cast out,
and the stench of their corpses shall rise;
the mountains shall flow with their blood.
4 All the host of heaven shall rot away,
and the skies roll up like a scroll.
All their host shall wither
like a leaf withering on a vine,
or fruit withering on a fig tree.

5 When my sword has drunk its fill in the heavens,
lo, it will descend upon Edom,
upon the people I have doomed to judgment.
6 The LORD has a sword; it is sated with blood,
it is gorged with fat,
with the blood of lambs and goats,
with the fat of the kidneys of rams.
For the LORD has a sacrifice in Bozrah,
a great slaughter in the land of Edom.
7 Wild oxen shall fall with them,
and young steers with the mighty bulls.
Their land shall be soaked with blood,
and their soil made rich with fat.

8 For the LORD has a day of vengeance,
a year of vindication by Zion's cause.[a]
9 And the streams of Edom[b] shall be turned into pitch,
and her soil into sulfur;
her land shall become burning pitch.
10 Night and day it shall not be quenched;
its smoke shall go up forever.
From generation to generation it shall lie waste;
no one shall pass through it forever and ever.
11 But the hawk[c] and the hedgehog[c] shall possess it;
the owl[c] and the raven shall live in it.
He shall stretch the line of confusion over it,
and the plummet of chaos over[d] its nobles.
12 They shall name it No Kingdom There,
and all its princes shall be nothing.
13 Thorns shall grow over its strongholds,
nettles and thistles in its fortresses.

34:12, 16 No Kingdom There... book of the LORD: "No Kingdom" is a name to make fun of the defeated Edom. The "book of the LORD" may refer to a scroll that contained a prophecy against Babylon (see 13:19-22).

[a] Or *of recompense by Zion's defender* [b] Heb *her streams* [c] Identification uncertain [d] Heb lacks *over*

It shall be the haunt of jackals,
an abode for ostriches.
14 Wildcats shall meet with hyenas,
goat-demons shall call to each other;
there too Lilith shall repose,
and find a place to rest.
15 There shall the owl nest
and lay and hatch and brood in its shadow;
there too the buzzards shall gather,
each one with its mate.
16 Seek and read from the book of the LORD:
Not one of these shall be missing;
none shall be without its mate.
For the mouth of the LORD has commanded,
and his spirit has gathered them.
17 He has cast the lot for them,
his hand has portioned it out to them with the line;
they shall possess it forever,
from generation to generation they shall live in it.

The Return of the Redeemed to Zion

35:1-10 The wilderness and the dry land shall be glad…sorrow and sighing shall flee away: This beautiful oracle pictures a joyful return of God's people to Zion (Jerusalem). It is similar to God's promises in chapters 40–55 (especially chapter 40) and deliberately looks forward to them. As in chapter 40, the wilderness is restored and the glory of the Lord is revealed (35:1-2; 40:3-5). God comes with both vengeance and comfort (35:4; 40:1, 10-11), and a highway appears in the desert (35:8-10; 40:3-5). Lebanon, Carmel, and Sharon (35:2) are fertile areas that even the desert will be made to resemble. Now eyes are opened and ears unstopped; the judgment of 6:9-10 is reversed. The highway is for the redeemed (35:8), whereas in chapter 40 it is for God (40:3). Throughout Isaiah, the highway theme is used in a variety of ways as a symbol of divine deliverance (11:16; 42:16; 45:13; 49:11; 51:10; 57:14; 62:10; see also Jer 31:7-9). All of these probably relate back to God's providing a way through the sea and through the desert at the exodus (Exod 13:17-18, 21; Deut 1:30-33).

35 The wilderness and the dry land shall be glad,
the desert shall rejoice and blossom;
like the crocus 2 it shall blossom abundantly,
and rejoice with joy and singing.
The glory of Lebanon shall be given to it,
the majesty of Carmel and Sharon.
They shall see the glory of the LORD,
the majesty of our God.

3 Strengthen the weak hands,
and make firm the feeble knees.
4 Say to those who are of a fearful heart,
"Be strong, do not fear!
Here is your God.
He will come with vengeance,
with terrible recompense.
He will come and save you."

5 Then the eyes of the blind shall be opened,
and the ears of the deaf unstopped;
6 then the lame shall leap like a deer,
and the tongue of the speechless sing for joy.
For waters shall break forth in the wilderness,
and streams in the desert;

7 the burning sand shall become a pool,
and the thirsty ground springs of water;
the haunt of jackals shall become a swamp,[a]
the grass shall become reeds and rushes.

8 A highway shall be there,
and it shall be called the Holy Way;
the unclean shall not travel on it,[b]
but it shall be for God's people;[c]
no traveler, not even fools, shall go astray.
9 No lion shall be there,
nor shall any ravenous beast come up on it;
they shall not be found there,
but the redeemed shall walk there.
10 And the ransomed of the LORD shall return,
and come to Zion with singing;
everlasting joy shall be upon their heads;
they shall obtain joy and gladness,
and sorrow and sighing shall flee away.

Sennacherib Threatens Jerusalem

36 In the fourteenth year of King Hezekiah, King Sennacherib of Assyria came up against all the fortified cities of
Judah and captured them. 2 The king of Assyria sent the Rabshakeh
from Lachish to King Hezekiah at Jerusalem, with a great army. He
stood by the conduit of the upper pool on the highway to the Fuller's
Field. 3 And there came out to him Eliakim son of Hilkiah, who was in
charge of the palace, and Shebna the secretary, and Joah son of Asaph,
the recorder.
4 The Rabshakeh said to them, "Say to Hezekiah: Thus says the
great king, the king of Assyria: On what do you base this confidence
of yours? 5 Do you think that mere words are strategy and power for
war? On whom do you now rely, that you have rebelled against me?
6 See, you are relying on Egypt, that broken reed of a staff, which will
pierce the hand of anyone who leans on it. Such is Pharaoh king of
Egypt to all who rely on him. 7 But if you say to me, 'We rely on the
LORD our God,' is it not he whose high places and altars Hezekiah
has removed, saying to Judah and to Jerusalem, 'You shall worship
before this altar'? 8 Come now, make a wager with my master the king
of Assyria: I will give you two thousand horses, if you are able on your
part to set riders on them. 9 How then can you repulse a single captain
among the least of my master's servants, when you rely on Egypt for
chariots and for horsemen? 10 Moreover, is it without the LORD that I

---

[a] Cn: Heb *in the haunt of jackals is her resting place* [b] Or *pass it by* [c] Cn: Heb *for them*

36:1—39:8 In the fourteenth year of King Hezekiah: The material in these chapters parallels very closely 2 Kings 18:13—20:19. See the notes in that section of 2 Kings for additional background. Isaiah 36—39 are included here for at least two reasons: They provide the historical background of First Isaiah, especially the reign of Hezekiah and the Assyrian invasion under King Sennacherib; and they perform a pivotal function in the structure of the book, looking backward to the time of Isaiah of Jerusalem (Isa 36–38) and forward to the time of Isaiah of the exile (Isa 39).

36:1-30 King Sennacherib of Assyria…sent the Rabshakeh…to King Hezekiah: When the Rabshakeh (the chief steward of the Assyrian king) brings the king's message to Judah, he functions as the king's messenger or ambassador. He delivers a word not his own in the language of the hearers (36:13). "Hear the words of the great king, the king of Assyria! Thus says the king…"—which sounds exactly like the formula used by the prophets to speak the word of God: "Hear the word of the LORD: thus says the LORD…" (2 Kgs 7:1; Ezek 20:47; Jer 2:4-5). Like the Assyrian ambassador, the prophets are messengers who speak the word of another (God), "translating" it into language the people can understand.

Sennacherib's message is tempting. If the people of Judah make peace with Assyria, Sennacherib promises to take care of them. He tells them to ignore their own King Hezekiah, who is asking the people to trust in God.

have come up against this land to destroy it? The LORD said to me, Go
up against this land, and destroy it."

11 Then Eliakim, Shebna, and Joah said to the Rabshakeh, "Please
speak to your servants in Aramaic, for we understand it; do not speak
to us in the language of Judah within the hearing of the people who
are on the wall." 12 But the Rabshakeh said, "Has my master sent me to
speak these words to your master and to you, and not to the people
sitting on the wall, who are doomed with you to eat their own dung
and drink their own urine?"

13 Then the Rabshakeh stood and called out in a loud voice in
the language of Judah, "Hear the words of the great king, the king of
Assyria! 14 Thus says the king: 'Do not let Hezekiah deceive you, for
he will not be able to deliver you. 15 Do not let Hezekiah make you
rely on the LORD by saying, The LORD will surely deliver us; this city
will not be given into the hand of the king of Assyria.' 16 Do not listen
to Hezekiah; for thus says the king of Assyria: 'Make your peace with
me and come out to me; then every one of you will eat from your
own vine and your own fig tree and drink water from your own cistern, 17 until I come and take you away to a land like your own land,
a land of grain and wine, a land of bread and vineyards. 18 Do not let
Hezekiah mislead you by saying, The LORD will save us. Has any of
the gods of the nations saved their land out of the hand of the king of
Assyria? 19 Where are the gods of Hamath and Arpad? Where are the
gods of Sepharvaim? Have they delivered Samaria out of my hand?
20 Who among all the gods of these countries have saved their countries out of my hand, that the LORD should save Jerusalem out of my
hand?' "

21 But they were silent and answered him not a word, for the
king's command was, "Do not answer him." 22 Then Eliakim son of
Hilkiah, who was in charge of the palace, and Shebna the secretary,
and Joah son of Asaph, the recorder, came to Hezekiah with their
clothes torn, and told him the words of the Rabshakeh.

Hezekiah Consults Isaiah

37:1-2 Hezekiah . . . tore his clothes, covered himself with sackcloth: The king and other officials do these things to show sorrow and distress.

37 When King Hezekiah heard it, he tore his clothes, covered himself with sackcloth, and went into the house of the
LORD. 2 And he sent Eliakim, who was in charge of the palace, and
Shebna the secretary, and the senior priests, covered with sackcloth,
to the prophet Isaiah son of Amoz. 3 They said to him, "Thus says Hezekiah, This day is a day of distress, of rebuke, and of disgrace; children
have come to the birth, and there is no strength to bring them forth.
4 It may be that the LORD your God heard the words of the Rabshakeh,
whom his master the king of Assyria has sent to mock the living God,
and will rebuke the words that the LORD your God has heard; therefore lift up your prayer for the remnant that is left."

5 When the servants of King Hezekiah came to Isaiah, [6]Isaiah said to them, "Say to your master, 'Thus says the LORD: Do not be afraid because of the words that you have heard, with which the servants of the king of Assyria have reviled me. [7]I myself will put a spirit in him, so that he shall hear a rumor, and return to his own land; I will cause him to fall by the sword in his own land.' "

8 The Rabshakeh returned, and found the king of Assyria fighting against Libnah; for he had heard that the king had left Lachish. [9]Now the king[a] heard concerning King Tirhakah of Ethiopia,[b] "He has set out to fight against you." When he heard it, he sent messengers to Hezekiah, saying, [10]"Thus shall you speak to King Hezekiah of Judah: Do not let your God on whom you rely deceive you by promising that Jerusalem will not be given into the hand of the king of Assyria. [11]See, you have heard what the kings of Assyria have done to all lands, destroying them utterly. Shall you be delivered? [12]Have the gods of the nations delivered them, the nations that my predecessors destroyed, Gozan, Haran, Rezeph, and the people of Eden who were in Telassar? [13]Where is the king of Hamath, the king of Arpad, the king of the city of Sepharvaim, the king of Hena, or the king of Ivvah?"

Hezekiah's Prayer

14 Hezekiah received the letter from the hand of the messengers and read it; then Hezekiah went up to the house of the LORD and spread it before the LORD. [15]And Hezekiah prayed to the LORD, saying: [16]"O LORD of hosts, God of Israel, who are enthroned above the cherubim, you are God, you alone, of all the kingdoms of the earth; you have made heaven and earth. [17]Incline your ear, O LORD, and hear; open your eyes, O LORD, and see; hear all the words of Sennacherib, which he has sent to mock the living God. [18]Truly, O LORD, the kings of Assyria have laid waste all the nations and their lands, [19]and have hurled their gods into the fire, though they were no gods, but the work of human hands—wood and stone—and so they were destroyed. [20]So now, O LORD our God, save us from his hand, so that all the kingdoms of the earth may know that you alone are the LORD."

21 Then Isaiah son of Amoz sent to Hezekiah, saying: "Thus says the LORD, the God of Israel: Because you have prayed to me concerning King Sennacherib of Assyria, [22]this is the word that the LORD has spoken concerning him:

She despises you, she scorns you—
  virgin daughter Zion;
she tosses her head—behind your back,
  daughter Jerusalem.

---

[a] Heb *he* [b] Or *Nubia*; Heb *Cush*

23 “Whom have you mocked and reviled?
Against whom have you raised your voice
and haughtily lifted your eyes?
Against the Holy One of Israel!
24 By your servants you have mocked the Lord,
and you have said, ‘With my many chariots
I have gone up the heights of the mountains,
to the far recesses of Lebanon;
I felled its tallest cedars,
its choicest cypresses;
I came to its remotest height,
its densest forest.
25 I dug wells
and drank waters,
I dried up with the sole of my foot
all the streams of Egypt.’

26 “Have you not heard
that I determined it long ago?
I planned from days of old
what now I bring to pass,
that you should make fortified cities
crash into heaps of ruins,
27 while their inhabitants, shorn of strength,
are dismayed and confounded;
they have become like plants of the field
and like tender grass,
like grass on the housetops,
blighted[a] before it is grown.

28 “I know your rising up[b] and your sitting down,
your going out and coming in,
and your raging against me.
29 Because you have raged against me
and your arrogance has come to my ears,
I will put my hook in your nose
and my bit in your mouth;
I will turn you back on the way
by which you came.

30 “And this shall be the sign for you: This year eat what grows
of itself, and in the second year what springs from that; then in the
third year sow, reap, plant vineyards, and eat their fruit. 31 The surviv-

[a] With 2 Kings 19.26: Heb *field* [b] Q Ms Gk: MT lacks *your rising up*

ing remnant of the house of Judah shall again take root downward,
and bear fruit upward; [32]for from Jerusalem a remnant shall go out,
and from Mount Zion a band of survivors. The zeal of the LORD of
hosts will do this.

33 "Therefore thus says the LORD concerning the king of Assyria:
He shall not come into this city, shoot an arrow there, come before it
with a shield, or cast up a siege ramp against it. [34]By the way that he
came, by the same he shall return; he shall not come into this city, says
the LORD. [35]For I will defend this city to save it, for my own sake and
for the sake of my servant David."

Sennacherib's Defeat and Death

36 Then the angel of the LORD set out and struck down one hundred eighty-five thousand in the camp of the Assyrians; when morning dawned, they were all dead bodies. [37]Then King Sennacherib of
Assyria left, went home, and lived at Nineveh. [38]As he was worshiping
in the house of his god Nisroch, his sons Adrammelech and Sharezer
killed him with the sword, and they escaped into the land of Ararat.
His son Esar-haddon succeeded him.

Hezekiah's Illness

38 In those days Hezekiah became sick and was at the point of
death. The prophet Isaiah son of Amoz came to him, and
said to him, "Thus says the LORD: Set your house in order, for you
shall die; you shall not recover." [2]Then Hezekiah turned his face to
the wall, and prayed to the LORD: [3]"Remember now, O LORD, I implore you, how I have walked before you in faithfulness with a whole
heart, and have done what is good in your sight." And Hezekiah wept
bitterly.

4 Then the word of the LORD came to Isaiah: [5]"Go and say to
Hezekiah, Thus says the LORD, the God of your ancestor David: I
have heard your prayer, I have seen your tears; I will add fifteen years
to your life. [6]I will deliver you and this city out of the hand of the king
of Assyria, and defend this city.

7 "This is the sign to you from the LORD, that the LORD will do
this thing that he has promised: [8]See, I will make the shadow cast by
the declining sun on the dial of Ahaz turn back ten steps." So the sun
turned back on the dial the ten steps by which it had declined.[a]

9 A writing of King Hezekiah of Judah, after he had been sick and
had recovered from his sickness:

10 I said: In the noontide of my days
I must depart;

[a] Meaning of Heb uncertain

38:7-8 the sign...sun turned back on the dial: An unexplainable sign punctuates God's promise of protection.

38:9-20 A writing of King Hezekiah of Judah: This long prayer is not included in the parallel section of 2 Kings 20. It is a typical song of lament and thanksgiving, looking back at the time of illness (38:10-16) and giving thanks for healing (38:17-20). In hindsight, Hezekiah realizes his suffering "was for my welfare" (38:17). He also realizes he has been spared from death (Sheol), where he could no longer praise God. He is alive, so he can give thanks (38:18-19; see note on 26:1-19). According to the narrative (38:4-6), God responds to the king's prayer with healing and deliverance.

I am consigned to the gates of Sheol
for the rest of my years.
11 I said, I shall not see the LORD
in the land of the living;
I shall look upon mortals no more
among the inhabitants of the world.
12 My dwelling is plucked up and removed from me
like a shepherd's tent;
like a weaver I have rolled up my life;
he cuts me off from the loom;
from day to night you bring me to an end;[a]
13 I cry for help[b] until morning;
like a lion he breaks all my bones;
from day to night you bring me to an end.[a]

14 Like a swallow or a crane[a] I clamor,
I moan like a dove.
My eyes are weary with looking upward.
O Lord, I am oppressed; be my security!
15 But what can I say? For he has spoken to me,
and he himself has done it.
All my sleep has fled[c]
because of the bitterness of my soul.

16 O Lord, by these things people live,
and in all these is the life of my spirit.[a]
Oh, restore me to health and make me live!
17 Surely it was for my welfare
that I had great bitterness;
but you have held back[d] my life
from the pit of destruction,
for you have cast all my sins
behind your back.
18 For Sheol cannot thank you,
death cannot praise you;
those who go down to the Pit cannot hope
for your faithfulness.
19 The living, the living, they thank you,
as I do this day;
fathers make known to children
your faithfulness.

---

[a] Meaning of Heb uncertain [b] Cn: Meaning of Heb uncertain [c] Cn Compare Syr: Heb *I will walk slowly all my years* [d] Cn Compare Gk Vg: Heb *loved*

20 The LORD will save me,
and we will sing to stringed instruments[a]
all the days of our lives,
at the house of the LORD.

21 Now Isaiah had said, "Let them take a lump of figs, and apply
it to the boil, so that he may recover." 22 Hezekiah also had said, "What
is the sign that I shall go up to the house of the LORD?"

Envoys from Babylon Welcomed

39 At that time King Merodach-baladan son of Baladan of
Babylon sent envoys with letters and a present to Hezekiah,
for he heard that he had been sick and had recovered. 2 Hezekiah welcomed them; he showed them his treasure house, the silver, the gold,
the spices, the precious oil, his whole armory, all that was found in his
storehouses. There was nothing in his house or in all his realm that
Hezekiah did not show them. 3 Then the prophet Isaiah came to King
Hezekiah and said to him, "What did these men say? From where did
they come to you?" Hezekiah answered, "They have come to me from
a far country, from Babylon." 4 He said, "What have they seen in your
house?" Hezekiah answered, "They have seen all that is in my house;
there is nothing in my storehouses that I did not show them."
5 Then Isaiah said to Hezekiah, "Hear the word of the LORD of
hosts: 6 Days are coming when all that is in your house, and that which
your ancestors have stored up until this day, shall be carried to Babylon; nothing shall be left, says the LORD. 7 Some of your own sons
who are born to you shall be taken away; they shall be eunuchs in the
palace of the king of Babylon." 8 Then Hezekiah said to Isaiah, "The
word of the LORD that you have spoken is good." For he thought,
"There will be peace and security in my days."

God's People Are Comforted

40 Comfort, O comfort my people,
says your God.
2 Speak tenderly to Jerusalem,
and cry to her
that she has served her term,
that her penalty is paid,
that she has received from the LORD's hand
double for all her sins.

3 A voice cries out:
"In the wilderness prepare the way of the LORD,

---

[a] Heb *my stringed instruments*

39:1-8 King Merodach-baladan... sent envoys...to Hezekiah: Anticipating the second major part of the book (chapters 40–55), the historical material now looks ahead to the coming exile in Babylon. The mention here of eunuchs (39:7) is balanced by another reference in 56:3-4. These two chapters serve as bookends around the message of Second Isaiah in chapters 40–55.

From 721 to about 705 B.C.E. Merodach-baladon of Babylonia led successful revolts against Assyria and ruled over an independent Babylonia for a time. Hezekiah ruled Judah during this time, and he welcomed the Babylonians, who were enemies of the more powerful Assyrians. Isaiah warns that trusting Babylon is not a good idea and seems to refer to the events that would happen in 597 B.C.E. when Babylonia invaded Judah and forced a first wave of people into exile (see 2 Kgs 24:10-17).

40:1—55:13 Comfort, O comfort my people: The unidentified prophetic voice behind these chapters has traditionally been called Second Isaiah or Isaiah of the exile. For more, see the introduction to Isaiah.

40:1-6 Comfort...Speak...Cry out!: Here God is perhaps addressing members of God's heavenly council (see 6:2-3; 1 Kgs 22:19), who will provide the voices that cry a message overheard by prophet and people (40:3, 6). The theme of "comfort" will become a refrain throughout the chapters to follow (49:13; 51:3, 12, 19; 52:9; 54:11; 57:18; 61:2; 66:13).

40:2 Speak tenderly to Jerusalem...her penalty is paid: The Babylonian armies destroyed Jerusalem and the temple in 587 B.C.E. and forced many of the people of Judah and their leaders to go into exile in Babylonia. That horrible event was seen by the prophets as the penalty for their many sins, including trusting in foreign powers, worshiping idols, and neglecting the needs of the poor. "She has served her term," that is, the exile is over. Though not yet historically true, the matter is certain because of the promise made here through the prophet.

40:3-5 a highway for our God: In 35:8-10 the highway was for the people; here it is for God, who comes to free the captives. Some see here a play on the highways built for the processions of the Babylonian gods. Now the roadways lead not *into* Babylon for the divine festivals there, but *out* of Babylon for God's new exodus.

make straight in the desert a highway for our God.
4 Every valley shall be lifted up,
and every mountain and hill be made low;
the uneven ground shall become level,
and the rough places a plain.
5 Then the glory of the LORD shall be revealed,
and all people shall see it together,
for the mouth of the LORD has spoken."

6 A voice says, "Cry out!"
And I said, "What shall I cry?"
All people are grass,
their constancy is like the flower of the field.
7 The grass withers, the flower fades,
when the breath of the LORD blows upon it;
surely the people are grass.
8 The grass withers, the flower fades;
but the word of our God will stand forever.
9 Get you up to a high mountain,
O Zion, herald of good tidings;[a]
lift up your voice with strength,
O Jerusalem, herald of good tidings,[b]
lift it up, do not fear;
say to the cities of Judah,
"Here is your God!"
10 See, the Lord GOD comes with might,
and his arm rules for him;
his reward is with him,

[a] Or *O herald of good tidings to Zion* [b] Or *O herald of good tidings to Jerusalem*

40:6-8 the word of our God will stand forever: The reliability of God's word is contrasted with human life, which grows and then fades like grass or flowers (see also 55:8-11).

How can God's word do such great things? The Lutheran emphasis on the power of God's word is based in part on the statements in 40:8 and 55:10-11, which form a kind of bookend to Second Isaiah. We hear God's promise to perform the word that God speaks through the prophet. Like the earth itself in Genesis 1, the exiles in Babylon lived in chaos and darkness. As in Genesis 1, here God speaks everything new into existence. God's word has creative power! This same Word became flesh in Jesus (John 1:1-14). Lutherans understand that Scripture has authority in our lives not as a static collection of truths but because it bears witness to this active and life-giving Word of God. Though powerful, of course, words are also fully human and sometimes weak. Words invite dialogue and can be resisted. God's entry into the world through human speech is an aspect of God's incarnation in human form. Commenting on the power of God's word Martin Luther asks: How can the water [of baptism] bring forgiveness of sins and eternal salvation? "Clearly the water does not do it," he writes, "but the word of God... For without the word of God the water is plain water and not a baptism, but with the word of God it is a baptism, that is, a grace-filled water of life..." (*SC*:29). *Isaiah 40:8*

40:9-11 Zion, herald of good tidings...shepherd: A new voice is called to speak: Zion or Jerusalem as a "herald of good tidings." In the Greek Septuagint the word translated "herald" is *euangellizomenos* (eu-an-gel-ih-ZOH-menos) or "evangelist." The herald is the sentinel, watching for who would come—here, none other than God. Typically for this prophet, God comes with power and strength (40:10), but also with tender mercy (40:11—balancing the tender speaking of 40:1). In a deliberate wordplay, the mighty *arm* of the warrior God (40:10) becomes the embracing arm of the gentle shepherd (40:11).

The Cyrus Cylinder describes in the Akkadian language how King Cyrus of Persia defeated the Babylonians. It also tells about his policies toward the people he ruled and describes their gods. See the note on 44:23—45:8 (Cyrus).

and his recompense before him.
11 He will feed his flock like a shepherd;
he will gather the lambs in his arms,
and carry them in his bosom,
and gently lead the mother sheep.

12 Who has measured the waters in the hollow of his hand
and marked off the heavens with a span,
enclosed the dust of the earth in a measure,
and weighed the mountains in scales
and the hills in a balance?
13 Who has directed the spirit of the LORD,
or as his counselor has instructed him?
14 Whom did he consult for his enlightenment,
and who taught him the path of justice?
Who taught him knowledge,
and showed him the way of understanding?
15 Even the nations are like a drop from a bucket,
and are accounted as dust on the scales;
see, he takes up the isles like fine dust.
16 Lebanon would not provide fuel enough,
nor are its animals enough for a burnt offering.
17 All the nations are as nothing before him;
they are accounted by him as less than nothing and emptiness.

18 To whom then will you liken God,
or what likeness compare with him?
19 An idol? —A workman casts it,
and a goldsmith overlays it with gold,
and casts for it silver chains.
20 As a gift one chooses mulberry wood[a]
—wood that will not rot—
then seeks out a skilled artisan
to set up an image that will not topple.

21 Have you not known? Have you not heard?
Has it not been told you from the beginning?
Have you not understood from the foundations of the earth?
22 It is he who sits above the circle of the earth,
and its inhabitants are like grasshoppers;
who stretches out the heavens like a curtain,
and spreads them like a tent to live in;
23 who brings princes to naught,
and makes the rulers of the earth as nothing.

40:12-31 Who has measured the waters…those who wait for the LORD: The questions of 40:12-14 are asked with a clear answer already in mind. The answer is "God." The nations are like nothing before God (40:17), and no likeness, including idols, has the creative power and wisdom of God. It is interesting to note the use of "likeness" from Genesis 1:26 ("Let us make humankind in our image, according to our likeness"). There the human was in the "likeness" of God. In Second Isaiah, God will be compared to many human "likenesses"—shepherd (40:11) warrior (42:13), mother (45:10), father (45:10), friend (41:8), potter (45:9-10), redeemer (41:14; see note on 43:1-7), helper (41:10), lover (43:4), nurse (49:15), husband (54:5). God will allow being compared to things "below," that is, to human beings. But God will not allow being compared to things "above," that is, to other gods or spirits,—to idols (40:19-20), or to the stars or moon or sun that some worshiped (40:26). God alone is God, and there is no other (45:5). Despite its emphasis on God's creative power, this passage, too, ends with compassion and encouragement to the faint and the powerless (40:28-31).

[a] Meaning of Heb uncertain

24 Scarcely are they planted, scarcely sown,
scarcely has their stem taken root in the earth,
when he blows upon them, and they wither,
and the tempest carries them off like stubble.

25 To whom then will you compare me,
or who is my equal? says the Holy One.
26 Lift up your eyes on high and see:
Who created these?
He who brings out their host and numbers them,
calling them all by name;
because he is great in strength,
mighty in power,
not one is missing.

27 Why do you say, O Jacob,
and speak, O Israel,
"My way is hidden from the LORD,
and my right is disregarded by my God"?
28 Have you not known? Have you not heard?
The LORD is the everlasting God,
the Creator of the ends of the earth.
He does not faint or grow weary;
his understanding is unsearchable.
29 He gives power to the faint,
and strengthens the powerless.
30 Even youths will faint and be weary,
and the young will fall exhausted;
31 but those who wait for the LORD shall renew their
strength,
they shall mount up with wings like eagles,
they shall run and not be weary,
they shall walk and not faint.

Israel Assured of God's Help

41 Listen to me in silence, O coastlands;
let the peoples renew their strength;
let them approach, then let them speak;
let us together draw near for judgment.

2 Who has roused a victor from the east,
summoned him to his service?
He delivers up nations to him,
and tramples kings under foot;
he makes them like dust with his sword,

41:1-7 draw near for judgment: God summons the nations to trial to show who is truly God (also 41:21-29; 43:8-15; 44:6-8; 45:20-25). "Coastlands" (41:1) is used frequently in these chapters to describe the nations. The repeated verdict is that, unlike the idols, God can and does deliver on the divine promises. The "victor from the east" (41:2) is Cyrus of Persia (see 44:23—45:8 and note). The idol makers declare their work "good," just as God declares the work of creation "good" seven times in Genesis 1, but ironically the powerless idols must be nailed down to hold themselves upright.

like driven stubble with his bow.
3 He pursues them and passes on safely,
scarcely touching the path with his feet.
4 Who has performed and done this,
calling the generations from the beginning?
I, the LORD, am first,
and will be with the last.
5 The coastlands have seen and are afraid,
the ends of the earth tremble;
they have drawn near and come.
6 Each one helps the other,
saying to one another, "Take courage!"
7 The artisan encourages the goldsmith,
and the one who smooths with the hammer encourages the
one who strikes the anvil,
saying of the soldering, "It is good";
and they fasten it with nails so that it cannot be moved.
8 But you, Israel, my servant,
Jacob, whom I have chosen,
the offspring of Abraham, my friend;
9 you whom I took from the ends of the earth,
and called from its farthest corners,
saying to you, "You are my servant,
I have chosen you and not cast you off";
10 do not fear, for I am with you,
do not be afraid, for I am your God;
I will strengthen you, I will help you,
I will uphold you with my victorious right hand.

11 Yes, all who are incensed against you
shall be ashamed and disgraced;
those who strive against you
shall be as nothing and shall perish.
12 You shall seek those who contend with you,
but you shall not find them;
those who war against you
shall be as nothing at all.
13 For I, the LORD your God,
hold your right hand;
it is I who say to you, "Do not fear,
I will help you."

14 Do not fear, you worm Jacob,
you insect[a] Israel!

[a] Syr: Heb *men of*

41:10-16 do not fear: In two typically strong yet intimate oracles (41:8-13, 14-16), God promises to help Israel, whom God calls both "servant" and "friend" (41:8-9). God reassures the people that they have been chosen long ago, called and never cast off, despite the present disaster. "Do not fear" becomes a repeating formula of comfort (see also 40:9; 43:1, 5; 44:2, 8; 51:7; 54:4, 14). These comforting words were especially meaningful to people who were suffering separation from their homeland and the feeling that God had abandoned them.

What makes you afraid or fearful? Have you ever felt like God had abandoned you? What does that feel like?

I will help you, says the LORD;
  your Redeemer is the Holy One of Israel.
15 Now, I will make of you a threshing sledge,
  sharp, new, and having teeth;
you shall thresh the mountains and crush them,
  and you shall make the hills like chaff.
16 You shall winnow them and the wind shall carry them away,
  and the tempest shall scatter them.
Then you shall rejoice in the LORD;
  in the Holy One of Israel you shall glory.

17 When the poor and needy seek water,
  and there is none,
  and their tongue is parched with thirst,
I the LORD will answer them,
  I the God of Israel will not forsake them.
18 I will open rivers on the bare heights,[a]
  and fountains in the midst of the valleys;
I will make the wilderness a pool of water,
  and the dry land springs of water.
19 I will put in the wilderness the cedar,
  the acacia, the myrtle, and the olive;
I will set in the desert the cypress,
  the plane and the pine together,
20 so that all may see and know,
  all may consider and understand,
that the hand of the LORD has done this,
  the Holy One of Israel has created it.

The Futility of Idols

41:21-29 bring your proofs…their images are empty wind: In this trial speech (see note on 41:1-7) the point is clear: the gods can neither tell what is to happen nor can they do anything good or bad. They are "nothing," and their works are "empty wind,"—an image that plays with the language of Genesis 1:2: they are like a "formless wind" of chaos rather the creative "wind from God" (see note on 44:9-20).

21 Set forth your case, says the LORD;
  bring your proofs, says the King of Jacob.
22 Let them bring them, and tell us
  what is to happen.
Tell us the former things, what they are,
  so that we may consider them,
and that we may know their outcome;
  or declare to us the things to come.
23 Tell us what is to come hereafter,
  that we may know that you are gods;
do good, or do harm,
  that we may be afraid and terrified.
24 You, indeed, are nothing

[a] *Or trails*

and your work is nothing at all;
whoever chooses you is an abomination.

25 I stirred up one from the north, and he has come,
from the rising of the sun he was summoned by name.[a]
He shall trample[b] on rulers as on mortar,
as the potter treads clay.
26 Who declared it from the beginning, so that we might know,
and beforehand, so that we might say, "He is right"?
There was no one who declared it, none who proclaimed,
none who heard your words.
27 I first have declared it to Zion,[c]
and I give to Jerusalem a herald of good tidings.
28 But when I look there is no one;
among these there is no counselor
who, when I ask, gives an answer.
29 No, they are all a delusion;
their works are nothing;
their images are empty wind.

The Servant, a Light to the Nations

42 Here is my servant, whom I uphold,
my chosen, in whom my soul delights;
I have put my spirit upon him;
he will bring forth justice to the nations.
2 He will not cry or lift up his voice,
or make it heard in the street;
3 a bruised reed he will not break,
and a dimly burning wick he will not quench;
he will faithfully bring forth justice.
4 He will not grow faint or be crushed
until he has established justice in the earth;
and the coastlands wait for his teaching.

5 Thus says God, the LORD,
who created the heavens and stretched them out,
who spread out the earth and what comes from it,
who gives breath to the people upon it
and spirit to those who walk in it:
6 I am the LORD, I have called you in righteousness,
I have taken you by the hand and kept you;
I have given you as a covenant to the people,[d]

---

[a] Cn Compare Q Ms Gk: MT *and he shall call on my name* [b] Cn: Heb *come* [c] Cn: Heb *First to Zion—Behold, behold them* [d] Meaning of Heb uncertain

42:1-4: my servant: This is the first of the four traditional "servant songs" of Second Isaiah (see note below). Here God introduces an unnamed servant, chosen by God (like Israel, 41:8) and anointed with God's spirit (like Israel's kings, who had oil poured over their heads as a sign of being chosen). Like the messianic king, the servant will bring God's justice and teaching (Isa 9:7; 11:1-5). Yet the servant will do this quietly and gently, without lifting his voice and without quenching "a dimly burning wick," unlike the necessary violence of the first exodus (43:16-17).

42:1-4 my servant...my chosen: In the late-nineteenth century, scholars identified four texts from Second Isaiah as "servant songs" (42:1-4; 49:1-6; 50:4-11; 52:13-53:12), frequently interpreting them apart from the context of the book and attempting to discover the particular identity of the servant. Christians tended to see the servant as an individual and identified him with Jesus, who like the servant suffers, is rejected, and bears the sins of many (53:3-12). Jewish readers saw the servant corporately as Israel (49:3). It is now agreed that the four passages must be read in the context of the book and in relation to other texts that seem clearly to identify Israel as God's servant (41:8-9; 42:19; 43:10; 44:1-2, 21; 45:4; 48:20). Still, in the traditional four servant songs, the servant is given a particular commission or task that sometimes sounds quite individual. In 49:1-6 and 50:4-11, the servant speaks directly and sounds like the prophet. Certainly the servant is Israel, but it may also be true that sometimes a particular member of Israel represents the whole people.

42:5-9 I have called you in righteousness...a light to the nations: It is not certain whether these verses continue the servant song in verses 1-4. Is the unnamed "you," called here to be "a light to the nations" and "to bring out the prisoners from the dungeon," the servant, or Cyrus, or Israel? All these figures do similar work. The identity is best left open (as it is in the text), allowing the reader in any generation to hear it addressed to her or him.

a light to the nations,
7 to open the eyes that are blind,
to bring out the prisoners from the dungeon,
from the prison those who sit in darkness.
8 I am the LORD, that is my name;
my glory I give to no other,
nor my praise to idols.
9 See, the former things have come to pass,
and new things I now declare;
before they spring forth,
I tell you of them.

A Hymn of Praise

10 Sing to the LORD a new song,
his praise from the end of the earth!
Let the sea roar[a] and all that fills it,
the coastlands and their inhabitants.
11 Let the desert and its towns lift up their voice,
the villages that Kedar inhabits;
let the inhabitants of Sela sing for joy,
let them shout from the tops of the mountains.
12 Let them give glory to the LORD,
and declare his praise in the coastlands.
13 The LORD goes forth like a soldier,
like a warrior he stirs up his fury;
he cries out, he shouts aloud,
he shows himself mighty against his foes.

14 For a long time I have held my peace,
I have kept still and restrained myself;
now I will cry out like a woman in labor,
I will gasp and pant.
15 I will lay waste mountains and hills,
and dry up all their herbage;
I will turn the rivers into islands,
and dry up the pools.
16 I will lead the blind
by a road they do not know,
by paths they have not known
I will guide them.
I will turn the darkness before them into light,
the rough places into level ground.
These are the things I will do,

42:13-14 like a warrior...like a woman in labor: In two back-to-back verses, God is compared to a fierce warrior and a woman in labor. Both are images of strength, both crying out in the effort to accomplish God's mission. This blending of images is characteristic of Second Isaiah, as the prophet attempts to redefine God for a people in exile who have lost faith (40:10-11).

The second half of the book of Isaiah contains a surprising number of female images for God. God is compared to a woman in labor (42:14; 45:10), a nursing mother (49:15; 66:13), and possibly a midwife (46:3-4). These images of comfort and intimacy were perhaps given through the prophet as part of the "new thing" (43:19) that God was doing to break Israel out of the despair produced by years of exile. When all the historical and political institutions had been destroyed, the prophet appealed to an unbreakable and intimate relationship between Israel and God.

[a] Cn Compare Ps 96.11; 98.7: Heb *Those who go down to the sea*

and I will not forsake them.
17 They shall be turned back and utterly put to shame—
those who trust in carved images,
who say to cast images,
"You are our gods."

18 Listen, you that are deaf;
and you that are blind, look up and see!
19 Who is blind but my servant,
or deaf like my messenger whom I send?
Who is blind like my dedicated one,
or blind like the servant of the LORD?
20 He sees many things, but does[a] not observe them;
his ears are open, but he does not hear.

Israel's Disobedience

21 The LORD was pleased, for the sake of his righteousness,
to magnify his teaching and make it glorious.
22 But this is a people robbed and plundered,
all of them are trapped in holes
and hidden in prisons;
they have become a prey with no one to rescue,
a spoil with no one to say, "Restore!"
23 Who among you will give heed to this,
who will attend and listen for the time to come?
24 Who gave up Jacob to the spoiler,
and Israel to the robbers?
Was it not the LORD, against whom we have sinned,
in whose ways they would not walk,
and whose law they would not obey?
25 So he poured upon him the heat of his anger
and the fury of war;
it set him on fire all around, but he did not understand;
it burned him, but he did not take it to heart.

Restoration and Protection Promised

43 But now thus says the LORD,
he who created you, O Jacob,
he who formed you, O Israel:
Do not fear, for I have redeemed you;
I have called you by name, you are mine.
2 When you pass through the waters, I will be with you;
and through the rivers, they shall not overwhelm you;

[a] Heb *You see many things but do*

42:18-25 Who is blind but my servant: God's servant Israel remains blind and deaf (6:9-10), as the people sit helplessly as captives in Babylon, "trapped in holes and hidden in prisons" (42:22). Because of their disobedience, they cannot be the shining example of God's teaching among the nations. No one has been able to say "Restore!" (or return, 42:22), but God will do precisely that in the chapters to follow (see 49:5; 51:11; 52:8).

43:1-7 I have redeemed you: God is called Redeemer thirteen times in chapters 40–66, but not at all in chapters 1–39. In Old Testament civil law, the redeemer (in Hebrew *go'el* [go-'EL]) was one who bought back a relative's property that had been sold or a family member who had been forced into slavery (Lev 25:25-55). In the exodus, God was seen as the one who "redeemed" Israel from slavery in Egypt (Exod 6:6; 15:13). That role is now applied in Second Isaiah to God's redeeming Israel from Babylon. So God ransoms, buys back, Israel from the nations. Despite this political and economic understanding of God's work, the intimacy of the passage is striking: "I have called you by name, you are mine...you are precious in my sight...and I love you." Only here do we hear the simple "I love you" sentence from God's mouth (43:4; though see Jer 31:3; Mal 1:2). God will gather the exiles not only from Babylon, but from all four corners of the earth, no matter where they have strayed or been stolen. Typical of the careful poetry of Second Isaiah, this beautiful passage is framed with common vocabulary: "created" and "formed" in verses 1 and 7.

"I have called you by name, you are mine," says God through the prophet. This is why God can say, "Do not fear." Think about times this word has been or might be especially important for you. Think about someone who may need to hear this.

How is God both Creator and Redeemer? Second Isaiah closely connects God's work of creation and redemption. God's power to create provides Israel assurance that God has the power to redeem. In his *Small Catechism*, Martin Luther further clarifies this in his explanations to the Apostles' Creed. According to Luther, the First Article says, "I believe that God has created me together with all that exists. . . ." The meaning of the Second Article continues "I believe that Jesus Christ, true God, begotten of the Father in eternity, and also a true human being, born of the virgin Mary, is my Lord. He has redeemed me, a lost and condemned human being." God creates and Jesus redeems—but both are the work of God, because Jesus is "true God." *Isaiah 43:1-15*

43:8-13 Bring forth the people who are blind: Though still blind and deaf, Israel is nevertheless called to be God's witnesses, as in witnesses at a court trial. This term is related to the book's trial speeches (see 44:8-9 and the note on 1:2-20). The task of the witness is simply to tell who God is and what God has done. God does not fear being put to the test by opposing witnesses, such as opposing nations (43:9), because "besides me there is no savior" (43:11).

43:11 I am the Lord: Second Isaiah contains several "I am" statements in the mouth of God, ranging from the grand and glorious declaration of 48:12-13 ("I am He; I am the first, and I am the last. My hand laid the foundation of the earth, and my right hand spread out the heavens. . . .") to the intimate and personal assurance of 51:12 ("I, I am he who comforts you; why then are you afraid of a mere mortal who must die, a human being who fades like grass?"). There are perhaps twenty-four such statements in all. These self-descriptions of God proclaim not only the power and glory of God but also God's loving and personal care. Several of these statements are the Bible's clearest statements of Israel's faith in one God (known as *monotheism*): "I am the first and I am the last; besides me there is no god" (44:6); "I am the Lord, and there is no other" (45:5, 6, 18). In the Gospel of John the "I am" statements of Jesus ("I am the bread of life," John 6:35; "I am the way, and the truth, and the life" John 14:6) recall themes and images from God's "I am" statements in Second Isaiah.

when you walk through fire you shall not be burned,
 and the flame shall not consume you.
3 For I am the Lord your God,
 the Holy One of Israel, your Savior.
I give Egypt as your ransom,
 Ethiopia[a] and Seba in exchange for you.
4 Because you are precious in my sight,
 and honored, and I love you,
I give people in return for you,
 nations in exchange for your life.
5 Do not fear, for I am with you;
 I will bring your offspring from the east,
 and from the west I will gather you;
6 I will say to the north, "Give them up,"
 and to the south, "Do not withhold;
bring my sons from far away
 and my daughters from the end of the earth—
7 everyone who is called by my name,
 whom I created for my glory,
 whom I formed and made."

8 Bring forth the people who are blind, yet have eyes,
 who are deaf, yet have ears!
9 Let all the nations gather together,
 and let the peoples assemble.
Who among them declared this,
 and foretold to us the former things?
Let them bring their witnesses to justify them,
 and let them hear and say, "It is true."
10 You are my witnesses, says the Lord,
 and my servant whom I have chosen,
so that you may know and believe me
 and understand that I am he.
Before me no god was formed,
 nor shall there be any after me.
11 I, I am the Lord,
 and besides me there is no savior.
12 I declared and saved and proclaimed,
 when there was no strange god among you;
 and you are my witnesses, says the Lord.
13 I am God, and also henceforth I am He;
 there is no one who can deliver from my hand;
 I work and who can hinder it?

---

[a] Or *Nubia;* Heb *Cush*

14 Thus says the Lord,
your Redeemer, the Holy One of Israel:
For your sake I will send to Babylon
and break down all the bars,
and the shouting of the Chaldeans will be turned to
lamentation.[a]
15 I am the Lord, your Holy One,
the Creator of Israel, your King.
16 Thus says the Lord,
who makes a way in the sea,
a path in the mighty waters,
17 who brings out chariot and horse,
army and warrior;
they lie down, they cannot rise,
they are extinguished, quenched like a wick:
18 Do not remember the former things,
or consider the things of old.
19 I am about to do a new thing;
now it springs forth, do you not perceive it?
I will make a way in the wilderness
and rivers in the desert.
20 The wild animals will honor me,
the jackals and the ostriches;
for I give water in the wilderness,
rivers in the desert,
to give drink to my chosen people,
21 the people whom I formed for myself
so that they might declare my praise.

43:16-21 who makes a way in the sea, a path in the mighty waters: The passage first clearly defines the old exodus, when God led the Hebrew people through the Red Sea (Exod 14:15-31). Then it immediately calls upon Israel to forget it, because God is "about to do a new thing" (43:19). Now Israel's salvation lies not behind them but ahead of them. The old exodus was a dry way through the sea; the new one will be a wet way in the desert (43:19-20). The old involved snuffing out Pharaoh's armies like a candle wick is quenched (43:17; but see 42:3); the new one will quench the people's thirst for freedom (43:20). Here, "the former things" apparently refers to the first exodus; elsewhere, more negatively, it seems to refer to the time of judgment in First Isaiah, which is now being undone (42:9; 48:3).

22 Yet you did not call upon me, O Jacob;
but you have been weary of me, O Israel!
23 You have not brought me your sheep for burnt offerings,
or honored me with your sacrifices.
I have not burdened you with offerings,
or wearied you with frankincense.
24 You have not bought me sweet cane with money,
or satisfied me with the fat of your sacrifices.
But you have burdened me with your sins;
you have wearied me with your iniquities.

25 I, I am He
who blots out your transgressions for my own sake,
and I will not remember your sins.

43:22-28 you did not call upon me, O Jacob…I will not remember your sins: Israel (Jacob) is condemned for burdening (literally, "enslaving") God with its sins. This is why Jerusalem was destroyed (2 Kgs 23:26; 24:3) and the princes of the sanctuary (the priests) were profaned (2 Kgs 25:18-21). Yet, at the center of this passage, God is identified as "I am," the one who forgives for God's own sake—because, in this self-definition, this is who God is.

[a] Meaning of Heb uncertain

26 Accuse me, let us go to trial;
set forth your case, so that you may be proved right.
27 Your first ancestor sinned,
and your interpreters transgressed against me.
28 Therefore I profaned the princes of the sanctuary,
I delivered Jacob to utter destruction,
and Israel to reviling.

God's Blessing on Israel

44 But now hear, O Jacob my servant,
Israel whom I have chosen!
2 Thus says the LORD who made you,
who formed you in the womb and will help you:
Do not fear, O Jacob my servant,
Jeshurun whom I have chosen.
3 For I will pour water on the thirsty land,
and streams on the dry ground;
I will pour my spirit upon your descendants,
and my blessing on your offspring.
4 They shall spring up like a green tamarisk,
like willows by flowing streams.
5 This one will say, "I am the LORD's,"
another will be called by the name of Jacob,
yet another will write on the hand, "The LORD's,"
and adopt the name of Israel.

6 Thus says the LORD, the King of Israel,
and his Redeemer, the LORD of hosts:
I am the first and I am the last;
besides me there is no god.
7 Who is like me? Let them proclaim it,
let them declare and set it forth before me.
Who has announced from of old the things to come?[a]
Let them tell us[b] what is yet to be.
8 Do not fear, or be afraid;
have I not told you from of old and declared it?
You are my witnesses!
Is there any god besides me?
There is no other rock; I know not one.

The Absurdity of Idol Worship

9 All who make idols are nothing, and the things they delight in
do not profit; their witnesses neither see nor know. And so they will

[a] Cn: Heb *from my placing an eternal people and things to come* [b] Tg: Heb *them*

44:9-20 All who make idols are nothing: Several passages condemn or ridicule the gods, idols, and idol worship (40:19-20; 41:23; 42:8; 45:16; 46:1-7; 48:5; 57:13; 66:3). The human or religious point is the absurdity of worshiping a carved image. The theological point is that there is nothing behind the idols, for God alone is Lord and there is no other (see note on 43:11). Nowhere is the ridicule as strong as here. At their best, other religions did not worship the idols themselves, but the deities they represented, which were thought to be present through the idols. Still, the prophet denounces the absurd possibility that access to God can be captured in an object or artifact made by human hands.

How do things and possessions become like idols, objects of devotion or worship? In what ways do such things compete for our devotion to God alone?

be put to shame. [10]Who would fashion a god or cast an image that can
do no good? [11]Look, all its devotees shall be put to shame; the artisans too are merely human. Let them all assemble, let them stand up;
they shall be terrified, they shall all be put to shame.

12 The ironsmith fashions it[a] and works it over the coals, shaping it with hammers, and forging it with his strong arm; he becomes
hungry and his strength fails, he drinks no water and is faint. [13]The
carpenter stretches a line, marks it out with a stylus, fashions it with
planes, and marks it with a compass; he makes it in human form,
with human beauty, to be set up in a shrine. [14]He cuts down cedars
or chooses a holm tree or an oak and lets it grow strong among the
trees of the forest. He plants a cedar and the rain nourishes it. [15]Then
it can be used as fuel. Part of it he takes and warms himself; he kindles
a fire and bakes bread. Then he makes a god and worships it, makes it
a carved image and bows down before it. [16]Half of it he burns in the
fire; over this half he roasts meat, eats it and is satisfied. He also warms
himself and says, "Ah, I am warm, I can feel the fire!" [17]The rest of it he
makes into a god, his idol, bows down to it and worships it; he prays
to it and says, "Save me, for you are my god!"

18 They do not know, nor do they comprehend; for their eyes
are shut, so that they cannot see, and their minds as well, so that they
cannot understand. [19]No one considers, nor is there knowledge or
discernment to say, "Half of it I burned in the fire; I also baked bread
on its coals, I roasted meat and have eaten. Now shall I make the rest
of it an abomination? Shall I fall down before a block of wood?" [20]He
feeds on ashes; a deluded mind has led him astray, and he cannot save
himself or say, "Is not this thing in my right hand a fraud?"

Israel Is Not Forgotten

21 Remember these things, O Jacob,
and Israel, for you are my servant;
I formed you, you are my servant;
O Israel, you will not be forgotten by me.
22 I have swept away your transgressions like a cloud,
and your sins like mist;
return to me, for I have redeemed you.

23 Sing, O heavens, for the LORD has done it;
shout, O depths of the earth;
break forth into singing, O mountains,
O forest, and every tree in it!
For the LORD has redeemed Jacob,
and will be glorified in Israel.

44:23—45:8 Jerusalem . . . shall be inhabited . . . Cyrus . . . my shepherd: This oracle is set off and surrounded by hymns of praise (44:23; 45:8). The first half of this divine speech is simply a lengthy self-introduction (44:24-28), establishing the authority of God to make the striking claims in the words to follow (45:1-7). God cannot be known by omens or divination (fortunetelling), or by human wisdom. The word of prophecy makes God known (44:25-26). The God who creates all things now names Cyrus his "shepherd" (44:28), a metaphor for king (see Jer 23:1-6) and even his "anointed" (45:1). In Hebrew, the word for anointed is *messiah*. Cyrus is not the ideal messiah awaited later by the Jewish people, but one "anointed" by God for a specific task: to set free the exiles from Judah and to rebuild Jerusalem and the temple (44:28). The Cyrus Cylinder, a clay cylinder discovered in Babylon in 1879 (see photo on p. 1158), reports Cyrus' own account of his capture of Babylon and his freeing of the foreign captives there (see Ezra 1:1-4; 6:3-5). God uses this government leader to set people free so that Cyrus himself and all the world will know that this is God's work (45:3, 6).

[a] Cn: Heb *an ax*

[24] Thus says the LORD, your Redeemer,
who formed you in the womb:
I am the LORD, who made all things,
who alone stretched out the heavens,
who by myself spread out the earth;
[25] who frustrates the omens of liars,
and makes fools of diviners;
who turns back the wise,
and makes their knowledge foolish;
[26] who confirms the word of his servant,
and fulfills the prediction of his messengers;
who says of Jerusalem, "It shall be inhabited,"
and of the cities of Judah, "They shall be rebuilt,
and I will raise up their ruins";
[27] who says to the deep, "Be dry—
I will dry up your rivers";
[28] who says of Cyrus, "He is my shepherd,
and he shall carry out all my purpose";
and who says of Jerusalem, "It shall be rebuilt,"
and of the temple, "Your foundation shall be laid."

44:28 my purpose: At the center of the long Cyrus oracle is the announcement of God's "purpose": to rebuild Jerusalem and the temple, that is, to restore Israel and begin anew. This "purpose" plays a major role in these chapters. It is related to the "plan" of God described in chapters 1–39 (see note on 25:1-5). Both terms, "purpose" and "intention" (or "plan"), come together in 46:10. Cyrus is one agent of God's purpose to free the captives and rebuild Jerusalem (44:28; 48:14). This purpose will also be accomplished by the divine word (55:11) and, surprisingly, by the suffering of the servant (53:10, where God's "will" is the same Hebrew term as "purpose" here; see note on 52:13—53:12). When all is made new, Israel will be given a new name based on this same word: *Hephzibah* ("My Delight [purpose] is in Her," 62:4).

Cyrus, God's Instrument

45 Thus says the LORD to his anointed, to Cyrus,
whose right hand I have grasped
to subdue nations before him
and strip kings of their robes,
to open doors before him—
and the gates shall not be closed:
[2] I will go before you
and level the mountains,[a]
I will break in pieces the doors of bronze
and cut through the bars of iron,
[3] I will give you the treasures of darkness
and riches hidden in secret places,
so that you may know that it is I, the LORD,
the God of Israel, who call you by your name.
[4] For the sake of my servant Jacob,
and Israel my chosen,
I call you by your name,
I surname you, though you do not know me.
[5] I am the LORD, and there is no other;
besides me there is no god.
I arm you, though you do not know me,

[a] Q Ms Gk: MT *the swellings*

6 so that they may know, from the rising of the sun
and from the west, that there is no one besides me;
I am the LORD, and there is no other.
7 I form light and create darkness,
I make weal and create woe;
I the LORD do all these things.

8 Shower, O heavens, from above,
and let the skies rain down righteousness;
let the earth open, that salvation may spring up,[a]
and let it cause righteousness to sprout up also;
I the LORD have created it.

9 Woe to you who strive with your Maker,
earthen vessels with the potter![b]
Does the clay say to the one who fashions it, "What are you making"?
or "Your work has no handles"?
10 Woe to anyone who says to a father, "What are you begetting?"
or to a woman, "With what are you in labor?"
11 Thus says the LORD,
the Holy One of Israel, and its Maker:
Will you question me[c] about my children,
or command me concerning the work of my hands?
12 I made the earth,
and created humankind upon it;
it was my hands that stretched out the heavens,
and I commanded all their host.
13 I have aroused Cyrus[d] in righteousness,
and I will make all his paths straight;
he shall build my city
and set my exiles free,
not for price or reward,
says the LORD of hosts.
14 Thus says the LORD:
The wealth of Egypt and the merchandise of Ethiopia,[e]
and the Sabeans, tall of stature,
shall come over to you and be yours,
they shall follow you;
they shall come over in chains and bow down to you.
They will make supplication to you, saying,
"God is with you alone, and there is no other;

45:7 I form light...make weal and create woe: Sometimes "woe" is translated as "evil." One consequence of belief in one God is this: if there are no other gods, then everything that is thought be of divine origin—whether understood on earth as good or bad—comes from God. This does not mean, however, that God is the cause of everything that happens. Human beings may still act against God's will (47:6). God is not here seen as the origin of moral "evil" or sin.

What do you think of the idea that everything that is out of human control—whether good or bad—comes from God?

---

[a] Q Ms: MT *that they may bring forth salvation* [b] Cn: Heb *with the potsherds*, or *with the potters*
[c] Cn: Heb *Ask me of things to come* [d] Heb *him* [e] Or *Nubia*; Heb *Cush*

there is no god besides him."
15 Truly, you are a God who hides himself,
O God of Israel, the Savior.
16 All of them are put to shame and confounded,
the makers of idols go in confusion together.
17 But Israel is saved by the LORD
with everlasting salvation;
you shall not be put to shame or confounded
to all eternity.

18 For thus says the LORD,
who created the heavens
(he is God!),
who formed the earth and made it
(he established it;
he did not create it a chaos,
he formed it to be inhabited!):
I am the LORD, and there is no other.
19 I did not speak in secret,
in a land of darkness;
I did not say to the offspring of Jacob,
"Seek me in chaos."
I the LORD speak the truth,
I declare what is right.

Idols Cannot Save Babylon

45:20-25: a god that cannot save: This trial speech announces the main point behind all of them: sadly, the prophet notes how the idolaters "keep praying to a god that cannot save" (see 1 Sam 12:20-21). The God of Israel can save, however, and the invitation is open: "turn to me and be saved, all the ends of the earth" (45:22).

20 Assemble yourselves and come together,
draw near, you survivors of the nations!
They have no knowledge—
those who carry about their wooden idols,
and keep on praying to a god
that cannot save.
21 Declare and present your case;
let them take counsel together!
Who told this long ago?
Who declared it of old?
Was it not I, the LORD?
There is no other god besides me,
a righteous God and a Savior;
there is no one besides me.

22 Turn to me and be saved,
all the ends of the earth!
For I am God, and there is no other.
23 By myself I have sworn,

from my mouth has gone forth in righteousness
a word that shall not return:
"To me every knee shall bow,
every tongue shall swear."

24 Only in the LORD, it shall be said of me,
are righteousness and strength;
all who were incensed against him
shall come to him and be ashamed.
25 In the LORD all the offspring of Israel
shall triumph and glory.

46 Bel bows down, Nebo stoops,
their idols are on beasts and cattle;
these things you carry are loaded
as burdens on weary animals.
2 They stoop, they bow down together;
they cannot save the burden,
but themselves go into captivity.

3 Listen to me, O house of Jacob,
all the remnant of the house of Israel,
who have been borne by me from your birth,
carried from the womb;
4 even to your old age I am he,
even when you turn gray I will carry you.
I have made, and I will bear;
I will carry and will save.

5 To whom will you liken me and make me equal,
and compare me, as though we were alike?
6 Those who lavish gold from the purse,
and weigh out silver in the scales—
they hire a goldsmith, who makes it into a god;
then they fall down and worship!
7 They lift it to their shoulders, they carry it,
they set it in its place, and it stands there;
it cannot move from its place.
If one cries out to it, it does not answer
or save anyone from trouble.

8 Remember this and consider,[a]
recall it to mind, you transgressors,

46:1-13: Bel bows down, Nebo stoops . . . I will put salvation in Zion: Bel ("lord") is a name for Marduk, god of Babylon; Nebo was understood to be his son. These gods cannot even carry their own idols, but God can and will carry and save Israel. God *carries* God's people just as the servant *bears* their infirmities and iniquities (53:4, 11). In 43:18, Israel was told not to remember the former things; here, they *are* to remember (46:8). They are not to look back to a salvation past; but they are to look to the God who saves, then and now.

[a] Meaning of Heb uncertain

9 remember the former things of old;
for I am God, and there is no other;
I am God, and there is no one like me,
10 declaring the end from the beginning
and from ancient times things not yet done,
saying, "My purpose shall stand,
and I will fulfill my intention,"
11 calling a bird of prey from the east,
the man for my purpose from a far country.
I have spoken, and I will bring it to pass;
I have planned, and I will do it.

46:11 calling a bird of prey: Refers to Cyrus and his attack on Babylon being as swift as the attack of a hawk or eagle.

12 Listen to me, you stubborn of heart,
you who are far from deliverance:
13 I bring near my deliverance, it is not far off,
and my salvation will not tarry;
I will put salvation in Zion,
for Israel my glory.

The Humiliation of Babylon

47 Come down and sit in the dust,
virgin daughter Babylon!
Sit on the ground without a throne,
daughter Chaldea!
For you shall no more be called
tender and delicate.
2 Take the millstones and grind meal,
remove your veil,
strip off your robe, uncover your legs,
pass through the rivers.
3 Your nakedness shall be uncovered,
and your shame shall be seen.
I will take vengeance,
and I will spare no one.
4 Our Redeemer—the LORD of hosts is his name—
is the Holy One of Israel.

47:1-15: Sit on the ground . . . daughter Chaldea!: Though Babylon (Chaldea) was chosen by God to punish Israel, Babylon is held responsible for working more death and destruction than required (47:6). Even God's agent of punishment should know to show mercy. Babylon thought that it was in charge ("I shall be mistress forever"), rather than seeing itself as God's agent. Babylon insults God by taking God's own sentence into its mouth ("I am, and there is no one besides me," 47:8, 10).

5 Sit in silence, and go into darkness,
daughter Chaldea!
For you shall no more be called
the mistress of kingdoms.
6 I was angry with my people,
I profaned my heritage;
I gave them into your hand,
you showed them no mercy;

on the aged you made your yoke
exceedingly heavy.
7 You said, "I shall be mistress forever,"
so that you did not lay these things to heart
or remember their end.

8 Now therefore hear this, you lover of pleasures,
who sit securely,
who say in your heart,
"I am, and there is no one besides me;
I shall not sit as a widow
or know the loss of children"—
9 both these things shall come upon you
in a moment, in one day:
the loss of children and widowhood
shall come upon you in full measure,
in spite of your many sorceries
and the great power of your enchantments.

10 You felt secure in your wickedness;
you said, "No one sees me."
Your wisdom and your knowledge
led you astray,
and you said in your heart,
"I am, and there is no one besides me."
11 But evil shall come upon you,
which you cannot charm away;
disaster shall fall upon you,
which you will not be able to ward off;
and ruin shall come on you suddenly,
of which you know nothing.

12 Stand fast in your enchantments
and your many sorceries,
with which you have labored from your youth;
perhaps you may be able to succeed,
perhaps you may inspire terror.
13 You are wearied with your many consultations;
let those who study[a] the heavens
stand up and save you,
those who gaze at the stars,
and at each new moon predict
what[b] shall befall you.

---

[a] Meaning of Heb uncertain [b] Gk Syr Compare Vg: Heb *from what*

14 See, they are like stubble,
the fire consumes them;
they cannot deliver themselves
from the power of the flame.
No coal for warming oneself is this,
no fire to sit before!
15 Such to you are those with whom you have labored,
who have trafficked with you from your youth;
they all wander about in their own paths;
there is no one to save you.

God the Creator and Redeemer

48:1-13 Jacob . . . Israel . . . Judah . . . you are obstinate: God now turns to the people in exile in Babylon and warns them to listen carefully to what God is about to do. "Jacob" and "Israel" are used to describe God's people, but most of the exiles would have been from the southern kingdom of Judah. God reminds the people of their former stubborn attitude (48:4). Their time in Babylon has been a time of testing (48:10), somewhat like the process of refining silver or gold, which were purified by being heated. This process burned away impurities within the melted gold or silver. Israel's "impurities" are removed not by heat but by a time of adversity.

48 Hear this, O house of Jacob,
who are called by the name of Israel,
and who came forth from the loins[a] of Judah;
who swear by the name of the LORD,
and invoke the God of Israel,
but not in truth or right.
2 For they call themselves after the holy city,
and lean on the God of Israel;
the LORD of hosts is his name.

3 The former things I declared long ago,
they went out from my mouth and I made them known;
then suddenly I did them and they came to pass.
4 Because I know that you are obstinate,
and your neck is an iron sinew
and your forehead brass,
5 I declared them to you from long ago,
before they came to pass I announced them to you,
so that you would not say, "My idol did them,
my carved image and my cast image commanded them."

6 You have heard; now see all this;
and will you not declare it?
From this time forward I make you hear new things,
hidden things that you have not known.
7 They are created now, not long ago;
before today you have never heard of them,
so that you could not say, "I already knew them."
8 You have never heard, you have never known,
from of old your ear has not been opened.
For I knew that you would deal very treacherously,
and that from birth you were called a rebel.

[a] Cn: Heb *waters*

9 For my name's sake I defer my anger,
for the sake of my praise I restrain it for you,
so that I may not cut you off.
10 See, I have refined you, but not like[a] silver;
I have tested you in the furnace of adversity.
11 For my own sake, for my own sake, I do it,
for why should my name[b] be profaned?
My glory I will not give to another.

12 Listen to me, O Jacob,
and Israel, whom I called:
I am He; I am the first,
and I am the last.
13 My hand laid the foundation of the earth,
and my right hand spread out the heavens;
when I summon them,
they stand at attention.

14 Assemble, all of you, and hear!
Who among them has declared these things?
The LORD loves him;
he shall perform his purpose on Babylon,
and his arm shall be against the Chaldeans.
15 I, even I, have spoken and called him,
I have brought him, and he will prosper in his way.
16 Draw near to me, hear this!
From the beginning I have not spoken in secret,
from the time it came to be I have been there.
And now the Lord GOD has sent me and his spirit.

17 Thus says the LORD,
your Redeemer, the Holy One of Israel:
I am the LORD your God,
who teaches you for your own good,
who leads you in the way you should go.
18 O that you had paid attention to my commandments!
Then your prosperity would have been like a river,
and your success like the waves of the sea;
19 your offspring would have been like the sand,
and your descendants like its grains;
their name would never be cut off
or destroyed from before me.

[a] Cn: Heb *with* [b] Gk Old Latin: Heb *for why should it*

48:14-16: The LORD loves him . . . God has sent me: God again pronounces love for Cyrus, chosen to perform God's purpose (see note on 44:28). This, though, is the last mention of Cyrus in the book. The "me" in 48:16 is likely the servant. This anticipates the themes of the servant song in 49:1-6, where God works in a new way. The gentle justice of the servant (42:1-4) now comes to the fore and reaches its climax in the suffering of the servant (52:13—53:12).

48:14-16: justice and mercy. The move in this passage from Cyrus to the servant, from God's work of liberating vengeance against the enemies of God's people to God's work of saving compassion is not chronological. That is true here as well as in the move from Old Testament to New Testament. Compassion has always been present, and harsh justice will still be needed; the move is a theological one within God, as God moves always toward the mercy that is the primary divine characteristic (54:7-10; Exod 34:6-7).

48:20 **Go out from Babylon . . . The Lord has redeemed . . . Jacob:** The new exodus from Babylon is about to begin. Just as God provided water in the desert in the first exodus (Exod 17:1-7) the people will have water for the journey home through dry land.

49:1-6 **the Lord called me before I was born . . . I will give you as a light to the nations:** This second servant song sounds very much like a prophetic call (see Jer 1:5). The simplest reading would understand the "I" as the prophet, the author of the book. Here, the roles of the prophet and the servant and Israel (49:3) blend. The prophet adds an autobiographical dimension to his understanding of the work of the servant and the mission of Israel, a feature that continues in 50:4-11. In response to God's call, the prophet-servant makes the typical objection (49:4), here saying that he has already tried to reach the people of Israel and failed. God ignores the objection and presents a more difficult and broader mission: to be "a light to the nations, that my salvation may reach to the end of the earth" (see also 42:6; 45:22). Jesus picks up the title of light to the nations (or "I am the light of the world," see John 8:12; 9:5) and passes it on to his followers (see Matt 5:14).

In the liturgy of Baptism the baptized is welcomed with the invitation to "Let your light so shine before others." How does this invitation become real or visible in your life?

20 Go out from Babylon, flee from Chaldea,
declare this with a shout of joy, proclaim it,
send it forth to the end of the earth;
say, "The Lord has redeemed his servant Jacob!"
21 They did not thirst when he led them through the deserts;
he made water flow for them from the rock;
he split open the rock and the water gushed out.

22 "There is no peace," says the Lord, "for the wicked."

The Servant's Mission

49 Listen to me, O coastlands,
pay attention, you peoples from far away!
The Lord called me before I was born,
while I was in my mother's womb he named me.
2 He made my mouth like a sharp sword,
in the shadow of his hand he hid me;
he made me a polished arrow,
in his quiver he hid me away.
3 And he said to me, "You are my servant,
Israel, in whom I will be glorified."
4 But I said, "I have labored in vain,
I have spent my strength for nothing and vanity;
yet surely my cause is with the Lord,
and my reward with my God."

5 And now the Lord says,
who formed me in the womb to be his servant,
to bring Jacob back to him,
and that Israel might be gathered to him,
for I am honored in the sight of the Lord,
and my God has become my strength—
6 he says,
"It is too light a thing that you should be my servant
to raise up the tribes of Jacob
and to restore the survivors of Israel;
I will give you as a light to the nations,
that my salvation may reach to the end of the earth."

7 Thus says the Lord,
the Redeemer of Israel and his Holy One,
to one deeply despised, abhorred by the nations,
the slave of rulers,
"Kings shall see and stand up,
princes, and they shall prostrate themselves,

because of the LORD, who is faithful,
the Holy One of Israel, who has chosen you."

Zion's Children to Be Brought Home

8 Thus says the LORD:
In a time of favor I have answered you,
on a day of salvation I have helped you;
I have kept you and given you
as a covenant to the people,[a]
to establish the land,
to apportion the desolate heritages;
9 saying to the prisoners, "Come out,"
to those who are in darkness, "Show yourselves."
They shall feed along the ways,
on all the bare heights[b] shall be their pasture;
10 they shall not hunger or thirst,
neither scorching wind nor sun shall strike them down,
for he who has pity on them will lead them,
and by springs of water will guide them.
11 And I will turn all my mountains into a road,
and my highways shall be raised up.
12 Lo, these shall come from far away,
and lo, these from the north and from the west,
and these from the land of Syene.[c]

13 Sing for joy, O heavens, and exult, O earth;
break forth, O mountains, into singing!
For the LORD has comforted his people,
and will have compassion on his suffering ones.

14 But Zion said, "The LORD has forsaken me,
my Lord has forgotten me."
15 Can a woman forget her nursing child,
or show no compassion for the child of her womb?
Even these may forget,
yet I will not forget you.
16 See, I have inscribed you on the palms of my hands;
your walls are continually before me.
17 Your builders outdo your destroyers,[d]
and those who laid you waste go away from you.
18 Lift up your eyes all around and see;
they all gather, they come to you.

[a] Meaning of Heb uncertain [b] Or *the trails* [c] Q Ms: MT *Sinim* [d] Or *Your children come swiftly; your destroyers*

49:14-16 my LORD has forgotten me . . . I have inscribed you: In response to Zion's lament of having been forgotten, God again uses the comparison to a nursing mother who cannot forget her child. In reality God is neither male nor female. Humans beings may fail, but God will not (see Ps 27:10; Deut 4:15-18).

49:17-25 Your builders outdo your destroyers . . . I will save your children: God's will restore Israel beyond all expectation. The builders of Jerusalem will outdo those who destroyed it. Jerusalem, now destroyed and deserted, will be "too crowded" (49:19). The nations will help Jerusalem's sons and daughters return home (49:22; 62:10). And the leaders of those nations will bow down to Jerusalem and its people (49:23).

As I live, says the LORD,
    you shall put all of them on like an ornament,
    and like a bride you shall bind them on.

19 Surely your waste and your desolate places
    and your devastated land—
surely now you will be too crowded for your inhabitants,
    and those who swallowed you up will be far away.
20 The children born in the time of your bereavement
    will yet say in your hearing:
"The place is too crowded for me;
    make room for me to settle."
21 Then you will say in your heart,
    "Who has borne me these?
I was bereaved and barren,
    exiled and put away—
    so who has reared these?
I was left all alone—
    where then have these come from?"

22 Thus says the Lord GOD:
I will soon lift up my hand to the nations,
    and raise my signal to the peoples;
and they shall bring your sons in their bosom,
    and your daughters shall be carried on their shoulders.
23 Kings shall be your foster fathers,
    and their queens your nursing mothers.
With their faces to the ground they shall bow down to you,
    and lick the dust of your feet.
Then you will know that I am the LORD;
    those who wait for me shall not be put to shame.

49:24-26 prey...captives of a tyrant: Though Israel was Babylon's prey (captives), God will rescue the people. God's rescue will show everyone ("all flesh") that God is Israel's "Savior."

24 Can the prey be taken from the mighty,
    or the captives of a tyrant[a] be rescued?
25 But thus says the LORD:
Even the captives of the mighty shall be taken,
    and the prey of the tyrant be rescued;
for I will contend with those who contend with you,
    and I will save your children.
26 I will make your oppressors eat their own flesh,
    and they shall be drunk with their own blood as with
        wine.
Then all flesh shall know

[a] Q Ms Syr Vg: MT *of a righteous person*

that I am the LORD your Savior,
and your Redeemer, the Mighty One of Jacob.

50 Thus says the LORD:
Where is your mother's bill of divorce
with which I put her away?
Or which of my creditors is it
to whom I have sold you?
No, because of your sins you were sold,
and for your transgressions your mother was put away.
2 Why was no one there when I came?
Why did no one answer when I called?
Is my hand shortened, that it cannot redeem?
Or have I no power to deliver?
By my rebuke I dry up the sea,
I make the rivers a desert;
their fish stink for lack of water,
and die of thirst.[a]
3 I clothe the heavens with blackness,
and make sackcloth their covering.

50:1-3 bill of divorce…creditors…because of your sin you were sold: God reminds the people that God didn't divorce them or sell them to pay off a creditor. Their own sins led to their separation from their homeland and their suffering.

The Servant's Humiliation and Vindication

4 The Lord GOD has given me
the tongue of a teacher,[b]
that I may know how to sustain
the weary with a word.
Morning by morning he wakens—
wakens my ear
to listen as those who are taught.
5 The Lord GOD has opened my ear,
and I was not rebellious,
I did not turn backward.
6 I gave my back to those who struck me,
and my cheeks to those who pulled out the beard;
I did not hide my face
from insult and spitting.

7 The Lord GOD helps me;
therefore I have not been disgraced;
therefore I have set my face like flint,
and I know that I shall not be put to shame;
8 he who vindicates me is near.
Who will contend with me?

50:4-11 The LORD God has given me…helps me: See the note on the servant songs at 42:1-4. As in 48:16 and 49:1-6, the servant-prophet speaks in the first person ("I"). Here, too, the role is that of a prophet, one with "the tongue of a teacher," able "to sustain the weary with a word" (50:4). Even though attacked for speaking God's word, the servant does not strike back (50:6; see also Matt 5:39). Apparently the message of release was not greeted favorably by all. Perhaps some were afraid to make the dangerous trip home; others may have become resigned to life in Babylon, or may even have prospered there (see Jer 29:4-7). In fact, many Israelites never did return, but remained in Babylon and founded a Jewish community there. The servant's confidence is in God, no matter what happens (50:7-9). His tone is similar to that in the psalms of trust (see especially Pss 16; 23; 27:1-6; 91; 121). The Apostle Paul echoes this same confidence in Romans 8:31-39.

[a] Or *die on the thirsty ground* [b] Cn: Heb *of those who are taught*

Let us stand up together.
Who are my adversaries?
Let them confront me.
9 It is the Lord GOD who helps me;
who will declare me guilty?
All of them will wear out like a garment;
the moth will eat them up.

10 Who among you fears the LORD
and obeys the voice of his servant,
who walks in darkness
and has no light,
yet trusts in the name of the LORD
and relies upon his God?
11 But all of you are kindlers of fire,
lighters of firebrands.[a]
Walk in the flame of your fire,
and among the brands that you have kindled!
This is what you shall have from my hand:
you shall lie down in torment.

Blessings in Store for God's People

51 Listen to me, you that pursue righteousness,
you that seek the LORD.
Look to the rock from which you were hewn,
and to the quarry from which you were dug.
2 Look to Abraham your father
and to Sarah who bore you;
for he was but one when I called him,
but I blessed him and made him many.
3 For the LORD will comfort Zion;
he will comfort all her waste places,
and will make her wilderness like Eden,
her desert like the garden of the LORD;
joy and gladness will be found in her,
thanksgiving and the voice of song.

4 Listen to me, my people,
and give heed to me, my nation;
for a teaching will go out from me,
and my justice for a light to the peoples.
5 I will bring near my deliverance swiftly,
my salvation has gone out

51:4-6 a teaching will go out…my justice for a light: God takes up the mission of the servant described in 42:1-4, using much of the same language, bringing teaching (*torah*) and justice to the coastlands. God's teaching is based on the *torah*, which here refers to God's word or "instruction." Similarly, the "light to the peoples" image of 49:6 is repeated. The mission of God and the mission of the servant are one.

[a] Syr: Heb *you gird yourselves with firebrands*

and my arms will rule the peoples;
the coastlands wait for me,
and for my arm they hope.
6 Lift up your eyes to the heavens,
and look at the earth beneath;
for the heavens will vanish like smoke,
the earth will wear out like a garment,
and those who live on it will die like gnats;[a]
but my salvation will be forever,
and my deliverance will never be ended.

7 Listen to me, you who know righteousness,
you people who have my teaching in your hearts;
do not fear the reproach of others,
and do not be dismayed when they revile you.
8 For the moth will eat them up like a garment,
and the worm will eat them like wool;
but my deliverance will be forever,
and my salvation to all generations.

9 Awake, awake, put on strength,
O arm of the LORD!
Awake, as in days of old,
the generations of long ago!
Was it not you who cut Rahab in pieces,
who pierced the dragon?
10 Was it not you who dried up the sea,
the waters of the great deep;
who made the depths of the sea a way
for the redeemed to cross over?
11 So the ransomed of the LORD shall return,
and come to Zion with singing;
everlasting joy shall be upon their heads;
they shall obtain joy and gladness,
and sorrow and sighing shall flee away.

12 I, I am he who comforts you;
why then are you afraid of a mere mortal who must die,
a human being who fades like grass?
13 You have forgotten the LORD, your Maker,
who stretched out the heavens
and laid the foundations of the earth.
You fear continually all day long

51:9—52:10 O arm of the LORD: This lengthy passage is divided into three parts by the call to "awake" (51:9, 17; 52:1), and it begins and ends with a reference to God's *arm* (51:9; 52:11). Israel calls on God's arm to "Awake" and to act "as in days of old" (51:9). But then God turns the tables and calls on Jerusalem to "Rouse yourself" (51:17) and to "Awake" (52:1). God promises to act (51:5, 11, 14), but then the people are called to take their own courage (51:12-16) and "loose the bonds from your neck" (52:2). Apparently, loosing the external bonds of the Babylonian captives was God's job, but Zion had its own responsibility to shake off the internal bonds and to respond in faith.

How can you "loosen the bonds" that tie you up or weigh you down? How has God already acted to help you do this?

[a] Or *in like manner*

because of the fury of the oppressor,
who is bent on destruction.
But where is the fury of the oppressor?
14 The oppressed shall speedily be released;
they shall not die and go down to the Pit,
nor shall they lack bread.
15 For I am the LORD your God,
who stirs up the sea so that its waves roar—
the LORD of hosts is his name.
16 I have put my words in your mouth,
and hidden you in the shadow of my hand,
stretching out[a] the heavens
and laying the foundations of the earth,
and saying to Zion, "You are my people."

17 Rouse yourself, rouse yourself!
Stand up, O Jerusalem,
you who have drunk at the hand of the LORD
the cup of his wrath,
who have drunk to the dregs
the bowl of staggering.
18 There is no one to guide her
among all the children she has borne;
there is no one to take her by the hand
among all the children she has brought up.
19 These two things have befallen you
—who will grieve with you?—
devastation and destruction, famine and sword—
who will comfort you?[b]
20 Your children have fainted,
they lie at the head of every street
like an antelope in a net;
they are full of the wrath of the LORD,
the rebuke of your God.

21 Therefore hear this, you who are wounded,[c]
who are drunk, but not with wine:
22 Thus says your Sovereign, the LORD,
your God who pleads the cause of his people:
See, I have taken from your hand the cup of staggering;
you shall drink no more
from the bowl of my wrath.
23 And I will put it into the hand of your tormentors,

---

[a] Syr: Heb *planting* [b] Q Ms Gk Syr Vg: MT *how may I comfort you?* [c] Or *humbled*

who have said to you,
"Bow down, that we may walk on you";
and you have made your back like the ground
and like the street for them to walk on.

Let Zion Rejoice

52 Awake, awake,
put on your strength, O Zion!
Put on your beautiful garments,
O Jerusalem, the holy city;
for the uncircumcised and the unclean
shall enter you no more.
2 Shake yourself from the dust, rise up,
O captive[a] Jerusalem;
loose the bonds from your neck,
O captive daughter Zion!

3 For thus says the LORD: You were sold for nothing, and you
shall be redeemed without money. 4 For thus says the Lord GOD:
Long ago, my people went down into Egypt to reside there as aliens;
the Assyrian, too, has oppressed them without cause. 5 Now therefore
what am I doing here, says the LORD, seeing that my people are taken
away without cause? Their rulers howl, says the LORD, and continually, all day long, my name is despised. 6 Therefore my people shall
know my name; therefore in that day they shall know that it is I who
speak; here am I.

7 How beautiful upon the mountains
are the feet of the messenger who announces peace,
who brings good news,
who announces salvation,
who says to Zion, "Your God reigns."
8 Listen! Your sentinels lift up their voices,
together they sing for joy;
for in plain sight they see
the return of the LORD to Zion.
9 Break forth together into singing,
you ruins of Jerusalem;
for the LORD has comforted his people,
he has redeemed Jerusalem.
10 The LORD has bared his holy arm
before the eyes of all the nations;
and all the ends of the earth shall see
the salvation of our God.

52:7-10 good news... salvation: As in 40:9-11, the sentinels watch and bring good news to the people (see the note there). The sentinels in this passage are back in Jerusalem, awaiting and announcing the return of God and the exiles. The section begins with the "feet of the messenger" and ends with the "holy arm" of the Lord—both serving God's *salvation* for all. Now, the comfort promised in 40:1 has been delivered: "the LORD has comforted his people." All the nations have seen the power of God's arm in freeing the captives (45:6).

In your life, who is like the messenger who brings good news?

[a] Cn: Heb *rise up, sit*

52:11-12 Depart...Touch no unclean thing: God's people are called to leave Babylon and not take with them any type of Babylonian things, especially anything related to Babylonian gods. Like the original exodus, God will go before and also bring up the rear (see Exod 14:19-20), but unlike the old exodus (Exod 12:33-39), this one need not be done in haste.

52:13—53:12: my servant...bore the sin of many: In this fourth traditional servant song (see the note on the servant songs at 42:1-4) the reality of suffering stands out. God introduces the servant, announcing that he will astound the nations despite his disfigured appearance (52:13-15). God will have the last word, rewarding the servant because he gave himself for others (53:11b-12). The "we" of 53:1-6 is not clearly identified, though the connection between 53:1 and 52:10 suggests that these observers could be the nations. In that case, they recognize, to their great surprise, that the servant Israel had in fact suffered on their behalf. This would be surprising, because they would have despised Israel as insignificant, and they would have regarded its suffering and disgrace as the consequence of Israel's own failures. God now brings all people to himself by placing their sins, diseases, and failings on God's servant. This is why "it was the will [purpose] of the LORD to crush him with pain" (53:10)—not because God takes pleasure in being cruel but because of God's unparalleled grace. God would win over the nations not by military defeat but through the voluntary suffering of the servant that sets them free to see everything (including Israel and God) in a new way. (See the note on the divine purpose, at 44:28.)

More often, however, interpreters have understood the observers (the "we") to be Israel, in which case the servant is a faithful one (or faithful minority) among them who gives himself on behalf of the many. The New Testament sees the servant's suffering for others fulfilled in Jesus (Acts 8:32-35; 1 Pet 2:22-25), and Jesus sees himself as called to be such a servant (see Mark 8:31; 10:43-45). In the Gospels, he "carried our diseases" (53:4) is seen first as a pointer to Jesus' healing ministry rather than to the cross (Matt 8:17).

Ponder the words "Surely he has borne our infirmities and carried our diseases." Perhaps you have heard them sung in reference to Jesus in Handel's *Messiah* or heard them proclaimed on Good Friday. What have these words meant to you?

11 Depart, depart, go out from there!
Touch no unclean thing;
go out from the midst of it, purify yourselves,
you who carry the vessels of the LORD.
12 For you shall not go out in haste,
and you shall not go in flight;
for the LORD will go before you,
and the God of Israel will be your rear guard.

The Suffering Servant

13 See, my servant shall prosper;
he shall be exalted and lifted up,
and shall be very high.
14 Just as there were many who were astonished at him[a]
—so marred was his appearance, beyond human semblance,
and his form beyond that of mortals—
15 so he shall startle[b] many nations;
kings shall shut their mouths because of him;
for that which had not been told them they shall see,
and that which they had not heard they shall contemplate.

53 Who has believed what we have heard?
And to whom has the arm of the LORD been revealed?
2 For he grew up before him like a young plant,
and like a root out of dry ground;
he had no form or majesty that we should look at him,
nothing in his appearance that we should desire him.
3 He was despised and rejected by others;
a man of suffering[c] and acquainted with infirmity;
and as one from whom others hide their faces[d]
he was despised, and we held him of no account.

4 Surely he has borne our infirmities
and carried our diseases;
yet we accounted him stricken,
struck down by God, and afflicted.
5 But he was wounded for our transgressions,
crushed for our iniquities;
upon him was the punishment that made us whole,
and by his bruises we are healed.
6 All we like sheep have gone astray;
we have all turned to our own way,
and the LORD has laid on him
the iniquity of us all.

---

[a] Syr Tg: Heb *you* [b] Meaning of Heb uncertain [c] Or *a man of sorrows* [d] Or *as one who hides his face from us*

7 He was oppressed, and he was afflicted,
yet he did not open his mouth;
like a lamb that is led to the slaughter,
and like a sheep that before its shearers is silent,
so he did not open his mouth.
8 By a perversion of justice he was taken away.
Who could have imagined his future?
For he was cut off from the land of the living,
stricken for the transgression of my people.
9 They made his grave with the wicked
and his tomb[a] with the rich,[b]
although he had done no violence,
and there was no deceit in his mouth.

10 Yet it was the will of the LORD to crush him with pain.[c]
When you make his life an offering for sin,[d]
he shall see his offspring, and shall prolong his days;
through him the will of the LORD shall prosper.
11 Out of his anguish he shall see light;[e]
he shall find satisfaction through his knowledge.
The righteous one,[f] my servant, shall make many righteous,
and he shall bear their iniquities.
12 Therefore I will allot him a portion with the great,
and he shall divide the spoil with the strong;
because he poured out himself to death,
and was numbered with the transgressors;
yet he bore the sin of many,
and made intercession for the transgressors.

The Eternal Covenant of Peace

54 Sing, O barren one who did not bear;
burst into song and shout,
you who have not been in labor!
For the children of the desolate woman will be more
than the children of her that is married, says the LORD.
2 Enlarge the site of your tent,
and let the curtains of your habitations be stretched out;
do not hold back; lengthen your cords
and strengthen your stakes.
3 For you will spread out to the right and to the left,
and your descendants will possess the nations
and will settle the desolate towns.

54:1-2 O barren one...desolate woman...Enlarge the site of your tent: Jerusalem is compared to a woman who grieves because she cannot have children. When the exiles return, her tent will be filled to overflowing with her children.

[a] Q Ms: MT *and in his death* [b] Cn: Heb *with a rich person* [c] Or *by disease*; meaning of Heb uncertain [d] Meaning of Heb uncertain [e] Q Mss: MT lacks *light* [f] Or *and he shall find satisfaction. Through his knowledge, the righteous one*

54:5-6 your Maker is your husband . . . called you . . . like the wife of a man's youth when she is cast off: God has not abandoned the relationship with Israel. It may have seemed like that for a time, but God did not divorce them (see note on 50:1-3).

54:6-10 For a brief moment: God admits to briefly abandoning the people, so their laments are legitimate. Still, they have only been momentarily forsaken (49:14), that is, left to the consequences of their own rebellion (48:3-8). On the other hand, God's compassion is not momentary, but everlasting (54:10). The phrase "like the days of Noah" refers to Gen 8:20-22, where after the flood was over, God promised never again to "curse the ground" or "destroy every living creature." Now God calls to mind that covenant and renews its promise (see Gen 9:8-17).

4 Do not fear, for you will not be ashamed;
do not be discouraged, for you will not suffer disgrace;
for you will forget the shame of your youth,
and the disgrace of your widowhood you will remember no more.
5 For your Maker is your husband,
the LORD of hosts is his name;
the Holy One of Israel is your Redeemer,
the God of the whole earth he is called.
6 For the LORD has called you
like a wife forsaken and grieved in spirit,
like the wife of a man's youth when she is cast off,
says your God.
7 For a brief moment I abandoned you,
but with great compassion I will gather you.
8 In overflowing wrath for a moment
I hid my face from you,
but with everlasting love I will have compassion on you,
says the LORD, your Redeemer.

9 This is like the days of Noah to me:
Just as I swore that the waters of Noah
would never again go over the earth,
so I have sworn that I will not be angry with you
and will not rebuke you.
10 For the mountains may depart
and the hills be removed,
but my steadfast love shall not depart from you,
and my covenant of peace shall not be removed,
says the LORD, who has compassion on you.

11 O afflicted one, storm-tossed, and not comforted,
I am about to set your stones in antimony,
and lay your foundations with sapphires.[a]
12 I will make your pinnacles of rubies,
your gates of jewels,
and all your wall of precious stones.
13 All your children shall be taught by the LORD,
and great shall be the prosperity of your children.
14 In righteousness you shall be established;
you shall be far from oppression, for you shall not fear;
and from terror, for it shall not come near you.
15 If anyone stirs up strife,

[a] Or *lapis lazuli*

it is not from me;
whoever stirs up strife with you
shall fall because of you.
16 See it is I who have created the smith
who blows the fire of coals,
and produces a weapon fit for its purpose;
I have also created the ravager to destroy.
17 No weapon that is fashioned against you shall prosper,
and you shall confute every tongue that rises against you in judgment.
This is the heritage of the servants of the LORD
and their vindication from me, says the LORD.

An Invitation to Abundant Life

55 Ho, everyone who thirsts,
come to the waters;
and you that have no money,
come, buy and eat!
Come, buy wine and milk
without money and without price.
2 Why do you spend your money for that which is not bread,
and your labor for that which does not satisfy?
Listen carefully to me, and eat what is good,
and delight yourselves in rich food.
3 Incline your ear, and come to me;
listen, so that you may live.
I will make with you an everlasting covenant,
my steadfast, sure love for David.
4 See, I made him a witness to the peoples,
a leader and commander for the peoples.
5 See, you shall call nations that you do not know,
and nations that do not know you shall run to you,
because of the LORD your God, the Holy One of Israel,
for he has glorified you.

6 Seek the LORD while he may be found,
call upon him while he is near;
7 let the wicked forsake their way,
and the unrighteous their thoughts;
let them return to the LORD, that he may have mercy on them,
and to our God, for he will abundantly pardon.
8 For my thoughts are not your thoughts,
nor are your ways my ways, says the LORD.
9 For as the heavens are higher than the earth,

55:1-13 come to the waters… come, buy and eat!: Like a street vendor, God invites all to a free and rich banquet (25:6; see Prov 9:1-5; John 7:37). With the words "I will make with you an everlasting covenant" (55:3), God not only renews the covenant with Noah (54:9-10), but also restates the one with David (2 Sam 7:4-17). This surprisingly extends the promise made to David to the entire people. Now, all Israel shares in God's royal messianic mission to all nations (55:5). Later, the priesthood is also opened to all (61:6). Both acts are signs of the remarkable universality of God's work in this portion of Isaiah.

55:6-13 seek the LORD…For you shall go out in joy: The words "Seek" and "call" continue the invitation begun in 55:1. Now is the time for Israel to repent and return to the Lord. Why? The clauses that begin with "for" provide an answer (55:7c, 8, 9, 10, 12). God wants to pardon those who return (55:7). God's ways and thoughts are not the same as the people's ways (55:8-9), and that is good news for God's people. According to God's law, the human response to a rebellious child is harsh (48:8; see Deut 21:18-21), but God's response is mercy (see Hos 11:9). God's word is as life-giving and nourishing as rain (55:10), and it will certainly accomplish God's purpose (55:11). God will lead the people in joy out of exile in Babylon and back home in peace to Judah (55:12). This affirmation of God's strong word balances the one in 40:8, closing this section of the book that began in chapter 40 (see the notes on 40:6-8). With the new exodus, not just Israel but all creation is transformed (55:12-13; see note on 24:5).

How have you experienced God's word accomplishing God's purpose? How is God's word like food or water?

56:1—66:24 **Maintain justice, and do what is right:** These chapters comprise the third major portion of the book, sometimes called Third Isaiah. However, few scholars think that a single prophetic voice was behind these words. The prophetic messages apparently reflect the difficult conditions and tensions faced by the people who returned to Jerusalem following the exile. (Recall that they were allowed to return after Cyrus conquered Babylon in 538 B.C.E.) The challenges they faced included the ongoing problem of worshiping the gods of the neighboring peoples (chapters 57–58) and failing to treat others with justice and fairness (59:6-21; 61:8).

56:1-8 **Maintain justice…I will gather others to them:** Third Isaiah begins with the same kind of openness exhibited in Second Isaiah. Here, foreigners and eunuchs who "maintain justice" (56:1), "keep my sabbaths" (56:4), and "hold fast my covenant" (56:6) are fully admitted to the community of God's people. To them is extended the "everlasting sign" promised forever to Israel (55:13). Biblical law had excluded eunuchs (males whose sexual organs had been removed) from the assembly (see Deut 23:1; Lev 21:18-20), but that prohibition is now surprisingly lifted. And foreigners are now assured of their welcome in God's house, "a house of prayer for all peoples" (56:7; see also Mark 11:17). Here, membership in God's people is a matter of commitment, not merely of heritage. During the exile, when temple worship was impossible, keeping the Sabbath had gained in importance as a mark of God's people (58:13-14).

so are my ways higher than your ways
and my thoughts than your thoughts.

10 For as the rain and the snow come down from heaven,
and do not return there until they have watered the earth,
making it bring forth and sprout,
giving seed to the sower and bread to the eater,
11 so shall my word be that goes out from my mouth;
it shall not return to me empty,
but it shall accomplish that which I purpose,
and succeed in the thing for which I sent it.

12 For you shall go out in joy,
and be led back in peace;
the mountains and the hills before you
shall burst into song,
and all the trees of the field shall clap their hands.
13 Instead of the thorn shall come up the cypress;
instead of the brier shall come up the myrtle;
and it shall be to the LORD for a memorial,
for an everlasting sign that shall not be cut off.

The Covenant Extended to All Who Obey

56 Thus says the LORD:
Maintain justice, and do what is right,
for soon my salvation will come,
and my deliverance be revealed.

2 Happy is the mortal who does this,
the one who holds it fast,
who keeps the sabbath, not profaning it,
and refrains from doing any evil.

3 Do not let the foreigner joined to the LORD say,
"The LORD will surely separate me from his people";
and do not let the eunuch say,
"I am just a dry tree."
4 For thus says the LORD:
To the eunuchs who keep my sabbaths,
who choose the things that please me
and hold fast my covenant,
5 I will give, in my house and within my walls,
a monument and a name
better than sons and daughters;

I will give them an everlasting name
that shall not be cut off.

6 And the foreigners who join themselves to the LORD,
to minister to him, to love the name of the LORD,
and to be his servants,
all who keep the sabbath, and do not profane it,
and hold fast my covenant—
7 these I will bring to my holy mountain,
and make them joyful in my house of prayer;
their burnt offerings and their sacrifices
will be accepted on my altar;
for my house shall be called a house of prayer
for all peoples.
8 Thus says the Lord GOD,
who gathers the outcasts of Israel,
I will gather others to them
besides those already gathered.[a]

The Corruption of Israel's Rulers

9 All you wild animals,
all you wild animals in the forest, come to devour!
10 Israel's[b] sentinels are blind,
they are all without knowledge;
they are all silent dogs
that cannot bark;
dreaming, lying down,
loving to slumber.
11 The dogs have a mighty appetite;
they never have enough.
The shepherds also have no understanding;
they have all turned to their own way,
to their own gain, one and all.
12 "Come," they say, "let us[c] get wine;
let us fill ourselves with strong drink.
And tomorrow will be like today,
great beyond measure."

Israel's Futile Idolatry

57 The righteous perish,
and no one takes it to heart;
the devout are taken away,
while no one understands.

[a] Heb *besides his gathered ones* [b] Heb *His* [c] Q Ms Syr Vg Tg: MT *me*

56:8 who gathers the outcasts of Israel: The Israelites are reminded that they were "outcasts" themselves when God saved them. So, they are to remember this when God gather "others," such as the foreigners and eunuchs to be part of the worshiping community. See also the note on 39:1-8.

Who might be considered outcasts today? How do we in the church reach out to them and invite them to be part of the community of faith?

56:9-12 wild animals...Israel's sentinels: This oracle is a warning to Israel's leaders (sentinels), who can't keep watch because they are blinded by their own appetites and have gone "their own way" (and not followed God). The "wild animals" are foreign nations who can come and devour Judah again (see 5:26-30, where Assyria is compared to a devouring lion).

57:1-4 righteous perish...enter into peace...Whom are you mocking?: Not only the nations practice the kind of idolatry denounced in chapters 40–55 (see note on 44:9-20), but now so does Israel. The righteous (those who follow God) are mocked by those who are worshiping idols.

For the righteous are taken away from calamity,
2 and they enter into peace;
those who walk uprightly
will rest on their couches.
3 But as for you, come here,
you children of a sorceress,
you offspring of an adulterer and a whore.[a]
4 Whom are you mocking?
Against whom do you open your mouth wide
and stick out your tongue?
Are you not children of transgression,
the offspring of deceit—
5 you that burn with lust among the oaks,
under every green tree;
you that slaughter your children in the valleys,
under the clefts of the rocks?
6 Among the smooth stones of the valley is your portion;
they, they, are your lot;
to them you have poured out a drink offering,
you have brought a grain offering.
Shall I be appeased for these things?
7 Upon a high and lofty mountain
you have set your bed,
and there you went up to offer sacrifice.
8 Behind the door and the doorpost
you have set up your symbol;
for, in deserting me,[b] you have uncovered your bed,
you have gone up to it,
you have made it wide;
and you have made a bargain for yourself with them,
you have loved their bed,
you have gazed on their nakedness.[c]
9 You journeyed to Molech[d] with oil,
and multiplied your perfumes;
you sent your envoys far away,
and sent down even to Sheol.
10 You grew weary from your many wanderings,
but you did not say, "It is useless."
You found your desire rekindled,
and so you did not weaken.

11 Whom did you dread and fear
so that you lied,

57:5-13 burn with lust among the oaks . . . let your collection of idols deliver you!: Several kinds of idolatry are named in these verses. Some of the people may be following sexual practices connected to old fertility cults (57:5); worshiping other gods with offerings (57:6-7) and individual idols in their homes (57:8); or presenting offerings to the god Molech, who was presented living children as sacrifices (Lev 18:21; 2 Kgs 23:10). But these gods cannot deliver anyone. Only those who trust in God can "possess the land" and "inherit [God's] holy mountain" (that is, be part of Israel's true worshiping community).

---

[a] Heb *an adulterer and she plays the whore* [b] Meaning of Heb uncertain [c] Or *their phallus*; Heb *the hand* [d] Or *the king*

and did not remember me
    or give me a thought?
Have I not kept silent and closed my eyes,[a]
    and so you do not fear me?
12 I will concede your righteousness and your works,
    but they will not help you.
13 When you cry out, let your collection of idols deliver you!
    The wind will carry them off,
    a breath will take them away.
But whoever takes refuge in me shall possess the land
    and inherit my holy mountain.

A Promise of Help and Healing

14 It shall be said,
"Build up, build up, prepare the way,
    remove every obstruction from my people's way."
15 For thus says the high and lofty one
    who inhabits eternity, whose name is Holy:
I dwell in the high and holy place,
    and also with those who are contrite and humble in spirit,
to revive the spirit of the humble,
    and to revive the heart of the contrite.
16 For I will not continually accuse,
    nor will I always be angry;
for then the spirits would grow faint before me,
    even the souls that I have made.
17 Because of their wicked covetousness I was angry;
    I struck them, I hid and was angry;
    but they kept turning back to their own ways.
18 I have seen their ways, but I will heal them;
    I will lead them and repay them with comfort,
    creating for their mourners the fruit of the lips.[b]
19 Peace, peace, to the far and the near, says the LORD;
    and I will heal them.
20 But the wicked are like the tossing sea
    that cannot keep still;
    its waters toss up mire and mud.
21 There is no peace, says my God, for the wicked.

False and True Worship

58 Shout out, do not hold back!
Lift up your voice like a trumpet!
Announce to my people their rebellion,

[a] Gk Vg: Heb *silent even for a long time* [b] Meaning of Heb uncertain

57:14-21 Build up . . . remove every obstruction from my people's way . . . I will heal them: In spite of the actions of some who are worshiping idols, God's mercy will prevail for "those who are contrite and humble in spirit" (57:15). Those who admit their wrongs and return to worshiping God alone will be forgiven. But the wicked will not have peace. The assurance that God is both "high and lofty" (57:15) and also present with the humble is a central theme in the Bible (66:1-2; see Ps 113:5-6).

58:1-9 Announce to my people their rebellion . . . loose the bonds of injustice: In the tradition of all the prophets, the speaker rejects the hypocrisy of focusing on worship practices while not living out faith by serving the neighbor, especially the poor. For other examples, see 1:10-17; 1 Sam 15:22; Hos 6:6; Amos 5:21-27; Mic 6:6-8; Jer 6:19-20; Joel 2:12-13; Mal 1:6-14; Mark 12:32-34; Matt 9:13. The phrases "Shout out" and "Lift up your voice" (58:1) sound like the invitations used to introduce the comforting message of Second Isaiah (40:1-2, 9), but ironically, here they announce judgment.

The people fast (58:3-4) and even wear sackcloth and cover themselves in ashes (58:5) as a show of their faith, but even in their complaint, the people betray the problem: they fast to "serve your own interest," which includes oppressing their own workers. On the other hand, "the fast that I [God] choose" is not a mere ritual but giving one's food and even one's self to the other. It is sharing food with the hungry and giving shelter to the homeless (58:7). If the people act with justice, then God will answer their cries for help (58:8-9).

to the house of Jacob their sins.
2 Yet day after day they seek me
and delight to know my ways,
as if they were a nation that practiced righteousness
and did not forsake the ordinance of their God;
they ask of me righteous judgments,
they delight to draw near to God.
3 "Why do we fast, but you do not see?
Why humble ourselves, but you do not notice?"
Look, you serve your own interest on your fast day,
and oppress all your workers.
4 Look, you fast only to quarrel and to fight
and to strike with a wicked fist.
Such fasting as you do today
will not make your voice heard on high.
5 Is such the fast that I choose,
a day to humble oneself?
Is it to bow down the head like a bulrush,
and to lie in sackcloth and ashes?
Will you call this a fast,
a day acceptable to the LORD?

6 Is not this the fast that I choose:
to loose the bonds of injustice,
to undo the thongs of the yoke,
to let the oppressed go free,
and to break every yoke?
7 Is it not to share your bread with the hungry,
and bring the homeless poor into your house;
when you see the naked, to cover them,
and not to hide yourself from your own kin?
8 Then your light shall break forth like the dawn,
and your healing shall spring up quickly;
your vindicator[a] shall go before you,
the glory of the LORD shall be your rear guard.
9 Then you shall call, and the LORD will answer;
you shall cry for help, and he will say, Here I am.

If you remove the yoke from among you,
the pointing of the finger, the speaking of evil,
10 if you offer your food to the hungry
and satisfy the needs of the afflicted,
then your light shall rise in the darkness

[a] Or *vindication*

58:9 Here I am: This phrase is generally the response that humans give when called by God or a superior. First Isaiah says this at his call (see note on 6:1-13). Now, in the latter part of the book (and only there in the Bible), God says these words three times (see also 52:6; 65:1). Now, as a sign of great compassion, God becomes totally available and vulnerable to God's people.

58:10 if you offer your food: The phrase "if you offer your food to the hungry" is based on the Greek Septuagint text. The Hebrew text supports the RSV translation, "if you pour yourself out for the hungry," and provides the richer meaning. The wordplay here is deliberate: If you pour out your *nephesh* [NE-phesh], Hebrew for "self" or "soul," and satisfy the *nephesh* of the afflicted (58:10), the LORD will satisfy your *nephesh* (58:11). This is not a bargain but a promise: as you give yourself for the sake of the other you find your true self (Matt 10:39). The gift of self will provide for the needs of the other (58:6-7) but will go beyond mere food (Matt 4:4; Acts 3:6).

and your gloom be like the noonday.
11 The LORD will guide you continually,
and satisfy your needs in parched places,
and make your bones strong;
and you shall be like a watered garden,
like a spring of water,
whose waters never fail.
12 Your ancient ruins shall be rebuilt;
you shall raise up the foundations of many generations;
you shall be called the repairer of the breach,
the restorer of streets to live in.

13 If you refrain from trampling the sabbath,
from pursuing your own interests on my holy day;
if you call the sabbath a delight
and the holy day of the LORD honorable;
if you honor it, not going your own ways,
serving your own interests, or pursuing your own affairs;[a]
14 then you shall take delight in the LORD,
and I will make you ride upon the heights of the earth;
I will feed you with the heritage of your ancestor Jacob,
for the mouth of the LORD has spoken.

Injustice and Oppression to Be Punished

59 See, the LORD's hand is not too short to save,
nor his ear too dull to hear.
2 Rather, your iniquities have been barriers
between you and your God,
and your sins have hidden his face from you
so that he does not hear.
3 For your hands are defiled with blood,
and your fingers with iniquity;
your lips have spoken lies,
your tongue mutters wickedness.
4 No one brings suit justly,
no one goes to law honestly;
they rely on empty pleas, they speak lies,
conceiving mischief and begetting iniquity.
5 They hatch adders' eggs,
and weave the spider's web;
whoever eats their eggs dies,
and the crushed egg hatches out a viper.
6 Their webs cannot serve as clothing;

[a] Heb *or speaking words*

Have you sometimes practiced fasting as a spiritual exercise? Or contemplated doing so? How does this passage help you think about the meaning of such fasting?

58:13-14 sabbath: Observing or keeping the Sabbath was an important part of true worship and not to be used for pursuing self-interests. See also the note on 56:1-8.

The Sabbath is called the "holy day of the LORD" (58:13). What makes this day holy? Why is such a day important to Christians as well?

59:1—64:12 Arise, shine; for your light has come: The central portion of Third Isaiah is carefully structured. At its core are the words of promise in chapters 60–62. Surrounding this core are two prayers of mourning called community laments (59:1-15a and 63:7—64:12). Within these laments are two oracles about the judgment of God, who is pictured as the divine warrior and Redeemer (59:15b-20 and 63:1-6). So, the movement in these chapters is from lament to warrior to promise to warrior to lament. As is often the case in biblical poetry and narrative, this structure serves to highlight the material at the center. The strong promises of deliverance in chapters 60–62 answer the surrounding laments and temper the sharp judgment of the warrior oracles.

59:1-15a your iniquities have been barriers…Justice is turned back: The section begins in verses 1-8 with a typical word of prophetic judgment against Israel's sins and failures, reminiscent of First Isaiah and the other eighth-century prophets (1:2-20). The sins (iniquities) include dealing unjustly and dishonestly with one another. Lies and unjust actions are compared to the poisonous bites of adders or vipers. The words of judgment (59:1-8) lead to the words of the lament, which sounds like a confession of sin (59:9-15a). The lack of justice for Israel was not God's fault (59:1), but their own (59:12-13).

they cannot cover themselves with what they make.
Their works are works of iniquity,
and deeds of violence are in their hands.
7 Their feet run to evil,
and they rush to shed innocent blood;
their thoughts are thoughts of iniquity,
desolation and destruction are in their highways.
8 The way of peace they do not know,
and there is no justice in their paths.
Their roads they have made crooked;
no one who walks in them knows peace.

9 Therefore justice is far from us,
and righteousness does not reach us;
we wait for light, and lo! there is darkness;
and for brightness, but we walk in gloom.
10 We grope like the blind along a wall,
groping like those who have no eyes;
we stumble at noon as in the twilight,
among the vigorous[a] as though we were dead.
11 We all growl like bears;
like doves we moan mournfully.
We wait for justice, but there is none;
for salvation, but it is far from us.
12 For our transgressions before you are many,
and our sins testify against us.
Our transgressions indeed are with us,
and we know our iniquities:
13 transgressing, and denying the LORD,
and turning away from following our God,
talking oppression and revolt,
conceiving lying words and uttering them from the heart.
14 Justice is turned back,
and righteousness stands at a distance;
for truth stumbles in the public square,
and uprightness cannot enter.
15 Truth is lacking,
and whoever turns from evil is despoiled.

The LORD saw it, and it displeased him
that there was no justice.
16 He saw that there was no one,
and was appalled that there was no one to intervene;

59:15b-20 The LORD…put on righteousness like a breastplate: Though Israel itself turned back justice (59:14), the enemies also denied justice to God's people. For this, only God's intervention as the divine warrior will provide the remedy (34:1-17; 63:1-6). God puts on armor in the battle against the nations (see also Eph 6:14-17).

[a] Meaning of Heb uncertain

so his own arm brought him victory,
and his righteousness upheld him.
17 He put on righteousness like a breastplate,
and a helmet of salvation on his head;
he put on garments of vengeance for clothing,
and wrapped himself in fury as in a mantle.
18 According to their deeds, so will he repay;
wrath to his adversaries, requital to his enemies;
to the coastlands he will render requital.
19 So those in the west shall fear the name of the LORD,
and those in the east, his glory;
for he will come like a pent-up stream
that the wind of the LORD drives on.

20 And he will come to Zion as Redeemer,
to those in Jacob who turn from transgression, says the LORD.
21 And as for me, this is my covenant with them, says the LORD: my
spirit that is upon you, and my words that I have put in your mouth,
shall not depart out of your mouth, or out of the mouths of your children, or out of the mouths of your children's children, says the LORD,
from now on and forever.

The Ingathering of the Dispersed

60 Arise, shine; for your light has come,
and the glory of the LORD has risen upon you.
2 For darkness shall cover the earth,
and thick darkness the peoples;
but the LORD will arise upon you,
and his glory will appear over you.
3 Nations shall come to your light,
and kings to the brightness of your dawn.

4 Lift up your eyes and look around;
they all gather together, they come to you;
your sons shall come from far away,
and your daughters shall be carried on their nurses' arms.
5 Then you shall see and be radiant;
your heart shall thrill and rejoice,[a]
because the abundance of the sea shall be brought to you,
the wealth of the nations shall come to you.
6 A multitude of camels shall cover you,
the young camels of Midian and Ephah;
all those from Sheba shall come.

---

[a] Heb *be enlarged*

60:1—62:12 the LORD will arise upon you: These chapters at the center of Third Isaiah are similar in tone to the good news of Second Isaiah (chapters 40–55). They reaffirm God's promises to the people following the exile (see the note on structure at 59:1—64:12). Restoration, abundance, blessing, and grace were assurances that the rebuilding community needed. There are also strong economic promises, which would have been very important for the returning exiles, who were pioneers in their own homeland.

60:1-22 your light has come . . . call you the City of the LORD: God promises the renewal of Jerusalem and the rebuilding of the temple. The two-fold command "Arise, shine" is typical of Second Isaiah (40:1; 51:9, 17; 52:1, 11)). The restored Jerusalem is pictured by several images. Nations and kings will come to the light of Jerusalem (60:3; see also 2:2-4; 11:2, 10; 42:6-7; 49:6), bringing gifts (60:5), flocks (60:6), silver and gold (60:9), and building materials for the temple, such as trees from Lebanon (60:13). Matthew uses this passage as background for the gifts of the wise men (Matt 2:11). The nations will come, bringing Zion's children (60:4) and even bow at its feet (60:14). When Jerusalem is restored, God "will be your everlasting light" (60:19; see 60:1-3; Rev 21:23).

60:3 Nations: Along with other biblical books, Isaiah reports a progression of God's treatment of the nations. When they come as the destroying enemy, they are totally defeated (34:1-17; 59:15b-19; 63:1-6). When they recognize the presence of God's light in Israel, they come first as servants of Israel (60:1-16; 61:5). But then they become part of God's people as converts, receiving God's salvation (2:1-4; 45:22; 49:5). With the recognition that all are outcasts (Israel and foreigners alike), there is full mutual recognition of one another as participants in God's covenant (56:1-8). The Apostle Paul speaks of the new community of Christ in a similar way: "There is no longer Jew or Greek, there is no longer slave or free, there is no longer male or female; for all of you are one in Christ Jesus." (Gal 3:28).

They shall bring gold and frankincense,
and shall proclaim the praise of the LORD.
7 All the flocks of Kedar shall be gathered to you,
the rams of Nebaioth shall minister to you;
they shall be acceptable on my altar,
and I will glorify my glorious house.

8 Who are these that fly like a cloud,
and like doves to their windows?
9 For the coastlands shall wait for me,
the ships of Tarshish first,
to bring your children from far away,
their silver and gold with them,
for the name of the LORD your God,
and for the Holy One of Israel,
because he has glorified you.
10 Foreigners shall build up your walls,
and their kings shall minister to you;
for in my wrath I struck you down,
but in my favor I have had mercy on you.
11 Your gates shall always be open;
day and night they shall not be shut,
so that nations shall bring you their wealth,
with their kings led in procession.
12 For the nation and kingdom
that will not serve you shall perish;
those nations shall be utterly laid waste.
13 The glory of Lebanon shall come to you,
the cypress, the plane, and the pine,
to beautify the place of my sanctuary;
and I will glorify where my feet rest.
14 The descendants of those who oppressed you
shall come bending low to you,
and all who despised you
shall bow down at your feet;
they shall call you the City of the LORD,
the Zion of the Holy One of Israel.
15 Whereas you have been forsaken and hated,
with no one passing through,
I will make you majestic forever,
a joy from age to age.
16 You shall suck the milk of nations,
you shall suck the breasts of kings;
and you shall know that I, the LORD, am your Savior
and your Redeemer, the Mighty One of Jacob.

17 Instead of bronze I will bring gold,
instead of iron I will bring silver;
instead of wood, bronze,
instead of stones, iron.
I will appoint Peace as your overseer
and Righteousness as your taskmaster.
18 Violence shall no more be heard in your land,
devastation or destruction within your borders;
you shall call your walls Salvation,
and your gates Praise.

God the Glory of Zion

19 The sun shall no longer be
your light by day,
nor for brightness shall the moon
give light to you by night;[a]
but the LORD will be your everlasting light,
and your God will be your glory.
20 Your sun shall no more go down,
or your moon withdraw itself;
for the LORD will be your everlasting light,
and your days of mourning shall be ended.
21 Your people shall all be righteous;
they shall possess the land forever.
They are the shoot that I planted, the work of my hands,
so that I might be glorified.
22 The least of them shall become a clan,
and the smallest one a mighty nation;
I am the LORD;
in its time I will accomplish it quickly.

The Good News of Deliverance

61 The spirit of the Lord GOD is upon me,
because the LORD has anointed me;
he has sent me to bring good news to the oppressed,
to bind up the brokenhearted,
to proclaim liberty to the captives,
and release to the prisoners;
2 to proclaim the year of the LORD's favor,
and the day of vengeance of our God;
to comfort all who mourn;
3 to provide for those who mourn in Zion—
to give them a garland instead of ashes,

[a] Q Ms Gk Old Latin Tg: MT lacks *by night*

61:1-4 good news to the oppressed... liberty to the captives: The prophet or servant (see note on 42:1-4) speaks in the first person. The phrase "The spirit of the Lord God is upon me" (61:1; also 11:2; 42:1; 44:3; 48:16) describes the anointing by the spirit that empowers the prophet's mission. The mission is defined— to bring good news, to bind up, to proclaim liberty, to proclaim the year of God's favor, to comfort, to provide, to give (60:1-3). Seven is often a symbolic number of completeness in the Bible. The point is that *everything* is opened and transformed. This extravagant work of liberation defines the work of Israel, of the servant, of God's messiah, and of God—all of which come together here and in the servant poems of Isaiah. Increasingly in the Bible, setting free those who are captive defines who God is and what God desires (43:14; see Exod 20:2; Lev 26:13; Pss 68:5-6; 107:10-16; 146:5-10; Ezek 34:27). Jesus accepts this role in his first sermon (see Luke 4:16-21). "The year of the LORD's favor" (61:2) is Israel's year of jubilee (every fifty years). In that year debts were to be cancelled and slaves set free (see Lev 25:10).

the oil of gladness instead of mourning,
the mantle of praise instead of a faint spirit.
They will be called oaks of righteousness,
the planting of the LORD, to display his glory.
4 They shall build up the ancient ruins,
they shall raise up the former devastations;
they shall repair the ruined cities,
the devastations of many generations.

5 Strangers shall stand and feed your flocks,
foreigners shall till your land and dress your vines;
6 but you shall be called priests of the LORD,
you shall be named ministers of our God;
you shall enjoy the wealth of the nations,
and in their riches you shall glory.
7 Because their[a] shame was double,
and dishonor was proclaimed as their lot,
therefore they shall possess a double portion;
everlasting joy shall be theirs.

8 For I the LORD love justice,
I hate robbery and wrongdoing;[b]
I will faithfully give them their recompense,
and I will make an everlasting covenant with them.
9 Their descendants shall be known among the nations,
and their offspring among the peoples;
all who see them shall acknowledge
that they are a people whom the LORD has blessed.
10 I will greatly rejoice in the LORD,
my whole being shall exult in my God;
for he has clothed me with the garments of salvation,
he has covered me with the robe of righteousness,
as a bridegroom decks himself with a garland,
and as a bride adorns herself with her jewels.
11 For as the earth brings forth its shoots,
and as a garden causes what is sown in it to spring up,
so the Lord GOD will cause righteousness and praise
to spring up before all the nations.

The Vindication and Salvation of Zion

62 For Zion's sake I will not keep silent,
and for Jerusalem's sake I will not rest,
until her vindication shines out like the dawn,

61:6 you shall be called priests of the LORD: As in the Davidic covenant in 55:3, the priesthood will be opened to all (see 1 Pet 2:9).

61:10 covered me with the robe of righteousness: Just as God was clothed in righteousness as battle armor (59:17), God clothes Zion or Israel in the same righteousness as the special clothing or jewels worn by a bridegroom and bride being married.

62:1-12: no more be termed Forsaken...Desolate: When God restores Zion (Jerusalem), new names are given that overturn the judgment of 6:9-13. There the land was only "emptiness" (6:12; same Hebrew word as "forsaken"). But now they "shall no more be termed Forsaken." In the judgment, the land was "desolate" (6:11), but now it "shall no more be termed Desolate." One new name for Zion is "My Delight [Purpose] Is in Her" (in Hebrew, *Hephzibah*, which incorporates the term for "purpose" so important in Second Isaiah; see note on 44:28). The second name is "Married" (in Hebrew, *Beulah*), for God will rejoice over Zion as a bride and will overcome the desolation of childlessness brought by the exile (54:1). When all is restored, the promises of Second Isaiah are fulfilled (62:10-12; see 35:4; 40:3-5, 10). Just as Israel was called to "seek the LORD" (55:6), now they themselves are those "Sought Out" (62:12).

[a] Heb *your* [b] Or *robbery with a burnt offering*

and her salvation like a burning torch.
2 The nations shall see your vindication,
and all the kings your glory;
and you shall be called by a new name
that the mouth of the LORD will give.
3 You shall be a crown of beauty in the hand of the LORD,
and a royal diadem in the hand of your God.
4 You shall no more be termed Forsaken,[a]
and your land shall no more be termed Desolate;[b]
but you shall be called My Delight Is in Her,[c]
and your land Married;[d]
for the LORD delights in you,
and your land shall be married.
5 For as a young man marries a young woman,
so shall your builder[e] marry you,
and as the bridegroom rejoices over the bride,
so shall your God rejoice over you.
6 Upon your walls, O Jerusalem,
I have posted sentinels;
all day and all night
they shall never be silent.
You who remind the LORD,
take no rest,
7 and give him no rest
until he establishes Jerusalem
and makes it renowned throughout the earth.
8 The LORD has sworn by his right hand
and by his mighty arm:
I will not again give your grain
to be food for your enemies,
and foreigners shall not drink the wine
for which you have labored;
9 but those who garner it shall eat it
and praise the LORD,
and those who gather it shall drink it
in my holy courts.

10 Go through, go through the gates,
prepare the way for the people;
build up, build up the highway,
clear it of stones,
lift up an ensign over the peoples.
11 The LORD has proclaimed

---

[a] Heb *Azubah* [b] Heb *Shemamah* [c] Heb *Hephzibah* [d] Heb *Beulah* [e] Cn: Heb *your sons*

to the end of the earth:
Say to daughter Zion,
"See, your salvation comes;
his reward is with him,
and his recompense before him."
12 They shall be called, "The Holy People,
The Redeemed of the LORD";
and you shall be called, "Sought Out,
A City Not Forsaken."

Vengeance on Edom

63:1-6 from Edom, from Bozrah . . . I poured out their lifeblood: This is perhaps the harshest of the divine warrior passages (see 59:15b-20 and note). God is pictured as coming from Edom and its major city, Bozrah, as a conquering warrior. Edom was a symbol of foreign enemy nations (see Jer 49:7-22). God's robe is spattered with the blood of the enemy, an image reversed in Rev 7:14, where the robes of the redeemed are made white in the blood of the Lamb.

63 "Who is this that comes from Edom,
from Bozrah in garments stained crimson?
Who is this so splendidly robed,
marching in his great might?"

"It is I, announcing vindication,
mighty to save."

2 "Why are your robes red,
and your garments like theirs who tread the wine press?"

3 "I have trodden the wine press alone,
and from the peoples no one was with me;
I trod them in my anger
and trampled them in my wrath;
their juice spattered on my garments,
and stained all my robes.
4 For the day of vengeance was in my heart,
and the year for my redeeming work had come.
5 I looked, but there was no helper;
I stared, but there was no one to sustain me;
so my own arm brought me victory,
and my wrath sustained me.
6 I trampled down peoples in my anger,
I crushed them in my wrath,
and I poured out their lifeblood on the earth."

63:7—64:12 I will recount the gracious deeds of the LORD: This community lament balances the earlier one in 59:1-15a (see notes there). The two laments surround but are answered by the promises of chapters 60–62. The mercy sought here is promised there. The appeal here is made to God as "father" (63:16; 64:8), the only time this title is applied directly to God in Isaiah (though it is perhaps implied in 45:10). Like the many appeals to God as "mother" in the latter part of Isaiah (see note at 42:13-14), the assumption is that a father, too, will recognize and help his children, no matter what might try to separate them.

God's Mercy Remembered

7 I will recount the gracious deeds of the LORD,
the praiseworthy acts of the LORD,
because of all that the LORD has done for us,
and the great favor to the house of Israel
that he has shown them according to his mercy,
according to the abundance of his steadfast love.

8 For he said, "Surely they are my people,
children who will not deal falsely";
and he became their savior
9 in all their distress.
It was no messenger[a] or angel
but his presence that saved them;[b]
in his love and in his pity he redeemed them;
he lifted them up and carried them all the days of old.

10 But they rebelled
and grieved his holy spirit;
therefore he became their enemy;
he himself fought against them.
11 Then they[c] remembered the days of old,
of Moses his servant.[d]
Where is the one who brought them up out of the sea
with the shepherds of his flock?
Where is the one who put within them
his holy spirit,
12 who caused his glorious arm
to march at the right hand of Moses,
who divided the waters before them
to make for himself an everlasting name,
13 who led them through the depths?
Like a horse in the desert,
they did not stumble.
14 Like cattle that go down into the valley,
the spirit of the LORD gave them rest.
Thus you led your people,
to make for yourself a glorious name.

A Prayer of Penitence

15 Look down from heaven and see,
from your holy and glorious habitation.
Where are your zeal and your might?
The yearning of your heart and your compassion?
They are withheld from me.
16 For you are our father,
though Abraham does not know us
and Israel does not acknowledge us;
you, O LORD, are our father;
our Redeemer from of old is your name.

---

[a] Gk: Heb *anguish* [b] Or *savior.* [9] *In all their distress he was distressed; the angel of his presence saved them;*
[c] Heb *he* [d] Cn: Heb *his people*

17 Why, O LORD, do you make us stray from your ways
and harden our heart, so that we do not fear you?
Turn back for the sake of your servants,
for the sake of the tribes that are your heritage.
18 Your holy people took possession for a little while;
but now our adversaries have trampled down your sanctuary.
19 We have long been like those whom you do not rule,
like those not called by your name.

64:1-3 tear open the heavens... mountains would quake at your presence: God is called to show awesome power as in the past when God came in earthquake and fire (see Exod 19:16-19; Judg 5:4-5). God's physical appearance in fire, thunder, and shaking earth is known as a theophany.

64 O that you would tear open the heavens and come down,
so that the mountains would quake at your presence—
2[a] as when fire kindles brushwood
and the fire causes water to boil—
to make your name known to your adversaries,
so that the nations might tremble at your presence!
3 When you did awesome deeds that we did not expect,
you came down, the mountains quaked at your presence.
4 From ages past no one has heard,
no ear has perceived,
no eye has seen any God besides you,
who works for those who wait for him.
5 You meet those who gladly do right,
those who remember you in your ways.
But you were angry, and we sinned;
because you hid yourself we transgressed.[b]
6 We have all become like one who is unclean,
and all our righteous deeds are like a filthy cloth.
We all fade like a leaf,
and our iniquities, like the wind, take us away.
7 There is no one who calls on your name,
or attempts to take hold of you;
for you have hidden your face from us,
and have delivered[c] us into the hand of our iniquity.
8 Yet, O LORD, you are our Father;
we are the clay, and you are our potter;
we are all the work of your hand.
9 Do not be exceedingly angry, O LORD,
and do not remember iniquity forever.
Now consider, we are all your people.
10 Your holy cities have become a wilderness,
Zion has become a wilderness,
Jerusalem a desolation.
11 Our holy and beautiful house,

---

[a] Ch 64.1 in Heb [b] Meaning of Heb uncertain [c] Gk Syr Old Latin Tg: Heb *melted*

where our ancestors praised you,
has been burned by fire,
and all our pleasant places have become ruins.
12 After all this, will you restrain yourself, O LORD?
Will you keep silent, and punish us so severely?

The Righteousness of God's Judgment

65 I was ready to be sought out by those who did not ask,
to be found by those who did not seek me.
I said, "Here I am, here I am,"
to a nation that did not call on my name.
2 I held out my hands all day long
to a rebellious people,
who walk in a way that is not good,
following their own devices;
3 a people who provoke me
to my face continually,
sacrificing in gardens
and offering incense on bricks;
4 who sit inside tombs,
and spend the night in secret places;
who eat swine's flesh,
with broth of abominable things in their vessels;
5 who say, "Keep to yourself,
do not come near me, for I am too holy for you."
These are a smoke in my nostrils,
a fire that burns all day long.
6 See, it is written before me:
I will not keep silent, but I will repay;
I will indeed repay into their laps
7 their[a] iniquities and their[a] ancestors' iniquities together,
says the LORD;
because they offered incense on the mountains
and reviled me on the hills,
I will measure into their laps
full payment for their actions.
8 Thus says the LORD:
As the wine is found in the cluster,
and they say, "Do not destroy it,
for there is a blessing in it,"
so I will do for my servants' sake,
and not destroy them all.
9 I will bring forth descendants[b] from Jacob,

65:1-6 I was ready to be sought out…Here I am: The different themes of this chapter are a sign of the complex process of formation of the material of Third Isaiah. The passages are not nearly so uniform in tone as the enduring message of comfort in chapters 40–55. In the first part of the chapter, God wants to be sought and found ("Here I am"; see note on 58:9). The words of judgment here apply to some members of the community of God's people, but not to all. There is a distinction between "my servants" (65:9, 13-14) and "you who forsake the LORD" (65:11-15). Apparently after the exile there are those who have accepted the invitation to "seek the LORD" (55:6; see 65:10) and those who have not. "My servants shall eat, but you shall be hungry" recalls the invitation in 55:1 for "everyone" to eat and drink. God had invited all, but some have refused or have proved unfaithful (see also Matt 22:1-14), and they are addressed here directly. The hope behind this word of warning is that they, too, might yet seek God and be restored (65:1-2).

[a] Gk Syr: Heb *your* [b] Or *a descendant*

and from Judah inheritors[a] of my mountains;
my chosen shall inherit it,
and my servants shall settle there.
10 Sharon shall become a pasture for flocks,
and the Valley of Achor a place for herds to lie down,
for my people who have sought me.
11 But you who forsake the LORD,
who forget my holy mountain,
who set a table for Fortune
and fill cups of mixed wine for Destiny;
12 I will destine you to the sword,
and all of you shall bow down to the slaughter;
because, when I called, you did not answer,
when I spoke, you did not listen,
but you did what was evil in my sight,
and chose what I did not delight in.
13 Therefore thus says the Lord GOD:
My servants shall eat,
but you shall be hungry;
my servants shall drink,
but you shall be thirsty;
my servants shall rejoice,
but you shall be put to shame;
14 my servants shall sing for gladness of heart,
but you shall cry out for pain of heart,
and shall wail for anguish of spirit.
15 You shall leave your name to my chosen to use as a curse,
and the Lord GOD will put you to death;
but to his servants he will give a different name.
16 Then whoever invokes a blessing in the land
shall bless by the God of faithfulness,
and whoever takes an oath in the land
shall swear by the God of faithfulness;
because the former troubles are forgotten
and are hidden from my sight.

The Glorious New Creation

17 For I am about to create new heavens
and a new earth;
the former things shall not be remembered
or come to mind.
18 But be glad and rejoice forever
in what I am creating;

65:17-25 new heavens and a new earth: The chapter ends with a beautiful vision of God's new heavens and new earth where the past things will be no more. The dark days of Jerusalem's destruction and the exile will be forgotten. And the sounds of weeping or cries of distress will be gone (65:19). This is clearly a description of the new age to come, where death is pushed back (65:20; see 25:7-8) and the "wolf and the lamb shall feed together" (65:25). The language here is borrowed from Isaiah 11:6-9. One curious difference here is that the serpent is not restored along with the other creatures (as it is in 11:8), but still suffers under the curse of Genesis 3:14-15.

[a] Or *an inheritor*

for I am about to create Jerusalem as a joy,
and its people as a delight.
19 I will rejoice in Jerusalem,
and delight in my people;
no more shall the sound of weeping be heard in it,
or the cry of distress.
20 No more shall there be in it
an infant that lives but a few days,
or an old person who does not live out a lifetime;
for one who dies at a hundred years will be considered a youth,
and one who falls short of a hundred will be considered
accursed.
21 They shall build houses and inhabit them;
they shall plant vineyards and eat their fruit.
22 They shall not build and another inhabit;
they shall not plant and another eat;
for like the days of a tree shall the days of my people be,
and my chosen shall long enjoy the work of their hands.
23 They shall not labor in vain,
or bear children for calamity;[a]
for they shall be offspring blessed by the LORD—
and their descendants as well.
24 Before they call I will answer,
while they are yet speaking I will hear.
25 The wolf and the lamb shall feed together,
the lion shall eat straw like the ox;
but the serpent—its food shall be dust!
They shall not hurt or destroy
on all my holy mountain,
says the LORD.

The Worship God Demands

66 Thus says the LORD:
Heaven is my throne
and the earth is my footstool;
what is the house that you would build for me,
and what is my resting place?
2 All these things my hand has made,
and so all these things are mine,[b]
says the LORD.
But this is the one to whom I will look,
to the humble and contrite in spirit,
who trembles at my word.

[a] Or *sudden terror* [b] Gk Syr: Heb *these things came to be*

What would God's new heaven and earth look like to you? What role do visions like this play in hope or faith?

66:1-4 the house you would build for me...chose what did not please me: This prophetic criticism seems to focus on the rebuilding of the temple and the sacrifices offered there. It continues the criticism in 58:1-9 (see note there). The reminder is that God seeks those who are humble and live according to God's word (66:2) even more than the sacrifices connected to worship.

3 Whoever slaughters an ox is like one who kills a human being;
whoever sacrifices a lamb, like one who breaks a dog's neck;
whoever presents a grain offering, like one who offers swine's
blood;[a]
whoever makes a memorial offering of frankincense, like one
who blesses an idol.
These have chosen their own ways,
and in their abominations they take delight;
4 I also will choose to mock[b] them,
and bring upon them what they fear;
because, when I called, no one answered,
when I spoke, they did not listen;
but they did what was evil in my sight,
and chose what did not please me.

The LORD Vindicates Zion

5 Hear the word of the LORD,
you who tremble at his word:
Your own people who hate you
and reject you for my name's sake
have said, "Let the LORD be glorified,
so that we may see your joy";
but it is they who shall be put to shame.

66:6-16 Listen, an uproar from the city!…you shall be comforted in Jerusalem: Another announcement of the restoration of Jerusalem. Mother Zion will give quick and painless birth to new children (49:17-21; 54:1-3). There are many miraculous births in the Bible, to mothers ranging from Sarah (Gen 18:14) to Mary (Luke 1:34). In this new birth, without labor pains, even the consequence of the sin in the garden is overcome (Gen 3:16). Now everything is new—including the image of God. The passage invites the hearer to rejoice with Jerusalem, to be nursed and carried by her, but then God applies this image to God's own work: "As a mother comforts her child, so I will comfort you" (66:13). The comfort announced in 40:1 is now delivered through God as a loving mother.

6 Listen, an uproar from the city!
A voice from the temple!
The voice of the LORD,
dealing retribution to his enemies!

7 Before she was in labor
she gave birth;
before her pain came upon her
she delivered a son.
8 Who has heard of such a thing?
Who has seen such things?
Shall a land be born in one day?
Shall a nation be delivered in one moment?
Yet as soon as Zion was in labor
she delivered her children.
9 Shall I open the womb and not deliver?
says the LORD;
shall I, the one who delivers, shut the womb?
says your God.

---

[a] Meaning of Heb uncertain [b] Or *to punish*

10 Rejoice with Jerusalem, and be glad for her,
all you who love her;
rejoice with her in joy,
all you who mourn over her—
11 that you may nurse and be satisfied
from her consoling breast;
that you may drink deeply with delight
from her glorious bosom.

12 For thus says the LORD:
I will extend prosperity to her like a river,
and the wealth of the nations like an overflowing stream;
and you shall nurse and be carried on her arm,
and dandled on her knees.
13 As a mother comforts her child,
so I will comfort you;
you shall be comforted in Jerusalem.

The Reign and Indignation of God

14 You shall see, and your heart shall rejoice;
your bodies[a] shall flourish like the grass;
and it shall be known that the hand of the LORD is with his
servants,
and his indignation is against his enemies.
15 For the LORD will come in fire,
and his chariots like the whirlwind,
to pay back his anger in fury,
and his rebuke in flames of fire.
16 For by fire will the LORD execute judgment,
and by his sword, on all flesh;
and those slain by the LORD shall be many.

17 Those who sanctify and purify themselves to go into the gardens, following the one in the center, eating the flesh of pigs, vermin, and rodents, shall come to an end together, says the LORD.

18 For I know[b] their works and their thoughts, and I am[c] coming
to gather all nations and tongues; and they shall come and shall see
my glory, 19and I will set a sign among them. From them I will send
survivors to the nations, to Tarshish, Put,[d] and Lud—which draw the
bow—to Tubal and Javan, to the coastlands far away that have not
heard of my fame or seen my glory; and they shall declare my glory
among the nations. 20They shall bring all your kindred from all the

[a] Heb *bones* [b] Gk Syr: Heb lacks *know* [c] Gk Syr Vg Tg: Heb *it is* [d] Gk: Heb *Pul*

66:17, 24 Those who sanctify and purify themselves…eating flesh of pigs…they shall be an abhorrence: The book of Isaiah ends with a mixture of promised punishment and reward. Those who follow unclean practices (66:17; see also 65:3-4) will be judged and punished. The final warning to "people who have rebelled against me" picks up the same Hebrew phrase that begins the book (1:2; see note there).

66:18-23 I am coming to gather all nations and tongues…all flesh shall come to worship before me: Distant nations such as Tarshish (in southern Spain), Put (in Libya), and Lud (Lydia in Asia Minor) will hear of God's glory. In the new heaven and new earth that God makes (see also 65:17), God's people will worship the LORD along with all flesh.

As you reflect on the words of judgment and hope in the book of Isaiah, what particular verse or passage stands out? Why?

nations as an offering to the LORD, on horses, and in chariots, and in
litters, and on mules, and on dromedaries, to my holy mountain Jerusalem, says the LORD, just as the Israelites bring a grain offering in a
clean vessel to the house of the LORD. [21] And I will also take some of
them as priests and as Levites, says the LORD.

22 For as the new heavens and the new earth,
which I will make,
shall remain before me, says the LORD;
so shall your descendants and your name remain.
23 From new moon to new moon,
and from sabbath to sabbath,
all flesh shall come to worship before me,
says the LORD.

24 And they shall go out and look at the dead bodies of the people who have rebelled against me; for their worm shall not die, their fire shall not be quenched, and they shall be an abhorrence to all flesh.

Jeremiah 19:11

JEREMIAH

Background File

Jeremiah was "only a boy" (1:6) when God called him to be a prophet in 626 B.C.E. About twenty years later he started to put his earlier and current sermons in writing. When Jeremiah died about 586 B.C.E., his secretary, Baruch, retold some of Jeremiah's sermons. Baruch also wrote some biographical information (chapters 26–45). Someone else wrote the oracles (messages from God) against the nations found in chapters 46–51. Yet another person wrote the final chapter.

What's the Story?

The first three verses of the book set the historical stage for Jeremiah's prophecy. Jeremiah was "only a boy" (no one knows exactly how old he was) when God called him to be a prophet, to speak God's messages. Throughout his life, much of the Middle East (an area that included Egypt, Israel/Judah, Syria, Assyria, and Babylonia) was at war (see Map 9, p. 2106). In 640 B.C.E., Josiah became king of Judah. Josiah was only eight years old. He ruled until Neco II (the pharaoh of Egypt) killed him in 609 B.C.E. Pharaoh Neco had come north to help the Assyrians fight against the Babylonians.

Then Josiah's son, Jehoahaz, became king. He lasted only three months. Pharaoh Neco took him to Egypt and installed as king another son of Josiah, named Jehoiakim. While Jehoiakim was king, Babylon defeated Egypt and Assyria in the Battle at Carchemish in Syria. This battle took place in 605 B.C.E. Babylon's victory ended Assyrian and Egyptian power. Control over the little country of Judah changed from Egypt to Babylon.

Eventually the Babylonian king Nebuchadrezzar made Jehoiachin king. Jehoiachin was Jehoiakim's son. Only a few months later (597 B.C.E.), Nebuchadrezzar forced Jehoiachin and some of Jerusalem's leading citizens to leave Judah and live in exile in Babylonia. Nebuchadrezzar named a new king. He chose Jehoiachin's uncle Mattaniah (another son of Josiah). Nebuchadrezzar gave him a new name, Zedekiah. Ten years later, in 587, Zedekiah rebelled. Nebuchadrezzar responded by destroying Jerusalem and the temple of the LORD. He also sent more people into exile.

In ten years (597–587 B.C.E.) the Babylonian king had destroyed three traditions that helped the people of Jerusalem believe God was with them. First, Nebuchadrezzar destroyed the kingly succession that God had promised to David four hundred years earlier (2 Sam 7:1-14). Second, Nebuchadrezzar destroyed the temple in Jerusalem, the center of Israel's worship life that Solomon had built in 960 B.C.E. Third, Nebuchadrezzar destroyed the belief that Jerusalem was invincible. Ever since the time of David (about 1000) the people believed no one could conquer Jerusalem. Now the people wondered if God was as faithful and powerful as they had thought.

What's the Message?

The situation in which Jeremiah prophesied—that is, spoke God's messages—was one of disaster and uncertainty. God called Jeremiah "to pluck up and to pull down, to destroy and to overthrow" (1:10). Most of Jeremiah's sermons announce the destruction as God's doing—on the people of Jerusalem (chapters 2–29) and on the other nations around Israel and Judah (46–51). His prophecies explain that this chaos was God's divine judgment on the people of Judah because they were unfaithful to God. Most of Jeremiah's listeners thought he was a heretic who opposed the popular religious understandings and practices of the day. Some people thought he was insane. His friends and family stayed away. Religious leaders called for his death. Jeremiah was depressed, angry, and insecure. But he endured all of the persecution and rejection. From "only a boy" through adulthood—about forty years—Jeremiah faithfully preached God's word.

The word of God is why we study the book of Jeremiah. We might feel sorry for the conflicted prophet and even empathize with him. Jeremiah would have us listen to God's word. That word shows the LORD's heartbreak over the unfaithfulness of the chosen people. Jeremiah often called the people God's spouse and children and threatened divorce and disinheritance. He delivered this message in hopes of bringing people back to the waiting arms of God. The people's refusal led to divine judgment. By accomplishing the promised judgment, God's word revealed the power to deliver another promise: to restore the people. The God who judges is the only one who can save.

Christians find comfort in this word. The impact of God's word on us is perhaps not so globally evident as the fates and fortunes of biblical Israel. God's people, the church, are not the citizens of any particular nation. We are a family of baptized children residing in many countries around the globe. Yet God knows heartbreak over our sin and separation. At the same time, God continually welcomes us into his loving presence. In that word, the gospel of Jesus Christ, God gives us hope.

1:2 to whom the word of the LORD came: God spoke words of judgment and comfort through people called prophets. The word *prophet* comes from a Greek word meaning "speak on behalf of." The Hebrew word for a prophet means "one who is called [for a task]." The call to speak on God's behalf always occurs in specific situations in the life of the people of Israel and Judah.

1 The words of Jeremiah son of Hilkiah, of the priests who were
in Anathoth in the land of Benjamin, 2 to whom the word of the
LORD came in the days of King Josiah son of Amon of Judah, in the
thirteenth year of his reign. 3 It came also in the days of King Jehoiakim son of Josiah of Judah, and until the end of the eleventh year of
King Zedekiah son of Josiah of Judah, until the captivity of Jerusalem
in the fifth month.

Jeremiah's Call and Commission

4 Now the word of the LORD came to me saying,
5 "Before I formed you in the womb I knew you,

and before you were born I consecrated you;
I appointed you a prophet to the nations."
6 Then I said, "Ah, Lord GOD! Truly I do not know how to speak, for I
am only a boy." 7 But the LORD said to me,
"Do not say, 'I am only a boy';
for you shall go to all to whom I send you,
and you shall speak whatever I command you.
8 Do not be afraid of them,
for I am with you to deliver you,
says the LORD."
9 Then the LORD put out his hand and touched my mouth; and the
LORD said to me,
"Now I have put my words in your mouth.
10 See, today I appoint you over nations and over kingdoms,
to pluck up and to pull down,
to destroy and to overthrow,
to build and to plant."
11 The word of the LORD came to me, saying, "Jeremiah, what
do you see?" And I said, "I see a branch of an almond tree."[a] 12 Then
the LORD said to me, "You have seen well, for I am watching[b] over my
word to perform it." 13 The word of the LORD came to me a second
time, saying, "What do you see?" And I said, "I see a boiling pot, tilted
away from the north."
14 Then the LORD said to me: Out of the north disaster shall
break out on all the inhabitants of the land. 15 For now I am calling
all the tribes of the kingdoms of the north, says the LORD; and they
shall come and all of them shall set their thrones at the entrance of
the gates of Jerusalem, against all its surrounding walls and against
all the cities of Judah. 16 And I will utter my judgments against them,
for all their wickedness in forsaking me; they have made offerings to
other gods, and worshiped the works of their own hands. 17 But you,
gird up your loins; stand up and tell them everything that I command
you. Do not break down before them, or I will break you before them.
18 And I for my part have made you today a fortified city, an iron pillar,
and a bronze wall, against the whole land—against the kings of Judah, its princes, its priests, and the people of the land. 19 They will fight
against you; but they shall not prevail against you, for I am with you,
says the LORD, to deliver you.

God Pleads with Israel to Repent

2 The word of the LORD came to me, saying: 2 Go and proclaim in
the hearing of Jerusalem, Thus says the LORD:
I remember the devotion of your youth,

[a] Heb *shaqed* [b] Heb *shoqed*

1:6 I am only a boy: His age was the excuse Jeremiah used to persuade God that someone else would make a better prophet. Other people in the Old Testament had excuses, too. Moses told God that he was not a good public speaker (Exod 4:10). Gideon argued that he was too insignificant to be God's agent (Judg 6:15). God would have none of it. God responded to every objection with the promise "I will be with you."

1:10 to pluck up and to pull down…to build and to plant: God called Jeremiah to bring the word of judgment both to the people of Jerusalem (chapters 1–29) and to other nations in the area (chapters 46–51). Jeremiah continued to address sermons about "plucking" or judgment to Israel until Nebuchadrezzar destroyed Jerusalem in 587 B.C.E. This was also when the people went into exile. His sermons about "planting" or promise begin in chapter 30. These sermons promise the people they will be able to return to their homeland. In 538 B.C.E. the Persian king Cyrus allowed the exiles to return home and rebuild their temple and city (Ezra 1:1-4).

Who are God's prophets today? What messages are they speaking?

1:11 what do you see?: Jeremiah brings together seeing and hearing to announce the word and will of the LORD.

1:11-12 almond…watching: These words make no connection in English. The Hebrew words *shaqed* (sha-KAYD) and *shoqad* (shoh-KAD) are similar in sound. Even biblical writers used puns.

1:14 Out of the north: We do not know what nation Jeremiah had in mind, but Babylon soon destroyed Judah.

1:16 in forsaking me: God's judgment is coming. The people have been worshiping human-made idols rather than the LORD, the First Commandment (Exod 20:3).

2:2 the devotion of your youth, your love as a bride…in the wilderness: The Israelite people had spent forty years in the wilderness after the LORD delivered the people from Egypt and before they entered Canaan. Jeremiah thinks of this time in the wilderness as a time of special relationship between the LORD and Israel. Other prophets also thought this way (Hos 2:14-15).

your love as a bride,
how you followed me in the wilderness,
in a land not sown.
3 Israel was holy to the LORD,
the first fruits of his harvest.
All who ate of it were held guilty;
disaster came upon them,
says the LORD.

4 Hear the word of the LORD, O house of Jacob, and all the families of the house of Israel. 5 Thus says the LORD:
What wrong did your ancestors find in me
that they went far from me,
and went after worthless things, and became worthless themselves?
6 They did not say, "Where is the LORD
who brought us up from the land of Egypt,
who led us in the wilderness,
in a land of deserts and pits,
in a land of drought and deep darkness,
in a land that no one passes through,
where no one lives?"
7 I brought you into a plentiful land
to eat its fruits and its good things.
But when you entered you defiled my land,
and made my heritage an abomination.
8 The priests did not say, "Where is the LORD?"
Those who handle the law did not know me;
the rulers[a] transgressed against me;
the prophets prophesied by Baal,
and went after things that do not profit.

9 Therefore once more I accuse you,
says the LORD,
and I accuse your children's children.
10 Cross to the coasts of Cyprus and look,
send to Kedar and examine with care;
see if there has ever been such a thing.
11 Has a nation changed its gods,
even though they are no gods?
But my people have changed their glory
for something that does not profit.
12 Be appalled, O heavens, at this,
be shocked, be utterly desolate,
says the LORD,

2:9 I accuse you: The LORD is taking the people of Israel to court. God sues the people because they have forsaken the LORD. They have had relationships with the idols of Canaan.

[a] Heb *shepherds*

13 for my people have committed two evils:
they have forsaken me,
the fountain of living water,
and dug out cisterns for themselves,
cracked cisterns
that can hold no water.

14 Is Israel a slave? Is he a homeborn servant?
Why then has he become plunder?
15 The lions have roared against him,
they have roared loudly.
They have made his land a waste;
his cities are in ruins, without inhabitant.
16 Moreover, the people of Memphis and Tahpanhes
have broken the crown of your head.
17 Have you not brought this upon yourself
by forsaking the LORD your God,
while he led you in the way?
18 What then do you gain by going to Egypt,
to drink the waters of the Nile?
Or what do you gain by going to Assyria,
to drink the waters of the Euphrates?
19 Your wickedness will punish you,
and your apostasies will convict you.
Know and see that it is evil and bitter
for you to forsake the LORD your God;
the fear of me is not in you,
says the Lord GOD of hosts.

20 For long ago you broke your yoke
and burst your bonds,
and you said, "I will not serve!"
On every high hill
and under every green tree
you sprawled and played the whore.
21 Yet I planted you as a choice vine,
from the purest stock.
How then did you turn degenerate
and become a wild vine?
22 Though you wash yourself with lye
and use much soap,
the stain of your guilt is still before me,
says the Lord GOD.

23 How can you say, "I am not defiled,
I have not gone after the Baals"?

2:16 the people of Memphis and Tahpanhes: Memphis was the capital of Egypt, and Tahpanhes was an Egyptian border town known as a commercial center (see Map 9, p. 2106). The people of Israel were placing their trust in Pharaoh Neco rather than in the LORD.

2:19 the LORD . . . of hosts: This name for God occurs nearly three hundred times in the Old Testament, eighty times in Jeremiah alone. The word *hosts* originally meant armies (for example, "the army of King Jabin," 1 Sam 12:9). In the period of the judges (1200–1000 B.C.E.) the name applied to the LORD sitting on the ark of the covenant that the Israelite armies carried into war. When Solomon brought the ark to reside in the Holy of Holies in the Jerusalem temple, the military slant disappeared. The hosts then came to be the total of powers in the heavens (celestial bodies—sun, moon, and stars—as well as angels, spirits, and lesser gods). The LORD reigned supreme over these hosts. See note on 23:18.

2:20 On every high hill . . . played the whore: The people have been worshiping Canaanite idols. Worshiping those deities may have involved sexual rites.

Look at your way in the valley;
know what you have done—
a restive young camel interlacing her tracks,
24 a wild ass at home in the wilderness,
in her heat sniffing the wind!
Who can restrain her lust?
None who seek her need weary themselves;
in her month they will find her.
25 Keep your feet from going unshod
and your throat from thirst.
But you said, "It is hopeless,
for I have loved strangers,
and after them I will go."

26 As a thief is shamed when caught,
so the house of Israel shall be shamed—
they, their kings, their officials,
their priests, and their prophets,
27 who say to a tree, "You are my father,"
and to a stone, "You gave me birth."
For they have turned their backs to me,
and not their faces.
But in the time of their trouble they say,
"Come and save us!"
28 But where are your gods
that you made for yourself?
Let them come, if they can save you,
in your time of trouble;
for you have as many gods
as you have towns, O Judah.

29 Why do you complain against me?
You have all rebelled against me,
says the LORD.
30 In vain I have struck down your children;
they accepted no correction.
Your own sword devoured your prophets
like a ravening lion.
31 And you, O generation, behold the word of the LORD![a]
Have I been a wilderness to Israel,
or a land of thick darkness?
Why then do my people say, "We are free,
we will come to you no more"?

---

[a] Meaning of Heb uncertain

32 Can a girl forget her ornaments,
or a bride her attire?
Yet my people have forgotten me,
days without number.

33 How well you direct your course
to seek lovers!
So that even to wicked women
you have taught your ways.
34 Also on your skirts is found
the lifeblood of the innocent poor,
though you did not catch them breaking in.
Yet in spite of all these things[a]
35 you say, "I am innocent;
surely his anger has turned from me."
Now I am bringing you to judgment
for saying, "I have not sinned."
36 How lightly you gad about,
changing your ways!
You shall be put to shame by Egypt
as you were put to shame by Assyria.
37 From there also you will come away
with your hands on your head;
for the LORD has rejected those in whom you trust,
and you will not prosper through them.

Unfaithful Israel

3 If[b] a man divorces his wife
and she goes from him
and becomes another man's wife,
will he return to her?
Would not such a land be greatly polluted?
You have played the whore with many lovers;
and would you return to me?
says the LORD.
2 Look up to the bare heights,[c] and see!
Where have you not been lain with?
By the waysides you have sat waiting for lovers,
like a nomad in the wilderness.
You have polluted the land
with your whoring and wickedness.
3 Therefore the showers have been withheld,
and the spring rain has not come;

[a] Meaning of Heb uncertain [b] Q Ms Gk Syr: MT *Saying, If* [c] Or *the trails*

3:1-4: If a man divorces his wife: In several books of the Old Testament, family metaphors or images describe the relationship between the LORD and the people of Israel. Sometimes the image is of marriage. Another family relationship that appears frequently is that of parent and children. Jeremiah uses this imagery when God cries, "I thought you would call me, My Father" (3:19). God's pain was that the people gave the title "father" to the fertility gods (2:27).

3:3 Therefore: In speeches by most of the prophets, the word *therefore* is important. When the word follows a description of the people's actions, "therefore" introduces God's judgment. Usually when "therefore" follows a description of God or action of God, the word introduces God's salvation. The pattern shows that people bring disaster on themselves and that God alone brings salvation.

3:3 Therefore the showers have been withheld, and the spring rain has not come: Canaanite cults were supposed to bring rain and help the earth flourish. The LORD shows who is in charge by causing a drought.

yet you have the forehead of a whore,
you refuse to be ashamed.
4 Have you not just now called to me,
"My Father, you are the friend of my youth—
5 will he be angry forever,
will he be indignant to the end?"
This is how you have spoken,
but you have done all the evil that you could.

A Call to Repentance

6 The LORD said to me in the days of King Josiah: Have you seen
what she did, that faithless one, Israel, how she went up on every high
hill and under every green tree, and played the whore there? 7 And I
thought, "After she has done all this she will return to me"; but she did
not return, and her false sister Judah saw it. 8 She[a] saw that for all the
adulteries of that faithless one, Israel, I had sent her away with a decree of divorce; yet her false sister Judah did not fear, but she too went
and played the whore. 9 Because she took her whoredom so lightly,
she polluted the land, committing adultery with stone and tree. 10 Yet
for all this her false sister Judah did not return to me with her whole
heart, but only in pretense, says the LORD.

11 Then the LORD said to me: Faithless Israel has shown herself
less guilty than false Judah. 12 Go, and proclaim these words toward
the north, and say:

Return, faithless Israel,
says the LORD.
I will not look on you in anger,
for I am merciful,
says the LORD;
I will not be angry forever.
13 Only acknowledge your guilt,
that you have rebelled against the LORD your God,
and scattered your favors among strangers under every green tree,
and have not obeyed my voice,
says the LORD.
14 Return, O faithless children,
says the LORD,
for I am your master;
I will take you, one from a city and two from a family,
and I will bring you to Zion.

15 I will give you shepherds after my own heart, who will feed
you with knowledge and understanding. 16 And when you have mul-

[a] Q Ms Gk Mss Syr: MT *I*

tiplied and increased in the land, in those days, says the LORD, they
shall no longer say, "The ark of the covenant of the LORD." It shall not
come to mind, or be remembered, or missed; nor shall another one
be made. 17 At that time Jerusalem shall be called the throne of the
LORD, and all nations shall gather to it, to the presence of the LORD in
Jerusalem, and they shall no longer stubbornly follow their own evil
will. 18 In those days the house of Judah shall join the house of Israel,
and together they shall come from the land of the north to the land
that I gave your ancestors for a heritage.

19 I thought
how I would set you among my children,
and give you a pleasant land,
the most beautiful heritage of all the nations.
And I thought you would call me, My Father,
and would not turn from following me.
20 Instead, as a faithless wife leaves her husband,
so you have been faithless to me, O house of Israel,
says the LORD.

21 A voice on the bare heights[a] is heard,
the plaintive weeping of Israel's children,
because they have perverted their way,
they have forgotten the LORD their God:
22 Return, O faithless children,
I will heal your faithlessness.

"Here we come to you;
for you are the LORD our God.
23 Truly the hills are[b] a delusion,
the orgies on the mountains.
Truly in the LORD our God
is the salvation of Israel.

24 "But from our youth the shameful thing has devoured all for
which our ancestors had labored, their flocks and their herds, their
sons and their daughters. 25 Let us lie down in our shame, and let our
dishonor cover us; for we have sinned against the LORD our God, we
and our ancestors, from our youth even to this day; and we have not
obeyed the voice of the LORD our God."

4 If you return, O Israel,
says the LORD,
if you return to me,
if you remove your abominations from my presence,

3:22 Return, O faithless children, I will heal your faithlessness: The LORD pleads with the people to repent. God wants the people to turn around and come back. God's will is to heal the broken relationship.

[a] Or *the trails* [b] Gk Syr Vg: Heb *Truly from the hills is*

and do not waver,
2 and if you swear, "As the LORD lives!"
in truth, in justice, and in uprightness,
then nations shall be blessed[a] by him,
and by him they shall boast.

3 For thus says the LORD to the people of Judah and to the inhabitants of Jerusalem:
Break up your fallow ground,
and do not sow among thorns.
4 Circumcise yourselves to the LORD,
remove the foreskin of your hearts,
O people of Judah and inhabitants of Jerusalem,
or else my wrath will go forth like fire,
and burn with no one to quench it,
because of the evil of your doings.

Invasion and Desolation of Judah Threatened

5 Declare in Judah, and proclaim in Jerusalem, and say:
Blow the trumpet through the land;
shout aloud[b] and say,
"Gather together, and let us go
into the fortified cities!"
6 Raise a standard toward Zion,
flee for safety, do not delay,
for I am bringing evil from the north,
and a great destruction.
7 A lion has gone up from its thicket,
a destroyer of nations has set out;
he has gone out from his place
to make your land a waste;
your cities will be ruins
without inhabitant.
8 Because of this put on sackcloth,
lament and wail:
"The fierce anger of the LORD
has not turned away from us."

9 On that day, says the LORD, courage shall fail the king and the officials; the priests shall be appalled and the prophets astounded. 10 Then
I said, "Ah, Lord GOD, how utterly you have deceived this people and
Jerusalem, saying, 'It shall be well with you,' even while the sword is
at the throat!"

---

[a] Or *shall bless themselves* [b] Or *shout, take your weapons:* Heb *shout, fill* (your hand)

11 At that time it will be said to this people and to Jerusalem:
A hot wind comes from me out of the bare heights[a] in the desert toward my poor people, not to winnow or cleanse— 12 a wind too strong
for that. Now it is I who speak in judgment against them.

13 Look! He comes up like clouds,
his chariots like the whirlwind;
his horses are swifter than eagles—
woe to us, for we are ruined!
14 O Jerusalem, wash your heart clean of wickedness
so that you may be saved.
How long shall your evil schemes
lodge within you?
15 For a voice declares from Dan
and proclaims disaster from Mount Ephraim.
16 Tell the nations, "Here they are!"
Proclaim against Jerusalem,
"Besiegers come from a distant land;
they shout against the cities of Judah.
17 They have closed in around her like watchers of a field,
because she has rebelled against me,
says the LORD.
18 Your ways and your doings
have brought this upon you.
This is your doom; how bitter it is!
It has reached your very heart."

Sorrow for a Doomed Nation

19 My anguish, my anguish! I writhe in pain!
Oh, the walls of my heart!
My heart is beating wildly;
I cannot keep silent;
for I[b] hear the sound of the trumpet,
the alarm of war.
20 Disaster overtakes disaster,
the whole land is laid waste.
Suddenly my tents are destroyed,
my curtains in a moment.
21 How long must I see the standard,
and hear the sound of the trumpet?
22 "For my people are foolish,
they do not know me;
they are stupid children,
they have no understanding.

4:15 from Dan...from Mount Ephraim: Dan was the northernmost city in Israel. Mount Ephraim probably refers to the hill country just north of Jerusalem. The "enemy from the north" is on the way to Jerusalem (see Map 4, p. 2102).

---

[a] Or *the trails* [b] Another reading is *for you, O my soul,*

They are skilled in doing evil,
but do not know how to do good."

4:23 waste and void: Jeremiah uses two Hebrew words to describe his vision of the land following God's judgment. These words are *tōhû wābōhû* (TOH-hoo-va-VOH-hoo). These words are the same ones used in Genesis 1:2. They mean "a formless void" (NRSV). These words describe the chaos that existed before God's word brought order and creation into being.

23 I looked on the earth, and lo, it was waste and void;
and to the heavens, and they had no light.
24 I looked on the mountains, and lo, they were
quaking,
and all the hills moved to and fro.
25 I looked, and lo, there was no one at all,
and all the birds of the air had fled.
26 I looked, and lo, the fruitful land was a desert,
and all its cities were laid in ruins
before the LORD, before his fierce anger.

27 For thus says the LORD: The whole land shall be a desolation;
yet I will not make a full end.
28 Because of this the earth shall mourn,
and the heavens above grow black;
for I have spoken, I have purposed;
I have not relented nor will I turn back.

29 At the noise of horseman and archer
every town takes to flight;
they enter thickets; they climb among rocks;
all the towns are forsaken,
and no one lives in them.
30 And you, O desolate one,
what do you mean that you dress in crimson,
that you deck yourself with ornaments of gold,
that you enlarge your eyes with paint?
In vain you beautify yourself.
Your lovers despise you;
they seek your life.
31 For I heard a cry as of a woman in labor,
anguish as of one bringing forth her first child,
the cry of daughter Zion gasping for breath,
stretching out her hands,
"Woe is me! I am fainting before killers!"

4:31 the cry of daughter Zion: Mount Zion is the hill in Jerusalem where the temple stood. The name "daughter Zion" is a symbol for the people of Jerusalem.

The Utter Corruption of God's People

5 Run to and fro through the streets of Jerusalem,
look around and take note!
Search its squares and see
if you can find one person
who acts justly
and seeks truth—

5:1 one person . . . so that I may pardon Jerusalem: Long before this time, the LORD promised Abraham to save the cities of Sodom and Gomorrah if the angels could find ten righteous people living there (Gen 18:32). Now the LORD commands Jeremiah to see if he can find even one. If so, the LORD would pardon the city.

so that I may pardon Jerusalem.[a]
2 Although they say, “As the Lord lives,”
yet they swear falsely.
3 O Lord, do your eyes not look for truth?
You have struck them,
but they felt no anguish;
you have consumed them,
but they refused to take correction.
They have made their faces harder than rock;
they have refused to turn back.

4 Then I said, “These are only the poor,
they have no sense;
for they do not know the way of the Lord,
the law of their God.
5 Let me go to the rich[b]
and speak to them;
surely they know the way of the Lord,
the law of their God.”
But they all alike had broken the yoke,
they had burst the bonds.

6 Therefore a lion from the forest shall kill them,
a wolf from the desert shall destroy them.
A leopard is watching against their cities;
everyone who goes out of them shall be torn in pieces—
because their transgressions are many,
their apostasies are great.

7 How can I pardon you?
Your children have forsaken me,
and have sworn by those who are no gods.
When I fed them to the full,
they committed adultery
and trooped to the houses of prostitutes.
8 They were well-fed lusty stallions,
each neighing for his neighbor’s wife.
9 Shall I not punish them for these things?
says the Lord;
and shall I not bring retribution
on a nation such as this?

10 Go up through her vine-rows and destroy,
but do not make a full end;

---

[a] Heb *it* [b] Or *the great*

strip away her branches,
for they are not the LORD's.
11 For the house of Israel and the house of Judah
have been utterly faithless to me,
says the LORD.
12 They have spoken falsely of the LORD,
and have said, "He will do nothing.
No evil will come upon us,
and we shall not see sword or famine."
13 The prophets are nothing but wind,
for the word is not in them.
Thus shall it be done to them!

14 Therefore thus says the LORD, the God of hosts:
Because they[a] have spoken this word,
I am now making my words in your mouth a fire,
and this people wood, and the fire shall devour them.
15 I am going to bring upon you
a nation from far away, O house of Israel,
says the LORD.
It is an enduring nation,
it is an ancient nation,
a nation whose language you do not know,
nor can you understand what they say.
16 Their quiver is like an open tomb;
all of them are mighty warriors.
17 They shall eat up your harvest and your food;
they shall eat up your sons and your daughters;
they shall eat up your flocks and your herds;
they shall eat up your vines and your fig trees;
they shall destroy with the sword
your fortified cities in which you trust.

18 But even in those days, says the LORD, I will not make a full
end of you. 19 And when your people say, "Why has the LORD our
God done all these things to us?" you shall say to them, "As you have
forsaken me and served foreign gods in your land, so you shall serve
strangers in a land that is not yours."

20 Declare this in the house of Jacob,
proclaim it in Judah:
21 Hear this, O foolish and senseless people,
who have eyes, but do not see,

---

[a] Heb *you*

who have ears, but do not hear.
22 Do you not fear me? says the LORD;
Do you not tremble before me?
I placed the sand as a boundary for the sea,
a perpetual barrier that it cannot pass;
though the waves toss, they cannot prevail,
though they roar, they cannot pass over it.
23 But this people has a stubborn and rebellious heart;
they have turned aside and gone away.
24 They do not say in their hearts,
"Let us fear the LORD our God,
who gives the rain in its season,
the autumn rain and the spring rain,
and keeps for us
the weeks appointed for the harvest."
25 Your iniquities have turned these away,
and your sins have deprived you of good.
26 For scoundrels are found among my people;
they take over the goods of others.
Like fowlers they set a trap;[a]
they catch human beings.
27 Like a cage full of birds,
their houses are full of treachery;
therefore they have become great and rich,
28 they have grown fat and sleek.
They know no limits in deeds of wickedness;
they do not judge with justice
the cause of the orphan, to make it prosper,
and they do not defend the rights of the needy.
29 Shall I not punish them for these things?
says the LORD,
and shall I not bring retribution
on a nation such as this?

30 An appalling and horrible thing
has happened in the land:
31 the prophets prophesy falsely,
and the priests rule as the prophets direct;[b]
my people love to have it so,
but what will you do when the end comes?

The Imminence and Horror of the Invasion

6 Flee for safety, O children of Benjamin,
from the midst of Jerusalem!

[a] Meaning of Heb uncertain [b] Or *rule by their own authority*

5:22 I placed the sand as a boundary for the sea: In the ancient world, the sea was a common symbol for the chaos that threatened life. The Canaanites called both the sea and the chaos monster "Yamm." That name is also the Hebrew word for "sea." The Babylonian story about creation tells that the god Marduk defeated a monster named *Tiamat* (in Hebrew, "the deep"). Marduk set a barrier so that the chaotic waters might not escape. Jeremiah uses this same image to show God's power as the basis for awe and worship (see also Isa 50:2; 51:9-10; Ps 74:12-14; 89:9-10).

5:28 they do not judge with justice…the rights of the needy: God gives responsibility for care of the most vulnerable (widows, orphans, the needy, and sojourners) to the king, as well as the people of God.

6:1 in Tekoa... on Beth-haccherem: Tekoa (teh-KOH-ah) is about ten miles south of Jerusalem. It is the hometown of the prophet Amos (Amos 1:1). Beth-haccherem (BAIT-ha-KEH-rem) is about five miles from Jerusalem. See Map 7, p. 2105.

Blow the trumpet in Tekoa,
and raise a signal on Beth-haccherem;
for evil looms out of the north,
and great destruction.
2 I have likened daughter Zion
to the loveliest pasture.[a]
3 Shepherds with their flocks shall come against her.
They shall pitch their tents around her;
they shall pasture, all in their places.
4 "Prepare war against her;
up, and let us attack at noon!"
"Woe to us, for the day declines,
the shadows of evening lengthen!"
5 "Up, and let us attack by night,
and destroy her palaces!"
6 For thus says the LORD of hosts:
Cut down her trees;
cast up a siege ramp against Jerusalem.
This is the city that must be punished;[b]
there is nothing but oppression within her.
7 As a well keeps its water fresh,
so she keeps fresh her wickedness;
violence and destruction are heard within her;
sickness and wounds are ever before me.
8 Take warning, O Jerusalem,
or I shall turn from you in disgust,
and make you a desolation,
an uninhabited land.

9 Thus says the LORD of hosts:
Glean[c] thoroughly as a vine
the remnant of Israel;
like a grape-gatherer, pass your hand again
over its branches.

10 To whom shall I speak and give warning,
that they may hear?
See, their ears are closed,[d]
they cannot listen.
The word of the LORD is to them an object of scorn;
they take no pleasure in it.
11 But I am full of the wrath of the LORD;
I am weary of holding it in.

---

[a] Or *I will destroy daughter Zion, the loveliest pasture* [b] Or *the city of license* [c] Cn: Heb *They shall glean*
[d] Heb *are uncircumcised*

Pour it out on the children in the street,
and on the gatherings of young men as well;
both husband and wife shall be taken,
the old folk and the very aged.
12 Their houses shall be turned over to others,
their fields and wives together;
for I will stretch out my hand
against the inhabitants of the land,
says the LORD.

13 For from the least to the greatest of them,
everyone is greedy for unjust gain;
and from prophet to priest,
everyone deals falsely.
14 They have treated the wound of my people carelessly,
saying, "Peace, peace,"
when there is no peace.
15 They acted shamefully, they committed abomination;
yet they were not ashamed,
they did not know how to blush.
Therefore they shall fall among those who fall;
at the time that I punish them, they shall be overthrown,
says the LORD.

16 Thus says the LORD:
Stand at the crossroads, and look,
and ask for the ancient paths,
where the good way lies; and walk in it,
and find rest for your souls.
But they said, "We will not walk in it."
17 Also I raised up sentinels for you:
"Give heed to the sound of the trumpet!"
But they said, "We will not give heed."
18 Therefore hear, O nations,
and know, O congregation, what will happen to them.
19 Hear, O earth; I am going to bring disaster on this people,
the fruit of their schemes,
because they have not given heed to my words;
and as for my teaching, they have rejected it.
20 Of what use to me is frankincense that comes from Sheba,
or sweet cane from a distant land?
Your burnt offerings are not acceptable,
nor are your sacrifices pleasing to me.
21 Therefore thus says the LORD:
See, I am laying before this people
stumbling blocks against which they shall stumble;

6:16 find rest for your souls: In several places in the Bible, God promises "rest" for the people of faith. In Deuteronomy and Joshua, God's promised rest is the land of Canaan and within that land security from enemies (see Deut 12:10; 25:19; Josh 1:13, 15; 21:44; 22:4; 23:1). God gave rest to King David (2 Sam 7:1, 11) and his son Solomon (1 Kgs 5:4). Jesus promised rest for the weary (Matt 11:28). Through Jesus, God promises rest for people of faith (see Heb 4:1-11).

6:18 hear, O nations, and know, O congregations, what will happen to them: Whether God's actions for Israel result in disaster or in salvation, others will observe and understand the power of God.

The nation Israel was God's people in biblical times. Christians are not citizens of only one country. Jesus refused to get involved in political and military affairs (see John 6:15). His "kingdom is not from this world" (John 18:36). The fates or fortunes of any nation, therefore, are not obviously the results of God's actions. How might people outside of the church know God's love and power today?

6:20 frankincense that comes from Sheba: Ancient people burned frankincense (a gum or resin from a tree) in temple rites to add a pleasing smell. The smoke also added an atmosphere of mystery to worship. God is angry that the people substitute the burning of such fragrances, along with burnt offerings and sacrifices, for obedience to God's word and instruction (see also Isa 1:10-11; Mic 6:6-8).

parents and children together,
neighbor and friend shall perish.

22 Thus says the LORD:
See, a people is coming from the land of the north,
a great nation is stirring from the farthest parts of the earth.
23 They grasp the bow and the javelin,
they are cruel and have no mercy,
their sound is like the roaring sea;
they ride on horses,
equipped like a warrior for battle,
against you, O daughter Zion!

24 "We have heard news of them,
our hands fall helpless;
anguish has taken hold of us,
pain as of a woman in labor.
25 Do not go out into the field,
or walk on the road;
for the enemy has a sword,
terror is on every side."

26 O my poor people, put on sackcloth,
and roll in ashes;
make mourning as for an only child,
most bitter lamentation:
for suddenly the destroyer
will come upon us.

27 I have made you a tester and a refiner[a] among my people
so that you may know and test their ways.
28 They are all stubbornly rebellious,
going about with slanders;
they are bronze and iron,
all of them act corruptly.
29 The bellows blow fiercely,
the lead is consumed by the fire;
in vain the refining goes on,
for the wicked are not removed.
30 They are called "rejected silver,"
for the LORD has rejected them.

Jeremiah Proclaims God's Judgment on the Nation

7 The word that came to Jeremiah from the LORD: 2Stand in the gate of the LORD's house, and proclaim there this word, and say,

[a] Or *a fortress*

7:1—8:3 the LORD's house: This section is called the Temple Sermon. Jeremiah criticizes an old tradition about Jerusalem's invincibility—that it could not be conquered. The people sang about Jerusalem as "the city of God" and the temple as "the holy habitation of the Most High" (Ps 46:4). They also sang, "Within its citadels God has shown himself a sure defense" (Ps 48:3). The people cared a lot about the city and the building. They cared little about defenseless people (7:5-6) or keeping the LORD's commandments (7:8-9). The people also worshiped idols (7:9). The fate of the city (7:12-14) would be like that of Shiloh (SHY-loh). Six centuries earlier Joshua had set up a sanctuary in Shiloh (Josh 18:1). About 1050 B.C.E. the Philistines (phi-LIS-teens) destroyed the city.

Hear the word of the Lord, all you people of Judah, you that enter
these gates to worship the Lord. 3 Thus says the Lord of hosts, the
God of Israel: Amend your ways and your doings, and let me dwell
with you[a] in this place. 4 Do not trust in these deceptive words: "This
is[b] the temple of the Lord, the temple of the Lord, the temple of the
Lord."

5 For if you truly amend your ways and your doings, if you truly
act justly one with another, 6 if you do not oppress the alien, the orphan, and the widow, or shed innocent blood in this place, and if you
do not go after other gods to your own hurt, 7 then I will dwell with
you in this place, in the land that I gave of old to your ancestors forever and ever.

8 Here you are, trusting in deceptive words to no avail. 9 Will you
steal, murder, commit adultery, swear falsely, make offerings to Baal,
and go after other gods that you have not known, 10 and then come
and stand before me in this house, which is called by my name, and
say, "We are safe!"—only to go on doing all these abominations?
11 Has this house, which is called by my name, become a den of robbers in your sight? You know, I too am watching, says the Lord. 12 Go
now to my place that was in Shiloh, where I made my name dwell at
first, and see what I did to it for the wickedness of my people Israel.
13 And now, because you have done all these things, says the Lord,
and when I spoke to you persistently, you did not listen, and when I
called you, you did not answer, 14 therefore I will do to the house that
is called by my name, in which you trust, and to the place that I gave to
you and to your ancestors, just what I did to Shiloh. 15 And I will cast
you out of my sight, just as I cast out all your kinsfolk, all the offspring
of Ephraim.

The People's Disobedience

16 As for you, do not pray for this people, do not raise a cry or
prayer on their behalf, and do not intercede with me, for I will not
hear you. 17 Do you not see what they are doing in the towns of Judah
and in the streets of Jerusalem? 18 The children gather wood, the fathers kindle fire, and the women knead dough, to make cakes for the
queen of heaven; and they pour out drink offerings to other gods, to
provoke me to anger. 19 Is it I whom they provoke? says the Lord. Is
it not themselves, to their own hurt? 20 Therefore thus says the Lord
God: My anger and my wrath shall be poured out on this place, on
human beings and animals, on the trees of the field and the fruit of the
ground; it will burn and not be quenched.

21 Thus says the Lord of hosts, the God of Israel: Add your
burnt offerings to your sacrifices, and eat the flesh. 22 For in the day

---

[a] Or *and I will let you dwell* [d] Heb *They are*

that I brought your ancestors out of the land of Egypt, I did not speak
to them or command them concerning burnt offerings and sacrifices.
23 But this command I gave them, "Obey my voice, and I will be your
God, and you shall be my people; and walk only in the way that I
command you, so that it may be well with you." 24 Yet they did not
obey or incline their ear, but, in the stubbornness of their evil will,
they walked in their own counsels, and looked backward rather than
forward. 25 From the day that your ancestors came out of the land
of Egypt until this day, I have persistently sent all my servants the
prophets to them, day after day; 26 yet they did not listen to me, or pay
attention, but they stiffened their necks. They did worse than their
ancestors did.

27 So you shall speak all these words to them, but they will not
listen to you. You shall call to them, but they will not answer you.
28 You shall say to them: This is the nation that did not obey the voice
of the LORD their God, and did not accept discipline; truth has perished; it is cut off from their lips.

29 Cut off your hair and throw it away;
    raise a lamentation on the bare heights,[a]
for the LORD has rejected and forsaken
    the generation that provoked his wrath.

30 For the people of Judah have done evil in my sight, says the
LORD; they have set their abominations in the house that is called
by my name, defiling it. 31 And they go on building the high place[b] of
Topheth, which is in the valley of the son of Hinnom, to burn their
sons and their daughters in the fire—which I did not command, nor
did it come into my mind. 32 Therefore, the days are surely coming,
says the LORD, when it will no more be called Topheth, or the valley
of the son of Hinnom, but the valley of Slaughter: for they will bury
in Topheth until there is no more room. 33 The corpses of this people
will be food for the birds of the air, and for the animals of the earth;
and no one will frighten them away. 34 And I will bring to an end the
sound of mirth and gladness, the voice of the bride and bridegroom
in the cities of Judah and in the streets of Jerusalem; for the land shall
become a waste.

8 At that time, says the LORD, the bones of the kings of Judah,
the bones of its officials, the bones of the priests, the bones of
the prophets, and the bones of the inhabitants of Jerusalem shall be
brought out of their tombs; 2 and they shall be spread before the sun
and the moon and all the host of heaven, which they have loved and
served, which they have followed, and which they have inquired of
and worshiped; and they shall not be gathered or buried; they shall
be like dung on the surface of the ground. 3 Death shall be preferred to

[a] Or *the trails* [b] Gk Tg: Heb *high places*

7:31 the high place of Topheth, which is in the valley of the son of Hinnom: The Hinnom (HIN-nohm) Valley lies immediately south of Jerusalem's walls (see Map 6, p. 2104). According to Jeremiah (and the books of Kings and Chronicles) the Canaanites and some Israelites sacrificed children to the Canaanite gods Baal and Molech (MOH-lek). By the first century B.C.E. the two Hebrew words for the Valley of Hinnom became one word: Gehenna (geh-HEN-nah). This word became the mythical place for the fires of judgment at the last day. Topheth (TOH-pheth) was a part of the valley where the Canaanites had built their sanctuaries or high places. The young King Josiah had destroyed the sanctuary of Topheth during his religious reforms (2 Kgs 23:10). Jeremiah prophesied that after the coming judgment of God, the names Topheth and Hinnom would change to "the valley of Slaughter" (7:32).

8:2 before the sun and the moon and all the host of heaven, which they have loved and served: The Canaanites, the Assyrians, and the Egyptians worshiped the stars and planets as gods and goddesses. As the people of Israel wandered away from the LORD, symbols from these religions found their way into the temple in Jerusalem.

life by all the remnant that remains of this evil family in all the places
where I have driven them, says the LORD of hosts.

The Blind Perversity of the Whole Nation

4 You shall say to them, Thus says the LORD:
When people fall, do they not get up again?
If they go astray, do they not turn back?
5 Why then has this people[a] turned away
in perpetual backsliding?
They have held fast to deceit,
they have refused to return.
6 I have given heed and listened,
but they do not speak honestly;
no one repents of wickedness,
saying, "What have I done!"
All of them turn to their own course,
like a horse plunging headlong into battle.
7 Even the stork in the heavens
knows its times;
and the turtledove, swallow, and crane[b]
observe the time of their coming;
but my people do not know
the ordinance of the LORD.

8 How can you say, "We are wise,
and the law of the LORD is with us,"
when, in fact, the false pen of the scribes
has made it into a lie?
9 The wise shall be put to shame,
they shall be dismayed and taken;
since they have rejected the word of the LORD,
what wisdom is in them?
10 Therefore I will give their wives to others
and their fields to conquerors,
because from the least to the greatest
everyone is greedy for unjust gain;
from prophet to priest
everyone deals falsely.
11 They have treated the wound of my people carelessly,
saying, "Peace, peace,"
when there is no peace.
12 They acted shamefully, they committed abomination;
yet they were not at all ashamed,

8:7-9 the ordinance of the LORD... the law of the LORD...the word of the LORD: These three phrases mean almost the same thing. *Ordinance* in Hebrew means "justice" and "judgment of justice." The Hebrew word for *law* is torah (to-RAH); it means "instruction." When used about God, *the word* means not simply speaking but accomplishing what it says, like the creation of the universe in Genesis 1. Together, the three words here indicate that the people have been rejecting God's will.

8:8-9 wise...wisdom: In the ancient Near East "wisdom" was the attempt to understand the world by listing living and nonliving things in categories. We call this practice "list science" when we assign plants and animals to certain species or identify rocks by their composition and their geological era. The goal of such listings for ancient people was to participate in the orders of the world and to live successfully. Those who did not learn and behave accordingly were fools.

[a] One Ms Gk: MT *this people, Jerusalem,* [b] Meaning of Heb uncertain

they did not know how to blush.
Therefore they shall fall among those who fall;
at the time when I punish them, they shall be overthrown,
says the LORD.

13 When I wanted to gather them, says the LORD,
there are[a] no grapes on the vine,
nor figs on the fig tree;
even the leaves are withered,
and what I gave them has passed away from them.[b]

14 Why do we sit still?
Gather together, let us go into the fortified cities
and perish there;
for the LORD our God has doomed us to perish,
and has given us poisoned water to drink,
because we have sinned against the LORD.
15 We look for peace, but find no good,
for a time of healing, but there is terror instead.

16 The snorting of their horses is heard from Dan;
at the sound of the neighing of their stallions
the whole land quakes.
They come and devour the land and all that fills it,
the city and those who live in it.
17 See, I am letting snakes loose among you,
adders that cannot be charmed,
and they shall bite you,
says the LORD.

The Prophet Mourns for the People

18 My joy is gone, grief is upon me,
my heart is sick.
19 Hark, the cry of my poor people
from far and wide in the land:
"Is the LORD not in Zion?
Is her King not in her?"
("Why have they provoked me to anger with their images,
with their foreign idols?")
20 "The harvest is past, the summer is ended,
and we are not saved."
21 For the hurt of my poor people I am hurt,
I mourn, and dismay has taken hold of me.

8:19-21 My joy is gone, grief is upon me: Jeremiah mourns for the people on whom he pronounces judgment. This earns him the name "the weeping prophet."

[a] Or *I will make an end of them, says the LORD. There are* [b] Meaning of Heb uncertain

22 Is there no balm in Gilead?
Is there no physician there?
Why then has the health of my poor people
not been restored?

9

[a] O that my head were a spring of water,
and my eyes a fountain of tears,
so that I might weep day and night
for the slain of my poor people!
2[b] O that I had in the desert
a traveler's lodging place,
that I might leave my people
and go away from them!
For they are all adulterers,
a band of traitors.
3 They bend their tongues like bows;
they have grown strong in the land for falsehood, and not for truth;
for they proceed from evil to evil,
and they do not know me, says the LORD.

4 Beware of your neighbors,
and put no trust in any of your kin;[c]
for all your kin[d] are supplanters,
and every neighbor goes around like a slanderer.
5 They all deceive their neighbors,
and no one speaks the truth;
they have taught their tongues to speak lies;
they commit iniquity and are too weary to repent.[e]
6 Oppression upon oppression, deceit[f] upon deceit!
They refuse to know me, says the LORD.

7 Therefore thus says the LORD of hosts:
I will now refine and test them,
for what else can I do with my sinful people?[g]
8 Their tongue is a deadly arrow;
it speaks deceit through the mouth.
They all speak friendly words to their neighbors,
but inwardly are planning to lay an ambush.
9 Shall I not punish them for these things? says the LORD;
and shall I not bring retribution
on a nation such as this?

---

[a] Ch 8.23 in Heb [b] Ch 9.1 in Heb [c] Heb *in a brother* [d] Heb *for every brother* [e] Cn Compare Gk: Heb *they weary themselves with iniquity. 6Your dwelling* [f] Cn: Heb *Your dwelling in the midst of deceit* [g] Or *my poor people*

10 Take up[a] weeping and wailing for the mountains,
and a lamentation for the pastures of the wilderness,
because they are laid waste so that no one passes through,
and the lowing of cattle is not heard;
both the birds of the air and the animals
have fled and are gone.
11 I will make Jerusalem a heap of ruins,
a lair of jackals;
and I will make the towns of Judah a desolation,
without inhabitant.

9:11 I will make Jerusalem a heap of ruins: A century before Jeremiah, the prophet Micah uttered the same words of judgment. This connection to Micah will save Jeremiah's life (see Jer 26:16-19).

12 Who is wise enough to understand this? To whom has the
mouth of the LORD spoken, so that they may declare it? Why is the
land ruined and laid waste like a wilderness, so that no one passes
through? 13 And the LORD says: Because they have forsaken my law
that I set before them, and have not obeyed my voice, or walked in
accordance with it, 14 but have stubbornly followed their own hearts
and have gone after the Baals, as their ancestors taught them. 15 Therefore thus says the LORD of hosts, the God of Israel: I am feeding this
people with wormwood, and giving them poisonous water to drink.
16 I will scatter them among nations that neither they nor their ancestors have known; and I will send the sword after them, until I have
consumed them.

9:15 I am feeding this people with wormwood: Wormwood is a bitter plant, not wormy.

The People Mourn in Judgment

17 Thus says the LORD of hosts:
Consider, and call for the mourning women to come;
send for the skilled women to come;
18 let them quickly raise a dirge over us,
so that our eyes may run down with tears,
and our eyelids flow with water.
19 For a sound of wailing is heard from Zion:
"How we are ruined!
We are utterly shamed,
because we have left the land,
because they have cast down our dwellings."

20 Hear, O women, the word of the LORD,
and let your ears receive the word of his mouth;
teach to your daughters a dirge,
and each to her neighbor a lament.
21 "Death has come up into our windows,
it has entered our palaces,

[a] Gk Syr: Heb *I will take up*

to cut off the children from the streets
and the young men from the squares."
22 Speak! Thus says the LORD:
"Human corpses shall fall
like dung upon the open field,
like sheaves behind the reaper,
and no one shall gather them."

23 Thus says the LORD: Do not let the wise boast in their wisdom, do not let the mighty boast in their might, do not let the wealthy
boast in their wealth; 24 but let those who boast boast in this, that they
understand and know me, that I am the LORD; I act with steadfast
love, justice, and righteousness in the earth, for in these things I delight, says the LORD.
25 The days are surely coming, says the LORD, when I will attend
to all those who are circumcised only in the foreskin: 26 Egypt, Judah,
Edom, the Ammonites, Moab, and all those with shaven temples who
live in the desert. For all these nations are uncircumcised, and all the
house of Israel is uncircumcised in heart.

Idolatry Has Brought Ruin on Israel

10 Hear the word that the LORD speaks to you, O house of
Israel. 2 Thus says the LORD:
Do not learn the way of the nations,
or be dismayed at the signs of the heavens;
for the nations are dismayed at them.
3 For the customs of the peoples are false:
a tree from the forest is cut down,
and worked with an ax by the hands of an artisan;
4 people deck it with silver and gold;
they fasten it with hammer and nails
so that it cannot move.
5 Their idols[a] are like scarecrows in a cucumber field,
and they cannot speak;
they have to be carried,
for they cannot walk.
Do not be afraid of them,
for they cannot do evil,
nor is it in them to do good.

6 There is none like you, O LORD;
you are great, and your name is great in might.
7 Who would not fear you, O King of the nations?

[a] Heb *They*

9:24 I am the LORD; I act with steadfast love, justice, and righteousness: Knowledge of God means understanding the LORD's ways. God's "steadfast love" means loyalty within a covenant (pledge or promise) relationship. "Justice" describes a community in harmony. "Righteousness" is the activity that brings harmony to the community.

9:25-26 circumcised only in the foreskin…uncircumcised in heart: God instructed Abraham to circumcise every male child among his offspring as "a sign of the covenant" (Gen 17:9-14). This became a symbol of what it meant to be Israel, the LORD's covenant people. Some of Israel's neighbors practiced circumcision, too, but it did not have the same meaning for them. Jeremiah feared that circumcision no longer had the original meaning for Israel. Jeremiah described this broken relationship with God as "uncircumcised in heart."

10:2-16 Do not learn the ways of the nations…Israel is the tribe of his inheritance: Ancient Israelites sang this hymn that warns the people about idols (see Ps 97:7) and shows how ridiculous idols are. The hymn praises the LORD as the creator of the universe. Similar hymns appear at Pss 8; 93; 95–99. Ancient Israel believed that God created the universe "by his power…by his wisdom…by his understanding…when he utters his voice" (10:12-13). All those "tools" for creating have much the same meaning (see Gen 1; Prov 3:19-20; Ps 33:6). The people confess that God is "the living God and the everlasting King" (10:10). God deserves the praise because God provides order to sustain life and gives life meaning.

Christians confess their faith in God as "Creator of heaven and earth." Scientific theory develops from principles that are observable and measurable. Faith "is the assurance of things hoped for, the conviction of things not seen" (Heb 11:1). What do you think about proving or disproving faith by scientific theory? What do you think about establishing scientific theory based on faith?

For that is your due;
among all the wise ones of the nations
and in all their kingdoms
there is no one like you.
8 They are both stupid and foolish;
the instruction given by idols
is no better than wood![a]
9 Beaten silver is brought from Tarshish,
and gold from Uphaz.
They are the work of the artisan and of the hands of the goldsmith;
their clothing is blue and purple;
they are all the product of skilled workers.
10 But the LORD is the true God;
he is the living God and the everlasting King.
At his wrath the earth quakes,
and the nations cannot endure his indignation.

11 Thus shall you say to them: The gods who did not make the heavens and the earth shall perish from the earth and from under the heavens.[b]

12 It is he who made the earth by his power,
who established the world by his wisdom,
and by his understanding stretched out the heavens.
13 When he utters his voice, there is a tumult of waters in the heavens,
and he makes the mist rise from the ends of the earth.
He makes lightnings for the rain,
and he brings out the wind from his storehouses.
14 Everyone is stupid and without knowledge;
goldsmiths are all put to shame by their idols;
for their images are false,
and there is no breath in them.
15 They are worthless, a work of delusion;
at the time of their punishment they shall perish.
16 Not like these is the LORD,[c] the portion of Jacob,
for he is the one who formed all things,
and Israel is the tribe of his inheritance;
the LORD of hosts is his name.

The Coming Exile

17 Gather up your bundle from the ground,
O you who live under siege!

---

[a] Meaning of Heb uncertain [b] This verse is in Aramaic [c] Heb lacks *the LORD*

18 For thus says the LORD:
I am going to sling out the inhabitants of the land
at this time,
and I will bring distress on them,
so that they shall feel it.

19 Woe is me because of my hurt!
My wound is severe.
But I said, "Truly this is my punishment,
and I must bear it."
20 My tent is destroyed,
and all my cords are broken;
my children have gone from me,
and they are no more;
there is no one to spread my tent again,
and to set up my curtains.
21 For the shepherds are stupid,
and do not inquire of the LORD;
therefore they have not prospered,
and all their flock is scattered.

22 Hear, a noise! Listen, it is coming—
a great commotion from the land of the north
to make the cities of Judah a desolation,
a lair of jackals.

23 I know, O LORD, that the way of human beings is not in their
control,
that mortals as they walk cannot direct their steps.
24 Correct me, O LORD, but in just measure;
not in your anger, or you will bring me to nothing.

25 Pour out your wrath on the nations that do not know you,
and on the peoples that do not call on your name;
for they have devoured Jacob;
they have devoured him and consumed him,
and have laid waste his habitation.

Israel and Judah Have Broken the Covenant

11 The word that came to Jeremiah from the LORD: 2Hear the
words of this covenant, and speak to the people of Judah and
the inhabitants of Jerusalem. 3You shall say to them, Thus says the
LORD, the God of Israel: Cursed be anyone who does not heed the
words of this covenant, 4which I commanded your ancestors when I
brought them out of the land of Egypt, from the iron-smelter, saying,

11:5 that I may perform the oath that I swore to your ancestors: The LORD makes promises and fulfills them, so God is trustworthy and praiseworthy. God first promised the land of Canaan to Abraham (Gen 12:7), Isaac (Gen 26:1-5), and Jacob (Gen 28:13). God repeated the promise to Moses (Exod 3:8). God fulfilled that promise in the days of Joshua. God expects from Israel the same kind of faithfulness to the covenant relationship.

Listen to my voice, and do all that I command you. So shall you be my people, and I will be your God, [5]that I may perform the oath that I swore to your ancestors, to give them a land flowing with milk and honey, as at this day. Then I answered, "So be it, LORD."

6 And the LORD said to me: Proclaim all these words in the cities of Judah, and in the streets of Jerusalem: Hear the words of this covenant and do them. [7]For I solemnly warned your ancestors when I brought them up out of the land of Egypt, warning them persistently, even to this day, saying, Obey my voice. [8]Yet they did not obey or incline their ear, but everyone walked in the stubbornness of an evil will. So I brought upon them all the words of this covenant, which I commanded them to do, but they did not.

9 And the LORD said to me: Conspiracy exists among the people of Judah and the inhabitants of Jerusalem. [10]They have turned back to the iniquities of their ancestors of old, who refused to heed my words; they have gone after other gods to serve them; the house of Israel and the house of Judah have broken the covenant that I made with their ancestors. [11]Therefore, thus says the LORD, assuredly I am going to bring disaster upon them that they cannot escape; though they cry out to me, I will not listen to them. [12]Then the cities of Judah and the inhabitants of Jerusalem will go and cry out to the gods to whom they make offerings, but they will never save them in the time of their trouble. [13]For your gods have become as many as your towns, O Judah; and as many as the streets of Jerusalem are the altars to shame you have set up, altars to make offerings to Baal.

14 As for you, do not pray for this people, or lift up a cry or prayer on their behalf, for I will not listen when they call to me in the time of their trouble. [15]What right has my beloved in my house, when she has done vile deeds? Can vows[a] and sacrificial flesh avert your doom? Can you then exult? [16]The LORD once called you, "A green olive tree, fair with goodly fruit"; but with the roar of a great tempest he will set fire to it, and its branches will be consumed. [17]The LORD of hosts, who planted you, has pronounced evil against you, because of the evil that the house of Israel and the house of Judah have done, provoking me to anger by making offerings to Baal.

Jeremiah's Life Threatened

18 It was the LORD who made it known to me, and I knew;
then you showed me their evil deeds.
19 But I was like a gentle lamb
led to the slaughter.
And I did not know it was against me
that they devised schemes, saying,

[a] Gk: Heb *Can many*

"Let us destroy the tree with its fruit,
let us cut him off from the land of the living,
so that his name will no longer be remembered!"
20 But you, O LORD of hosts, who judge righteously,
who try the heart and the mind,
let me see your retribution upon them,
for to you I have committed my cause.
21 Therefore thus says the LORD concerning the people of Anathoth, who seek your life, and say, "You shall not prophesy in the
name of the LORD, or you will die by our hand"— 22 therefore thus
says the LORD of hosts: I am going to punish them; the young men
shall die by the sword; their sons and their daughters shall die by famine; 23 and not even a remnant shall be left of them. For I will bring
disaster upon the people of Anathoth, the year of their punishment.

Jeremiah Complains to God

12 You will be in the right, O LORD,
when I lay charges against you;
but let me put my case to you.
Why does the way of the guilty prosper?
Why do all who are treacherous thrive?
2 You plant them, and they take root;
they grow and bring forth fruit;
you are near in their mouths
yet far from their hearts.
3 But you, O LORD, know me;
You see me and test me—my heart is with you.
Pull them out like sheep for the slaughter,
and set them apart for the day of slaughter.
4 How long will the land mourn,
and the grass of every field wither?
For the wickedness of those who live in it
the animals and the birds are swept away,
and because people said, "He is blind to our ways."[a]

God Replies to Jeremiah

5 If you have raced with foot-runners and they have wearied you,
how will you compete with horses?
And if in a safe land you fall down,
how will you fare in the thickets of the Jordan?
6 For even your kinsfolk and your own family,
even they have dealt treacherously with you;
they are in full cry after you;

[a] Gk: Heb *to our future*

11:21 the people of Anathoth: Anathoth was Jeremiah's hometown, and Jeremiah's father was a priest there. Jeremiah was unpopular when he preached about Anathoth's destruction. The citizens tried to kill him, and his own family turned against him (12:5-6). Parts of the report sound like Jesus' experience in his hometown of Nazareth (Luke 4:16-30).

12:1-4 when I lay charges against you...How long?: Jeremiah often complains against the LORD. We call these complaints "laments." The book of Psalms contains many laments against God for failing to appear when people looked for God's help. Sometimes individuals make complaints. See Psalm 22. Jesus quoted this psalm on the cross. At other times, the whole community of Israel cries out to God because God seems absent (like Ps 74). Almost all laments in the book of Psalms end with praise and thanksgiving to God for hearing the cries for help. God had established a reputation as one who hears and responds to such pleas (Exod 3:7-8).

What is your reaction to this complaining to God that is so common in the Bible? Read a few laments, like Psalms 7; 10; 13; 22; and 74, and try to put yourself in the positions of those who used the laments centuries ago. If you were praying a lament to God, what would you say? How does it help to know that God hears laments as well as other kinds of prayers?

How can we make sense of life when God seems to desert us? Luther taught that the more God-forsaken we feel, the closer we are to the crucified Christ. Theologians call this teaching of Luther "the theology of the cross." Its opposite, the theology of glory, focuses on success. *Jeremiah 12:1-4*

do not believe them,
though they speak friendly words to you.

12:7-17 I have forsaken my house, I have abandoned my heritage: God admits to forsaking the people. Jeremiah says in the sermon that the people brought this disaster upon themselves. They abandoned the LORD. The words "house" and "heritage" refer not to the temple but to the land. At 12:14-17, however, God promises one day to restore the land to Israel. The nations who destroyed Israel will also become heirs.

7 I have forsaken my house,
I have abandoned my heritage;
I have given the beloved of my heart
into the hands of her enemies.
8 My heritage has become to me
like a lion in the forest;
she has lifted up her voice against me—
therefore I hate her.
9 Is the hyena greedy[a] for my heritage at my command?
Are the birds of prey all around her?
Go, assemble all the wild animals;
bring them to devour her.
10 Many shepherds have destroyed my vineyard,
they have trampled down my portion,
they have made my pleasant portion
a desolate wilderness.
11 They have made it a desolation;
desolate, it mourns to me.
The whole land is made desolate,
but no one lays it to heart.
12 Upon all the bare heights[b] in the desert
spoilers have come;
for the sword of the LORD devours
from one end of the land to the other;
no one shall be safe.
13 They have sown wheat and have reaped thorns,
they have tired themselves out but profit nothing.
They shall be ashamed of their[c] harvests
because of the fierce anger of the LORD.

14 Thus says the LORD concerning all my evil neighbors who
touch the heritage that I have given my people Israel to inherit: I am
about to pluck them up from their land, and I will pluck up the house
of Judah from among them. 15 And after I have plucked them up, I will
again have compassion on them, and I will bring them again to their
heritage and to their land, every one of them. 16 And then, if they will
diligently learn the ways of my people, to swear by my name, "As the
LORD lives," as they taught my people to swear by Baal, then they shall
be built up in the midst of my people. 17 But if any nation will not listen, then I will completely uproot it and destroy it, says the LORD.

---

[a] Cn: Heb *Is the hyena, the bird of prey* [b] Or *the trails* [c] Heb *your*

The Linen Loincloth

13 Thus said the LORD to me, "Go and buy yourself a linen loincloth, and put it on your loins, but do not dip it in water." [2]So
I bought a loincloth according to the word of the LORD, and put it on
my loins. [3]And the word of the LORD came to me a second time, saying, [4]"Take the loincloth that you bought and are wearing, and go now
to the Euphrates,[a] and hide it there in a cleft of the rock." [5]So I went,
and hid it by the Euphrates,[a] as the LORD commanded me. [6]And after
many days the LORD said to me, "Go now to the Euphrates,[a] and take
from there the loincloth that I commanded you to hide there." [7]Then
I went to the Euphrates,[a] and dug, and I took the loincloth from the
place where I had hidden it. But now the loincloth was ruined; it was
good for nothing.

8 Then the word of the LORD came to me: [9]Thus says the LORD:
Just so I will ruin the pride of Judah and the great pride of Jerusalem.
[10]This evil people, who refuse to hear my words, who stubbornly follow their own will and have gone after other gods to serve them and
worship them, shall be like this loincloth, which is good for nothing.
[11]For as the loincloth clings to one's loins, so I made the whole house
of Israel and the whole house of Judah cling to me, says the LORD, in
order that they might be for me a people, a name, a praise, and a glory.
But they would not listen.

Symbol of the Wine-Jars

12 You shall speak to them this word: Thus says the LORD, the
God of Israel: Every wine-jar should be filled with wine. And they
will say to you, "Do you think we do not know that every wine-jar
should be filled with wine?" [13]Then you shall say to them: Thus says
the LORD: I am about to fill all the inhabitants of this land—the kings
who sit on David's throne, the priests, the prophets, and all the inhabitants of Jerusalem—with drunkenness. [14]And I will dash them one
against another, parents and children together, says the LORD. I will
not pity or spare or have compassion when I destroy them.

Exile Threatened

15 Hear and give ear; do not be haughty,
    for the LORD has spoken.
16 Give glory to the LORD your God
    before he brings darkness,
and before your feet stumble
    on the mountains at twilight;
while you look for light,
    he turns it into gloom

[a] Or *to Parah*; Heb *perath*

13:1-11 Go and buy yourself a linen loincloth: Could this have really happened? A round trip between Jerusalem and the Euphrates River on the western edge of Babylonia (modern Iraq) is 700–800 miles (see Map 9, p. 2106). In those days, this journey would take several months. Some scholars think the incident is a dramatic parable. Jeremiah gathered an audience, set out the locations on a stage, and carried his dirty loincloth from one spot on stage to another. In other words, he dramatized his message that the people of Jerusalem go off to exile and there become "good for nothing" (13:7).

The message Jeremiah delivered was bad news. Ancient people believed that a divine word did not simply inform the audience about coming judgment or salvation. The spoken word *accomplished* what it promised. For a beautiful expression of that spoken power, read Isaiah 55:10-11. Hearing Jeremiah's word of judgment and seeing it enacted, the people responded with anger, disbelief, and fear.

How do you feel about words accomplishing what they say? Think of the promises made by politicians as an election approaches. Think of the words of a pastor who pronounces, "God forgives you of all your sins."

13:11 that they might be for me a people, a name, a praise, and a glory. But they would not listen: The LORD lamented over the people's calling the Canaanite gods "father" (2:27) and their refusal to call the LORD "My Father" (3:19). Now the LORD is heartbroken because the people refuse to remain faithful to their God. Israel has dishonored God and their intimate relationship with the LORD.

How does it make you feel knowing God is heartbroken when God's people are unfaithful?

and makes it deep darkness.
17 But if you will not listen,
my soul will weep in secret for your pride;
my eyes will weep bitterly and run down with tears,
because the LORD's flock has been taken captive.

13:18 Say to the king and the queen mother: King Jehoiachin and the queen mother Nehushta have lost their crowns. The people have gone into exile (see 2 Kgs 24:8-17 for the story). Jehoiachin was only eighteen years old at the time.

18 Say to the king and the queen mother:
"Take a lowly seat,
for your beautiful crown
has come down from your head."[a]
19 The towns of the Negeb are shut up
with no one to open them;
all Judah is taken into exile,
wholly taken into exile.

20 Lift up your eyes and see
those who come from the north.
Where is the flock that was given you,
your beautiful flock?
21 What will you say when they set as head over you
those whom you have trained
to be your allies?
Will not pangs take hold of you,
like those of a woman in labor?
22 And if you say in your heart,
"Why have these things come upon me?"
it is for the greatness of your iniquity
that your skirts are lifted up,
and you are violated.
23 Can Ethiopians[b] change their skin
or leopards their spots?
Then also you can do good
who are accustomed to do evil.
24 I will scatter you[c] like chaff
driven by the wind from the desert.
25 This is your lot,
the portion I have measured out to you, says the LORD,
because you have forgotten me
and trusted in lies.
26 I myself will lift up your skirts over your face,
and your shame will be seen.
27 I have seen your abominations,
your adulteries and neighings, your shameless prostitutions
on the hills of the countryside.

13:27 I have seen your abominations, your adulteries and neighings, your shameless prostitutions on the hills of the countryside: The word "abominations" refers to Canaanite religious practices. The "adulteries" are relationships with fertility deities. The "neighings" are the strong desires for fertility worship. The "prostitutions" are the acts committed at the sites of this shameful worship.

---

[a] Gk Syr Vg: Meaning of Heb uncertain [b] Or *Nubians*; Heb *Cushites* [c] Heb *them*

Woe to you, O Jerusalem!
How long will it be
before you are made clean?

The Great Drought

14 The word of the LORD that came to Jeremiah concerning the drought:

2 Judah mourns
and her gates languish;
they lie in gloom on the ground,
and the cry of Jerusalem goes up.
3 Her nobles send their servants for water;
they come to the cisterns,
they find no water,
they return with their vessels empty.
They are ashamed and dismayed
and cover their heads,
4 because the ground is cracked.
Because there has been no rain on the land
the farmers are dismayed;
they cover their heads.
5 Even the doe in the field forsakes her newborn fawn
because there is no grass.
6 The wild asses stand on the bare heights,[a]
they pant for air like jackals;
their eyes fail
because there is no herbage.

7 Although our iniquities testify against us,
act, O LORD, for your name's sake;
our apostasies indeed are many,
and we have sinned against you.
8 O hope of Israel,
its savior in time of trouble,
why should you be like a stranger in the land,
like a traveler turning aside for the night?
9 Why should you be like someone confused,
like a mighty warrior who cannot give help?
Yet you, O LORD, are in the midst of us,
and we are called by your name;
do not forsake us!

10 Thus says the LORD concerning this people:
Truly they have loved to wander,

[a] Or *the trails*

14:1—15:21 The LORD said to me... Then I said: In this conversation between Jeremiah and God, Jeremiah speaks both his own words and those of the people. He also hears the words God speaks to the people, so that he might repeat them in his sermons. Jeremiah speaks in 14:2-10; God in 14:11-12; Jeremiah in 14:13; God in 14:14-18; Jeremiah in 14:19-22; God in 15:1-9; Jeremiah in 15:10; God in 15:11-14; Jeremiah in 15:15-18; God in 15:19-21.

Imagine you are eavesdropping on the conversation between God and Jeremiah in these chapters. What are your reactions to the speeches of God in these verses? How do you feel about the prophet in this conversation?

14:8 O hope of Israel, its savior in time of trouble: The Bible uses the word *hope* in the LORD as the only legitimate source of trust. The people of Israel express their hope *in* the LORD (as in 14:22; Ps 39:7). Sometimes the LORD *is* the hope of Israel (Jer 17:13; 50:7). The Hebrew word translated *savior* comes from a word meaning "spacious" or "broad." It refers to freedom to move about or to live in a broad place (see the description of the promised land at Exodus 3:8; geographically, Israel is a narrow strip).

What does it mean for you to hope in God?

they have not restrained their feet;
therefore the LORD does not accept them,
now he will remember their iniquity
and punish their sins.

11 The LORD said to me: Do not pray for the welfare of this people. [12]Although they fast, I do not hear their cry, and although they
offer burnt offering and grain offering, I do not accept them; but by
the sword, by famine, and by pestilence I consume them.

Denunciation of Lying Prophets

13 Then I said: "Ah, Lord GOD! Here are the prophets saying to
them, 'You shall not see the sword, nor shall you have famine, but I
will give you true peace in this place.'" [14]And the LORD said to me:
The prophets are prophesying lies in my name; I did not send them,
nor did I command them or speak to them. They are prophesying to
you a lying vision, worthless divination, and the deceit of their own
minds. [15]Therefore thus says the LORD concerning the prophets
who prophesy in my name though I did not send them, and who say,
"Sword and famine shall not come on this land": By sword and famine
those prophets shall be consumed. [16]And the people to whom they
prophesy shall be thrown out into the streets of Jerusalem, victims of
famine and sword. There shall be no one to bury them—themselves,
their wives, their sons, and their daughters. For I will pour out their
wickedness upon them.

17 You shall say to them this word:
Let my eyes run down with tears night and day,
and let them not cease,
for the virgin daughter—my people—is struck down with a crushing blow,
with a very grievous wound.
18 If I go out into the field,
look—those killed by the sword!
And if I enter the city,
look—those sick with[a] famine!
For both prophet and priest ply their trade throughout the land,
and have no knowledge.

The People Plead for Mercy

19 Have you completely rejected Judah?
Does your heart loathe Zion?
Why have you struck us down

14:19-22 Have you completely rejected Judah?: Jeremiah's main role in the first twenty-nine chapters of the book is to announce God's judgment on the people. Here Jeremiah serves as the spokesperson for the people to God. He pleads on their behalf.

Have you ever prayed for the welfare of people you feel acted in ways that dishonor God? What were the circumstances?

[a] Heb *look—the sicknesses of*

so that there is no healing for us?
We look for peace, but find no good;
for a time of healing, but there is terror instead.
20 We acknowledge our wickedness, O LORD,
the iniquity of our ancestors,
for we have sinned against you.
21 Do not spurn us, for your name's sake;
do not dishonor your glorious throne;
remember and do not break your covenant with us.
22 Can any idols of the nations bring rain?
Or can the heavens give showers?
Is it not you, O LORD our God?
We set our hope on you,
for it is you who do all this.

Punishment Is Inevitable

15 Then the LORD said to me: Though Moses and Samuel stood
before me, yet my heart would not turn toward this people.
Send them out of my sight, and let them go! 2And when they say
to you, "Where shall we go?" you shall say to them: Thus says the
LORD:

Those destined for pestilence, to pestilence,
and those destined for the sword, to the sword;
those destined for famine, to famine,
and those destined for captivity, to captivity.

3And I will appoint over them four kinds of destroyers, says the LORD:
the sword to kill, the dogs to drag away, and the birds of the air and the
wild animals of the earth to devour and destroy. 4I will make them a
horror to all the kingdoms of the earth because of what King Manasseh son of Hezekiah of Judah did in Jerusalem.

5 Who will have pity on you, O Jerusalem,
or who will bemoan you?
Who will turn aside
to ask about your welfare?
6 You have rejected me, says the LORD,
you are going backward;
so I have stretched out my hand against you and destroyed
you—
I am weary of relenting.
7 I have winnowed them with a winnowing fork
in the gates of the land;
I have bereaved them, I have destroyed my people;
they did not turn from their ways.
8 Their widows became more numerous

15:1 Though Moses and Samuel stood before me: God's words here are harsh. God rejects Jeremiah's attempts to intervene on the people's behalf. This is not because Jeremiah is young or unable. Even Moses and Samuel (Ps 99:6) could not persuade God to withhold the coming judgment for Israel's unfaithfulness. Moses pleaded for God's forgiveness for the people when they made the golden calf (Exod 32:11-14, 30-32). Samuel led the prayers of the people so that the LORD might make them victorious over the Philistines (1 Sam 7:5-11).

How seriously do you think God takes our prayers of intercession for others? When have you prayed for other people? When have other people prayed for you?

than the sand of the seas;
I have brought against the mothers of youths
a destroyer at noonday;
I have made anguish and terror
fall upon her suddenly.
9 She who bore seven has languished;
she has swooned away;
her sun went down while it was yet day;
she has been shamed and disgraced.
And the rest of them I will give to the sword
before their enemies,
says the LORD.

Jeremiah Complains Again and Is Reassured

10 Woe is me, my mother, that you ever bore me, a man of strife
and contention to the whole land! I have not lent, nor have I borrowed, yet all of them curse me. 11 The LORD said: Surely I have intervened in your life[a] for good, surely I have imposed enemies on you
in a time of trouble and in a time of distress.[b] 12 Can iron and bronze
break iron from the north?

13 Your wealth and your treasures I will give as plunder, without
price, for all your sins, throughout all your territory. 14 I will make you
serve your enemies in a land that you do not know, for in my anger a
fire is kindled that shall burn forever.

15 O LORD, you know;
remember me and visit me,
and bring down retribution for me on my persecutors.
In your forbearance do not take me away;
know that on your account I suffer insult.
16 Your words were found, and I ate them,
and your words became to me a joy
and the delight of my heart;
for I am called by your name,
O LORD, God of hosts.
17 I did not sit in the company of merrymakers,
nor did I rejoice;
under the weight of your hand I sat alone,
for you had filled me with indignation.
18 Why is my pain unceasing,
my wound incurable,
refusing to be healed?
Truly, you are to me like a deceitful brook,
like waters that fail.

---

[a] Heb *intervened with you* [b] Meaning of Heb uncertain

19 Therefore thus says the LORD:
If you turn back, I will take you back,
and you shall stand before me.
If you utter what is precious, and not what is worthless,
you shall serve as my mouth.
It is they who will turn to you,
not you who will turn to them.
20 And I will make you to this people
a fortified wall of bronze;
they will fight against you,
but they shall not prevail over you,
for I am with you
to save you and deliver you,
says the LORD.
21 I will deliver you out of the hand of the wicked,
and redeem you from the grasp of the ruthless.

15:19-20 says the LORD...for I am with you to save you and deliver you: God had promised Jeremiah this same saving presence (1:8). Now after Jeremiah's experiences of rejection and isolation, the prophet must have found God's promise even more essential for his life.

When you feel you are facing overwhelming odds, what comfort do you receive from the promise of God's presence, especially when it comes from the crucified and risen Christ (Matt 28:19-20)?

Jeremiah's Celibacy and Message

16 The word of the LORD came to me: 2You shall not take a wife,
nor shall you have sons or daughters in this place. 3For thus
says the LORD concerning the sons and daughters who are born in
this place, and concerning the mothers who bear them and the fathers
who beget them in this land: 4They shall die of deadly diseases. They
shall not be lamented, nor shall they be buried; they shall become like
dung on the surface of the ground. They shall perish by the sword and
by famine, and their dead bodies shall become food for the birds of
the air and for the wild animals of the earth.
5 For thus says the LORD: Do not enter the house of mourning,
or go to lament, or bemoan them; for I have taken away my peace
from this people, says the LORD, my steadfast love and mercy. 6Both
great and small shall die in this land; they shall not be buried, and
no one shall lament for them; there shall be no gashing, no shaving
of the head for them. 7No one shall break bread[a] for the mourner, to
offer comfort for the dead; nor shall anyone give them the cup of consolation to drink for their fathers or their mothers. 8You shall not go
into the house of feasting to sit with them, to eat and drink. 9For thus
says the LORD of hosts, the God of Israel: I am going to banish from
this place, in your days and before your eyes, the voice of mirth and
the voice of gladness, the voice of the bridegroom and the voice of
the bride.
10 And when you tell this people all these words, and they say
to you, "Why has the LORD pronounced all this great evil against us?
What is our iniquity? What is the sin that we have committed against

16:1 You shall not take a wife, nor shall you have sons or daughters in this place: Jeremiah now seems to be old enough to consider marriage and children. Since his family has rejected him, it seems they have not arranged a marriage for him. Bad times are ahead for families.

16:5 I have taken away my peace... my steadfast love and mercy: The LORD's steadfast love (covenant or promised loyalty) and acts of mercy gave the people peace (security, well-being, wholeness). Now God threatens to end this harmony, because the people have rejected the LORD by worshiping other gods.

---

[a] Two Mss Gk: MT *break for them*

the LORD our God?" 11 then you shall say to them: It is because your
ancestors have forsaken me, says the LORD, and have gone after other
gods and have served and worshiped them, and have forsaken me and
have not kept my law; 12 and because you have behaved worse than
your ancestors, for here you are, every one of you, following your
stubborn evil will, refusing to listen to me. 13 Therefore I will hurl you
out of this land into a land that neither you nor your ancestors have
known, and there you shall serve other gods day and night, for I will
show you no favor.

God Will Restore Israel

14 Therefore, the days are surely coming, says the LORD, when
it shall no longer be said, "As the LORD lives who brought the people
of Israel up out of the land of Egypt," 15 but "As the LORD lives who
brought the people of Israel up out of the land of the north and out of
all the lands where he had driven them." For I will bring them back to
their own land that I gave to their ancestors.

16 I am now sending for many fishermen, says the LORD, and
they shall catch them; and afterward I will send for many hunters, and
they shall hunt them from every mountain and every hill, and out of
the clefts of the rocks. 17 For my eyes are on all their ways; they are
not hidden from my presence, nor is their iniquity concealed from my
sight. 18 And[a] I will doubly repay their iniquity and their sin, because
they have polluted my land with the carcasses of their detestable idols,
and have filled my inheritance with their abominations.

19 O LORD, my strength and my stronghold,
  my refuge in the day of trouble,
to you shall the nations come
  from the ends of the earth and say:
Our ancestors have inherited nothing but lies,
  worthless things in which there is no profit.
20 Can mortals make for themselves gods?
  Such are no gods!

21 "Therefore I am surely going to teach them, this time I am going to teach them my power and my might, and they shall know that
my name is the LORD."

Judah's Sin and Punishment

17 The sin of Judah is written with an iron pen; with a diamond
point it is engraved on the tablet of their hearts, and on the
horns of their altars, 2 while their children remember their altars and
their sacred poles,[b] beside every green tree, and on the high hills, 3 on

[a] Gk: Heb *And first* [b] Heb *Asherim*

16:14 Therefore, the days are surely coming: The prophets had different ways to talk about when the LORD would establish the divine kingdom over Israel and over the whole world. Here Jeremiah uses "the days are surely coming." In other places we read "in those days" (Jer 31:29; Joel 2:29; 3:1), "in/on that day" (Isa 7:18-23; 26:1; 27:1, 2, 12; 28:5), or "at that time" (Jer 31:1). All the phrases show that "the day of the LORD" has two divine purposes. It brings judgment on the evil that stands in God's way for good. It also brings the salvation and peace that fulfills God's purposes for the world. Some of these phrases are used in the New Testament to show that in Jesus we see the nearness of God's day (Mark 1:15; 4:35).

16:14-15 As the LORD lives who brought the people of Israel up . . . I will bring them back to their own land: The same message appears at 23:7-8, where it fits better. This little sermon offers hope in the midst of the prophecies of doom. Jeremiah announces God's promise to restore the people from their exile in Babylon to their own land. This future event will be even better than the time God used Moses to lead the people out of the land of Egypt (see also Isa 43:14-21).

17:1 The sin of Judah is written . . . on the horns of their altars: The ancient priests smeared the blood of a sacrificial goat on the protruding corners of the altar (Lev 4:1-7; 16:18). The Israelites called these corners "horns." The ritual removed the sins of the people. It was called atonement.

the mountains in the open country. Your wealth and all your treasures
I will give for spoil as the price of your sin[a] throughout all your territory. 4By your own act you shall lose the heritage that I gave you, and I
will make you serve your enemies in a land that you do not know, for
in my anger a fire is kindled[b] that shall burn forever.

5 Thus says the LORD:
Cursed are those who trust in mere mortals
and make mere flesh their strength,
whose hearts turn away from the LORD.
6 They shall be like a shrub in the desert,
and shall not see when relief comes.
They shall live in the parched places of the wilderness,
in an uninhabited salt land.

7 Blessed are those who trust in the LORD,
whose trust is the LORD.
8 They shall be like a tree planted by water,
sending out its roots by the stream.
It shall not fear when heat comes,
and its leaves shall stay green;
in the year of drought it is not anxious,
and it does not cease to bear fruit.

9 The heart is devious above all else;
it is perverse—
who can understand it?
10 I the LORD test the mind
and search the heart,
to give to all according to their ways,
according to the fruit of their doings.

11 Like the partridge hatching what it did not lay,
so are all who amass wealth unjustly;
in mid-life it will leave them,
and at their end they will prove to be fools.

12 O glorious throne, exalted from the beginning,
shrine of our sanctuary!
13 O hope of Israel! O LORD!
All who forsake you shall be put to shame;
those who turn away from you[c] shall be recorded in the
underworld,[d]
for they have forsaken the fountain of living water, the LORD.

[a] Cn: Heb *spoil your high places for sin* [b] Two Mss Theodotion: *you kindled* [c] Heb *me* [d] Or *in the earth*

17:5-13 like a shrub: Jeremiah (and other prophets) sometimes used proverbs, short sayings that taught a lesson in life. Here Jeremiah writes (or quotes) several proverbs: 17:5-8, 9-10, 11, 12-13. In them he uses images called similes: "like a shrub," "like a tree," and "like the partridge." Verses 5-8 sound like Psalm 1:1-3, a "wisdom psalm" that teaches the different fates that await those who trust in human values and those who trust in the LORD.

17:14-18 Heal me, O Lord, and I shall be healed: Jeremiah expresses his dismay to God in the form of a lament (a prayer of complaint to God). The people have been ridiculing him. They have heard his sermons of doom, but nothing has happened yet. Only the Lord can heal him, by delivering the prophet from this public humiliation. He was certain the Lord had commanded him to announce the words of judgment. Or was he?

17:19 Go and stand in the People's Gate: The name for this gate appears nowhere else in the Bible. We do not know which gate Jeremiah (or the Lord) means.

17:19-27 keep the sabbath day holy, as I commanded your ancestors: Observing the Sabbath was one of the Ten Commandments that God gave to Israel through Moses (Exod 20:8; Deut 5:12). In the middle of the eighth century B.C.E., the prophet Amos spoke of Israel's disregard for the Sabbath. The people wanted to get on with the business of cheating the poor (Amos 8:4-6). Shortly after Amos, the prophet Isaiah gave little importance to Sabbaths and other assemblies. Isaiah considered Sabbaths as one of the religious formalities that kept the people of Jerusalem from their responsibility to "seek justice, rescue the oppressed, defend the orphan, plead for the widow" (Isa 1:13, 17).

This passage in Jeremiah 17 introduces the neglect of the Sabbath as one of the reasons for the Lord's judgment on the people. A decade or two after Jeremiah's sermon, Ezekiel preached that God gave the Sabbath "so that they might know that I the Lord sanctify them" (Ezek 20:12). Between the time of Isaiah's little regard for the Sabbath on the one hand and the importance it had for Jeremiah and Ezekiel on the other hand, someone found the scroll of Deuteronomy hidden in the temple. When the young King Josiah heard the long-lost book read aloud, he immediately began religious reforms (2 Kgs 23). In that document the Sabbath observance, along with the other commandments, took on special importance. In the New Testament, Jesus favors healing and eating (Matt 12:1-14) over the strict rules about Sabbath observance. In the book of Acts the apostles preached the word of God in the synagogues on Sabbaths (Acts 13:14, 44; 18:4). Eventually Christians set aside Sunday, the first day of the week, to celebrate the resurrection of Jesus and to hear the word of God.

Jeremiah Prays for Vindication

14 Heal me, O Lord, and I shall be healed;
save me, and I shall be saved;
for you are my praise.
15 See how they say to me,
"Where is the word of the Lord?
Let it come!"
16 But I have not run away from being a shepherd[a] in your service,
nor have I desired the fatal day.
You know what came from my lips;
it was before your face.
17 Do not become a terror to me;
you are my refuge in the day of disaster;
18 Let my persecutors be shamed,
but do not let me be shamed;
let them be dismayed,
but do not let me be dismayed;
bring on them the day of disaster;
destroy them with double destruction!

Hallow the Sabbath Day

19 Thus said the Lord to me: Go and stand in the People's Gate,
by which the kings of Judah enter and by which they go out, and in all
the gates of Jerusalem, 20 and say to them: Hear the word of the Lord,
you kings of Judah, and all Judah, and all the inhabitants of Jerusalem,
who enter by these gates. 21 Thus says the Lord: For the sake of your
lives, take care that you do not bear a burden on the sabbath day or
bring it in by the gates of Jerusalem. 22 And do not carry a burden out
of your houses on the sabbath or do any work, but keep the sabbath
day holy, as I commanded your ancestors. 23 Yet they did not listen
or incline their ear; they stiffened their necks and would not hear or
receive instruction.

24 But if you listen to me, says the Lord, and bring in no burden by the gates of this city on the sabbath day, but keep the sabbath
day holy and do no work on it, 25 then there shall enter by the gates
of this city kings[b] who sit on the throne of David, riding in chariots
and on horses, they and their officials, the people of Judah and the inhabitants of Jerusalem; and this city shall be inhabited forever. 26 And
people shall come from the towns of Judah and the places around Jerusalem, from the land of Benjamin, from the Shephelah, from the
hill country, and from the Negeb, bringing burnt offerings and sacrifices, grain offerings and frankincense, and bringing thank offerings
to the house of the Lord. 27 But if you do not listen to me, to keep the

[a] Meaning of Heb uncertain [b] Cn: Heb *kings and officials*

sabbath day holy, and to carry in no burden through the gates of Jerusalem on the sabbath day, then I will kindle a fire in its gates; it shall devour the palaces of Jerusalem and shall not be quenched.

The Potter and the Clay

18 The word that came to Jeremiah from the LORD: [2]"Come, go
down to the potter's house, and there I will let you hear my
words." [3]So I went down to the potter's house, and there he was working at his wheel. [4]The vessel he was making of clay was spoiled in the potter's hand, and he reworked it into another vessel, as seemed good to him.

5 Then the word of the LORD came to me: [6]Can I not do with you,
O house of Israel, just as this potter has done? says the LORD. Just like the clay in the potter's hand, so are you in my hand, O house of Israel.
[7]At one moment I may declare concerning a nation or a kingdom, that I will pluck up and break down and destroy it, [8]but if that nation,
concerning which I have spoken, turns from its evil, I will change my mind about the disaster that I intended to bring on it. [9]And at another
moment I may declare concerning a nation or a kingdom that I will build and plant it, [10]but if it does evil in my sight, not listening to my
voice, then I will change my mind about the good that I had intended to do to it. [11]Now, therefore, say to the people of Judah and the inhab-
itants of Jerusalem: Thus says the LORD: Look, I am a potter shaping evil against you and devising a plan against you. Turn now, all of you from your evil way, and amend your ways and your doings.

Israel's Stubborn Idolatry

12 But they say, "It is no use! We will follow our own plans, and
each of us will act according to the stubbornness of our evil will."

13 Therefore thus says the LORD:
Ask among the nations:
  Who has heard the like of this?
The virgin Israel has done
  a most horrible thing.
14 Does the snow of Lebanon leave
  the crags of Sirion?[a]
Do the mountain[b] waters run dry,[c]
  the cold flowing streams?
15 But my people have forgotten me,
  they burn offerings to a delusion;
they have stumbled[d] in their ways,

[a] Cn: Heb *of the field* [b] Cn: Heb *foreign* [c] Cn: Heb *Are . . . plucked up?* [d] Gk Syr Vg: Heb *they made them stumble*

How should we observe the Sabbath? In explaining the commandment about the Sabbath, Luther speaks not of the day at all but of the holiness of God's word and our commitment to hear and learn it (*SC*:5). We make the day holy "not when we sit behind the stove and refrain from work, or place a garland on our head and dress up in our best clothes, but...when we make use of God's Word and exercise ourselves in it" (*BC*:398). *Jeremiah 17:19-27*

18:1-11 go down to the potter's house: Jeremiah watches the potter rework the spoiled clay into a different object. This leads Jeremiah to a sermon about the LORD's willingness to rework plans for destruction or deliverance. The message gives Israel the opportunity to avoid the judgment if the people repent.

in the ancient roads,
and have gone into bypaths,
not the highway,
16 making their land a horror,
a thing to be hissed at forever.
All who pass by it are horrified
and shake their heads.
17 Like the wind from the east,
I will scatter them before the enemy.
I will show them my back, not my face,
in the day of their calamity.

18:17 Like the wind from the east: The east wind is a specific phenomenon in the Middle East. This wind, the *sirocco,* begins in the Sahara desert. It is hot, dusty, and can make people sick. It can be devastating (4:11-12; 13:24). The east wind is the instrument God uses to dry up the sea and stop the Egyptian army (Exod 14:21).

A Plot against Jeremiah

18 Then they said, "Come, let us make plots against Jeremiah—
for instruction shall not perish from the priest, nor counsel from the
wise, nor the word from the prophet. Come, let us bring charges
against him,[a] and let us not heed any of his words."

18:18 let us make plots against Jeremiah: This chapter is all about plotting. The Lord plots harm against the people for their idolatry (18:11). The people insist on following their own plots (18:12). Now the plotters are the groups of leaders against whom Jeremiah has announced judgment: the priest, the wise, and the prophet (8:8-10).

19 Give heed to me, O Lord,
and listen to what my adversaries say!
20 Is evil a recompense for good?
Yet they have dug a pit for my life.
Remember how I stood before you
to speak good for them,
to turn away your wrath from them.
21 Therefore give their children over to famine;
hurl them out to the power of the sword,
let their wives become childless and widowed.
May their men meet death by pestilence,
their youths be slain by the sword in battle.
22 May a cry be heard from their houses,
when you bring the marauder suddenly upon them!
For they have dug a pit to catch me,
and laid snares for my feet.
23 Yet you, O Lord, know
all their plotting to kill me.
Do not forgive their iniquity,
do not blot out their sin from your sight.
Let them be tripped up before you;
deal with them while you are angry.

18:19-23 Do not forgive their iniquity: Jeremiah offers another lament. He is afraid of the plots and is frustrated that the people have rejected his message. He asks God not to forgive their evil deeds or sins (iniquities).

The Broken Earthenware Jug

19 Thus said the Lord: Go and buy a potter's earthenware jug.
Take with you[b] some of the elders of the people and some of

[a] Heb *strike him with the tongue* [b] Syr Tg Compare Gk: Heb lacks *take with you*

the senior priests, [2]and go out to the valley of the son of Hinnom at the entry of the Potsherd Gate, and proclaim there the words that I tell you. [3]You shall say: Hear the word of the LORD, O kings of Judah and inhabitants of Jerusalem. Thus says the LORD of hosts, the God of Israel: I am going to bring such disaster upon this place that the ears of everyone who hears of it will tingle. [4]Because the people have forsaken me, and have profaned this place by making offerings in it to other gods whom neither they nor their ancestors nor the kings of Judah have known, and because they have filled this place with the blood of the innocent, [5]and gone on building the high places of Baal to burn their children in the fire as burnt offerings to Baal, which I did not command or decree, nor did it enter my mind; [6]therefore the days are surely coming, says the LORD, when this place shall no more be called Topheth, or the valley of the son of Hinnom, but the valley of Slaughter. [7]And in this place I will make void the plans of Judah and Jerusalem, and will make them fall by the sword before their enemies, and by the hand of those who seek their life. I will give their dead bodies for food to the birds of the air and to the wild animals of the earth. [8]And I will make this city a horror, a thing to be hissed at; everyone who passes by it will be horrified and will hiss because of all its disasters. [9]And I will make them eat the flesh of their sons and the flesh of their daughters, and all shall eat the flesh of their neighbors in the siege, and in the distress with which their enemies and those who seek their life afflict them.

10 Then you shall break the jug in the sight of those who go with you, [11]and shall say to them: Thus says the LORD of hosts: So will I break this people and this city, as one breaks a potter's vessel, so that it can never be mended. In Topheth they shall bury until there is no more room to bury. [12]Thus will I do to this place, says the LORD, and to its inhabitants, making this city like Topheth. [13]And the houses of Jerusalem and the houses of the kings of Judah shall be defiled like the place of Topheth—all the houses upon whose roofs offerings have been made to the whole host of heaven, and libations have been poured out to other gods.

14 When Jeremiah came from Topheth, where the LORD had sent him to prophesy, he stood in the court of the LORD's house and said to all the people: [15]Thus says the LORD of hosts, the God of Israel: I am now bringing upon this city and upon all its towns all the disaster that I have pronounced against it, because they have stiffened their necks, refusing to hear my words.

Jeremiah Persecuted by Pashhur

20 Now the priest Pashhur son of Immer, who was chief officer in the house of the LORD, heard Jeremiah prophesying these things. [2]Then Pashhur struck the prophet Jeremiah, and put him

19:2 the Potsherd Gate: The gate in the wall of the southeast section of Jerusalem received its name from its use. There the potters in the area discarded their rejects and broken parts, called potsherds. See Map 6, p. 2104.

19:10-11 break the jug…So I will break this people and this city: Jeremiah again enacts in drama the words he is preaching.

19:15 they have stiffened their necks: The expression describes Israel's stubborn rebellion against God (Exod 32:9; 33:3, 5; Deut 9:6, 13; Jer 17:23).

20:1-6 Pashhur son of Immer, who was chief officer in the house of the LORD: Pashhur (PAWSH-hur) held an office something like a head administrator in the temple. Jeremiah raged against the priest and even changed the administrator's name to words meaning "Terror-all-around" (20:3). In ancient times a person's name reflected one's origin, character, or destiny. Sara and Abraham named their son Isaac ("he laughs"), because, she said, "God has brought laughter for me" (Gen 21:6). Pashhur's new name describes the horrible future that awaits him, the temple, and the people of Jerusalem (2 Kgs 24:13-17).

in the stocks that were in the upper Benjamin Gate of the house of the
LORD. [3]The next morning when Pashhur released Jeremiah from the
stocks, Jeremiah said to him, The LORD has named you not Pashhur
but "Terror-all-around." [4]For thus says the LORD: I am making you
a terror to yourself and to all your friends; and they shall fall by the
sword of their enemies while you look on. And I will give all Judah
into the hand of the king of Babylon; he shall carry them captive to
Babylon, and shall kill them with the sword. [5]I will give all the wealth
of this city, all its gains, all its prized belongings, and all the treasures
of the kings of Judah into the hand of their enemies, who shall plunder
them, and seize them, and carry them to Babylon. [6]And you, Pashhur,
and all who live in your house, shall go into captivity, and to Babylon
you shall go; there you shall die, and there you shall be buried, you
and all your friends, to whom you have prophesied falsely.

Jeremiah Denounces His Persecutors

20:7-13 O LORD, you have enticed me: Jeremiah's laments become more shocking. Because he has fulfilled the LORD's call to "pluck up and to pull down" (1:10), Jeremiah is the object of a conspiracy. Even so, Jeremiah believes that the LORD is present and will deliver. This is like other laments in the Bible (see Pss 7; 10; 13; 22).

7 O LORD, you have enticed me,
and I was enticed;
you have overpowered me,
and you have prevailed.
I have become a laughingstock all day long;
everyone mocks me.
8 For whenever I speak, I must cry out,
I must shout, "Violence and destruction!"
For the word of the LORD has become for me
a reproach and derision all day long.
9 If I say, "I will not mention him,
or speak any more in his name,"
then within me there is something like a burning fire
shut up in my bones;
I am weary with holding it in,
and I cannot.
10 For I hear many whispering:
"Terror is all around!
Denounce him! Let us denounce him!"
All my close friends
are watching for me to stumble.
"Perhaps he can be enticed,
and we can prevail against him,
and take our revenge on him."
11 But the LORD is with me like a dread warrior;
therefore my persecutors will stumble,
and they will not prevail.
They will be greatly shamed,
for they will not succeed.

Their eternal dishonor
will never be forgotten.
12 O LORD of hosts, you test the righteous,
you see the heart and the mind;
let me see your retribution upon them,
for to you I have committed my cause.

13 Sing to the LORD;
praise the LORD!
For he has delivered the life of the needy
from the hands of evildoers.

14 Cursed be the day
on which I was born!
The day when my mother bore me,
let it not be blessed!
15 Cursed be the man
who brought the news to my father, saying,
"A child is born to you, a son,"
making him very glad.
16 Let that man be like the cities
that the LORD overthrew without pity;
let him hear a cry in the morning
and an alarm at noon,
17 because he did not kill me in the womb;
so my mother would have been my grave,
and her womb forever great.
18 Why did I come forth from the womb
to see toil and sorrow,
and spend my days in shame?

Jerusalem Will Fall to Nebuchadrezzar

21 This is the word that came to Jeremiah from the LORD, when
King Zedekiah sent to him Pashhur son of Malchiah and the
priest Zephaniah son of Maaseiah, saying, 2"Please inquire of the
LORD on our behalf, for King Nebuchadrezzar of Babylon is making
war against us; perhaps the LORD will perform a wonderful deed for
us, as he has often done, and will make him withdraw from us."
3 Then Jeremiah said to them: 4Thus you shall say to Zedekiah:
Thus says the LORD, the God of Israel: I am going to turn back the
weapons of war that are in your hands and with which you are fighting
against the king of Babylon and against the Chaldeans who are besieging you outside the walls; and I will bring them together into the
center of this city. 5I myself will fight against you with outstretched
hand and mighty arm, in anger, in fury, and in great wrath. 6And I will

In 20:14-18, Jeremiah curses the day he was born. What might bring hope to a person who is this depressed?

21:1—24:10 the word that came to Jeremiah: In these four chapters Jeremiah and other writers blame the kings and the prophets for the coming disaster. These two groups of leaders have failed in their responsibilities to the LORD and to the people. The material is not in chronological sequence.

21:1 when King Zedekiah sent to [Jeremiah] Pashhur son of Malchiah and the priest Zephaniah son of Maaseiah: This situation occurred in 588–587 B.C.E., just before, or during, the Babylonian attack on Jerusalem. This Pashhur is not the same person as in 20:1; this man is probably a prince.

21:2 King Nebuchadrezzar of Babylon: Nebuchadrezzar had been a military commander. He became king of Babylon in 605 B.C.E., after the death of his father, King Nabopolassar (NA-boh-pol-LAS-sar). In 597 he captured Jerusalem and took King Jehoiachin as an exile to Babylon. In 588 Nebuchadrezzar returned to Jerusalem to punish the city for its rebellion. Because of this threat, the delegation from King Zedekiah inquires of Jeremiah.

21:5 I myself will fight against you with outstretched hand and mighty arm: In the past, the people believed, the LORD fought *for* them with "outstretched hand and mighty arm" (see Deut 26:8). Now the LORD has chosen Nebuchadrezzar as "my servant" (see Jer 25:9; 27:6). The LORD fights with Nebuchadrezzar against the people of Israel to punish them for their unfaithfulness.

strike down the inhabitants of this city, both human beings and animals; they shall die of a great pestilence. [7]Afterward, says the LORD,
I will give King Zedekiah of Judah, and his servants, and the people
in this city—those who survive the pestilence, sword, and famine—
into the hands of King Nebuchadrezzar of Babylon, into the hands of
their enemies, into the hands of those who seek their lives. He shall
strike them down with the edge of the sword; he shall not pity them,
or spare them, or have compassion.
8 And to this people you shall say: Thus says the LORD: See, I am
setting before you the way of life and the way of death. [9]Those who
stay in this city shall die by the sword, by famine, and by pestilence;
but those who go out and surrender to the Chaldeans who are besieging you shall live and shall have their lives as a prize of war. [10]For
I have set my face against this city for evil and not for good, says the
LORD: it shall be given into the hands of the king of Babylon, and he
shall burn it with fire.

Message to the House of David

21:11-12: Hear the word of the LORD, O house of David!: Jeremiah addresses King Zedekiah, who was a member of the dynasty that had ruled in Jerusalem since the days of King David (about 1000 B.C.E.). The dynasty began when the LORD promised David that his descendants would always rule over God's people (2 Sam 7: 1-17). David, and every succeeding king from the royal family, was "the LORD's anointed one" (in Hebrew, *messiah*; in Greek, *Christ*). In Jeremiah's time the LORD's promise seemed questionable. Nebuchadrezzar removed several kings from David's line until he installed Zedekiah as king. (Zedekiah was not legitimate, because he was not a descendant of the previous king but a brother of Josiah and uncle of Jehoiachin.) In 587 B.C.E. Nebuchadrezzar killed Zedekiah. The only surviving member of David's line was a prisoner in Babylon: Jehoiachin.

11 To the house of the king of Judah say: Hear the word of the
LORD, [12]O house of David! Thus says the LORD:

Execute justice in the morning,
  and deliver from the hand of the oppressor
  anyone who has been robbed,
or else my wrath will go forth like fire,
  and burn, with no one to quench it,
  because of your evil doings.

13 See, I am against you, O inhabitant of the valley,
  O rock of the plain,
    says the LORD;
you who say, "Who can come down against us,
  or who can enter our places of refuge?"
14 I will punish you according to the fruit of your doings,
    says the LORD;
  I will kindle a fire in its forest,
  and it shall devour all that is around it.

Exhortation to Repent

22 Thus says the LORD: Go down to the house of the king of
Judah, and speak there this word, [2]and say: Hear the word of
the LORD, O King of Judah sitting on the throne of David—you, and
your servants, and your people who enter these gates. [3]Thus says the
LORD: Act with justice and righteousness, and deliver from the hand
of the oppressor anyone who has been robbed. And do no wrong
or violence to the alien, the orphan, and the widow, or shed inno-

22:3-5 Act with justice and righteousness: The king was responsible for justice and defense of the most vulnerable people (Ps 72:1-4, 12-14). This assignment was nothing less than the work of God (Pss 9:9-10; 82; 97).

cent blood in this place. [4]For if you will indeed obey this word, then
through the gates of this house shall enter kings who sit on the throne
of David, riding in chariots and on horses, they, and their servants,
and their people. [5]But if you will not heed these words, I swear by
myself, says the LORD, that this house shall become a desolation. [6]For
thus says the LORD concerning the house of the king of Judah:

You are like Gilead to me,
    like the summit of Lebanon;
but I swear that I will make you a desert,
    an uninhabited city.[a]
7 I will prepare destroyers against you,
    all with their weapons;
they shall cut down your choicest cedars
    and cast them into the fire.

8 And many nations will pass by this city, and all of them will say
one to another, "Why has the LORD dealt in this way with that great
city?" [9]And they will answer, "Because they abandoned the covenant
of the LORD their God, and worshiped other gods and served them."

10 Do not weep for him who is dead,
    nor bemoan him;
weep rather for him who goes away,
    for he shall return no more
    to see his native land.

Message to the Sons of Josiah

11 For thus says the LORD concerning Shallum son of King Josiah of Judah, who succeeded his father Josiah, and who went away
from this place: He shall return here no more, [12]but in the place where
they have carried him captive he shall die, and he shall never see this
land again.

13 Woe to him who builds his house by unrighteousness,
    and his upper rooms by injustice;
who makes his neighbors work for nothing,
    and does not give them their wages;
14 who says, "I will build myself a spacious house
    with large upper rooms,"
and who cuts out windows for it,
    paneling it with cedar,
    and painting it with vermilion.
15 Are you a king
    because you compete in cedar?

22:8-9 Why... Because: The question-and-answer format was a common way of teaching. Look at some examples in Deuteronomy 6:20-21 and 1 Kings 9:8-9.

22:10-12 Do not weep for him who is dead, nor bemoan him; weep rather for him who goes away: The poem in 22:10 might have been originally about the people who were exiled in 597 and 587 B.C.E., but here the poem is more specific. The one who has died was Josiah (Pharaoh Neco II executed him in 609). The one who is going away is Josiah's son Shallum (his throne name was Jehoahaz). Neco took Jehoahaz to Egypt three months after Josiah's death, and he died there (2 Kgs 23:34).

22:13-23 Woe to him who builds his house by unrighteousness: This section of the chapter describes the extravagance and the fate of Jehoiakim, who ruled from 609 to 597 B.C.E.

[a] Cn: Heb *uninhabited cities*

Did not your father eat and drink
and do justice and righteousness?
Then it was well with him.
16 He judged the cause of the poor and needy;
then it was well.
Is not this to know me?
says the LORD.
17 But your eyes and heart
are only on your dishonest gain,
for shedding innocent blood,
and for practicing oppression and violence.

18 Therefore thus says the LORD concerning King Jehoiakim son
of Josiah of Judah:

They shall not lament for him, saying,
"Alas, my brother!" or "Alas, sister!"
They shall not lament for him, saying,
"Alas, lord!" or "Alas, his majesty!"
19 With the burial of a donkey he shall be buried—
dragged off and thrown out beyond the gates of
Jerusalem.

20 Go up to Lebanon, and cry out,
and lift up your voice in Bashan;
cry out from Abarim,
for all your lovers are crushed.
21 I spoke to you in your prosperity,
but you said, "I will not listen."
This has been your way from your youth,
for you have not obeyed my voice.
22 The wind shall shepherd all your shepherds,
and your lovers shall go into captivity;
then you will be ashamed and dismayed
because of all your wickedness.
23 O inhabitant of Lebanon,
nested among the cedars,
how you will groan[a] when pangs come upon you,
pain as of a woman in labor!

22:24-30 King Coniah son of Jehoiakim: Jehoiakim's eighteen-year-old son Jeconiah (abbreviated as Coniah) became king. His three-month reign meant he could select a royal name. He chose the name Jehoiachin. Nebuchadrezzar exiled him to Babylon, and Jehoiachin spent thirty-seven years in prison (Jer 52:31-34). Since "none of his offspring shall succeed in sitting on the throne of David" (22:30), King Coniah's short reign marks the end of the four-hundred-year reign of David and his descendants.

Judgment on Coniah (Jehoiachin)

24 As I live, says the LORD, even if King Coniah son of Jehoiakim of Judah were the signet ring on my right hand, even from there
I would tear you off [25]and give you into the hands of those who seek
your life, into the hands of those of whom you are afraid, even into

[a] Gk Vg Syr: Heb *will be pitied*

the hands of King Nebuchadrezzar of Babylon and into the hands of
the Chaldeans. 26I will hurl you and the mother who bore you into another country, where you were not born, and there you shall die. 27But
they shall not return to the land to which they long to return.

28 Is this man Coniah a despised broken pot,
a vessel no one wants?
Why are he and his offspring hurled out
and cast away in a land that they do not know?
29 O land, land, land,
hear the word of the LORD!
30 Thus says the LORD:
Record this man as childless,
a man who shall not succeed in his days;
for none of his offspring shall succeed
in sitting on the throne of David,
and ruling again in Judah.

Restoration after Exile

23 Woe to the shepherds who destroy and scatter the sheep of
my pasture! says the LORD. 2Therefore thus says the LORD,
the God of Israel, concerning the shepherds who shepherd my people: It is you who have scattered my flock, and have driven them away,
and you have not attended to them. So I will attend to you for your
evil doings, says the LORD. 3Then I myself will gather the remnant of
my flock out of all the lands where I have driven them, and I will bring
them back to their fold, and they shall be fruitful and multiply. 4I will
raise up shepherds over them who will shepherd them, and they shall
not fear any longer, or be dismayed, nor shall any be missing, says the
LORD.

The Righteous Branch of David

5 The days are surely coming, says the LORD, when I will raise
up for David a righteous Branch, and he shall reign as king and deal
wisely, and shall execute justice and righteousness in the land. 6In
his days Judah will be saved and Israel will live in safety. And this is
the name by which he will be called: "The LORD is our righteousness."

7 Therefore, the days are surely coming, says the LORD, when it
shall no longer be said, "As the LORD lives who brought the people
of Israel up out of the land of Egypt," 8but "As the LORD lives who
brought out and led the offspring of the house of Israel out of the land
of the north and out of all the lands where he[a] had driven them." Then
they shall live in their own land.

[a] Gk: Heb *I*

23:1-2 Woe to the shepherds who destroy and scatter the sheep of my pasture!: In ancient texts from Babylon and Assyria, kings often called themselves shepherds. They led and protected their flocks of people. In this oracle, or speech, Jeremiah blames the king as well as the other leaders of Judah, who have failed their flocks.

23:3-4 Then I myself will gather the remnant of my flock: The LORD will reverse the fate of the people and restore them to their land. They will "be fruitful and multiply." Read God's blessing on all humankind in Genesis 1:28.

23:5-6 I shall raise up for David: Christians often think of Jesus when reading about God's promises for a future king from David's line who will rule the land, execute justice, and promote peace and security (Isa 9:2-7; 11:1-10; Jer 33:14-16; Mic 5:2-4; Zech 9:9-10). Jesus' ancestry shows that he is from the line of David (see Matt 1:1-17; Luke 3:23-38). Jesus was born in a stable, spent his adult years as a traveling preacher, and finally suffered death at the hands of religious and government leaders. This does not fit the picture of a Davidic king. Christians believe that in Jesus' suffering, death, and resurrection God proved to be faithful to the promises of the divine reign. In Jesus, God acted in an unexpected way to establish a reign that spread far beyond the land of Israel to include all people in every country. In their promises for a new time, the Old Testament passages about a future Davidic king take on a new and profound meaning in light of Jesus.

False Prophets of Hope Denounced

23:9-32 I did not send the prophets: The writers of the Bible struggled with how to distinguish between true prophecy and false prophecy. Jeremiah lists the traits of false prophets: They prophesied or preached in the name of Baal and led the people astray (23:13). They say what people want to hear (23:16-17). They have not stood in God's council to hear the word (23:18, 22). They have relied on their own dreams instead of God's word (23:23-32). The test, says the writer of Deuteronomy, is to distinguish whether or not a prophet is leading the people away from the LORD, even if that prophet's predictions come true (Deut 13:1-5). Jesus warns against false prophets who will reveal themselves by "their fruits," the outcome of their good or evil nature (Matt 7:15-20). The apostle Paul identifies false preachers of the gospel as those who require the Jewish rite of circumcision for Christians (Gal 1:6—2:21).

23:14 all of them have become like Sodom to me, and its inhabitants like Gomorrah: The story about Sodom and Gomorrah in Genesis 19 leads us to think that sexual immorality was the major problem in those two cities. Other prophets refer to the immorality in other ways. Isaiah uses the names of Sodom and Gomorrah as metaphors (symbolic language) for Jerusalem. Isaiah accuses the citizens of meaningless worship and prayers. He pleads with them to "cease to do evil; learn to do good; seek justice, rescue the oppressed, defend the orphan, plead for the widow" (Isa 1:9-17). Ezekiel says Sodom "had pride, excess of food, and prosperous ease, but did not aid the poor and needy" (Ezek 16:49).

9 Concerning the prophets:
My heart is crushed within me,
all my bones shake;
I have become like a drunkard,
like one overcome by wine,
because of the LORD
and because of his holy words.
10 For the land is full of adulterers;
because of the curse the land mourns,
and the pastures of the wilderness are dried up.
Their course has been evil,
and their might is not right.
11 Both prophet and priest are ungodly;
even in my house I have found their wickedness,
says the LORD.
12 Therefore their way shall be to them
like slippery paths in the darkness,
into which they shall be driven and fall;
for I will bring disaster upon them
in the year of their punishment,
says the LORD.
13 In the prophets of Samaria
I saw a disgusting thing:
they prophesied by Baal
and led my people Israel astray.
14 But in the prophets of Jerusalem
I have seen a more shocking thing:
they commit adultery and walk in lies;
they strengthen the hands of evildoers,
so that no one turns from wickedness;
all of them have become like Sodom to me,
and its inhabitants like Gomorrah.
15 Therefore thus says the LORD of hosts concerning the prophets:
"I am going to make them eat wormwood,
and give them poisoned water to drink;
for from the prophets of Jerusalem
ungodliness has spread throughout the land."

16 Thus says the LORD of hosts: Do not listen to the words of the
prophets who prophesy to you; they are deluding you. They speak
visions of their own minds, not from the mouth of the LORD. 17 They
keep saying to those who despise the word of the LORD, "It shall be
well with you"; and to all who stubbornly follow their own stubborn
hearts, they say, "No calamity shall come upon you."

18 For who has stood in the council of the LORD
so as to see and to hear his word?
Who has given heed to his word so as to proclaim it?
19 Look, the storm of the LORD!
Wrath has gone forth,
a whirling tempest;
it will burst upon the head of the wicked.
20 The anger of the LORD will not turn back
until he has executed and accomplished
the intents of his mind.
In the latter days you will understand it clearly.

21 I did not send the prophets,
yet they ran;
I did not speak to them,
yet they prophesied.
22 But if they had stood in my council,
then they would have proclaimed my words to my people,
and they would have turned them from their evil way,
and from the evil of their doings.

23 Am I a God near by, says the LORD, and not a God far off?
[24]Who can hide in secret places so that I cannot see them? says the
LORD. Do I not fill heaven and earth? says the LORD. [25]I have heard
what the prophets have said who prophesy lies in my name, saying, "I
have dreamed, I have dreamed!" [26]How long? Will the hearts of the
prophets ever turn back—those who prophesy lies, and who prophesy the deceit of their own heart? [27]They plan to make my people forget my name by their dreams that they tell one another, just as their
ancestors forgot my name for Baal. [28]Let the prophet who has a dream
tell the dream, but let the one who has my word speak my word faithfully. What has straw in common with wheat? says the LORD. [29]Is not
my word like fire, says the LORD, and like a hammer that breaks a rock
in pieces? [30]See, therefore, I am against the prophets, says the LORD,
who steal my words from one another. [31]See, I am against the prophets, says the LORD, who use their own tongues and say, "Says the
LORD." [32]See, I am against those who prophesy lying dreams, says the
LORD, and who tell them, and who lead my people astray by their lies
and their recklessness, when I did not send them or appoint them; so
they do not profit this people at all, says the LORD.

33 When this people, or a prophet, or a priest asks you, "What
is the burden of the LORD?" you shall say to them, "You are the
burden,[a] and I will cast you off, says the LORD." [34]And as for the

23:18 who has stood in the council of the LORD: Writers of the Bible believed that God ruled over an assembly of lesser gods or other beings (Job 1). Jeremiah uses this image to question the authority of the false prophets (23:22).

---

[a] Gk Vg: Heb *What burden*

prophet, priest, or the people who say, "The burden of the LORD," I will punish them and their households. 35 Thus shall you say to one another, among yourselves, "What has the LORD answered?" or "What has the LORD spoken?" 36 But "the burden of the LORD" you shall mention no more, for the burden is everyone's own word, and so you pervert the words of the living God, the LORD of hosts, our God. 37 Thus you shall ask the prophet, "What has the LORD answered you?" or "What has the LORD spoken?" 38 But if you say, "the burden of the LORD," thus says the LORD: Because you have said these words, "the burden of the LORD," when I sent to you, saying, You shall not say, "the burden of the LORD," 39 therefore, I will surely lift you up[a] and cast you away from my presence, you and the city that I gave to you and your ancestors. 40 And I will bring upon you everlasting disgrace and perpetual shame, which shall not be forgotten.

The Good and the Bad Figs

24:1-10 The LORD showed me... What do you see, Jeremiah?: The reason for distinguishing between the good figs that went into exile and the bad figs that stayed behind in the city is not clear. Perhaps Jeremiah thought that the first group of exiles (who went with the last Davidic king, Jehoiachin, in 597 B.C.E.) were the best in Jerusalem, and that those who stayed with Zedekiah, the one who broke the Davidic line of descent, were unworthy leaders.

24 The LORD showed me two baskets of figs placed before the temple of the LORD. This was after King Nebuchadrezzar of Babylon had taken into exile from Jerusalem King Jeconiah son of Jehoiakim of Judah, together with the officials of Judah, the artisans, and the smiths, and had brought them to Babylon. 2 One basket had very good figs, like first-ripe figs, but the other basket had very bad figs, so bad that they could not be eaten. 3 And the LORD said to me, "What do you see, Jeremiah?" I said, "Figs, the good figs very good, and the bad figs very bad, so bad that they cannot be eaten."

4 Then the word of the LORD came to me: 5 Thus says the LORD, the God of Israel: Like these good figs, so I will regard as good the exiles from Judah, whom I have sent away from this place to the land of the Chaldeans. 6 I will set my eyes upon them for good, and I will bring them back to this land. I will build them up, and not tear them down; I will plant them, and not pluck them up. 7 I will give them a heart to know that I am the LORD; and they shall be my people and I will be their God, for they shall return to me with their whole heart.

24:7 I will give them a new heart to know that I am the LORD: Like Ezekiel (Ezek 11:14-21), Jeremiah recognizes that a change of heart is necessary for the people to know the LORD. In the Old Testament, "to know" someone meant to have an intimate relationship (of the heart). Knowing was more than simply gathering information in the head (see Gen 4:1; Amos 3:2).

8 But thus says the LORD: Like the bad figs that are so bad they cannot be eaten, so will I treat King Zedekiah of Judah, his officials, the remnant of Jerusalem who remain in this land, and those who live in the land of Egypt. 9 I will make them a horror, an evil thing, to all the kingdoms of the earth—a disgrace, a byword, a taunt, and a curse in all the places where I shall drive them. 10 And I will send sword, famine, and pestilence upon them, until they are utterly destroyed from the land that I gave to them and their ancestors.

---

[a] Heb Mss Gk Vg: MT *forget you*

The Babylonian Captivity Foretold

25 The word that came to Jeremiah concerning all the people
of Judah, in the fourth year of King Jehoiakim son of Josiah
of Judah (that was the first year of King Nebuchadrezzar of Babylon),
2 which the prophet Jeremiah spoke to all the people of Judah and all
the inhabitants of Jerusalem: 3 For twenty-three years, from the thirteenth year of King Josiah son of Amon of Judah, to this day, the word
of the LORD has come to me, and I have spoken persistently to you,
but you have not listened. 4 And though the LORD persistently sent
you all his servants the prophets, you have neither listened nor inclined your ears to hear 5 when they said, "Turn now, every one of you,
from your evil way and wicked doings, and you will remain upon the
land that the LORD has given to you and your ancestors from of old
and forever; 6 do not go after other gods to serve and worship them,
and do not provoke me to anger with the work of your hands. Then
I will do you no harm." 7 Yet you did not listen to me, says the LORD,
and so you have provoked me to anger with the work of your hands
to your own harm.

8 Therefore thus says the LORD of hosts: Because you have not
obeyed my words, 9 I am going to send for all the tribes of the north,
says the LORD, even for King Nebuchadrezzar of Babylon, my servant, and I will bring them against this land and its inhabitants, and
against all these nations around; I will utterly destroy them, and make
them an object of horror and of hissing, and an everlasting disgrace.[a]
10 And I will banish from them the sound of mirth and the sound of
gladness, the voice of the bridegroom and the voice of the bride, the
sound of the millstones and the light of the lamp. 11 This whole land
shall become a ruin and a waste, and these nations shall serve the king
of Babylon seventy years. 12 Then after seventy years are completed, I
will punish the king of Babylon and that nation, the land of the Chaldeans, for their iniquity, says the LORD, making the land an everlasting waste. 13 I will bring upon that land all the words that I have uttered
against it, everything written in this book, which Jeremiah prophesied
against all the nations. 14 For many nations and great kings shall make
slaves of them also; and I will repay them according to their deeds and
the work of their hands.

The Cup of God's Wrath

15 For thus the LORD, the God of Israel, said to me: Take from
my hand this cup of the wine of wrath, and make all the nations to
whom I send you drink it. 16 They shall drink and stagger and go out of
their minds because of the sword that I am sending among them.

17 So I took the cup from the LORD's hand, and made all the

---

[a] Gk Compare Syr: Heb *and everlasting desolations*

25:9 King Nebuchadrezzar of Babylon, my servant: God uses foreign rulers who don't worship Israel's God to carry out God's plans. Nebuchadrezzar is the agent of God's judgment on the people of Judah (27:6). Years later, Cyrus, king of Persia, will become God's choice ("anointed one" or messiah) to deliver the people of Judah from the bondage in Babylon (Isa 45:1-7). The apostle Paul calls the governing authorities of Rome "God's servant for your good," even though the emperor at the time was Nero (Rom 13:1-7).

How important do you think it is for our governing authorities to be Christians? Why?

25:11-12 This whole land shall become a ruin and a waste...seventy years: The number is confusing. It recurs at 29:10. Perhaps we need to round up the sixty-six years from 605 B.C.E. (the beginning of Babylonian rule over Judah) to the conquest of Babylon by King Cyrus of Persia (539). Or the number might be symbolic for the period in which a country feels forsaken or abandoned by its god (Isa 23:15, 17). In any case, the number points to a long time of exile before deliverance will occur.

25:15 Take from my hand this cup of the wine of wrath: Drinking from "the cup" of wine of wrath is a metaphor for God's judgment. It is "a cup of horror and desolation" (Ezek 23:32-34), "the cup of his wrath" (Isa 51:17), and "a cup of reeling" (Zech 12:2). (See also Jer 51:7; Obad 16; Hab 2:16; Lam 4:21; Ps 75:8.) Christians know this imagery from the words of Jesus (Mark 10:38-39; Luke 22:42).

nations to whom the LORD sent me drink it: [18]Jerusalem and the
towns of Judah, its kings and officials, to make them a desolation and
a waste, an object of hissing and of cursing, as they are today; [19]Pha-
raoh king of Egypt, his servants, his officials, and all his people; [20]all
the mixed people;[a] all the kings of the land of Uz; all the kings of the
land of the Philistines—Ashkelon, Gaza, Ekron, and the remnant of
Ashdod; [21]Edom, Moab, and the Ammonites; [22]all the kings of Tyre,
all the kings of Sidon, and the kings of the coastland across the sea;
[23]Dedan, Tema, Buz, and all who have shaven temples; [24]all the kings
of Arabia and all the kings of the mixed peoples[a] that live in the desert;
[25]all the kings of Zimri, all the kings of Elam, and all the kings of Media; [26]all the kings of the north, far and near, one after another, and all
the kingdoms of the world that are on the face of the earth. And after
them the king of Sheshach[b] shall drink.

27 Then you shall say to them, Thus says the LORD of hosts, the
God of Israel: Drink, get drunk and vomit, fall and rise no more, because of the sword that I am sending among you.

28 And if they refuse to accept the cup from your hand to drink,
then you shall say to them: Thus says the LORD of hosts: You must
drink! [29]See, I am beginning to bring disaster on the city that is called
by my name, and how can you possibly avoid punishment? You shall
not go unpunished, for I am summoning a sword against all the inhabitants of the earth, says the LORD of hosts.

30 You, therefore, shall prophesy against them all these words,
and say to them:

The LORD will roar from on high,
    and from his holy habitation utter his voice;
he will roar mightily against his fold,
    and shout, like those who tread grapes,
    against all the inhabitants of the earth.
31 The clamor will resound to the ends of the earth,
    for the LORD has an indictment against the nations;
he is entering into judgment with all flesh,
    and the guilty he will put to the sword,
                says the LORD.

32 Thus says the LORD of hosts:
See, disaster is spreading
    from nation to nation,
and a great tempest is stirring
    from the farthest parts of the earth!

33 Those slain by the LORD on that day shall extend from one
end of the earth to the other. They shall not be lamented, or gathered,
or buried; they shall become dung on the surface of the ground.

---

[a] Meaning of Heb uncertain [b] *Sheshach* is a cryptogram for *Babel*, Babylon

34 Wail, you shepherds, and cry out;
roll in ashes, you lords of the flock,
for the days of your slaughter have come—and your dispersions,[a]
and you shall fall like a choice vessel.
35 Flight shall fail the shepherds,
and there shall be no escape for the lords of the flock.
36 Hark! the cry of the shepherds,
and the wail of the lords of the flock!
For the LORD is despoiling their pasture,
37 and the peaceful folds are devastated,
because of the fierce anger of the LORD.
38 Like a lion he has left his covert;
for their land has become a waste
because of the cruel sword,
and because of his fierce anger.

Jeremiah's Prophecies in the Temple

26 At the beginning of the reign of King Jehoiakim son of
Josiah of Judah, this word came from the LORD: 2Thus says
the LORD: Stand in the court of the LORD's house, and speak to all
the cities of Judah that come to worship in the house of the LORD;
speak to them all the words that I command you; do not hold back a
word. 3It may be that they will listen, all of them, and will turn from
their evil way, that I may change my mind about the disaster that I
intend to bring on them because of their evil doings. 4You shall say
to them: Thus says the LORD: If you will not listen to me, to walk in
my law that I have set before you, 5and to heed the words of my servants the prophets whom I send to you urgently—though you have
not heeded— 6then I will make this house like Shiloh, and I will make
this city a curse for all the nations of the earth.

7 The priests and the prophets and all the people heard Jeremiah
speaking these words in the house of the LORD. 8And when Jeremiah
had finished speaking all that the LORD had commanded him to speak
to all the people, then the priests and the prophets and all the people
laid hold of him, saying, "You shall die! 9Why have you prophesied
in the name of the LORD, saying, 'This house shall be like Shiloh, and
this city shall be desolate, without inhabitant'?" And all the people
gathered around Jeremiah in the house of the LORD.

10 When the officials of Judah heard these things, they came up
from the king's house to the house of the LORD and took their seat
in the entry of the New Gate of the house of the LORD. 11Then the
priests and the prophets said to the officials and to all the people,
"This man deserves the sentence of death because he has prophesied
against this city, as you have heard with your own ears."

26:1—45:5 At the beginning: This long section of the book of Jeremiah is a collection of sayings of Jeremiah and events in his life. The collection seems to be the work of Baruch. He wanted to continue the memory and contributions of the prophet after Jeremiah died.

26:1-6 At the beginning of the reign of King Jehoiakim: The speech is similar to the temple sermon in 7:1-15. Jehoiakim was king of Judah 609–598 B.C.E. Jeremiah attacks cherished traditions of Jerusalem: the city and the holiness of the temple.

26:10-11 took their seat in the entry of the New Gate of the house of the LORD: In ancient cities, the large openings at various gates provided the only space for public meetings and court cases. The priests and the prophets proposed the death sentence for Jeremiah's speaking against the city.

[a] Meaning of Heb uncertain

12 Then Jeremiah spoke to all the officials and all the people, saying, "It is the LORD who sent me to prophesy against this house and this city all the words you have heard. 13 Now therefore amend your ways and your doings, and obey the voice of the LORD your God, and the LORD will change his mind about the disaster that he has pronounced against you. 14 But as for me, here I am in your hands. Do with me as seems good and right to you. 15 Only know for certain that if you put me to death, you will be bringing innocent blood upon yourselves and upon this city and its inhabitants, for in truth the LORD sent me to you to speak all these words in your ears."

16 Then the officials and all the people said to the priests and the prophets, "This man does not deserve the sentence of death, for he has spoken to us in the name of the LORD our God." 17 And some of the elders of the land arose and said to all the assembled people, 18 "Micah of Moresheth, who prophesied during the days of King Hezekiah of Judah, said to all the people of Judah: 'Thus says the LORD of hosts,

Zion shall be plowed as a field;
  Jerusalem shall become a heap of ruins,
  and the mountain of the house a wooded height.'

19 Did King Hezekiah of Judah and all Judah actually put him to death? Did he not fear the LORD and entreat the favor of the LORD, and did not the LORD change his mind about the disaster that he had pronounced against them? But we are about to bring great disaster on ourselves!"

20 There was another man prophesying in the name of the LORD, Uriah son of Shemaiah from Kiriath-jearim. He prophesied against this city and against this land in words exactly like those of Jeremiah. 21 And when King Jehoiakim, with all his warriors and all the officials, heard his words, the king sought to put him to death; but when Uriah heard of it, he was afraid and fled and escaped to Egypt. 22 Then King Jehoiakim sent[a] Elnathan son of Achbor and men with him to Egypt, 23 and they took Uriah from Egypt and brought him to King Jehoiakim, who struck him down with the sword and threw his dead body into the burial place of the common people.

24 But the hand of Ahikam son of Shaphan was with Jeremiah so that he was not given over into the hands of the people to be put to death.

The Sign of the Yoke

27 In the beginning of the reign of King Zedekiah[b] son of Josiah of Judah, this word came to Jeremiah from the LORD. 2 Thus the LORD said to me: Make yourself a yoke of straps and bars, and put them on your neck. 3 Send word[c] to the king of Edom, the king

[a] Heb adds *men to Egypt* [b] Another reading is *Jehoiakim* [c] Cn: Heb *send them*

26:24 But the hand of Ahikam son of Shaphan was with Jeremiah: Jeremiah had friends in high places. Shaphan was a secretary during the reign of Josiah (2 Kgs 22:3). Ahikam (Shaphan's son) was a member of Josiah's representatives who looked for God's guidance from the prophetess Huldah (2 Kgs 22:12-14). Later, Jeremiah did not go with the exiles to Babylon (40:5—41:3). He decided to stay in Judah under the protection of Gedaliah (Ahikam's son), who became governor of Judah.

27:2 Make yourself a yoke of straps and bars, and put them on your neck: Jeremiah uses a visual device to demonstrate submitting to the service of the king of Babylon, Nebuchadnezzar. (Note the alternate spelling the text uses for the king's name.) The message extends beyond Zedekiah to representatives of all the kings who have gathered in Jerusalem. They have come to discuss plans for an alliance against the king of Babylon. A yoke is a wooden collar that fit on the neck of oxen. Using leather straps tied to the yoke, a driver steered the oxen as they plowed a field or pulled other equipment.

of Moab, the king of the Ammonites, the king of Tyre, and the king of
Sidon by the hand of the envoys who have come to Jerusalem to King
Zedekiah of Judah. 4 Give them this charge for their masters: Thus
says the LORD of hosts, the God of Israel: This is what you shall say
to your masters: 5 It is I who by my great power and my outstretched
arm have made the earth, with the people and animals that are on the
earth, and I give it to whomever I please. 6 Now I have given all these
lands into the hand of King Nebuchadnezzar of Babylon, my servant,
and I have given him even the wild animals of the field to serve him.
7 All the nations shall serve him and his son and his grandson, until the
time of his own land comes; then many nations and great kings shall
make him their slave.

8 But if any nation or kingdom will not serve this king, Nebuchadnezzar of Babylon, and put its neck under the yoke of the king
of Babylon, then I will punish that nation with the sword, with famine, and with pestilence, says the LORD, until I have completed its[a]
destruction by his hand. 9 You, therefore, must not listen to your
prophets, your diviners, your dreamers,[b] your soothsayers, or your
sorcerers, who are saying to you, "You shall not serve the king of Babylon." 10 For they are prophesying a lie to you, with the result that you
will be removed far from your land; I will drive you out, and you will
perish. 11 But any nation that will bring its neck under the yoke of the
king of Babylon and serve him, I will leave on its own land, says the
LORD, to till it and live there.

12 I spoke to King Zedekiah of Judah in the same way: Bring your
necks under the yoke of the king of Babylon, and serve him and his
people, and live. 13 Why should you and your people die by the sword,
by famine, and by pestilence, as the LORD has spoken concerning any
nation that will not serve the king of Babylon? 14 Do not listen to the
words of the prophets who are telling you not to serve the king of
Babylon, for they are prophesying a lie to you. 15 I have not sent them,
says the LORD, but they are prophesying falsely in my name, with the
result that I will drive you out and you will perish, you and the prophets who are prophesying to you.

16 Then I spoke to the priests and to all this people, saying, Thus
says the LORD: Do not listen to the words of your prophets who are
prophesying to you, saying, "The vessels of the LORD's house will
soon be brought back from Babylon," for they are prophesying a lie to
you. 17 Do not listen to them; serve the king of Babylon and live. Why
should this city become a desolation? 18 If indeed they are prophets,
and if the word of the LORD is with them, then let them intercede
with the LORD of hosts, that the vessels left in the house of the LORD,
in the house of the king of Judah, and in Jerusalem may not go to

27:5 It is I who by my great power and my outstretched arm have made the earth: God has created the earth and all its inhabitants, and so God has the right to give the land even to Nebuchadnezzar. God calls him "my servant." Almost sixty years later, the LORD uses the same argument to justify the appointment of Cyrus, king of Persia, as "my shepherd" to fulfill the divine plans for the people's return to Jerusalem (Isa 44:24-28).

---

[a] Heb *their* [b] Gk Syr Vg: Heb *dreams*

Babylon. [19]For thus says the LORD of hosts concerning the pillars,
the sea, the stands, and the rest of the vessels that are left in this city,
[20]which King Nebuchadnezzar of Babylon did not take away when he
took into exile from Jerusalem to Babylon King Jeconiah son of Jehoiakim of Judah, and all the nobles of Judah and Jerusalem— [21]thus
says the LORD of hosts, the God of Israel, concerning the vessels left
in the house of the LORD, in the house of the king of Judah, and in Jerusalem: [22]They shall be carried to Babylon, and there they shall stay,
until the day when I give attention to them, says the LORD. Then I will
bring them up and restore them to this place.

Hananiah Opposes Jeremiah and Dies

28:1-17 when the word of that prophet comes true: Read the note on 23:9-32 about true and false prophets. Hananiah was a false prophet. He was not sent by God and his words did not come true. Jeremiah's prophecies did come true, and so his preaching became part of the Bible.

28 In that same year, at the beginning of the reign of King Zedekiah of Judah, in the fifth month of the fourth year, the
prophet Hananiah son of Azzur, from Gibeon, spoke to me in the
house of the LORD, in the presence of the priests and all the people,
saying, [2]"Thus says the LORD of hosts, the God of Israel: I have broken
the yoke of the king of Babylon. [3]Within two years I will bring back to
this place all the vessels of the LORD's house, which King Nebuchadnezzar of Babylon took away from this place and carried to Babylon.
[4]I will also bring back to this place King Jeconiah son of Jehoiakim of
Judah, and all the exiles from Judah who went to Babylon, says the
LORD, for I will break the yoke of the king of Babylon."

5 Then the prophet Jeremiah spoke to the prophet Hananiah in
the presence of the priests and all the people who were standing in the
house of the LORD; [6]and the prophet Jeremiah said, "Amen! May the
LORD do so; may the LORD fulfill the words that you have prophesied, and bring back to this place from Babylon the vessels of the
house of the LORD, and all the exiles. [7]But listen now to this word that
I speak in your hearing and in the hearing of all the people. [8]The
prophets who preceded you and me from ancient times prophesied
war, famine, and pestilence against many countries and great kingdoms. [9]As for the prophet who prophesies peace, when the word of
that prophet comes true, then it will be known that the LORD has
truly sent the prophet."

10 Then the prophet Hananiah took the yoke from the neck of
the prophet Jeremiah, and broke it. [11]And Hananiah spoke in the
presence of all the people, saying, "Thus says the LORD: This is how
I will break the yoke of King Nebuchadnezzar of Babylon from the
neck of all the nations within two years." At this, the prophet Jeremiah
went his way.

12 Sometime after the prophet Hananiah had broken the yoke
from the neck of the prophet Jeremiah, the word of the LORD came
to Jeremiah: [13]Go, tell Hananiah, Thus says the LORD: You have broken wooden bars only to forge iron bars in place of them! [14]For thus

says the LORD of hosts, the God of Israel: I have put an iron yoke on
the neck of all these nations so that they may serve King Nebuchadnezzar of Babylon, and they shall indeed serve him; I have even given
him the wild animals. [15]And the prophet Jeremiah said to the prophet
Hananiah, "Listen, Hananiah, the LORD has not sent you, and you
made this people trust in a lie. [16]Therefore thus says the LORD: I am
going to send you off the face of the earth. Within this year you will be
dead, because you have spoken rebellion against the LORD."

17 In that same year, in the seventh month, the prophet Hananiah died.

Jeremiah's Letter to the Exiles in Babylon

29 These are the words of the letter that the prophet Jeremiah
sent from Jerusalem to the remaining elders among the exiles, and to the priests, the prophets, and all the people, whom Nebuchadnezzar had taken into exile from Jerusalem to Babylon. [2]This
was after King Jeconiah, and the queen mother, the court officials, the
leaders of Judah and Jerusalem, the artisans, and the smiths had departed from Jerusalem. [3]The letter was sent by the hand of Elasah son
of Shaphan and Gemariah son of Hilkiah, whom King Zedekiah of
Judah sent to Babylon to King Nebuchadnezzar of Babylon. It said:
[4]Thus says the LORD of hosts, the God of Israel, to all the exiles whom
I have sent into exile from Jerusalem to Babylon: [5]Build houses and
live in them; plant gardens and eat what they produce. [6]Take wives
and have sons and daughters; take wives for your sons, and give your
daughters in marriage, that they may bear sons and daughters; multiply there, and do not decrease. [7]But seek the welfare of the city where
I have sent you into exile, and pray to the LORD on its behalf, for in its
welfare you will find your welfare. [8]For thus says the LORD of hosts,
the God of Israel: Do not let the prophets and the diviners who are
among you deceive you, and do not listen to the dreams that they
dream,[a] [9]for it is a lie that they are prophesying to you in my name; I
did not send them, says the LORD.

10 For thus says the LORD: Only when Babylon's seventy years
are completed will I visit you, and I will fulfill to you my promise and
bring you back to this place. [11]For surely I know the plans I have for
you, says the LORD, plans for your welfare and not for harm, to give
you a future with hope. [12]Then when you call upon me and come and
pray to me, I will hear you. [13]When you search for me, you will find
me; if you seek me with all your heart, [14]I will let you find me, says the
LORD, and I will restore your fortunes and gather you from all the nations and all the places where I have driven you, says the LORD, and I
will bring you back to the place from which I sent you into exile.

[a] Cn: Heb *your dreams that you cause to dream*

29:1-23 the words of the letter that the prophet Jeremiah sent: Jeremiah's audience is in Babylon (about four hundred miles from Jerusalem). Jeremiah must preach God's word through writing rather than through oral sermons.

29:7 But seek the welfare of the city: Jeremiah encourages the people in exile to pray for Babylon. The Hebrew word *shalom* is translated here as "welfare." Shalom means wholeness, health, well-being, and peace.

Think about your prayers, both private and as part of a faith community. When do they include petitions, or requests, for the world and the peoples of various nations, whether Christian or not? How do you understand prayers for your own country?

29:10 Only when Babylon's seventy years are completed: The number seventy probably only means a long time. See note on 25:11-12.

29:11 I know the plans I have for you...plans for your welfare and not for harm, to give you a future with hope: As in 29:7, the Hebrew word for welfare is *shalom*. Earlier, the LORD claimed to be "a potter shaping evil against you and devising a plan against you" (18:11). Now that the promised judgment is upon the people, God devises plans for "a future with hope."

God's promise to the people exiled in Babylon that they would be able to return to Jerusalem would take years to be fulfilled. How would you respond to a promise of good news when you hear at the same time that its fulfillment is a long way off?

15 Because you have said, "The LORD has raised up prophets for us in Babylon,"— 16 Thus says the LORD concerning the king who sits on the throne of David, and concerning all the people who live in this city, your kinsfolk who did not go out with you into exile: 17 Thus says the LORD of hosts, I am going to let loose on them sword, famine, and pestilence, and I will make them like rotten figs that are so bad they cannot be eaten. 18 I will pursue them with the sword, with famine, and with pestilence, and will make them a horror to all the kingdoms of the earth, to be an object of cursing, and horror, and hissing, and a derision among all the nations where I have driven them, 19 because they did not heed my words, says the LORD, when I persistently sent to you my servants the prophets, but they[a] would not listen, says the LORD. 20 But now, all you exiles whom I sent away from Jerusalem to Babylon, hear the word of the LORD: 21 Thus says the LORD of hosts, the God of Israel, concerning Ahab son of Kolaiah and Zedekiah son of Maaseiah, who are prophesying a lie to you in my name: I am going to deliver them into the hand of King Nebuchadrezzar of Babylon, and he shall kill them before your eyes. 22 And on account of them this curse shall be used by all the exiles from Judah in Babylon: "The LORD make you like Zedekiah and Ahab, whom the king of Babylon roasted in the fire," 23 because they have perpetrated outrage in Israel and have committed adultery with their neighbors' wives, and have spoken in my name lying words that I did not command them; I am the one who knows and bears witness, says the LORD.

The Letter of Shemaiah

24 To Shemaiah of Nehelam you shall say: 25 Thus says the LORD of hosts, the God of Israel: In your own name you sent a letter to all the people who are in Jerusalem, and to the priest Zephaniah son of Maaseiah, and to all the priests, saying, 26 The LORD himself has made you priest instead of the priest Jehoiada, so that there may be officers in the house of the LORD to control any madman who plays the prophet, to put him in the stocks and the collar. 27 So now why have you not rebuked Jeremiah of Anathoth who plays the prophet for you? 28 For he has actually sent to us in Babylon, saying, "It will be a long time; build houses and live in them, and plant gardens and eat what they produce."

29 The priest Zephaniah read this letter in the hearing of the prophet Jeremiah. 30 Then the word of the LORD came to Jeremiah: 31 Send to all the exiles, saying, Thus says the LORD concerning Shemaiah of Nehelam: Because Shemaiah has prophesied to you, though I did not send him, and has led you to trust in a lie, 32 therefore thus says the LORD: I am going to punish Shemaiah of Nehelam and his

---

[a] Syr: Heb *you*

descendants; he shall not have anyone living among this people to see[a] the good that I am going to do to my people, says the LORD, for he has spoken rebellion against the LORD.

Restoration Promised for Israel and Judah

30 The word that came to Jeremiah from the LORD: ²Thus says the LORD, the God of Israel: Write in a book all the words that I have spoken to you. ³For the days are surely coming, says the LORD, when I will restore the fortunes of my people, Israel and Judah, says the LORD, and I will bring them back to the land that I gave to their ancestors and they shall take possession of it.

4 These are the words that the LORD spoke concerning Israel and Judah:

5 Thus says the LORD:
We have heard a cry of panic,
of terror, and no peace.
6 Ask now, and see,
can a man bear a child?
Why then do I see every man
with his hands on his loins like a woman in labor?
Why has every face turned pale?
7 Alas! that day is so great
there is none like it;
it is a time of distress for Jacob;
yet he shall be rescued from it.

8 On that day, says the LORD of hosts, I will break the yoke from off his[b] neck, and I will burst his[b] bonds, and strangers shall no more make a servant of him. ⁹But they shall serve the LORD their God and David their king, whom I will raise up for them.

10 But as for you, have no fear, my servant Jacob, says the LORD,
and do not be dismayed, O Israel;
for I am going to save you from far away,
and your offspring from the land of their captivity.
Jacob shall return and have quiet and ease,
and no one shall make him afraid.
11 For I am with you, says the LORD, to save you;
I will make an end of all the nations
among which I scattered you,
but of you I will not make an end.
I will chastise you in just measure,
and I will by no means leave you unpunished.

---

[a] Gk: Heb *and he shall not see* [b] Cn: Heb *your*

30:1—31:40 The word that came to Jeremiah from the LORD: Scholars have named this section The Book of Comfort. The LORD's word through Jeremiah announces the building and planting we were expecting since the prophet's call at 1:4-10. Many scholars believe that someone other than Jeremiah wrote this section in the prophet's name to balance his many sermons of doom. In either case, now that the word has afflicted (troubled) the comfortable, it is time to comfort the afflicted.

Why does God's word sometimes seem to give us hope and other times leave us with a feeling of gloom? Luther spoke of the word of God as law and as gospel. He meant that God confronts us in our sinfulness and accuses us of our rebellion. That action of God is the law. On the other hand, when we are accused and helpless, God reaches out to us with the word of good news called the gospel. This action of God forgives us and restores us to live freely as God's children. This dynamic word of God comes to us in sermons, in the sacraments, and in our consoling one another in times of trouble. *Jeremiah 30:1—31:40*

30:3 I will restore the fortunes of my people . . . and I will bring them back to the land: The people of God in the Old Testament were the people of the nation Israel. The territory where they lived was the land God had promised to Abraham (Gen 12:7) and delivered through Joshua (Josh 1–24). Exile was the means of God's judgment. Salvation was the LORD's act of restoring the people to the promised land.

30:9 But they shall serve the LORD their God and David their king, whom I will raise up for them: People will have a renewed commitment to the LORD and a new king from David's line. With Jehoiachin's removal from the throne to exile in 597 B.C.E., the hopes for continuing David's dynasty were fragile. Nevertheless, God will raise up the "righteous Branch" promised at 23:5.

30:10 my servant Jacob . . . O Israel: The people are called Jacob and Israel, just like the two names for the ancient patriarch (Gen 32:28).

12 For thus says the LORD:
Your hurt is incurable,
your wound is grievous.
13 There is no one to uphold your cause,
no medicine for your wound,
no healing for you.
14 All your lovers have forgotten you;
they care nothing for you;
for I have dealt you the blow of an enemy,
the punishment of a merciless foe,
because your guilt is great,
because your sins are so numerous.
15 Why do you cry out over your hurt?
Your pain is incurable.
Because your guilt is great,
because your sins are so numerous,
I have done these things to you.
16 Therefore all who devour you shall be devoured,
and all your foes, every one of them, shall go into captivity;
those who plunder you shall be plundered,
and all who prey on you I will make a prey.
17 For I will restore health to you,
and your wounds I will heal,
says the LORD,
because they have called you an outcast:
"It is Zion; no one cares for her!"

18 Thus says the LORD:
I am going to restore the fortunes of the tents of Jacob,
and have compassion on his dwellings;
the city shall be rebuilt upon its mound,
and the citadel set on its rightful site.
19 Out of them shall come thanksgiving,
and the sound of merrymakers.
I will make them many, and they shall not be few;
I will make them honored, and they shall not be disdained.
20 Their children shall be as of old,
their congregation shall be established before me;
and I will punish all who oppress them.
21 Their prince shall be one of their own,
their ruler shall come from their midst;
I will bring him near, and he shall approach me,
for who would otherwise dare to approach me?
says the LORD.

22 And you shall be my people,
and I will be your God.

23 Look, the storm of the LORD!
Wrath has gone forth,
a whirling[a] tempest;
it will burst upon the head of the wicked.
24 The fierce anger of the LORD will not turn back
until he has executed and accomplished
the intents of his mind.
In the latter days you will understand this.

The Joyful Return of the Exiles

31 At that time, says the LORD, I will be the God of all the families of Israel, and they shall be my people.
2 Thus says the LORD:
The people who survived the sword
found grace in the wilderness;
when Israel sought for rest,
3 the LORD appeared to him[b] from far away.[c]
I have loved you with an everlasting love;
therefore I have continued my faithfulness to you.
4 Again I will build you, and you shall be built,
O virgin Israel!
Again you shall take[d] your tambourines,
and go forth in the dance of the merrymakers.
5 Again you shall plant vineyards
on the mountains of Samaria;
the planters shall plant,
and shall enjoy the fruit.
6 For there shall be a day when sentinels will call
in the hill country of Ephraim:
"Come, let us go up to Zion,
to the LORD our God."

7 For thus says the LORD:
Sing aloud with gladness for Jacob,
and raise shouts for the chief of the nations;
proclaim, give praise, and say,
"Save, O LORD, your people,
the remnant of Israel."
8 See, I am going to bring them from the land of the north,
and gather them from the farthest parts of the earth,

31:3 I have loved you with an everlasting love: Israel has not been faithful to God, but God's love is everlasting and does not depend on human help.

God's love for you is as enduring as it was for the people of Israel. How do you respond to this unconditional promise of divine love and faithfulness?

[a] One Ms: Meaning of MT uncertain [b] Gk: Heb *me* [c] Or *to him long ago* [d] Or *adorn yourself with*

among them the blind and the lame,
    those with child and those in labor, together;
    a great company, they shall return here.
9 With weeping they shall come,
    and with consolations[a] I will lead them back,
I will let them walk by brooks of water,
    in a straight path in which they shall not stumble;
for I have become a father to Israel,
    and Ephraim is my firstborn.

10 Hear the word of the LORD, O nations,
    and declare it in the coastlands far away;
say, "He who scattered Israel will gather him,
    and will keep him as a shepherd a flock."
11 For the LORD has ransomed Jacob,
    and has redeemed him from hands too strong for him.
12 They shall come and sing aloud on the height of Zion,
    and they shall be radiant over the goodness of the LORD,
over the grain, the wine, and the oil,
    and over the young of the flock and the herd;
their life shall become like a watered garden,
    and they shall never languish again.
13 Then shall the young women rejoice in the dance,
    and the young men and the old shall be merry.
I will turn their mourning into joy,
    I will comfort them, and give them gladness for
        sorrow.
14 I will give the priests their fill of fatness,
    and my people shall be satisfied with my bounty,
                                        says the LORD.

15 Thus says the LORD:
A voice is heard in Ramah,
    lamentation and bitter weeping.
Rachel is weeping for her children;
    she refuses to be comforted for her children,
    because they are no more.
16 Thus says the LORD:
Keep your voice from weeping,
    and your eyes from tears;
for there is a reward for your work,
                                        says the LORD:
    they shall come back from the land of the enemy;

31:11 For the LORD has ransomed Jacob, and has redeemed him: The two actions (ransomed and redeemed) are the same. In the Old Testament, a redeemer was a person's nearest family member who paid the damages (ransom) so that the accused person could go free. The LORD acts as the next of kin (father of Jacob/Israel) and redeems the people from exile.

[a] Gk Compare Vg Tg: Heb *supplications*

17 there is hope for your future,
says the LORD:
your children shall come back to their own country.

18 Indeed I heard Ephraim pleading:
"You disciplined me, and I took the discipline;
I was like a calf untrained.
Bring me back, let me come back,
for you are the LORD my God.
19 For after I had turned away I repented;
and after I was discovered, I struck my thigh;
I was ashamed, and I was dismayed
because I bore the disgrace of my youth."
20 Is Ephraim my dear son?
Is he the child I delight in?
As often as I speak against him,
I still remember him.
Therefore I am deeply moved for him;
I will surely have mercy on him,
says the LORD.

21 Set up road markers for yourself,
make yourself signposts;
consider well the highway,
the road by which you went.
Return, O virgin Israel,
return to these your cities.
22 How long will you waver,
O faithless daughter?
For the LORD has created a new thing on the earth:
a woman encompasses[a] a man.

23 Thus says the LORD of hosts, the God of Israel: Once more
they shall use these words in the land of Judah and in its towns when
I restore their fortunes:
"The LORD bless you, O abode of righteousness,
O holy hill!"
24 And Judah and all its towns shall live there together, and the farmers
and those who wander[b] with their flocks.
25 I will satisfy the weary,
and all who are faint I will replenish.
26 Thereupon I awoke and looked, and my sleep was pleasant
to me.

---

[a] Meaning of Heb uncertain [b] Cn Compare Syr Vg Tg: Heb *and they shall wander*

Individual Retribution

27 The days are surely coming, says the LORD, when I will sow
the house of Israel and the house of Judah with the seed of humans
and the seed of animals. 28 And just as I have watched over them to
pluck up and break down, to overthrow, destroy, and bring evil, so I
will watch over them to build and to plant, says the LORD. 29 In those
days they shall no longer say:

"The parents have eaten sour grapes,
 and the children's teeth are set on edge."

30 But all shall die for their own sins; the teeth of everyone who eats
sour grapes shall be set on edge.

A New Covenant

31 The days are surely coming, says the LORD, when I will make a
new covenant with the house of Israel and the house of Judah. 32 It will
not be like the covenant that I made with their ancestors when I took
them by the hand to bring them out of the land of Egypt—a covenant
that they broke, though I was their husband,[a] says the LORD. 33 But
this is the covenant that I will make with the house of Israel after those
days, says the LORD: I will put my law within them, and I will write it
on their hearts; and I will be their God, and they shall be my people.
34 No longer shall they teach one another, or say to each other, "Know
the LORD," for they shall all know me, from the least of them to the
greatest, says the LORD; for I will forgive their iniquity, and remember
their sin no more.

35 Thus says the LORD,
who gives the sun for light by day
 and the fixed order of the moon and the stars for light by
 night,
who stirs up the sea so that its waves roar—
 the LORD of hosts is his name:
36 If this fixed order were ever to cease
 from my presence, says the LORD,
then also the offspring of Israel would cease
 to be a nation before me forever.

37 Thus says the LORD:
If the heavens above can be measured,
 and the foundations of the earth below can be explored,
then I will reject all the offspring of Israel
 because of all they have done,
 says the LORD.

31:31 The days are surely coming: This notice of time points to the undetermined future when God will establish the promised kingdom over the whole earth.

31:31-34 I will make a new covenant: Christians believe God made this new covenant in the death and resurrection of Jesus. "This cup is the new covenant in my blood" (1 Cor 11:25). Its content is not the law but the message about God's unconditional love. This love is demonstrated and accomplished in the crucifixion of God's Son. The recipient of this new covenant is all humankind. The LORD's promise to wipe away sin comes to fulfillment on the cross and reaches out to all people.

31:31-32 new covenant…not be like the covenant: The earlier covenant was the one God made with the people of Israel through Moses (Exod 20–24). God gave the people the Ten Commandments to guide them in their life together. The people broke that covenant (Exod 32).

31:34 I will forgive their iniquity, and remember their sin no more: What a profound understanding of forgiveness! God wipes away the memory of past sins.

How might this understanding of forgiveness (wiping away the memory of past sins) challenge you when dealing with people who have offended or even dishonored you?

---

[a] Or *master*

Jerusalem to Be Enlarged

38 The days are surely coming, says the LORD, when the city shall
be rebuilt for the LORD from the tower of Hananel to the Corner
Gate. 39 And the measuring line shall go out farther, straight to the hill
Gareb, and shall then turn to Goah. 40 The whole valley of the dead
bodies and the ashes, and all the fields as far as the Wadi Kidron, to
the corner of the Horse Gate toward the east, shall be sacred to the
LORD. It shall never again be uprooted or overthrown.

Jeremiah Buys a Field During the Siege

32 The word that came to Jeremiah from the LORD in the tenth
year of King Zedekiah of Judah, which was the eighteenth
year of Nebuchadrezzar. 2 At that time the army of the king of Babylon was besieging Jerusalem, and the prophet Jeremiah was confined
in the court of the guard that was in the palace of the king of Judah,
3 where King Zedekiah of Judah had confined him. Zedekiah had said,
"Why do you prophesy and say: Thus says the LORD: I am going to
give this city into the hand of the king of Babylon, and he shall take
it; 4 King Zedekiah of Judah shall not escape out of the hands of the
Chaldeans, but shall surely be given into the hands of the king of Babylon, and shall speak with him face to face and see him eye to eye;
5 and he shall take Zedekiah to Babylon, and there he shall remain until I attend to him, says the LORD; though you fight against the Chaldeans, you shall not succeed?"

6 Jeremiah said, The word of the LORD came to me: 7 Hanamel
son of your uncle Shallum is going to come to you and say, "Buy my
field that is at Anathoth, for the right of redemption by purchase is
yours." 8 Then my cousin Hanamel came to me in the court of the
guard, in accordance with the word of the LORD, and said to me, "Buy
my field that is at Anathoth in the land of Benjamin, for the right of
possession and redemption is yours; buy it for yourself." Then I knew
that this was the word of the LORD.

9 And I bought the field at Anathoth from my cousin Hanamel,
and weighed out the money to him, seventeen shekels of silver. 10 I
signed the deed, sealed it, got witnesses, and weighed the money
on scales. 11 Then I took the sealed deed of purchase, containing the
terms and conditions, and the open copy; 12 and I gave the deed of
purchase to Baruch son of Neriah son of Mahseiah, in the presence
of my cousin Hanamel, in the presence of the witnesses who signed
the deed of purchase, and in the presence of all the Judeans who were
sitting in the court of the guard. 13 In their presence I charged Baruch,
saying, 14 Thus says the LORD of hosts, the God of Israel: Take these
deeds, both this sealed deed of purchase and this open deed, and put
them in an earthenware jar, in order that they may last for a long time.

31:38-40 when the city shall be rebuilt: The future city will include the Kidron and Hinnom valleys. The whole city, even areas polluted by death and pagan sacrifice (see the note at 7:31), will "be sacred to the LORD." One can understand the hope that the new city would not "be uprooted or overthrown," but realities of time betray a different history.

Although 31:40 says the new city would not "be uprooted or overthrown," today the city of Jerusalem is divided. How do you respond to the realization that some prophecies of the Bible proved to be wrong?

32:1 in the tenth year of King Zedekiah of Judah, which was the eighteenth year of Nebuchadrezzar: Baruch (Jeremiah's secretary) describes an incident in 587 B.C.E. and explains how Jeremiah came to his imprisonment in the court of the guard of Zedekiah's palace.

32:6-25 Then my cousin Hanamel came to me: According to ancient law (Lev 25:25), a person selling property had to give first rights of purchase to a family member. This was to assure that property remained within the family. Hanamel, Jeremiah's cousin, needed to sell the family property in the hometown of Anathoth (1:1). Jeremiah had the "right of possession and redemption" (32:8). The prophet purchased the property as a way to strengthen his message: The LORD would one day bring back the exiles and restore the people to their homes.

15 For thus says the LORD of hosts, the God of Israel: Houses and fields
and vineyards shall again be bought in this land.

Jeremiah Prays for Understanding

16 After I had given the deed of purchase to Baruch son of Neriah,
I prayed to the LORD, saying: 17 Ah Lord GOD! It is you who made the
heavens and the earth by your great power and by your outstretched
arm! Nothing is too hard for you. 18 You show steadfast love to the
thousandth generation,[a] but repay the guilt of parents into the laps
of their children after them, O great and mighty God whose name
is the LORD of hosts, 19 great in counsel and mighty in deed; whose
eyes are open to all the ways of mortals, rewarding all according to
their ways and according to the fruit of their doings. 20 You showed
signs and wonders in the land of Egypt, and to this day in Israel and
among all humankind, and have made yourself a name that continues
to this very day. 21 You brought your people Israel out of the land of
Egypt with signs and wonders, with a strong hand and outstretched
arm, and with great terror; 22 and you gave them this land, which you
swore to their ancestors to give them, a land flowing with milk and
honey; 23 and they entered and took possession of it. But they did
not obey your voice or follow your law; of all you commanded them
to do, they did nothing. Therefore you have made all these disasters
come upon them. 24 See, the siege ramps have been cast up against
the city to take it, and the city, faced with sword, famine, and pestilence, has been given into the hands of the Chaldeans who are fighting against it. What you spoke has happened, as you yourself can see.
25 Yet you, O Lord GOD, have said to me, "Buy the field for money and
get witnesses"—though the city has been given into the hands of the
Chaldeans.

God's Assurance of the People's Return

26 The word of the LORD came to Jeremiah: 27 See, I am the
LORD, the God of all flesh; is anything too hard for me? 28 Therefore,
thus says the LORD: I am going to give this city into the hands of the
Chaldeans and into the hand of King Nebuchadrezzar of Babylon,
and he shall take it. 29 The Chaldeans who are fighting against this city
shall come, set it on fire, and burn it, with the houses on whose roofs
offerings have been made to Baal and libations have been poured out
to other gods, to provoke me to anger. 30 For the people of Israel and
the people of Judah have done nothing but evil in my sight from their
youth; the people of Israel have done nothing but provoke me to anger by the work of their hands, says the LORD. 31 This city has aroused
my anger and wrath, from the day it was built until this day, so that I

---

[a] Or *to thousands*

will remove it from my sight 32 because of all the evil of the people of
Israel and the people of Judah that they did to provoke me to anger—
they, their kings and their officials, their priests and their prophets,
the citizens of Judah and the inhabitants of Jerusalem. 33 They have
turned their backs to me, not their faces; though I have taught them
persistently, they would not listen and accept correction. 34 They set
up their abominations in the house that bears my name, and defiled
it. 35 They built the high places of Baal in the valley of the son of Hinnom, to offer up their sons and daughters to Molech, though I did not
command them, nor did it enter my mind that they should do this
abomination, causing Judah to sin.

36 Now therefore thus says the LORD, the God of Israel, concerning this city of which you say, "It is being given into the hand of the
king of Babylon by the sword, by famine, and by pestilence": 37 See, I
am going to gather them from all the lands to which I drove them in
my anger and my wrath and in great indignation; I will bring them
back to this place, and I will settle them in safety. 38 They shall be my
people, and I will be their God. 39 I will give them one heart and one
way, that they may fear me for all time, for their own good and the
good of their children after them. 40 I will make an everlasting covenant with them, never to draw back from doing good to them; and I
will put the fear of me in their hearts, so that they may not turn from
me. 41 I will rejoice in doing good to them, and I will plant them in this
land in faithfulness, with all my heart and all my soul.

42 For thus says the LORD: Just as I have brought all this great
disaster upon this people, so I will bring upon them all the good fortune that I now promise them. 43 Fields shall be bought in this land
of which you are saying, It is a desolation, without human beings or
animals; it has been given into the hands of the Chaldeans. 44 Fields
shall be bought for money, and deeds shall be signed and sealed and
witnessed, in the land of Benjamin, in the places around Jerusalem,
and in the cities of Judah, of the hill country, of the Shephelah, and of
the Negeb; for I will restore their fortunes, says the LORD.

Healing after Punishment

33 The word of the LORD came to Jeremiah a second time,
while he was still confined in the court of the guard: 2 Thus
says the LORD who made the earth,[a] the LORD who formed it to establish it—the LORD is his name: 3 Call to me and I will answer you,
and will tell you great and hidden things that you have not known.
4 For thus says the LORD, the God of Israel, concerning the houses of
this city and the houses of the kings of Judah that were torn down to
make a defense against the siege ramps and before the sword:[b] 5 The

[a] Gk: Heb *it* [b] Meaning of Heb uncertain

32:40 I will make an everlasting covenant with them: When God made an everlasting covenant, God assumed all responsibility for its continuation.

32:40 I will put the fear of me in their hearts: The word *fear* in the Bible has more to do with "being in awe" than "afraid." The LORD "will rejoice in doing good to them" (32:41), so the people need not be afraid of God.

32:42 Just as I have brought all this great disaster…so I will bring upon them all the good fortune that I now promise them: This is part of a tradition in the Old Testament that "the LORD gave, and the LORD has taken away" (Job 1:21) and "the LORD kills and brings to life" (1 Sam 2:6-7). This tradition, in spite of its dangers, intended to bring hope to the people.

Chaldeans are coming in to fight[a] and to fill them with the dead bodies of those whom I shall strike down in my anger and my wrath, for
I have hidden my face from this city because of all their wickedness.
6 I am going to bring it recovery and healing; I will heal them and reveal to them abundance[b] of prosperity and security. 7 I will restore the
fortunes of Judah and the fortunes of Israel, and rebuild them as they
were at first. 8 I will cleanse them from all the guilt of their sin against
me, and I will forgive all the guilt of their sin and rebellion against me.
9 And this city[c] shall be to me a name of joy, a praise and a glory before
all the nations of the earth who shall hear of all the good that I do for
them; they shall fear and tremble because of all the good and all the
prosperity I provide for it.

10 Thus says the Lord: In this place of which you say, "It is a
waste without human beings or animals," in the towns of Judah and
the streets of Jerusalem that are desolate, without inhabitants, human
or animal, there shall once more be heard 11 the voice of mirth and the
voice of gladness, the voice of the bridegroom and the voice of the
bride, the voices of those who sing, as they bring thank offerings to
the house of the Lord:

"Give thanks to the Lord of hosts,
for the Lord is good,
for his steadfast love endures forever!"

For I will restore the fortunes of the land as at first, says the Lord.

12 Thus says the Lord of hosts: In this place that is waste, without human beings or animals, and in all its towns there shall again be
pasture for shepherds resting their flocks. 13 In the towns of the hill
country, of the Shephelah, and of the Negeb, in the land of Benjamin, the places around Jerusalem, and in the towns of Judah, flocks
shall again pass under the hands of the one who counts them, says
the Lord.

The Righteous Branch and the Covenant with David

14 The days are surely coming, says the Lord, when I will fulfill
the promise I made to the house of Israel and the house of Judah. 15 In
those days and at that time I will cause a righteous Branch to spring
up for David; and he shall execute justice and righteousness in the
land. 16 In those days Judah will be saved and Jerusalem will live in
safety. And this is the name by which it will be called: "The Lord is
our righteousness."

17 For thus says the Lord: David shall never lack a man to sit on
the throne of the house of Israel, 18 and the levitical priests shall never
lack a man in my presence to offer burnt offerings, to make grain
offerings, and to make sacrifices for all time.

33:7 I will restore the fortunes of Judah and the fortunes of Israel, and rebuild them as they were at first: The series of sermons in this chapter, still placed in the time Jeremiah was in prison, promises the renewal of all that had been and all that would be destroyed. Nebuchadrezzar destroyed Jerusalem (which people had believed was invincible), the temple of the Lord, and the Davidic lineage (see introduction). The Lord will rebuild the city (33:9-13), restore the house of the Lord (33:11), and restore the royal line of David's descendants (33:14-26).

33:16 And this is the name by which it will be called: "The Lord is our righteousness": The prophecy about a future restoration of the line of rulers from David's family is almost identical with 23:5-6. One major difference is that here the future name refers to the city of Jerusalem; in the earlier passage the name was that of the coming king.

---

[a] Cn: Heb *They are coming in to fight against the Chaldeans* [b] Meaning of Heb uncertain [c] Heb *And it*

19 The word of the LORD came to Jeremiah: 20 Thus says the
LORD: If any of you could break my covenant with the day and my
covenant with the night, so that day and night would not come at
their appointed time, 21 only then could my covenant with my servant David be broken, so that he would not have a son to reign on his
throne, and my covenant with my ministers the Levites. 22 Just as the
host of heaven cannot be numbered and the sands of the sea cannot
be measured, so I will increase the offspring of my servant David, and
the Levites who minister to me.

23 The word of the LORD came to Jeremiah: 24 Have you not observed how these people say, "The two families that the LORD chose
have been rejected by him," and how they hold my people in such
contempt that they no longer regard them as a nation? 25 Thus says the
LORD: Only if I had not established my covenant with day and night
and the ordinances of heaven and earth, 26 would I reject the offspring
of Jacob and of my servant David and not choose any of his descendants as rulers over the offspring of Abraham, Isaac, and Jacob. For I
will restore their fortunes, and will have mercy upon them.

Death in Captivity Predicted for Zedekiah

34 The word that came to Jeremiah from the LORD, when
King Nebuchadrezzar of Babylon and all his army and all
the kingdoms of the earth and all the peoples under his dominion
were fighting against Jerusalem and all its cities: 2 Thus says the LORD,
the God of Israel: Go and speak to King Zedekiah of Judah and say
to him: Thus says the LORD: I am going to give this city into the hand
of the king of Babylon, and he shall burn it with fire. 3 And you yourself shall not escape from his hand, but shall surely be captured and
handed over to him; you shall see the king of Babylon eye to eye and
speak with him face to face; and you shall go to Babylon. 4 Yet hear the
word of the LORD, O King Zedekiah of Judah! Thus says the LORD
concerning you: You shall not die by the sword; 5 you shall die in
peace. And as spices were burned[a] for your ancestors, the earlier kings
who preceded you, so they shall burn spices[b] for you and lament for
you, saying, "Alas, lord!" For I have spoken the word, says the LORD.

6 Then the prophet Jeremiah spoke all these words to Zedekiah
king of Judah, in Jerusalem, 7 when the army of the king of Babylon
was fighting against Jerusalem and against all the cities of Judah that
were left, Lachish and Azekah; for these were the only fortified cities
of Judah that remained.

Treacherous Treatment of Slaves

8 The word that came to Jeremiah from the LORD, after King Zedekiah had made a covenant with all the people in Jerusalem to make

[a] Heb *as there was burning* [b] Heb *shall burn*

34:4-5 You shall not die by the sword; you shall die in peace: Zedekiah does not die by the sword, but he experiences something worse. He sees his sons killed, is then blinded, and finally put into prison (52:9-11; 2 Kgs 25:6-7).

34:7 Lachish and Azekah; for these were the only fortified cities of Judah that remained: Lachish (LA-kish) was an ancient city, almost thirty miles southwest of Jerusalem. The Assyrian king Sennacherib destroyed Lachish about 701 B.C.E. Josiah's father, Manasseh (king of Judah), rebuilt the city in the seventh century B.C.E. Archaeologists have discovered eight letters written on pieces of broken pottery. Some of the letters report the fear prior to the city's destruction by Nebuchadrezzar in 588–586 B.C.E. Azekah (a-ZEE-ka), mentioned in several of these letters, was ten miles north of Lachish. See Map 7, p. 2105.

a proclamation of liberty to them— [9]that all should set free their Hebrew slaves, male and female, so that no one should hold another Judean in slavery. [10]And they obeyed, all the officials and all the people who had entered into the covenant that all would set free their slaves, male or female, so that they would not be enslaved again; they obeyed and set them free. [11]But afterward they turned around and took back the male and female slaves they had set free, and brought them again into subjection as slaves. [12]The word of the LORD came to Jeremiah from the LORD: [13]Thus says the LORD, the God of Israel: I myself made a covenant with your ancestors when I brought them out of the land of Egypt, out of the house of slavery, saying, [14]"Every seventh year each of you must set free any Hebrews who have been sold to you and have served you six years; you must set them free from your service." But your ancestors did not listen to me or incline their ears to me. [15]You yourselves recently repented and did what was right in my sight by proclaiming liberty to one another, and you made a covenant before me in the house that is called by my name; [16]but then you turned around and profaned my name when each of you took back your male and female slaves, whom you had set free according to their desire, and you brought them again into subjection to be your slaves. [17]Therefore, thus says the LORD: You have not obeyed me by granting a release to your neighbors and friends; I am going to grant a release to you, says the LORD—a release to the sword, to pestilence, and to famine. I will make you a horror to all the kingdoms of the earth. [18]And those who transgressed my covenant and did not keep the terms of the covenant that they made before me, I will make like[a] the calf when they cut it in two and passed between its parts: [19]the officials of Judah, the officials of Jerusalem, the eunuchs, the priests, and all the people of the land who passed between the parts of the calf [20]shall be handed over to their enemies and to those who seek their lives. Their corpses shall become food for the birds of the air and the wild animals of the earth. [21]And as for King Zedekiah of Judah and his officials, I will hand them over to their enemies and to those who seek their lives, to the army of the king of Babylon, which has withdrawn from you. [22]I am going to command, says the LORD, and will bring them back to this city; and they will fight against it, and take it, and burn it with fire. The towns of Judah I will make a desolation without inhabitant.

34:14 Every seventh year each of you must set free any Hebrews [slaves]: The law regarding Hebrew slaves appears at Exodus 21:2 and Deuteronomy 15:12. The LORD commanded that after "seven weeks of years" (meaning fifty years) "you shall proclaim liberty throughout the land to all its inhabitants" (Lev 25:8-12). The people ignored the law for many years, but the threat of the Babylonians shocked them into obedience. When the people felt the threat was over, they reclaimed their slaves.

34:18 I will make like the calf when they cut in two and passed between its parts: One way to make a covenant was to cut a calf down the middle, place its parts on the ground, and walk between the pieces. Jeremiah uses an expression that means literally "cut a covenant" (32:40). In most English translations the expression is "make a covenant." Walking between the parts might be a ritual for committing one's own body to being cut in two if one proves unfaithful to the covenant. By refusing to free the slaves, the people have brought the death sentence on themselves.

The Rechabites Commended

35 The word that came to Jeremiah from the LORD in the days of King Jehoiakim son of Josiah of Judah: [2]Go to the house of the Rechabites, and speak with them, and bring them to the house

35:1-19 Go to the house of the Rechabites: The prior chapters dated from the last year or two of Zedekiah (588–587 B.C.E.). The name *Jehoiakim* may be a mistake for Zedekiah. If this is not an error, this incident takes us back ten years. In 597 Nebuchadrezzar invaded the areas where the Rechabites pitched their tents. The Rechabites impressed Jeremiah because they kept their commitments to their tribe.

[a] Cn: Heb lacks *like*

of the Lord, into one of the chambers; then offer them wine to drink. [3]So I took Jaazaniah son of Jeremiah son of Habazziniah, and his brothers, and all his sons, and the whole house of the Rechabites. [4]I brought them to the house of the Lord into the chamber of the sons of Hanan son of Igdaliah, the man of God, which was near the chamber of the officials, above the chamber of Maaseiah son of Shallum, keeper of the threshold. [5]Then I set before the Rechabites pitchers full of wine, and cups; and I said to them, "Have some wine." [6]But they answered, "We will drink no wine, for our ancestor Jonadab son of Rechab commanded us, 'You shall never drink wine, neither you nor your children; [7]nor shall you ever build a house, or sow seed; nor shall you plant a vineyard, or even own one; but you shall live in tents all your days, that you may live many days in the land where you reside.' [8]We have obeyed the charge of our ancestor Jonadab son of Rechab in all that he commanded us, to drink no wine all our days, ourselves, our wives, our sons, or our daughters, [9]and not to build houses to live in. We have no vineyard or field or seed; [10]but we have lived in tents, and have obeyed and done all that our ancestor Jonadab commanded us. [11]But when King Nebuchadrezzar of Babylon came up against the land, we said, 'Come, and let us go to Jerusalem for fear of the army of the Chaldeans and the army of the Arameans.' That is why we are living in Jerusalem."

12 Then the word of the Lord came to Jeremiah: [13]Thus says the Lord of hosts, the God of Israel: Go and say to the people of Judah and the inhabitants of Jerusalem, Can you not learn a lesson and obey my words? says the Lord. [14]The command has been carried out that Jonadab son of Rechab gave to his descendants to drink no wine; and they drink none to this day, for they have obeyed their ancestor's command. But I myself have spoken to you persistently, and you have not obeyed me. [15]I have sent to you all my servants the prophets, sending them persistently, saying, "Turn now every one of you from your evil way, and amend your doings, and do not go after other gods to serve them, and then you shall live in the land that I gave to you and your ancestors." But you did not incline your ear or obey me. [16]The descendants of Jonadab son of Rechab have carried out the command that their ancestor gave them, but this people has not obeyed me. [17]Therefore, thus says the Lord, the God of hosts, the God of Israel: I am going to bring on Judah and on all the inhabitants of Jerusalem every disaster that I have pronounced against them; because I have spoken to them and they have not listened, I have called to them and they have not answered.

18 But to the house of the Rechabites Jeremiah said: Thus says the Lord of hosts, the God of Israel: Because you have obeyed the command of your ancestor Jonadab, and kept all his precepts, and done all that he commanded you, [19]therefore thus says the Lord of

hosts, the God of Israel: Jonadab son of Rechab shall not lack a descendant to stand before me for all time.

The Scroll Read in the Temple

36:1-32 Take a scroll and write on it: Baruch reports how most of the book of Jeremiah came to be. The fourth year of Jehoiakim was about 606 B.C.E., when power was shifting between Egypt and Babylon.

36 In the fourth year of King Jehoiakim son of Josiah of Judah, this word came to Jeremiah from the LORD: [2]Take a scroll and write on it all the words that I have spoken to you against Israel and Judah and all the nations, from the day I spoke to you, from the days of Josiah until today. [3]It may be that when the house of Judah hears of all the disasters that I intend to do to them, all of them may turn from their evil ways, so that I may forgive their iniquity and their sin.

4 Then Jeremiah called Baruch son of Neriah, and Baruch wrote on a scroll at Jeremiah's dictation all the words of the LORD that he had spoken to him. [5]And Jeremiah ordered Baruch, saying, "I am prevented from entering the house of the LORD; [6]so you go yourself, and on a fast day in the hearing of the people in the LORD's house you shall read the words of the LORD from the scroll that you have written at my dictation. You shall read them also in the hearing of all the people of Judah who come up from their towns. [7]It may be that their plea will come before the LORD, and that all of them will turn from their evil ways, for great is the anger and wrath that the LORD has pronounced against this people." [8]And Baruch son of Neriah did all that the prophet Jeremiah ordered him about reading from the scroll the words of the LORD in the LORD's house.

9 In the fifth year of King Jehoiakim son of Josiah of Judah, in the ninth month, all the people in Jerusalem and all the people who came from the towns of Judah to Jerusalem proclaimed a fast before the LORD. [10]Then, in the hearing of all the people, Baruch read the words of Jeremiah from the scroll, in the house of the LORD, in the chamber of Gemariah son of Shaphan the secretary, which was in the upper court, at the entry of the New Gate of the LORD's house.

The Scroll Read in the Palace

11 When Micaiah son of Gemariah son of Shaphan heard all the words of the LORD from the scroll, [12]he went down to the king's house, into the secretary's chamber; and all the officials were sitting there: Elishama the secretary, Delaiah son of Shemaiah, Elnathan son of Achbor, Gemariah son of Shaphan, Zedekiah son of Hananiah, and all the officials. [13]And Micaiah told them all the words that he had heard, when Baruch read the scroll in the hearing of the people. [14]Then all the officials sent Jehudi son of Nethaniah son of Shelemiah son of Cushi to say to Baruch, "Bring the scroll that you read in the hearing of the people, and come." So Baruch son of Neriah took the scroll in his hand and came to them. [15]And they said to him, "Sit down

and read it to us." So Baruch read it to them. [16]When they heard all the words, they turned to one another in alarm, and said to Baruch, "We certainly must report all these words to the king." [17]Then they questioned Baruch, "Tell us now, how did you write all these words? Was it at his dictation?" [18]Baruch answered them, "He dictated all these words to me, and I wrote them with ink on the scroll." [19]Then the officials said to Baruch, "Go and hide, you and Jeremiah, and let no one know where you are."

Jehoiakim Burns the Scroll

20 Leaving the scroll in the chamber of Elishama the secretary, they went to the court of the king; and they reported all the words to the king. [21]Then the king sent Jehudi to get the scroll, and he took it from the chamber of Elishama the secretary; and Jehudi read it to the king and all the officials who stood beside the king. [22]Now the king was sitting in his winter apartment (it was the ninth month), and there was a fire burning in the brazier before him. [23]As Jehudi read three or four columns, the king[a] would cut them off with a penknife and throw them into the fire in the brazier, until the entire scroll was consumed in the fire that was in the brazier. [24]Yet neither the king, nor any of his servants who heard all these words, was alarmed, nor did they tear their garments. [25]Even when Elnathan and Delaiah and Gemariah urged the king not to burn the scroll, he would not listen to them. [26]And the king commanded Jerahmeel the king's son and Seraiah son of Azriel and Shelemiah son of Abdeel to arrest the secretary Baruch and the prophet Jeremiah. But the LORD hid them.

Jeremiah Dictates Another

27 Now, after the king had burned the scroll with the words that Baruch wrote at Jeremiah's dictation, the word of the LORD came to Jeremiah: [28]Take another scroll and write on it all the former words that were in the first scroll, which King Jehoiakim of Judah has burned. [29]And concerning King Jehoiakim of Judah you shall say: Thus says the LORD, You have dared to burn this scroll, saying, Why have you written in it that the king of Babylon will certainly come and destroy this land, and will cut off from it human beings and animals? [30]Therefore thus says the LORD concerning King Jehoiakim of Judah: He shall have no one to sit upon the throne of David, and his dead body shall be cast out to the heat by day and the frost by night. [31]And I will punish him and his offspring and his servants for their iniquity; I will bring on them, and on the inhabitants of Jerusalem, and on the people of Judah, all the disasters with which I have threatened them—but they would not listen.

---

[a] Heb *he*

32 Then Jeremiah took another scroll and gave it to the secretary
Baruch son of Neriah, who wrote on it at Jeremiah's dictation all the
words of the scroll that King Jehoiakim of Judah had burned in the
fire; and many similar words were added to them.

Zedekiah's Vain Hope

37 Zedekiah son of Josiah, whom King Nebuchadrezzar of
Babylon made king in the land of Judah, succeeded Coniah
son of Jehoiakim. [2]But neither he nor his servants nor the people of
the land listened to the words of the LORD that he spoke through the
prophet Jeremiah.

3 King Zedekiah sent Jehucal son of Shelemiah and the priest
Zephaniah son of Maaseiah to the prophet Jeremiah saying, "Please
pray for us to the LORD our God." [4]Now Jeremiah was still going in
and out among the people, for he had not yet been put in prison.
[5]Meanwhile, the army of Pharaoh had come out of Egypt; and when
the Chaldeans who were besieging Jerusalem heard news of them,
they withdrew from Jerusalem.

6 Then the word of the LORD came to the prophet Jeremiah:
[7]Thus says the LORD, God of Israel: This is what the two of you shall
say to the king of Judah, who sent you to me to inquire of me: Pharaoh's army, which set out to help you, is going to return to its own
land, to Egypt. [8]And the Chaldeans shall return and fight against this
city; they shall take it and burn it with fire. [9]Thus says the LORD: Do
not deceive yourselves, saying, "The Chaldeans will surely go away
from us," for they will not go away. [10]Even if you defeated the whole
army of Chaldeans who are fighting against you, and there remained
of them only wounded men in their tents, they would rise up and
burn this city with fire.

Jeremiah Is Imprisoned

11 Now when the Chaldean army had withdrawn from Jerusalem
at the approach of Pharaoh's army, [12]Jeremiah set out from Jerusalem
to go to the land of Benjamin to receive his share of property[a] among
the people there. [13]When he reached the Benjamin Gate, a sentinel
there named Irijah son of Shelemiah son of Hananiah arrested the
prophet Jeremiah saying, "You are deserting to the Chaldeans." [14]And
Jeremiah said, "That is a lie; I am not deserting to the Chaldeans." But
Irijah would not listen to him, and arrested Jeremiah and brought him
to the officials. [15]The officials were enraged at Jeremiah, and they beat
him and imprisoned him in the house of the secretary Jonathan, for it
had been made a prison. [16]Thus Jeremiah was put in the cistern house,
in the cells, and remained there many days.

---

[a] Meaning of Heb uncertain

37:1-2 Zedekiah son of Josiah... succeeded Coniah son of Jehoiakim: These verses place the following series of events in the last days of Zedekiah, or about 587 B.C.E., some two decades after the events of the previous chapter.

37:3—38:28 King Zedekiah sent Jehucal...and the priest Zephaniah...to the prophet Jeremiah: These two chapters describe several meetings between Zedekiah and Jeremiah, some through the king's agents and others face-to-face. The result of all the encounters is the same: The LORD will use the Babylonians to destroy Jerusalem.

37:5 the army of Pharaoh: The pharaoh at this time was Hophra (588–569 B.C.E.). He succeeded his father, Psammeticus II (595–588), the son of Neco II (609–595).

37:10 wounded men...would rise up and burn this city with fire: The author uses irony. Even wounded Chaldeans can destroy Jerusalem, a city the people thought was invincible.

17 Then King Zedekiah sent for him, and received him. The king
questioned him secretly in his house, and said, "Is there any word
from the LORD?" Jeremiah said, "There is!" Then he said, "You shall
be handed over to the king of Babylon." [18]Jeremiah also said to King
Zedekiah, "What wrong have I done to you or your servants or this
people, that you have put me in prison? [19]Where are your prophets
who prophesied to you, saying, 'The king of Babylon will not come
against you and against this land'? [20]Now please hear me, my lord
king: be good enough to listen to my plea, and do not send me back
to the house of the secretary Jonathan to die there." [21]So King Zedekiah gave orders, and they committed Jeremiah to the court of the
guard; and a loaf of bread was given him daily from the bakers' street,
until all the bread of the city was gone. So Jeremiah remained in the
court of the guard.

Jeremiah in the Cistern

38 Now Shephatiah son of Mattan, Gedaliah son of Pashhur,
Jucal son of Shelemiah, and Pashhur son of Malchiah heard
the words that Jeremiah was saying to all the people, [2]Thus says the
LORD, Those who stay in this city shall die by the sword, by famine,
and by pestilence; but those who go out to the Chaldeans shall live;
they shall have their lives as a prize of war, and live. [3]Thus says the
LORD, This city shall surely be handed over to the army of the king of
Babylon and be taken. [4]Then the officials said to the king, "This man
ought to be put to death, because he is discouraging the soldiers who
are left in this city, and all the people, by speaking such words to them.
For this man is not seeking the welfare of this people, but their harm."
[5]King Zedekiah said, "Here he is; he is in your hands; for the king is
powerless against you." [6]So they took Jeremiah and threw him into
the cistern of Malchiah, the king's son, which was in the court of the
guard, letting Jeremiah down by ropes. Now there was no water in the
cistern, but only mud, and Jeremiah sank in the mud.

Jeremiah Is Rescued by Ebed-melech

7 Ebed-melech the Ethiopian,[a] a eunuch in the king's house, heard
that they had put Jeremiah into the cistern. The king happened to be
sitting at the Benjamin Gate, [8]So Ebed-melech left the king's house
and spoke to the king, [9]"My lord king, these men have acted wickedly
in all they did to the prophet Jeremiah by throwing him into the cistern to die there of hunger, for there is no bread left in the city." [10]Then
the king commanded Ebed-melech the Ethiopian,[a] "Take three men
with you from here, and pull the prophet Jeremiah up from the cistern before he dies." [11]So Ebed-melech took the men with him and

[a] Or *Nubian*; Heb *Cushite*

38:7-13 Ebed-melech the Ethiopian, a eunuch in the king's house: People from Ethiopia (Cush in Hebrew) appear in other Bible stories. Moses married an Ethiopian woman, which angered his brother Aaron and his sister Miriam (Num 12:1-2). An Ethiopian eunuch opened his heart to the preaching of the apostle Philip and was baptized in some nearby water (Acts 8:26-40).

Why do you think the ancient biblical writers used stories about people from Ethiopia?

went to the house of the king, to a wardrobe of[a] the storehouse, and
took from there old rags and worn-out clothes, which he let down to
Jeremiah in the cistern by ropes. [12]Then Ebed-melech the Ethiopian[b]
said to Jeremiah, "Just put the rags and clothes between your armpits
and the ropes." Jeremiah did so. [13]Then they drew Jeremiah up by the
ropes and pulled him out of the cistern. And Jeremiah remained in
the court of the guard.

Zedekiah Consults Jeremiah Again

14 King Zedekiah sent for the prophet Jeremiah and received
him at the third entrance of the temple of the LORD. The king said to
Jeremiah, "I have something to ask you; do not hide anything from
me." [15]Jeremiah said to Zedekiah, "If I tell you, you will put me to
death, will you not? And if I give you advice, you will not listen to
me." [16]So King Zedekiah swore an oath in secret to Jeremiah, "As the
LORD lives, who gave us our lives, I will not put you to death or hand
you over to these men who seek your life."

17 Then Jeremiah said to Zedekiah, "Thus says the LORD, the
God of hosts, the God of Israel, If you will only surrender to the officials of the king of Babylon, then your life shall be spared, and this city
shall not be burned with fire, and you and your house shall live. [18]But
if you do not surrender to the officials of the king of Babylon, then
this city shall be handed over to the Chaldeans, and they shall burn
it with fire, and you yourself shall not escape from their hand." [19]King
Zedekiah said to Jeremiah, "I am afraid of the Judeans who have deserted to the Chaldeans, for I might be handed over to them and they
would abuse me." [20]Jeremiah said, "That will not happen. Just obey
the voice of the LORD in what I say to you, and it shall go well with
you, and your life shall be spared. [21]But if you are determined not to
surrender, this is what the LORD has shown me— [22]a vision of all the
women remaining in the house of the king of Judah being led out to
the officials of the king of Babylon and saying,

'Your trusted friends have seduced you
    and have overcome you;
Now that your feet are stuck in the mud,
    they desert you.'

[23]All your wives and your children shall be led out to the Chaldeans,
and you yourself shall not escape from their hand, but shall be seized
by the king of Babylon; and this city shall be burned with fire."

24 Then Zedekiah said to Jeremiah, "Do not let anyone else know
of this conversation, or you will die. [25]If the officials should hear that
I have spoken with you, and they should come and say to you, 'Just
tell us what you said to the king; do not conceal it from us, or we will

---

[a] Cn: Heb *to under* [b] Or *Nubian;* Heb *Cushite*

put you to death. What did the king say to you?' [26]then you shall say to them, 'I was presenting my plea to the king not to send me back to the house of Jonathan to die there.' " [27]All the officials did come to Jeremiah and questioned him; and he answered them in the very words the king had commanded. So they stopped questioning him, for the conversation had not been overheard. [28]And Jeremiah remained in the court of the guard until the day that Jerusalem was taken.

The Fall of Jerusalem

39 In the ninth year of King Zedekiah of Judah, in the tenth month, King Nebuchadrezzar of Babylon and all his army came against Jerusalem and besieged it; [2]in the eleventh year of Zedekiah, in the fourth month, on the ninth day of the month, a breach was made in the city. [3]When Jerusalem was taken,[a] all the officials of the king of Babylon came and sat in the middle gate: Nergal-sharezer, Samgar-nebo, Sarsechim the Rabsaris, Nergal-sharezer the Rabmag, with all the rest of the officials of the king of Babylon. [4]When King Zedekiah of Judah and all the soldiers saw them, they fled, going out of the city at night by way of the king's garden through the gate between the two walls; and they went toward the Arabah. [5]But the army of the Chaldeans pursued them, and overtook Zedekiah in the plains of Jericho; and when they had taken him, they brought him up to King Nebuchadrezzar of Babylon, at Riblah, in the land of Hamath; and he passed sentence on him. [6]The king of Babylon slaughtered the sons of Zedekiah at Riblah before his eyes; also the king of Babylon slaughtered all the nobles of Judah. [7]He put out the eyes of Zedekiah, and bound him in fetters to take him to Babylon. [8]The Chaldeans burned the king's house and the houses of the people, and broke down the walls of Jerusalem. [9]Then Nebuzaradan the captain of the guard exiled to Babylon the rest of the people who were left in the city, those who had deserted to him, and the people who remained. [10]Nebuzaradan the captain of the guard left in the land of Judah some of the poor people who owned nothing, and gave them vineyards and fields at the same time.

39:1-10 When Jerusalem was taken: Nebuchadrezzar's forces conquered Jerusalem. The conquest resulted in what Jeremiah had prophesied. The Babylonians destroyed the city, burned down the temple, executed Zedekiah's sons (the last event he would ever see), blinded him, and carried him and most of the remaining citizens away to a long exile in Babylon. The account appears also at 2 Kings 25:1-12.

39:10 Nebuzaradan the captain of the guard left in the land of Judah some of the poor people who owned nothing: The military commander Nebuzaradan (ne-BOO-za-RA-dan) sends many people into exile, but at the same time he helps the poor. He gives them fields and vineyards. Nebuzaradan, acting on orders from his king, released Jeremiah from the court of the guard and allowed him to stay in Judah under the newly appointed governor, Gedaliah (39:11-14).

Jeremiah, Set Free, Remembers Ebed-melech

11 King Nebuchadrezzar of Babylon gave command concerning Jeremiah through Nebuzaradan, the captain of the guard, saying, [12]"Take him, look after him well and do him no harm, but deal with him as he may ask you." [13]So Nebuzaradan the captain of the guard, Nebushazban the Rabsaris, Nergal-sharezer the Rabmag, and all the chief officers of the king of Babylon sent [14]and took Jeremiah from the court of the guard. They entrusted him to Gedaliah son of

[a] This clause has been transposed from 38.28

Ahikam son of Shaphan to be brought home. So he stayed with his
own people.

15 The word of the LORD came to Jeremiah while he was confined in the court of the guard: 16 Go and say to Ebed-melech the Ethiopian:[a] Thus says the LORD of hosts, the God of Israel: I am going to
fulfill my words against this city for evil and not for good, and they
shall be accomplished in your presence on that day. 17 But I will save
you on that day, says the LORD, and you shall not be handed over to
those whom you dread. 18 For I will surely save you, and you shall not
fall by the sword; but you shall have your life as a prize of war, because
you have trusted in me, says the LORD.

Jeremiah with Gedaliah the Governor

40 The word that came to Jeremiah from the LORD after Nebuzaradan the captain of the guard had let him go from
Ramah, when he took him bound in fetters along with all the captives of Jerusalem and Judah who were being exiled to Babylon. 2 The
captain of the guard took Jeremiah and said to him, "The LORD your
God threatened this place with this disaster; 3 and now the LORD has
brought it about, and has done as he said, because all of you sinned
against the LORD and did not obey his voice. Therefore this thing has
come upon you. 4 Now look, I have just released you today from the
fetters on your hands. If you wish to come with me to Babylon, come,
and I will take good care of you; but if you do not wish to come with
me to Babylon, you need not come. See, the whole land is before you;
go wherever you think it good and right to go. 5 If you remain,[b] then
return to Gedaliah son of Ahikam son of Shaphan, whom the king of
Babylon appointed governor of the towns of Judah, and stay with him
among the people; or go wherever you think it right to go." So the captain of the guard gave him an allowance of food and a present, and let
him go. 6 Then Jeremiah went to Gedaliah son of Ahikam at Mizpah,
and stayed with him among the people who were left in the land.

7 When all the leaders of the forces in the open country and their
troops heard that the king of Babylon had appointed Gedaliah son
of Ahikam governor in the land, and had committed to him men,
women, and children, those of the poorest of the land who had not
been taken into exile to Babylon, 8 they went to Gedaliah at Mizpah—
Ishmael son of Nethaniah, Johanan son of Kareah, Seraiah son of
Tanhumeth, the sons of Ephai the Netophathite, Jezaniah son of the
Maacathite, they and their troops. 9 Gedaliah son of Ahikam son of
Shaphan swore to them and their troops, saying, "Do not be afraid to
serve the Chaldeans. Stay in the land and serve the king of Babylon,

40:6 Then Jeremiah went to Gedaliah . . . and stayed with him among the people who were left in the land: Baruch's biography portrays Jeremiah as a man "among the people" (37:4, 12; 39:14; 42:1-2). The prophet who had lost all his friends as a result of his call to preach the word of the LORD now finds his joy living among them.

40:8 they went to Gedaliah at Mizpah: Gedaliah was appointed governor of Judah. Judah was now a Babylonian province. Gedaliah made Mizpah the center of the new community. The people of Judah who had fled to various lands found hope in this community at Mizpah and returned home.

---

[a] Or *Nubian;* Heb *Cushite* [b] Syr: Meaning of Heb uncertain

and it shall go well with you. [10]As for me, I am staying at Mizpah to represent you before the Chaldeans who come to us; but as for you, gather wine and summer fruits and oil, and store them in your vessels, and live in the towns that you have taken over." [11]Likewise, when all the Judeans who were in Moab and among the Ammonites and in Edom and in other lands heard that the king of Babylon had left a remnant in Judah and had appointed Gedaliah son of Ahikam son of Shaphan as governor over them, [12]then all the Judeans returned from all the places to which they had been scattered and came to the land of Judah, to Gedaliah at Mizpah; and they gathered wine and summer fruits in great abundance.

13 Now Johanan son of Kareah and all the leaders of the forces in the open country came to Gedaliah at Mizpah [14]and said to him, "Are you at all aware that Baalis king of the Ammonites has sent Ishmael son of Nethaniah to take your life?" But Gedaliah son of Ahikam would not believe them. [15]Then Johanan son of Kareah spoke secretly to Gedaliah at Mizpah, "Please let me go and kill Ishmael son of Nethaniah, and no one else will know. Why should he take your life, so that all the Judeans who are gathered around you would be scattered, and the remnant of Judah would perish?" [16]But Gedaliah son of Ahikam said to Johanan son of Kareah, "Do not do such a thing, for you are telling a lie about Ishmael."

40:13—41:18 Baalis king of the Ammonites…Ishmael son of Nethaniah: The motives for Gedaliah's murder do not appear in Baruch's report. Behind the scheme was Baalis, king of the Ammonites, a group of people living in the desert east of the Jordan River. See Map 7, p. 2105.

Insurrection against Gedaliah

41 In the seventh month, Ishmael son of Nethaniah son of Elishama, of the royal family, one of the chief officers of the king, came with ten men to Gedaliah son of Ahikam, at Mizpah. As they ate bread together there at Mizpah, [2]Ishmael son of Nethaniah and the ten men with him got up and struck down Gedaliah son of Ahikam son of Shaphan with the sword and killed him, because the king of Babylon had appointed him governor in the land. [3]Ishmael also killed all the Judeans who were with Gedaliah at Mizpah, and the Chaldean soldiers who happened to be there.

4 On the day after the murder of Gedaliah, before anyone knew of it, [5]eighty men arrived from Shechem and Shiloh and Samaria, with their beards shaved and their clothes torn, and their bodies gashed, bringing grain offerings and incense to present at the temple of the LORD. [6]And Ishmael son of Nethaniah came out from Mizpah to meet them, weeping as he came. As he met them, he said to them, "Come to Gedaliah son of Ahikam." [7]When they reached the middle of the city, Ishmael son of Nethaniah and the men with him slaughtered them, and threw them[a] into a cistern. [8]But there were ten men among them who said to Ishmael, "Do not kill us, for we have stores

41:5 and their bodies gashed: The Canaanites practiced ritual self-mutilation in the worship of Baal (1 Kgs 18:28), but the law of the LORD forbade the practice for Israelites (Lev 19:28; 21:5).

[a] Syr: Heb lacks *and threw them*; compare verse 9

of wheat, barley, oil, and honey hidden in the fields." So he refrained, and did not kill them along with their companions.

9 Now the cistern into which Ishmael had thrown all the bodies of the men whom he had struck down was the large cistern[a] that King Asa had made for defense against King Baasha of Israel; Ishmael son of Nethaniah filled that cistern with those whom he had killed. 10 Then Ishmael took captive all the rest of the people who were in Mizpah, the king's daughters and all the people who were left at Mizpah, whom Nebuzaradan, the captain of the guard, had committed to Gedaliah son of Ahikam. Ishmael son of Nethaniah took them captive and set out to cross over to the Ammonites.

11 But when Johanan son of Kareah and all the leaders of the forces with him heard of all the crimes that Ishmael son of Nethaniah had done, 12 they took all their men and went to fight against Ishmael son of Nethaniah. They came upon him at the great pool that is in Gibeon. 13 And when all the people who were with Ishmael saw Johanan son of Kareah and all the leaders of the forces with him, they were glad. 14 So all the people whom Ishmael had carried away captive from Mizpah turned around and came back, and went to Johanan son of Kareah. 15 But Ishmael son of Nethaniah escaped from Johanan with eight men, and went to the Ammonites. 16 Then Johanan son of Kareah and all the leaders of the forces with him took all the rest of the people whom Ishmael son of Nethaniah had carried away captive[b] from Mizpah after he had slain Gedaliah son of Ahikam—soldiers, women, children, and eunuchs, whom Johanan brought back from Gibeon.[c] 17 And they set out, and stopped at Geruth Chimham near Bethlehem, intending to go to Egypt 18 because of the Chaldeans; for they were afraid of them, because Ishmael son of Nethaniah had killed Gedaliah son of Ahikam, whom the king of Babylon had made governor over the land.

Jeremiah Advises Survivors Not to Migrate

42 Then all the commanders of the forces, and Johanan son of Kareah and Azariah[d] son of Hoshaiah, and all the people from the least to the greatest, approached 2 the prophet Jeremiah and said, "Be good enough to listen to our plea, and pray to the LORD your God for us—for all this remnant. For there are only a few of us left out of many, as your eyes can see. 3 Let the LORD your God show us where we should go and what we should do." 4 The prophet Jeremiah said to them, "Very well: I am going to pray to the LORD your God as you request, and whatever the LORD answers you I will tell you; I will keep nothing back from you." 5 They in their turn said to Jeremiah, "May

41:10 all the rest of the people who were in Mizpah: The group must have included Jeremiah and Baruch, because the prophet is among those Johanan (joh-HA-nan) rescued and took to Geruth Chimham, near Bethlehem (41:17; 42:1-2).

41:12 the great pool that is in Gibeon: The pool was the site of the battle between David's forces and those of Saul (2 Sam 2:12-17). At the shrine of Gibeon, King Solomon had his dream in which he asked the LORD for wisdom (1 Kgs 3:4-15).

---

[a] Gk: Heb *whom he had killed by the hand of Gedaliah* [b] Cn: Heb *whom he recovered from Ishmael son of Nethaniah* [c] Meaning of Heb uncertain [d] Gk: Heb *Jezaniah*

the LORD be a true and faithful witness against us if we do not act according to everything that the LORD your God sends us through you.
6 Whether it is good or bad, we will obey the voice of the LORD our
God to whom we are sending you, in order that it may go well with us
when we obey the voice of the LORD our God."

7 At the end of ten days the word of the LORD came to Jeremiah.
8 Then he summoned Johanan son of Kareah and all the commanders
of the forces who were with him, and all the people from the least to
the greatest, 9 and said to them, "Thus says the LORD, the God of Israel, to whom you sent me to present your plea before him: 10 If you
will only remain in this land, then I will build you up and not pull you
down; I will plant you, and not pluck you up; for I am sorry for the
disaster that I have brought upon you. 11 Do not be afraid of the king
of Babylon, as you have been; do not be afraid of him, says the LORD,
for I am with you, to save you and to rescue you from his hand. 12 I
will grant you mercy, and he will have mercy on you and restore you
to your native soil. 13 But if you continue to say, 'We will not stay in
this land,' thus disobeying the voice of the LORD your God 14 and saying, 'No, we will go to the land of Egypt, where we shall not see war,
or hear the sound of the trumpet, or be hungry for bread, and there
we will stay,' 15 then hear the word of the LORD, O remnant of Judah.
Thus says the LORD of hosts, the God of Israel: If you are determined
to enter Egypt and go to settle there, 16 then the sword that you fear
shall overtake you there, in the land of Egypt; and the famine that you
dread shall follow close after you into Egypt; and there you shall die.
17 All the people who have determined to go to Egypt to settle there
shall die by the sword, by famine, and by pestilence; they shall have no
remnant or survivor from the disaster that I am bringing upon them.

18 "For thus says the LORD of hosts, the God of Israel: Just as
my anger and my wrath were poured out on the inhabitants of Jerusalem, so my wrath will be poured out on you when you go to Egypt.
You shall become an object of execration and horror, of cursing and
ridicule. You shall see this place no more. 19 The LORD has said to you,
O remnant of Judah, Do not go to Egypt. Be well aware that I have
warned you today 20 that you have made a fatal mistake. For you yourselves sent me to the LORD your God, saying, 'Pray for us to the LORD
our God, and whatever the LORD our God says, tell us and we will do
it.' 21 So I have told you today, but you have not obeyed the voice of
the LORD your God in anything that he sent me to tell you. 22 Be well
aware, then, that you shall die by the sword, by famine, and by pestilence in the place where you desire to go and settle."

Taken to Egypt, Jeremiah Warns of Judgment

43 When Jeremiah finished speaking to all the people all these
words of the LORD their God, with which the LORD their

God had sent him to them, 2Azariah son of Hoshaiah and Johanan
son of Kareah and all the other insolent men said to Jeremiah, “You
are telling a lie. The LORD our God did not send you to say, ‘Do not go
to Egypt to settle there’; 3but Baruch son of Neriah is inciting you
against us, to hand us over to the Chaldeans, in order that they may
kill us or take us into exile in Babylon.” 4So Johanan son of Kareah and
all the commanders of the forces and all the people did not obey the
voice of the LORD, to stay in the land of Judah. 5But Johanan son of
Kareah and all the commanders of the forces took all the remnant of
Judah who had returned to settle in the land of Judah from all the
nations to which they had been driven— 6the men, the women, the
children, the princesses, and everyone whom Nebuzaradan the captain of the guard had left with Gedaliah son of Ahikam son of Shaphan; also the prophet Jeremiah and Baruch son of Neriah. 7And they
came into the land of Egypt, for they did not obey the voice of the
LORD. And they arrived at Tahpanhes.

8 Then the word of the LORD came to Jeremiah in Tahpanhes:
9Take some large stones in your hands, and bury them in the clay
pavement[a] that is at the entrance to Pharaoh’s palace in Tahpanhes.
Let the Judeans see you do it, 10and say to them, Thus says the LORD
of hosts, the God of Israel: I am going to send and take my servant
King Nebuchadrezzar of Babylon, and he[b] will set his throne above
these stones that I have buried, and he will spread his royal canopy
over them. 11He shall come and ravage the land of Egypt, giving

those who are destined for pestilence, to pestilence,
and those who are destined for captivity, to captivity,
and those who are destined for the sword, to the sword.

12He[c] shall kindle a fire in the temples of the gods of Egypt; and he
shall burn them and carry them away captive; and he shall pick clean
the land of Egypt, as a shepherd picks his cloak clean of vermin; and
he shall depart from there safely. 13He shall break the obelisks of Heliopolis, which is in the land of Egypt; and the temples of the gods of
Egypt he shall burn with fire.

Denunciation of Persistent Idolatry

44 The word that came to Jeremiah for all the Judeans living
in the land of Egypt, at Migdol, at Tahpanhes, at Memphis,
and in the land of Pathros, 2Thus says the LORD of hosts, the God of
Israel: You yourselves have seen all the disaster that I have brought on
Jerusalem and on all the towns of Judah. Look at them; today they are
a desolation, without an inhabitant in them, 3because of the wickedness that they committed, provoking me to anger, in that they went to
make offerings and serve other gods that they had not known, neither

[a] Meaning of Heb uncertain [b] Gk Syr: Heb *I* [c] Gk Syr Vg: Heb *I*

43:5-7 But Johanan…took all the remnant of Judah…also the prophet Jeremiah and Baruch son of Neriah. And they came into the land of Egypt: Jeremiah and Baruch will live in Egypt for the rest of the prophet’s ministry. Many other Judeans also settle in Egypt, where they will prosper for about four centuries.

43:7-9 Tahpanhes: The city is mentioned earlier in the book at 2:16. Tahpanhes (TAH-pa-neez) was located on the eastern frontier in northern Egypt and would have been the first stop as people traveled from Judah.

43:10-11 King Nebuchadrezzar…shall come and ravage the land of Egypt: Jeremiah prophesied against Egypt, but no historical records show that such a Babylonian destruction ever occurred.

43:13 He shall break the obelisks of Heliopolis: Heliopolis (HEE-lee-OP-o-lis), City of the Sun, was one of the most important religious sites in ancient Egypt. It is located just north of Cairo on the Nile River (see Map 1, p. 2098). An obelisk is a tall four-sided pillar covered with symbols and writings; it tapers as it rises toward the top.

44:2-14 Thus says the LORD of hosts, the God of Israel: The sermon has three parts. Verses 2-6 describe the past idolatries of the people. Verses 7-10 portray the present as they continue their unfaithfulness. Verses 11-14 tell of God’s future judgment.

they, nor you, nor your ancestors. 4 Yet I persistently sent to you all
my servants the prophets, saying, "I beg you not to do this abominable thing that I hate!" 5 But they did not listen or incline their ear, to
turn from their wickedness and make no offerings to other gods. 6 So
my wrath and my anger were poured out and kindled in the towns of
Judah and in the streets of Jerusalem; and they became a waste and
a desolation, as they still are today. 7 And now thus says the LORD
God of hosts, the God of Israel: Why are you doing such great harm
to yourselves, to cut off man and woman, child and infant, from the
midst of Judah, leaving yourselves without a remnant? 8 Why do you
provoke me to anger with the works of your hands, making offerings
to other gods in the land of Egypt where you have come to settle? Will
you be cut off and become an object of cursing and ridicule among
all the nations of the earth? 9 Have you forgotten the crimes of your
ancestors, of the kings of Judah, of their[a] wives, your own crimes and
those of your wives, which they committed in the land of Judah and
in the streets of Jerusalem? 10 They have shown no contrition or fear
to this day, nor have they walked in my law and my statutes that I set
before you and before your ancestors.

11 Therefore thus says the LORD of hosts, the God of Israel: I am
determined to bring disaster on you, to bring all Judah to an end. 12 I
will take the remnant of Judah who are determined to come to the
land of Egypt to settle, and they shall perish, everyone; in the land of
Egypt they shall fall; by the sword and by famine they shall perish;
from the least to the greatest, they shall die by the sword and by famine; and they shall become an object of execration and horror, of cursing and ridicule. 13 I will punish those who live in the land of Egypt,
as I have punished Jerusalem, with the sword, with famine, and with
pestilence, 14 so that none of the remnant of Judah who have come to
settle in the land of Egypt shall escape or survive or return to the land
of Judah. Although they long to go back to live there, they shall not go
back, except some fugitives.

15 Then all the men who were aware that their wives had been
making offerings to other gods, and all the women who stood by,
a great assembly, all the people who lived in Pathros in the land of
Egypt, answered Jeremiah: 16 "As for the word that you have spoken
to us in the name of the LORD, we are not going to listen to you. 17 Instead, we will do everything that we have vowed, make offerings to
the queen of heaven and pour out libations to her, just as we and our
ancestors, our kings and our officials, used to do in the towns of Judah
and in the streets of Jerusalem. We used to have plenty of food, and
prospered, and saw no misfortune. 18 But from the time we stopped
making offerings to the queen of heaven and pouring out libations to

---

[a] Heb *his*

her, we have lacked everything and have perished by the sword and by
famine.” 19 And the women said,[a] “Indeed we will go on making offerings to the queen of heaven and pouring out libations to her; do you
think that we made cakes for her, marked with her image, and poured
out libations to her without our husbands’ being involved?”

20 Then Jeremiah said to all the people, men and women, all the
people who were giving him this answer: 21 “As for the offerings that
you made in the towns of Judah and in the streets of Jerusalem, you
and your ancestors, your kings and your officials, and the people of
the land, did not the LORD remember them? Did it not come into his
mind? 22 The LORD could no longer bear the sight of your evil doings,
the abominations that you committed; therefore your land became
a desolation and a waste and a curse, without inhabitant, as it is to
this day. 23 It is because you burned offerings, and because you sinned
against the LORD and did not obey the voice of the LORD or walk
in his law and in his statutes and in his decrees, that this disaster has
befallen you, as is still evident today.”

24 Jeremiah said to all the people and all the women, “Hear the
word of the LORD, all you Judeans who are in the land of Egypt, 25 Thus
says the LORD of hosts, the God of Israel: You and your wives have accomplished in deeds what you declared in words, saying, ‘We are determined to perform the vows that we have made, to make offerings
to the queen of heaven and to pour out libations to her.’ By all means,
keep your vows and make your libations! 26 Therefore hear the word
of the LORD, all you Judeans who live in the land of Egypt: Lo, I swear
by my great name, says the LORD, that my name shall no longer be
pronounced on the lips of any of the people of Judah in all the land
of Egypt, saying, ‘As the Lord GOD lives.’ 27 I am going to watch over
them for harm and not for good; all the people of Judah who are in
the land of Egypt shall perish by the sword and by famine, until not
one is left. 28 And those who escape the sword shall return from the
land of Egypt to the land of Judah, few in number; and all the remnant
of Judah, who have come to the land of Egypt to settle, shall know
whose words will stand, mine or theirs! 29 This shall be the sign to you,
says the LORD, that I am going to punish you in this place, in order
that you may know that my words against you will surely be carried
out: 30 Thus says the LORD, I am going to give Pharaoh Hophra, king
of Egypt, into the hands of his enemies, those who seek his life, just as
I gave King Zedekiah of Judah into the hand of King Nebuchadrezzar
of Babylon, his enemy who sought his life.”

A Word of Comfort to Baruch

45 The word that the prophet Jeremiah spoke to Baruch son
of Neriah, when he wrote these words in a scroll at the dic-

[a] Compare Syr: Heb lacks *And the women said*

44:28 shall know whose word will stand, mine or theirs!: God’s word accomplishes what it says it will (Isa 55:10-11). God’s word brought into being all that exists (Gen 1). God’s word brought about the exile of the people of Judah and Jerusalem’s destruction (the subject of most of Jeremiah’s preaching), and God’s word would bring them home (Jer 29:10-14). This dynamic word makes God different from the idols (Isa 44:6-8). Eventually the word became flesh and dwelled among us (John 1:1-14).

45:1-5 The word that the prophet Jeremiah spoke to Baruch…in the fourth year of King Jehoiakim: The previous chapters described life for the Judeans in Egypt following the destruction of Jerusalem in 587 B.C.E. Now we suddenly read about an event that occurred eighteen years earlier. Like Jeremiah, Baruch laments his situation, but the LORD answers him with a promise.

tation of Jeremiah, in the fourth year of King Jehoiakim son of Josiah
of Judah: [2]Thus says the LORD, the God of Israel, to you, O Baruch:
[3]You said, "Woe is me! The LORD has added sorrow to my pain; I
am weary with my groaning, and I find no rest." [4]Thus you shall say
to him, "Thus says the LORD: I am going to break down what I have
built, and pluck up what I have planted—that is, the whole land. [5]And
you, do you seek great things for yourself? Do not seek them; for I am
going to bring disaster upon all flesh, says the LORD; but I will give
you your life as a prize of war in every place to which you may go."

Judgment on Egypt

46 The word of the LORD that came to the prophet Jeremiah concerning the nations.

2 Concerning Egypt, about the army of Pharaoh Neco, king of Egypt, which was by the river Euphrates at Carchemish and which King Nebuchadrezzar of Babylon defeated in the fourth year of King Jehoiakim son of Josiah of Judah:

3 Prepare buckler and shield,
and advance for battle!
4 Harness the horses;
mount the steeds!
Take your stations with your helmets,
whet your lances,
put on your coats of mail!
5 Why do I see them terrified?
They have fallen back;
their warriors are beaten down,
and have fled in haste.
They do not look back—
terror is all around!
says the LORD.
6 The swift cannot flee away,
nor can the warrior escape;
in the north by the river Euphrates
they have stumbled and fallen.

7 Who is this, rising like the Nile,
like rivers whose waters surge?
8 Egypt rises like the Nile,
like rivers whose waters surge.
It said, Let me rise, let me cover the earth,
let me destroy cities and their inhabitants.
9 Advance, O horses,
and dash madly, O chariots!
Let the warriors go forth:

45:5 your life as a prize of war: The word of the LORD to offer life as a booty or spoil of war goes out ironically to those who surrender to the Babylonians (21:9; 38:2). Likewise, the LORD offers the same spoil of life to Ebed-melech, the Ethiopian who saved Jeremiah's life (39:18). Now Baruch receives the promise of deliverance from disaster for his faithful service to the word of God. To him we owe the record of Jeremiah's preaching.

46:1—51:64 The word of the LORD: Disciples of the prophets, and later editors, gathered into one section of the book the messages the prophet spoke (or might have spoken) against foreign nations.

46:2 Concerning Egypt...at Carchemish: The Babylonians defeated the Egyptians at Carchemish (KAR-ke-mish) in 605 B.C.E., one of the great battles in history.

46:3-12 Prepare buckler and shield, and advance for battle!: We expect to read about the Babylonians driving back the Egyptians. Instead it is the LORD who causes panic among the Egyptian warriors and defeats them (Exod 14:27).

Ethiopia[a] and Put who carry the shield,
the Ludim, who draw[b] the bow.

10 That day is the day of the Lord GOD of hosts,
a day of retribution,
to gain vindication from his foes.
The sword shall devour and be sated,
and drink its fill of their blood.
For the Lord GOD of hosts holds a sacrifice
in the land of the north by the river Euphrates.

11 Go up to Gilead, and take balm,
O virgin daughter Egypt!
In vain you have used many medicines;
there is no healing for you.

12 The nations have heard of your shame,
and the earth is full of your cry;
for warrior has stumbled against warrior;
both have fallen together.

46:10 That day is the day of the LORD GOD of hosts: See the note on 31:31 ("days are surely coming"). In order for God to establish the divine reign, God becomes the divine warrior who defeats various forces of chaos (Exod 15:3, 18).

Babylonia Will Strike Egypt

13 The word that the LORD spoke to the prophet Jeremiah about
the coming of King Nebuchadrezzar of Babylon to attack the land of
Egypt:

14 Declare in Egypt, and proclaim in Migdol;
proclaim in Memphis and Tahpanhes;
Say, "Take your stations and be ready,
for the sword shall devour those around you."

15 Why has Apis fled?[c]
Why did your bull not stand?
—because the LORD thrust him down.

16 Your multitude stumbled[d] and fell,
and one said to another,[e]
"Come, let us go back to our own people
and to the land of our birth,
because of the destroying sword."

17 Give Pharaoh, king of Egypt, the name
"Braggart who missed his chance."

18 As I live, says the King,
whose name is the LORD of hosts,
one is coming
like Tabor among the mountains,
and like Carmel by the sea.

46:13-26 the coming of King Nebuchadrezzar of Babylon to attack the land of Egypt: The collection of sayings in 46:14-26 describes one of three situations. These sayings might describe the situation in 605 B.C.E. after the battle of Carchemish. They might report the days after the Babylonians destroyed Jerusalem while Jeremiah and the other Judeans were in Egypt. Or the sayings might portray Nebuchadrezzar's invasion of Egypt in 568–67 B.C.E. In any case, the message is clear: The LORD will bring the "servant" Nebuchadrezzar to destroy them all.

46:15 Why has Apis fled?: The Egyptians portrayed their gods as animals. Apis (AH-pis), a bull, was a form of the god Ptah, later called Osiris.

46:18 the King, whose name is the LORD of hosts: For LORD of hosts, see note on 2:19. The title *King* for the LORD here is unusual in Jeremiah. In contrast to the pharaoh, king of Egypt, the "Braggart who missed his chance" (46:17), the LORD is the ideal king, who takes advantage of the opportunity. In the Jerusalem temple, worshipers had praised the LORD as "a great King above all gods" (Ps 95:3). That is the reason Samuel was reluctant to grant the people's desire for "a king to govern us, like other nations" (1 Sam 8:4-22). One of the promises for the future day of the LORD was that the LORD's kingship would be over the world (Isa 24:23).

[a] Or *Nubia*; Heb *Cush* [b] Cn: Heb *who grasp, who draw* [c] Gk: Heb *Why was it swept away*
[d] Gk: Meaning of Heb uncertain [e] Gk: Heb *and fell one to another and they said*

19 Pack your bags for exile,
sheltered daughter Egypt!
For Memphis shall become a waste,
a ruin, without inhabitant.

20 A beautiful heifer is Egypt—
a gadfly from the north lights upon her.
21 Even her mercenaries in her midst
are like fatted calves;
they too have turned and fled together,
they did not stand;
for the day of their calamity has come upon them,
the time of their punishment.

22 She makes a sound like a snake gliding away;
for her enemies march in force,
and come against her with axes,
like those who fell trees.
23 They shall cut down her forest,
says the LORD,
though it is impenetrable,
because they are more numerous
than locusts;
they are without number.
24 Daughter Egypt shall be put to shame;
she shall be handed over to a people from the north.

25 The LORD of hosts, the God of Israel, said: See, I am bringing
punishment upon Amon of Thebes, and Pharaoh, and Egypt and her
gods and her kings, upon Pharaoh and those who trust in him. 26 I will
hand them over to those who seek their life, to King Nebuchadrezzar
of Babylon and his officers. Afterward Egypt shall be inhabited as in
the days of old, says the LORD.

46:25 Amon of Thebes: Amon (AHM-on), the chief god of Egypt, reigned from the temple of Karnak in Thebes, the capital of Egypt 2000–661 B.C.E.

God Will Save Israel

27 But as for you, have no fear, my servant Jacob,
and do not be dismayed, O Israel;
for I am going to save you from far away,
and your offspring from the land of their captivity.
Jacob shall return and have quiet and ease,
and no one shall make him afraid.
28 As for you, have no fear, my servant Jacob,
says the LORD,
for I am with you.
I will make an end of all the nations

46:28 have no fear…for I am with you: The promise of God to "my servant Jacob" promises deliverance for all the people of Judah and Israel who had been exiled to other lands between 721 (by Assyria) and 587 B.C.E. (by Babylon).

among which I have banished you,
but I will not make an end of you!
I will chastise you in just measure,
and I will by no means leave you unpunished.

Judgment on the Philistines

47:1 concerning the Philistines: The Philistines (fi-LIS-teens), the so-called Sea Peoples, moved into the area along the coast of the Mediterranean Sea as they conquered many other countries, including Egypt, about 1200 B.C.E. After the Egyptians drove them out, they settled in the coastal area east of Jerusalem. The introduction to the following verses sets the historical situation in 609 B.C.E., when Neco II had been returning from his victory at Megiddo, where he killed Judah's king Josiah.

47:2-7 waters are rising out of the north: We might assume this northern enemy is Babylon. But there is no reference to that country or any other. The destructive enemy is the LORD, armed with a sword dedicated to judgment (47:6-7).

47:4 the remnant of the coastland of Caphtor: According to the biblical tradition, the Philistines were descendants of Caphtor (KAF-tohr), which is Crete (see Ezek 25:16; Zeph 2:5). See Map 10, p. 2107.

47:5 Baldness has come upon Gaza, Ashkelon is silenced: The Philistine territory included five major cities: Gaza (GAH-za), Ashkelon (ASH-ke-lon), Ashdod (ASH-dod), Gath, and Ekron. The baldness, silence, and gashing are part of the mourning rites over their coming destruction.

47 The word of the LORD that came to the prophet Jeremiah concerning the Philistines, before Pharaoh attacked Gaza:
2 Thus says the LORD:
See, waters are rising out of the north
and shall become an overflowing torrent;
they shall overflow the land and all that fills it,
the city and those who live in it.
People shall cry out,
and all the inhabitants of the land shall wail.
3 At the noise of the stamping of the hoofs of his stallions,
at the clatter of his chariots, at the rumbling of their wheels,
parents do not turn back for children,
so feeble are their hands,
4 because of the day that is coming
to destroy all the Philistines,
to cut off from Tyre and Sidon
every helper that remains.
For the LORD is destroying the Philistines,
the remnant of the coastland of Caphtor.
5 Baldness has come upon Gaza,
Ashkelon is silenced.
O remnant of their power![a]
How long will you gash yourselves?
6 Ah, sword of the LORD!
How long until you are quiet?
Put yourself into your scabbard,
rest and be still!
7 How can it[b] be quiet,
when the LORD has given it an order?
Against Ashkelon and against the seashore—
there he has appointed it.

Judgment on Moab

48:1-47 Concerning Moab: During the thirteenth century B.C.E., desert tribes established the Kingdom of Moab in the lower half of the eastern side of the Dead Sea. Moab apparently mocked, or made fun of, Israel over the years.

48 Concerning Moab.

Thus says the LORD of hosts, the God of Israel:
Alas for Nebo, it is laid waste!

---

[a] Gk: Heb *their valley* [b] Gk Vg: Heb *you*

Kiriathaim is put to shame, it is taken;
the fortress is put to shame and broken down;
2 the renown of Moab is no more.
In Heshbon they planned evil against her:
"Come, let us cut her off from being a nation!"
You also, O Madmen, shall be brought to silence;[a]
the sword shall pursue you.

3 Hark! a cry from Horonaim,
"Desolation and great destruction!"
4 "Moab is destroyed!"
her little ones cry out.
5 For at the ascent of Luhith
they go[b] up weeping bitterly;
for at the descent of Horonaim
they have heard the distressing cry of anguish.
6 Flee! Save yourselves!
Be like a wild ass[c] in the desert!

7 Surely, because you trusted in your strongholds[d] and your treasures,
you also shall be taken;
Chemosh shall go out into exile,
with his priests and his attendants.
8 The destroyer shall come upon every town,
and no town shall escape;
the valley shall perish,
and the plain shall be destroyed,
as the LORD has spoken.

9 Set aside salt for Moab,
for she will surely fall;
her towns shall become a desolation,
with no inhabitant in them.

10 Accursed is the one who is slack in doing the work of the LORD; and accursed is the one who keeps back the sword from bloodshed.

11 Moab has been at ease from his youth,
settled like wine[e] on its dregs;
he has not been emptied from vessel to vessel,
nor has he gone into exile;

---

[a] The place-name *Madmen* sounds like the Hebrew verb *to be silent* [b] Cn: Heb *he goes* [c] Gk Aquila: Heb *like Aroer* [d] Gk: Heb *works* [e] Heb lacks *like wine*

therefore his flavor has remained
and his aroma is unspoiled.

12 Therefore, the time is surely coming, says the LORD, when I
shall send to him decanters to decant him, and empty his vessels, and
break his[a] jars in pieces. 13 Then Moab shall be ashamed of Chemosh,
as the house of Israel was ashamed of Bethel, their confidence.

14 How can you say, "We are heroes
and mighty warriors"?
15 The destroyer of Moab and his towns has come up,
and the choicest of his young men have gone down to slaughter,
says the King, whose name is the LORD of hosts.
16 The calamity of Moab is near at hand
and his doom approaches swiftly.
17 Mourn over him, all you his neighbors,
and all who know his name;
say, "How the mighty scepter is broken,
the glorious staff!"

18 Come down from glory,
and sit on the parched ground,
enthroned daughter Dibon!
For the destroyer of Moab has come up against you;
he has destroyed your strongholds.
19 Stand by the road and watch,
you inhabitant of Aroer!
Ask the man fleeing and the woman escaping;
say, "What has happened?"
20 Moab is put to shame, for it is broken down;
wail and cry!
Tell it by the Arnon,
that Moab is laid waste.

21 Judgment has come upon the tableland, upon Holon, and Jahzah, and Mephaath, 22 and Dibon, and Nebo, and Beth-diblathaim,
23 and Kiriathaim, and Beth-gamul, and Beth-meon, 24 and Kerioth,
and Bozrah, and all the towns of the land of Moab, far and near. 25 The
horn of Moab is cut off, and his arm is broken, says the LORD.

26 Make him drunk, because he magnified himself against the
LORD; let Moab wallow in his vomit; he too shall become a laughingstock. 27 Israel was a laughingstock for you, though he was not
caught among thieves; but whenever you spoke of him you shook
your head!

---

[a] Gk Aquila: Heb *their*

28 Leave the towns, and live on the rock,
O inhabitants of Moab!
Be like the dove that nests
on the sides of the mouth of a gorge.
29 We have heard of the pride of Moab—
he is very proud—
of his loftiness, his pride, and his arrogance,
and the haughtiness of his heart.
30 I myself know his insolence, says the LORD;
his boasts are false,
his deeds are false.
31 Therefore I wail for Moab;
I cry out for all Moab;
for the people of Kir-heres I mourn.
32 More than for Jazer I weep for you,
O vine of Sibmah!
Your branches crossed over the sea,
reached as far as Jazer;[a]
upon your summer fruits and your vintage
the destroyer has fallen.
33 Gladness and joy have been taken away
from the fruitful land of Moab;
I have stopped the wine from the wine presses;
no one treads them with shouts of joy;
the shouting is not the shout of joy.

34 Heshbon and Elealeh cry out;[b] as far as Jahaz they utter their
voice, from Zoar to Horonaim and Eglath-shelishiyah. For even the
waters of Nimrim have become desolate. 35 And I will bring to an end
in Moab, says the LORD, those who offer sacrifice at a high place and
make offerings to their gods. 36 Therefore my heart moans for Moab
like a flute, and my heart moans like a flute for the people of Kir-heres;
for the riches they gained have perished.
37 For every head is shaved and every beard cut off; on all the
hands there are gashes, and on the loins sackcloth. 38 On all the housetops of Moab and in the squares there is nothing but lamentation; for
I have broken Moab like a vessel that no one wants, says the LORD.
39 How it is broken! How they wail! How Moab has turned his back
in shame! So Moab has become a derision and a horror to all his
neighbors.

40 For thus says the LORD:
Look, he shall swoop down like an eagle,
and spread his wings against Moab;

---

[a] Two Mss and Isa 16.8: MT *the sea of Jazer* [b] Cn: Heb *From the cry of Heshbon to Elealeh*

41 the towns[a] shall be taken
and the strongholds seized.
The hearts of the warriors of Moab, on that day,
shall be like the heart of a woman in labor.
42 Moab shall be destroyed as a people,
because he magnified himself against the LORD.
43 Terror, pit, and trap
are before you, O inhabitants of Moab!
says the LORD.
44 Everyone who flees from the terror
shall fall into the pit,
and everyone who climbs out of the pit
shall be caught in the trap.
For I will bring these things[b] upon Moab
in the year of their punishment,
says the LORD.

45 In the shadow of Heshbon
fugitives stop exhausted;
for a fire has gone out from Heshbon,
a flame from the house of Sihon;
it has destroyed the forehead of Moab,
the scalp of the people of tumult.[c]
46 Woe to you, O Moab!
The people of Chemosh have perished,
for your sons have been taken captive,
and your daughters into captivity.
47 Yet I will restore the fortunes of Moab
in the latter days, says the LORD.
Thus far is the judgment on Moab.

48:47 I will restore the fortunes of Moab: The Moabites will experience the same restoration promised to Israel and Judah.

How does this promise (48:47) of God's grace to the nations, like Moab, even those that do not worship the LORD, influence your prayers, attitudes, and actions?

49:1-6 Concerning the Ammonites: The territory of Ammon lay north of Moab and east of the Jordan River from Israel. The Israelite tribes of Reuben and Gad lost their territory to the Ammonites and their god Milcom (or Molech; see note on 7:31).

49:2 Rabbah: The ancient name of the capital of Ammon, known today as Amman.

Judgment on the Ammonites

49 Concerning the Ammonites.

Thus says the LORD:
Has Israel no sons?
Has he no heir?
Why then has Milcom dispossessed Gad,
and his people settled in its towns?
2 Therefore, the time is surely coming,
says the LORD,
when I will sound the battle alarm
against Rabbah of the Ammonites;

[a] Or *Kerioth* [b] Gk Syr: Heb *bring upon it* [c] Or *of Shaon*

it shall become a desolate mound,
and its villages shall be burned with fire;
then Israel shall dispossess those who dispossessed him,
says the LORD.

3 Wail, O Heshbon, for Ai is laid waste!
Cry out, O daughters[a] of Rabbah!
Put on sackcloth,
lament, and slash yourselves with whips![b]
For Milcom shall go into exile,
with his priests and his attendants.
4 Why do you boast in your strength?
Your strength is ebbing,
O faithless daughter.
You trusted in your treasures, saying,
"Who will attack me?"
5 I am going to bring terror upon you,
says the Lord GOD of hosts,
from all your neighbors,
and you will be scattered, each headlong,
with no one to gather the fugitives.
6 But afterward I will restore the fortunes of the Ammonites, says the LORD.

Judgment on Edom

7 Concerning Edom.

Thus says the LORD of hosts:
Is there no longer wisdom in Teman?
Has counsel perished from the prudent?
Has their wisdom vanished?
8 Flee, turn back, get down low,
inhabitants of Dedan!
For I will bring the calamity of Esau upon him,
the time when I punish him.
9 If grape-gatherers came to you,
would they not leave gleanings?
If thieves came by night,
even they would pillage only what they wanted.
10 But as for me, I have stripped Esau bare,
I have uncovered his hiding places,
and he is not able to conceal himself.
His offspring are destroyed, his kinsfolk
and his neighbors; and he is no more.

49:7-22 Concerning Edom: According to the biblical tradition, the Edomites traced their family tree to Esau (Gen 36). Their territory was located south of Moab. The Edomites cheered on the destroyers of Jerusalem in 587 B.C.E. See Map 4, p. 2102.

49:7 no longer wisdom in Teman?: One of Job's three friends who talked about wisdom was Eliphaz the Temanite (Job 2:11).

49:8 inhabitants of Dedan!: Dedan (DEE-dan) is the name of a people rather than a place. They lived southeast of Edom. They had a reputation as merchants and caravan traders (Isa 21:13; Ezek 27:20; 38:13).

[a] Or *villages* [b] Cn: Meaning of Heb uncertain

11 Leave your orphans, I will keep them alive;
and let your widows trust in me.
12 For thus says the LORD: If those who do not deserve to drink
the cup still have to drink it, shall you be the one to go unpunished?
You shall not go unpunished; you must drink it. 13 For by myself I have
sworn, says the LORD, that Bozrah shall become an object of horror
and ridicule, a waste, and an object of cursing; and all her towns shall
be perpetual wastes.

14 I have heard tidings from the LORD,
and a messenger has been sent among the nations:
"Gather yourselves together and come against her,
and rise up for battle!"
15 For I will make you least among the nations,
despised by humankind.
16 The terror you inspire
and the pride of your heart have deceived you,
you who live in the clefts of the rock,[a]
who hold the height of the hill.
Although you make your nest as high as the eagle's,
from there I will bring you down,
says the LORD.

17 Edom shall become an object of horror; everyone who passes
by it will be horrified and will hiss because of all its disasters. 18 As
when Sodom and Gomorrah and their neighbors were overthrown,
says the LORD, no one shall live there, nor shall anyone settle in it.
19 Like a lion coming up from the thickets of the Jordan against a
perennial pasture, I will suddenly chase Edom[b] away from it; and I
will appoint over it whomever I choose.[c] For who is like me? Who
can summon me? Who is the shepherd who can stand before me?
20 Therefore hear the plan that the LORD has made against Edom and
the purposes that he has formed against the inhabitants of Teman:
Surely the little ones of the flock shall be dragged away; surely their
fold shall be appalled at their fate. 21 At the sound of their fall the earth
shall tremble; the sound of their cry shall be heard at the Red Sea.[d]
22 Look, he shall mount up and swoop down like an eagle, and spread
his wings against Bozrah, and the heart of the warriors of Edom in
that day shall be like the heart of a woman in labor.

Judgment on Damascus

23 Concerning Damascus.

Hamath and Arpad are confounded,
for they have heard bad news;

49:22 Bozrah: Known for its strength as a fortified Edomite city, Bozrah (BOZ-ra) was located about twenty miles southeast of the southern tip of the Dead Sea.

49:23-27 Concerning Damascus: Damascus (da-MAS-kus) was the capital of the Aramean kingdom (Gen 14:15; 1 Kgs 11:24; 2 Kgs 8:7, 9) and is now the capital of Syria.

49:23 Hamath and Arpad: Both cities were located north of Damascus.

[a] Or *of Sela* [b] Heb *him* [c] Or *and I will single out the choicest of his rams*: Meaning of Heb uncertain
[d] Or *Sea of Reeds*

they melt in fear, they are troubled like the sea[a]
that cannot be quiet.
24 Damascus has become feeble, she turned to flee,
and panic seized her;
anguish and sorrows have taken hold of her,
as of a woman in labor.
25 How the famous city is forsaken,[b]
the joyful town![c]
26 Therefore her young men shall fall in her squares,
and all her soldiers shall be destroyed in that day,
says the LORD of hosts.
27 And I will kindle a fire at the wall of Damascus,
and it shall devour the strongholds of Ben-hadad.

Judgment on Kedar and Hazor

28 Concerning Kedar and the kingdoms of Hazor that King Nebuchadrezzar of Babylon defeated.

Thus says the LORD:
Rise up, advance against Kedar!
Destroy the people of the east!
29 Take their tents and their flocks,
their curtains and all their goods;
carry off their camels for yourselves,
and a cry shall go up: "Terror is all around!"
30 Flee, wander far away, hide in deep places,
O inhabitants of Hazor!
says the LORD.
For King Nebuchadrezzar of Babylon
has made a plan against you
and formed a purpose against you.

31 Rise up, advance against a nation at ease,
that lives secure,
says the LORD,
that has no gates or bars,
that lives alone.
32 Their camels shall become booty,
their herds of cattle a spoil.
I will scatter to every wind
those who have shaven temples,
and I will bring calamity

49:27 the strongholds of Ben-hadad: Ben-hadad (ben-HA-dad) was the founder of a dynasty that began about 900 B.C.E. His treaties and conflicts with Judah and Israel make him a popular name in the Old Testament (see 1 Kgs 15:18-21; 20:1-34).

49:28-33 Concerning Kedar and the kingdoms of Hazor: Kedar (KEE-dar) was the name for tribes who lived in black tents (Song 1:5), inhabited villages (Isa 42:11), and shepherded flocks (Isa 60:7). Mentioned previously at Jeremiah 2:10, Kedar's territory seems to have been in northwestern Arabia between Moab and Dedan. Hazor (ha-TSOR) is not the Hazor of northern Galilee but a center for nomadic tribes in Arabia.

[a] Cn: Heb *there is trouble in the sea* [b] Vg: Heb *is not forsaken* [c] Syr Vg Tg: Heb *the town of my joy*

against them from every side,
says the LORD.

33 Hazor shall become a lair of jackals,
an everlasting waste;
no one shall live there,
nor shall anyone settle in it.

Judgment on Elam

49:34-39 concerning Elam: Elam lay to the east of Babylon. Its warriors had a reputation as archers (Isa 22:6) who rode on chariots.

34 The word of the LORD that came to the prophet Jeremiah concerning Elam, at the beginning of the reign of King Zedekiah of Judah.

35 Thus says the LORD of hosts: I am going to break the bow of
Elam, the mainstay of their might; 36 and I will bring upon Elam the
four winds from the four quarters of heaven; and I will scatter them to
all these winds, and there shall be no nation to which the exiles from
Elam shall not come. 37 I will terrify Elam before their enemies, and
before those who seek their life; I will bring disaster upon them, my
fierce anger, says the LORD. I will send the sword after them, until I
have consumed them; 38 and I will set my throne in Elam, and destroy
their king and officials, says the LORD.

39 But in the latter days I will restore the fortunes of Elam, says
the LORD.

Judgment on Babylon

50:1—51:64 concerning Babylon: These prophecies are two long chapters about Babylon's destruction. The Babylonians have brought on their own destruction because they "challenged the LORD" (50:24) and "arrogantly defied the LORD" (50:29). The oracles, or speeches, against Babylon collected here must have originated during the exile (597–538 B.C.E.). In 539 King Cyrus of Persia conquered but did not damage the city.

50:2 Bel is put to shame, Merodach is dismayed: God will humble Bel (BALE), also known as Merodach (Marduk), Babylon's chief god.

50:3 out of the north: Jeremiah's sermons gave the impression that Nebuchadrezzar was the foe from the north. Now that northern warrior comes against Babylon itself. Readers can sense that the warrior is, and has always been, the LORD.

50 The word that the LORD spoke concerning Babylon, concerning the land of the Chaldeans, by the prophet Jeremiah:

2 Declare among the nations and proclaim,
set up a banner and proclaim,
do not conceal it, say:
Babylon is taken,
Bel is put to shame,
Merodach is dismayed.
Her images are put to shame,
her idols are dismayed.

3 For out of the north a nation has come up against her; it shall
make her land a desolation, and no one shall live in it; both human
beings and animals shall flee away.

4 In those days and in that time, says the LORD, the people of
Israel shall come, they and the people of Judah together; they shall
come weeping as they seek the LORD their God. 5 They shall ask the
way to Zion, with faces turned toward it, and they shall come and
join[a] themselves to the LORD by an everlasting covenant that will
never be forgotten.

---

[a] Gk: Heb *toward it. Come! They shall join*

6 My people have been lost sheep; their shepherds have led them
astray, turning them away on the mountains; from mountain to hill
they have gone, they have forgotten their fold. 7 All who found them
have devoured them, and their enemies have said, "We are not guilty,
because they have sinned against the LORD, the true pasture, the
LORD, the hope of their ancestors."

8 Flee from Babylon, and go out of the land of the Chaldeans,
and be like male goats leading the flock. 9 For I am going to stir up
and bring against Babylon a company of great nations from the land
of the north; and they shall array themselves against her; from there
she shall be taken. Their arrows are like the arrows of a skilled warrior
who does not return empty-handed. 10 Chaldea shall be plundered; all
who plunder her shall be sated, says the LORD.

11 Though you rejoice, though you exult,
O plunderers of my heritage,
though you frisk about like a heifer on the grass,
and neigh like stallions,
12 your mother shall be utterly shamed,
and she who bore you shall be disgraced.
Lo, she shall be the last of the nations,
a wilderness, dry land, and a desert.
13 Because of the wrath of the LORD she shall not be
inhabited,
but shall be an utter desolation;
everyone who passes by Babylon shall be appalled
and hiss because of all her wounds.
14 Take up your positions around Babylon,
all you that bend the bow;
shoot at her, spare no arrows,
for she has sinned against the LORD.
15 Raise a shout against her from all sides,
"She has surrendered;
her bulwarks have fallen,
her walls are thrown down."
For this is the vengeance of the LORD:
take vengeance on her,
do to her as she has done.
16 Cut off from Babylon the sower,
and the wielder of the sickle in time of harvest;
because of the destroying sword
all of them shall return to their own people,
and all of them shall flee to their own land.

50:17-20 Israel is a hunted sheep driven away by lions: These verses present the history of Israel and Judah 721–539 B.C.E. The Assyrians, who destroyed the northern kingdom of Israel in 721, suffered defeat by the Egyptians in 612. The Babylonian involvement and destruction of Judah was 605–539 B.C.E.

50:21 the land of Merathaim…the inhabitants of Pekod: These are all invented names for Babylon. Merathaim (MAY-ra-THA-im) means "double rebellion," and Pekod (PEE-kod) means "punishment."

50:28 the vengeance of the LORD our God, vengeance for his temple: Jeremiah's judgment on the temple was negative (chapter 7) because the people used the building itself for false optimism. Now God is repaying the Babylonians for destroying the temple. Here the word *vengeance* means payment or compensation, not "get even." God's promised action is just, not based merely on anger (see also 51:6, 11, 36).

17 Israel is a hunted sheep driven away by lions. First the king
of Assyria devoured it, and now at the end King Nebuchadrezzar of
Babylon has gnawed its bones. 18 Therefore, thus says the LORD of
hosts, the God of Israel: I am going to punish the king of Babylon
and his land, as I punished the king of Assyria. 19 I will restore Israel
to its pasture, and it shall feed on Carmel and in Bashan, and on the
hills of Ephraim and in Gilead its hunger shall be satisfied. 20 In those
days and at that time, says the LORD, the iniquity of Israel shall be
sought, and there shall be none; and the sins of Judah, and none shall
be found; for I will pardon the remnant that I have spared.

21 Go up to the land of Merathaim;[a]
go up against her,
and attack the inhabitants of Pekod[b]
and utterly destroy the last of them,[c]
says the LORD;
do all that I have commanded you.
22 The noise of battle is in the land,
and great destruction!
23 How the hammer of the whole earth
is cut down and broken!
How Babylon has become
a horror among the nations!
24 You set a snare for yourself and you were caught, O Babylon,
but you did not know it;
you were discovered and seized,
because you challenged the LORD.
25 The LORD has opened his armory,
and brought out the weapons of his wrath,
for the Lord GOD of hosts has a task to do
in the land of the Chaldeans.
26 Come against her from every quarter;
open her granaries;
pile her up like heaps of grain, and destroy her utterly;
let nothing be left of her.
27 Kill all her bulls,
let them go down to the slaughter.
Alas for them, their day has come,
the time of their punishment!

28 Listen! Fugitives and refugees from the land of Babylon are
coming to declare in Zion the vengeance of the LORD our God, vengeance for his temple.

---

[a] Or *of Double Rebellion* [b] Or *of Punishment* [c] Tg: Heb *destroy after them*

29 Summon archers against Babylon, all who bend the bow. Encamp all around her; let no one escape. Repay her according to her
deeds; just as she has done, do to her—for she has arrogantly defied
the LORD, the Holy One of Israel. 30 Therefore her young men shall
fall in her squares, and all her soldiers shall be destroyed on that day,
says the LORD.

31 I am against you, O arrogant one,
says the Lord GOD of hosts;
for your day has come,
the time when I will punish you.
32 The arrogant one shall stumble and fall,
with no one to raise him up,
and I will kindle a fire in his cities,
and it will devour everything around him.

33 Thus says the LORD of hosts: The people of Israel are oppressed, and so too are the people of Judah; all their captors have held
them fast and refuse to let them go. 34 Their Redeemer is strong; the
LORD of hosts is his name. He will surely plead their cause, that he
may give rest to the earth, but unrest to the inhabitants of Babylon.

35 A sword against the Chaldeans, says the LORD,
and against the inhabitants of Babylon,
and against her officials and her sages!
36 A sword against the diviners,
so that they may become fools!
A sword against her warriors,
so that they may be destroyed!
37 A sword against her[a] horses and against her[a] chariots,
and against all the foreign troops in her midst,
so that they may become women!
A sword against all her treasures,
that they may be plundered!
38 A drought[b] against her waters,
that they may be dried up!
For it is a land of images,
and they go mad over idols.

39 Therefore wild animals shall live with hyenas in Babylon,[c] and
ostriches shall inhabit her; she shall never again be peopled, or inhabited for all generations. 40 As when God overthrew Sodom and Gomorrah and their neighbors, says the LORD, so no one shall live there,
nor shall anyone settle in her.

---

[a] Cn: Heb *his* [b] Another reading is *A sword* [c] Heb lacks *in Babylon*

41 Look, a people is coming from the north;
a mighty nation and many kings
are stirring from the farthest parts of the earth.
42 They wield bow and spear,
they are cruel and have no mercy.
The sound of them is like the roaring sea;
they ride upon horses,
set in array as a warrior for battle,
against you, O daughter Babylon!

43 The king of Babylon heard news of them,
and his hands fell helpless;
anguish seized him,
pain like that of a woman in labor.

44 Like a lion coming up from the thickets of the Jordan against
a perennial pasture, I will suddenly chase them away from her; and I
will appoint over her whomever I choose.[a] For who is like me? Who
can summon me? Who is the shepherd who can stand before me?
45 Therefore hear the plan that the LORD has made against Babylon,
and the purposes that he has formed against the land of the Chaldeans: Surely the little ones of the flock shall be dragged away; surely
their[b] fold shall be appalled at their fate. 46 At the sound of the capture
of Babylon the earth shall tremble, and her cry shall be heard among
the nations.

51 Thus says the LORD:
I am going to stir up a destructive wind[c]
against Babylon
and against the inhabitants of Leb-qamai;[d]
2 and I will send winnowers to Babylon,
and they shall winnow her.
They shall empty her land
when they come against her from every side
on the day of trouble.
3 Let not the archer bend his bow,
and let him not array himself in his coat of mail.
Do not spare her young men;
utterly destroy her entire army.
4 They shall fall down slain in the land of the Chaldeans,
and wounded in her streets.
5 Israel and Judah have not been forsaken

51:5 Israel and Judah have not been forsaken by their God, the LORD of hosts: God has not abandoned the people, contrary to their laments.

[a] Or *and I will single out the choicest of her rams*: Meaning of Heb uncertain [b] Syr Gk Tg Compare 49.20: Heb lacks *their* [c] Or *stir up the spirit of a destroyer* [d] *Leb-qamai* is a cryptogram for *Kasdim*, Chaldea

by their God, the LORD of hosts,
though their land is full of guilt
before the Holy One of Israel.

6 Flee from the midst of Babylon,
save your lives, each of you!
Do not perish because of her guilt,
for this is the time of the LORD's vengeance;
he is repaying her what is due.
7 Babylon was a golden cup in the LORD's hand,
making all the earth drunken;
the nations drank of her wine,
and so the nations went mad.
8 Suddenly Babylon has fallen and is shattered;
wail for her!
Bring balm for her wound;
perhaps she may be healed.
9 We tried to heal Babylon,
but she could not be healed.
Forsake her, and let each of us go
to our own country;
for her judgment has reached up to heaven
and has been lifted up even to the skies.
10 The LORD has brought forth our vindication;
come, let us declare in Zion
the work of the LORD our God.

11 Sharpen the arrows!
Fill the quivers!
The LORD has stirred up the spirit of the kings of the Medes, because
his purpose concerning Babylon is to destroy it, for that is the vengeance of the LORD, vengeance for his temple.
12 Raise a standard against the walls of Babylon;
make the watch strong;
post sentinels;
prepare the ambushes;
for the LORD has both planned and done
what he spoke concerning the inhabitants of Babylon.
13 You who live by mighty waters,
rich in treasures,
your end has come,
the thread of your life is cut.
14 The LORD of hosts has sworn by himself:
Surely I will fill you with troops like a swarm of locusts,
and they shall raise a shout of victory over you.

51:11 The LORD has stirred up the spirit of the kings of the Medes: The Medes joined with the Persians to bring down the Babylonian Empire in 539 B.C.E. See Map 10, p. 2107.

51:15-19 It is he who made the earth by his power: The passage is identical to 10:12-16. As in Psalm 135, God puts human-made idols to shame and claims the people of Israel as God's protected possession (Exod 19:5-6).

15 It is he who made the earth by his power,
who established the world by his wisdom,
and by his understanding stretched out the heavens.
16 When he utters his voice there is a tumult of waters in the heavens,
and he makes the mist rise from the ends of the earth.
He makes lightnings for the rain,
and he brings out the wind from his storehouses.
17 Everyone is stupid and without knowledge;
goldsmiths are all put to shame by their idols;
for their images are false,
and there is no breath in them.
18 They are worthless, a work of delusion;
at the time of their punishment they shall perish.
19 Not like these is the LORD,[a] the portion of Jacob,
for he is the one who formed all things,
and Israel is the tribe of his inheritance;
the LORD of hosts is his name.

Israel the Creator's Instrument

20 You are my war club, my weapon of battle:
with you I smash nations;
with you I destroy kingdoms;
21 with you I smash the horse and its rider;
with you I smash the chariot and the charioteer;
22 with you I smash man and woman;
with you I smash the old man and the boy;
with you I smash the young man and the girl;
23 with you I smash shepherds and their flocks;
with you I smash farmers and their teams;
with you I smash governors and deputies.

The Doom of Babylon

24 I will repay Babylon and all the inhabitants of Chaldea before your very eyes for all the wrong that they have done in Zion, says the LORD.

25 I am against you, O destroying mountain,
says the LORD,
that destroys the whole earth;
I will stretch out my hand against you,
and roll you down from the crags,
and make you a burned-out mountain.

[a] Heb lacks *the LORD*

26 No stone shall be taken from you for a corner
and no stone for a foundation,
but you shall be a perpetual waste,
says the LORD.

27 Raise a standard in the land,
blow the trumpet among the nations;
prepare the nations for war against her,
summon against her the kingdoms,
Ararat, Minni, and Ashkenaz;
appoint a marshal against her,
bring up horses like bristling locusts.
28 Prepare the nations for war against her,
the kings of the Medes, with their governors and deputies,
and every land under their dominion.
29 The land trembles and writhes,
for the LORD's purposes against Babylon stand,
to make the land of Babylon a desolation,
without inhabitant.
30 The warriors of Babylon have given up fighting,
they remain in their strongholds;
their strength has failed,
they have become women;
her buildings are set on fire,
her bars are broken.
31 One runner runs to meet another,
and one messenger to meet another,
to tell the king of Babylon
that his city is taken from end to end:
32 the fords have been seized,
the marshes have been burned with fire,
and the soldiers are in panic.
33 For thus says the LORD of hosts, the God of Israel:
Daughter Babylon is like a threshing floor
at the time when it is trodden;
yet a little while
and the time of her harvest will come.

34 "King Nebuchadrezzar of Babylon has devoured me,
he has crushed me;
he has made me an empty vessel,
he has swallowed me like a monster;
he has filled his belly with my delicacies,
he has spewed me out.
35 May my torn flesh be avenged on Babylon,"

51:27 summon against her the kingdoms, Ararat, Minni, and Ashkenaz: Ararat first appears in the Bible at Genesis 8:4, where Noah's ark "came to rest on the mountains of Ararat." The ancient land became Armenia. Minni does not appear elsewhere in the Bible. Scholars think it was north of Assyria. Minni's people, the Manneans, fought alongside the Ashkenaz warriors against Assyria in the seventh century B.C.E.

the inhabitants of Zion shall say.
"May my blood be avenged on the inhabitants of Chaldea,"
Jerusalem shall say.
36 Therefore thus says the LORD:
I am going to defend your cause
and take vengeance for you.
I will dry up her sea
and make her fountain dry;
37 and Babylon shall become a heap of ruins,
a den of jackals,
an object of horror and of hissing,
without inhabitant.

38 Like lions they shall roar together;
they shall growl like lions' whelps.
39 When they are inflamed, I will set out their drink
and make them drunk, until they become merry
and then sleep a perpetual sleep
and never wake, says the LORD.
40 I will bring them down like lambs to the slaughter,
like rams and goats.

41 How Sheshach[a] is taken,
the pride of the whole earth seized!
How Babylon has become
an object of horror among the nations!
42 The sea has risen over Babylon;
she has been covered by its tumultuous waves.
43 Her cities have become an object of horror,
a land of drought and a desert,
a land in which no one lives,
and through which no mortal passes.
44 I will punish Bel in Babylon,
and make him disgorge what he has swallowed.
The nations shall no longer stream to him;
the wall of Babylon has fallen.

45 Come out of her, my people!
Save your lives, each of you,
from the fierce anger of the LORD!
46 Do not be fainthearted or fearful
at the rumors heard in the land—
one year one rumor comes,
the next year another,

---

[a] *Sheshach* is a cryptogram for *Babel*, Babylon

rumors of violence in the land
    and of ruler against ruler.

47 Assuredly, the days are coming
    when I will punish the images of Babylon;
her whole land shall be put to shame,
    and all her slain shall fall in her midst.
48 Then the heavens and the earth,
    and all that is in them,
shall shout for joy over Babylon;
    for the destroyers shall come against them out of the north,
        says the LORD.
49 Babylon must fall for the slain of Israel,
    as the slain of all the earth have fallen because of Babylon.

50 You survivors of the sword,
    go, do not linger!
Remember the LORD in a distant land,
    and let Jerusalem come into your mind:
51 We are put to shame, for we have heard insults;
    dishonor has covered our face,
for aliens have come
    into the holy places of the LORD's house.

52 Therefore the time is surely coming, says the LORD,
    when I will punish her idols,
and through all her land
    the wounded shall groan.
53 Though Babylon should mount up to heaven,
    and though she should fortify her strong height,
from me destroyers would come upon her,
    says the LORD.

54 Listen!—a cry from Babylon!
    A great crashing from the land of the Chaldeans!
55 For the LORD is laying Babylon waste,
    and stilling her loud clamor.
Their waves roar like mighty waters,
    the sound of their clamor resounds;
56 for a destroyer has come against her,
    against Babylon;
her warriors are taken,
    their bows are broken;
for the LORD is a God of recompense,
    he will repay in full.

51:51 for aliens have come into the holy places of the LORD's house: The Holy of Holies, the most holy place, was the innermost room of the temple, where the ark of the covenant rested (1 Kgs 8:6). Only the high priest was allowed in this room. The invasion by foreigners (aliens) must have been appalling.

57 I will make her officials and her sages drunk,
also her governors, her deputies, and her warriors;
they shall sleep a perpetual sleep and never wake,
says the King, whose name is the LORD of hosts.

58 Thus says the LORD of hosts:
The broad wall of Babylon
shall be leveled to the ground,
and her high gates
shall be burned with fire.
The peoples exhaust themselves for nothing,
and the nations weary themselves only for fire.[a]

Jeremiah's Command to Seraiah

51:59-64 The word that the prophet Jeremiah commanded Seraiah son of Neriah: This narrative ends the section about judgment against the nations (chapters 46–51). It brings us back to the dramatic prophecies earlier in the book. The setting is 594 B.C.E., seven years prior to the fall of Jerusalem and fifty-five years before the fall of Babylon.

59 The word that the prophet Jeremiah commanded Seraiah son of Neriah son of Mahseiah, when he went with King Zedekiah of Judah to Babylon, in the fourth year of his reign. Seraiah was the quartermaster. 60 Jeremiah wrote in a[b] scroll all the disasters that would come on Babylon, all these words that are written concerning Babylon. 61 And Jeremiah said to Seraiah: "When you come to Babylon, see that you read all these words, 62 and say, 'O LORD, you yourself threatened to destroy this place so that neither human beings nor animals shall live in it, and it shall be desolate forever.' 63 When you finish reading this scroll, tie a stone to it, and throw it into the middle of the Euphrates, 64 and say, 'Thus shall Babylon sink, to rise no more, because of the disasters that I am bringing on her.' "[c]

Thus far are the words of Jeremiah.

The Destruction of Jerusalem Reviewed

52:1-34 Zedekiah was twenty-one…as long as [Jehoiachin] lived: This historical appendix is almost identical to 2 Kings 24:18—25:30. An ancient editor felt it necessary to insert this summary of history. The final paragraph offers a sense of hope and dignity. When Nebuchadrezzar died in 562 B.C.E., his son Evil-merodach ("man of Marduk") succeeded him. The new king released Jehoiachin, the surviving king of David's line, from his thirty-seven-year imprisonment. Jehoiachin enjoyed the rest of his days as a royal guest at the court of Babylon. The restoration of the Davidic line was still a possibility.

52 Zedekiah was twenty-one years old when he began to reign; he reigned eleven years in Jerusalem. His mother's name was Hamutal daughter of Jeremiah of Libnah. 2 He did what was evil in the sight of the LORD, just as Jehoiakim had done. 3 Indeed, Jerusalem and Judah so angered the LORD that he expelled them from his presence.

Zedekiah rebelled against the king of Babylon. 4 And in the ninth year of his reign, in the tenth month, on the tenth day of the month, King Nebuchadrezzar of Babylon came with all his army against Jerusalem, and they laid siege to it; they built siegeworks against it all around. 5 So the city was besieged until the eleventh year of King Zedekiah. 6 On the ninth day of the fourth month the famine became so severe in the city that there was no food for the people of the land.

---

[a] Gk Syr Compare Hab 2.13: Heb *and the nations for fire, and they are weary* [b] Or *one* [c] Gk: Heb *on her. And they shall weary themselves*

7 Then a breach was made in the city wall;[a] and all the soldiers fled and
went out from the city by night by the way of the gate between the
two walls, by the king's garden, though the Chaldeans were all around
the city. They went in the direction of the Arabah. 8 But the army of
the Chaldeans pursued the king, and overtook Zedekiah in the plains
of Jericho; and all his army was scattered, deserting him. 9 Then they
captured the king, and brought him up to the king of Babylon at Riblah in the land of Hamath, and he passed sentence on him. 10 The king
of Babylon killed the sons of Zedekiah before his eyes, and also killed
all the officers of Judah at Riblah. 11 He put out the eyes of Zedekiah,
and bound him in fetters, and the king of Babylon took him to Babylon, and put him in prison until the day of his death.

12 In the fifth month, on the tenth day of the month—which
was the nineteenth year of King Nebuchadrezzar, king of Babylon—
Nebuzaradan the captain of the bodyguard who served the king of
Babylon, entered Jerusalem. 13 He burned the house of the LORD, the
king's house, and all the houses of Jerusalem; every great house he
burned down. 14 All the army of the Chaldeans, who were with the
captain of the guard, broke down all the walls around Jerusalem.
15 Nebuzaradan the captain of the guard carried into exile some of the
poorest of the people and the rest of the people who were left in the
city and the deserters who had defected to the king of Babylon, together with the rest of the artisans. 16 But Nebuzaradan the captain of
the guard left some of the poorest people of the land to be vinedressers and tillers of the soil.

17 The pillars of bronze that were in the house of the LORD, and
the stands and the bronze sea that were in the house of the LORD,
the Chaldeans broke in pieces, and carried all the bronze to Babylon.
18 They took away the pots, the shovels, the snuffers, the basins, the
ladles, and all the vessels of bronze used in the temple service. 19 The
captain of the guard took away the small bowls also, the firepans,
the basins, the pots, the lampstands, the ladles, and the bowls for libation, both those of gold and those of silver. 20 As for the two pillars,
the one sea, the twelve bronze bulls that were under the sea, and the
stands,[b] which King Solomon had made for the house of the LORD,
the bronze of all these vessels was beyond weighing. 21 As for the pillars, the height of the one pillar was eighteen cubits, its circumference
was twelve cubits; it was hollow and its thickness was four fingers.
22 Upon it was a capital of bronze; the height of the capital was five cubits; latticework and pomegranates, all of bronze, encircled the top of
the capital. And the second pillar had the same, with pomegranates.
23 There were ninety-six pomegranates on the sides; all the pomegranates encircling the latticework numbered one hundred.

---

[a] Heb lacks *wall* [b] Cn: Heb *that were under the stands*

24 The captain of the guard took the chief priest Seraiah, the second priest Zephaniah, and the three guardians of the threshold; [25]and
from the city he took an officer who had been in command of the soldiers, and seven men of the king's council who were found in the city;
the secretary of the commander of the army who mustered the people of the land; and sixty men of the people of the land who were
found inside the city. [26]Then Nebuzaradan the captain of the guard
took them, and brought them to the king of Babylon at Riblah. [27]And
the king of Babylon struck them down, and put them to death at Riblah in the land of Hamath. So Judah went into exile out of its land.

28 This is the number of the people whom Nebuchadrezzar took
into exile: in the seventh year, three thousand twenty-three Judeans;
[29]in the eighteenth year of Nebuchadrezzar he took into exile from Jerusalem eight hundred thirty-two persons; [30]in the twenty-third year
of Nebuchadrezzar, Nebuzaradan the captain of the guard took into
exile of the Judeans seven hundred forty-five persons; all the persons
were four thousand six hundred.

Jehoiachin Favored in Captivity

31 In the thirty-seventh year of the exile of King Jehoiachin of
Judah, in the twelfth month, on the twenty-fifth day of the month,
King Evil-merodach of Babylon, in the year he began to reign, showed
favor to King Jehoiachin of Judah and brought him out of prison; [32]he
spoke kindly to him, and gave him a seat above the seats of the other
kings who were with him in Babylon. [33]So Jehoiachin put aside his
prison clothes, and every day of his life he dined regularly at the king's
table. [34]For his allowance, a regular daily allowance was given him by
the king of Babylon, as long as he lived, up to the day of his death.

Lamentations 3:41-42

LAMENTATIONS

Background File

The book of Lamentations is a collection of five poems. All of them mourn the destruction of the city of Jerusalem by the Babylonians in 586 B.C.E. The writer of the poems was long believed to be the prophet Jeremiah, probably because 2 Chronicles 35:25 mentions that his laments were recorded. Second Chronicles, however, reports that Jeremiah mourned the death of King Josiah (609 B.C.E.), not the fall of Jerusalem. In the end, the author of Lamentations remains unknown.

What's the Story?

The Hebrew alphabet guides the first four poems in Lamentations. Twenty-two stanzas in each poem begin with consecutive Hebrew letters, forming what is called an acrostic. This does not happen in the fifth poem or chapter, although there still are twenty-two lines. The reason for using an acrostic pattern in the poems is unclear. It may signal completeness as the poet or writer laments from "A to Z," or it may indicate the human need for form and pattern in times of grief.

What's the Message?

The poet who wrote Lamentations was convinced that the LORD had brought about the devastating victory of the Babylonians over Jerusalem. The LORD had "destroyed without mercy" (2:2; see also 2:21) and demolished and killed "without pity" (2:17; 3:43), becoming "like an enemy" (2:5). The poet believed that the LORD could act in ways that did not demonstrate steadfast love and could work "good and bad" (3:38). That was not in question for this writer. The LORD's silence in the face of the people's horrific suffering, however, launched these poems or laments. The writer cries out for the pain to stop, for God to ease the suffering and seek revenge on those human beings who brought destruction. The final poem ends on a note of uncertainty: God's mercy and future restoration are left in question (5:22).

To us, lament often sounds like despair, the opposite of faith. Yet Martin Luther taught that it is precisely in places where we would least expect to find God, in suffering, pain, disaster, catastrophe—and in the cross—that God is clearly present. Lamentations, then, does more than simply express despair. It shows us that in the most difficult of times and places, God is present and hears our desperate cries for help.

The Deserted City

1:1-6 She weeps bitterly in the night: The city of Jerusalem is pictured as a woman, an abandoned widow. The city has gone from full to empty, "princess" to slave, friends to enemies. It is completely destroyed, and the people have been taken captive.

1:1 like a widow: In ancient times, widows without adult sons did not have any form of protection or income. God shows concern for widows, along with orphans (Deut 10:17-18; Ps 146:9), and they have special protection under the law (Exod 22:22-24; Deut 14:28-29; 24:19-22; 26:12; 27:19). The prophets often say God is angry about the mistreatment of widows and orphans (Isa 1:17; 10:1-2; Jer 7:6-7; 22:3; Ezek 22:7; Zech 7:10; Mal 3:5; see Ps 94:6). The ministries of Jesus and the early church also include care for widows (Luke 7:11-15; Acts 6:1; 1 Tim 5:3-4; Jas 1:27).

In the world today, who is like the widows and orphans of ancient times? How do communities of faith serve these people?

1:2 she has no one to comfort her: This is the first of several references to Jerusalem's utter abandonment in the midst of suffering (see 1:9, 16, 17, 21). The belief that the LORD has not only been unmoved by this suffering (1:9, 11), but directed the activities of the enemies (1:5, 17, 21) only increases the agony in Jerusalem.

The book of Lamentations raises difficult questions that people of faith have struggled with for centuries. Do you think sin plays a role in disasters and wars? Does God play a role?

1 How lonely sits the city
that once was full of people!
How like a widow she has become,
she that was great among the nations!
She that was a princess among the provinces
has become a vassal.

2 She weeps bitterly in the night,
with tears on her cheeks;
among all her lovers
she has no one to comfort her;
all her friends have dealt treacherously with her,
they have become her enemies.

3 Judah has gone into exile with suffering
and hard servitude;
she lives now among the nations,
and finds no resting place;
her pursuers have all overtaken her
in the midst of her distress.

4 The roads to Zion mourn,
for no one comes to the festivals;
all her gates are desolate,
her priests groan;
her young girls grieve,[a]
and her lot is bitter.

5 Her foes have become the masters,
her enemies prosper,
because the LORD has made her suffer
for the multitude of her transgressions;
her children have gone away,
captives before the foe.

6 From daughter Zion has departed
all her majesty.
Her princes have become like stags
that find no pasture;
they fled without strength
before the pursuer.

[a] Meaning of Heb uncertain

[7] Jerusalem remembers,
in the days of her affliction and wandering,
all the precious things
that were hers in days of old.
When her people fell into the hand of the foe,
and there was no one to help her,
the foe looked on mocking
over her downfall.

[8] Jerusalem sinned grievously,
so she has become a mockery;
all who honored her despise her,
for they have seen her nakedness;
she herself groans,
and turns her face away.

[9] Her uncleanness was in her skirts;
she took no thought of her future;
her downfall was appalling,
with none to comfort her.
"O LORD, look at my affliction,
for the enemy has triumphed!"

[10] Enemies have stretched out their hands
over all her precious things;
she has even seen the nations
invade her sanctuary,
those whom you forbade
to enter your congregation.

[11] All her people groan
as they search for bread;
they trade their treasures for food
to revive their strength.
Look, O LORD, and see
how worthless I have become.

[12] Is it nothing to you,[a] all you who pass by?
Look and see
if there is any sorrow like my sorrow,
which was brought upon me,
which the LORD inflicted
on the day of his fierce anger.

1:10 the nations invade her sanctuary: During the Babylonian invasion of Jerusalem in 586 B.C.E., the temple is plundered. See 2 Kings 25:8-15; Jeremiah 52:12-23.

[a] Meaning of Heb uncertain

13 From on high he sent fire;
it went deep into my bones;
he spread a net for my feet;
he turned me back;
he has left me stunned,
faint all day long.

14 My transgressions were bound[a] into a yoke;
by his hand they were fastened together;
they weigh on my neck,
sapping my strength;
the Lord handed me over
to those whom I cannot withstand.

15 The LORD has rejected
all my warriors in the midst of me;
he proclaimed a time against me
to crush my young men;
the Lord has trodden as in a wine press
the virgin daughter Judah.

16 For these things I weep;
my eyes flow with tears;
for a comforter is far from me,
one to revive my courage;
my children are desolate,
for the enemy has prevailed.

17 Zion stretches out her hands,
but there is no one to comfort her;
the LORD has commanded against Jacob
that his neighbors should become his foes;
Jerusalem has become
a filthy thing among them.

18 The LORD is in the right,
for I have rebelled against his word;
but hear, all you peoples,
and behold my suffering;
my young women and young men
have gone into captivity.

19 I called to my lovers
but they deceived me;

---

[a] Meaning of Heb uncertain

my priests and elders
    perished in the city
while seeking food
    to revive their strength.

20 See, O Lord, how distressed I am;
    my stomach churns,
my heart is wrung within me,
    because I have been very rebellious.
In the street the sword bereaves;
    in the house it is like death.

21 They heard how I was groaning,
    with no one to comfort me.
All my enemies heard of my trouble;
    they are glad that you have done it.
Bring on the day you have announced,
    and let them be as I am.

22 Let all their evil doing come before you;
    and deal with them
as you have dealt with me
    because of all my transgressions;
for my groans are many
    and my heart is faint.

God's Warnings Fulfilled

2 How the Lord in his anger
    has humiliated[a] daughter Zion!
He has thrown down from heaven to earth
    the splendor of Israel;
he has not remembered his footstool
    in the day of his anger.

2 The Lord has destroyed without mercy
    all the dwellings of Jacob;
in his wrath he has broken down
    the strongholds of daughter Judah;
he has brought down to the ground in dishonor
    the kingdom and its rulers.

3 He has cut down in fierce anger
    all the might of Israel;

2:1, 6-7 has not remembered his footstool: The poet or writer blames the Lord not only for forgetting the "footstool" (referring to the ark of the covenant or the sanctuary; see 1 Chr 28:2; Ps 99:5; 132:7), but also for destroying the temple. (The ark of the covenant contained the stone tablets inscribed with the Ten Commandments.)

[a] Meaning of Heb uncertain

he has withdrawn his right hand from them
in the face of the enemy;
he has burned like a flaming fire in Jacob,
consuming all around.

4 He has bent his bow like an enemy,
with his right hand set like a foe;
he has killed all in whom we took pride
in the tent of daughter Zion;
he has poured out his fury like fire.

5 The Lord has become like an enemy;
he has destroyed Israel.
He has destroyed all its palaces,
laid in ruins its strongholds,
and multiplied in daughter Judah
mourning and lamentation.

2:6-7 spurned king and priest: God had promised to maintain the line of kings from David's family and protect Jerusalem, also known as Zion (2 Sam 7; Ps 46, 48; 132; Isa 31:4). The total destruction of Jerusalem, then, was devastating, even though prophets had warned the people in advance (for example, Jer 7:1-15; Mic 3:12).

The suffering of babies (2:11, 19) is another difficult issue raised in Lamentations. Can this kind of suffering be explained? What would you say about it?

6 He has broken down his booth like a garden,
he has destroyed his tabernacle;
the LORD has abolished in Zion
festival and sabbath,
and in his fierce indignation has spurned
king and priest.

7 The Lord has scorned his altar,
disowned his sanctuary;
he has delivered into the hand of the enemy
the walls of her palaces;
a clamor was raised in the house of the LORD
as on a day of festival.

8 The LORD determined to lay in ruins
the wall of daughter Zion;
he stretched the line;
he did not withhold his hand from destroying;
he caused rampart and wall to lament;
they languish together.

9 Her gates have sunk into the ground;
he has ruined and broken her bars;
her king and princes are among the nations;
guidance is no more,
and her prophets obtain
no vision from the LORD.

10 The elders of daughter Zion
sit on the ground in silence;
they have thrown dust on their heads
and put on sackcloth;
the young girls of Jerusalem
have bowed their heads to the ground.

11 My eyes are spent with weeping;
my stomach churns;
my bile is poured out on the ground
because of the destruction of my people,
because infants and babes faint
in the streets of the city.

12 They cry to their mothers,
"Where is bread and wine?"
as they faint like the wounded
in the streets of the city,
as their life is poured out
on their mothers' bosom.

13 What can I say for you, to what compare you,
O daughter Jerusalem?
To what can I liken you, that I may comfort you,
O virgin daughter Zion?
For vast as the sea is your ruin;
who can heal you?

14 Your prophets have seen for you
false and deceptive visions;
they have not exposed your iniquity
to restore your fortunes,
but have seen oracles for you
that are false and misleading.

15 All who pass along the way
clap their hands at you;
they hiss and wag their heads
at daughter Jerusalem;
"Is this the city that was called
the perfection of beauty,
the joy of all the earth?"

16 All your enemies
open their mouths against you;

they hiss, they gnash their teeth,
they cry: "We have devoured her!
Ah, this is the day we longed for;
at last we have seen it!"

2:17 he has demolished without pity: This verse summarizes several themes, including the painful claim that the devastation of the city was God's will. In spite of this, the writer calls for an appeal to the LORD (2:18-19). Jerusalem responds (2:20-22) because there is no one else to go to (see Hos 6:1).

17 The LORD has done what he purposed,
he has carried out his threat;
as he ordained long ago,
he has demolished without pity;
he has made the enemy rejoice over you,
and exalted the might of your foes.

18 Cry aloud[a] to the Lord!
O wall of daughter Zion!
Let tears stream down like a torrent
day and night!
Give yourself no rest,
your eyes no respite!

19 Arise, cry out in the night,
at the beginning of the watches!
Pour out your heart like water
before the presence of the Lord!
Lift your hands to him
for the lives of your children,
who faint for hunger
at the head of every street.

2:20 women eat their offspring: See Lamentations 4:10; 2 Kings 6:24-29; and Deuteronomy 28:53-57 on humans eating other humans in ancient times during a siege. In a siege, enemies would set up a military blockade around a city to force surrender. Among other things, the blockade would not allow food and water into the city.

20 Look, O LORD, and consider!
To whom have you done this?
Should women eat their offspring,
the children they have borne?
Should priest and prophet be killed
in the sanctuary of the Lord?

21 The young and the old are lying
on the ground in the streets;
my young women and my young men
have fallen by the sword;
in the day of your anger you have killed them,
slaughtering without mercy.

22 You invited my enemies from all around
as if for a day of festival;

---

[a] Cn: Heb *Their heart cried*

and on the day of the anger of the LORD
no one escaped or survived;
those whom I bore and reared
my enemy has destroyed.

God's Steadfast Love Endures

3 I am one who has seen affliction
under the rod of God's[a] wrath;
2 he has driven and brought me
into darkness without any light;
3 against me alone he turns his hand,
again and again, all day long.

4 He has made my flesh and my skin waste away,
and broken my bones;
5 he has besieged and enveloped me
with bitterness and tribulation;
6 he has made me sit in darkness
like the dead of long ago.

7 He has walled me about so that I cannot escape;
he has put heavy chains on me;
8 though I call and cry for help,
he shuts out my prayer;
9 he has blocked my ways with hewn stones,
he has made my paths crooked.

10 He is a bear lying in wait for me,
a lion in hiding;
11 he led me off my way and tore me to pieces;
he has made me desolate;
12 he bent his bow and set me
as a mark for his arrow.

13 He shot into my vitals
the arrows of his quiver;
14 I have become the laughingstock of all my people,
the object of their taunt-songs all day long.
15 He has filled me with bitterness,
he has sated me with wormwood.

16 He has made my teeth grind on gravel,
and made me cower in ashes;

3:1-21 I am one who has seen: In this third poem in Lamentations, an unnamed speaker reports painful experiences, using images of being surrounded by the LORD (3:2, 5, 6-8). The escape route is hopelessly twisted (3:9) and, in any event, it leads him to be ambushed by the LORD (3:10-13). Images of being surrounded or trapped pick up again in verses 43-47 and 52-54.

---

[a] Heb *his*

17 my soul is bereft of peace;
I have forgotten what happiness is;
18 so I say, "Gone is my glory,
and all that I had hoped for from the LORD."

19 The thought of my affliction and my homelessness
is wormwood and gall!
20 My soul continually thinks of it
and is bowed down within me.
21 But this I call to mind,
and therefore I have hope:

22 The steadfast love of the LORD never ceases,[a]
his mercies never come to an end;
23 they are new every morning;
great is your faithfulness.
24 "The LORD is my portion," says my soul,
"therefore I will hope in him."

25 The LORD is good to those who wait for him,
to the soul that seeks him.
26 It is good that one should wait quietly
for the salvation of the LORD.
27 It is good for one to bear
the yoke in youth,
28 to sit alone in silence
when the Lord has imposed it,
29 to put one's mouth to the dust
(there may yet be hope),
30 to give one's cheek to the smiter,
and be filled with insults.

31 For the Lord will not
reject forever.
32 Although he causes grief, he will have compassion
according to the abundance of his steadfast love;
33 for he does not willingly afflict
or grieve anyone.

34 When all the prisoners of the land
are crushed under foot,
35 when human rights are perverted
in the presence of the Most High,

3:22-39 The steadfast love of the LORD: These verses are often seen as the only message of hope in Lamentations. They may be an effort by the writer, however, to encourage the LORD to act with steadfast love and faithfulness to the promises made to Israel. Similar tactics are used by Abraham (Gen 18:24-25) and the psalmists (Ps 44:1-8; 74:12-17).

[a] Syr Tg: Heb *LORD, we are not cut off*

36 when one's case is subverted
—does the Lord not see it?

37 Who can command and have it done,
if the Lord has not ordained it?
38 Is it not from the mouth of the Most High
that good and bad come?
39 Why should any who draw breath complain
about the punishment of their sins?

40 Let us test and examine our ways,
and return to the LORD.
41 Let us lift up our hearts as well as our hands
to God in heaven.
42 We have transgressed and rebelled,
and you have not forgiven.

43 You have wrapped yourself with anger and
pursued us,
killing without pity;
44 you have wrapped yourself with a cloud
so that no prayer can pass through.
45 You have made us filth and rubbish
among the peoples.

46 All our enemies
have opened their mouths against us;
47 panic and pitfall have come upon us,
devastation and destruction.
48 My eyes flow with rivers of tears
because of the destruction of my people.

49 My eyes will flow without ceasing,
without respite,
50 until the LORD from heaven
looks down and sees.
51 My eyes cause me grief
at the fate of all the young women in my city.

52 Those who were my enemies without cause
have hunted me like a bird;
53 they flung me alive into a pit
and hurled stones on me;
54 water closed over my head;
I said, "I am lost."

3:36 does the Lord not see it?: This can also be translated "the Lord does not see." Those opposed to the LORD's purposes use the statement elsewhere (Ps 94:7; Ezek 8:12; 9:9).

3:37-39, 43-44 if the Lord has not ordained it? That the LORD's actions could be in conflict with God's steadfast love and faithfulness was not the issue (Exod 34:6; Num 14:8; Lam 3:22). The LORD *could* demolish and kill (2:2, 17, 21; 3:43) and the LORD *could* work "good and bad" (3:38). But the persistence of pain and the shocking silence of the LORD in response to suffering drove the poet to write these poems or laments.

[55] I called on your name, O LORD,
from the depths of the pit;
[56] you heard my plea, "Do not close your ear
to my cry for help, but give me relief!"
[57] You came near when I called on you;
you said, "Do not fear!"

3:58-66 Pay them back: The writer asks God to take revenge on the enemies (see also Lam 1:21; Ps 3:7; 17:13-14; 35:26; 59:11-13; Jer 11:20-23; 18:21-22).

What kind of prayers are appropriate to pray in times of devastation and destruction?

[58] You have taken up my cause, O Lord,
you have redeemed my life.
[59] You have seen the wrong done to me, O LORD;
judge my cause.
[60] You have seen all their malice,
all their plots against me.

[61] You have heard their taunts, O LORD,
all their plots against me.
[62] The whispers and murmurs of my assailants
are against me all day long.
[63] Whether they sit or rise—see,
I am the object of their taunt-songs.

[64] Pay them back for their deeds, O LORD,
according to the work of their hands!
[65] Give them anguish of heart;
your curse be on them!
[66] Pursue them in anger and destroy them
from under the LORD's heavens.

The Punishment of Zion

4:1-9 the gold has grown dim: The poem describes the reversal of fortunes experienced by Jerusalem's children (4:1-4), the wealthy (4:5, 7-8), and the general population (4:6). All suffer from the famine brought on by the Babylonian siege of Jerusalem.

4 How the gold has grown dim,
how the pure gold is changed!
The sacred stones lie scattered
at the head of every street.

[2] The precious children of Zion,
worth their weight in fine gold—
how they are reckoned as earthen pots,
the work of a potter's hands!

[3] Even the jackals offer the breast
and nurse their young,
but my people has become cruel,
like the ostriches in the wilderness.

[4] The tongue of the infant sticks
to the roof of its mouth for thirst;

the children beg for food,
    but no one gives them anything.

5 Those who feasted on delicacies
    perish in the streets;
those who were brought up in purple
    cling to ash heaps.

6 For the chastisement[a] of my people has been greater
    than the punishment[b] of Sodom,
which was overthrown in a moment,
    though no hand was laid on it.[c]

7 Her princes were purer than snow,
    whiter than milk;
their bodies were more ruddy than coral,
    their hair[c] like sapphire.[d]

8 Now their visage is blacker than soot;
    they are not recognized in the streets.
Their skin has shriveled on their bones;
    it has become as dry as wood.

9 Happier were those pierced by the sword
    than those pierced by hunger,
whose life drains away, deprived
    of the produce of the field.

10 The hands of compassionate women
    have boiled their own children;
they became their food
    in the destruction of my people.

11 The Lord gave full vent to his wrath;
    he poured out his hot anger,
and kindled a fire in Zion
    that consumed its foundations.

12 The kings of the earth did not believe,
    nor did any of the inhabitants of the world,
that foe or enemy could enter
    the gates of Jerusalem.

---

[a] Or *iniquity* [b] Or *sin* [c] Meaning of Heb uncertain [d] Or *lapis lazuli*

13 It was for the sins of her prophets
and the iniquities of her priests,
who shed the blood of the righteous
in the midst of her.

14 Blindly they wandered through the streets,
so defiled with blood
that no one was able
to touch their garments.

15 "Away! Unclean!" people shouted at them;
"Away! Away! Do not touch!"
So they became fugitives and wanderers;
it was said among the nations,
"They shall stay here no longer."

4:16 The LORD himself has scattered: The Hebrew text refers to "the face of the LORD" here. This phrase signals God's point of view toward someone, either for ill, when God's face is turned away (see Pss 30:7; 34:16; 88:14; 143:7; Isa 8:17; 54:8; Ezek 14:8; 15:7; Mic 3:4), or for good (see Num 6:25; 2 Chr 30:9; Pss 4:6; 11:7; 27:8; 80:19; Ezek 39:29).

16 The LORD himself has scattered them,
he will regard them no more;
no honor was shown to the priests,
no favor to the elders.

17 Our eyes failed, ever watching
vainly for help;
we were watching eagerly
for a nation that could not save.

18 They dogged our steps
so that we could not walk in our streets;
our end drew near; our days were numbered;
for our end had come.

4:20 The LORD's anointed...was taken: The "LORD's anointed" (or messiah) refers to the ritual of pouring olive oil on the king's head when he came to power (see 1 Sam 16:13; 1 Kgs 1:39; 2 Kgs 9:3, 6). Though unnamed here, the king in 4:20 is likely Zedekiah. He attempted to escape out of Jerusalem, but in the end that only caused him to be captured sooner by Babylonian king Nebuchadnezzar (2 Kgs 25:1-7).

19 Our pursuers were swifter
than the eagles in the heavens;
they chased us on the mountains,
they lay in wait for us in the wilderness.

20 The LORD's anointed, the breath of our life,
was taken in their pits—
the one of whom we said, "Under his shadow
we shall live among the nations."

What does it mean to trust in God? In explaining the First Commandment, "You shall have no other gods," Martin Luther wrote, "We are to fear, love, and trust God above all things" (*SC*). In stark contrast to this, the poet or writer of Lamentations describes how the people relied on the nation and their leader, rather than on God, during the invasion of the city. They waited for the nation to help. The king was the "breath" of their lives, and they trusted that they could continue to live under his rule. *Lamentations 4:17-20*

21 Rejoice and be glad, O daughter Edom,
you that live in the land of Uz;
but to you also the cup shall pass;
you shall become drunk and strip yourself bare.

22 The punishment of your iniquity, O daughter Zion, is accomplished,
he will keep you in exile no longer;
but your iniquity, O daughter Edom, he will punish,
he will uncover your sins.

A Plea for Mercy

5 Remember, O LORD, what has befallen us;
look, and see our disgrace!
2 Our inheritance has been turned over to strangers,
our homes to aliens.
3 We have become orphans, fatherless;
our mothers are like widows.
4 We must pay for the water we drink;
the wood we get must be bought.
5 With a yoke[a] on our necks we are hard driven;
we are weary, we are given no rest.
6 We have made a pact with[b] Egypt and Assyria,
to get enough bread.
7 Our ancestors sinned; they are no more,
and we bear their iniquities.
8 Slaves rule over us;
there is no one to deliver us from their hand.
9 We get our bread at the peril of our lives,
because of the sword in the wilderness.
10 Our skin is black as an oven
from the scorching heat of famine.
11 Women are raped in Zion,
virgins in the towns of Judah.
12 Princes are hung up by their hands;
no respect is shown to the elders.
13 Young men are compelled to grind,
and boys stagger under loads of wood.
14 The old men have left the city gate,
the young men their music.
15 The joy of our hearts has ceased;
our dancing has been turned to mourning.
16 The crown has fallen from our head;
woe to us, for we have sinned!
17 Because of this our hearts are sick,
because of these things our eyes have grown dim:
18 because of Mount Zion, which lies desolate;
jackals prowl over it.

5:1-22 what has befallen us: The acrostic (alphabetic) form used in the first four poems in Lamentations 1–4 falls apart in these twenty-two lines. Perhaps the disappearing structure reflects the writer's fading hope.

---

[a] Symmachus: Heb lacks *With a yoke* [b] Heb *have given the hand to*

5:19-22 unless you have utterly rejected us: The statement that God rules forever makes the questions and pleas in 5:20-21 all the more agonizing. The book ends in anguish and uncertainty as the poet or writer considers the possibility that the LORD's rejection truly is the final word. This possibility is raised again as Jesus dies on the cross (see Matt 27:46; Mark 15:34).

What do you think about the way this book ends?

19 But you, O LORD, reign forever;
your throne endures to all generations.
20 Why have you forgotten us completely?
Why have you forsaken us these many days?
21 Restore us to yourself, O LORD, that we may be restored;
renew our days as of old—
22 unless you have utterly rejected us,
and are angry with us beyond measure.

Ezekiel 47:12

EZEKIEL

Background File

While in captivity in Babylon, Ezekiel, the son of Buzi (1:3) and an Israelite priest, possibly a descendant of Zadok (40:46), prophesied to his fellow exiles. Little is known of the details of his life other than that his wife died while in exile (24:15-27). His prophetic activity began in 593 B.C.E. (1:1) and extended at least to 571. Like Jeremiah, Ezekiel prophesied before and after the destruction of Jerusalem and the temple in 587. While there was editing of his material, much of the book in its present form likely comes from Ezekiel himself.

What's the Story?

The political back-story for the book of Ezekiel begins after the first time Jerusalem submitted to King Nebuchadnezzar of Babylon in 597 B.C.E. Many of Israel's political and religious leaders, including the young Davidic king Jehoiachin, were deported or exiled to Babylon. Ezekiel was likely among them. Zedekiah, uncle of Jehoiachin and the last of the line of David to rule, was set up by Nebuchadnezzar to be a puppet ruler over Israel. Midway through the book, Jerusalem falls to the Babylonians (33:21). Zedekiah is captured while attempting to escape (12:12). After seeing his sons and officials slaughtered at Riblah, he is blinded, taken to Babylon, and not heard from again. The concluding chapters of the book are set after Jerusalem and Solomon's Temple are reduced to rubble.

Many of Ezekiel's prophecies are dated and flow chronologically, providing a historical backbone to the book. There are four primary sections:

- Judgments against Jerusalem and Israel (chapters 1–24)
- Judgments against foreign nations (chapters 25–32)
- Promises of restoration (chapters 33-39)
- A vision of a reestablished temple and order in Jerusalem and Israel (chapters 40–48)

Ezekiel's prophecies take a variety of forms, from poetry to visions to dramatic, symbolic physical actions. His words of judgment are biting and often troubling and violent. Particularly troubling are the images of women (chapters 16; 23).

The book of Ezekiel is a rich mix of priestly concerns and prophetic activity. His priestly concerns, which are informed in part by a portion of Israel's laws called the Holiness Code (see Lev 17–26), focus on idolatry, ritual purity, and the temple. His prophetic activity includes oracles of judgment similar to other prophets and symbolic visions that are so mysterious that heavenly beings must help interpret them. From these visions sprout the earliest shoots of apocalyptic literature. His transportation by the spirit of the LORD from Babylon to Jerusalem (8:3; 40:1), his encounters with heavenly guides that show him things other humans cannot see (8:2; 40:3), his vision of the LORD's victory in an final end-times battle (chapters 38–39), and his visions of the glory of the LORD (chapters 1; 10–11; 43) inform much later apocalyptic literature, such as the book of Revelation.

Set in Babylon and deeply concerned with Jerusalem, in Ezekiel there is a wider worldly awareness of life in Tyre (chapters 26–28), Egypt (chapters 29–32), and other countries in the region (chapter 25), including trade that extends from the Mediterranean region to West Africa and the subcontinent of India (chapter 27).

What's the Message?

Ezekiel boldly confronts Israel's unfaithfulness and idolatry and emphasizes the absolute holiness of the LORD. Set in the hopelessness of exile, the book is a swirl of scolding judgments, mind-blowing visions, and hopeful promises, all of which have inspired the creative imagination of Christian writers through the centuries, including those who have written a number of African American spirituals.

The book of Ezekiel addresses difficult questions about why God would allow God's people to be removed from Jerusalem and the temple to be destroyed. How could God go back on the promises of giving Israel the land and establishing the temple in Jerusalem as God's dwelling place? If the LORD is the God of Israel, how could God allow the prolonged crisis of the exile to happen?

Ezekiel's response is to announce the singular holiness of the one God of the cosmos. In spite of Israel's consistent idolatrous rebellion, the LORD acts to preserve the holiness of the LORD's name (36:16-38). The exile is the LORD's just judgment of Israel's unholiness. These unholy actions include contamination of the LORD's temple and the violence of its rulers and people (8:1-18; 22:23-31). The people of Israel, in particular its religious and political rulers, are held fully responsible for their own actions (chapter 18). The victory of the LORD (chapters 38–39) and the envisioned restoration of the people, Jerusalem, and the temple are solely the LORD's action. Why? So that the holiness of the LORD's name can be restored and that "they shall know that I am the LORD" (6:14). There is hope in the promise that the LORD does not take pleasure in the death of the wicked (33:11).

Ezekiel's language and images are from a distinctly priestly point of view. The focus of the book begins and ends at the temple, the place where the LORD's presence resided and the center of Israel's worship. The glory of the LORD rides a chariot that can move seamlessly in any direction and go anywhere, even abandoning the temple, which had been made unholy (chapters 1; 10–11; 43). On a human level, Ezekiel exhibits a concern that the distinction between the holy and the common be maintained (22:1-31; 44:23). This is something the Levite priests failed to do, with the exception of the descendants of Zadok (44:10-31).

Against any attempt to tame God, the book of Ezekiel is a testimony that God is holy beyond our understanding and control.

The Vision of the Chariot

1 In the thirtieth year, in the fourth month, on the fifth day of the
month, as I was among the exiles by the river Chebar, the heavens
were opened, and I saw visions of God. 2 On the fifth day of the month
(it was the fifth year of the exile of King Jehoiachin), 3 the word of the
LORD came to the priest Ezekiel son of Buzi, in the land of the Chaldeans by the river Chebar; and the hand of the LORD was on him there.
4 As I looked, a stormy wind came out of the north: a great cloud
with brightness around it and fire flashing forth continually, and in
the middle of the fire, something like gleaming amber. 5 In the middle of it was something like four living creatures. This was their appearance: they were of human form. 6 Each had four faces, and each
of them had four wings. 7 Their legs were straight, and the soles of
their feet were like the sole of a calf's foot; and they sparkled like burnished bronze. 8 Under their wings on their four sides they had human
hands. And the four had their faces and their wings thus: 9 their wings
touched one another; each of them moved straight ahead, without
turning as they moved. 10 As for the appearance of their faces: the four
had the face of a human being, the face of a lion on the right side, the
face of an ox on the left side, and the face of an eagle; 11 such were
their faces. Their wings were spread out above; each creature had two
wings, each of which touched the wing of another, while two covered
their bodies. 12 Each moved straight ahead; wherever the spirit would
go, they went, without turning as they went. 13 In the middle of[a] the
living creatures there was something that looked like burning coals of
fire, like torches moving to and fro among the living creatures; the fire
was bright, and lightning issued from the fire. 14 The living creatures
darted to and fro, like a flash of lightning.
15 As I looked at the living creatures, I saw a wheel on the earth
beside the living creatures, one for each of the four of them.[b] 16 As for
the appearance of the wheels and their construction: their appearance
was like the gleaming of beryl; and the four had the same form, their
construction being something like a wheel within a wheel. 17 When
they moved, they moved in any of the four directions without veering
as they moved. 18 Their rims were tall and awesome, for the rims of all
four were full of eyes all around. 19 When the living creatures moved,
the wheels moved beside them; and when the living creatures rose
from the earth, the wheels rose. 20 Wherever the spirit would go, they
went, and the wheels rose along with them; for the spirit of the living
creatures was in the wheels. 21 When they moved, the others moved;
when they stopped, the others stopped; and when they rose from the
earth, the wheels rose along with them; for the spirit of the living creatures was in the wheels.

---

[a] Gk OL: Heb *And the appearance of* [b] Heb *of their faces*

According to Luther, what important things does Ezekiel teach Christian readers? Luther's reading of Ezekiel, as with most of his reading of the Old Testament, included both the plain sense of the text and a reading of the text from the vantage point of Christ. "These two things Ezekiel teaches us when he comforts the people concerning the return from Babylon, but even more when he prophesies the new Israel and the kingdom of Christ. That is his vision of the chariot (1:4-28) and also really his temple, in the last part of his book (chs.40-48)" (*LW* 35:290). *Ezekiel 1:1*

1:1—24:27 I saw visions of God: The visions and judgments presented in the first half of the book focus on God's judgments against Jerusalem and Israel. The first three chapters describe Ezekiel's call to be a prophet. Compare his experience to that of Isaiah (Isa 6:1-13) and Jeremiah (Jer 1:1-19).

1:1-2 In the thirtieth year: Along with the king Jehoiachin (2 Kgs 24:1-17) and other religious and political leaders, Ezekiel was taken into exile in Babylon in 597 B.C.E. The date of the vision and Ezekiel's call to be a prophet is in the fifth year of the exile, June 6, 593.

1:3 the priest Ezekiel son of Buzi . . . river Chebar: Ezekiel was likely a priest, though it is possible this refers to his father, Buzi. The "land of the Chaldeans" refers to the empire of the Babylonians (see Map 9, p. 2106), present day Iraq. The river Chebar was a canal that flowed south from the Euphrates River toward Nippur.

1:4-28 As I looked: Ezekiel's first vision is a mind-blowing picture of the four living creatures and the wheels upon wheels with eyes in the rims. This vision is often called the *merkabah* (Hebrew for "chariot") vision. At the heart of the vision is "the glory of the LORD" (1:13, 26-28).

1:5-14 four living creatures: These likely were cherubs (10:1-22; similar to seraphs, Isa 6:2-7) that minister in the presence of the LORD. Revelation uses Ezekiel's imagery (Rev 4:6-8) to describe the creatures around the heavenly throne. The early Christian church began using the four faces of each creature—human, lion, ox, and eagle—to represent the four New Testament Gospels.

22 Over the heads of the living creatures there was something
like a dome, shining like crystal,[a] spread out above their heads. 23 Under the dome their wings were stretched out straight, one toward
another; and each of the creatures had two wings covering its body.
24 When they moved, I heard the sound of their wings like the sound
of mighty waters, like the thunder of the Almighty,[b] a sound of tumult like the sound of an army; when they stopped, they let down
their wings. 25 And there came a voice from above the dome over their
heads; when they stopped, they let down their wings.

26 And above the dome over their heads there was something like
a throne, in appearance like sapphire;[c] and seated above the likeness
of a throne was something that seemed like a human form. 27 Upward
from what appeared like the loins I saw something like gleaming amber, something that looked like fire enclosed all around; and downward from what looked like the loins I saw something that looked like
fire, and there was a splendor all around. 28 Like the bow in a cloud on
a rainy day, such was the appearance of the splendor all around. This
was the appearance of the likeness of the glory of the LORD.

When I saw it, I fell on my face, and I heard the voice of someone
speaking.

The Vision of the Scroll

2 He said to me: O mortal,[d] stand up on your feet, and I will speak
with you. 2 And when he spoke to me, a spirit entered into me
and set me on my feet; and I heard him speaking to me. 3 He said to
me, Mortal, I am sending you to the people of Israel, to a nation[e] of
rebels who have rebelled against me; they and their ancestors have
transgressed against me to this very day. 4 The descendants are impudent and stubborn. I am sending you to them, and you shall say
to them, "Thus says the Lord GOD." 5 Whether they hear or refuse to
hear (for they are a rebellious house), they shall know that there has
been a prophet among them. 6 And you, O mortal, do not be afraid of
them, and do not be afraid of their words, though briers and thorns
surround you and you live among scorpions; do not be afraid of their
words, and do not be dismayed at their looks, for they are a rebellious
house. 7 You shall speak my words to them, whether they hear or refuse to hear; for they are a rebellious house.

8 But you, mortal, hear what I say to you; do not be rebellious
like that rebellious house; open your mouth and eat what I give you.
9 I looked, and a hand was stretched out to me, and a written scroll
was in it. 10 He spread it before me; it had writing on the front and on
the back, and written on it were words of lamentation and mourning
and woe.

---

[a] Gk: Heb *like the awesome crystal* [b] Traditional rendering of Heb *Shaddai* [c] Or *lapis lazuli* [d] Or *son of man*; Heb *ben adam* (and so throughout the book when Ezekiel is addressed) [e] Syr: Heb *to nations*

"Ezekiel Saw the Wheel," an African-American spiritual, sees Ezekiel's vision of the wheels as a hopeful glimpse of God's liberating power—a power greater than slavery— "De big wheel run by faith / Little wheel run by the grace of God." How does this imagery engage the imagination of your faith?

1:22-26 something like a dome: This same Hebrew word is used in the second day of creation (Gen 1:6-8).

1:24-25 like the sound of mighty waters: With the quieting of the wings (43:2), the vision climaxes at the divine throne (1:26) and "the likeness of the glory of the LORD" (1:28; Isa 6:5). Because the holiness of the LORD is too much for people to experience directly (Exod 33:20), Ezekiel speaks of the likeness of the glory of the LORD, which he likens to both fire and a rainbow.

2:1-3:27 Mortal, I am sending you to the people of Israel: In this section, Ezekiel is called to be a prophet.

2:1 mortal: Throughout, Ezekiel is called "mortal" (in Hebrew, "son of man"). This shows the difference between the LORD as holy God and Ezekiel as created human being.

2:2 a spirit: The meaning of "spirit" is not clear, though the prophet does not stand or prophesy of his own power (3:12, 14; 8:3, 11:1, 24; 37:1; 43:5).

2:3 a nation of rebels: Ezekiel's call is to the children of Israel who have been rebelling against the LORD for many generations (20:38). That rebellion included worshiping other gods and treating one another unjustly.

2:4 Thus says the LORD GOD: This phrase, used commonly in prophetic books, indicates that the prophets' words are not theirs but the LORD's (2 Sam 7:5; Jer 2:2; Amos 1:3).

Being a prophet is not an easy (2:6-7; Heb 11:32-38), because prophets bring difficult words, especially to people in power, and call people to faithfulness. What prophetic voices are needed in the church and in the world today? What would it mean for you to be prophetic?

3 He said to me, O mortal, eat what is offered to you; eat this
scroll, and go, speak to the house of Israel. 2So I opened my
mouth, and he gave me the scroll to eat. 3He said to me, Mortal, eat
this scroll that I give you and fill your stomach with it. Then I ate it;
and in my mouth it was as sweet as honey.

4 He said to me: Mortal, go to the house of Israel and speak my
very words to them. 5For you are not sent to a people of obscure
speech and difficult language, but to the house of Israel— 6not to
many peoples of obscure speech and difficult language, whose words
you cannot understand. Surely, if I sent you to them, they would listen
to you. 7But the house of Israel will not listen to you, for they are not
willing to listen to me; because all the house of Israel have a hard forehead and a stubborn heart. 8See, I have made your face hard against
their faces, and your forehead hard against their foreheads. 9Like
the hardest stone, harder than flint, I have made your forehead; do
not fear them or be dismayed at their looks, for they are a rebellious
house. 10He said to me: Mortal, all my words that I shall speak to you
receive in your heart and hear with your ears; 11then go to the exiles,
to your people, and speak to them. Say to them, "Thus says the Lord
GOD"; whether they hear or refuse to hear.

Ezekiel at the River Chebar

12 Then the spirit lifted me up, and as the glory of the LORD rose[a]
from its place, I heard behind me the sound of loud rumbling; 13it
was the sound of the wings of the living creatures brushing against
one another, and the sound of the wheels beside them, that sounded
like a loud rumbling. 14The spirit lifted me up and bore me away; I
went in bitterness in the heat of my spirit, the hand of the LORD being
strong upon me. 15I came to the exiles at Tel-abib, who lived by the
river Chebar.[b] And I sat there among them, stunned, for seven days.

16 At the end of seven days, the word of the LORD came to me:
17Mortal, I have made you a sentinel for the house of Israel; whenever
you hear a word from my mouth, you shall give them warning from
me. 18If I say to the wicked, "You shall surely die," and you give them
no warning, or speak to warn the wicked from their wicked way, in
order to save their life, those wicked persons shall die for their iniquity; but their blood I will require at your hand. 19But if you warn the
wicked, and they do not turn from their wickedness, or from their
wicked way, they shall die for their iniquity; but you will have saved
your life. 20Again, if the righteous turn from their righteousness and
commit iniquity, and I lay a stumbling block before them, they shall
die; because you have not warned them, they shall die for their sin,

[a] Cn: Heb *and blessed be the glory of the LORD* [b] Two Mss Syr: Heb *Chebar, and to where they lived.* Another reading is *Chebar, and I sat where they sat*

2:8—3:3 eat what I give you: Ezekiel is told to eat the scroll covered with bad, sad news (2:10) about Israel's judgment. The eaten scroll becomes part of him (see also Isa 6:6-7; Jer 1:9). Ironically, the bad news of the scroll tastes as "sweet as honey" (3:3).

2:9 scroll: Ancient documents were primarily written on animal skins. Scrolls made from animal skins or leather often had many pieces sewn together and rolled between two spindles. All Old Testament "books" were first scrolls. Books with individual pages were not often used until the first century C.E.

What do we mean when we speak of God's "living Word"? Ezekiel eating the scroll in preparation for his prophesying is an interesting image to consider next to a Lutheran understanding of the Living Word. When Lutherans speak of the Word of God, we mean first that the Living Word is Jesus Christ, the Word of God incarnate, meaning alive in human form (John 1), by whose crucifixion and resurrection God fashions a new creation. Second, the Word is also alive when it is proclaimed. And third, the Living Word is the written Word of God, Scripture, the Bible. Through the Scriptures, God's Spirit speaks to us to create and sustain Christian faith. *Ezekiel 3:1-11*

3:4-11 go to the house of Israel: Ezekiel is sent to his own people who speak the same language as he does, Hebrew.

3:14-15 I came to the exiles: Upon his spirited return, Ezekiel is to be shocked into a state of devastated silence (see Ezra 9:3-4) for seven days.

3:16-21 made you a sentinel: A sentinel is one who keeps watch and is responsible for warning the people in the event of danger (also 33:1-9; Hos 9:8; Hab 2:1). But the stakes are high for Ezekiel. If he does not warn the righteous (those who walk in faith in God) and they sin, they will be punished, and God will require their blood at Ezekiel's hand (3:20). The opposite is also true. If they don't turn to sin, Ezekiel will have saved his life by proclaiming the message.

and their righteous deeds that they have done shall not be remembered; but their blood I will require at your hand. [21]If, however, you
warn the righteous not to sin, and they do not sin, they shall surely
live, because they took warning; and you will have saved your life.

Ezekiel Isolated and Silenced

3:22-27 the hand of the LORD... The spirit: These verses suggest that Ezekiel received personal revelations. "The hand of the LORD" describes the LORD's presence with Ezekiel. It also refers to the power of the LORD (20:33) that informs (8:1) and transports Ezekiel in his visions (3:22; 8:3; 37:1; 40:1). Ezekiel is "bound" (3:25) to his role as prophet, and it is the LORD who opens the prophet's mouth to prophesy (3:27; 33:22).

How do you hear the word of the LORD calling you to faithfulness?

22 Then the hand of the LORD was upon me there; and he said
to me, Rise up, go out into the valley, and there I will speak with you.
[23]So I rose up and went out into the valley; and the glory of the LORD
stood there, like the glory that I had seen by the river Chebar; and I
fell on my face. [24]The spirit entered into me, and set me on my feet;
and he spoke with me and said to me: Go, shut yourself inside your
house. [25]As for you, mortal, cords shall be placed on you, and you
shall be bound with them, so that you cannot go out among the people; [26]and I will make your tongue cling to the roof of your mouth,
so that you shall be speechless and unable to reprove them; for they
are a rebellious house. [27]But when I speak with you, I will open your
mouth, and you shall say to them, "Thus says the Lord GOD"; let those
who will hear, hear; and let those who refuse to hear, refuse; for they
are a rebellious house.

The Siege of Jerusalem Portrayed

4:1-3 take a brick: Like a child playing with blocks, Ezekiel is commanded to create a model of the siege of Jerusalem, a symbol without words. Throughout 4:1—5:4, the prophet uses actions and objects to get the people's attention (37:15-28).

4 And you, O mortal, take a brick and set it before you. On it portray a city, Jerusalem; [2]and put siegeworks against it, and build
a siege wall against it, and cast up a ramp against it; set camps also
against it, and plant battering rams against it all around. [3]Then take
an iron plate and place it as an iron wall between you and the city; set
your face toward it, and let it be in a state of siege, and press the siege
against it. This is a sign for the house of Israel.

4:4-8 bear their punishment: Ezekiel was likely a priest (1:3; Lev 16:17), so he symbolically bears the sins of Israel and Judah (see Lev 16:20-22).

4 Then lie on your left side, and place the punishment of the
house of Israel upon it; you shall bear their punishment for the number of the days that you lie there. [5]For I assign to you a number of days,
three hundred ninety days, equal to the number of the years of their
punishment; and so you shall bear the punishment of the house of
Israel. [6]When you have completed these, you shall lie down a second
time, but on your right side, and bear the punishment of the house
of Judah; forty days I assign you, one day for each year. [7]You shall set
your face toward the siege of Jerusalem, and with your arm bared you
shall prophesy against it. [8]See, I am putting cords on you so that you
cannot turn from one side to the other until you have completed the
days of your siege.

4:9-17 make bread: The variety of ingredients for this bread-baking, a task normally reserved for women in the ancient world, likely symbolizes the shortages of both the earlier siege of Jerusalem and the current exile in Babylon. This is the only place in the Scripture that speaks of cooking with human dung; such cooking methods likely were considered impure (Deut 23:12-14). At Ezekiel's complaint the LORD allows him to use cow dung for the fire.

4:9-17 twenty shekels... one-sixth of a hin: Twenty shekels equals about one-half pound. One-sixth of a hin would be a little more than a twelve-ounce can of soda pop.

9 And you, take wheat and barley, beans and lentils, millet and
spelt; put them into one vessel, and make bread for yourself. During
the number of days that you lie on your side, three hundred ninety
days, you shall eat it. [10]The food that you eat shall be twenty shekels a

day by weight; at fixed times you shall eat it. [11]And you shall drink water by measure, one-sixth of a hin; at fixed times you shall drink. [12]You shall eat it as a barley-cake, baking it in their sight on human dung. [13]The LORD said, "Thus shall the people of Israel eat their bread, unclean, among the nations to which I will drive them." [14]Then I said, "Ah Lord GOD! I have never defiled myself; from my youth up until now I have never eaten what died of itself or was torn by animals, nor has carrion flesh come into my mouth." [15]Then he said to me, "See, I will let you have cow's dung instead of human dung, on which you may prepare your bread."

16 Then he said to me, Mortal, I am going to break the staff of bread in Jerusalem; they shall eat bread by weight and with fearfulness; and they shall drink water by measure and in dismay. [17]Lacking bread and water, they will look at one another in dismay, and waste away under their punishment.

A Sword against Jerusalem

5 And you, O mortal, take a sharp sword; use it as a barber's razor and run it over your head and your beard; then take balances for weighing, and divide the hair. [2]One third of the hair you shall burn in the fire inside the city, when the days of the siege are completed; one third you shall take and strike with the sword all around the city;[a] and one third you shall scatter to the wind, and I will unsheathe the sword after them. [3]Then you shall take from these a small number, and bind them in the skirts of your robe. [4]From these, again, you shall take some, throw them into the fire and burn them up; from there a fire will come out against all the house of Israel.

5 Thus says the Lord GOD: This is Jerusalem; I have set her in the center of the nations, with countries all around her. [6]But she has rebelled against my ordinances and my statutes, becoming more wicked than the nations and the countries all around her, rejecting my ordinances and not following my statutes. [7]Therefore thus says the Lord GOD: Because you are more turbulent than the nations that are all around you, and have not followed my statutes or kept my ordinances, but have acted according to the ordinances of the nations that are all around you; [8]therefore thus says the Lord GOD: I, I myself, am coming against you; I will execute judgments among you in the sight of the nations. [9]And because of all your abominations, I will do to you what I have never yet done, and the like of which I will never do again. [10]Surely, parents shall eat their children in your midst, and children shall eat their parents; I will execute judgments on you, and any of you who survive I will scatter to every wind. [11]Therefore, as I live, says the Lord GOD, surely, because you have defiled my sanctuary

---

[a] Heb *it*

5:1-4 a sharp sword: Ezekiel used the hair shaved from his head and beard to act out the LORD's humiliation of Israel (see Isa 7:20). When the Babylonians defeated Jerusalem, they burned parts of the city, divided the people and took some away ("scattered to the wind") into exile. This humiliating defeat and exile were punishment for Israel's unfaithfulness. No part of Israel will escape the punishment.

5:5-17 Jerusalem...in the center of the nations...she has rebelled: Next come God's words of judgment against Jerusalem because of her sins against the LORD. The action shifts from symbolic prophetic actions to a prophetic speech. Jerusalem not only enjoys a privileged position among the nations but is considered the "center" (see note on 38.12). Even though Jerusalem enjoyed privileged status and had been given God's laws, it behaved worse than the nations around it.

5:8-17 I will execute judgments among you: The focus here is on the central sin against the LORD, defiling the sanctuary (5:11), meaning the temple in Jerusalem. The LORD's judgments (5:8) will include horrible punishments, such as parents eating their children (see Lev 26:29; Jer 19:9) as well as children eating their parents, a punishment not found elsewhere. The third that survive will be scattered into exile, shamed among the nations, and forced to face famine and violence.

How do we understand God's judgment in the Bible? The LORD's violent fury with the people's sinfulness challenges the believer who wants to know God completely. With texts such as this, we are reminded that as creatures we cannot know all of God's ways. At the same time, in the face of horrors in our world today, we ought to be very hesitant to claim to know and understand the hiddenness of God. Luther reminds us that it is in Christ and in him on the cross that God is revealed most clearly for us. This may be and remain in conflict with other pictures of God in Scripture. *Ezekiel 5*

with all your detestable things and with all your abominations—
therefore I will cut you down;[a] my eye will not spare, and I will have
no pity. 12 One third of you shall die of pestilence or be consumed by
famine among you; one third shall fall by the sword around you; and
one third I will scatter to every wind and will unsheathe the sword
after them.

13 My anger shall spend itself, and I will vent my fury on them
and satisfy myself; and they shall know that I, the LORD, have spoken in my jealousy, when I spend my fury on them. 14 Moreover I will
make you a desolation and an object of mocking among the nations
around you, in the sight of all that pass by. 15 You shall be[b] a mockery
and a taunt, a warning and a horror, to the nations around you, when I
execute judgments on you in anger and fury, and with furious punishments—I, the LORD, have spoken— 16 when I loose against you[c] my
deadly arrows of famine, arrows for destruction, which I will let loose
to destroy you, and when I bring more and more famine upon you,
and break your staff of bread. 17 I will send famine and wild animals
against you, and they will rob you of your children; pestilence and
bloodshed shall pass through you; and I will bring the sword upon
you. I, the LORD, have spoken.

Judgment on Idolatrous Israel

6 The word of the LORD came to me: 2 O mortal, set your face toward the mountains of Israel, and prophesy against them, 3 and
say, You mountains of Israel, hear the word of the Lord GOD! Thus
says the Lord GOD to the mountains and the hills, to the ravines and
the valleys: I, I myself will bring a sword upon you, and I will destroy
your high places. 4 Your altars shall become desolate, and your incense
stands shall be broken; and I will throw down your slain in front of
your idols. 5 I will lay the corpses of the people of Israel in front of
their idols; and I will scatter your bones around your altars. 6 Wherever you live, your towns shall be waste and your high places ruined,
so that your altars will be waste and ruined,[d] your idols broken and
destroyed, your incense stands cut down, and your works wiped out.
7 The slain shall fall in your midst; then you shall know that I am the
LORD.

8 But I will spare some. Some of you shall escape the sword
among the nations and be scattered through the countries. 9 Those of
you who escape shall remember me among the nations where they
are carried captive, how I was crushed by their wanton heart that
turned away from me, and their wanton eyes that turned after their
idols. Then they will be loathsome in their own sight for the evils that
they have committed, for all their abominations. 10 And they shall

6:2-3 You mountains of Israel . . . I will destroy your high places: The scope broadens from Jerusalem to all of Israel including its geography, a move that is later reversed (36:1-15). The high places were locations outside Jerusalem where Israelites worshiped idols (36:13-15).

6:4 idols: The Hebrew word translated here as "idols" and used often throughout Ezekiel is *gillulim* (gil-loo-LEEM), which means "dung heaps." The LORD judged not only these cultic objects of worship but also those who worshiped them as "vile abominations" (6:11).

---

[a] Another reading is *I will withdraw* [b] Gk Syr Vg Tg: Heb *It shall be* [c] Heb *them* [d] Syr Vg Tg: Heb *and be made guilty*

know that I am the LORD; I did not threaten in vain to bring this disaster upon them.
11 Thus says the Lord GOD: Clap your hands and stamp your
foot, and say, Alas for all the vile abominations of the house of Israel!
For they shall fall by the sword, by famine, and by pestilence. 12 Those
far off shall die of pestilence; those nearby shall fall by the sword; and
any who are left and are spared shall die of famine. Thus I will spend
my fury upon them. 13 And you shall know that I am the LORD, when
their slain lie among their idols around their altars, on every high hill,
on all the mountain tops, under every green tree, and under every
leafy oak, wherever they offered pleasing odor to all their idols. 14 I
will stretch out my hand against them, and make the land desolate
and waste, throughout all their settlements, from the wilderness to
Riblah.[a] Then they shall know that I am the LORD.

Impending Disaster

7 The word of the LORD came to me: 2 You, O mortal, thus says
the Lord GOD to the land of Israel:

An end! The end has come
upon the four corners of the land.
3 Now the end is upon you,
I will let loose my anger upon you;
I will judge you according to your ways,
I will punish you for all your abominations.
4 My eye will not spare you, I will have no pity.
I will punish you for your ways,
while your abominations are among you.
Then you shall know that I am the LORD.

5 Thus says the Lord GOD:
Disaster after disaster! See, it comes.
6 An end has come, the end has come.
It has awakened against you; see, it comes!
7 Your doom[b] has come to you,
O inhabitant of the land.
The time has come, the day is near—
of tumult, not of reveling on the mountains.
8 Soon now I will pour out my wrath upon you;
I will spend my anger against you.
I will judge you according to your ways,
and punish you for all your abominations.
9 My eye will not spare; I will have no pity.
I will punish you according to your ways,
while your abominations are among you.

[a] Another reading is *Diblah* [b] Meaning of Heb uncertain

6:13 you shall know I am the LORD: The LORD's concern is that the people come to know that the LORD is Lord of all, and that idolatry, that is, worshiping anything other than the LORD, leads to destruction and death.

6:14 from the wilderness to Riblah: The LORD's judgment extends through all of Israel from the southernmost (the desert wilderness south of Jerusalem) to northernmost (Riblah in Syria, though the Hebrew reads *Diblah*). See Map 9, p. 2106. Riblah was the site (588–587 B.C.E.) where Nebuchadrezzar king of Babylon slaughtered the sons and officials of Judah's king Zedekiah. After the slaughter Zedekiah was blinded and taken into exile (2 Kgs 25; Jer 39; 52).

7:1-27 The end has come…Disaster after disaster!: This prophetic speech is a poetic description of the day of the LORD (7:7; Amos 5:18-20, Mal 4:1, Heb 10:25). The ancient Greek version of Ezekiel 7:10 reads day "of the LORD." See note on 30:3.

7:6 An end has come, the end has come: The repetition emphasizes the seriousness of the judgment.

Then you shall know that it is I the LORD who strike.
10 See, the day! See, it comes!
Your doom[a] has gone out.
The rod has blossomed, pride has budded.
11 Violence has grown into a rod of wickedness.
None of them shall remain,
not their abundance, not their wealth;
no pre-eminence among them.[a]
12 The time has come, the day draws near;
let not the buyer rejoice, nor the seller mourn,
for wrath is upon all their multitude.
13 For the sellers shall not return to what has been sold as long as they
remain alive. For the vision concerns all their multitude; it shall not be
revoked. Because of their iniquity, they cannot maintain their lives.[a]
14 They have blown the horn and made everything ready;
but no one goes to battle,
for my wrath is upon all their multitude.
15 The sword is outside, pestilence and famine are inside;
those in the field die by the sword;
those in the city—famine and pestilence devour them.
16 If any survivors escape,
they shall be found on the mountains
like doves of the valleys,
all of them moaning over their iniquity.
17 All hands shall grow feeble,
all knees turn to water.
18 They shall put on sackcloth,
horror shall cover them.
Shame shall be on all faces,
baldness on all their heads.
19 They shall fling their silver into the streets,
their gold shall be treated as unclean.
Their silver and gold cannot save them on the day of the wrath of the
LORD. They shall not satisfy their hunger or fill their stomachs with it.
For it was the stumbling block of their iniquity. 20 From their[b] beautiful ornament, in which they took pride, they made their abominable
images, their detestable things; therefore I will make of it an unclean
thing to them.
21 I will hand it over to strangers as booty,
to the wicked of the earth as plunder;
they shall profane it.
22 I will avert my face from them,
so that they may profane my treasured[c] place;

[a] Meaning of Heb uncertain [b] Syr Symmachus: Heb *its* [c] Or *secret*

7:15 sword is outside, pestilence and famine are inside: Describes the scene of a city under siege. The army outside the walls won't allow people to go out to get food and water or to get rid of human or animal waste.

7:18-19 put on sackcloth…treated as unclean: Things will be so bad in the city that people will put on sackcloth and shave their heads, both signs of mourning and distress. They will toss away their money as if it were unclean, meaning ritually impure, since the money is useless in stopping the people's hunger and thirst. The word for "unclean" here refers to menstruation, which was considered to make one "unclean" in Israel's law (Lev 15:19-33). Later, Israel's disregard for the LORD is comparable to such menstrual impurity (36:17).

Israel sought safety and nourishment by worshiping idols, but that brought only death. What things in our culture are worshiped, bringing death instead of life?

7:22 they may profane my treasured place: God's treasured place is the temple in Jerusalem. The people profaned it (made it unholy) in various ways (see chapter 8). The desecration of the temple was only possible because the LORD allowed it to happen. "I will avert my face from them" refers to God allowing Judah's enemies to attack.

the violent shall enter it,
they shall profane it.
23 Make a chain![a]
For the land is full of bloody crimes;
the city is full of violence.
24 I will bring the worst of the nations
to take possession of their houses.
I will put an end to the arrogance of the strong,
and their holy places shall be profaned.
25 When anguish comes, they will seek peace,
but there shall be none.
26 Disaster comes upon disaster,
rumor follows rumor;
they shall keep seeking a vision from the prophet;
instruction shall perish from the priest,
and counsel from the elders.
27 The king shall mourn,
the prince shall be wrapped in despair,
and the hands of the people of the land shall tremble.
According to their way I will deal with them;
according to their own judgments I will judge them.
And they shall know that I am the LORD.

Abominations in the Temple

8 In the sixth year, in the sixth month, on the fifth day of the
month, as I sat in my house, with the elders of Judah sitting
before me, the hand of the Lord GOD fell upon me there. 2I looked,
and there was a figure that looked like a human being;[b] below what
appeared to be its loins it was fire, and above the loins it was like the
appearance of brightness, like gleaming amber. 3It stretched out the
form of a hand, and took me by a lock of my head; and the spirit lifted
me up between earth and heaven, and brought me in visions of God
to Jerusalem, to the entrance of the gateway of the inner court that
faces north, to the seat of the image of jealousy, which provokes to
jealousy. 4And the glory of the God of Israel was there, like the vision
that I had seen in the valley.
5 Then God[c] said to me, "O mortal, lift up your eyes now in the
direction of the north." So I lifted up my eyes toward the north, and
there, north of the altar gate, in the entrance, was this image of jealousy. 6He said to me, "Mortal, do you see what they are doing, the
great abominations that the house of Israel are committing here, to
drive me far from my sanctuary? Yet you will see still greater abominations."

[a] Meaning of Heb uncertain [b] Gk: Heb *like fire* [c] Heb *he*

7:26 Disaster comes upon disaster: In this time of turmoil, there is a breakdown of religious practices. Prophets had no visions and the priests' instruction (*torah*) perishes (22:26; 44:23).

8:1—11:25 brought me in visions of God to Jerusalem: In this section, Ezekiel reports a second vision to the elders of Judah. This vision focuses on the temple in Jerusalem and the sinful things done there.

8:1 the sixth year: This new vision is about fourteen months after the first vision (592 B.C.E.). While sitting in his home with other exiled leaders (see also 14:1, 20:1), Ezekiel is transported (37:1) by his hair (8:3) to Jerusalem and the gateway of the inner temple courts.

8:2 a figure: This is a heavenly guide (40:3), though resembling one seated on the throne (1:26).

8:3 the image of jealousy: This likely refers to an image of another god, an idol (6:4; Deut 4:16; 2 Chr 33:7, 15) set up in the temple courtyard.

8:4 glory of the God of Israel: Here the LORD's presence is experienced again (3:22-23). The same "glory of the LORD" appears in Exodus as a "devouring fire" within which God revealed the details of the tabernacle, the dwelling of God with the people in the wilderness (Exod 24:15-18). See also the LORD's presence in the temple (1 Kgs 8:11).

8:5-18 lift up your eyes: In these verses, four episodes build like a dramatic crescendo as the prophet moves closer to the center of the temple. Each episode is punctuated by "you will see greater abominations." This highlights the distressing state of Israel's worship that leads to God's punishment (chapter 9).

8:6 to drive me far from my sanctuary?: This foreshadows God's judgment of Israel, which climaxes when the glory leaves the temple (10:18; 11:22-25).

7 And he brought me to the entrance of the court; I looked, and there was a hole in the wall. [8]Then he said to me, "Mortal, dig through the wall"; and when I dug through the wall, there was an entrance. [9]He said to me, "Go in, and see the vile abominations that they are committing here." [10]So I went in and looked; there, portrayed on the wall all around, were all kinds of creeping things, and loathsome animals, and all the idols of the house of Israel. [11]Before them stood seventy of the elders of the house of Israel, with Jaazaniah son of Shaphan standing among them. Each had his censer in his hand, and the fragrant cloud of incense was ascending. [12]Then he said to me, "Mortal, have you seen what the elders of the house of Israel are doing in the dark, each in his room of images? For they say, 'The LORD does not see us, the LORD has forsaken the land.'" [13]He said also to me, "You will see still greater abominations that they are committing."

14 Then he brought me to the entrance of the north gate of the house of the LORD; women were sitting there weeping for Tammuz. [15]Then he said to me, "Have you seen this, O mortal? You will see still greater abominations than these."

16 And he brought me into the inner court of the house of the LORD; there, at the entrance of the temple of the LORD, between the porch and the altar, were about twenty-five men, with their backs to the temple of the LORD, and their faces toward the east, prostrating themselves to the sun toward the east. [17]Then he said to me, "Have you seen this, O mortal? Is it not bad enough that the house of Judah commits the abominations done here? Must they fill the land with violence, and provoke my anger still further? See, they are putting the branch to their nose! [18]Therefore I will act in wrath; my eye will not spare, nor will I have pity; and though they cry in my hearing with a loud voice, I will not listen to them."

The Slaughter of the Idolaters

9 Then he cried in my hearing with a loud voice, saying, "Draw near, you executioners of the city, each with his destroying weapon in his hand." [2]And six men came from the direction of the upper gate, which faces north, each with his weapon for slaughter in his hand; among them was a man clothed in linen, with a writing case at his side. They went in and stood beside the bronze altar.

3 Now the glory of the God of Israel had gone up from the cherub on which it rested to the threshold of the house. The LORD called to the man clothed in linen, who had the writing case at his side; [4]and said to him, "Go through the city, through Jerusalem, and put a mark on the foreheads of those who sigh and groan over all the abominations that are committed in it." [5]To the others he said in my hearing, "Pass through the city after him, and kill; your eye shall not spare, and you shall show no pity. [6]Cut down old men, young men and young

8:8-13 Mortal, dig...each in his room of images?: Though what happens behind the wall is not visible to those outside, it is seen by God (8:12). The prophet sees a space with images of idols and filled with elders of the Israelite community, including Jaazaniah son of Shaphan (2 Kgs 22), all involved in idol worship.

8:14 weeping for Tammuz: This is worship of Tammuz, a Mesopotamian god likely associated with fertility.

8:16 the inner court: At the threshold of the Holy of Holies (43:5), "between the porch and the altar" (see also Joel 2:17), there is ritual worship of the sun by Israelites, probably priests, with their backs to the LORD (see Jer 23:11). See the illustration of the temple, p. 1404.

8:17 Is it not bad enough: With a twist, the prophet's focus suddenly shifts from abominations in the temple to the violence in the land, which kindles the LORD's anger even further. This violence may refer to various ways the people and leaders treated one another unjustly (see 12:19).

The people turn their backs, ritually (8:16) and ethically (8:17), toward the LORD. How do you, your community, or your country turn away from the LORD?

9:1-4 executioners...put a mark on: The LORD's response to Israel's abominations (chapter 8) is the extermination of sinners. Seven men appear in the center of the temple—six executioners and a scribe who is dressed in linen (see also 44:17-22). The scribe is charged with putting a mark on the forehead of all who sigh and groan over the abominations of Israel. It is not stated that any received the mark.

9:5 Pass through the city: Turning upside down the Passover (Exod 12), the executioners are sent out with gruesome matter-of-factness to kill all who have not received the mark. This included women and men, elders, and children. The executioners are to begin at the temple, the center of Israel's abominations.

women, little children and women, but touch no one who has the
mark. And begin at my sanctuary." So they began with the elders who
were in front of the house. [7]Then he said to them, "Defile the house,
and fill the courts with the slain. Go!" So they went out and killed in
the city. [8]While they were killing, and I was left alone, I fell prostrate
on my face and cried out, "Ah Lord GOD! will you destroy all who remain of Israel as you pour out your wrath upon Jerusalem?" [9]He said
to me, "The guilt of the house of Israel and Judah is exceedingly great;
the land is full of bloodshed and the city full of perversity; for they say,
'The LORD has forsaken the land, and the LORD does not see.' [10]As for
me, my eye will not spare, nor will I have pity, but I will bring down
their deeds upon their heads."
11 Then the man clothed in linen, with the writing case at his side,
brought back word, saying, "I have done as you commanded me."

God's Glory Leaves Jerusalem

10 Then I looked, and above the dome that was over the heads
of the cherubim there appeared above them something like
a sapphire,[a] in form resembling a throne. [2]He said to the man clothed
in linen, "Go within the wheelwork underneath the cherubim; fill
your hands with burning coals from among the cherubim, and scatter
them over the city." He went in as I looked on. [3]Now the cherubim
were standing on the south side of the house when the man went in;
and a cloud filled the inner court. [4]Then the glory of the LORD rose
up from the cherub to the threshold of the house; the house was filled
with the cloud, and the court was full of the brightness of the glory of
the LORD. [5]The sound of the wings of the cherubim was heard as far
as the outer court, like the voice of God Almighty[b] when he speaks.
6 When he commanded the man clothed in linen, "Take fire
from within the wheelwork, from among the cherubim," he went in
and stood beside a wheel. [7]And a cherub stretched out his hand from
among the cherubim to the fire that was among the cherubim, took
some of it and put it into the hands of the man clothed in linen, who
took it and went out. [8]The cherubim appeared to have the form of a
human hand under their wings.
9 I looked, and there were four wheels beside the cherubim, one
beside each cherub; and the appearance of the wheels was like gleaming beryl. [10]And as for their appearance, the four looked alike, something like a wheel within a wheel. [11]When they moved, they moved
in any of the four directions without veering as they moved; but in
whatever direction the front wheel faced, the others followed without
veering as they moved. [12]Their entire body, their rims, their spokes,
their wings, and the wheels—the wheels of the four of them—were

[a] Or *lapis lazuli* [b] Traditional rendering of Heb *El Shaddai*

9:7 Defile the house: The LORD commands that the dead bodies be dumped in the temple, which makes the house of the LORD ritually unclean (see Num 19:10-13). This is like putting an exclamation point to the temple defilements (chapter 8). It could also be a way of keeping the people away from the temple.

In the face of overwhelming death, the prophet falls on his face and cries out to God, perhaps trying to get God to stop the awful judgment. The LORD does not give in to Ezekiel's request. Can you recall times when you have cried out to God, hoping to change God's mind, to convince God to relent? What response did you get?

9:10 my eye will not spare: Even though the leaders assumed God did not see their shameful idol worship (8:12), all the abominations of the people are visible to God and will be judged.

10:1-14 Then I looked: Another throne vision of the chariot and the four cherubim (1:4-28; see note on 1:5-14). The glory of the LORD rides the throne-chariot (10:4).

10:2 the man clothed in linen: The scribe charged with marking those to be spared from the sweep of God's wrath (9:2-11) is charged with scattering burning coals throughout Jerusalem. He is handed the coals by one of the cherubim from within the chariot (see 10:7).

full of eyes all around. [13]As for the wheels, they were called in my
hearing "the wheelwork." [14]Each one had four faces: the first face was
that of the cherub, the second face was that of a human being, the
third that of a lion, and the fourth that of an eagle.
15 The cherubim rose up. These were the living creatures that I
saw by the river Chebar. [16]When the cherubim moved, the wheels
moved beside them; and when the cherubim lifted up their wings to
rise up from the earth, the wheels at their side did not veer. [17]When
they stopped, the others stopped, and when they rose up, the others
rose up with them; for the spirit of the living creatures was in them.
18 Then the glory of the LORD went out from the threshold of
the house and stopped above the cherubim. [19]The cherubim lifted up
their wings and rose up from the earth in my sight as they went out
with the wheels beside them. They stopped at the entrance of the east
gate of the house of the LORD; and the glory of the God of Israel was
above them.
20 These were the living creatures that I saw underneath the God
of Israel by the river Chebar; and I knew that they were cherubim.
[21]Each had four faces, each four wings, and underneath their wings
something like human hands. [22]As for what their faces were like, they
were the same faces whose appearance I had seen by the river Chebar.
Each one moved straight ahead.

Judgment on Wicked Counselors

11 The spirit lifted me up and brought me to the east gate of the
house of the LORD, which faces east. There, at the entrance of
the gateway, were twenty-five men; among them I saw Jaazaniah son
of Azzur, and Pelatiah son of Benaiah, officials of the people. [2]He said
to me, "Mortal, these are the men who devise iniquity and who give
wicked counsel in this city; [3]they say, 'The time is not near to build
houses; this city is the pot, and we are the meat.' [4]Therefore prophesy
against them; prophesy, O mortal."
5 Then the spirit of the LORD fell upon me, and he said to me,
"Say, Thus says the LORD: This is what you think, O house of Israel;
I know the things that come into your mind. [6]You have killed many
in this city, and have filled its streets with the slain. [7]Therefore thus
says the Lord GOD: The slain whom you have placed within it are the
meat, and this city is the pot; but you shall be taken out of it. [8]You
have feared the sword; and I will bring the sword upon you, says the
Lord GOD. [9]I will take you out of it and give you over to the hands of
foreigners, and execute judgments upon you. [10]You shall fall by the
sword; I will judge you at the border of Israel. And you shall know
that I am the LORD. [11]This city shall not be your pot, and you shall not
be the meat inside it; I will judge you at the border of Israel. [12]Then
you shall know that I am the LORD, whose statutes you have not fol-

10:18 the glory of the LORD went out . . . from the . . . house: God's judgment reaches a pinnacle as the glory of the LORD abandons the temple (see 11:22-23).

10:19 the east gate: This was the main ceremonial gate of the temple (Ps 118:19-20), which has not been dishonored in the same way as the north gate (8:3-5). It is also the gate through which the glory of the LORD returns (43:4-5).

10:20 living creatures . . . by the river Chebar: See 1:3-14 and related notes.

11:1 officials of the people: Twenty-five men (possibly the same ones mentioned in 8:16) are judged for their inappropriate civic leadership. They abused their offices to "devise iniquity" and "give wicked counsel." Jaazaniah son of Azzur and Pelatiah son of Benaiah, are called "officials of the people," a term that likely means they were lay leaders (Neh 11:1).

What is the duty of public officials? Ezekiel speaks against unjust actions by civic officials, as they have led their people into wickedness rather than goodness. In his explanation to the Fourth Petition (give us this day our daily bread) of the Lord's Prayer in the Large Catechism, Martin Luther speaks of the duties of the civil leaders of his day: "It would therefore be fitting if the coat of arms of every upright prince were emblazoned with a loaf of bread instead of a lion" (*BC*: 450). According to Luther, it is the duty of princes (civil leaders) to care faithfully for their subjects *and* for the subjects to honor and hold their princes in prayer. *Ezekiel 11:1-4*

11:5 Say, Thus says the LORD: Ezekiel has been transported again (8:1) to the place where the glory of the LORD is exiting the temple (11:22-25) in judgment of Israel. For the first time in the temple vision (8:1—11:25), Ezekiel is called to function as a prophet by speaking God's words. The walls of Jerusalem—"your pot" (11:11; 24:1-14)—will not provide protection from the judgment.

11:9 I will take you out of it: Those left alive will be taken into exile, removed from the promised land because they have not lived according to God's law ("statutes" and "ordinances," 11:12; see also Exod 12:25, Deut 8:1).

lowed, and whose ordinances you have not kept, but you have acted
according to the ordinances of the nations that are around you."
13 Now, while I was prophesying, Pelatiah son of Benaiah died.
Then I fell down on my face, cried with a loud voice, and said, "Ah
Lord GOD! will you make a full end of the remnant of Israel?"

God Will Restore Israel

14 Then the word of the LORD came to me: 15Mortal, your kinsfolk, your own kin, your fellow exiles,[a] the whole house of Israel, all of
them, are those of whom the inhabitants of Jerusalem have said, "They
have gone far from the LORD; to us this land is given for a possession."
16Therefore say: Thus says the Lord GOD: Though I removed them
far away among the nations, and though I scattered them among the
countries, yet I have been a sanctuary to them for a little while[b] in the
countries where they have gone. 17Therefore say: Thus says the Lord
GOD: I will gather you from the peoples, and assemble you out of the
countries where you have been scattered, and I will give you the land
of Israel. 18When they come there, they will remove from it all its detestable things and all its abominations. 19I will give them one[c] heart,
and put a new spirit within them; I will remove the heart of stone
from their flesh and give them a heart of flesh, 20so that they may follow my statutes and keep my ordinances and obey them. Then they
shall be my people, and I will be their God. 21But as for those whose
heart goes after their detestable things and their abominations,[d] I will
bring their deeds upon their own heads, says the Lord GOD.
22 Then the cherubim lifted up their wings, with the wheels beside them; and the glory of the God of Israel was above them. 23And
the glory of the LORD ascended from the middle of the city, and
stopped on the mountain east of the city. 24The spirit lifted me up
and brought me in a vision by the spirit of God into Chaldea, to the
exiles. Then the vision that I had seen left me. 25And I told the exiles
all the things that the LORD had shown me.

Judah's Captivity Portrayed

12 The word of the LORD came to me: 2Mortal, you are living in
the midst of a rebellious house, who have eyes to see but do
not see, who have ears to hear but do not hear; 3for they are a rebellious house. Therefore, mortal, prepare for yourself an exile's baggage,
and go into exile by day in their sight; you shall go like an exile from
your place to another place in their sight. Perhaps they will understand, though they are a rebellious house. 4You shall bring out your
baggage by day in their sight, as baggage for exile; and you shall go

---

[a] Gk Syr: Heb *people of your kindred* [b] Or *to some extent* [c] Another reading is *a new* [d] Cn: Heb *And to the heart of their detestable things and their abominations their heart goes*

11:13 Pelatiah…the remnant of Israel?: Though Ezekiel had said Pelatiah and the others would die by the sword when the nation was invaded (11:1-9), Pelatiah suddenly dies. This causes Ezekiel to cry out to God again (9:8) on behalf of the "remnant," those of Israel who remain alive (see also Zech 8:11-12).

11:14-21 the word of the LORD came to me: The LORD makes it clear that the remnant of Israel (11:13) is not those Ezekiel sees in Jerusalem. Rather, it is the faithful in exile in Babylon that are the remnant. The LORD has been a "sanctuary" for them (11:16). This prophesy also clarifies that the exiles have a right to the land of Israel when they return.

11:17-21 I will gather you: These words to the exiles are a fresh break from overwhelming judgment. God will give them the gift of one heart and place within them a new spirit (11:19). (See also 18:31; 36:26; Jer 31:33-34; 32:37-41.) The state of one's heart, not geographical location, is what is most important to the LORD (11:21).

11:22-23 the cherubim…glory of the LORD: Again the throne-chariot appears (see also 1:4-28; 10:1-22). The vision concludes with the glory of the God of Israel leaving the temple and Jerusalem and stopping east of the city.

11:24-25 the spirit lifted me up: When the vision is completed, Ezekiel is returned to the exiles in Babylon to share what he has seen.

12:1-16 The word of the LORD came to me: Ezekiel is commanded to communicate not only with words but also with symbolic actions (4:1—5:17). Here he acts out the exile in the sight of the people in Babylon (12:3). He is not allowed to speak until the exiles ask the prophet about his actions (12:9).

How would you react to Ezekiel's behavior if you were his neighbor? What message do you think the world needs to hear or see? How might you help share this message?

out yourself at evening in their sight, as those do who go into exile. [5]Dig through the wall in their sight, and carry the baggage through it. [6]In their sight you shall lift the baggage on your shoulder, and carry it out in the dark; you shall cover your face, so that you may not see the land; for I have made you a sign for the house of Israel.

7 I did just as I was commanded. I brought out my baggage by day, as baggage for exile, and in the evening I dug through the wall with my own hands; I brought it out in the dark, carrying it on my shoulder in their sight.

8 In the morning the word of the LORD came to me: [9]Mortal, has not the house of Israel, the rebellious house, said to you, "What are you doing?" [10]Say to them, "Thus says the Lord GOD: This oracle concerns the prince in Jerusalem and all the house of Israel in it." [11]Say, "I am a sign for you: as I have done, so shall it be done to them; they shall go into exile, into captivity." [12]And the prince who is among them shall lift his baggage on his shoulder in the dark, and shall go out; he[a] shall dig through the wall and carry it through; he shall cover his face, so that he may not see the land with his eyes. [13]I will spread my net over him, and he shall be caught in my snare; and I will bring him to Babylon, the land of the Chaldeans, yet he shall not see it; and he shall die there. [14]I will scatter to every wind all who are around him, his helpers and all his troops; and I will unsheathe the sword behind them. [15]And they shall know that I am the LORD, when I disperse them among the nations and scatter them through the countries. [16]But I will let a few of them escape from the sword, from famine and pestilence, so that they may tell of all their abominations among the nations where they go; then they shall know that I am the LORD.

Judgment Not Postponed

17 The word of the LORD came to me: [18]Mortal, eat your bread with quaking, and drink your water with trembling and with fearfulness; [19]and say to the people of the land, Thus says the Lord GOD concerning the inhabitants of Jerusalem in the land of Israel: They shall eat their bread with fearfulness, and drink their water in dismay, because their land shall be stripped of all it contains, on account of the violence of all those who live in it. [20]The inhabited cities shall be laid waste, and the land shall become a desolation; and you shall know that I am the LORD.

21 The word of the LORD came to me: [22]Mortal, what is this proverb of yours about the land of Israel, which says, "The days are prolonged, and every vision comes to nothing"? [23]Tell them therefore, "Thus says the Lord GOD: I will put an end to this proverb, and they shall use it no more as a proverb in Israel." But say to them, The

[a] Gk Syr: Heb *they*

12:12 the prince: This likely refers to Zedekiah, who was placed upon the throne of Judah by the Babylonians as puppet ruler in 597 B.C.E. "Prince" indicates his humiliated status under the rule of the Babylon king. The phrase "in the dark" (12:6, 12) refers to the fact that Zedekiah fled Jerusalem under the cover of darkness, only to be captured at Riblah, where his sons were slaughtered in his sight, and then he was blinded (Jer 39:1-10; 2 Kgs 25:3-7).

12:14-16 I will scatter...they shall know that I am the LORD: Some are allowed to survive the attack of the Babylonians and exile, so they can tell the story of what happened. This will show God's power to the nations and be a reminder to themselves that God spared them for a purpose.

12:17-20 eat your bread with quaking: With another symbolic action, the prophet represents the fear of the coming destruction and displacement, which results from the people's violence (12:19).

12:21-28 every vision comes to nothing...many years ahead: The people question the word of the LORD, which Ezekiel receives in visions. They play down Ezekiel's vision because they think that like other visions they have heard his will come to nothing (12:22). They also play it down because they think if it happens it will only do so far in the future (12:27).

days are near, and the fulfillment of every vision. 24 For there shall no
longer be any false vision or flattering divination within the house of
Israel. 25 But I the LORD will speak the word that I speak, and it will be
fulfilled. It will no longer be delayed; but in your days, O rebellious
house, I will speak the word and fulfill it, says the Lord GOD.
26 The word of the LORD came to me: 27 Mortal, the house of
Israel is saying, "The vision that he sees is for many years ahead; he
prophesies for distant times." 28 Therefore say to them, Thus says the
Lord GOD: None of my words will be delayed any longer, but the
word that I speak will be fulfilled, says the Lord GOD.

False Prophets Condemned

13 The word of the LORD came to me: 2 Mortal, prophesy against
the prophets of Israel who are prophesying; say to those
who prophesy out of their own imagination: "Hear the word of the
LORD!" 3 Thus says the Lord GOD, Alas for the senseless prophets who
follow their own spirit, and have seen nothing! 4 Your prophets have
been like jackals among ruins, O Israel. 5 You have not gone up into
the breaches, or repaired a wall for the house of Israel, so that it might
stand in battle on the day of the LORD. 6 They have envisioned falsehood and lying divination; they say, "Says the LORD," when the LORD
has not sent them, and yet they wait for the fulfillment of their word!
7 Have you not seen a false vision or uttered a lying divination, when
you have said, "Says the LORD," even though I did not speak?
8 Therefore thus says the Lord GOD: Because you have uttered
falsehood and envisioned lies, I am against you, says the Lord GOD.
9 My hand will be against the prophets who see false visions and utter
lying divinations; they shall not be in the council of my people, nor be
enrolled in the register of the house of Israel, nor shall they enter the
land of Israel; and you shall know that I am the Lord GOD. 10 Because,
in truth, because they have misled my people, saying, "Peace," when
there is no peace; and because, when the people build a wall, these
prophets[a] smear whitewash on it. 11 Say to those who smear whitewash on it that it shall fall. There will be a deluge of rain,[b] great hailstones will fall, and a stormy wind will break out. 12 When the wall
falls, will it not be said to you, "Where is the whitewash you smeared
on it?" 13 Therefore thus says the Lord GOD: In my wrath I will make
a stormy wind break out, and in my anger there shall be a deluge of
rain, and hailstones in wrath to destroy it. 14 I will break down the wall
that you have smeared with whitewash, and bring it to the ground,
so that its foundation will be laid bare; when it falls, you shall perish
within it; and you shall know that I am the LORD. 15 Thus I will spend
my wrath upon the wall, and upon those who have smeared it with

[a] Heb *they* [b] Heb *rain and you*

13:1-16 prophesy against the prophets of Israel: Ezekiel is called to condemn false prophets who "prophesy out of their own imagination" (13:2) and "follow their own spirit" (13:3).

13:9 enrolled in the register: A public written record of citizenship in the house of Israel (see Ps 87:6, Ezra 2:62).

13:10-16 saying, "Peace," when there is no peace...you have smeared with whitewash: The biggest charge against the false prophets is lying to the people about reality (Jer 23:16-17). The image of a weak wall is a symbol of reality, which is made to look far stronger than it actually is by the whitewash applied by false prophets.

How and why do we whitewash things in our lives, our church, our world? What is the danger of whitewashing things?

whitewash; and I will say to you, The wall is no more, nor those who smeared it— [16]the prophets of Israel who prophesied concerning Jerusalem and saw visions of peace for it, when there was no peace, says the Lord God.

17 As for you, mortal, set your face against the daughters of your people, who prophesy out of their own imagination; prophesy against them [18]and say, Thus says the Lord God: Woe to the women who sew bands on all wrists, and make veils for the heads of persons of every height, in the hunt for human lives! Will you hunt down lives among my people, and maintain your own lives? [19]You have profaned me among my people for handfuls of barley and for pieces of bread, putting to death persons who should not die and keeping alive persons who should not live, by your lies to my people, who listen to lies.

20 Therefore thus says the Lord God: I am against your bands with which you hunt lives;[a] I will tear them from your arms, and let the lives go free, the lives that you hunt down like birds. [21]I will tear off your veils, and save my people from your hands; they shall no longer be prey in your hands; and you shall know that I am the Lord. [22]Because you have disheartened the righteous falsely, although I have not disheartened them, and you have encouraged the wicked not to turn from their wicked way and save their lives; [23]therefore you shall no longer see false visions or practice divination; I will save my people from your hand. Then you will know that I am the Lord.

God's Judgments Justified

14 Certain elders of Israel came to me and sat down before me. [2]And the word of the Lord came to me: [3]Mortal, these men have taken their idols into their hearts, and placed their iniquity as a stumbling block before them; shall I let myself be consulted by them? [4]Therefore speak to them, and say to them, Thus says the Lord God: Any of those of the house of Israel who take their idols into their hearts and place their iniquity as a stumbling block before them, and yet come to the prophet—I the Lord will answer those who come with the multitude of their idols, [5]in order that I may take hold of the hearts of the house of Israel, all of whom are estranged from me through their idols.

6 Therefore say to the house of Israel, Thus says the Lord God: Repent and turn away from your idols; and turn away your faces from all your abominations. [7]For any of those of the house of Israel, or of the aliens who reside in Israel, who separate themselves from me, taking their idols into their hearts and placing their iniquity as a stumbling block before them, and yet come to a prophet to inquire of me by him, I the Lord will answer them myself. [8]I will set my face against

[a] Gk Syr: Heb *lives for birds*

13:17-23 the daughters of your people: While there are positive examples of female prophets, such as Miriam (Exod 15:20) and Huldah (2 Kgs 22:14), the women here are false prophets who sew wristbands and make veils that may have to do with practicing magic and sorcery, things associated with the religious practice of foreigners and disgusting to the Lord (Deut 18:9-14).

13:19 handfuls of barley and for pieces of bread: The payment the false prophetesses received for services is small (see also 1 Sam 9:7).

13:22 Because you have disheartened: Similar to the whitewashed wall (13:10), judgment comes because these "daughters" have taken hope from the righteous and not called the wicked to task for their wickedness.

14:1-11 Certain elders of Israel: Ezekiel is again (8:1) approached by elders. This time they do not understand that the Lord expects worship of the Lord alone. The word of the Lord that comes to them likely is *not* what they wanted to hear.

14:3-5 have taken their idols into their hearts: An "idol" here is not merely a statue that is worshiped but something that has become part of the elders' hearts, causing them to be strangers to God and God to them (Isa 1:4).

How do the idols of our hearts cause us to be strangers to God?

14:6-8 Repent and turn away from your idols: Idolatry is not the final word. The elders and any who are still worshiping idols are commanded to turn away from their idols and toward the Lord.

14:7 aliens: This could refer to non-Israelites who lived in Israelite territory and had certain rights (see Deut 14: 29). See also the notes on 22:6-7 and 47:14.

them; I will make them a sign and a byword and cut them off from the
midst of my people; and you shall know that I am the LORD.
9 If a prophet is deceived and speaks a word, I, the LORD, have
deceived that prophet, and I will stretch out my hand against him,
and will destroy him from the midst of my people Israel. 10 And they
shall bear their punishment—the punishment of the inquirer and the
punishment of the prophet shall be the same— 11 so that the house
of Israel may no longer go astray from me, nor defile themselves any
more with all their transgressions. Then they shall be my people, and
I will be their God, says the Lord GOD.
12 The word of the LORD came to me: 13 Mortal, when a land
sins against me by acting faithlessly, and I stretch out my hand against
it, and break its staff of bread and send famine upon it, and cut off
from it human beings and animals, 14 even if Noah, Daniel,[a] and Job,
these three, were in it, they would save only their own lives by their
righteousness, says the Lord GOD. 15 If I send wild animals through
the land to ravage it, so that it is made desolate, and no one may pass
through because of the animals; 16 even if these three men were in it,
as I live, says the Lord GOD, they would save neither sons nor daughters; they alone would be saved, but the land would be desolate. 17 Or
if I bring a sword upon that land and say, "Let a sword pass through
the land," and I cut off human beings and animals from it; 18 though
these three men were in it, as I live, says the Lord GOD, they would
save neither sons nor daughters, but they alone would be saved. 19 Or
if I send a pestilence into that land, and pour out my wrath upon it
with blood, to cut off humans and animals from it; 20 even if Noah,
Daniel,[a] and Job were in it, as I live, says the Lord GOD, they would
save neither son nor daughter; they would save only their own lives
by their righteousness.
21 For thus says the Lord GOD: How much more when I send
upon Jerusalem my four deadly acts of judgment, sword, famine, wild
animals, and pestilence, to cut off humans and animals from it! 22 Yet,
survivors shall be left in it, sons and daughters who will be brought
out; they will come out to you. When you see their ways and their
deeds, you will be consoled for the evil that I have brought upon Jerusalem, for all that I have brought upon it. 23 They shall console you,
when you see their ways and their deeds; and you shall know that it
was not without cause that I did all that I have done in it, says the
Lord GOD.

The Useless Vine

15 The word of the LORD came to me:
2 O mortal, how does the wood of the vine surpass all other
wood—

[a] Or, as otherwise read, *Danel*

14:9-11 If a prophet is deceived: Under the threat of severe punishment, the LORD warns the true prophet to speak as instructed against the elders and their idolatry (14:3), because the repentance of the elders and their people is key to mending the broken relationship between God and God's people.

14:14 even if Noah, Daniel, and Job . . . were in it: These characters are named because they were above criticism for their faithfulness. The words "even if" are used three times (verses 14, 16, 20), building to a climax (14:21) that states that not even the presence of such faithful people would protect faithless Jerusalem from the LORD's judgment.

14:14 Daniel: This does not likely refer to the hero of the Old Testament book of Daniel, as that Daniel and the book come from a later time. More likely it is a reference to the wise and righteous king Dan'el in the ancient Ugaritic epic, *Aqhat.* See also 28:3.

14:21 sword, famine, wild animals, and pestilence: Four judgments, now aimed at Jerusalem, repeat the same judgments given in a different order in 5:16.

14:22-23 survivors: In a surprising turn toward hope, it is said that there will be survivors of God's judgment against Jerusalem. This may refer to the second wave of exiles, who came to Babylon after Jerusalem and the temple were completely destroyed in 586 B.C.E. The appearance of these survivors will "console" (14:23) Ezekiel's hearers, perhaps because they will be a glimmer of hope that God did not destroy every one of them. And they will recognize God's power.

15:1-8 the vine . . . I have given to the fire: This parable-like poem compares the dead, burnt wood of a useless grapevine to the people of Jerusalem (see 17:3-10; Isa 5:1-7). When grape vines no longer produce fruit they are cut down and burned.

the vine branch that is among the trees of the forest?
3 Is wood taken from it to make anything?
Does one take a peg from it on which to hang any object?
4 It is put in the fire for fuel;
when the fire has consumed both ends of it
and the middle of it is charred,
is it useful for anything?
5 When it was whole it was used for nothing;
how much less—when the fire has consumed it,
and it is charred—
can it ever be used for anything!
6 Therefore thus says the Lord GOD: Like the wood of the vine
among the trees of the forest, which I have given to the fire for fuel, so
I will give up the inhabitants of Jerusalem. 7 I will set my face against
them; although they escape from the fire, the fire shall still consume
them; and you shall know that I am the LORD, when I set my face
against them. 8 And I will make the land desolate, because they have
acted faithlessly, says the Lord GOD.

God's Faithless Bride

16 The word of the LORD came to me: 2 Mortal, make known
to Jerusalem her abominations, 3 and say, Thus says the Lord
GOD to Jerusalem: Your origin and your birth were in the land of the
Canaanites; your father was an Amorite, and your mother a Hittite.
4 As for your birth, on the day you were born your navel cord was not
cut, nor were you washed with water to cleanse you, nor rubbed with
salt, nor wrapped in cloths. 5 No eye pitied you, to do any of these
things for you out of compassion for you; but you were thrown out in
the open field, for you were abhorred on the day you were born.
6 I passed by you, and saw you flailing about in your blood. As
you lay in your blood, I said to you, "Live! 7 and grow up[a] like a plant
of the field." You grew up and became tall and arrived at full woman-
hood;[b] your breasts were formed, and your hair had grown; yet you
were naked and bare.
8 I passed by you again and looked on you; you were at the age
for love. I spread the edge of my cloak over you, and covered your
nakedness: I pledged myself to you and entered into a covenant with
you, says the Lord GOD, and you became mine. 9 Then I bathed you
with water and washed off the blood from you, and anointed you with
oil. 10 I clothed you with embroidered cloth and with sandals of fine
leather; I bound you in fine linen and covered you with rich fabric.[c]
11 I adorned you with ornaments: I put bracelets on your arms, a chain

[a] Gk Syr: Heb *Live! I made you a myriad* [b] Cn: Heb *ornament of ornaments* [c] Meaning of Heb uncertain

16:1-63 make known to Jerusalem her abominations...Adulterous wife: Told in the first-person ("I") voice of the LORD, this allegory describes Jerusalem as the LORD's unfaithful wife. The relationship is broken by Jerusalem's adulterous betrayal and is marked by abuse. The allegory *should not* be taken as a model or justification for similar actions and reactions between partners today. Ancient cities were at times considered female partners of male deities (Isa 47:1-15).

16:3 Your origin and your birth: Jerusalem's ancestry is outside the Abrahamic covenant (Gen 11:31) and instead located among foreigners, enemies of Israel (Deut 20:17, 1 Kgs 9:20-21) who had lived in the land prior to their occupation: the Canaanites (Josh 17:13), the Amorites (Josh 24:18, Amos 2:10), and the Hittites (Josh 3:10). The child, Jerusalem, in effect is a foreigner.

16:5 you were thrown out: Within certain ancient social systems baby girls were considered of little social or monetary worth, and so on occasion they were not cared for at birth and left out in the open to die.

16:6-8 you flailing: The LORD rescues Jerusalem, and she grows into a woman.

16:9-14 the age for love: Graphic language describing the LORD's courtship of and consummated marriage ("spread the edge of my cloak over you") with the young woman Jerusalem. God then bathed her, clothed her in beautiful clothing and jewelry, and gave her fine food to eat.

16:10 fine leather: The Hebrew word used here and elsewhere is only used for material that covers the tabernacle (Exod 39:34) or the ark of the covenant (Num 4:5-28), emphasizing that Jerusalem houses the temple (Ps 26:8).

on your neck, 12 a ring on your nose, earrings in your ears, and a beautiful crown upon your head. 13 You were adorned with gold and silver,
while your clothing was of fine linen, rich fabric,[a] and embroidered
cloth. You had choice flour and honey and oil for food. You grew exceedingly beautiful, fit to be a queen. 14 Your fame spread among the
nations on account of your beauty, for it was perfect because of my
splendor that I had bestowed on you, says the Lord GOD.

15 But you trusted in your beauty, and played the whore because
of your fame, and lavished your whorings on any passer-by.[b] 16 You
took some of your garments, and made for yourself colorful shrines,
and on them played the whore; nothing like this has ever been or ever
shall be.[a] 17 You also took your beautiful jewels of my gold and my silver that I had given you, and made for yourself male images, and with
them played the whore; 18 and you took your embroidered garments
to cover them, and set my oil and my incense before them. 19 Also
my bread that I gave you—I fed you with choice flour and oil and
honey—you set it before them as a pleasing odor; and so it was, says
the Lord GOD. 20 You took your sons and your daughters, whom you
had borne to me, and these you sacrificed to them to be devoured.
As if your whorings were not enough! 21 You slaughtered my children
and delivered them up as an offering to them. 22 And in all your abominations and your whorings you did not remember the days of your
youth, when you were naked and bare, flailing about in your blood.

23 After all your wickedness (woe, woe to you! says the Lord
GOD), 24 you built yourself a platform and made yourself a lofty place
in every square; 25 at the head of every street you built your lofty place
and prostituted your beauty, offering yourself to every passer-by, and
multiplying your whoring. 26 You played the whore with the Egyptians, your lustful neighbors, multiplying your whoring, to provoke
me to anger. 27 Therefore I stretched out my hand against you, reduced
your rations, and gave you up to the will of your enemies, the daughters of the Philistines, who were ashamed of your lewd behavior.
28 You played the whore with the Assyrians, because you were insatiable; you played the whore with them, and still you were not satisfied.
29 You multiplied your whoring with Chaldea, the land of merchants;
and even with this you were not satisfied.

30 How sick is your heart, says the Lord GOD, that you did all
these things, the deeds of a brazen whore; 31 building your platform at
the head of every street, and making your lofty place in every square!
Yet you were not like a whore, because you scorned payment. 32 Adulterous wife, who receives strangers instead of her husband! 33 Gifts are
given to all whores; but you gave your gifts to all your lovers, brib-
ing them to come to you from all around for your whorings. 34 So you

16:15-34 you trusted in your beauty: The courtship quickly goes bad as the young wife Jerusalem is accused of breaking the promise of her marriage with the LORD by acting as a prostitute with the Egyptians (16:26), Assyrians (16:28), and Chaldeans/Babylonians (16:29). At various times leading up to the destruction of Jerusalem, Judah's kings had made treaties with or paid bribes to each of these nations to gain protection against one of the other powers (see Isa 7; 20; 31; 39).

16:20 your sons and your daughters…you sacrificed: Part of Jerusalem's sins are said to include the sacrifice of her children. In this case it may be metaphorical. Child sacrifice was likely practiced during Israel's history. For example, such sacrifices were said to be made to the Canaanite god Baal (Jer 19:5; 32:35), to the god Molech (see Lev 18:21; 2 Kgs 23:10), and to the LORD (20:26, 23:39; Exod 22:29).

[a] Meaning of Heb uncertain [b] Heb adds *let it be his*

16:35-43 Therefore, O whore…I will deliver you into their hands: God will allow Jerusalem's foreign "lovers" (see note on 16:15-34) to execute God's judgments on Jerusalem, the unfaithful wife. This violent depiction of Jerusalem's punishment represents the violence of warfare and *should not* be confused with any condoning of violence against women (Gen 1:26-27).

16:38 as women who commit adultery: Central to the LORD's judgment is Jerusalem's infidelity, or unfaithfulness, to God. Missing from this image of adultery is the participation of the adulterous man. Too often the burden of adultery is placed unequally upon the woman.

16:44-58 Like mother, like daughter: Samaria and Sodom, two cities destroyed for their wickedness, are portrayed as sisters of Jerusalem and sinners like their mother, the Hittite (16:45). Samaria was the capital city of the northern kingdom of Israel, which Assyria defeated in 721 B.C.E. Neither Samaria nor Sodom (see Gen 19:24-28) was as sinful as Jerusalem (16:51).

were different from other women in your whorings: no one solicited
you to play the whore; and you gave payment, while no payment was
given to you; you were different.
35 Therefore, O whore, hear the word of the LORD: [36]Thus says
the Lord GOD, Because your lust was poured out and your nakedness
uncovered in your whoring with your lovers, and because of all your
abominable idols, and because of the blood of your children that you
gave to them, [37]therefore, I will gather all your lovers, with whom you
took pleasure, all those you loved and all those you hated; I will gather
them against you from all around, and will uncover your nakedness
to them, so that they may see all your nakedness. [38]I will judge you as
women who commit adultery and shed blood are judged, and bring
blood upon you in wrath and jealousy. [39]I will deliver you into their
hands, and they shall throw down your platform and break down your
lofty places; they shall strip you of your clothes and take your beautiful objects and leave you naked and bare. [40]They shall bring up a mob
against you, and they shall stone you and cut you to pieces with their
swords. [41]They shall burn your houses and execute judgments on you
in the sight of many women; I will stop you from playing the whore,
and you shall also make no more payments. [42]So I will satisfy my fury
on you, and my jealousy shall turn away from you; I will be calm, and
will be angry no longer. [43]Because you have not remembered the days
of your youth, but have enraged me with all these things; therefore, I
have returned your deeds upon your head, says the Lord GOD.
Have you not committed lewdness beyond all your abominations?
[44]See, everyone who uses proverbs will use this proverb about you,
"Like mother, like daughter." [45]You are the daughter of your mother,
who loathed her husband and her children; and you are the sister
of your sisters, who loathed their husbands and their children. Your
mother was a Hittite and your father an Amorite. [46]Your elder sister
is Samaria, who lived with her daughters to the north of you; and
your younger sister, who lived to the south of you, is Sodom with her
daughters. [47]You not only followed their ways, and acted according to
their abominations; within a very little time you were more corrupt
than they in all your ways. [48]As I live, says the Lord GOD, your sister Sodom and her daughters have not done as you and your daughters have done. [49]This was the guilt of your sister Sodom: she and her
daughters had pride, excess of food, and prosperous ease, but did not
aid the poor and needy. [50]They were haughty, and did abominable
things before me; therefore I removed them when I saw it. [51]Samaria
has not committed half your sins; you have committed more abominations than they, and have made your sisters appear righteous by
all the abominations that you have committed. [52]Bear your disgrace,
you also, for you have brought about for your sisters a more favorable
judgment; because of your sins in which you acted more abominably

than they, they are more in the right than you. So be ashamed, you
also, and bear your disgrace, for you have made your sisters appear
righteous.
53 I will restore their fortunes, the fortunes of Sodom and her
daughters and the fortunes of Samaria and her daughters, and I will
restore your own fortunes along with theirs, 54 in order that you may
bear your disgrace and be ashamed of all that you have done, becoming a consolation to them. 55 As for your sisters, Sodom and her daughters shall return to their former state, Samaria and her daughters shall
return to their former state, and you and your daughters shall return
to your former state. 56 Was not your sister Sodom a byword in your
mouth in the day of your pride, 57 before your wickedness was uncovered? Now you are a mockery to the daughters of Aram[a] and all her
neighbors, and to the daughters of the Philistines, those all around
who despise you. 58 You must bear the penalty of your lewdness and
your abominations, says the LORD.

An Everlasting Covenant

59 Yes, thus says the Lord GOD: I will deal with you as you have
done, you who have despised the oath, breaking the covenant; 60 yet I
will remember my covenant with you in the days of your youth, and
I will establish with you an everlasting covenant. 61 Then you will remember your ways, and be ashamed when I[b] take your sisters, both
your elder and your younger, and give them to you as daughters, but
not on account of my[c] covenant with you. 62 I will establish my covenant with you, and you shall know that I am the LORD, 63 in order
that you may remember and be confounded, and never open your
mouth again because of your shame, when I forgive you all that you
have done, says the Lord GOD.

The Two Eagles and the Vine

17 The word of the LORD came to me: 2 O mortal, propound a
riddle, and speak an allegory to the house of Israel. 3 Say: Thus
says the Lord GOD:

A great eagle, with great wings and long pinions,
rich in plumage of many colors,
came to the Lebanon.
He took the top of the cedar,
4 broke off its topmost shoot;
he carried it to a land of trade,
set it in a city of merchants.
5 Then he took a seed from the land,
placed it in fertile soil;

[a] Another reading is *Edom* [b] Syr: Heb *you* [c] Heb lacks *my*

16:53-58 I will restore: In what might first appear to be good news, the LORD promises to restore Sodom, Samaria, and Jerusalem. However, Jerusalem is restored "in order that you may bear your disgrace and be ashamed of all that you have done" (16:54)—that Jerusalem might be shamed in front of its neighbors.

16:59-63 I will remember my covenant: As the story draws to a close, the LORD's tone shifts from anger and vengeance to forgiveness, promising to remember (16:60) in order that Jerusalem may remember (16:63).

It is likely that the images used throughout chapter 16 were meant to shock and offend. How do you think about such assaulting images of God and of God's relationship with God's people?

17:1-10 A great eagle…became a vine: This poem (17:3-10) is both a riddle and an allegory (as in chapter 15). Such poems or sayings can also be called parables or proverbs (see 12:22-23; 16:44; 18:2-3). The characters represent historical figures during the time of the first and second waves of the Babylonian exile (597 and 587 B.C.E.). This becomes clear in the explanation (17:11-21).

17:3-5 great eagle…topmost shoot…seed: The Babylonian king Nebuchadnezzar is the great eagle. He took into exile King Jehoiachin of Judah, the topmost shoot of the long line of kings from the family of David. The tall cedar tree of Lebanon stands for the Davidic monarchy (Jer 22:6-7). In place of Jehoiachin, Nebuchadnezzar set up the "seed," Zedekiah, on the throne as a puppet king (see the note on 6:14), and he became the vine.

a plant[a] by abundant waters,
he set it like a willow twig.
6 It sprouted and became a vine
spreading out, but low;
its branches turned toward him,
its roots remained where it stood.
So it became a vine;
it brought forth branches,
put forth foliage.

17:7 another great eagle: This eagle is the Egyptian pharaoh Psammetichus II. The "vine," Zedekiah, stretched out his roots toward him, meaning that he transferred ("transplanted") his loyalty from Nebuchadnezzar. But this failed to repair the problem of Judah's unfaithfulness in a new political solution.

7 There was another great eagle,
with great wings and much plumage.
And see! This vine stretched out
its roots toward him;
it shot out its branches toward him,
so that he might water it.
From the bed where it was planted
8 it was transplanted
to good soil by abundant waters,
so that it might produce branches
and bear fruit
and become a noble vine.
9 Say: Thus says the Lord GOD:
Will it prosper?
Will he not pull up its roots,
cause its fruit to rot[a] and wither,
its fresh sprouting leaves to fade?
No strong arm or mighty army will be needed
to pull it from its roots.
10 When it is transplanted, will it thrive?
When the east wind strikes it,
will it not utterly wither,
wither on the bed where it grew?

17:9-10 Will it prosper?...When the east wind strikes it: These questions point to the inevitable end of Zedekiah's reign. They point to the eighteen-month siege of Jerusalem (588–587 B.C.E.) by Nebuchadnezzar ("the east wind"), which resulted in the second wave of exile and the destruction of Jerusalem and the temple (33:21-22).

11 Then the word of the LORD came to me: 12 Say now to the rebellious house: Do you not know what these things mean? Tell them:
The king of Babylon came to Jerusalem, took its king and its officials,
and brought them back with him to Babylon. 13 He took one of the
royal offspring and made a covenant with him, putting him under
oath (he had taken away the chief men of the land), 14 so that the kingdom might be humble and not lift itself up, and that by keeping his
covenant it might stand. 15 But he rebelled against him by sending ambassadors to Egypt, in order that they might give him horses and a
large army. Will he succeed? Can one escape who does such things?

17:11-21 what these things mean: The poem in 17:1-10 is explained.

---

[a] Meaning of Heb uncertain

Can he break the covenant and yet escape? [16]As I live, says the Lord
God, surely in the place where the king resides who made him king,
whose oath he despised, and whose covenant with him he broke—in
Babylon he shall die. [17]Pharaoh with his mighty army and great company will not help him in war, when ramps are cast up and siege walls
built to cut off many lives. [18]Because he despised the oath and broke
the covenant, because he gave his hand and yet did all these things, he
shall not escape. [19]Therefore thus says the Lord God: As I live, I will
surely return upon his head my oath that he despised, and my covenant that he broke. [20]I will spread my net over him, and he shall be
caught in my snare; I will bring him to Babylon and enter into judgment with him there for the treason he has committed against me.
[21]All the pick[a] of his troops shall fall by the sword, and the survivors
shall be scattered to every wind; and you shall know that I, the Lord,
have spoken.

17:19 my oath that he despised: Zedekiah breaking his oath to Nebuchadnezzar is understood as breaking an oath to the Lord (Jer 27:6-8).

Israel Exalted at Last

22 Thus says the Lord God:
I myself will take a sprig
from the lofty top of a cedar;
I will set it out.
I will break off a tender one
from the topmost of its young twigs;
I myself will plant it
on a high and lofty mountain.
23 On the mountain height of Israel
I will plant it,
in order that it may produce boughs and bear fruit,
and become a noble cedar.
Under it every kind of bird will live;
in the shade of its branches will nest
winged creatures of every kind.
24 All the trees of the field shall know
that I am the Lord.
I bring low the high tree,
I make high the low tree;
I dry up the green tree
and make the dry tree flourish.
I the Lord have spoken;
I will accomplish it.

17:22-24 I myself will take a sprig … plant it: Just as the eagle plucked the topmost shoot (17:3-4), now God will replant a sprig on a mountain height. This is likely a reference to God planting or restoring the temple on Mount Zion in Jerusalem (see Ps 48:1-2; Mic 4:1). With this action, every tree (leader or nation) will know the Lord's power (17:24). The image of the growth of a sapling ("a sprig") into a "noble cedar" implies a lengthy time.

Individual Retribution

18 The word of the Lord came to me: [2]What do you mean by
repeating this proverb concerning the land of Israel, "The

18:2-4 parents have eaten sour grapes: This familiar saying (see Jer 31:29-30) blames the problems of children on the actions of parents. But the Lord tells the exiles in this section (18:2-32) that they cannot blame previous generations for the problems that have come about because of their own lack of faithfulness. Each generation is responsible for its own actions (Deut 24:16).

It is clear in this text that all lives are God's (18:4). How can this impact how you relate with others and how communities relate with one another?

[a] Another reading is *fugitives*

parents have eaten sour grapes, and the children's teeth are set on edge"? [3]As I live, says the Lord GOD, this proverb shall no more be used by you in Israel. [4]Know that all lives are mine; the life of the parent as well as the life of the child is mine: it is only the person who sins that shall die.

18:5-9 If a man is righteous: Righteousness includes following God's law and right conduct within community ("acting faithfully," 18:9). But those who eat upon the mountains— meaning those who eat food that has been sacrificed to idols—or commit adultery or treat others unjustly are not righteous.

5 If a man is righteous and does what is lawful and right— [6]if he does not eat upon the mountains or lift up his eyes to the idols of the house of Israel, does not defile his neighbor's wife or approach a woman during her menstrual period, [7]does not oppress anyone, but restores to the debtor his pledge, commits no robbery, gives his bread to the hungry and covers the naked with a garment, [8]does not take advance or accrued interest, withholds his hand from iniquity, executes true justice between contending parties, [9]follows my statutes, and is careful to observe my ordinances, acting faithfully—such a one is righteous; he shall surely live, says the Lord GOD.

18:10-18 If he has a son: Ezekiel explores what it means if generations display opposite ways of living within God's expectations—son to father (18:10-13) and father to son (18:14-18). The sins and righteousness of each generation belong to it alone.

18:10 shedder of blood: Meaning a murderer (22:6, 9, 12; Gen 9:6).

10 If he has a son who is violent, a shedder of blood, [11]who does any of these things (though his father[a] does none of them), who eats upon the mountains, defiles his neighbor's wife, [12]oppresses the poor and needy, commits robbery, does not restore the pledge, lifts up his eyes to the idols, commits abomination, [13]takes advance or accrued interest; shall he then live? He shall not. He has done all these abominable things; he shall surely die; his blood shall be upon himself.

14 But if this man has a son who sees all the sins that his father has done, considers, and does not do likewise, [15]who does not eat upon the mountains or lift up his eyes to the idols of the house of Israel, does not defile his neighbor's wife, [16]does not wrong anyone, exacts no pledge, commits no robbery, but gives his bread to the hungry and covers the naked with a garment, [17]withholds his hand from iniquity,[b] takes no advance or accrued interest, observes my ordinances, and follows my statutes; he shall not die for his father's iniquity; he shall surely live. [18]As for his father, because he practiced extortion, robbed his brother, and did what is not good among his people, he dies for his iniquity.

18:19-20 Yet you say: Another saying (like 18:2) that is used as an excuse to dodge responsibility for one's own righteousness is taken apart.

19 Yet you say, "Why should not the son suffer for the iniquity of the father?" When the son has done what is lawful and right, and has been careful to observe all my statutes, he shall surely live. [20]The person who sins shall die. A child shall not suffer for the iniquity of a parent, nor a parent suffer for the iniquity of a child; the righteousness of the righteous shall be his own, and the wickedness of the wicked shall be his own.

18:21-24 if the wicked turn away from all their sins: Forgiveness is possible. Contrary to the idea of "fate," there is freedom in one's life choices. One can turn away from wickedness to righteousness—and vice versa (see also Jer 3:6-7; Amos 5:14-15).

21 But if the wicked turn away from all their sins that they have committed and keep all my statutes and do what is lawful and right, they shall surely live; they shall not die. [22]None of the transgressions

---

[a] Heb *he* [b] Gk: Heb *the poor*

that they have committed shall be remembered against them; for the
righteousness that they have done they shall live. 23 Have I any pleasure in the death of the wicked, says the Lord GOD, and not rather
that they should turn from their ways and live? 24 But when the righteous turn away from their righteousness and commit iniquity and do
the same abominable things that the wicked do, shall they live? None
of the righteous deeds that they have done shall be remembered; for
the treachery of which they are guilty and the sin they have committed, they shall die.

25 Yet you say, "The way of the Lord is unfair." Hear now, O house
of Israel: Is my way unfair? Is it not your ways that are unfair? 26 When
the righteous turn away from their righteousness and commit iniquity, they shall die for it; for the iniquity that they have committed
they shall die. 27 Again, when the wicked turn away from the wickedness they have committed and do what is lawful and right, they shall
save their life. 28 Because they considered and turned away from all the
transgressions that they had committed, they shall surely live; they
shall not die. 29 Yet the house of Israel says, "The way of the Lord is
unfair." O house of Israel, are my ways unfair? Is it not your ways that
are unfair?

30 Therefore I will judge you, O house of Israel, all of you according to your ways, says the Lord GOD. Repent and turn from all your
transgressions; otherwise iniquity will be your ruin.[a] 31 Cast away
from you all the transgressions that you have committed against me,
and get yourselves a new heart and a new spirit! Why will you die,
O house of Israel? 32 For I have no pleasure in the death of anyone,
says the Lord GOD. Turn, then, and live.

Israel Degraded

19 As for you, raise up a lamentation for the princes of Israel,
2 and say:

What a lioness was your mother
among lions!
She lay down among young lions,
rearing her cubs.
3 She raised up one of her cubs;
he became a young lion,
and he learned to catch prey;
he devoured humans.
4 The nations sounded an alarm against him;
he was caught in their pit;
and they brought him with hooks
to the land of Egypt.
5 When she saw that she was thwarted,

[a] Or *so that they shall not be a stumbling block of iniquity to you*

18:25-29 Yet you say: For a third time in the chapter (also 18: 2, 19), the people have a comeback to God's call to faithfulness. This time they suggest that the LORD is unfair (33:17). And consistent with previous times, the people's saying is turned back upon them.

18:30-32 Repent and turn…get yourselves a new heart and a new spirit!: The possibility of "a new heart and a new spirit" is a repeated theme in Ezekiel (11:19; 36:26). Compare this to the new covenant that God will write on the people's hearts (Jer 31:31-34). The statement "I have no pleasure in the death of anyone" is especially hopeful and does not draw a distinction between wicked and righteous (18:23; 33:11). The call to "Turn, then, and live" is an invitation to start over fresh (see also Amos 5:4, 6).

How do you hear the words "Turn, then, and live"?

19:1 a lamentation: A lamentation can be a prayer of sorrow or a funeral song, as it is here. For "the princes of Israel," see the note on 12:12.

19:2-14 a lioness…mother was like a vine: Two lamentations over the "lioness" (19:2-9) and over the "vine" (19:10-14). Similar to the allegory in 17.3-10, the elements of these laments correspond to figures in Judah's political history, and both end in exile and the "death" of the Davidic dynasty, with no hope for the future.

19:3-4 one of her cubs: Possibly refers to Jehoahaz, an evil king and son of Josiah and Hamutal, who was taken to Egypt by Pharaoh Neco in 609 B.C.E. (2 Kgs 23:30-34).

19:5 **another of her cubs:** This could be either Jehoiachin, who ruled briefly and was among the first wave of exiles after the fall of Jerusalem to the Babylonian king Nebuchadnezzar in 597 B.C.E. (2 Kgs 24:8-16), or Zedekiah, the Babylonian puppet ruler, the last of the line of David to reign and taken into exile in 586 B.C.E. (2 Kgs 24:17—25:7; Jer 39:7).

19:10-14 **like a vine:** The vine (chapters 15, 17) grows into a scepter, likely a reference to the Davidic dynasty. The vine is dried up by an "east wind," Nebuchadnezzar, and "transplanted into the wilderness," meaning taken into exile in Babylon. This effectively ended the dynasty, leaving no scepter for ruling (Jer 52:1-11).

that her hope was lost,
she took another of her cubs
and made him a young lion.
6 He prowled among the lions;
he became a young lion,
and he learned to catch prey;
he devoured people.
7 And he ravaged their strongholds,[a]
and laid waste their towns;
the land was appalled, and all in it,
at the sound of his roaring.
8 The nations set upon him
from the provinces all around;
they spread their net over him;
he was caught in their pit.
9 With hooks they put him in a cage,
and brought him to the king of Babylon;
they brought him into custody,
so that his voice should be heard no more
on the mountains of Israel.
10 Your mother was like a vine in a vineyard[b]
transplanted by the water,
fruitful and full of branches
from abundant water.
11 Its strongest stem became
a ruler's scepter;[c]
it towered aloft
among the thick boughs;
it stood out in its height
with its mass of branches.
12 But it was plucked up in fury,
cast down to the ground;
the east wind dried it up;
its fruit was stripped off,
its strong stem was withered;
the fire consumed it.
13 Now it is transplanted into the wilderness,
into a dry and thirsty land.
14 And fire has gone out from its stem,
has consumed its branches and fruit,
so that there remains in it no strong stem,
no scepter for ruling.

This is a lamentation, and it is used as a lamentation.

[a] Heb *his widows* [b] Cn: Heb *in your blood* [c] Heb *Its strongest stems became rulers' scepters*

Israel's Continuing Rebellion

20 In the seventh year, in the fifth month, on the tenth day of the month, certain elders of Israel came to consult the LORD, and sat down before me. [2]And the word of the LORD came to me: [3]Mortal, speak to the elders of Israel, and say to them: Thus says the Lord GOD: Why are you coming? To consult me? As I live, says the Lord GOD, I will not be consulted by you. [4]Will you judge them, mortal, will you judge them? Then let them know the abominations of their ancestors, [5]and say to them: Thus says the Lord GOD: On the day when I chose Israel, I swore to the offspring of the house of Jacob—making myself known to them in the land of Egypt—I swore to them, saying, I am the LORD your God. [6]On that day I swore to them that I would bring them out of the land of Egypt into a land that I had searched out for them, a land flowing with milk and honey, the most glorious of all lands. [7]And I said to them, Cast away the detestable things your eyes feast on, every one of you, and do not defile yourselves with the idols of Egypt; I am the LORD your God. [8]But they rebelled against me and would not listen to me; not one of them cast away the detestable things their eyes feasted on, nor did they forsake the idols of Egypt.

Then I thought I would pour out my wrath upon them and spend my anger against them in the midst of the land of Egypt. [9]But I acted for the sake of my name, that it should not be profaned in the sight of the nations among whom they lived, in whose sight I made myself known to them in bringing them out of the land of Egypt. [10]So I led them out of the land of Egypt and brought them into the wilderness. [11]I gave them my statutes and showed them my ordinances, by whose observance everyone shall live. [12]Moreover I gave them my sabbaths, as a sign between me and them, so that they might know that I the LORD sanctify them. [13]But the house of Israel rebelled against me in the wilderness; they did not observe my statutes but rejected my ordinances, by whose observance everyone shall live; and my sabbaths they greatly profaned.

Then I thought I would pour out my wrath upon them in the wilderness, to make an end of them. [14]But I acted for the sake of my name, so that it should not be profaned in the sight of the nations, in whose sight I had brought them out. [15]Moreover I swore to them in the wilderness that I would not bring them into the land that I had given them, a land flowing with milk and honey, the most glorious of all lands, [16]because they rejected my ordinances and did not observe my statutes, and profaned my sabbaths; for their heart went after their idols. [17]Nevertheless my eye spared them, and I did not destroy them or make an end of them in the wilderness.

18 I said to their children in the wilderness, Do not follow the statutes of your parents, nor observe their ordinances, nor defile

20:1-32 speak to the elders of Israel...go astray after their detestable things: Ezekiel is called not just to relay the LORD's message but to judge (20:4; 22:2; 23:36) them and their history.

20:1 In the seventh year: For the first time since 8:1, Ezekiel's prophesy is dated (see note on 1:1-2). The date of this prophecy is August 14, 591 B.C.E. Again, Ezekiel is consulted by "certain elders," leaders of the exile community in Babylon (8:1; 14:1).

20:5 when I chose: This language is reminiscent of the choosing of the people Israel (Deut 7:6); Eli the priest (1 Sam 2:28); King David (2 Sam 6:21); and Jerusalem as site of the temple (2 Chr 6:6). The phrase "I am the LORD your God" recalls the giving of the First Commandment (Exod 20:2-3).

20:7-8 detestable things: Israel is commanded to abandon their worship of Egyptian gods (7:20).

20:9 for the sake of my name: The LORD is gracious to the rebellious Israelites not because of Israel's merits but for the sake of the LORD's holy name (20:14; 22, 44; 36:21-23, 39:7-8, 25).

20:12 my sabbaths: From God's blessing of the seventh day of creation (Gen 2:2-3), keeping the sabbath is central to maintaining Israel's faithfulness to God (Exod 20:8-11; Deut 6:12-15). Ezekiel retells how Israel rebelled against God, especially by breaking the Sabbath (20:13, 16, 20, 21, 24; also see 23:38; Jer 17:19-27).

Consider the differences between keeping the Sabbath and the Christian celebration of the Lord's day, Sunday.

yourselves with their idols. [19]I the LORD am your God; follow my
statutes, and be careful to observe my ordinances, [20]and hallow my
sabbaths that they may be a sign between me and you, so that you
may know that I the LORD am your God. [21]But the children rebelled
against me; they did not follow my statutes, and were not careful to
observe my ordinances, by whose observance everyone shall live;
they profaned my sabbaths.

Then I thought I would pour out my wrath upon them and spend
my anger against them in the wilderness. [22]But I withheld my hand,
and acted for the sake of my name, so that it should not be profaned
in the sight of the nations, in whose sight I had brought them out.
[23]Moreover I swore to them in the wilderness that I would scatter
them among the nations and disperse them through the countries,
[24]because they had not executed my ordinances, but had rejected my
statutes and profaned my sabbaths, and their eyes were set on their
ancestors' idols. [25]Moreover I gave them statutes that were not good
and ordinances by which they could not live. [26]I defiled them through
their very gifts, in their offering up all their firstborn, in order that I
might horrify them, so that they might know that I am the LORD.

27 Therefore, mortal, speak to the house of Israel and say to them,
Thus says the Lord GOD: In this again your ancestors blasphemed
me, by dealing treacherously with me. [28]For when I had brought
them into the land that I swore to give them, then wherever they saw
any high hill or any leafy tree, there they offered their sacrifices and
presented the provocation of their offering; there they sent up their
pleasing odors, and there they poured out their drink offerings. [29](I
said to them, What is the high place to which you go? So it is called
Bamah[a] to this day.) [30]Therefore say to the house of Israel, Thus says
the Lord GOD: Will you defile yourselves after the manner of your
ancestors and go astray after their detestable things? [31]When you offer your gifts and make your children pass through the fire, you defile
yourselves with all your idols to this day. And shall I be consulted by
you, O house of Israel? As I live, says the Lord GOD, I will not be consulted by you.

32 What is in your mind shall never happen—the thought, "Let
us be like the nations, like the tribes of the countries, and worship
wood and stone."

God Will Restore Israel

33 As I live, says the Lord GOD, surely with a mighty hand and an
outstretched arm, and with wrath poured out, I will be king over you.
[34]I will bring you out from the peoples and gather you out of the countries where you are scattered, with a mighty hand and an outstretched

---

[a] That is *High Place*

20:25-26 offering up all their firstborn: This text suggests that God instituted an ordinance of child sacrifice to make the people unclean (20:31, see note on 16:20).

How do Lutherans understand a passage where God commands such a thing? There are no easy answers. Luther understood that God in God's majesty is hidden or masked. This he captured in the Latin phrase *deus absconditus* ("God hidden"). But it is in the cross of Christ, the crucifixion of the eternal Word made flesh (1 Cor 1:23), that God's self is revealed most clearly. This Luther called *deus revelatis* ("God revealed"). As it says in the *Apology of the Augsburg Confession*: "God cannot be dealt with and cannot be grasped in any other way than through the Word" (*BC* 131.67). *Ezekiel 20:25-26*

20:32 worship wood and stone: Central to Israel's rebellion is worshiping idols, gods other than the LORD, like their neighbors did (6:13; Ps 115:3-8).

20:33-44 As I live: In the face of the Israelites' idolatry, the living God declares God's true reign over the people. With all the downfalls of the kings of David's line (chapters 17, 19), the LORD pronounces that the LORD "will be king." God will be a holy and just king who will hold the people responsible for their transgressions *and* restore them to the land.

arm, and with wrath poured out; 35 and I will bring you into the wilderness of the peoples, and there I will enter into judgment with you
face to face. 36 As I entered into judgment with your ancestors in the
wilderness of the land of Egypt, so I will enter into judgment with
you, says the Lord God. 37 I will make you pass under the staff, and
will bring you within the bond of the covenant. 38 I will purge out the
rebels among you, and those who transgress against me; I will bring
them out of the land where they reside as aliens, but they shall not enter the land of Israel. Then you shall know that I am the LORD.

39 As for you, O house of Israel, thus says the Lord GOD: Go
serve your idols, every one of you now and hereafter, if you will not
listen to me; but my holy name you shall no more profane with your
gifts and your idols.

40 For on my holy mountain, the mountain height of Israel, says
the Lord GOD, there all the house of Israel, all of them, shall serve me
in the land; there I will accept them, and there I will require your contributions and the choicest of your gifts, with all your sacred things.
41 As a pleasing odor I will accept you, when I bring you out from the
peoples, and gather you out of the countries where you have been
scattered; and I will manifest my holiness among you in the sight of
the nations. 42 You shall know that I am the LORD, when I bring you
into the land of Israel, the country that I swore to give to your ancestors. 43 There you shall remember your ways and all the deeds by
which you have polluted yourselves; and you shall loathe yourselves
for all the evils that you have committed. 44 And you shall know that
I am the LORD, when I deal with you for my name's sake, not according to your evil ways, or corrupt deeds, O house of Israel, says the
Lord GOD.

A Prophecy against the Negeb

45[a] The word of the LORD came to me: 46 Mortal, set your face
toward the south, preach against the south, and prophesy against the
forest land in the Negeb; 47 say to the forest of the Negeb, Hear the
word of the LORD: Thus says the Lord GOD, I will kindle a fire in you,
and it shall devour every green tree in you and every dry tree; the blazing flame shall not be quenched, and all faces from south to north
shall be scorched by it. 48 All flesh shall see that I the LORD have kindled it; it shall not be quenched. 49 Then I said, "Ah Lord GOD! they
are saying of me, 'Is he not a maker of allegories?'"

The Drawn Sword of God

21[b] The word of the LORD came to me: 2 Mortal, set your face
toward Jerusalem and preach against the sanctuaries;

[a] Ch 21.1 in Heb [b] Ch 21.6 in Heb

20:40-44 my holy mountain: The setting for the LORD's restoration of Israel is the Jerusalem temple (Isa 56:7; 66:20), where Israel will be a priestly people. The holiness of the LORD's name ("for my name's sake") and *not* the wickedness of the people will guide how the LORD deals with the people (20:9).

This passage is not a fairy-tale ending for the people of Israel. Hope is based in God being God, the living LORD, who deals with Israel *not* based on their sins but for the sake of God's name. In spite of their sins the people of Israel "shall know that I am the LORD." What does it mean to you that God will really be God? According to this text, what role do our deeds and sins play in our standing before God?

20:45-49 set your face toward the south . . . Negeb: The first oracle of judgment is against the Negeb, an area to the south of Judah (See Map 5, p. 2103). This likely refers to the southern kingdom of Judah. The unquenchable and consuming fire from the LORD will sweep the land from the far south to the north (20:47).

20:49 maker of allegories: Ezekiel complains that the people taunt him as a mere storyteller; what they do not understand is that these allegories or parables (17:2) are from the LORD GOD.

21:1-32 will draw my sword: Four prophecies include images of God's sword of judgment.

prophesy against the land of Israel 3and say to the land of Israel, Thus
says the LORD: I am coming against you, and will draw my sword out
of its sheath, and will cut off from you both righteous and wicked.
4Because I will cut off from you both righteous and wicked, therefore my sword shall go out of its sheath against all flesh from south to
north; 5and all flesh shall know that I the LORD have drawn my sword
out of its sheath; it shall not be sheathed again. 6Moan therefore, mortal; moan with breaking heart and bitter grief before their eyes. 7And
when they say to you, "Why do you moan?" you shall say, "Because
of the news that has come. Every heart will melt and all hands will
be feeble, every spirit will faint and all knees will turn to water. See, it
comes and it will be fulfilled," says the Lord GOD.

8 And the word of the LORD came to me: 9Mortal, prophesy and
say: Thus says the Lord; Say:

A sword, a sword is sharpened,
 it is also polished;
10 it is sharpened for slaughter,
 honed to flash like lightning!
How can we make merry?
 You have despised the rod,
 and all discipline.[a]
11 The sword[b] is given to be polished,
 to be grasped in the hand;
it is sharpened, the sword is polished,
 to be placed in the slayer's hand.
12 Cry and wail, O mortal,
 for it is against my people;
it is against all Israel's princes;
 they are thrown to the sword,
 together with my people.
 Ah! Strike the thigh!

13For consider: What! If you despise the rod, will it not happen?[a] says
the Lord GOD.

14 And you, mortal, prophesy;
 strike hand to hand.
Let the sword fall twice, thrice;
 it is a sword for killing.
A sword for great slaughter—
 it surrounds them;
15 therefore hearts melt
 and many stumble.
At all their gates I have set
 the point[a] of the sword.

[a] Meaning of Heb uncertain [b] Heb *It*

21:4 against all flesh: Overwhelming destruction by the sword of the LORD will cut off "both righteous and wicked" (see also chapters 9; 18).

21:6-7 moan with breaking heart: A symbolic public act of lament draws attention to the coming destruction (see also 4:1—5:4; 6:11-14).

21:8-17 a sword is sharpened: In this second judgment oracle, the gleaming sword of the LORD will strike all Israel's princes "together with my people" (21:12). The sword of the foreign invader *is* that of the LORD.

21:12 Ah! Strike the thigh!: An exclamation of grief (see Jer 31:19), possibly Ezekiel's.

Ah! It is made for flashing,
it is polished[a] for slaughter.
16 Attack to the right!
Engage to the left!
—wherever your edge is directed.
17 I too will strike hand to hand,
I will satisfy my fury;
I the LORD have spoken.

18 The word of the LORD came to me: 19 Mortal, mark out two
roads for the sword of the king of Babylon to come; both of them shall
issue from the same land. And make a signpost, make it for a fork in
the road leading to a city; 20 mark out the road for the sword to come
to Rabbah of the Ammonites or to Judah and to[b] Jerusalem the fortified. 21 For the king of Babylon stands at the parting of the way, at the
fork in the two roads, to use divination; he shakes the arrows, he consults the teraphim,[c] he inspects the liver. 22 Into his right hand comes
the lot for Jerusalem, to set battering rams, to call out for slaughter,
for raising the battle cry, to set battering rams against the gates, to cast
up ramps, to build siege towers. 23 But to them it will seem like a false
divination; they have sworn solemn oaths; but he brings their guilt to
remembrance, bringing about their capture.

24 Therefore thus says the Lord GOD: Because you have brought your guilt to remembrance, in that your transgressions are uncovered, so that in all your deeds your sins appear—because you have come to remembrance, you shall be taken in hand.[d]

25 As for you, vile, wicked prince of Israel,
you whose day has come,
the time of final punishment,
26 thus says the Lord GOD:
Remove the turban, take off the crown;
things shall not remain as they are.
Exalt that which is low,
abase that which is high.
27 A ruin, a ruin, a ruin—
I will make it!
(Such has never occurred.)
Until he comes whose right it is;
to him I will give it.

28 As for you, mortal, prophesy, and say, Thus says the Lord GOD concerning the Ammonites, and concerning their reproach; say:
A sword, a sword! Drawn for slaughter,
polished to consume,[e] to flash like lightning.

21:18-27 mark out two roads for the sword: The third judgment oracle is devastatingly clear. The sword of the king of Babylon is identified with the sword of the LORD. Ezekiel is told to guide the foreign invaders to Jerusalem, even as the foreign king uses "divination" to discern which fork of the road to take.

21:21 shakes the arrows...consults the teraphim...inspects the liver: The Babylonian king uses various methods of fortunetelling or divination to make a decision. Shaking the arrows was similar to casting lots or flipping a coin (see Num 33:54). The "teraphim" were household gods (Gen 31:19; 34-35; 2 Kgs 23:24; Zech 10:2). In ancient Babylon, livers were understood to the have power to reveal the proper choice or action to take.

21:25-27 as for you: Zedekiah (see notes on 6:14; 12:12).

21:28-32 Drawn for slaughter: The fourth judgment oracle is a poem against the Ammonites, Nebuchadnezzar's other fork in the road (21:19-21). This foreshadows the oracles against the nations (chapters 25—32).

---

[a] Tg: Heb *wrapped up* [b] Gk Syr: Heb *Judah in* [c] Or *the household gods* [d] Or *be taken captive*
[e] Cn: Heb *to contain*

21:30-32 I will judge you: Likely a warning for Nebuchadnezzar and Babylon, which the LORD to this point has used as instruments of judgment against Israel, of their eventual destruction (2 Chr 36:20-21).

22:1-16 the bloody city: Jerusalem is charged with its sins against the LORD and one another. Central to Jerusalem's sin is that it has "forgotten" (22:12) the LORD and turned to idols. Compare to God's judgment of Nineveh in Nahum 3:1.

How do Lutherans understand idolatry? Martin Luther writes in the Large Catechism: "Idolatry does not consist merely of erecting an image and praying to it, but it is primarily a matter of the heart, which fixes its gaze upon other things and seeks help and consolation from creatures, saints, or devils" (*BC* 388.21). Idolatry is placing one's ultimate trust in anything that is not God. *Ezekiel 22:3*

22:6-7 princes of Israel . . . bent on shedding blood: Charges are directed against Jerusalem's princes of Israel, who have forgotten the LORD and thus used their "power" (in Hebrew "his strong arm") improperly. The results affect the whole land and people, as parents are treated with contempt (Exod. 20:12, Deut 5:16), foreigners in the land are cheated (Exod 22:21; Deut 10:18; Lev 19:33-34), and orphans and widows are mistreated (Exod 22:22-24; Deut 10:18).

How do you and your community use power properly to honor and treat justly those around you who have less power, such as immigrants, the homeless, orphans, widows, the poor?

22:8-12 despised my holy things . . . take bribes: The list of abuses continues. The princes of Israel despise God's "holy things" (20:40; 44:13; Num 18:8); profaned "my sabbaths" (see note on 20:12); "eat upon the mountains, where people ate meat that had been sacrificed to idols or other gods (18:6; Hos 4:13). They engage in inappropriate sexual relations (Lev 18 and 20) and use forbidden business practices that cause great pain to others, including bribes to shed blood (Deut 16:19; Mic 3:11), charging interest (Exod 22:25; Lev 25:36; Deut 23:20), and extortion (Lev 19:13; Hos 12:8).

22:12 you have forgotten me: Remembering the LORD is not only a private matter but makes a difference in how people relate to one another, especially to those without power.

29 Offering false visions for you,
divining lies for you,
they place you over the necks
of the vile, wicked ones—
those whose day has come,
the time of final punishment.
30 Return it to its sheath!
In the place where you were created,
in the land of your origin,
I will judge you.
31 I will pour out my indignation upon you,
with the fire of my wrath
I will blow upon you.
I will deliver you into brutish hands,
those skillful to destroy.
32 You shall be fuel for the fire,
your blood shall enter the earth;
you shall be remembered no more,
for I the LORD have spoken.

The Bloody City

22 The word of the LORD came to me: [2]You, mortal, will you
judge, will you judge the bloody city? Then declare to it all
its abominable deeds. [3]You shall say, Thus says the Lord GOD: A city!
Shedding blood within itself; its time has come; making its idols,
defiling itself. [4]You have become guilty by the blood that you have
shed, and defiled by the idols that you have made; you have brought
your day near, the appointed time of your years has come. Therefore I
have made you a disgrace before the nations, and a mockery to all the
countries. [5]Those who are near and those who are far from you will
mock you, you infamous one, full of tumult.
6 The princes of Israel in you, everyone according to his power,
have been bent on shedding blood. [7]Father and mother are treated
with contempt in you; the alien residing within you suffers extortion;
the orphan and the widow are wronged in you. [8]You have despised my
holy things, and profaned my sabbaths. [9]In you are those who slander
to shed blood, those in you who eat upon the mountains, who commit lewdness in your midst. [10]In you they uncover their fathers' nakedness; in you they violate women in their menstrual periods. [11]One
commits abomination with his neighbor's wife; another lewdly defiles his daughter-in-law; another in you defiles his sister, his father's
daughter. [12]In you, they take bribes to shed blood; you take both advance interest and accrued interest, and make gain of your neighbors
by extortion; and you have forgotten me, says the Lord GOD.
13 See, I strike my hands together at the dishonest gain you have

made, and at the blood that has been shed within you. [14]Can your courage endure, or can your hands remain strong in the days when I shall deal with you? I the LORD have spoken, and I will do it. [15]I will scatter you among the nations and disperse you through the countries, and I will purge your filthiness out of you. [16]And I[a] shall be profaned through you in the sight of the nations; and you shall know that I am the LORD.

17 The word of the LORD came to me: [18]Mortal, the house of Israel has become dross to me; all of them, silver,[b] bronze, tin, iron, and lead. In the smelter they have become dross. [19]Therefore thus says the Lord GOD: Because you have all become dross, I will gather you into the midst of Jerusalem. [20]As one gathers silver, bronze, iron, lead, and tin into a smelter, to blow the fire upon them in order to melt them; so I will gather you in my anger and in my wrath, and I will put you in and melt you. [21]I will gather you and blow upon you with the fire of my wrath, and you shall be melted within it. [22]As silver is melted in a smelter, so you shall be melted in it; and you shall know that I the LORD have poured out my wrath upon you.

23 The word of the LORD came to me: [24]Mortal, say to it: You are a land that is not cleansed, not rained upon in the day of indignation. [25]Its princes[c] within it are like a roaring lion tearing the prey; they have devoured human lives; they have taken treasure and precious things; they have made many widows within it. [26]Its priests have done violence to my teaching and have profaned my holy things; they have made no distinction between the holy and the common, neither have they taught the difference between the unclean and the clean, and they have disregarded my sabbaths, so that I am profaned among them. [27]Its officials within it are like wolves tearing the prey, shedding blood, destroying lives to get dishonest gain. [28]Its prophets have smeared whitewash on their behalf, seeing false visions and divining lies for them, saying, "Thus says the Lord GOD," when the LORD has not spoken. [29]The people of the land have practiced extortion and committed robbery; they have oppressed the poor and needy, and have extorted from the alien without redress. [30]And I sought for anyone among them who would repair the wall and stand in the breach before me on behalf of the land, so that I would not destroy it; but I found no one. [31]Therefore I have poured out my indignation upon them; I have consumed them with the fire of my wrath; I have returned their conduct upon their heads, says the Lord GOD.

Oholah and Oholibah

23 The word of the LORD came to me: [2]Mortal, there were two women, the daughters of one mother; [3]they played the

[a] Gk Syr Vg: Heb *you* [b] Transposed from the end of the verse; compare verse 20 [c] Gk: Heb *indignation.* [25]*A conspiracy of its prophets*

22:13-16 I strike my hands: The LORD's word proves good, because the sins of the princes of Israel bring God's judgment and punishment. "I will scatter" (22:15), refers to the exile the LORD will use to cleanse Israel.

22:17-22 Israel has become dross: An image of smelting metal is introduced. Dross is the worthless materials removed with intense heat, leaving behind (purifying) the valuable metals (see Jer 9:7; Mal 3:2-3).

22:23-31 Its princes...priests...officials...prophets...anyone among them: A complete failure of faithful leadership is condemned. The LORD found no one who would stand up for God and try to repair what was broken (22:30), resulting in the fire of God's wrath (22:31). See the note on 13:10-16 (whitewash).

23:1-49 two women, daughters of one mother: Again using explicit, violent, and belittling images of women (see chapter 16), a story of the two sisters is told to describe the unfaithfulness of God's people. Oholah, the elder, is the city of Samaria, the capital city of the northern kingdom of Israel, which fell to the Assyrians in 721 B.C.E. Oholibah, the younger, is Jerusalem, the capital city of the southern kingdom of Judah. Oholah ("her tent") and Oholibah ("my tent is in her") refers to the places of worship in these cities. While Samaria did have a place of worship, *the* place of worship was "in" Jerusalem.

23:3-4 played the whore in Egypt: The actions of both sisters are described as whoring—lustful unfaithfulness to their marriage covenant with the LORD ("they became mine," 23:4). See also notes in chapter 16.

While the violent images in chapter 23 stand for the brokenness of the relationship between God and God's people, they are problematic because the victim of the abuse and violence is blamed. How do you respond to these images?

whore in Egypt; they played the whore in their youth; their breasts
were caressed there, and their virgin bosoms were fondled. 4 Oholah
was the name of the elder and Oholibah the name of her sister. They
became mine, and they bore sons and daughters. As for their names,
Oholah is Samaria, and Oholibah is Jerusalem.

23:5-10 Oholah: Samaria's political alliance with Assyria (2 Kgs 17:1-6) is described as "adultery" against the LORD, Oholah's true spouse (see Hos 8:9-10). This resulted in her rape, the seizure of her children, and her execution (23:10).

5 Oholah played the whore while she was mine; she lusted after
her lovers the Assyrians, warriors[a] 6 clothed in blue, governors and
commanders, all of them handsome young men, mounted horsemen.
7 She bestowed her favors upon them, the choicest men of Assyria all of
them; and she defiled herself with all the idols of everyone for whom
she lusted. 8 She did not give up her whorings that she had practiced
since Egypt; for in her youth men had lain with her and fondled her
virgin bosom and poured out their lust upon her. 9 Therefore I delivered her into the hands of her lovers, into the hands of the Assyrians,
for whom she lusted. 10 These uncovered her nakedness; they seized her
sons and her daughters; and they killed her with the sword. Judgment
was executed upon her, and she became a byword among women.

23:11-35 Oholibah: After witnessing the violent end of her sister, Oholibah (Jerusalem) is accused of even greater unfaithfulness with Assyria (23:12), Babylonia (also called Chaldea; 23:14), and Egypt (23:19-20). Jerusalem's lewdness (23:28-30) included seeking political alliances with these nations and paying them bribe money, while not trusting in God's protection (see also the note on 16:15-34) and ultimately "forgetting" the LORD (23:35).

11 Her sister Oholibah saw this, yet she was more corrupt than
she in her lusting and in her whorings, which were worse than those of
her sister. 12 She lusted after the Assyrians, governors and commanders, warriors[a] clothed in full armor, mounted horsemen, all of them
handsome young men. 13 And I saw that she was defiled; they both
took the same way. 14 But she carried her whorings further; she saw
male figures carved on the wall, images of the Chaldeans portrayed in
vermilion, 15 with belts around their waists, with flowing turbans on
their heads, all of them looking like officers—a picture of Babylonians
whose native land was Chaldea. 16 When she saw them she lusted after
them, and sent messengers to them in Chaldea. 17 And the Babylonians came to her into the bed of love, and they defiled her with their
lust; and after she defiled herself with them, she turned from them in
disgust. 18 When she carried on her whorings so openly and flaunted
her nakedness, I turned in disgust from her, as I had turned from her
sister. 19 Yet she increased her whorings, remembering the days of her
youth, when she played the whore in the land of Egypt 20 and lusted
after her paramours there, whose members were like those of donkeys, and whose emission was like that of stallions. 21 Thus you longed
for the lewdness of your youth, when the Egyptians[b] fondled your
bosom and caressed[c] your young breasts.

22 Therefore, O Oholibah, thus says the Lord GOD: I will rouse
against you your lovers from whom you turned in disgust, and I will
bring them against you from every side: 23 the Babylonians and all
the Chaldeans, Pekod and Shoa and Koa, and all the Assyrians with
them, handsome young men, governors and commanders all of them,

---

[a] Meaning of Heb uncertain [b] Two Mss: MT *from Egypt* [c] Cn: Heb *for the sake of*

officers and warriors,[a] all of them riding on horses. 24 They shall come against you from the north[b] with chariots and wagons and a host of peoples; they shall set themselves against you on every side with buckler, shield, and helmet, and I will commit the judgment to them, and they shall judge you according to their ordinances. 25 I will direct my indignation against you, in order that they may deal with you in fury. They shall cut off your nose and your ears, and your survivors shall fall by the sword. They shall seize your sons and your daughters, and your survivors shall be devoured by fire. 26 They shall also strip you of your clothes and take away your fine jewels. 27 So I will put an end to your lewdness and your whoring brought from the land of Egypt; you shall not long for them, or remember Egypt any more. 28 For thus says the Lord God: I will deliver you into the hands of those whom you hate, into the hands of those from whom you turned in disgust; 29 and they shall deal with you in hatred, and take away all the fruit of your labor, and leave you naked and bare, and the nakedness of your whorings shall be exposed. Your lewdness and your whorings 30 have brought this upon you, because you played the whore with the nations, and polluted yourself with their idols. 31 You have gone the way of your sister; therefore I will give her cup into your hand. 32 Thus says the Lord God:

You shall drink your sister's cup,
    deep and wide;
you shall be scorned and derided,
    it holds so much.
33 You shall be filled with drunkenness and sorrow.
A cup of horror and desolation
    is the cup of your sister Samaria;
34 you shall drink it and drain it out,
    and gnaw its sherds,
    and tear out your breasts;

for I have spoken, says the Lord God. 35 Therefore thus says the Lord God: Because you have forgotten me and cast me behind your back, therefore bear the consequences of your lewdness and whorings.

36 The Lord said to me: Mortal, will you judge Oholah and Oholibah? Then declare to them their abominable deeds. 37 For they have committed adultery, and blood is on their hands; with their idols they have committed adultery; and they have even offered up to them for food the children whom they had borne to me. 38 Moreover this they have done to me: they have defiled my sanctuary on the same day and profaned my sabbaths. 39 For when they had slaughtered their children for their idols, on the same day they came into my sanctuary to profane it. This is what they did in my house.

23:32-34 your sister's cup: The younger sister Jerusalem will drink from the older sister Samaria's cup, meaning it will receive the same punishment. Drunk on the same wine as the elder sister Samaria, the younger sister Jerusalem is unable to get enough, possibly to dull the pain, to the point that she tears out her breasts (compare to Isa 51:17, 22; Jer 25:15-28).

23:36-49 their abominable deeds: The sisters' unfaithfulness included child sacrifice (see note on 16:20), defiling the temple and the Sabbath (23:38-39), and drunken orgies with foreign nations (23:40-45), which lead to public stoning and execution (23:47; see Lev 20:10) and a problematic object lesson for Israelite women (23:48).

[a] Compare verses 6 and 12: Heb *officers and called ones* [b] Gk: Meaning of Heb uncertain

40 They even sent for men to come from far away, to whom a
messenger was sent, and they came. For them you bathed yourself,
painted your eyes, and decked yourself with ornaments; 41 you sat
on a stately couch, with a table spread before it on which you had
placed my incense and my oil. 42 The sound of a raucous multitude
was around her, with many of the rabble brought in drunken from the
wilderness; and they put bracelets on the arms[a] of the women, and
beautiful crowns upon their heads.

43 Then I said, Ah, she is worn out with adulteries, but they carry
on their sexual acts with her. 44 For they have gone in to her, as one
goes in to a whore. Thus they went in to Oholah and to Oholibah,
wanton women. 45 But righteous judges shall declare them guilty of
adultery and of bloodshed; because they are adulteresses and blood
is on their hands.

46 For thus says the Lord GOD: Bring up an assembly against
them, and make them an object of terror and of plunder. 47 The assembly shall stone them and with their swords they shall cut them down;
they shall kill their sons and their daughters, and burn up their houses.
48 Thus will I put an end to lewdness in the land, so that all women
may take warning and not commit lewdness as you have done. 49 They
shall repay you for your lewdness, and you shall bear the penalty for
your sinful idolatry; and you shall know that I am the Lord GOD.

The Boiling Pot

24 In the ninth year, in the tenth month, on the tenth day of
the month, the word of the LORD came to me: 2 Mortal,
write down the name of this day, this very day. The king of Babylon
has laid siege to Jerusalem this very day. 3 And utter an allegory to the
rebellious house and say to them, Thus says the Lord GOD:

Set on the pot, set it on,
    pour in water also;
4 put in it the pieces,
    all the good pieces, the thigh and the shoulder;
    fill it with choice bones.
5 Take the choicest one of the flock,
    pile the logs[b] under it;
boil its pieces,[c]
    seethe[d] also its bones in it.

6 Therefore thus says the Lord GOD:
Woe to the bloody city,
    the pot whose rust is in it,

24:1-14 king of Baylon has laid siege to Jerusalem: The image of a pot boiling over a fire is used to describe Nebuchadnezzar's siege of Jerusalem, which began on January 15, 588 B.C.E. In the allegory (see note on 17:1-10) Jerusalem is a boiling pot (11:3; Jer 1:13) filled with cooking flesh and bone (24:3-5; Mic 3:2-3).

24:6-13 the pot whose rust is in it: Jerusalem, the bloody city (22:1-16), is as a pot that is rusted (the Hebrew can also mean "scummy") and bloody, making it unclean (Lev 7:26-27; 15:19) and needing purification by fire (Ezek 22:17-22). That fire is Nebuchadnezzar's siege. The second-person pronouns ("you") are all feminine, extending earlier female images (chapters 16, 23).

---

[a] Heb *hands* [b] Compare verse 10: Heb *the bones* [c] Two Mss: Heb *its boilings* [d] Cn: Heb *its bones seethe*

whose rust has not gone out of it!
Empty it piece by piece,
making no choice at all.[a]
7 For the blood she shed is inside it;
she placed it on a bare rock;
she did not pour it out on the ground,
to cover it with earth.
8 To rouse my wrath, to take vengeance,
I have placed the blood she shed
on a bare rock,
so that it may not be covered.
9 Therefore thus says the Lord GOD:
Woe to the bloody city!
I will even make the pile great.
10 Heap up the logs, kindle the fire;
boil the meat well, mix in the spices,
let the bones be burned.
11 Stand it empty upon the coals,
so that it may become hot, its copper glow,
its filth melt in it, its rust be consumed.
12 In vain I have wearied myself;[b]
its thick rust does not depart.
To the fire with its rust![c]
13 Yet, when I cleansed you in your filthy lewdness,
you did not become clean from your filth;
you shall not again be cleansed
until I have satisfied my fury upon you.
14 I the LORD have spoken; the time is coming, I will act. I will not
refrain, I will not spare, I will not relent. According to your ways and
your doings I will judge you, says the Lord GOD.

Ezekiel's Bereavement

15 The word of the LORD came to me: 16 Mortal, with one blow
I am about to take away from you the delight of your eyes; yet you
shall not mourn or weep, nor shall your tears run down. 17 Sigh, but
not aloud; make no mourning for the dead. Bind on your turban, and
put your sandals on your feet; do not cover your upper lip or eat the
bread of mourners.[d] 18 So I spoke to the people in the morning, and at
evening my wife died. And on the next morning I did as I was commanded.

19 Then the people said to me, "Will you not tell us what these
things mean for us, that you are acting this way?" 20 Then I said to

24:15-24 with one blow…my wife died: At the death of his wife, "the delight of your eyes" (24:16), Ezekiel is instructed to avoid traditional mourning rituals as a symbolic act like his earlier one (4:1—5:4). Ezekiel's wife's death is compared to the destruction of the temple in Jerusalem (24:21).

[a] Heb *piece, no lot has fallen on it* [b] Cn: Meaning of Heb uncertain [c] Meaning of Heb uncertain
[d] Vg Tg: Heb *of men*

them: The word of the LORD came to me: 21 Say to the house of Israel, Thus says the Lord GOD: I will profane my sanctuary, the pride of your power, the delight of your eyes, and your heart's desire; and your sons and your daughters whom you left behind shall fall by the sword. 22 And you shall do as I have done; you shall not cover your upper lip or eat the bread of mourners.[a] 23 Your turbans shall be on your heads and your sandals on your feet; you shall not mourn or weep, but you shall pine away in your iniquities and groan to one another. 24 Thus Ezekiel shall be a sign to you; you shall do just as he has done. When this comes, then you shall know that I am the Lord GOD.

25 And you, mortal, on the day when I take from them their stronghold, their joy and glory, the delight of their eyes and their heart's affection, and also[b] their sons and their daughters, 26 on that day, one who has escaped will come to you to report to you the news. 27 On that day your mouth shall be opened to the one who has escaped, and you shall speak and no longer be silent. So you shall be a sign to them; and they shall know that I am the LORD.

24:25-27 on the day: When he hears the news of Jerusalem's fall and the temple's destruction, "the delight of their eyes" (24:25), the prophet's mouth will open (33:21-22; also 3:22-27), signaling a change in the prophet's message.

Proclamation against Ammon

25 The word of the LORD came to me: 2 Mortal, set your face toward the Ammonites and prophesy against them. 3 Say to the Ammonites, Hear the word of the Lord GOD: Thus says the Lord GOD, Because you said, "Aha!" over my sanctuary when it was profaned, and over the land of Israel when it was made desolate, and over the house of Judah when it went into exile; 4 therefore I am handing you over to the people of the east for a possession. They shall set their encampments among you and pitch their tents in your midst; they shall eat your fruit, and they shall drink your milk. 5 I will make Rabbah a pasture for camels and Ammon a fold for flocks. Then you shall know that I am the LORD. 6 For thus says the Lord GOD: Because you have clapped your hands and stamped your feet and rejoiced with all the malice within you against the land of Israel, 7 therefore I have stretched out my hand against you, and will hand you over as plunder to the nations. I will cut you off from the peoples and will make you perish out of the countries; I will destroy you. Then you shall know that I am the LORD.

25:1—32:32 set your face toward the Ammonites . . . Egypt: As a break from the word of judgment against Israel, the oracles and laments in this section are a bridge between the news of the siege of Jerusalem (24:2) and its fall (33:21). Babylon is glaringly absent.

25:1-7 set your face toward the Ammonites: This is a second oracle against Ammon (21:28-32; see also Jer 49:1-6, Amos 1:13-15; see Map 7, p. 2105). They are to be judged for their jeering "Aha!" (25:3), and for their dancing, clapping, and rejoicing (25:6) at the destruction of the temple and Israel. They will be given over (conquered) by "people of the east," Babylon (25:4).

Proclamation against Moab

8 Thus says the Lord GOD: Because Moab[c] said, The house of Judah is like all the other nations, 9 therefore I will lay open the flank of Moab from the towns[d] on its frontier, the glory of the country, Beth-jeshimoth, Baal-meon, and Kiriathaim. 10 I will give it along with

25:8-11 Moab: Moabites were traditional descendants of Lot (Gen 19:36-38). Moab (see Map 7, p. 2105) is judged for suggesting that "Judah is like all the other nations," a phrase that implies a negative slight. Moab too will become a possession of Babylon, the people of the east (25:10), like Ammon (25:4). See also Jer 48:1-47 and Amos 2:1-3 for other judgments against Moab.

[a] Vg Tg: Heb *of men* [b] Heb lacks *and also* [c] Gk Old Latin: Heb *Moab and Seir* [d] Heb *towns from its towns*

Ammon to the people of the east as a possession. Thus Ammon shall
be remembered no more among the nations, [11]and I will execute
judgments upon Moab. Then they shall know that I am the LORD.

Proclamation against Edom

12 Thus says the Lord GOD: Because Edom acted revengefully
against the house of Judah and has grievously offended in taking vengeance upon them, [13]therefore thus says the Lord GOD, I will stretch
out my hand against Edom, and cut off from it humans and animals,
and I will make it desolate; from Teman even to Dedan they shall fall
by the sword. [14]I will lay my vengeance upon Edom by the hand of
my people Israel; and they shall act in Edom according to my anger
and according to my wrath; and they shall know my vengeance, says
the Lord GOD.

Proclamation against Philistia

15 Thus says the Lord GOD: Because with unending hostilities
the Philistines acted in vengeance, and with malice of heart took
revenge in destruction; [16]therefore thus says the Lord GOD, I will
stretch out my hand against the Philistines, cut off the Cherethites,
and destroy the rest of the seacoast. [17]I will execute great vengeance
on them with wrathful punishments. Then they shall know that I am
the LORD, when I lay my vengeance on them.

Proclamation against Tyre

26 In the eleventh year, on the first day of the month, the word
of the LORD came to me: [2]Mortal, because Tyre said concerning Jerusalem,

"Aha, broken is the gateway of the peoples;
it has swung open to me;
I shall be replenished,
now that it is wasted,"

[3]therefore, thus says the Lord GOD:

See, I am against you, O Tyre!
I will hurl many nations against you,
as the sea hurls its waves.
4 They shall destroy the walls of Tyre
and break down its towers.
I will scrape its soil from it
and make it a bare rock.
5 It shall become, in the midst of the sea,
a place for spreading nets.

I have spoken, says the Lord GOD.

It shall become plunder for the nations,
6 and its daughter-towns in the country
shall be killed by the sword.

25:12-14 Edom: The traditional descendants of Esau (Gen 25:23-26), Edom (see Map 7, p. 2105) is judged for revengeful behavior toward Judah and will be punished directly by God (25:13-14). See also Jeremiah 49:7-22 and Amos 1:11-12 for other judgments against Edom.

25:15-17 Philistines acted in vengeance: The Philistines, who lived in the area of Gaza along the Mediterranean Sea coast (see Map 7, p. 2105), are judged because of "unending hostilities" over many centuries (Judg 15—16; 1 Sam 17; 2 Sam 5:17-25; 1 Kgs 16:15-20). They will be punished directly by the LORD (25:17).

26:1—28:19 Tyre: The extra attention given to Tyre (see Map 7, p. 2105) may be because the city abandoned alliance talks with Jerusalem during Zedekiah's rule (Jer 27:3) or because, unlike Judah, it was able to resist Babylon, the LORD's instrument of judgment. Nebuchadnezzar besieged Tyre for thirteen years (586–573 B.C.E.) without a clear victory. See other oracles against and laments over the island city-state of Tyre (Isa 23; Amos 1:9-10).

26:1 In the eleventh year: Probably 587 B.C.E., the eleventh year of Johoiachin (see note on 1:1-2).

26:2 Aha: As the Ammonites heckled (25:3), so did Tyre (36:2; Ps 35:21, 25).

26:3-21 thus says the Lord GOD: Four different oracles, each introduced by this common phrase (26:3, 7, 15, 19) are filled with sea imagery, since Tyre was an important seaport.

26:6 daughter-towns: Towns on the mainland that Tyre ruled.

26:7 Nebuchadrezzar of Babylon: This variant spelling of Nebuchadnezzar may mean "may Nabu defend my children." Nabu was the Babylonian god of wisdom and son of Marduk.

26:8-14 He shall set up a siege... make you a bare rock: This destruction ("make you a bare rock," 26:14) never came at the hand of Nebuchadnezzar. Tyre, which also means "rock," was not conquered until 322 B.C.E., by Alexander the Great.

26:15-18 the sound of your fall: Upon hearing of the "death" of Tyre, the "princes of the sea" (26:16)—possibly Tyre's trading partners and allies—raised a "lamentation" (see note on 19:1) over the city.

Then they shall know that I am the LORD.

7 For thus says the Lord GOD: I will bring against Tyre from the north King Nebuchadrezzar of Babylon, king of kings, together with horses, chariots, cavalry, and a great and powerful army.

8 Your daughter-towns in the country
he shall put to the sword.
He shall set up a siege wall against you,
cast up a ramp against you,
and raise a roof of shields against you.
9 He shall direct the shock of his battering rams against your walls
and break down your towers with his axes.
10 His horses shall be so many
that their dust shall cover you.
At the noise of cavalry, wheels, and chariots
your very walls shall shake,
when he enters your gates
like those entering a breached city.
11 With the hoofs of his horses
he shall trample all your streets.
He shall put your people to the sword,
and your strong pillars shall fall to the ground.
12 They will plunder your riches
and loot your merchandise;
they shall break down your walls
and destroy your fine houses.
Your stones and timber and soil
they shall cast into the water.
13 I will silence the music of your songs;
the sound of your lyres shall be heard no more.
14 I will make you a bare rock;
you shall be a place for spreading nets.
You shall never again be rebuilt,
for I the LORD have spoken,
says the Lord GOD.

15 Thus says the Lord GOD to Tyre: Shall not the coastlands shake
at the sound of your fall, when the wounded groan, when slaughter
goes on within you? 16 Then all the princes of the sea shall step down
from their thrones; they shall remove their robes and strip off their
embroidered garments. They shall clothe themselves with trembling,
and shall sit on the ground; they shall tremble every moment, and be
appalled at you. 17 And they shall raise a lamentation over you, and
say to you:

How you have vanished[a] from the seas,

[a] Gk OL Aquila: Heb *have vanished, O inhabited one,*

O city renowned,
once mighty on the sea,
you and your inhabitants,[a]
who imposed your[b] terror
on all the mainland![c]
18 Now the coastlands tremble
on the day of your fall;
the coastlands by the sea
are dismayed at your passing.

19 For thus says the Lord GOD: When I make you a city laid
waste, like cities that are not inhabited, when I bring up the deep over
you, and the great waters cover you, 20then I will thrust you down
with those who descend into the Pit, to the people of long ago, and
I will make you live in the world below, among primeval ruins, with
those who go down to the Pit, so that you will not be inhabited or
have a place[d] in the land of the living. 21I will bring you to a dreadful
end, and you shall be no more; though sought for, you will never be
found again, says the Lord GOD.

26:19-21 when I bring up the deep over you…the Pit: Tyre will go down into the "deep," the primordial sea (31:15; Gen 1:2; Ps 77:16) and the "Pit" (26:20), also known as Sheol, the abode of the dead (31:15-17; 32:17-31; Ps 88:3-7).

Lamentation over Tyre

27 The word of the LORD came to me: 2Now you, mortal, raise
a lamentation over Tyre, 3and say to Tyre, which sits at the
entrance to the sea, merchant of the peoples on many coastlands,
Thus says the Lord GOD:
O Tyre, you have said,
"I am perfect in beauty."
4 Your borders are in the heart of the seas;
your builders made perfect your beauty.
5 They made all your planks
of fir trees from Senir;
they took a cedar from Lebanon
to make a mast for you.
6 From oaks of Bashan
they made your oars;
they made your deck of pines[e]
from the coasts of Cyprus,
inlaid with ivory.
7 Of fine embroidered linen from Egypt
was your sail,
serving as your ensign;
blue and purple from the coasts of Elishah
was your awning.

27:1-36 raise a lamentation over Tyre: Appropriate to an island city-state, Tyre is compared to a beautiful and richly cargoed ship that sinks in the high seas, the result of the "east wind," Babylon (27:26). The lament does not contain any specific judgment of the LORD.

27:3 I am perfect in beauty: No judgment is made of Tyre's arrogance (28:2-10).

27:4-25 your beauty: Here is a catalog of ancient international trade of goods and services.

27:5-11 Senir…Gamad: Several locations are mentioned. See Maps 7 and 11, pp. 2105 and 2108. Mount Hermon is in eastern Lebanon. Bashan is a region east of the Sea of Galilee. Cyprus is an island in the eastern Mediterranean. The ivory inlaid in the decking is material from the tusks of elephants or hippopotami of Asia or Africa. The location of Elishah is unclear, but may possibly be Cyprus. According to the first-century C.E. Roman historian Pliny, Tyre was a center of the production of purple dye, made from sea snails; purple indicates luxury. Sidon, Arvad, Zemer, Gebal are coastal cities of Phoenicia. Paras is Persia, and Lud is Lydia in western Asia Minor. Put is a region of Libya, and Helech is possibly Cilicia. The location of Gamad is uncertain.

[a] Heb *it and its inhabitants* [b] Heb *their* [c] Cn: Heb *its inhabitants* [d] Gk: Heb *I will give beauty*
[e] Or *boxwood*

8 The inhabitants of Sidon and Arvad
were your rowers;
skilled men of Zemer[a] were within you,
they were your pilots.
9 The elders of Gebal and its artisans were within you,
caulking your seams;
all the ships of the sea with their mariners were within you,
to barter for your wares.
10 Paras[b] and Lud and Put
were in your army,
your mighty warriors;
they hung shield and helmet in you;
they gave you splendor.
11 Men of Arvad and Helech[c]
were on your walls all around;
men of Gamad were at your towers.
They hung their quivers all around your walls;
they made perfect your beauty.

12 Tarshish did business with you out of the abundance of your
great wealth; silver, iron, tin, and lead they exchanged for your wares.
13 Javan, Tubal, and Meshech traded with you; they exchanged human beings and vessels of bronze for your merchandise. 14 Beth-
togarmah exchanged for your wares horses, war horses, and mules.
15 The Rhodians[d] traded with you; many coastlands were your own
special markets; they brought you in payment ivory tusks and ebony.
16 Edom[e] did business with you because of your abundant goods; they
exchanged for your wares turquoise, purple, embroidered work, fine
linen, coral, and rubies. 17 Judah and the land of Israel traded with you;
they exchanged for your merchandise wheat from Minnith, millet,[f]
honey, oil, and balm. 18 Damascus traded with you for your abundant
goods—because of your great wealth of every kind—wine of Helbon, and white wool. 19 Vedan and Javan from Uzal[f] entered into trade
for your wares; wrought iron, cassia, and sweet cane were bartered
for your merchandise. 20 Dedan traded with you in saddlecloths for
riding. 21 Arabia and all the princes of Kedar were your favored dealers
in lambs, rams, and goats; in these they did business with you. 22 The
merchants of Sheba and Raamah traded with you; they exchanged
for your wares the best of all kinds of spices, and all precious stones,
and gold. 23 Haran, Canneh, Eden, the merchants of Sheba, Asshur,
and Chilmad traded with you. 24 These traded with you in choice garments, in clothes of blue and embroidered work, and in carpets of
colored material, bound with cords and made secure; in these they

[a] Cn Compare Gen 10.18: Heb *your skilled men, O Tyre* [b] Or *Persia* [c] Or *and your army* [d] Gk: Heb *The Dedanites* [e] Another reading is *Aram* [f] Meaning of Heb uncertain

27:12-25 business with you: With a shift from poetry to prose, the description of the ship and crew moves to a description of the ship's cargo. More trading partners are named.

27:12-24 Tarshish...Chilmad: Tarshish is likely Tartessos, a port on the southeast coast of Spain (Jonah 1:3). Javan is Greece, and Tubal is Cilicia in south Asia Minor. Meshech is west-central Asia Minor (32:26-28; 38:2), and Beth-togarmah is eastern Asia Minor. Rhodes is an island in the Aegean Sea off southwestern Asia Minor. Ivory tusks (see note on 27:5-11) and ebony, wood native to south India or west Africa, are goods that show the scope of ancient trade.

Judah and Israel traded in agricultural goods. This passing reference to many other nations may suggest that chapter 27 was later inserted into Ezekiel.

Helbon is a city north of Damascus, and Uzal is in Yemen on the Arabian Peninsula. Dedan is in northwestern Arabia (38:13; Jer 49:8). Kedar refers to tribes in northwestern Arabia traditionally descended from Ishmael (Gen 25:13). Sheba was in southwestern Arabia and Raamah in southeastern Arabia. Haran, Canneh, Eden, Asshur, and Chilmad were Mesopotamian cities.

This chapter includes an offhand reference to trade of human beings (27:13), a reference to slavery alongside bronze ware. What does this tell you about the world of the Bible at this time? What does this say, if anything, about our reading or understanding of such a text today? How would you describe the Christian's duty regarding basic human dignity?

traded with you.[a] 25The ships of Tarshish traveled for you in your
trade.

So you were filled and heavily laden
in the heart of the seas.

26 Your rowers have brought you
into the high seas.
The east wind has wrecked you
in the heart of the seas.

27 Your riches, your wares, your merchandise,
your mariners and your pilots,
your caulkers, your dealers in merchandise,
and all your warriors within you,
with all the company
that is with you,
sink into the heart of the seas
on the day of your ruin.

28 At the sound of the cry of your pilots
the countryside shakes,

29 and down from their ships
come all that handle the oar.
The mariners and all the pilots of the sea
stand on the shore

30 and wail aloud over you,
and cry bitterly.
They throw dust on their heads
and wallow in ashes;

31 they make themselves bald for you,
and put on sackcloth,
and they weep over you in bitterness of soul,
with bitter mourning.

32 In their wailing they raise a lamentation for you,
and lament over you:
"Who was ever destroyed[b] like Tyre
in the midst of the sea?

33 When your wares came from the seas,
you satisfied many peoples;
with your abundant wealth and merchandise
you enriched the kings of the earth.

34 Now you are wrecked by the seas,
in the depths of the waters;
your merchandise and all your crew
have sunk with you.

35 All the inhabitants of the coastlands

[a] Cn: Heb *in your market* [b] Tg Vg: Heb *like silence*

27:25-36 So were you filled: The poem continues. The east wind Babylon wrecked the ship (27:26), and the ship, crew, and cargo are lost at sea (27:27, 34). The sailors (mariners) are mourned by other sailors on the shore by wailing and putting on sackcloth and ashes (27:29-32). Merchants whose goods sank with the ship hiss at Tyre in anger (27:36).

are appalled at you;
and their kings are horribly afraid,
their faces are convulsed.
36 The merchants among the peoples hiss at you;
you have come to a dreadful end
and shall be no more forever."

Proclamation against the King of Tyre

28:1-10 to the prince of Tyre: In spite of the prince's greatness (28:3-5), he is condemned because he portrays himself as a god (28:2, 6; Dan 11:36-39). He will suffer defeat at the hand of a foreign power (see note on 26:8-14).

28:3 Daniel: (see note on 14:14).

28:10 the death of the uncircumcised: Israelite men were to be circumcised (see Gen 17:10-14). This and the Sabbath (Exod 31:12-17) were to be signs of God's covenant with Israel. The "uncircumcised" refers to non-Israelites.

28 The word of the LORD came to me: [2]Mortal, say to the prince of Tyre, Thus says the Lord GOD:
Because your heart is proud
and you have said, "I am a god;
I sit in the seat of the gods,
in the heart of the seas,"
yet you are but a mortal, and no god,
though you compare your mind
with the mind of a god.
3 You are indeed wiser than Daniel;[a]
no secret is hidden from you;
4 by your wisdom and your understanding
you have amassed wealth for yourself,
and have gathered gold and silver
into your treasuries.
5 By your great wisdom in trade
you have increased your wealth,
and your heart has become proud in your wealth.
6 Therefore thus says the Lord GOD:
Because you compare your mind
with the mind of a god,
7 therefore, I will bring strangers against you,
the most terrible of the nations;
they shall draw their swords against the beauty of your wisdom
and defile your splendor.
8 They shall thrust you down to the Pit,
and you shall die a violent death
in the heart of the seas.
9 Will you still say, "I am a god,"
in the presence of those who kill you,
though you are but a mortal, and no god,
in the hands of those who wound you?
10 You shall die the death of the uncircumcised
by the hand of foreigners;
for I have spoken, says the Lord GOD.

[a] Or, as otherwise read, *Danel*

Lamentation over the King of Tyre

11 Moreover the word of the LORD came to me: [12]Mortal, raise
a lamentation over the king of Tyre, and say to him, Thus says the
Lord GOD:

You were the signet of perfection,[a]
full of wisdom and perfect in beauty.
13 You were in Eden, the garden of God;
every precious stone was your covering,
carnelian, chrysolite, and moonstone,
beryl, onyx, and jasper,
sapphire,[b] turquoise, and emerald;
and worked in gold were your settings
and your engravings.[a]
On the day that you were created
they were prepared.
14 With an anointed cherub as guardian I placed you;[a]
you were on the holy mountain of God;
you walked among the stones of fire.
15 You were blameless in your ways
from the day that you were created,
until iniquity was found in you.
16 In the abundance of your trade
you were filled with violence, and you sinned;
so I cast you as a profane thing from the mountain of God,
and the guardian cherub drove you out
from among the stones of fire.
17 Your heart was proud because of your beauty;
you corrupted your wisdom for the sake of your splendor.
I cast you to the ground;
I exposed you before kings,
to feast their eyes on you.
18 By the multitude of your iniquities,
in the unrighteousness of your trade,
you profaned your sanctuaries.
So I brought out fire from within you;
it consumed you,
and I turned you to ashes on the earth
in the sight of all who saw you.
19 All who know you among the peoples
are appalled at you;
you have come to a dreadful end
and shall be no more forever.

28:11-19 a lamentation over the king of Tyre: The poem recalls the garden of Eden (28:13; Gen 2:10-12). The king, a 'signet of perfection," wears a jeweled garment similar to the high priest of Israel (see Exod 28:17-20; 39:10-13; also Rev 21:19-20). He is protected by "an anointed cherub" (this can also read "you are a cherub anointed for guardianship") and placed on God's holy mountain. But the king sinned (28:16, 18) and so was thrown from God's mountain.

---

[a] Meaning of Heb uncertain [b] Or *lapis lazuli*

28:20-24 Sidon: A city north of Tyre on the Mediterranean coast (see Map 7, p. 2105) receives judgment with no specific charge. Tyre and Sidon are often named together (Jer 47:4; Zech 9:2).

Proclamation against Sidon

20 The word of the LORD came to me: 21 Mortal, set your face
toward Sidon, and prophesy against it, 22 and say, Thus says the Lord
GOD:

I am against you, O Sidon,
  and I will gain glory in your midst.
They shall know that I am the LORD
  when I execute judgments in it,
  and manifest my holiness in it;
23 for I will send pestilence into it,
  and bloodshed into its streets;
and the dead shall fall in its midst,
  by the sword that is against it on every side.
And they shall know that I am the LORD.

28:24-26 pricking brier or a piercing thorn...They shall live in safety: Concluding the first set of judgments of Israel's neighbors (the briers and thorns) is a promise of the return of the LORD's holiness and of Israel's return to the land to live in safety (34:28; Jer 23:6; Zech 14:11).

24 The house of Israel shall no longer find a pricking brier or a piercing thorn among all their neighbors who have treated them with contempt. And they shall know that I am the Lord GOD.

Future Blessing for Israel

25 Thus says the Lord GOD: When I gather the house of Israel
from the peoples among whom they are scattered, and manifest
my holiness in them in the sight of the nations, then they shall settle on their own soil that I gave to my servant Jacob. 26 They shall live
in safety in it, and shall build houses and plant vineyards. They shall
live in safety, when I execute judgments upon all their neighbors who
have treated them with contempt. And they shall know that I am the
LORD their God.

29:1–32:32 against all Egypt: In these chapters are seven oracles against Egypt and its rulers; six of the seven are dated.

29:1 the tenth year: January 7, 587 B.C.E.

29:1-5 Pharaoh king of Egypt...the great dragon: Likely Hophra (589–587 B.C.E.), the king of Egypt is compared to the large crocodile that lives in the Nile River channels (see Map 1, p. 2098). He claims to have created the Nile (29:3), implying he is as powerful as a god (compare to 28:9). Egyptian kings were honored with large funerals and placed in ornate tombs, including the pyramids, but this pharaoh will die in an open field and not receive an honorable burial.

Proclamation against Egypt

29 In the tenth year, in the tenth month, on the twelfth day of
the month, the word of the LORD came to me: 2 Mortal, set
your face against Pharaoh king of Egypt, and prophesy against him
and against all Egypt; 3 speak, and say, Thus says the Lord GOD:

I am against you,
  Pharaoh king of Egypt,
the great dragon sprawling
  in the midst of its channels,
saying, "My Nile is my own;
  I made it for myself."
4 I will put hooks in your jaws,
  and make the fish of your channels stick to your scales.
I will draw you up from your channels,
  with all the fish of your channels
  sticking to your scales.

[5] I will fling you into the wilderness,
you and all the fish of your channels;
you shall fall in the open field,
and not be gathered and buried.
To the animals of the earth and to the birds of the air
I have given you as food.
[6] Then all the inhabitants of Egypt shall know
that I am the LORD
because you[a] were a staff of reed
to the house of Israel;
[7] when they grasped you with the hand, you broke,
and tore all their shoulders;
and when they leaned on you, you broke,
and made all their legs unsteady.[b]

8 Therefore, thus says the Lord GOD: I will bring a sword upon
you, and will cut off from you human being and animal; [9] and the land
of Egypt shall be a desolation and a waste. Then they shall know that
I am the LORD.

Because you[c] said, "The Nile is mine, and I made it," [10] therefore, I
am against you, and against your channels, and I will make the land of
Egypt an utter waste and desolation, from Migdol to Syene, as far as
the border of Ethiopia.[d] [11] No human foot shall pass through it, and no
animal foot shall pass through it; it shall be uninhabited forty years.
[12] I will make the land of Egypt a desolation among desolated countries; and her cities shall be a desolation forty years among cities that
are laid waste. I will scatter the Egyptians among the nations, and disperse them among the countries.

13 Further, thus says the Lord GOD: At the end of forty years I
will gather the Egyptians from the peoples among whom they were
scattered; [14] and I will restore the fortunes of Egypt, and bring them
back to the land of Pathros, the land of their origin; and there they
shall be a lowly kingdom. [15] It shall be the most lowly of the kingdoms,
and never again exalt itself above the nations; and I will make them
so small that they will never again rule over the nations. [16] The Egyptians[e] shall never again be the reliance of the house of Israel; they will
recall their iniquity, when they turned to them for aid. Then they shall
know that I am the Lord GOD.

Babylonia Will Plunder Egypt

17 In the twenty-seventh year, in the first month, on the first
day of the month, the word of the LORD came to me: [18] Mortal, King
Nebuchadrezzar of Babylon made his army labor hard against Tyre;
every head was made bald and every shoulder was rubbed bare; yet
neither he nor his army got anything from Tyre to pay for the labor

[a] Gk Syr Vg: Heb *they* [b] Syr: Heb *stand* [c] Gk Syr Vg: Heb *he* [d] Or *Nubia*; Heb *Cush* [e] Heb *It*

29:7-12 they grasped you with the hand…I will scatter the Egyptians: "They" in 29:7 refers to King Zedekiah of Judah's attempt to make alliance with Egypt in 589 B.C.E. against the Babylonian threat (see Jer 37:1-10). The destruction of Egypt will be widespread.

29:10 from Migdol to Syene: Meaning from one end of the Nile to the other. Migdol is likely at the north and Syene at the south near the border of Ethiopia (Hebrew, *Cush*). Pathros (29:14) was in upper (southern) Egypt.

29:13-16 I will gather: The LORD promises to return the scattered Egyptians to their land after forty years, just as the people of Judah are promised a return to their land after the exile (4:6). It actually took nearly fifty years before the exile in Babylon ended.

29:17-21 the twenty-seventh year: By the date of this oracle (April 26, 571 B.C.E.), it is the latest of Ezekiel's oracles. Nebuchadnezzar's failed siege of Tyre (see note on 26:8-14) is compensated by his plunder of Egypt (29:19-20). The horn (29:21) likely refers to a return of rulers in the line of David (Ps 132:17).

that he had expended against it. [19]Therefore thus says the Lord GOD: I will give the land of Egypt to King Nebuchadrezzar of Babylon; and he shall carry off its wealth and despoil it and plunder it; and it shall be the wages for his army. [20]I have given him the land of Egypt as his payment for which he labored, because they worked for me, says the Lord GOD.

21 On that day I will cause a horn to sprout up for the house of Israel, and I will open your lips among them. Then they shall know that I am the LORD.

Lamentation for Egypt

30 The word of the LORD came to me: [2]Mortal, prophesy, and say, Thus says the Lord GOD:

Wail, "Alas for the day!"
3 For a day is near,
the day of the LORD is near;
it will be a day of clouds,
a time of doom[a] for the nations.
4 A sword shall come upon Egypt,
and anguish shall be in Ethiopia,[b]
when the slain fall in Egypt,
and its wealth is carried away,
and its foundations are torn down.

[5]Ethiopia,[b] and Put, and Lud, and all Arabia, and Libya,[c] and the people of the allied land[d] shall fall with them by the sword.

6 Thus says the LORD:
Those who support Egypt shall fall,
and its proud might shall come down;
from Migdol to Syene
they shall fall within it by the sword,
says the Lord GOD.
7 They shall be desolated among other desolated countries,
and their cities shall lie among cities laid waste.
8 Then they shall know that I am the LORD,
when I have set fire to Egypt,
and all who help it are broken.

9 On that day, messengers shall go out from me in ships to terrify the unsuspecting Ethiopians;[e] and anguish shall come upon them on the day of Egypt's doom;[f] for it is coming!

10 Thus says the Lord GOD:
I will put an end to the hordes of Egypt,

30:1-19 Wail…the slain fall in Egypt: The prophet commands his hearers to lament the coming destruction of Egypt. This is the only oracle against Egypt without a date.

30:3 day of the LORD: This phrase is common in prophetic texts. It refers to a dark day when the LORD intervenes decisively in earthly affairs. It is often directed at Israel (7:7; Amos 5:18-20) but also, as here, at other nations (38:18; Isa 13:6-19; Obad 1:15).

30:9-19 terrify…unsuspecting Ethiopians…the hordes of Egypt: The LORD's agent, Nebuchadnezzar, will destroy all corners of Egypt. Many of its major cities are mentioned, including Memphis, Zoan, On (Heliopolis) and Tehaphnehes. For locations see Maps 1 and 2, pp.2098-2099. Specific Egyptian gods were associated with many of these cities ("I will destroy the idols," 30:13).

[a] Heb lacks *of doom* [b] Or *Nubia;* Heb *Cush* [c] Compare Gk Syr Vg: Heb *Cub* [d] Meaning of Heb uncertain [e] Or *Nubians;* Heb *Cush* [f] Heb *the day of Egypt*

by the hand of King Nebuchadrezzar of Babylon.
11 He and his people with him, the most terrible of the nations,
shall be brought in to destroy the land;
and they shall draw their swords against Egypt,
and fill the land with the slain.
12 I will dry up the channels,
and will sell the land into the hand of evildoers;
I will bring desolation upon the land and everything in it
by the hand of foreigners;
I the LORD have spoken.

13 Thus says the Lord GOD:
I will destroy the idols
and put an end to the images in Memphis;
there shall no longer be a prince in the land of Egypt;
so I will put fear in the land of Egypt.
14 I will make Pathros a desolation,
and will set fire to Zoan,
and will execute acts of judgment on Thebes.
15 I will pour my wrath upon Pelusium,
the stronghold of Egypt,
and cut off the hordes of Thebes.
16 I will set fire to Egypt;
Pelusium shall be in great agony;
Thebes shall be breached,
and Memphis face adversaries by day.
17 The young men of On and of Pi-beseth shall fall by the sword;
and the cities themselves[a] shall go into captivity.
18 At Tehaphnehes the day shall be dark,
when I break there the dominion of Egypt,
and its proud might shall come to an end;
the city[b] shall be covered by a cloud,
and its daughter-towns shall go into captivity.
19 Thus I will execute acts of judgment on Egypt.
Then they shall know that I am the LORD.

Proclamation against Pharaoh

20 In the eleventh year, in the first month, on the seventh day of
the month, the word of the LORD came to me: 21 Mortal, I have broken the arm of Pharaoh king of Egypt; it has not been bound up for
healing or wrapped with a bandage, so that it may become strong to
wield the sword. 22 Therefore thus says the Lord GOD: I am against
Pharaoh king of Egypt, and will break his arms, both the strong arm

30:20-26 In the eleventh year… broken the arm of Pharaoh: The oracle dated April 29, 587 B.C.E. may speak of an encounter between the Babylonians and the Egyptians led by pharaoh Hophra, who had come to the aid of Judah's King Zedekiah (Jer 37:5-10). See the note on 29:1-5.

[a] Heb *and they* [b] Heb *she*

and the one that was broken; and I will make the sword fall from his hand. [23]I will scatter the Egyptians among the nations, and disperse them throughout the lands. [24]I will strengthen the arms of the king of Babylon, and put my sword in his hand; but I will break the arms of Pharaoh, and he will groan before him with the groans of one mortally wounded. [25]I will strengthen the arms of the king of Babylon, but the arms of Pharaoh shall fall. And they shall know that I am the LORD, when I put my sword into the hand of the king of Babylon. He shall stretch it out against the land of Egypt, [26]and I will scatter the Egyptians among the nations and disperse them throughout the countries. Then they shall know that I am the LORD.

The Lofty Cedar

31:1-18 say to Pharaoh: This oracle is dated June 21, 587 B.C.E. It compares Pharaoh/Egypt with the once great Assyria, which has now also been defeated by Babylon.

31:3-9 Assyria, a cedar of Lebanon: Assyria is compared to a cedar tree of Lebanon. These trees were known for their height, beauty, and valuable wood. God made this tree of mythic proportions. It is watered by the deep (31:4; see Gen 1:2; Prov 8:24, 27; Isa 51:9-11) and exceeds the greatness of any trees in the garden of God (31:8-9; Gen 2:8-9; 3:6).

31 In the eleventh year, in the third month, on the first day of the month, the word of the LORD came to me: [2]Mortal, say to Pharaoh king of Egypt and to his hordes:

Whom are you like in your greatness?
3 Consider Assyria, a cedar of Lebanon,
with fair branches and forest shade,
and of great height,
its top among the clouds.[a]
4 The waters nourished it,
the deep made it grow tall,
making its rivers flow[b]
around the place it was planted,
sending forth its streams
to all the trees of the field.
5 So it towered high
above all the trees of the field;
its boughs grew large
and its branches long,
from abundant water in its shoots.
6 All the birds of the air
made their nests in its boughs;
under its branches all the animals of the field
gave birth to their young;
and in its shade
all great nations lived.
7 It was beautiful in its greatness,
in the length of its branches;
for its roots went down
to abundant water.
8 The cedars in the garden of God could not rival it,

[a] Gk: Heb *thick boughs* [b] Gk: Heb *rivers going*

nor the fir trees equal its boughs;
the plane trees were as nothing
compared with its branches;
no tree in the garden of God
was like it in beauty.
9 I made it beautiful
with its mass of branches,
the envy of all the trees of Eden
that were in the garden of God.

10 Therefore thus says the Lord GOD: Because it[a] towered high
and set its top among the clouds,[b] and its heart was proud of its height,
11 I gave it into the hand of the prince of the nations; he has dealt with
it as its wickedness deserves. I have cast it out. 12 Foreigners from the
most terrible of the nations have cut it down and left it. On the mountains and in all the valleys its branches have fallen, and its boughs lie
broken in all the watercourses of the land; and all the peoples of the
earth went away from its shade and left it.

31:10-14 Because it towered... heart was proud: The tree is guilty of taking too much pride in its height, so it is brought low by the prince of nations (31:11), probably Nebuchadnezzar, king of Babylon.

13 On its fallen trunk settle
all the birds of the air,
and among its boughs lodge
all the wild animals.
14 All this is in order that no trees by the waters may grow to lofty height
or set their tops among the clouds,[b] and that no trees that drink water
may reach up to them in height.
For all of them are handed over to death,
to the world below;
along with all mortals,
with those who go down to the Pit.

15 Thus says the Lord GOD: On the day it went down to Sheol
I closed the deep over it and covered it; I restrained its rivers, and
its mighty waters were checked. I clothed Lebanon in gloom for it,
and all the trees of the field fainted because of it. 16 I made the nations
quake at the sound of its fall, when I cast it down to Sheol with those
who go down to the Pit; and all the trees of Eden, the choice and best
of Lebanon, all that were well watered, were consoled in the world
below. 17 They also went down to Sheol with it, to those killed by the
sword, along with its allies,[c] those who lived in its shade among the
nations.

31:15 Sheol: See the note on 26:19-21.

18 Which among the trees of Eden was like you in glory and in
greatness? Now you shall be brought down with the trees of Eden to
the world below; you shall lie among the uncircumcised, with those
who are killed by the sword. This is Pharaoh and all his horde, says
the Lord GOD.

31:18 Pharaoh and all his horde: Returning to the beginning (31:2), Ezekiel clarifies the object of this oracle. They lie among the uncircumcised (see the note on 28:10).

[a] Syr Vg: Heb *you* [b] Gk: Heb *thick boughs* [c] Heb *its arms*

32:1-16 **a lamentation over Pharaoh:** This oracle is dated March 3, 585 B.C.E.

32:2-8 **you are like a dragon...will throw my net over you:** Pharaoh is compared to a sea dragon, perhaps meaning the great sea monster that roamed the deep (see 31:4). This dragon reference probably is not the same as the Nile "crocodile" of 29:3. The image of netting the dragon may have been a comparison to the Babylonia myth in which the god Marduk netted Tiamat, the sea dragon. The complete darkness that accompanies the punishment (32:7) is a theme common to the judgment day of the LORD (see also 30:3; Joel 2:1-2; Zeph 1:15).

32:9-16 **carry you captive among the nations:** The oracle shifts its focus to the impact on the surrounding nations of the LORD's judgment upon and humiliation of Pharaoh, here the great sea monster. The reference to being taken captive sounds like being taken into exile (see also 29:11-12).

32:11 **king of Babylon:** Nebuchadnezzar (29:19).

Many times throughout Ezekiel, the LORD's judgment is all-consuming and has the purpose of knowing that the LORD is the LORD (see 32:15). How does this feel in relation to your understanding of Jesus?

Lamentation over Pharaoh and Egypt

32 In the twelfth year, in the twelfth month, on the first day
of the month, the word of the LORD came to me: 2 Mortal,
raise a lamentation over Pharaoh king of Egypt, and say to him:

You consider yourself a lion among the nations,
but you are like a dragon in the seas;
you thrash about in your streams,
trouble the water with your feet,
and foul your[a] streams.
3 Thus says the Lord GOD:
In an assembly of many peoples
I will throw my net over you;
and I[b] will haul you up in my dragnet.
4 I will throw you on the ground,
on the open field I will fling you,
and will cause all the birds of the air to settle on you,
and I will let the wild animals of the whole earth gorge
themselves with you.
5 I will strew your flesh on the mountains,
and fill the valleys with your carcass.[c]
6 I will drench the land with your flowing blood
up to the mountains,
and the watercourses will be filled with you.
7 When I blot you out, I will cover the heavens,
and make their stars dark;
I will cover the sun with a cloud,
and the moon shall not give its light.
8 All the shining lights of the heavens
I will darken above you,
and put darkness on your land,
says the Lord GOD.
9 I will trouble the hearts of many peoples,
as I carry you captive[d] among the nations,
into countries you have not known.
10 I will make many peoples appalled at you;
their kings shall shudder because of you.
When I brandish my sword before them,
they shall tremble every moment
for their lives, each one of them,
on the day of your downfall.
11 For thus says the Lord GOD:
The sword of the king of Babylon shall come against you.

[a] Heb *their* [b] Gk Vg: Heb *they* [c] Symmachus Syr Vg: Heb *your height* [d] Gk: Heb *bring your destruction*

12 I will cause your hordes to fall
by the swords of mighty ones,
all of them most terrible among the nations.
They shall bring to ruin the pride of Egypt,
and all its hordes shall perish.
13 I will destroy all its livestock
from beside abundant waters;
and no human foot shall trouble them any more,
nor shall the hoofs of cattle trouble them.
14 Then I will make their waters clear,
and cause their streams to run like oil, says the Lord GOD.
15 When I make the land of Egypt desolate
and when the land is stripped of all that fills it,
when I strike down all who live in it,
then they shall know that I am the LORD.
16 This is a lamentation; it shall be chanted.
The women of the nations shall chant it.
Over Egypt and all its hordes they shall chant it,
says the Lord GOD.

Dirge over Egypt

17 In the twelfth year, in the first month,[a] on the fifteenth day of
the month, the word of the LORD came to me:
18 Mortal, wail over the hordes of Egypt,
and send them down,
with Egypt[b] and the daughters of majestic nations,
to the world below,
with those who go down to the Pit.
19 "Whom do you surpass in beauty?
Go down! Be laid to rest with the uncircumcised!"
20 They shall fall among those who are killed by the sword. Egypt[c] has
been handed over to the sword; carry away both it and its hordes.
21 The mighty chiefs shall speak of them, with their helpers, out of the
midst of Sheol: "They have come down, they lie still, the uncircumcised, killed by the sword."
22 Assyria is there, and all its company, their graves all around it,
all of them killed, fallen by the sword. 23 Their graves are set in the ut-
termost parts of the Pit. Its company is all around its grave, all of them
killed, fallen by the sword, who spread terror in the land of the living.
24 Elam is there, and all its hordes around its grave; all of them
killed, fallen by the sword, who went down uncircumcised into the
world below, who spread terror in the land of the living. They bear
their shame with those who go down to the Pit. 25 They have made

32:16 women of the nations: Women played a central role in ancient mourning rituals (32:18). The image is of a haunting global, communal lament.

32:17-32 send them down: This final oracle against Egypt is dated April 7, 586 B.C.E. Ezekiel's wailing/lamenting sends Egypt into the Pit (32:18, 21). In Ezekiel, the Pit is the lowest level of the underworld. The uncircumcised are there, including Egypt and other great nations (see also 26:20). It may be that the Pit also includes "those slain by the sword," but it may also be that "those slain by the sword" is a portion of the uncircumcised in the Pit (32:21 and note on 31:18). Sheol, on the other hand, is the place where honored warriors lie in death (32:21, 27).

32:22-30 Assyria . . . Sidonians: Several places are mentioned in these verses: Assyria (see also 31:15); Elam east of Babylon (Jer 49:34-38); Meshech and Tubal in Asia Minor (27:13; 38:2); Edom (25:12-14); and Sidon (28:20-24). See Maps 7–9, pp. 2105-2106.

---

[a] Gk: Heb lacks *in the first month* [b] Heb *it* [c] Heb *It*

Elam[a] a bed among the slain with all its hordes, their graves all around
it, all of them uncircumcised, killed by the sword; for terror of them
was spread in the land of the living, and they bear their shame with
those who go down to the Pit; they are placed among the slain.

26 Meshech and Tubal are there, and all their multitude, their
graves all around them, all of them uncircumcised, killed by the
sword; for they spread terror in the land of the living. 27And they do
not lie with the fallen warriors of long ago[b] who went down to Sheol
with their weapons of war, whose swords were laid under their heads,
and whose shields[c] are upon their bones; for the terror of the warriors
was in the land of the living. 28So you shall be broken and lie among
the uncircumcised, with those who are killed by the sword.

29 Edom is there, its kings and all its princes, who for all their
might are laid with those who are killed by the sword; they lie with
the uncircumcised, with those who go down to the Pit.

30 The princes of the north are there, all of them, and all the Sidonians, who have gone down in shame with the slain, for all the terror
that they caused by their might; they lie uncircumcised with those
who are killed by the sword, and bear their shame with those who go
down to the Pit.

31 When Pharaoh sees them, he will be consoled for all his
hordes—Pharaoh and all his army, killed by the sword, says the Lord
God. 32For he[d] spread terror in the land of the living; therefore he shall
be laid to rest among the uncircumcised, with those who are slain by
the sword—Pharaoh and all his multitude, says the Lord God.

Ezekiel Israel's Sentry

33 The word of the LORD came to me: 2O Mortal, speak to
your people and say to them, If I bring the sword upon a
land, and the people of the land take one of their number as their sentinel; 3and if the sentinel sees the sword coming upon the land and
blows the trumpet and warns the people; 4then if any who hear the
sound of the trumpet do not take warning, and the sword comes and
takes them away, their blood shall be upon their own heads. 5They
heard the sound of the trumpet and did not take warning; their blood
shall be upon themselves. But if they had taken warning, they would
have saved their lives. 6But if the sentinel sees the sword coming and
does not blow the trumpet, so that the people are not warned, and the
sword comes and takes any of them, they are taken away in their iniquity, but their blood I will require at the sentinel's hand.

7 So you, mortal, I have made a sentinel for the house of Israel;
whenever you hear a word from my mouth, you shall give them warning from me. 8If I say to the wicked, "O wicked ones, you shall surely

33:1—39:29 The word of the LORD came to me: This major section in Ezekiel focuses on the promise of restoration for the exiles in Babylon. After Jerusalem's fall, Ezekiel's calling as a "sentinel for the house of Israel" (33:7) is renewed and his prophecy turns more hopeful.

33:2-7 speak to your people…as their sentinel: This section renews God's original calling of Ezekiel. As sentinel, Ezekiel is obligated to warn the people of coming danger. In the same way, Ezekiel is expected to warn the people of their sinfulness. If he doesn't, he will be held responsible (see 3:16-21 and note).

God charges Ezekiel with being a sentinel (33:1-9), a guard who keeps watch over God's people. Where do you hear sentinels for the church today, and what do they say? How are you a sentinel?

---

[a] Heb *it* [b] Gk Old Latin: Heb *of the uncircumcised* [c] Cn: Heb *iniquities* [d] Cn: Heb *I*

die," and you do not speak to warn the wicked to turn from their ways, the wicked shall die in their iniquity, but their blood I will require at your hand. [9]But if you warn the wicked to turn from their ways, and they do not turn from their ways, the wicked shall die in their iniquity, but you will have saved your life.

God's Justice and Mercy

10 Now you, mortal, say to the house of Israel, Thus you have said: "Our transgressions and our sins weigh upon us, and we waste away because of them; how then can we live?" [11] Say to them, As I live, says the Lord God, I have no pleasure in the death of the wicked, but that the wicked turn from their ways and live; turn back, turn back from your evil ways; for why will you die, O house of Israel? [12]And you, mortal, say to your people, The righteousness of the righteous shall not save them when they transgress; and as for the wickedness of the wicked, it shall not make them stumble when they turn from their wickedness; and the righteous shall not be able to live by their righteousness[a] when they sin. [13]Though I say to the righteous that they shall surely live, yet if they trust in their righteousness and commit iniquity, none of their righteous deeds shall be remembered; but in the iniquity that they have committed they shall die. [14]Again, though I say to the wicked, "You shall surely die," yet if they turn from their sin and do what is lawful and right— [15]if the wicked restore the pledge, give back what they have taken by robbery, and walk in the statutes of life, committing no iniquity—they shall surely live, they shall not die. [16]None of the sins that they have committed shall be remembered against them; they have done what is lawful and right, they shall surely live.

17 Yet your people say, "The way of the Lord is not just," when it is their own way that is not just. [18]When the righteous turn from their righteousness, and commit iniquity, they shall die for it.[b] [19]And when the wicked turn from their wickedness, and do what is lawful and right, they shall live by it.[b] [20]Yet you say, "The way of the Lord is not just." O house of Israel, I will judge all of you according to your ways!

The Fall of Jerusalem

21 In the twelfth year of our exile, in the tenth month, on the fifth day of the month, someone who had escaped from Jerusalem came to me and said, "The city has fallen." [22]Now the hand of the Lord had been upon me the evening before the fugitive came; but he had opened my mouth by the time the fugitive came to me in the morning; so my mouth was opened, and I was no longer unable to speak.

33:10-20 say to the house of Israel: This oracle mirrors much of the content of chapter 18. In spite of their complaints that "the way of the Lord is not just" (33:17), the people of Israel, whether they are righteous or wicked, will be held responsible for their own "ways" (33:20).

Which Ezekiel passage was a favorite of Luther and why? "As I live, says the Lord God, I have no pleasure in the death of the wicked, but that the wicked turn from their ways and live." Of the whole of Ezekiel, this is the favorite verse of Luther and the Lutheran Confessions. Luther understands that God does not desire the death of sinners (the wicked) but rather God hopes that we sinners might turn in faith and receive not what we deserve (death) but what God desires (life). *Ezekiel 33:11*

33:21-22 The city has fallen: From the testimony of a survivor, news is received in Babylon (January 19, 585 B.C.E) of Jerusalem's fall (2 Kgs 25:8-12). Ezekiel likely was unable to speak from the night before the news until the survivor from Jerusalem arrived (33:22).

---

[a] Heb *by it* [b] Heb *them*

The Survivors in Judah

23 The word of the LORD came to me: [24]Mortal, the inhabitants
of these waste places in the land of Israel keep saying, "Abraham was
only one man, yet he got possession of the land; but we are many; the
land is surely given us to possess." [25]Therefore say to them, Thus says
the Lord GOD: You eat flesh with the blood, and lift up your eyes to
your idols, and shed blood; shall you then possess the land? [26]You
depend on your swords, you commit abominations, and each of you
defiles his neighbor's wife; shall you then possess the land? [27]Say this
to them, Thus says the Lord GOD: As I live, surely those who are in
the waste places shall fall by the sword; and those who are in the open
field I will give to the wild animals to be devoured; and those who are
in strongholds and in caves shall die by pestilence. [28]I will make the
land a desolation and a waste, and its proud might shall come to an
end; and the mountains of Israel shall be so desolate that no one will
pass through. [29]Then they shall know that I am the LORD, when I have
made the land a desolation and a waste because of all their abominations that they have committed.

30 As for you, mortal, your people who talk together about you
by the walls, and at the doors of the houses, say to one another, each
to a neighbor, "Come and hear what the word is that comes from the
LORD." [31]They come to you as people come, and they sit before you as
my people, and they hear your words, but they will not obey them. For
flattery is on their lips, but their heart is set on their gain. [32]To them
you are like a singer of love songs,[a] one who has a beautiful voice and
plays well on an instrument; they hear what you say, but they will not
do it. [33]When this comes—and come it will!—then they shall know
that a prophet has been among them.

Israel's False Shepherds

34 The word of the LORD came to me: [2]Mortal, prophesy
against the shepherds of Israel: prophesy, and say to them—
to the shepherds: Thus says the Lord GOD: Ah, you shepherds of Israel who have been feeding yourselves! Should not shepherds feed
the sheep? [3]You eat the fat, you clothe yourselves with the wool, you
slaughter the fatlings; but you do not feed the sheep. [4]You have not
strengthened the weak, you have not healed the sick, you have not
bound up the injured, you have not brought back the strayed, you
have not sought the lost, but with force and harshness you have ruled
them. [5]So they were scattered, because there was no shepherd; and
scattered, they became food for all the wild animals. [6]My sheep were
scattered, they wandered over all the mountains and on every high

[a] Cn: Heb *like a love song*

33:23-29 inhabitants of these waste places: Those who remain in Judah after it is destroyed are claiming the land (33:24) and are reminded of their sins (33:25-26) and punishments (33:27-29; see also Lev 26:14-45).

The people speak of how beautiful Ezekiel's words are, but they don't take the words to heart and act on them (33:30-32). They miss the full force of his words, which include both justice and the loving-kindness of the living God. They hear only what they want to hear. How is this also true of us? How might we open our hearts to hear the words of the living God?

34:1-31 prophesy, and say…to the shepherds: This oracle condemns the false shepherds (leaders) of Israel (34:1-10) and describes God as the good and just shepherd (34:11-31; see Ps 23; John 10:1-21).

34:2-6 you shepherds of Israel… with force and harshness you have ruled them: The image of shepherd was used regularly for kings in the ancient Near East (2 Sam 5:2; Isa 44:28). Israel's shepherds have not treated people with justice and kindness. They are like shepherds who do not keep guard over their flocks. The result is that the LORD's sheep are scattered (Ezek 34:6; Jer 23:1-4).

The phrase "I will rescue my sheep from their mouths" (34:10) is vivid and strong language, condemning unjust leadership that preys on those being led. As Christians called to servant leadership in church and community, how can these words inform our leadership?

hill; my sheep were scattered over all the face of the earth, with no one
to search or seek for them.
7 Therefore, you shepherds, hear the word of the LORD: 8 As I
live, says the Lord GOD, because my sheep have become a prey, and
my sheep have become food for all the wild animals, since there was
no shepherd; and because my shepherds have not searched for my
sheep, but the shepherds have fed themselves, and have not fed my
sheep; 9 therefore, you shepherds, hear the word of the LORD: 10 Thus
says the Lord GOD, I am against the shepherds; and I will demand
my sheep at their hand, and put a stop to their feeding the sheep; no
longer shall the shepherds feed themselves. I will rescue my sheep
from their mouths, so that they may not be food for them.

God, the True Shepherd

11 For thus says the Lord GOD: I myself will search for my sheep,
and will seek them out. 12 As shepherds seek out their flocks when
they are among their scattered sheep, so I will seek out my sheep. I
will rescue them from all the places to which they have been scattered
on a day of clouds and thick darkness. 13 I will bring them out from
the peoples and gather them from the countries, and will bring them
into their own land; and I will feed them on the mountains of Israel,
by the watercourses, and in all the inhabited parts of the land. 14 I will
feed them with good pasture, and the mountain heights of Israel shall
be their pasture; there they shall lie down in good grazing land, and
they shall feed on rich pasture on the mountains of Israel. 15 I myself
will be the shepherd of my sheep, and I will make them lie down, says
the Lord GOD. 16 I will seek the lost, and I will bring back the strayed,
and I will bind up the injured, and I will strengthen the weak, but the
fat and the strong I will destroy. I will feed them with justice.

34:11-13 I myself…they have been scattered: The LORD promises to fulfill the role of shepherd for the people fully and justly. The people scattered to foreign lands in the exile will be brought back into their own land (34:13).

34:12 clouds and thick darkness: A reference to the day of the LORD, which has already happened (see 30:3 and note).

17 As for you, my flock, thus says the Lord GOD: I shall judge
between sheep and sheep, between rams and goats: 18 Is it not enough
for you to feed on the good pasture, but you must tread down with
your feet the rest of your pasture? When you drink of clear water,
must you foul the rest with your feet? 19 And must my sheep eat what
you have trodden with your feet, and drink what you have fouled with
your feet?
20 Therefore, thus says the Lord GOD to them: I myself will judge
between the fat sheep and the lean sheep. 21 Because you pushed with
flank and shoulder, and butted at all the weak animals with your horns
until you scattered them far and wide, 22 I will save my flock, and they
shall no longer be ravaged; and I will judge between sheep and sheep.

34:17-22 between sheep and sheep, between rams and goats: The LORD will judge the animals of the flock. Some of the sheep within the flock were fat and used their size to bully the weaker ones (34:21). As a result, the flock is scattered. Jesus uses similar language of separating the sheep from the goats when he speaks of judging between those who served the weak and those who ignored them (see Matt 25:31-46).

23 I will set up over them one shepherd, my servant David, and
he shall feed them: he shall feed them and be their shepherd. 24 And
I, the LORD, will be their God, and my servant David shall be prince
among them; I, the LORD, have spoken.

34:23-24 one shepherd, my servant David: This points to re-establishment of David's royal house. But the leader will be demoted to a prince, as the LORD is the true king/shepherd.

25 I will make with them a covenant of peace and banish wild animals from the land, so that they may live in the wild and sleep in the
woods securely. 26 I will make them and the region around my hill a
blessing; and I will send down the showers in their season; they shall
be showers of blessing. 27 The trees of the field shall yield their fruit,
and the earth shall yield its increase. They shall be secure on their
soil; and they shall know that I am the LORD, when I break the bars
of their yoke, and save them from the hands of those who enslaved
them. 28 They shall no more be plunder for the nations, nor shall the
animals of the land devour them; they shall live in safety, and no one
shall make them afraid. 29 I will provide for them a splendid vegetation
so that they shall no more be consumed with hunger in the land, and
no longer suffer the insults of the nations. 30 They shall know that I, the
LORD their God, am with them, and that they, the house of Israel, are
my people, says the Lord GOD. 31 You are my sheep, the sheep of my
pasture[a] and I am your God, says the Lord GOD.

Judgment on Mount Seir

35 The word of the LORD came to me: 2 Mortal, set your face
against Mount Seir, and prophesy against it, 3 and say to it,
Thus says the Lord GOD:

I am against you, Mount Seir;
  I stretch out my hand against you
  to make you a desolation and a waste.
4 I lay your towns in ruins;
  you shall become a desolation,
  and you shall know that I am the LORD.

5 Because you cherished an ancient enmity, and gave over the people
of Israel to the power of the sword at the time of their calamity, at the
time of their final punishment; 6 therefore, as I live, says the Lord GOD,
I will prepare you for blood, and blood shall pursue you; since you did
not hate bloodshed, bloodshed shall pursue you. 7 I will make Mount
Seir a waste and a desolation; and I will cut off from it all who come
and go. 8 I will fill its mountains with the slain; on your hills and in
your valleys and in all your watercourses those killed with the sword
shall fall. 9 I will make you a perpetual desolation, and your cities shall
never be inhabited. Then you shall know that I am the LORD.

10 Because you said, "These two nations and these two countries
shall be mine, and we will take possession of them,"—although the
LORD was there— 11 therefore, as I live, says the Lord GOD, I will deal
with you according to the anger and envy that you showed because of
your hatred against them; and I will make myself known among you,[b]
when I judge you. 12 You shall know that I, the LORD, have heard all

[a] Gk OL: Heb *pasture, you are people* [b] Gk: Heb *them*

34:25-31 a covenant of peace: God's covenant of peace includes many blessings, including rescue from dangers, return to Jerusalem (my hill) as a center of blessing, freedom from enslavement to other nations, and abundant harvests (see also Lev 26:4-6; Jer 31:31-34; Heb 13:20-21).

34:31 You are...the sheep of my pasture: God's shepherd relationship with the people is confirmed (see also 11:20; 14:11; 36:28; 37:23, 27).

35:1-15 set your face against Mount Seir...gave over the people of Israel: An oracle of judgment against the land of Edom (25:2-14; 32:29), symbolized by Mount Seir. The conflict between Israel and Edom ("ancient enmity") possibly refers to the conflict between Jacob and Esau, whose descendants were Edomites (Gen 25:27-34; 27:30-45; Jer 49:7-22). The prophet Obadiah describes Edom's role in the defeat of Judah (Obad 10–14).

It is said that violence ("bloodshed" in 35:6) only gives birth to more violence. How do these words in Ezekiel cause you to think about relating to other people, other faiths, other nations?

35:11 I will deal with you. . . your hatred against them: See 35:5 and note on 35:1-15. Compare this judgment to Jesus' words in the Lord's Prayer, where he encourages his followers to forgive others (Matt 6:12; Luke 11:4).

the abusive speech that you uttered against the mountains of Israel,
saying, "They are laid desolate, they are given us to devour." 13And
you magnified yourselves against me with your mouth, and multiplied your words against me; I heard it. 14Thus says the Lord GOD: As
the whole earth rejoices, I will make you desolate. 15As you rejoiced
over the inheritance of the house of Israel, because it was desolate, so
I will deal with you; you shall be desolate, Mount Seir, and all Edom,
all of it. Then they shall know that I am the LORD.

Blessing on Israel

36 And you, mortal, prophesy to the mountains of Israel, and
say: O mountains of Israel, hear the word of the LORD.
2Thus says the Lord GOD: Because the enemy said of you, "Aha!" and,
"The ancient heights have become our possession," 3therefore prophesy, and say: Thus says the Lord GOD: Because they made you desolate indeed, and crushed you from all sides, so that you became the
possession of the rest of the nations, and you became an object of
gossip and slander among the people; 4therefore, O mountains of Israel, hear the word of the Lord GOD: Thus says the Lord GOD to the
mountains and the hills, the watercourses and the valleys, the desolate wastes and the deserted towns, which have become a source of
plunder and an object of derision to the rest of the nations all around;
5therefore thus says the Lord GOD: I am speaking in my hot jealousy
against the rest of the nations, and against all Edom, who, with wholehearted joy and utter contempt, took my land as their possession, because of its pasture, to plunder it. 6Therefore prophesy concerning the
land of Israel, and say to the mountains and hills, to the watercourses
and valleys, Thus says the Lord GOD: I am speaking in my jealous
wrath, because you have suffered the insults of the nations; 7therefore
thus says the Lord GOD: I swear that the nations that are all around
you shall themselves suffer insults.

8 But you, O mountains of Israel, shall shoot out your branches,
and yield your fruit to my people Israel; for they shall soon come
home. 9See now, I am for you; I will turn to you, and you shall be tilled
and sown; 10and I will multiply your population, the whole house of
Israel, all of it; the towns shall be inhabited and the waste places rebuilt; 11and I will multiply human beings and animals upon you. They
shall increase and be fruitful; and I will cause you to be inhabited as
in your former times, and will do more good to you than ever before.
Then you shall know that I am the LORD. 12I will lead people upon
you—my people Israel—and they shall possess you, and you shall be
their inheritance. No longer shall you bereave them of children.

13 Thus says the Lord GOD: Because they say to you, "You devour people, and you bereave your nation of children," 14therefore
you shall no longer devour people and no longer bereave your nation

36:1-7 prophesy to the mountains of Israel…the nations…around you shall themselves suffer insults: Earlier Israel's mountains heard the LORD's condemnation (6:1-11). Now the same mountains are told that the LORD's jealousy (36:5-6) is directed at the nations who jeered ("Aha!") and slandered God's people (see 25:3; 26:2; Ps 35:21).

36:8 they shall soon come home: Refers to a homecoming for those in exile in Babylon.

36:13-15 you shall no longer devour: The mountains stand for the land of Israel, which had experienced many battles and the death of many of its people. See also Numbers 13:32, where Israel's spies talked of the land of Canaan as a place where its mountains devour its people. God promises a time of peace.

of children, says the Lord God; [15]and no longer will I let you hear
the insults of the nations, no longer shall you bear the disgrace of the
peoples; and no longer shall you cause your nation to stumble, says
the Lord God.

The Renewal of Israel

16 The word of the Lord came to me: [17]Mortal, when the house
of Israel lived on their own soil, they defiled it with their ways and
their deeds; their conduct in my sight was like the uncleanness of a
woman in her menstrual period. [18]So I poured out my wrath upon
them for the blood that they had shed upon the land, and for the idols
with which they had defiled it. [19]I scattered them among the nations,
and they were dispersed through the countries; in accordance with
their conduct and their deeds I judged them. [20]But when they came
to the nations, wherever they came, they profaned my holy name, in
that it was said of them, "These are the people of the Lord, and yet
they had to go out of his land." [21]But I had concern for my holy name,
which the house of Israel had profaned among the nations to which
they came.

22 Therefore say to the house of Israel, Thus says the Lord God:
It is not for your sake, O house of Israel, that I am about to act, but
for the sake of my holy name, which you have profaned among the
nations to which you came. [23]I will sanctify my great name, which
has been profaned among the nations, and which you have profaned
among them; and the nations shall know that I am the Lord, says
the Lord God, when through you I display my holiness before their
eyes. [24]I will take you from the nations, and gather you from all the
countries, and bring you into your own land. [25]I will sprinkle clean
water upon you, and you shall be clean from all your uncleannesses,
and from all your idols I will cleanse you. [26]A new heart I will give
you, and a new spirit I will put within you; and I will remove from
your body the heart of stone and give you a heart of flesh. [27]I will put
my spirit within you, and make you follow my statutes and be careful to observe my ordinances. [28]Then you shall live in the land that I
gave to your ancestors; and you shall be my people, and I will be your
God. [29]I will save you from all your uncleannesses, and I will summon the grain and make it abundant and lay no famine upon you. [30]I
will make the fruit of the tree and the produce of the field abundant,
so that you may never again suffer the disgrace of famine among the
nations. [31]Then you shall remember your evil ways, and your dealings
that were not good; and you shall loathe yourselves for your iniquities
and your abominable deeds. [32]It is not for your sake that I will act, says
the Lord God; let that be known to you. Be ashamed and dismayed
for your ways, O house of Israel.

33 Thus says the Lord God: On the day that I cleanse you from

36:16-38 the house of Israel: This oracle promises that Israel will be purified and restored *not* because of Israel's merit but for the sake of God's holy name (36:21-23, 32).

36:17 defiled it…like the uncleanness of a woman in her menstrual period: From Ezekiel's background as a priest and consistent with the image of Jerusalem as God's wife (chapters 16, 23), he compares the impurity caused by Israel's sins with a menstruating woman whose blood was said to make her ritually unclean (see 7:19; Lev 15:19-33). The power of blood to make unclean was related to the ancient belief that blood was the sacred source of life. Calling menstruation unclean and comparing it to Israel's evil deeds may be troubling for us today. We know menstruation is an involuntary fact of life. But Israel voluntarily chose to sin.

36:24-28 I will gather you…give you a heart of flesh: In this vision of renewal, God will gather the people who have been scattered to the nations and give the people a fresh start with a new heart (see the note on 11:17-21; Jer 31:31-34; Ps 51:10).

Amid promises of purification and restoration, Israel is reminded that it is not their goodness that initiates God's actions (36:32). How does this inform your understanding of God's relationship with you and the world?

all your iniquities, I will cause the towns to be inhabited, and the
waste places shall be rebuilt. 34The land that was desolate shall be
tilled, instead of being the desolation that it was in the sight of all who
passed by. 35And they will say, "This land that was desolate has become like the garden of Eden; and the waste and desolate and ruined
towns are now inhabited and fortified." 36Then the nations that are
left all around you shall know that I, the LORD, have rebuilt the ruined
places, and replanted that which was desolate; I, the LORD, have spoken, and I will do it.

37 Thus says the Lord GOD: I will also let the house of Israel
ask me to do this for them: to increase their population like a flock.
38Like the flock for sacrifices,[a] like the flock at Jerusalem during her
appointed festivals, so shall the ruined towns be filled with flocks of
people. Then they shall know that I am the LORD.

The Valley of Dry Bones

37 The hand of the LORD came upon me, and he brought me
out by the spirit of the LORD and set me down in the middle of a valley; it was full of bones. 2He led me all around them; there
were very many lying in the valley, and they were very dry. 3He said
to me, "Mortal, can these bones live?" I answered, "O Lord GOD, you
know." 4Then he said to me, "Prophesy to these bones, and say to
them: O dry bones, hear the word of the LORD. 5Thus says the Lord
GOD to these bones: I will cause breath[b] to enter you, and you shall
live. 6I will lay sinews on you, and will cause flesh to come upon you,
and cover you with skin, and put breath[b] in you, and you shall live;
and you shall know that I am the LORD."

7 So I prophesied as I had been commanded; and as I prophesied,
suddenly there was a noise, a rattling, and the bones came together,
bone to its bone. 8I looked, and there were sinews on them, and flesh
had come upon them, and skin had covered them; but there was no
breath in them. 9Then he said to me, "Prophesy to the breath, prophesy, mortal, and say to the breath:[c] Thus says the Lord GOD: Come
from the four winds, O breath,[c] and breathe upon these slain, that they
may live." 10I prophesied as he commanded me, and the breath came
into them, and they lived, and stood on their feet, a vast multitude.

11 Then he said to me, "Mortal, these bones are the whole house
of Israel. They say, 'Our bones are dried up, and our hope is lost; we
are cut off completely.' 12Therefore prophesy, and say to them, Thus
says the Lord GOD: I am going to open your graves, and bring you up
from your graves, O my people; and I will bring you back to the land
of Israel. 13And you shall know that I am the LORD, when I open your
graves, and bring you up from your graves, O my people. 14I will put

---

[a] Heb *flock of holy things* [b] Or *spirit* [c] Or *wind* or *spirit*

36:33-36 shall be rebuilt: The land that has been turned into a wasteland (36:4) by battle will be restored beyond its earlier beauty. It will be as perfectly beautiful and life-giving as the Garden of Eden (see also 47:1-12; Isa 51:3). This will happen so that the nations may know that God is God.

36:37-38 increase their population like a flock: Returning to the image in chapter 34, Israel will ask to increase the size of its flock (population) when it returns to the land.

37:1-14 a valley…full of bones: The prophet is transported (see 1:3) to a plain (3:22) where he has a vision of God's life-giving power in the reassembling and restoring of dead, dry bones to life. Compare this to the opposite image of bones in Jeremiah 8:1-3.

The vision of the dry bones (37:1-14) freed the faith-filled imagination of African American slaves, who created the spiritual "Dem Bones." How does this vision free your imagination? How does it help your faith "sing"?

37:5 breath: The Hebrew word *ruach* [ROO-ahk] used throughout 37:1-14 can be read as "wind," "breath," or "spirit" (see Gen 1:2).

37:13 when I open your graves: The "dry bones" of Ezekiel's vision are the community of exiles in Babylon, who have felt dead in exile but are now promised life. Christians have often understood the vision to point to the resurrection of the dead.

my spirit within you, and you shall live, and I will place you on your own soil; then you shall know that I, the LORD, have spoken and will act, says the LORD."

The Two Sticks

15 The word of the LORD came to me: 16 Mortal, take a stick and write on it, "For Judah, and the Israelites associated with it"; then take another stick and write on it, "For Joseph (the stick of Ephraim) and all the house of Israel associated with it"; 17 and join them together into one stick, so that they may become one in your hand. 18 And when your people say to you, "Will you not show us what you mean by these?" 19 say to them, Thus says the Lord GOD: I am about to take the stick of Joseph (which is in the hand of Ephraim) and the tribes of Israel associated with it; and I will put the stick of Judah upon it,[a] and make them one stick, in order that they may be one in my hand. 20 When the sticks on which you write are in your hand before their eyes, 21 then say to them, Thus says the Lord GOD: I will take the people of Israel from the nations among which they have gone, and will gather them from every quarter, and bring them to their own land. 22 I will make them one nation in the land, on the mountains of Israel; and one king shall be king over them all. Never again shall they be two nations, and never again shall they be divided into two kingdoms. 23 They shall never again defile themselves with their idols and their detestable things, or with any of their transgressions. I will save them from all the apostasies into which they have fallen,[b] and will cleanse them. Then they shall be my people, and I will be their God.

24 My servant David shall be king over them; and they shall all have one shepherd. They shall follow my ordinances and be careful to observe my statutes. 25 They shall live in the land that I gave to my servant Jacob, in which your ancestors lived; they and their children and their children's children shall live there forever; and my servant David shall be their prince forever. 26 I will make a covenant of peace with them; it shall be an everlasting covenant with them; and I will bless[c] them and multiply them, and will set my sanctuary among them forevermore. 27 My dwelling place shall be with them; and I will be their God, and they shall be my people. 28 Then the nations shall know that I the LORD sanctify Israel, when my sanctuary is among them forevermore.

Invasion by Gog

38 The word of the LORD came to me: 2 Mortal, set your face toward Gog, of the land of Magog, the chief prince of Meshech and Tubal. Prophesy against him 3 and say: Thus says the Lord

[a] Heb *I will put them upon it* [b] Another reading is *from all the settlements in which they have sinned*
[c] Tg: Heb *give*

37:15-28 take a stick: With another symbolic action (see also 4:1-5:4), the prophet proclaims that two sticks, the Northern (Ephraim) and Southern (Judah) kingdoms, both destroyed, will be reunited into one stick (37:17, 19).

37:21-28 I will take . . . gather . . . set my sanctuary: This promise of return, new life, and a covenant of peace (37:26) is similar to the promise of 34:23-31. The reuniting of the divided nation under one king (37:22) may refer to God's kingship (see 20:33-40. It envisions reestablishing David's royal house (34:23-24). The use of "king" for the Davidic house is unusual after the declaration that the LORD is king (see note on 20:33-44). "My sanctuary" looks ahead to the rebuilding of the Jerusalem temple (chapters 40–48) and the LORD's return to the temple (10:1-22; 11:22; 43:1-5).

38:1—39:29 Gog, of the land of Magog: This oracle provides a graphic and gory picture of a final battle between the one holy LORD GOD and the forces that would conquer God's people. With no historical nation of Magog or a ruler named Gog, it is likely that these are meant to be unclear. This picture then portrays God's ultimate victory against these forces and provides hope for those who have not yet experienced the victory of God's holiness. This vision is sandwiched between the promised restoration of the temple (37:26-28) and the visions of the new temple (chapters 40-48). Its clear emphasis on God's holiness shows how Israel's priestly tradition influences this picture of God's ultimate victory. These chapters provided imagery for later apocalyptic texts (Dan 11:40-45; Rev 20.7-10) that describe God's ultimate victory over the forces of evil.

38:2 Meshech and Tubal: These are cities in Lydia in Asia Minor (27:13; 32:26-28). This has led some to say Gog may be Lydia's ruler Gyges.

God: I am against you, O Gog, chief prince of Meshech and Tubal;
[4]I will turn you around and put hooks into your jaws, and I will lead
you out with all your army, horses and horsemen, all of them clothed
in full armor, a great company, all of them with shield and buckler,
wielding swords. [5]Persia, Ethiopia,[a] and Put are with them, all of them
with buckler and helmet; [6]Gomer and all its troops; Beth-togarmah
from the remotest parts of the north with all its troops—many peoples are with you.
7 Be ready and keep ready, you and all the companies that are assembled around you, and hold yourselves in reserve for them. [8]Af-
ter many days you shall be mustered; in the latter years you shall go
against a land restored from war, a land where people were gathered
from many nations on the mountains of Israel, which had long lain
waste; its people were brought out from the nations and now are living in safety, all of them. [9]You shall advance, coming on like a storm;
you shall be like a cloud covering the land, you and all your troops,
and many peoples with you.
10 Thus says the Lord God: On that day thoughts will come into
your mind, and you will devise an evil scheme. [11]You will say, "I will
go up against the land of unwalled villages; I will fall upon the quiet
people who live in safety, all of them living without walls, and having
no bars or gates"; [12]to seize spoil and carry off plunder; to assail the
waste places that are now inhabited, and the people who were gathered from the nations, who are acquiring cattle and goods, who live
at the center[b] of the earth. [13]Sheba and Dedan and the merchants of
Tarshish and all its young warriors[c] will say to you, "Have you come
to seize spoil? Have you assembled your horde to carry off plunder,
to carry away silver and gold, to take away cattle and goods, to seize a
great amount of booty?"
14 Therefore, mortal, prophesy, and say to Gog: Thus says the
Lord God: On that day when my people Israel are living securely, you
will rouse yourself[d] [15]and come from your place out of the remotest
parts of the north, you and many peoples with you, all of them riding
on horses, a great horde, a mighty army; [16]you will come up against
my people Israel, like a cloud covering the earth. In the latter days
I will bring you against my land, so that the nations may know me,
when through you, O Gog, I display my holiness before their eyes.

Judgment on Gog

17 Thus says the Lord God: Are you he of whom I spoke in former days by my servants the prophets of Israel, who in those days
prophesied for years that I would bring you against them? [18]On that
day, when Gog comes against the land of Israel, says the Lord God,

[a] Or *Nubia;* Heb *Cush* [b] Heb *navel* [c] Heb *young lions* [d] Gk: Heb *will you not know?*

38:4 hooks into your jaws: As had been done to Israel (19:4, 9).

38:5-6 Persia, Ethiopia, and Put... Gomer...Bethtogarmah: Magog's forces are international (27:10-14).

38:8 in the latter years: This is a time in the future after the exiles have been restored to the land and live in safety. The forces of Magog attack with the suddenness of a storm (38:9), setting the stage for God's ultimate victory.

38.12 center of the earth: Here "center" is better translated as "navel." Jerusalem and possibly the Temple Mount are pictured as the belly button of the world (5.5; see also 1 Enoch 26:1; Jubilees 8:12 and chart "Different Canons of the Hebrew Bible [Old Testament]," pp. 28-29).

38:18 on that day: The day of the Lord (see note on 30:3).

38:20 fish of the sea…creeping things: The list sounds like the language of the first creation story (Gen 1:20-31), said by many scholars to be influenced by the priestly tradition.

38:22-23 pestilence and bloodshed: The LORD is a divine warrior, armed with the forces of nature, conquering Gog's forces.

39:1-10 prophesy against Gog: The LORD completely destroys Gog, his forces, and their weapons (Isa 2:4; Mic 4:3). The picture of God's victory is gruesome, in that Gog's forces are left exposed as food for bird and beast (39:4; see also 39:17-20). Those coastland nations that support Magog will also be destroyed by God's fire (39:6).

39:7 My holy name: Making known the holiness of God's name is *the* reason for this massive display of power (39:29; see note on 20:9).

39:11-16 a place for burial in Israel, the Valley of the Travelers… Hamon-gog: The location of the site is unclear, though it may refer to a valley east of the Dead Sea in Moab, outside the boundaries of Israel's land. Proper burial is important so that the land might be cleansed (39:12, 16) from the contamination of the dead bodies (Num 19:10-20; 31:19). Like blood (see note at 36:17), dead things also carry ritual uncleanness.

my wrath shall be aroused. 19 For in my jealousy and in my blazing
wrath I declare: On that day there shall be a great shaking in the land
of Israel; 20 the fish of the sea, and the birds of the air, and the animals
of the field, and all creeping things that creep on the ground, and all
human beings that are on the face of the earth, shall quake at my presence, and the mountains shall be thrown down, and the cliffs shall fall,
and every wall shall tumble to the ground. 21 I will summon the sword
against Gog[a] in[b] all my mountains, says the Lord GOD; the swords of
all will be against their comrades. 22 With pestilence and bloodshed
I will enter into judgment with him; and I will pour down torrential
rains and hailstones, fire and sulfur, upon him and his troops and the
many peoples that are with him. 23 So I will display my greatness and
my holiness and make myself known in the eyes of many nations.
Then they shall know that I am the LORD.

Gog's Armies Destroyed

39 And you, mortal, prophesy against Gog, and say: Thus says
the Lord GOD: I am against you, O Gog, chief prince of
Meshech and Tubal! 2 I will turn you around and drive you forward,
and bring you up from the remotest parts of the north, and lead you
against the mountains of Israel. 3 I will strike your bow from your left
hand, and will make your arrows drop out of your right hand. 4 You
shall fall on the mountains of Israel, you and all your troops and the
peoples that are with you; I will give you to birds of prey of every kind
and to the wild animals to be devoured. 5 You shall fall in the open
field; for I have spoken, says the Lord GOD. 6 I will send fire on Magog
and on those who live securely in the coastlands; and they shall know
that I am the LORD.

7 My holy name I will make known among my people Israel; and
I will not let my holy name be profaned any more; and the nations
shall know that I am the LORD, the Holy One in Israel. 8 It has come!
It has happened, says the Lord GOD. This is the day of which I have
spoken.

9 Then those who live in the towns of Israel will go out and make
fires of the weapons and burn them—bucklers and shields, bows
and arrows, handpikes and spears—and they will make fires of them
for seven years. 10 They will not need to take wood out of the field or
cut down any trees in the forests, for they will make their fires of the
weapons; they will despoil those who despoiled them, and plunder
those who plundered them, says the Lord GOD.

The Burial of Gog

11 On that day I will give to Gog a place for burial in Israel, the
Valley of the Travelers[c] east of the sea; it shall block the path of the

---

[a] Heb *him* [b] Heb *to* or *for* [c] Or *of the Abarim*

travelers, for there Gog and all his horde will be buried; it shall be called the Valley of Hamon-gog.[a] [12]Seven months the house of Israel shall spend burying them, in order to cleanse the land. [13]All the people of the land shall bury them; and it will bring them honor on the day that I show my glory, says the Lord GOD. [14]They will set apart men to pass through the land regularly and bury any invaders[b] who remain on the face of the land, so as to cleanse it; for seven months they shall make their search. [15]As the searchers[b] pass through the land, anyone who sees a human bone shall set up a sign by it, until the buriers have buried it in the Valley of Hamon-gog.[a] [16](A city Hamonah[c] is there also.) Thus they shall cleanse the land.

17 As for you, mortal, thus says the Lord GOD: Speak to the birds of every kind and to all the wild animals: Assemble and come, gather from all around to the sacrificial feast that I am preparing for you, a great sacrificial feast on the mountains of Israel, and you shall eat flesh and drink blood. [18]You shall eat the flesh of the mighty, and drink the blood of the princes of the earth—of rams, of lambs, and of goats, of bulls, all of them fatlings of Bashan. [19]You shall eat fat until you are filled, and drink blood until you are drunk, at the sacrificial feast that I am preparing for you. [20]And you shall be filled at my table with horses and charioteers,[d] with warriors and all kinds of soldiers, says the Lord GOD.

Israel Restored to the Land

21 I will display my glory among the nations; and all the nations shall see my judgment that I have executed, and my hand that I have laid on them. [22]The house of Israel shall know that I am the LORD their God, from that day forward. [23]And the nations shall know that the house of Israel went into captivity for their iniquity, because they dealt treacherously with me. So I hid my face from them and gave them into the hand of their adversaries, and they all fell by the sword. [24]I dealt with them according to their uncleanness and their transgressions, and hid my face from them.

25 Therefore thus says the Lord GOD: Now I will restore the fortunes of Jacob, and have mercy on the whole house of Israel; and I will be jealous for my holy name. [26]They shall forget[e] their shame, and all the treachery they have practiced against me, when they live securely in their land with no one to make them afraid, [27]when I have brought them back from the peoples and gathered them from their enemies' lands, and through them have displayed my holiness in the sight of many nations. [28]Then they shall know that I am the LORD their God because I sent them into exile among the nations, and then gathered

[a] That is, *the Horde of Gog* [b] Heb *travelers* [c] That is *The Horde* [d] Heb *chariots* [e] Another reading is *They shall bear*

39:17-20: the wild animals...a great sacrificial feast: Ezekiel calls wild animals to come and devour the flesh and blood of the enemy troops, which he compared to animals used by Israel's priests for sacrifices. Though Israelites are forbidden from consuming any blood or fat (44:7, 15; Lev 3:16-17), the wild animals can eat and drink them.

39:18 Bashan: Bashan is a region east of Lake Gennesaret (Sea of Galilee) known for its cattle (Ps 22:12; Amos 4:1). See Map 7, p. 2105.

39:21-29 I will display my glory among the nations: A summary of the whole of Ezekiel to this point. God's judgments and God's action to restore serve the same purpose.

39:29 pour out my spirit: God's spirit will return to the people. This promise concludes God's ultimate victory (36:26-27; see also Joel 2:28-29).

40:1–48:35 in visions of God: The concluding section of the book contains a detailed vision of a new temple and a newly ordered Israel that is centered upon the return of God's glory to the temple (43:1-12). An overwhelming concern is the place and role of priests and the instruction of the Torah. It is not clear exactly how this new temple is connected to Solomon's Temple (which was destroyed by the Babylonians) or the Second Temple, rebuilt after the exile and completed in 515 B.C.E. (Ezra 6:15). Most of the detail in this section likely represents a hopeful priestly vision that was never fully realized. Compare this vision to the temple vision in chapters 8–11.

40:1 the twenty-fifth year of our exile: This vision came twenty years after Ezekiel's first prophecy in 597 B.C.E. (1:2) and about fourteen years after Jerusalem's destruction (see note on 33:21-22; 2 Kgs 25:8-12). The date is April 28, 573 B.C.E. Ezekiel is again (8:3) transported by the hand of the LORD (1:3) to the temple in Jerusalem.

40:3 a man...like bronze: The bronze appearance suggests a heavenly being (1:7) who guides Ezekiel from the outside into the innermost parts of the temple and then to areas surrounding Jerusalem.

40:4 declare all that you see: The prophet's vision is meant to be shared.

40:5 the measuring reed: Measurements done by the heavenly being come throughout chapters 40–48. The reed was approximately 10 feet or 3 meters. The "long cubit" was approximately 20.5 inches or 51.8 centimeters. Added together the six cubits would have equaled the length of the reed. The wall's thickness and height were both ten feet. See the diagram of the temple on this page.

them into their own land. I will leave none of them behind; 29 and I
will never again hide my face from them, when I pour out my spirit
upon the house of Israel, says the Lord GOD.

The Vision of the New Temple

40 In the twenty-fifth year of our exile, at the beginning of
the year, on the tenth day of the month, in the fourteenth
year after the city was struck down, on that very day, the hand of the
LORD was upon me, and he brought me there. 2 He brought me, in visions of God, to the land of Israel, and set me down upon a very high
mountain, on which was a structure like a city to the south. 3 When
he brought me there, a man was there, whose appearance shone
like bronze, with a linen cord and a measuring reed in his hand; and
he was standing in the gateway. 4 The man said to me, "Mortal, look
closely and listen attentively, and set your mind upon all that I shall
show you, for you were brought here in order that I might show it to
you; declare all that you see to the house of Israel."

5 Now there was a wall all around the outside of the temple area.
The length of the measuring reed in the man's hand was six long cubits, each being a cubit and a handbreadth in length; so he measured
the thickness of the wall, one reed; and the height, one reed. 6 Then he
went into the gateway facing east, going up its steps, and measured the
threshold of the gate, one reed deep.[a] There were 7 recesses, and each
recess was one reed wide and one reed deep; and the space between
the recesses, five cubits; and the threshold of the gate by the vestibule
of the gate at the inner end was one reed deep. 8 Then he measured

[a] Heb *deep, and one threshold, one reed deep*

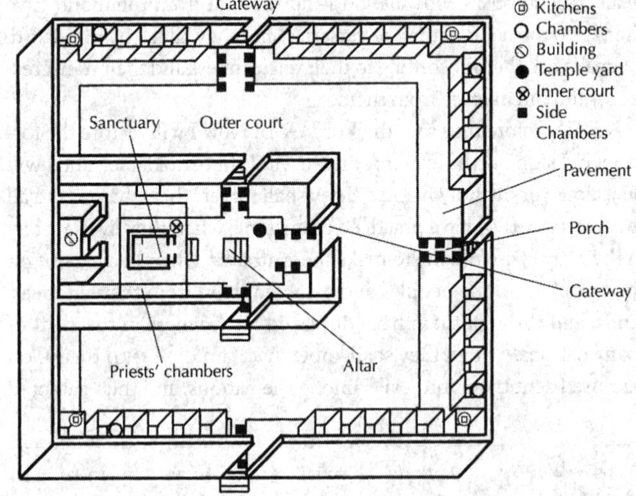

the inner vestibule of the gateway, one cubit. 9 Then he measured the
vestibule of the gateway, eight cubits; and its pilasters, two cubits;
and the vestibule of the gate was at the inner end. 10 There were three
recesses on either side of the east gate; the three were of the same
size; and the pilasters on either side were of the same size. 11 Then he
measured the width of the opening of the gateway, ten cubits; and the
width of the gateway, thirteen cubits. 12 There was a barrier before the
recesses, one cubit on either side; and the recesses were six cubits on
either side. 13 Then he measured the gate from the back[a] of the one
recess to the back[a] of the other, a width of twenty-five cubits, from
wall to wall.[b] 14 He measured[c] also the vestibule, twenty cubits; and
the gate next to the pilaster on every side of the court.[d] 15 From the
front of the gate at the entrance to the end of the inner vestibule of the
gate was fifty cubits. 16 The recesses and their pilasters had windows,
with shutters[d] on the inside of the gateway all around, and the vestibules also had windows on the inside all around; and on the pilasters
were palm trees.

17 Then he brought me into the outer court; there were chambers
there, and a pavement, all around the court; thirty chambers fronted
on the pavement. 18 The pavement ran along the side of the gates, corresponding to the length of the gates; this was the lower pavement.
19 Then he measured the distance from the inner front of[e] the lower
gate to the outer front of the inner court, one hundred cubits.[f]

20 Then he measured the gate of the outer court that faced
north—its depth and width. 21 Its recesses, three on either side, and
its pilasters and its vestibule were of the same size as those of the first
gate; its depth was fifty cubits, and its width twenty-five cubits. 22 Its
windows, its vestibule, and its palm trees were of the same size as
those of the gate that faced toward the east. Seven steps led up to it;
and its vestibule was on the inside.[g] 23 Opposite the gate on the north,
as on the east, was a gate to the inner court; he measured from gate to
gate, one hundred cubits.

24 Then he led me toward the south, and there was a gate on the
south; and he measured its pilasters and its vestibule; they had the
same dimensions as the others. 25 There were windows all around in
it and in its vestibule, like the windows of the others; its depth was
fifty cubits, and its width twenty-five cubits. 26 There were seven steps
leading up to it; its vestibule was on the inside.[g] It had palm trees on
its pilasters, one on either side. 27 There was a gate on the south of the
inner court; and he measured from gate to gate toward the south, one
hundred cubits.

28 Then he brought me to the inner court by the south gate, and

40:16 on the pilasters were palm trees: The engraved palm trees on the pilasters (pillars built into walls, often next to doorways or window openings) may reflect a return to the decorations in Solomon's Temple (1 Kgs 6:29, 32, 35; see also 1 Kgs 7:36)—in contrast to later idolatrous images (Ezek 8).

40:17-18 outer court...thirty chambers: These chambers were likely meeting or storage rooms.

---

[a] Gk: Heb *roof* [b] Heb *opening facing opening* [c] Heb *made* [d] Meaning of Heb uncertain
[e] Compare Gk: Heb *from before* [f] Heb adds *the east and the north* [g] Gk: Heb *before them*

he measured the south gate; it was of the same dimensions as the
others. 29 Its recesses, its pilasters, and its vestibule were of the same
size as the others; and there were windows all around in it and in its
vestibule; its depth was fifty cubits, and its width twenty-five cubits.
30 There were vestibules all around, twenty-five cubits deep and five
cubits wide. 31 Its vestibule faced the outer court, and palm trees were
on its pilasters, and its stairway had eight steps.

32 Then he brought me to the inner court on the east side, and he
measured the gate; it was of the same size as the others. 33 Its recesses,
its pilasters, and its vestibule were of the same dimensions as the others; and there were windows all around in it and in its vestibule; its
depth was fifty cubits, and its width twenty-five cubits. 34 Its vestibule
faced the outer court, and it had palm trees on its pilasters, on either
side; and its stairway had eight steps.

40:35-43 north gate…chamber: This chamber room in the north gate area was the place where animals were prepared for sacrificial offerings. See the chart Offerings in Israel, p. 197.

35 Then he brought me to the north gate, and he measured it; it
had the same dimensions as the others. 36 Its recesses, its pilasters, and
its vestibule were of the same size as the others;[a] and it had windows
all around. Its depth was fifty cubits, and its width twenty-five cubits.
37 Its vestibule[b] faced the outer court, and it had palm trees on its pilasters, on either side; and its stairway had eight steps.

38 There was a chamber with its door in the vestibule of the gate,[c]
where the burnt offering was to be washed. 39 And in the vestibule of
the gate were two tables on either side, on which the burnt offering
and the sin offering and the guilt offering were to be slaughtered. 40 On
the outside of the vestibule[d] at the entrance of the north gate were
two tables; and on the other side of the vestibule of the gate were two
tables. 41 Four tables were on the inside, and four tables on the outside
of the side of the gate, eight tables, on which the sacrifices were to be
slaughtered. 42 There were also four tables of hewn stone for the burnt
offering, a cubit and a half long, and one cubit and a half wide, and
one cubit high, on which the instruments were to be laid with which
the burnt offerings and the sacrifices were slaughtered. 43 There were
pegs, one handbreadth long, fastened all around the inside. And on
the tables the flesh of the offering was to be laid.

40:45-46 priests who have charge of the temple…altar…descendants of Zadok: As the exile came to an end and for about 350 years thereafter, control of the Jerusalem priesthood was maintained by the descendants of Zadok. He was a descendant of Aaron, understood to be Israel's first high priest (Exod 29:26-29; 1 Chr 6:1-8), a priest of David (2 Sam 8:17), and the one who anointed Solomon as king (1 Kgs 1:32-46). This section of Ezekiel supported the authority of the Zadokite priests. It suggests that they remained faithful while the other priests and the rest of Israel did not (44:13; 48:11).

44 On the outside of the inner gateway there were chambers for
the singers in the inner court, one[e] at the side of the north gate facing
south, the other at the side of the east gate facing north. 45 He said to
me, "This chamber that faces south is for the priests who have charge
of the temple, 46 and the chamber that faces north is for the priests
who have charge of the altar; these are the descendants of Zadok, who
alone among the descendants of Levi may come near to the LORD to
minister to him." 47 He measured the court, one hundred cubits deep,

[a] One Ms: Compare verses 29 and 33: MT lacks *were of the same size as the others* [b] Gk Vg Compare verses 26, 31, 34: Heb *pilasters* [c] Cn: Heb *at the pilasters of the gates* [d] Cn: Heb *to him who goes up* [e] Heb lacks *one*

and one hundred cubits wide, a square; and the altar was in front of
the temple.

The Temple

48 Then he brought me to the vestibule of the temple and measured the pilasters of the vestibule, five cubits on either side; and the
width of the gate was fourteen cubits; and the sidewalls of the gate
were three cubits[a] on either side. 49The depth of the vestibule was
twenty cubits, and the width twelve[b] cubits; ten steps led up[c] to it;
and there were pillars beside the pilasters on either side.
41 Then he brought me to the nave, and measured the pilasters;
on each side six cubits was the width of the pilasters.[d] 2The
width of the entrance was ten cubits; and the sidewalls of the entrance were five cubits on either side. He measured the length of the
nave, forty cubits, and its width, twenty cubits. 3Then he went into the
inner room and measured the pilasters of the entrance, two cubits;
and the width of the entrance, six cubits; and the sidewalls[e] of the
entrance, seven cubits. 4He measured the depth of the room, twenty
cubits, and its width, twenty cubits, beyond the nave. And he said to
me, This is the most holy place.
5 Then he measured the wall of the temple, six cubits thick; and
the width of the side chambers, four cubits, all around the temple.
6The side chambers were in three stories, one over another, thirty in
each story. There were offsets[f] all around the wall of the temple to
serve as supports for the side chambers, so that they should not be
supported by the wall of the temple. 7The passageway[g] of the side
chambers widened from story to story; for the structure was supplied
with a stairway all around the temple. For this reason the structure became wider from story to story. One ascended from the bottom story
to the uppermost story by way of the middle one. 8I saw also that the
temple had a raised platform all around; the foundations of the side
chambers measured a full reed of six long cubits. 9The thickness of
the outer wall of the side chambers was five cubits; and the free space
between the side chambers of the temple 10and the chambers of the
court was a width of twenty cubits all around the temple on every
side. 11The side chambers opened onto the area left free, one door toward the north, and another door toward the south; and the width of
the part that was left free was five cubits all around.
12 The building that was facing the temple yard on the west side
was seventy cubits wide; and the wall of the building was five cubits
thick all around, and its depth ninety cubits.
13 Then he measured the temple, one hundred cubits deep; and

[a] Gk: Heb *and the width of the gate was three cubits* [b] Gk: Heb *eleven* [c] Gk: Heb *and by steps that went up* [d] Compare Gk: Heb *tent* [e] Gk: Heb *width* [f] Gk Compare 1 Kings 6.6: Heb *they entered* [g] Cn: Heb *it was surrounded*

40:48-41:4 the temple…the most holy place: The temple building itself was a structure with three major divisions (1 Kgs 6): the vestibule (the entrance), the nave (the great hall), and the inner room ("most holy place"), which the heavenly being enters but Ezekiel does not. This inner room was also known as the Holy of Holies (1 Kgs 8:6). The movement toward the Holy of Holies in this description parallels Ezekiel's earlier vision of the abominations in the temple (8:5-18).

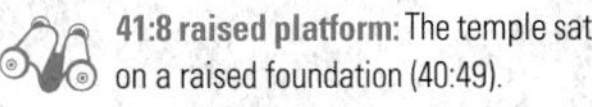

41:8 raised platform: The temple sat on a raised foundation (40:49).

the yard and the building with its walls, one hundred cubits deep; [14]also the width of the east front of the temple and the yard, one hundred cubits.

15 Then he measured the depth of the building facing the yard at the west, together with its galleries[a] on either side, one hundred cubits.

The nave of the temple and the inner room and the outer[b] vestibule [16]were paneled,[c] and, all around, all three had windows with recessed[d] frames. Facing the threshold the temple was paneled with wood all around, from the floor up to the windows (now the windows were covered), [17]to the space above the door, even to the inner room, and on the outside. And on all the walls all around in the inner room and the nave there was a pattern.[e] [18]It was formed of cherubim and palm trees, a palm tree between cherub and cherub. Each cherub had two faces: [19]a human face turned toward the palm tree on the one side, and the face of a young lion turned toward the palm tree on the other side. They were carved on the whole temple all around; [20]from the floor to the area above the door, cherubim and palm trees were carved on the wall.[f]

21 The doorposts of the nave were square. In front of the holy place was something resembling [22]an altar of wood, three cubits high, two cubits long, and two cubits wide;[g] its corners, its base,[h] and its walls were of wood. He said to me, "This is the table that stands before the LORD." [23]The nave and the holy place had each a double door. [24]The doors had two leaves apiece, two swinging leaves for each door. [25]On the doors of the nave were carved cherubim and palm trees, such as were carved on the walls; and there was a canopy of wood in front of the vestibule outside. [26]And there were recessed windows and palm trees on either side, on the sidewalls of the vestibule.[i]

The Holy Chambers and the Outer Wall

42 Then he led me out into the outer court, toward the north, and he brought me to the chambers that were opposite the temple yard and opposite the building on the north. [2]The length of the building that was on the north side[j] was[k] one hundred cubits, and the width fifty cubits. [3]Across the twenty cubits that belonged to the inner court, and facing the pavement that belonged to the outer court, the chambers rose[l] gallery[m] by gallery[m] in three stories. [4]In front of the chambers was a passage on the inner side, ten cubits wide and one hundred cubits deep,[n] and its[o] entrances were on the north. [5]Now

41:19 cherubim and palm trees: Decoration on the walls and doors of the nave and inner room of the temple portray the four living creatures (cherubim) of Ezekiel's earlier visions (see 1:5-14 and note; 10:1-22).

41:22 altar of wood...the table: Possibly for the "bread of the presence" (Exod 25:23-30; Lev 24:5-9).

42:1-14 chambers that were opposite the temple yard: These two chambers (40:45-47) are for priests who approach the LORD (42:13). In the chambers they eat and store their portion of the sacrificial offerings and their priestly robes (vestments) (42:14), which they wear when ministering in the temple.

---

[a] Cn: Meaning of Heb uncertain [b] Gk: Heb *of the court* [c] Gk: Heb *the thresholds* [d] Cn Compare Gk 1 Kings 6.4: Meaning of Heb uncertain [e] Heb *measures* [f] Cn Compare verse 25: Heb *and the wall* [g] Gk: Heb lacks *two cubits wide* [h] Gk: Heb *length* [i] Cn: Heb *vestibule. And the side chambers of the temple and the canopies* [j] Gk: Heb *door* [k] Gk: Heb *before the length* [l] Heb lacks *the chambers rose* [m] Meaning of Heb uncertain [n] Gk Syr: Heb *a way of one cubit* [o] Heb *their*

the upper chambers were narrower, for the galleries[a] took more away from them than from the lower and middle chambers in the building. 6 For they were in three stories, and they had no pillars like the pillars of the outer[b] court; for this reason the upper chambers were set back from the ground more than the lower and the middle ones. 7 There was a wall outside parallel to the chambers, toward the outer court, opposite the chambers, fifty cubits long. 8 For the chambers on the outer court were fifty cubits long, while those opposite the temple were one hundred cubits long. 9 At the foot of these chambers ran a passage that one entered from the east in order to enter them from the outer court. 10 The width of the passage[c] was fixed by the wall of the court.

On the south[d] also, opposite the vacant area and opposite the building, there were chambers 11 with a passage in front of them; they were similar to the chambers on the north, of the same length and width, with the same exits[e] and arrangements and doors. 12 So the entrances of the chambers to the south were entered through the entrance at the head of the corresponding passage, from the east, along the matching wall.[a]

13 Then he said to me, "The north chambers and the south chambers opposite the vacant area are the holy chambers, where the priests who approach the LORD shall eat the most holy offerings; there they shall deposit the most holy offerings—the grain offering, the sin offering, and the guilt offering—for the place is holy. 14 When the priests enter the holy place, they shall not go out of it into the outer court without laying there the vestments in which they minister, for these are holy; they shall put on other garments before they go near to the area open to the people."

15 When he had finished measuring the interior of the temple area, he led me out by the gate that faces east, and measured the temple area all around. 16 He measured the east side with the measuring reed, five hundred cubits by the measuring reed. 17 Then he turned and measured[f] the north side, five hundred cubits by the measuring reed. 18 Then he turned and measured[f] the south side, five hundred cubits by the measuring reed. 19 Then he turned to the west side and measured, five hundred cubits by the measuring reed. 20 He measured it on the four sides. It had a wall around it, five hundred cubits long and five hundred cubits wide, to make a separation between the holy and the common.

The Divine Glory Returns to the Temple

43 Then he brought me to the gate, the gate facing east. 2 And there, the glory of the God of Israel was coming from the

[a] Meaning of Heb uncertain [b] Gk: Heb lacks *outer* [c] Heb lacks *of the passage* [d] Gk: Heb *east* [e] Heb *and all their exits* [f] Gk: Heb *measuring reed all around. He measured*

42:20 a separation between the holy and the common: The wall around the temple compound separates the sacred from the common, a central concern of priests. Sacred or holy things were not to come into contact with unholy or common things, because the holy things would become ritually unclean.

43:1-12 the glory of the God of Israel: As the glory of the LORD left the temple going east (11:22-23), now the glory returns from the east (43:2) to reclaim and bless a new temple with the LORD's holy presence.

east; the sound was like the sound of mighty waters; and the earth shone with his glory. 3 The[a] vision I saw was like the vision that I had seen when he came to destroy the city, and[b] like the vision that I had seen by the river Chebar; and I fell upon my face. 4 As the glory of the LORD entered the temple by the gate facing east, 5 the spirit lifted me up, and brought me into the inner court; and the glory of the LORD filled the temple.

6 While the man was standing beside me, I heard someone speaking to me out of the temple. 7 He said to me: Mortal, this is the place of my throne and the place for the soles of my feet, where I will reside among the people of Israel forever. The house of Israel shall no more defile my holy name, neither they nor their kings, by their whoring, and by the corpses of their kings at their death.[c] 8 When they placed their threshold by my threshold and their doorposts beside my doorposts, with only a wall between me and them, they were defiling my holy name by their abominations that they committed; therefore I have consumed them in my anger. 9 Now let them put away their idolatry and the corpses of their kings far from me, and I will reside among them forever.

10 As for you, mortal, describe the temple to the house of Israel, and let them measure the pattern; and let them be ashamed of their iniquities. 11 When they are ashamed of all that they have done, make known to them the plan of the temple, its arrangement, its exits and its entrances, and its whole form—all its ordinances and its entire plan and all its laws; and write it down in their sight, so that they may observe and follow the entire plan and all its ordinances. 12 This is the law of the temple: the whole territory on the top of the mountain all around shall be most holy. This is the law of the temple.

The Altar

13 These are the dimensions of the altar by cubits (the cubit being one cubit and a handbreadth): its base shall be one cubit high,[d] and one cubit wide, with a rim of one span around its edge. This shall be the height of the altar: 14 From the base on the ground to the lower ledge, two cubits, with a width of one cubit; and from the smaller ledge to the larger ledge, four cubits, with a width of one cubit; 15 and the altar hearth, four cubits; and from the altar hearth projecting upward, four horns. 16 The altar hearth shall be square, twelve cubits long by twelve wide. 17 The ledge also shall be square, fourteen cubits long by fourteen wide, with a rim around it half a cubit wide, and its surrounding base, one cubit. Its steps shall face east.

18 Then he said to me: Mortal, thus says the Lord GOD: These are the ordinances for the altar: On the day when it is erected for

43:2 mighty waters: This is the sound of the living creatures who minister in the presence of the LORD (1:24; Rev 1:15; 14:2; 19:6).

43:3 destroy the city: Ezekiel refers to his vision in 8:1–11:25 by the river Chebar in Babylonia (see the note on 1:3).

43:7 He said to me: It is no longer the heavenly being (40:3) addressing the prophet but the LORD directly.

43:7 the place of my throne: God is Israel's ruler and the temple is God's throne (1:26; 10:1) and footrest (Isa 60:13). The "place for the soles of my feet" may refer to the ark of covenant (1 Chr 28:2).

43:10-12 describe the temple... make known... all its laws: In light of Israel's earlier abominations (8:5-18), the LORD is clear that the new temple is only for sacred purposes. Ezekiel is supposed to write down the temple plans and the law (Hebrew, *torah)* of the temple. It is unclear if this is a completely new law, since Israel already had received the book of the law (2 Kgs 22:8).

43:13-27 the altar...ordinances for the altar: The dimensions for the altar are given (43:13-17). The ordinances describe the initial offering and seven-day ceremony to purify the altar (43:18-27). These are similar to other dedication rituals (see Exod 29:36-37; Lev 8:14-15). These offerings were to be performed by priests from the family of Zadok (43:18-19; see note on 40:45-46).

[a] Gk: Heb *Like the vision* [b] Syr: Heb *and the visions* [c] Or *on their high places* [d] Gk: Heb lacks *high*

offering burnt offerings upon it and for dashing blood against it, 19 you
shall give to the levitical priests of the family of Zadok, who draw near
to me to minister to me, says the Lord GOD, a bull for a sin offering.
20 And you shall take some of its blood, and put it on the four horns
of the altar, and on the four corners of the ledge, and upon the rim
all around; thus you shall purify it and make atonement for it. 21 You
shall also take the bull of the sin offering, and it shall be burnt in the
appointed place belonging to the temple, outside the sacred area.

22 On the second day you shall offer a male goat without blemish for a sin offering; and the altar shall be purified, as it was purified
with the bull. 23 When you have finished purifying it, you shall offer a
bull without blemish and a ram from the flock without blemish. 24 You
shall present them before the LORD, and the priests shall throw salt on
them and offer them up as a burnt offering to the LORD. 25 For seven
days you shall provide daily a goat for a sin offering; also a bull and a
ram from the flock, without blemish, shall be provided. 26 Seven days
shall they make atonement for the altar and cleanse it, and so consecrate it. 27 When these days are over, then from the eighth day onward
the priests shall offer upon the altar your burnt offerings and your
offerings of well-being; and I will accept you, says the Lord GOD.

The Closed Gate

44 Then he brought me back to the outer gate of the sanctuary, which faces east; and it was shut. 2 The LORD said to
me: This gate shall remain shut; it shall not be opened, and no one
shall enter by it; for the LORD, the God of Israel, has entered by it;
therefore it shall remain shut. 3 Only the prince, because he is a prince,
may sit in it to eat food before the LORD; he shall enter by way of the
vestibule of the gate, and shall go out by the same way.

Admission to the Temple

4 Then he brought me by way of the north gate to the front of the
temple; and I looked, and lo! the glory of the LORD filled the temple
of the LORD; and I fell upon my face. 5 The LORD said to me: Mortal,
mark well, look closely, and listen attentively to all that I shall tell you
concerning all the ordinances of the temple of the LORD and all its
laws; and mark well those who may be admitted to[a] the temple and
all those who are to be excluded from the sanctuary. 6 Say to the rebellious house,[b] to the house of Israel, Thus says the Lord GOD: O house
of Israel, let there be an end to all your abominations 7 in admitting
foreigners, uncircumcised in heart and flesh, to be in my sanctuary,
profaning my temple when you offer to me my food, the fat and the
blood. You[c] have broken my covenant with all your abominations.

43:27 offerings of well-being: After the initial seven-day dedication ceremony was over, the priest would offer regular burnt offerings and offerings of well-being (see Lev 1–3 and the chart Offerings in Israel, p. 197).

44:1-3 it was shut: The east gate, where the glory of the LORD returned to the temple (43:1-5), is off limits and will remain closed. The "prince" refers to the civil head of state in the new community. This leader is able to use the gate area to eat a portion of the sacrifice of well-being. For more regulations related to the prince, see 46:1-18.

44:4-31 mark well…the ordinances of the temple: This section describes who can enter the temple and what duties different groups have.

44:6-9 foreigners uncircumcised in heart and flesh: Foreigners are forbidden to enter the temple (Lev 22:25; Neh 13:30). But compare this with Isaiah 56:3-8. See also the note on 28:10 (uncircumcised).

[a] Cn: Heb *the entrance of* [b] Gk: Heb lacks *house* [c] Gk Syr Vg: Heb *They*

[8]And you have not kept charge of my sacred offerings; but you have appointed foreigners[a] to act for you in keeping my charge in my sanctuary.

9 Thus says the Lord GOD: No foreigner, uncircumcised in heart and flesh, of all the foreigners who are among the people of Israel, shall enter my sanctuary. [10]But the Levites who went far from me, going astray from me after their idols when Israel went astray, shall bear their punishment. [11]They shall be ministers in my sanctuary, having oversight at the gates of the temple, and serving in the temple; they shall slaughter the burnt offering and the sacrifice for the people, and they shall attend on them and serve them. [12]Because they ministered to them before their idols and made the house of Israel stumble into iniquity, therefore I have sworn concerning them, says the Lord GOD, that they shall bear their punishment. [13]They shall not come near to me, to serve me as priest, nor come near any of my sacred offerings, the things that are most sacred; but they shall bear their shame, and the consequences of the abominations that they have committed. [14]Yet I will appoint them to keep charge of the temple, to do all its chores, all that is to be done in it.

The Levitical Priests

15 But the levitical priests, the descendants of Zadok, who kept the charge of my sanctuary when the people of Israel went astray from me, shall come near to me to minister to me; and they shall attend me to offer me the fat and the blood, says the Lord GOD. [16]It is they who shall enter my sanctuary, it is they who shall approach my table, to minister to me, and they shall keep my charge. [17]When they enter the gates of the inner court, they shall wear linen vestments; they shall have nothing of wool on them, while they minister at the gates of the inner court, and within. [18]They shall have linen turbans on their heads, and linen undergarments on their loins; they shall not bind themselves with anything that causes sweat. [19]When they go out into the outer court to the people, they shall remove the vestments in which they have been ministering, and lay them in the holy chambers; and they shall put on other garments, so that they may not communicate holiness to the people with their vestments. [20]They shall not shave their heads or let their locks grow long; they shall only trim the hair of their heads. [21]No priest shall drink wine when he enters the inner court. [22]They shall not marry a widow, or a divorced woman, but only a virgin of the stock of the house of Israel, or a widow who is the widow of a priest. [23]They shall teach my people the difference between the holy and the common, and show them how to distinguish between the unclean and the clean. [24]In a controversy they shall act as

[a] Heb lacks *foreigners*

44:10-14 Levites: Traditional priests of the temple (Num 1:48-53). As a lasting punishment for "going astray from me after their idols when Israel went astray" (44:10), the temple service of most of the Levites is limited and lower than for the Levitical family known as the Zadokites (44:15).

44:15-31 descendants of Zadok: They alone (see note on 40:45-46) enter the sanctuary and approach the table, the sacrificial altar, or the table for the bread of the presence (41:22).

44:17-22 linen...nothing of wool: The clothing of the priests is described (see also Exod 28:39; Lev 6:10). The heavenly beings also wore linen (Ezek 9:2; Dan 10:5). Mixing linen and wool was prohibited (Deut 22:11).

44:19-22 remove the vestments... shall not marry a widow: The priest had to remove the holy vestments when exiting the inner court and place them in the holy chambers (42:14). This was to keep them from getting contaminated or from passing on their holiness to common things or people (see the note on 42:20; Exod 28). Cutting hair or beard was also forbidden, possibly because of an association with death (Lev 21:5). Priests were not to drink wine while on duty in the temple (Lev 10:9) or marry a widow or divorced woman (Lev 21:7; 13-15).

44:23 between the holy and the common: The Zadokite priests are responsible for teaching the people about purity so that the common does not defile the holy (22:26; 42:20)—which had been an earlier failure (7:26).

44:24-31 act as judges...anything...that died of itself: More regulations for priests include acting as judges if necessary (Deut 21:5); not touching a corpse, with the exception of family members (Lev 21:1-3; Num 19). Even then, the priest has to go through a seven-day purification ritual to resume his duties in the temple. Eating an animal that was killed by another or died on its own was forbidden (Lev 22:8).

judges, and they shall decide it according to my judgments. They shall keep my laws and my statutes regarding all my appointed festivals, and they shall keep my sabbaths holy. [25]They shall not defile themselves by going near to a dead person; for father or mother, however, and for son or daughter, and for brother or unmarried sister they may defile themselves. [26]After he has become clean, they shall count seven days for him. [27]On the day that he goes into the holy place, into the inner court, to minister in the holy place, he shall offer his sin offering, says the Lord GOD.

28 This shall be their inheritance: I am their inheritance; and you shall give them no holding in Israel; I am their holding. [29]They shall eat the grain offering, the sin offering, and the guilt offering; and every devoted thing in Israel shall be theirs. [30]The first of all the first fruits of all kinds, and every offering of all kinds from all your offerings, shall belong to the priests; you shall also give to the priests the first of your dough, in order that a blessing may rest on your house. [31]The priests shall not eat of anything, whether bird or animal, that died of itself or was torn by animals.

The Holy District

45 When you allot the land as an inheritance, you shall set aside for the LORD a portion of the land as a holy district, twenty-five thousand cubits long and twenty[a] thousand cubits wide; it shall be holy throughout its entire extent. [2]Of this, a square plot of five hundred by five hundred cubits shall be for the sanctuary, with fifty cubits for an open space around it. [3]In the holy district you shall measure off a section twenty-five thousand cubits long and ten thousand wide, in which shall be the sanctuary, the most holy place. [4]It shall be a holy portion of the land; it shall be for the priests, who minister in the sanctuary and approach the LORD to minister to him; and it shall be both a place for their houses and a holy place for the sanctuary. [5]Another section, twenty-five thousand cubits long and ten thousand cubits wide, shall be for the Levites who minister at the temple, as their holding for cities to live in.[b]

6 Alongside the portion set apart as the holy district you shall assign as a holding for the city an area five thousand cubits wide, and twenty-five thousand cubits long; it shall belong to the whole house of Israel.

7 And to the prince shall belong the land on both sides of the holy district and the holding of the city, alongside the holy district and the holding of the city, on the west and on the east, corresponding in length to one of the tribal portions, and extending from the western to the eastern boundary [8]of the land. It is to be his property in Israel.

45:1-9 a holy district: The allotment of the land as an inheritance for the people is an important focus for those in exile in Babylon (see 47:13—48:35). But first a holy district is to be set up for the temple and sanctuary, which is also the place for the priests to live. Alongside the holy district is the city itself, which the prince will govern.

How would you describe where God "lives" in the world? How do you see God's presence reflected in the world around you?

[a] Gk: Heb *ten* [b] Gk: Heb *as their holding, twenty chambers*

And my princes shall no longer oppress my people; but they shall let the house of Israel have the land according to their tribes.

45:9 Put away violence and oppression: Rulers in the new restored community are called to be just and peaceful (Jer 22:3, 15; compare the note on 34:2-6).

9 Thus says the Lord GOD: Enough, O princes of Israel! Put away violence and oppression, and do what is just and right. Cease your evictions of my people, says the Lord GOD.

Weights and Measures

45:10-12 honest balances: In the new community, merchants will use honest scales. One of the unjust ways people had acted was in using false weights to cheat customers (see Amos 8:5, Mic 6:10).

10 You shall have honest balances, an honest ephah, and an honest bath.[a] 11 The ephah and the bath shall be of the same measure, the bath containing one-tenth of a homer, and the ephah one-tenth of a homer; the homer shall be the standard measure. 12 The shekel shall be twenty gerahs. Twenty shekels, twenty-five shekels, and fifteen shekels shall make a mina for you.

Offerings

45:13-17 the offering that you shall make: The size and weight of proper offerings from all the people and the prince are given (compare Exod 30:11-16). The prince is subject to greater obligations.

13 This is the offering that you shall make: one-sixth of an ephah from each homer of wheat, and one-sixth of an ephah from each homer of barley, 14 and as the fixed portion of oil,[b] one-tenth of a bath from each cor (the cor,[c] like the homer, contains ten baths); 15 and one sheep from every flock of two hundred, from the pastures of Israel. This is the offering for grain offerings, burnt offerings, and offerings of well-being, to make atonement for them, says the Lord GOD. 16 All the people of the land shall join with the prince in Israel in making this offering. 17 But this shall be the obligation of the prince regarding the burnt offerings, grain offerings, and drink offerings, at the festivals, the new moons, and the sabbaths, all the appointed festivals of the house of Israel: he shall provide the sin offerings, grain offerings, the burnt offerings, and the offerings of well-being, to make atonement for the house of Israel.

Festivals

45:18-20 purify the sanctuary... make atonement: Two rites of purification are given—one for the temple (45:18-19) and one for anyone who has sinned through error or ignorance (45:20). Compare some similarities in the description of the Day of Atonement (Lev 16).

18 Thus says the Lord GOD: In the first month, on the first day of the month, you shall take a young bull without blemish, and purify the sanctuary. 19 The priest shall take some of the blood of the sin offering and put it on the doorposts of the temple, the four corners of the ledge of the altar, and the posts of the gate of the inner court. 20 You shall do the same on the seventh day of the month for anyone who has sinned through error or ignorance; so you shall make atonement for the temple.

45:21-25 festival: Passover (45:21-24) and Succoth or the Festival of Booths (45:25) are the only festivals named. See the chart Jewish Festivals and Feasts, p. 227. (Also compare Lev 23; Deut 16:1-17).

21 In the first month, on the fourteenth day of the month, you shall celebrate the festival of the passover, and for seven days unleavened bread shall be eaten. 22 On that day the prince shall provide for himself and all the people of the land a young bull for a sin offering.

---

[a] A Heb measure of volume [b] Cn: Heb *oil, the bath the oil* [c] Vg: Heb *homer*

23 And during the seven days of the festival he shall provide as a burnt offering to the LORD seven young bulls and seven rams without blemish, on each of the seven days; and a male goat daily for a sin offering. 24 He shall provide as a grain offering an ephah for each bull, an ephah for each ram, and a hin of oil to each ephah. 25 In the seventh month, on the fifteenth day of the month and for the seven days of the festival, he shall make the same provision for sin offerings, burnt offerings, and grain offerings, and for the oil.

Miscellaneous Regulations

46 Thus says the Lord GOD: The gate of the inner court that faces east shall remain closed on the six working days; but on the sabbath day it shall be opened and on the day of the new moon it shall be opened. 2 The prince shall enter by the vestibule of the gate from outside, and shall take his stand by the post of the gate. The priests shall offer his burnt offering and his offerings of well-being, and he shall bow down at the threshold of the gate. Then he shall go out, but the gate shall not be closed until evening. 3 The people of the land shall bow down at the entrance of that gate before the LORD on the sabbaths and on the new moons. 4 The burnt offering that the prince offers to the LORD on the sabbath day shall be six lambs without blemish and a ram without blemish; 5 and the grain offering with the ram shall be an ephah, and the grain offering with the lambs shall be as much as he wishes to give, together with a hin of oil to each ephah. 6 On the day of the new moon he shall offer a young bull without blemish, and six lambs and a ram, which shall be without blemish; 7 as a grain offering he shall provide an ephah with the bull and an ephah with the ram, and with the lambs as much as he wishes, together with a hin of oil to each ephah. 8 When the prince enters, he shall come in by the vestibule of the gate, and he shall go out by the same way.

46:1-15 gate of the inner court that faces east: These are regulations about access and sacrifices of the prince and the people and their worship of the LORD. The inner east gate is distinguished from the outer east gate, which is sealed (44:1-3). The inner gate is opened each Sabbath and each new moon (46:1). (Compare with the Sabbath and new moon offerings as described in Num 28:9-15.)

9 When the people of the land come before the LORD at the appointed festivals, whoever enters by the north gate to worship shall go out by the south gate; and whoever enters by the south gate shall go out by the north gate: they shall not return by way of the gate by which they entered, but shall go out straight ahead. 10 When they come in, the prince shall come in with them; and when they go out, he shall go out.

46:9-10 whoever enters: This is ancient crowd control, as the people must file past coming in one door and out another. The prince was not to separate himself from the people (46:10).

11 At the festivals and the appointed seasons the grain offering with a young bull shall be an ephah, and with a ram an ephah, and with the lambs as much as one wishes to give, together with a hin of oil to an ephah. 12 When the prince provides a freewill offering, either a burnt offering or offerings of well-being as a freewill offering to the LORD, the gate facing east shall be opened for him; and he shall offer his burnt offering or his offerings of well-being as he does on the

sabbath day. Then he shall go out, and after he has gone out the gate shall be closed.

13 He shall provide a lamb, a yearling, without blemish, for a burnt offering to the LORD daily; morning by morning he shall provide it. [14]And he shall provide a grain offering with it morning by morning regularly, one-sixth of an ephah, and one-third of a hin of oil to moisten the choice flour, as a grain offering to the LORD; this is the ordinance for all time. [15]Thus the lamb and the grain offering and the oil shall be provided, morning by morning, as a regular burnt offering.

16 Thus says the Lord GOD: If the prince makes a gift to any of his sons out of his inheritance,[a] it shall belong to his sons, it is their holding by inheritance. [17]But if he makes a gift out of his inheritance to one of his servants, it shall be his to the year of liberty; then it shall revert to the prince; only his sons may keep a gift from his inheritance. [18]The prince shall not take any of the inheritance of the people, thrusting them out of their holding; he shall give his sons their inheritance out of his own holding, so that none of my people shall be dispossessed of their holding.

19 Then he brought me through the entrance, which was at the side of the gate, to the north row of the holy chambers for the priests; and there I saw a place at the extreme western end of them. [20]He said to me, "This is the place where the priests shall boil the guilt offering and the sin offering, and where they shall bake the grain offering, in order not to bring them out into the outer court and so communicate holiness to the people."

21 Then he brought me out to the outer court, and led me past the four corners of the court; and in each corner of the court there was a court— [22]in the four corners of the court were small[b] courts, forty cubits long and thirty wide; the four were of the same size. [23]On the inside, around each of the four courts[c] was a row of masonry, with hearths made at the bottom of the rows all around. [24]Then he said to me, "These are the kitchens where those who serve at the temple shall boil the sacrifices of the people."

Water Flowing from the Temple

47 Then he brought me back to the entrance of the temple; there, water was flowing from below the threshold of the temple toward the east (for the temple faced east); and the water was flowing down from below the south end of the threshold of the temple, south of the altar. [2]Then he brought me out by way of the north gate, and led me around on the outside to the outer gate that faces toward the east;[d] and the water was coming out on the south side.

[a] Gk: Heb *it is his inheritance* [b] Gk Syr Vg: Meaning of Heb uncertain [c] Heb *the four of them* [d] Meaning of Heb uncertain

46:16-18 inheritance: Regulations are given concerning the prince's royal property. A servant could receive royal property for "the year of liberty" (Lev 25:8-17). The prince is not to take the inheritance of the people as his own (46:18).

46:19-24 through the entrance: The guide shows Ezekiel kitchens for preparing sacrifices (42:13-14), set back so as not to communicate holiness, which is extremely dangerous (see 42:20 and note; 44:19; Lev 10:1-2; 2 Sam 6:7).

47:1-12 water was flowing from below the threshold of the temple: Unconcerned with degrees of holiness (44:1-31), Ezekiel's vision shows a sacred river flowing from the temple (Ps 46:4; Joel 3:18) to give life to all. This image was meant to ignite the imaginations of all its hearers. The same imagery is found in Revelation 22:1-5. Similar sacred river images are found in the ancient stories of Israel's neighbors.

Ezekiel uses words to paint pictures, some pleasant (1:4-28; 37:1-14), others not (16:1-58; 21:8-17). How does this image of the sacred river ignite the imagination of your faith?

3 Going on eastward with a cord in his hand, the man measured
one thousand cubits, and then led me through the water; and it was
ankle-deep. 4 Again he measured one thousand, and led me through
the water; and it was knee-deep. Again he measured one thousand,
and led me through the water; and it was up to the waist. 5 Again he
measured one thousand, and it was a river that I could not cross, for
the water had risen; it was deep enough to swim in, a river that could
not be crossed. 6 He said to me, "Mortal, have you seen this?"

Then he led me back along the bank of the river. 7 As I came back,
I saw on the bank of the river a great many trees on the one side and
on the other. 8 He said to me, "This water flows toward the eastern region and goes down into the Arabah; and when it enters the sea, the
sea of stagnant waters, the water will become fresh. 9 Wherever the
river goes,[a] every living creature that swarms will live, and there will
be very many fish, once these waters reach there. It will become fresh;
and everything will live where the river goes. 10 People will stand fishing beside the sea[b] from En-gedi to En-eglaim; it will be a place for the
spreading of nets; its fish will be of a great many kinds, like the fish of
the Great Sea. 11 But its swamps and marshes will not become fresh;
they are to be left for salt. 12 On the banks, on both sides of the river,
there will grow all kinds of trees for food. Their leaves will not wither
nor their fruit fail, but they will bear fresh fruit every month, because
the water for them flows from the sanctuary. Their fruit will be for
food, and their leaves for healing."

The New Boundaries of the Land

13 Thus says the Lord GOD: These are the boundaries by which
you shall divide the land for inheritance among the twelve tribes of
Israel. Joseph shall have two portions. 14 You shall divide it equally;
I swore to give it to your ancestors, and this land shall fall to you as
your inheritance.

15 This shall be the boundary of the land: On the north side,
from the Great Sea by way of Hethlon to Lebo-hamath, and on to
Zedad,[c] 16 Berothah, Sibraim (which lies between the border of Damascus and the border of Hamath), as far as Hazer-hatticon, which is
on the border of Hauran. 17 So the boundary shall run from the sea to
Hazar-enon, which is north of the border of Damascus, with the border of Hamath to the north.[d] This shall be the north side.

18 On the east side, between Hauran and Damascus; along the
Jordan between Gilead and the land of Israel; to the eastern sea and as
far as Tamar.[e] This shall be the east side.

19 On the south side, it shall run from Tamar as far as the waters

[a] Gk Syr Vg Tg: Heb *the two rivers go* [b] Heb *it* [c] Gk: Heb *Lebo-zedad, 16 Hamath* [d] Meaning of Heb uncertain [e] Compare Syr: Heb *you shall measure*

47:8 Arabah: The valley of the Dead Sea (see Map 7, p. 2105) is called here "the sea of stagnant waters," because its salt concentration is so high that no fish and little life can survive in its waters. En-gedi and likely En-eglaim (47:10) are sites around the Dead Sea. Even the otherwise lifeless waters of the Dead Sea are life-giving because of the sacred river.

47:12 all kinds of trees for food: Life-giving trees are an image often found with a stream of life-giving water (see Ps 1:3; Rev 22: 1-2).

47:13—48:29 boundaries: This detailed description of the boundaries and portioning of the land is a hopeful vision of return for Ezekiel's hearers still in exile in Babylon. It defines the whole land (47:13-23) and the portions of each tribe (48:1-29).

47:14 divide it equally: A command to divide the land among all people in a fair way. The recipients of land include the "aliens who reside among you" (47:21-23; 22:29; also Lev 19:33-34; Num 15:29; 2 Chr 30:25).

of Meribath-kadesh, from there along the Wadi of Egypt[a] to the Great Sea. This shall be the south side.

20 On the west side, the Great Sea shall be the boundary to a point opposite Lebo-hamath. This shall be the west side.

21 So you shall divide this land among you according to the tribes of Israel. 22 You shall allot it as an inheritance for yourselves and for the aliens who reside among you and have begotten children among you. They shall be to you as citizens of Israel; with you they shall be allotted an inheritance among the tribes of Israel. 23 In whatever tribe aliens reside, there you shall assign them their inheritance, says the Lord GOD.

The Tribal Portions

48:1-29 tribes: Each tribe (48:1-7, 23-39) receives an equal portion of land between the Mediterranean and the Jordan River. Adjoining the territory of Judah is "the portion that you shall set apart" (48:8-22; also 45:1-9). The Zadokites (48:10-12, see note on 40:45-46) receive the Temple Mount, with the Levites (48:13-14) and others of Jerusalem receiving portions nearby.

48 These are the names of the tribes: Beginning at the northern border, on the Hethlon road,[b] from Lebo-hamath, as far as Hazar-enon (which is on the border of Damascus, with Hamath to the north), and[c] extending from the east side to the west,[d] Dan, one portion. 2 Adjoining the territory of Dan, from the east side to the west, Asher, one portion. 3 Adjoining the territory of Asher, from the east side to the west, Naphtali, one portion. 4 Adjoining the territory of Naphtali, from the east side to the west, Manasseh, one portion. 5 Adjoining the territory of Manasseh, from the east side to the west, Ephraim, one portion. 6 Adjoining the territory of Ephraim, from the east side to the west, Reuben, one portion. 7 Adjoining the territory of Reuben, from the east side to the west, Judah, one portion.

8 Adjoining the territory of Judah, from the east side to the west, shall be the portion that you shall set apart, twenty-five thousand cubits in width, and in length equal to one of the tribal portions, from the east side to the west, with the sanctuary in the middle of it. 9 The portion that you shall set apart for the LORD shall be twenty-five thousand cubits in length, and twenty[e] thousand in width. 10 These shall be the allotments of the holy portion: the priests shall have an allotment measuring twenty-five thousand cubits on the northern side, ten thousand cubits in width on the western side, ten thousand in width on the eastern side, and twenty-five thousand in length on the southern side, with the sanctuary of the LORD in the middle of it. 11 This shall be for the consecrated priests, the descendants[f] of Zadok, who kept my charge, who did not go astray when the people of Israel went astray, as the Levites did. 12 It shall belong to them as a special portion from the holy portion of the land, a most holy place, adjoining the territory of the Levites. 13 Alongside the territory of the priests, the Levites shall have an allotment twenty-five thousand cubits in

---

[a] Heb lacks *of Egypt* [b] Compare 47.15: Heb *by the side of the way* [c] Cn: Heb *and they shall be his* [d] Gk Compare verses 2–8: Heb *the east side the west* [e] Compare 45.1: Heb *ten* [f] One Ms Gk: Heb *of the descendants*

length and ten thousand in width. The whole length shall be twenty-
five thousand cubits and the width twenty[a] thousand. [14]They shall
not sell or exchange any of it; they shall not transfer this choice portion of the land, for it is holy to the LORD.

15 The remainder, five thousand cubits in width and twenty-five
thousand in length, shall be for ordinary use for the city, for dwellings
and for open country. In the middle of it shall be the city; [16]and these
shall be its dimensions: the north side four thousand five hundred
cubits, the south side four thousand five hundred, the east side four
thousand five hundred, and the west side four thousand five hundred.
[17]The city shall have open land: on the north two hundred fifty cubits, on the south two hundred fifty, on the east two hundred fifty,
on the west two hundred fifty. [18]The remainder of the length alongside the holy portion shall be ten thousand cubits to the east, and ten
thousand to the west, and it shall be alongside the holy portion. Its
produce shall be food for the workers of the city. [19]The workers of the
city, from all the tribes of Israel, shall cultivate it. [20]The whole portion
that you shall set apart shall be twenty-five thousand cubits square,
that is, the holy portion together with the property of the city.

21 What remains on both sides of the holy portion and of the
property of the city shall belong to the prince. Extending from the
twenty-five thousand cubits of the holy portion to the east border,
and westward from the twenty-five thousand cubits to the west border, parallel to the tribal portions, it shall belong to the prince. The
holy portion with the sanctuary of the temple in the middle of it,
[22]and the property of the Levites and of the city, shall be in the middle
of that which belongs to the prince. The portion of the prince shall lie
between the territory of Judah and the territory of Benjamin.

23 As for the rest of the tribes: from the east side to the west, Benjamin, one portion. [24]Adjoining the territory of Benjamin, from the
east side to the west, Simeon, one portion. [25]Adjoining the territory
of Simeon, from the east side to the west, Issachar, one portion. [26]Ad-
joining the territory of Issachar, from the east side to the west, Zebulun, one portion. [27]Adjoining the territory of Zebulun, from the east
side to the west, Gad, one portion. [28]And adjoining the territory of
Gad to the south, the boundary shall run from Tamar to the waters of
Meribath-kadesh, from there along the Wadi of Egypt[b] to the Great
Sea. [29]This is the land that you shall allot as an inheritance among the
tribes of Israel, and these are their portions, says the Lord GOD.

30 These shall be the exits of the city: On the north side, which
is to be four thousand five hundred cubits by measure, [31]three gates,
the gate of Reuben, the gate of Judah, and the gate of Levi, the gates
of the city being named after the tribes of Israel. [32]On the east side,

[a] Gk: Heb *ten* [b] Heb lacks *of Egypt*

48:30-35 exits...name of the city: Twelve gates, three facing each direction, suggest that the renewed city is the center of the earth (48:30-34; Rev 21:12-13). Compare the arrangement and names of the gates to the arrangement of Israel's tribes as they camped in the wilderness (see Num 2:1-31 and the illustration "Israel's Wilderness Encampment," p. 242). The city's name, *adonai shamah* (a-doe-NAI sha-MAH) —"The LORD is There"—punctuates the LORD's dramatic life-giving return to Jerusalem (43:1-12).

Which of Ezekiel's images, visions, or prophecies trouble you most? Which strengthen your faith? Why?

which is to be four thousand five hundred cubits, three gates, the gate
of Joseph, the gate of Benjamin, and the gate of Dan. 33 On the south
side, which is to be four thousand five hundred cubits by measure,
three gates, the gate of Simeon, the gate of Issachar, and the gate of
Zebulun. 34 On the west side, which is to be four thousand five hundred cubits, three gates,[a] the gate of Gad, the gate of Asher, and the
gate of Naphtali. 35 The circumference of the city shall be eighteen
thousand cubits. And the name of the city from that time on shall be,
The LORD is There.

---

[a] One Ms Gk Syr: MT *their gates three*

Daniel 6:22

DANIEL

Background File

In Christian tradition, Daniel appears in the Prophets section of the Bible, following Ezekiel, another book that contains symbolic visions. In Jewish tradition, Daniel follows Esther, which also narrates the experiences of exiles—people displaced from Judah and Jerusalem. The book of Daniel focuses on Daniel, Shadrach, Meshach, and Abednego, not on other exiled people of God. The book was written in two languages. While 1:1–2:4a and 8:1–12:13 were written in Hebrew, 2:4b–7:28 were composed in Aramaic. This division does not match the common division of the book between chapters 1-6 and 7-12.

What's the Story?

The first six chapters of Daniel are stories, some of which include visions. The last six chapters are primarily visions. Daniel, Shadrach, Meshach, and Abednego interact with various kings in the first half of the book. Daniel, with help from God, interprets the dreams of others. These dreams are about the destiny of kings. The evil of the kings has an immediate impact on Daniel and his friends. Daniel's work takes place during the rule of several kings, but life does not improve for him as we move from one ruler to the next. God blesses Daniel and his friends, abides with them, and rescues them from the jealousy and violence directed against them. But the chaos continues and evil persists.

In the second half of the book, Daniel speaks with heavenly beings as he seeks to interpret his own visions. These visions concern the future of God's people ("the holy ones of the Most High," according to 7:25). They cover more than the time of the exile (587-538 B.C.E.) and the world of the Babylonians, Medes, and Persians. The main action moves back to Judah and Jerusalem. The final scenes take place in the centuries after Alexander the Great (d. 323 B.C.E.). With ever-increasing intensity, the chaos and violence are beyond comparison. Even the faithful will die, but God's abiding faithfulness is extended to life after death (12:1-4).

Several puzzles in this book have not been resolved. The language of the visions has been interpreted in many ways. For example, the final king or kingdom (the last "horn" in 7:20, the "little" horn in 8:9, and the "king of the north" in chapter 11) has been interpreted various ways, from political powers such as the Romans to figures such as the Antichrist. Smaller puzzles include where Daniel is when Shadrach, Meshach, and Abednego face the fiery furnace (chapter 3) or where the three men are when Daniel refuses to bow to Nebuchadnezzar's statue (chapter 2).

What's the Message?

Daniel is a book of consolation. The message is clear: evil will not have the last word. Usually seen here in the form of arrogant kings and kingdoms, evil is both upended in the stories and foreseen in the visions. Kingdoms collapse from overextension or are directly defeated by other kingdoms. Ultimately they face God's judgment, but in the short term the people of God live in a chaotic and even violent world.

Daniel also gives us a model for prayer. When he is puzzled by Jeremiah's reference to seventy years, he turns to prayer (chapter 9). He confesses his and his people's sin, then makes several requests of God: listen, open your eyes, hear, forgive, act, do not delay, and more.

Four Young Israelites at the Babylonian Court

1 In the third year of the reign of King Jehoiakim of Judah, King
Nebuchadnezzar of Babylon came to Jerusalem and besieged it.
2 The Lord let King Jehoiakim of Judah fall into his power, as well as
some of the vessels of the house of God. These he brought to the land
of Shinar,[a] and placed the vessels in the treasury of his gods.
3 Then the king commanded his palace master Ashpenaz to bring
some of the Israelites of the royal family and of the nobility, 4 young
men without physical defect and handsome, versed in every branch
of wisdom, endowed with knowledge and insight, and competent to
serve in the king's palace; they were to be taught the literature and
language of the Chaldeans. 5 The king assigned them a daily portion
of the royal rations of food and wine. They were to be educated for
three years, so that at the end of that time they could be stationed in
the king's court. 6 Among them were Daniel, Hananiah, Mishael, and
Azariah, from the tribe of Judah. 7 The palace master gave them other
names: Daniel he called Belteshazzar, Hananiah he called Shadrach,
Mishael he called Meshach, and Azariah he called Abednego.
8 But Daniel resolved that he would not defile himself with the
royal rations of food and wine; so he asked the palace master to allow him not to defile himself. 9 Now God allowed Daniel to receive
favor and compassion from the palace master. 10 The palace master
said to Daniel, "I am afraid of my lord the king; he has appointed
your food and your drink. If he should see you in poorer condition
than the other young men of your own age, you would endanger my
head with the king." 11 Then Daniel asked the guard whom the palace
master had appointed over Daniel, Hananiah, Mishael, and Azariah:
12 "Please test your servants for ten days. Let us be given vegetables to

[a] Gk Theodotion: Heb adds *to the house of his own gods*

1:1-2 In the third year: King Jehoiakim of Judah rebelled against King Nebuchadnezzar of Babylon in 601 B.C.E., but the first report of Babylonians taking away people and seizing items from the temple is during the reign of King Jehoiachin (597 B.C.E.). See 2 Kings 23:31—24:17.

1:2 The Lord let…fall: The deportation or exile of the people of Judah to Babylon is not simply a matter of bad political luck. Although Nebuchadnezzar undoubtedly assumes that the victory over Judah is a credit to his own greatness, the truth is that God gave him the victory.

1:3-7 competent to serve: Daniel and his three friends are chosen to learn a new language and government system in order to serve in the royal administration (the book of Daniel does not mention what happens to the rest of the Judeans in exile). It is not brutal work, but they are expected to alter their diet and their names. Their new names include references to various Babylonian gods.

1:8 he would not defile himself with the royal rations: Old Testament dietary laws do not demand vegetarianism (see Lev 11:4-12 and Deut 12:23-25), but Daniel believes that what he eats and drinks is the dividing line between obedience and disobedience to God's law.

eat and water to drink. [13]You can then compare our appearance with the appearance of the young men who eat the royal rations, and deal with your servants according to what you observe." [14]So he agreed to this proposal and tested them for ten days. [15]At the end of ten days it was observed that they appeared better and fatter than all the young men who had been eating the royal rations. [16]So the guard continued to withdraw their royal rations and the wine they were to drink, and gave them vegetables. [17]To these four young men God gave knowledge and skill in every aspect of literature and wisdom; Daniel also had insight into all visions and dreams.

18 At the end of the time that the king had set for them to be brought in, the palace master brought them into the presence of Nebuchadnezzar, [19]and the king spoke with them. And among them all, no one was found to compare with Daniel, Hananiah, Mishael, and Azariah; therefore they were stationed in the king's court. [20]In every matter of wisdom and understanding concerning which the king inquired of them, he found them ten times better than all the magicians and enchanters in his whole kingdom. [21]And Daniel continued there until the first year of King Cyrus.

Nebuchadnezzar's Dream

2 In the second year of Nebuchadnezzar's reign, Nebuchadnezzar dreamed such dreams that his spirit was troubled and his sleep left him. [2]So the king commanded that the magicians, the enchanters, the sorcerers, and the Chaldeans be summoned to tell the king his dreams. When they came in and stood before the king, [3]he said to them, "I have had such a dream that my spirit is troubled by the desire to understand it." [4]The Chaldeans said to the king (in Aramaic),[a] "O king, live forever! Tell your servants the dream, and we will reveal the interpretation." [5]The king answered the Chaldeans, "This is a public decree: if you do not tell me both the dream and its interpretation, you shall be torn limb from limb, and your houses shall be laid in ruins. [6]But if you do tell me the dream and its interpretation, you shall receive from me gifts and rewards and great honor. Therefore tell me the dream and its interpretation." [7]They answered a second time, "Let the king first tell his servants the dream, then we can give its interpretation." [8]The king answered, "I know with certainty that you are trying to gain time, because you see I have firmly decreed: [9]if you do not tell me the dream, there is but one verdict for you. You have agreed to speak lying and misleading words to me until things take a turn. Therefore, tell me the dream, and I shall know that you can give me its interpretation." [10]The Chaldeans answered the king, "There is no one on earth who can reveal what the king demands! In fact no

[a] The text from this point to the end of chapter 7 is in Aramaic

1:17 God gave knowledge and skill: God is actively at work in this story. Daniel and his companions have central roles, but as the story continues the focus is increasingly on the contest between the violent evil of the rulers and God's actions to challenge, limit, and defeat evil.

1:20 ten times better: God's action (1:2, 9, 17) causes the situation to turn out well for Daniel and his friends.

2:1-13 Nebuchadnezzar dreamed such dreams: This chapter is filled with ironic twists, as Nebuchadnezzar and the Chaldean astrologers do the opposite of what they want to do. Despite all that he controls, Nebuchadnezzar cannot control what disturbs his sleep or command a cure. The Chaldeans unwittingly state the message of the chapter: only a god could reveal what the king demands. The humorous bickering undercuts the king's power and control. Daniel and his companions become trapped in this test of wills as the king orders their execution.

king, however great and powerful, has ever asked such a thing of any
magician or enchanter or Chaldean. [11]The thing that the king is asking
is too difficult, and no one can reveal it to the king except the gods,
whose dwelling is not with mortals."

12 Because of this the king flew into a violent rage and commanded that all the wise men of Babylon be destroyed. [13]The decree
was issued, and the wise men were about to be executed; and they
looked for Daniel and his companions, to execute them. [14]Then Daniel responded with prudence and discretion to Arioch, the king's chief
executioner, who had gone out to execute the wise men of Babylon;
[15]he asked Arioch, the royal official, "Why is the decree of the king
so urgent?" Arioch then explained the matter to Daniel. [16]So Daniel
went in and requested that the king give him time and he would tell
the king the interpretation.

2:14-23 Daniel responded with prudence and discretion: Daniel and his companions do not automatically assume that God will deliver. Daniel uses his God-given wisdom, but he gives control of the situation to God by asking for mercy. When the dream is revealed, Daniel praises God before reporting to the king.

God Reveals Nebuchadnezzar's Dream

17 Then Daniel went to his home and informed his companions,
Hananiah, Mishael, and Azariah, [18]and told them to seek mercy from
the God of heaven concerning this mystery, so that Daniel and his
companions with the rest of the wise men of Babylon might not perish. [19]Then the mystery was revealed to Daniel in a vision of the night,
and Daniel blessed the God of heaven.

20 Daniel said:

"Blessed be the name of God from age to age,
for wisdom and power are his.

21 He changes times and seasons,
deposes kings and sets up kings;
he gives wisdom to the wise
and knowledge to those who have understanding.

22 He reveals deep and hidden things;
he knows what is in the darkness,
and light dwells with him.

23 To you, O God of my ancestors,
I give thanks and praise,
for you have given me wisdom and power,
and have now revealed to me what we asked of you,
for you have revealed to us what the king ordered."

2:20-23 thanks and praise: This thanksgiving prayer looks at the past (the king's dream and the death threat) and at the future (God will set up kings and overthrow them).

Daniel Interprets the Dream

24 Therefore Daniel went to Arioch, whom the king had appointed to destroy the wise men of Babylon, and said to him, "Do not
destroy the wise men of Babylon; bring me in before the king, and I
will give the king the interpretation."

25 Then Arioch quickly brought Daniel before the king and said
to him: "I have found among the exiles from Judah a man who can tell

2:25 among the exiles from Judah: Although successful in revealing the king's dream, Daniel is and will continue to be displaced.

the king the interpretation." [26]The king said to Daniel, whose name
was Belteshazzar, "Are you able to tell me the dream that I have seen
and its interpretation?" [27]Daniel answered the king, "No wise men,
enchanters, magicians, or diviners can show to the king the mystery
that the king is asking, [28]but there is a God in heaven who reveals mysteries, and he has disclosed to King Nebuchadnezzar what will happen
at the end of days. Your dream and the visions of your head as you lay
in bed were these: [29]To you, O king, as you lay in bed, came thoughts
of what would be hereafter, and the revealer of mysteries disclosed to
you what is to be. [30]But as for me, this mystery has not been revealed
to me because of any wisdom that I have more than any other living
being, but in order that the interpretation may be known to the king
and that you may understand the thoughts of your mind.

31 "You were looking, O king, and lo! there was a great statue.
This statue was huge, its brilliance extraordinary; it was standing before you, and its appearance was frightening. [32]The head of that statue
was of fine gold, its chest and arms of silver, its middle and thighs of
bronze, [33]its legs of iron, its feet partly of iron and partly of clay. [34]As
you looked on, a stone was cut out, not by human hands, and it struck
the statue on its feet of iron and clay and broke them in pieces. [35]Then
the iron, the clay, the bronze, the silver, and the gold, were all broken
in pieces and became like the chaff of the summer threshing floors;
and the wind carried them away, so that not a trace of them could be
found. But the stone that struck the statue became a great mountain
and filled the whole earth.

36 "This was the dream; now we will tell the king its interpretation. [37]You, O king, the king of kings—to whom the God of heaven
has given the kingdom, the power, the might, and the glory, [38]into
whose hand he has given human beings, wherever they live, the wild
animals of the field, and the birds of the air, and whom he has established as ruler over them all—you are the head of gold. [39]After you
shall arise another kingdom inferior to yours, and yet a third kingdom
of bronze, which shall rule over the whole earth. [40]And there shall be
a fourth kingdom, strong as iron; just as iron crushes and smashes
everything,[a] it shall crush and shatter all these. [41]As you saw the feet
and toes partly of potter's clay and partly of iron, it shall be a divided
kingdom; but some of the strength of iron shall be in it, as you saw the
iron mixed with the clay. [42]As the toes of the feet were part iron and
part clay, so the kingdom shall be partly strong and partly brittle. [43]As
you saw the iron mixed with clay, so will they mix with one another
in marriage,[b] but they will not hold together, just as iron does not mix
with clay. [44]And in the days of those kings the God of heaven will set
up a kingdom that shall never be destroyed, nor shall this kingdom

2:30 that you may understand: God grants the king understanding, but the king is still in a series of kings and kingdoms that will rise and fall. The reign of God holds the kingdoms of this world in check and continues after all other kingdoms are gone.

---

[a] Gk Theodotion Syr Vg: Aram adds *and like iron that crushes* [b] Aram *by human seed*

be left to another people. It shall crush all these kingdoms and bring
them to an end, and it shall stand forever; 45 just as you saw that a stone
was cut from the mountain not by hands, and that it crushed the iron,
the bronze, the clay, the silver, and the gold. The great God has informed the king what shall be hereafter. The dream is certain, and its
interpretation trustworthy."

Daniel and His Friends Promoted

46 Then King Nebuchadnezzar fell on his face, worshiped Daniel, and commanded that a grain offering and incense be offered to
him. 47 The king said to Daniel, "Truly, your God is God of gods and
Lord of kings and a revealer of mysteries, for you have been able to reveal this mystery!" 48 Then the king promoted Daniel, gave him many
great gifts, and made him ruler over the whole province of Babylon
and chief prefect over all the wise men of Babylon. 49 Daniel made a
request of the king, and he appointed Shadrach, Meshach, and Abednego over the affairs of the province of Babylon. But Daniel remained
at the king's court.

The Golden Image

3 King Nebuchadnezzar made a golden statue whose height was
sixty cubits and whose width was six cubits; he set it up on the
plain of Dura in the province of Babylon. 2 Then King Nebuchadnezzar sent for the satraps, the prefects, and the governors, the counselors, the treasurers, the justices, the magistrates, and all the officials of
the provinces, to assemble and come to the dedication of the statue
that King Nebuchadnezzar had set up. 3 So the satraps, the prefects,
and the governors, the counselors, the treasurers, the justices, the
magistrates, and all the officials of the provinces, assembled for the
dedication of the statue that King Nebuchadnezzar had set up. When
they were standing before the statue that Nebuchadnezzar had set up,
4 the herald proclaimed aloud, "You are commanded, O peoples, nations, and languages, 5 that when you hear the sound of the horn, pipe,
lyre, trigon, harp, drum, and entire musical ensemble, you are to fall
down and worship the golden statue that King Nebuchadnezzar has
set up. 6 Whoever does not fall down and worship shall immediately
be thrown into a furnace of blazing fire." 7 Therefore, as soon as all the
peoples heard the sound of the horn, pipe, lyre, trigon, harp, drum,
and entire musical ensemble, all the peoples, nations, and languages
fell down and worshiped the golden statue that King Nebuchadnezzar had set up.

8 Accordingly, at this time certain Chaldeans came forward and
denounced the Jews. 9 They said to King Nebuchadnezzar, "O king,
live forever! 10 You, O king, have made a decree, that everyone who
hears the sound of the horn, pipe, lyre, trigon, harp, drum, and en-

2:47 your God is God of gods: In another ironic twist, the king unknowingly speaks the truth when he says that God is the "Lord of kings."

2:48 the king promoted Daniel: Although Nebuchadnezzar promotes Daniel and his companions, this will not protect them from dangers to come.

Is there any conflict between working under a ruler like Nebuchadnezzar and being a person of faith? Why or why not?

3:1 King Nebuchadnezzar made a golden statue: Like the statue in a horrifying dream (chapter 2), the king now makes his own statue. He forgets that his kingdom is not permanent and demands total loyalty from the entire population.

3:8 denounced the Jews: The king's decree challenges the faithfulness of the Jewish people living in exile in Babylonia, who worship only God. Ironically, the king himself appointed those who do not obey (2:49; see also chapter 6), but the core conflict is between the king and God (3:15).

tire musical ensemble, shall fall down and worship the golden statue,
[11]and whoever does not fall down and worship shall be thrown into
a furnace of blazing fire. [12]There are certain Jews whom you have appointed over the affairs of the province of Babylon: Shadrach, Meshach, and Abednego. These pay no heed to you, O king. They do not
serve your gods and they do not worship the golden statue that you
have set up."

13 Then Nebuchadnezzar in furious rage commanded that Shadrach, Meshach, and Abednego be brought in; so they brought those
men before the king. [14]Nebuchadnezzar said to them, "Is it true,
O Shadrach, Meshach, and Abednego, that you do not serve my gods
and you do not worship the golden statue that I have set up? [15]Now if
you are ready when you hear the sound of the horn, pipe, lyre, trigon,
harp, drum, and entire musical ensemble to fall down and worship
the statue that I have made, well and good.[a] But if you do not worship,
you shall immediately be thrown into a furnace of blazing fire, and
who is the god that will deliver you out of my hands?"

16 Shadrach, Meshach, and Abednego answered the king,
"O Nebuchadnezzar, we have no need to present a defense to you in
this matter. [17]If our God whom we serve is able to deliver us from the
furnace of blazing fire and out of your hand, O king, let him deliver
us.[b] [18]But if not, be it known to you, O king, that we will not serve
your gods and we will not worship the golden statue that you have
set up."

3:17-18 If...if not: Shadrach, Meshach, and Abednego do not presume that God will rescue them. They let God be God, even if it will cost them their lives. (Compare Mark 8:34-35.)

How can we support those who, like Shadrach, Meshach, and Abednego, put their lives at risk by remaining faithful to God?

The Fiery Furnace

19 Then Nebuchadnezzar was so filled with rage against Shadrach, Meshach, and Abednego that his face was distorted. He ordered the furnace heated up seven times more than was customary,
[20]and ordered some of the strongest guards in his army to bind Shadrach, Meshach, and Abednego and to throw them into the furnace of
blazing fire. [21]So the men were bound, still wearing their tunics,[c] their
trousers,[c] their hats, and their other garments, and they were thrown
into the furnace of blazing fire. [22]Because the king's command was
urgent and the furnace was so overheated, the raging flames killed the
men who lifted Shadrach, Meshach, and Abednego. [23]But the three
men, Shadrach, Meshach, and Abednego, fell down, bound, into the
furnace of blazing fire.

24 Then King Nebuchadnezzar was astonished and rose up
quickly. He said to his counselors, "Was it not three men that we
threw bound into the fire?" They answered the king, "True, O king."
[25]He replied, "But I see four men unbound, walking in the middle of

3:24-27 was astonished and rose up quickly: Nebuchadnezzar, seeking total control, unleashes all his destructive powers, but loses control in the process. In addition, the officials who stood before the king's statue (3:3) now gather to observe the failure of the king's fire.

---

[a] Aram lacks *well and good* [b] Or *If our God whom we serve is able to deliver us, he will deliver us from the furnace of blazing fire and out of your hand, O king.* [c] Meaning of Aram word uncertain

the fire, and they are not hurt; and the fourth has the appearance of a god."[a] 26 Nebuchadnezzar then approached the door of the furnace of blazing fire and said, "Shadrach, Meshach, and Abednego, servants of the Most High God, come out! Come here!" So Shadrach, Meshach, and Abednego came out from the fire. 27 And the satraps, the prefects, the governors, and the king's counselors gathered together and saw that the fire had not had any power over the bodies of those men; the hair of their heads was not singed, their tunics[b] were not harmed, and not even the smell of fire came from them. 28 Nebuchadnezzar said, "Blessed be the God of Shadrach, Meshach, and Abednego, who has sent his angel and delivered his servants who trusted in him. They disobeyed the king's command and yielded up their bodies rather than serve and worship any god except their own God. 29 Therefore I make a decree: Any people, nation, or language that utters blasphemy against the God of Shadrach, Meshach, and Abednego shall be torn limb from limb, and their houses laid in ruins; for there is no other god who is able to deliver in this way." 30 Then the king promoted Shadrach, Meshach, and Abednego in the province of Babylon.

3:28-29 I make a decree: The new decree is as broad as the first (3:4-6). The king, portrayed in exaggerated terms, apparently forgets about his golden image and his first decree.

Nebuchadnezzar's Second Dream

4[c] King Nebuchadnezzar to all peoples, nations, and languages that live throughout the earth: May you have abundant prosperity! 2 The signs and wonders that the Most High God has worked for me I am pleased to recount.

3 How great are his signs,
how mighty his wonders!
His kingdom is an everlasting kingdom,
and his sovereignty is from generation to generation.

4[d] I, Nebuchadnezzar, was living at ease in my home and prospering in my palace. 5 I saw a dream that frightened me; my fantasies in bed and the visions of my head terrified me. 6 So I made a decree that all the wise men of Babylon should be brought before me, in order that they might tell me the interpretation of the dream. 7 Then the magicians, the enchanters, the Chaldeans, and the diviners came in, and I told them the dream, but they could not tell me its interpretation. 8 At last Daniel came in before me—he who was named Belteshazzar after the name of my god, and who is endowed with a spirit of the holy gods[e]—and I told him the dream: 9 "O Belteshazzar, chief of the magicians, I know that you are endowed with a spirit of the holy gods[e] and that no mystery is too difficult for you. Hear[f] the dream that I saw; tell me its interpretation.

10[g] Upon my bed this is what I saw;

4:1-37 I saw a dream: Daniel retells this chapter in 5:18-21.

4:3 his sovereignty is from generation to generation: The opening words of Nebuchadnezzar's decree anticipate the conclusion of the story. The king learns again the message of his earlier vision (chapter 2).

4:4-17 its height was great…he gives it to whom he will: Nebuchadnezzar's contentment and prosperity may have provided for many, but his power was *given* to him, not earned by his accomplishments. The heavenly figure's announcement turns the king's view of the world upside down.

---

[a] Aram *a son of the gods* [b] Meaning of Aram word uncertain [c] Ch 3.31 in Aram [d] Ch 4.1 in Aram [e] Or *a holy, divine spirit* [f] Theodotion: Aram *The visions of* [g] Theodotion Syr Compare Gk: Aram adds *The visions of my head*

there was a tree at the center of the earth,
and its height was great.
11 The tree grew great and strong,
its top reached to heaven,
and it was visible to the ends of the whole earth.
12 Its foliage was beautiful,
its fruit abundant,
and it provided food for all.
The animals of the field found shade under it,
the birds of the air nested in its branches,
and from it all living beings were fed.

13 "I continued looking, in the visions of my head as I lay in bed,
and there was a holy watcher, coming down from heaven. 14 He cried
aloud and said:

'Cut down the tree and chop off its branches,
strip off its foliage and scatter its fruit.
Let the animals flee from beneath it
and the birds from its branches.
15 But leave its stump and roots in the ground,
with a band of iron and bronze,
in the tender grass of the field.
Let him be bathed with the dew of heaven,
and let his lot be with the animals of the field
in the grass of the earth.
16 Let his mind be changed from that of a human,
and let the mind of an animal be given to him.
And let seven times pass over him.
17 The sentence is rendered by decree of the watchers,
the decision is given by order of the holy ones,
in order that all who live may know
that the Most High is sovereign over the kingdom of mortals;
he gives it to whom he will
and sets over it the lowliest of human beings.'

18 "This is the dream that I, King Nebuchadnezzar, saw. Now
you, Belteshazzar, declare the interpretation, since all the wise men
of my kingdom are unable to tell me the interpretation. You are able,
however, for you are endowed with a spirit of the holy gods."[a]

Daniel Interprets the Second Dream

19 Then Daniel, who was called Belteshazzar, was severely
distressed for a while. His thoughts terrified him. The king said,

4:18 the wise men of my kingdom are unable to tell me the interpretation: The message of the king's dream begins to take shape, even before it is interpreted to him. He can command his earthly kingdom, but he cannot approach the heavenly realm to understand his dream.

[a] Or *a holy, divine spirit*

"Belteshazzar, do not let the dream or the interpretation terrify you." Belteshazzar answered, "My lord, may the dream be for those who hate you, and its interpretation for your enemies! [20]The tree that you saw, which grew great and strong, so that its top reached to heaven and was visible to the end of the whole earth, [21]whose foliage was beautiful and its fruit abundant, and which provided food for all, under which animals of the field lived, and in whose branches the birds of the air had nests— [22]it is you, O king! You have grown great and strong. Your greatness has increased and reaches to heaven, and your sovereignty to the ends of the earth. [23]And whereas the king saw a holy watcher coming down from heaven and saying, 'Cut down the tree and destroy it, but leave its stump and roots in the ground, with a band of iron and bronze, in the grass of the field; and let him be bathed with the dew of heaven, and let his lot be with the animals of the field, until seven times pass over him'— [24]this is the interpretation, O king, and it is a decree of the Most High that has come upon my lord the king: [25]You shall be driven away from human society, and your dwelling shall be with the wild animals. You shall be made to eat grass like oxen, you shall be bathed with the dew of heaven, and seven times shall pass over you, until you have learned that the Most High has sovereignty over the kingdom of mortals, and gives it to whom he will. [26]As it was commanded to leave the stump and roots of the tree, your kingdom shall be re-established for you from the time that you learn that Heaven is sovereign. [27]Therefore, O king, may my counsel be acceptable to you: atone for[a] your sins with righteousness, and your iniquities with mercy to the oppressed, so that your prosperity may be prolonged."

Nebuchadnezzar's Humiliation

28 All this came upon King Nebuchadnezzar. [29]At the end of twelve months he was walking on the roof of the royal palace of Babylon, [30]and the king said, "Is this not magnificent Babylon, which I have built as a royal capital by my mighty power and for my glorious majesty?" [31]While the words were still in the king's mouth, a voice came from heaven: "O King Nebuchadnezzar, to you it is declared: The kingdom has departed from you! [32]You shall be driven away from human society, and your dwelling shall be with the animals of the field. You shall be made to eat grass like oxen, and seven times shall pass over you, until you have learned that the Most High has sovereignty over the kingdom of mortals and gives it to whom he will." [33]Immediately the sentence was fulfilled against Nebuchadnezzar. He was driven away from human society, ate grass like oxen, and his body was bathed with the dew of heaven, until his hair grew as long as eagles' feathers and his nails became like birds' claws.

4:25 until you have learned: Daniel's interpretation emphasizes the chapter's repeated contrast between earthly and heavenly rule.

4:27 atone: Acts of righteousness and mercy for the oppressed can be a cry for mercy, but they are not a formula for holding onto God's gifts. These acts are not at all like those of the king, who presumes he has all power and control.

4:29-34 At the end of twelve months: Nebuchadnezzar now moves from basking in his accomplishments to leaving human society. Finally, the king shifts from praising himself (4:30) to praising God (4:34).

Why is it difficult for us to shift from praising ourselves to praising God?

[a] Aram *break off*

Nebuchadnezzar Praises God

34 When that period was over, I, Nebuchadnezzar, lifted my eyes
to heaven, and my reason returned to me.

I blessed the Most High,
    and praised and honored the one who lives forever.
For his sovereignty is an everlasting sovereignty,
    and his kingdom endures from generation to generation.
35 All the inhabitants of the earth are accounted as nothing,
    and he does what he wills with the host of heaven
    and the inhabitants of the earth.
There is no one who can stay his hand
    or say to him, "What are you doing?"

36 At that time my reason returned to me; and my majesty and splendor were restored to me for the glory of my kingdom. My counselors
and my lords sought me out, I was re-established over my kingdom,
and still more greatness was added to me. 37 Now I, Nebuchadnezzar,
praise and extol and honor the King of heaven,

for all his works are truth,
    and his ways are justice;
and he is able to bring low
    those who walk in pride.

Belshazzar's Feast

5 King Belshazzar made a great festival for a thousand of his lords,
and he was drinking wine in the presence of the thousand.
2 Under the influence of the wine, Belshazzar commanded that
they bring in the vessels of gold and silver that his father Nebuchadnezzar had taken out of the temple in Jerusalem, so that the king and
his lords, his wives, and his concubines might drink from them. 3 So
they brought in the vessels of gold and silver[a] that had been taken out
of the temple, the house of God in Jerusalem, and the king and his
lords, his wives, and his concubines drank from them. 4 They drank
the wine and praised the gods of gold and silver, bronze, iron, wood,
and stone.

The Writing on the Wall

5 Immediately the fingers of a human hand appeared and began
writing on the plaster of the wall of the royal palace, next to the lampstand. The king was watching the hand as it wrote. 6 Then the king's
face turned pale, and his thoughts terrified him. His limbs gave way,
and his knees knocked together. 7 The king cried aloud to bring in the
enchanters, the Chaldeans, and the diviners; and the king said to the
wise men of Babylon, "Whoever can read this writing and tell me its

[a] Theodotion Vg: Aram lacks *and silver*

4:35 All the inhabitants of the earth are accounted as nothing: These words appear in contrast to human pride. Jesus' declaration that we are more valuable than the birds of the air (Matt 6:26) is set against the dishonoring of one person by another. Both statements are biblical and true.

When have you needed the message from Daniel 4:35? When have you needed the message from Matthew 6:26?

4:36 At that time my reason returned to me: The king's focus returns to himself ("my reason," "my majesty and splendor," "my kingdom," and so on) and undercuts his sincerity. See also 4:30.

5:1-4 King Belshazzar: The pride and vanity of a new king, Belshazzar, trigger his downfall. His pride is indicated with numbers (a thousand lords) and repetition ("his lords, his wives, and his concubines").

5:2 his father Nebuchadnezzar: Historians debate whether Belshazzar was Nebuchadnezzar's son, but this claim emphasizes Belshazzar's failure to learn from history.

5:3-4 drank from them……praised the gods: Belshazzar's pride leads to drinking from containers taken from the temple, as well as praising other gods.

5:5-9 the fingers of a human hand appeared: Though the king is able to command wise men, host a thousand nobles, and offer huge rewards, he is not in control of his destiny.

interpretation shall be clothed in purple, have a chain of gold around
his neck, and rank third in the kingdom." 8 Then all the king's wise
men came in, but they could not read the writing or tell the king the
interpretation. 9 Then King Belshazzar became greatly terrified and
his face turned pale, and his lords were perplexed.
10 The queen, when she heard the discussion of the king and his
lords, came into the banqueting hall. The queen said, "O king, live
forever! Do not let your thoughts terrify you or your face grow pale.
11 There is a man in your kingdom who is endowed with a spirit of the
holy gods.[a] In the days of your father he was found to have enlightenment, understanding, and wisdom like the wisdom of the gods.
Your father, King Nebuchadnezzar, made him chief of the magicians,
enchanters, Chaldeans, and diviners,[b] 12 because an excellent spirit,
knowledge, and understanding to interpret dreams, explain riddles,
and solve problems were found in this Daniel, whom the king named
Belteshazzar. Now let Daniel be called, and he will give the interpretation."

The Writing on the Wall Interpreted

13 Then Daniel was brought in before the king. The king said to
Daniel, "So you are Daniel, one of the exiles of Judah, whom my father the king brought from Judah? 14 I have heard of you that a spirit
of the gods[c] is in you, and that enlightenment, understanding, and
excellent wisdom are found in you. 15 Now the wise men, the enchanters, have been brought in before me to read this writing and tell me its
interpretation, but they were not able to give the interpretation of the
matter. 16 But I have heard that you can give interpretations and solve
problems. Now if you are able to read the writing and tell me its interpretation, you shall be clothed in purple, have a chain of gold around
your neck, and rank third in the kingdom."
17 Then Daniel answered in the presence of the king, "Let your
gifts be for yourself, or give your rewards to someone else! Nevertheless I will read the writing to the king and let him know the interpretation. 18 O king, the Most High God gave your father Nebuchadnezzar
kingship, greatness, glory, and majesty. 19 And because of the greatness that he gave him, all peoples, nations, and languages trembled
and feared before him. He killed those he wanted to kill, kept alive
those he wanted to keep alive, honored those he wanted to honor,
and degraded those he wanted to degrade. 20 But when his heart was
lifted up and his spirit was hardened so that he acted proudly, he was
deposed from his kingly throne, and his glory was stripped from him.
21 He was driven from human society, and his mind was made like that
of an animal. His dwelling was with the wild asses, he was fed grass

5:18-19 God gave: Daniel's statement restates the message of chapter 4: God's power and authority endures beyond the power and authority that God grants to human rulers.

5:21 the Most High God has sovereignty over the kingdom of mortals: The king holds the destiny of many in his hands but does not recognize that his fate is in God's hands. He does not know the truth about his position in life.

---

[a] Or *a holy, divine spirit* [b] Aram adds *the king your father* [c] Or *a divine spirit*

like oxen, and his body was bathed with the dew of heaven, until he
learned that the Most High God has sovereignty over the kingdom
of mortals, and sets over it whomever he will. 22 And you, Belshazzar
his son, have not humbled your heart, even though you knew all this!
23 You have exalted yourself against the Lord of heaven! The vessels of
his temple have been brought in before you, and you and your lords,
your wives and your concubines have been drinking wine from them.
You have praised the gods of silver and gold, of bronze, iron, wood,
and stone, which do not see or hear or know; but the God in whose
power is your very breath, and to whom belong all your ways, you
have not honored.

24 "So from his presence the hand was sent and this writing was
inscribed. 25 And this is the writing that was inscribed: MENE, MENE,
TEKEL, and PARSIN. 26 This is the interpretation of the matter: MENE,
God has numbered the days of[a] your kingdom and brought it to an
end; 27 TEKEL, you have been weighed on the scales and found wanting; 28 PERES,[b] your kingdom is divided and given to the Medes and
Persians."

29 Then Belshazzar gave the command, and Daniel was clothed
in purple, a chain of gold was put around his neck, and a proclamation
was made concerning him that he should rank third in the kingdom.

30 That very night Belshazzar, the Chaldean king, was killed.
31[c] And Darius the Mede received the kingdom, being about sixty-two
years old.

5:22 even though you knew all this!: Belshazzar knows all the facts but fails to order his life accordingly. The book of Daniel notes that generation after generation repeat—and even multiply—acts of pride and violence.

5:23-30 the interpretation of the matter: The writing that Belshazzar cannot control or interpret signals his personal and political end.

The Plot against Daniel

6 It pleased Darius to set over the kingdom one hundred twenty
satraps, stationed throughout the whole kingdom, 2 and over
them three presidents, including Daniel; to these the satraps gave
account, so that the king might suffer no loss. 3 Soon Daniel distinguished himself above all the other presidents and satraps because an
excellent spirit was in him, and the king planned to appoint him over
the whole kingdom. 4 So the presidents and the satraps tried to find
grounds for complaint against Daniel in connection with the kingdom. But they could find no grounds for complaint or any corruption, because he was faithful, and no negligence or corruption could
be found in him. 5 The men said, "We shall not find any ground for
complaint against this Daniel unless we find it in connection with the
law of his God."

6 So the presidents and satraps conspired and came to the king
and said to him, "O King Darius, live forever! 7 All the presidents of
the kingdom, the prefects and the satraps, the counselors and the
governors are agreed that the king should establish an ordinance and

6:1-9 the king planned: A contest of plans and a test of faithfulness intertwine in this chapter. Ironically, those who set out to trap others are themselves trapped. The king, no doubt out of vanity and pride, falls in line with the plot and becomes trapped in his own system.

---

[a] Aram lacks *the days of* [b] The singular of *Parsin* [c] Ch 6.1 in Aram

enforce an interdict, that whoever prays to anyone, divine or human,
for thirty days, except to you, O king, shall be thrown into a den of
lions. 8 Now, O king, establish the interdict and sign the document, so
that it cannot be changed, according to the law of the Medes and the
Persians, which cannot be revoked." 9 Therefore King Darius signed
the document and interdict.

6:8 the law of the Medes and Persians, which cannot be revoked: This claim is repeated in 6:12 and 15. The king demands total allegiance, placing himself in the position of a god, but he cannot alter a single law. The author and enforcer of the law becomes its victim.

6:10-11 praise him…seeking mercy: Daniel praises God and makes a request (a similar combination occurs in chapter 9). Daniel does not use God simply to bail himself out of trouble. No matter what his condition, he knows that as God's creature he owes God honor and praise. As Shadrach, Meshach, and Abednego acknowledged earlier (3:17-18), Daniel knows that he needs to be loyal to God, whether he lives or dies.

Daniel in the Lions' Den

10 Although Daniel knew that the document had been signed, he
continued to go to his house, which had windows in its upper room
open toward Jerusalem, and to get down on his knees three times
a day to pray to his God and praise him, just as he had done previously. 11 The conspirators came and found Daniel praying and seeking mercy before his God. 12 Then they approached the king and said
concerning the interdict, "O king! Did you not sign an interdict, that
anyone who prays to anyone, divine or human, within thirty days except to you, O king, shall be thrown into a den of lions?" The king
answered, "The thing stands fast, according to the law of the Medes
and Persians, which cannot be revoked." 13 Then they responded to
the king, "Daniel, one of the exiles from Judah, pays no attention to
you, O king, or to the interdict you have signed, but he is saying his
prayers three times a day."

14 When the king heard the charge, he was very much distressed.
He was determined to save Daniel, and until the sun went down he
made every effort to rescue him. 15 Then the conspirators came to the
king and said to him, "Know, O king, that it is a law of the Medes and
Persians that no interdict or ordinance that the king establishes can
be changed."

16 Then the king gave the command, and Daniel was brought and
thrown into the den of lions. The king said to Daniel, "May your God,
whom you faithfully serve, deliver you!" 17 A stone was brought and
laid on the mouth of the den, and the king sealed it with his own signet and with the signet of his lords, so that nothing might be changed
concerning Daniel. 18 Then the king went to his palace and spent the
night fasting; no food was brought to him, and sleep fled from him.

6:18 sleep fled from him: The world of a king is again totally turned upside down (see 2:1 and 4:5). The basic need for a night's sleep is beyond his control.

How are powers of the world "turned upside down" by God today?

Daniel Saved from the Lions

19 Then, at break of day, the king got up and hurried to the den
of lions. 20 When he came near the den where Daniel was, he cried out
anxiously to Daniel, "O Daniel, servant of the living God, has your
God whom you faithfully serve been able to deliver you from the lions?" 21 Daniel then said to the king, "O king, live forever! 22 My God
sent his angel and shut the lions' mouths so that they would not hurt
me, because I was found blameless before him; and also before you,
O king, I have done no wrong." 23 Then the king was exceedingly glad

and commanded that Daniel be taken up out of the den. So Daniel was taken up out of the den, and no kind of harm was found on him, because he had trusted in his God. 24 The king gave a command, and those who had accused Daniel were brought and thrown into the den of lions—they, their children, and their wives. Before they reached the bottom of the den the lions overpowered them and broke all their bones in pieces.

25 Then King Darius wrote to all peoples and nations of every language throughout the whole world: "May you have abundant prosperity! 26 I make a decree, that in all my royal dominion people should tremble and fear before the God of Daniel:

For he is the living God,
enduring forever.
His kingdom shall never be destroyed,
and his dominion has no end.
27 He delivers and rescues,
he works signs and wonders in heaven and on earth;
for he has saved Daniel
from the power of the lions."

28 So this Daniel prospered during the reign of Darius and the reign of Cyrus the Persian.

Visions of the Four Beasts

7 In the first year of King Belshazzar of Babylon, Daniel had a dream and visions of his head as he lay in bed. Then he wrote down the dream:[a] 2 I,[b] Daniel, saw in my vision by night the four winds of heaven stirring up the great sea, 3 and four great beasts came up out of the sea, different from one another. 4 The first was like a lion and had eagles' wings. Then, as I watched, its wings were plucked off, and it was lifted up from the ground and made to stand on two feet like a human being; and a human mind was given to it. 5 Another beast appeared, a second one, that looked like a bear. It was raised up on one side, had three tusks[c] in its mouth among its teeth and was told, "Arise, devour many bodies!" 6 After this, as I watched, another appeared, like a leopard. The beast had four wings of a bird on its back and four heads; and dominion was given to it. 7 After this I saw in the visions by night a fourth beast, terrifying and dreadful and exceedingly strong. It had great iron teeth and was devouring, breaking in pieces, and stamping what was left with its feet. It was different from all the beasts that preceded it, and it had ten horns. 8 I was considering the horns, when another horn appeared, a little one coming up among them; to make room for it, three of the earlier horns were

6:26 his dominion has no end: The king makes a new decree that is as broad as the earlier one (6:6-9). Darius "the Mede" (5:31) issues a decree for all of his "royal dominion" (6:26) to acknowledge God's everlasting power and authority.

Daniel was saved from death in the lions' den. How do you explain it when faithful servants of God are not saved from death caused by unfaithful people?

7:1-8 lion...bear...leopard...a fourth beast: The vision moves quickly through three animals, then lingers on the fourth beast (7:7-8). The ten horns indicate a series of kings within the period of the fourth kingdom. Daniel 2, 8, and 11 also focus on the last kingdom.

---

[a] Q Ms Theodotion: MT adds *the beginning of the words; he said* [b] Theodotion: Aram *Daniel answered and said, "I* [c] Or *ribs*

plucked up by the roots. There were eyes like human eyes in this horn, and a mouth speaking arrogantly.

Judgment before the Ancient One

9 As I watched,
thrones were set in place,
and an Ancient One[a] took his throne,
his clothing was white as snow,
and the hair of his head like pure wool;
his throne was fiery flames,
and its wheels were burning fire.
10 A stream of fire issued
and flowed out from his presence.
A thousand thousands served him,
and ten thousand times ten thousand stood attending him.
The court sat in judgment,
and the books were opened.
11 I watched then because of the noise of the arrogant words that the
horn was speaking. And as I watched, the beast was put to death, and
its body destroyed and given over to be burned with fire. 12 As for
the rest of the beasts, their dominion was taken away, but their lives
were prolonged for a season and a time. 13 As I watched in the night
visions,
I saw one like a human being[b]
coming with the clouds of heaven.
And he came to the Ancient One[c]
and was presented before him.
14 To him was given dominion
and glory and kingship,
that all peoples, nations, and languages
should serve him.
His dominion is an everlasting dominion
that shall not pass away,
and his kingship is one
that shall never be destroyed.

7:9-14 Ancient One: This term, used only in this chapter in Daniel, emphasizes the enduring character of God. The reign of the Ancient One lasts, even as each earthly kingdom is destroyed. The Ancient One has everlasting power and authority!

7:13 one like a human being: This phrase, often translated as "one like the son of man," may simply refer to a heavenly figure that looked like a human being.

Daniel's Visions Interpreted

15 As for me, Daniel, my spirit was troubled within me,[d] and the
visions of my head terrified me. 16 I approached one of the attendants
to ask him the truth concerning all this. So he said that he would disclose to me the interpretation of the matter: 17 "As for these four great
beasts, four kings shall arise out of the earth. 18 But the holy ones of

7:15 my spirit was troubled: Daniel and King Nebuchadnezzar both have troubled spirits after their dreams (see 2:1). After hearing the interpretation, Daniel is shocked at the prospect of future outbursts of violence and persecution (7:28).

---

[a] Aram *an Ancient of Days* [b] Aram *one like a son of man* [c] Aram *the Ancient of Days* [d] Aram *troubled in its sheath*

the Most High shall receive the kingdom and possess the kingdom forever—forever and ever."

19 Then I desired to know the truth concerning the fourth beast, which was different from all the rest, exceedingly terrifying, with its teeth of iron and claws of bronze, and which devoured and broke in pieces, and stamped what was left with its feet; [20]and concerning the ten horns that were on its head, and concerning the other horn, which came up and to make room for which three of them fell out—the horn that had eyes and a mouth that spoke arrogantly, and that seemed greater than the others. [21]As I looked, this horn made war with the holy ones and was prevailing over them, [22]until the Ancient One[a] came; then judgment was given for the holy ones of the Most High, and the time arrived when the holy ones gained possession of the kingdom.

23 This is what he said: "As for the fourth beast,
there shall be a fourth kingdom on earth
that shall be different from all the other kingdoms;
it shall devour the whole earth,
and trample it down, and break it to pieces.
24 As for the ten horns,
out of this kingdom ten kings shall arise,
and another shall arise after them.
This one shall be different from the former ones,
and shall put down three kings.
25 He shall speak words against the Most High,
shall wear out the holy ones of the Most High,
and shall attempt to change the sacred seasons and the law;
and they shall be given into his power
for a time, two times,[b] and half a time.
26 Then the court shall sit in judgment,
and his dominion shall be taken away,
to be consumed and totally destroyed.
27 The kingship and dominion
and the greatness of the kingdoms under the whole heaven
shall be given to the people of the holy ones of the Most High;
their kingdom shall be an everlasting kingdom,
and all dominions shall serve and obey them."

28 Here the account ends. As for me, Daniel, my thoughts greatly terrified me, and my face turned pale; but I kept the matter in my mind.

Vision of a Ram and a Goat

8 In the third year of the reign of King Belshazzar a vision appeared to me, Daniel, after the one that had appeared to me at

[a] Aram *the Ancient of Days* [b] Aram *a time, times*

7:19-27 this horn made war: While the exact historical references are disputed, it is certain that the violence of the kingdoms, especially the last one, will be put to an end. The saints of God will be in for some hard times (7:21, 25), but they need not fear, for God's kingdom will prevail (7:27).

7:21 made war with the holy ones: The violence inflicted on the people of God is part of the last ruler's attack against God. This opposition to God is part of a long history of resistance, which reaches its climax in the crucifixion of Jesus, the ultimate rejection of God.

How do you experience the powers of the world moving against God and God's people?

7:25 attempt to change: While all the kingdoms are described as being violent (7:4-5, 7), the fourth kingdom is also boastful (7:8, 20) and targets the saints of the Most High by changing worship times and laws (7:25).

first. 2 In the vision I was looking and saw myself in Susa the capital, in
the province of Elam,[a] and I was by the river Ulai.[b] 3 I looked up and
saw a ram standing beside the river.[c] It had two horns. Both horns
were long, but one was longer than the other, and the longer one
came up second. 4 I saw the ram charging westward and northward
and southward. All beasts were powerless to withstand it, and no one
could rescue from its power; it did as it pleased and became strong.
5 As I was watching, a male goat appeared from the west, coming across the face of the whole earth without touching the ground.
The goat had a horn[d] between its eyes. 6 It came toward the ram with
the two horns that I had seen standing beside the river,[c] and it ran
at it with savage force. 7 I saw it approaching the ram. It was enraged
against it and struck the ram, breaking its two horns. The ram did not
have power to withstand it; it threw the ram down to the ground and
trampled upon it, and there was no one who could rescue the ram
from its power. 8 Then the male goat grew exceedingly great; but at the
height of its power, the great horn was broken, and in its place there
came up four prominent horns toward the four winds of heaven.
9 Out of one of them came another[e] horn, a little one, which grew
exceedingly great toward the south, toward the east, and toward the
beautiful land. 10 It grew as high as the host of heaven. It threw down
to the earth some of the host and some of the stars, and trampled on
them. 11 Even against the prince of the host it acted arrogantly; it took
the regular burnt offering away from him and overthrew the place of
his sanctuary. 12 Because of wickedness, the host was given over to it
together with the regular burnt offering;[f] it cast truth to the ground,
and kept prospering in what it did. 13 Then I heard a holy one speaking, and another holy one said to the one that spoke, "For how long
is this vision concerning the regular burnt offering, the transgression
that makes desolate, and the giving over of the sanctuary and host
to be trampled?"[f] 14 And he answered him,[g] "For two thousand three
hundred evenings and mornings; then the sanctuary shall be restored
to its rightful state."

Gabriel Interprets the Vision

15 When I, Daniel, had seen the vision, I tried to understand it.
Then someone appeared standing before me, having the appearance
of a man, 16 and I heard a human voice by the Ulai, calling, "Gabriel,
help this man understand the vision." 17 So he came near where I
stood; and when he came, I became frightened and fell prostrate. But
he said to me, "Understand, O mortal,[h] that the vision is for the time
of the end."

---

[a] Gk Theodotion: MT Q Ms repeat *in the vision I was looking* [b] Or *the Ulai Gate* [c] Or *gate* [d] Theodotion: Gk *one horn;* Heb *a horn of vision* [e] Cn Compare 7.8: Heb *one* [f] Meaning of Heb uncertain [g] Gk Theodotion Syr Vg: Heb *me* [h] Heb *son of man*

8:2 Susa: In this vision, Daniel, while still working for Belshazzar, a Chaldean king, sees himself in Susa, the winter capital of the Persian Empire.

8:3-12 ram...two horns...male goat...four prominent horns...a little one: As in chapter 7, animals symbolize succeeding kingdoms, but now the interpretation (8:19-22) provides the names of nations. The ram with two horns is Media and Persia. The male goat is the king of Greece. Individual rulers, however, are not named. Alexander the Great, referred to as the male goat (8:5), quickly moves from Greece to conquer the former Persian Empire, but dies suddenly at the height of his power. His empire is divided into Macedonia, Asia Minor, Syria, and Egypt. The horn that emerges from among the other four refers to Antiochus IV Epiphanes (175–163 B.C.E.).

8:5 As I was watching: Before Daniel can figure out the ram, the next empire comes on the scene. The vision moves quickly from one kingdom to the next, collapsing many decades into a short period of time and emphasizing the impermanence of each empire.

8:10 grew as high as the host of heaven: Unlike Daniel 7, the last violent king does more than speak arrogant words against the Most High (7:25). He acts arrogantly. He directly challenges God by attacking the "beautiful land" (Israel), desecrating the temple, and abolishing the daily sacrifice.

8:13 For how long: This agonizing question grows out of faith that the wickedness presently holding power will not endure forever. The question is not *whether* the wickedness will end but *when* it will end.

18 As he was speaking to me, I fell into a trance, face to the
ground; then he touched me and set me on my feet. [19]He said, "Listen, and I will tell you what will take place later in the period of wrath;
for it refers to the appointed time of the end. [20]As for the ram that you
saw with the two horns, these are the kings of Media and Persia. [21]The
male goat[a] is the king of Greece, and the great horn between its eyes
is the first king. [22]As for the horn that was broken, in place of which
four others arose, four kingdoms shall arise from his[b] nation, but not
with his power.

23 At the end of their rule,
when the transgressions have reached their full measure,
a king of bold countenance shall arise,
skilled in intrigue.
24 He shall grow strong in power,[c]
shall cause fearful destruction,
and shall succeed in what he does.
He shall destroy the powerful
and the people of the holy ones.
25 By his cunning
he shall make deceit prosper under his hand,
and in his own mind he shall be great.
Without warning he shall destroy many
and shall even rise up against the Prince of princes.
But he shall be broken, and not by human hands.

[26]The vision of the evenings and the mornings that has been told is
true. As for you, seal up the vision, for it refers to many days from
now."

27 So I, Daniel, was overcome and lay sick for some days; then I
arose and went about the king's business. But I was dismayed by the
vision and did not understand it.

Daniel's Prayer for the People

9 In the first year of Darius son of Ahasuerus, by birth a Mede,
who became king over the realm of the Chaldeans— [2]in the
first year of his reign, I, Daniel, perceived in the books the number
of years that, according to the word of the LORD to the prophet Jeremiah, must be fulfilled for the devastation of Jerusalem, namely, seventy years.

3 Then I turned to the Lord God, to seek an answer by prayer
and supplication with fasting and sackcloth and ashes. [4]I prayed to the
LORD my God and made confession, saying,

"Ah, Lord, great and awesome God, keeping covenant and steadfast love with those who love you and keep your commandments,

[a] Or *shaggy male goat* [b] Gk Theodotion Vg: Heb *the* [c] Theodotion and one Gk Ms: Heb repeats (from 8.22) *but not with his power*

8:23 when the transgressions have reached their full measure: The days of wickedness have a limit. God does not directly destroy each evil empire. Some are allowed to exhaust themselves.

8:23 a king of bold countenance shall arise: The name of the last oppressive ruler or tyrant is not given. This figure, however, is generally seen as a type rather than a specific person. The early Christian church saw this last ruler as a kind of Antichrist.

8:25 make deceit prosper under his hand: The destructive force of the last king moves beyond physical violence. He attacks integrity or honor.

In what ways does "deceit prosper" in our world? How does our own dishonesty or deception inflict suffering, destruction, and desolation on others—and perhaps on ourselves as well?

8:25 But he shall be broken, and not by human hands: One simple sentence announces the end of arrogant power, extensive violence, and skillful deceit. As in Daniel 2:34-35, God alone will be responsible for the end of evil.

8:27 went about the king's business: Daniel returns to the service of the king, even though he is severely shaken by this dream. Knowing that the triumph of God is certain, Daniel can return to his earthly work.

9:2 Seventy years: This number of years, a full lifetime, may be a traditional number for massive devastation.

9:4-5 I prayed to the LORD my God and made confession...we have sinned and done wrong: The Bible does not consider sin to be merely a personal matter. The very fabric of life is threatened by sin's existence. Daniel does not confess any personal sins in his prayer, and he does not separate himself from any of the nation's sins (see 9:20). The pronouns "we," "our," and "us" include past and present generations.

Why should we come together to confess the sins of the community?

5 we have sinned and done wrong, acted wickedly and rebelled, turning aside from your commandments and ordinances. 6 We have not
listened to your servants the prophets, who spoke in your name to
our kings, our princes, and our ancestors, and to all the people of the
land.

7 "Righteousness is on your side, O Lord, but open shame, as at
this day, falls on us, the people of Judah, the inhabitants of Jerusalem,
and all Israel, those who are near and those who are far away, in all the
lands to which you have driven them, because of the treachery that
they have committed against you. 8 Open shame, O LORD, falls on us,
our kings, our officials, and our ancestors, because we have sinned
against you. 9 To the Lord our God belong mercy and forgiveness, for
we have rebelled against him, 10 and have not obeyed the voice of the
LORD our God by following his laws, which he set before us by his
servants the prophets.

11 "All Israel has transgressed your law and turned aside, refusing
to obey your voice. So the curse and the oath written in the law of
Moses, the servant of God, have been poured out upon us, because
we have sinned against you. 12 He has confirmed his words, which he
spoke against us and against our rulers, by bringing upon us a calamity so great that what has been done against Jerusalem has never before been done under the whole heaven. 13 Just as it is written in the
law of Moses, all this calamity has come upon us. We did not entreat
the favor of the LORD our God, turning from our iniquities and reflecting on his[a] fidelity. 14 So the LORD kept watch over this calamity
until he brought it upon us. Indeed, the LORD our God is right in all
that he has done; for we have disobeyed his voice.

15 "And now, O Lord our God, who brought your people out of
the land of Egypt with a mighty hand and made your name renowned
even to this day—we have sinned, we have done wickedly. 16 O Lord,
in view of all your righteous acts, let your anger and wrath, we pray,
turn away from your city Jerusalem, your holy mountain; because of
our sins and the iniquities of our ancestors, Jerusalem and your people have become a disgrace among all our neighbors. 17 Now therefore,
O our God, listen to the prayer of your servant and to his supplication,
and for your own sake, Lord,[b] let your face shine upon your desolated
sanctuary. 18 Incline your ear, O my God, and hear. Open your eyes
and look at our desolation and the city that bears your name. We do
not present our supplication before you on the ground of our righteousness, but on the ground of your great mercies. 19 O Lord, hear;
O Lord, forgive; O Lord, listen and act and do not delay! For your
own sake, O my God, because your city and your people bear your
name!"

9:17-19 listen…let your face shine upon…Incline your ear…hear…Open your eyes…look at…hear…forgive…listen and act…do not delay!: The intensity of the prayer is shown in these repeated calls for God to act. The bold, demanding tone of the prayer is a sign of faith. Daniel asks God to act and forgive, despite what the people have done, for the sake of God's mercy. God chose the people and the city (Jerusalem), so Daniel claims that God's reputation is now on the line.

---

[a] Heb *your* [b] Theodotion Vg Compare Syr: Heb *for the Lord's sake*

The Seventy Weeks

20 While I was speaking, and was praying and confessing my sin and the sin of my people Israel, and presenting my supplication before the LORD my God on behalf of the holy mountain of my God— 21 while I was speaking in prayer, the man Gabriel, whom I had seen before in a vision, came to me in swift flight at the time of the evening sacrifice. 22 He came[a] and said to me, "Daniel, I have now come out to give you wisdom and understanding. 23 At the beginning of your supplications a word went out, and I have come to declare it, for you are greatly beloved. So consider the word and understand the vision:

24 "Seventy weeks are decreed for your people and your holy city: to finish the transgression, to put an end to sin, and to atone for iniquity, to bring in everlasting righteousness, to seal both vision and prophet, and to anoint a most holy place.[b] 25 Know therefore and understand: from the time that the word went out to restore and rebuild Jerusalem until the time of an anointed prince, there shall be seven weeks; and for sixty-two weeks it shall be built again with streets and moat, but in a troubled time. 26 After the sixty-two weeks, an anointed one shall be cut off and shall have nothing, and the troops of the prince who is to come shall destroy the city and the sanctuary. Its[c] end shall come with a flood, and to the end there shall be war. Desolations are decreed. 27 He shall make a strong covenant with many for one week, and for half of the week he shall make sacrifice and offering cease; and in their place[d] shall be an abomination that desolates, until the decreed end is poured out upon the desolator."

9:24 to finish the transgression: In Gabriel's interpretation, the hardship shifts from punishment to an affliction that comes for other reasons. As previous visions have indicated (chapters 2, 7, 8), an evil will emerge that is worse than Israel's disobedience before the exile to Babylonia.

Conflict of Nations and Heavenly Powers

10 In the third year of King Cyrus of Persia a word was revealed to Daniel, who was named Belteshazzar. The word was true, and it concerned a great conflict. He understood the word, having received understanding in the vision.

10:1 a word was revealed to Daniel: The long introduction in this chapter to the actual report of the next vision and its meaning builds to a devastating and decisive announcement in the next chapter.

2 At that time I, Daniel, had been mourning for three weeks. 3 I had eaten no rich food, no meat or wine had entered my mouth, and I had not anointed myself at all, for the full three weeks. 4 On the twenty-fourth day of the first month, as I was standing on the bank of the great river (that is, the Tigris), 5 I looked up and saw a man clothed in linen, with a belt of gold from Uphaz around his waist. 6 His body was like beryl, his face like lightning, his eyes like flaming torches, his arms and legs like the gleam of burnished bronze, and the sound of his words like the roar of a multitude. 7 I, Daniel, alone saw the vision; the people who were with me did not see the vision, though a great trembling fell upon them, and they fled and hid themselves. 8 So I was left alone to see this great vision. My strength left me, and my

10:8-19 My strength left me... touched me: The repeated references to Daniel's reactions (10:9, 11, 15, 17) point out the significance of the vision. The three acts of touching (10:10, 16, 18) occur before Daniel is even able to say, "Let my lord speak."

---

[a] Gk Syr: Heb *He made to understand* [b] Or *thing* or *one* [c] Or *His* [d] Cn: Meaning of Heb uncertain

complexion grew deathly pale, and I retained no strength. [9]Then
I heard the sound of his words; and when I heard the sound of his
words, I fell into a trance, face to the ground.

10 But then a hand touched me and roused me to my hands and
knees. [11]He said to me, “Daniel, greatly beloved, pay attention to the
words that I am going to speak to you. Stand on your feet, for I have
now been sent to you.” So while he was speaking this word to me, I
stood up trembling. [12]He said to me, “Do not fear, Daniel, for from
the first day that you set your mind to gain understanding and to
humble yourself before your God, your words have been heard, and
I have come because of your words. [13]But the prince of the kingdom
of Persia opposed me twenty-one days. So Michael, one of the chief
princes, came to help me, and I left him there with the prince of the
kingdom of Persia,[a] [14]and have come to help you understand what is
to happen to your people at the end of days. For there is a further vision for those days.”

15 While he was speaking these words to me, I turned my face
toward the ground and was speechless. [16]Then one in human form
touched my lips, and I opened my mouth to speak, and said to the one
who stood before me, “My lord, because of the vision such pains have
come upon me that I retain no strength. [17]How can my lord’s servant
talk with my lord? For I am shaking,[b] no strength remains in me, and
no breath is left in me.”

18 Again one in human form touched me and strengthened me.
[19]He said, “Do not fear, greatly beloved, you are safe. Be strong and
courageous!” When he spoke to me, I was strengthened and said,
“Let my lord speak, for you have strengthened me.” [20]Then he said,
“Do you know why I have come to you? Now I must return to fight
against the prince of Persia, and when I am through with him, the
prince of Greece will come. [21]But I am to tell you what is inscribed
in the book of truth. There is no one with me who contends against

11 these princes except Michael, your prince. [1]As for me, in
the first year of Darius the Mede, I stood up to support and
strengthen him.

2 “Now I will announce the truth to you. Three more kings shall
arise in Persia. The fourth shall be far richer than all of them, and when
he has become strong through his riches, he shall stir up all against the
kingdom of Greece. [3]Then a warrior king shall arise, who shall rule
with great dominion and take action as he pleases. [4]And while still
rising in power, his kingdom shall be broken and divided toward the
four winds of heaven, but not to his posterity, nor according to the dominion with which he ruled; for his kingdom shall be uprooted and
go to others besides these.

11:2 I will announce the truth to you: The truth of the vision comes in an announcement. It is not a matter for speculation.

11:2-4 Persia: Daniel’s vision moves quickly from the Persian Empire to the conquest of the ancient Near East by Alexander the Great, then to the breakup of Alexander’s empire into four parts.

---

[a] Gk Theodotion: Heb *I was left there with the kings of Persia* [b] Gk: Heb *from now*

5 “Then the king of the south shall grow strong, but one of his
officers shall grow stronger than he and shall rule a realm greater than
his own realm. [6]After some years they shall make an alliance, and the
daughter of the king of the south shall come to the king of the north
to ratify the agreement. But she shall not retain her power, and his offspring shall not endure. She shall be given up, she and her attendants
and her child and the one who supported her.

“In those times [7]a branch from her roots shall rise up in his place.
He shall come against the army and enter the fortress of the king of
the north, and he shall take action against them and prevail. [8]Even
their gods, with their idols and with their precious vessels of silver
and gold, he shall carry off to Egypt as spoils of war. For some years
he shall refrain from attacking the king of the north; [9]then the latter
shall invade the realm of the king of the south, but will return to his
own land.

10 “His sons shall wage war and assemble a multitude of great
forces, which shall advance like a flood and pass through, and again
shall carry the war as far as his fortress. [11]Moved with rage, the king of
the south shall go out and do battle against the king of the north, who
shall muster a great multitude, which shall, however, be defeated by
his enemy. [12]When the multitude has been carried off, his heart shall
be exalted, and he shall overthrow tens of thousands, but he shall not
prevail. [13]For the king of the north shall again raise a multitude, larger
than the former, and after some years[a] he shall advance with a great
army and abundant supplies.

14 “In those times many shall rise against the king of the south.
The lawless among your own people shall lift themselves up in order
to fulfill the vision, but they shall fail. [15]Then the king of the north shall
come and throw up siegeworks, and take a well-fortified city. And the
forces of the south shall not stand, not even his picked troops, for
there shall be no strength to resist. [16]But he who comes against him
shall take the actions he pleases, and no one shall withstand him. He
shall take a position in the beautiful land, and all of it shall be in his
power. [17]He shall set his mind to come with the strength of his whole
kingdom, and he shall bring terms of peace[b] and perform them. In order to destroy the kingdom,[c] he shall give him a woman in marriage;
but it shall not succeed or be to his advantage. [18]Afterward he shall
turn to the coastlands, and shall capture many. But a commander shall
put an end to his insolence; indeed,[d] he shall turn his insolence back
upon him. [19]Then he shall turn back toward the fortresses of his own
land, but he shall stumble and fall, and shall not be found.

20 “Then shall arise in his place one who shall send an official for

11:5-28 In those times: These verses are filled with plots and revolutions (11:21, 25), strength (11:5-6, 10), disrespect (11:18), and deceit (11:23). The references to specific historical events are debated, but it is clear that the sins of humans and oppressive kingdoms will continue.

---

[a] Heb *and at the end of the times years* [b] Gk: Heb *kingdom, and upright ones with him* [c] Heb *it*
[d] Meaning of Heb uncertain

the glory of the kingdom; but within a few days he shall be broken,
though not in anger or in battle. [21]In his place shall arise a contemptible person on whom royal majesty had not been conferred; he shall
come in without warning and obtain the kingdom through intrigue.
[22]Armies shall be utterly swept away and broken before him, and the
prince of the covenant as well. [23]And after an alliance is made with
him, he shall act deceitfully and become strong with a small party.
[24]Without warning he shall come into the richest parts[a] of the province and do what none of his predecessors had ever done, lavishing
plunder, spoil, and wealth on them. He shall devise plans against
strongholds, but only for a time. [25]He shall stir up his power and
determination against the king of the south with a great army, and
the king of the south shall wage war with a much greater and stronger army. But he shall not succeed, for plots shall be devised against
him [26]by those who eat of the royal rations. They shall break him, his
army shall be swept away, and many shall fall slain. [27]The two kings,
their minds bent on evil, shall sit at one table and exchange lies. But
it shall not succeed, for there remains an end at the time appointed.
[28]He shall return to his land with great wealth, but his heart shall be
set against the holy covenant. He shall work his will, and return to his
own land.

11:29 this time it shall not be as it was before: The ruler will act against the faithful and some will die. Others will flatter the oppressor and make a pact with him. The picture is one of painful turmoil within the community of faith.

29 "At the time appointed he shall return and come into the south,
but this time it shall not be as it was before. [30]For ships of Kittim shall
come against him, and he shall lose heart and withdraw. He shall be
enraged and take action against the holy covenant. He shall turn back
and pay heed to those who forsake the holy covenant. [31]Forces sent
by him shall occupy and profane the temple and fortress. They shall
abolish the regular burnt offering and set up the abomination that
makes desolate. [32]He shall seduce with intrigue those who violate
the covenant; but the people who are loyal to their God shall stand
firm and take action. [33]The wise among the people shall give understanding to many; for some days, however, they shall fall by sword
and flame, and suffer captivity and plunder. [34]When they fall victim,
they shall receive a little help, and many shall join them insincerely.
[35]Some of the wise shall fall, so that they may be refined, purified, and
cleansed,[b] until the time of the end, for there is still an interval until
the time appointed.

11:35-45 until the time of the end…until the period of wrath is completed…At the time of the end…to his end: The oppressive ruler or tyrant will not only challenge God, but will abandon his own religious traditions and set himself up as a god. The repeated references to the end emphasize that God will put an end to evil.

36 "The king shall act as he pleases. He shall exalt himself and
consider himself greater than any god, and shall speak horrendous
things against the God of gods. He shall prosper until the period of
wrath is completed, for what is determined shall be done. [37]He shall
pay no respect to the gods of his ancestors, or to the one beloved by
women; he shall pay no respect to any other god, for he shall consider

---

[a] Or *among the richest men* [b] Heb *made them white*

himself greater than all. [38]He shall honor the god of fortresses instead
of these; a god whom his ancestors did not know he shall honor with
gold and silver, with precious stones and costly gifts. [39]He shall deal
with the strongest fortresses by the help of a foreign god. Those who
acknowledge him he shall make more wealthy, and shall appoint them
as rulers over many, and shall distribute the land for a price.

The Time of the End

40 "At the time of the end the king of the south shall attack him.
But the king of the north shall rush upon him like a whirlwind, with
chariots and horsemen, and with many ships. He shall advance
against countries and pass through like a flood. [41]He shall come into
the beautiful land, and tens of thousands shall fall victim, but Edom
and Moab and the main part of the Ammonites shall escape from his
power. [42]He shall stretch out his hand against the countries, and the
land of Egypt shall not escape. [43]He shall become ruler of the treasures of gold and of silver, and all the riches of Egypt; and the Libyans
and the Ethiopians[a] shall follow in his train. [44]But reports from the
east and the north shall alarm him, and he shall go out with great fury
to bring ruin and complete destruction to many. [45]He shall pitch his
palatial tents between the sea and the beautiful holy mountain. Yet he
shall come to his end, with no one to help him.

The Resurrection of the Dead

12 "At that time Michael, the great prince, the protector of your
people, shall arise. There shall be a time of anguish, such as
has never occurred since nations first came into existence. But at that
time your people shall be delivered, everyone who is found written
in the book. [2]Many of those who sleep in the dust of the earth[b] shall
awake, some to everlasting life, and some to shame and everlasting
contempt. [3]Those who are wise shall shine like the brightness of the
sky,[c] and those who lead many to righteousness, like the stars forever
and ever. [4]But you, Daniel, keep the words secret and the book sealed
until the time of the end. Many shall be running back and forth, and
evil[d] shall increase."

5 Then I, Daniel, looked, and two others appeared, one standing
on this bank of the stream and one on the other. [6]One of them said
to the man clothed in linen, who was upstream, "How long shall it be
until the end of these wonders?" [7]The man clothed in linen, who was
upstream, raised his right hand and his left hand toward heaven. And
I heard him swear by the one who lives forever that it would be for a
time, two times, and half a time,[e] and that when the shattering of the

---

[a] Or *Nubians;* Heb *Cushites* [b] Or *the land of dust* [c] Or *dome* [d] Cn Compare Gk: Heb *knowledge*
[e] Heb *a time, times, and a half*

11:44-45 reports...shall alarm him: Destruction and desperation escalate, and rumors send the ruler scurrying east and then north. The tyrant is not safe. When his end comes, everyone will abandon him.

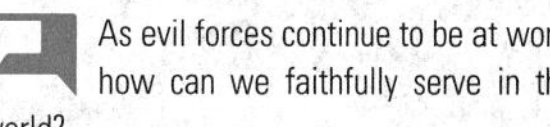

As evil forces continue to be at work, how can we faithfully serve in the world?

12:1 Michael: God has put the "great prince," Michael, in charge. When evil reaches levels never before seen, Michael acts to bring final deliverance.

12:2-4 everlasting life: These verses are the clearest statement in the Old Testament about the resurrection of the dead. The faithful can defy the demands of the tyrants of this world because these rulers do not, in the end, control the future. As Paul says in 1 Corinthians 15:58, the people of God can be *immovable* in this promise, and then keep *moving* forward with the work of the Lord.

12:6 How long: This question comes up again (see 8:13). Various numbers are given in the speech of the heavenly messenger (the man clothed in linen): three and one-half years (12:7); 1,290 days (12:11); and 1,335 days (12:12). In 7:25 the figure is three and one-half years; in 8:14 it is 1,150 days (or 2,300 "evenings and mornings"). Given this range of numbers, it is not surprising that the question "How long?" becomes an expression of agonizing lament in the Bible (see, for example, Ps 13).

power of the holy people comes to an end, all these things would be
accomplished. [8]I heard but could not understand; so I said, "My lord,
what shall be the outcome of these things?" [9]He said, "Go your way,
Daniel, for the words are to remain secret and sealed until the time
of the end. [10]Many shall be purified, cleansed, and refined, but the
wicked shall continue to act wickedly. None of the wicked shall understand, but those who are wise shall understand. [11]From the time
that the regular burnt offering is taken away and the abomination that
desolates is set up, there shall be one thousand two hundred ninety
days. [12]Happy are those who persevere and attain the thousand three
hundred thirty-five days. [13]But you, go your way,[a] and rest; you shall
rise for your reward at the end of the days."

The book of Daniel repeatedly claims that the evil powers and tyrannical kingdoms of the world will end—only the kingdom of God will go on. What do Lutherans say about this? In the hymn "A Mighty Fortress Is Our God," Martin Luther writes, "Were they to take our house, goods, honor, child, or spouse, though life be wrenched away, they cannot win the day. The kingdom's ours forever!" (*ELW* 504, Text and music: Martin Luther, 1483–1546. Tr. *LBW*). *Daniel 12*

[a] Gk Theodotion: Heb adds *to the end*

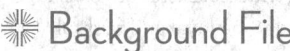

Hosea 14:6

HOSEA

Background File

The prophet Hosea was active during the reigns of five kings who ruled Judah (the southern kingdom) and Israel (the northern kingdom) approximately 769–697 B.C.E. Hosea's actions and messages from God were probably preserved and transmitted through northern circles. Eventually they were also directed to a southern audience.

What's the Story?

The worship rituals practiced by surrounding peoples were tempting to the Israelites. Canaanite fertility religion was especially tempting. It used sexual activity at outdoor shrines to encourage the gods to grant productive crops, livestock, and families. Canaanite gods were represented by stone pillars, trees planted beside altars, and statues of idols. These rituals or worship practices were clearly forbidden in the religion of Israel. The God of Israel had commanded the people not to have other gods or worship idols. This God could not be manipulated by humans. To observe the Canaanite fertility rituals, then, demonstrated a lack of trust in God, which Hosea calls "no knowledge of God" (4:1).

The small nations of Israel and Judah were at this time subjects of the more powerful nations of Assyria to the east or Egypt to the south. The people asked for military help from these nations when needed, rather than relying on God's help alone. This also indicated "no knowledge of God."

The book of Hosea can be divided into two unequal parts. Chapters 1–3 provide Hosea's personal story of his first years of marriage to Gomer, the birth of three children, and then his marriage to a woman who was unfaithful to him. Chapters 4–13, poetic in style, accuse Israel of ungodly behavior and announce the resulting punishment. Intended to bring Israel to its senses and convince the people to return to God, there are glimpses of hope here and there among the harsh accusations. Chapter 14, also poetic in style, holds out the promise of restored life with God.

To describe the extent of Israel's sinful behavior, Hosea uses vivid imagery from many areas of life. From public life, the prophet uses military imagery (bow, sword, horses) and courtroom imagery (listing of crimes, an arrest warrant). From nature the prophet uses farming imagery (sow, reap, plow), plant imagery (grapes, thorn, lily, olive tree), and hunting imagery (snare, net, lion, birds). Religious life is compared to family life as Israel is accused of spiritual adultery, or being unfaithful to God by worshiping other gods.

What's the Message?

Hosea's main message is God's desire for a relationship with the chosen people, and how far God will go to woo Israel back into this relationship. Through a covenant or promises God made with Israel to provide a land, many descendants, and blessings, the relationship was established out of grace and love. This means that when the people practice religious rituals connected to other gods, turn to other nations for military help, and do not promote justice and righteousness in society, they have betrayed or turned their backs on their covenant relationship with God.

First, Hosea acts out in his own life the way God continues to seek and love one who has proven to be unfaithful. Then, Hosea announces the punishment that is coming as a result of Israel's unfaithfulness, and also God's unfailing love for this unfaithful people. In the book of Hosea, God calls Israel to a relationship marked by loyal commitment and faithful worship. We also are called to be loyal and faithful to God in worship and in life.

1:1 The word of the Lord: This phrase, which serves as a title for the book, is the typical way prophets introduce their messages. It also shows that prophets understood themselves to be speaking and acting under God's direction.

1:2-3 whoredom: Going against accepted standards for sexual conduct was a serious sin in ancient Israel. Women who had sex outside of marriage could be subject to the death penalty for sinning against family, society, and God (see Deut 22:21). At the same time, worship by the Canaanite people often involved sex with "sacred prostitutes" as a way of encouraging the gods to bring about fertility, especially productive crops, livestock, and families.

1:4-9 Name: In ancient societies, personal names reflected actual or desired character traits. Hosea ("Salvation") marries Gomer ("End") and the harsh names of the children ("God-sows [seed]," "No pity," and "Not my people") illustrate the broken covenant relationship with God.

What name would you choose for yourself (or others) that would reflect actual or desired character traits?

1:10—2:1 Yet: Although prophets' messages announce mostly doom and punishment, almost every one includes some hope, based on God's unfailing love. Here, Hosea holds out hope for numerous descendants, a reuniting of the two kingdoms, and reinstatement of the covenant.

1 The word of the LORD that came to Hosea son of Beeri, in the
days of Kings Uzziah, Jotham, Ahaz, and Hezekiah of Judah, and
in the days of King Jeroboam son of Joash of Israel.

The Family of Hosea

2 When the LORD first spoke through Hosea, the LORD said to
Hosea, "Go, take for yourself a wife of whoredom and have children
of whoredom, for the land commits great whoredom by forsaking the
LORD." 3 So he went and took Gomer daughter of Diblaim, and she
conceived and bore him a son.
4 And the LORD said to him, "Name him Jezreel;[a] for in a little
while I will punish the house of Jehu for the blood of Jezreel, and I will
put an end to the kingdom of the house of Israel. 5 On that day I will
break the bow of Israel in the valley of Jezreel."
6 She conceived again and bore a daughter. Then the LORD said
to him, "Name her Lo-ruhamah,[b] for I will no longer have pity on the
house of Israel or forgive them. 7 But I will have pity on the house of
Judah, and I will save them by the LORD their God; I will not save
them by bow, or by sword, or by war, or by horses, or by horsemen."
8 When she had weaned Lo-ruhamah, she conceived and bore a
son. 9 Then the LORD said, "Name him Lo-ammi,[c] for you are not my
people and I am not your God."[d]

The Restoration of Israel

10[e] Yet the number of the people of Israel shall be like the sand
of the sea, which can be neither measured nor numbered; and in the

---

[a] That is *God sows* [b] That is *Not pitied* [c] That is *Not my people* [d] Heb *I am not yours* [e] Ch 2.1 in Heb

place where it was said to them, "You are not my people," it shall be
said to them, "Children of the living God." 11 The people of Judah and
the people of Israel shall be gathered together, and they shall appoint
for themselves one head; and they shall take possession of[a] the land,
for great shall be the day of Jezreel.

2 [b] Say to your brother,[c] Ammi,[d] and to your sister,[e] Ruhamah.[f]

Israel's Infidelity, Punishment, and Redemption

2 Plead with your mother, plead—
for she is not my wife,
and I am not her husband—
that she put away her whoring from her face,
and her adultery from between her breasts,
3 or I will strip her naked
and expose her as in the day she was born,
and make her like a wilderness,
and turn her into a parched land,
and kill her with thirst.
4 Upon her children also I will have no pity,
because they are children of whoredom.
5 For their mother has played the whore;
she who conceived them has acted shamefully.
For she said, "I will go after my lovers;
they give me my bread and my water,
my wool and my flax, my oil and my drink."
6 Therefore I will hedge up her[g] way with thorns;
and I will build a wall against her,
so that she cannot find her paths.
7 She shall pursue her lovers,
but not overtake them;
and she shall seek them,
but shall not find them.
Then she shall say, "I will go
and return to my first husband,
for it was better with me then than now."
8 She did not know
that it was I who gave her
the grain, the wine, and the oil,
and who lavished upon her silver
and gold that they used for Baal.
9 Therefore I will take back
my grain in its time,

2:2-15 I will punish her: Using his wife, Gomer, as an illustration of how Israel has been unfaithful to God, Hosea announces God's punishment of this unfaithfulness, in the hope that God can woo Israel back into relationship.

What do you think about the idea that God inflicts punishment to bring about a change in behavior?

---

[a] Heb *rise up from* [b] Ch 2.3 in Heb [c] Gk: Heb *brothers* [d] That is *My people* [e] Gk Vg: Heb *sisters*
[f] That is *Pitied* [g] Gk Syr: Heb *your*

and my wine in its season;
and I will take away my wool and my flax,
which were to cover her nakedness.
10 Now I will uncover her shame
in the sight of her lovers,
and no one shall rescue her out of my hand.
11 I will put an end to all her mirth,
her festivals, her new moons, her sabbaths,
and all her appointed festivals.
12 I will lay waste her vines and her fig trees,
of which she said,
"These are my pay,
which my lovers have given me."
I will make them a forest,
and the wild animals shall devour them.
13 I will punish her for the festival days of the Baals,
when she offered incense to them
and decked herself with her ring and jewelry,
and went after her lovers,
and forgot me, says the LORD.

14 Therefore, I will now allure her,
and bring her into the wilderness,
and speak tenderly to her.
15 From there I will give her her vineyards,
and make the Valley of Achor a door of hope.
There she shall respond as in the days of her youth,
as at the time when she came out of the land of Egypt.
16 On that day, says the LORD, you will call me, "My husband," and no
longer will you call me, "My Baal."[a] 17 For I will remove the names of
the Baals from her mouth, and they shall be mentioned by name no
more. 18 I will make for you[b] a covenant on that day with the wild animals, the birds of the air, and the creeping things of the ground; and
I will abolish[c] the bow, the sword, and war from the land; and I will
make you lie down in safety. 19 And I will take you for my wife forever;
I will take you for my wife in righteousness and in justice, in steadfast
love, and in mercy. 20 I will take you for my wife in faithfulness; and
you shall know the LORD.
21 On that day I will answer, says the LORD,
I will answer the heavens
and they shall answer the earth;
22 and the earth shall answer the grain, the wine, and the oil,
and they shall answer Jezreel;[d]

[a] That is, *"My master"* [b] Heb *them* [c] Heb *break* [d] That is *God sows*

2:16-23 You are my people: With language that sounds much like the everlasting covenant or promise with Noah (Gen 9), God promises to "marry" Israel forever. The relationship will be marked by righteousness, justice, steadfast love, and mercy (2:19), concepts regularly used to define God's nature and kingdom. The children's names will be changed to reflect the restored relationship.

**2:16 My husband... My Ba`al:** The original text in Hebrew contains a wordplay. Ba`al is the name of the chief god of Canaan (and Israel's "lover," Hosea says) and one of the Hebrew words for master/owner or husband. The translation "My husband" uses the typical Hebrew word for man ('ish), for whom woman ('ishah) is named in Genesis 2:23. God longs for an intimate relationship ('ish and 'ishah) with Israel ("My husband"), rather than a relationship of unfaithfulness and power ("My Ba`al").

23 and I will sow him[a] for myself in the land.
And I will have pity on Lo-ruhamah,[b]
and I will say to Lo-ammi,[c] "You are my people";
and he shall say, "You are my God."

Further Assurances of God's Redeeming Love

3 The LORD said to me again, "Go, love a woman who has a lover
and is an adulteress, just as the LORD loves the people of Israel,
though they turn to other gods and love raisin cakes." 2So I bought
her for fifteen shekels of silver and a homer of barley and a measure
of wine.[d] 3And I said to her, "You must remain as mine for many days;
you shall not play the whore, you shall not have intercourse with a
man, nor I with you." 4For the Israelites shall remain many days without king or prince, without sacrifice or pillar, without ephod or teraphim. 5Afterward the Israelites shall return and seek the LORD their
God, and David their king; they shall come in awe to the LORD and to
his goodness in the latter days.

God Accuses Israel

4 Hear the word of the LORD, O people of Israel;
for the LORD has an indictment against the inhabitants of the land.
There is no faithfulness or loyalty,
and no knowledge of God in the land.
2 Swearing, lying, and murder,
and stealing and adultery break out;
bloodshed follows bloodshed.
3 Therefore the land mourns,
and all who live in it languish;
together with the wild animals
and the birds of the air,
even the fish of the sea are perishing.

4 Yet let no one contend,
and let none accuse,
for with you is my contention, O priest.[e]
5 You shall stumble by day;
the prophet also shall stumble with you by night,
and I will destroy your mother.
6 My people are destroyed for lack of knowledge;
because you have rejected knowledge,
I reject you from being a priest to me.

[a] Cn: Heb *her* [b] That is *Not pitied* [c] That is *Not my people* [d] Gk: Heb *a homer of barley and a lethech of barley* [e] Cn: Meaning of Heb uncertain

3:1-5 The LORD said to me: These five verses follow the typical structure of prophetic writings: God's command (3:1), action to fulfill the command (3:2-3), and the prophet's interpretation of the action (3:4-5). Hosea's action of living with his wife without regular sexual intimacy is compared to Israel's life without regular government or worship. Scholars debate whether or not Gomer is the adulteress in this chapter.

3:1 raisin cakes: Raisin cakes were commonly offered to the gods worshiped by the Canaanite people.

3:4 without sacrifice or pillar: Everything mentioned here was a way into the realm of the gods. Sacrifices were offerings to gods. Pillars represented the male deity's presence. The ephod, a garment made of fine linen and designed for priests (see Exod 35:19), may have been used to clothe small figurines of gods or goddesses (teraphim) set in a household shrine (see Judg 17:5).

4:1-3 an indictment: The rest of the book of Hosea is presented as a legal case. Here God is both the plaintiff, who brings a lawsuit against Israel, and the judge. Worse than specific acts of disobeying the Ten Commandments, the main charge is that Israel does not trust God. In Hosea's words, there is "no knowledge of God in the land" (4:1; see introduction).

4:4-19 O priest...the prophet: Priests and prophets are singled out because of their special roles in communicating God's will to the people. Holy or sacred sites have become places for rituals and idols of the Canaanite people. Note how the punishment reflects the wrongdoing: "because you have rejected knowledge, I reject you" and "since you have forgotten...I also will forget."

And since you have forgotten the law of your God,
I also will forget your children.

7 The more they increased,
the more they sinned against me;
they changed[a] their glory into shame.
8 They feed on the sin of my people;
they are greedy for their iniquity.
9 And it shall be like people, like priest;
I will punish them for their ways,
and repay them for their deeds.
10 They shall eat, but not be satisfied;
they shall play the whore, but not multiply;
because they have forsaken the LORD
to devote themselves to 11 whoredom.

The Idolatry of Israel

Wine and new wine
take away the understanding.
12 My people consult a piece of wood,
and their divining rod gives them oracles.
For a spirit of whoredom has led them astray,
and they have played the whore, forsaking their God.
13 They sacrifice on the tops of the mountains,
and make offerings upon the hills,
under oak, poplar, and terebinth,
because their shade is good.

Therefore your daughters play the whore,
and your daughters-in-law commit adultery.
14 I will not punish your daughters when they play the whore,
nor your daughters-in-law when they commit adultery;
for the men themselves go aside with whores,
and sacrifice with temple prostitutes;
thus a people without understanding comes to ruin.

15 Though you play the whore, O Israel,
do not let Judah become guilty.
Do not enter into Gilgal,
or go up to Beth-aven,
and do not swear, "As the LORD lives."
16 Like a stubborn heifer,
Israel is stubborn;

---

[a] Ancient Heb tradition: MT *I will change*

can the LORD now feed them
like a lamb in a broad pasture?

17 Ephraim is joined to idols—
let him alone.
18 When their drinking is ended, they indulge in sexual orgies;
they love lewdness more than their glory.[a]
19 A wind has wrapped them[b] in its wings,
and they shall be ashamed because of their altars.[c]

Impending Judgment on Israel and Judah

5 Hear this, O priests!
Give heed, O house of Israel!
Listen, O house of the king!
For the judgment pertains to you;
for you have been a snare at Mizpah,
and a net spread upon Tabor,
2 and a pit dug deep in Shittim;[d]
but I will punish all of them.

3 I know Ephraim,
and Israel is not hidden from me;
for now, O Ephraim, you have played the whore;
Israel is defiled.
4 Their deeds do not permit them
to return to their God.
For the spirit of whoredom is within them,
and they do not know the LORD.

5 Israel's pride testifies against him;
Ephraim[e] stumbles in his guilt;
Judah also stumbles with them.
6 With their flocks and herds they shall go
to seek the LORD,
but they will not find him;
he has withdrawn from them.
7 They have dealt faithlessly with the LORD;
for they have borne illegitimate children.
Now the new moon shall devour them along with their fields.

8 Blow the horn in Gibeah,
the trumpet in Ramah.

[a] Cn Compare Gk: Meaning of Heb uncertain [b] Heb *her* [c] Gk Syr: Heb *sacrifices* [d] Cn: Meaning of Heb uncertain [e] Heb *Israel and Ephraim*

5:1-7 the judgment: Hunting imagery (snare, net) illustrates how the priests and political leaders have hunted and captured the people of Israel like prey, causing them to turn aside from God.

5:8-15 Sound the alarm: The prophet laments or mourns the total corruption of Israel (also called Ephraim) and Judah. One symptom of Israel's "sickness" is turning to the powerful Assyrian Empire for a "cure," rather than to God.

Sound the alarm at Beth-aven;
look behind you, Benjamin!
9 Ephraim shall become a desolation
in the day of punishment;
among the tribes of Israel
I declare what is sure.
10 The princes of Judah have become
like those who remove the landmark;
on them I will pour out
my wrath like water.
11 Ephraim is oppressed, crushed in judgment,
because he was determined to go after vanity.[a]
12 Therefore I am like maggots to Ephraim,
and like rottenness to the house of Judah.
13 When Ephraim saw his sickness,
and Judah his wound,
then Ephraim went to Assyria,
and sent to the great king.[b]
But he is not able to cure you
or heal your wound.
14 For I will be like a lion to Ephraim,
and like a young lion to the house of Judah.
I myself will tear and go away;
I will carry off, and no one shall rescue.
15 I will return again to my place
until they acknowledge their guilt and seek my face.
In their distress they will beg my favor:

A Call to Repentance

6 "Come, let us return to the LORD;
for it is he who has torn, and he will heal us;
he has struck down, and he will bind us up.
2 After two days he will revive us;
on the third day he will raise us up,
that we may live before him.
3 Let us know, let us press on to know the LORD;
his appearing is as sure as the dawn;
he will come to us like the showers,
like the spring rains that water the earth."

Impenitence of Israel and Judah

4 What shall I do with you, O Ephraim?
What shall I do with you, O Judah?
Your love is like a morning cloud,

[a] Gk: Meaning of Heb uncertain [b] Cn: Heb *to a king who will contend*

6:1-3 return to the LORD: These verses make up a penitential song expressing the desire to restore the relationship with God. They draw from a part of the liturgy when priests called worshipers to return to the LORD for healing.

6:2 on the third day: Originally, "three days" would have meant "a short time" or "a little while." After Jesus was raised from the dead, early Christians interpreted these words as a prediction of the resurrection.

6:4-6 sacrifice: Ancient Israelite worship included various types of sacrifices (see "Offerings in Israel," p. 197; and Lev 1–7). In a society that depended on livestock and crops, offering animals or grains in worship was a sacrifice of valuable goods as well as an act of devotion to God. Here God announces that observing worship rituals is meaningless without loving both God and neighbor. Jesus would remind people of this in Matthew 9:13 and 12:7.

like the dew that goes away early.
5 Therefore I have hewn them by the prophets,
I have killed them by the words of my mouth,
and my[a] judgment goes forth as the light.
6 For I desire steadfast love and not sacrifice,
the knowledge of God rather than burnt offerings.

7 But at[b] Adam they transgressed the covenant;
there they dealt faithlessly with me.
8 Gilead is a city of evildoers,
tracked with blood.
9 As robbers lie in wait[c] for someone,
so the priests are banded together;[d]
they murder on the road to Shechem,
they commit a monstrous crime.
10 In the house of Israel I have seen a horrible thing;
Ephraim's whoredom is there, Israel is defiled.

11 For you also, O Judah, a harvest is appointed.

When I would restore the fortunes of my people,
7 1 when I would heal Israel,
the corruption of Ephraim is revealed,
and the wicked deeds of Samaria;
for they deal falsely,
the thief breaks in,
and the bandits raid outside.
2 But they do not consider
that I remember all their wickedness.
Now their deeds surround them,
they are before my face.
3 By their wickedness they make the king glad,
and the officials by their treachery.
4 They are all adulterers;
they are like a heated oven,
whose baker does not need to stir the fire,
from the kneading of the dough until it is leavened.
5 On the day of our king the officials
became sick with the heat of wine;
he stretched out his hand with mockers.
6 For they are kindled[e] like an oven, their heart burns within them;
all night their anger smolders;
in the morning it blazes like a flaming fire.

How do the Bible, worship, baptism, and communion make a difference in your daily life in the world?

6:7—7:16 I will discipline them: Hosea announces that Israel's wickedness will bring about God's discipline.

---

[a] Gk Syr: Heb *your* [b] Cn: Heb *like* [c] Cn: Meaning of Heb uncertain [d] Syr: Heb *are a company*
[e] Gk Syr: Heb *brought near*

7 All of them are hot as an oven,
and they devour their rulers.
All their kings have fallen;
none of them calls upon me.

8 Ephraim mixes himself with the peoples;
Ephraim is a cake not turned.
9 Foreigners devour his strength,
but he does not know it;
gray hairs are sprinkled upon him,
but he does not know it.
10 Israel's pride testifies against[a] him;
yet they do not return to the LORD their God,
or seek him, for all this.

Futile Reliance on the Nations

11 Ephraim has become like a dove,
silly and without sense;
they call upon Egypt, they go to Assyria.
12 As they go, I will cast my net over them;
I will bring them down like birds of the air;
I will discipline them according to the report made to their assembly.[b]
13 Woe to them, for they have strayed from me!
Destruction to them, for they have rebelled against me!
I would redeem them,
but they speak lies against me.

14 They do not cry to me from the heart,
but they wail upon their beds;
they gash themselves for grain and wine;
they rebel against me.
15 It was I who trained and strengthened their arms,
yet they plot evil against me.
16 They turn to that which does not profit;[c]
they have become like a defective bow;
their officials shall fall by the sword
because of the rage of their tongue.
So much for their babbling in the land of Egypt.

Israel's Apostasy

8 Set the trumpet to your lips!
One like a vulture[b] is over the house of the LORD,

8:1-6 they made idols: Israel is guilty of making idols for worship in the form of calves. The bull or calf was a sign of strength and fertility throughout the ancient world. (See also 10:5, Exod 32:1-6; 1 Kgs 12:28-30.)

[a] Or *humbles* [b] Meaning of Heb uncertain [c] Cn: Meaning of Heb uncertain

because they have broken my covenant,
and transgressed my law.
2 Israel cries to me,
"My God, we—Israel—know you!"
3 Israel has spurned the good;
the enemy shall pursue him.

4 They made kings, but not through me;
they set up princes, but without my knowledge.
With their silver and gold they made idols
for their own destruction.
5 Your calf is rejected, O Samaria.
My anger burns against them.
How long will they be incapable of innocence?
6 For it is from Israel,
an artisan made it;
it is not God.
The calf of Samaria
shall be broken to pieces.[a]

7 For they sow the wind,
and they shall reap the whirlwind.
The standing grain has no heads,
it shall yield no meal;
if it were to yield,
foreigners would devour it.
8 Israel is swallowed up;
now they are among the nations
as a useless vessel.
9 For they have gone up to Assyria,
a wild ass wandering alone;
Ephraim has bargained for lovers.
10 Though they bargain with the nations,
I will now gather them up.
They shall soon writhe
under the burden of kings and princes.

11 When Ephraim multiplied altars to expiate sin,
they became to him altars for sinning.
12 Though I write for him the multitude of my instructions,
they are regarded as a strange thing.
13 Though they offer choice sacrifices,[b]
though they eat flesh,

[a] Or *shall go up in flames* [b] Cn: Meaning of Heb uncertain

8:7-14 Israel is swallowed up: Israel's sin will cause unintended outcomes in all aspects of life: food (standing grain) is not edible; the holy nation Israel is useless; altars are places for sinning; instructions from God are considered strange; and the nation created and chosen by God has forgotten the Creator.

the LORD does not accept them.
Now he will remember their iniquity,
and punish their sins;
they shall return to Egypt.
14 Israel has forgotten his Maker,
and built palaces;
and Judah has multiplied fortified cities;
but I will send a fire upon his cities,
and it shall devour his strongholds.

Punishment for Israel's Sin

9:1-9 days of punishment: Because of Israel's unfaithfulness, the people will be removed from the land and unable to offer proper worship to God.

9:3 in the land of the LORD: Land was a key component of the covenant or promise God made with Israel. In the Bible, to be "in the land" is concrete evidence of the covenant relationship with God. Not remaining in the land is a sign of not remaining in this relationship.

9 Do not rejoice, O Israel!
Do not exult[a] as other nations do;
for you have played the whore, departing from your God.
You have loved a prostitute's pay
on all threshing floors.
2 Threshing floor and wine vat shall not feed them,
and the new wine shall fail them.
3 They shall not remain in the land of the LORD;
but Ephraim shall return to Egypt,
and in Assyria they shall eat unclean food.

4 They shall not pour drink offerings of wine to the LORD,
and their sacrifices shall not please him.
Such sacrifices shall be like mourners' bread;
all who eat of it shall be defiled;
for their bread shall be for their hunger only;
it shall not come to the house of the LORD.

5 What will you do on the day of appointed festival,
and on the day of the festival of the LORD?
6 For even if they escape destruction,
Egypt shall gather them,
Memphis shall bury them.
Nettles shall possess their precious things of silver;[b]
thorns shall be in their tents.

7 The days of punishment have come,
the days of recompense have come;
Israel cries,[c]
"The prophet is a fool,
the man of the spirit is mad!"
Because of your great iniquity,

---

[a] Gk: Heb *To exultation* [b] Meaning of Heb uncertain [c] Cn Compare Gk: Heb *shall know*

your hostility is great.
8 The prophet is a sentinel for my God over Ephraim,
yet a fowler's snare is on all his ways,
and hostility in the house of his God.
9 They have deeply corrupted themselves
as in the days of Gibeah;
he will remember their iniquity,
he will punish their sins.

10 Like grapes in the wilderness,
I found Israel.
Like the first fruit on the fig tree,
in its first season,
I saw your ancestors.
But they came to Baal-peor,
and consecrated themselves to a thing of shame,
and became detestable like the thing they loved.
11 Ephraim's glory shall fly away like a bird—
no birth, no pregnancy, no conception!
12 Even if they bring up children,
I will bereave them until no one is left.
Woe to them indeed
when I depart from them!
13 Once I saw Ephraim as a young palm planted in a lovely
meadow,[a]
but now Ephraim must lead out his children for slaughter.
14 Give them, O LORD—
what will you give?
Give them a miscarrying womb
and dry breasts.

15 Every evil of theirs began at Gilgal;
there I came to hate them.
Because of the wickedness of their deeds
I will drive them out of my house.
I will love them no more;
all their officials are rebels.

16 Ephraim is stricken,
their root is dried up,
they shall bear no fruit.
Even though they give birth,
I will kill the cherished offspring of their womb.

9:10-17 Like the first fruit on the fig tree: Israel is like a tender plant that God wanted to care for and nurture for life. Instead, Israel's shameful behavior has brought about death. The prophet Hosea cries "woe," a word used to mourn the reality of death.

[a] Meaning of Heb uncertain

17 Because they have not listened to him,
my God will reject them;
they shall become wanderers among the nations.

Israel's Sin and Captivity

10:1-15 break down their altars: Israel is engaged in false worship by making empty oaths and setting up idols on altars that should be dedicated to the worship of God.

10:1 luxuriant vine: In the ancient Near East, garden imagery is often associated with temples (for example, the Hanging Gardens of Babylon) and with royal palaces. A king would cultivate a park called a "paradise," with sample plants from all over the empire, as a sign of his dominion or rule over the territory. Israel, the vine, is under the lordship of God, the King.

10 Israel is a luxuriant vine
that yields its fruit.
The more his fruit increased
the more altars he built;
as his country improved,
he improved his pillars.
2 Their heart is false;
now they must bear their guilt.
The LORD[a] will break down their altars,
and destroy their pillars.

3 For now they will say:
"We have no king,
for we do not fear the LORD,
and a king—what could he do for us?"
4 They utter mere words;
with empty oaths they make covenants;
so litigation springs up like poisonous weeds
in the furrows of the field.
5 The inhabitants of Samaria tremble
for the calf[b] of Beth-aven.
Its people shall mourn for it,
and its idolatrous priests shall wail[c] over it,
over its glory that has departed from it.
6 The thing itself shall be carried to Assyria
as tribute to the great king.[d]
Ephraim shall be put to shame,
and Israel shall be ashamed of his idol.[e]

7 Samaria's king shall perish
like a chip on the face of the waters.
8 The high places of Aven, the sin of Israel,
shall be destroyed.
Thorn and thistle shall grow up
on their altars.
They shall say to the mountains, Cover us,
and to the hills, Fall on us.

---

[a] Heb *he* [b] Gk Syr: Heb *calves* [c] Cn: Heb *exult* [d] Cn: Heb *to a king who will contend*
[e] Cn: Heb *counsel*

9 Since the days of Gibeah you have sinned, O Israel;
there they have continued.
Shall not war overtake them in Gibeah?
10 I will come[a] against the wayward people to punish them;
and nations shall be gathered against them
when they are punished[b] for their double iniquity.

11 Ephraim was a trained heifer
that loved to thresh,
and I spared her fair neck;
but I will make Ephraim break the ground;
Judah must plow;
Jacob must harrow for himself.
12 Sow for yourselves righteousness;
reap steadfast love;
break up your fallow ground;
for it is time to seek the LORD,
that he may come and rain righteousness upon you.

13 You have plowed wickedness,
you have reaped injustice,
you have eaten the fruit of lies.
Because you have trusted in your power
and in the multitude of your warriors,
14 therefore the tumult of war shall rise against your people,
and all your fortresses shall be destroyed,
as Shalman destroyed Beth-arbel on the day of battle
when mothers were dashed in pieces with their children.
15 Thus it shall be done to you, O Bethel,
because of your great wickedness.
At dawn the king of Israel
shall be utterly cut off.

God's Compassion Despite Israel's Ingratitude

11 When Israel was a child, I loved him,
and out of Egypt I called my son.
2 The more I[c] called them,
the more they went from me;[d]
they kept sacrificing to the Baals,
and offering incense to idols.

3 Yet it was I who taught Ephraim to walk,
I took them up in my[e] arms;

---

[a] Cn Compare Gk: Heb *In my desire* [b] Gk: Heb *bound* [c] Gk: Heb *they* [d] Gk: Heb *them*
[e] Gk Syr Vg: Heb *his*

10:12 seek the LORD: Amid harsh judgment, Hosea holds out a slim ray of hope that disaster may be avoided if the people "seek the LORD." Seeds of righteousness will yield a harvest of steadfast love. The apostle Paul echoes Hosea in calling for a "harvest of your righteousness" to come from people's generosity (2 Cor 9:10).

11:1-11 When Israel was a child: In this moving passage, God fondly remembers raising Israel like a young child. Despite the people's lack of knowledge of God, in the end the Holy One cannot abandon the covenant relationship with Israel, "my son."

11:1 out of Egypt I called my son: Originally this would have referred to the Israelites' exodus out of slavery in Egypt (see Exod 4:21-22). Later, the escape of Jesus' family to Egypt (Matt 2:14-15) would be seen as fulfillment of these words in Hosea.

Does the way God is pictured in Hosea 11:1-11 help you understand who God is and how God forms a relationship with us? Why or why not?

but they did not know that I healed them.
4 I led them with cords of human kindness,
with bands of love.
I was to them like those
who lift infants to their cheeks.[a]
I bent down to them and fed them.

5 They shall return to the land of Egypt,
and Assyria shall be their king,
because they have refused to return to me.
6 The sword rages in their cities,
it consumes their oracle-priests,
and devours because of their schemes.
7 My people are bent on turning away from me.
To the Most High they call,
but he does not raise them up at all.[b]

8 How can I give you up, Ephraim?
How can I hand you over, O Israel?
How can I make you like Admah?
How can I treat you like Zeboiim?
My heart recoils within me;
my compassion grows warm and tender.
9 I will not execute my fierce anger;
I will not again destroy Ephraim;
for I am God and no mortal,
the Holy One in your midst,
and I will not come in wrath.[b]

10 They shall go after the LORD,
who roars like a lion;
when he roars,
his children shall come trembling from the west.
11 They shall come trembling like birds from Egypt,
and like doves from the land of Assyria;
and I will return them to their homes, says the LORD.

12[c] Ephraim has surrounded me with lies,
and the house of Israel with deceit;
but Judah still walks[d] with God,
and is faithful to the Holy One.

12 Ephraim herds the wind,
and pursues the east wind all day long;

12:1-14 Ephraim…Judah: Although Ephraim or Israel (the northern kingdom) has broken the covenant with God, Hosea holds out some hope that Judah (the southern kingdom) will remain faithful. By recounting the history of Jacob's relationship with God, the prophet criticizes the northern kingdom for abandoning that relationship.

---

[a] Or *who ease the yoke on their jaws* [b] Meaning of Heb uncertain [c] Ch 12.1 in Heb [d] Heb *roams* or *rules*

they multiply falsehood and violence;
they make a treaty with Assyria,
and oil is carried to Egypt.

The Long History of Rebellion

2 The LORD has an indictment against Judah,
and will punish Jacob according to his ways,
and repay him according to his deeds.
3 In the womb he tried to supplant his brother,
and in his manhood he strove with God.
4 He strove with the angel and prevailed,
he wept and sought his favor;
he met him at Bethel,
and there he spoke with him.[a]
5 The LORD the God of hosts,
the LORD is his name!
6 But as for you, return to your God,
hold fast to love and justice,
and wait continually for your God.

7 A trader, in whose hands are false balances,
he loves to oppress.
8 Ephraim has said, "Ah, I am rich,
I have gained wealth for myself;
in all of my gain
no offense has been found in me
that would be sin."[b]
9 I am the LORD your God
from the land of Egypt;
I will make you live in tents again,
as in the days of the appointed festival.

10 I spoke to the prophets;
it was I who multiplied visions,
and through the prophets I will bring destruction.
11 In Gilead[c] there is iniquity,
they shall surely come to nothing.
In Gilgal they sacrifice bulls,
so their altars shall be like stone heaps
on the furrows of the field.
12 Jacob fled to the land of Aram,
there Israel served for a wife,
and for a wife he guarded sheep.[d]

---

[a] Gk Syr: Heb *us* [b] Meaning of Heb uncertain [c] Compare Syr: Heb *Gilead* [d] Heb lacks *sheep*

13 By a prophet the LORD brought Israel up from Egypt,
and by a prophet he was guarded.
14 Ephraim has given bitter offense,
so his Lord will bring his crimes down on him
and pay him back for his insults.

Relentless Judgment on Israel

13:1-6 kissing calves!: The people are sinning by crafting idols of silver in the shape of calves. Their behavior is baffling to God, who brought them out of Egypt and fed them in the wilderness.

13 When Ephraim spoke, there was trembling;
he was exalted in Israel;
but he incurred guilt through Baal and died.
2 And now they keep on sinning
and make a cast image for themselves,
idols of silver made according to their understanding,
all of them the work of artisans.
"Sacrifice to these," they say.[a]
People are kissing calves!
3 Therefore they shall be like the morning mist
or like the dew that goes away early,
like chaff that swirls from the threshing floor
or like smoke from a window.

4 Yet I have been the LORD your God
ever since the land of Egypt;
you know no God but me,
and besides me there is no savior.
5 It was I who fed[b] you in the wilderness,
in the land of drought.
6 When I fed[c] them, they were satisfied;
they were satisfied, and their heart was proud;
therefore they forgot me.
7 So I will become like a lion to them,
like a leopard I will lurk beside the way.
8 I will fall upon them like a bear robbed of her cubs,
and will tear open the covering of their heart;
there I will devour them like a lion,
as a wild animal would mangle them.

13:7-15 Sheol…Death?: The unavoidable outcome of Israel's behavior is death and banishment to Sheol, the place of the dead. The questions at the beginning of 13:14 anticipate the answer "no" and seem to be calling for Death and Sheol to bring on plagues and destruction! The apostle Paul puts the same questions to a different use, taunting Death and Sheol to bring death and destruction without any result, since Jesus has conquered them both (see 1 Cor 15:55-57).

9 I will destroy you, O Israel;
who can help you?[d]
10 Where now is[e] your king, that he may save you?
Where in all your cities are your rulers,
of whom you said,

---

[a] Cn Compare Gk: Heb *To these they say sacrifices of people* [b] Gk Syr: Heb *knew* [c] Cn: Heb *according to their pasture* [d] Gk Syr: Heb *for in me is your help* [e] Gk Syr Vg: Heb *I will be*

"Give me a king and rulers"?
11 I gave you a king in my anger,
and I took him away in my wrath.

12 Ephraim's iniquity is bound up;
his sin is kept in store.
13 The pangs of childbirth come for him,
but he is an unwise son;
for at the proper time he does not present himself
at the mouth of the womb.

14 Shall I ransom them from the power of Sheol?
Shall I redeem them from Death?
O Death, where are[a] your plagues?
O Sheol, where is[a] your destruction?
Compassion is hidden from my eyes.

15 Although he may flourish among rushes,[b]
the east wind shall come, a blast from the LORD,
rising from the wilderness;
and his fountain shall dry up,
his spring shall be parched.
It shall strip his treasury
of every precious thing.
16[c] Samaria shall bear her guilt,
because she has rebelled against her God;
they shall fall by the sword,
their little ones shall be dashed in pieces,
and their pregnant women ripped open.

A Plea for Repentance

14 Return, O Israel, to the LORD your God,
for you have stumbled because of your iniquity.
2 Take words with you
and return to the LORD;
say to him,
"Take away all guilt;
accept that which is good,
and we will offer
the fruit[d] of our lips.
3 Assyria shall not save us;
we will not ride upon horses;
we will say no more, 'Our God,'

14:1-8 return to the LORD: The prophet pleads with Israel to return to God, who is longing to heal and love them, so that they "flourish as a garden," a universal image of wholeness.

[a] Gk Syr: Heb *I will be* [b] Or *among brothers* [c] Ch 14.1 in Heb [d] Gk Syr: Heb *bulls*

to the work of our hands.
In you the orphan finds mercy."

Assurance of Forgiveness

4 I will heal their disloyalty;
I will love them freely,
for my anger has turned from them.
5 I will be like the dew to Israel;
he shall blossom like the lily,
he shall strike root like the forests of Lebanon.[a]
6 His shoots shall spread out;
his beauty shall be like the olive tree,
and his fragrance like that of Lebanon.
7 They shall again live beneath my[b] shadow,
they shall flourish as a garden;[c]
they shall blossom like the vine,
their fragrance shall be like the wine of Lebanon.

8 O Ephraim, what have I[d] to do with idols?
It is I who answer and look after you.[e]
I am like an evergreen cypress;
your faithfulness[f] comes from me.
9 Those who are wise understand these things;
those who are discerning know them.
For the ways of the LORD are right,
and the upright walk in them,
but transgressors stumble in them.

14:9 Those who are wise: The final verse encourages the wise reader to understand and walk in the ways of God as described in the book of Hosea. Jesus encourages people in a similar way: "Let anyone with ears to hear listen!" (Mark 4:9; Luke 8:8.)

---

[a] Cn: Heb *like Lebanon* [b] Heb *his* [c] Cn: Heb *they shall grow grain* [d] Or *What more has Ephraim*
[e] Heb *him* [f] Heb *your fruit*

Joel 2:25

JOEL

Background File

The name "Joel" means "Yah [an abbreviation of Yahweh] is my God." What we know about the prophet Joel comes from this book. A reference to Tyre (3:4), which was destroyed in 348 B.C.E., and the language of restoration for Judah and Jerusalem (3:1-2) suggest that Joel was largely written after the time of the exile and before Tyre's destruction. The audience for Joel's "word," then, is the community of Israelites during the period of reconstruction (or about the time of the events in Ezra and Nehemiah).

What's the Story?

Unlike Amos, Hosea, and Micah, Joel is not at all critical of religious practices or organization. This has led some scholars to suggest that Joel himself was a temple prophet, although this is far from certain. Joel's call to worship centers around lamenting and mourning Israel's difficult situation (1:5-20; 2:3) and returning to the LORD (2:12-13).

The book of Joel contains strong imagery. For example, Joel uses the lack of offerings (of grain or drink, see 1:9, 13) as a powerful image of being cut off from the blessings which flow from worship (3:18). Joel also reflects on the promised "day of the LORD;" the locusts, real or symbolic, as the LORD's agents; and the garden of Eden as a fitting description of what Israel was like before God's judgment.

What's the Message?

While the image of the locust is strong in Joel, what the locusts *point to* is more important. Along with the "blood and fire and columns of smoke" in 2:30, the locusts are "portents," which in Hebrew is the same word used for the "wonders" or "signs" of the plagues in the exodus story. These signs show that it is the LORD who is God and the LORD who is in control of Israel. The repeated phrase "you shall know" in 2:27 and 3:17 again echoes the exodus story, which also intends to show that the LORD is God.

Joel shows the LORD using and exercising power in the natural world and promises an outpouring of the Spirit. All of this makes a case for a God acting in the world on behalf of God's people. The message to the troubled and struggling people of the time was that the LORD is "gracious and merciful, slow to anger, and abounding in steadfast love, and relents from punishing" (2:13).

1:1-3 word of the Lord: The book of Joel is a "word" or message that comes to the prophet. Verses 2-3 introduce the book with two commands to pay attention to this word and one to share this word: "Hear this," "give ear," and "tell."

1:4 locust: The image of the locust is one of Joel's most compelling features. Here and again in 2:25, there are four kinds of locusts. What one kind does not eat, the next will, until everything is devoured. It is not clear whether these are actual locusts or an image for invading enemies. It is clear, however, that these swarms are a "powerful army" sent by God (2:4-9).

1:5-20 Wake up…weep: The word "wail" occurs three times (1:5, 11, 13), along with calls to lament (1:8), put on sackcloth (1:13), and "sanctify a fast" (1:14), all worship practices for times of mourning, complaint, and trouble. Because the nation had been laid waste, there is no produce for offering (1:10-12), joy withers like the failed crops (1:12, 16), and the people, priests, and domestic animals (1:18), as well as wild animals (1:20) and even the earth itself (1:10) all mourn.

Sin has consequences. What is at stake when the effects of sin, of being out of right relationship with God, are felt even by the ground?

1 The word of the LORD that came to Joel son of Pethuel:

Lament over the Ruin of the Country

2 Hear this, O elders,
give ear, all inhabitants of the land!
Has such a thing happened in your days,
or in the days of your ancestors?
3 Tell your children of it,
and let your children tell their children,
and their children another generation.

4 What the cutting locust left,
the swarming locust has eaten.
What the swarming locust left,
the hopping locust has eaten,
and what the hopping locust left,
the destroying locust has eaten.

5 Wake up, you drunkards, and weep;
and wail, all you wine-drinkers,
over the sweet wine,
for it is cut off from your mouth.
6 For a nation has invaded my land,
powerful and innumerable;
its teeth are lions' teeth,
and it has the fangs of a lioness.
7 It has laid waste my vines,
and splintered my fig trees;
it has stripped off their bark and thrown it down;
their branches have turned white.

8 Lament like a virgin dressed in sackcloth
for the husband of her youth.
9 The grain offering and the drink offering are cut off
from the house of the LORD.
The priests mourn,
the ministers of the LORD.
10 The fields are devastated,
the ground mourns;
for the grain is destroyed,
the wine dries up,
the oil fails.

11 Be dismayed, you farmers,
wail, you vinedressers,

over the wheat and the barley;
  for the crops of the field are ruined.
12 The vine withers,
  the fig tree droops.
Pomegranate, palm, and apple—
  all the trees of the field are dried up;
surely, joy withers away
  among the people.

A Call to Repentance and Prayer

13 Put on sackcloth and lament, you priests;
  wail, you ministers of the altar.
Come, pass the night in sackcloth,
  you ministers of my God!
Grain offering and drink offering
  are withheld from the house of your God.

14 Sanctify a fast,
  call a solemn assembly.
Gather the elders
  and all the inhabitants of the land
to the house of the LORD your God,
  and cry out to the LORD.

15 Alas for the day!
For the day of the LORD is near,
  and as destruction from the Almighty[a] it comes.
16 Is not the food cut off
  before our eyes,
joy and gladness
  from the house of our God?

17 The seed shrivels under the clods,[b]
  the storehouses are desolate;
the granaries are ruined
  because the grain has failed.
18 How the animals groan!
  The herds of cattle wander about
because there is no pasture for them;
  even the flocks of sheep are dazed.[c]

19 To you, O LORD, I cry.
For fire has devoured

[a] Traditional rendering of Heb *Shaddai* [b] Meaning of Heb uncertain [c] Compare Gk Syr Vg: Meaning of Heb uncertain

1:15 the day of the LORD: The "day of the LORD" (2:1, 11, 31; 3:14; see also Isa 13:6, 9; Jer 46:10; Ezek 30:3; Obad 15; Zeph 1:7, 14; Mal 3:2-3) is a major theme in Joel, as in other prophetic books, but perhaps even more so here. The LORD's day is described as a day of "destruction," a day of darkness, and a day that will usher in an age of prophecy—of speaking the LORD's word—by all people (see Peter quoting Joel, Acts 2:16).

the pastures of the wilderness,
and flames have burned
all the trees of the field.
20 Even the wild animals cry to you
because the watercourses are dried up,
and fire has devoured
the pastures of the wilderness.

2 Blow the trumpet in Zion;
sound the alarm on my holy mountain!
Let all the inhabitants of the land tremble,
for the day of the LORD is coming, it is near—
2 a day of darkness and gloom,
a day of clouds and thick darkness!
Like blackness spread upon the mountains
a great and powerful army comes;
their like has never been from of old,
nor will be again after them
in ages to come.

2:3 Eden: The garden of creation is used here as an image for what the land looked like before the ravaging army of locusts (2:4-11). In other prophetic material Eden is used as an image for restored Israel (see Isa 51:3; Ezek 36:35), but for Joel the image is reversed. For a similar reversal of prophetic imagery, see Joel 3:10, Micah 4:3, and Isaiah 2:4.

3 Fire devours in front of them,
and behind them a flame burns.
Before them the land is like the garden of Eden,
but after them a desolate wilderness,
and nothing escapes them.

4 They have the appearance of horses,
and like war-horses they charge.
5 As with the rumbling of chariots,
they leap on the tops of the mountains,
like the crackling of a flame of fire
devouring the stubble,
like a powerful army
drawn up for battle.

6 Before them peoples are in anguish,
all faces grow pale.[a]
7 Like warriors they charge,
like soldiers they scale the wall.
Each keeps to its own course,
they do not swerve from[b] their paths.
8 They do not jostle one another,
each keeps to its own track;
they burst through the weapons

[a] Meaning of Heb uncertain [b] Gk Syr Vg: Heb *they do not take a pledge along*

and are not halted.
9 They leap upon the city,
they run upon the walls;
they climb up into the houses,
they enter through the windows like a thief.

10 The earth quakes before them,
the heavens tremble.
The sun and the moon are darkened,
and the stars withdraw their shining.
11 The LORD utters his voice
at the head of his army;
how vast is his host!
Numberless are those who obey his command.
Truly the day of the LORD is great;
terrible indeed—who can endure it?

12 Yet even now, says the LORD,
return to me with all your heart,
with fasting, with weeping, and with mourning;
13 rend your hearts and not your clothing.
Return to the LORD, your God,
for he is gracious and merciful,
slow to anger, and abounding in steadfast love,
and relents from punishing.
14 Who knows whether he will not turn and relent,
and leave a blessing behind him,
a grain offering and a drink offering
for the LORD, your God?

15 Blow the trumpet in Zion;
sanctify a fast;
call a solemn assembly;
16 gather the people.
Sanctify the congregation;
assemble the aged;
gather the children,
even infants at the breast.
Let the bridegroom leave his room,
and the bride her canopy.

17 Between the vestibule and the altar
let the priests, the ministers of the LORD, weep.
Let them say, "Spare your people, O LORD,
and do not make your heritage a mockery,

2:12-27 Yet even now: An abrupt shift takes places here, moving from reflections on trouble and suffering to hope. A return to God will mean a reversal of fortunes—soil, animals, and people now rejoice and are glad (see 1:5-20); the years of locusts will be repaid (1:4; 2:25).

2:13-14 gracious and merciful: These verses describe God in five ways: gracious, merciful, slow to anger, steadfast in love, and relenting from punishing. Jonah 4:2 is the only other place in the Old Testament that describes God in all these ways. Notice also the question "Who knows . . . ?" and compare Jonah 3:9.

2:17 Where is their God?: This question is raised at other times (see Pss 79:10; 115:2). Joel says God's reputation is at stake. Believers in other gods may see Israel's trials and conclude that Yahweh is not supreme.

a byword among the nations.
Why should it be said among the peoples,
'Where is their God?'"

God's Response and Promise

18 Then the LORD became jealous for his land,
and had pity on his people.
19 In response to his people the LORD said:
I am sending you
grain, wine, and oil,
and you will be satisfied;
and I will no more make you
a mockery among the nations.

20 I will remove the northern army far from you,
and drive it into a parched and desolate land,
its front into the eastern sea,
and its rear into the western sea;
its stench and foul smell will rise up.
Surely he has done great things!

21 Do not fear, O soil;
be glad and rejoice,
for the LORD has done great things!
22 Do not fear, you animals of the field,
for the pastures of the wilderness are green;
the tree bears its fruit,
the fig tree and vine give their full yield.

23 O children of Zion, be glad
and rejoice in the LORD your God;
for he has given the early rain[a] for your vindication,
he has poured down for you abundant rain,
the early and the later rain, as before.
24 The threshing floors shall be full of grain,
the vats shall overflow with wine and oil.

25 I will repay you for the years
that the swarming locust has eaten,
the hopper, the destroyer, and the cutter,
my great army, which I sent against you.

26 You shall eat in plenty and be satisfied,
and praise the name of the LORD your God,

[a] Meaning of Heb uncertain

who has dealt wondrously with you.
And my people shall never again be put to shame.
27 You shall know that I am in the midst of Israel,
and that I, the LORD, am your God and there is no other.
And my people shall never again be put to shame.

God's Spirit Poured Out

28[a] Then afterward
I will pour out my spirit on all flesh;
your sons and your daughters shall prophesy,
your old men shall dream dreams,
and your young men shall see visions.
29 Even on the male and female slaves,
in those days, I will pour out my spirit.

30 I will show portents in the heavens and on the earth, blood
and fire and columns of smoke. 31 The sun shall be turned to darkness,
and the moon to blood, before the great and terrible day of the LORD
comes. 32 Then everyone who calls on the name of the LORD shall be
saved; for in Mount Zion and in Jerusalem there shall be those who
escape, as the LORD has said, and among the survivors shall be those
whom the LORD calls.

3[b] For then, in those days and at that time, when I restore the fortunes of Judah and Jerusalem, 2 I will gather all the nations and
bring them down to the valley of Jehoshaphat, and I will enter into
judgment with them there, on account of my people and my heritage
Israel, because they have scattered them among the nations. They
have divided my land, 3 and cast lots for my people, and traded boys
for prostitutes, and sold girls for wine, and drunk it down.
4 What are you to me, O Tyre and Sidon, and all the regions of
Philistia? Are you paying me back for something? If you are paying
me back, I will turn your deeds back upon your own heads swiftly and
speedily. 5 For you have taken my silver and my gold, and have carried
my rich treasures into your temples.[c] 6 You have sold the people of Judah and Jerusalem to the Greeks, removing them far from their own
border. 7 But now I will rouse them to leave the places to which you
have sold them, and I will turn your deeds back upon your own heads.
8 I will sell your sons and your daughters into the hand of the people
of Judah, and they will sell them to the Sabeans, to a nation far away;
for the LORD has spoken.

Judgment in the Valley of Jehoshaphat

9 Proclaim this among the nations:
Prepare war,[d]

2:27 You shall know that I am... the LORD: All the action—both in Israel's troubles and its restoration—is said to be due to God's activity, and it points to the knowledge of God. Compare Exodus (6:7; 7:5; 14:4) and Ezekiel (5:13; 7:4; 25:5). See also 3:17 and Psalm 46:10.

3:2-3 I will gather all the nations: The valley of Jehoshaphat is an unknown place, probably used here for a play on words (Jehoshaphat means "the LORD has judged," which might play off "I will enter into judgment" in 3:2.) The nations that "divided," "cast lots," "traded," and "sold" Israel might be similar to the four kinds of locusts in 1:4.

---

[a] Ch 3.1 in Heb [b] Ch 4.1 in Heb [c] Or *palaces* [d] Heb *sanctify war*

stir up the warriors.
Let all the soldiers draw near,
let them come up.
10 Beat your plowshares into swords,
and your pruning hooks into spears;
let the weakling say, "I am a warrior."

3:10 plowshares into swords: This image is reversed in Micah 4:3 and Isaiah 2:4.

The LORD judges the nations in Joel 3. How does this fit with the description of the LORD in 2:13?

11 Come quickly,[a]
all you nations all around,
gather yourselves there.
Bring down your warriors, O LORD.
12 Let the nations rouse themselves,
and come up to the valley of Jehoshaphat;
for there I will sit to judge
all the neighboring nations.

13 Put in the sickle,
for the harvest is ripe.
Go in, tread,
for the wine press is full.
The vats overflow,
for their wickedness is great.

14 Multitudes, multitudes,
in the valley of decision!
For the day of the LORD is near
in the valley of decision.
15 The sun and the moon are darkened,
and the stars withdraw their shining.

16 The LORD roars from Zion,
and utters his voice from Jerusalem,
and the heavens and the earth shake.
But the LORD is a refuge for his people,
a stronghold for the people of Israel.

The Glorious Future of Judah

17 So you shall know that I, the LORD your God,
dwell in Zion, my holy mountain.
And Jerusalem shall be holy,
and strangers shall never again pass through it.

3:18-21 In that day: Joel ends with a word of judgment against Israel's neighbors. This is the final and full reversal of fortunes—Israel will be restored and avenged, and Egypt and Edom (see the book of Obadiah) will be made into wastelands.

18 In that day
the mountains shall drip sweet wine,

[a] Meaning of Heb uncertain

the hills shall flow with milk,
and all the stream beds of Judah
shall flow with water;
a fountain shall come forth from the house of the LORD
and water the Wadi Shittim.

19 Egypt shall become a desolation
and Edom a desolate wilderness,
because of the violence done to the people of Judah,
in whose land they have shed innocent blood.
20 But Judah shall be inhabited forever,
and Jerusalem to all generations.
21 I will avenge their blood, and I will not clear the guilty,[a]
for the LORD dwells in Zion.

---

[a] Gk Syr: Heb *I will hold innocent their blood that I have not held innocent*

Amos 5:24

AMOS

Background File

Amos told one of his opponents that he was not a prophet but a farmer who raised sheep and tended fig trees (7:10-14). Though he may not have been part of a prophetic guild that served the king, he speaks in the language of a prophet. His arguments are among the most well-constructed of all the prophets, and his elegant use of the Hebrew language is rivaled only by the psalmists. Amos' prophecies date to the first half of the eighth century B.C.E., making him one of the earliest of the prophets whose writings appear in the Bible.

What's the Story?

According Amos 1:1, Amos was active as a prophet during the time of King Uzziah (783–742 B.C.E.) of the southern kingdom (Judah) and King Jeroboam (786–746 B.C.E.) of the northern kingdom (Israel). Though Amos was from Tekoa, about ten miles south of Jerusalem, he seems to have prophesied mainly at Bethel (7:13), one of the royal sanctuaries of the northern kingdom. It was located about eleven miles north of Jerusalem. Though Amos never mentions the Assyrians by name, he warned that the northern kingdom would be judged on the dark day of the LORD and that the people would be taken into exile beyond Damascus (5:18-27). Amos' prophecies came to pass when the Assyrians defeated Israel and captured its capital, Samaria, in 722 B.C.E. (see 2 Kgs 17:1-6).

Why did Amos bring his message of judgment to the north? Like the other eighth-century prophets, Amos wanted to invite the ten northern tribes (Israel) back into communion with their God (Yahweh) and with their two southern "brothers," Judah and Benjamin. The northern tribes of Israel disrupted the brotherhood that existed under the reign of kings David and Solomon. In 921 B.C.E., after the death of Solomon, the northern tribes worshiped in the wrong places, such as Samaria and Bethel, using rituals regarded as improper by the two southern tribes. While the history of this epic family separation is rich and nuanced, it can be told quite simply.

Judahite interpreters from the southern tribes blamed the north and its leaders for the broken relationship. They pointed to the northerners' rebellious spirit, which was fueled by the polluting influence of Canaanite and Phoenician politics and religious practices. The worship of other gods in addition to Yahweh was a severe offense. Also mentioned frequently was the issue of economic inequality. The mistreatment of the poor and disenfranchised was a key offense. Southerners accused the northerners of abandoning their shared core value, equality among siblings, based in their equality before God.

The book of Amos can be outlined as follows:

- Introduction (1:1-2)
- Oracles condemning Judah, Israel, and neighboring nations (1:3–2:16)
- Oracles against Israel (3:1–6:14)
- Visions of judgment (7:1–9:10)
- Vision of a restored kingdom (9:11-15)

What's the Message?

Amos clearly announces God's concern for justice. Properly observing worship practices, festivals, and sacrifices had little meaning if the people did not treat others with justice and righteousness (5:21-24). Even though the people of the northern kingdom lived in a time that was relatively peaceful and prosperous, they used their wealth for personal comforts, not to help others. Unfair business practices and oppressive taxes that squeezed the poor were common.

Poverty and landlessness were conditions that never should have come to exist in ancient Israel and Judah. The land, a visible sign of God's presence and promise, was a trust from God for the sake of all Israel and Judah. Laws and customs described in Leviticus and Deuteronomy prohibited the accumulation of land and goods in ways that would impoverish a fellow descendant of Abraham and Sarah. Regular land redistribution was a part of the ideal religious landscape.

The message of Amos is a challenge to people and nations caught up in the pursuit of material wealth and comfort. Societies driven by consumerism can lose sight of faithful stewardship of wealth and the just distribution of goods. Amos reminded the people that true faithfulness is trusting in God alone and treating the neighbor with justice.

---

1 The words of Amos, who was among the shepherds of Tekoa, which he saw concerning Israel in the days of King Uzziah of Judah and in the days of King Jeroboam son of Joash of Israel, two years[a] before the earthquake.

Judgment on Israel's Neighbors

2 And he said:

The LORD roars from Zion,
and utters his voice from Jerusalem;
the pastures of the shepherds wither,
and the top of Carmel dries up.

[a] Or *during two years*

1:1 The words of Amos...which he saw concerning Israel: These introductory words establish Amos' authority as a prophet or spokesperson for God.

1:1 in the days of King Uzziah of Judah and...King Jeroboam...of Israel: These clauses establish the time, two years before the earthquake during the reign of Jeroboam of Israel (786–746 B.C.E.) and the solitary reign of Uzziah of Judah (782–743 B.C.E.). The earthquake may have been the one reported to have happened in 760.

1:2—2:3 The LORD roars from Zion: In the first two chapters of Amos, the neighboring nations are condemned to endure harsh judgments and penalties for their actions that the LORD refuses to forget or forgive. These crimes against fellow human beings demonstrate a lack of solidarity, a refusal to acknowledge the basic humanity of Israel, or any of their neighbors. Zion refers to God's holy mountain, the place of the temple, in Jerusalem. For the locations of the places mentioned, see Map 7, p. 2105.

1:3-5 Damascus: The capital of Aram (modern Syria), immediately northeast of Israel, will be punished for treating Gilead harshly after defeating it in battle.

1:6-8 transgressions of Gaza...the Philistines: The Philistines were perennial rivals of Judah and Israel for control of the southwestern regions of Canaan. They are guilty of selling their captives into slavery in Edom.

1:9-10 Tyre: Many years earlier, this Phoenician city-state provided Solomon with cut stone and skilled labor for the construction of the first temple. Tyre was also guilty of selling entire families into slavery in Edom. In addition, the people of Tyre did not respect their family ties with Israel, which dated back to the days of the King David's empire (see 1 Kgs 7:14).

1:11-12 Edom...Bozrah: The Edomites were considered the offspring of Isaac's son Esau (Gen 36:1-14). Israel's distant cousin is guilty of using war captives as slaves in their copper mines.

3 Thus says the LORD:
For three transgressions of Damascus,
and for four, I will not revoke the punishment;[a]
because they have threshed Gilead
with threshing sledges of iron.
4 So I will send a fire on the house of Hazael,
and it shall devour the strongholds of Ben-hadad.
5 I will break the gate bars of Damascus,
and cut off the inhabitants from the Valley of Aven,
and the one who holds the scepter from Beth-eden;
and the people of Aram shall go into exile to Kir,
says the LORD.

6 Thus says the LORD:
For three transgressions of Gaza,
and for four, I will not revoke the punishment;[a]
because they carried into exile entire communities,
to hand them over to Edom.
7 So I will send a fire on the wall of Gaza,
fire that shall devour its strongholds.
8 I will cut off the inhabitants from Ashdod,
and the one who holds the scepter from Ashkelon;
I will turn my hand against Ekron,
and the remnant of the Philistines shall perish,
says the Lord GOD.

9 Thus says the LORD:
For three transgressions of Tyre,
and for four, I will not revoke the punishment;[a]
because they delivered entire communities over to Edom,
and did not remember the covenant of kinship.
10 So I will send a fire on the wall of Tyre,
fire that shall devour its strongholds.

11 Thus says the LORD:
For three transgressions of Edom,
and for four, I will not revoke the punishment;[a]
because he pursued his brother with the sword
and cast off all pity;
he maintained his anger perpetually,[b]
and kept his wrath[c] forever.
12 So I will send a fire on Teman,
and it shall devour the strongholds of Bozrah.

---

[a] Heb *cause it to return* [b] Syr Vg: Heb *and his anger tore perpetually* [c] Gk Syr Vg: Heb *and his wrath kept*

13 Thus says the LORD:
For three transgressions of the Ammonites,
and for four, I will not revoke the punishment;[a]
because they have ripped open pregnant women in Gilead
in order to enlarge their territory.
14 So I will kindle a fire against the wall of Rabbah,
fire that shall devour its strongholds,
with shouting on the day of battle,
with a storm on the day of the whirlwind;
15 then their king shall go into exile,
he and his officials together,
says the LORD.

1:13-15 Ammonites: Israel's odd distant cousins (see Gen 19) are also judged for vicious practices in time of war.

2 Thus says the LORD:
For three transgressions of Moab,
and for four, I will not revoke the punishment;[a]
because he burned to lime
the bones of the king of Edom.
2 So I will send a fire on Moab,
and it shall devour the strongholds of Kerioth,
and Moab shall die amid uproar,
amid shouting and the sound of the trumpet;
3 I will cut off the ruler from its midst,
and will kill all its officials with him,
says the LORD.

2:1-3 Moab: The other strange cousins, whose family line begins in Genesis 19, are judged guilty of disrespecting the remains of the king of Edom.

These first oracles of Amos reveal judgment for mistreatment and many different violations of human rights. What do you make of the idea that God will not allow these kinds of things to go unpunished ("not revoke the punishment")? What is the proper response to such attacks? Do you believe that God approves of vengeance? Why or why not?

Judgment on Judah

4 Thus says the LORD:
For three transgressions of Judah,
and for four, I will not revoke the punishment;[a]
because they have rejected the law of the LORD,
and have not kept his statutes,
but they have been led astray by the same lies
after which their ancestors walked.
5 So I will send a fire on Judah,
and it shall devour the strongholds of Jerusalem.

2:4-5 Judah . . . rejected the law of the LORD: This oracle against the southern kingdom, Judah, is almost certainly a sixth-century addition to the original oracles against the nations that surrounded Israel. Judah was defeated and Jerusalem was destroyed by the Babylonians in 587 B.C.E., more than 150 years after Amos delivered his oracles of judgment. The phrase "rejected the law of the LORD" is similar to language found in Deuteronomy, which was completed in final form after the people returned from exile in Babylon.

Judgment on Israel

6 Thus says the LORD:
For three transgressions of Israel,
and for four, I will not revoke the punishment;[a]
because they sell the righteous for silver,
and the needy for a pair of sandals—

2:6-8 transgressions of Israel: This list of God's judgments now turns to Israel, the main target of Amos' words. Honest ("righteous") people who could not pay their debts were being sold into slavery. Poor people were also sold for as little as a pair of sandals. Some Israelites engaged in sexual relations forbidden in God's law (Lev 18:6-17; 20:11-12). The "garments taken in pledge" refers to a coat taken as security for a loan.

[a] Heb *cause it to return*

What is a godly way of doing business? How can we protect the dignity of workers by the way we compensate them? What is the proper relationship between work and family?

7 they who trample the head of the poor into the dust of the earth,
and push the afflicted out of the way;
father and son go in to the same girl,
so that my holy name is profaned;
8 they lay themselves down beside every altar
on garments taken in pledge;
and in the house of their God they drink
wine bought with fines they imposed.

2:9-11 Amorite...Egypt: Israel's inhumane treatment of covenant brothers and sisters proved to be no better than any of its neighbors, many of whom God had defeated to protect Judah and Israel and to deliver the promised land to them. For the defeat of the Amorites, see Numbers 21:21-31. For Israel's deliverance from slavery in Egypt, see Exodus 12–14.

9 Yet I destroyed the Amorite before them,
whose height was like the height of cedars,
and who was as strong as oaks;
I destroyed his fruit above,
and his roots beneath.
10 Also I brought you up out of the land of Egypt,
and led you forty years in the wilderness,
to possess the land of the Amorite.
11 And I raised up some of your children to be prophets
and some of your youths to be nazirites.[a]
Is it not indeed so, O people of Israel?
says the LORD.

12 But you made the nazirites[a] drink wine,
and commanded the prophets,
saying, "You shall not prophesy."

13 So, I will press you down in your place,
just as a cart presses down
when it is full of sheaves.[b]
14 Flight shall perish from the swift,
and the strong shall not retain their strength,
nor shall the mighty save their lives;
15 those who handle the bow shall not stand,
and those who are swift of foot shall not save themselves,
nor shall those who ride horses save their lives;
16 and those who are stout of heart among the mighty
shall flee away naked in that day,
says the LORD.

Israel's Guilt and Punishment

3:1—6:14 O people of Israel: The oracles in these chapters are against Israel. The first Israelites to hear the prophecies of Amos must have been surprised and perhaps irritated to find themselves being criticized and mixed-up with unchosen nations in the prophet's net.

3 Hear this word that the LORD has spoken against you, O people
of Israel, against the whole family that I brought up out of the
land of Egypt:

[a] That is, *those separated* or *those consecrated* [b] Meaning of Heb uncertain

2 You only have I known
of all the families of the earth;
therefore I will punish you
for all your iniquities.

3 Do two walk together
unless they have made an appointment?
4 Does a lion roar in the forest,
when it has no prey?
Does a young lion cry out from its den,
if it has caught nothing?
5 Does a bird fall into a snare on the earth,
when there is no trap for it?
Does a snare spring up from the ground,
when it has taken nothing?
6 Is a trumpet blown in a city,
and the people are not afraid?
Does disaster befall a city,
unless the LORD has done it?
7 Surely the Lord GOD does nothing,
without revealing his secret
to his servants the prophets.
8 The lion has roared;
who will not fear?
The Lord GOD has spoken;
who can but prophesy?

9 Proclaim to the strongholds in Ashdod,
and to the strongholds in the land of Egypt,
and say, "Assemble yourselves on Mount[a] Samaria,
and see what great tumults are within it,
and what oppressions are in its midst."
10 They do not know how to do right, says the LORD,
those who store up violence and robbery in their strongholds.
11 Therefore thus says the Lord GOD:
An adversary shall surround the land,
and strip you of your defense;
and your strongholds shall be plundered.

12 Thus says the LORD: As the shepherd rescues from the mouth
of the lion two legs, or a piece of an ear, so shall the people of Israel
who live in Samaria be rescued, with the corner of a couch and part[b]
of a bed.

[a] Gk Syr: Heb *the mountains of* [b] Meaning of Heb uncertain

3:3-8 unless the LORD has done it?: These questions point to cause and effect. The LORD chooses to speak through prophets.

3:7 Lord GOD: The ways the NRSV translation spells the names of God are relatively simple, but they can be confusing. There are three names for God in the most-used Hebrew text of Amos: *yhwh* (YAH-way), *'lhym* (Eh-low-HEEM), and *'dny* (AH-do-NIGH). (Elsewhere in this Bible these names may appear in notes as Yahweh, Elohim, and Adonai).

Amos frequently uses these names in combinations such as *'dny yhwh*, translated Lord GOD (note the use of all capitals); *yhwh*, translated as LORD; and *yhwh 'lhy tsb't* translated as the LORD, the God of hosts. In short, the reader should be aware that *yhwh* is being translated and spelled as LORD when it stands alone and as GOD when it directly follows *`dny* (Lord). While it is too much to say that the translators have taken liberties in representing these words in English, this is evidence that good translation can seldom consist of a simple one-to-one transfer. Even the best translation is, in some ways, an interpretation.

3:9 Samaria: The capital of Israel.

3:13-15 house of Jacob...altars of Bethel...summer house: "Jacob" is another name for Israel. The holy sanctuary at Bethel and the houses of the wealthy (who have both summer and winter homes) will be destroyed.

4:1 cows of Bashan: The wealthy women of Samaria are compared to the well-fed cows that roamed the pastures of Bashan (see Map 7, p. 2105). These "cows" lie on beds of ivory and call out to their husbands to fetch them drinks. These greedy people should expect a reversal of their fortunes. God cares most for those who are in greatest need.

4:4 Come to Bethel...Gilgal...bring your sacrifices...tithes: These places were traditional worship sites (Gen 28:10-22; Josh 5:2-9; Amos 7:10-17). This call to bring offerings mocks those who are hypocrites, who don't really live according to God's justice.

4:6-10 cleanness of teeth...pestilence: "Cleanness of teeth" refers to going hungry because of famine. Other natural disasters accompany God's judgment—drought, blighted crops, locust swarms, and pestilence, probably referring to one of the plagues that God used to strike Egypt (see Exod 9:3-7, 15, for example).

13 Hear, and testify against the house of Jacob,
says the Lord God, the God of hosts:
14 On the day I punish Israel for its transgressions,
I will punish the altars of Bethel,
and the horns of the altar shall be cut off
and fall to the ground.
15 I will tear down the winter house as well as the summer house;
and the houses of ivory shall perish,
and the great houses[a] shall come to an end,
says the LORD.

4 Hear this word, you cows of Bashan
who are on Mount Samaria,
who oppress the poor, who crush the needy,
who say to their husbands, "Bring something to drink!"
2 The Lord GOD has sworn by his holiness:
The time is surely coming upon you,
when they shall take you away with hooks,
even the last of you with fishhooks.
3 Through breaches in the wall you shall leave,
each one straight ahead;
and you shall be flung out into Harmon,[b]
says the LORD.

4 Come to Bethel—and transgress;
to Gilgal—and multiply transgression;
bring your sacrifices every morning,
your tithes every three days;
5 bring a thank offering of leavened bread,
and proclaim freewill offerings, publish them;
for so you love to do, O people of Israel!
says the Lord GOD.

Israel Rejects Correction

6 I gave you cleanness of teeth in all your cities,
and lack of bread in all your places,
yet you did not return to me,
says the LORD.

7 And I also withheld the rain from you
when there were still three months to the harvest;
I would send rain on one city,
and send no rain on another city;

[a] Or *many houses* [b] Meaning of Heb uncertain

one field would be rained upon,
and the field on which it did not rain withered;
8 so two or three towns wandered to one town
to drink water, and were not satisfied;
yet you did not return to me,
says the LORD.

9 I struck you with blight and mildew;
I laid waste[a] your gardens and your vineyards;
the locust devoured your fig trees and your olive trees;
yet you did not return to me,
says the LORD.

10 I sent among you a pestilence after the manner of Egypt;
I killed your young men with the sword;
I carried away your horses;[b]
and I made the stench of your camp go up into your nostrils;
yet you did not return to me,
says the LORD.

11 I overthrew some of you,
as when God overthrew Sodom and Gomorrah,
and you were like a brand snatched from the fire;
yet you did not return to me,
says the LORD.

4:11 Sodom and Gomorrah: Ancient cities that God destroyed because they were evil (Gen 19:12-29; Jer 49:18).

12 Therefore thus I will do to you, O Israel;
because I will do this to you,
prepare to meet your God, O Israel!

13 For lo, the one who forms the mountains, creates the wind,
reveals his thoughts to mortals,
makes the morning darkness,
and treads on the heights of the earth—
the LORD, the God of hosts, is his name!

A Lament for Israel's Sin

5 Hear this word that I take up over you in lamentation, O house
of Israel:
2 Fallen, no more to rise,
is maiden Israel;
forsaken on her land,
with no one to raise her up.

5:1-3 lamentation…Fallen, no more to rise, is maiden Israel: Amos delivers a lamentation, or song of mourning and despair, for Israel, whose last chance has been squandered.

[a] Cn: Heb *the multitude of* [b] Heb *with the captivity of your horses*

3 For thus says the Lord GOD:
The city that marched out a thousand
shall have a hundred left,
and that which marched out a hundred
shall have ten left.[a]

5:4-5 do not seek Bethel: Israel should seek God, but not in the same places that have led to its ruin. The Bethel, Gilgal and Beer-sheba sanctuaries were the sites of spiritual rebellion against the temple in Jerusalem.

4 For thus says the LORD to the house of Israel:
Seek me and live;
5 but do not seek Bethel,
and do not enter into Gilgal
or cross over to Beer-sheba;
for Gilgal shall surely go into exile,
and Bethel shall come to nothing.

5:6 house of Joseph: Another name for the northern kingdom of Israel.

6 Seek the LORD and live,
or he will break out against the house of Joseph like fire,
and it will devour Bethel, with no one to quench it.
7 Ah, you that turn justice to wormwood,
and bring righteousness to the ground!

5:7 turn justice to wormwood: Wormwood is a bitter-tasting plant that symbolizes sorrow and bitterness in the Bible (see Prov 5:4; Lam 3:15, 19). Israel displaced justice and righteousness for personal gain. Israel has turned justice on its head, apparently believing that the creator of the universe would not notice.

5:8 Pleiades and Orion: These are constellations that God made along with light and darkness.

8 The one who made the Pleiades and Orion,
and turns deep darkness into the morning,
and darkens the day into night,
who calls for the waters of the sea,
and pours them out on the surface of the earth,
the LORD is his name,
9 who makes destruction flash out against the strong,
so that destruction comes upon the fortress.

10 They hate the one who reproves in the gate,
and they abhor the one who speaks the truth.
11 Therefore because you trample on the poor
and take from them levies of grain,
you have built houses of hewn stone,
but you shall not live in them;
you have planted pleasant vineyards,
but you shall not drink their wine.
12 For I know how many are your transgressions,
and how great are your sins—
you who afflict the righteous, who take a bribe,
and push aside the needy in the gate.
13 Therefore the prudent will keep silent in such a time;
for it is an evil time.

5:11-13 trample on the poor . . . take a bribe: Military force and corrupt officials pass for strength in this inverted system. Pushing aside the needy at the gate refers to using legal proceedings that often took place near the city gate to take advantage of the poor. God will return the situation to normal by taking away what the rich and powerful gained unjustly. See also the note on 2:6-8.

[a] Heb adds *to the house of Israel*

14 Seek good and not evil,
    that you may live;
and so the LORD, the God of hosts, will be with you,
    just as you have said.
15 Hate evil and love good,
    and establish justice in the gate;
it may be that the LORD, the God of hosts,
    will be gracious to the remnant of Joseph.

16 Therefore thus says the LORD, the God of hosts, the Lord:
In all the squares there shall be wailing;
    and in all the streets they shall say, "Alas! alas!"
They shall call the farmers to mourning,
    and those skilled in lamentation, to wailing;
17 in all the vineyards there shall be wailing,
    for I will pass through the midst of you,
says the LORD.

The Day of the LORD a Dark Day

18 Alas for you who desire the day of the LORD!
    Why do you want the day of the LORD?
It is darkness, not light;
19 as if someone fled from a lion,
    and was met by a bear;
or went into the house and rested a hand against the wall,
    and was bitten by a snake.
20 Is not the day of the LORD darkness, not light,
    and gloom with no brightness in it?

21 I hate, I despise your festivals,
    and I take no delight in your solemn assemblies.
22 Even though you offer me your burnt offerings and grain
        offerings,
    I will not accept them;
and the offerings of well-being of your fatted animals
    I will not look upon.
23 Take away from me the noise of your songs;
    I will not listen to the melody of your harps.
24 But let justice roll down like waters,
    and righteousness like an ever-flowing stream.

25 Did you bring to me sacrifices and offerings the forty years in
the wilderness, O house of Israel? 26You shall take up Sakkuth your
king, and Kaiwan your star-god, your images,[a] which you made for

[a] Heb *your images, your star-god*

5:14-15 Seek good…establish justice in the gate: God calls for the flow of justice and righteousness to be restored through divine and human collaboration. The rich and powerful will no longer dominate the poor and the weak.

5:18 the day of the LORD!: This common phrase in the prophetic writings refers to God's dark day of judgment (see also Isa 13:6-19; Ezek 30:1-4; Joel 2:1-2; Zeph 1:14-18).

5:21 I hate, I despise your festivals: All of the eighth-century prophets link social justice with proper worship of the one true God. Life and worship are a balance like a fair properly-weighted scale. Worship of other gods and oppression of the poor and the weak are the immoral acts that are most criticized by Amos. Unfaithfulness to Yahweh is all the same. It breaks the communion with covenantal partners both human and divine.

5:23-24 I will not listen to the melody of your harps. But let justice roll down like waters: God rejects the gifts of sacrifice and songs of praise when offered by those who oppress weaker persons in society by legal or illegal means. If God's justice were to roll down like waters and God's righteousness like an ever-flowing stream, there would be room and a place for everyone. Sometimes we act as if we believe that God's righteousness and the justification of creation through Christ have limits. Amos suggests otherwise. God's justice cannot be separated from God's love, which is like limitless waters raging toward us to restore us to wholeness. We are invited back into oneness with God and with one another.

How do Lutherans describe the neighbor? At the heart of Lutheran theology is the neighbor. Luther reminded Christians that the neighbor bore the face of Christ and that they bore the face of Christ to the neighbor. Perhaps he remembered those powerful words from Matthew's gospel: "Truly I tell you, just as you did it to one of the least of these who are members of my family, you did it to me" (see Matt 25:37-40). *Amos 5:24*

What are some of the ways that Christians around the world can work together to seize the opportunity to construct a world according to God's justice and righteousness?

6:1-2 Zion...Gath of the Philistines: This oracle of judgment also includes the leaders in Jerusalem (Zion), capital of the southern kingdom of Judah. See note on 3:9 (Samaria). Calneh and Hamath are cities in Syria. Gath is in the land of the Philistines. See Map 7, p. 2105.

6:4-7 lie on beds of ivory...anoint themselves with the finest oils: The wealthy of Israel lounge around and don't pay any attention to the coming ruin of Joseph (Israel), which their actions are bringing on.

yourselves; [27]therefore I will take you into exile beyond Damascus,
says the LORD, whose name is the God of hosts.

Complacent Self-Indulgence Will Be Punished

6 Alas for those who are at ease in Zion,
and for those who feel secure on Mount Samaria,
the notables of the first of the nations,
to whom the house of Israel resorts!
2 Cross over to Calneh, and see;
from there go to Hamath the great;
then go down to Gath of the Philistines.
Are you better[a] than these kingdoms?
Or is your[b] territory greater than their[c] territory,
3 O you that put far away the evil day,
and bring near a reign of violence?

4 Alas for those who lie on beds of ivory,
and lounge on their couches,
and eat lambs from the flock,
and calves from the stall;
5 who sing idle songs to the sound of the harp,
and like David improvise on instruments of music;
6 who drink wine from bowls,
and anoint themselves with the finest oils,
but are not grieved over the ruin of Joseph!
7 Therefore they shall now be the first to go into exile,
and the revelry of the loungers shall pass away.

8 The Lord GOD has sworn by himself
(says the LORD, the God of hosts):
I abhor the pride of Jacob
and hate his strongholds;
and I will deliver up the city and all that is in it.

9 If ten people remain in one house, they shall die. [10]And if a relative, one who burns the dead,[d] shall take up the body to bring it out
of the house, and shall say to someone in the innermost parts of the
house, "Is anyone else with you?" the answer will come, "No." Then
the relative[e] shall say, "Hush! We must not mention the name of the
LORD."

11 See, the LORD commands,
and the great house shall be shattered to bits,

[a] Or *Are they better* [b] Heb *their* [c] Heb *your* [d] Or *who makes a burning for him* [e] Heb *he*

and the little house to pieces.
12 Do horses run on rocks?
Does one plow the sea with oxen?[a]
But you have turned justice into poison
and the fruit of righteousness into wormwood—
13 you who rejoice in Lo-debar,[b]
who say, "Have we not by our own strength
taken Karnaim[c] for ourselves?"
14 Indeed, I am raising up against you a nation,
O house of Israel, says the LORD, the God of hosts,
and they shall oppress you from Lebo-hamath
to the Wadi Arabah.

6:12 turned justice into poison... wormwood: See note on 5:7.

6:13 Lo-debar...Karnaim: Cities conquered by Israel's Jeroboam II (2 Kgs 14:25). Israel mistakenly boasts that it conquered these cities by its own strength.

6:14 oppress you from Lebohamath to the Wadi Arabah: God will send a nation to oppress the whole land from its northern borders (Lebohamath) to its southern borders (Wadi Arabah).

Locusts, Fire, and a Plumb Line

7 This is what the Lord GOD showed me: he was forming locusts
at the time the latter growth began to sprout (it was the latter
growth after the king's mowings). 2 When they had finished eating the
grass of the land, I said,
"O Lord GOD, forgive, I beg you!
How can Jacob stand?
He is so small!"
3 The LORD relented concerning this;
"It shall not be," said the LORD.

4 This is what the Lord GOD showed me: the Lord GOD was call-
ing for a shower of fire,[d] and it devoured the great deep and was eating
up the land. 5 Then I said,
"O Lord GOD, cease, I beg you!
How can Jacob stand?
He is so small!"
6 The LORD relented concerning this;
"This also shall not be," said the Lord GOD.

7 This is what he showed me: the Lord was standing beside a wall
built with a plumb line, with a plumb line in his hand. 8 And the LORD
said to me, "Amos, what do you see?" And I said, "A plumb line." Then
the Lord said,
"See, I am setting a plumb line
in the midst of my people Israel;
I will never again pass them by;
9 the high places of Isaac shall be made desolate,
and the sanctuaries of Israel shall be laid waste,
and I will rise against the house of Jeroboam with the sword."

7:1—9:15 This is what the Lord God showed me: Chapters 7–9 are comprised of a series of visions intended to warn the Israelites to return to Yahweh before all patience is exhausted. These visions are usually introduced with a phrase that indicates that the LORD is showing Amos a sign.

7:1-9 forming locusts...shower of fire...plumb line: Locust swarms that eat the vegetation of the land and a cosmic fire that boils away the great deep (the waters that were thought to surround the earth and heavens) bring horrible disaster to Israel. Plumb lines are used in construction to make sure walls are built in a straight line. This may refer to God's judgment of whether Israel has been living according to God's perfect righteousness.

[a] Or *Does one plow them with oxen* [b] Or *in a thing of nothingness* [c] Or *horns* [d] Or *for a judgment by fire*

7:10-17 Amaziah, the priest of Bethel, sent to King Jeroboam: See note on 1:1 (Jeroboam). Amos warns the Israelites to repair the breaches in their covenant with their southern brothers. And he says that Israel's King Jeroboam will die by the sword as Israel is taken into exile. Because of his words, Amos finds himself confronted with a deportation order delivered by the priest Amaziah. He is told to go home to Judah and leave the people of Israel in peace. Amos was stirring up revolution against the king. Most Israelites regarded Jeroboam II to be the legitimate king, established by God. Amos also delivers words of judgment against Amaziah and his family (7:16-17).

8:1-2 a basket of summer fruit: Summer fruit harvested at the end of the season here is used to symbolize the end that is coming for the people of Israel. A play on the Hebrew words for "end" and "fruit" is "eternal winter."

8:3 songs of the temple shall become wailings: False worship at Israel's sanctuaries will be silenced by the judgment to come. The judgment will replace the songs of praise with suffering, agony, and silence.

8:4 trample on the needy, and bring to ruin the poor: The abuse of covenantal brothers and sisters is illustrated by the oppression of the poor and the weak.

Amaziah Complains to the King

10 Then Amaziah, the priest of Bethel, sent to King Jeroboam of
Israel, saying, "Amos has conspired against you in the very center of
the house of Israel; the land is not able to bear all his words. 11 For thus
Amos has said,

'Jeroboam shall die by the sword,
and Israel must go into exile
away from his land.' "

12 And Amaziah said to Amos, "O seer, go, flee away to the land of
Judah, earn your bread there, and prophesy there; 13 but never again
prophesy at Bethel, for it is the king's sanctuary, and it is a temple of
the kingdom."

14 Then Amos answered Amaziah, "I am[a] no prophet, nor a
prophet's son; but I am[a] a herdsman, and a dresser of sycamore trees,
15 and the LORD took me from following the flock, and the LORD said
to me, 'Go, prophesy to my people Israel.'

16 "Now therefore hear the word of the LORD.
You say, 'Do not prophesy against Israel,
and do not preach against the house of Isaac.'
17 Therefore thus says the LORD:
'Your wife shall become a prostitute in the city,
and your sons and your daughters shall fall by the sword,
and your land shall be parceled out by line;
you yourself shall die in an unclean land,
and Israel shall surely go into exile away from its land.' "

The Basket of Fruit

8 This is what the Lord GOD showed me—a basket of summer
fruit.[b] 2 He said, "Amos, what do you see?" And I said, "A basket
of summer fruit."[b] Then the LORD said to me,

"The end[c] has come upon my people Israel;
I will never again pass them by.
3 The songs of the temple[d] shall become wailings in that day,"
says the Lord GOD;
"the dead bodies shall be many,
cast out in every place. Be silent!"

4 Hear this, you that trample on the needy,
and bring to ruin the poor of the land,
5 saying, "When will the new moon be over
so that we may sell grain;
and the sabbath,
so that we may offer wheat for sale?

[a] Or *was* [b] Heb *qayits* [c] Heb *qets* [d] Or *palace*

We will make the ephah small and the shekel great,
and practice deceit with false balances,
6 buying the poor for silver
and the needy for a pair of sandals,
and selling the sweepings of the wheat."

7 The LORD has sworn by the pride of Jacob:
Surely I will never forget any of their deeds.
8 Shall not the land tremble on this account,
and everyone mourn who lives in it,
and all of it rise like the Nile,
and be tossed about and sink again, like the Nile of Egypt?

9 On that day, says the Lord GOD,
I will make the sun go down at noon,
and darken the earth in broad daylight.
10 I will turn your feasts into mourning,
and all your songs into lamentation;
I will bring sackcloth on all loins,
and baldness on every head;
I will make it like the mourning for an only son,
and the end of it like a bitter day.

11 The time is surely coming, says the Lord GOD,
when I will send a famine on the land;
not a famine of bread, or a thirst for water,
but of hearing the words of the LORD.
12 They shall wander from sea to sea,
and from north to east;
they shall run to and fro, seeking the word of the LORD,
but they shall not find it.

13 In that day the beautiful young women and the young men
shall faint for thirst.
14 Those who swear by Ashimah of Samaria,
and say, "As your god lives, O Dan,"
and, "As the way of Beer-sheba lives"—
they shall fall, and never rise again.

The Destruction of Israel

9 I saw the LORD standing beside[a] the altar, and he said:
Strike the capitals until the thresholds shake,
and shatter them on the heads of all the people;[b]

[a] Or *on* [b] Heb *all of them*

8:5 new moon be over…false balances…sweepings of the wheat: The crooked business owners in Israel can hardly wait for the new moon festival and Sabbath to be over so they can make money again—often by corrupt business practices. They falsify the usual weights and measures (ephah and shekel) in their favor when they balance out wheat, to which they also add the sweepings (chaff). This kind of practice was forbidden by the law of Moses (Exod 20:15; Deut 25:13-16). See also the note on 2:6-8 (selling the poor into slavery).

8:7-14 by the pride of Jacob…they shall fall, and never rise again: God's word of life will be withdrawn from the faithless and disobedient in Jacob (Israel) who swear by the Ashima of Samaria (8:14). The "Ashima" may refer to the name of a god or to false gods in general. Even though God is still committed to the covenant with Israel, the word of life will be withdrawn for a time. This will lead to sorrowful mourning, which included the wearing of coarse clothing (sackcloth) and shaving the head (8:10).

9:1-8 beside the altar…Strike the capitals…will destroy it: This judgment vision describes the "un-creation" of Israel! No way out remains, whether they dig down to the dark place of the dead (Sheol) or climb a high mountain (Carmel). The abandoned God of Israel is the Creator who knows every hiding place, and every mythic power (such as the sea-serpent) in the universe follows God's commands. This imagery recalls the foundations of the earth and the sea monsters mentioned in Job 38 and 41 and Genesis 1:21.

and those who are left I will kill with the sword;
not one of them shall flee away,
not one of them shall escape.

2 Though they dig into Sheol,
from there shall my hand take them;
though they climb up to heaven,
from there I will bring them down.
3 Though they hide themselves on the top of Carmel,
from there I will search out and take them;
and though they hide from my sight at the bottom of the sea,
there I will command the sea-serpent, and it shall bite them.
4 And though they go into captivity in front of their enemies,
there I will command the sword, and it shall kill them;
and I will fix my eyes on them
for harm and not for good.

5 The Lord, GOD of hosts,
he who touches the earth and it melts,
and all who live in it mourn,
and all of it rises like the Nile,
and sinks again, like the Nile of Egypt;
6 who builds his upper chambers in the heavens,
and founds his vault upon the earth;
who calls for the waters of the sea,
and pours them out upon the surface of the earth—
the LORD is his name.

9:7-8 Ethiopians...Philistines... Arameans: God compares the Israelites' migration from Egypt to the migration of other neighboring peoples. The Philistines migrated to the Mediterranean coastlands from Caphtor (Crete); the Arameans came from Kir, which may refer to Syria.

9:8 not utterly destroy the house of Jacob: Though the northern kingdom of Israel will be destroyed, the house of Jacob (Judah) will be spared in the end. This is likely a later addition.

7 Are you not like the Ethiopians[a] to me,
O people of Israel? says the LORD.
Did I not bring Israel up from the land of Egypt,
and the Philistines from Caphtor and the Arameans from Kir?
8 The eyes of the Lord GOD are upon the sinful kingdom,
and I will destroy it from the face of the earth
—except that I will not utterly destroy the house of Jacob,
says the LORD.

9 For lo, I will command,
and shake the house of Israel among all the nations
as one shakes with a sieve,
but no pebble shall fall to the ground.
10 All the sinners of my people shall die by the sword,
who say, "Evil shall not overtake or meet us."

---

[a] Or *Nubians;* Heb *Cushites*

The Restoration of David's Kingdom

11 On that day I will raise up
the booth of David that is fallen,
and repair its[a] breaches,
and raise up its[b] ruins,
and rebuild it as in the days of old;
12 in order that they may possess the remnant of Edom
and all the nations who are called by my name,
says the LORD who does this.

13 The time is surely coming, says the LORD,
when the one who plows shall overtake the one who reaps,
and the treader of grapes the one who sows the seed;
the mountains shall drip sweet wine,
and all the hills shall flow with it.
14 I will restore the fortunes of my people Israel,
and they shall rebuild the ruined cities and inhabit them;
they shall plant vineyards and drink their wine,
and they shall make gardens and eat their fruit.
15 I will plant them upon their land,
and they shall never again be plucked up
out of the land that I have given them,
says the LORD your God.

[a] Gk: Heb *their* [b] Gk: Heb *his*

9:11-15 I will raise up the booth of David that is fallen…and rebuild it as in the days of old: The restoration of the relationship between Yahweh and the remnant of the chosen people begins. Israel was destroyed, and the southern kingdom of Judah later was defeated and experienced exile as well (see note on 2:4-5). After a radical cleansing, a new beginning is possible. The optimistic tone of these final verses leads some to see them as an addition during the time of Judah's exile in Babylon, intended to remind the southern tribes that their time of judgment and purification is at an end.

What parallels do you see between Israel in Amos' time and modern society? What primary message do you take away from reading Amos?

Obadiah v. 18

OBADIAH

Background File

The name "Obadiah" means "Servant of Yah" (an abbreviation of Yahweh). Teachers of the Jewish faith traditionally connected this prophet with an administrator in King Ahab's court (1 Kgs 18:3-4), but it is more likely that the Obadiah of this book is another person. An exact date for the book is difficult to determine, yet it seems likely that it was written after the destruction of Jerusalem (see v. 11). Obadiah's vision, then, is delivered to a people mourning the loss of their kingdom, stinging from the betrayal of a neighboring country (Edom), and needing a word of hope.

What's the Story?

The first word in the book, in Hebrew, is "vision." God often communicates a message through visions or dreams (see also Isa 1:1; Nah 1:1; Hab 2:2; Dan 1:17). The message to Obadiah is for Edom, a country to the east and south of Israel (see Map 7, p. 2105). Edom was understood to be a "brother" to Israel. In the Old Testament Edom's roots are traced back to Esau, the twin brother of Israel's ancestor Jacob (see Gen 25:19-34; Amos 1:11-12). In Obadiah both Edom and Esau are used to talk about the same nation (vv. 6, 8, 9, 18, 19, 21). "House of" (vv. 17-18) is an expression for a nation or kingdom. In addition to addressing the house of Edom, Obadiah refers to the houses of Joseph and Judah (in other words, Israel).

Obadiah is unique among the prophets in that it is a single chapter and a single address or speech. Scholars have traditionally recognized two distinctive sections (vv. 1-14 and 16-21, with 15 serving as a link between the two). However, the book as it now stands is better read as a single vision with three scenes:

An oracle of judgment condemning Edom (vv. 1-7)
A catalogue reminding Edom of its past offenses (vv. 8-14)
The day of the LORD, when Israel will be restored (vv. 15-21)

What's the Message?

Obadiah's vision is about justice and hope. All that Edom should not have done (an accusation made eight times in vv. 12-14) to Israel "on the day of distress" is reviewed and will be turned back on Edom on "the day of the LORD" (v. 15). In other words, what Edom first did to Israel now will be done to Edom. This concept of punishing with an "eye for an eye" is called *retributive justice*.

But the punishment of Edom is not all that Obadiah envisions. The climax of the book, vv. 19-20, records a list of nations, places, and peoples that surround Israel: the Negeb and Mount Esau to the south, Shephelah and the Philistines to the west; Benjamin and Gilead to the east; Phoenicia and Zarephath to the north (see Map 7, p. 2105). This list reflects the extent of the nation of Israel when it had been at its height—all that Israel possessed then will be returned. Obadiah's message is that Israel will be restored, its glory will be renewed, and Edom will be punished.

Proud Edom Will Be Brought Low

1 The vision of Obadiah.

Thus says the Lord GOD concerning Edom:
We have heard a report from the LORD,
and a messenger has been sent among the nations:
"Rise up! Let us rise against it for battle!"
2 I will surely make you least among the nations;
you shall be utterly despised.
3 Your proud heart has deceived you,
you that live in the clefts of the rock,[a]
whose dwelling is in the heights.
You say in your heart,
"Who will bring me down to the ground?"
4 Though you soar aloft like the eagle,
though your nest is set among the stars,
from there I will bring you down,
says the LORD.

Pillage and Slaughter Will Repay Edom's Cruelty

5 If thieves came to you,
if plunderers by night
—how you have been destroyed!—
would they not steal only what they wanted?
If grape-gatherers came to you,
would they not leave gleanings?
6 How Esau has been pillaged,
his treasures searched out!
7 All your allies have deceived you,
they have driven you to the border;

1 The vision of Obadiah: Obadiah is one of three prophetic books introduced as a "vision" (see also Isa 1:1; Nah 1:1).

2-3 proud heart: Edom's pride is a problem. Edom takes pride in its "rock," its national strength and mountainous land that provides a position of safety. (In verse 7, Edom also takes pride in its alliances with other countries.) Edom's pride is in contrast with what the Psalms say about finding safety in God as our "rock" (Pss 18:2; 31:3; 71:3).

How does pride separate us from both God and our neighbors?

5-9 how you have been destroyed!: These verses may be read as a lament (a song of mourning or pity) spoken over Edom as it is destroyed, but it is more likely that the intent is to ridicule the prideful and treacherous country (see also Ezek 26:15-21; Amos 1:11-12).

Read verses 5-9 aloud in a harsh, sarcastic tone. Does that change the way you hear or understand the words?

[a] Or *clefts of Sela*

your confederates have prevailed against you;
those who ate[a] your bread have set a trap for you—
there is no understanding of it.
8 On that day, says the LORD,
I will destroy the wise out of Edom,
and understanding out of Mount Esau.
9 Your warriors shall be shattered, O Teman,
so that everyone from Mount Esau will be cut off.

Edom Mistreated His Brother

10 For the slaughter and violence done to your brother Jacob,
shame shall cover you,
and you shall be cut off forever.
11 On the day that you stood aside,
on the day that strangers carried off his wealth,
and foreigners entered his gates
and cast lots for Jerusalem,
you too were like one of them.
12 But you should not have gloated[b] over[c] your brother
on the day of his misfortune;
you should not have rejoiced over the people of Judah
on the day of their ruin;
you should not have boasted
on the day of distress.
13 You should not have entered the gate of my people
on the day of their calamity;
you should not have joined in the gloating over Judah's[d] disaster
on the day of his calamity;
you should not have looted his goods
on the day of his calamity.
14 You should not have stood at the crossings
to cut off his fugitives;
you should not have handed over his survivors
on the day of distress.

15 For the day of the LORD is near against all the nations.
As you have done, it shall be done to you;
your deeds shall return on your own head.
16 For as you have drunk on my holy mountain,
all the nations around you shall drink;
they shall drink and gulp down,[e]
and shall be as though they had never been.

11-16 On the day: Everything that Edom did to Israel is listed. Verses 15-16 describe the "day of the LORD" (see also Isa 13:6, 9; Jer 46:10; Ezek 30:3; Joel 2:1, 11; Zeph 1:7, 14; Mal 3:2-3), when Edom itself will experience what it did to Israel (see Lev 24:19-20; Matt 5:38-42).

The sins we commit and the mistakes we make often come back to haunt us. What can we do about those mistakes and our sin?

[a] Cn: Heb lacks *those who ate* [b] Heb *But do not gloat* (and similarly through verse 14) [c] Heb *on the day of* [d] Heb *his* [e] Meaning of Heb uncertain

Israel's Final Triumph

17 But on Mount Zion there shall be those that escape,
and it shall be holy;
and the house of Jacob shall take possession of those who
dispossessed them.
18 The house of Jacob shall be a fire,
the house of Joseph a flame,
and the house of Esau stubble;
they shall burn them and consume them,
and there shall be no survivor of the house of Esau;
for the LORD has spoken.
19 Those of the Negeb shall possess Mount Esau,
and those of the Shephelah the land of the Philistines;
they shall possess the land of Ephraim and the land of Samaria,
and Benjamin shall possess Gilead.
20 The exiles of the Israelites who are in Halah[a]
shall possess[b] Phoenicia as far as Zarephath;
and the exiles of Jerusalem who are in Sepharad
shall possess the towns of the Negeb.
21 Those who have been saved[c] shall go up to Mount Zion
to rule Mount Esau;
and the kingdom shall be the LORD's.

19-21 the kingdom shall be the LORD's: Everything that is returned to Israel (vv. 17, 19, 20) really belongs to God (see also Ps 135:4). Israel will return to glory, but the true king of Israel is the LORD (1 Sam 8:7; Ps 99), and every kingdom belongs to God.

Why do Lutherans say our possessions belong to God? All that we have, as individual believers and as the church, comes from the Lord. Martin Luther writes, "God daily and abundantly provides shoes and clothing, food and drink, house and farm, spouse and children, fields, livestock, and all property—along with all the necessities and nourishment for this body and life" (*SC*:13). God blesses us with these gifts and calls upon us to use them wisely and graciously. *Obadiah vv. 19-21*

---

[a] Cn: Heb *in this army* [b] Cn: Meaning of Heb uncertain [c] Or *Saviors*

Jonah 1:4

JONAH

Background File

The book of Jonah is listed among the books of the prophets, but it is more like a short story. The story's title character, Jonah, son of Amittai, is never called a prophet, though God calls him to deliver the kind of message prophets deliver. We don't know who wrote the book, and it is difficult to pinpoint exactly when this story was written. But certain clues in the book provide hints (see below).

What's the Story?

Jonah is unique among the prophetic books of the Bible. While the others are mostly made up of prophetic speeches, Jonah contains only one short prophetic speech (3:4). The rest of the book is about Jonah himself. Jonah openly disobeys God's command to go to Nineveh. He tries to run far away from God. God pursues him and causes a great fish to swallow him. Jonah calls out to God and recognizes God as his deliverer. After God has the fish vomit Jonah out, he then goes to Nineveh as God first asked him to do. But when his prophetic message causes the people of Nineveh to repent, Jonah becomes so angry that he wishes for death. Why? That's the plot twist that is key to understanding the story and why it was written.

The LORD calls Jonah to speak a prophetic word of judgment to the powerful city of Nineveh, the capital of Assyria. Assyria had been a feared enemy of the people of Israel. In 722 B.C.E. it defeated the northern kingdom of Israel and forced many of its people to leave their homes. So when God called Jonah to deliver his message to the hated Assyrians in Nineveh, Jonah wanted no part of it. He runs away, not because he is afraid to do what he is called to do, but because he knows what might happen. He knew that the LORD is a "gracious God and merciful, slow to anger, . . . and ready to relent from punishing" (4:2). In other words, he knew that if he warned the Ninevites to repent, God was likely to forgive them.

The story is making a clear point about God's love extending even to Israel's enemies. This is not common among the books of the prophets. This message also contrasts with the attitude that fueled the religious and social reforms found in such books as Ezra and Nehemiah. Those books describe life for Israel in the time following the exile in Babylon (after 539 B.C.E.), when God's people returned to rebuild Jerusalem and the temple. Ezra's religious reforms called for strict measures, such as Israelite men divorcing foreign wives. The religious community was especially concerned about being influenced by other religions, and this made them less open to those who did not live according to Jewish law and worship Israel's God. For this reason, many scholars think the story of Jonah was written sometime after the exile in Babylon ended, and long after Nineveh's reign of terror ended. Nineveh itself was defeated and destroyed in 612 B.C.E. Another hint about when this story may have been written relates to that date. Jonah 3:3 states that Nineveh *was* a great city, perhaps signaling that at the time the story was written, Nineveh had already been destroyed.

What's the Message?

Jonah, like the book of Ruth, offers a vision in which God's love and mercy is not only available to the people of Israel, but to other peoples as well. That message comes through in the story's plot twists, irony, and even comedy. The message of the book of Jonah is not about what kind of fish swallowed Jonah, nor about how he was able to survive inside the fish for three days. Nor is the message to be found in knowing just how big Nineveh was at the time, or what kind of plant grew up overnight to shade Jonah from the sun.

Instead, we must look for the message of Jonah in the gracious action of God in the history of God's people, and in relationship to God's creation. Jonah paints a picture of a God who pushes God's people to go beyond religious and ethnic boundaries to share the love and mercy of God with all nations, even those who were the traditional enemies of Israel. In Jonah, we see a concrete example of God's desire to save all people. The story uses irony when it shows the non-Hebrews (the sailors on the boat and the Ninevites) as the ones who end up praying to God and asking for God's mercy. Even though the destruction of Nineveh would have seemed justified to the original readers, the story takes a surprising twist. When the Ninevites express remorse for their evil actions, God decides to spare Nineveh, its people, and even its animals.

We also learn from Jonah that God is a God of surprises. God often has different things in store for us than what we had planned or imagined for ourselves. In relationship with such a God, the calling for us today is the same as it was for Jonah: to trust God always in all things, and believe that God knows better what we need than we do ourselves.

Finally, the book of Jonah illustrates how difficult it is for us to follow God's will, when we would so much rather follow our own desires. The relationship between Jonah and God shows a prophet who seems to want to control God and resists when God asks something of him that he does not want to do. In the end, however, God shows Jonah the wisdom of God's actions and the necessity of obeying God in all things. Like Jonah, we want to control God. But the story of Jonah shows how God is in control—of wind and waves, of swimming fish, and, most importantly, of helping us see the way of mercy and forgiveness.

Jonah Tries to Run Away from God

1:2 Go at once to Nineveh, that great city: Nineveh was the capital city of Assyria, a hated enemy of Israel. It was located on the Tigris River in Mesopotamia (modern-day Iraq). See Map 8, p. 2106. At the height of its power, Nineveh was one of the most powerful cities in the world, and its people did not know or fear Israel's God.

1:2-3 But Jonah set out to flee to Tarshish: Tarshish was about as far from Nineveh as one could get. It was located somewhere on the far coast of the Mediterranean, perhaps on the coast of modern-day Spain, while Nineveh was located in modern-day Iraq. See the map below. Jonah decided it was better to disobey the Lord than deliver a message that would save one of Israel's arch-enemies.

When have you run from God in your own life? Are you still running? How did God bring you back?

1:9 I am a Hebrew…I worship the Lord: At the time, monotheism, the worship of only one god, was unique among Near Eastern cultures. By identifying himself

1 Now the word of the Lord came to Jonah son of Amittai, saying,
2“Go at once to Nineveh, that great city, and cry out against it; for
their wickedness has come up before me.” 3But Jonah set out to flee to
Tarshish from the presence of the Lord. He went down to Joppa and
found a ship going to Tarshish; so he paid his fare and went on board,
to go with them to Tarshish, away from the presence of the Lord.

4 But the Lord hurled a great wind upon the sea, and such a
mighty storm came upon the sea that the ship threatened to break up.
5Then the mariners were afraid, and each cried to his god. They threw
the cargo that was in the ship into the sea, to lighten it for them. Jonah, meanwhile, had gone down into the hold of the ship and had lain
down, and was fast asleep. 6The captain came and said to him, “What
are you doing sound asleep? Get up, call on your god! Perhaps the
god will spare us a thought so that we do not perish.”

7 The sailors[a] said to one another, “Come, let us cast lots, so that
we may know on whose account this calamity has come upon us.” So
they cast lots, and the lot fell on Jonah. 8Then they said to him, “Tell
us why this calamity has come upon us. What is your occupation?
Where do you come from? What is your country? And of what people are you?” 9“I am a Hebrew,” he replied. “I worship the Lord, the

[a] Heb *They*

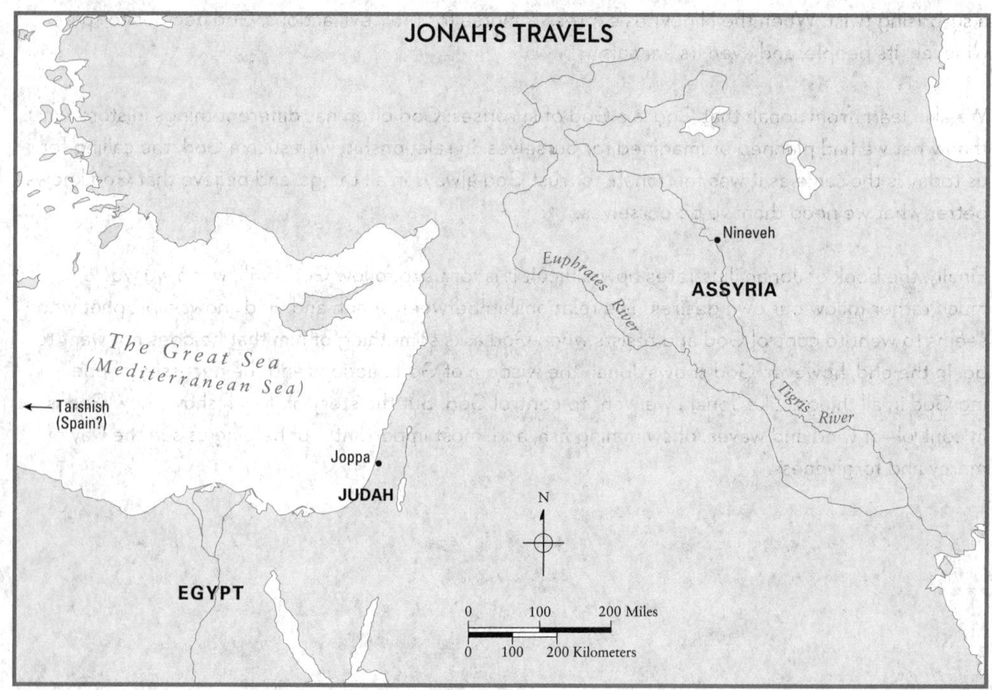

God of heaven, who made the sea and the dry land." [10]Then the men
were even more afraid, and said to him, "What is this that you have
done!" For the men knew that he was fleeing from the presence of the
LORD, because he had told them so.
11 Then they said to him, "What shall we do to you, that the sea
may quiet down for us?" For the sea was growing more and more
tempestuous. [12]He said to them, "Pick me up and throw me into the
sea; then the sea will quiet down for you; for I know it is because of
me that this great storm has come upon you." [13]Nevertheless the men
rowed hard to bring the ship back to land, but they could not, for the
sea grew more and more stormy against them. [14]Then they cried out
to the LORD, "Please, O LORD, we pray, do not let us perish on account of this man's life. Do not make us guilty of innocent blood; for
you, O LORD, have done as it pleased you." [15]So they picked Jonah up
and threw him into the sea; and the sea ceased from its raging. [16]Then
the men feared the LORD even more, and they offered a sacrifice to
the LORD and made vows.
17[a] But the LORD provided a large fish to swallow up Jonah; and
Jonah was in the belly of the fish three days and three nights.

A Psalm of Thanksgiving

2 Then Jonah prayed to the LORD his God from the belly of the
fish, [2]saying,

"I called to the LORD out of my distress,
and he answered me;
out of the belly of Sheol I cried,
and you heard my voice.
3 You cast me into the deep,
into the heart of the seas,
and the flood surrounded me;
all your waves and your billows
passed over me.
4 Then I said, 'I am driven away
from your sight;
how[b] shall I look again
upon your holy temple?'
5 The waters closed in over me;
the deep surrounded me;
weeds were wrapped around my head
6 at the roots of the mountains.
I went down to the land
whose bars closed upon me forever;
yet you brought up my life from the Pit,

[a] Ch 2.1 in Heb [b] Theodotion: Heb *surely*

this way, Jonah contrasted himself with the sailors, who worshiped a variety of gods. One of the story's ironic moments follows. When the storm came, all the sailors were praying to their gods for help, while Jonah, the only one whose God could actually save them, was sleeping.

1:14-16 they cried out to the LORD...offered a sacrifice: Here is an example of irony in the story. The non-Hebrew sailors pray to and worship Jonah's God, the God of Israel.

What does Luther say about God's alien work? God's "alien work" is a technical theological term that refers to the work of God's judgment done in response to human sin. Because God's true nature is love, God's words or action of judgment are always in service to God's "proper" work of love and forgiveness. When God causes the fish to swallow Jonah, it is in response to Jonah's disobedience to God. Through this "alien work," God calls Jonah back into right relationship with God, and renews his faith in God's purpose for his life. From our perspective, this work of God sometimes seems harsh. But God's judgment makes us aware of our sins and our need for God's saving mercy in Jesus Christ. *Jonah 1:17*

1:17 Jonah was in the belly of the fish three days and three nights: Christians may recall here the words of Matthew 12:38-40 and be reminded of Christ's three days in the tomb. In this story we see another example of God bringing life out of death. For all practical purposes, Jonah was dead while inside the fish. God's bringing him up out of the depths and the darkness symbolizes a rebirth for Jonah and the gift of new life.

2:1-10 Jonah prayed to the LORD: Jonah's prayer is like a song (psalm) of thanksgiving. It looks like Jonah is in danger in the fish's belly, but perhaps Jonah realizes that God is with him, using the fish to save him from drowning. This is why he gives thanks and claims God to be the one who delivers (2:10).

2:1 Have you ever prayed to God in a time of great distress? What did you say? How did God answer you?

2:2 Sheol: This is the dark underground world of the dead, a shadowy place of isolation, but not what Christians would consider hell.

2:4, 7 your holy temple: Prayers and sacrifices were offered to God at Israel's temple in Jerusalem. Though Jonah was far from this place of worship, he knew that God would hear his prayers.

3:3 exceedingly large city: A city that took three days to walk across would have been huge. This is probably an example of how the story uses exaggeration to make a point. Jonah travels only one day into the city to deliver his message (3:4).

3:4 And [Jonah] cried out, "Forty days more, and Nineveh shall be overthrown": A briefer prophetic word would be hard to find in the Bible. Even though Jonah has obeyed the Lord and come to Nineveh, he presents God's message as briefly as possible. Perhaps he was hoping his words would be ignored.

3:4 [Jonah] cried out: In Luke 11:29-30, Jesus reminds his followers that he is a sign of God's judgment, just as Jonah served as a sign of God's judgment to Nineveh.

3:6-8 sackcloth...sat in ashes: Sackcloth was rough cloth made of goat or camel hair. When people wanted to express extreme sadness, they put on this clothing, rubbed ashes or dirt on their bodies, and went without eating or drinking. Even the animals got into the act (3:8).

3:10 God saw...God changed: Sometimes we think that the will of God is set and can't be influenced or altered. This verse reminds us that God's loving kindness and mercy towards God's creation is stronger than God's determination to punish. God is not deaf to the cries of God's people, and God listens when we call.

4:2 That is why I fled...you are a gracious God: Now it becomes clear why Jonah ran away in the first place. He knew God would forgive the people of Nineveh if they showed they were sorry for their evil actions.

What does Luther say about how we are to treat our neighbors? Though the words of this commandment say only that we should not slander or gossip about our neighbors, Luther argues that the Eighth Commandment demands that we go a step further. We are to "come to their defense, speak well of them, and interpret everything they do in the best possible light" (*SC*:8). Jonah illus-

O Lord my God.
7 As my life was ebbing away,
I remembered the Lord;
and my prayer came to you,
into your holy temple.
8 Those who worship vain idols
forsake their true loyalty.
9 But I with the voice of thanksgiving
will sacrifice to you;
what I have vowed I will pay.
Deliverance belongs to the Lord!"

[10]Then the Lord spoke to the fish, and it spewed Jonah out upon the
dry land.

Conversion of Nineveh

3 The word of the Lord came to Jonah a second time, saying,
[2]"Get up, go to Nineveh, that great city, and proclaim to it the
message that I tell you." [3]So Jonah set out and went to Nineveh, according to the word of the Lord. Now Nineveh was an exceedingly
large city, a three days' walk across. [4]Jonah began to go into the city,
going a day's walk. And he cried out, "Forty days more, and Nineveh
shall be overthrown!" [5]And the people of Nineveh believed God; they
proclaimed a fast, and everyone, great and small, put on sackcloth.

6 When the news reached the king of Nineveh, he rose from his
throne, removed his robe, covered himself with sackcloth, and sat in
ashes. [7]Then he had a proclamation made in Nineveh: "By the decree
of the king and his nobles: No human being or animal, no herd or
flock, shall taste anything. They shall not feed, nor shall they drink
water. [8]Human beings and animals shall be covered with sackcloth,
and they shall cry mightily to God. All shall turn from their evil ways
and from the violence that is in their hands. [9]Who knows? God may
relent and change his mind; he may turn from his fierce anger, so that
we do not perish."

10 When God saw what they did, how they turned from their evil
ways, God changed his mind about the calamity that he had said he
would bring upon them; and he did not do it.

Jonah's Anger

4 But this was very displeasing to Jonah, and he became angry.
[2]He prayed to the Lord and said, "O Lord! Is not this what I
said while I was still in my own country? That is why I fled to Tarshish
at the beginning; for I knew that you are a gracious God and merciful,
slow to anger, and abounding in steadfast love, and ready to relent
from punishing. [3]And now, O Lord, please take my life from me, for
it is better for me to die than to live." [4]And the Lord said, "Is it right

for you to be angry?" 5 Then Jonah went out of the city and sat down
east of the city, and made a booth for himself there. He sat under it in
the shade, waiting to see what would become of the city.
6 The LORD God appointed a bush,[a] and made it come up over
Jonah, to give shade over his head, to save him from his discomfort;
so Jonah was very happy about the bush. 7 But when dawn came up
the next day, God appointed a worm that attacked the bush, so that it
withered. 8 When the sun rose, God prepared a sultry east wind, and
the sun beat down on the head of Jonah so that he was faint and asked
that he might die. He said, "It is better for me to die than to live."

Jonah Is Reproved

9 But God said to Jonah, "Is it right for you to be angry about the
bush?" And he said, "Yes, angry enough to die." 10 Then the LORD said,
"You are concerned about the bush, for which you did not labor and
which you did not grow; it came into being in a night and perished in
a night. 11 And should I not be concerned about Nineveh, that great
city, in which there are more than a hundred and twenty thousand
persons who do not know their right hand from their left, and also
many animals?"

---

[a] Heb *qiqayon,* possibly *the castor bean plant*

trates that this is one of the hardest commandments for us to keep, especially when our neighbors are people we don't like very much. Jonah is not happy when the Ninevites repent and are spared, much as we are not always happy when God seems to favor someone we don't think deserves it. *Jonah 4:1*

4:6 God appointed a bush: Just as God sent the fish to save Jonah from the sea, here the plant gives Jonah shade. See NRSV footnote *a* for the possible identity of the plant.

4:11 should I not be concerned about Nineveh...and also many animals: Here we see that animals also matter to God, and that God cares about their welfare, too. The loving covenant God has made with creation includes not only human life but all life. The message would have been clear: God's love and mercy are not limited to the people of Israel.

Who is the main actor in the story of Jonah—God or Jonah? Why? How can the message of the story influence the way you live?

Micah 6:8

MICAH

Background File

During much of the eighth century B.C.E., leaders in Israel (the northern kingdom) and Judah (the southern kingdom) lived comfortably. They seemed unaware of the threatening situation developing in surrounding countries. Four prophets responded to the situation. At mid-century, Amos and Hosea warned leaders in the north. Later Isaiah prophesied in Jerusalem to warn leaders in the southern kingdom. During this time, the prophet Micah came from a small village called Moresheth (twenty-five miles southwest of Jerusalem) to speak out against problems in both kingdoms.

What's the Story?

In the mid-eighth century B.C.E., the Assyrian Empire (see Map 8, p. 2106) began expanding westward. By 732 B.C.E., Tiglath-pileser III had conquered the city of Damascus. Then he surrounded Samaria, Israel's capital city, for three years. Finally, in 722, he forced the city to surrender (See 2 Kgs 17). The cities and countryside of Israel were laid waste. The people were removed to live in exile in various locations in Mesopotamia.

In 711 a new Assyrian king, Sargon II, defeated the coastal city of Ashdod (see Map 7, p. 2105). His successor, Sennacherib, terrorized the countryside of the southern kingdom. Forty-six towns and villages in Judah were destroyed, including many near Micah's home at Moresheth. By 701, Sennacherib's army surrounded Jerusalem, Judah's capital city.

Archaeologists have uncovered layers of burnt material at many places, especially Lachish. A large stone tablet from Nineveh, known as the Sennacherib Prism, gives the Assyrian side of the story. It describes the final stage of this invasion as Jerusalem was surrounded. Judah's King Hezekiah was like a bird in a cage, it says. The situation looked hopeless for the residents of Jerusalem. The future of the people and the kingdom was at risk.

Sennacherib eventually retreated, and Jerusalem was spared (Isaiah 37:36-37). The prophet Isaiah praised the leadership of King Hezekiah. He set the people to work repairing the city walls. He also dug a water canal, known still today as Hezekiah's tunnel (see Map 6, p. 2104). It winds nearly one-third of a mile underground to carry fresh water from the Gihon spring to the pool of Siloam. Most of all, Isaiah recognized Hezekiah's faithful worship of God. All proclaimed "God is with us" in the city (Isaiah 7:14; see NRSV footnote *c*).

This victory for Jerusalem came after Micah's career, when the outcome was uncertain, yet Micah's call had led him to speak out boldly.

What's the Message?

The words of Micah can be divided into two categories: oracles or messages of judgment and oracles of hope. These oracles were not written out ahead of time. Micah spoke the words, and one of his followers wrote them down later. Rather than arranging the oracles in historical order, they appear in a contrasting pattern in the book of Micah. Condemning words are followed by good news for the future. This is shown in the following outline of the book:

Oracles of judgment (1:2–2:11)
Oracles of hope (2:12-13)

Oracles of judgment (3:1-12)
Oracles of hope (4:1–5:15)

Oracles of judgment (6:1–7:7)
Oracles of hope (7:8-20)

In general, Micah's words of judgment are directed toward powerful leaders, including politicians, priests, and greedy traders. The words of hope are reserved for the people without power who remained faithful to God's covenant or promise to Abraham. In all three sections of Micah, hope wins out in the end.

---

1 The word of the LORD that came to Micah of Moresheth in the
days of Kings Jotham, Ahaz, and Hezekiah of Judah, which he saw
concerning Samaria and Jerusalem.

Judgment Pronounced against Samaria

2 Hear, you peoples, all of you;
listen, O earth, and all that is in it;
and let the Lord GOD be a witness against you,
the Lord from his holy temple.
3 For lo, the LORD is coming out of his place,
and will come down and tread upon the high places of the earth.
4 Then the mountains will melt under him
and the valleys will burst open,
like wax near the fire,
like waters poured down a steep place.
5 All this is for the transgression of Jacob

1:1 The word of the LORD: Micah's name means "Who is like the LORD?" In the book of Micah, the answer to the question clearly is *not* the powerful. Micah's home, Moresheth, was a small village twenty-five miles southwest of Jerusalem. Yet his call took him to Samaria and Jerusalem, the capital cities of the northern and southern kingdoms. There he stood face-to-face before kings.

1:2-7 Hear, you peoples: The first oracle of judgment begins here (see introduction). Jacob, Israel, and Samaria are all names for the northern kingdom. The southern kingdom is also called Judah and Jerusalem. Note the image of a courtroom (see also 6:1-8). Here God brings charges against people who have not kept the covenant relationship (1:2-3) with God, which began with Abraham and Sarah. Mountains and valleys testify to God's power (1:4). The verdict or judgment announces that Assyria will destroy Samaria (1:6-7).

and for the sins of the house of Israel.
What is the transgression of Jacob?
Is it not Samaria?
And what is the high place[a] of Judah?
Is it not Jerusalem?
6 Therefore I will make Samaria a heap in the open country,
a place for planting vineyards.
I will pour down her stones into the valley,
and uncover her foundations.
7 All her images shall be beaten to pieces,
all her wages shall be burned with fire,
and all her idols I will lay waste;
for as the wages of a prostitute she gathered them,
and as the wages of a prostitute they shall again be used.

1:8-16 I will lament: This passage is similar to a psalm of lament or grief. Typical mourning practices of the time included going barefoot and naked (1: 8) and shaving the head (1:16). Micah's wailing sounds like the cries of desert animals (1:8). Ten towns near Jerusalem will soon be destroyed. In Hebrew, the various words of destruction for each location sound like that village's name.

The Doom of the Cities of Judah

8 For this I will lament and wail;
I will go barefoot and naked;
I will make lamentation like the jackals,
and mourning like the ostriches.
9 For her wound[b] is incurable.
It has come to Judah;
it has reached to the gate of my people,
to Jerusalem.

10 Tell it not in Gath,
weep not at all;
in Beth-leaphrah
roll yourselves in the dust.
11 Pass on your way,
inhabitants of Shaphir,
in nakedness and shame;
the inhabitants of Zaanan
do not come forth;
Beth-ezel is wailing
and shall remove its support from you.
12 For the inhabitants of Maroth
wait anxiously for good,
yet disaster has come down from the LORD
to the gate of Jerusalem.
13 Harness the steeds to the chariots,
inhabitants of Lachish;
it was the beginning of sin

---

[a] Heb *what are the high places* [b] Gk Syr Vg: Heb *wounds*

to daughter Zion,
for in you were found
the transgressions of Israel.
14 Therefore you shall give parting gifts
to Moresheth-gath;
the houses of Achzib shall be a deception
to the kings of Israel.
15 I will again bring a conqueror upon you,
inhabitants of Mareshah;
the glory of Israel
shall come to Adullam.
16 Make yourselves bald and cut off your hair
for your pampered children;
make yourselves as bald as the eagle,
for they have gone from you into exile.

Social Evils Denounced

2 Alas for those who devise wickedness
and evil deeds[a] on their beds!
When the morning dawns, they perform it,
because it is in their power.
2 They covet fields, and seize them;
houses, and take them away;
they oppress householder and house,
people and their inheritance.
3 Therefore thus says the LORD:
Now, I am devising against this family an evil
from which you cannot remove your necks;
and you shall not walk haughtily,
for it will be an evil time.
4 On that day they shall take up a taunt song against you,
and wail with bitter lamentation,
and say, "We are utterly ruined;
the LORD[b] alters the inheritance of my people;
how he removes it from me!
Among our captors[c] he parcels out our fields."
5 Therefore you will have no one to cast the line by lot
in the assembly of the LORD.

6 "Do not preach"—thus they preach—
"one should not preach of such things;
disgrace will not overtake us."
7 Should this be said, O house of Jacob?

2:1-11 Alas for those who devise wickedness: Micah condemns the confiscation of family land by the wealthy and greedy. Verse 4 is a lament to be sung by victims when the Assyrians attack and the landgrabbers (2:1) stand helpless. The powerful will not be in "the assembly of the LORD" (2:5). They oppose Micah (2:8), who reminds them of God's care for those who have limited power and few possessions, especially orphans and widows. Verse 11 has a note of sarcasm about so-called prophets who distract from greater problems with accusations about drinking.

[a] Cn: Heb *work evil* [b] Heb *he* [c] Cn: Heb *the rebellious*

Is the LORD's patience exhausted?
Are these his doings?
Do not my words do good
to one who walks uprightly?
8 But you rise up against my people[a] as an enemy;
you strip the robe from the peaceful,[b]
from those who pass by trustingly
with no thought of war.
9 The women of my people you drive out
from their pleasant houses;
from their young children you take away
my glory forever.
10 Arise and go;
for this is no place to rest,
because of uncleanness that destroys
with a grievous destruction.[c]
11 If someone were to go about uttering empty falsehoods,
saying, "I will preach to you of wine and strong drink,"
such a one would be the preacher for this people!

A Promise for the Remnant of Israel

2:12-13 I will surely gather: This is Micah's first oracle of hope (see introduction). It uses the image of a good shepherd for God, who will gather faithful survivors from Israel, the northern kingdom.

12 I will surely gather all of you, O Jacob,
I will gather the survivors of Israel;
I will set them together
like sheep in a fold,
like a flock in its pasture;
it will resound with people.
13 The one who breaks out will go up before them;
they will break through and pass the gate,
going out by it.
Their king will pass on before them,
the LORD at their head.

Wicked Rulers and Prophets

3:1-12 Listen: This second oracle of judgment (see introduction) criticizes self-centered political leaders (3:1), rulers, chiefs (3:9), priests, and so-called prophets (3:11). They control both the north (Jacob and Israel) and the south (Zion and Jerusalem). Many prophets become popular by making light of the sins of society while blaming the victims (3:5). Unlike these prophets, who are profit-motivated, prophets like Micah proclaim justice (3:8). Micah is not as optimistic as the prophet Isaiah about the role of King Hezekiah (715–687 B.C.E.; see 3:12). In some ways Micah was wrong. Jerusalem was in fact spared in 701 B.C.E. when the Assyrian Sennacherib retreated. However, eventually corruption caught up with Jerusalem. A century later, the prophet Jeremiah (Jer 26:18-19) quoted Micah to judge Jerusalem in the face of threats from Babylonia.

3 And I said:
Listen, you heads of Jacob
and rulers of the house of Israel!
Should you not know justice?—
2 you who hate the good and love the evil,
who tear the skin off my people,[d]
and the flesh off their bones;
3 who eat the flesh of my people,

---

[a] Cn: Heb *But yesterday my people rose* [b] Cn: Heb *from before a garment* [c] Meaning of Heb uncertain
[d] Heb *from them*

flay their skin off them,
break their bones in pieces,
and chop them up like meat[a] in a kettle,
like flesh in a caldron.

4 Then they will cry to the LORD,
but he will not answer them;
he will hide his face from them at that time,
because they have acted wickedly.

5 Thus says the LORD concerning the prophets
who lead my people astray,
who cry "Peace"
when they have something to eat,
but declare war against those
who put nothing into their mouths.
6 Therefore it shall be night to you, without vision,
and darkness to you, without revelation.
The sun shall go down upon the prophets,
and the day shall be black over them;
7 the seers shall be disgraced,
and the diviners put to shame;
they shall all cover their lips,
for there is no answer from God.
8 But as for me, I am filled with power,
with the spirit of the LORD,
and with justice and might,
to declare to Jacob his transgression
and to Israel his sin.

9 Hear this, you rulers of the house of Jacob
and chiefs of the house of Israel,
who abhor justice
and pervert all equity,
10 who build Zion with blood
and Jerusalem with wrong!
11 Its rulers give judgment for a bribe,
its priests teach for a price,
its prophets give oracles for money;
yet they lean upon the LORD and say,
"Surely the LORD is with us!
No harm shall come upon us."
12 Therefore because of you

---

[a] Gk: Heb *as*

Zion shall be plowed as a field;
Jerusalem shall become a heap of ruins,
and the mountain of the house a wooded height.

Peace and Security through Obedience

4 In days to come
the mountain of the LORD's house
shall be established as the highest of the mountains,
and shall be raised up above the hills.
Peoples shall stream to it,
2 and many nations shall come and say:
"Come, let us go up to the mountain of the LORD,
to the house of the God of Jacob;
that he may teach us his ways
and that we may walk in his paths."
For out of Zion shall go forth instruction,
and the word of the LORD from Jerusalem.
3 He shall judge between many peoples,
and shall arbitrate between strong nations far away;
they shall beat their swords into plowshares,
and their spears into pruning hooks;
nation shall not lift up sword against nation,
neither shall they learn war any more;
4 but they shall all sit under their own vines and under their own fig trees,
and no one shall make them afraid;
for the mouth of the LORD of hosts has spoken.

5 For all the peoples walk,
each in the name of its god,
but we will walk in the name of the LORD our God
forever and ever.

Restoration Promised after Exile

6 In that day, says the LORD,
I will assemble the lame
and gather those who have been driven away,
and those whom I have afflicted.
7 The lame I will make the remnant,
and those who were cast off, a strong nation;
and the LORD will reign over them in Mount Zion
now and forevermore.

8 And you, O tower of the flock,
hill of daughter Zion,

4:1-13 In days to come: Compare this second oracle of hope (see introduction) or peace poem with Isaiah 4:1-5. In the book of Joel, farm tools are converted into weapons of war (Joel 3:10), but in Micah a return to farming brings prosperity. "Tower of the flock" (4:8) was a nickname for Jerusalem. Micah's vision is inclusive. A woman in childbirth symbolizes hope that makes such a change possible (4:10). Shepherd-like leadership will unite, rather than divide, the community. The reference to Babylon in 4:10 is unexpected. Micah's original words will be remembered when Babylon attacks Jerusalem a century later.

4:3 swords into plowshares: Peace or *shalom* is not a bandage that simply covers up conflict, like the false cries of "peace" that silence support for people who are powerless (3:5). Shalom is a state of wholeness and well-being. In Micah's description of shalom, weapons are destroyed (4:3), everyone finds enough food (4:4), and strangers are welcomed (4:2).

to you it shall come,
the former dominion shall come,
the sovereignty of daughter Jerusalem.

9 Now why do you cry aloud?
Is there no king in you?
Has your counselor perished,
that pangs have seized you like a woman in labor?
10 Writhe and groan,[a] O daughter Zion,
like a woman in labor;
for now you shall go forth from the city
and camp in the open country;
you shall go to Babylon.
There you shall be rescued,
there the LORD will redeem you
from the hands of your enemies.

11 Now many nations
are assembled against you,
saying, "Let her be profaned,
and let our eyes gaze upon Zion."
12 But they do not know
the thoughts of the LORD;
they do not understand his plan,
that he has gathered them as sheaves to the threshing floor.
13 Arise and thresh,
O daughter Zion,
for I will make your horn iron
and your hoofs bronze;
you shall beat in pieces many peoples,
and shall[b] devote their gain to the LORD,
their wealth to the Lord of the whole earth.

5 [c] Now you are walled around with a wall;[d]
siege is laid against us;
with a rod they strike the ruler of Israel
upon the cheek.

The Ruler from Bethlehem

2[e] But you, O Bethlehem of Ephrathah,
who are one of the little clans of Judah,
from you shall come forth for me

[a] Meaning of Heb uncertain [b] Gk Syr Tg: Heb *and I will* [c] Ch 4.14 in Heb [d] Cn Compare Gk: Meaning of Heb uncertain [e] Ch 5.1 in Heb

5:1-15 you, O Bethlehem: When the Assyrian king Sennacherib lays siege to Jerusalem, the situation looks hopeless. Micah, however, remembers God's promise that David's family would provide servant leaders (2 Sam 7). The shepherd David came from the humble village of Bethlehem, and Jesus would later be born there. Micah is quoted in Matthew, with an unusual twist: the once humble village of Bethlehem will be elevated among the cities of Judah (Matt 2:6). The name *Ephrathah,* meaning "fertile," promises that the hungry will be fed (5:2). Nimrod (5:6) was an ancient ruler of Assyria (Gen 10:9).

one who is to rule in Israel,
whose origin is from of old,
from ancient days.
3 Therefore he shall give them up until the time
when she who is in labor has brought forth;
then the rest of his kindred shall return
to the people of Israel.
4 And he shall stand and feed his flock in the strength of the LORD,
in the majesty of the name of the LORD his God.
And they shall live secure, for now he shall be great
to the ends of the earth;
5 and he shall be the one of peace.

If the Assyrians come into our land
and tread upon our soil,[a]
we will raise against them seven shepherds
and eight installed as rulers.
6 They shall rule the land of Assyria with the sword,
and the land of Nimrod with the drawn sword;[b]
they[c] shall rescue us from the Assyrians
if they come into our land
or tread within our border.

The Future Role of the Remnant

7 Then the remnant of Jacob,
surrounded by many peoples,
shall be like dew from the LORD,
like showers on the grass,
which do not depend upon people
or wait for any mortal.
8 And among the nations the remnant of Jacob,
surrounded by many peoples,
shall be like a lion among the animals of the forest,
like a young lion among the flocks of sheep,
which, when it goes through, treads down
and tears in pieces, with no one to deliver.
9 Your hand shall be lifted up over your adversaries,
and all your enemies shall be cut off.

5:10-14 the work of your hands: Instead of trusting God, people trusted in equipment for battle, fortified cities, predictions of the future, and other gods (represented by the "images," "pillars," and "sacred poles" used to worship Canaanite gods).

Instead of trusting God, what kinds of things do we trust?

10 In that day, says the LORD,
I will cut off your horses from among you
and will destroy your chariots;
11 and I will cut off the cities of your land

[a] Gk: Heb *in our palaces* [b] Cn: Heb *in its entrances* [c] Heb *he*

and throw down all your strongholds;
12 and I will cut off sorceries from your hand,
and you shall have no more soothsayers;
13 and I will cut off your images
and your pillars from among you,
and you shall bow down no more
to the work of your hands;
14 and I will uproot your sacred poles[a] from among you
and destroy your towns.
15 And in anger and wrath I will execute vengeance
on the nations that did not obey.

God Challenges Israel

6 Hear what the LORD says:
Rise, plead your case before the mountains,
and let the hills hear your voice.
2 Hear, you mountains, the controversy of the LORD,
and you enduring foundations of the earth;
for the LORD has a controversy with his people,
and he will contend with Israel.

3 "O my people, what have I done to you?
In what have I wearied you? Answer me!
4 For I brought you up from the land of Egypt,
and redeemed you from the house of slavery;
and I sent before you Moses,
Aaron, and Miriam.
5 O my people, remember now what King Balak of Moab devised,
what Balaam son of Beor answered him,
and what happened from Shittim to Gilgal,
that you may know the saving acts of the LORD."

What God Requires

6 "With what shall I come before the LORD,
and bow myself before God on high?
Shall I come before him with burnt offerings,
with calves a year old?
7 Will the LORD be pleased with thousands of rams,
with ten thousands of rivers of oil?
Shall I give my firstborn for my transgression,
the fruit of my body for the sin of my soul?"
8 He has told you, O mortal, what is good;
and what does the LORD require of you

[a] Heb *Asherim*

6:1-8 Hear: This third oracle of judgment (see introduction) continues through 7:7. It includes a courtroom scene, like 1:2-7. Again nature witnesses to the power of God (6:1-2). God accuses the people of neglecting the covenant. They have forgotten Moses, Aaron, and Miriam, leaders from the Exodus (6:4), and the prophet Balaam, who was bribed by King Balak to curse Israel (Num 22–24). Israel traveled from Shittim to Gilgal after crossing the Jordan (Josh 3–4). The defense makes a case on the basis of religious practices (6:6-7). However, like Amos (Amos 5:21-24), Micah despises false religious actions that ignore the neighbor. The verdict is introduced with the simple question: What does the LORD require of you?

6:8 justice...kindness: "Justice" (*mishpat* in Hebrew) is about fairness and equality (Isa 1:27; Amos 5:24). "Kindness" (*chesed* in Hebrew) describes merciful actions such as loyalty and integrity. "Walking humbly" is set in contrast with the rapid strides of the powerful.

What does the LORD require of us? God's word comes to us as law and gospel. Law shows us that we have fallen short of God's ways and are in drastic need of God's help. Gospel is God's merciful intervention. This concept fits well with the prophets' messages or oracles of judgment and hope. So, for example, Micah 6:8 is part of a judgment oracle. The question "What does the LORD require?" points out our shortcomings, but it does not provide a way to salvation. *Micah 6:8*

6:9-16 wicked scales . . . dishonest weights?: The judgment oracle in 6:9-16 is a warning to people who take advantage of the poor through dishonest practices, like Kings Omri (876-869 B.C.E.) and Ahab of Samaria (869–850). The prophet Elijah confronted King Ahab for confiscating a vineyard that belonged to man named Naboth (1 Kgs 21).

but to do justice, and to love kindness,
and to walk humbly with your God?

Cheating and Violence to Be Punished

9 The voice of the LORD cries to the city
(it is sound wisdom to fear your name):
Hear, O tribe and assembly of the city![a]
10 Can I forget[b] the treasures of wickedness in the house of the wicked,
and the scant measure that is accursed?
11 Can I tolerate wicked scales
and a bag of dishonest weights?
12 Your[c] wealthy are full of violence;
your[d] inhabitants speak lies,
with tongues of deceit in their mouths.
13 Therefore I have begun[e] to strike you down,
making you desolate because of your sins.
14 You shall eat, but not be satisfied,
and there shall be a gnawing hunger within you;
you shall put away, but not save,
and what you save, I will hand over to the sword.
15 You shall sow, but not reap;
you shall tread olives, but not anoint yourselves with oil;
you shall tread grapes, but not drink wine.
16 For you have kept the statutes of Omri[f]
and all the works of the house of Ahab,
and you have followed their counsels.
Therefore I will make you a desolation, and your[g] inhabitants an object of hissing;
so you shall bear the scorn of my people.

The Total Corruption of the People

7:1-7 your enemies are members of your own household: This judgment oracle is a lament. The people's relationships with God and neighbors have suffered. Family relationships now break down too (see Matt 10:35-36 and Luke 12:53). The mention of God three times in 7:7 shows confidence in the face of despair, making the transition to end on a word of hope.

7 Woe is me! For I have become like one who,
after the summer fruit has been gathered,
after the vintage has been gleaned,
finds no cluster to eat;
there is no first-ripe fig for which I hunger.
2 The faithful have disappeared from the land,
and there is no one left who is upright;
they all lie in wait for blood,
and they hunt each other with nets.
3 Their hands are skilled to do evil;

---

[a] Cn Compare Gk: Heb *tribe, and who has appointed it yet?* [b] Cn: Meaning of Heb uncertain [c] Heb *Whose* [d] Heb *whose* [e] Gk Syr Vg: Heb *have made sick* [f] Gk Syr Vg Tg: Heb *the statutes of Omri are kept* [g] Heb *its*

the official and the judge ask for a bribe,
and the powerful dictate what they desire;
thus they pervert justice.[a]

4 The best of them is like a brier,
the most upright of them a thorn hedge.
The day of their[b] sentinels, of their[b] punishment, has come;
now their confusion is at hand.

5 Put no trust in a friend,
have no confidence in a loved one;
guard the doors of your mouth
from her who lies in your embrace;

6 for the son treats the father with contempt,
the daughter rises up against her mother,
the daughter-in-law against her mother-in-law;
your enemies are members of your own household.

7 But as for me, I will look to the LORD,
I will wait for the God of my salvation;
my God will hear me.

Penitence and Trust in God

8 Do not rejoice over me, O my enemy;
when I fall, I shall rise;
when I sit in darkness,
the LORD will be a light to me.

9 I must bear the indignation of the LORD,
because I have sinned against him,
until he takes my side
and executes judgment for me.
He will bring me out to the light;
I shall see his vindication.

10 Then my enemy will see,
and shame will cover her who said to me,
"Where is the LORD your God?"
My eyes will see her downfall;[c]
now she will be trodden down
like the mire of the streets.

A Prophecy of Restoration

11 A day for the building of your walls!
In that day the boundary shall be far extended.

12 In that day they will come to you
from Assyria to[d] Egypt,
and from Egypt to the River,

7:8-20 the LORD will be a light to me: This is the third oracle of hope (see introduction). Restoration will occur amid two superpowers, Egypt, and Assyria with its Euphrates River (7:12; see Map 8, p. 2106). Bashan and Gilead (7:14) were fertile lands to the east of Israel. Verse 18—"Who is a God like you . . . ?"—returns to a play on Micah's name ("Who is like the LORD?"; see note on 1:1). God's nature is compassion and faithfulness.

---

[a] Cn: Heb *they weave it* [b] Heb *your* [c] Heb lacks *downfall* [d] One Ms: MT *Assyria and cities of*

from sea to sea and from mountain to mountain.
13 But the earth will be desolate
because of its inhabitants,
for the fruit of their doings.

14 Shepherd your people with your staff,
the flock that belongs to you,
which lives alone in a forest
in the midst of a garden land;
let them feed in Bashan and Gilead
as in the days of old.
15 As in the days when you came out of the land of Egypt,
show us[a] marvelous things.
16 The nations shall see and be ashamed
of all their might;
they shall lay their hands on their mouths;
their ears shall be deaf;
17 they shall lick dust like a snake,
like the crawling things of the earth;
they shall come trembling out of their fortresses;
they shall turn in dread to the LORD our God,
and they shall stand in fear of you.

God's Compassion and Steadfast Love

18 Who is a God like you, pardoning iniquity
and passing over the transgression
of the remnant of your[b] possession?
He does not retain his anger forever,
because he delights in showing clemency.
19 He will again have compassion upon us;
he will tread our iniquities under foot.
You will cast all our[c] sins
into the depths of the sea.
20 You will show faithfulness to Jacob
and unswerving loyalty to Abraham,
as you have sworn to our ancestors
from the days of old.

---

[a] Cn: Heb *I will show him* [b] Heb *his* [c] Gk Syr Vg Tg: Heb *their*

Nahum 1:7-8

NAHUM

Background File

The unknown prophet Nahum appeared around 612 B.C.E. to a troubled Jewish community under great stress. His sayings (oracles) encouraged the people to celebrate the destruction of Nineveh, the capital city of Assyria. According to Nahum, the fall of the city was God's judgment against the oppressive Assyrian superpower.

What's the Story?

In the seventh century B.C.E. Assyria was a mighty military empire headquartered in areas today mostly known as Syria and northern Iraq. Assyria was known for the brutal way it ruled its many conquered territories. It seemed unbeatable until the nation of Media (roughly north of modern Iran) and the rising Babylonian Empire (roughly present Iraq) joined together and managed to defeat Assyria and destroy its capital, Nineveh. Communities throughout the ancient Near East celebrated the fall of Nineveh. In those times, each nation worshiped a national warrior god. People believed that a nation's victory proved the power of its god. A nation's defeat demonstrated that god's lack of power. Using military language easily understood in his time, Nahum describes Israel's God as the divine warrior. Unlike the gods of other nations, Israel's God holds oppressive nations accountable for their acts and rescues people suffering under their oppressive rule. In a series of incredibly colorful sayings (oracles), Nahum proclaims that Assyria's fall is due to God's intervention against the oppressive superpower.

What's the Message?

To the Jewish community of Nahum's time, the message was clear: God has heard the cry of those who were afflicted and suffered and is acting to break the oppressor's back. It is time to celebrate and rejoice. To us in our time, however, the message may seem less clear. Unlike in ancient times, God is not pictured primarily as a divine warrior. Generally, as Christians we do not assume that the victories and defeats of nations reflect the victories or defeats of their particular gods.

The sometimes vicious and vengeful language of Nahum is troubling. What do we do with texts like this? How can we hear the message God intends us to hear in these pages? Lutherans make sense of texts like these by bringing them into conversation with other biblical texts. Only two biblical books end with questions—Nahum and Jonah. While Nahum's final question emphasizes Nineveh's never-ending cruelty (3:19), God's final question to Jonah emphasizes God's concern even for the people of that wicked city (4:11). Reading these two books together helps us to see more clearly that God is both just (Nahum) and merciful (Jonah) toward oppressors and oppressed alike.

1:2-5 A jealous and avenging God is the Lord: This is an example of the language of Israel's God as the divine warrior. Troubling though the language may be, in the ancient world it signified God's commitment to maintain justice on earth.

Note how God is described in 1:2-8. What thoughts do you have about these descriptions? For example, are you comforted, frightened, confused, or something else? Why?

1:3 The Lord is slow to anger… will by no means clear the guilty: This phrase, repeated often throughout the Old Testament, reminds us that God waits patiently for guilty persons and nations to repent, but also calls them to accountability. God is both just and merciful.

1:7 The Lord is good, a stronghold: The prophet Nahum reminds the faithful that God holds them close and will never let them go, even when they suffer greatly. Despite chaos all around, and perhaps within, they can take refuge and protection in God!

How can the words in 1:15 ("one who brings good tidings, who proclaims peace") give you strength when you are going through hard times?

1 An oracle concerning Nineveh. The book of the vision of Nahum of Elkosh.

The Consuming Wrath of God

2 A jealous and avenging God is the Lord,
the Lord is avenging and wrathful;
the Lord takes vengeance on his adversaries
and rages against his enemies.
3 The Lord is slow to anger but great in power,
and the Lord will by no means clear the guilty.

His way is in whirlwind and storm,
and the clouds are the dust of his feet.
4 He rebukes the sea and makes it dry,
and he dries up all the rivers;
Bashan and Carmel wither,
and the bloom of Lebanon fades.
5 The mountains quake before him,
and the hills melt;
the earth heaves before him,
the world and all who live in it.

6 Who can stand before his indignation?
Who can endure the heat of his anger?
His wrath is poured out like fire,
and by him the rocks are broken in pieces.
7 The Lord is good,
a stronghold in a day of trouble;
he protects those who take refuge in him,
8 even in a rushing flood.
He will make a full end of his adversaries,[a]
and will pursue his enemies into darkness.
9 Why do you plot against the Lord?
He will make an end;
no adversary will rise up twice.
10 Like thorns they are entangled,
like drunkards they are drunk;
they are consumed like dry straw.
11 From you one has gone out

---

[a] Gk: Heb *of her place*

who plots evil against the LORD,
one who counsels wickedness.

Good News for Judah

12 Thus says the LORD,
"Though they are at full strength and many,[a]
they will be cut off and pass away.
Though I have afflicted you,
I will afflict you no more.
13 And now I will break off his yoke from you
and snap the bonds that bind you."

14 The LORD has commanded concerning you:
"Your name shall be perpetuated no longer;
from the house of your gods I will cut off
the carved image and the cast image.
I will make your grave, for you are worthless."

15[b] Look! On the mountains the feet of one
who brings good tidings,
who proclaims peace!
Celebrate your festivals, O Judah,
fulfill your vows,
for never again shall the wicked invade you;
they are utterly cut off.

The Destruction of the Wicked City

2 A shatterer[c] has come up against you.
Guard the ramparts;
watch the road;
gird your loins;
collect all your strength.

2 (For the LORD is restoring the majesty of Jacob,
as well as the majesty of Israel,
though ravagers have ravaged them
and ruined their branches.)

3 The shields of his warriors are red;
his soldiers are clothed in crimson.
The metal on the chariots flashes
on the day when he musters them;
the chargers[d] prance.

2:1-14 A shatterer has come up against you: In colorful language, the oracles (sayings) of this chapter announce God's judgment against the cruel Assyrian king and his capital city, Nineveh. For Nineveh's location, see Map 8, p. 2106.

2:2 restoring the majesty of Jacob . . . Israel: Jacob is another name for Judah, the southern kingdom of Israel. The names of Israel's twelve tribes came from the names of Jacob's sons and two of his grandsons (see Gen 48–49).

[a] Meaning of Heb uncertain [b] Ch 2.1 in Heb [c] Cn:Heb *scatterer* [d] Cn Compare Gk Syr: Heb *cypresses*

4 The chariots race madly through the streets,
they rush to and fro through the squares;
their appearance is like torches,
they dart like lightning.
5 He calls his officers;
they stumble as they come forward;
they hasten to the wall,
and the mantelet[a] is set up.
6 The river gates are opened,
the palace trembles.
7 It is decreed[a] that the city[b] be exiled,
its slave women led away,
moaning like doves
and beating their breasts.
8 Nineveh is like a pool
whose waters[c] run away.
"Halt! Halt!"—
but no one turns back.
9 "Plunder the silver,
plunder the gold!
There is no end of treasure!
An abundance of every precious thing!"

10 Devastation, desolation, and destruction!
Hearts faint and knees tremble,
all loins quake,
all faces grow pale!
11 What became of the lions' den,
the cave[d] of the young lions,
where the lion goes,
and the lion's cubs, with no one to disturb them?
12 The lion has torn enough for his whelps
and strangled prey for his lionesses;
he has filled his caves with prey
and his dens with torn flesh.

13 See, I am against you, says the LORD of hosts, and I will burn
your[e] chariots in smoke, and the sword shall devour your young lions;
I will cut off your prey from the earth, and the voice of your messengers shall be heard no more.

2:6 river gates are opened: Canals from the Tigris River brought water into Nineveh. The evacuation of the city is like water rushing out of an overflowing pond. Compare to 1:8, which emphasizes God's protection in a time of rushing flood.

Ruin Imminent and Inevitable

3 Ah! City of bloodshed,
utterly deceitful, full of booty—

3:1-19 Ah! City of bloodshed: The language of this chapter is that of an insulting song (taunt). The purpose of such songs is to mock the enemy and to jeer at them. The great pain the prophet feels because of his people's suffering gets expressed in vengeful language toward the nation oppressing them.

[a] Meaning of Heb uncertain [b] Heb *it* [c] Cn Compare Gk: Heb *a pool, from the days that she has become, and they* [d] Cn: Heb *pasture* [e] Heb *her*

no end to the plunder!
2 The crack of whip and rumble of wheel,
galloping horse and bounding chariot!
3 Horsemen charging,
flashing sword and glittering spear,
piles of dead,
heaps of corpses,
dead bodies without end—
they stumble over the bodies!
4 Because of the countless debaucheries of the prostitute,
gracefully alluring, mistress of sorcery,
who enslaves[a] nations through her debaucheries,
and peoples through her sorcery,
5 I am against you,
says the LORD of hosts,
and will lift up your skirts over your face;
and I will let nations look on your nakedness
and kingdoms on your shame.
6 I will throw filth at you
and treat you with contempt,
and make you a spectacle.
7 Then all who see you will shrink from you and say,
"Nineveh is devastated; who will bemoan her?"
Where shall I seek comforters for you?

8 Are you better than Thebes[b]
that sat by the Nile,
with water around her,
her rampart a sea,
water her wall?
9 Ethiopia[c] was her strength,
Egypt too, and that without limit;
Put and the Libyans were her[d] helpers.

10 Yet she became an exile,
she went into captivity;
even her infants were dashed in pieces
at the head of every street;
lots were cast for her nobles,
all her dignitaries were bound in fetters.
11 You also will be drunken,
you will go into hiding;[e]
you will seek

[a] Heb *sells* [b] Heb *No-amon* [c] Or *Nubia;* Heb *Cush* [d] Gk: Heb *your* [e] Meaning of Heb uncertain

3:4 Because of the countless debaucheries of the prostitute: In ancient times, the picture of a prostitute was used to condemn sinful nations and leaders. Prophets often used this kind of language to shame oppressive male leaders by comparing them to these "loose women."

Imagine that you are a Jew who has suffered greatly at the hands of the Assyrians. How would the words in 3:5-7 ("I am against you . . . I will throw filth at you") make you feel? Why? How do you respond to being attacked or put down?

3:8-9 Are you better than Thebes: Thebes was an Egyptian capital city that had been destroyed by the Assyrians. Now, says Nahum, Assyria's capital, Nineveh, has suffered the same fate.

3:12-14 first-ripe figs . . . brick mold: Nineveh's walls would fall as easily as figs shaken from a tree, so the Ninevites try to strengthen the walls with newly made bricks.

3:19 For who has ever escaped your endless cruelty? The book ends with a question rather than a statement. Nahum's anguish and anger is great. See Jonah 4:11 for a concluding question that emphasizes God's mercy rather than judgment. Reading the texts together shows that God is both just and merciful.

The book of Nahum contains some of the most vengeful language in the Old Testament. How do you understand the presence of such language in the Bible? Is there a place for such language in today's world? Why or why not?

a refuge from the enemy.
12 All your fortresses are like fig trees
with first-ripe figs—
if shaken they fall
into the mouth of the eater.
13 Look at your troops:
they are women in your midst.
The gates of your land
are wide open to your foes;
fire has devoured the bars of your gates.

14 Draw water for the siege,
strengthen your forts;
trample the clay,
tread the mortar,
take hold of the brick mold!
15 There the fire will devour you,
the sword will cut you off.
It will devour you like the locust.

Multiply yourselves like the locust,
multiply like the grasshopper!
16 You increased your merchants
more than the stars of the heavens.
The locust sheds its skin and flies away.
17 Your guards are like grasshoppers,
your scribes like swarms[a] of locusts
settling on the fences
on a cold day—
when the sun rises, they fly away;
no one knows where they have gone.

18 Your shepherds are asleep,
O king of Assyria;
your nobles slumber.
Your people are scattered on the mountains
with no one to gather them.
19 There is no assuaging your hurt,
your wound is mortal.
All who hear the news about you
clap their hands over you.
For who has ever escaped
your endless cruelty?

[a] Meaning of Heb uncertain

MARTIN LUTHER
on the Bible

Portrait of Martin Luther by Lucas Cranach the Elder (1472-1553). 1529.

Martin Luther's deep engagement with Scripture caused the Lutheran Reformation. Writing in 1545, a year before his death, Luther recalled how his meditation on Romans 1:17 had affected him. The words of the apostle Paul, "He who through faith is righteous shall live," led Luther to a new understanding of the righteousness or justice of God. Luther remembered that "a totally other face of the entire Scripture showed itself to me." He no longer saw God's righteousness as the righteousness by which God judges us but rather as the way God justifies us, that is, puts us in right relationship with God.

Luther then "ran through the Scripture from memory," he later said, and found similar passages about "the work of God, that is, what God does in us, the power of God, with which he makes us strong, the wisdom of God, with which he makes us wise . . . ." In his "Reformation breakthrough" he came to recognize that God acted in the gospel to give away his righteousness. That was profoundly different from God acting in the law to demand righteousness from us. Luther's insight had tremendous implications for how we read the Bible, how we engage with the Bible's message, and how we live as Christians in the world.

How Luther Read the Bible

For Luther, God's two ways of dealing with humans—law and gospel—gave both content and shape to the biblical message and provided the proper lens for reading the Bible. He recognized that truly understanding the biblical text always rested on fundamental principles of Christian teaching or doctrine. But he also understood these principles to arise from the Bible itself rather than from the mind of the reader. Today we may struggle with the idea that certain core Christian beliefs shape the way we read the biblical text. But Luther and other theologians through the centuries recognized that this is true. Luther always tried to make his presuppositions clear, to show his readers that they originated in the Bible itself, and to show that they truly helped the hearer and reader to understand the biblical message.

Law and Gospel in the Bible

Luther recognized both law and gospel as God's good ways of working in the lives of humans. Sometimes he equated the Old Testament with law and the New Testament with gospel, but more often he recognized that law and gospel were found in both parts of the Bible. God gives us the law to teach us to fear, love, and trust in God above all. The law also helps us to order society, to curb evil, and to provide a standard of righteousness that guides human life. God gives the law so that we may know what good works please God. Luther recognized that some laws in the Bible were outdated or did not apply in his time and place. But he never dismissed biblical laws lightly and never merely because they were inconvenient or difficult. He taught that the biblical laws were one valid expression of the natural law governing humanity, law that could vary according to time and place. Most importantly for Luther, our failure to live up to God's law also reveals our sin and puts to shame all our assumptions about our own human ability.[1] This function (or "use") of the law drove humans to the promise of the gospel.

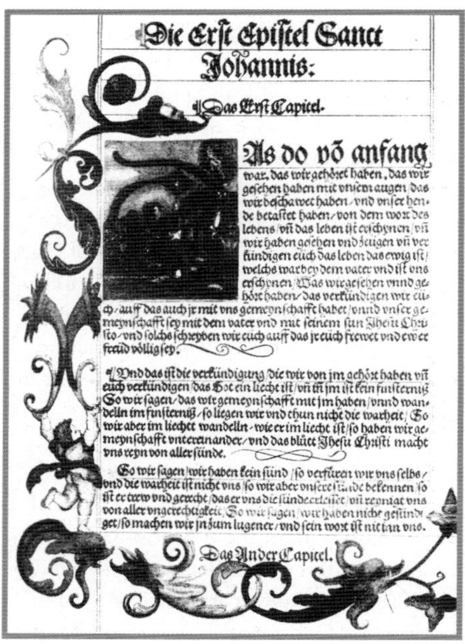

Die Erſt Epiſtel Sanct Johannis:

Das Erſt Capitel.

Als do võ anfang war, das wir gehöret haben, das wir geſehen haben mit vnſern augen, das wir beſchawet haben, vnd vnſer hende betaſtet haben, von dem wort des lebens, vñ das leben iſt erſchynen, vñ wir haben geſehen vnd zeugen vñ verkündigen euch das leben das ewig iſt, welchs war bey dem vater vnd iſt vns erſchynen, Was wir geſehen vnnd gehört haben, das verkündigen wir euch, auff das auch jr mit vns gemeynſchafft habet, vnnd vnſer gemeynſchafft ſey mit dem vater vnd mit ſeinem ſun Jheſu Chriſto, vnd ſolchs ſchreyben wir euch auff das jr euch frewet vnd ewer freud völlig ſey.

Vnd das iſt die verkündigung, die wir von jm gehört haben vñ euch verkündigen, das Got ein liecht iſt, vñ in jm iſt kein finſternis. So wir ſagen, das wir gemeynſchafft mit jm haben, vnnd wandelln im finſternis, ſo liegen wir vnd thun nicht die warheit, So wir aber im liecht wandelln, wie er im liecht iſt, ſo haben wir gemeynſchafft vntereinander, vnd das blüt Jheſu Chriſti macht vns reyn von aller ſünde.

So wir ſagen, wir haben kein ſünd, ſo verfüren wir vns ſelbs, vnd die warheit iſt nicht vns, ſo wir aber vnſere ſünde bekennen, ſo iſt er trew vnd gerecht, das er vns die ſünde erlaſſet, vñ reynigt vns von aller vngerechtigkeit, So wir ſagen, wir haben nicht geſündiget, ſo machen wir jn zum lugener, vnd ſein wort iſt nit in vns.

Das Ander Capitel.

Facsimile of a page of the New Testament printed in 1523.

The gospel is the gracious promise of God in Christ. It grants forgiveness of sin, life, and salvation to the fallen and unworthy sinner. To read the Bible with the gospel as its heart is to "urge Christ" in each biblical text. "The Scriptures," Luther stated, "must be understood in favor of Christ, not against him. For that reason they must either refer to him or must not be held to be true Scriptures." And again: "If one of them had to be parted with, Christ or the law, the law would have to be let go, not Christ."[2] Like Christian interpreters since the earliest era of the church, Luther understood Jesus Christ to be the center of Scripture. Christ was found throughout Scripture, not just in the New Testament. For many prior interpreters Christ was primarily an example to be imitated. But Luther saw Christ first and foremost as gift (gospel) and only secondarily as example (law). For him, this carried very personal implications:

> The chief article and foundation of the gospel is that before you take Christ as an example, you . . . recognize him as a gift, as a present that God has given you and that is your own. This means that when you see or hear of Christ doing or suffering something, you do not doubt that Christ himself, with his deeds and suffering, belongs to you . . . . This is the great fire of the love of God for us, whereby the heart and conscience become happy, secure, and content . . . Now when you

have Christ as the foundation and chief blessing of your salvation, then the other part follows: that you take him as your example, giving yourself in service to your neighbor just as you see that Christ has given himself for you . . . Therefore make note of this, that Christ as a gift nourishes your faith and makes you a Christian. But Christ as an example exercises your works. These do not make you a Christian. Actually they come forth from you because you have already been made a Christian.[3]

Is the Bible the Word of God?

Repeatedly, Luther warned against confusing law and gospel, demand and promise, example and gift, when interpreting Scripture: "It is not yet knowledge of the gospel when you know these doctrines and commandments, but only when the voice comes that says, 'Christ is your own, with his life, teaching, works, death, resurrection, and all that he is, has, does, and can do.'"[4]

So Luther never simply equated the Word of God (both law and gospel) with the written Scriptures. On the contrary, he taught that the word of God is essentially oral in character; it is a "living voice." In a famous passage from the *Church Postil* of 1522, Luther contrasts Moses as a writer of "doctrine" with Christ, who commanded that his teaching "should be orally continued giving no command that it should be written." That the New Testament finally took written form is, for Luther, evidence of "a serious decline and a lack of the Spirit which necessity forced upon us...."[5]

Genesis. Fontispiece Depicting the Creation. From the Luther Bible, 1st edition, 1534.

Where is the Word then? Luther believed that all humanity, all institutions, including the church, are affected by the hurly-burly of events and infected with sin. God's Word is mingled with and hidden under the forces that oppress the church at all times and places. God's Word is realized in the community of faith only because the Word itself acts in us. It forms in us confession of faith, a loving response to divine grace. Although that has been true from Adam to the present day, knowledge and proper understanding of God's Word are not a continuous, unbroken achievement of the church. Rather, our knowledge of God is best understood as God's gift, which draws the spontaneous response of the Christian community to the gospel. It is a response created within the hearts of believers by the Holy Spirit's work in the Word. God, not doctrinal propositions, a pope, or a succession of bishops, provides faithfulness in the church. Therefore, under the guidance of the Spirit, responsible faith requires critical discernment of the text of Scripture, not just listening to the traditions of the church.[6]

Discerning the Scriptures

Luther sought to discern or understand the meaning of biblical texts within his overall theological framework. At the same time he paid close attention to a number of factors, including historical context and literary style. "For before one learns the reason and the motive for what a man says, it is only letters, the shouts of choristers or the songs of nuns. . . .There are many passages in Holy Scripture that are contradictory according to the letters; but when that which motivates them is pointed out, everything is all right."[7] This sense of context even extends to individual authors of Scripture and their differences. In speaking of understanding Paul, for example, Luther declares:

> The histories in the Scriptures are often concise and confused so that they cannot be easily harmonized, as, for example, the denials of Peter and the history of Christ's Passion, etc. Thus Paul is not reciting the entire history here. Therefore I do not expend any labor or concern on harmonizing these things, but here pay attention to Paul's purpose and intention.[8]

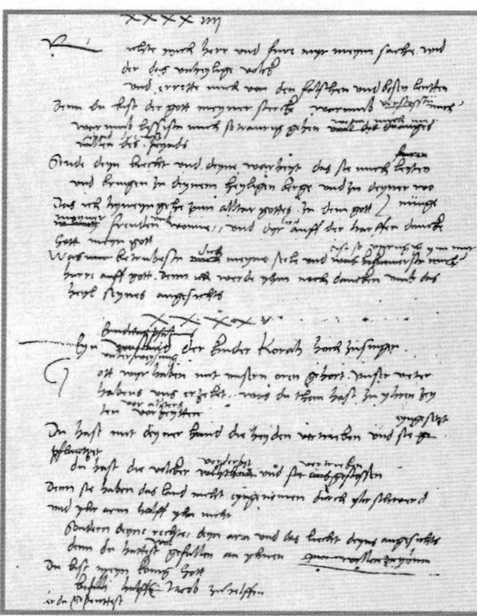

Luther's manuscript of Psalm 43 from his translation of the Bible.

Luther generally rejected the medieval method of interpreting Scripture, which sought four meanings—literal, allegorical, moral, and eschatological—in every text. He used and encouraged others to use the latest and best critical tools for understanding Scripture and making it available to everyone. His own translations of the Bible from the original Hebrew and Greek texts into German are one of the greatest achievements of his age. But while emphasizing the literal meaning, Luther was open to understanding texts in other ways when necessary, and he was willing to admit that he did not fully understand some biblical texts. He realized his readers might have trouble with the style of some texts, but he encouraged them to persevere in understanding Scripture, confident that Christ, the true center and treasure of Scripture, will shine forth. In his *Preface to the Old Testament* he wrote:

> I beg and really caution every pious Christian not to be offended by the simplicity of the language and stories frequently encountered there, but fully realize that, however simple they may seem, these are the very words, works, judgments, and deeds of the majesty, power, and wisdom of the most high God. For these are the Scriptures which make fools of all the wise and understanding, and are open only to the small and simple . . . Therefore dismiss your own opinions and feelings, and think of the Scriptures as the loftiest and noblest of holy things, as the richest of mines which can never be sufficiently explored, in order that you may find that divine wisdom which God here lays before you in such simple guise as to quench all pride. Here you will find the swaddling cloths

and the manger in which Christ lies, and to which the angel points the shepherds [Luke 2:12]. Simple and lowly are these swaddling cloths, but dear is the treasure, Christ, who lies in them.[9]

Luther's focus on Christ as the true treasure of Scripture and the Bible as the "swaddling cloths" that contain Christ does not in any way demean Scripture or lessen its importance. Luther exalted the authority of Scripture in no uncertain terms. The Word of God was his primary weapon against all the powers that threatened him—whether the cosmic powers of sin, death, and the devil, or the earthly powers of a corrupted church, scheming politicians, or inept or heretical theologians. Leaders of the church, regardless of rank, must subordinate themselves to its witness: "The Pope, Luther, Augustine, Paul, an angel from heaven—these should not be masters, judges, or arbiters but only witnesses, disciples, and confessors of Scripture."[10]

Scripture Interprets Itself

Luther believed that Scripture was clear. If humans do not understand it, the problem is the interpreter, not Scripture. His belief in the clarity of Scripture had two important aspects. First, the literal sense of Scripture is identical with its historical content. There is no going behind the text in order to discover a different event than the event reported. Indeed, the question does not even arise. Second, the Bible has a universal and immediate sense, granted by the Holy Spirit and recognized by the eyes of faith that rises above historical conditions and events. Luther heard biblical texts as speaking both to the time in which they were written and to his own time. On the basis of these assumptions, especially the second, Luther attacked the theology of his time and the church of the papacy. He did so with the confidence that his doctrine was identical with the doctrine of Scripture, which is the doctrine of God. "Doctrine is heaven; life is earth."[11]

Babylon burning. From the Apocalypse of Saint John (Rev. 18).
Luther Bible. First edition, ca. 1530.

According to Luther's view of revelation, history—or at least "true" history, the history that brings knowledge of God, is sure and certain. This is the *historia sacra* (sacred history) of Bible and church that is eternal, unchanging, and ever-present. It is the word of God contained in the Scriptures and the community of those who respond to this word. It may be hidden because of the ways of the world and even the power of the church, but it is there for the eyes of faith.

Scripture for the People

Luther wanted all Christians to hear, read, learn, and understand the Bible. He worked hard to aid them in this endeavor. He wrote his *Small Catechism,* in part, as an introduction to the Scriptures. He wrote prefaces for the Old and New Testaments as well as prefaces for biblical books to help readers focus on the central themes concerning law and gospel.[12] He inserted marginal notes; some of these simply identified persons, places, and terms while others dealt with theological issues, chiefly "issues of law and gospel, faith and works, Christian freedom and promise."[13] Illustrations (woodcuts) with teaching themes furthered the reader's understanding.

Gottes wort bleibt ewig.
Biblia/das ist/ die
gantze Heilige Schrifft Deudsch.
Mart. Luth.
Wittemberg.
Begnadet mit Kürfurstlicher zu Sachsen
freiheit.
Gedruckt durch Hans Lufft.
M. D. XXXIIII.

Title page of the first edition of Luther's translation of the Bible, 1534.

Luther made clear that some parts of the Bible were more important and/or clear than others; Luther suggested that Christians devote themselves especially to John's Gospel, Paul's epistles (especially Romans), and 1 Peter, remarking:

> They ought properly to be the foremost books, and it would be advisable for every Christian to read them first and most, and by daily reading to make them as much his own as his daily bread. For in them you do not find many works and miracles of Christ described, but you do find depicted in masterly fashion how faith in Christ overcomes sin, death, and hell, and gives life, righteousness, and salvation. This is the real nature of the gospel, as you have heard.[14]

Luther worked on and completed his translation of the New Testament into German while in hiding at the Wartburg Castle in 1521–22. He translated from Erasmus' Greek text, rather than the Latin Vulgate used by medieval scholars. After returning to Wittenberg, he and other reformers worked on the translation of the Old Testament. They published portions of it as they finished them; the entire Old Testament was not completed until 1535. Luther's was not the first translation of the Bible into German, but it was the first to gain wide acceptance. This was due largely to Luther's skill as a translator and his desire to make his translation truly speak the language of the people:

> We do not have to inquire of the literal Latin, how we are to speak German. . . . Rather we must inquire about this of the mother in the home, the children on the street, the common man in the marketplace. We must be guided by their language, the way they speak, and do our translating accordingly. That way they will understand it and recognize that we are speaking German to them.[15]

Luther was convinced that God would continue to use Scripture to speak to and work among individuals and communities. As he wrote in his *Large Catechism:*

> God's Word is the treasure that makes everything holy . . . At whatever time God's Word is taught, preached, heard, read, or pondered, there the person, the day, and the work is hallowed, not on account of the external work but on account of the Word that makes us all saints.[16]

Luther and his last elector John Frederick kneel at the foot of Christ's cross. Color woodcut from the 1546 Wittenberg edition of the New Testament, which Luther had himself edited. The top line is in Latin: "He prayed, he taught, Christ the Victor gave himself as victim." At the bottom, also in Latin, are the obviously handwritten words: "The Old and New Testaments are font and light."

1 Preface to the Old Testament (1545); *Luther's Works* (*LW*) 35: 242.

2 Theses concerning Faith and Law (1535); *LW* 34: 112.

3 A Brief Instruction on What to Look for and Expect in the Gospels (1521); *LW* 35: 119-120.

4 Preface to the New Testament (1546); *LW* 35: 360-361.

5 Church Postil, Sermon on the Gospel for the Festival of the Epiphany, Matthew 2[:1-12] (1521), *LW* 52: 205-206.

6 On the Councils and the Church (1539), *LW* 41: 139.

7 *LW* 41: 53-54.

8 Lectures on Galatians (1535), *LW* 26: 62.

9 *LW* 35: 236.

10 Lectures on Galatians (1535); *LW* 26: 58.

11 Lectures on Galatians (1535); *LW* 27: 41.

12 Mark U. Edwards, Jr., *Printing, Propaganda, and Martin Luther* (Berkeley: University of California Press, 1994), 116.

13 Edwards, 118.

14 Preface to the New Testament (1522); *LW* 35: 362.

15 On Translating: An Open Letter (1530); *LW* 35: 189.

16 The Large Catechism, in *The Book of Concord: The Confessions of the Evangelical Lutheran Church*, ed. Robert Kolb and Timothy J. Wengert (Minneapolis: Fortress Press, 2000), 399.

CHRONOLOGY
Luther and the Bible

1483 November 10: Born in Eisleben, Germany

1502 September: Is awarded a Bachelor of Arts degree

1505 May: Receives his Master of Arts degree and begins study of law

July: Enters Augustinian cloister in Erfurt

1507 Is ordained and celebrates his first Mass

1512 October: Receives Doctor of Theology degree and becomes Professor of Bible at Wittenberg

1513 Fall: Begins lectures on Psalms

1515 Fall: Begins lectures on Romans

1516 Fall: Begins lectures on Galatians

1517 April: Completes first biblical translation of seven penitential psalms

Fall: Begins lectures on Hebrews

October 31: Posts 95 Theses

1521 April: Appears at Diet of Worms

May: Begins his stay at the Wartburg Castle

Luther's commentary on the gospel texts appointed for Advent, the Advent Postil in Latin

December: Begins translation of the New Testament

1522 March: Sends completed translation to Philip Melanchthon for proof and correction

Summer: Translation of New Testament printed
Begins translation of Old Testament

September: New Testament translation published

December: Revised and improved New Testament translation published

1523 July: First part of Old Testament translation—the Five Books of Moses (Genesis to Deuteronomy)—published

At Luther's insistence, a printer in Haguenau, France, publishes Philip Melanchthon's lectures on the Gospel of John

Sermons on 1 Peter from 1522 are published

Lectures on Deuteronomy

1524 January: Old Testament translation—Joshua to Esther—published

Luther's sermons on 2 Peter and Jude from 1523 published

September: Psalms published

October: Job and Song of Songs published

1524–26: Lectures on the minor prophets

1526 March: Jonah published

June: Habakkuk published

Lectures on Ecclesiastes

1526–28: Luther's Postil on the Gospel and epistle texts for the church year and festivals appear

1527 February: Begins translation on Isaiah
Lectures on 1 John, Titus, Philemon

1528 January: Publication of Zechariah

October: Isaiah and revised Psalm translation published

Lectures on 1 Timothy

Begins lectures on Isaiah (completed 1530)

1529 June: Wisdom of Solomon published
Provides preface to the German translation of Philip Melanchthon's commentary on Colossians

1530 Daniel published

1530–31: Lectures on Song of Solomon

1531 Lectures on Galatians

1532 Complete translation of Old Testament Prophets published

1532–35 Lectures on selected Psalms

1533 Apocryphal books Sirach, Susanna, Bel and the Dragon, and First Maccabees published

1534 September: Full Bible with most of the Apocrypha published in Wittenberg

1534-45 Eleven editions of the full Bible in High German published

1535–45 Lectures—with interruptions—on Genesis

1544 A revised edition of Luther's Postil on the Gospel and epistle texts for the church year published

1546 February 18: Dies at age 62 in his hometown of Eisleben, Germany

For information in the chronology see, James M. Kittelson, *Luther the Reformer* (Minneapolis: Augsburg, 1986) 21-28; D. Martin Luther, *Die gantze Heilige Schrifft Deudsch*, Wittenberg 1545, ed. Hans Volz, Heinz Blanke, Friedrich Kur (Darmstadt: Wissenschaftliche Buchgesellschaft, 1972) 138-142.

THE SMALL CATECHISM
A Simple Guide for the Book of Faith

Revised edition of Luther's Catechism with cover picture of its author.

In 1529 Martin Luther, a pastor in the German town of Wittenberg and teacher at the university there, published explanations to the chief parts of the Christian faith. These explanations were first produced on individual sheets and sold for a few pennies each. By the middle of 1529 printers in Wittenberg and elsewhere had collected them into what they called an "enchiridion" or handbook. Luther added a preface, which told pastors how to use the book, and he also attached several other sections to the end of it. In this printing the handbook received a title by which we know it today, The Small Catechism of Martin Luther. The printers used the word "small" because in the same year Luther published a set of his sermons on the same topics. This book of sermons, then called The German Catechism, is now known as the Large Catechism.[1]

In 1580, Lutheran theologians included the Small and Large Catechisms of Martin Luther in *The Book of Concord* because, in their words, they were "the Laity's Bible."[2] As we read the Bible today, *Luther's Small Catechism* still offers assistance.[3] The *Small Catechism* provides adults and young people with three useful tools to approach Scripture: experiencing what the Scripture as God's Word does to us (Law and Gospel); encountering the Triune God's work to make believers out of us; and receiving the God who comes to us in weakness (Christ crucified and risen).

Lutheran Glasses: Diagnosis, Cure, Medicine

The genius of Martin Luther's catechetical instruction involved changing the order in which a person encountered the three traditional chief parts of the catechism: The Ten Commandments, the Apostles' Creed, and the Lord's Prayer.[4] In 1522, in the preface to the Personal Prayer Book, a forerunner of the *Small Catechism*, Luther compared this order to recovery from illness. First, one receives the diagnosis (the Ten Commandments), then one is told the source for healing (God's grace revealed in the Creed), and finally one calls the pharmacist to fill this gracious prescription (Lord's Prayer).[5] In the

Large Catechism, Luther reminded the reader of the same basic movement in the Christian life: our inability to fulfill the Ten Commandments, God's mercy revealed in the creed, and our cry for that very mercy in the Lord's Prayer.[6]

Even individual sections of the catechisms echo this same movement from law to gospel. In the *Large Catechism*, Luther wrote of the command to pray and the promise to be heard (a sentiment echoed in his explanation to "Amen" in the *Small Catechism*). In the *Small Catechism*'s explanation of both Baptism and the Lord's Supper, the first question touches on institution of the sacraments (command), and the second question describes the benefits (promise). Moreover, the fourth question on Baptism connected this order (moving from law to gospel) to our daily drowning and rising in baptism itself. When in 1531 Luther added a section on private confession and absolution, he again used the Ten Commandments to reveal a person's sins and concluded with the comfort of the gospel in absolution (the forgiveness of sins).[7]

This basic catechetical principle of interpretation (from law to gospel) unlocks the center of the Scripture. The distinction between law and gospel was never intended to divide the Old Testament from the New Testament or simply to distinguish commands from promises. Instead, this distinction arises from the biblical conviction that God's word *does* something to its hearers. The law—in addition to providing good order in this world and its institutions and restraining evil—breaks down, strips bare, destroys, terrifies, and puts to death by unmasking our lust for control of God and salvation. The gospel, as God's answer to our human predicament, builds up, clothes in righteousness, creates, comforts, and brings new life by announcing God's unconditional promise. The law is thus any word that does the former set of things (even the word of the cross); the gospel is similarly any word that does the latter (even a word that "sounds" like a command but is heard by faith as pure, loving invitation).

Moreover, hearing "law" does not simply call to mind guilt or shame, nor does the gospel remove such feelings. This guilt-ridden approach to the distinction distorts the catechism's point. God's Word that kills and makes alive does not send us inside ourselves to find or manufacture the appropriate religious feelings. Instead, the preacher or teacher of Scripture or even the reader of Scripture discovers two words in Scripture: one that tells the truth about the human condition (law) and the other that tells the truth about God (gospel). The truth about the human condition is not that we feel guilty but that we *are* guilty and are ashamed. Indeed, trying to manufacture the proper "spiritual" feelings is a part of our sinful condition that the law reveals. The Holy Spirit (not the preacher, teacher, or reader) then takes those very truths and does what only God can do—destroys the unbelieving Old Creature and creates the New Creature of faith by revealing the truth about God: that God is gracious and merciful.

Discovering this approach to reading Scripture in the *Small Catechism* means that we are suddenly spared from falling into two of the worst Bible-reading traps. First, we no longer need view the commandments as "doable." Quite the contrary! Instead of revealing what we can do to create or maintain our relation to God, the commandments remove all of our religious posturing or posing, so that we can beg God for mercy. Luther's explanations to the commandments state that we "*are to* fear and love God" with certain results, but it does not imply that we can. Indeed, as Luther once admonished his opponent, Erasmus of Rotterdam, regarding the latter's reading of Scripture, an "ought" never implies a "can."

Second, the promises of God are always unconditional: "God created me;" "Jesus . . . is my Lord;" "I . . . cannot believe . . . but the Holy Spirit calls." This means that the subject of the Bible is never us and our works but God and God's works. The question posed to us by Scripture is continuously: What is God doing to the people in the text and to us? Scriptural promises that are conditional ("*If* you do this, you will live") simply function as law, either as a means to maintain order and restrain evil or as "killing letter," to use St. Paul's word for it (2 Cor 3:6), exposing our sin. The promises of Scripture are, as gospel, like a gift given without strings attached, and so they always include an unconditional "for you." This is why the Bible functions best as law and gospel when proclaimed to us and not simply read alone. There must always be an interpreter and witness, that is, a preacher or teacher (or, in an emergency, an angel), who is under orders to announce: "*To you* is born this day."[8] Otherwise, we will never hear that it is truly for us. Of course, in the *Small Catechism*, Luther is that very teacher.

A woodcut depicting Pentecost scene: The Holy Spirit descends upon the believers in the form of a dove and as flames. From *Deutsch Catechismus* (German Catechism, 1531).

The Trinitarian Heart of the Bible

The central texts in the *Small Catechism* are the explanations to the creed. Seen from the perspective of law and gospel, these creedal texts reveal what defines the Christian faith and makes it different from all other religions: God at work in creating, redeeming, and making holy.[9] Christians encounter this triune God backwards, so to speak, so that first the Holy Spirit uses the Word (law and gospel) to put to death and make alive, creating and strengthening faith and forgiving sin. The Spirit does this so that we believe Jesus is our Lord. At the same time, having been led to Jesus Christ the Redeemer by the Holy Spirit, we suddenly encounter the mercy of God the Creator, since Jesus is, in Luther's words in the *Large Catechism*, "the mirror of the Father's heart."[10]

This Trinity is the heart of the Bible's message. In Scripture, God encounters us: the Holy Spirit uses God's Word (law and gospel) to put the old creature to death and raise us up as true believers in Christ, who is the mirror of the Father's heart. There are many other interesting things in Scripture, to be sure, but the readers' interest in observing and learning such things will always be informed by two activities: first, hearing and experiencing the law and gospel in the text and, second, being led by the Spirit to faith in the Son who is one with the Father. Or, to collapse these two into one: the single point of Scripture is to make believers out of us, that is, people who no longer trust themselves (and judge others) but people who trust in God who alone judges and saves.

Luther's simple confession of his faith in God, as expressed in his paraphrase of the Apostles' Creed in the *Small Catechism*, witnesses to this very action of God. In it we hear him testifying to his three-year-old son Hans and all of the simple folk in his congregation just what happened to him when God's Word hit him. "I believe that God created me, . . ." the First Article begins, and then piles up a host of verbs where God, not Luther, is the subject: [God] "has given . . . still preserves . . . provides . . . protects . . . shields and preserves." In case the readers do not get the point, Luther states the obvious (to the believing New Creature): "And all this is done out of pure, fatherly, and divine goodness and mercy, without any merit or worthiness of mine at all."[11] Of course, Luther also admits in the *Small Catechism* that he ought to "thank and praise, serve and obey" this God. But an "ought" never implies a "can," so that in the *Large Catechism* he admits that this article "should humble and terrify all of us," given the way we sin with all of these gifts of creation.[12]

When the First Article still sounds in us as law, the Second and Third Articles come to our rescue. "I believe that Jesus Christ . . . is my Lord." Realizing that Luther knew that his sixteenth-century hearers and readers understood the responsibility of their lords to ransom them if kidnapped by an evil rogue prince, he then piles up another set of verbs designed to reveal God's work in Christ, who "redeemed . . . purchased and freed" with his very sufferings and death. The result, as his hearers would have expected, caused the ransomed believer to "belong to [this true Lord], live under him in his kingdom, and serve him."

Finally, Luther witnessed to the Word in terms of the Holy Spirit, confessing that faith is not our work but God's gift: "I believe that by my own understanding or strength I cannot believe in Jesus Christ my Lord or come to him." Suddenly, all the verbs reside in God's grace and mercy and not our works. Instead of claiming that we can choose Jesus, Luther confesses that God is in charge not only of our creation and redemption but also of our very believing. Again, Luther piles up the verbs to testify to God's unbelievable mercy. The Holy Spirit "has called . . . enlightened . . . made me holy and kept me." Then, just when individualists may want to retreat into their private biblical religion, the same set of verbs (with one addition: "gathers") takes a curtain call for the church: "just as [the Holy Spirit] calls, gathers, enlightens, and makes holy the whole Christian church on earth and keeps it with Jesus Christ in the one common, true faith." Not content with this, the church becomes the location for one more verb where the Holy Spirit "*forgives* all sins—mine and those of all believers." Then, this same Spirit will raise the dead and give eternal life.

This trinitarian reading of Scripture, where God is the subject of the sentence, simply turns our Bible reading on its head. We no longer need to open the Bible to find out what *we* must do. Instead, we come away amazed by what *God* has been, is, and will be doing. Indeed, the entire Scripture is all about God and faith.[13] This same Trinity is revealed in Luther's explanations to the petitions of the Lord's Prayer. The explanation to the words "Our Father," first added to the *Small Catechism* in 1531, is a continuation of the creed itself and reveals God as reflected by Jesus, the "mirror of the Father's heart": God as a *loving* (not judging) parent. The petitions begin with a prayer for the Word ("Hallowed be your name"), which is the first medicine any believer needs to take. The Second Petition prays for faith brought by the Holy Spirit. The Third Petition prays for the very victory won by Christ the Redeemer, and the fourth prays for the blessings of the Creator. Thus, the Christian, when ordering medicine at the divine pharmacy, prays for the Trinity in reverse. The last three petitions pray again for the very things promised in the Third Article of the creed: forgiveness, strengthened faith in the face of attacks, and deliverance in this life and the next.

The Sacramental Scripture: God Revealed in Flesh

The *Small Catechism* helps us read the Bible in a third way. Early in his career, Luther developed what he called the "theology of the cross," a term that does not designate a theory about why Christ died but instead reveals the God who appears in the last place we would think to look. Building on what Paul said in 1 Corinthians 1:18-25, Luther discovered this "theology" in God's surprising blessing of Abraham and Sarah, in God's choosing Moses and the Israelites, and even in God using Paul, a former persecutor of the church, to be an apostle. This "weak and foolish" God is most clearly revealed in Jesus Christ, who came not in power but in the last place we would reasonably look: in the manger and on the cross.

In the Small Catechism there are hints of this theology all over the place. In the Second Article, Christ rescues us from our kidnappers—sin, death, and the devil—not with what we might expect (silver and gold) but with "his holy, precious blood and . . . innocent suffering and death." This unexpected action of God is already foreshadowed in the First Article of the Apostles' Creed, where God creates and preserves us, "out of pure, fatherly, and divine goodness and mercy, without any merit or worthiness of mine at all!" Mercy without merit is surely a foolish thing for God to do, and it makes the self-giving of the *Lord* Jesus even more remarkable—as if God just cannot stop giving. The Third Article continues this "foolishness" with the surprising confession of the believer's unbelief: "I believe that . . . I cannot believe." Here echoes one of Luther's favorite verses, the line of the father in Mark 9:24, "I believe; help my unbelief!"

The crucifixion of Jesus depicted in *Deutsch Catechismus* (German Catechism), 1531.

Scripture—functioning as the Word of God—proclaims (for all with ears to hear) a God of self-emptying mercy for foolish, weak followers. This is the basic theme of the Bible: a merciful Shepherd God who gathers sheep that love to wander. However, our "Old Creature" looks to Scripture for rules it is sure it can follow and for a God who will do its bidding. So, too, it creates "theologies of glory," centered in God's power and honor and in the human being's ability to measure up to God's rules.

The other place where the Small Catechism gives a glimpse of this foolish, weak God comes in the questions on Baptism and the Lord's Supper, where Luther asks the question that finally takes the sacraments far more seriously (and at God's Word) than his opponents: "How can water [or eating and drinking] do such great things?" Luther answers that it is not the water but the Word with the water; it is not the eating and drinking but the Word of promise ("for you") with the bread and wine that does the trick.[14]

No wonder that in the Gospels true believers are those who take this carpenter from Nazareth at his word: the centurion with a sick servant and the Syro-Phoenecian woman (who accepts Jesus' judgment that she is a dog and then begs for crumbs). No wonder so few people these days read the Bible this way! Instead, there is only a seeking for power, for wealth, or for a blessing on one's own "self-chosen spirituality" (see Col 2:23). Who wants a god who comes in the dust? The other centurion in Mark's gospel stands under the Crucified (Mark 15:39) and does not worry about being left behind or having a purpose or thinking positively. Instead, he recognizes "God's Son" in the last place anyone (ourselves included) would reasonably look: on the Roman gallows, breathing his last, crying out to God for help. This is truly good news for those who are left behind, who have no purpose, and who are themselves losers, but it remains a puzzling mystery—foolish and weak—to everyone else.

Turning the Bible Loose on Us

In the *Small Catechism*, Luther provided a guide for reading Scripture. It witnesses to the fact that the Scripture, as God's Word, does something to us: it puts to death the Old Creature with its schemes and guilt and shame and brings to life the New Creature of faith. As we hear and read Scripture, we will witness to and experience this same dying and rising. This same Word brings us directly into the heart of the Bible, that is, into the presence of the Trinity, who is forever creating, redeeming, and making holy or—taking the Trinity in its proper, reverse order—through the Spirit making us believers in the Lord Jesus who is the mirror of the Father's heart. At the same time, the Word comes to us not in strength but in weakness and foolishness and so overturns our thirst for power and wisdom in the brokenness of the Word made flesh. Armed with these three central scriptural claims of the *Small Catechism*—distinguishing law and gospel, encountering the self-giving Trinity for us, receiving God in the last place we would reasonably look—the Bible will suddenly sound like the thing it truly is: Book of Faith.

[1] From LUTHER'S SMALL CATECHISM with Evangelical Lutheran Worship texts. Copyright © 2008 Augsburg Fortress, Publishers. Original copyright © 1994, 2000 Augsburg Fortress, Publishers. Introduction and translation by Timothy J. Wengert.

[2] See the Epitome of the Formula of Concord, trans. Robert Kolb, "Binding Summary," par. 5 in: *The Book of Concord*, ed. Robert Kolb and Timothy J. Wengert (Minneapolis: Fortress, 2000), 487 [henceforth cited as: *BC* 2000].

[3] The idea for this connection was first suggested to the author by a student, Allison Wilcox, in a seminar paper on using the Small Catechism to introduce eighth-graders to the Bible.

[4] See Timothy J. Wengert, "Forming the Faith Today through Luther's Catechisms," Lutheran Quarterly, 11 (1997): 379–95.

[5] *Luther's Works* [American edition], ed. Helmut Lehmann and Jaroslav Pelikan, 55 vols. (Philadelphia: Fortress and St. Louis: Concordia, 1955–86), 43:13–14.

[6] *The Large Catechism* [henceforth cited as *LC*], trans. James Schaaf, Ten Commandments, par. 315–318, The Creed, par. 1–4, the Lord's Prayer, par. 2–3, in *BC* 2000: 428–29, 431, 440–41.

[7] See the *Small Catechism* [henceforth cited as *SC*], trans. Timothy J. Wengert, Baptism par. 1–8, 12, 20, 28–29 and the Lord's Supper, par. 1–2, 5–6, in *BC* 2000: 359–63.

[8] Not only Luke 2 but the story of the Ethiopian official in Acts 8 and Paul's comments in Romans 10:17 show how widespread in Scripture the office of preacher, teacher, or evangelist is for interpreting Scripture. The individualized piety of our culture actually destroys the gospel and replaces it with a distorted post-modern solipsism: what I feel is right for me; God as I understand it.

[9] See Luther's headings for the three articles in *SC*, Creed, 1, 3 and 5, in *BC* 2000: 354–55.

[10] *LC*, Creed, 63–69, here 65, in *BC* 2000: 439–40.

[11] *SC*, Creed, 2, in *BC* 2000: 354–55.

[12] *LC*, Creed, 22, in *BC* 2000: 433.

[13] See Luther's comments on the first commandment in *LC*, Ten Commandments, 324–25, in *BC* 2000: 429–30.

[14] See also Luther's comments in the *LC*, Lord's Supper, 12–14, in: *BC* 2000: 468.

LUTHER'S SEAL
and Daily Blessings

Martin Luther asked for a symbol to be designed as a visual summary of his theology. He explained the meaning of this symbol in a letter to his friend Lazarus Spengler, who worked as a town clerk in Nürnberg, Germany, and was an early supporter of the Reformation. Faith in Christ the Crucified One, Luther wrote, saves us and brings us joy, comfort, and peace—now in the present day and fully in the life to come.

In the Morning and Evening Blessings, Luther encourages us to begin and end each day joyfully with prayers and thanksgiving for all that Christ has done for us.

The Luther Rose

Letter to Lazarus Spengler, Coburg, July 8, 1530[1]

Grace and peace in Christ!

Honorable, kind, dear Sir and Friend! Since you ask whether my seal has come out correctly, I shall answer most amiably and tell you of those thoughts which [now] come to my mind about my seal as a symbol of my theology.

There is first to be a cross, black [and placed] in a heart, which should be of its natural color, so that I myself would be reminded that faith in the Crucified saves us. For if one believes from the heart he will be justified. Even though it is a black cross, [which] mortifies and [which] also should hurt us, yet it leaves the heart in its [natural] color [and] does not ruin nature; that is, [the cross] does not kill but keeps [man] alive. For the just man lives by faith, but by faith in the Crucified One. Such a heart is to be in the midst of a white rose, to symbolize that faith gives joy, comfort, and peace; in a word it places the believer into a white joyful rose; for [this faith] does not give peace and joy as the world gives and, therefore, the rose is to be white and not red, for white is the color of the spirits and of all the angels. Such a rose is to be in a sky-blue field, [symbolizing] that such joy in the Spirit and in faith is a beginning of the future heavenly joy; it is already a part [of faith], and is grasped through hope, even though not yet manifest. And around this field is a golden ring, [symbolizing] that in heaven such blessedness lasts forever and has no end, and in addition is precious beyond all joy and goods, just as gold is the most valuable and precious metal.

May Christ, our dear Lord, be with your spirit until the life to come. Amen.

The Morning Blessing[2]

In the morning, as soon as you get out of bed, you are to make the sign of the holy cross and say:

God the Father, Son, and Holy Spirit watch over me. Amen.

Then, kneeling or standing, say the Apostles' Creed and the Lord's Prayer. If you wish, you may recite this little prayer as well:

I give thanks to you, heavenly Father, through Jesus Christ your dear Son, that you have protected me through the night from all harm and danger. I ask that you would also protect me today from sin and all evil, so that my life and actions may please you. Into your hands I commend myself: my body, my soul, and all that is mine. Let your holy angel be with me, so that the wicked foe may have no power over me. Amen.

After singing a hymn, or whatever else may serve your devotion, you are to go to your work joyfully.

The Evening Blessing[3]

In the evening, when you go to bed, you are to make the sign of the holy cross and say:

God the Father, Son, and Holy Spirit watch over me. Amen.

Then, kneeling or standing, say the Apostles' Creed and the Lord's Prayer. If you wish, you may recite this little prayer as well:

I give thanks to you, heavenly Father, through Jesus Christ your dear Son, that you have graciously protected me today. I ask you to forgive me all my sins, where I have done wrong, and graciously to protect me tonight. Into your hands I commend myself: my body, my soul, and all that is mine. Let your holy angel be with me, so that the wicked foe may have no power over me. Amen.

Then you are to go to sleep quickly and cheerfully.

[1] *LW* 49:356-359.

[2] SC 36-37.

[3] SC 38.

LUTHERAN INSIGHTS that Open the Bible*

Lutherans are not *peculiar* in how they understand the Bible. Most of what we do is pretty similar to what other Christians do, but we sometimes do put a little different spin on things. We have our priorities and our preferences, and these sometimes lead us to understand Scripture differently.

The Word of God

Perhaps the first and last thing we should say about Lutherans and the Bible is this: *Lutherans believe the Bible is the Word of God.* Of course, almost all Christians would say this—and they might mean all sorts of different things by it. So we have to ask: What does it mean to say the Bible is the Word of God? Simply put, we Lutherans believe that the Bible tells us what God wants to say to us.

For the most part, Lutherans are more interested in *understanding* the Bible than they are in *defending* it. We don't think that we have to *prove* the Bible is the word of God—we just believe that it is the Word of God and then we focus on asking, "What *does* God have to say to us?" When we read the Bible, it tells us what God wants to say to us.

Lutherans have more to say about the Word of God. The Word of God is, first, Jesus Christ (the Incarnate Word); second, the message of law and gospel (the proclaimed Word); and, third, the Bible (the written Word). It isn't just Lutherans who speak of "the Word of God" this way. The Bible itself does so.

First, the Bible speaks of *Jesus Christ* as the Word of God. In John's Gospel, we read, "In the beginning was the Word and the Word was with God and the Word was God (John 1:1). And, then, a little bit later, John's Gospel says, "The Word became flesh and lived among us" (John 1:14). Obviously, the Bible did not become flesh and live among us. Jesus Christ did. So Jesus Christ is the Word of God.

Second, the Bible speaks of *preaching* as the word of God. In the book of Acts, we often hear about Peter or Paul or some other missionary preaching "the word of God" (see, for example, Acts 13:5; 18:11). What did they do? They didn't just read the Bible to people: they proclaimed a message that convicted people of their sin and offered them hope of salvation. Lutherans call this "the message of law

* Adapted from "How Can Lutheran Insights Open Up the Bible?" by Mark Allan Powell in *Opening the Book of Faith: Lutheran Insights for Bible Study.* (Minneapolis: Augsburg Fortress, 2008).

and gospel," and we will say more about it later. The message of law and gospel may also be identified as "the word of God."

And, third, the Bible identifies the Scriptures as the Word of God. For example, when Jesus believes that some people are failing to abide by one of the Ten Commandments, he tells them that they are "making void the word of God" (Mark 7:13). Jesus did not just regard Scripture as ancient testimony, as a collection of old traditions that ought to be valued for their historical significance. He believed that the writings of Scripture continued to express what God had to say to people centuries after they were written. The writings of Scripture may be identified as the Word of God.

Another phrase important to Lutherans is the Latin expression *sola scriptura ("scripture alone")*. So, what do Lutherans mean by *sola scriptura*? They mean that "scripture alone" has authority to serve as a source of divine revelation. Not councils. Not popes. Not churchwide assemblies. Not bishops or seminary professors. Only the Bible has the authority of divine revelation. Lutherans do not view the Bible as the only source for knowing what is true in this world, but they do claim that the Bible is the only authoritative source for knowing divine truth that God reveals to us.

Understanding the Bible

We are going to look at some principles that Lutherans have come up with to guide them in understanding the Bible. But, first, let's consider a basic question: "Where did we get the Bible?" Where does the Bible come from? We can answer the question, "Where does the Bible come from?" in three ways: two simple answers and one complicated answer.

The first simple answer is "The Bible comes from God." Of course, the Bible did not just fall out of heaven, all bound in leather with the words of Jesus printed in red. But it *is* the Word of God, and it does convey what God wants to say to us in a way that no other book or collection of books ever could. Lutherans have no trouble saying, "This book comes from God."

And the second simple answer is, "The Bible comes from the church." The church (meaning the historic Christian church) put the Bible together, preserved it, translated it, and made sure that people like you and I could have copies of the Bible today. The Bible is the church's gift to us and to the world.

And, finally, a third, more complicated answer is that the individual books of the Bible were written by human beings. In order to understand any particular book of the Bible, we need to know something about the circumstances in which it was written. This is important for Lutherans, because we believe the Bible must be studied and interpreted if we are going to understand it and receive God's truth. There is a famous bumper sticker that reads, "God said it, I believe it, and that settles it." Lutherans would want it to be a little bit longer: we would want to say something about *understanding* what God has said. It doesn't do any good to believe what you think the Bible teaches if you have misunderstood what the Bible teaches. What would we want the bumper sticker to say? "God speaks to us through the Bible, we interpret the Bible to understand what God wants to say, and then we believe it—and *that* settles it." But, of course, that is much too long. Lutherans have never been very good at bumper stickers.

Five Key Lutheran Principles

Here are five key principles that Lutherans follow when they study or interpret the Bible. The principles are easier to describe than they are to practice, but we have discovered over the years that when we do manage to follow these principles, we usually get things right.

1. Law and Gospel

Lutherans say that the Word of God speaks both law and gospel and that both must be held together for God's Word to be fulfilled. One way to describe these important terms is:

- the *law* is that which accuses us and judges us;
- the *gospel* is that which comforts us and saves us.

This message of law and gospel is at the heart of Scripture. One common misunderstanding sometimes equates "the law" with the Old Testament and "the gospel" with the New Testament. This is not right. There is a lot of material in the New Testament that accuses and judges people (law), and there is a lot of material in the *Old* Testament that comforts, saves, and heals (gospel). The whole Bible is both law and gospel.

A similar misunderstanding often tries to categorize Bible passages as *either* law *or* gospel. Some people develop lists: law texts and gospel texts. The law is usually associated with commandments and the gospel with promises. But this is not always right. The *same* text may function as *both* law and gospel: which *function* it has in any given situation may depend upon who is reading it and on what they need to hear.

Lutherans look for both messages in the Bible: law *and* gospel. This is part of what makes us love the Bible. We don't just believe the Bible; we treasure it—promises and commandments alike.

2. What Shows Forth Christ

When we Lutherans say the Bible is the Word of God we mean, above all, that the Bible is the book that reveals Jesus Christ to us. And by that we mean the whole Bible—not just the Gospels or the New Testament.

The Jesus we know and love is the Messiah of Israel, so the Scriptures of Israel—the Old Testament—also reveal him to us. Sometimes, I admit, this happens in a kind of a roundabout fashion. But, eventually, everything in the Bible brings us to Jesus Christ. Everything in the Bible points us toward Christ and helps us to know Christ and to love Christ and to have a relationship with Christ, who is risen from the dead.

Martin Luther used to say the Bible is like the manger that held the Christ child. In many Christmas scenes, we see people kneeling before the manger to worship, but they are not worshiping the manger. They are worshiping the Christ child who is in the manger. So, also, we do not worship the Bible. We worship the Christ who is found in the Bible.

I like to put it this way: *Lutherans are Jesus people, and they understand the Bible to be a Jesus book.* This is my own language—a contemporary way of expressing what I think is typical and traditional for Lutheranism.

3. Scripture Interprets Scripture

Lutherans believe that difficult passages of Scripture are to be interpreted in light of those passages that are more readily understandable, and that all of Scripture is to be interpreted in light of the Bible's central themes and motifs. We often try to reconcile what is said in one part of Scripture with what is said in other parts of Scripture, sometimes recognizing that there is tension between texts that seem to say different things. We try to be faithful to the entire Bible rather than just picking some parts and leaving others alone.

In practice, interpreting Scripture in light of Scripture means that Lutherans must do some initial work at defining the teaching of "Scripture as a whole" so that they will be able to interpret individual passages in light of the broader themes and overall message. When we do this, people who are not Lutheran often think that we are interpreting the Bible in light of our own theology. We understand why they think that, but *we* think that we are interpreting Scripture (individual passages) in light of Scripture (the Bible as a whole).

Let's look at a few examples:

Theology of the Cross. Lutherans believe that the death of Jesus Christ on the cross is an ultimate focal point of Scripture that reveals something profound about God's love for us and also about God's expectation for how we are to love and treat others. Jesus calls us to deny ourselves, take up *our* crosses, and follow him (Mark 8:34). The Apostle Paul calls us to have the same mind as Jesus Christ, who "humbled himself and became obedient to the point of death—even death on a cross" (Phil 2:5, 8). Lutherans try to read all of Scripture in this light. We believe we are called to love others with unselfish devotion and to do what we can to make the world a better place—loftier goals than simply expanding our own borders (see 1 Chr 4:10) or feathering our own nest. In the same vein, a theology of the cross (taught in Scripture as a whole) tells us that God has special concern for the most vulnerable people of the earth (Isa 61:1; Luke 6:20; Jas 2:5) and that pure religion must be fundamentally oriented toward them (Jas 1:27).

Justification by Grace through Faith. Lutherans believe that the Bible as a whole presents God as gracious and merciful and "abounding in steadfast love" (Exod 34:6; Ps 103:8; Joel 2:13). We are unworthy sinners, but we have been reconciled with God through the death and resurrection of Jesus Christ. God sent Jesus to die for our sins, and we can be put right with God by trusting in God's grace (Rom 5:1-11; Eph 2:8). Since Scripture as a whole teaches this, we know better than to think that our own efforts or merit will improve our status with God or increase God's love for us. There are many passages of Scripture that encourage us to do good works, and we take those seriously, but we do not think that those works will enable us to earn favor with God. Interpreting Scripture in light of Scripture leads us to view the call to good works as an invitation for people redeemed by God's grace to act as the transformed, spirit-filled "new creations" that God has made them to be (2 Cor 5:17; Gal 5:22-23).

4. The Plain Meaning of the Text

Lutherans say that Scripture is to be interpreted in line with its "plain sense." This means that passages are to be understood in the sense that would have seemed obvious to their original readers. They are not to be taken out of context or twisted to be read in a sense that never would have occurred to their original readers.

This comes straight from the teaching of Martin Luther and, when he talked about this, he had something specific in mind. It was popular in his day for interpreters to come up with creative ways of understanding the Bible that never would have been intended by the author. This was done by finding "secret meaning" in the Bible that no one had ever noticed before. The more creative the better!

Luther hated this way of interpreting the Bible. Luther would claim, if you allow this sort of thing to go on, people will find that they can make the Bible say anything they want it to say. We should stick to the plain sense of Scripture—the meaning it had for its original readers.

What about today? Do people still read the Bible in ways that ignore its "plain sense"? One example in our modern world might be the way that the book of Revelation gets treated at a certain popular level. Some books that are written about Revelation claim that modern authors are able to understand the book in a way that it never would have been understood in the first century. They do this by developing a creative system of codes and dispensations—some of them based on things they find in other books of the Bible and some based on current events or things that have happened in church history. Then, when these are applied to the book of Revelation, we get a picture of what is going to happen at the end of time.

If you have grown up Lutheran, you may not have heard much about this—or, you may have only heard about it as something that people in *other* churches believe. Why? Do we think it's *wrong*? Do we think there *won't* be a rapture, or a tribulation, or an Antichrist?

No. That would be going too far. Lutherans have no doctrine on this—though of course, we have *opinions*, and the opinions of individual Lutherans on such matters will vary. Basically, we recognize that the book of Revelation is a difficult book to understand, and we know that intelligent, responsible people understand it in different ways. But our tendency—what is typical and traditional for Lutherans—is to focus on how the book would have been understood by its original readers. This book was written for Christians who had suffered terrible persecution. Why had they suffered persecution? And how would this book have comforted them and helped them in their trials? Those are the questions we want to ask.

If you spend time in Lutheran circles, when you hear a sermon or Bible study on the book of Revelation, you will probably not hear about how certain things in that book match up with things that are happening in the world today, nor will you hear about what things are going to happen next, or *when* those things will happen. More likely, you will hear about how the hope of Christ's coming strengthens us and allows to persevere and to remain faithful to God in a troubled world. The reason is that this is what we get out of the book when we pay attention to its *plain sense*—what it would have meant to its original readers.

5. Public Interpretation

Lutherans say that the interpretation of Scripture is a public act rather than a private one. Through the Bible, God speaks to Israel and to the church. God does not speak directly or privately to individuals. What God says to Israel and to the church may have specific application for individual lives, but the meaning of Scripture for individuals is to be in harmony with its universal meaning for the community of faith.

This principle is difficult for some people to grasp. We *do* encourage personal and private Bible reading, and we do believe that the Bible speaks to people as a living Word with relevance to their individual lives. But Lutherans do not believe that this just happens automatically in a magical sort of way. People do not just open their Bibles to find private messages from God, words that would apply to them in a way that they would probably never apply to anyone else.

There is an old preacher joke about a man who opened the Bible every morning to let God speak to him, and one day it said, "Judas went out and hanged himself." Hmm, he thought. I don't know what God is saying to me. So he closed the Bible and opened it again. This time it said, "Go thou and do likewise."

I actually know someone—this is *not* a joke—who was a college student and read Isaiah 55:12 for his morning devotions. It says, "You shall go out with joy." So he decided to ask a girl named Joy for a date. He was serious. He thought God had given him a private message through the Bible.

The point, I think, is that Lutherans do not treat the Bible like some kind of magic book. We don't use the Bible the way that some people use Ouija boards or horoscopes or Tarot cards. But this does *not* mean that we think the Bible has no personal application to individual lives. Of course it does. What we recommend is that individuals first seek the *general* meaning—what the text would mean to all people—and then ask about personal application to their own particular circumstances. What the Bible means for you should be consistent or compatible with what it means for everyone.

Some Final Words

Since we are talking about a Lutheran approach to the Bible, we should perhaps conclude by noting that many Lutherans do not approach the Bible nearly enough. This is very un-Lutheran. Martin Luther translated the entire Bible, Old and New Testaments, into the language of the common people so that every family in Germany would be able to read the Scriptures in their homes. He was one of the first people to do this. It was a lot of work, and he did it because *he wanted Lutherans to read their Bibles in their homes.*

We should read the Bible, we should study the Bible, we should believe the Bible, we should treasure the Bible . . . and, I think, we should even memorize Bible passages, chapter and verse. Why? Because the Bible is the Word of God. The Bible tells us what God wants to say to us.

More than that, the Bible *does* things to us. In Scripture itself, we often hear about the Word of God as an active, dynamic force: the Word of God cleanses; it heals; it creates; it judges; it saves. One thing it does *not* do is sit unopened on bed stands or coffee tables. Rather, the Word of God is a force that never returns void but accomplishes what God intends (Isa 55:11).

So, the Bible is actually *more* than a book that says what God wants to say; it is also a book that *does* what God wants to do: a book that affects us, that transforms us.

Best of all, the Bible reveals Christ to us. It draws us into a living relationship with Jesus Christ, who is risen from the dead. Through the Bible, we come to know Jesus and love Jesus and to experience his love for us.

The Bible opens the very heart of God to us. It shows us what God has done for us—what God still does for us—what God always will do for us.

That's the first and the last thing we Lutherans want to say about the Bible: the Bible is the Word of God.

WHAT SHOULD WE EXPECT
When We Read the Bible?

All of us bring expectations with us when we open the pages of the Bible. The Lutheran understanding of Scripture is that we need to find ways for it to break through our expectations and to challenge us. Martin Luther opposed those who let their view of what was in the Bible keep it from speaking anew to them. So, what should we expect when we read and study the Bible? Here are ten things to consider:

1. We should expect to encounter God. The Bible is like a window. It is not intended to call attention to itself. It is intended to allow us to look through it and see what God is like. The words of Scripture are like windows to help us see even more than they can say. Most basically, we should expect to find Christ there—that is, to hear what God has done for us, how God has adopted us, and how God has promised to be with us into the future.

2. We should expect to discover what can be called "the first language of faith." The Bible supplies us with a vocabulary to talk about God and what it means to be the people of God. It supplies us with a vocabulary for talking with God through prayer and worship. Biblical language conveys a different understanding of the world than does nonbiblical language. For example, think about how we describe nature or the natural world we live in. The Bible says that God created it. The Bible helps us view the world as a gift from God, and we are called to take care of that gift, for the benefit of others.

3. We should expect a language rich in metaphor. In the Bible we find many metaphors, such as the "lamb of God," the "rock of our salvation," the "bread of life," and the "way." We should not expect to read the Bible simply as a textbook. The Bible uses language and stories rich in metaphors that point to God. That lively language enlivens our sense of ourselves in relation to our neighbors and the world.

4. We should expect to be challenged. The Bible provides a picture of what it means to live as a child of God and as a follower of Jesus. For example, one in ten verses in the Gospels are about wealth and our use of it. We hear, "Blessed are you who are poor" (Luke 6:20). To the rich young man Jesus says, "Go, sell what you own, and give the money to the poor" (Mark 10:21). It is important that we not too quickly say—oh, all of this just affects one's attitude toward riches. That insulates us from the challenge of these texts, from the challenge of doing justice. We need to let the challenge confront us.

5. We should expect to find meaningful answers for life, but we should not expect to find in the Bible an answer for every ethical decision we face. In the Bible we discover how God in Christ Jesus reveals a message of new life and true wisdom. By "wisdom" I mean the skill of putting knowledge to work in such a way that humans benefit. I mean by it our understanding of what makes humans tick and what benefits them and how communities work and what benefits them. We face many ethical challenges as we seek to live in the world as God's people. We don't expect to read the Bible to find a detailed list of do's and don'ts. Luther did not read the Bible that way. Just as Jesus had done and the apostle Paul had done, Luther urged people to love their neighbors. Then Luther expected that they would use their wisdom to decide what this entailed. So, on the one hand, we need to take what we find in the Bible seriously enough to let it challenge us. But, on the other hand, we also have been freed by the gospel ("for freedom Christ has set us free," Gal 5:1). We are not to be enslaved by the instructions found in the Bible but rather to use our God-given wisdom to serve our neighbor.

6. We should also not expect to have every question about God answered. For Luther, God remains hidden even as God's will for us is revealed. What God has revealed to us in Jesus the Christ is surprising enough and troubling enough so that we need to be cautious about our expectations. From the Bible we learn about God's grace and mercy and God's will for a restored world, but we do not have all our questions answered. Even with Christ and even with the Bible, we still see through a glass dimly (see 1 Cor 13:12).

7. We should expect to find out about God's here-and-now relationship with us. The Bible does talk about life after death. By faith we trust that God who has been so very loving and generous with us in the present will continue to be gracious to us—even beyond death. But that expectation grows out of the relationship. It is not the core of what is believed or of what the Bible is about. Luther almost never talked about hell and seldom talked about heaven. He rejected the idea he had been taught—that salvation was the end goal of life. He thought instead that being saved was the same thing as being in right relationship with God here and now. Whatever one says about life after death, one thing is for sure. For Luther it is not a reward. It is an extra gift from a gift-giving God.

8. We should expect to be left with tensions. God is described in many ways in the Bible—as Creator, as righteous judge, as ruler, as shepherd, as tender father or mother, as Savior. God is both this and that. God's people display great faith, and they display great evil. The Christian life is both this and that. The Bible does not resolve all these tensions. It reveals life's beauty and life's messiness. The purpose of the Bible is to invite us into a living relationship that is more than can be captured in a single proposition. There is more to God than any single portrait can convey. Human beings cannot be captured in a single description either. Tensions remind us of the inadequacy of labels when dealing with God or when dealing with human beings.

9. We should expect that each book of the Bible was written for a particular purpose and has a particular message. Though the overall message of the Bible is consistent, we can read each book to try to discover questions such as: When was it written? By whom? To whom? For what purpose? For example, it would be good if we could say to ourselves on a Sunday morning when the Gospel is read—oh, yes, that's from Luke—and here's what is distinctive about Luke's Gospel. Or, when Jeremiah is read—oh, yes, this is what was going on in Jeremiah's day. What were his primary concerns, and how does this passage express those concerns? When we discover the purpose and message of the book in the context of when it was originally written, we are better able to discover the

message it holds for today and the future. What it meant provides a kind of anchor for our interpretation of what it means now.

10. We should expect the Bible to say something to us now. That is, it is not just giving us information about the past, though it is doing that. It is not making predictions about the future, though it does make promises that carry into the future. It is calling us here and now to a deeper relationship with God and to a deeper understanding of our calling in this life.

"These are written so that you may come to believe that Jesus is the Messiah, the Son of God, and that through believing you may have life in his name." *John 20:31*

THE BIBLE AND GOD'S MISSION

God's Word in the Bible has come to us shaped by and bearing marks of a diversity of cultures, competing religious worldviews, and tribal and ethnic distinctiveness and intermixing. Much in Scripture presents the reader with the reality that God has spoken and speaks through such distinctive human marks. Both the content of Scripture and the way the Scriptures have been passed on call for us to use special lenses in reading and interpreting Scripture. These lenses take into account both cultural and religious differences. When we read and interpret the Bible with this in mind, we pay attention to, highlight, and value diversity in listening to God's Word speak to the individual reader and the community.

Faithful Reading through Cross-Cultural and Inter-Religious Lenses

Neither the individual reader nor community can avoid reading Scripture through particular cultural lenses. Every reader comes with a framework of interpretation, a tendency to see and understand the Bible in certain ways. So, it is important that we keep in mind that the biography of the reader-interpreter plays a critical role, sometimes the decisive role, in the interpretation of Scripture. Of course, if all we see in the biblical text or story is what we bring with us to the text, then our personal biography can get in the way of hearing what Scripture may be saying. We may read the Bible as if it were written only for a person, or people, like me. We may miss that God's Word is normative, meaning it is a standard for all who encounter it.

Scripture is also God's authoritative word to us. Even though the Bible is God's word, God speaks to human beings through created means, namely through human language that is stamped by various religions and cultures. The Bible was inspired by God but written down in languages other than our own and by people whose cultural situation was very different from our own. When we read the Bible, we remember that it was created by diverse people. The marks of cultural, religious, and ethnic diversity that permeate the Bible's structure and content do not make it less God's word to us. God is God of all the nations. The differences in ethnicity, for example, do not constitute any basis for considering the Israelites as being better suited for faithfulness to Yahweh (the LORD). Indeed, we need and have stories in Scripture that are centered in God's graciousness to the culturally, religiously, and ethnically other.

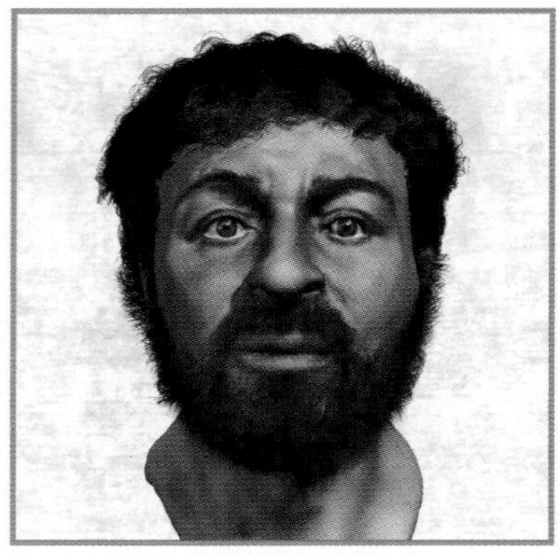

Jesus, a Scientific Reconstruction. The December 2002 issue of *Popular Mechanics* offered a portrait of Jesus created by forensic anthropologist Richard Neave, in its article "The Real Face of Jesus." Neave sought to base his image on an objective, scientific basis rather than on the cultural predispositions of artists' imaginations. He relied on archaeological discoveries of Galilean skeletons from the first century C.E. According to the Gospels, Jesus' appearance was so similar to that of his disciples that he had to be singled out by Judas Iscariot (see Matt 26:48-50).

God speaks to us in the diversity of languages, peoples, cultures, and even religious expressions. This means that we should be sensitive to these dimensions in Scripture, in history, and in ourselves. For example, it is helpful to bear in mind the many ways that Jesus of Nazareth, the Emmanuel (God-with-us) is depicted in art. He has been painted or drawn to look like a Middle-Easterner, a blond European, an Indian, African, African American, Native American, Japanese, to name a few. These depictions stem both from the context of the reader-interpreter as well as from the multicultural and ethnically diverse worlds that are presented in the very Scripture itself.

Not only should Scripture be read in light of those who are at the center of the story, but it should be read from the standpoint of those on the margins. In the Bible, God is the decisive maker of history, and one important way God acts in history is by showing surprising generosity, grace, and mercy to those on the margins. God offers to those on the margins a new identity in God's rule. To get at these dynamics, we can read the Bible attending to those at the center, those at the margins, or those at the boundaries or intersections of its stories and other texts.

Nativity, 1993, by Chinese artist Lu Lan. Jesus and his family have been portrayed as members of many cultures.

Reading the Bible through the eyes of the *other*

When we recognize that the Bible is a product of diverse voices and is intended to speak to all people, we need to consider how important it is to read Scripture through the eyes of the *other*. We can best do this by reading and interpreting some examples from the Bible itself—the books of Ruth and Jonah, and stories of Peter and Cornelius the Centurion (Acts 10), and the Apostle Paul in Athens (Acts 17:16-34). These stories bring us face to face with inter-cultural and inter-religious questions and issues.

The Book of Ruth—From the margins to the center

In the very opening verses of the Book of Ruth the family that is affected by the famine in Bethlehem is identified: "and a certain man of Bethlehem in Judah went to live in the country of Moab, he and his wife and two sons. The name of the man was Elimelech and the name of his wife Naomi, and the names of his two sons were Mahlon and Chilion; they were Ephrathites from Bethlehem in Judah" (1:1-2). To survive the famine they moved to "the country of Moab and remained there" (1:3). This meant moving to live among a foreign people with whom the Israelites have not had good relations (see Deut 23:3-6). In spite of the religious and ethnic differences with the locals—the Moabites—the two sons marry Moabite wives: Orpah and Ruth (1:4). The family does experience survival in this foreign land, but death comes for the father Elimelech and his sons Mahlon and Chilion (see 1:3, 5). Hopelessness and bitterness characterize the life of the lone survivor, Naomi, who is left with two foreign daughters-in-law, who come from a people who worship other gods, not the LORD.

Good news arrives from Bethlehem that "the LORD had considered his people and given them food" (1:6). This encourages Naomi to leave the foreign land of Moab and return home. She tells her Moabite daughters-in-law to return to their "mother's house," where they might have a future, but they persist in going with her to her homeland of Judah. While Naomi praises her Moabite daughters-in-law and wishes God's blessings upon them (see 1:8-9), she is bitter about how the LORD had treated her (1:13). She could not forsee that the LORD would open new life-giving opportunities for Ruth in Naomi's home country. The young widows defy Naomi's wishes—a very bold and unthinkable act then and in many cultures today! They both say, "No, we will return with you to your people."

The reader is ever aware that cultural, religious, and ethnic differences among them are never far from their consciousness, and it is central to a faithful reading of the story to keep that in mind. In the face of Naomi's pleas to return to her mother's house, Orpah agrees, modeling the obedience of a daughter-in-law to her mother-in-law in that setting. Ruth, however, persists in "disobeying" Naomi. She refuses to go back, and pledges that Naomi's future will be her future. Naomi's home and Naomi's people will become Ruth's home and people (1:16-18). Just as Naomi became a foreigner in Moab, Ruth will become a foreigner in Naomi's land of Judah. How are we to interpret what this means?

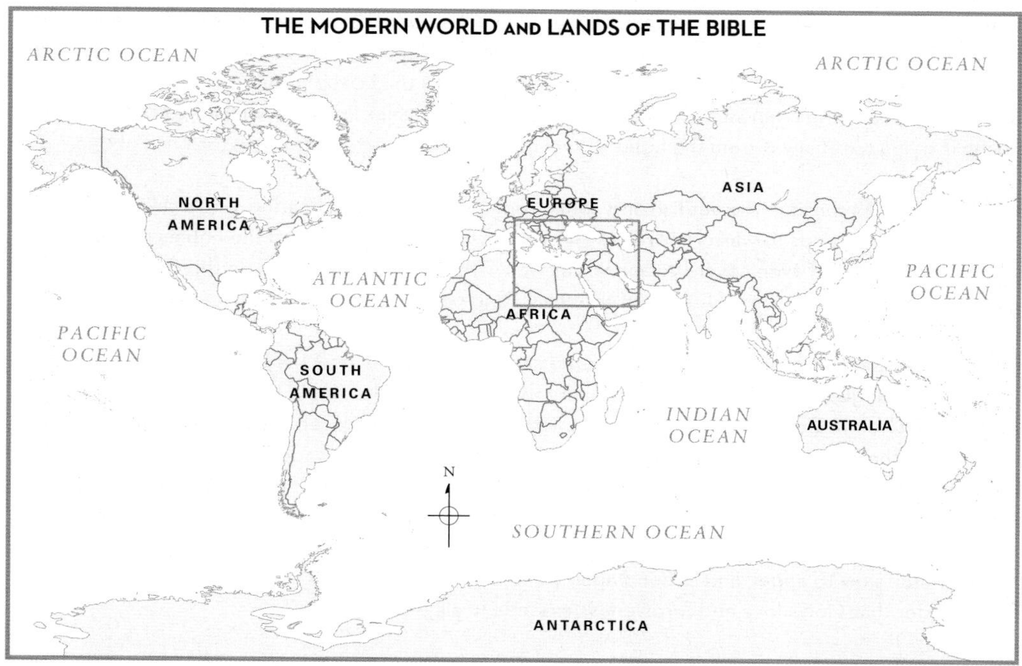

It comes as no surprise that as the story progresses in Naomi's home country references to Ruth repeatedly note her foreignness—Moabite (see 1:22; 2:2, 6, 10, 21); foreigner (see 2:10 for her own self-identification). In spite of Ruth's amazing pledge to Naomi (1:16-17), the reader rightly is left to wonder: what does Ruth have to offer that is life-giving and hope-filled? What role can she have in God's economy? The story ends on the note that Ruth bears a son who gives Naomi (who wished to be called *Mara*, "bitter"; see 1:20) new life. And "the women of neighborhood" recognize this new joy for Naomi, as they declare concerning Ruth's son Obed, "A son has been born to Naomi" (4:17).

The reader is expected to note that Ruth, the Moabite, the foreigner, is the Great Grandmother of the great King David (4:18-21). For the writer of the Gospel of Matthew, Jesus, the Emmanuel (Matt 1:23), is born of the line of Ruth (Matt 1:5). Ruth is lifted up as an example of the kind of faithfulness to the LORD that should characterize the Israelites. Human cultural and ethnic boundaries will not define God's faithful promise of liberation and righteous rule. Paying attention to Ruth as outsider to Israel, as culturally and religiously other, is key to faithfully reading and interpreting the story of God's faithfulness to all.

The Book of Jonah—from the center to the margins

Ruth the Moabite, the outsider from the margins, plays a critical role in the life of Naomi of Bethlehem. Jonah is called by the LORD to go to Nineveh, to a city inhabited by people who are not only the religious other but also enemies of the Israelites, the chosen people to which Jonah belonged. The LORD calls Jonah to speak God's Word of judgment and bring a call to repentance to the people of Nineveh in Assyria. Instead of going northeastward to Nineveh, Jonah flees in a ship going westward, in the opposite direction. A shipboard drama unfolds because of Jonah's disobedience. God sends a violent storm on the sea, and the sailors on the ship, all religious others (see 1:4; 14, 16), as well as Jonah, discover that their lives are threatened by the storm because of Jonah. Jonah's disobedience has consequences, not only for him, but for the sailors who prayed and worshiped their own gods (see 1:4). The sailors did not promptly throw Jonah overboard (1:13), and they even seek the LORD's forgiveness for their act (1:14) and seek to pacify the LORD after throwing Jonah overboard (1:15-16). Ironically, while the LORD's prophet Jonah is trying to run away from the LORD, the religiously other sailors are turning to Jonah's LORD.

God saves Jonah through a great fish and Jonah repents (2:1-10). Upon hearing God's call a second time (3:1-2) he proceeds to warn Nineveh (3:3-4). All the people, the king, and the nobles repent, and put on sackcloth, and even cover the animals as well with sackcloth (see 3:5-8). In this inter-religious world, the king expresses a real sense of the reality and power of Jonah's LORD.

The reader is amazed to learn that "[w]hen God saw what they did, how they turned from their evil ways, God changed his mind about the calamity that he had said he would bring upon them; and he did not do it" (3:10). God's mind is changed on account of the genuine repentance of a people who were not of the chosen people. This challenges Jonah's and likely his readers' predisposition to place narrow boundaries on God's graciousness. Jonah is angry that God's graciousness is widened to include the people of Nineveh, Israel's enemies. Jonah had been afraid that God's word would do its work in Nineveh and, consequently, God's plans would change. "I knew that you are a gracious God and merciful, slow to anger, and abounding in steadfast love . . ." (4:1-2). The story of Jonah is a powerful reminder that God's love and forgiveness extends to all, even our enemies.

Peter and Cornelius—from the center or the margins: Who possessses the right interpretation?

In our approach to Scripture, we come with cultural and religious lenses that may cause us to overlook or downplay internal religious and cultural-ethnic features in the story. In Acts 10, we learn that Cornelius, a centurion of the Italian Cohort "was a devout man who feared God with all his household; he gave alms generously to the people and prayed constantly to God" (10:2). Cornelius was part of the Roman imperial structure that regarded Caesar as a god among a pantheon of gods. Cornelius and his soldiers were expected to ensure that the Jews kept their place and the peace as a subject people. What is decisively noteworthy about Cornelius is that he finds favor with God. In the vision, he is instructed to send for Simon Peter (who is both a member of God's chosen people and Rome's subject peoples).

While at Simon the tanner's home in Joppa, Peter is hungry. In that state, he has a vision and is commanded by the Lord to "kill and eat" (10:9-13). But Peter, who was a Jew, followed the laws in the Hebrew Scriptures against eating anything that was categorized as profane or unclean. So in the dream he refuses to eat the unclean things (10:14). But a voice from heaven overrides his protests, by saying, "What God has made clean, you must not call profane" (10:15). Meanwhile, Cornelius has sent three representatives to see Peter. While still perplexed about the meaning of this vision, the Spirit instructs Peter to meet the three whom Cornelius has sent. It is critical to the interpretation of the text that the reader sees Cornelius through the lenses of the three who describe Cornelius as "an upright and God-fearing man, who is well spoken of by the whole Jewish nation" (10:22).

The reader cannot but note that Peter has begun to cross boundaries, for he "invited [the men] in and gave them lodging" (10:23). The next day, the meeting with Cornelius is curious. In the presence of his relatives and close friends Cornelius meets Peter and falls at his feet and worships him (see 10:24-25). Who has the power, we wonder? In Cornelius' home, Peter finds an even larger assembly and proceeds to speak of his own conversion: "You yourselves know that it is unlawful for a Jew to associate with or to visit a Gentile; but God has shown me that I should not call anyone profane or unclean" (10:28). In the exchange with Cornelius, Peter tells his audience that he "truly understand[s] that God shows no partiality..." (10:36). Peter explains this crossing of boundaries in terms of Jesus Christ—his death and resurrection, and his commissioning of the disciples to preach about God's work in and through him (10:37-43). The story closes with the gift of the Holy Spirit given to the Gentiles (to the surprise of the circumcised believers), with the baptism of Cornelius and his household, and with Peter's stay with them "for several days" (10:44-48).

The Apostle Paul in Athens—seeing the religious other in light of the gospel

In Acts 17:16-33, Paul "argued in the synagogue with the Jews" (17:17) and "debated" (17:18) Epicurean and Stoic philosophers and other foreigners in Athens, Greece. The text says that he was moved to do so because "he was deeply distressed to see that the city was full of idols" (17:16). In that inter-religious and cross-cultural setting, Paul notes how religious the Athenians are and then makes a bold move to point out a correlation between "an unknown god" they worship and the God whom he was proclaiming to them! He sounds a common note concerning creation—"The God who made the world and everything in it, he who is Lord of heaven and earth, does not live in shrines made by human hands, nor is he served by human hands..." (17:24). And without naming Jesus, Paul points to his decisive role in God's judgment. He tells them that God "has fixed a day on which he will have the world judged in righteousness by a man whom he has appointed, and of this he has given assurance to all by raising him from the dead" (see 17:22-31). Here we see Paul's authentic witness making connections between the deepest insights and longings of every culture and religious tradition and the gospel of Jesus Christ and its transforming power.

The Bible and God's Mission

Paying close attention to the dynamics and diversity of human cultures opens up the Bible in new, helpful, and even revealing ways. We learn about ancient peoples, of course, but also about ourselves and what God is trying to tell us. We can better hear the living voice of God in the Scriptures if we keep in mind that both the Hebrew Bible/Old Testament and the New Testament are written from the standpoint of minority communities. God calls Israel to witness to God's identity and unrelenting justice and righteousness, mercy and goodness. The church is called to bear witness to God's new creation in Jesus Christ through faith in him. The church was born of a persecuted community whose body and life bear the marks of suffering on account of their witness to Jesus Christ as Lord and Savior. In a cross-cultural and inter-religious reading of Scripture, this minority status needs to be in the center. It is a vital and essential reminder that God alone is the source of life, healing, and forgiveness. In this way of reading, the individual reader and community remember and listen for the story to hear that it is God through Jesus Christ, the Lord and the Spirit of life, who meets us in the concrete reality of the cultural, ethnic/racial, socio-economic particularities of human beings and human community.

A SHORT GUIDE
to Personal Bible Reading

Looking Up a Bible Passage

Use the Bible's table of contents to locate the beginning of a book. Chapter numbers are in large type, usually at the beginning of paragraphs. Verse numbers are in smaller type.

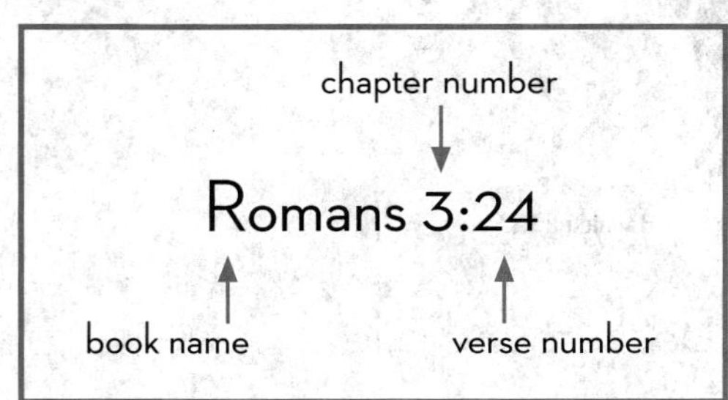

Getting Started

You can start reading anywhere in the Bible, or follow a list of selected readings. For three different lists of readings, see the Bible Reading Plan on pp. 2081-2093.

PRAY Begin by praying for God's Spirit to lead you. As Luther once said, "This book, the Holy Scripture, is the Holy Spirit's book."

SEARCH As you read, note key words and phrases. Ask: What can I learn from these faithful storytellers, prophets, and apostles?

CONFESS What do these words lead me to believe and confess—about God and myself?

THANK In times when you receive new strength, hope, or insight—and in times when understanding is clouded and insights are few—give thanks to God for the opportunity to encounter Scripture.

LIVE Luther said, "No one understands Scripture unless it is brought home to him [her], that is unless he [she] experiences it." Bring your experience with Scripture into your life experiences—at work, at play, at school, with family, friends, and neighbors.

Going Deeper

Questions that might help you go deeper into a Bible passage include:

- What in the passage scares, surprises, confuses, or challenges me?
- What stories or memories does this text stir in me?
- Who is speaking in this passage?
- Who is being addressed in this passage? How am I like or different from that person or group?
- Why was this text written, or what situation is being addressed?
- What does this passage say to me, my church, my community, the nation, the world?
- If I took these words seriously, what person or situation would I see differently than I do now?
- What new possibility is God offering me?

Marking Your Bible

Make notes about the questions and insights you have as you read your Bible.
The following symbols might be helpful.

*	A chapter or verse important to me	Ⓟ	A promise from God
!	A new idea	≈	Something that connects with my experience
√	A passage to memorize	†	My relationship with God
?	Something not clear to me	↔	My relationships with others
∞	God's love		

Habakkuk 3:17-18

HABAKKUK

Background File

Habakkuk was a prophet living in Judah around 600 B.C.E. He sees his small country of Judah sandwiched between the colliding superpowers of Babylon and Egypt. Habakkuk calls out to God to rescue God's faithful people.

What's the Story?

The ancient Near East was in a time of turmoil. The once mighty Assyria (roughly modern Syria and northern Iraq) had fallen. Egypt and the growing empire of Babylon (roughly modern Iraq) were on the rise (see Map 9, p. 2106). Caught between these two competing world powers, the people of Judah were anxious about what the superpower collision would mean for them. Making matters even worse, corruption was on the increase in Jerusalem. The rich were getting richer and the poor poorer. For the faithful Jewish community, times were bad all over.

Feeling the sting of hard times, God's people are suffering. Habakkuk questions God for allowing so much evil to last so long. Waiting like a watchman for answers to his questions, Habakkuk sees a vision of the day when God will act to save God's faithful people. The vision gives him the hope he needs to remain faithful to God's promises, even though his *why* questions are not answered.

What's the Message?

The book follows Habakkuk's journey from crisis to calm. It begins with Habakkuk's angry questions to God and ends with his sure hope in the future promised to God's people. Habakkuk's journey invites us to trust that it is okay to ask God hard questions. From the opening conversation between Habakkuk and God (chapter 1) through the vision Habakkuk reports in the form of a prayer (chapter 3), God is willing to listen. God comforts and gives hope, despite the questions that remain unanswered.

Each of the three chapters traces a step in Habakkuk's movement from fear to hope.

In his opening heated conversation with God, Habakkuk expresses dismay that God remains silent in the face of the violence, damage, and wrongdoing all around (1:1-4). Habakkuk refuses to be comforted by the statement that God will use the Babylonians as fierce messengers of God's judgment (1:5-11). Claiming that God makes people like fish and allows the powerful to hook and trap them in nets, Habakkuk announces that he is going to keep watch like a watchman to see what God will answer (1:12–2:1).

God responds by instructing Habakkuk to write the vision of a judgment against the powerful yet to come (2:3). Trusting that the vision he sees is true, Habakkuk proclaims that the righteous shall "live by their faith" (2:4).

Habakkuk takes a risk and trusts that the vision is true (God keeps God's promises). This trust frees Habakkuk to see the bigger picture and rest secure that God remains his strength and his salvation (3:18-19). For Habakkuk, God's faithfulness makes all the difference. Living by faith in God's faithfulness transforms his fear into hope.

---

1 The oracle that the prophet Habakkuk saw.

The Prophet's Complaint

2 O LORD, how long shall I cry for help,
and you will not listen?
Or cry to you "Violence!"
and you will not save?
3 Why do you make me see wrongdoing
and look at trouble?
Destruction and violence are before me;
strife and contention arise.
4 So the law becomes slack
and justice never prevails.
The wicked surround the righteous—
therefore judgment comes forth perverted.

5 Look at the nations, and see!
Be astonished! Be astounded!
For a work is being done in your days
that you would not believe if you were told.
6 For I am rousing the Chaldeans,
that fierce and impetuous nation,
who march through the breadth of the earth
to seize dwellings not their own.
7 Dread and fearsome are they;
their justice and dignity proceed from themselves.
8 Their horses are swifter than leopards,
more menacing than wolves at dusk;

1:2-4 O LORD, how long: Habakkuk begins an angry conversation with God about God's slowness to take action against those who do wrong.

1:4 So the law: *Law* is a translation of the Hebrew word *Torah.* More than dry rules and regulations, Torah means "instruction" and includes joyful response to God's grace through acts of justice and mercy.

1:5-11 Look at the nations: Instead of answering Habakkuk's questions, God changes the subject. This will lead Habakkuk to raise even more angry questions.

1:6 For I am rousing the Chaldeans: Known as fierce warriors, the Chaldeans were part of the rising empire of Babylon. Verses 5-11 proclaim that God is unleashing their military might on the earth.

1:5-11 For I am rousing the Chaldeans...their own might is their god: Some parts of the Old Testament understand Israel's sufferings and defeats as God's judgment against Israel. In 1:12-17, Habakkuk will disagree with this view.

their horses charge.
Their horsemen come from far away;
they fly like an eagle swift to devour.
9 They all come for violence,
with faces pressing[a] forward;
they gather captives like sand.
10 At kings they scoff,
and of rulers they make sport.
They laugh at every fortress,
and heap up earth to take it.
11 Then they sweep by like the wind;
they transgress and become guilty;
their own might is their god!

1:12-17 Are you not from of old: Angry at God's response, Habakkuk expresses his dismay that the pure God would use the evil enemy to bring judgment on wrongdoers among the people of Judah.

1:13 why do you look: Here Habakkuk raises the question of how the just God can allow the faithful to suffer so unjustly while the wicked do well in life. The technical term for this question is *theodicy*.

When have you wondered why God seems to remain totally silent when really bad things happen to faithful people?

12 Are you not from of old,
O LORD my God, my Holy One?
You[b] shall not die.
O LORD, you have marked them for judgment;
and you, O Rock, have established them for punishment.
13 Your eyes are too pure to behold evil,
and you cannot look on wrongdoing;
why do you look on the treacherous,
and are silent when the wicked swallow
those more righteous than they?
14 You have made people like the fish of the sea,
like crawling things that have no ruler.

15 The enemy[c] brings all of them up with a hook;
he drags them out with his net,
he gathers them in his seine;
so he rejoices and exults.
16 Therefore he sacrifices to his net
and makes offerings to his seine;
for by them his portion is lavish,
and his food is rich.
17 Is he then to keep on emptying his net,
and destroying nations without mercy?

God's Reply to the Prophet's Complaint

2:1 I will stand at my watchpost...I will keep watch: In ancient times, watchmen usually were looking for signs of danger. Habakkuk says he will keep watching until God answers his questions in a way that makes sense to him.

2 I will stand at my watchpost,
and station myself on the rampart;
I will keep watch to see what he will say to me,
and what he[d] will answer concerning my complaint.

[a] Meaning of Heb uncertain [b] Ancient Heb tradition: MT *We* [c] Heb *He* [d] Syr: Heb *I*

2 Then the LORD answered me and said:
Write the vision;
make it plain on tablets,
so that a runner may read it.
3 For there is still a vision for the appointed time;
it speaks of the end, and does not lie.
If it seems to tarry, wait for it;
it will surely come, it will not delay.
4 Look at the proud!
Their spirit is not right in them,
but the righteous live by their faith.[a]
5 Moreover, wealth[b] is treacherous;
the arrogant do not endure.
They open their throats wide as Sheol;
like Death they never have enough.
They gather all nations for themselves,
and collect all peoples as their own.

The Woes of the Wicked

6 Shall not everyone taunt such people and, with mocking riddles, say about them,
"Alas for you who heap up what is not your own!"
How long will you load yourselves with goods taken in pledge?
7 Will not your own creditors suddenly rise,
and those who make you tremble wake up?
Then you will be booty for them.
8 Because you have plundered many nations,
all that survive of the peoples shall plunder you—
because of human bloodshed, and violence to the earth,
to cities and all who live in them.

9 "Alas for you who get evil gain for your house,
setting your nest on high
to be safe from the reach of harm!"
10 You have devised shame for your house
by cutting off many peoples;
you have forfeited your life.
11 The very stones will cry out from the wall,
and the plaster[c] will respond from the woodwork.

12 "Alas for you who build a town by bloodshed,
and found a city on iniquity!"

2:2-4 Write the vision...the righteous live by their faith: Often prophets hear a message about events taking place in the near future. Here Habakkuk learns that the vision he is to record will be fulfilled, but later than he might wish. By trusting that God's promises are true and will come to pass in God's time, Habakkuk has courage to wait patiently, despite his questions and anxieties.

Why is the phrase "the righteous live by their faith" important to Lutherans? Habakkuk's words cited in Romans 1:17 and Galatians 3:11 capture the heart of the Lutheran conviction that God makes us right (justifies us) by grace through faith. Like Habakkuk, we live by faith in a promise. For us, the promise is that in Jesus Christ, God has acted to claim us as God's beloved people. Speaking in his *Lectures on Habakkuk,* Martin Luther comments on this verse: "The godly people are waiting for the Lord; therefore they live, therefore they are saved, therefore they receive what has been promised. They receive it by faith, because they give glory to the God of truth, because they hold the hand of the Lord" (*LW* 19:123). *Habakkuk 2:2-4*

2:6-19 Alas for you: Here, God replies to Habakkuk with five statements ("woes") against the wicked. This includes God's judgment against those who rob and cheat others (2:6-8); those who take care of their own needs at the expense of others in the community (2:9-11); those who build or govern cities through violence (2:12-14); those who use strong drink to tempt people into immoral or compromising situations (2:15-17); and those who make and worship idols (2:18-19).

What do you think about the "woes" listed above? How do they continue to speak to people of faith?

[a] Or *faithfulness* [b] Other Heb Mss read *wine* [c] Or *beam*

13 Is it not from the LORD of hosts
that peoples labor only to feed the flames,
and nations weary themselves for nothing?
14 But the earth will be filled
with the knowledge of the glory of the LORD,
as the waters cover the sea.

15 "Alas for you who make your neighbors drink,
pouring out your wrath[a] until they are drunk,
in order to gaze on their nakedness!"
16 You will be sated with contempt instead of glory.
Drink, you yourself, and stagger![b]
The cup in the LORD's right hand
will come around to you,
and shame will come upon your glory!
17 For the violence done to Lebanon will overwhelm you;
the destruction of the animals will terrify you—[c]
because of human bloodshed and violence to the earth,
to cities and all who live in them.

18 What use is an idol
once its maker has shaped it—
a cast image, a teacher of lies?
For its maker trusts in what has been made,
though the product is only an idol that cannot speak!
19 Alas for you who say to the wood, "Wake up!"
to silent stone, "Rouse yourself!"
Can it teach?
See, it is gold and silver plated,
and there is no breath in it at all.

20 But the LORD is in his holy temple;
let all the earth keep silence before him!

3 A prayer of the prophet Habakkuk according to Shigionoth.

The Prophet's Prayer

3:2-16 O LORD, I have heard: The picture of God as a divine warrior proclaims that God will soon save the suffering and hold accountable nations and persons who misuse power to hurt others.

2 O LORD, I have heard of your renown,
and I stand in awe, O LORD, of your work.
In our own time revive it;
in our own time make it known;
in wrath may you remember mercy.

[a] Or *poison* [b] Q Ms Gk: MT *be uncircumcised* [c] Gk Syr: Meaning of Heb uncertain

3 God came from Teman,
the Holy One from Mount Paran. *Selah*
His glory covered the heavens,
and the earth was full of his praise.
4 The brightness was like the sun;
rays came forth from his hand,
where his power lay hidden.
5 Before him went pestilence,
and plague followed close behind.
6 He stopped and shook the earth;
he looked and made the nations tremble.
The eternal mountains were shattered;
along his ancient pathways
the everlasting hills sank low.
7 I saw the tents of Cushan under affliction;
the tent-curtains of the land of Midian trembled.
8 Was your wrath against the rivers,[a] O LORD?
Or your anger against the rivers,[a]
or your rage against the sea,[b]
when you drove your horses,
your chariots to victory?
9 You brandished your naked bow,
sated[c] were the arrows at your command.[d] *Selah*
You split the earth with rivers.
10 The mountains saw you, and writhed;
a torrent of water swept by;
the deep gave forth its voice.
The sun[e] raised high its hands;
11 the moon[f] stood still in its exalted place,
at the light of your arrows speeding by,
at the gleam of your flashing spear.
12 In fury you trod the earth,
in anger you trampled nations.
13 You came forth to save your people,
to save your anointed.
You crushed the head of the wicked house,
laying it bare from foundation to roof.[d] *Selah*
14 You pierced with their[g] own arrows the head[h] of his warriors,[i]
who came like a whirlwind to scatter us,[j]
gloating as if ready to devour the poor who were in hiding.
15 You trampled the sea with your horses,
churning the mighty waters.

3:3 Teman . . . Mount Paran: Teman is an area in Edom, and Paran is in the hill country along the western border of the Gulf of Aqabah (see Map 2, p. 2099).

---

[a] Or *against River* [b] Or *against Sea* [c] Cn: Heb *oaths* [d] Meaning of Heb uncertain [e] Heb *It* [f] Heb *sun, moon* [g] Heb *his* [h] Or *leader* [i] Vg Compare Gk Syr: Meaning of Heb uncertain [j] Heb *me*

16 I hear, and I tremble within;
my lips quiver at the sound.
Rottenness enters into my bones,
and my steps tremble[a] beneath me.
I wait quietly for the day of calamity
to come upon the people who attack us.

Trust and Joy in the Midst of Trouble

17 Though the fig tree does not blossom,
and no fruit is on the vines;
though the produce of the olive fails,
and the fields yield no food;
though the flock is cut off from the fold,
and there is no herd in the stalls,
18 yet I will rejoice in the LORD;
I will exult in the God of my salvation.
19 GOD, the Lord, is my strength;
he makes my feet like the feet of a deer,
and makes me tread upon the heights.[b]

To the leader: with stringed[c] instruments.

In 3:18-19, Habakkuk says, "Yet I will rejoice in the LORD," even though he doesn't have answers for all his questions, and life continues to be difficult. What do these verses say about comfort and inspiration for going through hard times? Have you experienced such difficult times and such comfort?

[a] Cn Compare Gk: Meaning of Heb uncertain [b] Heb *my heights* [c] Heb *my stringed*

Zephaniah 3:14

ZEPHANIAH

Background File

The opening of the book of Zephaniah suggests that it takes place during the reign of Josiah, king of Judah from 640-609 B.C.E. (1:1). Josiah stands out as one of two kings praised for their religious reform and national expansion (2 Kings 23:1-20). Given the strong note of condemnation of idolatry in the book, the presumed setting may belong to a time before Josiah began his reforms. The lack of mention of these reforms, the nature of punishments prescribed, and the celebratory notes of victory suggest another historical setting for the book. Nonetheless, the literary setting of the reign of Josiah recalls that glory period even while the text itself draws attention to the transforming work of God. The book's setting appears to say that while Josiah's efforts end abruptly with his death (2 Kings 23:28-30), God's transformation will find completion.

What's the Story?

Like several prophetic books Zephaniah begins angrily but ends with serenity after several movements between notes of judgment and salvation. The book starts out with strong words of judgment against the priests who have been worshiping or allowing the worship of other gods (1:4-6); against officials and the king's sons pandering to foreign tastes (1:8); and against the wealthy who care only for their needs (1:12-13) and not for the poor. These evils contribute to making Judah's capital Jerusalem a defiled oppressing city (3:1).

In response to the wrongs described in Jerusalem, Zephaniah offers a full description of the destruction in the form of the Day of the LORD (1:14-18). This "Day" is the LORD's dark and destructive day of judgment. At the end of the description the reader lies panting from the onslaught of nouns loaded with harsh language (1:14-16). The divine declaration of complete destruction of creation (1:18) also leaves the reader gasping at the thought of a devastated earth. The picture of creation systematically being undone (1:3) contrasts with the picture of the creation unfolding (see Gen 1:1—2:4a). Zephaniah resembles books like Amos and Micah. Like Micah it uses the phrase "cut off" to speak of the destruction of foreign religions in Israel (1:4-6; see Mic 5:9-13). And it draws on the same elements as Amos in describing the Day of the LORD (See Amos 5:18-20).

Unlike the beginning, the book literally ends with singing. A renewed Jerusalem is called to rejoice over the removal of fear (1:15-17), disaster (1:18), and oppression (1:19). The negative Day of the LORD in chapter 1 gives way to a day of restoration and rejoicing in chapter 3 (see 3:14-20). Apart from God being the king in this new age and not a human figure, this time is marked by the absence of oppression. As in the book of Amos so too the book of Zephaniah calls attention to economic inequalities and sees the wealthy's inability to enjoy their possessions as their punishment (1:13; see Amos 5:11). Zephaniah identifies the wealthy and powerful as the target of the pending doom. Like Amos, he accuses them of great failures, such as participation in foreign cults (1:8), extortion (1:9), economic dishonesty (1:11), and complacency (1:12). (See Amos 6:1-8; 8:4-6.) Zephaniah, like Amos, mocks them for their trust in their wealth (1:18; see Amos 6:1). On the other hand, he proclaims that the humble and those that seek God's righteousness, including the poor, may escape the doom (2:3). They would form the core of the renewed city (3:11-13). Zephaniah's "humble and lowly" are essentially the poor and oppressed in the society. His song of renewal promises help and security to groups like "the lame" and "the outcast" (3:19).

What's the Message?

Zephaniah makes a call for trust in God as the sole guarantor of faithfulness and security. Those who have trusted in wealth, in power, or in other gods will face God's judgment. The wealthy and powerful of Judah have misplaced their trust, so they cannot bring justice and security to the land. God's judgment on other nations in chapter 2 implies that they too cannot bring security and justice to Judah. Rather, God stands as "king of Israel" (3:15). God alone can promise protection from disaster (3:15-19), the removal of the shame of foreign worship, and security from oppression. The book of Zephaniah affirms the power of God and God's claim to rule in Israel and the world.

1:1 Cushi...Hezekiah...Josiah: Zephaniah's father's name, Cushi, could be either his actual name or a way of saying that he is a Cushite or Ethiopian, in the same way someone from Texas might be called Tex. Ethiopians appear in several places in the Bible (see Num 12:1 and Jer 36:14; 38:7). The name Hezekiah in the list of Zephaniah's ancestors most likely refers to someone other than King Hezekiah. In the case where it is King Hezekiah an explicit reference appears (see Isa 1:1; Hos 1:1). Similarly, Gedaliah here may not be the Babylonian appointed governor of Jerusalem after the destruction of the city (see 2 Kings 25:22-26; Jer 40-41). The names of the ancestors all end in "-iah" a shortened form of Yahweh. This suggests an attempt to affirm Zephaniah as a Judean should his father's name suggest otherwise.

1:2-3 sweep away everything... cut off humanity: God's judgment results in un-creating creation of the major living beings listed in creation (see Gen 1:20-28). Similarly descriptions of undoing creation appear in the flood story (see Gen 6:7; 7:21-23).

1 The word of the LORD that came to Zephaniah son of Cushi son of Gedaliah son of Amariah son of Hezekiah, in the days of King Josiah son of Amon of Judah.

The Coming Judgment on Judah

2 I will utterly sweep away everything
from the face of the earth, says the LORD.
3 I will sweep away humans and animals;
I will sweep away the birds of the air
and the fish of the sea.
I will make the wicked stumble.[a]
I will cut off humanity
from the face of the earth, says the LORD.
4 I will stretch out my hand against Judah,
and against all the inhabitants of Jerusalem;
and I will cut off from this place every remnant of Baal
and the name of the idolatrous priests;[b]

[a] Cn: Heb *sea, and those who cause the wicked to stumble* [b] Compare Gk: Heb *the idolatrous priests with the priests*

5 those who bow down on the roofs
to the host of the heavens;
those who bow down and swear to the LORD,
but also swear by Milcom;[a]
6 those who have turned back from following the LORD,
who have not sought the LORD or inquired of him.

7 Be silent before the Lord GOD!
For the day of the LORD is at hand;
the LORD has prepared a sacrifice,
he has consecrated his guests.
8 And on the day of the LORD's sacrifice
I will punish the officials and the king's sons
and all who dress themselves in foreign attire.
9 On that day I will punish
all who leap over the threshold,
who fill their master's house
with violence and fraud.

10 On that day, says the LORD,
a cry will be heard from the Fish Gate,
a wail from the Second Quarter,
a loud crash from the hills.
11 The inhabitants of the Mortar wail,
for all the traders have perished;
all who weigh out silver are cut off.
12 At that time I will search Jerusalem with lamps,
and I will punish the people
who rest complacently[b] on their dregs,
those who say in their hearts,
"The LORD will not do good,
nor will he do harm."
13 Their wealth shall be plundered,
and their houses laid waste.
Though they build houses,
they shall not inhabit them;
though they plant vineyards,
they shall not drink wine from them.

The Great Day of the LORD

14 The great day of the LORD is near,
near and hastening fast;
the sound of the day of the LORD is bitter,

[a] Gk Mss Syr Vg: Heb *Malcam* (or, *their king*) [b] Heb *who thicken*

1:4 every remnant of Baal: The worship of the Canaanite fertility god Baal continued among the residents of Judah despite repeated efforts to wipe it out (see 1 Kgs 18:16-40; Jer 7:8-11; Hos 2:8). The idolatrous priests may refer to those priests who encouraged the practice of worshiping multiple gods.

1:5 bow down on the roofs to the host of the heavens: This refers to the worship of heavenly entities such as stars and the moon. A location on the tops of buildings provides greater access and visibility to the objects of worship. This type of worship occurred frequently among Babylonians.

1:5 also swear by Milcom: Milcom is the Ammonite deity or perhaps any foreign god. However, the Hebrew reads as "their king (see NRSV footnote *a*). In that case, this can be read as a sarcastic comment about trust in an illegitimate deity.

1:7, 14-18 the day of the LORD: This concept continues the set of ideas expressed by other prophets such as Isaiah (see Isa 13:6) and Joel (see Joel 1:15).

Is the "day of the LORD" meant to scare people into changing their lives? How does it work for you when you read it?

1:8 dress themselves in foreign attire: This refers to those who will be punished by God for wearing foreign clothes. This is not simply a matter of fashion tastes for things foreign. These clothes represent a culture that is unfit for those who would participate in the LORD's sacrifice.

1:10-12 Fish Gate...Second Quarter...the Mortar: These are locations within the city of Jerusalem. The Fish Gate, situated along the northern wall of the city, is named for the fish market located there (see Neh 13:16), which provided easy access to northern roads and towns. The Second Quarter, or Mishneh, houses newer settlements in the city in the period after the destruction of the northern city of Samaria. It is located on the western hills of the city. The Mortar refers to a section of the city found in a natural hollow shaped like a mortar. See Map 6, p. 2104.

1:12 I will punish the people: This notion of Jerusalem's invulnerability is seen in Psalms and attacked by Jeremiah (see Ps 48:4-7; 125; and Jer 7:5-7).

1:13 build houses, they shall not inhabit them: The threats relating to housing construction and vineyard plantings reverse blessings using these two elements. These normally represent settlement and blessing in the land (Deut 28:30-34; Jer 29:5-6). The failure to live in the houses and reap the produce not only denies the wealthy access to their gains but marks their absence from the benefits of being in the land.

How can the Lutheran teaching known as "grace alone" (sola gratia) be found in the words of prophets such as Zephaniah? With the language of disaster and impending destruction the prophet encourages the righteous to seek the Lord as a means of preventing the disaster falling on them (2:3). Here, as in other prophets, it appears that obedience to the Lord's commands is what ensures being saved from destruction. The Lutheran teaching of grace alone emphasizes that God's salvation is an act of grace on God's part. No one claims righteousness before God but require God's action in order to be right with God (Rom 3:23-25). Even in Zephaniah, the righteous can only depend upon God's decision to "hide" them from the destruction. *Zephaniah 2:3*

2:4-7 Gaza, Ashkelon, Ashdod, Ekron: These are four of five major Philistine cities that lie close to Israel (also mentioned in Amos 1:7-8; Jer 25:20; and Zech 9:5-6). See Map 7, p. 2105.

2:5 Cherethites: Along with the Pelethites, this group joined David's army after he defeated the Philistines (See 2 Sam 8:18). Their origins appear to be similar to those of the Philistines who are called Sea Peoples. However, it is not clear whether they settled the area with other Philistine groups or existed as a subgroup of outlaws for hire in the region. Like the other Philistine cities they receive condemnation given to foreign nations in this chapter, where they may be seen as a synonym of Philistines.

the warrior cries aloud there.
15 That day will be a day of wrath,
a day of distress and anguish,
a day of ruin and devastation,
a day of darkness and gloom,
a day of clouds and thick darkness,
16 a day of trumpet blast and battle cry
against the fortified cities
and against the lofty battlements.

17 I will bring such distress upon people
that they shall walk like the blind;
because they have sinned against the LORD,
their blood shall be poured out like dust,
and their flesh like dung.
18 Neither their silver nor their gold
will be able to save them
on the day of the LORD's wrath;
in the fire of his passion
the whole earth shall be consumed;
for a full, a terrible end
he will make of all the inhabitants of the earth.

Judgment on Israel's Enemies

2 Gather together, gather,
O shameless nation,
2 before you are driven away
like the drifting chaff,[a]
before there comes upon you
the fierce anger of the LORD,
before there comes upon you
the day of the LORD's wrath.
3 Seek the LORD, all you humble of the land,
who do his commands;
seek righteousness, seek humility;
perhaps you may be hidden
on the day of the LORD's wrath.
4 For Gaza shall be deserted,
and Ashkelon shall become a desolation;
Ashdod's people shall be driven out at noon,
and Ekron shall be uprooted.

5 Ah, inhabitants of the seacoast,
you nation of the Cherethites!

[a] Cn Compare Gk Syr: Heb *before a decree is born; like chaff a day has passed away*

The word of the LORD is against you,
O Canaan, land of the Philistines;
and I will destroy you until no inhabitant is left.
6 And you, O seacoast, shall be pastures,
meadows for shepherds
and folds for flocks.
7 The seacoast shall become the possession
of the remnant of the house of Judah,
on which they shall pasture,
and in the houses of Ashkelon
they shall lie down at evening.
For the LORD their God will be mindful of them
and restore their fortunes.

8 I have heard the taunts of Moab
and the revilings of the Ammonites,
how they have taunted my people
and made boasts against their territory.
9 Therefore, as I live, says the LORD of hosts,
the God of Israel,
Moab shall become like Sodom
and the Ammonites like Gomorrah,
a land possessed by nettles and salt pits,
and a waste forever.
The remnant of my people shall plunder them,
and the survivors of my nation shall possess them.
10 This shall be their lot in return for their pride,
because they scoffed and boasted
against the people of the LORD of hosts.
11 The LORD will be terrible against them;
he will shrivel all the gods of the earth,
and to him shall bow down,
each in its place,
all the coasts and islands of the nations.

12 You also, O Ethiopians,[a]
shall be killed by my sword.

13 And he will stretch out his hand against the north,
and destroy Assyria;
and he will make Nineveh a desolation,
a dry waste like the desert.
14 Herds shall lie down in it,

[a] Or *Nubians;* Heb *Cushites*

2:9 remnant of my people: This is a reference to those who would survive the disaster and would normally be seen in a positive light. In this case the prophet speaks of a small group picking up the pieces from ruined foreign cities.

2:12 Ethiopians: Unlike other nations in the list, no reason appears for the destruction of the Ethiopians, called "Cush" in the Bible. Ethiopia generally lies south of Egypt covering sections of east Africa in modern day Sudan. In other sources the region appears as "Nubia" whose leaders broke away from Egypt around 1000 B.C.E. but later ruled Egypt from 715-663 B.C.E. Hezekiah partners with one of their leaders who ruled Egypt, Taharka (Tirhakah in the Bible) in rebellion against the Assyrians (Isa 37:9). The third mention of Ethiopia in the book envisions it as the place from which worshipers of God will come with offerings. This suggests that Judeans may have found refuge in Ethiopia after the several devastating wars in their homeland. The inclination to read the reference to Ethiopia in 2:12 and 3:10 as symbolic markers of a distant place needs to pay attention to the specific references to other nations. Additionally, the reference in 1:1 points to a specific preoccupation with Ethiopia in Zephaniah.

2:13 Assyria . . . Nineveh a desolation: The Assyrian empire ruled the various parts of the region stretching from the Persian Gulf in a westward arc up to Egypt for most of the 8th to the end of the seventh century B.C.E. Its capital city Nineveh fell to the Babylonians and Medes in 612 B.C.E.

every wild animal;[a]
the desert owl[b] and the screech owl[b]
shall lodge on its capitals;
the owl[c] shall hoot at the window,
the raven[d] croak on the threshold;
for its cedar work will be laid bare.
15 Is this the exultant city
that lived secure,
that said to itself,
"I am, and there is no one else"?
What a desolation it has become,
a lair for wild animals!
Everyone who passes by it
hisses and shakes the fist.

The Wickedness of Jerusalem

3:1 Ah, soiled...oppressing city: The opening word, "Ah" (better heard here as "woe"), introduces the prophetic speech of accusations against various classes of leaders in the city. The prophets commonly use these speeches, in which they direct the word of misery against the city as if to a person. Most likely the unnamed city refers to Judah's capital Jerusalem.

3:3-4 officials...are roaring lions ...priests have profaned: Like other prophets Zephaniah accuses Judah's leaders of misleading the people (see Jer 2:26; Hos 9:15; Mic 3:1-12). The list normally includes officials, prophets, and priests for various offenses including injustice, improper sacrifices, and offering complacent answers to the people. The punishment for the leaders already appears in 1:8.

3 Ah, soiled, defiled,
oppressing city!
2 It has listened to no voice;
it has accepted no correction.
It has not trusted in the Lord;
it has not drawn near to its God.

3 The officials within it
are roaring lions;
its judges are evening wolves
that leave nothing until the morning.
4 Its prophets are reckless,
faithless persons;
its priests have profaned what is sacred,
they have done violence to the law.
5 The Lord within it is righteous;
he does no wrong.
Every morning he renders his judgment,
each dawn without fail;
but the unjust knows no shame.

6 I have cut off nations;
their battlements are in ruins;
I have laid waste their streets
so that no one walks in them;
their cities have been made desolate,

---

[a] Tg Compare Gk: Heb *nation* [b] Meaning of Heb uncertain [c] Cn: Heb *a voice* [d] Gk Vg: Heb *desolation*

without people, without inhabitants.
7 I said, "Surely the city[a] will fear me,
it will accept correction;
it will not lose sight[b]
of all that I have brought upon it."
But they were the more eager
to make all their deeds corrupt.

Punishment and Conversion of the Nations

8 Therefore wait for me, says the LORD,
for the day when I arise as a witness.
For my decision is to gather nations,
to assemble kingdoms,
to pour out upon them my indignation,
all the heat of my anger;
for in the fire of my passion
all the earth shall be consumed.

9 At that time I will change the speech of the peoples
to a pure speech,
that all of them may call on the name of the LORD
and serve him with one accord.
10 From beyond the rivers of Ethiopia[c]
my suppliants, my scattered ones,
shall bring my offering.

11 On that day you shall not be put to shame
because of all the deeds by which you have rebelled
against me;
for then I will remove from your midst
your proudly exultant ones,
and you shall no longer be haughty
in my holy mountain.
12 For I will leave in the midst of you
a people humble and lowly.
They shall seek refuge in the name of the LORD—
13 the remnant of Israel;
they shall do no wrong
and utter no lies,
nor shall a deceitful tongue
be found in their mouths.
Then they will pasture and lie down,
and no one shall make them afraid.

---

[a] Heb *it* [b] Gk Syr: Heb *its dwelling will not be cut off* [c] Or *Nubia*; Heb *Cush*

3:7 Surely the city…will accept correction: The self-reflective comment from God comes after the long list of nations destroyed and the statement of God's power against nations in 3:6. The expected outcome of the action against the nations lies in the turn around in Judah, which appears not to happen.

3:12-13 a people humble and lowly…the remnant of Israel: The humble and the lowly seem to be the core group from which the new nation will emerge, called here the remnant of Israel. At times these terms take on socio-economic meanings and can be rendered as "the afflicted and the poor." This group contrasts with the proud, removed from God's mountain for their rebellious deeds (3:11). A catalog of these deeds does not appear here but can be inferred from the various references in the book. The issues go beyond those of pride as character flaw but speak to haughty actions that disdain God and others, particularly the weak and defenseless. While only the words "afflicted and poor" suggest socio-economic categories of the remnant, these should not be erased by treating the terms as abstract concepts.

3:14-20 Sing... Rejoice... when I restore your fortunes: Sometimes the prophets follow up speeches against a city or kingdom with a word of salvation to another city. Zephaniah directs the song of salvation to Jerusalem addressing it in the typical feminine fashion as "daughter Zion." God's concern for justice is shown especially in the promise that those who are oppressed and outcast will be saved.

What would you rejoice about if you had the chance to be made over by God? What changes in the face of your church or your community would make you rejoice? Why?

A Song of Joy

14 Sing aloud, O daughter Zion;
shout, O Israel!
Rejoice and exult with all your heart,
O daughter Jerusalem!
15 The LORD has taken away the judgments against you,
he has turned away your enemies.
The king of Israel, the LORD, is in your midst;
you shall fear disaster no more.
16 On that day it shall be said to Jerusalem:
Do not fear, O Zion;
do not let your hands grow weak.
17 The LORD, your God, is in your midst,
a warrior who gives victory;
he will rejoice over you with gladness,
he will renew you[a] in his love;
he will exult over you with loud singing
18 as on a day of festival.[b]
I will remove disaster from you,[c]
so that you will not bear reproach for it.
19 I will deal with all your oppressors
at that time.
And I will save the lame
and gather the outcast,
and I will change their shame into praise
and renown in all the earth.
20 At that time I will bring you home,
at the time when I gather you;
for I will make you renowned and praised
among all the peoples of the earth,
when I restore your fortunes
before your eyes, says the LORD.

[a] Gk Syr: Heb *he will be silent* [b] Gk Syr: Meaning of Heb uncertain [c] Cn: Heb *I will remove from you; they were*

Haggai 2:9

HAGGAI

Background File

The book of Ezra credits the prophet Haggai along with Zechariah for their role in the rebuilding of the temple and advance of the community (See Ezra 5:1; 6:13-15). From the dates given, Haggai delivers these messages from mid-August to mid-December 520 B.C.E., almost eighteen years after the first group of exiles returned to Judah from Babylon. With the early excitement of the home-coming fading, the community experiences the difficulties of reconstruction and slumps into depression. Haggai's brief but pointed career works like a shot in the arm to get the community moving once again.

What's the Story?

The period starting with 538 B.C.E., when King Cyrus of Persia took over the Babylonian Empire without much of a struggle, marks a new turning point for the Judeans in Jerusalem and in Babylon. At its height the Babylonian Empire controlled territories and people in lands stretching from the Persian Gulf in a westward arc as far as Egypt and North Africa. In building their empire and controlling conquered nations, the Babylonians deported skilled persons and elite leadership to their chief cities. By this means they drained resources from local areas to build up their imperial center.

Judah and Jerusalem came under the control of the Babylonians in 597 B.C.E. By 586 the Babylonians had destroyed the major buildings and institutions in Jerusalem and deported the royal family, elite leadership and skilled workers to Babylon in successive waves. They left behind a cooperative group of leaders but mostly poor and unskilled persons (See 2 Kgs 25:12; Jer 40:7-8). With the rise of Cyrus comes a new policy to return conquered peoples to their homelands as a means for strengthening the Persian Empire (see Cyrus Cylinder, p. 1158; also 2 Chr 36:22-23, Ezra 1:2-4). Judeans appear to benefit from this new policy and slowly make their way back to Jerusalem to rebuild their ruined city. This period of reconstruction, known also as the postexilic period, marks a period of great promise but intense struggle and difficulty.

The book of Haggai takes place during the time of the Persian Empire and marks significant events by the reign of Darius (1:1; 2:1; 2:10). Darius I ruled over the Persian Empire from 521-485 B.C.E. This empire included Jerusalem as part of the province of Yehud (Judah). Haggai's singular purpose offers encouragement to the stalled temple rebuilding project. He appeals directly to the leadership and the people in the community (1:1). Zerubbabel, appointed governor by the Persians and Joshua, the high priest, appear to share leadership in the community. Both Zerubbabel and Joshua have links with Jerusalem's past. Zerubbabel's grandfather, King Jehoiachin (1 Chron 3:17-18) and Joshua's grandfather, the chief priest Seraiah (2 Kgs 25:9; Jer 52:24) both served the Jerusalem establishment before the Babylonians invaded Judah and eventually destroyed Jerusalem and the temple (586 B.C.E.).

In three dated oracles, Haggai advocates for action to be taken on the temple. The first oracle (1:2-11) describes the difficulties of the community and the people's decision to focus on their own houses. Haggai insists that the neglect of the temple resulted in the economic downturn in the region. The prophet's efforts pay quick returns as the leadership and the people stir themselves to action on the temple (1:12-15). In the second oracle (2:1-9), Haggai offers encouragement to continue the work. Echoing God's assurances for the leaders and the people, Haggai predicts that the project will end in success and glory much like the glory of the first temple. The third oracle (2:10-19) returns to the rebuking tone of the first. Armed with a priestly ruling, the prophet chastises the people for the spread of cultic impurity based in large part on the absence of the temple. He notes that the laying of the temple's foundation marked a turning point in the economic fortunes of the people.

The fourth oracle (2:20-23) in the book relates exclusively to Zerubbabel. Using some of the language of the second oracle, the prophet predicts a future for the governor. While in the second oracle the "shaking" language anticipates the completed temple, in this oracle it anticipates the complete reign of God over all the earth with Zerubbabel as God's representative. Haggai describes Zerubbabel in terms used for early kings—"my servant," "signet ring," "I have chosen you." Although these phrases heap praise upon Zerubbabel, the new reign will not be Zerubbabel's achievement. God destroys the kingdoms and their armies, then makes Zerubbabel God's representative on earth.

What's the Message?

Haggai's vision of the future reign of God is tied to his passion about the place of the temple in the restoration of the community. In the ancient world temples functioned as the center of communities in economic, social, and religious ways. The temple plays a significant role in rebuilding the community. Its role in restoring identity and a sense of place in the world comes out in Haggai's final oracle. The dislocated and dispirited community dedicate the temple to God who they dared to believe would create a future of strength for them. Even as empires pass away this vision of the temple seems to remain. In Haggai we see a vision of God and God's temple in the center of the new community of God's people. Faithful people of all generations are encouraged to consider what it means to put God in the center of all life.

The Command to Rebuild the Temple

1 In the second year of King Darius, in the sixth month, on the first
day of the month, the word of the LORD came by the prophet Haggai to Zerubbabel son of Shealtiel, governor of Judah, and to Joshua
son of Jehozadak, the high priest: 2 Thus says the LORD of hosts: These
people say the time has not yet come to rebuild the LORD's house.

1:1 second year of King Darius: Darius became king of Persia in 522 and ruled until 486 B.C.E. With this information we can accurately date Haggai's first prophecy to August 29, 520 B.C.E.

1:1 Zerubbabel son of Shealtiel, governor of Judah: The Persians appointed Zerubbabel, a grandson of King Jehoi-

[3]Then the word of the LORD came by the prophet Haggai, saying: [4]Is
it a time for you yourselves to live in your paneled houses, while this
house lies in ruins? [5]Now therefore thus says the LORD of hosts: Consider how you have fared. [6]You have sown much, and harvested little;
you eat, but you never have enough; you drink, but you never have
your fill; you clothe yourselves, but no one is warm; and you that earn
wages earn wages to put them into a bag with holes.
7 Thus says the LORD of hosts: Consider how you have fared. [8]Go
up to the hills and bring wood and build the house, so that I may take
pleasure in it and be honored, says the LORD. [9]You have looked for
much, and, lo, it came to little; and when you brought it home, I blew
it away. Why? says the LORD of hosts. Because my house lies in ruins,
while all of you hurry off to your own houses. [10]Therefore the heavens
above you have withheld the dew, and the earth has withheld its produce. [11]And I have called for a drought on the land and the hills, on
the grain, the new wine, the oil, on what the soil produces, on human
beings and animals, and on all their labors.
12 Then Zerubbabel son of Shealtiel, and Joshua son of Jehozadak, the high priest, with all the remnant of the people, obeyed the
voice of the LORD their God, and the words of the prophet Haggai, as
the LORD their God had sent him; and the people feared the LORD.
[13]Then Haggai, the messenger of the LORD, spoke to the people with
the LORD's message, saying, I am with you, says the LORD. [14]And the
LORD stirred up the spirit of Zerubbabel son of Shealtiel, governor of
Judah, and the spirit of Joshua son of Jehozadak, the high priest, and
the spirit of all the remnant of the people; and they came and worked
on the house of the LORD of hosts, their God, [15]on the twenty-fourth
day of the month, in the sixth month.

The Future Glory of the Temple

2 In the second year of King Darius, [1]in the seventh month, on
the twenty-first day of the month, the word of the LORD came
by the prophet Haggai, saying: [2]Speak now to Zerubbabel son of Shealtiel, governor of Judah, and to Joshua son of Jehozadak, the high
priest, and to the remnant of the people, and say, [3]Who is left among
you that saw this house in its former glory? How does it look to you
now? Is it not in your sight as nothing? [4]Yet now take courage, O Zerubbabel, says the LORD; take courage, O Joshua, son of Jehozadak,
the high priest; take courage, all you people of the land, says the
LORD; work, for I am with you, says the LORD of hosts, [5]according to
the promise that I made you when you came out of Egypt. My spirit
abides among you; do not fear. [6]For thus says the LORD of hosts:
Once again, in a little while, I will shake the heavens and the earth
and the sea and the dry land; [7]and I will shake all the nations, so that
the treasure of all nations shall come, and I will fill this house with

achin of Judah, presumably to win support from the community for a leader from a respected family.

1:1 Joshua son of Jehozadak, the high priest: Joshua occupies a prominent role alongside of the royal figure Zerubbabel. In Haggai as well as Ezra and Zechariah, he seems to share leadership of the community with Zechariah (see Ezra 5:1; 6:13-15; Zech 3:1-5; 4:1-10). This indicates the new role that priests played after the destruction of Jerusalem, during the period of exile and continuing.

1:2 rebuild the LORD's house: The temple in Jerusalem needed to be rebuilt because the Babylonians destroyed it in 587 B.C.E. The rebuilding efforts started slowly and the second temple reached completion in 515 B.C.E.

1:12 remnant of the people: In Haggai the "remnant" means those who remained in Jerusalem and survived the disaster there.

2:1 seventh month, on the twenty-first day: Based on the dating system of the reign of Darius, Haggai's second message comes about seven weeks after the first (1:1) on October 17, 520 B.C.E.

How important should church buildings be? What connections exist between faith and the building dedicated to the worship of God?

2:4 people of the land: Haggai uses two terms to designate the community: remnant of the people and people of the land. This usage contrasts with the use of "people of the land" in Ezra (see Ezra 4:1-5), where this group consists of those who remained in the land and formed opposition to the returnees. While Ezra presumes intra-group conflict, no such conflict appears in Haggai.

2:6 shake the heavens and the earth: Movements of the earth are associated in the Bible with God's presence. Because God contains such awesome power, the presence of God causes the earth to shake (see Judg 5:4; 2 Sam 22:8; Ps 29:1-9). At other times the language of shaking speaks to God's judgment and destruction of the world (see Ps 18:7; Isa 13:13; Joel 3:16). Here Haggai invokes the shaking language to speak to the return of God's presence to the temple.

2:10 twenty-fourth day of the ninth month: Based on the dating system of the reign of Darius, Haggai's third message occurs December 18, 520 B.C.E.

2:13-14 does it become unclean: The priests established zones around sacred space as outlined in Lev 13–15 and 22. This forms the basis of the response to Haggai's question. The first part of the question deals with the ability of consecrated objects to transfer holiness to things that touch them. The second part of the question inquires about unclean things communicating uncleanness. The specific response to the second part of the question draws from Numbers 19:11-13, the case of touching a dead body. The priests argue that while holiness is not communicable, uncleanness transfers easily to things it contacts. Haggai accepts the ruling as the basis for his argument that ritual purity would be restored with the rebuilt temple (2:15-19).

2:15 stone placed upon a stone: This refers to the laying of the foundation of the temple. The assumption that Haggai speaks at an event marking the laying of the foundation in December 520 B.C.E. seems correct. Yet it will be another five years before the work on the temple reaches completion. .

2:20 word of the LORD came a second time: A second message comes to Haggai on the same day as the third message (see note on 2:10).

2:23 signet ring: Kings wore rings or seals about their necks or fingers as markers of authority. As a descendant of King David, Zerubbabel receiving the signet ring suggests the return of David's family as rulers over Israel.

In what way is worship to be regarded as a gift? Haggai's passion for the reconstruction of the temple demonstrates the urgency for human communication with God. In the absence of the temple and its worship the people experience significant lack in their lives. Worship stands as God's gift to God's people and every opportunity should be used to take advantage of this gift. Luther says this about worship: "We cannot *give* God anything but praise and thanks, for everything else we *receive* from [God]—be it grace, words, works, Gospel, faith, and all things." (*WLS* 1545-46). *Haggai 2:23*

Based on Luther's quote above, does our worship enable us to gain God's favor? Why or why not? What is true worship?

splendor, says the LORD of hosts. 8 The silver is mine, and the gold is
mine, says the LORD of hosts. 9 The latter splendor of this house shall
be greater than the former, says the LORD of hosts; and in this place I
will give prosperity, says the LORD of hosts.

A Rebuke and a Promise

10 On the twenty-fourth day of the ninth month, in the second
year of Darius, the word of the LORD came by the prophet Haggai,
saying: 11 Thus says the LORD of hosts: Ask the priests for a ruling: 12 If
one carries consecrated meat in the fold of one's garment, and with
the fold touches bread, or stew, or wine, or oil, or any kind of food,
does it become holy? The priests answered, "No." 13 Then Haggai said,
"If one who is unclean by contact with a dead body touches any of
these, does it become unclean?" The priests answered, "Yes, it becomes unclean." 14 Haggai then said, So is it with this people, and with
this nation before me, says the LORD; and so with every work of their
hands; and what they offer there is unclean. 15 But now, consider what
will come to pass from this day on. Before a stone was placed upon a
stone in the LORD's temple, 16 how did you fare?[a] When one came to
a heap of twenty measures, there were but ten; when one came to the
wine vat to draw fifty measures, there were but twenty. 17 I struck you
and all the products of your toil with blight and mildew and hail; yet
you did not return to me, says the LORD. 18 Consider from this day on,
from the twenty-fourth day of the ninth month. Since the day that
the foundation of the LORD's temple was laid, consider: 19 Is there any
seed left in the barn? Do the vine, the fig tree, the pomegranate, and
the olive tree still yield nothing? From this day on I will bless you.

God's Promise to Zerubbabel

20 The word of the LORD came a second time to Haggai on the
twenty-fourth day of the month: 21 Speak to Zerubbabel, governor of
Judah, saying, I am about to shake the heavens and the earth, 22 and to
overthrow the throne of kingdoms; I am about to destroy the strength
of the kingdoms of the nations, and overthrow the chariots and their
riders; and the horses and their riders shall fall, every one by the sword
of a comrade. 23 On that day, says the LORD of hosts, I will take you,
O Zerubbabel my servant, son of Shealtiel, says the LORD, and make
you like a signet ring; for I have chosen you, says the LORD of hosts.

---

[a] Gk: Heb *since they were*

Zechariah 6:12

ZECHARIAH

Background File

The dates in the book place Zechariah as a contemporary of Haggai (1:1, 7; 7:1; compare Hag 1:1; 2:1, 10, 20). While the book of Haggai mentions Zechariah as a partner, Haggai is not mentioned in the book of Zechariah. The setting assumes the process for the reconstruction of the temple in Jerusalem after the exile. The book of Zechariah offers visions of restoration of the nation and in particular the life of the temple. Some of Zechariah's visions rise above the nation to incorporate the whole cosmos. Zechariah's visions of restoration offer fewer specifics about the physical plan of the temple than those of Ezekiel (Ezek 40–48). Yet, they provide more details about a more inclusive community that rises up around the temple. The two critical figures of Joshua the high priest and Zerubbabel the Persian-appointed governor of the province appear in this book as they do in Haggai. Only, Joshua receives the title high priest while Zerubbabel receives no title except the honor of laying the foundation of the temple. As leaders in the restoration community Joshua and Zerubbabel appear to share responsibility for the reconstruction of Jerusalem.

What's the Story?

The book of Zechariah divides neatly into two parts. The first part (chapters1–8) consists of a series of eight visions (chapters 1–6); a prophetic answer to a question (7:1-7); and statements from God on the nature of the future community (7:8–8:23). The prophet's visions in chapters 1–6 focus upon real personalities and events on earth even while presenting a mystical picture of extraterrestrial travels. In the book, these obscure visions require an interpreter (1:9). The series of vision-question-interpretations reinforces God's intervention into the events of history. From the patrolling presence of the four horsemen (1:7-17) to the horns (1:18-21) and measuring line (2:1-5); from the cleansing (3:1-5) and crowning (6:9-14) of Joshua to the ridding of the land of abominations, these visions paint pictures of renewal for Jerusalem. Set within these visions are promises of God's presence and help for real people. Jerusalem will be rebuilt and repopulated (2:4) and God shall become its city wall (2:5). The law of God will be effective in the land (5:1-4). Zerubbabel receives strength to complete the temple (4:8-10). The eight visions in the first part of Zechariah (1–8) are capped off by God's promise of a restored Jerusalem where peace, fertility, and security will flow to Jerusalem, making it attractive to the nations (8:1-23).

The second part of Zechariah (chapters 9–14, known as Second Zechariah) lacks specific references to the prophet and has no dates. This has led some to suggest that this portion was written later by another author. The content of Zechariah 9–14 is completely taken up with messages or oracles spoken by the LORD. The excitement of the first part of the book quickly gives way to harsh language of destruction at the start of chapter 9. Militaristic images and the condemnation of foreign nations (9:1-8) are balanced with words of encouragement, mostly for persons returning to Jerusalem (9:9–10:12). The fatalistic note of corrupt leadership (11:4-17) moves into noisy images of Jerusalem's victory over neighboring states (12:1-9). Yet, the fluctuations do not end there. A further attack on Jerusalem by "all the nations" results in destruction, rape, and deportation, but this time God comes to the rescue (14:1-11). God saves Jerusalem as the mighty warrior (14:3-5), becomes king (14:9), and changes the landscape to emphasize Jerusalem's loftiness (14:10-11). The second part of the book ends like the first, with eternal security promised to Jerusalem and the world streaming to it (14:16-19). The two parts of Zechariah offers two different visions of the future. First Zechariah (1–8) reflects confidence in the dual leadership of Joshua and Zerubbabel (4:14), while Second Zechariah (9–14) is at best cynical about human leaders (11:4-17). Royal honor is given to Joshua in the first part (6:9-14), while the second part equates the glory of the house of David with God's glory (12:7-9). In chapters 1–8, the nations are attracted to Jerusalem because of the way God has blessed its people with peace and prosperity. But in 9–14 the nations are threatened with punishment if they do not keep Israel's festival (14:18-19). For Second Zechariah, only God guarantees the peace and security of Jerusalem. But together these two sections reflect certainty in Jerusalem's restoration.

What's the Message?

As a whole, the book offers an ideal of restoration that makes Jerusalem the center of the world. The rebuilt temple is led by priests who are blessed and rededicated to lead the people in proper worship. The nation is cleansed of worthless leaders, and wicked nations are removed. These actions form the core of Zechariah's blueprint of the future. Like other books in the Old Testament, Zechariah's images and concepts provide a source from which writers of the New Testament draw to explain their understanding of Jesus. The image of the triumphant king entering Zion (9:9-10) helps to draw the picture of Jesus entering Jerusalem ahead of the events that lead to his death (Matt 21:5; Mark 14:27; John 12:15). Other aspects of the book, such as the thirty pieces of silver, are referred to indirectly in the New Testament (Matt 26:15, 28). Similarly, the book of Revelation shares with Zechariah visions of God's victory over all enemies and the creation of a new Jerusalem where God stands as ruler (compare Zech 14:8-11 and Rev 22:1-3). The New Testament writers continue the theme that from God's restored community in Jerusalem will come hope for the whole world.

Israel Urged to Repent

1 In the eighth month, in the second year of Darius, the word of
the LORD came to the prophet Zechariah son of Berechiah son of
Iddo, saying: [2]The LORD was very angry with your ancestors. [3]There-
fore say to them, Thus says the LORD of hosts: Return to me, says
the LORD of hosts, and I will return to you, says the LORD of hosts.
[4]Do not be like your ancestors, to whom the former prophets proclaimed, "Thus says the LORD of hosts, Return from your evil ways

1:1 the eighth month, in the second year of Darius: This date sets the book in the Persian period during the reign of Darius I, similar to that of Haggai (See Hag 1:1 and note). This places Zechariah one month before Haggai's last oracle (See Hag 2:10), precisely in November 520 B.C.E.

1:4-6 Return from your evil ways…So they repented: Many prophets call on the people of Israel and Judah

and from your evil deeds." But they did not hear or heed me, says the
LORD. 5Your ancestors, where are they? And the prophets, do they
live forever? 6But my words and my statutes, which I commanded my
servants the prophets, did they not overtake your ancestors? So they
repented and said, "The LORD of hosts has dealt with us according to
our ways and deeds, just as he planned to do."

First Vision: The Horsemen

7 On the twenty-fourth day of the eleventh month, the month of
Shebat, in the second year of Darius, the word of the LORD came to
the prophet Zechariah son of Berechiah son of Iddo; and Zechariah[a]
said, 8In the night I saw a man riding on a red horse! He was standing
among the myrtle trees in the glen; and behind him were red, sorrel,
and white horses. 9Then I said, "What are these, my lord?" The angel
who talked with me said to me, "I will show you what they are." 10So
the man who was standing among the myrtle trees answered, "They
are those whom the LORD has sent to patrol the earth." 11Then they
spoke to the angel of the LORD who was standing among the myrtle
trees, "We have patrolled the earth, and lo, the whole earth remains at
peace." 12Then the angel of the LORD said, "O LORD of hosts, how long
will you withhold mercy from Jerusalem and the cities of Judah, with
which you have been angry these seventy years?" 13Then the LORD
replied with gracious and comforting words to the angel who talked
with me. 14So the angel who talked with me said to me, Proclaim this
message: Thus says the LORD of hosts; I am very jealous for Jerusalem
and for Zion. 15And I am extremely angry with the nations that are at
ease; for while I was only a little angry, they made the disaster worse.
16Therefore, thus says the LORD, I have returned to Jerusalem with
compassion; my house shall be built in it, says the LORD of hosts, and
the measuring line shall be stretched out over Jerusalem. 17Proclaim
further: Thus says the LORD of hosts: My cities shall again overflow
with prosperity; the LORD will again comfort Zion and again choose
Jerusalem.

Second Vision: The Horns and the Smiths

18[b] And I looked up and saw four horns. 19I asked the angel who
talked with me, "What are these?" And he answered me, "These are
the horns that have scattered Judah, Israel, and Jerusalem." 20Then the
LORD showed me four blacksmiths. 21And I asked, "What are they
coming to do?" He answered, "These are the horns that scattered Judah, so that no head could be raised; but these have come to terrify
them, to strike down the horns of the nations that lifted up their horns
against the land of Judah to scatter its people."[c]

[a] Heb *and he* [b] Ch 2.1 in Heb [c] Heb *it*

to repent from their wrongdoing ("return to the LORD"). The list includes from time to time evils such as idolatry, breaking of commandments, oppression of the poor, injustice, and lack of faith in God. The people do not always follow this advice (see Jer 18:11; Ezek 14:6; Amos 5:14-15).

1:7 the twenty-fourth day of the eleventh month, the month of Shebat, in the second year of Darius: This represents the most precise dating in the text and includes day, month and year—February 15, 519 B.C.E. The date places the event on the eve of New Year celebrations normally associated with temple buildings. The name of the month, Shebat, comes from the Babylonian calendar, as does Chislev (7:1). The date formula using the Babylonian system and the Persian king emphasizes how much foreign powers controlled the region.

1:8-11 a man riding on a red horse!: The divine messenger appears riding the horse (see 1:11). The color of this horse and the others may not symbolize anything in particular. These colors reflect normal horses in the ancient world. The horses draw attention to the place where they are pastured—a fertile, peaceful place. The horses form part of a heavenly troop sent to patrol the earth.

1:12 these seventy years?: References to seventy-year periods in biblical sources often appear to indicate symbolic periods (see Isa 23:15-17; Jer 25:11-12; 29:10). Seventy years seems to be a standard period of divine anger and national humiliation. Zechariah draws upon Jeremiah (Jer 29:10) for this notion, but inverts it from the period of Babylonian rule to God's anger (7:4).

1:18-21 four horns: Horns symbolically represent nations or powers (see Jer 48:25; Dan 7:8), while the number four represents totality. The interpretation suggests that all the nations of the earth contributed to the destruction of Judah, Israel, and Jerusalem.

Third Vision: The Man with a Measuring Line

2 [a] I looked up and saw a man with a measuring line in his hand.
2Then I asked, "Where are you going?" He answered me, "To
measure Jerusalem, to see what is its width and what is its length."
3Then the angel who talked with me came forward, and another angel
came forward to meet him, 4and said to him, "Run, say to that young
man: Jerusalem shall be inhabited like villages without walls, because
of the multitude of people and animals in it. 5For I will be a wall of fire
all around it, says the LORD, and I will be the glory within it."

Interlude: An Appeal to the Exiles

6 Up, up! Flee from the land of the north, says the LORD; for I
have spread you abroad like the four winds of heaven, says the LORD.
7Up! Escape to Zion, you that live with daughter Babylon. 8For thus
said the LORD of hosts (after his glory[b] sent me) regarding the nations
that plundered you: Truly, one who touches you touches the apple
of my eye.[c] 9See now, I am going to raise[d] my hand against them, and
they shall become plunder for their own slaves. Then you will know
that the LORD of hosts has sent me. 10Sing and rejoice, O daughter
Zion! For lo, I will come and dwell in your midst, says the LORD.
11Many nations shall join themselves to the LORD on that day, and
shall be my people; and I will dwell in your midst. And you shall know
that the LORD of hosts has sent me to you. 12The LORD will inherit Judah as his portion in the holy land, and will again choose Jerusalem.
13 Be silent, all people, before the LORD; for he has roused himself from his holy dwelling.

Fourth Vision: Joshua and Satan

3 Then he showed me the high priest Joshua standing before
the angel of the LORD, and Satan[e] standing at his right hand to
accuse him. 2And the LORD said to Satan,[e] "The LORD rebuke you,
O Satan![e] The LORD who has chosen Jerusalem rebuke you! Is not
this man a brand plucked from the fire?" 3Now Joshua was dressed
with filthy clothes as he stood before the angel. 4The angel said to
those who were standing before him, "Take off his filthy clothes." And
to him he said, "See, I have taken your guilt away from you, and I will
clothe you with festal apparel." 5And I said, "Let them put a clean turban on his head." So they put a clean turban on his head and clothed
him with the apparel; and the angel of the LORD was standing by.
6 Then the angel of the LORD assured Joshua, saying 7"Thus says
the LORD of hosts: If you will walk in my ways and keep my requirements, then you shall rule my house and have charge of my courts,

[a] Ch 2.5 in Heb [b] Cn: Heb *after glory he* [c] Heb *his eye* [d] Or *wave* [e] Or *the Accuser;* Heb *the Adversary*

2:1 man with a measuring line: Builders use measuring lines, also known as a plumb line, to make sure walls are straight and correctly sized. Here the plumb line's use suggests the need to ensure an accurate rebuilding of the city.

2:6-7 Escape to Zion, you that live with daughter Babylon: The twice repeated invitation to leave calls upon the exiled people of Judah who live in Babylonia to return to Zion (Jerusalem). This return ends in celebration with rejoicing and with God dwelling with the people (2:10). The expression "daughter Babylon" refers to the Babylonian empire (Isa 47:1).

2:11 Many nations shall join themselves to the LORD: In the period after the exile the idea of foreigners becoming a part of Israel finds expression (see 8:20-23; 14:16; Isa 56:6-7).

3:1 high priest Joshua: Joshua appears to have priestly lineage (see 2 Kgs 25:18; Jer 52:24; 1 Chr 6:15). He functions as the main priest for the exilic community. The descriptions of him as a branding iron plucked from the fire and filthily dressed speak to his life as an exile. His ritual purification in this vision represents the first level of cleansing necessary for a renewed temple.

3:1 Satan: This same Satan appears in the book of Job as "the Satan" (the accuser). As in Job, this accuser belongs to the divine court under God's control (Job 1:6-12). The Satan is prevented from performing his role of accuser against Joshua. In later understanding the Satan will become the personification of evil and enemy of God.

3:5 clean turban on his head: The headgear forms part of the vestments of the priests (see Exod 29:5-9; Lev 8:7-9). The word used here comes from a list detailing losses on the day of the LORD (see Isa 3:23). Its usage here suggests the end of punishment associated with exile. The ritual and moral purity of the turban also enforces the idea of renewal.

3:8 my servant the Branch: While this promise is given to Joshua, it may not be about him and could possibly refer to Zerubbabel, who is a descendant of David. The later description of the Branch as the temple builder (6:13) connects with the previous portrayal of Zerubbabel as the temple builder (4:9).

and I will give you the right of access among those who are standing
here. 8Now listen, Joshua, high priest, you and your colleagues who
sit before you! For they are an omen of things to come: I am going to
bring my servant the Branch. 9For on the stone that I have set before
Joshua, on a single stone with seven facets, I will engrave its inscription, says the LORD of hosts, and I will remove the guilt of this land
in a single day. 10On that day, says the LORD of hosts, you shall invite
each other to come under your vine and fig tree."

Fifth Vision: The Lampstand and Olive Trees

4 The angel who talked with me came again, and wakened me,
as one is wakened from sleep. 2He said to me, "What do you
see?" And I said, "I see a lampstand all of gold, with a bowl on the
top of it; there are seven lamps on it, with seven lips on each of the
lamps that are on the top of it. 3And by it there are two olive trees, one
on the right of the bowl and the other on its left." 4I said to the angel
who talked with me, "What are these, my lord?" 5Then the angel who
talked with me answered me, "Do you not know what these are?" I
said, "No, my lord." 6He said to me, "This is the word of the LORD to
Zerubbabel: Not by might, nor by power, but by my spirit, says the
LORD of hosts. 7What are you, O great mountain? Before Zerubbabel
you shall become a plain; and he shall bring out the top stone amid
shouts of 'Grace, grace to it!' "

8 Moreover the word of the LORD came to me, saying, 9"The
hands of Zerubbabel have laid the foundation of this house; his hands
shall also complete it. Then you will know that the LORD of hosts has
sent me to you. 10For whoever has despised the day of small things
shall rejoice, and shall see the plummet in the hand of Zerubbabel.

"These seven are the eyes of the LORD, which range through the
whole earth." 11Then I said to him, "What are these two olive trees on
the right and the left of the lampstand?" 12And a second time I said to
him, "What are these two branches of the olive trees, which pour out
the oil[a] through the two golden pipes?" 13He said to me, "Do you not
know what these are?" I said, "No, my lord." 14Then he said, "These are
the two anointed ones who stand by the Lord of the whole earth."

Sixth Vision: The Flying Scroll

5 Again I looked up and saw a flying scroll. 2And he said to me,
"What do you see?" I answered, "I see a flying scroll; its length
is twenty cubits, and its width ten cubits." 3Then he said to me, "This
is the curse that goes out over the face of the whole land; for everyone
who steals shall be cut off according to the writing on one side, and
everyone who swears falsely[b] shall be cut off according to the writing

---

[a] Cn: Heb *gold* [b] The word *falsely* added from verse 4

3:9 single stone with seven facets: A unique stone that forms part of the priest's headpiece (see Exod 28:36-38). The message on the stone could be the words "Holy to the LORD" (Exod 28:36), a phrase that could be written in seven Hebrew letters.

3:9 remove the guilt of this land: The purified high priest becomes able to perform the sacrifice of atonement to forgive the people (see Lev 16:1-34 and note). With the return of the temple and proper worship, the land could once again be purified.

4:6 Zerubbabel: See the note on Haggai 1:1.

4:7 O great mountain…top stone: The mountain may refer to the hill where the temple is built. In this context it speaks of the mountain as an obstacle and may refer either to an actual adversary or the rubble on the ruined temple site.

In ancient temple reconstruction, a stone from the old temple was placed into the new one to ensure continuity with the old temple. Perhaps one of the stones from the top of the old temple would be used as the cornerstone for the new temple.

4:9 hands of Zerubbabel have laid the foundation: Zerubbabel receives the credit for the foundation work on the temple. In Ezra he appears to work in concert with Joshua on the start of the temple (Ezra 5:2). Here Joshua's role seems diminished.

4:10 the plummet: The leaden object that Zerubbabel holds appears to be a ceremonial metal incorporated into the new temple. Its exact purposes remain unknown except that ancient cultures seem to use metal in temple construction.

4:10 these seven are the eyes of the LORD: The answer to the question of "What are these" in 4:4 occurs here, since 4:5-10a appears to interrupt the earlier part of the passage. The lamp stand may distantly resemble the seven-branched lamp stand described in Exod 25:31-40, but this one consists of a bowl with seven wicks.

4:14 these are the two anointed ones: The Hebrew word translated "anointed" can also be rendered as "messiah." The vision points to the two representatives of God on earth, without naming them. In the context they refer to the high priest and the governor, providing dual leadership.

5:2 flying scroll…twenty cubits: This turns out to be a supersized scroll measuring 33 feet by 15 feet. The unusual scroll consists of writing on both sides. It swiftly and effectively condemns the houses of thieves and false witness it enters. The scroll relates legal texts that forbid stealing and false witness (see Exod 20:15; Lev 19:11-12; Deut 5:19; 6:13). It serves to complement the temple as a hallmark of the reconstructed community.

5:6-8 This is a basket…Wickedness: The personification of the sinfulness of the land as a woman called Wickedness recalls the practice of goddess worship. Worship of Asherah (2 Kgs 23:4), the queen of heaven (Jer 44:11-19), Tammuz (Ezek 8:14) and other female deities continued despite the protests of the prophets.

5:11 land of Shinar: Another name for Babylon. Perhaps the basket containing "wickedness" here represents Babylon as a place of abominations or simply refers to the fact that "wickedness" has been driven out to a foreign land.

6:5 four winds of heaven: The interpretation of the eighth vision identifies the four chariots with the four winds. These winds are regarded as the four basic winds from each compass point. As such they represent a total coverage of the earth (see Jer 49:36; Ezek 37:9; Dan 8:8; 11:4).

6:10 from the exiles: The only instance in Zechariah where members of the community are referred to as exiles. This usage relates specifically to those who returned from Babylon and excludes those who remained behind in the land.

on the other side. 4I have sent it out, says the LORD of hosts, and it
shall enter the house of the thief, and the house of anyone who swears
falsely by my name; and it shall abide in that house and consume it,
both timber and stones."

Seventh Vision: The Woman in a Basket

5 Then the angel who talked with me came forward and said to
me, "Look up and see what this is that is coming out." 6I said, "What
is it?" He said, "This is a basket[a] coming out." And he said, "This is
their iniquity[b] in all the land." 7Then a leaden cover was lifted, and
there was a woman sitting in the basket![a] 8And he said, "This is Wickedness." So he thrust her back into the basket,[a] and pressed the leaden
weight down on its mouth. 9Then I looked up and saw two women
coming forward. The wind was in their wings; they had wings like the
wings of a stork, and they lifted up the basket[a] between earth and sky.
10Then I said to the angel who talked with me, "Where are they taking
the basket?"[a] 11He said to me, "To the land of Shinar, to build a house
for it; and when this is prepared, they will set the basket[a] down there
on its base."

Eighth Vision: Four Chariots

6 And again I looked up and saw four chariots coming out from
between two mountains—mountains of bronze. 2The first
chariot had red horses, the second chariot black horses, 3the third
chariot white horses, and the fourth chariot dappled gray[c] horses.
4Then I said to the angel who talked with me, "What are these, my
lord?" 5The angel answered me, "These are the four winds[d] of heaven
going out, after presenting themselves before the Lord of all the earth.
6The chariot with the black horses goes toward the north country, the
white ones go toward the west country,[e] and the dappled ones go toward the south country." 7When the steeds came out, they were impatient to get off and patrol the earth. And he said, "Go, patrol the earth."
So they patrolled the earth. 8Then he cried out to me, "Lo, those who
go toward the north country have set my spirit at rest in the north
country."

The Coronation of the Branch

9 The word of the LORD came to me: 10Collect silver and gold[f]
from the exiles—from Heldai, Tobijah, and Jedaiah—who have arrived from Babylon; and go the same day to the house of Josiah son
of Zephaniah. 11Take the silver and gold and make a crown,[g] and set it
on the head of the high priest Joshua son of Jehozadak; 12say to him:

---

[a] Heb *ephah* [b] Gk Compare Syr: Heb *their eye* [c] Compare Gk: Meaning of Heb uncertain [d] Or *spirits* [e] Cn: Heb *go after them* [f] Cn Compare verse 11: Heb lacks *silver and gold* [g] Gk Mss Syr Tg: Heb *crowns*

Thus says the LORD of hosts: Here is a man whose name is Branch:
for he shall branch out in his place, and he shall build the temple of
the LORD. [13]It is he that shall build the temple of the LORD; he shall
bear royal honor, and shall sit upon his throne and rule. There shall be
a priest by his throne, with peaceful understanding between the two
of them. [14]And the crown[a] shall be in the care of Heldai,[b] Tobijah,
Jedaiah, and Josiah[c] son of Zephaniah, as a memorial in the temple
of the LORD.

15 Those who are far off shall come and help to build the temple
of the LORD; and you shall know that the LORD of hosts has sent me
to you. This will happen if you diligently obey the voice of the LORD
your God.

Hypocritical Fasting Condemned

7 In the fourth year of King Darius, the word of the LORD came to
Zechariah on the fourth day of the ninth month, which is Chislev.
[2]Now the people of Bethel had sent Sharezer and Regem-melech and
their men, to entreat the favor of the LORD, [3]and to ask the priests of
the house of the LORD of hosts and the prophets, "Should I mourn
and practice abstinence in the fifth month, as I have done for so many
years?" [4]Then the word of the LORD of hosts came to me: [5]Say to all
the people of the land and the priests: When you fasted and lamented
in the fifth month and in the seventh, for these seventy years, was it
for me that you fasted? [6]And when you eat and when you drink, do
you not eat and drink only for yourselves? [7]Were not these the words
that the LORD proclaimed by the former prophets, when Jerusalem
was inhabited and in prosperity, along with the towns around it, and
when the Negeb and the Shephelah were inhabited?

Punishment for Rejecting God's Demands

8 The word of the LORD came to Zechariah, saying: [9]Thus says the
LORD of hosts: Render true judgments, show kindness and mercy to
one another; [10]do not oppress the widow, the orphan, the alien, or the
poor; and do not devise evil in your hearts against one another. [11]But
they refused to listen, and turned a stubborn shoulder, and stopped
their ears in order not to hear. [12]They made their hearts adamant in order not to hear the law and the words that the LORD of hosts had sent
by his spirit through the former prophets. Therefore great wrath came
from the LORD of hosts. [13]Just as, when I[d] called, they would not hear,
so, when they called, I would not hear, says the LORD of hosts, [14]and I
scattered them with a whirlwind among all the nations that they had
not known. Thus the land they left was desolate, so that no one went
to and fro, and a pleasant land was made desolate.

---

[a] Gk Syr: Heb *crowns* [b] Syr Compare verse 10: Heb *Helem* [c] Syr Compare verse 10: Heb *Hen*
[d] Heb *he*

6:11-15 make a crown . . . as a memorial in the temple of the LORD: The Hebrew indicates two crowns are to be made. While it appears that one crown is placed upon the head of Joshua, no other person wears the second crown. This leads many to suspect that only one crown is intended. That Joshua wears the crown and appears to receive the name Branch contradicts 3:8. Further, Zerubbabel is honored for laying the foundation of the temple (see 4:8), but now "Branch" seems to get the honor of building the temple. The similarities between the confirmation of the promises relating to the building of the temple in 4:9 and 6:15 suggest that the same person is intended in both cases. Joshua receives authentication as high priest with the promise of sharing rule alongside the royal figure. This reflects the vision of shared leadership in the reconstituted community.

How does Luther describe the relationship between spiritual authority and civil authority? Luther spoke of the twofold reign of God, identifying the spiritual and the civil as God's twofold way of ruling in the world. God works through the Holy Spirit to rule the hearts of believers; God works through civil authorities to order common life. Luther's thinking on the twofold reign of God is like a theological geography in which he situates the whole of Christian life. Every Christian stands under both spiritual and temporal authority simultaneously. The twofold reign of God is often referred to as "two kingdoms." God reigns in both spiritual and temporal authorities, until that time when "God may be all in all" (1 Cor 15:28). *Zechariah 6:11-14*

How would you describe the proper interaction between church and government? To what degree do you believe our country is or should be under the rule of God?

7:1 fourth year of King Darius: According to the dating system of the Babylonian month of Chislev, December 7, 518 B.C.E. marks the precise date of the receipt of this message.

7:5 fasted and lamented in the fifth month . . . seventh, for these seventy years: The observance of the fifth month commemorates the destruction of Jerusalem (see 2 Kgs 25:8) in 587 B.C.E. The seventh month marks the assassination of the Babylonian-appointed governor Gedaliah some years later (2 Kgs 25:25).

God's Promises to Zion

8 The word of the LORD of hosts came to me, saying: [2]Thus says the LORD of hosts: I am jealous for Zion with great jealousy, and I am jealous for her with great wrath. [3]Thus says the LORD: I will return to Zion, and will dwell in the midst of Jerusalem; Jerusalem shall be called the faithful city, and the mountain of the LORD of hosts shall be called the holy mountain. [4]Thus says the LORD of hosts: Old men and old women shall again sit in the streets of Jerusalem, each with staff in hand because of their great age. [5]And the streets of the city shall be full of boys and girls playing in its streets. [6]Thus says the LORD of hosts: Even though it seems impossible to the remnant of this people in these days, should it also seem impossible to me, says the LORD of hosts? [7]Thus says the LORD of hosts: I will save my people from the east country and from the west country; [8]and I will bring them to live in Jerusalem. They shall be my people and I will be their God, in faithfulness and in righteousness.

9 Thus says the LORD of hosts: Let your hands be strong—you that have recently been hearing these words from the mouths of the prophets who were present when the foundation was laid for the rebuilding of the temple, the house of the LORD of hosts. [10]For before those days there were no wages for people or for animals, nor was there any safety from the foe for those who went out or came in, and I set them all against one another. [11]But now I will not deal with the remnant of this people as in the former days, says the LORD of hosts. [12]For there shall be a sowing of peace; the vine shall yield its fruit, the ground shall give its produce, and the skies shall give their dew; and I will cause the remnant of this people to possess all these things. [13]Just as you have been a cursing among the nations, O house of Judah and house of Israel, so I will save you and you shall be a blessing. Do not be afraid, but let your hands be strong.

14 For thus says the LORD of hosts: Just as I purposed to bring disaster upon you, when your ancestors provoked me to wrath, and I did not relent, says the LORD of hosts, [15]so again I have purposed in these days to do good to Jerusalem and to the house of Judah; do not be afraid. [16]These are the things that you shall do: Speak the truth to one another, render in your gates judgments that are true and make for peace, [17]do not devise evil in your hearts against one another, and love no false oath; for all these are things that I hate, says the LORD.

Joyful Fasting

18 The word of the LORD of hosts came to me, saying: [19]Thus says the LORD of hosts: The fast of the fourth month, and the fast of the fifth, and the fast of the seventh, and the fast of the tenth, shall

8:1 I am jealous for Zion with great jealousy: The start of the chapter parallels the first chapter. While God's jealousy for Jerusalem in 1:14 leads to divine rage, here God's jealousy leads to restoration of the city.

8:3 Jerusalem shall be called the faithful city: Several prophetic visions of the restored Jerusalem offer new names for the city (see Isa 62:4; Ezek 48:35). The renaming of the city indicates its new status and recovery of qualities lost during the time of its destruction.

8:4-5 old men and old women… boys and girls: The depiction of the restored community contrasts with descriptions of desolation like the immediate one in 7:14. Modern conceptions of old age as a time of retirement and childhood as a time of play ought not to be read here. Life expectancy in the ancient world did not allow many to live beyond their forties. Additionally, both old and young engaged in productive labor. The picture speaks of new births, abundant prosperity so that no one needs to work, and of happiness in the future.

8:6 remnant of this people: The community that survives to live in the restored Jerusalem takes this name in several books (see Ezra 9:8-15; Isa 37:31-32; 46:3; Jer 40:11, 15; Haggai 1:12, 14; 2:2). Whether that means both those who return to Jerusalem and those who continued to live there is not always clear in the texts. Here the text (8:7) means those who return to Jerusalem. This suggests that no one remained behind in Jerusalem. This view at times put the group returning to Jerusalem and the ones already there at odds with each other, as seen in Ezra and Nehemiah (see Ezra 4:1-5; Neh 4; 6).

8:8 They shall be my people: The restored community becomes one with God in covenant. The simple transaction in the language of being God's people and God becoming their Lord represents the heart of the covenant (see Exod 29:45; Jer 31:33; Ezek 37:26-28).

8:14-17 Speak the truth to one another, render in your gates: Compare the list of actions expected from the reconstituted community to those called for in Amos 5:15. They revolve around social norms that require proper treatment for all persons in the community. As the hallmarks of justice

be seasons of joy and gladness, and cheerful festivals for the house of Judah: therefore love truth and peace.

Many Peoples Drawn to Jerusalem

20 Thus says the LORD of hosts: Peoples shall yet come, the inhabitants of many cities; [21]the inhabitants of one city shall go to another, saying, "Come, let us go to entreat the favor of the LORD, and to
seek the LORD of hosts; I myself am going." [22]Many peoples
and strong nations shall come to seek the LORD of hosts in Jerusalem,
and to entreat the favor of the LORD. [23]Thus says the LORD of hosts:
In those days ten men from nations of every language shall take hold
of a Jew, grasping his garment and saying, "Let us go with you, for we
have heard that God is with you."

Judgment on Israel's Enemies

9 An Oracle.

The word of the LORD is against the land of Hadrach
  and will rest upon Damascus.
For to the LORD belongs the capital[a] of Aram,[b]
  as do all the tribes of Israel;
2 Hamath also, which borders on it,
  Tyre and Sidon, though they are very wise.
3 Tyre has built itself a rampart,
  and heaped up silver like dust,
  and gold like the dirt of the streets.
4 But now, the Lord will strip it of its possessions
  and hurl its wealth into the sea,
  and it shall be devoured by fire.

5 Ashkelon shall see it and be afraid;
  Gaza too, and shall writhe in anguish;
  Ekron also, because its hopes are withered.
The king shall perish from Gaza;
  Ashkelon shall be uninhabited;
6 a mongrel people shall settle in Ashdod,
  and I will make an end of the pride of Philistia.
7 I will take away its blood from its mouth,
  and its abominations from between its teeth;
it too shall be a remnant for our God;
  it shall be like a clan in Judah,
  and Ekron shall be like the Jebusites.
8 Then I will encamp at my house as a guard,

[a] Heb *eye* [b] Cn: Heb *of Adam* (or *of humankind*)

these actions belong "in your gates" since the city gates served as the courthouses in the ancient world. However, these actions of justice extend beyond the realms of legal justice into the realm of everyday human interaction.

8:18-19 fast of the fourth month: Two fasts in addition to the ones mentioned in 7:3-7 appear to suggest gloomy commemorative events around the destruction of Jerusalem. The dates of the first two fasts mark major events easily identified. The fasts in the fourth and tenth month may mark the breaching of the wall of Jerusalem (Jer 39:2) and the start of the Babylonian siege of the city (2 Kings 25:1; Jer 39:1). A full answer to the question of 7:3 occurs here with a resounding no. In the reconstructed city feasting replaces fasting.

8:20-23 People shall yet come... take hold of a Jew: Rarely do we find the term "Jew" in the Old Testament. When it does appear, it refers more to residents of the Persian province of Yehud than to the religious and ethnic identities that emerge in later usage. Here the term draws attention to those who live in Jerusalem and worship God, serving as the impetus for the world to gather in Jerusalem.

What about your faith can make you attractive to others who wish to know about God? What would make others want to take hold of you because they have heard or seen that "God is with you"?

9:1-8 The word of the LORD: The second part of Zechariah (see the introduction) begins with the word "an oracle," which means a message. It describes the nature of the rest of the chapter, essentially words of judgment against Israel's enemies. God acts as a divine warrior moving against the enemies from north (Damascus in Syria) through the cities of Philistia (see Map 7, p. 2105). A similar word appears at the opening of Nahum (Nah 1:1) and Malachi (Mal 1:1).

9:9 Rejoice…daughter Zion…your king comes to you: The divine warrior image (9:10) follows the image of the divine king entering into Jerusalem (9:9). The LORD serves as king of Jerusalem (Zion). The LORD as divine warrior rules over large parts of the earth and in the process ushers in peace. Two of the Gospels use this passage in their accounts of Jesus riding into Jerusalem in the days before his crucifixion (Matt 21:2-7; John 12:14-15).

9:10 from the River to the ends of the earth: This normally refers to the Euphrates River. Jerusalem falls within the province that the Persians call "Beyond the River." The expanse of land imagined here assigns a greater territory to God than the Persians control.

9:11 the blood of my covenant with you: Blood sacrifices sealed the covenant relationship between God and the people (see Exod 24:8). New Testament writers would later interpret Jesus as the mediator of a new covenant relationship with God through the shedding of his own blood (see Heb 9:11-22).

9:13 Ephraim: Refers to the northern kingdom of Israel (see note on 10:10-11).

9:13 your sons, O Greece: In 333 B.C.E. the Persian Empire fell to the forces of Alexander the Great. Even before this time a number of military encounters between the Greeks and the Persians made it necessary for the Persians to move forces close to the area of Jerusalem. The presence of large numbers of Persian forces meant limited chances of Jerusalem acting independent of Persia. This may account for the antagonism towards the Greeks.

9:15 they shall drink their blood: The Hebrew lacks the word "blood," but its presence here makes sense. The extent of the bloodshed in warfare conducted by the divine warrior appears in two images, the drinking of blood like wine from an overflowing bowl and the excess of blood splattered in rituals on the altar. (Images of drinking blood at the end of warfare also appear in Isa 49:26 and Ezek 39:17-19.) Here the image may reflect ritual activity associated with the collected blood of sacrificed animals (see Exod 27:3; 38:3; Num 4:14). The blood on the corners of the altar points to the practice of smearing blood on the four corners of a horned-altar (Lev 1:5).

so that no one shall march to and fro;
no oppressor shall again overrun them,
for now I have seen with my own eyes.

The Coming Ruler of God's People

9 Rejoice greatly, O daughter Zion!
Shout aloud, O daughter Jerusalem!
Lo, your king comes to you;
triumphant and victorious is he,
humble and riding on a donkey,
on a colt, the foal of a donkey.
10 He[a] will cut off the chariot from Ephraim
and the war-horse from Jerusalem;
and the battle bow shall be cut off,
and he shall command peace to the nations;
his dominion shall be from sea to sea,
and from the River to the ends of the earth.

11 As for you also, because of the blood of my covenant with you,
I will set your prisoners free from the waterless pit.
12 Return to your stronghold, O prisoners of hope;
today I declare that I will restore to you double.
13 For I have bent Judah as my bow;
I have made Ephraim its arrow.
I will arouse your sons, O Zion,
against your sons, O Greece,
and wield you like a warrior's sword.

14 Then the LORD will appear over them,
and his arrow go forth like lightning;
the Lord GOD will sound the trumpet
and march forth in the whirlwinds of the south.
15 The LORD of hosts will protect them,
and they shall devour and tread down the slingers;[b]
they shall drink their blood[c] like wine,
and be full like a bowl,
drenched like the corners of the altar.

16 On that day the LORD their God will save them
for they are the flock of his people;
for like the jewels of a crown
they shall shine on his land.
17 For what goodness and beauty are his!

---

[a] Gk: Heb *I* [b] Cn: Heb *the slingstones* [c] Gk: Heb *shall drink*

Grain shall make the young men flourish,
and new wine the young women.

Restoration of Judah and Israel

10 Ask rain from the LORD
in the season of the spring rain,
from the LORD who makes the storm clouds,
who gives showers of rain to you,[a]
the vegetation in the field to everyone.
2 For the teraphim[b] utter nonsense,
and the diviners see lies;
the dreamers tell false dreams,
and give empty consolation.
Therefore the people wander like sheep;
they suffer for lack of a shepherd.

3 My anger is hot against the shepherds,
and I will punish the leaders;[c]
for the LORD of hosts cares for his flock, the house of Judah,
and will make them like his proud war-horse.
4 Out of them shall come the cornerstone,
out of them the tent peg,
out of them the battle bow,
out of them every commander.
5 Together they shall be like warriors in battle,
trampling the foe in the mud of the streets;
they shall fight, for the LORD is with them,
and they shall put to shame the riders on horses.

6 I will strengthen the house of Judah,
and I will save the house of Joseph.
I will bring them back because I have compassion on them,
and they shall be as though I had not rejected them;
for I am the LORD their God and I will answer them.
7 Then the people of Ephraim shall become like warriors,
and their hearts shall be glad as with wine.
Their children shall see it and rejoice,
their hearts shall exult in the LORD.

8 I will signal for them and gather them in,
for I have redeemed them,
and they shall be as numerous as they were before.
9 Though I scattered them among the nations,

---

[a] Heb *them* [b] Or *household gods* [c] Or *male goats*

9:15 The LORD of hosts: This title often describes God as the Divine Warrior who commands a large heavenly army (hosts).

10:2 teraphim: The practice of making and worshiping individual household gods seemed to exist within Israel–Judah (see Gen 31; 1 Sam 19:13). These household deities represented deceased family members and were believed to provide guidance and answers to the living. The practice is condemned (2 Kgs 23:24), together with divination, widely seen as a source of false prophecy (Jer 14:14).

10:3 hot against the shepherds: Sometimes ancient leaders such as kings are referred to as shepherds. Prophets accuse leaders of gross failure in their duty (see Jer 23:2; Ezek 34). Similar ideas surface in Zechariah, where leaders fail miserably in their task of rebuilding the devastated community (11:4-17).

10:4 out of them shall come the cornerstone: The LORD's anger against the shepherds results in transformation for the flock. Several metaphors describe the change in the people. These range from construction images of cornerstone and tent peg, communicating stability, to military images of war horse and battle bow, indicating their power.

10:10-11 gather them from Assyria...Nile dried up: The Assyrians destroyed the northern kingdom of Israel in 722 B.C.E. and deported the inhabitants to the heartland of Assyria (2 Kgs 17:5-6). Here the deportation refers to the Babylonian captivity. However, the texts points to a wide-scale return of God's people from various places, including the long-forgotten Assyrian deportation. The reference to passing through the sea and the Nile (10:11) recalls the events of the Exodus (Exod 15). This may also refer to those who fled to Egypt after the destruction of Jerusalem (Jer 42-44). The verses anticipate a comprehensive gathering of people back to Jerusalem in such large numbers to exceed the capacity of the land.

11:1 Lebanon...your cedars: The destruction of the highly regarded cedars of Lebanon (see Ps 104:16; Isa 2:13; 14:8; Jer 22:23) forms the basis of a painful poem of woe. A similar claim for the oaks of Bashan as a destroyed valuable resource emphasizes the enormity of the devastation that opens this chapter.

11:4-17 Be a shepherd of the flock doomed to slaughter...my worthless shepherd: This vision is hard to explain with certainty. It probably has to do with judgment against the shepherd leaders, who did not properly lead the people (see 10:3 and note).

11:4-6 Be a shepherd of the flock doomed to slaughter: A different shepherd theme turns up here where the prophet becomes an uncaring shepherd. The shepherds, those who sell and those who slaughter the sheep, display no concern for the sheep. Profit appears to be their main concern. In a similar way the LORD acts like those shepherds and hands the people over to destruction. The prophet then reports carrying out the command from 11:4 in 11:7.

11:7-14 I became the shepherd of the flock: The prophet performs an attention-getting public action here. Normally these actions are followed with an explanation (see Jer 13:1-11; 18:1-11; 19:1-13; Ezek4:1-15; 12:1-16). The action consists of the prophet actually taking over the flock from the shepherds. In addition he enacts the breaking of the covenant and the separation of Judah and Israel with two sticks. The breaking of the two sticks contrasts with a prophetic action by Ezekiel that joins two sticks to symbolize reunification (see Ezek 37:15-28).

yet in far countries they shall remember me,
and they shall rear their children and return.
10 I will bring them home from the land of Egypt,
and gather them from Assyria;
I will bring them to the land of Gilead and to Lebanon,
until there is no room for them.
11 They[a] shall pass through the sea of distress,
and the waves of the sea shall be struck down,
and all the depths of the Nile dried up.
The pride of Assyria shall be laid low,
and the scepter of Egypt shall depart.
12 I will make them strong in the LORD,
and they shall walk in his name,
says the LORD.

11 Open your doors, O Lebanon,
so that fire may devour your cedars!
2 Wail, O cypress, for the cedar has fallen,
for the glorious trees are ruined!
Wail, oaks of Bashan,
for the thick forest has been felled!
3 Listen, the wail of the shepherds,
for their glory is despoiled!
Listen, the roar of the lions,
for the thickets of the Jordan are destroyed!

Two Kinds of Shepherds

4 Thus said the LORD my God: Be a shepherd of the flock
doomed to slaughter. 5Those who buy them kill them and go unpunished; and those who sell them say, "Blessed be the LORD, for I have
become rich"; and their own shepherds have no pity on them. 6For I
will no longer have pity on the inhabitants of the earth, says the LORD.
I will cause them, every one, to fall each into the hand of a neighbor,
and each into the hand of the king; and they shall devastate the earth,
and I will deliver no one from their hand.

7 So, on behalf of the sheep merchants, I became the shepherd
of the flock doomed to slaughter. I took two staffs; one I named Favor, the other I named Unity, and I tended the sheep. 8In one month
I disposed of the three shepherds, for I had become impatient with
them, and they also detested me. 9So I said, "I will not be your shepherd. What is to die, let it die; what is to be destroyed, let it be destroyed; and let those that are left devour the flesh of one another!"
10I took my staff Favor and broke it, annulling the covenant that I had

[a] Gk: Heb *He*

made with all the peoples. 11 So it was annulled on that day, and the
sheep merchants, who were watching me, knew that it was the word
of the LORD. 12 I then said to them, "If it seems right to you, give me
my wages; but if not, keep them." So they weighed out as my wages
thirty shekels of silver. 13 Then the LORD said to me, "Throw it into the
treasury"[a]—this lordly price at which I was valued by them. So I took
the thirty shekels of silver and threw them into the treasury[a] in the
house of the LORD. 14 Then I broke my second staff Unity, annulling
the family ties between Judah and Israel.

15 Then the LORD said to me: Take once more the implements
of a worthless shepherd. 16 For I am now raising up in the land a shepherd who does not care for the perishing, or seek the wandering,[b] or
heal the maimed, or nourish the healthy,[c] but devours the flesh of the
fat ones, tearing off even their hoofs.

17 Oh, my worthless shepherd,
who deserts the flock!
May the sword strike his arm
and his right eye!
Let his arm be completely withered,
his right eye utterly blinded!

Jerusalem's Victory

12

An Oracle.

The word of the LORD concerning Israel: Thus says the LORD,
who stretched out the heavens and founded the earth and formed the
human spirit within: 2 See, I am about to make Jerusalem a cup of reeling for all the surrounding peoples; it will be against Judah also in the
siege against Jerusalem. 3 On that day I will make Jerusalem a heavy
stone for all the peoples; all who lift it shall grievously hurt themselves. And all the nations of the earth shall come together against it.
4 On that day, says the LORD, I will strike every horse with panic, and
its rider with madness. But on the house of Judah I will keep a watch-
ful eye, when I strike every horse of the peoples with blindness. 5 Then
the clans of Judah shall say to themselves, "The inhabitants of Jerusalem have strength through the LORD of hosts, their God."

6 On that day I will make the clans of Judah like a blazing pot
on a pile of wood, like a flaming torch among sheaves; and they shall
devour to the right and to the left all the surrounding peoples, while
Jerusalem shall again be inhabited in its place, in Jerusalem.

7 And the LORD will give victory to the tents of Judah first, that
the glory of the house of David and the glory of the inhabitants of Jerusalem may not be exalted over that of Judah. 8 On that day the LORD

[a] Syr: Heb *it to the potter* [b] Syr Compare Gk Vg: Heb *the youth* [c] Meaning of Heb uncertain

11:12 thirty shekels of silver: From the context it is hard to tell whether thirty shekels of silver was too low or too high a sum to pay. This amount represents the price used to buy a person out of slavery (Exod 21:32) and Hosea's purchase price for the adulteress (Hos 3:2). Possibly this was a large sum and suggests the prophet's outrage over the price paid for incompetence. In the New Testament the allusion to this verse will be incorrectly attributed to Jeremiah (see Matt 27:9).

11:15-17 Take once more the implements of a worthless shepherd: The prophet resumes with unclear actions that point to the presence of an uncaring leader. Unlike 11:4-6 that makes no reference to leadership, 11:15-17 speaks to a human leader. Whether these verses recall the history of the nation's failed leaders or envision a future uncaring leader remains unclear.

12:2 a cup of reeling for the surrounding peoples: The image of nations becoming drunk after drinking from a cup appears in Jeremiah (Jer 25:15-31). The list there includes Jerusalem. Here Jerusalem will be the cause of drunkenness for other nations.

12:3-8 On that day . . . the house of David shall be like God: Meaning the day of God's victory, when Judah will be victorious over its enemies. The house of David refers to the descendants of King David (see also 2 Sam 7:16; Isa 9:1-7; 11:1-10). But here it seems God takes the role of ruler.

12:8 the house of David shall be like God, like the angel of the LORD: The Hebrew translated "God" could easily read as "gods." Later translations avoid the stunning declaration that humans can become like God through the use of a less direct word. A similar declaration appears in the description of the relationship between Moses and Aaron (Exod 4:16). No clear belief in human beings being divine occurs in Zechariah. The comparison, however, gives status to the future inhabitants of Jerusalem and the descendants of David.

12:10 the one whom they have pierced: The identities of the individual attacked and the attackers remain obscure. Presumably, a prophet, even a false prophet, can be inferred, based upon 13:3. New Testament writers use this phrase to highlight one of the aspects of the suffering of Jesus, being pierced in the side (John 19:37; Rev 1:7).

12:12-14 the land shall mourn, each family by itself: In the list of mourning families, the family of David stands out clearly. Nathan may refer to several persons. The prophet (2 Sam 11–12) and one of David's sons (2 Sam 5:14; 1 Chr 3:5; 14:4) seem like good candidates. If Levi (Deut 18:1) and Shimei (1 Chr 25:3; 2 Chr 29:14) represent priestly figures, then the list deals with royal and priestly families. The mourning in the families takes place in gender categories. This separation may point to the special role of women as mourners (Jer 9:16-25; Ezek 32:16).

13:4 a hairy mantle in order to deceive: Prophetic dress seems to include a distinctive mantle (see 1 Kgs 19:13, 19; 2 Kgs 2:8, 13). Elijah, known for passing his mantle to Elisha (2 Kgs 2:8), is described as a "hairy man" (2 Kgs 1:8), perhaps as a result of his garb. It also recalls the deception of Jacob, who covered himself with animal hair to trick his father (Gen 27:11-29).

13:5 I am no prophet: This denial echoes that by the prophet Amos when challenged by Amaziah (see Amos 7:14). While Amos denies being a prophet in order to distance himself from the professional class of prophets, these professional prophets deny their office as a means of hiding their shame over the quality of their work.

How does Luther understand Zechariah's message? For Martin Luther the message of Zechariah points toward the Messiah. He says this in his "Lectures on Zechariah" (1526): "This purpose [of the book] obviously involved especially one matter—to comfort the remnant of a dispersed people wretchedly afflicted by captivity and to encourage them not to despair. They should not lose confidence that the divine promises made to them about their coming King would be fulfilled: that Christ their King would finally come in spite of their totally desperate situation, in spite of their devastated land, in spite of a dispersed people facing a miserable death." (*LW* 20:3)

will shield the inhabitants of Jerusalem so that the feeblest among
them on that day shall be like David, and the house of David shall be
like God, like the angel of the LORD, at their head. 9 And on that day I
will seek to destroy all the nations that come against Jerusalem.

Mourning for the Pierced One

10 And I will pour out a spirit of compassion and supplication on
the house of David and the inhabitants of Jerusalem, so that, when
they look on the one[a] whom they have pierced, they shall mourn for
him, as one mourns for an only child, and weep bitterly over him, as
one weeps over a firstborn. 11 On that day the mourning in Jerusalem
will be as great as the mourning for Hadad-rimmon in the plain of
Megiddo. 12 The land shall mourn, each family by itself; the family of
the house of David by itself, and their wives by themselves; the family
of the house of Nathan by itself, and their wives by themselves; 13 the
family of the house of Levi by itself, and their wives by themselves;
the family of the Shimeites by itself, and their wives by themselves;
14 and all the families that are left, each by itself, and their wives by
themselves.

13 On that day a fountain shall be opened for the house of David
and the inhabitants of Jerusalem, to cleanse them from sin
and impurity.

Idolatry Cut Off

2 On that day, says the LORD of hosts, I will cut off the names of
the idols from the land, so that they shall be remembered no more;
and also I will remove from the land the prophets and the unclean
spirit. 3 And if any prophets appear again, their fathers and mothers
who bore them will say to them, "You shall not live, for you speak lies
in the name of the LORD"; and their fathers and their mothers who
bore them shall pierce them through when they prophesy. 4 On that
day the prophets will be ashamed, every one, of their visions when
they prophesy; they will not put on a hairy mantle in order to deceive,
5 but each of them will say, "I am no prophet, I am a tiller of the soil;
for the land has been my possession[b] since my youth." 6 And if anyone
asks them, "What are these wounds on your chest?"[c] the answer will
be "The wounds I received in the house of my friends."

The Shepherd Struck, the Flock Scattered

7 "Awake, O sword, against my shepherd,
against the man who is my associate,"
says the LORD of hosts.
Strike the shepherd, that the sheep may be scattered;

[a] Heb *on me* [b] Cn: Heb *for humankind has caused me to possess* [c] Heb *wounds between your hands*

I will turn my hand against the little ones.
8 In the whole land, says the LORD,
two-thirds shall be cut off and perish,
and one-third shall be left alive.
9 And I will put this third into the fire,
refine them as one refines silver,
and test them as gold is tested.
They will call on my name,
and I will answer them.
I will say, "They are my people";
and they will say, "The LORD is our God."

Future Warfare and Final Victory

14 See, a day is coming for the LORD, when the plunder taken
from you will be divided in your midst. 2For I will gather all
the nations against Jerusalem to battle, and the city shall be taken and
the houses looted and the women raped; half the city shall go into exile, but the rest of the people shall not be cut off from the city. 3Then
the LORD will go forth and fight against those nations as when he
fights on a day of battle. 4On that day his feet shall stand on the Mount
of Olives, which lies before Jerusalem on the east; and the Mount of
Olives shall be split in two from east to west by a very wide valley; so
that one half of the Mount shall withdraw northward, and the other
half southward. 5And you shall flee by the valley of the LORD's mountain,[a] for the valley between the mountains shall reach to Azal;[b] and
you shall flee as you fled from the earthquake in the days of King Uzziah of Judah. Then the LORD my God will come, and all the holy
ones with him.
6 On that day there shall not be[c] either cold or frost.[d] 7And there
shall be continuous day (it is known to the LORD), not day and not
night, for at evening time there shall be light.
8 On that day living waters shall flow out from Jerusalem, half of
them to the eastern sea and half of them to the western sea; it shall
continue in summer as in winter.
9 And the LORD will become king over all the earth; on that day
the LORD will be one and his name one.
10 The whole land shall be turned into a plain from Geba to Rimmon south of Jerusalem. But Jerusalem shall remain aloft on its site
from the Gate of Benjamin to the place of the former gate, to the Corner Gate, and from the Tower of Hananel to the king's wine presses.
11And it shall be inhabited, for never again shall it be doomed to destruction; Jerusalem shall abide in security.

---

[a] Heb *my mountains* [b] Meaning of Heb uncertain [c] Cn: Heb *there shall not be light* [d] Compare Gk Syr Vg Tg: Meaning of Heb uncertain

Luther understands how the book of Zechariah works for the displaced community that rebuilds Jerusalem. In common with other readers of the Bible at that time, he sees promises awaiting fulfillment in the time of Jesus. Luther seems sensitive to the fact that God responds to each generation's crises. God's ultimate act of deliverance experienced in Christ need not suggest that the people of Zechariah's time went without help from God. *Zechariah 13:9*

14:2 I will gather all the nations against Jerusalem to battle: The theme of a final great battle against the nations is common in the prophets (Isa 63:1-6; Ezek 38:14-23), as well as in literature known as apocalyptic (Joel 3:11-14; Rev 14:14-20). In this case the nations will be gathered to fight against Jerusalem.

14:2 the women raped: The practice of raping women as part of war may not have occurred in the ancient world as it does in modern conflict. However, women from conquered nations, as part of the booty, most likely are given over to men from the victorious armies.

14:3 Then the LORD will go forth and fight: The image of the divine warrior emerges here (see Isa 26:21; 42:13). The LORD engages in the actual fight against the enemies of the people. The picture of a giant with huge feet that stands aside the mountains dominates the verse. The mere steps of the giant create new valleys. The image of the giant links with the mythic figures of ancient Near Eastern traditions.

14:7 On that day...it is known to the LORD: The expression "on that day" occurs eighteen times in the second part of the book. It speaks to a future day in much the same way as the term Day of the LORD, as a time of judgment. The final conclusion to the problems in the world occurs on this day.

14:8 living waters shall flow out from Jerusalem: The expression living waters refers to flowing water, as distinct from stagnant water. The descriptive phrase connects with the images of Jerusalem and the temple as the center of the earth. In those pictures water flows from Jerusalem bringing life to the earth (Ps 84:5-6; 46:4; Ezek 47:1-12).

12 This shall be the plague with which the LORD will strike all
the peoples that wage war against Jerusalem: their flesh shall rot while
they are still on their feet; their eyes shall rot in their sockets, and
their tongues shall rot in their mouths. 13 On that day a great panic
from the LORD shall fall on them, so that each will seize the hand of
a neighbor, and the hand of the one will be raised against the hand
of the other; 14 even Judah will fight at Jerusalem. And the wealth of
all the surrounding nations shall be collected—gold, silver, and garments in great abundance. 15 And a plague like this plague shall fall on
the horses, the mules, the camels, the donkeys, and whatever animals
may be in those camps.

16 Then all who survive of the nations that have come against Jerusalem shall go up year after year to worship the King, the LORD of
hosts, and to keep the festival of booths.[a] 17 If any of the families of
the earth do not go up to Jerusalem to worship the King, the LORD
of hosts, there will be no rain upon them. 18 And if the family of Egypt
do not go up and present themselves, then on them shall[b] come the
plague that the LORD inflicts on the nations that do not go up to keep
the festival of booths.[a] 19 Such shall be the punishment of Egypt and
the punishment of all the nations that do not go up to keep the festival
of booths.[a]

20 On that day there shall be inscribed on the bells of the horses,
"Holy to the LORD." And the cooking pots in the house of the LORD
shall be as holy as[c] the bowls in front of the altar; 21 and every cooking pot in Jerusalem and Judah shall be sacred to the LORD of hosts,
so that all who sacrifice may come and use them to boil the flesh of
the sacrifice. And there shall no longer be traders[d] in the house of the
LORD of hosts on that day.

---

[a] Or *tabernacles*; Heb *succoth* [b] Gk Syr: Heb *shall not* [c] Heb *shall be like* [d] Or *Canaanites*

14:16 the festival of booths: This observance, also known as Sukkoth, commemorates the harvest ingathering and lasts for seven days (Deut 16:13-17; Lev 23:39-43). In the period after the exile, Sukkoth observances take place (Neh 8:13-18). Its title as simply "the festival" testifies to its importance in this period (Ezek 45:22-25; Lev 23:39). Apart from being a celebration of the harvest, Sukkoth observances celebrate the enthronement of God in the ark of the covenant (1 Kgs 8:1-2). Zechariah incorporates these elements, suggesting Sukkoth as the singular religious observance in the future that would draw diverse groups of people. At the same time, however, it undercuts the idea of unconditional openness by enforcing participation in this observance. Nations that do not go to celebrate this festival face punishment (14:17-19).

14:20-21 there shall be inscribed... cooking pots...sacred to the LORD of hosts: This list of objects used in and out of the temple speaks to the new state of holiness for all things in Jerusalem. The pots used for minor ceremonial purposes will become as holy as the bowls in which offerings are presented. The spread of holiness continues into the everyday part of Jerusalem and Judah where similar pots are used in sacrifices. Every ceremonial pot, whether used in the temple or not, becomes holy. By extension every sacrifice becomes acceptable to the LORD.

14:21 there shall no longer be traders in the house of the LORD: The Hebrew uses the word "Canaanite," translated here as "traders." In several places the term Canaanite appears in contexts relating to trading activity (see Hos 12:7; Zeph 1:11). The negative associations with Canaanites as distinct ethnic groups from earlier books such as Deuteronomy may not apply here (Deut 7:1-6). Equally, the prohibition of traders from the new temple because of corrupt or disruptive practices, as in the Gospels, seems not to be the case here (see Mark 11:15-17; John 2:13-17). The idea of increased holiness in the verse may suggest that the absence of "traders" results from the incorporation of everything into the full holiness of the temple. The distinctions of buyers and sellers, insiders and outsiders will fall away on that day.

How do you imagine world peace taking place? Would everyone be the same, or would people learn to live with their differences? How might we share our vision of everyone worshiping our God with those who do not believe in our God?

Malachi 4:6

MALACHI

Background File

We have no biographical details about a prophet named Malachi. In Hebrew *malachi* simply means "my messenger," so the title here may not be a proper name. Set in the period after the return to Jerusalem, the book calls for reforms in the priesthood and a revival in devotion to God. These calls became necessary because the people's commitment to worshiping and serving God were at a low point. The expectations raised by earlier prophets remained unfulfilled. Taking the form of a courtroom drama, Malachi lays out God's case to the priests and the people.

What's the Story?

The book of Malachi appears to have been written sometime after Haggai and Zechariah 1–8 (see the Introductions to those books) which deal with the reconstruction of the temple. The temple has been rebuilt and rededicated in 515 B.C.E., and priests are offering sacrifices again (1:6-14). Malachi's concerns revolve around the quality of ritual practices. This differs from a book like Amos that fusses over excess religious activity. While the book of Jeremiah speaks against the empty certainty of the temple system, Malachi assumes that sacrifices when offered correctly can be powerful. The book makes a case for treating God with respect deserving of a supreme ruler, avoiding participation in other religions, and remaining confident in God even if things appear bleak.

The prophet contends with priests over inappropriate sacrifices (1:6-14) and with worshipers for their neglect of paying proper tithes (3:8-9). In Malachi, the priests bear the blame for the depression in the community. The priests' failures consist of the dual and related offenses of shoddy ritual (2:1-3) and lack of instruction (2:7-9). This results in unacceptable offerings by the people, idolatry, and disobedience to the law. When the priesthood is reformed and their service is acceptable to God, then God's judgment can reasonably be handed out to others who offend God and God's law (3:5-7). Malachi argues that acceptable sacrifices, diligence over tithes, and proper instruction will lead to faithful action.

At the heart of the text lies the coming messenger of God ahead of the day of the LORD, a day of judgment (3:1-7). The promised messenger, the day of the LORD, and God's own word assure the faithful of their reward (3:16-18). The final chapter not only closes the book but also the Old Testament. In looking towards the future day of the LORD, it also looks backwards. The future day holds punishment for offenders (4:1) and reward for the faithful (4:2-3). Malachi appeals to past leaders, Moses (4:4) and

Elijah (4:5-6), who both experienced God on Mount Horeb (Deut 4:9-14; 1 Kgs 19:9-18) to call the people to return to following God.

What's the Message?

A key to understanding the message of the book lies in the many rhetorical questions asked by God and the people through the messenger, Malachi. God asks: "If I am a master, where is the honor due me?" (1:6). The people wonder: "Has not one God created us? Why then are we faithless to one another, profaning the covenant of our ancestors?" (2:10). These questions lay the groundwork for ongoing disputes with imagined persons that lead to rebuke, accusation, contradiction and the word of God. The book's core question, "Where is the God of justice" (2:17) gets to the heart of the anxiety affecting the people.

The people wonder why their difficult life has not really changed. After the temple was built, they expected that the promises and visions of prophets such as Zechariah (Zech 8), Isaiah (Isa 61:1-6), and Ezekiel (Ezek 47–48) would be fulfilled. But visions of a bright future appear dim. The people question the value of serving God when those who do not serve God continue to prosper (3:13-15). Apathy exists among the people over the lack of justice. In response, the prophet confronts those needing to be reassured that their faith in God is not misplaced. God will be faithful, but God expects the people to be faithful as well. That faithfulness includes proper worship and treating others with justice. Ending on the promise of Elijah, Christian readers continue into the New Testament with the challenge to demonstrate clear loyalty to God. They will hear Jesus as another call from God to firm faith.

1:2-4 Esau…Edom: Jacob rather than Esau the first-born receives the blessing of their father Isaac (Gen 25:19-34; 27:21-29). Jacob here stands for Israel. Esau is identified with the land of Edom, and his descendants are the Edomites (Gen 36:1). Esau's exclusion from the father's blessing finds expression in the negativity associated with his descendants. Several prophetic oracles announce judgment on Edom (see Isa 34; Jer 49:7-22; Ezek 25:12-14; Obadiah 1-16).

1:6-7 where is the honor due me?…How have we despised your name?: Throughout the book of Malachi these rhetorical questions introduce the message to come. In response to the charge contained in the questions, the priests who have dishonored and disrespected God (1:8-14) ask for evidence to support the charge. A direct answer follows describing the priests' disrespect of God (1:7-8).

1 An oracle. The word of the LORD to Israel by Malachi.[a]

Israel Preferred to Edom

2 I have loved you, says the LORD. But you say, "How have you
loved us?" Is not Esau Jacob's brother? says the LORD. Yet I have loved
Jacob [3]but I have hated Esau; I have made his hill country a desolation
and his heritage a desert for jackals. [4]If Edom says, "We are shattered
but we will rebuild the ruins," the LORD of hosts says: They may build,
but I will tear down, until they are called the wicked country, the people with whom the LORD is angry forever. [5]Your own eyes shall see
this, and you shall say, "Great is the LORD beyond the borders of
Israel!"

Corruption of the Priesthood

6 A son honors his father, and servants their master. If then I am a
father, where is the honor due me? And if I am a master, where is the
respect due me? says the LORD of hosts to you, O priests, who despise
my name. You say, "How have we despised your name?" [7]By offering

[a] Or *by my messenger*

polluted food on my altar. And you say, "How have we polluted it?"[a]
By thinking that the LORD's table may be despised. 8When you offer blind animals in sacrifice, is that not wrong? And when you offer
those that are lame or sick, is that not wrong? Try presenting that to
your governor; will he be pleased with you or show you favor? says
the LORD of hosts. 9And now implore the favor of God, that he may
be gracious to us. The fault is yours. Will he show favor to any of you?
says the LORD of hosts. 10Oh, that someone among you would shut
the temple[b] doors, so that you would not kindle fire on my altar in
vain! I have no pleasure in you, says the LORD of hosts, and I will not
accept an offering from your hands. 11For from the rising of the sun
to its setting my name is great among the nations, and in every place
incense is offered to my name, and a pure offering; for my name is
great among the nations, says the LORD of hosts. 12But you profane it
when you say that the Lord's table is polluted, and the food for it[c] may
be despised. 13"What a weariness this is," you say, and you sniff at me,[d]
says the LORD of hosts. You bring what has been taken by violence
or is lame or sick, and this you bring as your offering! Shall I accept
that from your hand? says the LORD. 14Cursed be the cheat who has
a male in the flock and vows to give it, and yet sacrifices to the Lord
what is blemished; for I am a great King, says the LORD of hosts, and
my name is reverenced among the nations.

2 And now, O priests, this command is for you. 2If you will not
listen, if you will not lay it to heart to give glory to my name, says
the LORD of hosts, then I will send the curse on you and I will curse
your blessings; indeed I have already cursed them,[e] because you do
not lay it to heart. 3I will rebuke your offspring, and spread dung on
your faces, the dung of your offerings, and I will put you out of my
presence.[f]

4 Know, then, that I have sent this command to you, that my
covenant with Levi may hold, says the LORD of hosts. 5My covenant
with him was a covenant of life and well-being, which I gave him; this
called for reverence, and he revered me and stood in awe of my name.
6True instruction was in his mouth, and no wrong was found on his
lips. He walked with me in integrity and uprightness, and he turned
many from iniquity. 7For the lips of a priest should guard knowledge,
and people should seek instruction from his mouth, for he is the messenger of the LORD of hosts. 8But you have turned aside from the way;
you have caused many to stumble by your instruction; you have corrupted the covenant of Levi, says the LORD of hosts, 9and so I make
you despised and abased before all the people, inasmuch as you have
not kept my ways but have shown partiality in your instruction.

[a] Gk: Heb *you* [b] Heb lacks *temple* [c] Compare Syr Tg: Heb *its fruit, its food* [d] Another reading is *at it* [e] Heb *it* [f] Cn Compare Gk Syr: Heb *and he shall bear you to it*

1:8 blind animals in sacrifice... lame or sick: Instructions in Deut 15:21; 17:1 and Lev 22:22 prohibit the use of blemished (Mal 1:14) animals in sacrifices. The prophet accuses the priests of offering improper sacrifices, animals that are blind, lame, sick, or in some other way unacceptable. In the same way that they are unsuitable gifts for the emperor, they are unsuitable as a sacrifice for God.

What does it say about God that God demands the sacrifice of the best animals? What would your best sacrifice look like?

1:10 kindle fire on my altar in vain: Sacrifices are burned on an altar as a symbolic offering of the gift of animal, grain or other offering to God. Shutting down temple sacrifices ("fire on my altar") altogether would be better than offering improper sacrifices and offerings. The demand repeats the challenge to ensure that sacrifices are offered in a way worthy of God.

2:2 I will curse your blessings: Priests are expected to pronounce blessings on the people (Num 6:22-27), but because of their actions, God will turn their blessings into curses.

2:4 covenant with Levi: Various priestly groups trace their family line back to an early descendant of Levi, much as kings can be traced back to David. While descendants of Levi such as Aaron and Phineas functioned as priests, these should not be confused with the Levites who later became assistants to the priests. No specific declaration relating to a covenant with Levi appears in the Bible, although Numbers 25:11-13 hints at the grant of a perpetual priesthood to Phineas and his descendants in the form of a "covenant of peace."

The Covenant Profaned by Judah

10 Have we not all one father? Has not one God created us?
Why then are we faithless to one another, profaning the covenant of
our ancestors? 11 Judah has been faithless, and abomination has been
committed in Israel and in Jerusalem; for Judah has profaned the
sanctuary of the LORD, which he loves, and has married the daughter
of a foreign god. 12 May the LORD cut off from the tents of Jacob anyone who does this—any to witness[a] or answer, or to bring an offering
to the LORD of hosts.

13 And this you do as well: You cover the LORD's altar with tears,
with weeping and groaning because he no longer regards the offering
or accepts it with favor at your hand. 14 You ask, "Why does he not?"
Because the LORD was a witness between you and the wife of your
youth, to whom you have been faithless, though she is your companion and your wife by covenant. 15 Did not one God make her?[b] Both
flesh and spirit are his.[c] And what does the one God[d] desire? Godly
offspring. So look to yourselves, and do not let anyone be faithless to
the wife of his youth. 16 For I hate[e] divorce, says the LORD, the God
of Israel, and covering one's garment with violence, says the LORD of
hosts. So take heed to yourselves and do not be faithless.

17 You have wearied the LORD with your words. Yet you say,
"How have we wearied him?" By saying, "All who do evil are good in
the sight of the LORD, and he delights in them." Or by asking, "Where
is the God of justice?"

The Coming Messenger

3 See, I am sending my messenger to prepare the way before me,
and the Lord whom you seek will suddenly come to his temple.
The messenger of the covenant in whom you delight—indeed, he is
coming, says the LORD of hosts. 2 But who can endure the day of his
coming, and who can stand when he appears?

For he is like a refiner's fire and like fullers' soap; 3 he will sit as a refiner and purifier of silver, and he will purify the descendants of Levi
and refine them like gold and silver, until they present offerings to the
LORD in righteousness.[f] 4 Then the offering of Judah and Jerusalem
will be pleasing to the LORD as in the days of old and as in former
years.

5 Then I will draw near to you for judgment; I will be swift to bear
witness against the sorcerers, against the adulterers, against those who
swear falsely, against those who oppress the hired workers in their
wages, the widow and the orphan, against those who thrust aside the
alien, and do not fear me, says the LORD of hosts.

[a] Cn Compare Gk: Heb *arouse* [b] Or *Has he not made one?* [c] Cn: Heb *and a remnant of spirit was his* [d] Heb *he* [e] Cn: Heb *he hates* [f] Or *right offerings to the LORD*

2:11 has married the daughter of a foreign god: The language in the verse can be taken two ways. It may suggest a case of idolatry. The worship of goddesses like Asherah continued in Israel and Judah for a long time (see 1 Kgs 15:9-13; 18:19). Or it may refer to marriage to a foreign woman. This issue appears to threaten Israel's identity in Ezra (9:1-4; 10:6-44) and Nehemiah (13:23-30).

2:14 wife of your youth...your wife by covenant: These two terms refer to the same person, in this case God and the worship of God. Judah's unfaithfulness with the goddess (2:11) breaches the covenant of marriage to its first love, God.

2:16 I hate divorce: The Hebrew word translated "divorce" literally means, "sending." The cause for divorce lies in the breaches of covenant loyalty outlined in 2:13-15 and refers to the worship of a foreign goddess (2:11). The rejection of divorce finds justification in the fact that it will only cover over Judah's sins like a garment. Prophets use the image of marriage to speak about religious unfaithfulness, but this time the unfaithful spouse is male (see also Hos 1–3; Isa 5:1-7; Jer 3:1-5). The outburst against divorce here hinders a further injustice to the wronged party, namely God. Provisions for a man to divorce his wife (Deut 24:1-2) are not nullified by this verse.

2:17 All who do evil are good... Where is the God of justice?: The people question why those who do wrong seem to be prospering, while those who are faithful to God find no success. They call for God to be fair to them, since they are playing by the rules. The perception that God is not fair to them leads the people to offer less than quality offerings and to stray in their duty to God.

3:1-3 sending my messenger...of the covenant: The messenger is not clearly identified, but it is one who will prepare the people for the LORD's return by making sure the priest and the people bring and offer proper sacrifices to God. In the New Testament, Malachi's messenger language is used to describe John the Baptist (see Matt 11:10; Mark 1:2). The "refiner's fire" refers to heating precious metals such as gold and silver to burn away impurities.

3:5 I will be swift to bear witness against: If the priests and people return to true worship of God, God will punish those who live outside God's law and justice.

6 For I the LORD do not change; therefore you, O children of
Jacob, have not perished. [7]Ever since the days of your ancestors you
have turned aside from my statutes and have not kept them. Return
to me, and I will return to you, says the LORD of hosts. But you say,
"How shall we return?"

Do Not Rob God

8 Will anyone rob God? Yet you are robbing me! But you say,
"How are we robbing you?" In your tithes and offerings! [9]You are
cursed with a curse, for you are robbing me—the whole nation of
you! [10]Bring the full tithe into the storehouse, so that there may be
food in my house, and thus put me to the test, says the LORD of hosts;
see if I will not open the windows of heaven for you and pour down
for you an overflowing blessing. [11]I will rebuke the locust[a] for you, so
that it will not destroy the produce of your soil; and your vine in the
field shall not be barren, says the LORD of hosts. [12]Then all nations
will count you happy, for you will be a land of delight, says the LORD
of hosts.

13 You have spoken harsh words against me, says the LORD. Yet
you say, "How have we spoken against you?" [14]You have said, "It is
vain to serve God. What do we profit by keeping his command or by
going about as mourners before the LORD of hosts? [15]Now we count
the arrogant happy; evildoers not only prosper, but when they put
God to the test they escape."

The Reward of the Faithful

16 Then those who revered the LORD spoke with one another.
The LORD took note and listened, and a book of remembrance was
written before him of those who revered the LORD and thought on
his name. [17]They shall be mine, says the LORD of hosts, my special
possession on the day when I act, and I will spare them as parents
spare their children who serve them. [18]Then once more you shall see
the difference between the righteous and the wicked, between one
who serves God and one who does not serve him.

The Great Day of the LORD

4 [b] See, the day is coming, burning like an oven, when all the arrogant and all evildoers will be stubble; the day that comes
shall burn them up, says the LORD of hosts, so that it will leave them
neither root nor branch. [2]But for you who revere my name the sun
of righteousness shall rise, with healing in its wings. You shall go
out leaping like calves from the stall. [3]And you shall tread down the
wicked, for they will be ashes under the soles of your feet, on the day
when I act, says the LORD of hosts.

[a] Heb *devourer* [b] Ch 4.1-6 are Ch 3.19-24 in Heb

3:10 full tithe: The expectation of a tithe refers to one-tenth of the agricultural yield of the people. Deuteronomy instructs worshipers to bring the tithes to the central sanctuary (Deut 12:5-19) while Numbers teaches that the tithe be given to the Levites who in turn would give a further tithe (Num 18: 21-32).

In what way does the giving of tithes reflect one's relationship with God? Do you think that paying tithes can be linked to any guarantees of blessings? If our offerings do not guarantee God's blessings, why do we give them?

3:16 book of remembrance: Various kinds of books of judgment are mentioned in the Bible (see Ps 139:16; Dan 7:10; 10:21; Rev 13:8; 20:15; 21:27). An actual book that keeps records of wrongs may not exist, contrary to images in Exodus 32:32-33 and Revelation 3:5. The reference here emphasizes the idea that God recognizes those who have honored God and live righteous lives.

How do Lutherans speak of the role of good works? The book of Malachi defines the difference between the righteous and the wicked as one of proper reverence for God. The righteous also are described as those who serve God. This service does not earn them God's favor but rather reflects their reverence for God (3:16-18). For Lutherans, works can be *bad* or *good*: it depends on what they are for. Works are *bad* when the Christian labors under the illusion that these deeds earn salvation. Such "good works" offend a God who provides a way of salvation through Christ. Christ is God's greatest work in our midst; we do not have to do anything else to earn God's favor. "Works" are *good* when they follow from the joyous affirmation of God's good work in Christ. Faith in God's promise of salvation acts in gratitude to serve the neighbor. *Malachi 3:18*

4:2 sun of righteousness: The image draws upon a representation of the Babylonian god of justice (Shamash) as a winged solar disk. Shamash's movements were believed to bring life and light to the world. Here, God will rise to bring healing to the righteous on the great day of the LORD.

What do you think of the idea that God will rise with healing for those who "revere" God's name, but punish those who do not live right lives? How have you experienced God's healing? Do you believe healing came because you deserved it? Why or why not?

4:4-6 Moses...Elijah: In Exodus (19–40) Moses received God's law on Mount Horeb (Sinai). The prophet Elijah met God at Horeb (1 Kgs 19:4-18) and is regarded as a powerful servant of God. Since Elijah did not really die but was carried away into heaven (2 Kgs 2:11), he serves as a fitting person to return to announce the coming Day of the Lord. Although not given the title messenger here he performs the role of messenger.

4 Remember the teaching of my servant Moses, the statutes and
ordinances that I commanded him at Horeb for all Israel.

5 Lo, I will send you the prophet Elijah before the great and terrible day of the LORD comes. 6 He will turn the hearts of parents to their
children and the hearts of children to their parents, so that I will not
come and strike the land with a curse.[a]

[a] Or *a ban of utter destruction*

THE NEW TESTAMENT

NEW TESTAMENT OVERVIEW

The New Testament is the second and shortest part of the Christian Bible. It is the part of the Bible that has stories about Jesus Christ, his teachings, his deeds, and his importance. It is only in the New Testament, too, that the writings of early Christians concerning Jesus and the Christian life are to be found.

The New Testament contains twenty-seven "books." Some are hardly books in the modern sense, since they are only a page or two long. But others are as long as fifty or sixty pages in most copies of the Bible in English. The books can be grouped into four types of writings.

The first four books of the New Testament are the Gospels (Matthew, Mark, Luke, and John). The modern word *gospel* comes from an Old English word (*godspel*) that meant "good news." So the four Gospels tell the "good news" of Jesus Christ. There are differences among them, but they are alike in that they tell about Jesus' life and ministry. Two of them (Matthew and Luke) have stories about Jesus' parents and his birth. All four tell about his baptism by John the Baptist in the Jordan River, the call of his disciples, his teachings, his miraculous deeds, and his arrest in Jerusalem, followed by his suffering, death, and resurrection. No single gospel tells all that can be known about Jesus. More will be said about the differences among the four Gospels in The Gospels and Acts introduction, p. 1599-1600.

Following the Gospels and closely related to them is one book that stands by itself—the book known as Acts. Its full name is the Acts of the Apostles, and it tells of the activities of the apostles and other disciples of Jesus after his death and resurrection. It continues the "orderly account of the events" initially begun in the Gospel of Luke (see Luke 1:1-4; Acts 1:1) and covers the story of the early church from about 30 to 60 C.E. The first two chapters tell the stories of Jesus going from earth into heaven (his ascension) and the Holy Spirit coming to Jesus' followers on the day that is celebrated by Christians as Pentecost. The next six chapters have stories of early Christians and the growth of the church in its earliest years. Most attention is given to Peter and Stephen. The rest of the book, chapters 9–28, is mostly about the apostle Paul, his travels, and his other activities.

The four Gospels and Acts tell stories, but they also contain important teachings. In addition, they provide the basis for all the major Christian celebrations, such as Christmas, Easter, and Pentecost. It is because Easter and Pentecost happened on a Sunday that Christians have gathered for worship on Sunday since the beginning of Christianity.

Following the Gospels and Acts come twenty-one letters or epistles (a formal name for letters). Whether one calls them letters or epistles, they make up about one-third of the content of the New Testament. The letters can be divided into sub-groups. Thirteen are "Pauline Letters," because they were written by the apostle Paul or by one of his associates. The Letter to the Hebrews reads like a letter but it is not addressed to anyone in particular. The seven that follow are called the "General Letters." These have traditionally been called the "Catholic Letters" (*catholic* here means "general" or "universal"). They are called general letters because they were written not to a specific person or community of believers but to the ancient churches in general.

The last book of the New Testament is called Revelation or, more fully, the Revelation to John. Sometimes the book is called the *Apocalypse* of John, because that is a Greek word for Revelation. Though it contains letters addressed to seven different churches, Revelation is a type of literature known as *apocalyptic,* writings that describe symbolic visions of current or future events and what those visions mean.

The twenty-seven books of the New Testament were all written in Greek, because that was the language the authors and the early readers used throughout the then-known world. The New Testament in English Bibles of today is translated from ancient Greek texts, of which over five thousand exist in libraries in various parts of the world. Though the "original" hand-written texts from actual authors no longer exist, translators use very old copies of manuscripts dating back to 300 C.E. and some fragments of manuscripts that are even earlier. The most important texts used are located in libraries in Rome and London. Using various methods, scholars have worked to get as close to the original texts as possible.

THE GOSPELS AND ACTS

The four Gospels (Matthew, Mark, Luke, and John) provide accounts of the life, ministry, and teachings of Jesus. The book of Acts tells the story of the early church.

The word *gospel* means "good news." The four Gospels in the New Testament tell the "good news" of Jesus Christ. The four are often divided into two groups. Matthew, Mark, and Luke are called the Synoptic Gospels. The word *synoptic* is made up of two smaller words that come into English from Greek: *syn,* meaning "together," and *optic* having to do with "seeing." These three gospels "see together" or have a "common perspective" on the life and ministry of Jesus. That is not to say that they are identical, but the three are quite different from the Gospel of John. For example, the Synoptic Gospels include things that are not in the Gospel of John, such as the parables of Jesus, the story of Jesus' transfiguration, and the Last Supper scene. The Gospel of John also follows a different order of events. These and other differences have been noticed for a long time. One ancient writer, Clement of Alexandria, in Egypt, noticed the differences. At some time between 180 and 200 C.E. he remarked that Matthew, Mark, and Luke wrote about the "outward facts" of Jesus' life, while John wrote a "spiritual gospel."

It is commonly thought that the four Gospels, as we have them today, were all written in the last third of the first century. That means that several decades passed between the final days of Jesus' life, death, and resurrection (about 30 C.E.) and the writing of the Gospels. According to most leading scholars today, the Gospel of Mark was probably the first to be written, around 70 C.E. or perhaps a few years earlier. The Gospels of Matthew and Luke are based in part on the Gospel of Mark and were written between 80 and 90 C.E. There were no rules in those days against using other people's work.

The authors of Matthew and Luke also made use of other sources and traditions known to them (see Luke 1:1-4). The commonly held view is that both made use of a document, now known as "Q." The Q document does not exist intact among ancient texts available, but its existence is a theory that has had strong support. The letter Q is an abbreviation given to the document by German scholars in the nineteenth century. It is shorthand for the German word *quelle*, meaning "source." The Q document would have been the source for more than two hundred verses in Matthew and Luke (but not in Mark) that are nearly identical (see, for example, Matt 6:25-33 and Luke 12:22-31). In addition, Matthew used his own special traditions, called "M," and Luke used his special traditions, known as "L." The relationship between the three gospels can be diagrammed as follows:

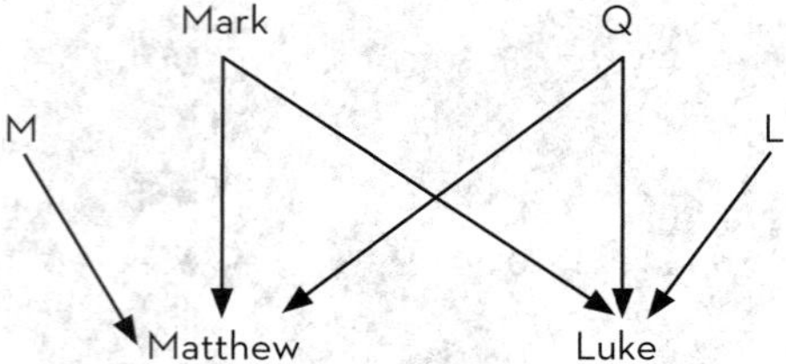

The Gospel of John is based on yet other sources and traditions and was likely the last to be written, probably near the end of the first century.

It is best to think of the four Gospels as giving four portraits of Jesus. That is to say, each gospel writer emphasized different facets and features of Jesus' ministry, just as different portrait painters would highlight different features of the person being portrayed.

The Gospel of Mark, the oldest and shortest of the Gospels, highlights the activities of Jesus. When it is compared with the other gospels, it does not provide as much of his teachings. Jesus is shown to be the strong Son of God who moves about quickly (the Greek word for "immediately" shows up forty times in the Greek text of Mark). He performs miracles, but he also calls upon his disciples and others not to speak about him to others until after his death and resurrection (9:9). Only then could people truly understand who he is. The Gospel of Matthew follows the general outline of Mark, but its author has inserted a lot of teaching material into the outline. The Gospel of Luke follows the outline as well, but its author has inserted some of the most memorable traditions about Jesus, showing his care for the poor, for Gentiles (non-Jews), and women. The Gospel of John portrays Jesus as the Son of God who has come into the world to reveal God and to identify himself as the one who brings eternal life to all believers.

The Acts of the Apostles is a bridge between the four Gospels and the letters of Paul that follow. The book is devoted largely to Paul's missionary journeys and ministry. Its author also wrote the Gospel of Luke, a fact made clear by comparing Luke 1:1-4 and Acts 1:1-2. Whoever wrote Luke-Acts wrote about one-fourth of the pages of the New Testament.

The *order* of the Gospels in the New Testament may be due to ancient ideas about the sequence in which they were written (Matthew earliest, John latest). But there may be other reasons. Matthew's gospel may come first because of its popularity in the early church for preaching and teaching. It offers the most in teaching material. The Gospel of John may come last because of its more spiritual or "theological" interpretation of Jesus, making a link to the rest of the New Testament. That the other two were placed in their present order may be due to the ancient view of their time of writing, and going from the shorter to the longer.

Questions about the authorship of these five books, the time and place they were written, and other details are dealt with in the introductions to each.

Jesus' Ministry

Miracles	
Healing of Individuals	
Man with leprosy	Matt 8:1-4; Mark 1:40-44; Luke 5:12-14
Roman centurion's servant	Matt 8:5-13; Luke 7:1-10
Peter's mother-in-law	Matt 8:14-17; Mark 1:29-34; Luke 4:38-39
Two demon-possessed men from Gadara	Matt 8:28-34
Paralyzed man	Matt 9:1-8; Mark 2:1-12; Luke 5:17-26
Two blind men	Matt 9:27-31
Man mute and possessed	Matt 9:32-33
Man with a withered hand	Matt 12:9-13; Mark 3:1-6; Luke 6:6-11
Man blind, mute, and possessed	Matt 12:22
Canaanite woman's daughter	Matt 15:21-28
Boy with epilepsy	Matt 17:14-18
Two blind men	Matt 20:29-34
Man with an evil spirit	Mark 1:23-26; Luke 4:33-36
Deaf man	Mark 7:31-37
Blind man	Mark 8:22-26
Bartimaeus, or one blind man	Mark 10:46-52; Luke 18:35-43
Woman with bleeding	Luke 8:43-48
Crippled woman	Luke 13:11-13
Man with dropsy	Luke 14:1-4
Ten men with leprosy	Luke 17:11-19
The high priest's servant	Luke 22:50-51
Royal official's son	John 4:46-54
Man at the pool of Bethesda	John 5:1-9
Man born blind	John 9:1-41
Control of nature	
Calming of storm	Matt 8:22-27; Mark 4:35-41; Luke 8:22-25
Feeding of 5,000	Matt 14:1-21; Mark 6:35-44; Luke 9:12-17; John 6:5-15
Walking on water	Matt 14:22-23; Mark 6:45-52; John 6:16-21
Feeding of 4,000	Matt 15:29-39; Mark 8:1-9
Fig tree withers	Matt 21:18-22; Mark 11:12-14, 20-25
Huge catch of fish	Luke 5:1-11; John 21:1-11

Water into wine	John 2:1-11
Raising the dead	
Jairus's daughter	Mark 5:22-42
Widow at Nain's son	Luke 7:11-15
Lazarus	John 11:1-44
Parables	
Light of the world	Matt 5:14-15
Wise and foolish builders	Matt 7:24-27; Luke 6:47-49
New wine in old wineskins	Matt 9:16-17; Mark 2:21-22; Luke 5:36-39
Sower	Matt 13:1-8, 18-23; Mark 4:3-8, 14-20; Luke 8:5-8, 11-15
Weeds	Matt 13:24-30, 36-43
Mustard seed	Matt 13:31-32
Yeast	Matt 13:33; Luke 13:20-21
Hidden treasure and pearl	Matt 13:44-46
Net	Matt 13:47-50
Lost sheep	Matt 18:12-14; Luke 15:3-7
Unforgiving servant	Matt 18:23-34
Laborers in the vineyard	Matt 20:1-16
Two sons	Matt 21:28-31
Tenants	Matt 21:33-44; Mark 12:1-12; Luke 20:9-18
Wedding banquet	Matt 22:2-14
Fig tree	Matt 24:32-35; Mark 13:28-29; Luke 21:29-31
Ten bridesmaids	Matt 25:1-13
Talents	Matt 25:14-30
Sheep and the goats	Matt 25:31-46
Growing seed	Mark 4:26-29
Canceled debts	Luke 7:41-43
Good Samaritan	Luke 10:30-37
Persistent friend	Luke 11:5-8
Rich fool	Luke 12:16-21
Watchful slaves	Luke 12:35-40
Faithful servant	Luke 12:42-48
Unfruitful fig tree	Luke 13:6-9
Honor at a banquet	Luke 14:7-14
The great dinner	Luke 14:16-24

Cost of discipleship	Luke 14:28-33
Lost coin	Luke 15:8-10
Prodigal (or lost) son	Luke 15:11-32
Dishonest manager	Luke 16:1-8
Rich man and Lazarus	Luke 16:19-31
Obedient servants	Luke 17:7-10
Persistent widow	Luke 18:2-8
Pharisee and the tax collector	Luke 18:10-14
Ten pounds	Luke 19:11-27
Teachings	
Beatitudes	Matt 5:1-12
Sermon on the Mount	Matt 5–7
Lord's Prayer	Matt 6:5-15
Sending out the Twelve	Matt 10
Wealth	Matt 19:16-30
Greatest commandment	Matt 22:34-40
Give to Caesar	Mark 12:13-17
Golden rule	Luke 6:31
Worry	Luke 12:22-34
Discipleship	Luke 14:25-35
Born again	John 3:1-21
Living water	John 4:1-26
Bread of life	John 6:25-59
Good shepherd	John 10:1-21
The way and the truth and the life	John 14:5-14
Vine and branches	John 15:1-17

Matthew 5:14, 16

MATTHEW

Background File

The Gospel of Matthew was probably written in the mid-80s C.E. The unknown author used the Gospel of Mark plus other oral and written sources, including a document that scholars refer to as "Q." The name *Matthew* was attached to the gospel early in the second century. Where Matthew was written is also unknown. Possibilities include Antioch in Syria or someplace in Galilee.

What's the Story?

After the temple in Jerusalem was destroyed by the Romans in 70 C.E., Judaism wrestled with its identity. Christians participated in that debate, along with other Jewish movements. Rabbinic Judaism and Christianity emerged as distinct-but-related movements. Each claimed Israel's heritage.

Christians also debated their relation to Judaism, the inclusion of Gentiles, and the relation between Jews and Gentiles within the church. Some followed Jewish traditions that identified Gentiles (non-Jews) as sinners. For them, Gentile believers needed to become Jewish. Others followed Jewish traditions that saw Gentiles in light of God's covenant with Noah (Gen 9:1-17). For them, Gentile believers need not become Jewish. The one body of Christ included both Jews and Gentiles (see Gal 3:28; Acts 15).

Matthew uses material that reflects these debates. Passages affirm the permanence of God's covenant with Israel (5:18-19) and restrict mission to Israel (10:5-6). Others include Gentiles and exclude some in Israel (8:5-13; 21:42-43). Both sides have their place in Matthew.

The author builds on Mark's basic framework. Matthew adds birth stories, resurrection appearances, and sayings. The sayings primarily occur in five blocks. Each ends with some variation of the phrase "When Jesus had finished saying these things" (7:28; 11:1; 13:53; 19:1; 26:1).

To focus its message, Matthew rearranges the sequence of stories and often shortens them. Sometimes Matthew adds to a story. This indicates a particular interest. Comparing Matthew with Mark is often helpful for understanding Matthew.

Matthew sets individual passages in the context of long sequences of stories and sayings. Each text must be seen in the light of this larger whole. The Sermon on the Mount, for example, includes things

Jesus may have said at different times. Yet it is a single sermon. Each saying needs to be read in light of its place in the whole. Often this dramatically influences its meaning. The Sermon on the Mount, in turn, is part of a larger context that runs from 4:12 through 9:34.

Themes often overlap. In the Sermon on the Mount, for example, righteousness is a central theme in 5:3–7:6. A second theme, the exclusive alternative between two ways, begins in 6:1 and comes into the foreground in 7:13-27.

Matthew develops parallel structures in telling the story. For example, Matthew 8 and 9 each open with a miracle, touch the question of outsiders, and end with an exorcism leading to opposition. The Gospel of Matthew can be outlined this way:

Jesus, the promised Son (1:1–4:11)
Light dawns in the darkness (4:12–9:34)
The kingdom's power in the midst of opposition and questions (9:35–16:12)
God's Son will suffer death and be raised (16:13–20:34)
Jesus in Jerusalem (21:1–25:46)
Jesus' death and resurrection (26:1–28:20)

What's the Message?

Jesus announces that God's rule has drawn near. Its power is already breaking into our world in his authority to teach, to cast out demons and heal, and to forgive sins. Instead of "kingdom of God," Matthew prefers the phrase "kingdom of heaven." This may reflect Jewish reservations about using God's name.

Matthew emphasizes that Jesus fulfills prophecy. Both God's promises to Israel and their history with God are treated as prophecy. Prophecy interprets the story of Jesus. The fulfillment transforms what the prophecies mean.

The story of Jesus moves toward his death. Hostility begins with his birth and climaxes in his crucifixion. On the other hand, Jesus is popular with the crowds. They come to listen and be healed, and they respond with amazement. Those hostile to Jesus are the religious and political leaders.

Matthew stresses forgiveness and the need to forgive (6:9-15; 9:10-13; 18:15-35; 26:27-28). Jesus forbids judging and seeking a visible righteousness of one's own (Matt 6:1; 7:1-6). Throughout the Gospel, Jesus rejected teaching that could be used to condemn others or exalt oneself, even if based on his teaching.

Some important themes are emphasized early, disappear, and then reappear in a cluster in Matthew 21:21-32.

"Righteousness" is linked to John's baptism in 3:15 and 21:32. It appears five times in chapters 5–6.

Jesus' authority is emphasized in chapters 5–9. The word itself occurs five times in 7:29–10:1. It appears three times in 21:23-27 and again, very importantly, in 28:18.

The words "faith" or "believe" occur six times in chapters 8–9. They are interpreted as turning to Jesus for help when in need. That theme occurs throughout these chapters. The words then appear seven times in 21:21-32 and also in 15:28, 23:23, and 27:42. "Do not believe" is used twice in warnings against false messengers (24:23-27). While others are commended for their faith, the disciples are scolded throughout the gospel for their "little faith" (6:30; 8:26; 14:31; 16:8; 17:20). Two Gentiles are praised for their great faith (8:10; 15:28).

The Genealogy of Jesus the Messiah

1 An account of the genealogy[a] of Jesus the Messiah,[b] the son of
David, the son of Abraham.
2 Abraham was the father of Isaac, and Isaac the father of Jacob,
and Jacob the father of Judah and his brothers, 3 and Judah the father
of Perez and Zerah by Tamar, and Perez the father of Hezron, and
Hezron the father of Aram, 4 and Aram the father of Aminadab, and
Aminadab the father of Nahshon, and Nahshon the father of Salmon, 5 and Salmon the father of Boaz by Rahab, and Boaz the father
of Obed by Ruth, and Obed the father of Jesse, 6 and Jesse the father
of King David.
And David was the father of Solomon by the wife of Uriah, 7 and
Solomon the father of Rehoboam, and Rehoboam the father of Abijah, and Abijah the father of Asaph,[c] 8 and Asaph[c] the father of Jehoshaphat, and Jehoshaphat the father of Joram, and Joram the father of
Uzziah, 9 and Uzziah the father of Jotham, and Jotham the father
of Ahaz, and Ahaz the father of Hezekiah, 10 and Hezekiah the father
of Manasseh, and Manasseh the father of Amos,[d] and Amos[d] the father of Josiah, 11 and Josiah the father of Jechoniah and his brothers, at
the time of the deportation to Babylon.
12 And after the deportation to Babylon: Jechoniah was the father of Salathiel, and Salathiel the father of Zerubbabel, 13 and Zerubbabel the father of Abiud, and Abiud the father of Eliakim, and
Eliakim the father of Azor, 14 and Azor the father of Zadok, and Zadok the father of Achim, and Achim the father of Eliud, 15 and Eliud
the father of Eleazar, and Eleazar the father of Matthan, and Matthan
the father of Jacob, 16 and Jacob the father of Joseph the husband of
Mary, of whom Jesus was born, who is called the Messiah.[e]
17 So all the generations from Abraham to David are fourteen
generations; and from David to the deportation to Babylon, fourteen generations; and from the deportation to Babylon to the Messiah,[e] fourteen generations.

[a] Or *birth* [b] Or *Jesus Christ* [c] Other ancient authorities read *Asa* [d] Other ancient authorities read *Amon* [e] Or *the Christ*

1:1-17 the genealogy of Jesus the Messiah: See Luke 3:23-38. Jesus Christ is the promised son of David, the Messiah, whose rule will be identical with God's rule (see 2 Sam 7:12-16; Ps 89:19-29; Gen 12:1-3). *Messiah* comes from a Hebrew word meaning "anointed one." He is also the son promised to Abraham, through whom the nations will be blessed (see Gen 12:1-3; Gal 3:16).

1:3-6 Tamar…wife of Uriah: It is unusual that four women are mentioned in this ancient genealogy, along with Mary, the mother of Jesus (1:16). Tamar had twins by her father-in-law (Gen 38). Rahab was a Canaanite prostitute who helped the Israelite spies in Jericho (Josh 2). Ruth, a Moabite, was a model of faithfulness and married into the Jewish people (Ruth). David committed adultery with Uriah's wife, Bathsheba, and had Uriah murdered (2 Sam 11–12).

What does Jesus' family tree have to do with Luther's theology of the cross? The genealogies recorded in the Bible are "patrilineal," meaning though the father's line. Matthew's record of Jesus' ancestry is unique in that it includes four women: Tamar, Rahab, Ruth, and Bathsheba. These women are not part of the history of God's promise because of their pedigree or purity. It's one more reminder that God uses unlikely people and circumstances to bring about the divine plan. Luther's theology of the cross says as much: that God's work gets done through those people and places that we least expect. *Matthew 1:1-17*

1:17 fourteen generations: Matthew lists three periods of fourteen generations, perhaps because fourteen is the numerical value of David's name in Hebrew.

1:18-25 the birth of Jesus: Joseph is troubled by Mary's pregnancy, which would have brought him dishonor before they were married. Before he follows through on his plan to stop the marriage, the angel sets him straight.

The Birth of Jesus the Messiah

18 Now the birth of Jesus the Messiah[a] took place in this way.
When his mother Mary had been engaged to Joseph, but before they
lived together, she was found to be with child from the Holy Spirit.
19 Her husband Joseph, being a righteous man and unwilling to expose her to public disgrace, planned to dismiss her quietly. 20 But just
when he had resolved to do this, an angel of the Lord appeared to
him in a dream and said, "Joseph, son of David, do not be afraid to
take Mary as your wife, for the child conceived in her is from the
Holy Spirit. 21 She will bear a son, and you are to name him Jesus, for
he will save his people from their sins." 22 All this took place to fulfill
what had been spoken by the Lord through the prophet:

23 "Look, the virgin shall conceive and bear a son,
and they shall name him Emmanuel,"

which means, "God is with us." 24 When Joseph awoke from sleep, he
did as the angel of the Lord commanded him; he took her as his wife,
25 but had no marital relations with her until she had borne a son;[b] and
he named him Jesus.

The Visit of the Wise Men

2 In the time of King Herod, after Jesus was born in Bethlehem
of Judea, wise men[c] from the East came to Jerusalem, 2 asking,
"Where is the child who has been born king of the Jews? For we
observed his star at its rising,[d] and have come to pay him homage."
3 When King Herod heard this, he was frightened, and all Jerusalem
with him; 4 and calling together all the chief priests and scribes of
the people, he inquired of them where the Messiah[e] was to be born.
5 They told him, "In Bethlehem of Judea; for so it has been written by
the prophet:

6 'And you, Bethlehem, in the land of Judah,
are by no means least among the rulers of Judah;
for from you shall come a ruler
who is to shepherd[f] my people Israel.'"

7 Then Herod secretly called for the wise men[c] and learned
from them the exact time when the star had appeared. 8 Then he sent
them to Bethlehem, saying, "Go and search diligently for the child;
and when you have found him, bring me word so that I may also
go and pay him homage." 9 When they had heard the king, they set
out; and there, ahead of them, went the star that they had seen at its
rising,[d] until it stopped over the place where the child was. 10 When
they saw that the star had stopped,[g] they were overwhelmed with
joy. 11 On entering the house, they saw the child with Mary his

---

[a] Or *Jesus Christ* [b] Other ancient authorities read *her firstborn son* [c] Or *astrologers;* Gk *magi* [d] Or *in the East* [e] Or *the Christ* [f] Or *rule* [g] Gk *saw the star*

1:23 the virgin shall conceive: In Isaiah 7:14, the Hebrew speaks of a "young woman." Matthew quotes the Greek translation of the Isaiah passage which speaks of a "virgin." The Gospel of Matthew begins with this Emmanuel promise, "God is with us." It ends with Jesus' promise to his disciples, "I am with you" (28:20).

1:23 the virgin: In the Bible the most important analogy to Jesus' miraculous birth is the birth of Isaac (Gen 18:1-15; 21:1-7). Jesus is linked in the genealogy (Matt 1:1-2) to Isaac, son of Abraham, the son of God's promise, and so is linked to the origin, of Israel. In this context, the story of Jesus' birth says three things. First he is fully human, like us. Second, like Isaac, Jesus is born from the power of God's promise, not from human possibilities. Third, his birth is the dawn of a new era in God's history with the world. In addition it says that Jesus is God's Son from conception. God and God's purpose for the world is the source of Jesus and everything he does.

What is the importance of the story of Jesus' birth? For Luther, God comes down to meet us here in this world filled with sin, suffering, and death. God's Son comes in weakness: in a baby and a crucified man. God's Son takes on all that we are to share with us all that he is. *Matthew 1:18-25*

2:1 King Herod . . . wise men: Herod, king of Judea 37–4 B.C.E., was an ally of Rome. He rebuilt the temple in Jerusalem to restore its glory. The wise men (magi) were probably Zoroastrian priests from Parthia or Persia.

2:4 chief priests and scribes: The chief priests were leaders of the priests in the Jerusalem temple, where they were in charge of temple sacrifices and purification rights. The scribes were scholars whose work often involved writing. They tend to be connected with the Pharisees in Matthew's Gospel.

2:5-6 Bethlehem: Like David, the Messiah was to come from Bethlehem (see Mic 5:2; 1 Sam 16:1-13). This small city was located just south of Jerusalem (see Map 12, p. 2109).

2:11 gold, frankincense, and myrrh: Three gifts are mentioned but the number of wise men is not. Frankincense and myrrh were sweet-smelling resins used for burning (Isa 6:4-6), anointing (Exod 30:23-32), and preparing a body for burial (John 19:39-40).

2:13-23 flee to Egypt: The non-Jewish wise men came to honor Jesus. Herod, king of the Jewish people, tried to kill him. This calls to mind Israel in Egypt. The Egyptian pharaoh tried to kill every male Hebrew child (see Exod 1:16, 22). Moses escaped and led Israel out of Egypt. Jesus' family fled to Egypt. Then they moved to Nazareth, which was under a different king.

2:15, 17-18 to fulfill what had been spoken...through the prophet: A key feature of Matthew's Gospel is the use of prophetic passages from Israel's Scriptures (Old Testament) to express that God's purpose has been fulfilled in Jesus. Jesus was called out of Egypt as God called Israel out of Egypt (Hos 11:1). Sorrow over the children in Bethlehem mirrors Rachel weeping over her children (Jer 31:15). Israel's history became prophecy.

2:22 Archelaus was ruling over Judea: After Herod died in 4 B.C.E. his kingdom was divided among his three sons. His son Archelaus ruled over Judea, Samaria, and Idumea for about ten years, until 6 C.E. Because he had no authority in Galilee, which was ruled by another son, Herod Antipas, Joseph could settle safely there. See Map 12, p. 2109.

2:23 Nazareth...Nazorean: Jesus' family settled in the northern province of Galilee, in the town of Nazareth. The prophecy Matthew intends is unclear. The strongest possibility is Judges 13:5, 7; 16:17. A less likely possibility is that it refers to the messianic branch from David's line, which in Hebrew is *netzer* (see Isa 11:1; Zech 3:8) which Mathew's readers would not know. In the area where Matthew may have been written, Christians were called Nazoreans.

3:1-10 John the Baptist: See Mark 1:1-11; Luke 3:1-22. Notice that Matthew summarizes John's and Jesus' message in the same words (3:2; 4:17). In the desert, John prepares the way (see Isa 40:3) by calling the people to be baptized for repentance.

3:2 Repent, for the kingdom of heaven has come near: The Greek word for repent means "change your mind." For John this means to confess sins, be baptized, and live a life that "bears fruit." For Jesus it means to live in the new world of God's rule. The "kingdom of heaven" means that God comes as God to rule. People do not bring it about. It is God's gift. God's rule is connected with creation and the promise of a new creation.

mother; and they knelt down and paid him homage. Then, opening their treasure chests, they offered him gifts of gold, frankincense,
and myrrh. 12 And having been warned in a dream not to return to
Herod, they left for their own country by another road.

The Escape to Egypt

13 Now after they had left, an angel of the Lord appeared to Joseph in a dream and said, "Get up, take the child and his mother,
and flee to Egypt, and remain there until I tell you; for Herod is
about to search for the child, to destroy him." 14 Then Joseph[a] got up,
took the child and his mother by night, and went to Egypt, 15 and
remained there until the death of Herod. This was to fulfill what had
been spoken by the Lord through the prophet, "Out of Egypt I have
called my son."

The Massacre of the Infants

16 When Herod saw that he had been tricked by the wise men,[b]
he was infuriated, and he sent and killed all the children in and
around Bethlehem who were two years old or under, according to
the time that he had learned from the wise men.[b] 17 Then was fulfilled what had been spoken through the prophet Jeremiah:
18 "A voice was heard in Ramah,
wailing and loud lamentation,
Rachel weeping for her children;
she refused to be consoled, because they are no more."

The Return from Egypt

19 When Herod died, an angel of the Lord suddenly appeared
in a dream to Joseph in Egypt and said, 20 "Get up, take the child and
his mother, and go to the land of Israel, for those who were seeking the child's life are dead." 21 Then Joseph[a] got up, took the child
and his mother, and went to the land of Israel. 22 But when he heard
that Archelaus was ruling over Judea in place of his father Herod, he
was afraid to go there. And after being warned in a dream, he went
away to the district of Galilee. 23 There he made his home in a town
called Nazareth, so that what had been spoken through the prophets
might be fulfilled, "He will be called a Nazorean."

The Proclamation of John the Baptist

3 In those days John the Baptist appeared in the wilderness of
Judea, proclaiming, 2 "Repent, for the kingdom of heaven has
come near."[c] 3 This is the one of whom the prophet Isaiah spoke when
he said,

---

[a] Gk *he* [b] Or *astrologers*; Gk *magi* [c] Or *is at hand*

"The voice of one crying out in the wilderness:
'Prepare the way of the Lord,
make his paths straight.'"
4 Now John wore clothing of camel's hair with a leather belt around
his waist, and his food was locusts and wild honey. 5 Then the people
of Jerusalem and all Judea were going out to him, and all the region
along the Jordan, 6 and they were baptized by him in the river Jordan,
confessing their sins.
7 But when he saw many Pharisees and Sadducees coming for
baptism, he said to them, "You brood of vipers! Who warned you to
flee from the wrath to come? 8 Bear fruit worthy of repentance. 9 Do
not presume to say to yourselves, 'We have Abraham as our ancestor'; for I tell you, God is able from these stones to raise up children
to Abraham. 10 Even now the ax is lying at the root of the trees; every
tree therefore that does not bear good fruit is cut down and thrown
into the fire.
11 "I baptize you with[a] water for repentance, but one who is
more powerful than I is coming after me; I am not worthy to carry
his sandals. He will baptize you with[a] the Holy Spirit and fire. 12 His
winnowing fork is in his hand, and he will clear his threshing floor
and will gather his wheat into the granary; but the chaff he will burn
with unquenchable fire."

The Baptism of Jesus

13 Then Jesus came from Galilee to John at the Jordan, to be
baptized by him. 14 John would have prevented him, saying, "I need
to be baptized by you, and do you come to me?" 15 But Jesus answered him, "Let it be so now; for it is proper for us in this way to
fulfill all righteousness." Then he consented. 16 And when Jesus had
been baptized, just as he came up from the water, suddenly the
heavens were opened to him and he saw the Spirit of God descending like a dove and alighting on him. 17 And a voice from heaven said,
"This is my Son, the Beloved,[b] with whom I am well pleased."

The Temptation of Jesus

4 Then Jesus was led up by the Spirit into the wilderness to be
tempted by the devil. 2 He fasted forty days and forty nights,
and afterwards he was famished. 3 The tempter came and said to him,
"If you are the Son of God, command these stones to become loaves
of bread." 4 But he answered, "It is written,
'One does not live by bread alone,
but by every word that comes from the mouth of God.'"

[a] Or *in* [b] Or *my beloved Son*

3:7 Pharisees and Sadducees: The Pharisees dedicated themselves to teaching the Jewish Scriptures and applying the law to everyday living. The Sadducees were a wealthy and powerful group that included many priests; they were connected to Jerusalem and the temple there. Often these two groups clashed with each other. In the Gospels they are often described as opposing Jesus.

3:7-12 baptize you with the Holy Spirit and fire: Fire is an image of cleansing or purifying (see 1 Cor 3:12-15). In Isaiah 4:2-6, God will cleanse people "by a spirit of judgment and . . . of burning." The Holy Spirit both cleanses and gives new life. In Numbers 31:21-24, Israel purified items captured in battle by passing them through fire and water. They passed what could not withstand the fire through water. John passed sinners, who could not withstand the fire, through water.

3:13-17 Jesus came from Galilee to John: By being baptized, Jesus identified with sinners who could not withstand the fire. Then God's Spirit descended on him, and the voice from heaven declared him God's beloved Son (see Ps 2:7; Isa 42:1).

3:15 righteousness: "Righteousness" in Matthew appears properly to refer to God's righteousness, which is identified with God's rule, not to human righteousness (5:20; 6:1, 33). By being baptized, Jesus fulfills and reveals God's righteousness by identifying with sinners. This identification reaches its climax in his death on the cross. See also the note on 6:33.

What does Jesus' baptism mean for our baptism?

4:1-11 into the wilderness to be tempted by the devil: The Spirit led Jesus into the desert to be tempted. The temptations drew on his identity: "If you are the Son of God" (see Gen 1:26-27; 3:4-5). Jesus answered with Scripture (see Deut 8:3; 6:16; 16:13). The second temptation used Scripture (see Ps 91:11-12) to ask Jesus whether he really trusted God's promise.

4:1, 3 the devil . . . tempter: In the New Testament the devil is generally seen as the leader of evil forces opposed to God. See also 6:13 (the evil one).

How do temptations draw on our identity as children or people of God? How do Jesus' responses to temptation help you think about your own response to temptations?

4:12—9:34 Jesus . . . withdrew to Galilee: This section is made up of two major units: the Sermon on the Mount (5–7) and Jesus' authority as transforming power (8:1—9:34). It sets the theme: light dawns in the darkness (4:12-17). It moves to rejection by the Pharisees, who claim that the power at work in Jesus is demonic (9:34). Both units place forgiveness at the center (6:8-15; 9:2-13). Both speak of God's love for sinners and those outside God's covenant with Israel (5:3, 43-45; 8:5-13; 9:10-13). Jesus' authority to teach parallels his authority to do acts of power and forgive sins. The amazement of the crowds at his authority to teach and do acts of power has its counterpart in the rejection of this authority by the Pharisees (7:28-29; 9:33-34).

4:13-17 left Nazareth . . . Capernaum: After John's arrest, Jesus moved to Capernaum in Galilee, an area that had been given to the Israelite tribes of Zebulun and Naphtali (see Maps 4 and 12, pp. 2102 and 2109). This fulfilled the prophecy: "in Galilee of the Gentiles, light has dawned on people who sat in darkness" (Isa 9:1-2; see also John 1:4-5). The Greek word translated "Gentiles" here is the same word that is translated "nations" in Matt 28:19. The beginning of Jesus' ministry anticipates the mission of the disciples at the end of the Gospel.

4:18-22 by the Sea of Galilee: Jesus sees two pairs of brothers, Peter and Andrew and James and John. They are fishers. He calls them to follow. His call is the only reason they follow. See also Mark 1:16-20; Luke 5:1-11 and the note on Matthew 16:13-20.

5 Then the devil took him to the holy city and placed him on the
pinnacle of the temple, 6 saying to him, "If you are the Son of God,
throw yourself down; for it is written,

'He will command his angels concerning you,'
and 'On their hands they will bear you up,
so that you will not dash your foot against a stone.' "

7 Jesus said to him, "Again it is written, 'Do not put the Lord your God
to the test.' "

8 Again, the devil took him to a very high mountain and showed
him all the kingdoms of the world and their splendor; 9 and he said
to him, "All these I will give you, if you will fall down and worship
me." 10 Jesus said to him, "Away with you, Satan! for it is written,

'Worship the Lord your God,
and serve only him.' "

11 Then the devil left him, and suddenly angels came and waited
on him.

Jesus Begins His Ministry in Galilee

12 Now when Jesus[a] heard that John had been arrested, he
withdrew to Galilee. 13 He left Nazareth and made his home in Capernaum by the sea, in the territory of Zebulun and Naphtali, 14 so
that what had been spoken through the prophet Isaiah might be fulfilled:

15 "Land of Zebulun, land of Naphtali,
on the road by the sea, across the Jordan, Galilee of the Gentiles—
16 the people who sat in darkness
have seen a great light,
and for those who sat in the region and shadow of death
light has dawned."

17 From that time Jesus began to proclaim, "Repent, for the kingdom
of heaven has come near."[b]

Jesus Calls the First Disciples

18 As he walked by the Sea of Galilee, he saw two brothers,
Simon, who is called Peter, and Andrew his brother, casting a net
into the sea—for they were fishermen. 19 And he said to them, "Follow me, and I will make you fish for people." 20 Immediately they
left their nets and followed him. 21 As he went from there, he saw
two other brothers, James son of Zebedee and his brother John,
in the boat with their father Zebedee, mending their nets, and he
called them. 22 Immediately they left the boat and their father, and
followed him.

[a] Gk *he* [b] Or *is at hand*

Jesus Ministers to Crowds of People

23 Jesus[a] went throughout Galilee, teaching in their synagogues
and proclaiming the good news[b] of the kingdom and curing every
disease and every sickness among the people. 24 So his fame spread
throughout all Syria, and they brought to him all the sick, those who
were afflicted with various diseases and pains, demoniacs, epilep-
tics, and paralytics, and he cured them. 25 And great crowds followed
him from Galilee, the Decapolis, Jerusalem, Judea, and from beyond the Jordan.

The Beatitudes

5 When Jesus[a] saw the crowds, he went up the mountain; and after he sat down, his disciples came to him. 2 Then he began to
speak, and taught them, saying:

3 "Blessed are the poor in spirit, for theirs is the kingdom of
heaven.

4 "Blessed are those who mourn, for they will be comforted.

5 "Blessed are the meek, for they will inherit the earth.

6 "Blessed are those who hunger and thirst for righteousness,
for they will be filled.

7 "Blessed are the merciful, for they will receive mercy.

8 "Blessed are the pure in heart, for they will see God.

9 "Blessed are the peacemakers, for they will be called children
of God.

10 "Blessed are those who are persecuted for righteousness'
sake, for theirs is the kingdom of heaven.

11 "Blessed are you when people revile you and persecute you
and utter all kinds of evil against you falsely[c] on my account. 12 Rejoice and be glad, for your reward is great in heaven, for in the same
way they persecuted the prophets who were before you.

Salt and Light

13 "You are the salt of the earth; but if salt has lost its taste, how
can its saltiness be restored? It is no longer good for anything, but is
thrown out and trampled under foot.

14 "You are the light of the world. A city built on a hill cannot
be hid. 15 No one after lighting a lamp puts it under the bushel basket, but on the lampstand, and it gives light to all in the house. 16 In
the same way, let your light shine before others, so that they may see
your good works and give glory to your Father in heaven.

The Law and the Prophets

17 "Do not think that I have come to abolish the law or the
prophets; I have come not to abolish but to fulfill. 18 For truly I tell

---

[a] Gk *He* [b] Gk *gospel* [c] Other ancient authorities lack *falsely*

5:1–7:29 Jesus...went up the mountain: This section is known as the Sermon on the Mount. While it includes things Jesus may have said at different times, in Matthew it is to be read as a single sermon. Like Sinai or the temple mount, mountains are often places of significant religious events (14:23: 15:29; 17:1, 2; 28:16).

5:3-12 Blessed are: This section is known as the Beatitudes. The word *blessed* also can be translated as "happy." So Jesus now declares people blessed in light of God's coming rule. The Beatitudes create what they declare. Jesus makes the new world of God's rule actual now in this broken world. Yet it also remains a promised future.

5:3 Blessed are the poor in spirit: "Poor in spirit" means to lack spirit. Spirit has to do with life and life beyond self. Jesus includes the spiritually poor in the kingdom. His friendship with sinners interprets this beatitude (8:5-13; 9:9-13; 21:32; see 1 Cor 1:27-29; Rom 5:6-10).

How does Luther understand God's spoken word? Luther understands God's spoken word as creative power, not information. When God speaks, God's word creates what it declares. God's word called the universe and everything in it into existence. The beatitudes create reality. *Matthew 5:3-12*

If Jesus teaches *who* to bless, not *how* to be blessed, how would that change your life?

What do you think it means to be salt and light in the world?

5:17-21 abolish the law or the prophets: Jesus has come to fulfill, not abolish, Israel's Scriptures (see Rom 3:31). God's covenant with Israel will not end. The scribes were interpreters of the law; the Pharisees applied the law to ordinary, daily life. Yet this righteousness is not enough. God's will goes beyond what the law requires (5:20).

5:17 law: The law, or Torah, is God's covenant with Israel at Sinai. Its basis is their election as God's people. The Torah also includes God's covenant with Noah, the nations, and all living things (see Gen 9:1-17).

you, until heaven and earth pass away, not one letter,[a] not one stroke
of a letter, will pass from the law until all is accomplished. [19]There-
fore, whoever breaks[b] one of the least of these commandments, and
teaches others to do the same, will be called least in the kingdom
of heaven; but whoever does them and teaches them will be called
great in the kingdom of heaven. [20]For I tell you, unless your righteousness exceeds that of the scribes and Pharisees, you will never
enter the kingdom of heaven.

Concerning Anger

21 "You have heard that it was said to those of ancient times,
'You shall not murder'; and 'whoever murders shall be liable to
judgment.' [22]But I say to you that if you are angry with a brother or
sister,[c] you will be liable to judgment; and if you insult[d] a brother
or sister,[e] you will be liable to the council; and if you say, 'You fool,'
you will be liable to the hell[f] of fire. [23]So when you are offering your
gift at the altar, if you remember that your brother or sister[g] has
something against you, [24]leave your gift there before the altar and
go; first be reconciled to your brother or sister,[g] and then come and
offer your gift. [25]Come to terms quickly with your accuser while you
are on the way to court[h] with him, or your accuser may hand you
over to the judge, and the judge to the guard, and you will be thrown
into prison. [26]Truly I tell you, you will never get out until you have
paid the last penny.

5:21-48 You have heard that it was said...But I say to you: This is a typical form of debate over interpretations of Scripture. Jesus, however, debates the interpretation of God's will in the law itself. Notice that Jesus deepens the demand of the first three commands concerning anger, adultery, and divorce (Deut 5:17, 18; Deut 24:1-4). The other two—regarding making oaths and getting back at someone who has caused harm—he seems to reject altogether (Deut 24:1-4; 19:21).

Concerning Adultery

27 "You have heard that it was said, 'You shall not commit adultery.' [28]But I say to you that everyone who looks at a woman with
lust has already committed adultery with her in his heart. [29]If your
right eye causes you to sin, tear it out and throw it away; it is better
for you to lose one of your members than for your whole body to be
thrown into hell.[f] [30]And if your right hand causes you to sin, cut it off
and throw it away; it is better for you to lose one of your members
than for your whole body to go into hell.[f]

Concerning Divorce

31 "It was also said, 'Whoever divorces his wife, let him give
her a certificate of divorce.' [32]But I say to you that anyone who divorces his wife, except on the ground of unchastity, causes her to
commit adultery; and whoever marries a divorced woman commits
adultery.

[a] Gk *one iota* [b] Or *annuls* [c] Gk *a brother*; other ancient authorities add *without cause* [d] Gk *say Raca to* (an obscure term of abuse) [e] Gk *a brother* [f] Gk *Gehenna* [g] Gk *your brother* [h] Gk lacks *to court*

Concerning Oaths

33 "Again, you have heard that it was said to those of ancient
times, 'You shall not swear falsely, but carry out the vows you have
made to the Lord.' [34]But I say to you, Do not swear at all, either by
heaven, for it is the throne of God, [35]or by the earth, for it is his
footstool, or by Jerusalem, for it is the city of the great King. [36]And
do not swear by your head, for you cannot make one hair white or
black. [37]Let your word be 'Yes, Yes' or 'No, No'; anything more than
this comes from the evil one.[a]

Concerning Retaliation

38 "You have heard that it was said, 'An eye for an eye and a
tooth for a tooth.' [39]But I say to you, Do not resist an evildoer. But if
anyone strikes you on the right cheek, turn the other also; [40]and if
anyone wants to sue you and take your coat, give your cloak as well;
[41]and if anyone forces you to go one mile, go also the second mile.
[42]Give to everyone who begs from you, and do not refuse anyone
who wants to borrow from you.

Love for Enemies

43 "You have heard that it was said, 'You shall love your neighbor and hate your enemy.' [44]But I say to you, Love your enemies and
pray for those who persecute you, [45]so that you may be children of
your Father in heaven; for he makes his sun rise on the evil and on
the good, and sends rain on the righteous and on the unrighteous.
[46]For if you love those who love you, what reward do you have? Do
not even the tax collectors do the same? [47]And if you greet only your
brothers and sisters,[b] what more are you doing than others? Do not
even the Gentiles do the same? [48]Be perfect, therefore, as your heavenly Father is perfect.

Concerning Almsgiving

6 "Beware of practicing your piety before others in order to be
seen by them; for then you have no reward from your Father
in heaven.

2 "So whenever you give alms, do not sound a trumpet before you, as the hypocrites do in the synagogues and in the streets,
so that they may be praised by others. Truly I tell you, they have
received their reward. [3]But when you give alms, do not let your
left hand know what your right hand is doing, [4]so that your alms
may be done in secret; and your Father who sees in secret will reward you.[c]

---

[a] Or *evil* [b] Gk *your brothers* [c] Other ancient authorities add *openly*

5:43-48 Love your enemies and pray for those who persecute you: The command to love your neighbor (see Lev 19:18) does not exclude hating enemies (see Deut 7:2). Jesus commands, "Love your enemies." The basis is God's love, which has no boundaries or limits. To be perfect is to live in the power of God's love for the righteous, sinners, and enemies. To do so is to love as God loves (Rom 12:14-21).

Why is this idea of loving enemies so radical? What examples of such love have you experienced or seen?

6:1 Beware of practicing your piety before others: Literally the Greek speaks of "righteousness," not "piety." For now, Matthew 6 concludes the topic of righteousness by contrasting visible human righteousness with God's righteousness. People are to seek God's rule and God's righteousness (6:33), rather than human righteousness that can be seen by themselves or others (6:1, 3). See also Romans 10:1-4; Philippians 3:2-9.

6:2 give alms: "Alms" given to the poor were an important element of religious life. Doing acts of love for attention or even for one's own satisfaction is a form of self-love. One cannot use the needs of others to make oneself righteous. By excluding that possibility, Jesus frees people to act simply because the other needs it.

Concerning Prayer

5 "And whenever you pray, do not be like the hypocrites; for
they love to stand and pray in the synagogues and at the street corners, so that they may be seen by others. Truly I tell you, they have
received their reward. [6]But whenever you pray, go into your room
and shut the door and pray to your Father who is in secret; and your
Father who sees in secret will reward you.[a]

6:5 pray…at the street corners: Commonly, Jewish men prayed in public while standing or bowing down. Again, the purpose of prayer is not to make a show for others but to communicate with God.

7 "When you are praying, do not heap up empty phrases as the
Gentiles do; for they think that they will be heard because of their
many words. [8]Do not be like them, for your Father knows what you
need before you ask him.

9 "Pray then in this way:
Our Father in heaven,
    hallowed be your name.
10 Your kingdom come.
    Your will be done,
        on earth as it is in heaven.
11 Give us this day our daily bread.[b]
12 And forgive us our debts,
        as we also have forgiven our debtors.
13 And do not bring us to the time of trial,[c]
        but rescue us from the evil one.[d]
[14]For if you forgive others their trespasses, your heavenly Father will
also forgive you; [15]but if you do not forgive others, neither will your
Father forgive your trespasses.

6:9-15 Pray then in this way: Our Father: The term translated "Father" is from the Aramaic word *Abba,* which is an intimate term like "Daddy." Matthew uses the Lord's Prayer (6:9-13; also Luke 11:2-4) to highlight forgiveness. Being forgiven requires forgiving (18:21-35; see Mark 11:25; Col 3:13). God's forgiveness is a field of power that includes the world. One either does or does not live in God's forgiveness.

Concerning Fasting

16 "And whenever you fast, do not look dismal, like the hypocrites, for they disfigure their faces so as to show others that they are
fasting. Truly I tell you, they have received their reward. [17]But when
you fast, put oil on your head and wash your face, [18]so that your fasting may be seen not by others but by your Father who is in secret;
and your Father who sees in secret will reward you.[a]

6:16 whenever you fast: Fasting, or going without eating, was an important religious practice associated with particular festivals, repentance for sins, and awareness of the need for God's help in times of struggle and suffering. Ashes were used to express mourning.

Concerning Treasures

19 "Do not store up for yourselves treasures on earth, where
moth and rust[e] consume and where thieves break in and steal; [20]but
store up for yourselves treasures in heaven, where neither moth nor
rust[e] consumes and where thieves do not break in and steal. [21]For
where your treasure is, there your heart will be also.

6:19-24 Do not store…but store: See Luke 11:34-36; 12:33-34; 16:13. In the context of Matthew 6, treasures serve as a metaphor for righteousness. Treasures on earth are visible human righteousness; treasures in heaven are God's righteousness. People seek one or the other. They live in light or in darkness. They can never serve two masters. One either seeks God's righteousness or visible human righteousness, but never both.

---

[a] Other ancient authorities add *openly* [b] Or *our bread for tomorrow* [c] Or *us into temptation*
[d] Or *from evil.* Other ancient authorities add, in some form, *For the kingdom and the power and the glory are yours forever. Amen.* [e] Gk *eating*

The Sound Eye

22 “The eye is the lamp of the body. So, if your eye is healthy,
your whole body will be full of light; 23 but if your eye is unhealthy,
your whole body will be full of darkness. If then the light in you is
darkness, how great is the darkness!

Serving Two Masters

24 “No one can serve two masters; for a slave will either hate
the one and love the other, or be devoted to the one and despise the
other. You cannot serve God and wealth.[a]

Do Not Worry

25 “Therefore I tell you, do not worry about your life, what you
will eat or what you will drink,[b] or about your body, what you will
wear. Is not life more than food, and the body more than clothing?
26 Look at the birds of the air; they neither sow nor reap nor gather
into barns, and yet your heavenly Father feeds them. Are you not
of more value than they? 27 And can any of you by worrying add a
single hour to your span of life?[c] 28 And why do you worry about
clothing? Consider the lilies of the field, how they grow; they neither toil nor spin, 29 yet I tell you, even Solomon in all his glory was
not clothed like one of these. 30 But if God so clothes the grass of the
field, which is alive today and tomorrow is thrown into the oven,
will he not much more clothe you—you of little faith? 31 Therefore
do not worry, saying, ‘What will we eat?’ or ‘What will we drink?’ or
‘What will we wear?’ 32 For it is the Gentiles who strive for all these
things; and indeed your heavenly Father knows that you need all
these things. 33 But strive first for the kingdom of God[d] and his[e] righteousness, and all these things will be given to you as well.

34 “So do not worry about tomorrow, for tomorrow will bring
worries of its own. Today’s trouble is enough for today.

Judging Others

7 “Do not judge, so that you may not be judged. 2 For with the
judgment you make you will be judged, and the measure you
give will be the measure you get. 3 Why do you see the speck in your
neighbor’s[f] eye, but do not notice the log in your own eye? 4 Or how
can you say to your neighbor,[g] ‘Let me take the speck out of your eye,’
while the log is in your own eye? 5 You hypocrite, first take the log out
of your own eye, and then you will see clearly to take the speck out of
your neighbor’s[f] eye.

[a] Gk *mammon* [b] Other ancient authorities lack *or what you will drink* [c] Or *add one cubit to your height* [d] Other ancient authorities lack *of God* [e] Or *its* [f] Gk *brother’s* [g] Gk *brother*

6:25-32 do not worry: This speaks about material needs. In this context it also points to deeper needs that consume people with worry. How can they be all they can? What makes their life count? How can they live in a way that is right and life-giving? How can they be righteous? Our heavenly Father knows what we need (see Luke 12:22-31).

It is difficult to eliminate worry completely. What makes you worry? How can you reduce worry? How do Jesus’ words help?

6:33 strive first for the kingdom of God and…righteousness: “Seek” better fits the context. When people seek God’s righteousness, rather than their own, everything will be given to them. Like God’s rule, God’s righteousness is God’s divine power being manifested in the world. What does this look like? It looks like the Beatitudes and God’s forgiving love for the righteous and the unrighteous.

How does Luther understand God’s righteousness? Luther discovered that God’s righteousness is the righteousness God grants through Jesus Christ. It is not the righteousness God demands. The reality that God is God is made visible in justifying sinners and the ungodly (see Rom 4:5, 17). *Matthew 6:33*

7:1-5 Do not judge: People judge when they define who are righteous or unrighteous, good or evil (compare Gen 3:5). This does not exclude ethical awareness. Jesus warns us that those who judge others fall under that same judgment (see Rom 2:1; 14:4, 10, 13; Jas 2:13; 4:11-12).

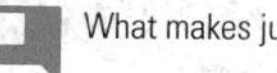

What makes judging such a sin?

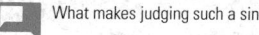

Profaning the Holy

7:6 dogs…pearls before swine: The image of giving something to dogs or swine was an image of contempt (see 15:26-27). In Matthew 13:45, "pearls" are a metaphor for persons. In this context, those who judge others are giving what is holy to dogs and casting pearls before swine.

6 "Do not give what is holy to dogs; and do not throw your
pearls before swine, or they will trample them under foot and turn
and maul you.

Ask, Search, Knock

7:7-11 Ask, and it will be given: God gives good things to those who ask, even when it does not seem like it, just as earthly parents want to give good things to their children (see Luke 11:9-13).

What would you pray for if you were first seeking God's rule and God's righteousness?

7 "Ask, and it will be given you; search, and you will find; knock,
and the door will be opened for you. 8 For everyone who asks receives, and everyone who searches finds, and for everyone who
knocks, the door will be opened. 9 Is there anyone among you who,
if your child asks for bread, will give a stone? 10 Or if the child asks
for a fish, will give a snake? 11 If you then, who are evil, know how to
give good gifts to your children, how much more will your Father in
heaven give good things to those who ask him!

The Golden Rule

7:12 do to others as you would have them do to you: This passage is often called "the Golden Rule."

12 "In everything do to others as you would have them do to
you; for this is the law and the prophets.

The Narrow Gate

13 "Enter through the narrow gate; for the gate is wide and the
road is easy[a] that leads to destruction, and there are many who take
it. 14 For the gate is narrow and the road is hard that leads to life, and
there are few who find it.

A Tree and Its Fruit

7:15-27 know them by their fruits: There is no middle path. Even people who act in Jesus' name and claim him as Lord can seek the easy way. False prophets are easy to spot. Claiming to speak for God, they justify limits to love, promote visible righteousness, and judge others. People seek God's rule and righteousness by living in God's love and forgiveness. No one does so without struggle. But any easier path leads to destruction (see Rom 2:13).

15 "Beware of false prophets, who come to you in sheep's clothing but inwardly are ravenous wolves. 16 You will know them by their
fruits. Are grapes gathered from thorns, or figs from thistles? 17 In the
same way, every good tree bears good fruit, but the bad tree bears
bad fruit. 18 A good tree cannot bear bad fruit, nor can a bad tree bear
good fruit. 19 Every tree that does not bear good fruit is cut down and
thrown into the fire. 20 Thus you will know them by their fruits.

Concerning Self-Deception

21 "Not everyone who says to me, 'Lord, Lord,' will enter the
kingdom of heaven, but only the one who does the will of my Father in heaven. 22 On that day many will say to me, 'Lord, Lord, did
we not prophesy in your name, and cast out demons in your name,
and do many deeds of power in your name?' 23 Then I will declare to
them, 'I never knew you; go away from me, you evildoers.'

---

[a] Other ancient authorities read *for the road is wide and easy*

Hearers and Doers

24 "Everyone then who hears these words of mine and acts on
them will be like a wise man who built his house on rock. [25]The rain
fell, the floods came, and the winds blew and beat on that house, but
it did not fall, because it had been founded on rock. [26]And everyone
who hears these words of mine and does not act on them will be like
a foolish man who built his house on sand. [27]The rain fell, and the
floods came, and the winds blew and beat against that house, and it
fell—and great was its fall!"

28 Now when Jesus had finished saying these things, the crowds
were astounded at his teaching, [29]for he taught them as one having
authority, and not as their scribes.

Jesus Cleanses a Leper

8 When Jesus[a] had come down from the mountain, great crowds
followed him; [2]and there was a leper[b] who came to him and
knelt before him, saying, "Lord, if you choose, you can make me
clean." [3]He stretched out his hand and touched him, saying, "I do
choose. Be made clean!" Immediately his leprosy[b] was cleansed.
[4]Then Jesus said to him, "See that you say nothing to anyone; but go,
show yourself to the priest, and offer the gift that Moses commanded,
as a testimony to them."

Jesus Heals a Centurion's Servant

5 When he entered Capernaum, a centurion came to him, appealing to him [6]and saying, "Lord, my servant is lying at home paralyzed, in terrible distress." [7]And he said to him, "I will come and cure
him." [8]The centurion answered, "Lord, I am not worthy to have you
come under my roof; but only speak the word, and my servant will
be healed. [9]For I also am a man under authority, with soldiers under
me; and I say to one, 'Go,' and he goes, and to another, 'Come,' and
he comes, and to my slave, 'Do this,' and the slave does it." [10]When
Jesus heard him, he was amazed and said to those who followed
him, "Truly I tell you, in no one[c] in Israel have I found such faith.
[11]I tell you, many will come from east and west and will eat with
Abraham and Isaac and Jacob in the kingdom of heaven, [12]while the
heirs of the kingdom will be thrown into the outer darkness, where
there will be weeping and gnashing of teeth." [13]And to the centurion
Jesus said, "Go; let it be done for you according to your faith." And
the servant was healed in that hour.

---

[a] Gk *he* [b] The terms *leper* and *leprosy* can refer to several diseases [c] Other ancient authorities read *Truly I tell you, not even*

7:28–9:34 as one having authority: Matthew interweaves three themes in this section: Jesus' authority, forgiveness, and faith. Jesus' authority has to do with the power of his word and forgiving sins. Notice the parallels between chapters 8 and 9. In 8:4 and 9:30, Jesus commands silence. Both 8:19-22 and 9:9 deal with following Jesus. Jesus includes Gentiles (8:5-13) and sinners (9:9-13) in God's rule. Jesus' power has cosmic dimensions (8:23-27; 9:18-26). Both end with exorcisms and rejection (8:28-34; 9:32-34). Notice especially how Matthew uses Mark's Gospel to give his own Gospel a distinctive voice.

8:1-4 a leper…show yourself to the priest: See Mark 1:40-45; Luke 5:12-16. Notice the leper's confidence and the command to be silent. Jesus tells him to do what the law requires (see Lev 14:2-32). Skin diseases like leprosy made a person ritually unclean. Once clean, the person would offer a proper sacrifice and then be allowed to again be part of the worshiping community.

8:5-13 a centurion…my servant will be healed: See Luke 7:1-10. A centurion was an officer in the Roman army. He saw Jesus' authority as the power of his word to heal, even at a distance. Amazed, Jesus praised this Gentile's faith, in contrast to Israel. Jesus applies prophecies that say God's gathering of the scattered people will include Gentiles (Isa 2:2-4; 49:12; Zech 8:20-23). Notice that the centurion has faith, and his servant is healed.

8:13 according to your faith: By "faith" Jesus means turning to him in need with confidence in his power to help. In this light, all the stories in Matthew 8:1—9:34 are about faith. Notice that one person's faith often leads to healing for another.

How does Luther connect faith and our understanding of what a "god" is? In his explanation of the First Commandment in the Large Catechism, Luther defines the word "god" in terms of faith. Whatever you turn to for help in time of need is your god. *Matthew 8:13*

8:14-17 fever...took our infirmities: See Mark 1:29-34; Luke 4:38-41. Jesus' healing power fulfills Isaiah 53:4.

8:18-22 scribe...said..."I will follow you": See Luke 9:57-60. The scribes were scholars who studied, copied, interpreted, and taught the Scriptures. They tend to be connected with the Pharisees in Matthew's Gospel. If one wants to follow Jesus, nothing else can matter. He has no home in this world. That points to Jesus' death on the cross. Whether it is also biographical is not clear. Matthew speaks of Jesus' home in Capernaum (4:13; 9:1). See 2 Corinthians 8:9, which also interprets his death.

8:23-27 windstorm arose...winds and the sea obey him: See Mark 4:36-41; Luke 8:23-25. The Old Testament links God's rule to the defeat of the sea and creation (see Ps 93; 89:5-14). The promised king will share in God's power over the sea (Ps 89:24-27). The disciples recognize that Jesus acts with power that belongs only to God. When the disciples turn to Jesus for help, he scolds them for their little faith.

8:28-34 Gadarenes, two demoniacs: See Mark 5:1-17; Luke 8:26-37. The exact location is in question (see NRSV footnote *a*). Jesus sends the demons into a herd of pigs. They perish in the sea. The man is healed; the owner of the pigs pays a high price. It is no surprise that these people want Jesus to leave.

Jesus Heals Many at Peter's House

14 When Jesus entered Peter's house, he saw his mother-in-law
lying in bed with a fever; 15he touched her hand, and the fever left
her, and she got up and began to serve him. 16That evening they
brought to him many who were possessed with demons; and he
cast out the spirits with a word, and cured all who were sick. 17This
was to fulfill what had been spoken through the prophet Isaiah, "He
took our infirmities and bore our diseases."

Would-Be Followers of Jesus

18 Now when Jesus saw great crowds around him, he gave orders to go over to the other side. 19A scribe then approached and
said, "Teacher, I will follow you wherever you go." 20And Jesus said
to him, "Foxes have holes, and birds of the air have nests; but the
Son of Man has nowhere to lay his head." 21Another of his disciples
said to him, "Lord, first let me go and bury my father." 22But Jesus
said to him, "Follow me, and let the dead bury their own dead."

Jesus Stills the Storm

23 And when he got into the boat, his disciples followed him.
24A windstorm arose on the sea, so great that the boat was being
swamped by the waves; but he was asleep. 25And they went and
woke him up, saying, "Lord, save us! We are perishing!" 26And he
said to them, "Why are you afraid, you of little faith?" Then he got
up and rebuked the winds and the sea; and there was a dead calm.
27They were amazed, saying, "What sort of man is this, that even the
winds and the sea obey him?"

Jesus Heals the Gadarene Demoniacs

28 When he came to the other side, to the country of the Gadarenes,[a] two demoniacs coming out of the tombs met him. They were
so fierce that no one could pass that way. 29Suddenly they shouted,
"What have you to do with us, Son of God? Have you come here to
torment us before the time?" 30Now a large herd of swine was feeding at some distance from them. 31The demons begged him, "If you
cast us out, send us into the herd of swine." 32And he said to them,
"Go!" So they came out and entered the swine; and suddenly, the
whole herd rushed down the steep bank into the sea and perished
in the water. 33The swineherds ran off, and on going into the town,
they told the whole story about what had happened to the demoniacs.
34Then the whole town came out to meet Jesus; and when they saw
9 him, they begged him to leave their neighborhood. 1And after
getting into a boat he crossed the sea and came to his own town.

[a] Other ancient authorities read *Gergesenes*; others, *Gerasenes*

Jesus Heals a Paralytic

2 And just then some people were carrying a paralyzed man lying on a bed. When Jesus saw their faith, he said to the paralytic,
"Take heart, son; your sins are forgiven." 3Then some of the scribes
said to themselves, "This man is blaspheming." 4But Jesus, perceiv-
ing their thoughts, said, "Why do you think evil in your hearts? 5For
which is easier, to say, 'Your sins are forgiven,' or to say, 'Stand up and
walk'? 6But so that you may know that the Son of Man has authority
on earth to forgive sins"—he then said to the paralytic—"Stand up,
take your bed and go to your home." 7And he stood up and went to
his home. 8When the crowds saw it, they were filled with awe, and
they glorified God, who had given such authority to human beings.

9:2-17 your sins are forgiven: See Mark 2:1-22; Luke 5:17-38. Healing the paralytic confirms Jesus' authority to forgive sins now, here on earth, not just in the ultimate future (9:2-8). The scribes believed in God's boundless mercy and forgiveness. What they know at present, however, is God's law, while the scope of God's mercy is hidden. Jesus reveals God's mercy now. God's judgment is hidden.

The Call of Matthew

9 As Jesus was walking along, he saw a man called Matthew sitting at the tax booth; and he said to him, "Follow me." And he got
up and followed him.

10 And as he sat at dinner[a] in the house, many tax collectors and
sinners came and were sitting[b] with him and his disciples. 11When
the Pharisees saw this, they said to his disciples, "Why does your
teacher eat with tax collectors and sinners?" 12But when he heard
this, he said, "Those who are well have no need of a physician, but
those who are sick. 13Go and learn what this means, 'I desire mercy,
not sacrifice.' For I have come to call not the righteous but sinners."

9:9-13 tax collectors and sinners: Matthew is a tax collector. Along with sinners (those who disregarded the law), tax collectors were considered outcasts in Israel's society and religion. In Israel's culture, sharing a meal establishes a close bond between people. When Jesus eats with tax collectors and sinners, he identifies with them and includes them in God's rule.

If Jesus' authority to forgive sins now has such power, what difference would that make for how we live and think of others?

The Question about Fasting

14 Then the disciples of John came to him, saying, "Why do we
and the Pharisees fast often,[c] but your disciples do not fast?" 15And
Jesus said to them, "The wedding guests cannot mourn as long as
the bridegroom is with them, can they? The days will come when
the bridegroom is taken away from them, and then they will fast.
16No one sews a piece of unshrunk cloth on an old cloak, for the
patch pulls away from the cloak, and a worse tear is made. 17Neither
is new wine put into old wineskins; otherwise, the skins burst, and
the wine is spilled, and the skins are destroyed; but new wine is put
into fresh wineskins, and so both are preserved."

9:14-17 the disciples of John... fast...old wineskins: Disciples are followers or pupils of a teacher. Like the Pharisees, John the Baptist's disciples regularly fast (see the note on 6:16). Jesus' disciples do not. When Jesus is present, it is a time to celebrate, not fast. In this context, the new that Jesus brings is his authority to forgive sins now. This does not fit with the old. When turning to wine, juice produces gas that stretches wineskins. Old dry wineskins were prone to split when newly fermenting juice was poured into them.

A Girl Restored to Life and a Woman Healed

18 While he was saying these things to them, suddenly a leader
of the synagogue[d] came in and knelt before him, saying, "My daughter has just died; but come and lay your hand on her, and she will
live." 19And Jesus got up and followed him, with his disciples. 20Then
suddenly a woman who had been suffering from hemorrhages for

9:18-26 leader of the synagogue: See Mark 5:21-43; Luke 8:40-56. In Mark, this leader, called Jairus, comes to Jesus when his daughter is dying. She dies as Jesus is on the way. Jesus raises her when no one believes help is possible. In Matthew the leader comes to Jesus for help after his daughter has died. What is the difference between how these two passages speak of faith and Jesus' power to help?

---

[a] Gk *reclined* [b] Gk *were reclining* [c] Other ancient authorities lack *often* [d] Gk lacks *of the synagogue*

9:32-34 a demoniac . . . By the ruler of the demons: The Pharisees (see the note on 3:7) claim Jesus' power comes from Satan, also known as Beelzebul, the prince of demons. This accusation, with no response, ends this secton of the Gospel (see the note on 4:12-9:34). It also sets the context for what follows (see 10:25; 12:24). It highlights the ambiguity of Jesus' ministry, especially his claim to authority now, on earth, to forgive sins. Ultimately it receives its answer only when God raises Jesus from the dead (28:18).

9:35—16:12 Jesus went about . . . teaching . . . proclaiming the good news: This section interweaves Jesus' compassion for the crowds with conflict. The conflict moves from claiming that Jesus' power is demonic (9:34; 10:25; 12:14) to asking for signs (12:38; 16:1). Second, the mystery of the kingdom is openly revealed, yet hidden from the wise (10:26-27; 11:25-27; 13:10-16, 34-35). Both move toward the question of Jesus' identity.

9:35 good news of the kingdom: This "good news" has to do with the reality that the power of God's rule is already breaking into this broken world in Jesus and his activity; it is not a matter of information.

9:35-38 ask the Lord to send out laborers: See 4:23-25; Luke 10:2. Using the image of a landowner (Lord) sending laborers out to harvest grain, Jesus speaks of the need for messengers to bring the good news in a world longing for God's rule.

10:1-15 Jesus summoned the twelve disciples: See Mark 3:16-19; 6:8-11; Luke 6:13-16; 9:1-6; 10:1-12). The twelve disciples are later compared to the twelve tribes of Israel (19:28). Jesus gives the twelve authority to continue his activity, restricting them to Israel (also 10:23). Bringing nothing, they depend on the hospitality of those who listen. Otherwise, they leave people to God's judgment.

twelve years came up behind him and touched the fringe of his
cloak, 21 for she said to herself, "If I only touch his cloak, I will be
made well." 22 Jesus turned, and seeing her he said, "Take heart,
daughter; your faith has made you well." And instantly the woman
was made well. 23 When Jesus came to the leader's house and saw
the flute players and the crowd making a commotion, 24 he said, "Go
away; for the girl is not dead but sleeping." And they laughed at him.
25 But when the crowd had been put outside, he went in and took
her by the hand, and the girl got up. 26 And the report of this spread
throughout that district.

Jesus Heals Two Blind Men

27 As Jesus went on from there, two blind men followed him,
crying loudly, "Have mercy on us, Son of David!" 28 When he entered the house, the blind men came to him; and Jesus said to them,
"Do you believe that I am able to do this?" They said to him, "Yes,
Lord." 29 Then he touched their eyes and said, "According to your
faith let it be done to you." 30 And their eyes were opened. Then Jesus
sternly ordered them, "See that no one knows of this." 31 But they
went away and spread the news about him throughout that district.

Jesus Heals One Who Was Mute

32 After they had gone away, a demoniac who was mute was
brought to him. 33 And when the demon had been cast out, the one
who had been mute spoke; and the crowds were amazed and said,
"Never has anything like this been seen in Israel." 34 But the Pharisees said, "By the ruler of the demons he casts out the demons."[a]

The Harvest Is Great, the Laborers Few

35 Then Jesus went about all the cities and villages, teaching
in their synagogues, and proclaiming the good news of the kingdom, and curing every disease and every sickness. 36 When he saw
the crowds, he had compassion for them, because they were harassed and helpless, like sheep without a shepherd. 37 Then he said
to his disciples, "The harvest is plentiful, but the laborers are few;
38 therefore ask the Lord of the harvest to send out laborers into his
harvest."

The Twelve Apostles

10 Then Jesus[b] summoned his twelve disciples and gave them
authority over unclean spirits, to cast them out, and to cure
every disease and every sickness. 2 These are the names of the twelve
apostles: first, Simon, also known as Peter, and his brother Andrew;

---

[a] Other ancient authorities lack this verse [b] Gk *he*

James son of Zebedee, and his brother John; [3]Philip and Bartholomew; Thomas and Matthew the tax collector; James son of Alphaeus,
and Thaddaeus;[a] [4]Simon the Cananaean, and Judas Iscariot, the one
who betrayed him.

The Mission of the Twelve

5 These twelve Jesus sent out with the following instructions:
"Go nowhere among the Gentiles, and enter no town of the Samaritans, [6]but go rather to the lost sheep of the house of Israel. [7]As
you go, proclaim the good news, 'The kingdom of heaven has come
near.'[b] [8]Cure the sick, raise the dead, cleanse the lepers,[c] cast out demons. You received without payment; give without payment. [9]Take
no gold, or silver, or copper in your belts, [10]no bag for your journey,
or two tunics, or sandals, or a staff; for laborers deserve their food.
[11]Whatever town or village you enter, find out who in it is worthy,
and stay there until you leave. [12]As you enter the house, greet it. [13]If
the house is worthy, let your peace come upon it; but if it is not
worthy, let your peace return to you. [14]If anyone will not welcome
you or listen to your words, shake off the dust from your feet as you
leave that house or town. [15]Truly I tell you, it will be more tolerable
for the land of Sodom and Gomorrah on the day of judgment than
for that town.

Coming Persecutions

16 "See, I am sending you out like sheep into the midst of
wolves; so be wise as serpents and innocent as doves. [17]Beware of
them, for they will hand you over to councils and flog you in their
synagogues; [18]and you will be dragged before governors and kings
because of me, as a testimony to them and the Gentiles. [19]When
they hand you over, do not worry about how you are to speak or
what you are to say; for what you are to say will be given to you at
that time; [20]for it is not you who speak, but the Spirit of your Father
speaking through you. [21]Brother will betray brother to death, and a
father his child, and children will rise against parents and have them
put to death; [22]and you will be hated by all because of my name. But
the one who endures to the end will be saved. [23]When they persecute you in one town, flee to the next; for truly I tell you, you will
not have gone through all the towns of Israel before the Son of Man
comes.

24 "A disciple is not above the teacher, nor a slave above the master; [25]it is enough for the disciple to be like the teacher, and the slave
like the master. If they have called the master of the house Beelzebul,
how much more will they malign those of his household!

---

[a] Other ancient authorities read *Lebbaeus*, or *Lebbaeus called Thaddaeus* [b] Or *is at hand* [c] The terms *leper* and *leprosy* can refer to several diseases

10:15 Sodom and Gomorrah: These two ancient cities were judged and destroyed by God for their wickedness (Gen 19:1-28).

10:16-25 sending you out...When they persecute you: The warning parallels the story of Jesus and reflects the experience of the early church (see Mark 13:9-13). Notice that active hostility replaces not listening. The "councils" (10:17) probably refers to local courts in Israel. The disciples will even be hated by their own families (10:35-38; 12:46-50; 13:54-58). Haste is necessary: the Son of Man will come soon.

10:24-25 Beelzebul: Beelzebul comes from the name "Prince Ba`al," the title of the Canaanite fertility god. This name later was used for the prince of demons, and here it is a name for Satan. See 9:34; 12:24.

Whom to Fear

26 "So have no fear of them; for nothing is covered up that will
not be uncovered, and nothing secret that will not become known.
27 What I say to you in the dark, tell in the light; and what you hear
whispered, proclaim from the housetops. 28 Do not fear those who
kill the body but cannot kill the soul; rather fear him who can destroy both soul and body in hell.[a] 29 Are not two sparrows sold for a
penny? Yet not one of them will fall to the ground apart from your
Father. 30 And even the hairs of your head are all counted. 31 So do
not be afraid; you are of more value than many sparrows.

32 "Everyone therefore who acknowledges me before others,
I also will acknowledge before my Father in heaven; 33 but whoever denies me before others, I also will deny before my Father in
heaven.

Not Peace, but a Sword

34 "Do not think that I have come to bring peace to the earth; I
have not come to bring peace, but a sword.

35 For I have come to set a man against his father,
and a daughter against her mother,
and a daughter-in-law against her mother-in-law;
36 and one's foes will be members of one's own household.

37 Whoever loves father or mother more than me is not worthy of me;
and whoever loves son or daughter more than me is not worthy of
me; 38 and whoever does not take up the cross and follow me is not
worthy of me. 39 Those who find their life will lose it, and those who
lose their life for my sake will find it.

Rewards

40 "Whoever welcomes you welcomes me, and whoever welcomes me welcomes the one who sent me. 41 Whoever welcomes
a prophet in the name of a prophet will receive a prophet's reward;
and whoever welcomes a righteous person in the name of a righteous person will receive the reward of the righteous; 42 and whoever
gives even a cup of cold water to one of these little ones in the name
of a disciple—truly I tell you, none of these will lose their reward."

11 Now when Jesus had finished instructing his twelve disciples,
he went on from there to teach and proclaim his message in
their cities.

Messengers from John the Baptist

2 When John heard in prison what the Messiah[b] was doing, he
sent word by his[c] disciples 3 and said to him, "Are you the one who is

---

[a] Gk *Gehenna* [b] Or *the Christ* [c] Other ancient authorities read *two of his*

10:26-31 have no fear of them: Jesus tells the disciples to proclaim publicly, without fear, what they have learned. Only God can destroy people. They can count on God's care (see 6:26).

Consider the potential danger that Jesus' early followers faced when they went out to share the good news of God's kingdom. How did they find the courage and strength to do this work? What if you were called to such a mission? How is the mission the same or different for Jesus' followers today?

10:32-39 Everyone . . . who acknowledges me . . . take up the cross and follow me: There is no middle ground (6:24). Jesus brings division, not peace. To be identified with Jesus was politically and religiously dangerous. Breaks over a family's traditions could also cause painful breaks with one's family. A decision for or against Jesus is a decision for life or death before God. Those who seek their own life lose it; those who lose their life for Jesus' sake find it.

What temptations do you face to deny Jesus and seek life apart from him?

10:40-42 whoever welcomes you welcomes me: To receive Jesus is to receive the one who sent him; to receive the disciples is to receive Jesus himself (also 25:31-46).

11:1-6 John heard in prison: See Luke 7:18-35. John was arrested and put in prison by Herod Antipas (see 14:1-3). While in prison he wonders about Jesus; he is not what John expected (3:7-12). Jesus' activity of healing, bringing the dead to life, and bringing good news to the poor fulfills prophecies of new life (Isa 29:18-19; 35:5-6). See the note on 9:35 (good news).

to come, or are we to wait for another?" 4Jesus answered them, "Go
and tell John what you hear and see: 5the blind receive their sight,
the lame walk, the lepers[a] are cleansed, the deaf hear, the dead are
raised, and the poor have good news brought to them. 6And blessed
is anyone who takes no offense at me."

Jesus Praises John the Baptist

7 As they went away, Jesus began to speak to the crowds about
John: "What did you go out into the wilderness to look at? A reed
shaken by the wind? 8What then did you go out to see? Someone[b]
dressed in soft robes? Look, those who wear soft robes are in royal
palaces. 9What then did you go out to see? A prophet?[c] Yes, I tell
you, and more than a prophet. 10This is the one about whom it is
written,

'See, I am sending my messenger ahead of you,
who will prepare your way before you.'

11Truly I tell you, among those born of women no one has arisen
greater than John the Baptist; yet the least in the kingdom of heaven
is greater than he. 12From the days of John the Baptist until now the
kingdom of heaven has suffered violence,[d] and the violent take it by
force. 13For all the prophets and the law prophesied until John came;
14and if you are willing to accept it, he is Elijah who is to come. 15Let
anyone with ears[e] listen!

16 "But to what will I compare this generation? It is like children sitting in the marketplaces and calling to one another,

17 'We played the flute for you, and you did not dance;
we wailed, and you did not mourn.'

18For John came neither eating nor drinking, and they say, 'He has
a demon'; 19the Son of Man came eating and drinking, and they say,
'Look, a glutton and a drunkard, a friend of tax collectors and sinners!' Yet wisdom is vindicated by her deeds."[f]

Woes to Unrepentant Cities

20 Then he began to reproach the cities in which most of his
deeds of power had been done, because they did not repent. 21"Woe
to you, Chorazin! Woe to you, Bethsaida! For if the deeds of power
done in you had been done in Tyre and Sidon, they would have repented long ago in sackcloth and ashes. 22But I tell you, on the day of
judgment it will be more tolerable for Tyre and Sidon than for you.
23And you, Capernaum,
will you be exalted to heaven?
No, you will be brought down to Hades.

[a] The terms *leper* and *leprosy* can refer to several diseases [b] Or *Why then did you go out? To see someone* [c] Other ancient authorities read *Why then did you go out? To see a prophet?* [d] Or *has been coming violently* [e] Other ancient authorities add *to hear* [f] Other ancient authorities read *children*

11:9-15 more than a prophet: As the messenger sent to prepare the way (see Mal 3:1; Isa 40:3), John the Baptist begins the transition from prophecy to fulfillment, a time when the kingdom suffers violence. Elijah, the prophet taken into heaven (2 Kgs 2:9-12), was expected to prepare for the Lord's coming (Mal 4:5-6).

11:16-19 this generation?: This generation, led by the religious leaders, especially the Pharisees (see 12:23-30, 38-39), is warned. John's life (11:18) fit his message of warning, but he was called demon-possessed. Jesus' life fit his message of salvation (11:19), but his actions were questioned. Both were rejected and eventually killed.

11:20-24 he began to reproach the cities: See Luke 10:13-15. Jesus lived in Capernaum (4:13). Matthew says nothing else about Chorazin and Bethsaida (see Mark 8:22-26; Luke 9:10-17; John 1:44, 12:21). Tyre and Sidon were non-Israelite cities in Phoenicia (Lebanon). God destroyed Sodom because of its people's sins (see Gen 19:24-25). Jesus compares Capernaum with the idolatrous pride of Babylon (Isa 14:14-15).

Why do you think it is hard for those who know Jesus to repent?

For if the deeds of power done in you had been done in Sodom, it
would have remained until this day. [24]But I tell you that on the day
of judgment it will be more tolerable for the land of Sodom than for
you."

Jesus Thanks His Father

25 At that time Jesus said, "I thank[a] you, Father, Lord of heaven
and earth, because you have hidden these things from the wise and
the intelligent and have revealed them to infants; [26]yes, Father, for
such was your gracious will.[b] [27]All things have been handed over to
me by my Father; and no one knows the Son except the Father, and
no one knows the Father except the Son and anyone to whom the
Son chooses to reveal him.

28 "Come to me, all you that are weary and are carrying heavy
burdens, and I will give you rest. [29]Take my yoke upon you, and learn
from me; for I am gentle and humble in heart, and you will find rest
for your souls. [30]For my yoke is easy, and my burden is light."

Plucking Grain on the Sabbath

12 At that time Jesus went through the grainfields on the sabbath; his disciples were hungry, and they began to pluck
heads of grain and to eat. [2]When the Pharisees saw it, they said to him,
"Look, your disciples are doing what is not lawful to do on the sabbath." [3]He said to them, "Have you not read what David did when he
and his companions were hungry? [4]He entered the house of God and
ate the bread of the Presence, which it was not lawful for him or his
companions to eat, but only for the priests. [5]Or have you not read in
the law that on the sabbath the priests in the temple break the sabbath
and yet are guiltless? [6]I tell you, something greater than the temple is
here. [7]But if you had known what this means, 'I desire mercy and not
sacrifice,' you would not have condemned the guiltless. [8]For the Son
of Man is lord of the sabbath."

The Man with a Withered Hand

9 He left that place and entered their synagogue; [10]a man was
there with a withered hand, and they asked him, "Is it lawful to cure
on the sabbath?" so that they might accuse him. [11]He said to them,
"Suppose one of you has only one sheep and it falls into a pit on the
sabbath; will you not lay hold of it and lift it out? [12]How much more
valuable is a human being than a sheep! So it is lawful to do good on
the sabbath." [13]Then he said to the man, "Stretch out your hand." He
stretched it out, and it was restored, as sound as the other. [14]But the
Pharisees went out and conspired against him, how to destroy him.

---

[a] Or *praise* [b] Or *for so it was well-pleasing in your sight*

11:25-28 I thank you, Father: See the note on 6:9-15 (Our Father). The knowledge that only Jesus can bring is hidden from the wise and revealed to children (see Luke 10:21-22; 1 Cor 1:27-29; Jer 8:8-9).

11:29 Take my yoke upon you: A yoke is a carved collar made of leather and wood. It is placed on a pair of oxen to keep them working together as they pull a plow or something else. The teachers (rabbis) also described the task of obeying the Torah (God's instruction or law) as a yoke. Here Jesus invites his followers to put on Jesus' yoke, or teaching, which is not heavy but easy and light.

12:1-50 At that time: In chapters 8–9, Matthew used stories from Mark and elsewhere to focus Jesus' power and opposition to him around his authority to forgive sins. Matthew now picks up other elements of Mark's story.

12:1-14 Jesus went through the grainfields on the sabbath… Pharisees…conspired against him: See Mark 2:23—3:6.The law of Israel did not permit gathering food on the sabbath (see Exod 16:22-26). Neither David (see 1 Sam 21:1-6) nor the exception made for priests (Lev 23:3-8) seem to justify the disciples' action. The story of healing the man with a withered hand is a typical Jewish debate. To help a person in an emergency was permitted, but a chronic illness should wait (see Luke 13:14). Jesus uses a typical argument from the lesser to the greater. If everyone would pull a sheep out of a well on the sabbath, how much more important it is to help a human being. Jesus claims authority over the Sabbath and gives priority to God's desire for mercy. The issue of the sabbath provides a second reason the Pharisees want to destroy Jesus.

12:1 the sabbath: The sabbath and circumcision were the two signs of God's covenant with Israel. They symbolized submission to the whole of the law. The penalty for violating the Sabbath was death (Exod 31:12-16; 35:2)! Sabbath rules were intended to make keeping it easy. Through keeping the sabbath, Israel participated in God's rest on the seventh day. This relates to the promise of sharing in God's ultimate rest beyond the power of sin, suffering, and death.

God's Chosen Servant

15 When Jesus became aware of this, he departed. Many
crowds[a] followed him, and he cured all of them, 16and he ordered
them not to make him known. 17This was to fulfill what had been
spoken through the prophet Isaiah:

18 "Here is my servant, whom I have chosen,
    my beloved, with whom my soul is well pleased.
I will put my Spirit upon him,
    and he will proclaim justice to the Gentiles.
19 He will not wrangle or cry aloud,
    nor will anyone hear his voice in the streets.
20 He will not break a bruised reed
    or quench a smoldering wick
until he brings justice to victory.
21 And in his name the Gentiles will hope."

12:15-21 he cured all of them: The prophecy interprets the power at work in Jesus as the power of God's Spirit (see Isa 42:1-4). Notice the emphasis on benefit to the Gentiles.

Jesus and Beelzebul

22 Then they brought to him a demoniac who was blind and
mute; and he cured him, so that the one who had been mute could
speak and see. 23All the crowds were amazed and said, "Can this be
the Son of David?" 24But when the Pharisees heard it, they said, "It is
only by Beelzebul, the ruler of the demons, that this fellow casts out
the demons." 25He knew what they were thinking and said to them,
"Every kingdom divided against itself is laid waste, and no city or
house divided against itself will stand. 26If Satan casts out Satan, he
is divided against himself; how then will his kingdom stand? 27If I
cast out demons by Beelzebul, by whom do your own exorcists[b] cast
them out? Therefore they will be your judges. 28But if it is by the
Spirit of God that I cast out demons, then the kingdom of God has
come to you. 29Or how can one enter a strong man's house and plunder his property, without first tying up the strong man? Then indeed
the house can be plundered. 30Whoever is not with me is against
me, and whoever does not gather with me scatters. 31Therefore I tell
you, people will be forgiven for every sin and blasphemy, but blasphemy against the Spirit will not be forgiven. 32Whoever speaks a
word against the Son of Man will be forgiven, but whoever speaks
against the Holy Spirit will not be forgiven, either in this age or in
the age to come.

12:22-32 brought to him a demoniac…"Can this be the Son of David?": See Mark 3:19b-30; Luke 11:14-23. Jesus heals another person possessed by a demon. The crowds are amazed and wonder if Jesus is the "Son of David," the long-awaited Messiah (see note on 1:1-17). The Pharisees, in contrast, again claim that it is by Satan's power that Jesus casts out demons (9:34). It makes no sense to think that Satan casts out Satan, and some Pharisees also do exorcisms. By whose power? If Jesus does so by God's Spirit, then God's rule has come. Again there is no middle ground (see Matt 9:34).

12:31-32 blasphemy against the Spirit: See Mark 3:28-30. Here the sin against the Holy Spirit is that the Pharisees identify Jesus' power as demonic. By doing so, they close themselves to forgiveness and God's mercy. The Pharisee named Saul (later Paul the apostle) persecuted Christians because he believed the power of the message about Jesus was demonic. Then Jesus met him. The end of our possibilities is not the end of God's.

A Tree and Its Fruit

33 "Either make the tree good, and its fruit good; or make the
tree bad, and its fruit bad; for the tree is known by its fruit. 34You
brood of vipers! How can you speak good things, when you are evil?

12:33-37 tree good, and its fruit good: See 7:15-20; Luke 6:43-45. We often think words do not matter. Jesus says they matter ultimately.

How do we use words in a way that contradicts God's forgiveness in Jesus Christ?

---

[a] Other ancient authorities lack *crowds* [b] Gk *sons*

For out of the abundance of the heart the mouth speaks. 35 The good
person brings good things out of a good treasure, and the evil person brings evil things out of an evil treasure. 36 I tell you, on the day
of judgment you will have to give an account for every careless word
you utter; 37 for by your words you will be justified, and by your
words you will be condemned."

The Sign of Jonah

12:38-42 see a sign from you . . . sign of the prophet Jonah: The scribes and Pharisees ask for signs. See the note on 11:16-19 (this generation). The only sign will be Jesus' death and resurrection, like Jonah's three days and three nights in the belly of the sea monster (Jonah 1:17–2:10). This sign means judgment on this generation. Again, Gentiles are more attentive and ready to repent. See 16:1-4; Luke 11:29-32.

12:42 queen of the South: This refers to the queen of Sheba, who came to visit the wise king Solomon (1 Kgs 10:1-13).

38 Then some of the scribes and Pharisees said to him, "Teacher,
we wish to see a sign from you." 39 But he answered them, "An evil
and adulterous generation asks for a sign, but no sign will be given
to it except the sign of the prophet Jonah. 40 For just as Jonah was
three days and three nights in the belly of the sea monster, so for
three days and three nights the Son of Man will be in the heart of the
earth. 41 The people of Nineveh will rise up at the judgment with this
generation and condemn it, because they repented at the proclamation of Jonah, and see, something greater than Jonah is here! 42 The
queen of the South will rise up at the judgment with this generation
and condemn it, because she came from the ends of the earth to
listen to the wisdom of Solomon, and see, something greater than
Solomon is here!

The Return of the Unclean Spirit

12:43-45 unclean spirit: See Luke 11:24-26. Unless the evil cast out is replaced with something positive, the end is worse than the beginning.

43 "When the unclean spirit has gone out of a person, it wanders through waterless regions looking for a resting place, but it
finds none. 44 Then it says, 'I will return to my house from which
I came.' When it comes, it finds it empty, swept, and put in order.
45 Then it goes and brings along seven other spirits more evil than itself, and they enter and live there; and the last state of that person is
worse than the first. So will it be also with this evil generation."

The True Kindred of Jesus

12:46-50 his mother and his brothers: See Mark 3:31-35. Jesus makes the point that those who are inside listening to Jesus, not those outside, are doing the will of God.

46 While he was still speaking to the crowds, his mother and his
brothers were standing outside, wanting to speak to him. 47 Someone
told him, "Look, your mother and your brothers are standing outside, wanting to speak to you."[a] 48 But to the one who had told him
this, Jesus[b] replied, "Who is my mother, and who are my brothers?"
49 And pointing to his disciples, he said, "Here are my mother and
my brothers! 50 For whoever does the will of my Father in heaven is
my brother and sister and mother."

The Parable of the Sower

13 That same day Jesus went out of the house and sat beside the
sea. 2 Such great crowds gathered around him that he got into

[a] Other ancient authorities lack verse 47 [b] Gk *he*

a boat and sat there, while the whole crowd stood on the beach. 3And
he told them many things in parables, saying: "Listen! A sower went
out to sow. 4And as he sowed, some seeds fell on the path, and the
birds came and ate them up. 5Other seeds fell on rocky ground, where
they did not have much soil, and they sprang up quickly, since they
had no depth of soil. 6But when the sun rose, they were scorched; and
since they had no root, they withered away. 7Other seeds fell among
thorns, and the thorns grew up and choked them. 8Other seeds fell on
good soil and brought forth grain, some a hundredfold, some sixty,
some thirty. 9Let anyone with ears[a] listen!"

The Purpose of the Parables

10 Then the disciples came and asked him, "Why do you speak
to them in parables?" 11He answered, "To you it has been given to
know the secrets[b] of the kingdom of heaven, but to them it has not
been given. 12For to those who have, more will be given, and they
will have an abundance; but from those who have nothing, even
what they have will be taken away. 13The reason I speak to them in
parables is that 'seeing they do not perceive, and hearing they do not
listen, nor do they understand.' 14With them indeed is fulfilled the
prophecy of Isaiah that says:

'You will indeed listen, but never understand,
and you will indeed look, but never perceive.
15 For this people's heart has grown dull,
and their ears are hard of hearing,
and they have shut their eyes;
so that they might not look with their eyes,
and listen with their ears,
and understand with their heart and turn—
and I would heal them.'

16But blessed are your eyes, for they see, and your ears, for they hear.
17Truly I tell you, many prophets and righteous people longed to see
what you see, but did not see it, and to hear what you hear, but did
not hear it.

The Parable of the Sower Explained

18 "Hear then the parable of the sower. 19When anyone hears
the word of the kingdom and does not understand it, the evil one
comes and snatches away what is sown in the heart; this is what was
sown on the path. 20As for what was sown on rocky ground, this is
the one who hears the word and immediately receives it with joy;
21yet such a person has no root, but endures only for a while, and
when trouble or persecution arises on account of the word, that person immediately falls away.[c] 22As for what was sown among thorns,

[a] Other ancient authorities add *to hear* [b] Or *mysteries* [c] Gk *stumbles*

13:3-23 A sower went out to sow: See Mark 4:1-20. Jesus tells a parable about the sower, a farmer who is careless with seed. He does not worry about where it lands. Seed is expensive. No farmer plants that way. While much produces nothing, some produces a great harvest. Jesus explains the parable in 13:16-23 as a story that is really about the "word of the kingdom" and people. The parable interprets Jesus' activity. It is about the sower and the power of the word of the kingdom, not about the soil.

13:10-17 Why do you speak to them in parables?: That Jesus teaches in parables is itself a parable. The mystery of the kingdom is revealed to disciples and hidden from others. Jesus teaches in parables because people see and hear but do not perceive, understand, or repent, fulfilling Isaiah 6:9-10. The parable is about Jesus. He heals and teaches all, without regard for whether they are righteous or sinners, whether they understand or not. Farmers are more careful about their seed; we also tend to be more careful about where we sow the kingdom.

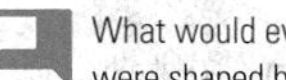

What would evangelism look like if it were shaped by this parable?

this is the one who hears the word, but the cares of the world and
the lure of wealth choke the word, and it yields nothing. 23 But as for
what was sown on good soil, this is the one who hears the word and
understands it, who indeed bears fruit and yields, in one case a hundredfold, in another sixty, and in another thirty."

The Parable of Weeds among the Wheat

24 He put before them another parable: "The kingdom of
heaven may be compared to someone who sowed good seed in his
field; 25 but while everybody was asleep, an enemy came and sowed
weeds among the wheat, and then went away. 26 So when the plants
came up and bore grain, then the weeds appeared as well. 27 And the
slaves of the householder came and said to him, 'Master, did you not
sow good seed in your field? Where, then, did these weeds come
from?' 28 He answered, 'An enemy has done this.' The slaves said to
him, 'Then do you want us to go and gather them?' 29 But he replied,
'No; for in gathering the weeds you would uproot the wheat along
with them. 30 Let both of them grow together until the harvest; and
at harvest time I will tell the reapers, Collect the weeds first and bind
them in bundles to be burned, but gather the wheat into my barn.'"

The Parable of the Mustard Seed

31 He put before them another parable: "The kingdom of
heaven is like a mustard seed that someone took and sowed in his
field; 32 it is the smallest of all the seeds, but when it has grown it is
the greatest of shrubs and becomes a tree, so that the birds of the air
come and make nests in its branches."

The Parable of the Yeast

33 He told them another parable: "The kingdom of heaven is
like yeast that a woman took and mixed in with[a] three measures of
flour until all of it was leavened."

The Use of Parables

34 Jesus told the crowds all these things in parables; without a
parable he told them nothing. 35 This was to fulfill what had been
spoken through the prophet:[b]

"I will open my mouth to speak in parables;
I will proclaim what has been hidden from the foundation of
the world."[c]

Jesus Explains the Parable of the Weeds

36 Then he left the crowds and went into the house. And his
disciples approached him, saying, "Explain to us the parable of the

13:24-30, 36-43 weeds among the wheat: Again the farmer is unusual. With *people*, it seems natural to separate the weeds from the wheat, to distinguish the good from the evil. But that is not how the *kingdom* works. People cannot correctly distinguish the good and the evil (7:1-5). There will always be weeds among wheat, but we will always get it wrong. Judgment is reserved for the Son of Man at the end of the ages.

How do you interpret the meaning of the short parable about the mustard seed (13:31-32)?

13:31-35 I will proclaim what has been hidden: See Mark 4:30-32; Ezekiel 17:23-24; Psalm 78:2. Like the mustard seed and yeast, the transforming power of the kingdom of heaven is hidden now. The tiny mustard seed becomes a tree far greater than the mustard plant. The picture of the tree is drawn from the widespread picture of the cosmic tree of life. Notice the contrast between hiding (13:10-17) and revealing what has been hidden from the foundation of the world (13:35; see also 11:25-27).

---

[a] Gk *hid in* [b] Other ancient authorities read *the prophet Isaiah* [c] Other ancient authorities lack *of the world*

weeds of the field." [37]He answered, "The one who sows the good
seed is the Son of Man; [38]the field is the world, and the good seed
are the children of the kingdom; the weeds are the children of the
evil one, [39]and the enemy who sowed them is the devil; the harvest
is the end of the age, and the reapers are angels. [40]Just as the weeds
are collected and burned up with fire, so will it be at the end of the
age. [41]The Son of Man will send his angels, and they will collect out
of his kingdom all causes of sin and all evildoers, [42]and they will
throw them into the furnace of fire, where there will be weeping and
gnashing of teeth. [43]Then the righteous will shine like the sun in the
kingdom of their Father. Let anyone with ears[a] listen!

Three Parables

44 "The kingdom of heaven is like treasure hidden in a field, which someone found and hid; then in his joy he goes and sells all that he has and buys that field.

45 "Again, the kingdom of heaven is like a merchant in search of
fine pearls; [46]on finding one pearl of great value, he went and sold all
that he had and bought it.

47 "Again, the kingdom of heaven is like a net that was thrown
into the sea and caught fish of every kind; [48]when it was full, they
drew it ashore, sat down, and put the good into baskets but threw
out the bad. [49]So it will be at the end of the age. The angels will come
out and separate the evil from the righteous [50]and throw them into
the furnace of fire, where there will be weeping and gnashing of
teeth.

13:44-45 kingdom of heaven is like treasure . . . pearl: These sound alike but have a different point of comparison. In the first, the kingdom is like the treasure. In the second, the kingdom is like the merchant. The pearl is a metaphor for the human person. The parable speaks of what God has done for us in Jesus Christ.

Treasures New and Old

51 "Have you understood all this?" They answered, "Yes." [52]And
he said to them, "Therefore every scribe who has been trained for
the kingdom of heaven is like the master of a household who brings
out of his treasure what is new and what is old." [53]When Jesus had
finished these parables, he left that place.

The Rejection of Jesus at Nazareth

54 He came to his hometown and began to teach the people[b]
in their synagogue, so that they were astounded and said, "Where
did this man get this wisdom and these deeds of power? [55]Is not
this the carpenter's son? Is not his mother called Mary? And are
not his brothers James and Joseph and Simon and Judas? [56]And are
not all his sisters with us? Where then did this man get all this?"
[57]And they took offense at him. But Jesus said to them, "Prophets
are not without honor except in their own country and in their own

13:54-58 his hometown . . . took offense at him: See the note on 2:23 (Nazareth). Opposition to Jesus includes his own hometown. Jesus' brothers named Joseph and Simon are not mentioned anywhere else in the Bible. Judas is mentioned in Jude 1. James likely is the same person who becomes a leader in the early church (Acts 12:17; 21:18; 1 Cor 15:7; James 1:1). See also Mark 6:1-6; John 1:11.

---

[a] Other ancient authorities add *to hear*   [b] Gk *them*

house." 58 And he did not do many deeds of power there, because of their unbelief.

The Death of John the Baptist

14:1-12 Herod had arrested John: Oddly, Herod thinks Jesus is John the Baptist raised from the dead (11:1-6)! Herod Antipas ruled Galilee and Perea (see Map 12, p. 2109). He was a son of Herod the Great, the Judean king when Jesus was born. Philip ruled an area east of Galilee and the Jordan. The law prohibits marrying a brother's wife (see Lev 18:16; 20:21).

14 At that time Herod the ruler[a] heard reports about Jesus; 2 and he said to his servants, "This is John the Baptist; he has been raised from the dead, and for this reason these powers are at work in him." 3 For Herod had arrested John, bound him, and put him in prison on account of Herodias, his brother Philip's wife,[b] 4 because John had been telling him, "It is not lawful for you to have her." 5 Though Herod[c] wanted to put him to death, he feared the crowd, because they regarded him as a prophet. 6 But when Herod's birthday came, the daughter of Herodias danced before the company, and she pleased Herod 7 so much that he promised on oath to grant her whatever she might ask. 8 Prompted by her mother, she said, "Give me the head of John the Baptist here on a platter." 9 The king was grieved, yet out of regard for his oaths and for the guests, he commanded it to be given; 10 he sent and had John beheaded in the prison. 11 The head was brought on a platter and given to the girl, who brought it to her mother. 12 His disciples came and took the body and buried it; then they went and told Jesus.

Feeding the Five Thousand

14:13-21 Jesus...withdrew...to a deserted place...those who ate were about five thousand: See Mark 6:30-44. The crowd follows Jesus into the desert. In compassion, Jesus heals them and feeds them in a feast that anticipates God's salvation (see Isa 35), in contrast with Herod's birthday feast (14:6). Where Jesus is, there is plenty, even in the desert.

13 Now when Jesus heard this, he withdrew from there in a boat to a deserted place by himself. But when the crowds heard it, they followed him on foot from the towns. 14 When he went ashore, he saw a great crowd; and he had compassion for them and cured their sick. 15 When it was evening, the disciples came to him and said, "This is a deserted place, and the hour is now late; send the crowds away so that they may go into the villages and buy food for themselves." 16 Jesus said to them, "They need not go away; you give them something to eat." 17 They replied, "We have nothing here but five loaves and two fish." 18 And he said, "Bring them here to me." 19 Then he ordered the crowds to sit down on the grass. Taking the five loaves and the two fish, he looked up to heaven, and blessed and broke the loaves, and gave them to the disciples, and the disciples gave them to the crowds. 20 And all ate and were filled; and they took up what was left over of the broken pieces, twelve baskets full. 21 And those who ate were about five thousand men, besides women and children.

Jesus Walks on the Water

22 Immediately he made the disciples get into the boat and go on ahead to the other side, while he dismissed the crowds. 23 And

---

[a] Gk *tetrarch* [b] Other ancient authorities read *his brother's wife* [c] Gk *he*

after he had dismissed the crowds, he went up the mountain by himself to pray. When evening came, he was there alone, [24]but by this
time the boat, battered by the waves, was far from the land,[a] for the
wind was against them. [25]And early in the morning he came walking
toward them on the sea. [26]But when the disciples saw him walking
on the sea, they were terrified, saying, "It is a ghost!" And they cried
out in fear. [27]But immediately Jesus spoke to them and said, "Take
heart, it is I; do not be afraid."

28 Peter answered him, "Lord, if it is you, command me to
come to you on the water." [29]He said, "Come." So Peter got out of
the boat, started walking on the water, and came toward Jesus. [30]But
when he noticed the strong wind,[b] he became frightened, and beginning to sink, he cried out, "Lord, save me!" [31]Jesus immediately
reached out his hand and caught him, saying to him, "You of little
faith, why did you doubt?" [32]When they got into the boat, the wind
ceased. [33]And those in the boat worshiped him, saying, "Truly you
are the Son of God."

14:24-33 he came walking toward them on the sea: See Mark 6:45-52. Jesus prays in solitude and comes to the disciples walking on the water. He tells them not to fear. Peter meets Jesus on the water, becomes afraid, and starts to sink. Jesus scolds him for his little faith. In Israel's Scriptures, the sea often symbolized destructive powers on a cosmic, political, or personal level. Creation and God's rule were linked with God's power over the sea (see Pss 89:5-18; 93; 69; Isa 17:12-14). The promised king will share this power (see Ps 89:25-27). This is the first time human beings use the title Son of God (also 16:16; 27:54). It is used by Satan and demons (4:3, 6; 8:29) and as false in the story of Jesus' death (26:63; 27:40, 43).

Jesus Heals the Sick in Gennesaret

34 When they had crossed over, they came to land at Gennesaret. [35]After the people of that place recognized him, they sent word
throughout the region and brought all who were sick to him, [36]and
begged him that they might touch even the fringe of his cloak; and
all who touched it were healed.

The Tradition of the Elders

15 Then Pharisees and scribes came to Jesus from Jerusalem
and said, [2]"Why do your disciples break the tradition of the
elders? For they do not wash their hands before they eat." [3]He answered them, "And why do you break the commandment of God for
the sake of your tradition? [4]For God said,[c] 'Honor your father and
your mother,' and, 'Whoever speaks evil of father or mother must
surely die.' [5]But you say that whoever tells father or mother, 'Whatever support you might have had from me is given to God,'[d] then that
person need not honor the father.[e] [6]So, for the sake of your tradition,
you make void the word[f] of God. [7]You hypocrites! Isaiah prophesied
rightly about you when he said:

8 'This people honors me with their lips,
but their hearts are far from me;
9 in vain do they worship me,
teaching human precepts as doctrines.'"

15:1-20 they do not wash their hands: See Mark 7:1-23; Isa 29:13. The tradition of the elders included interpretations of the law and rules not directly stated in the law in Israel's Scriptures. In later Judaism, the oral Torah was understood as God's word. Later rabbinic tradition agrees with Jesus about the priority of the commandment to honor parents over such vows.

Speaking to the crowd, Jesus shifts the subject to what defiles a person or makes a person ritually unclean. It is not what we eat, but what comes out of our mouths, which comes from our hearts. For the Bible, the heart is the center of a person's will and action, not the center of emotion.

---

[a] Other ancient authorities read *was out on the sea* [b] Other ancient authorities read *the wind* [c] Other ancient authorities read *commanded, saying* [d] Or *is an offering* [e] Other ancient authorities add *or the mother* [f] Other ancient authorities read *law*; others, *commandment*

Things That Defile

10 Then he called the crowd to him and said to them, "Listen and understand: 11 it is not what goes into the mouth that defiles a person, but it is what comes out of the mouth that defiles." 12 Then the disciples approached and said to him, "Do you know that the Pharisees took offense when they heard what you said?" 13 He answered, "Every plant that my heavenly Father has not planted will be uprooted. 14 Let them alone; they are blind guides of the blind.[a] And if one blind person guides another, both will fall into a pit." 15 But Peter said to him, "Explain this parable to us." 16 Then he said, "Are you also still without understanding? 17 Do you not see that whatever goes into the mouth enters the stomach, and goes out into the sewer? 18 But what comes out of the mouth proceeds from the heart, and this is what defiles. 19 For out of the heart come evil intentions, murder, adultery, fornication, theft, false witness, slander. 20 These are what defile a person, but to eat with unwashed hands does not defile."

The Canaanite Woman's Faith

15:21-28 district of Tyre and Sidon . . . a Canaanite woman: The cities mentioned are in the north (see Map 12, p. 2109). The Canaanite woman who is a Gentile, not an Israelite, looks for mercy for her daughter, who is possessed by a demon. She encounters rejection and insult from Jesus and the disciples. Jesus was sent only for Israelites. She persists, even accepting the insult. Recognizing her great faith, Jesus heals her daughter.

What does Jesus' encounter with the Canaanite woman say to you about his mission? How did she affect his vision of his mission?

21 Jesus left that place and went away to the district of Tyre and Sidon. 22 Just then a Canaanite woman from that region came out and started shouting, "Have mercy on me, Lord, Son of David; my daughter is tormented by a demon." 23 But he did not answer her at all. And his disciples came and urged him, saying, "Send her away, for she keeps shouting after us." 24 He answered, "I was sent only to the lost sheep of the house of Israel." 25 But she came and knelt before him, saying, "Lord, help me." 26 He answered, "It is not fair to take the children's food and throw it to the dogs." 27 She said, "Yes, Lord, yet even the dogs eat the crumbs that fall from their masters' table." 28 Then Jesus answered her, "Woman, great is your faith! Let it be done for you as you wish." And her daughter was healed instantly.

Jesus Cures Many People

15:29-39 Those who had eaten were four thousand: See Mark 8:1-10 and the note on Matt 14:13-21.

29 After Jesus had left that place, he passed along the Sea of Galilee, and he went up the mountain, where he sat down. 30 Great crowds came to him, bringing with them the lame, the maimed, the blind, the mute, and many others. They put them at his feet, and he cured them, 31 so that the crowd was amazed when they saw the mute speaking, the maimed whole, the lame walking, and the blind seeing. And they praised the God of Israel.

Feeding the Four Thousand

32 Then Jesus called his disciples to him and said, "I have compassion for the crowd, because they have been with me now for

---

[a] Other ancient authorities lack *of the blind*

three days and have nothing to eat; and I do not want to send them away hungry, for they might faint on the way." 33 The disciples said to him, "Where are we to get enough bread in the desert to feed so great a crowd?" 34 Jesus asked them, "How many loaves have you?" They said, "Seven, and a few small fish." 35 Then ordering the crowd to sit down on the ground, 36 he took the seven loaves and the fish; and after giving thanks he broke them and gave them to the disciples, and the disciples gave them to the crowds. 37 And all of them ate and were filled; and they took up the broken pieces left over, seven baskets full. 38 Those who had eaten were four thousand men, besides women and children. 39 After sending away the crowds, he got into the boat and went to the region of Magadan.[a]

The Demand for a Sign

16 The Pharisees and Sadducees came, and to test Jesus[b] they asked him to show them a sign from heaven. 2 He answered them, "When it is evening, you say, 'It will be fair weather, for the sky is red.' 3 And in the morning, 'It will be stormy today, for the sky is red and threatening.' You know how to interpret the appearance of the sky, but you cannot interpret the signs of the times.[c] 4 An evil and adulterous generation asks for a sign, but no sign will be given to it except the sign of Jonah." Then he left them and went away.

16:1-4 no sign will be given: See 12:38-42 and note; Mark 8:11-13. The Pharisees and Sadducees can read the signs regarding weather, but they cannot read the signs Jesus does, even though they see them (see 13:10-17).

The Yeast of the Pharisees and Sadducees

5 When the disciples reached the other side, they had forgotten to bring any bread. 6 Jesus said to them, "Watch out, and beware of the yeast of the Pharisees and Sadducees." 7 They said to one another, "It is because we have brought no bread." 8 And becoming aware of it, Jesus said, "You of little faith, why are you talking about having no bread? 9 Do you still not perceive? Do you not remember the five loaves for the five thousand, and how many baskets you gathered? 10 Or the seven loaves for the four thousand, and how many baskets you gathered? 11 How could you fail to perceive that I was not speaking about bread? Beware of the yeast of the Pharisees and Sadducees!" 12 Then they understood that he had not told them to beware of the yeast of bread, but of the teaching of the Pharisees and Sadducees.

16:5-12 beware of the yeast of the Pharisees and Sadducees: See the note on 3:7. The teaching of the Pharisees and Sadducees, as well as Jesus' teaching, works like yeast, which makes bread dough rise. These teachings leaven the whole (13:33).

Peter's Declaration about Jesus

13 Now when Jesus came into the district of Caesarea Philippi, he asked his disciples, "Who do people say that the Son of Man is?" 14 And they said, "Some say John the Baptist, but others

16:13—20:34 Jesus came into the district of Caesarea Philippi: This begins a section that circles around the question of who Jesus is and what that means.

16:13-20 Who do people say that the Son of Man is?: Jesus asks the disciples what others say and what they themselves say. Oddly, people identify him as someone risen from the dead. That leads some to wonder if this was originally a resurrection story (see 14:1-2; 27:52-53). Peter's confession that Jesus is the Messiah, the Son of God, is revealed to him directly by God, not human insight. Simon Peter's name (*Petros*) is the rock (*petra*) on which Jesus will build his church. In Rabbinic Judaism, authority to bind and loose had to do with deciding what was permitted or prohibited. In 18:18, it has to do with forgiveness.

---

[a] Other ancient authorities read *Magdala* or *Magdalan* [b] Gk *him* [c] Other ancient authorities lack [2]*When it is... of the time*

How have Christians interpreted Peter as the rock? Roman Catholics have understood Peter himself and his successors to be the rock. This provides the basis for the pope as leader of the church. For Protestants the important thing is what Peter confesses—that Jesus is the son of the living God. The continuity of the church then is based on its message and on continuing to tell that message. Peter struggled to understand the meaning of his confession and of Jesus' death for the world (see 16:22-23; 26:69-75). Even after Jesus' resurrection, Peter still continued to struggle to understand the full meaning of Jesus' death and resurrection. (Acts 10:1—11:18; Gal 2:11-14). Jesus' promise makes Peter who he is. It was important to Luther that we not idealize the apostles. Jesus sends people who still wrestle to understand what it is all about to spread the good news throughout the nations. Jesus makes more of people than they can make of themselves. *Matthew 16:18*

16:21-23 he must go to Jerusalem and undergo great suffering: Jesus tells his disciples about what lies ahead: he must go to Jerusalem, suffer, die, and be raised on the third day. Peter does not like what it means for Jesus to be God's Son. He falls into the role of Satan, the tempter (4:1-11).

In what ways are you tempted to make Jesus what you want him to be?

16:24-28 take up their cross: See Mark 8:34—9:1; Luke 9:23-27. Disciples cannot seek life in this world, which is passing away. Only in losing it for Jesus' sake do they find life. Jesus speaks of the end coming within their lifetime (10:23; 24:34).

What does it mean to you to take up Jesus' cross and follow?

17:1-13 led them up a high mountain...he was transfigured: See Mark 9:2-13. The odd reference to six days may suggest Moses at Sinai (see Exod 24:15-18; 34:29-35). High mountains like Sinai and Zion (see Ps 68:16; Isa 2:2-3) often were seen as sacred places where God and God's power are present. The story is a conversation between God and the disciples. Jesus appears in glory. He speaks with Moses and Elijah (see the note on 11:9-15), who represent the law and the prophets. Peter wants to honor the three. But God identifies Jesus as God's Son. The disciples are to listen to him. Then they see only Jesus, who speaks of his death and resurrection.

Elijah, and still others Jeremiah or one of the prophets." 15He said
to them, "But who do you say that I am?" 16Simon Peter answered,
"You are the Messiah,[a] the Son of the living God." 17And Jesus answered him, "Blessed are you, Simon son of Jonah! For flesh and
blood has not revealed this to you, but my Father in heaven. 18And
I tell you, you are Peter,[b] and on this rock[c] I will build my church,
and the gates of Hades will not prevail against it. 19I will give you the
keys of the kingdom of heaven, and whatever you bind on earth will
be bound in heaven, and whatever you loose on earth will be loosed
in heaven." 20Then he sternly ordered the disciples not to tell anyone
that he was[d] the Messiah.[a]

Jesus Foretells His Death and Resurrection

21 From that time on, Jesus began to show his disciples that he
must go to Jerusalem and undergo great suffering at the hands of the
elders and chief priests and scribes, and be killed, and on the third
day be raised. 22And Peter took him aside and began to rebuke him,
saying, "God forbid it, Lord! This must never happen to you." 23But
he turned and said to Peter, "Get behind me, Satan! You are a stumbling block to me; for you are setting your mind not on divine things
but on human things."

The Cross and Self-Denial

24 Then Jesus told his disciples, "If any want to become my followers, let them deny themselves and take up their cross and follow
me. 25For those who want to save their life will lose it, and those who
lose their life for my sake will find it. 26For what will it profit them
if they gain the whole world but forfeit their life? Or what will they
give in return for their life?
27 "For the Son of Man is to come with his angels in the glory of
his Father, and then he will repay everyone for what has been done.
28Truly I tell you, there are some standing here who will not taste
death before they see the Son of Man coming in his kingdom."

The Transfiguration

17 Six days later, Jesus took with him Peter and James and his
brother John and led them up a high mountain, by themselves. 2And he was transfigured before them, and his face shone like
the sun, and his clothes became dazzling white. 3Suddenly there appeared to them Moses and Elijah, talking with him. 4Then Peter said
to Jesus, "Lord, it is good for us to be here; if you wish, I[e] will make
three dwellings[f] here, one for you, one for Moses, and one for Elijah."
5While he was still speaking, suddenly a bright cloud overshadowed

[a] Or *the Christ* [b] Gk *Petros* [c] Gk *petra* [d] Other ancient authorities add *Jesus* [e] Other ancient authorities read *we* [f] Or *tents*

them, and from the cloud a voice said, "This is my Son, the Beloved;[a]
with him I am well pleased; listen to him!" [6]When the disciples heard
this, they fell to the ground and were overcome by fear. [7]But Jesus
came and touched them, saying, "Get up and do not be afraid." [8]And
when they looked up, they saw no one except Jesus himself alone.
9 As they were coming down the mountain, Jesus ordered them,
"Tell no one about the vision until after the Son of Man has been
raised from the dead." [10]And the disciples asked him, "Why, then,
do the scribes say that Elijah must come first?" [11]He replied, "Elijah
is indeed coming and will restore all things; [12]but I tell you that Elijah has already come, and they did not recognize him, but they did
to him whatever they pleased. So also the Son of Man is about to
suffer at their hands." [13]Then the disciples understood that he was
speaking to them about John the Baptist.

Jesus Cures a Boy with a Demon

14 When they came to the crowd, a man came to him, knelt
before him, [15]and said, "Lord, have mercy on my son, for he is an
epileptic and he suffers terribly; he often falls into the fire and often
into the water. [16]And I brought him to your disciples, but they could
not cure him." [17]Jesus answered, "You faithless and perverse generation, how much longer must I be with you? How much longer must
I put up with you? Bring him here to me." [18]And Jesus rebuked the
demon,[b] and it[c] came out of him, and the boy was cured instantly.
[19]Then the disciples came to Jesus privately and said, "Why could
we not cast it out?" [20]He said to them, "Because of your little faith.
For truly I tell you, if you have faith the size of a[d] mustard seed,
you will say to this mountain, 'Move from here to there,' and it will
move; and nothing will be impossible for you."[e]

17:14-21 my son...an epileptic: People often saw illness as an expression of demonic power. Jesus' power over the demons gave him power to heal. The disciples were unable to do anything, because of their little faith. Yet even the smallest faith transforms the world (13:31-32; 21:21-22; see 1 Cor 13:2).

Jesus Again Foretells His Death and Resurrection

22 As they were gathering[f] in Galilee, Jesus said to them, "The
Son of Man is going to be betrayed into human hands, [23]and they
will kill him, and on the third day he will be raised." And they were
greatly distressed.

17:22-23 Son of Man is going to be betrayed: Jesus predicts his coming death a second time (see 16:21-23; Mark 9:30-32).

Jesus and the Temple Tax

24 When they reached Capernaum, the collectors of the temple tax[g] came to Peter and said, "Does your teacher not pay the
temple tax?"[g] [25]He said, "Yes, he does." And when he came home,
Jesus spoke of it first, asking, "What do you think, Simon? From
whom do kings of the earth take toll or tribute? From their children

17:24-27 the temple tax: This annual temple tax was required of every Israelite (see Exod 30:11-13). The passage focuses on Jesus' identity. As God's Son, he is not obligated to pay the temple tax. To avoid giving offense, Jesus provides the tax for himself and Peter by means of a fish.

---

[a] Or *my beloved Son* [b] Gk *it* or *him* [c] Gk *the demon* [d] Gk *faith as a grain of* [e] Other ancient authorities add verse 21, *But this kind does not come out except by prayer and fasting* [f] Other ancient authorities read *living* [g] Gk *didrachma*

or from others?" 26 When Peter[a] said, "From others," Jesus said to
him, "Then the children are free. 27 However, so that we do not give
offense to them, go to the sea and cast a hook; take the first fish that
comes up; and when you open its mouth, you will find a coin;[b] take
that and give it to them for you and me."

18:1-7 Who is the greatest in the kingdom of heaven?: See Mark 9:33-37, 42-47. The disciples want to know about greatness. Jesus directs them to a child. Anyone who welcomes a child in Jesus' name welcomes Jesus (10:40-42). No one should despise or cause a child to stumble, for the Father cares for them (see Luke 15:4-7). A millstone is a large circular stone used to crush grain into flour.

True Greatness

18 At that time the disciples came to Jesus and asked, "Who is
the greatest in the kingdom of heaven?" 2 He called a child,
whom he put among them, 3 and said, "Truly I tell you, unless you
change and become like children, you will never enter the kingdom
of heaven. 4 Whoever becomes humble like this child is the greatest
in the kingdom of heaven. 5 Whoever welcomes one such child in my
name welcomes me.

Temptations to Sin

6 "If any of you put a stumbling block before one of these little
ones who believe in me, it would be better for you if a great millstone were fastened around your neck and you were drowned in the
depth of the sea. 7 Woe to the world because of stumbling blocks!
Occasions for stumbling are bound to come, but woe to the one by
whom the stumbling block comes!

18:8-9 If your hand...your eye causes you to stumble: Jesus uses intentional exaggeration to emphasize his point.

8 "If your hand or your foot causes you to stumble, cut it off and
throw it away; it is better for you to enter life maimed or lame than
to have two hands or two feet and to be thrown into the eternal fire.
9 And if your eye causes you to stumble, tear it out and throw it away;
it is better for you to enter life with one eye than to have two eyes
and to be thrown into the hell[c] of fire.

The Parable of the Lost Sheep

10 "Take care that you do not despise one of these little ones;
for, I tell you, in heaven their angels continually see the face of my
Father in heaven.[d] 12 What do you think? If a shepherd has a hundred
sheep, and one of them has gone astray, does he not leave the ninety-
nine on the mountains and go in search of the one that went astray?
13 And if he finds it, truly I tell you, he rejoices over it more than over
the ninety-nine that never went astray. 14 So it is not the will of your[e]
Father in heaven that one of these little ones should be lost.

18:15-20 If another member of the church sins against you: Jesus instructs the disciples about dealing with sin. The Greek in 18:15 does not restrict the question to sin between members of the church, but the church plays a role in what follows. The sending of witnesses (18:16) follows the Law (Deut 19:15; see also Matt 26:60). Those who do not repent and refuse to listen are to be treated as Gentiles and tax collectors. One ought not miss the irony of that, since Jesus is a friend of tax collectors and sinners. Binding and loosing has to do with authority to forgive sins (see John 20:22-23). Its basis is Jesus' presence and the Father's agreement. Peter, the head of the church, asks how often to forgive before binding. Jesus answers with the parable of the two slaves (18:23-35; see 6:14-15). Those who are forgiven cannot bind others.

Reproving Another Who Sins

15 "If another member of the church[f] sins against you,[g] go and
point out the fault when the two of you are alone. If the member

[a] Gk *he* [b] Gk *stater;* the stater was worth two didrachmas [c] Gk *Gehenna* [d] Other ancient authorities add verse 11, *For the Son of Man came to save the lost* [e] Other ancient authorities read *my* [f] Gk *If your brother* [g] Other ancient authorities lack *against you*

listens to you, you have regained that one.[a] [16]But if you are not listened to, take one or two others along with you, so that every word may be confirmed by the evidence of two or three witnesses. [17]If the member refuses to listen to them, tell it to the church; and if the offender refuses to listen even to the church, let such a one be to you as a Gentile and a tax collector. [18]Truly I tell you, whatever you bind on earth will be bound in heaven, and whatever you loose on earth will be loosed in heaven. [19]Again, truly I tell you, if two of you agree on earth about anything you ask, it will be done for you by my Father in heaven. [20]For where two or three are gathered in my name, I am there among them."

Forgiveness

21 Then Peter came and said to him, "Lord, if another member of the church[b] sins against me, how often should I forgive? As many as seven times?" [22]Jesus said to him, "Not seven times, but, I tell you, seventy-seven[c] times.

The Parable of the Unforgiving Servant

23 "For this reason the kingdom of heaven may be compared to a king who wished to settle accounts with his slaves. [24]When he began the reckoning, one who owed him ten thousand talents[d] was brought to him; [25]and, as he could not pay, his lord ordered him to be sold, together with his wife and children and all his possessions, and payment to be made. [26]So the slave fell on his knees before him, saying, 'Have patience with me, and I will pay you everything.' [27]And out of pity for him, the lord of that slave released him and forgave him the debt. [28]But that same slave, as he went out, came upon one of his fellow slaves who owed him a hundred denarii;[e] and seizing him by the throat, he said, 'Pay what you owe.' [29]Then his fellow slave fell down and pleaded with him, 'Have patience with me, and I will pay you.' [30]But he refused; then he went and threw him into prison until he would pay the debt. [31]When his fellow slaves saw what had happened, they were greatly distressed, and they went and reported to their lord all that had taken place. [32]Then his lord summoned him and said to him, 'You wicked slave! I forgave you all that debt because you pleaded with me. [33]Should you not have had mercy on your fellow slave, as I had mercy on you?' [34]And in anger his lord handed him over to be tortured until he would pay his entire debt. [35]So my heavenly Father will also do to every one of you, if you do not forgive your brother or sister[f] from your heart."

---

[a] Gk *the brother* [b] Gk *if my brother* [c] Or *seventy times seven* [d] A talent was worth more than fifteen years' wages of a laborer [e] The denarius was the usual day's wage for a laborer [f] Gk *brother*

Who has authority to forgive sins? For Luther, every believer has authority to forgive sins in Jesus' name, by virtue of Jesus' death for all. *Matthew 18:18*

18:22 seventy-seven times: See NRSV footnote *c* ("seventy times seven"). Because the number *seven* symbolized completeness, this comment is meant not to limit to a certain number but rather to suggest "as often as necessary."

18:23-35 a king who wished to settle accounts: This parable continued Jesus' answer to Peter's question about forgiving (18:21-22). The servant owed the enormous sum of ten thousand talents. According to NRSV footnote *d*, one talent was worth more than fifteen years' wages of a laborer. The debt the king forgave was huge. The debt owed the slave was small in comparison. Our sins, which God forgives, are far greater than any sin against us we refuse to forgive. We cannot live from God's mercy and forgiveness without extending that forgiveness to others.

Teaching about Divorce

19 When Jesus had finished saying these things, he left Galilee and went to the region of Judea beyond the Jordan. 2Large crowds followed him, and he cured them there.

3 Some Pharisees came to him, and to test him they asked, "Is it lawful for a man to divorce his wife for any cause?" 4He answered, "Have you not read that the one who made them at the beginning 'made them male and female,' 5and said, 'For this reason a man shall leave his father and mother and be joined to his wife, and the two shall become one flesh'? 6So they are no longer two, but one flesh. Therefore what God has joined together, let no one separate." 7They said to him, "Why then did Moses command us to give a certificate of dismissal and to divorce her?" 8He said to them, "It was because you were so hard-hearted that Moses allowed you to divorce your wives, but from the beginning it was not so. 9And I say to you, whoever divorces his wife, except for unchastity, and marries another commits adultery."[a]

10 His disciples said to him, "If such is the case of a man with his wife, it is better not to marry." 11But he said to them, "Not everyone can accept this teaching, but only those to whom it is given. 12For there are eunuchs who have been so from birth, and there are eunuchs who have been made eunuchs by others, and there are eunuchs who have made themselves eunuchs for the sake of the kingdom of heaven. Let anyone accept this who can."

Jesus Blesses Little Children

13 Then little children were being brought to him in order that he might lay his hands on them and pray. The disciples spoke sternly to those who brought them; 14but Jesus said, "Let the little children come to me, and do not stop them; for it is to such as these that the kingdom of heaven belongs." 15And he laid his hands on them and went on his way.

The Rich Young Man

16 Then someone came to him and said, "Teacher, what good deed must I do to have eternal life?" 17And he said to him, "Why do you ask me about what is good? There is only one who is good. If you wish to enter into life, keep the commandments." 18He said to him, "Which ones?" And Jesus said, "You shall not murder; You shall not commit adultery; You shall not steal; You shall not bear false witness; 19Honor your father and mother; also, You shall love your neighbor as yourself." 20The young man said to him, "I have

[a] Other ancient authorities read *except on the ground of unchastity, causes her to commit adultery*; others add at the end of the verse *and he who marries a divorced woman commits adultery*

19:1 went to the region of Judea beyond the Jordan: Jesus starts to move south from Galilee with his disciples, toward Jerusalem (see Map 12, p. 2109).

19:3-12 Is it lawful for a man to divorce his wife: See Mark 10:1-12. The Pharisee's question is not to be seen as hostile. Such questions belong in rabbinic debates. The law permitted a man to divorce his wife (Deut 24:1). But knowing what the law says does not answer the question. Jesus points to God's will in creation: divorce is not what God intended. Women and children were especially at risk in a society that allowed men to divorce wives for reasons other than unfaithfulness. In the law, God accommodates the reality of human sin, rather than sticking with principles. Divorce cannot be a righteous act, even when permitted. God's forgiveness is necessary. The disciples wonder if it is better not to marry. But Jesus tells them not to make that a general principle.

19:13-15 Let the little children come: See 18:1-7 and note; Mark 10:13-16.

19:16-26 what good deed must I do to have eternal life?...who can be saved?: Jesus answers the question with a question. "What must I do?" is like "Is it lawful?" No answer can ever satisfy either question. The young man knows that keeping the commandments does not satisfy the question. Jesus asks the young man to give up what he is most attached to—his possessions. He leaves in sorrow. But even that does not end the question, "What must I do?" Jesus says it is impossible for a rich person to enter the kingdom. The disciples then wonder if anyone can be saved! The question moves beyond deeds and possessions. It ends with impossibility—but not for God. See Mark 10:17-31; Luke 18:18-30; 1 Timothy 6:9-10.

How attached are you to your riches or possessions? What non-material possessions do you cling to? How do you respond to Jesus' words in 19:16-26? What is most challenging about what he says?

kept all these;[a] what do I still lack?" 21 Jesus said to him, "If you wish
to be perfect, go, sell your possessions, and give the money[b] to the
poor, and you will have treasure in heaven; then come, follow me."
22 When the young man heard this word, he went away grieving, for
he had many possessions.
23 Then Jesus said to his disciples, "Truly I tell you, it will be
hard for a rich person to enter the kingdom of heaven. 24 Again I tell
you, it is easier for a camel to go through the eye of a needle than for
someone who is rich to enter the kingdom of God." 25 When the disciples heard this, they were greatly astounded and said, "Then who
can be saved?" 26 But Jesus looked at them and said, "For mortals it is
impossible, but for God all things are possible."
27 Then Peter said in reply, "Look, we have left everything and
followed you. What then will we have?" 28 Jesus said to them, "Truly
I tell you, at the renewal of all things, when the Son of Man is seated
on the throne of his glory, you who have followed me will also sit on
twelve thrones, judging the twelve tribes of Israel. 29 And everyone
who has left houses or brothers or sisters or father or mother or children or fields, for my name's sake, will receive a hundredfold,[c] and
will inherit eternal life. 30 But many who are first will be last, and the
last will be first.

The Laborers in the Vineyard

20 "For the kingdom of heaven is like a landowner who went
out early in the morning to hire laborers for his vineyard.
2 After agreeing with the laborers for the usual daily wage,[d] he sent
them into his vineyard. 3 When he went out about nine o'clock, he
saw others standing idle in the marketplace; 4 and he said to them,
'You also go into the vineyard, and I will pay you whatever is right.'
So they went. 5 When he went out again about noon and about three
o'clock, he did the same. 6 And about five o'clock he went out and
found others standing around; and he said to them, 'Why are you
standing here idle all day?' 7 They said to him, 'Because no one has
hired us.' He said to them, 'You also go into the vineyard.' 8 When evening came, the owner of the vineyard said to his manager, 'Call the
laborers and give them their pay, beginning with the last and then going to the first.' 9 When those hired about five o'clock came, each of
them received the usual daily wage.[d] 10 Now when the first came, they
thought they would receive more; but each of them also received the
usual daily wage.[d] 11 And when they received it, they grumbled against
the landowner, 12 saying, 'These last worked only one hour, and you
have made them equal to us who have borne the burden of the day
and the scorching heat.' 13 But he replied to one of them, 'Friend, I am

19:27-30 when the Son of Man is seated on the throne of his glory: The disciples have left everything. Is there a reward? When all things are renewed, they will share Christ's rule. All who have left everything will be richly rewarded. Yet many of the first will be last and the last first.

20:1-16 kingdom of heaven is like a landowner: The parable of the workers in the vineyard develops the reversal of our expectations in the kingdom of heaven in 19:30 (20:16). Workers are to be paid on the same day they do the work (Lev 19:13; Deut 24:15). Those who worked hard all day think it unjust that those who have hardly worked receive the same pay. God's mercy breaks human ideas of what is right.

---

[a] Other ancient authorities add *from my youth* [b] Gk lacks *the money* [c] Other ancient authorities read *manifold* [d] Gk *a denarius*

doing you no wrong; did you not agree with me for the usual daily wage?[a] 14 Take what belongs to you and go; I choose to give to this last the same as I give to you. 15 Am I not allowed to do what I choose with what belongs to me? Or are you envious because I am generous?'[b] 16 So the last will be first, and the first will be last."[c]

A Third Time Jesus Foretells His Death and Resurrection

17 While Jesus was going up to Jerusalem, he took the twelve disciples aside by themselves, and said to them on the way, 18 "See, we are going up to Jerusalem, and the Son of Man will be handed over to the chief priests and scribes, and they will condemn him to death; 19 then they will hand him over to the Gentiles to be mocked and flogged and crucified; and on the third day he will be raised."

The Request of the Mother of James and John

20 Then the mother of the sons of Zebedee came to him with her sons, and kneeling before him, she asked a favor of him. 21 And he said to her, "What do you want?" She said to him, "Declare that these two sons of mine will sit, one at your right hand and one at your left, in your kingdom." 22 But Jesus answered, "You do not know what you are asking. Are you able to drink the cup that I am about to drink?"[d] They said to him, "We are able." 23 He said to them, "You will indeed drink my cup, but to sit at my right hand and at my left, this is not mine to grant, but it is for those for whom it has been prepared by my Father."

24 When the ten heard it, they were angry with the two brothers. 25 But Jesus called them to him and said, "You know that the rulers of the Gentiles lord it over them, and their great ones are tyrants over them. 26 It will not be so among you; but whoever wishes to be great among you must be your servant, 27 and whoever wishes to be first among you must be your slave; 28 just as the Son of Man came not to be served but to serve, and to give his life a ransom for many."

Jesus Heals Two Blind Men

29 As they were leaving Jericho, a large crowd followed him. 30 There were two blind men sitting by the roadside. When they heard that Jesus was passing by, they shouted, "Lord,[e] have mercy on us, Son of David!" 31 The crowd sternly ordered them to be quiet; but they shouted even more loudly, "Have mercy on us, Lord, Son of David!" 32 Jesus stood still and called them, saying, "What do you

---

[a] Gk *a denarius* [b] Gk *is your eye evil because I am good?* [c] Other ancient authorities add *for many are called but few are chosen* [d] Other ancient authorities add *or to be baptized with the baptism that I am baptized with?* [e] Other ancient authorities lack *Lord*

20:17-28 the Son of Man will be handed over to the chief priest and scribes: Jesus predicts his death a third time, in even greater detail (16:21-23; 17:22-23; see Mark 10:32-45). See the note on 2:4 (chief priests and scribes). Jesus moves toward the cross, but the disciples are interested in greatness. Here, the cup Jesus drinks refers to his suffering and death. For the disciples to drink this cup means martyrdom. The most literal translation of 20:26-27 would be: "Whoever wants to be great among you shall be your servant, and whoever wants to be first among you shall be your slave." It is a proverb stating the consequences of trying to be great or first. Jesus is not teaching them how to become great. He is rejecting that desire as inappropriate for his followers. As a proverb, it is even true of Jesus.

20:20 mother of the sons of Zebedee: She is a follower of Jesus and is present when Jesus is crucified (27:55-56).

20:29 Jericho: See Map 12, p. 2109.

20:30-34 two blind men...regained their sight: See Mark 10:46-52. Jesus again acts out of compassion.

want me to do for you?" [33]They said to him, "Lord, let our eyes be
opened." [34]Moved with compassion, Jesus touched their eyes. Immediately they regained their sight and followed him.

Jesus' Triumphal Entry into Jerusalem

21 When they had come near Jerusalem and had reached Bethphage, at the Mount of Olives, Jesus sent two disciples, [2]say-
ing to them, "Go into the village ahead of you, and immediately you
will find a donkey tied, and a colt with her; untie them and bring them
to me. [3]If anyone says anything to you, just say this, 'The Lord needs
them.' And he will send them immediately.[a]" [4]This took place to fulfill
what had been spoken through the prophet, saying,
5 "Tell the daughter of Zion,
Look, your king is coming to you,
humble, and mounted on a donkey,
and on a colt, the foal of a donkey."
[6]The disciples went and did as Jesus had directed them; [7]they brought
the donkey and the colt, and put their cloaks on them, and he sat on
them. [8]A very large crowd[b] spread their cloaks on the road, and others cut branches from the trees and spread them on the road. [9]The
crowds that went ahead of him and that followed were shouting,
"Hosanna to the Son of David!
Blessed is the one who comes in the name of the Lord!
Hosanna in the highest heaven!"
[10]When he entered Jerusalem, the whole city was in turmoil, asking,
"Who is this?" [11]The crowds were saying, "This is the prophet Jesus
from Nazareth in Galilee."

21:1—25:46 Jerusalem: This section describes Jesus' activity and teaching when he arrives in Jerusalem with his disciples.

21:1-11 come near Jerusalem...Bethphage, at the Mount of Olives: See Map 13, p. 2110. Jesus enters Jerusalem as the king, promised in the prophets (see Isa 62:11; Zech 9:9), and the crowd hails him as such (see Ps 118:26-27). Hosanna was an appeal to God to save, but it could also be used as praise. The prophecy in Zechariah reflects the royal humility associated with coronations in Israel (see 1 Kgs 1:32-37). This procession is a dangerous political act. Perhaps that is why the crowds refer to him as a prophet. See Mark 11:1-10.

Jesus Cleanses the Temple

12 Then Jesus entered the temple[c] and drove out all who were
selling and buying in the temple, and he overturned the tables of the
money changers and the seats of those who sold doves. [13]He said to
them, "It is written,
'My house shall be called a house of prayer';
but you are making it a den of robbers."
14 The blind and the lame came to him in the temple, and he
cured them. [15]But when the chief priests and the scribes saw the
amazing things that he did, and heard[d] the children crying out in the
temple, "Hosanna to the Son of David," they became angry [16]and
said to him, "Do you hear what these are saying?" Jesus said to them,
"Yes; have you never read,
'Out of the mouths of infants and nursing babies
you have prepared praise for yourself'?"

[a] Or *'The Lord needs them and will send them back immediately.'* [b] Or *Most of the crowd* [c] Other ancient authorities add *of God* [d] Gk lacks *heard*

21:12-17 Jesus entered the temple...money changers: See Mark 11:11, 15-19; Luke 19:45-46; John 2:13-17. The money changers and those who sold doves were essential to the sacrifice rituals of the temple. Roman coins bore the image of Caesar. They could not be used on the temple grounds. People who traveled to Jerusalem needed animals for the sacrifices. Jesus halted the sacrificial life of the temple that had been commanded by God! Jesus made the temple a place of prayer and healing. See the diagrams of the Jerusalem temple in Jesus' time, pp. 1696 and 1697.

How did Luther understand the place of sacrifice in worship? Luther understood worship primarily in terms of bringing our need and praise to God and receiving God's promise in Christ. He rejected ideas of worship that made it a sacrifice we offer to God. *Matthew 21:12-16*

[17]He left them, went out of the city to Bethany, and spent the night there.

21:18-22 a fig tree: See Mark 11:12-14, 20-24. This story is symbolic of God's judgment on the temple and its leadership. Matthew uses it to highlight the power of faith and prayer. Notice how strong the promise is.

What does it mean to pray with faith? How can this promise be true?

Jesus Curses the Fig Tree

18 In the morning, when he returned to the city, he was hungry. [19]And seeing a fig tree by the side of the road, he went to it and found nothing at all on it but leaves. Then he said to it, "May no fruit ever come from you again!" And the fig tree withered at once. [20]When the disciples saw it, they were amazed, saying, "How did the fig tree wither at once?" [21]Jesus answered them, "Truly I tell you, if you have faith and do not doubt, not only will you do what has been done to the fig tree, but even if you say to this mountain, 'Be lifted up and thrown into the sea,' it will be done. [22]Whatever you ask for in prayer with faith, you will receive."

21:23-32 By what authority are you doing these things: Not surprisingly, the chief priests and elders question Jesus' authority. See note on 2:4 (chief priests). Jesus links his authority with that of John the Baptist. Instead of answering directly, he tells the parable of the two brothers. The sign of John's authority, which should have led the chief priest and elders to believe, was that prostitutes and tax collectors believed him (see Rom 11:25-36; 1 Cor 1:26-31). Notice the cluster of themes important to the first nine chapters of Matthew: righteousness, faith, authority.

If this is the sign of God's power at work, what would that mean for our congregations?

The Authority of Jesus Questioned

23 When he entered the temple, the chief priests and the elders of the people came to him as he was teaching, and said, "By what authority are you doing these things, and who gave you this authority?" [24]Jesus said to them, "I will also ask you one question; if you tell me the answer, then I will also tell you by what authority I do these things. [25]Did the baptism of John come from heaven, or was it of human origin?" And they argued with one another, "If we say, 'From heaven,' he will say to us, 'Why then did you not believe him?' [26]But if we say, 'Of human origin,' we are afraid of the crowd; for all regard John as a prophet." [27]So they answered Jesus, "We do not know." And he said to them, "Neither will I tell you by what authority I am doing these things.

The Parable of the Two Sons

28 "What do you think? A man had two sons; he went to the first and said, 'Son, go and work in the vineyard today.' [29]He answered, 'I will not'; but later he changed his mind and went. [30]The father[a] went to the second and said the same; and he answered, 'I go, sir'; but he did not go. [31]Which of the two did the will of his father?" They said, "The first." Jesus said to them, "Truly I tell you, the tax collectors and the prostitutes are going into the kingdom of God ahead of you. [32]For John came to you in the way of righteousness and you did not believe him, but the tax collectors and the prostitutes believed him; and even after you saw it, you did not change your minds and believe him.

21:33-46 a landowner who planted a vineyard: See Mark 12:1-12. In this parable the vineyard refers to Israel (Isa 5:9-10; 27:2-11). Jesus' parable is directed against the leaders, not against the people. The suffering of the martyrs throughout history reaches its climax in the death of the Son. The parable anticipates Jesus' death and the destruction of Jerusalem and the temple by the Romans in 70 C.E. For the image of the rejected stone that becomes the cornerstone, see Psalm 118:22-23; Isaiah 8:14; 28:16; Acts 4:11; 1 Peter 2:6-8;

The Parable of the Wicked Tenants

33 "Listen to another parable. There was a landowner who planted a vineyard, put a fence around it, dug a wine press in it, and

[a] Gk *He*

built a watchtower. Then he leased it to tenants and went to another
country. 34 When the harvest time had come, he sent his slaves to the
tenants to collect his produce. 35 But the tenants seized his slaves and
beat one, killed another, and stoned another. 36 Again he sent other
slaves, more than the first; and they treated them in the same way.
37 Finally he sent his son to them, saying, 'They will respect my son.'
38 But when the tenants saw the son, they said to themselves, 'This
is the heir; come, let us kill him and get his inheritance.' 39 So they
seized him, threw him out of the vineyard, and killed him. 40 Now
when the owner of the vineyard comes, what will he do to those tenants?" 41 They said to him, "He will put those wretches to a miserable
death, and lease the vineyard to other tenants who will give him the
produce at the harvest time."

42 Jesus said to them, "Have you never read in the scriptures:

'The stone that the builders rejected
has become the cornerstone;[a]
this was the Lord's doing,
and it is amazing in our eyes'?

43 Therefore I tell you, the kingdom of God will be taken away from
you and given to a people that produces the fruits of the kingdom.[b]
44 The one who falls on this stone will be broken to pieces; and it will
crush anyone on whom it falls."[c]

45 When the chief priests and the Pharisees heard his parables,
they realized that he was speaking about them. 46 They wanted to
arrest him, but they feared the crowds, because they regarded him
as a prophet.

The Parable of the Wedding Banquet

22 Once more Jesus spoke to them in parables, saying: 2 "The
kingdom of heaven may be compared to a king who gave
a wedding banquet for his son. 3 He sent his slaves to call those who
had been invited to the wedding banquet, but they would not come.
4 Again he sent other slaves, saying, 'Tell those who have been invited: Look, I have prepared my dinner, my oxen and my fat calves
have been slaughtered, and everything is ready; come to the wedding
banquet.' 5 But they made light of it and went away, one to his farm,
another to his business, 6 while the rest seized his slaves, mistreated
them, and killed them. 7 The king was enraged. He sent his troops, destroyed those murderers, and burned their city. 8 Then he said to his
slaves, 'The wedding is ready, but those invited were not worthy. 9 Go
therefore into the main streets, and invite everyone you find to the
wedding banquet.' 10 Those slaves went out into the streets and gathered all whom they found, both good and bad; so the wedding hall
was filled with guests.

[a] Or *keystone* [b] Gk *the fruits of it* [c] Other ancient authorities lack verse 44

Romans 9:33.

22:1-14 king who gave a wedding banquet: See Luke 14:16-24; Revelation 19:6-9; Matthew 9:14-15. This parable also anticipates the destruction of Jerusalem and the temple. The invited guests choose not to come. They mistreat and kill the king's slaves. Then the king's slaves invite everyone they can find in the streets, good and bad. The last section about the guest without a wedding garment is puzzling. Many interpretations have been offered, but none has a clear basis in the text. It is best left as a warning without explanation.

11 "But when the king came in to see the guests, he noticed a
man there who was not wearing a wedding robe, [12]and he said to
him, 'Friend, how did you get in here without a wedding robe?' And
he was speechless. [13]Then the king said to the attendants, 'Bind him
hand and foot, and throw him into the outer darkness, where there
will be weeping and gnashing of teeth.' [14]For many are called, but
few are chosen."

The Question about Paying Taxes

15 Then the Pharisees went and plotted to entrap him in what
he said. [16]So they sent their disciples to him, along with the Herodians, saying, "Teacher, we know that you are sincere, and teach
the way of God in accordance with truth, and show deference to
no one; for you do not regard people with partiality. [17]Tell us, then,
what you think. Is it lawful to pay taxes to the emperor, or not?"
[18]But Jesus, aware of their malice, said, "Why are you putting me to
the test, you hypocrites? [19]Show me the coin used for the tax." And
they brought him a denarius. [20]Then he said to them, "Whose head
is this, and whose title?" [21]They answered, "The emperor's." Then he
said to them, "Give therefore to the emperor the things that are the
emperor's, and to God the things that are God's." [22]When they heard
this, they were amazed; and they left him and went away.

The Question about the Resurrection

23 The same day some Sadducees came to him, saying there is
no resurrection;[a] and they asked him a question, saying, [24]"Teacher,
Moses said, 'If a man dies childless, his brother shall marry the
widow, and raise up children for his brother.' [25]Now there were
seven brothers among us; the first married, and died childless, leaving the widow to his brother. [26]The second did the same, so also the
third, down to the seventh. [27]Last of all, the woman herself died. [28]In
the resurrection, then, whose wife of the seven will she be? For all of
them had married her."

29 Jesus answered them, "You are wrong, because you know neither the scriptures nor the power of God. [30]For in the resurrection
they neither marry nor are given in marriage, but are like angels[b] in
heaven. [31]And as for the resurrection of the dead, have you not read
what was said to you by God, [32]'I am the God of Abraham, the God
of Isaac, and the God of Jacob'? He is God not of the dead, but of
the living." [33]And when the crowd heard it, they were astounded at
his teaching.

The Greatest Commandment

34 When the Pharisees heard that he had silenced the Sadducees, they gathered together, [35]and one of them, a lawyer, asked him

---

[a] Other ancient authorities read *who say that there is no resurrection* [b] Other ancient authorities add *of God*

22:15-16 Pharisees...Herodians: See the note on 3:7 (Pharisees). No one knows who the Herodians were, although there has been a lot of speculation over the centuries. Apparently they sometimes were associated with the Pharisees in their opposition to Jesus (see Mark 3:6).

22:17-22 pay taxes to the emperor: See Mark 12:13-17. Politics made this a tricky question. Most Israelites opposed the tax, while Rome and Rome's emperor required it. The question of taxes paid to Caesar provided the spark for the Jewish revolt in 66 C.E. Jesus' answer avoids offending the Israelites or opposing Roman authority. Jesus asks whose image is on the coin. The image on the coin identifies its owner. Since it bears the emperor's image, it belongs to him.

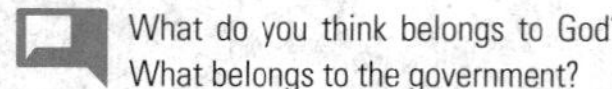

What do you think belongs to God? What belongs to the government?

22:23-33 Sadducees...no resurrection: See Mark 12:18-27. The resurrection was a matter of debate within Israel. The Sadducees (see note on 3:7) denied the resurrection; the Pharisees looked for the resurrection of the dead. Jesus makes two points. First, resurrection gives rise to a radically transformed reality. Second, God's identity is tied to particular people: Abraham, Isaac, and Jacob. Therefore, they cannot remain dead (see Exod 3:4-15).

22:34-40 which commandment in the law is the greatest?: See Mark 12:28-34; Luke 10:25-28. This third question also is not a challenge. It is like an exam question to see if Jesus understands the law. Jesus' answer is not new. It is in the Hebrew Scriptures (Deut 6:5; Lev 19:18). Notice that in Luke's Gospel the lawyer gives this answer.

a question to test him. 36 "Teacher, which commandment in the law
is the greatest?" 37 He said to him, " 'You shall love the Lord your
God with all your heart, and with all your soul, and with all your
mind.' 38 This is the greatest and first commandment. 39 And a second
is like it: 'You shall love your neighbor as yourself.' 40 On these two
commandments hang all the law and the prophets."

The Question about David's Son

41 Now while the Pharisees were gathered together, Jesus
asked them this question: 42 "What do you think of the Messiah?[a]
Whose son is he?" They said to him, "The son of David." 43 He said
to them, "How is it then that David by the Spirit[b] calls him Lord,
saying,

44 'The Lord said to my Lord,
"Sit at my right hand,
until I put your enemies under your feet" '?

45 If David thus calls him Lord, how can he be his son?" 46 No one was
able to give him an answer, nor from that day did anyone dare to ask
him any more questions.

Jesus Denounces Scribes and Pharisees

23 Then Jesus said to the crowds and to his disciples, 2 "The
scribes and the Pharisees sit on Moses' seat; 3 therefore, do
whatever they teach you and follow it; but do not do as they do, for
they do not practice what they teach. 4 They tie up heavy burdens,
hard to bear,[c] and lay them on the shoulders of others; but they themselves are unwilling to lift a finger to move them. 5 They do all their
deeds to be seen by others; for they make their phylacteries broad
and their fringes long. 6 They love to have the place of honor at banquets and the best seats in the synagogues, 7 and to be greeted with
respect in the marketplaces, and to have people call them rabbi. 8 But
you are not to be called rabbi, for you have one teacher, and you are
all students.[d] 9 And call no one your father on earth, for you have one
Father—the one in heaven. 10 Nor are you to be called instructors, for
you have one instructor, the Messiah.[e] 11 The greatest among you will
be your servant. 12 All who exalt themselves will be humbled, and all
who humble themselves will be exalted.

13 "But woe to you, scribes and Pharisees, hypocrites! For you
lock people out of the kingdom of heaven. For you do not go in
yourselves, and when others are going in, you stop them.[f] 15 Woe to
you, scribes and Pharisees, hypocrites! For you cross sea and land to

[a] Or *Christ* [b] Gk *in spirit* [c] Other ancient authorities lack *hard to bear* [d] Gk *brothers*
[e] Or *the Christ* [f] Other authorities add here (or after verse 12) verse 14, *Woe to you, scribes and Pharisees, hypocrites! For you devour widows' houses and for the sake of appearance you make long prayers; therefore you will receive the greater condemnation*

22:41-46 the Messiah?...Whose son is he?: See Mark 12:35-37. Jesus then asks the Pharisees how to interpret Psalm 110:1. It speaks of the Messiah, David's son, as greater than David. That ends the discussion. See also the note on 1:1-17.

23:1-36 scribes and the Pharisees sit on Moses' seat...do not do what they do: See Mark 12:38-40; Luke 11:39-52; 20:45-47. Jesus affirms what the scribes and Pharisees teach. The issue is that they want their devotion to God and obedience to be seen by others (6:1). This results in an emphasis on what is external rather than the inner substance of God's commands. Phylacteries were small cases worn on the arm and forehead containing quotations from Scripture (see Deut 6:4-9). Fringes, with a blue cord at each corner, were to remind people of the commandments (Num 15:37-41). While the scribes and Pharisees may teach correctly, they like to set themselves above others. Disciples are not to do so. The theme of this chapter is summarized in 23:12.

The scribes and Pharisees close the kingdom to others and do not themselves enter, yet they aggressively seek converts (23:13-15). They are like blind guides, who emphasize the trivial and miss what matters (23:24). They focus on the surface, not the substance (23:25-28). The scariest passage is 23:29-36. They honor the tombs of the martyred prophets and righteous, and claim that they would not have done what their ancestors did—shedding the blood of the prophets. But Jesus says their words demonstrate that they are just like their ancestors who murdered the prophets! All this suffering in history is gathered up into Jesus' suffering and death.

In what ways are you tempted to be like the scribes and Pharisees?

make a single convert, and you make the new convert twice as much
a child of hell[a] as yourselves.
16 "Woe to you, blind guides, who say, 'Whoever swears by the
sanctuary is bound by nothing, but whoever swears by the gold of
the sanctuary is bound by the oath.' 17 You blind fools! For which is
greater, the gold or the sanctuary that has made the gold sacred?
18 And you say, 'Whoever swears by the altar is bound by nothing,
but whoever swears by the gift that is on the altar is bound by the
oath.' 19 How blind you are! For which is greater, the gift or the altar
that makes the gift sacred? 20 So whoever swears by the altar, swears
by it and by everything on it; 21 and whoever swears by the sanctuary, swears by it and by the one who dwells in it; 22 and whoever
swears by heaven, swears by the throne of God and by the one who
is seated upon it.
23 "Woe to you, scribes and Pharisees, hypocrites! For you
tithe mint, dill, and cummin, and have neglected the weightier matters of the law: justice and mercy and faith. It is these you ought to
have practiced without neglecting the others. 24 You blind guides!
You strain out a gnat but swallow a camel!
25 "Woe to you, scribes and Pharisees, hypocrites! For you
clean the outside of the cup and of the plate, but inside they are full
of greed and self-indulgence. 26 You blind Pharisee! First clean the
inside of the cup,[b] so that the outside also may become clean.
27 "Woe to you, scribes and Pharisees, hypocrites! For you are
like whitewashed tombs, which on the outside look beautiful, but
inside they are full of the bones of the dead and of all kinds of filth.
28 So you also on the outside look righteous to others, but inside you
are full of hypocrisy and lawlessness.
29 "Woe to you, scribes and Pharisees, hypocrites! For you
build the tombs of the prophets and decorate the graves of the righteous, 30 and you say, 'If we had lived in the days of our ancestors,
we would not have taken part with them in shedding the blood
of the prophets.' 31 Thus you testify against yourselves that you are
descendants of those who murdered the prophets. 32 Fill up, then,
the measure of your ancestors. 33 You snakes, you brood of vipers!
How can you escape being sentenced to hell?[a]e 34 Therefore I send
you prophets, sages, and scribes, some of whom you will kill and
crucify, and some you will flog in your synagogues and pursue
from town to town, 35 so that upon you may come all the righteous
blood shed on earth, from the blood of righteous Abel to the blood
of Zechariah son of Barachiah, whom you murdered between the
sanctuary and the altar. 36 Truly I tell you, all this will come upon
this generation.

23:37 as a hen gathers her chicks: Using a motherly image (see also Deut 32:10-12; Ps 61:4), Jesus weeps over Jerusalem (see Luke 13:34-35).

23:38 your house: Jesus here speaks of the temple, but as "your house," not "God's house (21:13). This reflects a widespread tradition that before the Babylonians destroyed the temple, God had left the temple and the city (see Ezek 9:3; 10:18-19; 11:23). Josephus, the first-century Jewish historian, reports signs that God had left the temple be-

[a] Gk *Gehenna* [b] Other ancient authorities add *and of the plate*

The Lament over Jerusalem

37 "Jerusalem, Jerusalem, the city that kills the prophets and
stones those who are sent to it! How often have I desired to gather
your children together as a hen gathers her brood under her wings,
and you were not willing! 38See, your house is left to you, desolate.[a]
39For I tell you, you will not see me again until you say, 'Blessed is
the one who comes in the name of the Lord.' "

The Destruction of the Temple Foretold

24 As Jesus came out of the temple and was going away, his
disciples came to point out to him the buildings of the temple. 2Then he asked them, "You see all these, do you not? Truly I tell
you, not one stone will be left here upon another; all will be thrown
down."

Signs of the End of the Age

3 When he was sitting on the Mount of Olives, the disciples
came to him privately, saying, "Tell us, when will this be, and what
will be the sign of your coming and of the end of the age?" 4Jesus answered them, "Beware that no one leads you astray. 5For many will
come in my name, saying, 'I am the Messiah!'[b] and they will lead
many astray. 6And you will hear of wars and rumors of wars; see that
you are not alarmed; for this must take place, but the end is not yet.
7For nation will rise against nation, and kingdom against kingdom,
and there will be famines[c] and earthquakes in various places: 8all
this is but the beginning of the birth pangs.

Persecutions Foretold

9 "Then they will hand you over to be tortured and will put you
to death, and you will be hated by all nations because of my name.
10Then many will fall away,[d] and they will betray one another and
hate one another. 11And many false prophets will arise and lead
many astray. 12And because of the increase of lawlessness, the love
of many will grow cold. 13But the one who endures to the end will
be saved. 14And this good news[e] of the kingdom will be proclaimed
throughout the world, as a testimony to all the nations; and then the
end will come.

The Desolating Sacrilege

15 "So when you see the desolating sacrilege standing in the
holy place, as was spoken of by the prophet Daniel (let the reader
understand), 16then those in Judea must flee to the mountains; 17the
one on the housetop must not go down to take what is in the house;

[a] Other ancient authorities lack *desolate* [b] Or *the Christ* [c] Other ancient authorities add *and pestilences*
[d] Or *stumble* [e] Or *gospel*

fore the Romans destroyed it in 70 C.E. The temple, the place of God's life-giving presence, becomes a place of desolation and death.

24:1-35 not one stone will be left here upon another . . . this generation will not pass away until: See Mark 13:1-31. Jesus can see the temple from where he sits on the Mount of Olives (24:3; see Map 13, p. 2110). The temple and its sacrificial life participated in the stable order of the world. The language of this passage reflects the experiences of the Jewish revolt that led to the destruction of the temple in 70 C.E. When this Gospel was written, the temple had been destroyed. This event symbolized the reality that everything in this world will pass away, no matter how enduring it seems to be. Notice how ordinary the signs are: conflict among nations, wars, famines, earthquakes. This vision of a world under God's judgment draws on Israel's prophetic traditions (see Jer 28:8; Isa 13:10; 34:4).

Daniel also plays an important role: the Son of Man coming in the clouds (see Dan 7:13-27), the intense suffering (see Dan 12:1), and the desolating sacrilege set up in the temple (Matt 24:15; see Dan 9:27; 11:31; 12:11). This desolating sacrilege in Daniel was the image of the Seleucid emperor, Antiochus IV Epiphanes. Hanukkah is the celebration of the purification of the temple when the Jewish people removed the image and purified the temple. As the suffering increases, false prophets and false messiahs will arise, offering false promises of salvation. Hatred of Jesus' followers will intensify (Matt 10:16-24, 34-39). Every generation of Christians has been able to see these signs in their time. We all live in the midst of signs that this world, to which we cling, is passing away.

24:13-35 the one who endures . . . will be saved: Notice the four promises in this section. The one who endures to the end will be saved (24:13; 10:22). The gospel will be preached throughout the world (24:14). The coming of the Son of Man to gather his people will be visible to all, not hidden (24:27-31). Jesus' word endures when everything else passes away (24:35). On Jesus' expectation that these things were to be fulfilled within the lifetime of that generation (24:34), see also 10:23.

How do events in today's world seem to match the "signs of the end" mentioned in Matthew 24? Which give you most concern? Which give you hope?

18 the one in the field must not turn back to get a coat. 19 Woe to those
who are pregnant and to those who are nursing infants in those
days! 20 Pray that your flight may not be in winter or on a sabbath.
21 For at that time there will be great suffering, such as has not been
from the beginning of the world until now, no, and never will be.
22 And if those days had not been cut short, no one would be saved;
but for the sake of the elect those days will be cut short. 23 Then if
anyone says to you, 'Look! Here is the Messiah!'[a] or 'There he is!'—
do not believe it. 24 For false messiahs[b] and false prophets will appear
and produce great signs and omens, to lead astray, if possible, even
the elect. 25 Take note, I have told you beforehand. 26 So, if they say
to you, 'Look! He is in the wilderness,' do not go out. If they say,
'Look! He is in the inner rooms,' do not believe it. 27 For as the lightning comes from the east and flashes as far as the west, so will be
the coming of the Son of Man. 28 Wherever the corpse is, there the
vultures will gather.

The Coming of the Son of Man

29 "Immediately after the suffering of those days
the sun will be darkened,
    and the moon will not give its light;
the stars will fall from heaven,
    and the powers of heaven will be shaken.

30 Then the sign of the Son of Man will appear in heaven, and then all
the tribes of the earth will mourn, and they will see 'the Son of Man
coming on the clouds of heaven' with power and great glory. 31 And he
will send out his angels with a loud trumpet call, and they will gather
his elect from the four winds, from one end of heaven to the other.

The Lesson of the Fig Tree

32 "From the fig tree learn its lesson: as soon as its branch becomes tender and puts forth its leaves, you know that summer is
near. 33 So also, when you see all these things, you know that he[c] is
near, at the very gates. 34 Truly I tell you, this generation will not pass
away until all these things have taken place. 35 Heaven and earth will
pass away, but my words will not pass away.

The Necessity for Watchfulness

36 "But about that day and hour no one knows, neither the angels of heaven, nor the Son,[d] but only the Father. 37 For as the days
of Noah were, so will be the coming of the Son of Man. 38 For as in
those days before the flood they were eating and drinking, marrying
and giving in marriage, until the day Noah entered the ark, 39 and
they knew nothing until the flood came and swept them all away,

24:36 about that day and hour no one knows: See Mark 14:32-37. None of these signs provides a way of calculating the times. Not even Jesus knows the day or the hour.

24:37–25:30 the coming of the Son of Man: Jesus uses a series of sayings and parables to encourage his followers to endure as they face suffering. Since the hour is unexpected, they need to keep awake and be ready. Note that this passage provides no basis for the nonbiblical idea of the rapture. It speaks simply of suddenness and separation. There is no hint as to whether those taken are saved or destroyed. Also, all will see his coming (24:27-31). It will not be hidden. What watching and being ready mean is surprisingly simple. Faithfully carry out the tasks set before you (24:45-51), and use the gifts God gives you wisely and fruitfully (25:1-30).

[a] Or *the Christ* [b] Or *christs* [c] Or *it* [d] Other ancient authorities lack *nor the Son*

so too will be the coming of the Son of Man. [40]Then two will be in the field; one will be taken and one will be left. [41]Two women will be grinding meal together; one will be taken and one will be left. [42]Keep awake therefore, for you do not know on what day[a] your Lord is coming. [43]But understand this: if the owner of the house had known in what part of the night the thief was coming, he would have stayed awake and would not have let his house be broken into. [44]Therefore you also must be ready, for the Son of Man is coming at an unexpected hour.

The Faithful or the Unfaithful Slave

45 "Who then is the faithful and wise slave, whom his master has put in charge of his household, to give the other slaves[b] their allowance of food at the proper time? [46]Blessed is that slave whom his master will find at work when he arrives. [47]Truly I tell you, he will put that one in charge of all his possessions. [48]But if that wicked slave says to himself, 'My master is delayed,' [49]and he begins to beat his fellow slaves, and eats and drinks with drunkards, [50]the master of that slave will come on a day when he does not expect him and at an hour that he does not know. [51]He will cut him in pieces[c] and put him with the hypocrites, where there will be weeping and gnashing of teeth.

The Parable of the Ten Bridesmaids

25 "Then the kingdom of heaven will be like this. Ten bridesmaids[d] took their lamps and went to meet the bridegroom.[e] [2]Five of them were foolish, and five were wise. [3]When the foolish took their lamps, they took no oil with them; [4]but the wise took flasks of oil with their lamps. [5]As the bridegroom was delayed, all of them became drowsy and slept. [6]But at midnight there was a shout, 'Look! Here is the bridegroom! Come out to meet him.' [7]Then all those bridesmaids[d] got up and trimmed their lamps. [8]The foolish said to the wise, 'Give us some of your oil, for our lamps are going out.' [9]But the wise replied, 'No! there will not be enough for you and for us; you had better go to the dealers and buy some for yourselves.' [10]And while they went to buy it, the bridegroom came, and those who were ready went with him into the wedding banquet; and the door was shut. [11]Later the other bridesmaids[d] came also, saying, 'Lord, lord, open to us.' [12]But he replied, 'Truly I tell you, I do not know you.' [13]Keep awake therefore, for you know neither the day nor the hour.[f]

The Parable of the Talents

14 "For it is as if a man, going on a journey, summoned his slaves and entrusted his property to them; [15]to one he gave five talents,[g] to

[a] Other ancient authorities read *at what hour* [b] Gk *to give them* [c] Or *cut him off* [d] Gk *virgins* [e] Other ancient authorities add *and the bride* [f] Other ancient authorities add *in which the Son of Man is coming* [g] A talent was worth more than fifteen years' wages of a laborer

25:15 talents: It would take a laborer more than fifteen years to earn a talent (see NRSV footnote *g*). See also the note on 18:23-35.

another two, to another one, to each according to his ability. Then
he went away. [16]The one who had received the five talents went off
at once and traded with them, and made five more talents. [17]In the
same way, the one who had the two talents made two more talents.
[18]But the one who had received the one talent went off and dug a
hole in the ground and hid his master's money. [19]After a long time
the master of those slaves came and settled accounts with them.
[20]Then the one who had received the five talents came forward,
bringing five more talents, saying, 'Master, you handed over to me
five talents; see, I have made five more talents.' [21]His master said to
him, 'Well done, good and trustworthy slave; you have been trustworthy in a few things, I will put you in charge of many things; enter
into the joy of your master.' [22]And the one with the two talents also
came forward, saying, 'Master, you handed over to me two talents;
see, I have made two more talents.' [23]His master said to him, 'Well
done, good and trustworthy slave; you have been trustworthy in a
few things, I will put you in charge of many things; enter into the
joy of your master.' [24]Then the one who had received the one talent
also came forward, saying, 'Master, I knew that you were a harsh
man, reaping where you did not sow, and gathering where you did
not scatter seed; [25]so I was afraid, and I went and hid your talent in
the ground. Here you have what is yours.' [26]But his master replied,
'You wicked and lazy slave! You knew, did you, that I reap where I
did not sow, and gather where I did not scatter? [27]Then you ought
to have invested my money with the bankers, and on my return I
would have received what was my own with interest. [28]So take the
talent from him, and give it to the one with the ten talents. [29]For to
all those who have, more will be given, and they will have an abundance; but from those who have nothing, even what they have will
be taken away. [30]As for this worthless slave, throw him into the outer
darkness, where there will be weeping and gnashing of teeth.'

The Judgment of the Nations

31 "When the Son of Man comes in his glory, and all the angels with him, then he will sit on the throne of his glory. [32]All the
nations will be gathered before him, and he will separate people
one from another as a shepherd separates the sheep from the goats,
[33]and he will put the sheep at his right hand and the goats at the
left. [34]Then the king will say to those at his right hand, 'Come, you
that are blessed by my Father, inherit the kingdom prepared for you
from the foundation of the world; [35]for I was hungry and you gave
me food, I was thirsty and you gave me something to drink, I was
a stranger and you welcomed me, [36]I was naked and you gave me
clothing, I was sick and you took care of me, I was in prison and you
visited me.' [37]Then the righteous will answer him, 'Lord, when was

25:31-46 Son of Man . . . nations will be gathered before him: The coming of the Son of Man here includes a final judgment. Scholars have argued the identity of the "nations" in this parable. Matthew may be following the Jewish tendency to distinguish between non-Jewish "nations" and Israel as God's "people." That distinction is sometimes reflected when the word for "nations" is translated as "Gentiles." If this is so, the "nations" here are in contrast with God's "people" and the little ones (see Matt 18:6) who belong to Jesus. And the parable could refer to how the nations respond to the needs of God's people.

More likely, the meaning is much broader. All are judged by how they treat those in need. This means that both Jesus' followers and the unbelieving nations are invited to help those who suffer and are broken. What they do to these little ones they do to Jesus. Jesus' word is a promise that creates what it declares. Jesus makes those who suffer and are broken the place of his presence in our world, even for those who do not claim to be Jesus' followers. In this way the parable speaks of the surprising way in which the unbelieving nations have a relationship to Jesus, who is present in all the little, insignificant ones, whose suffering Jesus took into himself in his own suffering and death. At the same time, those who believe in Jesus need to guard against the temptation to make serving others a means to achieve salvation.

it that we saw you hungry and gave you food, or thirsty and gave you something to drink? [38]And when was it that we saw you a stranger and welcomed you, or naked and gave you clothing? [39]And when was it that we saw you sick or in prison and visited you?' [40]And the king will answer them, 'Truly I tell you, just as you did it to one of the least of these who are members of my family,[a] you did it to me.' [41]Then he will say to those at his left hand, 'You that are accursed, depart from me into the eternal fire prepared for the devil and his angels; [42]for I was hungry and you gave me no food, I was thirsty and you gave me nothing to drink, [43]I was a stranger and you did not welcome me, naked and you did not give me clothing, sick and in prison and you did not visit me.' [44]Then they also will answer, 'Lord, when was it that we saw you hungry or thirsty or a stranger or naked or sick or in prison, and did not take care of you?' [45]Then he will answer them, 'Truly I tell you, just as you did not do it to one of the least of these, you did not do it to me.' [46]And these will go away into eternal punishment, but the righteous into eternal life."

The Plot to Kill Jesus

26 When Jesus had finished saying all these things, he said to his disciples, [2]"You know that after two days the Passover is coming, and the Son of Man will be handed over to be crucified."

3 Then the chief priests and the elders of the people gathered in the palace of the high priest, who was called Caiaphas, [4]and they conspired to arrest Jesus by stealth and kill him. [5]But they said, "Not during the festival, or there may be a riot among the people."

The Anointing at Bethany

6 Now while Jesus was at Bethany in the house of Simon the leper,[b] [7]a woman came to him with an alabaster jar of very costly ointment, and she poured it on his head as he sat at the table. [8]But when the disciples saw it, they were angry and said, "Why this waste? [9]For this ointment could have been sold for a large sum, and the money given to the poor." [10]But Jesus, aware of this, said to them, "Why do you trouble the woman? She has performed a good service for me. [11]For you always have the poor with you, but you will not always have me. [12]By pouring this ointment on my body she has prepared me for burial. [13]Truly I tell you, wherever this good news[c] is proclaimed in the whole world, what she has done will be told in remembrance of her."

Judas Agrees to Betray Jesus

14 Then one of the twelve, who was called Judas Iscariot, went to the chief priests [15]and said, "What will you give me if I betray him

[a] Gk *these my brothers* [b] The terms *leper* and *leprosy* can refer to several diseases [c] Or *gospel*

26:1—28:20 Son of Man will be handed over to be crucified: The final section of Matthew's Gospel tells the story of Jesus' crucifixion and his resurrection.

26:1-2 When Jesus had finished saying all these things: The story of Jesus' death and resurrection begins by calling attention to all that Jesus taught. It ends with the command to teach people to obey Jesus' commands (28:16-20).

26:2 after two days the Passover is coming: It is two days before the Jewish festival of Passover (see the note on 26:17-29). Jesus will die on the third day. Jewish tradition says the third day is the day of salvation. One reason is Isaac's deliverance from death on the third day (see Gen 22:1-19). Another is God's descent on Sinai on the third day (see Exod 19). Jesus' resurrection on the third day fulfills this tradition. Matthew 26:2 and Luke 13:31-33 speak of the third day as the day of Jesus' death, interpreting this as the day of salvation (see 27:50-54).

26:3 chief priests and the elders... Caiaphas: See the notes on 2:4 and 21:23-32 (chief priests and elders). Caiaphas served as high priest 18–37 C.E.

26:6-16 at Bethany...a woman... poured it on his head: See Mark 14:1-11; John 12:1-8. Bethany was a short distance southeast of Jerusalem. The woman's action of pouring expensive ointment on Jesus' head is compared by Jesus to the use of ointment to prepare a body for burial. This story leads to Judas' betrayal (26:14-16). In 26:5 the chief priests want to kill Jesus, but not during the festival. But after the woman's extravagant act, Judas decides to betray Jesus (26:14-16). We know nothing about the woman or what she thought she was doing. The disciples interpret the woman's act negatively by setting it in the context of the needs of the poor (19:21). Jesus defends her and transforms what she does by setting it in the context of his death. In the movement of the story, Judas betrays Jesus because Jesus defends the woman and makes himself more important than the poor (see 6:24). Jesus dies because he defends the woman against her accusers, and his death redeems her action by giving it a positive meaning.

to you?" They paid him thirty pieces of silver. 16And from that moment he began to look for an opportunity to betray him.

The Passover with the Disciples

17 On the first day of Unleavened Bread the disciples came to Jesus, saying, "Where do you want us to make the preparations for you to eat the Passover?" 18He said, "Go into the city to a certain man, and say to him, 'The Teacher says, My time is near; I will keep the Passover at your house with my disciples.' " 19So the disciples did as Jesus had directed them, and they prepared the Passover meal.

20 When it was evening, he took his place with the twelve;[a] 21and while they were eating, he said, "Truly I tell you, one of you will betray me." 22And they became greatly distressed and began to say to him one after another, "Surely not I, Lord?" 23He answered, "The one who has dipped his hand into the bowl with me will betray me. 24The Son of Man goes as it is written of him, but woe to that one by whom the Son of Man is betrayed! It would have been better for that one not to have been born." 25Judas, who betrayed him, said, "Surely not I, Rabbi?" He replied, "You have said so."

26:17-29 the first day of Unleavened Bread…this is my blood of the covenant: See Mark 14:12-25; Luke 22:7-23; 1 Corinthians 11:23-26. The seven-day Jewish festival of Unleavened Bread was combined with Passover, which celebrated the Hebrew people's escape from Egypt (Exod 12:1—13:10). Notice that everything happens according to plan. The upper room is prepared and ready for Jesus and the disciples. In this version of "the last supper," Matthew alone includes the words "for the forgiveness of sins."

How does Luther understand the words of institution? In his Small Catechism, Luther says that God's word creates what it declares. "It is the true body and blood of our Lord Jesus Christ under the bread and wine." This is not some abstract presence. As we eat the bread and drink the wine, we eat and drink his body and his blood given in his death for our sins and for our forgiveness. *Matthew 26:26-28*

The Institution of the Lord's Supper

26 While they were eating, Jesus took a loaf of bread, and after blessing it he broke it, gave it to the disciples, and said, "Take, eat; this is my body." 27Then he took a cup, and after giving thanks he gave it to them, saying, "Drink from it, all of you; 28for this is my blood of the[b] covenant, which is poured out for many for the forgiveness of sins. 29I tell you, I will never again drink of this fruit of the vine until that day when I drink it new with you in my Father's kingdom."

30 When they had sung the hymn, they went out to the Mount of Olives.

26:30-35 You will all become deserters: See Mark 14:26-31. Notice that the disciples will desert Jesus because that is what the prophecy says (26:31; see Zech 13:7), not because they are weak. Peter thinks he can resist the prophecy, and he falls farther.

Peter's Denial Foretold

31 Then Jesus said to them, "You will all become deserters because of me this night; for it is written,

'I will strike the shepherd,
and the sheep of the flock will be scattered.'

32But after I am raised up, I will go ahead of you to Galilee." 33Peter said to him, "Though all become deserters because of you, I will never desert you." 34Jesus said to him, "Truly I tell you, this very night, before the cock crows, you will deny me three times." 35Peter said to him, "Even though I must die with you, I will not deny you." And so said all the disciples.

---

[a] Other ancient authorities add *disciples* [b] Other ancient authorities add *new*

Jesus Prays in Gethsemane

36 Then Jesus went with them to a place called Gethsemane; and he said to his disciples, "Sit here while I go over there and pray." 37 He took with him Peter and the two sons of Zebedee, and began to be grieved and agitated. 38 Then he said to them, "I am deeply grieved, even to death; remain here, and stay awake with me." 39 And going a little farther, he threw himself on the ground and prayed, "My Father, if it is possible, let this cup pass from me; yet not what I want but what you want." 40 Then he came to the disciples and found them sleeping; and he said to Peter, "So, could you not stay awake with me one hour? 41 Stay awake and pray that you may not come into the time of trial;[a] the spirit indeed is willing, but the flesh is weak." 42 Again he went away for the second time and prayed, "My Father, if this cannot pass unless I drink it, your will be done." 43 Again he came and found them sleeping, for their eyes were heavy. 44 So leaving them again, he went away and prayed for the third time, saying the same words. 45 Then he came to the disciples and said to them, "Are you still sleeping and taking your rest? See, the hour is at hand, and the Son of Man is betrayed into the hands of sinners. 46 Get up, let us be going. See, my betrayer is at hand."

26:36-46 Gethsemane: See Mark 14:32-42. See Map 13, p. 2110, for the location of Gethsemane. This is a conversation between Jesus and the Father. Three times Jesus asks Peter and the disciples to watch with him while he prays. Three times he finds them sleeping, unable to keep awake. This anticipates the disciples' flight and Peter's three denials. Notice the progression from Jesus' first prayer through the other two. After the third, Jesus knows the answer.

The Betrayal and Arrest of Jesus

47 While he was still speaking, Judas, one of the twelve, arrived; with him was a large crowd with swords and clubs, from the chief priests and the elders of the people. 48 Now the betrayer had given them a sign, saying, "The one I will kiss is the man; arrest him." 49 At once he came up to Jesus and said, "Greetings, Rabbi!" and kissed him. 50 Jesus said to him, "Friend, do what you are here to do." Then they came and laid hands on Jesus and arrested him. 51 Suddenly, one of those with Jesus put his hand on his sword, drew it, and struck the slave of the high priest, cutting off his ear. 52 Then Jesus said to him, "Put your sword back into its place; for all who take the sword will perish by the sword. 53 Do you think that I cannot appeal to my Father, and he will at once send me more than twelve legions of angels? 54 But how then would the scriptures be fulfilled, which say it must happen in this way?" 55 At that hour Jesus said to the crowds, "Have you come out with swords and clubs to arrest me as though I were a bandit? Day after day I sat in the temple teaching, and you did not arrest me. 56 But all this has taken place, so that the scriptures of the prophets may be fulfilled." Then all the disciples deserted him and fled.

26:47-56 Judas...arrived...with him was a large crowd: See Mark 14:43-50. Judas' action will fulfill Jesus' prediction (26:20-25). Notice that Matthew adds the point that even now things could be different if Jesus asked. But it is necessary that Scripture be fulfilled (26:53-54, 56).

---

[a] Or *into temptation*

Jesus before the High Priest

57 Those who had arrested Jesus took him to Caiaphas the high
priest, in whose house the scribes and the elders had gathered. 58 But
Peter was following him at a distance, as far as the courtyard of the
high priest; and going inside, he sat with the guards in order to see
how this would end. 59 Now the chief priests and the whole council
were looking for false testimony against Jesus so that they might put
him to death, 60 but they found none, though many false witnesses
came forward. At last two came forward 61 and said, "This fellow
said, 'I am able to destroy the temple of God and to build it in three
days.'" 62 The high priest stood up and said, "Have you no answer?
What is it that they testify against you?" 63 But Jesus was silent. Then
the high priest said to him, "I put you under oath before the living
God, tell us if you are the Messiah,[a] the Son of God." 64 Jesus said to
him, "You have said so. But I tell you,

From now on you will see the Son of Man
  seated at the right hand of Power
  and coming on the clouds of heaven."

65 Then the high priest tore his clothes and said, "He has blasphemed!
Why do we still need witnesses? You have now heard his blasphemy.
66 What is your verdict?" They answered, "He deserves death." 67 Then
they spat in his face and struck him; and some slapped him, 68 saying,
"Prophesy to us, you Messiah![a] Who is it that struck you?"

26:57-68 arrested Jesus took him to Caiaphas the high priest: See Mark 14:53-65. First, Jesus goes on trial before Caiaphas, the high priest of Israel and the council (26:59), or "Sanhedrin," a court that oversaw internal cases. The priests played an important role, but it also was made up of Pharisees and other lay religious leaders. The law required two witnesses (see Deut 17:6; 19:15). The trial focuses on two issues. The first is the strange saying about the temple (26:61; 27:40). Only later in John 2:19 is a similar saying directly attributed to Jesus. John interprets it as a prediction of Jesus' death and resurrection, which the disciples understood only after his resurrection (see John 2:21-22). The second issue is whether Jesus claims to be the Messiah. Jesus answers the high priest's question positively by referring to the high priest's own words. But then Jesus identifies himself with the Son of Man seated at God's right hand and coming to judge the world (Dan 7:13-14). For the high priest this touches God's honor, and he tears his clothes (26:65), a practice Judaism prescribed when one hears blasphemy. The punishment for blasphemy was death (Lev 24:10-23). The chief priests and elders turn Jesus over to the Romans, along with the accusation that he claims to be king (27:1-2).

Peter's Denial of Jesus

69 Now Peter was sitting outside in the courtyard. A servant-
girl came to him and said, "You also were with Jesus the Galilean."
70 But he denied it before all of them, saying, "I do not know what
you are talking about." 71 When he went out to the porch, another
servant-girl saw him, and she said to the bystanders, "This man was
with Jesus of Nazareth."[b] 72 Again he denied it with an oath, "I do not
know the man." 73 After a little while the bystanders came up and
said to Peter, "Certainly you are also one of them, for your accent
betrays you." 74 Then he began to curse, and he swore an oath, "I do
not know the man!" At that moment the cock crowed. 75 Then Peter
remembered what Jesus had said: "Before the cock crows, you will
deny me three times." And he went out and wept bitterly.

26:69-75 Peter was sitting outside in the courtyard: Peter's three denials have to be seen in light of 10:32-33. It shows that God's possibilities for mercy exceed God's judgment.

Jesus Brought before Pilate

27 When morning came, all the chief priests and the elders
of the people conferred together against Jesus in order to
bring about his death. 2 They bound him, led him away, and handed
him over to Pilate the governor.

27:1-2 handed him over to Pilate the governor: The chief priests and elders (see the notes on 2:4 and 21:23-32) bring Jesus to Pontius Pilate for his second trial. Pilate was the Roman governor of the province of Judea 26–36 C.E. The governor usually stayed in the city during the time of the Jewish festivals.

---

[a] Or *Christ* [b] Gk *the Nazorean*

The Suicide of Judas

3 When Judas, his betrayer, saw that Jesus[a] was condemned, he
repented and brought back the thirty pieces of silver to the chief
priests and the elders. 4 He said, "I have sinned by betraying innocent[b] blood." But they said, "What is that to us? See to it yourself."
5 Throwing down the pieces of silver in the temple, he departed; and
he went and hanged himself. 6 But the chief priests, taking the pieces
of silver, said, "It is not lawful to put them into the treasury, since
they are blood money." 7 After conferring together, they used them
to buy the potter's field as a place to bury foreigners. 8 For this reason
that field has been called the Field of Blood to this day. 9 Then was
fulfilled what had been spoken through the prophet Jeremiah,[c] "And
they took[d] the thirty pieces of silver, the price of the one on whom
a price had been set,[e] on whom some of the people of Israel had
set a price, 10 and they gave[f] them for the potter's field, as the Lord
commanded me."

Pilate Questions Jesus

11 Now Jesus stood before the governor; and the governor
asked him, "Are you the King of the Jews?" Jesus said, "You say so."
12 But when he was accused by the chief priests and elders, he did not
answer. 13 Then Pilate said to him, "Do you not hear how many accusations they make against you?" 14 But he gave him no answer, not
even to a single charge, so that the governor was greatly amazed.

Barabbas or Jesus?

15 Now at the festival the governor was accustomed to release
a prisoner for the crowd, anyone whom they wanted. 16 At that time
they had a notorious prisoner, called Jesus[g] Barabbas. 17 So after they
had gathered, Pilate said to them, "Whom do you want me to release for you, Jesus[g] Barabbas or Jesus who is called the Messiah?"[h]
18 For he realized that it was out of jealousy that they had handed
him over. 19 While he was sitting on the judgment seat, his wife sent
word to him, "Have nothing to do with that innocent man, for today
I have suffered a great deal because of a dream about him." 20 Now
the chief priests and the elders persuaded the crowds to ask for Barabbas and to have Jesus killed. 21 The governor again said to them,
"Which of the two do you want me to release for you?" And they
said, "Barabbas." 22 Pilate said to them, "Then what should I do with
Jesus who is called the Messiah?"[h] All of them said, "Let him be crucified!" 23 Then he asked, "Why, what evil has he done?" But they
shouted all the more, "Let him be crucified!"

27:3-10 Judas...repented...hanged himself: Compare this with the story in Acts 1:15-20. Matthew's story fits the prophecy, but Matthew also puts the prophecy together out of various pieces to fit his story: thirty pieces of silver cast into the treasury in the temple (Zech 11:12-13); a potter (Jer 18:1-11; 19:1-13); and buying a field (Jer 32:6-15).

27:11-26 Jesus stood before the governor: See Mark 15:1-15. The title "king of the Jews" represents a Roman, political perspective, not an Israelite one. Two things are stressed. First, Pilate knew that Jesus was innocent. Second, Pilate, with the power of Rome behind him, is intimidated by a small crowd, who demand that Pilate release a prisoner, supposedly according to the custom of the day. The crowd chooses Barabbas, whom Mark associates with an uprising (Mark 15:7). Pilate gives in and hands over Jesus to be crucified. Members of the crowd speak only for themselves, not for all Jews. Crucifixion was a penalty for political criminals. The early Christians wanted to accent Jesus' innocence of the political charges.

We see Jesus' death as the event of salvation (see John 11:45-53). In light of this, how might we judge the actions of Judas, Caiaphas, Pilate, and others differently? Why?

---

[a] Gk *he* [b] Other ancient authorities read *righteous* [c] Other ancient authorities read *Zechariah* or *Isaiah* [d] Or *I took* [e] Or *the price of the precious One* [f] Other ancient authorities read *I gave* [g] Other ancient authorities lack *Jesus* [h] Or *the Christ*

Pilate Hands Jesus over to Be Crucified

24 So when Pilate saw that he could do nothing, but rather that
a riot was beginning, he took some water and washed his hands before the crowd, saying, "I am innocent of this man's blood;[a] see to it
yourselves." 25 Then the people as a whole answered, "His blood be
on us and on our children!" 26 So he released Barabbas for them; and
after flogging Jesus, he handed him over to be crucified.

The Soldiers Mock Jesus

27 Then the soldiers of the governor took Jesus into the governor's headquarters,[b] and they gathered the whole cohort around
him. 28 They stripped him and put a scarlet robe on him, 29 and after
twisting some thorns into a crown, they put it on his head. They put
a reed in his right hand and knelt before him and mocked him, saying, "Hail, King of the Jews!" 30 They spat on him, and took the reed
and struck him on the head. 31 After mocking him, they stripped him
of the robe and put his own clothes on him. Then they led him away
to crucify him.

27:27-31 soldiers…put a scarlet robe on him: The governor's guards took Jesus either to Herod's palace, where the governor was likely staying, or to the Antonia Fortress next to the temple (see Map 13, p. 2110), where Roman guards were stationed. The scarlet robe was meant to mock the claim to be king of the Jews. Purple was a color reserved for royalty.

The Crucifixion of Jesus

32 As they went out, they came upon a man from Cyrene
named Simon; they compelled this man to carry his cross. 33 And
when they came to a place called Golgotha (which means Place
of a Skull), 34 they offered him wine to drink, mixed with gall; but
when he tasted it, he would not drink it. 35 And when they had crucified him, they divided his clothes among themselves by casting
lots;[c] 36 then they sat down there and kept watch over him. 37 Over
his head they put the charge against him, which read, "This is Jesus,
the King of the Jews."

38 Then two bandits were crucified with him, one on his right
and one on his left. 39 Those who passed by derided[d] him, shaking
their heads 40 and saying, "You who would destroy the temple and
build it in three days, save yourself! If you are the Son of God, come
down from the cross." 41 In the same way the chief priests also, along
with the scribes and elders, were mocking him, saying, 42 "He saved
others; he cannot save himself.[e] He is the King of Israel; let him
come down from the cross now, and we will believe in him. 43 He
trusts in God; let God deliver him now, if he wants to; for he said,
'I am God's Son.'" 44 The bandits who were crucified with him also
taunted him in the same way.

27:32-33 man from Cyrene named Simon…Golgotha: Cyrene was the capital of the Roman province of Cyrenaica, which is modern Libya. Golgotha was a hill just outside the city walls that may have resembled a skull.

27:34-44 when they had crucified him: See Mark 15:16-39. Matthew follows Mark in telling the story of Jesus' death in the framework of Psalm 22. References to that psalm include the mockery (Ps 22:6-8). Ironically, in the Psalm and here, the mockers say what is true about Jesus! "King of the Jews" (27:29, 37) would be a Roman political title. Jews would speak of the Messiah as the "King of Israel" (27:42). Other parallels from Psalm 22 include crucifixion (22:16 in Greek Septuagint: "they pierced my hands and feet"), dividing his garments (Ps 22:18), thirst (Ps 22:15), Jesus' cry of abandonment (see Ps 22:1), death and deliverance (Ps 22:15, 21b-24), and the Gentiles who confess him as God's Son (Ps 22:27). In Psalm 22, the fate of this person leads to establishing God's rule, a meal of thanksgiving, deliverance and praise to God from all the nations, future generations, and even the dead (Ps 22:25-31). For the wine mixed with gall (27:34, 48), see Psalm 69:19-21.

---

[a] Other ancient authorities read *this righteous blood*, or *this righteous man's blood* [b] Gk *the praetorium*
[c] Other ancient authorities add *in order that what had been spoken through the prophet might be fulfilled, "They divided my clothes among themselves, and for my clothing they cast lots."* [d] Or *blasphemed* [e] Or *is he unable to save himself?*

The Death of Jesus

45 From noon on, darkness came over the whole land[a] until
three in the afternoon. 46And about three o'clock Jesus cried with
a loud voice, "Eli, Eli, lema sabachthani?" that is, "My God, my
God, why have you forsaken me?" 47When some of the bystanders
heard it, they said, "This man is calling for Elijah." 48At once one
of them ran and got a sponge, filled it with sour wine, put it on a
stick, and gave it to him to drink. 49But the others said, "Wait, let us
see whether Elijah will come to save him."[b] 50Then Jesus cried again
with a loud voice and breathed his last.[c] 51At that moment the curtain of the temple was torn in two, from top to bottom. The earth
shook, and the rocks were split. 52The tombs also were opened, and
many bodies of the saints who had fallen asleep were raised. 53After
his resurrection they came out of the tombs and entered the holy
city and appeared to many. 54Now when the centurion and those
with him, who were keeping watch over Jesus, saw the earthquake
and what took place, they were terrified and said, "Truly this man
was God's Son!"[d]

55 Many women were also there, looking on from a distance;
they had followed Jesus from Galilee and had provided for him.
56Among them were Mary Magdalene, and Mary the mother of
James and Joseph, and the mother of the sons of Zebedee.

27:45-54 darkness came over the whole land . . . "Truly this man was God's Son!": The darkness (see Amos 8:9) is a symbol of God's judgment on the earth and of mourning. Jesus' cry of abandonment (27:46) needs to be taken seriously. For our sake, Jesus experienced the complete abandonment by God that is hell. The curtain in the temple protected people from the dangerous presence of God (see Deut 4:24; 18:16; Exod 19:7-25). The tearing of the curtain is a sign that God is no longer present in the temple (see note on 23:38). God is present in Jesus, forsaken by God and crucified by human beings. At his death, many of the dead saints came out of their tombs and appeared to many. Matthew places this at the point of Jesus' death, but he also says it took place after his resurrection (27:53). Apparently this was originally part of a resurrection story (see 28:2). By placing it here, Matthew says that Jesus' death is the source of resurrection life for others. The Roman centurion and those watching with him recognize that Jesus was God's Son.

27:55-61 Many women . . . had provided for him . . . sitting opposite the tomb: See Mark 15:40-47. Women who had followed Jesus were the witnesses to his suffering, death, and burial. Notice that they provided support for Jesus' ministry activity, and now they are present to provide for Jesus in death, when the other disciples have disappeared. Another follower, Joseph of Arimathea, buried Jesus in his own tomb.

The Burial of Jesus

57 When it was evening, there came a rich man from Arimathea, named Joseph, who was also a disciple of Jesus. 58He went to
Pilate and asked for the body of Jesus; then Pilate ordered it to be
given to him. 59So Joseph took the body and wrapped it in a clean
linen cloth 60and laid it in his own new tomb, which he had hewn in
the rock. He then rolled a great stone to the door of the tomb and
went away. 61Mary Magdalene and the other Mary were there, sitting opposite the tomb.

The Guard at the Tomb

62 The next day, that is, after the day of Preparation, the chief
priests and the Pharisees gathered before Pilate 63and said, "Sir, we
remember what that impostor said while he was still alive, 'After
three days I will rise again.' 64Therefore command the tomb to be
made secure until the third day; otherwise his disciples may go and
steal him away, and tell the people, 'He has been raised from the
dead,' and the last deception would be worse than the first." 65Pilate
said to them, "You have a guard[e] of soldiers; go, make it as secure as

27:62 after the day of Preparation: Meaning the day of preparation for the weekly Sabbath. Interestingly, Matthew does not note that they go to Pilate on the sabbath. That would violate the sabbath and make them unclean.

---

[a] Or *earth* [b] Other ancient authorities add *And another took a spear and pierced his side, and out came water and blood* [c] Or *gave up his spirit* [d] Or *a son of God* [e] Or *Take a guard*

you can."[a] [66]So they went with the guard and made the tomb secure
by sealing the stone.

28:1-15 He has been raised: See Mark 16:1-8. Matthew interweaves two stories of the empty tomb: the soldiers guarding the tomb for fear someone would steal Jesus' body (27:62-66; 28:2-4; 28:11-15); and the women at the tomb. Jesus appears first to the women, and they are the first messengers sent to tell of his resurrection. Meanwhile, the priests and elders bribed the soldiers guarding the tomb with money, so they wouldn't say anything about Jesus' resurrection.

The Resurrection of Jesus

28 After the sabbath, as the first day of the week was dawning,
Mary Magdalene and the other Mary went to see the tomb.
[2]And suddenly there was a great earthquake; for an angel of the Lord,
descending from heaven, came and rolled back the stone and sat on
it. [3]His appearance was like lightning, and his clothing white as snow.
[4]For fear of him the guards shook and became like dead men. [5]But
the angel said to the women, "Do not be afraid; I know that you are
looking for Jesus who was crucified. [6]He is not here; for he has been
raised, as he said. Come, see the place where he[b] lay. [7]Then go quickly
and tell his disciples, 'He has been raised from the dead,[c] and indeed
he is going ahead of you to Galilee; there you will see him.' This is my
message for you." [8]So they left the tomb quickly with fear and great
joy, and ran to tell his disciples. [9]Suddenly Jesus met them and said,
"Greetings!" And they came to him, took hold of his feet, and worshiped him. [10]Then Jesus said to them, "Do not be afraid; go and tell
my brothers to go to Galilee; there they will see me."

The Report of the Guard

11 While they were going, some of the guard went into the
city and told the chief priests everything that had happened. [12]Af-
ter the priests[d] had assembled with the elders, they devised a plan
to give a large sum of money to the soldiers, [13]telling them, "You
must say, 'His disciples came by night and stole him away while we
were asleep.' [14]If this comes to the governor's ears, we will satisfy
him and keep you out of trouble." [15]So they took the money and did
as they were directed. And this story is still told among the Jews to
this day.

28:16-20 the eleven disciples went to Galilee: The eleven meet Jesus on a mountain in Galilee. Even when the eleven see him, some doubt. Jesus' resurrection returns to the question of his authority in 7:28—9:34; 21:23-32. Through the resurrection, God has given Jesus all authority in heaven and on earth. This does not mean that only now does Jesus have authority. It establishes his authority exercised throughout his life and ministry (28:20). The end of the Gospel sends the reader back to the beginning (4:12—9:34), and it gives God's answer to the Pharisees' charge (9:34). In contrast to 10:5-6, 23, Jesus now sends the disciples to make disciples of all nations. Disciples are students, called for the sake of the world to learn from Jesus and to bear witness to the kingdom. They are salt and light (5:13-16). Jesus promises to be with them always as they carry out this mission. Previously, Jesus promised to be present in the exercise of forgiveness (18:18-20) and in the "least of these" who suffer (25:31-45).

The Commissioning of the Disciples

16 Now the eleven disciples went to Galilee, to the mountain
to which Jesus had directed them. [17]When they saw him, they worshiped him; but some doubted. [18]And Jesus came and said to them,
"All authority in heaven and on earth has been given to me. [19]Go
therefore and make disciples of all nations, baptizing them in the
name of the Father and of the Son and of the Holy Spirit, [20]and
teaching them to obey everything that I have commanded you. And
remember, I am with you always, to the end of the age."[e]

---

[a] Gk *you know how* [b] Other ancient authorities read *the Lord* [c] Other ancient authorities lack *from the dead* [d] Gk *they* [e] Other ancient authorities add *Amen*

Mark 15:39

MARK

Background File

The writer of this Gospel, according to tradition, is Mark (a companion of Peter and Paul mentioned in Acts 12:12, 25; 15:37-39; Col 4:10, 2 Tim 4:11, and Phlm 24), who would have written in Rome during the 60s C.E. We cannot be certain of this claim, but evidence from the Gospel itself suggests that it was written for a community of Christians situated within the Roman Empire but outside of Palestine, sometime around the destruction of Jerusalem in 70 C.E.

What's the Story?

Mark was the first to assemble the various stories that were being told about Jesus and compose a written document that he calls a "gospel." He not only had to figure out a way to bring the pieces together to tell the story, but also to provide a faithful perspective for understanding Jesus Christ, the Son of God, in a way that spoke to the people's situation.

Mark's Gospel is structured around three key scenes: Jesus' baptism, transfiguration, and crucifixion. In each of these scenes, Jesus is declared to be God's Son, but it is only with that final confession by the centurion at the cross that Jesus is fully revealed as the crucified Messiah.

The story begins in the wilderness near the Jordan River, but most of Jesus' ministry occurs in the northern region of Galilee (see Map 12, p. 2109). The story has a fast pace as Mark reports events "immediately" happening one after another. Jesus occasionally ventures into Gentile (non-Jewish) regions to the east and north. At Caesarea Philippi, far to the north, Peter confesses Jesus to be the Messiah (8:29). This high point is matched by the first of Jesus' three predictions regarding his death and resurrection. By 10:1 Jesus is back in the Judean wilderness, east of the Jordan River, and in 11:1 he is approaching Jerusalem. While chapters 1–10 may reflect up to three years of ministry, chapters 11–16 record the events of a single week. The pace slows, but the action intensifies. The entire story leads to the cross, but it also leads from the cross back into mission, as the disciples are directed to return to Galilee, where they will again see Jesus.

What's the Message?

This book is the only one in the Bible to clearly label itself as a "gospel" (the "good news" of 1:1). It provides one way that we understand this term—as a *story* about Jesus' life, death, and resurrection.

This Gospel, however, is not meant to simply convey information about Jesus. It is also intended to create and strengthen faith in Jesus, to develop true disciples of Jesus. It was written at a time when Christians needed to define who they were in connection to their Jewish heritage. They were also experiencing challenges, if not outright persecution, from the prevailing Greco-Roman culture. In effect, Christians were struggling with a question we often face today: If Jesus Christ did such wonderful things and has overcome death in his resurrection, why can things often be so bad for us today?

It is tempting to respond to this question by highlighting the glorious aspects of Jesus' ministry: his authority, his miracles, and the transfiguration. Mark, however, consistently focuses our attention on the cross. Jesus is indeed the Son of God, but this is not truly realized except in his serving, suffering, and death. Jesus is indeed the hoped-for Messiah, but we only fully realize *how* he is making God's kingdom present when we experience him as the crucified Messiah.

This Gospel also serves as *good news* that the story of Jesus' ministry, death, and resurrection provides shape and meaning for the faith and life of Mark's first readers as well as for us. As faithful disciples of Jesus, it is precisely in serving, in being last, even in dying for Christ's sake, that we discover the true meaning of life.

The Proclamation of John the Baptist

1 The beginning of the good news[a] of Jesus Christ, the Son of God.[b]

2 As it is written in the prophet Isaiah,[c]

"See, I am sending my messenger ahead of you,[d]
who will prepare your way;
3 the voice of one crying out in the wilderness:
'Prepare the way of the Lord,
make his paths straight,'"

[4]John the baptizer appeared[e] in the wilderness, proclaiming a baptism of repentance for the forgiveness of sins. [5]And people from the
whole Judean countryside and all the people of Jerusalem were going
out to him, and were baptized by him in the river Jordan, confessing
their sins. [6]Now John was clothed with camel's hair, with a leather belt
around his waist, and he ate locusts and wild honey. [7]He proclaimed,
"The one who is more powerful than I is coming after me; I am not
worthy to stoop down and untie the thong of his sandals. [8]I have baptized you with[f] water; but he will baptize you with[f] the Holy Spirit."

The Baptism of Jesus

9 In those days Jesus came from Nazareth of Galilee and was
baptized by John in the Jordan. [10]And just as he was coming up out

[a] Or *gospel* [b] Other ancient authorities lack *the Son of God* [c] Other ancient authorities read *in the prophets* [d] Gk *before your face* [e] Other ancient authorities read *John was baptizing* [f] Or *in*

1:1 good news... Christ: The good news or gospel can refer to the message Jesus preached, the message about Jesus, God's saving news for us preached by Jesus and all Christians. "Christ" is the Greek term for the Hebrew word *Messiah* which means "Anointed One." Pouring oil on someone's head was a way of designating that person as one chosen by God to rule over Israel (see 1 Sam 9:16, 16:3; Ps 89:20).

1:2-3 Prepare the way of the Lord: The quoted words are from Malachi 3:1 and Isaiah 40:3.

1:4 baptism: There were a variety of Jewish baptisms or washings before baptism became a Christian sacrament. John the Baptist is unique in that he connects baptism with repentance and offers it to all people as a sign of commitment.

1:6 John was clothed: The description of John's clothing connects him to the prophet Elijah (see 2 Kgs 1:8).

What is baptism? Martin Luther writes, "Baptism is not simply plain water. Instead, it is water used according to God's command and connected with God's word." It is, says Luther, "a grace-filled water

of the water, he saw the heavens torn apart and the Spirit descending like a dove on him. 11 And a voice came from heaven, "You are
my Son, the Beloved;[a] with you I am well pleased."

The Temptation of Jesus

12 And the Spirit immediately drove him out into the wilderness. 13 He was in the wilderness forty days, tempted by Satan; and
he was with the wild beasts; and the angels waited on him.

The Beginning of the Galilean Ministry

14 Now after John was arrested, Jesus came to Galilee, proclaiming the good news[b] of God,[c] 15 and saying, "The time is fulfilled, and
the kingdom of God has come near;[d] repent, and believe in the good
news."[b]

Jesus Calls the First Disciples

16 As Jesus passed along the Sea of Galilee, he saw Simon and
his brother Andrew casting a net into the sea—for they were fishermen. 17 And Jesus said to them, "Follow me and I will make you
fish for people." 18 And immediately they left their nets and followed
him. 19 As he went a little farther, he saw James son of Zebedee and
his brother John, who were in their boat mending the nets. 20 Immediately he called them; and they left their father Zebedee in the boat
with the hired men, and followed him.

The Man with an Unclean Spirit

21 They went to Capernaum; and when the sabbath came, he
entered the synagogue and taught. 22 They were astounded at his
teaching, for he taught them as one having authority, and not as the
scribes. 23 Just then there was in their synagogue a man with an unclean spirit, 24 and he cried out, "What have you to do with us, Jesus
of Nazareth? Have you come to destroy us? I know who you are, the
Holy One of God." 25 But Jesus rebuked him, saying, "Be silent, and
come out of him!" 26 And the unclean spirit, convulsing him and crying with a loud voice, came out of him. 27 They were all amazed, and
they kept on asking one another, "What is this? A new teaching—
with authority! He[e] commands even the unclean spirits, and they
obey him." 28 At once his fame began to spread throughout the surrounding region of Galilee.

Jesus Heals Many at Simon's House

29 As soon as they[f] left the synagogue, they entered the house
of Simon and Andrew, with James and John. 30 Now Simon's

[a] Or *my beloved Son* [b] Or *gospel* [c] Other ancient authorities read *of the kingdom* [d] Or *is at hand*
[e] Or *A new teaching! With authority he* [f] Other ancient authorities read *he*

of life and a 'bath of the new birth in the Holy Spirit,' as St. Paul says to Titus in chapter 3, 'through the water of rebirth and renewal by the Holy Spirit. This Spirit he poured out on us richly through Jesus Christ our Savior, so that, having been justified by his grace, we might become heirs according to the hope of eternal life'" (*SC*:28-29). In baptism God forgives us, rescues us, and gives us new life. *Mark 1:8*

1:9-11 Jesus . . . was baptized: The "heavens torn apart," the Spirit's presence, the voice declaring Jesus to be God's Son—match up with details in the transfiguration (9:2-9) and crucifixion (15:33-39).

1:12-13 in the wilderness forty days: This is a time of testing for Jesus, like the forty days of preparation for Moses (Exod 34:28) and Elijah (1 Kgs 19:8), and forty years in the wilderness for Israel (Deut 8:2-6). Satan is the ruler of the demons (see note at 3:22).

1:14 John was arrested: The arrest—and John's death—will not be described until 6:17-29.

1:15 the kingdom of God: This is a way to talk about God's presence in the world. Throughout the Gospel, there is a sharp contrast between the rule or dominion of God and the dominion of Rome, the ruling political power at that time.

How do you experience that the kingdom of God has come near?

1:21 Capernaum: See Map 12, p. 2109. This town becomes a base for Jesus' ministry. Jews gathered on the Sabbath (Saturday) for Scripture reading, instruction, and prayer.

1:23 unclean spirit: Also known as "demons," in Mark the unclean spirits are part of the forces of evil.

1:25 Be silent: Jesus commands the unclean spirit to be silent about his identity. This is the first instance of what is known as the "Messianic Secret" in Mark. Jesus will regularly tell people to keep quiet about what he has done or who he is, and the disciples will consistently fail to understand. This secrecy is only for "outsiders" in the story; readers of the Gospel are given all the "inside" information about Jesus.

1:32 demons: See note on 1:23.

1:34 would not permit the demons to speak: See note on 1:25.

1:40 A leper: Leprosy in Jesus' time could refer to a variety of skin diseases. It was a condition that meant the person would make others unclean by touching them.

1:44 show yourself to the priest: Priests determined if someone was cleansed of leprosy, and they presided over the required sacrifice (Lev 14).

2:1-12 a paralyzed man: This healing of a paralyzed man is paired with the healing of a man with a paralyzed hand in 3:1-6. The events between these two healings focus attention on Jesus' identity and raise questions among Jewish leaders about his authority.

2:5 your sins are forgiven: Many people at the time believed that physical problems were punishment for a person's sins. This does not seem to be the case for Jesus, however. He handles the situation so that he can show he has the authority to heal and forgive sins.

Are physical healing and forgiveness of sins connected? If so, in what ways?

2:6 scribes: The scribes in Mark are legal experts working with religious and political authorities.

2:7 blasphemy!: This is a severe charge, indicating lack of respect for God or a claim to have divine powers.

mother-in-law was in bed with a fever, and they told him about her
at once. 31 He came and took her by the hand and lifted her up. Then
the fever left her, and she began to serve them.

32 That evening, at sunset, they brought to him all who were
sick or possessed with demons. 33 And the whole city was gathered
around the door. 34 And he cured many who were sick with various
diseases, and cast out many demons; and he would not permit the
demons to speak, because they knew him.

A Preaching Tour in Galilee

35 In the morning, while it was still very dark, he got up and
went out to a deserted place, and there he prayed. 36 And Simon and
his companions hunted for him. 37 When they found him, they said
to him, "Everyone is searching for you." 38 He answered, "Let us go
on to the neighboring towns, so that I may proclaim the message
there also; for that is what I came out to do." 39 And he went throughout Galilee, proclaiming the message in their synagogues and casting out demons.

Jesus Cleanses a Leper

40 A leper[a] came to him begging him, and kneeling[b] he said to
him, "If you choose, you can make me clean." 41 Moved with pity,[c]
Jesus[d] stretched out his hand and touched him, and said to him, "I
do choose. Be made clean!" 42 Immediately the leprosy[a] left him, and
he was made clean. 43 After sternly warning him he sent him away at
once, 44 saying to him, "See that you say nothing to anyone; but go,
show yourself to the priest, and offer for your cleansing what Moses
commanded, as a testimony to them." 45 But he went out and began
to proclaim it freely, and to spread the word, so that Jesus[d] could
no longer go into a town openly, but stayed out in the country; and
people came to him from every quarter.

Jesus Heals a Paralytic

2 When he returned to Capernaum after some days, it was reported
that he was at home. 2 So many gathered around that there was no
longer room for them, not even in front of the door; and he was speaking the word to them. 3 Then some people[e] came, bringing to him a paralyzed man, carried by four of them. 4 And when they could not bring
him to Jesus because of the crowd, they removed the roof above him;
and after having dug through it, they let down the mat on which the
paralytic lay. 5 When Jesus saw their faith, he said to the paralytic, "Son,
your sins are forgiven." 6 Now some of the scribes were sitting there,
questioning in their hearts, 7 "Why does this fellow speak in this way?

[a] The terms *leper* and *leprosy* can refer to several diseases [b] Other ancient authorities lack *kneeling*
[c] Other ancient authorities read *anger* [d] Gk *he* [e] Gk *they*

It is blasphemy! Who can forgive sins but God alone?" 8 At once Jesus
perceived in his spirit that they were discussing these questions among
themselves; and he said to them, "Why do you raise such questions in
your hearts? 9 Which is easier, to say to the paralytic, 'Your sins are forgiven,' or to say, 'Stand up and take your mat and walk'? 10 But so that
you may know that the Son of Man has authority on earth to forgive
sins"—he said to the paralytic— 11 "I say to you, stand up, take your mat
and go to your home." 12 And he stood up, and immediately took the
mat and went out before all of them; so that they were all amazed and
glorified God, saying, "We have never seen anything like this!"

Jesus Calls Levi

13 Jesus[a] went out again beside the sea; the whole crowd gathered around him, and he taught them. 14 As he was walking along, he
saw Levi son of Alphaeus sitting at the tax booth, and he said to him,
"Follow me." And he got up and followed him.
15 And as he sat at dinner[b] in Levi's[c] house, many tax collectors
and sinners were also sitting[d] with Jesus and his disciples—for there
were many who followed him. 16 When the scribes of[e] the Pharisees
saw that he was eating with sinners and tax collectors, they said to
his disciples, "Why does he eat[f] with tax collectors and sinners?"
17 When Jesus heard this, he said to them, "Those who are well have
no need of a physician, but those who are sick; I have come to call
not the righteous but sinners."

The Question about Fasting

18 Now John's disciples and the Pharisees were fasting; and
people[g] came and said to him, "Why do John's disciples and the disciples of the Pharisees fast, but your disciples do not fast?" 19 Jesus
said to them, "The wedding guests cannot fast while the bridegroom
is with them, can they? As long as they have the bridegroom with
them, they cannot fast. 20 The days will come when the bridegroom
is taken away from them, and then they will fast on that day.
21 "No one sews a piece of unshrunk cloth on an old cloak; otherwise, the patch pulls away from it, the new from the old, and a
worse tear is made. 22 And no one puts new wine into old wineskins;
otherwise, the wine will burst the skins, and the wine is lost, and so
are the skins; but one puts new wine into fresh wineskins."[h]

Pronouncement about the Sabbath

23 One sabbath he was going through the grainfields; and as
they made their way his disciples began to pluck heads of grain.

[a] Gk *He* [b] Gk *reclined* [c] Gk *his* [d] Gk *reclining* [e] Other ancient authorities read *and* [f] Other ancient authorities add *and drink* [g] Gk *they* [h] Other ancient authorities lack *but one puts new wine into fresh wineskins*

2:10 Son of Man: Mark uses this term in three different but overlapping ways: Jesus uses it to refer to himself (2:28; 10:45); Jesus uses it when talking about his suffering, death, and resurrection (8:31; 9:12, 31; 10:33; 14:21, 41); and it is a title that draws on the book of Daniel 7:13-14, which Jesus uses to refer to his future role when he returns in power and glory (8:38; 13:26; 14:62). An important emphasis for Mark is that the last two uses stand in sharp contrast, but both are realized in Jesus.

2:14-15 tax booth . . . tax collectors: Tax collectors were generally despised by the Jewish people, because they functioned as agents of the occupying Roman government.

2:16 Pharisees: The Pharisees were influential and learned Jewish leaders who emphasized strict obedience to the law for all Jews. By eating with "tax collectors and sinners," Jesus was not simply being friendly, but risking becoming unclean like them. Rather than being infected by their sin, however, Jesus gives them his righteousness.

2:18 fasting: This was the practice of not eating food for a period of time, as a sign of repentance or commitment to God.

2:23 sabbath: See note on 1:21. According to Jewish law, no work, including plucking heads of grain, was to be done on the Sabbath.

24The Pharisees said to him, "Look, why are they doing what is not
lawful on the sabbath?" 25And he said to them, "Have you never read
what David did when he and his companions were hungry and in
need of food? 26He entered the house of God, when Abiathar was
high priest, and ate the bread of the Presence, which it is not lawful
for any but the priests to eat, and he gave some to his companions."
27Then he said to them, "The sabbath was made for humankind, and
not humankind for the sabbath; 28so the Son of Man is lord even of
the sabbath."

The Man with a Withered Hand

3 Again he entered the synagogue, and a man was there who had
a withered hand. 2They watched him to see whether he would
cure him on the sabbath, so that they might accuse him. 3And he said
to the man who had the withered hand, "Come forward." 4Then he
said to them, "Is it lawful to do good or to do harm on the sabbath, to
save life or to kill?" But they were silent. 5He looked around at them
with anger; he was grieved at their hardness of heart and said to the
man, "Stretch out your hand." He stretched it out, and his hand was
restored. 6The Pharisees went out and immediately conspired with
the Herodians against him, how to destroy him.

A Multitude at the Seaside

7 Jesus departed with his disciples to the sea, and a great multitude from Galilee followed him; 8hearing all that he was doing,
they came to him in great numbers from Judea, Jerusalem, Idumea,
beyond the Jordan, and the region around Tyre and Sidon. 9He told
his disciples to have a boat ready for him because of the crowd, so
that they would not crush him; 10for he had cured many, so that all
who had diseases pressed upon him to touch him. 11Whenever the
unclean spirits saw him, they fell down before him and shouted,
"You are the Son of God!" 12But he sternly ordered them not to
make him known.

Jesus Appoints the Twelve

13 He went up the mountain and called to him those whom he
wanted, and they came to him. 14And he appointed twelve, whom he
also named apostles,[a] to be with him, and to be sent out to proclaim
the message, 15and to have authority to cast out demons. 16So he
appointed the twelve:[b] Simon (to whom he gave the name Peter);
17James son of Zebedee and John the brother of James (to whom
he gave the name Boanerges, that is, Sons of Thunder); 18and Andrew, and Philip, and Bartholomew, and Matthew, and Thomas, and

---

[a] Other ancient authorities lack *whom he also named apostles* [b] Other ancient authorities lack *So he appointed the twelve*

2:25-26 what David did: Jesus is referring to the story about King David in 1 Samuel 21:1-6.

2:27-28 lord even of the Sabbath: Jesus indirectly asserts his authority to pluck and eat grain on the Sabbath, and, as a general statement, he claims that observing the Sabbath is not a burden we perform for God, but a gift that God has given to us. See note on Son of Man at 2:10.

3:1-6 a man . . . who had a withered hand: This story is paired with the healing of the paralyzed man in 2:1-12. See note on 2:1-12.

3:2 sabbath: See notes on 1:21; 2:23. According to Jewish law, to perform a cure was regarded as work and was not to be done on the Sabbath.

3:6 Pharisees: See note on 2:16.

3:6 Herodians: Herod Antipas, son of King Herod the Great, ruled over Galilee at this time. Here, Herodians means a political group supporting the family's reign.

3:8 they came to him in great numbers: The list of places covers almost all of Palestine and even extends into Gentile (non-Jewish) territory.

3:12 not to make him known: See note on 1:25.

3:14 twelve: The choosing of twelve apostles corresponds to the twelve tribes that make up Israel (see Gen 49). Here, an apostle is someone chosen by a leader to do a certain job.

James son of Alphaeus, and Thaddaeus, and Simon the Cananaean,
[19]and Judas Iscariot, who betrayed him.

3:19 who betrayed him: Jesus' life is already threatened (2:20; 3:6), but describing Judas as the one who betrays him introduces tension into the story.

Jesus and Beelzebul

Then he went home; [20]and the crowd came together again, so that
they could not even eat. [21]When his family heard it, they went out to
restrain him, for people were saying, "He has gone out of his mind."
[22]And the scribes who came down from Jerusalem said, "He has Beelzebul, and by the ruler of the demons he casts out demons." [23]And he
called them to him, and spoke to them in parables, "How can Satan
cast out Satan? [24]If a kingdom is divided against itself, that kingdom
cannot stand. [25]And if a house is divided against itself, that house will
not be able to stand. [26]And if Satan has risen up against himself and is
divided, he cannot stand, but his end has come. [27]But no one can enter a strong man's house and plunder his property without first tying
up the strong man; then indeed the house can be plundered.
28 "Truly I tell you, people will be forgiven for their sins and
whatever blasphemies they utter; [29]but whoever blasphemes against
the Holy Spirit can never have forgiveness, but is guilty of an eternal
sin"— [30]for they had said, "He has an unclean spirit."

3:22 Beelzebul: This title, which traces back to 2 Kings 1:2-16, means "lord of flies" or "lord of filth" and refers to Satan, the "ruler of the demons."

3:23 parables: Jesus' parables or stories use everyday examples, but there is usually some uncommon element that makes each one more than a simple observation. Some parables may make a particular point, and others are like allegories with symbolic meanings. Jesus uses parables to engage listeners and challenge what they believe to be true.

3:28-30 blasphemies: See note on 2:7.

The True Kindred of Jesus

31 Then his mother and his brothers came; and standing outside, they sent to him and called him. [32]A crowd was sitting around
him; and they said to him, "Your mother and your brothers and sisters[a] are outside, asking for you." [33]And he replied, "Who are my
mother and my brothers?" [34]And looking at those who sat around
him, he said, "Here are my mother and my brothers! [35]Whoever
does the will of God is my brother and sister and mother."

The Parable of the Sower

4 Again he began to teach beside the sea. Such a very large crowd
gathered around him that he got into a boat on the sea and sat
there, while the whole crowd was beside the sea on the land. [2]He began to teach them many things in parables, and in his teaching he said
to them: [3]"Listen! A sower went out to sow. [4]And as he sowed, some
seed fell on the path, and the birds came and ate it up. [5]Other seed fell
on rocky ground, where it did not have much soil, and it sprang up
quickly, since it had no depth of soil. [6]And when the sun rose, it was
scorched; and since it had no root, it withered away. [7]Other seed fell
among thorns, and the thorns grew up and choked it, and it yielded no
grain. [8]Other seed fell into good soil and brought forth grain, growing
up and increasing and yielding thirty and sixty and a hundredfold."
[9]And he said, "Let anyone with ears to hear listen!"

4:2 parables: See note on 3:23.

[a] Other ancient authorities lack *and sisters*

The Purpose of the Parables

4:12 look, but not perceive: Jesus cites Isaiah 6:9-10 here.

10 When he was alone, those who were around him along with
the twelve asked him about the parables. [11]And he said to them, "To
you has been given the secret[a] of the kingdom of God, but for those
outside, everything comes in parables; [12]in order that

'they may indeed look, but not perceive,
    and may indeed listen, but not understand;
so that they may not turn again and be forgiven.' "

13 And he said to them, "Do you not understand this parable? Then how will you understand all the parables? [14]The sower
sows the word. [15]These are the ones on the path where the word
is sown: when they hear, Satan immediately comes and takes away
the word that is sown in them. [16]And these are the ones sown on
rocky ground: when they hear the word, they immediately receive
it with joy. [17]But they have no root, and endure only for a while;
then, when trouble or persecution arises on account of the word,
immediately they fall away.[b] [18]And others are those sown among the
thorns: these are the ones who hear the word, [19]but the cares of the
world, and the lure of wealth, and the desire for other things come in
and choke the word, and it yields nothing. [20]And these are the ones
sown on the good soil: they hear the word and accept it and bear
fruit, thirty and sixty and a hundredfold."

A Lamp under a Bushel Basket

21 He said to them, "Is a lamp brought in to be put under the
bushel basket, or under the bed, and not on the lampstand? [22]For
there is nothing hidden, except to be disclosed; nor is anything secret, except to come to light. [23]Let anyone with ears to hear listen!"
[24]And he said to them, "Pay attention to what you hear; the measure
you give will be the measure you get, and still more will be given
you. [25]For to those who have, more will be given; and from those
who have nothing, even what they have will be taken away."

4:26, 30 kingdom of God: See note on 1:15.

Does the parable in 4:26-29 reflect on what God does or what we do? How does this affect our belief in God?

4:30-34 a mustard seed: The strange detail in this parable is that Jesus would choose a lowly mustard seed as a symbol of the kingdom of God. The contrasting symbol people were probably expecting is the mighty cedar tree as described in a text such as Ezekiel 17:22-23. See Lutheran Perspectives note on 8:33-37.

The Parable of the Growing Seed

26 He also said, "The kingdom of God is as if someone would
scatter seed on the ground, [27]and would sleep and rise night and day,
and the seed would sprout and grow, he does not know how. [28]The
earth produces of itself, first the stalk, then the head, then the full
grain in the head. [29]But when the grain is ripe, at once he goes in
with his sickle, because the harvest has come."

The Parable of the Mustard Seed

30 He also said, "With what can we compare the kingdom of
God, or what parable will we use for it? [31]It is like a mustard seed,

---

[a] Or *mystery* [b] Or *stumble*

which, when sown upon the ground, is the smallest of all the seeds on earth; [32]yet when it is sown it grows up and becomes the greatest of all shrubs, and puts forth large branches, so that the birds of the air can make nests in its shade."

The Use of Parables

33 With many such parables he spoke the word to them, as they were able to hear it; [34]he did not speak to them except in parables, but he explained everything in private to his disciples.

Jesus Stills a Storm

35 On that day, when evening had come, he said to them, "Let us go across to the other side." [36]And leaving the crowd behind, they took him with them in the boat, just as he was. Other boats were with him. [37]A great windstorm arose, and the waves beat into the boat, so that the boat was already being swamped. [38]But he was in the stern, asleep on the cushion; and they woke him up and said to him, "Teacher, do you not care that we are perishing?" [39]He woke up and rebuked the wind, and said to the sea, "Peace! Be still!" Then the wind ceased, and there was a dead calm. [40]He said to them, "Why are you afraid? Have you still no faith?" [41]And they were filled with great awe and said to one another, "Who then is this, that even the wind and the sea obey him?"

4:41 Who then is this: As part of the Messianic Secret (see note on 1:25), here is another example of the disciples not understanding what readers of the Gospel have already been told.

Jesus Heals the Gerasene Demoniac

5 They came to the other side of the sea, to the country of the Gerasenes.[a] [2]And when he had stepped out of the boat, immediately a man out of the tombs with an unclean spirit met him. [3]He lived among the tombs; and no one could restrain him any more, even with a chain; [4]for he had often been restrained with shackles and chains, but the chains he wrenched apart, and the shackles he broke in pieces; and no one had the strength to subdue him. [5]Night and day among the tombs and on the mountains he was always howling and bruising himself with stones. [6]When he saw Jesus from a distance, he ran and bowed down before him; [7]and he shouted at the top of his voice, "What have you to do with me, Jesus, Son of the Most High God? I adjure you by God, do not torment me." [8]For he had said to him, "Come out of the man, you unclean spirit!" [9]Then Jesus[b] asked him, "What is your name?" He replied, "My name is Legion; for we are many." [10]He begged him earnestly not to send them out of the country. [11]Now there on the hillside a great herd of swine was feeding; [12]and the unclean spirits[c] begged him, "Send us into the swine; let us enter them." [13]So he gave them permission. And the unclean spirits came out and entered the swine; and the herd, numbering

5:2 unclean spirit: See note on 1:23.

5:9 Legion: This was also the term for a Roman military unit of about six thousand soldiers.

5:11 swine: Jews considered swine to be unclean animals.

[a] Other ancient authorities read *Gergesenes;* others, *Gadarenes* [b] Gk *he* [c] Gk *they*

about two thousand, rushed down the steep bank into the sea, and were drowned in the sea.

14 The swineherds ran off and told it in the city and in the country. Then people came to see what it was that had happened. [15]They came to Jesus and saw the demoniac sitting there, clothed and in his right mind, the very man who had had the legion; and they were afraid. [16]Those who had seen what had happened to the demoniac and to the swine reported it. [17]Then they began to beg Jesus[a] to leave their neighborhood. [18]As he was getting into the boat, the man who had been possessed by demons begged him that he might be with him. [19]But Jesus[b] refused, and said to him, "Go home to your friends, and tell them how much the Lord has done for you, and what mercy he has shown you." [20]And he went away and began to proclaim in the Decapolis how much Jesus had done for him; and everyone was amazed.

5:17-20 beg Jesus to leave: In contrast to previous stories in Mark, the people want Jesus to leave, and he asks the restored man to tell others about what has happened.

A Girl Restored to Life and a Woman Healed

21 When Jesus had crossed again in the boat[c] to the other side, a great crowd gathered around him; and he was by the sea. [22]Then one of the leaders of the synagogue named Jairus came and, when he saw him, fell at his feet [23]and begged him repeatedly, "My little daughter is at the point of death. Come and lay your hands on her, so that she may be made well, and live." [24]So he went with him.

And a large crowd followed him and pressed in on him. [25]Now there was a woman who had been suffering from hemorrhages for twelve years. [26]She had endured much under many physicians, and had spent all that she had; and she was no better, but rather grew worse. [27]She had heard about Jesus, and came up behind him in the crowd and touched his cloak, [28]for she said, "If I but touch his clothes, I will be made well." [29]Immediately her hemorrhage stopped; and she felt in her body that she was healed of her disease. [30]Immediately aware that power had gone forth from him, Jesus turned about in the crowd and said, "Who touched my clothes?" [31]And his disciples said to him, "You see the crowd pressing in on you; how can you say, 'Who touched me?' " [32]He looked all around to see who had done it. [33]But the woman, knowing what had happened to her, came in fear and trembling, fell down before him, and told him the whole truth. [34]He said to her, "Daughter, your faith has made you well; go in peace, and be healed of your disease."

35 While he was still speaking, some people came from the leader's house to say, "Your daughter is dead. Why trouble the teacher any further?" [36]But overhearing[d] what they said, Jesus said to the leader of the synagogue, "Do not fear, only believe." [37]He allowed

5:21-43 My little daughter...a woman: As in other places in this Gospel (for example, 6:6-32; 11:12-25), Mark here sandwiches one story (5:25-34) within another (5:21-24, 35-43), so that the two stories shed light on each other.

5:25 a woman...suffering from hemorrhages: This woman would have been considered unclean (see Lev 15:25), along with anything she touched.

5:34 your faith has made you well: In the original Greek, the word translated here as "has made you well" expresses the idea of "has saved you" (from your disease). The concepts of health, wholeness, and salvation are closely related in the Bible.

[a] Gk *him* [b] Gk *he* [c] Other ancient authorities lack *in the boat* [d] Or *ignoring;* other ancient authorities read *hearing*

no one to follow him except Peter, James, and John, the brother of
James. 38When they came to the house of the leader of the synagogue,
he saw a commotion, people weeping and wailing loudly. 39When
he had entered, he said to them, "Why do you make a commotion
and weep? The child is not dead but sleeping." 40And they laughed
at him. Then he put them all outside, and took the child's father and
mother and those who were with him, and went in where the child
was. 41He took her by the hand and said to her, "Talitha cum," which
means, "Little girl, get up!" 42And immediately the girl got up and
began to walk about (she was twelve years of age). At this they were
overcome with amazement. 43He strictly ordered them that no one
should know this, and told them to give her something to eat.

5:41 Talitha cum: Jesus spoke Aramaic, a language related to Hebrew, which was commonly spoken by Jews in Palestine at that time. Here and in 7:34, 14:36, and 15:34, Mark makes a point of citing Jesus' actual words.

5:43 no one should know this: See note on 1:25.

The Rejection of Jesus at Nazareth

6 He left that place and came to his hometown, and his disciples
followed him. 2On the sabbath he began to teach in the synagogue,
and many who heard him were astounded. They said, "Where
did this man get all this? What is this wisdom that has been given to
him? What deeds of power are being done by his hands! 3Is not this
the carpenter, the son of Mary[a] and brother of James and Joses and
Judas and Simon, and are not his sisters here with us?" And they took
offense[b] at him. 4Then Jesus said to them, "Prophets are not without
honor, except in their hometown, and among their own kin, and in
their own house." 5And he could do no deed of power there, except
that he laid his hands on a few sick people and cured them. 6And he
was amazed at their unbelief.

6:1 his hometown: This apparently refers to Nazareth (see Map 12, p. 2109).

6:3 the son of Mary: It is unusual and perhaps even insulting that Jesus is identified as "the son of Mary" rather than as the son of his father.

The Mission of the Twelve

Then he went about among the villages teaching. 7He called the
twelve and began to send them out two by two, and gave them authority
over the unclean spirits. 8He ordered them to take nothing for
their journey except a staff; no bread, no bag, no money in their belts;
9but to wear sandals and not to put on two tunics. 10He said to them,
"Wherever you enter a house, stay there until you leave the place. 11If
any place will not welcome you and they refuse to hear you, as you
leave, shake off the dust that is on your feet as a testimony against
them." 12So they went out and proclaimed that all should repent.
13They cast out many demons, and anointed with oil many who were
sick and cured them.

6:12-13 they went out: The disciples imitate Jesus by calling for repentance (see 1:15), casting out demons, and healing (see 1:34).

The Death of John the Baptist

14 King Herod heard of it, for Jesus'[c] name had become known.
Some were[d] saying, "John the baptizer has been raised from the

6:14-29 John the baptizer: The reader only now learns what happened to John when he had been arrested in 1:14. See note on Herodians (and Herod) at 3:6.

[a] Other ancient authorities read *son of the carpenter and of Mary* [b] Or *stumbled* [c] Gk *his* [d] Other ancient authorities read *He was*

dead; and for this reason these powers are at work in him." 15 But
others said, "It is Elijah." And others said, "It is a prophet, like one
of the prophets of old." 16 But when Herod heard of it, he said, "John,
whom I beheaded, has been raised."

17 For Herod himself had sent men who arrested John, bound
him, and put him in prison on account of Herodias, his brother
Philip's wife, because Herod[a] had married her. 18 For John had been
telling Herod, "It is not lawful for you to have your brother's wife."
19 And Herodias had a grudge against him, and wanted to kill him.
But she could not, 20 for Herod feared John, knowing that he was a
righteous and holy man, and he protected him. When he heard him,
he was greatly perplexed;[b] and yet he liked to listen to him. 21 But
an opportunity came when Herod on his birthday gave a banquet
for his courtiers and officers and for the leaders of Galilee. 22 When
his daughter Herodias[c] came in and danced, she pleased Herod and
his guests; and the king said to the girl, "Ask me for whatever you
wish, and I will give it." 23 And he solemnly swore to her, "Whatever
you ask me, I will give you, even half of my kingdom." 24 She went
out and said to her mother, "What should I ask for?" She replied,
"The head of John the baptizer." 25 Immediately she rushed back to
the king and requested, "I want you to give me at once the head of
John the Baptist on a platter." 26 The king was deeply grieved; yet out
of regard for his oaths and for the guests, he did not want to refuse
her. 27 Immediately the king sent a soldier of the guard with orders
to bring John's[d] head. He went and beheaded him in the prison,
28 brought his head on a platter, and gave it to the girl. Then the girl
gave it to her mother. 29 When his disciples heard about it, they came
and took his body, and laid it in a tomb.

Feeding the Five Thousand

30 The apostles gathered around Jesus, and told him all that they
had done and taught. 31 He said to them, "Come away to a deserted
place all by yourselves and rest a while." For many were coming and
going, and they had no leisure even to eat. 32 And they went away in
the boat to a deserted place by themselves. 33 Now many saw them
going and recognized them, and they hurried there on foot from
all the towns and arrived ahead of them. 34 As he went ashore, he
saw a great crowd; and he had compassion for them, because they
were like sheep without a shepherd; and he began to teach them
many things. 35 When it grew late, his disciples came to him and said,
"This is a deserted place, and the hour is now very late; 36 send them
away so that they may go into the surrounding country and villages
and buy something for themselves to eat." 37 But he answered them,

---

[a] Gk *he* [b] Other ancient authorities read *he did many things* [c] Other ancient authorities read *the daughter of Herodias herself* [d] Gk *his*

6:15 Elijah: Many Jews expected Elijah to appear before the coming of the Messiah (see Mal 4:5 and the note on 1:6). Others were looking for a prophet like Moses (see Deut 18:15).

6:26 The king was deeply grieved: Herod follows through on his promise, even though it goes against his own wishes. Pilate will do the same in 15:15 in dealing with Jesus.

6:29 they came and took his body: After John's death, his disciples take his body and lay it in a tomb. Jesus' disciples fail to do this after he dies (15:42-47).

6:31 to a deserted place: The disciples imitate the actions of Jesus listed in 1:35.

6:37 two hundred denarii: A laborer at the time would be paid about one denarius a day.

"You give them something to eat." They said to him, "Are we to go and buy two hundred denarii[a] worth of bread, and give it to them to eat?" 38 And he said to them, "How many loaves have you? Go and see." When they had found out, they said, "Five, and two fish." 39 Then he ordered them to get all the people to sit down in groups on the green grass. 40 So they sat down in groups of hundreds and of fifties. 41 Taking the five loaves and the two fish, he looked up to heaven, and blessed and broke the loaves, and gave them to his disciples to set before the people; and he divided the two fish among them all. 42 And all ate and were filled; 43 and they took up twelve baskets full of broken pieces and of the fish. 44 Those who had eaten the loaves numbered five thousand men.

Jesus Walks on the Water

45 Immediately he made his disciples get into the boat and go on ahead to the other side, to Bethsaida, while he dismissed the crowd. 46 After saying farewell to them, he went up on the mountain to pray.

47 When evening came, the boat was out on the sea, and he was alone on the land. 48 When he saw that they were straining at the oars against an adverse wind, he came towards them early in the morning, walking on the sea. He intended to pass them by. 49 But when they saw him walking on the sea, they thought it was a ghost and cried out; 50 for they all saw him and were terrified. But immediately he spoke to them and said, "Take heart, it is I; do not be afraid." 51 Then he got into the boat with them and the wind ceased. And they were utterly astounded, 52 for they did not understand about the loaves, but their hearts were hardened.

Healing the Sick in Gennesaret

53 When they had crossed over, they came to land at Gennesaret and moored the boat. 54 When they got out of the boat, people at once recognized him, 55 and rushed about that whole region and began to bring the sick on mats to wherever they heard he was. 56 And wherever he went, into villages or cities or farms, they laid the sick in the marketplaces, and begged him that they might touch even the fringe of his cloak; and all who touched it were healed.

The Tradition of the Elders

7 Now when the Pharisees and some of the scribes who had come from Jerusalem gathered around him, 2 they noticed that some of his disciples were eating with defiled hands, that is, without washing them. 3 (For the Pharisees, and all the Jews, do not eat unless they thoroughly wash their hands,[b] thus observing the tradition of the

[a] The denarius was the usual day's wage for a laborer [b] Meaning of Gk uncertain

6:43 twelve baskets: The "twelve baskets" of leftovers is symbolically important, suggesting that Jesus provides enough for all twelve tribes of Israel.

6:47-51 walking on the sea: The disciples are "terrified," but Jesus is in control of the wind and water. Compare this scene, especially the disciples' response, with 4:35-41.

6:52 did not understand about the loaves: The disciples are astounded at Jesus walking on the water, because they do not understand "the loaves"—in other words, the feeding of the five thousand (6:35-44).

What do you make of the disciples' response to Jesus' actions? How do you respond?

7:1-23 the tradition of the elders: The elders were authorities on the traditional interpretation and application of Jewish law. The issue here is the role of the tradition of the elders (7:3) as it relates to matters of ritual purity and our relationship with God. The Pharisees (see note at 2:16), who were particularly concerned about such matters, promoted these teachings (see a similar dispute about Sabbath observance in 2:23—3:6).

elders; [4]and they do not eat anything from the market unless they wash
it;[a] and there are also many other traditions that they observe, the
washing of cups, pots, and bronze kettles.[b]) [5]So the Pharisees and
the scribes asked him, "Why do your disciples not live[c] according to
the tradition of the elders, but eat with defiled hands?" [6]He said to
them, "Isaiah prophesied rightly about you hypocrites, as it is written,

7:6-7 their hearts are far from me: Jesus quotes Isaiah 29:13 from the Greek version.

'This people honors me with their lips,
but their hearts are far from me;
7 in vain do they worship me,
teaching human precepts as doctrines.'

[8]You abandon the commandment of God and hold to human tradition."

7:10 Moses said: Jesus quotes Exodus 20:12, 21:17; Leviticus 20:9; and Deuteronomy 5:16.

9 Then he said to them, "You have a fine way of rejecting the
commandment of God in order to keep your tradition! [10]For Moses
said, 'Honor your father and your mother'; and, 'Whoever speaks
evil of father or mother must surely die.' [11]But you say that if anyone
tells father or mother, 'Whatever support you might have had from
me is Corban' (that is, an offering to God[d])— [12]then you no longer
permit doing anything for a father or mother, [13]thus making void
the word of God through your tradition that you have handed on.
And you do many things like this."

7:14-23 can defile: The issue of ritually clean foods continued to be a concern in the early church (see Acts 10:9-16; 15:28-29; Rom 14:20), because it was a key distinction between Jews and Gentiles (non-Jews).

14 Then he called the crowd again and said to them, "Listen to
me, all of you, and understand: [15]there is nothing outside a person
that by going in can defile, but the things that come out are what
defile."[e]

17 When he had left the crowd and entered the house, his disciples asked him about the parable. [18]He said to them, "Then do you
also fail to understand? Do you not see that whatever goes into a
person from outside cannot defile, [19]since it enters, not the heart
but the stomach, and goes out into the sewer?" (Thus he declared
all foods clean.) [20]And he said, "It is what comes out of a person that
defiles. [21]For it is from within, from the human heart, that evil intentions come: fornication, theft, murder, [22]adultery, avarice, wickedness, deceit, licentiousness, envy, slander, pride, folly. [23]All these evil
things come from within, and they defile a person."

The Syrophoenician Woman's Faith

7:24-26 the region of Tyre: Jesus leaves Galilee and goes north to Tyre, a town on the Mediterranean Sea, near the Gentile (non-Jewish) region of Syria and Phoenicia (see Map 12, p. 2109).

24 From there he set out and went away to the region of Tyre.[f]
He entered a house and did not want anyone to know he was there.
Yet he could not escape notice, [25]but a woman whose little daughter
had an unclean spirit immediately heard about him, and she came

---

[a] Other ancient authorities read *and when they come from the marketplace, they do not eat unless they purify themselves* [b] Other ancient authorities add *and beds* [c] Gk *walk* [d] Gk lacks *to God* [e] Other ancient authorities add verse 16, *"Let anyone with ears to hear listen"* [f] Other ancient authorities add *and Sidon*

and bowed down at his feet. [26]Now the woman was a Gentile, of
Syrophoenician origin. She begged him to cast the demon out of her
daughter. [27]He said to her, "Let the children be fed first, for it is not
fair to take the children's food and throw it to the dogs." [28]But she
answered him, "Sir,[a] even the dogs under the table eat the children's
crumbs." [29]Then he said to her, "For saying that, you may go—the
demon has left your daughter." [30]So she went home, found the child
lying on the bed, and the demon gone.

Jesus Cures a Deaf Man

31 Then he returned from the region of Tyre, and went by
way of Sidon towards the Sea of Galilee, in the region of the Decapolis. [32]They brought to him a deaf man who had an impediment
in his speech; and they begged him to lay his hand on him. [33]He
took him aside in private, away from the crowd, and put his fingers
into his ears, and he spat and touched his tongue. [34]Then looking
up to heaven, he sighed and said to him, "Ephphatha," that is, "Be
opened." [35]And immediately his ears were opened, his tongue was
released, and he spoke plainly. [36]Then Jesus[b] ordered them to tell no
one; but the more he ordered them, the more zealously they proclaimed it. [37]They were astounded beyond measure, saying, "He has
done everything well; he even makes the deaf to hear and the mute
to speak."

Feeding the Four Thousand

8 In those days when there was again a great crowd without anything to eat, he called his disciples and said to them, [2]"I have
compassion for the crowd, because they have been with me now
for three days and have nothing to eat. [3]If I send them away hungry to their homes, they will faint on the way—and some of them
have come from a great distance." [4]His disciples replied, "How can
one feed these people with bread here in the desert?" [5]He asked
them, "How many loaves do you have?" They said, "Seven." [6]Then
he ordered the crowd to sit down on the ground; and he took the
seven loaves, and after giving thanks he broke them and gave them
to his disciples to distribute; and they distributed them to the crowd.
[7]They had also a few small fish; and after blessing them, he ordered
that these too should be distributed. [8]They ate and were filled; and
they took up the broken pieces left over, seven baskets full. [9]Now
there were about four thousand people. And he sent them away.
[10]And immediately he got into the boat with his disciples and went
to the district of Dalmanutha.[c]

[a] Or *Lord*; other ancient authorities prefix *Yes* [b] Gk *he* [c] Other ancient authorities read *Mageda* or *Magdala*

7:27-30 throw it to the dogs: Since dogs were scavenging animals, comparing someone to a dog could be seen as an insult. In any case, the woman is determined to get Jesus to help her daughter.

7:31 Decapolis: Located east of Galilee and Samaria, Decapolis included ten cities (see Map 12, p. 2109). After Jesus sent unclean spirits out of a man and into a herd of swine, the man went to Decapolis and told people what had happened (5:1-20).

7:32-37 a deaf man: This healing of a deaf man who has a speech impediment is paired with the healing of a blind man in 8:22-26. The events between these two healing stories deal with seeing, hearing, and understanding who Jesus is.

7:34 Ephphatha: This is another Aramaic word (see note at 5:41) included by the writer of Mark.

7:36 tell no one: See note on 1:25.

8:1-10 a great crowd without anything to eat: This story is similar to the account in 6:30-44. In light of what happened there, the disciples' lack of understanding (8:4) here is stunning. The disciples still do not know who Jesus is (see note on 1:25).

The Demand for a Sign

11 The Pharisees came and began to argue with him, asking him
for a sign from heaven, to test him. 12 And he sighed deeply in his
spirit and said, "Why does this generation ask for a sign? Truly I tell
you, no sign will be given to this generation." 13 And he left them,
and getting into the boat again, he went across to the other side.

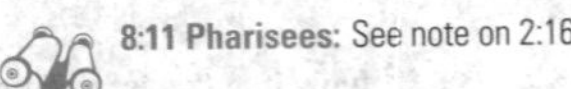

8:11 Pharisees: See note on 2:16.

The Yeast of the Pharisees and of Herod

14 Now the disciples[a] had forgotten to bring any bread; and
they had only one loaf with them in the boat. 15 And he cautioned
them, saying, "Watch out—beware of the yeast of the Pharisees
and the yeast of Herod."[b] 16 They said to one another, "It is because we have no bread." 17 And becoming aware of it, Jesus said to
them, "Why are you talking about having no bread? Do you still
not perceive or understand? Are your hearts hardened? 18 Do you
have eyes, and fail to see? Do you have ears, and fail to hear? And
do you not remember? 19 When I broke the five loaves for the five
thousand, how many baskets full of broken pieces did you collect?"
They said to him, "Twelve." 20 "And the seven for the four thousand,
how many baskets full of broken pieces did you collect?" And they
said to him, "Seven." 21 Then he said to them, "Do you not yet understand?"

8:15 Herod: See note on Herodians at 3:6.

8:17-21 Do you not yet understand?: See note on 1:25.

8:19-21 five loaves: "Five loaves" refers to the event in 6:35-44 and "the seven" loaves to 8:1-9. The meaning of the different numbers is unclear, but may be symbolic. See 4:11-13.

Jesus Cures a Blind Man at Bethsaida

22 They came to Bethsaida. Some people[c] brought a blind man
to him and begged him to touch him. 23 He took the blind man by
the hand and led him out of the village; and when he had put saliva
on his eyes and laid his hands on him, he asked him, "Can you see
anything?" 24 And the man[d] looked up and said, "I can see people,
but they look like trees, walking." 25 Then Jesus[d] laid his hands on his
eyes again; and he looked intently and his sight was restored, and he
saw everything clearly. 26 Then he sent him away to his home, saying,
"Do not even go into the village."[e]

8:22-26 a blind man: See the note at 7:32-37 for how this healing of a blind man pairs up with the previous healing of a deaf man. The two-stage healing here (8:24-25) may also foresee Peter's two-stage recognition of Jesus' identity and mission (8:27-38).

Peter's Declaration about Jesus

27 Jesus went on with his disciples to the villages of Caesarea
Philippi; and on the way he asked his disciples, "Who do people
say that I am?" 28 And they answered him, "John the Baptist; and
others, Elijah; and still others, one of the prophets." 29 He asked
them, "But who do you say that I am?" Peter answered him, "You
are the Messiah."[f] 30 And he sternly ordered them not to tell anyone about him.

8:27 Caesarea Philippi: This city was in a mixed Jewish-Gentile (non-Jewish) area north of Galilee (see Map 12, p. 2109).

8:28 John the Baptist…Elijah…one of the prophets: See 6:14-16 and note on 6:15.

In your own words, who is Jesus?

8:29 the Messiah: The writer of this Gospel identifies Jesus as the Christ (1:1; see also note on "Christ" at 1:1), which is the Greek word for the Hebrew title "Messiah." This is the first time, however, that someone other than the writer recognizes Jesus in this way.

8:30 not to tell anyone: See note on 1:25.

---

[a] Gk *they* [b] Other ancient authorities read *the Herodians* [c] Gk *They* [d] Gk *he* [e] Other ancient authorities add *or tell anyone in the village* [f] Or *the Christ*

Jesus Foretells His Death and Resurrection

31 Then he began to teach them that the Son of Man must undergo great suffering, and be rejected by the elders, the chief priests,
and the scribes, and be killed, and after three days rise again. 32 He
said all this quite openly. And Peter took him aside and began to rebuke him. 33 But turning and looking at his disciples, he rebuked Peter and said, "Get behind me, Satan! For you are setting your mind
not on divine things but on human things."

34 He called the crowd with his disciples, and said to them, "If
any want to become my followers, let them deny themselves and
take up their cross and follow me. 35 For those who want to save their
life will lose it, and those who lose their life for my sake, and for the
sake of the gospel,[a] will save it. 36 For what will it profit them to gain
the whole world and forfeit their life? 37 Indeed, what can they give
in return for their life? 38 Those who are ashamed of me and of my
words[b] in this adulterous and sinful generation, of them the Son of
Man will also be ashamed when he comes in the glory of his Father
9 with the holy angels." 1 And he said to them, "Truly I tell you,
there are some standing here who will not taste death until they
see that the kingdom of God has come with[c] power."

The Transfiguration

2 Six days later, Jesus took with him Peter and James and John,
and led them up a high mountain apart, by themselves. And he was
transfigured before them, 3 and his clothes became dazzling white,
such as no one[d] on earth could bleach them. 4 And there appeared
to them Elijah with Moses, who were talking with Jesus. 5 Then Peter said to Jesus, "Rabbi, it is good for us to be here; let us make
three dwellings,[e] one for you, one for Moses, and one for Elijah."
6 He did not know what to say, for they were terrified. 7 Then a cloud
overshadowed them, and from the cloud there came a voice, "This is
my Son, the Beloved;[f] listen to him!" 8 Suddenly when they looked
around, they saw no one with them any more, but only Jesus.

The Coming of Elijah

9 As they were coming down the mountain, he ordered them
to tell no one about what they had seen, until after the Son of Man
had risen from the dead. 10 So they kept the matter to themselves,
questioning what this rising from the dead could mean. 11 Then they
asked him, "Why do the scribes say that Elijah must come first?"
12 He said to them, "Elijah is indeed coming first to restore all things.
How then is it written about the Son of Man, that he is to go through

[a] Other ancient authorities read *lose their life for the sake of the gospel* [b] Other ancient authorities read *and of mine* [c] Or *in* [d] Gk *no fuller* [e] Or *tents* [f] Or *my beloved Son*

8:31 the Son of Man must undergo great suffering: This is the first of three predictions (see 9:31; 10:33-34) Jesus makes about the suffering, death, and resurrection of the Son of Man (see note at 2:10). Jesus' main foes are the elders (see note on 7:1-23), chief priests, and scribes (see note on 2:6).

8:33 Satan!: See note on 3:22.

How does God work in the world? In the world today, most people value power, wealth, and fame, and those who have these things are able to impose their will on those who do not. Peter was hoping that Jesus, with Peter at his side, would have this kind of power, wealth, and fame and turn out to be the one on top. Martin Luther called this way of God working through things that are powerful a *theology of glory*. Jesus, however, reveals that God often works through weakness—even shame and death. Luther called this the *theology of the cross*. As followers of Christ (see note on 1:17-20), taking up a cross is not simply about putting up with bad things. It is about serving others, perhaps even dying for others, because Christ died for us. *Mark 8:33-37*

What does following Jesus and taking up a cross mean in your life?

8:38 Son of Man: See note at 2:10.

9:1 kingdom of God: See note on 1:15.

9:2 a high mountain: It is not clear what mountain this is, but God is revealed here. In the book of Exodus, God is also revealed on a mountain (Exod 3:1-6; 24:16-18.)

9:4 Elijah with Moses: See note on 6:15.

9:7 This is my Son: Details in this scene match up with Jesus' baptism and crucifixion (see note on 1:9-11).

9:9, 12 Son of Man: See note on 2:10.

9:11, 14 scribes: See note on 2:6.

9:13 Elijah has come: See note at 6:15. Mark indicates here that John the Baptist has played the role of Elijah by preparing the way for the Messiah.

A man says to Jesus, "I believe; help my unbelief!" (9:24). Is faith an either/or matter? How can someone have faith and doubts at the same time?

many sufferings and be treated with contempt? 13But I tell you that
Elijah has come, and they did to him whatever they pleased, as it is
written about him."

The Healing of a Boy with a Spirit

14 When they came to the disciples, they saw a great crowd
around them, and some scribes arguing with them. 15When the
whole crowd saw him, they were immediately overcome with awe,
and they ran forward to greet him. 16He asked them, "What are you
arguing about with them?" 17Someone from the crowd answered
him, "Teacher, I brought you my son; he has a spirit that makes
him unable to speak; 18and whenever it seizes him, it dashes him
down; and he foams and grinds his teeth and becomes rigid; and I
asked your disciples to cast it out, but they could not do so." 19He answered them, "You faithless generation, how much longer must I be
among you? How much longer must I put up with you? Bring him
to me." 20And they brought the boy[a] to him. When the spirit saw
him, immediately it convulsed the boy,[a] and he fell on the ground
and rolled about, foaming at the mouth. 21Jesus[b] asked the father,
"How long has this been happening to him?" And he said, "From
childhood. 22It has often cast him into the fire and into the water,
to destroy him; but if you are able to do anything, have pity on us
and help us." 23Jesus said to him, "If you are able!—All things can be
done for the one who believes." 24Immediately the father of the child
cried out,[c] "I believe; help my unbelief!" 25When Jesus saw that a
crowd came running together, he rebuked the unclean spirit, saying
to it, "You spirit that keeps this boy from speaking and hearing, I
command you, come out of him, and never enter him again!" 26Af-
ter crying out and convulsing him terribly, it came out, and the boy
was like a corpse, so that most of them said, "He is dead." 27But Jesus
took him by the hand and lifted him up, and he was able to stand.
28When he had entered the house, his disciples asked him privately,
"Why could we not cast it out?" 29He said to them, "This kind can
come out only through prayer."[d]

9:25 unclean spirit: See note on 1:23.

Jesus Again Foretells His Death and Resurrection

30 They went on from there and passed through Galilee. He did
not want anyone to know it; 31for he was teaching his disciples, saying to them, "The Son of Man is to be betrayed into human hands,
and they will kill him, and three days after being killed, he will rise
again." 32But they did not understand what he was saying and were
afraid to ask him.

9:30-32 He did not want anyone to know it…they did not understand: See note on 1:25.

9:31 they will kill him: This is the second of Jesus' three predictions of the death and resurrection of the Son of Man (see note on 8:31).

[a] Gk *him* [b] Gk *He* [c] Other ancient authorities add *with tears* [d] Other ancient authorities add *and fasting*

Who Is the Greatest?

33 Then they came to Capernaum; and when he was in the
house he asked them, "What were you arguing about on the way?"
[34]But they were silent, for on the way they had argued with one another who was the greatest. [35]He sat down, called the twelve, and
said to them, "Whoever wants to be first must be last of all and servant of all." [36]Then he took a little child and put it among them; and
taking it in his arms, he said to them, [37]"Whoever welcomes one
such child in my name welcomes me, and whoever welcomes me
welcomes not me but the one who sent me."

Another Exorcist

38 John said to him, "Teacher, we saw someone[a] casting out demons in your name, and we tried to stop him, because he was not
following us." [39]But Jesus said, "Do not stop him; for no one who
does a deed of power in my name will be able soon afterward to
speak evil of me. [40]Whoever is not against us is for us. [41]For truly I
tell you, whoever gives you a cup of water to drink because you bear
the name of Christ will by no means lose the reward.

Temptations to Sin

42 "If any of you put a stumbling block before one of these little
ones who believe in me,[b] it would be better for you if a great millstone were hung around your neck and you were thrown into the
sea. [43]If your hand causes you to stumble, cut it off; it is better for
you to enter life maimed than to have two hands and to go to hell,[c]
to the unquenchable fire.[d] [45]And if your foot causes you to stumble,
cut it off; it is better for you to enter life lame than to have two feet
and to be thrown into hell.[c,d] [47]And if your eye causes you to stumble, tear it out; it is better for you to enter the kingdom of God with
one eye than to have two eyes and to be thrown into hell,[c] [48]where
their worm never dies, and the fire is never quenched.
49 "For everyone will be salted with fire.[e] [50]Salt is good; but if
salt has lost its saltiness, how can you season it?[f] Have salt in yourselves, and be at peace with one another."

Teaching about Divorce

10 He left that place and went to the region of Judea and[g] beyond the Jordan. And crowds again gathered around him;
and, as was his custom, he again taught them.

9:33-35 who was the greatest: See Lutheran Perspectives note on 8:33-37. This discussion about greatness and service is revisited in 10:35-45. Compare 9:35 with 10:31 and 10:43-44.

9:36-37 a little child: Children at this time were considered to be weak and insignificant, and they had low status in society. This scene is similar to another in 10:13-16.

9:42-47 stumbling block: Jesus gives both promise and warning to those who wish to bear his name. The extreme examples emphasize that—whether we cause others to stumble or put ourselves in jeopardy—participating in the life of the kingdom of God is a matter of total commitment.

9:43, 45, 47 hell: The Greek word is *Gehenna*, also the name of a valley south of Jerusalem where garbage was dumped. It became a term that designated the place of final judgment and punishment.

9:47 kingdom of God: See note on 1:15.

9:48 their worm never dies: This phrase refers to Isaiah 66:24. It emphasizes the horror and finality of not being part of the kingdom of God.

9:49-50 saltiness: The meaning of these verses is unclear, but the point seems to be about purification and commitment to the purpose of God's kingdom.

10:1 beyond the Jordan: Jesus has left Galilee in the north and returns to the wilderness where Mark's Gospel begins (1:4-13). See Map 12, p. 2109.

---

[a] Other ancient authorities add *who does not follow us* [b] Other ancient authorities lack *in me*
[c] Gk *Gehenna* [d] Verses 44 and 46 (which are identical with verse 48) are lacking in the best ancient authorities [e] Other ancient authorities either add or substitute *and every sacrifice will be salted with salt*
[f] Or *how can you restore its saltiness?* [g] Other ancient authorities lack *and*

10:2-12 Is it lawful: The Pharisees (see note at 2:16) try to trap Jesus in a dispute going on among Jews. Based on how one interprets the law (Deut 24:1-4), what are proper grounds for divorce? Some said a man could divorce for any reason. Others said adultery was the only reason allowed for divorce (see Matt 5:32; 19:9). Jesus, however, avoids legal arguments entirely by stating God's purpose for marriage from the beginning.

10:6 God made them male and female: See Genesis 1:27; 5:2.

10:7-8 the two shall become one: See Genesis 2:24.

10:10-12 divorces his wife…her husband: In Jewish society at that time, only the husband had the power to decide on divorce. Here Mark also includes Roman society, where a woman could divorce her husband.

10:13-16 Let the little children come: This scene is a follow-up to 9:36-37. There the disciples were told to welcome children. See note on 9:36-37.

10:14-16 receive the kingdom of God as a little child: Jesus' point is not that his followers are to be like children. Rather, in welcoming children—seen as weak and unimportant by society—they correctly understand what the kingdom of God (see note at 1:15) is like and receive it.

10:17-31 what must I do: This passage starts with a man's question about what he must *do* to inherit eternal life (10:17) and ends with Jesus telling how his followers *receive* eternal life (10:29-30).

10:19 the commandments: This is a summary of the commandments from Exodus 20:12-16 and Deuteronomy 5:16.-20. (The command to "not defraud" refers to cheating workers as in Deuteronomy 24:14.) Note that this list does not include the commands dealing with our relationship with God.

10:21 follow me: Throughout Mark, following Jesus is the mark of a disciple.

10:23-27 kingdom of God: See note on 1:15.

10:26 They were greatly astounded: The disciples probably

2 Some Pharisees came, and to test him they asked, "Is it lawful for a man to divorce his wife?" 3He answered them, "What did
Moses command you?" 4They said, "Moses allowed a man to write
a certificate of dismissal and to divorce her." 5But Jesus said to them,
"Because of your hardness of heart he wrote this commandment for
you. 6But from the beginning of creation, 'God made them male and
female.' 7'For this reason a man shall leave his father and mother and
be joined to his wife,[a] 8and the two shall become one flesh.' So they
are no longer two, but one flesh. 9Therefore what God has joined
together, let no one separate."

10 Then in the house the disciples asked him again about this
matter. 11He said to them, "Whoever divorces his wife and marries
another commits adultery against her; 12and if she divorces her husband and marries another, she commits adultery."

Jesus Blesses Little Children

13 People were bringing little children to him in order that he
might touch them; and the disciples spoke sternly to them. 14But
when Jesus saw this, he was indignant and said to them, "Let the little children come to me; do not stop them; for it is to such as these
that the kingdom of God belongs. 15Truly I tell you, whoever does
not receive the kingdom of God as a little child will never enter it."
16And he took them up in his arms, laid his hands on them, and
blessed them.

The Rich Man

17 As he was setting out on a journey, a man ran up and knelt
before him, and asked him, "Good Teacher, what must I do to inherit eternal life?" 18Jesus said to him, "Why do you call me good?
No one is good but God alone. 19You know the commandments:
'You shall not murder; You shall not commit adultery; You shall not
steal; You shall not bear false witness; You shall not defraud; Honor
your father and mother.' " 20He said to him, "Teacher, I have kept all
these since my youth." 21Jesus, looking at him, loved him and said,
"You lack one thing; go, sell what you own, and give the money[b] to
the poor, and you will have treasure in heaven; then come, follow
me." 22When he heard this, he was shocked and went away grieving,
for he had many possessions.

23 Then Jesus looked around and said to his disciples, "How
hard it will be for those who have wealth to enter the kingdom of
God!" 24And the disciples were perplexed at these words. But Jesus
said to them again, "Children, how hard it is[c] to enter the kingdom
of God! 25It is easier for a camel to go through the eye of a needle

---

[a] Other ancient authorities lack *and be joined to his wife* [b] Gk lacks *the money* [c] Other ancient authorities add *for those who trust in riches*

than for someone who is rich to enter the kingdom of God." 26 They
were greatly astounded and said to one another,[a] "Then who can be
saved?" 27 Jesus looked at them and said, "For mortals it is impossible, but not for God; for God all things are possible."
28 Peter began to say to him, "Look, we have left everything and
followed you." 29 Jesus said, "Truly I tell you, there is no one who has
left house or brothers or sisters or mother or father or children or
fields, for my sake and for the sake of the good news,[b] 30 who will
not receive a hundredfold now in this age—houses, brothers and
sisters, mothers and children, and fields, with persecutions—and in
the age to come eternal life. 31 But many who are first will be last, and
the last will be first."

A Third Time Jesus Foretells His Death and Resurrection

32 They were on the road, going up to Jerusalem, and Jesus was
walking ahead of them; they were amazed, and those who followed
were afraid. He took the twelve aside again and began to tell them
what was to happen to him, 33 saying, "See, we are going up to Jerusalem, and the Son of Man will be handed over to the chief priests
and the scribes, and they will condemn him to death; then they
will hand him over to the Gentiles; 34 they will mock him, and spit
upon him, and flog him, and kill him; and after three days he will
rise again."

The Request of James and John

35 James and John, the sons of Zebedee, came forward to him
and said to him, "Teacher, we want you to do for us whatever we
ask of you." 36 And he said to them, "What is it you want me to do
for you?" 37 And they said to him, "Grant us to sit, one at your right
hand and one at your left, in your glory." 38 But Jesus said to them,
"You do not know what you are asking. Are you able to drink the
cup that I drink, or be baptized with the baptism that I am baptized
with?" 39 They replied, "We are able." Then Jesus said to them, "The
cup that I drink you will drink; and with the baptism with which I
am baptized, you will be baptized; 40 but to sit at my right hand or at
my left is not mine to grant, but it is for those for whom it has been
prepared."
41 When the ten heard this, they began to be angry with James
and John. 42 So Jesus called them and said to them, "You know that
among the Gentiles those whom they recognize as their rulers lord
it over them, and their great ones are tyrants over them. 43 But it is
not so among you; but whoever wishes to become great among you

[a] Other ancient authorities read *to him* [b] Or *gospel*

shared the general understanding that wealth was a sign of God's blessing (see Prov 8:20-21), so they are surprised by Jesus' words about the rich and the kingdom of God.

10:31 first will be last: Compare this with 9:35 and 10:43-44.

10:32 going up to Jerusalem: Up to this time, Jesus' ministry has taken place outside the southern region of Judea. This marks an important turning point in the Gospel as Jesus now heads to Jerusalem.

10:33-34 after three days he will rise again: This is Jesus' third prediction of the death and resurrection of the Son of Man (see note on 8:31).

10:35-45 Grant us to sit: Two disciples, James and John, show that they do not understand what Jesus just said (10:32-34). In kingdoms at the time, the most powerful people would sit next to the king. See note on 9:33-35. Those who will be on each side of Jesus are revealed in 15:27.

10:38-39 cup . . . baptism: These are images for experiences of suffering (see 14:36). James (see Acts 12:2) and John, according to tradition, eventually are killed because of their faith.

10:43-44 first among you must be slave of all: Compare this with 10:31 and 9:35.

10:45 a ransom for many: Here Jesus gives the only direct explanation in this Gospel for his death. Although he is the glorious Son of Man (see note at 2:10), he comes as a servant, even to the point of giving his life. This is reflected in the "Servant Song" (Isa 53) and the "Christ Hymn" (Phil 2:5-11). "Ransom" describes a payment made to get something or someone back. It can also be a way of making things right again. By giving his life, Jesus demonstrates what it means to serve, and he changes everything so that we can experience the kingdom of God in our lives.

10:46-52 Bartimaeus: The healing of Bartimaeus is similar to the earlier healing of a blind man (see note at 8:22-26). It shows the contrast between the crowd and the disciples, who do not yet see Jesus clearly, with Bartimaeus and his ability to see who Jesus really is.

10:46 Jericho: See Map 12, p. 2109.

10:47-48 Son of David: This title recognizes Jesus as the anticipated heir of King David (see 2 Sam 7:12-16), in other words, as the Christ or Messiah (see 12:35-37).

Jesus asks Bartimaeus, "What do you want me to do for you?" What do you want Jesus to do for you?

10:52 made you well: See note on 5:34.

10:52 followed him: See note on 10:21.

11:3 The Lord: The Greek word translated as "Lord" (*kurios*) in the New Testament can refer to either God as Lord or to an owner as lord.

11:7-10 they brought the colt to Jesus: Unlike processions for kings and other important figures intended to display their power, Jesus rides on a colt. The people, however, greet him as the Davidic king described in Zechariah 9:9.

11:9-10 Hosanna!: This is a Hebrew word that means "Save now!" (see Ps 118:25).

11:11 temple: The Jerusalem temple was the religious, cultural, and economic center for Jews.

must be your servant, [44]and whoever wishes to be first among you
must be slave of all. [45]For the Son of Man came not to be served but
to serve, and to give his life a ransom for many."

The Healing of Blind Bartimaeus

46 They came to Jericho. As he and his disciples and a large
crowd were leaving Jericho, Bartimaeus son of Timaeus, a blind beggar, was sitting by the roadside. [47]When he heard that it was Jesus of
Nazareth, he began to shout out and say, "Jesus, Son of David, have
mercy on me!" [48]Many sternly ordered him to be quiet, but he cried
out even more loudly, "Son of David, have mercy on me!" [49]Jesus
stood still and said, "Call him here." And they called the blind man,
saying to him, "Take heart; get up, he is calling you." [50]So throwing
off his cloak, he sprang up and came to Jesus. [51]Then Jesus said to
him, "What do you want me to do for you?" The blind man said to
him, "My teacher,[a] let me see again." [52]Jesus said to him, "Go; your
faith has made you well." Immediately he regained his sight and followed him on the way.

Jesus' Triumphal Entry into Jerusalem

11 When they were approaching Jerusalem, at Bethphage and
Bethany, near the Mount of Olives, he sent two of his disciples [2]and said to them, "Go into the village ahead of you, and immediately as you enter it, you will find tied there a colt that has never
been ridden; untie it and bring it. [3]If anyone says to you, 'Why are
you doing this?' just say this, 'The Lord needs it and will send it back
here immediately.'" [4]They went away and found a colt tied near a
door, outside in the street. As they were untying it, [5]some of the
bystanders said to them, "What are you doing, untying the colt?"
[6]They told them what Jesus had said; and they allowed them to
take it. [7]Then they brought the colt to Jesus and threw their cloaks
on it; and he sat on it. [8]Many people spread their cloaks on the
road, and others spread leafy branches that they had cut in the
fields. [9]Then those who went ahead and those who followed were
shouting,

"Hosanna!
Blessed is the one who comes in the name of the Lord!
10 Blessed is the coming kingdom of our ancestor David!
Hosanna in the highest heaven!"

11 Then he entered Jerusalem and went into the temple; and
when he had looked around at everything, as it was already late, he
went out to Bethany with the twelve.

[a] Aramaic *Rabbouni*

Jesus Curses the Fig Tree

12 On the following day, when they came from Bethany, he
was hungry. [13]Seeing in the distance a fig tree in leaf, he went to see
whether perhaps he would find anything on it. When he came to it,
he found nothing but leaves, for it was not the season for figs. [14]He
said to it, "May no one ever eat fruit from you again." And his disciples heard it.

Jesus Cleanses the Temple

15 Then they came to Jerusalem. And he entered the temple
and began to drive out those who were selling and those who were
buying in the temple, and he overturned the tables of the money
changers and the seats of those who sold doves; [16]and he would not
allow anyone to carry anything through the temple. [17]He was teaching and saying, "Is it not written,

'My house shall be called a house of prayer for all the nations'?
But you have made it a den of robbers."

[18]And when the chief priests and the scribes heard it, they kept looking for a way to kill him; for they were afraid of him, because the
whole crowd was spellbound by his teaching. [19]And when evening
came, Jesus and his disciples[a] went out of the city.

The Lesson from the Withered Fig Tree

20 In the morning as they passed by, they saw the fig tree withered away to its roots. [21]Then Peter remembered and said to him,
"Rabbi, look! The fig tree that you cursed has withered." [22]Jesus answered them, "Have[b] faith in God. [23]Truly I tell you, if you say to this
mountain, 'Be taken up and thrown into the sea,' and if you do not
doubt in your heart, but believe that what you say will come to pass,
it will be done for you. [24]So I tell you, whatever you ask for in prayer,
believe that you have received[c] it, and it will be yours.

25 "Whenever you stand praying, forgive, if you have anything
against anyone; so that your Father in heaven may also forgive you
your trespasses."[d]

Jesus' Authority Is Questioned

27 Again they came to Jerusalem. As he was walking in the temple, the chief priests, the scribes, and the elders came to him [28]and
said, "By what authority are you doing these things? Who gave you
this authority to do them?" [29]Jesus said to them, "I will ask you one
question; answer me, and I will tell you by what authority I do these
things. [30]Did the baptism of John come from heaven, or was it of

---

[a] Gk *they*: other ancient authorities read *he* [b] Other ancient authorities read *"If you have* [c] Other ancient authorities read *are receiving* [d] Other ancient authorities add verse 26, *"But if you do not forgive, neither will your Father in heaven forgive your trespasses."*

11:12-14 fig tree: That Jesus would condemn the fig tree for not having any figs out of season indicates that he was performing a symbolic action. The fruitless fig tree represents a "fruitless" Israel that is not ready for its Lord. This situation becomes clear in the next scene, when Jesus drives out the temple merchants. Mark 11:19-25 continues and tells the outcome of the fig-tree story.

11:15-18 temple: In Jesus' time, the temple grounds had been expanded and included an area for merchants involved in providing animals for sacrifice. Money changers were also needed near the temple, because people could not use coins with images on them (see Exod 20:4; Mark 12:13-17) to pay the temple tax. Jesus is opposed to the conducting of this kind of business in the holy space.

11:17 house of prayer…den of robbers: Jesus is quoting from Isaiah 56:7 and Jeremiah 7:11.

11:18 chief priests and the scribes: See note on 8:31.

11:20-22 fig tree: See note on 11:12-14.

11:23-24 whatever you ask for in prayer: The point is not that if you pray for something and it does not happen, you did not have enough faith. Rather, when you have faith, your prayers tend to line up with those things that God wants to happen (see 1 Cor 13:2). God wants us to pray, hears our prayers, and responds to them.

11:25 forgive: Compare this with a similar statement about forgiveness in the Lord's Prayer in Matthew 6:14.

11:27 chief priests, the scribes, and the elders: See note on 8:31.

11:28 authority: Jesus' authority will be an issue throughout his ministry (see 1:22).

human origin? Answer me." [31]They argued with one another, "If we
say, 'From heaven,' he will say, 'Why then did you not believe him?'
[32]But shall we say, 'Of human origin'?"—they were afraid of the
crowd, for all regarded John as truly a prophet. [33]So they answered
Jesus, "We do not know." And Jesus said to them, "Neither will I tell
you by what authority I am doing these things."

The Parable of the Wicked Tenants

12 Then he began to speak to them in parables. "A man planted
a vineyard, put a fence around it, dug a pit for the wine press,
and built a watchtower; then he leased it to tenants and went to another country. [2]When the season came, he sent a slave to the tenants
to collect from them his share of the produce of the vineyard. [3]But
they seized him, and beat him, and sent him away empty-handed.
[4]And again he sent another slave to them; this one they beat over the
head and insulted. [5]Then he sent another, and that one they killed.
And so it was with many others; some they beat, and others they
killed. [6]He had still one other, a beloved son. Finally he sent him to
them, saying, 'They will respect my son.' [7]But those tenants said to
one another, 'This is the heir; come, let us kill him, and the inheritance will be ours.' [8]So they seized him, killed him, and threw him
out of the vineyard. [9]What then will the owner of the vineyard do?
He will come and destroy the tenants and give the vineyard to others.
[10]Have you not read this scripture:

'The stone that the builders rejected
has become the cornerstone;[a]
11 this was the Lord's doing,
and it is amazing in our eyes'?"

12 When they realized that he had told this parable against
them, they wanted to arrest him, but they feared the crowd. So they
left him and went away.

The Question about Paying Taxes

13 Then they sent to him some Pharisees and some Herodians to trap him in what he said. [14]And they came and said to him,
"Teacher, we know that you are sincere, and show deference to no
one; for you do not regard people with partiality, but teach the way
of God in accordance with truth. Is it lawful to pay taxes to the emperor, or not? [15]Should we pay them, or should we not?" But knowing their hypocrisy, he said to them, "Why are you putting me to the
test? Bring me a denarius and let me see it." [16]And they brought one.
Then he said to them, "Whose head is this, and whose title?" They
answered, "The emperor's." [17]Jesus said to them, "Give to the em-

[a] Or *keystone*

12:1-9 the tenants: The practice of tenants farming land for an owner was common at the time. This parable (see note at 3:23) is an allegory, or symbolic story. The vineyard represents Israel (see Isa 5:1-2), the tenants are the Jewish leaders (see Mark 12:12), the slaves are the prophets who spoke God's messages, and the beloved son is Jesus (see 1:11; 9:7).

12:10-11 cornerstone: Jesus quotes Psalm 118:22-23, a passage the early church used to talk about Christ as the cornerstone. A cornerstone is a large stone near the foundation of a building that joins two or more rows of stones together (see Acts 4:11; Eph 2:20; 1 Pet 2:6-8.)

12:13 Pharisees and some Herodians: See notes on 2:16 and 3:6. Here these opponents of Jesus try to trap him into being disloyal to the emperor.

12:14-17 taxes to the emperor: This issue was controversial for the Jews, because paying taxes to Rome validated and helped support the government occupying the land. A denarius was a coin worth about one day's pay for a laborer. It was inscribed with the Roman emperor's name and his picture.

Illustration of silver Roman denarius of the first century, showing Tiberius Caesar (14-37 C.E.).

peror the things that are the emperor's, and to God the things that
are God's." And they were utterly amazed at him.

The Question about the Resurrection

18 Some Sadducees, who say there is no resurrection, came to
him and asked him a question, saying, 19 "Teacher, Moses wrote for
us that if a man's brother dies, leaving a wife but no child, the man[a]
shall marry the widow and raise up children for his brother. 20 There
were seven brothers; the first married and, when he died, left no
children; 21 and the second married the widow[b] and died, leaving no
children; and the third likewise; 22 none of the seven left children.
Last of all the woman herself died. 23 In the resurrection[c] whose wife
will she be? For the seven had married her."

24 Jesus said to them, "Is not this the reason you are wrong,
that you know neither the scriptures nor the power of God? 25 For
when they rise from the dead, they neither marry nor are given in
marriage, but are like angels in heaven. 26 And as for the dead being
raised, have you not read in the book of Moses, in the story about
the bush, how God said to him, 'I am the God of Abraham, the God
of Isaac, and the God of Jacob'? 27 He is God not of the dead, but of
the living; you are quite wrong."

The First Commandment

28 One of the scribes came near and heard them disputing with
one another, and seeing that he answered them well, he asked him,
"Which commandment is the first of all?" 29 Jesus answered, "The
first is, 'Hear, O Israel: the Lord our God, the Lord is one; 30 you
shall love the Lord your God with all your heart, and with all your
soul, and with all your mind, and with all your strength.' 31 The second is this, 'You shall love your neighbor as yourself.' There is no
other commandment greater than these." 32 Then the scribe said to
him, "You are right, Teacher; you have truly said that 'he is one, and
besides him there is no other'; 33 and 'to love him with all the heart,
and with all the understanding, and with all the strength,' and 'to
love one's neighbor as oneself,'—this is much more important than
all whole burnt offerings and sacrifices." 34 When Jesus saw that he
answered wisely, he said to him, "You are not far from the kingdom
of God." After that no one dared to ask him any question.

The Question about David's Son

35 While Jesus was teaching in the temple, he said, "How can the
scribes say that the Messiah[d] is the son of David? 36 David himself, by
the Holy Spirit, declared,

What is the Lutheran doctrine of the Two Kingdoms? Luther tried to explain the relationship between God and emperor by talking about the "Two Kingdoms." There is a secular, worldly realm or kingdom that uses governments and laws to keep order. There is also a spiritual realm directed by God and the gospel. Christians live in both kingdoms, but our first allegiance or commitment is always to the kingdom of God. *Mark 12:14-17*

12:18 Sadducees: The Sadducees were a Jewish group and rivals of the Pharisees (see Acts 23:6-10). They rejected the tradition of the elders (see note on 7:1-23) and only accepted laws from the five "books of Moses" (Gen–Deut).

12:19 children for his brother: This refers to the practice of *levirate marriage,* described in Deuteronomy 25:5-10. A man would marry his brother's widow to preserve the family name through children.

12:24-27 like angels in heaven: In addressing the issue of marriage in heaven, Jesus says people are like angels, who were considered to be nonsexual beings. The Sadducees, however, did not believe in angels' existence (see Acts 23:8). To address the real issue of resurrection or life after death, Jesus quotes Moses (Exod 3:6) and points out that God said, "I *am*"—not *was*—the God of ancestors who had been long dead.

12:28 scribes: See note on 2:6.

12:29-31 love the Lord your God: The first quote Jesus uses is from Deuteronomy 6:4-5 and the Greek version of Joshua 22:5. The second quote is from Leviticus 19:18.

12:34 kingdom of God: See note on 1:15.

12:35-37 the Messiah is the son of David?: The scribes claim that the Messiah is the son of David on the basis of passages such as 2 Samuel 7:12, and Mark appears to agree with this (see note at 10:47). But Jesus' argument, based on Psalm 110:1, is about the son of David's authority and role. This psalm was important in the early church for talking about Jesus' resurrection and superior position to angels (see Acts 2:34-36; Heb 1:13).

---

[a] Gk *his brother* [b] Gk *her* [c] Other ancient authorities add *when they rise* [d] Or *the Christ*

'The Lord said to my Lord,
"Sit at my right hand,
until I put your enemies under your feet."'
[37]David himself calls him Lord; so how can he be his son?" And the
large crowd was listening to him with delight.

Jesus Denounces the Scribes

38 As he taught, he said, "Beware of the scribes, who like to walk
around in long robes, and to be greeted with respect in the marketplaces, [39]and to have the best seats in the synagogues and places of
honor at banquets! [40]They devour widows' houses and for the sake
of appearance say long prayers. They will receive the greater condemnation."

The Widow's Offering

41 He sat down opposite the treasury, and watched the crowd
putting money into the treasury. Many rich people put in large sums.
[42]A poor widow came and put in two small copper coins, which
are worth a penny. [43]Then he called his disciples and said to them,
"Truly I tell you, this poor widow has put in more than all those who
are contributing to the treasury. [44]For all of them have contributed
out of their abundance; but she out of her poverty has put in everything she had, all she had to live on."

The Destruction of the Temple Foretold

13 As he came out of the temple, one of his disciples said to him,
"Look, Teacher, what large stones and what large buildings!"
[2]Then Jesus asked him, "Do you see these great buildings? Not one
stone will be left here upon another; all will be thrown down."

3 When he was sitting on the Mount of Olives opposite the temple, Peter, James, John, and Andrew asked him privately, [4]"Tell us,
when will this be, and what will be the sign that all these things are
about to be accomplished?" [5]Then Jesus began to say to them, "Beware that no one leads you astray. [6]Many will come in my name and
say, 'I am he!'[a] and they will lead many astray. [7]When you hear of
wars and rumors of wars, do not be alarmed; this must take place, but
the end is still to come. [8]For nation will rise against nation, and kingdom against kingdom; there will be earthquakes in various places;
there will be famines. This is but the beginning of the birth pangs.

Persecution Foretold

9 "As for yourselves, beware; for they will hand you over to
councils; and you will be beaten in synagogues; and you will stand
before governors and kings because of me, as a testimony to them.

12:38 scribes: See note on 2:6.

12:41-44 treasury: The treasury or place for collecting money was probably located near the temple's entrance. The widow's coins were the smallest unit of money in use at the time.

13:1-37 when will this be: In this chapter, Jesus reveals events that would happen in the future. These events were experienced by Mark's readers and also by other Christians throughout history. Jesus warns against thinking either that the end is coming very soon or at some very distant time.

13:2 Not one stone will be left: Jesus' statement anticipates the destruction of the temple by the Romans in 70 C.E.

13:7, 13 the end: This refers to the end of time, when judgment and resurrection happens (see 1 Cor 1:8; 15:24).

13:9-13 they will hand you over: The book of Acts will describe the events listed here as happening to the disciples and Paul.

[a] Gk *I am*

10And the good news[a] must first be proclaimed to all nations.
11When they bring you to trial and hand you over, do not worry beforehand about what you are to say; but say whatever is given you at
that time, for it is not you who speak, but the Holy Spirit. 12Brother
will betray brother to death, and a father his child, and children will
rise against parents and have them put to death; 13and you will be
hated by all because of my name. But the one who endures to the
end will be saved.

The Desolating Sacrilege

14 "But when you see the desolating sacrilege set up where it
ought not to be (let the reader understand), then those in Judea
must flee to the mountains; 15the one on the housetop must not go
down or enter the house to take anything away; 16the one in the field
must not turn back to get a coat. 17Woe to those who are pregnant
and to those who are nursing infants in those days! 18Pray that it may
not be in winter. 19For in those days there will be suffering, such as
has not been from the beginning of the creation that God created
until now, no, and never will be. 20And if the Lord had not cut short
those days, no one would be saved; but for the sake of the elect,
whom he chose, he has cut short those days. 21And if anyone says
to you at that time, 'Look! Here is the Messiah!'[b] or 'Look! There
he is!'—do not believe it. 22False messiahs[c] and false prophets will
appear and produce signs and omens, to lead astray, if possible, the
elect. 23But be alert; I have already told you everything.

13:14 the desolating sacrilege: This is a concept shared with Daniel 9:27 and 11:31. It also appears in 1 Maccabees 1:54, which is in the Apocrypha, a group of books outside of the Old and New Testaments (see the chart "Different Canons of the Hebrew Bible (Old Testament)," pp. 14-15). It is not certain what is meant by "the desolating sacrilege," but it probably refers to the destruction of the temple in 70 C.E. (see 13:2).

13:20, 22, 27 elect: The "elect" is a term used in the Old and New Testaments to refer to those chosen by God to be the people of God.

The Coming of the Son of Man

24 "But in those days, after that suffering,
the sun will be darkened,
and the moon will not give its light,
25 and the stars will be falling from heaven,
and the powers in the heavens will be shaken.
26Then they will see 'the Son of Man coming in clouds' with great
power and glory. 27Then he will send out the angels, and gather his
elect from the four winds, from the ends of the earth to the ends of
heaven.

13:26 Son of Man: See note on 2:10. The language here clearly draws on Daniel 7:13-14.

The Lesson of the Fig Tree

28 "From the fig tree learn its lesson: as soon as its branch becomes tender and puts forth its leaves, you know that summer is
near. 29So also, when you see these things taking place, you know
that he[d] is near, at the very gates. 30Truly I tell you, this generation
will not pass away until all these things have taken place. 31Heaven
and earth will pass away, but my words will not pass away.

13:30-33 this generation: Mark apparently expected Jesus to return during his lifetime, but as Jesus says, no one other than God the Father knows when this will occur.

---

[a] Gk *gospel* [b] Or *the Christ* [c] Or *christs* [d] Or *it*

The Necessity for Watchfulness

32 "But about that day or hour no one knows, neither the angels
in heaven, nor the Son, but only the Father. 33Beware, keep alert;[a]
for you do not know when the time will come. 34It is like a man going on a journey, when he leaves home and puts his slaves in charge,
each with his work, and commands the doorkeeper to be on the
watch. 35Therefore, keep awake—for you do not know when the
master of the house will come, in the evening, or at midnight, or
at cockcrow, or at dawn, 36or else he may find you asleep when he
comes suddenly. 37And what I say to you I say to all: Keep awake."

The Plot to Kill Jesus

14 It was two days before the Passover and the festival of Unleavened Bread. The chief priests and the scribes were looking for a way to arrest Jesus[b] by stealth and kill him; 2for they said,
"Not during the festival, or there may be a riot among the people."

The Anointing at Bethany

3 While he was at Bethany in the house of Simon the leper,[c] as
he sat at the table, a woman came with an alabaster jar of very costly
ointment of nard, and she broke open the jar and poured the ointment on his head. 4But some were there who said to one another in
anger, "Why was the ointment wasted in this way? 5For this ointment could have been sold for more than three hundred denarii,[d]
and the money given to the poor." And they scolded her. 6But Jesus
said, "Let her alone; why do you trouble her? She has performed a
good service for me. 7For you always have the poor with you, and
you can show kindness to them whenever you wish; but you will
not always have me. 8She has done what she could; she has anointed
my body beforehand for its burial. 9Truly I tell you, wherever the
good news[e] is proclaimed in the whole world, what she has done
will be told in remembrance of her."

Judas Agrees to Betray Jesus

10 Then Judas Iscariot, who was one of the twelve, went to the
chief priests in order to betray him to them. 11When they heard it,
they were greatly pleased, and promised to give him money. So he
began to look for an opportunity to betray him.

The Passover with the Disciples

12 On the first day of Unleavened Bread, when the Passover
lamb is sacrificed, his disciples said to him, "Where do you want

14:1 the Passover and the festival of Unleavened Bread: This was a combined celebration recalling the exodus out of slavery from Egypt (see Exod 12:1—13:16). According to Mark, in this particular year it started on a Friday (which happened in 30 or 33 C.E.), so the events described here are on a Wednesday. See note on 8:31.

14:3 Simon the leper: Presumably Simon was now cured of his leprosy. See note at 1:40. Pouring ointment on someone's head, or anointing, was a way of designating that person as the chief priest (Exod 29:7; Lev 8:12; 21:10) or king (1 Sam 10:1; 2 Kgs 9:3). See note on "Christ" at 1:1.

14:5 three hundred denarii: A denarius was worth about one day's wage for a laborer.

14:8 anointed my body beforehand for its burial: See 16:1-2.

14:9 good news: See note on "good news" at 1:1.

14:10 betray him: The Greek word translated as "betray" can also be translated as "hand over." Jesus had already said that he would be betrayed (9:31) to the chief priests and scribes (10:33). Also see note on 3:19.

14:12-16 first day of Unleavened Bread: See note on 14:1. This would be a Thursday, and the Passover meal would be eaten that evening. Compare Jesus' directions here with the similar story in 11:1-6.

---

[a] Other ancient authorities add *and pray* [b] Gk *him* [c] The terms *leper* and *leprosy* can refer to several diseases [d] The denarius was the usual day's wage for a laborer [e] Or *gospel*

us to go and make the preparations for you to eat the Passover?"
[13]So he sent two of his disciples, saying to them, "Go into the city,
and a man carrying a jar of water will meet you; follow him, [14]and
wherever he enters, say to the owner of the house, 'The Teacher
asks, Where is my guest room where I may eat the Passover with my
disciples?' [15]He will show you a large room upstairs, furnished and
ready. Make preparations for us there." [16]So the disciples set out and
went to the city, and found everything as he had told them; and they
prepared the Passover meal.

17 When it was evening, he came with the twelve. [18]And when
they had taken their places and were eating, Jesus said, "Truly I tell
you, one of you will betray me, one who is eating with me." [19]They
began to be distressed and to say to him one after another, "Surely,
not I?" [20]He said to them, "It is one of the twelve, one who is dipping
bread[a] into the bowl[b] with me. [21]For the Son of Man goes as it is written of him, but woe to that one by whom the Son of Man is betrayed!
It would have been better for that one not to have been born."

The Institution of the Lord's Supper

22 While they were eating, he took a loaf of bread, and after
blessing it he broke it, gave it to them, and said, "Take; this is my
body." [23]Then he took a cup, and after giving thanks he gave it to
them, and all of them drank from it. [24]He said to them, "This is my
blood of the[c] covenant, which is poured out for many. [25]Truly I tell
you, I will never again drink of the fruit of the vine until that day
when I drink it new in the kingdom of God."

Peter's Denial Foretold

26 When they had sung the hymn, they went out to the Mount
of Olives. [27]And Jesus said to them, "You will all become deserters;
for it is written,

'I will strike the shepherd,
and the sheep will be scattered.'

[28]But after I am raised up, I will go before you to Galilee." [29]Peter said
to him, "Even though all become deserters, I will not." [30]Jesus said to
him, "Truly I tell you, this day, this very night, before the cock crows
twice, you will deny me three times." [31]But he said vehemently, "Even
though I must die with you, I will not deny you." And all of them said
the same.

Jesus Prays in Gethsemane

32 They went to a place called Gethsemane; and he said to his
disciples, "Sit here while I pray." [33]He took with him Peter and James

[a] Gk lacks *bread* [b] Other ancient authorities read *same bowl* [c] Other ancient authorities add *new*

14:21 Son of Man: See note on 2:10.

What is the Lord's Supper? The Lord's Supper is also called Holy Communion, the Eucharist, and the Sacrament of the Altar. As a sacrament, it uses earthly elements (bread and wine) with God's word, at Christ's command. Although the Lord's Supper began with Jesus and the twelve disciples, it is more than a remembrance of that event. When we celebrate the sacrament, we are in the presence of Christ. Martin Luther writes, "It is the true body and blood of our Lord Jesus Christ under the bread and wine, instituted by Christ himself for us Christians to eat and to drink" (SC:33). *Mark 14:22-24*

14:22-26 bread ... cup: Eating unleavened bread, drinking a cup of wine, and singing a hymn are parts of the traditional Passover meal. A covenant or promise was agreed to with blood (see Exod 24:8; see also Jer 31:31). For the possible location of the Last Supper, see Map 13, p. 2110.

14:25 kingdom of God: See note on 1:15.

14:27 strike the shepherd: Jesus quotes Zechariah 13:7.

14:28 Galilee: See 16:7.

14:30 three times: See 14:66-72.

14:32 Gethsemane: This was a garden on the Mount of Olives. The name comes from the Aramaic for "oil press." See Map 13, p. 2110, for the possible location.

and John, and began to be distressed and agitated. 34 And he said to
them, "I am deeply grieved, even to death; remain here, and keep
awake." 35 And going a little farther, he threw himself on the ground
and prayed that, if it were possible, the hour might pass from him.
36 He said, "Abba,[a] Father, for you all things are possible; remove
this cup from me; yet, not what I want, but what you want." 37 He
came and found them sleeping; and he said to Peter, "Simon, are you
asleep? Could you not keep awake one hour? 38 Keep awake and pray
that you may not come into the time of trial;[b] the spirit indeed is
willing, but the flesh is weak." 39 And again he went away and prayed,
saying the same words. 40 And once more he came and found them
sleeping, for their eyes were very heavy; and they did not know what
to say to him. 41 He came a third time and said to them, "Are you still
sleeping and taking your rest? Enough! The hour has come; the Son
of Man is betrayed into the hands of sinners. 42 Get up, let us be going.
See, my betrayer is at hand."

The Betrayal and Arrest of Jesus

43 Immediately, while he was still speaking, Judas, one of the
twelve, arrived; and with him there was a crowd with swords and
clubs, from the chief priests, the scribes, and the elders. 44 Now the
betrayer had given them a sign, saying, "The one I will kiss is the
man; arrest him and lead him away under guard." 45 So when he
came, he went up to him at once and said, "Rabbi!" and kissed him.
46 Then they laid hands on him and arrested him. 47 But one of those
who stood near drew his sword and struck the slave of the high
priest, cutting off his ear. 48 Then Jesus said to them, "Have you come
out with swords and clubs to arrest me as though I were a bandit?
49 Day after day I was with you in the temple teaching, and you did
not arrest me. But let the scriptures be fulfilled." 50 All of them deserted him and fled.

51 A certain young man was following him, wearing nothing
but a linen cloth. They caught hold of him, 52 but he left the linen
cloth and ran off naked.

Jesus before the Council

53 They took Jesus to the high priest; and all the chief priests,
the elders, and the scribes were assembled. 54 Peter had followed
him at a distance, right into the courtyard of the high priest; and
he was sitting with the guards, warming himself at the fire. 55 Now
the chief priests and the whole council were looking for testimony
against Jesus to put him to death; but they found none. 56 For many
gave false testimony against him, and their testimony did not agree.
57 Some stood up and gave false testimony against him, saying, 58 "We

[a] Aramaic for *Father* [b] Or *into temptation*

14:36-38 Abba: This is the Aramaic term for "father" (see note on 5:41). Jesus' words are similar to the Lord's Prayer (Matt 6:9-13): "Our Father . . . Your will be done . . . do not bring us to the time of trial."

What helps you get through difficult situations when you are torn between what you think you should do and what you are tempted to do?

14:41 Son of Man: See note on 2:10.

14:42-44 betrayer: Jesus has already talked about being betrayed. See 14:10-11, 18-21.

14:45 Rabbi!: This title means "teacher." It was a respectful form of addressing someone. A kiss on the cheek was a common greeting at the time.

14:49-50 scriptures: See 14:27.

14:51-52 A certain young man: No one is sure what this incident is about, but a young man dressed in a white robe is at the tomb (16:5).

14:53 high priest . . . chief priests, the elders, and the scribes: See note at 8:31. See Map 13, p. 2110, for the location of the trial before the high priests.

14:55 council: The council or Sanhedrin was the highest Jewish court.

14:58 I will destroy this temple: There is no record in Mark that Jesus ever said this (but see 15:29 and John 2:19). Yet the statement is true at another level when referring to Jesus' body or to the church.

heard him say, 'I will destroy this temple that is made with hands,
and in three days I will build another, not made with hands.' " 59 But
even on this point their testimony did not agree. 60 Then the high
priest stood up before them and asked Jesus, "Have you no answer?
What is it that they testify against you?" 61 But he was silent and did
not answer. Again the high priest asked him, "Are you the Messiah,[a]
the Son of the Blessed One?" 62 Jesus said, "I am; and

'you will see the Son of Man
seated at the right hand of the Power,'
and 'coming with the clouds of heaven.' "

63 Then the high priest tore his clothes and said, "Why do we still need
witnesses? 64 You have heard his blasphemy! What is your decision?"
All of them condemned him as deserving death. 65 Some began to spit
on him, to blindfold him, and to strike him, saying to him, "Prophesy!" The guards also took him over and beat him.

Peter Denies Jesus

66 While Peter was below in the courtyard, one of the servant-
girls of the high priest came by. 67 When she saw Peter warming
himself, she stared at him and said, "You also were with Jesus, the
man from Nazareth." 68 But he denied it, saying, "I do not know or
understand what you are talking about." And he went out into the
forecourt.[b] Then the cock crowed.[c] 69 And the servant-girl, on seeing him, began again to say to the bystanders, "This man is one of
them." 70 But again he denied it. Then after a little while the bystanders again said to Peter, "Certainly you are one of them; for you are a
Galilean." 71 But he began to curse, and he swore an oath, "I do not
know this man you are talking about." 72 At that moment the cock
crowed for the second time. Then Peter remembered that Jesus had
said to him, "Before the cock crows twice, you will deny me three
times." And he broke down and wept.

Jesus before Pilate

15 As soon as it was morning, the chief priests held a consulta-
tion with the elders and scribes and the whole council. They
bound Jesus, led him away, and handed him over to Pilate. 2 Pilate asked
him, "Are you the King of the Jews?" He answered him, "You say so."
3 Then the chief priests accused him of many things. 4 Pilate asked him
again, "Have you no answer? See how many charges they bring against
you." 5 But Jesus made no further reply, so that Pilate was amazed.

Pilate Hands Jesus over to Be Crucified

6 Now at the festival he used to release a prisoner for them,
anyone for whom they asked. 7 Now a man called Barabbas was in

[a] Or *the Christ* [b] Or *gateway* [c] Other ancient authorities lack *Then the cock crowed*

14:61 Messiah: See note on 1:1. "Blessed One" is a Jewish way of referring to God without speaking God's holy name.

14:62 I am: This is the first time in Mark that Jesus openly declares himself to be the Messiah and Son of God. See note on Son of Man at 2:10.

14:64 blasphemy!: See note on 2:7. The Jewish leaders decide that Jesus deserves to die, but because Rome had greater authority, they are not officially able to put Jesus to death.

14:72 Peter remembered: See 14:30.

15:1-15 council: See note on council at 14:55. Pilate was the highest ranking Roman official, known as a prefect, in charge of Judea 26–36 C.E. He is interested in Jesus' possible political role—"King of the Jews"—rather than a religious role, although for the Jews the Messiah's main role was as king.

15:7 Barabbas: This is an Aramaic name meaning "son of the father." This scene raises the question of whether or not the true Son of God is one with a political agenda, like Barabbas, who is willing to use violence against Roman oppression.

prison with the rebels who had committed murder during the insurrection. 8 So the crowd came and began to ask Pilate to do for them
according to his custom. 9 Then he answered them, "Do you want
me to release for you the King of the Jews?" 10 For he realized that it
was out of jealousy that the chief priests had handed him over. 11 But
the chief priests stirred up the crowd to have him release Barabbas
for them instead. 12 Pilate spoke to them again, "Then what do you
wish me to do[a] with the man you call[b] the King of the Jews?" 13 They
shouted back, "Crucify him!" 14 Pilate asked them, "Why, what evil
has he done?" But they shouted all the more, "Crucify him!" 15 So
Pilate, wishing to satisfy the crowd, released Barabbas for them; and
after flogging Jesus, he handed him over to be crucified.

The Soldiers Mock Jesus

16 Then the soldiers led him into the courtyard of the palace
(that is, the governor's headquarters[c]); and they called together the
whole cohort. 17 And they clothed him in a purple cloak; and after
twisting some thorns into a crown, they put it on him. 18 And they
began saluting him, "Hail, King of the Jews!" 19 They struck his head
with a reed, spat upon him, and knelt down in homage to him. 20 After mocking him, they stripped him of the purple cloak and put his
own clothes on him. Then they led him out to crucify him.

The Crucifixion of Jesus

21 They compelled a passer-by, who was coming in from the
country, to carry his cross; it was Simon of Cyrene, the father of
Alexander and Rufus. 22 Then they brought Jesus[d] to the place called
Golgotha (which means the place of a skull). 23 And they offered
him wine mixed with myrrh; but he did not take it. 24 And they crucified him, and divided his clothes among them, casting lots to decide what each should take.

25 It was nine o'clock in the morning when they crucified him.
26 The inscription of the charge against him read, "The King of the
Jews." 27 And with him they crucified two bandits, one on his right
and one on his left.[e] 29 Those who passed by derided[f] him, shaking
their heads and saying, "Aha! You who would destroy the temple
and build it in three days, 30 save yourself, and come down from the
cross!" 31 In the same way the chief priests, along with the scribes,
were also mocking him among themselves and saying, "He saved
others; he cannot save himself. 32 Let the Messiah,[g] the King of Israel, come down from the cross now, so that we may see and believe." Those who were crucified with him also taunted him.

15:13 Crucify him!: The Romans only crucified the worst criminals, especially ones who threatened the Roman order. This horrible type of execution was carried out in public as a way of discouraging others from committing similar crimes.

15:14-15 what evil has he done?: Pilate's role in the death of Jesus matches Herod's role in the death of John the Baptist (see 6:17-29).

15:22 Golgotha: This was located at a prominent place outside the walls of Jerusalem (see Map 13, p. 2110). It is also known as Calvary, the Latin word for "skull."

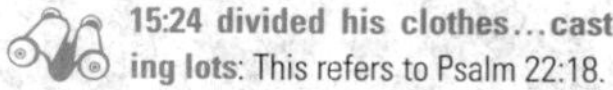

15:24 divided his clothes…casting lots: This refers to Psalm 22:18.

15:26 The King of the Jews: Note that while the Romans intend this inscription to be a *warning* to anyone else who might try to be "King of the Jews," it also displays the *truth* that this is how Jesus reigns.

15:27 his right…his left: See note on 10:35-45.

15:29-32 destroy the temple: See note at 14:58. The mocking is highly ironic and draws upon the language of Psalm 22:7-8.

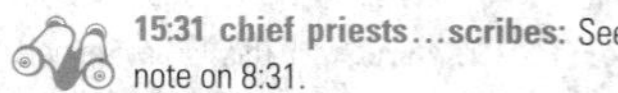

15:31 chief priests…scribes: See note on 8:31.

15:32 Messiah: See note on 1:1.

[a] Other ancient authorities read *what should I do* [b] Other ancient authorities lack *the man you call* [c] Gk *the praetorium* [d] Gk *him* [e] Other ancient authorities add verse 28, *And the scripture was fulfilled that says, "And he was counted among the lawless."* [f] Or *blasphemed* [g] Or *the Christ*

The Death of Jesus

33 When it was noon, darkness came over the whole land[a] until
three in the afternoon. 34 At three o'clock Jesus cried out with a loud
voice, "Eloi, Eloi, lema sabachthani?" which means, "My God, my
God, why have you forsaken me?"[b] 35 When some of the bystanders
heard it, they said, "Listen, he is calling for Elijah." 36 And someone
ran, filled a sponge with sour wine, put it on a stick, and gave it to
him to drink, saying, "Wait, let us see whether Elijah will come to
take him down." 37 Then Jesus gave a loud cry and breathed his last.
38 And the curtain of the temple was torn in two, from top to bottom.
39 Now when the centurion, who stood facing him, saw that in this
way he[c] breathed his last, he said, "Truly this man was God's Son!"[d]

40 There were also women looking on from a distance; among
them were Mary Magdalene, and Mary the mother of James the
younger and of Joses, and Salome. 41 These used to follow him and
provided for him when he was in Galilee; and there were many
other women who had come up with him to Jerusalem.

The Burial of Jesus

42 When evening had come, and since it was the day of Preparation, that is, the day before the sabbath, 43 Joseph of Arimathea,
a respected member of the council, who was also himself waiting
expectantly for the kingdom of God, went boldly to Pilate and asked
for the body of Jesus. 44 Then Pilate wondered if he were already
dead; and summoning the centurion, he asked him whether he had
been dead for some time. 45 When he learned from the centurion
that he was dead, he granted the body to Joseph. 46 Then Joseph[e]
bought a linen cloth, and taking down the body,[f] wrapped it in the
linen cloth, and laid it in a tomb that had been hewn out of the rock.
He then rolled a stone against the door of the tomb. 47 Mary Magdalene and Mary the mother of Joses saw where the body[f] was laid.

The Resurrection of Jesus

16 When the sabbath was over, Mary Magdalene, and Mary
the mother of James, and Salome bought spices, so that they
might go and anoint him. 2 And very early on the first day of the week,
when the sun had risen, they went to the tomb. 3 They had been saying to one another, "Who will roll away the stone for us from the entrance to the tomb?" 4 When they looked up, they saw that the stone,
which was very large, had already been rolled back. 5 As they entered
the tomb, they saw a young man, dressed in a white robe, sitting on
the right side; and they were alarmed. 6 But he said to them, "Do not

---

[a] Or *earth* [b] Other ancient authorities read *made me a reproach* [c] Other ancient authorities add *cried out and* [d] Or *a son of God* [e] Gk *he* [f] Gk *it*

15:34-35 Eloi, Eloi, lema sabachthani?: This is a quote from Psalm 22:1, spoken in Aramaic (see the note at 5:41). The bystanders confuse *Eloi* with *Elijah* (see note on 6:15).

15:37-39 gave a loud cry and breathed his last: This tells how Jesus expired or released his spirit. See note at 1:9-11 for how this scene is matched with Jesus' baptism and transfiguration. The "curtain of the temple" probably refers to the veil that shielded the Holy of Holies area, where God was symbolically understood to dwell.

15:39 the centurion: A centurion was an officer in the Roman army. It is possible that he says sarcastically, "Truly this man was a son of a god!" More likely, his statement is intended as a declaration of faith. In this moment, the Messianic Secret (see note on 1:25) is revealed, and we fully see what it means for Jesus to be the Son of God.

15:42-47 Joseph of Arimathea: As a respected member of the highest Jewish court, making sure that Jesus is buried properly is a risky move for this man. Arimathea was a village about twenty miles northwest of Jerusalem (see Map 12, p. 2109). Joseph and the two women want the work of getting the body into the tomb to be done before the Sabbath (see note at 2:23) starts on Friday evening.

15:43 kingdom of God: See note on 1:15.

15:46 linen cloth: The burial practice at the time was to wrap the body in linen cloth, treat it with spices, and place it in a cave-like tomb. After a year, when the body had decomposed, the bones would be gathered, placed in a container, and left in the tomb.

16:1-2 When the sabbath was over: The Sabbath ended Saturday evening. The women purchase the spices then, and go to the tomb on Sunday morning.

16:5 a young man, dressed in a white robe: It is not clear whether this young man is considered to be an angel.

16:6 was crucified: The Greek wording here emphasizes the crucifixion: "You are looking for Jesus of Nazareth, who has been crucified [*or* the Crucified One]. He was raised."

be alarmed; you are looking for Jesus of Nazareth, who was crucified. He has been raised; he is not here. Look, there is the place they laid him. [7]But go, tell his disciples and Peter that he is going ahead of you to Galilee; there you will see him, just as he told you." [8]So they went out and fled from the tomb, for terror and amazement had seized them; and they said nothing to anyone, for they were afraid.[a]

The Shorter Ending of Mark

⟦And all that had been commanded them they told briefly to those around Peter. And afterward Jesus himself sent out through them, from east to west, the sacred and imperishable proclamation of eternal salvation.[b]⟧

The Longer Ending of Mark

Jesus Appears to Mary Magdalene

9 ⟦Now after he rose early on the first day of the week, he appeared first to Mary Magdalene, from whom he had cast out seven demons. [10]She went out and told those who had been with him, while they were mourning and weeping. [11]But when they heard that he was alive and had been seen by her, they would not believe it.

Jesus Appears to Two Disciples

12 After this he appeared in another form to two of them, as they were walking into the country. [13]And they went back and told the rest, but they did not believe them.

Jesus Commissions the Disciples

14 Later he appeared to the eleven themselves as they were sitting at the table; and he upbraided them for their lack of faith and stubbornness, because they had not believed those who saw him after he had risen.[c] [15]And he said to them, "Go into all the world and proclaim the good news[d] to the whole creation. [16]The one who believes and is baptized will be saved; but the one who does not believe will be condemned. [17]And these signs will accompany those

16:7 Peter: The last mention of Peter before this is at 14:72, when the cock crows a second time. Jesus had spoken about being in Galilee after he was raised up (14:28).

16:8 terror and amazement: The most reliable manuscripts for Mark's Gospel end at 16:8. The ending works well because it shows this story is indeed just the "beginning of the good news" (1:1).

If the women say nothing (16:8), how is anyone going to find out that Jesus, the crucified Messiah, was raised?

16:9-20 he appeared: It is clear by the variety of endings here that some people did not like leaving the story so open-ended at 16:8. The details included in this longer ending of Mark are for the most part drawn from the other Gospels (Matt 28:9-20; Luke 24:10-53; John 20:11-29).

---

[a] Some of the most ancient authorities bring the book to a close at the end of verse 8. One authority concludes the book with the shorter ending; others include the shorter ending and then continue with verses 9–20. In most authorities verses 9–20 follow immediately after verse 8, though in some of these authorities the passage is marked as being doubtful. [b] Other ancient authorities add *Amen* [c] Other ancient authorities add, in whole or in part, *And they excused themselves, saying, "This age of lawlessness and unbelief is under Satan, who does not allow the truth and power of God to prevail over the unclean things of the spirits. Therefore reveal your righteousness now"—thus they spoke to Christ. And Christ replied to them, "The term of years of Satan's power has been fulfilled, but other terrible things draw near. And for those who have sinned I was handed over to death, that they may return to the truth and sin no more, that they may inherit the spiritual and imperishable glory of righteousness that is in heaven."* [d] Or *gospel*

who believe: by using my name they will cast out demons; they will
speak in new tongues; 18 they will pick up snakes in their hands,[a] and
if they drink any deadly thing, it will not hurt them; they will lay
their hands on the sick, and they will recover."

The Ascension of Jesus

19 So then the Lord Jesus, after he had spoken to them, was
taken up into heaven and sat down at the right hand of God. 20 And
they went out and proclaimed the good news everywhere, while the
Lord worked with them and confirmed the message by the signs
that accompanied it.[b]]]

---

[a] Other ancient authorities lack *in their hands* [b] Other ancient authorities add *Amen*

Luke 2:12, 16

LUKE

Background File

The Gospel of Luke tells the story of Jesus. It follows the same storyline as the Gospels of Mark and Matthew, with some differences in the arrangement and use of Jesus' teachings. As it was recited and performed orally for decades in formal and informal settings, it developed a distinctive flavor and focus. The account was written down in the late first century C.E., sometime after the First Jewish Revolt against Rome failed and the Jewish temple in Jerusalem was destroyed (66–70 C.E.)—perhaps between 80 and 90 C.E.

What's the Story?

The Gospel writer goes to great lengths to point out the Jewish character of all the central actors in this story and to emphasize how the coming of a messiah fit into ancient Jewish beliefs and expectations. Luke begins and ends in the temple (see diagrams, pp. 1696 and 1697). There we meet Zechariah, husband of Elizabeth, burning incense. He and Elizabeth are faithful, devoted Jews. We meet Mary, soon-to-be mother of Jesus, a relative of Elizabeth, a daughter of Aaron. After John (son of Elizabeth) and Jesus are born, they are circumcised, marked as Jews forever. When the infant Jesus is presented at the temple, he is welcomed by Simeon and Anna, old faithful Jews waiting for God to rescue the people of Israel. When we next meet Jesus, he is twelve years old and is in Jerusalem, participating in the annual Passover pilgrimage. At the end of the festival, Jesus stays behind and is found, days later, again in the temple. Jesus later travels, teaches, heals, and points to a day when all God's promises will be kept. He acts out the words of Mary's *Magnificat*, or song of praise (1:46-55). In the end, Jesus is crucified by Pilate, a senior Roman official who will not allow the powerful to be brought down from their thrones—or the lowly to be lifted up (see 1:52). Jesus rises and ascends into heaven. The last scene in Luke's story (24:53) takes place in the temple, with the disciples gathered to bless God.

Rome, still in power, destroys both Jerusalem and the temple forty years later. The writer of Luke and his readers know this, and that adds tension to the story.

The Gospel of Luke can be outlined as follows:

Beginning, mainly in Jerusalem (1:1–2:52)

Teaching, mainly in Galilee (3:1–9:50)

Last journey to Jerusalem (9:51–19:28)

Dying, rising, and ascending; return to the temple (19:29–24:53)

What's the Message?

Luke's story of Jesus relates closely to the Jewish world and its beliefs, expectations, and hopes. Jesus is presented as an obedient—if sometimes puzzling—Jew. As the story develops, it becomes clear that God is acting for the good of all of creation, for Jews and Gentiles together. Samaritans, for instance, are shown rejecting Jesus because he is Jewish, yet the storyteller presents them in other settings as examples of neighborliness and gratitude. The Jewish faith has always expected that when God's glory is revealed, all people will see it (see Isa 40:5). That is the point of Luke's story: the Messiah is good news for all people and all of creation.

In the background of the story, the Roman Empire, which would destroy Jerusalem and the temple in 70 C.E., is always lurking. Mary, Jesus' mother, sings her hope that the powerful and abusive will be overturned, thrown down from their thrones. Jesus reads aloud Isaiah's words about good news for the poor, release for the captives, sight for the blind, and freedom for the oppressed (4:16-20). Luke and his readers know that these promises have not been completely fulfilled, but Luke does not explain them away or forget them. He leaves readers to ponder these things, just as Mary pondered what the shepherds said about her child.

Dedication to Theophilus

1 Since many have undertaken to set down an orderly account of
the events that have been fulfilled among us, 2just as they were
handed on to us by those who from the beginning were eyewitnesses
and servants of the word, 3I too decided, after investigating everything
carefully from the very first,[a] to write an orderly account for you, most
excellent Theophilus, 4so that you may know the truth concerning the
things about which you have been instructed.

The Birth of John the Baptist Foretold

5 In the days of King Herod of Judea, there was a priest named
Zechariah, who belonged to the priestly order of Abijah. His wife was
a descendant of Aaron, and her name was Elizabeth. 6Both of them
were righteous before God, living blamelessly according to all the
commandments and regulations of the Lord. 7But they had no children, because Elizabeth was barren, and both were getting on in years.
8 Once when he was serving as priest before God and his section was on duty, 9he was chosen by lot, according to the custom of
the priesthood, to enter the sanctuary of the Lord and offer incense.
10Now at the time of the incense offering, the whole assembly of the
people was praying outside. 11Then there appeared to him an angel
of the Lord, standing at the right side of the altar of incense. 12When

[a] Or *for a long time*

1:1-4 orderly account: Luke writes his own account of Jesus' life for Theophilus, a name meaning "friend of God" in Greek. Theophilus might refer to a certain person or to any friend or follower of Jesus.

1:5 King Herod of Judea: Herod, also called Herod the Great, became king in 37 B.C.E. Zechariah and his wife, Elizabeth, are both members of priestly families.

1:6 righteous before God: This phrase identifies Elizabeth and Zechariah as Jews who observe the Torah or God's teachings and laws. It does not mean they had somehow earned their salvation. Jewish faith (then and now) understands that God's grace always comes first, that God always chooses us before we choose God. Elizabeth and Zechariah are living witnesses to the steady and orderly love of God for all of creation.

1:9 the sanctuary of the Lord: Zechariah is in the temple in Jerusalem. Jews in the first century C.E. viewed the temple as the safe, secure center of a world that was chaotic and dangerous. In their view, the world was structured in concentric circles of holiness and safety that radiated out from the Holy of Holies, out to the Temple itself, out to the city of Jerusalem, out to the historic land of promise, then to the rest of the world—and danger.

1:11-20 **angel:** The angel Gabriel (1:19) appears to Zechariah. Gabriel also appeared to the prophet Daniel (Dan 8:16; 9:21) and later to Mary (1:26-38).

1:13 **John:** This name means "The Lord is kind."

Zechariah saw him, he was terrified; and fear overwhelmed him.
13But the angel said to him, "Do not be afraid, Zechariah, for your
prayer has been heard. Your wife Elizabeth will bear you a son, and
you will name him John. 14You will have joy and gladness, and many
will rejoice at his birth, 15for he will be great in the sight of the Lord.
He must never drink wine or strong drink; even before his birth he
will be filled with the Holy Spirit. 16He will turn many of the people of
Israel to the Lord their God. 17With the spirit and power of Elijah he
will go before him, to turn the hearts of parents to their children, and
the disobedient to the wisdom of the righteous, to make ready a people prepared for the Lord." 18Zechariah said to the angel, "How will I
know that this is so? For I am an old man, and my wife is getting on
in years." 19The angel replied, "I am Gabriel. I stand in the presence of
God, and I have been sent to speak to you and to bring you this good
news. 20But now, because you did not believe my words, which will
be fulfilled in their time, you will become mute, unable to speak, until
the day these things occur."

21 Meanwhile the people were waiting for Zechariah, and wondered at his delay in the sanctuary. 22When he did come out, he could
not speak to them, and they realized that he had seen a vision in the
sanctuary. He kept motioning to them and remained unable to speak.
23When his time of service was ended, he went to his home.

24 After those days his wife Elizabeth conceived, and for five
months she remained in seclusion. She said, 25"This is what the Lord
has done for me when he looked favorably on me and took away the
disgrace I have endured among my people."

The Birth of Jesus Foretold

1:26-28 **Nazareth:** This was a small town in southern Galilee, a region in northern Palestine that included the Sea of Galilee (see Map 12, p. 2109). Most of Jesus' ministry takes place in this region. Joseph is a descendant of David, the youngest son of Jesse, who became King of Israel. God had promised that David's throne or kingship would go on forever (see 2 Sam 7; Isa 11:1-3).

The Gospel of Luke begins and ends in the temple. See the introduction, pp. 1694–1695.

26 In the sixth month the angel Gabriel was sent by God to a
town in Galilee called Nazareth, 27to a virgin engaged to a man whose
name was Joseph, of the house of David. The virgin's name was Mary.

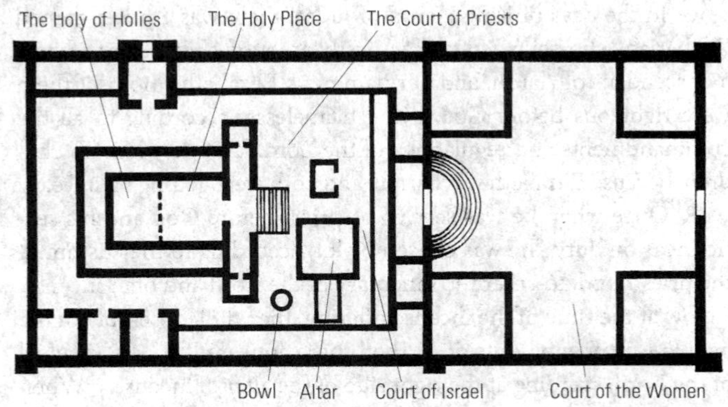

The Interior of the Temple in Jerusalem, New Testament Times

28 And he came to her and said, "Greetings, favored one! The Lord is
with you."[a] 29 But she was much perplexed by his words and pondered
what sort of greeting this might be. 30 The angel said to her, "Do not be
afraid, Mary, for you have found favor with God. 31 And now, you will
conceive in your womb and bear a son, and you will name him Jesus.
32 He will be great, and will be called the Son of the Most High, and
the Lord God will give to him the throne of his ancestor David. 33 He
will reign over the house of Jacob forever, and of his kingdom there
will be no end." 34 Mary said to the angel, "How can this be, since I am
a virgin?"[b] 35 The angel said to her, "The Holy Spirit will come upon
you, and the power of the Most High will overshadow you; therefore
the child to be born[c] will be holy; he will be called Son of God. 36 And
now, your relative Elizabeth in her old age has also conceived a son;
and this is the sixth month for her who was said to be barren. 37 For
nothing will be impossible with God." 38 Then Mary said, "Here am
I, the servant of the Lord; let it be with me according to your word."
Then the angel departed from her.

Mary Visits Elizabeth

39 In those days Mary set out and went with haste to a Judean
town in the hill country, 40 where she entered the house of Zechariah and greeted Elizabeth. 41 When Elizabeth heard Mary's greeting, the child leaped in her womb. And Elizabeth was filled with the
Holy Spirit 42 and exclaimed with a loud cry, "Blessed are you among
women, and blessed is the fruit of your womb. 43 And why has this
happened to me, that the mother of my Lord comes to me? 44 For as

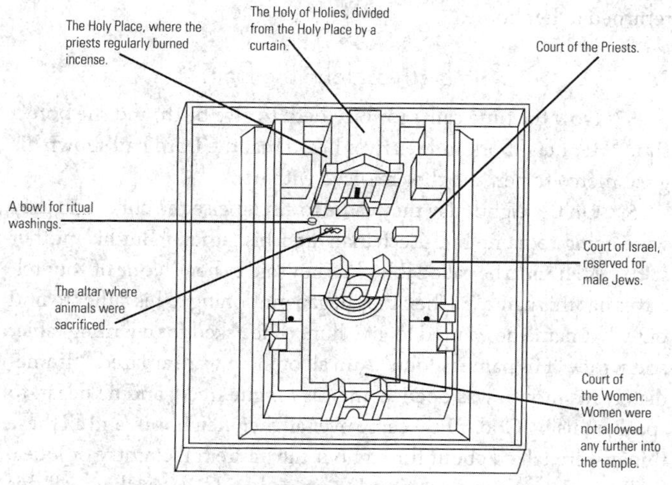
The Holy Place, where the priests regularly burned incense.
The Holy of Holies, divided from the Holy Place by a curtain.
Court of the Priests.
A bowl for ritual washings.
Court of Israel, reserved for male Jews.
The altar where animals were sacrificed.
Court of the Women. Women were not allowed any further into the temple.

The Exterior of the Temple in Jerusalem, New Testament Times

[a] Other ancient authorities add *Blessed are you among women* [b] Gk *I do not know a man* [c] Other ancient authorities add *of you*

1:31 Jesus: This name means "The Lord saves" in Hebrew.

1:36 your relative Elizabeth: The word translated as "relative" does not indicate the exact relationship between Mary and Elizabeth, it only establishes them as "kinswomen." Elizabeth is clearly older, and Mary is likely a very young woman, perhaps as young as thirteen. Luke is the only Gospel writer to suggest that the mothers of John and Jesus are related. Luke might be suggesting that Mary is also Aaron's descendant, which would make Jesus part of a priestly line. In any case, Luke shows that Jesus is born into a family of faithful Jews.

1:39 went with haste: Luke does not give reasons for Mary's quick departure. Some texts from around this period suggest that a woman in Mary's position might be stoned to death. If Mary is a member of a priestly family (see the note on 1:36), the penalty for an untimely pregnancy would have been even more severe: she would have been burned.

soon as I heard the sound of your greeting, the child in my womb
leaped for joy. 45 And blessed is she who believed that there would be[a]
a fulfillment of what was spoken to her by the Lord."

Mary's Song of Praise

46 And Mary[b] said,
"My soul magnifies the Lord,
47 and my spirit rejoices in God my Savior,
48 for he has looked with favor on the lowliness of his servant.
Surely, from now on all generations will call me blessed;
49 for the Mighty One has done great things for me,
and holy is his name.
50 His mercy is for those who fear him
from generation to generation.
51 He has shown strength with his arm;
he has scattered the proud in the thoughts of their
hearts.
52 He has brought down the powerful from their thrones,
and lifted up the lowly;
53 he has filled the hungry with good things,
and sent the rich away empty.
54 He has helped his servant Israel,
in remembrance of his mercy,
55 according to the promise he made to our ancestors,
to Abraham and to his descendants forever."

56 And Mary remained with her about three months and then
returned to her home.

The Birth of John the Baptist

57 Now the time came for Elizabeth to give birth, and she bore a
son. 58 Her neighbors and relatives heard that the Lord had shown his
great mercy to her, and they rejoiced with her.

59 On the eighth day they came to circumcise the child, and they
were going to name him Zechariah after his father. 60 But his mother
said, "No; he is to be called John." 61 They said to her, "None of your relatives has this name." 62 Then they began motioning to his father to find
out what name he wanted to give him. 63 He asked for a writing tablet
and wrote, "His name is John." And all of them were amazed. 64 Immediately his mouth was opened and his tongue freed, and he began to
speak, praising God. 65 Fear came over all their neighbors, and all these
things were talked about throughout the entire hill country of Judea.
66 All who heard them pondered them and said, "What then will this
child become?" For, indeed, the hand of the Lord was with him.

---

[a] Or *believed, for there will be* [b] Other ancient authorities read *Elizabeth*

1:46-55 My soul magnifies the Lord, and my spirit rejoices in God my Savior: Mary's song, often called the *Magnificat* ("magnify," in Latin), reveals key themes in Luke's story. Faithful Jews had been waiting for God to keep ancient promises and repair the damaged creation (see 2:25-38; 23:50-51). This would require putting down the powerful, lifting up the lowly, feeding the hungry, and sending the rich away empty (6:20-31). Mary's song begins by naming God twice, first as "the Lord," then as "God." Hebrew poetry rhymes ideas, not words, so this pattern of repetition is part of a recognizable poetic structure. The rabbis identify the unpronounceable divine name *YHWH*, translated into Greek as *kurios* (KUR-ee-os) and here as "Lord," with God acting toward creation with forgiveness, tenderness, and mercy. They identify *Elohim*, translated into Greek as *theos* (theh-OS) and here as "God," with God acting to bring about justice, either by protecting the weak or by punishing the abusive. Mary's song, then, expresses hope that God will act in both mercy and justice.

What did Martin Luther believe about Mary, the Mother of Jesus? Martin Luther had great admiration for Mary, the "Mother of God" (Mary's official title since 431 C.E.). As a monk, he was initially devoted to Mary as a saint who spoke with God on behalf of people. As Luther grew older, he no longer understood Mary in this way but continued to point out Mary's life of faithful witness. In his commentary on Mary's song, Luther said, "Here, the tender mother of Christ teaches us, with her words and by the example of her experience, how to know, love, and praise God" (*LW* 21:301). *Luke 1:46-55*

How do Lutherans describe the way God works in the world? Martin Luther's "theology of the cross" describes the way God often works through the unexpected, unlikely, and lowly. God chooses Mary, a young girl in an unknown place, to be the mother of the long-awaited Savior. God takes down the proud and powerful and sends away the rich, but lifts up the lowly, fills the hungry, and keeps promises to the people of Israel. *Luke 2:1-7*

Zechariah's Prophecy

67 Then his father Zechariah was filled with the Holy Spirit and spoke this prophecy:

68 "Blessed be the Lord God of Israel,
for he has looked favorably on his people and redeemed them.
69 He has raised up a mighty savior[a] for us
in the house of his servant David,
70 as he spoke through the mouth of his holy prophets from of old,
71 that we would be saved from our enemies and from the hand of all who hate us.
72 Thus he has shown the mercy promised to our ancestors,
and has remembered his holy covenant,
73 the oath that he swore to our ancestor Abraham,
to grant us 74 that we, being rescued from the hands of our enemies,
might serve him without fear, 75 in holiness and righteousness
before him all our days.
76 And you, child, will be called the prophet of the Most High;
for you will go before the Lord to prepare his ways,
77 to give knowledge of salvation to his people
by the forgiveness of their sins.
78 By the tender mercy of our God,
the dawn from on high will break upon[b] us,
79 to give light to those who sit in darkness and in the shadow of death,
to guide our feet into the way of peace."

80 The child grew and became strong in spirit, and he was in the wilderness until the day he appeared publicly to Israel.

The Birth of Jesus

2 In those days a decree went out from Emperor Augustus that
all the world should be registered. 2 This was the first registration and was taken while Quirinius was governor of Syria. 3 All went
to their own towns to be registered. 4 Joseph also went from the town
of Nazareth in Galilee to Judea, to the city of David called Bethlehem, because he was descended from the house and family of David.
5 He went to be registered with Mary, to whom he was engaged and
who was expecting a child. 6 While they were there, the time came for
her to deliver her child. 7 And she gave birth to her firstborn son and
wrapped him in bands of cloth, and laid him in a manger, because
there was no place for them in the inn.

[a] Gk *a horn of salvation* [b] Other ancient authorities read *has broken upon*

2:1-2 In those days: Emperor Augustus, also called Caesar Augustus, was the Roman emperor at the time Jesus was born. The registration or listing was done so that the people could be taxed by the Roman government.

2:4 Bethlehem: This means "house of bread" in Hebrew. Bethlehem is located south of Jerusalem (see Map 12, p. 2109).

2:7 no place for them in the inn: The word translated as "inn" is translated as "guest room" in 22:11. The exact meaning remains uncertain, but it may refer to a guest room in a house. Bethlehem was Joseph's hometown, so family members may have lived there. If so, the guest room might well have been in one of their houses. According to some researchers, families at that time may have shared their living quarters with valued livestock. In any case, Jesus is laid in a manger, a feed box for animals.

2:8-20 shepherds: Shepherds spent nearly all their time taking care of sheep and protecting them from thieves and wild animals. Others in society generally looked down on them.

2:11 city of David: This refers to Bethlehem, King David's hometown.

2:11 Messiah: This Hebrew name means "anointed one." Anointing involved pouring oil on someone's head to set that person apart. In Greek the name is *christos*, translated as Christ. Faithful Jews had waited centuries for the Messiah promised by God.

2:21 time to circumcise the child: Luke is the only Gospel that tells about the day of John's circumcision (1:59-66) and reports that Jesus is circumcised. Circumcision is a present-day Jewish practice that dates back to ancient times. In 163 B.C.E., an oppressive ruler named Antiochus IV Epiphanes banned circumcision. Those who continued the practice could be put to death. From that time on, circumcision became not just a religious ritual but an act of political resistance and defiant faithfulness. In Luke, Jesus and John both belong to families of devout Jews who are careful to mark their children as Jews.

2:22-38 When the time came: Jewish women participate in ritual washings to return to normal life after encountering the holy mystery of childbirth (see Lev 12). First-born sons were to be dedicated to God (see Exod 2, 12). Luke is the only Gospel that includes these events, including the encounters with Simeon and Anna.

The Shepherds and the Angels

8 In that region there were shepherds living in the fields, keeping watch over their flock by night. 9 Then an angel of the Lord stood
before them, and the glory of the Lord shone around them, and they
were terrified. 10 But the angel said to them, "Do not be afraid; for
see—I am bringing you good news of great joy for all the people: 11 to
you is born this day in the city of David a Savior, who is the Messiah,[a]
the Lord. 12 This will be a sign for you: you will find a child wrapped in
bands of cloth and lying in a manger." 13 And suddenly there was with
the angel a multitude of the heavenly host,[b] praising God and saying,

14 "Glory to God in the highest heaven,
and on earth peace among those whom he favors!"[c]

15 When the angels had left them and gone into heaven, the
shepherds said to one another, "Let us go now to Bethlehem and see
this thing that has taken place, which the Lord has made known to
us." 16 So they went with haste and found Mary and Joseph, and the
child lying in the manger. 17 When they saw this, they made known
what had been told them about this child; 18 and all who heard it were
amazed at what the shepherds told them. 19 But Mary treasured all
these words and pondered them in her heart. 20 The shepherds returned, glorifying and praising God for all they had heard and seen,
as it had been told them.

Jesus Is Named

21 After eight days had passed, it was time to circumcise the
child; and he was called Jesus, the name given by the angel before he
was conceived in the womb.

Jesus Is Presented in the Temple

22 When the time came for their purification according to the
law of Moses, they brought him up to Jerusalem to present him to the
Lord 23 (as it is written in the law of the Lord, "Every firstborn male
shall be designated as holy to the Lord"), 24 and they offered a sacrifice
according to what is stated in the law of the Lord, "a pair of turtledoves or two young pigeons."

25 Now there was a man in Jerusalem whose name was Simeon;[d]
this man was righteous and devout, looking forward to the consolation of Israel, and the Holy Spirit rested on him. 26 It had been revealed
to him by the Holy Spirit that he would not see death before he had
seen the Lord's Messiah.[e] 27 Guided by the Spirit, Simeon[f] came into
the temple; and when the parents brought in the child Jesus, to do for
him what was customary under the law, 28 Simeon[g] took him in his
arms and praised God, saying,

---

[a] Or *the Christ* [b] Gk *army* [c] Other ancient authorities read *peace, goodwill among people*
[d] Gk *Symeon* [e] Or *the Lord's Christ* [f] Gk *In the Spirit, he* [g] Gk *he*

29 “Master, now you are dismissing your servant[a] in peace,
according to your word;
30 for my eyes have seen your salvation,
31 which you have prepared in the presence of all peoples,
32 a light for revelation to the Gentiles
and for glory to your people Israel.”

33 And the child’s father and mother were amazed at what was
being said about him. 34 Then Simeon[b] blessed them and said to his
mother Mary, “This child is destined for the falling and the rising of
many in Israel, and to be a sign that will be opposed 35 so that the inner thoughts of many will be revealed—and a sword will pierce your
own soul too.”

36 There was also a prophet, Anna[c] the daughter of Phanuel, of
the tribe of Asher. She was of a great age, having lived with her husband seven years after her marriage, 37 then as a widow to the age of
eighty-four. She never left the temple but worshiped there with fasting and prayer night and day. 38 At that moment she came, and began
to praise God and to speak about the child[d] to all who were looking
for the redemption of Jerusalem.

The Return to Nazareth

39 When they had finished everything required by the law of the
Lord, they returned to Galilee, to their own town of Nazareth. 40 The
child grew and became strong, filled with wisdom; and the favor of
God was upon him.

The Boy Jesus in the Temple

41 Now every year his parents went to Jerusalem for the festival
of the Passover. 42 And when he was twelve years old, they went up as
usual for the festival. 43 When the festival was ended and they started
to return, the boy Jesus stayed behind in Jerusalem, but his parents
did not know it. 44 Assuming that he was in the group of travelers, they
went a day’s journey. Then they started to look for him among their
relatives and friends. 45 When they did not find him, they returned to
Jerusalem to search for him. 46 After three days they found him in the
temple, sitting among the teachers, listening to them and asking them
questions. 47 And all who heard him were amazed at his understanding
and his answers. 48 When his parents[e] saw him they were astonished;
and his mother said to him, “Child, why have you treated us like this?
Look, your father and I have been searching for you in great anxiety.”
49 He said to them, “Why were you searching for me? Did you not
know that I must be in my Father’s house?”[f] 50 But they did not understand what he said to them. 51 Then he went down with them and

[a] Gk *slave* [b] Gk *Symeon* [c] Gk *Hanna* [d] Gk *him* [e] Gk *they* [f] Or *be about my Father’s interests?*

2:32 a light for revelation to the Gentiles: Jesus will reveal God’s glory not only to the Jews, but to non-Jews (Gentiles). See Isaiah 42:6; 49:6; 52:10.

2:36 a prophet, Anna: A prophet is someone called to deliver God’s message. Anna is one of many women in Luke who meet Jesus and spread the good news.

2:41 every year his parents went to Jerusalem: Jesus’ family goes to Jerusalem each year for the pilgrimage festival of Passover, showing their passion for Jewish faith, tradition, and practice. See Jewish Festivals and Feasts, p. 227.

2:41-51 he was twelve years old: Jesus is at the age when a young Jewish boy is expected to show the ability to enter into living and studying Torah or God’s teachings. This is active learning that includes questioning and arguing. Jewish faith, in fact, expects respectful study to involve hard questions and faithful arguments.

What questions do you have about God, faith, or the Bible? Where can you go to ask hard questions and argue faithfully?

came to Nazareth, and was obedient to them. His mother treasured
all these things in her heart.

52 And Jesus increased in wisdom and in years,[a] and in divine
and human favor.

The Proclamation of John the Baptist

3:1-3 In the fifteenth year: Tiberius Claudius Caesar was emperor of Rome 14–37 C.E. He appointed Pontius Pilate as the Judean governor. Pilate was in this office for ten years, 26–36 C.E. Herod Antipas, son of Herod the Great, ruled Galilee 4 B.C.E.–39 C.E. Annas and Caiaphas were Jewish high priests. The Jordan is the main river in Palestine. See Map 12, p. 2109, for locations.

3 In the fifteenth year of the reign of Emperor Tiberius, when
Pontius Pilate was governor of Judea, and Herod was ruler[b]
of Galilee, and his brother Philip ruler[b] of the region of Ituraea and
Trachonitis, and Lysanias ruler[b] of Abilene, 2 during the high priest-
hood of Annas and Caiaphas, the word of God came to John son of
Zechariah in the wilderness. 3 He went into all the region around the
Jordan, proclaiming a baptism of repentance for the forgiveness of
sins, 4 as it is written in the book of the words of the prophet Isaiah,

"The voice of one crying out in the wilderness:
'Prepare the way of the Lord,
make his paths straight.
5 Every valley shall be filled,
and every mountain and hill shall be made low,
and the crooked shall be made straight,
and the rough ways made smooth;
6 and all flesh shall see the salvation of God.' "

7 John said to the crowds that came out to be baptized by him,
"You brood of vipers! Who warned you to flee from the wrath to
come? 8 Bear fruits worthy of repentance. Do not begin to say to yourselves, 'We have Abraham as our ancestor'; for I tell you, God is able
from these stones to raise up children to Abraham. 9 Even now the ax
is lying at the root of the trees; every tree therefore that does not bear
good fruit is cut down and thrown into the fire."

10 And the crowds asked him, "What then should we do?" 11 In
reply he said to them, "Whoever has two coats must share with anyone who has none; and whoever has food must do likewise." 12 Even
tax collectors came to be baptized, and they asked him, "Teacher,
what should we do?" 13 He said to them, "Collect no more than the
amount prescribed for you." 14 Soldiers also asked him, "And we, what
should we do?" He said to them, "Do not extort money from anyone
by threats or false accusation, and be satisfied with your wages."

15 As the people were filled with expectation, and all were questioning in their hearts concerning John, whether he might be the
Messiah,[c] 16 John answered all of them by saying, "I baptize you with
water; but one who is more powerful than I is coming; I am not worthy to untie the thong of his sandals. He will baptize you with[d] the
Holy Spirit and fire. 17 His winnowing fork is in his hand, to clear his

3:16 baptize: Baptism with water represented washing away the old way of life. Baptism with fire could represent judgment (see 3:17) or the Holy Spirit (see Acts 2).

3:16 untie the thong of his sandals: This would have been a slave's duty.

[a] Or *in stature* [b] Gk *tetrarch* [c] Or *the Christ* [d] Or *in*

threshing floor and to gather the wheat into his granary; but the chaff he will burn with unquenchable fire."

18 So, with many other exhortations, he proclaimed the good news to the people. 19 But Herod the ruler,[a] who had been rebuked by him because of Herodias, his brother's wife, and because of all the evil things that Herod had done, 20 added to them all by shutting up John in prison.

3:19-20 John in prison: Among other evil things Herod did, he took his sister-in-law, Herodias, as his wife. After John pointed out to Herod what he had done wrong, Herod sent him to prison.

The Baptism of Jesus

21 Now when all the people were baptized, and when Jesus also had been baptized and was praying, the heaven was opened, 22 and the Holy Spirit descended upon him in bodily form like a dove. And a voice came from heaven, "You are my Son, the Beloved;[b] with you I am well pleased."[c]

The Ancestors of Jesus

23 Jesus was about thirty years old when he began his work. He was the son (as was thought) of Joseph son of Heli, 24 son of Matthat, son of Levi, son of Melchi, son of Jannai, son of Joseph, 25 son of Mattathias, son of Amos, son of Nahum, son of Esli, son of Naggai, 26 son of Maath, son of Mattathias, son of Semein, son of Josech, son of Joda, 27 son of Joanan, son of Rhesa, son of Zerubbabel, son of Shealtiel,[d] son of Neri, 28 son of Melchi, son of Addi, son of Cosam, son of Elmadam, son of Er, 29 son of Joshua, son of Eliezer, son of Jorim, son of Matthat, son of Levi, 30 son of Simeon, son of Judah, son of Joseph, son of Jonam, son of Eliakim, 31 son of Melea, son of Menna, son of Mattatha, son of Nathan, son of David, 32 son of Jesse, son of Obed, son of Boaz, son of Sala,[e] son of Nahshon, 33 son of Amminadab, son of Admin, son of Arni,[f] son of Hezron, son of Perez, son of Judah, 34 son of Jacob, son of Isaac, son of Abraham, son of Terah, son of Nahor, 35 son of Serug, son of Reu, son of Peleg, son of Eber, son of Shelah, 36 son of Cainan, son of Arphaxad, son of Shem, son of Noah, son of Lamech, 37 son of Methuselah, son of Enoch, son of Jared, son of Mahalaleel, son of Cainan, 38 son of Enos, son of Seth, son of Adam, son of God.

3:23-38 son of David: The Jews believed the Messiah would come from David's family line (Isa 11:1-11). See also the list of Jesus' ancestors in Matthew 1:1-17.

The Temptation of Jesus

4 Jesus, full of the Holy Spirit, returned from the Jordan and was led by the Spirit in the wilderness, 2 where for forty days he was tempted by the devil. He ate nothing at all during those days, and when they were over, he was famished. 3 The devil said to him, "If you are the Son of God, command this stone to become a loaf of bread." 4 Jesus answered him, "It is written, 'One does not live by bread alone.'"

4:2 forty days: Jesus, Moses (Exod 24:18; 34:28), and Elijah (1 Kgs 19:8) all spend forty days preparing for their work.

4:2 tempted by the devil: The word translated as "tempted" might be better translated as "tested." The tester (here called "the devil") developed out of the character in the book of Job, the satan (no capital letter), who examines all of creation to check construction quality. It is his job to make sure that everything is up to code. He pokes and prods to make sure everything is as solid as God wants it to be. If more weight is going to be carried, more testing is required. In Luke, Jesus is going to carry great weight: he is the Messiah and carries the weight of centuries of Jewish hope for justice in the world.

4:3-12 bread . . . authority . . . throw yourself down: These tests echo the tests the first humans failed. Adam was offered food and ate it without question. Eve was offered a chance to be like God and took it (see Gen 3). The tester offers Jesus food, power, and even the opportunity to live without the limits of gravity. Jesus responds to each test with Scripture (see Deut 8:3; 6:13, 16).

---

[a] Gk *tetrarch* [b] Or *my beloved Son* [c] Other ancient authorities read *You are my Son, today I have begotten you* [d] Gk *Salathiel* [e] Other ancient authorities read *Salmon* [f] Other ancient authorities read *Amminadab, son of Aram*; others vary widely

Jesus faced the test to keep appetites (his wants and desires) under control and aspirations (for Jesus, his work or ministry) in balance. What would your life be like if you "fed" all of your wants and desires? What are your hopes, goals, and callings? How do you keep all of these things in balance?

4:13 an opportune time: The testing of Jesus is over—for now. See note on 22:3-6.

4:16-20 The Spirit of the Lord is upon me: A synagogue is a Jewish gathering place. The Sabbath day for Jews is a day of rest, observed on the seventh day of the week, the day God rested after creating the world (see Gen 2:2-3). Jesus reads from Isaiah 61:1-2 from a scroll, which would have been made of parchment or leather. (Compare 4:18-19 with 1:46-55 and 1:67-79.)

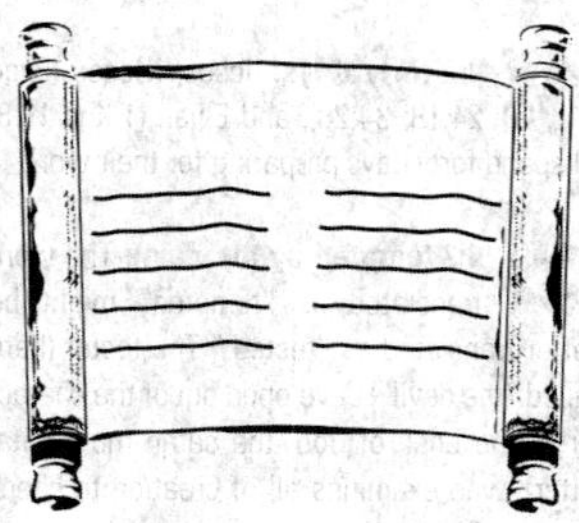

4:19 the year of the Lord's favor: This refers to the Year of Jubilee (see Lev 25:1-17). Any land that had been sold was to be returned. Any person held as a slave was to be freed. Over the centuries, the notion of "return" intensified, so that the passage from Isaiah also included the overturning of blindness and oppression. Compare this with the songs of Mary (1:46-55) and Zechariah (1:68-79).

4:22-30 All spoke well of him: The people gathered in the synagogue approve of what Jesus has said. The question ("Is not this Joseph's son?") does not imply rejection, only amazement. This makes Jesus' words in 4:24 puzzling.

5 Then the devil[a] led him up and showed him in an instant all the
kingdoms of the world. 6 And the devil[a] said to him, "To you I will give
their glory and all this authority; for it has been given over to me, and
I give it to anyone I please. 7 If you, then, will worship me, it will all be
yours." 8 Jesus answered him, "It is written,

'Worship the Lord your God,
    and serve only him.'"

9 Then the devil[a] took him to Jerusalem, and placed him on the
pinnacle of the temple, saying to him, "If you are the Son of God,
throw yourself down from here, 10 for it is written,

'He will command his angels concerning you,
    to protect you,'

11 and

'On their hands they will bear you up,
    so that you will not dash your foot against a stone.'"

12 Jesus answered him, "It is said, 'Do not put the Lord your God to the
test.'" 13 When the devil had finished every test, he departed from him
until an opportune time.

The Beginning of the Galilean Ministry

14 Then Jesus, filled with the power of the Spirit, returned to
Galilee, and a report about him spread through all the surrounding
country. 15 He began to teach in their synagogues and was praised by
everyone.

The Rejection of Jesus at Nazareth

16 When he came to Nazareth, where he had been brought up,
he went to the synagogue on the sabbath day, as was his custom. He
stood up to read, 17 and the scroll of the prophet Isaiah was given to
him. He unrolled the scroll and found the place where it was written:

18 "The Spirit of the Lord is upon me,
    because he has anointed me
        to bring good news to the poor.
He has sent me to proclaim release to the captives
    and recovery of sight to the blind,
        to let the oppressed go free,
19 to proclaim the year of the Lord's favor."

20 And he rolled up the scroll, gave it back to the attendant, and sat
down. The eyes of all in the synagogue were fixed on him. 21 Then he
began to say to them, "Today this scripture has been fulfilled in your
hearing." 22 All spoke well of him and were amazed at the gracious
words that came from his mouth. They said, "Is not this Joseph's son?"
23 He said to them, "Doubtless you will quote to me this proverb, 'Doctor, cure yourself!' And you will say, 'Do here also in your hometown

---

[a] Gk *he*

the things that we have heard you did at Capernaum.' " 24 And he said, "Truly I tell you, no prophet is accepted in the prophet's hometown. 25 But the truth is, there were many widows in Israel in the time of Elijah, when the heaven was shut up three years and six months, and there was a severe famine over all the land; 26 yet Elijah was sent to none of them except to a widow at Zarephath in Sidon. 27 There were also many lepers[a] in Israel in the time of the prophet Elisha, and none of them was cleansed except Naaman the Syrian." 28 When they heard this, all in the synagogue were filled with rage. 29 They got up, drove him out of the town, and led him to the brow of the hill on which their town was built, so that they might hurl him off the cliff. 30 But he passed through the midst of them and went on his way.

The Man with an Unclean Spirit

31 He went down to Capernaum, a city in Galilee, and was teaching them on the sabbath. 32 They were astounded at his teaching, because he spoke with authority. 33 In the synagogue there was a man who had the spirit of an unclean demon, and he cried out with a loud voice, 34 "Let us alone! What have you to do with us, Jesus of Nazareth? Have you come to destroy us? I know who you are, the Holy One of God." 35 But Jesus rebuked him, saying, "Be silent, and come out of him!" When the demon had thrown him down before them, he came out of him without having done him any harm. 36 They were all amazed and kept saying to one another, "What kind of utterance is this? For with authority and power he commands the unclean spirits, and out they come!" 37 And a report about him began to reach every place in the region.

4:33-37 unclean spirits: Demons and unclean spirits were thought to cause many illnesses.

Healings at Simon's House

38 After leaving the synagogue he entered Simon's house. Now Simon's mother-in-law was suffering from a high fever, and they asked him about her. 39 Then he stood over her and rebuked the fever, and it left her. Immediately she got up and began to serve them.

40 As the sun was setting, all those who had any who were sick with various kinds of diseases brought them to him; and he laid his hands on each of them and cured them. 41 Demons also came out of many, shouting, "You are the Son of God!" But he rebuked them and would not allow them to speak, because they knew that he was the Messiah.[b]

4:38-41 Simon's house: Simon, also called Peter, was one of Jesus' first disciples (see 5:3-11).

Jesus Preaches in the Synagogues

42 At daybreak he departed and went into a deserted place. And the crowds were looking for him; and when they reached him, they wanted to prevent him from leaving them. 43 But he said to them, "I

---

[a] The terms *leper* and *leprosy* can refer to several diseases [b] Or *the Christ*

4:43 the kingdom of God: God's kingdom is not in one location. It exists wherever God's will is done.

must proclaim the good news of the kingdom of God to the other cities also; for I was sent for this purpose." 44 So he continued proclaiming the message in the synagogues of Judea.[a]

Jesus Calls the First Disciples

5:3 sat down: Teachers at the time were usually seated as they taught.

5 Once while Jesus[b] was standing beside the lake of Gennesaret, and the crowd was pressing in on him to hear the word of God, 2 he saw two boats there at the shore of the lake; the fishermen had gone out of them and were washing their nets. 3 He got into one of the boats, the one belonging to Simon, and asked him to put out a little way from the shore. Then he sat down and taught the crowds from the boat. 4 When he had finished speaking, he said to Simon, "Put out into the deep water and let down your nets for a catch." 5 Simon answered, "Master, we have worked all night long but have caught nothing. Yet if you say so, I will let down the nets." 6 When they had done this, they caught so many fish that their nets were beginning to break. 7 So they signaled their partners in the other boat to come and help them. And they came and filled both boats, so that they began to sink. 8 But when Simon Peter saw it, he fell down at Jesus' knees, saying, "Go away from me, Lord, for I am a sinful man!" 9 For he and all who were with him were amazed at the catch of fish that they had taken; 10 and so also were James and John, sons of Zebedee, who were partners with Simon. Then Jesus said to Simon, "Do not be afraid; from now on you will be catching people." 11 When they had brought their boats to shore, they left everything and followed him.

Jesus Cleanses a Leper

5:12-14 leprosy: The word translated here as "leprosy" could refer to several types of skin diseases. Because people with leprosy were seen as "unclean," and anyone who touched them became unclean as well, they usually lived away from others. Healing of leprosy had to be confirmed by a priest before a person could rejoin the community. (See Lev 13–14.)

12 Once, when he was in one of the cities, there was a man covered with leprosy.[c] When he saw Jesus, he bowed with his face to the ground and begged him, "Lord, if you choose, you can make me clean." 13 Then Jesus[b] stretched out his hand, touched him, and said, "I do choose. Be made clean." Immediately the leprosy[c] left him. 14 And he ordered him to tell no one. "Go," he said, "and show yourself to the priest, and, as Moses commanded, make an offering for your cleansing, for a testimony to them." 15 But now more than ever the word about Jesus[d] spread abroad; many crowds would gather to hear him and to be cured of their diseases. 16 But he would withdraw to deserted places and pray.

Jesus Heals a Paralytic

5:17 Pharisees and teachers of the law: The Pharisees were devoted, faithful Jews who practiced living as if the stable orderly love of God were the most important thing in the universe. They conducted their lives, in fact, as if they were living in the temple. The teachers studied God's teachings and worked to help people shape their everyday lives according to tradition and Scripture.

17 One day, while he was teaching, Pharisees and teachers of the law were sitting near by (they had come from every village of Galilee and Judea and from Jerusalem); and the power of the Lord was with

---

[a] Other ancient authorities read *Galilee* [b] Gk *he* [c] The terms *leper* and *leprosy* can refer to several diseases [d] Gk *him*

him to heal.[a] 18 Just then some men came, carrying a paralyzed man
on a bed. They were trying to bring him in and lay him before Jesus;[b]
19 but finding no way to bring him in because of the crowd, they went
up on the roof and let him down with his bed through the tiles into
the middle of the crowd[c] in front of Jesus. 20 When he saw their faith,
he said, "Friend,[d] your sins are forgiven you." 21 Then the scribes and
the Pharisees began to question, "Who is this who is speaking blasphemies? Who can forgive sins but God alone?" 22 When Jesus perceived their questionings, he answered them, "Why do you raise
such questions in your hearts? 23 Which is easier, to say, 'Your sins are
forgiven you,' or to say, 'Stand up and walk'? 24 But so that you may
know that the Son of Man has authority on earth to forgive sins"—he
said to the one who was paralyzed—"I say to you, stand up and take
your bed and go to your home." 25 Immediately he stood up before
them, took what he had been lying on, and went to his home, glorifying God. 26 Amazement seized all of them, and they glorified God and
were filled with awe, saying, "We have seen strange things today."

5:19 up on the roof: Houses in Palestine at this time generally had flat roofs covered with packed dirt or occasionally clay tiles.

Jesus Calls Levi

27 After this he went out and saw a tax collector named Levi, sitting at the tax booth; and he said to him, "Follow me." 28 And he got
up, left everything, and followed him.

29 Then Levi gave a great banquet for him in his house; and there
was a large crowd of tax collectors and others sitting at the table[e] with
them. 30 The Pharisees and their scribes were complaining to his disciples, saying, "Why do you eat and drink with tax collectors and
sinners?" 31 Jesus answered, "Those who are well have no need of a
physician, but those who are sick; 32 I have come to call not the righteous but sinners to repentance."

5:27-32 tax collector named Levi: Tax collectors were Jews who collaborated with the occupying Roman forces and brought in taxes for them.

The Question about Fasting

33 Then they said to him, "John's disciples, like the disciples of the
Pharisees, frequently fast and pray, but your disciples eat and drink."
34 Jesus said to them, "You cannot make wedding guests fast while the
bridegroom is with them, can you? 35 The days will come when the
bridegroom will be taken away from them, and then they will fast in
those days." 36 He also told them a parable: "No one tears a piece from
a new garment and sews it on an old garment; otherwise the new will
be torn, and the piece from the new will not match the old. 37 And no
one puts new wine into old wineskins; otherwise the new wine will
burst the skins and will be spilled, and the skins will be destroyed.
38 But new wine must be put into fresh wineskins. 39 And no one after
drinking old wine desires new wine, but says, 'The old is good.' "[f]

---

[a] Other ancient authorities read *was present to heal them* [b] Gk *him* [c] Gk *into the midst* [d] Gk *Man*
[e] Gk *reclining* [f] Other ancient authorities read *better*; others lack verse 39

The Question about the Sabbath

6 One sabbath[a] while Jesus[b] was going through the grainfields,
his disciples plucked some heads of grain, rubbed them in their
hands, and ate them. 2 But some of the Pharisees said, "Why are you
doing what is not lawful[c] on the sabbath?" 3 Jesus answered, "Have
you not read what David did when he and his companions were hungry? 4 He entered the house of God and took and ate the bread of the
Presence, which it is not lawful for any but the priests to eat, and gave
some to his companions?" 5 Then he said to them, "The Son of Man is
lord of the sabbath."

6:1 plucked some heads of grain: Jewish practice seeks to preserve Sabbath as a monument to life, so rest is the order of the day, unless a life needs saving. In that case, all commands to rest are suspended, both in the ancient world and now.

6:2 what is not lawful on the sabbath: The Pharisees say that Jesus' disciples are breaking the law against working on the Sabbath (Exod 20:10; Deut 5:14).

The Man with a Withered Hand

6 On another sabbath he entered the synagogue and taught, and
there was a man there whose right hand was withered. 7 The scribes
and the Pharisees watched him to see whether he would cure on the
sabbath, so that they might find an accusation against him. 8 Even
though he knew what they were thinking, he said to the man who
had the withered hand, "Come and stand here." He got up and stood
there. 9 Then Jesus said to them, "I ask you, is it lawful to do good or to
do harm on the sabbath, to save life or to destroy it?" 10 After looking
around at all of them, he said to him, "Stretch out your hand." He did
so, and his hand was restored. 11 But they were filled with fury and discussed with one another what they might do to Jesus.

Jesus Chooses the Twelve Apostles

12 Now during those days he went out to the mountain to pray;
and he spent the night in prayer to God. 13 And when day came, he
called his disciples and chose twelve of them, whom he also named
apostles: 14 Simon, whom he named Peter, and his brother Andrew,
and James, and John, and Philip, and Bartholomew, 15 and Matthew,
and Thomas, and James son of Alphaeus, and Simon, who was called
the Zealot, 16 and Judas son of James, and Judas Iscariot, who became
a traitor.

6:12 mountain: In Luke, mountains are often connected to important events in Jesus' ministry (4:5; 9:28; 19:29).

6:13-16 chose twelve: Jews see twelve as a sacred number. There were also twelve tribes of Israel. A disciple is someone who follows a teacher. An apostle is someone sent to carry a message.

Jesus Teaches and Heals

17 He came down with them and stood on a level place, with a
great crowd of his disciples and a great multitude of people from all
Judea, Jerusalem, and the coast of Tyre and Sidon. 18 They had come
to hear him and to be healed of their diseases; and those who were
troubled with unclean spirits were cured. 19 And all in the crowd were
trying to touch him, for power came out from him and healed all of
them.

---

[a] Other ancient authorities read *On the second first sabbath* [b] Gk *he* [c] Other ancient authorities add *to do*

Blessings and Woes

20 Then he looked up at his disciples and said:
"Blessed are you who are poor,
for yours is the kingdom of God.
21 "Blessed are you who are hungry now,
for you will be filled.
"Blessed are you who weep now,
for you will laugh.
22 "Blessed are you when people hate you, and when they exclude you, revile you, and defame you[a] on account of the Son of Man.
23 Rejoice in that day and leap for joy, for surely your reward is great in
heaven; for that is what their ancestors did to the prophets.
24 "But woe to you who are rich,
for you have received your consolation.
25 "Woe to you who are full now,
for you will be hungry.
"Woe to you who are laughing now,
for you will mourn and weep.
26 "Woe to you when all speak well of you, for that is what their
ancestors did to the false prophets.

Love for Enemies

27 "But I say to you that listen, Love your enemies, do good to
those who hate you, 28 bless those who curse you, pray for those who
abuse you. 29 If anyone strikes you on the cheek, offer the other also;
and from anyone who takes away your coat do not withhold even
your shirt. 30 Give to everyone who begs from you; and if anyone takes
away your goods, do not ask for them again. 31 Do to others as you
would have them do to you.
32 "If you love those who love you, what credit is that to you?
For even sinners love those who love them. 33 If you do good to those
who do good to you, what credit is that to you? For even sinners do
the same. 34 If you lend to those from whom you hope to receive, what
credit is that to you? Even sinners lend to sinners, to receive as much
again. 35 But love your enemies, do good, and lend, expecting nothing
in return.[b] Your reward will be great, and you will be children of the
Most High; for he is kind to the ungrateful and the wicked. 36 Be merciful, just as your Father is merciful.

Judging Others

37 "Do not judge, and you will not be judged; do not condemn,
and you will not be condemned. Forgive, and you will be forgiven;
38 give, and it will be given to you. A good measure, pressed down,

[a] Gk *cast out your name as evil* [b] Other ancient authorities read *despairing of no one*

6:20-26 Blessed are you who are poor: The situation of the poor, hungry, and weeping will be reversed. The lowly are lifted up, and the powerful are brought down, the hungry are filled, and the rich are sent away empty. (Compare with 1:46-55 and 4:18-19.)

The way things usually are in the world is turned upside-down in Luke 6:20-26. What might be dangerous about thinking the world needs to be turned upside down (or maybe right-side-up) like this? What might be dangerous about thinking that this should *not* happen?

6:20 the kingdom of God: See note on 4:43.

6:35 children of the Most High: Believers are God's children, and they are to be loving, kind, and merciful like God.

shaken together, running over, will be put into your lap; for the measure you give will be the measure you get back."

39 He also told them a parable: "Can a blind person guide a blind person? Will not both fall into a pit? 40 A disciple is not above the teacher, but everyone who is fully qualified will be like the teacher. 41 Why do you see the speck in your neighbor's[a] eye, but do not notice the log in your own eye? 42 Or how can you say to your neighbor,[b] 'Friend,[b] let me take out the speck in your eye,' when you yourself do not see the log in your own eye? You hypocrite, first take the log out of your own eye, and then you will see clearly to take the speck out of your neighbor's[a] eye.

A Tree and Its Fruit

43 "No good tree bears bad fruit, nor again does a bad tree bear good fruit; 44 for each tree is known by its own fruit. Figs are not gathered from thorns, nor are grapes picked from a bramble bush. 45 The good person out of the good treasure of the heart produces good, and the evil person out of evil treasure produces evil; for it is out of the abundance of the heart that the mouth speaks.

The Two Foundations

46 "Why do you call me 'Lord, Lord,' and do not do what I tell you? 47 I will show you what someone is like who comes to me, hears my words, and acts on them. 48 That one is like a man building a house, who dug deeply and laid the foundation on rock; when a flood arose, the river burst against that house but could not shake it, because it had been well built.[c] 49 But the one who hears and does not act is like a man who built a house on the ground without a foundation. When the river burst against it, immediately it fell, and great was the ruin of that house."

Jesus Heals a Centurion's Servant

7:1 Capernaum: This was a fishing town and Roman military base.

7:2 centurion: A centurion was a Roman military leader of one hundred men.

7:3 Jewish elders: This probably refers to respected local leaders.

7 After Jesus[d] had finished all his sayings in the hearing of the people, he entered Capernaum. 2 A centurion there had a slave whom he valued highly, and who was ill and close to death. 3 When he heard about Jesus, he sent some Jewish elders to him, asking him to come and heal his slave. 4 When they came to Jesus, they appealed to him earnestly, saying, "He is worthy of having you do this for him, 5 for he loves our people, and it is he who built our synagogue for us." 6 And Jesus went with them, but when he was not far from the house, the centurion sent friends to say to him, "Lord, do not trouble yourself, for I am not worthy to have you come under my roof; 7 therefore I did not presume to come to you. But only speak the word, and let my servant be healed. 8 For I also am a man set under authority, with soldiers

---

[a] Gk *brother's* [b] Gk *brother* [c] Other ancient authorities read *founded upon the rock* [d] Gk *he*

under me; and I say to one, 'Go,' and he goes, and to another, 'Come,'
and he comes, and to my slave, 'Do this,' and the slave does it." 9When
Jesus heard this he was amazed at him, and turning to the crowd that
followed him, he said, "I tell you, not even in Israel have I found such
faith." 10When those who had been sent returned to the house, they
found the slave in good health.

Jesus Raises the Widow's Son at Nain

11 Soon afterwards[a] he went to a town called Nain, and his disciples and a large crowd went with him. 12As he approached the gate
of the town, a man who had died was being carried out. He was his
mother's only son, and she was a widow; and with her was a large
crowd from the town. 13When the Lord saw her, he had compassion
for her and said to her, "Do not weep." 14Then he came forward and
touched the bier, and the bearers stood still. And he said, "Young man,
I say to you, rise!" 15The dead man sat up and began to speak, and
Jesus[b] gave him to his mother. 16Fear seized all of them; and they glorified God, saying, "A great prophet has risen among us!" and "God
has looked favorably on his people!" 17This word about him spread
throughout Judea and all the surrounding country.

Messengers from John the Baptist

18 The disciples of John reported all these things to him. So John
summoned two of his disciples 19and sent them to the Lord to ask, "Are
you the one who is to come, or are we to wait for another?" 20When
the men had come to him, they said, "John the Baptist has sent us to
you to ask, 'Are you the one who is to come, or are we to wait for another?' " 21Jesus[c] had just then cured many people of diseases, plagues,
and evil spirits, and had given sight to many who were blind. 22And he
answered them, "Go and tell John what you have seen and heard: the
blind receive their sight, the lame walk, the lepers[d] are cleansed, the
deaf hear, the dead are raised, the poor have good news brought to
them. 23And blessed is anyone who takes no offense at me."

24 When John's messengers had gone, Jesus[b] began to speak to
the crowds about John:[e] "What did you go out into the wilderness
to look at? A reed shaken by the wind? 25What then did you go out
to see? Someone[f] dressed in soft robes? Look, those who put on fine
clothing and live in luxury are in royal palaces. 26What then did you go
out to see? A prophet? Yes, I tell you, and more than a prophet. 27This
is the one about whom it is written,

'See, I am sending my messenger ahead of you,
who will prepare your way before you.'

28I tell you, among those born of women no one is greater than John;

[a] Other ancient authorities read *Next day* [b] Gk *he* [c] Gk *He* [d] The terms *leper* and *leprosy* can refer to several diseases [e] Gk *him* [f] Or *Why then did you go out? To see someone*

7:12 man who had died: According to Jewish custom, a dead body was usually carried to a tomb the same day the person died.

7:14-17 rise: The prophet Elijah also raised a widow's dead son (1 Kgs 17:8-24). Jesus would also raise Jairus's daughter (8:40-56) and Lazarus (John 11:38-44).

yet the least in the kingdom of God is greater than he." 29 (And all the
people who heard this, including the tax collectors, acknowledged
the justice of God,[a] because they had been baptized with John's baptism. 30 But by refusing to be baptized by him, the Pharisees and the
lawyers rejected God's purpose for themselves.)

31 "To what then will I compare the people of this generation,
and what are they like? 32 They are like children sitting in the marketplace and calling to one another,

'We played the flute for you, and you did not dance;
we wailed, and you did not weep.'

33 For John the Baptist has come eating no bread and drinking no wine,
and you say, 'He has a demon'; 34 the Son of Man has come eating and
drinking, and you say, 'Look, a glutton and a drunkard, a friend of tax
collectors and sinners!' 35 Nevertheless, wisdom is vindicated by all
her children."

A Sinful Woman Forgiven

36 One of the Pharisees asked Jesus[b] to eat with him, and he
went into the Pharisee's house and took his place at the table. 37 And
a woman in the city, who was a sinner, having learned that he was eating in the Pharisee's house, brought an alabaster jar of ointment. 38 She
stood behind him at his feet, weeping, and began to bathe his feet with
her tears and to dry them with her hair. Then she continued kissing
his feet and anointing them with the ointment. 39 Now when the Pharisee who had invited him saw it, he said to himself, "If this man were a
prophet, he would have known who and what kind of woman this is
who is touching him—that she is a sinner." 40 Jesus spoke up and said
to him, "Simon, I have something to say to you." "Teacher," he replied,
"speak." 41 "A certain creditor had two debtors; one owed five hundred
denarii,[c] and the other fifty. 42 When they could not pay, he canceled
the debts for both of them. Now which of them will love him more?"
43 Simon answered, "I suppose the one for whom he canceled the
greater debt." And Jesus[d] said to him, "You have judged rightly." 44 Then
turning toward the woman, he said to Simon, "Do you see this woman?
I entered your house; you gave me no water for my feet, but she has
bathed my feet with her tears and dried them with her hair. 45 You gave
me no kiss, but from the time I came in she has not stopped kissing my
feet. 46 You did not anoint my head with oil, but she has anointed my
feet with ointment. 47 Therefore, I tell you, her sins, which were many,
have been forgiven; hence she has shown great love. But the one to
whom little is forgiven, loves little." 48 Then he said to her, "Your sins
are forgiven." 49 But those who were at the table with him began to say
among themselves, "Who is this who even forgives sins?" 50 And he
said to the woman, "Your faith has saved you; go in peace."

7:37 alabaster jar: Alabaster is a very soft, valuable stone.

7:41 denarii: One of these coins, a denarius, equaled about one day's pay for a common laborer.

7:44-46 entered your house: Guests in a Jewish home were welcomed with a kiss on the cheek, water to wash their feet, and often olive oil poured on their heads.

---

[a] Or *praised God* [b] Gk *him* [c] The denarius was the usual day's wage for a laborer [d] Gk *he*

Some Women Accompany Jesus

8 Soon afterwards he went on through cities and villages, proclaiming and bringing the good news of the kingdom of God.
The twelve were with him, 2 as well as some women who had been
cured of evil spirits and infirmities: Mary, called Magdalene, from
whom seven demons had gone out, 3 and Joanna, the wife of Herod's
steward Chuza, and Susanna, and many others, who provided for
them[a] out of their resources.

8:2 Mary, called Magdalene: The name "Magdalene" indicates that Mary was from a small town next to the Sea of Galilee. She is present when Jesus dies, is buried, and is raised from the dead (23:49, 55; 24:1, 8-10). (See also Mark 15:40-41, 47; 16:1, 9.)

8:3 Joanna...Susanna: It was not unusual for women to provide Jewish teachers with money. These women and others seem to have traveled with Jesus and helped support his ministry. Susanna is not mentioned again, but Joanna is named as one of the women at Jesus' empty tomb (24:10). Joanna's husband, Chuza, worked for Herod Antipas, ruler of Galilee.

The Parable of the Sower

4 When a great crowd gathered and people from town after town
came to him, he said in a parable: 5 "A sower went out to sow his seed;
and as he sowed, some fell on the path and was trampled on, and the
birds of the air ate it up. 6 Some fell on the rock; and as it grew up,
it withered for lack of moisture. 7 Some fell among thorns, and the
thorns grew with it and choked it. 8 Some fell into good soil, and when
it grew, it produced a hundredfold." As he said this, he called out, "Let
anyone with ears to hear listen!"

The Purpose of the Parables

9 Then his disciples asked him what this parable meant. 10 He
said, "To you it has been given to know the secrets[b] of the kingdom of
God; but to others I speak[c] in parables, so that

'looking they may not perceive,
and listening they may not understand.'

8:10 the kingdom of God: See note on 4:43.

The Parable of the Sower Explained

11 "Now the parable is this: The seed is the word of God. 12 The
ones on the path are those who have heard; then the devil comes and
takes away the word from their hearts, so that they may not believe
and be saved. 13 The ones on the rock are those who, when they hear
the word, receive it with joy. But these have no root; they believe only
for a while and in a time of testing fall away. 14 As for what fell among
the thorns, these are the ones who hear; but as they go on their way,
they are choked by the cares and riches and pleasures of life, and their
fruit does not mature. 15 But as for that in the good soil, these are the
ones who, when they hear the word, hold it fast in an honest and good
heart, and bear fruit with patient endurance.

A Lamp under a Jar

16 "No one after lighting a lamp hides it under a jar, or puts it
under a bed, but puts it on a lampstand, so that those who enter may
see the light. 17 For nothing is hidden that will not be disclosed, nor

---

[a] Other ancient authorities read *him* [b] Or *mysteries* [c] Gk lacks *I speak*

is anything secret that will not become known and come to light.
[18]Then pay attention to how you listen; for to those who have, more
will be given; and from those who do not have, even what they seem
to have will be taken away."

The True Kindred of Jesus

19 Then his mother and his brothers came to him, but they could
not reach him because of the crowd. [20]And he was told, "Your mother
and your brothers are standing outside, wanting to see you." [21]But he
said to them, "My mother and my brothers are those who hear the
word of God and do it."

Jesus Calms a Storm

22 One day he got into a boat with his disciples, and he said to
them, "Let us go across to the other side of the lake." So they put out,
[23]and while they were sailing he fell asleep. A windstorm swept down
on the lake, and the boat was filling with water, and they were in danger. [24]They went to him and woke him up, shouting, "Master, Master,
we are perishing!" And he woke up and rebuked the wind and the
raging waves; they ceased, and there was a calm. [25]He said to them,
"Where is your faith?" They were afraid and amazed, and said to one
another, "Who then is this, that he commands even the winds and the
water, and they obey him?"

Jesus Heals the Gerasene Demoniac

8:26 country of the Gerasenes: The people, architecture, and lifestyle in this area east of the Jordan River were mainly Greek.

8:27-39 demons: See note on 4:33-37.

26 Then they arrived at the country of the Gerasenes,[a] which is
opposite Galilee. [27]As he stepped out on land, a man of the city who
had demons met him. For a long time he had worn[b] no clothes, and
he did not live in a house but in the tombs. [28]When he saw Jesus, he
fell down before him and shouted at the top of his voice, "What have
you to do with me, Jesus, Son of the Most High God? I beg you, do
not torment me"— [29]for Jesus[c] had commanded the unclean spirit
to come out of the man. (For many times it had seized him; he was
kept under guard and bound with chains and shackles, but he would
break the bonds and be driven by the demon into the wilds.) [30]Jesus
then asked him, "What is your name?" He said, "Legion"; for many
demons had entered him. [31]They begged him not to order them to go
back into the abyss.

32 Now there on the hillside a large herd of swine was feeding;
and the demons[d] begged Jesus[e] to let them enter these. So he gave
them permission. [33]Then the demons came out of the man and entered the swine, and the herd rushed down the steep bank into the
lake and was drowned.

---

[a] Other ancient authorities read *Gadarenes;* others, *Gergesenes* [b] Other ancient authorities read *a man of the city who had had demons for a long time met him. He wore* [c] Gk *he* [d] Gk *they* [e] Gk *him*

34 When the swineherds saw what had happened, they ran off
and told it in the city and in the country. 35 Then people came out to
see what had happened, and when they came to Jesus, they found
the man from whom the demons had gone sitting at the feet of Jesus,
clothed and in his right mind. And they were afraid. 36 Those who had
seen it told them how the one who had been possessed by demons
had been healed. 37 Then all the people of the surrounding country
of the Gerasenes[a] asked Jesus[b] to leave them; for they were seized
with great fear. So he got into the boat and returned. 38 The man from
whom the demons had gone begged that he might be with him; but
Jesus[c] sent him away, saying, 39 "Return to your home, and declare how
much God has done for you." So he went away, proclaiming throughout the city how much Jesus had done for him.

A Girl Restored to Life and a Woman Healed

40 Now when Jesus returned, the crowd welcomed him, for they
were all waiting for him. 41 Just then there came a man named Jairus, a
leader of the synagogue. He fell at Jesus' feet and begged him to come
to his house, 42 for he had an only daughter, about twelve years old,
who was dying.

As he went, the crowds pressed in on him. 43 Now there was a
woman who had been suffering from hemorrhages for twelve years;
and though she had spent all she had on physicians,[d] no one could
cure her. 44 She came up behind him and touched the fringe of his
clothes, and immediately her hemorrhage stopped. 45 Then Jesus
asked, "Who touched me?" When all denied it, Peter[e] said, "Master, the crowds surround you and press in on you." 46 But Jesus said,
"Someone touched me; for I noticed that power had gone out from
me." 47 When the woman saw that she could not remain hidden, she
came trembling; and falling down before him, she declared in the
presence of all the people why she had touched him, and how she had
been immediately healed. 48 He said to her, "Daughter, your faith has
made you well; go in peace."

49 While he was still speaking, someone came from the leader's
house to say, "Your daughter is dead; do not trouble the teacher any
longer." 50 When Jesus heard this, he replied, "Do not fear. Only believe, and she will be saved." 51 When he came to the house, he did
not allow anyone to enter with him, except Peter, John, and James,
and the child's father and mother. 52 They were all weeping and wailing
for her; but he said, "Do not weep; for she is not dead but sleeping."
53 And they laughed at him, knowing that she was dead. 54 But he took
her by the hand and called out, "Child, get up!" 55 Her spirit returned,

8:51 Peter, John, and James: John and James were brothers (5:1-10). All three were fishermen called to follow Jesus. They would also be with Jesus when his glory was revealed on a mountaintop (see 9:28-36). (See also Mark 14:33.)

---

[a] Other ancient authorities read *Gadarenes;* others, *Gergesenes* [b] Gk *him* [c] Gk *he* [d] Other ancient authorities lack *and though she had spent all she had on physicians* [e] Other ancient authorities add *and those who were with him*

and she got up at once. Then he directed them to give her something
to eat. 56 Her parents were astounded; but he ordered them to tell no
one what had happened.

The Mission of the Twelve

9 Then Jesus[a] called the twelve together and gave them power
and authority over all demons and to cure diseases, 2 and he
sent them out to proclaim the kingdom of God and to heal. 3 He said
to them, "Take nothing for your journey, no staff, nor bag, nor bread,
nor money—not even an extra tunic. 4 Whatever house you enter,
stay there, and leave from there. 5 Wherever they do not welcome you,
as you are leaving that town shake the dust off your feet as a testimony
against them." 6 They departed and went through the villages, bringing
the good news and curing diseases everywhere.

9:5 shake the dust off your feet: This was a way to reject someone.

Herod's Perplexity

7 Now Herod the ruler[b] heard about all that had taken place, and
he was perplexed, because it was said by some that John had been
raised from the dead, 8 by some that Elijah had appeared, and by others that one of the ancient prophets had arisen. 9 Herod said, "John I
beheaded; but who is this about whom I hear such things?" And he
tried to see him.

Feeding the Five Thousand

10 On their return the apostles told Jesus[c] all they had done. He
took them with him and withdrew privately to a city called Bethsaida.
11 When the crowds found out about it, they followed him; and he
welcomed them, and spoke to them about the kingdom of God, and
healed those who needed to be cured.

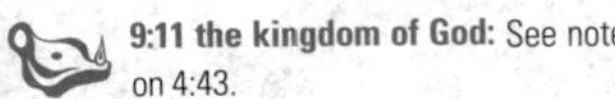

9:11 the kingdom of God: See note on 4:43.

12 The day was drawing to a close, and the twelve came to him
and said, "Send the crowd away, so that they may go into the surrounding villages and countryside, to lodge and get provisions; for
we are here in a deserted place." 13 But he said to them, "You give
them something to eat." They said, "We have no more than five
loaves and two fish—unless we are to go and buy food for all these
people." 14 For there were about five thousand men. And he said to
his disciples, "Make them sit down in groups of about fifty each."
15 They did so and made them all sit down. 16 And taking the five
loaves and the two fish, he looked up to heaven, and blessed and
broke them, and gave them to the disciples to set before the crowd.
17 And all ate and were filled. What was left over was gathered up,
twelve baskets of broken pieces.

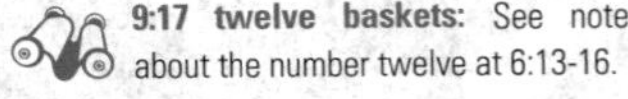

9:17 twelve baskets: See note about the number twelve at 6:13-16.

[a] Gk *he* [b] Gk *tetrarch* [c] Gk *him*

Peter's Declaration about Jesus

18 Once when Jesus[a] was praying alone, with only the disciples
near him, he asked them, "Who do the crowds say that I am?" 19 They
answered, "John the Baptist; but others, Elijah; and still others, that
one of the ancient prophets has arisen." 20 He said to them, "But who
do you say that I am?" Peter answered, "The Messiah[b] of God."

Jesus Foretells His Death and Resurrection

21 He sternly ordered and commanded them not to tell anyone,
22 saying, "The Son of Man must undergo great suffering, and be rejected by the elders, chief priests, and scribes, and be killed, and on
the third day be raised."

23 Then he said to them all, "If any want to become my followers,
let them deny themselves and take up their cross daily and follow me.
24 For those who want to save their life will lose it, and those who lose
their life for my sake will save it. 25 What does it profit them if they
gain the whole world, but lose or forfeit themselves? 26 Those who
are ashamed of me and of my words, of them the Son of Man will be
ashamed when he comes in his glory and the glory of the Father and
of the holy angels. 27 But truly I tell you, there are some standing here
who will not taste death before they see the kingdom of God."

9:27 the kingdom of God: See note on 4:43.

The Transfiguration

28 Now about eight days after these sayings Jesus[a] took with him
Peter and John and James, and went up on the mountain to pray. 29 And
while he was praying, the appearance of his face changed, and his
clothes became dazzling white. 30 Suddenly they saw two men, Moses
and Elijah, talking to him. 31 They appeared in glory and were speaking of his departure, which he was about to accomplish at Jerusalem.
32 Now Peter and his companions were weighed down with sleep; but
since they had stayed awake,[c] they saw his glory and the two men who
stood with him. 33 Just as they were leaving him, Peter said to Jesus,
"Master, it is good for us to be here; let us make three dwellings,[d] one
for you, one for Moses, and one for Elijah"—not knowing what he said.
34 While he was saying this, a cloud came and overshadowed them; and
they were terrified as they entered the cloud. 35 Then from the cloud
came a voice that said, "This is my Son, my Chosen;[e] listen to him!"
36 When the voice had spoken, Jesus was found alone. And they kept
silent and in those days told no one any of the things they had seen.

9:30-31 departure: This word could also be translated as "exodus." Jesus, Moses, and Elijah discuss Jesus' approaching "exodus," which will take place in Jerusalem. In the first century C.E., Moses (leader of the Israelites' exodus out of slavery in Egypt) and the prophet Elijah were understood never to have died and never to have been buried, so that they could reenter human history as representatives of God's interests.

Moses led the Israelites out of Egypt, out of slavery, and on to the promised land. What does Jesus lead us out of? What can we leave behind when we follow Jesus? Where are we headed?

Jesus Heals a Boy with a Demon

37 On the next day, when they had come down from the mountain, a great crowd met him. 38 Just then a man from the crowd shouted,

9:37-43 demon: See note on 4:33-37.

[a] Gk *he* [b] Or *The Christ* [c] Or *but when they were fully awake* [d] Or *tents* [e] Other ancient authorities read *my Beloved*

"Teacher, I beg you to look at my son; he is my only child. [39]Sud-
denly a spirit seizes him, and all at once he[a] shrieks. It convulses him
until he foams at the mouth; it mauls him and will scarcely leave
him. [40]I begged your disciples to cast it out, but they could not."
[41]Jesus answered, "You faithless and perverse generation, how much
longer must I be with you and bear with you? Bring your son here."
[42]While he was coming, the demon dashed him to the ground in
convulsions. But Jesus rebuked the unclean spirit, healed the boy,
and gave him back to his father. [43]And all were astounded at the
greatness of God.

Jesus Again Foretells His Death

While everyone was amazed at all that he was doing, he said to
his disciples, [44]"Let these words sink into your ears: The Son of Man
is going to be betrayed into human hands." [45]But they did not understand this saying; its meaning was concealed from them, so that
they could not perceive it. And they were afraid to ask him about
this saying.

True Greatness

46 An argument arose among them as to which one of them was
the greatest. [47]But Jesus, aware of their inner thoughts, took a little
child and put it by his side, [48]and said to them, "Whoever welcomes
this child in my name welcomes me, and whoever welcomes me welcomes the one who sent me; for the least among all of you is the
greatest."

Another Exorcist

49 John answered, "Master, we saw someone casting out demons
in your name, and we tried to stop him, because he does not follow
with us." [50]But Jesus said to him, "Do not stop him; for whoever is not
against you is for you."

A Samaritan Village Refuses to Receive Jesus

9:51-56 they did not receive him: On the way to Jerusalem, the center of the Jewish world, Jesus enters a Samaritan village. Jews and Samaritans had a strained relationship, stretching back to the time when the Assyrians and then the Babylonians attacked and conquered the people of Israel (722 B.C.E. and 587 B.C.E., respectively). Because of this, it is no surprise when the villagers do not welcome Jesus.

51 When the days drew near for him to be taken up, he set his face
to go to Jerusalem. [52]And he sent messengers ahead of him. On their
way they entered a village of the Samaritans to make ready for him;
[53]but they did not receive him, because his face was set toward Jerusalem. [54]When his disciples James and John saw it, they said, "Lord,
do you want us to command fire to come down from heaven and consume them?"[b] [55]But he turned and rebuked them. [56]Then[c] they went
on to another village.

---

[a] Or *it* [b] Other ancient authorities add *as Elijah did* [c] Other ancient authorities read *rebuked them, and said, "You do not know what spirit you are of, [56] for the Son of Man has not come to destroy the lives of human beings but to save them." Then*

Would-Be Followers of Jesus

57 As they were going along the road, someone said to him, "I
will follow you wherever you go." 58 And Jesus said to him, "Foxes
have holes, and birds of the air have nests; but the Son of Man has
nowhere to lay his head." 59 To another he said, "Follow me." But he
said, "Lord, first let me go and bury my father." 60 But Jesus[a] said to
him, "Let the dead bury their own dead; but as for you, go and proclaim the kingdom of God." 61 Another said, "I will follow you, Lord;
but let me first say farewell to those at my home." 62 Jesus said to him,
"No one who puts a hand to the plow and looks back is fit for the
kingdom of God."

The Mission of the Seventy

10 After this the Lord appointed seventy[b] others and sent them
on ahead of him in pairs to every town and place where he
himself intended to go. 2 He said to them, "The harvest is plentiful,
but the laborers are few; therefore ask the Lord of the harvest to send
out laborers into his harvest. 3 Go on your way. See, I am sending you
out like lambs into the midst of wolves. 4 Carry no purse, no bag, no
sandals; and greet no one on the road. 5 Whatever house you enter,
first say, 'Peace to this house!' 6 And if anyone is there who shares in
peace, your peace will rest on that person; but if not, it will return to
you. 7 Remain in the same house, eating and drinking whatever they
provide, for the laborer deserves to be paid. Do not move about from
house to house. 8 Whenever you enter a town and its people welcome
you, eat what is set before you; 9 cure the sick who are there, and say
to them, 'The kingdom of God has come near to you.'[c] 10 But whenever you enter a town and they do not welcome you, go out into its
streets and say, 11 'Even the dust of your town that clings to our feet,
we wipe off in protest against you. Yet know this: the kingdom of God
has come near.'[d] 12 I tell you, on that day it will be more tolerable for
Sodom than for that town.

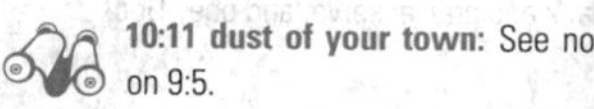

10:11 dust of your town: See note on 9:5.

Woes to Unrepentant Cities

13 "Woe to you, Chorazin! Woe to you, Bethsaida! For if the
deeds of power done in you had been done in Tyre and Sidon, they
would have repented long ago, sitting in sackcloth and ashes. 14 But
at the judgment it will be more tolerable for Tyre and Sidon than for
you. 15 And you, Capernaum,
will you be exalted to heaven?
No, you will be brought down to Hades.
16 "Whoever listens to you listens to me, and whoever rejects
you rejects me, and whoever rejects me rejects the one who sent me."

10:13 sackcloth and ashes: Wearing sackcloth and putting ashes on their heads was a way for people to express sadness or show they were sorry for their sins (see Esth 4:1; Job 2:8; Jonah 3).

10:13-15 Chorazin!...Bethsaida!...Tyre and Sidon...Capernaum: Chorazin, Bethsaida, and Capernaum were Jewish towns at the northern end of the Sea of Galilee. Tyre and Sidon were non-Jewish cities on the Mediterranean Sea coast.

[a] Gk *he* [b] Other ancient authorities read *seventy-two* [c] Or *is at hand for you* [d] Or *is at hand*

The Return of the Seventy

10:17 demons: See note on 4:33-37.

17 The seventy[a] returned with joy, saying, "Lord, in your name
even the demons submit to us!" 18 He said to them, "I watched Satan
fall from heaven like a flash of lightning. 19 See, I have given you authority to tread on snakes and scorpions, and over all the power of
the enemy; and nothing will hurt you. 20 Nevertheless, do not rejoice
at this, that the spirits submit to you, but rejoice that your names are
written in heaven."

Jesus Rejoices

21 At that same hour Jesus[b] rejoiced in the Holy Spirit[c] and said,
"I thank[d] you, Father, Lord of heaven and earth, because you have
hidden these things from the wise and the intelligent and have revealed them to infants; yes, Father, for such was your gracious will.[e]
22 All things have been handed over to me by my Father; and no one
knows who the Son is except the Father, or who the Father is except
the Son and anyone to whom the Son chooses to reveal him."

23 Then turning to the disciples, Jesus[b] said to them privately,
"Blessed are the eyes that see what you see! 24 For I tell you that many
prophets and kings desired to see what you see, but did not see it, and
to hear what you hear, but did not hear it."

The Parable of the Good Samaritan

10:25-29 wanting to justify himself: This phrase could indicate that the man is trying to make himself righteous before God, or simply win an argument. It could also mean he is serious about observing God's teachings, not to earn favor with God, but to thank and praise, serve, and obey God.

25 Just then a lawyer stood up to test Jesus.[f] "Teacher," he said,
"what must I do to inherit eternal life?" 26 He said to him, "What is
written in the law? What do you read there?" 27 He answered, "You
shall love the Lord your God with all your heart, and with all your
soul, and with all your strength, and with all your mind; and your
neighbor as yourself." 28 And he said to him, "You have given the right
answer; do this, and you will live."

10:30 Jerusalem to Jericho: Jericho is located about sixteen miles northeast of Jerusalem (see Map 12, p. 2109).

10:33 a Samaritan: This is a story about being a neighbor, and it is also about the important contributions made by outsiders. The last time Samaritans were mentioned in Luke (9:51-56), they refused to welcome Jesus. The fact that a Samaritan stopped to help the man who was beaten would have surprised (and perhaps angered) first-century readers.

29 But wanting to justify himself, he asked Jesus, "And who is my
neighbor?" 30 Jesus replied, "A man was going down from Jerusalem
to Jericho, and fell into the hands of robbers, who stripped him, beat
him, and went away, leaving him half dead. 31 Now by chance a priest
was going down that road; and when he saw him, he passed by on the
other side. 32 So likewise a Levite, when he came to the place and saw
him, passed by on the other side. 33 But a Samaritan while traveling
came near him; and when he saw him, he was moved with pity. 34 He
went to him and bandaged his wounds, having poured oil and wine
on them. Then he put him on his own animal, brought him to an inn,
and took care of him. 35 The next day he took out two denarii,[g] gave

---

[a] Other ancient authorities read *seventy-two* [b] Gk *he* [c] Other authorities read *in the spirit* [d] Or *praise* [e] Or *for so it was well-pleasing in your sight* [f] Gk *him* [g] The denarius was the usual day's wage for a laborer

them to the innkeeper, and said, ‘Take care of him; and when I come back, I will repay you whatever more you spend.’ 36 Which of these three, do you think, was a neighbor to the man who fell into the hands of the robbers?” 37 He said, “The one who showed him mercy.” Jesus said to him, “Go and do likewise.”

10:37 The one who showed him mercy: The man’s answer is the key to the parable: Being a neighbor is about what you actually *do* for a person in need.

Jesus Visits Martha and Mary

38 Now as they went on their way, he entered a certain village, where a woman named Martha welcomed him into her home. 39 She had a sister named Mary, who sat at the Lord’s feet and listened to what he was saying. 40 But Martha was distracted by her many tasks; so she came to him and asked, “Lord, do you not care that my sister has left me to do all the work by myself? Tell her then to help me.” 41 But the Lord answered her, “Martha, Martha, you are worried and distracted by many things; 42 there is need of only one thing.[a] Mary has chosen the better part, which will not be taken away from her.”

10:38-42 Martha...Mary: In John 11:1-44, sisters Martha and Mary have a brother named Lazarus and live in the village of Bethany.

The Lord’s Prayer

11 He was praying in a certain place, and after he had finished, one of his disciples said to him, “Lord, teach us to pray, as John taught his disciples.” 2 He said to them, “When you pray, say:

Father,[b] hallowed be your name.
Your kingdom come.[c]
3 Give us each day our daily bread.[d]
4 And forgive us our sins,
for we ourselves forgive everyone indebted to us.
And do not bring us to the time of trial.”[e]

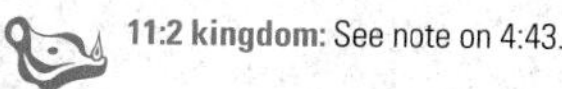

11:2 kingdom: See note on 4:43.

Perseverance in Prayer

5 And he said to them, “Suppose one of you has a friend, and you go to him at midnight and say to him, ‘Friend, lend me three loaves of bread; 6 for a friend of mine has arrived, and I have nothing to set before him.’ 7 And he answers from within, ‘Do not bother me; the door has already been locked, and my children are with me in bed; I cannot get up and give you anything.’ 8 I tell you, even though he will not get up and give him anything because he is his friend, at least because of his persistence he will get up and give him whatever he needs.

9 “So I say to you, Ask, and it will be given you; search, and you will find; knock, and the door will be opened for you. 10 For everyone who asks receives, and everyone who searches finds, and for everyone who knocks, the door will be opened. 11 Is there anyone among

[a] Other ancient authorities read *few things are necessary, or only one* [b] Other ancient authorities read *Our Father in heaven* [c] A few ancient authorities read *Your Holy Spirit come upon us and cleanse us.* Other ancient authorities add *Your will be done, on earth as in heaven* [d] Or *our bread for tomorrow* [e] Or *us into temptation.* Other ancient authorities add *but rescue us from the evil one* (or *from evil*)

you who, if your child asks for[a] a fish, will give a snake instead of a
fish? 12Or if the child asks for an egg, will give a scorpion? 13If you
then, who are evil, know how to give good gifts to your children, how
much more will the heavenly Father give the Holy Spirit[b] to those who
ask him!"

Jesus and Beelzebul

14 Now he was casting out a demon that was mute; when the
demon had gone out, the one who had been mute spoke, and the
crowds were amazed. 15But some of them said, "He casts out demons
by Beelzebul, the ruler of the demons." 16Others, to test him, kept
demanding from him a sign from heaven. 17But he knew what they
were thinking and said to them, "Every kingdom divided against itself becomes a desert, and house falls on house. 18If Satan also is divided against himself, how will his kingdom stand? —for you say that
I cast out the demons by Beelzebul. 19Now if I cast out the demons
by Beelzebul, by whom do your exorcists[c] cast them out? Therefore
they will be your judges. 20But if it is by the finger of God that I cast
out the demons, then the kingdom of God has come to you. 21When
a strong man, fully armed, guards his castle, his property is safe. 22But
when one stronger than he attacks him and overpowers him, he takes
away his armor in which he trusted and divides his plunder. 23Who-
ever is not with me is against me, and whoever does not gather with
me scatters.

11:15 Beelzebul: This title, which traces back to 2 Kings 1:2-16 (Baal-zebub), means "lord of flies" or "lord of filth" and refers to the "ruler of the demons."

The Return of the Unclean Spirit

24 "When the unclean spirit has gone out of a person, it wanders
through waterless regions looking for a resting place, but not finding
any, it says, 'I will return to my house from which I came.' 25When it
comes, it finds it swept and put in order. 26Then it goes and brings
seven other spirits more evil than itself, and they enter and live there;
and the last state of that person is worse than the first."

True Blessedness

27 While he was saying this, a woman in the crowd raised her
voice and said to him, "Blessed is the womb that bore you and the
breasts that nursed you!" 28But he said, "Blessed rather are those who
hear the word of God and obey it!"

The Sign of Jonah

29 When the crowds were increasing, he began to say, "This generation is an evil generation; it asks for a sign, but no sign will be given
to it except the sign of Jonah. 30For just as Jonah became a sign to

11:29-30 the sign of Jonah: When the prophet Jonah refused to go to Nineveh with God's message, a big fish swallowed him up. He was inside the fish for three days. Jesus would die and then be raised after three days. The "sign of Jonah" might also refer to the unexpected and wholehearted repentance of the people of Nineveh, which echoes an important theme in Luke.

---

[a] Other ancient authorities add *bread, will give a stone; or if your child asks for* [b] Other ancient authorities read *the Father give the Holy Spirit from heaven* [c] Gk *sons*

the people of Nineveh, so the Son of Man will be to this generation.
31 The queen of the South will rise at the judgment with the people of
this generation and condemn them, because she came from the ends
of the earth to listen to the wisdom of Solomon, and see, something
greater than Solomon is here! 32 The people of Nineveh will rise up at
the judgment with this generation and condemn it, because they repented at the proclamation of Jonah, and see, something greater than
Jonah is here!

The Light of the Body

33 "No one after lighting a lamp puts it in a cellar,[a] but on the
lampstand so that those who enter may see the light. 34 Your eye is the
lamp of your body. If your eye is healthy, your whole body is full of
light; but if it is not healthy, your body is full of darkness. 35 Therefore
consider whether the light in you is not darkness. 36 If then your whole
body is full of light, with no part of it in darkness, it will be as full of
light as when a lamp gives you light with its rays."

Jesus Denounces Pharisees and Lawyers

37 While he was speaking, a Pharisee invited him to dine with
him; so he went in and took his place at the table. 38 The Pharisee was
amazed to see that he did not first wash before dinner. 39 Then the
Lord said to him, "Now you Pharisees clean the outside of the cup
and of the dish, but inside you are full of greed and wickedness. 40 You
fools! Did not the one who made the outside make the inside also?
41 So give for alms those things that are within; and see, everything
will be clean for you.

42 "But woe to you Pharisees! For you tithe mint and rue and
herbs of all kinds, and neglect justice and the love of God; it is these
you ought to have practiced, without neglecting the others. 43 Woe
to you Pharisees! For you love to have the seat of honor in the synagogues and to be greeted with respect in the marketplaces. 44 Woe to
you! For you are like unmarked graves, and people walk over them
without realizing it."

45 One of the lawyers answered him, "Teacher, when you say
these things, you insult us too." 46 And he said, "Woe also to you lawyers! For you load people with burdens hard to bear, and you yourselves do not lift a finger to ease them. 47 Woe to you! For you build
the tombs of the prophets whom your ancestors killed. 48 So you are
witnesses and approve of the deeds of your ancestors; for they killed
them, and you build their tombs. 49 Therefore also the Wisdom of
God said, 'I will send them prophets and apostles, some of whom
they will kill and persecute,' 50 so that this generation may be charged
with the blood of all the prophets shed since the foundation of the

[a] Other ancient authorities add *or under the bushel basket*

11:42 tithe: Pharisees tithed or gave one-tenth of everything—including spices—back to God, and did this to remember that all of life was a gift from God to be received with thanksgiving. Jesus makes the point that choosing justice shows real thankfulness. Faithful Jews then and now would agree.

11:44 unmarked graves: Touching a tomb or dead body made a person unclean, so tombs were whitewashed to make them noticeable and prevent this from happening.

world, 51 from the blood of Abel to the blood of Zechariah, who perished between the altar and the sanctuary. Yes, I tell you, it will be
charged against this generation. 52 Woe to you lawyers! For you have
taken away the key of knowledge; you did not enter yourselves, and
you hindered those who were entering."

53 When he went outside, the scribes and the Pharisees began
to be very hostile toward him and to cross-examine him about many
things, 54 lying in wait for him, to catch him in something he might say.

A Warning against Hypocrisy

12:1 hypocrisy: In Jewish writings, a small amount of yeast can make things go bad. Jesus compares hypocrisy to yeast—a small amount can make things go bad.

Jesus uses humor in the unlikely comparison between humans and sparrows in 12:6-7. Are you surprised to find humor in the Bible? Why or why not?

12 Meanwhile, when the crowd gathered by the thousands, so
that they trampled on one another, he began to speak first to
his disciples, "Beware of the yeast of the Pharisees, that is, their hypocrisy. 2 Nothing is covered up that will not be uncovered, and nothing secret that will not become known. 3 Therefore whatever you have
said in the dark will be heard in the light, and what you have whispered behind closed doors will be proclaimed from the housetops.

Exhortation to Fearless Confession

4 "I tell you, my friends, do not fear those who kill the body, and
after that can do nothing more. 5 But I will warn you whom to fear:
fear him who, after he has killed, has authority[a] to cast into hell.[b] Yes,
I tell you, fear him! 6 Are not five sparrows sold for two pennies? Yet
not one of them is forgotten in God's sight. 7 But even the hairs of your
head are all counted. Do not be afraid; you are of more value than
many sparrows.

8 "And I tell you, everyone who acknowledges me before others,
the Son of Man also will acknowledge before the angels of God; 9 but
whoever denies me before others will be denied before the angels of
God. 10 And everyone who speaks a word against the Son of Man will
be forgiven; but whoever blasphemes against the Holy Spirit will not
be forgiven. 11 When they bring you before the synagogues, the rulers, and the authorities, do not worry about how[c] you are to defend
yourselves or what you are to say; 12 for the Holy Spirit will teach you
at that very hour what you ought to say."

The Parable of the Rich Fool

13 Someone in the crowd said to him, "Teacher, tell my brother to
divide the family inheritance with me." 14 But he said to him, "Friend,
who set me to be a judge or arbitrator over you?" 15 And he said to
them, "Take care! Be on your guard against all kinds of greed; for
one's life does not consist in the abundance of possessions." 16 Then
he told them a parable: "The land of a rich man produced abundantly.

---

[a] Or *power* [b] Gk *Gehenna* [c] Other ancient authorities add *or what*

[17]And he thought to himself, 'What should I do, for I have no place to store my crops?' [18]Then he said, 'I will do this: I will pull down my barns and build larger ones, and there I will store all my grain and my goods. [19]And I will say to my soul, Soul, you have ample goods laid up for many years; relax, eat, drink, be merry.' [20]But God said to him, 'You fool! This very night your life is being demanded of you. And the things you have prepared, whose will they be?' [21]So it is with those who store up treasures for themselves but are not rich toward God."

Do Not Worry

22 He said to his disciples, "Therefore I tell you, do not worry about your life, what you will eat, or about your body, what you will wear. [23]For life is more than food, and the body more than clothing. [24]Consider the ravens: they neither sow nor reap, they have neither storehouse nor barn, and yet God feeds them. Of how much more value are you than the birds! [25]And can any of you by worrying add a single hour to your span of life?[a] [26]If then you are not able to do so small a thing as that, why do you worry about the rest? [27]Consider the lilies, how they grow: they neither toil nor spin;[b] yet I tell you, even Solomon in all his glory was not clothed like one of these. [28]But if God so clothes the grass of the field, which is alive today and tomorrow is thrown into the oven, how much more will he clothe you—you of little faith! [29]And do not keep striving for what you are to eat and what you are to drink, and do not keep worrying. [30]For it is the nations of the world that strive after all these things, and your Father knows that you need them. [31]Instead, strive for his[c] kingdom, and these things will be given to you as well.

32 "Do not be afraid, little flock, for it is your Father's good pleasure to give you the kingdom. [33]Sell your possessions, and give alms. Make purses for yourselves that do not wear out, an unfailing treasure in heaven, where no thief comes near and no moth destroys. [34]For where your treasure is, there your heart will be also.

Watchful Slaves

35 "Be dressed for action and have your lamps lit; [36]be like those who are waiting for their master to return from the wedding banquet, so that they may open the door for him as soon as he comes and knocks. [37]Blessed are those slaves whom the master finds alert when he comes; truly I tell you, he will fasten his belt and have them sit down to eat, and he will come and serve them. [38]If he comes during the middle of the night, or near dawn, and finds them so, blessed are those slaves.

39 "But know this: if the owner of the house had known at what

12:25 add a single hour to your span of life? Jesus again uses humor to make a point (see 12:6-7). As the NRSV footnote *a* indicates, the original Greek might be translated as "add a cubit to your stature." A cubit equals eighteen to twenty-one inches or forty-six to fifty-three centimeters. In other words, Jesus says, "Can you make yourself taller by worrying?"

12:27 Solomon in all his glory: King Solomon of Israel was seen as the richest person to ever live.

12:33 purses…that do not wear out: The rabbis say that anyone who gives to the poor, lends to God. That is the point Jesus is making here.

---

[a] Or *add a cubit to your stature* [b] Other ancient authorities read *Consider the lilies; they neither spin nor weave*
[c] Other ancient authorities read *God's*

hour the thief was coming, he[a] would not have let his house be broken into. 40You also must be ready, for the Son of Man is coming at an
unexpected hour."

The Faithful or the Unfaithful Slave

41 Peter said, "Lord, are you telling this parable for us or for
everyone?" 42And the Lord said, "Who then is the faithful and prudent manager whom his master will put in charge of his slaves, to give
them their allowance of food at the proper time? 43Blessed is that slave
whom his master will find at work when he arrives. 44Truly I tell you,
he will put that one in charge of all his possessions. 45But if that slave
says to himself, 'My master is delayed in coming,' and if he begins to
beat the other slaves, men and women, and to eat and drink and get
drunk, 46the master of that slave will come on a day when he does not
expect him and at an hour that he does not know, and will cut him
in pieces,[b] and put him with the unfaithful. 47That slave who knew
what his master wanted, but did not prepare himself or do what was
wanted, will receive a severe beating. 48But the one who did not know
and did what deserved a beating will receive a light beating. From
everyone to whom much has been given, much will be required; and
from the one to whom much has been entrusted, even more will be
demanded.

Jesus the Cause of Division

49 "I came to bring fire to the earth, and how I wish it were already kindled! 50I have a baptism with which to be baptized, and what
stress I am under until it is completed! 51Do you think that I have
come to bring peace to the earth? No, I tell you, but rather division!
52From now on five in one household will be divided, three against
two and two against three; 53they will be divided:

father against son
    and son against father,
mother against daughter
    and daughter against mother,
mother-in-law against her daughter-in-law
    and daughter-in-law against mother-in-law."

Interpreting the Time

54 He also said to the crowds, "When you see a cloud rising in
the west, you immediately say, 'It is going to rain'; and so it happens.
55And when you see the south wind blowing, you say, 'There will be
scorching heat'; and it happens. 56You hypocrites! You know how to
interpret the appearance of earth and sky, but why do you not know
how to interpret the present time?

---

[a] Other ancient authorities add *would have watched and* [b] Or *cut him off*

Settling with Your Opponent

57 "And why do you not judge for yourselves what is right? 58 Thus, when you go with your accuser before a magistrate, on the way make an effort to settle the case,[a] or you may be dragged before the judge, and the judge hand you over to the officer, and the officer throw you in prison. 59 I tell you, you will never get out until you have paid the very last penny."

Repent or Perish

13 At that very time there were some present who told him about the Galileans whose blood Pilate had mingled with their sacrifices. 2 He asked them, "Do you think that because these Galileans suffered in this way they were worse sinners than all other Galileans? 3 No, I tell you; but unless you repent, you will all perish as they did. 4 Or those eighteen who were killed when the tower of Siloam fell on them—do you think that they were worse offenders than all the others living in Jerusalem? 5 No, I tell you; but unless you repent, you will all perish just as they did."

13:1 Pilate: Pontius Pilate was the Roman governor of Judea and reportedly a cruel leader with little respect for Jewish religious practices.

The Parable of the Barren Fig Tree

6 Then he told this parable: "A man had a fig tree planted in his vineyard; and he came looking for fruit on it and found none. 7 So he said to the gardener, 'See here! For three years I have come looking for fruit on this fig tree, and still I find none. Cut it down! Why should it be wasting the soil?' 8 He replied, 'Sir, let it alone for one more year, until I dig around it and put manure on it. 9 If it bears fruit next year, well and good; but if not, you can cut it down.' "

Jesus Heals a Crippled Woman

10 Now he was teaching in one of the synagogues on the sabbath. 11 And just then there appeared a woman with a spirit that had crippled her for eighteen years. She was bent over and was quite unable to stand up straight. 12 When Jesus saw her, he called her over and said, "Woman, you are set free from your ailment." 13 When he laid his hands on her, immediately she stood up straight and began praising God. 14 But the leader of the synagogue, indignant because Jesus had cured on the sabbath, kept saying to the crowd, "There are six days on which work ought to be done; come on those days and be cured, and not on the sabbath day." 15 But the Lord answered him and said, "You hypocrites! Does not each of you on the sabbath untie his ox or his donkey from the manger, and lead it away to give it water? 16 And ought not this woman, a daughter of Abraham whom Satan bound for eighteen long years, be set free from this bondage on the sabbath

13:16-17 daughter of Abraham: This phrase emphasizes that the woman is Jewish. Being Jewish makes a difference. Paul makes the same point (see Rom 3:2). Jews, he says, have been entrusted with God's revelations and have received God's irrevocable gifts and call (Romans 11:29). Those listening to Jesus also appear to agree, because they are ashamed when they absorb the point of his argument.

---

[a] Gk *settle with him*

day?" 17 When he said this, all his opponents were put to shame; and
the entire crowd was rejoicing at all the wonderful things that he was
doing.

The Parable of the Mustard Seed

13:18-19 a mustard seed…sowed in the garden: This story is one of Jesus' parables, which use everyday examples to make a point or describe something. The Greek word translated as "sowed" could refer to planting a seed on purpose or accidentally. Either way, the idea of sowing a mustard seed would have surprised and even amused Jews in the first century C.E. They did not plant mustard in their gardens, because its uncontrollable growth weakened their witness to the stable and orderly love of God.

18 He said therefore, "What is the kingdom of God like? And
to what should I compare it? 19 It is like a mustard seed that someone took and sowed in the garden; it grew and became a tree, and the
birds of the air made nests in its branches."

The Parable of the Yeast

20 And again he said, "To what should I compare the kingdom
of God? 21 It is like yeast that a woman took and mixed in with[a] three
measures of flour until all of it was leavened."

The Narrow Door

22 Jesus[b] went through one town and village after another, teaching as he made his way to Jerusalem. 23 Someone asked him, "Lord,
will only a few be saved?" He said to them, 24 "Strive to enter through
the narrow door; for many, I tell you, will try to enter and will not
be able. 25 When once the owner of the house has got up and shut
the door, and you begin to stand outside and to knock at the door,
saying, 'Lord, open to us,' then in reply he will say to you, 'I do not
know where you come from.' 26 Then you will begin to say, 'We ate
and drank with you, and you taught in our streets.' 27 But he will say,
'I do not know where you come from; go away from me, all you evildoers!' 28 There will be weeping and gnashing of teeth when you see
Abraham and Isaac and Jacob and all the prophets in the kingdom of
God, and you yourselves thrown out. 29 Then people will come from
east and west, from north and south, and will eat in the kingdom of
God. 30 Indeed, some are last who will be first, and some are first who
will be last."

The Lament over Jerusalem

13:31 Pharisees came: The Pharisees do not act only as hypocritical opponents (12:1-3) in Luke. Jesus argues with them, a sign of sincere respect in Jewish culture. In this scene, some Pharisees act to protect Jesus, warning him of Herod's murderous intentions.

31 At that very hour some Pharisees came and said to him, "Get
away from here, for Herod wants to kill you." 32 He said to them, "Go
and tell that fox for me,[c] 'Listen, I am casting out demons and performing cures today and tomorrow, and on the third day I finish my
work. 33 Yet today, tomorrow, and the next day I must be on my way,
because it is impossible for a prophet to be killed outside of Jerusalem.' 34 Jerusalem, Jerusalem, the city that kills the prophets and stones
those who are sent to it! How often have I desired to gather your children together as a hen gathers her brood under her wings, and you
were not willing! 35 See, your house is left to you. And I tell you, you

---

[a] Gk *hid in* [b] Gk *He* [c] Gk lacks *for me*

will not see me until the time comes when[a] you say, 'Blessed is the
one who comes in the name of the Lord.' "

Jesus Heals the Man with Dropsy

14 On one occasion when Jesus[b] was going to the house of a
leader of the Pharisees to eat a meal on the sabbath, they
were watching him closely. 2 Just then, in front of him, there was a man
who had dropsy. 3 And Jesus asked the lawyers and Pharisees, "Is it
lawful to cure people on the sabbath, or not?" 4 But they were silent.
So Jesus[b] took him and healed him, and sent him away. 5 Then he said
to them, "If one of you has a child[c] or an ox that has fallen into a well,
will you not immediately pull it out on a sabbath day?" 6 And they
could not reply to this.

Humility and Hospitality

7 When he noticed how the guests chose the places of honor, he
told them a parable. 8 "When you are invited by someone to a wedding banquet, do not sit down at the place of honor, in case someone
more distinguished than you has been invited by your host; 9 and the
host who invited both of you may come and say to you, 'Give this
person your place,' and then in disgrace you would start to take the
lowest place. 10 But when you are invited, go and sit down at the lowest
place, so that when your host comes, he may say to you, 'Friend, move
up higher'; then you will be honored in the presence of all who sit at
the table with you. 11 For all who exalt themselves will be humbled,
and those who humble themselves will be exalted."

14:8 wedding banquet: Wedding banquets were elaborate celebrations for the entire community, lasting as long as a week.

12 He said also to the one who had invited him, "When you give
a luncheon or a dinner, do not invite your friends or your brothers or
your relatives or rich neighbors, in case they may invite you in return,
and you would be repaid. 13 But when you give a banquet, invite the
poor, the crippled, the lame, and the blind. 14 And you will be blessed,
because they cannot repay you, for you will be repaid at the resurrection of the righteous."

14:13 invite the poor: Again, Jesus makes the point that anyone who gives to the poor, lends to God (see note on 12:33).

The Parable of the Great Dinner

15 One of the dinner guests, on hearing this, said to him, "Blessed
is anyone who will eat bread in the kingdom of God!" 16 Then Jesus[b]
said to him, "Someone gave a great dinner and invited many. 17 At the
time for the dinner he sent his slave to say to those who had been invited, 'Come; for everything is ready now.' 18 But they all alike began to
make excuses. The first said to him, 'I have bought a piece of land, and
I must go out and see it; please accept my regrets.' 19 Another said, 'I
have bought five yoke of oxen, and I am going to try them out; please
accept my regrets.' 20 Another said, 'I have just been married, and

---

[a] Other ancient authorities lack *the time comes when* [b] Gk *he* [c] Other ancient authorities read *a donkey*

therefore I cannot come.' 21 So the slave returned and reported this to
his master. Then the owner of the house became angry and said to his
slave, 'Go out at once into the streets and lanes of the town and bring
in the poor, the crippled, the blind, and the lame.' 22 And the slave said,
'Sir, what you ordered has been done, and there is still room.' 23 Then
the master said to the slave, 'Go out into the roads and lanes, and
compel people to come in, so that my house may be filled. 24 For I tell
you,[a] none of those who were invited will taste my dinner.'"

The Cost of Discipleship

14:25-33 cross: The Roman government executed criminals by crucifixion (death on a cross).

25 Now large crowds were traveling with him; and he turned and
said to them, 26 "Whoever comes to me and does not hate father and
mother, wife and children, brothers and sisters, yes, and even life itself, cannot be my disciple. 27 Whoever does not carry the cross and
follow me cannot be my disciple. 28 For which of you, intending to
build a tower, does not first sit down and estimate the cost, to see
whether he has enough to complete it? 29 Otherwise, when he has laid
a foundation and is not able to finish, all who see it will begin to ridicule him, 30 saying, 'This fellow began to build and was not able to finish.' 31 Or what king, going out to wage war against another king, will
not sit down first and consider whether he is able with ten thousand
to oppose the one who comes against him with twenty thousand? 32 If
he cannot, then, while the other is still far away, he sends a delegation
and asks for the terms of peace. 33 So therefore, none of you can become my disciple if you do not give up all your possessions.

About Salt

34 "Salt is good; but if salt has lost its taste, how can its saltiness
be restored?[b] 35 It is fit neither for the soil nor for the manure pile; they
throw it away. Let anyone with ears to hear listen!"

The Parable of the Lost Sheep

15 Now all the tax collectors and sinners were coming near to
listen to him. 2 And the Pharisees and the scribes were grumbling and saying, "This fellow welcomes sinners and eats with them."
3 So he told them this parable: 4 "Which one of you, having a hundred sheep and losing one of them, does not leave the ninety-nine in
the wilderness and go after the one that is lost until he finds it? 5 When
he has found it, he lays it on his shoulders and rejoices. 6 And when
he comes home, he calls together his friends and neighbors, saying
to them, 'Rejoice with me, for I have found my sheep that was lost.'
7 Just so, I tell you, there will be more joy in heaven over one sinner
who repents than over ninety-nine righteous persons who need no
repentance.

15:2 the Pharisees and the scribes were grumbling: The Pharisees are not happy that Jesus draws crowds of tax collectors and sinners. See note on 5:27-32 about tax collectors.

15:4-7 Which one of you: The answer to Jesus' question is that no one would do this. Sheep left unattended in the wilderness could scatter and be attacked and eaten by wild animals. This shepherd will do anything to bring one sheep home.

---

[a] The Greek word for *you* here is plural [b] Or *how can it be used for seasoning?*

The Parable of the Lost Coin

8 "Or what woman having ten silver coins,[a] if she loses one of
them, does not light a lamp, sweep the house, and search carefully until she finds it? 9When she has found it, she calls together her friends
and neighbors, saying, 'Rejoice with me, for I have found the coin
that I had lost.' 10Just so, I tell you, there is joy in the presence of the
angels of God over one sinner who repents."

15:8-10 ten silver coins: These coins are drachmas, each worth about one day's wage. Even if these are the only coins she has, could a woman in the ancient world set aside all other tasks to look for one lost coin? The answer is "no." This woman will do anything to find one lost coin.

The Parable of the Prodigal and His Brother

11 Then Jesus[b] said, "There was a man who had two sons. 12The
younger of them said to his father, 'Father, give me the share of the
property that will belong to me.' So he divided his property between
them. 13A few days later the younger son gathered all he had and traveled to a distant country, and there he squandered his property in dis-
solute living. 14When he had spent everything, a severe famine took
place throughout that country, and he began to be in need. 15So he
went and hired himself out to one of the citizens of that country, who
sent him to his fields to feed the pigs. 16He would gladly have filled
himself with[c] the pods that the pigs were eating; and no one gave him
anything. 17But when he came to himself he said, 'How many of my
father's hired hands have bread enough and to spare, but here I am dying of hunger! 18I will get up and go to my father, and I will say to him,
"Father, I have sinned against heaven and before you; 19I am no longer
worthy to be called your son; treat me like one of your hired hands."'
20So he set off and went to his father. But while he was still far off, his
father saw him and was filled with compassion; he ran and put his
arms around him and kissed him. 21Then the son said to him, 'Father,
I have sinned against heaven and before you; I am no longer worthy to
be called your son.'[d] 22But the father said to his slaves, 'Quickly, bring
out a robe—the best one—and put it on him; put a ring on his finger
and sandals on his feet. 23And get the fatted calf and kill it, and let us
eat and celebrate; 24for this son of mine was dead and is alive again; he
was lost and is found!' And they began to celebrate.

25 "Now his elder son was in the field; and when he came and
approached the house, he heard music and dancing. 26He called one
of the slaves and asked what was going on. 27He replied, 'Your brother
has come, and your father has killed the fatted calf, because he has
got him back safe and sound.' 28Then he became angry and refused
to go in. His father came out and began to plead with him. 29But he
answered his father, 'Listen! For all these years I have been working
like a slave for you, and I have never disobeyed your command; yet
you have never given me even a young goat so that I might celebrate

15:12 share of the property: In Jewish families, sons inherited goods and property from their fathers, with the oldest son generally receiving a larger share of the inheritance. Apparently an inheritance was divided up only after a father's death, so the younger son's request is unusual.

15:17 when he came to himself: This phrase does not necessarily imply that the son repents. He does not think about how he has wronged his father—that comes later, perhaps in 15:21. Literally, his first thought is, "How many of the hired workers of my father have *too much* bread?"

The father had no advance notice, yet at a distance he immediately sees and recognizes his son (15:20). What things could he have recognized? What do you think he had been doing before the son appeared?

---

[a] Gk *drachmas,* each worth about a day's wage for a laborer [b] Gk *he* [c] Other ancient authorities read *filled his stomach with* [d] Other ancient authorities add *Treat me like one of your hired servants*

with my friends. 30 But when this son of yours came back, who has
devoured your property with prostitutes, you killed the fatted calf for
him!' 31 Then the father[a] said to him, 'Son, you are always with me, and
all that is mine is yours. 32 But we had to celebrate and rejoice, because
this brother of yours was dead and has come to life; he was lost and
has been found.'"

15:32 this brother of yours was dead: This statement might be like one person cutting off a relationship with another by saying, "You are dead to me." It could also mean that the son, who was starving even before he started to return home, looked like a dead person when he arrived home.

The Parable of the Dishonest Manager

16 Then Jesus[a] said to the disciples, "There was a rich man who
had a manager, and charges were brought to him that this
man was squandering his property. 2 So he summoned him and said
to him, 'What is this that I hear about you? Give me an accounting of
your management, because you cannot be my manager any longer.'
3 Then the manager said to himself, 'What will I do, now that my master is taking the position away from me? I am not strong enough to
dig, and I am ashamed to beg. 4 I have decided what to do so that,
when I am dismissed as manager, people may welcome me into their
homes.' 5 So, summoning his master's debtors one by one, he asked
the first, 'How much do you owe my master?' 6 He answered, 'A hundred jugs of olive oil.' He said to him, 'Take your bill, sit down quickly,
and make it fifty.' 7 Then he asked another, 'And how much do you
owe?' He replied, 'A hundred containers of wheat.' He said to him,
'Take your bill and make it eighty.' 8 And his master commended the
dishonest manager because he had acted shrewdly; for the children of
this age are more shrewd in dealing with their own generation than
are the children of light. 9 And I tell you, make friends for yourselves
by means of dishonest wealth[b] so that when it is gone, they may welcome you into the eternal homes.[c]

10 "Whoever is faithful in a very little is faithful also in much; and
whoever is dishonest in a very little is dishonest also in much. 11 If then
you have not been faithful with the dishonest wealth,[b] who will entrust to you the true riches? 12 And if you have not been faithful with
what belongs to another, who will give you what is your own? 13 No
slave can serve two masters; for a slave will either hate the one and
love the other, or be devoted to the one and despise the other. You
cannot serve God and wealth."[b]

The Law and the Kingdom of God

14 The Pharisees, who were lovers of money, heard all this, and
they ridiculed him. 15 So he said to them, "You are those who justify
yourselves in the sight of others; but God knows your hearts; for what
is prized by human beings is an abomination in the sight of God.

16 "The law and the prophets were in effect until John came;
since then the good news of the kingdom of God is proclaimed, and

---

[a] Gk *he* [b] Gk *mammon* [c] Gk *tents*

everyone tries to enter it by force.[a] 17 But it is easier for heaven and
earth to pass away, than for one stroke of a letter in the law to be
dropped.

18 "Anyone who divorces his wife and marries another commits
adultery, and whoever marries a woman divorced from her husband
commits adultery.

The Rich Man and Lazarus

19 "There was a rich man who was dressed in purple and fine
linen and who feasted sumptuously every day. 20 And at his gate lay
a poor man named Lazarus, covered with sores, 21 who longed to satisfy his hunger with what fell from the rich man's table; even the dogs
would come and lick his sores. 22 The poor man died and was carried
away by the angels to be with Abraham.[b] The rich man also died and
was buried. 23 In Hades, where he was being tormented, he looked up
and saw Abraham far away with Lazarus by his side.[c] 24 He called out,
'Father Abraham, have mercy on me, and send Lazarus to dip the tip
of his finger in water and cool my tongue; for I am in agony in these
flames.' 25 But Abraham said, 'Child, remember that during your lifetime you received your good things, and Lazarus in like manner evil
things; but now he is comforted here, and you are in agony. 26 Besides
all this, between you and us a great chasm has been fixed, so that those
who might want to pass from here to you cannot do so, and no one
can cross from there to us.' 27 He said, 'Then, father, I beg you to send
him to my father's house— 28 for I have five brothers—that he may
warn them, so that they will not also come into this place of torment.'
29 Abraham replied, 'They have Moses and the prophets; they should
listen to them.' 30 He said, 'No, father Abraham; but if someone goes
to them from the dead, they will repent.' 31 He said to him, 'If they do
not listen to Moses and the prophets, neither will they be convinced
even if someone rises from the dead.' "

Some Sayings of Jesus

17 Jesus[d] said to his disciples, "Occasions for stumbling are
bound to come, but woe to anyone by whom they come! 2 It
would be better for you if a millstone were hung around your neck
and you were thrown into the sea than for you to cause one of these
little ones to stumble. 3 Be on your guard! If another disciple[e] sins, you
must rebuke the offender, and if there is repentance, you must forgive.
4 And if the same person sins against you seven times a day, and turns
back to you seven times and says, 'I repent,' you must forgive."

5 The apostles said to the Lord, "Increase our faith!" 6 The Lord
replied, "If you had faith the size of a[f] mustard seed, you could say to

[a] Or *everyone is strongly urged to enter it* [b] Gk *to Abraham's bosom* [c] Gk *in his bosom* [d] Gk *He*
[e] Gk *your brother* [f] Gk *faith as a grain of*

16:19 a rich man who was dressed in purple and fine linen: Fine linen would have been expensive, and purple was a color reserved for people of wealth, royalty, or connections to the Roman Empire. The rich man could be one of the colonizers, who built new cities for themselves from taxes and tributes imposed on the Jews. Colonizers were also known to drive people off their farms, making former landowners their servants. Original readers of Luke would not have felt sorry for this man.

16:20 at his gate lay a poor man named Lazarus: The Greek may be translated as "thrown at the rich man's door."

16:24 send Lazarus: The rich man believes he can give commands from Hades and Lazarus will obey. Notice that he speaks to Abraham and not directly to Lazarus.

this mulberry tree, 'Be uprooted and planted in the sea,' and it would
obey you.
7 "Who among you would say to your slave who has just come in
from plowing or tending sheep in the field, 'Come here at once and
take your place at the table'? 8Would you not rather say to him, 'Prepare supper for me, put on your apron and serve me while I eat and
drink; later you may eat and drink'? 9Do you thank the slave for doing
what was commanded? 10So you also, when you have done all that
you were ordered to do, say, 'We are worthless slaves; we have done
only what we ought to have done!' "

Jesus Cleanses Ten Lepers

17:11-19 he was a Samaritan: This is a story about gratitude and also about the important contributions made by outsiders. The first Samaritans mentioned in Luke's story reject Jesus (9:51-53). The next Samaritan acts like a neighbor to the man who was beaten (10:25-37). This Samaritan is the only one to return and thank Jesus for healing him. (As an outsider, the Samaritan is also the only one who does not need to go and show himself to the priests.)

11 On the way to Jerusalem Jesus[a] was going through the region
between Samaria and Galilee. 12As he entered a village, ten lepers[b]
approached him. Keeping their distance, 13they called out, saying,
"Jesus, Master, have mercy on us!" 14When he saw them, he said to
them, "Go and show yourselves to the priests." And as they went, they
were made clean. 15Then one of them, when he saw that he was healed,
turned back, praising God with a loud voice. 16He prostrated himself
at Jesus'[c] feet and thanked him. And he was a Samaritan. 17Then Jesus
asked, "Were not ten made clean? But the other nine, where are they?
18Was none of them found to return and give praise to God except
this foreigner?" 19Then he said to him, "Get up and go on your way;
your faith has made you well."

The Coming of the Kingdom

17:20-37 one will be taken and the other left: This likely refers to people taken from nearly every family when the First Jewish Revolt against Rome failed (66–70 C.E.). Some ancient sources suggest that as many as one million Jews were killed during this time.

20 Once Jesus[a] was asked by the Pharisees when the kingdom of
God was coming, and he answered, "The kingdom of God is not coming with things that can be observed; 21nor will they say, 'Look, here it
is!' or 'There it is!' For, in fact, the kingdom of God is among[d] you."
22 Then he said to the disciples, "The days are coming when you
will long to see one of the days of the Son of Man, and you will not
see it. 23They will say to you, 'Look there!' or 'Look here!' Do not go,
do not set off in pursuit. 24For as the lightning flashes and lights up
the sky from one side to the other, so will the Son of Man be in his
day.[e] 25But first he must endure much suffering and be rejected by
this generation. 26Just as it was in the days of Noah, so too it will be
in the days of the Son of Man. 27They were eating and drinking, and
marrying and being given in marriage, until the day Noah entered the
ark, and the flood came and destroyed all of them. 28Likewise, just as
it was in the days of Lot: they were eating and drinking, buying and
selling, planting and building, 29but on the day that Lot left Sodom,
it rained fire and sulfur from heaven and destroyed all of them 30—it

17:28-29 Sodom: This was an evil city destroyed by God. God saved Abraham's nephew, Lot, from this destruction (see Gen 18:16—19:29).

---

[a] Gk *he* [b] The terms *leper* and *leprosy* can refer to several diseases [c] Gk *his* [d] Or *within* [e] Other ancient authorities lack *in his day*

will be like that on the day that the Son of Man is revealed. 31On that
day, anyone on the housetop who has belongings in the house must
not come down to take them away; and likewise anyone in the field
must not turn back. 32Remember Lot's wife. 33Those who try to make
their life secure will lose it, but those who lose their life will keep it. 34I
tell you, on that night there will be two in one bed; one will be taken
and the other left. 35There will be two women grinding meal together;
one will be taken and the other left."[a] 37Then they asked him, "Where,
Lord?" He said to them, "Where the corpse is, there the vultures will
gather."

17:32 Lot's wife: God told Lot and his family not to look back when they left Sodom. Lot's wife disobeyed and became a pillar of salt (Gen 19:26).

The Parable of the Widow and the Unjust Judge

18 Then Jesus[b] told them a parable about their need to pray always and not to lose heart. 2He said, "In a certain city there
was a judge who neither feared God nor had respect for people. 3In
that city there was a widow who kept coming to him and saying,
'Grant me justice against my opponent.' 4For a while he refused; but
later he said to himself, 'Though I have no fear of God and no respect
for anyone, 5yet because this widow keeps bothering me, I will grant
her justice, so that she may not wear me out by continually coming.'"[c]
6And the Lord said, "Listen to what the unjust judge says. 7And will
not God grant justice to his chosen ones who cry to him day and
night? Will he delay long in helping them? 8I tell you, he will quickly
grant justice to them. And yet, when the Son of Man comes, will he
find faith on earth?"

The Parable of the Pharisee and the Tax Collector

9 He also told this parable to some who trusted in themselves
that they were righteous and regarded others with contempt: 10"Two
men went up to the temple to pray, one a Pharisee and the other a tax
collector. 11The Pharisee, standing by himself, was praying thus, 'God,
I thank you that I am not like other people: thieves, rogues, adulterers, or even like this tax collector. 12I fast twice a week; I give a tenth
of all my income.' 13But the tax collector, standing far off, would not
even look up to heaven, but was beating his breast and saying, 'God,
be merciful to me, a sinner!' 14I tell you, this man went down to his
home justified rather than the other; for all who exalt themselves will
be humbled, but all who humble themselves will be exalted."

18:9-14 one a Pharisee and the other a tax collector: Notice that in this scene both men tell the truth. The Pharisee does exactly what he says. Jesus does not criticize his deeds, but the way he despises other people. The tax collector also tells the truth about himself. Jesus does not excuse his behavior.

Jesus Blesses Little Children

15 People were bringing even infants to him that he might touch
them; and when the disciples saw it, they sternly ordered them not
to do it. 16But Jesus called for them and said, "Let the little children

---

[a] Other ancient authorities add verse 36, *"Two will be in the field; one will be taken and the other left."* [b] Gk *he*

[c] Or *so that she may not finally come and slap me in the face*

come to me, and do not stop them; for it is to such as these that the
kingdom of God belongs. 17 Truly I tell you, whoever does not receive
the kingdom of God as a little child will never enter it."

The Rich Ruler

18 A certain ruler asked him, "Good Teacher, what must I do to
inherit eternal life?" 19 Jesus said to him, "Why do you call me good?
No one is good but God alone. 20 You know the commandments: 'You
shall not commit adultery; You shall not murder; You shall not steal;
You shall not bear false witness; Honor your father and mother.'"
21 He replied, "I have kept all these since my youth." 22 When Jesus
heard this, he said to him, "There is still one thing lacking. Sell all that
you own and distribute the money[a] to the poor, and you will have
treasure in heaven; then come, follow me." 23 But when he heard this,
he became sad; for he was very rich. 24 Jesus looked at him and said,
"How hard it is for those who have wealth to enter the kingdom of
God! 25 Indeed, it is easier for a camel to go through the eye of a needle
than for someone who is rich to enter the kingdom of God."

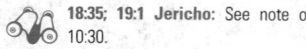

18:22 treasure in heaven: Once again, the person who gives to the poor lends to God (see notes on 12:33; 14:13).

26 Those who heard it said, "Then who can be saved?" 27 He replied, "What is impossible for mortals is possible for God."

28 Then Peter said, "Look, we have left our homes and followed
you." 29 And he said to them, "Truly I tell you, there is no one who has
left house or wife or brothers or parents or children, for the sake of the
kingdom of God, 30 who will not get back very much more in this age,
and in the age to come eternal life."

A Third Time Jesus Foretells His Death and Resurrection

31 Then he took the twelve aside and said to them, "See, we are
going up to Jerusalem, and everything that is written about the Son of
Man by the prophets will be accomplished. 32 For he will be handed
over to the Gentiles; and he will be mocked and insulted and spat
upon. 33 After they have flogged him, they will kill him, and on the
third day he will rise again." 34 But they understood nothing about all
these things; in fact, what he said was hidden from them, and they did
not grasp what was said.

Jesus Heals a Blind Beggar Near Jericho

18:35; 19:1 Jericho: See note on 10:30.

35 As he approached Jericho, a blind man was sitting by the roadside begging. 36 When he heard a crowd going by, he asked what was
happening. 37 They told him, "Jesus of Nazareth[b] is passing by." 38 Then
he shouted, "Jesus, Son of David, have mercy on me!" 39 Those who
were in front sternly ordered him to be quiet; but he shouted even
more loudly, "Son of David, have mercy on me!" 40 Jesus stood still

---

[a] Gk lacks *the money* [b] Gk *the Nazorean*

and ordered the man to be brought to him; and when he came near,
he asked him, 41 "What do you want me to do for you?" He said, "Lord,
let me see again." 42 Jesus said to him, "Receive your sight; your faith
has saved you." 43 Immediately he regained his sight and followed him,
glorifying God; and all the people, when they saw it, praised God.

Jesus and Zacchaeus

19 He entered Jericho and was passing through it. 2 A man was
there named Zacchaeus; he was a chief tax collector and
was rich. 3 He was trying to see who Jesus was, but on account of the
crowd he could not, because he was short in stature. 4 So he ran ahead
and climbed a sycamore tree to see him, because he was going to pass
that way. 5 When Jesus came to the place, he looked up and said to
him, "Zacchaeus, hurry and come down; for I must stay at your house
today." 6 So he hurried down and was happy to welcome him. 7 All who
saw it began to grumble and said, "He has gone to be the guest of one
who is a sinner." 8 Zacchaeus stood there and said to the Lord, "Look,
half of my possessions, Lord, I will give to the poor; and if I have
defrauded anyone of anything, I will pay back four times as much."
9 Then Jesus said to him, "Today salvation has come to this house, because he too is a son of Abraham. 10 For the Son of Man came to seek
out and to save the lost."

The Parable of the Ten Pounds

11 As they were listening to this, he went on to tell a parable,
because he was near Jerusalem, and because they supposed that the
kingdom of God was to appear immediately. 12 So he said, "A nobleman went to a distant country to get royal power for himself and then
return. 13 He summoned ten of his slaves, and gave them ten pounds,[a]
and said to them, 'Do business with these until I come back.' 14 But the
citizens of his country hated him and sent a delegation after him, saying, 'We do not want this man to rule over us.' 15 When he returned,
having received royal power, he ordered these slaves, to whom he had
given the money, to be summoned so that he might find out what
they had gained by trading. 16 The first came forward and said, 'Lord,
your pound has made ten more pounds.' 17 He said to him, 'Well done,
good slave! Because you have been trustworthy in a very small thing,
take charge of ten cities.' 18 Then the second came, saying, 'Lord, your
pound has made five pounds.' 19 He said to him, 'And you, rule over
five cities.' 20 Then the other came, saying, 'Lord, here is your pound.
I wrapped it up in a piece of cloth, 21 for I was afraid of you, because
you are a harsh man; you take what you did not deposit, and reap
what you did not sow.' 22 He said to him, 'I will judge you by your own
words, you wicked slave! You knew, did you, that I was a harsh man,

19:2 Zacchaeus: This name means "pure, clean, innocent."

19:8 pay back four times as much: This goes beyond what would have been required of Zacchaeus, and if he is corrupt, the amount to be repaid could be staggeringly high. In Greek the verb tense is not future but present—not "I will give/repay" but "I [already]] give/repay." This might imply that he is not corrupt and is acting justly.

19:9 He too is a son of Abraham: When Jesus healed the woman bent double, he noted that she was a daughter of Abraham (13:16). Now Jesus carefully notes that Zacchaeus is a son of Abraham. The writer of this Gospel makes it clear that it is important to be Jewish.

19:11 the kingdom of God: See note on 4:43.

[a] The mina, rendered here by *pound*, was about three months' wages for a laborer

taking what I did not deposit and reaping what I did not sow? [23]Why
then did you not put my money into the bank? Then when I returned,
I could have collected it with interest.' [24]He said to the bystanders,
'Take the pound from him and give it to the one who has ten pounds.'
[25](And they said to him, 'Lord, he has ten pounds!') [26]'I tell you, to all
those who have, more will be given; but from those who have nothing, even what they have will be taken away. [27]But as for these enemies
of mine who did not want me to be king over them—bring them here
and slaughter them in my presence.'"

Jesus' Triumphal Entry into Jerusalem

28 After he had said this, he went on ahead, going up to Jerusalem.

29 When he had come near Bethphage and Bethany, at the place
called the Mount of Olives, he sent two of the disciples, [30]saying, "Go
into the village ahead of you, and as you enter it you will find tied
there a colt that has never been ridden. Untie it and bring it here. [31]If
anyone asks you, 'Why are you untying it?' just say this, 'The Lord
needs it.'" [32]So those who were sent departed and found it as he had
told them. [33]As they were untying the colt, its owners asked them,
"Why are you untying the colt?" [34]They said, "The Lord needs it."
[35]Then they brought it to Jesus; and after throwing their cloaks on the
colt, they set Jesus on it. [36]As he rode along, people kept spreading
their cloaks on the road. [37]As he was now approaching the path down
from the Mount of Olives, the whole multitude of the disciples began
to praise God joyfully with a loud voice for all the deeds of power that
they had seen, [38]saying,

"Blessed is the king
who comes in the name of the Lord!
Peace in heaven,
and glory in the highest heaven!"

[39]Some of the Pharisees in the crowd said to him, "Teacher, order
your disciples to stop." [40]He answered, "I tell you, if these were silent,
the stones would shout out."

19:29 Mount of Olives: Bethphage and Bethany were small villages near Jerusalem. The Mount of Olives is in the Kidron Valley outside Jerusalem (see Map 13, p. 2110).

19:31 The Lord needs it: This may be another instance of giving to the poor and, therefore, lending to God (see notes on 12:33; 14:13; and 18:22). If the owner of the colt lets it go because he sees the disciples as poor people who need help, then he is yet another faithful Jew who gives without expecting to receive anything in return.

19:36 spreading their cloaks on the road: This was a way to welcome an important person (2 Kgs 9:13).

Jesus Weeps over Jerusalem

41 As he came near and saw the city, he wept over it, [42]saying, "If
you, even you, had only recognized on this day the things that make
for peace! But now they are hidden from your eyes. [43]Indeed, the days
will come upon you, when your enemies will set up ramparts around
you and surround you, and hem you in on every side. [44]They will
crush you to the ground, you and your children within you, and they
will not leave within you one stone upon another; because you did
not recognize the time of your visitation from God."[a]

19:41-44 the city: Jerusalem's city walls and the temple were destroyed by the Romans in 70 C.E.

[a] Gk lacks *from God*

Jesus Cleanses the Temple

45 Then he entered the temple and began to drive out those who
were selling things there; 46and he said, "It is written,

'My house shall be a house of prayer';
but you have made it a den of robbers."

47 Every day he was teaching in the temple. The chief priests, the
scribes, and the leaders of the people kept looking for a way to kill
him; 48but they did not find anything they could do, for all the people
were spellbound by what they heard.

The Authority of Jesus Questioned

20 One day, as he was teaching the people in the temple and
telling the good news, the chief priests and the scribes
came with the elders 2and said to him, "Tell us, by what authority are
you doing these things? Who is it who gave you this authority?" 3He
answered them, "I will also ask you a question, and you tell me: 4Did
the baptism of John come from heaven, or was it of human origin?"
5They discussed it with one another, saying, "If we say, 'From heaven,'
he will say, 'Why did you not believe him?' 6But if we say, 'Of human
origin,' all the people will stone us; for they are convinced that John
was a prophet." 7So they answered that they did not know where it
came from. 8Then Jesus said to them, "Neither will I tell you by what
authority I am doing these things."

The Parable of the Wicked Tenants

9 He began to tell the people this parable: "A man planted a vineyard, and leased it to tenants, and went to another country for a long
time. 10When the season came, he sent a slave to the tenants in order
that they might give him his share of the produce of the vineyard;
but the tenants beat him and sent him away empty-handed. 11Next he
sent another slave; that one also they beat and insulted and sent away
empty-handed. 12And he sent still a third; this one also they wounded
and threw out. 13Then the owner of the vineyard said, 'What shall I
do? I will send my beloved son; perhaps they will respect him.' 14But
when the tenants saw him, they discussed it among themselves and
said, 'This is the heir; let us kill him so that the inheritance may be
ours.' 15So they threw him out of the vineyard and killed him. What
then will the owner of the vineyard do to them? 16He will come and
destroy those tenants and give the vineyard to others." When they
heard this, they said, "Heaven forbid!" 17But he looked at them and
said, "What then does this text mean:

'The stone that the builders rejected
has become the cornerstone'?[a]

19:47 looking for a way to kill him: Temple authorities, chosen by Rome to represent the empire to the Jewish population, would have had reasons for wanting Jesus dead. They may have been jealous (see the people's reaction to Jesus in 19:48). They were also forced by Rome to maintain order and turn over anyone who might become a troublemaker. If they did not do this, and trouble broke out, Pilate would punish the Jewish people. When Jesus disrupted the practices of the temple (19:45-46), it was clear that things could get out of hand.

---

[a] Or *keystone*

18 Everyone who falls on that stone will be broken to pieces; and it will crush anyone on whom it falls." 19 When the scribes and chief priests realized that he had told this parable against them, they wanted to lay hands on him at that very hour, but they feared the people.

The Question about Paying Taxes

20 So they watched him and sent spies who pretended to be honest, in order to trap him by what he said, so as to hand him over to the jurisdiction and authority of the governor. 21 So they asked him, "Teacher, we know that you are right in what you say and teach, and you show deference to no one, but teach the way of God in accordance with truth. 22 Is it lawful for us to pay taxes to the emperor, or not?" 23 But he perceived their craftiness and said to them, 24 "Show me a denarius. Whose head and whose title does it bear?" They said, "The emperor's." 25 He said to them, "Then give to the emperor the things that are the emperor's, and to God the things that are God's." 26 And they were not able in the presence of the people to trap him by what he said; and being amazed by his answer, they became silent.

20:22 taxes to the emperor: Judea at this time was under the rule of the Roman Empire, which imposed taxes on the people.

The Question about the Resurrection

20:27 Sadducees: These Jews, who did not believe in life after death, worked with the temple priests.

27 Some Sadducees, those who say there is no resurrection, came to him 28 and asked him a question, "Teacher, Moses wrote for us that if a man's brother dies, leaving a wife but no children, the man[a] shall marry the widow and raise up children for his brother. 29 Now there were seven brothers; the first married, and died childless; 30 then the second 31 and the third married her, and so in the same way all seven died childless. 32 Finally the woman also died. 33 In the resurrection, therefore, whose wife will the woman be? For the seven had married her."

34 Jesus said to them, "Those who belong to this age marry and are given in marriage; 35 but those who are considered worthy of a place in that age and in the resurrection from the dead neither marry nor are given in marriage. 36 Indeed they cannot die anymore, because they are like angels and are children of God, being children of the resurrection. 37 And the fact that the dead are raised Moses himself showed, in the story about the bush, where he speaks of the Lord as the God of Abraham, the God of Isaac, and the God of Jacob. 38 Now he is God not of the dead, but of the living; for to him all of them are alive." 39 Then some of the scribes answered, "Teacher, you have spoken well." 40 For they no longer dared to ask him another question.

The Question about David's Son

41 Then he said to them, "How can they say that the Messiah[b] is David's son? 42 For David himself says in the book of Psalms,

---

[a] Gk *his brother* [b] Or *the Christ*

'The Lord said to my Lord,
"Sit at my right hand,
43 until I make your enemies your footstool." '
44 David thus calls him Lord; so how can he be his son?"

Jesus Denounces the Scribes

45 In the hearing of all the people he said to the[a] disciples, 46 "Beware of the scribes, who like to walk around in long robes, and love
to be greeted with respect in the marketplaces, and to have the best
seats in the synagogues and places of honor at banquets. 47 They devour widows' houses and for the sake of appearance say long prayers.
They will receive the greater condemnation."

The Widow's Offering

21 He looked up and saw rich people putting their gifts into the
treasury; 2 he also saw a poor widow put in two small copper
coins. 3 He said, "Truly I tell you, this poor widow has put in more
than all of them; 4 for all of them have contributed out of their abundance, but she out of her poverty has put in all she had to live on."

The Destruction of the Temple Foretold

5 When some were speaking about the temple, how it was
adorned with beautiful stones and gifts dedicated to God, he said,
6 "As for these things that you see, the days will come when not one
stone will be left upon another; all will be thrown down."

Signs and Persecutions

7 They asked him, "Teacher, when will this be, and what will be
the sign that this is about to take place?" 8 And he said, "Beware that

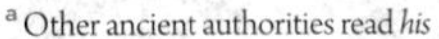

[a] Other ancient authorities read *his*

21:1-4 two small copper coins: The *lepton* was the smallest Greek coin. Two of these coins would have had little if any value.

21:5 how it was adorned with beautiful stones: See illustration below. The beauty of the temple was both a source of delight and cause for offense for faithful Jews at the time of Jesus. The temple was beautiful and magnificent, a testimony to the holiness of God and a reminder of the presence of God in a chaotic world. But the adornments that made it beautiful were the work of Herod, a brutal king who killed his own children.

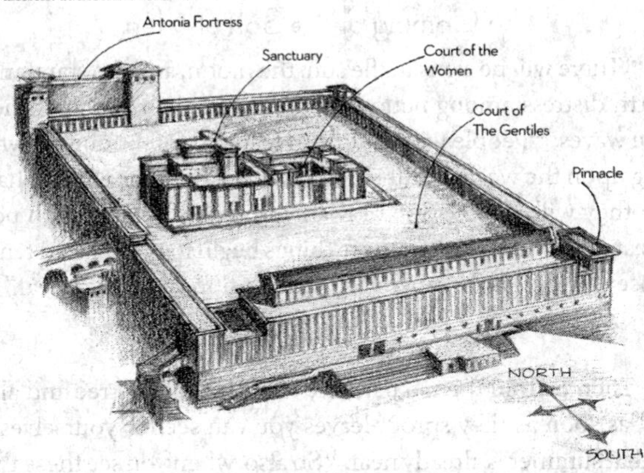

The Temple in Jerusalem and Antonia Fortress, New Testament Times. Roman soldiers were stationed at the Antonia Fortress.

you are not led astray; for many will come in my name and say, 'I am
he!'[a] and, 'The time is near!'[b] Do not go after them.
9 "When you hear of wars and insurrections, do not be terrified;
for these things must take place first, but the end will not follow immediately." 10 Then he said to them, "Nation will rise against nation,
and kingdom against kingdom; 11 there will be great earthquakes, and
in various places famines and plagues; and there will be dreadful portents and great signs from heaven.
12 "But before all this occurs, they will arrest you and persecute
you; they will hand you over to synagogues and prisons, and you will
be brought before kings and governors because of my name. 13 This
will give you an opportunity to testify. 14 So make up your minds not
to prepare your defense in advance; 15 for I will give you words[c] and
a wisdom that none of your opponents will be able to withstand or
contradict. 16 You will be betrayed even by parents and brothers, by
relatives and friends; and they will put some of you to death. 17 You
will be hated by all because of my name. 18 But not a hair of your head
will perish. 19 By your endurance you will gain your souls.

The Destruction of Jerusalem Foretold

20 "When you see Jerusalem surrounded by armies, then know
that its desolation has come near.[d] 21 Then those in Judea must flee to
the mountains, and those inside the city must leave it, and those out
in the country must not enter it; 22 for these are days of vengeance, as
a fulfillment of all that is written. 23 Woe to those who are pregnant
and to those who are nursing infants in those days! For there will be
great distress on the earth and wrath against this people; 24 they will
fall by the edge of the sword and be taken away as captives among all
nations; and Jerusalem will be trampled on by the Gentiles, until the
times of the Gentiles are fulfilled.

The Coming of the Son of Man

25 "There will be signs in the sun, the moon, and the stars, and on
the earth distress among nations confused by the roaring of the sea
and the waves. 26 People will faint from fear and foreboding of what is
coming upon the world, for the powers of the heavens will be shaken.
27 Then they will see 'the Son of Man coming in a cloud' with power
and great glory. 28 Now when these things begin to take place, stand up
and raise your heads, because your redemption is drawing near."

The Lesson of the Fig Tree

29 Then he told them a parable: "Look at the fig tree and all the
trees; 30 as soon as they sprout leaves you can see for yourselves and
know that summer is already near. 31 So also, when you see these things

---

[a] Gk *I am* [b] Or *at hand* [c] Gk *a mouth* [d] Or *is at hand*

taking place, you know that the kingdom of God is near. 32 Truly I tell
you, this generation will not pass away until all things have taken place.
33 Heaven and earth will pass away, but my words will not pass away.

Exhortation to Watch

34 "Be on guard so that your hearts are not weighed down with
dissipation and drunkenness and the worries of this life, and that day
does not catch you unexpectedly, 35 like a trap. For it will come upon
all who live on the face of the whole earth. 36 Be alert at all times, praying that you may have the strength to escape all these things that will
take place, and to stand before the Son of Man."

37 Every day he was teaching in the temple, and at night he would
go out and spend the night on the Mount of Olives, as it was called.
38 And all the people would get up early in the morning to listen to him
in the temple.

The Plot to Kill Jesus

22 Now the festival of Unleavened Bread, which is called the
Passover, was near. 2 The chief priests and the scribes were
looking for a way to put Jesus[a] to death, for they were afraid of the
people.

3 Then Satan entered into Judas called Iscariot, who was one of
the twelve; 4 he went away and conferred with the chief priests and
officers of the temple police about how he might betray him to them.
5 They were greatly pleased and agreed to give him money. 6 So he consented and began to look for an opportunity to betray him to them
when no crowd was present.

The Preparation of the Passover

7 Then came the day of Unleavened Bread, on which the Passover
lamb had to be sacrificed. 8 So Jesus[b] sent Peter and John, saying, "Go
and prepare the Passover meal for us that we may eat it." 9 They asked
him, "Where do you want us to make preparations for it?" 10 "Listen,"
he said to them, "when you have entered the city, a man carrying a
jar of water will meet you; follow him into the house he enters 11 and
say to the owner of the house, 'The teacher asks you, "Where is the
guest room, where I may eat the Passover with my disciples?" ' 12 He
will show you a large room upstairs, already furnished. Make preparations for us there." 13 So they went and found everything as he had told
them; and they prepared the Passover meal.

The Institution of the Lord's Supper

14 When the hour came, he took his place at the table, and the
apostles with him. 15 He said to them, "I have eagerly desired to eat

22:3-6 Then Satan entered into Judas: Luke links this scene with the testing of Jesus in the wilderness in 4:1-13, when Satan left "until an opportune time." The Greek spelling of the Hebrew name "Judah" is Judas, which might indicate that this disciple was from Judea. The name "Iscariot" could mean "a man from Kerioth" (located in Judea), "a man who was a betrayer," or "a man who was a liar."

22:4 chief priests and officers of the temple police: Rome allowed the chief priests to manage local matters. The temple police were Jewish guards of the temple and surrounding area.

22:7 Passover: See Jewish Festivals and Feasts, p. 227.

22:10-12 a man carrying a jar of water . . . large room upstairs: This man might stand out, because women usually did this work. The "large room upstairs" is often called the "Upper Room" (see Map 13, p. 2110).

[a] Gk *him* [b] Gk *he*

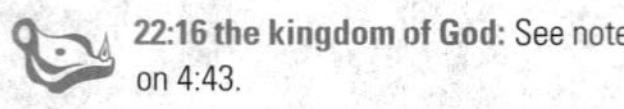

22:16 the kingdom of God: See note on 4:43.

22:19-20 new covenant: God had made a covenant or agreement with Moses (Exod 24:1-8). This new covenant is made through Jesus' body and blood.

this Passover with you before I suffer; 16 for I tell you, I will not eat
it[a] until it is fulfilled in the kingdom of God." 17 Then he took a cup,
and after giving thanks he said, "Take this and divide it among yourselves; 18 for I tell you that from now on I will not drink of the fruit
of the vine until the kingdom of God comes." 19 Then he took a loaf
of bread, and when he had given thanks, he broke it and gave it to
them, saying, "This is my body, which is given for you. Do this in
remembrance of me." 20 And he did the same with the cup after supper, saying, "This cup that is poured out for you is the new covenant
in my blood.[b] 21 But see, the one who betrays me is with me, and his
hand is on the table. 22 For the Son of Man is going as it has been
determined, but woe to that one by whom he is betrayed!" 23 Then
they began to ask one another which one of them it could be who
would do this.

The Dispute about Greatness

24 A dispute also arose among them as to which one of them was
to be regarded as the greatest. 25 But he said to them, "The kings of the
Gentiles lord it over them; and those in authority over them are called
benefactors. 26 But not so with you; rather the greatest among you
must become like the youngest, and the leader like one who serves.
27 For who is greater, the one who is at the table or the one who serves? Is
it not the one at the table? But I am among you as one who serves.

28 "You are those who have stood by me in my trials; 29 and I confer on you, just as my Father has conferred on me, a kingdom, 30 so
that you may eat and drink at my table in my kingdom, and you will
sit on thrones judging the twelve tribes of Israel.

Jesus Predicts Peter's Denial

31 "Simon, Simon, listen! Satan has demanded[c] to sift all of you
like wheat, 32 but I have prayed for you that your own faith may not fail;
and you, when once you have turned back, strengthen your brothers."
33 And he said to him, "Lord, I am ready to go with you to prison and
to death!" 34 Jesus[d] said, "I tell you, Peter, the cock will not crow this
day, until you have denied three times that you know me."

Purse, Bag, and Sword

22:35-36 purse...bag...sword: People in Jesus' time would have taken these things along on a dangerous trip.

35 He said to them, "When I sent you out without a purse, bag,
or sandals, did you lack anything?" They said, "No, not a thing." 36 He
said to them, "But now, the one who has a purse must take it, and
likewise a bag. And the one who has no sword must sell his cloak and
buy one. 37 For I tell you, this scripture must be fulfilled in me, 'And he
was counted among the lawless'; and indeed what is written about me

---

[a] Other ancient authorities read *never eat it again* [b] Other ancient authorities lack, in whole or in part, verses 19b-20 (*which is given ... in my blood*) [c] Or *has obtained permission* [d] Gk *He*

is being fulfilled." [38]They said, "Lord, look, here are two swords." He
replied, "It is enough."

Jesus Prays on the Mount of Olives

39 He came out and went, as was his custom, to the Mount of
Olives; and the disciples followed him. [40]When he reached the place,
he said to them, "Pray that you may not come into the time of trial."[a]
[41]Then he withdrew from them about a stone's throw, knelt down,
and prayed, [42]"Father, if you are willing, remove this cup from me;
yet, not my will but yours be done." ⟦[43]Then an angel from heaven
appeared to him and gave him strength. [44]In his anguish he prayed
more earnestly, and his sweat became like great drops of blood falling
down on the ground.⟧[b] [45]When he got up from prayer, he came to
the disciples and found them sleeping because of grief, [46]and he said
to them, "Why are you sleeping? Get up and pray that you may not
come into the time of trial."[a]

22:39-53 Mount of Olives: See Map 13, p. 2110. Jesus comes here to pray, and Judas hands him over to the chief priests, temple police, and other leaders.

The Betrayal and Arrest of Jesus

47 While he was still speaking, suddenly a crowd came, and the
one called Judas, one of the twelve, was leading them. He approached
Jesus to kiss him; [48]but Jesus said to him, "Judas, is it with a kiss that
you are betraying the Son of Man?" [49]When those who were around
him saw what was coming, they asked, "Lord, should we strike with
the sword?" [50]Then one of them struck the slave of the high priest
and cut off his right ear. [51]But Jesus said, "No more of this!" And he
touched his ear and healed him. [52]Then Jesus said to the chief priests,
the officers of the temple police, and the elders who had come for
him, "Have you come out with swords and clubs as if I were a bandit?
[53]When I was with you day after day in the temple, you did not lay
hands on me. But this is your hour, and the power of darkness!"

Peter Denies Jesus

54 Then they seized him and led him away, bringing him into
the high priest's house. But Peter was following at a distance. [55]When
they had kindled a fire in the middle of the courtyard and sat down
together, Peter sat among them. [56]Then a servant-girl, seeing him in
the firelight, stared at him and said, "This man also was with him."
[57]But he denied it, saying, "Woman, I do not know him." [58]A little later
someone else, on seeing him, said, "You also are one of them." But Peter said, "Man, I am not!" [59]Then about an hour later still another kept
insisting, "Surely this man also was with him; for he is a Galilean."
[60]But Peter said, "Man, I do not know what you are talking about!"
At that moment, while he was still speaking, the cock crowed. [61]The
Lord turned and looked at Peter. Then Peter remembered the word of

22:54 the high priest's house: See Map 13, p. 2110. Jesus may have been brought to the home of Caiaphas (see note on 3:1-3).

[a] Or *into temptation* [b] Other ancient authorities lack verses 43 and 44

the Lord, how he had said to him, "Before the cock crows today, you
will deny me three times." 62 And he went out and wept bitterly.

The Mocking and Beating of Jesus

63 Now the men who were holding Jesus began to mock him and
beat him; 64 they also blindfolded him and kept asking him, "Prophesy! Who is it that struck you?" 65 They kept heaping many other insults on him.

Jesus before the Council

22:66-71 council: The council could hear cases that involved Jewish religious laws.

66 When day came, the assembly of the elders of the people, both
chief priests and scribes, gathered together, and they brought him to
their council. 67 They said, "If you are the Messiah,[a] tell us." He replied,
"If I tell you, you will not believe; 68 and if I question you, you will not
answer. 69 But from now on the Son of Man will be seated at the right
hand of the power of God." 70 All of them asked, "Are you, then, the
Son of God?" He said to them, "You say that I am." 71 Then they said,
"What further testimony do we need? We have heard it ourselves
from his own lips!"

Jesus before Pilate

23:1 Pilate: Pontius Pilate, as governor of Judea, was a senior official for Rome.

23:2 forbidding us to pay taxes: Jesus did not do what he is accused of here. See 20:22-26.

23:1-3 Are you the king of the Jews?: Pilate asks this question, and Jesus answers it in each of the four Gospels (see Matt 27:11; Mark 15:2; John 18:33-38), but only Luke provides information on what led up to it. The authorities handing Jesus over explain that he is a troublemaker (see 23:2). Their accusations before Pilate are not the same as the case heard by the Jewish council (22:66-71), but Pilate would not have understood those charges or cared about them. The authorities, however, know that Pilate will retaliate if trouble should break out because of Jesus, so they are forced to turn Jesus over and charge him with things Pilate would understand as dangerous. In Greek, Pilate's question is a mocking statement: "You are the king of the Jews," and this is repeated on the inscription placed over Jesus on the cross (23:38). Historical sources show Pilate's contempt and mockery of the Jews and their faith and give this as a reason why he was removed from office by the Romans a few years later.

23 Then the assembly rose as a body and brought Jesus[b] before Pilate. 2 They began to accuse him, saying, "We found
this man perverting our nation, forbidding us to pay taxes to the emperor, and saying that he himself is the Messiah, a king."[c] 3 Then Pilate
asked him, "Are you the king of the Jews?" He answered, "You say so."
4 Then Pilate said to the chief priests and the crowds, "I find no basis
for an accusation against this man." 5 But they were insistent and said,
"He stirs up the people by teaching throughout all Judea, from Galilee
where he began even to this place."

Jesus before Herod

23:6-12 Herod: Herod Antipas, son of Herod the Great, ruled Galilee at this time.

6 When Pilate heard this, he asked whether the man was a Galilean. 7 And when he learned that he was under Herod's jurisdiction,
he sent him off to Herod, who was himself in Jerusalem at that time.
8 When Herod saw Jesus, he was very glad, for he had been wanting
to see him for a long time, because he had heard about him and was
hoping to see him perform some sign. 9 He questioned him at some
length, but Jesus[d] gave him no answer. 10 The chief priests and the
scribes stood by, vehemently accusing him. 11 Even Herod with his
soldiers treated him with contempt and mocked him; then he put
an elegant robe on him, and sent him back to Pilate. 12 That same day
Herod and Pilate became friends with each other; before this they
had been enemies.

---

[a] Or *the Christ* [b] Gk *him* [c] Or *is an anointed king* [d] Gk *he*

Jesus Sentenced to Death

13 Pilate then called together the chief priests, the leaders, and the people, [14]and said to them, “You brought me this man as one who was perverting the people; and here I have examined him in your presence and have not found this man guilty of any of your charges against him. [15]Neither has Herod, for he sent him back to us. Indeed, he has done nothing to deserve death. [16]I will therefore have him flogged and release him.”[a]

18 Then they all shouted out together, “Away with this fellow! Release Barabbas for us!” [19](This was a man who had been put in prison for an insurrection that had taken place in the city, and for murder.) [20]Pilate, wanting to release Jesus, addressed them again; [21]but they kept shouting, “Crucify, crucify him!” [22]A third time he said to them, “Why, what evil has he done? I have found in him no ground for the sentence of death; I will therefore have him flogged and then release him.” [23]But they kept urgently demanding with loud shouts that he should be crucified; and their voices prevailed. [24]So Pilate gave his verdict that their demand should be granted. [25]He released the man they asked for, the one who had been put in prison for insurrection and murder, and he handed Jesus over as they wished.

The Crucifixion of Jesus

26 As they led him away, they seized a man, Simon of Cyrene, who was coming from the country, and they laid the cross on him, and made him carry it behind Jesus. [27]A great number of the people followed him, and among them were women who were beating their breasts and wailing for him. [28]But Jesus turned to them and said, “Daughters of Jerusalem, do not weep for me, but weep for yourselves and for your children. [29]For the days are surely coming when they will say, ‘Blessed are the barren, and the wombs that never bore, and the breasts that never nursed.’ [30]Then they will begin to say to the mountains, ‘Fall on us’; and to the hills, ‘Cover us.’ [31]For if they do this when the wood is green, what will happen when it is dry?”

32 Two others also, who were criminals, were led away to be put to death with him. [33]When they came to the place that is called The Skull, they crucified Jesus[b] there with the criminals, one on his right and one on his left. ⟦[34]Then Jesus said, “Father, forgive them; for they do not know what they are doing.”⟧[c] And they cast lots to divide his clothing. [35]And the people stood by, watching; but the leaders scoffed at him, saying, “He saved others; let him save himself if he is the Messiah[d] of God, his chosen one!” [36]The soldiers also mocked him,

[a] Here, or after verse 19, other ancient authorities add verse 17, *Now he was obliged to release someone for them at the festival* [b] Gk *him* [c] Other ancient authorities lack the sentence *Then Jesus . . . what they are doing* [d] Or *the Christ*

23:13 the people: This may refer to a crowd, but not to all the Jews or all the people in Jerusalem.

23:26 Cyrene: This was a city in northern Africa (see Map 11, p. 2108).

23:27-28 women who were beating their breasts and wailing for him: Again, Jesus is surrounded with Jews who support him. These “Daughters of Jerusalem” are mourning for Jesus as they would for members of their own families.

23:31 if they do this when the wood is green, what will happen when it is dry?: Although local officials handed Jesus over to the Roman authorities, only Rome had the authority to crucify someone. This power to torture people to death in public allowed Rome to demonstrate, when necessary, that it had no moral limits on what it would do to maintain “peace.” The saying, therefore, means something like: “If Rome puts one Jew to death when there is no rebellion, just think what they will do when there is rebellion.” The original readers of Luke would have witnessed Rome’s response to the First Jewish Revolt in 66–70 C.E. Some sources say that one million Jews were killed. Jerusalem was besieged and defeated, and the temple was burned and leveled.

23:33 The Skull: Also called Golgotha, this place may have been named for a skull-shaped rock, or for the crucifixions that took place there. See Map 13, p. 2110.

coming up and offering him sour wine, 37 and saying, "If you are the
King of the Jews, save yourself!" 38 There was also an inscription over
him,[a] "This is the King of the Jews."

39 One of the criminals who were hanged there kept deriding[b]
him and saying, "Are you not the Messiah?[c] Save yourself and us!"
40 But the other rebuked him, saying, "Do you not fear God, since you
are under the same sentence of condemnation? 41 And we indeed have
been condemned justly, for we are getting what we deserve for our
deeds, but this man has done nothing wrong." 42 Then he said, "Jesus,
remember me when you come into[d] your kingdom." 43 He replied,
"Truly I tell you, today you will be with me in Paradise."

The Death of Jesus

44 It was now about noon, and darkness came over the whole
land[e] until three in the afternoon, 45 while the sun's light failed;[f] and
the curtain of the temple was torn in two. 46 Then Jesus, crying with a
loud voice, said, "Father, into your hands I commend my spirit." Having said this, he breathed his last. 47 When the centurion saw what
had taken place, he praised God and said, "Certainly this man was
innocent."[g] 48 And when all the crowds who had gathered there for
this spectacle saw what had taken place, they returned home, beating
their breasts. 49 But all his acquaintances, including the women who
had followed him from Galilee, stood at a distance, watching these
things.

The Burial of Jesus

50 Now there was a good and righteous man named Joseph, who,
though a member of the council, 51 had not agreed to their plan and
action. He came from the Jewish town of Arimathea, and he was waiting expectantly for the kingdom of God. 52 This man went to Pilate
and asked for the body of Jesus. 53 Then he took it down, wrapped it
in a linen cloth, and laid it in a rock-hewn tomb where no one had
ever been laid. 54 It was the day of Preparation, and the sabbath was
beginning.[h] 55 The women who had come with him from Galilee followed, and they saw the tomb and how his body was laid. 56 Then they
returned, and prepared spices and ointments.

On the sabbath they rested according to the commandment.

The Resurrection of Jesus

24 But on the first day of the week, at early dawn, they came
to the tomb, taking the spices that they had prepared.
2 They found the stone rolled away from the tomb, 3 but when they

---

[a] Other ancient authorities add *written in Greek and Latin and Hebrew* (that is, *Aramaic*) [b] Or *blaspheming* [c] Or *the Christ* [d] Other ancient authorities read *in* [e] Or *earth* [f] Or *the sun was eclipsed.* Other ancient authorities read *the sun was darkened* [g] Or *righteous* [h] Gk *was dawning*

23:40-43 Jesus, remember me: Again in Luke's story, Jesus meets a faithful Jew, even as he is nailed to a cross.

23:45 curtain of the temple: A curtain separated the Holy Place from the Holy of Holies inside the temple. The high priest was the only person who went behind the curtain, and then only once a year to perform essential acts. See note on 1:9.

23:47 Certainly this man was innocent: The word translated here as "innocent" is translated elsewhere in Luke as "righteous," referring to the actions of people who faithfully observed God's teachings (see note on 1:6). The centurion's announcement shows that Jesus held his faith to the last.

23:49 all his acquaintances: Even as he is being tortured to death, Jesus is surrounded and supported by family and acquaintances, Jewish women and men who had followed him from the beginning. The crowds return home mourning for Jesus (23:48). In Luke's Gospel, Jesus comes to his own people and they welcome and support him to the very end.

23:50-53 Joseph...of Arimathea: The Gospel writer notes again that there are faithful Jews who are waiting for the kingdom of God. Handling the burial of Jesus' body was a risky move for someone on the Jewish council. Arimathea was about twenty miles from Jerusalem (see Map 12, p. 2109).

23:56 On the sabbath they rested: Even in the shocking aftermath of Jesus' death, the faithful Jewish women who have followed him testify to their reverence for the gift of the Sabbath by resting on it.

24:1 on the first day of the week, at early dawn: The Jewish Sabbath ends at sunset Saturday evening. The women waited to bring spices to the tomb until early Sunday morning.

went in, they did not find the body.[a] [4]While they were perplexed
about this, suddenly two men in dazzling clothes stood beside
them. [5]The women[b] were terrified and bowed their faces to the
ground, but the men[c] said to them, "Why do you look for the living
among the dead? He is not here, but has risen.[d] [6]Remember how he
told you, while he was still in Galilee, [7]that the Son of Man must be
handed over to sinners, and be crucified, and on the third day rise
again." [8]Then they remembered his words, [9]and returning from the
tomb, they told all this to the eleven and to all the rest. [10]Now it was
Mary Magdalene, Joanna, Mary the mother of James, and the other
women with them who told this to the apostles. [11]But these words
seemed to them an idle tale, and they did not believe them. [12]But
Peter got up and ran to the tomb; stooping and looking in, he saw
the linen cloths by themselves; then he went home, amazed at what
had happened.[e]

The Walk to Emmaus

13 Now on that same day two of them were going to a village
called Emmaus, about seven miles[f] from Jerusalem, [14]and talking with
each other about all these things that had happened. [15]While they
were talking and discussing, Jesus himself came near and went with
them, [16]but their eyes were kept from recognizing him. [17]And he said
to them, "What are you discussing with each other while you walk
along?" They stood still, looking sad.[g] [18]Then one of them, whose
name was Cleopas, answered him, "Are you the only stranger in Jerusalem who does not know the things that have taken place there
in these days?" [19]He asked them, "What things?" They replied, "The
things about Jesus of Nazareth,[h] who was a prophet mighty in deed
and word before God and all the people, [20]and how our chief priests
and leaders handed him over to be condemned to death and crucified him. [21]But we had hoped that he was the one to redeem Israel.[i]
Yes, and besides all this, it is now the third day since these things took
place. [22]Moreover, some women of our group astounded us. They
were at the tomb early this morning, [23]and when they did not find his
body there, they came back and told us that they had indeed seen a
vision of angels who said that he was alive. [24]Some of those who were
with us went to the tomb and found it just as the women had said;
but they did not see him." [25]Then he said to them, "Oh, how foolish
you are, and how slow of heart to believe all that the prophets have
declared! [26]Was it not necessary that the Messiah[j] should suffer these
things and then enter into his glory?" [27]Then beginning with Moses

24:9 the eleven: There are eleven apostles instead of twelve, because Judas is not with them now.

24:10 Mary Magdalene, Joanna, Mary the mother of James: See notes on 8:2 and 8:3. Mary, the mother of James, may be the mother of one of the two disciples named James, but this is unclear.

24:13 Emmaus: This small village was in Judea (see Map 12, p. 2109).

24:26 Was it not necessary that the Messiah should suffer these things: For believing Jews at the time of Jesus, the answer to this question simply would have been "no." The Messiah was expected to defend them against their enemies, restore balance to all creation by feeding the hungry and raising up the poor, bring peace on earth, and rule forever (see 1:46-55). After Jesus' suffering, death, and resurrection, his followers searched the Scriptures to find passages that dealt with suffering and the Messiah.

24:27, 32 scriptures: This would have been the Jewish Scriptures, what Christians call the Old Testament.

[a] Other ancient authorities add *of the Lord Jesus* [b] Gk *They* [c] Gk *but they* [d] Other ancient authorities lack *He is not here, but has risen* [e] Other ancient authorities lack verse 12 [f] Gk *sixty stadia;* other ancient authorities read *a hundred sixty stadia* [g] Other ancient authorities read *walk along, looking sad?"* [h] Other ancient authorities read *Jesus the Nazorean* [i] Or *to set Israel free* [j] Or *the Christ*

and all the prophets, he interpreted to them the things about himself
in all the scriptures.
28 As they came near the village to which they were going, he
walked ahead as if he were going on. 29 But they urged him strongly,
saying, "Stay with us, because it is almost evening and the day is now
nearly over." So he went in to stay with them. 30 When he was at the
table with them, he took bread, blessed and broke it, and gave it to
them. 31 Then their eyes were opened, and they recognized him; and
he vanished from their sight. 32 They said to each other, "Were not our
hearts burning within us[a] while he was talking to us on the road, while
he was opening the scriptures to us?" 33 That same hour they got up
and returned to Jerusalem; and they found the eleven and their companions gathered together. 34 They were saying, "The Lord has risen
indeed, and he has appeared to Simon!" 35 Then they told what had
happened on the road, and how he had been made known to them in
the breaking of the bread.

Jesus Appears to His Disciples

36 While they were talking about this, Jesus himself stood among
them and said to them, "Peace be with you."[b] 37 They were startled and
terrified, and thought that they were seeing a ghost. 38 He said to them,
"Why are you frightened, and why do doubts arise in your hearts?
39 Look at my hands and my feet; see that it is I myself. Touch me
and see; for a ghost does not have flesh and bones as you see that I
have." 40 And when he had said this, he showed them his hands and his
feet.[c] 41 While in their joy they were disbelieving and still wondering,
he said to them, "Have you anything here to eat?" 42 They gave him a
piece of broiled fish, 43 and he took it and ate in their presence.
44 Then he said to them, "These are my words that I spoke to you
while I was still with you—that everything written about me in the
law of Moses, the prophets, and the psalms must be fulfilled." 45 Then
he opened their minds to understand the scriptures, 46 and he said to
them, "Thus it is written, that the Messiah[d] is to suffer and to rise from
the dead on the third day, 47 and that repentance and forgiveness of
sins is to be proclaimed in his name to all nations, beginning from Jerusalem. 48 You are witnesses[e] of these things. 49 And see, I am sending
upon you what my Father promised; so stay here in the city until you
have been clothed with power from on high."

24:39 my hands and my feet: People put to death on a cross sometimes had nails driven through their wrists and feet.

24:49 what my Father promised: The apostles would be filled with God's Holy Spirit (see Acts 2).

The Ascension of Jesus

50 Then he led them out as far as Bethany, and, lifting up his
hands, he blessed them. 51 While he was blessing them, he withdrew

---

[a] Other ancient authorities lack *within us* [b] Other ancient authorities lack *and said to them, "Peace be with you."* [c] Other ancient authorities lack verse 40 [d] Or *the Christ* [e] Or *nations. Beginning from Jerusalem* [48] *you are witnesses*

from them and was carried up into heaven.[a] [52]And they worshiped
him, and[b] returned to Jerusalem with great joy; [53]and they were continually in the temple blessing God.[c]

---

[a] Other ancient authorities lack *and was carried up into heaven* [b] Other ancient authorities lack *worshiped him, and* [c] Other ancient authorities add *Amen*

24:53 they were continually in the temple: The first scene in Luke (1:8-23) takes place in the temple, the stable, safe center of the Jewish universe. Now the last scene returns there. By the time this Gospel was written and read, however, the temple would lie in ruins.

John 20:30-31

JOHN

Background File

It is clear from the beginning of the Gospel of John that it has a different feel than the Gospels of Matthew, Mark, and Luke. While the first three Gospels have a lot of the same stories and events in Jesus' life, John's Gospel gives us an altogether different Jesus. John's Gospel begins with a hymn of praise for the Word of God made flesh (1:1-18). It includes events in Jesus' ministry, but the order is not like that of the other Gospels, and much new material focuses on who Jesus is, including the way he describes himself in "I am" statements. Like the other Gospels, the authorship of John's Gospel is unknown. Early traditions credit John the son of Zebedee as its author. The "beloved disciple" mentioned in the book (19:26; 21:20-24) has been identified with John. There are clues in the Gospel that lead scholars to believe that it was written for Jewish Christians who, because they were followers of Jesus, experienced hostility within their Jewish communities.

What's the Story?

This gospel includes two larger sections after the prologue (1:1-18). Frequently called the Book of Signs, the first of the larger sections (1:19–12:50) tells of Jesus' public ministry. He is described as performing seven miracles, or signs, as they are called in this gospel. The second section (chapters 13–21) describes the events of Jesus' last meal with his disciples and his crucifixion, resurrection, and post-resurrection appearances. This last half of story is sometimes referred to as the "Book of Glory."

An early-church father, Clement of Alexandria, described the Gospel of John as a "spiritual account" of Jesus' life and teaching. Often considered more theological than historical, the portrait of Jesus in the Gospel of John is very different from the other Gospels. John includes stories about Jesus that do not appear in Matthew, Mark, or Luke, among them his first sign at the wedding in Cana (2:1-11); his encounters with Nicodemus (3:1-21); the Samaritan woman (4:1-41); the woman caught in adultery (7:53—8:11); his raising of Lazarus (11:17-44); and his post-resurrection appearances to Thomas (20:24-29) and Mary Magdalene (20:11-18). Also unique to John's Gospel are the various "I am" images of Jesus (see the chart The "I AM" Sayings of Jesus in John's Gospel, p. 1773). On the other hand, John's gospel does not include some familiar events in the story of Jesus. There are no parables, Sermon on the Mount, institution of the Lord's Supper, or nativity story.

What's the Message?

The first words of the Gospel, "In the beginning was the Word, and the Word was with God, and the Word was God," make it clear that the Gospel is not concerned with Jesus' family tree but with his true identity as the Word of God made flesh. Jesus is portrayed as being one with the Father, and he is in absolute control of and aware of his purpose. The central claim of this Gospel is that, in Jesus, the Word that in the beginning was with God, and was God, became human. This claim is firmly established in the prologue (1:1-18), and we can use this lens to read the whole gospel. The prologue introduces the Gospel's main themes: light and darkness, belief, truth, witness, and the identity of Jesus. Jesus is the one who makes God known (1:18). In Jesus' words and actions, God is revealed to us. For the Gospel of John, Jesus is not the suffering Messiah but the very presence of the divine "I AM" (see Exod 3:14 and NRSV footnote *a*) who has chosen to come into the world.

The writer also makes it clear that the Gospel was written for a very specific purpose: "Now Jesus did many other signs. . . . But these are written so that you may come to believe that Jesus is the Messiah, the Son of God, and that through believing you may have life in his name" (20:30-31). The reader is invited into this story to have an encounter with Jesus and to abide in the Word (8:31-32). We receive the same promises as Jesus' first disciples: abundant life and unity with Jesus and God the Father. The Gospel continues to call Jesus' followers to witness to the presence of the Word in the world even after Jesus has returned to the Father.

The Word Became Flesh

1 In the beginning was the Word, and the Word was with God,
and the Word was God. 2 He was in the beginning with God. 3 All
things came into being through him, and without him not one thing
came into being. What has come into being 4 in him was life,[a] and the
life was the light of all people. 5 The light shines in the darkness, and
the darkness did not overcome it.

6 There was a man sent from God, whose name was John. 7 He
came as a witness to testify to the light, so that all might believe
through him. 8 He himself was not the light, but he came to testify to
the light. 9 The true light, which enlightens everyone, was coming into
the world.[b]

10 He was in the world, and the world came into being through
him; yet the world did not know him. 11 He came to what was his own,[c]
and his own people did not accept him. 12 But to all who received him,
who believed in his name, he gave power to become children of God,
13 who were born, not of blood or of the will of the flesh or of the will
of man, but of God.

14 And the Word became flesh and lived among us, and we have

---

[a] Or *3 through him. And without him not one thing came into being that has come into being. 4 In him was life*
[b] Or *He was the true light that enlightens everyone coming into the world*
[c] Or *to his own home*

1:1 the Word: The Greek term for "word" is *logos* (LOW-gohs), which has roots in Greek thought as the ordering plan of the universe and in Judaism as divine Wisdom.

1:1 In the beginning: The first words of John's Gospel recall the first words of Genesis (Gen 1:1). In contrast to the stories of Jesus' birth in Matthew and Luke, here Jesus' origin is outside of time, space, and history.

1:7 so that all might believe: This is the first occurrence of the verb "to believe." Belief is always active in John's Gospel—it is something one does, not what one has.

1:14 the Word became flesh and lived among us: That God chose to take on human form is the central claim of this Gospel. The word *lived* can also be translated as "tabernacled" or "dwelt."

seen his glory, the glory as of a father's only son,[a] full of grace and
truth. 15 (John testified to him and cried out, "This was he of whom I
said, 'He who comes after me ranks ahead of me because he was before me.' ") 16 From his fullness we have all received, grace upon grace.
17 The law indeed was given through Moses; grace and truth came
through Jesus Christ. 18 No one has ever seen God. It is God the only
Son,[b] who is close to the Father's heart,[c] who has made him known.

The Testimony of John the Baptist

19 This is the testimony given by John when the Jews sent priests
and Levites from Jerusalem to ask him, "Who are you?" 20 He confessed and did not deny it, but confessed, "I am not the Messiah."[d]
21 And they asked him, "What then? Are you Elijah?" He said, "I am
not." "Are you the prophet?" He answered, "No." 22 Then they said to
him, "Who are you? Let us have an answer for those who sent us.
What do you say about yourself?" 23 He said,

"I am the voice of one crying out in the wilderness,
'Make straight the way of the Lord,'"

as the prophet Isaiah said.

24 Now they had been sent from the Pharisees. 25 They asked him,
"Why then are you baptizing if you are neither the Messiah,[d] nor Elijah, nor the prophet?" 26 John answered them, "I baptize with water.
Among you stands one whom you do not know, 27 the one who is
coming after me; I am not worthy to untie the thong of his sandal."
28 This took place in Bethany across the Jordan where John was baptizing.

The Lamb of God

29 The next day he saw Jesus coming toward him and declared,
"Here is the Lamb of God who takes away the sin of the world! 30 This
is he of whom I said, 'After me comes a man who ranks ahead of me
because he was before me.' 31 I myself did not know him; but I came
baptizing with water for this reason, that he might be revealed to Israel." 32 And John testified, "I saw the Spirit descending from heaven
like a dove, and it remained on him. 33 I myself did not know him, but
the one who sent me to baptize with water said to me, 'He on whom
you see the Spirit descend and remain is the one who baptizes with
the Holy Spirit.' 34 And I myself have seen and have testified that this
is the Son of God."[e]

The First Disciples of Jesus

35 The next day John again was standing with two of his disciples,
36 and as he watched Jesus walk by, he exclaimed, "Look, here is the

---

[a] Or *the Father's only Son* [b] Other ancient authorities read *It is an only Son, God,* or *It is the only Son*
[c] Gk *bosom* [d] Or *the Christ* [e] Other ancient authorities read *is God's chosen one*

What difference does it make to your faith that God chose to become human?

How do Lutherans understand God's grace? That we are saved by grace through no effort of our own is central to Lutheran theology. John tells us that we receive "grace upon grace" because of Jesus. The word *grace* never again appears in the Gospel of John, but the whole of the Gospel shows what grace upon grace looks like because of God's presence in Jesus. *John 1:16*

What does it mean to confess that Jesus Christ is truly God? John 1:18 provides biblical support for claiming that Jesus is true God. The second part of the Nicene Creed reflects this confession of the church, "We believe in one Lord, Jesus Christ, the only Son of God, eternally begotten of the Father, God from God, Light from Light, true God from true God, begotten, not made, of one Being with the Father; through him all things were made." (See also the Lutheran Perspectives note on Prov 8:22-24.) *John 1:18*

1:29 Lamb of God: This title for Jesus, one of many in John's Gospel, links Jesus' crucifixion with the slaughter of lambs in preparation for the Israelites' celebration of the festival of Passover (Exod 12:21-27). Although the lamb was not a sacrifice for sin in Jewish celebrations of Passover, Jesus' death is linked to this belief in the early church.

Note that Jesus takes away the sin (singular) of the world, not plural, "sins." What is the difference? How do you define sin?

1:35-51 What are you looking for? Jesus' first words to his disciples are critical for this Gospel (see 18:4; 20:15). When the disciples ask, "where are you staying?" the verb is "remain" or "abide." The Gospel of John uses this term more than any other writer in the New Testament. By remaining or abiding with Jesus one comes to believe in Jesus and is given life by being in his presence. It denotes the intimate relationship that Jesus has with his "own."

Lamb of God!" 37 The two disciples heard him say this, and they followed Jesus. 38 When Jesus turned and saw them following, he said to
them, "What are you looking for?" They said to him, "Rabbi" (which
translated means Teacher), "where are you staying?" 39 He said to
them, "Come and see." They came and saw where he was staying, and
they remained with him that day. It was about four o'clock in the afternoon. 40 One of the two who heard John speak and followed him was
Andrew, Simon Peter's brother. 41 He first found his brother Simon
and said to him, "We have found the Messiah" (which is translated
Anointed[a]). 42 He brought Simon[b] to Jesus, who looked at him and
said, "You are Simon son of John. You are to be called Cephas" (which
is translated Peter[c]).

Jesus Calls Philip and Nathanael

43 The next day Jesus decided to go to Galilee. He found Philip
and said to him, "Follow me." 44 Now Philip was from Bethsaida, the
city of Andrew and Peter. 45 Philip found Nathanael and said to him,
"We have found him about whom Moses in the law and also the
prophets wrote, Jesus son of Joseph from Nazareth." 46 Nathanael said
to him, "Can anything good come out of Nazareth?" Philip said to
him, "Come and see." 47 When Jesus saw Nathanael coming toward
him, he said of him, "Here is truly an Israelite in whom there is no
deceit!" 48 Nathanael asked him, "Where did you get to know me?"
Jesus answered, "I saw you under the fig tree before Philip called you."
49 Nathanael replied, "Rabbi, you are the Son of God! You are the King
of Israel!" 50 Jesus answered, "Do you believe because I told you that
I saw you under the fig tree? You will see greater things than these."
51 And he said to him, "Very truly, I tell you,[d] you will see heaven
opened and the angels of God ascending and descending upon the
Son of Man."

The Wedding at Cana

2 On the third day there was a wedding in Cana of Galilee, and the
mother of Jesus was there. 2 Jesus and his disciples had also been
invited to the wedding. 3 When the wine gave out, the mother of Jesus
said to him, "They have no wine." 4 And Jesus said to her, "Woman,
what concern is that to you and to me? My hour has not yet come."
5 His mother said to the servants, "Do whatever he tells you." 6 Now
standing there were six stone water jars for the Jewish rites of purification, each holding twenty or thirty gallons. 7 Jesus said to them, "Fill
the jars with water." And they filled them up to the brim. 8 He said to
them, "Now draw some out, and take it to the chief steward." So they

[a] Or *Christ* [b] Gk *him* [c] From the word for *rock* in Aramaic (*kepha*) and Greek (*petra*), respectively
[d] Both instances of the Greek word for *you* in this verse are plural

1:39 Come and see: Jesus invites his first disciples to know him through "abiding" with him and witnessing for themselves his active presence in the world. See also 4:29, where the Samaritan woman at the well invites the people in her city to "Come and see." As a result, they also "abide" with Jesus (4:40) and believe in him.

Jesus' words to his disciples to "come and see" suggest that one way to witness to your faith is by invitation to experience Jesus for oneself. When you think of sharing your faith, what comes to mind? Why would you encourage someone to come and see Jesus?

2:1-11 the first of his signs: Changing water into wine is the first of seven "signs" that Jesus performs in John's Gospel, and only John includes this event. The author of the Gospel does not use the term "miracle" but "sign," because they *point* to some truth about Jesus beyond the event itself.

2:3 the mother of Jesus: Jesus' mother, Mary, is mentioned only twice in this Gospel: here and at Jesus' crucifixion (19:25-27). While never named, her presence in John's Gospel frames Jesus' ministry.

took it. 9When the steward tasted the water that had become wine, and did not know where it came from (though the servants who had drawn the water knew), the steward called the bridegroom 10and said to him, “Everyone serves the good wine first, and then the inferior wine after the guests have become drunk. But you have kept the good wine until now.” 11Jesus did this, the first of his signs, in Cana of Galilee, and revealed his glory; and his disciples believed in him.

12 After this he went down to Capernaum with his mother, his brothers, and his disciples; and they remained there a few days.

Jesus Cleanses the Temple

13 The Passover of the Jews was near, and Jesus went up to Jerusalem. 14In the temple he found people selling cattle, sheep, and doves, and the money changers seated at their tables. 15Making a whip of cords, he drove all of them out of the temple, both the sheep and the cattle. He also poured out the coins of the money changers and overturned their tables. 16He told those who were selling the doves, “Take these things out of here! Stop making my Father’s house a marketplace!” 17His disciples remembered that it was written, “Zeal for your house will consume me.” 18The Jews then said to him, “What sign can you show us for doing this?” 19Jesus answered them, “Destroy this temple, and in three days I will raise it up.” 20The Jews then said, “This temple has been under construction for forty-six years, and will you raise it up in three days?” 21But he was speaking of the temple of his body. 22After he was raised from the dead, his disciples remembered that he had said this; and they believed the scripture and the word that Jesus had spoken.

23 When he was in Jerusalem during the Passover festival, many believed in his name because they saw the signs that he was doing. 24But Jesus on his part would not entrust himself to them, because he knew all people 25and needed no one to testify about anyone; for he himself knew what was in everyone.

Nicodemus Visits Jesus

3 Now there was a Pharisee named Nicodemus, a leader of the Jews. 2He came to Jesus[a] by night and said to him, “Rabbi, we know that you are a teacher who has come from God; for no one can do these signs that you do apart from the presence of God.” 3Jesus answered him, “Very truly, I tell you, no one can see the kingdom of God without being born from above.”[b] 4Nicodemus said to him, “How can anyone be born after having grown old? Can one enter a second time into the mother’s womb and be born?” 5Jesus answered, “Very truly, I tell you, no one can enter the kingdom of God without

[a] Gk *him* [b] Or *born anew*

2:13 Passover of the Jews: John records that Jesus made three annual pilgrimages to Jerusalem for the Passover festival (2:13; 6:4; 11:55). In the other Gospels the adult Jesus travels to Jerusalem only once for Passover, in the last week of his life, after his ministry in Galilee is done. In John, Jesus goes back and forth between Galilee and Jerusalem. The three-year ministry of Jesus is based on the number of times Jesus attended Passover according to John’s Gospel.

2:13-22 In the temple . . . Stop making my Father’s house a marketplace! This event, described as Jesus’ cleansing of the temple, is included in all four Gospels. In John, it takes place at the beginning of Jesus’ ministry. In Matthew, Mark, and Luke, it happens just before he is crucified.

2:19-21 Destroy this temple: This temple is the second temple. The first was destroyed by the Babylonians in 587 B.C.E. The second temple, constructed after the Jews returned to their land from exile in Babylonia in 539 B.C.E., was leveled by the Romans in 70 C.E. and never again rebuilt.

What do you think Jesus means by connecting the temple to his body?

2:23 Passover festival: Jewish festivals have a central role in this Gospel. Passover, an eight-day festival in the months of March–April, commemorates Israel’s escape from slavery in Egypt (see Exod 12). The Festival of Booths (John 7:1—8:59), at first a harvest festival held in September–October, commemorates God’s care for Israel in the wilderness following the escape from Egypt. The Festival of Dedication (John 10:22-42) observed the rededication of the temple in 165–164 B.C.E., after its desecration by the Seleucid king, Antiochus Epiphanes (see 1 Macc 4:36-61). Celebrated in November–December, it is known today as Hanukkah.

3:1 Nicodemus: Nicodemus isn’t mentioned in the other Gospels, but he appears here and two other times in John’s Gospel (see 7:50-52; 19:38-42).

3:2 by night: That this encounter takes place “by night” is significant, because in this Gospel night/darkness symbolize unbelief and day/light symbolize belief. Nicodemus’s last words to Jesus, “How can these things be?” suggest that he does not yet believe who Jesus is or understand what Jesus is able to offer him.

being born of water and Spirit. 6 What is born of the flesh is flesh, and what is born of the Spirit is spirit.[a] 7 Do not be astonished that I said to you, 'You[b] must be born from above.'[c] 8 The wind[a] blows where it chooses, and you hear the sound of it, but you do not know where it comes from or where it goes. So it is with everyone who is born of the Spirit." 9 Nicodemus said to him, "How can these things be?" 10 Jesus answered him, "Are you a teacher of Israel, and yet you do not understand these things?

11 "Very truly, I tell you, we speak of what we know and testify to what we have seen; yet you[d] do not receive our testimony. 12 If I have told you about earthly things and you do not believe, how can you believe if I tell you about heavenly things? 13 No one has ascended into heaven except the one who descended from heaven, the Son of Man.[e] 14 And just as Moses lifted up the serpent in the wilderness, so must the Son of Man be lifted up, 15 that whoever believes in him may have eternal life.[f]

16 "For God so loved the world that he gave his only Son, so that everyone who believes in him may not perish but may have eternal life.

17 "Indeed, God did not send the Son into the world to condemn the world, but in order that the world might be saved through him. 18 Those who believe in him are not condemned; but those who do not believe are condemned already, because they have not believed in the name of the only Son of God. 19 And this is the judgment, that the light has come into the world, and people loved darkness rather than light because their deeds were evil. 20 For all who do evil hate the light and do not come to the light, so that their deeds may not be exposed. 21 But those who do what is true come to the light, so that it may be clearly seen that their deeds have been done in God."[f]

Jesus and John the Baptist

22 After this Jesus and his disciples went into the Judean countryside, and he spent some time there with them and baptized. 23 John also was baptizing at Aenon near Salim because water was abundant there; and people kept coming and were being baptized 24 —John, of course, had not yet been thrown into prison.

25 Now a discussion about purification arose between John's disciples and a Jew.[g] 26 They came to John and said to him, "Rabbi, the one who was with you across the Jordan, to whom you testified, here he is baptizing, and all are going to him." 27 John answered, "No one can receive anything except what has been given from heaven. 28 You

[a] The same Greek word means both *wind* and *spirit* [b] The Greek word for *you* here is plural [c] Or *anew* [d] The Greek word for *you* here and in verse 12 is plural [e] Other ancient authorities add *who is in heaven* [f] Some interpreters hold that the quotation concludes with verse 15 [g] Other ancient authorities read *the Jews*

3:3 born from above: The word translated "from above" can also be translated "anew" or "again." Nicodemus initially takes Jesus' words literally, but the term is deliberately ambiguous.

Have you heard others speak of their faith as being "born again"? What do you think they mean? What do you think Jesus means when he speaks of being born again, or being born from above?

3:8 wind: The Greek word translated here as "wind" is the same word used for "spirit," and can also be translated "breath." The Hebrew word for "spirit," *ruah* (ROO-ah), has similar meanings.

3:14 as Moses lifted up the serpent: This is a reference to Numbers 21:8-9, where Moses lifts up the bronze serpent to give life to God's people in the wilderness. In the context of John's Gospel, "lifted up" can have at least three different meanings: lifted up on the cross, lifted up to resurrected life from the tomb, and lifted up at the ascension when Jesus returns to the Father.

John 3:16 is one of the most well-known verses in the Bible. When and where have you heard this verse? How would you explain what it means to someone who had never before heard it?

3:17-19 judgment: The words *judgment* and *condemn* have the same root in Greek. In John, the concept of judgment is not connected with a future time but is a present reality. Judgment occurs in the moment when one rejects Jesus.

yourselves are my witnesses that I said, 'I am not the Messiah,[a] but
I have been sent ahead of him.' 29 He who has the bride is the bridegroom. The friend of the bridegroom, who stands and hears him, rejoices greatly at the bridegroom's voice. For this reason my joy has
been fulfilled. 30 He must increase, but I must decrease."[b]

The One Who Comes from Heaven

31 The one who comes from above is above all; the one who is
of the earth belongs to the earth and speaks about earthly things. The
one who comes from heaven is above all. 32 He testifies to what he has
seen and heard, yet no one accepts his testimony. 33 Whoever has accepted his testimony has certified[c] this, that God is true. 34 He whom
God has sent speaks the words of God, for he gives the Spirit without
measure. 35 The Father loves the Son and has placed all things in his
hands. 36 Whoever believes in the Son has eternal life; whoever disobeys the Son will not see life, but must endure God's wrath.

Jesus and the Woman of Samaria

4 Now when Jesus[d] learned that the Pharisees had heard, "Jesus is
making and baptizing more disciples than John" 2 —although it
was not Jesus himself but his disciples who baptized— 3 he left Judea
and started back to Galilee. 4 But he had to go through Samaria. 5 So he
came to a Samaritan city called Sychar, near the plot of ground that
Jacob had given to his son Joseph. 6 Jacob's well was there, and Jesus,
tired out by his journey, was sitting by the well. It was about noon.

7 A Samaritan woman came to draw water, and Jesus said to her,
"Give me a drink." 8 (His disciples had gone to the city to buy food.)
9 The Samaritan woman said to him, "How is it that you, a Jew, ask
a drink of me, a woman of Samaria?" (Jews do not share things in
common with Samaritans.)[e] 10 Jesus answered her, "If you knew the
gift of God, and who it is that is saying to you, 'Give me a drink,' you
would have asked him, and he would have given you living water."
11 The woman said to him, "Sir, you have no bucket, and the well is
deep. Where do you get that living water? 12 Are you greater than our
ancestor Jacob, who gave us the well, and with his sons and his flocks
drank from it?" 13 Jesus said to her, "Everyone who drinks of this water
will be thirsty again, 14 but those who drink of the water that I will give
them will never be thirsty. The water that I will give will become in
them a spring of water gushing up to eternal life." 15 The woman said
to him, "Sir, give me this water, so that I may never be thirsty or have
to keep coming here to draw water."

16 Jesus said to her, "Go, call your husband, and come back."

---

[a] Or *the Christ* [b] Some interpreters hold that the quotation continues through verse 36 [c] Gk *set a seal to* [d] Other ancient authorities read *the Lord* [e] Other ancient authorities lack this sentence

4:1-42 The Samaritan woman: This story is only found in John's Gospel. The Samaritan woman's interaction with Jesus ends up being very different than the response of Nicodemus.

4:4 he had to go through Samaria: See Map 12, p. 2109. The most direct route from Judea to Galilee is through Samaria, but the outcome of Jesus' encounter with the Samaritan woman suggests a theological rather than a geographical reason for going through Samaria.

4:6 Jacob's well...about noon: The well is often an important meeting place in the Old Testament (see Gen 24:1-51; 29:1-14; Exod 2:15-22).

4:9 Jews do not share things in common with Samaritans: There was great disagreement between Samaritans and Jews in Jesus' time. Though both were descended from ancient Israel, because of longstanding hostility and concern for ritual purity, Jews and Samaritans went out of their way to avoid contact with each other. That Jesus would initiate contact with a Samaritan, particularly a woman, is surprising, as is Jesus' parable of the Good Samaritan in Luke (10:29-37).

For many reasons, the Samaritan woman is not someone we would expect to become a witness for Jesus. How do our judgments of people prevent us from seeing them as our neighbors in Christ?

17 The woman answered him, "I have no husband." Jesus said to her, "You are right in saying, 'I have no husband'; 18 for you have had five husbands, and the one you have now is not your husband. What you have said is true!" 19 The woman said to him, "Sir, I see that you are a prophet. 20 Our ancestors worshiped on this mountain, but you[a] say that the place where people must worship is in Jerusalem." 21 Jesus said to her, "Woman, believe me, the hour is coming when you will worship the Father neither on this mountain nor in Jerusalem. 22 You worship what you do not know; we worship what we know, for salvation is from the Jews. 23 But the hour is coming, and is now here, when the true worshipers will worship the Father in spirit and truth, for the Father seeks such as these to worship him. 24 God is spirit, and those who worship him must worship in spirit and truth." 25 The woman said to him, "I know that Messiah is coming" (who is called Christ). "When he comes, he will proclaim all things to us." 26 Jesus said to her, "I am he,[b] the one who is speaking to you."

27 Just then his disciples came. They were astonished that he was speaking with a woman, but no one said, "What do you want?" or, "Why are you speaking with her?" 28 Then the woman left her water jar and went back to the city. She said to the people, 29 "Come and see a man who told me everything I have ever done! He cannot be the Messiah,[c] can he?" 30 They left the city and were on their way to him.

31 Meanwhile the disciples were urging him, "Rabbi, eat something." 32 But he said to them, "I have food to eat that you do not know about." 33 So the disciples said to one another, "Surely no one has brought him something to eat?" 34 Jesus said to them, "My food is to do the will of him who sent me and to complete his work. 35 Do you not say, 'Four months more, then comes the harvest'? But I tell you, look around you, and see how the fields are ripe for harvesting. 36 The reaper is already receiving[d] wages and is gathering fruit for eternal life, so that sower and reaper may rejoice together. 37 For here the saying holds true, 'One sows and another reaps.' 38 I sent you to reap that for which you did not labor. Others have labored, and you have entered into their labor."

39 Many Samaritans from that city believed in him because of the woman's testimony, "He told me everything I have ever done." 40 So when the Samaritans came to him, they asked him to stay with them; and he stayed there two days. 41 And many more believed because of his word. 42 They said to the woman, "It is no longer because of what you said that we believe, for we have heard for ourselves, and we know that this is truly the Savior of the world."

---

[a] The Greek word for *you* here and in verses 21 and 22 is plural [b] Gk *I am* [c] Or *the Christ*

[d] Or [35] *... the fields are already ripe for harvesting.* [36] *The reaper is receiving*

4:18 the one you have now is not your husband: While we tend to think that Jesus is questioning the woman's morals, her marital history is not the point and most likely not her fault. The reason Jesus asks her about her husband is to get her to move to another level of understanding, because she then sees Jesus as a prophet.

The Samaritan woman grows in her understanding of Jesus. Where do you see places of growth in your own faith life?

4:20 this mountain: The critical debate between the Jews and the Samaritans was about the proper place to worship God. The Jews believed that Jerusalem was the center of worship, but the Samaritans contended that it was at Mount Gerizim. To this day, there are still Samaritans who celebrate festival days on Mount Gerizim.

4:25 Messiah is coming: Both the Jews and the Samaritans expected a Messiah to come. Messiah means "anointed one." In the Old Testament, kings were anointed with oil as a symbol of their calling. For example, see Saul (1 Sam 10:1), David (1 Sam 16:1-13), and Solomon (1 Kgs 1:32-40). The high priest was also anointed (see Aaron, Exod 29:1-9).

4:26 I am he: The pronoun "he" is not included in the original Greek text. Jesus' response, "I am," recalls the name of God revealed to Moses (Exod 3:14).

Even though the Samaritan woman is not completely sure that Jesus is the Christ (see 4:29), she does not let that stop her from being a witness. What keeps you from witnessing to your faith?

4:42 Savior of the world: This is the only occurrence of "savior" in the Gospel of John. We believe that Jesus is our "Savior," but only Luke (2:11) and John describe Jesus as savior, which can also be translated "deliverer" or "preserver." God is also described as "savior" (Luke 1:47).

Jesus Returns to Galilee

43 When the two days were over, he went from that place to Galilee 44 (for Jesus himself had testified that a prophet has no honor in the
prophet's own country). 45 When he came to Galilee, the Galileans
welcomed him, since they had seen all that he had done in Jerusalem
at the festival; for they too had gone to the festival.

Jesus Heals an Official's Son

46 Then he came again to Cana in Galilee where he had changed
the water into wine. Now there was a royal official whose son lay ill
in Capernaum. 47 When he heard that Jesus had come from Judea to
Galilee, he went and begged him to come down and heal his son, for
he was at the point of death. 48 Then Jesus said to him, "Unless you[a]
see signs and wonders you will not believe." 49 The official said to him,
"Sir, come down before my little boy dies." 50 Jesus said to him, "Go;
your son will live." The man believed the word that Jesus spoke to him
and started on his way. 51 As he was going down, his slaves met him
and told him that his child was alive. 52 So he asked them the hour
when he began to recover, and they said to him, "Yesterday at one in
the afternoon the fever left him." 53 The father realized that this was the
hour when Jesus had said to him, "Your son will live." So he himself
believed, along with his whole household. 54 Now this was the second
sign that Jesus did after coming from Judea to Galilee.

Jesus Heals on the Sabbath

5 After this there was a festival of the Jews, and Jesus went up to
Jerusalem.

2 Now in Jerusalem by the Sheep Gate there is a pool, called in
Hebrew[b] Beth-zatha,[c] which has five porticoes. 3 In these lay many
invalids—blind, lame, and paralyzed.[d] 5 One man was there who had
been ill for thirty-eight years. 6 When Jesus saw him lying there and
knew that he had been there a long time, he said to him, "Do you want
to be made well?" 7 The sick man answered him, "Sir, I have no one
to put me into the pool when the water is stirred up; and while I am
making my way, someone else steps down ahead of me." 8 Jesus said to
him, "Stand up, take your mat and walk." 9 At once the man was made
well, and he took up his mat and began to walk.

Now that day was a sabbath. 10 So the Jews said to the man who
had been cured, "It is the sabbath; it is not lawful for you to carry your
mat." 11 But he answered them, "The man who made me well said to

5:1-47 Do you want to be made well?: Chapter 5 and the third of Jesus' signs is a good example of an important pattern in this gospel: Jesus performs a sign, a dialogue follows, and then Jesus explains the sign (see 6:1-71; 9:1—10:21).

5:9 a sabbath: According to the law of Moses, there were specific instructions for keeping the Sabbath holy. With the exception of certain necessary duties, no work was to be done on the Sabbath. We learn only after Jesus heals the man that it happened on the Sabbath (see also 7:14-24; 9:14).

How do we keep the Sabbath holy? Luther thought that the Ten Commandments were so important for the life of faith that he included them with explanation in the *Small Catechism*. Luther explains the Third Commandment, "Remember the sabbath day, and keep it holy," like this: "We are to fear and love God, so that we do not despise preaching or God's word, but instead keep that word holy and gladly hear and learn it." *John 5:9-18*

---

[a] Both instances of the Greek word for *you* in this verse are plural [b] That is, *Aramaic* [c] Other ancient authorities read *Bethesda*, others *Bethsaida* [d] Other ancient authorities add, wholly or in part, *waiting for the stirring of the water; [4]for an angel of the Lord went down at certain seasons into the pool, and stirred up the water; whoever stepped in first after the stirring of the water was made well from whatever disease that person had.*

me, 'Take up your mat and walk.'" [12]They asked him, "Who is the
man who said to you, 'Take it up and walk'?" [13]Now the man who had
been healed did not know who it was, for Jesus had disappeared in[a]
the crowd that was there. [14]Later Jesus found him in the temple and
said to him, "See, you have been made well! Do not sin any more, so
that nothing worse happens to you." [15]The man went away and told
the Jews that it was Jesus who had made him well. [16]Therefore the
Jews started persecuting Jesus, because he was doing such things on
the sabbath. [17]But Jesus answered them, "My Father is still working,
and I also am working." [18]For this reason the Jews were seeking all the
more to kill him, because he was not only breaking the sabbath, but
was also calling God his own Father, thereby making himself equal
to God.

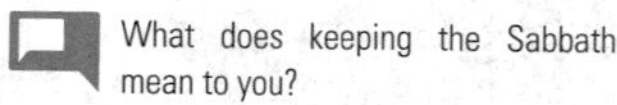
What does keeping the Sabbath mean to you?

5:18 the Jews: The term "the Jews" in the Gospel of John is best understood as the Jewish authorities, including the Pharisees, rather than the Jewish people as a whole.

The Authority of the Son

19 Jesus said to them, "Very truly, I tell you, the Son can do nothing on his own, but only what he sees the Father doing; for whatever
the Father[b] does, the Son does likewise. [20]The Father loves the Son
and shows him all that he himself is doing; and he will show him
greater works than these, so that you will be astonished. [21]Indeed,
just as the Father raises the dead and gives them life, so also the Son
gives life to whomever he wishes. [22]The Father judges no one but has
given all judgment to the Son, [23]so that all may honor the Son just
as they honor the Father. Anyone who does not honor the Son does
not honor the Father who sent him. [24]Very truly, I tell you, anyone
who hears my word and believes him who sent me has eternal life, and
does not come under judgment, but has passed from death to life.

25 "Very truly, I tell you, the hour is coming, and is now here,
when the dead will hear the voice of the Son of God, and those who
hear will live. [26]For just as the Father has life in himself, so he has
granted the Son also to have life in himself; [27]and he has given him authority to execute judgment, because he is the Son of Man. [28]Do not
be astonished at this; for the hour is coming when all who are in their
graves will hear his voice [29]and will come out—those who have done
good, to the resurrection of life, and those who have done evil, to the
resurrection of condemnation.

Witnesses to Jesus

30 "I can do nothing on my own. As I hear, I judge; and my judgment is just, because I seek to do not my own will but the will of him
who sent me.

31 "If I testify about myself, my testimony is not true. [32]There is
another who testifies on my behalf, and I know that his testimony to

[a] Or *had left because of* [b] Gk *that one*

me is true. [33]You sent messengers to John, and he testified to the truth.
[34]Not that I accept such human testimony, but I say these things so
that you may be saved. [35]He was a burning and shining lamp, and you
were willing to rejoice for a while in his light. [36]But I have a testimony
greater than John's. The works that the Father has given me to complete, the very works that I am doing, testify on my behalf that the Father has sent me. [37]And the Father who sent me has himself testified
on my behalf. You have never heard his voice or seen his form, [38]and
you do not have his word abiding in you, because you do not believe
him whom he has sent.

39 "You search the scriptures because you think that in them you
have eternal life; and it is they that testify on my behalf. [40]Yet you refuse to come to me to have life. [41]I do not accept glory from human
beings. [42]But I know that you do not have the love of God in[a] you. [43]I
have come in my Father's name, and you do not accept me; if another
comes in his own name, you will accept him. [44]How can you believe
when you accept glory from one another and do not seek the glory
that comes from the one who alone is God? [45]Do not think that I will
accuse you before the Father; your accuser is Moses, on whom you
have set your hope. [46]If you believed Moses, you would believe me,
for he wrote about me. [47]But if you do not believe what he wrote, how
will you believe what I say?"

Feeding the Five Thousand

6:1-14 they sat down, about five thousand in all: This event, the feeding of the five thousand, is recorded in all four Gospels (see Matt 14:13-21; Mark 6:32-44; Luke 9:10-17). Only in John does Jesus, not the disciples, distribute the bread and the fish to the crowd.

6 After this Jesus went to the other side of the Sea of Galilee, also
called the Sea of Tiberias.[b] [2]A large crowd kept following him,
because they saw the signs that he was doing for the sick. [3]Jesus went
up the mountain and sat down there with his disciples. [4]Now the
Passover, the festival of the Jews, was near. [5]When he looked up and
saw a large crowd coming toward him, Jesus said to Philip, "Where
are we to buy bread for these people to eat?" [6]He said this to test him,
for he himself knew what he was going to do. [7]Philip answered him,
"Six months' wages[c] would not buy enough bread for each of them
to get a little." [8]One of his disciples, Andrew, Simon Peter's brother,
said to him, [9]"There is a boy here who has five barley loaves and two
fish. But what are they among so many people?" [10]Jesus said, "Make
the people sit down." Now there was a great deal of grass in the place;
so they[d] sat down, about five thousand in all. [11]Then Jesus took the
loaves, and when he had given thanks, he distributed them to those
who were seated; so also the fish, as much as they wanted. [12]When
they were satisfied, he told his disciples, "Gather up the fragments left
over, so that nothing may be lost." [13]So they gathered them up, and

---

[a] Or *among* [b] Gk *of Galilee of Tiberias* [c] Gk *Two hundred denarii*; the denarius was the usual day's wage for a laborer [d] Gk *the men*

from the fragments of the five barley loaves, left by those who had
eaten, they filled twelve baskets. 14 When the people saw the sign that
he had done, they began to say, "This is indeed the prophet who is to
come into the world."

15 When Jesus realized that they were about to come and take
him by force to make him king, he withdrew again to the mountain
by himself.

Jesus Walks on the Water

16 When evening came, his disciples went down to the sea, 17 got
into a boat, and started across the sea to Capernaum. It was now dark,
and Jesus had not yet come to them. 18 The sea became rough because
a strong wind was blowing. 19 When they had rowed about three or
four miles,[a] they saw Jesus walking on the sea and coming near the
boat, and they were terrified. 20 But he said to them, "It is I;[b] do not
be afraid." 21 Then they wanted to take him into the boat, and immediately the boat reached the land toward which they were going.

6:15-21 they saw Jesus walking on the sea: In John's telling of this gospel story, Jesus does not command the storm to be still, as he does in Matthew 14:22-27 and Mark 6:45-51. For the writer of John's Gospel, this miracle is another sign pointing to Jesus as the divine "I am." See notes on 4:26 and 6:20.

6:20 It is I: See NRSV footnote *b*. The "I am" statements are unique to John and appear in two forms: the absolute "I am" that stands by itself (for example, 4:26; see NRSV footnote *b*) and those that include an image or figure after the "I am" statement, as in "I am the bread of life" (see 6:35). When Jesus uses "I am" by itself, he uses the divine name of God (see Exod 3:14). See the chart The "I AM" Sayings of Jesus in John's Gospel, p. 1773.

The Bread from Heaven

22 The next day the crowd that had stayed on the other side of the
sea saw that there had been only one boat there. They also saw that
Jesus had not got into the boat with his disciples, but that his disciples
had gone away alone. 23 Then some boats from Tiberias came near
the place where they had eaten the bread after the Lord had given
thanks.[c] 24 So when the crowd saw that neither Jesus nor his disciples
were there, they themselves got into the boats and went to Capernaum looking for Jesus.

25 When they found him on the other side of the sea, they said
to him, "Rabbi, when did you come here?" 26 Jesus answered them,
"Very truly, I tell you, you are looking for me, not because you saw
signs, but because you ate your fill of the loaves. 27 Do not work for the
food that perishes, but for the food that endures for eternal life, which
the Son of Man will give you. For it is on him that God the Father
has set his seal." 28 Then they said to him, "What must we do to perform the works of God?" 29 Jesus answered them, "This is the work of
God, that you believe in him whom he has sent." 30 So they said to him,
"What sign are you going to give us then, so that we may see it and
believe you? What work are you performing? 31 Our ancestors ate the
manna in the wilderness; as it is written, 'He gave them bread from
heaven to eat.'" 32 Then Jesus said to them, "Very truly, I tell you, it was
not Moses who gave you the bread from heaven, but it is my Father
who gives you the true bread from heaven. 33 For the bread of God

6:32 bread from heaven: This phrase reminds us of God's gift of manna to the Israelites in the wilderness (Exod 16). In the Gospel of John, Jesus is the true bread from heaven.

---

[a] Gk *about twenty-five or thirty stadia* [b] Gk *I am* [c] Other ancient authorities lack *after the Lord had given thanks*

How is the bread of the Lord's Supper "bread of life"? In the Lutheran church, the Lord's Supper or Holy Communion is connected to the last supper Jesus had with his disciples as told by Matthew (26:26-29), Mark (14:22-25), and Luke (22:14-20; see also 1 Cor 11:23-26). John's Gospel connects this event to the feeding of the 5,000 and focuses on Jesus' teaching that he is the true bread of life (6:51-58) who provides relationship with and life forever in him. Luther's explanation of the Sacrament of the Altar (Lord's Supper) in the *Small Catechism* focuses on Jesus' words "for you" and "for the forgiveness of sins." And "where there is forgiveness of sin," Luther continues, "there is also life and salvation." *John 6:35*

How do you understand Jesus as the bread of life? What does the sacrament of Holy Communion mean to you?

Lord, to whom can we go? You have the words of eternal life: Peter's words are often used as part of the Gospel Acclamation in the Lutheran liturgy. *John 6:68*

is that which[a] comes down from heaven and gives life to the world."
34 They said to him, "Sir, give us this bread always."

35 Jesus said to them, "I am the bread of life. Whoever comes to
me will never be hungry, and whoever believes in me will never be
thirsty. 36 But I said to you that you have seen me and yet do not believe. 37 Everything that the Father gives me will come to me, and anyone who comes to me I will never drive away; 38 for I have come down
from heaven, not to do my own will, but the will of him who sent me.
39 And this is the will of him who sent me, that I should lose nothing of
all that he has given me, but raise it up on the last day. 40 This is indeed
the will of my Father, that all who see the Son and believe in him may
have eternal life; and I will raise them up on the last day."

41 Then the Jews began to complain about him because he said,
"I am the bread that came down from heaven." 42 They were saying, "Is
not this Jesus, the son of Joseph, whose father and mother we know?
How can he now say, 'I have come down from heaven'?" 43 Jesus answered them, "Do not complain among yourselves. 44 No one can
come to me unless drawn by the Father who sent me; and I will raise
that person up on the last day. 45 It is written in the prophets, 'And they
shall all be taught by God.' Everyone who has heard and learned from
the Father comes to me. 46 Not that anyone has seen the Father except
the one who is from God; he has seen the Father. 47 Very truly, I tell
you, whoever believes has eternal life. 48 I am the bread of life. 49 Your
ancestors ate the manna in the wilderness, and they died. 50 This is the
bread that comes down from heaven, so that one may eat of it and not
die. 51 I am the living bread that came down from heaven. Whoever
eats of this bread will live forever; and the bread that I will give for the
life of the world is my flesh."

52 The Jews then disputed among themselves, saying, "How can
this man give us his flesh to eat?" 53 So Jesus said to them, "Very truly,
I tell you, unless you eat the flesh of the Son of Man and drink his
blood, you have no life in you. 54 Those who eat my flesh and drink my
blood have eternal life, and I will raise them up on the last day; 55 for
my flesh is true food and my blood is true drink. 56 Those who eat my
flesh and drink my blood abide in me, and I in them. 57 Just as the living Father sent me, and I live because of the Father, so whoever eats
me will live because of me. 58 This is the bread that came down from
heaven, not like that which your ancestors ate, and they died. But the
one who eats this bread will live forever." 59 He said these things while
he was teaching in the synagogue at Capernaum.

The Words of Eternal Life

60 When many of his disciples heard it, they said, "This teaching
is difficult; who can accept it?" 61 But Jesus, being aware that his disci-

[a] Or *he who*

ples were complaining about it, said to them, "Does this offend you?
[62]Then what if you were to see the Son of Man ascending to where
he was before? [63]It is the spirit that gives life; the flesh is useless. The
words that I have spoken to you are spirit and life. [64]But among you
there are some who do not believe." For Jesus knew from the first who
were the ones that did not believe, and who was the one that would
betray him. [65]And he said, "For this reason I have told you that no one
can come to me unless it is granted by the Father."

66 Because of this many of his disciples turned back and no
longer went about with him. [67]So Jesus asked the twelve, "Do you also
wish to go away?" [68]Simon Peter answered him, "Lord, to whom can
we go? You have the words of eternal life. [69]We have come to believe
and know that you are the Holy One of God."[a] [70]Jesus answered them,
"Did I not choose you, the twelve? Yet one of you is a devil." [71]He was
speaking of Judas son of Simon Iscariot,[b] for he, though one of the
twelve, was going to betray him.

The Unbelief of Jesus' Brothers

7 After this Jesus went about in Galilee. He did not wish[c] to go
about in Judea because the Jews were looking for an opportunity to kill him. [2]Now the Jewish festival of Booths[d] was near. [3]So his
brothers said to him, "Leave here and go to Judea so that your disciples also may see the works you are doing; [4]for no one who wants[e] to
be widely known acts in secret. If you do these things, show yourself
to the world." [5](For not even his brothers believed in him.) [6]Jesus said
to them, "My time has not yet come, but your time is always here.
[7]The world cannot hate you, but it hates me because I testify against
it that its works are evil. [8]Go to the festival yourselves. I am not[f] going
to this festival, for my time has not yet fully come." [9]After saying this,
he remained in Galilee.

Jesus at the Festival of Booths

10 But after his brothers had gone to the festival, then he also
went, not publicly but as it were[g] in secret. [11]The Jews were looking
for him at the festival and saying, "Where is he?" [12]And there was
considerable complaining about him among the crowds. While some
were saying, "He is a good man," others were saying, "No, he is deceiving the crowd." [13]Yet no one would speak openly about him for
fear of the Jews.

14 About the middle of the festival Jesus went up into the temple
and began to teach. [15]The Jews were astonished at it, saying, "How

7:1—8:59 looking for an opportunity to kill him: These chapters represent a significant break in the story plot of the Gospel. They tell of the increasing tension between Jesus and the Jewish authorities and include some of Jesus' harshest words to the Jewish rulers.

Chapters 7 and 8 in John's Gospel have frequently been misinterpreted to support anti-Semitism, or prejudice against the Jewish people. Can you recall a time when you heard someone make a negative statement about Jews? How does knowing the context of Jesus' comments help you know how to respond to such statements?

7:2 festival of Booths: The Festival of Booths was one of three pilgrimage festivals, when Jews living outside of Jerusalem were required to come to the city. The festival included two major ceremonies, one for light and one for water. Jesus presents himself as the source of living water (7:37-38) and light (8:12).

[a] Other ancient authorities read *the Christ, the Son of the living God* [b] Other ancient authorities read *Judas Iscariot son of Simon;* others, *Judas son of Simon from Karyot* (Kerioth) [c] Other ancient authorities read *was not at liberty* [d] Or *Tabernacles* [e] Other ancient authorities read *wants it* [f] Other ancient authorities add *yet* [g] Other ancient authorities lack *as it were*

does this man have such learning,[a] when he has never been taught?”
16 Then Jesus answered them, “My teaching is not mine but his who
sent me. 17 Anyone who resolves to do the will of God will know
whether the teaching is from God or whether I am speaking on my
own. 18 Those who speak on their own seek their own glory; but the
one who seeks the glory of him who sent him is true, and there is
nothing false in him.

19 “Did not Moses give you the law? Yet none of you keeps the
law. Why are you looking for an opportunity to kill me?” 20 The crowd
answered, “You have a demon! Who is trying to kill you?” 21 Jesus answered them, “I performed one work, and all of you are astonished.
22 Moses gave you circumcision (it is, of course, not from Moses, but
from the patriarchs), and you circumcise a man on the sabbath. 23 If
a man receives circumcision on the sabbath in order that the law of
Moses may not be broken, are you angry with me because I healed
a man’s whole body on the sabbath? 24 Do not judge by appearances,
but judge with right judgment.”

Is This the Christ?

25 Now some of the people of Jerusalem were saying, “Is not
this the man whom they are trying to kill? 26 And here he is, speaking
openly, but they say nothing to him! Can it be that the authorities
really know that this is the Messiah?[b] 27 Yet we know where this man
is from; but when the Messiah[b] comes, no one will know where he is
from.” 28 Then Jesus cried out as he was teaching in the temple, “You
know me, and you know where I am from. I have not come on my
own. But the one who sent me is true, and you do not know him. 29 I
know him, because I am from him, and he sent me.” 30 Then they tried
to arrest him, but no one laid hands on him, because his hour had not
yet come. 31 Yet many in the crowd believed in him and were saying,
“When the Messiah[b] comes, will he do more signs than this man has
done?”[c]

Officers Are Sent to Arrest Jesus

32 The Pharisees heard the crowd muttering such things about
him, and the chief priests and Pharisees sent temple police to arrest
him. 33 Jesus then said, “I will be with you a little while longer, and
then I am going to him who sent me. 34 You will search for me, but you
will not find me; and where I am, you cannot come.” 35 The Jews said
to one another, “Where does this man intend to go that we will not
find him? Does he intend to go to the Dispersion among the Greeks
and teach the Greeks? 36 What does he mean by saying, ‘You will
search for me and you will not find me’ and ‘Where I am, you cannot
come’?”

---

[a] Or *this man know his letters* [b] Or *the Christ* [c] Other ancient authorities read *is doing*

Rivers of Living Water

37 On the last day of the festival, the great day, while Jesus was
standing there, he cried out, "Let anyone who is thirsty come to me,
[38]and let the one who believes in me drink. As[a] the scripture has said,
'Out of the believer's heart[b] shall flow rivers of living water.' " [39]Now
he said this about the Spirit, which believers in him were to receive;
for as yet there was no Spirit,[c] because Jesus was not yet glorified.

Division among the People

40 When they heard these words, some in the crowd said, "This
is really the prophet." [41]Others said, "This is the Messiah."[d] But some
asked, "Surely the Messiah[d] does not come from Galilee, does he?
[42]Has not the scripture said that the Messiah[d] is descended from
David and comes from Bethlehem, the village where David lived?"
[43]So there was a division in the crowd because of him. [44]Some of them
wanted to arrest him, but no one laid hands on him.

The Unbelief of Those in Authority

45 Then the temple police went back to the chief priests and Pharisees, who asked them, "Why did you not arrest him?" [46]The police
answered, "Never has anyone spoken like this!" [47]Then the Pharisees
replied, "Surely you have not been deceived too, have you? [48]Has any
one of the authorities or of the Pharisees believed in him? [49]But this
crowd, which does not know the law—they are accursed." [50]Nicode-
mus, who had gone to Jesus[e] before, and who was one of them, asked,
[51]"Our law does not judge people without first giving them a hearing
to find out what they are doing, does it?" [52]They replied, "Surely you
are not also from Galilee, are you? Search and you will see that no
prophet is to arise from Galilee."

The Woman Caught in Adultery

8 ⟦[53]Then each of them went home, [1]while Jesus went to the
Mount of Olives. [2]Early in the morning he came again to the
temple. All the people came to him and he sat down and began to
teach them. [3]The scribes and the Pharisees brought a woman who
had been caught in adultery; and making her stand before all of them,
[4]they said to him, "Teacher, this woman was caught in the very act of
committing adultery. [5]Now in the law Moses commanded us to stone
such women. Now what do you say?" [6]They said this to test him, so
that they might have some charge to bring against him. Jesus bent
down and wrote with his finger on the ground. [7]When they kept on
questioning him, he straightened up and said to them, "Let anyone

7:53—8:11 woman…caught in adultery: This story is not included in the earliest and most reliable manuscripts of the Gospel of John.

The story of the woman caught in adultery includes one of the most famous sayings of Jesus: "Let anyone among you who is without sin be the first to throw a stone. . . ." When have you heard this saying used? What do you think it means?

---

[a] Or *come to me and drink.* [38]*The one who believes in me, as* [b] Gk *out of his belly* [c] Other ancient authorities read *for as yet the Spirit* (others, *Holy Spirit*) *had not been given* [d] Or *the Christ* [e] Gk *him*

among you who is without sin be the first to throw a stone at her." 8And once again he bent down and wrote on the ground.[a] 9When they heard it, they went away, one by one, beginning with the elders; and Jesus was left alone with the woman standing before him. 10Jesus straightened up and said to her, "Woman, where are they? Has no one condemned you?" 11She said, "No one, sir."[b] And Jesus said, "Neither do I condemn you. Go your way, and from now on do not sin again."⟧[c]

Jesus the Light of the World

12 Again Jesus spoke to them, saying, "I am the light of the world. Whoever follows me will never walk in darkness but will have the light of life." 13Then the Pharisees said to him, "You are testifying on your own behalf; your testimony is not valid." 14Jesus answered, "Even if I testify on my own behalf, my testimony is valid because I know where I have come from and where I am going, but you do not know where I come from or where I am going. 15You judge by human standards;[d] I judge no one. 16Yet even if I do judge, my judgment is valid; for it is not I alone who judge, but I and the Father[e] who sent me. 17In your law it is written that the testimony of two witnesses is valid. 18I testify on my own behalf, and the Father who sent me testifies on my behalf." 19Then they said to him, "Where is your Father?" Jesus answered, "You know neither me nor my Father. If you knew me, you would know my Father also." 20He spoke these words while he was teaching in the treasury of the temple, but no one arrested him, because his hour had not yet come.

8:20 his hour had not yet come: By "hour" the Gospel writer means Jesus' death, resurrection, and ascension (see 7:30; 13:1).

Jesus Foretells His Death

21 Again he said to them, "I am going away, and you will search for me, but you will die in your sin. Where I am going, you cannot come." 22Then the Jews said, "Is he going to kill himself? Is that what he means by saying, 'Where I am going, you cannot come'?" 23He said to them, "You are from below, I am from above; you are of this world, I am not of this world. 24I told you that you would die in your sins, for you will die in your sins unless you believe that I am he."[f] 25They said to him, "Who are you?" Jesus said to them, "Why do I speak to you at all?[g] 26I have much to say about you and much to condemn; but the one who sent me is true, and I declare to the world what I have heard from him." 27They did not understand that he was speaking to them about the Father. 28So Jesus said, "When you have lifted up the Son of Man, then you will realize that I am he,[f] and that I do nothing on

---

[a] Other ancient authorities add *the sins of each of them* [b] Or *Lord* [c] The most ancient authorities lack 7.53—8.11; other authorities add the passage here or after 7.36 or after 21.25 or after Luke 21.38, with variations of text; some mark the passage as doubtful. [d] Gk *according to the flesh* [e] Other ancient authorities read *he* [f] Gk *I am* [g] Or *What I have told you from the beginning*

my own, but I speak these things as the Father instructed me. [29]And
the one who sent me is with me; he has not left me alone, for I always
do what is pleasing to him." [30]As he was saying these things, many
believed in him.

True Disciples

31 Then Jesus said to the Jews who had believed in him, "If you
continue in my word, you are truly my disciples; [32]and you will know
the truth, and the truth will make you free." [33]They answered him,
"We are descendants of Abraham and have never been slaves to anyone. What do you mean by saying, 'You will be made free'?"
34 Jesus answered them, "Very truly, I tell you, everyone who
commits sin is a slave to sin. [35]The slave does not have a permanent
place in the household; the son has a place there forever. [36]So if the
Son makes you free, you will be free indeed. [37]I know that you are
descendants of Abraham; yet you look for an opportunity to kill me,
because there is no place in you for my word. [38]I declare what I have
seen in the Father's presence; as for you, you should do what you have
heard from the Father."[a]

8:32 the truth will make you free: Jesus calls himself the truth (14:6) and he testifies to the truth (18:37).

How does the truth make a person free? What does that kind of freedom look like?

Jesus and Abraham

39 They answered him, "Abraham is our father." Jesus said to
them, "If you were Abraham's children, you would be doing[b] what
Abraham did, [40]but now you are trying to kill me, a man who has told
you the truth that I heard from God. This is not what Abraham did.
[41]You are indeed doing what your father does." They said to him, "We
are not illegitimate children; we have one father, God himself." [42]Jesus
said to them, "If God were your Father, you would love me, for I came
from God and now I am here. I did not come on my own, but he sent
me. [43]Why do you not understand what I say? It is because you cannot accept my word. [44]You are from your father the devil, and you
choose to do your father's desires. He was a murderer from the beginning and does not stand in the truth, because there is no truth in him.
When he lies, he speaks according to his own nature, for he is a liar
and the father of lies. [45]But because I tell the truth, you do not believe
me. [46]Which of you convicts me of sin? If I tell the truth, why do you
not believe me? [47]Whoever is from God hears the words of God. The
reason you do not hear them is that you are not from God."
48 The Jews answered him, "Are we not right in saying that you
are a Samaritan and have a demon?" [49]Jesus answered, "I do not have
a demon; but I honor my Father, and you dishonor me. [50]Yet I do
not seek my own glory; there is one who seeks it and he is the judge.

---

[a] Other ancient authorities read *you do what you have heard from your father* [b] Other ancient authorities read *If you are Abraham's children, then do*

51 Very truly, I tell you, whoever keeps my word will never see death."
52 The Jews said to him, "Now we know that you have a demon. Abraham died, and so did the prophets; yet you say, 'Whoever keeps my
word will never taste death.' 53 Are you greater than our father Abraham, who died? The prophets also died. Who do you claim to be?"
54 Jesus answered, "If I glorify myself, my glory is nothing. It is my Father who glorifies me, he of whom you say, 'He is our God,' 55 though
you do not know him. But I know him; if I would say that I do not
know him, I would be a liar like you. But I do know him and I keep his
word. 56 Your ancestor Abraham rejoiced that he would see my day; he
saw it and was glad." 57 Then the Jews said to him, "You are not yet fifty
years old, and have you seen Abraham?"[a] 58 Jesus said to them, "Very
truly, I tell you, before Abraham was, I am." 59 So they picked up stones
to throw at him, but Jesus hid himself and went out of the temple.

A Man Born Blind Receives Sight

9:1—10:21 These verses form a single section that includes a sign by Jesus (healing of a man born blind) followed by interpretation of that sign. When seen this way, the man who gains his sight becomes one of the sheep who knows the shepherd's voice (9:7; 10:3, 5) and receives abundant life (10:10).

9:2 who sinned: In biblical times, people believed that disease, physical disabilities, and mental illness were due to sin or sins committed by the individual or the parents of the one afflicted.

9 As he walked along, he saw a man blind from birth. 2 His disciples asked him, "Rabbi, who sinned, this man or his parents,
that he was born blind?" 3 Jesus answered, "Neither this man nor his
parents sinned; he was born blind so that God's works might be revealed in him. 4 We[b] must work the works of him who sent me[c] while
it is day; night is coming when no one can work. 5 As long as I am in
the world, I am the light of the world." 6 When he had said this, he
spat on the ground and made mud with the saliva and spread the mud
on the man's eyes, 7 saying to him, "Go, wash in the pool of Siloam"
(which means Sent). Then he went and washed and came back able
to see. 8 The neighbors and those who had seen him before as a beggar
began to ask, "Is this not the man who used to sit and beg?" 9 Some
were saying, "It is he." Others were saying, "No, but it is someone
like him." He kept saying, "I am the man." 10 But they kept asking him,
"Then how were your eyes opened?" 11 He answered, "The man called
Jesus made mud, spread it on my eyes, and said to me, 'Go to Siloam
and wash.' Then I went and washed and received my sight." 12 They
said to him, "Where is he?" He said, "I do not know."

The Pharisees Investigate the Healing

13 They brought to the Pharisees the man who had formerly
been blind. 14 Now it was a sabbath day when Jesus made the mud
and opened his eyes. 15 Then the Pharisees also began to ask him how
he had received his sight. He said to them, "He put mud on my eyes.
Then I washed, and now I see." 16 Some of the Pharisees said, "This
man is not from God, for he does not observe the sabbath." But others

---

[a] Other ancient authorities read *has Abraham seen you?* [b] Other ancient authorities read *I* [c] Other ancient authorities read *us*

said, "How can a man who is a sinner perform such signs?" And they
were divided. 17 So they said again to the blind man, "What do you say
about him? It was your eyes he opened." He said, "He is a prophet."

18 The Jews did not believe that he had been blind and had received his sight until they called the parents of the man who had received his sight 19 and asked them, "Is this your son, who you say was
born blind? How then does he now see?" 20 His parents answered,
"We know that this is our son, and that he was born blind; 21 but we
do not know how it is that now he sees, nor do we know who opened
his eyes. Ask him; he is of age. He will speak for himself." 22 His parents said this because they were afraid of the Jews; for the Jews had
already agreed that anyone who confessed Jesus[a] to be the Messiah[b]
would be put out of the synagogue. 23 Therefore his parents said, "He
is of age; ask him."

24 So for the second time they called the man who had been
blind, and they said to him, "Give glory to God! We know that this
man is a sinner." 25 He answered, "I do not know whether he is a sinner.
One thing I do know, that though I was blind, now I see." 26 They said
to him, "What did he do to you? How did he open your eyes?" 27 He
answered them, "I have told you already, and you would not listen.
Why do you want to hear it again? Do you also want to become his
disciples?" 28 Then they reviled him, saying, "You are his disciple, but
we are disciples of Moses. 29 We know that God has spoken to Moses,
but as for this man, we do not know where he comes from." 30 The man
answered, "Here is an astonishing thing! You do not know where he
comes from, and yet he opened my eyes. 31 We know that God does
not listen to sinners, but he does listen to one who worships him and
obeys his will. 32 Never since the world began has it been heard that
anyone opened the eyes of a person born blind. 33 If this man were
not from God, he could do nothing." 34 They answered him, "You were
born entirely in sins, and are you trying to teach us?" And they drove
him out.

Spiritual Blindness

35 Jesus heard that they had driven him out, and when he found
him, he said, "Do you believe in the Son of Man?"[c] 36 He answered,
"And who is he, sir?[d] Tell me, so that I may believe in him." 37 Jesus
said to him, "You have seen him, and the one speaking with you is he."
38 He said, "Lord,[d] I believe." And he worshiped him. 39 Jesus said, "I
came into this world for judgment so that those who do not see may
see, and those who do see may become blind." 40 Some of the Pharisees near him heard this and said to him, "Surely we are not blind, are

9:22 put out of the synagogue: Most scholars think that the people for whom this Gospel was written were experiencing some sort of conflict with the established Jewish community and synagogue (see 12:42; 16:2).

9:35 Jesus…found him: Jesus has been absent during the man's interrogation by the Pharisees. When Jesus finds him (compare to 1:43) the man confesses his faith as a true disciple.

"I was blind, now I see" (9:25) is a phrase in the well-known and much loved hymn "Amazing Grace." What is your favorite hymn or faith song? What do you love about it? What do you think it means to gain "spiritual" sight?

---

[a] Gk *him* [b] Or *the Christ* [c] Other ancient authorities read *the Son of God* [d] *Sir* and *Lord* translate the same Greek word

we?" [41]Jesus said to them, "If you were blind, you would not have sin. But now that you say, 'We see,' your sin remains.

Jesus the Good Shepherd

10 "Very truly, I tell you, anyone who does not enter the sheepfold by the gate but climbs in by another way is a thief and a bandit. [2]The one who enters by the gate is the shepherd of the sheep. [3]The gatekeeper opens the gate for him, and the sheep hear his voice. He calls his own sheep by name and leads them out. [4]When he has brought out all his own, he goes ahead of them, and the sheep follow him because they know his voice. [5]They will not follow a stranger, but they will run from him because they do not know the voice of strangers." [6]Jesus used this figure of speech with them, but they did not understand what he was saying to them.

7 So again Jesus said to them, "Very truly, I tell you, I am the gate for the sheep. [8]All who came before me are thieves and bandits; but the sheep did not listen to them. [9]I am the gate. Whoever enters by me will be saved, and will come in and go out and find pasture. [10]The thief comes only to steal and kill and destroy. I came that they may have life, and have it abundantly.

11 "I am the good shepherd. The good shepherd lays down his life for the sheep. [12]The hired hand, who is not the shepherd and does not own the sheep, sees the wolf coming and leaves the sheep and runs away—and the wolf snatches them and scatters them. [13]The hired hand runs away because a hired hand does not care for the sheep. [14]I am the good shepherd. I know my own and my own know me, [15]just as the Father knows me and I know the Father. And I lay down my life for the sheep. [16]I have other sheep that do not belong to this fold. I must bring them also, and they will listen to my voice. So there will be one flock, one shepherd. [17]For this reason the Father loves me, because I lay down my life in order to take it up again. [18]No one takes[a] it from me, but I lay it down of my own accord. I have power to lay it down, and I have power to take it up again. I have received this command from my Father."

19 Again the Jews were divided because of these words. [20]Many of them were saying, "He has a demon and is out of his mind. Why listen to him?" [21]Others were saying, "These are not the words of one who has a demon. Can a demon open the eyes of the blind?"

Jesus Is Rejected by the Jews

22 At that time the festival of the Dedication took place in Jerusalem. It was winter, [23]and Jesus was walking in the temple, in the portico of Solomon. [24]So the Jews gathered around him and said to him,

[a] Other ancient authorities read *has taken*

10:3 the sheep hear his voice: Jesus' own are able to recognize his voice. The man born blind responds to Jesus' voice and is healed (9:7). Lazarus was dead four days (11:39) but hears Jesus call him by name and comes out from his tomb (11:43-44). Mary Magdalene, mourning the death of Jesus, hears Jesus call her name and recognizes that she is in the presence of the risen Lord (20:16).

10:6 Jesus used this figure of speech: Many commentators suggest that 10:1-5 is a parable followed by its explanation (10:7-18; see Mark 4:1-20), but John refers to it as a "figure of speech." Jesus does not so much offer an explanation in 10:7-18 as he continues his discourse by introducing new words and figures.

10:7, 9 I am the gate: Jesus identifies himself as the gate through which to enter the sheepfold and therefore have a relationship with Jesus. Jesus as the gate also provides access to pasture for the sheep, which means salvation and abundant life.

10:10 The thief comes only to steal: The only other time *thief* is used in the Gospel is to describe Judas, the disciple who betrayed Jesus (12:4-6). The term *bandit* is used to describe Barabbas, whom the Jews chose over Jesus to be set free (18:40).

10:11 the good shepherd: Shepherd imagery is used to describe the activity of God in the Old Testament (see Psalm 23; Ezek 34; Zech 11).

Jesus the good shepherd is a popular image in art and music. How do you picture Jesus? What words do you use to describe him?

The "I AM" Sayings of Jesus in John's Gospel

Two Kinds of "I AM" sayings appear in the Gospel of John (see the note on 6:20).

Absolute "I AM" Sayings	"I AM" Sayings with a Descriptive Image
4:26 "I am he, the one who is speaking to you."	**6:35** "I am the bread of life."
6:20 "It is I; do not be afraid."	**6:51** "I am the living bread that came down from heaven."
8:24 "I told you that you would die in your sins, for you will die in your sins unless you believe that I am he."	**8:12** "I am the light of the world."
8:28 "When you have lifted up the Son of Man, then you will realize that I am he, and that I do nothing on my own, but I speak these things as the Father instructed me."	**9:5** "I am the light of the world."
8:58 "Very truly, I tell you, before Abraham was, I am."	**10:7** "I am the gate for the sheep."
13:19 "I tell you this now, before it occurs, so that when it does occur, you may believe that I am he."	**10:9** "I am the gate."
18:5, 8 "I am he."	**10:11, 14** "I am the good shepherd."
	11:25-26 "I am the resurrection and the life."
	14:6 "I am the way, and the truth, and the life."
	15:1 "I am the true vine."
	15:5 "I am the vine, you are the branches."

"How long will you keep us in suspense? If you are the Messiah,[a] tell
us plainly." 25 Jesus answered, "I have told you, and you do not believe.
The works that I do in my Father's name testify to me; 26 but you do
not believe, because you do not belong to my sheep. 27 My sheep hear
my voice. I know them, and they follow me. 28 I give them eternal life,
and they will never perish. No one will snatch them out of my hand.
29 What my Father has given me is greater than all else, and no one can
snatch it out of the Father's hand.[b] 30 The Father and I are one."

31 The Jews took up stones again to stone him. 32 Jesus replied,
"I have shown you many good works from the Father. For which of
these are you going to stone me?" 33 The Jews answered, "It is not for a
good work that we are going to stone you, but for blasphemy, because
you, though only a human being, are making yourself God." 34 Jesus
answered, "Is it not written in your law,[c] 'I said, you are gods'? 35 If
those to whom the word of God came were called 'gods'—and the
scripture cannot be annulled— 36 can you say that the one whom the
Father has sanctified and sent into the world is blaspheming because
I said, 'I am God's Son'? 37 If I am not doing the works of my Father,

---

[a] Or *the Christ* [b] Other ancient authorities read *My Father who has given them to me is greater than all, and no one can snatch them out of the Father's hand* [c] Other ancient authorities read *in the law*

then do not believe me. [38]But if I do them, even though you do not
believe me, believe the works, so that you may know and understand[a]
that the Father is in me and I am in the Father." [39]Then they tried to
arrest him again, but he escaped from their hands.

40 He went away again across the Jordan to the place where John
had been baptizing earlier, and he remained there. [41]Many came to
him, and they were saying, "John performed no sign, but everything
that John said about this man was true." [42]And many believed in him
there.

The Death of Lazarus

11:1-44 The dead man came out: The raising of Lazarus happens only in the Gospel of John and is the last of Jesus' signs. The pattern of sign–dialogue–explanation used throughout the Gospel (see note on 5:1-9) is modified in this instance. Here Jesus interprets the sign *before* it happens.

11:2 Mary was the one who anointed the Lord: Mary will not anoint Jesus until 12:1-8, but referring to this event yet to come in the context of Lazarus' death is a reminder that Jesus' own death is fast approaching.

11 Now a certain man was ill, Lazarus of Bethany, the village of
Mary and her sister Martha. [2]Mary was the one who anointed
the Lord with perfume and wiped his feet with her hair; her brother
Lazarus was ill. [3]So the sisters sent a message to Jesus,[b] "Lord, he
whom you love is ill." [4]But when Jesus heard it, he said, "This illness
does not lead to death; rather it is for God's glory, so that the Son of
God may be glorified through it." [5]Accordingly, though Jesus loved
Martha and her sister and Lazarus, [6]after having heard that Lazarus[c]
was ill, he stayed two days longer in the place where he was.

7 Then after this he said to the disciples, "Let us go to Judea again."
[8]The disciples said to him, "Rabbi, the Jews were just now trying to
stone you, and are you going there again?" [9]Jesus answered, "Are there
not twelve hours of daylight? Those who walk during the day do not
stumble, because they see the light of this world. [10]But those who
walk at night stumble, because the light is not in them." [11]After saying
this, he told them, "Our friend Lazarus has fallen asleep, but I am going there to awaken him." [12]The disciples said to him, "Lord, if he has
fallen asleep, he will be all right." [13]Jesus, however, had been speaking about his death, but they thought that he was referring merely to
sleep. [14]Then Jesus told them plainly, "Lazarus is dead. [15]For your sake
I am glad I was not there, so that you may believe. But let us go to
him." [16]Thomas, who was called the Twin,[d] said to his fellow disciples,
"Let us also go, that we may die with him."

Jesus the Resurrection and the Life

17 When Jesus arrived, he found that Lazarus[c] had already been
in the tomb four days. [18]Now Bethany was near Jerusalem, some two
miles[e] away, [19]and many of the Jews had come to Martha and Mary
to console them about their brother. [20]When Martha heard that Jesus
was coming, she went and met him, while Mary stayed at home.
[21]Martha said to Jesus, "Lord, if you had been here, my brother would

---

[a] Other ancient authorities lack *and understand;* others read *and believe* [b] Gk *him* [c] Gk *he*
[d] Gk *Didymus* [e] Gk *fifteen stadia*

not have died. 22 But even now I know that God will give you whatever you ask of him." 23 Jesus said to her, "Your brother will rise again."
24 Martha said to him, "I know that he will rise again in the resurrection on the last day." 25 Jesus said to her, "I am the resurrection and the
life.[a] Those who believe in me, even though they die, will live, 26 and
everyone who lives and believes in me will never die. Do you believe
this?" 27 She said to him, "Yes, Lord, I believe that you are the Messiah,[b] the Son of God, the one coming into the world."

Jesus Weeps

28 When she had said this, she went back and called her sister
Mary, and told her privately, "The Teacher is here and is calling for
you." 29 And when she heard it, she got up quickly and went to him.
30 Now Jesus had not yet come to the village, but was still at the place
where Martha had met him. 31 The Jews who were with her in the
house, consoling her, saw Mary get up quickly and go out. They followed her because they thought that she was going to the tomb to
weep there. 32 When Mary came where Jesus was and saw him, she
knelt at his feet and said to him, "Lord, if you had been here, my
brother would not have died." 33 When Jesus saw her weeping, and the
Jews who came with her also weeping, he was greatly disturbed in
spirit and deeply moved. 34 He said, "Where have you laid him?" They
said to him, "Lord, come and see." 35 Jesus began to weep. 36 So the
Jews said, "See how he loved him!" 37 But some of them said, "Could
not he who opened the eyes of the blind man have kept this man from
dying?"

Jesus Raises Lazarus to Life

38 Then Jesus, again greatly disturbed, came to the tomb. It was
a cave, and a stone was lying against it. 39 Jesus said, "Take away the
stone." Martha, the sister of the dead man, said to him, "Lord, already
there is a stench because he has been dead four days." 40 Jesus said to
her, "Did I not tell you that if you believed, you would see the glory
of God?" 41 So they took away the stone. And Jesus looked upward
and said, "Father, I thank you for having heard me. 42 I knew that you
always hear me, but I have said this for the sake of the crowd standing
here, so that they may believe that you sent me." 43 When he had said
this, he cried with a loud voice, "Lazarus, come out!" 44 The dead man
came out, his hands and feet bound with strips of cloth, and his face
wrapped in a cloth. Jesus said to them, "Unbind him, and let him go."

The Plot to Kill Jesus

45 Many of the Jews therefore, who had come with Mary and had
seen what Jesus did, believed in him. 46 But some of them went to the

[a] Other ancient authorities lack *and the life* [b] Or *the Christ*

11:25 and the life: Some ancient sources lack "and the life," perhaps suggesting that some scribes thought Jesus was repeating himself. Verses 25-26 imply, however, that Jesus means both the future resurrection and living and believing in Jesus' presence today.

How do you think of the resurrection?

11:39 dead four days: Jewish belief held that the soul left the body after three days. The reference to four days emphasizes that Lazarus was truly dead.

11:45-53 they planned to put him to death: The resurrection of Lazarus is the event that brings about the plan to kill Jesus. In the other Gospels, the temple incident is the impetus for the plot to kill Jesus. In John, raising Lazarus to life causes the desire to put him to death. And not only Jesus, they also want to kill Lazarus (12:10-11). In other words, bringing Lazarus to life brings about Jesus' death.

Pharisees and told them what he had done. 47 So the chief priests and the Pharisees called a meeting of the council, and said, "What are we to do? This man is performing many signs. 48 If we let him go on like this, everyone will believe in him, and the Romans will come and destroy both our holy place[a] and our nation." 49 But one of them, Caiaphas, who was high priest that year, said to them, "You know nothing at all! 50 You do not understand that it is better for you to have one man die for the people than to have the whole nation destroyed." 51 He did not say this on his own, but being high priest that year he prophesied that Jesus was about to die for the nation, 52 and not for the nation only, but to gather into one the dispersed children of God. 53 So from that day on they planned to put him to death.

54 Jesus therefore no longer walked about openly among the Jews, but went from there to a town called Ephraim in the region near the wilderness; and he remained there with the disciples.

55 Now the Passover of the Jews was near, and many went up from the country to Jerusalem before the Passover to purify themselves. 56 They were looking for Jesus and were asking one another as they stood in the temple, "What do you think? Surely he will not come to the festival, will he?" 57 Now the chief priests and the Pharisees had given orders that anyone who knew where Jesus[b] was should let them know, so that they might arrest him.

12:1-8 Mary...anointed Jesus' feet: The Gospel of John, along with Matthew (26:1-13) and Mark (14:3-9), connects Jesus' anointing with his death, when spices and precious ointments were used to prepare bodies for burial. Luke, however, uses the episode to focus on forgiveness (see Luke 7:36-50).

In John's Gospel, Mary's act of discipleship is contrasted with Judas, the disciple who will betray Jesus. Mary's anointing of Jesus' feet looks forward to Jesus' washing of the disciples' feet (13:1-11) and highlights the meaning of true discipleship. What do you think it means to be a disciple of Jesus?

12:6 because he was a thief: That Judas is called a thief recalls the thief who tries to get into the sheepfold by some other way (10:1, 8, 10). Judas as the thief also foreshadows his appearance in the garden, where Jesus comes out (18:4) so as not to allow Judas into the "fold."

12:9-11 planned to put Lazarus to death: This brief passage about the plot to kill Lazarus is found only in this Gospel. It links the plot to the one that began to be hatched against Jesus after he raised Lazarus from the dead (11:45-57).

Mary Anoints Jesus

12 Six days before the Passover Jesus came to Bethany, the home of Lazarus, whom he had raised from the dead. 2 There they gave a dinner for him. Martha served, and Lazarus was one of those at the table with him. 3 Mary took a pound of costly perfume made of pure nard, anointed Jesus' feet, and wiped them[c] with her hair. The house was filled with the fragrance of the perfume. 4 But Judas Iscariot, one of his disciples (the one who was about to betray him), said, 5 "Why was this perfume not sold for three hundred denarii[d] and the money given to the poor?" 6 (He said this not because he cared about the poor, but because he was a thief; he kept the common purse and used to steal what was put into it.) 7 Jesus said, "Leave her alone. She bought it[e] so that she might keep it for the day of my burial. 8 You always have the poor with you, but you do not always have me."

The Plot to Kill Lazarus

9 When the great crowd of the Jews learned that he was there, they came not only because of Jesus but also to see Lazarus, whom he had raised from the dead. 10 So the chief priests planned to put Laza-

[a] Or *our temple;* Greek *our place* [b] Gk *he* [c] Gk *his feet* [d] Three hundred denarii would be nearly a year's wages for a laborer [e] Gk lacks *She bought it*

rus to death as well, 11 since it was on account of him that many of the
Jews were deserting and were believing in Jesus.

Jesus' Triumphal Entry into Jerusalem

12 The next day the great crowd that had come to the festival
heard that Jesus was coming to Jerusalem. 13 So they took branches of
palm trees and went out to meet him, shouting,

"Hosanna!
Blessed is the one who comes in the name of the Lord—
the King of Israel!"

14 Jesus found a young donkey and sat on it; as it is written:

15 "Do not be afraid, daughter of Zion.
Look, your king is coming,
sitting on a donkey's colt!"

16 His disciples did not understand these things at first; but when Jesus
was glorified, then they remembered that these things had been written of him and had been done to him. 17 So the crowd that had been
with him when he called Lazarus out of the tomb and raised him from
the dead continued to testify.[a] 18 It was also because they heard that he
had performed this sign that the crowd went to meet him. 19 The Pharisees then said to one another, "You see, you can do nothing. Look,
the world has gone after him!"

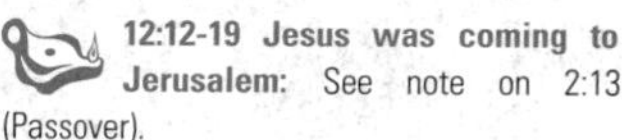

12:12-19 Jesus was coming to Jerusalem: See note on 2:13 (Passover).

Some Greeks Wish to See Jesus

20 Now among those who went up to worship at the festival
were some Greeks. 21 They came to Philip, who was from Bethsaida in
Galilee, and said to him, "Sir, we wish to see Jesus." 22 Philip went and
told Andrew; then Andrew and Philip went and told Jesus. 23 Jesus answered them, "The hour has come for the Son of Man to be glorified.
24 Very truly, I tell you, unless a grain of wheat falls into the earth and
dies, it remains just a single grain; but if it dies, it bears much fruit.
25 Those who love their life lose it, and those who hate their life in this
world will keep it for eternal life. 26 Whoever serves me must follow
me, and where I am, there will my servant be also. Whoever serves
me, the Father will honor.

Jesus Speaks about His Death

27 "Now my soul is troubled. And what should I say—'Father,
save me from this hour'? No, it is for this reason that I have come
to this hour. 28 Father, glorify your name." Then a voice came from
heaven, "I have glorified it, and I will glorify it again." 29 The crowd
standing there heard it and said that it was thunder. Others said, "An
angel has spoken to him." 30 Jesus answered, "This voice has come for

[a] Other ancient authorities read *with him began to testify that he had called . . . from the dead*

your sake, not for mine. [31]Now is the judgment of this world; now
the ruler of this world will be driven out. [32]And I, when I am lifted
up from the earth, will draw all people[a] to myself." [33]He said this to
indicate the kind of death he was to die. [34]The crowd answered him,
"We have heard from the law that the Messiah[b] remains forever. How
can you say that the Son of Man must be lifted up? Who is this Son
of Man?" [35]Jesus said to them, "The light is with you for a little longer.
Walk while you have the light, so that the darkness may not overtake
you. If you walk in the darkness, you do not know where you are going. [36]While you have the light, believe in the light, so that you may
become children of light."

The Unbelief of the People

After Jesus had said this, he departed and hid from them. [37]Al-
though he had performed so many signs in their presence, they
did not believe in him. [38]This was to fulfill the word spoken by the
prophet Isaiah:

"Lord, who has believed our message,
 and to whom has the arm of the Lord been revealed?"

[39]And so they could not believe, because Isaiah also said,

40 "He has blinded their eyes
 and hardened their heart,
so that they might not look with their eyes,
 and understand with their heart and turn—
 and I would heal them."

[41]Isaiah said this because[c] he saw his glory and spoke about him.
[42]Nevertheless many, even of the authorities, believed in him. But because of the Pharisees they did not confess it, for fear that they would
be put out of the synagogue; [43]for they loved human glory more than
the glory that comes from God.

Summary of Jesus' Teaching

44 Then Jesus cried aloud: "Whoever believes in me believes not
in me but in him who sent me. [45]And whoever sees me sees him who
sent me. [46]I have come as light into the world, so that everyone who
believes in me should not remain in the darkness. [47]I do not judge
anyone who hears my words and does not keep them, for I came not
to judge the world, but to save the world. [48]The one who rejects me
and does not receive my word has a judge; on the last day the word
that I have spoken will serve as judge, [49]for I have not spoken on my
own, but the Father who sent me has himself given me a commandment about what to say and what to speak. [50]And I know that his commandment is eternal life. What I speak, therefore, I speak just as the
Father has told me."

---

[a] Other ancient authorities read *all things* [b] Or *the Christ* [c] Other ancient witnesses read *when*

Jesus Washes the Disciples' Feet

13 Now before the festival of the Passover, Jesus knew that his
hour had come to depart from this world and go to the Father. Having loved his own who were in the world, he loved them to
the end. 2 The devil had already put it into the heart of Judas son of
Simon Iscariot to betray him. And during supper 3 Jesus, knowing that
the Father had given all things into his hands, and that he had come
from God and was going to God, 4 got up from the table,[a] took off his
outer robe, and tied a towel around himself. 5 Then he poured water
into a basin and began to wash the disciples' feet and to wipe them
with the towel that was tied around him. 6 He came to Simon Peter,
who said to him, "Lord, are you going to wash my feet?" 7 Jesus answered, "You do not know now what I am doing, but later you will
understand." 8 Peter said to him, "You will never wash my feet." Jesus
answered, "Unless I wash you, you have no share with me." 9 Simon
Peter said to him, "Lord, not my feet only but also my hands and my
head!" 10 Jesus said to him, "One who has bathed does not need to
wash, except for the feet,[b] but is entirely clean. And you[c] are clean,
though not all of you." 11 For he knew who was to betray him; for this
reason he said, "Not all of you are clean."

12 After he had washed their feet, had put on his robe, and had
returned to the table, he said to them, "Do you know what I have
done to you? 13 You call me Teacher and Lord—and you are right,
for that is what I am. 14 So if I, your Lord and Teacher, have washed
your feet, you also ought to wash one another's feet. 15 For I have set
you an example, that you also should do as I have done to you. 16 Very
truly, I tell you, servants[d] are not greater than their master, nor are
messengers greater than the one who sent them. 17 If you know these
things, you are blessed if you do them. 18 I am not speaking of all of
you; I know whom I have chosen. But it is to fulfill the scripture, 'The
one who ate my bread[e] has lifted his heel against me.' 19 I tell you this
now, before it occurs, so that when it does occur, you may believe
that I am he.[f] 20 Very truly, I tell you, whoever receives one whom
I send receives me; and whoever receives me receives him who
sent me."

Jesus Foretells His Betrayal

21 After saying this Jesus was troubled in spirit, and declared,
"Very truly, I tell you, one of you will betray me." 22 The disciples
looked at one another, uncertain of whom he was speaking. 23 One of
his disciples—the one whom Jesus loved—was reclining next to him;
24 Simon Peter therefore motioned to him to ask Jesus of whom he

---

[a] Gk *from supper* [b] Other ancient authorities lack *except for the feet* [c] The Greek word for *you* here is plural [d] Gk *slaves* [e] Other ancient authorities read *ate bread with me* [f] Gk *I am*

13:1 Jesus knew that his hour had come: This chapter marks a significant shift in the Gospel story. The previous chapter ends with a summary of Jesus' teaching (12:44-50). Now, with his public ministry over and the hour of his death fast approaching, Jesus gathers privately with his disciples for what will be their final meal together.

13:1-11 began to wash the disciples' feet: Foot washing was a gesture of hospitality that hosts provided to guests when they entered their homes after traveling the dusty roads of Palestine. Usually, however, household servants, not homeowners, performed the task. In John's Gospel, Jesus washes his disciples' feet before they eat together. It is this loving act, rather than the meal, that becomes the central event of Jesus' farewell supper with his disciples.

Have you ever experienced a foot-washing? How would you describe it and the impact it had on you? What else may foot washing symbolize?

13:21-30 one of you will betray me: Judas appears for the last time before he participates in Jesus' arrest in the garden later in the evening. The Gospel indicates that Jesus knew that Judas would be the one who would betray him (see 13:26).

How do you make sense of the fact that the one who betrayed Jesus was one of Jesus' own disciples? What difference does Satan's involvement and timing make?

13:23 the one whom Jesus loved: This is the first time that the Gospel mentions this unnamed disciple. While some commentators suggest that the beloved disciple is the author of the Gospel, the more important literary function of this character seems to be to describe what discipleship looks like.

was speaking. 25 So while reclining next to Jesus, he asked him, "Lord, who is it?" 26 Jesus answered, "It is the one to whom I give this piece of bread when I have dipped it in the dish."[a] So when he had dipped the piece of bread, he gave it to Judas son of Simon Iscariot.[b] 27 After he received the piece of bread,[c] Satan entered into him. Jesus said to him, "Do quickly what you are going to do." 28 Now no one at the table knew why he said this to him. 29 Some thought that, because Judas had the common purse, Jesus was telling him, "Buy what we need for the festival"; or, that he should give something to the poor. 30 So, after receiving the piece of bread, he immediately went out. And it was night.

13:30 And it was night: Like Nicodemus coming "by night" (3:2), Judas also leaves at night, indicating that Judas remains in the realm of darkness, or unbelief.

The New Commandment

31 When he had gone out, Jesus said, "Now the Son of Man has been glorified, and God has been glorified in him. 32 If God has been glorified in him,[d] God will also glorify him in himself and will glorify him at once. 33 Little children, I am with you only a little longer. You will look for me; and as I said to the Jews so now I say to you, 'Where I am going, you cannot come.' 34 I give you a new commandment, that you love one another. Just as I have loved you, you also should love one another. 35 By this everyone will know that you are my disciples, if you have love for one another."

Jesus Foretells Peter's Denial

36 Simon Peter said to him, "Lord, where are you going?" Jesus answered, "Where I am going, you cannot follow me now; but you will follow afterward." 37 Peter said to him, "Lord, why can I not follow you now? I will lay down my life for you." 38 Jesus answered, "Will you lay down your life for me? Very truly, I tell you, before the cock crows, you will have denied me three times.

Jesus the Way to the Father

14 "Do not let your hearts be troubled. Believe[e] in God, believe also in me. 2 In my Father's house there are many dwelling places. If it were not so, would I have told you that I go to prepare a place for you?[f] 3 And if I go and prepare a place for you, I will come again and will take you to myself, so that where I am, there you may be also. 4 And you know the way to the place where I am going."[g] 5 Thomas said to him, "Lord, we do not know where you are going. How can we know the way?" 6 Jesus said to him, "I am the way, and the truth, and the life. No one comes to the Father except through me. 7 If

14:1—16:33 Do not let your hearts be troubled...I have conquered the world: These three chapters include Jesus' final words to his disciples before his arrest. In these chapters, Jesus prepares his disciples for his departure and return to the Father.

14:2 many dwelling places: This verse has sometimes been translated "many mansions" or "many rooms," but "dwelling places" better captures the intended meaning of the original Greek. Described here is the intimate relationship with Jesus that is ours as we abide in Jesus' presence here and now, and the promise of dwelling with God forever in the life to come.

---

[a] Gk *dipped it* [b] Other ancient authorities read *Judas Iscariot son of Simon*; others, *Judas son of Simon from Karyot* (Kerioth) [c] Gk *After the piece of bread* [d] Other ancient authorities lack *If God has been glorified in him* [e] Or *You believe* [f] Or *If it were not so, I would have told you; for I go to prepare a place for you* [g] Other ancient authorities read *Where I am going you know, and the way you know*

you know me, you will know[a] my Father also. From now on you do
know him and have seen him."
8 Philip said to him, "Lord, show us the Father, and we will be satisfied." [9]Jesus said to him, "Have I been with you all this time, Philip,
and you still do not know me? Whoever has seen me has seen the
Father. How can you say, 'Show us the Father'? [10]Do you not believe
that I am in the Father and the Father is in me? The words that I say to
you I do not speak on my own; but the Father who dwells in me does
his works. [11]Believe me that I am in the Father and the Father is in me;
but if you do not, then believe me because of the works themselves.
[12]Very truly, I tell you, the one who believes in me will also do the
works that I do and, in fact, will do greater works than these, because
I am going to the Father. [13]I will do whatever you ask in my name, so
that the Father may be glorified in the Son. [14]If in my name you ask
me[b] for anything, I will do it.

What is works-righteousness? Jesus speaks of his followers doing even greater works than Jesus did himself. Lutherans believe that a person is not saved by doing good works but by having faith in Christ Jesus. Yet, throughout John's Gospel, Jesus understands his followers to be participants in his own work (9:4; 14:12). How can Lutherans understand Jesus' words here? Luther writes in his preface to the book of Romans, "It is impossible to separate works from faith, quite as impossible as to separate heat and light from fire." The works that we do are in response to what God has already done for us. *John 14:12*

What do you think it means "to do the works of Jesus"?

The Promise of the Holy Spirit

15 "If you love me, you will keep[c] my commandments. [16]And I
will ask the Father, and he will give you another Advocate,[d] to be with
you forever. [17]This is the Spirit of truth, whom the world cannot receive, because it neither sees him nor knows him. You know him, because he abides with you, and he will be in[e] you.
18 "I will not leave you orphaned; I am coming to you. [19]In a little
while the world will no longer see me, but you will see me; because
I live, you also will live. [20]On that day you will know that I am in my
Father, and you in me, and I in you. [21]They who have my commandments and keep them are those who love me; and those who love me
will be loved by my Father, and I will love them and reveal myself to
them." [22]Judas (not Iscariot) said to him, "Lord, how is it that you will
reveal yourself to us, and not to the world?" [23]Jesus answered him,
"Those who love me will keep my word, and my Father will love them,
and we will come to them and make our home with them. [24]Whoever
does not love me does not keep my words; and the word that you hear
is not mine, but is from the Father who sent me.
25 "I have said these things to you while I am still with you. [26]But
the Advocate,[d] the Holy Spirit, whom the Father will send in my
name, will teach you everything, and remind you of all that I have
said to you. [27]Peace I leave with you; my peace I give to you. I do not
give to you as the world gives. Do not let your hearts be troubled, and
do not let them be afraid. [28]You heard me say to you, 'I am going away,
and I am coming to you.' If you loved me, you would rejoice that I am
going to the Father, because the Father is greater than I. [29]And now

14:16 another Advocate: This name for the Spirit is unique to John's Gospel. In Greek, the word is *paraclete,* which means "one who is called alongside." The word can also be translated "helper," "comforter," "encourager," and "intercessor."

14:17 the Spirit of truth: In the Bible, the role of the Holy Spirit varies considerably. John's Gospel provides a unique understanding of the meaning and function of the Spirit as one who comes to walk alongside and guide the followers in the way of truth (see 14:16-17, 26; 15:26; 16:7-15).

How have you or do you experience the Holy Spirit in your life? What words would you use to describe the Holy Spirit in your experience?

What is the Trinity? Along with other Christians, Lutherans believe in the doctrine of the Trinity, which says that God is one, yet three persons. These "persons" are traditionally described as Father, Son, and Holy Spirit. Each of the three sections of the Apostles' Creed confesses the activity of one person of the Trinity. Though the term "Trinity" is not found in the Bible, it is based on biblical texts upon which the church, after the New Testament was written, based the official doctrine of the Trinity. *John 14:26*

---

[a] Other ancient authorities read *If you had known me, you would have known* [b] Other ancient authorities lack *me* [c] Other ancient authorities read *me, keep* [d] Or *Helper* [e] Or *among*

I have told you this before it occurs, so that when it does occur, you
may believe. 30 I will no longer talk much with you, for the ruler of this
world is coming. He has no power over me; 31 but I do as the Father
has commanded me, so that the world may know that I love the Father. Rise, let us be on our way.

Jesus the True Vine

15 "I am the true vine, and my Father is the vinegrower. 2 He removes every branch in me that bears no fruit. Every branch
that bears fruit he prunes[a] to make it bear more fruit. 3 You have already been cleansed[a] by the word that I have spoken to you. 4 Abide in
me as I abide in you. Just as the branch cannot bear fruit by itself unless it abides in the vine, neither can you unless you abide in me. 5 I am
the vine, you are the branches. Those who abide in me and I in them
bear much fruit, because apart from me you can do nothing. 6 Whoever does not abide in me is thrown away like a branch and withers;
such branches are gathered, thrown into the fire, and burned. 7 If you
abide in me, and my words abide in you, ask for whatever you wish,
and it will be done for you. 8 My Father is glorified by this, that you
bear much fruit and become[b] my disciples. 9 As the Father has loved
me, so I have loved you; abide in my love. 10 If you keep my commandments, you will abide in my love, just as I have kept my Father's commandments and abide in his love. 11 I have said these things to you so
that my joy may be in you, and that your joy may be complete.

12 "This is my commandment, that you love one another as I have
loved you. 13 No one has greater love than this, to lay down one's life
for one's friends. 14 You are my friends if you do what I command you.
15 I do not call you servants[c] any longer, because the servant[d] does not
know what the master is doing; but I have called you friends, because
I have made known to you everything that I have heard from my Father. 16 You did not choose me but I chose you. And I appointed you
to go and bear fruit, fruit that will last, so that the Father will give you
whatever you ask him in my name. 17 I am giving you these commands
so that you may love one another.

The World's Hatred

18 "If the world hates you, be aware that it hated me before it
hated you. 19 If you belonged to the world,[e] the world would love you
as its own. Because you do not belong to the world, but I have chosen
you out of the world—therefore the world hates you. 20 Remember
the word that I said to you, 'Servants[f] are not greater than their master.' If they persecuted me, they will persecute you; if they kept my

15:1-11 I am the true vine...you are the branches: These verses continue to develop the important theme in John's Gospel of abiding in Jesus.

15:1 vine...vinegrower: The vine is a common image in the Bible and is used to represent the relationship between God and God's people (see Isa 5:1-7).

15:13 lay down one's life for one's friends: This verse recalls Jesus' words in 10:17-18 about giving up his own life. It also looks forward to 21:15-19, where Jesus' words to Peter hint that Peter, too, will lay down his life for his friends.

Jesus chose his followers (15:16) and calls them friends (15:14). How do they remain friends, and why are they chosen (15:14-17)? Does this seem like "conditional" friendship? Why or why not? How do Jesus' words about friendship affect your understanding of friendship?

15:18-25 If the world hates you: The love that is shared between Jesus, his disciples, and the Father is contrasted with the response of the world (see 1:10). The "world" represents anyone who does not believe or recognize who Jesus is or where Jesus comes from.

---

[a] The same Greek root refers to pruning and cleansing [b] Or *be* [c] Gk *slaves* [d] Gk *slave*
[e] Gk *were of the world* [f] Gk *Slaves*

word, they will keep yours also. 21 But they will do all these things to
you on account of my name, because they do not know him who sent
me. 22 If I had not come and spoken to them, they would not have sin;
but now they have no excuse for their sin. 23 Whoever hates me hates
my Father also. 24 If I had not done among them the works that no one
else did, they would not have sin. But now they have seen and hated
both me and my Father. 25 It was to fulfill the word that is written in
their law, 'They hated me without a cause.'

26 "When the Advocate[a] comes, whom I will send to you from
the Father, the Spirit of truth who comes from the Father, he will testify on my behalf. 27 You also are to testify because you have been with
me from the beginning.

16 "I have said these things to you to keep you from stumbling.
2 They will put you out of the synagogues. Indeed, an hour is
coming when those who kill you will think that by doing so they are
offering worship to God. 3 And they will do this because they have
not known the Father or me. 4 But I have said these things to you so
that when their hour comes you may remember that I told you about
them.

15:26-27 testify on my behalf: The theme of testimony or witness is central to John's Gospel. The Advocate will also be sent to testify for Jesus.

What do you think it means to witness or give testimony of your faith?

The Work of the Spirit

"I did not say these things to you from the beginning, because I
was with you. 5 But now I am going to him who sent me; yet none of
you asks me, 'Where are you going?' 6 But because I have said these
things to you, sorrow has filled your hearts. 7 Nevertheless I tell you
the truth: it is to your advantage that I go away, for if I do not go away,
the Advocate[a] will not come to you; but if I go, I will send him to you.
8 And when he comes, he will prove the world wrong about[b] sin and
righteousness and judgment: 9 about sin, because they do not believe
in me; 10 about righteousness, because I am going to the Father and
you will see me no longer; 11 about judgment, because the ruler of this
world has been condemned.

12 "I still have many things to say to you, but you cannot bear
them now. 13 When the Spirit of truth comes, he will guide you into
all the truth; for he will not speak on his own, but will speak whatever
he hears, and he will declare to you the things that are to come. 14 He
will glorify me, because he will take what is mine and declare it to you.
15 All that the Father has is mine. For this reason I said that he will take
what is mine and declare it to you.

16:5 I am going to him who sent me: Jesus' work is not complete until he returns to God the Father.

16:7-15 I will send him to you: These verses say more about the work of the Spirit. Jesus will send the Spirit after his resurrection and before he returns to God the Father (see 20:22).

What do you think Jesus means when he says, "I will see you again" (16:22)?

Sorrow Will Turn into Joy

16 "A little while, and you will no longer see me, and again a little
while, and you will see me." 17 Then some of his disciples said to one

[a] Or *Helper* [b] Or *convict the world of*

another, "What does he mean by saying to us, 'A little while, and you
will no longer see me, and again a little while, and you will see me';
and 'Because I am going to the Father'?" 18 They said, "What does he
mean by this 'a little while'? We do not know what he is talking about."
19 Jesus knew that they wanted to ask him, so he said to them, "Are
you discussing among yourselves what I meant when I said, 'A little
while, and you will no longer see me, and again a little while, and you
will see me'? 20 Very truly, I tell you, you will weep and mourn, but the
world will rejoice; you will have pain, but your pain will turn into joy.
21 When a woman is in labor, she has pain, because her hour has come.
But when her child is born, she no longer remembers the anguish because of the joy of having brought a human being into the world. 22 So
you have pain now; but I will see you again, and your hearts will rejoice, and no one will take your joy from you. 23 On that day you will
ask nothing of me.[a] Very truly, I tell you, if you ask anything of the
Father in my name, he will give it to you.[b] 24 Until now you have not
asked for anything in my name. Ask and you will receive, so that your
joy may be complete.

Peace for the Disciples

16:25, 29 figures of speech: Speaking in figures of speech (see 10:6) is contrasted to plain speaking. Yet the disciples are still not able to "bear" all that Jesus has to say (16:12).

25 "I have said these things to you in figures of speech. The hour
is coming when I will no longer speak to you in figures, but will tell
you plainly of the Father. 26 On that day you will ask in my name. I do
not say to you that I will ask the Father on your behalf; 27 for the Father
himself loves you, because you have loved me and have believed that
I came from God.[c] 28 I came from the Father and have come into the
world; again, I am leaving the world and am going to the Father."

29 His disciples said, "Yes, now you are speaking plainly, not in
any figure of speech! 30 Now we know that you know all things, and
do not need to have anyone question you; by this we believe that you
came from God." 31 Jesus answered them, "Do you now believe? 32 The
hour is coming, indeed it has come, when you will be scattered, each
one to his home, and you will leave me alone. Yet I am not alone because the Father is with me. 33 I have said this to you, so that in me you
may have peace. In the world you face persecution. But take courage;
I have conquered the world!"

16:33 I have conquered the world! Jesus' last words to his disciples are a sweeping claim of what he has accomplished.

Jesus Prays for His Disciples

17:1-26 Jesus...looked up to heaven: Jesus prays for his followers in this chapter. Jesus prays to the Father in a location very different from those in the other Gospels. Jesus doesn't pray in the garden or at Gethsemane. Nor does Jesus grieve or ask for this cup to pass. And there is no mention made of the disciples sleeping while Jesus prays (see Matt 26:36-46; Mark 14:32-41; Luke 22:39-46).

The Lord's Prayer isn't found in the Gospel of John, but aspects of Jesus' final prayer mirror the Lord's Prayer. For example, compare 17:15 to Luke 11:4b.

17 After Jesus had spoken these words, he looked up to heaven
and said, "Father, the hour has come; glorify your Son so that
the Son may glorify you, 2 since you have given him authority over all
people,[d] to give eternal life to all whom you have given him. 3 And this

---

[a] Or *will ask me no question* [b] Other ancient authorities read *Father, he will give it to you in my name*
[c] Other ancient authorities read *the Father* [d] Gk *flesh*

is eternal life, that they may know you, the only true God, and Jesus
Christ whom you have sent. 4 I glorified you on earth by finishing the
work that you gave me to do. 5 So now, Father, glorify me in your own
presence with the glory that I had in your presence before the world
existed.
6 "I have made your name known to those whom you gave me
from the world. They were yours, and you gave them to me, and they
have kept your word. 7 Now they know that everything you have given
me is from you; 8 for the words that you gave to me I have given to
them, and they have received them and know in truth that I came
from you; and they have believed that you sent me. 9 I am asking on
their behalf; I am not asking on behalf of the world, but on behalf
of those whom you gave me, because they are yours. 10 All mine are
yours, and yours are mine; and I have been glorified in them. 11 And
now I am no longer in the world, but they are in the world, and I am
coming to you. Holy Father, protect them in your name that you
have given me, so that they may be one, as we are one. 12 While I was
with them, I protected them in your name that[a] you have given me. I
guarded them, and not one of them was lost except the one destined
to be lost,[b] so that the scripture might be fulfilled. 13 But now I am
coming to you, and I speak these things in the world so that they may
have my joy made complete in themselves.[c] 14 I have given them your
word, and the world has hated them because they do not belong to
the world, just as I do not belong to the world. 15 I am not asking you
to take them out of the world, but I ask you to protect them from the
evil one.[d] 16 They do not belong to the world, just as I do not belong to
the world. 17 Sanctify them in the truth; your word is truth. 18 As you
have sent me into the world, so I have sent them into the world. 19 And
for their sakes I sanctify myself, so that they also may be sanctified in
truth.
20 "I ask not only on behalf of these, but also on behalf of those
who will believe in me through their word, 21 that they may all be one.
As you, Father, are in me and I am in you, may they also be in us,[e] so
that the world may believe that you have sent me. 22 The glory that
you have given me I have given them, so that they may be one, as we
are one, 23 I in them and you in me, that they may become completely
one, so that the world may know that you have sent me and have
loved them even as you have loved me. 24 Father, I desire that those
also, whom you have given me, may be with me where I am, to see
my glory, which you have given me because you loved me before the
foundation of the world.
25 "Righteous Father, the world does not know you, but I know

17:20 also on behalf of those: Jesus prays for his disciples and also for those who will come to believe in Jesus because of the disciples' work after Jesus' ascension.

In this prayer, Jesus specifically prays for his disciples. Do you ever think about Jesus praying to the Father for you? How does that make you feel? How does his prayer inform your praying?

---

[a] Other ancient authorities read *protected in your name those whom* [b] Gk *except the son of destruction*
[c] Or *among themselves* [d] Or *from evil* [e] Other ancient authorities read *be one in us*

you; and these know that you have sent me. 26 I made your name known to them, and I will make it known, so that the love with which you have loved me may be in them, and I in them."

The Betrayal and Arrest of Jesus

18 After Jesus had spoken these words, he went out with his disciples across the Kidron valley to a place where there was a garden, which he and his disciples entered. 2 Now Judas, who betrayed him, also knew the place, because Jesus often met there with his disciples. 3 So Judas brought a detachment of soldiers together with police from the chief priests and the Pharisees, and they came there with lanterns and torches and weapons. 4 Then Jesus, knowing all that was to happen to him, came forward and asked them, "Whom are you looking for?" 5 They answered, "Jesus of Nazareth."[a] Jesus replied, "I am he."[b] Judas, who betrayed him, was standing with them. 6 When Jesus[c] said to them, "I am he,"[b] they stepped back and fell to the ground. 7 Again he asked them, "Whom are you looking for?" And they said, "Jesus of Nazareth."[a] 8 Jesus answered, "I told you that I am he.[b] So if you are looking for me, let these men go." 9 This was to fulfill the word that he had spoken, "I did not lose a single one of those whom you gave me." 10 Then Simon Peter, who had a sword, drew it, struck the high priest's slave, and cut off his right ear. The slave's name was Malchus. 11 Jesus said to Peter, "Put your sword back into its sheath. Am I not to drink the cup that the Father has given me?"

Jesus before the High Priest

12 So the soldiers, their officer, and the Jewish police arrested Jesus and bound him. 13 First they took him to Annas, who was the father-in-law of Caiaphas, the high priest that year. 14 Caiaphas was the one who had advised the Jews that it was better to have one person die for the people.

Peter Denies Jesus

15 Simon Peter and another disciple followed Jesus. Since that disciple was known to the high priest, he went with Jesus into the courtyard of the high priest, 16 but Peter was standing outside at the gate. So the other disciple, who was known to the high priest, went out, spoke to the woman who guarded the gate, and brought Peter in. 17 The woman said to Peter, "You are not also one of this man's disciples, are you?" He said, "I am not." 18 Now the slaves and the police had made a charcoal fire because it was cold, and they were standing around it and warming themselves. Peter also was standing with them and warming himself.

---

[a] Gk *the Nazorean* [b] Gk *I am* [c] Gk *he*

18:1 Kidron valley…there was a garden: This is the only mention in the New Testament of this area (see Map 13, p. 2110). John alone places Jesus' arrest in a garden, not Gethsemane (Matt 26:36; Mark 14:32) or the more general location of the Mount of Olives (Luke 22:39).

18:2 Judas…also knew the place: Last mentioned in 13:30, Judas now returns. He knows the location of the garden, a place where Jesus and his disciples often met. This knowledge underscores that Judas was in the inner circle of Jesus' disciples.

18:3 detachment of soldiers: A detachment was about six hundred Roman soldiers. Mention of other arresting authorities indicates that both Roman and Jewish soldiers are present at the arrest.

18:3 lanterns and torches and weapons: The lanterns and torches suggest a nighttime arrest (see 13:30) but also highlight the significance of Jesus, the Light of the World, being arrested by soldiers dependent upon the illumination of torches (see 8:12; 9:5). The weapons are an exaggerated show of force for the arrest of only one man, Jesus.

18:4 knowing all: Jesus is in total control of the situation. He does not wait for Judas to kiss him (Matt 26:47-50; Mark 14:43-46; Luke 22:47-48) but comes forward to meet the soldiers. In the Greek text, Jesus "comes out" of the garden, which suggests that the disciples are left inside, protected from the arresting mob, and Judas is not allowed in (see 10:1).

18:4 Whom are you looking for?: This question echoes Jesus' first words to his disciples (see 1:38) and anticipates his words to Mary after his resurrection, also in a garden (20:15).

18:5 I am he: See NRSV footnote *b*. The "I am" statement is an absolute "I am" (see chart The "I AM" Sayings of Jesus in John's Gospel, p. 1773). At Jesus' word, the soldiers fall to the ground, typical of what happens when people come into contact with the God elsewhere in the Bible (see Ezek 1:28; Dan 10:9; Acts 9:3-4; Rev 1:17).

18:5 Judas…was standing with them: The last time Judas appears in John's Gospel, he stands not with Jesus but with the army that has come to arrest him.

The High Priest Questions Jesus

19 Then the high priest questioned Jesus about his disciples and
about his teaching. 20 Jesus answered, "I have spoken openly to the
world; I have always taught in synagogues and in the temple, where
all the Jews come together. I have said nothing in secret. 21 Why do
you ask me? Ask those who heard what I said to them; they know
what I said." 22 When he had said this, one of the police standing
nearby struck Jesus on the face, saying, "Is that how you answer the
high priest?" 23 Jesus answered, "If I have spoken wrongly, testify to the
wrong. But if I have spoken rightly, why do you strike me?" 24 Then
Annas sent him bound to Caiaphas the high priest.

Peter Denies Jesus Again

25 Now Simon Peter was standing and warming himself. They
asked him, "You are not also one of his disciples, are you?" He denied
it and said, "I am not." 26 One of the slaves of the high priest, a relative
of the man whose ear Peter had cut off, asked, "Did I not see you in
the garden with him?" 27 Again Peter denied it, and at that moment
the cock crowed.

Jesus before Pilate

28 Then they took Jesus from Caiaphas to Pilate's headquarters.[a]
It was early in the morning. They themselves did not enter the headquarters,[a] so as to avoid ritual defilement and to be able to eat the
Passover. 29 So Pilate went out to them and said, "What accusation
do you bring against this man?" 30 They answered, "If this man were
not a criminal, we would not have handed him over to you." 31 Pilate
said to them, "Take him yourselves and judge him according to your
law." The Jews replied, "We are not permitted to put anyone to death."
32 (This was to fulfill what Jesus had said when he indicated the kind
of death he was to die.)

33 Then Pilate entered the headquarters[a] again, summoned Jesus,
and asked him, "Are you the King of the Jews?" 34 Jesus answered, "Do
you ask this on your own, or did others tell you about me?" 35 Pilate
replied, "I am not a Jew, am I? Your own nation and the chief priests
have handed you over to me. What have you done?" 36 Jesus answered,
"My kingdom is not from this world. If my kingdom were from this
world, my followers would be fighting to keep me from being handed
over to the Jews. But as it is, my kingdom is not from here." 37 Pilate
asked him, "So you are a king?" Jesus answered, "You say that I am a
king. For this I was born, and for this I came into the world, to testify
to the truth. Everyone who belongs to the truth listens to my voice."
38 Pilate asked him, "What is truth?"

---

[a] Gk *the praetorium*

The Gospel of John doesn't provide a reason for Judas' betrayal (see Matt 26:14-16) or mention his suicide (Matt 27:3-10). What do you make of this difference?

18:10 cut off his right ear: This event is found in all four Gospels (see Matt 26:51; Mark 14:47; Luke 22:50), but each recounts it differently. In Luke, Jesus heals the servant's ear (22:51); in Matthew and Mark the episode is the occasion for Jesus' teaching on the nature of his arrest and the flight of the disciples (Matt 26:52-56; Mark 14:48-50). In John, the name of the disciple (Simon Peter) and the name of the servant (Malchus) are both given.

18:11 Am I not to drink the cup: In John's Gospel, Jesus willingly takes the cup that the Father has given him, unlike in the other Gospels (Matt 20:22; Mark 10:38-39; Luke 22:42). Jesus freely accepts this gift because it is central to complete the work God has given him (3:27, 35; 5:22, 26-27; 6:37; 12:49).

18:15-18, 25-27 Peter was standing outside the gate…Peter denied it: This section and chapter 10 share the terminology of fold, door/gate, and gatekeeper. The word for "door" and "gate" is the same in Greek, and is translated as "gate" in both chapters.

Compare Peter's denial of Jesus in John with the other Gospels (Matt 26:69-75; Mark 14:66-72; Luke 22:56-62). What is the nature of Peter's denial in John?

18:19-24 the high priest questioned Jesus…Annas sent him bound to Caiaphas: Annas had been the high priest of the Jews 6–15 C.E. He probably remained influential with his son, Caiaphas, who held the position at this time (11:49). Caiaphas was high priest 18–26 C.E.

18:28—19:16 they took Jesus from Caiaphas to Pilate's headquarters: Jesus' trial by Pilate is typically divided into seven scenes, as Pilate moves back and forth between Jesus inside Pilate's headquarters and the Jewish authorities outside. Pilate's headquarters may have been at the Fortress Antonia (see Map 13, p. 2110), which included Pilate's residence when visiting Jerusalem, barracks for his guards, and the open courtyard where he made his judgments (19:13). He was the Roman governor of the region 26–36 C.E.

18:38 What is truth?: Jesus is tried before Pilate, while Pilate is "on trial" for whether or not he will believe in Jesus.

Jesus Sentenced to Death

After he had said this, he went out to the Jews again and told them,
"I find no case against him. 39 But you have a custom that I release
someone for you at the Passover. Do you want me to release for you
the King of the Jews?" 40 They shouted in reply, "Not this man, but
Barabbas!" Now Barabbas was a bandit.

19 Then Pilate took Jesus and had him flogged. 2 And the soldiers wove a crown of thorns and put it on his head, and they
dressed him in a purple robe. 3 They kept coming up to him, saying,
"Hail, King of the Jews!" and striking him on the face. 4 Pilate went
out again and said to them, "Look, I am bringing him out to you to let
you know that I find no case against him." 5 So Jesus came out, wearing
the crown of thorns and the purple robe. Pilate said to them, "Here
is the man!" 6 When the chief priests and the police saw him, they
shouted, "Crucify him! Crucify him!" Pilate said to them, "Take him
yourselves and crucify him; I find no case against him." 7 The Jews answered him, "We have a law, and according to that law he ought to die
because he has claimed to be the Son of God."

8 Now when Pilate heard this, he was more afraid than ever.
9 He entered his headquarters[a] again and asked Jesus, "Where are
you from?" But Jesus gave him no answer. 10 Pilate therefore said to
him, "Do you refuse to speak to me? Do you not know that I have
power to release you, and power to crucify you?" 11 Jesus answered
him, "You would have no power over me unless it had been given you
from above; therefore the one who handed me over to you is guilty of
a greater sin." 12 From then on Pilate tried to release him, but the Jews
cried out, "If you release this man, you are no friend of the emperor.
Everyone who claims to be a king sets himself against the emperor."

13 When Pilate heard these words, he brought Jesus outside and
sat[b] on the judge's bench at a place called The Stone Pavement, or in
Hebrew[c] Gabbatha. 14 Now it was the day of Preparation for the Passover; and it was about noon. He said to the Jews, "Here is your King!"
15 They cried out, "Away with him! Away with him! Crucify him!"
Pilate asked them, "Shall I crucify your King?" The chief priests answered, "We have no king but the emperor." 16 Then he handed him
over to them to be crucified.

The Crucifixion of Jesus

So they took Jesus; 17 and carrying the cross by himself, he went
out to what is called The Place of the Skull, which in Hebrew[c] is called
Golgotha. 18 There they crucified him, and with him two others, one
on either side, with Jesus between them. 19 Pilate also had an inscription written and put on the cross. It read, "Jesus of Nazareth,[d] the King

19:9 Where are you from?: Pilate's question is central for this Gospel. Knowing where Jesus is from is essential for believing who he is.

19:14 day of Preparation: Jesus dies on the first day of Passover in the Gospels of Matthew, Mark, and Luke. In John, however, Jesus dies on the Day of Preparation for Passover, at the same time the sacrificial lambs for the Passover meal are being slaughtered.

19:17 carrying the cross by himself: Jesus carried only the horizontal bar of the cross. The upright posts would have already been at the crucifixion site, which was located outside the city gates. Jesus carries his own cross alone in John. In the other Gospels, Simon of Cyrene is made to carry it for him (Matt 27:32; Mark 15:21; Luke 23:26).

Why is it significant that, according to the Gospel of John, Jesus carried his own cross to his death?

[a] Gk *the praetorium* [b] Or *seated him* [c] That is, *Aramaic* [d] Gk *the Nazorean*

of the Jews." 20 Many of the Jews read this inscription, because the place
where Jesus was crucified was near the city; and it was written in Hebrew,[a] in Latin, and in Greek. 21 Then the chief priests of the Jews said
to Pilate, "Do not write, 'The King of the Jews,' but, 'This man said, I
am King of the Jews.' " 22 Pilate answered, "What I have written I have
written." 23 When the soldiers had crucified Jesus, they took his clothes
and divided them into four parts, one for each soldier. They also took
his tunic; now the tunic was seamless, woven in one piece from the
top. 24 So they said to one another, "Let us not tear it, but cast lots for it
to see who will get it." This was to fulfill what the scripture says,

"They divided my clothes among themselves,
    and for my clothing they cast lots."

25 And that is what the soldiers did.
Meanwhile, standing near the cross of Jesus were his mother, and
his mother's sister, Mary the wife of Clopas, and Mary Magdalene.
26 When Jesus saw his mother and the disciple whom he loved standing beside her, he said to his mother, "Woman, here is your son."
27 Then he said to the disciple, "Here is your mother." And from that
hour the disciple took her into his own home.
28 After this, when Jesus knew that all was now finished, he said
(in order to fulfill the scripture), "I am thirsty." 29 A jar full of sour wine
was standing there. So they put a sponge full of the wine on a branch
of hyssop and held it to his mouth. 30 When Jesus had received the
wine, he said, "It is finished." Then he bowed his head and gave up
his spirit.

Jesus' Side Is Pierced

31 Since it was the day of Preparation, the Jews did not want the
bodies left on the cross during the sabbath, especially because that
sabbath was a day of great solemnity. So they asked Pilate to have the
legs of the crucified men broken and the bodies removed. 32 Then the
soldiers came and broke the legs of the first and of the other who had
been crucified with him. 33 But when they came to Jesus and saw that
he was already dead, they did not break his legs. 34 Instead, one of the
soldiers pierced his side with a spear, and at once blood and water
came out. 35 (He who saw this has testified so that you also may believe. His testimony is true, and he knows[b] that he tells the truth.)
36 These things occurred so that the scripture might be fulfilled, "None
of his bones shall be broken." 37 And again another passage of scripture
says, "They will look on the one whom they have pierced."

The Burial of Jesus

38 After these things, Joseph of Arimathea, who was a disciple of
Jesus, though a secret one because of his fear of the Jews, asked Pilate

---

[a] That is, *Aramaic*   [b] Or *there is one who knows*

19:25-27 When Jesus saw his mother: The mother of Jesus appears in John's Gospel on two occasions (see note on 2:3). Here Jesus makes sure that both his mother and the disciple whom he loves will be cared for. Jesus' words to them, "Woman, here is your son. Here is your mother" are the first of the three Seven Last Words of Christ that occur in John. The others are "I thirst" and "It is finished."

19:28 I am thirsty: In contrast to the other Gospels, Jesus is not first offered the sour wine but initiates the action with own his words, "I am thirsty."

19:30 It is finished: Jesus' words can also be translated "It has been completed." What has been finished or completed is the work that Jesus came to do as the Word made flesh.

19:33 they did not break his legs: The soldiers did not have to break Jesus' legs, because he was already dead. In crucifixion, the cause of death was suffocation. The longer a person hung on the cross, gravity pulled on the body, compressing the lungs and making it more and more difficult to breathe. Breaking the victim's legs made this even more difficult and, consequently, accelerated death.

Compare John's account of Jesus' crucifixion with that of the other Gospels (Matt 27:33-54; Mark 15:22-39; Luke 23:33-48). What are the similarities and differences? How do you understand the purpose of Jesus' death?

19:38-42 Joseph of Arimathea: In all four Gospels, Joseph of Arimathea is named as the one who buries Jesus, but in John's account, Nicodemus also helps (see 3:1-21).

What do Lutherans mean when they confess that they "believe in Jesus Christ, God's only Son, our Lord"? Along with other Christians, Lutherans have confessed in the Apostles' Creed that to know Jesus as Lord means to know that he is, as Luther said in his *Small Catechism*, "true God, begotten of the Father in eternity, and also a true human being, born of the virgin Mary." Lutherans also confess that this Jesus "has redeemed me, a lost and condemned human being. He has purchased and freed me from all sins, from death, and from the power of the devil, not with gold or silver but with his holy, precious blood and with his innocent suffering and death. He has done all this in order that I may belong to him, live under him in his kingdom, and serve him in eternal righteousness, innocence and blessedness, just as he is risen from the dead and lives and rules eternally. This is most certainly true" (*SC*:15). *John 19:28-37*

to let him take away the body of Jesus. Pilate gave him permission; so
he came and removed his body. 39 Nicodemus, who had at first come
to Jesus by night, also came, bringing a mixture of myrrh and aloes,
weighing about a hundred pounds. 40 They took the body of Jesus and
wrapped it with the spices in linen cloths, according to the burial custom of the Jews. 41 Now there was a garden in the place where he was
crucified, and in the garden there was a new tomb in which no one
had ever been laid. 42 And so, because it was the Jewish day of Preparation, and the tomb was nearby, they laid Jesus there.

The Resurrection of Jesus

20 Early on the first day of the week, while it was still dark,
Mary Magdalene came to the tomb and saw that the stone
had been removed from the tomb. 2 So she ran and went to Simon
Peter and the other disciple, the one whom Jesus loved, and said to
them, "They have taken the Lord out of the tomb, and we do not
know where they have laid him." 3 Then Peter and the other disciple
set out and went toward the tomb. 4 The two were running together,
but the other disciple outran Peter and reached the tomb first. 5 He
bent down to look in and saw the linen wrappings lying there, but he
did not go in. 6 Then Simon Peter came, following him, and went into
the tomb. He saw the linen wrappings lying there, 7 and the cloth that
had been on Jesus' head, not lying with the linen wrappings but rolled
up in a place by itself. 8 Then the other disciple, who reached the tomb
first, also went in, and he saw and believed; 9 for as yet they did not
understand the scripture, that he must rise from the dead. 10 Then the
disciples returned to their homes.

Jesus Appears to Mary Magdalene

11 But Mary stood weeping outside the tomb. As she wept, she
bent over to look[a] into the tomb; 12 and she saw two angels in white,
sitting where the body of Jesus had been lying, one at the head and
the other at the feet. 13 They said to her, "Woman, why are you weeping?" She said to them, "They have taken away my Lord, and I do not
know where they have laid him." 14 When she had said this, she turned
around and saw Jesus standing there, but she did not know that it was
Jesus. 15 Jesus said to her, "Woman, why are you weeping? Whom are
you looking for?" Supposing him to be the gardener, she said to him,
"Sir, if you have carried him away, tell me where you have laid him,
and I will take him away." 16 Jesus said to her, "Mary!" She turned and
said to him in Hebrew,[b] "Rabbouni!" (which means Teacher). 17 Jesus
said to her, "Do not hold on to me, because I have not yet ascended to
the Father. But go to my brothers and say to them, 'I am ascending to

20:16 Jesus said to her, "Mary!": Mary does not recognize Jesus until he calls her name. See note on 10:3.

Mary recognizes Jesus when he calls her by name. Why do you think she doesn't recognize Jesus when she sees him? What do you think is the relationship between seeing and hearing and believing?

20:17 Do not hold on to me: The events of the hour are still not complete. Jesus must return to the Father. Here Jesus sends Mary to witness to his ascension, not his resurrection.

Why do you think Mary wants to hold on to Jesus?

---

[a] Gk lacks *to look* [b] That is, *Aramaic*

my Father and your Father, to my God and your God.' " 18 Mary Magdalene went and announced to the disciples, "I have seen the Lord";
and she told them that he had said these things to her.

Jesus Appears to the Disciples

19 When it was evening on that day, the first day of the week, and
the doors of the house where the disciples had met were locked for
fear of the Jews, Jesus came and stood among them and said, "Peace
be with you." 20 After he said this, he showed them his hands and his
side. Then the disciples rejoiced when they saw the Lord. 21 Jesus said
to them again, "Peace be with you. As the Father has sent me, so I
send you." 22 When he had said this, he breathed on them and said to
them, "Receive the Holy Spirit. 23 If you forgive the sins of any, they
are forgiven them; if you retain the sins of any, they are retained."

Jesus and Thomas

24 But Thomas (who was called the Twin[a]), one of the twelve,
was not with them when Jesus came. 25 So the other disciples told him,
"We have seen the Lord." But he said to them, "Unless I see the mark
of the nails in his hands, and put my finger in the mark of the nails and
my hand in his side, I will not believe."

26 A week later his disciples were again in the house, and Thomas
was with them. Although the doors were shut, Jesus came and stood
among them and said, "Peace be with you." 27 Then he said to Thomas,
"Put your finger here and see my hands. Reach out your hand and put
it in my side. Do not doubt but believe." 28 Thomas answered him, "My
Lord and my God!" 29 Jesus said to him, "Have you believed because
you have seen me? Blessed are those who have not seen and yet have
come to believe."

The Purpose of This Book

30 Now Jesus did many other signs in the presence of his disciples, which are not written in this book. 31 But these are written so that
you may come to believe[b] that Jesus is the Messiah,[c] the Son of God,
and that through believing you may have life in his name.

Jesus Appears to Seven Disciples

21 After these things Jesus showed himself again to the disciples by the Sea of Tiberias; and he showed himself in this
way. 2 Gathered there together were Simon Peter, Thomas called the
Twin,[a] Nathanael of Cana in Galilee, the sons of Zebedee, and two
others of his disciples. 3 Simon Peter said to them, "I am going fishing."
They said to him, "We will go with you." They went out and got into
the boat, but that night they caught nothing.

---

[a] Gk *Didymus* [b] Other ancient authorities read *may continue to believe* [c] Or *the Christ*

20:18 Mary Magdalene . . . announced: The Greek word used here for "announce" has the same root as "angel." Mary is the first to carry the message of Jesus' resurrection and ascension.

20:19 the doors of the house: The word "house" does not appear in the Greek text. Rather, there is a more ambiguous location: "where they were." The emphasis here is on the disciples hiding out in fear behind locked doors. Yet Jesus enters and stands among them with the doors shut. This is not merely a supernatural act but evidence of the truth of Jesus' claim: "I am the gate" (10:7, 9).

20:24-28 Unless I see the mark of the nails: This story about "doubting" Thomas is only found in John's Gospel. It is the appointed Gospel reading for the second Sunday of Easter.

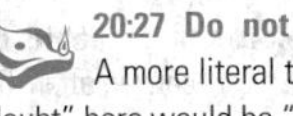

20:27 Do not doubt but believe: A more literal translation of the word "doubt" here would be "unbelieving."

What do you think is the difference between doubt and unbelief?

20:28 My Lord and my God: Thomas's statement is the unique claim of John's Gospel, that Jesus is both Lord and God. It recalls Jesus' words to Mary Magdalene: "I am ascending to my Father and your Father, to my God and your God" (20:17).

20:31 come to believe: The purpose of the Gospel is clearly stated. This phrase can also be translated "continue to believe," "come to faith," or "continue in faith." Our earliest and best manuscripts of the Greek text attest to any of these possibilities: that the Gospel was written to bring others to faith and to help believers remain faithful.

21:1-25 Jesus showed himself again: This chapter is frequently cited as an epilogue to the narrative and a later addition to or revision of the Gospel, perhaps by the same author. There is no manuscript evidence to suggest that the Gospel circulated without this ending, and there are a number of important connections between this last chapter and the rest of the Gospel.

4 Just after daybreak, Jesus stood on the beach; but the disciples
did not know that it was Jesus. 5 Jesus said to them, "Children, you
have no fish, have you?" They answered him, "No." 6 He said to them,
"Cast the net to the right side of the boat, and you will find some." So
they cast it, and now they were not able to haul it in because there
were so many fish. 7 That disciple whom Jesus loved said to Peter, "It
is the Lord!" When Simon Peter heard that it was the Lord, he put
on some clothes, for he was naked, and jumped into the sea. 8 But the
other disciples came in the boat, dragging the net full of fish, for they
were not far from the land, only about a hundred yards[a] off.

9 When they had gone ashore, they saw a charcoal fire there,
with fish on it, and bread. 10 Jesus said to them, "Bring some of the fish
that you have just caught." 11 So Simon Peter went aboard and hauled
the net ashore, full of large fish, a hundred fifty-three of them; and
though there were so many, the net was not torn. 12 Jesus said to them,
"Come and have breakfast." Now none of the disciples dared to ask
him, "Who are you?" because they knew it was the Lord. 13 Jesus came
and took the bread and gave it to them, and did the same with the fish.
14 This was now the third time that Jesus appeared to the disciples after
he was raised from the dead.

21:11 full of large fish, a hundred fifty-three of them: The specific number of fish caught is another example of the abundance that Jesus provides (see 1:16; 2:6-8; 4:14; 10:10).

Jesus appears to the disciples after they have returned to their former job—fishing. How do you think of Jesus appearing to you in your everyday life?

Jesus and Peter

15 When they had finished breakfast, Jesus said to Simon Peter,
"Simon son of John, do you love me more than these?" He said to
him, "Yes, Lord; you know that I love you." Jesus said to him, "Feed
my lambs." 16 A second time he said to him, "Simon son of John, do
you love me?" He said to him, "Yes, Lord; you know that I love you."
Jesus said to him, "Tend my sheep." 17 He said to him the third time,
"Simon son of John, do you love me?" Peter felt hurt because he said
to him the third time, "Do you love me?" And he said to him, "Lord,
you know everything; you know that I love you." Jesus said to him,
"Feed my sheep. 18 Very truly, I tell you, when you were younger, you
used to fasten your own belt and to go wherever you wished. But
when you grow old, you will stretch out your hands, and someone
else will fasten a belt around you and take you where you do not wish
to go." 19 (He said this to indicate the kind of death by which he would
glorify God.) After this he said to him, "Follow me."

21:15-17 Simon son of John, do you love me: The conversation between Jesus and Peter recalls Peter's three-fold denial of Jesus (18:15-18, 25-27) and Jesus' own identity and work as the Good Shepherd (10:1-18). While some scholars focus on this conversation as Peter's redemption, Peter is more than redeemed; he is charged with the work of Jesus—to shepherd his sheep.

21:18-19 you will stretch out your hands: These verses foreshadow Peter's death by crucifixion and recall Jesus' words to his disciples: "No one has greater love than this, to lay down one's life for one's friends. You are my friends if you do what I command you" (15:13-14; see also 13:37).

Jesus and the Beloved Disciple

20 Peter turned and saw the disciple whom Jesus loved following
them; he was the one who had reclined next to Jesus at the supper and
had said, "Lord, who is it that is going to betray you?" 21 When Peter
saw him, he said to Jesus, "Lord, what about him?" 22 Jesus said to him,

[a] Gk *two hundred cubits*

"If it is my will that he remain until I come, what is that to you? Follow me!" [23]So the rumor spread in the community[a] that this disciple would not die. Yet Jesus did not say to him that he would not die, but, "If it is my will that he remain until I come, what is that to you?"[b]

24 This is the disciple who is testifying to these things and has written them, and we know that his testimony is true. [25]But there are also many other things that Jesus did; if every one of them were written down, I suppose that the world itself could not contain the books that would be written.

[a] Gk *among the brothers* [b] Other ancient authorities lack *what is that to you*

21:24-25 the disciple...has written them: This claim does not necessarily argue for who wrote the Gospel, but suggests that the witness of the beloved disciple (21:20) became the tradition on which the gospel was based.

The last verses of John's Gospel refer to "many other things that Jesus did" that were not written down in this Gospel. What does that mean to you? Why do you think this was included here? What would you want someone to write about you after you were gone?

Acts 2:1-4

ACTS

Background File

The full title of this book is The Acts of the Apostles. The word *apostle* comes from a Greek word meaning "one who is sent out," or a person sent to deliver a message. In Acts, *apostles* refers to the disciples Jesus chooses to carry on his teaching and ministry. Acts records the activities of certain apostles—including Peter, Paul, and Stephen—after the resurrection and ascension of Jesus. It was likely written around 80–85 C.E.

The books of Luke and Acts were written by the same person. Acts continues the story started in Luke. We don't know much about this writer, as there is no mention of the writer's own background or life story. Because of the skillful writing and the number of speeches by Jewish followers of Jesus, scholars think the writer was a well-educated Jew who had come to faith in Jesus Christ.

Both Luke and Acts are addressed to "Theophilus" (1:1; Luke 1:3). This name means "friend of God." Some scholars think this name is used to stand for all who follow Jesus. Others believe Theophilus was a wealthy person, perhaps a Roman official, who paid for the recording and copying of this work. Either way, the book is intended for a large audience. It is likely that the first readers of Acts were Gentiles and Jews living on the northern coast of the Mediterranean Sea (see Map 15, p. 2112).

What's the Story?

The Gospel of Luke ends with an account of Jesus ascended into heaven (see Luke 24:50-53). Acts begins with the same event (Acts 1:9-11). Acts tells the story of the early days of the Christian church. It traces the growth of the church from a small group of Jewish believers in Jerusalem to a worldwide movement that included both Jews and Gentiles.

In Acts, the writer continues to provide an "orderly account" (Luke 1:3) of the events surrounding the life, death, and resurrection of Jesus Christ. This account in Acts tells about the ministry of the early Christians, forming a framework that helps readers understand the issues and conflicts addressed by the remaining books in the New Testament. The writer tells this story of the early church by focusing on the stories of key leaders, Peter and Paul in particular. It is quite possible that some of the first readers of Acts were Jews who were critical of the apostle Paul and the believers who were taught by him. By detailing many of Paul's journeys and speeches, the writer positions Paul as a faithful Jew who believed in Jesus.

Speeches make up nearly one-third of the content in Acts. Most of the twenty-eight speeches are given by Jewish followers who believe Jesus is God's Messiah. From these speeches, readers gain insight into how different groups wrestled with what it means to follow Jesus.

The book is sometimes called "The Acts of the Holy Spirit," because of the writer's strong emphasis on the work of the Holy Spirit. Acts tells how the Spirit formed and guided the new church. Those who came to believe in Jesus did so because of the Spirit.

The outline of this book follows Jesus' words in Acts 1:8: "But you will receive power when the Holy Spirit has come upon you; and you will be my witnesses in Jerusalem, in all Judea and Samaria, and to the ends of the earth."

Preparation for Christian witness (1:1–2:13)
Witnessing in Jerusalem (2:14–8:3)
Witnessing in Judea and Samaria (8:4–9:43)
Witnessing to the Gentiles (10:1–15:35)
Witnessing to the "ends of the earth" (15:36–28:31)

What's the Message?

The writer of Luke and Acts clearly desires to tell the story of God's redeeming and saving love in Jesus Christ. Acts continues on from Luke, giving a systematic presentation of the growth of the Christian church from its beginnings in Jerusalem. This account is presented with many details about people and places.

The writer, trying to do more than tell the history of the early church, offers a defense of faith in Jesus Christ, including arguments that the faith is meant for both Jews and Gentiles. The writer also strives to show how and why the Christian church became a movement that included both Jews and Gentiles. The stories and speeches by key leaders demonstrate how quickly Christianity spread beyond Jerusalem. The writer also seeks to show the work of the Holy Spirit in the lives of the early believers as they face persecution and opposition to their witness.

The Promise of the Holy Spirit

1 In the first book, Theophilus, I wrote about all that Jesus did and
taught from the beginning 2 until the day when he was taken up to
heaven, after giving instructions through the Holy Spirit to the apostles whom he had chosen. 3 After his suffering he presented himself
alive to them by many convincing proofs, appearing to them during
forty days and speaking about the kingdom of God. 4 While staying[a]

[a] Or *eating*

1:1 In the first book, Theophilus: The writer refers to the Gospel of Luke and positions this book as a continuation of that story. He writes to Theophilus, a name that means "friend of God." This may have been a person by that name or the writer's name for all friends of God.

1:2 instructions through the Holy Spirit: In both Luke and Acts, the writer consistently emphasizes the Holy Spirit acting with and through the disciples (for example, 1:8; 2:4; 4:8, 31; 6:3, 5; 8:16; 10:44).

1:4 the promise of the Father: Jesus often used "Father" to refer to God. This promise refers to the coming of the Holy Spirit (see John 14:16-17). An account of this event is given in Acts 2. Jesus describes this coming of the Spirit as being "baptized with the Holy Spirit" (1:5).

1:6 restore the kingdom to Israel? Some of the disciples were still hoping Jesus would set up an earthly kingdom, like the one King David ruled. Jesus dismisses the question by saying that what will happen in the future is in God's hands and not for them to know (1:7).

1:8 be my witnesses: The disciples are named as witnesses—people who bear testimony to the truthfulness of what has been said or done. The work of Jesus' witnesses is mentioned often in Acts (2:32, 3:15; 5:32; 10:39; 13:31; 22:15).

In what ways have you been a witness for Jesus Christ?

1:12 mount called Olivet: This location is also called Mount of Olives (see Map 13, p. 2110). Jesus' ascension took place on this large hill that was about halfway between Jerusalem and Bethany.

1:12 a sabbath day's journey away: This was the distance that the rabbis said one could travel on the Sabbath without breaking the law against work on the Sabbath.

1:14 with certain women…his brothers: These women, including Jesus' mother, traveled and worked with the disciples (see Luke 8:1-3). The group may have included wives and relatives of the disciples. Mary and Joseph had sons, who would have been Jesus' half-brothers (see Mark 6:3).

1:18 man acquired a field: This is a reference to Judas Iscariot, who was paid thirty pieces of silver to betray Jesus. After Jesus was condemned to death, Judas returned the silver to the chief priests who had given it to him. They used the money to buy land as a burial ground for poor people. Judas took his own life (see Matt 26:14-16; 27:3-10).

1:20 written in the book of Psalms: The quotations here are from Psalm 69:25 and Psalm 109:8.

with them, he ordered them not to leave Jerusalem, but to wait there
for the promise of the Father. "This," he said, "is what you have heard
from me; 5 for John baptized with water, but you will be baptized with[a]
the Holy Spirit not many days from now."

The Ascension of Jesus

6 So when they had come together, they asked him, "Lord, is this
the time when you will restore the kingdom to Israel?" 7 He replied, "It
is not for you to know the times or periods that the Father has set by
his own authority. 8 But you will receive power when the Holy Spirit
has come upon you; and you will be my witnesses in Jerusalem, in all
Judea and Samaria, and to the ends of the earth." 9 When he had said
this, as they were watching, he was lifted up, and a cloud took him out
of their sight. 10 While he was going and they were gazing up toward
heaven, suddenly two men in white robes stood by them. 11 They said,
"Men of Galilee, why do you stand looking up toward heaven? This
Jesus, who has been taken up from you into heaven, will come in the
same way as you saw him go into heaven."

Matthias Chosen to Replace Judas

12 Then they returned to Jerusalem from the mount called Olivet, which is near Jerusalem, a sabbath day's journey away. 13 When
they had entered the city, they went to the room upstairs where they
were staying, Peter, and John, and James, and Andrew, Philip and
Thomas, Bartholomew and Matthew, James son of Alphaeus, and Simon the Zealot, and Judas son of[b] James. 14 All these were constantly
devoting themselves to prayer, together with certain women, including Mary the mother of Jesus, as well as his brothers.

15 In those days Peter stood up among the believers[c] (together
the crowd numbered about one hundred twenty persons) and said,
16 "Friends,[d] the scripture had to be fulfilled, which the Holy Spirit
through David foretold concerning Judas, who became a guide for
those who arrested Jesus— 17 for he was numbered among us and was
allotted his share in this ministry." 18 (Now this man acquired a field
with the reward of his wickedness; and falling headlong,[e] he burst
open in the middle and all his bowels gushed out. 19 This became
known to all the residents of Jerusalem, so that the field was called in
their language Hakeldama, that is, Field of Blood.) 20 "For it is written
in the book of Psalms,

'Let his homestead become desolate,
and let there be no one to live in it';

and

'Let another take his position of overseer.'

---

[a] Or *by* [b] Or *the brother of* [c] Gk *brothers* [d] Gk *Men, brothers* [e] Or *swelling up*

21 So one of the men who have accompanied us during all the time
that the Lord Jesus went in and out among us, 22 beginning from the
baptism of John until the day when he was taken up from us—one
of these must become a witness with us to his resurrection." 23 So
they proposed two, Joseph called Barsabbas, who was also known as
Justus, and Matthias. 24 Then they prayed and said, "Lord, you know
everyone's heart. Show us which one of these two you have chosen
25 to take the place[a] in this ministry and apostleship from which Judas
turned aside to go to his own place." 26 And they cast lots for them, and
the lot fell on Matthias; and he was added to the eleven apostles.

The Coming of the Holy Spirit

2 When the day of Pentecost had come, they were all together in
one place. 2 And suddenly from heaven there came a sound like
the rush of a violent wind, and it filled the entire house where they
were sitting. 3 Divided tongues, as of fire, appeared among them, and a
tongue rested on each of them. 4 All of them were filled with the Holy
Spirit and began to speak in other languages, as the Spirit gave them
ability.

5 Now there were devout Jews from every nation under heaven
living in Jerusalem. 6 And at this sound the crowd gathered and was

1:26 cast lots...added to the eleven apostles: In the process of casting lots marked stones or twigs were thrown or drawn to determine an answer to a question. The apostles probably cast lots to be sure the decision was God's and not theirs. As twelve was considered a holy number, the apostles sought someone to replace Judas Iscariot, preserving the group of twelve apostles appointed by Jesus.

2:1 day of Pentecost: The word *pentecost* means fifty. Pentecost is the Jewish festival that comes fifty days after Passover (see Lev 23:15-16). It is also called the Feast of Weeks, and originally celebrated the wheat harvest (see Exod 23:16; Deut 16:9-10). Many Jews would have gathered in Jerusalem to celebrate Pentecost. (See Jewish Festivals and Feasts, p. 227.)

2:4 filled with the Holy Spirit: This is a fulfillment of Jesus' promise in Luke 24:49. The disciples are led by the Spirit—not only in what they say, but also in the languages they speak. This miracle is sometimes seen as the reversal of what happened at the Tower of Babel (see Gen 11:1-9), when God confused the languages to curb human pride.

[a] Other ancient authorities read *the share*

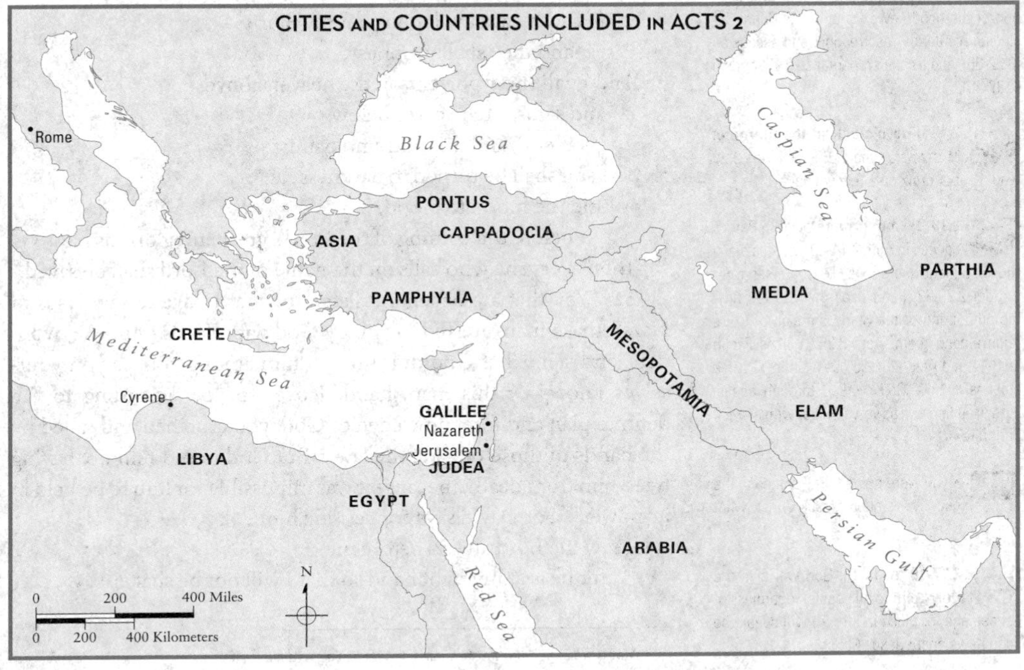

2:5-11 devout Jews: The people gathered in Jerusalem for the festival of Pentecost came from all over the known world. (See map, p. 1797). The miracle was the many languages that were spoken and heard.

What is the work of the Holy Spirit? Lutherans believe that we come to faith, remain in the faith, and live our lives of faith by the power of the Holy Spirit. In his explanation to the Third Article of the Apostles' Creed, Martin Luther taught: "... the Holy Spirit has called me through the gospel, enlightened me with his gifts, made me holy and kept me in the true faith, just as he calls, gathers, enlightens, and makes holy the whole Christian church on earth and keeps it with Jesus Christ in the one common, true faith" (*SC*:16). *Acts 1—2*

How do you see the Holy Spirit at work in your life?

2:14-40 Peter...raised his voice and addressed them: A number of speeches in Acts begin with a misunderstanding that the speaker corrects. Acts 2:13 is explained in 2:15. Peter's sermon follows a pattern that is common in the teaching and preaching of the early disciples: an explanation of what was happening (2:14-21); a presentation of the good news about Jesus Christ, including his death, resurrection, and ascension (2:22-36); and a call to repentance and baptism (2:37-40).

2:15 nine o'clock in the morning: This was a time of day when no Jew would eat or drink on a festival day.

2:16-21 the prophet Joel: Peter's speech in Acts 2:14-40 includes many Old Testament quotations. These verses refer to Joel 2:28-32. Peter uses them to tell how the outpouring of the Spirit is a sign of God's reign among them. Acts 2:25-31 uses Psalm 16:8-11 and Acts 2:34-35 uses Psalm 110:1 to emphasize how God worked through Jesus. Peter's audience was very familiar with Jewish Scripture.

If you were going to tell someone the good news about Jesus Christ, what would you say?

2:17-18 all flesh: God will give the Holy Spirit to all people, regardless of gender, age, or place in life. All will speak the good news about Jesus Christ.

bewildered, because each one heard them speaking in the native language of each. 7 Amazed and astonished, they asked, "Are not all these
who are speaking Galileans? 8 And how is it that we hear, each of us, in
our own native language? 9 Parthians, Medes, Elamites, and residents
of Mesopotamia, Judea and Cappadocia, Pontus and Asia, 10 Phrygia
and Pamphylia, Egypt and the parts of Libya belonging to Cyrene,
and visitors from Rome, both Jews and proselytes, 11 Cretans and
Arabs—in our own languages we hear them speaking about God's
deeds of power." 12 All were amazed and perplexed, saying to one another, "What does this mean?" 13 But others sneered and said, "They
are filled with new wine."

Peter Addresses the Crowd

14 But Peter, standing with the eleven, raised his voice and addressed them, "Men of Judea and all who live in Jerusalem, let this be
known to you, and listen to what I say. 15 Indeed, these are not drunk,
as you suppose, for it is only nine o'clock in the morning. 16 No, this is
what was spoken through the prophet Joel:

17 'In the last days it will be, God declares,
that I will pour out my Spirit upon all flesh,
and your sons and your daughters shall prophesy,
and your young men shall see visions,
and your old men shall dream dreams.
18 Even upon my slaves, both men and women,
in those days I will pour out my Spirit;
and they shall prophesy.
19 And I will show portents in the heaven above
and signs on the earth below,
blood, and fire, and smoky mist.
20 The sun shall be turned to darkness
and the moon to blood,
before the coming of the Lord's great and glorious day.
21 Then everyone who calls on the name of the Lord shall be saved.'

22 "You that are Israelites,[a] listen to what I have to say: Jesus of
Nazareth,[b] a man attested to you by God with deeds of power, wonders, and signs that God did through him among you, as you yourselves know— 23 this man, handed over to you according to the
definite plan and foreknowledge of God, you crucified and killed by
the hands of those outside the law. 24 But God raised him up, having
freed him from death,[c] because it was impossible for him to be held in
its power. 25 For David says concerning him,

'I saw the Lord always before me,
for he is at my right hand so that I will not be shaken;

---

[a] Gk *Men, Israelites* [b] Gk *the Nazorean* [c] Gk *the pains of death*

26 therefore my heart was glad, and my tongue rejoiced;
moreover my flesh will live in hope.
27 For you will not abandon my soul to Hades,
or let your Holy One experience corruption.
28 You have made known to me the ways of life;
you will make me full of gladness with your presence.'
29 "Fellow Israelites,[a] I may say to you confidently of our ancestor David that he both died and was buried, and his tomb is with us
to this day. 30 Since he was a prophet, he knew that God had sworn
with an oath to him that he would put one of his descendants on his
throne. 31 Foreseeing this, David[b] spoke of the resurrection of the
Messiah,[c] saying,
'He was not abandoned to Hades,
nor did his flesh experience corruption.'
32 This Jesus God raised up, and of that all of us are witnesses. 33 Being
therefore exalted at[d] the right hand of God, and having received from
the Father the promise of the Holy Spirit, he has poured out this that
you both see and hear. 34 For David did not ascend into the heavens,
but he himself says,
'The Lord said to my Lord,
"Sit at my right hand,
35 until I make your enemies your footstool." '
36 Therefore let the entire house of Israel know with certainty that
God has made him both Lord and Messiah,[e] this Jesus whom you
crucified."

The First Converts

37 Now when they heard this, they were cut to the heart and said
to Peter and to the other apostles, "Brothers,[a] what should we do?"
38 Peter said to them, "Repent, and be baptized every one of you in
the name of Jesus Christ so that your sins may be forgiven; and you
will receive the gift of the Holy Spirit. 39 For the promise is for you, for
your children, and for all who are far away, everyone whom the Lord
our God calls to him." 40 And he testified with many other arguments
and exhorted them, saying, "Save yourselves from this corrupt generation." 41 So those who welcomed his message were baptized, and
that day about three thousand persons were added. 42 They devoted
themselves to the apostles' teaching and fellowship, to the breaking of
bread and the prayers.

Life among the Believers

43 Awe came upon everyone, because many wonders and signs
were being done by the apostles. 44 All who believed were together

2:38 Repent, and be baptized: To repent means to turn back to God or to change one's mind. Repentance is an important theme in John's preaching (see Mark 1:4) and in Jesus' preaching (see Mark 1:15). So is baptism (see Mark 1:4 and Matt 28:18-19).

2:42 teaching and fellowship... breaking of bread...prayers: These words describe the daily life of these followers of Jesus. "Fellowship" probably means worship. "Breaking of bread" may mean sharing meals or the Lord's Supper.

---

[a] Gk *Men, brothers* [b] Gk *he* [c] Or *the Christ* [d] Or *by* [e] Or *Christ*

and had all things in common; 45 they would sell their possessions and
goods and distribute the proceeds[a] to all, as any had need. 46 Day by
day, as they spent much time together in the temple, they broke bread
at home[b] and ate their food with glad and generous[c] hearts, 47 praising
God and having the goodwill of all the people. And day by day the
Lord added to their number those who were being saved.

Peter Heals a Crippled Beggar

3 One day Peter and John were going up to the temple at the hour
of prayer, at three o'clock in the afternoon. 2 And a man lame
from birth was being carried in. People would lay him daily at the gate
of the temple called the Beautiful Gate so that he could ask for alms
from those entering the temple. 3 When he saw Peter and John about
to go into the temple, he asked them for alms. 4 Peter looked intently
at him, as did John, and said, "Look at us." 5 And he fixed his attention
on them, expecting to receive something from them. 6 But Peter said,
"I have no silver or gold, but what I have I give you; in the name of
Jesus Christ of Nazareth,[d] stand up and walk." 7 And he took him by
the right hand and raised him up; and immediately his feet and ankles
were made strong. 8 Jumping up, he stood and began to walk, and he
entered the temple with them, walking and leaping and praising God.
9 All the people saw him walking and praising God, 10 and they recognized him as the one who used to sit and ask for alms at the Beautiful
Gate of the temple; and they were filled with wonder and amazement
at what had happened to him.

Peter Speaks in Solomon's Portico

11 While he clung to Peter and John, all the people ran together
to them in the portico called Solomon's Portico, utterly astonished.
12 When Peter saw it, he addressed the people, "You Israelites,[e] why
do you wonder at this, or why do you stare at us, as though by our
own power or piety we had made him walk? 13 The God of Abraham,
the God of Isaac, and the God of Jacob, the God of our ancestors has
glorified his servant[f] Jesus, whom you handed over and rejected in the
presence of Pilate, though he had decided to release him. 14 But you
rejected the Holy and Righteous One and asked to have a murderer
given to you, 15 and you killed the Author of life, whom God raised
from the dead. To this we are witnesses. 16 And by faith in his name,
his name itself has made this man strong, whom you see and know;
and the faith that is through Jesus[g] has given him this perfect health in
the presence of all of you.

17 "And now, friends,[h] I know that you acted in ignorance, as

[a] Gk *them* [b] Or *from house to house* [c] Or *sincere* [d] Gk *the Nazorean* [e] Gk *Men, Israelites*
[f] Or *child* [g] Gk *him* [h] Gk *brothers*

2:45 sell their possessions: While the verse describes how this group of early Christians sold their possessions and shared the proceeds, some believers in Acts continued to own property. Lydia, for example, owns a house and shows hospitality to Paul and Silas by having them stay with her (16:14-15).

3:2 at the gate of the temple... ask for alms: There were several gates into the temple in Jerusalem. Those in need often gathered at the gates to ask for gifts from the worshipers. See the diagrams of the Temple in Jesus' Day, pp. 1696-1697.

3:6 in the name of Jesus Christ of Nazareth: Peter was very clear that the power of healing comes from God. Because many Jewish men were named Jesus, naming Jesus' hometown of Nazareth makes it clear that this is Jesus the Christ.

3:12-26 addressed the people: This is Peter's second sermon, given in the temple. It follows the same pattern as his Pentecost sermon: explanation of what was happening, presentation of the gospel of Jesus, and a call to repentance. Peter corrects misunderstandings about the healing the crowd witnessed (3:1-11).

3:15 you killed... God raised... we are witnesses: These are often-repeated phrases in Acts (4:10; 5:30-32; 10:39-41). Peter, a Jew, is blaming his Jewish brothers and sisters. Since both Peter and his audience are Jewish, this is a family fight within Judaism. Modern day Gentile (non-Jewish) readers of the book of Acts need to be careful not to blame Jews in general for the death of Jesus. The Gospels and Acts tend to focus the blame on Jewish leaders in Jerusalem (see 4:1-3).

did also your rulers. 18 In this way God fulfilled what he had foretold
through all the prophets, that his Messiah[a] would suffer. 19 Repent
therefore, and turn to God so that your sins may be wiped out, 20 so
that times of refreshing may come from the presence of the Lord, and
that he may send the Messiah[b] appointed for you, that is, Jesus, 21 who
must remain in heaven until the time of universal restoration that
God announced long ago through his holy prophets. 22 Moses said,
'The Lord your God will raise up for you from your own people[c] a
prophet like me. You must listen to whatever he tells you. 23 And it
will be that everyone who does not listen to that prophet will be utterly rooted out of the people.' 24 And all the prophets, as many as have
spoken, from Samuel and those after him, also predicted these days.
25 You are the descendants of the prophets and of the covenant that
God gave to your ancestors, saying to Abraham, 'And in your descendants all the families of the earth shall be blessed.' 26 When God raised
up his servant,[d] he sent him first to you, to bless you by turning each
of you from your wicked ways."

3:22 Moses said: Peter refers to Jesus as the fulfillment of Moses' promise that God would raise up a new prophet from among the Jewish people (see Deut 18:15-20).

Peter and John before the Council

4 While Peter and John[e] were speaking to the people, the priests,
the captain of the temple, and the Sadducees came to them,
2 much annoyed because they were teaching the people and proclaiming that in Jesus there is the resurrection of the dead. 3 So they arrested
them and put them in custody until the next day, for it was already
evening. 4 But many of those who heard the word believed; and they
numbered about five thousand.

4:1 Sadducees: The Sadducees were one of the groups of Jewish leaders. They did not believe in bodily resurrection.

4:3 evening: The offering of sacrifices ended at about 4:00 p.m., when the temple gates were closed.

5 The next day their rulers, elders, and scribes assembled in Jerusalem, 6 with Annas the high priest, Caiaphas, John,[f] and Alexander,
and all who were of the high-priestly family. 7 When they had made
the prisoners[g] stand in their midst, they inquired, "By what power
or by what name did you do this?" 8 Then Peter, filled with the Holy
Spirit, said to them, "Rulers of the people and elders, 9 if we are questioned today because of a good deed done to someone who was sick
and are asked how this man has been healed, 10 let it be known to all
of you, and to all the people of Israel, that this man is standing before
you in good health by the name of Jesus Christ of Nazareth,[h] whom
you crucified, whom God raised from the dead. 11 This Jesus[i] is

'the stone that was rejected by you, the builders;
it has become the cornerstone.'[j]

12 There is salvation in no one else, for there is no other name under
heaven given among mortals by which we must be saved."

13 Now when they saw the boldness of Peter and John and

4:5 rulers, elders, and scribes: These were the leaders who made up the Sanhedrin, a group of seventy to one hundred men, the ruling high court of the Jews.

4:8-12 filled with the Holy Spirit: Peter's powerful witness is inspired and guided by the Holy Spirit. Peter's words respond to the question asked in 4:7.

4:11 the stone that was rejected by you, the builders . . . the cornerstone: Peter refers to Psalm 118:21-25, as did Jesus (see Matt 21:42).

---

[a] Or *his Christ* [b] Or *the Christ* [c] Gk *brothers* [d] Or *child* [e] Gk *While they* [f] Other ancient authorities read *Jonathan* [g] Gk *them* [h] Gk *the Nazorean* [i] Gk *This* [j] Or *keystone*

realized that they were uneducated and ordinary men, they were
amazed and recognized them as companions of Jesus. 14 When they
saw the man who had been cured standing beside them, they had
nothing to say in opposition. 15 So they ordered them to leave the
council while they discussed the matter with one another. 16 They
said, "What will we do with them? For it is obvious to all who live in
Jerusalem that a notable sign has been done through them; we cannot deny it. 17 But to keep it from spreading further among the people,
let us warn them to speak no more to anyone in this name." 18 So they
called them and ordered them not to speak or teach at all in the name
of Jesus. 19 But Peter and John answered them, "Whether it is right in
God's sight to listen to you rather than to God, you must judge; 20 for
we cannot keep from speaking about what we have seen and heard."
21 After threatening them again, they let them go, finding no way to
punish them because of the people, for all of them praised God for
what had happened. 22 For the man on whom this sign of healing had
been performed was more than forty years old.

The Believers Pray for Boldness

23 After they were released, they went to their friends[a] and reported what the chief priests and the elders had said to them. 24 When
they heard it, they raised their voices together to God and said, "Sovereign Lord, who made the heaven and the earth, the sea, and everything in them, 25 it is you who said by the Holy Spirit through our
ancestor David, your servant:[b]

'Why did the Gentiles rage,
and the peoples imagine vain things?
26 The kings of the earth took their stand,
and the rulers have gathered together
against the Lord and against his Messiah.'[c]

27 For in this city, in fact, both Herod and Pontius Pilate, with the
Gentiles and the peoples of Israel, gathered together against your
holy servant[b] Jesus, whom you anointed, 28 to do whatever your hand
and your plan had predestined to take place. 29 And now, Lord, look
at their threats, and grant to your servants[d] to speak your word with
all boldness, 30 while you stretch out your hand to heal, and signs
and wonders are performed through the name of your holy servant[b]
Jesus." 31 When they had prayed, the place in which they were gathered together was shaken; and they were all filled with the Holy Spirit
and spoke the word of God with boldness.

The Believers Share Their Possessions

32 Now the whole group of those who believed were of one heart
and soul, and no one claimed private ownership of any possessions,

[a] Gk *their own* [b] Or *child* [c] Or *his Christ* [d] Gk *slaves*

4:24-30 raised their voices together to God: The disciples' prayer emphasizes God's power and authority ("Sovereign Lord") and asks for courage and power to continue to preach the good news about Jesus.

What does it mean to pray for boldness in faith? When might you offer such a prayer?

4:32-37 was held in common: Jesus' followers chose to live in a close community and share everything. Barnabas is shown as a good example of that sharing. (See note at 2:42.)

In what ways might the daily life of the first Christian community be a model for us?

but everything they owned was held in common. 33 With great power
the apostles gave their testimony to the resurrection of the Lord Jesus,
and great grace was upon them all. 34 There was not a needy person
among them, for as many as owned lands or houses sold them and
brought the proceeds of what was sold. 35 They laid it at the apostles'
feet, and it was distributed to each as any had need. 36 There was a Levite, a native of Cyprus, Joseph, to whom the apostles gave the name
Barnabas (which means "son of encouragement"). 37 He sold a field
that belonged to him, then brought the money, and laid it at the apostles' feet.

Ananias and Sapphira

5 But a man named Ananias, with the consent of his wife Sapphira, sold a piece of property; 2 with his wife's knowledge, he
kept back some of the proceeds, and brought only a part and laid it at
the apostles' feet. 3 "Ananias," Peter asked, "why has Satan filled your
heart to lie to the Holy Spirit and to keep back part of the proceeds
of the land? 4 While it remained unsold, did it not remain your own?
And after it was sold, were not the proceeds at your disposal? How
is it that you have contrived this deed in your heart? You did not lie
to us[a] but to God!" 5 Now when Ananias heard these words, he fell
down and died. And great fear seized all who heard of it. 6 The young
men came and wrapped up his body,[b] then carried him out and buried him.

7 After an interval of about three hours his wife came in, not
knowing what had happened. 8 Peter said to her, "Tell me whether
you and your husband sold the land for such and such a price." And
she said, "Yes, that was the price." 9 Then Peter said to her, "How is it
that you have agreed together to put the Spirit of the Lord to the test?
Look, the feet of those who have buried your husband are at the door,
and they will carry you out." 10 Immediately she fell down at his feet
and died. When the young men came in they found her dead, so they
carried her out and buried her beside her husband. 11 And great fear
seized the whole church and all who heard of these things.

The Apostles Heal Many

12 Now many signs and wonders were done among the people
through the apostles. And they were all together in Solomon's Portico. 13 None of the rest dared to join them, but the people held them
in high esteem. 14 Yet more than ever believers were added to the Lord,
great numbers of both men and women, 15 so that they even carried
out the sick into the streets, and laid them on cots and mats, in order that Peter's shadow might fall on some of them as he came by.

5:1-11 Ananias and Sapphira: This husband and wife are shown as bad examples of sharing. They had a right to the money they got for their property, but lied about their gift. Judgment was swift and a warning to others.

5:11 church: This is the first use of "church" to mean the fellowship of those who follow Jesus. The word means literally "the called-out ones," indicating that believers are called out from the world.

5:12-16 held them in high esteem: The popularity of the disciples is a tribute to their courage in continuing to speak the gospel and to the many healings they perform. Some of the people are fearful of socializing with the Jesus-believing Jews (5:13), probably for fear that the religious leaders might persecute them (4:17-18).

[a] Gk *to men* [b] Meaning of Gk uncertain

16 A great number of people would also gather from the towns around
Jerusalem, bringing the sick and those tormented by unclean spirits,
and they were all cured.

The Apostles Are Persecuted

17 Then the high priest took action; he and all who were with
him (that is, the sect of the Sadducees), being filled with jealousy,
18 arrested the apostles and put them in the public prison. 19 But during the night an angel of the Lord opened the prison doors, brought
them out, and said, 20 "Go, stand in the temple and tell the people the
whole message about this life." 21 When they heard this, they entered
the temple at daybreak and went on with their teaching.

When the high priest and those with him arrived, they called together the council and the whole body of the elders of Israel, and sent
to the prison to have them brought. 22 But when the temple police
went there, they did not find them in the prison; so they returned
and reported, 23 "We found the prison securely locked and the guards
standing at the doors, but when we opened them, we found no one
inside." 24 Now when the captain of the temple and the chief priests
heard these words, they were perplexed about them, wondering what
might be going on. 25 Then someone arrived and announced, "Look,
the men whom you put in prison are standing in the temple and
teaching the people!" 26 Then the captain went with the temple police
and brought them, but without violence, for they were afraid of being
stoned by the people.

27 When they had brought them, they had them stand before
the council. The high priest questioned them, 28 saying, "We gave you
strict orders not to teach in this name,[a] yet here you have filled Jerusalem with your teaching and you are determined to bring this man's
blood on us." 29 But Peter and the apostles answered, "We must obey
God rather than any human authority.[b] 30 The God of our ancestors
raised up Jesus, whom you had killed by hanging him on a tree. 31 God
exalted him at his right hand as Leader and Savior that he might give
repentance to Israel and forgiveness of sins. 32 And we are witnesses to
these things, and so is the Holy Spirit whom God has given to those
who obey him."

33 When they heard this, they were enraged and wanted to kill
them. 34 But a Pharisee in the council named Gamaliel, a teacher of
the law, respected by all the people, stood up and ordered the men to
be put outside for a short time. 35 Then he said to them, "Fellow Israelites,[c] consider carefully what you propose to do to these men. 36 For
some time ago Theudas rose up, claiming to be somebody, and a num-

5:28: you are determined to bring this man's blood on us: This charge refers to the disciples' repeated accusation that some of the Jewish leaders are responsible for crucifying Jesus (2:23; 3:13-15; 4:10-11). Another reason the religious leaders are antagonistic is that many people are responding to the miracles of healing by following the apostles.

5:34 Gamaliel: This respected teacher and leader was, at one time, one of Paul's teachers (22:3).

[a] Other ancient authorities read *Did we not give you strict orders not to teach in this name?* [b] Gk *than men*
[c] Gk *Men, Israelites*

ber of men, about four hundred, joined him; but he was killed, and all
who followed him were dispersed and disappeared. 37 After him Judas
the Galilean rose up at the time of the census and got people to follow
him; he also perished, and all who followed him were scattered. 38 So
in the present case, I tell you, keep away from these men and let them
alone; because if this plan or this undertaking is of human origin, it
will fail; 39 but if it is of God, you will not be able to overthrow them—
in that case you may even be found fighting against God!"

They were convinced by him, 40 and when they had called in the
apostles, they had them flogged. Then they ordered them not to speak
in the name of Jesus, and let them go. 41 As they left the council, they
rejoiced that they were considered worthy to suffer dishonor for the
sake of the name. 42 And every day in the temple and at home[a] they did
not cease to teach and proclaim Jesus as the Messiah.[b]

Seven Chosen to Serve

6 Now during those days, when the disciples were increasing in
number, the Hellenists complained against the Hebrews because their widows were being neglected in the daily distribution of
food. 2 And the twelve called together the whole community of the
disciples and said, "It is not right that we should neglect the word
of God in order to wait on tables.[c] 3 Therefore, friends,[d] select from
among yourselves seven men of good standing, full of the Spirit and
of wisdom, whom we may appoint to this task, 4 while we, for our part,
will devote ourselves to prayer and to serving the word." 5 What they
said pleased the whole community, and they chose Stephen, a man
full of faith and the Holy Spirit, together with Philip, Prochorus, Ni-
canor, Timon, Parmenas, and Nicolaus, a proselyte of Antioch. 6 They
had these men stand before the apostles, who prayed and laid their
hands on them.

7 The word of God continued to spread; the number of the disciples increased greatly in Jerusalem, and a great many of the priests
became obedient to the faith.

6:1 the Hellenists complained against the Hebrews: At this time in the early church, nearly all the believers are Jews. However, some are Hellenists, Jews born outside of Israel and who speak Greek. The rest were born in Judea and speak Aramaic or Hebrew.

The Arrest of Stephen

8 Stephen, full of grace and power, did great wonders and signs
among the people. 9 Then some of those who belonged to the synagogue of the Freedmen (as it was called), Cyrenians, Alexandrians,
and others of those from Cilicia and Asia, stood up and argued with
Stephen. 10 But they could not withstand the wisdom and the Spirit[e]
with which he spoke. 11 Then they secretly instigated some men to
say, "We have heard him speak blasphemous words against Moses
and God." 12 They stirred up the people as well as the elders and the

6:8-15 some...argued with Stephen: The jealousy and plotting of the leaders are reminiscent of Jesus' arrest and trial before the Sanhedrin (see Matt 26:59-66).

[a] Or *from house to house* [b] Or *the Christ* [c] Or *keep accounts* [d] Gk *brothers* [e] Or *spirit*

7:1-54 Stephen replied: This is the longest speech in Acts. Stephen's detailed sermon recalls many events in the history of the Jews, in order to "prove" to the leaders that Jesus is indeed God's chosen one, the Messiah.

scribes; then they suddenly confronted him, seized him, and brought
him before the council. [13]They set up false witnesses who said, "This
man never stops saying things against this holy place and the law;
[14]for we have heard him say that this Jesus of Nazareth[a] will destroy
this place and will change the customs that Moses handed on to us."
[15]And all who sat in the council looked intently at him, and they saw
that his face was like the face of an angel.

Stephen's Speech to the Council

7 Then the high priest asked him, "Are these things so?" [2]And Stephen replied:

"Brothers[b] and fathers, listen to me. The God of glory appeared to
our ancestor Abraham when he was in Mesopotamia, before he lived
in Haran, [3]and said to him, 'Leave your country and your relatives and
go to the land that I will show you.' [4]Then he left the country of the
Chaldeans and settled in Haran. After his father died, God had him
move from there to this country in which you are now living. [5]He did
not give him any of it as a heritage, not even a foot's length, but promised to give it to him as his possession and to his descendants after
him, even though he had no child. [6]And God spoke in these terms,
that his descendants would be resident aliens in a country belonging to others, who would enslave them and mistreat them during four
hundred years. [7]'But I will judge the nation that they serve,' said God,
'and after that they shall come out and worship me in this place.' [8]Then
he gave him the covenant of circumcision. And so Abraham[c] became
the father of Isaac and circumcised him on the eighth day; and Isaac
became the father of Jacob, and Jacob of the twelve patriarchs.

9 "The patriarchs, jealous of Joseph, sold him into Egypt; but
God was with him, [10]and rescued him from all his afflictions, and
enabled him to win favor and to show wisdom when he stood before Pharaoh, king of Egypt, who appointed him ruler over Egypt
and over all his household. [11]Now there came a famine throughout
Egypt and Canaan, and great suffering, and our ancestors could find
no food. [12]But when Jacob heard that there was grain in Egypt, he
sent our ancestors there on their first visit. [13]On the second visit Joseph made himself known to his brothers, and Joseph's family became
known to Pharaoh. [14]Then Joseph sent and invited his father Jacob
and all his relatives to come to him, seventy-five in all; [15]so Jacob went
down to Egypt. He himself died there as well as our ancestors, [16]and
their bodies[d] were brought back to Shechem and laid in the tomb that
Abraham had bought for a sum of silver from the sons of Hamor in
Shechem.

17 "But as the time drew near for the fulfillment of the promise

---

[a] Gk *the Nazorean* [b] Gk *Men, brothers* [c] Gk *he* [d] Gk *they*

that God had made to Abraham, our people in Egypt increased and
multiplied 18 until another king who had not known Joseph ruled over
Egypt. 19 He dealt craftily with our race and forced our ancestors to
abandon their infants so that they would die. 20 At this time Moses
was born, and he was beautiful before God. For three months he was
brought up in his father's house; 21 and when he was abandoned, Pharaoh's daughter adopted him and brought him up as her own son.
22 So Moses was instructed in all the wisdom of the Egyptians and was
powerful in his words and deeds.

23 "When he was forty years old, it came into his heart to visit his
relatives, the Israelites.[a] 24 When he saw one of them being wronged,
he defended the oppressed man and avenged him by striking down
the Egyptian. 25 He supposed that his kinsfolk would understand that
God through him was rescuing them, but they did not understand.
26 The next day he came to some of them as they were quarreling and
tried to reconcile them, saying, 'Men, you are brothers; why do you
wrong each other?' 27 But the man who was wronging his neighbor
pushed Moses[b] aside, saying, 'Who made you a ruler and a judge over
us? 28 Do you want to kill me as you killed the Egyptian yesterday?'
29 When he heard this, Moses fled and became a resident alien in the
land of Midian. There he became the father of two sons.

30 "Now when forty years had passed, an angel appeared to him in
the wilderness of Mount Sinai, in the flame of a burning bush. 31 When
Moses saw it, he was amazed at the sight; and as he approached to
look, there came the voice of the Lord: 32 'I am the God of your ancestors, the God of Abraham, Isaac, and Jacob.' Moses began to tremble
and did not dare to look. 33 Then the Lord said to him, 'Take off the
sandals from your feet, for the place where you are standing is holy
ground. 34 I have surely seen the mistreatment of my people who are in
Egypt and have heard their groaning, and I have come down to rescue
them. Come now, I will send you to Egypt.'

35 "It was this Moses whom they rejected when they said, 'Who
made you a ruler and a judge?' and whom God now sent as both
ruler and liberator through the angel who appeared to him in the
bush. 36 He led them out, having performed wonders and signs in
Egypt, at the Red Sea, and in the wilderness for forty years. 37 This
is the Moses who said to the Israelites, 'God will raise up a prophet
for you from your own people[c] as he raised me up.' 38 He is the one
who was in the congregation in the wilderness with the angel who
spoke to him at Mount Sinai, and with our ancestors; and he received living oracles to give to us. 39 Our ancestors were unwilling to
obey him; instead, they pushed him aside, and in their hearts they
turned back to Egypt, 40 saying to Aaron, 'Make gods for us who will

---

[a] Gk *his brothers, the sons of Israel* [b] Gk *him* [c] Gk *your brothers*

lead the way for us; as for this Moses who led us out from the land
of Egypt, we do not know what has happened to him.' 41 At that time
they made a calf, offered a sacrifice to the idol, and reveled in the
works of their hands. 42 But God turned away from them and handed
them over to worship the host of heaven, as it is written in the book
of the prophets:

'Did you offer to me slain victims and sacrifices
    forty years in the wilderness, O house of Israel?
43 No; you took along the tent of Moloch,
    and the star of your god Rephan,
        the images that you made to worship;
so I will remove you beyond Babylon.'

44 "Our ancestors had the tent of testimony in the wilderness, as
God[a] directed when he spoke to Moses, ordering him to make it according to the pattern he had seen. 45 Our ancestors in turn brought
it in with Joshua when they dispossessed the nations that God drove
out before our ancestors. And it was there until the time of David,
46 who found favor with God and asked that he might find a dwelling
place for the house of Jacob.[b] 47 But it was Solomon who built a house
for him. 48 Yet the Most High does not dwell in houses made with human hands;[c] as the prophet says,

49 'Heaven is my throne,
    and the earth is my footstool.
What kind of house will you build for me, says the Lord,
    or what is the place of my rest?
50 Did not my hand make all these things?'

51 "You stiff-necked people, uncircumcised in heart and ears,
you are forever opposing the Holy Spirit, just as your ancestors used
to do. 52 Which of the prophets did your ancestors not persecute?
They killed those who foretold the coming of the Righteous One,
and now you have become his betrayers and murderers. 53 You are
the ones that received the law as ordained by angels, and yet you have
not kept it."

The Stoning of Stephen

54 When they heard these things, they became enraged and
ground their teeth at Stephen.[d] 55 But filled with the Holy Spirit, he
gazed into heaven and saw the glory of God and Jesus standing at
the right hand of God. 56 "Look," he said, "I see the heavens opened
and the Son of Man standing at the right hand of God!" 57 But they
covered their ears, and with a loud shout all rushed together against
him. 58 Then they dragged him out of the city and began to stone him;
and the witnesses laid their coats at the feet of a young man named

---

[a] Gk *he* [b] Other ancient authorities read *for the God of Jacob* [c] Gk *with hands* [d] Gk *him*

The Conversion of Saul

9 Meanwhile Saul, still breathing threats and murder against the disciples of the Lord, went to the high priest 2 and asked him for letters to the synagogues at Damascus, so that if he found any who belonged to the Way, men or women, he might bring them bound to Jerusalem. 3 Now as he was going along and approaching Damascus, suddenly a light from heaven flashed around him. 4 He fell to the ground and heard a voice saying to him, "Saul, Saul, why do you persecute me?" 5 He asked, "Who are you, Lord?" The reply came, "I am Jesus, whom you are persecuting. 6 But get up and enter the city, and you will be told what you are to do." 7 The men who were traveling with him stood speechless because they heard the voice but saw no one. 8 Saul got up from the ground, and though his eyes were open, he could see nothing; so they led him by the hand and brought him into Damascus. 9 For three days he was without sight, and neither ate nor drank.

10 Now there was a disciple in Damascus named Ananias. The Lord said to him in a vision, "Ananias." He answered, "Here I am, Lord." 11 The Lord said to him, "Get up and go to the street called Straight, and at the house of Judas look for a man of Tarsus named Saul. At this moment he is praying, 12 and he has seen in a vision[a] a man named Ananias come in and lay his hands on him so that he might regain his sight." 13 But Ananias answered, "Lord, I have heard from many about this man, how much evil he has done to your saints in Jerusalem; 14 and here he has authority from the chief priests to bind all who invoke your name." 15 But the Lord said to him, "Go, for he is an instrument whom I have chosen to bring my name before Gentiles and kings and before the people of Israel; 16 I myself will show him how much he must suffer for the sake of my name." 17 So Ananias went and entered the house. He laid his hands on Saul[b] and said, "Brother Saul, the Lord Jesus, who appeared to you on your way here, has sent me so that you may regain your sight and be filled with the Holy Spirit." 18 And immediately something like scales fell from his eyes, and his sight was restored. Then he got up and was baptized, 19 and after taking some food, he regained his strength.

Saul Preaches in Damascus

For several days he was with the disciples in Damascus, 20 and immediately he began to proclaim Jesus in the synagogues, saying, "He is the Son of God." 21 All who heard him were amazed and said, "Is not this the man who made havoc in Jerusalem among those who invoked this name? And has he not come here for the purpose of bringing them bound before the chief priests?" 22 Saul became increasingly

[a] Other ancient authorities lack *in a vision* [b] Gk *him*

9:1-19 suddenly a light from heaven flashed around him: This dramatic "calling" of Saul (Paul) indicates the Holy Spirit's power to change hearts and lives.

9:2 the Way: This is another name for the fellowship of believers, based on Jesus naming himself "the way" (see John 14:6).

What is vocation? Paul was called and chosen for a new way of life—a life as a witness for Jesus. Yet, for the early church to have grown as fast as it did, many ordinary believers must have taken the initiative to share the good news about Jesus. They didn't depend on leaders to do most of the work. Martin Luther taught that all Christians are called through baptism to be "priests" in Christ's church. Luther named this the "priesthood of all believers" and said that "being a good and honest butcher or shoemaker" is as holy a vocation as being a priest of the church. Lutherans teach that believers are called to live out their calling to serve God and others as they carry out their daily occupations. Vocation is the call for all believers to proclaim the gospel through daily life and work. *Acts 9*

How do you live out your calling to follow Jesus in your home, school, workplace, and/or neighborhood?

more powerful and confounded the Jews who lived in Damascus by
proving that Jesus[a] was the Messiah.[b]

Saul Escapes from the Jews

23 After some time had passed, the Jews plotted to kill him, 24 but
their plot became known to Saul. They were watching the gates day
and night so that they might kill him; 25 but his disciples took him by
night and let him down through an opening in the wall,[c] lowering him
in a basket.

Saul in Jerusalem

26 When he had come to Jerusalem, he attempted to join the disciples; and they were all afraid of him, for they did not believe that he
was a disciple. 27 But Barnabas took him, brought him to the apostles,
and described for them how on the road he had seen the Lord, who
had spoken to him, and how in Damascus he had spoken boldly in
the name of Jesus. 28 So he went in and out among them in Jerusalem,
speaking boldly in the name of the Lord. 29 He spoke and argued with
the Hellenists; but they were attempting to kill him. 30 When the believers[d] learned of it, they brought him down to Caesarea and sent
him off to Tarsus.

9:30 Caesarea: This busy port city was built by Herod (see Map 14, page 2111).

31 Meanwhile the church throughout Judea, Galilee, and Samaria had peace and was built up. Living in the fear of the Lord and in
the comfort of the Holy Spirit, it increased in numbers.

The Healing of Aeneas

32 Now as Peter went here and there among all the believers,[e] he
came down also to the saints living in Lydda. 33 There he found a man
named Aeneas, who had been bedridden for eight years, for he was
paralyzed. 34 Peter said to him, "Aeneas, Jesus Christ heals you; get up
and make your bed!" And immediately he got up. 35 And all the residents of Lydda and Sharon saw him and turned to the Lord.

Peter in Lydda and Joppa

36 Now in Joppa there was a disciple whose name was Tabitha,
which in Greek is Dorcas.[f] She was devoted to good works and acts
of charity. 37 At that time she became ill and died. When they had
washed her, they laid her in a room upstairs. 38 Since Lydda was near
Joppa, the disciples, who heard that Peter was there, sent two men to
him with the request, "Please come to us without delay." 39 So Peter
got up and went with them; and when he arrived, they took him to

9:37 When they had washed her, they laid her in a room upstairs: Both the Jews and Greeks prepared bodies for burial by washing. It was the custom in Jerusalem to bury on the day of death. In outlying areas, sometimes up to three days passed before burial.

---

[a] Gk *that this* [b] Or *the Christ* [c] Gk *through the wall* [d] Gk *brothers* [e] Gk *all of them*
[f] The name Tabitha in Aramaic and the name Dorcas in Greek mean *a gazelle*

the room upstairs. All the widows stood beside him, weeping and
showing tunics and other clothing that Dorcas had made while she
was with them. 40Peter put all of them outside, and then he knelt
down and prayed. He turned to the body and said, "Tabitha, get up."
Then she opened her eyes, and seeing Peter, she sat up. 41He gave her
his hand and helped her up. Then calling the saints and widows, he
showed her to be alive. 42This became known throughout Joppa, and
many believed in the Lord. 43Meanwhile he stayed in Joppa for some
time with a certain Simon, a tanner.

Peter and Cornelius

10 In Caesarea there was a man named Cornelius, a centurion
of the Italian Cohort, as it was called. 2He was a devout man
who feared God with all his household; he gave alms generously to
the people and prayed constantly to God. 3One afternoon at about
three o'clock he had a vision in which he clearly saw an angel of God
coming in and saying to him, "Cornelius." 4He stared at him in terror
and said, "What is it, Lord?" He answered, "Your prayers and your
alms have ascended as a memorial before God. 5Now send men to
Joppa for a certain Simon who is called Peter; 6he is lodging with Simon, a tanner, whose house is by the seaside." 7When the angel who
spoke to him had left, he called two of his slaves and a devout soldier from the ranks of those who served him, 8and after telling them
everything, he sent them to Joppa.

9 About noon the next day, as they were on their journey and approaching the city, Peter went up on the roof to pray. 10He became
hungry and wanted something to eat; and while it was being prepared,
he fell into a trance. 11He saw the heaven opened and something like
a large sheet coming down, being lowered to the ground by its four
corners. 12In it were all kinds of four-footed creatures and reptiles and
birds of the air. 13Then he heard a voice saying, "Get up, Peter; kill
and eat." 14But Peter said, "By no means, Lord; for I have never eaten
anything that is profane or unclean." 15The voice said to him again, a
second time, "What God has made clean, you must not call profane."
16This happened three times, and the thing was suddenly taken up to
heaven.

17 Now while Peter was greatly puzzled about what to make of
the vision that he had seen, suddenly the men sent by Cornelius appeared. They were asking for Simon's house and were standing by the
gate. 18They called out to ask whether Simon, who was called Peter,
was staying there. 19While Peter was still thinking about the vision,
the Spirit said to him, "Look, three[a] men are searching for you. 20Now
get up, go down, and go with them without hesitation; for I have sent

[a] One ancient authority reads *two*; others lack the word

9:40 Peter put all of them outside: The raising of Dorcas is reminiscent of Jesus raising Jairus's daughter (see Luke 8:51-55). Peter, however, prays rather than simply taking her by the hand and bringing her to life.

10:1-2 centurion...devout man who feared God: A centurion was a Roman military officer in charge of about one hundred men. Cornelius is also identified as a "God-fearer," a Gentile who was associated with a Jewish synagogue. "God-fearers" respected Jewish teachings such as Sabbath observance and may have followed Jewish food laws.

10:3 about three o'clock: This note of the time indicates that Cornelius follows Jewish customs, as three in the afternoon is a traditional hour of prayer.

10:9 roof to pray: Many houses in that day had flat roofs and an outside stairway to reach them. The rooftops were used as places of relaxation and prayer.

10:12 all kinds of...creatures: These included animals considered ritually clean and ritually unclean (see Lev 11). Peter later realizes (10:15, 28) that these visions indicate the divisions between Jew and Gentile are being overcome.

them." 21 So Peter went down to the men and said, "I am the one you
are looking for; what is the reason for your coming?" 22 They answered,
"Cornelius, a centurion, an upright and God-fearing man, who is well
spoken of by the whole Jewish nation, was directed by a holy angel to
send for you to come to his house and to hear what you have to say."
23 So Peter[a] invited them in and gave them lodging.

The next day he got up and went with them, and some of the believers[b] from Joppa accompanied him. 24 The following day they came
to Caesarea. Cornelius was expecting them and had called together
his relatives and close friends. 25 On Peter's arrival Cornelius met him,
and falling at his feet, worshiped him. 26 But Peter made him get up,
saying, "Stand up; I am only a mortal." 27 And as he talked with him, he
went in and found that many had assembled; 28 and he said to them,
"You yourselves know that it is unlawful for a Jew to associate with or
to visit a Gentile; but God has shown me that I should not call anyone
profane or unclean. 29 So when I was sent for, I came without objection. Now may I ask why you sent for me?"

30 Cornelius replied, "Four days ago at this very hour, at three
o'clock, I was praying in my house when suddenly a man in dazzling
clothes stood before me. 31 He said, 'Cornelius, your prayer has been
heard and your alms have been remembered before God. 32 Send
therefore to Joppa and ask for Simon, who is called Peter; he is staying in the home of Simon, a tanner, by the sea.' 33 Therefore I sent for
you immediately, and you have been kind enough to come. So now all
of us are here in the presence of God to listen to all that the Lord has
commanded you to say."

Gentiles Hear the Good News

34 Then Peter began to speak to them: "I truly understand that
God shows no partiality, 35 but in every nation anyone who fears him
and does what is right is acceptable to him. 36 You know the message
he sent to the people of Israel, preaching peace by Jesus Christ—he
is Lord of all. 37 That message spread throughout Judea, beginning in
Galilee after the baptism that John announced: 38 how God anointed
Jesus of Nazareth with the Holy Spirit and with power; how he went
about doing good and healing all who were oppressed by the devil,
for God was with him. 39 We are witnesses to all that he did both in
Judea and in Jerusalem. They put him to death by hanging him on a
tree; 40 but God raised him on the third day and allowed him to appear, 41 not to all the people but to us who were chosen by God as witnesses, and who ate and drank with him after he rose from the dead.
42 He commanded us to preach to the people and to testify that he is
the one ordained by God as judge of the living and the dead. 43 All

10:23 invited them in and gave them lodging: Jewish customs prohibited Jews from table fellowship with Gentiles who were not sensitive to Jewish food laws and community events that may have included worship of idols. Peter, however, invites Cornelius in and later visits Cornelius in his home (see 10:27). This shows Peter's willingness to accept and reach out to Gentiles.

What is Christian freedom? In *The Freedom of a Christian* (1520), Luther wrote: "A Christian is a perfectly free lord of all, subject to none. A Christian is a perfectly dutiful servant of all, subject to all." Jesus Christ is a Christian's only Lord—a Lord who commands us to love our neighbor as we love ourselves. *Acts 10*

---

[a] Gk *he* [b] Gk *brothers*

the prophets testify about him that everyone who believes in him receives forgiveness of sins through his name."

Gentiles Receive the Holy Spirit

44 While Peter was still speaking, the Holy Spirit fell upon all
who heard the word. 45 The circumcised believers who had come with
Peter were astounded that the gift of the Holy Spirit had been poured
out even on the Gentiles, 46 for they heard them speaking in tongues
and extolling God. Then Peter said, 47 "Can anyone withhold the water for baptizing these people who have received the Holy Spirit just
as we have?" 48 So he ordered them to be baptized in the name of Jesus
Christ. Then they invited him to stay for several days.

Peter's Report to the Church at Jerusalem

11 Now the apostles and the believers[a] who were in Judea heard
that the Gentiles had also accepted the word of God. 2 So when
Peter went up to Jerusalem, the circumcised believers[b] criticized him,
3 saying, "Why did you go to uncircumcised men and eat with them?"
4 Then Peter began to explain it to them, step by step, saying, 5 "I was
in the city of Joppa praying, and in a trance I saw a vision. There was
something like a large sheet coming down from heaven, being lowered by its four corners; and it came close to me. 6 As I looked at it
closely I saw four-footed animals, beasts of prey, reptiles, and birds of
the air. 7 I also heard a voice saying to me, 'Get up, Peter; kill and eat.'
8 But I replied, 'By no means, Lord; for nothing profane or unclean
has ever entered my mouth.' 9 But a second time the voice answered
from heaven, 'What God has made clean, you must not call profane.'
10 This happened three times; then everything was pulled up again to
heaven. 11 At that very moment three men, sent to me from Caesarea,
arrived at the house where we were. 12 The Spirit told me to go with
them and not to make a distinction between them and us.[c] These six
brothers also accompanied me, and we entered the man's house. 13 He
told us how he had seen the angel standing in his house and saying,
'Send to Joppa and bring Simon, who is called Peter; 14 he will give
you a message by which you and your entire household will be saved.'
15 And as I began to speak, the Holy Spirit fell upon them just as it had
upon us at the beginning. 16 And I remembered the word of the Lord,
how he had said, 'John baptized with water, but you will be baptized
with the Holy Spirit.' 17 If then God gave them the same gift that he
gave us when we believed in the Lord Jesus Christ, who was I that I
could hinder God?" 18 When they heard this, they were silenced. And
they praised God, saying, "Then God has given even to the Gentiles
the repentance that leads to life."

11:1-18 the apostles . . . heard that the Gentiles had also accepted the word of God: Peter tells how the Spirit is leading the Gentiles to faith. This helps the Jews who believe in Jesus Christ to drop their objections and accept Gentiles into the fellowship of believers.

---

[a] Gk *brothers* [b] Gk lacks *believers* [c] Or *not to hesitate*

The Church in Antioch

19 Now those who were scattered because of the persecution
that took place over Stephen traveled as far as Phoenicia, Cyprus,
and Antioch, and they spoke the word to no one except Jews. [20]But
among them were some men of Cyprus and Cyrene who, on coming
to Antioch, spoke to the Hellenists[a] also, proclaiming the Lord Jesus.
[21]The hand of the Lord was with them, and a great number became
believers and turned to the Lord. [22]News of this came to the ears of
the church in Jerusalem, and they sent Barnabas to Antioch. [23]When
he came and saw the grace of God, he rejoiced, and he exhorted them
all to remain faithful to the Lord with steadfast devotion; [24]for he was
a good man, full of the Holy Spirit and of faith. And a great many people were brought to the Lord. [25]Then Barnabas went to Tarsus to look
for Saul, [26]and when he had found him, he brought him to Antioch.
So it was that for an entire year they met with[b] the church and taught
a great many people, and it was in Antioch that the disciples were first
called "Christians."

27 At that time prophets came down from Jerusalem to Antioch.
[28]One of them named Agabus stood up and predicted by the Spirit
that there would be a severe famine over all the world; and this took
place during the reign of Claudius. [29]The disciples determined that according to their ability, each would send relief to the believers[c] living in
Judea; [30]this they did, sending it to the elders by Barnabas and Saul.

James Killed and Peter Imprisoned

12 About that time King Herod laid violent hands upon some
who belonged to the church. [2]He had James, the brother of
John, killed with the sword. [3]After he saw that it pleased the Jews, he
proceeded to arrest Peter also. (This was during the festival of Unleavened Bread.) [4]When he had seized him, he put him in prison and
handed him over to four squads of soldiers to guard him, intending to
bring him out to the people after the Passover. [5]While Peter was kept
in prison, the church prayed fervently to God for him.

Peter Delivered from Prison

6 The very night before Herod was going to bring him out, Peter, bound with two chains, was sleeping between two soldiers, while
guards in front of the door were keeping watch over the prison. [7]Sud-
denly an angel of the Lord appeared and a light shone in the cell. He
tapped Peter on the side and woke him, saying, "Get up quickly." And
the chains fell off his wrists. [8]The angel said to him, "Fasten your belt
and put on your sandals." He did so. Then he said to him, "Wrap your
cloak around you and follow me." [9]Peter[d] went out and followed him;

---

[a] Other ancient authorities read *Greeks* [b] Or *were guests of* [c] Gk *brothers* [d] Gk *He*

11:22 sent Barnabas to Antioch: It was apparently the practice of the church leaders in Jerusalem to send someone to check on new communities of faith as they heard of them.

11:26 Christians: This is the first use of "Christians" to describe believers in Jesus Christ. It is not clear whether the name was first used by the enemies of the church or by the believers themselves.

What does it mean to you to be called a Christian?

12:2 James, the brother of John: This is James the disciple, who was with Jesus during significant events of his ministry on earth.

12:6-19 the chains fell off his wrists: Miraculous escape from prison—Peter's, in this case—is a repeated theme in Acts (see 5:17-20; 16:16-26).

he did not realize that what was happening with the angel's help was
real; he thought he was seeing a vision. 10 After they had passed the
first and the second guard, they came before the iron gate leading into
the city. It opened for them of its own accord, and they went outside
and walked along a lane, when suddenly the angel left him. 11 Then
Peter came to himself and said, "Now I am sure that the Lord has sent
his angel and rescued me from the hands of Herod and from all that
the Jewish people were expecting."

12 As soon as he realized this, he went to the house of Mary, the
mother of John whose other name was Mark, where many had gathered and were praying. 13 When he knocked at the outer gate, a maid
named Rhoda came to answer. 14 On recognizing Peter's voice, she
was so overjoyed that, instead of opening the gate, she ran in and announced that Peter was standing at the gate. 15 They said to her, "You
are out of your mind!" But she insisted that it was so. They said, "It
is his angel." 16 Meanwhile Peter continued knocking; and when they
opened the gate, they saw him and were amazed. 17 He motioned to
them with his hand to be silent, and described for them how the Lord
had brought him out of the prison. And he added, "Tell this to James
and to the believers."[a] Then he left and went to another place.

18 When morning came, there was no small commotion among
the soldiers over what had become of Peter. 19 When Herod had
searched for him and could not find him, he examined the guards and
ordered them to be put to death. Then he went down from Judea to
Caesarea and stayed there.

The Death of Herod

20 Now Herod[b] was angry with the people of Tyre and Sidon. So
they came to him in a body; and after winning over Blastus, the king's
chamberlain, they asked for a reconciliation, because their country
depended on the king's country for food. 21 On an appointed day
Herod put on his royal robes, took his seat on the platform, and delivered a public address to them. 22 The people kept shouting, "The voice
of a god, and not of a mortal!" 23 And immediately, because he had not
given the glory to God, an angel of the Lord struck him down, and he
was eaten by worms and died.

24 But the word of God continued to advance and gain adherents. 25 Then after completing their mission Barnabas and Saul returned to[c] Jerusalem and brought with them John, whose other name
was Mark.

Barnabas and Saul Commissioned

13 Now in the church at Antioch there were prophets and
teachers: Barnabas, Simeon who was called Niger, Lucius of

[a] Gk *brothers* [b] Gk *he* [c] Other ancient authorities read *from*

12:19-23 Herod: This is Herod Agrippa I. He is the grandson of Herod the Great, who ruled when Jesus was born.

13:1—14:28 being sent out by the Holy Spirit: These chapters describe the first missionary journey of Paul (see Map 14, page 2111).

13:1 Simeon . . . Lucius . . . Manaen: The church in Antioch includes several prophets and teachers. *Niger* is the Greek word for "black," which may mean that Simeon had dark skin. Lucius came from Cyrene (11:20), and Manaen had served Herod Antipas, the ruler of Galilee in the time of Jesus. This diversity is an example of how the gospel is spreading.

Cyrene, Manaen a member of the court of Herod the ruler,[a] and Saul.
2 While they were worshiping the Lord and fasting, the Holy Spirit
said, "Set apart for me Barnabas and Saul for the work to which I have
called them." 3 Then after fasting and praying they laid their hands on
them and sent them off.

The Apostles Preach in Cyprus

4 So, being sent out by the Holy Spirit, they went down to Seleucia; and from there they sailed to Cyprus. 5 When they arrived at Salamis, they proclaimed the word of God in the synagogues of the Jews.
And they had John also to assist them. 6 When they had gone through
the whole island as far as Paphos, they met a certain magician, a Jewish false prophet, named Bar-Jesus. 7 He was with the proconsul, Ser-
gius Paulus, an intelligent man, who summoned Barnabas and Saul
and wanted to hear the word of God. 8 But the magician Elymas (for
that is the translation of his name) opposed them and tried to turn the
proconsul away from the faith. 9 But Saul, also known as Paul, filled
with the Holy Spirit, looked intently at him 10 and said, "You son of the
devil, you enemy of all righteousness, full of all deceit and villainy, will
you not stop making crooked the straight paths of the Lord? 11 And
now listen—the hand of the Lord is against you, and you will be blind
for a while, unable to see the sun." Immediately mist and darkness
came over him, and he went about groping for someone to lead him
by the hand. 12 When the proconsul saw what had happened, he believed, for he was astonished at the teaching about the Lord.

Paul and Barnabas in Antioch of Pisidia

13 Then Paul and his companions set sail from Paphos and came
to Perga in Pamphylia. John, however, left them and returned to Jerusalem; 14 but they went on from Perga and came to Antioch in Pisidia.
And on the sabbath day they went into the synagogue and sat down.
15 After the reading of the law and the prophets, the officials of the synagogue sent them a message, saying, "Brothers, if you have any word
of exhortation for the people, give it." 16 So Paul stood up and with a
gesture began to speak:

"You Israelites,[b] and others who fear God, listen. 17 The God of this
people Israel chose our ancestors and made the people great during
their stay in the land of Egypt, and with uplifted arm he led them out
of it. 18 For about forty years he put up with[c] them in the wilderness.
19 After he had destroyed seven nations in the land of Canaan, he gave
them their land as an inheritance 20 for about four hundred fifty years.
After that he gave them judges until the time of the prophet Samuel.
21 Then they asked for a king; and God gave them Saul son of Kish, a

13:5 proclaimed the word of God in the synagogues of the Jews: Jews had scattered to many countries and often established new communities and built synagogues—places of learning and worship. Paul's mission work is done primarily in synagogues, where he encounters both Jews and God-fearing Gentiles (14:1; 17:1, 10, 17; 18:4; 19:8).

13:5-6 Salamis...Paphos: These towns were on the Island of Crete, about one hundred miles apart. Paul and Barnabas make the journey on foot.

13:9 Saul...Paul: It is noted here that Saul is also known as *Paul,* which means "little" in Greek. From this point in the book of Acts, Saul is referred to as Paul. Perhaps using his Greek name helps Paul to be better received in Greek-speaking areas.

13:15 reading of the law and the prophets, the officials: It was customary in synagogue worship to read portions of the Old Testament. The officials are those charged with planning and leading worship. They would often invite visiting teachers to speak.

13:16-41 Paul stood up and...began to speak: Paul's sermon is shaped to reach the Jews. He quotes the Hebrew Bible several times (13:33-35, 41).

---

[a] Gk *tetrarch* [b] Gk *Men, Israelites* [c] Other ancient authorities read *cared for*

man of the tribe of Benjamin, who reigned for forty years. 22When he
had removed him, he made David their king. In his testimony about
him he said, 'I have found David, son of Jesse, to be a man after my
heart, who will carry out all my wishes.' 23Of this man's posterity God
has brought to Israel a Savior, Jesus, as he promised; 24before his coming John had already proclaimed a baptism of repentance to all the
people of Israel. 25And as John was finishing his work, he said, 'What
do you suppose that I am? I am not he. No, but one is coming after
me; I am not worthy to untie the thong of the sandals[a] on his feet.'

26 "My brothers, you descendants of Abraham's family, and others
who fear God, to us[b] the message of this salvation has been sent. 27Be-
cause the residents of Jerusalem and their leaders did not recognize
him or understand the words of the prophets that are read every sabbath, they fulfilled those words by condemning him. 28Even though
they found no cause for a sentence of death, they asked Pilate to have
him killed. 29When they had carried out everything that was written
about him, they took him down from the tree and laid him in a tomb.
30But God raised him from the dead; 31and for many days he appeared
to those who came up with him from Galilee to Jerusalem, and they
are now his witnesses to the people. 32And we bring you the good news
that what God promised to our ancestors 33he has fulfilled for us, their
children, by raising Jesus; as also it is written in the second psalm,

'You are my Son;
    today I have begotten you.'

34As to his raising him from the dead, no more to return to corruption, he has spoken in this way,

'I will give you the holy promises made to David.'

35Therefore he has also said in another psalm,

'You will not let your Holy One experience corruption.'

36For David, after he had served the purpose of God in his own generation, died,[c] was laid beside his ancestors, and experienced corruption; 37but he whom God raised up experienced no corruption. 38Let
it be known to you therefore, my brothers, that through this man forgiveness of sins is proclaimed to you; 39by this Jesus[d] everyone who
believes is set free from all those sins[e] from which you could not be
freed by the law of Moses. 40Beware, therefore, that what the prophets
said does not happen to you:

41 'Look, you scoffers!
    Be amazed and perish,
for in your days I am doing a work,
    a work that you will never believe, even if someone tells you.' "

42 As Paul and Barnabas[f] were going out, the people urged them

---

[a] Gk *untie the sandals* [b] Other ancient authorities read *you* [c] Gk *fell asleep* [d] Gk *this* [e] Gk *all*
[f] Gk *they*

to speak about these things again the next sabbath. 43 When the meeting of the synagogue broke up, many Jews and devout converts to Judaism followed Paul and Barnabas, who spoke to them and urged them to continue in the grace of God.

44 The next sabbath almost the whole city gathered to hear the word of the Lord.[a] 45 But when the Jews saw the crowds, they were filled with jealousy; and blaspheming, they contradicted what was spoken by Paul. 46 Then both Paul and Barnabas spoke out boldly, saying, "It was necessary that the word of God should be spoken first to you. Since you reject it and judge yourselves to be unworthy of eternal life, we are now turning to the Gentiles. 47 For so the Lord has commanded us, saying,

'I have set you to be a light for the Gentiles,
so that you may bring salvation to the ends of the earth.' "

48 When the Gentiles heard this, they were glad and praised the word of the Lord; and as many as had been destined for eternal life became believers. 49 Thus the word of the Lord spread throughout the region. 50 But the Jews incited the devout women of high standing and the leading men of the city, and stirred up persecution against Paul and Barnabas, and drove them out of their region. 51 So they shook the dust off their feet in protest against them, and went to Iconium. 52 And the disciples were filled with joy and with the Holy Spirit.

Paul and Barnabas in Iconium

14 The same thing occurred in Iconium, where Paul and Barnabas[b] went into the Jewish synagogue and spoke in such a way that a great number of both Jews and Greeks became believers. 2 But the unbelieving Jews stirred up the Gentiles and poisoned their minds against the brothers. 3 So they remained for a long time, speaking boldly for the Lord, who testified to the word of his grace by granting signs and wonders to be done through them. 4 But the residents of the city were divided; some sided with the Jews, and some with the apostles. 5 And when an attempt was made by both Gentiles and Jews, with their rulers, to mistreat them and to stone them, 6 the apostles[b] learned of it and fled to Lystra and Derbe, cities of Lycaonia, and to the surrounding country; 7 and there they continued proclaiming the good news.

Paul and Barnabas in Lystra and Derbe

8 In Lystra there was a man sitting who could not use his feet and had never walked, for he had been crippled from birth. 9 He listened to Paul as he was speaking. And Paul, looking at him intently and seeing that he had faith to be healed, 10 said in a loud voice, "Stand upright on your feet." And the man[c] sprang up and began to walk. 11 When

[a] Other ancient authorities read *God* [b] Gk *they* [c] Gk *he*

13:45 Jews: This refers to the Jews who did not accept what Paul was teaching about Jesus. It does not refer to all Jews.

13:46-47 be spoken first to you: Paul feels an obligation to speak first to the Jews, because Paul loves his people and because Jesus had come from Jewish roots. Paul quotes Isaiah 49:6 to convince the audience that there ought to be a mission to Gentiles.

13:50 incited...stirred up persecution...drove them out of their region: The Jews who do not accept Jesus as Messiah consider Paul a false teacher and a threat. These people harass Paul during his missionary journeys.

13:51 shook the dust off their feet: This action is a way of showing rejection.

14:1-7 both Jews and Greeks became believers: This section identifies many of the key groups in the stories of Acts: Jews who believe in Jesus and Jews who do not believe; Gentiles who believe in Jesus and Gentiles who do not. In the first century, a person could be a Jew and a believer in Jesus at the same time.

14:4 apostles: Paul and Barnabas are called "apostles." Here the word means not only Jesus' original twelve disciples, but all those sent on a mission to preach and teach the good news about Jesus Christ.

Who can be an apostle today? What might an apostle do in your community?

the crowds saw what Paul had done, they shouted in the Lycaonian
language, "The gods have come down to us in human form!" 12 Barnabas they called Zeus, and Paul they called Hermes, because he was
the chief speaker. 13 The priest of Zeus, whose temple was just outside
the city,[a] brought oxen and garlands to the gates; he and the crowds
wanted to offer sacrifice. 14 When the apostles Barnabas and Paul heard
of it, they tore their clothes and rushed out into the crowd, shouting,
15 "Friends,[b] why are you doing this? We are mortals just like you, and
we bring you good news, that you should turn from these worthless
things to the living God, who made the heaven and the earth and the
sea and all that is in them. 16 In past generations he allowed all the nations to follow their own ways; 17 yet he has not left himself without
a witness in doing good—giving you rains from heaven and fruitful
seasons, and filling you with food and your hearts with joy." 18 Even
with these words, they scarcely restrained the crowds from offering
sacrifice to them.

19 But Jews came there from Antioch and Iconium and won over
the crowds. Then they stoned Paul and dragged him out of the city,
supposing that he was dead. 20 But when the disciples surrounded
him, he got up and went into the city. The next day he went on with
Barnabas to Derbe.

The Return to Antioch in Syria

21 After they had proclaimed the good news to that city and had
made many disciples, they returned to Lystra, then on to Iconium and
Antioch. 22 There they strengthened the souls of the disciples and encouraged them to continue in the faith, saying, "It is through many
persecutions that we must enter the kingdom of God." 23 And after
they had appointed elders for them in each church, with prayer and
fasting they entrusted them to the Lord in whom they had come to
believe.

24 Then they passed through Pisidia and came to Pamphylia.
25 When they had spoken the word in Perga, they went down to Attalia. 26 From there they sailed back to Antioch, where they had been
commended to the grace of God for the work[c] that they had completed. 27 When they arrived, they called the church together and related all that God had done with them, and how he had opened a door
of faith for the Gentiles. 28 And they stayed there with the disciples for
some time.

The Council at Jerusalem

15 Then certain individuals came down from Judea and were
teaching the brothers, "Unless you are circumcised according

[a] Or *The priest of Zeus-Outside-the-City* [b] Gk *Men* [c] Or *committed in the grace of God to the work*

14:12 Barnabas they called Zeus, and Paul they called Hermes: Zeus, the chief Greek god, was honored with a temple in the city of Lystra. Hermes, the messenger of the Greek gods, was said to bring messages to humankind.

14:14 tore their clothes: This act is an expression of great sorrow or anguish.

14:15-17 We are mortals: Paul responds to the group's misunderstanding (14:12) in this speech directed to a Gentile audience. The main topic is prohibition of idolatry.

14:23 appointed elders: The elders are to oversee the church and arrange for worship and teaching. Paul and Barnabas may feel a need to appoint elders because these new churches have many Gentile members.

15:1-35 The apostles and the elders met together: This chapter tells of an important conflict in the early church. Some devout Jews are teaching that Gentiles who become Christian must also accept and obey all of the Old Testament laws, including circumcision. The resolution of the conflict makes it clear that Gentiles may come into the fellowship of believers without keeping the rules and customs of the Jewish community (see Rom 3:21-31 and Gal 3:26-29). This decision did not end the conflict. Some believing Jews, who assume that the Jewish law applies to believing Gentiles, are called Judaizers. They continue to oppose Paul and others who are reaching out to Gentiles.

to the custom of Moses, you cannot be saved.” 2 And after Paul and
Barnabas had no small dissension and debate with them, Paul and
Barnabas and some of the others were appointed to go up to Jerusalem to discuss this question with the apostles and the elders. 3 So
they were sent on their way by the church, and as they passed through
both Phoenicia and Samaria, they reported the conversion of the
Gentiles, and brought great joy to all the believers.[a] 4 When they came
to Jerusalem, they were welcomed by the church and the apostles and
the elders, and they reported all that God had done with them. 5 But
some believers who belonged to the sect of the Pharisees stood up
and said, “It is necessary for them to be circumcised and ordered to
keep the law of Moses.”

6 The apostles and the elders met together to consider this matter. 7 After there had been much debate, Peter stood up and said to
them, “My brothers,[b] you know that in the early days God made a
choice among you, that I should be the one through whom the Gentiles would hear the message of the good news and become believers. 8 And God, who knows the human heart, testified to them by
giving them the Holy Spirit, just as he did to us; 9 and in cleansing
their hearts by faith he has made no distinction between them and
us. 10 Now therefore why are you putting God to the test by placing on
the neck of the disciples a yoke that neither our ancestors nor we have
been able to bear? 11 On the contrary, we believe that we will be saved
through the grace of the Lord Jesus, just as they will.”

12 The whole assembly kept silence, and listened to Barnabas
and Paul as they told of all the signs and wonders that God had done
through them among the Gentiles. 13 After they finished speaking,
James replied, “My brothers,[b] listen to me. 14 Simeon has related how
God first looked favorably on the Gentiles, to take from among them
a people for his name. 15 This agrees with the words of the prophets,
as it is written,

16 ‘After this I will return,
and I will rebuild the dwelling of David, which has fallen;
from its ruins I will rebuild it,
and I will set it up,
17 so that all other peoples may seek the Lord—
even all the Gentiles over whom my name has been called.
Thus says the Lord, who has been making these things
18 known from long ago.’[c]

19 Therefore I have reached the decision that we should not trouble
those Gentiles who are turning to God, 20 but we should write to them
to abstain only from things polluted by idols and from fornication

---

[a] Gk *brothers* [b] Gk *Men, brothers* [c] Other ancient authorities read *things.* 18 *Known to God from of old are all his works.’*

15:7 Peter stood up: Peter is a leader in the church and the first apostle sent to the Gentiles (Acts 10).

15:8 giving [the Gentiles] the Holy Spirit: The coming of the Spirit is proof that God accepts the Gentiles.

15:10 yoke: This refers to the burden of keeping the law (see Gal 5:1). More specifically, it probably refers here to circumcision.

15:11 we will be saved through the grace of the Lord Jesus: The belief that salvation is a free gift of God’s grace is at the heart of the preaching of the gospel.

What does it mean to be “saved by grace”? “The Law says, ‘do this,’ and it’s never done. Grace says, ‘believe in this,’ and everything is already done,” Martin Luther said in his *Heidelberg Disputation* (1518). *Grace* means that the Lord gives us forgiveness, love, and life with God forever, as free gifts. Since God has given us all this through Jesus, we don’t have to do anything to earn God’s favor (see Eph 2:8-9). This grace drives us to worship God and share grace with our neighbor in word and deed. *Acts 15:11*

and from whatever has been strangled[a] and from blood. 21 For in every
city, for generations past, Moses has had those who proclaim him, for
he has been read aloud every sabbath in the synagogues."

The Council's Letter to Gentile Believers

22 Then the apostles and the elders, with the consent of the whole
church, decided to choose men from among their members[b] and to
send them to Antioch with Paul and Barnabas. They sent Judas called
Barsabbas, and Silas, leaders among the brothers, 23 with the following letter: "The brothers, both the apostles and the elders, to the believers[c] of Gentile origin in Antioch and Syria and Cilicia, greetings.
24 Since we have heard that certain persons who have gone out from
us, though with no instructions from us, have said things to disturb
you and have unsettled your minds,[d] 25 we have decided unanimously
to choose representatives[e] and send them to you, along with our beloved Barnabas and Paul, 26 who have risked their lives for the sake of
our Lord Jesus Christ. 27 We have therefore sent Judas and Silas, who
themselves will tell you the same things by word of mouth. 28 For it
has seemed good to the Holy Spirit and to us to impose on you no
further burden than these essentials: 29 that you abstain from what has
been sacrificed to idols and from blood and from what is strangled[f]
and from fornication. If you keep yourselves from these, you will do
well. Farewell."

30 So they were sent off and went down to Antioch. When they
gathered the congregation together, they delivered the letter. 31 When
its members[g] read it, they rejoiced at the exhortation. 32 Judas and
Silas, who were themselves prophets, said much to encourage and
strengthen the believers.[c] 33 After they had been there for some time,
they were sent off in peace by the believers[c] to those who had sent
them.[h] 35 But Paul and Barnabas remained in Antioch, and there, with
many others, they taught and proclaimed the word of the Lord.

Paul and Barnabas Separate

36 After some days Paul said to Barnabas, "Come, let us return
and visit the believers[c] in every city where we proclaimed the word of
the Lord and see how they are doing." 37 Barnabas wanted to take with
them John called Mark. 38 But Paul decided not to take with them one
who had deserted them in Pamphylia and had not accompanied them
in the work. 39 The disagreement became so sharp that they parted
company; Barnabas took Mark with him and sailed away to Cyprus.
40 But Paul chose Silas and set out, the believers[c] commending him to

15:29 abstain from: For groups of believers that include both Jews and Gentiles, this is a sensitive matter. Gentile believers are expected to follow Jewish food laws in order to allow table fellowship with Jewish believers. Those who eat food sacrificed to idols are seen as worshiping those idols. Eating blood (including that of strangled animals) is forbidden by Jewish law (see Lev 17:10-12) and would be offensive to Jews who believe in Jesus.

15:32 prophets: This was one of the offices or positions in the early church and included speaking for God, offering instruction and encouragement.

15:39 parted company: Even though Barnabas is mentioned in Paul's first letter to the Corinthians (1 Cor 9:6) as a good example, he never again travels with Paul. Paul joins with Silas to begin his second missionary journey (15:40—18:23). See Map 14, p. 2111.

---

[a] Other ancient authorities lack *and from whatever has been strangled* [b] Gk *from among them*
[c] Gk *brothers* [d] Other ancient authorities add *saying, 'You must be circumcised and keep the law,'*
[e] Gk *men* [f] Other ancient authorities lack *and from what is strangled* [g] Gk *When they* [h] Other ancient authorities add verse 34, *But it seemed good to Silas to remain there*

the grace of the Lord. 41 He went through Syria and Cilicia, strengthening the churches.

Timothy Joins Paul and Silas

16 Paul[a] went on also to Derbe and to Lystra, where there was a
disciple named Timothy, the son of a Jewish woman who was
a believer; but his father was a Greek. 2 He was well spoken of by the
believers[b] in Lystra and Iconium. 3 Paul wanted Timothy to accompany him; and he took him and had him circumcised because of the
Jews who were in those places, for they all knew that his father was a
Greek. 4 As they went from town to town, they delivered to them for
observance the decisions that had been reached by the apostles and
elders who were in Jerusalem. 5 So the churches were strengthened in
the faith and increased in numbers daily.

Paul's Vision of the Man of Macedonia

6 They went through the region of Phrygia and Galatia, having
been forbidden by the Holy Spirit to speak the word in Asia. 7 When
they had come opposite Mysia, they attempted to go into Bithynia,
but the Spirit of Jesus did not allow them; 8 so, passing by Mysia, they
went down to Troas. 9 During the night Paul had a vision: there stood
a man of Macedonia pleading with him and saying, "Come over to
Macedonia and help us." 10 When he had seen the vision, we immediately tried to cross over to Macedonia, being convinced that God had
called us to proclaim the good news to them.

The Conversion of Lydia

11 We set sail from Troas and took a straight course to Samo-
thrace, the following day to Neapolis, 12 and from there to Philippi,
which is a leading city of the district[c] of Macedonia and a Roman colony. We remained in this city for some days. 13 On the sabbath day
we went outside the gate by the river, where we supposed there was
a place of prayer; and we sat down and spoke to the women who had
gathered there. 14 A certain woman named Lydia, a worshiper of God,
was listening to us; she was from the city of Thyatira and a dealer in
purple cloth. The Lord opened her heart to listen eagerly to what was
said by Paul. 15 When she and her household were baptized, she urged
us, saying, "If you have judged me to be faithful to the Lord, come and
stay at my home." And she prevailed upon us.

Paul and Silas in Prison

16 One day, as we were going to the place of prayer, we met a
slave-girl who had a spirit of divination and brought her owners a

[a] Gk *He* [b] Gk *brothers* [c] Other authorities read *a city of the first district*

16:1 disciple named Timothy: Timothy was probably very young at this time. His mother was a faithful believer (see 2 Tim 1:5). His father was probably not a Christian.

16:3 Paul…had him circumcised: Timothy is circumcised according to Jewish law so that he can work more effectively with the Jews, who know that his father is Greek.

It is challenging to reconcile this action with Paul's own words about circumcision in Galatians 5:1-6. Perhaps this is reported as a defense against accusations by believing Jews that Paul has abandoned Jewish law (21:21).

16:9 vision…man of Macedonia: God sometimes chooses to communicate in visions.

16:10 we immediately tried to cross over: The writer's use of "we" here may suggest that he is telling about a personal experience, or that he is working from someone else's diary or account of travels with Paul.

16:13 place of prayer: Apparently there are so few Jews in Philippi that they have no synagogue. They follow the custom of finding a quiet place by water for prayer.

16:14-15 Lydia: Lydia is a Gentile and a devout seeker after God. She is able to offer hospitality to Paul and the others, so she probably is wealthy. God opens her heart, and the Spirit brings her to faith in Jesus.

16:16 spirit of divination…fortune-telling: The Greek words used here indicate that the girl has a "python" spirit, associated with the prophet or Oracle at Delphi, in Greece. People believe that this spirit speaks through her, allowing her to tell the future. The girl's owners charge people for this information.

Key People in Acts

Name	Brief description	Description	References
James, the son of Zebedee	Son of Thunder	With his brother John, called by Jesus as a disciple. In the Gospel of Mark (10:35-45), he and his brother ask Jesus for places of honor in the kingdom (it is their mother's request in Matthew 20:20-28). Herod Agrippa orders his beheading.	Acts 12:2
Rhoda	Mary's maid	The maid of Mary, John Mark's mother, Rhoda hears Peter, miraculously freed from prison, knocking at the door. She recognizes his voice and runs to tell the others, "Peter is at the door!" They think she is crazy until they open the gate and see Peter for themselves.	Acts 12:12-17
Silas	Apostle	One of the leaders of the Jerusalem church and also mentioned in Paul's letters (as Silvanus, the Latin form), Silas is Paul's companion on the second missionary journey to Macedonia.	Acts 15:22-18:5
Timothy	Emissary of Paul	Already a disciple when Paul meets him and invites him to join the mission in progress, Paul sends Timothy to churches as his representative.	Acts 16:1-5
Lydia	Merchant of purple cloth	A trader in purple-dyed cloth from the city of Thyatira, Acts describes her as a "worshiper of God" whose heart God opens to hear Paul. She and her whole household are baptized.	Acts 16:14-15
Aquila and Priscilla	Paul's coworkers	Sought out by Paul as fellow tentmakers, they work with him and also instruct Apollos, who has incomplete information about Jesus, in the Way of God.	Acts 18:1-4, 24-28
Apollos	Eloquent man	A Jew from Alexandria known for his eloquence and knowledge of scriptures, Apollos is recruited for Paul's mission in Corinth.	Acts 18:24-28

great deal of money by fortune-telling. 17While she followed Paul
and us, she would cry out, "These men are slaves of the Most High
God, who proclaim to you[a] a way of salvation." 18She kept doing this
for many days. But Paul, very much annoyed, turned and said to the
spirit, "I order you in the name of Jesus Christ to come out of her."
And it came out that very hour.

19 But when her owners saw that their hope of making money
was gone, they seized Paul and Silas and dragged them into the marketplace before the authorities. 20When they had brought them before the magistrates, they said, "These men are disturbing our city;
they are Jews 21and are advocating customs that are not lawful for
us as Romans to adopt or observe." 22The crowd joined in attacking

[a] Other ancient authorities read *to us*

16:21 customs that are not lawful for us as Romans: Religions that did not have Roman approval were considered illegal. Judaism was recognized; Christianity was not.

How do you hope you would respond if you were imprisoned because of your faith? What might prepare you for this?

them, and the magistrates had them stripped of their clothing and
ordered them to be beaten with rods. 23 After they had given them a
severe flogging, they threw them into prison and ordered the jailer to
keep them securely. 24 Following these instructions, he put them in
the innermost cell and fastened their feet in the stocks.

25 About midnight Paul and Silas were praying and singing
hymns to God, and the prisoners were listening to them. 26 Suddenly
there was an earthquake, so violent that the foundations of the prison
were shaken; and immediately all the doors were opened and everyone's chains were unfastened. 27 When the jailer woke up and saw
the prison doors wide open, he drew his sword and was about to kill
himself, since he supposed that the prisoners had escaped. 28 But Paul
shouted in a loud voice, "Do not harm yourself, for we are all here."
29 The jailer[a] called for lights, and rushing in, he fell down trembling
before Paul and Silas. 30 Then he brought them outside and said, "Sirs,
what must I do to be saved?" 31 They answered, "Believe on the Lord
Jesus, and you will be saved, you and your household." 32 They spoke
the word of the Lord[b] to him and to all who were in his house. 33 At the
same hour of the night he took them and washed their wounds; then
he and his entire family were baptized without delay. 34 He brought
them up into the house and set food before them; and he and his entire household rejoiced that he had become a believer in God.

35 When morning came, the magistrates sent the police, saying,
"Let those men go." 36 And the jailer reported the message to Paul, saying, "The magistrates sent word to let you go; therefore come out now
and go in peace." 37 But Paul replied, "They have beaten us in public,
uncondemned, men who are Roman citizens, and have thrown us
into prison; and now are they going to discharge us in secret? Certainly not! Let them come and take us out themselves." 38 The police
reported these words to the magistrates, and they were afraid when
they heard that they were Roman citizens; 39 so they came and apologized to them. And they took them out and asked them to leave the
city. 40 After leaving the prison they went to Lydia's home; and when
they had seen and encouraged the brothers and sisters[c] there, they
departed.

16:27 about to kill himself: A jailer who allowed prisoners to escape was expected to pay with his life (see 12:19).

16:34 he and his entire household rejoiced: Those who come to faith are consistently filled with joy (8:39).

16:37 Roman citizens: Those who were given citizenship because of some service to Rome, who were born Roman citizens, or who purchased Roman citizenship were entitled to special treatment by the authorities. They were protected from imprisonment without conviction, from torture, and from public humiliation.

16:39 apologized to them: Paul is interested in establishing his innocence, not only for his own sake, but for the sake of the church at Philippi.

The Uproar in Thessalonica

17 After Paul and Silas[d] had passed through Amphipolis and Apollonia, they came to Thessalonica, where there was a synagogue of the Jews. 2 And Paul went in, as was his custom, and on three
sabbath days argued with them from the scriptures, 3 explaining and
proving that it was necessary for the Messiah[e] to suffer and to rise
from the dead, and saying, "This is the Messiah,[e] Jesus whom I am

---

[a] Gk *He* [b] Other ancient authorities read *word of God* [c] Gk *brothers* [d] Gk *they* [e] Or *the Christ*

proclaiming to you." [4]Some of them were persuaded and joined Paul
and Silas, as did a great many of the devout Greeks and not a few of
the leading women. [5]But the Jews became jealous, and with the help
of some ruffians in the marketplaces they formed a mob and set the
city in an uproar. While they were searching for Paul and Silas to bring
them out to the assembly, they attacked Jason's house. [6]When they
could not find them, they dragged Jason and some believers[a] before
the city authorities,[b] shouting, "These people who have been turning
the world upside down have come here also, [7]and Jason has entertained them as guests. They are all acting contrary to the decrees of
the emperor, saying that there is another king named Jesus." [8]The people and the city officials were disturbed when they heard this, [9]and
after they had taken bail from Jason and the others, they let them go.

Paul and Silas in Beroea

10 That very night the believers[a] sent Paul and Silas off to Beroea;
and when they arrived, they went to the Jewish synagogue. [11]These
Jews were more receptive than those in Thessalonica, for they welcomed the message very eagerly and examined the scriptures every
day to see whether these things were so. [12]Many of them therefore believed, including not a few Greek women and men of high standing.
[13]But when the Jews of Thessalonica learned that the word of God
had been proclaimed by Paul in Beroea as well, they came there too,
to stir up and incite the crowds. [14]Then the believers[a] immediately
sent Paul away to the coast, but Silas and Timothy remained behind.
[15]Those who conducted Paul brought him as far as Athens; and after
receiving instructions to have Silas and Timothy join him as soon as
possible, they left him.

Paul in Athens

16 While Paul was waiting for them in Athens, he was deeply
distressed to see that the city was full of idols. [17]So he argued in the
synagogue with the Jews and the devout persons, and also in the
marketplace[c] every day with those who happened to be there. [18]Also
some Epicurean and Stoic philosophers debated with him. Some
said, "What does this babbler want to say?" Others said, "He seems to
be a proclaimer of foreign divinities." (This was because he was telling
the good news about Jesus and the resurrection.) [19]So they took him
and brought him to the Areopagus and asked him, "May we know
what this new teaching is that you are presenting? [20]It sounds rather
strange to us, so we would like to know what it means." [21]Now all the
Athenians and the foreigners living there would spend their time in
nothing but telling or hearing something new.

17:7 acting contrary to the decrees of the emperor: Acting against Caesar's laws would be considered treason and could be punished by death.

17:9 taken bail from Jason: Jason posts a money bond. But if Jason does not control his guests he is liable to lose his property and even his life.

17:15 Athens: For centuries this important Greek city was known as a center for art, culture, and philosophy. It boasted a leading university in Paul's day.

17:18 Epicurean and Stoic philosophers: These men represent two of the philosophical schools in Athens. Epicureans believe in finding joy and pleasure in life. The Stoics teach that it is important to live quietly, in harmony with life and nature.

17:19 Areopagus: This was a meeting place near the Acropolis in Athens, where matters of religion and morals were often discussed.

---

[a] Gk *brothers* [b] Gk *politarchs* [c] Or *civic center;* Gk *agora*

17:23 To an unknown god: The Greeks were afraid to offend any god, so they sought to make up for any omission by crafting an altar and giving it this label.

17:24-27 The God who made the world...allotted the times of their existence and the...places where they would live: Paul challenges both the Stoics, who think that God is a sort of force in all nature, and the Epicureans, who think that all times, places, and events are by chance.

17:28 as even some of your own poets have said: Paul shows his education by quoting Greek poets who seem to agree with him—in this case Epimenides and Aratus.

17:32 resurrection of the dead: Many Greeks accepted the immortality of the soul but not the resurrection of the dead.

17:34 Dionysius: Tradition says he later becomes bishop of Athens, but this claim cannot be proven.

18:1-2 Aquila...Priscilla...Claudius had ordered all Jews to leave Rome: Priscilla and Aquila are probably Jews who believe in Jesus. They left Rome because Claudius, the emperor, had ordered the Jews to leave. A Roman historian, Suetonius, reports that the Jews were causing disturbances in Rome, probably because of the conflict between Jews who believed in Jesus and those who did not.

22 Then Paul stood in front of the Areopagus and said, "Athenians, I see how extremely religious you are in every way. 23 For as I went
through the city and looked carefully at the objects of your worship,
I found among them an altar with the inscription, 'To an unknown
god.' What therefore you worship as unknown, this I proclaim to you.
24 The God who made the world and everything in it, he who is Lord
of heaven and earth, does not live in shrines made by human hands,
25 nor is he served by human hands, as though he needed anything,
since he himself gives to all mortals life and breath and all things.
26 From one ancestor[a] he made all nations to inhabit the whole earth,
and he allotted the times of their existence and the boundaries of the
places where they would live, 27 so that they would search for God[b]
and perhaps grope for him and find him—though indeed he is not
far from each one of us. 28 For 'In him we live and move and have our
being'; as even some of your own poets have said,

'For we too are his offspring.'

29 Since we are God's offspring, we ought not to think that the deity
is like gold, or silver, or stone, an image formed by the art and imagination of mortals. 30 While God has overlooked the times of human
ignorance, now he commands all people everywhere to repent, 31 because he has fixed a day on which he will have the world judged in
righteousness by a man whom he has appointed, and of this he has
given assurance to all by raising him from the dead."

32 When they heard of the resurrection of the dead, some scoffed;
but others said, "We will hear you again about this." 33 At that point
Paul left them. 34 But some of them joined him and became believers,
including Dionysius the Areopagite and a woman named Damaris,
and others with them.

Paul in Corinth

18 After this Paul[c] left Athens and went to Corinth. 2 There he
found a Jew named Aquila, a native of Pontus, who had recently come from Italy with his wife Priscilla, because Claudius had
ordered all Jews to leave Rome. Paul[d] went to see them, 3 and, because
he was of the same trade, he stayed with them, and they worked together—by trade they were tentmakers. 4 Every sabbath he would argue in the synagogue and would try to convince Jews and Greeks.

5 When Silas and Timothy arrived from Macedonia, Paul was
occupied with proclaiming the word,[e] testifying to the Jews that the
Messiah[f] was Jesus. 6 When they opposed and reviled him, in protest
he shook the dust from his clothes[g] and said to them, "Your blood
be on your own heads! I am innocent. From now on I will go to the

[a] Gk *From one;* other ancient authorities read *From one blood* [b] Other ancient authorities read *the Lord*
[c] Gk *he* [d] Gk *He* [e] Gk *with the word* [f] Or *the Christ* [g] Gk *reviled him, he shook out his clothes*

Gentiles." 7 Then he left the synagogue[a] and went to the house of a
man named Titius[b] Justus, a worshiper of God; his house was next
door to the synagogue. 8 Crispus, the official of the synagogue, became a believer in the Lord, together with all his household; and
many of the Corinthians who heard Paul became believers and were
baptized. 9 One night the Lord said to Paul in a vision, "Do not be
afraid, but speak and do not be silent; 10 for I am with you, and no one
will lay a hand on you to harm you, for there are many in this city who
are my people." 11 He stayed there a year and six months, teaching the
word of God among them.

12 But when Gallio was proconsul of Achaia, the Jews made a
united attack on Paul and brought him before the tribunal. 13 They
said, "This man is persuading people to worship God in ways that are
contrary to the law." 14 Just as Paul was about to speak, Gallio said to
the Jews, "If it were a matter of crime or serious villainy, I would be
justified in accepting the complaint of you Jews; 15 but since it is a matter of questions about words and names and your own law, see to it
yourselves; I do not wish to be a judge of these matters." 16 And he dismissed them from the tribunal. 17 Then all of them[c] seized Sosthenes,
the official of the synagogue, and beat him in front of the tribunal. But
Gallio paid no attention to any of these things.

Paul's Return to Antioch

18 After staying there for a considerable time, Paul said farewell
to the believers[d] and sailed for Syria, accompanied by Priscilla and
Aquila. At Cenchreae he had his hair cut, for he was under a vow.
19 When they reached Ephesus, he left them there, but first he himself
went into the synagogue and had a discussion with the Jews. 20 When
they asked him to stay longer, he declined; 21 but on taking leave of
them, he said, "I[e] will return to you, if God wills." Then he set sail
from Ephesus.

22 When he had landed at Caesarea, he went up to Jerusalem[f] and
greeted the church, and then went down to Antioch. 23 After spending
some time there he departed and went from place to place through
the region of Galatia[g] and Phrygia, strengthening all the disciples.

Ministry of Apollos

24 Now there came to Ephesus a Jew named Apollos, a native of
Alexandria. He was an eloquent man, well-versed in the scriptures.
25 He had been instructed in the Way of the Lord; and he spoke with
burning enthusiasm and taught accurately the things concerning
Jesus, though he knew only the baptism of John. 26 He began to speak

[a] Gk *left there* [b] Other ancient authorities read *Titus* [c] Other ancient authorities read *all the Greeks*
[d] Gk *brothers* [e] Other ancient authorities read *I must at all costs keep the approaching festival in Jerusalem, but I* [f] Gk *went up* [g] Gk *the Galatian region*

18:13 contrary to the law: The Jews are accusing Paul of treason (see note on 17:7).

18:15 a matter of questions about words and names and your own law: Gallio identifies the dispute as a matter of Jewish law and rejects the charge that Paul has broken Roman law. Gallio turns the matter back to the Jewish community to settle.

18:17 seized Sosthenes, the official of the synagogue, and beat him: It seems that the Jews who lose their case against Paul turn on the ruler of the synagogue because he also is a "believing Jew." Paul mentions him in 1 Corinthians 1:1.

18:23 he departed: This is the start of Paul's third missionary journey (see Map 14, p. 2111). It follows much of the same route as the second journey, as Paul revisits and strengthens the new churches.

18:25 knew only the baptism of John: John's baptism was a baptism of repentance that looked forward to Jesus, rather than a baptism based on faith in Jesus (see Luke 3:3, 16).

boldly in the synagogue; but when Priscilla and Aquila heard him,
they took him aside and explained the Way of God to him more accurately. 27 And when he wished to cross over to Achaia, the believers[a]
encouraged him and wrote to the disciples to welcome him. On his
arrival he greatly helped those who through grace had become believers, 28 for he powerfully refuted the Jews in public, showing by the
scriptures that the Messiah[b] is Jesus.

Paul in Ephesus

19 While Apollos was in Corinth, Paul passed through the interior regions and came to Ephesus, where he found some
disciples. 2 He said to them, "Did you receive the Holy Spirit when
you became believers?" They replied, "No, we have not even heard
that there is a Holy Spirit." 3 Then he said, "Into what then were you
baptized?" They answered, "Into John's baptism." 4 Paul said, "John
baptized with the baptism of repentance, telling the people to believe
in the one who was to come after him, that is, in Jesus." 5 On hearing
this, they were baptized in the name of the Lord Jesus. 6 When Paul
had laid his hands on them, the Holy Spirit came upon them, and
they spoke in tongues and prophesied— 7 altogether there were about
twelve of them.

19:6 Holy Spirit came upon them...spoke in tongues and prophesied: The coming of the Spirit shows that these people are accepted by God. They receive the same gifts from the Spirit as those in Caesarea (10:44-46) and Jerusalem (2:4).

8 He entered the synagogue and for three months spoke out
boldly, and argued persuasively about the kingdom of God. 9 When
some stubbornly refused to believe and spoke evil of the Way before
the congregation, he left them, taking the disciples with him, and argued daily in the lecture hall of Tyrannus.[c] 10 This continued for two
years, so that all the residents of Asia, both Jews and Greeks, heard the
word of the Lord.

19:9 left them...hall of Tyrannus: Paul leaves the synagogue, where he usually teaches, because of strong opposition. He begins to teach in a public building where Gentiles would be welcome, the place where the philosopher Tyrannus taught.

The Sons of Sceva

11 God did extraordinary miracles through Paul, 12 so that when
the handkerchiefs or aprons that had touched his skin were brought
to the sick, their diseases left them, and the evil spirits came out of
them. 13 Then some itinerant Jewish exorcists tried to use the name of
the Lord Jesus over those who had evil spirits, saying, "I adjure you by
the Jesus whom Paul proclaims." 14 Seven sons of a Jewish high priest
named Sceva were doing this. 15 But the evil spirit said to them in reply, "Jesus I know, and Paul I know; but who are you?" 16 Then the man
with the evil spirit leaped on them, mastered them all, and so overpowered them that they fled out of the house naked and wounded.
17 When this became known to all residents of Ephesus, both Jews and
Greeks, everyone was awestruck; and the name of the Lord Jesus was

19:12 handkerchiefs or aprons: Paul likely wore these when he worked as a tentmaker, one around his head and the other around his waist.

---

[a] Gk *brothers* [b] Or *the Christ* [c] Other ancient authorities read *of a certain Tyrannus, from eleven o'clock in the morning to four in the afternoon*

praised. [18]Also many of those who became believers confessed and
disclosed their practices. [19]A number of those who practiced magic
collected their books and burned them publicly; when the value of
these books[a] was calculated, it was found to come to fifty thousand
silver coins. [20]So the word of the Lord grew mightily and prevailed.

19:19 books . . . fifty thousand silver coins: Each coin was worth about one day's wage. The value of the books was in the powers they supposedly offered.

The Riot in Ephesus

21 Now after these things had been accomplished, Paul resolved
in the Spirit to go through Macedonia and Achaia, and then to go on
to Jerusalem. He said, "After I have gone there, I must also see Rome."
[22]So he sent two of his helpers, Timothy and Erastus, to Macedonia,
while he himself stayed for some time longer in Asia.

23 About that time no little disturbance broke out concerning
the Way. [24]A man named Demetrius, a silversmith who made silver
shrines of Artemis, brought no little business to the artisans. [25]These
he gathered together, with the workers of the same trade, and said,
"Men, you know that we get our wealth from this business. [26]You also
see and hear that not only in Ephesus but in almost the whole of Asia
this Paul has persuaded and drawn away a considerable number of
people by saying that gods made with hands are not gods. [27]And there
is danger not only that this trade of ours may come into disrepute but
also that the temple of the great goddess Artemis will be scorned, and
she will be deprived of her majesty that brought all Asia and the world
to worship her."

19:24 Demetrius, a silversmith . . . Artemis: Demetrius was probably a leader in the guild of silversmiths. Artemis is the Greek name for the goddess Diana. The temple to Artemis in Ephesus was famous, and many came to visit it and to purchase the wares of the silversmiths.

28 When they heard this, they were enraged and shouted, "Great
is Artemis of the Ephesians!" [29]The city was filled with the confusion;
and people[b] rushed together to the theater, dragging with them Gaius
and Aristarchus, Macedonians who were Paul's travel companions.
[30]Paul wished to go into the crowd, but the disciples would not let
him; [31]even some officials of the province of Asia,[c] who were friendly
to him, sent him a message urging him not to venture into the theater.
[32]Meanwhile, some were shouting one thing, some another; for the
assembly was in confusion, and most of them did not know why they
had come together. [33]Some of the crowd gave instructions to Alexander, whom the Jews had pushed forward. And Alexander motioned
for silence and tried to make a defense before the people. [34]But when
they recognized that he was a Jew, for about two hours all of them
shouted in unison, "Great is Artemis of the Ephesians!" [35]But when
the town clerk had quieted the crowd, he said, "Citizens of Ephesus,
who is there that does not know that the city of the Ephesians is the
temple keeper of the great Artemis and of the statue that fell from
heaven?[d] [36]Since these things cannot be denied, you ought to be quiet

19:33 Alexander: He was apparently a leader among the Jews who believed in Jesus.

19:35 statue that fell from heaven?: Some believed that the statue of Artemis fell into the temple from the sky.

---

[a] Gk *them* [b] Gk *they* [c] Gk *some of the Asiarchs* [d] Meaning of Gk uncertain

and do nothing rash. 37You have brought these men here who are neither temple robbers nor blasphemers of our[a] goddess. 38If therefore Demetrius and the artisans with him have a complaint against anyone, the courts are open, and there are proconsuls; let them bring charges there against one another. 39If there is anything further[b] you want to know, it must be settled in the regular assembly. 40For we are in danger of being charged with rioting today, since there is no cause that we can give to justify this commotion." 41When he had said this, he dismissed the assembly.

19:40 charged with rioting: Causing a riot was a serious crime. Such a charge could have brought punishment by Roman authorities and occupation of the area by Roman soldiers.

Paul Goes to Macedonia and Greece

20 After the uproar had ceased, Paul sent for the disciples; and after encouraging them and saying farewell, he left for Macedonia. 2When he had gone through those regions and had given the believers[c] much encouragement, he came to Greece, 3where he stayed for three months. He was about to set sail for Syria when a plot was made against him by the Jews, and so he decided to return through Macedonia. 4He was accompanied by Sopater son of Pyrrhus from Beroea, by Aristarchus and Secundus from Thessalonica, by Gaius from Derbe, and by Timothy, as well as by Tychicus and Trophimus from Asia. 5They went ahead and were waiting for us in Troas; 6but we sailed from Philippi after the days of Unleavened Bread, and in five days we joined them in Troas, where we stayed for seven days.

20:3-4 return through Macedonia: The men listed accompany Paul back to Jerusalem with money collected for those who were poor (see 2 Cor 8:1-2).

Paul's Farewell Visit to Troas

7 On the first day of the week, when we met to break bread, Paul was holding a discussion with them; since he intended to leave the next day, he continued speaking until midnight. 8There were many lamps in the room upstairs where we were meeting. 9A young man named Eutychus, who was sitting in the window, began to sink off into a deep sleep while Paul talked still longer. Overcome by sleep, he fell to the ground three floors below and was picked up dead. 10But Paul went down, and bending over him took him in his arms, and said, "Do not be alarmed, for his life is in him." 11Then Paul went upstairs, and after he had broken bread and eaten, he continued to converse with them until dawn; then he left. 12Meanwhile they had taken the boy away alive and were not a little comforted.

20:10 his life is in him: As Peter raised Tabitha (9:40), now Paul raises Eutychus.

The Voyage from Troas to Miletus

13 We went ahead to the ship and set sail for Assos, intending to take Paul on board there; for he had made this arrangement, intending to go by land himself. 14When he met us in Assos, we took him on board and went to Mitylene. 15We sailed from there, and on the

20:14-16 eager to be in Jerusalem: Paul is anxious to get to Jerusalem, perhaps because he knows the money they are bringing is badly needed. Trace Paul's journey from Macedonia to Jerusalem on Map 14, p. 2111.

20:15 Miletus: This port city was about thirty miles from Ephesus.

[a] Other ancient authorities read *your* [b] Other ancient authorities read *about other matters*
[c] Gk *given them*

following day we arrived opposite Chios. The next day we touched
at Samos, and[a] the day after that we came to Miletus. 16 For Paul had
decided to sail past Ephesus, so that he might not have to spend time
in Asia; he was eager to be in Jerusalem, if possible, on the day of Pentecost.

Paul Speaks to the Ephesian Elders

17 From Miletus he sent a message to Ephesus, asking the elders of the church to meet him. 18 When they came to him, he said
to them:
"You yourselves know how I lived among you the entire time from
the first day that I set foot in Asia, 19 serving the Lord with all humility
and with tears, enduring the trials that came to me through the plots
of the Jews. 20 I did not shrink from doing anything helpful, proclaiming the message to you and teaching you publicly and from house
to house, 21 as I testified to both Jews and Greeks about repentance
toward God and faith toward our Lord Jesus. 22 And now, as a captive to the Spirit,[b] I am on my way to Jerusalem, not knowing what
will happen to me there, 23 except that the Holy Spirit testifies to me
in every city that imprisonment and persecutions are waiting for me.
24 But I do not count my life of any value to myself, if only I may finish
my course and the ministry that I received from the Lord Jesus, to testify to the good news of God's grace.
25 "And now I know that none of you, among whom I have gone
about proclaiming the kingdom, will ever see my face again. 26 Therefore I declare to you this day that I am not responsible for the blood
of any of you, 27 for I did not shrink from declaring to you the whole
purpose of God. 28 Keep watch over yourselves and over all the flock,
of which the Holy Spirit has made you overseers, to shepherd the
church of God[c] that he obtained with the blood of his own Son.[d] 29 I
know that after I have gone, savage wolves will come in among you,
not sparing the flock. 30 Some even from your own group will come
distorting the truth in order to entice the disciples to follow them.
31 Therefore be alert, remembering that for three years I did not cease
night or day to warn everyone with tears. 32 And now I commend you
to God and to the message of his grace, a message that is able to build
you up and to give you the inheritance among all who are sanctified.
33 I coveted no one's silver or gold or clothing. 34 You know for yourselves that I worked with my own hands to support myself and my
companions. 35 In all this I have given you an example that by such
work we must support the weak, remembering the words of the Lord
Jesus, for he himself said, 'It is more blessed to give than to receive.' "

[a] Other ancient authorities add *after remaining at Trogyllium* [b] Or *And now, bound in the spirit* [c] Other ancient authorities read *of the Lord* [d] Or *with his own blood;* Gk *with the blood of his Own*

20:17 elders of the church: Leaders in the church were selected by election or appointment. They also were called overseers (20:28).

20:22-23 captive to the Spirit . . . imprisonment and persecutions are waiting: Paul feels compelled by the Spirit to go to Jerusalem, even though he believes that imprisonment awaits him there.

What is the "theology of the cross"? Lutherans teach that discipleship—following Jesus—often calls a person to make a sacrifice or "bear a cross," especially for the sake of others. Paul did this for the sake of the believers in the early church. Some teach that coming to faith brings success, fulfillment, wealth, and other rewards. Martin Luther called this the "theology of glory" and warned that trusting such a message leads to disappointment and despair when success and wealth do not come. The "theology of the cross" calls us to follow Jesus, to be "little Christs" to our neighbors in need, and to be ready to bear a cross as we live out our faith life. *Acts 20:22-23*

When have you been a "little Christ" to a person in need?

20:34 support myself: Paul often worked as a tentmaker as he traveled and taught (18:3). Tents in Paul's day were made of leather or cloth.

36 When he had finished speaking, he knelt down with them all
and prayed. [37]There was much weeping among them all; they embraced Paul and kissed him, [38]grieving especially because of what he
had said, that they would not see him again. Then they brought him
to the ship.

Paul's Journey to Jerusalem

21 When we had parted from them and set sail, we came by a
straight course to Cos, and the next day to Rhodes, and from
there to Patara.[a] [2]When we found a ship bound for Phoenicia, we
went on board and set sail. [3]We came in sight of Cyprus; and leaving
it on our left, we sailed to Syria and landed at Tyre, because the ship
was to unload its cargo there. [4]We looked up the disciples and stayed
there for seven days. Through the Spirit they told Paul not to go on to
Jerusalem. [5]When our days there were ended, we left and proceeded
on our journey; and all of them, with wives and children, escorted us
outside the city. There we knelt down on the beach and prayed [6]and
said farewell to one another. Then we went on board the ship, and
they returned home.

21:7-8 Tyre...Ptolemais...Caesarea: These cities were ports along the coast of Judea (see Map 15, p. 2112).

21:9 daughters... gift of prophesy: These four women may have been set apart for the work of preaching the gospel. Prophecy (see note on 15:32) is one of the gifts of the Spirit (1 Cor 12:8-10).

7 When we had finished[b] the voyage from Tyre, we arrived at Ptolemais; and we greeted the believers[c] and stayed with them for one
day. [8]The next day we left and came to Caesarea; and we went into
the house of Philip the evangelist, one of the seven, and stayed with
him. [9]He had four unmarried daughters[d] who had the gift of prophecy. [10]While we were staying there for several days, a prophet named
Agabus came down from Judea. [11]He came to us and took Paul's belt,
bound his own feet and hands with it, and said, "Thus says the Holy
Spirit, 'This is the way the Jews in Jerusalem will bind the man who
owns this belt and will hand him over to the Gentiles.'" [12]When we
heard this, we and the people there urged him not to go up to Jerusalem. [13]Then Paul answered, "What are you doing, weeping and
breaking my heart? For I am ready not only to be bound but even to
die in Jerusalem for the name of the Lord Jesus." [14]Since he would
not be persuaded, we remained silent except to say, "The Lord's will
be done."

15 After these days we got ready and started to go up to Jerusalem. [16]Some of the disciples from Caesarea also came along and
brought us to the house of Mnason of Cyprus, an early disciple, with
whom we were to stay.

Paul Visits James at Jerusalem

17 When we arrived in Jerusalem, the brothers welcomed us
warmly. [18]The next day Paul went with us to visit James; and all the

[a] Other ancient authorities add *and Myra* [b] Or *continued* [c] Gk *brothers* [d] Gk *four daughters, virgins,*

elders were present. 19 After greeting them, he related one by one the
things that God had done among the Gentiles through his ministry.
20 When they heard it, they praised God. Then they said to him, "You
see, brother, how many thousands of believers there are among the
Jews, and they are all zealous for the law. 21 They have been told about
you that you teach all the Jews living among the Gentiles to forsake
Moses, and that you tell them not to circumcise their children or observe the customs. 22 What then is to be done? They will certainly
hear that you have come. 23 So do what we tell you. We have four men
who are under a vow. 24 Join these men, go through the rite of purification with them, and pay for the shaving of their heads. Thus all
will know that there is nothing in what they have been told about
you, but that you yourself observe and guard the law. 25 But as for the
Gentiles who have become believers, we have sent a letter with our
judgment that they should abstain from what has been sacrificed to
idols and from blood and from what is strangled[a] and from fornication." 26 Then Paul took the men, and the next day, having purified
himself, he entered the temple with them, making public the completion of the days of purification when the sacrifice would be made
for each of them.

Paul Arrested in the Temple

27 When the seven days were almost completed, the Jews from
Asia, who had seen him in the temple, stirred up the whole crowd.
They seized him, 28 shouting, "Fellow Israelites, help! This is the man
who is teaching everyone everywhere against our people, our law, and
this place; more than that, he has actually brought Greeks into the
temple and has defiled this holy place." 29 For they had previously seen
Trophimus the Ephesian with him in the city, and they supposed that
Paul had brought him into the temple. 30 Then all the city was aroused,
and the people rushed together. They seized Paul and dragged him
out of the temple, and immediately the doors were shut. 31 While they
were trying to kill him, word came to the tribune of the cohort that all
Jerusalem was in an uproar. 32 Immediately he took soldiers and centurions and ran down to them. When they saw the tribune and the
soldiers, they stopped beating Paul. 33 Then the tribune came, arrested
him, and ordered him to be bound with two chains; he inquired who
he was and what he had done. 34 Some in the crowd shouted one thing,
some another; and as he could not learn the facts because of the uproar, he ordered him to be brought into the barracks. 35 When Paul[b]
came to the steps, the violence of the mob was so great that he had to
be carried by the soldiers. 36 The crowd that followed kept shouting,
"Away with him!"

21:24 rite of purification: Jews who had become ritually unclean (as Paul had by associating with Gentiles) needed to go through a ritual to be made clean or pure again. Paul is accused of abandoning Jewish law (21:21). Here the writer makes sure that readers view Paul as a faithful Jew by telling how he goes beyond what is required by Jewish law.

21:28-29 brought Greeks into the temple: There is no evidence that Paul violates the temple law prohibiting Gentiles from entering the temple, except the area called the Court of the Gentiles. Breaking this rule could result in the death of the Gentile. See the diagrams depicting The Temple in Paul's day, pp. 1696-1697.

21:34 barracks: The Fortress of Antonia in Jerusalem was near the temple. The barracks were the living quarters for the soldiers in the fortress. See Map 13, p. 2110, for the location of the Antonia Fortress.

---

[a] Other ancient authorities lack *and from what is strangled* [b] Gk *he*

Paul Defends Himself

37 Just as Paul was about to be brought into the barracks, he said
to the tribune, "May I say something to you?" The tribune[a] replied,
"Do you know Greek? 38 Then you are not the Egyptian who recently
stirred up a revolt and led the four thousand assassins out into the wilderness?" 39 Paul replied, "I am a Jew, from Tarsus in Cilicia, a citizen
of an important city; I beg you, let me speak to the people." 40 When
he had given him permission, Paul stood on the steps and motioned
to the people for silence; and when there was a great hush, he addressed them in the Hebrew[b] language, saying:

22 "Brothers and fathers, listen to the defense that I now make
before you."

2 When they heard him addressing them in Hebrew,[b] they became even more quiet. Then he said:

3 "I am a Jew, born in Tarsus in Cilicia, but brought up in this
city at the feet of Gamaliel, educated strictly according to our ancestral law, being zealous for God, just as all of you are today. 4 I persecuted this Way up to the point of death by binding both men and
women and putting them in prison, 5 as the high priest and the whole
council of elders can testify about me. From them I also received letters to the brothers in Damascus, and I went there in order to bind
those who were there and to bring them back to Jerusalem for punishment.

Paul Tells of His Conversion

6 "While I was on my way and approaching Damascus, about
noon a great light from heaven suddenly shone about me. 7 I fell to the
ground and heard a voice saying to me, 'Saul, Saul, why are you persecuting me?' 8 I answered, 'Who are you, Lord?' Then he said to me,
'I am Jesus of Nazareth[c] whom you are persecuting.' 9 Now those who
were with me saw the light but did not hear the voice of the one who
was speaking to me. 10 I asked, 'What am I to do, Lord?' The Lord said
to me, 'Get up and go to Damascus; there you will be told everything
that has been assigned to you to do.' 11 Since I could not see because
of the brightness of that light, those who were with me took my hand
and led me to Damascus.

12 "A certain Ananias, who was a devout man according to the
law and well spoken of by all the Jews living there, 13 came to me; and
standing beside me, he said, 'Brother Saul, regain your sight!' In that
very hour I regained my sight and saw him. 14 Then he said, 'The God
of our ancestors has chosen you to know his will, to see the Righteous
One and to hear his own voice; 15 for you will be his witness to all the
world of what you have seen and heard. 16 And now why do you de-

21:39 I am a Jew: Paul both claims to be a Jew and criticizes the Jews (see 25:8-11).

22:2-3 addressing them in Hebrew: The writer wants to show how faithful Paul is to his Jewish faith, including speaking the language of the Jews. Acts 22:3 is like a resumé, listing notable qualifications that identify Paul as a highly respected Jewish leader.

22:3-21 I am a Jew: In this speech, Paul does not follow the usual pattern of explanation, proclamation of the gospel, and call to repentance. Rather, he makes a personal appeal, telling about his life and coming to faith in Jesus Christ.

---

[a] Gk *He* [b] That is, *Aramaic* [c] Gk *the Nazorean*

lay? Get up, be baptized, and have your sins washed away, calling on his name.'

Paul Sent to the Gentiles

17 "After I had returned to Jerusalem and while I was praying in the temple, I fell into a trance [18]and saw Jesus[a] saying to me, 'Hurry and get out of Jerusalem quickly, because they will not accept your testimony about me.' [19]And I said, 'Lord, they themselves know that in every synagogue I imprisoned and beat those who believed in you. [20]And while the blood of your witness Stephen was shed, I myself was standing by, approving and keeping the coats of those who killed him.' [21]Then he said to me, 'Go, for I will send you far away to the Gentiles.'"

Paul and the Roman Tribune

22 Up to this point they listened to him, but then they shouted, "Away with such a fellow from the earth! For he should not be allowed to live." [23]And while they were shouting, throwing off their cloaks, and tossing dust into the air, [24]the tribune directed that he was to be brought into the barracks, and ordered him to be examined by flogging, to find out the reason for this outcry against him. [25]But when they had tied him up with thongs,[b] Paul said to the centurion who was standing by, "Is it legal for you to flog a Roman citizen who is uncondemned?" [26]When the centurion heard that, he went to the tribune and said to him, "What are you about to do? This man is a Roman citizen." [27]The tribune came and asked Paul,[a] "Tell me, are you a Roman citizen?" And he said, "Yes." [28]The tribune answered, "It cost me a large sum of money to get my citizenship." Paul said, "But I was born a citizen." [29]Immediately those who were about to examine him drew back from him; and the tribune also was afraid, for he realized that Paul was a Roman citizen and that he had bound him.

22:24 examined by flogging: It was customary to flog a prisoner to get information or a confession. Flogging involved beating the prisoner with a braided whip, which often had pieces of bone or metal attached to it.

22:28 born a citizen: How Paul became a Roman citizen is not known. His father may have purchased citizenship (see note on 16:37).

Paul before the Council

30 Since he wanted to find out what Paul[c] was being accused of by the Jews, the next day he released him and ordered the chief priests and the entire council to meet. He brought Paul down and had him stand before them.

23 While Paul was looking intently at the council he said, "Brothers,[d] up to this day I have lived my life with a clear conscience before God." [2]Then the high priest Ananias ordered those standing near him to strike him on the mouth. [3]At this Paul said to him, "God will strike you, you whitewashed wall! Are you sitting there to judge me according to the law, and yet in violation of the law

23:3 whitewashed wall!: The phrase indicates a hypocrite, someone who appears good on the outside, but really isn't.

[a] Gk *him* [b] Or *up for the lashes* [c] Gk *he* [d] Gk *Men, brothers*

23:5 I did not realize...he was high priest: Paul may be using irony, indicating that a real high priest would not order someone to be struck.

23:6 Sadducees...Pharisees: These were the two main parties among the ruling Jews. Paul knows how to get them arguing by bringing up the resurrection, which the Pharisees accepted but the Sadducees did not. Paul, himself a Pharisee (26:5), quickly gets many of the Pharisees on his side (23:9-10).

23:12 bound themselves by an oath: These individuals were likely Zealots, an extremist group of that day. They later led the revolt against Rome.

you order me to be struck?" 4 Those standing nearby said, "Do you
dare to insult God's high priest?" 5 And Paul said, "I did not realize,
brothers, that he was high priest; for it is written, 'You shall not speak
evil of a leader of your people.'"

6 When Paul noticed that some were Sadducees and others were
Pharisees, he called out in the council, "Brothers, I am a Pharisee, a
son of Pharisees. I am on trial concerning the hope of the resurrection[a] of the dead." 7 When he said this, a dissension began between the
Pharisees and the Sadducees, and the assembly was divided. 8 (The
Sadducees say that there is no resurrection, or angel, or spirit; but
the Pharisees acknowledge all three.) 9 Then a great clamor arose, and
certain scribes of the Pharisees' group stood up and contended, "We
find nothing wrong with this man. What if a spirit or an angel has
spoken to him?" 10 When the dissension became violent, the tribune,
fearing that they would tear Paul to pieces, ordered the soldiers to go
down, take him by force, and bring him into the barracks.

11 That night the Lord stood near him and said, "Keep up your
courage! For just as you have testified for me in Jerusalem, so you
must bear witness also in Rome."

The Plot to Kill Paul

12 In the morning the Jews joined in a conspiracy and bound
themselves by an oath neither to eat nor drink until they had killed
Paul. 13 There were more than forty who joined in this conspiracy.
14 They went to the chief priests and elders and said, "We have strictly
bound ourselves by an oath to taste no food until we have killed Paul.
15 Now then, you and the council must notify the tribune to bring him
down to you, on the pretext that you want to make a more thorough
examination of his case. And we are ready to do away with him before
he arrives."

16 Now the son of Paul's sister heard about the ambush; so he
went and gained entrance to the barracks and told Paul. 17 Paul called
one of the centurions and said, "Take this young man to the tribune,
for he has something to report to him." 18 So he took him, brought him
to the tribune, and said, "The prisoner Paul called me and asked me
to bring this young man to you; he has something to tell you." 19 The
tribune took him by the hand, drew him aside privately, and asked,
"What is it that you have to report to me?" 20 He answered, "The Jews
have agreed to ask you to bring Paul down to the council tomorrow,
as though they were going to inquire more thoroughly into his case.
21 But do not be persuaded by them, for more than forty of their men
are lying in ambush for him. They have bound themselves by an oath
neither to eat nor drink until they kill him. They are ready now and are

[a] Gk *concerning hope and resurrection*

waiting for your consent." 22So the tribune dismissed the young man,
ordering him, "Tell no one that you have informed me of this."

Paul Sent to Felix the Governor

23 Then he summoned two of the centurions and said, "Get
ready to leave by nine o'clock tonight for Caesarea with two hundred
soldiers, seventy horsemen, and two hundred spearmen. 24Also provide mounts for Paul to ride, and take him safely to Felix the governor." 25He wrote a letter to this effect:
26 "Claudius Lysias to his Excellency the governor Felix, greetings. 27This man was seized by the Jews and was about to be killed by
them, but when I had learned that he was a Roman citizen, I came
with the guard and rescued him. 28Since I wanted to know the charge
for which they accused him, I had him brought to their council. 29I
found that he was accused concerning questions of their law, but was
charged with nothing deserving death or imprisonment. 30When I
was informed that there would be a plot against the man, I sent him to
you at once, ordering his accusers also to state before you what they
have against him.[a]"
31 So the soldiers, according to their instructions, took Paul and
brought him during the night to Antipatris. 32The next day they let
the horsemen go on with him, while they returned to the barracks.
33When they came to Caesarea and delivered the letter to the governor, they presented Paul also before him. 34On reading the letter, he
asked what province he belonged to, and when he learned that he was
from Cilicia, 35he said, "I will give you a hearing when your accusers arrive." Then he ordered that he be kept under guard in Herod's
headquarters.[b]

23:23-24 soldiers...horsemen...spearmen: The "tribune"—a Roman official—wants to make sure that Paul will be safe because he is a Roman citizen. Paul is sent out at night, with 470 armed men.

23:31 Antipatris: This Roman military base was named after the father of Herod the Great. It was located between Samaria and Judea, about thirty miles from Jerusalem.

Paul before Felix at Caesarea

24 Five days later the high priest Ananias came down with
some elders and an attorney, a certain Tertullus, and they
reported their case against Paul to the governor. 2When Paul[c] had
been summoned, Tertullus began to accuse him, saying:
"Your Excellency,[d] because of you we have long enjoyed peace,
and reforms have been made for this people because of your fore-
sight. 3We welcome this in every way and everywhere with utmost
gratitude. 4But, to detain you no further, I beg you to hear us briefly
with your customary graciousness. 5We have, in fact, found this man a
pestilent fellow, an agitator among all the Jews throughout the world,
and a ringleader of the sect of the Nazarenes.[e] 6He even tried to profane the temple, and so we seized him.[f] 8By examining him yourself

24:1 Ananias: The fact that the high priest travels to oversee the trial shows how important it is to the Jewish leaders.

---

[a] Other ancient authorities add *Farewell* [b] Gk *praetorium* [c] Gk *he* [d] Gk lacks *Your Excellency*
[e] Gk *Nazoreans* [f] Other ancient authorities add *and we would have judged him according to our law. 7But the chief captain Lysias came and with great violence took him out of our hands, 8commanding his accusers to come before you.*

you will be able to learn from him concerning everything of which we accuse him."

9 The Jews also joined in the charge by asserting that all this was true.

Paul's Defense before Felix

10 When the governor motioned to him to speak, Paul replied:

"I cheerfully make my defense, knowing that for many years you have been a judge over this nation. [11]As you can find out, it is not more than twelve days since I went up to worship in Jerusalem. [12]They did not find me disputing with anyone in the temple or stirring up a crowd either in the synagogues or throughout the city. [13]Neither can they prove to you the charge that they now bring against me. [14]But this I admit to you, that according to the Way, which they call a sect, I worship the God of our ancestors, believing everything laid down according to the law or written in the prophets. [15]I have a hope in God—a hope that they themselves also accept—that there will be a resurrection of both[a] the righteous and the unrighteous. [16]Therefore I do my best always to have a clear conscience toward God and all people. [17]Now after some years I came to bring alms to my nation and to offer sacrifices. [18]While I was doing this, they found me in the temple, completing the rite of purification, without any crowd or disturbance. [19]But there were some Jews from Asia—they ought to be here before you to make an accusation, if they have anything against me. [20]Or let these men here tell what crime they had found when I stood before the council, [21]unless it was this one sentence that I called out while standing before them, 'It is about the resurrection of the dead that I am on trial before you today.'"

24:14 the Way . . . God of our ancestors: Paul admits to being a Jew who believes in Jesus Christ. Believing Jews are called the "sect of the Nazarenes" in 24:5.

22 But Felix, who was rather well informed about the Way, adjourned the hearing with the comment, "When Lysias the tribune comes down, I will decide your case." [23]Then he ordered the centurion to keep him in custody, but to let him have some liberty and not to prevent any of his friends from taking care of his needs.

24:22 well informed about the Way: This trial is not the first time the governor, Felix, has dealt with the growing Christian community. See the note on 9:2 (the Way).

Paul Held in Custody

24 Some days later when Felix came with his wife Drusilla, who was Jewish, he sent for Paul and heard him speak concerning faith in Christ Jesus. [25]And as he discussed justice, self-control, and the coming judgment, Felix became frightened and said, "Go away for the present; when I have an opportunity, I will send for you." [26]At the same time he hoped that money would be given him by Paul, and for that reason he used to send for him very often and converse with him.

24:26 money would be given him: Felix apparently thinks Paul has money, perhaps because of the gifts he delivered to Jerusalem. In fact, Paul is unable and unwilling to offer a bribe.

---

[a] Other ancient authorities read *of the dead, both of*

27 After two years had passed, Felix was succeeded by Porcius
Festus; and since he wanted to grant the Jews a favor, Felix left Paul
in prison.

24:27 left Paul in prison: Actually, Paul is under house arrest (24:23), probably because he is a Roman citizen and hasn't been convicted of any crime.

Paul Appeals to the Emperor

25 Three days after Festus had arrived in the province, he went
up from Caesarea to Jerusalem [2]where the chief priests and
the leaders of the Jews gave him a report against Paul. They appealed
to him [3]and requested, as a favor to them against Paul,[a] to have him
transferred to Jerusalem. They were, in fact, planning an ambush to
kill him along the way. [4]Festus replied that Paul was being kept at
Caesarea, and that he himself intended to go there shortly. [5]"So," he
said, "let those of you who have the authority come down with me,
and if there is anything wrong about the man, let them accuse him."

6 After he had stayed among them not more than eight or ten
days, he went down to Caesarea; the next day he took his seat on the
tribunal and ordered Paul to be brought. [7]When he arrived, the Jews
who had gone down from Jerusalem surrounded him, bringing many
serious charges against him, which they could not prove. [8]Paul said
in his defense, "I have in no way committed an offense against the
law of the Jews, or against the temple, or against the emperor." [9]But
Festus, wishing to do the Jews a favor, asked Paul, "Do you wish to
go up to Jerusalem and be tried there before me on these charges?"
[10]Paul said, "I am appealing to the emperor's tribunal; this is where
I should be tried. I have done no wrong to the Jews, as you very well
know. [11]Now if I am in the wrong and have committed something for
which I deserve to die, I am not trying to escape death; but if there
is nothing to their charges against me, no one can turn me over to
them. I appeal to the emperor." [12]Then Festus, after he had conferred
with his council, replied, "You have appealed to the emperor; to the
emperor you will go."

25:11 I appeal to the emperor: Roman citizens had the right to have their case heard by Caesar or his representative, the highest court in the empire. The appeal meant Paul would have to travel to Rome.

Festus Consults King Agrippa

13 After several days had passed, King Agrippa and Bernice arrived at Caesarea to welcome Festus. [14]Since they were staying there
several days, Festus laid Paul's case before the king, saying, "There is
a man here who was left in prison by Felix. [15]When I was in Jerusalem, the chief priests and the elders of the Jews informed me about
him and asked for a sentence against him. [16]I told them that it was
not the custom of the Romans to hand over anyone before the accused had met the accusers face to face and had been given an opportunity to make a defense against the charge. [17]So when they met here,
I lost no time, but on the next day took my seat on the tribunal and

[a] Gk *him*

ordered the man to be brought. 18When the accusers stood up, they
did not charge him with any of the crimes[a] that I was expecting. 19In-
stead they had certain points of disagreement with him about their
own religion and about a certain Jesus, who had died, but whom Paul
asserted to be alive. 20Since I was at a loss how to investigate these
questions, I asked whether he wished to go to Jerusalem and be tried
there on these charges.[b] 21But when Paul had appealed to be kept in
custody for the decision of his Imperial Majesty, I ordered him to be
held until I could send him to the emperor." 22Agrippa said to Festus,
"I would like to hear the man myself." "Tomorrow," he said, "you will
hear him."

Paul Brought before Agrippa

23 So on the next day Agrippa and Bernice came with great
pomp, and they entered the audience hall with the military tribunes
and the prominent men of the city. Then Festus gave the order and
Paul was brought in. 24And Festus said, "King Agrippa and all here
present with us, you see this man about whom the whole Jewish community petitioned me, both in Jerusalem and here, shouting that he
ought not to live any longer. 25But I found that he had done nothing
deserving death; and when he appealed to his Imperial Majesty, I decided to send him. 26But I have nothing definite to write to our sovereign about him. Therefore I have brought him before all of you, and
especially before you, King Agrippa, so that, after we have examined
him, I may have something to write— 27for it seems to me unreasonable to send a prisoner without indicating the charges against him."

Paul Defends Himself before Agrippa

26:1-31 defend himself: Both the previous governor, Felix (23:29), and the present governor, Festus (25:24-25), found Paul to be innocent. In this speech before King Agrippa, Paul again tells his personal story and urges Agrippa to believe in Jesus Christ (26:27-29).

26 Agrippa said to Paul, "You have permission to speak for
yourself." Then Paul stretched out his hand and began to
defend himself:

2 "I consider myself fortunate that it is before you, King Agrippa,
I am to make my defense today against all the accusations of the Jews,
3because you are especially familiar with all the customs and controversies of the Jews; therefore I beg of you to listen to me patiently.

4 "All the Jews know my way of life from my youth, a life spent
from the beginning among my own people and in Jerusalem. 5They
have known for a long time, if they are willing to testify, that I have belonged to the strictest sect of our religion and lived as a Pharisee. 6And
now I stand here on trial on account of my hope in the promise made
by God to our ancestors, 7a promise that our twelve tribes hope to
attain, as they earnestly worship day and night. It is for this hope, your
Excellency,[c] that I am accused by Jews! 8Why is it thought incredible
by any of you that God raises the dead?

---

[a] Other ancient authorities read *with anything* [b] Gk *on them* [c] Gk *O king*

9 “Indeed, I myself was convinced that I ought to do many things
against the name of Jesus of Nazareth.[a] 10 And that is what I did in Jerusalem; with authority received from the chief priests, I not only
locked up many of the saints in prison, but I also cast my vote against
them when they were being condemned to death. 11 By punishing
them often in all the synagogues I tried to force them to blaspheme;
and since I was so furiously enraged at them, I pursued them even to
foreign cities.

Paul Tells of His Conversion

12 “With this in mind, I was traveling to Damascus with the authority and commission of the chief priests, 13 when at midday along
the road, your Excellency,[b] I saw a light from heaven, brighter than the
sun, shining around me and my companions. 14 When we had all fallen
to the ground, I heard a voice saying to me in the Hebrew[c] language,
‘Saul, Saul, why are you persecuting me? It hurts you to kick against
the goads.’ 15 I asked, ‘Who are you, Lord?’ The Lord answered, ‘I am
Jesus whom you are persecuting. 16 But get up and stand on your feet;
for I have appeared to you for this purpose, to appoint you to serve
and testify to the things in which you have seen me[d] and to those in
which I will appear to you. 17 I will rescue you from your people and
from the Gentiles—to whom I am sending you 18 to open their eyes
so that they may turn from darkness to light and from the power of
Satan to God, so that they may receive forgiveness of sins and a place
among those who are sanctified by faith in me.’

Paul Tells of His Preaching

19 “After that, King Agrippa, I was not disobedient to the heavenly vision, 20 but declared first to those in Damascus, then in Jerusalem and throughout the countryside of Judea, and also to the Gentiles,
that they should repent and turn to God and do deeds consistent with
repentance. 21 For this reason the Jews seized me in the temple and
tried to kill me. 22 To this day I have had help from God, and so I stand
here, testifying to both small and great, saying nothing but what the
prophets and Moses said would take place: 23 that the Messiah[e] must
suffer, and that, by being the first to rise from the dead, he would proclaim light both to our people and to the Gentiles.”

Paul Appeals to Agrippa to Believe

24 While he was making this defense, Festus exclaimed, “You are
out of your mind, Paul! Too much learning is driving you insane!”
25 But Paul said, “I am not out of my mind, most excellent Festus, but

---

[a] Gk *the Nazorean* [b] Gk *O king* [c] That is, *Aramaic* [d] Other ancient authorities read *the things that you have seen* [e] Or *the Christ*

I am speaking the sober truth. [26]Indeed the king knows about these things, and to him I speak freely; for I am certain that none of these things has escaped his notice, for this was not done in a corner. [27]King Agrippa, do you believe the prophets? I know that you believe." [28]Agrippa said to Paul, "Are you so quickly persuading me to become a Christian?"[a] [29]Paul replied, "Whether quickly or not, I pray to God that not only you but also all who are listening to me today might become such as I am—except for these chains."

30 Then the king got up, and with him the governor and Bernice and those who had been seated with them; [31]and as they were leaving, they said to one another, "This man is doing nothing to deserve death or imprisonment." [32]Agrippa said to Festus, "This man could have been set free if he had not appealed to the emperor."

26:32 could have been set free: Paul's defense is effective. Neither Festus nor Agrippa finds him guilty of any of the charges against him.

Paul Sails for Rome

27:1-44 sail for Italy: Paul travels by ship to Rome (see Map 14, p. 2111). Ordinarily the trip would have taken about two weeks.

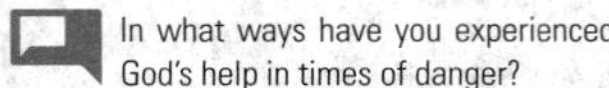
In what ways have you experienced God's help in times of danger?

27 When it was decided that we were to sail for Italy, they transferred Paul and some other prisoners to a centurion of the Augustan Cohort, named Julius. [2]Embarking on a ship of Adramyttium that was about to set sail to the ports along the coast of Asia, we put to sea, accompanied by Aristarchus, a Macedonian from Thessalonica. [3]The next day we put in at Sidon; and Julius treated Paul kindly, and allowed him to go to his friends to be cared for. [4]Putting out to sea from there, we sailed under the lee of Cyprus, because the winds were against us. [5]After we had sailed across the sea that is off Cilicia and Pamphylia, we came to Myra in Lycia. [6]There the centurion found an Alexandrian ship bound for Italy and put us on board. [7]We sailed slowly for a number of days and arrived with difficulty off Cnidus, and as the wind was against us, we sailed under the lee of Crete off Salmone. [8]Sailing past it with difficulty, we came to a place called Fair Havens, near the city of Lasea.

9 Since much time had been lost and sailing was now dangerous, because even the Fast had already gone by, Paul advised them, [10]saying, "Sirs, I can see that the voyage will be with danger and much heavy loss, not only of the cargo and the ship, but also of our lives." [11]But the centurion paid more attention to the pilot and to the owner of the ship than to what Paul said. [12]Since the harbor was not suitable for spending the winter, the majority was in favor of putting to sea from there, on the chance that somehow they could reach Phoenix, where they could spend the winter. It was a harbor of Crete, facing southwest and northwest.

The Storm at Sea

13 When a moderate south wind began to blow, they thought they could achieve their purpose; so they weighed anchor and began

---

[a] Or *Quickly you will persuade me to play the Christian*

to sail past Crete, close to the shore. [14]But soon a violent wind, called
the northeaster, rushed down from Crete.[a] [15]Since the ship was caught
and could not be turned head-on into the wind, we gave way to it and
were driven. [16]By running under the lee of a small island called Cauda[b]
we were scarcely able to get the ship's boat under control. [17]After hoisting it up they took measures[c] to undergird the ship; then, fearing that
they would run on the Syrtis, they lowered the sea anchor and so were
driven. [18]We were being pounded by the storm so violently that on
the next day they began to throw the cargo overboard, [19]and on the
third day with their own hands they threw the ship's tackle overboard.
[20]When neither sun nor stars appeared for many days, and no small
tempest raged, all hope of our being saved was at last abandoned.

21 Since they had been without food for a long time, Paul then
stood up among them and said, "Men, you should have listened to me
and not have set sail from Crete and thereby avoided this damage and
loss. [22]I urge you now to keep up your courage, for there will be no
loss of life among you, but only of the ship. [23]For last night there stood
by me an angel of the God to whom I belong and whom I worship,
[24]and he said, 'Do not be afraid, Paul; you must stand before the emperor; and indeed, God has granted safety to all those who are sailing
with you.' [25]So keep up your courage, men, for I have faith in God that
it will be exactly as I have been told. [26]But we will have to run aground
on some island."

27 When the fourteenth night had come, as we were drifting
across the sea of Adria, about midnight the sailors suspected that they
were nearing land. [28]So they took soundings and found twenty fathoms; a little farther on they took soundings again and found fifteen
fathoms. [29]Fearing that we might run on the rocks, they let down four
anchors from the stern and prayed for day to come. [30]But when the
sailors tried to escape from the ship and had lowered the boat into the
sea, on the pretext of putting out anchors from the bow, [31]Paul said to
the centurion and the soldiers, "Unless these men stay in the ship, you
cannot be saved." [32]Then the soldiers cut away the ropes of the boat
and set it adrift.

33 Just before daybreak, Paul urged all of them to take some food,
saying, "Today is the fourteenth day that you have been in suspense
and remaining without food, having eaten nothing. [34]Therefore I urge
you to take some food, for it will help you survive; for none of you
will lose a hair from your heads." [35]After he had said this, he took
bread; and giving thanks to God in the presence of all, he broke it and
began to eat. [36]Then all of them were encouraged and took food for
themselves. [37](We were in all two hundred seventy-six[d] persons in the

---

[a] Gk *it* [b] Other ancient authorities read *Clauda* [c] Gk *helps* [d] Other ancient authorities read *seventy-six*; others, *about seventy-six*

ship.) 38 After they had satisfied their hunger, they lightened the ship
by throwing the wheat into the sea.

The Shipwreck

39 In the morning they did not recognize the land, but they
noticed a bay with a beach, on which they planned to run the ship
ashore, if they could. 40 So they cast off the anchors and left them in
the sea. At the same time they loosened the ropes that tied the steer-
ing-oars; then hoisting the foresail to the wind, they made for the
beach. 41 But striking a reef,[a] they ran the ship aground; the bow stuck
and remained immovable, but the stern was being broken up by the
force of the waves. 42 The soldiers' plan was to kill the prisoners, so that
none might swim away and escape; 43 but the centurion, wishing to
save Paul, kept them from carrying out their plan. He ordered those
who could swim to jump overboard first and make for the land, 44 and
the rest to follow, some on planks and others on pieces of the ship.
And so it was that all were brought safely to land.

27:42 The soldiers' plan was to kill the prisoners: The soldiers and prisoners were shipwrecked near an unfamiliar beach. The soldiers would have been held responsible if the prisoners had escaped.

Paul on the Island of Malta

28 After we had reached safety, we then learned that the island
was called Malta. 2 The natives showed us unusual kindness. Since it had begun to rain and was cold, they kindled a fire and
welcomed all of us around it. 3 Paul had gathered a bundle of brushwood and was putting it on the fire, when a viper, driven out by the
heat, fastened itself on his hand. 4 When the natives saw the creature
hanging from his hand, they said to one another, "This man must be
a murderer; though he has escaped from the sea, justice has not allowed him to live." 5 He, however, shook off the creature into the fire
and suffered no harm. 6 They were expecting him to swell up or drop
dead, but after they had waited a long time and saw that nothing unusual had happened to him, they changed their minds and began to
say that he was a god.

28:3-4 viper…murderer: The islanders apparently knew the snake to be poisonous and assumed it bit Paul to bring justice because he was guilty.

7 Now in the neighborhood of that place were lands belonging to
the leading man of the island, named Publius, who received us and entertained us hospitably for three days. 8 It so happened that the father
of Publius lay sick in bed with fever and dysentery. Paul visited him
and cured him by praying and putting his hands on him. 9 After this
happened, the rest of the people on the island who had diseases also
came and were cured. 10 They bestowed many honors on us, and when
we were about to sail, they put on board all the provisions we needed.

Paul Arrives at Rome

11 Three months later we set sail on a ship that had wintered at
the island, an Alexandrian ship with the Twin Brothers as its figure-

28:11 Three months later: They had to wait until the sailing season opened, in February or March.

[a] Gk *place of two seas*

head. 12We put in at Syracuse and stayed there for three days; 13then
we weighed anchor and came to Rhegium. After one day there a south
wind sprang up, and on the second day we came to Puteoli. 14There
we found believers[a] and were invited to stay with them for seven days.
And so we came to Rome. 15The believers[a] from there, when they
heard of us, came as far as the Forum of Appius and Three Taverns to
meet us. On seeing them, Paul thanked God and took courage.
16 When we came into Rome, Paul was allowed to live by himself, with the soldier who was guarding him.

28:15 Forum of Appius...Three Taverns: These towns were forty-three and thirty-three miles from Rome. The leaders were eager to meet Paul. *Tavern* refers to any kind of shop.

28:16-17 lived by himself: Again Paul is under house arrest. He immediately makes plans to continue his preaching of the gospel, this time to Jewish leaders in Rome. His preaching has mixed results (28:24).

Paul and Jewish Leaders in Rome

17 Three days later he called together the local leaders of the
Jews. When they had assembled, he said to them, "Brothers, though
I had done nothing against our people or the customs of our ancestors, yet I was arrested in Jerusalem and handed over to the Romans.
18When they had examined me, the Romans[b] wanted to release me,
because there was no reason for the death penalty in my case. 19But
when the Jews objected, I was compelled to appeal to the emperor—
even though I had no charge to bring against my nation. 20For this
reason therefore I have asked to see you and speak with you,[c] since it
is for the sake of the hope of Israel that I am bound with this chain."
21They replied, "We have received no letters from Judea about you,
and none of the brothers coming here has reported or spoken anything evil about you. 22But we would like to hear from you what you
think, for with regard to this sect we know that everywhere it is spoken against."

Paul Preaches in Rome

23 After they had set a day to meet with him, they came to him
at his lodgings in great numbers. From morning until evening he explained the matter to them, testifying to the kingdom of God and trying to convince them about Jesus both from the law of Moses and
from the prophets. 24Some were convinced by what he had said, while
others refused to believe. 25So they disagreed with each other; and as
they were leaving, Paul made one further statement: "The Holy Spirit
was right in saying to your ancestors through the prophet Isaiah,
26 'Go to this people and say,
You will indeed listen, but never understand,
and you will indeed look, but never perceive.
27 For this people's heart has grown dull,
and their ears are hard of hearing,
and they have shut their eyes;
so that they might not look with their eyes,

[a] Gk *brothers* [b] Gk *they* [c] Or *I have asked you to see me and speak with me*

28:30-31 **two whole years:** The book of Acts ends with Paul still under house arrest. The writer does not tell what happens to Paul. Paul may have been executed in Rome, but it is more likely that he was released. Some say that Paul returned to the churches he had started in Asia. Others say he went to preach in Spain.

and listen with their ears,
and understand with their heart and turn—
and I would heal them.'
28 Let it be known to you then that this salvation of God has been sent
to the Gentiles; they will listen."[a]

30 He lived there two whole years at his own expense[b] and welcomed all who came to him, 31 proclaiming the kingdom of God and
teaching about the Lord Jesus Christ with all boldness and without
hindrance.

---

[a] Other ancient authorities add verse 29, *And when he had said these words, the Jews departed, arguing vigorously among themselves* [b] Or *in his own hired dwelling*

THE LETTERS OF PAUL

Romans to Philemon

Thirteen letters, or "epistles," in the New Testament claim to have been written by the apostle Paul. Each names Paul as author in the very first verse. *Epistle,* a formal word for *letter*, is an English word that comes from the Greek word *epistolē* (eh-pist-o-LAY).

Who was Paul?

Paul lived at the time of Jesus, but as far as we know he never met him. He was born of a Jewish family in Tarsus, in Cilicia (Acts 21:39; 22:3), in the eastern part of today's Turkey. He was likely educated in his hometown, which had a large Jewish population. Schools were commonly created so that Jewish boys could attend. Later, in Jerusalem, Paul studied under a well-known Jewish teacher of the day known as Gamaliel (Acts 22:3). Early in his career, Paul was a persecutor of the church. He refers to this several times in his letters (1 Cor 15:9; Gal 1:13, 23; Phil 3:6). But sometime in the early 30s of the first century (perhaps as early as 32 or 33 C.E.), the risen Christ appeared to him, and he became an apostle (Acts 9:1-9; Gal 1:15-17).

Paul was a missionary for much of his career, founding churches in Galatia and Ephesus in Asia Minor (parts of Turkey today), Corinth in Greece, and Philippi and Thessalonica in Macedonia (within Greece today). Most of our information on his travels and other activities comes from the book of Acts. According to that source, Paul was arrested in Jerusalem about 56 C.E. (or perhaps later), for bringing Gentile (non-Jewish) companions into the temple there (Acts 21:28-29). He was imprisoned for at least two years in Caesarea, along the Mediterranean sea coast (Acts 24:27), then was taken to Rome, where he was imprisoned for another two years (Acts 28:16-31). According to information from early Christian writers, he was executed on orders of Emperor Nero in the early part of the 60s of the first century.

Paul and his letters

Paul wrote many of the letters in the New Testament. They are extremely important for their teachings about the meaning of Christ and for their instructions on how Christians are to think of themselves and their lives in the church and the world. Not all of the thirteen letters attributed to Paul were necessarily written by him, even though they bear his name. The issue of authorship is especially important whenever a person seeks to know what Paul thought about a particular matter.

There is no doubt that Paul wrote at least seven of the thirteen. These are Romans, 1–2 Corinthians, Galatians, Philippians, 1 Thessalonians, and Philemon. Except for the last mentioned, these letters were written to congregations at cities (Rome, Corinth, Philippi, and Thessalonica) or territories (Galatia). Paul had founded all of the congregations except the one at Rome, and he wrote to them about concerns they had or issues he had heard about. The shortest of all, Philemon, was written to a friend by that name. From indications we have in the letters themselves, Paul used secretaries or scribes to help write his letters (see Rom 16:22; 1 Cor 16:21; Gal 6:11). His letters were often carried by trusted friends to their destinations (see Rom 16:1; Phil 2:25). The friends also returned from those places with news and information for Paul (see 1 Cor 16:17; 2 Cor 7:6).

The other six letters attributed to Paul may not have been written or dictated by him in a literal sense. Many scholars believe that their authors were associates of Paul who felt authorized to speak for him and who may have continued to speak and write in his name for some years after his death. This would explain why these six letters are so different from the other seven letters of Paul in vocabulary and style. It would also explain why some concepts in these six letters differ from those in the other seven, and why some major concepts found in the seven letters certainly written by Paul are missing from these six. In any case, these six letters have been included within the New Testament without any reservations regarding their status as Christian Scripture. They express teachings and ideas that the church has always found inspiring.

Of the six "disputed" letters, three (1–2 Timothy, and Titus) are called the "Pastoral Letters," or "Pastoral Epistles," because they deal with issues around leadership in congregations. These and the other three (Ephesians, Colossians, and 2 Thessalonians) are commonly thought by leading scholars to reflect situations and concerns not faced by Paul, since those things are not evident in other sources having to do with Paul (Acts and the "undisputed" letters of Paul).

The order in which the Letters of Paul appear in the New Testament is not based on when they were written. The nine addressed to churches come first (Romans—2 Thessalonians), and then come the four addressed to individuals (1 Timothy—Philemon). Within those two large groupings, the letters in each case are arranged according to length, the longest first, the shortest at the end. One exception: although Ephesians is slightly longer than Galatians, the former has been placed after Galatians. One theory is that Ephesians may have been considered a general letter and a summary of the others, so it was placed at the end of that group.

Details on the circumstances and authorship of each of the thirteen letters attributed to Paul are discussed in the introductions to each.

Romans 10:17

ROMANS

Background File

Paul is the author of Romans, a letter written to believers in Christ in the capital city of the Roman Empire. He writes from Corinth, in southern Greece, during the winter of 56–57 C.E. (see Map 14, p. 2111). He has been a missionary for twenty years and is at the height of his career. Each of his other letters is written to a congregation he founded or a person he converted. Romans is the exception.

What's the Story?

Paul is at a transition point in his ministry, preparing to do new things. He has begun many congregations in Greece, in areas of Asia that are now in Turkey, and elsewhere. He wants to make three important moves in the near future:

- Take a collection, gathered from his mainly Gentile (non-Jewish) congregations, to the mother church in Jerusalem as a sign of unity between Gentile and Jewish believers.
- Next, stop in Rome.
- Finally, go to Spain to do missionary work in the western part of the Roman Empire.

The Roman congregations are in transition too. In 49 C.E. Emperor Claudius expelled Jews, including Jewish Christians, from Rome. While all did not leave, many did. When Claudius died and they returned, Jewish Christians found a church now run by Gentile Christians, whose numbers had increased. Tensions were inevitable.

Romans is a *letter*, organized like this:

Introduction (1:1-17)
Why God needs to reveal God's righteousness (1:18—3:20)
God's righteousness revealed (3:21—5:21)
God frees us from the power of sin (6:1-23)
The Spirit ends the law as a way of salvation (7:1—8:39)

Israel's place in God's salvation plan (9:1—11:36)
Righteousness in daily Christian life (12:1—15:13)
Travel plans (15:14-33)
Letter of recommendation and greetings (16:1-27)

What's the Message?

Paul has four goals in writing this letter:

To ask the Roman congregations to help support his new missionary work in Spain.
To heal divisions between Christians who are Jewish and those who are not.
To ask for prayers for his trip to Jerusalem and, possibly, help resolving issues with Christians there.
To resolve any misunderstandings about his view of the gospel.

The theme of the letter is in 1:16-17. Paul is an apostle, a representative, of the gospel. That gospel, or good news, is God's power for salvation for people who believe. When Paul and others announce the gospel, God is present as the righteous God who is reclaiming the world from the power of sin that now controls it. Those who believe have a restored relationship with God. They are justified apart from works of the law, and freed from sin and everything else that keeps people from being less than God created them to be. The gospel is God's power of salvation for individuals, for the church, and for all of creation too.

The message of Romans would become a turning point for Martin Luther and his work as a teacher, writer, and reformer. In his *Preface to Romans* Luther writes, "This epistle is really the chief part of the New Testament, and is truly the purest gospel. . . . It is a bright light, almost sufficient to illuminate the entire Holy Scriptures" (*Martin Luther's Basic Theological Writings*, second ed., Fortress, 2005, pp. 98-99).

Salutation

1 Paul, a servant[a] of Jesus Christ, called to be an apostle, set apart for
the gospel of God, [2]which he promised beforehand through his
prophets in the holy scriptures, [3]the gospel concerning his Son, who
was descended from David according to the flesh [4]and was declared
to be Son of God with power according to the spirit[b] of holiness by
resurrection from the dead, Jesus Christ our Lord, [5]through whom
we have received grace and apostleship to bring about the obedience
of faith among all the Gentiles for the sake of his name, [6]including
yourselves who are called to belong to Jesus Christ,

[a] Gk *slave* [b] Or *Spirit*

1:1-7 To all God's beloved: Ancient letters begin with the sender's name (Paul), followed by the people to whom the letter is sent (To all . . . in Rome), and conclude with a greeting (Grace . . . and peace). In Romans, the beginning of the letter is unusually long because Paul needs to introduce himself.

1:1 Paul, a servant of Jesus Christ: A better translation for "servant" here is "slave." The emperor's slaves in Rome proudly called themselves "slaves of Caesar." Paul is proud to be a slave of Jesus Christ.

1:1 apostle: An apostle is someone sent with a message.

1:1 gospel: Paul's message is the gospel, which means "good news." It

7 To all God's beloved in Rome, who are called to be saints:
Grace to you and peace from God our Father and the Lord Jesus
Christ.

Prayer of Thanksgiving

8 First, I thank my God through Jesus Christ for all of you, because your faith is proclaimed throughout the world. 9 For God,
whom I serve with my spirit by announcing the gospel[a] of his Son,
is my witness that without ceasing I remember you always in my
prayers, 10 asking that by God's will I may somehow at last succeed
in coming to you. 11 For I am longing to see you so that I may share
with you some spiritual gift to strengthen you— 12 or rather so that
we may be mutually encouraged by each other's faith, both yours and
mine. 13 I want you to know, brothers and sisters,[b] that I have often
intended to come to you (but thus far have been prevented), in order
that I may reap some harvest among you as I have among the rest of
the Gentiles. 14 I am a debtor both to Greeks and to barbarians, both
to the wise and to the foolish 15 —hence my eagerness to proclaim the
gospel to you also who are in Rome.

The Power of the Gospel

16 For I am not ashamed of the gospel; it is the power of God for
salvation to everyone who has faith, to the Jew first and also to the
Greek. 17 For in it the righteousness of God is revealed through faith
for faith; as it is written, "The one who is righteous will live by faith."[c]

The Guilt of Humankind

18 For the wrath of God is revealed from heaven against all ungodliness and wickedness of those who by their wickedness sup-
press the truth. 19 For what can be known about God is plain to them,
because God has shown it to them. 20 Ever since the creation of the
world his eternal power and divine nature, invisible though they are,
have been understood and seen through the things he has made. So
they are without excuse; 21 for though they knew God, they did not
honor him as God or give thanks to him, but they became futile in
their thinking, and their senseless minds were darkened. 22 Claiming
to be wise, they became fools; 23 and they exchanged the glory of the
immortal God for images resembling a mortal human being or birds
or four-footed animals or reptiles.
24 Therefore God gave them up in the lusts of their hearts to impurity, to the degrading of their bodies among themselves, 25 because
they exchanged the truth about God for a lie and worshiped and
served the creature rather than the Creator, who is blessed forever!
Amen.

---

[a] Gk *my spirit in the gospel* [b] Gk *brothers* [c] Or *The one who is righteous through faith will live*

is the wonderful good news that God has acted through Jesus to forgive and save (1:16).

1:5 Gentiles: Paul has special responsibility for telling Gentiles (non-Jewish people) about Jesus.

1:8-10 I thank my God: After the salutation, Paul usually gives thanks to God for those receiving the letter.

1:13 brothers and sisters: Part of Paul's missionary strategy is to put believers into a family in which people are related by faith, not necessarily by blood.

1:16 I am not ashamed: In a world deeply concerned about honor and shame, Paul is not ashamed of God's good news.

1:16-17 salvation: Paul states the major theme of Romans—the good news of Jesus is a powerful message that saves everyone who believes.

1:17 righteousness of God: To be "righteous" means to meet all the conditions of a covenant or agreement. God has made various covenants with humanity (for example, Gen 12:1-3; Exod 19:1-9). Humanity has broken these covenants by sinning, but God refuses to end the relationship. God's righteousness comes to humanity through faith and reclaims the world from the power of sin.

1:18 wrath of God: This refers to God's righteous response to sin. It does not mean anger. Here Paul begins a section on the universal sinfulness of humanity.

Apart from Christ, what is humanity's relationship with God? All people, without exception, are sinners and have broken their relationship with God. *Evangelical Lutheran Worship* states: "We confess that we are captive to sin and cannot free ourselves" (p. 95). *Romans 1:18—3:23*

1:19-21 without excuse: God has revealed enough to all humanity that people should have honored God as God.

1:24, 26, 28 God gave them up: In response to human sin, God handed over humanity to destructive behavior that alienated people from God, themselves, and others.

1:25 served the creature: The basic sin of humanity is confusing the creation with the Creator (see Exod 32).

26 For this reason God gave them up to degrading passions.
Their women exchanged natural intercourse for unnatural, 27 and
in the same way also the men, giving up natural intercourse with
women, were consumed with passion for one another. Men committed shameless acts with men and received in their own persons the
due penalty for their error.

28 And since they did not see fit to acknowledge God, God gave
them up to a debased mind and to things that should not be done.
29 They were filled with every kind of wickedness, evil, covetousness,
malice. Full of envy, murder, strife, deceit, craftiness, they are gossips,
30 slanderers, God-haters,[a] insolent, haughty, boastful, inventors of
evil, rebellious toward parents, 31 foolish, faithless, heartless, ruthless.
32 They know God's decree, that those who practice such things deserve to die—yet they not only do them but even applaud others who
practice them.

The Righteous Judgment of God

2:1 no excuse: Paul turns the tables on anyone who has been judging the people he described in chapter 1. Those who judge are doing the very things they condemn (2:1-5).

2 Therefore you have no excuse, whoever you are, when you
judge others; for in passing judgment on another you condemn
yourself, because you, the judge, are doing the very same things.
2 You say,[b] "We know that God's judgment on those who do such
things is in accordance with truth." 3 Do you imagine, whoever you
are, that when you judge those who do such things and yet do them
yourself, you will escape the judgment of God? 4 Or do you despise
the riches of his kindness and forbearance and patience? Do you not
realize that God's kindness is meant to lead you to repentance? 5 But
by your hard and impenitent heart you are storing up wrath for yourself on the day of wrath, when God's righteous judgment will be revealed. 6 For he will repay according to each one's deeds: 7 to those
who by patiently doing good seek for glory and honor and immortality, he will give eternal life; 8 while for those who are self-seeking
and who obey not the truth but wickedness, there will be wrath and
fury. 9 There will be anguish and distress for everyone who does evil,
the Jew first and also the Greek, 10 but glory and honor and peace for
everyone who does good, the Jew first and also the Greek. 11 For God
shows no partiality.

2:12 apart from the law: "The law" is the Law of Moses. Paul allows no escape from judgment.

12 All who have sinned apart from the law will also perish apart
from the law, and all who have sinned under the law will be judged
by the law. 13 For it is not the hearers of the law who are righteous in
God's sight, but the doers of the law who will be justified. 14 When
Gentiles, who do not possess the law, do instinctively what the law
requires, these, though not having the law, are a law to themselves.
15 They show that what the law requires is written on their hearts, to

---

[a] Or *God-hated* [b] Gk lacks *You say*

which their own conscience also bears witness; and their conflicting
thoughts will accuse or perhaps excuse them [16]on the day when, according to my gospel, God, through Jesus Christ, will judge the secret
thoughts of all.

The Jews and the Law

17 But if you call yourself a Jew and rely on the law and boast of
your relation to God [18]and know his will and determine what is best
because you are instructed in the law, [19]and if you are sure that you are
a guide to the blind, a light to those who are in darkness, [20]a corrector
of the foolish, a teacher of children, having in the law the embodiment
of knowledge and truth, [21]you, then, that teach others, will you not
teach yourself? While you preach against stealing, do you steal? [22]You
that forbid adultery, do you commit adultery? You that abhor idols,
do you rob temples? [23]You that boast in the law, do you dishonor God
by breaking the law? [24]For, as it is written, "The name of God is blasphemed among the Gentiles because of you."

25 Circumcision indeed is of value if you obey the law; but if you
break the law, your circumcision has become uncircumcision. [26]So, if
those who are uncircumcised keep the requirements of the law, will
not their uncircumcision be regarded as circumcision? [27]Then those
who are physically uncircumcised but keep the law will condemn you
that have the written code and circumcision but break the law. [28]For
a person is not a Jew who is one outwardly, nor is true circumcision
something external and physical. [29]Rather, a person is a Jew who is
one inwardly, and real circumcision is a matter of the heart—it is spiritual and not literal. Such a person receives praise not from others but
from God.

3 Then what advantage has the Jew? Or what is the value of circumcision? [2]Much, in every way. For in the first place the Jews[a]
were entrusted with the oracles of God. [3]What if some were unfaithful? Will their faithlessness nullify the faithfulness of God? [4]By no
means! Although everyone is a liar, let God be proved true, as it is
written,

"So that you may be justified in your words,
and prevail in your judging."[b]

[5]But if our injustice serves to confirm the justice of God, what should
we say? That God is unjust to inflict wrath on us? (I speak in a human
way.) [6]By no means! For then how could God judge the world? [7]But
if through my falsehood God's truthfulness abounds to his glory, why
am I still being condemned as a sinner? [8]And why not say (as some
people slander us by saying that we say), "Let us do evil so that good
may come"? Their condemnation is deserved!

2:25-29 circumcision: For males, circumcision is a symbol of being part of the people of Israel. Paul redefines circumcision as fulfilling the intent of the law, which he sees as more important than being physically circumcised.

God is faithful, even when we are not (3:3-4). In what ways do you experience God's faithfulness to you, even when you are not faithful to God?

---

[a] Gk *they* [b] Gk *when you are being judged*

None Is Righteous

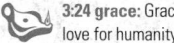

3:9 power of sin: Sin for Paul is more than individual sins. It is also a power that overtakes people's lives.

9 What then? Are we any better off?[a] No, not at all; for we have
already charged that all, both Jews and Greeks, are under the power
of sin, 10 as it is written:

"There is no one who is righteous, not even one;
11 there is no one who has understanding,
there is no one who seeks God.
12 All have turned aside, together they have become worthless;
there is no one who shows kindness,
there is not even one."
13 "Their throats are opened graves;
they use their tongues to deceive."
"The venom of vipers is under their lips."
14 "Their mouths are full of cursing and bitterness."
15 "Their feet are swift to shed blood;
16 ruin and misery are in their paths,
17 and the way of peace they have not known."
18 "There is no fear of God before their eyes."

19 Now we know that whatever the law says, it speaks to those
who are under the law, so that every mouth may be silenced, and the
whole world may be held accountable to God. 20 For "no human being will be justified in his sight" by deeds prescribed by the law, for
through the law comes the knowledge of sin.

3:20 justified: In Greek, to be "righteous" and to be "justified" are from the same word family (see also 1:17). "Justify" is language from courts of law. The prisoner stands before the judge and is guilty. But the judge declares the prisoner innocent—or "justifies" the prisoner.

Righteousness through Faith

21 But now, apart from law, the righteousness of God has been
disclosed, and is attested by the law and the prophets, 22 the righteousness of God through faith in Jesus Christ[b] for all who believe.
For there is no distinction, 23 since all have sinned and fall short of the
glory of God; 24 they are now justified by his grace as a gift, through
the redemption that is in Christ Jesus, 25 whom God put forward as a
sacrifice of atonement[c] by his blood, effective through faith. He did
this to show his righteousness, because in his divine forbearance he
had passed over the sins previously committed; 26 it was to prove at
the present time that he himself is righteous and that he justifies the
one who has faith in Jesus.[d]

27 Then what becomes of boasting? It is excluded. By what law?
By that of works? No, but by the law of faith. 28 For we hold that a per-
son is justified by faith apart from works prescribed by the law. 29 Or is
God the God of Jews only? Is he not the God of Gentiles also? Yes, of
Gentiles also, 30 since God is one; and he will justify the circumcised
on the ground of faith and the uncircumcised through that same faith.

3:23 all have sinned: Paul believes that every person has broken the positive relationship that God wants to have with humanity; see 1:18—3:20.

3:24 grace: Grace is God's unmerited love for humanity.

3:24 redemption: This word refers to buying back someone who has been kidnapped or taken as a prisoner of war. It also refers to buying a slave in order to set the slave free. In Deuteronomy 7:8, the Israelites are "redeemed" from slavery in Egypt.

3:25 sacrifice of atonement: God gave stone tablets of the law to Moses. The people of Israel placed the tablets into a box called the Ark of the Covenant. The "sacrifice of atonement" refers to the *lid* on the box. At the lid, God met humanity (see Exod 25:16-22; "mercy seat" means "lid"). In addition, to forgive sins, priests sprinkled an animal's blood on the lid (Lev 16:15). Jesus, then, is where God meets humanity, forgives sin, and heals the broken relationship with humanity.

[a] Or *at any disadvantage?* [b] Or *through the faith of Jesus Christ* [c] Or *a place of atonement* [d] Or *who has the faith of Jesus*

[31]Do we then overthrow the law by this faith? By no means! On the contrary, we uphold the law.

The Example of Abraham

4 What then are we to say was gained by[a] Abraham, our ancestor according to the flesh? [2]For if Abraham was justified by works, he has something to boast about, but not before God. [3]For what does the scripture say? "Abraham believed God, and it was reckoned to him as righteousness." [4]Now to one who works, wages are not reckoned as a gift but as something due. [5]But to one who without works trusts him who justifies the ungodly, such faith is reckoned as righteousness. [6]So also David speaks of the blessedness of those to whom God reckons righteousness apart from works:

7 "Blessed are those whose iniquities are forgiven,
and whose sins are covered;
8 blessed is the one against whom the Lord will not reckon sin."

9 Is this blessedness, then, pronounced only on the circumcised, or also on the uncircumcised? We say, "Faith was reckoned to Abraham as righteousness." [10]How then was it reckoned to him? Was it before or after he had been circumcised? It was not after, but before he was circumcised. [11]He received the sign of circumcision as a seal of the righteousness that he had by faith while he was still uncircumcised. The purpose was to make him the ancestor of all who believe without being circumcised and who thus have righteousness reckoned to them, [12]and likewise the ancestor of the circumcised who are not only circumcised but who also follow the example of the faith that our ancestor Abraham had before he was circumcised.

God's Promise Realized through Faith

13 For the promise that he would inherit the world did not come to Abraham or to his descendants through the law but through the righteousness of faith. [14]If it is the adherents of the law who are to be the heirs, faith is null and the promise is void. [15]For the law brings wrath; but where there is no law, neither is there violation.

16 For this reason it depends on faith, in order that the promise may rest on grace and be guaranteed to all his descendants, not only to the adherents of the law but also to those who share the faith of Abraham (for he is the father of all of us, [17]as it is written, "I have made you the father of many nations")—in the presence of the God in whom he believed, who gives life to the dead and calls into existence the things that do not exist. [18]Hoping against hope, he believed that he would become "the father of many nations," according to what was said, "So numerous shall your descendants be." [19]He did not weaken

[a] Other ancient authorities read *say about*

How are people made right with God? People do not make themselves right with God and cannot bridge the gap created by sin. But God, through Jesus, does. People are invited to trust and live out that message by believing it, and so a person is justified by faith. Luther writes, "I believe that Jesus Christ... has redeemed me, a lost and condemned human being. He has purchased and freed me from all sins, from death, and from the power of the devil... with his holy, precious blood and with his innocent suffering and death" (SC). *Romans 3:21-26, 28*

4:3 Abraham: Abraham is Paul's prime example of the believer (see also Gal 3). He had no proof that God would keep God's promise (Gen 15:1-6), but still Abraham believed (4:19-21).

Name some people who have believed without proof. What proof would make it easier for you to believe God?

in faith when he considered his own body, which was already[a] as good
as dead (for he was about a hundred years old), or when he considered the barrenness of Sarah's womb. 20 No distrust made him waver
concerning the promise of God, but he grew strong in his faith as he
gave glory to God, 21 being fully convinced that God was able to do
what he had promised. 22 Therefore his faith[b] "was reckoned to him
as righteousness." 23 Now the words, "it was reckoned to him," were
written not for his sake alone, 24 but for ours also. It will be reckoned
to us who believe in him who raised Jesus our Lord from the dead,
25 who was handed over to death for our trespasses and was raised for
our justification.

Results of Justification

5 Therefore, since we are justified by faith, we[c] have peace with
God through our Lord Jesus Christ, 2 through whom we have
obtained access[d] to this grace in which we stand; and we[e] boast in
our hope of sharing the glory of God. 3 And not only that, but we[e]
also boast in our sufferings, knowing that suffering produces endurance, 4 and endurance produces character, and character produces
hope, 5 and hope does not disappoint us, because God's love has been
poured into our hearts through the Holy Spirit that has been given
to us.

6 For while we were still weak, at the right time Christ died for
the ungodly. 7 Indeed, rarely will anyone die for a righteous person—
though perhaps for a good person someone might actually dare to
die. 8 But God proves his love for us in that while we still were sinners
Christ died for us. 9 Much more surely then, now that we have been
justified by his blood, will we be saved through him from the wrath
of God.[f] 10 For if while we were enemies, we were reconciled to God
through the death of his Son, much more surely, having been reconciled, will we be saved by his life. 11 But more than that, we even boast
in God through our Lord Jesus Christ, through whom we have now
received reconciliation.

Adam and Christ

12 Therefore, just as sin came into the world through one man,
and death came through sin, and so death spread to all because all
have sinned— 13 sin was indeed in the world before the law, but sin
is not reckoned when there is no law. 14 Yet death exercised dominion
from Adam to Moses, even over those whose sins were not like the
transgression of Adam, who is a type of the one who was to come.

15 But the free gift is not like the trespass. For if the many died

---

[a] Other ancient authorities lack *already* [b] Gk *Therefore it* [c] Other ancient authorities read *let us*
[d] Other ancient authorities add *by faith* [e] Or *let us* [f] Gk *the wrath*

5:3-4 sufferings...character...hope: "Sufferings" refers especially to the suffering that is to occur before the end of time, but it can also mean everyday suffering. Character results from experiences and attitudes not unlike the process of refining metals in fire to burn off impurities. Enduring suffering refines people. People who have been refined have hope because they place their future into God's hands, not their own.

5:5 hope does not disappoint: "Disappoint" also means "put to shame" (see 1:16).

5:5 poured: The reason hope does not put us to shame is the outpouring of God's love through the Holy Spirit. God holds nothing back!

5:6-8 while we were still weak...Christ died for the ungodly...while we still were sinners Christ died for us: Part of the wonder of God's love is that Christ does not wait for humanity to become perfect before dying for us. And so he died for us when we were weak, sinners, and ungodly (see also 4:5).

5:9-10 justified...will we be saved...reconciled...will we be saved: Paul distinguishes between the justification and reconciliation that have already occurred and the salvation that is still in the future (see also 6:5, 8; 8:11; 9:27; 10:9, 13; 11:26). Paul's model is "already—but not yet." Already much has happened, but we do not yet have everything.

5:12, 14 one man: Adam is the "one man" (Gen 1–3). As the first human being, Adam stands at the beginning of the human family, and in his sin all of humanity is implicated. Jesus also stands at the beginning of a new humanity, but without the sin that corrupted humanity after Adam.

5:15 the free gift...abounded: No matter how much humanity sins, God's free gift of grace is always greater.

through the one man's trespass, much more surely have the grace of God and the free gift in the grace of the one man, Jesus Christ, abounded for the many. [16]And the free gift is not like the effect of the one man's sin. For the judgment following one trespass brought condemnation, but the free gift following many trespasses brings justification. [17]If, because of the one man's trespass, death exercised dominion through that one, much more surely will those who receive the abundance of grace and the free gift of righteousness exercise dominion in life through the one man, Jesus Christ.

18 Therefore just as one man's trespass led to condemnation for all, so one man's act of righteousness leads to justification and life for all. [19]For just as by the one man's disobedience the many were made sinners, so by the one man's obedience the many will be made righteous. [20]But law came in, with the result that the trespass multiplied; but where sin increased, grace abounded all the more, [21]so that, just as sin exercised dominion in death, so grace might also exercise dominion through justification[a] leading to eternal life through Jesus Christ our Lord.

Dying and Rising with Christ

6 What then are we to say? Should we continue in sin in order that grace may abound? [2]By no means! How can we who died to sin go on living in it? [3]Do you not know that all of us who have been baptized into Christ Jesus were baptized into his death? [4]Therefore we have been buried with him by baptism into death, so that, just as Christ was raised from the dead by the glory of the Father, so we too might walk in newness of life.

5 For if we have been united with him in a death like his, we will certainly be united with him in a resurrection like his. [6]We know that our old self was crucified with him so that the body of sin might be destroyed, and we might no longer be enslaved to sin. [7]For whoever has died is freed from sin. [8]But if we have died with Christ, we believe that we will also live with him. [9]We know that Christ, being raised from the dead, will never die again; death no longer has dominion over him. [10]The death he died, he died to sin, once for all; but the life he lives, he lives to God. [11]So you also must consider yourselves dead to sin and alive to God in Christ Jesus.

12 Therefore, do not let sin exercise dominion in your mortal bodies, to make you obey their passions. [13]No longer present your members to sin as instruments[b] of wickedness, but present yourselves to God as those who have been brought from death to life, and present your members to God as instruments[b] of righteousness. [14]For sin will have no dominion over you, since you are not under law but under grace.

---

[a] Or *righteousness* [b] Or *weapons*

6:1-2 continue in sin: Some might conclude that since God's grace is always greater than our sin, we should keep sinning. Paul rejects that idea.

6:3 baptized into: Baptism is the ceremony in which a believer enters into the rule of Jesus as Lord and becomes part of the church. Baptism identifies the believer with the fate of Jesus, including his saving death.

6:4 walk in newness of life: "Walk" refers to how people live in relationship to others. Baptized believers have a new quality of life.

How does Baptism affect daily life? While baptism itself is a one-time action, the struggle with sin is so great that we need to return to the waters of baptism every day as we remember that God has made us God's own. Baptism "signifies that the old person in us with all sins and evil desires is to be drowned and die through daily sorrow for sin and through repentance, and on the other hand that daily a new person is to come forth and rise up to live before God in righteousness and purity forever" (*ELW*, p. 1165). And in his *Large Catechism* Luther writes, "Thus a Christian life is nothing else than a daily Baptism, begun once and continuing ever after." (*BC*, p. 465). *Romans 6:4-6*

6:12 do not let sin exercise dominion: Sin, for Paul, is a power that rules in our lives (see 3:9).

Slaves of Righteousness

6:15-23 slaves of sin...slaves of righteousness: To contrast sin's power and God's gift, Paul uses the image of slavery. Paul believes all people are slaves of some kind. The only question is who or what we will serve as slaves.

How do Lutherans understand God's law? The law has two main functions or "uses." Under the first use (generally called the "civil use"), the law provides rules to show humans how to live with God and neighbor, and it provides consequences when those rules are broken. The second use (called the "theological" or "pedagogical use") reveals the extent of our sin and our need for a savior. Some Lutherans and Christians from other traditions argue for a third use of the law, in which the law provides guidelines for Christian life. *Romans 7*

15 What then? Should we sin because we are not under law but
under grace? By no means! [16]Do you not know that if you present
yourselves to anyone as obedient slaves, you are slaves of the one
whom you obey, either of sin, which leads to death, or of obedience,
which leads to righteousness? [17]But thanks be to God that you, having once been slaves of sin, have become obedient from the heart to
the form of teaching to which you were entrusted, [18]and that you, having been set free from sin, have become slaves of righteousness. [19]I
am speaking in human terms because of your natural limitations.[a] For
just as you once presented your members as slaves to impurity and to
greater and greater iniquity, so now present your members as slaves to
righteousness for sanctification.

20 When you were slaves of sin, you were free in regard to righteousness. [21]So what advantage did you then get from the things of
which you now are ashamed? The end of those things is death. [22]But
now that you have been freed from sin and enslaved to God, the advantage you get is sanctification. The end is eternal life. [23]For the
wages of sin is death, but the free gift of God is eternal life in Christ
Jesus our Lord.

An Analogy from Marriage

7:1-6 discharged from the law: As a wife is released from the law of marriage when her husband dies, believers are freed from the Law of Moses as the way of salvation when they "die" in baptism (6:4-5).

7 Do you not know, brothers and sisters[b]—for I am speaking to
those who know the law—that the law is binding on a person
only during that person's lifetime? [2]Thus a married woman is bound
by the law to her husband as long as he lives; but if her husband dies,
she is discharged from the law concerning the husband. [3]Accordingly,
she will be called an adulteress if she lives with another man while her
husband is alive. But if her husband dies, she is free from that law, and
if she marries another man, she is not an adulteress.

4 In the same way, my friends,[b] you have died to the law through
the body of Christ, so that you may belong to another, to him who
has been raised from the dead in order that we may bear fruit for God.
[5]While we were living in the flesh, our sinful passions, aroused by the
law, were at work in our members to bear fruit for death. [6]But now
we are discharged from the law, dead to that which held us captive, so
that we are slaves not under the old written code but in the new life
of the Spirit.

7:5 living in the flesh: *Flesh* and *body* do not mean the same thing. For Paul, *flesh* means the body as it is misused and controlled by the power of sin (see 7:18; 8:3-9).

The Law and Sin

7:7-13 sin, seizing an opportunity: The law shows us how we have failed; at that point it is a positive gift of God. But the power of sin misuses the law for its own purposes, to make us desire what is not ours (see 8:3).

Make a list of gifts from God that humanity has misused. How can we use these gifts in the ways God intended?

7 What then should we say? That the law is sin? By no means!
Yet, if it had not been for the law, I would not have known sin. I would
not have known what it is to covet if the law had not said, "You shall

[a] Gk *the weakness of your flesh* [b] Gk *brothers*

not covet." [8]But sin, seizing an opportunity in the commandment,
produced in me all kinds of covetousness. Apart from the law sin lies
dead. [9]I was once alive apart from the law, but when the commandment came, sin revived [10]and I died, and the very commandment that
promised life proved to be death to me. [11]For sin, seizing an opportunity in the commandment, deceived me and through it killed me. [12]So
the law is holy, and the commandment is holy and just and good.

13 Did what is good, then, bring death to me? By no means! It
was sin, working death in me through what is good, in order that sin
might be shown to be sin, and through the commandment might become sinful beyond measure.

The Inner Conflict

14 For we know that the law is spiritual; but I am of the flesh,
sold into slavery under sin.[a] [15]I do not understand my own actions.
For I do not do what I want, but I do the very thing I hate. [16]Now if I
do what I do not want, I agree that the law is good. [17]But in fact it is
no longer I that do it, but sin that dwells within me. [18]For I know that
nothing good dwells within me, that is, in my flesh. I can will what is
right, but I cannot do it. [19]For I do not do the good I want, but the evil
I do not want is what I do. [20]Now if I do what I do not want, it is no
longer I that do it, but sin that dwells within me.

21 So I find it to be a law that when I want to do what is good,
evil lies close at hand. [22]For I delight in the law of God in my inmost
self, [23]but I see in my members another law at war with the law of my
mind, making me captive to the law of sin that dwells in my members.
[24]Wretched man that I am! Who will rescue me from this body of
death? [25]Thanks be to God through Jesus Christ our Lord!

So then, with my mind I am a slave to the law of God, but with my
flesh I am a slave to the law of sin.

7:14-25 I: Paul here uses and repeats the "I" to emphasize our common struggle with sin (7:15). This section may be another example of "already—but not yet." We are already justified, but not yet perfect.

How are Christians justified and sinners at the same time? As baptized believers, Christians live in the new age of Christ. But the old age of the power of sin has not disappeared, and so Christians are caught in the tension between the two ages. Lutherans express this with the phrase "at the same time justified and a sinner." *Romans 7:14-25*

Life in the Spirit

8 There is therefore now no condemnation for those who are in
Christ Jesus. [2]For the law of the Spirit[b] of life in Christ Jesus has
set you[c] free from the law of sin and of death. [3]For God has done what
the law, weakened by the flesh, could not do: by sending his own Son
in the likeness of sinful flesh, and to deal with sin,[d] he condemned
sin in the flesh, [4]so that the just requirement of the law might be fulfilled in us, who walk not according to the flesh but according to the
Spirit.[b] [5]For those who live according to the flesh set their minds on
the things of the flesh, but those who live according to the Spirit[b] set
their minds on the things of the Spirit.[b] [6]To set the mind on the flesh

8:3 in the likeness of sinful flesh: These words do not mean that Jesus was not a true human being. Rather, Jesus is not "flesh" because for Paul that means the body as misused and controlled by the power of sin. For Paul, then, Jesus was "in the likeness of sinful flesh" because he did not sin (see 2 Cor 5:21).

---

[a] Gk *sold under sin* [b] Or *spirit* [c] Here the Greek word *you* is singular number; other ancient authorities read *me* or *us* [d] Or *and as a sin offering*

is death, but to set the mind on the Spirit[a] is life and peace. [7]For this
reason the mind that is set on the flesh is hostile to God; it does not
submit to God's law—indeed it cannot, [8]and those who are in the
flesh cannot please God.

9 But you are not in the flesh; you are in the Spirit,[a] since the
Spirit of God dwells in you. Anyone who does not have the Spirit of
Christ does not belong to him. [10]But if Christ is in you, though the
body is dead because of sin, the Spirit[a] is life because of righteousness.
[11]If the Spirit of him who raised Jesus from the dead dwells in you, he
who raised Christ[b] from the dead will give life to your mortal bodies
also through[c] his Spirit that dwells in you.

12 So then, brothers and sisters,[d] we are debtors, not to the flesh,
to live according to the flesh— [13]for if you live according to the flesh,
you will die; but if by the Spirit you put to death the deeds of the
body, you will live. [14]For all who are led by the Spirit of God are children of God. [15]For you did not receive a spirit of slavery to fall back
into fear, but you have received a spirit of adoption. When we cry,
"Abba![e] Father!" [16]it is that very Spirit bearing witness[f] with our spirit
that we are children of God, [17]and if children, then heirs, heirs of God
and joint heirs with Christ—if, in fact, we suffer with him so that we
may also be glorified with him.

Future Glory

8:19-22 bondage to decay: Creation is affected by human sin and looks forward to release.

18 I consider that the sufferings of this present time are not worth
comparing with the glory about to be revealed to us. [19]For the creation
waits with eager longing for the revealing of the children of God; [20]for
the creation was subjected to futility, not of its own will but by the
will of the one who subjected it, in hope [21]that the creation itself will
be set free from its bondage to decay and will obtain the freedom of
the glory of the children of God. [22]We know that the whole creation
has been groaning in labor pains until now; [23]and not only the creation, but we ourselves, who have the first fruits of the Spirit, groan
inwardly while we wait for adoption, the redemption of our bodies.
[24]For in[g] hope we were saved. Now hope that is seen is not hope. For
who hopes[h] for what is seen? [25]But if we hope for what we do not see,
we wait for it with patience.

26 Likewise the Spirit helps us in our weakness; for we do not
know how to pray as we ought, but that very Spirit intercedes[i] with
sighs too deep for words. [27]And God,[j] who searches the heart, knows
what is the mind of the Spirit, because the Spirit[k] intercedes for the
saints according to the will of God.[l]

---

[a] Or *spirit* [b] Other ancient authorities read *the Christ* or *Christ Jesus* or *Jesus Christ* [c] Other ancient authorities read *on account of* [d] Gk *brothers* [e] Aramaic for *Father* [f] Or [15]*a spirit of adoption, by which we cry, 'Abba! Father!'* [16]*The Spirit itself bears witness* [g] Or *by* [h] Other ancient authorities read *awaits* [i] Other ancient authorities add *for us* [j] Gk *the one* [k] Gk *he* or *it* [l] Gk *according to God*

28 We know that all things work together for good[a] for those who
love God, who are called according to his purpose. 29For those whom
he foreknew he also predestined to be conformed to the image of his
Son, in order that he might be the firstborn within a large family.[b]
30And those whom he predestined he also called; and those whom he
called he also justified; and those whom he justified he also glorified.

God's Love in Christ Jesus

31 What then are we to say about these things? If God is for us,
who is against us? 32He who did not withhold his own Son, but gave
him up for all of us, will he not with him also give us everything else?
33Who will bring any charge against God's elect? It is God who justifies. 34Who is to condemn? It is Christ Jesus, who died, yes, who was
raised, who is at the right hand of God, who indeed intercedes for
us.[c] 35Who will separate us from the love of Christ? Will hardship, or
distress, or persecution, or famine, or nakedness, or peril, or sword?
36As it is written,

"For your sake we are being killed all day long;
we are accounted as sheep to be slaughtered."

37No, in all these things we are more than conquerors through him
who loved us. 38For I am convinced that neither death, nor life, nor
angels, nor rulers, nor things present, nor things to come, nor powers,
39nor height, nor depth, nor anything else in all creation, will be able
to separate us from the love of God in Christ Jesus our Lord.

God's Election of Israel

9 I am speaking the truth in Christ—I am not lying; my conscience confirms it by the Holy Spirit— 2I have great sorrow
and unceasing anguish in my heart. 3For I could wish that I myself
were accursed and cut off from Christ for the sake of my own people,[d]
my kindred according to the flesh. 4They are Israelites, and to them
belong the adoption, the glory, the covenants, the giving of the law,
the worship, and the promises; 5to them belong the patriarchs, and
from them, according to the flesh, comes the Messiah,[e] who is over
all, God blessed forever.[f] Amen.
6 It is not as though the word of God had failed. For not all Israelites truly belong to Israel, 7and not all of Abraham's children are his
true descendants; but "It is through Isaac that descendants shall be
named for you." 8This means that it is not the children of the flesh who
are the children of God, but the children of the promise are counted
as descendants. 9For this is what the promise said, "About this time
I will return and Sarah shall have a son." 10Nor is that all; something

8:28 all things work...for good: Paul's concern is the ultimate good, namely, salvation. Whatever evil happens, God is able to save.

List some ways that God has brought good out of bad in your life or in the lives of people you know. How might these examples help you deal with bad things that happen to you?

8:31-35 If God is for us, who is against us?: God is the judge, so who can successfully bring charges against believers? Answer: no one.

8:39 separate: The word translated as "separate" also means to "divorce." Nothing can divorce believers from God's love.

9:1—11:36 Israel: In chapters 9–11, Paul raises questions such as these: What about Jews who do not believe in Jesus? Has God abandoned them? If so, has God broken God's promises to Israel? And if God has done that, can God be trusted to keep the promises made to Gentile (non-Jewish) believers? Paul's final answers are in 11:26, 29. God does *not* break the promises to Israel or abandon the people. God is trustworthy.

9:1-5 my own people: The people of Israel have not believed in Jesus. What will happen to them? Paul's anguish for his own ethnic group drives chapters 9–11.

[a] Other ancient authorities read *God makes all things work together for good*, or *in all things God works for good*
[b] Gk *among many brothers* [c] Or *Is it Christ Jesus . . . for us?* [d] Gk *my brothers* [e] Or *the Christ*
[f] Or *Messiah, who is God over all, blessed forever*; or *Messiah. May he who is God over all be blessed forever*

similar happened to Rebecca when she had conceived children by
one husband, our ancestor Isaac. [11]Even before they had been born
or had done anything good or bad (so that God's purpose of election
might continue, [12]not by works but by his call) she was told, "The elder shall serve the younger." [13]As it is written,

"I have loved Jacob,
but I have hated Esau."

14 What then are we to say? Is there injustice on God's part? By
no means! [15]For he says to Moses,

"I will have mercy on whom I have mercy,
and I will have compassion on whom I have compassion."

[16]So it depends not on human will or exertion, but on God who shows
mercy. [17]For the scripture says to Pharaoh, "I have raised you up for
the very purpose of showing my power in you, so that my name may
be proclaimed in all the earth." [18]So then he has mercy on whomever
he chooses, and he hardens the heart of whomever he chooses.

God's Wrath and Mercy

19 You will say to me then, "Why then does he still find fault? For
who can resist his will?" [20]But who indeed are you, a human being,
to argue with God? Will what is molded say to the one who molds
it, "Why have you made me like this?" [21]Has the potter no right over
the clay, to make out of the same lump one object for special use and
another for ordinary use? [22]What if God, desiring to show his wrath
and to make known his power, has endured with much patience the
objects of wrath that are made for destruction; [23]and what if he has
done so in order to make known the riches of his glory for the objects
of mercy, which he has prepared beforehand for glory— [24]including
us whom he has called, not from the Jews only but also from the Gentiles? [25]As indeed he says in Hosea,

"Those who were not my people I will call 'my people,'
and her who was not beloved I will call 'beloved.' "

26 "And in the very place where it was said to them, 'You are not my
people,'
there they shall be called children of the living God."

27 And Isaiah cries out concerning Israel, "Though the number
of the children of Israel were like the sand of the sea, only a remnant
of them will be saved; [28]for the Lord will execute his sentence on the
earth quickly and decisively."[a] [29]And as Isaiah predicted,

"If the Lord of hosts had not left survivors[b] to us,
we would have fared like Sodom
and been made like Gomorrah."

---

[a] Other ancient authorities read *for he will finish his work and cut it short in righteousness, because the Lord will make the sentence shortened on the earth* [b] Or *descendants*; Gk *seed*

Israel's Unbelief

30 What then are we to say? Gentiles, who did not strive for righteousness, have attained it, that is, righteousness through faith; [31]but
Israel, who did strive for the righteousness that is based on the law,
did not succeed in fulfilling that law. [32]Why not? Because they did not
strive for it on the basis of faith, but as if it were based on works. They
have stumbled over the stumbling stone, [33]as it is written,

"See, I am laying in Zion a stone that will make people stumble, a
rock that will make them fall,
and whoever believes in him[a] will not be put to shame."

10 Brothers and sisters,[b] my heart's desire and prayer to God
for them is that they may be saved. [2]I can testify that they
have a zeal for God, but it is not enlightened. [3]For, being ignorant of
the righteousness that comes from God, and seeking to establish their
own, they have not submitted to God's righteousness. [4]For Christ is
the end of the law so that there may be righteousness for everyone
who believes.

Salvation Is for All

5 Moses writes concerning the righteousness that comes from
the law, that "the person who does these things will live by them."
[6]But the righteousness that comes from faith says, "Do not say in your
heart, 'Who will ascend into heaven?' " (that is, to bring Christ down)
[7]"or 'Who will descend into the abyss?' " (that is, to bring Christ up
from the dead). [8]But what does it say?

"The word is near you,
on your lips and in your heart"

(that is, the word of faith that we proclaim); [9]because[c] if you confess
with your lips that Jesus is Lord and believe in your heart that God
raised him from the dead, you will be saved. [10]For one believes with
the heart and so is justified, and one confesses with the mouth and so
is saved. [11]The scripture says, "No one who believes in him will be put
to shame." [12]For there is no distinction between Jew and Greek; the
same Lord is Lord of all and is generous to all who call on him. [13]For,
"Everyone who calls on the name of the Lord shall be saved."

14 But how are they to call on one in whom they have not believed? And how are they to believe in one of whom they have never
heard? And how are they to hear without someone to proclaim him?
[15]And how are they to proclaim him unless they are sent? As it is written, "How beautiful are the feet of those who bring good news!" [16]But
not all have obeyed the good news;[d] for Isaiah says, "Lord, who has
believed our message?" [17]So faith comes from what is heard, and what
is heard comes through the word of Christ.[e]

---

[a] Or *trusts in it* [b] Gk *Brothers* [c] Or *namely, that* [d] Or *gospel* [e] Or *about Christ;* other ancient authorities read *of God*

10:4 Christ is the end of the law: For everyone who believes, Christ is the "end" of the law, in the sense that it is no longer the way to establish a relationship with God.

10:5-21 righteousness that comes from faith: This section contrasts righteousness that comes from doing what the law requires (10:5) with righteousness that comes from hearing and believing (10:6-17).

10:12-13: no distinction: All people are saved in the same way—by calling on the one Lord.

10:12-17 the word of Christ: The spoken word of Christ is crucial. Paul carefully constructs this passage so that a key word or phrase is picked up later in the verse or in a subsequent one: "call on" (10:12b, 13, 14), "believe(d)" (10:14a, 14b), "hear(d)" (10:14b, 14c), "proclaim" (10:14c, 15a), "believed"/"faith" (10:16b, 17,), and "what is heard" (10:17a, 17b). "Word of Christ" (10:17b) goes back to "word" and "word of faith" (10:8). Note that "believed" and "faith" have the same Greek root.

How can we speak the word of Christ in our daily lives?

18 But I ask, have they not heard? Indeed they have; for
"Their voice has gone out to all the earth,
and their words to the ends of the world."
19 Again I ask, did Israel not understand? First Moses says,
"I will make you jealous of those who are not a nation;
with a foolish nation I will make you angry."
20 Then Isaiah is so bold as to say,
"I have been found by those who did not seek me;
I have shown myself to those who did not ask for me."
21 But of Israel he says, "All day long I have held out my hands to a disobedient and contrary people."

Israel's Rejection Is Not Final

11:1-7 has God rejected his people? A natural response would be "Yes, given everything you have said." But Paul has led his listeners to a false conclusion. He points to himself: he was an Israelite, and God obviously had not rejected him. Paul next turns to the Old Testament concept of *remnant* (11:2-6). Even when God judges, God often saves a small number (see 1 Kgs 19:14-18, which Paul quotes, and Isa 10:20-22).

11:7-14 hardened: Paul introduces the Old Testament concept of *hardening* (Exod 4:21; Isa 63:17). God hardens the hearts and minds of Israel so that most of them do not believe. Why? Paul thinks that if Israel as a people had believed in Jesus as Messiah, the message would have stayed inside Israel.

11:11, 14 jealous: In Mediterranean cultures, jealousy meant desiring something that a person (or people) had at one time but lost. Paul hopes to make Israel jealous of the righteousness that now belongs to believing Gentiles (non-Jews).

11 I ask, then, has God rejected his people? By no means! I myself am an Israelite, a descendant of Abraham, a member of the
tribe of Benjamin. 2 God has not rejected his people whom he foreknew. Do you not know what the scripture says of Elijah, how he
pleads with God against Israel? 3 "Lord, they have killed your prophets, they have demolished your altars; I alone am left, and they are
seeking my life." 4 But what is the divine reply to him? "I have kept for
myself seven thousand who have not bowed the knee to Baal." 5 So too
at the present time there is a remnant, chosen by grace. 6 But if it is by
grace, it is no longer on the basis of works, otherwise grace would no
longer be grace.[a]
7 What then? Israel failed to obtain what it was seeking. The elect
obtained it, but the rest were hardened, 8 as it is written,
"God gave them a sluggish spirit,
eyes that would not see
and ears that would not hear,
down to this very day."
9 And David says,
"Let their table become a snare and a trap,
a stumbling block and a retribution for them;
10 let their eyes be darkened so that they cannot see,
and keep their backs forever bent."

The Salvation of the Gentiles

11 So I ask, have they stumbled so as to fall? By no means! But
through their stumbling[b] salvation has come to the Gentiles, so as to
make Israel[c] jealous. 12 Now if their stumbling[b] means riches for the
world, and if their defeat means riches for Gentiles, how much more
will their full inclusion mean!
13 Now I am speaking to you Gentiles. Inasmuch then as I am an

---

[a] Other ancient authorities add *But if it is by works, it is no longer on the basis of grace, otherwise work would no longer be work* [b] Gk *transgression* [c] Gk *them*

apostle to the Gentiles, I glorify my ministry 14in order to make my
own people[a] jealous, and thus save some of them. 15For if their rejection is the reconciliation of the world, what will their acceptance be
but life from the dead! 16If the part of the dough offered as first fruits
is holy, then the whole batch is holy; and if the root is holy, then the
branches also are holy.

17 But if some of the branches were broken off, and you, a wild
olive shoot, were grafted in their place to share the rich root[b] of the olive tree, 18do not boast over the branches. If you do boast, remember
that it is not you that support the root, but the root that supports you.
19You will say, "Branches were broken off so that I might be grafted
in." 20That is true. They were broken off because of their unbelief, but
you stand only through faith. So do not become proud, but stand in
awe. 21For if God did not spare the natural branches, perhaps he will
not spare you.[c] 22Note then the kindness and the severity of God: severity toward those who have fallen, but God's kindness toward you,
provided you continue in his kindness; otherwise you also will be cut
off. 23And even those of Israel,[d] if they do not persist in unbelief, will
be grafted in, for God has the power to graft them in again. 24For if
you have been cut from what is by nature a wild olive tree and grafted,
contrary to nature, into a cultivated olive tree, how much more will
these natural branches be grafted back into their own olive tree.

All Israel Will Be Saved

25 So that you may not claim to be wiser than you are, brothers
and sisters,[e] I want you to understand this mystery: a hardening has
come upon part of Israel, until the full number of the Gentiles has
come in. 26And so all Israel will be saved; as it is written,

"Out of Zion will come the Deliverer;
he will banish ungodliness from Jacob."
27 "And this is my covenant with them,
when I take away their sins."

28As regards the gospel they are enemies of God[f] for your sake; but as
regards election they are beloved, for the sake of their ancestors; 29for
the gifts and the calling of God are irrevocable. 30Just as you were once
disobedient to God but have now received mercy because of their disobedience, 31so they have now been disobedient in order that, by the
mercy shown to you, they too may now[g] receive mercy. 32For God has
imprisoned all in disobedience so that he may be merciful to all.

33 O the depth of the riches and wisdom and knowledge of God!
How unsearchable are his judgments and how inscrutable his ways!
34 "For who has known the mind of the Lord?

---

[a] Gk *my flesh* [b] Other ancient authorities read *the richness* [c] Other ancient authorities read *neither will he spare you* [d] Gk lacks *of Israel* [e] Gk *brothers* [f] Gk lacks *of God* [g] Other ancient authorities lack *now*

11:17-24 olive tree: Paul uses the example of the olive tree to warn Gentiles not to become over-confident and look down on Israelites.

11:25 hardening: The hardening of Israel is temporary and will end when "the full number of the Gentiles has come in." Paul does not say what the full number is.

11:26 all Israel will be saved: Salvation comes through the "Deliverer," who is Jesus. Paul does not say exactly how this Deliverer will work, but he appears to envision a mission at the end of time by Jesus.

11:29 irrevocable: *Irrevocable* means "cannot be taken back or removed." So can this God be trusted—based on chapters 9–11 as a unit? Yes!

11:33-36 how inscrutable his ways! Paul admits that he does not understand how God will finally fulfill all promises.

Or who has been his counselor?"
35 "Or who has given a gift to him,
to receive a gift in return?"
36 For from him and through him and to him are all things. To him be
the glory forever. Amen.

The New Life in Christ

12 I appeal to you therefore, brothers and sisters,[a] by the mercies
of God, to present your bodies as a living sacrifice, holy and
acceptable to God, which is your spiritual[b] worship. 2 Do not be conformed to this world,[c] but be transformed by the renewing of your
minds, so that you may discern what is the will of God—what is good
and acceptable and perfect.[d]

3 For by the grace given to me I say to everyone among you not
to think of yourself more highly than you ought to think, but to think
with sober judgment, each according to the measure of faith that God
has assigned. 4 For as in one body we have many members, and not all
the members have the same function, 5 so we, who are many, are one
body in Christ, and individually we are members one of another. 6 We
have gifts that differ according to the grace given to us: prophecy, in
proportion to faith; 7 ministry, in ministering; the teacher, in teaching;
8 the exhorter, in exhortation; the giver, in generosity; the leader, in
diligence; the compassionate, in cheerfulness.

Marks of the True Christian

9 Let love be genuine; hate what is evil, hold fast to what is good;
10 love one another with mutual affection; outdo one another in showing honor. 11 Do not lag in zeal, be ardent in spirit, serve the Lord.[e]
12 Rejoice in hope, be patient in suffering, persevere in prayer. 13 Contribute to the needs of the saints; extend hospitality to strangers.

14 Bless those who persecute you; bless and do not curse them.
15 Rejoice with those who rejoice, weep with those who weep. 16 Live
in harmony with one another; do not be haughty, but associate with
the lowly;[f] do not claim to be wiser than you are. 17 Do not repay anyone evil for evil, but take thought for what is noble in the sight of all.
18 If it is possible, so far as it depends on you, live peaceably with all.
19 Beloved, never avenge yourselves, but leave room for the wrath of
God;[g] for it is written, "Vengeance is mine, I will repay, says the Lord."
20 No, "if your enemies are hungry, feed them; if they are thirsty, give
them something to drink; for by doing this you will heap burning
coals on their heads." 21 Do not be overcome by evil, but overcome
evil with good.

---

[a] Gk *brothers* [b] Or *reasonable* [c] Gk *age* [d] Or *what is the good and acceptable and perfect will of God*
[e] Other ancient authorities read *serve the opportune time* [f] Or *give yourselves to humble tasks*
[g] Gk *the wrath*

12:1—15:13 I appeal to you: Paul has laid the basis for Christian moral behavior (6:3-14). Now he devotes an entire section to how to live as a follower of Jesus ("the imperative"). This section comes only after he has discussed what God has done for humanity ("the indicative"). In the Bible, the pattern is what God has done, *then* how to live as a believer (indicative, only then the imperative). See Exodus 20:1-2, 3-17.

12:1 present your bodies: God's gifts are so great that the only proper response is for people to offer their entire lives to God.

12:2 Do not be conformed...be transformed: Paul calls believers to resist behaving the way nonbelievers want them to behave. The structure of the Greek verb here translated as "conformed" indicates an *ongoing* action—not conforming has to be done again and again. However, "be transformed," in Greek, also indicates an ongoing action. The Spirit works in believers to bring their moral thinking into God's new age.

What do you experience the world telling you to do? How do you resist? What activities and people help transform you?

12:2 you may discern: The word *you* here is used to indicate "you all" (*second* person plural). Discerning or detecting God's will is done by believers together.

12:4-8 one body in Christ: God calls Christians to live in community with one another. The one body in Christ needs the gifts of individuals in order to function properly (see 1 Cor 12:4-31).

What gifts do you bring to the one body in Christ?

12:9-21 Let love be genuine: Paul outlines in everyday, practical terms how Christians are to live as justified believers.

Being Subject to Authorities

13 Let every person be subject to the governing authorities; for there is no authority except from God, and those authorities that exist have been instituted by God. 2 Therefore whoever resists authority resists what God has appointed, and those who resist will incur judgment. 3 For rulers are not a terror to good conduct, but to bad. Do you wish to have no fear of the authority? Then do what is good, and you will receive its approval; 4 for it is God's servant for your good. But if you do what is wrong, you should be afraid, for the authority[a] does not bear the sword in vain! It is the servant of God to execute wrath on the wrongdoer. 5 Therefore one must be subject, not only because of wrath but also because of conscience. 6 For the same reason you also pay taxes, for the authorities are God's servants, busy with this very thing. 7 Pay to all what is due them—taxes to whom taxes are due, revenue to whom revenue is due, respect to whom respect is due, honor to whom honor is due.

13:1-7 authority: Part of Christian responsibility is living justly in relationship to the government. The government, in turn, is to act as God's servant (13:4).

Love for One Another

8 Owe no one anything, except to love one another; for the one who loves another has fulfilled the law. 9 The commandments, "You shall not commit adultery; You shall not murder; You shall not steal; You shall not covet"; and any other commandment, are summed up in this word, "Love your neighbor as yourself." 10 Love does no wrong to a neighbor; therefore, love is the fulfilling of the law.

13:8 love: The fundamental command Paul gives is to love. It underlies all Christian moral action (13:10).

An Urgent Appeal

11 Besides this, you know what time it is, how it is now the moment for you to wake from sleep. For salvation is nearer to us now than when we became believers; 12 the night is far gone, the day is near. Let us then lay aside the works of darkness and put on the armor of light; 13 let us live honorably as in the day, not in reveling and drunkenness, not in debauchery and licentiousness, not in quarreling and jealousy. 14 Instead, put on the Lord Jesus Christ, and make no provision for the flesh, to gratify its desires.

13:11-14 what time it is: Notice the words Paul chooses: "time," "moment" (in Greek, "hour"), "wake from sleep," "salvation is nearer," "night," "day," "works of darkness," and "armor of light." He expects the end of the world to come suddenly and soon.

13:13 as in the day: Paul encourages Christians to live as though the day of end-time judgment and salvation has already arrived.

Do Not Judge Another

14 Welcome those who are weak in faith,[b] but not for the purpose of quarreling over opinions. 2 Some believe in eating anything, while the weak eat only vegetables. 3 Those who eat must not despise those who abstain, and those who abstain must not pass judgment on those who eat; for God has welcomed them. 4 Who are you to pass judgment on servants of another? It is before their own lord that they stand or fall. And they will be upheld, for the Lord[c] is able to make them stand.

14:1—15:13 weak in faith: Christians in Rome were nearly divided over which foods believers should eat and which holy days they should celebrate. The "weak in faith," according to Paul, insist on the old rules. The "strong" (15:1) argue that the previous laws do not apply to those who believe in Christ.

---

[a] Gk *it* [b] Or *conviction* [c] Other ancient authorities read *for God*

5 Some judge one day to be better than another, while others judge all days to be alike. Let all be fully convinced in their own minds. [6]Those who observe the day, observe it in honor of the Lord. Also those who eat, eat in honor of the Lord, since they give thanks to God; while those who abstain, abstain in honor of the Lord and give thanks to God.

7 We do not live to ourselves, and we do not die to ourselves. [8]If we live, we live to the Lord, and if we die, we die to the Lord; so then, whether we live or whether we die, we are the Lord's. [9]For to this end Christ died and lived again, so that he might be Lord of both the dead and the living.

10 Why do you pass judgment on your brother or sister?[a] Or you, why do you despise your brother or sister?[a] For we will all stand before the judgment seat of God.[b] [11]For it is written,

"As I live, says the Lord, every knee shall bow to me,
and every tongue shall give praise to[c] God."

[12]So then, each of us will be accountable to God.[d]

Do Not Make Another Stumble

13 Let us therefore no longer pass judgment on one another, but resolve instead never to put a stumbling block or hindrance in the way of another.[e] [14]I know and am persuaded in the Lord Jesus that nothing is unclean in itself; but it is unclean for anyone who thinks it unclean. [15]If your brother or sister[a] is being injured by what you eat, you are no longer walking in love. Do not let what you eat cause the ruin of one for whom Christ died. [16]So do not let your good be spoken of as evil. [17]For the kingdom of God is not food and drink but righteousness and peace and joy in the Holy Spirit. [18]The one who thus serves Christ is acceptable to God and has human approval. [19]Let us then pursue what makes for peace and for mutual upbuilding. [20]Do not, for the sake of food, destroy the work of God. Everything is indeed clean, but it is wrong for you to make others fall by what you eat; [21]it is good not to eat meat or drink wine or do anything that makes your brother or sister[a] stumble.[f] [22]The faith that you have, have as your own conviction before God. Blessed are those who have no reason to condemn themselves because of what they approve. [23]But those who have doubts are condemned if they eat, because they do not act from faith;[g] for whatever does not proceed from faith[g] is sin.[h]

14:14-23 nothing is unclean in itself: For Paul, the correct view is that "nothing is unclean in itself," but those who agree with him need to understand that for other believers, the food laws still make sense. People who agree with Paul can offend the "weak" and hurt their faith.

14:19 mutual upbuilding: "Upbuilding" or "build up" is a construction term that Paul often uses (15:2; 1 Cor 8:1; 10:23; 14:4; 1 Thess 5:11). As a missionary he knows how difficult it is to build people up.

How can Christians with differing views be part of the same church? What can you do to build up the church?

Please Others, Not Yourselves

15 We who are strong ought to put up with the failings of the weak, and not to please ourselves. [2]Each of us must please

15:1-3 Christ did not please himself: Christ is the model, and so believers do not please themselves but others.

[a] Gk *brother* [b] Other ancient authorities read *of Christ* [c] Or *confess* [d] Other ancient authorities lack *to God* [e] Gk *of a brother* [f] Other ancient authorities add *or be upset or be weakened* [g] Or *conviction* [h] Other authorities, some ancient, add here 16.25–27

our neighbor for the good purpose of building up the neighbor. 3For Christ did not please himself; but, as it is written, "The insults of those who insult you have fallen on me." 4For whatever was written in former days was written for our instruction, so that by steadfastness and by the encouragement of the scriptures we might have hope. 5May the God of steadfastness and encouragement grant you to live in harmony with one another, in accordance with Christ Jesus, 6so that together you may with one voice glorify the God and Father of our Lord Jesus Christ.

The Gospel for Jews and Gentiles Alike

7 Welcome one another, therefore, just as Christ has welcomed you, for the glory of God. 8For I tell you that Christ has become a servant of the circumcised on behalf of the truth of God in order that he might confirm the promises given to the patriarchs, 9and in order that the Gentiles might glorify God for his mercy. As it is written,

"Therefore I will confess[a] you among the Gentiles,
and sing praises to your name";

10and again he says,

"Rejoice, O Gentiles, with his people";

11and again,

"Praise the Lord, all you Gentiles,
and let all the peoples praise him";

12and again Isaiah says,

"The root of Jesse shall come,
the one who rises to rule the Gentiles;
in him the Gentiles shall hope."

13May the God of hope fill you with all joy and peace in believing, so that you may abound in hope by the power of the Holy Spirit.

Paul's Reason for Writing So Boldly

14 I myself feel confident about you, my brothers and sisters,[b] that you yourselves are full of goodness, filled with all knowledge, and able to instruct one another. 15Nevertheless on some points I have written to you rather boldly by way of reminder, because of the grace given me by God 16to be a minister of Christ Jesus to the Gentiles in the priestly service of the gospel of God, so that the offering of the Gentiles may be acceptable, sanctified by the Holy Spirit. 17In Christ Jesus, then, I have reason to boast of my work for God. 18For I will not venture to speak of anything except what Christ has accomplished[c] through me to win obedience from the Gentiles, by word and deed, 19by the power of signs and wonders, by the power of the Spirit of

[a] Or *thank* [b] Gk *brothers* [c] Gk *speak of those things that Christ has not accomplished*

15:14-33 my brothers and sisters: Paul begins to conclude his letter. In 15:14-21, he states again his call and mission. In 15:22-33, he outlines his travel plans.

15:19 Illyricum: Illyricum was a Roman province across the Adriatic Sea from Italy (see Map 11, p. 2108). Paul has finished his work in the eastern part of the empire, where he has planted the church in different kinds of cities in different locations as part of his plan to claim the world for the gospel of Jesus.

God,[a] so that from Jerusalem and as far around as Illyricum I have fully proclaimed the good news[b] of Christ. 20 Thus I make it my ambition to proclaim the good news,[b] not where Christ has already been named, so that I do not build on someone else's foundation, 21 but as it is written,

"Those who have never been told of him shall see,
and those who have never heard of him shall understand."

Paul's Plan to Visit Rome

22 This is the reason that I have so often been hindered from coming to you. 23 But now, with no further place for me in these regions, I desire, as I have for many years, to come to you 24 when I go to Spain. For I do hope to see you on my journey and to be sent on by you, once I have enjoyed your company for a little while. 25 At present, however, I am going to Jerusalem in a ministry to the saints; 26 for Macedonia and Achaia have been pleased to share their resources with the poor among the saints at Jerusalem. 27 They were pleased to do this, and indeed they owe it to them; for if the Gentiles have come to share in their spiritual blessings, they ought also to be of service to them in material things. 28 So, when I have completed this, and have delivered to them what has been collected,[c] I will set out by way of you to Spain; 29 and I know that when I come to you, I will come in the fullness of the blessing[d] of Christ.

30 I appeal to you, brothers and sisters,[e] by our Lord Jesus Christ and by the love of the Spirit, to join me in earnest prayer to God on my behalf, 31 that I may be rescued from the unbelievers in Judea, and that my ministry[f] to Jerusalem may be acceptable to the saints, 32 so that by God's will I may come to you with joy and be refreshed in your company. 33 The God of peace be with all of you.[g] Amen.

Personal Greetings

16 I commend to you our sister Phoebe, a deacon[h] of the church at Cenchreae, 2 so that you may welcome her in the Lord as is fitting for the saints, and help her in whatever she may require from you, for she has been a benefactor of many and of myself as well.

3 Greet Prisca and Aquila, who work with me in Christ Jesus, 4 and who risked their necks for my life, to whom not only I give thanks, but also all the churches of the Gentiles. 5 Greet also the church in their house. Greet my beloved Epaenetus, who was the first convert[i] in Asia for Christ. 6 Greet Mary, who has worked very hard among you. 7 Greet Andronicus and Junia,[j] my relatives[k] who were in prison

[a] Other ancient authorities read *of the Spirit* or *of the Holy Spirit* [b] Or *gospel* [c] Gk *have sealed to them this fruit* [d] Other ancient authorities add *of the gospel* [e] Gk *brothers* [f] Other ancient authorities read *my bringing of a gift* [g] One ancient authority adds 16.25–27 here [h] Or *minister* [i] Gk *first fruits* [j] Or *Junias;* other ancient authorities read *Julia* [k] Or *compatriots*

15:23-24 Spain: Spain, at the western end of the Mediterranean Sea, was considered to be barbarian territory (see Map 11, p. 2108).

15:24 to be sent on by you: This phrase is technical language requesting the Romans' help in conducting the mission in Spain. Paul most likely needs money, people (including translators), and prayers.

15:25, 31 a ministry to the saints: "Ministry" in this case refers to a monetary collection Paul has been taking among his basically Gentile congregations (15:25-27; 1 Cor 16:1-2; 2 Cor 8–9). The collection will be given to Jewish Christians in Jerusalem to relieve suffering and to show unity between Gentile and Jewish Christians.

16:1-2 Phoebe: Paul writes a brief recommendation for Phoebe. Likely she is the one who will bring the letter to Rome, and she may be the one who is to read it aloud and interpret it. She lives in Cenchreae, one of Corinth's two port cities (see Map 14, p. 2111).

16:1 deacon: Phoebe is one of the decision-makers and ministers in the congregation.

16:2 benefactor: The word *benefactor,* the Greek term for "patron," indicates that Phoebe has helped many people. She is an example of the important role of women in Paul's churches.

16:3-16 Greet: Paul sends greetings, as he seeks to build connections with the Roman congregations.

16:3 Prisca and Aquila: This married couple was a missionary team. She was also known as Priscilla. When Emperor Claudius expelled Jews from Rome, this couple moved to Corinth. They also worked with Paul in Ephesus (1 Cor 16:19; Acts 18:2, 18, 26).

16:5 the church in their house: Early Christians usually met in apartments or private homes.

16:7 Junia: Junia is a female apostle. (See note on "apostle" at 1:1.)

with me; they are prominent among the apostles, and they were in
Christ before I was. [8]Greet Ampliatus, my beloved in the Lord. [9]Greet
Urbanus, our co-worker in Christ, and my beloved Stachys. [10]Greet
Apelles, who is approved in Christ. Greet those who belong to the
family of Aristobulus. [11]Greet my relative[a] Herodion. Greet those in
the Lord who belong to the family of Narcissus. [12]Greet those workers in the Lord, Tryphaena and Tryphosa. Greet the beloved Persis,
who has worked hard in the Lord. [13]Greet Rufus, chosen in the Lord;
and greet his mother—a mother to me also. [14]Greet Asyncritus, Phle-
gon, Hermes, Patrobas, Hermas, and the brothers and sisters[b] who
are with them. [15]Greet Philologus, Julia, Nereus and his sister, and
Olympas, and all the saints who are with them. [16]Greet one another
with a holy kiss. All the churches of Christ greet you.

Final Instructions

17 I urge you, brothers and sisters,[b] to keep an eye on those who cause dissensions and offenses, in opposition to the teaching that you have learned; avoid them. [18]For such people do not serve our Lord
Christ, but their own appetites,[c] and by smooth talk and flattery they deceive the hearts of the simple-minded. [19]For while your obedience
is known to all, so that I rejoice over you, I want you to be wise in what is good and guileless in what is evil. [20]The God of peace will shortly
crush Satan under your feet. The grace of our Lord Jesus Christ be with you.[d]

21 Timothy, my co-worker, greets you; so do Lucius and Jason and Sosipater, my relatives.[e]

22 I Tertius, the writer of this letter, greet you in the Lord.[f]

23 Gaius, who is host to me and to the whole church, greets you. Erastus, the city treasurer, and our brother Quartus, greet you.[g]

Final Doxology

25 Now to God[h] who is able to strengthen you according to my gospel and the proclamation of Jesus Christ, according to the revelation of the mystery that was kept secret for long ages [26]but is now
disclosed, and through the prophetic writings is made known to all the Gentiles, according to the command of the eternal God, to bring about the obedience of faith— [27]to the only wise God, through Jesus
Christ, to whom[i] be the glory forever! Amen.[j]

16:21-23 Tertius: Paul relays greetings from other believers, including his secretary, Tertius. Paul probably dictated the letter to him.

16:23 Erastus: An inscription found at Corinth honors someone named Erastus, who was a city official and patron. (See note at 16:2.) If this refers to the same man, Paul's message has spread to people with higher income levels and social status.

---

[a] Or *compatriot* [b] Gk *brothers* [c] Gk *their own belly* [d] Other ancient authorities lack this sentence [e] Or *compatriots* [f] Or *I Tertius, writing this letter in the Lord, greet you* [g] Other ancient authorities add verse 24, *The grace of our Lord Jesus Christ be with all of you. Amen* [h] Gk *the one* [i] Other ancient authorities lack *to whom*. The verse then reads, *to the only wise God be the glory through Jesus Christ forever. Amen.* [j] Other ancient authorities lack 16.25–27 or include it after 14.23 or 15.33; others put verse 24 after verse 27

1 Corinthians 11:23-26

1 CORINTHIANS

Background File

Paul wrote this letter to the Corinthian church around 53–55 C.E., from Ephesus (see 16:8). In it he responds to a letter that some in the church have written to him (7:1). But he is also responding to an *oral* report from "Chloe's people" (1:11; see 5:1), who have brought him disturbing news. The church is divided, and one of the points at issue seems to be Paul's own authority.

What's the Story?

Although we call this "First Corinthians," Paul wrote another, earlier letter (see 5:9), which is lost. First Corinthians is one more stage in a much longer back-and-forth between Paul and the Corinthian church. After Paul "planted" the community of believers in Christ in Corinth (3:6) and stayed there for a year and a half (Acts 18:1-11), he left to continue his work elsewhere. Another teacher, Apollos, came to Corinth and was successful, apparently baptizing many ("Apollos watered," 3:6). Paul writes that they are "working together" (3:9), so he scolds the Corinthians for being divided, siding with one apostle or another (1:10-17).

This complex letter gives us our best first-hand information about day-to-day realities in the early church. It is a bewildering mix of issues, involving competing claims to wisdom, wealth, power, and spiritual gifts. Apparently people disagree about specific practices: should Christians break off relationships, including marriages, with nonbelievers? Can they eat meat that has been offered to other gods? Paul brings up still other issues: sexual immorality (chapter 5), Christians taking each other to court (chapter 6), what Paul considers their abuse of the Lord's Supper (chapter 11) and of the charismatic gift of speaking in tongues (chapter 14).

Some influential scholars say that *control* is the central issue in the letter. They think Paul wrote to establish *his* authority over the church. The Corinthians had misunderstood the gospel, supposing that Paul's message of freedom in the gospel meant they could throw aside moral constraints and social roles of the time. For example, some Corinthian women had thrown off the veil, perhaps a symbol of subordination to their husbands (11:2-16). They were speaking up in church (14:34-35), and some may have declared their independence from nonbelieving husbands and fiancés (chapter 7). In short, they were acting as men would act and taking on roles normally reserved for men. Paul stepped in and reasserted what that society said was the rightful control exercised by men, God, and apostles—chiefly himself.

Paul certainly confronts bad behavior in the letter. Recent studies have suggested that Paul was angered by elite persons in the church, males mostly, who misused church meetings as opportunities to display social status. Persons in antiquity were intensely aware of rank. Gender, class, wealth, education, freeborn or slave, urban or rural dwelling—these were some of the factors that determined a person's standing. It was a social fact of life that gatherings were occasions when the honorable were honored and the humble reminded of their shameful position. Paul attacks those in the Corinthian church who turned the Christian assembly into such an event. He accuses them of celebrating their prosperity while he and the other apostles still appear "like the rubbish of the world" (4:13). He scolds them for ignoring the hungry at the Lord's Supper (11:20-22). Paul's answer to their identity crisis seems clear enough. The church's humble beginnings were no accident. "God chose what is foolish in the world to shame the wise," the weak to shame the strong, the "low and despised in the world, things that are not, to reduce to nothing things that are" (1:27-28).

What's the Message?

First Corinthians is primarily about love. That is why reading the letter as Paul's attempt to establish authority over the church misses the point. Love is not the same thing as control, nor is love the same as discipline. Control is power over others or even power on behalf of others. But love is communion. It is the sharing of all things between persons who are completely open to one another. It is mutuality and equality. Most of all, it is a desire for the presence of the other. It is sitting face to face and knowing as one is known. Love themes run throughout 1 Corinthians, indicating that Paul is up to something other than asserting his authority.

The structure of 1 Corinthians reflects Paul's strategy of replacing displays of social status with love. Paul ridicules power as it is normally interpreted and claims real power is Christ crucified (1:1—2:16). He redefines leadership as the distribution of the mystery of God's will to glorify humanity (3:1—4:21). He attacks the privileges of the elite and praises love as the better way for the church to live (5:1—14:40). In chapter 13, he speaks of love as the greatest of God's gifts. Finally, chapter 15 tells the good news of how God's love will be everything to everyone in the resurrection.

Salutation

1 Paul, called to be an apostle of Christ Jesus by the will of God, and
our brother Sosthenes,
2 To the church of God that is in Corinth, to those who are sanctified in Christ Jesus, called to be saints, together with all those who
in every place call on the name of our Lord Jesus Christ, both their
Lord[a] and ours:
3 Grace to you and peace from God our Father and the Lord
Jesus Christ.

1:1-2 apostle of Christ…Sosthenes…Corinth: Paul claims to be an "apostle," which means "one who is chosen and sent." It is not clear if Sosthenes is the same person who was leader of the Jewish synagogue in Corinth (see Acts 18:17). The city of Corinth, in Greece, was a center of culture and had many temples honoring Greek gods such as Aesclepius, the god of healing, and Aphrodite, the goddess of love.

[a] Gk *theirs*

4 I give thanks to my[a] God always for you because of the grace
of God that has been given you in Christ Jesus, [5]for in every way you
have been enriched in him, in speech and knowledge of every kind—
[6]just as the testimony of[b] Christ has been strengthened among you—
[7]so that you are not lacking in any spiritual gift as you wait for the
revealing of our Lord Jesus Christ. [8]He will also strengthen you to the
end, so that you may be blameless on the day of our Lord Jesus Christ.
[9]God is faithful; by him you were called into the fellowship of his Son,
Jesus Christ our Lord.

Divisions in the Church

10 Now I appeal to you, brothers and sisters,[c] by the name of our
Lord Jesus Christ, that all of you be in agreement and that there be
no divisions among you, but that you be united in the same mind
and the same purpose. [11]For it has been reported to me by Chloe's
people that there are quarrels among you, my brothers and sisters.[d]
[12]What I mean is that each of you says, "I belong to Paul," or "I belong
to Apollos," or "I belong to Cephas," or "I belong to Christ." [13]Has
Christ been divided? Was Paul crucified for you? Or were you baptized in the name of Paul? [14]I thank God[e] that I baptized none of you
except Crispus and Gaius, [15]so that no one can say that you were baptized in my name. [16](I did baptize also the household of Stephanas;
beyond that, I do not know whether I baptized anyone else.) [17]For
Christ did not send me to baptize but to proclaim the gospel, and not
with eloquent wisdom, so that the cross of Christ might not be emptied of its power.

Christ the Power and Wisdom of God

18 For the message about the cross is foolishness to those who
are perishing, but to us who are being saved it is the power of God.
[19]For it is written,

"I will destroy the wisdom of the wise,
and the discernment of the discerning I will thwart."

[20]Where is the one who is wise? Where is the scribe? Where is the
debater of this age? Has not God made foolish the wisdom of the
world? [21]For since, in the wisdom of God, the world did not know
God through wisdom, God decided, through the foolishness of our
proclamation, to save those who believe. [22]For Jews demand signs
and Greeks desire wisdom, [23]but we proclaim Christ crucified, a
stumbling block to Jews and foolishness to Gentiles, [24]but to those
who are the called, both Jews and Greeks, Christ the power of God
and the wisdom of God. [25]For God's foolishness is wiser than human
wisdom, and God's weakness is stronger than human strength.

---

[a] Other ancient authorities lack *my* [b] Or *to* [c] Gk *brothers* [d] Gk *my brothers* [e] Other ancient authorities read *I am thankful*

1:7 spiritual gift: See 12:1-11 and note.

1:9 fellowship: The Greek word translated here as "fellowship" is *koinonia* (koi-noh-NEE-ah). This *koinonia* is related to love, which figures prominently in the rest of the letter.

How does Luther speak of Christian fellowship or community as a "happy exchange"? Humans share with Christ all that Christ is and has, and Christ shares with us all that we are and have—like a bride and bridegroom, lovers, or two very close friends. The medieval teacher Bernard of Clairvaux described this as a "happy exchange." Luther used that term to describe the relationship between the believer and Christ. When the Christian grasps Christ in faith, that is, relies on him to be truthful and trustworthy, then he or she is joined to him like a bride to her bridegroom. All that belongs to the bride becomes his and all that is his is shared with her. *1 Corinthians 1:9*

1:10-12, 29-31 no divisions among you...boast in the Lord: Observing distinctions in social status diminishes the church. Apparently, high-ranking men accustomed to controlling those of lower social standing (women, children, slaves, and those who were poor) were using the assemblies of believers to show off their status. The lower-status people apparently let them do it, perhaps even taking pride in the status of the one who dominated them (see 4:6; 5:2, 6). Paul seeks to get rid of all forms of controlling power from church life. He attacks the privileges of the powerful elite and builds up the confidence of those who do not belong to the elite. If anyone boasts, it is to be about Christ crucified (1:23).

1:10-15 Chloe's people...Apollos...Crispus and Gaius...Stephanas: Members of Chloe's family, or perhaps her servants if she was a prominent person, bring news to Paul. Apollos had spent time in Corinth (Acts 18:24—19:1), perhaps continuing Paul's ministry there. Crispus and Gaius are also mentioned in Acts 18:8 and Romans 16:23, respectively; Stephanas also is mentioned in 1 Corinthians 16:15.

26 Consider your own call, brothers and sisters:[a] not many of you were wise by human standards,[b] not many were powerful, not many were of noble birth. 27But God chose what is foolish in the world to shame the wise; God chose what is weak in the world to shame the strong; 28God chose what is low and despised in the world, things that are not, to reduce to nothing things that are, 29so that no one[c] might boast in the presence of God. 30He is the source of your life in Christ Jesus, who became for us wisdom from God, and righteousness and sanctification and redemption, 31in order that, as it is written, "Let the one who boasts, boast in[d] the Lord."

Proclaiming Christ Crucified

2 When I came to you, brothers and sisters,[a] I did not come proclaiming the mystery[e] of God to you in lofty words or wisdom. 2For I decided to know nothing among you except Jesus Christ, and him crucified. 3And I came to you in weakness and in fear and in much trembling. 4My speech and my proclamation were not with plausible words of wisdom,[f] but with a demonstration of the Spirit and of power, 5so that your faith might rest not on human wisdom but on the power of God.

The True Wisdom of God

6 Yet among the mature we do speak wisdom, though it is not a wisdom of this age or of the rulers of this age, who are doomed to perish. 7But we speak God's wisdom, secret and hidden, which God decreed before the ages for our glory. 8None of the rulers of this age understood this; for if they had, they would not have crucified the Lord of glory. 9But, as it is written,

"What no eye has seen, nor ear heard,
　nor the human heart conceived,
what God has prepared for those who love him"—

10these things God has revealed to us through the Spirit; for the Spirit searches everything, even the depths of God. 11For what human being knows what is truly human except the human spirit that is within? So also no one comprehends what is truly God's except the Spirit of God. 12Now we have received not the spirit of the world, but the Spirit that is from God, so that we may understand the gifts bestowed on us by God. 13And we speak of these things in words not taught by human wisdom but taught by the Spirit, interpreting spiritual things to those who are spiritual.[g]

14 Those who are unspiritual[h] do not receive the gifts of God's Spirit, for they are foolishness to them, and they are unable to

[a] Gk *brothers* [b] Gk *according to the flesh* [c] Gk *no flesh* [d] Or *of* [e] Other ancient authorities read *testimony* [f] Other ancient authorities read *the persuasiveness of wisdom* [g] Or *interpreting spiritual things in spiritual language*, or *comparing spiritual things with spiritual* [h] Or *natural*

1:18-25 the cross is foolishness... God made foolish the wisdom of the world: Paul contrasts God's wisdom (shown in the foolishness of the cross) with human wisdom. *Sophia* (wisdom) meant two different things to ancient Greeks. Among philosophers, particularly Stoics, it meant knowledge of the world as a perfect system of cause and effect. To be wise was to know that everything happens for a reason and everything is just as it should be. To think otherwise insults the great cause of all things, God. The rich and powerful favored Stoic ideas about cosmic order—because those ideas preserved the social order.

If Christ crucified is the "power of God and the wisdom of God" (1:23-24), however, then the force that holds the universe together is not the rule of superiors over inferiors but the love that joyfully bears the burdens of others. Seeing God in Christ crucified means we can no longer use God to justify hierarchy and oppression.

2:2 Jesus Christ...crucified: The Greek here and in 1:23 is in the perfect tense, which means that *crucified* refers not simply to a past event but one that happened in the past and has ongoing significance. In other words, Christ is who he is right now by being the crucified one. The resurrection does not remove from his identity his dying and his complete solidarity with humans in their sin and death. Mark 16:6 makes the same point, as does John 20:24-29.

2:6-16 we speak God's wisdom: God's inventive wisdom, demonstrated by raising the crucified one from the dead, far surpasses human reason and imagination (2:10-11). Before all time, God resolved to glorify humanity (2:7; see also Romans 5:1-2 and 8:18). In time, the crucified Christ, the Son of God, shares all that he has, even himself, with humanity (see 1:9; 2:16). This divine wisdom is particularly mysterious to those who value power and control above love (2:8).

How does Luther describe the role of the Holy Spirit and faith? In his explanation to the Third Article of the Creed, Luther says that we cannot believe in Jesus through own understanding or strength. Instead, the Holy Spirit calls us through the gospel, gives us spiritual gifts, and keeps us in the faith. *1 Corinthians 2:11-15*

understand them because they are spiritually discerned. 15 Those who
are spiritual discern all things, and they are themselves subject to no
one else's scrutiny.

16 "For who has known the mind of the Lord
so as to instruct him?"
But we have the mind of Christ.

On Divisions in the Corinthian Church

3:1-23 I belong to Paul…Apollos… let no one boast about human leaders: Apparently a controversy over which leader was best arose in the Corinthian church (3:4). Paul reminds the Corinthians of his work among them as one who planted the gospel (3:6) and laid the foundation for the church (3:10-11). Apollos and others (3:22) watered and kept the church growing through their work. But Paul reminds them that the true foundation of the church is Jesus Christ (3:11). Since Christ is the true leader of the church, they shouldn't waste time arguing about which leader is best (3:21).

3 And so, brothers and sisters,[a] I could not speak to you as spiritual people, but rather as people of the flesh, as infants in Christ.
2 I fed you with milk, not solid food, for you were not ready for solid
food. Even now you are still not ready, 3 for you are still of the flesh.
For as long as there is jealousy and quarreling among you, are you
not of the flesh, and behaving according to human inclinations? 4 For
when one says, "I belong to Paul," and another, "I belong to Apollos,"
are you not merely human?

5 What then is Apollos? What is Paul? Servants through whom
you came to believe, as the Lord assigned to each. 6 I planted, Apollos
watered, but God gave the growth. 7 So neither the one who plants nor
the one who waters is anything, but only God who gives the growth.
8 The one who plants and the one who waters have a common purpose, and each will receive wages according to the labor of each. 9 For
we are God's servants, working together; you are God's field, God's
building.

10 According to the grace of God given to me, like a skilled master
builder I laid a foundation, and someone else is building on it. Each
builder must choose with care how to build on it. 11 For no one can
lay any foundation other than the one that has been laid; that foundation is Jesus Christ. 12 Now if anyone builds on the foundation with
gold, silver, precious stones, wood, hay, straw— 13 the work of each
builder will become visible, for the Day will disclose it, because it will
be revealed with fire, and the fire will test what sort of work each has
done. 14 If what has been built on the foundation survives, the builder
will receive a reward. 15 If the work is burned up, the builder will suffer
loss; the builder will be saved, but only as through fire.

16 Do you not know that you are God's temple and that God's
Spirit dwells in you?[b] 17 If anyone destroys God's temple, God will destroy that person. For God's temple is holy, and you are that temple.

18 Do not deceive yourselves. If you think that you are wise in
this age, you should become fools so that you may become wise. 19 For
the wisdom of this world is foolishness with God. For it is written,

"He catches the wise in their craftiness,"

20 and again,

---

[a] Gk *brothers* [b] In verses 16 and 17 the Greek word for *you* is plural

"The Lord knows the thoughts of the wise,
that they are futile."
21 So let no one boast about human leaders. For all things are yours,
22 whether Paul or Apollos or Cephas or the world or life or death
or the present or the future—all belong to you, 23 and you belong to
Christ, and Christ belongs to God.

The Ministry of the Apostles

4 Think of us in this way, as servants of Christ and stewards of
God's mysteries. 2 Moreover, it is required of stewards that
they be found trustworthy. 3 But with me it is a very small thing that
I should be judged by you or by any human court. I do not even
judge myself. 4 I am not aware of anything against myself, but I am not
thereby acquitted. It is the Lord who judges me. 5 Therefore do not
pronounce judgment before the time, before the Lord comes, who
will bring to light the things now hidden in darkness and will disclose
the purposes of the heart. Then each one will receive commendation
from God.

6 I have applied all this to Apollos and myself for your benefit,
brothers and sisters,[a] so that you may learn through us the meaning of
the saying, "Nothing beyond what is written," so that none of you will
be puffed up in favor of one against another. 7 For who sees anything
different in you?[b] What do you have that you did not receive? And if
you received it, why do you boast as if it were not a gift?

8 Already you have all you want! Already you have become rich!
Quite apart from us you have become kings! Indeed, I wish that you
had become kings, so that we might be kings with you! 9 For I think
that God has exhibited us apostles as last of all, as though sentenced to
death, because we have become a spectacle to the world, to angels and
to mortals. 10 We are fools for the sake of Christ, but you are wise in
Christ. We are weak, but you are strong. You are held in honor, but we
in disrepute. 11 To the present hour we are hungry and thirsty, we are
poorly clothed and beaten and homeless, 12 and we grow weary from
the work of our own hands. When reviled, we bless; when persecuted,
we endure; 13 when slandered, we speak kindly. We have become like
the rubbish of the world, the dregs of all things, to this very day.

Fatherly Admonition

14 I am not writing this to make you ashamed, but to admonish
you as my beloved children. 15 For though you might have ten thousand guardians in Christ, you do not have many fathers. Indeed, in
Christ Jesus I became your father through the gospel. 16 I appeal to
you, then, be imitators of me. 17 For this reason I sent[c] you Timothy,

[a] Gk *brothers* [b] Or *Who makes you different from another?* [c] Or *am sending*

4:1-13 Think of us...as servants of Christ: Some in the church may have been using their social status to put others down (4:6). Paul's understanding of power and leadership contradicts the usual definition. No longer are leaders to exercise power over people, even if it is for their own good. Using his own and Apollos's ministry as examples (3:1-15), Paul says that leaders should not be granted any honor or special recognition until the final judgment (3:3, 12-15). The people of the church in fact *possess* their leaders (3:22). And, most significantly, true leaders are "stewards of God's mysteries" (4:1). In the ancient household, some of which may have consisted of twenty or more people, stewards had a responsibility to distribute food, clothing, and other necessities of life. Leaders in the church have a similar duty: to make sure that all possess, even enjoy, the unimaginably good news of God's promise to glorify humanity (2:7).

Paul declares that he and his fellow apostles live as "the rubbish of the world" (4:13). How do you think this connects with his understanding of leadership in the church? Where do you see the signs of this kind of servant leadership in the church or in the world today?

who is my beloved and faithful child in the Lord, to remind you of my ways in Christ Jesus, as I teach them everywhere in every church. [18]But some of you, thinking that I am not coming to you, have become arrogant. [19]But I will come to you soon, if the Lord wills, and I will find out not the talk of these arrogant people but their power. [20]For the kingdom of God depends not on talk but on power. [21]What would you prefer? Am I to come to you with a stick, or with love in a spirit of gentleness?

Sexual Immorality Defiles the Church

5 It is actually reported that there is sexual immorality among you, and of a kind that is not found even among pagans; for a man is living with his father's wife. [2]And you are arrogant! Should you not rather have mourned, so that he who has done this would have been removed from among you?

3 For though absent in body, I am present in spirit; and as if present I have already pronounced judgment [4]in the name of the Lord Jesus on the man who has done such a thing.[a] When you are assembled, and my spirit is present with the power of our Lord Jesus, [5]you are to hand this man over to Satan for the destruction of the flesh, so that his spirit may be saved in the day of the Lord.[b]

6 Your boasting is not a good thing. Do you not know that a little yeast leavens the whole batch of dough? [7]Clean out the old yeast so that you may be a new batch, as you really are unleavened. For our paschal lamb, Christ, has been sacrificed. [8]Therefore, let us celebrate the festival, not with the old yeast, the yeast of malice and evil, but with the unleavened bread of sincerity and truth.

Sexual Immorality Must Be Judged

9 I wrote to you in my letter not to associate with sexually immoral persons— [10]not at all meaning the immoral of this world, or the greedy and robbers, or idolaters, since you would then need to go out of the world. [11]But now I am writing to you not to associate with anyone who bears the name of brother or sister[c] who is sexually immoral or greedy, or is an idolater, reviler, drunkard, or robber. Do not even eat with such a one. [12]For what have I to do with judging those outside? Is it not those who are inside that you are to judge? [13]God will judge those outside. "Drive out the wicked person from among you."

Lawsuits among Believers

6 When any of you has a grievance against another, do you dare to take it to court before the unrighteous, instead of taking it

[a] Or *on the man who has done such a thing in the name of the Lord Jesus* [b] Other ancient authorities add *Jesus*
[c] Gk *brother*

5:1—14:40 It is actually reported: In these chapters, Paul criticizes various practices in Corinth that show how the privileges of the elite have distorted the church's common life. The biggest obstacle to ministry, in Paul's view, is for the church to forget the values of love, communion, and equality and instead become a location for observing distinctions in social status. In one passage after another, by shaming, cajoling, and even with wit, Paul seeks to talk the church out of allowing worldly distinctions in social status to reappear within the church's assembly.

5:1, 9-10 there is sexual immorality among you: This phrase and "sexually immoral persons" are misleading translations, because they are too general and do not help us understand what Paul finds objectionable. Paul uses two words with the same root: *porneia* and *pornos*, from which comes the term "pornography." Greek words with *porn-* as their root referred to sex in a commercial setting, with one person buying the body of another. The Greek phrase in 5:1 for having sex, which the NRSV blandly translates as "living with," also has a commercial connotation: "to have (someone)."

5:7 our paschal lamb: Jesus is compared to the animal slaughtered for the Jewish Festival of Passover (Exod 12:1-27; see also John 1:29).

6:1-11 do you dare to take it to court before the unrighteous: Paul rejected taking disputes in the church community to the civil law courts. Law courts in antiquity dealt with matters of injury to property and reputation. For this reason, only the upper classes, who were owners of property and anxious to maintain prestige, had a need for the courts. From these classes also came court officials. By taking property disputes out of the church assembly and into the law courts, the elite reminded lower-status persons in the church of their social inferiority.

6:4 do you appoint as judges: The NRSV translates this verse as a question, but from a grammatical point of view it is more likely a command: "appoint judges." A command also makes better sense in the social context described above—in effect, "Establish as arbiters those in the church who are counted as nobodies." Nothing would shame the elite more than to put their petty problems, as Paul sees them, before the poor of the church, who possess neither property nor reputation, but do have the Holy Spirit.

before the saints? 2Do you not know that the saints will judge the
world? And if the world is to be judged by you, are you incompetent
to try trivial cases? 3Do you not know that we are to judge angels—to
say nothing of ordinary matters? 4If you have ordinary cases, then, do
you appoint as judges those who have no standing in the church? 5I
say this to your shame. Can it be that there is no one among you wise
enough to decide between one believer[a] and another, 6but a believer[a]
goes to court against a believer[a]—and before unbelievers at that?

7 In fact, to have lawsuits at all with one another is already a defeat
for you. Why not rather be wronged? Why not rather be defrauded?
8But you yourselves wrong and defraud—and believers[b] at that.

9 Do you not know that wrongdoers will not inherit the kingdom of God? Do not be deceived! Fornicators, idolaters, adulterers,
male prostitutes, sodomites, 10thieves, the greedy, drunkards, revilers,
robbers—none of these will inherit the kingdom of God. 11And this
is what some of you used to be. But you were washed, you were sanctified, you were justified in the name of the Lord Jesus Christ and in
the Spirit of our God.

Glorify God in Body and Spirit

12 "All things are lawful for me," but not all things are beneficial.
"All things are lawful for me," but I will not be dominated by anything.
13"Food is meant for the stomach and the stomach for food,"[c] and
God will destroy both one and the other. The body is meant not for
fornication but for the Lord, and the Lord for the body. 14And God
raised the Lord and will also raise us by his power. 15Do you not know
that your bodies are members of Christ? Should I therefore take the
members of Christ and make them members of a prostitute? Never!
16Do you not know that whoever is united to a prostitute becomes
one body with her? For it is said, "The two shall be one flesh." 17But
anyone united to the Lord becomes one spirit with him. 18Shun fornication! Every sin that a person commits is outside the body; but the
fornicator sins against the body itself. 19Or do you not know that your
body is a temple[d] of the Holy Spirit within you, which you have from
God, and that you are not your own? 20For you were bought with a
price; therefore glorify God in your body.

Directions concerning Marriage

7 Now concerning the matters about which you wrote: "It is well
for a man not to touch a woman." 2But because of cases of sexual immorality, each man should have his own wife and each woman
her own husband. 3The husband should give to his wife her conjugal
rights, and likewise the wife to her husband. 4For the wife does not

[a] Gk *brother* [b] Gk *brothers* [c] The quotation may extend to the word *other* [d] Or *sanctuary*

6:9-11 wrongdoers . . . sodomites. The last two examples of injustice in verse 9 stir controversy: the Greek words *malakoi* (literally, "soft ones") and *arsenokoitai* (literally, "the ones who 'bed' males"). Bible versions beyond the NRSV (here "male prostitutes") translate *malakoi* as "passive homosexual partners" (NET) and "homosexuals" (NKJV); *arsenokoitai* (here "sodomites") appears as "practicing homosexuals,"(TNIV) and "homosexual offenders" (NIV). Two Bible versions (RSV and ESV) even join the separate words; one reads "sexual perverts" and the other "men who practice homosexuality." Recently, scholars have asked how ancient, Greek-speaking audiences might have heard the two terms. "Softness" signified lack of self-control in matters including but not limited to sex, as reflected in the KJV's "effeminate" and NJB's "the self-indulgent." Some early Christians (Theophilus of Antioch, Eusebius, and Macarius) heard in *arsenokoitai* a male's desire to increase his reputation for power by shaming other males through coerced penetration. In a word, rape.

6:12-20 united to a prostitute: In Greek antiquity, elite, married males regularly maintained women for sexual relationships outside of marriage. Although Paul does not say so directly, this use of prostitutes or mistresses would have emphasized the social power of elite males even within the church. Readers will note that the arguments of 6:12-20 seem disconnected from each other. From Paul's viewpoint they are. Any argument that puts an end to the behavior will do. His stated concern is not for the economic and psychological ruin that prostitution might bring to women. Rather, he seeks to shame the men out of this behavior by appealing to a widespread male attitude that in a romantic affair a man subordinated himself to the authority of a woman (6:12, 14-16).

7:1-9 It is well for a man not to touch a woman: The quotation marks in 7:1, which imply that the enclosed phrase is not Paul's own opinion, are not in the Greek text. For Paul, marriage is a second-best option provided for those who "burn," that is, those unable to control their passion. Some scholars have seen a breakthrough to equality between husband and wife in 7:3-5, but the underlying metaphors are drawn from the world of ownership and commerce. Sex is described as a matter of mutual "use," a fairly typical attitude in the ancient world.

How do Paul's views on sex and marriage here compare with the best moral reflection in our culture and the experiences of the faithful today?

have authority over her own body, but the husband does; likewise
the husband does not have authority over his own body, but the wife
does. 5 Do not deprive one another except perhaps by agreement for
a set time, to devote yourselves to prayer, and then come together
again, so that Satan may not tempt you because of your lack of self-
control. 6 This I say by way of concession, not of command. 7 I wish
that all were as I myself am. But each has a particular gift from God,
one having one kind and another a different kind.

8 To the unmarried and the widows I say that it is well for them to
remain unmarried as I am. 9 But if they are not practicing self-control,
they should marry. For it is better to marry than to be aflame with
passion.

10 To the married I give this command—not I but the Lord—
that the wife should not separate from her husband 11 (but if she does
separate, let her remain unmarried or else be reconciled to her husband), and that the husband should not divorce his wife.

12 To the rest I say—I and not the Lord—that if any believer[a]
has a wife who is an unbeliever, and she consents to live with him, he
should not divorce her. 13 And if any woman has a husband who is an
unbeliever, and he consents to live with her, she should not divorce
him. 14 For the unbelieving husband is made holy through his wife,
and the unbelieving wife is made holy through her husband. Otherwise, your children would be unclean, but as it is, they are holy. 15 But
if the unbelieving partner separates, let it be so; in such a case the
brother or sister is not bound. It is to peace that God has called you.[b]
16 Wife, for all you know, you might save your husband. Husband, for
all you know, you might save your wife.

The Life that the Lord Has Assigned

17 However that may be, let each of you lead the life that the
Lord has assigned, to which God called you. This is my rule in all the
churches. 18 Was anyone at the time of his call already circumcised?
Let him not seek to remove the marks of circumcision. Was anyone
at the time of his call uncircumcised? Let him not seek circumcision.
19 Circumcision is nothing, and uncircumcision is nothing; but obeying the commandments of God is everything. 20 Let each of you remain in the condition in which you were called.

21 Were you a slave when called? Do not be concerned about it.
Even if you can gain your freedom, make use of your present condition now more than ever.[c] 22 For whoever was called in the Lord as
a slave is a freed person belonging to the Lord, just as whoever was
free when called is a slave of Christ. 23 You were bought with a price;
do not become slaves of human masters. 24 In whatever condition you
were called, brothers and sisters,[d] there remain with God.

7:17-20 circumcision . . . uncircumcision: Paul came from a Jewish family and so was circumcised according to Israel's law (Phil 3:5). He disagreed with other early church leaders who believed new Gentile converts to Christianity should be circumcised to show that they were part of God's chosen people (see Gal 2:1-14; Rom 2:25-29).

---

[a] Gk *brother* [b] Other ancient authorities read *us* [c] Or *avail yourself of the opportunity* [d] Gk *brothers*

The Unmarried and the Widows

25 Now concerning virgins, I have no command of the Lord, but
I give my opinion as one who by the Lord's mercy is trustworthy. 26 I
think that, in view of the impending[a] crisis, it is well for you to remain
as you are. 27 Are you bound to a wife? Do not seek to be free. Are you
free from a wife? Do not seek a wife. 28 But if you marry, you do not
sin, and if a virgin marries, she does not sin. Yet those who marry will
experience distress in this life,[b] and I would spare you that. 29 I mean,
brothers and sisters,[c] the appointed time has grown short; from now
on, let even those who have wives be as though they had none, 30 and
those who mourn as though they were not mourning, and those
who rejoice as though they were not rejoicing, and those who buy as
though they had no possessions, 31 and those who deal with the world
as though they had no dealings with it. For the present form of this
world is passing away.

32 I want you to be free from anxieties. The unmarried man is
anxious about the affairs of the Lord, how to please the Lord; 33 but
the married man is anxious about the affairs of the world, how to
please his wife, 34 and his interests are divided. And the unmarried
woman and the virgin are anxious about the affairs of the Lord, so
that they may be holy in body and spirit; but the married woman is
anxious about the affairs of the world, how to please her husband. 35 I
say this for your own benefit, not to put any restraint upon you, but to
promote good order and unhindered devotion to the Lord.

36 If anyone thinks that he is not behaving properly toward his
fiancée,[d] if his passions are strong, and so it has to be, let him marry as
he wishes; it is no sin. Let them marry. 37 But if someone stands firm
in his resolve, being under no necessity but having his own desire under control, and has determined in his own mind to keep her as his
fiancée,[d] he will do well. 38 So then, he who marries his fiancée[d] does
well; and he who refrains from marriage will do better.

39 A wife is bound as long as her husband lives. But if the husband dies,[e] she is free to marry anyone she wishes, only in the Lord.
40 But in my judgment she is more blessed if she remains as she is. And
I think that I too have the Spirit of God.

Food Offered to Idols

8 Now concerning food sacrificed to idols: we know that "all of
us possess knowledge." Knowledge puffs up, but love builds up.
2 Anyone who claims to know something does not yet have the necessary knowledge; 3 but anyone who loves God is known by him.

4 Hence, as to the eating of food offered to idols, we know that
"no idol in the world really exists," and that "there is no God but one."

[a] Or *present* [b] Gk *in the flesh* [c] Gk *brothers* [d] Gk *virgin* [e] Gk *falls asleep*

7:26 impending crisis: Paul apparently believed the time he was living in would soon pass away (7:29, 31). This seemed to color his views of whether or not to marry.

If you were certain that Jesus would return soon in your lifetime, how would that change the way you live? Why?

8:1—11:1 concerning food sacrificed to idols: Paul addresses yet another subject that was likely causing some concern or controversy. Could meat that had been ritually sacrificed and prepared as an offering to a god be eaten by Christ's followers? Temples to several gods existed in Corinth. Animals were sacrificed to those gods, and the sacred meat from the rituals was often eaten in communal meals in those temples. Though Paul saw those gods as powerless and the offerings as just food, he warned the believers that they had to consider how others who were weak in conscience might view such eating (8:10) and in so doing compromise their faith in Christ (8:13; 10:28-29). See also the note on 8:6.

8:1-13 Knowledge puffs up, but love builds up: Thus love trumps knowledge, even when knowledge is absolutely correct. This passage anticipates chapter 13, especially 13:8-13. For Paul, what was the problem with knowledge? Knowing requires subjects and objects. Love overcomes the distance between subjects and objects. With knowledge, lives are observed, studied, understood. With love, however, lives are shared and the communion mentioned in 1:9 happens.

8:6 Jesus Christ, through whom are all things and through whom we exist:. The idea of a single force originating and permeating the universe is from ancient Stoic philosophy. In this way of seeing the world, there is no such thing as clean or unclean, since God is present in *all* things as originator and guide. The elite within the church may have approached the question of idol meat with this kind of "knowledge." They may never have considered that their consumption of meat was a privilege afforded to them by their "better" knowledge and their wealth, which allowed them routinely to eat a relatively expensive food. Paul does not say they are incorrect about the inconsequential nature of meat, but that knowledge itself must take a back seat to love for the sake of the one for whom Christ died (8:11).

5 Indeed, even though there may be so-called gods in heaven or on
earth—as in fact there are many gods and many lords— 6 yet for us
there is one God, the Father, from whom are all things and for whom
we exist, and one Lord, Jesus Christ, through whom are all things and
through whom we exist.
7 It is not everyone, however, who has this knowledge. Since
some have become so accustomed to idols until now, they still think
of the food they eat as food offered to an idol; and their conscience,
being weak, is defiled. 8 "Food will not bring us close to God."[a] We
are no worse off if we do not eat, and no better off if we do. 9 But take
care that this liberty of yours does not somehow become a stumbling
block to the weak. 10 For if others see you, who possess knowledge,
eating in the temple of an idol, might they not, since their conscience
is weak, be encouraged to the point of eating food sacrificed to idols?
11 So by your knowledge those weak believers for whom Christ died
are destroyed.[b] 12 But when you thus sin against members of your
family,[c] and wound their conscience when it is weak, you sin against
Christ. 13 Therefore, if food is a cause of their falling,[d] I will never eat
meat, so that I may not cause one of them[e] to fall.

The Rights of an Apostle

9:1, 15 Am I not free?...I have made no use of any of these rights: Paul continues to speak of what it means to exercise Christian freedom, but the conversation takes a personal turn. Paul believes it is within his rights to freely ask for compensation for his work as an apostle of the gospel, but he has not chosen to exercise that right (9:15). Part of Paul's problem in Corinth was apparently that some in the church had very specific expectations of how an apostle should live, based perhaps on the example of other apostles or even on the words of Jesus (see Matt 10:5-14). They expected Paul to depend on them financially; perhaps some of them even wanted to "own" his ministry! He insisted on his right to be financially independent (9:18).

What can we expect from our leaders in the church? What expectations do we have about our ministers that have nothing to do with their ministry?

9 Am I not free? Am I not an apostle? Have I not seen Jesus our
Lord? Are you not my work in the Lord? 2 If I am not an apostle
to others, at least I am to you; for you are the seal of my apostleship
in the Lord.
3 This is my defense to those who would examine me. 4 Do we
not have the right to our food and drink? 5 Do we not have the right to
be accompanied by a believing wife,[f] as do the other apostles and the
brothers of the Lord and Cephas? 6 Or is it only Barnabas and I who
have no right to refrain from working for a living? 7 Who at any time
pays the expenses for doing military service? Who plants a vineyard
and does not eat any of its fruit? Or who tends a flock and does not
get any of its milk?
8 Do I say this on human authority? Does not the law also say
the same? 9 For it is written in the law of Moses, "You shall not muzzle an ox while it is treading out the grain." Is it for oxen that God is
concerned? 10 Or does he not speak entirely for our sake? It was indeed written for our sake, for whoever plows should plow in hope
and whoever threshes should thresh in hope of a share in the crop.
11 If we have sown spiritual good among you, is it too much if we reap
your material benefits? 12 If others share this rightful claim on you, do
not we still more?

---

[a] The quotation may extend to the end of the verse [b] Gk *the weak brother . . . is destroyed* [c] Gk *against the brothers* [d] Gk *my brother's falling* [e] Gk *cause my brother* [f] Gk *a sister as wife*

Nevertheless, we have not made use of this right, but we endure
anything rather than put an obstacle in the way of the gospel of Christ.
[13]Do you not know that those who are employed in the temple service get their food from the temple, and those who serve at the altar
share in what is sacrificed on the altar? [14]In the same way, the Lord
commanded that those who proclaim the gospel should get their living by the gospel.

15 But I have made no use of any of these rights, nor am I writing
this so that they may be applied in my case. Indeed, I would rather
die than that—no one will deprive me of my ground for boasting!
[16]If I proclaim the gospel, this gives me no ground for boasting, for
an obligation is laid on me, and woe to me if I do not proclaim the
gospel! [17]For if I do this of my own will, I have a reward; but if not of
my own will, I am entrusted with a commission. [18]What then is my
reward? Just this: that in my proclamation I may make the gospel free
of charge, so as not to make full use of my rights in the gospel.

19 For though I am free with respect to all, I have made myself a
slave to all, so that I might win more of them. [20]To the Jews I became
as a Jew, in order to win Jews. To those under the law I became as one
under the law (though I myself am not under the law) so that I might
win those under the law. [21]To those outside the law I became as one
outside the law (though I am not free from God's law but am under
Christ's law) so that I might win those outside the law. [22]To the weak
I became weak, so that I might win the weak. I have become all things
to all people, that I might by all means save some. [23]I do it all for the
sake of the gospel, so that I may share in its blessings.

24 Do you not know that in a race the runners all compete, but
only one receives the prize? Run in such a way that you may win it.
[25]Athletes exercise self-control in all things; they do it to receive a perishable wreath, but we an imperishable one. [26]So I do not run aimlessly, nor do I box as though beating the air; [27]but I punish my body
and enslave it, so that after proclaiming to others I myself should not
be disqualified.

What is the nature of Christian freedom? In an apparent contradiction, Paul says he is simultaneously a free person and a slave. This verse, along with Philippians 2:5-11, inspired Luther's treatise "On the Freedom of the Christian." In it he said: "A Christian is a perfectly free lord of all, subject to none. A Christian is a perfectly dutiful servant of all, subject to all." For the Christian, being a "slave" flows from consciousness of one's freedom. True freedom is power to bear another's suffering and even their death. *1 Corinthians 9:19*

How can a person be free and a servant at the same time?

Warnings from Israel's History

10 I do not want you to be unaware, brothers and sisters,[a]
that our ancestors were all under the cloud, and all passed
through the sea, [2]and all were baptized into Moses in the cloud and
in the sea, [3]and all ate the same spiritual food, [4]and all drank the same
spiritual drink. For they drank from the spiritual rock that followed
them, and the rock was Christ. [5]Nevertheless, God was not pleased
with most of them, and they were struck down in the wilderness.

6 Now these things occurred as examples for us, so that we might

10:1-11 our ancestors...do not complain as some of them did: Paul's ancestors are the people of Israel. God led them out of Egypt by a cloud and pillar of fire and opened the Red Sea for them to escape the Egyptians (Exod 13:3—14:31). Even though God saved them and took care of them in the wilderness, the people worshiped an idol (Exod 32) and complained, so God punished them (Num 14:1-16, 29-30; Heb 3:17). Paul warns the Corinthians about complaining (10:10) and worshiping idols (10:14).

[a] Gk *brothers*

not desire evil as they did. 7 Do not become idolaters as some of them
did; as it is written, "The people sat down to eat and drink, and they
rose up to play." 8 We must not indulge in sexual immorality as some
of them did, and twenty-three thousand fell in a single day. 9 We must
not put Christ[a] to the test, as some of them did, and were destroyed
by serpents. 10 And do not complain as some of them did, and were
destroyed by the destroyer. 11 These things happened to them to serve
as an example, and they were written down to instruct us, on whom
the ends of the ages have come. 12 So if you think you are standing,
watch out that you do not fall. 13 No testing has overtaken you that is
not common to everyone. God is faithful, and he will not let you be
tested beyond your strength, but with the testing he will also provide
the way out so that you may be able to endure it.

14 Therefore, my dear friends,[b] flee from the worship of idols. 15 I
speak as to sensible people; judge for yourselves what I say. 16 The cup
of blessing that we bless, is it not a sharing in the blood of Christ? The
bread that we break, is it not a sharing in the body of Christ? 17 Because
there is one bread, we who are many are one body, for we all partake
of the one bread. 18 Consider the people of Israel;[c] are not those who
eat the sacrifices partners in the altar? 19 What do I imply then? That
food sacrificed to idols is anything, or that an idol is anything? 20 No,
I imply that what pagans sacrifice, they sacrifice to demons and not
to God. I do not want you to be partners with demons. 21 You cannot
drink the cup of the Lord and the cup of demons. You cannot partake
of the table of the Lord and the table of demons. 22 Or are we provoking the Lord to jealousy? Are we stronger than he?

10:17 we who are many are one body: Paul describes the sharing of the cup (Christ's blood) and the bread (Christ's body) as a meal that unites Christ's followers with Christ as his one body. They don't need to participate in sacred meals honoring other gods, which Paul calls "demons" (10:20-21).

Do All to the Glory of God

23 "All things are lawful," but not all things are beneficial. "All
things are lawful," but not all things build up. 24 Do not seek your own
advantage, but that of the other. 25 Eat whatever is sold in the meat
market without raising any question on the ground of conscience,
26 for "the earth and its fullness are the Lord's." 27 If an unbeliever invites you to a meal and you are disposed to go, eat whatever is set
before you without raising any question on the ground of conscience.
28 But if someone says to you, "This has been offered in sacrifice," then
do not eat it, out of consideration for the one who informed you, and
for the sake of conscience— 29 I mean the other's conscience, not your
own. For why should my liberty be subject to the judgment of someone else's conscience? 30 If I partake with thankfulness, why should I
be denounced because of that for which I give thanks?

31 So, whether you eat or drink, or whatever you do, do everything for the glory of God. 32 Give no offense to Jews or to Greeks or

---

[a] Other ancient authorities read *the Lord* [b] Gk *my beloved* [c] Gk *Israel according to the flesh*

to the church of God, [33]just as I try to please everyone in everything I do, not seeking my own advantage, but that of many, so that they may be saved.

11 [1]Be imitators of me, as I am of Christ.

Head Coverings

2 I commend you because you remember me in everything and maintain the traditions just as I handed them on to you. [3]But I want you to understand that Christ is the head of every man, and the husband[a] is the head of his wife,[b] and God is the head of Christ. [4]Any man who prays or prophesies with something on his head disgraces his head, [5]but any woman who prays or prophesies with her head unveiled disgraces her head—it is one and the same thing as having her head shaved. [6]For if a woman will not veil herself, then she should cut off her hair; but if it is disgraceful for a woman to have her hair cut off or to be shaved, she should wear a veil. [7]For a man ought not to have his head veiled, since he is the image and reflection[c] of God; but woman is the reflection[c] of man. [8]Indeed, man was not made from woman, but woman from man. [9]Neither was man created for the sake of woman, but woman for the sake of man. [10]For this reason a woman ought to have a symbol of[d] authority on her head,[e] because of the angels. [11]Nevertheless, in the Lord woman is not independent of man or man independent of woman. [12]For just as woman came from man, so man comes through woman; but all things come from God. [13]Judge for yourselves: is it proper for a woman to pray to God with her head unveiled? [14]Does not nature itself teach you that if a man wears long hair, it is degrading to him, [15]but if a woman has long hair, it is her glory? For her hair is given to her for a covering. [16]But if anyone is disposed to be contentious—we have no such custom, nor do the churches of God.

Abuses at the Lord's Supper

17 Now in the following instructions I do not commend you, because when you come together it is not for the better but for the worse. [18]For, to begin with, when you come together as a church, I hear that there are divisions among you; and to some extent I believe it. [19]Indeed, there have to be factions among you, for only so will it become clear who among you are genuine. [20]When you come together, it is not really to eat the Lord's supper. [21]For when the time comes to eat, each of you goes ahead with your own supper, and one goes hungry and another becomes drunk. [22]What! Do you not have homes to eat and drink in? Or do you show contempt for the church of God and humiliate those who have nothing? What should I say to you? Should I commend you? In this matter I do not commend you!

---

[a] The same Greek word means *man* or *husband* [b] Or *head of the woman* [c] Or *glory* [d] Gk lacks *a symbol of* [e] Or *have freedom of choice regarding her head*

11:1-16 any woman who prays or prophesies with her head unveiled disgraces her head: Paul has usually been understood as trying here to reign in wayward women who have taken their freedom in the gospel *too* seriously and have thrown off the veil, a sign of their husbands' authority over them (11:10). But there is another way to interpret this text. The higher and more elaborate the arrangement of a woman's hair, the higher was her husband's wealth and social class. Paul's urging that women pray with their heads covered (11:13) would effectively hide the very thing elite husbands wished to display to their own advantage. On this reading, Paul is not putting women "in their place"—after all, what they wear on their heads is their own "authority" to pray and prophesy in church (see also Rom 16:1-2 and Phil 4:2-3). In 11:8-9, he qualifies what he has said in 11:4-7 to avoid a possible misunderstanding regarding the equality of men and women.

11:10 because of the angels: The translation adds "a symbol of" (see NRSV footnote *d*), but it is better to read this as "a woman ought to have authority over her head." Contrary to our ways of thinking, Paul's contemporaries thought of heavenly beings such as angels feeling sexual desire for humans (see Gen 6:1-4). Since hair was thought to be particularly attractive, women ought to have the right to protect themselves by keeping it from the sight of angels!

11:17-22 when you come together it is not for the better: The divisions and factions in the Corinthian church discussed earlier also were causing improper conduct when the people celebrated the Lord's Supper. Some drank too much wine, and some ate all the food before others got a share (11:21). Paul explains in 11:23-26 how this meal is supposed to happen.

How do Lutherans understand the body and blood in the Lord's Supper? Paul recites the words of Jesus in 11:23-26 (see also Matt 26:26-29; Luke 22:15-20). Central to the Lutheran understanding of the Lord's Supper are the words "This *is* my body . . . my blood." While some Christians tend to understand the bread and the wine as symbols for Jesus' body and blood, Lutherans follow Luther's belief that the words should be understood literally. But Lutherans prefer to talk about the "real presence of Christ" in or with the bread and wine of Holy Communion. For Lutherans, the bread and wine do not themselves become Christ's body and blood; instead, with the bread and wine, Christ gives himself entirely, that is, physically, to us. This "sacramental unity" is described concisely in Luther's *Small Catechism*: "It is the true body and blood of our Lord Jesus Christ under the bread and wine, instituted by Christ himself for us Christians to eat and to drink" (*SC*:33). *1 Corinthians 11:23-26*

The Institution of the Lord's Supper

23 For I received from the Lord what I also handed on to you,
that the Lord Jesus on the night when he was betrayed took a loaf of
bread, 24 and when he had given thanks, he broke it and said, "This
is my body that is for[a] you. Do this in remembrance of me." 25 In the
same way he took the cup also, after supper, saying, "This cup is the
new covenant in my blood. Do this, as often as you drink it, in remembrance of me." 26 For as often as you eat this bread and drink the cup,
you proclaim the Lord's death until he comes.

Partaking of the Supper Unworthily

27 Whoever, therefore, eats the bread or drinks the cup of the
Lord in an unworthy manner will be answerable for the body and
blood of the Lord. 28 Examine yourselves, and only then eat of the
bread and drink of the cup. 29 For all who eat and drink[b] without discerning the body,[c] eat and drink judgment against themselves. 30 For
this reason many of you are weak and ill, and some have died.[d] 31 But
if we judged ourselves, we would not be judged. 32 But when we are
judged by the Lord, we are disciplined[e] so that we may not be condemned along with the world.

33 So then, my brothers and sisters,[f] when you come together to
eat, wait for one another. 34 If you are hungry, eat at home, so that when
you come together, it will not be for your condemnation. About the
other things I will give instructions when I come.

Spiritual Gifts

12:1-11 Now concerning spiritual gifts: This phrase signals Paul's response to another concern or controversy: What are the spiritual gifts? And are some better than others, as some followers may have been claiming? Different gifts are given to different people, but they all come from the same source, God (12:6), and for one purpose, "the common good" (12:7).

12 Now concerning spiritual gifts,[g] brothers and sisters,[f] I do
not want you to be uninformed. 2 You know that when you
were pagans, you were enticed and led astray to idols that could not
speak. 3 Therefore I want you to understand that no one speaking by
the Spirit of God ever says "Let Jesus be cursed!" and no one can say
"Jesus is Lord" except by the Holy Spirit.

4 Now there are varieties of gifts, but the same Spirit; 5 and there
are varieties of services, but the same Lord; 6 and there are varieties of
activities, but it is the same God who activates all of them in everyone. 7 To each is given the manifestation of the Spirit for the common
good. 8 To one is given through the Spirit the utterance of wisdom,
and to another the utterance of knowledge according to the same
Spirit, 9 to another faith by the same Spirit, to another gifts of healing by the one Spirit, 10 to another the working of miracles, to another
prophecy, to another the discernment of spirits, to another various

---

[a] Other ancient authorities read *is broken for* [b] Other ancient authorities add *in an unworthy manner,* [c] Other ancient authorities read *the Lord's body* [d] Gk *fallen asleep* [e] Or *When we are judged, we are being disciplined by the Lord* [f] Gk *brothers* [g] Or *spiritual persons*

kinds of tongues, to another the interpretation of tongues. 11All these
are activated by one and the same Spirit, who allots to each one individually just as the Spirit chooses.

One Body with Many Members

12 For just as the body is one and has many members, and all the
members of the body, though many, are one body, so it is with Christ.
13For in the one Spirit we were all baptized into one body—Jews or
Greeks, slaves or free—and we were all made to drink of one Spirit.

14 Indeed, the body does not consist of one member but of
many. 15If the foot would say, "Because I am not a hand, I do not belong to the body," that would not make it any less a part of the body.
16And if the ear would say, "Because I am not an eye, I do not belong
to the body," that would not make it any less a part of the body. 17If the
whole body were an eye, where would the hearing be? If the whole
body were hearing, where would the sense of smell be? 18But as it
is, God arranged the members in the body, each one of them, as he
chose. 19If all were a single member, where would the body be? 20As
it is, there are many members, yet one body. 21The eye cannot say to
the hand, "I have no need of you," nor again the head to the feet, "I
have no need of you." 22On the contrary, the members of the body
that seem to be weaker are indispensable, 23and those members of
the body that we think less honorable we clothe with greater honor,
and our less respectable members are treated with greater respect;
24whereas our more respectable members do not need this. But God
has so arranged the body, giving the greater honor to the inferior
member, 25that there may be no dissension within the body, but the
members may have the same care for one another. 26If one member
suffers, all suffer together with it; if one member is honored, all rejoice together with it.

27 Now you are the body of Christ and individually members
of it. 28And God has appointed in the church first apostles, second
prophets, third teachers; then deeds of power, then gifts of healing,
forms of assistance, forms of leadership, various kinds of tongues.
29Are all apostles? Are all prophets? Are all teachers? Do all work miracles? 30Do all possess gifts of healing? Do all speak in tongues? Do all
interpret? 31But strive for the greater gifts. And I will show you a still
more excellent way.

The Gift of Love

13 If I speak in the tongues of mortals and of angels, but do not
have love, I am a noisy gong or a clanging cymbal. 2And if I
have prophetic powers, and understand all mysteries and all knowledge, and if I have all faith, so as to remove mountains, but do not
have love, I am nothing. 3If I give away all my possessions, and if I

12:12-30 the body is one and has many members: It is surprising that Paul calls the church a body, since Greek and Roman political speeches ordinarily used this metaphor to encourage social unity based on hierarchy. The healthy human body corresponded to a healthy social body. Health, for the upper classes, meant that every part of the body was in its place and doing its assigned function. The body was diseased when any part of the body failed to keep its place or perform its function in some way. But Paul says that even the weaker parts of the body are important, and when one part suffers, all suffer (12:22-26).

12:27 you are the body of Christ: In his letters, Paul does not describe Jesus as the head of the church, and he does not seem to indicate the need for a hierarchy of control within the church. Here he speaks of the church as the body of Christ as having many members who have a variety of gifts. Only after Paul's death did other New Testament authors, writing in Paul's name, identify Christ as the "head" of the church (see Eph 4:14-16; Col 2:19). This change seemed to suggest the idea of hierarchical control within the church.

12:31—13:13 a still more excellent way: Here Paul shows that the mutuality and equality of love is a more excellent way to be the church than the hierarchical relations implied by the analogy of the human body. Perhaps beginning as early as the fourth century B.C.E., friends gathering to dine together (at *symposia*) sometimes ended their evening with hymns to love. Similarly, Paul begins to bring 1 Corinthians to a close with praise of love, the underlying theme of the letter.

hand over my body so that I may boast,[a] but do not have love, I gain nothing.

4 Love is patient; love is kind; love is not envious or boastful or arrogant 5or rude. It does not insist on its own way; it is not irritable or resentful; 6it does not rejoice in wrongdoing, but rejoices in the truth. 7It bears all things, believes all things, hopes all things, endures all things.

8 Love never ends. But as for prophecies, they will come to an end; as for tongues, they will cease; as for knowledge, it will come to an end. 9For we know only in part, and we prophesy only in part; 10but when the complete comes, the partial will come to an end. 11When I was a child, I spoke like a child, I thought like a child, I reasoned like a child; when I became an adult, I put an end to childish ways. 12For now we see in a mirror, dimly,[b] but then we will see face to face. Now I know only in part; then I will know fully, even as I have been fully known. 13And now faith, hope, and love abide, these three; and the greatest of these is love.

Gifts of Prophecy and Tongues

14 Pursue love and strive for the spiritual gifts, and especially that you may prophesy. 2For those who speak in a tongue do not speak to other people but to God; for nobody understands them, since they are speaking mysteries in the Spirit. 3On the other hand, those who prophesy speak to other people for their upbuilding and encouragement and consolation. 4Those who speak in a tongue build up themselves, but those who prophesy build up the church. 5Now I would like all of you to speak in tongues, but even more to prophesy. One who prophesies is greater than one who speaks in tongues, unless someone interprets, so that the church may be built up.

6 Now, brothers and sisters,[c] if I come to you speaking in tongues, how will I benefit you unless I speak to you in some revelation or knowledge or prophecy or teaching? 7It is the same way with lifeless instruments that produce sound, such as the flute or the harp. If they do not give distinct notes, how will anyone know what is being played? 8And if the bugle gives an indistinct sound, who will get ready for battle? 9So with yourselves; if in a tongue you utter speech that is not intelligible, how will anyone know what is being said? For you will be speaking into the air. 10There are doubtless many different kinds of sounds in the world, and nothing is without sound. 11If then I do not know the meaning of a sound, I will be a foreigner to the speaker and the speaker a foreigner to me. 12So with yourselves; since you are eager for spiritual gifts, strive to excel in them for building up the church.

[a] Other ancient authorities read *body to be burned* [b] Gk *in a riddle* [c] Gk *brothers*

13:12 then we will see face to face: The tender scene of two lovers gazing at one another "face to face" occurs in ancient art and poetry as early as the seventh century B.C.E. With this picture of perfect mutuality, equality, and devotion, Paul portrays the communion of God and world in the end time. The church, through the power of the Spirit, anticipates God's future (see 2 Cor 3:18).

Paul's words in praise of love are often said, or sung, at weddings and other celebrations. He meant them, however, as a serious plea, urging people to stop competing with one another for power and prestige and to live in genuine service to one another. How might Paul's vision of love shape the way we think about belonging to a church?

14:1-33 those who speak in a tongue do not speak to other people: Speaking in tongues needs to be understood in the context of the mysterious or ecstatic speech that occurred at certain temples in the Greek and Roman worlds. The oracle at Delphi is the most famous example. Gas (*pneuma*) emitted from the earth was understood to enter the body of the young woman (the oracle) and to displace her mind temporarily. The occupying spirit used the body as an instrument, much as a musician plays a guitar. The spirit would then disclose the future in speech that was often nonsensical and ambiguous. Interpreters were therefore required. Note that Paul criticizes speaking in unintelligible tongues, unless it is accompanied by interpretation. He repeats the idea that the gifts are for "upbuilding" the church (14:3; see note on 12:1-11). Speaking in tongues builds up the speaker but cannot build up the church unless interpreted (14:4).

13 Therefore, one who speaks in a tongue should pray for the
power to interpret. [14]For if I pray in a tongue, my spirit prays but my
mind is unproductive. [15]What should I do then? I will pray with the
spirit, but I will pray with the mind also; I will sing praise with the
spirit, but I will sing praise with the mind also. [16]Otherwise, if you say
a blessing with the spirit, how can anyone in the position of an outsider say the "Amen" to your thanksgiving, since the outsider does not
know what you are saying? [17]For you may give thanks well enough,
but the other person is not built up. [18]I thank God that I speak in
tongues more than all of you; [19]nevertheless, in church I would rather
speak five words with my mind, in order to instruct others also, than
ten thousand words in a tongue.

20 Brothers and sisters,[a] do not be children in your thinking;
rather, be infants in evil, but in thinking be adults. [21]In the law it is
written,

"By people of strange tongues
    and by the lips of foreigners
I will speak to this people;
    yet even then they will not listen to me,"

says the Lord. [22]Tongues, then, are a sign not for believers but for unbelievers, while prophecy is not for unbelievers but for believers. [23]If,
therefore, the whole church comes together and all speak in tongues,
and outsiders or unbelievers enter, will they not say that you are out of
your mind? [24]But if all prophesy, an unbeliever or outsider who enters
is reproved by all and called to account by all. [25]After the secrets of
the unbeliever's heart are disclosed, that person will bow down before
God and worship him, declaring, "God is really among you."

Orderly Worship

26 What should be done then, my friends?[a] When you come together, each one has a hymn, a lesson, a revelation, a tongue, or an interpretation. Let all things be done for building up. [27]If anyone speaks
in a tongue, let there be only two or at most three, and each in turn;
and let one interpret. [28]But if there is no one to interpret, let them
be silent in church and speak to themselves and to God. [29]Let two
or three prophets speak, and let the others weigh what is said. [30]If a
revelation is made to someone else sitting nearby, let the first person
be silent. [31]For you can all prophesy one by one, so that all may learn
and all be encouraged. [32]And the spirits of prophets are subject to the
prophets, [33]for God is a God not of disorder but of peace.

(As in all the churches of the saints, [34]women should be silent
in the churches. For they are not permitted to speak, but should be
subordinate, as the law also says. [35]If there is anything they desire to

[a] Gk *brothers*

14:33b-36 women should be silent in the churches: These verses seem to contradict Paul's approval of women speaking in church in other passages (see 11:5). Some scholars believe this passage is a non-Pauline addition that is more like comments found in other Pastoral Letters (see 1 Tim 2:11-12; Titus 2:5; 1 Pet 3:1-6). Others think Paul is being inconsistent. There is another solution: perhaps it is the *kind* of speech the women engage in that is at issue. Everyday conversations were not to distract from the assembly's conversation, where *all* are empowered to speak by the Spirit.

know, let them ask their husbands at home. For it is shameful for a woman to speak in church.[a] [36]Or did the word of God originate with you? Or are you the only ones it has reached?)

37 Anyone who claims to be a prophet, or to have spiritual powers, must acknowledge that what I am writing to you is a command of the Lord. [38]Anyone who does not recognize this is not to be recognized. [39]So, my friends,[b] be eager to prophesy, and do not forbid speaking in tongues; [40]but all things should be done decently and in order.

15:1-11 good news that I proclaimed to you... For I handed on to you as of first importance what I in turn had received: Paul summarizes the gospel ("good news") that he had preached to the Corinthians earlier when he lived among them (see introduction). Paul's description of Christ's resurrection is the earliest written account of appearances of the risen Jesus and a summary of what Paul had preached to the Corinthians (see 2 Cor 1:19). Some of the details are not the same as in the Gospel accounts. It is possible that the accounts of the discovery of the empty tomb circulated only later, after Paul had "received" what he "handed on" to the Corinthians.

The Resurrection of Christ

15 Now I would remind you, brothers and sisters,[c] of the good news[d] that I proclaimed to you, which you in turn received, in which also you stand, [2]through which also you are being saved, if you hold firmly to the message that I proclaimed to you—unless you have come to believe in vain.

3 For I handed on to you as of first importance what I in turn had received: that Christ died for our sins in accordance with the scriptures, [4]and that he was buried, and that he was raised on the third day in accordance with the scriptures, [5]and that he appeared to Cephas, then to the twelve. [6]Then he appeared to more than five hundred brothers and sisters[c] at one time, most of whom are still alive, though some have died.[e] [7]Then he appeared to James, then to all the apostles. [8]Last of all, as to one untimely born, he appeared also to me. [9]For I am the least of the apostles, unfit to be called an apostle, because I persecuted the church of God. [10]But by the grace of God I am what I am, and his grace toward me has not been in vain. On the contrary, I worked harder than any of them—though it was not I, but the grace of God that is with me. [11]Whether then it was I or they, so we proclaim and so you have come to believe.

15:12 how can some of you say there is no resurrection of the dead? Probably the Corinthians did not deny that Jesus had been "raised," but took that language in a "spiritual" sense—the same sense in which they believed that they, too, had been "raised" to a place of greater wisdom and knowledge. Compare the language in Colossians and Ephesians of having been "raised with Christ" and "seated... with him in the heavenly places" (Col 3:1; Eph 2:6), language that some scholars take as evidence that Paul himself did not write those letters. Here he insists that Jesus was raised "from the dead," in a body that had died but was now transformed (15:35-40).

For some, the Christian religion is mainly concerned with what happens after we die. Paul's argument with some of the Corinthians seems to be more concerned with how one lives before death. What difference would it make if we lived as though we look forward to the end of "every ruler and every authority and power" (15:24)? In what way are we like the Corinthians, who seemed to imagine that the world they lived in and the way they lived would go on in much the same way indefinitely?

The Resurrection of the Dead

12 Now if Christ is proclaimed as raised from the dead, how can some of you say there is no resurrection of the dead? [13]If there is no resurrection of the dead, then Christ has not been raised; [14]and if Christ has not been raised, then our proclamation has been in vain and your faith has been in vain. [15]We are even found to be misrepresenting God, because we testified of God that he raised Christ—whom he did not raise if it is true that the dead are not raised. [16]For if the dead are not raised, then Christ has not been raised. [17]If Christ has not been raised, your faith is futile and you are still in your sins. [18]Then those also who have died[e] in Christ have perished. [19]If for this life only we have hoped in Christ, we are of all people most to be pitied.

---

[a] Other ancient authorities put verses 34-35 after verse 40 [b] Gk *my brothers* [c] Gk *brothers* [d] Or *gospel* [e] Gk *fallen asleep*

20 But in fact Christ has been raised from the dead, the first fruits
of those who have died.[a] 21 For since death came through a human
being, the resurrection of the dead has also come through a human
being; 22 for as all die in Adam, so all will be made alive in Christ. 23 But
each in his own order: Christ the first fruits, then at his coming those
who belong to Christ. 24 Then comes the end,[b] when he hands over
the kingdom to God the Father, after he has destroyed every ruler and
every authority and power. 25 For he must reign until he has put all
his enemies under his feet. 26 The last enemy to be destroyed is death.
27 For "God[c] has put all things in subjection under his feet." But when
it says, "All things are put in subjection," it is plain that this does not
include the one who put all things in subjection under him. 28 When
all things are subjected to him, then the Son himself will also be subjected to the one who put all things in subjection under him, so that God may be all in all.

29 Otherwise, what will those people do who receive baptism on behalf of the dead? If the dead are not raised at all, why are people baptized on their behalf?

30 And why are we putting ourselves in danger every hour? 31 I
die every day! That is as certain, brothers and sisters,[d] as my boasting
of you—a boast that I make in Christ Jesus our Lord. 32 If with merely
human hopes I fought with wild animals at Ephesus, what would I have gained by it? If the dead are not raised,

"Let us eat and drink,
for tomorrow we die."

33 Do not be deceived:

"Bad company ruins good morals."

34 Come to a sober and right mind, and sin no more; for some people have no knowledge of God. I say this to your shame.

The Resurrection Body

35 But someone will ask, "How are the dead raised? With what
kind of body do they come?" 36 Fool! What you sow does not come to
life unless it dies. 37 And as for what you sow, you do not sow the body
that is to be, but a bare seed, perhaps of wheat or of some other grain.
38 But God gives it a body as he has chosen, and to each kind of seed
its own body. 39 Not all flesh is alike, but there is one flesh for human
beings, another for animals, another for birds, and another for fish.
40 There are both heavenly bodies and earthly bodies, but the glory of
the heavenly is one thing, and that of the earthly is another. 41 There
is one glory of the sun, and another glory of the moon, and another glory of the stars; indeed, star differs from star in glory.

42 So it is with the resurrection of the dead. What is sown is

[a] Gk *fallen asleep* [b] Or *Then come the rest* [c] Gk *he* [d] Gk *brothers*

15:28 so that God may be all in all: This is another expression of love at the center of all reality. "So-and-so is all things to me" was a popular phrase in Paul's day, used by the lover to describe the beloved. Here God is the world's beloved. The world and God share all things in the future God brings. Sharing "all things" is also what the church has traditionally confessed about the relationship of God the Father and Christ the Son.

15:32-33 Let us eat and drink, for tomorrow we die: Paul refers to Greek philosophy and poetry. This shows the level of his own education and that of at least some in the audience at Corinth. Fighting with "wild animals" (15:32) is not to be taken literally. Philosophers in Paul's day used the expression to describe to the perennial battle between reason and the passions, especially when they were denouncing the Epicureans, a philosophical school unfairly stereotyped as pleasure seekers. Epicureans thought that the soul dissolved with the body at death, so their opponents accused them of thinking something like "let us eat, drink, and be merry." Paul uses the same tactic to urge the Corinthians not to live only for the moment.

15:42-44 resurrection of the dead... raised a spiritual body: Paul says the dead will be raised from the dead with new spiritual bodies that are transformed. This is more than a resurrection of the spirit alone (see note at 15:12). The church's confession of faith, the Apostles' Creed, speaks of belief in the "resurrection of the body," just as Jesus was resurrected (see Rom 6:5).

Notice that Paul says nothing here about final judgment, nothing about hell. Just as all were incorporated into Adam's death through no fault of our own, Paul says all will be made alive in Christ through no effort of their own. We will be dead, after all (15:21-22).

Paul speaks of us bearing the image of the man of heaven in the resurrection (15:45-49). What do you think that means? Have you ever thought of your future beyond death, or of the world's future, in these terms?

perishable, what is raised is imperishable. [43]It is sown in dishonor, it
is raised in glory. It is sown in weakness, it is raised in power. [44]It is
sown a physical body, it is raised a spiritual body. If there is a physical
body, there is also a spiritual body. [45]Thus it is written, "The first man,
Adam, became a living being"; the last Adam became a life-giving
spirit. [46]But it is not the spiritual that is first, but the physical, and then
the spiritual. [47]The first man was from the earth, a man of dust; the
second man is[a] from heaven. [48]As was the man of dust, so are those
who are of the dust; and as is the man of heaven, so are those who are
of heaven. [49]Just as we have borne the image of the man of dust, we
will[b] also bear the image of the man of heaven.

50 What I am saying, brothers and sisters,[c] is this: flesh and blood
cannot inherit the kingdom of God, nor does the perishable inherit
the imperishable. [51]Listen, I will tell you a mystery! We will not all
die,[d] but we will all be changed, [52]in a moment, in the twinkling of an
eye, at the last trumpet. For the trumpet will sound, and the dead will
be raised imperishable, and we will be changed. [53]For this perishable
body must put on imperishability, and this mortal body must put on
immortality. [54]When this perishable body puts on imperishability,
and this mortal body puts on immortality, then the saying that is written will be fulfilled:

"Death has been swallowed up in victory."
55 "Where, O death, is your victory?
Where, O death, is your sting?"

[56]The sting of death is sin, and the power of sin is the law. [57]But thanks
be to God, who gives us the victory through our Lord Jesus Christ.

58 Therefore, my beloved,[e] be steadfast, immovable, always excelling in the work of the Lord, because you know that in the Lord
your labor is not in vain.

The Collection for the Saints

16:1-3 the collection for the saints…take your gift to Jerusalem: Paul had committed to collecting offerings for the church in Jerusalem (Gal 2:10; 2 Cor 8–9).

16 Now concerning the collection for the saints: you should follow the directions I gave to the churches of Galatia. [2]On the
first day of every week, each of you is to put aside and save whatever
extra you earn, so that collections need not be taken when I come.
[3]And when I arrive, I will send any whom you approve with letters to
take your gift to Jerusalem. [4]If it seems advisable that I should go also,
they will accompany me.

Plans for Travel

16:5, 8 Macedonia…Ephesus: For these locations, see Map 14, p. 2111.

5 I will visit you after passing through Macedonia—for I intend
to pass through Macedonia— [6]and perhaps I will stay with you or

[a] Other ancient authorities add *the Lord* [b] Other ancient authorities read *let us* [c] Gk *brothers* [d] Gk *fall asleep* [e] Gk *beloved brothers*

even spend the winter, so that you may send me on my way, wherever
I go. 7I do not want to see you now just in passing, for I hope to spend
some time with you, if the Lord permits. 8But I will stay in Ephesus
until Pentecost, 9for a wide door for effective work has opened to me,
and there are many adversaries.
10 If Timothy comes, see that he has nothing to fear among you,
for he is doing the work of the Lord just as I am; 11therefore let no one
despise him. Send him on his way in peace, so that he may come to
me; for I am expecting him with the brothers.
12 Now concerning our brother Apollos, I strongly urged him to
visit you with the other brothers, but he was not at all willing[a] to come
now. He will come when he has the opportunity.

16:8 Pentecost: Early Christians likely observed this Jewish festival that came fifty days after Passover.

16:10 Timothy: Paul's young coworker in the mission of the gospel (Acts 16:1-4; 1 Thess 1:1; 1 Tim 1:1-3). Paul had sent Timothy to the Corinthians (1 Cor 4:17).

Final Messages and Greetings

13 Keep alert, stand firm in your faith, be courageous, be strong.
14Let all that you do be done in love.
15 Now, brothers and sisters,[b] you know that members of the
household of Stephanas were the first converts in Achaia, and they
have devoted themselves to the service of the saints; 16I urge you to
put yourselves at the service of such people, and of everyone who
works and toils with them. 17I rejoice at the coming of Stephanas
and Fortunatus and Achaicus, because they have made up for your
absence; 18for they refreshed my spirit as well as yours. So give recognition to such persons.
19 The churches of Asia send greetings. Aquila and Prisca, together with the church in their house, greet you warmly in the Lord.
20All the brothers and sisters[b] send greetings. Greet one another with
a holy kiss.

16:19 Aquila and Prisca: Paul's close friends (see also Acts 18:1-3; Rom 16:3-5).

21 I, Paul, write this greeting with my own hand. 22Let anyone
be accursed who has no love for the Lord. Our Lord, come![c] 23The
grace of the Lord Jesus be with you. 24My love be with all of you in
Christ Jesus.[d]

---

[a] Or *it was not at all God's will for him* [b] Gk *brothers* [c] Gk *Marana tha.* These Aramaic words can also be read *Maran atha,* meaning *Our Lord has come* [d] Other ancient authorities add *Amen*

2 Corinthians 5:17

2 CORINTHIANS

Background File

Second Corinthians begins with 1:1 and ends with 13:13. That seems obvious, but many scholars believe that 2 Corinthians was not originally a single letter. Rather, they believe this is a compilation of several separate letters from Paul to the Corinthian church, written over a period of time after 1 Corinthians.

What's the Story?

Many scholars contend that the letter we see before us today was the work of a late first- or early second-century editor who pieced these thirteen chapters together out of five or perhaps six letter fragments. This theory has little to recommend it, except for the undeniable fact that the letter includes several rough transitions. Readers have noted for centuries the abrupt change of tone between 9:15 and 10:1, for example. Many have commented that 6:14—7:1 seems completely out of place in its present context. Once we consider the possibility that the letter is a compilation, traces of more letter fragments are easier to see.

The matching geographical references at 2:13 and 7:5 perhaps originally lay next to each other in a letter that included 1:1–2:13 and 7:5-15. The second-century editor would have cut the letter after 2:13 and inserted different fragments, the material in 2:14—6:13 and 7:2-4 (6:14—7:1 was then added even later). Chapters 8 and 9, which concern the unrelated topic of the collection for Jerusalem, were originally freestanding (and may have been two different letters, according to one respected scholar who wonders why else Paul would have repeated himself).

But are the rough transitions really so problematic? Recent studies of letter writing in the ancient world suggest that jerky movement within letters was not unusual. Neither was repetition. If this is true, we have no need to imagine letter fragments and an ancient editor, and we can read 2 Corinthians from 1:1 to 13:13 without worrying that we are missing the sense of what Paul wrote. Nevertheless, readers will be richly rewarded for reading the letter in long stretches: 1:1—7:15; 8:1—9:15; and 10:1—13:13.

Whether read as a single letter or a roughly edited compilation of several letters, 2 Corinthians shows that the relationship between Paul and the Corinthians worsened after they received 1 Corinthians. He made a "painful visit" to Corinth (2:1). Then he decided not to make another visit (12:14; 13:1) because he thought it would only aggravate the situation. He then wrote another letter, the "letter of tears"

(2:4)—now lost, unless we have part of it in chapters 10–13. As soon as Paul sent that letter, he regretted it (7:8) and the remorse stuck with him (1:8-9 and 2:13). Having probably sent it to Corinth with Titus, he couldn't wait for Titus to return, so he left Ephesus to meet him in Troas; then, not finding him there, he traveled on to Macedonia (2:12-13). The news from Titus offered some relief (7:13-16).

What's the Message?

Each section of 2 Corinthians has its own treasures. In the first section (1:1—7:15), Paul defends his ministry against charges that he is plenty bold when writing letters but his delivery is weak when he speaks with them face to face (10:9-11). His accusers know that he is bold in letters, because he wrote a nasty one to the Corinthians, the "letter of tears." The anguish Paul felt about having written that letter and the charges against him drove him to reflect deeply about the meaning of ministry.

The middle section of the letter (8:1—9:15) deals with the collection for the Christians in Jerusalem. On the surface, the topic is money. Below the surface, however, Paul deals with the social meaning of money and the way gifts are often given to emphasize the social distance between giver and recipient. In the last section (10:1—13:13), Paul does battle for the allegiance of the church. Rival missionaries have come on to the scene and their severity impressed the church—which led them to hold Paul's gentleness in suspicion.

Salutation

1 Paul, an apostle of Christ Jesus by the will of God, and Timothy our brother,

To the church of God that is in Corinth, including all the saints throughout Achaia:

2 Grace to you and peace from God our Father and the Lord Jesus Christ.

Paul's Thanksgiving after Affliction

3 Blessed be the God and Father of our Lord Jesus Christ, the
Father of mercies and the God of all consolation,
4 who consoles us in all our affliction, so that we may be able to console those who are in any affliction with the consolation with which we ourselves are consoled by God.
5 For just as the sufferings of Christ are abundant for us, so also our consolation is abundant through Christ.
6 If we are being afflicted, it is for your consolation and salvation; if we are being consoled, it is for your consolation, which you experience when you patiently endure the same sufferings that we are also suffering.
7 Our hope for you is unshaken; for we know that as you share in our sufferings, so also you share in our consolation.

8 We do not want you to be unaware, brothers and sisters,[a] of the

[a] Gk *brothers*

1:1 Timothy…Achaia: Paul's co-worker Timothy helped establish the church in Corinth (Acts 18:5; 2 Cor 1:19). Corinth was the capital city of the Roman province of Achaia (see Map 14, p. 2111).

1:3-7 Father of mercies…who consoles us…sufferings that we are also suffering: The feelings of the Corinthian community have been injured. So have Paul's. He caused the church grief by writing a severe rebuke, the "letter of tears" (see 2:4 and 7:8). Paul had been injured by a critic of his ministry (see 2:5). At first the church did not discipline the critic, but then they went overboard in their rebuke (2:5-11). Furthermore, Paul claims to have brought emotional pain to himself (see 1:8-9 and note on 1:9) by writing the letter of tears that had hurt his beloved Corinthians. The occasion of 2 Corinthians is far more complex and painful than the soothing words of 1:3-8 might imply. One indication of this is the fact that Greek words for "grief" and "to grieve" occur sixteen times in the letter (2:2-5, 7; 6:10; 7:8-11).

1:9 we had received the sentence of death: Paul tells how he passed the "sentence of death" upon himself after he sent the letter of tears to the Corinthian church through Titus. In ancient literature, such self-condemnation was a common way of expressing regret and remorse. Paul lets his injured readers know that his journey up the eastern coast of modern-day Turkey to his rendezvous with Titus in Macedonia (see 2:12-13 and 7:5-8) was filled with sorrow for having written the letter of tears and apprehension about its effects on the church.

1:12 This is our boast...godly sincerity: Sometime after Timothy arrived in Corinth with the letter we know as 1 Corinthians, other Christian missionaries, who disapproved of Paul's adaptability in ministry (see 1 Cor 9 and 1 Thess 2), charged him with flattering the Corinthian church. We have no independent information about Paul's rivals, only Paul's very biased descriptions of those he calls "super-apostles" in 2 Corinthians 11:5. They were probably quite severe in their own ministries, believing that apostles of Christ ought to come down hard on human failings (see 11:20-21 and 13:2-3). The gentleness that Paul calls the "grace of God" they call "fleshy wisdom" (1:12; the NRSV translates it as "earthly wisdom"). Much of 2 Corinthians 1–7 is dedicated to a defense of Paul's form of ministry, which seeks to embody God's grace.

1:17 ready to say "Yes, yes" and "No, no" at the same time?: Flatterers say "yes" to the "yes" said by the persons they seek to please and "no" to their "no." This verse echoes a famous line from a lost work of the Roman playwright Terence, entitled "The Flatterer." The opposite of flattery is the frank speech of friends, a topic Paul pursues in 3:1-18.

1:21-22 giving us his Spirit in our hearts as a first installment: This is a powerful application of the language of friendship. There may even be wedding imagery in the term "first installment" (a better translation: "pledge"), a gift to the bride indicating the groom's intentions and anticipating the future wedding. Paul uses marriage imagery for the church's relationship to Christ in 2 Corinthians 11:2 and describes his own relationship with Christ this way in Philippians 3:7-12. The author of Ephesians (probably not Paul) takes the image of marriage in a different direction, stressing the subordination of the wife (the church) to her husband (Christ).

affliction we experienced in Asia; for we were so utterly, unbearably
crushed that we despaired of life itself. 9Indeed, we felt that we had
received the sentence of death so that we would rely not on ourselves
but on God who raises the dead. 10He who rescued us from so deadly
a peril will continue to rescue us; on him we have set our hope that he
will rescue us again, 11as you also join in helping us by your prayers, so
that many will give thanks on our[a] behalf for the blessing granted us
through the prayers of many.

The Postponement of Paul's Visit

12 Indeed, this is our boast, the testimony of our conscience: we
have behaved in the world with frankness[b] and godly sincerity, not by
earthly wisdom but by the grace of God—and all the more toward
you. 13For we write you nothing other than what you can read and
also understand; I hope you will understand until the end— 14as you
have already understood us in part—that on the day of the Lord Jesus
we are your boast even as you are our boast.

15 Since I was sure of this, I wanted to come to you first, so that
you might have a double favor;[c] 16I wanted to visit you on my way to
Macedonia, and to come back to you from Macedonia and have you
send me on to Judea. 17Was I vacillating when I wanted to do this?
Do I make my plans according to ordinary human standards,[d] ready
to say "Yes, yes" and "No, no" at the same time? 18As surely as God
is faithful, our word to you has not been "Yes and No." 19For the Son
of God, Jesus Christ, whom we proclaimed among you, Silvanus and
Timothy and I, was not "Yes and No"; but in him it is always "Yes."
20For in him every one of God's promises is a "Yes." For this reason it
is through him that we say the "Amen," to the glory of God. 21But it is
God who establishes us with you in Christ and has anointed us, 22by
putting his seal on us and giving us his Spirit in our hearts as a first
installment.

23 But I call on God as witness against me: it was to spare you
that I did not come again to Corinth. 24I do not mean to imply that
we lord it over your faith; rather, we are workers with you for your joy,

2 because you stand firm in the faith. 1So I made up my mind
not to make you another painful visit. 2For if I cause you pain,
who is there to make me glad but the one whom I have pained? 3And
I wrote as I did, so that when I came, I might not suffer pain from
those who should have made me rejoice; for I am confident about
all of you, that my joy would be the joy of all of you. 4For I wrote you
out of much distress and anguish of heart and with many tears, not
to cause you pain, but to let you know the abundant love that I have
for you.

---

[a] Other ancient authorities read *your* [b] Other ancient authorities read *holiness* [c] Other ancient authorities read *pleasure* [d] Gk *according to the flesh*

Forgiveness for the Offender

5 But if anyone has caused pain, he has caused it not to me, but to
some extent—not to exaggerate it—to all of you. 6 This punishment
by the majority is enough for such a person; 7 so now instead you
should forgive and console him, so that he may not be overwhelmed
by excessive sorrow. 8 So I urge you to reaffirm your love for him. 9 I
wrote for this reason: to test you and to know whether you are obedient in everything. 10 Anyone whom you forgive, I also forgive. What
I have forgiven, if I have forgiven anything, has been for your sake in
the presence of Christ. 11 And we do this so that we may not be outwit-
ted by Satan; for we are not ignorant of his designs.

Paul's Anxiety in Troas

12 When I came to Troas to proclaim the good news of Christ, a
door was opened for me in the Lord; 13 but my mind could not rest because I did not find my brother Titus there. So I said farewell to them
and went on to Macedonia.

14 But thanks be to God, who in Christ always leads us in triumphal procession, and through us spreads in every place the fragrance
that comes from knowing him. 15 For we are the aroma of Christ to
God among those who are being saved and among those who are perishing; 16 to the one a fragrance from death to death, to the other a
fragrance from life to life. Who is sufficient for these things? 17 For we
are not peddlers of God's word like so many;[a] but in Christ we speak
as persons of sincerity, as persons sent from God and standing in his
presence.

Ministers of the New Covenant

3 Are we beginning to commend ourselves again? Surely we do
not need, as some do, letters of recommendation to you or from
you, do we? 2 You yourselves are our letter, written on our[b] hearts,
to be known and read by all; 3 and you show that you are a letter of
Christ, prepared by us, written not with ink but with the Spirit of the
living God, not on tablets of stone but on tablets of human hearts.

4 Such is the confidence that we have through Christ toward God.
5 Not that we are competent of ourselves to claim anything as coming
from us; our competence is from God, 6 who has made us competent
to be ministers of a new covenant, not of letter but of spirit; for the
letter kills, but the Spirit gives life.

7 Now if the ministry of death, chiseled in letters on stone tablets,[c]
came in glory so that the people of Israel could not gaze at Moses'
face because of the glory of his face, a glory now set aside, 8 how much
more will the ministry of the Spirit come in glory? 9 For if there was

[a] Other ancient authorities read *like the others* [b] Other ancient authorities read *your* [c] Gk *on stones*

How does Luther use Paul's marriage imagery? Although Luther quotes the Ephesians passage, he develops wedding imagery as an illustration of the happy exchange between Christ and believers. Luther's marriage imagery is rooted in the authentic Paul. See notes on 1 Corinthians 1:9 ("happy exchange"). *2 Corinthians 1:21-22*

2:6-7 This punishment . . . is enough: Shame was a powerful force in antiquity. Public reprimands were known to cause excessive pain, leading even to suicide, as Paul warns the church here. Apparently, the church took too seriously Paul's demand in the letter of tears that the person who had injured him be disciplined.

2:14 thanks be to God, who in Christ always leads us in triumphal procession: This is a perplexing metaphor: it represents God as a victorious general, parading Paul in procession like the captured nobleman of a conquered land. It begins to make sense, however, if read in light of ancient love poetry. "Love conquers all" was a popular motif. The lover, when unsure of his beloved's response to his overtures, laments that love leads him in triumphal procession. Paul's rocky relationship with the Corinthians, worsened by the letter of tears, might be at issue here.

3:1 Are we beginning to commend ourselves again?: The passage 2:14—4:6 is one of the more difficult ones in Paul's letters, but perhaps the most intriguing. Paul seems to be defending himself against the charge made by the "super-apostles" that he is a flatterer and lacks frank speech. After an introduction filled with metaphors ("triumphal procession," "peddlers," "letters of recommendation") in 2:14—3:3, Paul offers two arguments (3:3-12 and 3:13-18) that he has the courage and freedom to speak his mind openly and completely.

glory in the ministry of condemnation, much more does the ministry
of justification abound in glory! 10Indeed, what once had glory has
lost its glory because of the greater glory; 11for if what was set aside
came through glory, much more has the permanent come in glory!
12 Since, then, we have such a hope, we act with great boldness,
13not like Moses, who put a veil over his face to keep the people of Israel from gazing at the end of the glory that[a] was being set aside. 14But
their minds were hardened. Indeed, to this very day, when they hear
the reading of the old covenant, that same veil is still there, since only
in Christ is it set aside. 15Indeed, to this very day whenever Moses is
read, a veil lies over their minds; 16but when one turns to the Lord,
the veil is removed. 17Now the Lord is the Spirit, and where the Spirit
of the Lord is, there is freedom. 18And all of us, with unveiled faces,
seeing the glory of the Lord as though reflected in a mirror, are being transformed into the same image from one degree of glory to another; for this comes from the Lord, the Spirit.

Treasure in Clay Jars

4 Therefore, since it is by God's mercy that we are engaged in this
ministry, we do not lose heart. 2We have renounced the shameful things that one hides; we refuse to practice cunning or to falsify
God's word; but by the open statement of the truth we commend ourselves to the conscience of everyone in the sight of God. 3And even
if our gospel is veiled, it is veiled to those who are perishing. 4In their
case the god of this world has blinded the minds of the unbelievers,
to keep them from seeing the light of the gospel of the glory of Christ,
who is the image of God. 5For we do not proclaim ourselves; we proclaim Jesus Christ as Lord and ourselves as your slaves for Jesus' sake.
6For it is the God who said, "Let light shine out of darkness," who has
shone in our hearts to give the light of the knowledge of the glory of
God in the face of Jesus Christ.
7 But we have this treasure in clay jars, so that it may be made
clear that this extraordinary power belongs to God and does not come
from us. 8We are afflicted in every way, but not crushed; perplexed,
but not driven to despair; 9persecuted, but not forsaken; struck down,
but not destroyed; 10always carrying in the body the death of Jesus,
so that the life of Jesus may also be made visible in our bodies. 11For
while we live, we are always being given up to death for Jesus' sake,
so that the life of Jesus may be made visible in our mortal flesh. 12So
death is at work in us, but life in you.
13 But just as we have the same spirit of faith that is in accordance with scripture—"I believed, and so I spoke"—we also believe,
and so we speak, 14because we know that the one who raised the Lord

[a] Gk *of what*

3:12 we act with great boldness: Paul concludes his first argument that he is a frank speaker and not a flatterer. A better translation of the Greek word *parrēsia* would be "we use much frank speech." See also the note on 7:4.

3:15-18 whenever Moses is read... unveiled faces: Here "reading Moses" refers to reading the Torah or Pentateuch, the first five books of the Hebrew Scriptures (Old Testament). Moses was traditionally described as the author (but see the Pentateuch introduction, pp. 45-46). In Exodus 34:33-35, Moses removes the veil as he meets the Lord. The church is defined by face-to-face relations, frank speech with one another, and transformation into Christ's image. Each aspect of the church's existence is created by the Spirit.

How does Luther describe the role of the Holy Spirit regarding the church? In his explanation to the Third Article of the Creed, Luther says that the Holy Spirit "calls, gathers, enlightens, and makes holy the whole Christian church on earth and keeps it with Jesus Christ in the one common, true faith" (*SC*:16). *2 Corinthians 3:17-18*

How do you approach God? How do you see God reflected in others? How might others see God reflected in you?

4:1-6 we proclaim Jesus Christ as Lord and ourselves as your slaves for Jesus' sake: Here Paul summarizes the arguments he has made in 2:14—3:18. He denies the charge of flattery (4:2), accuses the super-apostles of not understanding the gospel (4:3-4), and presents himself as the community's slave (4:5) in contrast to those who would lord it over the church with harsh leadership.

4:7-12 treasure in clay jars...We are afflicted in every way: The powerful treasure of the gospel is entrusted to human beings, who are fragile and breakable like clay jars. Lists of hardships like that in 4:8-12 were employed in ancient literature to illustrate the wise man's inner strength; to narrate the wise man's training in virtue (rather on the principle that "what doesn't kill you makes you stronger"); and to reveal the wise man's love

Jesus will raise us also with Jesus, and will bring us with you into his
presence. [15]Yes, everything is for your sake, so that grace, as it extends
to more and more people, may increase thanksgiving, to the glory of
God.

Living by Faith

16 So we do not lose heart. Even though our outer nature is wasting away, our inner nature is being renewed day by day. [17]For this
slight momentary affliction is preparing us for an eternal weight of
glory beyond all measure, [18]because we look not at what can be seen
but at what cannot be seen; for what can be seen is temporary, but
what cannot be seen is eternal.

5 For we know that if the earthly tent we live in is destroyed, we
have a building from God, a house not made with hands, eternal
in the heavens. [2]For in this tent we groan, longing to be clothed with
our heavenly dwelling— [3]if indeed, when we have taken it off[a] we will
not be found naked. [4]For while we are still in this tent, we groan under
our burden, because we wish not to be unclothed but to be further
clothed, so that what is mortal may be swallowed up by life. [5]He who
has prepared us for this very thing is God, who has given us the Spirit
as a guarantee.

6 So we are always confident; even though we know that while we
are at home in the body we are away from the Lord— [7]for we walk by
faith, not by sight. [8]Yes, we do have confidence, and we would rather
be away from the body and at home with the Lord. [9]So whether we
are at home or away, we make it our aim to please him. [10]For all of us
must appear before the judgment seat of Christ, so that each may receive recompense for what has been done in the body, whether good
or evil.

The Ministry of Reconciliation

11 Therefore, knowing the fear of the Lord, we try to persuade
others; but we ourselves are well known to God, and I hope that we
are also well known to your consciences. [12]We are not commending
ourselves to you again, but giving you an opportunity to boast about
us, so that you may be able to answer those who boast in outward
appearance and not in the heart. [13]For if we are beside ourselves, it
is for God; if we are in our right mind, it is for you. [14]For the love of
Christ urges us on, because we are convinced that one has died for
all; therefore all have died. [15]And he died for all, so that those who live
might live no longer for themselves, but for him who died and was
raised for them.

16 From now on, therefore, we regard no one from a human

[a] Other ancient authorities read *put it on*

for humanity (his *philanthrōpia*). Here Paul modifies the last theme to show that his ministry is motivated by love (5:14) and radical friendship (5:18—6:10).

4:15 everything is for your sake: In 4:7—6:13 Paul seeks to persuade the Corinthians to set aside the injured feelings his letter of tears caused.

Paul says that we "walk by faith, not by sight" (5:7; see also 4:18; Rom 8:24-25; 1 Pet 1:8). What does this phrase mean to you?

point of view;[a] even though we once knew Christ from a human
point of view,[a] we know him no longer in that way. 17 So if anyone is in
Christ, there is a new creation: everything old has passed away; see,
everything has become new! 18 All this is from God, who reconciled
us to himself through Christ, and has given us the ministry of reconciliation; 19 that is, in Christ God was reconciling the world to himself,[b] not counting their trespasses against them, and entrusting the
message of reconciliation to us. 20 So we are ambassadors for Christ,
since God is making his appeal through us; we entreat you on behalf
of Christ, be reconciled to God. 21 For our sake he made him to be sin
who knew no sin, so that in him we might become the righteousness
of God.

6 As we work together with him,[c] we urge you also not to accept
the grace of God in vain. 2 For he says,

"At an acceptable time I have listened to you,
and on a day of salvation I have helped you."

See, now is the acceptable time; see, now is the day of salvation! 3 We
are putting no obstacle in anyone's way, so that no fault may be found
with our ministry, 4 but as servants of God we have commended ourselves in every way: through great endurance, in afflictions, hardships,
calamities, 5 beatings, imprisonments, riots, labors, sleepless nights,
hunger; 6 by purity, knowledge, patience, kindness, holiness of spirit,
genuine love, 7 truthful speech, and the power of God; with the weapons of righteousness for the right hand and for the left; 8 in honor and
dishonor, in ill repute and good repute. We are treated as impostors,
and yet are true; 9 as unknown, and yet are well known; as dying, and
see—we are alive; as punished, and yet not killed; 10 as sorrowful, yet
always rejoicing; as poor, yet making many rich; as having nothing,
and yet possessing everything.

11 We have spoken frankly to you Corinthians; our heart is wide
open to you. 12 There is no restriction in our affections, but only in
yours. 13 In return—I speak as to children—open wide your hearts
also.

The Temple of the Living God

14 Do not be mismatched with unbelievers. For what partnership
is there between righteousness and lawlessness? Or what fellowship
is there between light and darkness? 15 What agreement does Christ
have with Beliar? Or what does a believer share with an unbeliever?
16 What agreement has the temple of God with idols? For we[d] are the
temple of the living God; as God said,

"I will live in them and walk among them,
and I will be their God,

---

[a] Gk *according to the flesh* [b] Or *God was in Christ reconciling the world to himself* [c] Gk *As we work together*
[d] Other ancient authorities read *you*

5:19 in Christ God was reconciling the world to himself: "Reconciliation" is a powerful theological idea, repeated throughout 5:17-20 in the NRSV. But is "reconciliation" the best translation? The *re-* at its beginning indicates restoration of an existing relationship. The Greek word, *katallassein,* meant "restoration" only occasionally. More often, as is probably the case here, it refers to the *initiation* of friendship, a relationship between persons in which all things are shared in common. In the new creation (5:17), God and world share all things in complete, loving communion, a point Paul expresses clearly in 5:21. In Luther's language, the "happy exchange" between Christ and humans (see notes on 1 Cor 1:9) extends to the relationship between God and all of God's creation. The perfect union of God and human in Jesus of Nazareth anticipates the world's future *and* God's.

What does it mean that God made Jesus to be sin? Another example of Luther's happy exchange (see notes on 1 Cor 1:9). Christ bears the sin of the world in his body and shares with us the righteousness he possesses as the Son of God. *2 Corinthians 5:21*

What do you think of the explanation given in the note (5:21)? What do you find most challenging or comforting about it?

6:3-10 as servants of God we have commended ourselves: Paul speaks of hardships, a commonplace in the philosophical talk of his day (see note at 4:7-12). But Paul never regards his hardships as demonstrating that he is a wise man; rather, his point here is that he has conducted himself with sincerity, not seeking to gain any advantage (see 6:11-12).

6:11-13 our heart is wide open to you... open wide your hearts also: To ancient Greeks, the internal organs (heart, lungs, gall bladder, and liver) did the feeling and thinking of a person; the brain functioned merely as the body's radiator, cooling the blood, which was heated in and around the heart. Emotions and thoughts were understood as the warming or cooling of the innards. So Paul writes here as if grief narrows the heart, while

and they shall be my people.
17 Therefore come out from them,
and be separate from them, says the Lord,
and touch nothing unclean;
then I will welcome you,
18 and I will be your father,
and you shall be my sons and daughters,
says the Lord Almighty."

7 Since we have these promises, beloved, let us cleanse ourselves
from every defilement of body and of spirit, making holiness
perfect in the fear of God.

Paul's Joy at the Church's Repentance

2 Make room in your hearts[a] for us; we have wronged no one, we
have corrupted no one, we have taken advantage of no one. 3 I do not
say this to condemn you, for I said before that you are in our hearts,
to die together and to live together. 4 I often boast about you; I have
great pride in you; I am filled with consolation; I am overjoyed in all
our affliction.

5 For even when we came into Macedonia, our bodies had no
rest, but we were afflicted in every way—disputes without and fears
within. 6 But God, who consoles the downcast, consoled us by the arrival of Titus, 7 and not only by his coming, but also by the consolation
with which he was consoled about you, as he told us of your longing,
your mourning, your zeal for me, so that I rejoiced still more. 8 For
even if I made you sorry with my letter, I do not regret it (though I
did regret it, for I see that I grieved you with that letter, though only
briefly). 9 Now I rejoice, not because you were grieved, but because
your grief led to repentance; for you felt a godly grief, so that you were
not harmed in any way by us. 10 For godly grief produces a repentance
that leads to salvation and brings no regret, but worldly grief produces death. 11 For see what earnestness this godly grief has produced
in you, what eagerness to clear yourselves, what indignation, what
alarm, what longing, what zeal, what punishment! At every point you
have proved yourselves guiltless in the matter. 12 So although I wrote
to you, it was not on account of the one who did the wrong, nor on account of the one who was wronged, but in order that your zeal for us
might be made known to you before God. 13 In this we find comfort.

In addition to our own consolation, we rejoiced still more at the
joy of Titus, because his mind has been set at rest by all of you. 14 For if
I have been somewhat boastful about you to him, I was not disgraced;
but just as everything we said to you was true, so our boasting to Titus
has proved true as well. 15 And his heart goes out all the more to you,

[a] Gk lacks *in your hearts*

joy expands it. We may also compare his plea with ancient love poetry. The idea of friends and loved ones existing, literally, in each other's hearts was not uncommon; so Paul pleads with the Corinthians to open themselves to him (see also Phil 1:7).

7:4 I have great pride in you: A better translation would be "great is my frank speech towards you." The Greek word is *parrēsia*, as in 3:12.

7:5-16 when we came into Macedonia…we rejoiced still more at the joy of Titus: This section appears to continue the message ended at 2:12-13. Apparently Titus met Paul in Macedonia and put his mind to rest concerning the way the Corinthians had taken his challenging letter (7:8-13).

Paul compares godly grief to worldly grief (7:10). One produces repentance, and the other produces death. For you, what is godly grief?

as he remembers the obedience of all of you, and how you welcomed him with fear and trembling. 16 I rejoice, because I have complete confidence in you.

Encouragement to Be Generous

8 We want you to know, brothers and sisters,[a] about the grace of God that has been granted to the churches of Macedonia; 2 for during a severe ordeal of affliction, their abundant joy and their extreme poverty have overflowed in a wealth of generosity on their part. 3 For, as I can testify, they voluntarily gave according to their means, and even beyond their means, 4 begging us earnestly for the privilege[b] of sharing in this ministry to the saints— 5 and this, not merely as we expected; they gave themselves first to the Lord and, by the will of God, to us, 6 so that we might urge Titus that, as he had already made a beginning, so he should also complete this generous undertaking[c] among you. 7 Now as you excel in everything—in faith, in speech, in knowledge, in utmost eagerness, and in our love for you[d]—so we want you to excel also in this generous undertaking.[c]

8:2 a severe ordeal of affliction: Exactly what the Macedonia churches have suffered is not certain. It may have to do with persecution (see also Phil 1:29-30; 1 Thess 1:6; 3:3-4).

8 I do not say this as a command, but I am testing the genuineness of your love against the earnestness of others. 9 For you know the generous act[e] of our Lord Jesus Christ, that though he was rich, yet for your sakes he became poor, so that by his poverty you might become rich. 10 And in this matter I am giving my advice: it is appropriate for you who began last year not only to do something but even to desire to do something— 11 now finish doing it, so that your eagerness may be matched by completing it according to your means. 12 For if the eagerness is there, the gift is acceptable according to what one has—not according to what one does not have. 13 I do not mean that there should be relief for others and pressure on you, but it is a question of a fair balance between 14 your present abundance and their need, so that their abundance may be for your need, in order that there may be a fair balance. 15 As it is written,

"The one who had much did not have too much,
and the one who had little did not have too little."

8:13-14 it is a question of a fair balance between your present abundance and their need: In 8:13—9:15 we get a glimpse of the economic relationships between Christian congregations. In an age before the church had synods and bishops, Paul sought to create unity among diverse and geographically separated congregations through the redistribution of wealth. But there were hazards. While Paul promotes the collection he is taking up for the church in Jerusalem, he knows that giving money is filled with danger. In the ancient world, gifts reinforced status differences, on the principle that some give because they can; others receive because they must. Paul seeks to protect the collection from these implied meanings by stressing equality and reciprocity (8:11-15) and the sharing of God's gifts and a common confession (9:6-15).

Commendation of Titus

16 But thanks be to God who put in the heart of Titus the same eagerness for you that I myself have. 17 For he not only accepted our appeal, but since he is more eager than ever, he is going to you of his own accord. 18 With him we are sending the brother who is famous among all the churches for his proclaiming the good news;[f] 19 and not only that, but he has also been appointed by the churches to travel

---

[a] Gk *brothers* [b] Gk *grace* [c] Gk *this grace* [d] Other ancient authorities read *your love for us*
[e] Gk *the grace* [f] Or *the gospel*

with us while we are administering this generous undertaking[a] for the
glory of the Lord himself[b] and to show our goodwill. [20]We intend that
no one should blame us about this generous gift that we are administering, [21]for we intend to do what is right not only in the Lord's sight
but also in the sight of others. [22]And with them we are sending our
brother whom we have often tested and found eager in many matters,
but who is now more eager than ever because of his great confidence
in you. [23]As for Titus, he is my partner and co-worker in your service;
as for our brothers, they are messengers[c] of the churches, the glory of
Christ. [24]Therefore openly before the churches, show them the proof
of your love and of our reason for boasting about you.

Economic relationships are a significant challenge in this letter. In the Roman world, those who enjoyed prosperity and prestige expected to be honored by their social inferiors. Paul struggles against these expectations in the church, not just as they affect the Corinthians' perception of him but also as they influence relationships between churches. How do economic relationships in our own day shape the way we perceive others, especially those in need? In 9:6-7, Paul appears to speak about both of the size of a gift and about the attitude of giving. Do you think either of these is more important than the other? Why or why not?

The Collection for Christians at Jerusalem

9 Now it is not necessary for me to write you about the ministry
to the saints, [2]for I know your eagerness, which is the subject of
my boasting about you to the people of Macedonia, saying that Achaia
has been ready since last year; and your zeal has stirred up most of
them. [3]But I am sending the brothers in order that our boasting about
you may not prove to have been empty in this case, so that you may be
ready, as I said you would be; [4]otherwise, if some Macedonians come
with me and find that you are not ready, we would be humiliated—to
say nothing of you—in this undertaking.[d] [5]So I thought it necessary
to urge the brothers to go on ahead to you, and arrange in advance for
this bountiful gift that you have promised, so that it may be ready as a
voluntary gift and not as an extortion.
6 The point is this: the one who sows sparingly will also reap
sparingly, and the one who sows bountifully will also reap bountifully. [7]Each of you must give as you have made up your mind, not
reluctantly or under compulsion, for God loves a cheerful giver. [8]And
God is able to provide you with every blessing in abundance, so that
by always having enough of everything, you may share abundantly in
every good work. [9]As it is written,

"He scatters abroad, he gives to the poor;
his righteousness[e] endures forever."

[10]He who supplies seed to the sower and bread for food will supply
and multiply your seed for sowing and increase the harvest of your
righteousness.[e] [11]You will be enriched in every way for your great generosity, which will produce thanksgiving to God through us; [12]for the
rendering of this ministry not only supplies the needs of the saints
but also overflows with many thanksgivings to God. [13]Through the
testing of this ministry you glorify God by your obedience to the confession of the gospel of Christ and by the generosity of your sharing

---

[a] Gk *this grace* [b] Other ancient authorities lack *himself* [c] Gk *apostles* [d] Other ancient authorities add *of boasting* [e] Or *benevolence*

with them and with all others, [14]while they long for you and pray for
you because of the surpassing grace of God that he has given you.
[15]Thanks be to God for his indescribable gift!

Paul Defends His Ministry

10 I myself, Paul, appeal to you by the meekness and gentleness
of Christ—I who am humble when face to face with you, but
bold toward you when I am away!— [2]I ask that when I am present
I need not show boldness by daring to oppose those who think we
are acting according to human standards.[a] [3]Indeed, we live as human
beings,[b] but we do not wage war according to human standards;[a] [4]for
the weapons of our warfare are not merely human,[c] but they have divine power to destroy strongholds. We destroy arguments [5]and every
proud obstacle raised up against the knowledge of God, and we take
every thought captive to obey Christ. [6]We are ready to punish every
disobedience when your obedience is complete.

7 Look at what is before your eyes. If you are confident that you
belong to Christ, remind yourself of this, that just as you belong to
Christ, so also do we. [8]Now, even if I boast a little too much of our
authority, which the Lord gave for building you up and not for tearing you down, I will not be ashamed of it. [9]I do not want to seem as
though I am trying to frighten you with my letters. [10]For they say, "His
letters are weighty and strong, but his bodily presence is weak, and his
speech contemptible." [11]Let such people understand that what we say
by letter when absent, we will also do when present.

12 We do not dare to classify or compare ourselves with some of
those who commend themselves. But when they measure themselves
by one another, and compare themselves with one another, they do
not show good sense. [13]We, however, will not boast beyond limits,
but will keep within the field that God has assigned to us, to reach out
even as far as you. [14]For we were not overstepping our limits when
we reached you; we were the first to come all the way to you with
the good news[d] of Christ. [15]We do not boast beyond limits, that is, in
the labors of others; but our hope is that, as your faith increases, our
sphere of action among you may be greatly enlarged, [16]so that we may
proclaim the good news[d] in lands beyond you, without boasting of
work already done in someone else's sphere of action. [17]"Let the one
who boasts, boast in the Lord." [18]For it is not those who commend
themselves that are approved, but those whom the Lord commends.

Paul and the False Apostles

11 I wish you would bear with me in a little foolishness. Do bear
with me! [2]I feel a divine jealousy for you, for I promised you in

[a] Gk *according to the flesh* [b] Gk *in the flesh* [c] Gk *fleshly* [d] Or *the gospel*

10:1-2 I myself, Paul, appeal to you by the meekness and gentleness of Christ—I who am humble...bold: In contrast to the more conciliatory tone of early chapters, 10:1—13:11 drips with sarcasm—one of the reasons some scholars consider these chapters to have originally come from a separate letter. Paul aims his sarcasm at the Corinthians' willingness to endure the severe practices of the super-apostles (see 11:4, 18-21). As best we can tell from Paul's response, these Christian missionaries, like some Cynic philosophers, condemned the people's moral failures publicly and without thought for feelings. Paul contrasts their harshness with his own ministry, which was marked by "meekness and gentleness."

10:12 We do not dare to classify or compare ourselves with some of those who commend themselves: Paul is engaged in a delicate balancing act: he does not want to compete with the rival "super-apostles" for prestige, but wants to draw a contrast between their approach and his own. His strategy is paradoxically to "boast" within limits (10:13-18).

11:1 a little foolishness: Paul's concern for the Corinthians drives him to engage in the sort of comparison that he realizes can be misunderstood, so he strives to make clear that he considers this kind of argument unworthy of himself—and of them. He calls himself a "fool" for stooping to the level of the "super-apostles" (see 11:16-19, 21-23).

marriage to one husband, to present you as a chaste virgin to Christ.
[3]But I am afraid that as the serpent deceived Eve by its cunning,
your thoughts will be led astray from a sincere and pure[a] devotion
to Christ. [4]For if someone comes and proclaims another Jesus than
the one we proclaimed, or if you receive a different spirit from the
one you received, or a different gospel from the one you accepted,
you submit to it readily enough. [5]I think that I am not in the least inferior to these super-apostles. [6]I may be untrained in speech, but not
in knowledge; certainly in every way and in all things we have made
this evident to you.

7 Did I commit a sin by humbling myself so that you might be exalted, because I proclaimed God's good news[b] to you free of charge?
[8]I robbed other churches by accepting support from them in order
to serve you. [9]And when I was with you and was in need, I did not
burden anyone, for my needs were supplied by the friends[c] who came
from Macedonia. So I refrained and will continue to refrain from burdening you in any way. [10]As the truth of Christ is in me, this boast of
mine will not be silenced in the regions of Achaia. [11]And why? Because I do not love you? God knows I do!

12 And what I do I will also continue to do, in order to deny an opportunity to those who want an opportunity to be recognized as our
equals in what they boast about. [13]For such boasters are false apostles,
deceitful workers, disguising themselves as apostles of Christ. [14]And
no wonder! Even Satan disguises himself as an angel of light. [15]So it
is not strange if his ministers also disguise themselves as ministers of
righteousness. Their end will match their deeds.

Paul's Sufferings as an Apostle

16 I repeat, let no one think that I am a fool; but if you do, then
accept me as a fool, so that I too may boast a little. [17]What I am saying
in regard to this boastful confidence, I am saying not with the Lord's
authority, but as a fool; [18]since many boast according to human standards,[d] I will also boast. [19]For you gladly put up with fools, being wise
yourselves! [20]For you put up with it when someone makes slaves of
you, or preys upon you, or takes advantage of you, or puts on airs, or
gives you a slap in the face. [21]To my shame, I must say, we were too
weak for that!

But whatever anyone dares to boast of—I am speaking as a fool—
I also dare to boast of that. [22]Are they Hebrews? So am I. Are they
Israelites? So am I. Are they descendants of Abraham? So am I. [23]Are
they ministers of Christ? I am talking like a madman—I am a better
one: with far greater labors, far more imprisonments, with countless
floggings, and often near death. [24]Five times I have received from the

[a] Other ancient authorities lack *and pure* [b] Gk *the gospel of God* [c] Gk *brothers* [d] Gk *according to the flesh*

11:7 Did I commit a sin by humbling myself...because I proclaimed God's good news to you free of charge? Here one of the issues between Paul and the "super-apostles" becomes clear. They apparently accepted financial support from the Corinthian church (perhaps citing words of Jesus like those in Matthew 10:9-15); he did not. He thus deprived more prosperous members of the Corinthian church of the opportunity to support him financially and then act as if they "owned" a part of him and his ministry. If Paul actually refused their financial support (patronage), it would have been taken as a grave insult, which might explain the almost desperate tone of his arguments here.

11:23 Are they ministers of Christ? I am talking like a madman—I am a better one: In 11:23-33 Paul offers yet another list of hardships he has endured (see 4:7-12 and 6:3-10). He now represents these hardships as his apostolic credentials—implying sarcastically that the "super-apostles" who have suffered less are less genuine.

Jews the forty lashes minus one. [25]Three times I was beaten with rods.
Once I received a stoning. Three times I was shipwrecked; for a night
and a day I was adrift at sea; [26]on frequent journeys, in danger from
rivers, danger from bandits, danger from my own people, danger from
Gentiles, danger in the city, danger in the wilderness, danger at sea,
danger from false brothers and sisters;[a] [27]in toil and hardship, through
many a sleepless night, hungry and thirsty, often without food, cold
and naked. [28]And, besides other things, I am under daily pressure because of my anxiety for all the churches. [29]Who is weak, and I am not
weak? Who is made to stumble, and I am not indignant?

30 If I must boast, I will boast of the things that show my weakness. [31]The God and Father of the Lord Jesus (blessed be he forever!)
knows that I do not lie. [32]In Damascus, the governor[b] under King Ar-
etas guarded the city of Damascus in order to[c] seize me, [33]but I was
let down in a basket through a window in the wall,[d] and escaped from
his hands.

11:28-29 my anxiety for all the churches: Paul softens the antagonistic tone of his argument by pleading that his tribulations include his constant concern and anxiety for the churches. He is still speaking ironically when he calls his love and anxiety "weakness" and declares he is quite proud of it (11:30). The word translated "I am indignant" means literally "I burn."

Paul's Visions and Revelations

12 It is necessary to boast; nothing is to be gained by it, but I will
go on to visions and revelations of the Lord. [2]I know a person
in Christ who fourteen years ago was caught up to the third heaven—
whether in the body or out of the body I do not know; God knows.
[3]And I know that such a person—whether in the body or out of the
body I do not know; God knows— [4]was caught up into Paradise and
heard things that are not to be told, that no mortal is permitted to
repeat. [5]On behalf of such a one I will boast, but on my own behalf I
will not boast, except of my weaknesses. [6]But if I wish to boast, I will
not be a fool, for I will be speaking the truth. But I refrain from it, so
that no one may think better of me than what is seen in me or heard
from me, [7]even considering the exceptional character of the revelations. Therefore, to keep[e] me from being too elated, a thorn was given
me in the flesh, a messenger of Satan to torment me, to keep me from
being too elated.[f] [8]Three times I appealed to the Lord about this, that
it would leave me, [9]but he said to me, "My grace is sufficient for you,
for power[g] is made perfect in weakness." So, I will boast all the more
gladly of my weaknesses, so that the power of Christ may dwell in
me. [10]Therefore I am content with weaknesses, insults, hardships, persecutions, and calamities for the sake of Christ; for whenever I am
weak, then I am strong.

12:1-10 visions and revelations of the Lord: Paul tells the strange story of an encounter with Christ so intimate that it cannot be disclosed. Some scholars find here Paul's own description of his vision of Christ, in contrast to the more "earthbound" story told in Acts 9:1-22; 22:4-16; 26:9-18. He was snatched, presumably by Christ, into a garden (*paradisos* in Greek, but originally a Persian word). That this happened in "the third heaven" may indicate that Paul shared the worldview of other apocalyptic or mystical Jewish visionaries of his day. But Paul means to tell how he came to love and care for the church (see 11:28-29). To keep him from remaining in this elevated state, a thorn was given to him in the flesh. In ancient literature, the piercing of flesh by thorns, goads, missiles, and arrows signified love's invasion of the body; this also explains the burning referred to in 11:28 (see the note on 11:28-29), since burning was another favorite theme in love poetry.

What do the phrases in 12:9 mean to you: "My grace is sufficient for you," and "power is made perfect in weakness"? If you have you ever experienced either or both, how would you describe the experience?

Paul's Concern for the Corinthian Church

11 I have been a fool! You forced me to it. Indeed you should
have been the ones commending me, for I am not at all inferior to

[a] Gk *brothers* [b] Gk *ethnarch* [c] Other ancient authorities read *and wanted to* [d] Gk *through the wall* [e] Other ancient authorities read *To keep* [f] Other ancient authorities lack *to keep me from being too elated* [g] Other ancient authorities read *my power*

these super-apostles, even though I am nothing. [12]The signs of a true
apostle were performed among you with utmost patience, signs and
wonders and mighty works. [13]How have you been worse off than the
other churches, except that I myself did not burden you? Forgive me
this wrong!

14 Here I am, ready to come to you this third time. And I will not
be a burden, because I do not want what is yours but you; for children
ought not to lay up for their parents, but parents for their children. [15]I
will most gladly spend and be spent for you. If I love you more, am I
to be loved less? [16]Let it be assumed that I did not burden you. Nevertheless (you say) since I was crafty, I took you in by deceit. [17]Did
I take advantage of you through any of those whom I sent to you?
[18]I urged Titus to go, and sent the brother with him. Titus did not
take advantage of you, did he? Did we not conduct ourselves with the
same spirit? Did we not take the same steps?

19 Have you been thinking all along that we have been defending
ourselves before you? We are speaking in Christ before God. Everything we do, beloved, is for the sake of building you up. [20]For I fear
that when I come, I may find you not as I wish, and that you may find
me not as you wish; I fear that there may perhaps be quarreling, jealousy, anger, selfishness, slander, gossip, conceit, and disorder. [21]I fear
that when I come again, my God may humble me before you, and that
I may have to mourn over many who previously sinned and have not
repented of the impurity, sexual immorality, and licentiousness that
they have practiced.

Further Warning

13 This is the third time I am coming to you. "Any charge must
be sustained by the evidence of two or three witnesses." [2]I
warned those who sinned previously and all the others, and I warn
them now while absent, as I did when present on my second visit,
that if I come again, I will not be lenient— [3]since you desire proof
that Christ is speaking in me. He is not weak in dealing with you, but
is powerful in you. [4]For he was crucified in weakness, but lives by the
power of God. For we are weak in him,[a] but in dealing with you we
will live with him by the power of God.

5 Examine yourselves to see whether you are living in the faith.
Test yourselves. Do you not realize that Jesus Christ is in you?—unless, indeed, you fail to meet the test! [6]I hope you will find out that we
have not failed. [7]But we pray to God that you may not do anything
wrong—not that we may appear to have met the test, but that you
may do what is right, though we may seem to have failed. [8]For we
cannot do anything against the truth, but only for the truth. [9]For we

13:2-3 I will not be lenient—since you desire proof that Christ is speaking in me: Here the more severe tone of chapters 10–13 reaches a climax. The aim of the "super-apostles" was to cause shame. To scold the people severely for their moral failures was a key sign of Christ speaking in them. Paul seeks to rebuke immorality among the Corinthians (12:21) that the church apparently tolerates even as they welcome rival apostles.

[a] Other ancient authorities read *with him*

rejoice when we are weak and you are strong. This is what we pray for, that you may become perfect. 10 So I write these things while I am away from you, so that when I come, I may not have to be severe in using the authority that the Lord has given me for building up and not for tearing down.

13:13 The grace of the Lord Jesus Christ...be with all of you: This benediction is often recited in Christian worship and may have had a liturgical role in Paul's churches as well.

How does Paul's final desire for the Corinthians (13:11) sum up his understanding of the nature of God and the nature of Christian community? How do the Pauline themes of communion and love inform your own understanding of God and the church?

Final Greetings and Benediction

11 Finally, brothers and sisters,[a] farewell.[b] Put things in order, listen to my appeal,[c] agree with one another, live in peace; and the God of love and peace will be with you. 12 Greet one another with a holy kiss. All the saints greet you.

13 The grace of the Lord Jesus Christ, the love of God, and the communion of[d] the Holy Spirit be with all of you.

---

[a] Gk *brothers* [b] Or *rejoice* [c] Or *encourage one another* [d] Or *and the sharing in*

Galatians 5:1

GALATIANS

Background File

The apostle Paul wrote "to the churches of Galatia" around 50–55 C.E., about twenty years after the death and resurrection of Jesus. These communities included non-Jews (Gentiles). Paul had announced God's mercy for them in Christ, and the believers had experienced the Holy Spirit. Paul's letter was probably read aloud in the congregations.

What's the Story?

Other Jewish leaders who were believers in Jesus had come to Galatia. They insisted that to be acceptable to God the non-Jewish believers must observe the laws of Moses. They claimed the authority of prominent leaders of the church in Jerusalem. In addition to Jewish food laws and festivals, they taught that the men and boys must be circumcised in accord with God's covenant with Israel.

Paul rejects their teaching strongly, clearly, and hopefully. After some brief opening words of greeting and blessing (1:1-5), he quickly goes on the attack, accusing the Galatians of "turning to a different gospel" and charging his opponents with perverting of the gospel of Christ (1:6-10). He first provides a strong defense of his authority as an apostle sent directly by Jesus Christ and God (1:11-24; see also 1:1). Paul then gives a detailed account of how the leaders in Jerusalem accepted his mission to the non-Jews (Gentiles). He also recounts the confrontation he had earlier with Peter when agreements about the full welcome of the Gentiles (see also Acts 15) were not honored (2:11-14). Paul insists that the grace of God itself is at stake in this dispute (2:15-21).

Paul then moves into his teaching. He appeals to the Galatians' experience of the Holy Spirit (3:1-5), draws deeply from the wells of Scripture (3:6-18), and interprets the place God's law held in the time before Christ came (3:19-29). He makes several direct appeals to the faith of the Galatians (4:1-31), and he announces a remarkable vision: For freedom, Christ has set believers free with full confidence of the blessing this freedom holds for the world (5:1-26). He concludes with gentle, pastoral counsel for the well being of the community, confident of the hope they share with him.

What's the Message?

Galatians has been called "the Magna Carta of Christian Freedom," in comparison to the great charter that guaranteed certain liberties in England in 1215. Martin Luther so loved Galatians that he called it "My Katie," in honor of the woman he married. This brief letter has called the church to reform and has inspired faith in millions.

Together with Paul's letter to the Romans, Galatians teaches God's *justification* by faith through grace in the clearest terms. Jews and Gentiles alike are acceptable to God through their trust (faith) in God's mercy through Christ. With the Acts of the Apostles, Galatians displays God's intentional inclusion through Christ Jesus of non-Jewish people within the chosen "Israel of God" (6:16). The mission of Jesus' apostles will move confidently within and beyond its Jewish roots.

Galatians testifies that the Holy Spirit is at work (3:1-5) and that Christ is alive in the believer (2:20). Faith in Christ receives Christ's faithfulness (2:16). The baptized are clothed with Christ (3:27). The law of Christ (6:2) is the gracious reign of Christ (6:16; see note on 6:11-18)). Galatians declares that Christians are free *from* both enslaving powers and attempts to save themselves. It also envisions Christian freedom *for* the callings of God's people to be a blessing to the neighbor and of trustworthy service in the world.

1:1 Paul an apostle—sent... through Jesus Christ: An apostle is "sent" as an official ambassador. Paul emphasizes that his orders came directly from the risen Jesus Christ and God. See also 1:11-12, 16: "I did not confer with any human being."

1:3-5 Grace to you and peace from God: Paul's greetings are not followed by his usual words of thanksgiving for the community (see Rom 1:1-15; 1 Cor 1:1-9, for example).

1:6-9 some who... want to pervert the gospel of Christ: Paul's harsh words ("deserting," "confusing you," "to pervert the gospel," "let that one be accursed!") express fear that God's gospel promise could be lost. His strong words of a "curse" express the depth of his warning to those who are perverting the gospel (5:12, but note the final blessing in 6:18).

Salutation

1 Paul an apostle—sent neither by human commission nor from
human authorities, but through Jesus Christ and God the Father,
who raised him from the dead— 2 and all the members of God's family[a] who are with me,
To the churches of Galatia:
3 Grace to you and peace from God our Father and the Lord Jesus
Christ, 4 who gave himself for our sins to set us free from the present
evil age, according to the will of our God and Father, 5 to whom be the
glory forever and ever. Amen.

There Is No Other Gospel

6 I am astonished that you are so quickly deserting the one who
called you in the grace of Christ and are turning to a different gospel— 7 not that there is another gospel, but there are some who are
confusing you and want to pervert the gospel of Christ. 8 But even if
we or an angel[b] from heaven should proclaim to you a gospel contrary
to what we proclaimed to you, let that one be accursed! 9 As we have
said before, so now I repeat, if anyone proclaims to you a gospel contrary to what you received, let that one be accursed!

---

[a] Gk *all the brothers* [b] Or *a messenger*

10 Am I now seeking human approval, or God's approval? Or am
I trying to please people? If I were still pleasing people, I would not be
a servant[a] of Christ.

Paul's Vindication of His Apostleship

11 For I want you to know, brothers and sisters,[b] that the gospel that was proclaimed by me is not of human origin; 12 for I did not
receive it from a human source, nor was I taught it, but I received it
through a revelation of Jesus Christ.
13 You have heard, no doubt, of my earlier life in Judaism. I was
violently persecuting the church of God and was trying to destroy it.
14 I advanced in Judaism beyond many among my people of the same
age, for I was far more zealous for the traditions of my ancestors. 15 But
when God, who had set me apart before I was born and called me
through his grace, was pleased 16 to reveal his Son to me,[c] so that I
might proclaim him among the Gentiles, I did not confer with any
human being, 17 nor did I go up to Jerusalem to those who were already apostles before me, but I went away at once into Arabia, and
afterwards I returned to Damascus.
18 Then after three years I did go up to Jerusalem to visit Cephas
and stayed with him fifteen days; 19 but I did not see any other apostle
except James the Lord's brother. 20 In what I am writing to you, before
God, I do not lie! 21 Then I went into the regions of Syria and Cilicia,
22 and I was still unknown by sight to the churches of Judea that are in
Christ; 23 they only heard it said, "The one who formerly was persecuting us is now proclaiming the faith he once tried to destroy." 24 And
they glorified God because of me.

Paul and the Other Apostles

2 Then after fourteen years I went up again to Jerusalem with Barnabas, taking Titus along with me. 2 I went up in response to a
revelation. Then I laid before them (though only in a private meeting
with the acknowledged leaders) the gospel that I proclaim among the
Gentiles, in order to make sure that I was not running, or had not run,
in vain. 3 But even Titus, who was with me, was not compelled to be
circumcised, though he was a Greek. 4 But because of false believers[d]
secretly brought in, who slipped in to spy on the freedom we have in
Christ Jesus, so that they might enslave us— 5 we did not submit to
them even for a moment, so that the truth of the gospel might always
remain with you. 6 And from those who were supposed to be acknowledged leaders (what they actually were makes no difference to me;
God shows no partiality)—those leaders contributed nothing to me.
7 On the contrary, when they saw that I had been entrusted with the

[a] Gk *slave* [b] Gk *brothers* [c] Gk *in me* [d] Gk *false brothers*

1:12 I received it through a revelation of Jesus Christ: See Acts 9:1-15; 1 Cor 15:3-7.

1:13-16 my earlier life in Judaism: "Judaism" here probably refers to Paul's training as a Pharisee (see Phil 3:4-6). According to the "traditions of my ancestors," faithfulness to God meant obeying all God's commandments. The "Gentiles" (1:16) are "the nations" or non-Jews. Paul's call was to proclaim Christ to all the nations. God has welcomed people who didn't keep all the laws God gave to the Jewish people.

1:17-24 to Jerusalem to visit Cephas...into the regions of Syria and Cilicia: At first Paul did not go to Jerusalem to meet with the other apostles, but later he did meet with the disciples Cephas (Peter) and James (see note on 2:1-10). See Map 14, p. 2111, for locations mentioned.

2:1-10 I went up again to Jerusalem: Paul admits that James, Cephas (Aramaic for "Rock," "Peter" in Greek; see Matt 16:18), and John are recognized as community "leaders" (2:2, 6) or "pillars" (2:9). Paul, however, claims his authority from Christ Jesus (2:4). This meeting recalls the debate in the "Jerusalem council" in Acts 15. The authorities in Jerusalem agreed that "it has seemed good to the Holy Spirit and to us" (Acts 15:28) and "recognized the grace that had been given to [Paul]" (2:9). To the surprise of prominent Jewish followers of Jesus, God had accepted Gentiles, without their keeping all the laws.

Who are the "Gentiles" in the eyes of respectable Christians in your community?

gospel for the uncircumcised, just as Peter had been entrusted with
the gospel for the circumcised [8](for he who worked through Peter
making him an apostle to the circumcised also worked through me in
sending me to the Gentiles), [9]and when James and Cephas and John,
who were acknowledged pillars, recognized the grace that had been
given to me, they gave to Barnabas and me the right hand of fellowship, agreeing that we should go to the Gentiles and they to the circumcised. [10]They asked only one thing, that we remember the poor,
which was actually what I was[a] eager to do.

Paul Rebukes Peter at Antioch

11 But when Cephas came to Antioch, I opposed him to his face,
because he stood self-condemned; [12]for until certain people came
from James, he used to eat with the Gentiles. But after they came, he
drew back and kept himself separate for fear of the circumcision faction. [13]And the other Jews joined him in this hypocrisy, so that even
Barnabas was led astray by their hypocrisy. [14]But when I saw that they
were not acting consistently with the truth of the gospel, I said to Cephas before them all, "If you, though a Jew, live like a Gentile and not
like a Jew, how can you compel the Gentiles to live like Jews?"[b]

Jews and Gentiles Are Saved by Faith

15 We ourselves are Jews by birth and not Gentile sinners; [16]yet
we know that a person is justified[c] not by the works of the law but
through faith in Jesus Christ.[d] And we have come to believe in Christ
Jesus, so that we might be justified by faith in Christ,[d] and not by doing the works of the law, because no one will be justified by the works
of the law. [17]But if, in our effort to be justified in Christ, we ourselves
have been found to be sinners, is Christ then a servant of sin? Certainly not! [18]But if I build up again the very things that I once tore
down, then I demonstrate that I am a transgressor. [19]For through the
law I died to the law, so that I might live to God. I have been crucified
with Christ; [20]and it is no longer I who live, but it is Christ who lives
in me. And the life I now live in the flesh I live by faith in the Son of
God,[e] who loved me and gave himself for me. [21]I do not nullify the
grace of God; for if justification[f] comes through the law, then Christ
died for nothing.

Law or Faith

3 You foolish Galatians! Who has bewitched you? It was before
your eyes that Jesus Christ was publicly exhibited as crucified!
[2]The only thing I want to learn from you is this: Did you receive the

[a] Or *had been* [b] Some interpreters hold that the quotation extends into the following paragraph
[c] Or *reckoned as righteous;* and so elsewhere [d] Or *the faith of Jesus Christ* [e] Or *by the faith of the Son of God* [f] Or *righteousness*

2:11-14 when Cephas came to Antioch, I opposed him: The circumcision faction were Jewish Christians who insisted on full obedience to God's law. They also observed the food laws. In Acts 10, Peter had a vision of being commanded by God to eat foods that were regarded as unclean, then preached in the house of the non-Jew Cornelius. In Galatia, Peter (Cephas) stopped eating with the non-Jews (Gentiles) when strict Jewish Christians arrived. Paul accused Peter of hypocrisy, claiming to believe one thing yet doing another.

2:15-21 a person is justified not by the works of the law but through faith: The good news (gospel) is that sinful people are acceptable to God not because they are "righteous" by the standard of God's law. They live trusting in what Jesus Christ has done for them and empowered by Christ living in them. When believers are tempted to rely on their own righteousness, they risk rejecting Christ.

How are we made acceptable to God? Many Christians think only people who keep all God's laws are acceptable to God. Martin Luther rejected the idea that God loves only people who keep the church's rules. Luther saw how clear Paul's letter to the Galatians was about God's love in Jesus Christ. *Galatians 2:16-17*

How do you feel knowing that God loves people who don't keep God's laws perfectly? What encouragement does such love give to you? How can the church welcome people whose lives are messy?

3:1-5 the Spirit: The Holy Spirit is experienced by believers in their hearing of the gospel (3:2), their empowered actions (3:5), and their confident prayers as God's children (4:6-7), which come to us by God's gift and promise (3:6-9, 14, 18, 21, 29).

Spirit by doing the works of the law or by believing what you heard?
3 Are you so foolish? Having started with the Spirit, are you now ending with the flesh? 4 Did you experience so much for nothing?—if it
really was for nothing. 5 Well then, does God[a] supply you with the
Spirit and work miracles among you by your doing the works of the
law, or by your believing what you heard?
6 Just as Abraham "believed God, and it was reckoned to him as
righteousness," 7 so, you see, those who believe are the descendants of
Abraham. 8 And the scripture, foreseeing that God would justify the
Gentiles by faith, declared the gospel beforehand to Abraham, saying,
"All the Gentiles shall be blessed in you." 9 For this reason, those who
believe are blessed with Abraham who believed.
10 For all who rely on the works of the law are under a curse; for
it is written, "Cursed is everyone who does not observe and obey all
the things written in the book of the law." 11 Now it is evident that no
one is justified before God by the law; for "The one who is righteous
will live by faith."[b] 12 But the law does not rest on faith; on the contrary,
"Whoever does the works of the law[c] will live by them." 13 Christ redeemed us from the curse of the law by becoming a curse for us—for
it is written, "Cursed is everyone who hangs on a tree"— 14 in order
that in Christ Jesus the blessing of Abraham might come to the Gentiles, so that we might receive the promise of the Spirit through faith.

The Promise to Abraham

15 Brothers and sisters,[d] I give an example from daily life: once a
person's will[e] has been ratified, no one adds to it or annuls it. 16 Now
the promises were made to Abraham and to his offspring;[f] it does
not say, "And to offsprings,"[g] as of many; but it says, "And to your offspring,"[f] that is, to one person, who is Christ. 17 My point is this: the
law, which came four hundred thirty years later, does not annul a covenant previously ratified by God, so as to nullify the promise. 18 For
if the inheritance comes from the law, it no longer comes from the
promise; but God granted it to Abraham through the promise.

The Purpose of the Law

19 Why then the law? It was added because of transgressions, until the offspring[f] would come to whom the promise had been made;
and it was ordained through angels by a mediator. 20 Now a mediator
involves more than one party; but God is one.
21 Is the law then opposed to the promises of God? Certainly not!
For if a law had been given that could make alive, then righteousness
would indeed come through the law. 22 But the scripture has imprisoned

3:6-9 Abraham "believed God... righteousness": Paul argues that Abraham, the father of God's chosen people, was righteous in God's eyes by his faith or trust in God (see Gen 15:6; Rom 3:21–4:25).

3:13-15 for it is written: Paul grounds his witness in the testimony of Scripture (see Deut 27:26; 28:58; Hab 2:4b; Lev 18:5; see also Rom 10:5; Gen 12:3; and, again, Deut 27:15-26; 28:15-68).

3:15—4:7 I give an example from daily life: Paul reads God's covenant with Abraham like a contract, word for word. "Offspring" (3:16) from the Greek *sperma,* "seed," can be a group or a person. Paul testifies that the "offspring" anticipates that God's promise will be kept in Christ, after the giving of the law. Adult heirs are liberated from legal guardians when they reach the appropriate age. Christian freedom is authorized by God's will and enacted when the promise of Christ is kept.

[a] Gk *he* [b] Or *The one who is righteous through faith will live* [c] Gk *does them* [d] Gk *Brothers*
[e] Or *covenant* (as in verse 17) [f] Gk *seed* [g] Gk *seeds*

all things under the power of sin, so that what was promised through
faith in Jesus Christ[a] might be given to those who believe.
23 Now before faith came, we were imprisoned and guarded under the law until faith would be revealed. 24 Therefore the law was our
disciplinarian until Christ came, so that we might be justified by faith.
25 But now that faith has come, we are no longer subject to a disciplinarian, 26 for in Christ Jesus you are all children of God through faith.
27 As many of you as were baptized into Christ have clothed yourselves
with Christ. 28 There is no longer Jew or Greek, there is no longer slave
or free, there is no longer male and female; for all of you are one in
Christ Jesus. 29 And if you belong to Christ, then you are Abraham's
offspring,[b] heirs according to the promise.

4 My point is this: heirs, as long as they are minors, are no better than slaves, though they are the owners of all the property;
2 but they remain under guardians and trustees until the date set by
the father. 3 So with us; while we were minors, we were enslaved to
the elemental spirits[c] of the world. 4 But when the fullness of time had
come, God sent his Son, born of a woman, born under the law, 5 in
order to redeem those who were under the law, so that we might receive adoption as children. 6 And because you are children, God has
sent the Spirit of his Son into our[d] hearts, crying, "Abba![e] Father!" 7 So
you are no longer a slave but a child, and if a child then also an heir,
through God.[f]

Paul Reproves the Galatians

8 Formerly, when you did not know God, you were enslaved to
beings that by nature are not gods. 9 Now, however, that you have
come to know God, or rather to be known by God, how can you turn
back again to the weak and beggarly elemental spirits?[g] How can you
want to be enslaved to them again? 10 You are observing special days,
and months, and seasons, and years. 11 I am afraid that my work for
you may have been wasted.
12 Friends,[h] I beg you, become as I am, for I also have become as
you are. You have done me no wrong. 13 You know that it was because of
a physical infirmity that I first announced the gospel to you; 14 though
my condition put you to the test, you did not scorn or despise me,
but welcomed me as an angel of God, as Christ Jesus. 15 What has become of the goodwill you felt? For I testify that, had it been possible,
you would have torn out your eyes and given them to me. 16 Have I
now become your enemy by telling you the truth? 17 They make much
of you, but for no good purpose; they want to exclude you, so that
you may make much of them. 18 It is good to be made much of for a

3:27-29 clothed yourselves with Christ: From the time of their baptisms, God's children share the identity and destiny of Christ (see also Rom 6:3-5). They are no longer defined by their race (Jew or Greek), social class (slave or free), or even their gender.

How does the church live out the statement in 3:28? What do you think it means to live as an heir of the promise (3:29)?

4:8-10 beings that by nature are not gods . . . elemental spirits: Paul compares the Galatians' interest in observing the Jewish festival days with following their former worship of natural elements.

What religious or secular beliefs, practices, values, and loyalties threaten to control our lives today? How can we worship our Creator in the care of nature?

4:12-20 welcomed me as an angel of God, as Christ Jesus: Like the Lord Jesus, Paul bears Christ's mercy to the Galatians in the midst of "physical infirmity" (4:13), "pain of childbirth" until Christ "is formed" in them (4:19), and perplexity (4:20). Exactly what sort of physical infirmity Paul was suffering is unclear (see 5:11; 6:17; 2 Cor 11:23-27; 12:7-10).

---

[a] Or *through the faith of Jesus Christ* [b] Gk *seed* [c] Or *the rudiments* [d] Other ancient authorities read *your* [e] Aramaic for *Father* [f] Other ancient authorities read *an heir of God through Christ* [g] Or *beggarly rudiments* [h] Gk *Brothers*

good purpose at all times, and not only when I am present with you.
19 My little children, for whom I am again in the pain of childbirth until Christ is formed in you, 20 I wish I were present with you now and
could change my tone, for I am perplexed about you.

The Allegory of Hagar and Sarah

21 Tell me, you who desire to be subject to the law, will you not
listen to the law? 22 For it is written that Abraham had two sons, one
by a slave woman and the other by a free woman. 23 One, the child of
the slave, was born according to the flesh; the other, the child of the
free woman, was born through the promise. 24 Now this is an allegory:
these women are two covenants. One woman, in fact, is Hagar, from
Mount Sinai, bearing children for slavery. 25 Now Hagar is Mount Sinai in Arabia[a] and corresponds to the present Jerusalem, for she is in
slavery with her children. 26 But the other woman corresponds to the
Jerusalem above; she is free, and she is our mother. 27 For it is written,

"Rejoice, you childless one, you who bear no children,
    burst into song and shout, you who endure no birth pangs;
for the children of the desolate woman are more numerous
    than the children of the one who is married."

28 Now you,[b] my friends,[c] are children of the promise, like Isaac. 29 But
just as at that time the child who was born according to the flesh persecuted the child who was born according to the Spirit, so it is now
also. 30 But what does the scripture say? "Drive out the slave and her
child; for the child of the slave will not share the inheritance with the
child of the free woman." 31 So then, friends,[c] we are children, not of
5 the slave but of the free woman. 1 For freedom Christ has set us
free. Stand firm, therefore, and do not submit again to a yoke of
slavery.

The Nature of Christian Freedom

2 Listen! I, Paul, am telling you that if you let yourselves be circumcised, Christ will be of no benefit to you. 3 Once again I testify to
every man who lets himself be circumcised that he is obliged to obey
the entire law. 4 You who want to be justified by the law have cut yourselves off from Christ; you have fallen away from grace. 5 For through
the Spirit, by faith, we eagerly wait for the hope of righteousness. 6 For
in Christ Jesus neither circumcision nor uncircumcision counts for
anything; the only thing that counts is faith working[d] through love.
7 You were running well; who prevented you from obeying the
truth? 8 Such persuasion does not come from the one who calls you.
9 A little yeast leavens the whole batch of dough. 10 I am confident

4:21-31 Abraham had two sons, one by a slave woman and the other by a free woman: Paul uses a metaphor or word picture to make his point. Centuries later, Islam also claimed Abraham's ancestry through Ishmael, son of Hagar (see Gen 16:1-15). Paul declared Christ and all who belong to him to be the free and full heirs of God's promises.

5:1-12 Christ has set us free... through the Spirit, by faith: Paul attacks the cutting of circumcision as a cutting off from Christ (5:4; see also 5:12, which literally means "those who unsettle you should cut it all off"). Through the Spirit and by faith, not by the law, we have access to God's righteousness (5:5; see note on 6:1-10). "Faith working through love" signals Christ at work among us.

---

[a] Other ancient authorities read *For Sinai is a mountain in Arabia* [b] Other ancient authorities read *we*
[c] Gk *brothers* [d] Or *made effective*

about you in the Lord that you will not think otherwise. But whoever it is that is confusing you will pay the penalty. 11 But my friends,[a] why am I still being persecuted if I am still preaching circumcision? In that case the offense of the cross has been removed. 12 I wish those who unsettle you would castrate themselves!

13 For you were called to freedom, brothers and sisters;[a] only do not use your freedom as an opportunity for self-indulgence,[b] but through love become slaves to one another. 14 For the whole law is summed up in a single commandment, "You shall love your neighbor as yourself." 15 If, however, you bite and devour one another, take care that you are not consumed by one another.

The Works of the Flesh

16 Live by the Spirit, I say, and do not gratify the desires of the flesh. 17 For what the flesh desires is opposed to the Spirit, and what the Spirit desires is opposed to the flesh; for these are opposed to each other, to prevent you from doing what you want. 18 But if you are led by the Spirit, you are not subject to the law. 19 Now the works of the flesh are obvious: fornication, impurity, licentiousness, 20 idolatry, sorcery, enmities, strife, jealousy, anger, quarrels, dissensions, factions, 21 envy,[c] drunkenness, carousing, and things like these. I am warning you, as I warned you before: those who do such things will not inherit the kingdom of God.

The Fruit of the Spirit

22 By contrast, the fruit of the Spirit is love, joy, peace, patience, kindness, generosity, faithfulness, 23 gentleness, and self-control. There is no law against such things. 24 And those who belong to Christ Jesus have crucified the flesh with its passions and desires. 25 If we live by the Spirit, let us also be guided by the Spirit. 26 Let us not become conceited, competing against one another, envying one another.

Bear One Another's Burdens

6 My friends,[d] if anyone is detected in a transgression, you who have received the Spirit should restore such a one in a spirit of gentleness. Take care that you yourselves are not tempted. 2 Bear one another's burdens, and in this way you will fulfill[e] the law of Christ. 3 For if those who are nothing think they are something, they deceive themselves. 4 All must test their own work; then that work, rather than their neighbor's work, will become a cause for pride. 5 For all must carry their own loads.

6 Those who are taught the word must share in all good things with their teacher.

---

[a] Gk *brothers* [b] Gk *the flesh* [c] Other ancient authorities add *murder* [d] Gk *Brothers* [e] Other ancient authorities read *in this way fulfill*

5:13-15 you were called to freedom...love your neighbor: Christian freedom means more than personal liberty. Believers are not only freed *from* enslaving powers and attempts to appease God, but they are freed *for* bearing Christ's love to the neighbor. Christ Jesus "did not regard equality with God as something to be exploited, but emptied himself, taking the form of a slave" (Phil 2:6-7). Freedom in Christ empowers self-giving service to others and to the world.

How is being freed to love the neighbor different from serving because the commandment says you should? Where have you sensed this freedom to serve in your life?

5:16-26 Live by the Spirit: Paul shares the biblical confidence in the goodness of God's creation, including human bodies and life in the flesh. Christ Jesus is God's Word in the flesh living among us (John 1:14). But gratifying "the desires of the flesh" (5:16) and doing "the works of the flesh" (5:19; see also Rom 1:29-31) reveals a self-centered life that is still enslaved to "passions and desires" (5:24). Being "led by the Spirit" (5:18) in Christian freedom yields the "fruit of the Spirit" (5:22; see also Rom 8:9-11; Phil 1:11). The power of Christ's ultimate reign (5:1, 24-25) is already at work.

6:1-10 fulfill the law of Christ: Paul has sharply warned the Galatians against claiming righteousness before God based on observance of the law, even God's law. Closing his letter, he recites practical sayings, confident that "we" remain eager to "work for the good of all, and especially for those of the family of faith" (6:9-10). Fulfilling "the law of Christ" is living humbly in the power and Spirit of Christ, not just keeping another set of rules.

7 Do not be deceived; God is not mocked, for you reap whatever
you sow. [8]If you sow to your own flesh, you will reap corruption from
the flesh; but if you sow to the Spirit, you will reap eternal life from
the Spirit. [9]So let us not grow weary in doing what is right, for we will
reap at harvest time, if we do not give up. [10]So then, whenever we have
an opportunity, let us work for the good of all, and especially for those
of the family of faith.

Final Admonitions and Benediction

11 See what large letters I make when I am writing in my own
hand! [12]It is those who want to make a good showing in the flesh
that try to compel you to be circumcised—only that they may not
be persecuted for the cross of Christ. [13]Even the circumcised do not
themselves obey the law, but they want you to be circumcised so that
they may boast about your flesh. [14]May I never boast of anything except the cross of our Lord Jesus Christ, by which[a] the world has been
crucified to me, and I to the world. [15]For[b] neither circumcision nor
uncircumcision is anything; but a new creation is everything! [16]As for
those who will follow this rule—peace be upon them, and mercy, and
upon the Israel of God.

17 From now on, let no one make trouble for me; for I carry the
marks of Jesus branded on my body.

18 May the grace of our Lord Jesus Christ be with your spirit,
brothers and sisters.[c] Amen.

---

[a] Or *through whom* [b] Other ancient authorities add *in Christ Jesus* [c] Gk *brothers*

How does Luther describe Paul's understanding of righteousness? Luther says that in Galatians Paul teaches how we receive Christ's righteousness as our own: "...this most excellent righteousness, the righteousness of faith, which God imputes to us through Christ without works, is neither political nor ceremonial nor legal nor work-righteousness but is quite the opposite.... For here we work nothing, render nothing to God; we only receive and permit someone else to work in us, namely, God." (*LW* 26:4-5) *Galatians 6:2*

6:11-18 a new creation is everything: These verses summarize the letter's themes in Paul's own voice and hand. "A new creation" (6:15) surpasses either circumcision or uncircumcision, both of which once meant much (see the same emphasis about "faith working through love" in 5:6). Through the cross of Christ, God launched Christ's new reign. The world itself "has been crucified" (6:12-14). The "rule" (6:16) to be followed, therefore, is filled with God's promise of peace and mercy. "The Israel of God" identifies all who belong to the reign of God's crucified Messiah, Jesus.

EPHESIANS

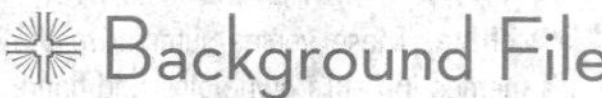
Ephesians 2:8

Background File

The city of Ephesus was an important center of the early Christian mission in Asia Minor. The book of Acts reports that the apostle Paul spent time teaching and preaching in the city of Ephesus (see Acts 18:18–20:1). Paul is listed as author in the greeting of the letter (1:1), but his authorship is debated (see below).

What's the Story?

Many of Paul's letters deal with specific issues or concerns in the local churches that Paul helped establish (see 1–2 Corinthians and Galatians, for example). However, the letter to the Ephesians does not have any such specific references. In fact, some reliable ancient manuscripts omit "Ephesus" in 1:1 (see NRSV footnote *a*). This has led to the notion that Ephesians is a general letter written to provide a message for the whole church.

The letter to the Ephesians summarizes key aspects of Paul's thought, but some scholars have also noted important differences in the content and writing style of Ephesians when compared with the other letters whose authorship by Paul is undisputed (see the introduction The Letters of Paul, p. 1817). For example, some sentences in Ephesians are unusually long. The passages 1:3-14 and 3:1-6 are each one long sentence in the Greek. Nearly ninety words appear in Ephesians that do not appear in other letters written by Paul. Jesus is called "the Beloved" (1:6) and described as the "head over all things for the church" (1:22). These are not found in Paul's other letters.

So how could a letter bear the name of a person who may not have written the letter? Over the centuries, customs regarding authorship have changed. Two thousand years ago, it was not uncommon for a disciple of a famous teacher to write a letter in the name of the teacher. This may strike us as being deceptive, but readers in ancient times understood the practice.

The letter does follow the form of Paul's letters. It begins with a greeting (1:1-2) and ends with a blessing 6:23-24). The following outline shows how the main sections of the letter are introduced by prayer:

Greeting and blessing (1:1-14)
Prayer for the saints (1:15-23)

The church is one in Christ (2:1-22)
Paul's mission and God's plan (3:1-13)
Prayer for strength and understanding (3:14-21)
Living out Christ's calling (4:1–6:20)
Final greetings and blessing (6:21-24)

What's the Message?

Ephesians is filled with praise for God, who is at work in Jesus Christ to put in place a plan for salvation. God destined us (the church) for adoption as children through Jesus Christ (1:5). Though we were dead because of sins (2:1), God has chosen to save us by grace through faith as a gift (2:8). Because salvation is a gift, no one can boast of being saved by works. But those who are saved are created for good works (2:9-10).

This letter describes the divisions between Jewish and Gentile followers of Jesus, apparent in many of Paul's letters, to be now broken down and reconciled in one body through the cross of Christ (2:11-16). This aligns Paul's mission of bringing the gospel to the Gentiles with God's plan (3:6-10). The church, Christ's body (1:22-23), is called to share this mission and to live a life worthy of this calling (4:1). The final three chapters provide several examples of how God's people, individually and as the church, can live out this calling. For example, the church has been given certain gifts (4:11) that are to be used to do ministry and build up the body of Christ in love (4:12-16).

Individual believers are encouraged to avoid living the old sinful life that was like living in the darkness. Instead, they are to live as children of light (5:3-9). Living in the light includes family members as well as masters and servants loving and respecting one another. Finally, because living in the light is challenging in a world of darkness, the letter encourages God's people to put on the "whole armor of God," including the breastplate of righteousness, shield of faith, and helmet of salvation (6:10-17).

Salutation

1 Paul, an apostle of Christ Jesus by the will of God,
To the saints who are in Ephesus and are faithful[a] in Christ Jesus:
2 Grace to you and peace from God our Father and the Lord
Jesus Christ.

Spiritual Blessings in Christ

3 Blessed be the God and Father of our Lord Jesus Christ, who
has blessed us in Christ with every spiritual blessing in the heavenly
places, 4just as he chose us in Christ[b] before the foundation of the
world to be holy and blameless before him in love. 5He destined us for

[a] Other ancient authorities lack *in Ephesus,* reading *saints who are also faithful* [b] Gk *in him*

1:1 apostle of Christ...by the will of God: An "apostle" is "sent" as an official ambassador. Paul's calling came directly from God through his encounter with Jesus (see Acts 9:1-22).

Who is a "saint"? This term is mentioned twelve times in Ephesians. In the Lutheran tradition, a saint is everybody who has been baptized, regardless of their economic affluence, prestige, power. Baptism clothes the Christian in the righteousness of Christ, filling her or him with the power of the Holy Spirit to do God's will in the world. At the same time, the believer continues to struggle with the power of sin. So, Luther said, we are both saint and sinner at the same time. *Ephesians 1:1*

1:5 destined us for adoption as his children: Those who are chosen by God in Christ Jesus are new children and heirs of the promise (see 2:11-13; Rom 8:28-32). God's chosen family makes all people worthy, in spite of human actions that devalue women, people of color, those who are economically poor, sick, or aging, and others. Christ breaks down the walls that divide (2:14).

1:7 redemption through his blood: Redemption had the meaning of freeing someone from slavery (see also Col 1:14).

1:14 to the praise of his glory: This phrase is a reminder of the words of the saintly Roman Catholic archbishop Arnulfo Romero: "the glory of God is a fully alive poor person."

1:22-23 head over all things for the church . . . his body: Ephesians introduces this description of Jesus as head of the church, an image not found in the undisputed letters of Paul (see also 4:15; 5:23; compare with 1 Cor 12:12-27).

How do we speak of God as Creator? In his explanation to the First Article of the Creed, Luther describes God as creator in this way: "I believe that God has created me together with all that exists" (*SC: 13*). He goes on to say that God abundantly provides what is needed for daily living and protects us against danger. Ephesians says that God has "put all things under [Christ's] feet." This is a confession of faith that reminds us of God's living power over the destroying powers. God doesn't abandon his creation in spite of its often sorry condition. Therefore, God's people are called in obedience to our Creator to do what we can to preserve our tiny planet. *Ephesians 1:20-22; 2:10*

2:3 we were by nature children of wrath: Before God acted in Christ, the believers followed the "ruler of the power of the air" (the devil) and lived by "desires of flesh."

Regarding Luther's words, "we are at the same time saints and sinners," do you think we sometimes overemphasize the sinful side? Why or why not? What may be the consequences of overemphasizing our sinful side? What happens if we underemphasize it?

adoption as his children through Jesus Christ, according to the good
pleasure of his will, [6]to the praise of his glorious grace that he freely
bestowed on us in the Beloved. [7]In him we have redemption through
his blood, the forgiveness of our trespasses, according to the riches of
his grace [8]that he lavished on us. With all wisdom and insight [9]he has
made known to us the mystery of his will, according to his good pleasure
that he set forth in Christ, [10]as a plan for the fullness of time, to
gather up all things in him, things in heaven and things on earth. [11]In
Christ we have also obtained an inheritance,[a] having been destined
according to the purpose of him who accomplishes all things according
to his counsel and will, [12]so that we, who were the first to set our
hope on Christ, might live for the praise of his glory. [13]In him you also,
when you had heard the word of truth, the gospel of your salvation,
and had believed in him, were marked with the seal of the promised
Holy Spirit; [14]this[b] is the pledge of our inheritance toward redemption
as God's own people, to the praise of his glory.

Paul's Prayer

15 I have heard of your faith in the Lord Jesus and your love[c] toward
all the saints, and for this reason [16]I do not cease to give thanks
for you as I remember you in my prayers. [17]I pray that the God of our
Lord Jesus Christ, the Father of glory, may give you a spirit of wisdom
and revelation as you come to know him, [18]so that, with the eyes of
your heart enlightened, you may know what is the hope to which he
has called you, what are the riches of his glorious inheritance among
the saints, [19]and what is the immeasurable greatness of his power for
us who believe, according to the working of his great power. [20]God[d]
put this power to work in Christ when he raised him from the dead
and seated him at his right hand in the heavenly places, [21]far above all
rule and authority and power and dominion, and above every name
that is named, not only in this age but also in the age to come. [22]And
he has put all things under his feet and has made him the head over
all things for the church, [23]which is his body, the fullness of him who
fills all in all.

From Death to Life

2 You were dead through the trespasses and sins [2]in which you
once lived, following the course of this world, following the
ruler of the power of the air, the spirit that is now at work among
those who are disobedient. [3]All of us once lived among them in the
passions of our flesh, following the desires of flesh and senses, and we
were by nature children of wrath, like everyone else. [4]But God, who

---

[a] Or *been made a heritage* [b] Other ancient authorities read *who* [c] Other ancient authorities lack *and your love* [d] Gk *He*

is rich in mercy, out of the great love with which he loved us 5even
when we were dead through our trespasses, made us alive together
with Christ[a]—by grace you have been saved— 6and raised us up with
him and seated us with him in the heavenly places in Christ Jesus, 7so
that in the ages to come he might show the immeasurable riches of
his grace in kindness toward us in Christ Jesus. 8For by grace you have
been saved through faith, and this is not your own doing; it is the gift
of God— 9not the result of works, so that no one may boast. 10For
we are what he has made us, created in Christ Jesus for good works,
which God prepared beforehand to be our way of life.

One in Christ

11 So then, remember that at one time you Gentiles by birth,[b]
called "the uncircumcision" by those who are called "the
circumcision"—a physical circumcision made in the flesh by human
hands— 12remember that you were at that time without Christ, being aliens from the commonwealth of Israel, and strangers to the covenants of promise, having no hope and without God in the world.
13But now in Christ Jesus you who once were far off have been brought
near by the blood of Christ. 14For he is our peace; in his flesh he has
made both groups into one and has broken down the dividing wall,
that is, the hostility between us. 15He has abolished the law with its
commandments and ordinances, that he might create in himself one
new humanity in place of the two, thus making peace, 16and might reconcile both groups to God in one body[c] through the cross, thus putting to death that hostility through it.[d] 17So he came and proclaimed
peace to you who were far off and peace to those who were near; 18for
through him both of us have access in one Spirit to the Father. 19So
then you are no longer strangers and aliens, but you are citizens with
the saints and also members of the household of God, 20built upon
the foundation of the apostles and prophets, with Christ Jesus himself
as the cornerstone.[e] 21In him the whole structure is joined together
and grows into a holy temple in the Lord; 22in whom you also are built
together spiritually[f] into a dwelling place for God.

Paul's Ministry to the Gentiles

3 This is the reason that I Paul am a prisoner for[g] Christ Jesus for
the sake of you Gentiles— 2for surely you have already heard
of the commission of God's grace that was given me for you, 3and how
the mystery was made known to me by revelation, as I wrote above
in a few words, 4a reading of which will enable you to perceive my
understanding of the mystery of Christ. 5In former generations this

[a] Other ancient authorities read *in Christ* [b] Gk *in the flesh* [c] Or *reconcile both of us in one body for God*
[d] Or *in him*, or *in himself* [e] Or *keystone* [f] Gk *in the Spirit* [g] Or *of*

2:5-10 by grace you have been saved...through faith: Though Paul's letters tend to speak of salvation as a future event (see Rom 5:9; 6:5; 1 Cor 15:21-22), here the believers have been saved already. What is consistent in Paul's teaching is that works or works based on law do not save (see Rom 3:24-37; 1 Cor 1:29-31).

What is the grace of God? God always takes the initiative in forgiving and recreating us. It is not our social status, the color of our skin, gender, citizenship, age, or good deeds that makes us worthy before God. The Holy Spirit is the first missionary who grants us salvation freely based solely on God's love. This powerful discovery led Luther to add a word in his translation of this verse into German: "For grace *alone* you have been saved." *Ephesians 2:5-10*

What difference does it make if we believe we are saved or if we look ahead "with fear and trembling" (Phil 2:12), trusting that salvation will take place in the future (Rom 8:24)?

2:11-22 Gentiles by birth, called "the uncircumcision"...strangers to the covenants of promise...joined together: In Judaism, circumcision was a physical sign of being part of God's people. It was based on God's covenant with the people of Israel (Gen 17:1-8; see also Col 2:11-13). But Christ brings both Jews and Gentiles together by the cross (2:16). Gentiles are no longer aliens but full citizens in the household of God (2:19).

2:14 has broken down the dividing wall: The Jerusalem temple had walls separating male and female, Jews and Gentiles (see the diagrams of the temple on pp. 1696-1697). Trespassers who crossed the lines could receive punishment. Jesus tears down such dividing walls of racism, sexism, social class, culture, and language that prevent us from loving and caring for the neighbors and those who may be described as aliens or foreigners. In the reign of God, "illegal aliens" do not exist.

3:1-13 prisoner...for the sake of you Gentiles...fellow heirs: Paul was imprisoned a number of times during his ministry travels (2 Cor 6:5; Phil 1:13-14; Phlm vv. 1, 9). His calling to bring the gospel to the Gentiles is in line with God's plan to reconcile all in the cross of Christ (2:11-22)

mystery[a] was not made known to humankind, as it has now been
revealed to his holy apostles and prophets by the Spirit: 6 that is, the
Gentiles have become fellow heirs, members of the same body, and
sharers in the promise in Christ Jesus through the gospel.
7 Of this gospel I have become a servant according to the gift of
God's grace that was given me by the working of his power. 8 Although
I am the very least of all the saints, this grace was given to me to bring
to the Gentiles the news of the boundless riches of Christ, 9 and to
make everyone see[b] what is the plan of the mystery hidden for ages in[c]
God who created all things; 10 so that through the church the wisdom
of God in its rich variety might now be made known to the rulers and
authorities in the heavenly places. 11 This was in accordance with the
eternal purpose that he has carried out in Christ Jesus our Lord, 12 in
whom we have access to God in boldness and confidence through
faith in him.[d] 13 I pray therefore that you[e] may not lose heart over my
sufferings for you; they are your glory.

Prayer for the Readers

14 For this reason I bow my knees before the Father,[f] 15 from
whom every family[g] in heaven and on earth takes its name. 16 I pray
that, according to the riches of his glory, he may grant that you may be
strengthened in your inner being with power through his Spirit, 17 and
that Christ may dwell in your hearts through faith, as you are being
rooted and grounded in love. 18 I pray that you may have the power
to comprehend, with all the saints, what is the breadth and length
and height and depth, 19 and to know the love of Christ that surpasses
knowledge, so that you may be filled with all the fullness of God.
20 Now to him who by the power at work within us is able to accomplish abundantly far more than all we can ask or imagine, 21 to him
be glory in the church and in Christ Jesus to all generations, forever
and ever. Amen.

Unity in the Body of Christ

4 I therefore, the prisoner in the Lord, beg you to lead a life worthy of the calling to which you have been called, 2 with all humility and gentleness, with patience, bearing with one another in love,
3 making every effort to maintain the unity of the Spirit in the bond of
peace. 4 There is one body and one Spirit, just as you were called to the
one hope of your calling, 5 one Lord, one faith, one baptism, 6 one God
and Father of all, who is above all and through all and in all.
7 But each of us was given grace according to the measure of
Christ's gift. 8 Therefore it is said,

---

[a] Gk *it* [b] Other ancient authorities read *to bring to light* [c] Or *by* [d] Or *the faith of him* [e] Or *I*
[f] Other ancient authorities add *of our Lord Jesus Christ* [g] Gk *fatherhood*

3:10 heavenly places: This phrase is unique to Ephesians and appears often in the letter (see also 1:3, 20; 2:6; 6:12).

3:17 Christ may dwell in your hearts: The apostle's prayer is that Christ would live in the hearts of all the believers, as God lived in the temple (2:20-22). Compare this to Col 3:16, where the prayer is for "the word of Christ" to dwell in the believers.

4:1—5:20 lead a life worthy of the calling: Those who are called according to God's plan are to live out that calling by being unified as Christ's body (4:3-6), using their gifts to build up one another and the church in love (4:7-16), and living as children of light (4:17—5:20).

How do we speak of calling as "vocation"? Vocation means that all who are baptized have been called by God to serve our neighbor individually and as members of communities and groups. Along with our love of the Word of God, Lutherans cherish the notion of calling or vocation. Luther believed that God's invitation to follow extended to everyone, not just professional church workers such as pastors or priests. All Christians had a "religious vocation," for God organized the world through an intricate network of roles. Fulfilling these various roles, people served both God and their neighbors. *Ephesians 4:1*

What do you think is the primary vocation or calling of a Christian? Why?

4:4-6 one body…one baptism…one God: The writer emphasizes unity (oneness), listing seven key things that define that unity. Compare to Galatians 3:28, where Paul describes one baptism in Christ as the source of unity: "There is no longer Jew or Greek, there is no longer slave or free, there is no longer male and female; for all of you are one in Christ Jesus."

"When he ascended on high he made captivity itself a captive;
he gave gifts to his people."
9 (When it says, "He ascended," what does it mean but that he had also
descended[a] into the lower parts of the earth? 10 He who descended is
the same one who ascended far above all the heavens, so that he might
fill all things.) 11 The gifts he gave were that some would be apostles,
some prophets, some evangelists, some pastors and teachers, 12 to
equip the saints for the work of ministry, for building up the body
of Christ, 13 until all of us come to the unity of the faith and of the
knowledge of the Son of God, to maturity, to the measure of the full
stature of Christ. 14 We must no longer be children, tossed to and fro
and blown about by every wind of doctrine, by people's trickery, by
their craftiness in deceitful scheming. 15 But speaking the truth in love,
we must grow up in every way into him who is the head, into Christ,
16 from whom the whole body, joined and knit together by every liga-
ment with which it is equipped, as each part is working properly, promotes the body's growth in building itself up in love.

The Old Life and the New

17 Now this I affirm and insist on in the Lord: you must no longer
live as the Gentiles live, in the futility of their minds. 18 They are darkened in their understanding, alienated from the life of God because of
their ignorance and hardness of heart. 19 They have lost all sensitivity
and have abandoned themselves to licentiousness, greedy to practice
every kind of impurity. 20 That is not the way you learned Christ! 21 For
surely you have heard about him and were taught in him, as truth is in
Jesus. 22 You were taught to put away your former way of life, your old
self, corrupt and deluded by its lusts, 23 and to be renewed in the spirit
of your minds, 24 and to clothe yourselves with the new self, created
according to the likeness of God in true righteousness and holiness.

Rules for the New Life

25 So then, putting away falsehood, let all of us speak the truth to
our neighbors, for we are members of one another. 26 Be angry but do
not sin; do not let the sun go down on your anger, 27 and do not make
room for the devil. 28 Thieves must give up stealing; rather let them labor and work honestly with their own hands, so as to have something
to share with the needy. 29 Let no evil talk come out of your mouths,
but only what is useful for building up,[b] as there is need, so that your
words may give grace to those who hear. 30 And do not grieve the Holy
Spirit of God, with which you were marked with a seal for the day of
redemption. 31 Put away from you all bitterness and wrath and anger
and wrangling and slander, together with all malice, 32 and be kind to

[a] Other ancient authorities add *first* [b] Other ancient authorities read *building up faith*

Why do you think unity in the church is important? On what key things should this unity be built?

4:11 apostles...teachers: This list of ministries of the early church is not meant to be a complete list (see also Rom 12:4-8; 1 Cor 12:28-30). For example, bishops and deacons are not included (see 1 Tim 3:1-13).

What do you think are your particular gifts for serving in the church? How would you define what an apostle or prophet is today? Where do we find apostles and prophets?

4:28—5:5 something to share with the needy: In Jesus' message and deeds, the poor played a central role. In the list of vices in 4:25—5:5, greediness means stealing but also refers to idolatry. When we trust in things or wealth more than God, we idolize money and are not open to sharing. Jesus encouraged sharing our abundance with the needy.

one another, tenderhearted, forgiving one another, as God in Christ
5 has forgiven you.[a] 1 Therefore be imitators of God, as beloved
children, 2 and live in love, as Christ loved us[b] and gave himself up
for us, a fragrant offering and sacrifice to God.

Renounce Pagan Ways

3 But fornication and impurity of any kind, or greed, must not
even be mentioned among you, as is proper among saints. 4 Entirely
out of place is obscene, silly, and vulgar talk; but instead, let there be
thanksgiving. 5 Be sure of this, that no fornicator or impure person,
or one who is greedy (that is, an idolater), has any inheritance in the
kingdom of Christ and of God.

6 Let no one deceive you with empty words, for because of these
things the wrath of God comes on those who are disobedient. 7 Therefore do not be associated with them. 8 For once you were darkness,
but now in the Lord you are light. Live as children of light— 9 for the
fruit of the light is found in all that is good and right and true. 10 Try to
find out what is pleasing to the Lord. 11 Take no part in the unfruitful
works of darkness, but instead expose them. 12 For it is shameful even
to mention what such people do secretly; 13 but everything exposed
by the light becomes visible, 14 for everything that becomes visible is
light. Therefore it says,

"Sleeper, awake!
Rise from the dead,
and Christ will shine on you."

15 Be careful then how you live, not as unwise people but as wise,
16 making the most of the time, because the days are evil. 17 So do not
be foolish, but understand what the will of the Lord is. 18 Do not get
drunk with wine, for that is debauchery; but be filled with the Spirit,
19 as you sing psalms and hymns and spiritual songs among yourselves, singing and making melody to the Lord in your hearts, 20 giving
thanks to God the Father at all times and for everything in the name
of our Lord Jesus Christ.

The Christian Household

21 Be subject to one another out of reverence for Christ.

22 Wives, be subject to your husbands as you are to the Lord.
23 For the husband is the head of the wife just as Christ is the head of
the church, the body of which he is the Savior. 24 Just as the church
is subject to Christ, so also wives ought to be, in everything, to their
husbands.

25 Husbands, love your wives, just as Christ loved the church
and gave himself up for her, 26 in order to make her holy by cleans-

[a] Other ancient authorities read *us* [b] Other ancient authorities read *you*

5:21-33 Be subject to one another: The writer compares ancient Roman society's view of the family or marriage hierarchy to the relationship between Christ and the church. In Paul's undisputed letters, he does not talk about wives being subject to husbands. The "subject to" language is tempered by a call for husbands to love wives as Christ loves the church (5:25).

5:25 just as Christ loved the church: The hierarchical (holy power) language can and has been used in a way that causes hardship for others, especially women, children, and servants. Though our society encourages mutual respect within marriage relationships and has laws to protect the most vulnerable in our society, some in positions of power or authority continue to abuse their power. For example, the battering of females, child abuse, and child slave labor continue around the globe.

How does the church work to be more hospitable to those with little or no status? How do we work to do away with abuses of power and authority that harm especially the most vulnerable?

ing her with the washing of water by the word, 27 so as to present the
church to himself in splendor, without a spot or wrinkle or anything
of the kind—yes, so that she may be holy and without blemish. 28 In
the same way, husbands should love their wives as they do their own
bodies. He who loves his wife loves himself. 29 For no one ever hates
his own body, but he nourishes and tenderly cares for it, just as Christ
does for the church, 30 because we are members of his body.[a] 31 "For
this reason a man will leave his father and mother and be joined to
his wife, and the two will become one flesh." 32 This is a great mystery,
and I am applying it to Christ and the church. 33 Each of you, however, should love his wife as himself, and a wife should respect her
husband.

Children and Parents

6 Children, obey your parents in the Lord,[b] for this is right.
2 "Honor your father and mother"—this is the first commandment with a promise: 3 "so that it may be well with you and you may
live long on the earth."

4 And, fathers, do not provoke your children to anger, but bring
them up in the discipline and instruction of the Lord.

Slaves and Masters

5 Slaves, obey your earthly masters with fear and trembling, in singleness of heart, as you obey Christ; 6 not only while being watched,
and in order to please them, but as slaves of Christ, doing the will of
God from the heart. 7 Render service with enthusiasm, as to the Lord
and not to men and women, 8 knowing that whatever good we do, we
will receive the same again from the Lord, whether we are slaves or
free.

9 And, masters, do the same to them. Stop threatening them, for
you know that both of you have the same Master in heaven, and with
him there is no partiality.

The Whole Armor of God

10 Finally, be strong in the Lord and in the strength of his power.
11 Put on the whole armor of God, so that you may be able to stand
against the wiles of the devil. 12 For our[c] struggle is not against enemies of blood and flesh, but against the rulers, against the authorities, against the cosmic powers of this present darkness, against the
spiritual forces of evil in the heavenly places. 13 Therefore take up the
whole armor of God, so that you may be able to withstand on that
evil day, and having done everything, to stand firm. 14 Stand therefore,

6:1-4 obey your parents: See that commandment (Exod 20:12) and also the teaching that encourages parents to instruct their children in God's commandments and decrees (Deut 6:4-9). Compare also to Colossians 3:20-21.

6:5-6 Slaves, obey your earthly masters: For centuries, slavery was blessed by the Christian church. While slavery has been abolished by law in our society, various forms of slavery still exist in many places. Ephesians encourages slaves to be slaves for Christ. Paul spoke of himself in this way (Rom 1:1, see NRSV footnote *a*; Phil 1:1, see NRSV footnote *a*), as well as those who are one with Christ (1 Cor 7:22).

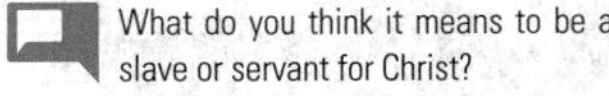

What do you think it means to be a slave or servant for Christ?

6:10-20 Put on the whole armor of God: This armor is the clothing of the new self (4:24) that the believer is to put on. Armor and tools of battle are used to show that the faithful face struggle against evil (6:13).

How is God's word like the sword of the Spirit? What other images would you use to describe God's word?

[a] Other ancient authorities add *of his flesh and of his bones*

[b] Other ancient authorities lack *in the Lord*

[c] Other ancient authorities read *your*

and fasten the belt of truth around your waist, and put on the breastplate of righteousness. [15]As shoes for your feet put on whatever will make you ready to proclaim the gospel of peace. [16]With all of these,[a] take the shield of faith, with which you will be able to quench all the flaming arrows of the evil one. [17]Take the helmet of salvation, and the sword of the Spirit, which is the word of God.

18 Pray in the Spirit at all times in every prayer and supplication.
To that end keep alert and always persevere in supplication for all
the saints. [19]Pray also for me, so that when I speak, a message may be
given to me to make known with boldness the mystery of the gospel,[b]
[20]for which I am an ambassador in chains. Pray that I may declare it
boldly, as I must speak.

Personal Matters and Benediction

21 So that you also may know how I am and what I am doing,
Tychicus will tell you everything. He is a dear brother and a faithful
minister in the Lord. [22]I am sending him to you for this very purpose,
to let you know how we are, and to encourage your hearts.

23 Peace be to the whole community,[c] and love with faith, from
God the Father and the Lord Jesus Christ. [24]Grace be with all who
have an undying love for our Lord Jesus Christ.[d]

---

[a] Or *In all circumstances* [b] Other ancient authorities lack *of the gospel* [c] Gk *to the brothers* [d] Other ancient authorities add *Amen*

PHILIPPIANS

Philippians 2:5

Background File

The first Christian church in Europe was established in the city of Philippi in Macedonia (modern-day Greece) by the apostle Paul (see Map 14, p. 2111). Paul first came to Philippi around 50 C.E, but he returned more than once during his ministry (Acts 20:6; 1 Cor 16:5-6; 2 Cor 2:13; 7:5). Lydia and her household were the first converts there (Acts 16:11-15). Paul and Silas were imprisoned in Philippi but released following an earthquake, resulting in their jailer becoming a convert (Acts 16:16-34).

Philip II of Macedonia (father of Alexander the Great) founded the city of Philippi in 356 B.C.E. After the battle of Philippi in 42 B.C.E., which took place during the Roman civil war, Marc Antony settled many of his soldiers there and made the city a Roman colony. In the time of the early church, Philippi was an important city on the *Via Egnatia*, a road used to transport goods and supplies between Rome and the eastern part of the empire. Citizens in Philippi enjoyed the same legal rights as those in Italian cities.

Excavations indicate that Roman, Greek, Egyptian, and other gods were worshiped in the city. A Jewish synagogue or place of prayer (Acts 16:13; 16) was located outside the city walls.

What's the Story?

The apostle Paul and Timothy, his fellow evangelist, sent this letter. Paul often wrote in conjunction with others (see 1 Cor 1:1; 2 Cor 1:1; Gal 1:2; 1 Thess 1:1; Phlm v. 1). Paul writes from prison (1:7, 14) but does not tell what city he is in. It may have been Ephesus, Caesarea, or Rome.

The Philippian church had "bishops [overseers] and deacons" and leaders such as Euodia, Syntyche, and Clement (1:1; 4:2-3). The Philippians had helped Paul "in the early days of the gospel" (4:15) and show a renewed concern for him (4:10). Epaphroditus, who delivered their gifts to Paul, is returning to them (see 2:25-30; 4:18). The development of the church and of the relationship between Paul and the Philippians indicates that this letter was not written very early in Paul's missionary career, perhaps in the mid-to-late 50s C.E. If Paul was in Ephesus, the date of the letter would be earlier (around 54-55 C.E.). If written from Caesarea or Rome, it would likely be dated three to six years later, respectively.

What's the Message?

This is Paul's most joyful letter. It is a letter of thanksgiving for the Philippians' material support of Paul's ministry. Paul's thanks, however, are combined with his belief in God's grace for both himself and the Philippians, and therefore God deserves ultimate thanks (1:3). Paul expresses his warmest feelings for the Philippians (1:7), the freedom of joy in the Lord even as he is in chains (1:12-14; 4:10-13), and he encourages them to be of one mind in Christ (2:5). He quotes an early Christian hymn (2:6-11), which summarizes beautifully the servant Savior who humbled himself on a cross, so that God and all people might exalt him.

Paul also warns the Philippians about the "dogs," and "evil workers" (3:2) and those who preach Christ from insincere motives (1:17). Paul stresses that the Philippians, though living in a favored city of the Roman Empire, have a higher citizenship in heaven (3:20). Theirs is the joy of knowing Christ and his resurrection, which provides Paul and the Philippians with a new perspective on life and enables them to rejoice, even in difficult circumstances (4:4-7).

1:1 Paul and Timothy: Paul's co-worker Timothy was from Lystra (Acts 16:1-4, see Map 14, p. 2111). Paul and Timothy are also listed as writers of 2 Corinthians, 1 Thessalonians, and Philemon.

Who can be a saint? Paul calls all baptized Christians saints, not just a few. The Apology of the Augsburg Confession says that we honor saints for three reasons. First, they are examples of God's mercy and show how much God wants to save humankind. Second, honoring saints strengthens our faith. For example, when we see Saint Peter forgiven after denying Jesus, we see how God's grace abounds. And third, they are examples of faith that encourage us in our own callings. (*BC*: 238) *Philippians 1:1*

How can the baptized be saints in the world today? How do we encourage one another in our own callings?

1:1 bishops and deacons: The Greek word translated as "bishops" could also be "overseers," and the Greek word for "deacons" could be translated as "officers." These were leaders in the church, not official positions or titles at the time.

1:2 God our Father: God is not domineering and abusive, but a kind and giving parent. See also Rom 1:7; 1 Cor 1:3; Gal 1:1-4.

Salutation

1 Paul and Timothy, servants[a] of Christ Jesus,
To all the saints in Christ Jesus who are in Philippi, with the
bishops[b] and deacons:[c]
2 Grace to you and peace from God our Father and the Lord
Jesus Christ.

Paul's Prayer for the Philippians

3 I thank my God every time I remember you, 4 constantly praying with joy in every one of my prayers for all of you, 5 because of your
sharing in the gospel from the first day until now. 6 I am confident of
this, that the one who began a good work among you will bring it to
completion by the day of Jesus Christ. 7 It is right for me to think this
way about all of you, because you hold me in your heart,[d] for all of you
share in God's grace[e] with me, both in my imprisonment and in the
defense and confirmation of the gospel. 8 For God is my witness, how
I long for all of you with the compassion of Christ Jesus. 9 And this is
my prayer, that your love may overflow more and more with knowledge and full insight 10 to help you to determine what is best, so that in
the day of Christ you may be pure and blameless, 11 having produced
the harvest of righteousness that comes through Jesus Christ for the
glory and praise of God.

---

[a] Gk *slaves* [b] Or *overseers* [c] Or *overseers and helpers* [d] Or *because I hold you in my heart* [e] Gk *in grace*

Paul's Present Circumstances

12 I want you to know, beloved,[a] that what has happened to me
has actually helped to spread the gospel, 13so that it has become known
throughout the whole imperial guard[b] and to everyone else that my
imprisonment is for Christ; 14and most of the brothers and sisters,[a]
having been made confident in the Lord by my imprisonment, dare
to speak the word[c] with greater boldness and without fear.
15 Some proclaim Christ from envy and rivalry, but others from
goodwill. 16These proclaim Christ out of love, knowing that I have
been put here for the defense of the gospel; 17the others proclaim
Christ out of selfish ambition, not sincerely but intending to increase
my suffering in my imprisonment. 18What does it matter? Just this,
that Christ is proclaimed in every way, whether out of false motives
or true; and in that I rejoice.

Yes, and I will continue to rejoice, 19for I know that through your
prayers and the help of the Spirit of Jesus Christ this will turn out for
my deliverance. 20It is my eager expectation and hope that I will not
be put to shame in any way, but that by my speaking with all boldness,
Christ will be exalted now as always in my body, whether by life or by
death. 21For to me, living is Christ and dying is gain. 22If I am to live in
the flesh, that means fruitful labor for me; and I do not know which
I prefer. 23I am hard pressed between the two: my desire is to depart
and be with Christ, for that is far better; 24but to remain in the flesh is
more necessary for you. 25Since I am convinced of this, I know that I
will remain and continue with all of you for your progress and joy in
faith, 26so that I may share abundantly in your boasting in Christ Jesus
when I come to you again.
27 Only, live your life in a manner worthy of the gospel of Christ,
so that, whether I come and see you or am absent and hear about you,
I will know that you are standing firm in one spirit, striving side by
side with one mind for the faith of the gospel, 28and are in no way
intimidated by your opponents. For them this is evidence of their destruction, but of your salvation. And this is God's doing. 29For he has
graciously granted you the privilege not only of believing in Christ,
but of suffering for him as well— 30since you are having the same
struggle that you saw I had and now hear that I still have.

Imitating Christ's Humility

2 If then there is any encouragement in Christ, any consolation
from love, any sharing in the Spirit, any compassion and sympathy, 2make my joy complete: be of the same mind, having the same
love, being in full accord and of one mind. 3Do nothing from selfish ambition or conceit, but in humility regard others as better than

[a] Gk *brothers* [b] Gk *whole praetorium* [c] Other ancient authorities read *word of God*

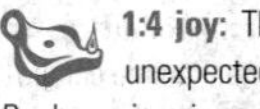

1:4 joy: This is a major and perhaps unexpected theme in Philippians, since Paul was in prison at the time (1:7; 3:1; 4:4).

1:6 the day of Jesus Christ: This refers to the second coming of Christ, an event Paul and the early church eagerly awaited (see 1 Cor 15:23; 1 Thess 2:19; 3:13; 4:15; 5:23.)

1:7 grace: The Greek word translated as "grace" means kindness, gift, favor, or goodwill (see also Rom 3:24; 1 Cor 15:10; Gal 2:21; and note at Eph 2:5-10). God's grace is freely given, without conditions, resulting in future salvation and present fellowship.

1:11 having produced the harvest of righteousness: "Having produced" may be translated as "having been filled with." Righteousness, God's saving power, is not something we can produce but something that God gives in Jesus Christ (see also Rom 1:17; 3:22; 2 Cor 5:21)

We are made right with God as a gift. How do you respond to this?

1:13 the whole imperial guard: This would have consisted of elite Roman soldiers who protected the emperor and his family and kept political unrest under control. The Philippians might have assumed that being in prison would prevent Paul from spreading the good news of Jesus Christ, but Paul says it has actually helped him to reach these soldiers and others.

1:15-18 Christ is proclaimed: This message does not depend on who proclaims it or their motives. (See also Mark 9:38-41; Luke 9:49-50.)

1:26 boasting in Christ Jesus: Paul writes about this several times (for examples, see 2:16 and Gal 6:14). For Paul, what God accomplished through the dying and rising of Christ goes beyond any human accomplishment. Christ Jesus, then, is the only reason for pride or boasting.

1:27 live your life: These words refer to life in community and its responsibilities. Christianity is more than a religion; believing in Christ is a way of life.

1:29 granted you the privilege: God grants faith (believing in Christ) as a gift, not a work (see Rom 3:24)..

2:5-11 Let the same mind be in you: If not an original Pauline composition, this passage may be the earliest Christian hymn still in existence.

2:6-8 emptied himself: Jesus gave up everything to become human. He fully obeyed God, all the way to dying on the cross. The hymn implies the spiritual emptiness of humanity without God.

2:10-11 every knee…every tongue: Jesus Christ is Lord of all (see Rom 8:19-22; 1 Cor 15:28.)

How can we "work out our own salvation"? God is the source of good will, works, obedience, and salvation. Paul is not commanding the Philippians to save themselves, but to live out the salvation they already have in Christ. This is possible because God promises to be at work in us. *Philippians 2:12-13*

2:17 libation: Jews followed God's law in offering sacrifices to God. Sometimes this included pouring out water or wine on the altar (see 2 Kgs 16:13). In other religions, people would pour wine on an altar or on the ground as a way of honoring their gods. Paul would be glad to have his life poured out, or even lose his life, as a sacrifice to God.

yourselves. [4]Let each of you look not to your own interests, but to the
interests of others. [5]Let the same mind be in you that was[a] in Christ
Jesus,

6 who, though he was in the form of God,
did not regard equality with God
as something to be exploited,
7 but emptied himself,
taking the form of a slave,
being born in human likeness.
And being found in human form,
8 he humbled himself
and became obedient to the point of death—
even death on a cross.

9 Therefore God also highly exalted him
and gave him the name
that is above every name,
10 so that at the name of Jesus
every knee should bend,
in heaven and on earth and under the earth,
11 and every tongue should confess
that Jesus Christ is Lord,
to the glory of God the Father.

Shining as Lights in the World

12 Therefore, my beloved, just as you have always obeyed me,
not only in my presence, but much more now in my absence, work
out your own salvation with fear and trembling; [13]for it is God who
is at work in you, enabling you both to will and to work for his good
pleasure.

14 Do all things without murmuring and arguing, [15]so that you
may be blameless and innocent, children of God without blemish in
the midst of a crooked and perverse generation, in which you shine
like stars in the world. [16]It is by your holding fast to the word of life
that I can boast on the day of Christ that I did not run in vain or labor in vain. [17]But even if I am being poured out as a libation over the
sacrifice and the offering of your faith, I am glad and rejoice with all
of you— [18]and in the same way you also must be glad and rejoice
with me.

Timothy and Epaphroditus

19 I hope in the Lord Jesus to send Timothy to you soon, so that
I may be cheered by news of you. [20]I have no one like him who will

[a] Or *that you have*

be genuinely concerned for your welfare. [21]All of them are seeking
their own interests, not those of Jesus Christ. [22]But Timothy's[a] worth
you know, how like a son with a father he has served with me in the
work of the gospel. [23]I hope therefore to send him as soon as I see
how things go with me; [24]and I trust in the Lord that I will also come
soon.

25 Still, I think it necessary to send to you Epaphroditus—my
brother and co-worker and fellow soldier, your messenger[b] and minister to my need; [26]for he has been longing for[c] all of you, and has
been distressed because you heard that he was ill. [27]He was indeed so
ill that he nearly died. But God had mercy on him, and not only on
him but on me also, so that I would not have one sorrow after another.
[28]I am the more eager to send him, therefore, in order that you may
rejoice at seeing him again, and that I may be less anxious. [29]Welcome
him then in the Lord with all joy, and honor such people, [30]because
he came close to death for the work of Christ,[d] risking his life to make
up for those services that you could not give me.

3 Finally, my brothers and sisters,[e] rejoice[f] in the Lord.

Breaking with the Past

To write the same things to you is not troublesome to me, and for
you it is a safeguard.

2 Beware of the dogs, beware of the evil workers, beware of those
who mutilate the flesh![g] [3]For it is we who are the circumcision, who
worship in the Spirit of God[h] and boast in Christ Jesus and have no
confidence in the flesh— [4]even though I, too, have reason for confidence in the flesh.

If anyone else has reason to be confident in the flesh, I have more:
[5]circumcised on the eighth day, a member of the people of Israel, of
the tribe of Benjamin, a Hebrew born of Hebrews; as to the law, a
Pharisee; [6]as to zeal, a persecutor of the church; as to righteousness
under the law, blameless.

7 Yet whatever gains I had, these I have come to regard as loss because of Christ. [8]More than that, I regard everything as loss because
of the surpassing value of knowing Christ Jesus my Lord. For his sake
I have suffered the loss of all things, and I regard them as rubbish, in
order that I may gain Christ [9]and be found in him, not having a righteousness of my own that comes from the law, but one that comes
through faith in Christ,[i] the righteousness from God based on faith.
[10]I want to know Christ[j] and the power of his resurrection and the
sharing of his sufferings by becoming like him in his death, [11]if somehow I may attain the resurrection from the dead.

---

[a] Gk *his* [b] Gk *apostle* [c] Other ancient authorities read *longing to see* [d] Other ancient authorities read *of the Lord* [e] Gk *my brothers* [f] Or *farewell* [g] Gk *the mutilation* [h] Other ancient authorities read *worship God in spirit* [i] Or *through the faith of Christ* [j] Gk *him*

3:2 mutilate the flesh!...the circumcision: This is a harsh reference to circumcision (similar to another in Gal 5:11-12). As in Galatians, Paul insists that one does not need to observe Jewish rituals in order to be a Christian. At the same time, Paul refers symbolically to Christians as "the circumcision," meaning they are now fully part of God's people and have access to God's promises (see Rom 2:25-28; Eph 2:11).

3:4-6 a Pharisee...blameless: The Pharisees were devoted, faithful Jews who were committed to following God's law. As a Pharisee, Paul believed he had fulfilled the law (see Gal 1:14). But faith in Christ gave him a different view of a righteousness based on the gift of faith, not human achievement.

3:11 if somehow I may attain: The word "attain," as Paul uses it here, refers to an arrival, not an achievement.

Your faith in Christ is a gift. What does this mean to you? What do you do with this gift?

3:17 imitating me: Paul speaks here as a good teacher encouraging his students to follow his example (see also 1 Cor 11:1).

3:20 our citizenship is in heaven: In Paul's time, few people were allowed to become Roman citizens. Being citizens of heaven is greater than being citizens of any earthly realm.

What do you think it means to be a "citizen of heaven"? How does that citizenship affect the way you live? How does it affect your allegiances?

4:2-3 women: Some of the congregations Paul started had female leaders (see Rom 16:3; 1 Cor 1:11).

Pressing toward the Goal

12 Not that I have already obtained this or have already reached
the goal;[a] but I press on to make it my own, because Christ Jesus has
made me his own. 13Beloved,[b] I do not consider that I have made it
my own;[c] but this one thing I do: forgetting what lies behind and
straining forward to what lies ahead, 14I press on toward the goal for
the prize of the heavenly[d] call of God in Christ Jesus. 15Let those of us
then who are mature be of the same mind; and if you think differently
about anything, this too God will reveal to you. 16Only let us hold fast
to what we have attained.

17 Brothers and sisters,[b] join in imitating me, and observe those
who live according to the example you have in us. 18For many live as
enemies of the cross of Christ; I have often told you of them, and now
I tell you even with tears. 19Their end is destruction; their god is the
belly; and their glory is in their shame; their minds are set on earthly
things. 20But our citizenship[e] is in heaven, and it is from there that we
are expecting a Savior, the Lord Jesus Christ. 21He will transform the
body of our humiliation[f] that it may be conformed to the body of his
glory,[g] by the power that also enables him to make all things subject
4 to himself. 1Therefore, my brothers and sisters,[h] whom I love
and long for, my joy and crown, stand firm in the Lord in this
way, my beloved.

Exhortations

2 I urge Euodia and I urge Syntyche to be of the same mind in
the Lord. 3Yes, and I ask you also, my loyal companion,[i] help these
women, for they have struggled beside me in the work of the gospel,
together with Clement and the rest of my co-workers, whose names
are in the book of life.

4 Rejoice[j] in the Lord always; again I will say, Rejoice.[j] 5Let your
gentleness be known to everyone. The Lord is near. 6Do not worry
about anything, but in everything by prayer and supplication with
thanksgiving let your requests be made known to God. 7And the
peace of God, which surpasses all understanding, will guard your
hearts and your minds in Christ Jesus.

8 Finally, beloved,[k] whatever is true, whatever is honorable, whatever is just, whatever is pure, whatever is pleasing, whatever is com-
mendable, if there is any excellence and if there is anything worthy of
praise, think about[l] these things. 9Keep on doing the things that you
have learned and received and heard and seen in me, and the God of
peace will be with you.

---

[a] Or *have already been made perfect* [b] Gk *Brothers* [c] Other ancient authorities read *my own yet* [d] Gk *upward* [e] Or *commonwealth* [f] Or *our humble bodies* [g] Or *his glorious body* [h] Gk *my brothers* [i] Or *loyal Syzygus* [j] Or *Farewell* [k] Gk *brothers* [l] Gk *take account of*

Acknowledgment of the Philippians' Gift

10 I rejoice[a] in the Lord greatly that now at last you have revived
your concern for me; indeed, you were concerned for me, but had no
opportunity to show it.[b] 11 Not that I am referring to being in need;
for I have learned to be content with whatever I have. 12 I know what
it is to have little, and I know what it is to have plenty. In any and all
circumstances I have learned the secret of being well-fed and of going
hungry, of having plenty and of being in need. 13 I can do all things
through him who strengthens me. 14 In any case, it was kind of you to
share my distress.

15 You Philippians indeed know that in the early days of the gospel, when I left Macedonia, no church shared with me in the matter of
giving and receiving, except you alone. 16 For even when I was in Thessalonica, you sent me help for my needs more than once. 17 Not that
I seek the gift, but I seek the profit that accumulates to your account.
18 I have been paid in full and have more than enough; I am fully satisfied, now that I have received from Epaphroditus the gifts you sent,
a fragrant offering, a sacrifice acceptable and pleasing to God. 19 And
my God will fully satisfy every need of yours according to his riches
in glory in Christ Jesus. 20 To our God and Father be glory forever and
ever. Amen.

4:10-19 the gifts you sent: The Philippians supported Paul's ministry through gifts delivered to Paul by Epaphroditus (1:5-7; 2:25). Paul attempted to support himself while doing his ministry (see Acts 18:3) and was cautious about receiving gifts from churches, so that no one could control his ministry (see 1 Cor 9:13-18). While in prison he couldn't make a living, so he welcomed the gifts.

4:10-19 I rejoice in the Lord . . . my God will fully satisfy every need: Ancient gift-giving was based on reciprocity—one is obligated to give in response to receiving a gift. Paul explodes this idea of gift-giving between Christians. Because God is the first giver, when we give gifts to others, we ought not regard those gifts as obligations upon those who receive the gifts. This is why Paul never thanks the Philippians directly, but only indirectly by thanking God.

Final Greetings and Benediction

21 Greet every saint in Christ Jesus. The friends[c] who are with me
greet you. 22 All the saints greet you, especially those of the emperor's
household.

23 The grace of the Lord Jesus Christ be with your spirit.[d]

4:22 emperor's household: This may refer to the emperor and his family, as well as servants, slaves, and others connected to the household. Paul was apparently making an impression for the sake of the gospel during his imprisonment.

---

[a] Gk *I rejoiced* [b] Gk lacks *to show it* [c] Gk *brothers* [d] Other ancient authorities add *Amen*

Colossians 3:16

COLOSSIANS

Background File

This letter appears to be written by the apostle Paul from prison to Christians living in the town of Colossae (1:1-2; 4:10, 18). Some scholars, however, think that perhaps Paul did not actually write this letter, because its style, wording, and theology are different from Paul's other letters. Possibly a disciple of Paul wrote in his name because Paul was unable to write it. If Paul wrote this letter, it was written around 55 B.C.E. If a disciple of Paul was the author, it may have been written 65–75 B.C.E

What's the Story?

Colossae was located about 125 miles from the sea in what is now western Turkey. Paul, or whoever wrote this letter, had not been to Colossae but had heard about the Colossians from a Christian minister named Epaphras (1:7-8; 4:12-13). Letters in the ancient world followed a regular pattern, beginning with greetings (1:1-2) and a prayer of thanks (1:3-8). The largest part of a letter was its body, which in Colossians has two parts. The first focuses on right and wrong Christian *teachings* (1:9—2:23). The second part focuses on right and wrong Christian *living* (3:1—4:9). Letters in the ancient pattern closed with a series of greetings and final thoughts (4:10-18).

What's the Message?

This letter emphasizes the important role Jesus Christ plays in God's plan of salvation and how Christians are now fully united with Christ. Evidently some false teachers were claiming that the Colossians were not yet fully united with Christ. They were teaching that the Colossians needed special knowledge and must live in very strict ways in order to be fully united with Christ (2:8, 16-23). The apostle rejects their claims. He reminds the Colossians that they have already received Christ and so are to continue to live as they had been taught (2:6-7). The foundation for this letter's understanding of God and Jesus is found in 1:15-20. These verses are a type of early hymn celebrating who Jesus is and what God has done through Jesus. Here Christ is called the image of the invisible God, the one through whom God created everything, the one who holds the universe together, and the one whose death brings peace throughout the universe.

Because Christians of all ages have already been united with Christ through baptism (2:11-15), we therefore let Christ's love, peace, and forgiveness guide our lives and our relationships with other Christians (3:1-5, 12-17), with members of our family (3:18–4:1), and with people who are not Christians (4:5-6).

Salutation

1 Paul, an apostle of Christ Jesus by the will of God, and Timothy
our brother,
2 To the saints and faithful brothers and sisters[a] in Christ in
Colossae:
Grace to you and peace from God our Father.

Paul Thanks God for the Colossians

3 In our prayers for you we always thank God, the Father of our
Lord Jesus Christ, 4for we have heard of your faith in Christ Jesus and
of the love that you have for all the saints, 5because of the hope laid
up for you in heaven. You have heard of this hope before in the word
of the truth, the gospel 6that has come to you. Just as it is bearing fruit
and growing in the whole world, so it has been bearing fruit among
yourselves from the day you heard it and truly comprehended the
grace of God. 7This you learned from Epaphras, our beloved fellow
servant.[b] He is a faithful minister of Christ on your[c] behalf, 8and he
has made known to us your love in the Spirit.
9 For this reason, since the day we heard it, we have not ceased
praying for you and asking that you may be filled with the knowledge
of God's[d] will in all spiritual wisdom and understanding, 10so that you
may lead lives worthy of the Lord, fully pleasing to him, as you bear
fruit in every good work and as you grow in the knowledge of God.
11May you be made strong with all the strength that comes from his
glorious power, and may you be prepared to endure everything with
patience, while joyfully 12giving thanks to the Father, who has enabled[e] you[f] to share in the inheritance of the saints in the light. 13He
has rescued us from the power of darkness and transferred us into the
kingdom of his beloved Son, 14in whom we have redemption, the forgiveness of sins.[g]

The Supremacy of Christ

15 He is the image of the invisible God, the firstborn of all creation; 16for in[h] him all things in heaven and on earth were created,
things visible and invisible, whether thrones or dominions or rulers

---

[a] Gk *brothers* [b] Gk *slave* [c] Other ancient authorities read *our* [d] Gk *his* [e] Other ancient authorities read *called* [f] Other ancient authorities read *us* [g] Other ancient authorities add *through his blood* [h] Or *by*

1:1 Timothy our brother...Colossae: Timothy was Paul's young partner in preaching and teaching the gospel (see Acts 16:1-4; 1 Thess 1:1; 1 Tim 1:1-3). Colossae was located some one hundred miles west of Ephesus, in Asia Minor. It was known for its wool making. Sometime after 60 C.E. it was destroyed by an earthquake.

1:7 Epaphras: Possibly the founder of the church in Colossae (4:12-13; Phlm v. 23).

What does it mean to lead lives worthy of the Lord? The letter to the Colossians invites us to "lead lives worthy of the Lord, fully pleasing to him, as you bear fruit in every good work." For Lutherans this does not mean that we have to earn Christ's love or prove through good words that we are worthy of his forgiveness. Because God first loves us and forgives us, we respond by loving God and gladly acting according to God's commands. *Colossians 1:10*

What does it mean to say that you have been "rescued...from the power of darkness and transferred...into the kingdom of [God's] beloved Son"? Where and what is that kingdom?

1:15-17 [Christ] is the image of the invisible God: False teachers were telling the Colossians that the created, physical world was bad, and they needed to escape from it through special knowledge and religious practices. Here the letter stresses that God created everything in heaven and on earth through Christ. Notice the emphasis that Christ exists before creation, and that Christ is the glue that holds all things together.

1:15, 18 the firstborn of all creation...the firstborn from the dead: While Christ existed before creation, at his birth he became fully human to carry out God's plan of salvation, so his birth is the most important birth in all creation (John 1:1-14; Phil 2:5-11; Heb 1:1-14). Christ's resurrection (firstborn from the dead) opens up the way to eternal life for us.

What does it mean for you to think about Christ as the image of the invisible God (1:15)?

1:18, 21-22, 24; 3:15 [Christ] is the head of the body, the church: Colossians refers to the body of Christ in two ways. First, the physical body of Christ was nailed to the cross as part of God's plan so that we would no longer be separated from God (1:21-22). Second, Colossians refers to the church as the body of Christ (1:18, 24; 3:15) to describe the full unity we have with Jesus and with all Christians.

1:19; 2:9 the fullness of God... dwells: Note how Colossians stresses that all of God's divine nature is completely and fully in Christ, so that Christ is fully divine and fully human.

2:2-4 God's mystery: The word *mystery* refers to God's hidden plan of salvation. Paul claims that God's secrets have been fully revealed in Christ's life, death, and resurrection, rather than through the secret traditions of the false teachers.

What secret traditions or misleading teachings are present in our modern world?

or powers—all things have been created through him and for him.
17He himself is before all things, and in[a] him all things hold together.
18He is the head of the body, the church; he is the beginning, the
firstborn from the dead, so that he might come to have first place in
everything. 19For in him all the fullness of God was pleased to dwell,
20and through him God was pleased to reconcile to himself all things,
whether on earth or in heaven, by making peace through the blood
of his cross.

21 And you who were once estranged and hostile in mind, doing evil deeds, 22he has now reconciled[b] in his fleshly body[c] through
death, so as to present you holy and blameless and irreproachable
before him— 23provided that you continue securely established and
steadfast in the faith, without shifting from the hope promised by the
gospel that you heard, which has been proclaimed to every creature
under heaven. I, Paul, became a servant of this gospel.

Paul's Interest in the Colossians

24 I am now rejoicing in my sufferings for your sake, and in my
flesh I am completing what is lacking in Christ's afflictions for the
sake of his body, that is, the church. 25I became its servant according
to God's commission that was given to me for you, to make the word
of God fully known, 26the mystery that has been hidden throughout
the ages and generations but has now been revealed to his saints. 27To
them God chose to make known how great among the Gentiles are
the riches of the glory of this mystery, which is Christ in you, the hope
of glory. 28It is he whom we proclaim, warning everyone and teaching
everyone in all wisdom, so that we may present everyone mature in
Christ. 29For this I toil and struggle with all the energy that he powerfully inspires within me.

2 For I want you to know how much I am struggling for you, and
for those in Laodicea, and for all who have not seen me face
to face. 2I want their hearts to be encouraged and united in love, so
that they may have all the riches of assured understanding and have
the knowledge of God's mystery, that is, Christ himself,[d] 3in whom
are hidden all the treasures of wisdom and knowledge. 4I am saying
this so that no one may deceive you with plausible arguments. 5For
though I am absent in body, yet I am with you in spirit, and I rejoice
to see your morale and the firmness of your faith in Christ.

Fullness of Life in Christ

6 As you therefore have received Christ Jesus the Lord, continue
to live your lives[e] in him, 7rooted and built up in him and established
in the faith, just as you were taught, abounding in thanksgiving.

---

[a] Or *by* [b] Other ancient authorities read *you have now been reconciled* [c] Gk *in the body of his flesh*
[d] Other ancient authorities read *of the mystery of God, both of the Father and of Christ* [e] Gk *to walk*

8 See to it that no one takes you captive through philosophy and
empty deceit, according to human tradition, according to the elemental spirits of the universe,[a] and not according to Christ. [9]For in him
the whole fullness of deity dwells bodily, [10]and you have come to fullness in him, who is the head of every ruler and authority. [11]In him also
you were circumcised with a spiritual circumcision,[b] by putting off
the body of the flesh in the circumcision of Christ; [12]when you were
buried with him in baptism, you were also raised with him through
faith in the power of God, who raised him from the dead. [13]And when
you were dead in trespasses and the uncircumcision of your flesh,
God[c] made you[d] alive together with him, when he forgave us all our
trespasses, [14]erasing the record that stood against us with its legal demands. He set this aside, nailing it to the cross. [15]He disarmed[e] the
rulers and authorities and made a public example of them, triumph-
ing over them in it.

16 Therefore do not let anyone condemn you in matters of food
and drink or of observing festivals, new moons, or sabbaths. [17]These
are only a shadow of what is to come, but the substance belongs to
Christ. [18]Do not let anyone disqualify you, insisting on self-abasement
and worship of angels, dwelling[f] on visions,[g] puffed up without cause
by a human way of thinking,[h] [19]and not holding fast to the head, from
whom the whole body, nourished and held together by its ligaments
and sinews, grows with a growth that is from God.

Warnings against False Teachers

20 If with Christ you died to the elemental spirits of the universe,[a]
why do you live as if you still belonged to the world? Why do you submit to regulations, [21]"Do not handle, Do not taste, Do not touch"?
[22]All these regulations refer to things that perish with use; they are
simply human commands and teachings. [23]These have indeed an appearance of wisdom in promoting self-imposed piety, humility, and
severe treatment of the body, but they are of no value in checking self-
indulgence.[i]

The New Life in Christ

3 So if you have been raised with Christ, seek the things that are
above, where Christ is, seated at the right hand of God. [2]Set
your minds on things that are above, not on things that are on earth,
[3]for you have died, and your life is hidden with Christ in God. [4]When
Christ who is your[j] life is revealed, then you also will be revealed with
him in glory.

[a] Or *the rudiments of the world* [b] Gk *a circumcision made without hands* [c] Gk *he* [d] Other ancient authorities read *made us*; others, *made* [e] Or *divested himself of* [f] Other ancient authorities read *not dwelling* [g] Meaning of Gk uncertain [h] Gk *by the mind of his flesh* [i] Or *are of no value, serving only to indulge the flesh* [j] Other authorities read *our*

2:11-13 a spiritual circumcision: In Judaism, a male was brought into a right relationship with God through the act of circumcision, the cutting off of the foreskin of the penis. Here baptism is described as a spiritual circumcision, meaning that through baptism we are brought into a right relationship with God.

What happens in baptism? In Colossians, we discover that in baptism we are included in Jesus' death, burial, and resurrection as God makes us alive with Christ and forgives us our trespasses. Similarly, in the Small Catechism Luther describes baptism as bringing us the forgiveness of sins, rescue from death, and the gift of eternal salvation. In Colossians 3:5, we are told to put to death whatever is earthly. This also recalls Luther's view that the old creature, or self, with its sins, is to be drowned by daily repentance, so that a new person will come forth daily and rise up to live before God. *Colossians 2:12-15*

2:16-20 elemental spirits of the universe: In the ancient world, some believed that divine spirits caused problems such as sickness, family arguments, and failures. The false teachers were promising protection from such spirits through their secret teachings and rituals. Note how Paul claims that in baptism we are united with Christ, and as Christ rules the universe so Christ rules over our lives. Therefore we do not fear such spirits.

5 Put to death, therefore, whatever in you is earthly: fornication,
impurity, passion, evil desire, and greed (which is idolatry). 6On account of these the wrath of God is coming on those who are disobedient.[a] 7These are the ways you also once followed, when you were
living that life.[b] 8But now you must get rid of all such things—anger,
wrath, malice, slander, and abusive[c] language from your mouth. 9Do
not lie to one another, seeing that you have stripped off the old self
with its practices 10and have clothed yourselves with the new self,
which is being renewed in knowledge according to the image of its
creator. 11In that renewal[d] there is no longer Greek and Jew, circumcised and uncircumcised, barbarian, Scythian, slave and free; but
Christ is all and in all!

12 As God's chosen ones, holy and beloved, clothe yourselves
with compassion, kindness, humility, meekness, and patience. 13Bear
with one another and, if anyone has a complaint against another, forgive each other; just as the Lord[e] has forgiven you, so you also must
forgive. 14Above all, clothe yourselves with love, which binds everything together in perfect harmony. 15And let the peace of Christ rule
in your hearts, to which indeed you were called in the one body. And
be thankful. 16Let the word of Christ[f] dwell in you richly; teach and
admonish one another in all wisdom; and with gratitude in your
hearts sing psalms, hymns, and spiritual songs to God.[g] 17And whatever you do, in word or deed, do everything in the name of the Lord
Jesus, giving thanks to God the Father through him.

Rules for Christian Households

18 Wives, be subject to your husbands, as is fitting in the Lord.
19Husbands, love your wives and never treat them harshly.

20 Children, obey your parents in everything, for this is your acceptable duty in the Lord. 21Fathers, do not provoke your children,
or they may lose heart. 22Slaves, obey your earthly masters[h] in everything, not only while being watched and in order to please them, but
wholeheartedly, fearing the Lord.[h] 23Whatever your task, put yourselves into it, as done for the Lord and not for your masters,[i] 24since
you know that from the Lord you will receive the inheritance as your
reward; you serve[j] the Lord Christ. 25For the wrongdoer will be paid
back for whatever wrong has been done, and there is no partiality.

4 1Masters, treat your slaves justly and fairly, for you know that
you also have a Master in heaven.

3:8-10, 12, 14: get rid of…stripped off…clothed yourselves: Notice how examples of taking off and putting on clothes are used to describe how Christians stop acting in old negative ways and now act according to the new ways of Christian life.

Colossians 3:8-14 provides examples of behaviors to get rid of and new ones to take on. What are some of the negative, old ways of living that you want to take off? What are some of the new ways of living you want to put on?

3:18—4:1 Wives…husbands… Children: In the ancient world, there were instructions that established proper conduct for the members of a household—for wives and husbands, children and parents, and slaves and masters. Here they are being modified for Christian households, so that love for each other and respect for the Lord become the guiding values for family life (see also Eph 5:21—6:9).

In 3:18—4:1 Paul describes some guidelines for how people of a household should treat one another. How does faith in Christ affect your family relationships?

---

[a] Other ancient authorities lack *on those who are disobedient* (Gk *the children of disobedience*) [b] Or *living among such people* [c] Or *filthy* [d] Gk *its creator, 11where* [e] Other ancient authorities read *just as Christ* [f] Other ancient authorities read *of God,* or *of the Lord* [g] Other ancient authorities read *to the Lord* [h] In Greek the same word is used for *master* and *Lord* [i] Gk *not for men* [j] Or *you are slaves of,* or *be slaves of*

Further Instructions

2 Devote yourselves to prayer, keeping alert in it with thanksgiving. 3 At the same time pray for us as well that God will open to us
a door for the word, that we may declare the mystery of Christ, for
which I am in prison, 4 so that I may reveal it clearly, as I should.
5 Conduct yourselves wisely toward outsiders, making the most
of the time.[a] 6 Let your speech always be gracious, seasoned with salt,
so that you may know how you ought to answer everyone.

Final Greetings and Benediction

7 Tychicus will tell you all the news about me; he is a beloved
brother, a faithful minister, and a fellow servant[b] in the Lord. 8 I have
sent him to you for this very purpose, so that you may know how we
are[c] and that he may encourage your hearts; 9 he is coming with Onesimus, the faithful and beloved brother, who is one of you. They will
tell you about everything here.
10 Aristarchus my fellow prisoner greets you, as does Mark the
cousin of Barnabas, concerning whom you have received instructions—if he comes to you, welcome him. 11 And Jesus who is called
Justus greets you. These are the only ones of the circumcision among
my co-workers for the kingdom of God, and they have been a comfort to me. 12 Epaphras, who is one of you, a servant[b] of Christ Jesus,
greets you. He is always wrestling in his prayers on your behalf, so that
you may stand mature and fully assured in everything that God wills.
13 For I testify for him that he has worked hard for you and for those
in Laodicea and in Hierapolis. 14 Luke, the beloved physician, and
Demas greet you. 15 Give my greetings to the brothers and sisters[d] in
Laodicea, and to Nympha and the church in her house. 16 And when
this letter has been read among you, have it read also in the church of
the Laodiceans; and see that you read also the letter from Laodicea.
17 And say to Archippus, "See that you complete the task that you have
received in the Lord."

18 I, Paul, write this greeting with my own hand. Remember my
chains. Grace be with you.[e]

---

[a] Or *opportunity* [b] Gk *slave* [c] Other authorities read *that I may know how you are* [d] Gk *brothers*
[e] Other ancient authorities add *Amen*

4:3 the mystery of Christ: See 1:26-27 and the note on 2:2-4.

How is God opening a door for you to share with others what God has done for the world through Jesus Christ (4:3-4)?

4:7-18 Tychicus...Archippus... with my own hand: The apostle mentions the names of several coworkers in the gospel in the final greetings of the letter. Onesimus (4:9) was a slave who became close to Paul while had had been imprisoned in Colossae (see Phlm vv. 8-16). Luke, the beloved physician (4:14), may be the same Luke who has been considered the author of both the Gospel of Luke and the book of Acts. The final line, "with my own hand," may suggest that the apostle wrote the final greeting in his own hand, while a scribe wrote down the rest of the letter. This was a common practice in ancient times.

1 THESSALONIANS

1 Thessalonians 4:15-17

Background File

Scholars date 1 Thessalonians back to 43–50 C.E. This is the earliest letter we have from Paul, and it may be the oldest writing we have from the early church. Paul traveled throughout the Roman Empire, sharing the good news about Jesus Christ and starting new churches. With his co-workers Timothy and Silvanus, Paul writes the letter to a church he started in Thessalonica, a city located in what now is northern Greece. At the time, Thessalonica was a trade center and the capital city of the Roman province of Macedonia (see Map 14, p. 2111). Ancient coins discovered in Thessalonica indicate that people in the city honored Julius Caesar as "God" and worshiped Emperor Octavian as a "son of God." As a result of this worship of other gods, the believers in the church at Thessalonica probably experienced some form of persecution for their faith (see 1:6; 3:4, 7).

What's the Story?

This letter can be outlined as follows:

Introduction and prayer (1:1-10)
Review of past events (2:1–3:10)
An intercessory prayer (3:11-13)
Specific advice (4:1–5:3)
Epilogue (5:4-22)
Concluding prayer (5:23-28)

The letter shows Paul's relationship with the young church in Thessalonica and his wish to visit it again. During a previous visit, Paul and his co-workers had been forced to leave. Following that unexpected exit, Paul sent Timothy to visit the congregation and learned that something was "lacking" in the people's faith (3:10).

In this letter, then, Paul praises the Thessalonian believers, because they "turned to God from idols, to serve a living and true God" (1:9). To believers in a city filled with worship of the emperor and other gods, Paul specifies that this God they serve is "God the Father and the Lord Jesus Christ" (1:1). He goes on to encourage the Thessalonians to live a life pleasing to God (4:1-12).

Paul also discusses the status of those who have already died in Christ, before the Lord's final coming. Persecution may have led to the premature death of the believers Paul refers to in 4:13-18. Here Paul shifts from writing "you know" and "you remember" to something new: "But we do not want you to be uninformed" (4:13). He urges the believers not to grieve "as others do who have no hope." He assures his readers that the dead in Christ are not forgotten and that on the last day they, in fact, "will rise first" (4:16).

What's the Message?

People throughout time have worshiped and served many gods, but there is only one living and true God. This God wants to save us and make us holy. By God's grace, we can "please God" (2:4; 4:1) and do God's will (4:3; 5:18). The one living and true God gives us hope in the face of death. Because Jesus Christ died for us and rose again, we live with him, whether we are alive or dead (5:10).

Salutation

1 Paul, Silvanus, and Timothy,
To the church of the Thessalonians in God the Father and the
Lord Jesus Christ:
Grace to you and peace.

The Thessalonians' Faith and Example

2 We always give thanks to God for all of you and mention you
in our prayers, constantly 3 remembering before our God and Father your work of faith and labor of love and steadfastness of hope
in our Lord Jesus Christ. 4 For we know, brothers and sisters[a] beloved
by God, that he has chosen you, 5 because our message of the gospel
came to you not in word only, but also in power and in the Holy Spirit
and with full conviction; just as you know what kind of persons we
proved to be among you for your sake. 6 And you became imitators of
us and of the Lord, for in spite of persecution you received the word
with joy inspired by the Holy Spirit, 7 so that you became an example
to all the believers in Macedonia and in Achaia. 8 For the word of the
Lord has sounded forth from you not only in Macedonia and Achaia,
but in every place your faith in God has become known, so that we
have no need to speak about it. 9 For the people of those regions[b] report about us what kind of welcome we had among you, and how you
turned to God from idols, to serve a living and true God, 10 and to wait
for his Son from heaven, whom he raised from the dead—Jesus, who
rescues us from the wrath that is coming.

[a] Gk *brothers* [b] Gk *For they*

1:1 the church of the Thessalonians: Paul and his coworkers, Silvanus and Timothy, write to the congregation in the city of Thessalonica (see Map 14, p. 2111).

1:1 God: Many gods were worshiped in Thessalonica, so Paul specifies the God of the believers: "God the Father and the Lord Jesus Christ."

1:2-10 give thanks to God for all of you: Paul is grateful for the Thessalonian church, the people's gifts, and their example. He is also concerned about the persecution faced by the congregation.

1:3 faith . . . love . . . hope: Paul gives thanks for the people's "work of faith," the living out of their faith in daily life; their "labor of love" toward one another; and their "steadfastness of hope."

1:4 chosen: Here Paul emphasizes the priority of God's call and grace.

1:5-8 gospel: The power of the gospel lies in the power of the Holy Spirit, so it is received with joy, despite persecution. The people imitate the Lord and Paul and are empowered to proclaim the gospel message boldly.

1:10 Jesus: Jesus' resurrection will protect these believers from God's future judgment (see Rom 1:18; 2:5).

Paul's Ministry in Thessalonica

2 You yourselves know, brothers and sisters,[a] that our coming to
you was not in vain, [2]but though we had already suffered and
been shamefully mistreated at Philippi, as you know, we had courage
in our God to declare to you the gospel of God in spite of great opposition. [3]For our appeal does not spring from deceit or impure motives
or trickery, [4]but just as we have been approved by God to be entrusted
with the message of the gospel, even so we speak, not to please mortals, but to please God who tests our hearts. [5]As you know and as God
is our witness, we never came with words of flattery or with a pretext
for greed; [6]nor did we seek praise from mortals, whether from you
or from others, [7]though we might have made demands as apostles of
Christ. But we were gentle[b] among you, like a nurse tenderly caring
for her own children. [8]So deeply do we care for you that we are determined to share with you not only the gospel of God but also our own
selves, because you have become very dear to us.

9 You remember our labor and toil, brothers and sisters;[a] we
worked night and day, so that we might not burden any of you while
we proclaimed to you the gospel of God. [10]You are witnesses, and
God also, how pure, upright, and blameless our conduct was toward
you believers. [11]As you know, we dealt with each one of you like a
father with his children, [12]urging and encouraging you and pleading
that you lead a life worthy of God, who calls you into his own kingdom and glory.

13 We also constantly give thanks to God for this, that when you
received the word of God that you heard from us, you accepted it not
as a human word but as what it really is, God's word, which is also at
work in you believers. [14]For you, brothers and sisters,[a] became imitators of the churches of God in Christ Jesus that are in Judea, for
you suffered the same things from your own compatriots as they did
from the Jews, [15]who killed both the Lord Jesus and the prophets,[c]
and drove us out; they displease God and oppose everyone [16]by hindering us from speaking to the Gentiles so that they may be saved.
Thus they have constantly been filling up the measure of their sins;
but God's wrath has overtaken them at last.[d]

Paul's Desire to Visit the Thessalonians Again

17 As for us, brothers and sisters,[a] when, for a short time, we
were made orphans by being separated from you—in person, not in
heart—we longed with great eagerness to see you face to face. [18]For
we wanted to come to you—certainly I, Paul, wanted to again and
again—but Satan blocked our way. [19]For what is our hope or joy or

---

[a] Gk *brothers* [b] Other ancient authorities read *infants* [c] Other ancient authorities read *their own prophets* [d] Or *completely* or *forever*

2:1-16 You remember our labor and toil: Paul describes his first visit to Thessalonica. The book of Acts reports that in Thessalonica, Paul and his associates were "acting contrary to the decrees of the emperor, saying that there is another king named Jesus" (Acts 17:7). Despite being mistreated, Paul continues to preach the gospel in a manner that is pleasing to God and not human beings. Similarly, believers need to lead a life worthy of God.

2:13 the word of God: This refers to the gospel, which originates with God and encourages believers.

2:14-16 hindering us from speaking to the Gentiles: Paul, himself a Jew, criticizes his fellow Jews for preventing the gospel from being shared with non-Jews (Gentiles).

2:17—3:10 see you face to face: Following a forced exit from Thessalonica, Paul sent Timothy back to see how the people were handling persecution. Despite a positive report, something is "lacking" in the people's faith, namely hope, and Paul wants to see them again in person.

crown of boasting before our Lord Jesus at his coming? Is it not you?
20 Yes, you are our glory and joy!

3 Therefore when we could bear it no longer, we decided to be
left alone in Athens; 2 and we sent Timothy, our brother and co-
worker for God in proclaiming[a] the gospel of Christ, to strengthen
and encourage you for the sake of your faith, 3 so that no one would be
shaken by these persecutions. Indeed, you yourselves know that this
is what we are destined for. 4 In fact, when we were with you, we told
you beforehand that we were to suffer persecution; so it turned out,
as you know. 5 For this reason, when I could bear it no longer, I sent to
find out about your faith; I was afraid that somehow the tempter had
tempted you and that our labor had been in vain.

3:2 for the sake of your faith: Faith is not static or unchanging. The gospel must constantly help "restore whatever is lacking" in faith (3:10).

Timothy's Encouraging Report

6 But Timothy has just now come to us from you, and has brought
us the good news of your faith and love. He has told us also that you
always remember us kindly and long to see us—just as we long to see
you. 7 For this reason, brothers and sisters,[b] during all our distress and
persecution we have been encouraged about you through your faith.
8 For we now live, if you continue to stand firm in the Lord. 9 How can
we thank God enough for you in return for all the joy that we feel before our God because of you? 10 Night and day we pray most earnestly
that we may see you face to face and restore whatever is lacking in
your faith.

11 Now may our God and Father himself and our Lord Jesus
direct our way to you. 12 And may the Lord make you increase and
abound in love for one another and for all, just as we abound in love
for you. 13 And may he so strengthen your hearts in holiness that you
may be blameless before our God and Father at the coming of our
Lord Jesus with all his saints.

3:11-13 Now may our God: Paul prays for the Thessalonians to increase in love, to be blameless, and to remain steadfast in hope.

A Life Pleasing to God

4 Finally, brothers and sisters,[b] we ask and urge you in the Lord
Jesus that, as you learned from us how you ought to live and to
please God (as, in fact, you are doing), you should do so more and
more. 2 For you know what instructions we gave you through the Lord
Jesus. 3 For this is the will of God, your sanctification: that you abstain from fornication; 4 that each one of you know how to control
your own body[c] in holiness and honor, 5 not with lustful passion, like
the Gentiles who do not know God; 6 that no one wrong or exploit
a brother or sister[d] in this matter, because the Lord is an avenger
in all these things, just as we have already told you beforehand and
solemnly warned you. 7 For God did not call us to impurity but in

4:1-8 to please God: Paul urges the people to abstain from unfaithful sexual behavior and to control their bodies. Rejecting this appeal, he says, means rejecting God's authority.

4:7 holiness: Paul uses this term, often translated as "sanctification," to describe what the new life in Christ was intended to look like.

[a] Gk lacks *proclaiming* [b] Gk *brothers* [c] Or *how to take a wife for himself* [d] Gk *brother*

4:9-12 love: Loving others is something God teaches us to do.

4:13—5:3 since we believe that Jesus died and rose again: Believers have hope because of Jesus' death and resurrection. On the final day, those who have already died in Christ will rise first. Until that time, some people may proclaim "peace and security," but the day of the Lord will come unexpectedly.

4:16 in Christ: This phrase, which indicates being a member and participant in the body of Christ, is a major theme in Paul's letters.

5:4-22 children of light: This refers to followers of Jesus (see Luke 16:8; John 12:36; Eph 5:8). Paul urges the Thessalonians—"children of light"—to fully live their new life in Christ, because God has "destined" them "for obtaining salvation" (5:9).

5:8-9 salvation: God saves us, but this is not fully realized in our lives on earth. It reaches completion in and through Christ.

holiness. 8 Therefore whoever rejects this rejects not human authority
but God, who also gives his Holy Spirit to you.

9 Now concerning love of the brothers and sisters,[a] you do not
need to have anyone write to you, for you yourselves have been taught
by God to love one another; 10 and indeed you do love all the brothers
and sisters[a] throughout Macedonia. But we urge you, beloved,[a] to do
so more and more, 11 to aspire to live quietly, to mind your own affairs,
and to work with your hands, as we directed you, 12 so that you may
behave properly toward outsiders and be dependent on no one.

The Coming of the Lord

13 But we do not want you to be uninformed, brothers and sisters,[a] about those who have died,[b] so that you may not grieve as others do who have no hope. 14 For since we believe that Jesus died and
rose again, even so, through Jesus, God will bring with him those who
have died.[b] 15 For this we declare to you by the word of the Lord, that
we who are alive, who are left until the coming of the Lord, will by no
means precede those who have died.[b] 16 For the Lord himself, with a
cry of command, with the archangel's call and with the sound of God's
trumpet, will descend from heaven, and the dead in Christ will rise first.
17 Then we who are alive, who are left, will be caught up in the clouds together with them to meet the Lord in the air; and so we will be with the
Lord forever. 18 Therefore encourage one another with these words.

5 Now concerning the times and the seasons, brothers and sisters,[a] you do not need to have anything written to you. 2 For you
yourselves know very well that the day of the Lord will come like a
thief in the night. 3 When they say, "There is peace and security," then
sudden destruction will come upon them, as labor pains come upon a
pregnant woman, and there will be no escape! 4 But you, beloved,[a] are
not in darkness, for that day to surprise you like a thief; 5 for you are
all children of light and children of the day; we are not of the night or
of darkness. 6 So then let us not fall asleep as others do, but let us keep
awake and be sober; 7 for those who sleep sleep at night, and those
who are drunk get drunk at night. 8 But since we belong to the day,
let us be sober, and put on the breastplate of faith and love, and for a
helmet the hope of salvation. 9 For God has destined us not for wrath
but for obtaining salvation through our Lord Jesus Christ, 10 who died
for us, so that whether we are awake or asleep we may live with him.
11 Therefore encourage one another and build up each other, as indeed you are doing.

Final Exhortations, Greetings, and Benediction

12 But we appeal to you, brothers and sisters,[a] to respect those
who labor among you, and have charge of you in the Lord and

[a] Gk *brothers* [b] Gk *fallen asleep*

admonish you; [13]esteem them very highly in love because of their
work. Be at peace among yourselves. [14]And we urge you, beloved,[a]
to admonish the idlers, encourage the fainthearted, help the weak, be
patient with all of them. [15]See that none of you repays evil for evil, but
always seek to do good to one another and to all. [16]Rejoice always,
[17]pray without ceasing, [18]give thanks in all circumstances; for this is
the will of God in Christ Jesus for you. [19]Do not quench the Spirit.
[20]Do not despise the words of prophets,[b] [21]but test everything; hold
fast to what is good; [22]abstain from every form of evil.

23 May the God of peace himself sanctify you entirely; and may
your spirit and soul and body be kept sound[c] and blameless at the
coming of our Lord Jesus Christ. [24]The one who calls you is faithful,
and he will do this.

25 Beloved,[d] pray for us.

26 Greet all the brothers and sisters[a] with a holy kiss. [27]I solemnly
command you by the Lord that this letter be read to all of them.[e]

28 The grace of our Lord Jesus Christ be with you.[f]

---

[a] Gk *brothers* [b] Gk *despise prophecies* [c] Or *complete* [d] Gk *Brothers* [e] Gk *to all the brothers*
[f] Other ancient authorities add *Amen*

5:16-18 Rejoice: To "rejoice," "pray," and "give thanks" are at the core of doing God's will.

5:23-28 sanctify you: Paul ends the letter with a prayer that the Thessalonians will live lives of holiness so that they will be blameless when the Lord comes again.

5:28 grace: This is the free gift of God that enables new life in Christ. It is included at the beginning and ending of this letter.

2 Thessalonians 3:5

2 THESSALONIANS

Background File

Paul was a missionary who traveled throughout the Roman Empire, sharing the good news about Jesus Christ and starting new churches. This letter, like 1 Thessalonians, is written to a church that Paul started in Thessalonica (see Map 14, p. 2111). At the time, Thessalonica was a trade center and the capital city of the Roman province of Macedonia. Although 2 Thessalonians is attributed to Paul, it is possible that one of his two co-workers, Timothy or Silvanus, wrote this letter. In any case, the church included it in the canon of the New Testament.

What's the Story?

This letter can be outlined as follows:

Introduction (1:1-2)
Thanksgiving prayer (1:3-10)
Intercessory prayer (1:11-12)
Summary and discussion of specific points (2:1-15)
Epilogue with exhortation (2:16—3:15)
Conclusion (3:16-18)

Although 1 and 2 Thessalonians have similar themes, the second letter is distinguished by its emphasis on the "day of the Lord." The day of the Lord was understood to be the day Jesus Christ would come again to the world. Some people, perhaps even in Paul's name, were arguing "that the day of the Lord is already here" (2:2). The writer of 2 Thessalonians corrects this false information and urges the people to stand firm against persecution and misleading claims that the day of the Lord has already arrived.

The persecution of believers, discussed in 1 Thessalonians, appears to have become more intense. In a major expansion of what 1 Thessalonians says about persecution, 2 Thessalonians 1:5-12 describes how those who are persecuting the believers will be punished when the Lord appears again (1:9). Those who "do not know God" and who "do not obey the gospel of our Lord Jesus" will be punished as well (1:8). The implication is that those who do not obey the gospel do not know God. While the theme of not knowing God is connected to the immoral behavior of the nonbelievers in 1 Thessalonians 4:5, here it describes aggressive persecution of believers. A similar theme appears in 2 Thessalonians 2:9-12.

What's the Message?

This is a letter of encouragement for believers. Some people will make false claims that the time of Christ's return is here, but there is no need for panic or alarm. Others will be hostile to the gospel message and will persecute believers, but the Lord gives eternal comfort and hope. In spite of false claims, hostility, and persecution, we can continue to grow in faith, love one another, and stay true to the teachings of the gospel.

Salutation

1 Paul, Silvanus, and Timothy,
To the church of the Thessalonians in God our Father and the
Lord Jesus Christ:
2 Grace to you and peace from God our[a] Father and the Lord
Jesus Christ.

1:1 Paul, Silvanus, and Timothy: The letter begins in the same way as 1 Thessalonians (see 1 Thess 1:1).

Thanksgiving

3 We must always give thanks to God for you, brothers and sisters,[b] as is right, because your faith is growing abundantly, and the
love of every one of you for one another is increasing. 4 Therefore we
ourselves boast of you among the churches of God for your steadfastness and faith during all your persecutions and the afflictions that you
are enduring.

1:3-10 give thanks to God for you: The writer thanks God for the way the Thessalonians are handling persecution and suffering.

1:4 faith: This is God's powerful, gracious gift that enables believers to endure persecution and suffering, remain steadfast, and receive "eternal comfort and good hope" (2:16).

The Judgment at Christ's Coming

5 This is evidence of the righteous judgment of God, and is intended to make you worthy of the kingdom of God, for which you
are also suffering. 6 For it is indeed just of God to repay with affliction
those who afflict you, 7 and to give relief to the afflicted as well as to us,
when the Lord Jesus is revealed from heaven with his mighty angels
8 in flaming fire, inflicting vengeance on those who do not know God
and on those who do not obey the gospel of our Lord Jesus. 9 These
will suffer the punishment of eternal destruction, separated from
the presence of the Lord and from the glory of his might, 10 when he
comes to be glorified by his saints and to be marveled at on that day
among all who have believed, because our testimony to you was believed. 11 To this end we always pray for you, asking that our God will
make you worthy of his call and will fulfill by his power every good

1:11-12 pray for you: This is a prayer for the Thessalonians' faith in action to glorify the Lord.

---

[a] Other ancient authorities read *the* [b] Gk *brothers*

resolve and work of faith, 12 so that the name of our Lord Jesus may be glorified in you, and you in him, according to the grace of our God and the Lord Jesus Christ.

The Man of Lawlessness

2:1-15 when his time comes: These verses suggest that misleading information was being conveyed in Paul's name. This letter is written to help set things right again.

2:3-12 that day will not come unless: So that the believers will not be deceived through the powerful delusions of Satan, here the letter lists events that must occur before "the day of the Lord" actually arrives.

2 As to the coming of our Lord Jesus Christ and our being gathered together to him, we beg you, brothers and sisters,[a] 2 not to be quickly shaken in mind or alarmed, either by spirit or by word or by letter, as though from us, to the effect that the day of the Lord is already here. 3 Let no one deceive you in any way; for that day will not come unless the rebellion comes first and the lawless one[b] is revealed, the one destined for destruction.[c] 4 He opposes and exalts himself above every so-called god or object of worship, so that he takes his seat in the temple of God, declaring himself to be God. 5 Do you not remember that I told you these things when I was still with you? 6 And you know what is now restraining him, so that he may be revealed when his time comes. 7 For the mystery of lawlessness is already at work, but only until the one who now restrains it is removed. 8 And then the lawless one will be revealed, whom the Lord Jesus[d] will destroy[e] with the breath of his mouth, annihilating him by the manifestation of his coming. 9 The coming of the lawless one is apparent in the working of Satan, who uses all power, signs, lying wonders, 10 and every kind of wicked deception for those who are perishing, because they refused to love the truth and so be saved. 11 For this reason God sends them a powerful delusion, leading them to believe what is false, 12 so that all who have not believed the truth but took pleasure in unrighteousness will be condemned.

Chosen for Salvation

2:13-15 belief: This passage picks up on the theme of holiness or a life that pleases God, also found in the first letter (1 Thess 4:1-12). Here the theme is expanded to include believing in the "truth" and holding to "the traditions that you were taught by us."

13 But we must always give thanks to God for you, brothers and sisters[a] beloved by the Lord, because God chose you as the first fruits[f] for salvation through sanctification by the Spirit and through belief in the truth. 14 For this purpose he called you through our proclamation of the good news,[g] so that you may obtain the glory of our Lord Jesus Christ. 15 So then, brothers and sisters,[a] stand firm and hold fast to the traditions that you were taught by us, either by word of mouth or by our letter.

2:16—3:15 strengthen them in every good work and word: This prayer asks God to strengthen and comfort the people amid terror, distortion of the truth, and persecution.

16 Now may our Lord Jesus Christ himself and God our Father, who loved us and through grace gave us eternal comfort and good hope, 17 comfort your hearts and strengthen them in every good work and word.

---

[a] Gk *brothers* [b] Gk *the man of lawlessness;* other ancient authorities read *the man of sin* [c] Gk *the son of destruction* [d] Other ancient authorities lack *Jesus* [e] Other ancient authorities read *consume* [f] Other ancient authorities read *from the beginnin* [g] Or *through our gospel*

Request for Prayer

3 Finally, brothers and sisters,[a] pray for us, so that the word of the
Lord may spread rapidly and be glorified everywhere, just as it
is among you, 2and that we may be rescued from wicked and evil people; for not all have faith. 3But the Lord is faithful; he will strengthen
you and guard you from the evil one.[b] 4And we have confidence in
the Lord concerning you, that you are doing and will go on doing the
things that we command. 5May the Lord direct your hearts to the love
of God and to the steadfastness of Christ.

Warning against Idleness

6 Now we command you, beloved,[a] in the name of our Lord Jesus
Christ, to keep away from believers who are[c] living in idleness and
not according to the tradition that they[d] received from us. 7For you
yourselves know how you ought to imitate us; we were not idle when
we were with you, 8and we did not eat anyone's bread without paying
for it; but with toil and labor we worked night and day, so that we
might not burden any of you. 9This was not because we do not have
that right, but in order to give you an example to imitate. 10For even
when we were with you, we gave you this command: Anyone unwilling to work should not eat. 11For we hear that some of you are living in
idleness, mere busybodies, not doing any work. 12Now such persons
we command and exhort in the Lord Jesus Christ to do their work
quietly and to earn their own living. 13Brothers and sisters,[e] do not be
weary in doing what is right.

14 Take note of those who do not obey what we say in this letter;
have nothing to do with them, so that they may be ashamed. 15Do not
regard them as enemies, but warn them as believers.[f]

Final Greetings and Benediction

16 Now may the Lord of peace himself give you peace at all times
in all ways. The Lord be with all of you.

17 I, Paul, write this greeting with my own hand. This is the mark
in every letter of mine; it is the way I write. 18The grace of our Lord
Jesus Christ be with all of you.[g]

---

[a] Gk *brothers* [b] Or *from evil* [c] Gk *from every brother who is* [d] Other ancient authorities read *you*
[e] Gk *Brothers* [f] Gk *a brother* [g] Other ancient authorities add *Amen*

3:1-4 pray for us: The letter includes a request for prayers for Paul, Silvanus, and Timothy so that they, too, may be "rescued from wicked and evil people."

3:5 love...steadfastness: This prayer for love and steadfastness relates back to the opening words about the Thessalonians' love for one another and steadfastness in the face of persecution and suffering (see 1:3-4).

3:6-15 we worked night and day: The believers in Thessalonica should imitate Paul, Silvanus, and Timothy in working for a living. (Note a similar emphasis in 1 Thess 2:9; 4:11; see also Acts 18:3; 1 Cor 9:1-18.)

3:17 with my own hand: Paul signed other letters (see 1 Cor 16:21), but here special attention is drawn to this.

1 Timothy 6:12

1 TIMOTHY

Background File

This letter starts with Paul's name. But that does not necessarily mean that Paul wrote the letter. In ancient times, people sometimes used the name of a famous person for their own letters. This might be compared to watching a new Walt Disney movie. Mr. Disney is no longer alive, yet movies continue to feature his name because the Walt Disney Company produces them. People at the company try to continue Disney's legacy. In a similar fashion, it is likely that an unknown person wrote 1 Timothy near the end of the first century C.E., many years after Paul had died. This person respected Paul and was familiar with his ideas. He wrote 1 Timothy—as well as 2 Timothy and Titus—to continue Paul's mission.

What's the Story?

This letter is addressed to Timothy, who had been close to Paul. The two men met in the city of Lystra (see Acts 16:1-4) and then worked together (see Rom 16:21; Phil 2:19-23). In this letter, Timothy appears as a leader and teacher of his local church (4:13, 16). Due to his position as a church leader, 1 and 2 Timothy and Titus are called the "pastoral epistles"—letters to pastors and other church leaders.

Paul leaves the city of Ephesus, but Timothy stays behind (1:3). Timothy is facing false teachers by himself. The background situation of this letter, however, is the church at the end of the first century. This is why 1 Timothy combines some ideas of Paul with ideas found in the Gospel of John, which likely was written around 90 C.E. At the time of this letter, Christian congregations had grown larger. Thus it was necessary to explain who could lead them and which teachings were false or true. First Timothy can be outlined in this way:

Directives to guide church life (1:1–3:13)
False teachings and faith (3:14–4:5)
Advice for church leaders (4:6–6:21)

Readers today may understand the name Timothy in a different way. "Timothy" can be each reader, as the intended audience of this letter is all people who respect Paul's message of God's grace and want to continue Paul's mission. The end of the letter reveals this. Here the original Greek text of the greeting "Grace be with you" (6:21) addresses not a single person but many people—the plural *you*.

What's the Message?

The main message of 1 Timothy is found in confessions about Jesus and God (2:5-6; 3:16), and in instructions to Timothy. The author encourages young people to have faith in Jesus Christ: "Let no one despise your youth, but set the believers an example in speech and conduct, in love, in faith, in purity" (4:12). This faith is more than theory and discussions. Jesus Christ lived in this world and deeply cared for it. Christianity starts with this story of Jesus Christ, and it leads to action in the world. The church is to be a place where Christ's love becomes visible. For this task, the church needs competent leaders who engage people to lead lives of *love* and *godliness*, two important words in 1 Timothy.

Salutation

1 Paul, an apostle of Christ Jesus by the command of God our
Savior and of Christ Jesus our hope,
2 To Timothy, my loyal child in the faith:
Grace, mercy, and peace from God the Father and Christ Jesus
our Lord.

Warning against False Teachers

3 I urge you, as I did when I was on my way to Macedonia, to remain in Ephesus so that you may instruct certain people not to teach
any different doctrine, 4and not to occupy themselves with myths and
endless genealogies that promote speculations rather than the divine
training[a] that is known by faith. 5But the aim of such instruction is
love that comes from a pure heart, a good conscience, and sincere
faith. 6Some people have deviated from these and turned to meaningless talk, 7desiring to be teachers of the law, without understanding either what they are saying or the things about which they make
assertions.
8 Now we know that the law is good, if one uses it legitimately.
9This means understanding that the law is laid down not for the innocent but for the lawless and disobedient, for the godless and sinful, for
the unholy and profane, for those who kill their father or mother, for
murderers, 10fornicators, sodomites, slave traders, liars, perjurers, and
whatever else is contrary to the sound teaching 11that conforms to the
glorious gospel of the blessed God, which he entrusted to me.

Gratitude for Mercy

12 I am grateful to Christ Jesus our Lord, who has strengthened
me, because he judged me faithful and appointed me to his service,
13even though I was formerly a blasphemer, a persecutor, and a man
of violence. But I received mercy because I had acted ignorantly in
unbelief, 14and the grace of our Lord overflowed for me with the faith

---

[a] Or *plan*

1:1 Paul, an apostle: The beginning of this letter resembles letters written by Paul, but the letter probably was not written by him. A person who knew Paul's main ideas probably wrote it after Paul died.

1:2 To Timothy: Timothy is Paul's "loyal child" because he has faith in Jesus Christ, distinguishing him from people mentioned in 1:3. The name Timothy represents all people who respect what Paul preached (see introduction).

1:3 Macedonia . . . Ephesus: Macedonia is a province in northern Greece. Ephesus is a harbor city in western Asia Minor, in modern Turkey (see Map 15, p. 2112). Paul visited Ephesus during his third missionary journey (see Acts 19:1-41).

1:3 certain people: The writer urges Timothy to correct people who teach "different doctrine" (possibly myths about Greek gods or popular books that retell and embellish parts of the Torah, the first five books of the Old Testament).

1:4 endless genealogies: This term might refer to ancestor lists like those in Matthew 1:1-17 or Luke 3:23-38. Both books were written in 80–90 C.E., only a few years before 1 Timothy.

What is "the law"? Here "law" refers to the Jewish Torah (the first five books of the Old Testament) or to additional Jewish laws based on the Torah. Paul called the law "holy and just and good" (Rom 7:12, 16), but also taught that Christians "have died to the law" (Rom 7:4, 6) and are "free from the law of sin and death" (Rom 8:2). As God's child, Martin Luther understood himself to be free from the law. As Lutherans, we understand ourselves to be free, as well. *1 Timothy 1:7-8*

and love that are in Christ Jesus. 15The saying is sure and worthy of full
acceptance, that Christ Jesus came into the world to save sinners—of
whom I am the foremost. 16But for that very reason I received mercy,
so that in me, as the foremost, Jesus Christ might display the utmost
patience, making me an example to those who would come to believe
in him for eternal life. 17To the King of the ages, immortal, invisible,
the only God, be honor and glory forever and ever.[a] Amen.

18 I am giving you these instructions, Timothy, my child, in accordance with the prophecies made earlier about you, so that by following them you may fight the good fight, 19having faith and a good
conscience. By rejecting conscience, certain persons have suffered
shipwreck in the faith; 20among them are Hymenaeus and Alexander,
whom I have turned over to Satan, so that they may learn not to blaspheme.

Instructions concerning Prayer

2 First of all, then, I urge that supplications, prayers, intercessions,
and thanksgivings be made for everyone, 2for kings and all who
are in high positions, so that we may lead a quiet and peaceable life in
all godliness and dignity. 3This is right and is acceptable in the sight of
God our Savior, 4who desires everyone to be saved and to come to the
knowledge of the truth. 5For

there is one God;
 there is also one mediator between God and humankind,
Christ Jesus, himself human,
6 who gave himself a ransom for all

—this was attested at the right time. 7For this I was appointed a herald and an apostle (I am telling the truth,[b] I am not lying), a teacher of
the Gentiles in faith and truth.

8 I desire, then, that in every place the men should pray, lifting up
holy hands without anger or argument; 9also that the women should
dress themselves modestly and decently in suitable clothing, not with
their hair braided, or with gold, pearls, or expensive clothes, 10but
with good works, as is proper for women who profess reverence for
God. 11Let a woman[c] learn in silence with full submission. 12I permit
no woman[c] to teach or to have authority over a man;[d] she is to keep
silent. 13For Adam was formed first, then Eve; 14and Adam was not
deceived, but the woman was deceived and became a transgressor.
15Yet she will be saved through childbearing, provided they continue
in faith and love and holiness, with modesty.

Qualifications of Bishops

3 The saying is sure:[e] whoever aspires to the office of bishop[f]
desires a noble task. 2Now a bishop[g] must be above reproach,

---

[a] Gk *to the ages of the ages* [b] Other ancient authorities add *in Christ* [c] Or *wife* [d] Or *her husband*
[e] Some interpreters place these words at the end of the previous paragraph. Other ancient authorities read *The saying is commonly accepted* [f] Or *overseer* [g] Or *an overseer*

1:12-17 the grace of our Lord: Paul's life is an example of how God's grace changes people. God's salvation has practical consequences for humans.

2:4 everyone to be saved . . . knowledge of the truth: God desires that all humans "be saved." For Christians, "knowledge of the truth" means knowing the story of Jesus Christ's life, death, and resurrection. Jesus demonstrated that God cares about those who are considered sinners. This good news is the "truth." Therefore Jesus calls himself "the truth" in John 14:6.

Why is it important for Christians to know the story of Jesus?

2:9 women should dress: The author of 1 Timothy adopts many customs or standards of his time regarding the status of men and women and proper ways of dressing. When Paul wrote about the issue of covering one's head, he also honored local customs (see 1 Cor 11:2-7). Paul knew that these were not universal standards, admitting that such customs did not exist in other churches (1 Cor 11:16).

2:12 she is to keep silent: A similar rule is found in 1 Corinthians 14:34. Before this time, women were not allowed to worship with men at the temple or in synagogues, so worshiping together was a major change. The Gospels emphasize the valuable contributions of women in supporting Jesus (see Luke 8:1-3) and being the first to proclaim the resurrection (see Matt 28:8; Luke 24:10; John 20:18).

2:13-14 but the woman was deceived: This statement contradicts Paul's teaching in Romans 5:12-14, which says sin entered the world because of one man (Adam).

3:1-13 bishop . . . Deacons . . . Women: All people in the church need to be moderate and respectable. Their behavior determines whether society will persecute or accept Christians. They also need good management skills to oversee their churches.

married only once,[a] temperate, sensible, respectable, hospitable, an
apt teacher, 3not a drunkard, not violent but gentle, not quarrelsome,
and not a lover of money. 4He must manage his own household well,
keeping his children submissive and respectful in every way— 5for if
someone does not know how to manage his own household, how can
he take care of God's church? 6He must not be a recent convert, or he
may be puffed up with conceit and fall into the condemnation of the
devil. 7Moreover, he must be well thought of by outsiders, so that he
may not fall into disgrace and the snare of the devil.

Qualifications of Deacons

8 Deacons likewise must be serious, not double-tongued, not indulging in much wine, not greedy for money; 9they must hold fast to
the mystery of the faith with a clear conscience. 10And let them first
be tested; then, if they prove themselves blameless, let them serve as
deacons. 11Women[b] likewise must be serious, not slanderers, but temperate, faithful in all things. 12Let deacons be married only once,[c] and
let them manage their children and their households well; 13for those
who serve well as deacons gain a good standing for themselves and
great boldness in the faith that is in Christ Jesus.

3:9 mystery of the faith: The mystery of Christianity is Jesus, the Son of God who lived in the world and cared for it (3:16). It is not easy to understand how Jesus can be both human and divine. Faith statements in 1 and 2 Timothy do not mention the cross, which is central in Paul's teachings (see 1 Cor 1:17-18; Phil 2:8; 3:18).

Which parts of the Christian faith are mysteries to you? Which parts are easier for you to explain to others?

The Mystery of Our Religion

14 I hope to come to you soon, but I am writing these instructions to you so that, 15if I am delayed, you may know how one ought
to behave in the household of God, which is the church of the living
God, the pillar and bulwark of the truth. 16Without any doubt, the
mystery of our religion is great:

He[d] was revealed in flesh,
vindicated[e] in spirit,[f]
seen by angels,
proclaimed among Gentiles,
believed in throughout the world,
taken up in glory.

False Asceticism

4 Now the Spirit expressly says that in later[g] times some will renounce the faith by paying attention to deceitful spirits and
teachings of demons, 2through the hypocrisy of liars whose consciences are seared with a hot iron. 3They forbid marriage and demand abstinence from foods, which God created to be received with
thanksgiving by those who believe and know the truth. 4For everything created by God is good, and nothing is to be rejected, provided

[a] Gk *the husband of one wife* [b] Or *Their wives*, or *Women deacons* [c] Gk *be husbands of one wife*
[d] Gk *Who*; other ancient authorities read *God*; others, *Which* [e] Or *justified* [f] Or *by the Spirit*
[g] Or *the last*

4:4 everything created by God is good: The false teachers said that one could be saved only by not marrying or by not eating certain foods (4:3). These teachings are rejected because God is the creator of everything and because "God's word," which here means Jesus (see John 1:1-18; Heb 4:12), makes this world holy or good.

it is received with thanksgiving; 5 for it is sanctified by God's word and by prayer.

A Good Minister of Jesus Christ

6 If you put these instructions before the brothers and sisters,[a] you will be a good servant[b] of Christ Jesus, nourished on the words of the faith and of the sound teaching that you have followed. 7 Have nothing to do with profane myths and old wives' tales. Train yourself in godliness, 8 for, while physical training is of some value, godliness is valuable in every way, holding promise for both the present life and the life to come. 9 The saying is sure and worthy of full acceptance. 10 For to this end we toil and struggle,[c] because we have our hope set on the living God, who is the Savior of all people, especially of those who believe.

11 These are the things you must insist on and teach. 12 Let no one despise your youth, but set the believers an example in speech and conduct, in love, in faith, in purity. 13 Until I arrive, give attention to the public reading of scripture,[d] to exhorting, to teaching. 14 Do not neglect the gift that is in you, which was given to you through prophecy with the laying on of hands by the council of elders.[e] 15 Put these things into practice, devote yourself to them, so that all may see your progress. 16 Pay close attention to yourself and to your teaching; continue in these things, for in doing this you will save both yourself and your hearers.

Duties toward Believers

5 Do not speak harshly to an older man,[f] but speak to him as to a father, to younger men as brothers, 2 to older women as mothers, to younger women as sisters—with absolute purity.

5:3—6:2 widows...elders...yoke of slavery: In the body of Christ, there is respect and honor for all.

3 Honor widows who are really widows. 4 If a widow has children or grandchildren, they should first learn their religious duty to their own family and make some repayment to their parents; for this is pleasing in God's sight. 5 The real widow, left alone, has set her hope on God and continues in supplications and prayers night and day; 6 but the widow[g] who lives for pleasure is dead even while she lives. 7 Give these commands as well, so that they may be above reproach. 8 And whoever does not provide for relatives, and especially for family members, has denied the faith and is worse than an unbeliever.

9 Let a widow be put on the list if she is not less than sixty years old and has been married only once;[h] 10 she must be well attested for her good works, as one who has brought up children, shown hospitality, washed the saints' feet, helped the afflicted, and devoted herself to doing good in every way. 11 But refuse to put younger widows on the list; for when their sensual desires alienate them from Christ, they want to marry, 12 and so they incur condemnation for having violated

---

[a] Gk *brothers* [b] Or *deacon* [c] Other ancient authorities read *suffer reproach* [d] Gk *to the reading*
[e] Gk *by the presbytery* [f] Or *an elder, or a presbyter* [g] Gk *she* [h] Gk *the wife of one husband*

their first pledge. 13 Besides that, they learn to be idle, gadding about from house to house; and they are not merely idle, but also gossips and busybodies, saying what they should not say. 14 So I would have younger widows marry, bear children, and manage their households, so as to give the adversary no occasion to revile us. 15 For some have already turned away to follow Satan. 16 If any believing woman[a] has relatives who are really widows, let her assist them; let the church not be burdened, so that it can assist those who are real widows.

17 Let the elders who rule well be considered worthy of double honor,[b] especially those who labor in preaching and teaching; 18 for the scripture says, "You shall not muzzle an ox while it is treading out the grain," and, "The laborer deserves to be paid." 19 Never accept any accusation against an elder except on the evidence of two or three witnesses. 20 As for those who persist in sin, rebuke them in the presence of all, so that the rest also may stand in fear. 21 In the presence of God and of Christ Jesus and of the elect angels, I warn you to keep these instructions without prejudice, doing nothing on the basis of partiality. 22 Do not ordain[c] anyone hastily, and do not participate in the sins of others; keep yourself pure.

23 No longer drink only water, but take a little wine for the sake of your stomach and your frequent ailments.

24 The sins of some people are conspicuous and precede them to judgment, while the sins of others follow them there. 25 So also good works are conspicuous; and even when they are not, they cannot remain hidden.

6 Let all who are under the yoke of slavery regard their masters as worthy of all honor, so that the name of God and the teaching may not be blasphemed. 2 Those who have believing masters must not be disrespectful to them on the ground that they are members of the church;[d] rather they must serve them all the more, since those who benefit by their service are believers and beloved.[e]

False Teaching and True Riches

Teach and urge these duties. 3 Whoever teaches otherwise and does not agree with the sound words of our Lord Jesus Christ and the teaching that is in accordance with godliness, 4 is conceited, understanding nothing, and has a morbid craving for controversy and for disputes about words. From these come envy, dissension, slander, base suspicions, 5 and wrangling among those who are depraved in mind and bereft of the truth, imagining that godliness is a means of gain.[f] 6 Of course, there is great gain in godliness combined with contentment; 7 for we brought nothing into the world, so that[g] we can take

[a] Other ancient authorities read *believing man or woman;* others, *believing man* [b] Or *compensation* [c] Gk *Do not lay hands on* [d] Gk *are brothers* [e] Or *since they are believers and beloved, who devote themselves to good deeds* [f] Other ancient authorities add *Withdraw yourself from such people* [g] Other ancient authorities read *world—it is certain that*

6:6-9 great gain in godliness... rich fall into temptation: Faith means putting one's trust in God. Temptation can come in the form of riches, if we put our trust in them (see Mark 10:17-27; Luke 16:13).

6:10 **the love of money is a root of all kinds of evil:** Money is not evil in and of itself. Love of money can draw us away from God and into selfish harmful actions.

What do you think it means to "be content"? What makes it hard for you to be content with your life?

6:20 **falsely called knowledge:** Some claimed to have special knowledge (Greek, *gnosis*). A religious movement called Gnosticism developed in the second century. People who followed it said that a divine being cannot die, and that the divine Christ left the human Jesus before the crucifixion.

nothing out of it; [8]but if we have food and clothing, we will be content
with these. [9]But those who want to be rich fall into temptation and
are trapped by many senseless and harmful desires that plunge people
into ruin and destruction. [10]For the love of money is a root of all kinds
of evil, and in their eagerness to be rich some have wandered away
from the faith and pierced themselves with many pains.

The Good Fight of Faith

11 But as for you, man of God, shun all this; pursue righteousness, godliness, faith, love, endurance, gentleness. [12]Fight the good
fight of the faith; take hold of the eternal life, to which you were called
and for which you made[a] the good confession in the presence of many
witnesses. [13]In the presence of God, who gives life to all things, and
of Christ Jesus, who in his testimony before Pontius Pilate made the
good confession, I charge you [14]to keep the commandment without
spot or blame until the manifestation of our Lord Jesus Christ, [15]which
he will bring about at the right time—he who is the blessed and only
Sovereign, the King of kings and Lord of lords. [16]It is he alone who has
immortality and dwells in unapproachable light, whom no one has
ever seen or can see; to him be honor and eternal dominion. Amen.

17 As for those who in the present age are rich, command them
not to be haughty, or to set their hopes on the uncertainty of riches,
but rather on God who richly provides us with everything for our enjoyment. [18]They are to do good, to be rich in good works, generous,
and ready to share, [19]thus storing up for themselves the treasure of a
good foundation for the future, so that they may take hold of the life
that really is life.

Personal Instructions and Benediction

20 Timothy, guard what has been entrusted to you. Avoid the profane chatter and contradictions of what is falsely called knowledge;
[21]by professing it some have missed the mark as regards the faith.

Grace be with you.[b]

---

[a] Gk *confessed* [b] The Greek word for *you* here is plural; in other ancient authorities it is singular. Other ancient authorities add *Amen*

2 Timothy 3:16

2 TIMOTHY

Background File

Second Timothy is similar to 1 Timothy in style, content, and vocabulary, but it is quite different from Paul's writings. As discussed in the introduction to 1 Timothy (p. 1952), Paul probably did not write these two letters to Timothy. Instead, it is likely that a person who wanted to continue Paul's mission wrote the letters near the end of the first century C.E.

What's the Story?

First Timothy and 2 Timothy differ in how Paul is depicted. In 2 Timothy, Paul is in prison in Rome (1:8, 16-17; 2:9), awaiting his death (4:6-8). Most of his co-workers and friends have left him (4:9-16). In this time of personal suffering, Paul is shown writing an affectionate letter to "Timothy, my beloved child" (1:2), urging him to carry on with ministry. To do this, he will need to oppose false teachings, as discussed in 1 Timothy.

Second Timothy provides few specifics about these false teachings. There is some dispute about words (2:14-16, 23-26; 3:6-9; 4:3-5), and some think that the resurrection of the dead has already taken place (2:18). Beyond that, the letter features a long and vivid list of immoral habits, or vices (3:2-5).

Several verses in 2 Timothy include quotations from Paul's letter to the Romans (find these connections in 2 Tim 1:7 and Rom 8:15; 2 Tim 2:8 and Rom 1:3-4; 2 Tim 2:11 and Rom 6:8; 2 Tim 2:20 and Rom 9:21; 2 Tim 4:14 and Rom 2:6; and 2 Tim 4:18 and Rom 16:27). It seems the writer studied Romans to better understand Paul's ideas and style of writing. This demonstrates the popularity of collections of Paul's writings in the early Christian church.

Second Timothy can be outlined as follows:

- Words of warning and encouragement (1:1—2:26)
- Living with faithfulness to the gospel (3:1—4:8)
- Last words and greetings (4:9-22)

What's the Message?

Second Timothy is a call to persist courageously in the ministry of Jesus Christ. Timothy was not only facing false teachings; it also seems he was struggling to fulfill his responsibilities. The writer encourages him: "I remind you to rekindle the gift of God that is within you through the laying on of my hands; for God did not give us a spirit of cowardice, but rather a spirit of power and of love and of self-discipline" (2 Tim 1:6-7; see also 4:1-2). To motivate Timothy, the writer depicts Paul's sufferings in graphic detail, hoping that Timothy will follow this example.

This letter teaches that there are practical consequences to faith in Jesus Christ. Dietrich Bonhoeffer, a Lutheran pastor, called faith that avoids practical consequences "cheap grace." In contrast to this, Bonhoeffer believed that God's grace and faith in Christ compelled him to fight the regime of Nazi Germany, which led to his arrest and execution.

Salutation

1 Paul, an apostle of Christ Jesus by the will of God, for the sake of
the promise of life that is in Christ Jesus,
2 To Timothy, my beloved child:
Grace, mercy, and peace from God the Father and Christ Jesus
our Lord.

Thanksgiving and Encouragement

3 I am grateful to God—whom I worship with a clear conscience,
as my ancestors did—when I remember you constantly in my prayers
night and day. 4 Recalling your tears, I long to see you so that I may be
filled with joy. 5 I am reminded of your sincere faith, a faith that lived
first in your grandmother Lois and your mother Eunice and now, I am
sure, lives in you. 6 For this reason I remind you to rekindle the gift of
God that is within you through the laying on of my hands; 7 for God
did not give us a spirit of cowardice, but rather a spirit of power and of
love and of self-discipline.
8 Do not be ashamed, then, of the testimony about our Lord or
of me his prisoner, but join with me in suffering for the gospel, relying
on the power of God, 9 who saved us and called us with a holy calling,
not according to our works but according to his own purpose and
grace. This grace was given to us in Christ Jesus before the ages began,
10 but it has now been revealed through the appearing of our Savior
Christ Jesus, who abolished death and brought life and immortality
to light through the gospel. 11 For this gospel I was appointed a herald and an apostle and a teacher,[a] 12 and for this reason I suffer as I
do. But I am not ashamed, for I know the one in whom I have put

[a] Other ancient authorities add *of the Gentiles*

1:1 Paul, an apostle of Christ Jesus: Like 1 Timothy, 2 Timothy mentions Paul as the writer. But 2 Timothy was probably written by someone else, years after Paul had died (see introduction).

1:2 To Timothy, my beloved child: From the letter's opening to its closing (4:19-22), an affectionate relationship between the writer and Timothy is apparent.

1:3-7 I am grateful to God: Following the typical pattern of Paul's letters, 2 Timothy features an initial thanksgiving and prayer.

1:5 faith that lived first in your grandmother Lois and your mother Eunice: Timothy appears as a Christian of the third generation. According to Acts 16:1, his family lived in Lystra. His mother was a Jew who believed in Jesus Christ, and his father was Greek. Timothy has been acquainted with the sacred writings from childhood (3:15).

What are some ways you might talk about faith and read the Bible with your family?

1:6-7 spirit of power…love…self-discipline: This summarizes the teaching task (see 4:1-2).

1:8 join with me in suffering for the gospel: Paul often talked of suffering for the gospel (see 1 Cor 4:9-13; Phil 1:27-30).

my trust, and I am sure that he is able to guard until that day what I
have entrusted to him.[a] 13 Hold to the standard of sound teaching that
you have heard from me, in the faith and love that are in Christ Jesus.
14 Guard the good treasure entrusted to you, with the help of the Holy
Spirit living in us.

15 You are aware that all who are in Asia have turned away from
me, including Phygelus and Hermogenes. 16 May the Lord grant
mercy to the household of Onesiphorus, because he often refreshed
me and was not ashamed of my chain; 17 when he arrived in Rome, he
eagerly[b] searched for me and found me 18 —may the Lord grant that
he will find mercy from the Lord on that day! And you know very
well how much service he rendered in Ephesus.

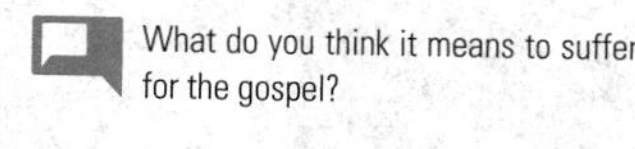

What do you think it means to suffer for the gospel?

1:18 Ephesus: The apostle Paul had visited Ephesus in Asia Minor during his journeys (see Acts 19).

A Good Soldier of Christ Jesus

2 You then, my child, be strong in the grace that is in Christ Jesus;
2 and what you have heard from me through many witnesses entrust to faithful people who will be able to teach others as well. 3 Share
in suffering like a good soldier of Christ Jesus. 4 No one serving in the
army gets entangled in everyday affairs; the soldier's aim is to please
the enlisting officer. 5 And in the case of an athlete, no one is crowned
without competing according to the rules. 6 It is the farmer who does
the work who ought to have the first share of the crops. 7 Think over
what I say, for the Lord will give you understanding in all things.

8 Remember Jesus Christ, raised from the dead, a descendant of
David—that is my gospel, 9 for which I suffer hardship, even to the
point of being chained like a criminal. But the word of God is not
chained. 10 Therefore I endure everything for the sake of the elect, so
that they may also obtain the salvation that is in Christ Jesus, with
eternal glory. 11 The saying is sure:

If we have died with him, we will also live with him;
12 if we endure, we will also reign with him;
if we deny him, he will also deny us;
13 if we are faithless, he remains faithful—
for he cannot deny himself.

2:5 crowned: Athletes sometimes received a crown of flowers or leaves as a reward for victory in a contest.

2:11-13 If we have died with him: The writer quotes part of Romans 6:3-11, where Paul compares dying with Christ to baptism.

A Worker Approved by God

14 Remind them of this, and warn them before God[c] that they
are to avoid wrangling over words, which does no good but only ruins
those who are listening. 15 Do your best to present yourself to God
as one approved by him, a worker who has no need to be ashamed,
rightly explaining the word of truth. 16 Avoid profane chatter, for it will
lead people into more and more impiety, 17 and their talk will spread
like gangrene. Among them are Hymenaeus and Philetus, 18 who have

2:14-18 avoid wrangling over words: The false teachings, which dominate much of this letter, are mentioned for the first time.

[a] Or *what has been entrusted to me* [b] Or *promptly* [c] Other ancient authorities read *the Lord*

2:21 dedicated and useful: A more literal translation of the original Greek text is "sanctified and useful." This statement contradicts how Paul understands sanctification. For Paul, sanctification is an act of purification that God performs for humans (see 1 Cor 6:11; 1 Thess 5:23; see also 1 Cor 7:14, where husband and wife can sanctify each other).

3:1 in the last days distressing times will come: The writer warns that a time is coming when faith will be tested, especially by false teachers (see also Mark 13:3-23; 1 Tim 4:1-5).

3:8 Jannes and Jambres: The *Damascus Document,* a Jewish source, gave these names to Pharaoh's magicians who challenged Moses (Exod 7:11, 22). Here, these two magicians embody human opposition to God.

3:10-12 observed my teaching: These verses describe how Paul suffered because of his teaching ministry and yet prevailed. This image stands in contrast to the false teachers, who are arrogant.

swerved from the truth by claiming that the resurrection has already
taken place. They are upsetting the faith of some. [19]But God's firm
foundation stands, bearing this inscription: "The Lord knows those
who are his," and, "Let everyone who calls on the name of the Lord
turn away from wickedness."

20 In a large house there are utensils not only of gold and silver
but also of wood and clay, some for special use, some for ordinary.
[21]All who cleanse themselves of the things I have mentioned[a] will
become special utensils, dedicated and useful to the owner of the
house, ready for every good work. [22]Shun youthful passions and pursue righteousness, faith, love, and peace, along with those who call
on the Lord from a pure heart. [23]Have nothing to do with stupid and
senseless controversies; you know that they breed quarrels. [24]And
the Lord's servant[b] must not be quarrelsome but kindly to everyone,
an apt teacher, patient, [25]correcting opponents with gentleness. God
may perhaps grant that they will repent and come to know the truth,
[26]and that they may escape from the snare of the devil, having been
held captive by him to do his will.[c]

Godlessness in the Last Days

3 You must understand this, that in the last days distressing times
will come. [2]For people will be lovers of themselves, lovers of
money, boasters, arrogant, abusive, disobedient to their parents, ungrateful, unholy, [3]inhuman, implacable, slanderers, profligates, brutes,
haters of good, [4]treacherous, reckless, swollen with conceit, lovers of
pleasure rather than lovers of God, [5]holding to the outward form
of godliness but denying its power. Avoid them! [6]For among them
are those who make their way into households and captivate silly
women, overwhelmed by their sins and swayed by all kinds of desires,
[7]who are always being instructed and can never arrive at a knowledge
of the truth. [8]As Jannes and Jambres opposed Moses, so these people, of corrupt mind and counterfeit faith, also oppose the truth. [9]But
they will not make much progress, because, as in the case of those two
men,[d] their folly will become plain to everyone.

Paul's Charge to Timothy

10 Now you have observed my teaching, my conduct, my aim in
life, my faith, my patience, my love, my steadfastness, [11]my persecutions, and my suffering the things that happened to me in Antioch,
Iconium, and Lystra. What persecutions I endured! Yet the Lord rescued me from all of them. [12]Indeed, all who want to live a godly life in
Christ Jesus will be persecuted. [13]But wicked people and impostors
will go from bad to worse, deceiving others and being deceived. [14]But
as for you, continue in what you have learned and firmly believed,

---

[a] Gk *of these things* [b] Gk *slave* [c] Or *by him, to do his* (that is, God's) *will* [d] Gk lacks *two men*

knowing from whom you learned it, 15and how from childhood you
have known the sacred writings that are able to instruct you for salvation through faith in Christ Jesus. 16All scripture is inspired by God
and is[a] useful for teaching, for reproof, for correction, and for training
in righteousness, 17so that everyone who belongs to God may be pro-
ficient, equipped for every good work.

4 In the presence of God and of Christ Jesus, who is to judge
the living and the dead, and in view of his appearing and his
kingdom, I solemnly urge you: 2proclaim the message; be persistent
whether the time is favorable or unfavorable; convince, rebuke, and
encourage, with the utmost patience in teaching. 3For the time is
coming when people will not put up with sound doctrine, but having
itching ears, they will accumulate for themselves teachers to suit their
own desires, 4and will turn away from listening to the truth and wander away to myths. 5As for you, always be sober, endure suffering, do
the work of an evangelist, carry out your ministry fully.

6 As for me, I am already being poured out as a libation, and the
time of my departure has come. 7I have fought the good fight, I have
finished the race, I have kept the faith. 8From now on there is reserved
for me the crown of righteousness, which the Lord, the righteous
judge, will give me on that day, and not only to me but also to all who
have longed for his appearing.

Personal Instructions

9 Do your best to come to me soon, 10for Demas, in love with this
present world, has deserted me and gone to Thessalonica; Crescens
has gone to Galatia,[b] Titus to Dalmatia. 11Only Luke is with me. Get
Mark and bring him with you, for he is useful in my ministry. 12I have
sent Tychicus to Ephesus. 13When you come, bring the cloak that I left
with Carpus at Troas, also the books, and above all the parchments.
14Alexander the coppersmith did me great harm; the Lord will pay
him back for his deeds. 15You also must beware of him, for he strongly
opposed our message.

16 At my first defense no one came to my support, but all deserted me. May it not be counted against them! 17But the Lord stood
by me and gave me strength, so that through me the message might
be fully proclaimed and all the Gentiles might hear it. So I was rescued from the lion's mouth. 18The Lord will rescue me from every evil
attack and save me for his heavenly kingdom. To him be the glory
forever and ever. Amen.

Final Greetings and Benediction

19 Greet Prisca and Aquila, and the household of Onesiphorus. 20Erastus remained in Corinth; Trophimus I left ill in Miletus.

[a] Or *Every scripture inspired by God is also* [b] Other ancient authorities read *Gaul*

3:16-17 All scripture is inspired by God: In the New Testament, the word *scripture* (*grafe,* in Greek) refers to the books of the Old Testament, not to the entire Bible. A literal translation of "inspired" (*theopnustos* [thee-oh-NOO-stows] in Greek) is "God-breathed." This term does not mean that the Bible is inerrant or free of contradictions. It implies instead that those who read the Old Testament, which was the Bible of early Christianity, will adopt godly behavior. This is expressly mentioned in 3:16, and it is the overall theme of 2 Timothy.

How do Lutherans understand Holy Scripture? Martin Luther recognizes the Old Testament as Holy Scripture and describes the gospel in this way: "The gospel should really not be something written, but a spoken word which brought forth the Scriptures, as Christ and the apostles have done" (*LW* 35:123). For Lutherans, then, the writings of the New Testament are voices that teach and preach about faith in Jesus Christ. *2 Timothy 3:16-17*

Do Christians actually believe in the Bible? If a friend asked what you believe about the Bible, what would you say?

4:6-8 crown of righteousness: Here the writer implies that one can earn the "crown of righteousness" through suffering. This concept is not typical of Paul's writings. For Paul, righteousness is God's free gift for people (see Rom 3:21-26; Gal 2:15-21; Phil 3:9).

4:9-21 Get Mark...bring the cloak... Greet: The letter ends with some personal instructions and final greetings. In addition to friends, the writer also mentions people who harmed and opposed Paul.

[21]Do your best to come before winter. Eubulus sends greetings to you,
as do Pudens and Linus and Claudia and all the brothers and sisters.[a]
22 The Lord be with your spirit. Grace be with you.[b]

---

[a] Gk *all the brothers* [b] The Greek word for *you* here is plural. Other ancient authorities add *Amen*

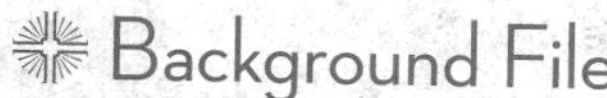
Titus 3:6-7

TITUS

Background File

Although attributed to Paul, the style, vocabulary, understanding of the church, and themes of the letter to Titus are very different from letters considered to be written by Paul himself. Most scholars believe this letter was written in Paul's name by an anonymous author. It was common practice in the first century for writers to do this. They would credit someone else as author in order to honor the person and give authority to the writing. The role of "elders" or "overseers," as described in this letter, was not a part of church structure until late in the first century C.E., so dates suggested for the writing of Titus are between 80 and 90. The letter, addressed to Titus on the island of Crete, also provides general instruction to the early church.

What's the Story?

The letter to Titus can be outlined as follows:

Salutation or greeting (1:1-4)
The role of elders or overseers as leaders of the church (1:5-16)
Expectations for various members of the community (2:1-15)
Encouragement to be good citizens and do good works (3:1-15)

The teachings in Titus are very similar to those in 1 Timothy. Titus and 1–2 Timothy are referred to collectively as the "Pastoral Epistles." They explain how Christians need to live together in harmony, in much the same way a pastor today encourages members of a congregation to care for one another.

What's the Message?

The writer of Titus teaches that all believers have a responsibility to live godly lives as individuals and as members of a Christian community. They are to resist false teaching, live together in love, and be productive citizens. These good works do not save believers, however. Salvation and the hope of eternal life are made possible only by the mercy and grace that comes to believers in the water of rebirth and renewal by the Holy Spirit.

Salutation

1 Paul, a servant[a] of God and an apostle of Jesus Christ, for the sake
of the faith of God's elect and the knowledge of the truth that is in
accordance with godliness, 2in the hope of eternal life that God, who
never lies, promised before the ages began— 3in due time he revealed
his word through the proclamation with which I have been entrusted
by the command of God our Savior,
4 To Titus, my loyal child in the faith we share:
Grace[b] and peace from God the Father and Christ Jesus our
Savior.

Titus in Crete

5 I left you behind in Crete for this reason, so that you should
put in order what remained to be done, and should appoint elders in
every town, as I directed you: 6someone who is blameless, married
only once,[c] whose children are believers, not accused of debauchery
and not rebellious. 7For a bishop,[d] as God's steward, must be blameless; he must not be arrogant or quick-tempered or addicted to wine
or violent or greedy for gain; 8but he must be hospitable, a lover of
goodness, prudent, upright, devout, and self-controlled. 9He must
have a firm grasp of the word that is trustworthy in accordance with
the teaching, so that he may be able both to preach with sound doctrine and to refute those who contradict it.
10 There are also many rebellious people, idle talkers and deceivers, especially those of the circumcision; 11they must be silenced,
since they are upsetting whole families by teaching for sordid gain
what it is not right to teach. 12It was one of them, their very own
prophet, who said,
"Cretans are always liars, vicious brutes, lazy gluttons."
13That testimony is true. For this reason rebuke them sharply, so that
they may become sound in the faith, 14not paying attention to Jewish
myths or to commandments of those who reject the truth. 15To the
pure all things are pure, but to the corrupt and unbelieving nothing is
pure. Their very minds and consciences are corrupted. 16They profess
to know God, but they deny him by their actions. They are detestable,
disobedient, unfit for any good work.

Teach Sound Doctrine

2 But as for you, teach what is consistent with sound doctrine.
2Tell the older men to be temperate, serious, prudent, and
sound in faith, in love, and in endurance.
3 Likewise, tell the older women to be reverent in behavior, not
to be slanderers or slaves to drink; they are to teach what is good, 4so

[a] Gk *slave* [b] Other ancient authorities read *Grace, mercy,* [c] Gk *husband of one wife* [d] Or *an overseer*

1:1 apostle . . . God's elect: An apostle is someone sent by God with the message or good news about Jesus Christ. The notion of believers as elected or chosen by God is prevalent throughout the Bible. The Hebrew Bible identifies the Israelites as God's chosen people. Some New Testament writers call Christians elect or chosen (see 1 Chr 16:13; Col 3:12; 1 Pet 2:9).

How do people become Christians?

1:1 for the sake of the faith: "Faith" is a difficult word to translate. The most useful English word may be "trust." The writer of Titus uses the word "faith" (in Greek, *pistis* [PIS-tis]) in describing healthy relationships with others.

How do Lutherans understand God's grace? Grace is God's gift to us in Jesus Christ, who redeems us, saving us from our sin. God's gift of a Savior calls us to do good works, but it is grace that saves us. *Titus 1:4*

1:5-9 elders: The writer instructs Titus to appoint people who live righteously and can be trusted to teach sound doctrine as elders or overseers in the church. These leaders will guard the community against false teachers and rebels who seek to deceive the believers. Other New Testament writers also call for the appointment of leaders (see Acts 14:23; 1 Tim 5:17).

How are leaders chosen in congregations and in the greater church today? What does it mean to be chosen for church leadership?

1:10-14 those of the circumcision: Some in the early church believed that circumcision was necessary for all believers. Here, the letter strongly urges Titus, a Gentile (non-Jew), to teach against circumcision (see Gal 2:3).

1:12-14 Cretans are always liars . . . Jewish myths: These verses display strong social and religious bias, including the use of a quotation from the Cretan poet Epimenides, from about 600 B.C.E.

Do we show unjust bias against anyone today?

that they may encourage the young women to love their husbands, to
love their children, [5]to be self-controlled, chaste, good managers of
the household, kind, being submissive to their husbands, so that the
word of God may not be discredited.
6 Likewise, urge the younger men to be self-controlled. [7]Show
yourself in all respects a model of good works, and in your teaching
show integrity, gravity, [8]and sound speech that cannot be censured;
then any opponent will be put to shame, having nothing evil to say
of us.
9 Tell slaves to be submissive to their masters and to give satisfaction in every respect; they are not to talk back, [10]not to pilfer, but to
show complete and perfect fidelity, so that in everything they may be
an ornament to the doctrine of God our Savior.
11 For the grace of God has appeared, bringing salvation to all,[a]
[12]training us to renounce impiety and worldly passions, and in the
present age to live lives that are self-controlled, upright, and godly,
[13]while we wait for the blessed hope and the manifestation of the
glory of our great God and Savior,[b] Jesus Christ. [14]He it is who gave
himself for us that he might redeem us from all iniquity and purify for
himself a people of his own who are zealous for good deeds.
15 Declare these things; exhort and reprove with all authority.[c]
Let no one look down on you.

Maintain Good Deeds

3 Remind them to be subject to rulers and authorities, to be obedient, to be ready for every good work, [2]to speak evil of no one,
to avoid quarreling, to be gentle, and to show every courtesy to everyone. [3]For we ourselves were once foolish, disobedient, led astray,
slaves to various passions and pleasures, passing our days in malice
and envy, despicable, hating one another. [4]But when the goodness
and loving kindness of God our Savior appeared, [5]he saved us, not because of any works of righteousness that we had done, but according
to his mercy, through the water[d] of rebirth and renewal by the Holy
Spirit. [6]This Spirit he poured out on us richly through Jesus Christ
our Savior, [7]so that, having been justified by his grace, we might become heirs according to the hope of eternal life. [8]The saying is sure.
I desire that you insist on these things, so that those who have
come to believe in God may be careful to devote themselves to good
works; these things are excellent and profitable to everyone. [9]But
avoid stupid controversies, genealogies, dissensions, and quarrels
about the law, for they are unprofitable and worthless. [10]After a first
and second admonition, have nothing more to do with anyone who

2:4-5, 9 being submissive: Women and slaves were expected to submit to husbands and masters in first-century society.

What kind of relationship does God call us to build with others? What kind of relationship does God call spouses to build with each other?

How are we reborn through the waters of baptism? Baptism is the way we become heirs or sons and daughters of God. In baptism, we are washed with water, and God rescues us and raises us up to new life. Our sins are washed away, and we become new through the Holy Spirit. *Titus 3:5*

---

[a] Or *has appeared to all, bringing salvation* [b] Or *of the great God and our Savior* [c] Gk *commandment*
[d] Gk *washing*

causes divisions, [11] since you know that such a person is perverted and
sinful, being self-condemned.

Final Messages and Benediction

12 When I send Artemas to you, or Tychicus, do your best to
come to me at Nicopolis, for I have decided to spend the winter there.
[13]Make every effort to send Zenas the lawyer and Apollos on their
way, and see that they lack nothing. [14]And let people learn to devote
themselves to good works in order to meet urgent needs, so that they
may not be unproductive.

15 All who are with me send greetings to you. Greet those who
love us in the faith.

Grace be with all of you.[a]

[a] Other ancient authorities add *Amen*

Philemon v. 10

PHILEMON

Background File

This is the shortest of Paul's letters in the New Testament, consisting of only twenty-five verses. It was written from jail at the same time as Paul's letter to the church at Colossae (see Map 14, p. 2111). (Compare Col 4:7-17 with Phlm vv. 2, 10, 23-24.) This letter is addressed primarily to Philemon, whose house evidently served as the gathering place for the Colossian church (Phlm v. 2).

What's the Story?

The purpose of this letter is to ask Philemon, and perhaps his wife, Apphia, and other members of his household and church, to welcome back Onesimus, who was Philemon's slave. Onesimus had apparently wronged Philemon in some way, probably by running away as a fugitive and perhaps by stealing from his master as well (Phlm v. 18). In the Roman Empire, where slavery was common, slave owners had the right to punish severely and even put to death a slave who had been caught after running away. During Paul's time in prison, Onesimus had become a believer in Christ and had begun to work with Paul in some way (Phlm vv. 10-14). However, Paul felt it necessary to send Onesimus back to Philemon, and wrote this letter to ask Philemon to welcome Onesimus "no longer as a slave but more than a slave, a beloved brother" (Phlm v. 16).

What's the Message?

This brief letter offers us a glimpse into the way the gospel proclaimed by Paul transformed the social relationships of the first believers. Distinctions of gender, race, and social ranking came to be viewed differently. As Paul wrote to the Galatians, "There is no longer Jew or Greek, there is no longer slave or free, there is no longer male and female; for all of you are one in Christ Jesus" (Gal 3:28). The identity of all people was now redefined in light of their relationship to God as their Father, to Christ as their Lord (Phlm v. 3), and to one another as sisters and brothers belonging to a single family and struggling together for the common cause of the gospel (Phlm vv. 1-2, 16, 20). So Paul urges Philemon to be transformed in the way he views Onesimus, by forgiving him for any wrongs he has committed and accepting him just as he would accept Paul—as a beloved brother, partner, and fellow worker in Christ. Paul realizes that this transformation cannot be forced upon someone. It must be the result of the faith and love that have been produced in a believer's heart by the gospel (Phlm vv. 8-9).

This letter invites us today to be transformed in the way we view our sisters and brothers in Christ, overcoming the social distinctions that often divide us, so that we may join together as a family and as co-workers in the common cause of the gospel.

Salutation

1 Paul, a prisoner of Christ Jesus, and Timothy our brother,[a]
To Philemon our dear friend and co-worker, 2to Apphia our sister,[b]
to Archippus our fellow soldier, and to the church in your house:
3 Grace to you and peace from God our Father and the Lord
Jesus Christ.

v. 2 the church in your house: The first Christians generally met either in a Jewish synagogue or in a fairly spacious house belonging to a wealthier member.

How do we come to have love and faith? Paul gives thanks *to God* for Philemon's love and faith, because, as Luther constantly stressed, these are gracious gifts of God alone. We cannot produce them in ourselves. *Philemon vv. 4-5*

Philemon's Love and Faith

4 When I remember you[c] in my prayers, I always thank my God
5because I hear of your love for all the saints and your faith toward the
Lord Jesus. 6I pray that the sharing of your faith may become effective
when you perceive all the good that we[d] may do for Christ. 7I have indeed received much joy and encouragement from your love, because
the hearts of the saints have been refreshed through you, my brother.

Paul's Plea for Onesimus

8 For this reason, though I am bold enough in Christ to command you to do your duty, 9yet I would rather appeal to you on the
basis of love—and I, Paul, do this as an old man, and now also as a
prisoner of Christ Jesus.[e] 10I am appealing to you for my child, Onesimus, whose father I have become during my imprisonment. 11For-
merly he was useless to you, but now he is indeed useful[f] both to you
and to me. 12I am sending him, that is, my own heart, back to you. 13I
wanted to keep him with me, so that he might be of service to me in
your place during my imprisonment for the gospel; 14but I preferred
to do nothing without your consent, in order that your good deed
might be voluntary and not something forced. 15Perhaps this is the
reason he was separated from you for a while, so that you might have
him back forever, 16no longer as a slave but more than a slave, a beloved brother—especially to me but how much more to you, both in
the flesh and in the Lord.
17 So if you consider me your partner, welcome him as you
would welcome me. 18If he has wronged you in any way, or owes you
anything, charge that to my account. 19I, Paul, am writing this with
my own hand: I will repay it. I say nothing about your owing me even
your own self. 20Yes, brother, let me have this benefit from you in the

v.11 useful: Here Paul offers a play on words. The name "Onesimus" means "useful" in Greek. It was a common name for a slave.

What is the source of good deeds? In Lutheran thought, good deeds by nature *cannot* be "something forced" (Phlm v. 14) but flow spontaneously and voluntarily from a transformed heart. As Martin Luther says, "O, it is a living, busy, active, mighty thing, this faith. It is impossible for it not to be doing good deeds incessantly" (Preface, Epistle to the Romans). *Philemon v. 14*

---

[a] Gk *the brother* [b] Gk *the sister* [c] From verse 4 through verse 21, *you* is singular [d] Other ancient authorities read *you* (plural) [e] Or *as an ambassador of Christ Jesus, and now also his prisoner* [f] The name Onesimus means *useful* or (compare verse 20) *beneficial*

Lord! Refresh my heart in Christ. [21]Confident of your obedience, I
am writing to you, knowing that you will do even more than I say.
22 One thing more—prepare a guest room for me, for I am hoping through your prayers to be restored to you.

Final Greetings and Benediction

23 Epaphras, my fellow prisoner in Christ Jesus, sends greetings
to you,[a] [24]and so do Mark, Aristarchus, Demas, and Luke, my fellow
workers.
25 The grace of the Lord Jesus Christ be with your spirit.[b]

---

[a] Here *you* is singular [b] Other ancient authorities add *Amen*

Paul hints that there was a divine purpose behind Onesimus's separation from Philemon and his return now to Philemon in a new and different relationship (Phlm v. 15). When have you done something wrong only to later see God graciously bring something good out of it that transforms your life and relationships with others?

GENERAL LETTERS AND REVELATION

Hebrews to Revelation

The last portion of the New Testament consists of eight letters, or "epistles," and the book of Revelation. Traditionally, the collection known as the "General Letters" has consisted of only seven letters, since the eighth (Hebrews) was at one time thought to be written by the apostle Paul. The King James Bible of 1611, for example, calls it "The Epistle of Paul the Apostle to the Hebrews." As a result, the reader of the King James Bible might think that there are fourteen Pauline letters. Modern scholars do not think Hebrews was written by Paul, and no one knows for certain who the author was. Today, Bibles typically provide a shorter title for the book, simply "The Letter to the Hebrews." It refers to itself as being rather like a sermon—a "word of exhortation" (13:22). It was written to Christians who had experienced persecution (10:32-39). The book encourages them to stay faithful to Christ, who has gone away to heaven where he speaks up for them in the heavenly sanctuary (7:25-28). Although most of Hebrews is more like a sermon than a letter, it does end like a letter (13:20-25).

The General Letters

The seven letters that remain are named after three of the most outstanding apostles (James, Peter, and John) and a lesser-known one (Jude). There is more than one person named James in the New Testament. The one intended here is no doubt James the brother of Jesus (Mark 6:3), who also became an apostle (Gal 1:19) and leader of the church in Jerusalem (Acts 15:13; 21:18; Gal 1:19; 2:9). In regard to Peter, there is only one person by that name, although he is also known more fully as Simon Peter in all four Gospels (Matt 4:18; Mark 3:16; Luke 5:8; John 6:68). Sometimes Peter is known as Cephas in the Gospel of John and the letters of Paul (John 1:42; Gal 1:18). His name comes first whenever the names of the twelve original apostles are listed (Matt 10:2; Mark 3:16; Luke 6:14; Acts 1:13). As with the name James, there is more than one person who bears the name John in the New Testament. But the person intended is undoubtedly John, son of Zebedee, one of the twelve (Matt 4:21; 10:2). Jude likely refers to one of the brothers of Jesus (Mark 6:3, where he is "Judas"), who became an apostle (1 Cor 9:5). The writer of the letter calls himself "brother of James" (Jude, verse 1), no doubt referring to the James who was also a brother of Jesus.

The seven letters are called "general" or "catholic" (meaning "universal") because they appear to be written not to any one church but for churches more generally. Many modern scholars do not think that these seven letters were literally written or dictated by the apostolic leaders whose names they bear. More often, the letters are thought to have been written by Christians who sought to express the *perspectives* of those leaders for believers a generation after the apostles had died.

The order of these letters in the New Testament at least seems transparent. Hebrews comes after Paul's letters, because it was associated with Paul, and some in the early church considered it to have been written by him. The letters of James, Peter, and John may be ordered after Galatians 2:9, where Paul lists the three in that sequence and speaks of them as "acknowledged pillars" of the church in Jerusalem. Jude must then come last.

The Book of Revelation

Revelation (also known as the Revelation to John) is the last book of the Bible and rightly so. Because it includes writing called "apocalyptic," it is difficult to understand. Some people have tried to interpret it in ways that have little to do with its actual message. A careful study of its contents leads to the conclusion that it was written to encourage Christians suffering persecution near the end of the first century. It uses symbolism to envision the final triumph of God over the forces of evil. It includes some magnificent hymns that celebrate God's triumph (see Rev 4:8, 11; 5:9-10, 12-13; 7:12).

The General Letters and Revelation bring to an end not only the New Testament but the entire Christian Bible. Each addresses believers in Christ who belong to the second and third generations of Christianity. But they continue to speak to believers of every age, offering hope and encouragement grounded in Jesus Christ, who came into the world to reveal God and to save humans from sin and death. This same Jesus continues to live and reign for all time and eternity.

Hebrews 12:1

HEBREWS

Background File

The Letter to the Hebrews is a sophisticated document, written in elegant Greek around 70 C.E., perhaps in Rome (13:24). From the time of the early church, many have questioned the tradition that claimed the apostle Paul wrote this letter. Martin Luther thought the author was perhaps Apollos (see Acts 18:24).

The traditional title of the work, "The Letter to the Hebrews," is also questioned. Hebrews is not really an "epistle" or letter, and it was not written to Hebrew-speaking Jews. Hebrews calls itself a "word of exhortation" (13:22), and its overall form and subject matter suggest that it is an extended sermon. It is written for a community of second-generation Greek-speaking Christians (2:3), though some may have had a Jewish background. This community has lived through a variety of trials (10:32-34). Because of the suffering of the people and what they perceived as a delay in the coming Day of the Lord (10:25, 37), some within the community are tempted to "drift away" (2:1) from their faith in the gospel (10:35-36). Hebrews is written to warn them of the dire consequences of turning their backs on Christ and to encourage them to persevere in faith to the end.

What's the Story?

Lutherans believe that the Word of God meets us as both law (judgment) and gospel (promise). Hebrews follows this pattern, often moving back and forth between severe warning and strong encouragement, as shown in these examples:

> Law: There is danger in an "unbelieving heart that turns away from the living God" (3:12).
> Gospel: "The promise of entering [God's] rest is still open" (4:1).
> Law: God's Word judges "the thoughts and intentions of the heart" (4:12).
> Gospel: Grace and mercy abound (4:14-16).

The "living and active" Word of God, then, is a "two-edged sword" (4:12), bringing about both God's judgment and God's mercy. This is important to remember as we read, study, or discuss individual verses within the law-gospel movement of Hebrews.

What's the Message?

Like other New Testament books, Hebrews often quotes and interprets Old Testament passages. These passages are understood to be the messages or "oracles of God" (5:12). Through them God speaks to the present concerns of the community of faith. Hebrews makes this clear in the ways Old Testament passages are introduced: God "says" (see 1:5, 7; 8:8); Jesus says (see 1:2; 10:5); and the Holy Spirit "testifies" (see 3:7; 9:8; 10:15). Hebrews, citing Jeremiah 31:31-34 (see Heb 8:8-12; 10:15-18), says that God extends the promise of a "new covenant" given, through the sacrifice of Christ, to the world. Hebrews often compares this new activity of God with God's dealings "long ago" with Israel (1:1). By doing this, Hebrews repeatedly makes the point that what was good has been made even "better," because it has been made perfect (or complete) in Christ (1:4; 11:40).

In the last chapter (13:10-16), Hebrews also makes one of the boldest statements of what Lutherans have called "theology of the cross." God is not revealed in sacrifices in the holy sanctuary but on the cross—the last place anyone would look for insight into God's will, purpose, and heart (see 1 Cor 1:18-25).

God Has Spoken by His Son

1 Long ago God spoke to our ancestors in many and various ways
by the prophets, 2but in these last days he has spoken to us by a
Son,[a] whom he appointed heir of all things, through whom he also
created the worlds. 3He is the reflection of God's glory and the exact
imprint of God's very being, and he sustains[b] all things by his powerful word. When he had made purification for sins, he sat down at the
right hand of the Majesty on high, 4having become as much superior
to angels as the name he has inherited is more excellent than theirs.

The Son Is Superior to Angels

5 For to which of the angels did God ever say,
"You are my Son;
today I have begotten you"?
Or again,
"I will be his Father,
and he will be my Son"?
6And again, when he brings the firstborn into the world, he says,
"Let all God's angels worship him."
7Of the angels he says,
"He makes his angels winds,
and his servants flames of fire."
8But of the Son he says,
"Your throne, O God, is[c] forever and ever,

---

[a] Or *the Son* [b] Or *bears along* [c] Or *God is your throne*

1:1-4 a Son: Jesus is divine, the Son of God (see John 1:1-3; 1 Cor 8:6; Col 1:15-20).

1:1-2 God spoke…has spoken: God "speaks" to create and sustain life (see Gen 1; John 1:1). God spoke in a variety of ways through Old Testament figures (see Heb 11). God speaks in a new—and final—way through Jesus. Through Scripture (which tells about Christ crucified and risen), God continues to speak to us today (3:7; 10:15).

1:3 purification for sins: Jesus' sacrificial death brings about this purification (9:14; 10:10). The phrase "at the right hand" comes from Psalm 110:1. Here it describes the exalted Son, who reigns with God (see 1:13; 8:1; 10:12; 12:2).

1:4 the name: The name Jesus inherited is "Son" (1:5-14), although the name "Lord" (*kyrios*, 2:3; see Phil 2:9-11) is also possible. In the Gospels, Jesus is declared "Son" at his baptism. The word *angel* means "messenger," one sent by God (1:14).

1:4 superior: Hebrews makes much use of the ancient technique of "comparison" (*synkrisis*, [SOON-kree-sis]) to show how the Christian message is superior—better or more honorable—to that which came before it (good or honorable). In this example, the comparison is between Christ and the angels. (See also 6:9; 7:7, 19, 22; 8:6; 9:23; 10:34; 11:16, 35, 40; 12:24.)

and the righteous scepter is the scepter of your[a] kingdom.
9 You have loved righteousness and hated wickedness;
therefore God, your God, has anointed you
with the oil of gladness beyond your companions."
10 And,
"In the beginning, Lord, you founded the earth,
and the heavens are the work of your hands;
11 they will perish, but you remain;
they will all wear out like clothing;
12 like a cloak you will roll them up,
and like clothing[b] they will be changed.
But you are the same,
and your years will never end."
13 But to which of the angels has he ever said,
"Sit at my right hand
until I make your enemies a footstool for your feet"?
14 Are not all angels[c] spirits in the divine service, sent to serve for the
sake of those who are to inherit salvation?

Warning to Pay Attention

2 Therefore we must pay greater attention to what we have heard,
so that we do not drift away from it. 2 For if the message declared
through angels was valid, and every transgression or disobedience received a just penalty, 3 how can we escape if we neglect so great a salvation? It was declared at first through the Lord, and it was attested to
us by those who heard him, 4 while God added his testimony by signs
and wonders and various miracles, and by gifts of the Holy Spirit, distributed according to his will.

Exaltation through Abasement

5 Now God[d] did not subject the coming world, about which we
are speaking, to angels. 6 But someone has testified somewhere,
"What are human beings that you are mindful of them,[e]
or mortals, that you care for them?[f]
7 You have made them for a little while lower[g] than the angels;
you have crowned them with glory and honor,[h]
8 subjecting all things under their feet."
Now in subjecting all things to them, God[d] left nothing outside
their control. As it is, we do not yet see everything in subjection to
them, 9 but we do see Jesus, who for a little while was made lower[i]
than the angels, now crowned with glory and honor because of the

[a] Other ancient authorities read *his* [b] Other ancient authorities lack *like clothing* [c] Gk *all of them* [d] Gk *he* [e] Gk *What is man that you are mindful of him?* [f] Gk *or the son of man that you care for him?* In the Hebrew of Psalm 8.4–6 both *man* and *son of man* refer to all humankind [g] Or *them only a little lower* [h] Other ancient authorities add *and set them over the works of your hands* [i] Or *who was made a little lower*

1:5-14 [God] says: Hebrews uses a series of Psalms (Pss 2:7; 104:4; 45:6-7; 102:25-27; 110:1) to refer to Christ. Note that Hebrews generally introduces Old Testament texts with some version of "God says," demonstrating that the living word of God (4:12) is actual speech directed to real hearers.

Do you read the Old Testament as Hebrews does, as referring to Christ? Why or why not?

1:6 firstborn: Jesus is called "firstborn" in the New Testament in two ways: firstborn of all creation (Col 1:15) and firstborn from the dead (Col 1:18; Rev 1:5).

1:8 God: The New Testament rarely calls the Son "God," as Hebrews does here (see Rom 9:5; Titus 2:13; John 1:1, 20:28; 2 Pet 1:1).

2:1 Drift away: Another image related to water and ships is used at 6:19. The writer of Hebrews calls it a "word of exhortation" (13:22). It is written in part to encourage those who are tempted to disregard the God's word to pay attention to it.

2:6-8 mortals: The Greek phrase translated as "mortals" is actually "Son of Man" (Jesus). Throughout this section what is singular in Greek has been translated as plural.

2:8 do not yet see: See 11:1.

2:9-18 made lower than the angels: While 1:5-14 reveals the Son's divinity, 2:9-18 stresses the Son's common humanity. The name *Jesus*, introduced in 2:9, is linked to "the suffering of death" (2:9-10). This suffering was on our account, that we might be freed from bondage to sin and the fear of death (2:15).

suffering of death, so that by the grace of God[a] he might taste death for everyone.

10 It was fitting that God,[b] for whom and through whom all things exist, in bringing many children to glory, should make the pioneer of their salvation perfect through sufferings. [11]For the one who sanctifies and those who are sanctified all have one Father.[c] For this reason Jesus[b] is not ashamed to call them brothers and sisters,[d] [12]saying,

"I will proclaim your name to my brothers and sisters,[d]
in the midst of the congregation I will praise you."

[13]And again,

"I will put my trust in him."

And again,

"Here am I and the children whom God has given me."

14 Since, therefore, the children share flesh and blood, he himself likewise shared the same things, so that through death he might destroy the one who has the power of death, that is, the devil, [15]and free those who all their lives were held in slavery by the fear of death. [16]For it is clear that he did not come to help angels, but the descendants of Abraham. [17]Therefore he had to become like his brothers and sisters[d] in every respect, so that he might be a merciful and faithful high priest in the service of God, to make a sacrifice of atonement for the sins of the people. [18]Because he himself was tested by what he suffered, he is able to help those who are being tested.

Moses a Servant, Christ a Son

3 Therefore, brothers and sisters,[d] holy partners in a heavenly calling, consider that Jesus, the apostle and high priest of our confession, [2]was faithful to the one who appointed him, just as Moses also "was faithful in all[e] God's[f] house." [3]Yet Jesus[g] is worthy of more glory than Moses, just as the builder of a house has more honor than the house itself. [4](For every house is built by someone, but the builder of all things is God.) [5]Now Moses was faithful in all God's[f] house as a servant, to testify to the things that would be spoken later. [6]Christ, however, was faithful over God's[f] house as a son, and we are his house if we hold firm[h] the confidence and the pride that belong to hope.

Warning against Unbelief

7 Therefore, as the Holy Spirit says,

"Today, if you hear his voice,
[8] do not harden your hearts as in the rebellion,
as on the day of testing in the wilderness,
[9] where your ancestors put me to the test,
though they had seen my works [10]for forty years.

[a] Other ancient authorities read *apart from God* [b] Gk *he* [c] Gk *are all of one* [d] Gk *brothers*
[e] Other ancient authorities lack *all* [f] Gk *his* [g] Gk *this one* [h] Other ancient authorities add *to the end*

2:10-18 brothers and sisters: Hebrews notes the specific ways Jesus is related to us, the "brothers and sisters" (2:11) for whom he died.

2:10 make... perfect: A central concept in Hebrews, "make perfect" means "make complete." Access to the presence of God brings "perfection" (6:1; 7:11). The word *pioneer* can also be translated as "author" or "leader." Jesus leads the way to God so that we may follow (see 10:19-22). He is our salvation as well as the promise of our *perfection.*

2:17 high priest: This is a special term used only in Hebrews to describe Christ. Jesus is repeatedly compared to the Jewish high priest who offered sacrifice for the sins of God's people on the Day of Atonement.

3:2 faithful: Jesus' faithfulness is grounded in trust (2:13), as well as loyalty and obedience to God (5:8).

3:2-6 just as Moses: Jesus is compared to Moses. See Bible Concepts note on 1:4.

3:7—4:1 Today, if you hear his voice: These verses make up a "sermon" that focuses on Psalm 95:7-8. The Holy Spirit (3:7) speaks to God's people through Scripture (10:15). In this case, the Spirit tells of the Israelites' trials (and rebellion) in the wilderness, events that convey both judgment and promise to the present time (4:1).

Therefore I was angry with that generation,
and I said, 'They always go astray in their hearts,
and they have not known my ways.'
11 As in my anger I swore,
'They will not enter my rest.' "
12 Take care, brothers and sisters,[a] that none of you may have an evil,
unbelieving heart that turns away from the living God. 13 But exhort
one another every day, as long as it is called "today," so that none of
you may be hardened by the deceitfulness of sin. 14 For we have become partners of Christ, if only we hold our first confidence firm to
the end. 15 As it is said,

"Today, if you hear his voice,
do not harden your hearts as in the rebellion."

16 Now who were they who heard and yet were rebellious? Was it not
all those who left Egypt under the leadership of Moses? 17 But with
whom was he angry forty years? Was it not those who sinned, whose
bodies fell in the wilderness? 18 And to whom did he swear that they
would not enter his rest, if not to those who were disobedient? 19 So
we see that they were unable to enter because of unbelief.

The Rest That God Promised

4 Therefore, while the promise of entering his rest is still open, let
us take care that none of you should seem to have failed to reach
it. 2 For indeed the good news came to us just as to them; but the message they heard did not benefit them, because they were not united by
faith with those who listened.[b] 3 For we who have believed enter that
rest, just as God[c] has said,

"As in my anger I swore,
'They shall not enter my rest,' "

though his works were finished at the foundation of the world. 4 For
in one place it speaks about the seventh day as follows, "And God
rested on the seventh day from all his works." 5 And again in this place
it says, "They shall not enter my rest." 6 Since therefore it remains open
for some to enter it, and those who formerly received the good news
failed to enter because of disobedience, 7 again he sets a certain day—
""today"—saying through David much later, in the words already
quoted,

"Today, if you hear his voice,
do not harden your hearts."

8 For if Joshua had given them rest, God[c] would not speak later about
another day. 9 So then, a sabbath rest still remains for the people of
God; 10 for those who enter God's rest also cease from their labors as
God did from his. 11 Let us therefore make every effort to enter that
rest, so that no one may fall through such disobedience as theirs.

---

[a] Gk *brothers* [b] Other ancient authorities read *it did not meet with faith in those who listened* [c] Gk *he*

3:14 our first confidence: The community of faith is reminded of its initial belief in the promises of God, as a way to encourage it through difficult times.

What is faith? The Lutheran tradition often describes faith as trust in God's promises (see 10:23; 11:1). *Hebrews 4:1-2*

What is the word of God? The word of God is like a "two-edged sword." Some Lutherans understand the two edges to be law and gospel. God's word comes to us both as judgment and life-giving promise. In 4:12-13, judgment is prominent, but the gospel creates life from what has been "killed" (judged) by the law (see 2 Cor 3:6). *Hebrews 4:12-13*

12 Indeed, the word of God is living and active, sharper than any two-edged sword, piercing until it divides soul from spirit, joints from marrow; it is able to judge the thoughts and intentions of the heart. [13]And before him no creature is hidden, but all are naked and laid bare to the eyes of the one to whom we must render an account.

Jesus the Great High Priest

14 Since, then, we have a great high priest who has passed through the heavens, Jesus, the Son of God, let us hold fast to our confession.
[15]For we do not have a high priest who is unable to sympathize with our weaknesses, but we have one who in every respect has been tested[a] as we are, yet without sin. [16]Let us therefore approach the throne of grace with boldness, so that we may receive mercy and find grace to help in time of need.

5 Every high priest chosen from among mortals is put in charge of things pertaining to God on their behalf, to offer gifts and sacrifices for sins. [2]He is able to deal gently with the ignorant and wayward, since he himself is subject to weakness; [3]and because of this he must offer sacrifice for his own sins as well as for those of the people. [4]And one does not presume to take this honor, but takes it only when called by God, just as Aaron was.

5 So also Christ did not glorify himself in becoming a high priest, but was appointed by the one who said to him,

"You are my Son,
today I have begotten you";

[6]as he says also in another place,

"You are a priest forever,
according to the order of Melchizedek."

7 In the days of his flesh, Jesus[b] offered up prayers and supplications, with loud cries and tears, to the one who was able to save him from death, and he was heard because of his reverent submission. [8]Although he was a Son, he learned obedience through what he suffered; [9]and having been made perfect, he became the source of eternal salvation for all who obey him, [10]having been designated by God a high priest according to the order of Melchizedek.

Warning against Falling Away

11 About this[c] we have much to say that is hard to explain, since you have become dull in understanding. [12]For though by this time you ought to be teachers, you need someone to teach you again the basic elements of the oracles of God. You need milk, not solid food; [13]for everyone who lives on milk, being still an infant, is unskilled in the word of righteousness. [14]But solid food is for the mature, for those

[a] Or *tempted* [b] Gk *he* [c] Or *him*

4:15 tested as we are: Here Hebrews lifts up Jesus' humanity (see 2:9-18). He fully shared our weakness and our sufferings (5:7-8), but he was without sin.

4:16 receive mercy and find grace: The word of God both judges us as law (4:12-13) and offers the gift of the gospel, which we experience as mercy and grace.

5:5 high priest: Jesus is compared to a line of high priests that begins with Aaron, the brother of Moses and Miriam.

5:6 Melchizedek: See Hebrews 7, which discusses this Old Testament figure at length.

5:7 with loud cries and tears: This phrase suggests that Jesus prayed psalms of lament (for example, Ps 22:1-2). See Types of Psalms, pp. 849-850.

5:9 eternal salvation: In Hebrews, eternal salvation is a gift given by God's grace, received by us through faith, and experienced as the promises of God.

What is your understanding of salvation? *From* what are we saved? *For* what are we saved?

5:12 oracles of God: This phrase refers to the Holy Scriptures (see Rom 3:2).

5:13 word of righteousness: This probably refers to ethical instruction that provides order and strengthens community.

whose faculties have been trained by practice to distinguish good
from evil.

The Peril of Falling Away

6 Therefore let us go on toward perfection,[a] leaving behind the
basic teaching about Christ, and not laying again the foundation: repentance from dead works and faith toward God, [2]instruc-
tion about baptisms, laying on of hands, resurrection of the dead,
and eternal judgment. [3]And we will do[b] this, if God permits. [4]For it is
impossible to restore again to repentance those who have once been
enlightened, and have tasted the heavenly gift, and have shared in the
Holy Spirit, [5]and have tasted the goodness of the word of God and the
powers of the age to come, [6]and then have fallen away, since on their
own they are crucifying again the Son of God and are holding him up
to contempt. [7]Ground that drinks up the rain falling on it repeatedly,
and that produces a crop useful to those for whom it is cultivated, receives a blessing from God. [8]But if it produces thorns and thistles, it
is worthless and on the verge of being cursed; its end is to be burned
over.

9 Even though we speak in this way, beloved, we are confident of
better things in your case, things that belong to salvation. [10]For God
is not unjust; he will not overlook your work and the love that you
showed for his sake[c] in serving the saints, as you still do. [11]And we
want each one of you to show the same diligence so as to realize the
full assurance of hope to the very end, [12]so that you may not become
sluggish, but imitators of those who through faith and patience inherit the promises.

The Certainty of God's Promise

13 When God made a promise to Abraham, because he had no
one greater by whom to swear, he swore by himself, [14]saying, "I will
surely bless you and multiply you." [15]And thus Abraham,[d] having patiently endured, obtained the promise. [16]Human beings, of course,
swear by someone greater than themselves, and an oath given as confirmation puts an end to all dispute. [17]In the same way, when God
desired to show even more clearly to the heirs of the promise the unchangeable character of his purpose, he guaranteed it by an oath, [18]so
that through two unchangeable things, in which it is impossible that
God would prove false, we who have taken refuge might be strongly
encouraged to seize the hope set before us. [19]We have this hope, a sure
and steadfast anchor of the soul, a hope that enters the inner shrine
behind the curtain, [20]where Jesus, a forerunner on our behalf, has entered, having become a high priest forever according to the order of
Melchizedek.

6:1-8 toward perfection: This is a passage of exhortation or warning, followed by words of encouragement (6:9-12).

6:1 dead works: This term is best understood as works that lead to death (in other words, immoral actions). It may also refer to Jewish regulations concerning worship and sacrifice. In that case, *dead* would mean "ineffective" (see 9:9-10; 14).

6:4-6 impossible to restore again: These verses, as well as 10:26-31 and 12:17, seem to suggest that repentance after baptism is impossible. Since the early church, however, these passages have been understood to prohibit a second baptism for the forgiveness of sin.

6:12 faith and patience: Faith and patience (persistence through adversity) are marks of those who live with the "assurance of hope" (6:11).

6:13-18 Abraham: In Hebrews, as in the writings of the apostle Paul, Abraham is a model of confidence in God's promises. His belief is his "righteousness" before God (11:8-19). See also 11:7, about Noah.

6:18 two unchangeable things: Most interpreters believe these two things are God's promise (6:13) and the oath that confirms it (6:17).

6:19 inner shrine behind the curtain: This is the inner sanctuary of the tabernacle, which the high priest entered once a year to offer sacrifice on the Day of Atonement (see 9:3, 24-26).

---

[a] Or *toward maturity* [b] Other ancient authorities read *let us do* [c] Gk *for his name* [d] Gk *he*

The Priestly Order of Melchizedek

7 This "King Melchizedek of Salem, priest of the Most High God,
met Abraham as he was returning from defeating the kings and
blessed him"; 2 and to him Abraham apportioned "one-tenth of everything." His name, in the first place, means "king of righteousness";
next he is also king of Salem, that is, "king of peace." 3 Without father,
without mother, without genealogy, having neither beginning of days
nor end of life, but resembling the Son of God, he remains a priest
forever.

4 See how great he is! Even[a] Abraham the patriarch gave him
a tenth of the spoils. 5 And those descendants of Levi who receive
the priestly office have a commandment in the law to collect tithes[b]
from the people, that is, from their kindred,[c] though these also are
descended from Abraham. 6 But this man, who does not belong to
their ancestry, collected tithes[b] from Abraham and blessed him who
had received the promises. 7 It is beyond dispute that the inferior is
blessed by the superior. 8 In the one case, tithes are received by those
who are mortal; in the other, by one of whom it is testified that he
lives. 9 One might even say that Levi himself, who receives tithes, paid
tithes through Abraham, 10 for he was still in the loins of his ancestor
when Melchizedek met him.

Another Priest, Like Melchizedek

11 Now if perfection had been attainable through the levitical
priesthood—for the people received the law under this priesthood—
what further need would there have been to speak of another priest
arising according to the order of Melchizedek, rather than one according to the order of Aaron? 12 For when there is a change in the
priesthood, there is necessarily a change in the law as well. 13 Now the
one of whom these things are spoken belonged to another tribe, from
which no one has ever served at the altar. 14 For it is evident that our
Lord was descended from Judah, and in connection with that tribe
Moses said nothing about priests.

15 It is even more obvious when another priest arises, resembling
Melchizedek, 16 one who has become a priest, not through a legal requirement concerning physical descent, but through the power of an
indestructible life. 17 For it is attested of him,

"You are a priest forever,
according to the order of Melchizedek."

18 There is, on the one hand, the abrogation of an earlier commandment because it was weak and ineffectual 19 (for the law made nothing perfect); there is, on the other hand, the introduction of a better
hope, through which we approach God.

[a] Other ancient authorities lack *Even* [b] Or *a tenth* [c] Gk *brothers*

7:1-28 Melchizedek: Here Hebrews looks at the mysterious Old Testament character Melchizedek—based on the two Old Testament texts that mention him (Gen 14; Ps 110:4)—as someone like Christ. Melchizedek is said to be greater than either Abraham (7:2, 4-10) or Levi (7:9). Because the Old Testament does not mention Melchizedek's ancestors or his death, Hebrews concludes that he has "neither beginning of days nor end of life" (7:3).

7:14-17 one who has become a priest: Jesus was of the nonpriestly tribe Judah. His priesthood came through the "order of Melchizedek" (7:11, 17) rather than through family line (7:16).

7:19-22 a better hope: Hebrews compares the old covenant or promise with the new. This continues in Hebrews 8–10. See Bible Concepts note on 1:4.

20 This was confirmed with an oath; for others who became
priests took their office without an oath, 21but this one became a
priest with an oath, because of the one who said to him,
"The Lord has sworn
and will not change his mind,
'You are a priest forever' "—
22accordingly Jesus has also become the guarantee of a better covenant.
23 Furthermore, the former priests were many in number, because they were prevented by death from continuing in office; 24but
he holds his priesthood permanently, because he continues forever.
25Consequently he is able for all time to save[a] those who approach
God through him, since he always lives to make intercession for
them.
26 For it was fitting that we should have such a high priest, holy,
blameless, undefiled, separated from sinners, and exalted above the
heavens. 27Unlike the other[b] high priests, he has no need to offer sacrifices day after day, first for his own sins, and then for those of the
people; this he did once for all when he offered himself. 28For the law
appoints as high priests those who are subject to weakness, but the
word of the oath, which came later than the law, appoints a Son who
has been made perfect forever.

Mediator of a Better Covenant

8 Now the main point in what we are saying is this: we have such
a high priest, one who is seated at the right hand of the throne of
the Majesty in the heavens, 2a minister in the sanctuary and the true
tent[c] that the Lord, and not any mortal, has set up. 3For every high
priest is appointed to offer gifts and sacrifices; hence it is necessary for
this priest also to have something to offer. 4Now if he were on earth,
he would not be a priest at all, since there are priests who offer gifts according to the law. 5They offer worship in a sanctuary that is a sketch
and shadow of the heavenly one; for Moses, when he was about to
erect the tent,[c] was warned, "See that you make everything according
to the pattern that was shown you on the mountain." 6But Jesus[d] has
now obtained a more excellent ministry, and to that degree he is the
mediator of a better covenant, which has been enacted through better
promises. 7For if that first covenant had been faultless, there would
have been no need to look for a second one.
8 God[e] finds fault with them when he says:
"The days are surely coming, says the Lord,
when I will establish a new covenant with the house of Israel
and with the house of Judah;

[a] Or *able to save completely* [b] Gk lacks *other* [c] Or *tabernacle* [d] Gk *he* [e] Gk *He*

7:27 once for all: Jesus' death on the cross was received by God as the sacrifice for sin (see 9:12, 26; 10:2, 10), once and for all. Jesus offered his life as an end of all such sacrifices to God. As a priest, he intercedes for humanity before God (7:25).

8:2 the true tent: This is the heavenly sanctuary. Jesus is the eternal high priest there.

8:3 something to offer: What Christ offers is himself (7:27).

8:5 the pattern: Israel's worship is patterned after the worship in heaven. A similar insight is found in the book of Revelation, where the worship of the church mirrors that in heaven (see Rev 4:8; 5:9-14; 7:9-12 for examples).

8:8-12 a new covenant: Jeremiah 31:31-34 is quoted here. The "new covenant" is made possible by the death of Jesus. The law will be written in the people's hearts, and God will no longer remember their sins.

[9] not like the covenant that I made with their ancestors,
on the day when I took them by the hand to lead them out of the land of Egypt;
for they did not continue in my covenant,
and so I had no concern for them, says the Lord.
[10] This is the covenant that I will make with the house of Israel
after those days, says the Lord:
I will put my laws in their minds,
and write them on their hearts,
and I will be their God,
and they shall be my people.
[11] And they shall not teach one another
or say to each other, 'Know the Lord,'
for they shall all know me,
from the least of them to the greatest.
[12] For I will be merciful toward their iniquities,
and I will remember their sins no more."
[13]In speaking of "a new covenant," he has made the first one obsolete.
And what is obsolete and growing old will soon disappear.

8:13 obsolete: A better translation of the Greek is "made the first old." Hebrews was written at a time when lines between "Christianity" and "Judaism" were much murkier than they would later become. Hebrews does not claim that Gentile (non-Jewish) Christianity has replaced Judaism, but that God is doing something new within a tradition that stretches back to Abraham and beyond.

The Earthly and the Heavenly Sanctuaries

9 Now even the first covenant had regulations for worship and an
earthly sanctuary. [2]For a tent[a] was constructed, the first one, in
which were the lampstand, the table, and the bread of the Presence;[b]
this is called the Holy Place. [3]Behind the second curtain was a tent[a]
called the Holy of Holies. [4]In it stood the golden altar of incense and
the ark of the covenant overlaid on all sides with gold, in which there
were a golden urn holding the manna, and Aaron's rod that budded,
and the tablets of the covenant; [5]above it were the cherubim of glory
overshadowing the mercy seat.[c] Of these things we cannot speak now
in detail.
6 Such preparations having been made, the priests go continually
into the first tent[a] to carry out their ritual duties; [7]but only the high
priest goes into the second, and he but once a year, and not without
taking the blood that he offers for himself and for the sins committed unintentionally by the people. [8]By this the Holy Spirit indicates
that the way into the sanctuary has not yet been disclosed as long as
the first tent[a] is still standing. [9]This is a symbol[d] of the present time,
during which gifts and sacrifices are offered that cannot perfect the
conscience of the worshiper, [10]but deal only with food and drink and
various baptisms, regulations for the body imposed until the time
comes to set things right.

9:1-5 earthly sanctuary: These verses describe the tent or tabernacle constructed as a portable sanctuary (see Exod 25–31, 36–40), not the later temple.

9:6-10 the priests: The activities carried out in the tabernacle by the priests are described here.

9:8 the way into the sanctuary: The death of Jesus pays for sins (see 9:12).

[a] Or *tabernacle* [b] Gk *the presentation of the loaves* [c] Or *the place of atonement* [d] Gk *parable*

11 But when Christ came as a high priest of the good things that
have come,[a] then through the greater and perfect[b] tent[c] (not made
with hands, that is, not of this creation), 12 he entered once for all into
the Holy Place, not with the blood of goats and calves, but with his
own blood, thus obtaining eternal redemption. 13 For if the blood of
goats and bulls, with the sprinkling of the ashes of a heifer, sanctifies those who have been defiled so that their flesh is purified, 14 how
much more will the blood of Christ, who through the eternal Spirit[d]
offered himself without blemish to God, purify our[e] conscience from
dead works to worship the living God!

15 For this reason he is the mediator of a new covenant, so that
those who are called may receive the promised eternal inheritance,
because a death has occurred that redeems them from the transgressions under the first covenant.[f] 16 Where a will[f] is involved, the death
of the one who made it must be established. 17 For a will[f] takes effect
only at death, since it is not in force as long as the one who made it
is alive. 18 Hence not even the first covenant was inaugurated without
blood. 19 For when every commandment had been told to all the people by Moses in accordance with the law, he took the blood of calves
and goats,[g] with water and scarlet wool and hyssop, and sprinkled
both the scroll itself and all the people, 20 saying, "This is the blood of
the covenant that God has ordained for you." 21 And in the same way
he sprinkled with the blood both the tent[c] and all the vessels used in
worship. 22 Indeed, under the law almost everything is purified with
blood, and without the shedding of blood there is no forgiveness
of sins.

Christ's Sacrifice Takes Away Sin

23 Thus it was necessary for the sketches of the heavenly things to
be purified with these rites, but the heavenly things themselves need
better sacrifices than these. 24 For Christ did not enter a sanctuary
made by human hands, a mere copy of the true one, but he entered
into heaven itself, now to appear in the presence of God on our behalf.
25 Nor was it to offer himself again and again, as the high priest enters
the Holy Place year after year with blood that is not his own; 26 for
then he would have had to suffer again and again since the foundation of the world. But as it is, he has appeared once for all at the end
of the age to remove sin by the sacrifice of himself. 27 And just as it is
appointed for mortals to die once, and after that the judgment, 28 so
Christ, having been offered once to bear the sins of many, will appear
a second time, not to deal with sin, but to save those who are eagerly
waiting for him.

---

[a] Other ancient authorities read *good things to come* [b] Gk *more perfect* [c] Or *tabernacle* [d] Other ancient authorities read *Holy Spirit* [e] Other ancient authorities read *your* [f] The Greek word used here means both *covenant* and *will* [g] Other ancient authorities lack *and goats*

9:11-28 But when Christ came: Hebrews compares (see Bible Concepts note on 1:4) the first tabernacle and its priestly activity (9:1-10) with the heavenly sanctuary and the forgiveness (9:22) that comes with Christ's priestly work.

9:14 the blood of Christ: The death of Jesus removes the guilt of sin from a person's "conscience," a term introduced in 9:9 and discussed elsewhere (10:2, 22; 13:18). This inner "spiritual" transformation also affects our relationship to the neighbor (for example, 13:1-9, 12-16).

What difference does it make that through Jesus' death you can have a purified conscience (9:14)?

9:23 the heavenly things themselves: This refers to the consciences of those who follow Christ (9:14).

Christ's Sacrifice Once for All

10 Since the law has only a shadow of the good things to come
and not the true form of these realities, it[a] can never, by the
same sacrifices that are continually offered year after year, make perfect those who approach. 2 Otherwise, would they not have ceased
being offered, since the worshipers, cleansed once for all, would no
longer have any consciousness of sin? 3 But in these sacrifices there is
a reminder of sin year after year. 4 For it is impossible for the blood of
bulls and goats to take away sins. 5 Consequently, when Christ[b] came
into the world, he said,

"Sacrifices and offerings you have not desired,
but a body you have prepared for me;
6 in burnt offerings and sin offerings
you have taken no pleasure.
7 Then I said, 'See, God, I have come to do your will, O God'
(in the scroll of the book[c] it is written of me)."

8 When he said above, "You have neither desired nor taken pleasure in
sacrifices and offerings and burnt offerings and sin offerings" (these
are offered according to the law), 9 then he added, "See, I have come
to do your will." He abolishes the first in order to establish the second.
10 And it is by God's will[d] that we have been sanctified through the
offering of the body of Jesus Christ once for all.

11 And every priest stands day after day at his service, offering
again and again the same sacrifices that can never take away sins. 12 But
when Christ[e] had offered for all time a single sacrifice for sins, "he sat
down at the right hand of God," 13 and since then has been waiting
"until his enemies would be made a footstool for his feet." 14 For by a
single offering he has perfected for all time those who are sanctified.
15 And the Holy Spirit also testifies to us, for after saying,

16 "This is the covenant that I will make with them
after those days, says the Lord:
I will put my laws in their hearts,
and I will write them on their minds,"

17 he also adds,

"I will remember[f] their sins and their lawless deeds no more."

18 Where there is forgiveness of these, there is no longer any offering
for sin.

A Call to Persevere

19 Therefore, my friends,[g] since we have confidence to enter the
sanctuary by the blood of Jesus, 20 by the new and living way that he
opened for us through the curtain (that is, through his flesh), 21 and

10:5-7 he said: For the second time in Hebrews, Jesus speaks by quoting Scripture, in this case Psalm 40:6-8 (see 1:13). Here Jesus speaks against worship that is more concerned with rituals than with doing God's will.

10:5 Christ came into the world: Christ offered his sacrifice in the world, not in the heavenly sanctuary where he now intercedes for those who follow him.

10:12 he sat down at the right hand of God: This is a quote from Psalm 110:1. See also 1:3, 13, and 8:1.

10:15 the Holy Spirit also testifies: Here the Holy Spirit, rather than Jesus (10:5-7), speaks through Scripture (see 3:7; 9:8). This is a paraphrase of Jeremiah 31:31-34 (quoted in full at 8:8-12).

10:20 through his flesh: The curtain (6:19; 9:3) to the heavenly sanctuary (8:2, 5; 9:8, 24; 10:19) is Christ's body.

[a] Other ancient authorities read *they* [b] Gk *he* [c] Meaning of Gk uncertain [d] Gk *by that will*
[e] Gk *this one* [f] Gk *on their minds and I will remember* [g] Gk *Therefore, brothers*

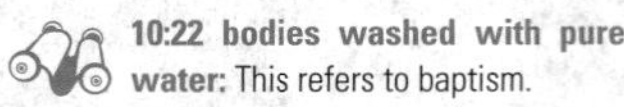

10:22 bodies washed with pure water: This refers to baptism.

since we have a great priest over the house of God, [22]let us approach with a true heart in full assurance of faith, with our hearts sprinkled clean from an evil conscience and our bodies washed with pure water. [23]Let us hold fast to the confession of our hope without wavering, for he who has promised is faithful. [24]And let us consider how to provoke one another to love and good deeds, [25]not neglecting to meet together, as is the habit of some, but encouraging one another, and all the more as you see the Day approaching.

26 For if we willfully persist in sin after having received the knowledge of the truth, there no longer remains a sacrifice for sins, [27]but a fearful prospect of judgment, and a fury of fire that will consume the adversaries. [28]Anyone who has violated the law of Moses dies without mercy "on the testimony of two or three witnesses." [29]How much worse punishment do you think will be deserved by those who have spurned the Son of God, profaned the blood of the covenant by which they were sanctified, and outraged the Spirit of grace? [30]For we know the one who said, "Vengeance is mine, I will repay." And again, "The Lord will judge his people." [31]It is a fearful thing to fall into the hands of the living God.

32 But recall those earlier days when, after you had been enlightened, you endured a hard struggle with sufferings, [33]sometimes being publicly exposed to abuse and persecution, and sometimes being partners with those so treated. [34]For you had compassion for those who were in prison, and you cheerfully accepted the plundering of your possessions, knowing that you yourselves possessed something better and more lasting. [35]Do not, therefore, abandon that confidence of yours; it brings a great reward. [36]For you need endurance, so that when you have done the will of God, you may receive what was promised. [37]For yet

"in a very little while,
the one who is coming will come and will not delay;
38 but my righteous one will live by faith.
My soul takes no pleasure in anyone who shrinks
back."

[39]But we are not among those who shrink back and so are lost, but among those who have faith and so are saved.

10:38 my righteous one will live by faith: This quote from Habakkuk 2:4 is also cited by Paul in Romans 1:17 and Galatians 3:11.

The Meaning of Faith

11 Now faith is the assurance of things hoped for, the conviction of things not seen. [2]Indeed, by faith[a] our ancestors received approval. [3]By faith we understand that the worlds were prepared by the word of God, so that what is seen was made from things that are not visible.[b]

11:1 the assurance...the conviction: Faith is confidence in the promises of God proclaimed in the gospel. These promises are "hoped for...not seen" (see 2:8; 4:1). The opposite of such confidence is fear (2:15).

---

[a] Gk *by this* [b] Or *was not made out of visible things*

The Examples of Abel, Enoch, and Noah

4 By faith Abel offered to God a more acceptable[a] sacrifice than
Cain's. Through this he received approval as righteous, God himself giving approval to his gifts; he died, but through his faith[b] he
still speaks. 5By faith Enoch was taken so that he did not experience
death; and "he was not found, because God had taken him." For it was
attested before he was taken away that "he had pleased God." 6And
without faith it is impossible to please God, for whoever would approach him must believe that he exists and that he rewards those who
seek him. 7By faith Noah, warned by God about events as yet unseen,
respected the warning and built an ark to save his household; by this
he condemned the world and became an heir to the righteousness
that is in accordance with faith.

11:4-38 By faith: This section of Hebrews describes various Old Testament figures as examples of faith, beginning with Abel (son of Adam and Eve) and ending with the prophets.

To sum up what God requires of us, Martin Luther often quoted Hebrews 11:6: "Without faith it is impossible to please God." How do you feel about this? What if faith itself is a gift from God?

The Faith of Abraham

8 By faith Abraham obeyed when he was called to set out for
a place that he was to receive as an inheritance; and he set out, not
knowing where he was going. 9By faith he stayed for a time in the
land he had been promised, as in a foreign land, living in tents, as did
Isaac and Jacob, who were heirs with him of the same promise. 10For
he looked forward to the city that has foundations, whose architect
and builder is God. 11By faith he received power of procreation, even
though he was too old—and Sarah herself was barren—because he
considered him faithful who had promised.[c] 12Therefore from one
person, and this one as good as dead, descendants were born, "as
many as the stars of heaven and as the innumerable grains of sand by
the seashore."

13 All of these died in faith without having received the promises, but from a distance they saw and greeted them. They confessed
that they were strangers and foreigners on the earth, 14for people who
speak in this way make it clear that they are seeking a homeland. 15If
they had been thinking of the land that they had left behind, they
would have had opportunity to return. 16But as it is, they desire a better country, that is, a heavenly one. Therefore God is not ashamed to
be called their God; indeed, he has prepared a city for them.

17 By faith Abraham, when put to the test, offered up Isaac. He
who had received the promises was ready to offer up his only son, 18of
whom he had been told, "It is through Isaac that descendants shall be
named for you." 19He considered the fact that God is able even to raise
someone from the dead—and figuratively speaking, he did receive
him back. 20By faith Isaac invoked blessings for the future on Jacob
and Esau. 21By faith Jacob, when dying, blessed each of the sons of

11:8-19 Abraham: In this list of people who lived by faith, Abraham (see 6:13-15) is given the most detailed description, which ends with him offering up Isaac (11:17-19; see Gen 22:1-18). The description of God as "able even to raise someone from the dead" is similar to the one in Romans 4:17.

---

[a] Gk *greater* [b] Gk *through it* [c] Or *By faith Sarah herself, though barren, received power to conceive, even when she was too old, because she considered him faithful who had promised.*

Joseph, "bowing in worship over the top of his staff." 22 By faith Joseph,
at the end of his life, made mention of the exodus of the Israelites and
gave instructions about his burial.[a]

The Faith of Moses

23 By faith Moses was hidden by his parents for three months after his birth, because they saw that the child was beautiful; and they
were not afraid of the king's edict.[b] 24 By faith Moses, when he was
grown up, refused to be called a son of Pharaoh's daughter, 25 choosing rather to share ill-treatment with the people of God than to enjoy
the fleeting pleasures of sin. 26 He considered abuse suffered for the
Christ[c] to be greater wealth than the treasures of Egypt, for he was
looking ahead to the reward. 27 By faith he left Egypt, unafraid of the
king's anger; for he persevered as though[d] he saw him who is invisible. 28 By faith he kept the Passover and the sprinkling of blood, so
that the destroyer of the firstborn would not touch the firstborn of
Israel.[e]

The Faith of Other Israelite Heroes

29 By faith the people passed through the Red Sea as if it were dry
land, but when the Egyptians attempted to do so they were drowned.
30 By faith the walls of Jericho fell after they had been encircled for
seven days. 31 By faith Rahab the prostitute did not perish with those
who were disobedient,[f] because she had received the spies in peace.

32 And what more should I say? For time would fail me to tell
of Gideon, Barak, Samson, Jephthah, of David and Samuel and the
prophets— 33 who through faith conquered kingdoms, administered
justice, obtained promises, shut the mouths of lions, 34 quenched raging fire, escaped the edge of the sword, won strength out of weakness, became mighty in war, put foreign armies to flight. 35 Women
received their dead by resurrection. Others were tortured, refusing
to accept release, in order to obtain a better resurrection. 36 Others
suffered mocking and flogging, and even chains and imprisonment.
37 They were stoned to death, they were sawn in two,[g] they were killed
by the sword; they went about in skins of sheep and goats, destitute,
persecuted, tormented— 38 of whom the world was not worthy. They
wandered in deserts and mountains, and in caves and holes in the
ground.

39 Yet all these, though they were commended for their faith, did
not receive what was promised, 40 since God had provided something
better so that they would not, apart from us, be made perfect.

11:39-40 made perfect: In this conclusion to the list of the faithful, Hebrews draws the reader into the story. The heroes of Israel are "made perfect" (brought into the presence of God) together with "us" by means of the sacrifice of the great high priest, Jesus.

---

[a] Gk *his bones* [b] Other ancient authorities add *By faith Moses, when he was grown up, killed the Egyptian, because he observed the humiliation of his people* (Gk *brothers*) [c] Or *the Messiah* [d] Or *because* [e] Gk *would not touch them* [f] Or *unbelieving* [g] Other ancient authorities add *they were tempted*

The Example of Jesus

12 Therefore, since we are surrounded by so great a cloud of witnesses, let us also lay aside every weight and the sin that clings
so closely,[a] and let us run with perseverance the race that is set before
us, 2 looking to Jesus the pioneer and perfecter of our faith, who for
the sake of[b] the joy that was set before him endured the cross, dis-
regarding its shame, and has taken his seat at the right hand of the
throne of God.

3 Consider him who endured such hostility against himself from
sinners,[c] so that you may not grow weary or lose heart. 4 In your struggle against sin you have not yet resisted to the point of shedding your
blood. 5 And you have forgotten the exhortation that addresses you
as children—

"My child, do not regard lightly the discipline of the Lord,
or lose heart when you are punished by him;
6 for the Lord disciplines those whom he loves,
and chastises every child whom he accepts."

7 Endure trials for the sake of discipline. God is treating you as children; for what child is there whom a parent does not discipline? 8 If
you do not have that discipline in which all children share, then you
are illegitimate and not his children. 9 Moreover, we had human parents to discipline us, and we respected them. Should we not be even
more willing to be subject to the Father of spirits and live? 10 For they
disciplined us for a short time as seemed best to them, but he disciplines us for our good, in order that we may share his holiness. 11 Now,
discipline always seems painful rather than pleasant at the time, but
later it yields the peaceful fruit of righteousness to those who have
been trained by it.

12 Therefore lift your drooping hands and strengthen your weak
knees, 13 and make straight paths for your feet, so that what is lame
may not be put out of joint, but rather be healed.

Warnings against Rejecting God's Grace

14 Pursue peace with everyone, and the holiness without which
no one will see the Lord. 15 See to it that no one fails to obtain the
grace of God; that no root of bitterness springs up and causes trouble,
and through it many become defiled. 16 See to it that no one becomes
like Esau, an immoral and godless person, who sold his birthright for
a single meal. 17 You know that later, when he wanted to inherit the
blessing, he was rejected, for he found no chance to repent,[d] even
though he sought the blessing[e] with tears.

18 You have not come to something[f] that can be touched, a

[a] Other ancient authorities read *sin that easily distracts* [b] Or *who instead of* [c] Other ancient authorities read *such hostility from sinners against themselves* [d] Or *no chance to change his father's mind* [e] Gk *it*
[f] Other ancient authorities read *a mountain*

12:1-13 run with perseverance the race: These verses use the image of an athletic contest to describe those who follow Jesus, the pioneer of their salvation (12:2). The "cloud of witnesses," described in Hebrews 11, is like a group of spectators observing a race. Painful struggle (12:4) and exhaustion (12:12) are part of the discipline (education or training in character) of those adopted as God's children (12:8).

12:14-29 that no one fails to obtain the grace of God: Instructions in discipleship and warnings against rejecting God's grace are interrupted by the consolation that comes in knowing that one has been brought to the "city of the living God" (12:22-24). The Word gathers the people of God into an "assembly" (12:23) that celebrates the new covenant God has established with humanity through the cross. God has promised to be present to that assembly, experienced in the worship life of the church, by means of the sacramental presence of Christ Jesus, crucified and risen.

blazing fire, and darkness, and gloom, and a tempest, [19]and the sound
of a trumpet, and a voice whose words made the hearers beg that not
another word be spoken to them. [20](For they could not endure the
order that was given, "If even an animal touches the mountain, it shall
be stoned to death." [21]Indeed, so terrifying was the sight that Moses
said, "I tremble with fear.") [22]But you have come to Mount Zion and
to the city of the living God, the heavenly Jerusalem, and to innumerable angels in festal gathering, [23]and to the assembly[a] of the firstborn
who are enrolled in heaven, and to God the judge of all, and to the
spirits of the righteous made perfect, [24]and to Jesus, the mediator of
a new covenant, and to the sprinkled blood that speaks a better word
than the blood of Abel.

25 See that you do not refuse the one who is speaking; for if
they did not escape when they refused the one who warned them on
earth, how much less will we escape if we reject the one who warns
from heaven! [26]At that time his voice shook the earth; but now he
has promised, "Yet once more I will shake not only the earth but also
the heaven." [27]This phrase, "Yet once more," indicates the removal
of what is shaken—that is, created things—so that what cannot be
shaken may remain. [28]Therefore, since we are receiving a kingdom
that cannot be shaken, let us give thanks, by which we offer to God
an acceptable worship with reverence and awe; [29]for indeed our God
is a consuming fire.

Service Well-Pleasing to God

13 Let mutual love continue. [2]Do not neglect to show hospitality to strangers, for by doing that some have entertained
angels without knowing it. [3]Remember those who are in prison, as
though you were in prison with them; those who are being tortured,
as though you yourselves were being tortured.[b] [4]Let marriage be held
in honor by all, and let the marriage bed be kept undefiled; for God
will judge fornicators and adulterers. [5]Keep your lives free from the
love of money, and be content with what you have; for he has said, "I
will never leave you or forsake you." [6]So we can say with confidence,

"The Lord is my helper;
I will not be afraid.
What can anyone do to me?"

7 Remember your leaders, those who spoke the word of God to
you; consider the outcome of their way of life, and imitate their faith.
[8]Jesus Christ is the same yesterday and today and forever. [9]Do not
be carried away by all kinds of strange teachings; for it is well for the
heart to be strengthened by grace, not by regulations about food,[c]
which have not benefited those who observe them. [10]We have an altar

12:28 acceptable worship: The most acceptable worship (or service) is thankful recognition of the blessings we have received from a gracious God. This insight leads into practical advice for discipleship in Hebrews 13. True worship of God results in active service to our neighbors.

13:1-9 Let mutual love continue: These verses give final practical instructions to those who follow Christ. In the midst of these instructions, Hebrews inserts a reminder of God's promises (13:5-6).

13:8 Jesus Christ is the same: Although the leaders of Christian community (13:7) may change or die, and teachings contrary to the gospel may arise (13:9), the basis of the enduring faith of the church is always the same: the life, death, and resurrection of Jesus Christ.

---

[a] Or *angels, and to the festal gathering* [23]*and assembly* [b] Gk *were in the body* [c] Gk *not by foods*

from which those who officiate in the tent[a] have no right to eat. 11For
the bodies of those animals whose blood is brought into the sanctuary by the high priest as a sacrifice for sin are burned outside the
camp. 12Therefore Jesus also suffered outside the city gate in order to
sanctify the people by his own blood. 13Let us then go to him outside
the camp and bear the abuse he endured. 14For here we have no lasting city, but we are looking for the city that is to come. 15Through him,
then, let us continually offer a sacrifice of praise to God, that is, the
fruit of lips that confess his name. 16Do not neglect to do good and to
share what you have, for such sacrifices are pleasing to God.

17 Obey your leaders and submit to them, for they are keeping watch over your souls and will give an account. Let them do this with joy and not with sighing—for that would be harmful to you.

18 Pray for us; we are sure that we have a clear conscience, desiring to act honorably in all things. 19I urge you all the more to do this,
so that I may be restored to you very soon.

Benediction

20 Now may the God of peace, who brought back from the dead
our Lord Jesus, the great shepherd of the sheep, by the blood of the
eternal covenant, 21make you complete in everything good so that
you may do his will, working among us[b] that which is pleasing in his
sight, through Jesus Christ, to whom be the glory forever and ever.
Amen.

Final Exhortation and Greetings

22 I appeal to you, brothers and sisters,[c] bear with my word of exhortation, for I have written to you briefly. 23I want you to know that
our brother Timothy has been set free; and if he comes in time, he will
be with me when I see you. 24Greet all your leaders and all the saints.
Those from Italy send you greetings. 25Grace be with all of you.[d]

---

[a] Or *tabernacle* [b] Other ancient authorities read *you* [c] Gk *brothers* [d] Other ancient authorities add *Amen*

What is the theology of the cross? Martin Luther pointed out that God often works in the most unlikely ways, showing strength in things that are seen as weak and showing glory in things seen as shameful. In Jesus, God is not revealed in the holy sanctuary but outside the city walls on a cross. This shameful way of dying becomes holy because of Christ's suffering and obedience. This sacrifice takes away sins once and for all. *Hebrews 13:10-16*

13:22 word of exhortation: Hebrews preaches both law and gospel. On one hand, it lays out the demands of discipleship, reminds us of the danger of "drifting away," and reveals the depth of human sinfulness. On the other hand, it describes the comfort that comes with following Christ, encourages us to "stay on course," and shows us the depth of God's compassion and mercy.

James 2:18

JAMES

Background File

The letter of James contains few details about authorship, dating, and recipients. Tradition identifies the author as James, the brother of Jesus and leader of the Jerusalem church until his martyrdom just prior to the Jewish war of 66–70 C.E. (see Gal 1:19; Acts 15:13-21). Still, many scholars see this as the work of a later author who was dedicating the letter to a hero of the faith, a practice common in the ancient world. They would place the writing as late as 130–140 C.E. The letter's address to "the twelve tribes in the Dispersion" (1:1) is also unclear. It probably refers to the early Christian community in its relation to the people of Israel.

What's the Story?

As even Martin Luther noted, it is difficult to outline this brief letter's 108 verses. Its opening verses (1:2-27) introduce themes which are then revisited in the rest of the letter: joy, wisdom, creation, word, first fruits, faith, blessing, growth, endurance. These themes give powerful encouragement for responsible Christian action amid the complex realities of daily life. Christians are urged to conduct their lives according to the wisdom "from above," from God who is the giver of "every perfect gift" (1:17). Empowered by God's "implanted word" (1:21), Christians are called to be not only "hearers" but "doers" (1:22), whose faith shows forth in specific acts of love that sustain the neighbor and community. The remainder of the letter illustrates aspects of this practical "wisdom from above" (3:17): showing mercy rather than partiality (2:1-13); using speech to bless rather than harm the neighbor (3:1-12); being humble before God and preventing conflicts and disputes (4:1-12); living by God's mercy today rather than worrying about tomorrow (4:13-17); working for justice for the poor and needy (5:1-6); and, finally, praying constantly and confidently for healing, forgiveness, and life in community (5:7-20).

What's the Message?

Martin Luther once characterized the letter of James as an "epistle of straw." As a result, Lutherans have not always appreciated the message of James. What was the basis for Luther's comment? He believed that Jesus Christ and his cross and resurrection were the heart of the Scriptures. For Luther, then, the two brief references to Jesus Christ (1:1; 2:1) in James and its lack of any reference to the death and resurrection didn't offer enough of what was centrally Christian, when James is compared with other New Testament books.

Many other Christian readers, however, have drawn comfort, strength, and power from the letter of James. William E. Hulme tells how the letter of James "spoke" to him when the tragic death of his oldest daughter immobilized him spiritually and emotionally: "James does not present the *techniques* for effective change. Rather, he affirms the *power* for change that is ours through the faith of our Lord Jesus Christ" (*The Fire of Little Jim: Power for Growth from the Letter of James* [Abingdon, 1976], pp. 9-13). That "implanted word" (1:21) of God's gift of wisdom affirms human freedom and the power to use God's gifts to change those things that can and should be changed.

Salutation

1 James, a servant[a] of God and of the Lord Jesus Christ,
To the twelve tribes in the Dispersion:
Greetings.

Faith and Wisdom

2 My brothers and sisters,[b] whenever you face trials of any kind,
consider it nothing but joy, 3because you know that the testing of your
faith produces endurance; 4and let endurance have its full effect, so
that you may be mature and complete, lacking in nothing.
5 If any of you is lacking in wisdom, ask God, who gives to all
generously and ungrudgingly, and it will be given you. 6But ask in
faith, never doubting, for the one who doubts is like a wave of the
sea, driven and tossed by the wind; 7, 8for the doubter, being double-
minded and unstable in every way, must not expect to receive anything from the Lord.

Poverty and Riches

9 Let the believer[c] who is lowly boast in being raised up, 10and the
rich in being brought low, because the rich will disappear like a flower
in the field. 11For the sun rises with its scorching heat and withers the
field; its flower falls, and its beauty perishes. It is the same way with
the rich; in the midst of a busy life, they will wither away.

Trial and Temptation

12 Blessed is anyone who endures temptation. Such a one has
stood the test and will receive the crown of life that the Lord[d] has
promised to those who love him. 13No one, when tempted, should
say, "I am being tempted by God"; for God cannot be tempted by
evil and he himself tempts no one. 14But one is tempted by one's own
desire, being lured and enticed by it; 15then, when that desire has

---

[a] Gk *slave* [b] Gk *brothers* [c] Gk *brother* [d] Gk *he;* other ancient authorities read *God*

1:1-8, 12 consider it nothing but joy: Some of this letter's appeal and power is due to the skillful writing and use of words. In these verses, key words are repeated to weave together the main themes: *greetings* and *joy* (1:1-2; these two words are the same in the original Greek); *endurance* and *endurance* (1:3-4); *lacking* and *lacking* (1:4-5); *ask* and *ask* (1:5-6); *doubts* and *doubter* (1:6-7). *Endures* and *temptation* (1:12) link to the same two words, *testing* and *endurance*, in 1:3-4 (*testing* and *temptation* translate the same original Greek word).

1:5-6, 17 lacking in wisdom... every perfect gift, is from above: In James, grace mainly takes shape in wisdom. Wisdom is the creative gift of God. Through this gift, God blesses people to live and grow in responsible maturity. God gives this "perfect" gift "generously and ungrudgingly" (1:17; 1:5) to those who ask in sincere trust. King Solomon, for example, prayed for wisdom (see 1 Kgs 3–4, especially 3:5-14). Psalm 111:10 and Proverbs 9:10 say that the "fear of the LORD is the beginning of wisdom."

Wisdom reminds us of God's gifts. What God-given gifts enable you to live daily in a complex world—to care for yourself, your family, your neighbor, and the world?

1:5-6 ask God...ask in faith: This letter begins and ends on the theme of the power of prayer (see 5:13-20). Those who lack wisdom only need to ask for it in prayer. God gives generously to those who ask in faithful expectation.

Think of times when someone prayed for you or you prayed for someone else. How was prayer a generous gift from God to you?

1:18-21 implanted word: With the gift of wisdom, God's word becomes "implanted" in us so that we become a kind of "first fruits" of creation. The first fruits of a harvest were offered to God to give thanks for God's rich blessings. They also held the promise of a rich harvest still to come.

God creates us anew, and God equips and encourages us to grow and produce fruit. What kind of "fruit" might come from God's word planted within you?

1:22-24 be doers of the word, and not merely hearers: James calls for "hearing" and "doing" to be in harmony. Jesus compares someone who hears his words and does them to a wise person who builds a house on a rock (see Matt 7:24–27). The "implanted word" (1:21) grows and bears fruit in both "hearing" and "doing."

1:25-27; 2:8-13 those who look into the perfect law: The "perfect law" (1:25), "law of liberty" (1:25; 2:12), and the "royal law" (2:8) of Scripture refer to Jesus' teaching in the Gospels that God's law is summarized in the command to "love your neighbor as yourself" (2:8). The freedom to love rests upon harmony between "hearing" and "doing" God's word, which is demonstrated in the "pure" religion of acts of mercy for those who are poor and needy (1:27; 2:12-13).

How are faith and works related? James says "faith without works is also dead" (2:26). We are new creations in Christ, and God is at work in us to bring our "will" and our "work" in line with the model of Jesus' own life (see Phil 2:12-13). Faith and works are both signs of a confident and unwavering trust in the power of God's wisdom in us—not only to weather the storms of life, but to grow in faith. *James 2:14-26*

conceived, it gives birth to sin, and that sin, when it is fully grown,
gives birth to death. 16 Do not be deceived, my beloved.[a]

17 Every generous act of giving, with every perfect gift, is from
above, coming down from the Father of lights, with whom there is no
variation or shadow due to change.[b] 18 In fulfillment of his own purpose he gave us birth by the word of truth, so that we would become
a kind of first fruits of his creatures.

Hearing and Doing the Word

19 You must understand this, my beloved:[a] let everyone be quick
to listen, slow to speak, slow to anger; 20 for your anger does not produce God's righteousness. 21 Therefore rid yourselves of all sordidness
and rank growth of wickedness, and welcome with meekness the implanted word that has the power to save your souls.

22 But be doers of the word, and not merely hearers who deceive
themselves. 23 For if any are hearers of the word and not doers, they
are like those who look at themselves[c] in a mirror; 24 for they look at
themselves and, on going away, immediately forget what they were
like. 25 But those who look into the perfect law, the law of liberty, and
persevere, being not hearers who forget but doers who act—they will
be blessed in their doing.

26 If any think they are religious, and do not bridle their tongues
but deceive their hearts, their religion is worthless. 27 Religion that is
pure and undefiled before God, the Father, is this: to care for orphans
and widows in their distress, and to keep oneself unstained by the
world.

Warning against Partiality

2 My brothers and sisters,[d] do you with your acts of favoritism
really believe in our glorious Lord Jesus Christ?[e] 2 For if a person with gold rings and in fine clothes comes into your assembly, and
if a poor person in dirty clothes also comes in, 3 and if you take notice of the one wearing the fine clothes and say, "Have a seat here,
please," while to the one who is poor you say, "Stand there," or, "Sit
at my feet,"[f] 4 have you not made distinctions among yourselves, and
become judges with evil thoughts? 5 Listen, my beloved brothers and
sisters.[g] Has not God chosen the poor in the world to be rich in faith
and to be heirs of the kingdom that he has promised to those who
love him? 6 But you have dishonored the poor. Is it not the rich who
oppress you? Is it not they who drag you into court? 7 Is it not they
who blaspheme the excellent name that was invoked over you?

8 You do well if you really fulfill the royal law according to the

[a] Gk *my beloved brothers* [b] Other ancient authorities read *variation due to a shadow of turning* [c] Gk *at the face of his birth* [d] Gk *My brothers* [e] Or *hold the faith of our glorious Lord Jesus Christ without acts of favoritism* [f] Gk *Sit under my footstool* [g] Gk *brothers*

scripture, "You shall love your neighbor as yourself." [9]But if you show
partiality, you commit sin and are convicted by the law as transgressors. [10]For whoever keeps the whole law but fails in one point has become accountable for all of it. [11]For the one who said, "You shall not
commit adultery," also said, "You shall not murder." Now if you do not
commit adultery but if you murder, you have become a transgressor
of the law. [12]So speak and so act as those who are to be judged by the
law of liberty. [13]For judgment will be without mercy to anyone who
has shown no mercy; mercy triumphs over judgment.

Faith without Works Is Dead

14 What good is it, my brothers and sisters,[a] if you say you have
faith but do not have works? Can faith save you? [15]If a brother or sister
is naked and lacks daily food, [16]and one of you says to them, "Go in
peace; keep warm and eat your fill," and yet you do not supply their
bodily needs, what is the good of that? [17]So faith by itself, if it has no
works, is dead.

18 But someone will say, "You have faith and I have works." Show
me your faith apart from your works, and I by my works will show
you my faith. [19]You believe that God is one; you do well. Even the
demons believe—and shudder. [20]Do you want to be shown, you
senseless person, that faith apart from works is barren? [21]Was not our
ancestor Abraham justified by works when he offered his son Isaac
on the altar? [22]You see that faith was active along with his works, and
faith was brought to completion by the works. [23]Thus the scripture
was fulfilled that says, "Abraham believed God, and it was reckoned
to him as righteousness," and he was called the friend of God. [24]You
see that a person is justified by works and not by faith alone. [25]Like-
wise, was not Rahab the prostitute also justified by works when she
welcomed the messengers and sent them out by another road? [26]For
just as the body without the spirit is dead, so faith without works is
also dead.

Taming the Tongue

3 Not many of you should become teachers, my brothers and
sisters,[a] for you know that we who teach will be judged with
greater strictness. [2]For all of us make many mistakes. Anyone who
makes no mistakes in speaking is perfect, able to keep the whole body
in check with a bridle. [3]If we put bits into the mouths of horses to
make them obey us, we guide their whole bodies. [4]Or look at ships:
though they are so large that it takes strong winds to drive them, yet
they are guided by a very small rudder wherever the will of the pilot
directs. [5]So also the tongue is a small member, yet it boasts of great
exploits.

3:1—5:6 the wisdom from above: Chapters 3, 4, and 5 give practical illustrations of life lived according to God's gift of reason. We use the gift of speech to bless others, not to harm them (3:1-12). With humility, we prevent conflicts and disputes by not always seeking our own way (4:1-12). We live life one day at a time, knowing that each day offers a new opportunity to do what we know is right (4:13-17). We share God's concern for justice and care of those who are poor and needy (5:1-6).

---

[a] Gk *brothers*

How great a forest is set ablaze by a small fire! [6]And the tongue is a fire. The tongue is placed among our members as a world of iniquity; it stains the whole body, sets on fire the cycle of nature,[a] and is itself set on fire by hell.[b] [7]For every species of beast and bird, of reptile and sea creature, can be tamed and has been tamed by the human species, [8]but no one can tame the tongue—a restless evil, full of deadly poison. [9]With it we bless the Lord and Father, and with it we curse those who are made in the likeness of God. [10]From the same mouth come blessing and cursing. My brothers and sisters,[c] this ought not to be so. [11]Does a spring pour forth from the same opening both fresh and brackish water? [12]Can a fig tree, my brothers and sisters,[d] yield olives, or a grapevine figs? No more can salt water yield fresh.

Two Kinds of Wisdom

13 Who is wise and understanding among you? Show by your good life that your works are done with gentleness born of wisdom. [14]But if you have bitter envy and selfish ambition in your hearts, do not be boastful and false to the truth. [15]Such wisdom does not come down from above, but is earthly, unspiritual, devilish. [16]For where there is envy and selfish ambition, there will also be disorder and wickedness of every kind. [17]But the wisdom from above is first pure, then peaceable, gentle, willing to yield, full of mercy and good fruits, without a trace of partiality or hypocrisy. [18]And a harvest of righteousness is sown in peace for[e] those who make peace.

Friendship with the World

4 Those conflicts and disputes among you, where do they come from? Do they not come from your cravings that are at war within you? [2]You want something and do not have it; so you commit murder. And you covet[f] something and cannot obtain it; so you engage in disputes and conflicts. You do not have, because you do not ask. [3]You ask and do not receive, because you ask wrongly, in order to spend what you get on your pleasures. [4]Adulterers! Do you not know that friendship with the world is enmity with God? Therefore whoever wishes to be a friend of the world becomes an enemy of God. [5]Or do you suppose that it is for nothing that the scripture says, "God[g] yearns jealously for the spirit that he has made to dwell in us"? [6]But he gives all the more grace; therefore it says,

"God opposes the proud,
but gives grace to the humble."

[7]Submit yourselves therefore to God. Resist the devil, and he will flee from you. [8]Draw near to God, and he will draw near to you. Cleanse

---

[a] Or *wheel of birth* [b] Gk *Gehenna* [c] Gk *My brothers* [d] Gk *my brothers* [e] Or *by* [f] Or *you murder and you covet* [g] Gk *He*

your hands, you sinners, and purify your hearts, you double-minded.
[9]Lament and mourn and weep. Let your laughter be turned into
mourning and your joy into dejection. [10]Humble yourselves before
the Lord, and he will exalt you.

Warning against Judging Another

11 Do not speak evil against one another, brothers and sisters.[a]
Whoever speaks evil against another or judges another, speaks evil
against the law and judges the law; but if you judge the law, you are
not a doer of the law but a judge. [12]There is one lawgiver and judge
who is able to save and to destroy. So who, then, are you to judge your
neighbor?

Boasting about Tomorrow

13 Come now, you who say, "Today or tomorrow we will go to
such and such a town and spend a year there, doing business and making money." [14]Yet you do not even know what tomorrow will bring.
What is your life? For you are a mist that appears for a little while and
then vanishes. [15]Instead you ought to say, "If the Lord wishes, we will
live and do this or that." [16]As it is, you boast in your arrogance; all such
boasting is evil. [17]Anyone, then, who knows the right thing to do and
fails to do it, commits sin.

Warning to Rich Oppressors

5 Come now, you rich people, weep and wail for the miseries that
are coming to you. [2]Your riches have rotted, and your clothes
are moth-eaten. [3]Your gold and silver have rusted, and their rust will
be evidence against you, and it will eat your flesh like fire. You have
laid up treasure[b] for the last days. [4]Listen! The wages of the laborers
who mowed your fields, which you kept back by fraud, cry out, and
the cries of the harvesters have reached the ears of the Lord of hosts.
[5]You have lived on the earth in luxury and in pleasure; you have fat-
tened your hearts in a day of slaughter. [6]You have condemned and
murdered the righteous one, who does not resist you.

Patience in Suffering

7 Be patient, therefore, beloved,[a] until the coming of the Lord.
The farmer waits for the precious crop from the earth, being patient
with it until it receives the early and the late rains. [8]You also must be
patient. Strengthen your hearts, for the coming of the Lord is near.[c]
[9]Beloved,[d] do not grumble against one another, so that you may not
be judged. See, the Judge is standing at the doors! [10]As an example of
suffering and patience, beloved,[a] take the prophets who spoke in the

5:7-20 Be patient...pray...powerful: The final verses of the letter draw together and summarize the letter's themes: patience, prayer, and power. Be patient in waiting for the Lord's return, because God has a purpose and shows enduring mercy and compassion (5:11). Pray for endurance in times of suffering, for the healing of those who are sick, and for mutual confession and forgiveness. Tell about the power of prayer to bring forgiveness and restore the Christian community (5:16).

[a] Gk *brothers* [b] Or *will eat your flesh, since you have stored up fire* [c] Or *is at hand* [d] Gk *Brothers*

name of the Lord. 11 Indeed we call blessed those who showed endurance. You have heard of the endurance of Job, and you have seen the
purpose of the Lord, how the Lord is compassionate and merciful.

12 Above all, my beloved,[a] do not swear, either by heaven or by
earth or by any other oath, but let your "Yes" be yes and your "No" be
no, so that you may not fall under condemnation.

The Prayer of Faith

13 Are any among you suffering? They should pray. Are any cheerful? They should sing songs of praise. 14 Are any among you sick? They
should call for the elders of the church and have them pray over them,
anointing them with oil in the name of the Lord. 15 The prayer of faith
will save the sick, and the Lord will raise them up; and anyone who
has committed sins will be forgiven. 16 Therefore confess your sins to
one another, and pray for one another, so that you may be healed.
The prayer of the righteous is powerful and effective. 17 Elijah was a
human being like us, and he prayed fervently that it might not rain,
and for three years and six months it did not rain on the earth. 18 Then
he prayed again, and the heaven gave rain and the earth yielded its
harvest.

19 My brothers and sisters,[b] if anyone among you wanders from
the truth and is brought back by another, 20 you should know that
whoever brings back a sinner from wandering will save the sinner's[c]
soul from death and will cover a multitude of sins.

---

[a] Gk *brothers* [b] Gk *My brothers* [c] Gk *his*

1 Peter 2:9

1 PETER

Background File

This letter carries the name of Peter, a disciple of Jesus who became a leader in the early church. Many scholars believe the letter was written some years after Peter's death, by someone who wrote in his name. This was an accepted practice in ancient times. The references to Peter (see 1:1, 5:12-13) would have been understood by the original readers as literary devices used in this type of writing. Like 2 Peter, this letter was probably written for a more general audience of churches, rather than for one specific church. It brings Peter's perspective to bear on issues and concerns that he did not have the opportunity to address during his lifetime.

What's the Story?

First Peter reflects the rapid expansion of the early church into Asia Minor. The writer explores issues of community, mission, and suffering—issues these young faith communities may have been facing. The letter may be outlined in this way:

- Greetings (1:1-2)
- A new birth (1:3-12)
- Living as God's people (1:13—3:22)
- Suffering because of faith (4:1—5:11)
- Final greetings (5:12-14)

What's the Message?

Jesus' suffering, death, and resurrection provide new life and living hope to believers. We are called to live as chosen people, God's servants, and stewards of grace. We are also called to the community of faith, which is a spiritual house of living stones, a holy priesthood, and God's own people. God brings this community "out of darkness" into "marvelous light" to carry out a mission—to tell others about God's "mighty acts" (2:4-10).

Jesus faced temptation, rejection, suffering, and death. It should be no surprise, then, if believers and the community suffer or are persecuted and rejected because of faith. We should not lose hope when we suffer for faith, because all is not lost. God who chooses us, saves us, and gives us new life will strengthen and support us as we live as God's chosen people and even suffer because of faith. The mission will keep moving forward.

1:1 Pontus, Galatia, Cappadocia, Asia, and Bithynia: These provinces were located in Asia Minor (see Map 15, p. 2112).

1:3 new birth: The gift of new life, made possible through Christ, has changed the identity of this community of believers.

1:6 various trials: Adopting a new identity means enduring the animosity of people who consider such a change to be contrary to God's will.

1:8-9 believe: The new birth and new identity are evident in the way the community lives.

Salutation

1 Peter, an apostle of Jesus Christ,
To the exiles of the Dispersion in Pontus, Galatia, Cappadocia,
Asia, and Bithynia, 2 who have been chosen and destined by God the
Father and sanctified by the Spirit to be obedient to Jesus Christ and
to be sprinkled with his blood:
May grace and peace be yours in abundance.

A Living Hope

3 Blessed be the God and Father of our Lord Jesus Christ! By his
great mercy he has given us a new birth into a living hope through the
resurrection of Jesus Christ from the dead, 4 and into an inheritance
that is imperishable, undefiled, and unfading, kept in heaven for you,
5 who are being protected by the power of God through faith for a salvation ready to be revealed in the last time. 6 In this you rejoice,[a] even
if now for a little while you have had to suffer various trials, 7 so that
the genuineness of your faith—being more precious than gold that,
though perishable, is tested by fire—may be found to result in praise
and glory and honor when Jesus Christ is revealed. 8 Although you
have not seen[b] him, you love him; and even though you do not see
him now, you believe in him and rejoice with an indescribable and
glorious joy, 9 for you are receiving the outcome of your faith, the salvation of your souls.
10 Concerning this salvation, the prophets who prophesied of
the grace that was to be yours made careful search and inquiry, 11 inquiring about the person or time that the Spirit of Christ within them
indicated when it testified in advance to the sufferings destined for
Christ and the subsequent glory. 12 It was revealed to them that they
were serving not themselves but you, in regard to the things that have
now been announced to you through those who brought you good
news by the Holy Spirit sent from heaven—things into which angels
long to look!

A Call to Holy Living

13 Therefore prepare your minds for action;[c] discipline yourselves; set all your hope on the grace that Jesus Christ will bring you

---

[a] Or *Rejoice in this* [b] Other ancient authorities read *known* [c] Gk *gird up the loins of your mind*

when he is revealed. 14 Like obedient children, do not be conformed
to the desires that you formerly had in ignorance. 15 Instead, as he who
called you is holy, be holy yourselves in all your conduct; 16 for it is
written, "You shall be holy, for I am holy."

17 If you invoke as Father the one who judges all people impar-
tially according to their deeds, live in reverent fear during the time
of your exile. 18 You know that you were ransomed from the futile
ways inherited from your ancestors, not with perishable things like
silver or gold, 19 but with the precious blood of Christ, like that of a
lamb without defect or blemish. 20 He was destined before the foundation of the world, but was revealed at the end of the ages for your
sake. 21 Through him you have come to trust in God, who raised him
from the dead and gave him glory, so that your faith and hope are set
on God.

22 Now that you have purified your souls by your obedience to
the truth[a] so that you have genuine mutual love, love one another
deeply[b] from the heart.[c] 23 You have been born anew, not of perishable
but of imperishable seed, through the living and enduring word of
God.[d] 24 For

"All flesh is like grass
and all its glory like the flower of grass.
The grass withers,
and the flower falls,
25 but the word of the Lord endures forever."

That word is the good news that was announced to you.

The Living Stone and a Chosen People

2 Rid yourselves, therefore, of all malice, and all guile, insincerity,
envy, and all slander. 2 Like newborn infants, long for the pure,
spiritual milk, so that by it you may grow into salvation— 3 if indeed
you have tasted that the Lord is good.

4 Come to him, a living stone, though rejected by mortals yet
chosen and precious in God's sight, and 5 like living stones, let yourselves be built[e] into a spiritual house, to be a holy priesthood, to offer spiritual sacrifices acceptable to God through Jesus Christ. 6 For it
stands in scripture:

"See, I am laying in Zion a stone,
a cornerstone chosen and precious;
and whoever believes in him[f] will not be put to shame."

7 To you then who believe, he is precious; but for those who do not
believe,

"The stone that the builders rejected
has become the very head of the corner,"

1:15-16 holy: What belongs solely to God is holy. The temple is holy, not because it is such a special building, but because it is reserved entirely for worship of God. A community of people is holy because the people are God's people.

1:21 trust: The saving gift that Christ brings is trust in God. This trust defines the faith of God's people.

2:5 a holy priesthood: This is the core of the letter. There is no turning back. There may still be doubts, but the focus is on the future. These "newborn" believers (see 2:2) are to become a community with a distinct identity and mission.

---

[a] Other ancient authorities add *through the Spirit* [b] Or *constantly* [c] Other ancient authorities read *a pure heart* [d] Or *through the word of the living and enduring God* [e] Or *you yourselves are being built* [f] Or *it*

[8]and

"A stone that makes them stumble,
and a rock that makes them fall."

They stumble because they disobey the word, as they were destined to do.

9 But you are a chosen race, a royal priesthood, a holy nation, God's own people,[a] in order that you may proclaim the mighty acts of him who called you out of darkness into his marvelous light.

10 Once you were not a people,
but now you are God's people;
once you had not received mercy,
but now you have received mercy.

Live as Servants of God

11 Beloved, I urge you as aliens and exiles to abstain from the desires of the flesh that wage war against the soul. [12]Conduct yourselves honorably among the Gentiles, so that, though they malign you as evildoers, they may see your honorable deeds and glorify God when he comes to judge.[b]

13 For the Lord's sake accept the authority of every human institution,[c] whether of the emperor as supreme, [14]or of governors, as sent by him to punish those who do wrong and to praise those who do right. [15]For it is God's will that by doing right you should silence the ignorance of the foolish. [16]As servants[d] of God, live as free people, yet do not use your freedom as a pretext for evil. [17]Honor everyone. Love the family of believers.[e] Fear God. Honor the emperor.

The Example of Christ's Suffering

18 Slaves, accept the authority of your masters with all deference, not only those who are kind and gentle but also those who are harsh. [19]For it is a credit to you if, being aware of God, you endure pain while suffering unjustly. [20]If you endure when you are beaten for doing wrong, what credit is that? But if you endure when you do right and suffer for it, you have God's approval. [21]For to this you have been called, because Christ also suffered for you, leaving you an example, so that you should follow in his steps.

22 "He committed no sin,
and no deceit was found in his mouth."

[23]When he was abused, he did not return abuse; when he suffered, he did not threaten; but he entrusted himself to the one who judges justly. [24]He himself bore our sins in his body on the cross,[f] so that, free from sins, we might live for righteousness; by his wounds[g] you have

---

[a] Gk *a people for his possession* [b] Gk *God on the day of visitation* [c] Or *every institution ordained for human beings* [d] Gk *slaves* [e] Gk *Love the brotherhood* [f] Or *carried up our sins in his body to the tree* [g] Gk *bruise*

2:9-10 proclaim the mighty acts: The new community is called to tell others about God's mighty acts.

What is the priesthood of all believers? This is a key concept for Martin Luther, who insists that all Christians are priests or God's messengers. Proclaiming God's mighty acts is not a job reserved for only a few people. God calls all believers—no matter what their vocation or standing—to share the gospel and serve their neighbors so that others come to know Christ. *1 Peter 2:9*

2:21 follow in his steps: As one of the stones in the house built on Christ (2:5), the community shares in all Christ's experiences, including unjust suffering, and becomes the present expression of Christ himself.

How important is the community of believers or church in a life of faith? The writer of 1 Peter believes that communities of believers are stones in the house of faith built on Christ. His identity, purpose, and belonging came from being a member of a faith community. Martin Luther emphasized that same point in his explanation of the Third Article of the Apostles' Creed: "The Holy Spirit has called me through the gospel, enlightened me with his gifts, made me holy and kept me in the true faith, just as he calls, gathers, enlightens, and makes holy the whole Christian church on earth and keeps it with Jesus Christ in the one common, true faith. Daily in this Christian church the Holy Spirit abundantly forgives all sins—mine and those of all believers. On the last day the Holy Spirit will raise me and all the dead and will give to me and all believers in Christ eternal life" (*SC*:16-17). *1 Peter 2:21*

been healed. [25]For you were going astray like sheep, but now you have
returned to the shepherd and guardian of your souls.

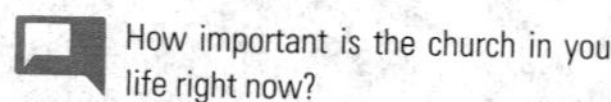
How important is the church in your life right now?

Wives and Husbands

3 Wives, in the same way, accept the authority of your husbands,
so that, even if some of them do not obey the word, they may
be won over without a word by their wives' conduct, [2]when they see
the purity and reverence of your lives. [3]Do not adorn yourselves outwardly by braiding your hair, and by wearing gold ornaments or fine
clothing; [4]rather, let your adornment be the inner self with the lasting
beauty of a gentle and quiet spirit, which is very precious in God's
sight. [5]It was in this way long ago that the holy women who hoped
in God used to adorn themselves by accepting the authority of their
husbands. [6]Thus Sarah obeyed Abraham and called him lord. You
have become her daughters as long as you do what is good and never
let fears alarm you.

7 Husbands, in the same way, show consideration for your wives
in your life together, paying honor to the woman as the weaker sex,[a]
since they too are also heirs of the gracious gift of life—so that nothing may hinder your prayers.

3:1-7 in your life together: Within the community, marriage and human sexuality reflect the overriding call to be God's people and proclaim the gospel (see note on 2:5).

Suffering for Doing Right

8 Finally, all of you, have unity of spirit, sympathy, love for one
another, a tender heart, and a humble mind. [9]Do not repay evil for
evil or abuse for abuse; but, on the contrary, repay with a blessing. It is
for this that you were called—that you might inherit a blessing. [10]For

"Those who desire life
  and desire to see good days,
let them keep their tongues from evil
  and their lips from speaking deceit;
11 let them turn away from evil and do good;
  let them seek peace and pursue it.
12 For the eyes of the Lord are on the righteous,
  and his ears are open to their prayer.
But the face of the Lord is against those who do evil."

13 Now who will harm you if you are eager to do what is good?
[14]But even if you do suffer for doing what is right, you are blessed.
Do not fear what they fear,[b] and do not be intimidated, [15]but in your
hearts sanctify Christ as Lord. Always be ready to make your defense to anyone who demands from you an accounting for the hope
that is in you; [16]yet do it with gentleness and reverence.[c] Keep your
conscience clear, so that, when you are maligned, those who abuse
you for your good conduct in Christ may be put to shame. [17]For it

---

[a] Gk *vessel* [b] Gk *their fear* [c] Or *respect*

is better to suffer for doing good, if suffering should be God's will,
than to suffer for doing evil. 18 For Christ also suffered[a] for sins once
for all, the righteous for the unrighteous, in order to bring you[b] to
God. He was put to death in the flesh, but made alive in the spirit,
19 in which also he went and made a proclamation to the spirits in
prison, 20 who in former times did not obey, when God waited patiently in the days of Noah, during the building of the ark, in which a
few, that is, eight persons, were saved through water. 21 And baptism,
which this prefigured, now saves you—not as a removal of dirt from
the body, but as an appeal to God for[c] a good conscience, through
the resurrection of Jesus Christ, 22 who has gone into heaven and is
at the right hand of God, with angels, authorities, and powers made
subject to him.

Good Stewards of God's Grace

4:1-2 by the will of God: Our actions bear witness to Christ, whose suffering frees us from sin.

4 Since therefore Christ suffered in the flesh,[d] arm yourselves
also with the same intention (for whoever has suffered in the
flesh has finished with sin), 2 so as to live for the rest of your earthly
life[e] no longer by human desires but by the will of God. 3 You have already spent enough time in doing what the Gentiles like to do, living
in licentiousness, passions, drunkenness, revels, carousing, and lawless idolatry. 4 They are surprised that you no longer join them in the
same excesses of dissipation, and so they blaspheme.[f] 5 But they will
have to give an accounting to him who stands ready to judge the living
and the dead. 6 For this is the reason the gospel was proclaimed even
to the dead, so that, though they had been judged in the flesh as everyone is judged, they might live in the spirit as God does.

7 The end of all things is near;[g] therefore be serious and discipline
yourselves for the sake of your prayers. 8 Above all, maintain constant
love for one another, for love covers a multitude of sins. 9 Be hospitable to one another without complaining. 10 Like good stewards of
the manifold grace of God, serve one another with whatever gift each
of you has received. 11 Whoever speaks must do so as one speaking
the very words of God; whoever serves must do so with the strength
that God supplies, so that God may be glorified in all things through
Jesus Christ. To him belong the glory and the power forever and ever.
Amen.

Suffering as a Christian

4:12-19 do not be surprised: Hardships are not unusual. You may suffer because of your faith. When you suffer, trust yourself and your community to God, who created you and remains faithful.

12 Beloved, do not be surprised at the fiery ordeal that is taking
place among you to test you, as though something strange were happening to you. 13 But rejoice insofar as you are sharing Christ's suffer-

---

[a] Other ancient authorities read *died* [b] Other ancient authorities read *us* [c] Or *a pledge to God from*
[d] Other ancient authorities add *for us;* others, *for you* [e] Gk *rest of the time in the flesh* [f] Or *they malign you* [g] Or *is at hand*

ings, so that you may also be glad and shout for joy when his glory is
revealed. [14]If you are reviled for the name of Christ, you are blessed,
because the spirit of glory,[a] which is the Spirit of God, is resting on
you.[b] [15]But let none of you suffer as a murderer, a thief, a criminal,
or even as a mischief maker. [16]Yet if any of you suffers as a Christian,
do not consider it a disgrace, but glorify God because you bear this
name. [17]For the time has come for judgment to begin with the household of God; if it begins with us, what will be the end for those who
do not obey the gospel of God? [18]And

"If it is hard for the righteous to be saved,
what will become of the ungodly and the sinners?"

[19]Therefore, let those suffering in accordance with God's will entrust
themselves to a faithful Creator, while continuing to do good.

Tending the Flock of God

5 Now as an elder myself and a witness of the sufferings of Christ,
as well as one who shares in the glory to be revealed, I exhort
the elders among you [2]to tend the flock of God that is in your charge,
exercising the oversight,[c] not under compulsion but willingly, as God
would have you do it[d]—not for sordid gain but eagerly. [3]Do not lord
it over those in your charge, but be examples to the flock. [4]And when
the chief shepherd appears, you will win the crown of glory that never
fades away. [5]In the same way, you who are younger must accept the
authority of the elders.[e] And all of you must clothe yourselves with
humility in your dealings with one another, for

"God opposes the proud,
but gives grace to the humble."

6 Humble yourselves therefore under the mighty hand of God, so
that he may exalt you in due time. [7]Cast all your anxiety on him, because he cares for you. [8]Discipline yourselves, keep alert.[f] Like a roaring lion your adversary the devil prowls around, looking for someone
to devour. [9]Resist him, steadfast in your faith, for you know that your
brothers and sisters[g] in all the world are undergoing the same kinds
of suffering. [10]And after you have suffered for a little while, the God of
all grace, who has called you to his eternal glory in Christ, will himself
restore, support, strengthen, and establish you. [11]To him be the power
forever and ever. Amen.

Final Greetings and Benediction

12 Through Silvanus, whom I consider a faithful brother, I have
written this short letter to encourage you and to testify that this is the

[a] Other ancient authorities add *and of power* [b] Other ancient authorities add *On their part he is blasphemed, but on your part he is glorified* [c] Other ancient authorities lack *exercising the oversight* [d] Other ancient authorities lack *as God would have you do it* [e] Or *of those who are older* [f] Or *be vigilant* [g] Gk *your brotherhood*

5:3-11 be examples: The temptation to grow powerful and "lord it over" others is a constant issue for any community. A community that suffers because of its faith appears to be unsuccessful, but it might be successful in its mission to proclaim the gospel. God has never-ending glory and power.

What do Lutherans say about suffering because of faith? Being a Christian and being a community of believers is not always easy. Like Martin Luther, Dietrich Bonhoeffer (a German pastor who was imprisoned and executed for his opposition to the Nazi regime during World War II) observed that the devil continues to hound every last shred of the church, the body of Christ, in hopes of destroying it. Jesus faced temptations, rejections, and suffering. As part of the body of Christ, we will do the same, but God is with us to support us and strengthen us. *1 Peter 5:3-11*

Many Christians from the early church on have faced persecution, suffering, and even death for their beliefs. What does this say about faith?

5:12-14 Greet one another: Silvanus (see 2 Cor 1:19; 1 Thess 1:1; 2 Thess 1:1) may be the same person as Silas (see Acts 15:22-41; 16:9—17:15). "Babylon" could refer to Rome, which destroyed the temple in Jerusalem in 70 C.E., just as Babylon destroyed an earlier temple in 587 B.C.E. Mark (or John, called Mark) traveled with Paul and Barnabas (Acts 12:12, 25; 13:13; 15:36-39).

true grace of God. Stand fast in it. 13Your sister church[a] in Babylon,
chosen together with you, sends you greetings; and so does my son
Mark. 14Greet one another with a kiss of love.

Peace to all of you who are in Christ.[b]

---

[a] Gk *She who is* [b] Other ancient authorities add *Amen*

2 Peter 1:19

2 PETER

Background File

This letter carries the name of Simeon (or Simon, see NRSV footnote *a*) Peter, a disciple of Jesus who became a leader in the early church. Many scholars believe the letter was written some years after Peter's death, by someone who wrote in his name. This was an accepted practice in ancient times. The references to Peter (see 1:1, 16-18; 3:1) would have been understood by the original readers as literary devices used in this type of writing. Like 1 Peter, this letter was probably written for a more general audience of churches, rather than for one specific church. It brings Peter's perspective to bear on issues and concerns that he did not have the opportunity to address during his lifetime.

What's the Story?

The writer of the letter believes he will die soon. He writes this letter to remind readers of things they already know, but are important for them to remember after his death (1:12-15). They will need to remember God's promises, support their faith, live out their call, faithfully interpret scripture, stay away from false prophets and false teachers, and prepare for the day of the Lord.

The letter may be outlined like this:

Greeting (1:1-2)
God's promises and call (1:3-21)
False prophets and false teachers (2:1-22)
The day of the Lord (3:1-17)
Blessing (3:18)

What's the Message?

This letter contains what the writer believed to be his final words. As a result, the words have a sense of urgency and importance for believers, then and now. Those who are faithful will face difficult challenges. There is corruption in the world. People impose their own interpretation on Scripture. False prophets and false teachers lure people with their promises, but their words are lies. Many people do not believe that the Lord is coming again. In spite of all this, the writer says, hold onto God's "precious and very great promises" (1:4). Grow in faith by practicing goodness, knowledge, self-control, endurance, godliness, mutual affection, and love (1:5-8). Treasure God's word revealed in Scripture (1:19-21; 3:2). Wait with faith and hope, because Christ is certainly coming again.

1:3-8 very great promises: God promises us future victory over the corruption in the world. Practicing goodness, knowledge, and self-control reminds us of God's promises and makes our lives rich and meaningful. Growing as a believer produces love.

1:8 Lord: *Kyrios*, the original Greek word, means "master." Using this title means that Jesus Christ has power and authority over everything.

1:9-11 confirm your call: The way we live our lives should reflect the fact that the Lord Jesus Christ cleanses us of our sins.

What is the relationship between salvation and good works? Being saved and entering God's heavenly kingdom does not depend on what we do but on what God has done for us. Because of God's grace in Christ, we receive forgiveness and God's heavenly kingdom. What we do and how we live are ways to give thanks for these incredible gifts, tell the good news about Jesus, and joyfully serve God and others. *2 Peter 1:3-11*

Salutation

1 Simeon[a] Peter, a servant[b] and apostle of Jesus Christ,
To those who have received a faith as precious as ours through the
righteousness of our God and Savior Jesus Christ:[c]
2 May grace and peace be yours in abundance in the knowledge
of God and of Jesus our Lord.

The Christian's Call and Election

3 His divine power has given us everything needed for life and
godliness, through the knowledge of him who called us by[d] his own
glory and goodness. 4 Thus he has given us, through these things, his
precious and very great promises, so that through them you may escape from the corruption that is in the world because of lust, and
may become participants of the divine nature. 5 For this very reason,
you must make every effort to support your faith with goodness, and
goodness with knowledge, 6 and knowledge with self-control, and
self-control with endurance, and endurance with godliness, 7 and godliness with mutual[e] affection, and mutual[e] affection with love. 8 For if
these things are yours and are increasing among you, they keep you
from being ineffective and unfruitful in the knowledge of our Lord
Jesus Christ. 9 For anyone who lacks these things is short-sighted and
blind, and is forgetful of the cleansing of past sins. 10 Therefore, brothers and sisters,[f] be all the more eager to confirm your call and election,
for if you do this, you will never stumble. 11 For in this way, entry into
the eternal kingdom of our Lord and Savior Jesus Christ will be richly
provided for you.
12 Therefore I intend to keep on reminding you of these things,
though you know them already and are established in the truth that
has come to you. 13 I think it right, as long as I am in this body,[g] to refresh your memory, 14 since I know that my death[h] will come soon, as
indeed our Lord Jesus Christ has made clear to me. 15 And I will make
every effort so that after my departure you may be able at any time to
recall these things.

---

[a] Other ancient authorities read *Simon* [b] Gk *slave* [c] Or *of our God and the Savior Jesus Christ* [d] Other ancient authorities read *through* [e] Gk *brotherly* [f] Gk *brothers* [g] Gk *tent* [h] Gk *the putting off of my tent*

Eyewitnesses of Christ's Glory

16 For we did not follow cleverly devised myths when we made
known to you the power and coming of our Lord Jesus Christ, but we
had been eyewitnesses of his majesty. 17 For he received honor and
glory from God the Father when that voice was conveyed to him by
the Majestic Glory, saying, "This is my Son, my Beloved,[a] with whom
I am well pleased." 18 We ourselves heard this voice come from heaven,
while we were with him on the holy mountain.
19 So we have the prophetic message more fully confirmed. You
will do well to be attentive to this as to a lamp shining in a dark place,
until the day dawns and the morning star rises in your hearts. 20 First
of all you must understand this, that no prophecy of scripture is a matter of one's own interpretation, 21 because no prophecy ever came by
human will, but men and women moved by the Holy Spirit spoke
from God.[b]

False Prophets and Their Punishment

2 But false prophets also arose among the people, just as there will
be false teachers among you, who will secretly bring in destructive opinions. They will even deny the Master who bought them—
bringing swift destruction on themselves. 2 Even so, many will follow
their licentious ways, and because of these teachers[c] the way of truth
will be maligned. 3 And in their greed they will exploit you with deceptive words. Their condemnation, pronounced against them long
ago, has not been idle, and their destruction is not asleep.
4 For if God did not spare the angels when they sinned, but cast
them into hell[d] and committed them to chains[e] of deepest darkness to
be kept until the judgment; 5 and if he did not spare the ancient world,
even though he saved Noah, a herald of righteousness, with seven
others, when he brought a flood on a world of the ungodly; 6 and if by
turning the cities of Sodom and Gomorrah to ashes he condemned
them to extinction[f] and made them an example of what is coming
to the ungodly;[g] 7 and if he rescued Lot, a righteous man greatly distressed by the licentiousness of the lawless 8 (for that righteous man,
living among them day after day, was tormented in his righteous soul
by their lawless deeds that he saw and heard), 9 then the Lord knows
how to rescue the godly from trial, and to keep the unrighteous under
punishment until the day of judgment 10 —especially those who indulge their flesh in depraved lust, and who despise authority.
Bold and willful, they are not afraid to slander the glorious ones,[h]

1:16-18 eyewitnesses: This passage refers to the transfiguration, when the fullness of God's glory was revealed in Jesus. Peter, James, and John were on the mountaintop with Jesus when this happened (see Matt 17:1-8; Mark 9:2-8,;Luke 9:28-36).

1:19 the day dawns…the morning star: A morning star appears in the sky just before or at sunrise. Jesus, the "morning star," will bring in a new day when he returns (see also Rev 22:16).

1:20-21 spoke from God: The prophets delivered God's messages, not their own. To interpret Scripture, we must, like the prophets, be led by the Holy Spirit.

How can we recognize a Spirit-led interpretation of Scripture from one that is not? How can the church encourage Spirit-led interpretation?

2:1-22 false prophets: The writer warns readers about false prophets and false teachings and compares the gospel of Jesus Christ to the myths and rituals organized around Greek and Roman gods. The myths are seen as works of fanciful imagination rather than truths about God and human society. The people in the worst situation are former believers who have changed their minds and returned to those myths.

How should believers in Christ regard the faith and religions of others?

2:1 Master: This refers to Jesus Christ (see note on 1:8).

2:5 Noah: God rescued Noah and his family from the flood (see Gen 6:9—9:17).

2:6-8 Sodom and Gomorrah: God rescued Lot, Abraham's nephew, when the cities of Sodom and Gomorrah were destroyed (see Gen 19:15-29).

---

[a] Other ancient authorities read *my beloved Son* [b] Other ancient authorities read *but moved by the Holy Spirit saints of God spoke* [c] Gk *because of them* [d] Gk *Tartaros* [e] Other ancient authorities read *pits* [f] Other ancient authorities lack *to extinction* [g] Other ancient authorities read *an example to those who were to be ungodly* [h] Or *angels;* Gk *glories*

2:15-16 **Balaam:** The king of Moab sent Balaam to curse the Israelites. God told Balaam not to go, but Balaam went anyway, and his donkey questioned him (see Num 22:1-35).

11 whereas angels, though greater in might and power, do not bring
against them a slanderous judgment from the Lord.[a] 12 These people,
however, are like irrational animals, mere creatures of instinct, born
to be caught and killed. They slander what they do not understand,
and when those creatures are destroyed,[b] they also will be destroyed,
13 suffering[c] the penalty for doing wrong. They count it a pleasure to
revel in the daytime. They are blots and blemishes, reveling in their
dissipation[d] while they feast with you. 14 They have eyes full of adultery, insatiable for sin. They entice unsteady souls. They have hearts
trained in greed. Accursed children! 15 They have left the straight road
and have gone astray, following the road of Balaam son of Bosor,[e]
who loved the wages of doing wrong, 16 but was rebuked for his own
transgression; a speechless donkey spoke with a human voice and restrained the prophet's madness.

17 These are waterless springs and mists driven by a storm; for
them the deepest darkness has been reserved. 18 For they speak bombastic nonsense, and with licentious desires of the flesh they entice
people who have just[f] escaped from those who live in error. 19 They
promise them freedom, but they themselves are slaves of corruption;
for people are slaves to whatever masters them. 20 For if, after they
have escaped the defilements of the world through the knowledge of
our Lord and Savior Jesus Christ, they are again entangled in them
and overpowered, the last state has become worse for them than the
first. 21 For it would have been better for them never to have known
the way of righteousness than, after knowing it, to turn back from the
holy commandment that was passed on to them. 22 It has happened to
them according to the true proverb,

"The dog turns back to its own vomit,"

and,

"The sow is washed only to wallow in the mud."

The Promise of the Lord's Coming

3 This is now, beloved, the second letter I am writing to you; in
them I am trying to arouse your sincere intention by reminding
you 2 that you should remember the words spoken in the past by the
holy prophets, and the commandment of the Lord and Savior spoken
through your apostles. 3 First of all you must understand this, that in
the last days scoffers will come, scoffing and indulging their own lusts
4 and saying, "Where is the promise of his coming? For ever since our
ancestors died,[g] all things continue as they were from the beginning
of creation!" 5 They deliberately ignore this fact, that by the word of
God heavens existed long ago and an earth was formed out of water

---

[a] Other ancient authorities read *before the Lord;* others lack the phrase [b] Gk *in their destruction* [c] Other ancient authorities read *receiving* [d] Other ancient authorities read *love-feasts* [e] Other ancient authorities read *Beor* [f] Other ancient authorities read *actually* [g] Gk *our fathers fell asleep*

and by means of water, [6]through which the world of that time was
deluged with water and perished. [7]But by the same word the present
heavens and earth have been reserved for fire, being kept until the day
of judgment and destruction of the godless.

8 But do not ignore this one fact, beloved, that with the Lord one
day is like a thousand years, and a thousand years are like one day.
[9]The Lord is not slow about his promise, as some think of slowness,
but is patient with you,[a] not wanting any to perish, but all to come to
repentance. [10]But the day of the Lord will come like a thief, and then
the heavens will pass away with a loud noise, and the elements will
be dissolved with fire, and the earth and everything that is done on it
will be disclosed.[b]

11 Since all these things are to be dissolved in this way, what sort
of persons ought you to be in leading lives of holiness and godliness,
[12]waiting for and hastening[c] the coming of the day of God, because of
which the heavens will be set ablaze and dissolved, and the elements
will melt with fire? [13]But, in accordance with his promise, we wait for
new heavens and a new earth, where righteousness is at home.

Final Exhortation and Doxology

14 Therefore, beloved, while you are waiting for these things,
strive to be found by him at peace, without spot or blemish; [15]and regard the patience of our Lord as salvation. So also our beloved brother
Paul wrote to you according to the wisdom given him, [16]speaking of
this as he does in all his letters. There are some things in them hard to
understand, which the ignorant and unstable twist to their own destruction, as they do the other scriptures. [17]You therefore, beloved,
since you are forewarned, beware that you are not carried away with
the error of the lawless and lose your own stability. [18]But grow in the
grace and knowledge of our Lord and Savior Jesus Christ. To him be
the glory both now and to the day of eternity. Amen.[d]

3:7-10 the day of the Lord: The Lord will return, and the present world will be judged to be godless. On the other hand, God is deliberately slow in bringing destruction, so that all have a chance to repent. The cosmos is not eternal, but will come to a definite end.

3:15-16 our beloved brother Paul: The apostle Paul wrote several letters that were circulated among churches and became part of Scripture. The writer warns that some people have "twisted" Paul's teachings.

---

[a] Other ancient authorities read *on your account* [b] Other ancient authorities read *will be burned up*
[c] Or *earnestly desiring* [d] Other ancient authorities lack *Amen*

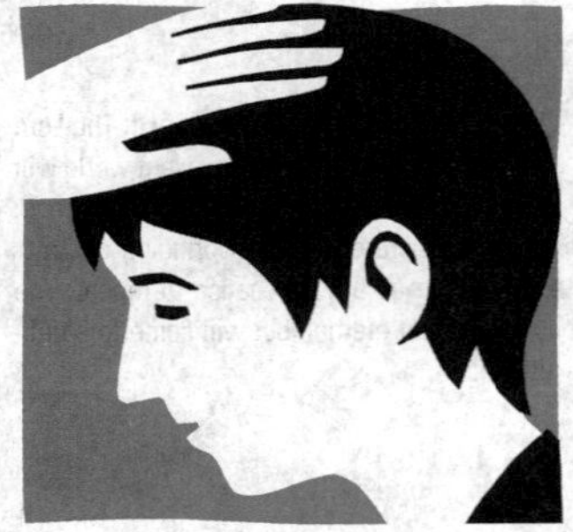
1 John 1:9

1 JOHN

Background File

Martin Luther, in his lectures on 1 John, said, "This is an outstanding epistle, . . . so beautifully and gently does it picture Christ to us" (*LW* 30:219). Although ancient tradition associated the book with the apostle John, no one can say for certain who wrote this book. Similarities with the other two letters of John lead some scholars to credit this book to a writer known as "the elder" (2 John 1, 3 John 1). According to some ancient traditions, the book was written in Ephesus.

What's the Story?

Most scholars agree that 1, 2, and 3 John and the Gospel of John share several themes, key phrases, and a common theological foundation. Many conclude that the three letters were generated by members of a faith community whose beliefs were deeply rooted in their understanding of the Gospel of John.

First John can be outlined as follows:

The word of life (1:1-7)
Sin and Christ's work of atonement (1:8—2:2)
Love one another (2:3—3:24)
God is love (4:1-21)
Love God (5:1-12)
Sin's power and God's power (5:13-21)

First John is the longest of the three letters of John, yet it is not really a letter. It reads more like testimony arguing for the truth of what the writer believes. This truth is nothing new. It has existed from the beginning of time and is a matter of "what we have heard, what we have seen" (1:1).

What's the Message?

The writer provides testimony for three main points. First, Jesus offered himself as the "atoning sacrifice" (2:2; 4:10) for human sin. In ancient practice this kind of sacrifice usually involved the shed blood of an animal. This blood cleansed the people and restored the damaged relationship between the people and their god. Jesus, the Lamb of God, shed his blood and gave up his life. His blood cleanses us from sin and restores us to new life with God.

Second, the writer argues against the teaching of some people at the time that Jesus was completely spiritual in nature and only seemed to be mortal. For the writer, anyone who denies the true nature of Jesus is an "antichrist" (2:18, 22; 4:3). Readers are urged instead to trust that Jesus was truly born in the flesh (4:2). That is the only way Jesus' sacrifice could accomplish its godly purpose.

Third, the writer insists that the words and actions of believers must go together (1:5-7). Loving the Lord extends naturally and necessarily into loving one another. When we hate another person, we are still in darkness, but God's light shines in those who love others (2:3-11).

The Word of Life

1 We declare to you what was from the beginning, what we have
heard, what we have seen with our eyes, what we have looked at
and touched with our hands, concerning the word of life— 2this life
was revealed, and we have seen it and testify to it, and declare to you
the eternal life that was with the Father and was revealed to us— 3we
declare to you what we have seen and heard so that you also may have
fellowship with us; and truly our fellowship is with the Father and
with his Son Jesus Christ. 4We are writing these things so that our[a] joy
may be complete.

God Is Light

5 This is the message we have heard from him and proclaim to
you, that God is light and in him there is no darkness at all. 6If we say
that we have fellowship with him while we are walking in darkness,
we lie and do not do what is true; 7but if we walk in the light as he
himself is in the light, we have fellowship with one another, and the
blood of Jesus his Son cleanses us from all sin. 8If we say that we have
no sin, we deceive ourselves, and the truth is not in us. 9If we confess
our sins, he who is faithful and just will forgive us our sins and cleanse
us from all unrighteousness. 10If we say that we have not sinned, we
make him a liar, and his word is not in us.

Christ Our Advocate

2 My little children, I am writing these things to you so that you
may not sin. But if anyone does sin, we have an advocate with
the Father, Jesus Christ the righteous; 2and he is the atoning sacrifice
for our sins, and not for ours only but also for the sins of the whole
world.

---

[a] Other ancient authorities read *your*

1:1-3 the word of life: This section shares key words with John 1:1-18: *beginning, see, word, testify, life, made known/revealed, Father, Son.*

1:3 Father... Son: Note that the Father and Son are mentioned here, but not the Holy Spirit. First John was probably written before Christians had developed a clear understanding of the Holy Trinity—God as Father, Son, and Holy Spirit.

1:4 joy: Joy cannot be contained but grows as it is shared. In the original Greek, the word means a final and complete fulfillment (see John 3:29; 15:11; and 16:24).

Tell about a time in your life when you experienced joy. How are faith and joy related?

1:5-7 light... darkness: The contrast between light and darkness is a common theme in the Bible. People can choose either to walk down dark alleys of their selfish interests or along pathways lit by the presence of God (see Isa 9:2; Luke 1:78-79; John 1:4-9, 8:12).

If Jesus' blood cleanses us from all sin (1 John 1:7), why do we need to confess our sins? We all fall short and continue to need forgiveness. Martin Luther says that we are in "bondage" or captivity to sin and we cannot break free from sin's hold on us. In confession we admit that we are still sin's captives and still need a Savior to set us free. *1 John 1:8-10*

2:3 by this we may be sure that we know: This is a phrase used throughout 1 John (3:19; 3:24; 4:2; 4:13; 5:2).

How can we be sure of something? What would you like to know about God?

2:4-11 a new commandment: It is easy to love someone who is lovable, but Jesus commands his followers to selflessly love even those who are difficult to love (see John 13:34-35).

Who is Jesus calling you to love with compassion, kindness, and grace?

3 Now by this we may be sure that we know him, if we obey his commandments. 4 Whoever says, "I have come to know him," but does not obey his commandments, is a liar, and in such a person the truth does not exist; 5 but whoever obeys his word, truly in this person the love of God has reached perfection. By this we may be sure that we are in him: 6 whoever says, "I abide in him," ought to walk just as he walked.

A New Commandment

7 Beloved, I am writing you no new commandment, but an old commandment that you have had from the beginning; the old commandment is the word that you have heard. 8 Yet I am writing you a new commandment that is true in him and in you, because[a] the darkness is passing away and the true light is already shining. 9 Whoever says, "I am in the light," while hating a brother or sister,[b] is still in the darkness. 10 Whoever loves a brother or sister[c] lives in the light, and in such a person[d] there is no cause for stumbling. 11 But whoever hates another believer[e] is in the darkness, walks in the darkness, and does not know the way to go, because the darkness has brought on blindness.

12 I am writing to you, little children,
because your sins are forgiven on account of his name.
13 I am writing to you, fathers,
because you know him who is from the beginning.
I am writing to you, young people,
because you have conquered the evil one.
14 I write to you, children,
because you know the Father.
I write to you, fathers,
because you know him who is from the beginning.
I write to you, young people,
because you are strong
and the word of God abides in you,
and you have overcome the evil one.

15 Do not love the world or the things in the world. The love of the Father is not in those who love the world; 16 for all that is in the world—the desire of the flesh, the desire of the eyes, the pride in riches—comes not from the Father but from the world. 17 And the world and its desire[f] are passing away, but those who do the will of God live forever.

Warning against Antichrists

18 Children, it is the last hour! As you have heard that antichrist is coming, so now many antichrists have come. From this we know

2:12-14 I am writing to you: The author interrupts his discussion of the new commandment to speak to three groups: little children, fathers, and young people (see 2:21).

2:15-17 passing away...live forever: Human desires and material things do not last, but those who do God's will have life everlasting.

2:18-20 the last hour: Many early Christians believed they were living in a time just before God would bring about Christ's reign on earth. The writer of 1 John says that the presence and activity of many "antichrists" signals these final days (see the following note on antichrists).

2:18-20 antichrists: This refers to all who undermine the understanding of Jesus as Christ or Messiah. The term does not appear often in the Bible. In the New Testament, it occurs only in 1 and 2 John (1 John 2:18, 22; 4:3; 2 John 7).

[a] Or *that* [b] Gk *hating a brother* [c] Gk *loves a brother* [d] Or *in it* [e] Gk *hates a brother* [f] Or *the desire for it*

that it is the last hour. 19 They went out from us, but they did not belong to us; for if they had belonged to us, they would have remained
with us. But by going out they made it plain that none of them belongs to us. 20 But you have been anointed by the Holy One, and all of
you have knowledge.[a] 21 I write to you, not because you do not know
the truth, but because you know it, and you know that no lie comes
from the truth. 22 Who is the liar but the one who denies that Jesus is
the Christ?[b] This is the antichrist, the one who denies the Father and
the Son. 23 No one who denies the Son has the Father; everyone who
confesses the Son has the Father also. 24 Let what you heard from the
beginning abide in you. If what you heard from the beginning abides
in you, then you will abide in the Son and in the Father. 25 And this is
what he has promised us,[c] eternal life.
26 I write these things to you concerning those who would deceive you. 27 As for you, the anointing that you received from him
abides in you, and so you do not need anyone to teach you. But as his
anointing teaches you about all things, and is true and is not a lie, and
just as it has taught you, abide in him.[d]
28 And now, little children, abide in him, so that when he is revealed we may have confidence and not be put to shame before him
at his coming.

2:21-29 the liar: This refers to one who denies that Jesus is the Messiah and denies the Father and the Son. Some scholars believe that the writer of 1 John is trying to disprove a teaching of the time—that Jesus was completely spiritual in nature and only seemed to be mortal. For the writer, anyone who denies the true identity of Jesus is an "antichrist" (2:18, 22; 4:3). Readers should trust that Jesus was truly born in the flesh (4:2). That is the only way the sacrifice of Jesus could accomplish its godly purpose.

What are some false teachings in today's world? How does 1 John help us face the challenges of false teachings?

Children of God

29 If you know that he is righteous, you may be sure that every-
3 one who does right has been born of him. 1 See what love the
Father has given us, that we should be called children of God;
and that is what we are. The reason the world does not know us is that
it did not know him. 2 Beloved, we are God's children now; what we
will be has not yet been revealed. What we do know is this: when he[d]
is revealed, we will be like him, for we will see him as he is. 3 And all
who have this hope in him purify themselves, just as he is pure.
4 Everyone who commits sin is guilty of lawlessness; sin is lawlessness. 5 You know that he was revealed to take away sins, and in him
there is no sin. 6 No one who abides in him sins; no one who sins has
either seen him or known him. 7 Little children, let no one deceive
you. Everyone who does what is right is righteous, just as he is righteous. 8 Everyone who commits sin is a child of the devil; for the devil
has been sinning from the beginning. The Son of God was revealed
for this purpose, to destroy the works of the devil. 9 Those who have
been born of God do not sin, because God's seed abides in them;[e]
they cannot sin, because they have been born of God. 10 The children
of God and the children of the devil are revealed in this way: all who

3:1-24 children of God: People are born with a tendency to be self-centered, to live apart from God, and to do evil. But being God's children and receiving the Spirit empowers us to love and do good.

Martin Luther says we are sinners (who love only ourselves) and saints (who love others and God) at the same time. Give examples of this from your own life.

[a] Other ancient authorities read *you know all things* [b] Or *the Messiah* [c] Other ancient authorities read *you* [d] Or *it* [e] Or *because the children of God abide in him*

do not do what is right are not from God, nor are those who do not
love their brothers and sisters.[a]

Love One Another

11 For this is the message you have heard from the beginning,
that we should love one another. 12 We must not be like Cain who was
from the evil one and murdered his brother. And why did he murder him? Because his own deeds were evil and his brother's righteous.
13 Do not be astonished, brothers and sisters,[b] that the world hates you.
14 We know that we have passed from death to life because we love
one another. Whoever does not love abides in death. 15 All who hate
a brother or sister[a] are murderers, and you know that murderers do
not have eternal life abiding in them. 16 We know love by this, that he
laid down his life for us—and we ought to lay down our lives for one
another. 17 How does God's love abide in anyone who has the world's
goods and sees a brother or sister[c] in need and yet refuses help?

18 Little children, let us love, not in word or speech, but in truth
and action. 19 And by this we will know that we are from the truth
and will reassure our hearts before him 20 whenever our hearts condemn us; for God is greater than our hearts, and he knows everything.
21 Beloved, if our hearts do not condemn us, we have boldness before
God; 22 and we receive from him whatever we ask, because we obey
his commandments and do what pleases him.

23 And this is his commandment, that we should believe in the
name of his Son Jesus Christ and love one another, just as he has commanded us. 24 All who obey his commandments abide in him, and he
abides in them. And by this we know that he abides in us, by the Spirit
that he has given us.

Testing the Spirits

4:1-6 test the spirits: Believers need to think carefully about what others say in God's name, so they are not misled by many conflicting voices.

How would you "test" something someone declares to be God's truth? How could your faith community help with this?

4 Beloved, do not believe every spirit, but test the spirits to see
whether they are from God; for many false prophets have gone
out into the world. 2 By this you know the Spirit of God: every spirit
that confesses that Jesus Christ has come in the flesh is from God,
3 and every spirit that does not confess Jesus[d] is not from God. And
this is the spirit of the antichrist, of which you have heard that it is
coming; and now it is already in the world. 4 Little children, you are
from God, and have conquered them; for the one who is in you is
greater than the one who is in the world. 5 They are from the world;
therefore what they say is from the world, and the world listens to
them. 6 We are from God. Whoever knows God listens to us, and
whoever is not from God does not listen to us. From this we know
the spirit of truth and the spirit of error.

---

[a] Gk *his brother* [b] Gk *brothers* [c] Gk *brother* [d] Other ancient authorities read *does away with Jesus* (Gk *dissolves Jesus*)

God Is Love

7 Beloved, let us love one another, because love is from God;
everyone who loves is born of God and knows God. 8Whoever does
not love does not know God, for God is love. 9God's love was revealed
among us in this way: God sent his only Son into the world so that we
might live through him. 10In this is love, not that we loved God but
that he loved us and sent his Son to be the atoning sacrifice for our
sins. 11Beloved, since God loved us so much, we also ought to love
one another. 12No one has ever seen God; if we love one another, God
lives in us, and his love is perfected in us.

13 By this we know that we abide in him and he in us, because
he has given us of his Spirit. 14And we have seen and do testify that
the Father has sent his Son as the Savior of the world. 15God abides
in those who confess that Jesus is the Son of God, and they abide in
God. 16So we have known and believe the love that God has for us.

God is love, and those who abide in love abide in God, and God
abides in them. 17Love has been perfected among us in this: that we
may have boldness on the day of judgment, because as he is, so are we
in this world. 18There is no fear in love, but perfect love casts out fear;
for fear has to do with punishment, and whoever fears has not reached
perfection in love. 19We love[a] because he first loved us. 20Those who
say, "I love God," and hate their brothers or sisters,[b] are liars; for those
who do not love a brother or sister[c] whom they have seen, cannot
love God whom they have not seen. 21The commandment we have
from him is this: those who love God must love their brothers and
sisters[b] also.

Faith Conquers the World

5 Everyone who believes that Jesus is the Christ[d] has been born
of God, and everyone who loves the parent loves the child. 2By
this we know that we love the children of God, when we love God and
obey his commandments. 3For the love of God is this, that we obey
his commandments. And his commandments are not burdensome,
4for whatever is born of God conquers the world. And this is the victory that conquers the world, our faith. 5Who is it that conquers the
world but the one who believes that Jesus is the Son of God?

Testimony concerning the Son of God

6 This is the one who came by water and blood, Jesus Christ, not
with the water only but with the water and the blood. And the Spirit
is the one that testifies, for the Spirit is the truth. 7There are three that
testify:[e] 8the Spirit and the water and the blood, and these three agree.

4:7-21 love God...brothers and sisters: Loving God and loving our neighbor cannot be separated (see Mark 12:29-31; John 15:1-17).

Where does love of God and love of neighbor come from? Our sin puts our own desires and needs above anything or anyone else, making it impossible for us to love God or neighbor on our own. But God loves us, even though we do not deserve it, and shows this love by sending the gift of a Savior to the world. God's love for us in Jesus Christ is so deep and powerful that we can even say God *is* love. The gift of God's love makes it possible for us to love God and our neighbors. We love God and one another because God, who is love, first loves us. *1 John 4:7-21*

5:1-12 commandments: Love is active. To love God is to obey God. God's laws are intended to guide our lives, not make us feel guilty. In fact, not following God's will can make our lives seem bleak or futile, while loving and obeying God leads to a life of joy and meaning.

Think of a time when loving and obeying God brought a sense of joy and meaning to you or to someone else.

---

[a] Other ancient authorities add *him;* others add *God* [b] Gk *brothers* [c] Gk *brother* [d] Or *the Messiah*
[e] A few other authorities read (with variations) *7There are three that testify in heaven, the Father, the Word, and the Holy Spirit, and these three are one. 8And there are three that testify on earth:*

[9]If we receive human testimony, the testimony of God is greater; for this is the testimony of God that he has testified to his Son. [10]Those who believe in the Son of God have the testimony in their hearts. Those who do not believe in God[a] have made him a liar by not believing in the testimony that God has given concerning his Son. [11]And this is the testimony: God gave us eternal life, and this life is in his Son. [12]Whoever has the Son has life; whoever does not have the Son of God does not have life.

Epilogue

13 I write these things to you who believe in the name of the Son of God, so that you may know that you have eternal life.

14 And this is the boldness we have in him, that if we ask anything according to his will, he hears us. [15]And if we know that he hears us in whatever we ask, we know that we have obtained the requests made of him. [16]If you see your brother or sister[b] committing what is not a mortal sin, you will ask, and God[c] will give life to such a one—to those whose sin is not mortal. There is sin that is mortal; I do not say that you should pray about that. [17]All wrongdoing is sin, but there is sin that is not mortal.

18 We know that those who are born of God do not sin, but the one who was born of God protects them, and the evil one does not touch them. [19]We know that we are God's children, and that the whole world lies under the power of the evil one. [20]And we know that the Son of God has come and has given us understanding so that we may know him who is true;[d] and we are in him who is true, in his Son Jesus Christ. He is the true God and eternal life.

21 Little children, keep yourselves from idols.[e]

---

[a] Other ancient authorities read *in the Son* [b] Gk *your brother* [c] Gk *he* [d] Other ancient authorities read *know the true God* [e] Other ancient authorities add *Amen*

5:13-17 so that you may know: The writer's purpose is to make sure readers know they have eternal life. Compare this purpose statement with John 20:30-31.

5:18-20 the Son of God has come: Although we should not take the powers of sin and evil lightly, they have no ultimate power over those protected by God. God is greater than all sin and evil.

5:19 evil one: The word translated here as "evil one" is the same word that appears in the Lord's Prayer (Matt 6:13). It can be translated either as "deliver us from *evil*" or "deliver us from the *evil one*."

5:21 idols: Instead of ending 1 John like an ancient letter, the writer includes an urgent warning to readers to guard against idols. "Idols" here refers to false gods—anything we value above God.

Think of how the word *idol* is used today. How might we guard ourselves against idols or false gods?

2 John v. 6

2 JOHN

Background File

This book follows the traditional pattern of ancient letters found in many New Testament epistles or letters. The letter appears to be written by the leader of one Christian community to the leader of another. Nothing in the book tells us the names of either these leaders or their communities. The writer identifies himself simply as "the elder." This implies that he was familiar to those to whom he wrote and that he held some position of respect among them.

Scholars often treat "the elect lady and her children" (v. 1) as an image for the congregation receiving the letter. It is equally possible, however, that the elder was addressing a female church leader and believers who met in her home. In those times women generally directed affairs in the home, and the earliest Christian fellowships met in houses, so it was common for women to hold positions of leadership and responsibility in faith communities. Phoebe the deacon, Paul's co-worker Priscilla (or Prisca), and Junia the apostle (Rom 16:1, 3, 7) are clear examples of this practice.

What's the Story?

Most scholars agree that 1, 2, and 3 John and the Gospel of John share several themes, key phrases, and a common theological foundation. Many conclude that the three letters were generated by members of a faith community whose beliefs were deeply rooted in their understanding of the Gospel of John.

This letter can be outlined as follows:

Salutation or greeting (vv. 1-3)
Love one another is not a new commandment (vv. 4-6)
Be on guard against false teaching (vv. 7-11)
Final greetings (vv. 12-13)

What's the Message?

In 2 John "truth" is like a good pair of hiking boots—it is something to walk in, not just think about. To walk in the truth means to "love one another" (v. 5). The writer defends his message to obey the call to love one another by insisting that this is no new commandment at all. It is really the chief commandment God has issued consistently from the very beginning of time. Love, however, is to be practiced with truth and caution. The author insists that showing hospitality to deceivers can be dangerous and sometimes promotes evil.

Salutation

1 The elder to the elect lady and her children, whom I love in the
truth, and not only I but also all who know the truth, 2 because of the
truth that abides in us and will be with us forever:
3 Grace, mercy, and peace will be with us from God the Father
and from[a] Jesus Christ, the Father's Son, in truth and love.

Truth and Love

4 I was overjoyed to find some of your children walking in the
truth, just as we have been commanded by the Father. 5 But now,
dear lady, I ask you, not as though I were writing you a new commandment, but one we have had from the beginning, let us love one
another. 6 And this is love, that we walk according to his commandments; this is the commandment just as you have heard it from the
beginning—you must walk in it.
7 Many deceivers have gone out into the world, those who do not
confess that Jesus Christ has come in the flesh; any such person is the
deceiver and the antichrist! 8 Be on your guard, so that you do not lose
what we[b] have worked for, but may receive a full reward. 9 Everyone
who does not abide in the teaching of Christ, but goes beyond it, does
not have God; whoever abides in the teaching has both the Father
and the Son. 10 Do not receive into the house or welcome anyone who
comes to you and does not bring this teaching; 11 for to welcome is to
participate in the evil deeds of such a person.

Final Greetings

12 Although I have much to write to you, I would rather not use
paper and ink; instead I hope to come to you and talk with you face to
face, so that our joy may be complete.
13 The children of your elect sister send you their greetings.[c]

---

[a] Other ancient authorities add *the Lord* [b] Other ancient authorities read *you* [c] Other ancient authorities add *Amen*

1 elder: This was probably a church leader (see 1 Tim 4:14; 5:17-22; 2 Tim 1:6; Titus 1:5-9). "The elect lady and her children" is an image for the congregation receiving the letter, or a female church leader and the believers who met in her home.

4-6 from the beginning: "Love one another" is not a *new* commandment, but the essence of all God's commandments. (See also 1 John 2:7; 3:11. Compare this with John 13:34-35.)

Do the ways you spend your time and treat others correspond to what you believe? What can you do to make your beliefs and behavior more in line with each other?

7-9 Be on your guard: The elder's call to his readers to be on guard echoes the warning in 1 John 5:21. Although God possesses final power over all evil, as long as deceivers walk the earth, believers need to draw strength from one another to stand against the persuasive power of evil.

7 antichrist!: On "antichrists," see notes on 1 John 2:18-20.

10-11 Do not receive: In biblical times, giving shelter to strangers was not just a matter of politeness. Harsh terrains and brutal bandits made travel difficult and potentially dangerous. The offer of shelter, food, water, and aid to travelers often saved lives. In spite of this, the elder prohibits the spread of false teaching by forbidding believers from giving shelter to those who teach that Jesus is not human (see Gal 1:6-9).

13 children of your elect sister: This most likely refers to another group of believers who send along greetings to those receiving this letter.

3 John v. 4

3 JOHN

Background File

Like 2 John, 3 John follows the traditional pattern of ancient letters found in many New Testament epistles or letters. The letter appears to be written by the leader of one Christian community to the leader of another. The writer identifies himself simply as "the elder." This implies that he was familiar to those to whom he wrote and that he held some position of respect among them. The letter is addressed to "the beloved Gaius."

What's the Story?

Most scholars agree that 1, 2, and 3 John and the Gospel of John share several themes, key phrases, and a common theological foundation. Many conclude that the three letters were generated by members of a faith community whose beliefs were deeply rooted in their understanding of the Gospel of John.

Third John can be outlined as follows:

Salutation and greeting (v. 1)
Words of praise (vv. 2-8)
Stern rebuke (vv. 9-11)
Positive testimony (v. 12)
Final greetings (vv. 13-15)

The letter features words of praise (vv. 2-8, 12) and a stern rebuke (vv. 9-11). First, the elder commends Gaius for the hospitality he has shown to some traveling missionaries. He declares that people who show support to those who work for Christ are themselves "co-workers with the truth" (v. 8).

Then the elder turns his attention to two others, Diotrephes and Demetrius. He reports that Diotrephes slanders him with false charges and refuses to be hospitable to his followers. On the other hand, the elder praises Demetrius for his faithful attitude and behavior.

What's the Message?

The letter's central theme is stated in verse 11: "Beloved, do not imitate what is evil but imitate what is good. Whoever does good is from God; whoever does evil has not seen God." We can be "co-workers with the truth" by offering hospitality and lending support when people do good and preach the gospel, and we can encourage others to be co-workers with the truth as well.

---

1 elder...Gaius: The name "Gaius" (GUY-us) occurs four other times in the New Testament (Acts 19:29; 20:4; Rom 16:23; 1 Cor 1:14). His identity here remains unknown. The way the writer addresses Gaius as one of "my children" (verse 4) implies that the author was his spiritual teacher or church leader.

2-8 truth: Third John demonstrates the emphasis on "truth" that runs through the letters of John as well as the Gospel of John.

3 walk in the truth: Here this means showing hospitality to Christian missionaries. By supporting those who are literally walking to preach the gospel, people become "co-workers with the truth."

9-10 Diotrephes: Based on this description, some scholars have wondered if Diotrephes (dee-UH-truh-phees) might be the one mentioned in 1 John 4:1-6 and 2 John 7 as one of the "false prophets" or "the deceiver."

11 Whoever does good: This is another example of testing the spirits (see note on 1 John 4:1-6). The one who does good is of God; the one who does evil does not know God.

13-15 Peace: The letter closes in a traditional fashion, with the desire for a personal visit, a request to pass on greetings, and hope for peace.

Salutation

1 The elder to the beloved Gaius, whom I love in truth.

Gaius Commended for His Hospitality

2 Beloved, I pray that all may go well with you and that you may
be in good health, just as it is well with your soul. [3]I was overjoyed
when some of the friends[a] arrived and testified to your faithfulness
to the truth, namely how you walk in the truth. [4]I have no greater joy
than this, to hear that my children are walking in the truth.
5 Beloved, you do faithfully whatever you do for the friends,[a] even
though they are strangers to you; [6]they have testified to your love before the church. You will do well to send them on in a manner worthy
of God; [7]for they began their journey for the sake of Christ,[b] accepting no support from non-believers.[c] [8]Therefore we ought to support
such people, so that we may become co-workers with the truth.

Diotrephes and Demetrius

9 I have written something to the church; but Diotrephes, who
likes to put himself first, does not acknowledge our authority. [10]So
if I come, I will call attention to what he is doing in spreading false
charges against us. And not content with those charges, he refuses to
welcome the friends,[a] and even prevents those who want to do so and
expels them from the church.
11 Beloved, do not imitate what is evil but imitate what is good.
Whoever does good is from God; whoever does evil has not seen
God. [12]Everyone has testified favorably about Demetrius, and so has
the truth itself. We also testify for him,[d] and you know that our testimony is true.

Final Greetings

13 I have much to write to you, but I would rather not write with
pen and ink; [14]instead I hope to see you soon, and we will talk together face to face.
15 Peace to you. The friends send you their greetings. Greet the
friends there, each by name.

---

[a] Gk *brothers* [b] Gk *for the sake of the name* [c] Gk *the Gentiles* [d] Gk lacks *for him*

Jude vv. 20-21

JUDE

Background File

Jude is a general letter, written to all Christian communities. The identity of the writer is unknown. Some scholars argue that the writer is Jude, the brother of James and Jesus, which would date the writing to the middle of the first century. This is unlikely, however, because references to false teachers in the last days and faith entrusted to the saints once for all (vv. 3, 18) indicate the writing is from late in the first century. The writer would like to provide instruction and encouragement in the faith to the early Christian church, but instead feels compelled to warn believers against false teachings (v. 3).

What's the Story?

The letter of Jude can be outlined as follows:

Salutation or greeting (vv. 1-2)
Proofs against false teachers (vv. 3-16)
Instructions for responding to false teachings (vv. 17-23)
Doxology (vv. 24-25)

The writer offers proof against false teachers from the Old Testament and from other ancient sources, then tells readers how to respond to false teachings by praying, living in God's love, and looking forward to God's mercy that leads to eternal life. The letter concludes with a doxology, words that offer glory and honor to God.

What's the Message?

The writer of Jude is concerned not only with false teachings but with the ungodly behavior that might result from them. This letter is a strong exhortation against bad behavior caused by a distorted understanding of God's grace in Jesus Christ. The ending doxology reassures believers that God is able to keep them safe from falling into these sins and that all praise belongs to God in Christ Jesus, not only at that time but "before all time and now and forever" (v. 25).

Salutation

1 Jude,[a] a servant[b] of Jesus Christ and brother of James,
To those who are called, who are beloved[c] in[d] God the Father and
kept safe for[d] Jesus Christ:
2 May mercy, peace, and love be yours in abundance.

Occasion of the Letter

3 Beloved, while eagerly preparing to write to you about the salvation we share, I find it necessary to write and appeal to you to contend for the faith that was once for all entrusted to the saints. 4 For
certain intruders have stolen in among you, people who long ago
were designated for this condemnation as ungodly, who pervert the
grace of our God into licentiousness and deny our only Master and
Lord, Jesus Christ.[e]

Judgment on False Teachers

5 Now I desire to remind you, though you are fully informed, that
the Lord, who once for all saved[f] a people out of the land of Egypt,
afterward destroyed those who did not believe. 6 And the angels who
did not keep their own position, but left their proper dwelling, he has
kept in eternal chains in deepest darkness for the judgment of the
great day. 7 Likewise, Sodom and Gomorrah and the surrounding cities, which, in the same manner as they, indulged in sexual immorality and pursued unnatural lust,[g] serve as an example by undergoing a
punishment of eternal fire.
8 Yet in the same way these dreamers also defile the flesh, reject
authority, and slander the glorious ones.[h] 9 But when the archangel Michael contended with the devil and disputed about the body of Moses,
he did not dare to bring a condemnation of slander[i] against him, but
said, "The Lord rebuke you!" 10 But these people slander whatever
they do not understand, and they are destroyed by those things that,
like irrational animals, they know by instinct. 11 Woe to them! For they
go the way of Cain, and abandon themselves to Balaam's error for the
sake of gain, and perish in Korah's rebellion. 12 These are blemishes[j] on
your love-feasts, while they feast with you without fear, feeding themselves.[k] They are waterless clouds carried along by the winds; autumn
trees without fruit, twice dead, uprooted; 13 wild waves of the sea,
casting up the foam of their own shame; wandering stars, for whom
the deepest darkness has been reserved forever.
14 It was also about these that Enoch, in the seventh generation

4 grace…licentiousness: Some were saying that because God is gracious, people can do whatever they want. New Testament writers often list licentiousness—immoral, ungodly behavior—as a sin (see Mark 7:22; Rom 13:13; 2 Cor 12:21; Gal 5:19; Eph 4:19; 1 Pet 4:3; 2 Pet 2:2, 7).

5 people out of the land of Egypt: The writer notes the fate of the Israelites who did not obey God. This refers to the story of exodus and the people who were rescued by God from slavery in Egypt.

6 angels: The writer refers to the fate of fallen angels, according to an ancient book called 1 Enoch.

7 Sodom and Gomorrah: The sin of the people of Sodom and Gomorrah is here described as sexual immorality, but many scholars find that sin to be inhospitality to strangers (see Gen 19).

How do we show hospitality and welcome strangers into our communities of faith?

9 Moses: This relates to a story from The Assumption of Moses, another ancient book, in which the devil falsely charges Moses as a murderer not worthy of burial.

11 rebellion: The writer uses the stories of Cain (Gen 4:8), Balaam (Num 22–24), and Korah (Num 16) as examples of the kinds of sins committed by false teachers.

12 love-feasts: Early Christians gathered for community meals that were similar to a gathering for Holy Communion (see 1 Cor 11:18-34; 2 Pet 2:13).

---

a Gk *Judas* b Gk *slave* c Other ancient authorities read *sanctified* d Or *by* e Or *the only Master and our Lord Jesus Christ* f Other ancient authorities read *though you were once for all fully informed, that Jesus (or Joshua) who saved* g Gk *went after other flesh* h Or *angels;* Gk *glories* i Or *condemnation for blasphemy* j Or *reefs* k Or *without fear. They are shepherds who care only for themselves*

from Adam, prophesied, saying, “See, the Lord is coming[a] with ten
thousands of his holy ones, [15]to execute judgment on all, and to convict everyone of all the deeds of ungodliness that they have committed in such an ungodly way, and of all the harsh things that ungodly
sinners have spoken against him.” [16]These are grumblers and malcon-
tents; they indulge their own lusts; they are bombastic in speech, flattering people to their own advantage.

Warnings and Exhortations

17 But you, beloved, must remember the predictions of the apostles of our Lord Jesus Christ; [18]for they said to you, “In the last time
there will be scoffers, indulging their own ungodly lusts.” [19]It is these
worldly people, devoid of the Spirit, who are causing divisions. [20]But
you, beloved, build yourselves up on your most holy faith; pray in the
Holy Spirit; [21]keep yourselves in the love of God; look forward to the
mercy of our Lord Jesus Christ that leads to[b] eternal life. [22]And have
mercy on some who are wavering; [23]save others by snatching them
out of the fire; and have mercy on still others with fear, hating even
the tunic defiled by their bodies.[c]

Benediction

24 Now to him who is able to keep you from falling, and to make
you stand without blemish in the presence of his glory with rejoicing,
[25]to the only God our Savior, through Jesus Christ our Lord, be glory,
majesty, power, and authority, before all time and now and forever.
Amen.

---

[a] Gk *came* [b] Gk *Christ to* [c] Gk *by the flesh*. The Greek text of verses 22–23 is uncertain at several points

What does Luther's *Small Catechism* say about Holy Communion? The sacrament was instituted by Christ himself (see Matt 26:17-29; Mark 14:12-25; Luke 22:7-20). The bread and wine are the true body and blood of our Lord Jesus Christ. Forgiveness of sins, life, and salvation are given to us in the eating and drinking. All that is required to receive Holy Communion is a believing heart. *Jude v. 12*

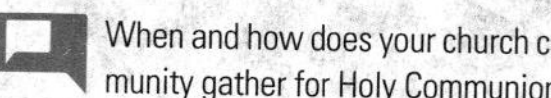
When and how does your church community gather for Holy Communion?

24-25 glory: This stern letter ends with a doxology (a prayer that offers all praise and glory to God).

What kind of doxology does your congregation say or sing?

Revelation 21:6

REVELATION

Background File

"John" is named as the author of Revelation. Legend claims that he was the beloved apostle of Jesus. The author of Revelation, however, identifies himself only as John. It was a common name, and he makes no claim to be an apostle or to have ever seen Jesus during his time on earth. This John likely was a leader of several Christian communities in what is now known as western Turkey.

Most scholars think Revelation was written late in the first century C.E. During this time Roman authorities demanded that emperors be worshiped as gods. Revelation 1:9 describes how John's activities on behalf of the gospel upset local authorities, who banished him to the small island of Patmos in the Aegean Sea. John wrote this letter to seven churches that were facing various challenges.

What's the Story?

John presents his message in an ancient style of writing known as *apocalypse*. The word is often used today to mean an end-of-the-world catastrophe. The Greek word *apokalypsis* (uh-POCK-uh-LIP-sis), however, simply means "revelation." It refers to an unveiling or revealing of something that was previously hidden.

In Scripture, an apocalypse tells of an experience with the supernatural world, in which the author is usually guided by a mystical being. It is filled with striking, fantastic images of conflict between good and evil, and ends in a glorious triumph of God's forces of good. See Daniel 7–12 for another example of apocalyptic writing.

Revelation does not have a story line that moves in a logical sequence from one scene to the next. Instead, it offers a series of visions. Some of these visions are repeated with slight alterations in other chapters. Some build upon previous visions. Revelation presents two kinds of visions: terrifying episodes of violence and glorious visions of victory and celebration. As in the writings of the Old Testament prophets, the terror always gives way to the promise of God's triumph. Revelation can be outlined in this way:

Opening words (1:1-8)
The seven churches (1:9–3:22)

Praise to God and the Lamb (4:1–5:14)
Seven seals and seven trumpets (6:1–11:19)
Opposition to God's kingdom (12:1–13:18)
God's judgment and victory (14:1–20:15)
New heaven and new earth (21:1–22:5)
Final words (22:6-21)

What's the Message?

Much of the controversy about Revelation revolves around the question: Who were the original readers for this revelation? A popular view of Revelation in our society assumes that this book is "history told in advance," written to warn readers about events that will happen during their lifetimes. According to this view, the book is a series of hidden clues that reveal exactly what will take place at the end of the world.

John, however, seems to have something more immediate in mind. He had worked with seven churches and now writes to them as they struggle to survive in a world dominated by the Roman Empire. Some faced persecution; some were being corrupted by society; some had stopped taking faith seriously.

The visions in Revelation address this question: Who or what is at the center of Christian life? John uses bold and dramatic images to drive home the point that Christian life centers on Jesus Christ alone. This message takes two forms. First, the terrifying visions are warnings to those who are falling away from the faith. Second, the glorious visions of triumph offer encouragement to those who are oppressed, persecuted, or feeling powerless in a hostile world.

Introduction and Salutation

1 The revelation of Jesus Christ, which God gave him to show his
servants[a] what must soon take place; he made[b] it known by sending his angel to his servant[c] John, 2who testified to the word of God
and to the testimony of Jesus Christ, even to all that he saw.
3 Blessed is the one who reads aloud the words of the prophecy,
and blessed are those who hear and who keep what is written in it; for
the time is near.

4 John to the seven churches that are in Asia:
Grace to you and peace from him who is and who was and who is
to come, and from the seven spirits who are before his throne, 5and
from Jesus Christ, the faithful witness, the firstborn of the dead, and
the ruler of the kings of the earth.

1:1 The revelation: The book's name comes from its first word. In Greek it is *apokalypsis*, which means a revealing or unveiling.

1:4 John to the seven churches that are in Asia: John uses the standard letter form of his time, addressing his readers and including words of welcome and blessing.

[a] Gk *slaves* [b] Gk *and he made* [c] Gk *slave*

1:7 Look! He is coming with the clouds: John introduces the two themes of his letter. Jesus' reign over creation forever is both a *warning* to the unfaithful and a *word of comfort* to the faithful.

1:8 Alpha and the Omega: Alpha and Omega are the first and last letters of the Greek alphabet. John builds on the concept of "the fear of the LORD is the beginning of knowledge" (Prov 1:7). The focus of the Christian community begins and ends with God, revealed in Jesus Christ.

1:9 I, John, your brother: John declares his relationship to the churches as a brother in Christ, and he explains his absence. The lands around the Mediterranean Sea were under the rule of the Roman Empire at this time. John's preaching of the gospel displeased local authorities, and they sent him into exile.

1:11 send it to the seven churches: John identifies the groups of Christians to whom he is writing.

1:12 seven golden lampstands: The number seven, a symbol of perfection in the ancient world, is repeated in many of John's visions.

To him who loves us and freed[a] us from our sins by his blood, 6and
made[b] us to be a kingdom, priests serving[c] his God and Father, to him
be glory and dominion forever and ever. Amen.

7 Look! He is coming with the clouds;
every eye will see him,
even those who pierced him;
and on his account all the tribes of the earth will wail.
So it is to be. Amen.

8 "I am the Alpha and the Omega," says the Lord God, who is and
who was and who is to come, the Almighty.

A Vision of Christ

9 I, John, your brother who share with you in Jesus the persecution and the kingdom and the patient endurance, was on the island called Patmos because of the word of God and the testimony of
Jesus.[d] 10I was in the spirit[e] on the Lord's day, and I heard behind me a
loud voice like a trumpet 11saying, "Write in a book what you see and
send it to the seven churches, to Ephesus, to Smyrna, to Pergamum,
to Thyatira, to Sardis, to Philadelphia, and to Laodicea."

12 Then I turned to see whose voice it was that spoke to me, and
on turning I saw seven golden lampstands, 13and in the midst of the

[a] Other ancient authorities read *washed* [b] Gk *and he made* [c] Gk *priests to* [d] Or *testimony to Jesus* [e] Or *in the Spirit*

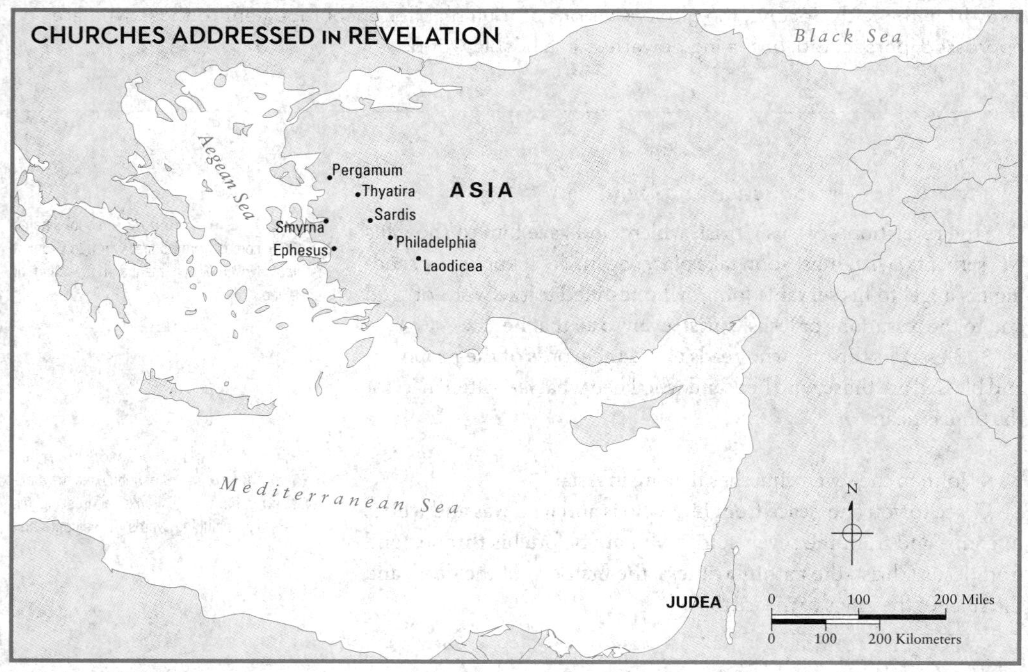

lampstands I saw one like the Son of Man, clothed with a long robe
and with a golden sash across his chest. [14]His head and his hair were
white as white wool, white as snow; his eyes were like a flame of fire,
[15]his feet were like burnished bronze, refined as in a furnace, and his
voice was like the sound of many waters. [16]In his right hand he held
seven stars, and from his mouth came a sharp, two-edged sword, and
his face was like the sun shining with full force.

17 When I saw him, I fell at his feet as though dead. But he placed
his right hand on me, saying, "Do not be afraid; I am the first and the
last, [18]and the living one. I was dead, and see, I am alive forever and
ever; and I have the keys of Death and of Hades. [19]Now write what
you have seen, what is, and what is to take place after this. [20]As for
the mystery of the seven stars that you saw in my right hand, and the
seven golden lampstands: the seven stars are the angels of the seven
churches, and the seven lampstands are the seven churches.

The Message to Ephesus

2 "To the angel of the church in Ephesus write: These are the
words of him who holds the seven stars in his right hand, who
walks among the seven golden lampstands:

2 "I know your works, your toil and your patient endurance. I
know that you cannot tolerate evildoers; you have tested those who
claim to be apostles but are not, and have found them to be false.
[3]I also know that you are enduring patiently and bearing up for the
sake of my name, and that you have not grown weary. [4]But I have this
against you, that you have abandoned the love you had at first. [5]Re-
member then from what you have fallen; repent, and do the works
you did at first. If not, I will come to you and remove your lampstand
from its place, unless you repent. [6]Yet this is to your credit: you hate
the works of the Nicolaitans, which I also hate. [7]Let anyone who has
an ear listen to what the Spirit is saying to the churches. To everyone
who conquers, I will give permission to eat from the tree of life that is
in the paradise of God.

2:1—3:22 To the angel of: John addresses each of the seven churches and identifies the challenge each church faces.

2:1-7 To the angel of the church in Ephesus: While believers in Ephesus have been faithful to works of the law, they have forgotten that love is the core of the Christian faith.

The Message to Smyrna

8 "And to the angel of the church in Smyrna write: These are the
words of the first and the last, who was dead and came to life:

9 "I know your affliction and your poverty, even though you are
rich. I know the slander on the part of those who say that they are Jews
and are not, but are a synagogue of Satan. [10]Do not fear what you are
about to suffer. Beware, the devil is about to throw some of you into
prison so that you may be tested, and for ten days you will have affliction. Be faithful until death, and I will give you the crown of life. [11]Let
anyone who has an ear listen to what the Spirit is saying to the churches.
Whoever conquers will not be harmed by the second death.

2:8-11 to the angel of the church in Smyrna: Smyrna is a prosperous community under attack from powerful, hostile adversaries. The Christians there face a time of severe persecution.

The Message to Pergamum

2:12-17 to the angel of the church in Pergamum: Pergamum is surrounded by a culture that is heavily influenced by Rome, and the Pergamum church has started to yield to these corrupting influences.

2:14 the teaching of Balaam: Balaam's story is told in Numbers 22–24.

12 "And to the angel of the church in Pergamum write: These are
the words of him who has the sharp two-edged sword:
13 "I know where you are living, where Satan's throne is. Yet you
are holding fast to my name, and you did not deny your faith in me[a]
even in the days of Antipas my witness, my faithful one, who was killed
among you, where Satan lives. 14 But I have a few things against you:
you have some there who hold to the teaching of Balaam, who taught
Balak to put a stumbling block before the people of Israel, so that they
would eat food sacrificed to idols and practice fornication. 15 So you
also have some who hold to the teaching of the Nicolaitans. 16 Repent
then. If not, I will come to you soon and make war against them with
the sword of my mouth. 17 Let anyone who has an ear listen to what
the Spirit is saying to the churches. To everyone who conquers I will
give some of the hidden manna, and I will give a white stone, and on
the white stone is written a new name that no one knows except the
one who receives it.

The Message to Thyatira

2:18-29 to the angel of the church in Thyatira: This group of Christians has been faithful but is falling under the influence of leaders who say that it is okay to compromise their values in order to fit in with the society.

18 "And to the angel of the church in Thyatira write: These are the
words of the Son of God, who has eyes like a flame of fire, and whose
feet are like burnished bronze:
19 "I know your works—your love, faith, service, and patient endurance. I know that your last works are greater than the first. 20 But
I have this against you: you tolerate that woman Jezebel, who calls
herself a prophet and is teaching and beguiling my servants[b] to practice fornication and to eat food sacrificed to idols. 21 I gave her time
to repent, but she refuses to repent of her fornication. 22 Beware, I am
throwing her on a bed, and those who commit adultery with her I am
throwing into great distress, unless they repent of her doings; 23 and I
will strike her children dead. And all the churches will know that I am
the one who searches minds and hearts, and I will give to each of you
as your works deserve. 24 But to the rest of you in Thyatira, who do not
hold this teaching, who have not learned what some call 'the deep
things of Satan,' to you I say, I do not lay on you any other burden;
25 only hold fast to what you have until I come. 26 To everyone who
conquers and continues to do my works to the end,

I will give authority over the nations;
27 to rule[c] them with an iron rod,
as when clay pots are shattered—

28 even as I also received authority from my Father. To the one who
conquers I will also give the morning star. 29 Let anyone who has an
ear listen to what the Spirit is saying to the churches.

---

[a] Or *deny my faith* [b] Gk *slaves* [c] Or *to shepherd*

The Message to Sardis

3 "And to the angel of the church in Sardis write: These are the
words of him who has the seven spirits of God and the seven
stars:
"I know your works; you have a name of being alive, but you are
dead. 2 Wake up, and strengthen what remains and is on the point of
death, for I have not found your works perfect in the sight of my God.
3 Remember then what you received and heard; obey it, and repent. If
you do not wake up, I will come like a thief, and you will not know at
what hour I will come to you. 4 Yet you have still a few persons in Sardis who have not soiled their clothes; they will walk with me, dressed
in white, for they are worthy. 5 If you conquer, you will be clothed like
them in white robes, and I will not blot your name out of the book of
life; I will confess your name before my Father and before his angels.
6 Let anyone who has an ear listen to what the Spirit is saying to the
churches.

3:1-6 to the angel of the church in Sardis: The Christians in Sardis are a faith community in name only. They meet and go through the motions of worship but show no real Christian commitment.

The Message to Philadelphia

7 "And to the angel of the church in Philadelphia write:
These are the words of the holy one, the true one,
who has the key of David,
who opens and no one will shut,
who shuts and no one opens:
8 "I know your works. Look, I have set before you an open door,
which no one is able to shut. I know that you have but little power,
and yet you have kept my word and have not denied my name. 9 I will
make those of the synagogue of Satan who say that they are Jews and
are not, but are lying—I will make them come and bow down before
your feet, and they will learn that I have loved you. 10 Because you have
kept my word of patient endurance, I will keep you from the hour of
trial that is coming on the whole world to test the inhabitants of the
earth. 11 I am coming soon; hold fast to what you have, so that no one
may seize your crown. 12 If you conquer, I will make you a pillar in the
temple of my God; you will never go out of it. I will write on you the
name of my God, and the name of the city of my God, the new Jerusalem that comes down from my God out of heaven, and my own new
name. 13 Let anyone who has an ear listen to what the Spirit is saying
to the churches.

3:7-13 to the angel of the church in Philadelphia: The Christian community in Philadelphia has little money or influence. They are persecuted by groups opposed to Christianity.

The Message to Laodicea

14 "And to the angel of the church in Laodicea write: The words
of the Amen, the faithful and true witness, the origin[a] of God's
creation:

3:14-22 to the angel of the church in Laodicea: The church in Laodicea is a wealthy, complacent congregation that thinks highly of itself because of its success.

Which of the attitudes of the seven churches seem most common among churches today? If John were to write a letter to your church, what concerns would he raise?

---

[a] Or *beginning*

15 “I know your works; you are neither cold nor hot. I wish that you were either cold or hot. [16]So, because you are lukewarm, and neither cold nor hot, I am about to spit you out of my mouth. [17]For you say, ‘I am rich, I have prospered, and I need nothing.’ You do not realize that you are wretched, pitiable, poor, blind, and naked. [18]Therefore I counsel you to buy from me gold refined by fire so that you may be rich; and white robes to clothe you and to keep the shame of your nakedness from being seen; and salve to anoint your eyes so that you may see. [19]I reprove and discipline those whom I love. Be earnest, therefore, and repent. [20]Listen! I am standing at the door, knocking; if you hear my voice and open the door, I will come in to you and eat with you, and you with me. [21]To the one who conquers I will give a place with me on my throne, just as I myself conquered and sat down with my Father on his throne. [22]Let anyone who has an ear listen to what the Spirit is saying to the churches.”

The Heavenly Worship

4 After this I looked, and there in heaven a door stood open! And the first voice, which I had heard speaking to me like a trumpet, said, “Come up here, and I will show you what must take place after this.” [2]At once I was in the spirit,[a] and there in heaven stood a throne, with one seated on the throne! [3]And the one seated there looks like jasper and carnelian, and around the throne is a rainbow that looks like an emerald. [4]Around the throne are twenty-four thrones, and seated on the thrones are twenty-four elders, dressed in white robes, with golden crowns on their heads. [5]Coming from the throne are flashes of lightning, and rumblings and peals of thunder, and in front of the throne burn seven flaming torches, which are the seven spirits of God; [6]and in front of the throne there is something like a sea of glass, like crystal.

Around the throne, and on each side of the throne, are four living creatures, full of eyes in front and behind: [7]the first living creature like a lion, the second living creature like an ox, the third living creature with a face like a human face, and the fourth living creature like a flying eagle. [8]And the four living creatures, each of them with six wings, are full of eyes all around and inside. Day and night without ceasing they sing,

“Holy, holy, holy,
the Lord God the Almighty,
who was and is and is to come.”

[9]And whenever the living creatures give glory and honor and thanks to the one who is seated on the throne, who lives forever and ever, [10]the twenty-four elders fall before the one who is seated on the

[a] Or *in the Spirit*

3:20 I am standing at the door: God seeks out all people and takes the initiative to be heard and welcomed by them.

What prevents people from responding to God’s invitation? When have you felt hesitant to accept God’s word and follow in God’s ways?

4:1 in heaven a door stood open!: Jesus opens the door to heaven for us; there is nothing we need to do to open it.

4:3 jasper and carnelian: By referencing these precious stones, John shows that the halls of heaven are far more splendid than the best that Rome has to offer. God is the ultimate power, not the Roman Empire.

4:2—22:19 I was in the spirit: John’s visions are filled with striking images, both horrible and wonderful. Images are a powerful means of providing new perspective on the situations of life. Images have the power to *recall* and to *reveal*. Many images in Revelation come from the Old Testament. They help readers recall the warnings and the promises in those books. Other images reveal truth about God by presenting it in a striking, sometimes exaggerated, way.

4:8 each of them with six wings: This mirrors the vision of seraphs, or angels, around God’s throne in Isaiah 6:1-3.

4:9-11 fall before the one who is seated on the throne: The image of kings who “cast their crowns before the throne” signifies that even the most powerful earthly rulers understand their place in God’s universe.

What do you learn about worship from Revelation 4:9-11?

throne and worship the one who lives forever and ever; they cast their crowns before the throne, singing,

11 "You are worthy, our Lord and God,
to receive glory and honor and power,
for you created all things,
and by your will they existed and were created."

The Scroll and the Lamb

5 Then I saw in the right hand of the one seated on the throne
a scroll written on the inside and on the back, sealed[a] with
seven seals; 2and I saw a mighty angel proclaiming with a loud voice,
"Who is worthy to open the scroll and break its seals?" 3And no one
in heaven or on earth or under the earth was able to open the scroll
or to look into it. 4And I began to weep bitterly because no one was
found worthy to open the scroll or to look into it. 5Then one of the
elders said to me, "Do not weep. See, the Lion of the tribe of Judah,
the Root of David, has conquered, so that he can open the scroll and
its seven seals."

6 Then I saw between the throne and the four living creatures and
among the elders a Lamb standing as if it had been slaughtered, having seven horns and seven eyes, which are the seven spirits of God
sent out into all the earth. 7He went and took the scroll from the right
hand of the one who was seated on the throne. 8When he had taken
the scroll, the four living creatures and the twenty-four elders fell before the Lamb, each holding a harp and golden bowls full of incense,
which are the prayers of the saints. 9They sing a new song:

"You are worthy to take the scroll
and to open its seals,
for you were slaughtered and by your blood you ransomed for God
saints from[b] every tribe and language and people and nation;
10 you have made them to be a kingdom and priests serving[c] our God,
and they will reign on earth."

11 Then I looked, and I heard the voice of many angels surrounding the throne and the living creatures and the elders; they numbered
myriads of myriads and thousands of thousands, 12singing with full
voice,

"Worthy is the Lamb that was slaughtered
to receive power and wealth and wisdom and might
and honor and glory and blessing!"

13Then I heard every creature in heaven and on earth and under the
earth and in the sea, and all that is in them, singing,

[a] Or *written on the inside, and sealed on the back* [b] Gk *ransomed for God from* [c] Gk *priests to*

What do Lutherans believe about Christ's "second coming" and the last days? Martin Luther, though not impressed with the book of Revelation, believed that the last days were just around the bend. Five hundred years later, hundreds of end-times predictions and predictors have come and gone. Lutherans—along with other Christians who hold to the ancient creeds—believe that Christ will come again, but have not spent much time worrying much about the details of Christ's return in glory. This might be because Lutherans proclaim that Christ, though seated at God's right hand, is ever-present in Word and Sacrament. That is, the crucified and risen Jesus has never really left his church. *Revelation 4:9-11*

5:1 a scroll: Scrolls were documents written on paper or animal skins then rolled and often sealed with a drop of melted wax. Some legal documents were closed with seven seals. John presents the scroll as a symbol of God's final intent and plan for creation. The seals symbolize authority and proof that the message is authentic.

5:2-4 worthy to open the scroll: There is mourning because there is no person worthy to understand God's plan and put it into action on earth.

5:5-10 he can open the scroll: Jesus, the Lamb of God (see John 1:29), steps forward to do what human beings cannot do for themselves. The Lamb refers to the Passover (see Exod 12), when a lamb was sacrificed to save the lives of God's people.

5:11-13 the voice of many angels: John's guide in this vision directs the focus. Here the guide reveals all heaven and earth united under God's reign and praising God and the Lamb.

"To the one seated on the throne and to the Lamb
be blessing and honor and glory and might
forever and ever!"

[14]And the four living creatures said, "Amen!" And the elders fell down
and worshiped.

The Seven Seals

6 Then I saw the Lamb open one of the seven seals, and I heard
one of the four living creatures call out, as with a voice of thunder, "Come!"[a] [2]I looked, and there was a white horse! Its rider had a
bow; a crown was given to him, and he came out conquering and to
conquer.
3 When he opened the second seal, I heard the second living
creature call out, "Come!"[a] [4]And out came[b] another horse, bright red;
its rider was permitted to take peace from the earth, so that people
would slaughter one another; and he was given a great sword.
5 When he opened the third seal, I heard the third living creature
call out, "Come!"[a] I looked, and there was a black horse! Its rider held
a pair of scales in his hand, [6]and I heard what seemed to be a voice in
the midst of the four living creatures saying, "A quart of wheat for a
day's pay,[c] and three quarts of barley for a day's pay,[c] but do not damage the olive oil and the wine!"
7 When he opened the fourth seal, I heard the voice of the fourth
living creature call out, "Come!"[a] [8]I looked and there was a pale green
horse! Its rider's name was Death, and Hades followed with him; they
were given authority over a fourth of the earth, to kill with sword,
famine, and pestilence, and by the wild animals of the earth.
9 When he opened the fifth seal, I saw under the altar the souls of
those who had been slaughtered for the word of God and for the testimony they had given; [10]they cried out with a loud voice, "Sovereign
Lord, holy and true, how long will it be before you judge and avenge
our blood on the inhabitants of the earth?" [11]They were each given a
white robe and told to rest a little longer, until the number would be
complete both of their fellow servants[d] and of their brothers and sisters,[e] who were soon to be killed as they themselves had been killed.
12 When he opened the sixth seal, I looked, and there came a
great earthquake; the sun became black as sackcloth, the full moon
became like blood, [13]and the stars of the sky fell to the earth as the
fig tree drops its winter fruit when shaken by a gale. [14]The sky vanished like a scroll rolling itself up, and every mountain and island was
removed from its place. [15]Then the kings of the earth and the magnates and the generals and the rich and the powerful, and everyone,
slave and free, hid in the caves and among the rocks of the mountains,

[a]Or *"Go!"* [b]Or *went* [c]Gk *a denarius* [d]Gk *slaves* [e]Gk *brothers*

6:1-2 I saw the Lamb open one of the seven seals: The opening of the seals reveals that what was predicted will happen. This action releases the nightmare commonly known as the Four Horsemen of the Apocalypse. This is similar to Zechariah's vision (see Zech 6:1-7). The first rider attacks and conquers, with the message that there is no security in strong national defense.

6:3-4 he opened the second: This rider creates war and rebellion within the people, showing that there is no security in the rule of society.

6:5-6 he opened the third: This rider spreads famine and poverty, showing that there is no security in wealth.

6:7-8 he opened the fourth: This rider brings death, with the message that there is no security in life. All will die some day.

6:9-11 he opened the fifth: This is a vision of martyrs, those who died because of their Christian faith. It offers a word of hope for those who are oppressed.

6:12-17 he opened the sixth: Opening this seal unleashes a vision of warning and terror that ends with the desperate question of who is worthy or "able to stand" in God's presence.

How might we understand the violence and the joy in this book? Revelation swings back and forth between grim destruction and heavenly celebration. These cycles of violence and joy bring to mind Martin Luther's description of the purpose of a sermon: "to comfort the afflicted and afflict the comfortable." Like the Hebrew prophets, Revelation flows between warning and promise. The warnings are intended to *afflict the comfortable*, to alert people to the consequences of their deteriorating relationship with God. The promises are intended to *comfort the afflicted*. They give assurance that, regardless of how strong the forces of evil appear to be, Christ will triumph in the end. Luther also taught that each Christian is simultaneously saint and sinner. Each of us has moments of being comfortable and moments of being afflicted. Each of us needs both God's challenge and God's promise. *Revelation 2—6*

16 calling to the mountains and rocks, "Fall on us and hide us from
the face of the one seated on the throne and from the wrath of the
Lamb; 17 for the great day of their wrath has come, and who is able to
stand?"

The 144,000 of Israel Sealed

7 After this I saw four angels standing at the four corners of the
earth, holding back the four winds of the earth so that no wind
could blow on earth or sea or against any tree. 2 I saw another angel
ascending from the rising of the sun, having the seal of the living God,
and he called with a loud voice to the four angels who had been given
power to damage earth and sea, 3 saying, "Do not damage the earth
or the sea or the trees, until we have marked the servants[a] of our God
with a seal on their foreheads."

4 And I heard the number of those who were sealed, one hundred
forty-four thousand, sealed out of every tribe of the people of Israel:

5 From the tribe of Judah twelve thousand sealed,
from the tribe of Reuben twelve thousand,
from the tribe of Gad twelve thousand,
6 from the tribe of Asher twelve thousand,
from the tribe of Naphtali twelve thousand,
from the tribe of Manasseh twelve thousand,
7 from the tribe of Simeon twelve thousand,
from the tribe of Levi twelve thousand,
from the tribe of Issachar twelve thousand,
8 from the tribe of Zebulun twelve thousand,
from the tribe of Joseph twelve thousand,
from the tribe of Benjamin twelve thousand sealed.

The Multitude from Every Nation

9 After this I looked, and there was a great multitude that no one
could count, from every nation, from all tribes and peoples and languages, standing before the throne and before the Lamb, robed in
white, with palm branches in their hands. 10 They cried out in a loud
voice, saying,

"Salvation belongs to our God who is seated on the throne, and
to the Lamb!"

11 And all the angels stood around the throne and around the elders
and the four living creatures, and they fell on their faces before the
throne and worshiped God, 12 singing,

"Amen! Blessing and glory and wisdom
and thanksgiving and honor
and power and might
be to our God forever and ever! Amen."

[a] Gk *slaves*

7:4-8 the number of those who were sealed: Suspense has been building toward the opening of the seventh seal. Instead, John pauses to describe "the servants of our God with a seal on their foreheads" (7:3). In the early church, *sealing* was another way of saying "baptism." In the Lutheran rite for Holy Baptism, the pastor makes the sign of the cross on the forehead of the baptized person and says "you have been sealed by the Holy Spirit and marked with the cross of Christ forever" (*ELW*, p. 231).

7:9 multitude that no one could count: Twelve is a special number in Christian tradition, symbolizing completeness. There were twelve tribes of Israel; Jesus had twelve disciples. One hundred forty-four thousand is twelve times twelve hundred, which symbolizes completeness on a grand scale. John hears that there are one hundred forty-four thousand servants of God (7:4), but then sees a multitude too enormous to count. God is greater than one can expect or imagine.

13 Then one of the elders addressed me, saying, "Who are these,
robed in white, and where have they come from?" 14 I said to him, "Sir,
you are the one that knows." Then he said to me, "These are they who
have come out of the great ordeal; they have washed their robes and
made them white in the blood of the Lamb.

7:15-17 For this reason they are before the throne: Revelation often refers to images from the Old Testament but does not always quote them directly. The images in these verses recall Isaiah 49:10; Psalm 121:6; Psalm 23:2; and Isaiah 25:8.

15 For this reason they are before the throne of God,
and worship him day and night within his temple,
and the one who is seated on the throne will shelter them.
16 They will hunger no more, and thirst no more;
the sun will not strike them,
nor any scorching heat;
17 for the Lamb at the center of the throne will be their shepherd,
and he will guide them to springs of the water of life,
and God will wipe away every tear from their eyes."

The Seventh Seal and the Golden Censer

8:1—11:19 When the lamb opened the seventh seal: Opening this seal unleashes seven even more devastating visions. The seven trumpets given to the seven angels represent God's judgments.

8 When the Lamb opened the seventh seal, there was silence in
heaven for about half an hour. 2 And I saw the seven angels who
stand before God, and seven trumpets were given to them.
3 Another angel with a golden censer came and stood at the altar;
he was given a great quantity of incense to offer with the prayers of
all the saints on the golden altar that is before the throne. 4 And the
smoke of the incense, with the prayers of the saints, rose before God
from the hand of the angel. 5 Then the angel took the censer and filled
it with fire from the altar and threw it on the earth; and there were
peals of thunder, rumblings, flashes of lightning, and an earthquake.

The Seven Trumpets

6 Now the seven angels who had the seven trumpets made ready
to blow them.
7 The first angel blew his trumpet, and there came hail and fire,
mixed with blood, and they were hurled to the earth; and a third of
the earth was burned up, and a third of the trees were burned up, and
all green grass was burned up.
8 The second angel blew his trumpet, and something like a great
mountain, burning with fire, was thrown into the sea. 9 A third of the
sea became blood, a third of the living creatures in the sea died, and a
third of the ships were destroyed.
10 The third angel blew his trumpet, and a great star fell from
heaven, blazing like a torch, and it fell on a third of the rivers and on
the springs of water. 11 The name of the star is Wormwood. A third of
the waters became wormwood, and many died from the water, because it was made bitter.
12 The fourth angel blew his trumpet, and a third of the sun was
struck, and a third of the moon, and a third of the stars, so that a third

of their light was darkened; a third of the day was kept from shining,
and likewise the night.

13 Then I looked, and I heard an eagle crying with a loud voice as
it flew in midheaven, "Woe, woe, woe to the inhabitants of the earth,
at the blasts of the other trumpets that the three angels are about to
blow!"

9 And the fifth angel blew his trumpet, and I saw a star that had
fallen from heaven to earth, and he was given the key to the
shaft of the bottomless pit; [2]he opened the shaft of the bottomless
pit, and from the shaft rose smoke like the smoke of a great furnace,
and the sun and the air were darkened with the smoke from the shaft.
[3]Then from the smoke came locusts on the earth, and they were given
authority like the authority of scorpions of the earth. [4]They were told
not to damage the grass of the earth or any green growth or any tree,
but only those people who do not have the seal of God on their foreheads. [5]They were allowed to torture them for five months, but not
to kill them, and their torture was like the torture of a scorpion when
it stings someone. [6]And in those days people will seek death but will
not find it; they will long to die, but death will flee from them.

7 In appearance the locusts were like horses equipped for battle.
On their heads were what looked like crowns of gold; their faces were
like human faces, [8]their hair like women's hair, and their teeth like
lions' teeth; [9]they had scales like iron breastplates, and the noise of
their wings was like the noise of many chariots with horses rushing
into battle. [10]They have tails like scorpions, with stingers, and in their
tails is their power to harm people for five months. [11]They have as
king over them the angel of the bottomless pit; his name in Hebrew is
Abaddon,[a] and in Greek he is called Apollyon.[b]

12 The first woe has passed. There are still two woes to come.

13 Then the sixth angel blew his trumpet, and I heard a voice from
the four[c] horns of the golden altar before God, [14]saying to the sixth
angel who had the trumpet, "Release the four angels who are bound
at the great river Euphrates." [15]So the four angels were released, who
had been held ready for the hour, the day, the month, and the year, to
kill a third of humankind. [16]The number of the troops of cavalry was
two hundred million; I heard their number. [17]And this was how I saw
the horses in my vision: the riders wore breastplates the color of fire
and of sapphire[d] and of sulfur; the heads of the horses were like lions'
heads, and fire and smoke and sulfur came out of their mouths. [18]By
these three plagues a third of humankind was killed, by the fire and
smoke and sulfur coming out of their mouths. [19]For the power of the
horses is in their mouths and in their tails; their tails are like serpents,
having heads; and with them they inflict harm.

---

[a] That is, *Destruction* [b] That is, *Destroyer* [c] Other ancient authorities lack *four* [d] Gk *hyacinth*

9:20-21 The rest of humankind, who were not killed: Scripture testifies that human sin is deep-rooted. Despite unspeakable consequences from their sin, those who survive the terrible plagues ignore the warning. They do not repent.

Do you think God actively punishes wrongdoing, or do you think that destruction and suffering are the logical and inevitable consequences of human sin? Or do you think it is some of each? Why?

20 The rest of humankind, who were not killed by these plagues,
did not repent of the works of their hands or give up worshiping demons and idols of gold and silver and bronze and stone and wood,
which cannot see or hear or walk. 21 And they did not repent of their
murders or their sorceries or their fornication or their thefts.

The Angel with the Little Scroll

10 And I saw another mighty angel coming down from heaven,
wrapped in a cloud, with a rainbow over his head; his face
was like the sun, and his legs like pillars of fire. 2 He held a little scroll
open in his hand. Setting his right foot on the sea and his left foot
on the land, 3 he gave a great shout, like a lion roaring. And when he
shouted, the seven thunders sounded. 4 And when the seven thunders
had sounded, I was about to write, but I heard a voice from heaven
saying, "Seal up what the seven thunders have said, and do not write it
down." 5 Then the angel whom I saw standing on the sea and the land
raised his right hand to heaven
6 and swore by him who lives forever and ever,
who created heaven and what is in it, the earth and what is in it, and
the sea and what is in it: "There will be no more delay, 7 but in the days
when the seventh angel is to blow his trumpet, the mystery of God
will be fulfilled, as he announced to his servants[a] the prophets."
8 Then the voice that I had heard from heaven spoke to me again,
saying, "Go, take the scroll that is open in the hand of the angel who is
standing on the sea and on the land." 9 So I went to the angel and told
him to give me the little scroll; and he said to me, "Take it, and eat;
it will be bitter to your stomach, but sweet as honey in your mouth."
10 So I took the little scroll from the hand of the angel and ate it; it was
sweet as honey in my mouth, but when I had eaten it, my stomach
was made bitter.
11 Then they said to me, "You must prophesy again about many
peoples and nations and languages and kings."

10:6 who created heaven and what is in it: In the midst of destruction, the angel proclaims that God's basic nature is creative, not destructive.

10:8-11 take the scroll that is open: The scroll contains God's plan for creation. The plan is revealed to John, who is told to "eat" it—internalize it—and then to proclaim it. This affirms John's call to prophesy in 1:10-11.

The Two Witnesses

11 Then I was given a measuring rod like a staff, and I was told,
"Come and measure the temple of God and the altar and those
who worship there, 2 but do not measure the court outside the temple; leave that out, for it is given over to the nations, and they will
trample over the holy city for forty-two months. 3 And I will grant my
two witnesses authority to prophesy for one thousand two hundred
sixty days, wearing sackcloth."
4 These are the two olive trees and the two lampstands that stand
before the Lord of the earth. 5 And if anyone wants to harm them, fire

11:1-2 measure the temple of God: John uses the image of the temple to refer to the community of God's true followers. Despite the threatening powers of the world, this community remains intact.

11:3-12 I will grant my two witnesses authority: The witnesses are God's faithful ones who call the world to repent from its evil ways. Their enemies appear to defeat them, but this is only temporary.

---

[a] Gk *slaves*

pours from their mouth and consumes their foes; anyone who wants to
harm them must be killed in this manner. 6 They have authority to shut
the sky, so that no rain may fall during the days of their prophesying,
and they have authority over the waters to turn them into blood, and to
strike the earth with every kind of plague, as often as they desire.
7 When they have finished their testimony, the beast that comes
up from the bottomless pit will make war on them and conquer them
and kill them, 8 and their dead bodies will lie in the street of the great
city that is prophetically[a] called Sodom and Egypt, where also their
Lord was crucified. 9 For three and a half days members of the peoples
and tribes and languages and nations will gaze at their dead bodies
and refuse to let them be placed in a tomb; 10 and the inhabitants of
the earth will gloat over them and celebrate and exchange presents,
because these two prophets had been a torment to the inhabitants of
the earth.
11 But after the three and a half days, the breath[b] of life from God
entered them, and they stood on their feet, and those who saw them
were terrified. 12 Then they[c] heard a loud voice from heaven saying to
them, "Come up here!" And they went up to heaven in a cloud while
their enemies watched them. 13 At that moment there was a great
earthquake, and a tenth of the city fell; seven thousand people were
killed in the earthquake, and the rest were terrified and gave glory to
the God of heaven.
14 The second woe has passed. The third woe is coming very
soon.

11:7 the beast that comes up from the bottomless pit: In writings like Revelation, terrible creatures—beasts and dragons—represent evil. Here John describes the beast in stark contrast to the Lamb, who opposes them.

The Seventh Trumpet

15 Then the seventh angel blew his trumpet, and there were loud
voices in heaven, saying,

"The kingdom of the world has become the kingdom of our Lord
and of his Messiah,[d]
and he will reign forever and ever."

16 Then the twenty-four elders who sit on their thrones before
God fell on their faces and worshiped God, 17 singing,

"We give you thanks, Lord God Almighty,
who are and who were,
for you have taken your great power
and begun to reign.
18 The nations raged,
but your wrath has come,
and the time for judging the dead,
for rewarding your servants,[e] the prophets
and saints and all who fear your name,

11:15-19 the seventh angel blew his trumpet: The trumpet blast signals another round of joyful praise of God, followed by more ominous rumblings in heaven. Whether or not this is the vision of "woe" mentioned in 11:14 depends on where one stands in this conflict.

[a] Or *allegorically*; Gk *spiritually* [b] Or *the spirit* [c] Other ancient authorities read *I* [d] Gk *Christ*
[e] Gk *slaves*

both small and great,
and for destroying those who destroy the earth."
19 Then God's temple in heaven was opened, and the ark of his
covenant was seen within his temple; and there were flashes of lightning, rumblings, peals of thunder, an earthquake, and heavy hail.

The Woman and the Dragon

12:1-6 A great portent appeared in heaven: Revelation 12 describes a cosmic battle between good and evil. The struggle is universal. God is working to restore justice to all creation. Some scholars think John adapted this story from a Greek myth. Others think it draws from stories of Jesus' birth and ascension, and from Old Testament stories of Satan. It may be that the woman refers to the community of believers, the child to Jesus, and the dragon to Satan.

12 A great portent appeared in heaven: a woman clothed with
the sun, with the moon under her feet, and on her head a
crown of twelve stars. 2She was pregnant and was crying out in birth
pangs, in the agony of giving birth. 3Then another portent appeared
in heaven: a great red dragon, with seven heads and ten horns, and
seven diadems on his heads. 4His tail swept down a third of the stars
of heaven and threw them to the earth. Then the dragon stood before the woman who was about to bear a child, so that he might devour her child as soon as it was born. 5And she gave birth to a son, a
male child, who is to rule[a] all the nations with a rod of iron. But her
child was snatched away and taken to God and to his throne; 6and the
woman fled into the wilderness, where she has a place prepared by
God, so that there she can be nourished for one thousand two hundred sixty days.

Michael Defeats the Dragon

12:7-11 war broke out in heaven: These verses are sometimes cited as evidence for the legend that Satan was a fallen angel that God cast out from heaven. Here, however, it is Michael, not the Messiah, who defeats "the dragon and his angels." This description is similar to Jesus' account in Luke 10:18.

7 And war broke out in heaven; Michael and his angels fought
against the dragon. The dragon and his angels fought back, 8but they
were defeated, and there was no longer any place for them in heaven.
9The great dragon was thrown down, that ancient serpent, who is called
the Devil and Satan, the deceiver of the whole world—he was thrown
down to the earth, and his angels were thrown down with him.
10 Then I heard a loud voice in heaven, proclaiming,
"Now have come the salvation and the power
and the kingdom of our God
and the authority of his Messiah,[b]
for the accuser of our comrades[c] has been thrown down,
who accuses them day and night before our God.
11 But they have conquered him by the blood of the Lamb
and by the word of their testimony,
for they did not cling to life even in the face of death.
12 Rejoice then, you heavens
and those who dwell in them!
But woe to the earth and the sea,
for the devil has come down to you
with great wrath,
because he knows that his time is short!"

12:12-17 Rejoice: The story of cosmic war gives hope to the persecuted. Evil reigns on earth not because it is powerful but because it has been defeated in heaven and has nowhere else to go. The dragon—evil—is now confined to a small range and rages in destructive fury at seeing its power curtailed.

[a] Or *to shepherd* [b] Gk *Christ* [c] Gk *brothers*

The Dragon Fights Again on Earth

13 So when the dragon saw that he had been thrown down to
the earth, he pursued[a] the woman who had given birth to the male
child. 14 But the woman was given the two wings of the great eagle, so
that she could fly from the serpent into the wilderness, to her place
where she is nourished for a time, and times, and half a time. 15 Then
from his mouth the serpent poured water like a river after the woman,
to sweep her away with the flood. 16 But the earth came to the help
of the woman; it opened its mouth and swallowed the river that the
dragon had poured from his mouth. 17 Then the dragon was angry
with the woman, and went off to make war on the rest of her children,
those who keep the commandments of God and hold the testimony
of Jesus.

The First Beast

18 Then the dragon[b] took his stand on the sand of the seashore.

13

1 And I saw a beast rising out of the sea, having ten horns and
seven heads; and on its horns were ten diadems, and on its
heads were blasphemous names. 2 And the beast that I saw was like
a leopard, its feet were like a bear's, and its mouth was like a lion's
mouth. And the dragon gave it his power and his throne and great authority. 3 One of its heads seemed to have received a death-blow, but
its mortal wound[c] had been healed. In amazement the whole earth
followed the beast. 4 They worshiped the dragon, for he had given his
authority to the beast, and they worshiped the beast, saying, "Who is
like the beast, and who can fight against it?"

5 The beast was given a mouth uttering haughty and blasphemous
words, and it was allowed to exercise authority for forty-two months.
6 It opened its mouth to utter blasphemies against God, blaspheming
his name and his dwelling, that is, those who dwell in heaven. 7 Also it
was allowed to make war on the saints and to conquer them.[d] It was
given authority over every tribe and people and language and nation,
8 and all the inhabitants of the earth will worship it, everyone whose
name has not been written from the foundation of the world in the
book of life of the Lamb that was slaughtered.[e]

9 Let anyone who has an ear listen:

10 If you are to be taken captive,
  into captivity you go;
if you kill with the sword,
  with the sword you must be killed.
Here is a call for the endurance and faith of the saints.

---

[a] Or *persecuted* [b] Gk *Then he*; other ancient authorities read *Then I stood* [c] Gk *the plague of its death* [d] Other ancient authorities lack this sentence [e] Or *written in the book of life of the Lamb that was slaughtered from the foundation of the world*

13:1 I saw a beast rising out of the sea: As the dragon exits the stage, other beasts appear. Evil is persistent and keeps reappearing in different forms. Here, the beast may refer to the Roman Empire. Roman armies traveled across the sea to conquer cities in Asia Minor.

13:3-8 One of its heads seemed to have received a death-blow: This beast displays remarkable similarities to the Lamb. It has been slain, yet lives (13:3), as did the Lamb (5:6). The beast conquers and has authority over every tribe and nation (13:7), as does the Lamb (5:9-10). Multitudes worship the beast (13:8), as is true of the Lamb (7:9-10). There are, however, huge differences. For example, this beast conquers by war (13:7), while the Lamb conquers by its innocent death (12:11). Perhaps John depicts evil in this way to jolt complacent readers out of the belief that the rule of Rome is compatible with Christianity.

13:4 who can fight against it? John voices the common complaint of those who feel powerless in the face of evil and wonder if there is any use in fighting it.

13:9-17 Let anyone who has an ear listen: John exhorts readers to listen to his message: stand with God or stand with the forces opposed to God. Just as the faithful are marked as servants of God (7:3), those who side with the beast are marked (13:16). There is no middle ground.

What do you think Christians need to "conquer" today? How might we do this?

The Second Beast

11 Then I saw another beast that rose out of the earth; it had two
horns like a lamb and it spoke like a dragon. 12 It exercises all the authority of the first beast on its behalf, and it makes the earth and its
inhabitants worship the first beast, whose mortal wound[a] had been
healed. 13 It performs great signs, even making fire come down from
heaven to earth in the sight of all; 14 and by the signs that it is allowed
to perform on behalf of the beast, it deceives the inhabitants of earth,
telling them to make an image for the beast that had been wounded
by the sword[b] and yet lived; 15 and it was allowed to give breath[c] to the
image of the beast so that the image of the beast could even speak and
cause those who would not worship the image of the beast to be killed.
16 Also it causes all, both small and great, both rich and poor, both free
and slave, to be marked on the right hand or the forehead, 17 so that no
one can buy or sell who does not have the mark, that is, the name of
the beast or the number of its name. 18 This calls for wisdom: let anyone with understanding calculate the number of the beast, for it is the
number of a person. Its number is six hundred sixty-six.[d]

The Lamb and the 144,000

14 Then I looked, and there was the Lamb, standing on Mount
Zion! And with him were one hundred forty-four thousand
who had his name and his Father's name written on their foreheads.
2 And I heard a voice from heaven like the sound of many waters and
like the sound of loud thunder; the voice I heard was like the sound of
harpists playing on their harps, 3 and they sing a new song before the
throne and before the four living creatures and before the elders. No
one could learn that song except the one hundred forty-four thousand who have been redeemed from the earth. 4 It is these who have
not defiled themselves with women, for they are virgins; these follow
the Lamb wherever he goes. They have been redeemed from humankind as first fruits for God and the Lamb, 5 and in their mouth no lie
was found; they are blameless.

The Messages of the Three Angels

6 Then I saw another angel flying in midheaven, with an eternal
gospel to proclaim to those who live[e] on the earth—to every nation
and tribe and language and people. 7 He said in a loud voice, "Fear
God and give him glory, for the hour of his judgment has come; and
worship him who made heaven and earth, the sea and the springs of
water."
8 Then another angel, a second, followed, saying, "Fallen, fallen is

---

[a] Gk *whose plague of its death* [b] Or *that had received the plague of the sword* [c] Or *spirit* [d] Other ancient authorities read *six hundred sixteen* [e] Gk *sit*

13:18 the number of the beast…is six hundred sixty-six: This number symbolizes imperfection; it is the sacred number seven minus one, repeated "a completeness" of three times. In popular interpretation, 666 is Satan's identifying number. John, however, appears to be using the practice of *gematria (guh-MAH-tree-uh)*, which was common in his time. Gematria is a form of code that assigns numerical values to different letters. Evidence is strong that 666 referred to the Roman emperor Nero. As a ruler known for ordering horrible torture and the slaughter of Christians, Nero stood as the symbol of the opposition to God in the world.

14:1 there was the Lamb: The visions of Revelation 14 revisit previous themes: good and evil are in constant struggle; people must choose which side to be on; and the forces of good will win in the end.

14:8 fallen is Babylon: Babylon was the powerful capital of an ancient empire, destroyed long before John's time. The name Babylon symbolizes Rome or any other worldly power. Its reign is always temporary.

Babylon the great! She has made all nations drink of the wine of the
wrath of her fornication."
9 Then another angel, a third, followed them, crying with a loud
voice, "Those who worship the beast and its image, and receive a mark
on their foreheads or on their hands, [10]they will also drink the wine of
God's wrath, poured unmixed into the cup of his anger, and they will
be tormented with fire and sulfur in the presence of the holy angels
and in the presence of the Lamb. [11]And the smoke of their torment
goes up forever and ever. There is no rest day or night for those who
worship the beast and its image and for anyone who receives the mark
of its name."
12 Here is a call for the endurance of the saints, those who keep
the commandments of God and hold fast to the faith of[a] Jesus.
13 And I heard a voice from heaven saying, "Write this: Blessed
are the dead who from now on die in the Lord." "Yes," says the Spirit,
"they will rest from their labors, for their deeds follow them."

Reaping the Earth's Harvest

14 Then I looked, and there was a white cloud, and seated on the
cloud was one like the Son of Man, with a golden crown on his head,
and a sharp sickle in his hand! [15]Another angel came out of the temple, calling with a loud voice to the one who sat on the cloud, "Use
your sickle and reap, for the hour to reap has come, because the harvest of the earth is fully ripe." [16]So the one who sat on the cloud swung
his sickle over the earth, and the earth was reaped.
17 Then another angel came out of the temple in heaven, and he
too had a sharp sickle. [18]Then another angel came out from the altar,
the angel who has authority over fire, and he called with a loud voice
to him who had the sharp sickle, "Use your sharp sickle and gather the
clusters of the vine of the earth, for its grapes are ripe." [19]So the angel
swung his sickle over the earth and gathered the vintage of the earth,
and he threw it into the great wine press of the wrath of God. [20]And
the wine press was trodden outside the city, and blood flowed from
the wine press, as high as a horse's bridle, for a distance of about two
hundred miles.[b]

The Angels with the Seven Last Plagues

15 Then I saw another portent in heaven, great and amazing:
seven angels with seven plagues, which are the last, for with
them the wrath of God is ended.
2 And I saw what appeared to be a sea of glass mixed with fire, and
those who had conquered the beast and its image and the number of
its name, standing beside the sea of glass with harps of God in their

---

[a] Or *to their faith in* [b] Gk *one thousand six hundred stadia*

15:3 sing the song: This vision of triumph recalls the joy of Moses and the Israelites upon being delivered by God from the Egyptians (see Exod 15:1-18).

15:4 All nations will come and worship before you: In the midst of terrifying visions of the destruction comes the reassurance that God's desire is not that nations be destroyed, but that they repent and follow God.

16:1 seven bowls of the wrath of God: In Revelation 16, the cycle of visions returns to the dire warnings. This repetition hammers relentlessly at the false security people build for themselves. Because the contents of a bowl can be dumped quickly, perhaps John's vision is saying that God's judgment will take place rapidly.

16:5 You are just, O Holy One: The vision affirms that, in the name of justice, God has every right to wreak the vengeance described in this vision.

hands. 3 And they sing the song of Moses, the servant[a] of God, and the
song of the Lamb:

"Great and amazing are your deeds,
Lord God the Almighty!
Just and true are your ways,
King of the nations![b]
4 Lord, who will not fear
and glorify your name?
For you alone are holy.
All nations will come
and worship before you,
for your judgments have been revealed."

5 After this I looked, and the temple of the tent[c] of witness in
heaven was opened, 6 and out of the temple came the seven angels
with the seven plagues, robed in pure bright linen,[d] with golden
sashes across their chests. 7 Then one of the four living creatures gave
the seven angels seven golden bowls full of the wrath of God, who
lives forever and ever; 8 and the temple was filled with smoke from the
glory of God and from his power, and no one could enter the temple
until the seven plagues of the seven angels were ended.

The Bowls of God's Wrath

16 Then I heard a loud voice from the temple telling the seven
angels, "Go and pour out on the earth the seven bowls of the
wrath of God."

2 So the first angel went and poured his bowl on the earth, and
a foul and painful sore came on those who had the mark of the beast
and who worshiped its image.

3 The second angel poured his bowl into the sea, and it became
like the blood of a corpse, and every living thing in the sea died.

4 The third angel poured his bowl into the rivers and the springs
of water, and they became blood. 5 And I heard the angel of the waters
say,

"You are just, O Holy One, who are and were,
for you have judged these things;
6 because they shed the blood of saints and prophets,
you have given them blood to drink.
It is what they deserve!"

7 And I heard the altar respond,

"Yes, O Lord God, the Almighty,
your judgments are true and just!"

---

[a] Gk *slave* [b] Other ancient authorities read *the ages* [c] Or *tabernacle* [d] Other ancient authorities read *stone*

8 The fourth angel poured his bowl on the sun, and it was allowed
to scorch people with fire; [9]they were scorched by the fierce heat, but
they cursed the name of God, who had authority over these plagues,
and they did not repent and give him glory.
10 The fifth angel poured his bowl on the throne of the beast, and
its kingdom was plunged into darkness; people gnawed their tongues
in agony, [11]and cursed the God of heaven because of their pains and
sores, and they did not repent of their deeds.
12 The sixth angel poured his bowl on the great river Euphrates,
and its water was dried up in order to prepare the way for the kings
from the east. [13]And I saw three foul spirits like frogs coming from
the mouth of the dragon, from the mouth of the beast, and from the
mouth of the false prophet. [14]These are demonic spirits, performing signs, who go abroad to the kings of the whole world, to assemble them for battle on the great day of God the Almighty. [15]("See, I
am coming like a thief! Blessed is the one who stays awake and is
clothed,[a] not going about naked and exposed to shame.") [16]And they
assembled them at the place that in Hebrew is called Harmagedon.
17 The seventh angel poured his bowl into the air, and a loud
voice came out of the temple, from the throne, saying, "It is done!"
[18]And there came flashes of lightning, rumblings, peals of thunder,
and a violent earthquake, such as had not occurred since people
were upon the earth, so violent was that earthquake. [19]The great city
was split into three parts, and the cities of the nations fell. God remembered great Babylon and gave her the wine-cup of the fury of
his wrath. [20]And every island fled away, and no mountains were to
be found; [21]and huge hailstones, each weighing about a hundred
pounds,[b] dropped from heaven on people, until they cursed God for
the plague of the hail, so fearful was that plague.

The Great Whore and the Beast

17 Then one of the seven angels who had the seven bowls came
and said to me, "Come, I will show you the judgment of the
great whore who is seated on many waters, [2]with whom the kings of
the earth have committed fornication, and with the wine of whose
fornication the inhabitants of the earth have become drunk." [3]So he
carried me away in the spirit[c] into a wilderness, and I saw a woman sitting on a scarlet beast that was full of blasphemous names, and it had
seven heads and ten horns. [4]The woman was clothed in purple and
scarlet, and adorned with gold and jewels and pearls, holding in her
hand a golden cup full of abominations and the impurities of her fornication; [5]and on her forehead was written a name, a mystery: "Babylon the great, mother of whores and of earth's abominations." [6]And

---

[a] Gk *and keeps his robes* [b] Gk *weighing about a talent* [c] Or *in the Spirit*

16:9 and they did not repent: Humankind continually brings about its own suffering by refusing to recognize that it is useless to oppose God.

16:16 at the place that in Hebrew is called Harmagedon: This is the name from which the term "armageddon" is taken. In modern usage, armageddon refers to a final, terrible battle that brings about the end of the world. This Hebrew name appears to be a combination of *har* ("mountain") and *Megiddo*, a place in northwest Palestine (see Map 12, p. 2109). The name Harmagedon appears nowhere else in Scripture. Megiddo was the site of some ancient battles (see Judg 5:19; 2 Kings 9:27; 2 Kings 23:29). Perhaps this inspires John's use of Harmagedon to mean a place where God's enemies are destroyed.

17:1-3 the judgment of the great whore: The "great whore" represents self-absorbed earthly powers, another symbol for Rome. She flaunts her wealth and power, and she leads people into destructive paths of materialism and selfishness.

When do you think it is appropriate to incorporate elements of popular culture into the Christian message in order to reach out to those who are not believers?

17:5-6 on her forehead was written a name...Babylon: John draws a clear distinction between those who are marked by God (7:3) and those who follow worldly leaders.

In what ways should believers be different from those who do not believe? In what ways should they be the same?

I saw that the woman was drunk with the blood of the saints and the
blood of the witnesses to Jesus.
When I saw her, I was greatly amazed. 7 But the angel said to me,
"Why are you so amazed? I will tell you the mystery of the woman,
and of the beast with seven heads and ten horns that carries her. 8 The
beast that you saw was, and is not, and is about to ascend from the
bottomless pit and go to destruction. And the inhabitants of
the earth, whose names have not been written in the book of life from
the foundation of the world, will be amazed when they see the beast,
because it was and is not and is to come.
9 "This calls for a mind that has wisdom: the seven heads are
seven mountains on which the woman is seated; also, they are seven
kings, 10 of whom five have fallen, one is living, and the other has not
yet come; and when he comes, he must remain only a little while. 11 As
for the beast that was and is not, it is an eighth but it belongs to the
seven, and it goes to destruction. 12 And the ten horns that you saw are
ten kings who have not yet received a kingdom, but they are to receive
authority as kings for one hour, together with the beast. 13 These are
united in yielding their power and authority to the beast; 14 they will
make war on the Lamb, and the Lamb will conquer them, for he is
Lord of lords and King of kings, and those with him are called and
chosen and faithful."
15 And he said to me, "The waters that you saw, where the whore
is seated, are peoples and multitudes and nations and languages. 16 And
the ten horns that you saw, they and the beast will hate the whore;
they will make her desolate and naked; they will devour her flesh and
burn her up with fire. 17 For God has put it into their hearts to carry
out his purpose by agreeing to give their kingdom to the beast, until
the words of God will be fulfilled. 18 The woman you saw is the great
city that rules over the kings of the earth."

The Fall of Babylon

18 After this I saw another angel coming down from heaven,
having great authority; and the earth was made bright with
his splendor. 2 He called out with a mighty voice,

"Fallen, fallen is Babylon the great!
  It has become a dwelling place of demons,
a haunt of every foul spirit,
  a haunt of every foul bird,
  a haunt of every foul and hateful beast.[a]
3 For all the nations have drunk[b]
  of the wine of the wrath of her fornication,

---

[a] Other ancient authorities lack the words *a haunt of every foul beast* and attach the words *and hateful* to the previous line so as to read *a haunt of every foul and hateful bird* [b] Other ancient authorities read *She has made all nations drink*

17:8 was, and is not, and is about to: This beast is in contrast to the Lamb and God, the one "who is and who was and who is to come" (1:8). Part of the phrase is repeated in 17:11, speaking about the beast.

17:9 the seven heads are seven mountains on which the woman is seated: The reference to the seven mountains would have been clear to John's readers. Rome was known as the city built on seven hills. John declares that the mighty Roman Empire is faithless and corrupt.

18:2 fallen is Babylon: Revelation 18 is a dirge, or funeral hymn, for Babylon, signifying Rome or any oppressive rule. While Babylon appears to be rich and powerful, that is an illusion. This vision is John's warning to those who admire and are attracted to the Roman Empire, and a message of hope to those who fear it. No matter how alluring and invincible it seems, the power of Rome is nothing compared to the power of God.

and the kings of the earth have committed fornication with her,
and the merchants of the earth have grown rich from the
power[a] of her luxury."

4 Then I heard another voice from heaven saying,
"Come out of her, my people,
so that you do not take part in her sins,
and so that you do not share in her plagues;
5 for her sins are heaped high as heaven,
and God has remembered her iniquities.
6 Render to her as she herself has rendered,
and repay her double for her deeds;
mix a double draught for her in the cup she mixed.
7 As she glorified herself and lived luxuriously,
so give her a like measure of torment and grief.
Since in her heart she says,
'I rule as a queen;
I am no widow,
and I will never see grief,'
8 therefore her plagues will come in a single day—
pestilence and mourning and famine—
and she will be burned with fire;
for mighty is the Lord God who judges her."

9 And the kings of the earth, who committed fornication and
lived in luxury with her, will weep and wail over her when they see
the smoke of her burning; 10 they will stand far off, in fear of her torment, and say,

"Alas, alas, the great city,
Babylon, the mighty city!
For in one hour your judgment has come."

11 And the merchants of the earth weep and mourn for her, since
no one buys their cargo anymore, 12 cargo of gold, silver, jewels and
pearls, fine linen, purple, silk and scarlet, all kinds of scented wood,
all articles of ivory, all articles of costly wood, bronze, iron, and marble, 13 cinnamon, spice, incense, myrrh, frankincense, wine, olive oil,
choice flour and wheat, cattle and sheep, horses and chariots, slaves—
and human lives.[b]

14 "The fruit for which your soul longed
has gone from you,
and all your dainties and your splendor
are lost to you,
never to be found again!"

15 The merchants of these wares, who gained wealth from her, will
stand far off, in fear of her torment, weeping and mourning aloud,

---

[a] Or *resources* [b] Or *chariots, and human bodies and souls*

16 "Alas, alas, the great city,
clothed in fine linen,
in purple and scarlet,
adorned with gold,
with jewels, and with pearls!
17 For in one hour all this wealth has been laid waste!"
And all shipmasters and seafarers, sailors and all whose trade is
on the sea, stood far off 18 and cried out as they saw the smoke of her
burning,
"What city was like the great city?"
19 And they threw dust on their heads, as they wept and mourned, crying out,
"Alas, alas, the great city,
where all who had ships at sea
grew rich by her wealth!
For in one hour she has been laid waste."
20 Rejoice over her, O heaven, you saints and apostles and prophets! For God has given judgment for you against her.
21 Then a mighty angel took up a stone like a great millstone and
threw it into the sea, saying,
"With such violence Babylon the great city
will be thrown down,
and will be found no more;
22 and the sound of harpists and minstrels and of flutists and
trumpeters
will be heard in you no more;
and an artisan of any trade
will be found in you no more;
and the sound of the millstone
will be heard in you no more;
23 and the light of a lamp
will shine in you no more;
and the voice of bridegroom and bride
will be heard in you no more;
for your merchants were the magnates of the earth,
and all nations were deceived by your sorcery.
24 And in you[a] was found the blood of prophets and of saints,
and of all who have been slaughtered on earth."

The Rejoicing in Heaven

19 After this I heard what seemed to be the loud voice of a great
multitude in heaven, saying,
"Hallelujah!

19:1-6 I heard what seemed to be the loud voice of a great multitude: John's vision returns to scenes of praise and worship, this time rejoicing at the fall of oppressive and faithless earthly powers. *Hallelujah* means "praise the Lord."

---

[a] Gk *her*

Salvation and glory and power to our God,
2 for his judgments are true and just;
he has judged the great whore
who corrupted the earth with her fornication,
and he has avenged on her the blood of his servants."[a]
3 Once more they said,
"Hallelujah!
The smoke goes up from her forever and ever."
4 And the twenty-four elders and the four living creatures fell down
and worshiped God who is seated on the throne, saying,
"Amen. Hallelujah!"
5 And from the throne came a voice saying,
"Praise our God,
all you his servants,[a]
and all who fear him,
small and great."
6 Then I heard what seemed to be the voice of a great multitude, like
the sound of many waters and like the sound of mighty thunderpeals,
crying out,
"Hallelujah!
For the Lord our God
the Almighty reigns.
7 Let us rejoice and exult
and give him the glory,
for the marriage of the Lamb has come,
and his bride has made herself ready;
8 to her it has been granted to be clothed
with fine linen, bright and pure"—
for the fine linen is the righteous deeds of the saints.
9 And the angel said[b] to me, "Write this: Blessed are those who
are invited to the marriage supper of the Lamb." And he said to me,
"These are true words of God." 10 Then I fell down at his feet to worship him, but he said to me, "You must not do that! I am a fellow servant[c] with you and your comrades[d] who hold the testimony of Jesus.[e]
Worship God! For the testimony of Jesus[e] is the spirit of prophecy."

The Rider on the White Horse

11 Then I saw heaven opened, and there was a white horse! Its
rider is called Faithful and True, and in righteousness he judges and
makes war. 12 His eyes are like a flame of fire, and on his head are many
diadems; and he has a name inscribed that no one knows but himself.
13 He is clothed in a robe dipped in[f] blood, and his name is called The

19:6-8 the marriage of the Lamb has come: In contrast to the "great whore" (17:1-6), the "great multitude" (19:6)—God's faithful people—is depicted as the bride of the Lamb. Elsewhere in Scripture, marriage also is used as an image of the relationship between God and God's people (see Isa 54:1-8; Jer 3:1-20; Hos 2:19-20; 2 Cor 11:2; Eph 5:25-32).

19:11 Then I saw heaven opened: The conflict between good and evil builds to a climax with this image of the return of Christ.

---

[a] Gk *slaves* [b] Gk *he said* [c] Gk *slave* [d] Gk *brothers* [e] Or *to Jesus* [f] Other ancient authorities read *sprinkled with*

Word of God. 14 And the armies of heaven, wearing fine linen, white
and pure, were following him on white horses. 15 From his mouth
comes a sharp sword with which to strike down the nations, and he
will rule[a] them with a rod of iron; he will tread the wine press of the
fury of the wrath of God the Almighty. 16 On his robe and on his thigh
he has a name inscribed, "King of kings and Lord of lords."

The Beast and Its Armies Defeated

17 Then I saw an angel standing in the sun, and with a loud voice
he called to all the birds that fly in midheaven, "Come, gather for the
great supper of God, 18 to eat the flesh of kings, the flesh of captains,
the flesh of the mighty, the flesh of horses and their riders—flesh of
all, both free and slave, both small and great." 19 Then I saw the beast
and the kings of the earth with their armies gathered to make war
against the rider on the horse and against his army. 20 And the beast
was captured, and with it the false prophet who had performed in
its presence the signs by which he deceived those who had received
the mark of the beast and those who worshiped its image. These two
were thrown alive into the lake of fire that burns with sulfur. 21 And the
rest were killed by the sword of the rider on the horse, the sword that
came from his mouth; and all the birds were gorged with their flesh.

The Thousand Years

20 Then I saw an angel coming down from heaven, holding
in his hand the key to the bottomless pit and a great chain.
2 He seized the dragon, that ancient serpent, who is the Devil and Satan, and bound him for a thousand years, 3 and threw him into the
pit, and locked and sealed it over him, so that he would deceive the
nations no more, until the thousand years were ended. After that he
must be let out for a little while.

4 Then I saw thrones, and those seated on them were given authority to judge. I also saw the souls of those who had been beheaded
for their testimony to Jesus[b] and for the word of God. They had not
worshiped the beast or its image and had not received its mark on
their foreheads or their hands. They came to life and reigned with
Christ a thousand years. 5 (The rest of the dead did not come to life
until the thousand years were ended.) This is the first resurrection.
6 Blessed and holy are those who share in the first resurrection. Over
these the second death has no power, but they will be priests of God
and of Christ, and they will reign with him a thousand years.

Satan's Doom

7 When the thousand years are ended, Satan will be released from
his prison 8 and will come out to deceive the nations at the four cor-

[a] Or *will shepherd* [b] Or *for the testimony of Jesus*

19:19-21 the beast and the kings of the earth: This depicts what is sometimes called the Battle of Armageddon. Many see it as a literal world war between military forces. However, this great battle is over before it starts. God accomplishes the victory, and the weapon used to annihilate evil is the Word of God (19:13, 15, 21).

What do you think it means for the Word of God to triumph in the world today? What does such victory look like?

20:1-3 Then I saw an angel coming down from heaven: The dragon, identified as Satan, is not annihilated at this great battle, but is locked away for a thousand years. John does not explain why evil exists. He simply accepts that it exists and that it stubbornly resists God's efforts to eliminate it. This long period of time suggests the final victory will not come during the lifetime of John or his readers. It suggests God's time. In God's time, the ultimate triumph will come.

What would you describe as evil in the world? What are the dangers of refusing to recognize and name evil in the world? What are the dangers of labeling people, places, or events as evil?

20:4-6 came to life and reigned with Christ a thousand years: This thousand-year reign is called the millennium (see note on 20:1-3). John's vision invites wonder and awe in considering God's ultimate victory over evil. Throughout the history of the church, some have taken this image literally, believing either that Christ will return to earth before the beginning of this period or that Christ will return one thousand years after this time of God's final reign begins.

20:7-10 When the thousand years are ended: Yet one more battle takes place after the great battle. Again, it is no contest. God accomplishes the final victory.

ners of the earth, Gog and Magog, in order to gather them for battle;
they are as numerous as the sands of the sea. 9 They marched up over
the breadth of the earth and surrounded the camp of the saints and
the beloved city. And fire came down from heaven[a] and consumed
them. 10 And the devil who had deceived them was thrown into the
lake of fire and sulfur, where the beast and the false prophet were, and
they will be tormented day and night forever and ever.

The Dead Are Judged

11 Then I saw a great white throne and the one who sat on it; the
earth and the heaven fled from his presence, and no place was found
for them. 12 And I saw the dead, great and small, standing before the
throne, and books were opened. Also another book was opened, the
book of life. And the dead were judged according to their works, as
recorded in the books. 13 And the sea gave up the dead that were in
it, Death and Hades gave up the dead that were in them, and all were
judged according to what they had done. 14 Then Death and Hades
were thrown into the lake of fire. This is the second death, the lake of
fire; 15 and anyone whose name was not found written in the book of
life was thrown into the lake of fire.

The New Heaven and the New Earth

21 Then I saw a new heaven and a new earth; for the first heaven
and the first earth had passed away, and the sea was no more.
2 And I saw the holy city, the new Jerusalem, coming down out of
heaven from God, prepared as a bride adorned for her husband. 3 And
I heard a loud voice from the throne saying,

"See, the home[b] of God is among mortals.
He will dwell[c] with them;
they will be his peoples,[d]
and God himself will be with them;[e]
4 he will wipe every tear from their eyes.
Death will be no more;
mourning and crying and pain will be no more,
for the first things have passed away."

5 And the one who was seated on the throne said, "See, I am making all things new." Also he said, "Write this, for these words are trustworthy and true." 6 Then he said to me, "It is done! I am the Alpha
and the Omega, the beginning and the end. To the thirsty I will give
water as a gift from the spring of the water of life. 7 Those who conquer will inherit these things, and I will be their God and they will be
my children. 8 But as for the cowardly, the faithless,[f] the polluted, the

[a] Other ancient authorities read *from God, out of heaven,* or *out of heaven from God* [b] Gk *the tabernacle* [c] Gk *will tabernacle* [d] Other ancient authorities read *people* [e] Other ancient authorities add *and be their God* [f] Or *the unbelieving*

20:11-15 I saw a great white throne: This description of God's final judgment, sometimes called Judgment Day, is John's vision of what the end of human history will be like. It speaks of two books. One includes works that people have done in their lifetimes and holds them responsible. The other is the book of life, which contains the names of God's people (see Exod 32:31-33; Ps 69:28; Dan 12:1; Phil 4:3; Rev 3:5, 13:8). Our names are in this book of life by God's grace alone. We cling to this promise, not to the effectiveness of our works.

21:1-5 I saw a new heaven and a new earth: The triumph of God over evil results in a new existence. John's vision is a fulfillment of what is promised in Isaiah 65:17-19. God does not start over. Rather, God makes "all things new" within God's good creation. "The new Jerusalem" is a vision of community—God's people will live together in peace and wholeness. "The home of God is among mortals" confirms God's ultimate desire to live among God's people.

murderers, the fornicators, the sorcerers, the idolaters, and all liars,
their place will be in the lake that burns with fire and sulfur, which is
the second death."

Vision of the New Jerusalem

9 Then one of the seven angels who had the seven bowls full of
the seven last plagues came and said to me, "Come, I will show you
the bride, the wife of the Lamb." 10 And in the spirit[a] he carried me
away to a great, high mountain and showed me the holy city Jerusalem coming down out of heaven from God. 11 It has the glory of God
and a radiance like a very rare jewel, like jasper, clear as crystal. 12 It has
a great, high wall with twelve gates, and at the gates twelve angels, and
on the gates are inscribed the names of the twelve tribes of the Israelites; 13 on the east three gates, on the north three gates, on the south
three gates, and on the west three gates. 14 And the wall of the city has
twelve foundations, and on them are the twelve names of the twelve
apostles of the Lamb.

15 The angel[b] who talked to me had a measuring rod of gold to
measure the city and its gates and walls. 16 The city lies foursquare,
its length the same as its width; and he measured the city with his
rod, fifteen hundred miles;[c] its length and width and height are equal.
17 He also measured its wall, one hundred forty-four cubits[d] by human
measurement, which the angel was using. 18 The wall is built of jasper,
while the city is pure gold, clear as glass. 19 The foundations of the wall
of the city are adorned with every jewel; the first was jasper, the second sapphire, the third agate, the fourth emerald, 20 the fifth onyx, the
sixth carnelian, the seventh chrysolite, the eighth beryl, the ninth to-
paz, the tenth chrysoprase, the eleventh jacinth, the twelfth amethyst.
21 And the twelve gates are twelve pearls, each of the gates is a single
pearl, and the street of the city is pure gold, transparent as glass.

22 I saw no temple in the city, for its temple is the Lord God the
Almighty and the Lamb. 23 And the city has no need of sun or moon to
shine on it, for the glory of God is its light, and its lamp is the Lamb.
24 The nations will walk by its light, and the kings of the earth will bring
their glory into it. 25 Its gates will never be shut by day—and there will
be no night there. 26 People will bring into it the glory and the honor
of the nations. 27 But nothing unclean will enter it, nor anyone who
practices abomination or falsehood, but only those who are written
in the Lamb's book of life.

The River of Life

22 Then the angel[e] showed me the river of the water of life,
bright as crystal, flowing from the throne of God and of the

[a] Or *in the Spirit* [b] Gk *He* [c] Gk *twelve thousand stadia* [d] That is, almost seventy-five yards [e] Gk *he*

21:9 I will show you the bride, the wife of the Lamb: The reference to the church as Christ's bride here and in 21:2 is a call to the church to be faithful. This is in contrast to the whore or harlot—described earlier in Revelation as the shallow deceit of earthly powers (see note on 17:1-3).

21:15 measuring rod of gold to measure the city: The city is described as a cube, whose sides each measure twelve thousand *stadia,* units of measurement each equaling about 202 yards. This would make the city nearly 1,400 miles long, 1,400 miles wide, and 1,400 miles high. Such dimensions symbolize the unimaginable splendor of our dwelling place with God.

21:25 Its gates will never be shut: John's vision declares that the gates of pearl are never shut. Living with God is an open invitation to all.

21:27 nothing unclean will enter it: There is tension between God's desire to bring all creation together and God's desire for a creation free from sin. Since we cannot free ourselves from sin, John's vision asks us to trust that Christ alone can accomplish this union and purity in us.

22:1-3 the angel showed me the river of the water of life: The image brings readers back to the image of the Garden of Eden from Genesis 2–3. John's vision is of God's creation unspoiled by human sin.

Lamb 2 through the middle of the street of the city. On either side of
the river is the tree of life[a] with its twelve kinds of fruit, producing
its fruit each month; and the leaves of the tree are for the healing of
the nations. 3 Nothing accursed will be found there any more. But the
throne of God and of the Lamb will be in it, and his servants[b] will
worship him; 4 they will see his face, and his name will be on their
foreheads. 5 And there will be no more night; they need no light of
lamp or sun, for the Lord God will be their light, and they will reign
forever and ever.
6 And he said to me, "These words are trustworthy and true, for
the Lord, the God of the spirits of the prophets, has sent his angel to
show his servants[b] what must soon take place."
7 "See, I am coming soon! Blessed is the one who keeps the words
of the prophecy of this book."

Epilogue and Benediction

8 I, John, am the one who heard and saw these things. And when
I heard and saw them, I fell down to worship at the feet of the angel
who showed them to me; 9 but he said to me, "You must not do that! I
am a fellow servant[c] with you and your comrades[d] the prophets, and
with those who keep the words of this book. Worship God!"
10 And he said to me, "Do not seal up the words of the prophecy
of this book, for the time is near. 11 Let the evildoer still do evil, and
the filthy still be filthy, and the righteous still do right, and the holy
still be holy."

12 "See, I am coming soon; my reward is with me, to repay according to everyone's work. 13 I am the Alpha and the Omega, the first
and the last, the beginning and the end."

14 Blessed are those who wash their robes,[e] so that they will have
the right to the tree of life and may enter the city by the gates. 15 Outside are the dogs and sorcerers and fornicators and murderers and
idolaters, and everyone who loves and practices falsehood.
16 "It is I, Jesus, who sent my angel to you with this testimony for
the churches. I am the root and the descendant of David, the bright
morning star."

17 The Spirit and the bride say, "Come."
And let everyone who hears say, "Come."
And let everyone who is thirsty come.
Let anyone who wishes take the water of life as a gift.

18 I warn everyone who hears the words of the prophecy of this

22:13 I am the Alpha and the Omega: John sums up the entire series of visions with this declaration. Many have tried to use the book of Revelation to determine the exact schedule of events at the end of the world. However, if Jesus Christ is the beginning (see John 1:1-2) and the end, then the end of the world is not a place or a time or a battle. The end is Jesus Christ. Whatever happens in the future, the Lamb will be there at the end of time, making all things new and living among God's people.

Why do we pray "Come, Lord Jesus"? In the *Small Catechism,* Martin Luther explains "your kingdom come," the second petition of the Lord's Prayer: "God's kingdom comes on its own without our prayer, but we ask in this prayer that it may also come to us" (*SC*:21). When we pray "Come, Lord Jesus!" we proclaim that we want to be part of God's kingdom now and for all time. *Revelation 22:20*

[a] Or *the Lamb.* [2] *In the middle of the street of the city, and on either side of the river, is the tree of life* [b] Gk *slaves* [c] Gk *slave* [d] Gk *brothers* [e] Other ancient authorities read *do his commandments*

book: if anyone adds to them, God will add to that person the plagues
described in this book; [19]if anyone takes away from the words of the
book of this prophecy, God will take away that person's share in the
tree of life and in the holy city, which are described in this book.

20 The one who testifies to these things says, "Surely I am coming soon."

Amen. Come, Lord Jesus!

21 The grace of the Lord Jesus be with all the saints. Amen.[a]

---

[a] Other ancient authorities lack *all*; others lack *the saints*; others lack *Amen*

SUBJECT GUIDE

Aaron
The brother of Moses who helped lead Israel
- Spokesman for Moses ... Exod 4:14
- Appears before Pharaoh ... Exod 5:1
- His rod becomes a serpent ... Exod 7:10
- Causes the plagues ... Exod 7–10
- Holds up Moses' hands ... Exod 17:12
- The first high priest ... Exod 28
- Makes the golden calf ... Exod 32:4
- His sons ... Lev 10
- Speaks against Moses ... Num 12
- His rod buds ... Num 17:8
- Excluded from the promised land ... Num 20:12
- His death ... Num 20:28
- Chosen by God ... Ps 105:26; Heb 5:4

Abba
The word for "father" in Aramaic
- We cry out "Abba, Father" ... Rom 8:15
- The Spirit calls "Abba, Father" ... Gal 4:6

Abel
The second son of Adam and Eve; murdered by his brother Cain
- Son of Adam and Eve ... Gen 4:1-2
- Offering accepted by God ... Gen 4:4
- Killed by Cain ... Gen 4:8
- Declared righteous ... Matt 23:35; 1 John 3:12
- His faith ... Heb 11:4

Abigail
The wife of Nabal
- Speaks wisely to David ... 1 Sam 25:23-35
- Becomes David's wife ... 1 Sam 25:39

Abraham
Called by God to become father of the people of Israel
- Leaves Ur ... Gen 11:31
- God calls him ... Gen 12:1-9
- God's covenant with ... Gen 15:18; Ps 105:9
- God promises him a son ... Gen 17:16
- Offers up Isaac ... Gen 22
- Abraham justified by faith ... Rom 4:3,10-22
- God's promise fulfilled ... Heb 6:13-15
- Abraham's faith ... Heb 11:8-12,17-19

Absalom
The son of David who led a revolt against him
- David's son ... 2 Sam 3:3
- Murders Amnon ... 2 Sam 13:28
- Revolt against King David ... 2 Sam 15
- Caught in tree ... 2 Sam 18:9
- Killed by Joab ... 2 Sam 18:14
- David mourns for ... 2 Sam 18:33

Abundance
- If we have, we're given more ... Matt 25:29
- Have life abundantly ... John 10:10
- Blessings in abundance ... 2 Cor 9:8
- Grace and peace in abundance ... 2 Pet 1:2

Acceptance
- Do not judge ... Matt 7:1-2
- The Golden Rule ... Luke 6:31
- God accepts people of all nations ... Acts 10:34-35
- Accept one another ... Rom 15:7
- We are one in Christ ... Gal 3:28
- Submit to one another ... Eph 5:21
- Love one another ... 1 Pet 4:8

Accountable
- We will account for our deeds ... Matt 12:36; Heb 4:13
- Whole world is accountable ... Rom 3:19
- We are accountable to God ... Rom 14:12
- We are accountable to the law ... Jas 2:10

See also Responsibility

Adam
The first human created by God
- Created by God ... Gen 2:7
- Blessed by God ... Gen 1:28
- Placed in garden ... Gen 2:15
- Names the animals ... Gen 2:20
- His disobedience and punishment ... Gen 3
- His death ... Gen 5:5
- His sin ... Rom 5:14
- The first Adam ... 1 Cor 15:45; 1 Tim 2:13
- In Adam all die ... 1 Cor 15:22

Adoption
- Moses is adopted ... Exod 2:10
- Ruth is accepted as a daughter ... Ruth 4:11-12
- Esther adopted by a cousin ... Esth 2:15
- We are adopted into God's family ... Eph 1:4-6

Adultery
- Judah and Tamar ... Gen 38:15-18
- Law against ... Exod 20:14
- David and Bathsheba ... 2 Sam 11
- Warning against ... Prov 6:20-29
- Sinful even in thought ... Matt 5:27-28
- Adultery starts in the heart ... Matt 15:19
- A sinful action ... Rom 7:2-3

Advice, *See* Guidance, Wisdom

Advocate
- He will come and teach everything ... John 14:26
- He will testify ... John 15:26
- The promise of his coming ... John 16:7
- Jesus Christ is our advocate ... 1 John 2:1

Age
- Honor your father and mother ... Exod 20:12
- Wisdom comes with age ... Job 12:12
- Declare God to the next generation ... Ps 71:18
- Bear fruit in old age ... Ps 92:14-15
- A promise of long life ... Ps 91:16
- A blessing ... Ps 128:5-6
- Keeping God's commands prolongs life ... Prov 3:1-2
- Fear of the Lord lengthens life ... Prov 10:27
- Gray hair is a crown ... Prov 16:31; 20:29
- Grandchildren are a crown ... Prov 17:6
- God sustains us through the ages ... Isa 46:4

Ahab
One of the most wicked kings of Israel
- King of Israel ... 1 Kgs 16:20
- He marries Jezebel ... 1 Kgs 16:31
- His worship of Baal ... 1 Kgs 16:32-34
- His confrontation with Elijah ... 1 Kgs 18:17-46
- He takes Naboth's vineyard ... 1 Kgs 21

Alcohol
- Raises tempers ... Prov 20:1
- Leads to problems ... Prov 23:21, 29-30
- Impairs judgment ... Prov 31:4-5
- Aids in happiness ... Eccl 10:19
- Jesus changes water into wine ... John 2:1-11
- Creates disunity in the church ... 1 Cor 11:18-21
- Used as medicine ... 1 Tim 5:23

Alien
- Do not mistreat ... Exod 22:21
- No longer called aliens ... Eph 2:19
- We are aliens in this world ... 1 Pet 2:11

Almighty
God's identity ... Gen 17:1
God is holy ... Isa 6:3
God's breath gives us life ... Job 33:4
God reigns over all ... Rev 19:6

Altar
Built by Noah ... Gen 8:20
Built by Abraham ... Gen 12:7
Built by Isaac ... Gen 26:25
Built by Jacob ... Gen 33:20
Description of God's altar ... Exod 27:1-8
Altar of stones ... Judg 6:19-23
The altar in Solomon's temple ... 2 Chr 4:1
The golden altar ... Rev 8:3

Ambition
Hezekiah's hard work ... 2 Chr 31:21
Recognition for skilled labor ... Prov 22:29
Setting priorities ... Matt 6:19-21
Rewards for work done ... Matt 16:26-27
Paul's ambition to preach ... Rom 15:20
We should show diligence ... Heb 6:10-11

Amen
So be it; let it become true
A response of the people ... Deut 27:15-26
A response of praise ... Ps 106:48
The ending to a prayer ... Rom 15:33
Jesus as the Amen ... 2 Cor 1:20; Rev 3:14
The close of a benediction ... Heb 13:21

Angel, angels
They protect God's people ... Ps 91:11
They protect Daniel from the lions ... Dan 6:22
An angel warns Joseph ... Matt 2:13
An angel at Jesus' tomb ... Matt 28:2-7
An angel speaks to Mary ... Luke 1:26-38
They announce Christ's birth ... Luke 2:8-20
They guide God's people ... Acts 27:23-24
They will return with Christ ... 2 Thess 1:7
They were created by God ... Col 1:16
They are not to be worshiped ... Col 2:18
They are spirits ... Heb 1:14

Anger
Moses responds in anger ... Num 20:7-13
Avoid anger, don't react ... Prov 14:17
A fool loses control to anger ... Prov 29:11
Anger leads to sinning ... Prov 29:22
Don't let anger escalate to sin ... Eph 4:26-27
Anger is not acceptable ... Col 3:8
Don't get angry quickly ... Jas 1:19-20

Animals
God creates the animals ... Gen 1:20-25
God gives humankind dominion over animals ... Genesis 1:26
Adam names them ... Gen 2:19-20
The talking donkey ... Num 22:21-38
David kills a lion and a bear ... 1 Sam 17:34-37
They live together in peace ... Isa 11:6-9

Anna
A prophet in the temple who praised God for the infant Jesus
Her longevity and joy ... Luke 2:36-38

Anoint, anointed
David anointed king ... 1 Sam 16:12
Head anointed with oil ... Ps 23:5
Mary anoints Christ ... Luke 7:46; John 11:2
The meaning of Messiah ... John 1:41
We are anointed with the Spirit ... 2 Cor 1:21-22

Antichrist
He is coming ... 1 John 2:18
He denies the Father ... 1 John 2:22
The spirit of ... 1 John 4:3
A deceiver is one ... 2 John 1:7

Anxiety
God's presence will bring peace ... Exod 33:14
God will give strength ... Ps 73:26
God will console us ... Ps 94:18-19
God's people must not worry ... Eccl 11:10
Everything is in God's control ... Isa 45:5-7
Don't worry about your life ... Luke 12:22-23
Bring your anxieties to God ... 1 Pet 5:7
See also Worry

Apostle
The twelve named ... Mark 3:14
Paul as an apostle to the Gentiles ... Rom 11:13
Appointed in the church ... 1 Cor 12:28
Paul as the least of them ... 1 Cor 15:9

Ark, Noah's
Built by Noah ... Gen 6:11-22
Rests on the mountains of Ararat ... Gen 8:4
Noah leaves the ark ... Gen 8:16

Ark of the Covenant
Contents of ... Exod 16:33-34; Num 17:10; Deut 10:2, 5
Description of ... Exod 25:10-22
Carried through the wilderness ... Josh 3:6-17
Carried around Jericho ... Josh 6:6-9
Brought to Jerusalem ... 2 Sam 6
Installed in the temple ... 1 Kgs 8

Armor
Of Goliath ... 1 Sam 17:5
For David ... 1 Sam 17:38
Of God ... Eph 6:11

Ascension
Jesus' ascension ... Mark 16:19; Luke 24:51; Acts 1:9

Ashamed
Not ashamed of nakedness ... Gen 2:25
A worker not ashamed ... 2 Tim 2:15
Paul not ashamed of the gospel ... Rom 1:16

Ask
Moses should ask for help ... Exod 18:17-18, 21-24
Call on God ... Jer 33:3
Call for help ... Jonah 2:2
Ask and you will receive ... Luke 11:9-10; 1 John 5:15
Help one another ... Gal 6:2
God will give us help ... Heb 4:16

Assurance
Of God's protection ... Ps 121
Of forgiveness ... Hos 14:4
Of salvation ... John 3:16; 1 Tim 1:15
Of God's love ... Rom 8:38-39
Of hope ... Heb 6:11-19
Of faith ... Heb 10:22
Definition of faith ... Heb 11:1

Atonement
Blood makes atonement ... Lev 17:11
Day of Atonement ... Lev 16
Christ as the atonement sacrifice ... Rom 3:25
Christ makes atonement for sins ... Heb 2:17

Attitude
Of hope ... Mic 7:7
The "servant" attitude ... Mark 10:43-45
A pleasing attitude for God ... Rom 12:1-2
Of love ... 1 Cor 16:13-14
Of rejoicing ... Phil 4:4-5
Thoughts form our attitude ... Phil 4:8
Copy Christ's attitude ... Phil 2:5-8; 1 Pet 4:1-2
Of humility ... 1 Pet 5:5-6

Authority
God's authority on earth ... Matt 9:6
Given to Christ ... Matt 28:18
Submit to ... Rom 13
In marriage ... 1 Cor 7:4

Awesome
God's splendor is awesome ... Exod 15:11
God will do awesome things ... Exod 34:10
God's name is awesome ... Ps 99:3; 111:9

Jesus breaks the bread ... Matt 26:26; 1 Cor 11:24
Christ's bones not broken ... John 19:36

Cain

The firstborn son of Adam and Eve
His occupation ... Gen 4:2
His anger ... Gen 4:5
Murders Abel ... Gen 4:8; 1 John 3:12
His punishment ... Gen 4:11; Jude 11

Call, calling

God calls us by name ... Ps 147:4; John 10:3
Voice calling in the wilderness ... Isa 40:3; Matt 3:3
Call on God ... Isa 55:6
Call and God will answer ... Jer 33:3; Rom 10:12
Jesus calls the first disciples ... Luke 5:1-11
Lead a life worthy of your calling ... Eph 4:1

Cana

A town in Galilee located northeast of Nazareth
Site of Jesus' first miracle ... John 2

Canaan

The land promised to Abraham and his descendants
Land inhabited by Abraham ... Gen 12:6
by Isaac and Jacob ... Gen 28
by Esau ... Gen 36
by Joseph ... Gen 37
Promised to Abraham ... Gen 12:7; 13:14-15; 17:8
God's warning to Israel about the people ... Lev 18:3,24
Spies visit, their report of the land ... Num 13
Moses views it before his death ... Num 27:12; Deut 3:27; 34:1-5
Given to the children of Israel ... Josh 14

Captive

Israel taken into captivity ... 2 Kgs 15:29
Judah taken into captivity ... 2 Kgs 24:10-17
Freedom for captives ... Isa 61:1; Luke 4:18
We are captive to sin ... Rom 7:23

Change

Jacob adjusts to change ... Gen 47
A time for everything ... Eccl 3:1-8
God changes his mind about Nineveh ... Jonah 3:10
God doesn't change ... Mal 3:6
Jesus is the same forever ... Heb 13:8
With the Father there is no variation ... Jas 1:17

Character

A man of character is blessed ... Ps 1:1-2
An example of good character ... Ps 112:5-6
God's requirements ... Mic 6:8
Suffering builds character ... Rom 5:3-4
Put others first ... Phil 2:3-4
A worker approved by God ... 2 Tim 2:15
Deeds should be done in humility ... Jas 3:13

Children

Teach your children ... Deut 4:9
A blessing for increase ... Ps 115:14-15
Children are a reward ... Ps 127:3-4
Train children in the right way ... Prov 22:6
Faith like a child's ... Matt 18:1-5
Jesus calls the children to him ... Matt 19:14
Children walk in truth ... 3 John 4

Children of God

Peacemakers are called ... Matt 5:9
They cannot die anymore ... Luke 20:36
They receive Christ and believe ... John 1:12
They are led by God's spirit ... Rom 8:14-21
They are in Christ through faith ... Gal 3:26
We are called this because of God's love ... 1 John 3:1

Chose, chosen

Many are called, few are chosen ... Matt 22:14
God chooses us ... John 15:16
Mercy for the chosen ... Rom 9:18
God chooses the foolish ... 1 Cor 1:27
A chosen race, a royal priesthood ... 1 Pet 2:9

Christ

A name meaning "the anointed one" given to the Son of God
His birth ... Luke 2
His baptism ... Matt 3:13-17
His temptation by the devil ... Matt 4:1-11
Peter's declaration ... Matt16:13-20
The Last Supper ... Matt 26:17-30
Judas betrays him ... Matt 26:14-16, 47-49
His death ... Mark 15:21-41
His resurrection ... Luke 24:1-10
His ascension ... Luke 24:50-53
See also Messiah; Jesus

Christian

First called Christian ... Acts 11:26
Do not be ashamed ... 1 Pet 4:16

Christian living

Making a choice ... Josh 24:15
Walk with God ... Ps 56:13
Do not conform to the world ... Rom 12:2
Behave discreetly ... Rom 13:13-14
We are God's people ... 2 Cor 6:16
Live by the Spirit ... Gal 5:16-26
Do good to all ... Gal 6:1-10
Live for God ... 1 Pet 4:1-3
Live in love and obedience ... 2 John 6
Live in truth ... 3 John 3-4

Church

Peter as the rock ... Matt 16:18
The early Christian church ... Acts 2:37-47
Orderly worship ... 1 Cor 14:26-40
Christ is the head of the church ... Eph 5:23
Christ's body is the church ... Col 1:24
A description of the church ... 1 Pet 2:9-10

Circumcision

A sign of the covenant ... Gen 17:10
Instituted to enter the promised land ... Josh 5:1-9
Jesus is circumcised ... Luke 2:21
An issue in the early church ... Acts 15:1-5; 1 Cor 7:17-20
The gospel for circumcised and uncircumcised alike ... Gal 2:7-9

Cities of refuge

Their purpose ... Num 35:9-15
Their location ... Josh 20:1-9

Clean, cleanse

Clean animals saved in the ark ... Gen 7:2
Clean hands, pure heart ... Ps 24:4
Request for cleansing ... Ps 51:2,7; 1 John 1:9
Jesus washes Peter's feet ... John 13:9-10
Peter's vision of clean and unclean ... Acts 10:9-16

Come, comes

Come and find rest ... Matt 11:28
Comes in the name of the Lord ... John 12:13
Comes to the Father through Jesus ... John 14:6
Until Christ comes again ... 1 Cor 11:26
Come, Lord Jesus ... Rev 22:20

Comfort

The Lord comforts ... Ps 71:19-21
Comfort in suffering ... Ps 119:50
Strength for the weary ... Isa 40:28-29, 31
Comfort as a mother ... Isa 66:13
I will give comfort ... Jer 31:13
There is comfort in mourning ... Matt 5:4
Trust in God ... John 14:1
The God of all comfort ... 2 Cor 1:3-4
God's grace is sufficient ... 2 Cor 12:9

Commandment

God gives the Ten Commandments ... Exod 20:6
The greatest commandment ... Matt 22:37-38
A new commandment ... John 15:12

Commission, the Great

Go, baptize, teach ... Matt 28:16-20
Jesus command to his disciples ... Mark 16:15-16

Dance, danced
- David danced before the Lord ... 2 Sam 6:14
- Praise God with dance ... Ps 150:4
- A time to dance ... Eccl 3:4
- Young women will dance ... Jer 31:4
- Herodias's daughter danced before Herod ... Matt 14:6

Daniel
A young man from Judah taken to Babylon as a captive
- His wise decision ... Dan 1
- He understands dreams ... Dan 1:17
- He interprets dreams ... Dan 2, 4
- His friends in the fiery furnace ... Dan 3:19-23
- He reads the writing on the wall ... Dan 5:17
- His stay in the lion's den ... Dan 6:16-23

Dark, darkness
- Darkness covered the deep ... Gen 1:2
- Plague of darkness ... Exod 10:21
- Things said in the dark are revealed ... Luke 12:3
- Jesus brings light to darkness ... John 12:35-46
- Never walk in darkness ... John 8:12
- The sun will turn to darkness ... Acts 2:20

David
The king of Israel, a man after God's own heart
- Anointed by Samuel ... 1 Sam 16:12-13
- Confronts Goliath ... 1 Sam 17:49
- His friendship with Jonathan ... 1 Sam 18:1; 20
- He becomes king of Israel ... 2 Sam 2:4; 5:3
- His kindness to Mephibosheth ... 2 Sam 9
- His adultery with Bathsheba ... 2 Sam 11; 12
- His confession of adultery and murder ... 2 Sam 12
- Absalom's rebellion ... 2 Sam 15
- He makes Solomon king ... 1 Kgs 1
- Named in Christ's genealogy ... Matt 1:6
- A man after God's heart ... Acts 13:22

Deacon
- The position instituted ... Acts 6:1-6
- The qualifications ... 1 Tim 3:8-13

Death
- Death is our destiny ... Eccl 7:2
- Christ will swallow up death ... Isa 25:8
- Death comes to all ... Isa 57:1-2
- The wages of sin is death ... Rom 6:23
- Death came through man ... 1 Cor 15:21
- Where, O death, is your sting? ... 1 Cor 15:55
- There will be no more death ... Rev 21:4

See also Grief; Loss

Deborah
A prophet and judge of Israel
- A judge of Israel ... Judg 4
- She encourages Barak ... Judg 4:6
- Her song ... Judg 5

Deceive
- Don't be deceived ... Gal 6:7
- Don't be deceived by unbelievers ... Eph 5:6
- If we think we're sinless we are deceived ... 1 John 1:8

Decision-making
- Solomon asks for wisdom ... 1 Kgs 3:5-15
- Solomon's good judgment ... 1 Kgs 3:16-28
- Listen to advice ... Prov 12:15
- Consult advisers ... Prov 15:22
- Accept instruction ... Prov 19:20
- Obtain guidance ... Prov 20:18
- Prayer for discernment ... Phil 1:9-11

Deeds
- We are repaid for our deeds ... Rom 2:6
- What you do in word or deed ... Col 3:17

Delilah
Samson's second wife
- She betrays Samson ... Judg 16:4

Deliver, deliverance
- The people are delivered from slavery ... Exod 3:8
- A plea for deliverance from suffering ... Ps 22
- Daniel is delivered from the lions ... Dan 6:20-22
- "Deliver us from evil" ... Matt 6:13

Demon
- Jesus casts out demons and heals people ... Matt 4:24; 8:16; 17:18; Mark 7:26-30; Luke 4:33-35; 11:18
- Don't become a partner with demons ... 1 Cor 10:20-21
- False teachings of ... 1 Tim 4:1
- Demons believe God is one ... Jas 2:19

Deny
- Deny yourself and take up the cross ... Matt 16:24
- Peter's denial of Jesus ... Matt 26:69-75

Depression
- The Lord brings light to darkness ... 2 Sam 22:29
- Elijah overcomes depression ... 1 Kgs 19:1-8
- Hope comes from God ... Ps 42
- God will reply to our cry ... Ps 143:7-8
- Words of encouragement ... Isa 41:10
- God will answer our call for help ... Jonah 2:2
- If we ask we will receive ... Matt 7:7-8
- Nothing is impossible for God ... Mark 10:27

Desire, desires
- God will give the desires of your heart ... Ps 37:4
- Do not gratify sinful desires ... Gal 5:16-17
- God desires everyone to be saved ... 1 Tim 2:3-4

Devil
- Jesus tempted by ... Matt 4:1-11
- He lies ... John 8:44
- We are to stand against him ... Eph 6:11
- If we resist him, he will go away ... Jas 4:7
- Christ destroys his work ... 1 John 3:8

See also Satan

Disciples
- Jesus calls them ... Matt 4:18-22
- The cost of being a disciple ... Luke 14:27
- Jesus washes their feet ... John 13:1-20
- An indication of who is a disciple ... John 13:35

Discipleship
- Speak the truth ... Ps 15:1-2
- Put words into practice ... Matt 7:24-25
- Take up the cross and follow ... Matt 10:37-39
- Live by the truth ... John 3:21
- Love one another ... John 13:35
- Remain in Christ ... John 15:4-5
- Live in accordance with the Spirit ... Rom 8:5
- Do not conform to the world ... Rom 12:1-2
- Do not become weary ... Gal 6:8-9
- Say no to worldly passions ... Titus 2:11-12

Discipline
- We are blessed if disciplined ... Ps 94:12-13
- Discipline is the way to life ... Prov 6:23; 10:17
- Love discipline ... Prov 12:1
- Heed discipline ... Prov 15:5
- Get discipline ... Prov 23:23
- The Lord's discipline ... Heb 12:5-7, 9-11
- Discipline for those God loves ... Rev 3:19

Disobey, disobedient
- God's anger if we disobey ... Eph 5:6
- We were once disobedient ... Titus 3:3
- We stumble if we disobey the word ... 1 Pet 2:8

Distress
- A request for help ... Ps 4:1
- A request for salvation ... Ps 69:29
- Comfort in distress ... Ps 119:143
- God answers ... Ps 120:1
- God's promise ... Jer 15:11
- A cry of distress ... Lam 1:20
- Jonah's call for help ... Jonah 2:2

Divorce
- Divorce is allowed, but regulated ... Deut 22:13-19, 28-29
- God hates divorce ... Mal 2:16

- Our assurance of ... 2 Tim 1:8-12
- Is in God's Son ... 1 John 5:11-13

Evangelist, evangelists
- Philip as an evangelist ... Acts 21:8
- The gift to become an evangelist ... Eph 4:11
- Do the work of an evangelist ... 2 Tim 4:5

Eve
The first woman, created from Adam's rib
- Created from Adam's rib ... Gen 2:21-23
- Tempted by the serpent ... Gen 3:1-5
- She eats the fruit ... Gen 3:6
- Her name is given ... Gen 3:20
- Banished from the garden ... Gen 3:24
- She gives birth ... Gen 4:1

Everlasting
- God's everlasting covenant ... Gen 9:16
- God from everlasting to everlasting ... Ps 90:2
- Everlasting Father, Prince of Peace ... Isa 9:6

Eye
- Their eyes were opened ... Gen 3:7
- God's eye views the earth ... 2 Chr 16:9
- The apple of the eye ... Ps 17:8
- Lift up my eyes to the hills ... Ps 121:1
- Eye for eye, tooth for tooth ... Matt 5:38
- Eye of a needle ... Mark 10:25
- In a twinkling of an eye ... 1 Cor 15:52

Ezekiel
A priest called by God to be a prophet to the exiles in Babylon
- His call ... Ezek 2
- The vision of dry bones ... Ezek 37
- His words of hope to Israel ... Ezek 37:20-28

Ezra
A Jewish exile who returned to Jerusalem to rebuild the temple
- A scribe in Babylon ... Ezra 7:6
- Commanded to rebuild the temple ... Ezra 7:11
- Institutes reforms ... Ezra 10
- Reads the book of the law ... Neh 8

Faith
- God tests Abraham's faith ... Gen 22
- It can move mountains ... Matt 17:20
- If we believe we will receive ... Matt 21:22
- Everything is possible ... Mark 9:23
- The righteous will live by faith ... Rom 1:17
- If you confess and believe ... Rom 10:9, 17
- Live by faith ... 2 Cor 5:7
- Have kept the faith ... 2 Tim 4:7
- The goal of faith ... 1 Pet 1:8-9
- Add to your faith ... 2 Pet 1:5-8
- Heroes of the faith ... Heb 11
- Definition of faith ... Heb 11:1, 6
- Faith and deeds ... Jas 2:17-18

Faithfulness of God
- Through generations ... Deut 7:9
- To those who are faithful to him ... 2 Sam22:22-26
- Is abundant ... Ps 57:3, 9-10
- It will protect us ... Ps 91:4
- His faithfulness continues ... Ps 100
- Is great ... Lam 3:19-24
- Is from the Spirit ... Gal 5:22-23
- God is faithful to forgive ... 1 John 1:9

Family
- The choice to serve God ... Josh 24:15
- God's blessing on ... Ps 128
- Live in unity ... Ps 133:1
- A noble wife ... Prov 31
- Be devoted to one another ... Rom 12:10
- Do good to all ... Gal 6:10
- The establishment of the family ... Eph 5:31
- Honor your father and mother ... Eph 6:2-3
- How to behave ... Col 3:12-14
- Love above all ... 1 Pet 4:8

Fast, fasting
- Jesus fasted 40 days ... Matt 4:2
- Instructions for ... Matt 6:16-17
- The pious Pharisee fasts ... Luke 18:12
- Combined with worship ... Acts 13:2

Father
- Our Father in heaven ... Matt 6:9
- The Father knows what we need ... Matt 6:32
- Father forgive them ... Luke 23:34
- A place for us in the Father's house ... John 14:2
- Perfect gifts are from the Father ... Jas 1:17

Fear
- God will be with us ... Josh 1:9
- Be strong ... Ps 27:13-14
- God is our strength ... Ps 46
- Trust in God ... Ps 56:3-4
- Rely on God ... Isa 50:10
- We are important to God ... Matt 10:29-31
- God gives peace ... John 14:27
- The Lord is our help ... Heb 13:5-6

Fellowship
- In the early church ... Acts 2:42
- Fellowship with the Son ... 1 Cor 1:9
- Do not have fellowship with unbelievers ... 2 Cor 6:14-18
- With the Father and the Son ... 1 John 1:3-7

Fight
- God fights our battles ... 2 Chr 32:8
- Fight the good fight ... 1 Tim 6:12
- Have fought the fight ... 2 Tim 4:7

Filled
- People are filled with the Spirit at Pentecost ... Acts 2:4
- Peter, filled with the Spirit, preaches ... Acts 4:8
- Let your life be filled ... Eph 5:15-20

Fish
- Fish die in the Nile River ... Exod 7:21
- A great fish swallows Jonah ... Jonah 1:17
- The disciples will fish for people ... Matt 4:19
- Jesus feeds 5,000 with two fish ... Mark 6:38-43
- The great catch of fish ... Mark 8:7

Flesh
- Eve created from Adam's flesh ... Gen 2:23
- United as one flesh ... Gen 2:24
- The spirit is strong, but the flesh is weak ... Matt 26:41
- The Word became flesh ... John 1:14
- A thorn in the flesh ... 2 Cor 12:7
- The sins of the flesh ... Gal 5:19-21

Flood
- The Great Flood ... Gen 6:9—9:17

Follow
- Goodness and mercy will follow me ... Ps 23:6
- The disciples follow Jesus ... Mark 1:17-18
- Take up the cross and follow ... Mark 8:34; Luke 9:23
- Sheep follow ... John 10:27

Forgiveness
- Joseph forgives his brothers ... Gen 50:15-21
- If we ask, God will forgive ... 2 Chr 7:14
- God doesn't record our sins ... Ps 130:3-4
- Don't get offended ... Prov 19:11
- Don't be happy over others' failures ... Prov 24:17
- A cry for forgiveness ... Dan 9:19
- Continually forgive ... Matt 18:21-22
- God forgives if we forgive ... Mark 11:25
- Be kind and forgive ... Eph 4:32
- We must forgive others ... Col 3:13

Free, freedom
- Truth makes you free ... John 8:31-44
- Salvation is a free gift ... Rom 6:23
- We are free from the law ... Rom 8:1-17
- No distinction of slave or free ... Gal 3:28
- Christ sets us free ... Gal 5:1,13

The good Samaritan
- The story of ... Luke 10:25-37

Gospel
- The power of ... Rom 1:16
- It is for everyone ... Rom 15:7
- Only one gospel ... Gal 1:6-9
- A summary of ... Eph 2:4-10

Gossip
- Don't lie ... Exod 23:1
- Keep a secret ... Prov 11:13
- It is wise to watch what you say ... Prov 16:23-24, 28
- Don't talk too much ... Prov 20:19
- Speak constructively ... Eph 4:29-32
- Refrain from idle talk and gossip ... 1 Tim 5:13
- A lesson in controlling our tongues ... Jas 3:1-12
- Do not return insults ... 1 Pet 3:8-9

Grace
- The Lord is gracious ... Ps 103:8-14
- We are justified by grace ... Rom 3:23-24
- A definition of grace ... Rom 5:8
- By grace we are saved ... Eph 2:4-5, 8
- God's grace brings salvation ... Titus 2:11
- Justified by grace, we become heirs ... Titus 3:4-7
- God gives grace to the humble ... 1 Pet 5:5

Grief
- Flesh and heart may fail ... Ps 73:24-26
- We belong to God ... Rom 14:7-8
- In Christ all are alive ... 1 Cor 15:19-22
- To die is gain ... Phil 1:21
- We will be with God forever ... 1 Thess 4:14-18
- Live together with Christ ... 1 Thess 5:10
- Blessed are the dead ... Rev 14:13
- No more death or crying ... Rev 21:3-4
- *See also* Comfort; Loss

Guidance
- God leads his people ... Exod 15:13
- The Lord is my shepherd ... Ps 23
- God guides the humble ... Ps 25:9
- A request for guidance ... Ps 25:5-6
- Guide with counsel ... Ps 73:23-24
- God's hand guides ... Ps 139:9-10
- God guides in wisdom ... Prov 4:11-12
- God will teach us his ways ... Isa 2:3

Guilt
- We can't hide our guilt ... Ps 69:5-6
- Don't carry the guilt ... Ps 103:12
- God forgives and forgets ... Isa 43:25
- Let go of your guilt—God does ... Mic 7:18-19
- God will punish the guilty ... Nah 1:3
- God takes away our guilt ... Heb 10:22-23

Hades
The place where the souls of the dead reside
- Its gates will not prevail ... Matt 16:18
- The keys of ... Rev 1:18
- Thrown into the lake of fire ... Rev 20:13-14

Hagar
The maidservant of Sarah
- Gives birth to Ishmael ... Gen 16
- An angel speaks to her ... Gen 16:10-11
- Sent away from Abraham's family ... Gen 21:14

Hannah
The mother of Samuel
- Prays for a child ... 1 Sam 1
- Her prayer answered ... 1 Sam 1:20
- Her prayer of thanksgiving ... 1 Sam 2:1-10

Hate
- Creates strife ... Prov 10:12
- Do not hate your enemies ... Luke 6:27
- Hate evil ... Rom 12:9
- Cannot love God and hate others ... 1 John 4:20

Healing
- A cry for healing ... Ps 6:2; Jer 17:14; Acts 4:30
- God is our strength ... Ps 46:1
- A recipe for health ... Prov 3:7-8
- Turn to God and be healed ... Isa 6:10
- God's promise for health ... Jer 33:6
- Be strong in the Lord ... Eph 6:10
- A prayer for good health ... 3 John 2

Healthy living
- Peace gives life ... Prov 14:30
- Power of good news ... Prov 15:30
- Daniel's wise decision ... Dan 1:8-20
- Train yourself ... 1 Tim 4:7-8
- Live a self-controlled life ... Titus 2:12

Hear, hearing
- Hear, O Israel, the Lord is God ... Deut 6:4; Mark 12:29
- God hears prayer ... Prov 15:29
- Ears to hear ... Mark 4:9
- Sheep hear his voice ... John 10:3

Heart
- Love God with your whole heart ... Mark 12:30
- Do not let your heart be troubled ... John 14:1
- Believe in your heart ... Rom 10:9
- God is greater than our hearts ... 1 John 3:20

Heaven
- Elijah goes to heaven ... 2 Kgs 2:1-12
- Keep your treasure in heaven ... Luke 12:33-34
- Jesus' promise to the criminal ... Luke 23:43
- The Father's house has many rooms ... John 14:2-3
- Jesus' ascension ... Acts 1:1-9
- Eternal glory ... 2 Cor 4:17
- Eternal house in heaven ... 2 Cor 5:1
- Looking to a new heaven ... 2 Pet 3:13
- Great multitude before the throne ... Rev 7:9
- The new heaven and new earth ... Rev 21:1-4

Heir
- Joint heirs with Christ ... Rom 8:17
- We are heirs through God ... Gal 4:7
- Noah an heir of righteousness ... Heb 11:7
- Heirs with hope of eternal life ... Titus 3:7

Hell
- Soul and body in hell ... Matt 10:28
- A place of fallen angels ... 2 Pet 2:4

Herod
The king of Judaea called Herod the Great
- He is ruler at Christ's birth ... Matt 2:1-3
- He kills the infants of Bethlehem ... Matt 2:16
- He beheads John the Baptist ... Matt 14:1-12
- He imprisons John the Baptist ... Luke 3:19-20
- He attempts to see Jesus ... Luke 9:7-9
- He questions Jesus ... Luke 23:6-12

Hezekiah
A righteous king of Judah who led a religious reform
- He becomes king of Judah ... 2 Kgs 16:19-20
- His reign ... 2 Kgs 18
- His prayer for deliverance from the enemy ... 2 Kgs 19:14-19
- His illness; given 15 more years ... 2 Kgs 20; Isa 38
- His death ... 2 Kgs 20:20
- His goodness ... 2 Chr 29

Holy
- What God asks ... Deut 10:12
- Serve God wholeheartedly ... 1 Chr 28:9
- Our bodies are a living sacrifice ... Rom 12:1
- Put off old self ... Eph 4:22-24
- Be blameless and holy ... 1 Thess 3:13
- Live a holy life ... 1 Thess 4:7
- Be holy ... Heb 12:14
- People belonging to God ... 1 Pet 2:9

Holy Spirit
The third person of the Trinity
- Baptism with ... Mark 1:8
- The promise to send the Spirit ... John 14:16-26

Honest, honesty

Honor

Hope

Hospitality

Humility

Hungry

Husband

Identity

Idols

Illness

Immanuel

Immoral, immorality

Immortality

Impossible

Inherit, inheritance

Inspired

Integrity

Interpret, interpretation

Isaac

The only son of Abraham and Sarah, born to them in their old age

Isaiah

An important prophet whose writings tell of the coming Messiah

Ishmael

The son of Abraham by Sarai's maidservant, Hagar

Israel, Israelites

The nation of people chosen by God

The scepter shall rise out of....Num 24:17
They are governed by Judges....Judg 1–16
Their wickedness and idolatry....Judg 2:11-23; 1 Kgs 12:28-33
They ask for a king....1 Sam 8
A great nation under David and Solomon....2 Sam 5; 1 Kgs 3
The kingdom is divided....1 Kgs 12
Their captivity....2 Kgs 17:5-23; 25
Their return from captivity....Ezra 1
Their future....Rom 11

Jacob
One of the twin sons of Isaac and Rebekah
His birth....Gen 25:19-28
He receives Esau's birthright....Gen 25:29-34
He receives his father's blessing....Gen 27:1-29
His dream at Bethel....Gen 28:10-22
He marries Leah and Rachel....Gen 29
His children....Gen 30:1-24
His name is changed to Israel....Gen 32:28
He goes to Egypt....Gen 46
He blesses his sons....Gen 48

James
Son of Zebedee, a disciple of Jesus, brother of John
His call to be a disciple....Matt 4:21
One of the twelve apostles....Matt 10:1-4
His presence at the transfiguration....Matt 17:1; Mark 9:2; Luke 9:28
With Jesus in the Garden....Matt 26:36-37
A fisherman by trade....Mark 1:19; Luke 5:10
Killed by Herod....Acts 12:2

James
Son of Alphaeus, a disciple of Jesus
One of the twelve apostles....Matt 10:1-4
Present after the ascension....Acts 1:13

James
The brother of Jesus
Listed as Jesus' brother....Matt 13:55; Gal 1:19
His speech about the Gentiles....Acts 15:13-21
A "pillar" of the church....Gal 2:9

Jealous, jealousy
Rachel is jealous....Gen 30:1
Joseph's brothers are jealous....Gen 37:11
Jealousy is powerful....Prov 27:4
High priests are jealous of the apostles....Acts 5:17-18
The Jews are jealous of Paul....Acts 13:45
Get rid of jealousy....Rom 13:13
It leads to quarreling....1 Cor 3:3-4
It is an act of the sinful nature....Gal 5:20-21

Jeremiah
A major prophet who foretold the destruction of Judah and was forced to flee from the Babylonians to Egypt
His call....Jer 1
He prophesies about the captivity....Jer 25:8-14
His promise of comfort and future hope....Jer 31
He writes a scroll that is read and burned....Jer 36
He is thrown into a cistern....Jer 38:1-13

Jericho
The first city captured in the promised land
Spies sent to the city....Josh 2:1
The home of Rahab....Josh 2:1-21
The wall of the city falls down....Josh 6:20
Mentioned in Hebrews....Heb 11:30

Jerusalem
The capital of David's kingdom; the religious center of Israel
The ark brought to Jerusalem....2 Sam 6
The temple built there....1 Kgs 5–8
The captives return to Jerusalem....Ezra 1–3; Neh 2
Jesus as a boy in Jerusalem....Luke 2:41-43
The triumphal entry....Luke 19:28-40
Apostles there at Pentecost....Acts 2:4-5
The new Jerusalem....Rev 21:2

Jesus
Sends out his disciples....Matt 28:18-20
Is with us always....Matt 28:20
Is equal with God....John 5:18
Is one with the Father....John 10:30
We must trust him....John 14:1
Every knee will bow at his name....Phil 2:10
See also chart Jesus' Ministry, pp. 1601-1603

Jews
Descendants of Abraham and Sarah; worshipers of God according to Jewish law and customs
First called by this name....Esth 3:13
Jesus: the king of the Jews....Matt 2:2; 27:11
Gospel given to the Jews first....Rom 1:16
Is God only the God of the Jews?....Rom 3:29
There is neither Jew nor Greek....Gal 3:28

Jezebel
The wicked wife of King Ahab
The wife of Ahab....1 Kgs 16:31
She kills the Lord's prophets....1 Kgs 18:4
She threatens Elijah....1 Kgs 19:1-3
Her violent death....2 Kgs 9:30-37

Joash
A righteous young king of Judah
He is saved by his aunt....2 Kgs 11:1-3
He becomes king as a child....2 Kgs 11:4-12
He repairs the temple....2 Kgs 12

Job
A righteous man who was tested by Satan and remained faithful to God
His losses....Job 1–2
His humility before God....Job 40:3-4; 42:1-6
His restoration....Job 42

John
A disciple of Jesus
He becomes a disciple....Matt 4:21
He is named as one of the twelve....Matt 10:2
He is called "the disciple whom Jesus loved"....John 13:23

John the Baptist
A forerunner to Jesus who preached of the Messiah's coming
Mentioned by the prophets....Isa 40:3; Mal 4:5
His teaching and lifestyle....Matt 3:1-12; Luke 3
He baptizes Christ....Matt 3:13-17
He is beheaded....Matt 14:1-12
His birth....Luke 1:57-66
He is put in prison....Luke 3:19-20

John of Patmos
The writer of the book of Revelation....Rev 1:9

Jonah
A prophet who ran from God's call to preach in Nineveh
His call by God....Jonah 1:1-2
He runs away....Jonah 1:3
He is swallowed by a large fish....Jonah 1:15-17
He goes to Nineveh....Jonah 3
Christ compared to....Matt 12:40-41

Jonathan
The son of King Saul; a close friend of David
He battles the Philistines....1 Sam 13:1-4; 19-23; 14
His friendship with David....1 Sam 18:1; 19–20
He reassures David....1 Sam 23:16
He is killed in battle....1 Sam 31:2
David mourns his death....2 Sam 1:17

Jordan
A river running north of the Sea of Galilee down to the Dead Sea
Israelites cross it on dry ground....Josh 3–4
Elijah crosses it on dry ground....2 Kgs 2:6-8
Elisha parts it....2 Kgs 2:13-14
Naaman washes in it....2 Kgs 5:10-14
John baptizes there....Matt 3

Joseph
A favorite son of Jacob who became a ruler in Egypt
The son of Jacob....Gen 30:24
His special robe....Gen 37:2-4
His dreams....Gen 37:5-11

Lydia
A woman in Thyatira who became a believer
Her conversion .... Acts 16:11-15
Paul and Silas go to her home .... Acts 16:40

Lying
Lying is always wrong .... Exod 20:16
Don't speak deceit .... Ps 34:13
The Lord hates lying .... Prov 6:16-17
Truth lasts, lying doesn't .... Prov 12:19
Telling the truth is important .... Eph 4:25
The truth is what God wants .... Col 3:9

Made
God made everything good .... Gen 1:31
Humans are made a little lower than God .... Ps 8:5
This is the day the Lord made .... Ps 118:24
We are wonderfully made .... Ps 139:14

Magic, witchcraft
A command against .... Lev 19:26
The detestable practices of .... Deut 18:10-12, 20-21
Saul and the witch of Endor .... 1 Sam 28
Warning against magic .... Ezek 13:18, 20
Simon the sorcerer .... Acts 8:9-13
The fortune teller .... Acts 16:16-18
Sorcery among works of the flesh .... Gal 5:19-20
The second death .... Rev 21:8

Make, maker
Let us make humans .... Gen 1:26
Make his face shine on us .... Num 6:25
Kneel before our Maker .... Ps 95:6
Make you "fishers of people" .... Mark 1:17

Manna
Provided in the wilderness .... Exod 16
Description of .... Exod 16:31
Sample placed in the ark .... Exod 16:33-34
No longer provided .... Josh 5:12
Referenced by Jesus .... John 6:49

Mark
A disciple of Jesus; a traveling companion of Paul
Travels with Paul and Barnabas .... Acts 12:25; 13:5
Disagreement about him .... Acts 15:36-41
Paul asks for him .... 2 Tim 4:11

Marriage
Marriage is designed by God .... Gen 2:21-24
Remain faithful to your spouse .... Exod 20:14
Two are stronger than one .... Eccl 4:9-12
Guidance for marriage .... 1 Cor 7:3-5
Criteria for marriage .... 2 Cor 6:14
Think of the other person .... Phil 2:3-4
Be faithful to your partner .... Heb 13:4

Martha
Lazarus's sister and a friend to Jesus
Jesus visits her home .... Luke 10:38-42
At Lazarus's death .... John 11:1-37
Loved by Jesus .... John 11:5

Mary
Lazarus's sister who anointed Jesus
Anoints Christ's head .... Matt 26:6-13; Mark 14:3-9
Jesus visits her home .... Luke 10:38-42
At Lazarus's death .... John 11:1-37
Loved by Jesus .... John 11:5
Anoints Christ's feet .... John 12:3

Mary
The mother of Jesus
Visited by Gabriel .... Luke 1:26-38
She visits Elizabeth .... Luke 1:39-45
Her Magnificat .... Luke 1:46-55
The birth of Christ .... Luke 2:1-7
She is anxious for her missing son .... Luke 2:48
At the wedding in Cana .... John 2:1
At Christ's crucifixion .... John 19:25

Mary Magdalene
The woman from Magdala who became a follower of Jesus
Present at the crucifixion .... Matt 27:56; Mark 15:40; John 19:25
Present at the tomb .... Matt 28:1-7
The risen Jesus speaks to her .... Matt 28:8-10
She is cured by Christ .... Luke 8:2
The risen Jesus says her name .... John 20:11-18

Matthew
A tax collector and one of Jesus' twelve disciples
Jesus calls him .... Matt 9:9
He is called Levi .... Mark 2:14; Luke 5:27
He is chosen as one of the twelve .... Luke 6:15

Meditate, meditation
Meditate on the law .... Ps 1:2
Meditations of the heart .... Ps 19:14
My meditation all day .... Ps 119:97

Meek
The meek inherit the earth .... Ps 37:11
The meek will have joy .... Isa 29:19
Blessed are the meek .... Matt 5:5

Melchizedek
The priest-king of Salem (Jerusalem)
Blesses Abraham .... Gen 14:18
His priesthood .... Ps 110:4
Christ compared to .... Heb 5:5-10
"According to the order of" .... Heb 6:20
A description of .... Heb 7

Mercy
A cry for God's mercy .... Ps 51:1
What the Lord requires .... Mic 6:8
God delights to show mercy .... Mic 7:18
Show mercy to one another .... Zech 7:9
Blessed are the merciful .... Matt 5:7
Shown through generations .... Luke 1:49-50
Be merciful .... Luke 6:36
The gift of showing mercy .... Rom 12:6-8
Mercy triumphs .... Jas 2:13
Wisdom shows mercy .... Jas 3:17

Messiah
The genealogy of Jesus .... Matt 1:1-17
His birth .... Matt 1:18
Peter's confession .... Matt 16:16
Jesus called this .... Luke 2:11, 26
Meaning of the name .... John 1:41

Midianites
The people of Midian, an enemy of Israel
Conquered by Israel .... Num 31:1-24
Their oppression of Israel .... Judg 6:1-10
Defeated by Gideon and his men .... Judg 7-8

Minister, ministry
Ministers of the new covenant .... 2 Cor 3:6
Ministry of reconciliation .... 2 Cor 5:18
Saints prepared for ministry .... Eph 4:12

Miracles
See chart Jesus' Ministry, pp. 1601-1603

Miriam
Sister of Moses and Aaron
Her identity .... Exod 15:20; Num 26:59
She watches over the baby Moses .... Exod 2:4-8
Her song .... Exod 15:21
Her jealousy of Moses .... Num 12:1-9
She becomes leprous .... Num 12:10-15

Money
Don't worship money .... Exod 20:22-23
Money doesn't satisfy .... Eccl 5:10
Invitation to buy without money .... Isa 55:1-2
Loving money leads to evil .... 1 Tim 6:6-10, 17
Keep away from loving money .... Heb 13:5
See also Riches; Treasure; Wealth

Obey God, not humans ... Acts 5:29
Listen and do ... Jas 1:22-24
Obey God's commands ... 1 John 5:2-3
Walk in obedience ... 2 John 6

Offer, offering
Offer right sacrifices ... Ps 4:5
Christ gave himself as an offering ... Eph 5:2
The offering of Jesus Christ ... Heb 10:10
Offer praise to God ... Heb 13:15

One
The Father and the Son are one ... John 10:30
May all be one ... John 17:21
Overcome the evil one ... 1 John 2:14

Orphans
God defends the orphan ... Deut 10:18
God helps the orphan ... Ps 10:14
How to behave toward the orphan ... Ps 82:3-4
God upholds the orphan ... Ps 146:9
Those who oppress the orphan ... Mal 3:5
Favor on those who care for orphans ... Jas 1:27

Parable
Of the sower and seed ... Mark 4:1-9
Of the Good Samaritan ... Luke 10:29-37
Of the lost sheep, coin, son ... Luke 15
See also chart Jesus' Ministry, pp. 1601-1603

Paradise
Jesus' promise to the criminal ... Luke 23:43
Vision of person caught up into paradise ... 2 Cor 12:4
The tree in the paradise of God ... Rev 2:7

Parents
Jacob's sons care for him ... Gen 46-47
Honor your parents ... Exod 20:12
Children will rebel against their parents ... Matt 10:21
Obey your parents ... Eph 6:1; Col 3:20

Passover
The first Passover ... Exod 12
Jesus' parents observe Passover ... Luke 2:41
Christ observes Passover ... Luke 22:7-23

Pastor
Gift to be a pastor ... Eph 4:11

Patience
Wait patiently for God ... Ps 40:1
Better to be patient than to be proud ... Eccl 7:8
Wait patiently ... Rom 8:25
Be patient during difficult times ... Rom 12:12
Patience leads to maturity ... Jas 1:4
God is patient with us ... 2 Pet 3:9

Paul
The apostle who preached the gospel to the Gentiles, writer of many New Testament letters
His persecution of the church ... Acts 8:1-3
His calling ... Acts 9:1-19
With Silas in prison ... Acts 16:16-40
His preaching ... Acts 18:1-11
His shipwreck ... Acts 27:39-44
His sufferings ... 2 Cor 11:21-29
His reason to be confident ... Phil 3:4-9
See also Saul

Peace
Sleep in peace ... Ps 4:8
God blesses his people with peace ... Ps 29:11
A time for peace ... Eccl 3:8
Keep in peace ... Isa 26:3
"Peace I leave with you" ... John 14:27
Peace a reward for doing good ... Rom 2:9-10
A fruit of the Spirit ... Gal 5:22
Blessing of peace ... Phil 4:7

Perfect
Be perfect like our heavenly Father ... Matt 5:48
Know what is good and perfect ... Rom 12:2
Power is perfect in weakness ... 2 Cor 12:9
Perfect love ... 1 John 4:18

Persecute, persecution
Pray for those who persecute ... Matt 5:44
Saul persecutes the early Christians ... Acts 8:1-3; 9:1-2
Persecution won't separate us from Christ's love ... Rom 8:35

Perseverance, persevere
Happy are those who persevere ... Dan 12:12
Keep on praying ... Rom 12:12
Pressing toward the goal ... Phil 3:14
Run the race with perseverance ... Heb 12:1

Perspective
The Lord looks at the heart ... 1 Sam 16:7
Good and bad times ... Eccl 7:14
Seek God's kingdom first ... Matt 6:33
Focus on the unseen ... 2 Cor 4:18
All that matters ... Gal 5:6
Consider others better than yourself ... Phil 2:2-5
Consider loss ... Phil 3:7
Fix your eyes on Jesus ... Heb 12:1-2

Peter
One of the twelve disciples of Jesus
Called by Jesus ... Matt 4:18; Mark 1:16
He tries to walk on water ... Matt 14:29
He confesses Jesus as the Christ ... Matt 16:16; Mark 8:29; Luke 9:20
At the Transfiguration ... Matt 17:1-13
Known as Simon Peter ... Luke 5:1-11
He denies Christ ... John 18:17
He professes his love for Jesus ... John 21:15-19
He heals the crippled beggar ... Acts 3:1-10
He escapes from prison ... Acts 12:1-19

Pharaoh
The ruler of Egypt
His dreams of cows and grain ... Gen 41
He welcomes Joseph's family ... Gen 47
Oppresses the Israelites ... Exod 1:8-14
His daughter saves Moses ... Exod 2:5, 10
His heart is hardened ... Exod 7:13, 22
The 10 plagues ... Exod 7-10
He lets the Israelites leave ... Exod 12:31-32
He pursues the Israelites ... Exod 14:5-9

Pharisees
A religious group during Jesus' time who strictly observed the Law and Jewish ceremonies
Their challenge about the Sabbath ... Matt 12:1-8
Their desire to kill Jesus ... Matt 12:12, 14
They question Jesus on divorce ... Matt 19:1-12
They attempt to entrap Jesus ... Matt 22:15-46
They are denounced by Jesus ... Matt 23:23-24; Luke 11:37-53
The parable about ... Luke 18:9-14
Paul as a Pharisee ... Acts 23:6-11

Philistines
The neighboring enemies of Israel
Their confrontations with Samson ... Judg 14-16
They capture the ark of God ... 1 Sam 5-6
Their confrontation with David ... 1 Sam 17-18
Their destruction predicted ... Jer 47

Pontius Pilate
The governor of Judaea who ordered Christ to be crucified
Governor of Judaea ... Luke 3:1
Christ brought before him ... Matt 27:1-2, 11-26; Mark 15:1-15; Luke 23:1-25; John 18:28–19:16

Poor
The poor in spirit are blessed ... Matt 5:3
If done to the least done to me ... Matt 25:31-46
Sell what you have, give to the poor ... Mark 10:21
The rich man and poor Lazarus ... Luke 16:19-31
The poor will always be with you ... John 12:8

Possessed
Jesus heals demon-possessed people ... Matt 8:16
Unclean spirits come out of the possessed ... Acts 8:7
We possess something better ... Heb 10:34

Possessions
Sell your possessions and follow me ... Matt 19:21
Life is more than possessions ... Luke 12:15
Early church shared their possessions ... Acts 4:32
If I give away possessions but have no love ... 1 Cor 13:3

Power
Not by might or power but by my spirit ... Zech 4:6
Coming of the Son in power ... Mark 13:26
Gospel is God's power for salvation ... Rom 1:16
Struggle against cosmic powers ... Eph 6:12
Power of Christ's resurrection ... Phil 3:10
God's power gives everything ... 2 Pet 1:3

Praise
Sing praise to God ... 2 Sam 22:47-50
Bless the Lord ... Ps 103
Let everything praise the Lord ... Ps 150
Angels and shepherds praise God ... Luke 2:13, 20
Offer a sacrifice of praise ... Heb 13:15
Praise of the great multitude in heaven ... Rev 19:6-7

Pray
If we pray, then God will hear ... 2 Chr 7:14
How to pray ... Matt 6:6-10; Luke 11:1-4
Jesus prays in Gethsemane ... Matt 26:36-39
Spirit helps when we can't pray ... Rom 8:26
Pray without ceasing ... 1 Thess 5:17
Pray with confidence ... Heb 4:16

Prayer
The Lord hears prayer ... Prov 15:29
God answers prayer ... Jer 33:3
The Lord's Prayer ... Matt 6:9-13
Ask in prayer ... Mark 11:24
Persist in prayer ... Luke 11:5-13
The power of prayer ... Jas 5:13-16
God is attentive to our prayers ... 1 Pet 3:12

Preach, preaching
Jonah is called to preach to Nineveh ... Jonah 1:1-2; 3:1
Proclaiming the good news ... Rom 10:14-17
Proclaim Christ crucified ... 1 Cor 1:23
Elders who labor in preaching ... 1 Tim 5:17
Preach sound doctrine ... Titus 1:9

Predestined
God called those chosen ... Rom 8:28-30

Prepare
Prepare a table before you ... Ps 23:5
Prepare the way for Christ ... Matt 3:3
Prepare a place for you ... John 14:2
What's prepared for those who love ... 1 Cor 2:9

Pride
God looks at the heart ... 1 Sam 16:7
Pride brings disgrace ... Prov 11:2
Pride goes before destruction ... Prov 16:18
The humble will be exalted ... Luke 18:14
Don't think too highly of yourself ... Rom 12:3
God opposes the proud ... Jas 4:6

Priesthood, priests
The vestments of the priests ... Exod 28
The privileges of the Levite priests ... Deut 18:1-8
A priest forever ... Ps 110:4
Zechariah chosen by the customs of ... Luke 1:9
Jesus, our great high priest ... Heb 4:14-16
A permanent priesthood ... Heb 7:24
A royal priesthood ... 1 Pet 2:5-9

Priorities
Seek God's kingdom first ... Matt 6:31-33
Fix our eyes on the unseen ... 2 Cor 4:18
Look at the interests of others ... Phil 2:2-5
Everything is a loss, gain is Christ ... Phil 3:7-8
Work for the Lord ... Col 3:23-24
Fix our eyes on Jesus ... Heb 12:1-2
See also Perspective

Problems
The Lord is our safe dwelling ... Ps 27:5
The Lord delivers us from trouble ... Ps 34:19
God is our refuge ... Isa 25:4
Jesus' promise ... John 16:33
When we are weak, God is strong ... 2 Cor 12:10
Struggle against evil ... Eph 6:12
We are blessed if insulted ... 1 Pet 4:14

Prodigal Son
The parable of the lost son ... Luke 15:11-32

Promise
God's promises never fail ... Josh 23:14
The promise of Immanuel ... Isa 7:14
The promise of the Prince of Peace ... Isa 9:6-7
God fulfills promises ... 2 Cor 1:18-20
God is faithful to promises ... Heb 10:23
God gives us promises ... 2 Pet 1:4
God keeps promises ... 2 Pet 3:9
The promise of eternal life ... 1 John 2:25

Promised land
God's promise to Abram ... Gen 17:8
The spies' exploration ... Num 13
The Israelites enter ... Josh 3–4

Prophecy, prophecies
Women with gift of prophecy ... Acts 21:9
A gift of the Spirit ... 1 Cor 12:10
Compared to gift of love ... 1 Cor 13:8

Prophesy
A vision of sons and daughters ... Joel 2:28

Prophet, prophets
All the Lord's people ... Num 11:29
Prophets of Baal killed ... 1 Kgs 18:40
God calls a prophet ... Jer 1:4-10
The basis of the law and the prophets ... Matt 22:40
A prophet is not accepted in his own town ... Luke 4:24
The words of the prophets must be fulfilled ... Luke 24:44

Provide, Provision
Food from heaven ... Exod 16
God provides for the poor ... Ps 68:10
God watches over us ... Ps 121:7-8
The Lord will sustain us ... Isa 46:4
God knows our needs ... Matt 6:8
Jesus feeds the five thousand ... Mark 6:32-44
God provides food ... Acts 14:17
God provides a way out ... 1 Cor 10:13
God provides everything ... 1 Tim 6:17
God will rescue ... 2 Tim 4:18
God's power gives us everything we need ... 2 Pet 1:3
Gifts are from above ... Jas 1:17

Pure
Keep your way pure ... Ps 119:9
Pure in heart are blessed ... Matt 5:8
Think about pure things ... Phil 4:8
To the pure everything is pure ... Titus 1:15

Purification
Mary's time of purification after birth ... Luke 2:22
Jars of water for ... John 2:6
Discussion about ... John 3:25
Paul's advice on ... Acts 21:24-26

Purify
By being obedient ... 1 Pet 1:22

Purpose
God's purpose can't be thwarted ... Job 42:2
God purpose fulfilled ... Ps 57:2; 138:8
God's purpose will be established ... Prov 19:21
Called according to God's purpose ... Rom 8:28

Rachel
One of Jacob's wives; mother of Joseph and Benjamin
She meets Jacob ... Gen 29:10
She is loved by Jacob ... Gen 29:28-30

Safe from the evil one ... 1 John 5:18
See also God's protection

Salvation, saved

My light and my salvation ... Ps 27:1
Simeon's song ... Luke 2:28-32
Salvation assured ... John 10:28
Salvation is only from Christ ... Acts 4:12
Repentance leads to salvation ... 2 Cor 7:10
Work out your salvation ... Phil 2:12
Saved by believing ... Rom 10:9
Saved by grace through faith ... Eph 2:8-9

Samaria

The capital city of the northern kingdom of Israel
The capital chosen ... 1 Kgs 16:29, 32
The twelve apostles told not to go there ... Matt 10:5
The people of Samaria refuse to receive Jesus ... Luke 9:51-53
Peter and John proclaim the gospel there ... Acts 8:25
Paul converts Gentiles there ... Acts 15:3

Samaritan

A person who lived in Samaria; a people disliked by their Jewish neighbors
The parable of the good Samaritan ... Luke 10:30-37
Jesus heals a leper ... Luke 17:11-19
Jesus talks with a Samaritan woman ... John 4:1-42

Samson

A judge of Israel who had great strength
His birth foretold ... Judg 13
He was a nazirite ... Judg 13:3-5
His birth ... Judg 13:24
He taunts the Philistines ... Judg 14–15
His relationship with Delilah ... Judg 16:1-20
He is captured by the Philistines ... Judg 16:21-27
His death ... Judg 16:28-31

Samuel

A leader and judge of Israel
His birth and dedication ... 1 Sam 1
His life as a boy ... 1 Sam 2:18-21, 26
His call from the Lord ... 1 Sam 3
He anoints Saul king ... 1 Sam 9:27—10:8
He anoints David king ... 1 Sam 16:1-13
His death ... 1 Sam 25:1

Sanctification

How God's Spirit calls people to holy living
In God we are sanctified ... Rom 6:22
Christ is the source ... 1 Cor 1:30
God's will for people ... 1 Thess 4:3
A prayer for ... 1 Thess 5:23

Sarah

Wife of Abraham
She was childless ... Gen 11:29
The plan with Hagar ... Gen 16:1-6
Her name is changed ... Gen 17:15
She is promised a son ... Gen 17:16-21
She laughs ... Gen 18:1-15
The birth of Isaac ... Gen 21:1-7
She sends Hagar and Ishmael away ... Gen 21:8-21

Satan

The one who tempts Eve ... Gen 3
Attacks Job ... Job 1–2
Commanded to "get behind me" ... Matt 16:23
Tempts Jesus ... Mark 1:12-13
Described by Jesus ... Mark 4:15
Enters Judas ... Luke 22:3; John 13:27
Causes Peter's denial ... Luke 22:31
Is disguised as an angel of light ... 2 Cor 11:14
Was thrown out of heaven ... Rev 12:9
Judged and doomed ... Rev 20:7

Saul

The first king of Israel
He becomes king ... 1 Sam 9:27—10:8
He is rejected by God ... 1 Sam 15:10-31
He is tormented by an evil spirit ... 1 Sam 16:14
He favors David ... 1 Sam 18:5
He attempts to kill David ... 1 Sam 18–24
With the medium at Endor ... 1 Sam 28:7
His death ... 1 Sam 31

Saul

Persecutor of the early Christian church
He persecutes Christians ... Acts 8:1-3
His call to serve Christ ... Acts 9:1-22
Also called Paul ... Acts 13:9
See also Paul

Savior

Know who is the Savior ... Isa 49:26
Christ will save his people ... Matt 1:21
Name given by angels ... Luke 2:11
Jesus' purpose: save the lost ... Luke 19:10
God is Savior of all people ... 1 Tim 4:10

Scripture(s)

Scriptures encourage and give hope ... Rom 15:4
Christ died and rose according to the scriptures ... 1 Cor 15:3-4
All scripture is inspired ... 2 Tim 3:16
See also Bible; Word of God

Sea of Galilee

A large, fresh-water lake in Galilee, known for its sudden and fierce storms
Jesus calls the disciples ... Matt 4:18; Mark 1:16
Jesus walks on the water ... Matt 14:22-33
Jesus heals many at the seaside ... Mark 3:7-12
Jesus stills the storm ... Mark 4:35-41
Called the lake of Gennesaret ... Luke 5:1
The miraculous catch of fish ... Luke 5:1-11
Feeding the five thousand ... John 6:1-15

Second Coming

Described by Jesus ... Matt 24—25; Mark 13
Jesus promises to come back ... John 14:1-4
The resurrection of the dead ... 1 Cor 15:12-28, 51-52
The Lord's coming ... 1 Thess 4:13—5:11

Seeking God

Elijah waits for God to appear ... 1 Kgs 19:9-18
If we seek, we will find ... 1 Chr 28:9
The Lord is with us ... 2 Chr 15:2
God is everywhere ... Ps 139:7-10
Seek the Lord ... Isa 55:6-7
God is not far away ... Acts 17:27
God is near ... Jas 4:8
God lives in us ... 1 John 4:12

Self-esteem

We are made in God's image ... Gen 1:26-27
God formed us and made us ... Ps 139:13-16
God chose us before we were born ... Jer 1:5
God takes delight in us ... Zeph 3:17
We were made for God's pleasure ... Eph 1:3-6
We are complete in Christ ... Col 2:9-10
You are a child of God ... 1 John 3:1

Sermon on the Mount

Delivered by Jesus ... Matt 5–7

Serve

Serve and obey the Lord ... Deut 13:4
Serve God wholeheartedly ... Josh 22:5
Choose whom you will serve ... Josh 24:15
Serve God only ... Matt 4:10
Greatest will serve ... Matt 23:11
The first must be a slave ... Mark 10:43-44
The good Samaritan ... Luke 10:33
"I am one who serves" ... Luke 22:26-27
Jesus washes his disciples' feet ... John 13:15-17
"Slave to everyone" ... 1 Cor 9:19-22
Serve in love ... Gal 5:13
Serve with God's strength ... 1 Pet 4:11

Shadrach, Meshach, and Abednego

Three young men from Judah who were held captive in Babylon
Their faith ... Dan 1
They refuse to worship the golden image ... Dan 3:8-18
They survive the fiery furnace ... Dan 3:19-30

Shepherd
The Lord is my shepherd ... Ps 23
The shepherds and the angels ... Luke 2:8-18
The parable of the lost sheep ... Luke 15:1-7
The good shepherd ... John 10:1-18

Simeon
One of the twelve sons of Jacob
Son of Jacob ... Gen 29:33
Joseph detains him in Egypt ... Gen 42:18-25
His descendants ... 1 Chr 4:24-42

Simeon
A righteous man who blessed Jesus as an infant
He blesses the infant Jesus ... Luke 2:25-35

Sin
Sin enters the world ... Gen 3
Everyone sins ... 1 Kgs 8:46
That I might not sin ... Ps 119:11
The lamb who takes away sin ... John 1:29
Who sinned? ... John 9:2-3
All have sinned ... Rom 3:23
Wages of sin is death ... Rom 6:23
Christ had no sin ... 2 Cor 5:21
Jesus forgives our sins ... 1 John 1:7

Sing, song
Sing praise to God ... Ps 47:6
Sing a new song ... Isa 42:10
Sing psalms in gratitude ... Col 3:16
Sing and make music to God ... Eph 5:19
If you're happy, you should sing ... Jas 5:13

Slander
A fool speaks slander ... Prov 10:18
Slander is evil ... Matt 15:19
Get rid of slander ... Eph 4:31; Col 3:8

Slave
Hagar, Sarah's slave ... Gen 16; 21:8-21
To be first you must be a slave ... Mark 10:44
No longer slave or free ... Gal 3:28; Col 3:11
Christ took on the form of a slave ... Phil 2:7

Snake
Moses' staff becomes a snake ... Exod 4:1-5
The bronze snake saves the people ... Num 21:4-9

Sodom and Gomorrah
Cities known for their extreme wickedness
Abraham's plea for ... Gen 18:16-33
Its wickedness ... Gen 19:1-11
Lot saved from ... Gen 19:12-23
Its destruction ... Gen 19:24-28
How God deals with the ungodly ... 2 Pet 2:6

Solomon
The son of David and Bathsheba; a great king of Israel
He becomes king ... 1 Kgs 1:28-48
He asks God for wisdom ... 1 Kgs 3:1-15
His child custody decision ... 1 Kgs 3:16-28
His wisdom and accomplishments ... 1 Kgs 4:29-34
He builds the temple ... 1 Kgs 6–7
Named as author ... Prov 1:1; Eccl 1:1; Song 1:1

Son, sons
"This is my Son" ... Matt 3:17
God gave his only Son ... John 3:16
Sons and daughters will prophesy ... Acts 2:17
We will be conformed to the Son's image ... Rom 8:29
We will be God's sons and daughters ... 2 Cor 6:18

Soul
Love God with soul, heart, might ... Deut 6:5; Josh 22:5
My soul longs for God ... Ps 42:1
Save the soul from death ... Jas 5:20
It is well with your soul ... 3 John 1:2

Speech
Moses lacks eloquence ... Exod 4:10-17
The speech of the heavens ... Ps 19:1-4
Guard your mouth ... Prov 13:3
No unwholesome talk ... Eph 4:29
Graceful conversation ... Col 4:6
Set an example in speech ... 1 Tim 4:12
Speech that cannot be condemned ... Titus 2:8
Control your speech ... Jas 1:26; 3:1-12
Stay away from deceitful speech ... 1 Pet 3:10

Spirit, spirits
The Spirit of God comes:
on Gideon ... Judg 6:34
on Samson ... Judg 14:19; 15:14
on Saul ... 1 Sam 10:10
on David ... 1 Sam 16:13
Elijah's spirit on Elisha ... 2 Kgs 2:9
A haughty spirit comes before a fall ... Prov 16:18
A new spirit within you ... Ezek 36:26
A helper in times of weakness ... Rom 8:26
Gives life ... 2 Cor 3:6
Fruits of the Spirit named ... Gal 5:22

Spiritual life
Put Jesus' words into practice ... Matt 7:24-27
Remain in Christ ... John 15:4-5, 7-8
The fruits of the Spirit ... Gal 5:22-25
Grow up in Christ ... Eph 4:14-15
Press on toward the goal ... Phil 3:13-14
Present yourself as one approved ... 2 Tim 2:15
Say no to worldly passions ... Titus 2:11-12
Grow in salvation ... 1 Pet 2:2-3
Add to your faith ... 2 Pet 1:6-8

Stars, constellations
Made by God ... Gen 1:16
Abraham's descendants as numerous as ... Gen 22:17
The ungodly worship the stars ... 2 Kgs 21:3
Constellations mentioned ... Job 9:9; Amos 5:8
They must praise God ... Ps 148:3
God knows their names ... Isa 40:26
The star of Bethlehem ... Matt 2:2,9

Stephen
The first Christian martyr
He is chosen to serve ... Acts 6:1-7
His accomplishments ... Acts 6:8-10
He faces opposition ... Acts 6:11-15
His speech to the council ... Acts 7:1-53
His stoning and death ... Acts 7:54-60

Stewards, Stewardship
The ability to be rich is from God ... Deut 8:18
Wealth comes from God ... 1 Chr 29:12
Everything comes from God ... 1 Chr 29:14
The parable of the talents ... Matt 25:14-16, 19-21
Give and it will be given to you ... Luke 6:38
Put your hope in God not wealth ... 1 Tim 6:17-19

Stone, stones
The stone builders rejected ... Ps 118:22; Mark 12:10
Dash your foot against a stone ... Matt 4:6
Roll away the stone ... Mark 16:3
The stones would shout ... Luke 19:40
We are like living stones ... 1 Pet 2:5
See also Cornerstone

Stranger
Love the stranger ... Deut 10:19
Support the cause of the stranger ... Job 29:16
I was a stranger and you took me in ... Matt 25:35
People don't follow a stranger ... John 10:5
Show hospitality to a stranger ... Rom 12:13

Strength
The joy of the Lord is strength ... Neh 8:10
God gives strength ... Ps 29:11
God is our strength and help ... Ps 46:1-3
Knowledge increases strength ... Prov 24:5
The Lord is my strength and might ... Isa 12:2
Strength will be renewed ... Isa 40:31
God promises to give strength ... Isa 41:10
The Lord is my strength ... Hab 3:19
God's power ... 2 Cor 12:9

Worry
Cast your cares on the Lord ... Ps 55:22
God cares for us ... Nah 1:7
Don't worry about your life ... Matt 6:25-26
Don't worry about food or drink ... Luke 12:29-31
Don't be troubled ... John 14:1
"Peace I leave with you" ... John 14:27
God gives relief ... 2 Thess 1:6-7
See also Anxiety

Worship
The Lord is my strength and might ... Exod 15:2
Praise the Lord with all your heart ... Ps 9:1-2
Worship the Lord ... Ps 29:2
Bow down in worship ... Ps 95:6-7
Worship with gladness ... Ps 100
The Lord is worthy of praise ... Ps 145:3
Worship in spirit and in truth ... John 4:23-24
Worship with reverence and awe ... Heb 12:28
Praise God continually ... Heb 13:15

Write, writings
Write the teachings on the doorposts ... Deut 6:9
Write on your heart ... Prov 7:3; Heb 8:10
Written in the book of life ... Rev 21:27

Youth, young
Youth is renewed ... Ps 103:5
Glory of youth is their strength ... Prov 20:29
Remember your creator ... Eccl 12:1
Young men will see visions ... Joel 2:28
Don't let others look down on you ... 1 Tim 4:12
Flee desires of youth ... 2 Tim 2:22

Zacchaeus
A tax collector who repents
Climbs a tree to see Jesus ... Luke 19:1-10

Zechariah
A minor prophet who presented a message of hope to the Jews returning from exile
His call to repentance ... Zech 1
His vision of the horsemen ... Zech 1:7-17
His vision of the measuring line ... Zech 2:1-5
His vision of the flying scroll ... Zech 5:1-4
His vision of a woman in the basket ... Zech 5:5-11
"The day of the Lord" ... Zech 12--14

Zechariah
The father of John the Baptist
A priest ... Luke 1:5-6
An angel appears to him ... Luke 1:11-20
He can't speak ... Luke 1:21-22
The birth of his son John ... Luke 1:57-66
His prophecy ... Luke 1:67-80

Zion
A reference to Jerusalem
David captures the hill ... 2 Sam 5:7
The location of the temple ... 1 Kgs 8:1
The holy hill ... Ps 2:6
It will produce a deliverer ... Rom 11:26
Where God is ... Heb 12:22
The Lamb stands on Mount Zion ... Rev 14:1

ACKNOWLEDGMENTS

22............. Erich Lessing/Art Resource, NY.

22............. Photo © Regents of the University of Michigan. Used by permission.

1521.......... Portrait of Martin Luther by Lucas Cranach the Elder (1472–1553). 1529. Uffizi, Florence, Italy. Photo © Scala/Art Resource, NY.

1522.......... Facsimile of New Testament page, as appeared in *Luther's Life*, Ingeborg Stolee, Augsburg, 1943.

1523.......... Art Resource, NY.

1524.......... Psalm 43 manuscript, as appeared in *Luther and the Reformation: An Illustrated Review*, Hanns Lilje, Fortress Press, 1967, p. 158.

1525.......... Art Resource, NY.

1526.......... Title page of Luther's translation of the Bible, as appeared in *Luther's Life*, p. 91.

1527.......... Woodcut from the 1546 Wittenberg edition of the New Testament, as appeared in *Reformation: A Picture Story of Martin Luther*, Dietrich Steinwede, Fortress Press, 1983, p. 52.

1530.......... Luther's Catechism, 1542. Photo © Bayerische Staatsbibliothek München. (Catech. 432). Used by permission.

1532.......... From Kessler Reformation Collection, Pitts Theological Library Digital Image Archive. Used by permission.

1534.......... From Kessler Reformation Collection, Pitts Theological Library Digital Image Archive. Used by permission.

1548.......... Portrait of Jesus from BBC One's documentary *Son of God,* based on forensic anthropologists' research; illustration © BBC Photo Library. Used by permission.

1548.......... *Nativity by Lu Lan;* © Lu Lan.

CHARTS AND FIGURES

Charts

Figures

BIBLE READING PLAN

Martin Luther once said, "For some years now . . . I have read through the Bible twice every year. If you picture the Bible to be a mighty tree and every word a little branch, I have shaken every one of these branches because I wanted to know what it was and what it meant" (*LW* 54:165).

Few of us will ever approach the time and energy Luther devoted to reading the Bible. Yet, as Luther's heirs, we carry his love for Scripture and affirm with him that God's Word alone holds the key to life and salvation. With Luther, we want to "shake each branch" to discover its meaning for our lives.

When Martin Luther lived in exile at the Wartburg Castle, with his own life as well as his reforming cause in jeopardy, he used his time for intensive Bible study. In addition, he began a monumental undertaking to translate the Bible into the common language of his country's people. If every believer was a priest before God, as Luther proclaimed, then he or she should be invited to read and study God's truth found in Scripture.

Using This Plan

This Bible reading companion provides a year-long interaction with the Holy Scriptures based on readings for an entire year. Each day offers three different "paths" through the Bible. This allows adults, youth, and children to choose the path most appropriate for their interests, their reading abilities, and the amount of daily time they are willing to dedicate to focusing on the Word of God.

The Challenge Path. Dig deeply into the Bible's riches. This path offers large sections of Scripture for thoughtful meditation. For six days of each week, read through about two to four chapters of a book of the Bible. These readings alternate between the New and Old Testaments. Sundays offer a different approach. Since three appointed Scripture readings are read at Sunday worship, those following the Challenge Path generally will study selections from a variety of biblical resources such as Psalms, Proverbs, and Ecclesiastes. In other instances, Sunday reading will focus on short books such as Ruth, Jonah, and Esther.

The Survey Path. Shorter scriptural references characterize the Survey Path. There is usually a close connection with the readings listed for the Challenge Path. However, from time to time related passages from both the Old and New Testaments are brought together to explore connections of key biblical ideas. Each week features a theme for your reading.

The Sampler Path. This path distills the Bible's message in a weekly series of memorable and quotable references. These passages are special treasures of Christian faith and can be used for memorization. For the most part, the Sampler Path uses shorter portions of the Challenge Path selections. Hopefully, this will encourage discussion and interaction between members of the same household who are reading different "paths."

Week 1

	Challenge	Survey: God with Us		Sampler	
S	Psalms 1, 2, 4; Proverbs 1:1-19	Luke 1:26-38	Announcement to Mary	Psalm 24:8-10	King of Glory
M	Luke 1:1—2:52	Luke 2:1-20	Birth of Jesus	Luke 2:1-7	Jesus Is Born
T	Luke 3:1—4:13	Luke 4:1-13	Jesus' Temptations	Luke 2:41-52	Jesus at Twelve
W	Luke 4:14—5:11	Luke 5:1-11	Calling Disciples	Luke 3:21-22	Jesus Is Baptized
T	Luke 5:12—6:11	Luke 5:12-26	Jesus the Healer	Luke 5:12-16	Jesus Heals
F	Luke 6:12—7:50	Luke 6:12-38	Jesus the Teacher	Luke 6:20-23	Jesus Teaches
S	Luke 8:1—9:50	Luke 9:10-27	Jesus the Christ	Luke 9:18-22	Jesus the Christ

Week 2

	Challenge	Survey: Paying Attention to Jesus		Sampler	
S	Psalms 5, 6; Proverbs 1:20—3:12	1 Corinthians 1:1-9	Called to Fellowship	Psalm 5:11-12	Sing for Joy
M	Luke 9:51—10:42	Luke 9:57-62	Half-Hearted Followers	Luke 10:29-37	The Good Samaritan
T	Luke 11:1—13:9	Luke 11:1-13	Power of Prayer	Luke 11:1-4	The Lord's Prayer
W	Luke 13:10—14:35	Luke 13:18-30	God's Kingdom	Luke 13:18-21	Growth in Faith
T	Luke 15:1-32	Luke 15:11-32	Forgiveness	Luke 15:3-7	The Lost Sheep
F	Luke 16:1—17:19	Luke 17:1-4	Learning to Forgive	Luke 16:10	Real Faithfulness
S	Luke 17:20—18:30	Luke 18:18-27	Wealth and Faithfulness	Luke 18:15-17	The Kingdom's Children

Week 3

	Challenge	Survey: Christ's Gifts to Us		Sampler	
S	Psalms 7, 8, 9, 10	Luke 18:35-43	Faith in the Lord	Psalm 9:1, 2	Giving Thanks
M	Luke 18:32—19:27	Luke 19:1-10	Zacchaeus	Luke 19:1-6	Getting a Better View
T	Luke 19:28—20:26	Luke 19:28-39	Blessed Is the King	Luke 19:36-38	The Triumphant Entry
W	Luke 20:27—21:38	Luke 21:1-4	A Widow's Coins	Luke 21:1-4	A Special Offering
T	Luke 22:1-71	Luke 22:14-23	The Last Supper	Luke 22:19-20	Preparing a Supper
F	Luke 23:1-56	Luke 23:26-56	The Crucifixion	Luke 23:38	King of the Jews
S	Luke 24:1-53	Luke 24:1-12	The Resurrection	Luke 24:1-9	The Resurrection

Week 4

	Challenge	Survey: Led by the Spirit		Sampler	
S	Proverbs 3:13—5:23	Proverbs 3:5-8, 11-14	Trust	Proverbs 3:5, 6	Trust in the Lord
M	Acts 1:1—2:42	Acts 1:1-11; 2:1-21	Promise, Presence	Acts 2:1-4	Day of Pentecost
T	Acts 2:43—4:4	Acts 2:2:43-47	Believers Together	Acts 2:46-47	Day by Day
W	Acts 4:5—5:11	Acts 4:32-37	Everything in Common	Acts 4:32-35	One Heart and Soul
T	Acts 5:12—6:7	Acts 6:1-7	Seven Appointed	Acts 5:12-16	Signs and Wonders
F	Acts 6:8—8:3	Acts 6:8-15; 7:58—8:3	Stephen	Acts 6:8	Stephen Serves
S	Acts 8:4-40	Acts 8:26-40	Philip and the Eunuch	Acts 8:35-38	The Eunuch Is Baptized

Week 5

	Challenge	Survey: Calls and Conversions		Sampler	
S	Ruth 1:1—4:22	Ruth 1:1-18	Ruth's Decision	Ruth 1:15-18	Ruth's Loyalty
M	Acts 9:1-43	Acts 9:1-9	Saul Is Called	Acts 9:20-22	Saul Preaches Christ
T	Acts 10:1—11:18	Acts 10:34-48	Conversion of Gentiles	Acts 10:34-35	Acceptable to God

W	Acts 11:19—12:25	Matthew 18:1-6	As Children in Faith	Acts 11:17-18	God's Spirit Is for All
T	Acts 13:1—14:7	Isaiah 55:6-9	Return to the Lord	Acts 13:48-49	God's Word Is Spread
F	Acts 14:8—15:35	Romans 1:16-17	Power of the Gospel	Acts 15:6-9	God Knows the Heart
S	Acts 15:36—16:40	Ephesians 4:22—5:2	Imitators of God	Acts 16:9-10	A Call to Go Forth

Week 6

	Challenge	Survey: Sharing the Good News		Sampler	
S	Psalms 11, 12, 15; Ecclesiastes 1:1—2:26	Isaiah 52:7-10	Good Tidings	Psalm 11:7	The Lord Is Righteous
M	Acts 17:1—18:11	Matthew 28:16-20	Making Disciples	Acts 18:8-11	Baptizing and Teaching
T	Acts 18:12—19:20	Acts 1:6-11	Witnesses for Christ	Acts 19:11-12	God Works Through Paul
W	Acts 19:21—20:16	Acts 17:16-34	Paul in Athens	Acts 20:35	Paul Shares a Teaching
T	Acts 20:17—21:14	2 Timothy 4:1-5	Being an Evangelist	Acts 21:13	To Die for Jesus
F	Acts 21:15—22:29	John 21:15-17	Doing the Lord's Work	Acts 21:39—22:1	Paul Defends Himself
S	Acts 22:30—23:35	Ephesians 4:11-16	The Saints Equipped	Acts 28:30-31	Paul in Rome At Last

Week 7

	Challenge	Survey: Life to Come		Sampler	
S	Proverbs 6:1—7:27; Ecclesiastes 3:1—4:16	John 14:1-11	Preparing for Our Future	Ecclesiastes 3:1-2	A Time to Be Born
M	Acts 24:1—25:12	Matthew 25:31-46	Serving the Lord	1 Thessalonians 1:1-3	Greetings
T	Acts 25:13—26:32	1 Corinthians 2:6-16	The Spirit	1 Thessalonians 2:13	Acceptance
W	Acts 27:1—28:31	1 Thessalonians 4:13-18	With the Lord	1 Thessalonians 3:11-13	Benediction
T	1 Thessalonians 1:1—3:13	1 Thessalonians 5:1-11	Be Watchful	1 Thessalonians 4:1	Pleasing to God
F	1 Thessalonians 4:1—5:28	2 Thessalonians 1:3-12	Live Worthily	1 Thessalonians 5:1-2	Day of the Lord
S	2 Thessalonians 1:1—3:18	Revelation 21:1-14	New Heaven, Earth	1 Thessalonians 5:15-18	Rejoice

Week 8

	Challenge	Survey: God the Creator		Sampler	
S	Psalms 16, 17; Ecclesiastes 5:1—6:12	Genesis 1:1-3	God Creates the World	Psalm 17:8	In God's Care
M	Genesis 1:1—2:3	Genesis 1:26-31	God Creates Humans	Genesis 1:1	God Created the World
T	Genesis 2:4—3:24	Psalm 8:3-9	The Value of Humans	Genesis 1:27	Created in God's Image
W	Genesis 4:1—5:32	John 1:1-5	The Incarnate Word	Genesis 5:1-2	In God's Likeness
T	Genesis 6:1—8:12	Proverbs 3:19-24	Creativity, Wisdom	Genesis 7:12-16	Noah and the Ark
F	Genesis 8:13—9:29	Ephesians 2:8-10	Created in Christ	Genesis 9:16-17	A Rainbow Promise
S	Genesis 10:1—11:32	Romans 11:33-36	All Things from God	Genesis 11:4-9	Tower of Babel

Week 9

	Challenge	Survey: Abraham—God's Chosen		Sampler	
S	Psalms 18, 19; Proverbs 8:1—9:18	Genesis 12:1-3	God Calls Abraham	Psalm 19:1-2	The Glory of God
M	Genesis 12:1—13:18	Genesis 17:1-8	God's Covenant	Genesis 12:1-2	Abram's Call
T	Genesis 14:1—5:11	Genesis 21:1-7	The Birth of Isaac	Genesis 15:5-6	God's Promise
W	Genesis 16:1—17:27	Genesis 22:1-14	God Tests Abraham	Genesis 17:15-16	A Child for Sarah
T	Genesis 18:1—19:38	Hebrews 11:8-12	Examples of Faith	Hebrews 11:8-12	Faith in God

F	Genesis 20:1—21:34	Galatians 3:6-9	Children of Abraham	Galatians 3:6-7	Abraham's Children
S	Genesis 22:1—23:20	John 8:52-59	Jesus and Abraham	John 8:58	I Am

Week 10					
	Challenge	**Survey: Jacob Becomes Israel**		**Sampler**	
S	Psalms 20, 22, 23, 24	Genesis 25:19-26	Isaac's Children	Psalm 23	The Shepherd Psalm
M	Genesis 24:1-67	Genesis 25:27-34	The Lost Birthright	Genesis 25:11	God Blesses Isaac
T	Genesis 25:1—26:35	Genesis 27:1-29	Jacob the Trickster	Genesis 27:41-45	Trouble Between Brothers
W	Genesis 27:1—28:22	Genesis 32:22-30	Wrestling an Angel	Genesis 28:10-13	Jacob's Stairway
T	Genesis 29:1—30:24	Genesis 33:1-11	Peace Returns	Genesis 33:4-5	The Brothers Meet Again
F	Genesis 30:25—31:54	Psalm 105:1-11	God's Faithfulness	Genesis 33:9-11	Peace Between Brothers
S	Genesis 31:55—33:20	Romans 9:6-16	Children of Promise	Psalm 105:1-6	God's Chosen Ones

Week 11					
	Challenge	**Survey: Joseph's Story**		**Sampler**	
S	Psalms 25, 26, 27; Proverbs 10:1-32	Genesis 37:1-11	Joseph's Dream	Psalm 27:14	Wait for the Lord
M	Genesis 34:1—35:29	Genesis 37:12-36	Joseph Sold as Slave	Genesis 37:1-4	Jacob's Favorite Son
T	Genesis 36:6-8; 38:1-30	Genesis 39:1-23	In Potiphar's Service	Genesis 37:23-24	Joseph in a Pit
W	Genesis 37:1-36; 39:1-23	Genesis 41:9-24	Joseph before Pharaoh	Genesis 37:28	Joseph Taken to Egypt
T	Genesis 40:1—41:45	Genesis 41:25-43	Appointed to Office	Genesis 39:20-21	Joseph in Prison
F	Genesis 41:46—42:38	Genesis 42:6-28	A Time of Famine	Genesis 41:38-40	Wise Joseph
S	Genesis 43:1—45:3	Genesis 43:1-34	Joseph's Brothers	Genesis 45:4-8	A Brotherly Surprise

Week 12					
	Challenge	**Survey: Good News, Bad News**		**Sampler**	
S	Proverbs 11:1—12:28; Ecclesiastes 7:1-8	Galatians 3:21-29	Heirs of Christ	Proverbs 12:15	Listening to Advice
M	Genesis 45:4—46:34	Genesis 45:4-28	Good News for Jacob	Genesis 45:4-10	A Caring Brother
T	Genesis 47:1—48:22	Genesis 47:13-26	Bad News for Egypt	Genesis 48:15-20	A Surprising Blessing
W	Genesis 49:1—50:26	Genesis 50:1-16	End of an Era	Genesis 50:15-21	No Revenge Intended
T	Romans 1:1—2:23	Romans 2:1-16	Sinful People	Romans 1:28-32	Worthless Thinking
F	Romans 2:24—3:31	Romans 3:21-31	Grace as a Gift	Romans 3:21-23	By Grace through Faith
S	Romans 4:1—5:21	Romans 5:1-21	Justified by Faith	Romans 5:18-21	Abundant Grace

Week 13					
	Challenge	**Survey: Living with Christ**		**Sampler**	
S	Psalms 28, 29, 30; Ecclesiastes 9:1—10:20	Romans 6:1-11	Alive in Christ	Psalm 30:4	Sing, You Saints
M	Romans 6:1—7:25	Romans 7:14-25	Inner Conflict	Romans 6:23	The Wages of Sin
T	Romans 8:1—9:5	Romans 8:28-39	No Separation	Romans 8:28	All Things Work for Good
W	Romans 9:6—10:10	Romans 10:1-13	Hearts and Voices	Romans 10:11-13	God Is Lord of All
T	Romans 10:11—12:8	Romans 12:1-8	Gifts that Differ	Romans 11:33-36	The Glory of God
F	Romans 12:9—14:23	Romans 12:9-21	Marks of a Christian	Romans 12:14-16	Living in Harmony
S	Romans 15:1—16:27	Romans 15:1-13	Set a Good Example	Romans 15:4-6, 13	Joy and Peace

Week 14	Challenge	Survey: Amazing Power of Life		Sampler	
S	Psalms 31, 32, 33; Proverbs 13:1-25	Philemon	Promote Knowledge of Good	Psalm 33:1-3	A New Song
M	Philemon; Mark 1:1-13	Mark 1:1-11	Prepare the Way	Mark 1:1-8	John Prepares the Way
T	Mark 1:14—3:6	Mark 1:14-45	Jesus Came Preaching	Mark 1:16-20	Fishermen Follow Jesus
W	Mark 3:7—4:41	Mark 4:1-29	The Sower and the Seeds	Mark 3:13-19	Jesus Calls the Twelve
T	Mark 5:1—6:13	Mark 5:1-43	Healing the Hurting	Mark 6:7-13	The Disciples Serve Jesus
F	Mark 6:14—7:13	Mark 6:30-56	Feeding the Multitudes	Mark 6:45-50	A Surprise on the Sea
S	Mark 7:14—8:26	Mark 7:14-37	Cleansing the Evil Within	Mark 8:1-10	Loaves and Fishes

Week 15	Challenge	Survey: Power in the Gospel		Sampler	
S	Psalms 34, 36; Ecclesiastes 11:1—12:14	Mark 8:27—9:1	Cost of Discipleship	Psalm 34:1-3	Praising the Lord
M	Mark 8:27—9:50	Mark 9:2-13	Jesus, Son of God	Mark 9:33-37	Servants of All
T	Mark 10:1—11:10	Mark 10:1-16	Blessings of Marriage	Mark 10:23-27	Easier for a Camel
W	Mark 11:11—12:27	Mark 11:12-25	Cleansing God's House	Mark 11:15-19	A House of Prayer
T	Mark 12:28—13:37	Mark 12:28-44	The Great Commandment	Mark 12:28-31	Love God First
F	Mark 14:1—15:20	Mark 14:12-31	The Last Supper	Mark 14:1-2	The Plotters
S	Mark 15:21—16:8 (9-20)	Mark 16:1-8	The First Easter	Mark 16:6-7	"He Has Been Raised"

Week 16	Challenge	Survey: A Man Named Moses		Sampler	
S	Psalms 40, 41, 42; Proverbs 14:1—15:33	Exodus 1:6-16; 2:1-10	Moses Is Saved	Proverbs 14:20-21	Happy Is the One
M	Exodus 1:1—3:12	Exodus 3:1-12	God Calls Moses	Exodus 2:1-10	Moses in the Bulrushes
T	Exodus 3:13—4:31	Exodus 4:1-18	The Reluctant Leader	Exodus 3:10-12	God Needs Moses
W	Exodus 5:1—7:24	Exodus 7:14-25	Struggle with Pharaoh	Exodus 6:6-8	Moses' Challenge
T	Exodus 7:25—10:29	Exodus 9:1-35	Terrible Plagues	Exodus 6:10-13	Aaron Helps, Too
F	Exodus 11:1—12:50	Exodus 12:1-32	The First Passover	Exodus 14:26-31	Crossing the Red Sea
S	Exodus 13:1—15:21	Exodus 13:17-22; 14:5-9, 15-31	Free!	Exodus 15:1-2	Singing Praises to God

Week 17	Challenge	Survey: Struggles in the Wilderness		Sampler	
S	Psalms 43, 44, 45; Proverbs 16:1—17:28	Hebrews 11:23-27	Moses' Faith	Psalm 43:3-5	God's Light and Truth
M	Exodus 15:22—17:7	Exodus 16:2-26	Wilderness Food	Exodus 15:19-21	A Time to Dance
T	Exodus 17:8—18:27	Exodus 18:1-23	Jethro's Advice	Exodus 18:25-26	Moses Chooses Leaders
W	Exodus 19:1—20:21	Exodus 19:17—20:17	Ten Commandments	Exodus 19:3-6	A Holy Nation
T	Exodus 31:18—33:23	Exodus 32:1-20	The Golden Calf	Exodus 20:1-17	God's Law Is Given
F	Exodus 34:1-10, 28-35	Exodus 33:12—34:10	Tables of the Law	Exodus 34:6-10	God's Steadfast Love
S	Deuteronomy 5:1-33; 6:1-25; 8:1-20	Deuteronomy 6:1-15	Moses' Instruction	Deuteronomy 6:4-7	Heart, Soul, Might

Week 18					
	Challenge	Survey: Into the Promised Land		Sampler	
S	Psalms 46, 47, 48, 49	Psalm 23	The Shepherd Lord	Psalm 46:1-3	Confidence in God
M	Deuteronomy 30:11—31:29; 32:48-52; 34:1-12	Deuteronomy 34:1-12	Death of Moses	Deuteronomy 30:15-16	Walk in God's Ways
T	Joshua 1:1—4:14	Joshua 1:1-9	Joshua Leads the Way	Joshua 1:1-2,9	God Is with the People
W	Joshua 5:13—7:26	Joshua 6:1-20	Jericho's Fall	Joshua 6:15, 20	The Walls of Jericho
T	Joshua 8:30—10:15	Joshua 8:30-35	An Altar to the Lord	Joshua 8:30-32	Offerings to God
F	Joshua 23:1—24:33	Joshua 24:1-15	Serve the Lord!	Joshua 24:14-15	A Promise to Serve
S	Judges 1:1—2:23	Judges 2:16-23	The First Judges	Judges 2:16	God Appoints Judges to Rule

Week 19					
	Challenge	Survey: Challenge of Faith		Sampler	
S	Psalms 50, 51, 53, 54	1 Peter 4:7-11	Love Conquers All	Psalm 53:1	What Fools They Are
M	Judges 4:1—5:31	Judges 4:1-24	Deborah's Victory	Judges 4:4-5	One of God's Judges
T	Judges 6:1—8:32	Judges 6:33-7:22	Gideon's Charge	Judges 8:22-23	Gideon Knows Who Rules
W	Judges 13:1—16:31	Judges 16:4-30	Samson's Story	Judges 16:27-30	Samson's Strength
T	1 Corinthians 1:1—4:21	1 Corinthians 3:18-23	Christ's Own	1 Corinthians 3:16	A Temple of God
F	1 Corinthians 5:1—7:40	1 Corinthians 6:12-20	Live in Honor	1 Corinthians 6:19-20	Glorify God
S	1 Corinthians 8:1—11:1	1 Corinthians 9:19-27	Self-Discipline	1 Corinthians 10:13	Endure Temptation

Week 20					
	Challenge	Survey: Living in Community		Sampler	
S	John 1—4	1 Corinthians 11:23-32	The Eucharist	1 Corinthians 11:23-26	Lord's Supper
M	1 Corinthians 11:2—13:13	1 Corinthians 13:1-13	Love's Greatness	1 Corinthians 13:1, 4-7, 13	Love Is First
T	1 Corinthians 14:1—16:24	1 Corinthians 15:12-28	Gift of New Life	1 Corinthians 16:13-14	Act in Love
W	2 Corinthians 1:1—3:18	2 Corinthians 3:1-6	Living Letters	2 Corinthians 3:1-6	Letter from Christ
T	2 Corinthians 4:1—7:16	2 Corinthians 5:17-21	Ambassadors	2 Corinthians 5:17	New Person in Christ
F	2 Corinthians 8:1—10:18	2 Corinthians 9:6-15	Cheerful Givers	2 Corinthians 8:9	In Christ
S	2 Corinthians 11:1—13:14	2 Corinthians 13:4-14	Test Yourselves	2 Corinthians 13:5-6	Meet the Test

Week 21					
	Challenge	Survey: Judgment and Forgiveness		Sampler	
S	Psalms 56, 57, 61; Proverbs 18:1-24	John 12:44-50	God the Judge	Psalm 61:1-5	Seeking Safety
M	Hosea 1:1—4:19	Romans 2:1-11	God Is Just	Proverbs 18:10	Safe with God
T	Hosea 5:1—9:7	Hosea 11:1-11	A Loving Parent	Hosea 6:1-2	Return to the Lord
W	Hosea 10:1-10; 11:1-11; 14:1-9	Amos 5:21-24	Call for Justice	Hosea 14:9	The Lord's Ways Are Right
T	Amos 1:1—4:13	Amos 9:13-15	Restoration	Amos 4:13	The Lord, the God of Hosts
F	Amos 5:1—9:15	Joel 2:12-19	Repentance	Amos 5:24	Let There Be Justice
S	Joel 1:1—3:21	Psalm 51:1-13	Plea for Forgiveness	Joel 2:12-13	With All Your Heart

Week 22	Challenge	Survey: Warnings and Promises		Sampler	
S	Psalms 62, 63; Proverbs 19:1—21:31	Psalm 63:1-8	You Are My God	Proverbs 21:3, 21	What Is Acceptable
M	Micah 1:1—4:5	Micah 4:1-5	Walking in God's Paths	Micah 4:5	Walk with God
T	Micah 4:6—7:20	Micah 7:18-20	No One Like Our God	Micah 7:7	Trust in God
W	Isaiah 1:1—4:6	Isaiah 1:11-20	Seeking Justice	Isaiah 1:16-17	Learn to Do Good
T	Isaiah 5:1—7:25	Isaiah 7:1-25	A Special Prophecy	Isaiah 7:14	A Sign from God
F	Isaiah 8:11—10:34	Isaiah 9:1-7	More Good News	Isaiah 9:6	A Child for Us
S	Isaiah 11:1—16:14	Isaiah 11:1-10	A Sign of Peace	Isaiah 11:6-7	Peace Will Come

Week 23	Challenge	Survey: Strength in Times of Testing		Sampler	
S	Psalms 65, 66, 67, 68	Psalm 67:1-7	God's Blessings	Psalm 67:1-7	Let All People Praise God
M	Isaiah 25:1—27:13	Isaiah 26:1-13	Victorious People of God	Isaiah 26:1-4	An Everlasting Rock
T	Isaiah 30:1—33:24	Isaiah 30:19-26	Help in Hard Times	Isaiah 30:19-21	God Hears and Answers
W	Isaiah 36:1—39:8	Isaiah 38:1-20	The King Is Healed	Isaiah 38:19-20	All Our Days
T	James 1:1—5:20	James 4:1-10	Come Close to God	James 4:8-10	Draw Near to God
F	1 Peter 1:1—2:25	1 Peter 2:1-12	Living Stones	1 Peter 2:9-10	God's Own People
S	1 Peter 3:1—5:14	1 Peter 4:1-11	Maintain Love	1 Peter 4:10-11	Using God's Gifts

Week 24	Challenge	Survey: Living in Love		Sampler	
S	2 Peter 1:1—3:18	2 Peter 1:1-21	How to Live	1 John 1:5-7	God Is Light
M	1 John 1:1—3:10	1 John 2:1-17	To Do God's Will	1 John 2:9-11	Walking in the Light
T	1 John 3:11—5:21	1 John 4:7-21	God Is Love	1 John 3:1-3	Children of God
W	Colossians 1:1—2:23	Colossians 1:9-23	Christ Above All	1 John 4:19-21	God First Loved Us
T	Colossians 3:1—4:18	Colossians 3:5—4:5	Christian Conduct	1 John 5:1-5	Love and Obey
F	Song of Solomon 1:1—4:16	1 Corinthians 12:4-26	Spiritual Gifts	Colossians 2:6	Live in Christ Jesus
S	Song of Solomon 5:1—8:14	John 15:12-21	Love One Another	Colossians 3:12-15	Put on Love

Week 25	Challenge	Survey: The Call to Loyalty		Sampler	
S	2 John; 3 John; Jude	2 John	Stand by Christ	Psalm 42:1-2, 11	Hope in God
M	Jeremiah 1:1—2:37	Jeremiah 1:4-10	A Young Prophet	Jeremiah 1:6-8	A Youth Called to Serve
T	Jeremiah 3:6—5:31	Jeremiah 3:12-18	Return to God	Jeremiah 3:12	God Is Merciful
W	Jeremiah 6:1—8:3	Jeremiah 7:1-11	False Religion	Jeremiah 7:1-3	Jeremiah Speaks for God
T	Jeremiah 11:1—12:13	Jeremiah 11:1-14	Keep the Covenant	Jeremiah 11:3-5	Listen to God
F	Jeremiah 18:1—20:6	Luke 15:11-31	Prodigal Son	Jeremiah 18:1-6	Like a Potter
S	Jeremiah 23:1—25:38	Hebrews 12:1-13	Run the Race	Jeremiah 23:23-24	God Is Near Us

Week 26	Challenge	Survey: God's Living Covenant		Sampler	
S	Psalms 37, 38, 39	Jeremiah 31:1-4	Restoring Israel	Psalm 37:40	Refuge with God
M	Jeremiah 26:1—28:17	Jeremiah 31:31-35	New Covenant	Jeremiah 31:7-8	Israel Will Return
T	Jeremiah 30:1—31:40	Hebrews 8:1-13	Christ Our Priest	Jeremiah 31:35	God's Good Order
W	Jeremiah 32:1—34:7	Galatians 3:15-29	Belonging to Christ	Jeremiah 33:10-11	God Will Restore
T	Jeremiah 34:8—37:21	1 Corinthians 11:23-32	Christ's Supper	Jeremiah 50:4-5	Joined to the Lord
F	Jeremiah 38:1—39:18	Acts 3:1-26	Heirs of the Covenant	Romans 12:18-21	Overcoming Evil
S	Jeremiah 40:1—42:17	Romans 12:1-21	Living Sacrifice	Romans 13:8	Fulfilling the Law

Week 27	Challenge	Survey: The Coming of Jesus		Sampler	
S	Psalms 70, 71, 72, 73	Matthew 1:18-25	God with Us	Psalm 70:4-5	God Is Great
M	Matthew 1:1—2:23	Matthew 2:1-12	Gifts of the Magi	Matthew 21:1-2, 10-12	Following a Star
T	Matthew 3:1—4:22	Matthew 4:1-11	Jesus' Temptations	Matthew 4:18-22	Fishing for Followers
W	Matthew 4:23—6:4	Matthew 5:1-12	The Beatitudes	Matthew 5:14-16	Let Your Light Shine
T	Matthew 6:5—7:29	Matthew 6:5-15	The Lord's Prayer	Matthew 6:5-6	When You Pray
F	Matthew 8:1—9:34	Matthew 7:24-29	The Two Houses	Matthew 9:27-31	The Blind See
S	Matthew 9:35—11:30	Matthew 9:35—10:9	Sending the Twelve	Matthew 9:35-38	Jesus Has Much to Do

Week 28	Challenge	Survey: Jesus and the Kingdom		Sampler	
S	Psalm 78; Proverbs 24:1-34	Proverbs 24:1-24	Wisdom's Values	Psalm 78:1	Listen to God
M	Matthew 12:1—13:52	Matthew 12:22-37	A Good Tree's Fruit	Matthew 13:1-9	Parable of the Sower
T	Matthew 13:53—15:39	Matthew 13:44-52	Kingdom Parables	Matthew 14:13-21	A Great Picnic
W	Matthew 16:1—17:27	Matthew 16:13-20	Jesus the Messiah	Matthew 16:24-25	A Hard Teaching
T	Matthew 18:1—19:30	Matthew 18:21-35	Forgiving Others	Matthew 18:12-14	A Good Shepherd
F	Matthew 20:1—21:22	Matthew 20:17-28	Selfless Service	Matthew 20:25-28	Servants All
S	Matthew 21:23—23:39	Matthew 22:15-33	Traps for Jesus	Matthew 22:34-40	Two Commandments

Week 29	Challenge	Survey: God's Plan for the World		Sampler	
S	Psalms 80, 81, 82, 84	Matthew 24:23-44	The Second Coming	Psalm 84:1-4	Finding Shelter
M	Matthew 23:37—24:51	Matthew 25:31-46	Time of Judgment	Matthew 23:11-12	Who Is the Greatest?
T	Matthew 25:1—26:46	Matthew 26:59-69	Jesus on Trial	Matthew 26:47-50	Judas Betrays Jesus
W	Matthew 26:47—27:61	Matthew 27:24-54	Words from the Cross	Matthew 28:5-10	Jesus Is Risen
T	Matthew 27:62—28:20	Matthew 28:1-20	Christ's Commission	Matthew 28:19-20	Go to All Nations
F	1 Samuel 1:1—2:36	1 Samuel 1:1-28	Samuel's Birth	1 Samuel 1:27-28	Hannah's Gift
S	1 Samuel 3:1—4:22	1 Samuel 3:1—4:1	Samuel's Call	1 Samuel 3:10	God Calls Samuel

Week 30	Challenge	Survey: The First King of Israel		Sampler	
S	Psalms 85, 86, 87, 88	Psalm 86:1-17	The Greatness of God	Psalm 86:15-17	God's Help and Comfort
M	1 Samuel 6:1—7:17	1 Samuel 7:2-17	Samuel the Judge	1 Samuel 7:3-4	Serve the Lord Only
T	1 Samuel 8:1—9:26	1 Samuel 10:1-24	Choosing Saul	1 Samuel 9:15-17	Here Is the Man
W	1 Samuel 10:1—11:15	1 Samuel 13:1-14	Saul the King	1 Samuel 11:15	Saul Becomes King

T	1 Samuel 12:1—14:52	1 Samuel 16:1-23	David Anointed	1 Samuel 14:52	Hard Fighting for Saul
F	1 Samuel 15:1—17:58	1 Samuel 17:12-58	David and Goliath	1 Samuel 15:26	Saul Rejects God's Word
S	1 Samuel 18:1—19:24	1 Samuel 18:1-16	David Is Popular	1 Samuel 16:1	God Will Choose a New King

Week 31

	Challenge	Survey: David – From Warrior to King		Sampler	
S	Psalm 89; Proverbs 25:1-28	Psalm 89:19-37	God's Covenant	Psalm 89:19-21	God Chose David
M	1 Samuel 20:1—21:15	1 Samuel 20:12-42	David and Jonathan	1 Samuel 16:6-12	David Is Chosen
T	1 Samuel 22:1—24:22	1 Samuel 24:1-22	Hiding from Saul	1 Samuel 16:21-23	David Helps Saul
W	1 Samuel 25:1—26:25	1 Samuel 26:1-25	David Spares Saul	1 Samuel 17:2-11	Goliath
T	1 Samuel 27:1—28:25	1 Samuel 28:3-19	The Witch of Endor	1 Samuel 17:25, 31-37	David Volunteers
F	1 Samuel 29:1—31:13	1 Samuel 31:1-13	Saul's Death	1 Samuel 17:38-47	In the Name of the Lord
S	2 Samuel 1:1—2:32	2 Samuel 1:17—2:7	David Is King	1 Samuel 17:48-49	David Defeats Goliath

Week 32

	Challenge	Survey: David – From the Heights to the Depths		Sampler	
S	Psalms 90, 91, 92, 93	2 Samuel 4:4-12	The Avenger	Psalm 91:1-2	Trusting in God
M	2 Samuel 3:1—4:12	2 Samuel 6:1-19	Moving the Ark	2 Samuel 5:1-3	David Anointed King
T	2 Samuel 5:1—6:23	2 Samuel 7:4-17	God's Promise	2 Samuel 7:16	A Kingdom Forever
W	2 Samuel 7:1—8:18	2 Samuel 9:1-13	David's Kindness	2 Samuel 7:22-24, 28-29	David's Prayer
T	2 Samuel 9:1—10:19	2 Samuel 11:2-27	David's Sin	2 Samuel 12:1-6	Nathan's Story
F	2 Samuel 11:1—12:25	2 Samuel 12:1-15	Nathan's Story	2 Samuel 12:7-10	David's Sin
S	2 Samuel 12:26—13:39	2 Samuel 13:1-19	Family Sins	2 Samuel 12:11-14	Judgment and Forgiveness

Week 33

	Challenge	Survey: David – A Time of Turmoil		Sampler	
S	Psalms 94, 95; Proverbs 26:1-28	Matthew 21:1-11; 22:41-46	Son of David	Psalm 95:1-7	A Song of Praise
M	2 Samuel 14:1—15:37	2 Samuel 15:1-18	Absalom's Rebellion	2 Samuel 22:1-4	David's Song
T	2 Samuel 16:1—17:29	2 Samuel 16:1-14	David on the Run	2 Samuel 22:47	Blessed Be My Rock
W	2 Samuel 18:1—19:43	2 Samuel 18:1-18	Absalom's Defeat	2 Samuel 23:1-5	David's Last Words
T	2 Samuel 20:1—21:22	2 Samuel 19:4-15	David Mourns	Psalm 24:1-2	The Earth Is the Lord's
F	2 Samuel 22:1–23:7	2 Samuel 21:1-14	Famine Strikes	Psalm 24:3-6	Who Shall Stand?
S	2 Samuel 23:8—24:25	2 Samuel 24:10-25	Averting the Plague	Psalm 24:7-10	King of Glory

Week 34

	Challenge	Survey: The People of God		Sampler	
S	Esther	Matthew 6:25-34	Seek God's Kingdom	Psalm 72:18-20	God's Glorious Name
M	Galatians 1:1—2:21	Galatians 2:11-21	Christ Lives in Me	Galatians 1:1-5	Letter to God's People
T	Galatians 3:1—5:1	Galatians 3:21-29	Equality in Christ	Galatians 3:27-29	All Are in Christ
W	Galatians 5:2—6:18	Galatians 5:13-25	Walk by the Spirit	Galatians 5:13-15	Serve One Another
T	Ephesians 1:1—2:22	Ephesians 2:1-10	Saved by Grace	Ephesians 2:8-10	A Gift of God
F	Ephesians 3:1—4:32	Ephesians 3:14-21	Rooted in Love	Ephesians 4:15-16	Growing Up
S	Ephesians 5:1—6:23	Ephesians 5:1-20	Imitators of God	Ephesians 5:1-2	Walk in Love

Week 35	Challenge	Survey: Christ, Our High Priest		Sampler	
S	Psalms 96, 97, 98, 99, 100	Psalm 100:1-5	Enduring Love	Psalm 100:1-5	A Joyful Noise
M	Hebrews 1:1—2:18	Hebrews 2:9-18	Our High Priest	Hebrews 1:1-4	God in Christ
T	Hebrews 3:1—5:14	Hebrews 4:1-13	God Promises Rest	Hebrews 4:14-16	Jesus Knows Our Needs
W	Hebrews 6:1—7:28	Hebrews 6:1-12	Hope to the End	Hebrews 7:26	Above All Others
T	Hebrews 8:1—9:28	Hebrews 8:1-13	A New Covenant	Hebrews 9:28	Eagerly Waiting
F	Hebrews 10:1—11:40	Hebrews 10:11-25	Assurance of Faith	Hebrews 11:1-3	Assured by Faith
S	Hebrews 12:1-13:25	Hebrews 13:1-16	The Constant Christ	Hebrews 13:5-6	Our Helper

Week 36	Challenge	Survey: Breakdown of a Dynasty		Sampler	
S	Nahum	1 Kings 1:28-40	The New King	Nahum 1:3	God's Ways
M	1 Kings 1:1—2:46	1 Kings 2:1-10	David's Death	1 Kings 2:10-12	Solomon on the Throne
T	1 Kings 3:3-28; 4:20-34	1 Kings 3:3-14	Prayers for Wisdom	1 Kings 3:10-14	God Is Pleased
W	1 Kings 5:1—7:51	1 Kings 5:1-12	Cedars for the Temple	1 Kings 5:5-6	A Plan to Build
T	1 Kings 8:1—9:25	1 Kings 8:12-26	God's House Dedicated	1 Kings 7:51	God's House Is Ready
F	1 Kings 9:26—11:43	1 Kings 11:1-13	The King's Great Evil	1 Kings 10:23-25	A Rich and Wise King
S	1 Kings 12:1—13:34	1 Kings 11:41—12:11, 17-20	Civil War	1 Kings 11:9-10	The King Turns Away

Week 37	Challenge	Survey: Troubles in Israel		Sampler	
S	Psalms 102, 103, 104	1 Kings 16:8-24	Samaria Is Built	Psalm 103:1	Bless the Lord
M	1 Kings 14:21—16:28	1 Kings 16:29—17:16	Ahab and Elijah	1 Kings 11:41-43	Solomon's Rule Ends
T	1 Kings 16:29—18:46	1 Kings 18:17-46	Mount Carmel Test	1 Kings 16:21	Wars Divide Israel
W	1 Kings 19:1—20:43	1 Kings 19:1-16	Elijah Flees	1 Kings 7:1	Elijah's Story Begins
T	1 Kings 21:1—22:53	1 Kings 21:1-19	Naboth's Vineyard	1 Kings 19:9-14	A Still Small Voice
F	2 Kings 1:1—2:25	2 Kings 2:1-14	Elisha Takes Over	2 Kings 2:15	Elisha is God's Prophet
S	2 Kings 4:1—7:20	2 Kings 4:8-17	Elisha's Room	2 Kings 5:1-3, 13-14	Naaman's Cure

Week 38	Challenge	Survey: War and Peace		Sampler	
S	Psalm 105, Proverbs 27:1-27	2 Kings 8:1-19	Prophetic Power	Psalm 105:1-4	Seek the Lord
M	2 Kings 8:1—9:37	2 Kings 9:1-3, 17-28	Violent Revolt	2 Kings 8:1-6	Elisha Helps a Woman
T	2 Kings 10:1—12:21	2 Kings 11:21—12:16	Temple Repair	2 Kings 12:10-16	God's House Repaired
W	2 Kings 13:1—15:38	2 Kings 13:14-25	Elisha's Death	2 Kings 13:14-19	Elisha's Last Act
T	2 Kings 16:1—17:41	2 Kings 17:1-18	Israel Is Conquered	2 Kings 17:5-8, 19-20	Cast Out of Sight
F	2 Kings 18:1—20:21	2 Kings 18:1-8, 15-34	Jerusalem Spared	2 Kings 19:29-31	Isaiah Speaks for God
S	2 Kings 21:1—22:20	2 Kings 22:1-13	Law Book Found	2 Kings 22:1-2, 8	Josiah Is King

Week 39	Challenge	Survey: Loyalty to God		Sampler	
S	Psalms 107, 109, 110	2 Kings 23:1-25	Josiah's Reforms	Psalm 107:23-32	God Hears the Cries
M	2 Kings 23:1—25:30	2 Kings 24:8-20	Judah in Captivity	2 Kings 23:21-25	A Good King
T	Philippians 1:1—2:30	Philippians 2:1-11	Have Christ's Mind	Philippians 2:5-11	Jesus, a Servant
W	Philippians 3:1—4:23	Philippians 4:4-13	Rejoice in the Lord	Philippians 4:4-9	God's Peace
T	Daniel 1:1—2:49	Daniel 2:25-48	A Dream Interpreted	Daniel 1:17-20	Four Youth

	Challenge	Survey		Sampler	
F	Daniel 3:1—4:37	Daniel 3:8-29	The Fiery Furnace	Daniel 6:16-18	Den of Lions
S	Daniel 5:1—6:28	Daniel 6:6-23	The Lions' Den	Daniel 6:19-23	Daniel Is Safe

Week 40

	Challenge	Survey: Who is Jesus		Sampler	
S	Psalms 111, 112, 113, 114, 115	John 1:1-18	Incarnate Word	Psalm 113	God Lifts Up the Needy
M	John 1:1-51	John 2:1-11	Cana Wedding	John 1:1-5	Jesus Is the Word
T	John 2:1—3:36	John 3:1-21	God So Loved	John 3:16	God's Wonderful Gift of Love
W	John 4:1—5:47	John 4:5-42	Water of Life	John 4:24-26	Jesus Is the Messiah
T	John 6:1-71	John 6:22-40	Bread of Life	John 6:35	Jesus Is the Bread of Life
F	John 7:1—8:20	John 8:8-20	Light of the World	John 8:12	Jesus Is the Light
S	John 8:21—9:41	John 9:1-41	A Blind Man Sees	John 8:31-32	Truth and Freedom

Week 41

	Challenge	Survey: Jesus, the Source of Life		Sampler	
S	Psalms 116, 117, 118; Proverbs 28:1-28	John 10:1-18	The Good Shepherd	Psalm 118:26-29	God Has Given Light
M	John 10:1-42	John 11:5-44	Lazarus Is Alive	John 10:14, 15	Jesus, the Shepherd
T	John 11:1—12:11	John 12:12-36	Hosanna!	John 11:21-27	Resurrection and Life
W	John 12:12—13:20	John 14:1-15	Way, Truth, Life	John 13:36-38	Peter's Promise
T	John 13:21—15:17	John 15:1-17	Vine and Branches	John 14:5-6	Jesus the Way
F	John 15:18—16:33	John 16:1-24	The Counselor Spirit	John 15:12-17	Love One Another
S	John 17:1—18:40	John 17:1-21	Jesus' Prayer	John 18:25-27	A Broken Promise

Week 42

	Challenge	Survey: Trust in God		Sampler	
S	Psalm 119	John 19:1-16	King of the Jews	Psalm 119:105	A Lamp to My Feet
M	John 19:1-42	John 19:17-42	Cross and Tomb	John 19:17-22	Jesus Is Crucified
T	John 20:1—21:25	John 20:1-17	The Risen Lord	John 20:1-10	An Empty Tomb
W	Job 1:1—3:26	John 20:19-29	Blessed Believers	John 20:30-31	So You May Believe
T	Job 4:1—6:30	John 21:1-17	Feed My Sheep	Job 1:1-5	An Upright Man
F	Job 7:1—8:22	Job 1:1-22	Job's Test	Job 3:23-26	Trouble Comes
S	Job 9:1—11:20	Job 2:1-10	Job Stands Firm	Job 8:1-10	God the Almighty

Week 43

	Challenge	Survey: Pessimism and Assurance		Sampler	
S	Psalm 121; Proverbs 19:1-27	Job 14:1-12	Job's Pessimism	Psalm 121:1-2	Help Comes from God
M	Job 12:1—14:22	Psalm 8:1-9	A Psalmist's Faith	Job 12:7-10	In God's Hands
T	Job 15:1—17:16	John 5:19-30	God Gives Life	Job 17:1-3	Troubles Increase
W	Job 18:1—19:29	1 Corinthians 15:20-28	Resurrection	Job 19:1-3	Job Blames God
T	Job 20:1—22:30	1 Corinthians 15:35-50	Raised in Glory	Job 23:1-6	If Job Were God
F	Job 23:1—26:14	1 Corinthians 15:51-58	The Victory	Job 26:14	Who Is Like God?
S	Job 27:1—28:28	Matthew 18:1-10	A Child's Faith	Job 28:20-28	Fear of the Lord

Week 44	Challenge	Survey: Let God Be God		Sampler	
S	Psalms 122, 123, 124, 125	Job 38:1-20	God Questions Job	Psalm 122:1	I Was Glad
M	Job 29:1—31:40	Psalm 104:1-13	Divine Greatness	Job 29:21-25	Remembering Good Days
T	Job 32:1—33:33	Psalm 128:1-6	True Happiness	Job 30:9, 10	Now the Bad Days
W	Job 34:1—37:24	Mark 12:13-17	Render to God	Job 37:14	God Is Great
T	Job 38:1—40:2	Luke 18:9-14	Humility	Job 38:1-4	God Answers Job
F	Job 40:3—41:34	Philippians 1:12-30	Encouragement	Job 40:1-9	God's Power
S	Job 42:1-17	Romans 6:1-11	United with Christ	Job 42:5-6, 10	A Happy Ending

Week 45	Challenge	Survey: Living a Godly Life		Sampler	
S	Psalms 126, 127, 128, 130	Psalm 1:1-3	The Lord's Way	Psalm 127:1	Depend on God
M	1 Timothy 1:1—2:15	1 Timothy 2:1-7	One God	1 Timothy 1:15-17	To Save the World
T	1 Timothy 3:1—4:16	1 Timothy 4:1-10	Godliness	1 Timothy 4:4-5	God's Good Creation
W	1 Timothy 5:1—6:21	1 Timothy 6:6-19	Contentment	1 Timothy 6:9-11	Aim for Godliness
T	2 Timothy 1:1—2:26	2 Timothy 2:1-13	Strong in Grace	2 Timothy 1:8-10	A Holy Calling
F	2 Timothy 3:1—4:22	2 Timothy 3:10-17	Continue Learning	2 Timothy 3:14-15	Equipped to Serve
S	Titus 1:1—3:15	Titus 2:1-14	A Model Life	2 Timothy 4:7-8	The Good Fight

Week 46	Challenge	Survey: God's Power to Save		Sampler	
S	Psalms 131, 132; Proverbs 30:1-33	Proverbs 3:5-12	Trust in the Lord	Psalm 133:1	Live in Harmony
M	Isaiah 40:1—41:29	Isaiah 40:3-11	God's Living Word	Isaiah 40:11	Like a Shepherd
T	Isaiah 42:1—43:28	Isaiah 42:5-12	The Lord Calls	Isaiah 42:5-7	A Light to the Nations
W	Isaiah 44:1—45:25	Isaiah 44:6-20	Foolish Idols	Isaiah 45:22-23	Turn to God
T	Isaiah 46:1—47:15	Isaiah 45:18-25	God Saves	Isaiah 46:8-11	None Other Like God
F	Isaiah 48:1—49:26	Isaiah 49:8-13	Break into Singing	Isaiah 49:13	Sing for Joy
S	Isaiah 50:1—51:23	Isaiah 51:4-8	Salvation Forever	Isaiah 51:15-16	In God's Hands

Week 47	Challenge	Survey: Fulfilling God's Plan		Sampler	
S	Psalms 133, 134, 135, 136	Isaiah 52:7-10	Good Tidings	Psalm 134:1-3	Lift Up Your Hands
M	Isaiah 52:1—53:12	Isaiah 53:1-12	Suffering Servant	Isaiah 52:7	Here's the Good News
T	Isaiah 54:1—55:13	Isaiah 55:1-13	Seek the Lord	Isaiah 55:6-9	Return to the Lord
W	Isaiah 56:1—58:14	Isaiah 58:6-12	Righteousness	Isaiah 58:13-14	Turn Back
T	Isaiah 59:1—61:11	Isaiah 61:1-11	Ministers of God	Isaiah 60:1-3	Arise, Shine
F	Isaiah 62:1—64:12	Isaiah 64:4-9	Our Father	Isaiah 64:8	The Work of God's Hand
S	Isaiah 65:1—66:24	Isaiah 65:17-25	New Worlds	Isaiah 65:17, 25	A Peaceful Kingdom

Week 48	Challenge	Survey: Ezekiel – Judgment and Promise		Sampler	
S	Psalms 138, 139	Psalm 138:1-8	Enduring Love	Psalm 139:22-24	Search Me, Know Me
M	Ezekiel 1:1—3:27	Ezekiel 1:4-28	The Vision	Ezekiel 1:26-28	Vision of God's Glory
T	Ezekiel 4:1—6:14	Ezekiel 2:1-3:3	Eaten Words	Ezekiel 2:1-3	Ezekiel Is Sent
W	Ezekiel 33:1—35:15	Ezekiel 34:11-16	Shepherd God	Ezekiel 18:30-32	Turn and Live
T	Ezekiel 36:1—37:28	Ezekiel 37:1-14	Dry Bones	Ezekiel 37:1-6	Called to Life

	Challenge	Survey		Sampler	
F	Ezekiel 39:21—40:4; 43:1—44:31	Ezekiel 37:15-28	All God's People	Ezekiel 39:28-29	The Lord Our God
S	Ezekiel 45:1—47:23	Ezekiel 39:21-29	God's Glory	Ezekiel 43:4-5	God's Glory Returns

Week 49

	Challenge	Survey: To Rebuild Jerusalem		Sampler	
S	Psalm 141; Proverbs 3:1-31	Psalm 141:1-10	Prayer for Goodness	Proverbs 3:5-10	Give Honor to God
M	Ezra 1:1-11; 3:13	Ecclesiastes 3:1-15	Proper Seasons	Ezra 2:1	Out of Captivity
T	Ezra 4:1—5:17	Ezra 1:1-11	Return Home	Ezra 3:10-13	Joy and Tears
W	Ezra 6:1—7:28	Ezra 3:8-13	Renew the Temple	Ezra 7:27-28	The Lord's House
T	Ezra 8:15—9:15	Ezra 7:21-28	Ezra the Judge	Ezra 9:15	Ezra Prays
F	Ezra 10:1-19	Nehemiah 2:1-8	Another Recruit	Nehemiah 2:3-8	Nehemiah's Request
S	Nehemiah 1:1—2:20	Nehemiah 2:11-20	Build the Walls	Nehemiah 2:17	A Good Work

Week 50

	Challenge	Survey: Work for the Lord		Sampler	
S	Psalms 142, 143, 145	Nehemiah 4:7-23	Under Pressure	Psalm 145:4-7	God's Mighty Acts
M	Nehemiah 3:1—4:23	Nehemiah 5:1-12	Internal Justice	Nehemiah 4:1-5	Despised and Taunted
T	Nehemiah 5:1—7:4	Nehemiah 5:14-19	Love in Action	Nehemiah 6:15-16	Rebuilt at Last
W	Nehemiah 8:1-18	Nehemiah 6:1-16	Task Completed	Nehemiah 8:1-3	Reading the Law
T	Nehemiah 9:1-38; 10:28-39	2 Thessalonians 3:5-13	Honest Work	Nehemiah 9:1-3	Confession
F	Nehemiah 11:1-2; 12:27-47	Ephesians 4:1-7	A Worthy Life	Nehemiah 12:27	The Dedication
S	Nehemiah 13:1-31	Psalm 84:1-12	Sing for Joy	Nehemiah 13:30-31	Duties and Offerings

Week 51

	Challenge	Survey: Prophetic Voices		Sampler	
S	Psalms 146, 147	Psalm 146:1-10	Praise the Lord	Psalm 147:1-6	Beyond Measure
M	Habakkuk 1:1—3:19	Habakkuk 2:1-4	Live by Faith	Habakkuk 2:4	Living by Faith
T	Zephaniah 1:1—3:20	Zephaniah 2:1-4	Chance to Change	Zephaniah 3:19-20	Fulfillment
W	Haggai 1:1—2:23	Haggai 1:1-15	The Lord's House	Haggai 2:6-7	Shake Up
T	Zechariah 8:20—11:3	Zechariah 14:1-9	Day of the Lord	Zechariah 10:8-9,12	Gathering Them In
F	Zechariah 11:4—14:21	Malachi 4:1-5	Evil Is Punished	Zechariah 14:9	Victory Will Come
S	Malachi 3:1—4:6	Matthew 24:3-14	End of Time	Malachi 2:10	One Creator of Us All

Week 52

	Challenge	Survey: Our God Forever		Sampler	
S	Psalms 148, 149, 150	Psalm 150:1-6	Praise the Lord	Psalm 150:1-6	Everyone Give Praise
M	Revelation 1:1-20	Revelation 1:1-8	Alpha and Omega	Revelation 1:1-3	John Bears Witness
T	Revelation 2:1—3:22	Revelation 3:14-22	Door of the Heart	Revelation 1:4-5a	To the Seven Churches
W	Revelation 4:1—5:14	Revelation 7:9-17	From Every Nation	Revelation 3:20	Jesus Stands Waiting
T	Revelation 6:1—7:17	Revelation 21:1-8, 22-27	God Among Mortals	Revelation 4:11	Glory, Honor, Power
F	Revelation 20:1—21:8	Ephesians 6:10-18a	Wear God's Armor	Revelation 21:1-4	God Will Be With Us
S	Revelation 21:9—22:21	Philippians 1:3-11	Abound in Love	Revelation 22:16	A Bright Morning Star

Thirty Key Old Testament Stories

Story	Bible Text	Key Verse
Creation	Genesis 1—2	Genesis 1:27
The Human Condition	Genesis 3—4	Genesis 3:5
The Flood and the First Covenant	Genesis 6—9	Genesis 9:8
The Tower of Babel and Abraham and Sarah	Genesis 11—12	Genesis 12:1
Sarah, Hagar, and Abraham	Genesis 12—25	Genesis 17:19
Isaac and Rebecca	Genesis 22—25	Genesis 24:67
Jacob and Esau	Genesis 25—36	Genesis 28:15
Joseph and God's Hidden Ways	Genesis 37—50	Genesis 50:20
Moses and Pharaoh	Exodus 1—15	Exodus 2:23
The Ten Commandments	Exodus 20	Exodus 20:2
From the Wilderness into the Promised Land	Exodus 16—18; Deuteronomy 1—6; Joshua 1—3, 24	Deuteronomy 6:4
Judges	Book of Judges	Judges 21:25
Ruth	Book of Ruth	Ruth 4:14
Samuel and Saul	1 Samuel 1—11	1 Samuel 3:1
King David	multiple books	1 Samuel 8:6
David, Nathan, and What Is a Prophet?	2 Samuel 11—12	2 Samuel 7:12
Solomon	1 Kings 1—11	1 Kings 6:12
Split of the Kingdom	1 Kings 11	1 Kings 12:16
Northern Kingdom, Its Prophets and Fate	1 Kings—2 Kings 17	Amos 5:21
Southern Kingdom, Its Prophets and Fate (Part 1)	multiple books	Isaiah 5:7
Southern Kingdom, Its Prophets and Fate (Part 2)	multiple books	Jeremiah 31:31
The Exile	Isaiah 40—55; Ezekiel	Isaiah 40:10
Return from Exile	multiple books	Ezra 1:1
Ezra and Nehemiah	Books of Ezra and Nehemiah	Ezra 3:10
Esther	Book of Esther	Esther 4:14
Job	Book of Job	Job 1:1
Daniel	Book of Daniel	Daniel 3:17
Psalms of Praise and Trust	Psalms 8, 30, 100, 113, 121	Psalm 121:1
Psalms for Help	various psalms	Psalm 22:1
Wisdom	Job, Proverbs, Ecclesiastes	Proverbs 1:7

Thirty Key New Testament Stories

Story	Bible Text	Key Verse
The Annunciation	Luke 1:26-56	Luke 1:31-33
Magi	Matthew 2:1-12	Matthew 2:2-3
Birth of Jesus	Luke 2:1-20	Luke 2:10-11
Simeon	Luke 2:25-35	Luke 2:30-32
Wilderness Temptations	Matthew 4:1-11; Mark 1:12-13; Luke 4:1-13	Luke 4:12-13
Jesus' Nazareth Sermon	Matthew 13:54-58; Mark 6:1-6: Luke 4:16-30	Luke 4:18-19, 21
Jesus Calls the First Disciples	Matthew 4:18-22; Mark 1:16-20; Luke 5:1-11	Luke 5:9-10
Beatitudes	Matthew 5:3-12	Luke 6:20-26
Gerasene Demoniac	Matthew 8:28-34; Mark 5:1-20; Luke 8:26-39	Luke 8:39
Feeding of the 5,000	Matthew 14:13-21; Mark 6:30-44; Luke 9:10-17; John 6:1-14	Luke 9:16-17
The Transfiguration	Matthew 17:1-8; Mark 9:2-8: Luke 9:28-36	Luke 9:34-35
Sending of the Seventy	Matthew 8:19-22; Luke 10:1-16	Luke 10:8, 16
Good Samaritan	Luke 10:25-37	Luke 10:27-28
Healing the Bent-Over Woman	Luke 13:10-17	Luke 13:16
Parables of Lost and Found	Luke 15:1-32	Luke 15:31-32
Rich Man and Lazarus	Luke 16:19-31	Luke 16:29-31
Zacchaeus	Luke 19:1-11	Luke 19:9
Sheep and Goats	Matthew 25:31-46	Matthew 25:40
Parable of the Vineyard	Matthew 21:33-46; Mark 12:1-12; Luke 20:9-19; (Isaiah 5:1-7)	Luke 20:14-16
The Last Supper	Matthew 26:20-29; Mark 14:12-16: Luke 22:14-38	Luke 22:19-20, 27
Crucifixion	Matthew 27; Mark 15; Luke 23; John 19	Luke 23:42-43, 46
Road to Emmaus	Luke 24	Luke 24:30-31
Pentecost	Acts 2:1-21	Acts 2:17-18
Healing the Lame Man	Acts 3—4	Acts 4:19
Baptism of the Ethiopian	Acts 8:26-39	Acts 8:35-37
Call of Saul	Acts 7:58—8:1, 9:1-30	Acts 9:15-16
Peter and Cornelius	Acts 10	Acts 10:34-35
Philippians' Humility	Philippians 2:1-13	Philippians 2:12-13
Love Hymn	1 Corinthians 13	1 Corinthians 13:4-7
Resurrection	1 Corinthians 15	1 Corinthians 15:51-55

Prayers in the Bible

Reference	Person	Concern or Request
Genesis 15:1-6	Abraham	To have a son
Genesis 24:12-52	Abraham's servant	Guidance
Genesis 25:22, 23	Rebekah	Understanding
Genesis 32:9-12	Jacob	Deliverance from Esau
Genesis 32:24-30	Jacob	Blessing
Exodus 32:31-35	Moses	Forgiveness of the people
Joshua 7:6-9	Joshua	Help and mercy
Judges 6:36-40	Gideon	Proof of his call
Judges 15:18, 19	Samson	Water
1 Samuel 1:10-17	Hannah	To have a son
2 Samuel 7:18-29	David	Blessing
1 Kings 3:6-14	Solomon	Wisdom
1 Kings 17:20-23	Elijah	The widow's son
1 Kings 18:36-38	Elijah	Triumph over Baal
2 Kings 19:15-19	Hezekiah	Deliverance
1 Chronicles 4:10	Jabez	Blessings
Ezra 9:5-15	Ezra	The people's sins
Nehemiah 1:4-11	Nehemiah	Mercy
Jeremiah 14:7-10	Jeremiah	Mercy
Daniel 2:17-23	Daniel	Knowledge
Jonah 2:1-10	Jonah	Thanksgiving
Habakkuk 1:1-4	Habakkuk	Justice
Matthew 6:9-13	Jesus	The Lord's Prayer
Matthew 26:39, 42, 44	Jesus	God's will to be done
Luke 18:13	Tax collector	Mercy
Luke 23:34	Jesus	Forgiveness for others
John 11:41-44	Jesus	Thanksgiving
John 12:27-28	Jesus	The Father's glory
John 17:1-26	Jesus	His followers
Acts 4:23-31	Disciples	Boldness

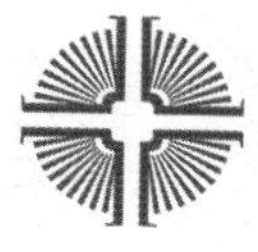

MAPS

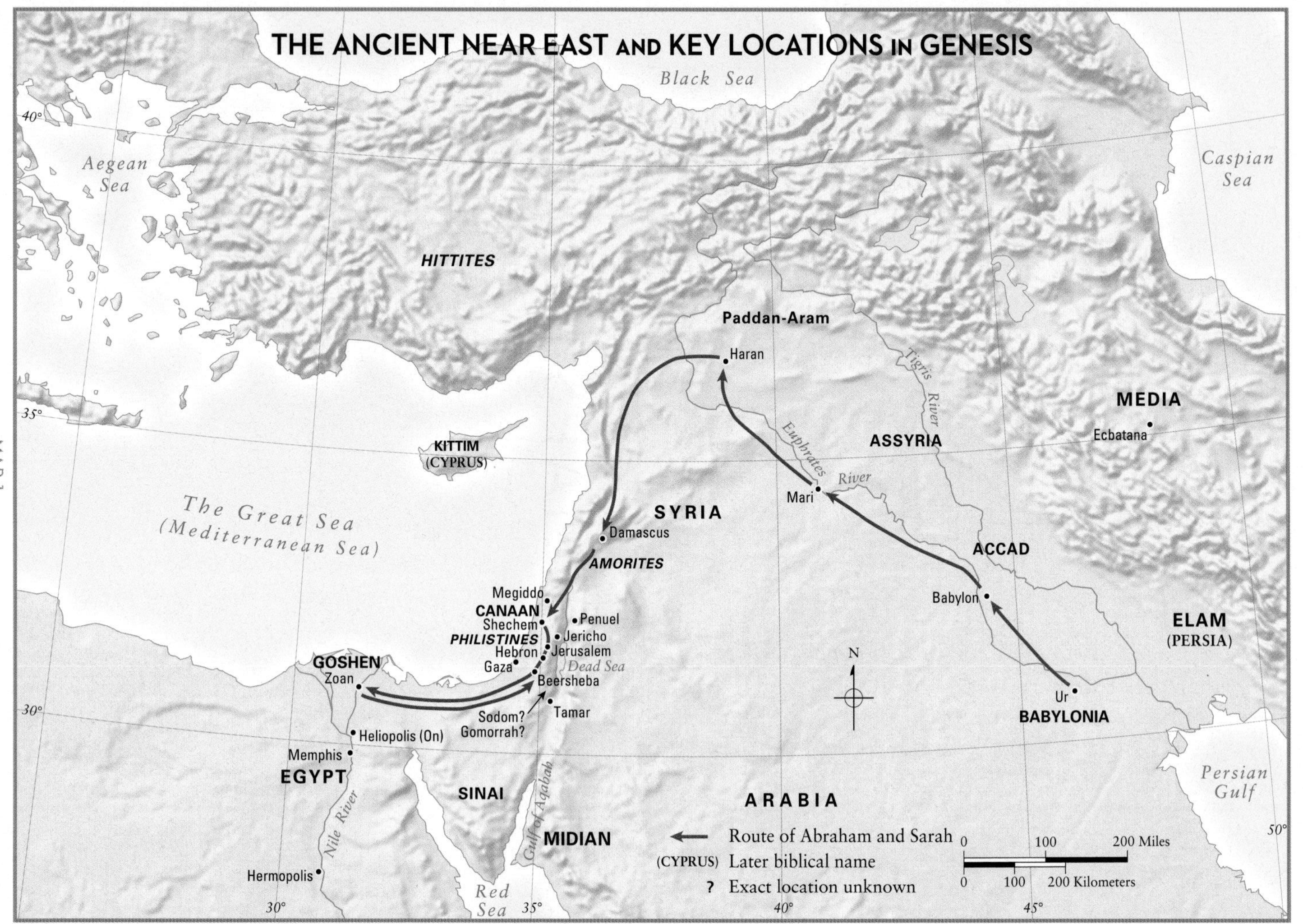
THE ANCIENT NEAR EAST AND KEY LOCATIONS IN GENESIS
Black Sea
Aegean Sea
Caspian Sea
HITTITES
Paddan-Aram
Haran
Tigris River
Euphrates River
MEDIA
Ecbatana
ASSYRIA
KITTIM (CYPRUS)
Mari
SYRIA
The Great Sea (Mediterranean Sea)
Damascus
AMORITES
ACCAD
Megiddo
CANAAN
Shechem
Penuel
PHILISTINES
Jericho
Hebron
Jerusalem
Gaza
Dead Sea
Babylon
ELAM (PERSIA)
GOSHEN
Zoan
Beersheba
Sodom?
Gomorrah?
Tamar
N
Ur
BABYLONIA
Heliopolis (On)
Memphis
EGYPT
SINAI
Gulf of Aqabah
ARABIA
Persian Gulf
Nile River
MIDIAN
Hermopolis
Red Sea
Route of Abraham and Sarah
(CYPRUS) Later biblical name
? Exact location unknown
0 100 200 Miles
0 100 200 Kilometers
30°
35°
40°
45°
50°

MAP 1

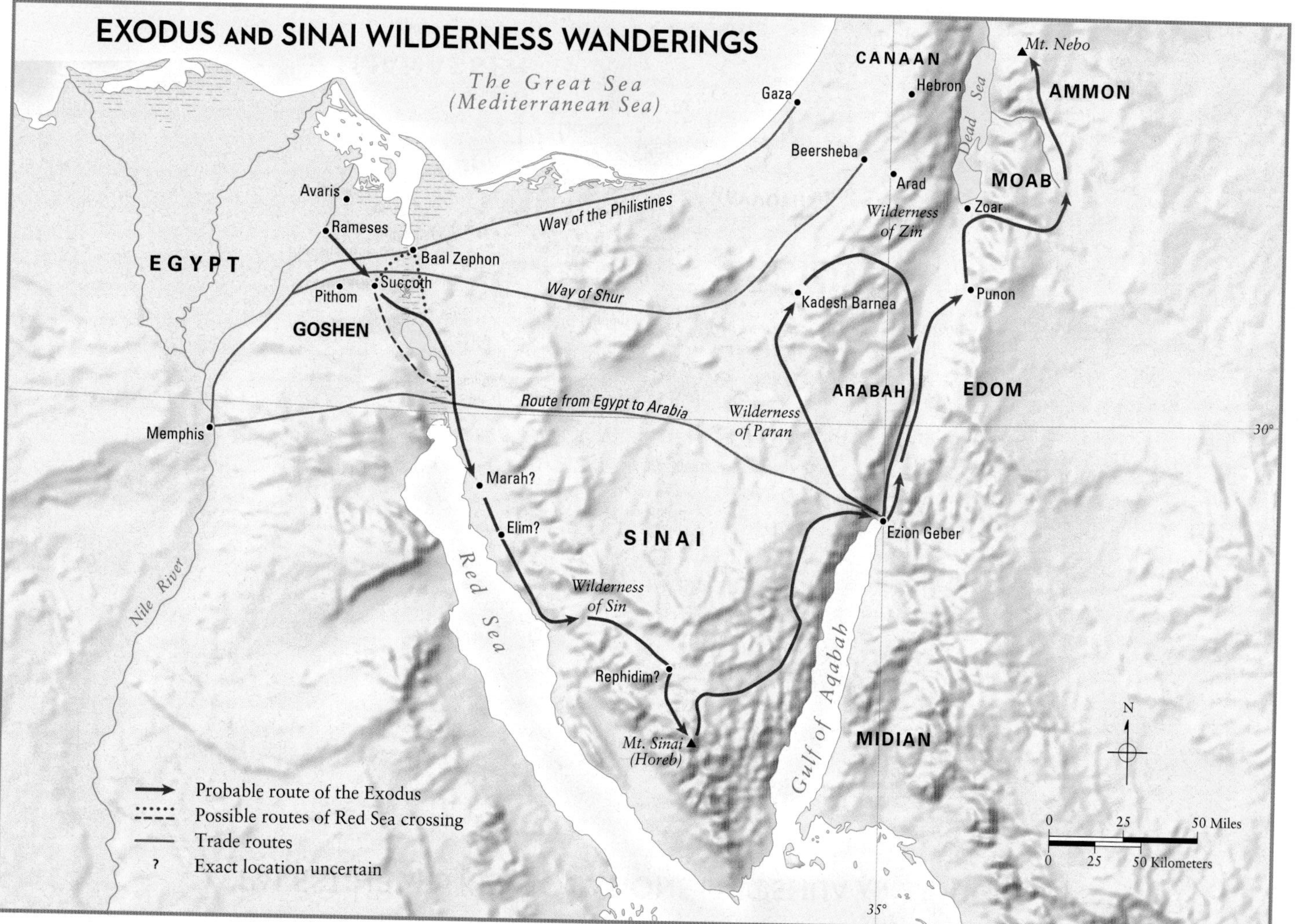

EXODUS AND SINAI WILDERNESS WANDERINGS
The Great Sea
(Mediterranean Sea)
EGYPT
GOSHEN
Avaris
Rameses
Pithom
Succoth
Baal Zephon
Memphis
Nile River
Way of the Philistines
Way of Shur
Route from Egypt to Arabia
Gaza
Beersheba
Arad
Hebron
CANAAN
Wilderness of Zin
Kadesh Barnea
Wilderness of Paran
ARABAH
Ezion Geber
Punon
Zoar
Dead Sea
MOAB
AMMON
Mt. Nebo
EDOM
MIDIAN
Gulf of Aqabah
SINAI
Marah?
Elim?
Wilderness of Sin
Rephidim?
Mt. Sinai (Horeb)
Red Sea
30°
35°
N
0 25 50 Miles
0 25 50 Kilometers
Probable route of the Exodus
Possible routes of Red Sea crossing
Trade routes
? Exact location uncertain

MAP 2

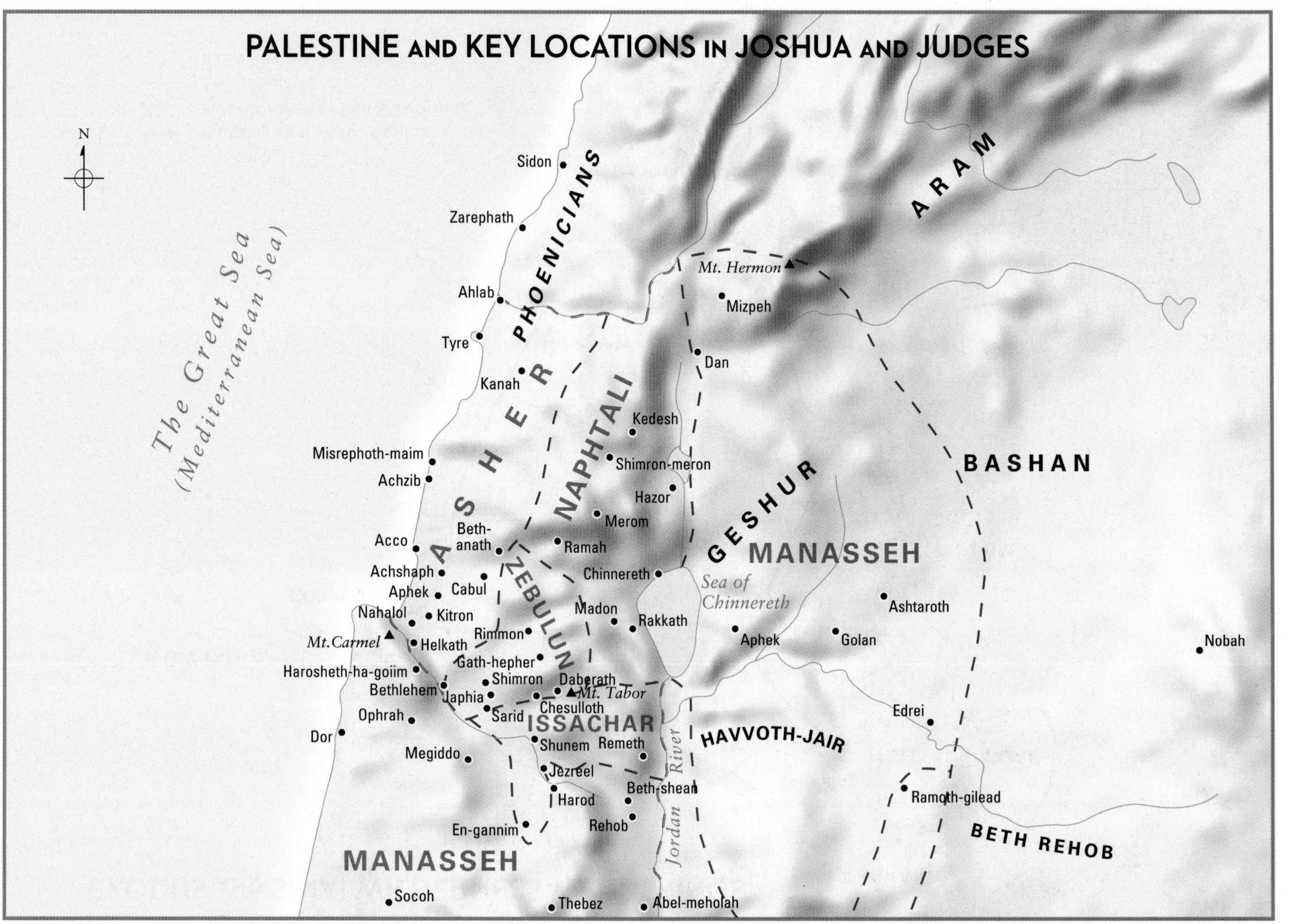
PALESTINE AND KEY LOCATIONS IN JOSHUA AND JUDGES
N
The Great Sea
(Mediterranean Sea)
PHOENICIANS
ARAM
BASHAN
ASHER
NAPHTALI
ZEBULUN
ISSACHAR
GESHUR
MANASSEH
HAVVOTH-JAIR
BETH REHOB
MANASSEH
Sidon
Zarephath
Ahlab
Tyre
Kanah
Misrephoth-maim
Achzib
Acco
Beth-
anath
Achshaph
Cabul
Aphek
Nahalol
Kitron
Mt. Carmel
Helkath
Rimmon
Gath-hepher
Harosheth-ha-goiim
Shimron
Bethlehem
Japhia
Daberath
Mt. Tabor
Chesulloth
Sarid
Ophrah
Dor
Megiddo
Shunem
Remeth
Jezreel
Beth-shean
Harod
Rehob
En-gannim
Socoh
Thebez
Abel-meholah
Jordan River
Mt. Hermon
Mizpeh
Dan
Kedesh
Shimron-meron
Hazor
Merom
Ramah
Chinnereth
Madon
Rakkath
Sea of
Chinnereth
Aphek
Golan
Ashtaroth
Edrei
Ramoth-gilead
Nobah

MAP 3

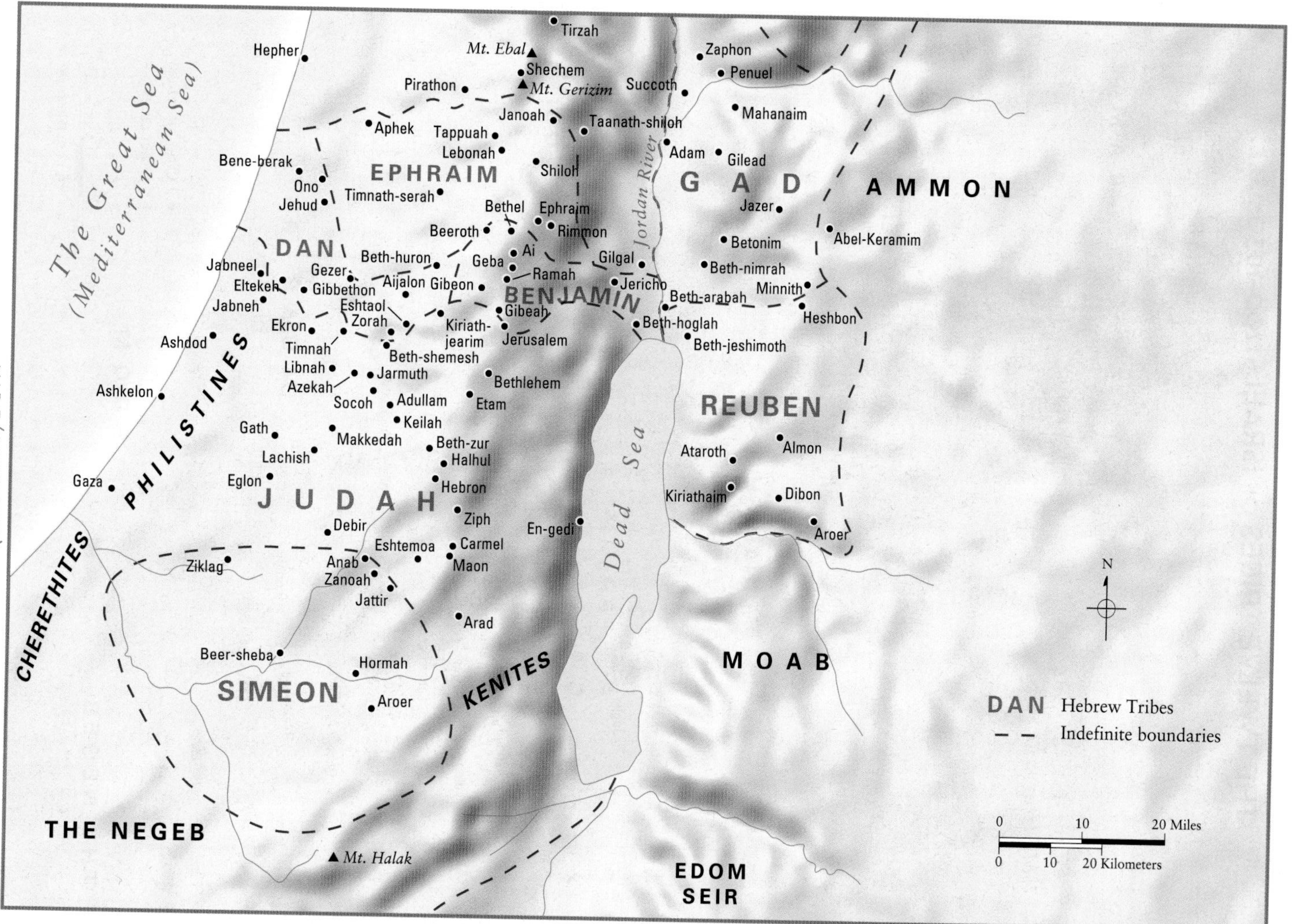

MAP 3 (CONTINUED)

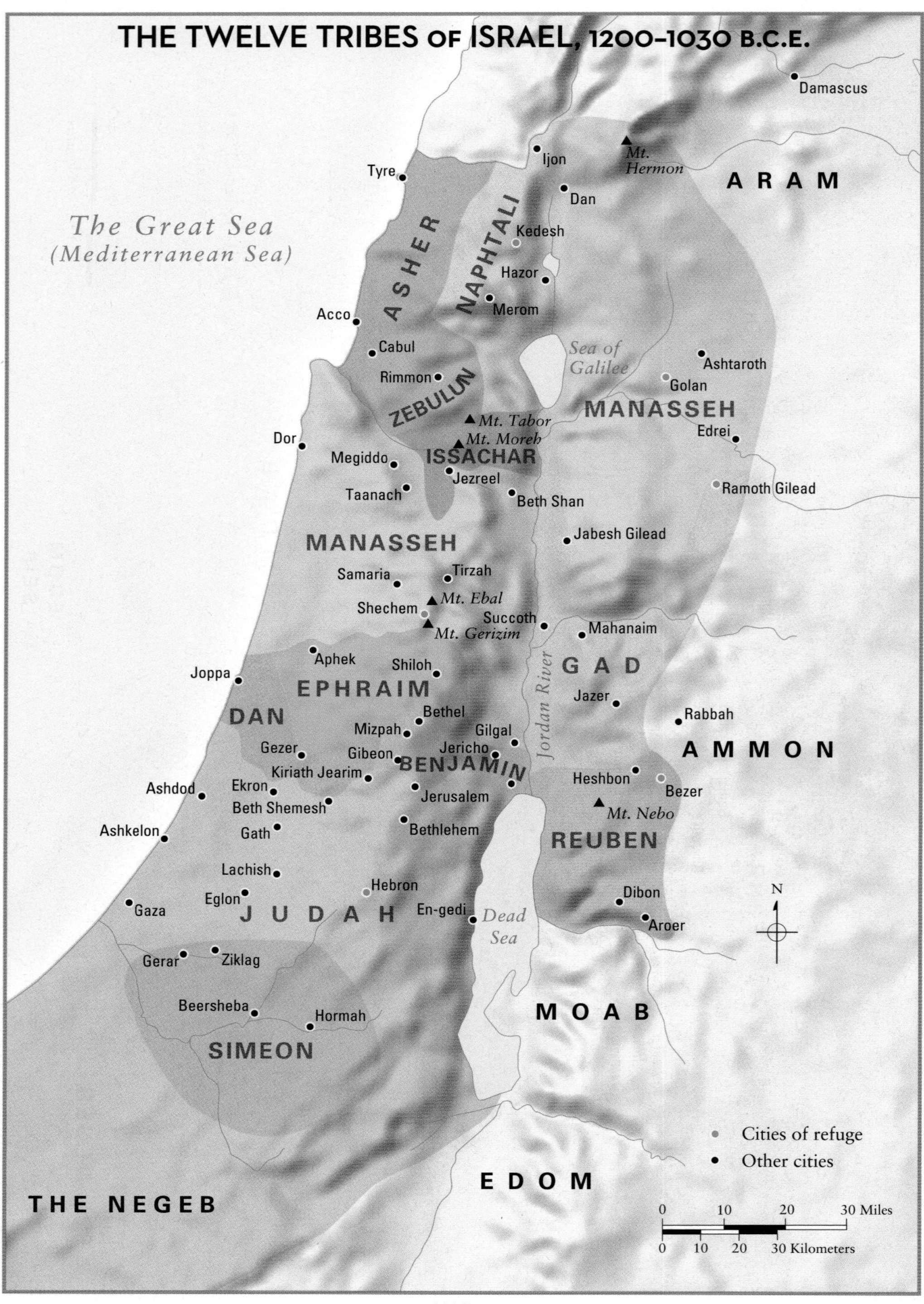
THE TWELVE TRIBES OF ISRAEL, 1200–1030 B.C.E.
Damascus
Ijon
Mt. Hermon
Tyre
Dan
ARAM
The Great Sea
(Mediterranean Sea)
ASHER
NAPHTALI
Kedesh
Hazor
Merom
Acco
Cabul
Sea of Galilee
Ashtaroth
Rimmon
Golan
ZEBULUN
MANASSEH
Mt. Tabor
Mt. Moreh
Edrei
Dor
Megiddo
ISSACHAR
Jezreel
Ramoth Gilead
Taanach
Beth Shan
Jabesh Gilead
MANASSEH
Samaria
Tirzah
Mt. Ebal
Shechem
Succoth
Mahanaim
Mt. Gerizim
Aphek
Shiloh
GAD
Joppa
EPHRAIM
Jordan River
Jazer
DAN
Bethel
Rabbah
Mizpah
Gilgal
Gezer
Jericho
AMMON
Gibeon
BENJAMIN
Kiriath Jearim
Heshbon
Bezer
Ashdod
Ekron
Jerusalem
Beth Shemesh
Mt. Nebo
Ashkelon
Gath
Bethlehem
REUBEN
Lachish
Hebron
Dibon
Gaza
Eglon
JUDAH
En-gedi
Dead Sea
Aroer
N
Gerar
Ziklag
Beersheba
Hormah
MOAB
SIMEON
Cities of refuge
Other cities
EDOM
THE NEGEB
0 10 20 30 Miles
0 10 20 30 Kilometers

MAP 4

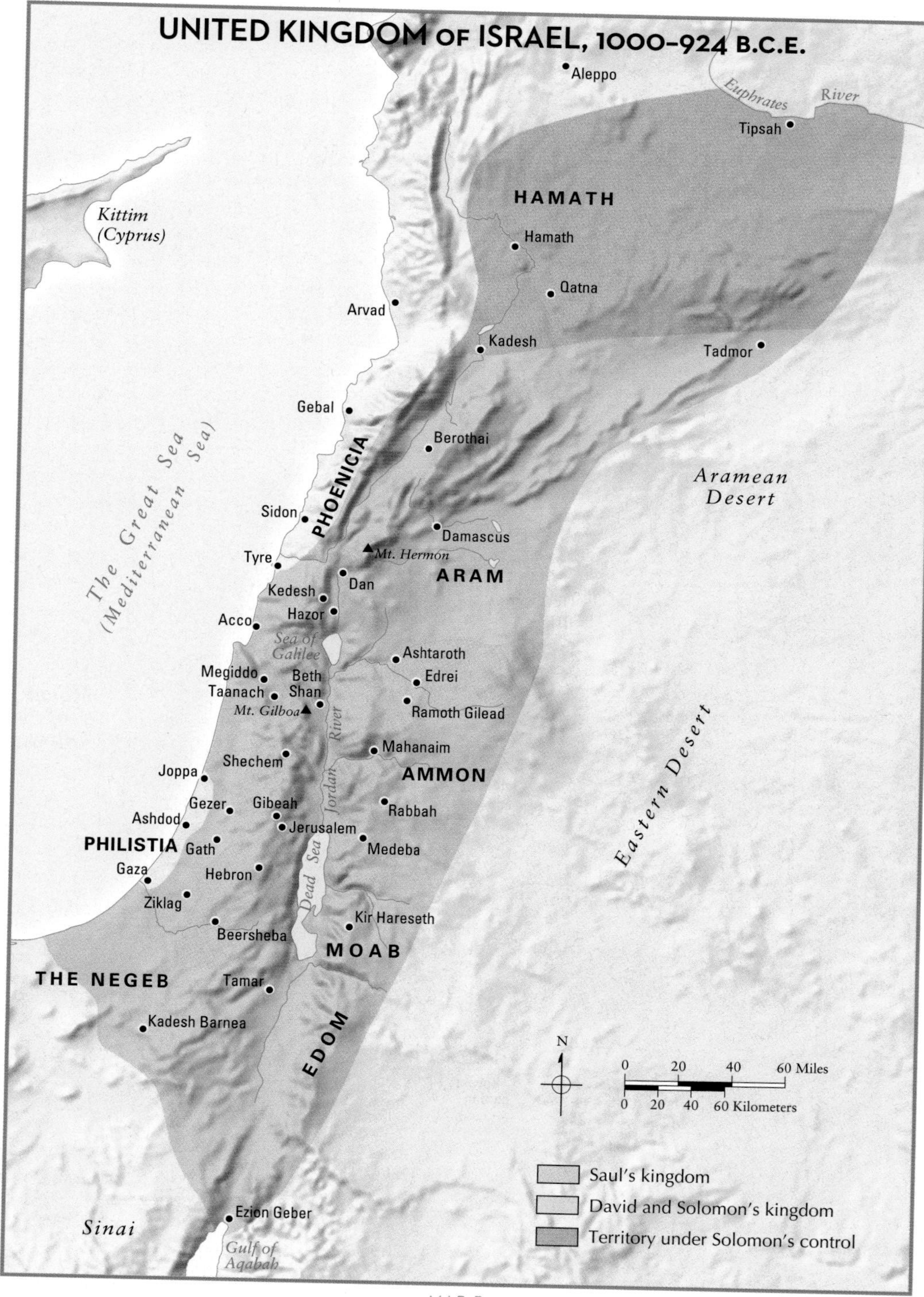
UNITED KINGDOM OF ISRAEL, 1000–924 B.C.E.
Aleppo
Euphrates River
Tipsah
HAMATH
Hamath
Qatna
Kittim (Cyprus)
Arvad
Kadesh
Tadmor
Gebal
Berothai
The Great Sea (Mediterranean Sea)
PHOENICIA
Aramean Desert
Sidon
Damascus
Mt. Hermon
Tyre
ARAM
Dan
Kedesh
Hazor
Acco
Sea of Galilee
Ashtaroth
Megiddo
Beth Shan
Edrei
Taanach
Mt. Gilboa
Ramoth Gilead
Jordan River
Mahanaim
Shechem
Joppa
AMMON
Eastern Desert
Gezer
Gibeah
Rabbah
Ashdod
Jerusalem
PHILISTIA
Gath
Medeba
Gaza
Hebron
Dead Sea
Ziklag
Kir Hareseth
Beersheba
MOAB
THE NEGEB
Tamar
Kadesh Barnea
EDOM
N
0 20 40 60 Miles
0 20 40 60 Kilometers
Saul's kingdom
David and Solomon's kingdom
Territory under Solomon's control
Ezion Geber
Sinai
Gulf of Aqabah

MAP 5

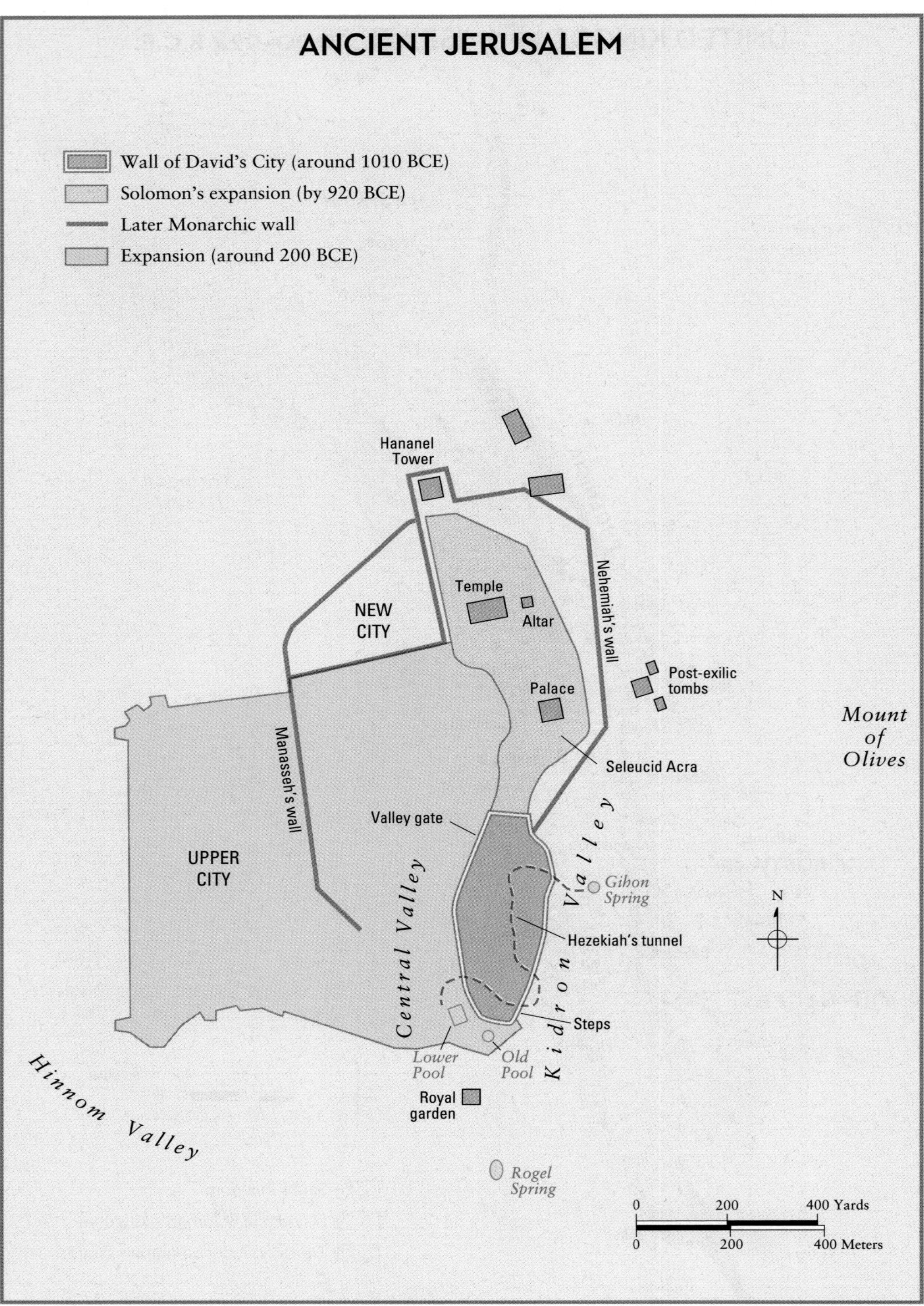

ANCIENT JERUSALEM
Wall of David's City (around 1010 BCE)
Solomon's expansion (by 920 BCE)
Later Monarchic wall
Expansion (around 200 BCE)
Hananel Tower
Temple
Altar
NEW CITY
Nehemiah's wall
Post-exilic tombs
Palace
Mount of Olives
Seleucid Acra
Manasseh's wall
Valley gate
UPPER CITY
Central Valley
Kidron Valley
Gihon Spring
Hezekiah's tunnel
Steps
Lower Pool
Old Pool
Royal garden
Hinnom Valley
Rogel Spring
N
0 200 400 Yards
0 200 400 Meters

MAP 6

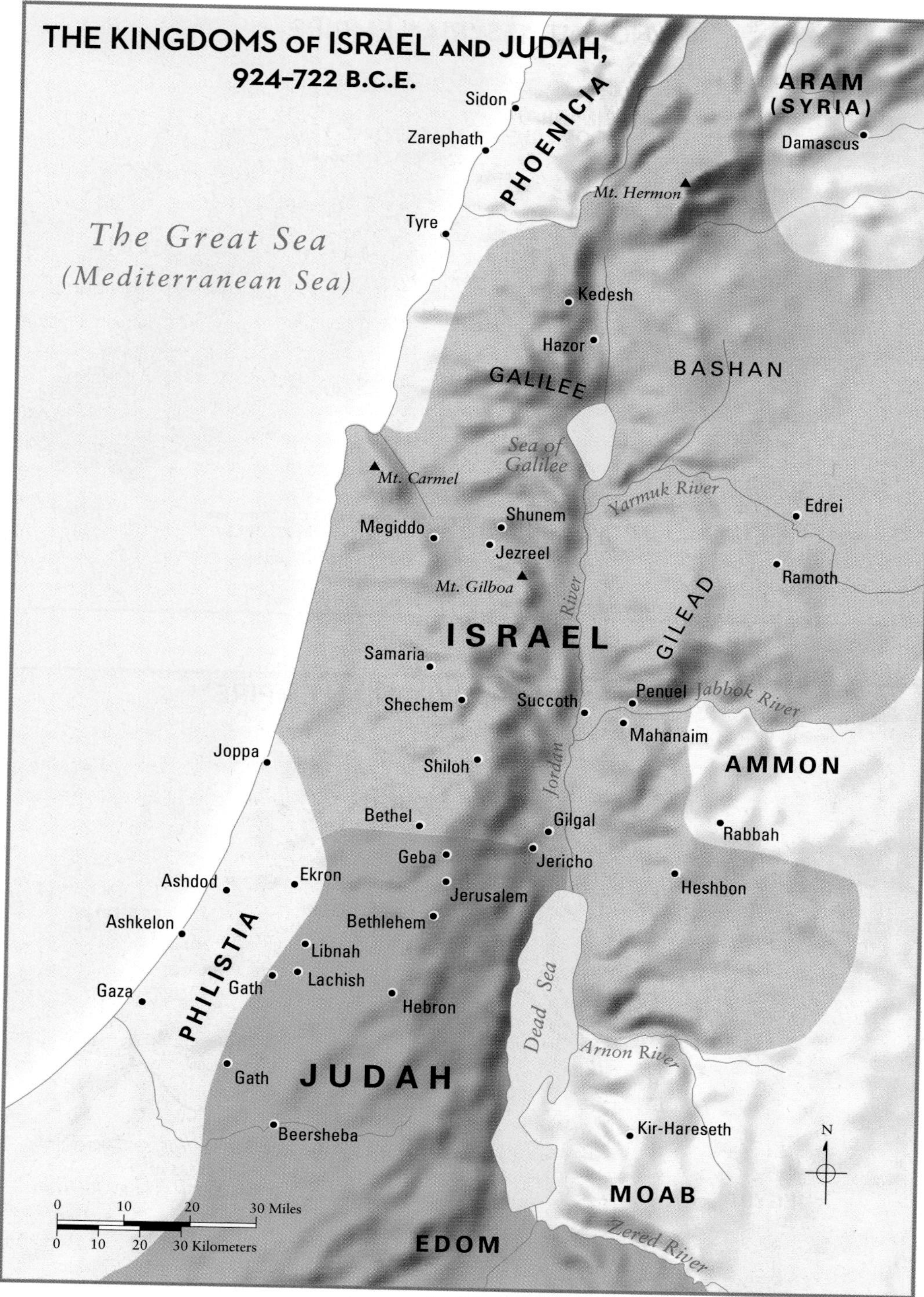
THE KINGDOMS OF ISRAEL AND JUDAH,
924–722 B.C.E.
The Great Sea
(Mediterranean Sea)
PHOENICIA
ARAM
(SYRIA)
Sidon
Zarephath
Damascus
Mt. Hermon
Tyre
Kedesh
Hazor
BASHAN
GALILEE
Sea of
Galilee
Mt. Carmel
Yarmuk River
Edrei
Shunem
Megiddo
Jezreel
Ramoth
Mt. Gilboa
River
GILEAD
ISRAEL
Samaria
Penuel
Jabbok River
Shechem
Succoth
Mahanaim
Joppa
Shiloh
Jordan
AMMON
Bethel
Gilgal
Rabbah
Geba
Jericho
Ashdod
Ekron
Heshbon
Jerusalem
Ashkelon
Bethlehem
PHILISTIA
Libnah
Lachish
Gath
Gaza
Hebron
Dead Sea
Arnon River
Gath
JUDAH
Beersheba
Kir-Hareseth
N
MOAB
0
10
20
30 Miles
0
10
20
30 Kilometers
EDOM
Zered River

MAP 7

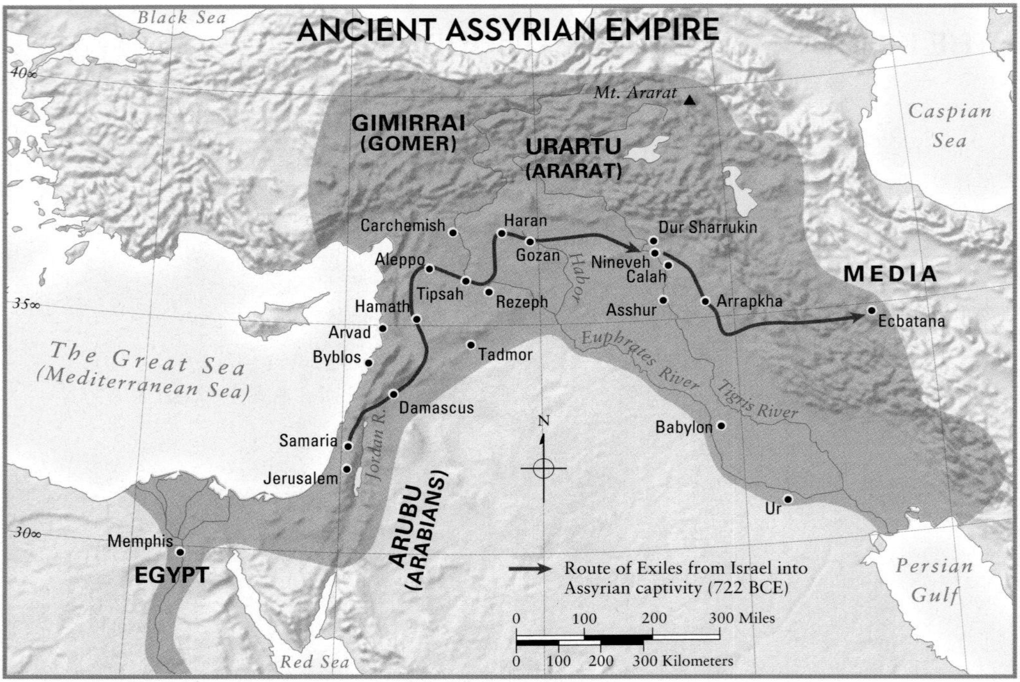

ANCIENT ASSYRIAN EMPIRE

Black Sea
Caspian Sea
Mt. Ararat
GIMIRRAI (GOMER)
URARTU (ARARAT)
MEDIA
Carchemish
Haran
Gozan
Dur Sharrukin
Nineveh
Calah
Aleppo
Tipsah
Rezeph
Habor
Asshur
Arrapkha
Ecbatana
Hamath
Arvad
Byblos
Tadmor
The Great Sea (Mediterranean Sea)
Euphrates River
Tigris River
Damascus
Babylon
Samaria
Jerusalem
Jordan R.
ARUBU (ARABIANS)
Ur
Memphis
EGYPT
Persian Gulf
Red Sea

Route of Exiles from Israel into Assyrian captivity (722 BCE)

0 100 200 300 Miles
0 100 200 300 Kilometers

MAP 8

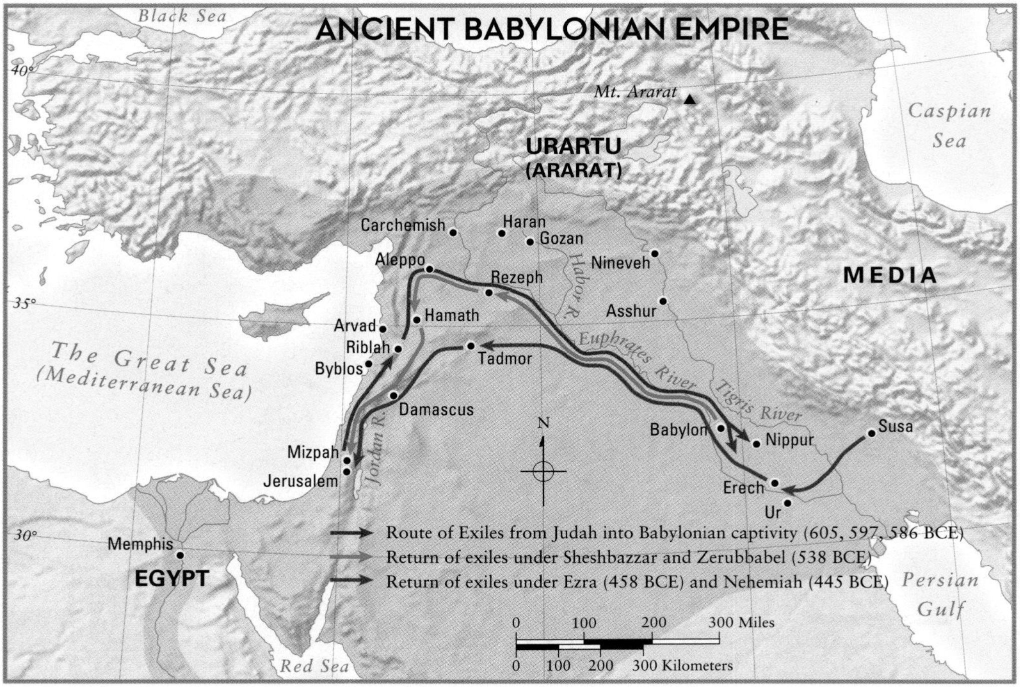

ANCIENT BABYLONIAN EMPIRE

Black Sea
Caspian Sea
Mt. Ararat
URARTU (ARARAT)
MEDIA
Carchemish
Haran
Gozan
Aleppo
Rezeph
Habor R.
Nineveh
Asshur
Hamath
Arvad
Riblah
Byblos
Tadmor
The Great Sea (Mediterranean Sea)
Euphrates River
Tigris River
Damascus
Babylon
Nippur
Susa
Mizpah
Jerusalem
Jordan R.
Erech
Ur
Memphis
EGYPT
Persian Gulf
Red Sea

Route of Exiles from Judah into Babylonian captivity (605, 597, 586 BCE)
Return of exiles under Sheshbazzar and Zerubbabel (538 BCE)
Return of exiles under Ezra (458 BCE) and Nehemiah (445 BCE)

0 100 200 300 Miles
0 100 200 300 Kilometers

MAP 9

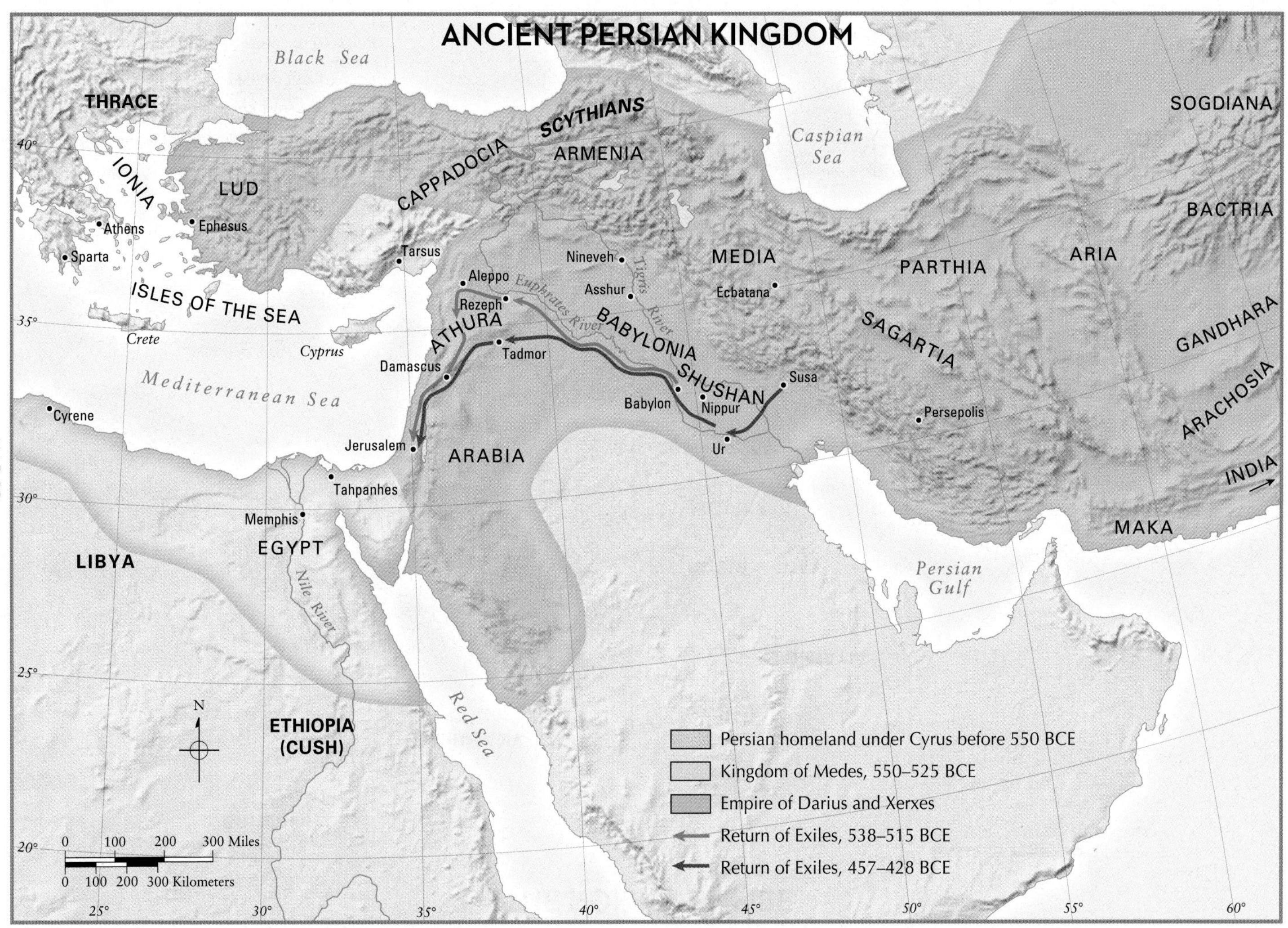
ANCIENT PERSIAN KINGDOM
SOGDIANA
BACTRIA
GANDHARA
ARACHOSIA
INDIA
ARIA
MAKA
PARTHIA
SAGARTIA
Persepolis
Persian Gulf
Caspian Sea
MEDIA
Ecbatana
Susa
SHUSHAN
Nippur
Ur
Babylon
BABYLONIA
Tigris River
Asshur
Nineveh
SCYTHIANS
ARMENIA
Euphrates River
Tadmor
Aleppo
Rezeph
ATHURA
ARABIA
Damascus
Jerusalem
Tahpanhes
CAPPADOCIA
Tarsus
Black Sea
Cyprus
Mediterranean Sea
Red Sea
Nile River
EGYPT
Memphis
ETHIOPIA (CUSH)
LUD
Ephesus
ISLES OF THE SEA
THRACE
IONIA
Athens
Sparta
Crete
LIBYA
Cyrene
Persian homeland under Cyrus before 550 BCE
Kingdom of Medes, 550–525 BCE
Empire of Darius and Xerxes
Return of Exiles, 538–515 BCE
Return of Exiles, 457–428 BCE
N
0 100 200 300 Miles
0 100 200 300 Kilometers
40°
35°
30°
25°
20°
25°
30°
35°
40°
45°
50°
55°
60°

MAP 10

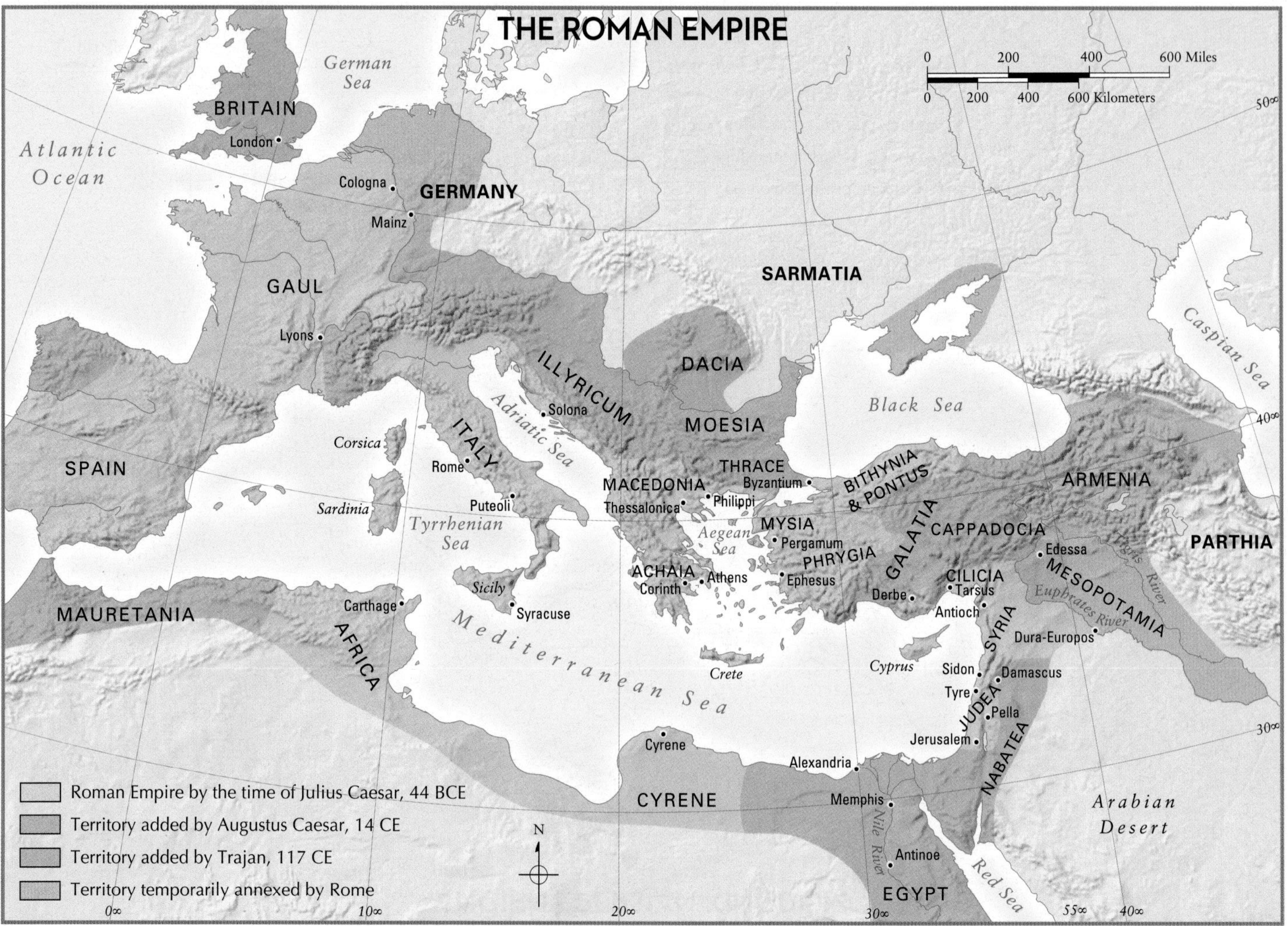

THE ROMAN EMPIRE
0
200
400
600 Miles
0
200
400
600 Kilometers
German Sea
BRITAIN
London
Atlantic Ocean
Cologna
GERMANY
Mainz
GAUL
Lyons
SARMATIA
Caspian Sea
DACIA
ILLYRICUM
Solona
Adriatic Sea
MOESIA
Black Sea
Corsica
ITALY
Rome
SPAIN
THRACE
Byzantium
MACEDONIA
Thessalonica
Philippi
BITHYNIA & PONTUS
ARMENIA
Sardinia
Puteoli
Tyrrhenian Sea
MYSIA
Aegean Sea
Pergamum
PHRYGIA
GALATIA
CAPPADOCIA
Edessa
PARTHIA
ACHAIA
Corinth
Athens
Ephesus
Derbe
CILICIA
Tarsus
Antioch
MESOPOTAMIA
Tigris River
Euphrates River
Sicily
Syracuse
MAURETANIA
Carthage
AFRICA
Mediterranean Sea
Crete
Cyprus
SYRIA
Dura-Europos
Sidon
Damascus
Tyre
JUDEA
Pella
Jerusalem
NABATEA
Cyrene
Alexandria
CYRENE
Memphis
Nile River
Antinoe
EGYPT
Red Sea
Arabian Desert
N
Roman Empire by the time of Julius Caesar, 44 BCE
Territory added by Augustus Caesar, 14 CE
Territory added by Trajan, 117 CE
Territory temporarily annexed by Rome

MAP 11

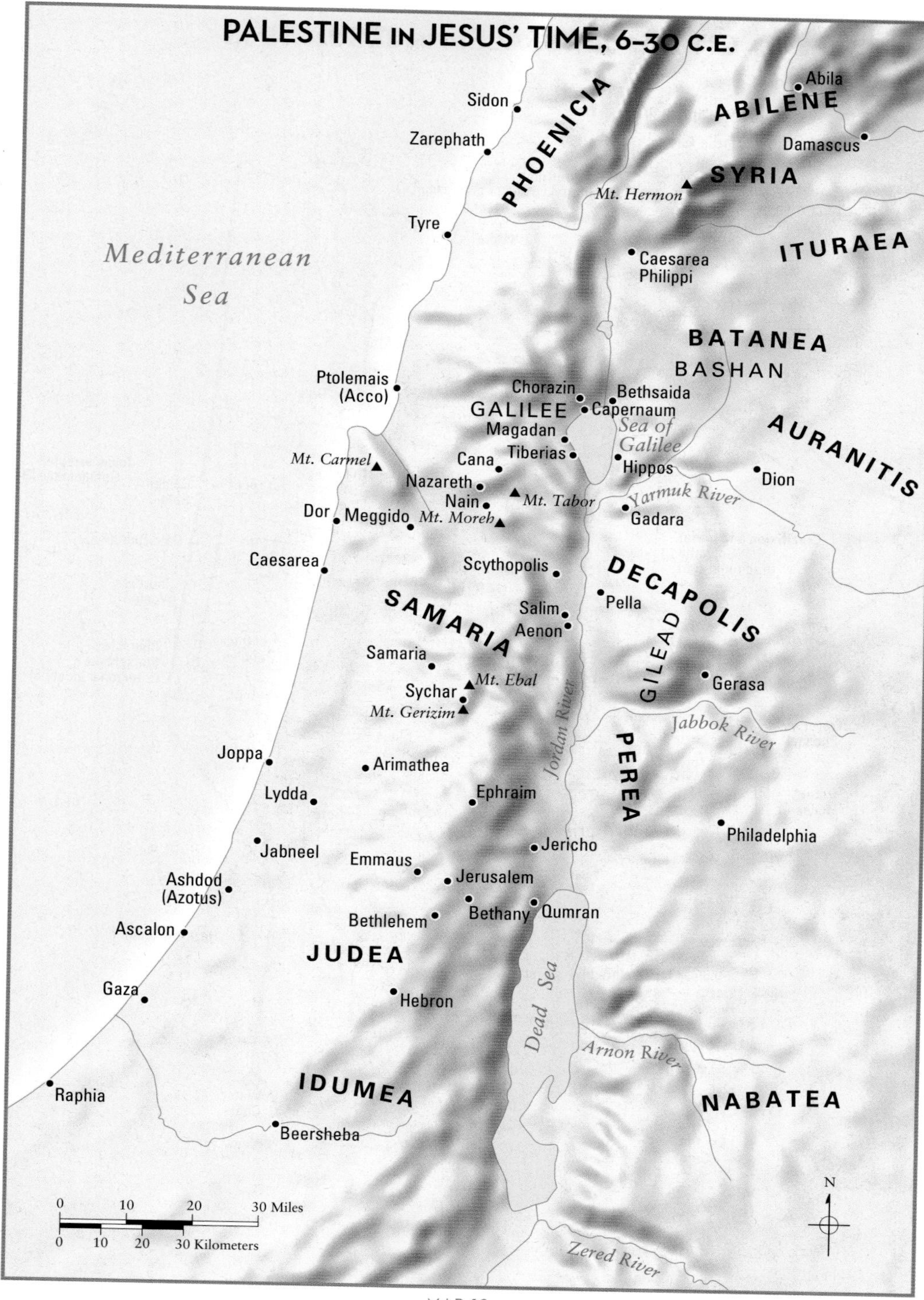
PALESTINE IN JESUS' TIME, 6–30 C.E.
Sidon
Zarephath
PHOENICIA
Abila
ABILENE
Damascus
SYRIA
Mt. Hermon
Tyre
Mediterranean Sea
Caesarea Philippi
ITURAEA
BATANEA
BASHAN
Ptolemais (Acco)
Chorazin
Bethsaida
GALILEE
Capernaum
Magadan
Sea of Galilee
AURANITIS
Mt. Carmel
Cana
Tiberias
Hippos
Dion
Nazareth
Nain
Mt. Tabor
Yarmuk River
Dor
Meggido
Mt. Moreh
Gadara
Caesarea
Scythopolis
DECAPOLIS
SAMARIA
Salim
Pella
Aenon
GILEAD
Samaria
Mt. Ebal
Sychar
Gerasa
Mt. Gerizim
Jordan River
Jabbok River
Joppa
Arimathea
PEREA
Lydda
Ephraim
Philadelphia
Jabneel
Jericho
Emmaus
Jerusalem
Ashdod (Azotus)
Bethany
Qumran
Bethlehem
Ascalon
JUDEA
Dead Sea
Gaza
Hebron
Arnon River
Raphia
IDUMEA
NABATEA
Beersheba
0 10 20 30 Miles
0 10 20 30 Kilometers
N
Zered River

MAP 12

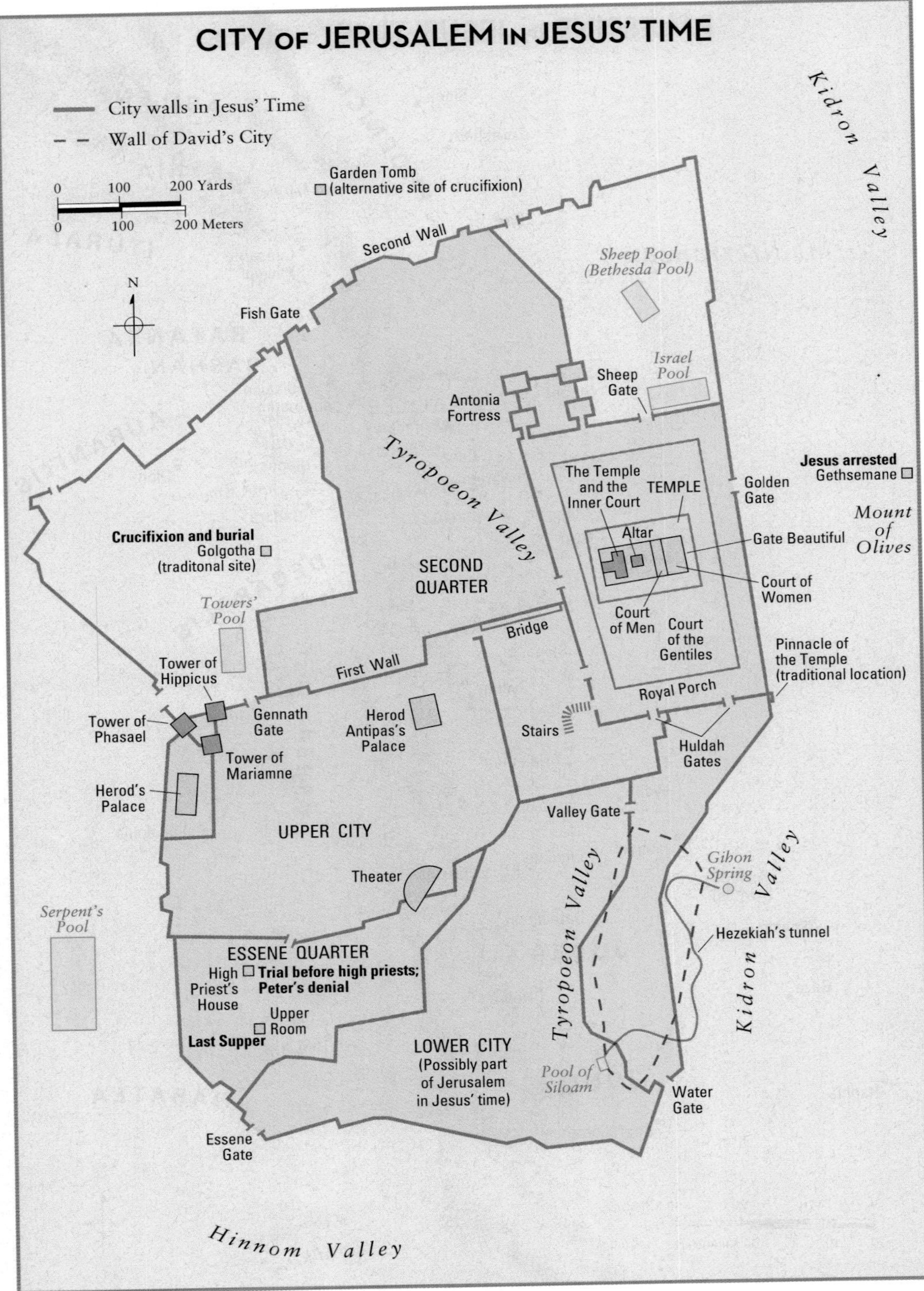
CITY OF JERUSALEM IN JESUS' TIME
City walls in Jesus' Time
Wall of David's City
0 100 200 Yards
0 100 200 Meters
N
Garden Tomb
(alternative site of crucifixion)
Second Wall
Fish Gate
Sheep Pool
(Bethesda Pool)
Kidron Valley
Israel Pool
Sheep Gate
Antonia Fortress
Tyropoeon Valley
Crucifixion and burial
Golgotha
(traditonal site)
Towers' Pool
SECOND QUARTER
The Temple and the Inner Court
TEMPLE
Altar
Golden Gate
Jesus arrested
Gethsemane
Mount of Olives
Gate Beautiful
Court of Women
Court of Men
Court of the Gentiles
Bridge
First Wall
Pinnacle of the Temple
(traditional location)
Tower of Hippicus
Tower of Phasael
Gennath Gate
Herod Antipas's Palace
Royal Porch
Stairs
Huldah Gates
Tower of Mariamne
Herod's Palace
UPPER CITY
Valley Gate
Theater
Gihon Spring
Serpent's Pool
ESSENE QUARTER
High Priest's House
Trial before high priests;
Peter's denial
Upper Room
Last Supper
Hezekiah's tunnel
LOWER CITY
(Possibly part of Jerusalem in Jesus' time)
Pool of Siloam
Water Gate
Essene Gate
Hinnom Valley

MAP 13

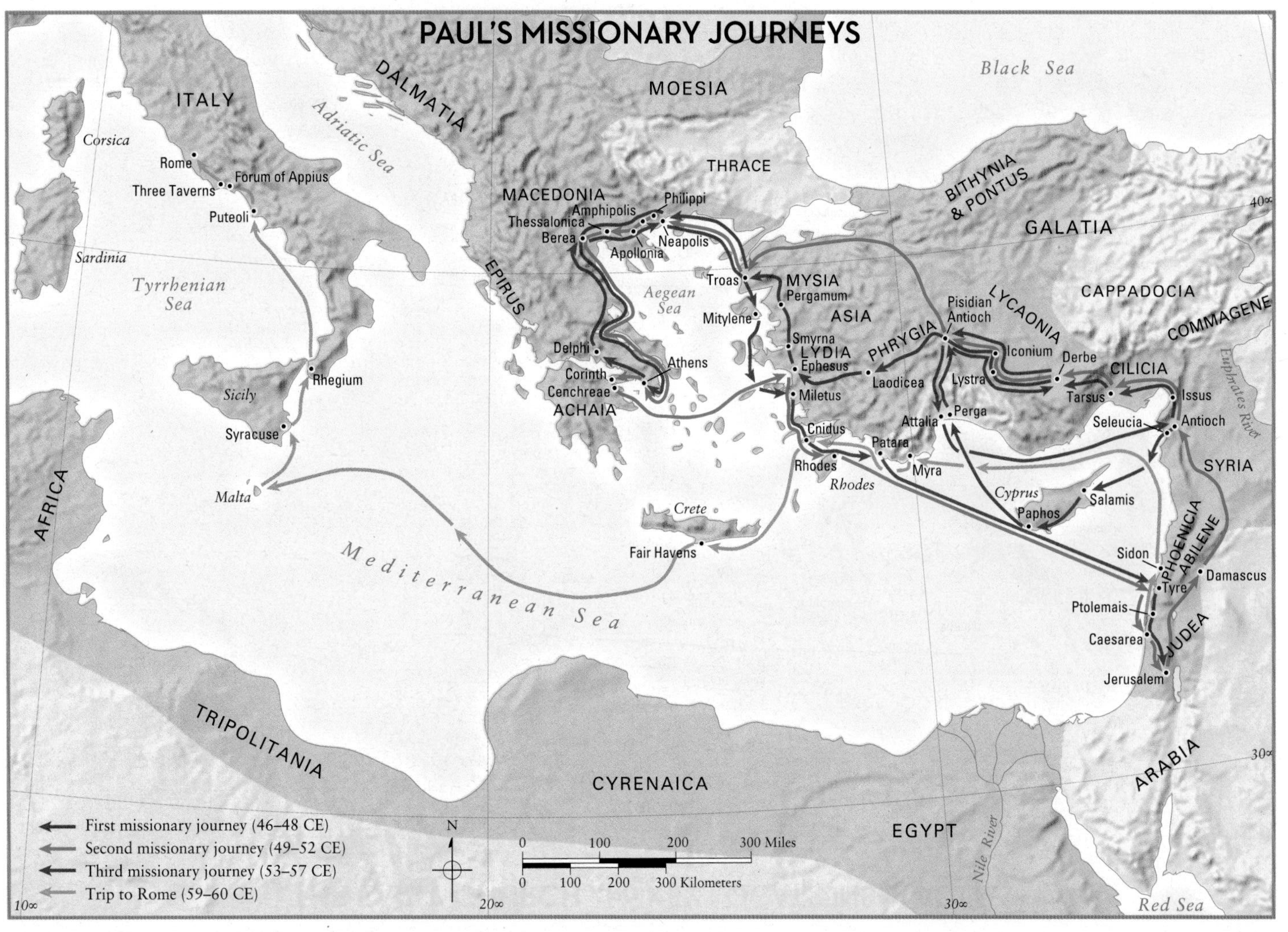
PAUL'S MISSIONARY JOURNEYS
Black Sea
MOESIA
DALMATIA
ITALY
Adriatic Sea
Corsica
Rome
Three Taverns
Forum of Appius
Puteoli
THRACE
BITHYNIA & PONTUS
MACEDONIA
Philippi
Amphipolis
Thessalonica
Berea
Neapolis
Apollonia
GALATIA
Sardinia
Tyrrhenian Sea
EPIRUS
Aegean Sea
Troas
MYSIA
Pergamum
Mitylene
ASIA
Pisidian Antioch
LYCAONIA
CAPPADOCIA
COMMAGENE
Euphrates River
Smyrna
LYDIA
Ephesus
PHRYGIA
Iconium
Derbe
CILICIA
Delphi
Athens
Corinth
Cenchreae
ACHAIA
Sicily
Rhegium
Syracuse
Laodicea
Lystra
Tarsus
Issus
Miletus
Attalia
Perga
Seleucia
Antioch
Cnidus
Patara
Rhodes
Myra
Rhodes
SYRIA
Malta
AFRICA
Crete
Fair Havens
Cyprus
Salamis
Paphos
PHOENICIA
ABILENE
Sidon
Tyre
Damascus
Ptolemais
Caesarea
JUDEA
Jerusalem
Mediterranean Sea
TRIPOLITANIA
CYRENAICA
EGYPT
ARABIA
Nile River
Red Sea
First missionary journey (46–48 CE)
Second missionary journey (49–52 CE)
Third missionary journey (53–57 CE)
Trip to Rome (59–60 CE)
N
0
100
200
300 Miles
0
100
200
300 Kilometers
10∞
20∞
30∞
40∞
30∞

MAP 14

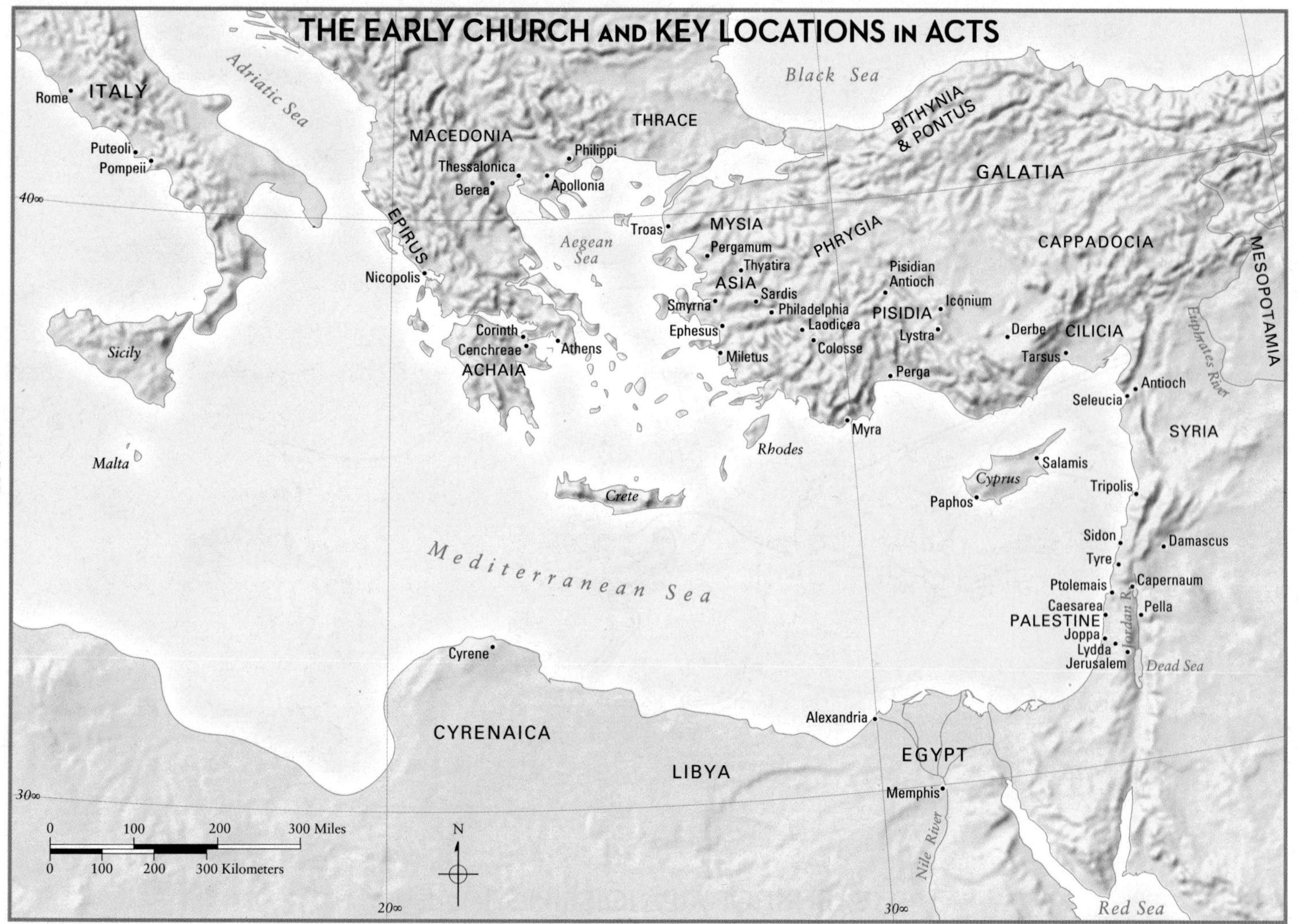
THE EARLY CHURCH AND KEY LOCATIONS IN ACTS
Black Sea
Adriatic Sea
Rome
ITALY
Puteoli
Pompeii
MACEDONIA
THRACE
BITHYNIA & PONTUS
Philippi
Thessalonica
Apollonia
Berea
GALATIA
40∞
EPIRUS
Troas
MYSIA
Aegean Sea
Pergamum
PHRYGIA
CAPPADOCIA
MESOPOTAMIA
Nicopolis
Thyatira
ASIA
Pisidian Antioch
Sardis
Smyrna
Philadelphia
PISIDIA
Iconium
Ephesus
Laodicea
Lystra
Derbe
CILICIA
Corinth
Athens
Cenchreae
Colosse
Tarsus
Sicily
Miletus
ACHAIA
Perga
Euphrates River
Antioch
Seleucia
Myra
SYRIA
Rhodes
Malta
Salamis
Cyprus
Tripolis
Crete
Paphos
Sidon
Damascus
Mediterranean Sea
Tyre
Ptolemais
Capernaum
Caesarea
Pella
PALESTINE
Jordan R.
Joppa
Lydda
Cyrene
Jerusalem
Dead Sea
Alexandria
CYRENAICA
EGYPT
LIBYA
Memphis
30∞
0
100
200
300 Miles
N
0
100
200
300 Kilometers
Nile River
20∞
30∞
Red Sea

MAP 15